A Genealogical and Heraldic History of the Extinct and Dormant Baronetcies of England, by J. and J.B. Burke

A

GENEALOGICAL AND HERALDIC

HISTORY

OF THE

EXTINCT AND DORMANT BARONETCIES

OF ENGLAND.

The Extinct & Dormant
BARONETCIES
of
England
by
JOHN : BURKE
&
JOHN · BERNARD · BURKE
London
Scott Webster and Geary
MDCCCXXXVIII

A GENEALOGICAL AND HERALDIC HISTORY OF THE EXTINCT AND DORMANT BARONETCIES OF ENGLAND.

BY

JOHN BURKE, ESQ.

AUTHOR OF THE PEERAGE AND BARONETAGE, HISTORY OF THE COMMONERS, ETC.

AND

JOHN BERNARD BURKE, ESQ.

OF THE MIDDLE TEMPLE.

LONDON:
PRINTED FOR SCOTT, WEBSTER, AND GEARY,
CHARTERHOUSE SQUARE.

MDCCCXXXVIII.

C. WHITTINGHAM, TOOKS COURT, CHANCERY LANE.

RABLE

ſ PHIPPS,

AVE, K.P.

:eland,

:RIBED.

C. WHITTINGHAM, TOOKS COU

TO THE RIGHT HONOURABLE

CONSTANTINE HENRY PHIPPS,

EARL OF MULGRAVE, K.P.

Lord Lieutenant of Ireland,

ETC. ETC. ETC.

THIS WORK

IS

MOST RESPECTFULLY INSCRIBED.

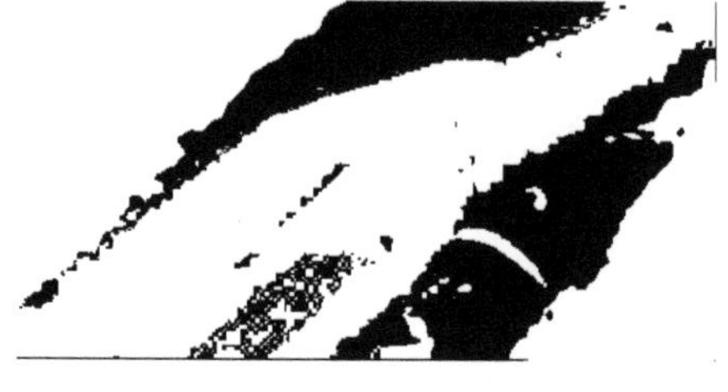

PREFACE.

King James the First instituted the order of Baronet in 1611, two hundred and twenty-seven years ago; and within that period, brief in the estimation of an antiquary, nearly a thousand patents have become obsolete; nearly a thousand Baronetcies have ceased to exist: not all, perhaps, become absolutely extinct, but all virtually so. The personages who enjoyed those honours have left behind them, however, numerous and widely spread connexions, who, although excluded by the tenour of the royal grant, from their dignity, inherit, in many instances, their name, in more their lands, in all, their blood:—to those this book especially belongs; to rescue them from the fate of their titled predecessors it is produced, and to their interests it is mainly devoted, under an impression, at the same time, that a work *directly* appertaining to so large and influential a portion of the community, must *indirectly* be of value to the whole: that it might prove so, much time and vast labour have been bestowed upon its composition; the public records have been carefully explored, private collections and private authorities referred to—in fine, nothing has been left undone to render its statements full, clear, and accurate.

In addition to these few prefatory words, the Authors have to express their acknowledgments for the facilities afforded them in every channel, public and private, through which it was necessary to seek for information; they would willingly express their thanks to many individuals, but so many occur, that they are obliged to forego the pleasure.

Note.—The red hand of Ulster, which is carried upon the shield of a Baronet, is omitted in the armorial ensigns of this work, from the necessity of the engravings being upon a narrow scale.

London, 1838.

EXTINCT AND DORMANT

BARONETAGE.

ABDY, OF ALBINS.

CREATED 9th June, 1660.  EXTINCT 2nd April, 1759.

Lineage.

This family, one of considerable antiquity, is presumed to have derived its surname from Abdy, in the county of York, where RICHARD ABDY was seated at a very remote period.

ANTHONY ABDY, a lineal descendant of the Yorkshire house, entering into commercial pursuits, established himself in London, and became an alderman of that city. He married Abigail, daughter of Sir Thomas Campbell, knt. and left at his decease, in 1640, three sons and one daughter, viz.

- I. THOMAS, of Felix Hall, Essex, created a BARONET in 1641, which honour is now enjoyed by his descendant,
  - SIR WILLIAM ABDY, bart. of Chobham Place, Surrey. See BURKE's *Peerage and Baronetage*.
- II. ROBERT.
- III. JOHN, see ABDY, OF MOORES.
- I. Alice, m. to Sir John Bramston, K.B. of Skreens, ancestor of the present Thomas William Bramston, esq. of Skreens, M.P. for Essex.

Mr. Alderman Abdy's second son,

ROBERT ABDY, esq. of Albins, in Essex, was created a BARONET 9th June, 1660. He m. Catherine, daughter of Sir John Gayer, knt. and by her, who died in 1662, had several sons and daughters, of whom the third daughter, Sarah, wedded John Pennington, esq. and the eldest son,

SIR JOHN ABDY, second baronet, of Albins, succeeded his father in 1670. He m. Jane, only daughter of George Nicholas, esq. youngest son of Sir Edward Nicholas, knt. secretary of state to Charles I., (one of the ill-fated monarch's most faithful adherents), and left at his decease a daughter, JANE, m. to the Rev. EDWARD CRANK, and a son and successor,

SIR ROBERT ABDY, third baronet, of Albins, whom Morant describes as "a man of deep knowledge in antiquity and natural history, a great connoisseur in medals, of which he had a fine collection; and, what is more valuable, a true patriot, and a person of unshaken integrity, and remarkable humanity." He was chosen M.P. for the county of Essex in 1727, and continued to represent that shire in parliament until his demise. He m. Theodosia, only daughter and heir of George Bramston, LL.D. and had, to survive youth, one son and one daughter, namely,

JOHN, his heir.

Theodosia, m. in 1752, to the Rev. Stotherd Abdy, rector of Theydon Gernon, a younger son of Sir William Abdy, fourth baronet, of Felix Hall. She died issueless in 1758.

Sir Robert died in 1748, and was succeeded by his son,

SIR JOHN ABDY, fourth baronet, of Albins, M.P. for Essex, who died unmarried 2nd April, 1759, when the BARONETCY became EXTINCT. He bequeathed his estates to his aunt, Mrs. Crank, for life, with remainder to Sir Anthony Thomas Abdy, bart. of Felix Hall, to the Rev. Stotherd Abdy, that gentleman's brother, and eventually, on failure of the issue of both, to Thomas, son of the Rev. Dr. Rutherford, by their sister, Charlotte Abdy. The last named devisee ultimately inherited, and, assuming the surname and arms of ABDY in 1775, became

The Rev. THOMAS ABDY ABDY, of Albins. He m. in 1778 a daughter of James Hayes, esq. of Holliport, bencher of the Middle Temple, and died in 1798, leaving issue,

- I. JOHN-RUTHERFORD-ABDY HATCH-ABDY, esq. of Albins, who m. Miss Hatch, daughter of Oliver Hatch, of Bromley.
- II. Anthony-Abdy, captain R. N. a widower with an only son, Neville.

III. Charles-Boyd Abdy, in holy orders, of Cooper-sall.
IV. James-Abdy, major in the East India Company's military service, married.
V. Edward-Strutt Abdy.

I. Harriet Abdy, m. to Mr. Sykes, the navy agent.
II. Caroline Abdy.

Arms—Or, two chevronels between three trefoils, slipped, sa.

ABDY, OF MOORES.

CREATED 22nd June, 1660.—EXTINCT about 1662.

Lineage.

JOHN ABDY, of Moores, in Salcot, Essex, third son of Alderman Anthony Abdy, was created a BARONET in 1660, but dying in two years after without issue, the title expired, while his estates passed to the ABDYS, of Albins.

Arms—See preceding article.

ABERCROMBIE, OF EDINBURGH.

CREATED in 1709. EXTINCT in 1724.

Lineage.

I. SIR JAMES ABERCROMBIE, of Edinburgh, captain in the Coldstream Guards, was created a BARONET in 1709, but dying without issue in 1724, the title became EXTINCT.

Arms—Ar. a chev. gu. between three boars' heads erased, az.

ACTON, OF LONDON.

CREATED 31st May, 1629. EXTINCT in 1651.

Lineage.

I. SIR WILLIAM ACTON, of London, the first and only baronet, died without male issue in 1651, when the title became EXTINCT.

Arms—Quarterly, per fesse indented arg. and gu.; in the first quarter a Cornish chough, sa.

ADAMS, OF LONDON.

CREATED 13th June, 1660. EXTINCT 12th April, 1770.

Lineage.

I. SIR THOMAS ADAMS, knt. sheriff of the city of London in 1644, and lord mayor in 1646, having suffered in the royal cause, by imprisonment in the Tower of London, and having further evinced his fidelity to his exiled sovereign by remitting to his majesty in his hour of need £10,000, was created a BARONET in a few days after the Restoration. Sir Thomas, although advanced in years, was deputed by the city to accompany General Monk to Breda, and to attend the exiled monarch to his restored realms. He endowed several schools, particularly that of Wem, in Shropshire, where he was born, and founded an Arabic lecture in Cambridge, of which University he had been a member. Sir Thomas died president of St. Thomas's Hospital and father of the city, 24th February, 1667, aged eighty-two, by a fall in stepping out of his coach. He m. Anne, daughter of Humphrey Mapstead, esq. of Trenton, in Essex, and was s. by his son,

II. SIR WILLIAM ADAMS, who wedded first, Anne, daughter of John Rushout, esq. and sister of Sir James Rushout, bart. of Northwick, by whom he had nine sons and a daughter. The eldest son,

WILLIAM, died in the lifetime of his father, leaving by his wife, Mary, daughter of Sir John Maynard, and relict of Captain Butler, of Saltash, in Cornwall, (she afterwards m. Sir Rushout Cullen, bart.), an only daughter,

JANE, who wedded Sir Erasmus Norwich, bart.

Sir William m. secondly, Jane, daughter of — Burnet, and widow of Alderman Allington, of London, but had no other issue. He d. in 1687, and was s. by his eldest surviving son,

III. SIR THOMAS ADAMS, who d. unmar. in August, 1690, and was s. by his brother,

IV. SIR CHARLES ADAMS. This gentleman, who was the sixth son of his father, resided at Sprowston Hall, in Norfolk. He m. Frances, one of the six daughters of Sir Francis Rolle, knt. and granddaughter of the Lord Chief Justice Rolle, but d. s. p. 12th August, 1726, when the estates passed to his niece, Jane, Lady Norwich, and the title devolved upon his only surviving brother,

V. SIR ROBERT ADAMS, who m. first, Dorothea, daughter and co-heir of Piercy Wiseman, esq. but by that lady had no issue. He wedded, secondly, Diana ——, and by her left at his decease, about the year 1754, a son and successor,

VI. SIR THOMAS ADAMS, Capt. R. N. who died on the Virginia station 12th April, 1770, issueless, when the BARONETCY became EXTINCT.

Arms—Erm. three cats passant in pale az.

AIRMINE, OF OSGODBY.

CREATED 28th Nov. 1619.  EXTINCT in 1668.

Lineage.

I. SIR WILLIAM AIRMINE, of Osgodby, the representative of an old Lincolnshire family, was created a BARONET in 1619. He m. first, Elizabeth, daughter of Sir Michael Hicks, knt.; and, secondly, Mary, daughter and co-heir of the Hon. Henry Talbot, fourth son of George, Earl of Shrewsbury. He died in 1651, leaving, by his first wife, a son and successor,

II. SIR WILLIAM AIRMINE, of Osgodby, who m. Anne, daughter and co-heir of Sir Robert Crane, bart. of Chilton, in Suffolk, and by her (who wedded, secondly, John, Lord Belasyse) had daughters, his co-heirs, one of whom,

ANNE, married Thomas, second Lord Crew, of Stene, and had four daughters, her co-heirs, viz.

1. JEMIMA CREW, m. to Henry De Grey, Duke of Kent, and had issue,
   - ANTHONY, Earl of Harold, summoned to parliament as Baron Lucas, of Crudwell, in 1719. He m. Lady Mary Tufton, but *d. s. p.* in 1723. His death is mentioned as having arisen from an ear of barley which his lordship had inadvertently put into his mouth, by which he was choked.
   - Henry, died unm.
   - Amabel, m. to John, Viscount Glenorchy, and hence descend the Earls DE GREY and RIPON.
   - Jemima, m. to John, third Lord Ashburnham, and was grandmother of the present peer.
   - Anne, m. to Lord Charles Cavendish.
   - Mary, m. to Dr. Gregory, dean of Christchurch.
2. Airmine Crew, m. to Thomas Cartwright, esq. of Aynho, great-grandfather of the present WILLIAM-RALPH CARTWRIGHT, esq. of Aynho, M.P. for Northamptonshire.
3. Catherine Crew, m. to Sir John Harper, bart. of Caulk Abbey, and the great-great-grand-son of this marriage is the present SIR GEORGE CREWE, bart. of Caulk Abbey.
4. Elizabeth Crew, m. to Charles Butler, Earl of Arran.

Arms—Erm. a saltire engr. gu. on a chief of the last a lion passant or, armed and langued az.

ALLAN, OF KINGSGATE.

CREATED 18th Sept. 1819.—EXTINCT 14th Sept. 1820.

Lineage.

I. LIEUT. COL. SIR ALEXANDER ALLAN, a director of the East India Company, and for some time M. P. for Berwick, was raised to the dignity of a baronet towards the close of 1819, and survived his elevation but the brief period of one year, dying issueless 14th September, 1820, aged fifty-six.

ALLEN, OF LONDON.

CREATED 14th June, 1660.—EXTINCT 19th June, 1730.

Lineage.

I. SIR THOMAS ALLEN, citizen of London, who was created a BARONET at the Restoration, m. Elizabeth Birch, daughter of a vintner, of the same place, and died 15th December, 1690, when he was *s.* by his son,

II. SIR THOMAS ALLEN, who wedded Elizabeth Angell, but leaving no surviving issue at his decease, 19th June, 1730, the title became EXTINCT.

ALLEYN, OF HATFIELD.

CREATED June 24, 1629.  EXTINCT Sept. 15, 1759.

Lineage.

RICHARD ALLEYN, descended from a family settled at Thaxtead, in Essex, died 23rd June, 1527, possessed of a considerable estate in the same county, and was *s.* by his eldest son,

SIR JOHN ALLEYN, an eminent citisen of London, who was sheriff in 1518, and lord mayor in 1525 and again in 1535. Dying unmarried in 1544, he devised to that city five hundred marks, as a stock for sea coal; the rents of his lands, purchased of the king, to be distributed to the poor for ever, beside many benefactions to the prisons and hospitals, and a rich collar of gold to be worn by the successive lord mayors. His next brother and successor,

JOHN ALLEYN, wedding Margaret, elder daughter and co-heir of Gyles Leigh, esq. of Walton Leigh, in Surrey, acquired with her the estate of Hatfield, in Essex, and had issue,

- JOHN, his heir.
- Christopher.
- Giles, of Hatfield Peverell, m. Christian, daughter of John West, and had one son and three daughters, namely,
  - John.
  - Catherine, m. to John Baker, esq. of Chesterford.
  - Elizabeth, m. to Thomas Barnaby, esq.
  - Agnes, m. to William Higham, esq.

John Alleyn died 22nd June, 1558, and was succeeded by his eldest son,

JOHN ALLEYN, of Hatfield Peverell, then aged twenty years, who married thrice, and had two sons, and as many daughters, viz.

- EDMUND, his heir,
- Thomas, who m. Mary Fairclough, of Herts.
- Elizabeth, m. to Christopher Goldingham, esq. of Bulmer.

Mary, *m.* to William Coys, of North Okingdon.

The elder son,

EDMUND ALLEYN, esq. of Hatfield Peverell, succeeded his father in 1572. He *m.* Martha, daughter and co-heir of John Glasscock, esq. of Powers Hall, in Witham, and had by her, who died in 1593, one son and two daughters, viz.

EDWARD, his heir.

Elizabeth, *m.* to Robert Castle, esq. of East Hatley, in Cambridgeshire.

Mary, *m.* to Henry Hall, esq. of Gratford, in Lincolnshire.

Mr. Alleyn died in 1616, and was *s.* by his son,

I. EDWARD ALLEYN, esq. of Hatfield Peverell, aged thirty at the period of inheritance. In 1629 he served as sheriff for Essex, and was created a BARONET on the 24th of June in that year. He *m.* Elizabeth, daughter and co-heir of George Scot, esq. of Little Lees, by whom he obtained considerable landed property in Essex, and had, with two daughters, Martha, *m.* to the Rev. Joshua Blower Rocke, and Mary, to Robert Clive, esq. of Styche, a son,

EDMUND, who died *v. p.* in 1633, leaving by Mary, his wife, daughter of Nicholas Miller, esq. of Wrotham, one son and one daughter,

EDMUND, successor to his grandfather.

Elizabeth, *m.* first, to John Robinson, esq. of Denston Hall, and, secondly, to Sir William Jones, attorney-general to CHARLES II.

GEORGE.

Sir Edward Alleyn died in November, 1638, and was succeeded by his grandson,

II. SIR EDMUND ALLEYN, of Hatfield, who wedded Frances, only daughter and heir of Thomas Gent, esq. of Moyns, in Essex, and had, by her, who died in 1657, an only daughter and heiress,

ARABELLA, who *m.* first, Francis Thompson, esq. of Hambleton, in Yorkshire, and, secondly, Lord George Howard, son of Henry, Duke of Norfolk. Between the years 1715 and 1720 her ladyship conveyed her estates to Arthur Dobbs, formerly clerk to Sir John Floyer, and he enjoyed them until his decease, 1750-1, when, by a reversionary clause in Lady Arabella's will, they passed to her kinsman, Sir Edmund Alleyn.

Sir Edmund died 2nd November, 1656, when his extensive estates devolved on his daughter, while the baronetcy reverted to his uncle,

III. SIR GEORGE ALLEYN, seated at Little Lees, in Essex, who married three wives. By the second, Martha, daughter of Roger Jones, esq. of the county of Monmouth, he left at his decease in 1664, with other issue, a daughter, Anne, *m.* to Henry Freeman, esq. of Higham Ferrers, and a son and successor,

IV. SIR GEORGE ALLEYN, who *m.* Mercy, youngest daughter of John Cloxton, esq. of Little Waltham, and had issue,

CLOPTON, } successive baronets.
GEORGE, }

Edward, who *m.* Mary, daughter of John or Thomas Trott, vicar of Saling Magna, and had

EDMUND, successor to his uncle.

Arabella, *m.* to the Rev. James Chalmers, M.A. vicar of Earl's Colne, and rector of Little Waltham.

John, who died unmarried.

Sir George died in 1702, and was succeeded by his eldest son,

V. SIR CLOPTON ALLEYN, at whose decease unmarried, in September, 1726, the title devolved on his brother,

VI. SIR GEORGE ALLEYN, who also died unm. and was succeeded by his nephew,

VII. SIR EDMUND ALLEYN, who dying unm. 15th September, 1759, the BARONETCY became extinct, while the estates passed to Sir Edmund's sister, ARABELLA, wife of the Rev. JAMES CHALMERS.

Arms—Sa. a cross potent or.

ALLIN, OF BLUNDESTON.

CREATED 7th Feb. 1673. EXTINCT in 1696.

Lineage.

ROBERT ALLIN left, with two daughters, Mary, who died in 1672, the wife of Rear Admiral Uther, and Alice, of Robert Ashby, esq. an only son,

I. SIR THOMAS ALLIN, knt. *b.* in 1612, who acquired and left behind the high reputation of a brave and distinguished naval officer. He served under the Commonwealth, and commanded one of the ships in that part of the fleet which revolted to the Prince of Wales. In 1660 he was appointed to the Dover, amongst the earliest vessels commissioned by the Duke of York. In 1663 he was constituted commander-in-chief (as commodore only) of the ships and vessels in the Downs, and invested on that occasion with the singular privilege of bearing at his main-top the Union flag, which he hoisted on board the St. Andrew. The next year he was commander-in-chief in the Mediterranean; and he soon afterwards achieved a victory over the Dutch fleet, for which he received the honour of knighthood, and was promoted to the rank of Admiral of the *Blue*. In 1666 he was advanced to the *White*, and again distinguished himself as commander of the Van or White squadron in a decisive action with the French and Dutch allied fleets. In consideration of these and subsequent equally gallant exploits Admiral Allin was created a BARONET, on the 7th July, 1673, and retired then to his seat at Somerleyton, in Suffolk, which estate and manor he had purchased from Thomas Garneys, esq. great grandson of John Wentworth, who acquired them from the Jernynghams of Cossey. Sir Thomas was at different periods comptroller of the navy, captain of Sandgate Castle, and master of the Trinity House. He *m.* first, Alice, daughter of W. Whiting, esq. of Lowestoff, Capt. R. N. and by her had issue,

THOMAS, his successor.

Anne, who *d.* 31st May, 1664, unm. aged twenty-seven.

ALICE, *m.* to EDMUND ANGUISH, esq. of Moulton, in Norfolk, and had three sons, viz.

RICHARD ANGUISH, who inherited the estates of his uncle Sir Thomas Allin.

Edmund Anguish.

Allin Anguish.

Sir Thomas wedded, secondly, Elizabeth, daughter of Thomas Anguish, esq. of Moulton, and sister of his son-in-law, but had no other issue. He *d.* in 1686, was interred at Somerleyton, and *s.* by his son,

II. SIR THOMAS ALLIN, of Somerleyton, who *m.* in

1671, Mary, daughter of John Caldwall, of London, but dying without issue in 1696, the BARONETCY EXPIRED, and the estates devolved upon his nephew, RICHARD ANGUISH, esq. of Moulton, who subsequently changed his name to ALLIN, and was created a baronet, (see ALLIN, of *Somerleyton*).

Arms—Gu. a cinquefoil pierced or.

ALLIN, OF SOMERLEYTON.

CREATED 14th Dec. 1699.—EXTINCT in 1794.

Lineage.

ALICE ALLIN, younger and only surviving daughter of Admiral Sir Thomas Allin, bart. of Blundeston, espoused EDMUND ANGUISH,* esq. of Moulton, in the county of Norfolk, and by him had issue,

I. RICHARD ANGUISH, of whom presently.
II. EDMUND ANGUISH, who *m.* Miss Mary Betts, and dying in 1708, left two sons and two daughters, viz.
    THOMAS ANGUISH, of Halesworth, in holy orders, who *m.* Miss Mary Eling, of Beccles, and dying 23rd April, 1763, was *s.* by his son,
        THOMAS ANGUISH, accountant-general to the Court of Chancery, who wedded Sarah, daughter of — Henley, esq. of Docking, in Norfolk, and dying 31st December, 1785, left issue,
            1. THOMAS ANGUISH, who inherited SOMERLEYTON and the other estates of his kinsman SIR THOMAS ALLIN, bart.
            2. GEORGE ANGUISH, in holy orders, who inherited at the decease of his elder brother.
            3. Charles Anguish, *d.* unm.
            1. Catherine Anguish, who *m.* in 1788, Francis-Godolphin, fifth Duke of Leeds, (his grace's second duchess), and had a son, Lord Sidney-Godolphin-Osborne, and a daughter, Lady Anne-Sarah-Osborne, who *m.* John Whyte Melville, esq.
            2. Anne Anguish.
            3. Charlotte Anguish.
    Edmund Anguish, *m.* Miss Rebecca Betts.
    Mary Anguish, of Beccles.
    Dorothy Anguish, *m.* to the Rev. Thomas Symonds.
III. Allin Anguish.

The eldest son,

I. RICHARD ANGUISH, esq. having inherited SOMERLEYTON, in Suffolk, and the other estates of his uncle, Sir Thomas Allin, assumed the surname and arms of ALLIN, and was created a BARONET 14th December, 1699. He *m.* Frances, only daughter of Sir Henry Ashurst, bart. of Waterstock, in the county of Oxford, and had issue,
    THOMAS, his heir.
    Henry, *d.* unm.
    Richard, *d.* unm.
    ASHURST, in holy orders, who became third baronet.
    Diana, *m.* to Thomas-Henry Ashurst, esq. of Waterstock.

Sir Richard *d.* 19th October, 1725, and was *s.* by his eldest son,

II. SIR THOMAS ALLIN, of Somerleyton. This gentleman was sheriff of Suffolk in 1730, and he was appointed serjeant-at-arms to the Treasury in 1733. He died unmar. 11th August, 1764, and was *s.* by his brother,

III. *The Rev.* SIR ASHURST ALLIN, rector of Blunston cum Flixton, who died 6th November, 1770, leaving a daughter, Frances, who *d.* unm. and a son and heir,

IV. SIR THOMAS ALLIN, who *d.* unm. in 1794, when the BARONETCY became EXTINCT, and Somerleyton with his other estates passed to his kinsman,

THOMAS ANGUISH, esq. who then became "of Somerleyton." He died unm. in 1810, and was *s.* by his brother,

The Rev. GEORGE ANGUISH, M. A. now of Somerleyton, in the county of Suffolk. (*Refer to* BURKE'S *Commoners*, vol. ii. p. 419).

Arms—Gu. a cinquefoil pierced or.

ALSTON, OF ODELL.

CREATED 13th June, 1642. 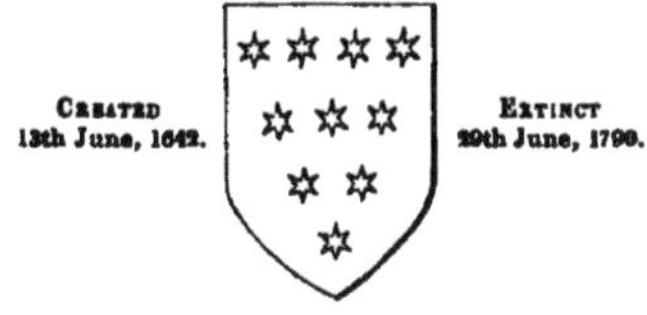 EXTINCT 29th June, 1790.

Lineage.

The family of ALSTON is upon record so early as the reign of EDWARD I. when "WILLIAM ALSTON, of Stisted, in Essex, for want of warranty of Brockscroft, in Stisted, did grant and confirm to John de Carpenter, of Naylinghurst, so much of the better land in Stisted, except his mansion-house there. In the time of EDWARD III. Hugh Alston bore for arms, 'azure, ten stars, or, four, three, two, one;' which was long before coat armour was granted by patent."

JOHN ALSTON, of Newton, in Suffolk, descended from the above-mentioned William, of Stisted, was father of

WILLIAM ALSTON, of Newton, who had by Ann his wife, daughter of Thomas Symons, a son and heir,

EDWARD or EDMUND ALSTON, of Saxham Hall, in Newton, who *m.* Elizabeth, daughter of John Coleman, and had two sons, viz.
    WILLIAM, his heir.
    Thomas, of Edwardston, in Suffolk, who *m.* first, Dorothy, daughter and co-heir of Henry Holmsted, esq. of Maplested, in Essex, and had a son,
        EDWARD, his successor.
    He wedded, secondly, ———, and had another son,
        Thomas, of Newton, *m.* to Elizabeth, daughter of Thomas West, of London, and was father of

---

* The family of ANGUISH came originally from the Isle of Angus, whence the name, and settling in Norfolk remained there for three hundred years. In 1600 Edmund Anguish held the manor of Moughton or Molton of the Earl of Northampton, as parcel of his lordship's manor of Fornat.

Thomas Alston, of Newton.
Thomas, of Edwardston, was *s.* by his elder son,
EDWARD ALSTON, esq. of Edwardston, who *m.* Margaret, daughter of Arthur Penning, esq. of Kettleborough, in Suffolk, and was father of
SIR EDWARD ALSTON, knt. of London, M. D. and President of the College of Physicians.*
JOSEPH ALSTON, esq. of Chelsea, created a baronet in 1681.
Penning Alston, esq. of London.

The elder son and heir,

WILLIAM ALSTON, esq. of Sayham Hall, *m.* Margery, daughter and co-heir of — Holmsted, esq. of Maplested, in Essex, by whom he had (with other children, whose lines all failed),

WILLIAM, who *m.* a daughter of — Neuce, esq. of Hadham, in Hertfordshire, and was father of
WILLIAM, of the Inner Temple, who was seated at Marlesford, in Suffolk. He *m.* Avise, daughter and co-heir of Jeffry Pitman, esq. of Woodbridge, and had issue,
SAMUEL, his heir.
Thomas, of the Inner Temple, who died *s. p.*
Avise, *m.* to Sir Thomas Foster, knt. son of the Lord Chief Justice Foster.
Elizabeth, *m.* to Thomas Mann, esq. of the Inner Temple, Usher of the Rolls.
Mary, who *d.* unm.
He *d.* in 1641, and with his wife lies interred in Marlesford Church. He was *s.* by his elder son,
SAMUEL ALSTON, esq. of Marlesford, who *m.* Alice, daughter of Francis Nicholson, esq. of Chapelle, in Essex, and had a son,
SAMUEL ALSTON, esq. of Marlesford, who wedded Elizabeth, daughter of Gregory Wescomb, esq. of Eltham, in Kent, and had a son and three daughters.
WILLIAM ALSTON, of Gray's Inn.

THOMAS.

The younger son,

THOMAS ALSTON, esq. of Polstead, in Suffolk, wedded Frances, daughter of Simon Blomevill, or Blomfield, esq. of Monk's Illey, in the same county, and by her (who survived him, and *m.* secondly, Sir John Temple, knt. of Stantonbury, Bucks.) had issue,

William, of the Inner Temple, *d.* unm. buried at Odell, 1637.
THOMAS, of the Inner Temple: of him presently.
Edward (Sir), of the Inner Temple, and of Strixton, in Northamptonshire. He had the honour of knighthood conferred upon him, and *m.* Esther, daughter of Sir William Ashcombe, of Ascot, in Oxfordshire, by whom he had
Thomas, *d.* unm.
John, *d.* unm.
Charles, in holy orders, D. D. archdeacon of Essex, *d.* in 1714, unm.
Catharine, *m.* to — Wiseman, of Northamptonshire.
John, of the Inner Temple, and of Pavenham, in Bedfordshire, *m.* Dorothy, daughter of Sir John Temple, knt. of Stanton, Bucks, and had
William, *m.* to a daughter of — Brooks, and *d. s. p.*
Thomas.
Edward.
John, *m.* Anne, daughter of — Wallis.
Frances, *m.* to Edward Reynolds.
Elizabeth, *m.* to William Crofts.
Mary, *m.* to John Leman.
Dorothy, *m.* to Thomas Wells.
Sarah.
Frances, *m.* to William Lord Monson.

The second but eldest surviving son,

I. SIR THOMAS ALSTON, knt. of Odell, in the county of Bedford, high sheriff in 1641, was created a BARONET by *King* CHARLES I. 13th June, 1642. He *m.* Elizabeth, daughter of Sir Rowland St. John, K. B. and had issue,

Thomas, who *d.* at Oxford in his father's lifetime, 2nd June, 1668, aged twenty-two, unm.
ROWLAND, successor to his father.
Frances, *m.* to Sir John Pickering, of Titchmarsh, in Northamptonshire.
Elizabeth, *m.* first, to Stavely Stanton, esq. of Birchmoor, in the county of Bedford; and, secondly, to Montague Pickering, esq. brother of Sir John.

He *d.* in 1678, and was *s.* by his only surviving son,

II. SIR ROWLAND ALSTON, who wedded Temperance, second daughter of Thomas, second Lord Crew, of Stene, by whom (who outlived him, and *m.* secondly, Sir John Wolstonholme, knt. of Forty Hill, in Enfield, Middlesex) he had issue,

THOMAS, his successor.
ROWLAND, heir to his brother.
Vere-John, in holy orders, rector of Odell, died in 1763, aged seventy-seven, having had, by Sarah his wife, who predeceased him, an only daughter,
TEMPERANCE, who *m.* the Rev. Arthur Bedford, vicar of Sharnbrook and Poddington, in Bedfordshire, and dying *vitâ patris*, in 1742, aged twenty-six, left two daughters, viz.
1. TEMPERANCE, who *m.* the Rev. Daniel Shipton, of Husborn Crawley, Bedfordshire, rector of Wavendon, Bucks, and had an only daughter and heiress,
CHARLOTTE SHIPTON, *m.* in 1807, Robert-Charles Orlebar, esq. and has six sons and three daughters.
2. Ann, *m.* to John Kent, esq. of Wavendon, and had a son, John Kent.
Mary, *m.* to Mr. Serjeant James Selby, of Wavendon, and was mother of Thomas-James Selby, esq. of Wavendon and Whaddon Hall, who died *s. p.*
Elizabeth, *m.* first, to General Stuart, and, secondly, to Mr. Rowe.
Anne, *m.* to Richard Mead, M. D. of Harrold, in Bedfordshire, and *d. s. p.*

Sir Rowland *d.* in 1698, and was *s.* by his eldest son,

III. SIR THOMAS ALSTON, who *d.* unm. in 1714, and was *s.* by his brother,

---

* This eminent person *m.* Susan, daughter of Christopher Hudson, esq. of Norwich, and had two daughters,
MARY, *m.* to Sir John Langham, second baronet of Cottesbroke, in Northamptonshire, and had an only child,
MARY LANGHAM, who wedded Henry Booth, Earl of Warrington. (See BURKE's *Extinct Peerage*).
SARAH, *m.* first, to George, eldest son of Sir Harbottle Grimstone, bart.; secondly, to John, fourth Duke of Somerset; and, thirdly, to Henry Lord Colerain, and died issueless.

IV. Sir Rowland Alston, M.P. for the county of Bedford in three parliaments. This gentleman wedded Elizabeth, only daughter of Capt. Thomas Raynes, and had two sons and two daughters, viz.

Thomas, his heir.

Rowland, successor to his brother.

Elizabeth, *d.* unmarried 5th May, 1756.

Anne, *m.* to the Rev. Robert Pye, rector of Odell, and had a daughter Anna, *m.* to — Fitzherbert, esq. but *d. s. p.*

The baronet *d.* 2nd January, 1759, and was *s.* by his son,

V. Sir Thomas Alston, M.P. for the county of Bedford, who *m.* Catherine Davis, daughter and heir of Doctor Bovey.

He *d.* 18th July, 1774, and was *s.* by his brother,

VI. Sir Rowland Alston. This gentleman *m.* Gertrude, sister of Stillingfleet Durnford, esq. of the Tower, but dying *s. p.* 29th June, 1790, aged sixty-four, the title became extinct. The family property, by the will of Sir Thomas Alston, his predecessor, devolved on Thomas Alston, that gentleman's illegitimate son. His widow survived until March, 1807.

Arms—Az. ten etoiles or, four, three, two, and one.

ALSTON, OF CHELSEA.

Created 20th Jan. 1681.—Extinct in 1783.

Lineage.

This was a branch of the family of Alston, baronets of Odell, in Bedfordshire, springing from

Thomas Alston, esq. of Edwardston, in Suffolk, second son of Edward Alston, of Sayham Hall, in the same county. This Thomas left by his first wife, Dorothy, daughter and coheir of — Holmsted, esq. of Mapleted, in Essex, an only son,

Edward Alston, esq. of Edwardston, who *m.* Margaret, daughter and heir of Arthur Penning, esq. of Kettleborough, in Suffolk, and had issue,

Edward, (Sir) of London, an eminent physician, and President of the College of Physicians, who *m.* Susan, daughter of Christopher Hudson, esq. of Norwich, and had two daughters, his coheirs, namely,

Mary, *m.* to Sir John Langham, (second) baronet of Cottesbroke, in Northamptonshire, and had an only child,

Mary Langham, who wedded Henry Booth, Earl of Warrington (see *Burke's Extinct Peerage*).

Sarah, *m.* first to George, eldest son of Sir Harbottle Grimstone, bart.; secondly, to John, fourth Duke of Somerset; and thirdly, to Henry, Lord Colerain. Her grace died without issue.

Joseph, of whom presently.

Penning, of London.

The second son, and eventual continuator of the male line,

I. Joseph Alston, esq. of Chelsea, was created a baronet 20th January, 1681. He *m.* Mary, daughter and coheir of Mr. Crookenberg, a Dutch merchant, residing at Bergen-op-zoom, with whom he obtained the large fortune at that period of £12,000. He subsequently purchased Bridewell Abbey, in the county of Bucks, and made it the residence of his family. He died in May, 1688, leaving issue,

Joseph, *his successor.*

Edward, *m.* Mary, daughter of Capt. Thompson, and had

Joseph

Isaac, *b.* at Edwardston, and commenced the erection of a new house there, but did not live to complete it. He *m.* Mary, daughter and coheir of Henry Seile, of London, and was *s.* by his son,

Joseph, of Edwardston, who wedded Laurentia, only daughter and heir of the Rev. Charles Trumbull, LL.D. and niece of Sir William Trumbull, knt.* secretary of state to King *William*, and left one son and three daughters, viz.

Joseph.

Margaret, *m.* to — Soame, esq.

Anne, *m.* to the Right Rev. Doctor Hare, Bishop of Chichester.

Charlotte.

Clare, *m.* to John Witterong, esq. eldest son of Sir John Witterong, bart. of Rothampstead, in Hertfordshire.

Mary, *m.* to James Clayton, esq. only son of Sir Thomas Clayton, knt. of La Vache, in the county of Buckingham, but had no issue.

The elder son and heir,

II. Sir Joseph Alston, was seated at Bradwell Abbey, in Bucks. He *m.* Elizabeth, daughter of Maurice Thompson, esq. and sister of John, first Lord Haversham, and had two sons, viz.

Joseph, *his heir.*

Edward, in holy orders, rector of Wivenhoe, *m.* Mrs. Elizabeth Wells, and had a daughter.

He *d.* 14th March, 1688-9, at the age of forty-nine, was buried in the chancel of the church at Bradwell, and *s.* by his elder son,

III. Sir Joseph Alston, who *m.* in 1690, Penelope, daughter and co-heir of Sir Edward Evelyn, bart. of Long Ditton, in Surrey, and had issue,

Joseph, } fourth and fifth baronets.
Evelyn, }

Penelope, *b.* in 1694.

Elizabeth, *b.* in 1701.

Theodosia.

Die Patris, a name given from the circumstance of the lady being born on her father's birth day.

He was buried 29th January, 1715-16, and *s.* by his elder son,

IV. Sir Joseph Alston, who *m.* Lucy, only daughter of Richard Thursby, esq. but dying issueless, was *s.* by his brother,

V. Sir Evelyn Alston, who *m.* in March, 1766, Mrs. May, of Mary la Bonne, but dying issueless in 1783, the Baronetcy became extinct. The manor of Long Ditton, in Surrey, which he had inherited from the Evelyns, Sir Evelyn sold, previously to 1721, to Sir Peter King, afterwards Lord King.

Arms—See preceding article.

---

* William Trumbull, esq. the secretary's son and heir, *m.* the Hon. Mary Blundell, one of the daughters and coheirs of Montagu, Viscount Blundell, in Ireland, and left a daughter,

Mary Trumbull, who wedded Col. the Hon. Martin Sandys, son of Samuel, Baron Sandys, of Ombersley, and had, with two sons, William and Edward, who both died unmarried, an only daughter,

Mary Sandys, who *m.* Arthur, Marquess of Downshire, and was created Baroness Sandys, of Ombersley in 1802, the former barony having become extinct in 1797, when the estates of the family devolved upon her ladyship.

ANDERSON, OF EYWORTH.

CREATED 13th July, 1664.

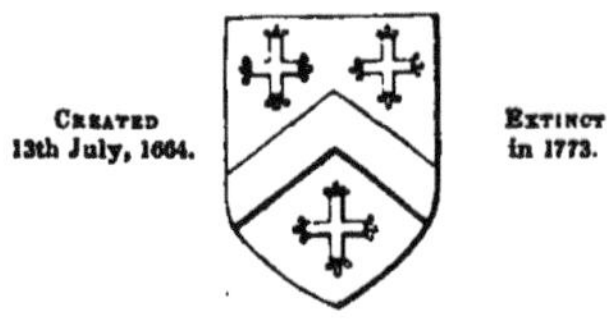

EXTINCT in 1773.

Lineage.

This family, which originally bore the name of L'ISLE, and was seated at Broughton, in the county of Lincoln, is thus spoken of by COLLIER, in his historical dictionary: "Lionel Anderson, esq. lineally descended from the ancient family of the Andersons of Northumberland (as appears by a grant from Clarencieux), afterwards settled in Lincolnshire, from whom this Lionel is in the genealogy the seventeenth. Their first name was (as Sir Richard Anderson, the antiquarian, relates) L'Isle; but marrying an heiress, were obliged to take her name of Anderson. The chief seat of the family is Broughton (now enjoyed by Sir Stephen Anderson, bart.) in Lincolnshire: there are likewise three other branches of it, as, Sir Edmund Anderson, in Hertfordshire, Sir Richard, in Buckinghamshire, and Sir John, of Newcastle." This family intermarried with several of the nobility, and a great many of the principal gentry of several counties; as that of Sheffield, Clinton, *alias* Fines, Sherwood, Butler, Beaumont, Booth, all noble houses, and as for commoners, they are related by marriage to the L'Estranges, Mounsons, Dallisons, Fitzwilliams, Cottons of Huntingdonshire, Constables of Yorkshire, Johnsons of Lancashire, and to several other families of figure and consideration.

Of the family of L'ISLE of Northumberland, was

ROBERT L'ISLE, who flourished in the reigns of HENRY IV. and HENRY V. and who, on marrying the heiress of ANDERSON, took the name in place of his own. He was ancestor of

HENRY ANDERSON, who settled at Wrawbray, in the county of Lincoln, and left an only son,

EDWARD ANDERSON, esq. of Flixborough, in the same county, who had three sons,

Thomas, whose line failed.

Richard, *d.* unm.

EDMUND.

The youngest son,

SIR EDMUND ANDERSON, knt. an eminent lawyer in the *time* of ELIZABETH, was lord chief justice of the Common Pleas from 1582 to 1605. He *m.* Magdalen, daughter of Christopher Smith, esq. of Annables, in Hertfordshire, and had issue,

Edmund, who *m.* Elizabeth, daughter of Thomas Inkpenn, esq. and died before his father, issueless. His widow wedded Sir Robert Bell, knt. of Upwell, in Norfolk.

FRANCIS, heir to his father.

WILLIAM, who *m.* Joan, daughter of Henry Essex, esq. of Lambourne, in Berks, and had an only son,

EDMUND, of Kilnwick Piercy, in the county of Lincoln, created a BARONET in 1660 as SIR EDMUND ANDERSON, of *Broughton*, and is now (1836) represented by the *Rev.* SIR CHARLES-JOHN ANDERSON, bart. of Broughton.

Margaret, *m.* to Sir Thomas Monson, knt. of Burton, in the county of Lincoln, master of the armory, and master falconer to *King* JAMES I. M.P. for Great Grimsby, who was created a BARONET in 1611, by whom she had, with other children,

SIR JOHN MONSON, second baronet, direct ancestor of the LORDS MONSON.

WILLIAM MONSON, who was created by CHARLES I. VISCOUNT CASTLEMAINE, in the peerage of Ireland, but being afterwards a party to the death of his royal master, he was degraded in 1661, and sentenced, with Sir Henry Mildmay and Sir Robert Wallop, to be drawn on a sledge with a rope about his neck, from the Tower to Tyburn and back again, and to be imprisoned in the Tower for life.

Catherine, *m.* to Sir George Booth, knt. of Dunham Massie, in the county of Chester, who was created a BARONET 22nd May, 1611. She was Sir George's second wife, but mother of all his children, the eldest of whom,

SIR GEORGE BOOTH, second baronet, was raised to the peerage 20th April, 1661, as BARON DELAMERE, of *Dunham Massie*. His lordship was one of the twelve members deputed by the House of Commons, in May, 1660, to convey the recall of *King* CHARLES II. to his majesty, and the house voted him, on the 13th July following, the sum of £10,000.

Griseld, *m.* to Sir John Sheffield, knt. son and heir of Edmund, second Baron Sheffield of Butterwike, and Earl of Mulgrave, by whom she was mother of

EDMUND SHEFFIELD, second Earl of Mulgrave.

The chief justice died 1st August, 1605, according to the following extract from the funeral certificate book of WILLIAM CAMDEN, *Clarencieux*: "The right worshippfull, Sir Edmund Andersonne, knight, lord chiefe-justice of the Common Pleas, departed this transitorie lyfe, the 1st August, 1605, in London, whose funeralls were solemnized the fifte of September, at Eyworth, in the countie of Bedford next following; Sir Francys Andersonne, knt. sonne and heyre to the defunct, being chiefe mourner, assisted by Sir Thomas Monson, Sir Stephen Some, Sir George Both, and Sir John Rotherham, knights; the standard borne by Mr. Robert Andersonne, the pennon by Mr. Roger Andersonn, esqs.; healme and crest, borne by Holland, Portcullis, deputie for Mercurye Patten, bluemantle, sword and targe, by Mr. St. George, Norroy, cote-armour, by Mr. Camden, Clarencieux, king of armes of the province." Sir Edmund's lady *d.* 9th January, 1622, and was buried in the church with him. He was *s.* by his elder surviving son,

SIR FRANCIS ANDERSON, who had received the honor of knighthood from *Queen* ELIZABETH. He *m.* first, Judith, daughter of Sir Stephen Soame, knt. lord mayor of London, and by her had two sons,

EDMUND, his heir, of Stratton, in the county of Bedford, *m.* Alice, daughter and sole heir of Sir John Constable, knt.* of Dromby, in Yorkshire, and had an only daughter and heir,

DOROTHY ANDERSON, *m.* to John Cotton, esq. of Conington, in the county of Huntingdon, afterwards Sir John Cotton, bart.

* By his wife, Dorothy, daughter and co-heir (with her sister Alice, wife of the celebrated Sir Francis Bacon, Viscount St. Albans) of Benedict Barnham, esq. an alderman of the city of London.

He died, and was buried at Eyworth; his wife surviving him, became afterwards the second wife of Sir Thomas Cotton, bart. of Conington, father of the above Sir John.

Stephen, of whom presently.

Sir Francis wedded, secondly, Audrey, eldest daughter of Sir John Butler, bart. of Hatfield Woodhall, in the county of Hertford, afterwards, by creation, Lord Butler of Bramfield (see Burke's *Extinct Peerage*), by whom (who survived him, and m. secondly, Francis Leigh, Earl of Chichester,) he had, with two daughters (Frances, who died unm. and —), a son,

John, of St. Ives, in Huntingdonshire, created a baronet 3rd January, 1628.

He d. 22nd December, 1616, and was interred at Eyworth. His second son and eventual heir,

Stephen Anderson, esq. of Eyworth, m. Catherine, daughter of Sir Edwyn Sandys, knt. of Ombersley, in the county of Worcester, and had issue,

Stephen, his heir.

Francis, of Manby, in the county of Lincoln, who m. Mary, daughter of Charles Pelham, esq. of Brocklesby, in the same shire, and sister and eventual heiress of Charles Pelham, esq. and had issue,

Francis, his heir.

Eliza-Maria, m. to Thomas Whichest, esq.

Charlotte, m. to Charles Reynolds, esq. of the Inner Temple.

His son and heir,

Francis Anderson, esq. of Manby, m. 2nd February, 1747, Eleanor, daughter of Thomas Carter, esq. of Bossavern, in the county of Denbigh, and by her (who m. secondly, Robert Vyner, esq. of Gautby, in Lincolnshire) had, with other issue,

Charles, who assumed the surname and arms of Pelham, as heir to his great uncle, Charles Pelham, of Brocklesby, and was raised to the peerage, as Baron Yarborough, 13th August, 1794 (refer to Burke's *Peerage and Baronetage*).

Edmund, d. 6th August, 1724, leaving issue.

Edwin, left two sons,

Edwin.

Henry, of Lincolnshire.

Penelope, m. to Sir William Glynne, bart. of Bisseter, in Oxfordshire.

Mary, d. young.

Catherine, } d. unm.
Elizabeth, }

Judith, m. to John Lister, esq. of Bawtrey, in the county of York.

Frances, d. unm.

He was s. by his eldest son,

i. Stephen Anderson, of Eyworth, in the county of Bedford, and Broughton, in Lincolnshire, who was created a baronet 13th July, 1664. Sir Stephen m. first, Mary, daughter of Sir John Glynne, knt. serjeant at law, and by that lady (who d. 25th February, 1667) had an only daughter,

Anne, m. to Sir Willoughby Hickman, bart. of Gainsborough, in the county of Lincoln.

He wedded, secondly, Judith, daughter of Sir John Lawrence, knt. an alderman of London, and had, with three daughters, Abigail, Penelope, and Catherine, who all died unm. an only son, his successor, at his decease, 9th January, 1707,

ii. Sir Stephen Anderson, who wedded Anne, only daughter of Sir Martin Lumley, bart. of Bradfield,* in Essex, and had issue,

Stephen, his successor.

Edmund, of Magdalen College, Cambridge, d. unm. 9th February, 1766.

Jonathan, d. unm.

Henry, of the Inner Temple, barrister-at-law, died 18th March, 1761, unm.

Anne, m. to the Rev. Doctor Anthony Ellis, rector of St. Olave's, Old Jewry, and prebendary of Gloucester, afterwards Bishop of Gloucester, who died 18th January, 1761. They had one daughter,

Elizabeth-Frances Ellis.

Judith, d. unm. 29th January, 1740-1.

Elizabeth, d. unm.

Mary, m. to Justinian Isham, esq. grandson of Sir Justinian Isham, bart. of Lamport, in Northamptonshire, and became a widow 28th March, 1742.

Frances, m. to Edward Radcliffe, esq. of Devonshire Square, London, a Turkey merchant, grandson of Sir Ralph Radcliffe, knt. of Hitchen, in Hertfordshire, and d. s. p.

He died 21st October, 1740, was buried at Eyworth, and s. by his eldest son,

iii. Sir Stephen Anderson, who wedded Elizabeth, only daughter of Miles Barne, esq. of London, merchant, and had a son, Stephen, who died young. Dying himself in 1773, the title became extinct. The estate of Eyworth reverted to the Andersons of Manby, whose representative is Lord Yarborough; and Broughton passed to Mr. Anderson Stephens.

Arms—Arg. a chev. between three crosses flory sa.

ANDERSON, OF ST. IVES.

Conferred 3rd Jan. 1628.—Extinct in 1630.

Lineage.

Sir Francis Anderson, knt. of Eyworth, eldest surviving son and heir of the lord chief justice Sir Edmund Anderson, married, for his second wife, Audrey, eldest daughter of Sir John Butler, bart. of Hatfield Woodhall, in the county of Hertford, subsequently, by creation, Lord Butler of Bramfield, by whom he had, with two daughters, an only son,

John Anderson, esq. of St. Ives, in Huntingdonshire, who was created a Baronet 3rd January, 1628, but dying without issue in 1630, the title became extinct.

Arms—As Anderson, of Eyworth.

ANDERSON, OF PENLEY.

Created 3rd July, 1643.—Extinct 16th Aug. 1699.

Lineage.

Sir Henry Anderson, knt. alderman of London, and sheriff in 1602, married Elizabeth, daughter of Sir William Bowyer, knt. and had issue,

Richard, his heir.

Catherine, m. to Sir John Dereham, knt.

Elizabeth, m. to Thomas Cowley, esq. of London, and d. s. p.

Frances, m. to Robert Needham, esq. of Sherington, Salop.

Sarah, m. to Sir Charles Wilmot, afterwards Viscount Athlone.

Mary, m. to Sir John Spencer, bart. of Offley.

* By his first wife, Elizabeth, daughter of Sir Jonathan Dawes, knt. alderman of London.

Sir Henry *d.* in 1695, and was *s.* by his son,

Sir Richard Anderson, who *m.* Mary, daughter of Robert, Lord Spencer of Wormleighton, and dying in 1653, was *s.* by his son,

I. Henry Anderson, esq. of Penley, in the county of Hertford, who was created a baronet by *King* Charles I. on the 3rd July, 1643. Sir Henry *m.* first, Jacomina, daughter of Sir Charles Cæsar, knt. of Benington, Herts; and, secondly, Mary, daughter of Sir William Lytton, knt. He *d.* aged forty-five, 7th July, 1658, was buried at Tring, and *s.* by his son,

II. Sir Richard Anderson, who *m.* first, Elizabeth, daughter of Sir Thomas Hewit, bart. of Pishiobury, in Hertfordshire, and sister and co-heir of George, Viscount Hewit, of the kingdom of Ireland, by whom he had issue,

- Richard, who *m.* Elizabeth, daughter of Richard Spencer, esq. of Derbyshire, but died *s. p.* in the lifetime of his father; his widow became the second wife of the Lord Chancellor (Simon first Viscount) Harcourt.
- Elizabeth, *m.* to Simon Harcourt, esq. clerk of the crown, eldest son of Vere Harcourt, D. D. archdeacon of Nottingham, and prebendary of Lincoln, by whom she had (with three daughters, who all *d.* unm.),
  1. Henry Harcourt, who *s.* his father 30th March, 1724, and became "of Penley;" he *m.* Frances, only daughter and heir of Nathaniel Bard, esq.* and had
     - Richard-Bard, his heir.
     - John, who *d.* 14th August, 1748.
     - Henry, rector of Warbleton and Crowhurst, in Sussex.
     - Elizabeth.
     - Ernestina.
     - Louisa.
     - Melusina.
     - Anne.
     - Persiana.

     Henry Harcourt *d.* 9th November, 1741, and was *s.* by his eldest son,

     Richard-Bard Harcourt, of Penley, who *m.* Rachel, daughter of Albert Nesbit, esq. and had a son,

     Henry Harcourt.
  2. Richard Harcourt, *m.* first, Elizabeth, daughter of Sir Richard Harcourt, knt. and had two children, viz.
     - Richard Harcourt, of Wigsel, in Sussex, who *m.* Phœby, daughter of Sir Charles Palmer, bart. of Dorney Court, Bucks, and had two daughters,
       - Phœby, *m.* to Anthony Sawyer, esq.
       - Elizabeth.
     - Anne Harcourt, *m.* to Sir Charles Palmer, bart. of Dorney Court.

     He wedded, secondly, a daughter of — Banister, esq. and by her had two other daughters, Elizabeth and Jane.
  3. Simon Harcourt.

Sir Richard Anderson wedded, secondly, Mary, elder daughter of the Right Hon. John Methuen, Lord Chancellor of Ireland, *temp. King* William and *Queen* Anne. She was widow of Humphrey Simpson, esq. and outliving Sir Richard, without issue by him, she *m.* thirdly, Sir Brownlow Sherrard, bart. Sir Richard *d.* 16th August, 1699, when the estate of Penley devolved upon his only surviving daughter, Elizabeth, who conveyed it to her husband, Simon Harcourt, and the title appears to have become extinct, although upon the death of Sir Richard it was assumed by the Andersons of East Meon, in the county of Hants.

Arms—As Anderson, of Eyworth.

ANDERSON, OF MILL HILL.

Created 14th May, 1798. Extinct 21st May, 1813.

Lineage.

William Anderson, esq. of Dantsic, merchant, born in Scotland, married Lucy, daughter of Sheldon, and had issue,

- Andrew, of Dantzic, who died in 1772, without issue.
- John-William, of whom presently.
- Anne, died unm.
- Elizabeth, *m.* to Lieutenant Colonel Gunther, of Dantsic.
- Lucy, *m.* to Andrew Scott, merchant, of Dantzic.
- Louisa, *m.* to John Simpson, merchant, of Berlin, and had a son, George.

Mr. Anderson died about the year 1749. His second son,

I. John-William Anderson, esq. of Mill Hill, in Middlesex, born at Dantzic in 1735-6, filled the civic chair of the city of London in 1796, and was created a baronet 14th May, 1798. He married, in 1762, Dorothy, daughter and co-heiress of Charles Simkins, esq. of Devizes, but dying without issue, in 1813, the honour became extinct.

Arms—Az. on a saltire erm. between three mullets, and in base a crescent arg. an antique key, or, and a sword ppr. hilted gold, in saltire, transfixed through the collar of the city chain.

ANDERTON, OF LOSTOCK.

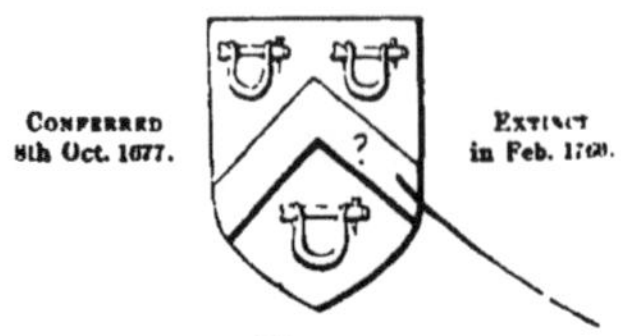

Conferred 8th Oct. 1677. Extinct in Feb. 1760.

Lineage.

From a third son of the Andertons, of Anderton,† descended

Lawrence Anderton, esq. who was seated at Lostock, and was father of

Christopher Anderton, esq. of Lostock, who *m.*

---

* By his wife, Persina, daughter and sole heir of Henry Bard, Viscount Belmont, in the peerage of Ireland.

† From a second son of the same family descend the Andertons, of Euxton, in Lancashire, now represented by William Ince Anderton, esq. (See Burke's *History of the Commoners.*)

Dorothy, daughter of Peter Anderton, esq. of Anderton, and had (with five daughters, of whom Elizabeth married Thomas Tildesley, and Ann, Roger Bradshaw, of Haigh) three sons, viz.

- I. James, who went abroad, and entered into orders of the church of Rome. He was a learned writer and eloquent preacher.
- II. Christopher, successor to his father.
- III. Roger, of Birchley, a recusant, who m. Ann, daughter of Edward Stafford, esq. and died in 1640.

Christopher Anderton died in 1593, and was s. by his son,

Christopher Anderton, esq. of Lostock, who m. Ann, daughter of W. Scarisbrick, esq. of Scarisbrick, and had one son and two daughters, viz.

- Christopher, his heir.
- Dorothy, m. to Anthony Munson, esq. of Carleton, in Lincolnshire.
- Margaret, m. to Henry Turvile, esq. of Aston Flamvile, but had no issue.

The son and successor,

Christopher Anderton, esq. of Lostock, succeeded his father in 1623. He m. first, a daughter of John Preston, esq. of the Manor in Furness, by whom he had an only child, Margaret, who died unmarried; and, secondly, Alathea, daughter of Sir Francis Smith, of Wolston Waven, in Warwickshire, by whom he had, with several other children,

- Francis (Sir), his heir.
- Mary, m. to William Jones, esq. of Trevon, in Monmouthshire.
- Ann, m. to John Tuberville, esq. of Penclin Castle, Glamorganshire.

He died about the year 1650, and was s. by his son,

I. Sir Francis Anderton, of Lostock, who was created a Baronet by Charles II. He m. Elizabeth, daughter of Sir Charles Somerset, second son of Edward, Earl of Worcester, lord privy seal, and dying at Paris 9th February, 1678, was interred in the church of the English Benedictine Monks, where an inscription is engraven to his memory. Sir Francis was s. by his eldest son,

II. Sir Charles Anderton, of Lostock, who m. a daughter of Ireland, of Lidiate, in Lancashire, and had four sons, successive baronets. The eldest,

III. Sir Charles Anderton, of Lostock, died young, as did his next brother,

IV. Sir James Anderton, of Lostock, to whom succeeded his brother,

V. Sir Lawrence Anderton, of Lostock, a monk, who died in London s. p. 30th September, 1724, and the title devolved on his brother,

VI. Sir Francis Anderton, of Lostock, who m. Margaret, daughter of Sir Henry Bedingfeld, bart. of Oxburgh, but by that lady he left no issue. Sir Francis had his estate sequestered for his participation in the rebellion at Preston, and dying issueless in 1760, the Baronetcy became extinct.

Arms—Sa. three shackbolts arg.

ANDRÉ, OF SOUTHAMPTON.

Created 4th March, 1781.—Extinct 11th Nov. 1802.

Lineage.

Major John André, (descended from a French refugee family, settled at Southampton, in the county of Hants,) adopted the military profession, and was appointed adjutant-general of the British army in America, under Sir Henry Clinton. There he became highly distinguished, and gave promise of one day taking a leading place among the military heroes of his country, but the hopes which the brightness of his early and brief career held out were destined to prove delusive. The gallant soldier—the idol of his comrades, the admiration of his superiors—fell a victim to one of those acts for which the excitement of war was the only and feeble excuse. In Sept. 1780, he was intrusted with the management of the negotiation with General Arnold, previously to that officer's joining the royal army; and being taken, within the American lines, in disguise, his case was referred by General Washington to a board of officers, who adjudged him to be a spy, and he suffered death on the 2nd October following. The melancholy event excited general grief on its announcement in England, and the exquisite lines of a poetic friend of the deceased, the gifted Miss Seward, consecrated the memory of the ill-fated soldier in a mournful and beautiful eulogium. Major André died unmarried, but in honour of his memory, *King* George III. conferred the dignity of a baronet upon his brother,

I. Sir William-Lewis André, at whose decease without issue, 11th November, 1802, the title became extinct.

ANDREWS, OF DODDINGTON, OR DENTON.

Created 11th Dec. 1641.

Extinct in 1804.

Lineage.

I. Sir William Andrews, of Denton, lineal descendant of Thomas Andrews, esq. a younger son of the family of Andrews, of Winwick, in Northamptonshire, who acquired by marriage the estate of Denton, was created a Baronet in 1641. He m. the daughter of Mr. Paris, of Linton, in the county of Cambridge, and had five sons, three of whom fell at the battle of Worcester, fighting under the royal banner. Sir William was buried at St. Edmund's Bury, and succeeded by his son,

II. Sir John Andrews, of Denton, who left at his decease an only daughter, who died unmarried. He was succeeded by his brother,

III. Sir William Andrews, of Denton, who wedded Helen, daughter and heir of Edward Attslow, esq. of Downham Hall, Essex, and had, with several other children,

- Francis, his heir.
- Catherine, m. to Joseph Petre, esq. of Fidlers, in Essex, and had a son,
  - John Petre, esq. of Fidlers, whose daughter and eventual heir, Mary, m. Francis Canning, esq. of Foxcote, in Warwickshire.

Sir William died 15th August, 1684, and was buried in the chancel at Downham. His son and successor,

IV. Sir Francis Andrews, of Denton, having obtained an act of parliament for the purpose in 1698, sold the estate of Downham, which he inherited from his materual ancestors, to Francis Platt, esq. of the Victualling Office, from whose sisters and co heirs it was purchased by Osmond Beauvoir, esq. of Balms. Sir Francis m. Bridget, only daughter of Sir Thomas Clifton, bart. of Lytham, in Lancashire, by Bridget, his second wife, daughter of Sir Edward Hussey, knt. of Hunnington, in the county of Lincoln, and left at his decease, which occurred at Chelsea, 3rd April, 1759, with two daughters, Bridget and Eleanor, an only son,

v. Sir William Andrews, of Denton, at whose demise in 1804, the title became extinct.

Arms—Gu. a saltire or, surmounted of another vert.

ANDREWS, OF LATHBURY.

Created 27th May, 1661.  Extinct in Aug. 1696.

Lineage.

i. Sir Henry Andrews, of Lathbury, in Buckinghamshire, was created a Baronet in 1661, but leaving no issue by either of his wives; the first, a daughter of the Kentish family of Browne, the second, Elizabeth, relict of John Drew, esq. of Devises: the title expired with him in 1696. The manor of Lathbury, purchased by his ancestor about the year 1599, was eventually disposed of by the baronet's representatives to the mother of Mrs. Jane Symes, who bequeathed it to Mansel Dawkins Mansel, esq. and Mrs. Margaret Dalway, in equal portions. The old mansion house of Lathbury, on the site of which the present has been built, was erected in the reign of James I. by Sir William Andrewes, knt.

Arms—Arg. on a bend cottised sa. three mullets of the field.

ANDREWS, OF SHAW PLACE.

Created 19th Aug. 1766.  Extinct in 1822.

Lineage.

Henry Andrewes removed, early in the seventeenth century, from Canterbury to London, where he died in 1665, a victim to the fatal pestilence which then raged there, and which cut off his whole household, with the exception of an infant son,

Henry Andrewes, who acquired some fortune by commercial pursuits, and had a grant of arms in 1720. His son,

Daniel Andrews, survived but for a brief period. He was father of

Joseph Andrews, esq. appointed paymaster to the forces serving in Scotland in 1718, who m. in 1725, Elizabeth, daughter of Samuel Beard, esq. of Newcastle-under-Lyne, and had by her a son,

Joseph, of whom presently.

He wedded, secondly, in 1736, Elizabeth, daughter of John Pettit, esq. of St. Botolph, Aldgate, by whom he had

James-Pettit, police magistrate at Queen Square, distinguished in the literary world as author of several admired publications; amongst others, of "Anecdotes, ancient and modern, with observations," and of "A History of Great Britain, connected with the Chronology of Europe, containing anecdotes of the Times, Lives of the Learned, with specimens of their Works, on the plan of the President Henault," &c. Mr. James Pettit Andrews m. Anne, daughter of the Rev. Mr. Penrose, rector of Newbury, and by her, who d. 1st September, 1785, had issue,

Joseph, who succeeded his uncle as second baronet.

Charles-Grey, R. N. d. in 1791, unm.

Elizabeth-Anne, m. to Charles Henry Hunt, esq. of Goldreoth, in Worcestershire.

Mr. Andrews, who purchased in 1700, from the representatives of the Duke of Chandos, the manor of Shaw, in Berks, d. in April 1753, aged sixty-two, and was s. by his son,

i. Joseph Andrews, esq. of Shaw, major of the Berkshire Militia, who was created a Baronet in 1766, with remainder to his half brother and his issue male. He m. in 1762, Elizabeth, daughter of Richard Phillips, esq. of Tarrington, in Herts, but dying issueless, 29th December, 1800, was s. by his nephew,

ii. Sir Joseph Andrews, of the Foot Guards, b. 22nd September, 1768, at whose decease s. p. in 1822, the title became extinct.

Arms—Gu. a saltire arg. surmounted by another az. charged in the centre with a bezant.

APPLETON, OF SOUTH BEMFLEET.

Created 29th June, 1611.  Extinct in 1709-10.

Lineage.

The Apyltons or Appletons, as the name was afterwards spelt, are supposed to be descended from a family long seated at Wadingfield Magna, in Norfolk. In the time of Henry VII.

Thomas Appleton, of the county of Suffolk, married Joice, daughter of Sir Robert Tyrrill, of Herons, in Essex, and thus acquired the estate of South Bemfled, in that shire. He was succeeded by his son,

Sir Roger Appleton, of Bemflet, who held at the period of his decease 26th February, 1557, considerable lands of the queen, of the dean and chapter of Westminster, and of the Earl of Sussex. He m. Anne, daughter of John Sulyard, esq. and had issue,

Henry, his heir.

Jane, m. first, to Sir John Wentworth, of North Elmsal, and, secondly, to Sir Thomas Gargrave, of Nostal. By her first husband she had three sons and as many daughters, viz.

- Thomas Wentworth, of Howley and Ashby, *m.* Elizabeth, daughter of Sir C. Danby, of Thorpe, and had several children. The eldest daughter, Elizabeth, *m.* William Ellerker, of Ellerker.
- Christopher Wentworth, of Sheffield; will dated 25th November, 1561.
- Hector Wentworth, living in 1561 and 1570.
- Elizabeth Wentworth, *m.* to Francis Haldenby, of Haldenby.
- Frances Wentworth, *m.* to Thomas Wombwell.
- Bridget Wentworth, *m.* to Nicholas Hague.

By her second husband she had no issue.

Sir Roger's son and successor,

HENRY APPLETON, esq. of Bemflet, married Margaret, daughter of John Roper, esq. of Eltham, attorney-general to HENRY VIII. by Jane, his wife, daughter of Sir John Pineaux, chief justice of England, and left, with a daughter, Margaret, the wife of John Bemflet, a son,

ROGER APPLETON, esq. of Bemflet, afterwards knighted, who wedded Agnes, sister and heir of Walter Clarke, esq. of Hadley, in Suffolk, and had

- I. HENRY, his heir.
- II. William, of Kettlebaston, in Suffolk, ancestor of the family settled at that place.
- III. Roger.
- IV. John.
- V. Edward.

- I. Mary, *m.* to Richard Ward.
- II. Alice, *m.* to Henry Barney.
- III. Anne.
- IV. Agnes.
- V. Margaret, *m.* to Peter Loone.

Roger Appleton died 27th February, 4 PHILIP and MARY, and was *s.* by his eldest son,

HENRY APPLETON, esq. who held the manor of South Bemfleet, with all its services and appurtenances, and a capital messuage or mansion-house, called Northmayes or Jarvis Hill, besides other estates. He *m.* Faith, daughter of William Cardinal, gent. of Great Bromley, in Essex, and had two sons, Roger and Edward, and a daughter, Edith. He *d.* 2nd Nov. 4 JAMES I. and was *s.* by his son,

I. SIR ROGER APPLETON, knt. of South Bemfleet, who was created a BARONET in 1611. He wedded Anne, daughter of Sir Thomas Mildmay, knt. of Moulsham, in Essex, and by her (who married, secondly, John Paschall, of Badow,) left at his decease, 16th January, 1614 (with two daughters, Frances, the wife of Francis Goldsmith, of Dartford, and Mary, of Thomas Henley, esq.) a son, his successor,

II. SIR HENRY APPLETON, bart. of South Bemfleet, who *m.* Joan, daughter of Edward Sheldon, esq. of Beoley, by Elizabeth, his wife, daughter of Thomas Markham, esq. of Ollerton, Notts, standard-bearer to the band of gentlemen pensioners, *temp.* ELIZABETH, and left a son and successor,

III. SIR HENRY APPLETON, of South Bemfleet, who *m.* first, Sarah, daughter of Sir Thomas Oldfield, of Spalding, in Lincolnshire, and, secondly, Mary, relict of Sir Thomas Wiseman, bart. of Rivenhall, Essex. He *d.* about the year 1670, and was succeeded by his son (by the first marriage),

IV. SIR HENRY APPLETON, of South Bemfleet, who *m.* Mary, daughter of John Rivet, merchant of London, but dying without male issue about 1680, the baronetcy devolved on his uncle (the son of the second baronet),

V. SIR WILLIAM APPLETON, of South Bemfleet, who *m.* Dorothy, daughter of Mr. Hatt, a solicitor in London, and by her, who died 16th December, 1710, aged eighty-four, had issue,

- William, who predeceased his father 28th April, 1685, aged twenty-eight.
- HENRY, heir.
- John, who *d. v. p.* 25th July, 1689, in his nineteenth year.
- ELIZABETH, *m.* to Richard Vaughan, esq. of Shenfeild Place, Essex.

Sir William *d.* 15th November, 1705, aged seventy-seven, and was *s.* by his only surviving son,

VI. SIR HENRY APPLETON, of South Bemfleet, who died *s. p.* in 1709-10, when the title became EXTINCT, but the large estates of the family passed to Sir Henry's sister, ELIZABETH, the wife of RICHARD VAUGHAN, esq.

Arms—Arg. a fess engrailed (originally plain) sa. between three apples leafed and slipped ppr. The Norfolk family bore three apples gu. the leaves and stalks vert; and the Appletons of the West of England, "Or, a fess between three apples vert."

ARMYTAGE, OF KIRKLEES.

CREATED 15th Dec. 1641.	EXTINCT 12th Oct. 1737.

Lineage.

The family of ARMYTAGE, of which there is still an existing branch enjoying the rank of baronet, is of considerable antiquity, being descended, according to a pedigree, attested by Sir Henry St. George, Norroy King of Arms, 2nd February, 1637, from

JOHN ARMYTAGE, of Wrigbowls, living in the 10th of *King* STEPHEN, which seat and his coat armour he is said to have had conferred upon him by Roger Omfynes, steward to Remigius, Bishop of Dorchester, and founder of Elsam Abbey, in Lincolnshire. Sixth in descent from this John was

WILLIAM ARMYTAGE, father of

JOHN ARMYTAGE, whose son and heir,

WILLIAM ARMYTAGE, living in the time of EDWARD VI. was of Kirklees, in the West Riding of the county of York. He *m.* Catherine, daughter of Henry Beaumont, esq. of Crossland, and left a son and heir,

JOHN ARMYTAGE, of Kirklees, who wedded Elizabeth, daughter of John Kaye, esq. of Lockwood, and was *s.* by his son,

JOHN ARMYTAGE, esq. in the commission of the peace for the West Riding, and treasurer in the 41st and 42nd of ELIZABETH, with Sir Robert Swift, for lame soldiers. This gentleman *m.* first, Jane, daughter of Mr. George Gregory, of Kingston-upon-Hull; and, secondly, Margery, daughter of Richard Beaumont, esq. By the former he had three sons and a daughter, viz.

- I. JOHN, his heir.
- II. Gregory, of Netherton, in Yorkshire, living in 1650, *m.* Elizabeth, daughter and co-heir of John Savile, esq. of Netherton, and left, with a daughter, Elizabeth, *m.* to Sir Thomas Beaumont, knt. of Whitley, an only son,
  - WILLIAM, of Netherton, who *m.* in 1631, Grace, daughter of Robert Rockley, esq. of Rock-

ley, and by her (who wedded, secondly, Thomas Metcalfe, esq.) left at his decease, in 1652, with other issue, a son and successor,

ROBERT, of Netherton, m. in 1660, Anne, daughter of Francis Stringer, esq. of Whiston, and was father of

JOHN, of Netherton, whose only daughter and heir, ELIZABETH, m. first, Sir William Thornton, knt. of Cottle; and, secondly, John Perkins, esq. of Fishlake.

III. EDWARD, of Kerresforth-hill, in the county of York, m. first, Elizabeth, daughter and heiress of Edward Hanson, esq. of Little Royd; and, secondly, Jane, daughter of John Popeley, of Moorehouse. By the former he was father of

JOHN, of Kerresforth-hill, b. in 1610, whose fifth son,

GEORGE, b. in 1661, was father of

SAMUEL, of Barnsley, who eventually succeeded to the Kirklees estates upon the demise of Sir John in 1732, and was created a BARONET. His great grandson is the present SIR JOHN ARMYTAGE, bart. of Kirklees.

I. Anne, m. to Sir Hugh Worrall, knt. of Loversall, in Yorkshire.

He was s. by his eldest son,

JOHN ARMYTAGE, esq. of Kirklees, sheriff of Yorkshire in the 13th of JAMES I. He m. Winifred, daughter of Henry Knight, esq. of Knighthill, and had surviving issue,

JOHN, his heir.

FRANCIS, successor to his brother.

Elizabeth, m. to Sir John Savile, knt. of Lupset, near Wakefield.

He was s. at his decease by his elder son,

JOHN ARMYTAGE, esq. who m. Dorothy, daughter of Cyrill Arthington, esq. of Arthington, but dying without issue, in 1624, was s. by his brother,

I. FRANCIS ARMYTAGE, esq. of Kirklees, who was created a BARONET by *King* CHARLES I. 15th December, 1641. Sir Francis m. Catharine, daughter of Christopher Danby, esq. of Farnley, near Leeds, and had three sons and five daughters, viz.

JOHN, his heir.

Francis, who m. Mary, daughter of Robert Trappe, esq. of Nidd, near Knaresborough, and had an only surviving son,

THOMAS, who succeeded as sixth baronet.

William, of Killinghall, living in 1660, m. Catherine Trapps, sister of his brother Francis's wife.

Catherine, d. unm.

Anne, m. to Mr. Smith, of London.

Prudence, Elizabeth, } d. unm.

Winifred, m. to Thomas Lacy, esq.

Sir Francis d. in 1646, and was s. by his eldest son,

II. SIR JOHN ARMYTAGE, of Kirklees, justice of the peace, deputy lieutenant and captain of a troop of Volunteer Horse. This gentleman m. Margaret, second daughter of Thomas Thornhill, esq. of Fixby, and had issue,

THOMAS, his successor.

JOHN, heir to his brother.

Michael, Francis, William, } d. unm.

Christopher, of Hartshead Hall, b. in 1658; m. Rebecca, daughter of Thomas Moore, esq. of Austrope, and had a son,

John, of Hartshead, who d. s. p. in 1732.

GEORGE, who succeeded his brother JOHN.

Charles, d. unm.

Margaret, m. to Francis Nevile, esq. of Chevet, and had issue.

Catharine, m. to Christopher Tancred, esq. of Westley, in the county of York, and had issue.

The baronet was s. by his eldest son,

III. SIR THOMAS ARMYTAGE, of Kirklees, b. in 1652, who d. s. p. in 1693, and was s. by his next brother,

IV. SIR JOHN ARMYTAGE, of Kirklees, who died a bachelor, at an advanced age, 11th December, 1732, and was s. by his only surviving brother,

V. SIR GEORGE ARMYTAGE, of Kirklees. This gentleman dying like his brothers unmarried, the BARONETCY devolved on his cousin,

VI. SIR THOMAS ARMYTAGE, of Kirklees, at whose decease unm. in 1737, the title became *Extinct*, while the estates passed under the will of Sir John, the fourth baronet, to his cousin (refer to EDWARD ARMYTAGE, of Kerresforth-hill, third son of JOHN ARMYTAGE, of Kirklees, treasurer for lame soldiers *temp.* ELIZABETH, and his wife Margery Beaumont)

SAMUEL ARMYTAGE, who then became "of Kirklees." He was grandfather of

SIR GEORGE ARMYTAGE, who m. first, Mary, eldest daughter of Sir Harbord Harbord, bart. by whom he had several children, all of whom d. unmar. He m. secondly, Mary, daughter of O. Bowles, esq. and left, *inter alios*, a son and successor, the present

SIR JOHN ARMYTAGE, bart. of Kirklees.

Arms—Gu. a lion's head erased between three cross crosslets arg.

ASGILL, OF LONDON.

CREATED 16th April, 1761.—EXTINCT in 1823.

Lineage.

CHARLES ASGILL, esq. an eminent merchant of London, was father of

I. SIR CHARLES ASGILL, knt. who was also bred to trade, and amassed a considerable fortune by commercial pursuits. He was an alderman of the city of London, served the office of sheriff in 1752, when he received the honour of knighthood, and filled the civic chair in 1757. Sir Charles was created a BARONET by *King* GEORGE III. 16th April, 1761. He m. first, a daughter of Henry Vanderstegen, a merchant in London, which lady d. 6th February, 1754, s. p. He wedded, secondly, Miss Pratviel, daughter of Daniel Pratviel, esq. secretary to Sir Benjamin Harris, ambassador at the court of Madrid, and had

CHARLES, his successor.

A daughter, m. to Robert Colville, esq. of Hemmington Hall, Suffolk.

A daughter, m. to Richard Legge, esq.

Sir Charles d. in 1778, and was s. by his son,

II. SIR CHARLES ASGILL, a general officer in the army, and colonel of the 11th regiment of foot, who m. Jemima Sophia, daughter of Admiral Sir Charles Ogle, but died issueless in 1823, when the BARONETCY became EXTINCT.

Sir Charles entered the service on the 27th of February, 1778, as an ensign in the 1st foot guards, and obtained a lieutenancy, with the rank of captain, in that regiment, on the 3rd of February, 1781. He went to America in the same year, joined the army under the command of the Marquis Cornwallis, served the whole of the campaigns, was taken prisoner with the army in October, at the siege of York Town, in Virginia, and sent up the country, where he remained till May, 1782, at which period all the captains of the army were ordered by General Washington to assemble and draw lots, that one might be selected to suffer death, by way of retaliation for the death of an American officer, Captain Hardy, whom our government refused to deliver up, for political reasons, although General Washington demanded it. The lot fell on Sir Charles Asgill, and he was, in consequence, conveyed under a strong escort, to the place intended for his execution, in the Jerseys, where he remained in prison enduring peculiar hardships for the space of six months, expecting daily that his execution would take place. Sir Charles was unexpectedly released from his confinement by an act of Congress passed at the intercession of the Queen of France, who, deeply affected by a most eloquent and pathetic appeal from his mother Lady Asgill, humanely interfered and obtained his release. He returned to England on parole, and shortly after went to Paris to make his acknowledgments to the Queen of France.

ASHBY, OF HAREFIELD.

CREATED 18th June, 1622.

EXTINCT 23rd Dec. 1623.

Lineage.

SIR ROBERT ASHBY, knt. of Breakspears, in Harefield, Middlesex, great-great great grandson of George Ashby, of Breakspears, clerk of the signet to Margaret of Anjou, Queen of HENRY VI. *m.* Dorothy, youngest daughter of Francis Haydon, esq. of the Grove, Watford, Herts, and had issue,

FRANCIS, his heir.

Edward, bapt. 17th Nov. 1596, died in 1642, leaving issue.

Robert of Breakspears, after the death of his brother, Sir Francis, bapt. 11th April, 1598, died in 1674-5, leaving with other issue, a son and heir,

FRANCIS, of Breakspears, bapt. at Harefield, 19th Nov. 1660, *m.* Judith, only daughter of Mr. William Turner, of Ickenham, Middlesex, and dying 10th April, 1743, left issue,

WILLIAM, of Breakspears, who *m.* first, Anne, daughter of John Aleyn, esq. and secondly, Anne, daughter of Whitlock Bulstrode, esq. of Hounslow. By the former he had three children, who died infants, and by the latter, he left, at his decease 18th April, 1769, three daughters, of whom the youngest, Charlotte, *m.* the Rev. William Williams, M.A.

ROBERT, of Breakspears, bapt. 30th Nov. 1690, *m.* Mary, sister of Rear Admiral Peter Tom, and died 2nd June, 1769, leaving an only daughter and heir,

ELIZABETH, who *m.* in 1770, Joseph Partridge, esq. of St. James's, and died in 1817, leaving with a daughter, Elizabeth, a son,

JOSEPH ASHBY PARTRIDGE, esq. of Breakspears, Middlesex, and of Cranfield, Bucks.

Judith, died unm.

Sarah, *m.* in 1711, to Edward Blackstone, citizen of London, and had a son, John Blackstone, of Fleet Street, whose only child, Sophia, *m.* in 1780, Hector Davies, esq. and was mother of the Rev. Hector Davies Morgan, A.M. of Castle Hedingham, Essex.

William, Ferdinando, } who both had issue.

Sir Robert died in 1617-18, and was *s.* by his eldest son,

I. SIR FRANCIS ASHBY, knt. of Breakspears, who was created a BARONET 18th June, 1622. By Joane, his wife, who was buried at Harefield, 17th March, 1634-5, he had an only daughter,

ALICE, bapt. at Harefield, 8th Nov. 1620, *m.* to Alexander Lynde, esq. of Rickmansworth, Herts.

Sir Francis died 23rd December, 1623, aged thirty one, and was buried at Harefield 22nd February following. The BARONETCY EXPIRED with him.

Arms—Az. a chev. or, between three double headed eagles, with wings displayed, arg.

ASHE, OF TWICKENHAM.

CREATED 19th Sept. 1660.

EXTINCT 8th Nov. 1731.

Lineage.

"The ancient and eminent family of Esse, Ashe, or D'Essecourt, which came over with WILLIAM the Conqueror, appears by certified extracts under the seal of Ulster King of Arms, by the authority of the College of Arms, and from the pages of our old historians, to have held large estates in the county of Devon, so early as the eleventh century."

SIR OLIVER D'ESSE or ASHE, a person of rank and influence in the beginning of the fourteenth century, was father of

HENRY ESSE or ASHE, who wedded in the time of EDWARD II. the daughter and heiress of Richard Fornyson, and acquired thereby, with other lands, the manor of Sowton, otherwise Clyst Fornyson, in Devon. Of this marriage there was a son and heir,

RICHARD ESSE or ASHE, of Clyst Fornyson, father of BALDWIN ASHE, of Clyst Fornyson, whose son,

JOHN ASHE, of Clyst Fornyson, *m.* and left a son,

WILLIAM ASHE, of Clyst Fornyson, to whom *s.* his son,

JOHN ASHE, of Clyst Fornyson, father of

NICHOLAS ASHE, of Clyst Fornyson, who wedded Johanna, daughter of Anthony Pollard, of Harwood, in Devon, and had three sons, viz.

I. RICHARD, who inherited Clyst Fornyson, and whose male line ceased with his grandson,

RICHARD, who had three daughters.

II. THOMAS, *m.* the daughter and heiress of Nicholas Bailey, esq. of the Abbey of St. John, in the county of Meath, and settling in Ireland, founded many of the numerous and highly respectable branches of the family fixed in that part of the United Kingdom, the principal of which—ASHE, of Ashefield—is now represented by CAPT. WELLESLEY ASHE. (For details refer to BURKE's History of the Commoners, vol. ii. p. 577).

III. JAMES.

The youngest son,

JAMES ASHE, esq. m. Anne, daughter of John Walrond, esq. of Bovey, and from him sprang

JOHN ASHE, esq. of Westcombe, in the county of Somerset, living in 1634, who m. Anne, daughter of Thomas Strode, esq. of Huxton Mallet, and had issue,

JAMES, his heir.

Alice, m. to John Pitt, esq. of Melcombe Regis.

Margaret, m. to John Mansel, esq. of Weymouth.

The son,

JAMES ASHE, esq. of Freshford, in Somersetshire, m. Grace, daughter of Richard Pitt, esq. of Melcombe Regis, and had five sons, viz.

I. JOHN, of Freshford, who sat in parliament *temp.* CHARLES I., and subsequently under the Protectorate. He was in favour with CROMWELL, but refused to sit in judgment upon the King. He possessed a landed property valued at £6000 a year, which he divided at his decease amongst his sons, by Elizabeth his wife, the daughter of Henry Davison, esq. viz.

1. JAMES, of Fifield, Wilts, whose son was seated at Heywood.
2. JOHN, of Teffont, Wilts, who had the manor of Beckington, in Somersetshire, and *d. s. p.*
3. EDWARD, of Freshford, who left an only daughter and heiress.
4. SAMUEL, of Challots, Wilts.
5. JOSEPH, of Longstreet, Wilts.
6. BENJAMIN, of Westcombe, in Somersetshire.
7. JONATHAN, of Clanwilliam, in the county of Tipperary, from whom the present Rev. Trevor-Lloyd Ashe, of Ashgrove, in the county of Limerick.
1. ANNE, m. to Sir John Shaw, bart. of Eltham, in Kent.
2. Grace, m. to Paul Methuen, esq. direct ancestor of the present Paul Methuen, esq. of Corsham.
3. Hester, m. to Samuel Creswick, esq. of Hanlam.
4. ——, m. to John Barnard, esq. of Surrey.
5. Mary, m. to Jacob Self, esq. of Beanacre.

II. Edward, of London, M.P. for Heytesbury in the 16th of CHARLES I. m. Elizabeth, daughter of Christopher Woodward, esq. and had a son and heir,

WILLIAM, of Heytesbury, who died in 1713, leaving by Anne his wife, daughter of Alexander Popham, esq. M.P. of Littlecoot, two sons, whose posterity became extinct, and an only daughter,

ELIZABETH ASHE, who m. Pierce A'Court, esq. of Ivychurch, and was great grandmother to William A'Court, now LORD HEYTESBURY.

III. JOSEPH, of whom presently.

IV. Jonathan, of London, merchant, whose daughter, Rebecca, m. Sir Francis Vincent, bart.

V. Samuel, of Langley Burrell, Wilts.

The third son,

I. JOSEPH ASHE, esq. of Twickenham, in the county of Middlesex, in consideration of the services he had rendered to the Crown, was created a BARONET by *King* CHARLES II. 19th September, 1660. Sir Joseph m. Mary, daughter of Robert Wilson, esq. of London, (who fined for alderman), and had issue,

JAMES, his successor.

CATHERINE, m. to William Wyndham, esq. of Fellbrigge, in Norfolk.

MARY, m. to Horatio, Viscount Townshend.

ANNE.

He *d.* 15th April, 1686, and was *s.* by his son,

II. SIR JAMES ASHE, who m. Catherine, daughter and co-heir of Sir Edmund Bowyer, knt. of Camberwell, in Surrey, but dying 1734, the BARONETCY became EXTINCT.

Arms—Arg. two chevronels sa.

ASHFIELD, OF NETHERHALL.

CREATED 27th July, 1626.

EXTINCT before 1727.

Lineage.

The ASHFIELDS were seated at Stowlangtoft, in Suffolk, from the time of EDWARD III. when they acquired that estate by purchase, until the 12th JAMES I. They subsequently were of Netherhall.

ROBERT DE ASHFIELD, great-grandson of the first proprietor of Stowlangtoft, living in 1455, married three wives; and by the second, Cicely, daughter of John Tendring, he had three sons, and a daughter, Margaret, m. to John Beaupre, of Wells. By the first, Eleanor Curson, he had a son and heir,

JOHN ASHFIELD, who flourished in the time of EDWARD IV. He wedded Florentia, daughter of John Butler, and was father of

JOHN ASHFIELD, who died 15 HEN. VII. 1499, leaving by Margaret, his wife, daughter of John Wentworth, of Gosfield, in Essex, a son and successor,

GEORGE ASHFIELD, of Pakenham, who m. Margery, daughter of Cheeke of Bludhall, in Debenham, and dying 9 HENRY VIII. left a son,

ROBERT ASHFIELD, who married two wives: by the first, Margaret, daughter of Simon Le Grosse, knt. he had no issue; but by the second, Alice, daughter of Sir Thomas Termin, he had six sons and three daughters, viz.

I. ROBERT, his heir. II. William.
III. Thomas. IV. George. V. John.
VI. Edmund, m. the daughter and heir of — Harvey, esq. of Suffolk.
I. Florence, m. to Edward Brooke, of Aspal.
II. Amye, m. to Reinold Rous, of Baddingham.
III. Anne, m. to John Sturt, of Highgate.

The eldest son and heir,

ROBERT ASHFIELD, m. first, Alice, daughter of William Clapton, of Lyston, in Essex, and had by her a son, ROBERT, his heir, and a daughter, Anne, the wife of Anthony Denny, esq. He espoused, secondly, Frances, daughter of Robert Spring, esq. of Lavenham, and had by her,

JOHN, of Wickham, who m. Margaret Cleare, of Stokesby.

Thomas, of Hopton, who m. Elen Holditch, relict of Thomas Prettiman, and had two daughters, Penelope and Dorothy. The latter m. Robert Wilmot, gent. of St. Giles, Middlesex.

William, } who both died "in expeditione Lusi-
Francis, } tania, 1589."

Dorothy, m. to Sir Richard Ogle, knt.

Robert Ashfield *d.* 10 JAMES I. and was *s.* by his son,

SIR ROBERT ASHFIELD, knt. who sold his inheritance at Stowlangtoft to Paul D'Ewes, esq. He m. Anne, daughter of Sir John Tasburgh, and was father of

I. SIR JOHN ASHFIELD, knt. gentleman of the privy

chamber to CHARLES I. created a BARONET in 1626. This gentleman wedded Elizabeth, daughter and heir of Sir Richard Sutton, knt. and dying in 1635, was *s.* by his son,

II. SIR RICHARD ASHFIELD, who *m.* first, the daughter and co-heir of Sir Richard Rogers, knt. of Eastwood, in Gloucestershire, and, secondly, Dorcas, daughter of James Hore, esq. of the Mint. He *d.* in [illegible], and was *s.* by his son,

III. SIR JOHN ASHFIELD, who *m.* Anne, daughter of James Hore, esq. of the Mint, and had issue. He was living in 1692, but his estate was destroyed. The baronetcy was EXTINCT in 1727.

Arms—Sa. a fesse between three fleurs-de-lys.

ASHHURST, OF WATERSTOCK.

CREATED 21st July, 1688.

EXPIRED 17th May, 1732.

Lineage.

This family had long been resident at a seat bearing their own name in the county of Lancaster. Soon after the Conquest, Roger de Leyland quitted all claim of lands in Dalton to

ADAM DE ASSHEHURST and his heirs. His son,

ROGER DE ASSHEHURST, is also mentioned in a deed, wherein he releases to John de Scarisbrick and the said John's heirs his whole right to the town of Scarisbrick. The son of this Roger,

HUGH DE ASSHEHURST, was father of

THOMAS DE ASSHEHURST, who was *s.* by his son,

WILLIAM DE ASSHEHURST, unto whom and his heirs, doing homage and fealty, Simon de Winstanley released his right in the town of Winstanley. His son and successor,

RALPH DE ASSHEHURST, had two sons, SIMON, his heir, and Henry, upon whom he conferred lands in Holland, in the county of Lancaster, the deed of gift being sealed with a cross, and in the dexter chief points one *fleur de lis*. The elder son,

SIMON DE ASSHEHURST, had also two sons,

I. ROBERT, who possessed lands in Dalton.

II. John, who had the manor and entire parish of Asshehurst, in the county of Kent, for homage and service, settled upon him.

ROBERT DE ASSHEHURST, the elder son and heir, was *s.* by his son,

RICHARD DE ASSHEHURST, living in the 28th of EDWARD I. who was father of

SIR ADAM DE ASSHEHURST, knt. who flourished in the reign of EDWARD III. and serving that monarch in his foreign wars, had letters patent, during his sojourn abroad, of royal protection and defence granted to his tenants; at the same time the king discharged him from all contributions emergent within the realm, and from all tenths, fifteenths, &c. witnessed by the king at Brussels 6th November, in the 13th year of his reign. Sir Adam was *s.* by his son,

SIR JOHN DE ASSHEHURST, knt. living in the 1st of RICHARD II., who *m.* Margaret, daughter of Henry de Orrell, and had three sons, ROGER, Geoffry, and John. This gallant knight was the first who sealed with a cross between four *fleurs de lis*, the latter having been conferred for his great services in the French wars. His eldest son and heir,

ROGER DE ASSHEHURST, is mentioned in the 19th of RICHARD II. and having *m.* Matilda, daughter of Hugh de Ince, left a son and successor,

ROBERT DE ASSHEHURST, who figured in the reign of HENRY V. He *m.* Ellen, daughter of Ralphe de Anderton, and was *s.* by his son,

JOHN DE ASSHEHURST, living in the 15th of HENRY VI., who wedded Catherine, daughter and co-heir of Roger Dalton, and was father of

ROBERT ASSHEHURST, esq. who was alive in the 38th of the same reign. He *m.* Margaret, daughter of Richard Byram, esq. of Byram, and was *s.* by his son,

JOHN ASSHEHURST, esq. This gentleman *m.* first, Martha, daughter of Sir William Leyland, knt.; and, secondly, Alice, daughter and heir of John Orrell, esq. By the latter he left a son and successor,

WILLIAM ASSHEHURST, esq. mentioned in the 8th of HENRY VIII., who intermarried with Elizabeth, daughter of John Ogle, esq. and had a son and heir,

WILLIAM ASSHEHURST, esq. living in the 1st of EDWARD VI. This gentleman wedded Cecily, daughter of Nicholas Taylor, gent. and was *s.* by his son,

WILLIAM ASSHEHURST, esq. who flourished in the time of ELIZABETH, and having *m.* Margaret, daughter of Thomas Wilton, esq. left a son and successor,

HENRY ASSHEHURST, esq. who wedded Cassandra, daughter of John Bradshaw, esq. of Bradshaw, and had issue,

I. WILLIAM, his heir. This gentleman served with great reputation in several parliaments before and at the commencement of the civil war, and opposed all parties whose views he deemed adverse to the institutions and freedom of the country so firmly as to have the motto, *Sed magis Amica Veritas*, placed under his portrait, from the pencil of Vandyke. He *m.* one of the daughters of Sir Thomas Ellys, knt. of Wyham, in Lincolnshire, and had three sons, THOMAS, William, and John, by the eldest of whom, (the two younger *d. s. p.*),

THOMAS ASSHHURST, esq. of Asshhurst, he was succeeded. This gentleman wedded Susanna, daughter and co-heir of Thomas Bosvile, esq. of Edlington, in Yorkshire, and *d.* in January, 1699, 1700.

II. John, from whom descended a family in Ireland, which became long since extinct in the male line.

III. HENRY, of whom presently.

IV. Robert, who *d. s. p.*

Henry Asshehurst, who was living in the 2nd of JAMES I., was *s.* in his paternal estate of Asshhurst, in Lancashire, by his eldest son, William. His second son, it would appear, emigrated to Ireland, while the third,

HENRY ASSHHURST, esq. settled in the city of London, and became a merchant there. He was eminent for great benevolence, humanity, and piety, was a chief person in founding the corporation for propagating the gospel in foreign parts, *temp.* CHARLES II., to which he acted as treasurer. He was likewise a promoter of translating the Bible into Hindostan. He fined for alderman, raised a considerable fortune, and left a high character behind him at his decease in 1680, when his remains were interred at St. Augustin's, in Watling-street. This worthy and opulent citizen *m.* Judith, daughter of — Reresby, esq. of the county of York, and by her had four sons and two daughters, viz.

I. HENRY, his heir.

II. WILLIAM (Sir), lord mayor of London in 1693, and one of the representatives of the city in several parliaments, who received the honour of knighthood from King William. He *m.* Elizabeth, daughter of Robert Thompson, esq. and had issue.

III. Joseph, *m.* the daughter of Henry Cornish, esq.
IV. Benjamin, *d.* unm.
I. Mary, *m.* to Sir Thomas Lane.
II. Judith, *m.* to Sir Robert Booth, knt. of London, merchant, and had an only daughter,
JUDITH BOOTH, heir of her father, who *m.* Sir William Cowper, first EARL COWPER, lord chancellor of England, but had no issue.

The eldest son and heir,

I. HENRY ASHHURST, esq. of Waterstock, in the county of Oxford, was created a BARONET by *King* JAMES II. 21st July, 1688. Sir Henry *m.* the Hon. Diana Paget, sixth daughter of William, fifth Lord Paget,* and had issue,

HENRY, his heir.
Frances, *m.* to Sir Richard Allin, bart. of Somerleyton, in the county of Suffolk, and had, with other issue, a son, Sir Ashhurst Allin, bart. whose line expired with his son, and a daughter, Diana, *m.* to Thomas Henry Ashhurst, esq.

Sir Henry Ashhurst sat in parliament in the reigns of CHARLES II. and WILLIAM III. for the boroughs of Truro, in Cornwall, and Wilton, in Wilts. He was the intimate friend of the Hon. Robert Boyle, to whom he was executor, and trustee for founding the lecture which bore that gentleman's name. He died at Waterstock 13th April, 1710, lies buried there, and was *s.* by his son,

II. SIR HENRY ASHHURST, M.P. for Windsor in 1714, who *m.* in 1712, Elizabeth, daughter and co-heir of Sir Thomas Draper, bart. of Sunning Hill, Berks, but dying *s. p.* 17th May, 1732, the BARONETCY *expired.*

Arms—Gu. a cross eng. or, in the dexter chief quarter a fleur-de-lis of the second.

ASHLEY, OF WINBOURNE ST. GILES.

Lineage.

The Ashleys came originally from Wiltshire, where they possessed the manor of Ashley, at a very early period.

BENEDICT ASHLEY, of Ashley, living in the reigns of HENRY III. and EDWARD I. was great-great-grandfather of

ROBERT ASHLEY, who flourished under HENRY IV. and his two immediate successors. He *m.* Egidia, only daughter and heiress of Sir John Hamelyn, by Joan Piecy, by whom he acquired the manor of Winbourne St. Giles, in the county of Dorset, and had a son and successor,

EDMUND ASHLEY, living *temp.* EDWARD IV. who *m.* Margaret, daughter of Robert Turgis, and was father of

HUGH ASHLEY, of Winbourne St. Giles, who died 29th April, 1493, leaving by Elizabeth, daughter of Raynold Walwyn, of Sussex, a daughter *m.* to Stephen Wallop, of Over Wallop, in Hampshire, ancestor to the EARLS OF PORTSMOUTH, and a son and successor,

HENRY ASHLEY, esq. of Winbourne, who *m.* Radegan, daughter of Robert Gilbert, of Somersetshire, and had issue,

I. HENRY (Sir), his heir.
II. Anthony of Damerham, who *m.* Dorothy, daughter of John Lyte, esq. of Lytes Carey, in Somersetshire, and had three sons, namely,
1. ANTHONY, of whom presently, as successor to his cousin at Winbourne.
2. Robert, chosen M.P. for Dorchester 39 ELIZABETH, *d. s. p.*
3. Francis (Sir), knt. of the Middle Temple, serjeant-at-law, and recorder of Dorchester, for which borough he was twice sent to parliament, *m.* Anne, eldest daughter and co-heir of Bernard Samwayes, esq. of Toller Fratrum, in Dorsetshire, and dying in 1635, left an only daughter and heiress,
DOROTHY, *m.* to Danzell Lord Holles, of Ifield, so conspicuous in the troubled times of CHARLES I. The grandson of this marriage, Danzell, last Lord Holles dying unm. in 1694, his estates passed to his heir at-law, John, Duke of Newcastle, the ancestor of the present noble houses of Portland, Newcastle, Chichester, and Cleveland.
I. Elisabeth, *m.* to — Percy, esq.
II. Anne, *m.* to John Osborne.
III. Margaret, *m.* to John Hales.

Henry Ashley, died in 1549, and was *s.* by his elder son,

SIR HENRY ASHLEY, of Winbourne St. Giles, M.P. for Dorsetshire, *b.* in 1519, knighted at the coronation of *Queen* MARY, and appointed ranger of Holt Forest. He *m.* Catharine, daughter of Sir John Basset, knt. and was *s.* at his decease, in 1588, by his son,

SIR HENRY ASHLEY, knt. of Winbourne St. Giles, *b.* in 1548, gentleman pensioner to *Queen* ELIZABETH; *m.* Anne, daughter of Lord Burgh, and had, with four daughters, three sons who died *s. p.* whereupon the family estates passed to his cousin,

I. SIR ANTHONY ASHLEY, of Winbourne St. Giles, who sat in several parliaments, and was highly distinguished by the favour of *Queen* ELIZABETH. He was secretary to her council of war, and received the honour of knighthood for his services at the capture of Calais; the account of which event he brought over to her majesty. He was subsequently secretary to the privy council in the reign of JAMES I. and was created a BARONET in 1622. Sir Anthony married, first, Jane, relict of Thomas Cokaine, esq. and daughter and co-heir of Philip Okeover, esq. of Okeover, in Staffordshire, by whom he had an only daughter and heiress,

ANNE, who marrying SIR JOHN COOPER, bart. conveyed the Ashley estates to the Cooper family, by which they are still possessed; she was mother of
SIR ANTHONY ASHLEY COOPER, EARL OF SHAFTESBURY,† the celebrated statesman.

* By his wife, the Lady Frances Rich, daughter of Henry, Earl of Holland.

† His lordship had, previously to his elevation to the earldom, been created in 1661, BARON ASHLEY, in accordance with a stipulation in his father's marriage settlement, that if the family ever attained the peerage, their title should be that of Ashley.

Sir Anthony Ashley married, secondly, a lady named Philippa, but by her had no child. He *d.* 13th January, 1626, and, as he left no male issue, the baronetcy became EXTINCT.

Arms—Ar. three bulls passant sa. armed, and unguled or.

ASSHETON, OF LEVER.

CREATED 28th June, 1620. 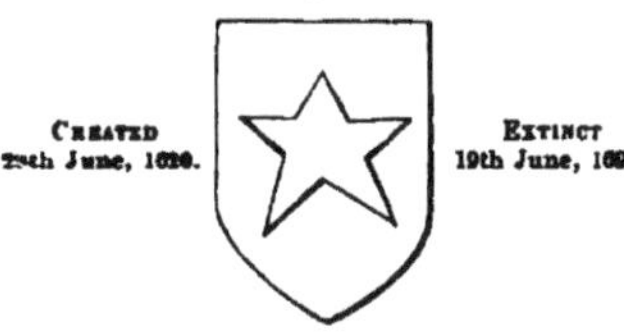 EXTINCT 19th June, 1697.

Lineage.

SIR RALPH ASSHETON, knight banneret, marrying Margaret, daughter of John Barton, esq. of Middleton, who was heir of her uncle, Richard Barton, acquired that estate, and had two sons, RICHARD (Sir) who inherited Middleton, and

SIR RALPH ASSHETON, who acquired the lordship of LEVER, in the county of Lancaster, by marrying MARGARET, the daughter and heir of ADAM LEVER, esq. of Great Lever. He had issue,

RALPH, his heir.
Robert.
John, *m.* Eleanor, daughter of Sir Robert Constable, of Masham, in the county of York, and left a daughter,
HELEN ASSHETON, who *m.* William Pickering, esq. and was mother of
JOHN PICKERING, keeper of the great seal, *temp.* ELIZABETH.

The eldest son,

RALPH ASSHETON, *m.* Eleanor, daughter of Adam Hulton, esq. of the Park, and had

RALPH, his successor.
Richard, who purchased Whalley Abbey, *m.* Jane, daughter and heir of Ralph Harbottle, esq. of Northumberland, and *d. s. p.* at Whalley, 9th September, 1561.
Nicholas, rector of Wickford, in the county of York.
Patricius.
Margaret.
Anne.

He was *s.* by his eldest son,

RALPH ASSHETON, esq. who wedded Margaret, daughter of William Orrell, esq. of Turton Tower, and had issue,

RALPH, his heir.
Andrew, rector of Mungewell, in the county of Oxford.

The eldest son,

RALPH ASSHETON, esq. of Great Lever, *m.* Alice, daughter of William Hulton, esq. of Farnworth, and was father of

RALPH ASSHETON, esq. of Great Lever, in the county of Lancaster, who *m.* first, Johanna, widow of Edward Radcliffe, esq. of Todmorden, and daughter and coheir of Thomas Radcliffe, esq. of Wimbersley. Of this lady there is a portrait painted on pannel at Towneley; she appears to have been of a fair complexion and handsome. By her Mr. Assheton had issue,

RALPH, his successor.
Ratcliffe, *b.* in 1582, from whom the Asshetons of Cuerdale and Downham.
Jane, *b.* in 1573, *m.* to Richard Towneley, esq. of Towneley, (ancestor of the present P. E. TOWNELEY, esq. of Towneley) and *d.* at Hapton Tower, in 1635.
Alice, *b.* in 1574, *m.* to Alexander Standish, esq. of Duxbury.
Eliza, *b.* in 1575, *m.* to George Preston, esq. of Holker.

He wedded, secondly, Anne, daughter of John Talbot, son of Sir Thomas Talbot, of Bashall, and relict of Edmund Assheton, esq. of Chatterton, and was *s.* at his decease by his elder son,

I. RALPH ASSHETON, esq. of Great Lever, and Whalley, *b.* in 1579, and created a BARONET 28th June, 1620. Sir Ralph *m.* first, Dorothy, daughter of Sir James Bellingham, knt. of Levens, in Westmoreland; and, secondly, Eleanor, daughter of Thomas Shuttleworth, esq. of Gawthorp, in Lancashire. By his first wife only he had issue, viz.

RALPH, second baronet.
Thomas, a merchant, *m.* Anne, daughter of Sir Sheffield Clapham, and had a son,
Thomas, commoner of Brasennose College, Oxford, buried 1670.
EDMUND, JOHN, } third and fourth baronets.
ANNE, *m.* to SIR RALPH ASSHETON, bart. of Middleton, and was mother of SIR RALPH ASSHETON, second baronet of Middleton, who inherited the estates of his uncle, SIR JOHN ASSHETON, bart. of Whalley.

Sir Ralph sold his paternal estate of Great Lever, to Bridgman, Bishop of Chester, about the year 1629. In the latter part of his life he complained of great oppression from Archbishop Laud, in breaking a lease of the rectory of Whalley, on which account he was compelled to make a journey to London, when very gouty and infirm. He *d.* 18th October, 1644, and was *s.* by his eldest son,

II. SIR RALPH ASSHETON, of Whalley, *b.* in 1680, *m.* first, Lady Dorothy Tufton, daughter of Nicholas, first Earl of Thanet; and, secondly, Elizabeth, daughter of Sir Sapcote Harrington, and had an only son, who *d.* young. He died in 1680, and was buried at Downham, where he built the family vault in the chancel: he pulled down the old Abbey Church and Tower at Whalley. Sir Ralph dying without surviving issue, was *s.* by his next surviving brother,

III. SIR EDMUND ASSHETON, of Whalley, *b.* in 1620, who *d.* issueless 31st October, 1695, and was *s.* by his brother,

IV. SIR JOHN ASSHETON, of Whalley, *b.* in 1621, *m.* Catherine, daughter of Sir Henry Fletcher, bart. of Hutton, in Cumberland and widow of Thomas Lister, esq. of Arnoldsbriggin, but dying *s. p.* 19th June, 1697, the estate of Whalley devolved upon (the son and heir of his sister) his nephew, SIR RALPH ASSHETON, bart. of Middleton, and the BARONETCY expired.

Arms—Arg. a mullet sa.

ASSHETON, OF MIDDLETON.

CREATED 17th Aug. 1660.—EXTINCT 31st Dec. 1765.

Lineage.

ASHTON-UNDER-LYNE, a market town, in Salford Hundred, county palatine of Lancaster, gave name to this ancient family, which was founded by

ORM FITZ EWARD, to whom Albert de Greslev gave

one carucate of land in Asheton, beside a knight's fee in Dalton Parbold and Wrightington, *temp.* HENRY III. This Orm *m.* Emma, daughter of the above-mentioned Albert de Gresley, and was grandfather of

SIR THOMAS DE ASSHETON, Lord of Assheton. His grandson,

SIR ROBERT DE ASSHETON, was vice chamberlain to *King* EDWARD III. and a commissioner to treat for peace with France. He was afterwards governor of Guynes, warden of the cinque ports, and admiral of the *Narrow Seas*. In the 43rd of the same reign he was made justice of Ireland; four years afterwards constituted treasurer of England; and lastly, appointed constable of Dover Castle. Sir Robert was one of the executors of the last will of his royal master, and he appears to have enjoyed the confidence of the succeeding monarch; for we find him in the 4th of RICHARD II. again warden of the cinque ports. He left at his decease a son and heir,

THOMAS DE ASSHETON, who captured the royal standard of Scotland at the battle of Durham, 17th October, 1346. He was father of

SIR JOHN DE ASSHETON, who represented the county of Lancaster in parliament 12th RICHARD II. He *m.* Margaret, daughter of Perkins de Legh, of Lyme, in the county of Chester, and had a son,

SIR JOHN DE ASHTON, drowned at Norham. He *m.* the daughter of Sir Robert Standish, of Standish, knt. and had two sons,

JOHN (Sir).

Nicholas (Sir), who was a knight of the order of St. John of Jerusalem, afterwards so well known as knights of Malta.

The elder son,

SIR JOHN DE ASSHETON was made a knight of the Bath at the coronation of *King* HENRY IV. and returned one of the knights of the shire for the county palatine of Lancaster to the first parliament of HENRY V. by which latter monarch he was made governor of Constance in France. He *m.* first, Jane, daughter of John Savile, of Tankersley, in the county of York, and had issue,

THOMAS (Sir), his heir, the alchemist, who *m.* Elizabeth, daughter of Sir John Byron, and had issue,

1. JOHN (Sir), knighted before the battle of Northampton, 10th July, 1460. He *m.* first, Dulcia, daughter of Sir Edmund Trafford, knt. of Trafford; and, secondly, Isabella, daughter of Elland, of Elland, in the county of York. He *d.* 23rd HENRY VII. leaving by his first wife,

THOMAS (Sir), knighted at Ripon 7th HENRY VII., *m.* first, Elizabeth, dau. and heiress of Ralph Staveleigh, of Stayley, and had issue,

Margaret, *m.* to Sir William Booth, of Dunham Massey, ancestor of the Earls of Stamford and Warrington.

Elizabeth, *m.* to Randle Ashton, of Barton.

Joan, *m.* to Sir John Leigh.

He *m.* secondly, Agnes, one of the ten daughters and co-heirs of Sir James Harrington, of Woolfage, Northamptonshire, and dying 8th HENRY VII., left by her,

John, *d. s. p. m.* Jane, daughter and heir of W. Stanley.

Alice, *m.* to Sir R. Hoghton, of Hoghton Tower.

2. Edmund, *m.* Johanna, daughter and heir of Richard Radcliffe, of Chadderton.

3. Geffrey, *m.* the daughter and heiress of Thomas Manners, of Shipley.

4. Nicholas, *m.* Mary, daughter of Lord Brook.

1. Dulcia, *m.* to Sir Thomas Gerrard, of Bryn.

2. Elizabeth, *m.* to Sir John Trafford.

And four other children.

Lucy, *m.* first, to Sir Bertoue Entwisle; secondly, to Richard Byron; and, thirdly, to Sir Ralph Shirley.

Margaret, *m.* to Thomas Laugley, of Edgecroft.

Katherine, *m.* to John Duckenfield.

Elizabeth, *m.* first, to Sir Ralph Harrington; secondly, to Sir Richard Hammerton.

Agnes, *m.* to Thomas Booth, of Barton.

Anne, *m.* to — Dutton, esq. of Cheshire.

Sir John wedded, secondly, Mary, daughter of Sir John Byron, of Clayton in Lancashire, and by that lady had a son,

SIR RALPH ASSHETON, who was page of honor to *King* HENRY VI. and marrying MARGARET, daughter of JOHN BARTON, esq. of MIDDLETON, in the county of Lancaster, and heir to her uncle, Richard Barton, became proprietor of that estate. He was knight marshal of England, lieutenant of the Tower of London, and sheriff of Yorkshire in the 12th and 13th of EDWARD IV. In the 24th of which monarch's reign, *anno* 1482, he was made KNIGHT BANNERET at Hatton field, in Scotland, whither he had attended the Duke of Gloucester to recover Berwick. He was afterwards appointed vice-constable of England, with the authority of constable; and *Holinshed* names him amongst the knights who rode in procession at the coronation of RICHARD III. which ceremony he did not long survive. He had, with other issue, two sons,

RICHARD (Sir), his heir.

RALPH (Sir), who marrying Margaret, daughter and heir of Adam Lever, esq. of Lever, in Lancashire, acquired that lordship. He was progenitor of

SIR RALPH ASSHETON, of Lever, created a BARONET by *King* JAMES I. 28th June, 1620. (*See* ASSHETON, of Lever.)

The eldest son and heir,

SIR RICHARD ASSHETON, of Middleton, in the county palatine of Laucaster received the honour of knighthood for his gallant services in the Scottish wars under the Lord Strange, and died 28th April, in 23rd HENRY VII. leaving by his wife, Isabel, daughter of John Talbot, esq. of Salisbury, one son and four daughters, viz.

RICHARD, his heir.

Margaret, *m.* to John Hopwood, esq. of Hopwood.

—, *m.* to Holte of Stubley.

Alice, *m.* first, to John Lawrence, esq.; secondly, to Richard Ratclyffe, esq. of Ratclyffe Tower; and, thirdly, to Thomas Booth, esq. of Hackensall.

Elizabeth, *m.* to Robert, son of Thurstan Holland, esq. of Denton.

SIR RICHARD ASSHETON, the only son and heir, was a distinguished warrior, and received the honor of knighthood for his valiant bearing on the celebrated FIELD of FLODDEN, where he took the Scottish standard bearer's sword, and made Sir John Foreman, the Scots' monarch's serjeant-porter, prisoner. On his return he dedicated to St. Leonard of Middleton his standard, having several privileges within the said manor allowed him by the king. He *m.* Anne, daughter of Sir Robert Foulshurst, of Crew, in Cheshire, and had issue,

RICHARD, his successor.

Thomas.

Edmund, rector of Middleton.

Anne, *m.* to George Atherton, of Atherton.

The eldest son and heir,

SIR RICHARD ASSHETON, knt. of Middleton, *m.* first, Anne, daughter of Sir Thomas Strickland, knt. of Kendale, in Cumberland, and had (with a younger son and daughter who both *d.* issueless),

RICHARD, his heir.

Robert, } both rectors of Middleton.
John, }

Ralph, who had issue.

Thomas, who had issue.

He *m.* secondly, Anne, Lady Bellingham, but by her had no issue. He *d.* in the 3rd of EDWARD VI. and was *s.* by his eldest son,

RICHARD ASSHETON, esq. of Middleton, who survived his father but one year. He *m.* first, Anne, daughter of Sir Thomas Gerrard, knt. of Bryn, in Lancashire, and had a son and two daughters, viz.

RICHARD, his successor.

Margaret, *m.* to William Davenport, esq. of Bramhall, in Cheshire.

Anne, *m.* to John Booth, esq. of Barton.

He *m.* secondly, Catherine, daughter of Sir Thomas Bellingham, by whom he had an only daughter, *m.* to Alexander Hoghton, of Hoghton. He was *s.* by his only son,

RICHARD ASSHETON, esq. sheriff of Lancashire in the 39th and 40th of ELIZABETH. He *m.* Elizabeth, daughter of Sir William Davenport, knt. of Bramhill, and was *s.* by his son,

SIR RICHARD ASSHETON, of Middleton, who was knighted at the coronation of JAMES I. and was sheriff of Lancashire in the fourth of that king's reign. He *m.* first, Mary, daughter of Sir John Byron, of Clayton, by whom he had surviving issue,

RICHARD, his successor.

Winefred, *m.* to John Holte, esq. of Stubley.

Mary, *m.* to Robert Holte, esq. of Ashworth.

Dorothy, *m.* to James Anderton, esq. of Clayton.

Sir Richard wedded, secondly, Mary, daughter of Robert Holte, esq. of Ashworth, and relict of John Greenhalgh, esq. of Brandlesom, and by that lady had

Ralph of Kirby, in the county of York, *m.* Catherine, daughter of William Brereton, esq. of Ashley, in Cheshire.

Susan, *d.* unm.

He *d.* 27th December, 1617, and was *s.* by his elder son,

RICHARD ASSHETON, of Middleton, who *d.* 7th November, in the year after his father, having had by Mary, daughter of Thomas Venables, Baron of Kinderton, in Cheshire, the following issue,

Richard, who predeceased him.

RALPH, his heir.

John, *d.* young.

James, accidentally killed.

William, rector of Middleton.

Thomas.

Dorothy, *m.* to John Legh, esq. of Booths, in Cheshire, ancestor of the present PETER LEGH, esq. of Booth's Hall.

Anne, *m.* to the Rev. Paul Latham, of Standish.

The eldest surviving son,

RALPH ASSHETON, esq. of Middleton, was elected to parliament for Chester, *temp.* CHARLES I. and represented the county in the last year of that eventful reign. He *m.* Elizabeth, daughter of John Kaye, esq. of Woodsome, in Yorkshire, and had surviving issue,

ASS

Richard, *d. vita patris* 25th March, 1631. His death was supposed to have been the effect of witchcraft, the work of one Utley, who in consequence was hanged at Lancaster.

RALPH, his successor.

John.

Elizabeth, *m.* to Adam Beaumont, esq. of Whitley, in the county of York.

Mary, *m.* to Christopher Banaster, esq. of Bank.

Anne, *d.* unm.

He *d.* 17th February, 1650, and was *s.* by his elder son,

I. SIR RALPH ASSHETON, knt. of Middleton, *b.* in 1626, who had received the honour of knighthood from *King* CHARLES I. and was created a BARONET soon after the Restoration by *King* CHARLES II. He *m.* Anne, daughter of Sir Ralph Assheton, bart.* of Whalley Abbey, and had

RALPH, his successor.

Richard, of Allerton-Gledow, in the county of York, *m.* Mary, daughter of John Parker, esq. of Extwisle, and relict of Benjamin Waddington, esq. of Allerton-Gledow, by whom he left, at his decease,

RALPH, successor to his uncle.

John, *d.* unm. Sept. 1758.

Richard, *d. s. p.* Nov. 1758.

Anne, *d.* unm.

Elizabeth, *m.* to Thomas Pigot, of Manchester, *d. s. p.*

Anne.

Mary, *m.* to Edward Thornicroft, esq. of Thornicroft, in Cheshire.

Sir Ralph represented Clithero in the Restoration parliament, and was *s.* at his decease by his eldest son,

II. SIR RALPH ASSHETON, of Middleton, *b.* 11th February, 1657, who inherited, at the decease of his maternal uncle, Sir John Assheton, fourth and last baronet of Lever, as heir in tail, 11th June, 1697, the estate of Whalley Abbey. Sir Ralph *m.* first, Mary, only daughter and heir of Thomas Vavasour, esq. of Spaldington, in Yorkshire, and by her, who *d.* in 1694, had issue,

1. RICHARD-VAVASOUR, who died at the age of eighteen, in 1707-8, his father then living.

1. ANNE ASSHETON, who enjoyed her mother's estate of Spaldington, under a decree of Chancery, *m.* to Humphrey Trafford, esq. of Trafford, and had issue,

HUMPHREY TRAFFORD, who died *s. p.* in 1779, having devised Trafford to John Trafford, esq. of Croston.

Cecil Trafford, } *d. s. p.*
Sigismund Trafford, }

Anne Trafford, *m.* to P. Barnes, esq. and *d. s. p.*

ELIZABETH TRAFFORD, who had her mother's estate of Spaldington, *m.* Maile Yates, esq. of Maghall, and dying in 1786, left three daughters, viz.

1. ANNE ASSHETON YATES, who had the estate of Spaldington, and marrying Lieutenant Colonel Henry Nooth, that gentleman, in compliance with the testamentary injunction of Thomas Vavasour, who *d.* in 1679, his wife's great-great-grandfather, assumed the surname and arms of VAVASOUR. He was created a BARO-

* First baronet of Lever.

NET 20th March, 1801, and his son is the present Sir HENRY VAVASOUR, of Spaldington.

2. Mary Yates, m. first, John Aspinall, esq. serjeant-at-law, and, secondly, Henry Aspinall, esq. but d. in 1794, s. p.

3. Catherine-Eleanor Yates, living in 1806, m. Robert Campbell, esq. and had issue.

II. Mary Assheton, m. to Sir Nathaniel Curzon, bart. of Kedleston, and had two sons (she d. in 1776, aged eighty-one),

NATHANIEL CURZON, created BARON SCARSDALE in 1761.

ASSHETON CURZON, created Baron Curzon in 1794, and VISCOUNT CURZON in 1802, which honors have merged in the earldom of Howe.*

III. CATHERINE ASSHETON, m. to Thomas Lister, esq. of Arnoldsbriggin, and had issue,

THOMAS LISTER, whose son, Thomas Lister, esq. of Gisburne Park, was raised to the peerage in 1797, as BARON RIBBLESDALE.

NATHANIEL LISTER, of Armitage Park, grandfather of the present THOMAS HENRY LISTER, esq.

Sir Ralph wedded, secondly, Mary, only daughter and heir of Robert Hyde, esq. of Denton, in Lancashire, but had no other issue. He died in May, 1716, when his daughters inherited all his fortune as co-heirs, with the exception of the paternal estate of Middleton, which with the baronetcy devolved upon his nephew, Ralph Assheton of Allerton Gledow, who then became

III. SIR RALPH ASSHETON, of Middleton. He m. first, Mary, daughter of Sir Holland Egerton, bart. and had two daughters, namely,

MARY, m. in 1760, Sir Harbord Harbord, bart. created BARON SUFFIELD in 1786, and her grandson, Edward-Vernon, fourth and present LORD SUFFIELD, enjoys the estate of MIDDLETON.

ELEANOR, m. in 1769, to Sir Thomas Egerton, bart. who was created in 1784, Baron Grey de Wilton, and in 1801, Viscount Grey de Wilton and EARL OF WILTON, by whom she had of several children one daughter only to survive, viz.

ELEANOR EGERTON, who m. 30th April, 1794, Robert Grosvenor, then Viscount Belgrave, now Marquess of Westminster, by whom she had three sons,

RICHARD, *Earl Grosvenor.*

THOMAS, *Earl of Wilton.*

Robert.

Sir Ralph wedded, secondly, Eleanor, daughter of the Rev. John Copley, of Bathely, and relict of John Hulton, esq. of Hulton, in the county of Lancaster. He died 31st December, 1765, when his daughters became his co-heirs, and the BARONETCY *expired.*

Arms—Arg. a mullet sa.

ASTLEY, OF MELTON CONSTABLE.

CREATED 21st Jan. 1642. EXTINCT 7th Sept. 1659.

Lineage.

The ASTLEYS, extinct and extant, derived their name from the manor of Astley, or as originally written Estley, in the county of Warwick, of which they were lords so early as the time of HENRY I.

PHILIP DE ESTLEY, grandson of the first proprietor, held three knights' fees, in the reign of HENRY II., (*anno* 1166), of William, Earl of Warwick, viz. Estley or Astley, in Warwickshire, Wedinton, Hillmorton, Melverton, and Merston Jabet, *de veteri feoffamento,* by the service "of laying hands on the earl's stirrup when he did get upon, or alight from horseback." His great-grandson,

SIR THOMAS DE ASTLEY, knt. was constituted, in the 26th of HENRY III., one of the king's justices for the gaol delivery at Warwick, and again the next year, when he paid £15 for his relief. Sir Thomas was afterwards one of the great leaders amongst the barons, and fell at Evesham in 1264, with Montford, Earl of Leicester, and other rebellious lords. By his first wife, Joane, daughter of Ehnald de Bois, a great man at that time in Leicestershire, Sir Thomas had a son, ANDREW ASTLEY, from whom sprang the *Extinct* Lords Astley, of Astley, and a daughter, Isabel, wife of William de Birmingham. By his second, Editha, daughter of Peter Constable, of Melton Constable, in Norfolk, and co-heir of her brother, Sir Robert Constable, knt., he left three sons, THOMAS, Ralph, and Stephen, with a daughter, Agnes. The eldest of these sons,

THOMAS DE ASTLEY, inherited Hill Morton, but died s. p. and was s. by his brother,

RALPH DE ASTLEY, of Hill Morton and Melton Constable. From whom we pass to his lineal descendant, (fifth in succession),

JOHN ASTLEY, esq. of Hill Morton and Melton Constable, who m. Frances, daughter and heir of John Cheyney, esq. of Sittingborne, in the county of Kent, and was s. by his only son,

ISAAC ASTLEY, esq. of Hill Morton and Melton Constable. This gentleman m. Mary, daughter of Edward Waldegrave, esq. of Borley, in Essex, and had

THOMAS, his heir.

JACOB (Sir), a distinguished cavalier officer, who for his eminent services was raised to the peerage in 1661 as Lord Astley, of Reading. (See BURKE's *Extinct Peerage.*)

---

* ASSHETON CURZON, Viscount Curzon, m. first, Esther, daughter of William Hanmer, esq. and had a son,

PEN-ASSHETON CURZON, who m. Sophia-Charlotte, Baroness Howe, and by her ladyship (who wedded, secondly, Sir Jonathan Wathen Waller, bart. and d. in 1835), left at his decease in 1797, an only surviving child,

RICHARD-WILLIAM-PEN CURZON, who inherited the honors of his grandfather, and was created EARL HOWE. His lordship is the present proprietor of WHALLEY ABBEY.

Lord Howe wedded, secondly, Dorothy, youngest child of Sir Robert Grosvenor, bart. and aunt of the Marquess of Westminster, and by that lady had

Assheton Curzon, b. in 1771.

Robert Curzon, b. in 1774, m. in 1808, to Henrietta-Anne, Baroness Zouche.

Elizabeth Curzon.

Charlotte Curzon, m. in 1799, to Dugdale Stratford Dugdale esq. of Merevale.

The elder son,

Thomas Astley, esq. of Hill Morton and Melton Constable, wedded Frances, daughter and co-heir of George Deane, esq. of Tilney, and had issue,

Francis (Sir), who *d. s. p.*

Isaac, heir to his father.

Edward (Sir), who *m.* the Hon. Elizabeth Astley, only daughter and eventual heiress of his uncle Jacob, first Lord Astley, of Reading, and was father of

Jacob Astley, who inherited the estates of his uncle, Sir Isaac Astley, bart. and being created a Baronet himself in 1660, founded the existing baronets of Hill Morton and Melton Constable.

The elder surviving son,

I. Isaac Astley, esq. of Hill Morton and Melton Constable, was created a Baronet by *King* Charles I. 21st January, 1642. Sir Isaac *m.* Rachel, daughter of Augustine Messinger, esq. of Hackford, in Norfolk; and, secondly, Bridget, daughter of John Coke, esq. of Holkham, and widow of Edward Doyley, esq. of Shottisham, but dying without issue 7th September, 1659, his estates devolved upon his nephew, as stated above, and the baronetcy became *Extinct*.

Arms—Az. a cinquefoil erm. within a bordure engrailed, or.

ASTLEY, OF PATSHULL.

Created 13th Aug. 1662.—Extinct 29th Dec. 1771.

Lineage.

Sir Thomas de Astley, third Lord Astley, of Astley, who was summoned to parliament from 1342 to 1349, *m.* the Lady Elizabeth de Beauchamp, daughter of Guy, second Earl of Warwick, and had issue,

William (Sir), his successor, as fourth lord.

Thomas (Sir).

Giles, from whom the Astleys, of Wolvey.

The second son,

Sir Thomas de Astley, knt. was in commission 2nd Richard II., *anno* 1379, for taxing a subsidy on the county of Warwick, and six years after, for collecting a fifteenth and tenth granted by parliament when he sat as one of the knights of the shire. He wedded Elizabeth, daughter and heir of Richard, son of Sir William Harcourt, and had issue,

Thomas (Sir), his heir.

John (Sir), one of the bravest and most eminent soldiers of the era in which he lived, and distinguished by his extraordinary personal prowess. Amongst his many exploits is recorded a duel fought by him on horseback with Peter de Massei, a Frenchman, on the 29th August, 1428, in the street St. Antoine at Paris before *King* Charles VII., when having pierced his antagonist through the head, he had the helmet, by agreement of the vanquished, to present to his lady. He subsequently fought Sir Philip Boyle, an Arragonian knight, in Smithfield, in the city of London, in the presence of Henry VI. and his court, which combat, it is related, was gallantly sustained on foot, with battle-axes, spears, swords and daggers: at its termination Astley was knighted by the king, and further rewarded with a pension of one hundred marks for his life. "Yea (saith Dugdale) so famous did John de Astley grow for his valour that he was elected a Knight of the Garter, and bore for his arms the coats of *Astley* and *Harecourt*, quarterly, with a *label of three points ermine.*" He was interred at Patshull under a handsome monument.

The eldest son,

Thomas Astley, esq. of Patshull, in the county of Stafford, *m.* Jane,* daughter of Sir Thomas Griesly, knt. of Colton, in the same shire, and had an only son,

Thomas Astley, esq. of Patshull, who wedded Margaret, daughter of Sir William Boteler, knt. of Warrington, in Lancashire, and dying in 1483, was *s.* by his eldest son,

Richard Astley, esq. of Patshull. This gentleman *m.* Joan, daughter of Thomas Oteley, esq. of Pitchford, in Salop, and had, with a daughter Jane, an only son, his successor at his decease in 1532,

Thomas Astley, esq. of Patshull, who *m.* Mary, daughter and co-heir of Sir Gilbert Talbot, knt.† and had two sons and a daughter, viz.

Gilbert, his heir.

John, from whom the Astleys, of Aston.

Elizabeth, *m.* to John Wrottesley, esq. of Wrottesley.

He was *s.* at his decease by his elder son,

Gilbert Astley, esq. of Patshull, who wedded Dorothy, daughter of Sir Thomas Giffard, knt. of Chillinton, in Staffordshire, and was *s.* by (the son of Thomas Astley, his only son, by Margery, daughter of Sir Walter Aston, knt. of Tixal, county of Stafford) his grandson,

Walter Astley, esq. of Patshull, who *m.* Grace, daughter of Francis Trentham, esq. of Roucester, in the county of Stafford, and had issue,

Richard, his heir.

Thomas, of East Court House, in the county of Warwick, *m.* Jane, daughter and heir of Joseph Carver, esq. of Hether, in Leicestershire, and left a son,

Richard Astley, of East Court House, who *m.* in 1706, Elizabeth, daughter of Stanislaus Browne, esq. of Eastbourne, and aunt of the last Viscount Montagu, by whom he left at his decease in 1718, a son and heir,

William-Francis Corbet Astley, *b.* in 1708; *m.* Mary, daughter of Francis Bickley, esq. (and his wife Judith, dau. and co-heir of William Dugdale, esq. of Blythe Hall). He *d.* in 1790, leaving issue.‡

---

* This lady was nurse to *King* Henry VI.

† By Anne, daughter and heir of Sir William Paston, knt. and the Lady Anne Beaufort his wife, daughter of Edmund, Duke of Somerset, and great-granddaughter of John of Gaunt.

‡ I. Francis-Dugdale Astley, his heir, who *m.* in 1775, Mary, second daughter and co-heir of William Buckler, esq. of Boreham, Wilts, and by her, who *d.* 28th September, 1804, had, with other issue,

John-Dugdale Astley, his heir, created a Baronet in 1821: the present Sir John-Dugdale Astley, of Everley, county of Wilts.

II. Richard Astley, of Oldstone, in the county of Leicester, *b.* in 1746; *m.* in 1784, Mary, daughter of John Boswell, esq. of Wilton, in Warwickshire, and had

Richard, who took the name and arms of Gough in 1815.

He *d.* in 1831.

I. Mary Astley.

He was *s.* by his eldest son,

I. Sir Richard Astley, knt. of Patshull, who for his devotion to the cause of royalty was knighted by *King* Charles II. and created a Baronet 13th August, 1662, soon after the Restoration. He *m.* first, Elizabeth, daughter of John Philipps, esq. of Picton Castle, in the county of Pembroke, but by her had no male issue to survive himself. Sir Richard wedded, secondly, Henrietta, daughter and co-heir of William Borlace, esq. of Great Marlow, in the county of Bucks, and by that lady had an only son, his successor, at his decease 24th February, 1687,

II. Sir John Astley, M.P. for Shrewsbury, who *m.* Mary, daughter and heir of Francis Prynce, esq.* of the county of Salop, and had issue,

- Richard-Prynce, who predeceased his father unm.
- Mary, *d.* unm.
- Henrietta, *m.* to Edward Daniell, esq.
- Alicia, *m.* to Charles, third Earl of Tankerville.
- Anne, *d.* unm.
- Arabella, *m.* first, to Anthony-Langley Swimmer, esq.; and, secondly, to Sir Francis Vincent, bart.
- Frances, *m.* to James O'Donnell, esq.

Sir John Astley *d.* 29th December, 1771, when his estates devolved upon his daughters as co-heirs, and the Baronetcy became *extinct*.

Arms—Az. a cinquefoil erm. within a bordure eng. or, a crescent for difference.

ASTON, OF ASTON.

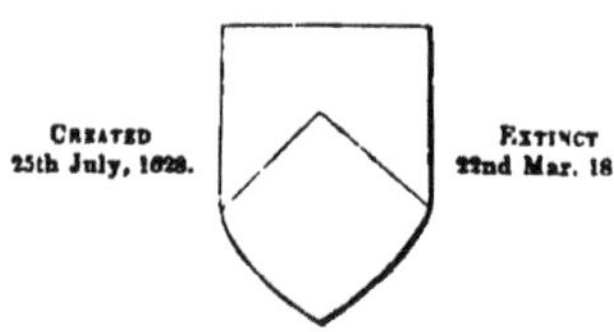

Created 25th July, 1628. — Extinct 22nd Mar. 1815.

Lineage.

In Domesday Book the town of Aston was held by Odard under William Fitznigell, Baron of Halton, A.D. 1086. At that time there appears to have been but one place of the name: it was subsequently divided into Aston-juxta Sutton, and Aston Grange.

About the reign of Henry II.

Gilbert de Aston was proprietor of Aston-juxta-Sutton, and was living in that reign, and in the subsequent reigns of Richard I. and *King* John. His son and heir,

Richard de Aston gave unto Hugh Dutton, of Dutton, *Sex Bovatas Terræ* in Aston, in the beginning of the reign of Henry III. His wife's name was Joan, and he left a son and heir,

Richard de Aston, who was *s.* by his son, another

Richard de Aston, who wedded, *temp.* Edward I., Rose, youngest daughter and co-heir of Roger Throssel, of Maxfield, in Cheshire, and had issue,

- Richard, his heir.
- Hugh, prior of Birkenhead Abbey.

This Richard died before his wife, (who was living a widow in the 18th of Edward III.) and was *s.* by his elder son,

Richard Aston, of Aston, who *m.* Anabella, daughter of Eva de Rode, and sister of William Rode, of Rode, in Cheshire, and had Robert (Sir), his heir, Thomas, living in the 7th of Edward III. but then very young, and Margery, *m.* to William Walensis, of Halton. His eldest son,

Sir Robert Aston, knt. of Aston, *m.* Felice, daughter of John Hawarden, citizen of Chester, about the year 1338, and had four sons, viz.

- Richard, his heir.
- Hugh, father, by Cicely (afterwards *m.* to —— Hocknell) his wife, of
  - Robert Aston,† of Ringey, whose son, by his wife, Fillote Hawarden,
    - Sir Richard Aston, continued the line of the family.
- Lawrence, } living 49th Edward III.
- James, }

Sir Robert died before the 29th Edward III. for in that year his eldest son,

Richard Aston, was lord of Aston, but he dying issueless about the 42nd or 43rd of the same reign, the estates passed to his grand-nephew,

Sir Richard Aston, knt. lord of Aston, who *m.* first, Jonet, daughter of John Hocknell, of Huxley, and had several children who with their mother all died of the plague at Ringey. He wedded, secondly, 9th Richard II. Ellen, daughter and heir of Geffrey Dutton,‡ and acquired lands thereby in Listark and Halton. Of this second marriage there was issue,

- Robert.
- Henry, living 10th Henry V.
- Eleanor, *m.* to Richard Priestland, of Priestland.
- Elizabeth, *m.* first, 17th Richard II. to Thomas, son of Thomas Boydell, of Caterich, without issue; secondly, 21st of the same reign, to Robert Massy, of Hale; and, thirdly, to Thomas Danyel, of Over-Tabley; she *d.* in 1410.

Sir Richard was treasurer to Philippa, Queen Consort of Edward III., of her lands and rents in Ambrage, in Wales, and steward of Hopesdale. He was in the wars in Spain, 12th Richard II., and was steward of Halton, 10th Henry IV. Sir Richard, who was lord of Aston forty years, was *s.* at his decease (Ellen, his widow, remarried John Rycroft) by his elder son,

Sir Robert Aston, of Aston, who wedded Isabel, daughter and heir of John Beeston, and had, Richard, his heir, David, living 23rd Henry VI., and Alice, wife of John Massy, of Sale. He died in 1417, leaving

---

* And Mary his wife, daughter and heir of Samuel Gilly, esq. of High Hall, in the county of Dorset, by Arabella, daughter of the Lord Chief Justice Bankes.

† It appears by the testimony of Robin Hocan, 5th Henry V. 1417, then aged seventy years, that he knew Robin, of Aston, son and heir of Hugh, to be married by Hugh his father to Fillote, daughter of Black John Hawarden, at that time steward of Hawarden, and that Robin and Fillote were enfeoffed of a parcel of land called Ringey, and had issue Sir Richard Aston and other children; and afterwards Robin died in Spain, in the lifetime of Hugh his father. This Hugh had to wife Cicely, afterwards married to Hocknell: and Hugh married Richard his grandson, son of Richard Aston of Ringey, unto Jonet, daughter of John Hocknell, of Huxley, and they had issue: but Jonet and her children, and Fillote, mother of Richard, died all of the pestilence at Ringey; and afterwards Sir Richard Aston married Ellen, daughter of Geffrey Dutton; and that he, Hocan, knew Sir Richard Aston, occupying the whole manor of Aston for forty years and more, and Sir Robert, his son, occupying it for seven years and more.

‡ Third son of Sir Hugh Dutton, of Dutton.

Isabel, his widow, who wedded, secondly, Sir John Carington, knt. of Carington, in Cheshire: she had the guardianship of her son,

Sir Richard Aston, of Aston, who m. 9 Henry V. Maude, daughter and heir of Peter Massy,* of Horton, in the county of Chester, by Margaret his wife, daughter and heir of William de Horton, and had issue,

Thomas, his heir; m. in 1467, Margaret, daughter and co-heir of Sir Thomas Dutton, of Dutton, by whom (who wedded, secondly, Ralph Vernon, esq. of Haslington, in Cheshire) he left at his decease, about 1484, a son,

Richard, successor to his grandfather.

John, living 19 Henry VII.

William, *d. s. p.* 20 Henry VII.

Maude, m. to John Done, of Flaxyoards, in Cheshire.

Joan, m. first, to Roger Dutton, who afterwards became heir to all Dutton's lands; and, secondly, to Sir Richard Strangeways.

Margery, m. 2 Henry VII. to John Wood, of Sutton.

He *d.* in 1492, and was *s.* by his grandson,

Richard Aston, esq. of Aston, who m. Douce, daughter of Piers Warburton, esq. (called *Wise Piers*) of Warburton and Arley, and had issue,

Thomas, his successor.

Richard, a priest, 26 Henry VIII.

Robert, of Grange, in the county of Stafford.

John, of Grange.

Catherine, m. to Richard Broughton, of Broughton, in Staffordshire.

Alice, m. 23 Henry VII. to Randle, son and heir of Randle Mainwaring, esq. of Karincham, in Cheshire.

Anne, m. 10 Henry VIII. to William Massy, esq. of Rixton, in Lancashire.

Richard Aston *d.* in 1529, and was *s.* by his eldest son,

Thomas Aston, esq. of Aston. This gentleman wedded, in 1512, Bridget, daughter of John Harewell, and sister and co-heir of Thomas Harewell, esq. of Shotery, in Warwickshire, and had five sons, viz.†

John, his heir.

Richard.

Peter, who had a bastard son, Thomas Aston, who was living in London in the 36 Henry VIII.

William, m. Anne, daughter of Thomas Ireland, esq. of the Hutt, in Lancashire.

Francis.

Thomas Aston was sheriff of Cheshire in 1551, 4 Edward VI. and dying in two years after was *s.* by his eldest son,

John Aston, esq. of Aston, who m. in 1546, Margaret, daughter of Thomas Ireland, esq. of the Hutt, in the county of Lancaster,‡ and by her (who wedded, secondly, Hugh Beeston, esq. of Torperley, in Cheshire) had issue,§

Thomas, his successor.

John, a lawyer, } *d. s. p.*
Edward, }

Bridget, m. to Thomas Bunbury, esq. of Stanney, in the county of Chester.

Elizabeth, m. to John Massy, esq. of Coughow, younger brother of George Massy, esq. of Podington, and afterwards heir to his brother.

Margaret, m. first, to Thomas Egerton, esq. of Walgreve; and, secondly, to Sir Edward Tirrel, of Thornton, Bucks.

Mary, *d. s. p.*

Eleanor, m. to James Whitlock.

Winifred, m. to Peter Derby, residing near Liverpool.

Ellen, m. to George Mainwaring, esq. a younger brother, of Ightfield, in Shropshire.

Ursula, m. to Geffrey Holcroft, of Hurst, in Lancashire.

He *d.* 5th August, 1573, and *s.* by his eldest son,

Sir Thomas Aston, of Aston, who received the honour of knighthood in 1603. He m. first, in 1569, Elizabeth, daughter of Sir Arthur Mainwaring, of Ightfield, and had issue,

John, his successor.

Arthur (Sir), of Fulham, in Middlesex, who had two sons, Richard Aston, and Sir Arthur Aston, a colonel in the army, and governor of Oxford for the king in 1644, who was put to death by the rebels at Tredagh, in Ireland, in 1655, after having surrendered the town on conditions. He left issue.

Thomas (Sir), m. Elizabeth, daughter of John Shuckburgh, esq. of Birdenbury, in Warwickshire, and had issue.

Frances, m. first, to John Hocknell, esq. of Hocknell; secondly, to Robert Davis, of Croughton; and, thirdly, to Owen Longford, of Burton, in Derbyshire.

Grace, *d. s. p.*

Margaret, m. to Sir Thomas Ireland, of Beusy, near Warrington, and was vice-chamberlain of Chester.

Elizabeth, m. to Richard Dod, esq. of Cloverley, in Shropshire.

Mary, m. first, to Richard Brown, gent. of Upton, near Chester; and, secondly, to Jaques Arnodio.

Anne, m. to Richard Allen, esq. of Greenhill, Cheshire.

Catherine, m. to Peter Leigh, gent. of Ridge.

He wedded, secondly, Mary, daughter of William Unton, esq. of Dracton, in Salop, but had no other issue. She survived him, and m. secondly, Edward Payler, esq. of York. Sir Thomas was sheriff of Cheshire in 1601. He *d.* in 1613, and was *s.* by his eldest son,

John Aston, esq. of Aston, sewer to Anne, Queen Consort of *King* James I. This gentleman m. in 1611, Maude, daughter of Robert Needham, esq. of Shenton, in Shropshire, and had three sons and three daughters, viz.

Thomas, his heir.

John, *d.* unm. in 1646.

Robert, *d.* young.

Maude, m. first, to Thomas Parsons, esq. of Cubbington, in Warwickshire; and, secondly, in

---

* Younger son of Richard Massy, esq. of Rixton, in Lancashire.

† *He* had beside an illegitimate son, called Roger, afterwards

Sir Roger Aston, knt. gentleman of the bedchamber to *King* James I. who m. first, Mary Stewart, daughter of Alexander, Lord Ochiltree, and had four daughters, his co-heirs, viz.

i. Margaret, m. to Sir Gilbert Houghton, bart. of Houghton Tower, and had issue.

ii. Mary, m. to Sir Samuel Peyton, bart. of Knowlton, in Kent.

iii. Elizabeth, m. to Sir Robert Winkfield, knt. of Upton, in Northamptonshire.

iv. Anne, m. to Sir Thomas Perient, knt. of Colchester.

He wedded, secondly, Cordelia, daughter of Sir John Stanhope, and sister of the first Earl of Chesterfield, but had no other issue.

‡ By Margaret his wife, daughter of Sir Richard Bold, knt. of Bold, in Lancashire.

§ He had beside an illegitimate son, Richard Aston, who lived at Rocksavage, and *d.* in 1616.

1666, to John Shuckburgh, of Upton, in Wirral, a younger son of the Shuckburghs, of Warwickshire.

Anne, *d.* young.

Elizabeth, *d.* unm. in 1628.

Mr. Aston *d.* 13th May, 1615, and was *s.* by his eldest son,

I. THOMAS ASTON, esq. of Aston, who was created a BARONET by *King* CHARLES I. 25th July, 1628, and was subsequently in the civil wars a zealous supporter of the Royal cause. He *m.* first, in 1627, Magdalene, daughter of Sir John Poultney, knt. of Misterton, in the county of Leicester, and co-heir of her brother, John Poultney, of the same place, by whom (who *d.* 2nd June, 1635) he had no surviving issue. He wedded, secondly, Anne, daughter and sole heir of Sir Henry Willoughby, bart. of Ridley, in the county of Derby, by his first wife, one of the daughters and co-heirs of Sir Thomas Knollys, knt. of Berks, and by that lady (who survived him, and *m.* in her widowhood the Hon. Anchetel Grey, second son of Henry, Earl of Stamford) had

WILLOUGHBY, his successor.

Magdalene, *m.* to Sir Robert Burdett, (third) baronet, of Foremark, in the county of Derby—his second wife, and had several children.

Mary, *m.* to — Biddulph, esq. of Polesworth, in the county of Warwick.

Sir Thomas Aston sustained a defeat from Sir William Brereton's party of parliamentarians near Nantwich, 28th January, 1642, but effected his escape: he was afterwards however made prisoner in another skirmish, and brought into Stafford, whence attempting again to escape, he was observed by a soldier who gave him a blow on the head, which, and his other wounds brought on a fever and occasioned his death in Stafford, 24th May, 1645. He was *s.* by his son,

II. SIR WILLOUGHBY ASTON. This gentleman erected a sumptuous mansion at Aston, a little distant from the old seat. He *m.* Mary, daughter of John Offley, esq. of Madeley Manor, in Staffordshire, and had eight sons and nine surviving daughters, viz.

THOMAS, his heir.

John, captain R.N. *d. s. p.*

Willoughby, *m.* and left two daughters.

Arthur, *d.* at Constantinople unmarried.

Gilbert, *d.* young.

RICHARD, *m.* Elizabeth, daughter of John Warren, esq. of Oxfordshire, and died 24th November, 1741, leaving issue,

WILLOUGHBY, who inherited as fifth baronet.

Richard, barrister-at-law, constituted one of the judges of the court of King's Bench in 1765, and received the honour of knighthood. Sir Richard *m.* first, Miss Eldred, and, secondly, the relict of Sir David Williams, bart.

Mary, *m.* to — Dawson, M.D.

Robert, a merchant in London.

Edward, *d.* young.

Mary, *m.* first, to Sir John Crew, knt. of Utkinton, in Cheshire; and, secondly, to Dr. Chamberlen, of Alderton and Hinton.

Magdalen, *m.* to Thomas Norris, esq. of Speke, in Lancashire.

Frances.

Dorothy.

Charlotte, *m.* to John Pickering, esq. of Thelwall, in Cheshire.

Catherine, died unmarried.

Purefoy, *m.* to Henry Wright, esq. of Mobberley, in Cheshire, and of this marriage the grandson is the present LAURENCE WRIGHT, esq. of Mottram St. Andrew. (See BURKE'S *Commoners*, vol. iii. p. 406.)

Helena, *m.* to Captain Pennington, who assumed the surname of Legh, and was great grandfather of the present PETER LEGH, esq. of Booths.

Letitia, *m.* to — Jenks, esq.

Sir Willoughby *d.* 14th December, 1702, and was *s.* by his eldest son,

III. SIR THOMAS ASTON, who wedded Catherine, daughter of William Widdrington, esq. and died 16th January, 1724, left, with eight daughters, of whom CATHERINE, *m.* in 1730, the Hon. and Rev. Henry Hervey, fourth son of John, Earl of Bristol, and Margery, became the wife of Gilbert Walmesly, esq. register of the diocese of Lichfield and Coventry, an only son and heir,

IV. SIR THOMAS ASTON, elected M.P. for Liverpool in the 1st of GEORGE II. and afterwards for St. Albans. He *m.* in March, 1735-6, Rebecca, daughter of John Shishe, esq. of Greenwich, by whom (who *d.* in May, 1737), having had no issue, he devised his estates, at his decease in France, 17th February, 1744, to his eldest sister, CATHERINE,* wife of the Hon. and Rev. JOHN HERVEY, D.D. who in consequence assumed, by act of parliament, the surname of ASTON. The baronetcy reverted to his cousin, (refer to RICHARD, sixth son of the second baronet).

V. SIR WILLOUGHBY ASTON, who wedded Elizabeth, daughter of Henry Pye, esq. of Farringdon, Berks, (by his wife Anne, sister of Lord Bathurst), and had issue,

WILLOUGHBY, his successor.

Elizabeth, *m.* to Admiral Cotton.

Purefoy, *m.* to the Hon. James Preston, brother of Lord Gormanston.

Mary, *m.* to Francis-Grant Gordon, esq. capt. R.N.

Selina, died unmarried in 1764.

Belinda, } died unmarried.
Sophia, }

Sir Willoughby was returned to parliament for Nottingham in 1754, and appointed colonel of the Berkshire militia in 1759. He *d.* 24th August, 1772, and was *s.* by his son,

VI. SIR WILLOUGHBY ASTON, who *m.* Lady Jane Henley, second daughter of Robert, Earl of Northington, LORD CHANCELLOR OF ENGLAND in 1761, but dying *s. p.* 22nd March, 1815, his sisters became his heirs, and the BARONETCY *expired*.

Arms—Party per chev. sa. and arg.

---

* CATHERINE ASTON, who inherited Aston Hall and the estates of her brother, had by her husband the Hon. and Rev. Dr. Hervey-Aston, who died in November, 1741, a son,

HENRY-HERVEY-ASTON, who *m.* Miss Dickinson, of Lancashire, and had a son and daughter, namely,

HENRY HERVEY-ASTON, a colonel in the army, who *m.* 16th September, 1780, the Hon. Harriet-Ingram Shepherd, fourth daughter and co-heir of Charles, ninth and last Viscount Irvine, of Scotland, and left at his decease (having fallen in a duel 23rd December, 1798) an only son,

HENRY-CHARLES HERVEY-ASTON, esq. of Aston Hall, who *m.*
and left at his decease,

HENRY HERVEY-ASTON, cornet 1st Life Guards.

Arthur Henry-Aston.

Harriet Hervey-Aston, *m.* 17th July, 1832, to the Hon. and Rev. Arthur Talbot.

Anna-Sophia Hervey-Aston, *m.* 2nd June, 1782, to Anthony Hodges, esq. which marriage was dissolved by parliament in 1795.

ATKINS, OF CLAPHAM.

CREATED 13th June, 1660. EXTINCT 19th June, 1756.

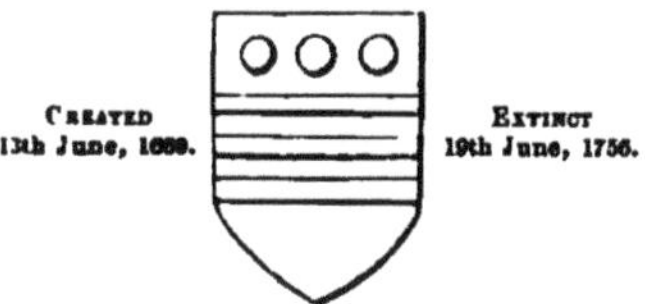

Lineage.

This family was originally of Great Berkhampsted, in Hertfordshire, where it was located in the time of ELIZABETH, but it rose into eminence through the professional success of

HENRY ATKINS, M.D. physician to *King* JAMES I. who was offered by his royal master the first baronet's patent, on the institution of the order, but he declined accepting the honor. His son and heir,

SIR HENRY ATKINS, received the honor of knighthood from the same monarch, and marrying Annabella, daughter of John Hawkins, esq. of Chiddingstone, in Kent, had a numerous family. He was *s.* at his decease by his eldest surviving son,

I. RICHARD ATKINS, esq. of Clapham, in the county of Surrey, who was created a BARONET by *King* CHARLES II. 13th June, 1660. He *m.* Rebecca, daughter of Sir Edmund Wright, of London, knt. and had issue,

Henry, who *d.* 15th February, 1677, aged twenty-four, unmarried.

RICHARD, successor to the title.

Annabella, } Rebecca, } *d.* unm.

Mary, *m.* to the Right Rev. William Moreton, D.D. Bishop of Meath, and had issue,

Richard Moreton, in holy orders, *d. s. p.*

ANNABELLA MORETON, *m.* to William Taylor, esq. of Dublin, barrister-at-law, and dying in 1774, left a son,

The Rev. RICHARD TAYLOR, who inherited the estate of Little Moreton, in the county of Chester, at the decease of his uncle of the half blood, Sir William Moreton, recorder of the city of London in 1763, and assumed the name and arms of MORETON. He was father of the *present* Rev. William-Moreton Moreton, of Little Moreton.

Agnes, *m.* to Edward Atkins, esq. brother of Sir Robert Atkins, K. B.

Elizabeth, *m.* to Thomas Tooke, esq. of Wormley.

Rebecca, *m.* to Sir Wolstan Dixie, bart. of Market Bosworth, in the county of Leicester.

Sir Richard *d.* 19th August, 1689, and was *s.* by his only surviving son,

II. SIR RICHARD ATKINS, who wedded Elizabeth, daughter of Sir Thomas Byde, knt. of Ware Park, in Hertfordshire, and had surviving issue,

HENRY, his successor.

Ralph.

Richard.

Annabella.

This gentleman, who was a colonel in the army, *d.* 28th November, 1696, and was *s.* by his eldest son,

III. SIR HENRY ATKINS, who *m.* Rebecca-Maria, eldest daughter of Sir Wolstan Dixie, bart. and had, with one surviving daughter, Rebecca-Maria, *m.* in 1730, to Thomas Polkes, esq. an only surviving son, his successor at his decease in 1712,

IV. SIR HENRY ATKINS. This gentleman *m.* in October 1723, Penelope, daughter of Sir John Stonhouse, bart. of Radley, in the county of Berks, by whom (who *rem.* 31st October, 1733, John, first Earl Gower*), he had

HENRY, } RICHARD, } fifth and sixth baronets.

Penelope, *m.* 5th January, 1745-6, George Pitt, first Lord Rivers, and was great-grandfather of the present peer.

He *d.* in France, in 1728, and was *s.* by his elder son,

V. SIR HENRY ATKINS, who *d.* at the age of sixteen, 1st September, 1742, and was *s.* by his brother,

VI. SIR RICHARD ATKINS. This gentleman *d.* unm. 19th June, 1756, when the representation of the family vested in the Pitt family, and the BARONETCY became *extinct.*

Arms—Az. three bars arg. in chief three bezants.

AUCHER, OF BISHOPSBOURNE.

CREATED 4th July, 1666. EXTINCT 20th May, 1726.

Lineage.

The family of AUCHER, eminent in ancient times in the counties of Essex, Kent, Sussex, and Nottingham, "derived" (we quote Hasted) from *Ealcher* or AUCHER, the first Earl of Kent, and among its earliest members we may mention Walter Fitz-Auger, a noble Briton, who flourished at the Conquest, and was a considerable benefactor to the Monks of St. Saviour, Bermondsey; Thomas Fitzaunger, who possessed the manor of Losenham, in Kent, *temp. King* JOHN; and Henry Fitzaucher, whose name occurs in the roll of those Kentish gentlemen who were with EDWARD I. at the siege of Carlaverock.

NICHOLAS AUCHER, son of Thomas, Lord of Losenham, in Kent, *temp.* EDWARD II. married the daughter of Oxenbridge of Bread, in Sussex, and had two sons. The younger, William, left an only daughter, Christina, the wife of Arnald de Alkham. The elder was father of

HENRY AUCHER, of Losenham, *m.* Elizabeth, daughter of John Diggs, of Barham, in Kent, and had a son and successor.

HENRY AUCHER, of Losenham, who wedded, first, Isabella At Towne, of Throwleigh, and had by her,

I. THOMAS, of Losenham, whose son, HENRY of Losenham, *m.* Elizabeth, daughter of Sir John Guldeford, knt. of Halden, and left an only daughter and heir,

ANNE, who espoused, *temp.* HENRY VII. Walter Colepeper, second son of Sir John Colepeper, knt. by Agnes, daughter and

* She was his lordship's second wife; by him she had a daughter, Penelope, *b.* at Trentham, in June 1734, who died in the seventh year of her age.

heir of John Bedgebery, esq. The grandson of this marriage, Sir John Colepeper, knt. of Wigsell, sold the manor of Losenham to Adrian Moore, esq. of Egham, in Surrey, in whose family it continued until alienated in 1702 to Nicholas Bishop.

II. Robert, ancestor of the Auchers of Westwell.

Henry Aucher married, secondly, Joan, daughter and heir of Thomas St. Leger, of Otterden, second son of Sir Ralph St. Leger, of Ulcomb, knight of the shire for Kent 51 Edward, and had an only son,

Henry Aucher, who succeeded to the manor of Otterden, his mother's inheritance, and seated himself there, where he was residing 19 Henry VI. He m. Alicia Boleyn, and left a son and successor,

John Aucher, of Otterden, who died 23rd April, 1503, and was buried in the north chapel of the parish church, leaving by Alice Church, his wife, three sons and two daughters, viz.

I. James, his heir.
II. William, *d. s. p.*
III. Marmaduke, *m.* a daughter of Gilbofe.

I. Elizabeth, *m.* to Thomas Berham, of Sisinghurst.
II. Jane, *m.* to Thomas Corbet.

The eldest son,

James Aucher, esq. of Otterden, wedded Alice, daughter of Thomas Hills, esq. of Eggarton, near Godmersham, and by her (who *m.* secondly, James Hardres, esq. of Hardres) had a son and daughter, Anthony, his heir, and Susan, *m.* to James Aucher. He died 6th January, 1508, was interred near his father, and succeeded by his son,

Sir Anthony Aucher, knt. of Otterden, who acquired from Thomas Colepeper, *temp.* Henry VIII. the manors of Bishopsborne and Hautsborne, in Kent. He wedded Affra, daughter of William Cornwallis, of Norfolk, and had issue,

I. John, of Otterden, *m.* Ann, daughter of Sir William Kellaway, knt. and left an only daughter and heiress,
   Joan, *m. temp. Queen* Elizabeth, to Sir Humphrey Gilbert, knt. by whom the manor of Otterden was sold to William Lewin, LL.D.
II. Edward, of whom presently.
III. Thomas, *d. s. p.*
IV. William, of Nonington.

I. Susannah.

The second son,

Edward Aucher, esq. inherited, under his father's will, the manors of Bishopsbourne and Hautsborne. He *m.* Mabel, daughter of Sir Thomas Wrothe, knt. and had

Anthony, his heir.

Elizabeth, *m.* to Sir William Lovelace, knt. of Bethersden, in Kent, and had by him, who died in 1629, with other issue, a son,
   Sir William Lovelace, of Woolwich, who *m.* Anne, daughter of Sir William Barnes, knt. and had a son,
      Richard (Sir), of Lovelace Place, in Kent, who *d.* in 1658, leaving an only daughter and heir,
         Margaret, *m.* to Henry, fifth son of Lord Chief Justice Coke.

The son and successor,

Anthony Aucher, esq. of Bishopsbourne, or Bourne, married two wives, but had issue only by the second, Margaret, daughter of Edwin Sandys, Archbishop of York, viz. two sons and as many daughters,

Anthony, his heir.

Edwin, of Willesborough, who *m.* Mary, daughter of John Gibbon, and by her, who *d.* in 1679, had a numerous issue. His son, the Rev. John Aucher, D.D. prebendary of Canterbury, died in 1701.

Elizabeth, *m.* first, to Sir William Hammond, knt. of St. Albans Court, in Kent, ancestor of the poet Hammond, and of the present William Osmund Hammond, esq. of St. Albans Court (see Burke's *History of the Commoners*). She wedded, secondly, in 1624, the Venerable Walter Balcanqual, Dean of Rochester.

Margaret, *m.* to Sir Roger James, knt.

He died 13th January, 1609-10, and was succeeded by his son,

Sir Anthony Aucher, knt. of Bourne, who served as sheriff of Kent in 12 James I. He *m.* Hester, daughter and co-heir of Peter Collet, of London, and dying in July 1637, was succeeded by his son,

I. Sir Anthony Aucher, of Bourne, who was created a baronet 4th July, 1666. He wedded, first, Elizabeth, daughter of Robert Hatton, esq. by whom (who died in 1648) he had no issue to survive him, and, secondly, Elizabeth, daughter of Sir Thomas Hewitt, knt. by whom he had,

I. Anthony, his heir.
II. Hewitt, successor to his brother.

I. Elizabeth, *m.* to John Corbett, LL.D. Of this lady presently as co-heiress to her brother, the last baronet.
II. Hester, *m.* to Ralph Blomer, D.D. prebendary of Canterbury, and had, with other issue, a daughter,
   Anne Blomer, who wedded James Teale, esq. and had a son, Isaac M. Teale, esq. and a daughter, Mary Teale, who *m.* Major General Sir Charles Shipley, and left three daughters,
      Katherine-Jane, *m.* to Colonel Edward Warner.
      Augusta-Mary, *m.* to Alexander Manning, esq.
      Elizabeth-Cole, *m.* to Henry, Earl of Buchan.

Sir Anthony died in May, 1692, and was *s.* by his son,

II. Sir Anthony Aucher, of Bourne, at whose decease in minority in 1694, the title passed to his brother,

III. Sir Hewitt Aucher, of Bourne, who died unmarried in 1726, when the Baronetcy expired. His elder sister and co-heir,

Elizabeth, the wife of John Corbett, LL.D. left five daughters and co-heirs, viz.

1. Catharine Corbett, who *m.* Stephen Beckingham, esq. (to whom she was second wife), and had a son,
   The Rev. John Charles Beckingham, who inherited the whole of the Bishopsbourne estate, his father having purchased, in 1752, the shares of his sisters-in-law in the property. Mr. Beckingham left at his decease an only daughter and heir,
      Louisa, *m.* in 1802, to Edward Taylor, esq. of Bifrons, in Kent, and has issue. (See Burke's *Commoners*, vol. iii. p. 107).
2. Elizabeth Corbett, *m.* to Thomas Dinward, esq. and *d. s. p.*
3. Frances Corbett, *m.* to Sir William Hardres, bart. of Hardres, who *d. s. p.* 31st Aug. 1764.
4. Antonina Corbett, *m.* to Ignatius Geoghegan, esq. and had issue.

3. MARGARET-HANNAH-ROBERTA CORBETT, m. to William Hougham, esq. of Barton Court, and had issue,

William Hougham, of Barton Court, d. in 1828, s. p.

Catharine Hougham, m. to the Rev. Richard Sandys, and had issue,

Richard-Edwin Sandys, lieut. R. N. killed in action off Copenhagen 2nd April, 1801, unm.

Catharina Sandys, m. in 1803, to John Chesshyre, esq. capt. R.N.

Arms—Erm. on a chief az. three lions rampt. or.

AUSTEN, OF BEXLEY.

CREATED 10th July, 1660.

EXTINCT 13th Feb. 1772.

Lineage.

WILLIAM AUSTEN, esq. of Herendon, in Tenterden, county of Kent, m. Elizabeth, daughter of Edward Hales, esq., also of Tenterden, by Margaret, his wife, daughter of John Honywood, esq. and had issue, viz.

EDWARD, of Herendon, m. Rebecca, daughter of Sir Edward Baston, knt. of Mersham, and had a son,

EDWARD, who wedded Jane, only daughter of Cheyney Selhurst, esq. of Tenterden, and d. s. p.

John d. unm. in 1655.

ROBERT.

Elizabeth, m. to Samuel Short, of Tenterden.

Mary, m. to Anthony Whetenhall, esq. of East Peckham.

Abigail, m. to Edward Jervis.

The youngest son,

I. ROBERT AUSTEN, esq. of Bexley, high sheriff of Kent in 1660 and 1661, was created a BARONET by *King* CHARLES II. on the 10th July in the former year. Sir Robert m. first, Margaret, daughter of William Williamson, of London, vintner, and had an only surviving child, Elizabeth, wife of Sir Thomas Dacres, knt. of Cheshunt, Herts. He m. secondly, Anne, daughter of Thomas Muns, esq. of Otteridge, in Kent, and by that lady had issue,

I. JOHN, his successor.

II. Robert, of Herendon, m. Judith, daughter and co-heir of Ralph Freke, esq. of Hanington, Wilts, and had

1. Robert, who wedded Jane, daughter of William Strode, esq. of Barrington, in the county of Somerset, and had three sons and one daughter, viz.

William.

EDWARD, who inherited as sixth baronet.

ROBERT, s. his brother as seventh baronet.

Jane-Grace, m. Richard Windsor, esq. of Tottenham, and had an only dau. Sarah Windsor, who m. first, Edward Constable, and, secondly, J. Bristow, and left by the former two daughters and co-heirs, viz.

MARY CONSTABLE, m. to the Rev. Thomas Roberts.

ANNE CONSTABLE, m. to Sir William Curtis, bart.

2. Edward, of Bexley, m. first, Mary, daughter of Edward Napier, esq. of Dorsetshire, but had no issue. He wedded, secondly, Elizabeth, daughter of Edward Manning, esq. of Kivington, in Kent, and had a son, John.

III. John, a merchant, who d. in Turkey.

I. Anne, m. to Sir Oliver Boteler, bart. of Treston, in Kent.

II. Ursula, m. first, to George Stawell, esq. of Cotherston, in the county of Somerset, son of Sir John Stawell, K.B. and, secondly, to Henry Seymour, esq. of Langley Park, in the county of Buckingham.

Sir Robert d. 30th October, 1666, and was s. by his eldest son,

II. SIR JOHN AUSTEN, M.P. for Rye, in several parliaments *temp.* WILLIAM III. and one of the commissioners of the Customs. He m. Rose, daughter and heir of Sir John Hale, knt. of Stagenhoe, in Hertfordshire, by whom (who d. in 1695) he had issue,

ROBERT, his heir.

Edward, colonel in the Guards, killed at the Battle of Almanza, d. s. p.

Elizabeth, d. unm.

Rose, m. to Comberford Brooke, Esq. of Madeley Court, in Shropshire, and of Comberford, in the county of Stafford.

Anne, m. to Robert Rod, esq. of Herefordshire.

He d. in 1698, and was s. by his son,

III. SIR ROBERT AUSTEN. This gentleman wedded Elizabeth, daughter and co-heir of George Stawell, esq. of Cotherston, in Somersetshire, and by her (who survived him, and wedded, secondly, William Wynd, esq. of Norfolk, chamberlain to the Princess Sophia, and d. in 1725) had issue,

ROBERT, his successor.

SHEFFIELD, heir to his brother.

John.

Rose, m. to Sherrington Grosvenor, esq. of Holt, in the county of Warwick.

Anne.

Mary.

Elizabeth.

Stawell.

Sir Robert d. in 1706, and was s. by his eldest son,

IV. SIR ROBERT AUSTEN, M.P. for New Romney, in Kent, m. in November 1738, Rachel, daughter of Sir Francis Dashwood, bart. of West Wycomb, Bucks, but dying without issue in 1743, was s. by his brother,

V. SIR SHEFFIELD AUSTEN. This gentleman dying s. p. about the year 1758, was s. by his kinsman (refer to line of Robert, second son of the first baronet),

VI. SIR EDWARD AUSTEN, who d. unm. 28th December, 1760, and was s. by his brother,

VII. SIR ROBERT, at whose decease s. p. 13th February, 1772, the BARONETCY EXPIRED.

Arms—Or, a chevron gu. between three lions' paws erect and erased sa.

AUSTEN, OF DERHAMS.

CREATED 16th Nov. 1714.

EXTINCT 22nd Mar. 1472.

Lineage.

I. JOHN AUSTEN, esq. of Derhams, in Middlesex, (of a family which had for a long time possessed considerable estates, at Islington, Hoxton, and other parts of the same county,) was created a BARONET 16th November, 1714. Sir John represented the county of Middlesex in parliament. He *d.* unm. 22nd March, 1742, when the BARONETCY became *extinct*.

Arms—Az. on a chev. or, three cinquefoils vert between as many doves of the second.

AYLOFFE, OF BRAXTED MAGNA, ESSEX.

CREATED 25th Nov. 1612.

EXTINCT 10th Apr. 1781.

Lineage.

The ancient seat of this family, one of Saxon extraction, was at Bocton Aloph, near Wye, in the county of Kent, which town they possessed in the reign of HENRY III., and which place, as Mr. Philpot observes, "had that appellative distinction united to its name to intimate to us, that in the Saxon time it owned the jurisdiction of one Alulphus, a Saxon." From this Alulphus descended ALUFF, a person of great note in the time of EDWARD the Confessor.

About the reign of HENRY VI.,

JOHN AYLOFF was seated at Hornchurch, in the county of Essex, and married to Anne, daughter of Thomas West, esq. by whom he had issue,

THOMAS AYLOFF, of the same place, and of Sudbury in Suffolk, holding large possessions in the counties of Essex and Suffolk *temp.* EDWARD IV., who had issue, by Agnes, his wife, daughter of William Birch (by Alice his wife, daughter of Roger Grice, of Norfolk), a son, William, and a daughter, Agnes, *m.* to Sir John Bruges, lord mayor of London, from whom the Barons Chandos descended, and Winifred Bruges, *m.* to Sir Richard Sackville, of Buckhurst, father of Sir Thomas Sackville, Baron Buckhurst, and Earl of Dorset.

The son,

WILLIAM AYLOFFE, *m.* Audrey, daughter of Sir John Shaw, knt. alderman of London, by whom he had three children, WILLIAM, THOMAS,* and Agnes.

The elder son,

WILLIAM AYLOFF, esq. was high sheriff of Essex and Hertfordshire 6th ELIZABETH, and left by Agnes, his wife, daughter of Sir Thomas Barnardiston, knt. of Ketton, in Suffolk (by Anne, daughter of Sir Thomas Lucas, knt. of Colchester, in Essex), a son and heir,

WILLIAM AYLOFFE, high sheriff of the county of Essex 36th ELIZABETH, and one of the judges of the King's Bench 20th of the same reign. He *m.* Jane, daughter of Eustace Sulyard, esq. of Flemings, in Suffolk, and had issue three sons and one daughter, viz.

I. WILLIAM.
II. Thomas, who *m.* Mary Guicciardine, and was father of Guicciardine Ayloff, secretary of the Duchy of Lancaster.
III. George, who *d. s. p.*
I. Margaret, wife of Edward Broom, esq. of Oxfordshire.

The eldest son,

I. SIR WILLIAM AYLOFFE, knt. *s.* to the estate, and residing at Braxted Magna, was knighted by *King* JAMES I. at the Charter-house with many more, on his first arrival in London, and afterwards advanced by the said king to the degree of a BARONET in 1612. He *m.* first, Catharine, daughter and co-heir of John Sterne, esq. of Melburne, in Cambridgeshire, and had by her three sons and four daughters,

William, died in the lifetime of his father in the West Indies.
BENJAMIN, his successor.
James, had his mother's estate at Melburne, in Cambridgeshire: from his first wife, Jane, dau. of Sir William Herris, knt. of Shenfield, in Essex, descended William Ayloffe, esq. of Basingburn, in Cambridgeshire; and by his second wife, Elizabeth, daughter of Thomas Penyston, esq. of Rochester, Thomas Ayloffe, D.C.L.
Mary, wife of Sir Anthony Thomas, knt. of Cobham, in Surrey.
Elizabeth, wife of Gervase Lee, of Norwell, in Nottinghamshire.
Anne, *d. s. p.*
Jane, *m.* to Edward Kighley, of Gray, in Essex.

Sir William *m.* secondly, Barbara, daughter and heir of Thomas Sexton, and had two sons,

Thomas, of Gray's Inn, who *m.* Elizabeth, daughter of Edward Wentworth, of Bocking, in Essex, and was father of Benjamin Ayloffe, esq. of Gray's Inn, who *m.* Victoria, daughter of Alexander Erskine, esq. son to John, Earl of Mar.
John, was a colonel in the West Indies, and *d. s. p.*

The baronet *m.* thirdly, Alice Stokes, and had issue,

Joseph, of Gray's Inn, *m.* Frances, daughter of Henry Ayscough, esq. and left two sons and five daughters. The elder son,
JOSEPH, of Gray's Inn, barrister-at-law, wedded Mary, daughter of Bryan Ayloffe, merchant, of London, and was father of
JOSEPH, who eventually inherited the baronetcy as sixth baronet.

---

* The younger son of William Ayloffe,

THOMAS AYLOFFE, was a merchant, free of the company of barber-surgeons in London, and when Bridge Ward was finished, 4th EDWARD VI, the first elected alderman of it. He was afterwards knighted, and died 2nd PHILIP and MARY. He left William, his son and heir, by his wife Elizabeth, (or Isabel), daughter of Thomas, and sister of Sir Edward Walsingham, knt., who had issue, a son of his own name, William Ayloffe, esq. who was brought up to the study of the law.

Sir William was *s.* at his decease by his eldest surviving son,

II. SIR BENJAMIN AYLOFFE, who adhered with eminent fidelity to *King* CHARLES I., and was appointed by that monarch high sheriff of Essex at the commencement of the civil war. He survived until after the Restoration, and served as knight of the shire for Essex in the first parliament succeeding that great event. He married three wives, but had issue only by the second, Margaret, daughter of Thomas Fanshaw, esq. remembrancer of the Exchequer, and aunt of Thomas, Lord Fanshaw, three sons and one daughter, viz.

I. WILLIAM, his successor.
II. BENJAMIN, heir to his brother.
III. Henry, who *m.* Dorothy, daughter and heir of Richard Bulkeley, esq. of Cheadle, and was father of
 JOHN, of Stanford Rivers, in Essex, who succeeded as fifth BARONET.
I. Catharine, *m.* to Thomas Hardwick, esq. of Leeds.

Sir Benjamin *d.* about the year 1663, and was *s.* by his eldest son,

III. SIR WILLIAM AYLOFFE, who wedded Anne, daughter of Peter Orbye, esq. of Burton Pedwarden, in Lincolnshire, and relict of Frederick de la Tremouille Comte de Laval and Benon, but had no surviving issue at his decease in 1675, when the title passed to his brother,

IV. SIR BENJAMIN AYLOFFE, an eminent merchant of the city of London, who *m.* Martha, daughter of Sir John Tyrrel, knt. of Heron, in Essex, and had
 John, who *d. v. p.* unm.
 Margaret, *m.* to the Rev. Mr. Jenks, minister of St. Dunstan's in the West, London.
 Martha, *m.* to John Preston, of London, merchant.

Sir Benjamin died 5th March, 1722, and leaving no male issue, was *s.* by his nephew,

V. THE REV. SIR JOHN AYLOFFE, at whose demise unm. 10th December, 1730, the dignity reverted to (the descendant of the third marriage of the first baronet) his cousin,

VI. SIR JOSEPH AYLOFFE, F.R.S. who *m.* Margaret, daughter and sole heir of Thomas Railton, esq. of Carlisle, but dying without surviving issue, 19th April, 1781, aged seventy-two, the BARONETCY expired.

Arms—Sa. a lion rampant or, between three crosses patee of the second.

BACKHOUSE, OF LONDON.

CREATED 9th Nov. 1660.

EXTINCT 22nd Aug. 1669.

Lineage.

I. SIR WILLIAM BACKHOUSE, of the city of London, was created a BARONET in 1660. He *m.* Flower, daughter and sole heir of William Backhouse, esq. of Swallowfield, in Berkshire, but dying *s. p.* the title became EXTINCT in less than nine years after its creation.

Arms—A saltire ermine.

BACON, OF GILLINGHAM.

CREATED 7th Feb. 1662.

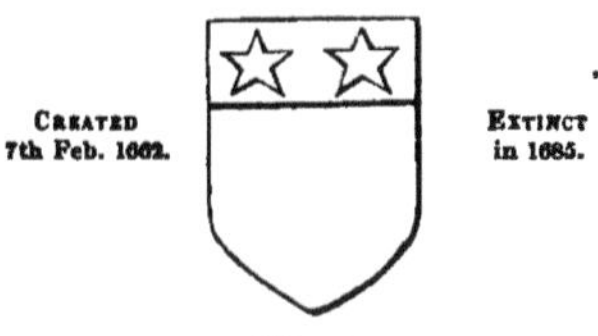

EXTINCT in 1685.

Lineage.

SIR NICHOLAS BACON, of Redgrave, eldest son of the Lord Keeper, was the first person advanced to the dignity of a BARONET on the institution of the order by JAMES I. in 1611. He *m.* Anne, only daughter and heir of Edmund Butts, esq. of Thornage, in Norfolk, by Anne his wife, daughter and co-heir of Henry Buers, esq. of Barrow, in Suffolk, and had issue,

I. EDMUND (Sir), who *s.* his father as second baronet of Redgrave, but *d. s. p.* in 1649.
II. ROBERT (Sir), whose male line terminated with SIR EDMUND BACON, the sixth baronet of Redgrave.
III. BACHEVELL, of Hockham, in Norfolk, who left three daughters his co-heirs, viz.
 Mary, *m.* to Sir Robert Baldock, knt. one of the judges of the Common Pleas.
 Philippa, *m.* to Robert Keddington, esq.
 Anne, *m.* to Nicholas Rookwood, esq.
IV. BUTTS, ancestor of the present SIR EDMUND BACON, bart. of Redgrave and Mildenhall. (See BURKE'S *Peerage and Baronetage*.)
V. NICHOLAS, of whom presently.
VI. NATHANIEL (Sir), of Culford, in Suffolk, K. B. who *m.* Jane, daughter of Hercules Meautys, esq. and widow of Sir William Cornwallis, by whom he had one son and two daughters, viz.
 Nicholas, who *d.* without male issue.
 Anne, *m.* first, to Sir Thomas Meautys, knt.; and, secondly, to Sir Harbottle Grimston, bart.
 Jane, *d.* unm.
I. Anne, *m.* to Sir Robert Drury, knt. of Hawsted, in Suffolk.
II. Dorothy, *m.* first, to Sir Bassingbourn Gawdey, knt. of Harling; and, secondly, to Philip Colby, esq.
III. Jemima, *m.* to Sir William Waldegrave, knt. of Smallbridge.

The fifth son,

NICHOLAS BACON, esq. of Gillingham, in Norfolk, *m.* first, a daughter of Sir James Weston, baron of the Exchequer, by whom he had an only daughter, *m.* to Sir John Rous, bart. of Henham; and, secondly, Margaret, daughter of Eustace D'Arcy, esq. of Norwich, by whom he had a son,

I. SIR NICHOLAS BACON, of Gillingham, who was created a BARONET 7th February, 1661; he *m.* Elizabeth, daughter and heir of Richard Freeston, esq. of Mendham, in Norfolk, and dying about the year 1666, was *s.* by his eldest son,

II. SIR EDMUND BACON, of Gillingham, at whose decease unmarried, in 1683, the title devolved on his brother,

III. SIR RICHARD BACON, of Gillingham, who *m.*

Anne, daughter of Sir Henry Bacon, bart. of Herringfleet, but dying *s. p.* in 1685, the BARONETCY became EXTINCT, but the estates passed to his brother-in-law, Sir Henry Bacon, bart. of Herringfleet, direct ancestor of the present SIR EDMUND BACON, bart. of Redgrave.

Arms—Gu. on a chief arg. two mullets sa.

BADD, OF CAMES OYSELLS.

CREATED 28th Feb. 1642.

EXTINCT 10th June, 1683.

Lineage.

I. SIR THOMAS BADD, of Cames Oysells, was created a BARONET in 1642, but dying without surviving issue, 10th June, 1683, aged seventy-six, the title ceased with himself.

Arms—Five fleurs-de-lys.

BAKER, OF SISINGHURST.

CREATED 29th June, 1611.

EXTINCT 28th Mar. 1661.

Lineage.

The family of Baker was settled at Cranbrooke, in Kent, so early as the reign of EDWARD III., and from one of its younger branches descended THOMAS BAKER, of Rushington, whose daughter and heiress, Margaret, *m.* to John Selden, was mother of the learned John Selden.

THOMAS BAKER, of Sisinghurst, Cranbrook, Kent, was father of

RICHARD BAKER, living *temp.* HENRY VII., whose son,

SIR JOHN BAKER, knt. of Sisinghurst, adopting the legal profession, attained considerable eminence, and when a young man was sent ambassador to Denmark. On his return he became Speaker of the House of Commons, and was soon after appointed attorney-general and sworn of the privy council, but gained no further preferment until 1545, when, having recommended himself to the king by his activity in forwarding a loan in London and other imposts, he was made chancellor of the Exchequer. HENRY VIII. constituted him an assistant trustee for the minor successor, after whose accession his name is scarcely mentioned in history, except in one instance, which ought not to be forgotten: he was the only privy counsellor who steadfastly denied his assent to the last will of that prince, by which Mary and Elizabeth were excluded from inheriting the crown. He was successively recorder of London, attorney and chancellor of the Exchequer. He was likewise a privy counsellor to HENRY VIII., EDWARD VI., MARY, and ELIZABETH. Sir Richard *m.* Elizabeth, daughter and heir of Thomas Dinley, and widow of George Barret, by whom he had issue,

RICHARD (Sir), his heir.

John, of London, who *m.* Catharine, daughter of Sir Reginald Scott, knt. of Scott's Hall, and left a son,

SIR RICHARD BAKER, *b.* about the year 1568, the celebrated CHRONICLER. This distinguished writer *m.* Margaret, daughter of Sir George Manwaring, of Ightfield, by whom he had two sons and three daughters. Sir Richard, who possessed the manor of Middle Aston, and other estates in Oxfordshire, served the office of high sheriff for that county in 1620, but having become surety for some of the debts of his wife's family, was thereby reduced to poverty and thrown into the Fleet prison, where he died 18th February, 1645, and was buried in St. Bride's Church, Fleet Street.

Elizabeth, *m.* to Sir Thomas Scott, knt. of Scott's Hall.

Cecilia, *m.* to the Lord Treasurer Dorset.

Mary, *m.* to George Tufton, of Heathfield, in Kent.

Sir Richard *d.* in 1558, and was interred at Sisinghurst, where he possessed a fine estate formerly belonging to the family of De Berham, and a noble mansion built by himself, Sisinghurst Castle, which remained for centuries with his descendants, but has since bowed down its battlements to the unfeeling taste of modern times. His eldest son and heir,

SIR RICHARD BAKER, knt. of Sisinghurst, entertained *Queen* ELIZABETH in her progress into Kent July, 1573. He *m.* first, Catherine, daughter and heir of John Tirrell, youngest son of Sir Thomas Tirrell, knt. and had

JOHN, his heir.

Thomas (Sir), knt. of Whittingham, in Suffolk, *m.* and had issue.

Anne, *m.* first, to John Goodwin; secondly, to — Drew; and, thirdly, to Baron Sandys, of the Vine, in Hampshire.

Sir Richard wedded, secondly, Mary, daughter of John Gifford, and had by her two daughters,

Grisagon, *m.* to Henry Lennard, Lord Dacre.

Cecilia, *m.* to Richard Blunt, son and heir of Sir Michael Blunt.

The elder son,

JOHN BAKER, esq. of Sisinghurst, succeeded his father in 1594. He *m.* Mary, daughter of Sir Thomas Guildford, knt. of Hempsted, in Kent, and had, with a daughter, Catharine, wife of Edward Yates, esq. of Buckland, two sons, Henry and Edward. The elder

I. HENRY BAKER, esq. of Sisinghurst, was created a BARONET 29th June, 1611. He *m.* Catharine, eldest daughter of Sir John Smith, knt. of Ostenhanger, and dying in 1623, was *s.* by his son,

II. SIR JOHN BAKER, of Sisinghurst, who *m.* Elizabeth, daughter of Sir Robert Parkhurst, knt. and by her, who died in 1639, left at his decease, in 1653, an only surviving child,

III. SIR JOHN BAKER, of Sisinghurst, who *m.* Elizabeth, daughter and heir of Sir Robert Newton, bart. of London, and by her (who wedded, secondly, Philip Howard, and died in 1693), had four daughters, his co-heirs, viz.

ANNE, *m.* to Edmund Beaghan, esq. and dying in 1685, left a son,

EDMUND-STUNGATE BEAGHAN, esq. of Sisinghurst, who sold in the year 1730, to the trustees of Sir Horace Mann, knt. his portion of the Sisinghurst estates.

Elizabeth, m. to Robert Spencer, esq. and *d. s. p.* in 1765.

Mary, m. to John Dowel, esq. of Over, in Gloucestershire, and had a son,

John-Baker Dowel, esq. of Over, who *d.* in 1738, and was *s.* by his son,

John-Baker-Bridges Dowel, esq. of Over, who *d.* in 1744, bequeathing his interest in the Baker estates to the Rev. Staunton Degge, who conveyed them to Galfridus Mann, esq. father of Sir Horace Mann.

Katherine, m. to Roger Kirkby, and *d.* in 1733.

Sir John Baker died in 1661, and leaving no male issue, the Baronetcy expired, while his estates passed to his daughters, from whose heirs they were purchased by Sir Horace Mann's family.

Arms—Az. on a fesse between three swans' heads erased and ducally gorged or, as many cinquefoils gu.

BAILLIE, OF PORTMAN SQUARE.

Created 11th Dec. 1812.—Extinct 21st Aug. 1820.

Lineage.

William Baillie, esq. son of Alexander Baillie, esq. of Dockfour, m. first, Elizabeth, daughter of Alexander Sutherland, esq. of Cleyn, in the county of Ross, by whom he had (with an elder and younger son) Ewen, of whom presently; and, secondly, Miss Margaret Mackay, of Biggens, in the county of Caithness, and had, with other children,

Catherine, who m. in 1769, Roderick Mackenzie, esq. of Fairburn, by whom she had

Alexander Mackenzie, the present baronet of Fairburn. (See Burke's *Peerage and Baronetage*.)

With other issue.

I. Ewen Baillie, esq. having attained the rank of major general in the army, with the colonelcy of the 23rd regiment of native infantry in Bengal, and being some time commander-in-chief of the forces there, was created a Baronet on the 11th December, 1812, but having no issue he obtained a second patent 26th May, 1819, with remainder to his nephew, Alexander Mackenzie. Sir Ewen *d. s. p.* in 1820, when the title under the first patent became extinct, while that under the second passed according to the limitation.

Arms—Az. a buck's head cabossed or, within a bordure embattled ar.

BALE, OF CARLETON CURLIEU.

Created 9th Nov. 1643.  Extinct About 1653.

Lineage.

Sir John Bale, knt. of Carleton Curlieu and Sadington, the representative of a respectable Leicestershire family, married Frances, daughter of Bernard Brocas, of Beaurepaire, in Hampshire, and by her, who *d.* in 1629, aged eighty, had issue,

George, his heir.

Robert, *d. s. p.*

John, of Sadington.

Francis, of London, merchant, who m. Margaret, daughter of John Maninge, also of London, merchant, and had issue,

Charles, *b.* in 1625.

Elizabeth, *b.* in 1614.

Margaret, *b.* in 1623.

Edmund, of Sadington, m. Joice, daughter of Sir Richard Roberts, of Sutton Cheynell, and had three sons, William, *b.* in 1610, John and Richard; and four daughters, Elizabeth, Frances, Dorothy, and Joice.

The eldest son,

George Bale, esq. of Carleton Curlieu, espoused Elizabeth, daughter of Valentine Hartopp, esq. of Burton Lazars, and by her (who m. secondly, Sir William Roberts, of Sutton Cheynell), had issue,

John (Sir), his heir.

Valentine, of Humberston, who m. Elizabeth, daughter and heir of Tobias Chippingdale, son and heir of John Chippingdale, doctor of civil law, and had a son, John, *b.* in 1618, and two daughters, Elizabeth and Emma.

Frances, m. to William Roberts, esq. of Barwell.

The elder son,

Sir John Bale, received the honour of knighthood from James I., and served as high sheriff for Leicestershire in 1624. He m. first, Emma, daughter of William Halford, of Welham, which lady died in 1630; and, secondly, a daughter of John Bainbrigge, esq. of Lockington. By the former he had issue,

John, his heir.

William, of Humberston, m. Elizabeth, daughter of William Jerveis, of Peatling, and was *s.* by his son,

Samuel, of Humberston, who m. Elizabeth, fourth daughter of George Faunt, esq. of Foston, but *d. s. p.* in 1687.

George, *d. s. p.*

Thomas, killed in the royal cause at Ashby-de-la-Zouch.

Samuel, *b.* in 1625.

Francis, *d.* in 1631.

Richard, *d.* in 1657.

Frances, m. to William Warner, esq. of Lubbenham.

The eldest son,

I. John Bale, esq. of Carleton Curlieu, one of the loyalists to whom the king's commission of array was addressed in June, 1642, was created a Baronet 9th November, 1643. During the civil wars he adhered with devoted attachment to the ill-fated king, and in 1645 his house at Carleton Curlieu was garrisoned in the royal cause. Sir John contributed also largely to the expenses of the war, by voluntary gifts to the monarch, and by the fines which were levied by parliament. He m. Anne, daughter and heir of Sir Thomas Puckering, bart. of Warwick, but having no issue at his decease about 1653, the Baronetcy became extinct, and his property at Carleton was purchased by a London scrivener named Prudham, who sold it in 1654 to Sir Geoffrey Palmer, of Carleton, in Northamptonshire.

Arms—Per pale vert and gu. an eagle displayed arg. armed and beaked or.

BAMBURGH, OF HOUGHTON.

CREATED 1st December, 1619.—EXTINCT ——.

Lineage.

I. SIR WILLIAM BAMBURGH, of Houghton, in Yorkshire, was created a Baronet by JAMES I., but leaving no male issue by his wife Mary, daughter of Sir Robert Foard, (which lady wedded, secondly, Thomas, first Viscount Fairfax), the title expired with him.

BANKS, OF REVESBY ABBEY.

CREATED 24th Mar. 1781.

EXTINCT 19th June, 1820.

Lineage.

This family is descended from Simon Banke, who *m.* the daughter and heiress of Caterton, of Newton, Yorkshire, 7th EDWARD III. By this marriage the manor of Newton, in the Wapentake of Staincliffe, came to the family of Banke, and was afterwards called Banke Newton. It was sold to Mr. Townley, of Royle, about the middle of the seventeenth century.

HENRY BANKE, of Banke Newton, the tenth in lineal descent from the said Simon, *m.* Isabella, daughter of William Lister, of Thornton and Medhope, in the county of York, by whom he had two sons, Henry and Robert. The elder son, Henry, of Banke Newton, living in 1612, *m.* first, Alicia, daughter of Robert Byncloes, of Bewick, in Lancashire, by whom he had Thomas, aged eleven, in 1612, and Isabella. He married, secondly, Johanna, daughter of Nicholas Parker, of Horracforth, in Lancashire, by whom he had four sons and two daughters,

Giles.
Stephen.
Michael.
Richard.
Anne.
Aurelia.

The second son,

ROBERT BANKES was an eminent attorney at Giggleswick, in Yorkshire, *temp.* ELIZABETH and JAC. I. and lived at Beck, *jure uxoris.* He *m.* Anne, daughter of Joseph Crake, of Beck Hall, in the parish of Giggleswick, by whom he had three sons and two daughters,

- I. Luke, died in the king's service in the civil wars: he *m.* Hester, daughter of Alan Bellingham, esq. by whom he had one daughter, Anne, who was the first wife of Roger Pepys, esq. of the Middle Temple, London. She *d.* about 1641, without issue: he was afterwards recorder of Cambridge, and *m.* a daughter of Judge Bacon, by whom he had several children.
- II. Robert, in holy orders, of whom hereafter.
- III. Joseph, a barrister-at-law, one of the six clerks in Chancery: he died without issue at Giggleswick.

- I. Anne, was wife of Ralph Baynes, gent. of Mewith-Head, of the parish of Bentham, in Yorkshire.
- II. Margaret, *m.* to William Pukering, A.M. rector of Swillington, in Yorkshire. He *d.* in 1646, and she in 1686.

REV. ROBERT BANKES, of Beck Hall, second son, living 16th February, 1641, 17th CAR. I. as per deed: he was heir to his niece, Anne Pepys, and *m.* Anne, daughter of Stephen Pudsey, esq. by whom he had a son,

REV. ROBERT BANKS, of Beck Hall, born there 27th March, 1630; *m.* Margaret, daughter of John Frankland, of Rathmell, and sister of the Rev. Richard Frankland, also of Rathmell, by whom he had two sons,* Robert, and

JOSEPH BANKS, esq. of Revesby Abbey, in Lincolnshire, sometime of Sheffield, M.P. for Grimsby, in Lincolnshire, and Totness, in Devonshire, born at Giggleswick 6th September, 1665, *d.* 27th September, 1727, buried at Revesby. He *m.* Mary, daughter of the Rev. Rowland Handcock, of Shircliffe Hall, in the parish of Ecclesfield, in Yorkshire, by whom he had one son, JOSEPH, and one daughter, Mary, wife of Sir Francis Whichcote, bart. of Aswarby, in Lincolnshire. She died *s. p.* and was buried at Chesham, in Buckinghamshire. The son and heir,

JOSEPH BANKS, esq. aged twenty-nine years 1719, was high sheriff of Lincolnshire 1736, and sometime

---

* Rev. Robert Banks, born 22nd June, 1650, vicar of Trinity, in Hull, and prebendary of York in 1712. He *m.* first, Margaret, daughter of the Rev. Robert Thornton, rector of Birkin, in Yorkshire, by whom he had four sons and three daughters,

- I. Robert Banks, of Bawtrey, in Yorkshire, attorney-at-law, and clerk of the peace for the county of Nottingham. He *m.* first, Jane, daughter of — Wharton, by whom he had one son,
  - Robert Banks, of Bawtrey, attorney-at-law, who *m.* Elizabeth, daughter of Francis Ward, of Wittington, in Derbyshire, by whom he had two sons, Robert and Joseph, who both died in their infancy.
- II. Rev. Joseph Banks, rector of Stooton-Roberts, in Yorkshire, and buried there. He *m.* Mary, daughter of Mr. Alderman Sykes, of Leeds (buried at Stooton-Roberts), by whom he had issue, three sons and one daughter,
  - Robert Banks, of London, merchant, who *m.* but died without surviving issue.
  - Joseph Banks, LL.B. of Mortlake, in Surrey, chancellor of the diocese of York 1780, barrister-at-law, of Lincoln, died at Walton upon Thames, in Surrey. He married his cousin Mary, daughter of the Rev. William Steer, who died at Margate, in Kent, 18th November, 1780, by whom he had an only daughter,
    - Anne, *m.* at Walton 29th November, 1784, to Henry-John Kearney, esq.
  - Samuel, governor of Vigapatam, in the East Indies, where he died *s. p.*
  - Mary, the daughter, was wife of the Rev. Mr. Wilkinson, vicar of Gargrave, in Yorkshire.
- III. Hamon, third son of Robert, *m.* Anne, daughter of — Rogers, and died *s. p.*
- IV. John, died *s. p.*

Of the daughters of Robert,

- I. Anne, was wife of William Steer, vicar of Ecclesfield, and prebendary of York, by whom she had one daughter,
  - Mary, wife of her cousin, Joseph Banks, above-mentioned.
- II. Elizabeth, was wife of the Rev. Mr. Wilkinson, vicar of Trinity church, Hull, and died *s. p.*

M.P. for Peterborough. He m. first, Anne, daughter and heiress of William Hodgkinson, esq. of Overton, in Derbyshire receiver-general of the customs, by whom he had three sons and four daughters,

I. Joseph, who *d. vita patris.*
II. William, of whom hereafter.
III. Robert-Hodgkinson, of Overton, succeeded to that estate by his grandfather's will, when his brother William succeeded to the Revesby estate, F.R.S and F.S.A. aged four 1726, high-sheriff for Carmarthenshire 1784, died 11th November, 1792, and was buried at Battersea. He m. 1st October, 1757, Bridget, daughter and co-heiress of Thomas Williams, esq. of Edwinsford, Carmarthenshire, chancellor and chamberlain of the counties of Carmarthen, Pembroke, and Cardigan.

I. Lettice-Mary, died unmarried at Revesby Abbey, 1787.
II. Elizabeth, died young.
III. Elizabeth, wife (1744) of James Hawley, M. D. of Brentford, in Middlesex, and of Leybourne Grange, Kent, died 1777, aged seventy-two.
IV. Margaret-Eleanor, wife of the Hon. Henry Grenville, uncle to the Marquess of Buckingham.

Joseph Banks m. secondly, Catherine, daughter of — Collingwood, esq. of Northumberland, relict of Newman Wallis, of Stamford, in Lincolnshire, and by her had two sons,

Collingwood, who died at Christchurch college, Oxford, a minor, and there buried.
George, b. 10th March, 1735-6, a lieutenant of the guards, died unmarried.

The son and heir,

William Banks, b. 1719, assumed the surname and arms of Hodgkinson for the Overton estate, before his eldest brother's death. He m. Sarah, daughter of William Bate, of Pausson, in Derbyshire, by the daughter and co-heiress (with her sister, Hannah-Sophia, wife of Brownlow, eighth Earl of Exeter) of Thomas Chambers, esq. of London, by whom he had one daughter, Sarah-Sophia, b. 17th October, 1744, and one son, Joseph. Mr. Banks d. 1761, and was s. by his son, the celebrated

I. Right Hon. Sir Joseph Banks, bart. president of the Royal Society, knight of the most honourable order of the Bath, and one of his majesty's most honourable privy council, b. 13th December, 1743. He m. 23rd March, 1779, Dorothea, daughter and co-heiress (with her sister Mary, wife of Sir Edward Knatchbull) of William-Weston Hugessen, esq. of Provender, in the parish of Norton, in Kent, but dying issueless, 19th June, 1820, the Baronetcy, which had been conferred on him in 1781, expired.

Arms—Sa. a cross or, betw. four fleurs-de-lis ar.

BANKS, OF LONDON.

Created 22d Aug. 1661. Extinct About 1699.

Lineage.

I. Sir John Banks, of London, who obtained a patent of Baronetcy shortly after the restoration, m. Elizabeth, daughter of Sir John Dethick, knt., Lord Mayor of London, but dying without male issue, about 1699, the title expired.

Arms—Sa., on a cross or, between four fleurs-de-lis, ar., five pellets.

BARD, OF STAINES.

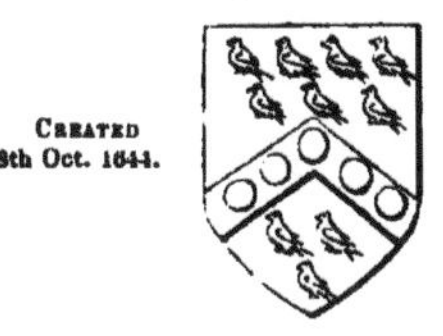

Created 8th Oct. 1644. Extinct in 1660.

Lineage.

I. Sir Henry Bard, colonel in the royal army during the civil commotions of the reign of Charles. I. was created a Baronet in 1644, and in two years after raised to the peerage of Ireland as *Baron Bard, of Drombey*, and Viscount Belmont. His lordship proceeding on an embassy from Charles II., then in exile, to the court of Persia, was overtaken in that country by a whirlwind and choked by the sand; the melancholy event occurred in the year 1660, when all his honours, including the Baronetcy, expired.

Arms—Sa., on a chevron, between ten martlets ar. five plates.

BARKER, OF GRIMSTON HALL.

Created 17th Mar. 1622. Extinct 3rd Jan. 1766.

Lineage.

This family resided at Ipswich from a very remote period, and so early as the time of Edward III. it gave its name to a street in that borough.

Robert Barker, of Ipswich, m. Anne, daughter of — Bestney, esq. of Cambridgeshire, and left by her a son and heir,

Robert Barker, a burgess of Ipswich in the 1st of Elizabeth. He m. a daughter of — Kempe, of Suffolk, and had a son,

John Barker, a burgess of Ipswich in the 26th and 30th of Elizabeth, who m. first, Willemina, daughter and heir of John Bomart, a merchant at Bremen, and by that lady had issue,

Robert (Sir), his heir.
John, a colonel in the army, m. a daughter of Paul Withypoole, esq. by the Honorable Dorothy Wentworth his wife, youngest daughter of Thomas, Lord Wentworth, and left two daughters, namely,

Dorothy, m. to — Knowles, esq. of Kenthorp, in the county of Warwick.
Willemina, m. to — Gerling, esq.

William.

Margery, *m.* to Thomas Clench, esq. son and heir of Mr. Justice Clench, of the court of King's Bench.

Thomasine, *m.* to Sir Robert Gardiner, knt. of the county of Suffolk, lord deputy of Ireland.

He wedded, secondly, Anne, daughter of Mr. Alderman Herdson, of London, and widow of George Stoddart, esq. by whom he had another daughter, Abigail, *m.* to Sir Edward Waterhouse, knt. of Halifax, in the county of York. He was *s.* at his decease by his eldest son,

Sir Robert Barker, M.P. for Ipswich 35th Elizabeth, who was made a Knight of the Bath at the coronation of *King* James I. (1603). This gentleman fixed the seat of the family at Grimston Hall, in the parish of Trinley St. Martin, eight miles south-east from Ipswich, whither he removed. He *m.* first, Judith, daughter of George Stoddard, esq. of Mottingham, in Kent, and by her had

John, his heir.

Robert, who *d. s. p.*

Anne, *m.* to Sir Arthur Jenney, knt. of Knotishall.

Sir Robert wedded, secondly, Susanna, daughter of Sir John Crofts, knt. of Saxham, in Suffolk, by whom he had

Thomas (Sir), heir of his mother, was of Besford, in the county of Suffolk, and marrying Penelope, daughter of Sir John Tasborough, knt. of the same shire, had several children.

Edward, *m.* first, Mary, daughter and sole heir of Edward Wigmore, esq. of Twickenham, and widow of Sir Thomas Holland, knt. of Quiddenham, in Norfolk; and, secondly, a daughter of James Pooley, esq. of Boxted.

William, an alderman of London, from whom the Barkers, of Bocking Hall.

The eldest son and heir,

I. John Barker, esq. of Grimston Hall, in the county of Suffolk, was created a Baronet by *King* James I. on the 17th March, 1621. He *m.* Frances, daughter of Sir John Jermy, knt. of Brightwell, in Suffolk, and had three sons,

John, his successor.

Thomas, *m.* a daughter of Sir Dudley Carleton, knt. of Imber Court, in Surrey.

Robert, *d. s. p.*

Sir John *d.* in 1652, and was *s.* by his eldest son,

II. Sir John Barker, of Grimston Hall, who wedded Winifrid, daughter of Sir Philip Parker, knt. of Arwarton, in Suffolk, and left at his decease, in 1664, three sons, viz.

Jermy, his heir.

John, successor to his brother.

Robert, who *m.* a daughter of Robert Marriot, esq. of Bradfield, and had two sons and five daughters: the sons both fell in the service of *Queen* Anne, one a naval officer, the other in the army.

The eldest son and heir,

III. Sir Jermy Barker, died unmarried about the year 1665, and was *s.* by his brother,

IV. Sir John Barker. This gentleman wedded Bridget, daughter of Sir Nicholas Bacon, K. B. of Shrubland, and had a son and daughter, namely,

William, his successor.

Grace, *m.* to Philip Bacon, esq. of Ipswich, grandson of Sir N. Bacon, of Shrubland.

Sir John returned back to Ipswich, and again made that the place of abode of the family. He represented the borough in several parliaments, in the reigns of Charles II., James II., and William and Mary. He *d.* in 1696, and was *s* by his son,

V. Sir William Barker, who *m.* first, Mary, only daughter of John Bence, esq. of Heveningham, in Suffolk, and by her, who *d.* 1st January, 1715-16, had an only child, John, his successor. He wedded, secondly, 9th February, 1731, Anne, relict of Edward Spencer, esq. of Rendlesham, in Suffolk, but had no issue by that lady. Sir William sat in parliament for Ipswich in the reign of *Queen* Anne, and he was one of the knights of the shire for Suffolk, in the reigns of George I. and of George II. He *d.* 23rd July, 1731, and was *s.* by his son,

VI. Sir John Barker. This gentleman *m.* 28th October, 1741, Alice, only daughter of Sir Comport Fytch, bart. of Mount Marksall, in Kent, and heir of her brother, Sir William, who died a minor in 1736, by this lady he had

John-Fytch, his heir, *b.* 25th July, 1741.

He *d.* 7th June, 1757, and was *s.* by his son,

VII. Sir John-Fytch Barker, who *m.* Lucy, daughter of Sir Richard Lloyd, of Hintlesham, in Suffolk, but *d. s. p.* 3rd January, 1766, when the Baronetcy became extinct.

Arms—Party per fess nebule vert and sa. three martlets or; a canton erm.

BARKER, OF HAMBLETON.

Created 9th Sept. 1665.—Expired in 1708.

Lineage.

Baldwin Barker, who died in 1603, married two wives: by the first wife he had a large family, and by the second, Elizabeth Taylor, he had two sons, namely,

Abel, his heir.

Samuel, of South Luffenham, who *m.* Dorothy Dixey, and was father of

Samuel, who *m.* Elizabeth Wildbore, widow of — Chaloner, esq. of Duffield, and died in 1676, when he was *s.* by his son,

Augustin, of South Luffenham, who *m.* Thomasin Tryst, of Maidford, Northamptonshire, and *d.* in 1680, leaving a son,

Samuel, *b.* in 1686, who *m.* in 1717, Sarah, daughter of the Rev. William Whiston, well known to the philosophers and controversialists of his time, and dying in 1759, was *s.* by his son,

Thomas, *b.* in 1722, who *m.* in 1751, Anne, daughter of John White, esq. of S. Iburn, Hants, and dying in 1809, left (with four daughters, Sarah, *m.* to Edward Brown, esq. of Walcot, Anne, Mary, and Elizabeth, who all died unmarried), a son,

Samuel, of Lyndon, in Rutlandshire, *b.* 21st January, 1757, who served the office of high sheriff for that county in 1815. He *m.* 2[illegible] October, 1786, Mary, daughter of the Rev. George Haggitt, rector of Rushton, Northamptonshire, and had one son and two daughters, viz.

Thomas, who *d.* in 1802, aged nine years.

Mary.

Anne.

The elder son,

Abel Barker, esq. of Hambleton, in the county of Rutland, *m.* Elizabeth Wright, and was *s.* by his son,

I. Abel Barker, esq. of Hambleton, *b.* in 16[illegible], who was created a Baronet 9th September, 1665. He *m.* first, Anne, daughter of Sir Thomas Burton, bart. of Stokerston, in Leicestershire; and, secondly, Mary, daughter of Alexander Noel, esq. of Whitwell, in Rutlandshire. By the latter he had no issue, but by the former he had a son, Thomas, his heir. Sir Abel purchased the estate of Lyndon, in the county of Rutland, soon after the Restoration, and erected the present mansion, which was completed in 1675. He *d.* in September, 1679, and was *s.* by his son,

II. SIR THOMAS BARKER, of Hambleton and Lyndon, who *d.* issueless in 1706, when the BARONETCY became EXTINCT, and the estate passed to the descendants of his grand-uncle, Samuel Barker, of South Luffenham.

Arms—Party nebulé or and az. three martlets counterchanged.

BARKER, OF BOCKING HALL.

CREATED 29th Mar. 1676.—EXTINCT 22nd Oct. 1818.

Lineage.

SIR ROBERT BARKER, K. B. of Grimston Hall, in the county of Suffolk, married for his second wife Susan, daughter of Sir John Crofts, of Saxham, and by her had three sons, viz.

THOMAS (Sir), who became heir to his mother, and was of Besford, in Suffolk. He *m.* Penelope, daughter of Sir John Tasborough, knt. and had several children.

Edward, *m.* first, Mary, daughter and sole heir of Sir Edward Wigmore, knt. of Twickenham, and widow of Sir Thomas Holland, knt. of Quidenham, in Norfolk; and, secondly, a daughter of James Pooley, esq. of Boxted.

WILLIAM.

The youngest son,

WILLIAM BARKER, esq. who was an alderman of London, *m.* Martha, daughter of William Turnor, of [illegible]worth, Wilts, and of London, merchant (relict of [illegible] Williams, also a merchant of London), by whom he left a son and heir,

I. WILLIAM BARKER, esq. of Bocking Hall, in the county of Essex, who was created a BARONET by *King* CHARLES II. 29th March, 1676. He *m.* Elizabeth, sixteenth child of Sir Jerome Alexander, knt. one of the justices of the court of Common Pleas in Ireland, by whom he acquired an estate of 1500*l.* per annum, and had issue,

WILLIAM, his successor.

Jerome, *d.* unmarried.

Robert, of Everley, in Wiltshire, who *m.* a daughter and one of the co-heirs of Samuel Keck, esq. of the Middle Temple.

Sir William died in Ireland, and was *s.* by his eldest son,

II. SIR WILLIAM BARKER, of Bocking Hall. This gentleman *m.* Catherine-Teresa, daughter and co-heir of Samuel Keck, esq. of the Middle Temple, and had issue,

WILLIAM, his heir.

Samuel.

Alexander.

Eleanor, *m.* to Thomas Vokes, esq. barrister-at-law.

Hannah-Martha.

Grace.

He *d.* 5th May, 1746, and was *s.* by his eldest son,

III. SIR WILLIAM BARKER of Bocking Hall, and Kilcooley Abbey. This gentleman wedded Mary, daughter of Valentine Quin, Esq. of Adare, in the county of Limerick, and had issue,

1. WILLIAM, his heir.

1. Mary, who *m.* first, Chambre-Brabazon Ponsonby, Esq., grandson of the first Viscount Besborough, and had issue,

1. Chambre-Brabazon Ponsonby, of Kilcooley Abbey, in the county of Tipperary, who assumed the additional surname of BARKER. He *m.* in 1791, Lady Henrietta Taylor, eldest daughter of Thomas, first Earl of Bective, and dying in 1834, left, with other issue, a son, the present WILLIAM-PONSONBY BARKER, Esq. of Kilcooley Abbey.

2. Frances, widow of George Lowther, Esq.

3. Sarah, *d.* at Llangollen, 8th Dec., 1831.

Mrs. Ponsonby wedded, secondly, Sir Robert Staples, Bart., of Dunmore, and had a son, Robert, and a daughter, Anne-Maria, *m.* to Ralph Smyth, esq. of Gaybrook.

II. Hannah-Maria, *m.* to Eland Mossom, Esq.

Sir William *d.* 20 March, 1770, and was *s.* by his son,

IV. SIR WILLIAM BARKER, of Bocking Hall, who *m.* Miss Lane, only daughter and heiress of William Lane, esq. of Dublin, but dying without issue, 22d October, 1818, the BARONETCY expired, while the estates devolved on his nephew, Charles-Brabazon Ponsonby, esq., father of the present Mr. PONSONBY BARKER, of Kilcooley Abbey.

Arms—See Barker of Grimston Hall.

BARKER, OF BUSHBRIDGE.

CREATED 24th Mar. 1781.—EXTINCT 14th Sept. 1789.

Lineage.

I. SIR ROBERT BARKER, knt. M. P. for the borough of Wallingford, and a general officer in the East Indies, where he performed eminent service as commander in chief of the artillery at the capture of Manilla in October, 1762, was created a BARONET 24th March, 1781. He purchased of the widow of Philip-Carteret Webb, esq. the estate of Bushbridge, in Surrey, and was thence designated. He *m.* in September, 1779, Ann, daughter of Brabazon Hallows, esq. of Glapwell, in Derbyshire, but had no issue.

Sir Robert *d.* 14th September, 1789, and was buried at Hammersmith, when the BARONETCY became EXTINCT. In 1791, the estate of Bushbridge was sold, under a decree of chancery, to Nathaniel Webb, esq. but he subsequently sold it to Henry-Hare Townsend, esq.

BARKHAM, OF SOUTH ACRE.

CREATED 28th June, 1623.

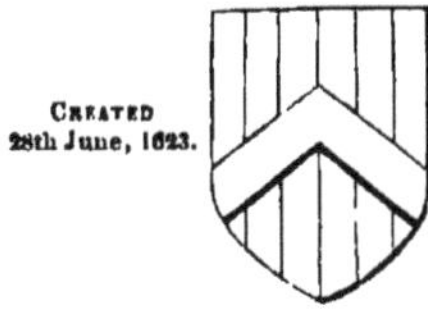

EXTINCT in Dec. 1695.

Lineage.

The family of Barkham was, for a long period, of influence and fortune, in the counties of Norfolk and Lincoln.

I. SIR EDWARD BARKHAM, of South Acre, in Norfolk, the first baronet of the family, *m.* Frances, daughter of Sir Thomas Hervey, knt. of Redham, in that county, and was *s.* by his son,

II. SIR EDWARD BARKHAM, of South Acre, who *m.* first, Grace, daughter of Lewis, first Lord Rockingham, which lady died without issue; and, secondly, Frances, daughter of Sir John Napier, bart. of Luton

Hoo, in the county of Bedford, by whom he had no issue. Sir Edward *d.* in 1688, and was *s.* by his brother,

III. Sir William Barkham, of South Acre, who *m.* Judith, daughter of Sir John Halsey, knt. of Gadesden, Herts, but *d. s. p. m.* in December, 1695, the Baronetcy expired.

Arms—Paly of six ar. and gu, a chevron or.

BARKHAM, OF WAINFLETE.

Created 21st July, 1661.

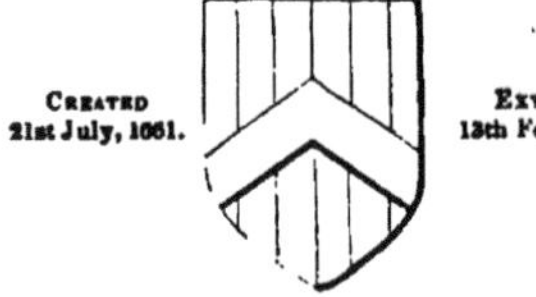

Extinct 13th Feb. 1711.

Lineage.

I. Sir Edward Barkham, of Wainflete, in Lincolnshire, received shortly after the restoration of Charles II. the dignity of Baronet. He *m.* Anne, daughter and heir of Sir Robert Lee, of Billerslee, in Warwickshire, and was father of

II. Sir Robert Barkham, of Wainflete, who *m.* the daughter of — Jeffry, of Wygtoft, in Lincolnshire, and *d.* about the year 1701, was *s.* by his son,

III. Sir Edward Barkham, of Wainflete, who *m.* Mary, daughter and heir of John Wolley, of Alford, in Lincolnshire, and *d. s. p.* 13th February, 1711, the Baronetcy became extinct.

Arms—Paly of six ar. and gu. a chevron or.

BARLOW, OF SLEBETCH.

Created 13th July, 1677.

Extinct before the year 1775.

Lineage.

This was a very ancient family, enjoying equestrian rank for many generations prior to its being raised to the baronetcy.

Sir Thomas Barlow, knt. of Barlow, in the county of Lancaster, was father of

James Barlow, of Barlow, who *m.* a daughter of Sir Robert Worsley, and was *s.* by his son,

Sir Richard Barlow, knt. of Barlow, who wedded the daughter of Thomas Antwisle, esq. and was father of

Sir Robert Barlow, who *m.* Ursula, daughter of Sir John Berron, knt. and left a son and heir,

Sir Christopher Barlow, whose wife was Margaret, daughter of Robert Gamble, esq. and his son and heir,

Henry Barlow, esq., wedded Anne, daughter of Sir Rowland Shirwood, knt. and was *s.* by his son.

Richard Barlow, esq. who *m.* the daughter of Sir John Townley, knt. and left a son and heir,

John Barlow, esq. who wedded Maryan, daughter of Sir Thomas Sherburn, knt. and was *s.* by his son,

Sir Thomas Barlow, knt. This gentleman *m.* Anne, daughter of Sir William Stanwidge, knt. and had a son and heir,

Sir John Barlow, knt. who *m.* Anne, daughter of Sir Ralph Langford, knt. by whom he had a daughter, Margaret, *m.* to Edward Stanley, Earl of Derby, and a son and heir,

Sir Thomas Barlow, knt. who wedded, according to Thoresby,* Christian, daughter of Edward Barley, esq. of Barley, in the county of Hertford, and had several children. His second son,

Thomas Barlow, esq. *m.* Margaret, daughter and heir of John Trussel, esq. and had a son,

John Barlow, esq. This gentleman *m.* Christian, daughter of Edward Barley, esq. of Barley, and had four sons and a daughter, who were thrown upon the world almost destitute, owing to the political misfortunes of their father. In the time of Henry VII. Mr. Barlow was committed close prisoner to the Tower, for harbouring at Barlow his brother-in-law Barley, and Sir Robert Clifford, who had married his wife's sister, the night before their departure for the court of Margaret, Duchess of Burgundy, and his whole estate being wrested from him was conferred upon Vere, Earl of Oxford, then recently created lord high chamberlain of England, while he himself was detained in prison until he fully and legally ratified the transfer, getting free at last, but with difficulty, from the penalties of high treason. Of his children,

- Thomas, became a secular priest, and was made chaplain to *Queen* Anne Boleyne.
- Roger, we shall treat of presently.
- John, was a student at Oxford, and fellow of Magdalen College.
- William, also of Oxford, and a fellow of Magdalen, was a canon regular and prior of Bisham in the 27th Henry VIII. he was constituted Bishop of St. Asaph, and two months afterwards translated to St. David's. In the 2nd Edward VI. (1547) he was translated to Bath and Wells, but in the 1st of Mary (1553) he was deprived and forced to fly the realm, and remained in exile until the accession of Elizabeth, when he was appointed Bishop of Chichester, and was the principal bishop of the four at the consecration of Archbishop Parker. He was the first Protestant bishop in England. He *m.* Agatha, daughter of John Wellesborne, esq. and had, with several sons, five daughters,† who all became the wives of bishops, namely,
  - Anne, of Herbert Westfaling, Bishop of Hereford.
  - Elizabeth, of William Day, Bishop of Winchester.
  - Margaret, of William Overton, Bishop of Lichfield and Coventry.
  - Frances, of Tobias Matthews,‡ Archbishop of York.

* Thoresby's Leeds, but this marriage was not mentioned in the family pedigree.

† In the marriages of these ladies Thoresby has been followed, but the family pedigree makes Anne to marry first, Augustus Bradbridge, and secondly, Bishop Westfaling; and Frances to marry first, Matthew Parker, son of Archbishop Parker, and secondly, Bishop Matthews.

‡ Toby Matthews, Archbishop of York, was a great favourite of *Queen* Elizabeth and *King* James I., an able and indefatigable preacher, who kept an account of all the sermons he preached, by which it appears he preached, while Dean of Durham, 721; whilst Bishop of Durham, 550, and whilst Archbishop of York, 7[illegible], in all, 1992 sermons.

Antonina, of W. Wickham, Bishop of Lincoln.

Bishop Barlow *d.* in 1569, and was interred in his own cathedral of Chichester.

Elizabeth, went as a companion with the Countess of Oxford into Scotland, and was maid of honour to Mary *Queen* of Scots: she *m.* first, Alexander, Lord Elphinstone; and, secondly, Lord Drummond, and was mother of the succeeding Lords Elphinstone and Drummond.

The second son,

Roger Barlow, esq. on his father's commitment to the Tower, went over to Spain, and was employed, at the recommendation of the Duke of Modena, by the *Emperor* Charles V. for the discovery of Peru; but having communicated his discovery to the English ambassador at Madrid, Sir Thomas Boleyne, he was ordered by his own sovereign, *King* Henry VIII., to return home, with a promise of preferment. He was afterwards appointed vice-admiral to Lord Seymour, and but for the death of the king, was to have undertaken the discovery of a north passage to the East Indies with three of his highness's ships from Milford Haven. This Roger was the first of the family who came into Pembrokeshire, and purchased an estate from the crown. He *m.* Julian, daughter and co-heir of Rees Daws, of Bristol, and was *s.* by his son,

John Barlow, esq. of Slebetch, in the county of Pembroke, who wedded Elizabeth, daughter of John Fisher, esq. and had a son and heir,

George Barlow, esq. who wedded Anne Vernon, niece of Viscount Hereford, and was *s.* by his son,

John Barlow, esq. of Slebetch, known as "Colonel Barlow," from holding that commission in the royalist army during the great rebellion. Colonel Barlow marched at the head of his corps, chiefly composed of his own tenantry, to the relief of the Marquess of Worcester at Ragland Castle, but his followers having been nearly cut to pieces, he was himself forced to abscond for several years, when his estates were conferred upon Cromwell's favourites, and his library, with a valuable collection of manuscripts, burnt at Slebetch by Colonel Horton, one of Cromwell's officers. This gentleman had six sons and three daughters, viz.

George, his successor.

John.

William, served for the Venetians against the Turks, and returned to England after the Restoration.

Lewis.

Charles, } entered the Venetian service with their
Thomas, } brother William, and fell in it.

Anne, *m.* to Lewis Wogan, esq. of Weston Castle.

——, } lady abbesses in France.
——, }

Colonel Barlow was *s.* by his eldest son,

George Barlow, esq. of Slebetch, who *m.* Joan, daughter and co-heir of David Lloyd, esq. of Kilykeithed, in Pembrokeshire, and had issue,

John, his successor.

William, who was introduced into the court of Charles II., and on the king's death was made captain of horse in Lord Peterborough's regiment; before *King* James's abdication he had attained the rank of colonel, and accompanied that monarch in his retirement. On his majesty's death he returned, and lived and died in Pembrokeshire in great esteem.

——, *m.* to Sir Herbert Perrot, knt. of Wellington, Herts.

He was *s.* by his elder son,

I. John Barlow, esq. of Slebetch, in the county of Pembroke, who was created a Baronet by *King* Charles II. 13th July, 1677. He *m.* first, Beatrice, daughter and eventually heir of Sir John Lloyd, bart. of Forrest, in Carmarthenshire, and had two daughters, viz.

Beatrice, *m.* first, to Sir Anthony Rudd, bart.; and, secondly, to Griffith Lloyd, esq.

Anne, *d.* unmarried.

Sir John wedded, secondly, Catherine, daughter of Christopher Middleton, esq. of Middleton Hall, in the county of Carmarthen, and by that lady had three sons, viz.

George, his successor.

John, *m.* first, Anne, daughter of Simon, Viscount Harcourt, Lord Chancellor of Great Britain, and had a son,

George, who wedded Anne, daughter of — Blundell, esq. of Haverfordwest.

Mr. John Barlow *m.* secondly, Anne, daughter of Richard Skrine, esq. and left by her a daughter, Anne. He *d.* in November, 1739.

William.

He *d.* about the year 1695, and was *s.* by his eldest son,

II. Sir George Barlow, who *m.* Winifred, daughter of George Heneage, esq. of Hainton, in the county of Lincoln, and had an only son, George. Sir George made over a great part of his estate to his brother, John Barlow, esq. He was *s.* at his decease by his son,

III. Sir George Barlow. This gentleman died in France without issue, when the Baronetcy became extinct. Administration to his effects was taken out in 1775.

Arms—Arg. on a chev. engrailed between three cross crosslets fitchée sa. two lions encounter of the first.

BARNARDISTON, OF KETTON.

Created 7th Apr. 1663.

Extinct about 1750.

Lineage.

This was one of the most ancient families of the equestrian order in the kingdom, having flourished in a direct line for twenty-seven generations at least. The name was assumed from the town of Barnarston or Barnston, contiguous to Ketton, of which the Barnardistons were proprietors from the Conquest.

By marrying the heiress of Willoughby, in the time of Edward II., the family obtained the noble manor of Great Cotes, in the county of Lincoln, which they held for several centuries.

Ketton Hall, or Kedyton Hall, they acquired with the heiress of the family of Newmarch, which surname it appears they adopted and anciently bore, in conjunction with that of Barnardiston, as exhibited on the monument of Anne, daughter of Sir Thomas Barnardiston, the wife of Sir Hugh Everard, in the church of Great Waltham, Essex. She died in 1609.

The estate of the Barnardistones amounted, in the time of Elizabeth, to 4000*l.* per annum.

Le Neve, in his MSS. begins the pedigree with

Roger Barnardiston, who *m.* the daughter and heir of Havering, and was father of

Sir Thomas Barnardiston, who wedded the daughter and co-heir of Sir William Franke, knt. of Grimsby, in the county of Lincoln,* and left a son,

Roger Barnardiston, father by his wife Isabel, relict of William Kelke, of Beverley, of

Thomas Barnardiston, who *m.* Alice, daughter of Henry Vavasor, of Haselwood, in the county of York, and left a son and heir,

Thomas Barnardiston, who wedded a daughter of Sir Thomas Waterton, knt. and was *s.* by his son,

Sir Thomas Barnardiston, knt. of Kedington, or Ketton, in Suffolk, who *m.* Elizabeth, daughter of Roger Newport, of Pelham, in Hertfordshire, by whom he had seven sons and seven daughters. In Kedington church, in the south window, there is to be seen, says Weaver, "a Barnardiston, kneeling, in his compleat armour, his coat armour on his breast, and behind him seven sons. In the next pane of the glass is Elizabeth, the daughter of Newport, kneeling, with her coat armour likewise on her breast, and seven daughters behind her, and under it is thus written, now much defaced:

> 'Orate pro Animabus Thome Barnardiston, Militis, et Elizabethe, uxoris ejus, qui istam Fenestram fieri fecerunt, anno Domini Mccccc . . . Anima . . . Deus, Amen.'

Over against the said south window, under the second arch of the said south side of the church, is the monument of the said Sir Thomas Barnardiston, in stone, at length, in his compleat armour, and the said Dame Elizabeth his wife by him: and in a table of stone, under their coat armours, this epitaph or inscription:

> 'This is the monument of Sir Thomas Barnardiston, knight, beying buryd in Cotys, in the countie of Lincolne, and of Dame Elizabeth, his Wyffe, buryd under this Tombe: whych Sir Thomas, by his last will, gave certen Londis in the Towne callyd Brokholes, of the yerly value of vii markis, towards the maintenens of a chantrie, in this church: and the seid Dame Elisabeth, aftyr his Deth, optened lycens to amortyse the seid Chantrie, perpetually, and made the possession thereof, to the yerly value of xii markis, and besyds buylt the church roif new, and coveryd it with Lede. Whych Dame Elisabeth, died the — day of — Anno Domini Mcccccxx.'"

The son and heir of Sir Thomas, by Elizabeth Newport, another

Sir Thomas Barnardiston, knt. *m.* Anne, daughter of Sir Thomas Lucas, of Saxham, in Suffolk, and was *s.* by his son,

Sir Thomas Barnardiston, knt. who wedded Mary, second daughter of Sir Edward Walsingham, knt. of Scadbury, in Kent, lieutenant of the Tower, by whom he left his successor,

Sir Thomas Barnardiston, knt. who *m.* first, Elizabeth,† daughter of Thomas Hanchet, esq. of Hertfordshire, and by her had a son, Thomas (Sir), his heir. He wedded, secondly, Anne, daughter of — Bygrave, esq. of Hertfordshire, and had another son, Giles, of Clare, in Suffolk, who left issue by his wife, Philippa, daughter of Sir William Waldgrave, knt. of Smallbridge. Sir Thomas *d.* 23rd December, 1619, and was *s.* by his elder son,

Sir Thomas Barnardiston, knt. of Witham, Essex, who *m.* first, Mary, daughter of Sir Richard Knightley, knt. of Fawsley, in the county of Northampton, and had issue,

- Nathaniel (Sir), his heir.
- Thomas, ancestor of the Barnardistons, of Bur[illegible], of which Mr. Serjeant Barnardiston was the lineal descendant and heir male.
- Arthur, *m.* Anne, daughter of James Harvey, esq. of Debden, in Suffolk, and relict of Sir R[illegible] Thornton, knt. of Snailswell, in Cambridgeshire.
- Stephen.
- Thomas, *m.* first, Mary, daughter of Henry Austin, of London, and had a daughter,
  - Margaret, *m.* to Richard Poulter.

  He wedded, secondly, a daughter of Henry P[illegible]sted, and left by her,
  - Thomas, who *m.* a daughter of John Clark.
- John.
- William, a Turkey merchant.
- A daughter, *m.* to Sir William Fish, knt.
- Hannah, *m.* to Sir John Brograve, knt. of Ha[illegible], in the county of Hertford.

He wedded, secondly, Catherine, daughter of Thomas Banks, esq. of London, but by that lady had no issue. She died 3rd March, 1632. Sir Thomas was *s.* at his decease by his eldest son,

Sir Nathaniel Barnardiston, knt. of Ketton, who was five times knight of the shire for the county of Suffolk, and sat once for Sudbury, in the same county. He *m.* Jane, daughter of Sir Peter Soame, knt. lord mayor of London, and by her had seven sons and [illegible] daughters, viz.

- Thomas, his successor.
- Nathaniel, of Hackney, in the county of Middlesex, who *m.* Elizabeth, daughter of Thomas Bacon, esq. of Friston,‡ in Suffolk, and had
  - Samuel, who inherited the baronetcy of Brightwell from his uncle, Sir Samuel Barnardiston, of *Brightwell Hall*, and *d.* [illegible] in 1712.
  - Pelethiah, successor to his brother, and th[illegible] baronet of Brightwell.
  - Jane, *m.* to Robert, son and heir of Mr. Alderman Man, of Norwich.
  - Elizabeth, *m.* to Samuel Blackerby, esq of Gray's Inn.
- Samuel, of Brightwell Hall, created a baronet 11th May, 1663, with remainder, default of [illegible] issue, to his elder brother Nathaniel Barnardiston, esq. of Hackney, and his heirs, d[illegible] of which, to his younger brother, Pelethiah Barnardiston, of Hackney, merchant, and his [illegible] male. (See Barnardiston, of Brightwell)
- Pelethiah, of Hackney, merchant, *m.* a daughter of Richard Turnor, esq. of Totteridge, in Hertfordshire, and sister of Sir William Turnor, knt. of Bromley, and had a son,
  - Nathaniel, who succeeded to the baronetcy of Brightwell at the decease of his [illegible] Sir Nathaniel Barnardiston, in 1712.

---

* By a daughter and co-heir of Sir Marmadake Tunstall, knt.

† On the north side of Kedington Church, is a very fair monument or tomb, with the portraiture of Sir Thomas Barnardiston, and his lady Elizabeth. In the second window of the north side of the church, is to be seen a Barnardiston kneeling, in his complete armour, and his coat armour on his breast, and upon both his shoulders; the writing under him is wholly perished: over him is written non peccata nostra—nobis— This seems to be very ancient.

‡ The eventual heiress of the Bacons of Friston married Dr. Hugh Chamberlen, and had three daughters, viz.

- Mary, *d.* unmarried.
- Anna-Maria, *m.* to the Rt. Hon. Edward Ho[illegible], and thence descends the present General No[illegible] Hopkins, of Oving.
- Charlotte, *m.* to Richard Luther, esq. great gra[illegible] father of Dr. Taylor, of Clifton.

William, } *d.* unm.
John, }

Arthur, who *m.* first, a daughter of Sir Richard Lloyd, knt. of Hallom, and had by her three sons and two daughters,

Samuel, of London, merchant, *m.* Anne, dau. of Samuel Blackerby, esq. of Gray's Inn.

Nathaniel, *d.* young.

Arthur, a merchant, at Smyrna.

Mary, *m.* to Sir Robert Clarke, bart. of Snailwell, in the county of Cambridge.

Jane, *d.* unmarried.

Mr. Arthur Barnardiston *m.* secondly, Mary, daughter of Samuel Luke, esq. of Woodend, in Bedfordshire, who surviving him, re-married in her widowhood Samuel Blackerby, esq.

Anne, *m.* to Sir John Rolt, knt. of Milton, in the county of Bedford.

Jane, *m.* to Sir William Blois, knt. of Coxfield Hall, Suffolk.

This Sir Nathaniel Barnardiston, esteemed the greatest ornament of his family, is styled by Fairclough, who wrote his life, and printed it with Clark's Lives, "one of the most eminent patriots of his time, and the twenty-third knight of his family." He died 25th July, 1653, and was *s.* by his eldest son,

I. Sir Thomas Barnardiston, of Ketton, M.P. for the county of Suffolk, who was created a Baronet by King Charles II. 7th April, 1663. He *m.* Anne, dau. and co-heir of Sir William Armine, bart. of Osgodby, in Lincolnshire, and had issue,

Nathaniel, *d. s. p.* in his father's lifetime.

Thomas, his successor.

William, }
Nathaniel, } all *d. s. p.*
Samuel, }

Michael, *d.* at Smyrna, unmarried.

John, *m.* Margaret, daughter of Sir Robert Cordell, bart. of Long Melford, in Suffolk.

Mary, *m.* to Sir Joseph Brand, knt. of Edwardstown, in Suffolk.

Anne, *m.* to Sir Philip Skippon, knt. of Wrentham, in the same county.

Elizabeth, *m.* to Thomas Williams, esq. of Stoke, also in Suffolk.

Sir Thomas *d.* 14th October, 1669, (his widow survived to the 25th August, 1671), and was *s.* by his eldest surviving son,

II. Sir Thomas Barnardiston, of Ketton, who *m.* Elizabeth, daughter and heir of Sir Robert King,* of Boyle, in Ireland, and by her, who *d.* in 1707, had, with two daughters, Sophia and Elizabeth, who both died in infancy, six sons, viz.

Thomas, his heir, *b.* 7th August, 1674.

Nathaniel, *d.* an infant.

Robert, successor to his elder brother.

Nathaniel, *d.* in the East Indies, unmarried.

Samuel, who inherited as fifth baronet.

John, *m.* Sophia, daughter of — Rich, esq. of Scotland, and relict of William, brother of the Lord Gray, by whom he left at his decease, in the lifetime of his brother Samuel, a son,

John, who succeeded that gentleman, and became sixth baronet.

Sir Thomas *d.* in 1698, was buried on the 15th October, in that year, and *s.* by his eldest son,

III. Sir Thomas Barnardiston. This gentleman *m.* Anne, daughter and co-heir of Sir Richard Rothwell, bart. of Stapleford, in the county of Lincoln, by whom (who *d.* 21st February, 1701) he had three daughters, his co-heirs, namely,

Elizabeth, *b.* 23rd January, 1694, *d.* in 1701.

Anna-Maria, *m.* in 1716, to Sir John Shaw, bart. of Eltham, in Kent.

Charlotte, *m.* in 1720, to Sir Anthony Abdy, bart. of Felix Hall.

Sir Thomas *d.* in November, 1700, was buried on the 21st of that month, and leaving no male issue, was *s.* in the baronetcy by his next surviving brother,

IV. Sir Robert Barnardiston, who *d.* unm. in July, 1728, when the title devolved upon his next brother,

V. Sir Samuel Barnardiston, who *m.* in August, 1730, Catherine, daughter of Sir Rowland Wynne, bart. of Nostel Abbey, in the county of York, but had no issue. He died at Ketton Hall 4th Feb. 1735-6, and was *s.* by his nephew,

VI. Sir John Barnardiston. This gentleman dying *s. p.* about the year 1750, the Baronetcy became extinct.

Arms—Azure, a fesse dancette, ermine, between six cross croslets, argent.

BARNARDISTON, OF BRIGHTWELL.

Created 11th May, 1663.

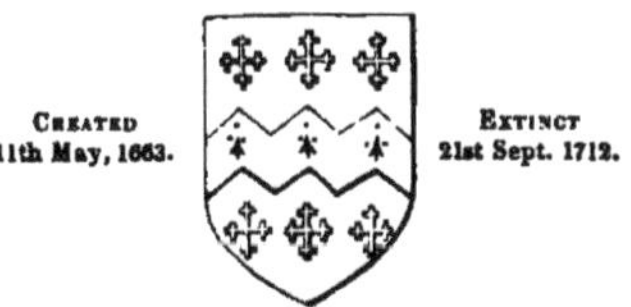

Extinct 21st Sept. 1712.

Lineage.

This was a scion from the ancient family of Barnardiston, of Ketton.

Sir Nathaniel Barnardiston, knt. of Ketton, M.P. for the county of Suffolk, and esteemed the most eminent of his knightly family, *m.* Jane, daughter of Sir Stephen Soame, lord mayor of London, and by that lady had, with other issue,

Thomas (Sir), his successor.

Nathaniel, of Hackney, who *m.* Elizabeth, dau. of Thomas Bacon, esq. of Fristow, in Suffolk, and had two sons and two daughters, viz.

Samuel, who inherited the title and estates of his uncle, Sir Samuel Barnardiston, of Brightwell Hall.

Peletiah, heir to his brother.

Jane, *m.* to Robert, son and heir of Mr. Alderman Man, of Norwich.

Elizabeth, *m.* to Samuel Blackerby, esq. of Gray's Inn.

Samuel, of whom presently.

Peletiah, who *m.* a daughter of Richard Turnor, esq. of Totteridge, in Hertfordshire, and had one son,

Nathaniel, who became fourth baronet of Brightwell, at the decease of his cousin, in 1712.

The third son,

I. Samuel Barnardiston, esq. of Brightwell Hall, in the county of Suffolk, was created a Baronet 11th May, 1663, with remainder, default of direct male issue, to his elder brother, Nathaniel Barnardiston, of Hackney, and his heirs male, default of which to his younger brother Peletiah Barnardiston, and his heirs male. Sir Samuel *m.* first, Thomasine, daughter of

* By Sophia, widow of Viscount Wimbleton, and daughter of Sir Edward Zouch, knt. of Woking, in Surrey.

Joseph Brand, esq. of Edwardston, in Suffolk; and, secondly, Mary, daughter of Sir Abraham Reynardson, knt. lord mayor of London, but having no issue, the title devolved according to the limitation upon his nephew,

II. SIR SAMUEL BARNARDISTON, who wedded a daughter and co-heir of Mr. Thomas Richmond, of London, apothecary, but died issueless 3rd January, 1709, and was *s.* by his brother,

III. SIR PELETIAH BARNARDISTON, who *d.* unm. 4th May, 1712, when the title devolved upon his cousin,

IV. SIR NATHANIEL BARNARDISTON. This gentleman dying, like his predecessor, issueless, 21st September, 1712, the BARONETCY became EXTINCT.

Arms—As Barnardiston, of Ketton.

BARNHAM, OF BOUGHTON MONCHELSEY.

CREATED 15th Aug. 1663.

EXTINCT in 1728.

Lineage.

STEPHEN BARNHAM, of Southwick, in Hampshire, of the privy chamber to HENRY VIII. had, with one dau. Dorothea, m. to Mr. Chapman, of London, two sons,

FRANCIS, his heir.

Thomas, who *m.* a daughter of — Gressey, and had issue.

The elder son,

FRANCIS BARNHAM, sheriff of London in 1570, married Alice, daughter and heir of — Brobridge, of Sussex, and dying in 1571 left issue,

MARTIN (Sir), his heir.

Anthony.

Stephen.

Benedict, sheriff of London in 1592, m. Dorothea, daughter of Ambrose Smith, of London, and by her, who wedded, secondly, Sir John Packington, knt. left at his decease in 1598 five daughters, viz.

Elizabeth, m. to Mervin, Earl of Castlehaven.

Dorothy, m. to Sir John Constable, knt.

Benedicta.

Bridget, m. to Sir William Soame, knt.

Alice, m. to Francis, Lord Verulam, lord high chancellor.

Etheldred, m. to William Cleybroke.

The eldest son,

SIR MARTIN BARNHAM, knt. of Hollingborne, sheriff of Kent 14 ELIZABETH, married, first, Ursula, daughter of Robert Rudstone, of Boughton Monchelsey, in the same county, and had by her a son,

FRANCIS (Sir), his heir.

Sir Martin espoused, secondly, Judith, daughter of Sir Martin Colthorp, knt. mayor of London, and by that lady had

Martin, of Hollingborne.

James, m. the daughter of Wood of Bromley, and had issue.

Thomas.

Elizabeth, m. Augustin Steward, esq. of Barking.

Anne, m. to Robert Honywood, esq. of Charing.

Catherine, m. to Sir Christopher Buckle, knt. of Banstead.

——, m. to Sir George Chute, knt.

Sir Martin *d.* in 1610, and was *s.* by his son,

SIR FRANCIS BARNHAM, knt. of Hollingborne, who m. Elizabeth, daughter of Sampson Leonard, esq. of Chevening, and had issue,

I. Dacres, *d. s. p.*

II. ROBERT, of whom presently.

III. Edward.

IV. Francis, of Maidstone.

V. William, mayor of Norwich in 1652, m. first, Elizabeth, daughter of William Windham, esq. of Stokesby, in Norfolk, and had by her a son.

William, barrister-at-law, who m. his cousin Elizabeth, daughter and co-heir of Charles Wyndham, esq. of Stokesby, but *d. s. p.* His widow wedded, secondly, Sir Francis Burdett, bart. grandfather of the present SIR CHARLES WYNDHAM BURDETT, bart.

Mr. William Barnham wedded, secondly, Sarah, granddaughter of Sir Hugh Middleton, bart. and by her had a daughter, Sarah, the wife of Charles Wood, esq. of London. He m. thirdly, Rebecca, daughter of Edward Bacon, of London, and had by that lady two daughters,

Mary, m. to Charles Wood.

Rebecca, m. Benjamin Wolleston, of London.

He m. fourthly, Mary Flowerdew, of Norwich, and had issue of his fourth marriage,

William, of Norwich, m. the sister of the Rev. Isaac Virtue, and had a son,

William, of Norwich, who m. Elizabeth, daughter of William Smith, esq. of Ramplingham, in Norfolk, and had

1. William, of Norwich, *b.* in 1756, m. Catherine-Barry, widow of John Gibbs Clarke, esq. of Barbadoes, daughter of James Hebert, of London, merchant, and granddaughter of Sir Hildebrand Jacob, bart. and had issue,

William, *b.* in 1788.

Hildebrand-Barry, captain in the army.

Charles-Windham, *b.* in 1794.

2. John, of Heyden, in Norfolk, m. Prudence Howlet, and has one son, George.

1. Mary, *d.* unm.

2. Hannah, m. to Charles Vercoral, of Rotterdam, merchant.

3. Margaret, m. to Thomas Hopking.

4. Elizabeth, *d.* unm.

VI. Dudley.

VII. Martin.

The eldest surviving son,

I. ROBERT BARNHAM, esq. of Boughton Monchelsey, was created a BARONET 15th August, 1663. He m. and had one son,

FRANCIS, who predeceased his father in 1668, leaving by Anne, his wife, sixth daughter of Sir Thomas Parker, knt. of Ratton, and widow of John Shirley, esq. of Isfield,

ROBERT, successor to his grandfather.

Sir Robert *d.* in 1685, and was *s.* by his grandson,

II. SIR ROBERT BARNHAM, of Boughton, who *d.* in 1728 without male issue, when the BARONETCY expired, and the estates devolved on his only daughter and heir, the wife of Thomas Rider, esq. and are now inherited by that lady's descendant, THOMAS RIDER, esq. of Boughton, in Kent.

Arms—Sa. a cross engrailed between four crescents arg.

BARRINGTON, OF BARRINGTON HALL.

CREATED 29th June, 1611.

EXTINCT 26th Sept. 1833.

Lineage.

Camden, in his Britannia, says, "Barrington Hall, (heretofore) the seat of that eminent family of the Barringtons, who in the time of *King* STEPHEN were greatly enriched with the estate of the Lord Montfichet; and in the memory of our fathers a match with the daughter and co-heir of Henry Pole, Lord Montacute, son and heir to Margaret, Countess of Salisbury, rendered them more illustrious, by an alliance with the royal blood."

Le Neve (Norroy king-of-arms) deduces the lineage of the Barringtons from BARENTONE, a Saxon, who had the custody of the forest of Hatfield-Regis, *temp.* WILLIAM the Conqueror, and whose son,

EUSTACHIUS DE BARENTONA, servant to *King* HENRY I., obtained grants of land from that monarch, with the custody of the forest. This Eustachius died in the reign of STEPHEN, and from him we pass to his (thirteenth) lineal descendant,

JOHN BARRINGTON, living in the 23th of HENRY VIII. who *m.* Elisabeth, daughter of Thomas Bonham, by his wife the Hon. Elisabeth Marney, daughter of Henry, first Lord Marney, of Marney, in the county of Essex, and was *s.* by his son,

THOMAS BARRINGTON, esq. This gentleman *m.* first, Alice, daughter of Henry Parker, Lord Morley, by whom he had an only daughter, Elisabeth, *m.* to Edward Harris, esq. He espoused, secondly, Winifred, relict of Sir Thomas Hastings, knt. youngest daughter and co-heiress of Henry Pole, Lord Montagu, granddaughter of Sir Richard Pole, K.G. by Margaret Plantagenet, Countess of Salisbury, and great granddaughter of George, Duke of Clarence, brother to *King* EDWARD IV. (see BURKE's *Extinct Peerage*); by which illustrious lady Mr. Barrington had, with a daughter, Catherine, *m.* to William Bourchier, esq. two sons, viz.

- FRANCIS (Sir), his heir.
- John, who had a very extensive grant of lands in Ireland from *Queen* ELIZABETH, in 1558, and was of Cullinagh, in the Queen's County, where his descendants remained seated until that property was sold, under an act of parliament, in 1796, by John's descendant,
  - JOHN BARRINGTON, esq. of Cullinagh, who left, besides four daughters, five sons, viz.
    1. John, *d. s. p.* 1834.
    2. French, *d. s. p.* 1836.
    3. Jonah (Sir), formerly judge of the high court of admiralty in Ireland, and M.P. for the cities of Tuam and Clogher, *d.* in 1833, leaving issue,
       - Edward, *b.* in 1796, *m.* and has issue.
       - Jane-Catherine, *m.* in 1815, to Thomas de Grenier de Fonblanque, K.H. an hereditary viscount of France, second son of the eminent king's counsel, and has issue.
       - Sybella, *m.* in 1815, to William Otway, esq.
       - Patricia, *m.* to Alexander Hunter, esq.
       - Arabella-Henrietta, *m.* in 1826, to Edward Hughes Lee, esq.
       - Margaret, *m.* 1829, to Capt. R. Worthy, of the H. E. I. Co.'s service.
    4. Wheeler, who *m.* Miss O'Neill, and had a daughter.
    5. Charles, *m.* and settled in Canada.

He was *s.* at his decease by the elder son,

I. SIR FRANCIS BARRINGTON, knt. member for the county of Essex, in the parliament assembled in the 43rd year of *Queen* ELIZABETH, and subsequently in all the parliaments of the reign of JAMES I. and in the three first of CHARLES I. who was created a BARONET the 29th June, 1611. Sir Francis *m.* Joan, daughter of Sir Henry Cromwell, of Hinchinbrook, in the county of Huntingdon, and aunt of the Protector Cromwell, and had issue,

- THOMAS, his heir.
- Robert, who *m.* Dorothy, daughter of Sir Thomas Eden, knt. and had issue.
- Francis, of London.
- John, *d.* in Germany.
- Elisabeth, *m.* to Sir James Altham, knt. and secondly, to Sir William Masham, bart.
- Mary, *m.* to Sir Gilbert Gerard.
- Winifred, *m.* to Sir William Mewes, or Meux.
- Ruth, *m.* to Sir George Lamplugh, knt.
- Joane, *m.* to Sir Richard Everard, bart.

Sir Francis dying in 1628, was *s.* by his eldest son,

II. SIR THOMAS BARRINGTON, who *m.* first, Frances, daughter and co-heir of John Gobart, esq. of Coventry, by whom he had (with a daughter, Lucy) two sons, viz.

- JOHN, his successor.
- Gobart (Sir), of Tofts, Essex, who *m.* Lucy, daughter of Sir Richard Wiseman, knt. of Torrel's Hall, Essex, by whom he had surviving issue,
  - Thomas, a colonel in the army, who *d. s. p.* having previously made over his estate to his brother.
  - Francis, who *m.* Elizabeth, daughter and co-heir of Samuel Shute, esq. of London, but had no issue. Mr. Barrington bequeathed his estate to his wife's cousin-german, John Shute, of Becket Park, Berks, who assumed the surname of BARRINGTON, and was elevated to the peerage of Ireland. (See BURKE's *Peerage*).

Sir Thomas espoused, secondly, Judith, daughter of Sir Rowland Lytton, knt. of Knebworth, in Hertfordshire, and widow of Sir George Smith, knt. of Annables, in the same shire, but had no other issue. He *d.* in 1644, and was *s.* by his elder son,

III. SIR JOHN BARRINGTON. This gentleman was M.P. in 1640, for the borough of Newport, and one of the parliamentary committee for Essex and the Isle of Wight; but when he observed the lengths to which the parliamentarians had determined to proceed, he declined to follow; although it is probable it was expected that he would go to the utmost extremity, as he was one of the members nominated to sit in the mock high court of justice, appointed to try his unhappy sovereign. Sir John, however, refused to attend any of its meetings, and peremptorily declined signing the warrant for *King* CHARLES's execution. He lived in retirement after the Restoration. Sir John *m.* Dorothy, daughter of Sir William Lytton, of Knebworth, and dying 24th March, 1682, was *s.* by the eldest son of Thomas Barrington, esq. by Anne, daughter and co-heiress of Robert Rich, Earl of Warwick, his grandson,

IV. SIR JOHN BARRINGTON. This gentleman dying unmarried, of the small-pox, in 1691, the title devolved upon his brother,

V. SIR CHARLES BARRINGTON, M.P. for the county of Essex; *m.* twice: but dying without issue, he devised his Essex estate to his sister Anne, wife of Charles Shales, esq. but the title descended to his cousin,

VI. SIR JOHN BARRINGTON, son and heir of John Barrington, esq. (third son of Sir John, third baronet) by Elizabeth, daughter of Edward Hawkins, esq. of Bishop-Stopford. This gentleman *m.* Susan, daughter of George Draper, esq. of Hitchen, in the county of Herts, and was *s.* in 1717, by his eldest son,

VII. SIR JOHN BARRINGTON, M.P.; at whose decease, issueless, 4th May, 1776, the title devolved upon his brother,

VIII. SIR FITZWILLIAM BARRINGTON, who *m.* first, in 1741, Sarah, daughter and sole heiress of Thomas Meades, captain R.N. but had no surviving issue: he *m.* secondly, in 1750, Jane, daughter of Matthew Hall, esq. and was *s.* at his decease, 24th September, 1792, by the elder of two sons,

IX. SIR JOHN BARRINGTON; at whose decease, unmarried, 5th August, 1818, the title devolved upon his brother,

X. SIR FITZWILLIAM BARRINGTON, *b.* 2nd March, 1755; *m.* 8th July, 1789, Edith-Mary, daughter of Sir Samuel Marshall, knt. R.N. and dying 26th September, 1833, leaving no male issue, the BARONETCY became EXTINCT. His daughters and co-heirs were,

LOUISA, *m.* in 1813, to Sir Richard Simeon, bart. and has issue.

JANE-ELIZABETH.

JULIA, *m.* in 1817, to Henry Philip Powys, esq. eldest son of P. L. Powys, esq. of Hardwick, in Berkshire.

ELLEN-FLACKE, *m.* in 1824, to John George Campbell, esq. second son of the late Colonel Campbell, of Islay.

MARY, *m.* in 1827, to Capt. Thomas Pakenham Vandeleur, third son of Col. I. O. Vandeleur.

Arms—Ar. three chevronels, gu. and a label of as many points, az.

BASSETT, OF TEHIDY.

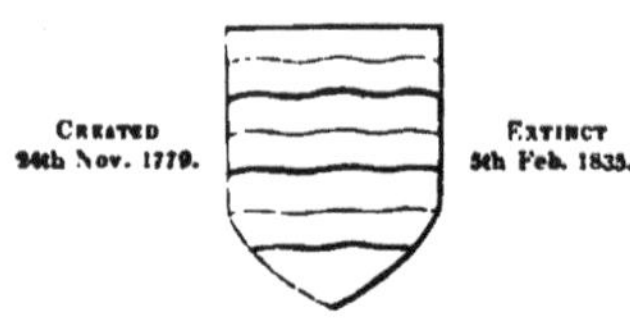

Lineage.

Immediately after the Norman conquest, arose into power and importance, particularly in the midland counties, the great baronial family of BASSETT, which gave a chief-justice to England in the reign of HENRY I. in the person of Ralph Basset; from whom sprung the Lords Basset, of Drayton, the Lords Basset, of Hedendon, &c. &c. About the middle of the twelfth century, the Basets, of Cornwall, obtained the estate of Tehidy by marriage with the heiress of the great house of De Dunstanville, from which period they appear to have enjoyed considerable wealth and influence until the civil wars. At that momentous crisis, there were three brothers of the Bassets, all eminently prominent in the royal cause,

Sir Francis Basset, sheriff of Cornwall.
Sir Thomas Basset, } both majors-general in the
Sir Arthur Basset, } royal army.

Sir Francis Basset, the sheriff, was with the king at Lestwithiel, when Essex's army surrendered; and his majesty, Sir Francis relates, in a letter to his wife, then said to him, "I now leave, Mr. Sheriff, the county of Cornwall to your protection." Owing, however, to the large sums of money disbursed in the unhappy struggle, the family became considerably reduced in circumstances; but its fortunes were at length retrieved by intermarriages with heiresses. The issue and heir of one of those, the heiress of Pendarves,

JOHN-PENDARVES BASSET, esq. *m.* Anne, daughter of Sir Edmund Prideaux, bart. and dying in 1739, was *s.* by his son,

JOHN-PRIDEAUX BASSET, esq. at whose decease in minority, 28th May, 1756, the estates reverted to his uncle,

FRANCIS BASSET, esq. who *m.* Margaret, daughter of Sir John St. Aubyn, bart. of Clowance, in the county of Cornwall, and had

FRANCIS, his heir.
John, in holy orders, *m.* Mary, daughter of George Wingfield, esq. and had a son,
John, of Lincoln's-inn.
Margaret, *m.* to John Rogers, esq. of Penrose, in Cornwall.
Cecilia.
Mary.
Catherine, *d.* unmarried, 2nd June, 1817.

The elder son,

I. FRANCIS BASSETT, esq. of Tehidy, *b.* 9th August, 1757, was created a BARONET 24th November, 1779, and advanced to the peerage as BARON DE DUNSTANVILLE 17th June, 1796. He was further created Baron Bassett, of Stratton, 7th November, 1797, with remainder to his only daughter. His lordship *m.* first, in 1780, Frances-Susannah, daughter of John Hippisley Coxe, esq. of Stone Easton, by whom (who *d.* in 1823) he had one daughter, FRANCES, BARONESS BASSETT, of Stratton. Lord de Dunstanville *m.* secondly, in 1824, Harriet, daughter of Sir William Lemon, bart. He *d.* in 1835, and leaving no male issue, the Barony of De Dunstanville and the BARONETCY became EXTINCT.

Arms—Or, three bars wavy gu.

BASTARD, OF KITLEY.

Lineage.

WILLIAM BASTARD, esq. of Kitley, descended from a very ancient Devonshire family, having during the war with France rendered essential service to government by conducting from Plymouth to Exeter a large number of French prisoners confined in the arsenal of the former place, for the removal of whom no troops could be spared from the garrison, already insufficient for the defence of the place, was created a BARONET by *King* GEORGE III. The title was gazetted in 1779, but has never been adopted. Had it been assumed by the family, Edmund Pollexfen Bastard, esq. of Kitley, in Devon, late M.P. for that county, would be the baronet. (See BURKE'S Commoners, vol. i. p. 17.)

Arms—Or a chev. az.

BATE, OF SLOANE STREET.

(See Bate-Dudley.)

BATEMAN, OF HOW HALL.

Created 31st Aug. 1664. Extinct

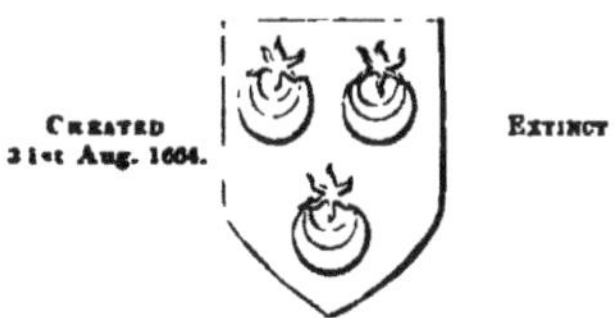

Lineage.

Richard Bateman, esq. of Hartington, living in 1561, son of William Bateman, and grandson of Robert Bateman, m. Ellen, daughter of William Topleyes, of Tissington, in Derbyshire, and had two sons,

I. Hugh, b. in 1554, ancestor of the Batemans of Hartington, whose representative, Hugh Bateman, esq. was created a Baronet in 1806, but d. s. p. m. when the baronetcy passed under the limitation to his grandson, the present Sir Francis-Edward Scott, bart. while the male representation of the Bateman family devolved on his nephew, the present Richard-Thomas Bateman, esq. (See Burke's *Commoners*, vol. iii. p. 349).

II. Richard.

The second son,

Richard Bateman, esq. bapt. at Hartington, 6th September, 1561, was chamberlain of London, and sometime one of the representatives in parliament of that city. He m. Elizabeth, daughter of John Westrow, esq. and had, with other issue,

William (Sir), of London.

Anthony (Sir), lord mayor of London in 1664, m. at Charlton, in Kent, in 1645, Elizabeth Russell.

Thomas (Sir), of whom we have to treat.

The third son,

I. Sir Thomas Bateman, a merchant of London, was created a Baronet in 1664, as Sir Thomas Bateman, of How Hall, Norfolk. In 1666 this gentleman and his two brothers, who all appear to have been engaged in commercial pursuits, sustained great losses by the dreadful fire of that year in London: many of their houses were burnt, and their property and papers destroyed. Sir Thomas's house in Coleman Street was so damaged that he left it and went to reside at Isleworth, and soon after at Chelsea, where he rented, in 1670, a house of Mr. Cheney, who married the Duke of Norfolk's daughter. He wedded the only daughter and heiress of Mr. Midleton, high sheriff of the counties of Cambridge and Huntingdon, but dying s. p. the Baronetcy expired.

Arms—Or, three crescents with an estoile of six points, above each crescent gu.

BATHURST, OF LEACHLADE.

Created 15th Dec. 1643. Extinct*

Lineage.

The family of Bathurst was originally of Bathurst, in the county of Sussex, whence they removed into Kent, and afterwards spread into various other counties.

Laurence Bathurst, who held lands in the time of Henry VI. at Cranbrook, in Kent, and had property in the city of Canterbury, was father of three sons,

I. Edward, from whom the noble house of Bathurst. (See Burke's *Peerage*).

II. Robert, of whom presently.

III. John, who had lands at Staplehurst, by gift of his father, m. Elizabeth, and left a son,

Edward Bathurst, esq. of Ockham, in the county of Southampton, who m. Mary, daughter of George Holland, of Augmering, in Sussex, and had three sons,

Edward.

John, alderman of London.

Anthony.

The second son,

Robert Bathurst, esq. of Horsmanden, in Kent, m. first, the daughter of William Saunders, esq. and had three sons,

I. John, his successor.

II. Paul, who wedded Elizabeth, daughter and coheir of Edward Hordon, esq. of Hordon and Finchcocks, in Kent, a member of the Board of Green Cloth *temp.* Edward VI., *Queen* Mary, and *Queen* Elizabeth, and had two sons, Richard, who was king's avener in 1620, and his heir,

Edward Bathurst, of Finchcocks, in the parish of Goudhurst, which he derived through his mother. This gentleman m. Nasaretha, sister of Sir John Levison, knt. and left issue,

Thomas, of Finchcocks.

Edward, gentleman harbinger to *King* Charles I.

William, merchant and alderman of London.

Richard, of Goodhurst.

Elizabeth, m. to Edward Maplesden.

Anna, m. to George Maplesden.

III. Stephen.

He m. secondly, and had three other sons, viz.

IV. Robert.

V. Timothy.

VI. John, of Goudhurst, in Kent, m. Dorothy, daughter of Edward Maplesden, esq. of Marden, in Kent, and had

Edward, who d. in 1673, aged seventy-seven, without issue.

* It is doubtful whether this title be extinct or not.

John, M.D. of Richmond, in the county of York, and of London, *d.* in 1659, leaving by his wife, Elizabeth, daughter and co-heir of Bryan Williams, esq. of Clints, eight sons and three daughters. Of the former all died *s. p.* but the fifth, THEODORE, of whom presently. The daughters were

Dorothy, *m.* to Moses Bathurst, esq. uncle of Lord Bathurst.
Elizabeth, *m.* to Sir Richard Blake, knt. of Clerkenwell, Middlesex, and left two daughters, co-heirs of their father, viz.
Elizabeth Blake, *m.* first, to Robert Berkley, esq.; and, secondly, to DR. GILBERT BURNET, Bishop of Salisbury.
Mary Blake, *m.* to Robert Dormer, one of the judges of the Common Pleas.

The eldest surviving son and heir of Dr. Bathurst,

Theodore Bathurst, esq. of Scutterskelf, Clints, and Arkendale, in Yorkshire, *m.* Lettice, daughter of Sir John Repington, knt. and was *s.* by his son,
Charles Bathurst, who wedded Frances, daughter and heir of Thomas Potter, of Leeds, and left issue,
Charles, high sheriff of Yorkshire, *d. s. p.*
Mary, *m.* Wm. Sleigh, esq. and was great-grandmother of the present GEORGE WILLIAM SUTTON, esq. of Elton, in Durham. (See BURKE's *Commoners*, vol. ii. p. 63.)
Jane, *m.* to Wm. Turner, esq.
Frances, *m.* to C. F. Forster, esq.

The eldest son and heir,

JOHN BATHURST, esq. having *m.* Mary,* daughter of Edward Dodge, esq. of Wrotham, in Kent, became seised thereby of the manor of Leachdale, and dying in the lifetime of his father, left a son and heir,

ROBERT BATHURST, esq. of Leachdale, in the county of Gloucester, high sheriff of that shire in 1611. This gentleman *m.* first, Benetta, daughter of Roger Twisden, esq. of Reydon Hall, in Kent, but by her had no issue. He wedded, secondly, Elizabeth, daughter and heir of Ralph Waller, esq. and widow of Sir John Laurence, knt. lord mayor of London, by which lady he had

ROBERT, his successor.
EDWARD, heir to his brother.
Mary, } *d.* unm.
Elizabeth, }

This Robert, at the visitation of 1623, applied for an alteration in his coat of arms, and obtained it. He was *s.* at his decease by his eldest son,

ROBERT BATHURST, esq. of Leachdale, who *d.* in minority in the 3rd of CHARLES I. and was *s.* by his brother,

I. EDWARD BATHURST, esq. of Leachdale, *b.* in 1615, who for his loyalty during the civil wars, having had his estate sequestered in the rebellion, and being obliged to compound for the same, was knighted in 1643, and created a BARONET on the 15th December, in the same year. Sir Edward *m.* first, Anne, daughter of Thomas Morris, esq. of Great Coxwell, in Berks, and had issue,

I. LAWRENCE, who *m.* Susan, daughter of Thomas Cook, esq. of Stanton, and by her (who wedded, secondly, Sir John Pettiplace, bart.; and, thirdly, Sir John Cutler, knt.) he left at his decease in 1670, his father then living,
EDWARD, second baronet.
Susannah, *d.* unmarried.
Anne, *m.* to Mr. John Greening, and *d. s. p.*
MARY, *m.* to George Coxeter, esq. of the Middle Temple, and of Kennington, Berks, and had issue,
THOMAS COXETER, who inherited eventually the manor of Leachdale from his mother and aunt, it having devolved upon them at the decease of his uncle SIR EDWARD BATHURST, in minority, 21st May, 1677.
II. EDWARD, third baronet.
III. Robert, *d. s. p.*
IV. Mary, *m.* to John Cook, of London, merchant.
V. Elizabeth, *m.* to Edward Gibbs, esq. of the county of Gloucester, deputy governor of Chepstow Castle.
VI. Anne, *d. s. p.*

Sir Edward wedded, secondly, Susan, daughter of Thomas Rich, esq. of North Cerney, in the county of Gloucester, and widow of Thomas Cook, esq. of Stanton, and by her had four other sons and four daughters, viz.

VII. Robert, who *m.* Mary, daughter of Robert Oatridge, gent. of Leachlade, and had issue,
Robert, who left two sons,
Robert and Edward.
Edmund.
John.
VIII. Lancelot, who went to Virginia, and his descendants settled in Jamaica.
IX. Edward, Fellow of Trinity College, Cambridge, *d.* unmarried.
X. Charles, a draper in London, *d. s. p.*
XI. Susan, *m.* first, to Robert Jordan, esq. of Leachlade; secondly, to the Rev. Mr. Orchard; and thirdly, to Richard Parsons, LL.D. chancellor of Gloucester.
XII. Annabella, *m.* first, to William Goodenough esq. of Broughton Poggs, in the county of Oxford; and, secondly, to the Rev. Thomas Kingdon, vicar of Burscote, Berks.
XIII. Elizabeth, *m.* to Henry Willet, of Leachlade
XIV. Maria, *d.* unmarried.

He *m.* thirdly, Mrs. Dorothy Nash, but had no other issue. He *d.* in August, 1674, and was *s.* by his grandson,

II. SIR EDWARD BATHURST, of Leachlade, who *d.* at the age of twelve in March, 1677, when the manor of Leachlade passed to his surviving sisters, Mrs. Greening and Mrs. Coxeter, and eventually devolved upon the son of the latter, Thomas Coxeter, esq. while the baronetcy reverted to his uncle,

III. SIR EDWARD BATHURST, who *m.* Mary, daughter of Francis Peacock, esq. of Chawley, in the county of Oxford, and had issue,

EDWARD, his successor.
Walter, *d. s. p.*
FRANCIS, successor to his brother.
Robert.
Charles, *d.* unmarried.
Mary.

* This lady wedded, secondly, Francis Champneys, esq.

He was *s.* at his decease by his eldest son,

IV. SIR EDWARD BATHURST, who *d.* unmarried, and was *s.* by his brother,

V. SIR FRANCIS BATHURST. This gentleman wedded Frances, daughter of the Rev. Mr. Peacock, and had two sons and three daughters, viz.

LAURENCE, his heir.

Robert, killed in an engagement with the Indians at Georgia.

Sir Francis and his lady, with part of his family, embarked for America with General Oglethorp to encourage the new settlement, and *d.* there about the year 1738, when he was *s.* by his son,

VI. SIR LAURENCE BATHURST, who resided at Georgia, and died there. The title is stated by some accounts to be EXTINCT, but by other to be vested in a gentleman still resident in America.

Arms—Sa. two bars erm. in chief three crosses pattee or.

BAYNING, OF BENTLEY PARVA.

CREATED 24th Sept. 1612.

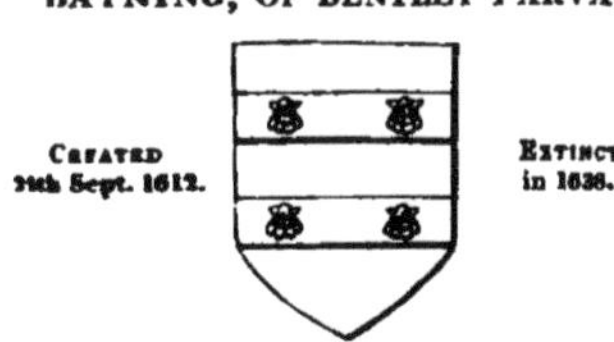

EXTINCT in 1638.

Lineage.

I. SIR PAUL BAYNING, of Bentley-Parva, in the county of Essex, (son of Paul Bayning, esq. one of the sheriffs of London in the reign of ELIZABETH, *anno* 1593. was created a BARONET 24th September, 1612, and elevated to the peerage on the 27th February, 1627, in the dignity of BARON BAYNING, of Horkesley-Bentley, in the county of Essex, and advanced to the rank of VISCOUNT BAYNING, of Sudbury, in the county of Suffolk, on the 8th of March, in the same year. His lordship m. Anne, daughter of Sir Henry Glemham, knt. of Glemham, in the county of Suffolk, and had issue,

PAUL, his successor.

Cecilia, m. Henry Viscount Newark, who succeeded his father, in 1643, in the earldom of Kingston, and was created MARQUESS OF DORCHESTER in the following year, by whom she had two surviving daughters, viz.

Anne, m. to John, Lord Ros, afterwards Earl of Rutland, a marriage dissolved by parliament in 1668.

Grace, died unmarried in 1703.

Anne, m. to Henry Murray, esq. one of the grooms of the bedchamber to *King* CHARLES I. This lady was created VISCOUNTESS BAYNING, of Foxley, for life. Her ladyship *d.* in 1698, when the dignity of course expired. Mr. Murray's eldest daughter and co-heiress, by Lady Bayning,

The Honourable Elizabeth Murray, m. Randolph Egerton, esq. and had a daughter,

ANNE EGERTON, (sole heiress of her father), who m. Lord William Paulet, second son of Charles, first Duke of Bolton, by whom she had an only daughter,

HENRIETTA PAULET, (heiress of her father), who m. the Honourable William Townshend, third son of Charles, second Viscount Townshend, K.G. and left a son,

CHARLES TOWNSHEND, who was created BARON BAYNING, of Foxley, on the 27th October, 1797, and was father of the present LORD BAYNING.

Mary, m. first, to William Viscount Grandison; and, secondly, to Christopher, Earl of Anglesey.

Elizabeth, m. to Francis Leonard, Lord Dacre.

The Viscount died "at his own house in Mark-lane, within the city of London," on the 29th July, 1629, and was *s.* by his son,

II. SIR PAUL BAYNING, bart. second viscount, who m. Penelope, only daughter and heiress of Sir Robert Naunton, knt. master of the court of ward and liveries, by whom (who m. secondly, Philip, Earl of Pembroke) he left two daughters, viz.

ANNE, m. to Aubrey de Vere, Earl of Oxford.

PENELOPE, m. to the Hon. John Herbert, youngest son of Philip, fourth Earl of Pembroke, and first Earl of Montgomery.

His lordship dying thus without male issue, all his honours, including the BARONETCY, EXPIRED.

Arms—Or, two bars sa. on each as many escallop shells of the first.

BAYNTUN, OF SPYE PARK.

(See BAYNTUN-ROLT).

BEALE, OF MAIDSTONE.

CREATED 16th Oct. 1660.

EXTINCT 13th Oct. 1684.

Lineage.

WILLIAM BEALE, son of John Beale, of Maidstone, who died in 1399, was portreve and one of the elder brethren of the fraternity of that borough. He died in 1429, and was buried in St. Faith's Church, leaving by Katherine his wife a son,

JOHN BEALE, of Maidstone, who married twice, and was *s.* at his decease, in 1461, by his son,

ROBERT BEALE, of Maidstone, whose wife's Christian name was Agnes, but of what family she came is not recorded. He *d.* in 1490, and was *s.* by his son,

WILLIAM BEALE, of Maidstone, who was twice portreve of that town. He m. Johanna ——, and dying in 1534, left issue,

I. JOHN, whose son,

RICHARD BEALE, a merchant in London, purchased several estates in Kent, and resided at Whaddon, in Surrey. He m. Bersheba, daughter of Thomas Gilbert, but leaving no surviving issue at his decease, in 1636, he devised his estates to his grand-nephew,

RICHARD BEALE, the son of Richard, and grandson of Alexander Beale, of Frittenden. This gentleman resided at Hayle Place, and was in the commission of the peace for Kent. He *m.* Susan, daughter of Edward Bennet, deputy to the Hamburgh company, and dying in 1664, was *s.* by his son,

RICHARD BEALE, a Hamburgh merchant, *b.* in 1645, who *d.* without issue in 1703, leaving his nephew,

RICHARD BEALE, esq. the son of his brother Alexander, his heir. This gentleman, who was a justice of the peace for Kent, *m.* in 1704, Mary, daughter of James Wittewronge, esq. of Lincoln's Inn, and by her (who wedded, secondly, the Rev. Thomas Taylor) left at his decease, in 1712, a daughter,

MARY BEALE, *b.* in 1705, who *m.* in 1728, William Post, esq. of London, and *d.* in 1768, leaving a son,

WILLIAM POST, esq. of Hayle Place, *b.* in 1738, who *m.* Mary, daughter of the Rev. T. M. Jordan, rector of Barming and Iden, and *d.* in 1806, leaving issue,

BEALE POST, in holy orders, LL.B. curate of Milsted, near Sittingbourne, *b.* in 1793, *m.* Mary-Jane, daughter of J. Cousens, gent. of Westbourn, and has issue.

Mary Anne Post, *m.* to Rear-Admiral George Montague Hamilton, of the Russian navy.

Frances Post, *m.* in 1814, to the Rev. Maurice Johnson, A.M.

II. William, *d.* in 1807.

III. THOMAS, of whom presently.

I. Margery, *m.* to John Clarke.

The youngest son,

THOMAS BEALE, was a jurat of the Maidstone Corporation and mayor in 1561 and 1574. He *m.* first, in 1547, Johanna Cobb, by whom he had one son and one daughter. He *m.* secondly, in 1553, Alice Wolgate, and by her, who *d.* in 1613, had with other issue,

Thomas, of Maidstone, *b.* in 1559, *m.* and *d.* in 1606, leaving issue.

JOHN, of whom presently.

Ambrose, of Maidstone, mayor thereof in 1624 and 1637, *m.* twice, and left issue.

The second son of the second marriage,

JOHN BEALE, esq. a merchant of London, living in 1633, married Anne, daughter of Allan Ducket, and was father of

I. SIR JOHN BEALE, of Farningham Court, in Kent, *b.* about the year 1621, who was created a BARONET in 1660, and served as high sheriff of Kent in 1665. He *m.* first, in 1655, Anne, daughter of Sir William Culpeper, bart. of Aylesford, but by that lady, who *d.* in 1657, had no issue; and, secondly, Jane, daughter of Richard Duke, esq. of Maidstone, by whom he left four daughters, his co-heirs, viz.

JANE, *m.* to Sir Thomas Roberts, bart. of Glassenbury, Kent.

ANNE, *m.* in 1688, to Sir George Hanger, knt. of Driffield, Gloucestershire.

ELIZABETH, *m.* in 1691, to William Emmerton, esq. of Chipsted House.

MARY, *m.* in 1695, to Thomas, eldest son of William Lambard, esq. of Seven Oaks.

Sir John Beale *d.* 3rd October, 1684, when the BARONETCY became EXTINCT.

Arms—Sa. on a chev. or between three griffins' heads erased arg. as many estoiles gu.

BEAUMONT, OF COLE ORTON.

CREATED 17th Sept. 1619. EXTINCT 11th June, 1702.

Lineage.

NICHOLAS BEAUMONT, esq. M.P. for the county of Leicester *temp.* ELIZABETH, (a member of the very ancient family of Beaumont, which deduces its pedigree paternally from the old monarchs of France, and maternally from HENRY III. King of England. See BURKE'S *Peerage and Baronetage*), married Anne, daughter of William Saunders, esq. of Welford, in Northamptonshire, and by her, who *d.* 7th September, 1582, and was buried in Christ Church, London, had four sons and two daughters, viz.

I. HENRY, his heir.

II. Francis, master of the Charter-house, *d. s. p.* in 1624.

III. THOMAS (Sir), knt. of Stoughton Grange, in Leicestershire, ancestor of the present SIR GEORGE-HOWLAND-WILLOUGHBY BEAUMONT, bart. of Stoughton Grange, who now resides at Cole Orton Hall, the seat of the extinct baronets.

IV. Huntington, who married and had issue.

I. Dorothy, *m.* to William Read, esq. of Barton, in Berkshire.

II. Catherine, *m.* to Sir Henry Berkeley, bart.

The eldest son,

SIR HENRY BEAUMONT, knt. of Cole Orton, M.P. for Leicestershire 31st ELIZABETH, and high sheriff of the county in the 36th of the same reign, presented a petition to JAMES I. but without success, praying for the revival in his favour of the Viscountcy of Beaumont, forfeited by the attainder of John, Viscount Beaumont, who was slain at the battle of Northampton fighting under the banner of Lancaster. Sir Henry *m.* Elizabeth, daughter and heiress of Thomas Lewis, and dying 31st March, 1607, was *s.* by his only son,

I. SIR THOMAS BEAUMONT, of Cole Orton, M.P. and high sheriff for Leicestershire, who was created a BARONET 17th September, 1619, and subsequently elevated to the peerage of Ireland as VISCOUNT BEAUMONT, of Swords. During the troubled period in which he lived, his lordship strenuously supported the Royal cause, and had in consequence to compound for his estates. He wedded Elizabeth, daughter and heir of Henry Sapcote, esq. of Elton, in Huntingdonshire, and left a son and successor,

II. SIR SAPCOTE BEAUMONT, second viscount Beaumont, who like his father suffered deeply by his fidelity to the king, and *d.* before the Restoration. His lordship *m.* Elizabeth, daughter of Sir Thomas Monson, knt. of Burton, in Lincolnshire, by Margaret his wife, daughter of Sir Edmond Anderson, knt. lord chief justice of the court of Common Pleas, and had issue,

THOMAS, his heir.

John, who attended CHARLES II. in exile, and held after the Restoration under that monarch and his brother JAMES II. several honourable

(102. V.)

Visit. Rutland p 29

Sr Robt
Treasr of

Breaste

Wm Sheely = Frances

Wm

R Gifford = Mary
d 1550

Ursula =

Sr

Wm Staveleye
d 1498 of Notts

Wm
Mary

e Fr. = Thos Sapcotte

p 46

Visit. Warw. 179

Robt Arden of

to mol... or

Wm Greville of Campden

" ... p 251 Horne of Bl...

3 ... on ...

5. arg chough ppr

7. qrly or & gu

... Sa ...

Thos Hord = ... Hor

Edw Raleigh = Frances d
of Farnegho

az lion tail forked or

... Vale

Chesterfield Glos

... chief ... or

Rs & Bees
Schuske 117
Whitaker Richd III 251

VCH Hants III ...

Rich Sapcote ... 1451 ...
Isabel Wolston widow of Sir ... of
Burley Rutland ... 1492 ...
... Dorothy ...

Note Ped. of Sheeley in Visit. ...
... out ... Visit

City of Oxford Education Committee.

....School,

....Dept.

....19

appointments, but on the landing of the Prince of Orange, joining the new king, he was constituted governor of Dover Castle and colonel of a regiment, with which he served for many years abroad. He *m.* first, Mary, daughter of Sir Halton Fermor, knt. of Easton Neston, in Northamptonshire, and relict of the Hon. Sir Charles Compton, knt.; and, secondly, Philipa, daughter of Sir Nicholas Carew, knt. of Beddington, in Surrey, but *d. s. p.* 3rd July, 1701.

Elizabeth, *m.* to Sir John Hotham, bart. of Scarborough.

The elder son,

III. Sir Thomas Beaumont, third viscount Beaumont, *m.* Mary, daughter of Sir Erasmus Fountain, knt. of Kerby Bellers, in Leicestershire, but had no issue. His lordship founded at Cole Orton an hospital for six widows and a free school, and endowed them bountifully, appointing for trustees his heir, the rector of the parish, and two others. Dying *s. p.* 11th June, 1702, the peerage, together with the baronetcy, became extinct, while all the estates passed, under his will, to his lordship's heir male, Sir George Beaumont, bart. of Stoughton.

Arms—Az. semée of fleurs-de-lys, a lion rampt. or.

BEAUMONT, OF GRACE-DIEU.

Created 29th Jan. 1627.—Extinct 7th July, 1686.

Lineage.

Thomas Beaumont, of Tringston, a scion of the Cole Orton family, *m.* Anne Harcourt, and dying 22nd Henry VIII. left two sons, viz.

John, his heir.

Edward, who settled at Barrow upon Trent, and founded the branch of the family there seated, and now represented by John Beaumont, esq. of Barrow upon Trent. (See Burke's *Commoners*, vol. iv.)

The elder son,

John Beaumont, master of the Rolls in 1550, purchased the site of the priory of Grace-Dieu, in 1539, and by Elizabeth, his wife, eldest daughter and co-heir of Sir William Hastings, knt. left a son and heir,

Sir Francis Beaumont, knt. of Grace-Dieu, judge of the Common Pleas, who *m.* Anne, daughter of Sir George Pierrepoint, of Home Pierrepoint, in Nottinghamshire, and relict of Thomas Thorold, esq. and had three sons, viz.

Henry (Sir), of Grace-Dieu, whose only daughter and heir,

Barbara, *m.* first, John Harpur, esq.; and secondly, Sir Wolstan Dixie, bart.

John, of whom presently.

Francis, the celebrated dramatic poet.

The second son,

I. John Beaumont, esq. of Grace-Dieu, was created a baronet in 1627. He *m.* Elizabeth, daughter of John Fortescue, esq. and great-granddaughter of Sir Richard Pole, K.G. by whom he left at his decease, in 1628, a son and successor,

II. Sir John Beaumont, of Grace-Dieu, colonel in the royal army, who gallantly distinguished himself in the cause of his ill-fated prince, and was slain at Gloucester in 1644. His brother and successor,

III. Sir Thomas Beaumont, of Grace-Dieu, married Vere, only daughter of Sir William Tufton, bart. of Vintners, in Kent, and by her (who *m.* secondly, George Lane) had issue,

Cicely, *m.* to Robert Beaumont, esq. of Barrow upon Trent.

Vere, *m.* to Sir John Rayney, bart.

Mary, *m.* to George Morton, esq. of Sileby.

Jane, *m.* to Charles Byerly, esq. of Belgrave.

Anne, *m.* to Robert Pawley, esq.

Sir Thomas died without male issue 7th July, 1686, aged sixty-six, when the Baronetcy expired. The site of the priory of Grace-Dieu was inherited by Cicely, wife of Robert Beaumont, esq. of Barrow-on-Trent, and from that gentleman was purchased by Sir Ambrose Phillipps, knt. of Garendon.

Arms—As Beaumont, of Cole Orton.

BEAUMONT, OF WHITLEY.

Created 19th Aug. 1628. Extinct 29th Oct. 1631.

Lineage.

I. Sir Richard Beaumont,* knt. of Whitley Beaumont, *b.* 2nd August, 1574, son of Edward Beaumont, esq. of Whitley, by Elizabeth his wife, daughter of John Ramsden, esq. was knighted by James I. on the 23rd July, 1609, and in 1613 had a commission to command two hundred of the train-band soldiers. In 1625 Pontefract returned him to parliament, and in three years after he was created a Baronet. He *d.* unm. 28th October, 1631, when the Baronetcy became extinct, and the estates devolved, under his will, upon his cousin, Sir Thomas Beaumont.

Arms—Gu. a lion rampant, arg. langued and armed az. between eight crescents.

BECK, OF LONDON.

Created 1st Nov. 1714. Extinct 12th Jan. 1764.

Lineage.

I. Justus Beck, esq. an eminent merchant of London, was raised to the Baronetage by *King* George I. (the first Baronetcy created by that monarch) on the 1st November, 1714. He *m.* Rachel, daughter of Mr. Alderman Chamberlayne, also of London, and by her (who *d.* 1st October, 1734) had issue,

* For details of the family of Beaumont of Whitley, refer to Burke's *Commoners*, vol. ii. p. 321.

CHAMBERLAYNE, his successor.
JUSTUS, third baronet.
George.
Rachel.

Sir Justus *d.* 15th December, 1722, and was *s.* by his eldest son,

II. SIR CHAMBERLAYNE BECK, who *d.* unmarried in August, 1730, and was *s.* by his brother,

III. SIR JUSTUS BECK, who *d.* unmarried 12th January, 1764, when the BARONETCY became EXTINCT.

Arms—Quarterly; first, or, a blackbird ppr.; second and third, az. a mullet or; fourth, az. a dolphin haurient or.

BECKWITH, OF ALDBOROUGH.

CREATED 15th April, 1681.

EXTINCT in May, 1743.

Lineage.

This was a very ancient family, and it bore originally the name of MALBIE, or MALBYSSE. Its pedigree was entered in the visitation of Yorkshire by Sir William Dugdale at Doncaster, 9th April, 1666.

SIR SYMON MALBIE, knt. lord of Cawton, in Craven, *m.* the daughter of John, lord of Methley, and had three sons, viz.

I. JOHN, his heir, who wedded a daughter of Sir Alan Zouch, knt. and had a son,

SIR JOHN MALBIE, knt. lord of Cowton, who *m.* the daughter of Sir John Aldburgh, of Aldburgh, and had a son and heir,

JOHN MALBIE, or MALBYSSE, lord of Malbie, who wedded the daughter of Sir Edward Willstrope, and had three daughters, of whom MARGARET, who eventually became sole heir, *m.* THOMAS FAIRFAX, of Walton, and had issue,

William Fairfax, of Walton, from whom the Fairfaxes of Gilling Castle. (See BURKE'S *Commoners*, vol. ii. page 113.)

Anne Fairfax, *m.* to — Maston.

Claricia Fairfax, *m.* to William Palmes, of Naburn. (See BURKE'S *Commoners*, vol. i. page 611.)

II. Roger, *m.* the daughter of Sir Hugh Haigh, and had a son,

Ambrose Malbie, who wedded Timothea, daughter of Sir John Pensax, knt. and had a son and heir,

Edward Malbie, who *m.* the daughter of Sir Hugh Coyney, knt. and *d. s. p.*

III. HERCULES.

The youngest son, (in whose descendants the representation of the family eventually merged),

HERCULES DE MALBIE, wedded a daughter of Sir John Ferrers, of Tamworth Castle, and had a son and heir,

HERCULES DE MALBIE, who *m.* Beckwith, one of the daughters of Sir William Bruce,* lord of Uglebarby, descended from Sir Robert Brus, lord of Skelton Castle, in Cleveland, a noble Norman knight, ancestor of the BRUCES, of SCOTLAND, and had a son and heir,

NICHOLAS BECKWITH, who changed his name in pursuance of the marriage contract between his father and Beckwith Bruce, wherein it was stipulated that he should do so, or adopt the coat armour of that family, and it appears by the following documents that he preferred the former.

" Be it known to all nobles where this present writing shall come, be seen or heard: whereas Hammon Beckwith, esq. son and heir of Nicholas Beckwith, was warned by the Earl Marshal of England, by a process that was dated from the aforesaid Earl Marshal's manor of Ryseing Castle, in the county of Norfolk, January 10th, in the thirteenth year of the reign of our sovereign lord the king, in the year of our Lord 1339, that the said Hamon Beckwith should usurp, and take unto him, a coat of arms, which was appertaining unto John, Lord Malbie; for which better use, by virtue of this process, we charge you, that you will appear at the now mansion-house, and manor of Saymor, before us, and bring with you all such evidence and records of arms, that we may allow, grant, and set our hands, to your teste and posterity for ever. And also that your appearance shall be the 14th day of October next coming, in the aforesaid year above written.

" And the said Orator did appear at the said day appointed, and did bring with him such evidence whereof one piece, bearing date from the 10th year of HENRY III., which was in the year of our Lord 1226, from one Hercules Malbie, the third son of Sir Simon Malbie, knt. which married the Lady Dame Beckwith Browse, one of the daughters of Sir William Browse, lord of Uglebarby, and certain lands in Pickering, that the said Hercules should change his name, or else his coat, and his posterity for ever; and so it was that the said Hercules changed his name from Malbie to Beckwith, and did hold his coat: whereof I, the said Earl Marshal, Peter Mawlam, lord of de Lake, lord chamberlain to our sovereign lord *King* EDWARD III. and Henry, Lord Percy, Sir Robert Boynton, knt. and Sir William Acton, did see and allow of it in due proof, and the aforesaid coat to be his own, lineally descended; whereof we have set our hands and seals to the aforesaid teste, the day and year above written, in the presence of many."

This Nicholas Beckwith *m.* the daughter of Sir John Chaworth, knt. and was *s.* by his son,

HAMON BECKWITH, esq. who was seised of the lordship of Clint, bounding of the north side of Nid juxta Hampesthwait, and of Uglebarby, in Whitby-strand, certain lands in Pickering and Roxbie, with the manor of Beckwith and Beckwithshaw, 13th EDWARD III. A. D. 1339. He *m.* the daughter of Sir Philip Tilney, knt. and had, with a daughter Anne, the wife of William Frevile, esq. a son and successor,

* This Sir William de Bruce appears to have inherited a considerable portion of the lands granted by WILLIAM the Conqueror to his ancestor, Sir Robert de Bruce, for we find that his daughter was heiress of Uggleharby and Roxby, both of which places are mentioned amongst the possessions originally granted to Sir Robert de Bruce. Amongst those possessions are also named lands in "Leverton," or "Levinton," which must also have formed part of the inheritance of Sir William de Bruce which was conveyed by his daughter's marriage to Sir Hercules de Malbie, and is now possessed by the lineal descendant of Sir Hercules, the present Colonel Beckwith of Trimdon. This estate is held by a feudal tenure, that the eldest son of the possessor should hold the king's stirrup whenever his majesty may come into the North Riding of Yorkshire.

WILLIAM BECKWITH, esq. of Beckwith in 1364, who m. a daughter of Sir Gerard Uffiet, and was s. by his son,

THOMAS BECKWITH, esq. who was seised of Clint, the manor of Magna Otrington, and of Horqby juxta Thurske, which lands were holden of John, Lord Mowbray, of the manor of Thurske, 4 RICHARD II. He m. a daughter of John Sawley, esq. of Saxton, and had issue,

WILLIAM, his heir.

John, m. Amye, daughter of Arthur Chambers, esq. and d. s. p. m.

Anne, m. to John Chancy, esq. and had

Thomas Chancy.

Julian Chancy.

Ellen, m. to John Vavasour, esq. of Weston. This lady made her will in the 2nd HENRY VII.

He was s. by his elder son,

WILLIAM BECKWITH, esq. of Clint, who m. a daughter of Sir John Baskervile, knt. and was s. by his son,

THOMAS BECKWITH, esq. of Clint, who m. the daughter and heir of Sir William Hasterton, knt. and in her right enjoyed the third part of the manors of Filey-Maston and Thorp. He had issue,

THOMAS, his successor.

WILLIAM (Sir), successor to his brother.

John, m. the daughter of Thomas Ratcliff, of Mulgrave, and had a son,

THOMAS, heir to his uncle SIR WILLIAM.

Adam, m. Amy, daughter of William Redman, esq. of Harwood Castle, and d. s. p.

Robert, m. Barbara, daughter of John Leventhorp, esq. of Leventhorp, and had, with a daughter Mary, an only son,

John, from whom descended Sir Leonard Beckwith and Ambrose Beckwith, of Stillingfleet.

Sir Leonard Beckwith was sheriff of Yorkshire in the 4th of EDWARD VI. He served *King* HENRY VIII. in his French wars, and was afterwards in the service of EDWARD VI., from which monarch he received a grant in the 4th year of the king's reign of the site of the Abbey of Selby. He m. Elizabeth, daughter and co-heir of Sir Roger Cholmley, knt. and had issue,

Roger, } both d. s. p.
Rancy, }

Elizabeth, m. to William Vavasour, of Weston, in the county of York.

Frances, m. to George Harvey, esq. of Markes, in Essex.

Thomas Beckwith was s. by his eldest son,

THOMAS BECKWITH, esq. of Clint, who m. Elizabeth, daughter of Thomas Ingleby, esq. of Ripley, in the county of York, but dying s. p. was s. by his brother,

SIR WILLIAM BECKWITH, knt. of Clint. This gentleman m. first, Elizabeth, daughter of Sir William Plumpton, knt. of Plumpton; and secondly, the daughter of Sir John Ratcliffe, knt. but had no issue. His next brother,

JOHN BECKWITH, married a daughter of Thomas Radcliffe, esq. of Mulgrave, and had two sons, viz.

I. THOMAS, heir to his uncle Sir William Beckwith, m. Maud, daughter of Henry Pudsey, esq. and was s. by his son,

WILLIAM, of Clint, who m. first, Anne, daughter of Sir John Lancaster, knt. of Westmoreland; and secondly, a daughter of Sir John Mallory, knt. of Studley, but by that lady had no issue. Dying thus s. p. he was s. by his brother,

THOMAS, of Clint, father, by Elizabeth Tyrrell, his wife, of

THOMAS, of Clint, who m. first, Maud, daughter of Bryan Palmes, esq. of Linley; and secondly, Catherine, daughter of William Tancred, esq. of Boroughbridge. He d. in 1575, and was s. by his son (by his first wife),

WILLIAM, of Clint, who m. first, Joanna, daughter of William Tancred, esq. of Boroughbridge, by whom he had a son, William, who died young. His second wife was Mary, daughter of Anthony Salmon, gent. of Ansley Woodhouse, Notts, and by her he had

HUNTINGDON, who m. 19th February, 1589, Margaret, daughter of Thomas Meering, esq.

William.

Henry.

Katherine.

Isabel.

II. ROBERT.

The second son,

ROBERT BECKWITH, esq. of Broxholm, who was father of

JOHN BECKWITH, esq. of Clint, who left a son and heir,

ROBERT BECKWITH, esq. of Clint, father of

MARMADUKE BECKWITH,* esq. of Aikton, who m. Anne, daughter of Robert Dyneley, esq. of Bramhope, in the county of York, and had issue,

I. THOMAS, of Aikton, living in 1612, m. Frances, daughter and heir of William Frost, esq. of Aikton, and had a son,

THOMAS, of Aikton, who left by his wife, the daughter of Henry Hunt, esq. of Carlton, a son and heir,

THOMAS, of Aikton, who wedded Barbara, daughter of John Milburne, esq. of Hinderskelf, and had (with a daughter, Mary, m. to Edward Ashton, of Methley)

THOMAS, of Aikton, who m. Murioll,† daughter of William Wandesford, esq. of Pickhill, in the county of York, and had two daughters, his co-heirs, viz.

ISABEL, m. to Nicholas Fairfax, esq. second brother of Thomas, Viscount Fairfax of the kingdom of Ireland.

BARBARA, m. to Matthew Lockwood, esq. of Sowerby.

II. ROGER.

III. Jane, m. at Wragby 6th August, 1635, to John Thorp, esq.

The younger son,

ROGER BECKWITH, esq. having sold his lands in Clint, purchased the estate of Aldborough, and settled

---

* This MARMADUKE sold Clint, and purchased lands in Fetherston and Aikton, which were sold by his grandson, Thomas Beckwith, to Langdale Sunderland, esq. whose grandson, Peter Sunderland, sold the greater part with the royalty about 1715 to Edmund Wince, esq.

† THOMAS BECKWITH is by another authority stated to have married three wives: first, Murioll, daughter of William Wandesford, which lady died without issue; secondly, Eleanor, the sister of his deceased wife, by whom he had the two daughters mentioned above as his co-heirs; and thirdly, Priscilla, daughter of Thomas Waterton, of Walton, by whom he had a son, Thomas, who died young.

there. He m. first, Dorothy, daughter of Mr. Currer, of Leeds, and had issue,

Thomas, of Beverley.
Katherine, m. to Thomas Norton, of Elveston.
Anne, m. to John Robinson, of Bolton upon Swale.

He wedded, secondly, Susanna, daughter of Mr. Brakenbury, of Denton and Sellaby, in the county of Durham, and by that lady had

Arthur, his successor.
Matthew, of Tanfield, in the county of York, m. Elizabeth, daughter of Sir John Buck, knt. of Filey, in the same county, and was ancestor of the Beckwiths of Thurcroft and Trimdon, now represented by William Beckwith, esq. (See Burke's *Commoners*, vol. ii. p. 636).
William, m. Margaret, daughter of Bernard Ellis, esq. recorder of York, and widow of Robert Mirfield, of Thurcroft. William Beckwith *d. s. p.* in 1678. and bequeathed Thurcroft to his nephew William.
Susan, m. to John Anlaby, esq. of Anlaby, in the county of York. Her daughter,
Susanna Anlaby, m. first, Arnold Colwell, esq.; and, secondly, Foot Onslow, esq. first commissioner of excise; by the latter she was mother of Mr. Speaker Onslow.
Judith, m. to William Parker, M.D. of London.
Hester, m. to Thomas Odingsells, esq. of Eperston, in Nottinghamshire.

Roger Beckwith *d.* 19th January, 1634, and was buried at Masham, in the North Riding, where in the choir of the church there was a monument erected to his memory, thus inscribed:

"In memory of Roger Beckwith, of Aldbrough, esq. who dyed on Monday the 19th of January, in the year 1634, and was buried near this place. He married Susanna, the daughter of Mr. Brakenbury, of Sellaby, in the county palatine of Durham, by whom he had Arthur, his successor, and seven other children, four sons and three daughters; she departed this life the 28th day of October, Anno Domini 1670, and lyes buried in the parish church of Skelborough. He was the son of Marmaduke Beckwith, of Acton, by Anne, daughter to Mr. Dynley, of Bramhope, which Marmaduke was the next in descent to Huntington Beckwith, of Clint, where the family had continued, from the tenth year of King Henry III. Anno Domini 1226, until the year 1597, when the aforesaid Roger Beckwith sold his lands in Clint, and purchased Aldbrough."

He was *s.* by his son,

Arthur Beckwith, esq. of Aldborough, who m. Mary, eldest daughter of Sir Marmaduke Wyvill, bart. of Constable Burton, in the county of York, and had issue,

Marmaduke, *d.* unm.
Roger, his heir.
Mary, Isabel, Susan, } *d.* all unm.

He *d.* in the service of his country in 1642, and was *s.* by his only surviving son,

I. Roger Beckwith, esq. of Aldborough, who was created a Baronet by *King* Charles II. on the 15th April, 1681. He m. first, Elizabeth, daughter of Sir Christopher Clapham, knt. of Beamsley, by whom he had a son, Arthur, who died beyond sea in 1700. Sir Roger wedded, secondly, Elizabeth, daughter of Sir Edmund Jenings, knt. of Ripon, and by that lady had

Roger, his heir.
Marmaduke, a Virginia merchant.

Sir Roger *d.* 6th December, 1700, and was *s.* by his son,

II. Sir Roger Beckwith, of Aldborough, high sheriff of Yorkshire in 1706. This gentleman m. 10th October, 1705, Jane, daughter and sole heir of Benjamin Waddington, esq. of Allerton Gledhow, and by her, who *d.* in 1713, had issue,

Roger, Edmund, } both *d.* unm.
Jane, eventual heiress, who m. Beilby Thompson, esq. of Micklethwaite Grange, in Yorkshire, and had a daughter, Jane Thompson, m. to Peregrine Wentworth, but *d. s. p.* Mr. Thompson, after the decease of his wife Jane Beckwith, espoused Sarah, widow of Sir Darcy Dawes, and daughter of Richard Roundell, esq. of Hutton Wandsley, and by her was grandfather of the present Paul Beilby Thompson, esq. of Escrick Park, M.P. for the East Riding of Yorkshire.

Sir Roger *d.* in May, 1743, when the title became extinct.

Arms—Arg. a chev. between three hinds' heads erased gu.

BEDELL, OF HAMERTON.

Created 3rd June, 1622.  Extinct in 1663.

Lineage.

I. Sir Capell Bedell, of Hamerton, in the county of Huntingdon, created a Baronet in 1622; leaving no male issue at his decease, in 1663, the title became extinct.

Arms—Gu. a chev. engrailed between three escallop shells arg.

BELASYSE, OF NEWBOROUGH.

Created 29th June, 1611.  Extinct in June, 1815.

Lineage.

I. Sir Henry Belasyse, of Newborough, in the county of York, (for the early descent see Burke's Extinct Peerage), having received the honour of knighthood from *King* James I. at York, in his majesty's journey to London, 17th April, 1603, was created a Baronet upon the institution of the order on the 29th June, 1611. Sir Henry m. Ursula, daughter of Sir Thomas Fairfax, of Denton, in the county of York, and had issue,

Thomas, his successor.
Dorothy, m. to Sir Conyers Darcy, knt. of Hornby.
Mary, m. to Sir William Lister, knt. of Thornton, in the county of York.

He was *s.* at his decease by his son,

II. Sir Thomas Belasyse, *b.* in 1587, who was advanced to the peerage by the title of Baron Fauconberg nasc, of Yarum, in the county of York, on the 26th May, 1627. His lordship, adhering to the fortunes of *King* CHARLES I., was created, on the 31st of January, 1642, VISCOUNT FAUCONBERG, of Henknowle, in the county palatine of Durham. He was subsequently at the siege of York, and at the battle of Marston Moor, under the Duke of Newcastle, with whom he fled to the continent after that unfortunate defeat. He *m.* Barbara, daughter of Sir Henry Cholmondley, bart. of Roxby, in the county of York, and had issue,

Henry, M. P. for the county of York; of whom Clarendon writes:—"Harry Belasis, with the Lord Fairfax, the two knights who served in parliament for Yorkshire, signed articles for a neutrality for that county, being nearly allied together, and of great kindness, till their several opinions and affections had divided them in this quarrel; the Lord Fairfax adhering to the parliament, and the other, with great courage and sobriety, to the king." Mr. Belasyse *m.* Grace, daughter and heiress of Sir Thomas Barron, of Smithells, in the county of Lancaster, and dying in the lifetime of his father, left issue,

THOMAS, successor to his grandfather.

Henry, *d.* unmarried.

Rowland (Sir), K. B. *m.* Anne, eldest daughter and sole heiress of J. Davenport, esq. of Sutton, in the county of Chester, and dying in 1699, left

THOMAS, who *s.* as third Viscount Fauconberg.

Henry, *d.* unmarried.

John, *d. s. p.*

Rowland, *m.* Frances, daughter of Christopher, Lord Teynham, by whom he had, with other issue,

Anthony, who *m.* Susannah, daughter of John Clarvet, esq. and had issue,

ROWLAND, who *s.* as sixth viscount.

CHARLES, D.D. of Sorbonne, who *s.* as seventh viscount.

Thomas, *m.* Marie Louise de Maneville, and had five daughters.

Frances.

Barbara.

Grace, *m.* to George, Viscount Castletown, in Ireland.

Frances, *m.* to Sir Henry Jones, knt. of Aston, in the county of Oxford, of which marriage there was an only daughter and heiress,

FRANCES JONES, *m.* to Richard, Earl of Scarborough.

Arabella, *m.* to Sir William Frankland, bart. of Thirkleby, in the county of York.

Barbara, *m.* first, to Walter Strickland, esq. son of Sir Robert Strickland, of Sizergh; and, secondly, to Sir Marmaduke Dalton, of Haxwell, Yorkshire.

John, created LORD BELASYSE, of Worlaby, whose grandson HENRY, second lord, *d. s. p.*

Margaret, *m.* to Sir Edward Osborn, of Kiveton.

Mary, *m.* to John, Lord Darcy, of Aston.

Barbara, *m.* to Sir Henry Slingsby, bart. of Scriven, in the county of York, who was put to death under Cromwell's usurpation, and died, as he said on the scaffold, "for being an honest man."

Ursula, *m.* to Sir Walter Vavasor, bart. of Haslewood.

Frances, *m.* to Thomas Ingram, esq. eldest son of Sir Arthur Ingram, of Temple Newsom, Yorkshire.

His lordship *d.* in 1652, and was *s.* by his grandson,

III. SIR THOMAS BELASYSE, second viscount, who *m.* first, Mildred, daughter of Nicholas, Viscount Castleton, by whom he had no issue; and, secondly, on the 18th of November, 1657, the LADY MARY CROMWELL, daughter of the PROTECTOR. Of this nobleman Lord Clarendon gives the following account:—"After Cromwell was declared protector, and in great power, he married his daughter to the Lord Fauconberg, the owner of a very great estate in Yorkshire, and descended of a family eminently loyal. There were many reasons to believe that this young gentleman, being then about three or four-and-twenty years of age, of great vigour and ambition, had many good purposes that he thought that alliance might qualify and enable him to perform. His marriage was celebrated at Whitehall (Wood has given the time at Hampton Court,) with all imaginable pomp and lustre. And it was observed, that, though it was performed in public, according to the rites and ceremonies then in use, they were presently afterwards, in private, married by ministers ordained by bishops, and according to the form in the book of Common Prayer, and this with the privity of Cromwell." In 1657, his lordship was made one of the council of state, and sent the next year, by his father-in-law, with a complimentary message to the court of Versailles. This was the only employment Lord Fauconberg had under the usurper; for, as the noble author before mentioned relates, "his domestic delights were lessened every day; he plainly discovered that his son Fauconberg's heart was set upon an interest destructive to his, and grew to hate him perfectly." Of Lady Fauconberg, Burnet writes:—"She was a wise and worthy woman, more likely to have maintained the post (of protector) than either of her brothers; according to a saying that went of her, 'that those who wore breeches deserved petticoats better; but if those in petticoats had been in breeches, they would have held faster.'" That his lordship forwarded the restoration, is evident from his being appointed, by the restored monarch, in 1660, lord-lieutenant of the bishopric of Durham, and in the same year, lord-lieutenant and custos rotulorum of the North Riding of Yorkshire. He was soon afterwards accredited ambassador to the state of Venice and the princes of Italy, and constituted captain of the band of gentleman pensioners. In 1679, Lord Fauconberg was sworn of the privy council; and, again, in 1689, upon the accession of *King* WILLIAM and *Queen* MARY, when his lordship was created EARL FAUCONBERG, by letters patent, dated on the 9th of April, in that year. He *d.* on the 31st December, 1700, and leaving no issue, the EARLDOM EXPIRED, while his other honours reverted to his nephew (refer to Sir Rowland Belasyse, K. B. third son of the first lord),

IV. SIR THOMAS BELASYSE, as fourth baronet, and third Viscount Fauconberg. His lordship *m.* Bridget, daughter of Sir John Gage, bart. of Firle, in the county of Sussex, and co-heiress of her mother, who was daughter of Thomas Middlesmore, esq. of Egbaston, in Warwickshire, by whom he had surviving issue,

THOMAS, his successor.

Rowland.

Mary, *m.* 9th April, 1721, to John Pitt, esq. third son of Thomas Pitt, esq. governor of Fort St. George.

His lordship *d.* 26th November, 1718, and was *s.* by his elder son,

V. SIR THOMAS BELASYSE, fourth viscount, who was created EARL FAUCONBERG, of Newborough, in the county of York, on the 15th June, 1756. His lordship *m.* in 1726, Catherine, daughter and heiress of John Betham, esq. of Rowington, in the county of Warwick, and co-heiress of William Fowler, esq. of St. Thomas, in the county of Stafford, by whom he had surviving issue,

HENRY, his successor.

Barbara, m. in 1752, to the Hon. George Barnewall, only brother of Henry Benedict, Viscount Kingsland.

Mary, m. in 1775, to Thomas Eyre, esq. of Hassop, in the county of Derby.

Anne, m. in 1761, to the Hon. Francis Talbot, brother of George, fourteenth Earl of Shrewsbury.

His lordship, who conformed to the established church, d. 4th February, 1774, and was s. by his son,

VI. SIR HENRY BELASYSE, second earl. His lordship m. first, in 1766, Charlotte, daughter of Sir Matthew Lamb, bart. of Brocket Hall, in the county of Hertford, and had four daughters, his co-heirs, viz.

CHARLOTTE, m. to Thomas Edward Wynn, esq. third son of Colonel Glynn Wynn, who assumed the surname and arms of BELASYSE, in addition to his own.

ANNE, m. to Sir George Wombwell, bart.

ELIZABETH, m. in 1789, to Bernard Howard, esq. (afterwards Duke of Norfolk), from whom she was divorced in 1794, when she remarried the Earl of Lucan. Her ladyship died in 1819.

HARRIOT.

The earl m. secondly, Miss Chesshyre, but had no other issue. He d. 23rd March, 1802, when the EARLDOM became EXTINCT, but the other honors devolved upon his kinsman (refer to descendants of the Hon. Henry Belasyse, eldest son of Sir Thomas Belasyse, the first viscount),

VII. SIR ROWLAND BELASYSE, as seventh baronet and sixth viscount, who d. s. p. in 1810, and was s. by his brother,

VIII. THE REV. SIR CHARLES BELASYSE, D.D. of the Roman catholic church, as eighth baronet, and seventh viscount, at whose decease in 1815, the Barony and Viscounty of Fauconberg and the ancient BARONETCY became EXTINCT.

Arms—Quarterly; first and fourth arg. a chev. gu. between three fleurs-de-lis az.; second and third arg. a pale ingrailed between two pallets plain sa.

BELLINGHAM, OF HILSINGTON.

CREATED 30th May, 1620.

EXTINCT in 1650.

Lineage.

SIR ROBERT BELLINGHAM, knt. tenth in descent from Alan de Bellingham, who lived "tempore CONQUESTORIS," flourished in the reigns of HENRY V. and HENRY VI. He m. Elizabeth, daughter of Sir Richard Tunstall, knt. and had two sons, namely,

HENRY (Sir), whose son, Sir Roger, was made a banneret at the battle of Stoke in 1487. He left an only son,

ROBERT (Sir), who died without male issue.

ALAN.

The second son,

ALAN BELLINGHAM, was father of

THOMAS BELLINGHAM, whose son,

ALAN BELLINGHAM, of Hilsington, in Westmoreland, was a bencher of the Middle Temple, and king's counsel. He represented the county of Northumberland in 1570, and died 7th May, 1577, leaving by Dorothy, his wife, daughter of Thomas Sandford, of Askham, a son,

SIR JAMES BELLINGHAM, of Hilsington, who received the honor of knighthood from *King* JAMES I. on his Majesty's journey into England. He m. Agnes, daughter of Sir Henry Curwen, knt. and had, *inter alios*,

HENRY (Sir), his heir.

Alan, of Levens, in Westmoreland, b. in 1588, m. Susan, daughter of Marmaduke Constable, esq. and was ancestor of the BELLINGHAMS of Castle Bellingham, in the county of Louth, now represented by SIR ALAN-EDWARD BELLINGHAM, bart. of Castle Bellingham.

The eldest son,

I. SIR HENRY BELLINGHAM, of Hilsington, was created a BARONET 30th May, 1620. He m. Dorothy, daughter of Sir Francis Boynton, knt. of Barmston, in the county of York, and was s. by his son,

II. SIR JAMES BELLINGHAM, of Hilsington, who m. Catherine, daughter and co-heir of Sir Henry Willoughby, of Risley, in Derbyshire, but by her, who m. secondly, George Purefoy, esq. of Whalley, in Berks. having no issue, the BARONETCY EXPIRED at his decease in 1650.

Arms—Arg. three bugle horns sa. stringed and garnished or.

BELLOT, OF MORETON.

CREATED 30th June, 1663.

EXTINCT 8th Feb. 1714.

Lineage.

JOHN BELLOT, of Moreton, in Cheshire (lineally descended from John Bellot, esq. who acquired the estate of Moreton in marriage with Katherine, sister and heiress of Ralph Moreton), m. Joan, daughter of Ralph Moreton, of Little Moreton, and had issue,

THOMAS, his heir.

Robert, who m. Ellen Sandford, and had issue.

Philip, who m. and had issue.

Blanche, m. to Roger Sparke.

Mary, m. to Roger Grene.

Margery, m. to Randle Thornton.

Ursula, m. to Edward Unwin, of Chaterley.

Elizabeth, m. to Roger Davenport, of Cherley

Emma, m. to John Comerford.

Catherine, m. to John Creswall.

The eldest son,

THOMAS BELLOT, esq. of Moreton, m. Alice, dau. and heir of William Roydon, of Denbighshire, and had a numerous family, viz.

EDWARD, who m. Anne, daughter of Edward Weston, esq. and d. v. p. leaving a son, EDWARD.

Thomas.

Hugh, bishop of Bangor and Chester.

John.

George.

Robert, had issue.

David.

Matthew.

Owen.

Cuthbert, archdeacon of Chester.

Dorothy, m. to John Drinkwater, of Chester.

Erasinia, m. first, to John Manley; and secondly, to Thomas Manley.

Mary, m. first, to Richard Minshull; and secondly, to Arthur Starkey.

Thomas Belliot was s. at his decease by his grandson,

EDWARD BELLOT, esq. of Moreton, who died 7th August, 1622, leaving by Amy, his wife, daughter and co-heir of Anthony Grosvenor, esq. of Dodleston, younger son of Richard Grosvenor, esq. of Eaton, three sons and four daughters, namely,

JOHN, his heir.

George, of Odd Rode, m. Eleanor, daughter of William Lawton, of Lawton, in Cheshire, and had two daughters, Amie and Mary.

Thomas, d. unm. in 1654.

Susan, m. to John Broughton, of Broughton.

Frances, m. Peter Legh, of Lyme.

Elizabeth, m. to Thomas Bromley, of Hampton.

Mary, m. to Thomas Gamull.

The eldest son,

JOHN BELLOT, esq. of Moreton, m. Ursula, daughter and sole heir of John Bentley, esq. of the Ashes, in Staffordshire, and dying in 1660, left, with four younger sons and two daughters, Anne, m. to William Ferne; and Ursula, m. to Thomas Stockton; a son and successor,

I. SIR JOHN BELLOT, of Moreton, b. in 1619, who was created a BARONET 30th June, 1663. He m. Anne, daughter of Roger Wilbraham, of Dorfold, in Cheshire, and dying 14th July, 1674, left an only surviving child,

II. SIR THOMAS BELLOT, of Moreton, b. 22nd October, 1651, who m. in 1674-5, Susanna, daughter of Christopher Pache, esq. of Cotes, in Leicestershire, and was s. by his son,

III. SIR JOHN BELLOT, of Moreton, b. 20th November, 1676; at whose decease, 8th February, 1714, the BARONETCY became EXTINCT. The manor of Moreton was soon after sold to the family of Powis of the county of Stafford, and subsequently purchased from Thomas Jelf Powis, esq. by HOLLAND ACKERS, esq.

Arms—Arg. on a chief gu. three cinquefoils of the first.

BENDISH, OF STEEPLE BUMSTEAD.

CREATED 29th June, 1611.

EXPIRED 4th Sept. 1717.

Lineage.

The surname, originally DE WESTLEY, was changed to that of BENDISH, from a considerable lordship in Radwinter, whereof the family became possessed some time in the twelfth century. The first whose name occurs in ancient writings that may be certainly depended upon is

PETER DE WESTLEY, alias BENDISH. He flourished about the reigns of *King* JOHN and of HENRY III. His son,

GEORGE, or GERRARD DE WESTLEY, alias BENDISH, m. Margaret, daughter and heir of Richard De Burghwell and had by her

RALPH DE WESTLEY, alias BENDISH, of Radwinter, who by his wife Agnes, daughter and heir of John de Grauncester, was direct ancestor of

THOMAS BENDISH, who was the first of the family who laid aside the surname of WESTLEY, and took up that of BENDISH. He was also the first of the family who purchased lands in Steeple Bumpstead, Essex, and marrying Alice, daughter of William Helion, of the adjoining parish, had two sons, JOHN and Robert. Departing this life about the year 1342, he was s. by his elder son,

JOHN BENDISH, who m. Alice, daughter of Sir Robert Rosse, and had a son,

EDMUND BENDYSHE, who accompanied EDWARD III. to the famous siege of Calais in 1347-8, and with John Wythorne, rector of Halsted, gave £100 to the university chest of Cambridge, founded by Walter Neale, about the year 1345. He died in 1392, leaving by Alice, his wife, sister, and at length heir, to William de Bennington, two sons, THOMAS, his heir, and Edmund, who died without issue in 1401.

THOMAS BENDISH, esq. the elder son, married, first, Margaret, daughter and co-heir of Thomas Bradfield, esq. of Barrington, in Cambridgeshire, and secondly, Alice, daughter and sole heir of Sir Walter Clopton, of Hadley, in Suffolk, Knight of Rhodes. By his second wife he had Thomas of Hadley, William, and John, founder of the Suffolk and Norfolk branches of Bendish; also two daughters, Elizabeth, married to John Huntingdon, and Alice, to Richard Ongar, of Yeldham. By his first wife he had EDMUND, from whom are descended the BENDISHES of BARRINGTON, now represented by JOHN BENDYSHE, esq. of that place; THOMAS, of whom presently; Joane, m. to W. Wilford, esq. of Crocheston, in the county of Southampton; and Alice, to Walter Gerard, of Essex, who had with her a portion of £40. Their father died in 1447-8, and was succeeded in the Bumpstead estate by

THOMAS BENDISH, his second son by his first wife. He m. first, Joane, daughter of — Fitzwilliams, by whom he had RICHARD and Thomas; and by his second wife, Joane, daughter of John de Thockeldon, he had Ralph, John, and Maud. He d. in 1484-5, and was s. by his eldest son,

RICHARD BENDISH, who, dying 27th February, 1486, was buried in the north aisle of Essan church, under a monument. He m. Anne, daughter of — Rawden, esq. of Royden Hall, Essex, by whom he had a daughter, Margaret, and a son and heir,

RICHARD BENDISH, who d. 22nd Sept. 1523, and was buried near his father. His wife was Margaret, daughter and heir of James Newport, Esq. of Herts. and by her he had JOHN and Margaret.

JOHN BENDISH, only son and successor to his father, departed this life 20th August, 1585, and lies interred near his ancestors. By his wife Margaret, daughter of Thomas Crawley, esq. he left a son and heir,

THOMAS BENDISH, who had four wives; first, Eleanor, daughter and co-heir of John Ford, of Hockesley, in Essex, by whom he had THOMAS, Richard, Barbara, m. to Thomas Smyth, of Walsoken, in Norfolk; Mary, Elizabeth, m. to James Pepys, of Cottenham, in Cambridgeshire; Eleanor, wife of Robert Bryan, of Bolinbroke, Margaret, and Elizabeth. His second wife was Thomasine, daughter of — Fincham, who was buried in this church. Alice was his third wife. His fourth wife was Margery, daughter of R. Greene, esq. of Little Stamford, but by the three last he had no issue. He d. 23rd Feb. 1603, aged 63 years, and lies buried at Frating.

I. THOMAS BENDISH, esq. of Steeple Bumstead, his eldest son and successor, was created a BARONET 22nd May, 1611, and served the office of high sheriff for his county in 1618 and 1630, and made a considerable addition to his estate. He m. Dorothy, daughter of

Richard Cutts, esq. of Arkesden, in Essex, by whom he had THOMAS; John, who died young; and two daughters, Dorothy, wife of Sir Thomas Hartop, knt. of Burton Lazers, Leicester; and Eliza, *m.* to John Fearnley, of Creting, in Suffolk. He *d.* in 1636, and was *s.* by his son,

II. SIR THOMAS BENDISH, then aged about twenty-nine years. "He was," says Morant, "a man of great sense and resolution, and steadfastly loyal to his prince, *King* CHARLES I. For at the beginning of the national troubles he had a chief hand in drawing up, 18th July, 1642, and presenting to the King a declaration, and afterwards petition, both to his Majesty and the parliament, recommending an amicable accommodation, in order to stop the distractions and bloody miseries wherein this nation was most unhappily involved. For which good office he was imprisoned twenty-two months in the Tower, by order of the House of Commons; and his estate being sequestered, he was forced to pay a composition of £1,000. He also sent £3,000 to his Royal master, when under restraint at Newcastle. However, though he fell at first under the displeasure of the prevailing powers, yet so considerable was he on account of his capacities and integrity, that afterwards they made choice of him to be their ambassador to the Ottoman Porte; but no arguments of theirs could prevail with him to accept of this honourable employ without the King's commission, which his Majesty readily granted him, and also leave to carry with him such seal as the Parliament had given him, and to make such use of it as he should think fit, and might conduce to the advantage of himself and the Turkey company. He entered on his embassy in 1647, and resided at the Turkish court about fourteen years, filling up that great post with admirable sufficiency. For besides his skill in languages, he was a gentleman of consummate prudence and invincible courage. How well he understood his character, and how jealous he was of his prince's and country's honour, appears from the instances set down as follows: first, when the grand visier would have publicly affronted him at an audience, in causing the chair to be removed out of the room that he might deliver his embassy standing, Sir Thomas made one of his gentlemen kneel down and lean on his hands, and then sat down upon him, before he would deliver his embassy. At another audience, when the grand visier would have placed the French ambassador above him, he jostled him from his chair, and took his place, telling him that he was ambassador from a crowned head who was king of France as well as England. Another time there happening some disputes between the grand visier and Sir Thomas, Sir Thomas rose up, and kicking from him the stool whereon he sate, said, his master was dishonored, and he would have reparation for the affront. This resolute and gallant behaviour made him only the more considerable. King CHARLES I. had such a sense of his gallant behaviour, and the eminent service he had done the Levant Company, beyond any other ambassador, that he wrote him a letter of thanks from the Isle of Wight, about November, 1648. After that King's tragical death, Sir Thomas continued firm to his son's interest, and renewed the capitulation between the Grand Signior and him, by the title of CHARLES II. King of England, Scotland, France, and Ireland, and this prince confirmed Sir Thomas in his commission of ambassador extraordinary. How he came to escape the resentment of the then usurping powers, and keep out of the reach of men whose hearts were found harder than those of most princes, we cannot explain, especially when Sir Henry Hyde, sent by King CHARLES II. as his agent to the Ottoman Porte, in 1649, was sentenced by the High Court of Justice March, 1650, to be beheaded. However, in 1653, Oliver, the Protector, dispatched Richard Laurence to Constantinople with letters of revocation for Sir Thomas, who shewed the value he had for the King's commission, by telling Laurence, that he was sent by the King, and would not deliver up his commission without his Majesty's order, upon which articles of high treason were exhibited to the parliament against him by one Paul Hagett, but without effect; for Sir Thomas appears to have continued in Turkey until recalled thence in 1662 by *King* CHARLES II., who gave him a very honourable testimonial of his loyalty and good affection, with promises of doing him service. This renowned gentleman, the chief glory and ornament of his family, after many years spent abroad, at last departed this life at Bower Hall, the place of his nativity, about the year 1674, aged 67 years. His lady, the faithful companion of his travels, died at Constantinople, and her body was brought over and buried here. She was Anne, daughter and co-heir of Henry Baker, of Shoebery, in this county. By her he had Thomas, John, Robert, Henry, Andrew, and six daughters, Dorothy, *m.* first, to —— Williams, secondly, to — Bowyer†; Abigail, *m.* to — Edwards; Anne, *m.* to Sir Jonathan Dawes, knt.; Elizabeth, *m.* to — Cartwright; Diana, *m.* to Sir Strensham Masters, knt.; and Susan, *m.* to Sir William Hooker, knt.

III. SIR JOHN BENDISH, the second but eldest surviving son and successor to his father, had by Martha his wife, daughter and heir of Richard Batson, of London, six sons, John, Richard, Charles, Robert, all of whom died young, and HENRY; also three daughters, Anne, Martha, and Sarah, wife of John Pyke Crouch, esq. He died 1706, and was *s.* by his only surviving son,

IV. SIR HENRY BENDISH, for many years a justice of the peace, and one of the deputy-lieutenants for Essex. He *m.* Catherine, daughter of Sir William Gosling, knt. one of the Sheriffs of London in [illegible], and by her had one son, named Henry, who lived only five months. Sir Henry *d.* 4th September, 1717, when the BARONETCY EXPIRED.

Arms—Argent, a chevron sable, between three rams' heads erased azure, armed or. In the reign of King EDWARD III. and HENRY IV. they gave a wild ram's head for their arms. They quartered the coats of Burghwell, Graunocstre, Bennington, Cal-leys, Beauchamp, Bradfield, Huntingdon, Clopton, Newport, Ford, Baker, Bateson.

BENNET, OF BECHAMPTON.

CREATED 17th July, 1627.

EXTINCT in 1631.

Lineage.

THOMAS BENNET, esq. of Clapcot, *m.* Anne Molins, of Mackney, in the county of Oxford, and had two sons,

RICHARD, ancestor of the BENNETS, Earls of Tankerville, and of the BENNETS of Babraham.

THOMAS, of whom presently.

The second son,

SIR THOMAS BENNET, knt. lord mayor of London in 1603, purchased in 1609 from Thomas Pigott the [illegible]

of Bechampton, in Buckinghamshire. He m. Mary, daughter of Robert Taylor, sheriff of London 34 ELIZABETH, and had issue,

SIMON, his heir.

Richard, an eminent merchant of London, who m. Elizabeth, daughter of William Cradock, esq. of Staffordshire, and by her, who wedded, secondly, Sir Heneage Finch, knt. left a son,

SIMON, of whom hereafter as heir to the estates of his uncle, Sir Simon, the baronet.

John, d. s. p.

Anne, m. to William Duncombe, esq. of Brickhill, Bucks.

Margaret, m. to Sir George Croke, knt. justice of the Common Pleas.

Sir Thomas was s. by his eldest son,

I. SIR SIMON BENNET, of Bechampton, in the county of Bucks, created a BARONET 17th July, 1627. He m. Elizabeth, daughter of Sir Arthur Ingram, knt. but dying s. p. about the year 1631, the BARONETCY became EXTINCT. The manor of Bechampton devolved on (the son of his brother Richard) his nephew, SIMON BENNET, esq. of Bechampton, who m. Grace, daughter of Gilbert Moorwood, merchant, of London, and died in 1682, leaving three daughters, his co-heirs,

ELIZABETH, m. to Edward Osborne, Lord Latimer, and d. s. p.

GRACE, m. to John Bennet, esq. of Abington, in Cambridgeshire.

FRANCES, m. to James Cecil, Earl of Salisbury.

Arms—Gu. a bezant, between three demi-lions rampant, arg.

BENNET, OF BABRAHAM.

CREATED 22nd Nov. 1660.—EXTINCT 23rd May, 1701.

Lineage.

THOMAS BENNET, alderman of London, younger brother of Sir John Bennet, ancestor of the Earls of Tankerville, purchased from Sir Toby Palavicini the estate of Babraham, in Cambridgeshire. He left two sons and a daughter, viz.

Richard, whose daughter, by his first wife, Jane, m. the Hon. James Scudamore, eldest son of Lord Scudamore, of the kingdom of Ireland,

THOMAS, of whom presently.

Rebecca, m. to Sir Bulstrode Whitlock, knt. created Lord Whitlock by CROMWELL.

The second son,

I. THOMAS BENNET, esq. of Babraham, in Cambridgeshire, was created a BARONET 22nd November, 1660. He m. Mary, daughter and co-heir of Levinus Monk, esq. and died in 1667, leaving a son and successor,

II. SIR LEVINUS BENNET, of Babraham, who m. Judith, daughter of William Boeve, merchant of London, and died 5th December, 1693, leaving a son and successor,

III. SIR RICHARD BENNET, of Babraham, who m. in 1694, Elizabeth, daughter of Sir Charles Adelmare Cæsar, knt. of Bennington Place, in Hertfordshire, M.P. and by her, who wedded, secondly, James Butler, esq. M.P. of Warminghurst Park, Sussex, having a daughter only, Judith, who d. unmarried; the BARONETCY became EXTINCT at his decease, 23rd May, 1701, aged twenty-eight.

The estates eventually devolved on BENNET ALEXANDER, esq. son of Edward Alexander, esq. of Ongar, by Levina, daughter of SIR LEVINUS BENNET, bart. Mr. Alexander assumed in consequence, by act of parliament in 1742, the surname and arms of BENNET. He m. Mary, daughter of Benjamin Ash, esq. and had by her, who m. secondly, Richard Bull, esq. son of Sir John Bull, knt. one son and one daughter, viz.

RICHARD-HENRY-ALEXANDER BENNET, esq. of Babraham, who sold the estate in 1765, and it ultimately became the property of General Adeane.

Levina, m. 16th January, 1762, to John Luther, esq. of Myles, in Essex, M.P. for that county. (See BURKE's *Commoners*, vol. iv. p. 7.)

Arms—Gu. a bezant between three demi lions rampant, arg.

BENSLEY, OF MARYLABONNE.

CREATED 25th June, 1801. EXTINCT 17th Dec. 1809.

Lineage.

I. SIR WILLIAM BENSLEY, son of Thomas Bensley, esq. of Norfolk, by Elizabeth, daughter of William Winter, esq. of the same county, entered the navy at an early age, but retiring from the service, repaired to the East Indies, whence returning in 1777, he was chosen one of the Company's directors, and created a BARONET in 1801. He m. Mary, daughter of Vincent Biscoe, esq. of London, but dying without issue, 17th December, 1809, aged seventy-two, the BARONETCY became EXTINCT.

Arms—Sa. a fess erminois, charged with a bomb bursting ppr. between three mullets of the second.

BERKELEY, OF BRUTON.

CREATED 2nd July, 1660. EXTINCT in 1690.

Lineage.

Descended from the BARONS BERKELEY, of BERKELEY CASTLE, was

SIR RICHARD BERKELEY, knt. of Stoke Gifford, in the county of Gloucester, who died in 1514, leaving issue by his wife, Elizabeth, daughter of Sir Humphrey Coningsby, knt. two sons, namely, Sir John Berkeley, of Stoke Gifford, ancestor to the Lord Botetort, and

SIR MAURICE BERKELEY, K.B. of Bruton, in the county of Somerset, standard-bearer to HENRY VIII. and EDWARD VI. and to *Queen* ELIZABETH. Of this gentleman it is mentioned, that, in the first year of *Queen* MARY, riding casually in London, he met with

Sir Thomas Wiat at Temple Bar, and persuading him to yield himself to the queen. Sir Thomas took his advice, and, mounting behind Sir Maurice, rode to the court. Sir Maurice Berkeley *m.* first, Catherine, daughter of William Blount, Lord Mountjoy, and had issue,

- HENRY, his heir.
- Edward.
- Gertrude, *m.* to Edward Horne, esq.
- Elizabeth, *m.* to James Percival, esq. of Weston Gordon, in the county of Somerset.
- Anne, *m.* to Nicholas Poynings, esq. of Adderley.
- Frances, *d.* unmarried.

Sir Maurice *m.* secondly, Elizabeth, daughter of Anthony Sands, esq. and by that lady had two other sons and a daughter. He was *s.* at his decease by his eldest son,

SIR HENRY BERKELEY, knt. of Bruton, who *m.* Margaret, daughter of William Lygon, esq. and had three sons, viz.

- MAURICE (Sir), his heir.
- Henry (Sir), ancestor of the BERKELEYS of Yarlington.
- Edward (Sir), of Pylle, ancestor of the present EDWARD-BERKELEY PORTMAN, LORD PORTMAN. (See BURKE'S *Peerage, and Commoners,* vol. i. p. 62.)

The eldest son,

SIR MAURICE BERKELEY, received the honor of knighthood from the Earl of Essex, while serving under that nobleman in the expedition to Calais, anno 1596. Sir Maurice *m.* Elizabeth, daughter of Sir Henry Killegrew, of Hanworth, in the county of Middlesex, and had issue five sons and two daughters, viz.

- CHARLES (Sir), his heir.
- Henry (Sir).
- Maurice (Sir).
- William (Sir).
- John (Sir), a distinguished cavalier, created BARON BERKELEY, of Stratton. (See BURKE'S *Extinct Peerage.*)
- Margaret.
- Jane.

The eldest son,

SIR CHARLES BERKELEY, received the honor of knighthood at Bewley in 1623, and, being eminently loyal to *King* CHARLES I., was sworn of the privy council upon the restoration of the monarchy, and appointed, first, comptroller, and then treasurer, of the household. Sir Charles *m.* Penelope, daughter of Sir William Godolphin, knt. of Godolphin, in Cornwall, and had issue,

I. MAURICE, his heir.

II. CHARLES, who, for his fidelity to *King* CHARLES II. during his majesty's exile, and other eminent services, was created a peer of Ireland, as *Baron Berkeley, of Rathdown,* and VISCOUNT FITZHARDINGE, with remainder to his father and his issue male; and a peer of England, on the 17th March, 1664, by the title of *Baron Botetort, of Langport, in the county of Somerset,* and EARL OF FALMOUTH. His lordship *m.* Elizabeth, daughter of Colonel Hervey Bagot, second son of Sir Henry Bagot, bart. of Blithfield, in the county of Stafford, and had an only daughter,

   Mary, *m.* to Gilbert Cosyn Gerrard, esq. eldest son of Sir Gilbert Gerrard, bart. of Fiskerton, in the county of Lincoln, from whom she was divorced in 1684, and *d.* in 1693.

   Lord Falmouth fell in a naval engagement with the Dutch, 3rd June, 1665, and his remains were honorably interred in Westminster Abbey. At the decease of his lordship, his English honors EXPIRED, while those of Ireland reverted, according to the patent, to his father, Sir Charles Berkeley.

III. William (Sir), governor of Portsmouth and vice-admiral of the White, killed at sea in 1666.

IV. John, who succeeded his eldest brother as VISCOUNT FITZHARDINGE, was treasurer of the chamber, and one of the tellers of the Exchequer, in the reign of *Queen* ANNE. He *m.* a daughter of Sir Edward Villiers, and sister to the Earl of Jersey, governess to his royal highness William, Duke of Gloucester, and had issue,

   Mary, *m.* to Walter Chetwynd, esq. of Ingestre, in the county of Stafford, who was created in 1717 Baron Rathdown and Viscount Chetwynd, with the remainder to the heirs male of his father.

   Frances, *m.* to Sir Thomas Clarges, bart.

   His lordship *d.* on the 19th December, 1712, and thus leaving no male issue, the Irish *Barony of Berkeley* and VISCOUNTCY OF FITZHARDINGE became EXTINCT.

Sir Charles Berkeley, upon the decease of his second son, Charles, Earl of Falmouth, succeeding to that nobleman's Irish honors, became *Baron Berkeley of Rathdown* and VISCOUNT FITZHARDINGE; and dying 12th June, 1668, those honors descended to his eldest son,

I. SIR MAURICE BERKELEY, third Viscount Fitzhardinge, who had been created a BARONET 2nd July, 1660. His lordship married Anne, daughter of Henry Lee, esq. of Quarendon, Bucks, but dying issueless in 1690, the BARONETCY became EXTINCT, while the Viscounty and Barony devolved on his brother.

Arms—Gu. a chev. erm. between ten crosses pattée arg.

BERKELEY, OF WYMONDHAM.

CREATED in 1611.—EXTINCT ....

Lineage.

SIR THOMAS BERKELEY, knt. Lord of Coston, second son of Thomas, Lord Berkeley, by Jane, his wife, daughter of William Ferrers, Earl of Derby, was living at the commencement of the fourteenth century. He *m.* Isabel, daughter and heir of Sir John Hamelin, Lord of Wymondham, in the county of Leicester, and was father of

SIR JOHN DE BERKELEY, of Wymondham, made a knight banneret 34 EDWARD I. He left by Joan, his wife, living in 1308, a son and successor,

SIR JOHN BERKELEY, knt. of Wymondham, who *d.* in 1374, leaving by Elizabeth, his wife, three sons, namely,

- JOHN, his heir.
- Thomas, whose daughter and heir, Elizabeth, *m.* Richard, fourth Earl of Warwick.
- Lawrence, living in 1374.

The eldest son,

SIR JOHN BERKELEY, knt. of Wymondham, living in 1403, was father of

SIR LAWRENCE BERKELEY, knt. of Wymondham, who *m.* Joan, sister of Sir Robert Woodford, knt and being slain in France in 1458, left, with two daughters, Elizabeth, *m.* to Sir William Hussey, lord chief justice, and Alice, *m.* to Thomas Woodford, esq. a son.

SIR THOMAS BERKELEY, knt. of Wymondham, who *m.* Petronell, daughter of William Brokesby, esq. and was *s.* at his decease in 1488 by his son,

SIR MAURICE BERKELEY, knt. of Wymondham, who m. Margaret, daughter of Sir John Byron, knt. of Over Colwich, and widow of Sir William Atherton, of Atherton, and left at his decease in 1522 a son and successor,

SIR THOMAS BERKELEY, knt. of Wymondham, who m. Margaret, eldest daughter and co-heir of Thomas de la Laund, by Katherine, his wife, daughter and co-heir of Lionel, Lord Welles, by Jane, daughter and heir of Sir Robert Waterton, and had two sons, MAURICE, his heir; and William, successor to his nephew. The elder,

MAURICE BERKELEY, esq. of Wymondham, m. Margaret, daughter of Sir John Harrington, bart., and left, with a daughter, Elizabeth, m. first, to Robert Pakenham, esq. clerk of the green cloth; and secondly, to Richard Levesey; a son,

JOHN BERKELEY, esq. of Wymondham, who *d. s. p.* and was *s.* by his uncle,

WILLIAM BERKELEY, esq. of Wymondham, who m. Mary, daughter of Robert Baude, of Hornby, in the county of Lincoln, and *d.* in 1536, leaving a son and successor,

MAURICE BERKELEY, esq. of Wymondham, who m. Mary, daughter of John Hall, esq. of Grantham, and died in 1600, aged seventy, leaving several children, who all *d.* unmarried, except one daughter, Eleanor, *b.* in 1563, who m. — Wingfield, esq. and one son,

I. SIR HENRY BERKELEY, of Wymondham, *b.* in 1566, created a BARONET in 1611. This gentleman m. first, Miss Mynne; and secondly, Katharine, daughter of Nicholas Beaumont, esq. of Cole Orton, and relict of Anthony Byron, esq.; but dying *s. p.* the title became EXTINCT. The estate of Wymondham Sir Henry sold to Sir William Sedley, bart. of Southfleet and Aylesford.

Arms—As BERKELEY, of Bruton.

BERNARD, OF HUNTINGDON.

CREATED 1st July, 1662. EXTINCT 2nd Jan. 1789.

Lineage.

The elder branch of this family, founded by GODFREY BERNARD, of Wanford, whose grandson, WILLIAM BERNARD, was living in the time of EDWARD III. terminated in a female heir, MARGARET BERNARD, who wedded SIR JOHN PEYTON, knt. and conveyed the paternal estate of Iselham to the Peytons. (Refer to PEYTON *of Iselham*, extinct baronet.)

Of the younger branch was

FRANCIS BERNARD, esq. of Abington,* near Northampton, of which manor his ancestors had been proprietors upwards of two hundred years. His second son,

I. FRANCIS BERNARD, esq. serjeant-at-law, was created a BARONET 1st July, 1662. Sir Francis m. first, Elizabeth, daughter of Sir John Tallakerne, and by her had issue,

- JOHN (Sir), his successor.
- Lucy, m. to Sir Nicholas Pedley, knt. M.P. for the borough of Huntingdon.
- Mary, m. to Laurence Torkington, esq. of Great Stewkley, in the county of Huntingdon.

He wedded, secondly, Elizabeth, daughter of Sir James Altham, of Oxey, Herts, but had no other issue. This lady died 3rd January, 1662, and was buried in Covent Garden Church, Middlesex. Sir Francis *d.* in his sixty-sixth year, anno 1666, and lies interred in the north aisle of Abington Church. He was *s.* by his son,

II. SIR JOHN BERNARD, knt. member for the borough of Huntingdon in the Restoration and the Long Parliaments. He m. first, Elizabeth, daughter of Oliver St. John, lord chief justice of the Common Pleas, and had (with five other daughters, who all died unmarried,)

- ROBERT, his successor.
- Mary, m. to Thomas Brown, esq. of Arlsey, in the county of Bedford.
- Johanna, m. to the celebrated Richard Bentley, archdeacon and prebendary of Ely, regius professor, and master of Trinity College, Cambridge, and had issue,
  - Richard Bentley, a writer of some distinction; *d.* 23rd October, 1782.
  - Elizabeth Bentley, m. first, to Humphrey Ridge, esq. of Portsmouth, and surviving him without issue, she m. secondly, the Rev. Dr. Favell.
  - Johanna Bentley, the Phœbe of Dr. Byron's well known pastoral, m. to the Rev. Dennison Cumberland, Bishop of Kilmore (son of the Rev. Richard Cumberland, archdeacon of Northampton, and grandson of Dr. Richard Cumberland, bishop of Peterborough), by whom she had
    - RICHARD CUMBERLAND, the dramatist.
    - Johanna Cumberland.
    - Elizabeth-Bentley Cumberland.

He wedded, secondly, Grace, daughter of Sir Richard Shuckburgh, knt. of Shuckburgh, in the county of Warwick, but by her had no issue. Sir John *d.* in June, 1679, and was buried in Brampton Church, where a marble monument records the event. He was *s.* by his only son,

III. SIR ROBERT BERNARD, M.P. for the county of Huntingdon in 1688. This gentleman m. Anne, dau. of Robert Weldon, esq. of London, and had issue,

- JOHN, his heir.
- Anne.
- Mary.

He *d.* about the year 1703, and his widow became the second wife of Thomas, *first* Lord Trevor, of Bromham.† Sir Robert was *s.* by his son,

IV. SIR JOHN BERNARD, who m. Mary, youngest daughter of Sir Francis St. John, bart. of Longthorpe, in the county of Northampton, and had issue,

- ROBERT, his successor.
- Mary.

He *d.* 15th December, 1766, and was *s.* by his son,

V. SIR ROBERT BERNARD; at whose decease unmarried, 2nd January, 1789, the BARONETCY became EXTINCT.

Arms—Arg. a bear rampant sa. muzzled or.

---

* The manor of Abington was sold in 1699 by Sir John Bernard, knt. to William Thursby, esq. and is now possessed by JOHN HARVEY THURSBY, esq. of Abington Abbey.

† By whom she had

ROBERT TREVOR, who succeeded as fourth Lord Trevor, and was created Viscount Hampden. (See BURKE's *Extinct Peerage.*)

RICHARD TREVOR, in holy orders, consecrated Bishop of St. David's in 1744, and translated to Durham in 1752, *d.* unmarried in 1771.

EDWARD TREVOR, *d.* young.

BERTIE.

CREATED 8th Dec. 1812.

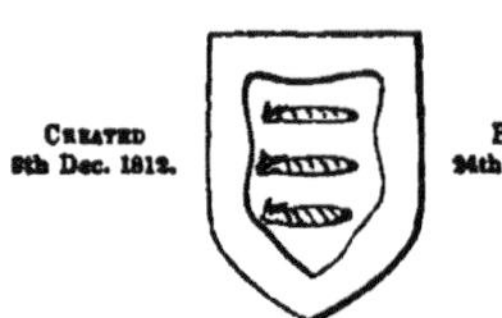

EXTINCT 24th Feb. 1824.

Lineage.

I. SIR ALBEMARLE BERTIE, admiral of the White, having distinguished himself in his gallant profession, was created a knight of the Bath, and subsequently made a BARONET in 1812. He m. Emma, daughter of James Modyford Heywood, esq. of Maristow, in Devon, but dying without surviving issue 24th Feb. 1824, aged seventy, the title became EXTINCT.

Arms—Arg. three battering rams ppr. within a bordure, az.

BETENSON, OF WIMBLEDON.

CREATED 7th Feb. 1666.

EXTINCT 15th June, 1786.

Lineage.

RICHARD BETENSON m. Elizabeth, daughter and co-heir of John Osborn, of Lackingdon, in Essex, and obtaining thereby the estate of Tiled Hall, in the same county, made it the place of his abode. He had by this lady (who survived him, and married, secondly, Arthur Breme, of Halsted,*) three sons, viz.

RICHARD, his heir.
Peter, *d. s. p.*
Edward, of Colne Engaine, in Essex, m. a daughter of Richard Lance, of Truro, and had issue,
Peter.
Joan, m. to John Plot, of Sparsholt, Berks.
Jane, m. to Thomas Tuke, of London.

The eldest son and heir,

RICHARD BETENSON, esq. who was of Layer de la Hay, in Essex, wedded Catherine, daughter of George Tuke, esq. of Layer-Marney, in the same county, and had two sons, viz.

RICHARD, his successor.
Thomas, m. Anne, daughter of Henry Lovell, esq. of Bletchingly, Surrey, and had issue,
Richard, *d.* young.
Thomas.
Anne.
Jane.

He was *s.* by his elder son,

I. SIR RICHARD BETENSON, knt. of Layer de la Hay, who was created a BARONET by *King* CHARLES II. 7th February, 1666. He m. Anne, daughter of Sir William Monyns, bart. of Waldershare, in Kent, and had issue,

RICHARD, who m. Albinia, daughter of Sir Christopher Wray, knt.† and dying in the lifetime of his father, left
EDWARD, successor to his grandfather.
Theodosia, m. to Major-General William Farrington, of Chiselhurst, and had
Thomas Farrington, commissioner of excise.
Albinia Farrington, who became second wife of Robert Bertie, first Duke of Ancaster.
Albinia, m. to William Selwin, esq. colonel of a regiment of foot and governor of Jamaica.
Frances, m. to Sir Thomas Hewet, knt. of Shire Oaks, Notts.
Dorothy, *d.* unmarried.
Edward, of Lincoln's Inn, m. Catherine, eldest daughter of Sir John Rayney, bart. of Wrotham, in Kent, and dying in 1700, left an only son,
EDWARD, who inherited as third baronet.

Sir Richard *d.* 29th August, 1679, was buried at Chiselhurst, in Kent, and *s.* by his grandson,

II. SIR EDWARD BETENSON, *b.* in 1675, who died unmarried 17th October, 1733, when his estates—comprising lands in Chiselhurst and Greenwich, in Kent, at Wimbledon, in Surrey; at several places in Essex, and an estate in London—devolved upon his sisters as co-heirs, and the Baronetcy reverted to his cousin,

III. SIR EDWARD BETENSON. This gentleman m. Ursula, daughter of John Nicks, esq. of Fort St. George, merchant, and had

RICHARD, his successor.
Helen.

He *d.* 24th November, 1762, and was *s.* by his son,

IV. SIR RICHARD BETENSON, who wedded Lucretia, daughter and co-heir of Martin Folkes, esq. of Hillington, in Norfolk, president of the Royal Society, but dying *s. p.* 15th June, 1786, the BARONETCY became EXTINCT.

Arms—Arg. a fess gu. in chief a lion passant, within a bordure engrailed erm.

BICKERTON, OF UPWOOD.

CREATED 29th May, 1778.

EXTINCT 9th Feb. 1832.

Lineage.

I. RICHARD BICKERTON, esq. (son of Captain Bick

* By whom she had one daughter,
JANE BREME (heir of her father), who became the wife of Sir Thomas Gardiner, knt. of Tottesbury, in Essex.

† By his wife, the Hon. Albinia Cecil, one of the daughters and co-heirs of Edward, Viscount Wimbledon. (See BURKE's *Extinct Peerage*.)

erton, of the fourth dragoon guards, by Miss Dowdal, of Carrickfergus, in Ireland,) *b.* the 22nd June 1727, received the honour of knighthood in 1773, upon the occasion of steering his late majesty's barge at a naval review off Portsmouth. Sir Richard had previously distinguished himself as a naval officer, and continued to acquire so much renown in his gallant profession, that he was created a BARONET, 19th May, 1778. He was, subsequently, a participator in the achievements of Sir Edward Hughes in the Indian Seas, and attained the rank of rear-admiral of the blue. He *m.* in 1758, Maria-Anne, daughter of Thomas Hussey, esq. of Wrexham, and heiress of her brother Lieut.-Gen. Vere Warner Hussey, of Wood Walton, and dying in 1792, left (with two daughters, Jane, who *d.* unm: in 1827, and MARIA, now of UPWOOD) a son,

II. SIR RICHARD BICKERTON, of Upwood, in the county of Huntingdon, K.C.B, K.C. and F.R.S. admiral of the white, lieutenant-general of marines, and a director of Greenwich Hospital; *b.* 11th October, 1759; *m.* 25th September, 1788, Anne, daughter of James Athill, esq. of the Island of Antigua, but had no issue. He assumed, by royal license, in 1823, his maternal surname and arms of "HUSSEY." Sir Richard Hussey-Bickerton dying *s. p.* in 1832, the Baronetcy EXPIRED, while the estate of Upwood (a property which formerly belonged to Henry Cromwell, uncle of the Protector) devolved on his only surviving sister, Miss BICKERTON, and that of Wood Walton passed to his cousin, (the second son of his aunt Arabella Warner and her husband Robert Moubray, esq. of Cockairny, rear-admiral Richard Hussey Moubray, the present SIR RICHARD HUSSEY HUSSEY, K.C.B. of Wood Walton. (See BURKE's *Commoners*, vol. ii. p. 358.)

Arms—Sa. on a chev. erminois three pheons az.

BICKLEY, OF ATTLEBOROUGH.

CREATED 3rd Sept. 1661.

EXTINCT ....

Lineage.

This family was anciently seated at Bickleigh, upon the river Ex, in Devonshire; the elder branch removed into Sussex, and settled at Chidham, in that county.

FRANCIS BICKLEY, of Lolworth, in Cambridgeshire, married Amy Mayor, a Huntingdonshire lady, and had issue,

- I. John, in holy orders, bachelor of divinity, and parson of Sandy, in the county of Bedford, *d. s. p.*
- II. Robert, of Caxton, in the county of Cambridge, *d. s. p.*
- III. FRANCIS, of whom presently.
- IV. Richard, of Halliston, in the county of Warwick, *m.* Sarah, daughter and co-heir of John Rugeley, esq. second brother of Ralph Rugeley, esq. of Dunton Hall, in the county of Warwick.
- I. Elizabeth, *m.* (his second wife) to Sir Rowland Rugeley, knt.
- II. ———, *m.* to — York.
- III. ———, *m.* to — Stallyon.

The third son,

I. FRANCIS BICKLEY, esq. of Dalston, in the county of Middlesex, having amassed a fortune, as a draper, in the city of London, purchased ATTLEBURGH HALL, in Norfolk, from John Ratcliffe, esq. about the year 1657. This gentleman was created a BARONET by *King* CHARLES II. 3rd September, 1661. He *m.* Mary, daughter of Richard Parsons, esq. of London, and had issue,

- I. FRANCIS, his heir.
- II. Thomas, } *d.* unm.
- III. John, } *d.* unm.
- I. Anne, *m.* to Mr. Richard Edisbury, of London, draper.
- II. Mary, *m.* to William Hoo, esq. of the Hoo, and had
  - Thomas Hoo, of the Hoo, in the county of Hertford, *d. s. p.* when his sister became his heir.
  - Susannah Hoo, who married Sir Jonathan Keate, bart. and carried the inheritance of Hoo to her husband. Doctor Kidder, afterwards Bishop of Bath and Wells, gives this lady a high character, for her great piety, humility, wisdom, discretion, &c. in a sermon he preached at her funeral, 19th June, 1673, at Kimpton, in Hertfordshire, and adds at the end of it, "Her extraction was honourable, in a direct line from the Lord of Hastings and Hoo, of whose family she was the heir general, and the sole inheretrix of those ancient possessions that remained to the barony; the Lord, her ancestor, being a person of that renown, that in the fatal quarrels between the houses of York and Lancaster, and when those quarrels were at the height, he was pitched upon to treat and mediate between the parties."
- III. Elizabeth, *m.* to Mr. Cotton, of London.
- IV. Amy, *d.* unm.

Sir Francis died at the advanced age of ninety, 11th August, 1670, and was interred in a vault of his own erecting, in Mortimer's chapel, in Attleburgh church. He was *s.* by his eldest son,

II. SIR FRANCIS BICKLEY, of Attleburgh Hall, in the county of Norfolk, who *m.* Mary, daughter of Mr. Alderman Mawe, of the city of Norwich, and had five sons and four daughters, viz.

- I. FRANCIS, his successor.
- II. Thomas, a mercer, in London, *d.* unm.
- III. John, of Magdalen College, Cambridge, *d.* unm.
- IV. Nathaniel, a lieutenant in the Duke of Norfolk's regiment, died unm. in Ireland.
- V. Charles, a lieutenant in the same regiment, who after the fatigues of the Irish war, came to visit his relations in England, and was barbarously murdered by one Hickford, at New Buckenham, in Norfolk. He died unm.
- I. Elizabeth, *m.* to Mr. Ware, of London.
- II. Amy, *m.* to the Rev. Thomas Church, rector of Hethersett, near Norwich.
- III. Mary, *m.* to her cousin, the Rev. Richard Bickley, rector of Attleburgh.
- IV. Jane, *m.* to Mr. Barnet, an apothecary, in London.

Sir Francis *d.* in 1681, and was *s.* by his eldest son,

III. SIR FRANCIS BICKLEY, of Attleburgh. This gentleman wedded first, Deborah, daughter of Sir Cornelius Vermuyden, knt. and had a son and daughter, viz.

- FRANCIS, his heir.
- Anne, *d.* unm.

Lady Bickley *d.* 6th March, 1669, and was buried at Attleburgh. Sir Francis wedded secondly, Mary, daughter of Sir Humphrey Winch, bart. of Braunston, in the county of Lincoln, and by that lady, had

John, captain in the army.
Humphrey, in holy orders, rector of Attleburgh.
Joseph, *m.* in Virginia, and had issue.
Elizabeth.

He *m.* thirdly, Mrs. Poynter, but had no other issue. He *d.* 1687, and was *s.* by his eldest son,

IV. Sir Francis Bickley, of Attleburgh, who *m.* Alathea, elder daughter and co-heir of Jacob Garrard, esq. son and heir of Sir Thomas Garrard, bart. of Longford Hall, in Norfolk, and by her, who *d.* in February, 1739-40, had issue,

John-Garrard, Charles, Alathea, } who all died *s. p.*

Sir Francis, who had served in the wars in Ireland, as captain in the Duke of Norfolk's regiment, died 4th July, 1746, and was *s.* by his elder surviving half-brother,

V. *The Rev.* Sir Humphry Bickley, who *d.* issueless 18th Sept. 1754, when the Baronetcy is supposed to have become extinct.

Arms—Arg. a chev. counter embattled between three griffins' heads erased sa. each charged with a plate, langued gu.

BIGG, OF LENCHWICK.

Created 26th May, 1620.  Extinct 11th June, 1621.

Lineage.

Thomas Bigg, son of John Bigg, of Sherborn and Radford, in Gloucestershire, was of Lenchwick, in the county of Worcester. He died 25th June, 1581, aged seventy-four, leaving by Magdalen, his wife, sister of Sir Philip Hoby, a son and successor,

Sir Thomas Bigg, of Lenchwick, who received the honor of knighthood 23rd July, 1603. This gentleman erected the mansion at Lenchwick. He wedded Ursula, fourth daughter of Clement Throckmorton, esq. of Haseley, in Warwickshire, and had issue,

I. Thomas, his heir.
II. Edward.
III. Clement.
IV. Samuel.
I. Catherine, *m.* to Michael Fox, esq. of Chacombe, in Northamptonshire, whose representative is the present Fiennes Wykeham Martin, esq. of Chacombe.
II. Ann, *m.* to John Wright, esq. of East Mayn, Hants.
III. Elizabeth, *m.* to Thomas Freme, esq. of Lippyate, Gloucestershire.

Sir Thomas died 4th May, 1613, and was *s.* by his son,

I. Sir Thomas Bigg, of Lenchwick, who was created a Baronet 26th May, 1620; but dying 11th June in the next year, the title became extinct. His widow, Anne, who was daughter of William Witham, esq. of Leadstone, in Yorkshire, wedded, secondly, Sir John Walter, chief baron of the Exchequer. Sir Thomas sold the estates of Lenchwick and Norton to the first Lord Craven, and from the Cravens they passed by purchase to Sir Edward Seymour, of Maiden Bradley, Wiltshire.

Arms—Arg. on a fesse between three martlets sa. as many annulets or.

BINDLOSSE, OF BORWICK.

Created 1641.  Extinct 1688.

Lineage.

Sir Robert Bindlosse, who died about the year 1629, was the first of the Bindlosse family who settled at Borwick Hall, in the county of Lancaster. He *m.* first, Alice, daughter and co-heir of Lancelot Dockwray, esq. of Dockwray Hall, in Kendal, and had by her two daughters, Anne, the wife of Henry Denton; and Alice, of Henry Bank, esq. of Bank Newton, in Yorkshire. Sir Robert *m.* secondly, Mary, daughter of Edmund Eltoft, esq. of Thornhill, and had by her one son and three daughters, namely,

Francis, his heir.
Dorothy, *m.* to Charles Middleton, esq. of Belsey, in Northumberland.
Mary, *m.* to Robert Holt, esq. of Castleton, in Lancashire.
Jane, *m.* to Sir William Carnaby, of Bothall, in Northumberland.

The only son and heir,

Sir Francis Bindlosse, knt. baptized 9th April, 1603, *m.* first, a daughter of Thomas Charnoke, esq. of Charnoke, by whom he had a daughter, Mary, *m.* to — Dene, esq. of Mansfield; and secondly, Cecilia, daughter of Thomas West, Lord Delaware, by whom (who *m.* secondly, Sir John Byron, knt.) he had

Robert, his heir.
Delaware, who *d.* unmarried before 1664.
Francis, of Brock Hall, in Lancashire, *d. s. p.*
Dorothy, *m.* to Sir Charles Wheler, bart. lieutenant-colonel of the Guards to Charles II.

The son and successor,

I. Sir Robert Bindlosse, of Borwick Hall, in the county of Lancaster, was created a Baronet 16th June, 1641. He *m.* Rebecca, daughter and co-heir of Sir Hugh Perry, knt. alderman of London, and had an only daughter and heiress,

Cecilia, *m.* to William Standish, esq. of Standish, in Lancashire, and is now represented by Charles Strickland Standish, esq. of Standish.

Sir Robert died in November, 1688, when the Baronetcy became extinct, but the estates descended to his daughter, Mrs. Standish.

Arms—Quarterly, per fesse indented or and gu. on a bend az. a cinquefoil between two martlets of the first.

BLACKET, OF NEWCASTLE.

CREATED 23rd Jan. 1685.

EXTINCT 25th Sept. 1728.

Lineage.

This family was seated at a remote period and for a long time at Wylam, in Northumberland.

NICHOLAS BLACKET, of Woodcroft, (lineally descended from Sir John Blackett, knt. of Woodcroft, one of the heroes of Agincourt) *m.* Alison, dau. and co-heir of Sir Rowland Tempest, of Holmside, in the county of Durham.* His great-grandson,

WILLIAM BLACKET, of Hoppyland, in Durham, who wedded Isabel, daughter of Crook, of Woolsingham, and had

- I. CHRISTOPHER, of Hoppyland, an officer in the army of CHARLES I. ancestor of the present head of the family, CHRISTOPHER BLACKETT, esq. of Wylam, in Northumberland. (See BURKE's *Commoners*, vol. i. p. 257.)
- II. Edward, whose line is extinct.
- III. WILLIAM, of whom we have to treat.

The third son,

WILLIAM BLACKETT, esq. M.P. for Newcastle upon Tyne, who amassed a considerable fortune by the product of his mines and collieries, and was created a BARONET by *King* CHARLES II. 12 December, 1673. Sir William *m.* first, Elizabeth, daughter of Michael Kirkley, of Newcastle, merchant, and had issue,

- I. EDWARD, his successor, from whom the extant baronets now represented by SIR WILLIAM BLACKETT descend.
- II. Michael, who *m.* Dorothy, daughter of —— Barnes, esq. of Darlington, in Durham, and had an only child, Elizabeth, who *d.* young. His wife survived him, and *m.* secondly, Sir Richard Brown, bart.; and thirdly, Dr. John Moor, Bishop of Ely.
- III. WILLIAM, of Wallington, in Northumberland, of whom presently.
- IV. Elizabeth, *m.* to Timothy Davison, esq. of Bemish, in Durham.
- V. Isabel, *m.* to Shem Bridges, esq. of Ember Court, Surrey.
- VI. Christian, *m.* to Robert Mitford, esq. of Seahill, in Northumberland.

He wedded, secondly, Mrs. Rogers, widow of Captain John Rogers, of Newcastle, and daughter of Mr. Cock, but had no other issue. His eldest son, EDWARD, succeeded him in the baronetcy. The youngest son,

I. WILLIAM BLACKET, esq. of Wallington, in Northumberland, where he erected a mansion-house, was created a BARONET by *King* JAMES II. 23rd January, 1685. Sir William distinguished himself in parliament as a popular speaker, and was offered public employment by *King* WILLIAM after the Revolution. He *m.* in 1684, Julia, daughter of Sir Christopher Conyers, bart. of Horden, in Durham, and by that lady (who wedded after his decease Sir William Thompson, one of the Barons of the Exchequer,) had issue,

- I. WILLIAM, his successor.
- II. Christopher, *d.* in infancy.
- III. JULIA, *m.* to Sir Walter Calverley, bart. and had
    - SIR WALTER CALVERLEY, bart. who eventually inherited the BLACKET estates.
    - Julia Calverley, *m.* to Sir George Trevelyan, bart. of Nettlecombe.
- IV. Elizabeth, *m.* to William Marshall, esq. of Reavley, in the county of Huntingdon, and had two daughters, who both *d. s. p.*
- V. Isabella, *d.* young.
- VI. Frances, *m.* in 1729, to Robert, only son of Charles, Lord Bruce, heir apparent of Thomas, Earl of Ailsbury, but had no issue.
- VII. Isabella, *m.* in 1743, to David, Earl of Buchan, and *d. s. p.* in 1763.
- VIII. Mary, *d.* young.
- IX. DIANA, *m.* to Sir William Wentworth, bart. of Bretton, in the county of York, and had issue,
    1. THOMAS WENTWORTH, who *s.* his father, and was fifth baronet of Bretton. He also inherited the estates and assumed the surname of BLACKETT. He *d.* unm. in 1792, and left his estates to his natural daughter, DIANA, wife of Thomas R. Beaumont, esq. of the Oaks, whose son, THOMAS WENTWORTH BEAUMONT, esq. M.P. of Bretton and Hexham Abbey, now possesses them. (*See* WENTWORTH *of West Bretton.*)
    2. Diana Wentworth, *m.* to Godfrey Bosvile, esq. of Gunthwaite, and had issue,
        - William Bosvile, of Gunthwaite, who devised his estate to his nephew,
            - Godfrey Macdonald, third Lord Macdonald, who assumed the additional surname of Bosvile.
        - Thomas Blacket Bosvile, Capt. Coldstream Guards, slain at Liencells.
        - Elizabeth Diana Bosvile, who *m.* Alexander, first Lord Macdonald. See BURKE's *Peerage and Baronetage.*
        - Julia Bosvile, *m.* to William Ward, Viscount Dudley.
    3. Elizabeth Wentworth, *m.* to James Watson, M.D. of Springhead.
    4. Julia Wentworth, *m.* in 1760, to the Rev. John De Chair, D.D. Rector of Rissington, and was grandmother of the Rev. Richard De Chair.
    5. Arabella Wentworth, *d.* unm.
- X. Anne, *m.* first, to John Trenchard, esq. of Abbots Leigh, in the county of Somerset, and secondly, to — Gordon, esq. She *d. s. p.*

Sir William *d.* in Dec. 1705, and was *s.* by his son,

II. SIR WILLIAM BLACKET, of Wallington, Member in several Parliaments for Newcastle on Tyne, who *m.* Lady Barbara Villiers, daughter of William, second Earl of Jersey, but dying without legitimate issue 25th September, 1728, (his widow *m.* Bussy Mansel, esq.) the BARONETCY became EXTINCT, but he bequeathed his estates to his illegitimate daughter, ELI-

* SIR RICHARD TEMPEST, of Studley, was father of SIR WILLIAM TEMPEST, of Studley, who *m.* Eleanor, daughter and sole heir of Sir William Washington, knt. and was ancestor of the TEMPESTS of *Holmside, Stella, Stanley, Studley,* and *Wynyard.* BURKE's *Commoners,* vol. i. page 474.

zabeth Orde, on condition that she should, within twelve months, intermarry with Sir William's nephew, Walter Calverley, and that Mr. Calverley should assume the surname of Blackett. These conditions being complied with, Mr. Calverley became (having inherited the baronetcy of his own family)

Sir Walter Calverley Blackett, bart. He *d.* in 1777, without surviving issue, (his only daughter, Elizabeth, predeceased him, unm. in 1752.) and the chief estates of the Blacketts are now possessed by Thomas Wentworth Beaumont, esq. M.P. for Northumberland. (See Burke's *Commoners*, vol. ii. p. 324.)

Arms—Arg. on a chevron between three mullets pierced sa. three escallops of the field.

BLACKHAM, OF LONDON.

Created 13th April, 1696. Extinct 2nd July, 1728.

Lineage.

i. Sir Richard Blackham, of London, Turkey merchant, descended of a family settled in Warwickshire and Staffordshire, was one of the greatest traders and promoters of the woollen manufactures in the kingdom, and in recompense for his meritorious public services was advanced to the degree of Baronet by William III, in 1696. He *m.* Elizabeth, daughter of Thomas Appleyard, esq. of Ulceby, in Lincolnshire, and niece of Sir John Boynton, of Rockliffe, in Yorkshire, by whom he left at his decease 29th June, 1728, a daughter Frances, and a son,

ii. Sir John Blackham, who survived his father but three days, and at his decease the Baronetcy expired.

Arms—Az. two bars between nine cross crosslets or.

BLACKWELL, OF SPROWSTON.

Created 16th July, 1718. Extinct 9th May, 1801.

Lineage.

This family was originally of the counties of Hertford and Surrey.

John Blackwell, esq. of Mortlake, in the latter, was Gentleman of the Board of Green Cloth to *King* Charles I. and served sheriff of his county in the year 1657. His son and heir,

John Blackwell, esq. of Mortlake, *m.* Elizabeth, daughter of James Smithsby, esq. and had seventeen children, one of the younger of whom,

i. Sir Lambert Blackwell, was appointed by *King* William, in 1697, knight harbinger and gentleman of the privy chamber. In the next year he was knighted, and accredited envoy extraordinary to the court of Tuscany, and republic of Genoa, and remained in office during the whole of *King* William's and the first three years of *Queen* Anne. In 1719 he was returned to parliament by the borough of Welton, in Wiltshire, and was created a Baronet by *King* George I. He *m.* Elizabeth, eldest daughter of Sir Joseph Herne, knt. and had issue,

- Charles, his successor.
- Elizabeth, *m.* to Sir Robert Lawley, and was grandmother of Sir Robert Lawley, bart. created Lord Wenlock in 1831.

He *d.* 27th October, 1727, and was *s.* by his son,

ii. Sir Charles Blackwell, who wedded Anne, daughter of Sir William Clayton, bart. of Merden, in Surrey, and by that lady, who wedded secondly, Doctor Thomas, Bishop of Rochester, left, with one daughter, at his decease 18th July, 1741, an only son,

iii. Sir Lambert Blackwell, who *d.* unmarried 9th May, 1801, aged sixty-nine, when the Baronetcy became extinct.

Arms—Paly of six, arg. and az. on a chief gu. a lion of England and a bordure ermine.

BLAKISTON, OF BLAKISTON.

Created 27th May, 1615. Extinct 1630.

Lineage.

"Few families of private gentry," says Surtees, "have spread more wide, or flourished fairer, than Blakiston; but all its branches, Gibside, Newton Hall, Old Malton, Seaton, and Thornton Hall, have perished like the original stock. One family alone remains within the county of Durham which can trace its blood, without hereditary possessions; and a dubious and a distant kindred to the old tree of Blakiston, is asserted by some families who bear the name in the south." The representative of this "long descended line" in the middle of the 16th century,

John Blakiston, esq. of Blakiston, aged twenty-two in 1557, *d.* in 1587, leaving by Elizabeth, his first wife, daughter and co-heir of Sir George Bowes, knt. of Streatlam, *inter alios,*

- William, his heir.
- Thomas, of Old Malton, in Yorkshire, whose male descendants became extinct in 1684.
- Christopher, of Coxhow, in Durham, whose only daughter and heir *m.* William Kennet, esq.
- Marmaduke, prebendary of Durham, ancestor of the Blakistons of Newton Hall, in Durham, and of Robert Blakiston, esq. of Bishop Wearmouth, who was living at Gateshead in 1821, married, with a numerous family.
- Muriel, *m.* to William Wyclyffe, esq. of Wyclyffe, in Yorkshire.

The eldest son,

Sir William Blakiston, knt. of Blakiston, *b.* in 1588, knighted at Whitehall, 23rd July, 1603, *m.* 26th

November, 1561, Alice, daughter and co-heir of William Claxton, esq. of Winyard, and had issue,

Thomas, his heir.

John, who m. Anne, daughter of Francis Trollop, of Eden, in Durham.

Elizabeth, m. to John Trollop, esq. of Thornley.

Anne, m. to Topp Heath, esq. of Little Eden.

Frances, d. unm.

The eldest son,

I. Sir Thomas Blakiston, of Blakiston, baptised at Norton, 8th July, 1582, was created a Baronet 27th May, 1615. He m. Mary, daughter of Sir Henry Constable, of Burton Constable, in Yorkshire, and sister to Henry, Viscount Dunbar, by whom he had two daughters, Margaret, b. in 1614, and Mary, m. to Sir Thomas Smith, knt. of Broxton, Notts, and had issue. Sir Thomas d. in 1630, when the Baronetcy became extinct. The estate he had sold in 1615, to Alexander Davison, of Newcastle, merchant, who afterwards died under arms in the service of *King* Charles, at the age of eighty-one, during the memorable siege of Newcastle, in 1644. His son, Sir Thomas Davison, inheritor of his father's spirit and loyalty, was high sheriff of Durham after the Restoration, and for a long series of generations his descendants continued to reside at Blakiston, until their marriage with the heiress of Bland induced them to desert their ancient residence for Kippax, the seat of the latter family. The manor of Blakiston was sold again some years since to William Russell, esq. of Brancepeth Castle, in Durham.

Arms—Arg. two bars, and in chief three cocks gu.

BLAKISTON, OF GIBSIDE.

Created 30th July, 1642.—Extinct 8th Oct. 1713.

Lineage.

William Blakiston, esq. a younger son of the very ancient house of Blakiston, of Blakiston, m. Eleanor Millot, of Whithill, in Durham, and left at his decease (his will bearing date 15th January, 1561), a daughter, Dorothy, wife of Christopher Fulthorpe, esq. of Tunstall, and a son,

Roger Blakiston, esq. who m. Elizabeth, daughter and sole heir of Richard Marley, esq. of Gibside, in Durham, and had issue,

I. William, of Gibside, who m. Jeane, daughter of Robert Lambton, esq. of Lambton, but d. s. p. 1606.

II. George, of whom presently.

III. Thomas.

I. Anne, m. to George Lumley, esq. of Axwell House, Durham.

II. Dorothy.

III. Mary.

IV. Isabel.

V. Grace, m. to Christopher Shafto, esq.

VI. Eleanor, m. to — Bennett.

VII. Barbara.

VIII. Mary, m. to — Hardcastle.

The second son,

George Blakiston, esq. of Hedley Hall, in Durham, wedded Eleanor, daughter of John Thaine, esq. of Swaffham, in Norfolk, and by her (who m. 2ndly, about 1597, Rev. Richard Fawcett, rector of Boldon,) had issue,

I. William, his heir.

II. Henry, of Archdeacon Newton, who left surviving issue, Sir William Blakiston, a distinguished loyalist, and Mary, m. to Stephen Thompson, of Humbleton, in Yorkshire.

I. Elizabeth.

II. Elinor.

III. Joane, m. to — Morell.

IV. Alice, m. to the Rev. John Hickes, rector of Whitburn.

The eldest son,

Sir William Blakiston, knt. of Gibside, m. Jane, daughter of Robert Lambton, esq. of Lambton, and had issue,

I. Ralph, his heir.

II. Nicholas, of Shieldrow, in Durham, m. Jane Porter, and had issue.

III. Lionel.

IV. John, who left issue.

V. Roger, of Hedley, m. Miss Cooke, of Newcastle, and had issue.

VI. William.

VII. Henry, m. and had issue.

I. Margaret, m. to Roger Fenwick, esq. of Shortflatt.

II. Jane, m. to Toby Dudley, esq. of Chopwell.

III. Dorothy.

IV. Barbara, m. Lindley Wren, esq. son and heir of Sir Charles Wren, knt.

Sir William d. in 1641, and was s. by his son,

I. Sir Ralph Blakiston, of Gibside, aged twenty-six in 1615, who was created a Baronet, 30th July, 1642. He m. Margaret, daughter of Sir William Fenwick, knt. of Wallington, in Northumberland, and had issue,

I. William, his heir.

II. Francis, successor to his brother.

III. Henry, d. young.

IV. George, of Lintz Hall, d. unm. will dated 1682.

V. Robert, d. s. p.

I. Margaret, m. to Thomas Moore, esq. of Angram Grange, in Yorkshire.

II. Mary, of New Elvet, d. unm. 1677.

Sir Ralph d. in 1651, and was s. by his eldest son,

II. Sir William Blakiston, of Gibside, who m. Mary, daughter of Cecil Calvert, Lord Baltimore, but leaving no surviving issue at his decease in 1692, was s. by his brother,

III. Sir Francis Blakiston, of Gibside, who m. Anne, daughter of Sir George Bowes, knt. of Bradley, and dying 8th Oct. 1713, the Baronetcy became extinct, but the estates descended to Sir Francis's only surviving child and heir,

Elizabeth, m. in 1693, to Sir William Bowes, knt. of Streatlam Castle.

Arms—Arg. two bars gu. in chief three cocks of the second.

BLAND, OF KIPPAX.

Created 30th Aug. 1642.

Extinct 16th Oct. 1756.

Lineage.

The family of Bland was anciently seated at Blands Gill, in the county of York, but the male line of the elder stock failing, the representation devolved upon the descendant of

ROBERT BLAND, of Leeming, in the North Riding, a younger son of Bland, of Blands Gill. This Robert wedded a daughter of Gale of Deighton, in the same county, and had, with two daughters, Margaret and Isabella, an only son, his successor,

RICHARD BLAND, of Leeming, who *m.* Grace, daughter of Thomas Pole, esq. and had several children. He directs by his will that his body be interred in the parish church of Bumestin, with his ancestors. He was *s.* at his decease by his eldest son,

ROBERT BLAND, of Leeming, who *m.* Anne, daughter of William Pepper, gent., and was father of

SIR THOMAS BLAND, knt. who settled at Kippax Park, in the time of ELIZABETH, and was in the commission of the peace for the county of York in the 32nd of that reign. He *m.* Elizabeth, daughter and heiress of Thomas Eastoft, of Redness, and had issue,

- THOMAS (Sir), his heir.
- Margaret, *m.* to Gilbert Nevile, esq. of Grove, Co. Notts.
- Elizabeth-Muriel, *m.* to Arthur Burgh, esq. lord mayor of York.

He *d.* on the 26th (was buried in St. George's church, London, 28th) December, 1612, and *s.* by his son,

SIR THOMAS BLAND, knt. of Kippax Park, a justice of the peace 13th JAMES I. He *m.* the Hon. Katherine Savile, eldest daughter of John, Lord Savile, and sister of Thomas, Earl of Sussex, by whom (who wedded, secondly, Walter Welsh, esq.), he had two sons and two daughters, viz.

- THOMAS (Sir), his successor.
- Adam, a major of horse in the royal army, and a devoted adherent to the royal cause in the wars of the Commonwealth. Major Bland was one of the Yorkshire gentlemen who seized the Castle of Pontefract for the king, and so boldly defended it; and he is stated, on good authority, to have been amongst those who made the remarkable sortie from the garrison to Doncaster, when the parliamentary general, Rainsborough, was killed. He *m.* Katherine, relict of Sir John Girlington, knt.
- Katherine, *m.* to Thomas Harrison, esq. of Dancers' Hill, Herts.
- Frances, *m.* to John Belton, of Rocliffe.

He was *s.* by his elder son,

I. SIR THOMAS BLAND, of Kippax Park, who was created a BARONET on the 30th August, 1642, by *King* CHARLES I. for his active zeal and devotion in the royal cause. He *m.* Rosamond, daughter of Francis Nevile, esq. of Chevet, in the county of York, and by her (who wedded, secondly, Walter Walsh, esq. of Houghton), had issue,

- FRANCIS, his heir.
- Adam, who *m.* a daughter of Sir Thomas Barnardiston, and relict of Ashcroft, by whom he had Adam, *m.* to the daughter of Edward Chetham, of Manchester, and Jane.
- Rosamond, *m.* to Martin Headly, an alderman of Leeds.
- Katherine, *m.* to John Frank, esq. of Pontefract.
- Frances.
- Dorothy.
- Elizabeth, *m.* to the Rev. Mr. Mitchell.

The baronet died in October, 1657, and was *s.* by his elder son,

II. SIR FRANCIS BLAND, bart. of Kippax Park. This gentleman *m.* Jane, daughter of Sir William Lowther, by whom (who survived him fifty years, dying 7th April, 1713, aged seventy-two), he left, at his decease 14th November, 1663, aged twenty-one, two sons,

THOMAS, } JOHN, } 3rd and 4th baronets.

The elder son,

III. SIR THOMAS BLAND, of Kippax Park, *d.* 14th December, 1667, aged five years, and was *s.* by his brother,

IV. SIR JOHN BLAND, of Kippax Park, *b.* 2nd November, 1663. This gentleman sate in parliament for Appleby, afterwards for Pontefract, and was member, at the time of his death, for the county of Lancaster. He *m.* 31st March, 1685, Anne, daughter and heiress of Sir Edward Mosley, of Hulm, in Lancashire, and had to survive infancy, one son and four daughters, viz.

1. JOHN, his heir.
2. ANNE, *m.* to Thomas Davison, esq. of Blackiston, in the county palatine of Durham,* and had one surviving son,
   - THOMAS DAVISON, esq. of Blackiston, baptised 19th June, 1712, who *m.* [illegible], daughter of William Hoar, esq. of [illegible] house, in the county of Middlesex, by whom (who *d.* in 1795), he left at his decease, 5th April, 1756,
     - THOMAS DAVISON, of whom presently, as inheritor of the estates of BLAND, and assumer of that name.
     - John Davison, barrister at law, *d.* [illegible] and was buried at Norton, in the county of Durham, 18th Nov. 17[illegible].
     - Martha-Anne Davison, *d. s. p.*
     - Anne-Catherine Davison, *d. s. p.*
   - Mrs. Davison *d.* 17th May, 1715, at the age of twenty-seven, and her widower re-married Theophila, daughter of [illegible] Turner, esq. of Kirkleatham, in the county of York, by whom he left, at his decease, 9th Sept. 1748,
     - William Davison, in holy orders, rector of Scruton, in the county of York, who *m.* 3rd June, 1750, Catherine, eldest daughter of George [illegible], esq. of Long Newton, in the county of Durham, by whom he had, with other issue,
       - The Rev. Thomas Davison, [illegible] of Hartburne, in Northumberland, who *m.* Elizabeth, daughter of William Webster, esq. of Stockton-upon-Tees, and had several children.
3. Elizabeth, *d.* at Bath, 3rd July, 17[illegible], unm. [illegible] aged sixteen.
4. Frances, *d.* 31st August, 1712.
5. Muriel, *m.* to Hildebrand Jacob, esq.

Sir John was *s.* at his decease, by his son,

V. SIR JOHN BLAND, bart. of Kippax Park, M.P. for Lancashire in 1714. He *m.* Lady Frances Finch, daughter of Heneage, first Earl of Aylesford, and had two sons and two daughters, viz.

JOHN, } HUNGERFORD, } 7th and 8th baronets.

Elizabeth, } Anne, } both *d.* unm. The elder 2nd June, 17[illegible] and the younger 28th January, 17[illegible]

The baronet was *s.* at his decease, in 1743, by his elder son,

---

* Great grandson of SIR THOMAS DAVISON, knt. of Blackiston, high sheriff of the county palatine of Durham, in 1661, by Alice, his wife, daughter of Sir William Lambton, knt. of Lambton.

Sir John Bland, of Kippax Park, who *d.* unm. in France, in 1755, and was *s.* by his brother,

Sir Hungerford Bland, eighth and last baronet, at whose decease, unm. in 1756, the title became extinct, while the estate passed to his two sisters, who both died unm. and devised their possessions to their cousin,

Thomas Davison, esq. who, assuming in 1786, the additional surname of Bland, became Thomas Davison Bland, esq. of Kippax Park, and was father of the present

Thomas Davison Bland, esq. of Kippax Park.

Arms—Arg. on a bend sa. three pheons or.

BLOUNT, OF TITTENHANGER.

Created 27th Jan. 1679.

Extinct 8th Oct. 1757.

Lineage.

This was a branch of the ancient house of Blount of *Sodington*, for which refer to Burke's *History of the Commoners*, vol. iii. p. 163.

Walter Blount, esq. second son of John Blount, esq. of Burton upon Trent, and Blount's Hall, in Staffordshire, and great-grandson of Peter Blount, the fourth son of Sir Walter Blount, knt. the standard-bearer, who was slain at Shrewsbury, *temp.* Henry IV.* *m.* Mary, elder daughter and co-heir of John Sutton, esq. of Osberston, in Leicestershire, and had issue,

- William.
- Elizabeth, who *m.* first, Anthony Beresford, esq. of Bentley, in Derbyshire; secondly, Sir Thomas Pope, of Tittenhanger, in the county of Hertford; and thirdly, Sir Hugh Pawlet, of Hinton St. George, in Somersetshire, but died without issue 7th October, 1593. Her second husband, Sir Thomas Pope, who was one of the visitors of the religious houses, and the first treasurer of the court of augmentations, and master of the king's jewel-house, *temp.* Henry VIII. a privy-councillor to *Queen* Mary, and founder of Trinity College, Oxford, dying issueless 29th January, 1558-9, left her his estate at Tittenhanger for life, and settled it subsequently upon her brother, William Blount's eldest son, Thomas Pope Blount.
- Mary, *m.* Sir — Sydenham, knt.

Walter Blount's son and heir,

William Blount, esq. who was of Osberston, county of Leicester, in right of his mother, *m.* Frances, daughter and heir of Edward Love, esq. of Eynsage, in Oxfordshire,† by Alice Pope, sister of Sir Thomas Pope above mentioned, and was father of

Sir Thomas Pope Blount, knt. of Tittenhanger, in the county of Hertford, which estate he inherited under the will of his great-uncle, Sir Thomas Pope, at the decease of his aunt Elizabeth, in 1593. This gentleman, one of the four deputy lieutenants of Hertfordshire, was sheriff of that county in 1598, and received the honour of knighthood from *King* James I. at Theobald's, 7th May, 1603, in his Majesty's journey from Scotland. He *m.* Frances, daughter of Sir Thomas Pigot, knt. of Doddershall, Bucks, and widow of Sir Thomas Nevil, knt. of Holt, in Leicestershire, by whom (who *d.* 23rd June, 1616,) he had two surviving sons, viz.

- Thomas-Pope, his successor.
- Henry, heir to his brother.

Sir Thomas *d.* 10th January, 1638-9, in the eighty-sixth year of his age, and was buried on the 13th of the same month in the family vault adjoining to the north side of the chancel of the church of Ridge. He was possessed of estates in the counties of Hertford, Middlesex, Bedford, Leicester, Stafford, and Derby, and was *s* by his elder son,

Thomas-Pope Blount, esq. of Tittenhanger, *b.* 7th February, 1598-9, who *m.* Mrs. Margaret Pate, but dying without issue 7th August, 1654, was *s.* by his brother,

Sir Henry Blount, knt. of Blount's Hall, who thus became "of Tittenhanger." This gentleman, *b.* 15th December, 1602, was educated in the free school of St. Albans, where his progress was so rapid that before he attained his fourteenth year he was enabled to enter Trinity College, Oxford, as a fellow-commoner. After he had taken a degree in Arts, he retired to Gray's Inn, and studied the municipal law. He subsequently travelled in France, Italy, and part of Spain, and embarked in 1634 at Venice for Constantinople, in order to make a voyage to the Levant. On his return he became one of the gentlemen-pensioners to *King* Charles I. and received the honor of knighthood at Whitehall, 21st March, 1639-40. He afterwards attended the King at York, and Edgehill, in which battle he is said to have had the care of the royal children. Sir Henry remained some time with the King at Oxford, but retiring and coming to London, he was summoned before Parliament for his adhesion to his Majesty, but pleading that he had only fulfilled the duties of his office, was acquitted. When the royal cause declined, accommodating himself to the state of affairs, he was appointed of the committee, 20th January, 1651, to regulate the abuses of the law, and at that time he evinced a determination against the payment of tythes, maintaining that no minister of the gospel should receive more than £100 per annum. In 1654, he was appointed, with the lord chief justice Rolles and others, of the commission of oyer and terminer, for the trial of Don Pantaleon Sa, the Portuguese ambassador's brother; and on the 5th and 6th of July in that year sat as a commissioner on the said trial in Westminster Hall. About this time he pulled down the old house of Tittenhanger, which, before the dissolution of the monasteries, had been the seat of the abbots of St. Albans, and erected a new mansion. In 1660, he was sheriff of the county of Hertford, and died, in his eightieth year, at Tittenhanger, 9th Oct. 1682. He was buried on the 11th in the family vault

* By his wife, Ellen, daughter and heir of John Hall, esq. of Dovebridge, in Derbyshire. The John Blount above mentioned *d.* in 1524, as appears by the probate of his will, dated 14th October, 1523, wherein he appoints his body to be buried in the abbey church of Burton upon Trent, with his wife Ellen, and leaves his manor of Blount's Hall, with other lands, in default of his own issue, to the use of the right heirs of Sir Edward Blount, of Solyngton, (alias Sodington aforesaid), and he makes the Lord Mountjoy (William Blount) supervisor of his testament.

† She was daughter of William Pope, gent. of Dedington, in Oxfordshire, father of Sir Thomas Pope, and ancestor of the Popes, who were Earls of Downe, in Ireland.

at Ridge, "esteemed," says an old writer, "by those who knew him, a gentleman of very clear judgment, great experience, much contemplation, and of a notable foresight in government. He was also a person of admirable conversation; in his younger years a great banterer, which, in his elder, he disused." He wrote and published, *in quarto*, "A Voyage into the Levant," which passed through several editions, and was, according to Anthony Wood, "so well esteemed abroad, that he was informed it was translated into French and Dutch." He is said to be author of a pamphlet, called "The Exchange Walk," printed about 1647; and he wrote to Walter Rumsey, esq. in praise of tobacco and coffee, which is printed before Rumsey's *Organon Salutis*, and of the virtue of those plants. Sir Henry Blount *m.* in 1647, Hester, elder daughter and co-heir of Christopher Wase, esq. of Upper Holloway, in Middlesex, and widow of Sir William Mainwaring, knt. of Chester, (who was slain on the king's side in the civil wars, in defence of that city), and by that lady, who *d.* in 1678, had surviving issue,

I. THOMAS-POPE, his successor.

II. Charles, *b.* 27th April, 1654, of Blount's Hall; a literary man of some reputation at the period in which he lived. His principal works were collected and published in two volumes, with an account of his life, by Charles Gildon, under the title of "The Miscellaneous Works of Charles Blount, esq." He *d.* in Catherine Street, London, in August, 1693, having had by his wife, Eleanor, fourth daughter of Sir Timothy Tyrrell, knt. of Shotover, in Oxfordshire,

Henry, lieutenant-colonel of the foot guards, killed at the head of the advanced guard in the battle of Schellenberg, *anno* 1704, unm.

Charles, of Blount's Hall, *b.* 12th September, 1681, *d. s. p.* in April, 1729.

Thomas-Pope, *b.* 25th March, 1683, lost at sea in 1702, unm.

Hester, *b.* 27th December, 1673; *m.* 21st October, 1692, in the church of Banbury, to Sir Harry Tyrrell, bart. and eventually inherited Blount's Hall, as heir to her brother. (*See* TYRRELL, *of Thornton.*)

Eleanor, *d.* young.

Charlotte, *b.* 13 May, 1684, *m.* — Smith, esq. and *d.* in 1707.

III. Ulysses, *b.* 7th April, 1664; had lands in Hertfordshire upon the death of his mother, and afterwards, on the decease of his father, an estate in Surrey. He *m.* 6th June, 1687, Hester, eldest daughter of Sir John Hewet, bart. and left at his decease in 1704, two daughters, his co-heirs, viz.

Hester, baptized 8th March, 1687, *m.* to Stephen Bateman, gent. of London.

Philippa, *m.* to Sir Henry Bateman, knt. of London, *d.* at Bath 22nd May, 1718, and was buried in the church of St. Pancras, London.

I. Frances, *b.* 25th October, 1648, *m.* in 1666, to Sir Thomas Tyrrell, bart. of Thornton, and *d.* 7th June, 1699.

The eldest son and heir,

I. SIR THOMAS-POPE BLOUNT, *b.* 12th September, 1649, succeeded to the seat of Tittenhanger, at the decease of his mother in 1678, his father having about four years before settled it upon her for life. He was created a BARONET by *King* CHARLES II. 27th January, 1679, his father being then alive. Sir Thomas *m.* in St. Olave's church, Hart Street, London, 22nd July, 1669, Jane, only daughter of Sir Henry Cæsar, knt. (*See* BURKE'S *Commoners*, vol. ii. p. 20), and by her (who *d.* 14th July, 1726,) had surviving issue,

THOMAS-POPE, his heir.

Charles, *b.* 21st August, 1683, captain in the army, killed in a dispute at the King's Arms Tavern, in the Strand, London, in July, 1714, and *d.* unm.

Cæsar, *b.* 5th March, 1687-8, an officer in the royal navy, *m.* Jane, daughter of — Hodges, esq.

Robert, *b.* 18th March, 1688-9, had been page of honor to *Queen* ANNE; was lieutenant of the Scotch regiment of guards; *d.* unm. in July, 1726.

Elizabeth, *b.* 15th December, 1673, *d.* unm. 25th October, 1734.

Judith, *b.* 28th December, 1674.

Susannah, *b.* 24th July, 1677, *m.* in the church of Sheuley, in Hertfordshire, 17th May, 1696, to Michael Arnall, esq. of Ampthill, and survived his widow.

Jane, *b.* 27th July, 1678, *d.* unm. 14th April, 1725.

Frances, *b.* 20th November, 1680, *d.* unm. 25th April, 1729.

Anne, *b.* 18th July, 1682, *m.* 16th February, 1712, to the Rev. James Mashborne, and *d.* 2nd June, 1718.

Mary, *b.* 17th April, 1685, *d.* unm. 25th January, 1737-8.

Christian, *b.* 19th August, 1690, *m.* 3rd May, 1733, to the Rev. Rowland Bowen.

Sir Thomas Blount served for St. Albans in the two last parliaments of *King* CHARLES II. and after the revolution was knight of the shire for the county of Hertford for three parliaments, the first of which was the convention parliament. He was chosen by the House of Commons three successive years a commissioner of public accounts; and dying 30th June, 1697, was buried 8th July, in the vault at Ridge. He was *s.* by his eldest son,

II. SIR THOMAS-POPE BLOUNT, of Tittenhanger, *b.* 19th April, 1670, *m.* 8th November, 1695, Catherine, eldest daughter of James Butler, esq. of Amberley Castle, in Sussex, and had issue,

HARRY-POPE, his successor.

James-Pope, *b.* 1st November, 1705, *d.* unm.

John-Pope, *b.* 15th October, 1707; was of Clare Hall, Cambridge; had taken deacon's orders; *d.* unm. 8th April, 1734.

Katharina, *b.* 9th April, 1704, *m.* 21st February, 1730-1, to William Freeman, esq. of Aspeden Hall, in Hertfordshire, eldest son and heir of Ralph Freeman, esq. of Hammels, in the same county, and had an only daughter and heiress,

KATHARINA FREEMAN, who *m.* 19th May, 1755, the Hon. Charles Yorke, second son of Philip, first Earl of Hardwicke, and died in 1759, leaving an only surviving child,

PHILIP YORKE, third EARL OF HARDWICKE.

He *d.* 17th October, 1731, and was *s.* by his eldest son.

III. SIR HARRY-POPE BLOUNT, of Tittenhanger, *b.* 13th September, 1702, *m.* 19th September, 1728, Anne, younger daughter and co-heir of Charles Cornwallis, esq. of Medlow, in Huntingdonshire, but *d. s. p.* 8th October, 1757, when the BARONETCY became EXTINCT, and the estates passed to the noble family of HARDWICKE.

Arms—Barry nebuly of six or and sa.

BOLLE, OF SCAMPTON.

CREATED in 1628.

EXTINCT in Dec. 1714.

Lineage.

The family of Bolles, of long standing in the county of Lincoln, was resident there so early as the reign of HENRY III. Its principal seat seems to have been Bolle Hall, in Swineshead, until the close of the reign of EDWARD IV. when, by an intermarriage with the heiress of the family of Hough, the elder branch became settled at Hough, near Alford, in Lincolnshire; while a younger established itself at Gosberkirke, now Gosberton, in the same county, and from this branch descended the Baronets of Scampton.

JOHN BOLLE, sheriff 16 EDWARD IV. m. Katherine, daughter and co-heir of Richard Hough, esq. of Hough, in Lincolnshire, and had, *inter alios*,

RICHARD, of Hough, who m. Isabel, sister and heir of Richard Nansant, of Cornwall, and had issue.
The descendant and representative of this line,
JOHN BOLLE, esq. of Thorpe Hall, left at his decease one son and two daughters, namely,
JOHN, *d. s. p.* in 1732, aged seventy-nine.
ELIZABETH, m. to the Rev. Thomas Bosvile, B. D. Rector of Ufford, and had three daughters, namely,
MARGARET BOSVILE, *b.* in 1710, *m.* 1734, to James Birch, esq. of Coventry, and had issue,
1. Thomas Birch, of Thorpe Hall, whose son, Thomas-James Birch, lt.-col. first life guards, assumed the surname of BOSVILE, on inheriting Ravenfield Park, in Yorkshire. He *d. s. p.* 22nd April, 1829.
2. James Birch, rector of Wishford, Wilts, *d.* in 1823, aged eighty-four.
3. Elizabeth Birch, m. to Robert Lee, esq. of Louth and Littlecoates, in Lincolnshire, and was grandmother of the present THOMAS BOSVILE BOSVILE, esq. of Ravenfield Park, Yorkshire.
ELIZABETH BOSVILE, m. first, to Alexander Emerson, esq. of West Retford, Notts; and secondly, to the Rev. Stephen Ashton, vicar of Louth.
BRIDGET BOSVILE, m. to Thomas Bosvile, esq. of Braithwell and of Ulverscroft Abbey, and had two sons, who both *d. s. p.*
SARAH, m. to Henry Eyre, esq. of Bramley Hall, and had an only daughter and heir,
MARGARET EYRE, m. in 1726, to William Spencer, esq. of Attercliffe Hall, Yorkshire, and was great-grandmother of the present REV. WILLIAM PAKENHAM SPENCER, of Bramley Grange. (See BURKE'S *Commoners*, vol. ii. p. 389.)
GODFREY.

The younger son,

GODFREY BOLLE, esq. was father of

THOMAS BOLLE, esq. of Gosberkirke, who m. Jane, daughter of George Winter, esq. of Workington, in Leicestershire, and was *s.* by his son,

SIR GEORGE BOLLE, knt. alderman of London, who served as sheriff of that city in 1608, and filled the civic chair in 1617. He m. Jane, daughter and co-heir of Sir John Hart, knt. lord mayor of London in 1590, by whom he acquired the estate of Scampton, in Lincolnshire, and had issue,

JOHN, his heir.
George, *d. s. p.*
Judith, who married.
Anne, m. to Humphrey Smith, of London, sheriff in 1639.

Sir George died 1st September, 1621, at the advanced age of eighty-three, and was buried on the 25th of that month in the family vault in St. Swithin's, London, where a monument was erected to his memory by his widow. The son and successor of this respected citizen,

I. SIR JOHN BOLLE, knt. inherited Scampton at the decease of his mother, served as high sheriff of Lincolnshire in 1627, and was created a BARONET in the following year. He m. Katherine, daughter of Thomas Conyers, esq. of Brodham, in the county of Nottingham, and dying 8th March, 1648, aged sixty-seven, was *s.* by his son,

II. SIR ROBERT BOLLE, of Scampton, M.P. for Lincoln in 1661, who m. in October, 1637, Mary, daughter of Sir Edward Hussey, knt. of Hunnington, and had two sons and five daughters, viz.

JOHN, his heir.
Robert.
Isabella, m. to Sir Edward Ayscough, knt.
Elizabeth, m. to Sir Peter Wych, knt. and was mother of Sir Cyril Wych, bart.
Katherine, m. to Thomas Washer, esq. and had a son,
John Washer, esq. of Lincoln's Inn.
Mary.
Anne, m. to George Antrobus, esq. and had an only daughter and heir,
Mary Antrobus, who m. John Hayes, esq. of Ashby-de-la-Zouche, and had an only surviving daughter,
MARY HAYES, m. to JOHN TURTON, M.D. of Birmingham.

Sir Robert Bolles, a munificent patron of the arts and literature, died in August, 1663, aged forty-four, and was *s.* by his son,

III. SIR JOHN BOLLE, of Scampton, who m. first, in November, 1663, Elizabeth, daughter of John Pynsent, esq. one of the prothonotaries of the Court of Common Pleas, by whom he had an only daughter, who died young; and secondly, in May, 1667, Elizabeth, eldest daughter of Sir Vincent Corbett, bart. of Morton Corbett, in Shropshire, by whom he had to survive him,

JOHN, his heir.
Sarah.

Sir John *d.* in 1685, and was *s.* by his son,

IV. SIR JOHN BOLLE, of Scampton, who represented the city of Lincoln in five successive parliaments, from 1690 to 1701, and is recorded to have lived in great splendour. He died unmarried in December, 1714, and was buried with his ancestors at St. Swithin's, London. At his decease the BARONETCY EXPIRED, and with him vanished all the grandeur and hospitality which the little village of Scampton had witnessed for more than a century and a half, during the existence of the much respected family of Bolle. Sir John dying intestate, the estate of Scampton vested in his sister, Mrs. Sarah Bolle, a maiden lady, who resided at Shrewsbury. On her demise, which occurred 7th November, 1746, the manor and estate of Scampton, together with a wood of about one hundred acres, called Ingleby Wood, descended to her three co-heirs,

Sir Cyril Wych, bart.*
John Wasner, esq.* of Lincoln's Inn,
Mrs. Mary Turton,* wife of John Turton M.D. of Birmingham,

who, in 1749, alienated the whole of the property to William Cayley, esq. grandson of Sir William Cayley, bart. of Brompton.

BOND, OF PECKHAM.

Lineage.

William Bond, of Buckland, in the county of Somerset, the first of this family who is mentioned in the pedigree proved at the visitation of London, in 1633, is there described as "descended of a younger house of Bond, of Cornwall."† He m. a daughter of — Hill, and had three sons,

I. William, of Crosby Palace, in the City of London, who was "a merchant adventurer, and most famous in his age for his great adventures both by sea and land." He was an alderman, and in 1568 sheriff of London. By Margaret, his wife, daughter of William Aldy, of Guildford, in Surrey, he had issue,

1. Daniel (Sir), who inherited Crosby Palace.

2. William, of London, m. Margaret, daughter of Thomas Gore, esq. of London, and had issue.

3. Martin, of London, who was a captain at Tilbury camp, in 1588, and chief captain of the train bands of the city of London. In 21 James I. he was M.P. for that city, and d. in May, 1645, aged eighty-five.

4. Nicholas.

5. Anne, m. first, to Robert King, and secondly, to William Whitmore, esq. of London.

II. Edward, who m. and had issue.

III. George (Sir), of whom presently.

I. Katherine, m. to Palmer, of Trull, in Somersetshire.

II. Avis, m. to Otto Wescombe.

III. Ann, m. to William Gifford.

IV. Agnes, m. to — Cade.

The third son,

Sir George Bond, b. at Buckland, filled the civic chair of the city of London, in 1587. He d. in 1592, leaving, by Winifred his wife, daughter of Sir Thomas Leigh, knt. of London, issue,

I. William (Sir), his heir.

II. George, of Bridgewater, m. Gertrude, daughter and heir of William Saunders, and left an only daughter and heir,

Mary, m. to Richard Musgrave, esq. of Nettlecomb.

III. Thomas (Sir), of Ogborn St. George, Wilts, received the honour of knighthood, and was secretary to the lord chancellor Egerton. m. Frances, second daughter of Edmund B[illegible], of Soddington, in Devon, and was father of

George, of Ogborne, whose name appears in the list of those gentlemen, of the county of Wilts, who were qualified to become knights of the royal oak. He m. Elizabeth, daughter of Charles Hoskins, of Barrow Green, in Surrey, and had one son,

George, who d. 22nd September, 17[illegible]2, aged forty.

Alice, m. first, to Walter Vaughan, esq. of Pembray, and secondly, to William B[illegible] esq.

I. Alice, m. to Sir William Quarles, knt. of Lancaster.

II. Ann, m. to Richard Martin.

III. Dronese, m. to Sir Henry Wenston, knt. of Standish, in Gloucestershire.

IV. Jane, m. to — Dare, of Devonshire.

V. Mary, m. to Hugh Hill, of Yard, near Taunton, Somersetshire.

VI. Rose, m. to William Hale, esq. of King's Walden, Herts, ancestor of the present

William Hale, esq. of King's Walden.

The eldest son,

Sir William Bond, knt. who was of Highgate, and received the honour of knighthood, 23rd July, 1[illegible] m. Catherine, daughter and sole heir of John P[illegible], gent. of Barnard's Inn, Holborn, and had two sons,

John, who died without issue, and

Thomas Bond, M. D. of Hoxton, in the county of Middlesex, who wedded Catherine, daughter and heir of John Osbaldeston, esq. of Harbens, in the county of Warwick, a younger branch of the Osbaldestons of Chadlington, and had issue,

I. Thomas.

II. John, who left issue by his wife, Elizabeth, second daughter of John Field, of London, John and Mary.

III. Edward.

IV. William, m. Mary, daughter of Sir Edward Gage, bart. of Hengrave, in Suffolk, and left issue, at his decease in 1696, two daughters, d. s. p.

I. Mary, m. to Sir Thomas Grymes, bart. of Peckham.

II. Catherine, m. to Sir William Compton, bart. of Hartpury, in Gloucestershire.

III. Elizabeth, m. to — Wynne, esq. of Wales.

Doctor Bond's eldest son,

I. Thomas Bond, esq. being introduced to court by

---

* The descendants of the daughters of Sir Robert Bolle, the second baronet.

† See family of Bond of Dorsetshire, Burke's Commoners, vol. i. p. 240.

Lord St. Albans, was made comptroller of the household to the Queen Mother of *King* CHARLES II. and advanced to a baronetcy 9th October, 1658. This gentleman appears to have been a considerable person and in great favour with *King* CHARLES II., and several sums of money were remitted to him, for his majesty's use, during the civil war. He purchased a considerable estate at Peckham, in Surrey, of his brother-in-law, Sir Thomas Crimes, bart. He married Marie, daughter of Mons. Charles Peliott, Sieur de la Gard, of Paris, whose sister, Madmoiselle de la Gard, was one of the maids of honour to the Queen of CHARLES II. By her he had issue,

- I. HENRY, his successor.
- II. Thomas, of Bury St. Edmond's, county of Suffolk, who, by Henrietta his wife, second daughter and co-heir of Thomas, Lord Jermyn, of St. Edmondsbury, was father of
    - Henry Jermyn Bond, esq. of Bury, who died 20th February, 1748, leaving, by Jane his wife, daughter of — Godfrey, (who remarried 20th Dec. 1750, Thomas, first Viscount Gage, and *d.* 1757), three sons, viz.
        - Charles Jermyn, of Bury, *d. s. p.* 1760.
        - Henry, *b.* 1726.
        - James, *b.* 1724, who *m.* and left issue.
    - Judith, *d.* unm. 1793.
- I. Mary-Charlotte, was brought up by Henrietta, Duchess of Orleans, daughter of *King* CHARLES I. and married Sir William Gage, bart. of Hengrave Hall, in the county of Suffolk. She *d.* in 1717.

The elder son,

II. SIR HENRY BOND, of Peckham, sold that estate, and lived chiefly in France. He married a French lady of the name of Noir, and had a son and successor,

III. SIR THOMAS BOND, who espoused Dorothea, daughter of — Wynne, of Wales, and dying in August, 1734, left issue,

IV. SIR CHARLES BOND, who is believed to have been the last baronet of this family. He was born in December, 1734, and was living 7th November, 1760, but the period of his death is unknown. He had an only sister, who was living unmarried 7th November, 1760.

Arms—Argent on a chevron sable three bezants, in dexter chief a crescent gules.

BOOTH, OF DUNHAM MASSEY.

CREATED 22nd May, 1611.

EXTINCT 7th Nov. 1797.

Lineage.

The family of BOOTH was of great repute and honorable station in the counties of Lancaster and Chester for several centuries before it arrived to the dignity of the peerage.

ADAM DE BOOTHS, so called from his place of abode in Lancashire, was father of

WILLIAM DE BOOTHS, living in 1275, who *m.* Sibel, daughter of Sir Ralph de Bereton, knt., and was *s.* by his son,

THOMAS DE BOOTHS, to whom *s.* his son,

JOHN DE BOUTHE, living *temp.* EDW. II., who *m.* Agnes, dau. and heiress of Sir Gilbert de Barton, and was *s.* by his son,

SIR THOMAS BOUTH, of Barton, called "Tomalin of the Boothes," *m.* Ellen, daughter of Thomas de Workesley, esq. of Workesley, now Worsley, in the county of Lancaster, and had issue,

- JOHN, his successor.
- Henry, left a son, John.
- Thomas, left a son, Robert.
- Alice, *m.* first, to William Leigh, esq. of Baguley, in the county of Chester, and secondly, to Thomas Duncalf, esq. of Foxwist.
- Catherine.
- Margaret.
- Anne, *m.* to Sir Edward Weever.

Sir Thomas was *s.* by his eldest son,

JOHN BOUTH, esq. of Barton, who lived in the reigns of RICHARD II. and HENRY IV. and *m.* first, Joan, daughter of Sir Henry Trafford, of Trafford, in the county of Lancaster, by whom he had issue,

- THOMAS, who received the honour of knighthood in the 14th HENRY VI. Sir Thomas *m.* a daughter of Sir George Carrington, knt. and widow of —— Weever, and had issue,
    - Sir John Bouth, knt. to whom *King* HENRY VII. granted an annuity of 10 marks sterling for his good services. Sir John fell at Flodden-Field in the 5th of HENRY VIII. and his male line ceased with his great-grandson, JOHN, who left, at his decease, three daughters, co-heiresses.
- Robert, of whom presently, as ancestor of the Lords Delamere.
- William, archbishop of York.
- Richard, of Strickland, near Ipswich, in the county of Suffolk.
- Roger, *m.* Catherine, daughter and heiress of Ralph Hatton, esq. of Mollington, near Chester, and had issue,
    - Robert Booth, esq. of Sawley, in the county of Derby.
        - Isabel, *m.* to Ralph Nevil, third earl of Westmoreland, and had issue,
            - ANNE, who *m.* William Lord Coniers.
- John, bishop of Exeter, anno 1465; buried in the church of St. Clement Danes, London, in 1478.
- Ralph, archdeacon of York.
- Margery, *m.* to John Byron, esq. of Clayton, in the county of Lancaster.
- Joan, *m.* first, to Thomas Sherborne, esq. of Stonyhurst, in the county of Lancaster, and secondly, to Sir Thomas Sudworth, knt.
- Catherine, *m.* to Thomas Ratcliffe, esq. of Wimmorley.
- Alice, *m.* to Sir Robert Clifton, knt. of Clifton, in the county of Nottingham.

Mr. Booth married a second wife, (but the lady's name is not known), and left a son,

- Laurence Booth, who was chancellor of the university of Cambridge, bishop of Durham, and afterwards archbishop of York. His Lordship was appointed keeper of the privy-seal in the 35th of HENRY VI., and LORD CHANCELLOR OF ENGLAND in the 12th of EDWARD IV. He *d.* in 1480.

The line of Sir Thomas Bouth, the eldest son, terminating, as stated above, in co-heiresses, we proceed with the second son,

SIR ROBERT BOUTH, knt. of Dunham Massie, in the

BOO

county of Chester, which seat he acquired by his wife, Douce, daughter and co-heiress of Sir William Venables, of Bollen, in the same shire; which Sir William was son of Joane, daughter and heir of Hamon Fitton, who was grandson of John Fitton, of Bollen, by Cicelie his wife, eldest daughter and co-heir of Sir Hamon de Massie, the sixth and last baron of Dunham Massie, one of the eight feudal lordships instituted by Hugh Lupus, Earl of Chester, in the time of the Conqueror. By this lady Sir Robert Bouth had no less than nine sons and five daughters. Of the former,

WILLIAM, the eldest, inherited the fortune.
Philip, the youngest, m. the daughter and heiress of Sir William Hampton, of Wellington, knt.

The daughters were,

Lucy, m. to William Chauntrell, esq. of the Bache, near Chester.
Ellen, m. to Robert Legh, esq. of Adlington, in the county of Chester.
Alice, m. to Robert Hesketh, esq. of Rufford, in the county of Lancaster, ancestor of the baronets Hesketh.
Joan, m. to Hamond Massie, esq. of Rixton, Lancashire.
Margery, m. to James Scarebrich, esq.

Sir Robert and his eldest son had a grant of the office of sheriff of Cheshire for both their lives, and to the surviver of them, by patent, dated at Chester on the 6th of March, in the 21st of HENRY VI., with all fees appertaining to the said office, and to execute its duties, either personally or by deputy. Sir Robert died on the 16th September, 1450, and was s. by his eldest son,

SIR WILLIAM BOTHE, who m. Maud, daughter of John Dutton, esq. of Dutton, in the county of Chester, by whom he had five sons and nine daughters, which daughters were,

Douce, m. to Thomas Leigh, esq. of West Hall, in the county of Chester.
Anne, m. first, to John Leigh, esq. of Booths, Cheshire, and secondly, to Geoffery Shakerly, of Shakerly, in the county of Lancaster.
Ellen, m. to Sir John Leigh, of Baguley, in the county of Chester.
Margery, m. John Hyde, esq. of Haighton, Lancashire.
Alice, m. to John Ashley, esq. of Ashley, in the county of Chester.
Elizabeth, m. to Thomas Fitton, esq. of Pownall, Cheshire.
Joane, m. to William Holt, esq.
Isabella.
Catherine.

Sir William d. in 1476, and was s. by his eldest son,

GEORGE BOTHE, esq. This gentleman m. Catherine, daughter and heiress of Robert Mountfort, esq. of Bescote, in the county of Stafford, and of Monkspath, Warwickshire, by whom he acquired considerable estates in the counties of Salop, Stafford, Warwick, Leicester, Wilts, Somerset, Cornwall, and Hereford, and had issue,

WILLIAM, his successor.
Laurence.
Roger.
Alice, m. to William Massie, esq. of Denfield, in the county of Chester.
Ellen, m. first, to Thomas Vaudrey, esq. and secondly, to Trafford, of Trafford.

Mr. Bothe d. in 1483, and was s. by his eldest son,

SIR WILLIAM BOTHE, knt. who m. first, Margaret, daughter and co-heir of Sir Thomas Ashton, of Ashton-under-Lyne, in the county of Lancaster, and of his wife Anne, daughter of Ralph, Lord Greystock, by which alliance a great accession of property came to the family of Bothe. He had issue of this marriage,

GEORGE, his successor.
John, m. to Margery, daughter of Sir Piers Dutton, of Dutton, in the county of Chester, and had two sons, William and Robert.

Sir William m. secondly, Ellen, daughter of Sir John Montgomery, of Trewly, in the county of Stafford, and had

William, m. a daughter of —— Smith, esq. of the county of Leicester.
Hammet, m. a daughter of Humphrey Newton, esq.
Edward, m. to Mary, daughter and co-heir of Roger Knutsford, esq. of Twemlow, in the county of Chester, from whom descended the Booths of Twemlow Hall.
Henry, m. to a daughter of — Bowdon, of the county of Chester.
Andrew.
Jane, m. first, to Hugh, son and heir of Sir Piers Dutton, of Dutton, in the county of Chester, and secondly, to Thomas Holford, esq. of Holford, in the same shire.
Dorothy, m. to Edward, son and heir of Laurence Warren, esq. of Pointon, in the county of Chester.
Anne, m. to Sir William Brereton, of Brereton, in Cheshire.

Sir William d. 9th November, in the 11th HEN. VIII. and was s. by his eldest son,

GEORGE BOTHE, esq. who m. Elizabeth, daughter of Sir Thomas Boteler, of Beausey, near Warrington, and had issue,

GEORGE, his successor.
John, m. to Elizabeth, daughter of John Dutton, esq. and left four sons,
William.
Robert.
Edmund.
Henry.
Robert, in holy orders, rector of Thornton-in-the-Moors, in the county of Chester.
Ellen, m. to John Carrington, esq. of Carrington.
Anne, m. to William Massie, esq. of Podingt[illegible].
Margaret, m. to Sir William Davenport, of Bramhall.
Elizabeth, m. Richard Sutton, esq. of Sutton, near Macclesfield.
Dorothy, m. to Robert Tatton, esq. of Withenshaw.
Alice, m. to Peter Daniel, esq. of Over-Tabley.
Cecilie, d. unmarried.

Mr. Bothe died in the 22d HENRY VIII. and was s. by his eldest son,

GEORGE BOTHE, esq. who left, at his decease in 1543, a son and three daughters, viz.

WILLIAM, his successor.
Elizabeth, m. to William Chauntrell, esq. of the Bache, near Chester.
Mary, m. to Randle Davenport, esq. of Henbury, in the county of Chester.
Anne, m. to — Wentworth, esq. of the county of York.

To this George Bothe, Queen Jane Seymour commanded a letter to be written, acquainting him with the birth of a son, (afterwards King EDWARD VI.) bearing date, at Hampton Court, the very day of her delivery, October 12th, 29th HENRY VIII., in these words:—

BY THE QUEEN.

"Trusty and welbeloved, we grete youe well. And for asmuche as by the inestimable goodness and grace of Almighty God, we be delivered and brought in childbed of a prince, conceived in most lawful matrimonie between my Lord the King's Majestye and us, doubting not but for the love and affection which ye beare unto us, and to the commyn wealth of this realme, the knowledge thereof shud be joyous and glad tidings unto youe, we have thought fit to certifie youe of the same. To thintent ye might not only rendre unto God condigne thanks and praise for soo great a benefit, but also pray for the long continuance and preservation of the same here in this lief, to the honor of God, joy and pleasor of my Lord the King, and us, and the universall weale, quiet, and tranquillyty of this hole realme. Gevyn under our signet, at my Lord's manor of Hampton-Cort, the xii. day of October.

"To our trusty and welbeloved,
"George Both,' Esq."

Mr. Bothe had also the honour of a letter from *King* Henry himself, dated at Westminster, 16th February, in the 34th year of his reign, concerning forces to be raised to war against the Scotch. Mr. Bothe was *s.* by his son,

William Bothe, or Bouthe, who, being then but three years old, was in ward to the king. He received the honour of knighthood in 1578. Sir William *m.* Elizabeth, daughter of Sir John Warburton, of Warburton and Arley, in the county of Chester, and had seven sons and six daughters.

Of the former,

- George succeeded his father.
- John, *m.* to a daughter of Prestwick, of Hulme, near Manchester, and had several children.
- Richard, *m.* the daughter and heiress of Massie, of Cogshull.

The married daughters were,

- Elizabeth, *m.* first, to William Basnet, esq. of Eaton, in the county of Denbigh, and secondly, to — Walsh, esq. of ———, Ireland.
- Dorothy, *m.* to Ralph Bunnington, esq. of Barrowcote, in the county of Derby.
- Alice, *m.* to — Panton, esq.
- Susan, *m.* first, to Sir Edward Warren, of Pointon, in the county of Chester, and secondly, to John Fitton, esq. of the city of Chester.

Sir William *d.* on the 28th Nov. 1579, and was *s.* by his eldest son,

Sir George Booth, whose extensive estates were seized by Queen Elizabeth during his minority, under the guardianship of her favourite, Robert Dudley, Earl of Leicester. In the latter end of her majesty's reign, Sir George received the honour of knighthood, and upon the institution of the order of baronet, he was one of the first raised to that dignity, on the 22d May, 1611. Sir George Booth *m.* first, his second cousin, Jane, only daughter, and heiress of John Carrington, esq. of Carrington, in the county of Chester; by whom he had no issue, nor did he live long with her, yet he inherited the lands of her father; the same being strictly so settled by that gentleman, before the marriage of his daughter, to descend to the family of Booth in which settlement, among other provisions, one particularly worthy of notice: "That if she, the said Jane, should, after marriage, be detected of incontinency, the estate should remain to the family of Booth." After the decease of this lady, Sir George *m.* Catherine, daughter of Chief Justice Anderson, of the Court of Common Pleas, and had several children, of whom,

- William, the eldest son, *m.* Vere, second daughter, and co-heir of Sir Thomas Egerton, Viscount Brackley, Lord Chancellor of England, and predeceasing his father, (26th April, 1636,) left issue,
  - George, of whom presently, as successor to the baronetcy.
  - Nathaniel, *m.* Anne, third daughter of Thomas Ravenscroft, esq. of Bretton, in the county of Flint, whose line terminated with his great-granddaughter, Hannah Vere Booth, in 1765.
  - Catherine, *m.* to Sir John Jackson, of Hickleton, in the county of York, baronet.
- John, the youngest son, having actively espoused the cause of *King* Charles II. received the honour of knighthood after the restoration, anno 1660. Sir John *m.* Dorothy, daughter of Sir Anthony St. John, younger son of Oliver, Earl of Bolingbroke, and left several children at his decease, in 1678.
- Alice, *m.* George Vernon, esq. of Haslinton, in the county of Chester.
- Susan, *m.* Sir William Brereton, of Handforth, in the county of Chester, baronet.
- Elizabeth, *m.* to Richard, Lord Byron, (his lordship's second wife,) and died without issue.

Sir George Booth, who served the office of sheriff of Cheshire twice, and as often of Lancashire, *d.* on the 24th October, 1652, and was *s.* in his title and estates by his grandson (whose guardianship he had purchased from the crown for £4000.),

II. Sir George Booth. This gentleman was committed prisoner to the Tower of London during the usurpation, for his zeal in the royal cause, and his efforts to restore the exiled prince. He had the pleasure eventually, however, of being chosen one of the twelve members deputed by the House of Commons, in May, 1660, to carry to that prince the recall of the house, in answer to his majesty's letters. And on Monday, 13th July, 1660, the House of Commons ordered, "that the sum of £10,000 be conferred on Sir George, as a mark of respect for his eminent services, and great sufferings in the public cause;" which order obtained the sanction of the House of Lords in the ensuing month. In addition to which honourable grant, the baronet was elevated to the Peerage, by letters patent, dated 20th April, 1661, as Baron Delamere, *of Dunham Massie, in the county of Chester*. His Lordship *m.* first, Lady Caroline Clinton, daughter and co-heir of Theophilus, Earl of Lincoln, by whom he had an only daughter, Vere, who *d.* unmarried, in 1717, in the 74th year of her age. He *m.* secondly, Lady Elizabeth Grey, eldest daughter of Henry, Earl of Stamford, by whom he had seven sons and five daughters, of whom,

- Henry, succeeded to the title.
- George, *m.* Lucy, daughter of the Right Hon. Robert Robartes, Viscount Bodmin, son and heir of John, Earl of Radnor, by whom he had an only son, Henry, who *d.* unmarried.
- Robert, in holy orders, Archdeacon of Durham, in 1691, and Dean of Bristol, in 1708. This gentleman *m.* first, Ann, daughter of Sir Robert Booth, chief justice of the Court of Common Pleas in Ireland, by whom he had a son, Henry, who died *s. p.* He *m.* secondly, Mary, daughter of Thomas Hales, esq. of Howlets, in the county of Kent, and had five sons and four daughters, of whom,
  - Nathaniel, the fourth and only surviving, succeeded to the Barony of Delamere, but of him hereafter.
  - Elizabeth, *m.* to Charlton Thrupp, esq. of Hampstead, Middlesex.

Vere, *m.* to George Tyndale, esq. of Bathford, Somersetshire, and had a son,

George Booth Tyndale, esq. Barrister at Law, of Bathford, father of the present George Booth Tyndale, esq. of Hayling, Hants. (See Burke's *Commoners*, vol. iv. p. 545.)

Elizabeth, *m.* to Edward, Earl of Conway.

Diana, *m.* to Sir Ralph Delavall, bart. of Seaton-Delavall, in the county of Northumberland, and after his decease to Sir Edward Blacket, bart. of Newby, in the county of York.

George, first Lord Delamere, *d.* on the 8th August, 1684, and was *s.* by his eldest surviving son,

III. Sir Henry Booth, second baron. This nobleman, who had been committed to the Tower prior to the death of *King* Charles II. was brought to trial, in the reign of *King* James, for high treason, before the Lord Chancellor Jeffreys, constituted high steward on the occasion, and a select number (27) of peers, but was most honourably acquitted. After which he lived in retirement until the revolution, when espousing the cause of the Prince of Orange, he was deputed with the Marquess of Halifax, and the Earl of Shrewsbury, upon the arrival of the prince at Windsor, 17th December, 1688, to bear a message to the fallen monarch, requiring that his majesty should remove from Whitehall. An office which his Lordship executed so delicately that *King* James was afterwards heard to remark; "that the Lord Delamere, whom he had used ill, treated him with much more regard, than those to whom he had been kind, and from whom he might better have expected it." His lordship was afterwards sworn of the privy council, and appointed chancellor of the exchequer, an office which he held but one year; when, upon his retirement, he was advanced to the dignity of Earl of Warrington, by letters patent, dated 17th April, 1690. The earl *m.* Mary, daughter, and sole heiress of Sir James Langham, bart. of Cottesbrooke, in the county of Northampton, by whom he had four sons and two daughters, which latter were,

Elizabeth, *m.* to Thomas Delves, esq. son and heir apparent of Sir Thomas Delves, bart. of Dodington, in the county of Chester, and died *s. p.* in 1697.

Mary, *m.* to the Hon. Russel Robartes, and had issue,

Henry, last Earl of Radnor of that family.

His lordship, who published a Vindication of his friend, Lord Russel, and other literary productions mentioned in Walpole's Catalogue, *d.* on the 2nd January, 1693-4, and was *s.* by his second, but eldest surviving son,

IV. Sir George Booth, second Earl of Warrington. This nobleman *m.* Mary, eldest daughter, and co-heiress of John Oldbury, esq. of London, merchant, by whom he had an only daughter,

Mary, who *m.* in 1736, Henry Grey, fourth Earl of Stamford, and left,

Henry, who *s.* to the Earldom of Stamford, upon the decease of his father, in 1768, and was created in 1796, Baron Delamere, and Earl of Warrington—(see those dignities in *Burke's Dictionary of the Peerage and Baronetage*).

His lordship *d.* on the 2nd August, 1758, when his estates passed to his daughter, Mary, Countess of Stamford; the Earldom of Warrington expired, while the baronetcy, with the barony reverted to his cousin, (refer to the Very Reverend Dean Robert Booth, son of the first Lord Delamere).

V. Nathaniel Booth, esq. as fourth Baron Delamere. His lordship *m.* Margaret, daughter of Richard Jones, esq. of Ramsbury Manor in the county of Wilts, by whom he had two sons, who both died young and a daughter, Elizabeth, who *d.* unmarried, in 1765. Lord Delamere was appointed chairman of the committees of the House of Lords in 1765, and *d.* in 1770 when the Baronetcy, together with the Barony of Delamere, became extinct.

Arms—Three boars' heads erect and erased sa.

BOOTHBY, OF CHINGFORD.

Created 9th Nov. 1660.

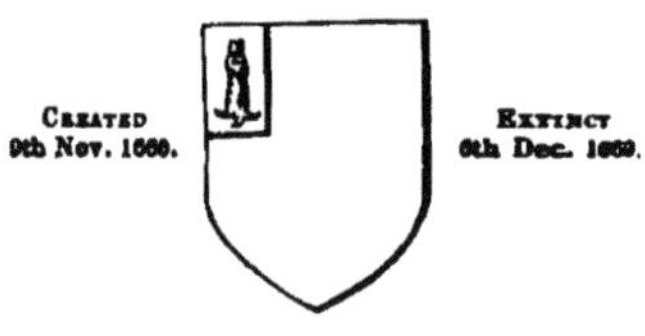

Extinct 6th Dec. 1669.

Lineage.

This family was originally settled in the county of Stafford, and had its seat at Marchanton, where Richard Boothby was living *temp.* Henry VIII. The first who established himself in Essex, and purchased the manor of Chingford, was

Thomas Boothby, esq. second son of William Boothby, merchant of London, who engaged himself in commercial pursuits. By his first wife, Anne Grafton, who died 16th December, 1622, he had two daughters and three sons, William and Richard, who both died unmarried, and Walter, seated at Tottenham, in Middlesex. By his second wife, Elizabeth Wright, he had two sons and as many daughters, namely,

Thomas, a merchant in Spain.

Robert, of whom presently.

Anne, *m.* to Matthew Bedell, esq.

Elizabeth, *m.* to — Styles, esq. of Westerham, in Kent.

The youngest son,

Robert Boothby, esq. of Friday Hill, *m.* Mary, daughter and heir of George Hyer, esq. of Weston, in Surrey, and had issue,

Thomas, his heir.

George, *d.* unm.

Robert, who succeeded to the estates of his eldest brother, Sir Thomas; and marrying Sarah, dau. of Samuel Jackson, esq. of Bicker, in the county of Lincoln, had a son, Thomas, who died 12th May, 1735, and a daughter, Sarah, who never married.

William, of Shere, in Surrey.

The eldest son,

I. Sir Thomas Boothby, of Chingford, was created a Baronet 9th November, 1660. He *m.* Elizabeth, daughter of — Styles, of Westerham, in Kent, and had

Thomas (Sir), knt. who *d. s. p.* 1st December, 1669, aged twenty-four.

Robert, died young.

Elizabeth, *m.* to Hugh Wood, of London, Turkey merchant.

Dying without surviving male issue, Sir Thomas Boothby left his estate to his next surviving brother. The Baronetcy became extinct.

Arms—Arg. on a canton sa. a lion's paw erased or.

BOREEL, OF AMSTERDAM.

Created 21st March, 1644.—Extinct ——.

Lineage.

Of this Baronetcy, conferred in 1644 on Sir William de Boreel, of Amsterdam, nothing appears on record.

BORLASE, OF BROCKMER.

Created 4th May, 1642. Extinct in 1688.

Lineage.

Edward Borlase, the ancestor of the first baronet, was the second son of Walter Borlase, the representative of an ancient Cornish family which had married an heiress of Moels.

Sir William Borlase, the descendant of the said Edward, was of Marlow and Brockmer, in the county of Buckingham. He m. Amy, daughter of Sir Francis Popham, knt. of Littlecot, in Wiltshire, and had issue,

I. John, his heir.

II. William, M.P. for Marlow 12 and 13 Charles II. d. in 1665, leaving three daughters,

- Henrietta, m. to Sir Richard Astley, bart.
- Anne, m. to Lieutenant-General Webb.
- Alicia, m. to John Wallop, esq.

III. Henry.

I. Anne, m. to Richard Grenville, esq.

II. Mary, d. unm.

Sir William was s. by his eldest son,

I. Sir John Borlase, of Brockmer, one of the lords justices of Ireland, who was created a Baronet 4th May, 1642. He d. in August, 1672, and was s. by his son,

II. Sir John Borlase, of Brockmer, M.P. who died in 1688, when the Baronetcy expired, leaving by Alice, his wife, an only daughter and heir,

Anne, m. to Arthur Warren, esq. of Stapleford, Notts, and was mother of

Borlase Warren, esq. of Little Marlow, father of the late

Admiral Sir John Borlase Warren, G. C. B. distinguished for his high professional abilities, who was created a Baronet in 1775. He was afterwards sworn of the privy council, and accredited ambassador extraordinary and plenipotentiary to the court of Russia. He married Caroline, daughter of General Sir John Clavering, K.C.B. and had (with a son, killed at the landing of the Bristol troops in Egypt) an only surviving daughter and heir,

Frances-Mary, m. to George Charles, fourth Lord Vernon, and was mother of the present (1838) Lord. (See *Baronetcy of* Warren, *of Little Marlow*.)

Arms—Erm. on a bend sa. two arms issuing from the clouds rending a horse-shoe, all ppr.

BOTELER, OF HATFIELD WOODHALL.

Created 12th Apr. 1620. Extinct in 1647.

Lineage.

From the Botelers or Butlers, Barons Boteler, of Wemme and Oversley, descended

I. Sir John Boteler, of Hatfield Woodhall, in the county of Hertford, who was created a Baronet in 1620, and advanced to the Peerage 20th September, 1628, as Baron Butler or Boteler, of Bramfield, in the same shire. His lordship m. Elizabeth, sister of George Villiers, Duke of Buckingham, by whom he had six sons, whereof five predeceased him unmarried, and six daughters, of whom

- Aubrey, m. first, Sir Francis Anderson; and secondly, Francis, Earl of Chichester.
- Helen, m. Sir John Drake, knt.
- Jane, m. to James Ley, Earl of Marlborough.
- Olivera, m. to Endymion Porter, esq.
- Mary, m. to Edward, Lord Howard of Escrick.
- Anne, m. first, to Mountjoy Blount, Earl of New port; and secondly, Thomas Weston, Earl of Portland.

His lordship d. in 1637, and was s. by his only surviving son,

II. William, second baron, at whose decease without issue in 1647, the Baronetcy, together with the Barony of Boteler of Bramfield, expired, while his lordship's estates devolved on his sisters or their representatives, and were purchased afterwards by George, Viscount Grandison in Ireland, who thereby obtained possession of the manor of Bramfield.

Arms—Gu. a fess checquy arg. and sa. between six cross crosslets or.

BOTELER, OF BRAMFIELD.

Created 7th Dec. 1643.—Extinct in June, 1657.

Lineage.

I. Sir George Boteler, half-brother of Sir John Boteler, of Hatfield Woodhall, the first peer, was created a Baronet in 1643. He m. Lady Bethell, but d. s. p. in 1657, when the title became extinct.

Arms—See Boteler, *of Hatfield Woodhall*.

BOTELER, OF TESTON.

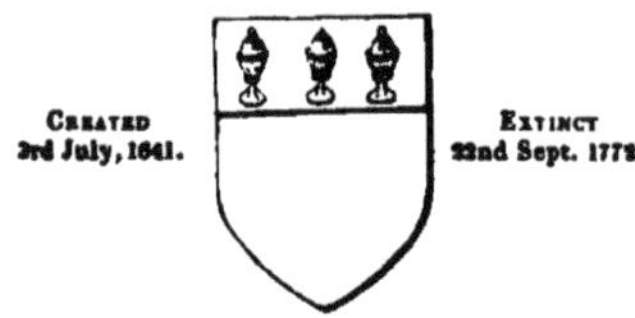

Lineage.

In the Visitation of the county of Kent *temp.* JAMES, this family is designated "right worshipful and ancient" by John Philipot, rouge-dragon, marshal, and deputy for said county to William Camden, clarencieux king of arms.

JOHN BOTELER, high sheriff of Kent 22 RICHARD II. and knight of the shire 1 HENRY V. *m.* the daughter and heir of Richard Feversham, and from that marriage lineally descended

SIR OLIVER BOTELER, who, in the time of *Queen* ELIZABETH, upon his marriage with Anne, daughter and heir of Thomas Berham, esq. of Teston, in Kent, removed from Sharnbroke, in Bedfordshire (where his grandfather came from Kent and settled), to that seat, and the family continued ever afterwards to reside there. He was subsequently knighted by *King* JAMES I. in 1604. He had issue

- John (Sir), who wedded Alice, daughter of Sir Edward Apsley, knt. of Sussex, but died in his father's lifetime *s. p.*
- James, *d. s. p.* also in the life of his father.
- WILLIAM, successor to the estate.
- Anne, *m.* to Sir George Fane, of Buston, in Kent, second son of Sir Thomas Fane by the Lady Mary Neville, only daughter and heiress of Henry, Lord Abergavenny. This lady was restored, by letters patent, to the dignity of Baroness Le Despencer, to which barony her eldest son, Francis, Earl of Westmoreland, succeeded at her decease. (See BURKE'S *Peerage and Baronetage.*)

Sir Oliver *d.* in 1632, and was *s.* by his third and only surviving son,

I. WILLIAM BOTELER, esq. of Teston, in the county of Kent, who inherited the estates at the decease of his father, and was created a BARONET by *King* CHARLES I. 3rd July, 1641. He *m.* in 1631, Joan, daughter of Sir Henry Fanshaw, knt. of Ware Park, Herts, and had an only son, OLIVER. At the breaking out of the civil war, Sir William raised a regiment at his own expense for the service of the king, and was killed at its head in the battle of Cropedy Bridge, 29th June, 1644, when he was *s.* by his son,

II. SIR OLIVER BOTELER, of Teston, who wedded Anne, daughter of Sir Robert Austen, bart. of Bexley, and had issue,

- PHILIP, his successor.
- John.
- Elizabeth, *d.* unm.
- Joane, *m.* to Christopher Rhodes, esq.

He *d.* about the year 1690, and was *s.* by his elder son,

III. SIR PHILIP BOTELER, of Teston, M.P. for Hythe *temp.* WILLIAM III. and *Queen* ANNE. He *m.* in 16[illegible], Anne, daughter of Sir Edward Desbouverie, knt. of Cheshunt, and dying in April, 1719, was *s.* by his only son,

IV. SIR PHILIP BOTELER, of Teston. This gentleman wedded, in May, 1720, Elizabeth, only daughter and heir of Thomas Williams, esq. of Cabalva, in Radnorshire, by whom he had an only daughter, Elizabeth, who predeceased him unmarried in 1737. He *d.* himself in 1772, when the title became EXTINCT. By his last will he bequeathed one moiety of all his estates, both real and personal, to Mrs. Elizabeth Bouverie, of Chart Sutton; and the other moiety to Elizabeth, Viscountess Dowager Folkstone, and her son, William, Earl of Radnor. Teston Manor became the property of Mrs. Elizabeth Bouveric.*

Arms—Arg. on a chief az. three cups or.

BOVEY, OF HILLFIELDS.

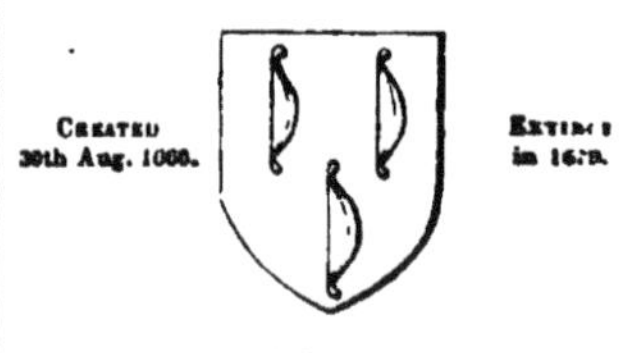

Lineage.

I. SIR RALPH BOVEY, of Hillfields, in the county of Warwick, who was created a BARONET 30th August 1660, *m.* Mary, daughter of William, Lord Maynard, but died without legitimate issue in 1679 when the title became EXTINCT, but the estates passed, under Sir Ralph's will, to his natural son.

Arms—Vert, three bows strung, or.

---

* The connexion of Sir Philip with the legatees was as follows:—

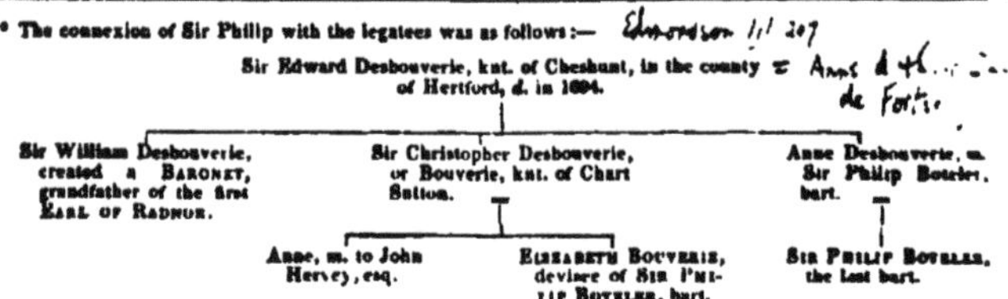

BOWYER, OF LEIGHTHORNE.

CREATED 23rd July, 1627. EXTINCT in 1678.

Lineage.

WILLIAM BOWYER, of Petworth, grandson of Thomas Bowyer, of Knipersley, in Staffordshire, *m.* Eliza Tredcroft, of Billinghurst, in Sussex, and had three sons and two daughters, namely,

THOMAS, his heir.

Robert, of Chichester, mayor in 1532, whose son, Alderman Francis Bowyer, was father of

SIR WILLIAM BOWYER, knt. who purchased the estate of Denham Court, Bucks, and was ancestor of the present

SIR GEORGE BOWYER, bart. of Denham Court and Radley. (See BURKE'S *Peerage and Baronetage.*)

John, of Petworth, whose granddaughter, Grace Bowyer, *m.* Robert Badger, of Wimbell.

Elizabeth, *m.* to Thomas Norton.

Katherine, *m.* to John Calcot.

The eldest son,

THOMAS BOWYER, esq. of London, *m.* Jane, daughter and heir of Robert Merry, of Hatfield, and by her, who wedded, secondly, Alexander Nowell, deane of Paules, had, *inter alios*, a son,

THOMAS BOWYER, esq. of Leighthorne, in Sussex, who left by Jane, his second wife, daughter of John Birch, baron of the Exchequer, a son,

I. SIR THOMAS BOWYER, of Leighthorne, who was created a BARONET in 1627. He *m.* first, Ann, daughter and co-heir of Adrian Stoughton, esq. of Stoke; and secondly, Jane, daughter and heir of Emery Cranley, relict of Samuel Austen, of Stratford, and of Sir George Stoughton. By the former only did Sir Thomas leave issue,

THOMAS, aged upwards of twenty-four in 1634, who predeceased his father in 1634, leaving a son,

JAMES, successor to his grandfather.

John, *d. s. p.*

ANNE, *m.* to Sir John Morley, knt. of Broomes and Chichester, and had an only daughter and heir,

CATHERINE, *m.* to Peter Bettesworth.

Sir Thomas was *s.* by his grandson,

II. SIR JAMES BOWYER, of Leighthorne, who surrendered his patent of Baronetcy, and procured a new one in 1678, with the precedency of the former, entailing the title on Henry Goring, esq. of Highden, in Sussex. Sir James Bowyer *d. s. p.*, when the DIGNITY under the first patent became EXTINCT.

Arms—Or, a bend vair cottised sa.

BOWYER, OF KNIPERSLEY.

CREATED 11th Sept. 1660. EXTINCT in 1701.

Lineage.

The pedigree of the Bowyers, of Knipersley, is traced by Sir William Dugdale up to Aldred Bowyer, *temp.* HENRY II. and is to be found recorded at full length in the Visitations of Staffordshire, preserved in the British Museum. Aldred's descendant,

THOMAS BOWYER, living 2 RICHARD II. married Katharine de Knipersley,* and thus acquired the estate of Knipersley. He was direct ancestor of

SIR JOHN BOWYER, knt. of Knipersley, living in 1598, whose grandson,

I. JOHN BOWYER, esq. of Knipersley, was created a BARONET in 1660, and the title remained with his children until the demise of SIR WILLIAM BOWYER, his youngest surviving son, the fourth baronet, in 1701. That gentleman had four daughters, his co-heirs, viz.

I. MARY, *m.* Charles Adderley, esq. of Hams Hall, Warwickshire, and from this marriage descend the present CHARLES BOWYER ADDERLEY, esq. of Hams Hall, RALPH ADDERLEY, esq. of Barlaston Hall, &c. &c. (See BURKE'S *Commoners*, vol. ii. p. 279.)

II. DOROTHY, *m.* to Sir Thomas Gresley, bart.

III. JANE, *m.* to Leftwich Oldfield, esq. of Leftwich, in Cheshire.

IV. Anne, *m.* first, to Sir John Bellot, bart. and secondly, to Rowland Port, esq. of Ilam, but dying *s. p.* left her share of the Knipersley estate to her nephew, Sir Nigel Gresley, bart.

Arms—A lion rampant, between three crosses crosslet, fitchée gu.

BRADSHAIGH, OF HAIGH.

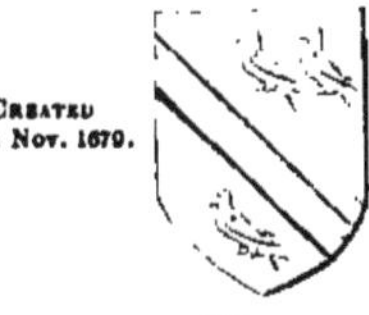

CREATED 17th Nov. 1679. EXTINCT before 1786.

Lineage.

This family lineally derived from

SIR JOHN BRADSHAW, of Bradshaw, a Saxon living at the time of the Conquest, who was reinvested in his

---

* She descended from Ormus le Guidon, who held in capite Biddulph and fifteen other manors. Ormus was son of Richard Forestarius, one of William the Conqueror's barons. Knipersley is a part of Biddulph which came (by a partition) to Alured Biddulph, who assumed, *temp.* HENRY III. the name of KNIPERSLEY, and was ancestor of KATHARINE KNIPERSLEY, who married Thomas Bowyer.

estate by the Norman. He *m.* the daughter and sole heir of Sir Robert Remington, knt. of Remington, and left a son and heir,

Sir Robert Bradshaw, who allied with the Conquerors, by marrying the daughter of Sir William Fitz-John, a Norman Knight; by her he had two sons,

- John, (Sir) his heir.
- George, (Sir) who seated himself in the county of Warwick, and wedded the daughter and heir of Humphry Atherston, of Atherston, by whom he left a son,
  - John,* from whom the Bradshaws of Atherston, and other places in Warwickshire.

The elder son and heir,

Sir John Bradshaw, living in the 13th of Henry I. *m.* a daughter of Sir John Molineux, knt. of Sephton, in Lancashire, and left a son and successor,

John Bradshaw, who was alive in the 8th of *King* Stephen, and marrying a daughter of Brackenbury, of Brackenbury, left a son and heir,

William Bradshaw, who wedded a daughter of Sir William Trollope, knt. of Thornley, his son,

Sir John Bradshaw, living in the 2nd of Richard I. took to wife the daughter of Sir Walter Harcourt knt. of Stanton, and left a son and heir,

Sir John Bradshaw, who *m.* a daughter of Sir Ralph Musgrave, knt. and had issue,

Thomas Bradshaw, living in the 23rd of Henry III. whose wife was a daughter of Adam Hoghton, of Hoghton Tower, in Lancashire, and whose son and heir,

Sir John Bradshaw, *m.* in the 10th of Edward I. the daughter and heir of Sir John Bromley, knt. of Bromley, in the county of Stafford, by whom he had three sons, viz.

- I. Thomas, (Sir) progenitor of the Bradshaws, of Bradshaw.
- II. William, (Sir) of whom presently.
- III. John, (Sir) who *m.* the daughter and heir of Langton, of Langton, but having no issue, settled his estate upon his elder brother,

The second son,

Sir William Bradshaw who is represented as a soldier and a traveller, assumed the Cross in the 8th of Edward II. and was absent from his lady ten years in the holy wars, which lady was Mabel, daughter and co-heir of Hugh Norris, Lord of Sutton, Raynhill, Whiston, Haigh, Blackrode, and Westleigh, six manors. Sir William possessed as "his property" Haigh and Blackrode, by a twelfth part of a knight's fee, as Hugh le Norris held the same, and as Mabel Bradshaigh, his wife held the same as heir of Hugh, for which they paid 2*s.* 8*d.* aid, *temp* Edward III. for making the King's eldest son a knight, as appears by the accounts of John Cockayne "*late* sheriff of that county. At that time Sir William made an alteration in the spelling of his name, changing the last syllable from shaw to shaigh," acquiring an addition of two martlets in his coat of arms, and a vine to his crest. During Sir William's protracted stay in Palestine, a report reached home that he had been slain, and on his return he found Mabel, his wife, acknowledging another lord, in the person of Sir Osmond Nevil, a Welch knight to whom she had been married. "Sir William returning," says an old writer, "came in a palmer's habit amongst the poor to Haigh, whom, as soon as his wife beheld, transported with the resembling idea of her former husband, fell a weeping, for which Sir Osmond gave her correction; Sir William thereupon withdrew, and made himself known to his tenants, and upon intelligence of the discovery, Sir Osmond fled towards Wales, but near to Newton Park, in Lancashire, Sir William overtook and slew him. Mabel was enjoyned by her confessor to do penance while she lived, by going once every week bare-footed, and bare-legged from Haigh to a cross near Wigan, which from that occasion is called Mab's Cross to this day. They now both lie buried in Wigan Church, under a fair stone tomb adorned with two prostrate figures the man in antique mail, cross-legged, unsheathing his sword, which hangs on his left side, and on his shoulder his shield, with two bends thereon; she is in a long robe, and veil'd, her hands elated, and conjoyned, in a praying posture; tho' they were formerly placed in a chapel on the south side of the chancel, belonging to the family, which chancel was in being in Mabel's time, as appears by ancient deeds. In the 13th of Edward II. Sir William, with John de Hornsby, were returned knights of the shire for the county of Lancaster, to serve in the Parliament then to be held at Westminster, having allowance of £7. 14*s.* for twenty-two days attendance; to Sir William, at the rate of 4*s.* per day, and John de Hornsby, 3*s.* Sir William served again for the said county, in the 2nd and 4th of Edward III. By Mabel, his wife, he had two sons,

- Richard, his heir.
- Thomas, who *m.* the daughter and heir of Sir John Twisden, of Twisden, in Kent, and founded the family of Bradshaigh, of Twisden.

The elder son and heir,

Richard Bradsheigh, esq. of Haigh, *m.* the daughter of Sir Robert Holcroft, knt. of Holcroft, in Cheshire, and was *s.* by his son,

Roger Bradsheigh, esq. of Heigh, who wedded in the 6th of Richard II. the daughter of John Osbaldston, esq. of Osbaldston, in Lancashire, and had a son and heir,

Sir Thomas Bradshaigh, knt. of Haigh, living in the 11th of Henry IV. who *m.* a daughter of Sir William Sherburne, of Stonyhurst, in Lancashire, and had, with a daughter, the wife of Sir John, St. John, of Bletso, a son and successor,

James Bradshaigh, Lord of Haigh, &c. in the 3rd of Henry VI. who wedded a daughter of Sir Robert Prescott, knt. and left a son and heir,

William Bradshaigh, living in the 1st of Richard III. and *s.* at his decease, by his son,

James Bradshaigh, esq. of Haigh, who died in the 20th of Henry VII. leaving three sons, Sir Roger and Sir Ralph, who both died without issue, and the continuator of the line,

William Bradshaigh, esq. who *m.* Maud, daughter of Sir Christopher Standish, knt. of Duxbury, in Lancashire, and had a son and heir,

Roger Bradshaigh, esq. of Haigh. This gentleman *m.* in 1567, Jane, daughter of Ralph Standish, of Standish in Lancashire, and had issue,

- James, his heir.
- Edward, surnamed the Deaf.
- Richard, serjeant at arms to Queen Elizabeth,
- Thomas, serjeant at arms to Queen Elizabeth and to *King* James I.
- Miles,
- John,
- Anne, *m.* to Richard Grosvenor, esq. of Eaton in the county of Chester.

* William Bradshaw, a younger son of this John Bradshaw, *m.* the daughter and heir of Bouler, of Bouler, in Gloucestershire, and settled there—whence the Bradshaws of Bouler, which line after four generations terminated in two daughters,

- Jane Bradshaw, who died a nun.
- Margaret Bradshaw, *m.* to Sir William Randolph, and conveyed to her husband the inheritance.

Mary, *m.* to Robert Berkenhead, esq. of Cheshire.
Ellen, *m.* to Ralph Houghton, esq. of Kirklees, in Cheshire.
Mabel, } *d.* young.
Alice, }

The eldest son and heir,

JAMES BRADSHAIGH, of Haigh, wedded first, Jane, only daughter and heir of Thomas Hoghton, esq. of Hoghton Tower, and in right of her grandmother, of Ashton under-Line,* by whom he had issue,

Roger, his heir.
John.
Jane, *m.* to Richard Emine, of London, merchant.
Catherine, *d. unm.*

He *m.* secondly, Dorothy, daughter of Robert Tatton, esq. of Wettenshaw, in the county of Chester, and by that lady had

William, who *d. s. p.*
Alexander, *m.* to Dorothy, daughter of William Jennings, esq. of Derbyshire.
Mabell, *m.* to Robert Goddard, esq. of Hargrave, in the county of Chester.
Maud, *d.* young.
Anne, *m.* to Richard Royle, esq. of Hargrave.

He (James) was *s.* at his decease by his eldest son,

ROGER BRADSHAIGH, esq. of Haigh, who *m.* Anne, daughter of Christopher Anderton, esq. of Lostock, in the county of Lancaster, and died in 1641, having had [illegible] sons and six daughters,

James, his heir, who acquired the reputation of a scholar and a poet. He had travelled over Europe, and was familiar with its languages and its letters. He died in the year 1631, before his father, leaving by Anne his wife, daughter of Sir William Norris, knt. of Speak, in the county of Lancaster,

Roger, (Sir) successor to his grandfather.
Eleanor, a nun at Graveline.
Anne, *m.* 1649, to Thomas Culcheth, esq. of Culcheth, in Lancashire.

Thomas, *d.* young.
Richard, an eminent scholar, living in Paris, in 1647.
Edward, likewise a scholar in France.
William, (Sir) who was knighted by King Charles I. for his good and faithful services, *m.* first, Dorothy, Lady Butler, but by her had no issue. Sir William wedded secondly, Margaret, daughter of Sir Francis Englefield, knt. of Berkshire, and relict of Hatton Berners, esq. of Whittlebury, in Northamptonshire, by whom he had a son,

William, who left by Troath, daughter of John Kennet, of Cockshaw, two daughters.

Thomas, student at Naples.
Roger, "who followed the wars."
Peter, living at St. Omers, in 1647.
Christopher, living at the same time in Italy.
Jane, *m.* to Nicholas Blundell, esq. of Crosby, in Lancashire, now represented by WILLIAM BLUNDELL, esq. of Crosby.
Dorothy, *m.* to Hamlet Massey, esq. of Rixton, in Lancashire.
Elizabeth, } nuns at Graveline.
Anne, }
Francis, *m.* to Edward Scarisbrick, esq. of Scarisbrick, in Lancashire.
Frances, a nun at Rouen.

Roger Bradshaigh was *s.* by his grandson,

I. SIR ROGER BRADSHAIGH, of Haigh, *b.* in 1627, and knighted in the 12th of CHARLES II. by which monarch he was created a BARONET 17th November, 1679. He *m.* in 1647, Elizabeth, daughter of William Pennington, esq. of Moncaster, in Cumberland, and had a son and daughter to survive, viz.

Roger, his successor.
Elizabeth, *m.* to Thomas Preston, esq. of Holker, in Lancashire, and had an only daughter,
CATHERINE PRESTON, heir of her father, who wedded Sir William Lowther, bart. of Marske.
(See BURKE'S *Commoners*, vol. i. p. 479.)

Sir Roger was the first of his family who embraced the Reformation, they had all previously been Catholics, and his conformation was attributable chiefly to his guardian, James, seventh Earl of Derby, under whom he had been educated. At the time, in the civil war, when that nobleman was beheaded at Bolton, Sir Roger fell into the hands of the Parliamentarians, and was consigned a prisoner to the castle of Chester, but nothing could induce him to swerve from his allegiance to his royal master. Doctor Wroe, in his "Memorials and Characters of eminent Persons, describes him as "remarkable for the chasteness of his conjugal love, the goodness of a father's care, and the sweetness of a master's rule. Plenty and welcome (continues the same authority) were never wanting at his table; no man entertained both acquaintance and strangers, with greater freedom and affability. His charity was extended to all who stood in need of it, and he had not only a cheerful heart, but a liberal hand; which I never knew contracted or shut up when any just occasion called to stretch it out; but I have often been a witness of his forward bounty, that he might provoke others by the example of his own cheerful liberality. For two things he is to be honoured: his religion to God, and his unshaken loyalty to his Prince. His religion was true Protestant, in which he was happily educated, and instructed in his greener years, by the care and direction of James, Earl of Derby, to whom he was entrusted by his faithful guardian, John Fleetwood, of Penwortham, esq. to whose religious designs, and the joint endeavours of his virtuous consort, he owed the early impressions of piety and in that family first commenced protestant, and was thence sent to the Isle of Man, where the principles he had already imbibed, were soon cultivated and improved under the umbrage of that religious, loyal, and great man. Next to his religion, his loyalty was most dear to him. In him both commenced together, and he gave early proofs of his loyalty, in an age wherein it was judged a crime; when rebellion looked gay with success, and sacrilege had providence to gild it over; yet even then, he judged not the cause by its success, but by the righteousness of it, and durst be honest spite of bad times. The king was well acquainted with his worth, and entrusted him with those offices, which witnessed the esteem he had both of his faithfulness and ability. His country judged him a true patriot, no less than a good subject, and therefore made choice of him for their representative in Parliament, in which station he served many years with great diligence and fidelity; and in the recesses of that public employ was not less serviceable to his country at home, than faithful to their interest abroad."

This eminent person, who had served in parliament the greater part of his life, either for the county of Lancaster, or Borough of Wigan, died at Chester, 31st March, 1684; was buried in the family vault at Wigan (where his widow erected a marble monument to his memory) and *s.* by his son,

* James Bradshaigh had a great contest about this lady's paternal estate, which he eventually lost, the decision being in favour of her uncle, Alexander Hoghton.

II. Sir Roger Bradshaigh, of Haigh, who had received the honour of knighthood from *King* Charles II. in the lifetime of his father. He *m.* 7th April, 1673, Mary, daughter and co-heir of Henry Murray, esq. gentleman of the bed chamber to *King* Charles I. by his wife, Anne, Viscountess Bayning, and had issue,

- Roger, his successor.
- Henry, a major in the army, and aid-de-camp to the Earl of Rivers, in Spain, afterwards M. P. for Wigan, *d.* in 1710, at Putney.
- James, *d.* young.
- William, captain in the army, *d.* in 1725, was buried in the chancel, the burial place of his family, in Wigan church.
- Richard, *d.* young.
- Thomas, in holy orders, rector of Stradford, in Suffolk, and Langham, Essex, *m.* Mary, daughter and sole heir of Robert Stephens, M. D. of Ardley-Week, in Essex, and had issue.
- Elizabeth, *m.* first to Job Yates, esq. and secondly, to Gabriel, Marquis Du Quesne.

Sir Roger was returned to parliament by the county palatine of Lancaster, in 1685, and dying 17th June, 1687, was *s.* by his eldest son,

III. Sir Roger Bradshaigh, of Haigh, who was returned to parliament by the borough of Wigan, in 1695, and continued to sit for that place full half a century. He was colonel of a regiment of foot, in the beginning of the reign of *Queen* Anne. Sir Roger wedded Rachel, second daughter of Sir John Guise, bart. of Ellmore, in Gloucestershire, and dying 25th February, 1746, left four sons and two daughters, viz.

- Roger, his heir.
- Charles.
- John.
- Richard.
- Elizabeth, *m.* to John Edwin, esq. son of Sir Humphrey Edwin.
- Rachel.

The eldest son,

IV. Sir Roger Bradshaigh, of Haigh, *m.* in April, 1731, Dorothy, daughter and co-heir of William Bellingham, esq. of Levens, in Westmoreland, but dying *s. p.* the Baronetcy became extinct.

Arms—Arg. two bendlets between three martlets sa.

BRAHAM, OF NEW WINDSOR.

Created 16th Apr. 1662. Extinct

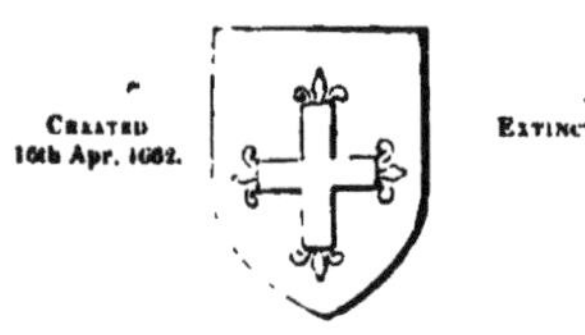

Lineage.

I. Sir Richard Braham, of New Windsor, in Berkshire, son of Richard Braham, esq. of Wandsworth, by Elizabeth, daughter of Nathaniel Giles, doctor of music, and great great-grandson of Sir John Braham, knt. of Braham Hall, Suffolk; was created a Baronet 16th April, 1662. He *m.* first, Susan, daughter of Sir George Southcott; secondly, Susan Michel, daughter of Sir Robert Gawsell, knt. of Watlington; and thirdly, Jane, daughter of Thomas Devenish, esq. of Langham, in Dorsetshire, but dying without surviving issue the Baronetcy became extinct.

Arms—Sa. a cross patonce, or.

BRAITHWAITE.

Created 18th Dec. 1802.—Extinct 9th March, 1809.

Lineage.

The family of Braithwaite has been for many years settled in the county of Westmoreland.

John Braithwaite, born in 1696, governor-in-chief of the African Company's factories on the south coast of Africa, was killed on board the Baltic merchantman in an engagement off Sicily with a Spanish privateer. He *m.* Silvia Cole, of Amsterdam, and had by her, who died in 1799, one son and two daughters, namely,

- John.
- Silvia, *m.* to Bonnel Thornton, esq. and was mother of the well known physician and botanist Robert John Thornton, M. D.
- Caroline, *m.* to Robert Armitage, esq.

The only son,

I. Sir John Braithwaite, *b.* in 1739, a major general in the army and commander-in-chief of the coast of Coromandel in 1793, was created a Baronet [illegible] December, 1802. He *m.* Elizabeth, daughter of [illegible] Brown, esq. by Elizabeth, his wife, daughter of Sir John Colleton, bart. and died in August, 1803, leaving a daughter, Silvia, wife of Charles Parkhurst, esq. and a son and successor,

II. Sir George-Charles Braithwaite, *b.* in [illegible] a colonel in the army, who *m.* in June, 1801, [illegible] Davis, illegitimate daughter of Sir Edward Boughton, bart. of Poston Court, in the county of Hereford, but dying *s. p.* 9th March, 1809, the Baronetcy became extinct.

BRERETON, OF HONFORD.

Created 10th Mar. 1627. Extinct 7th Jan. [illegible]

Lineage.

Sir Urian Brereton, ninth son of Sir R[illegible] Brereton, of Malpas Escheator, of Cheshire, and one of the grooms of the king's chamber 32 Henry VIII. died 19th March, 19 Elizabeth, leaving by Margaret, his first wife, daughter and sole heir of William Honford, of Honford, in Cheshire, and relict of Sir John Stanley, knt. several sons and two daughters, Jane *m.* to Edward Legh, esq. of Baggilegh, from whom she was divorced; and Sibilla, *m.* to Thomas Legh, esq. of Adlington. The second but eldest surviving son

William Brereton, esq. of Honford, *m.* in [illegible]

Katherine, daughter of Roger Hurleston, esq. of Chester, and dying 5th June, 1601, left, with a daughter, Dorothy, m. to Charles Wishes, esq. of Copgrove, in Yorkshire, a son and successor,

WILLIAM BRERETON, esq. of Honford or Hanford, who m. Margaret, daughter of Richard Holland, esq. of Denton, in Lancashire, and died 18th February, 1610, leaving a daughter, Margaret, wife of Richard Egerton, esq. of Ridley, and a son,

I. SIR WILLIAM BRERETON, of Honford. This distinguished soldier, incontestibly one of the greatest military characters which his country has produced, was in his sixth year at the period of his father's decease. His "notorious aversion for the government of the church," which Clarendon notices, was probably heightened in its effects on his political conduct by several casual circumstances: he was the friend and neighbour of Henry Bradshaw and Colonel Dukinfield, and son-in-law of Sir George Booth, who was considered the corner-stone of the Presbyterian interest in Cheshire. The best and greatest of his kinsmen, Sir William Brereton, of the Shocklach branch, had been sacrificed on the block but a few generations before to the fury of HENRY VIII., which would yet rankle in the breasts of his relatives; and many annoying circumstances attendant on the imposition of the ship money, which had brought him into active collision with the citizens of Chester, and a vexatious opposition by the municipal authorities of that place to his exemptions from tolls and murage in right of the lands of St. Mary's Nunnery, are supposed to have contributed towards making the severity with which he followed up the siege of that place, an act of premeditated vengeance.* In 1627, Mr. Brereton, shortly after he had attained majority, was raised to the degree of BARONET, and returned knight of the shire for Chester in the 3rd, 15th, and 16th of CHARLES I. At the outbreaking of the civil war, Sir William arrayed himself under the parliamentary banner, and received the appointment of commander-in-chief of the Cheshire forces. The scene of his action was, however, by no means limited to the palatine, and though the engagements in which he participated, were perhaps not the most distinguished in the history of the unhappy contentions of the era, still their influence and importance tended in no small degree to the final destruction of the royal cause. His early defence and final relief of Nantwich, and his reduction of Chester, deprived the cavaliers of their main point of shelter in the palatinate and the great centre for their exertions. By that fatal coincidence which generally attends civil contests, Sir William was opposed, both at Nantwich and Chester, to his near connexion, the gallant Lord Byron. After the termination of the war, he received a grant, subsequently to the death of Archbishop Laud, of the palace of Croydon, and there fixing his residence, he died a few months after the Restoration, 7th April, 1661. He m. first, Susan, daughter of Sir George Booth, bart. of Dunham, and had by her one son and three daughters, viz.

- THOMAS, his heir.
- Frances, m. to Edward, son and heir of Humble, Lord Ward.
- Susannah, m. to Edmund Lenthall, esq.
- Catherine, d. unm.

Sir William wedded, secondly, Cicely, daughter of Sir William Skeffington, bart. of Fisherwick, and relict of Edward Mitton, esq. of Weston, in Staffordshire, by whom he had two daughters,

- Cicely, m. to Edward Brabazon, younger son of the Earl of Meath.
- Mary.

The only son,

II. SIR THOMAS BRERETON, of Honford, b. in 1632, m. Theodosia, youngest daughter of Humble, Lord Ward, of Birmingham, but by her, who wedded, secondly, the Hon. Charles Brereton, had no issue. Sir Thomas d. 7th January, 1673, when the BARONETCY EXPIRED.

Arms—Arg. two bars sa. over all a cross formée fleury gu.

BRIDGEMAN, OF RIDLEY.

CREATED 13th Nov. 1673.

EXTINCT in Nov. or Dec. 1740.

Lineage.

This was a branch of the house of Bridgeman of Great Lever, in the county of Lancaster, now represented by the Earl of Bradford.

JOHN BRIDGEMAN, D.D. elected Bishop of Chester 15th March, 1618, m. Elizabeth, daughter of Dr. Helyar, canon of Exeter, and had five sons, viz.

- ORLANDO (Sir), his successor.
- Dove, in holy orders, prebendary of the cathedral church of Chester, m. Miss Bennet (who surviving him, m. secondly, Doctor Hacket, Bishop of Lichfield,) by whom he had an only son,
  - Charles, archdeacon of Richmond, in Yorkshire, d. unmarried in 1678.
- Henry, in holy orders, dean of Chester in 1660, consecrated Bishop of the Isle of Man in 1671, m. first, Catherine, daughter of Robert Lever, gent. of Lancashire, and had a daughter, the wife of Thomas Greenhalgh, esq. of Bundlesham, in the same county. His lordship wedded secondly, but the name of his wife is not known. He d. in May, 1682.
- James (Sir), m. Anne, daughter of Mr. Allen, of Cheshire, and had issue,
  - James, d. unmarried.
  - Frances, m. to William, Lord Howard of Escrick.
  - Magdalen, m. to William Wind, esq.
  - Anne.
- Richard, a merchant at Amsterdam, m. Catherine, daughter of Mr. Watson, a merchant of the same city, and had issue,
  - William, some time secretary of the Admiralty, and one of the clerks of the privy council, m. Diana, daughter of M. Vernatti, and had a son and daughter,
    - Orlando.
    - Catherine, m. her kinsman, Orlando, son of Sir John Bridgeman.
  - Elizabeth, m. to John Dove, esq. surveyor of the customs.

The Bishop of Chester, after filling the see for thirty years, d. at an advanced age in 1649. His eldest son,

SIR ORLANDO BRIDGEMAN, bart. an eminent lawyer, and lord chief baron of the Exchequer after the Restoration, m. first, Judith, daughter and heir of John

* Ormerod.

Kynaston, esq. of Morton, in Shropshire, and had a son, JOHN, his successor, from whom the EARLS OF BRADFORD. Sir Orlando wedded, secondly, Dorothy, daughter of Doctor Saunders, provost of Oriel College, Oxford, and widow of George Cradock, esq. of Carswell Castle, in Staffordshire, and by that lady had

ORLANDO, who purchased the estate of Ridley, in Cheshire, from the Egertons.

Francis (Sir), knighted by *King* CHARLES II. 15th November, 1673, *m.* Susanna, daughter and heir of Sir Richard Barker, of London, M.D. and *d.* issueless.

Charlotte, *m.* to Sir Thomas Myddleton, bart. of Chirk Castle, in Denbighshire.

The elder son of the second marriage,

I. ORLANDO BRIDGEMAN, esq. of Ridley, in the county of Chester, was created a BARONET by *King* CHARLES II. 12th November, 1673. He *m.* Mary, daughter of Sir Thomas Cave, bart. of Stamford, in the county of Northampton, and had issue,

ORLANDO, his successor.

Penelope, *m.* to Thomas Newport, Lord Torrington, (his second wife) and *d. s. p.*

Charlotte, *m.* to Richard Sims, esq. of Blackheath, (his second wife).

Sir Orlando was *s.* at his decease by his son,

II. SIR ORLANDO BRIDGEMAN, of Ridley, M.P. successively for Coventry (1705), for Calne, Lestwithiel, Blechingly, and Dunwich, auditor-general to the Prince of Wales, and eventually governor of Barbadoes. He *m.* Susanna, daughter of Sir Thomas Dashwood, bart. of Wickham, in Bucks, and had issue,

FRANCIS, *b.* in 1713.

Mary.

Sir Orlando was missing for some weeks in 1738, when at length his body was found in the Thames, in the June of that year. He was *s.* by his son,

III. SIR FRANCIS BRIDGEMAN, of Ridley, who went with Sir Charles Ogle to the West Indies, and died on board the fleet in November or December, 1740, unm. when the BARONETCY became EXTINCT.

Arms—Sa. ten plates, four, three, two and one: on a chief arg. a lion passant erm.

BRIGGES, OF HAUGHTON.

CREATED 12th Aug. 1641.

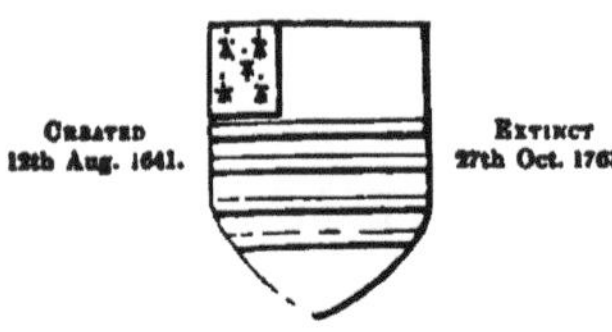

EXTINCT 27th Oct. 1767.

Lineage.

JOHN BRIGGES, of Saul, in the county of Norfolk, settled by deed, without date, but supposed to have been made in the time of EDWARD II. all his lands, tenements, and hereditaments, at Crastfont, in Westmoreland, upon his second son,

EDMUND BRIGGES, which estate descended lineally to the seventh inheritor,

OLIVER BRIGGES, esq. who having sold it in 1565, to William Knype, jun. of Carmellfell, in Lancashire, removed himself to Ernestry Park, near Ludlow, in Salop, in the beginning of *Queen* ELIZABETH's time, and in the seventh of the same reign purchased from GEORGE, Earl of Shrewsbury, the grant of the forest or free chase of Clees, or Clives, in that county, where he was then possessed of other good estates, as well as of lands in the shires of Warwick and Montgomery. He *d.* at an advanced age, in 1596, and was buried in Shiffnall church, Salop. The inscription on his tomb states that he *m.* Anne, daughter of Humphry Coningsby, esq. of Nemesoles, and that he was the son of Brian Brigges, of Crastfont, in Westmoreland, by Cecily, daughter and co-heir of Oliver Gilpin, of Yorkshire; which Brian was the son of Simon Brigges, by Catherine Bellingham, of the same county. Oliver Brigges by his wife had three sons, Humphry, Oliver, and Brian, who are mentioned on their father's tomb. The eldest,

HUMPHRY BRIGGES, esq. *s.* his father, and resided at Ernestry Park. He was high sheriff of the county in the year of the gunpowder plot, and *m.* Anne, eldest daughter and co-heir of Robert Moreton, esq. of Houghton. He was *s.* at his decease by his only surviving child,

I. MORETON BRIGGES, esq. of Haughton, in the county of Salop, who was created a BARONET by *King* CHARLES I. 12th August, 1641. He *m.* Crysogon, daughter of Edward Grey, esq. of Buildwas, in the same shire, by which lady, who lived in good health to the advanced age of ninety-seven, he had issue,

HUMPHREY, his successor.

Moreton, killed in the civil wars at Sturton Castle, in Staffordshire, on the side of the king, *d. s. p.*

Robert, *m.* Sarah, daughter of Thomas Moreton, esq. of Shiffnal, in Salop, and left an only child,

Martha, who wedded, first, Richard Spencer, esq. of London, a Turkey merchant, and secondly, Sir John Stonhouse, bart. of Radley, in Berks.

Priscilla, *m.* to Robert Dod, esq. of Petsey, in the county of Salop.

Anne, *m.* to Thomas Draper, esq. of Walton, also in Salop.

Elizabeth, *m.* to Edward Chapman, gent. of Greenwich.

Francis, *m.* to Ferrers Fowke, esq. of Brewood, in Staffordshire.

Martha, } both *d.* young.
Sarah, }

Sir Moreton was *s.* at his decease by his eldest son,

II. SIR HUMPHREY BRIGGES, knt. of Haughton. This gentleman *m.* no less than four wives; first, Elizabeth, daughter of Sir Philip Cary, knt. of Marylebone Park, in Middlesex, by whom he had two sons, Moreton and Edward, who both *d.* young. He wedded secondly, Elizabeth, youngest daughter of Sir Richard Wilbraham, bart. of Woodhey, in Cheshire, and by that lady had a son, HUMPHREY, his successor. His third wife was Anne, widow of Richard Moreton, esq. of Montgomeryshire, and the fourth, Magdalen, daughter of Sir John Corbet, bart. of Adderley. These ladies left no issue. He *d.* about the year 1691, and was *s.* by his only surviving son,

III. SIR HUMPHREY BRIGGES, of Haughton, who *m.* Barbara, daughter of Sir Wadham Wyndham, bart of Nonyngton, in Wilts, one of the judges of the court of king's bench, and had issue,

HUMPHREY, his heir.

HUGH, successor to his brother.

William.

Barbara, *m.* to the Rt. Rev. Edward Chandler, D.D. Bishop of Durham, and had issue.

Richard Chandler, solicitor of excise, and M.P. for Andover, who *m.* Elizabeth, daughter of Lord James Cavendish, and took the name of Cavendish, and *d. s. p.*

Wadham Chandler, vicar-general of the diocese of Durham, *d. s. p.*

Anne Chandler, *m.* to the Rev. Thomas Brotherton.

Catharine Chandler, *m.* to Wadham Wyndham, esq. of Eversley, Hants.

Barbara Chandler, *m.* first, to William, son of Lord James Cavendish, and secondly, to the Hon. John Fitzwilliam.

Elizabeth, *m.* to Leigh Brooke, esq. of Blacklands, Staffordshire, whose grandson,

THE REV. JOHN BROOKE, of Haughton, vicar of Shiffnal, *d.* in 1796, and devised his estates to his nephew, George Brooke Briggs Townshend, with an injunction to adopt the name of BROOKE only, and that gentleman is now possessor of Haughton. He *m.* Henrietta, daughter of William Massey, esq. of Moreton Hall, Cheshire, and had issue.

Anne, *d.* unm.

Frances, *m.* to the Rev. Dr. Chetham, of Derbyshire.

Magdalen, *d.* unm.

He *d.* in the forty-ninth year of his age, in 1699, and was *s.* by his eldest son,

IV. SIR HUMPHREY BRIGGES, of Haughton. This gentleman served in parliament for the county of Salop when the succession to the Crown was settled in the House of Hanover, and was member for Wenlock in the two parliaments of *King* GEORGE I. He *d.* unmarried 8th December, 1734, and was *s.* by his brother,

V. SIR HUGH BRIGGES, of Haughton, high sheriff of Salop in 1747, at whose decease unm. 27th October, 1767, the BARONETCY became EXTINCT,* the estates† passing to the descendants of his sisters. That of Haughton became the property of the family of BROOKE.

Arms—Gu. three bars gemels or, a canton sa.

BRIGHT, OF BADSWORTH.

CREATED 16th July, 1660.

EXTINCT 13th Sept. 1688.

Lineage.

THOMAS BRIGHT, of Bradway, in the parish of Norton, and of Carbrook, was father of

STEPHEN BRIGHT, esq. of Carbrook, lord of the manor of Ecclesall, baptized 27th December, 1563, *m.* first, Jane, sister of George Westbye, of Ravenfield, by whom he had,

JOHN (Sir), his heir.

Mary, *m.* to William Jessop, esq. of Broom Hall.

Ruth, *m.* to Edward Gill, esq. of Carhouse.

He wedded, secondly, Barbara, daughter of Ralph Hatfield, esq. and by her, who *m.* secondly, Thomas Westby, esq. of Ravenfield, had a daughter, Martha, the wife of William Lister, esq. of Thornton and Midhope. Stephen Bright *d.* 6th June, 1642, and was *s.* by his son,

I. SIR JOHN BRIGHT, of Carbrook, a very distinguished partisan of the parliament against CHARLES I. At the outbreaking of the civil war, we find him holding a captain's commission from Fairfax, actively exerting himself to raise forces to oppose the decisive measures adopted by the court, and in 1643, his name occurs as a commissioner for the West Riding for "sequestering the estates of notorious delinquents." In the military transactions which ensued, Capt. Bright took a prominent part, and was made colonel of a regiment of foot, for his gallant conduct in the attack which was made on the head quarters of the Earl of Newcastle, at Wakefield. Colonel Bright accompanied Sir Thomas Fairfax in his Cheshire expedition, and was with him till he joined the confederated armies before York. The battle of Marston Moor soon ensued, and its disastrous event proved fatal to the royal cause in the north. Several fortresses, garrisoned for the king, surrendered to the victorious army, and Colonel Bright was appointed governor of the castle of Sheffield. In 1644, he made a successful attack on a party of the king's forces under Sir William Cobb, and in the following year took Sir Charles Howard, of Naworth, prisoner. After an heroic struggle, the cause of royalty was now almost utterly defeated, and to the strife of arms negotiations succeeded. Colonel Bright continued to serve under Cromwell in Scotland, and at the second siege of Pontefract Castle, which the royalists had recovered by an ingenious but desperate stratagem. In 1650 he accompanied the army marching into Scotland, but threw up his commission in disgust, having solicited a fortnight's leave of absence, and been refused. During the commonwealth, Colonel Bright was successively governor of York and Hull, and one of the six representatives in parliament for the West Riding. He served the office of high sheriff for two years, 1654 and 1655. The measures for bringing about the restoration he appears to have supported, and so soon as the July following that great event, he was created a BARONET. He *m.* first, Catherine, daughter of Sir Richard Hawksworth, knt. of Hawksworth, and relict of William Lister, esq. of Thornton, who was slain at Tadcaster, in 1642. By this lady he had one son and one daughter,

JOHN, *b.* in 1660, *m.* the Lady Lucy Montague, daughter of Edward, Earl of Manchester, but predeceased his father, without issue.

CATHERINE, who *m.* Sir Henry Liddell, bart. of Ravensworth Castle, and dying 24th February, 1703, left issue,

1. THOMAS LIDDELL, who *d.* before his father in 1715, leaving by Jane, his wife, daughter of James Clavering, esq. of Greencroft, two sons,

HENRY, created BARON RAVENSWORTH, of Ravensworth Castle, in 1747, *m.* Anne, only daughter of Sir Peter Delme, and left an only daughter and heiress,

ANNE, *m.* first, to Augustus Henry, Duke of Grafton, and secondly, to the Earl of Upper Ossory.

* The baronetcy is said to have devolved on a younger branch of the family, and Sir John Briggs, bart. described as of Monmouthshire, was plaintiff in a cause tried at Hereford in 1795.

† In the year 1800 an act of parliament was obtained for a more regular partition of the Brigges' estate, which had then centred in three parties, George Brooke, esq. the Rev. Richard Huntley, of Boxwell, and Richard, Viscount Fitzwilliam. The last bequeathed his portion to George Augustus, Earl of Pembroke, with remainder to his second son, the Hon. Sydney Herbert.

Thomas, who m. Margaret, daughter of Sir William Bowes, knt. of Gibside, and was grandfather of

HENRY LIDDELL, present LORD RAVENSWORTH.

2. JOHN LIDDELL, who assumed, upon inheriting Badsworth and the principal portion of his grandfather's estates, the surname and arms of BRIGHT. He d. 6th October, 1737, leaving by Cordelia Clutterbuck, his wife, a daughter, Cordelia, m. to Clifton Wintringham, M.D. of York, and a son,

THOMAS BRIGHT, esq. of Badsworth, lord of the manor of Ecclesall, who m. Margaret, daughter and heir of William Norton, esq. of Sawley, by Margaret, his wife, sister and co-heir of John Lowther, esq. of Ackworth. By her, who m. secondly, in 1748, Sir John Ramsden, bart. Mr. Bright left an only daughter and heir,

MARY, m. in 1752, to Charles, Marquis of Rockingham, and d. without issue. The Badsworth and other estates of the Bright family passed to the Earl of Fitzwilliam.

3. HENRY LIDDELL, who had Carbrook settled on him. He d. s. p. and left that estate to his wife, Anne Liddell. This lady was the daughter of John Clavering, esq. of Chopwell, in Durham, by Susan, his wife, sister of Edward Thompson, esq. of Marston.

1. Elizabeth Liddell, m. to Robert Ellison, esq. of Hepburn, in Durham.

Colonel Bright m. secondly, Elizabeth, daughter of Sir Thomas Norcliffe, knt. of Langton, by whom he had an only child, who d. young; thirdly, Frances, daughter of Sir Thomas Liddell, bart. of Ravensworth Castle, and relict of Thomas Vane, esq. of Raby; and fourthly, Susanna, daughter of Michael Wharton, esq. of Beverley. The last survived her husband, and wedded, secondly, Sir John Newton, bart. of Bars Court, near Bath. Colonel Bright d. at Badsworth, 13th September, 1688, and leaving no surviving male issue, the BARONETCY became EXTINCT. His estates devolved on the LIDDELL family.

Arms—Party per pale az. and gu. a bend or, between two mullets arg.

BROGRAVE, OF HAMELLS.

Lineage.

WILLIAM BROGRAVE, esq. lord of the manor of Kelseys, in Beckenham, Kent, in 1479, descended from Sir Roger Brograve, of Warwickshire, living *temp.* EDWARD I. married Elizabeth, daughter of John Alphew, of Bear Place, and had issue,

I. JOHN, who m. Anne, daughter of Sir John Fogge, knt. and was father of William Brograve, of Mepenham, in Northamptonshire.

II. Robert, who m. Catherine Leventhorpe, and had two daughters, Margaret, m. to Robert Bridges; and Anne, to Thomas Hammond, of Ratwell.

III. Edward.

IV. Richard.

V. NICHOLAS.

The fifth son,

NICHOLAS BROGRAVE, esq. of Kelseys, in Kent, left issue,

RICHARD BROGRAVE, esq. whose son,

SIR JOHN BROGRAVE, of Gray's Inn, barrister-at-law, attorney-general to the duchy of Lancaster, and custos rotulorum of the county of Hertford, received the honour of knighthood from *Queen* ELIZABETH, and purchased from the Earl of Suffolk the manor of Hamells, in the latter shire. He m. Margaret, daughter of Simeon Steward, esq. of Lackenheath, in Suffolk, and had issue,

SIMEON, his heir.

John, barrister-at-law, *d. s. p.*

Charles, died young.

Joan, m. to Sir John Leventhorpe, bart. of Shingey Hall.

Bridget, m. to Sir Thomas Mead, of Lofts, in Essex.

Sir John d. 11th September, 1613, and was s. by his son,

SIMEON BROGRAVE, esq. of Hamells, who m. Dorothy, sister and co-heir of Thomas Leventhorpe, esq. of Albury, and had, with other issue, who died unmarried,

JOHN, his heir.

Edward, who m. Alice Burges, of Norfolk, an heiress, and had a numerous family. His youngest daughter, Joan, m. William Minors, rector of Digswell.

Dorothy, m. to Thomas Wright, esq. of Kilverstone, in Norfolk, but had no issue.

Bridget, m. to Humphrey Steward, esq. of Broughing.

Jane, m. to Charles Nodes, esq. of Shephall.

He d. 21st January, 1638-9, and was s. by his son,

JOHN BROGRAVE, esq. of Hamells, baptized 26th April, 1597, who m. Hannah, daughter of Sir Thomas Barnardiston, knt. of Ketton, in Suffolk, and had, with other children, who died unmarried, two daughters, Anne, m. to Philip Twisleton, esq.; and Jane, m. to the Rev. Dr. Fuller; and a son, his successor in 1670-1,

I. SIR THOMAS BROGRAVE, of Hamells, who served as sheriff of the county in 1660, and was created a BARONET 18th March, 1662-3. He m. Grace, daughter of Sir John Hewyt, bart. of Waresley, in Huntingdonshire, and dying in 1670, left, with two daughters, Jemima and Honora, two sons, successive baronets. The elder,

II. SIR JOHN BROGRAVE, of Hamells, baptized 31st March, 1664, died without issue in July, 1691, and was s. by his brother,

III. SIR THOMAS BROGRAVE, of Hamells, baptized 2nd March, 1670, who m. Elizabeth, daughter of William, Lord Maynard, but dying s. p. 6th June, 1707, the title became EXTINCT. The manor and estate of Hamells was afterwards sold by a decree of the Court of Chancery, and purchased by Ralph Freeman, esq. of Aspeden, by whose descendant, Katharine Freeman, it was conveyed to her husband, the Hon. Charles Yorke, whose son, Philip, third Earl of Hardwicke, sold Hamells to John Mellish, esq.

Arms—Arg. three lions passant, guardant in pale gu.

BROKE, OF NACTON.

CREATED 21st May, 1661. EXTINCT 25th Feb. 1693.

Lineage.

This family, one of importance for a long series of years, traces an uninterrupted male descent from ADAM, Lord of Leighton, in Cheshire, at the close of the twelfth century. The lineal descendant and representative of Adam,*

THOMAS BROKE, of Leighton, living in 1400, m. Agnes Venables, and had a son and successor,

THOMAS BROKE, of Leighton, who m. the daughter and heiress of John Parker, of Copen Hall, and had five sons, namely,

- I. JOHN, of Leighton, ancestor of the Brokes of Leighton; Norton (now represented by SIR RICHARD BROOKE, bart. of Norton Priory), and of Mere (whose present chief is PETER LANGFORD BROOKE, esq. of Mere, in Cheshire).
- II. Ralph, of Nantwich, governor of Calais, ancestor of the Brokes of Nantwich.
- III. Robert.
- IV. RICHARD, of whom presently.
- V. Henry, principal clerk to the board of green cloth.

The fourth son,

SIR RICHARD BROKE, knt. chief baron of the exchequer *temp.* HENRY VIII. erected the present mansion of Broke Hall, near Ipswich. He was father of

ROBERT BROKE, esq. of Nacton, in Suffolk, who m. Elizabeth, daughter and heiress of — Holgrave, of Sussex, and was s. by his son,

RICHARD BROKE, esq. of Nacton, who m. Elizabeth, daughter of Sir John Jermy, knt. of Brightwell, in Suffolk, and left a son and successor,

ROBERT BROKE, esq. of Nacton, who m. Elizabeth, daughter of William Waters, esq. of Wimbledon, in Surrey, and dying in 1608, was s. by his son,

SIR RICHARD BROKE, knt. of Nacton, who m. Maria, daughter of Sir John Packington, knt. of Hampton Lovett, in the county of Worcester, and had three sons, viz.

ROBERT, his heir.
Richard.
William, of Dartford, in Kent, whose son,
ROBERT, eventually inherited Nacton, and was ancestor of the present
SIR PHILIP BOWES VERE BROKE, bart. K.C.B. of Broke Hall, Suffolk, a highly distinguished naval officer. (See BURKE'S *Peerage and Baronetage.*)

Sir Richard *d.* in 1639, and was *s.* by his eldest son,

I. SIR ROBERT BROKE, of Nacton, who was created a BARONET 21st May, 1661. He m. Anne, daughter of Sir Lionel Talmash, bart. of Bentley, in Suffolk, and had three daughters, his co-heirs, viz.

ELIZABETH, m. to Edward Kynaston, esq. of the county of Salop.
MARY, m. to Thomas Walgrave, esq. of Smallbridge, in Kent.
ANNE, m. to ROBERT BROKE, esq. of Nacton.

Sir Robert *d.* 25th February, 1693, when the BARONETCY EXPIRED, and the estates devolved on his nephew and son-in-law, ROBERT BROKE, esq. the ancestor of the present SIR P. B. V. BROKE, bart.

Arms—Or, a cross eng. party per pale gu. and sa.

BROMFIELD, OF SOUTHWARK.

CREATED 20th Mar. 1660. EXTINCT 6th Sept. 1733.

Lineage.

This family claimed ancient Welch descent, its ancestor being, as alleged, LLEWELLYN AUR DORCHOCK, *Lord of Yale*, from whose descendant, GRIFFITH, *of Bromfield*, ap Cadwygan, proceeded

THOMAS BROMFIELD, of Odomer, in Sussex, father of

SIR EDWARD BROMFIELD, knt. sheriff of London in 1626, and lord mayor in 1636, who m. first, Joyce, daughter of Sir William Austin, of Clevers Hall, Essex, and by her had one son, EDWARD. He m. secondly, Elizabeth, daughter and co-heir of William Mitchelborne, of Westmaston, Sussex, and by that lady had Charles, George, Elizabeth, and Margaret. He wedded, thirdly, Anne, daughter of Christopher Woodward, of Lambeth, in Surrey, and by her had another son,

I. JOHN BROMFIELD, esq. of Southwark, who was created a BARONET by *King* CHARLES II. 20th March, 1660. This gentleman married and had issue,

EDWARD, his successor.
Charles, father of
CHARLES, who *s.* his uncle.

---

* The intervening descent was as follows:

Adam, Lord of Leighton, in Cheshire.
|
William del Broke.
|
William Broke, of Leighton, A.D. 1249.
|
Richard del Broke de Leighton, 1280-1299.
|
John del Broke, *d. vita patris.*
|
Thomas del Broke, of Leighton, m. Felicia, daughter of R. Crowmarsh, 1283-1316.
|
Richard del Broke, 1316-1332-1333.
|
Nicholas de la Broke, of Leighton, 1362.
|
Ralph de la Broke, of Leighton, 1374.
|
Roger de la Broke, of Leighton, 1404.
|
John Broke, *d. vita patris.*
|
Thomas Broke, of Leighton, 1400.

George, } *d. s. p.*
John, }

Sir John was *s.* by his eldest son,

II. Sir Edward Bromfield, who *d.* suddenly without issue male (his only daughter, Joyce, *m.* Thomas Lant, esq.), 17th February, 1703, and was *s.* in the baronetcy by his nephew,

III. Sir Charles Bromfield, who *m.* Theodosia daughter of John Steele, esq. of Orton on the Hill, in the county of Leicester, and sister and co-heir of Samuel Steele, esq. of the same place, but at his decease the Baronetcy expired.

Arms—Az. a lion passant, guardant, or.

BROOKES, OF YORK.

Created 13th June, 1676.

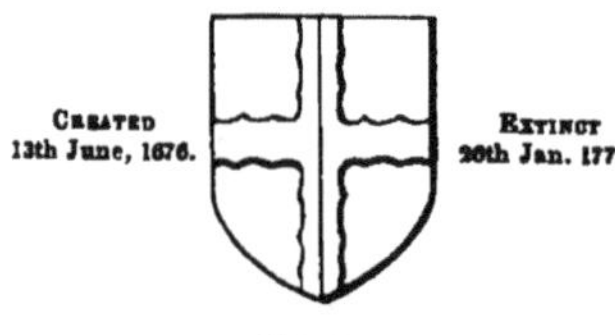

Extinct 26th Jan. 1770.

Lineage.

Alderman James Brookes, or Brooke, fined for sheriff of the city of London, and afterwards settled at York, in which county, as well as in Nottinghamshire, he acquired a considerable estate. He *m.* and had, with a daughter, Anne, *m.* to Sir William Wyvil, bart. of Constable Burton, in Yorkshire, a son and successor,

I. Sir John Brookes, of York, who was created a Baronet in 1676. He *m.* Mary, daughter of Sir Hardress Waller, knt. by Elizabeth, his wife, second daughter and co-heir of Sir John Dowdall, and had issue,

- James, his heir.
- John, of Breade, in Sussex, who *m.* first, Damaris Mulbank, and, secondly, Mrs. Mary Lulham, by the former of whom he had a daughter, Honora, Gatland.
- Thomas, a merchant in London.
- Henry.
- Elizabeth, *m.* to William Bethel, esq. of Swinden, in Yorkshire.
- Priscilla, *m.* to Rowland Place, esq. of Dinsdale, in Durham.
- Mary, *m.* to Alderman Proctor, of Newcastle on Tyne.
- Jane, *m.* to William Pigot, esq.
- Anne, who *d.* unmarried.
- Honoretta, *m.* to John Pratt, esq. of Dublin, by whom she had a daughter, Mary Pratt, *m.* to Sir George Savile, bart. of Thornhill.

Sir John *d.* in November, 1691, and was *s.* by his son,

II. Sir James Brookes, of York, who *m.* Bridget, daughter of Mr. Wright, of Hammersmith, in Middlesex, and was *s.* at his decease in March, 1735, aged sixty-seven, by his son,

III. Sir Job Brookes, of York, who *d.* unm. 26th January, 1770, a lunatic, when the title became extinct.

Arms—Or, a cross eng. per pale gu. and sa.

BROWN, OF DEPTFORD.

Created 1st Sept. 1649.—Extinct 12th Feb. 1683.

Lineage.

I. Sir Richard Brown, of Deptford, in Kent, some time resident at the court of France, and one of the clerks of the Privy Council, who was created a Baronet in 1649, *m.* Elizabeth, daughter of Sir John Prettyman, knt. of Dryfield, in Gloucestershire, but leaving no male issue at his decease, 12th Feb. 1683, the title expired.

BROWN, OF EDINBURGH.

Created 24th Feb. 1709.—Extinct (date unknown).

Lineage.

I. Sir Robert Brown, of Edinburgh, Lord Provost of Edinburgh, was created a Baronet in 1709, but of the honour nothing further is known.

BROWN, OF LONDON.

Created 22d July, 1699.—Extinct (date unknown).

Lineage.

I. William Brown, esq. of a Scottish family, acquired a large fortune as a merchant, residing in Dantzic, trading with London, and was created a Baronet, 14th Dec. 1699, in which dignity he was *s.* by his son,

II. Sir John Brown, who lived in Pall Mall, and had a seat on Kew Green, which was purchased from him by Caroline, Queen Consort of *King* George II. He had two wives, and left by the first a son and successor,

III. Sir — Brown, who lived and died in Poland, and of the family there are no further details, but there can be little doubt of the extinction of the Baronetcy.

BROWN, OF WESTMINSTER.

Created 11th Mar. 1731-2.

Extinct 20th Oct. [illegible]

Lineage.

I. Sir Robert Brown, a merchant at Venice, and some time his Majesty's resident there, was created a Baronet in 1731-2, with remainder, in default of male issue, to his brothers, Colonel James Brown, and Edward Brown. He *m.* Margaret, sister of Dr. Charles Cecil, bishop of Bangor, and had by her, who *d.* 1[illegible] February, 1782, two daughters, who *d.* unm. Sir Robert *d.* 5th October, 1760, and was *s.* by his nephew (the son of Colonel James Brown)

II. Sir James Brown, who *d.* 29th April, 1784, leaving a son and heir,

III. Sir William Augustus Brown, lieutenant 91st regiment, who *d.* issueless 20th Oct. 1830, aged sixty-six, having been many years insane. With him the Baronetcy expired.

Arms—Gu. a chev. erminois, between three fleurs de lys or.

BROWNE, OF BEECHWORTH.

Created 7th July, 1627.  Extinct 3rd Nov. 1690.

Lineage.

Sir Anthony Browne, created a knight of the Bath at the coronation of Richard II. married, and had two sons, Sir Richard, his heir, and Sir Stephen, lord mayor of London in 1439. The elder

Sir Robert Browne, living *temp.* Henry V. was father of

Sir Thomas Browne, treasurer of the household to Henry VI. and sheriff of Kent in 1444 and 1460. He *m.* Eleanor, daughter and sole heir of Sir Thomas Fitz-Alan, of Beechworth Castle, brother of John, Earl of Arundel, and had issue,

I. George (Sir), his heir.

II. William, whose son removed to Tavistock. This line is extinct.

III. Robert (Sir), knt. *m.* Mary, daughter of Sir William Mallet, knt., and had an only daughter and heiress, Eleanor, wife, first, of Sir Thomas Fogge, and secondly, of Sir William Kempe.

IV. Anthony (Sir), standard-bearer of England, esquire of the body, governor of Queenboro' Castle, and constable of the castle of Calais. From this eminent person derive the Lords Montagu, the heiress of which distinguished family, the Hon. Elizabeth Mary Brown, wedded William Stephen Poyntz, esq. M.P. (See Burke's *Extinct Peerage* and *Commoners.*)

I. Catherine, *m.* to Humphry Sackville, of Buckhurst.

Sir Thomas was *s.* by his eldest son,

Sir George Browne, knt. of Beechworth Castle, sheriff of Kent in 1481, who espousing the cause of the Earl of Richmond, was included in the proclamation for apprehending the Duke of Buckingham and his associates, and being soon after taken, suffered decapitation in London *anno* 1483. He *m.* Elizabeth, daughter of Sir William Paston, and widow of Richard Lord Poynings, and was *s.* by his son,

Sir Matthew Browne, knt., of Beechworth Castle, sheriff of Surrey in 1496, living in 1520, who *m.* Fridiswide, daughter of Sir Richard Guilford, K. G. of Hempsted, in Kent, and had issue,

Henry, who predeceased his father, leaving, by Catherine, his second wife, daughter of Sir William Shelley, of Michelgrove, a son,

Thomas, successor to his grandfather.

Jane, *m.* to Sir Edward Bray.

Catherine, *m.* to John Poyntz, esq. of Alderley, sheriff of Surrey 14th and 20th Elizabeth, and from this marriage lineally descends the present William Stephen Poyntz, esq. M.P. of Cowdray. (See Burke's *Commoners*, vol. iii.)

Sir Matthew was *s.* by his grandson,

Sir Thomas Browne, knt.* of Beechworth Castle, who *m.* Mabell, daughter and heir of Sir William Fitz-Williams, and had, with two daughters, Elizabeth, the wife of Robert Honywood, of Kent, and Jane, of Sir Oliff Leigh, of Addington, in Surrey, a son and successor,

Sir Matthew Browne, of Beechworth Castle, who *m.* Jane, daughter of Sir Thomas Vincent, of Stoke Dabernon, and dying in the 1st of James I. was *s.* by his son,

I. Sir Ambrose Browne, of Beechworth Castle, created a Baronet in 1727, who *m.* Elizabeth, daughter of William Adam, esq. of Saffron Waldon, and *d.* in 1661, leaving issue, two sons, Adam, his heir; and Ambrose, who predeceased his father unmarried, with two daughters, the elder *m.* to John Browne, esq. of Buckland, and the younger to — Jevon, esq. The surviving son,

II. Sir Adam Browne, of Beechworth, M.P. for Surrey, married Philippa, daughter of Sir John Cooper, bart. of Winbourn St. Giles, in Dorsetshire, and *d.* 3rd November, 1690, having had one son, Ambrose, who predeceased him unmarried in 1688, and an only daughter and heiress,

Margaret Browne, of Beechworth, who *m.* in 1691, William Fenwick, esq. high sheriff of Surrey in 1705, and died issueless in 1726. Shortly after her decease, the estate of Beechworth was sold to Abraham Tucker, esq. and eventually descended to Sir Henry Paulet St. John Mildmay, who, in 1798, disposed of the mansion, manor, &c. to Henry Peters, esq. At the death of Mrs. Fenwick the representation of the family is stated to have devolved on the descendants of Catharine Browne, who wedded John Poyntz, esq.

Arms—Sa. three lions passant in bend between two double cotises, arg.

BROWNE, OF CAVERSHAM.

Created 10th May, 1665.—Extinct in 1774.

Lineage.

Sir George Browne, of Wickham, in Kent, eldest son of the first Lord Montague, by Magdalen, his second wife, daughter of William Lord Dacre, of Gillesland, *m.* first, Eleanor, daughter and co-heir of Anthony Bridges, esq. of Shefford, in Berkshire, by whom he had no issue; and secondly, Mary, daughter of Sir Robert Terwhit, of Kettleby, in Lincolnshire, by whom he had one son and four daughters, viz.

George, his heir.

Mary, *m.* to Thomas Paston, esq. of Norfolk.

Jane, Elizabeth, Frances, } who all died unmarried.

The only son,

George Browne, esq. of Caversham, Oxfordshire, *m.* Elizabeth, second daughter of Sir Richard Blount, knt., of Maple Durham, and had nineteen children; three of the sons fell in the service of Charles I.

* He *m.* secondly, Helen Harding, and was father, by her, of Richard Browne, esq. of Shingleton, in Kent.

Of the daughters several died in infancy, three were nuns, and one *m.* a gentleman named Yates, of Berkshire. The only sons who married were,

GEORGE, (Sir) K. B. at the coronation of CHARLES II. He *m.* Elizabeth, daughter of Sir Francis Englefield, of Englefield, in the county of Berks, and left at his decease two daughters, his co-heirs, viz.

Winifrid, *m.* to Basil Brooke, esq. of Madeley, in Shropshire.

Eleanor, *m.* to Henry Fermor, esq. of Tusmore, in Oxfordshire.

JOHN, of whom presently.

The younger son,

I. JOHN BROWNE, esq., of Caversham, was created a BARONET, 10th May, 1665. He *m.* Mrs. Bradley, and had issue,

ANTHONY, } successive Baronets.
JOHN, }
GEORGE, }

Catherine, *m.* to Fortescue, of Cookhill, in Worcestershire.

Elizabeth, *m.* to — Morley, esq.

Magdalene, *d.* unmarried.

The eldest son,

II. SIR ANTHONY BROWNE, dying unm., was *s.* by his brother,

III. SIR JOHN BROWNE, who also died unm. and was *s.* by his brother,

IV. SIR JOHN BROWNE, who *m.* first, Gertrude Morley, esq. and left three sons,

JOHN, his heir.

Anthony, a military officer.

James, in the Empress's service.

Sir George wedded, secondly, Mary, sister of Sir George Thorold, bart., of Harmston, in Lincolnshire, by whom he had no issue. Sir George died 20th Feb. 1729-30, and was *s.* by his son,

V. SIR JOHN BROWNE, who *d. s. p.* in 1774, when the title became EXTINCT.

Arms—As BROWNE, OF BEECHWORTH.

BROWNE, OF KIDDINGTON.

CREATED 1st July, 1659.—EXTINCT 20th June, 1754.

Lineage.

This was a branch of the ennobled house of Brown, VISCOUNTS MONTAGUE.

SIR ANTHONY BROWNE, made knight of the bath at the coronation of *King* RICHARD II. left two sons,

ROBERT (Sir), his heir.

Stephen (Sir), lord mayor of London in 1439, 17 HENRY VI. During the mayoralty of Sir Stephen, a great scarcity of wheat occurring, he imported large cargoes of rye from Prussia, and distributed them amongst the poorer classes of people.

The elder son,

SIR ROBERT BROWNE, was father of

SIR THOMAS BROWNE, knt. who was treasurer of the household to *King* HENRY VI. and in the thirty-sixth year of that monarch, was in commission with others, to meet at the city of Rochester on the 29th of August, to summon persons and enquire upon oath into a certain disturbance that happened at sea, between Richard, Earl of Warwick, and his retinue, and certain persons of Lubyc, who were under a league of friendship with the king. Sir Thomas *m.* Eleanor, daughter and co-heir of Sir Thomas Fitz-Alan, and niece of John, Earl of Arundel, by which marriage he acquir the castle of Beechworth, in Surrey, and had issue,

GEORGE (Sir), of Beechworth Castle, from whe the baronets of Beechworth.

William, *d. s. p.*

ANTHONY.

Robert (Sir), *m.* Mary, daughter of Sir Willia Mallet, knt. and left an only daughter and hei

Eleanor, who wedded, first, Thomas Fog esq. and secondly, William Kempe, esq. Olantye, in Kent.

Catherine, *m.* to Humphrey Sackvile, esq. Buckhurst, in Surrey.

The third son,

SIR ANTHONY BROWNE, was appointed in the fir year of *King* HENRY VII. standard-bearer for th whole realm of England and elsewhere; and the nex year, being then one of the esquires of the king's body was constituted governor of Queenborough Castle, i Kent, in which year, being in the battle of Newark upo Trent, 16th June, when John de la Pole, Earl Lincoln, and the pretender, Lambert Simnell, su tained a signal defeat, he was knighted for his valia behaviour. In the eighteenth of the same reign, bein constable of the castle of Calais, he and Sir Richa Nansan, deputy-lieutenant of Calais, were commi sioned, in consideration of "their loyalty, industry foresight, and care," to receive the sum of 25,00 franks in gold, due 1st November, 1502, being an an nual payment from the French king, according agreement concluded 3rd November, 1492; and agai in two years afterwards he was commissioned to re ceive the same payment. His last will and testamen is dated at Calais, 25th September, 1505, and wa proved 19th November, 1506, wherein, being writte Sir Anthony Browne, knt. lieutenant of the castle Calais, he orders his body to be buried in the resu rection church, in St. Nicholas's Chapel, by his wif and bequeathes to every brotherhood within the sai church ten shillings, and to the lord prior of Chri Church, Canterbury, a standing cup of silver gilt; also two others, to Sir Edward Poyning and Sir Hug Conway, whom he constitutes overseers of his wil and Lucy, his wife, executrix, which Lucy was one the daughters and co-heirs of John Nevil, MARQUE OF MONTAGU, and widow of Sir Thomas Fitzwilliam of Aldwarke, in the county of York. By her he lef with two daughters, Elizabeth, the wife of Hen Somerset, Earl of Worcester, and Lucy, of Sir Thoma Clifford, knt. an only son, his successor,

SIR ANTHONY BROWNE, who was with the Earl Surry, lord high admiral, at Southampton, in the fou teenth HENRY VIII. when he conveyed the Empero from that port to Biscay; and after landing at Mo leis, in Brittany, was knighted for his valour in th assault and winning of that town. He *m.* Alice daughter of Sir John Gage, K.G. and had issue,

ANTHONY, his heir.

William, *m.* Anne, daughter and co-heir of Hug Hastings, esq. and thereby acquired Elsing, Norfolk, where his descendants have been seated

Henry.

Francis.

Mary, *m.* to John, second son of Thomas Grey Marquess of Dorset.

Mabel, *m.* to Gerard, Earl of Kildare.

Lucy, *m.* to Thomas Roper, esq. of Eltham, Kent.

He *d.* 6th May, 1546, and was *s.* by his eldest son,

SIR ANTHONY BROWNE, who was one of the forty knights made at the coronation of *King* EDWARD VI and was advanced to the peerage, as VISCOUNT MON TAGU, 2nd September, 1554, in which year he wa master of the horse to *Queen* MARY, and was subse quently a knight of the garter. His lordship, with Thomas Thurlby, Bishop of Ely, was deputed by parliament to the pope, to reconcile the realm to the holy see, and to make a tender of renewed allegiance, and after the accession of ELIZABETH, in whose privy council his name was omitted, he had the courage and consistency, with the Earl of Shrewsbury alone, to vote against the abolition of the papal ascendancy. He was afterwards, nevertheless, accredited ambassador to the court of Spain, by *Queen* ELIZABETH. Lord Montagu *m.* first, Jane, daughter of Robert Ratcliffe, Earl of Sussex, and by her ladyship had issue,

ANTHONY, who *d.* in the lifetime of the Viscount, 29th June, 1592, leaving by his wife, Mary, daughter of Sir William Dormer, knt.

ANTHONY, second Viscount.

John, *m.* Anne, daughter of — Gifford, esq. and had a son,

Stanislaus, whose grandson, MARK ANTHONY BROWNE, inherited as ninth VISCOUNT MONTAGU. (See BURKE's *Extinct Peerage.*)

Dorothy, *m.* to Edward Lee, esq. of Stanton Barry, Bucks.

Jane, *m.* to Sir George Englefield, bart.

Catherine, *m.* to — Treganian, esq.

Mary, *m.* first, to Henry Wriothesley, Earl of Southampton, secondly, to Sir Thomas Heneage, knt. and thirdly, to Sir William Hervey, bart. created Baron Hervey, of Ross, in the county of Wexford, in the peerage of Ireland, and Baron Hervey, of Kidbrook, in the county of Kent, in that of England.

His lordship wedded, secondly, Magdalen, daughter of William, Lord Dacre, of Gillesland, and by her had

George (Sir), of Wickham-Breus, in the county of Kent, *m.* Mary, daughter of Sir Robert Tyrwhitt, knt. of Ketilby, in Lincolnshire, and had issue. He was ancestor of the BROWNES, of Caversham.

Thomas, *d. unm.*

HENRY (Sir), of whom presently.

Anthony (Sir), of Effingham, who *m.* Anne, daughter of — Bell, esq. of Norfolk.

Elizabeth, *m.* to Sir Robert Dormer, afterwards Lord Dormer.

Mabel, *m.* to Sir Hugh Capel.

Jane, *m.* to Sir Francis Lacon, of Willey, in the county of Salop.

The Viscount, who sate on the trial of MARY, *Queen of Scots*, *d.* 19th October, 1592. The third son of his lordship's second marriage,

SIR HENRY BROWNE, knt. who was seated at Kiddington, in the county of Oxford, *m.* first, Anne, daughter of Sir William Catesby, knt. of Ashby Legers, and by that lady had two daughters, both nuns at Graveline. He wedded, secondly, Mary, daughter of Sir Philip Hungate, bart. of Saxton, in the county of York, by which lady he had a son,

SIR PETER BROWNE, knt. who *d.* at Oxford of his wounds received at the battle of Naseby, in the service of *King* CHARLES I. leaving, by Margaret, his wife, daughter of Sir Henry Knollys, knt. two sons, HENRY and FRANCIS; the elder,

I. HENRY BROWNE, esq. of Kiddington, was created a BARONET, with remainder to his brother, default his own male issue, by *King* CHARLES II. 1st July, 1659. (Letters patent dated at Brussels.) He *m.* Frances, third daughter and co-heir of Sir Charles Somerset, K. B. of Troy, in the county of Monmouth, sixth son of Edward, Earl of Worcester, and had issue, CHARLES, his successor, Henry, Peter, Mary, Frances, and Catherine. Sir Henry *d.* about 1690, and was *s.* by his eldest son,

II. SIR CHARLES BROWNE, of Kiddington, who wedded Mary, eldest daughter of George Pitt, esq. of Strathfieldsay, in the county of Southampton, and dying 20th December, 1751, was *s.* by his only son,

III. SIR GEORGE BROWNE, of Kiddington, (the *Sir Plume* of the *Rape of the Lock.*) This gentleman *m.* first, in 1725, Lady Barbara Lee, youngest daughter of Edward, first Earl of Litchfield, and widow of Colonel Lee, by which lady he had an only daughter and heiress,

BARBARA BROWNE, who wedded, first, in 1748, Sir Edward Mostyn, (fifth) bart. of Talacre, and had two sons,

PYERS, father of the present SIR EDWARD MOSTYN, of Talacre, Flintshire.

CHARLES, who assumed, pursuant to the will of Sir George Browne, bart. the name and arms of BROWNE, and became of KIDDINGTON. (See BURKE's *Commoners*, vol. iii. p. 381.)

Lady Mostyn *m.* secondly, Edward Gore, esq. of Barrow Court, in Somersetshire, and left by him two sons, Colonel Gore Langton, of Newton Park, and the Rev. Charles Gore.

Sir George *m.* secondly, Mrs. Holman, of Warkworth, and thirdly, Frances, sister of William Sheldon, esq. of Beoley, and widow of Henry Fermor, esq. of Tusmore, but had no issue by either of those ladies. He *d.* 20th June, 1754, when the BARONETCY became EXTINCT.

Arms—As BROWNE, OF BEECHWORTH.

BROWNE, OF WALCOT.

CREATED 21st Sept. 1621.—EXTINCT after 1647.

Lineage.

SIR JOHN BROWNE, knt. Lord Mayor of London in 1480, *m.* first, Alice, daughter and heir of William Swineshed, and secondly, Anne Betwood. By the latter he left a son, Sir William, Lord Mayor of London in 1507, and by the former, a successor,

ROBERT BROWNE, esq., Chamberlain of the Exchequer, who *m.* Isabel, daughter and heir of Sir John Sharpe, knt. and had two sons, Robert, his heir, and Edward, knt. of Rhodes, and one daughter, Isabel, *m.* to George Quarles, of Ufford. The elder son,

ROBERT BROWNE, esq. of Walcot, one of the Privy Chamber to HENRY VIII. *m.* Elizabeth, daughter of Sir Edward Palmer, of Augmering, in Sussex, and left, with a younger son, John, of Welley, in Wilts, a successor,

ROBERT BROWNE, esq. of Walcot, who *m.* Margaret, daughter and heir of Philip Barnard, esq. of Aldenham, and relict of Sir Barnard Whetstone, of Essex, by whom he left a son and heir,

SIR WILLIAM BROWNE, of Walcot, knight of the Bath, who *d.* in 1663, and was *s.* by his brother,

I. SIR ROBERT BROWNE, of Walcot, created a BARONET, 21st Sept., 1621. He *m.* first, Anne, daughter of Roger Capstock, who *d. s. p.* and secondly, Elizabeth, daughter of John Doyley, esq. of Chiselhampton, in Oxfordshire, by whom (who wedded secondly Sir Guy Palmes, knt. of Ashwell, in Rutlandshire,) he left at his decease, in 1623, a son,

II. SIR THOMAS BROWNE, of Walcot, who *m.* Anne, daughter of Sir Guy Palmes, knt. of Ashwell, and dying, in 1635, left issue,

Elizabeth.

Anne, *m.* to John Lord Poulett, of Hinton, St. George.

Sir Thomas was *s.* by his uncle,

III. SIR ROBERT BROWNE, of Walcot, who *d.* unmarried, and with him the BARONETCY EXPIRED.

BROWNLOW, OF BELTON.

CREATED 26th July, 1641.

EXTINCT in 1690.

Lineage.

RICHARD BROWNLOW, esq. of Belton, prothonotary of the Court of Common Pleas *temp.* ELIZABETH and JAMES I. *m.* Katherine, daughter of John Page, esq. of Wembly, a master in Chancery, and dying in 1638, left two sons,

JOHN (Sir), his heir.

William (Sir), of Great Humby, in Lincolnshire, who was created a BARONET 27th July, 1641. He *m.* Elizabeth, daughter and co-heir of William Duncombe, esq. and *d.* in 1666, leaving, with a daughter, Elizabeth, *m.* to Sir Charles Hussey, bart. a son and successor,

SIR RICHARD BROWNLOW, second baronet, of Humby, who *m.* Elizabeth, daughter of John Freke, esq. of Stretton, in Dorsetshire, and was *s.* by his son,

SIR JOHN BROWNLOW, third baronet, of Humby, who *m.* Alice, daughter of Richard Sherrard, esq. of Lopethorp, in Lincolnshire, and had four daughters, his co-heirs, viz. Jane, *m.* to Peregrine, Duke of Ancaster; Elizabeth, *m.* to John, Earl of Exeter; Alicia, *m.* to Francis, Lord Guilford; Eleanor, *m.* to John, Lord Tyrconnel. Sir John dying without male issue, 16th July, 1697, was *s.* by his brother,

SIR WILLIAM BROWNLOW, fourth baronet, of Humby, who *m.* Dorothy, eldest daughter and co-heir of Sir Richard Mason, knt. of Sutton, in Surrey, and dying 6th March, 1700, left issue,

JOHN, his heir.

William, who *d.* unm. in 1726.

ANNE (eventual heiress of the family), *m.* to Sir Richard Cust, bart. ancestor of JOHN, present EARL BROWNLOW.

Sir William was *s.* by his son,

SIR JOHN BROWNLOW, fifth bart. of Humby, M.P. for Lincolnshire, who was elevated to the peerage of Ireland, as Baron Charleville and VISCOUNT TYRCONNEL, in 1718. His lordship *m.* first, Eleanor, daughter and co-heir of his uncle, Sir John Brownlow, bart. and secondly, Elizabeth, daughter of William Cartwright, esq. of Marnham, Notts, but *d. s. p.* in 1754.

The elder son of Richard Brownlow, the prothonotary,

I. SIR JOHN BROWNLOW, of Belton, in the county of Lincoln, was created a BARONET 26th July, 1641, and served as high sheriff in 16th CHARLES I. He *m.* Alice, second daughter and eventual heir of Sir John Pulteney, of Misterton, and dying *s. p.* in 1690, the BARONETCY EXPIRED.

Arms—Or, an inescutcheon within an orle of eight martlets sa.

BROWNLOW, OF HUMBY.

CREATED 27th July, 1641.—EXTINCT in 1754.

(See BROWNLOW, OF BELTON.)

BRYDGES, OF WILTON.

CREATED 17th May, 1627.

EXTINCT 29th Sept. 1789.

Lineage.

CHARLES BRYDGES, of Wilton Castle, near Rose, in Herefordshire, (second son of Sir John Bruges, of Sudeley, created BARON CHANDOS, in 1554,) became cup-bearer to *King* PHILIP, and was deputy-lieutenant of the Tower to his father, Lord Chandos, when the warrant came for executing the Princess Elizabeth, which he refused to obey, until he should receive orders from the king and queen, and thereby was the means of saving her life; for the order being disowned at court a stop was put to the execution. Mr. Brydges lived to an advanced age, and was sheriff of Herefordshire, in the 32nd of ELIZABETH. He *m.* Jane daughter of Sir Edward Carne, of Wenny, in the county of Glamorgan, knt. and dying in 1619, was *s.* by his eldest son,

I. SIR GILES BRYDGES, of Wilton Castle, who was created a BARONET, 17th May, 1627. Sir Giles *m.* Mary, daughter of Sir James Scudamore, and was *s.* by his eldest son,

II. SIR JOHN BRYDGES, second baronet, who *m.* Mary, only daughter and heir of James Fearle, esq. of Dewsal and Anconbury, in the county of Hereford, and dying in 1651, was *s.* by his only son,

III. SIR JAMES BRYDGES, of Wilton Castle, who eventually succeeded his kinsman as eighth Baron Chandos. This noble was accredited ambassador to Constantinople, in 1680, where he resided for some years in great honor and esteem. His lordship *m.* Elizabeth, eldest daughter and co-heir of Sir Henry Bernard, knt. an eminent Turkey merchant. By this lady he had no less than twenty-two children, of which number fifteen only were christened, and seven of those dying young, the remainder were,

JAMES, his successor.

Henry, in holy orders, of Addlestrop, in Gloucestershire, archdeacon and prebendary of Rochester, and rector of Agmondesham, Bucks. Mr. Brydges *m.* Annabella, daughter of Henry, and grand-daughter of Sir Robert Atkins, lord chief baron of the exchequer, by whom he had a large family.

Francis, receiver general of the duties on malt, died *s. p.*

Mary, *m.* to Theophilus Leigh, esq. of Addlestrop, in the county of Gloucester.

Elizabeth, *m.* first, to Alexander Jacob, esq. and secondly, to the Rev. Dr. Thomas Dawson, vicar of Windsor.

Emma, *m.* to Edmund Chamberlain, esq. of Stow in the county of Gloucester.

Anne, m. to John Walcote, esq. of Walcote, in the county of Salop.

Catherine, m. first, to Brereton Bourchier, esq. of Barnsley Court, in the county of Gloucester, and secondly, to Henry Perrot, esq. of North Leigh, in the county of Oxford.

His lordship d. in 1714, and was s. by his eldest son,

IV. James Brydges, ninth baron, who, upon the accession of *King* George I. was created, by letters patent, dated 19th October, 1714, *Viscount Wilton*, and Earl of Caernarvon, with a collateral remainder to the issue male of his father; and in the November following, a patent passed the great seal, granting to his lordship and his two sons, John and Henry, the reversion of the office of clerk of the hanaper in chancery. In 1719, on the 30th April, his lordship was advanced to the *Marquisate of Caernarvon*, and Dukedom of Chandos, and he acquired by his magnificence the appellation of the *princely* Chandos. He espoused first, 26th February, 1696-7, Mary, only surviving daughter of Sir Thomas Lake, of Cannons, in the county of Middlesex, by whom he had two surviving sons,

John, Marquess of Caernarvon, m. in 1724, Lady Catharine Talmache, daughter of Lionel, Earl of Dysart, by whom he had issue,

Catherine, m. first, to William Berkeley Lyon, esq. of the horse guards, and secondly, to Edwin Francis Stanhope, esq. by whom she was grandmother of the present Sir Edwyn Francis Scudamore Stanhope, bart.

Jane, (a posthumous child,) m. to James Brydges, esq. of Pinner.

Lord Caernarvon d. 8th April, 1727.

Henry, Marquess of Caernarvon, after the decease of his brother.

His grace m. secondly, Cassandra, daughter of Francis Willoughby, esq. and sister of Thomas Willoughby, Lord Middleton; and thirdly, Lydia Catherine Van Hatten, widow of Sir Thomas Davall, knt. but had no issue by either of these ladies. He d. at his noble seat of Cannons,* 9th August, 1744, and was s. by his only surviving son,

V. Henry Brydges, second duke, who m. in 1728, Mary, eldest daughter and co-heir of Charles, Lord Bruce, only son and heir apparent of Thomas, Earl of Aylesbury, by whom he had issue,

James, Marquess of Caernarvon.

Caroline, m. to John Leigh, esq. of Addlestrop, in the county of Gloucester, and was grandmother of the present Chandos Leigh, esq. of Stoneleigh Abbey, in the county of Warwick.

His grace espoused, secondly, Anne Jeffreys, and by her he had a daughter, Augusta-Anne, m. to Henry John Kearney, esq. The duke m. thirdly, in 1767, Elizabeth, second daughter and co-heir of Sir John Major, bart. of Worlingworth Hall, in the county of Suffolk, by whom he had no issue. He d. 28th November, 1771, and was s. by his son,

VI. James Brydges, third duke, b. 27th December, 1731. This nobleman, upon the accession of his Majesty, King George III. was appointed one of the lords of his bed-chamber. In 1775, he was sworn of the privy council, and was afterwards constituted lord-steward of the household. His grace m. 22nd May, 1753, Mary, daughter and sole heiress of John Nicol, esq. of Southgate, Middlesex, by whom he acquired Minchenden House, at Southgate, together with the whole fortune of his father-in-law. By this lady, who d. in 1768, he had no issue. The duke espoused, secondly, 21st June, 1777, Anne-Eliza, daughter of Richard Gamon, esq. and widow of Roger Hope Elletson, esq. by whom he had a daughter and heiress,

Anne-Eliza, who m. in 1796, Richard, *Earl Temple*, now Duke of Buckingham and Chandos.

His grace d. without male issue 29th September, 1789, when all his honours, including the Baronetcy, became extinct, but the Barony of Chandos, which was immediately claimed by the Rev. Edward Tymewell Brydges, M.A. of Wootton Court, in Kent, as next heir male of the body of Sir John Brydges, Lord Chandos, the first grantee, who d. in 1557.

Arms—Arg. on a cross sa. a leopard's face or.

BUCK, OF HAMBY-GRANGE.

Created 22nd Dec. 1660. Extinct 7th June, 1782.

Lineage.

Sir John Bucke, of Hamby-Grange, in the county of Lincoln, served under the Lord Willoughby, in Holland, and was provost marshal of the army, under the Earl of Essex at Cadiz, where he was knighted. He purchased Hamby from the Lord-deputy, Sir Henry Sidney, in 1584. He m. Eleanor, daughter and heir of John Wymarke, esq. of Gretford, in Lincolnshire, and had issue,

John, his heir.

Edward, m. Elizabeth, daughter of John Claydon, of London.

Peregrine.

Anne.

Sir John d. 29th Nov., 1596,† and was s. by his eldest son,

---

* Cannons.—This most splendid palace stood on the road leading to Edgeware. The fronts were all of freestone, and the pillars of marble, as were also the steps of the great stair-case. The gilding was executed by the famous Pargotti, and the hall painted by Paolucci. The apartments were most exquisitely finished, and most richly furnished. The gardens, avenues, and offices, were proportionably grand. At night there was a constant watch kept, who walked the rounds and proclaimed the hours. The duke also maintained a full choir, and had divine service performed with the best music, in a chapel that could hardly be exceeded in the beauty of its workmanship. But all this terminated with his life; for on his decease this magnificent mansion was disposed of piecemeal. The stone obelisks, with copper lamps, which formed the approach from the Edgeware-road, were purchased for the Earl of Tilney, for his new building at Wanstead, in Essex, which has since experienced the fate of Cannons; the marble staircase was bought by the Earl of Chesterfield for his residence in May Fair. The ground and site whereon this magnificent edifice stood became the property of an opulent tradesman, who built thereon a neat habitation which still remains, after having passed into the hands of the well known Colonel O'Kelly of sporting celebrity.

† He was buried at St. Giles's, Cripplegate, as appears by the following certificate:

Ano. 1596,

Sir John Bucke, of Hembecke, als Hamby, in the parishe of Lynton, als Leventon, in the county of Lincolne, (who was knighted at Cales, in Spayn,) maryed Ellioner,

Sir John Buck, of Hamby-Grange, who was knighted by *King* James the 1st, with several others, at Whitehall, 23rd July, 1603, before his majesty's coronation. He wedded Elizabeth, daughter and heir of William Green, esq. of Filey, in Yorkshire, and had issue,

John, his successor.

Robert, of Flotmamby, in the county of York, *m.* Mary, daughter of Edward Skipwith, esq. of Grantham, in Lincolnshire.

Elizabeth, *m.* to William Wyvill, esq. of Osgoodby, in the county of York.

He *d.* in 1648, and was *s.* by his elder son,

I. John Buck, esq. of Hamby-Grange, who was created a Baronet by *King* Charles II. 22nd Dec. 1660. Sir John *m.* first, Anne, daughter of Sir John Style, bart. of Wateringbury, in Kent, but by her had no surviving issue. He wedded secondly, Mary, daughter and sole heir of William Ashton, esq. of Tingrey, in Bedfordshire, (by Mary, daughter and sole heir of Henry Ewer, esq. of South-Mims,) and by that lady (who *m.* after his decease, the Lord Chief Baron Turnor,) had

William, his successor.

Henry, *m.* Deborah, daughter of Mr. Thomas Salter, of London, draper, and died 9th Oct. 1737, aged 75, leaving two sons, Henry and William, and three daughters.

Mary, *m.* to the Right Honourable James Vernon, principal Secretary of State to *King* William the III.

He *d.* in 1668, and was *s.* by his elder son,

II. Sir William Buck, of Hamby-Grange. This gentleman *m.* Frances, daughter of Daniel Skinner, of London, merchant, and by her, who *d.* in 1712, had surviving issue,

Charles, his heir.

Mary, *m.* to Charles Hoar, esq. of Rushford, in Derbyshire.

Elisabeth, *m.* to Mr. Pusey, of London, merchant.

Alice.

Frances.

He *d.* 15th August, 1717, was buried at Watford, in Hertfordshire, and *s.* by his son,

III. Sir Charles Buck, of Hamby-Grange, who wedded Anne, daughter of Sir Edward Seabright, bart. of Besford, in the county of Worcester, by whom he had issue,

Charles, (Sir), his heir.

Anne, *m.* Ambrose Isted, esq. of Ecton, in Northamptonshire, and was grandmother of the present

Ambrose Isted, esq. of Ecton. (See Burke's *Commoners*.)

Catherine, *m.* to Sir Henry Englefield, bart. of Whiteknight.

He *d.* 20th June, 1729, and was *s.* by his son,

IV. Sir Charles Buck, of Hamby-Grange, who *m.* Mary, daughter of George Cartwright, esq. of Ossington, Notts, but dying *s. p.* 7th June, 1782, the Baronetcy expired.

Arms—Lozengy bendy of eight pieces or and az. a canton ermine.

BULLER, OF TRENANT PARK.

Created 3rd Oct. 1808.

Extinct 13th April, 1804.

Lineage.

John Francis Buller, esq. of Shillingham, representative of the ancient family of Buller, so long seated in the west of England, *m.* 22nd July, 1716, Rebecca, daughter and eventual co-heir of Sir Jonathan Trelawny, bart. bishop of Winchester, and dying in 1751, left issue,

I. James, of Shillingham, M.P. for Cornwall, who *m.* first, in 1739, Elizabeth, daughter and sole heir of William Gould, esq. of Downes, in Devonshire, by whom he had one son,

James, of Shillingham and Downes, father of

James, now of Shillingham and Downes, some time M.P. for Exeter.

He *m.* secondly, in 1744, Jane, third daughter of Allen, first Earl Bathurst, and had by her

John, of Morval, M.P. for West Looe, who *m.* Anne, daughter of William Lemon, esq. and *d.* in 1793, leaving a son,

John, of Morvall, some time M.P. for West Looe.

Francis, the celebrated Judge Buller, grandfather of the present Sir John Buller Yarde Buller, bart. of Lupton, in Devon.

Edward, who *m.* Harriet, daughter of John Hoskyns, esq. and had issue.

Jane, *m.* to the late Sir William Lemon, bart, M.P.

Mary, *m.* to James Templer, esq. of Stover, Devon.

Catherine, *m.* to lieut.-gen. William Macarmick.

II. Francis, M.P. for West Looe, *m.* Mary, daughter of Sir Copleston Warwick Bamfylde, bart. of Poltimore, and relict of Sir Coventry Carew, bart. of Anthony, but *d. s. p.* in 1764.

III. John, of whom presently.

IV. William, bishop of Exeter, *m.* in 1762, Anne, daughter and co-heir of Thomas, D.D. bishop of Winchester, and *d.* in 1796, leaving issue.

V. Rebecca, *m.* to Vice-Admiral Charles Watson.

VI. Anne, *m.* to Reginald Pole, esq. of Stoke.

VII. Mary, *m.* to Sir Joseph Copley, bart. of Sprotborough.

VIII. Elizabeth, *m.* to the Rev. John Sturges, D.D.

The third son,

John Buller, esq. sometime M.P. for East Looe

---

daughter of John Wymarke, of Getford, in the sayd countye, and had by her issue three sonnes, and one daughter, viz., John, the first son; Edward, the second; Peregrine, the thyrd; and Anne. The above sayd knight, departed this life on Saturday, the xxth of November, 1596, and was buryed in the parishe Churche of St. Gyles, without Criplegate, in London, on fryday, following, being the xxvith day of the sayd moneth; whose funerall was appoynted and served by Richard Lee *Clarenceux*, king of armes, and with him served at the said funerall, John Raven, *Rouge Dragon*, and Thomas Lant, *portcullis*, officers of Armes. In witness whereof we, the executors to the aforesayd knight, have herunto subscribed our names, the day and year above specifyed.

Eleanor Buck, Executrix.

Edward Coxsoon, John Rose, Francis Vincent.

and one of the lords of the treasury, *m.* first, 3rd March, 1760, Mary, daughter of Sir John St. Aubyn, bart. of Clowance, in Cornwall, by whom he had, *inter alios*, a son, EDWARD, of whom presently. He wedded, secondly, 4th November, 1768, Elizabeth-Caroline, daughter of John Hunter, esq. and had also issue by that lady, who *d.* 17th January, 1798. His son by his first marriage,

I. SIR EDWARD BULLER, of Trenant Park, Cornwall, vice-admiral of the red, was created a BARONET 3rd October, 1808. He *m.* Gertrude, daughter of Colonel Philip Van Cortlandt (for an account of the Van Cortlandt family, see BURKE'S *Commoners*, vol. iv.), and had issue,

John St. Aubyn, *d.* young.

ANNA-MARIA, who *m.* 25th February, 1824, Lieut.-Col. James Drummond Elphinstone, youngest son of the Hon. Fullerton Elphinstone, of East Lodge, Middlesex, and has, with other issue, a son and heir, William. Colonel Elphinstone has assumed the additional surname of BULLER.

Sir Edward, who was recorder of East Looe, died without male issue 15th April, 1824, when the BARONETCY became EXTINCT.

Arms—Sa. on a cross arg. quarterly pierced of the field, four eagles displayed of the first.

BURGES, OF EAST HAM.

CREATED 4th May, 1793.—EXTINCT 24th April, 1803.

Lineage.

I. SIR JOHN SMITH-BURGES, who *m.* Margaret, only daughter and heir of Ynyr Burges, esq. of East Ham and Thorpe Hall, Essex, was created a BARONET 4th May, 1793, but dying *s. p.* in 1803, the title expired.

BURROUGHS, OF CASTLE BAGSHAW.

CREATED 1st Dec. 1804.

EXTINCT in 1829.

Lineage.

The first settler of this family in Ireland, presumed to be descended from the Lincolnshire house of Burroughs, who was elevated to the peerage by *Queen* ELIZABETH, acquired a large landed property in the county of Wicklow, and was grandfather of

THOMAS BURROUGHS, esq. who *m.* Elizabeth Lewis, and had a son,

FRANCIS BURROUGHS, esq. who *m.* Miss Mushet, niece to the Bishop of Derry, and had issue,

THOMAS, who *m.* first, Miss Rainsford, and secondly, Miss Nugent. He *d.* leaving two sons,

Thomas, who *m.* Catherine, daughter of the Right Hon. Sir Henry Cavendish, bart. and had issue.

Francis.

LEWIS.

Mary.

The second son,

THE REV. LEWIS BURROUGHS, D.D. Archdeacon of Derry, *m.* Mary, daughter of Richard Cane, esq. of Larabrian, in Kildare, by Anne Lyons, of River Lyons, in the King's County, and had issue,

Medlicott, an officer in the army, who *m.* Mary Moorecroft, widow of Captain Morrison, and had issue.

Newburgh, Archdeacon of Derry, *m.* Anne Trevor, only child of Isaac Bomford, esq. of Tyrrellstown, in Meath, and had issue.

WILLIAM, of whom presently.

Thomas, who *d.* unm.

Mary-Anne.

Frances.

Selina-Frances.

The third son,

I. SIR WILLIAM BURROUGHS, barrister-at-law, went to India, and was appointed advocate-general of Bengal, by Lord Cornwallis. On his return he was created a BARONET, 1st December, 1804. Sir William *m.* Letitia, daughter of William Newburgh, esq. of Ballyhaise and Drumcarn, in Cavan, by Letitia, his wife, daughter and heir of Broghill Perrot, esq. of Ballyhugh, and had by her, who *d.* in 1803, one son and three daughters, viz.

William, *b.* 15th September, 1784, in the Coldstream regiment of foot guards, who *d.* of wounds received before Bayonne, 11th May, 1814.

Letitia, *m.* 4th September, 1820, to Rear-Admiral Sir Charles Ogle, bart. and *d.* 13th November, 1832, leaving a son, William Ogle.

Maria-Isabella, *d.* unm. in 1798.

Louisa.

Sir William dying in 1829, without surviving male issue, the BARONETCY EXPIRED.

Arms—Gu. the trunk of a laurel tree eradicated with two branches ppr.: on a chief or, an eastern coronet gu. between two annulets az.

BURTON, OF STOCKERSTON.

CREATED 22nd July, 1622.

EXTINCT (date unknown).

Lineage.

The first of this family on record is

HENRY, son of RICHARD DE BURTONE, who by his deed confirmed to the monks of Geronden, in the county of Leicester, the donations made by Reginald, son of Ingehulf, and Reginald, son of that Reginald, in Ybestoke.

NICHOLAS DE BURTON, was lord of Tolethorp, in the county of Rutland, in the 9th of EDWARD II. and in that year was knight of the shire. His son,

SIR WILLIAM DE BURTON, knt. of Tolethorp, was one of the justices of the king's bench from the 17th to the 36th of Edward III. Beside Tolethorp, Sir William was lord of Foxlin, and other lands in Leicestershire. He *d.* in the 49th of Edward III. and was *s.* by his son,

Sir Thomas de Burton, knight of the shire for Rutland in the 1st of Richard II. and sheriff for the same county in 1379. This gentleman, by deed dated at Tolethorp, on the Saturday next after the feast of St. Martin, the bishop, 50th Edward III. did convey unto John Brown, esq. of Stamford, the manor of Tolethorp, together with all its appurtenances, and the perpetual advowson of the chapel of the same; also all his lands, tenements, rents, and services, in the village of Little Casterton, with the reversion of the patronage of the church. Sir Thomas *d.* in the 8th of Richard II. leaving, by his wife, Margaret, daughter of Thomas Grenham, a son and heir,

Sir Thomas Burton, knt. who served as high sheriff for the county of Rutland four times, in the reigns of Henry V. and Henry VI. and was appointed in the former to receive such sums of money collected in the county, as should be lent to the king to enable him to carry on the war in France. Sir Thomas *m.* the daughter of Simon Louthe, and was *s.* by his son,

Thomas Burton, esq. who was sheriff of Rutland in the 19th of Henry VI. This gentleman *m.* first, a daughter of Sir Robert Brabeson, knt. and had one son, who died young. He wedded, secondly, a daughter of Sir Hugh Bushey, knt. and was *s.* by his son, by that lady,

William Burton, esq. who *m.* a daughter of John Folville, esq. of Ashby Folville, in the county of Leicester, and left a son and heir,

John Burton, esq. of Uppingham, in the county of Rutland, who, by his wife, a daughter of Thomas Basing, had a son and successor,

Sir Thomas Burton, who was knighted by *King* Henry VIII. This gentleman *m.* the daughter of Ralph Lowe, esq. of Denbigh, in the county of Derby, and was *s.* by his son,

John Burton, esq. of Braunston, who *m.* the daughter of — Blackwell, and dying in the 1st year of *Queen* Mary, left a son and heir,

William Burton, esq. of Braunston, who *m.* Alice, daughter of Richard Peck, of Ridlington, in Rutland, and had three sons, viz.

- John, his heir.
- Bertin, of Okeham, ancestor of the Burtons of that place, and of Exeter.
- Simon, of Braunston.

The eldest son,

John Burton, esq. of Stockerston, in the county of Leicester, *m.* Anne, daughter and heir of Thomas Digby, esq. of Coats,* and acquired thereby a considerable estate. He was *s.* by his son,

I. Sir Thomas Burton, knt. of Stockerston, who was created a Baronet by *King* James I. 22nd July, 1622. He *m.* first, Philippa, relict of Walter Calverley, of Calverley, in the county of York, and daughter of the Hon. Henry Brooke, son of George Brooke, Lord Cobham, by which lady he had three daughters, viz.

- Anne, *m.* to Sir Abel Barker, bart. of Hambleton, in the county of Rutland.
- Elizabeth, } *d. unm.*
- Frances, }

Sir Thomas wedded, secondly, Anne, daughter of Robert Reynolds, of London, gent. and widow of Thomas Havers, of the Custom-House. He *d.* in 1655, and was *s.* by his son,

II. Sir Thomas Burton, of Stockerston, a distinguished royalist in the time of Charles I. and a commissioner of array, with Sir George Villiers, Sir Henry Skipwith, and others, for the county of Leicester, on the breaking out of the rebellion in 1641. He *m.* Elizabeth, daughter of Sir John Prettyman, bart. of Lodington, and by that lady, who wedded, secondly Sir William Halford, knt. of Welham, in Leicestershire, had two sons,

- Thomas, his successor.
- John, *d. s. p.*

Sir Thomas, who suffered sequestration and imprisonment, *d.* 3rd April, 1669, and was *s.* by his elder son,

III. Sir Thomas Burton, of Stockerston, who *m.* Anne, eldest daughter of Sir Thomas Clutterbuck, knt. of London, and Blakesware, in the county of Hertford, and had two sons, Charles, his successor, and Thomas. Sir Thomas sold the estate of Stockerston to Sir Charles Duncomb, knt. and dying in 1768, left little more than the title to his son and heir,

IV. Sir Charles Burton, who appears to have been in great pecuniary distress, and a prisoner for debt in 1710. In two years afterwards he was tried at the Old Bailey sessions on a charge of stealing a ring, and being convicted sentenced to transportation.

Arms—Sa. a chev. between three owls arg. crowned or.

BUSWELL, OF CLIPSTON.

Created 7th July 1660.—Extinct 16th Mar. 1687

Lineage.

I. Sir George Buswell, of Clipston, in Northamptonshire, was created a Baronet, 7th July, 1660. He *m.* Jane, daughter and co-heir of Sir James Knyvet, bart. of Flowrie, in the same county, by whom (who wedded, secondly, Sir John Garrard, bart.) he had no issue. Sir George *d.* 16th March, 1687, when the title became extinct. (See Buswell-Pleasant.)

BUTTON, OF ALTON.

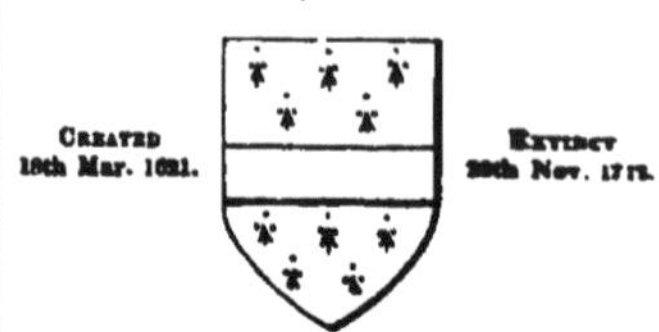

Created 18th Mar. 1621.

Extinct 20th Nov. 1712.

Lineage.

William Button, of Alton, (son of another William Button, of Alton, and a lineal descendant of Sir Walter de Button, knt. living 12th Henry III.) *m.* Mary, daughter of Sir William Kelway, knt. of Rockborne, in Wiltshire, and had issue,

- Ambrose (Sir), knt. *d. s. p.*
- William, of Alton.
- John, of Buckland, in Lymington, who *m.* Eleanor.

* Son of Lybeus Digby, esq. of Coats and Luffenham, fourth son of Sir Simon Digby, of Coleshill.

daughter of Sir Bernard Drake, of Ash, in Devonshire, and was father of

John Button, esq. of Buckland, who *d.* 7th March, 1666, leaving by Eleanor, his wife, daughter of Thomas South, esq. of South Badesley, Hants, an only son,

John Button, esq. of Buckland, who *m.* Mary, daughter of William Jesson, esq. of Coventry, and dying 1679, was buried at Lymington, leaving issue,

Elizabeth, *b.* 1651, *m.* to John Burrard, esq. M.P. for Lymington, and had issue.

Mary or Sarah, *b.* 1653, *m.* to Sir Richard Hopkyns, knt. of Coventry, ancestor of the present William-Richard Hopkyns-Northey, esq. Lady Hopkyns *d.* 1711.

Anne, *b.* 1656, *m.* to Paul Burrard, esq. of Walhampton, M.P. for Lymington: hence descend the Burrards, baronets.

Eleanor, *b.* 1658, *m.* to Thomas Dore, and had issue.

Cicely, *m.* to John Meux, esq. of Kingston, Isle of Wight.

Dorothy, *m.* to John Drake, esq. of Ashe, county Devon.

The second son,

William Button, of Alton, *m.* Jane, daughter of John Lamb, of Wiltshire, and had three sons and two daughters, viz.

William, his heir.

Martyn, living unm. 1649.

John, *d. s. p.*

Jane, *m.* to Walter Coningsby, D.D.

Martha, *m.* to Thomas Coningsby, esq. of North Mims, Herts.

The eldest son,

I. Sir William Button, of Alton, in Wiltshire, was created a Baronet in 1621. He *m.* Ruth, daughter of Walter Dunche, esq. of Avebury, Wilts, and had issue,

William, *m.* Anne, daughter of Sir Henry Rolle, knt. of Steventon, in Devonshire.

Thomas, *d.* unm.

Robert, of whom presently.

John, living 1649.

Mary, *m.* to Clement Walker, esq. of Charter-House London, in Somersetshire, usher of the Exchequer, and their representative is the present George Heneage Walker-Heneage, esq. of Compton Basset, in Wiltshire.

Jane, *m.* to Dr. Richard Steward, dean of the king's chapel.

Ruth, *m.* to Thomas Lambert, esq. son of Sir Thomas Lambert.

The third son,

II. Sir Robert Button, of Alton, *m.* Eleanor, daughter of William Compton, esq. of Hartbury, in Gloucestershire, and dying about 1679, was *s.* by his brother,

III. Sir John Button, of Alton, who *m.* twice, but *d. s. p.* in 1712, when the title expired.

Arms—Erm. a fess gu.

CAIRNES, OF MONAGHAN.

Created 6th May, 1708. Extinct 16th June, 1743.

Lineage.

The founder of this family,

Thomas Cairnes, of the Cairnes's, of Orchardtown, North Britain, went over to Ireland, with his kinsman, the Earl of Annandale, and settled there. He *m.* Jane, daughter of John Scott, of Colefadd,* in Scotland, and was father of

John Cairnes, of Donoghmore, in Ireland, who wedded Jane, daughter of James Miller, M.D. of Millhugh,† and was *s.* by his eldest son,

I. Alexander Cairnes, esq. of Monaghan, who was created a Baronet of England and Ireland‡ by *Queen* Anne, 6th May, 1708, with remainder, in default of his own male issue, to his brother Henry, and the heirs male of his body. Sir Alexander *m.* Elizabeth, sister of Sir Nathaniel Gould, knt. of Newington, Middlesex, and had an only daughter and heiress,

Mary, *m.* to Cadwallader, seventh Lord Blayney, but *d. s. p.*

He *d.* at Dublin, 30th October, 1732, and leaving no son, the title passed under the limitation to his brother,

II. Sir Henry Cairnes, of Monaghan, M.P. for that borough, who *m.* Frances, daughter of John Gould, esq. of Hackney, in Middlesex, brother of Sir Nathaniel Gould, but *d.* without issue, 16th June, 1743, when the Baronetcy became extinct.

Arms—Arg. three martlets gu. within a border or.

CALDER, OF SOUTHWICK.

Created 22nd Aug. 1798. Extinct in 1818.

Lineage.

Sir James Calder, third baronet of Muirtown, in North Britain, *m.* Alice, daughter of Admiral Robert Hughes, and had issue,

Henry, who *s.* his father as 4th baronet of Muirtoun, and was father of the present

Sir Henry Roddam Calder, bart. of Muirtoun.

Robert, of whom presently.

Alithea, *m.* to Admiral Robert Roddam, of Roddam.

* By his wife, Mary Anne, niece of the then Earl of Annandale.

† By Margaret, his wife, daughter of Mure, of Rowallan, by his wife, the Lady Elizabeth Stuart, daughter of the Duke of Lennox, and sister of the unhappy Earl of Darnley, James *the First's* father.

‡ Mr. Le Neve says, he was advanced to the dignity of baronet of Great Britain and Ireland, paying whole fees for the former, and half fees for the latter.

The second son,

I. Sir Robert Calder, K.C.B. of Southwick, in Hants, a distinguished naval commander, attained the rank of admiral of the white, and for his gallant professional services, had the honour of knighthood conferred upon him, and was subsequently created a Baronet in 1798. He *m.* Amelia, daughter of John Michell, esq. of Bayfield, in Norfolk, but *d.* without issue in 1818, when the Baronetcy expired.

Arms—Or, a hart's head, caboshed and sa. attired gu.

CALLANDER, OF WESTERTOWN.

Created 1st Aug. 1798.  Extinct 2nd Apr. 1812.

Lineage.

John Callander, *b.* in 1653, a near kinsman of James, fourth Earl of Callander, who inherited upon the demise of his uncle, George, third earl of Linlithgow, that title, and thus the two earldoms were united in his person. Enrolling himself, however, under the banner of the Chevalier in 1715, his lordship was attainted, and his lands and honours fell under the forfeiture. John Callander *m.* Janet, eldest daughter of John Buchanan, esq. and was father of

Alexander Callander, *b.* in 1719, who *m.* in 1734, Margaret, youngest daughter of David Ramsay, esq. and had issue,

- John.
- Alexander, *d. s. p.*
- David, *d.* unm.
- Euphemia, *d.* unm. in 1798.
- Janet, *m.* to John Higgins.

The eldest son,

I. Sir John Callander, of Westertown, in Stirlingshire, a colonel in the army, and M.P. for Berwick upon Tweed, *b.* in September, 1739, was created a Baronet 1st August, 1798. He *m.* 2nd February, 1786, Margaret, daughter of John Romer, esq. of Cherwick, in Northumberland, and relict of Bridges Kearney, esq. but dying *s. p.* 2nd April, 1812, the title became extinct.

Arms—Sa. a bend chequy or and gu. between six billets of the second.

CALVERLEY, OF CALVERLEY.

Created 11th Dec. 1611.  Extinct 11th Feb. 1777.

Lineage.

The original name of this family was Scott, and the first member of it who came into England from Scotland, *temp.* Henry I. was

John Scott, who *m.* Larderina, second daughter of Alphonsus Gospatrick, Lord of Calverley, and several other manors, and a person of great importance. His son, another

John Scott, lord of the manor of Calverley, in the county of York, in right of his mother, was steward of the house to the Empress Maud, and bore sometimes a lion rampant counterchanged, and sometimes a lion rampant, droit; inclosed in an ortogon, as affixed to his seal affixed to deeds in his time. He was living in 1st Stephen, *anno* 1136, and *m.* the daughter of Sir John Luttrell, knt. of Hooton Pannel, and had several sons, of whom the eldest,

William Scott, gave the vicarage of Calverley to the chapel of the Blessed Virgin Mary at York, founded by Roger, the archbishop, (whose right surname was Scott, in *King* Henry the Second's reign. He *m.* Joan, daughter of Sir John Swillington, and had issue,

- William, his heir.
- Roger (Sir), a person of great eminence.
- Henry, who held lands in Pudsey, which he gave to the Knights Templars.
- Thomas, from whom the Scotts of Newton descended; of which family was William Scott, who, in 1453, gave the vicarage house at Leeds, &c. by deed, dated that year, and sealed with an owl.
- Barnard, *d.* unm.
- Mary, *m.* Jeffrey, son of Peter de Arthington, with which lady her brother, Sir Roger Scott, gave lands in Calverley.

The eldest son and heir,

William Scott, living in 1217, *m.* Mabel, daughter of Sir Nicholas Stapleton, knt. and was father of

Walter Scott, living in 1273, *m.* the daughter of Sir John Normanville, and had several sons, from one of the younger of whom descended the Calverleys of Hayton, Clarebrough, Lound, &c. in Nottinghamshire. The eldest son and heir,

William Scott, *m.* the daughter of Sir John Goldsbrough, knt. of Goldsbrough, and had issue. This gentleman, who was living in 1355, was the last of the family who bore the name of Scott, his eldest son and heir being styled

John de Calverley. This John, whose wife's christian name was Margaret, had two sons and a daughter, viz.

- John (Sir).
- Simon.
- Elizabeth, the wife of Thomas Paitfyn, of Hedingley, who bequeathed her body to be buried at the priory of Esholt. This lady, by deed executed in her widowhood, 15th Edward . . granted the manor of Hedingley to her brother John Calverley: and the said John appears to have made a gift of the manor, in 1394, to the abbot and convent of Kirkstall.

His son and heir,

Sir John de Calverley, who bore for arms six or eight owls, *m.* Joanna, daughter or niece of Sir Simon Ward, and had issue, John, Walter, and Richard, and a daughter, Isabel, who was prioress of Esholt. He was *s.* by his eldest son,

John de Calverley, who was sheriff of the county of Rutland, and one of the esquires to the Queen in *King* Richard the Second's time, and being in the wars on the King's part, was made prisoner by the enemy and beheaded. He left no issue, and was *s.* in his estate by his brother,

Walter de Calverley, who *m.* first, a daughter of — Nevile, without issue, and secondly, Margaret, daughter of John de Dinsley, and had issue,

William (Sir), *m.* Eleanor, daughter of Sir John

Thornhill, knt. and *d. s. p.* in his father's life-time.
Walter (Sir), heir to his father.
John.

The second son,

Sir Walter de Calverley, knt. *s.* to the estate in consequence of the decease issueless of his elder brother. He wedded, *temp.* Richard II. Joanna, daughter of Sir John Bygot, knt. of Settrington, and had two sons, John and Walter. In the time of Sir Walter, Calverley church was rebuilt, and his arms, the owls, cut or plated in the wood-work there. His elder son,

Sir John de Calverley, was knighted and killed at the battle of Shrewsbury, fighting for *King* Henry IV. against Hotspur. His brother and heir,

Walter Calverley, living in 1429, *m.* Elizabeth, daughter of Sir Thomas Mackingfield, and had issue,

William, his heir.
Thomas, of Park House, in Byrill, had that and other lands settled upon him. He *m.* Agnes, daughter and heir of — Skargill, and acquired thereby a considerable estate. From him descended the Calverleys of Morley, and those of Cumberland.
Robert, who had lands at Baseford and Broxton, in Nottinghamshire.

Alice, *m.* to Gilbert, son and heir of Gilbert del Leigh, esq. of Middleton.
Isabel, *m.* to John, son and heir of William Slingsby, esq. of Scriven.
Margaret, *m.* to Thomas, son and heir of Thomas Clapham, esq. of Beamsley.
Beatrice, *m.* to Tristram, son and heir of Robert Bellyng, esq.
Amice, *m.* to Robert, son and heir of Nicholas Baildon.
Anne, *m.* to John Wentworth, esq. of Elmsall.
——, *m.* to William Scott, of Scott Hall, in Newton.
——, *m.* to Gilbert Tipcliffe.
Elizabeth, a nun at Esholt.

The eldest son,

William Calverley, esq. *m.* in the 29th Henry VI. Agnes, daughter of Sir John Tempest, and had several sons and daughters, viz.

i. William (Sir), his heir,
ii. John,
iii. Richard,
iv. Robert,
v. Thomas,
} all living in 1488.
vi. Nicholas, a priest, vicar of Battley, in 1499.

i. Margaret, *m.* to Mr. Popelay.
ii. Joan, *m.* to Christopher Lister, of Pontefract.
iii. Anne, *m.* to Mr. Ellis, of Kiddall.
iv. Isabel, *m.* to Mr. Mearing, of Wherdale.
v. Eleanor, *m.* to Mr. Leventhorpe, of Leventhorpe.
vi. Alice, a nun, at Esholt, in 1488.

He was *s.* by his eldest son,

Sir William Calverley, who was knighted on the field by the Earl of Surrey, 13th Henry VIII. in the expedition to Scotland. He *m.* Alice, daughter of Sir John Savile, of Thornhill, and had issue,

Walter (Sir), his successor.
William,
Robert,
Thomas,
} living in the 21st Henry VIII. and 10th Elizabeth.

Agnes, *m.* to John Vavasour, esq. of Weston.

The eldest son and heir,

Sir Walter Calverley, knt. *m.* first, *temp.* Henry VIII., Isabel, daughter and heir of John Drax, esq. and had

William (Sir), his heir.
Gilbert.
Thomas.
John.

Alice, *m.* to Robert Warcop, esq. of Warcop.
Margery, *m.* to Henry Radcliffe, esq.
Ellen, *m.* to Miles Hodson, esq. of Newcastle.
Isabel, *m.* to Gilbert Legh, esq.
Anne.
Jane.
Margaret, *m.* to Mr. Bollinge, of London.
Elizabeth.
Maud.

Sir Walter wedded, secondly, Anne, daughter of John Vavasor, esq. but had no other issue. He was *s.* by his eldest son,

Sir William Calverley, who was knighted about the 3rd Edward VI., and the next year was sheriff of Yorkshire. He *m.* first, Elizabeth, daughter of Sir William Middleton, knt. of Stockeld, and had a numerous progeny, viz.

Walter, his heir.
Thomas, *m.* Isabel, daughter of Mr. Anderson, of Newcastle, and was progenitor of the Calverleys of Ayreholm, in Durham.
William, *m.* Anne, daughter and heiress of Walter Calverley, of Park, and acquired thereby estates in Morley, Carlinghow, Seacroft, Bolton, &c.
Henry.
John, who *m.* the daughter of Mr. Leys, of Lincolnshire.
Ralph.
Michael.

Isabel, *m.* to Francis Passelew, esq. of Riddlesden.
Elizabeth, *m.* to Robert Beeston, esq. of Beeston.
Anne, *m.* to Thomas Ellis, esq. of Kiddall.
——— *m.* to William Wentworth, esq. of Kilnswick.
Dorothy, *m.* to Walter Furnes, of Mirfeild.
——— *m.* to John Cooper, alderman of Chester.

Sir William wedded, secondly, Elizabeth, daughter of Richard Sneyd, esq. and had three other daughters,

Beatrice, *m.* to Robert Hide, esq. of Norbury, in Cheshire.
Jane, *m.* to Mr. Anby.
Elizabeth, *m.* to Mr. Hallie.

He *d.* about the 13th of Elizabeth, and was *s.* by his eldest son,

Walter Calverley, esq. of Calverley, who wedded Anne, daughter of Sir Christopher Danby, knt. and had, with one daughter, three sons, viz.

William, his heir.
Christopher, living in 1568.
Edmund, whose grandson, Edmund Calverley, of the Broad, in Sussex, was ancestor of the present Thomas Calverley, esq. of the Broad, and of Ewell Castle.

He was *s.* by the eldest son,

William Calverley, esq. of Calverley, who *m.* Catherine,* daughter of Sir John Thornholm, knt. of Haystrope, and was *s.* by his eldest son,

Walter Calverley, esq. of Calverley, who wedded Philippa, sister of John Broke, Lord Cobham, and by that lady, (who *m.* secondly, Sir Thomas Burton, knt.) had a son and successor,

Henry Calverley, esq. of Calverley. This gentle-

* This lady, who was a zealous Catholic, suffered much for recusancy, the estate being sequestered, and some manors sold off.

man m. first, Elizabeth, daughter of Alexander More, esq. of Grantham, but by that lady had no surviving issue. He wedded, secondly, Joyce, daughter of Sir Walter Pye, knt. of the Mynde, in Herefordshire, attorney-general to the court of wards and liveries, and had, WALTER, his successor, and John, of Gray's inn, barrister-at-law. He was s. by the elder son,

WALTER CALVERLEY, esq. of Calverley, who espousing the cause of the king, suffered in person and estate during the civil wars. He m. Frances, daughter of Henry Thompson, esq. of Esholt and Bromfield, and had, with two daughters, Anne, wife of Benjamin Wade, esq. of New Grange, near Leeds; and Bridget, wife successively of John Ramsden, esq. and Walter Nevile, esq.; a son and successor,

I. WALTER CALVERLEY, esq. of Calverley, who was created a BARONET by *Queen* ANNE, 11th Dec. 1711. Sir Walter m. in January, 1706, Julia, eldest daughter of Sir William Blackett, of Newcastle-upon-Tyne, bart. and left at his decease in 1749, a daughter, JULIA, m. to Sir George Trevelyan, bart. and an only son,

II. SIR WALTER CALVERLEY, of Calverley, who wedded Elizabeth, daughter and heir of Sir William Blackett, bart. and thereupon assumed the surname and arms of BLACKETT. (See BLACKETT baronetcy.)

Arms—Sa. an inescutcheon arg. with an orle of eight horned owls of the second.

CAMBELL, OF CLAY HALL.

CREATED 12th Feb. 1664. — EXTINCT 23rd May, 1699.

Lineage.

SIR THOMAS CAMBELL, who was lord mayor of London in 1609, d. 13th February, 1613, aged seventy-eight, leaving by Alice, his wife, daughter of Edward Bugle, merchant, a son,

SIR ROBERT CAMBELL, alderman of London, who m. Alice, daughter of William Willington, and had two sons, JAMES, of Woodford, and THOMAS, of Clay Hall, who were both created BARONETS. The younger,

I. SIR THOMAS CAMBELL, of Clay Hall, in Essex, was so created in 1664. He m. first, a daughter of Nicholas Corsellis, merchant of London, and secondly, Mary, daughter of Thomas, Viscount Fanshawe. Sir Thomas d. in 1665, (his widow wedded, secondly, Robert Sheffield, esq.) and was s. by his son,

II. SIR THOMAS CAMBELL, at whose decease, unm. in 1668, the title passed to his brother,

III. SIR HARRY CAMBELL, who m. first, Katherine, daughter of Sir Anthony Chester, bart. of Chichley, in Buckinghamshire, and secondly, Katherine, daughter of Sir William Whorwood, of Sturton Castle, in Staffordshire, and relict of Captain Anthony Markham. Dying, however, without male issue, in 1699, the BARONETCY EXPIRED, but his property devolved on his only daughter, ANNE, m. to Thomas Price, esq. of Westbury, Bucks.

Arms—Sa. on a fess erm. three pellets between three tigers' heads erased or.

CAMBELL, OF WOODFORD.

CREATED 9th April, 1661.—EXTINCT May, 1662.

Lineage.

I. SIR JOHN CAMBELL, of Woodford, Essex, elder brother of the first baronet, of Clay Hall, was himself created a BARONET in 1661, but dying s. p. the following year, the title became EXTINCT.

Arms—As CAMBELL, of Clay Hall.

CAMPBELL, OF INVERNEIL.

CREATED 4th Dec. 1818.—EXTINCT in 1819.

Lineage.

I. Lieut.-Gen. SIR JAMES CAMPBELL, G.C.H., K.F.M., of Inverneil, in the county of Argylle, sometime chief commissioner to the Ionian Isles, and commander of the forces in the Adriatic, was created a BARONET 4th December, 1818, but dying shortly after, and leaving no issue, the title became EXTINCT.

CANN, OF COMPTON GREEN.

CREATED 13th Sept. 1662. — EXTINCT 20th July, 17..

Lineage.

WILLIAM CANN, esq. who was mayor of the city of Bristol in 1648, and bore for arms, "Azure, fretty argent, a fesse, gules," m. Margaret, sister of Robert Yeamans, esq.† and had issue,

ROBERT (Sir), his heir.

John.

Richard, who m. Eleanor, daughter of Henry Grove, esq. of Chiselburg, in the county Wilts, and had a daughter,

ANNE, m. to Thomas Wilkins, esq. of Llanblethian, in Glamorganshire, prothonotary for the counties of Glamorgan, Brecon, and Radnor, and had a son,

CANN WILKINS, esq. grandfather of the present

CANN WILKINS, esq. of Clifton. — BURKE'S *Commoners*, vol. iii. p. 3..

† ROBERT YEAMANS was one of the sheriffs of Bristol in 1642, and the next year (30th May, 1643,) was executed, with George Bouchier, by the command of Col. Fiennes, the new governor, opposite the Nagg's Head tavern, in Wine Street, in that city, for being concerned together in projecting a scheme, for letting Prince Rupert into the said city, and turning the governor and rebels ...

William.
Matthew.
Margaret, m. to Alderman Richard Streamert, of Bristol.
Martha, m. to John Lane, merchant, of Bristol.
Hester, m. to Sir Thomas Langton, knt. of Bristol.

The eldest son,

I. Sir Robert Cann, who was mayor of Bristol (1662 and 1675), and its representative in 1678, received the honour of knighthood from *King* Charles II. 22nd April, 1662, and was advanced to a Baronetcy on the 13th September, in the same year. In 1664, he had an addition to his arms from Sir Edward Walker, garter king of arms, viz. "on a fess, three leopards' faces, or." Sir Robert m. first, Cecily, daughter of Mr. Alderman Humphry Hooke, of Bristol, and by that lady had

William, his successor.
Anne, m. first, to Sir Robert Gunning, knt. of Cold Ashton, in the county of Somerset, and secondly, to Sir Dudley North, knt. brother of Charles, Lord North and Grey, to Sir Francis North, the lord-keeper, and to Lord Guildford. By the latter husband, she had a son,
Dudley North, of Glemham, in Suffolk, who m. Catherine, daughter of Elihu Yale, esq. a governor in the East Indies, and had a son,
Dudley North, of Glemham, who m. Lady Barbara Herbert.

He wedded, secondly, Anne, daughter of W. Popley, esq. and had another son, (with a daughter, m. to Col. Joseph Earle, M.P. for Bristol,) another son,

Thomas (Sir), knighted by *King* James II. in the second year of whose reign he was high sheriff of the county of Gloucester. He m. Miss Earle, daughter of Sir Thomas Earle, knt. and dying in the lifetime of his father, left
Robert, who inherited as fourth baronet.
William, town-clerk of Bristol, who s. his brother as 5th baronet.

Sir Robert d. in November, 1685, and was s. by his eldest son,

II. Sir William Cann, of Compton Green, in the county of Gloucester, who m. Elizabeth, daughter of Sir Thomas Langton, knt. of Bristol, and dying 16th July, 1697, was s. by his son,

III. Sir William Cann. This gentleman wedded Elizabeth, sister of Thomas Chester, M.P. for Gloucestershire, but dying s. p. 27th April, 1726, in his thirty-second year, was s. by his cousin,

IV. Sir Robert Cann, high sheriff for Gloucestershire in 1736, who d. unm. in 1748, and was s. by his brother,

V. Sir William Cann, who left an only son,

VI. Sir Robert Cann, who m. Anne, daughter of Henry Churchman, esq. of Aust, in Gloucestershire, but dying without issue 20th July, 1765, the Baronetcy became extinct, while the estates devolved on Sir Robert's only sister and heiress,

Catherine, who m. 10th February, 1774, Charles Jeffries, esq. by whom she had an only daughter,
Elizabeth Jeffries, m. to Henry Lippincott, esq. of Sydbury, Devon, who was created a Baronet 7th September, 1778, and d. in 1781, leaving an only son,
Sir Henry Cann Lippincott, bart. who d. unm. in 1829.

Arms—Az. fretty arg. a fesse gu. charged with three leopards' faces or.

CAREW, OF ANTHONY.

Created 9th Aug. 1641. Extinct 24th Mar. 1748.

Lineage.

This was a younger branch of the Carews of Haccombe, in the county of Devon, founded by

Alexander Carew, esq.* of East Anthony, in Cornwall, who m. Isabel, daughter of John Hatch, esq. of Woodleigh, in Devon, (by the heir of Dyrwin) and dying in the 11th Henry VIII. was s. by his son,

John Carew, esq. of Anthony, who m. Thomasine, daughter and co-heir of Roger Holland, esq. and had four sons, viz.

Wymond (Sir), his successor.
John, of Poole, who left two daughters, his co-heirs.
Thomas, m. Eleanor, daughter of Sir Giles Strangeways, knt. and from him sprang the Carews of Hamworth, in the county of Dorset.
Roger, master of one of the colleges in Oxford.

Mr. Carew, who was sheriff of Cornwall in the 6th of Henry VIII. was s. at his decease by his eldest son,

Sir Wymond Carew, knt. of Anthony, who was treasurer to *Queen* Catherine, in the time of Henry VIII. and was knighted at the coronation of *King* Edward, being one of the forty knights made instead of so many knights of the bath, the time not being sufficient to perform the ceremonies necessary to the latter creations. He m. Martha, daughter of Edward Denny, esq. king's remembrancer, *temp.* Henry VII., and had issue,

Thomas, his heir.
Roger, who left issue.
George (Sir),† LL.D. left issue.

---

* Sir Nicholas Carew, knt. who d. in 1449, m. Joan, daughter of Sir Hugh Courtenay, knt. of Haccombe, by Philippa, his wife, daughter and co-heir of Sir Warren Erchedeacon, knt.) and had five sons, viz.
Thomas (Sir), ancestor of George Carew, Earl of Totness.
Nicholas, of Haccombe, Ringmore, and Milton.
Hugh, of Lyhem, Manedon, Combhall, and Southawton, d. issueless, and his estates passed to Nicholas.
Alexander, of East Anthony, in Cornwall, Shoggebroke, and Landegy.
William (Sir), of Wichehand, Widebridge, Bokeland, and Bledenagh, ancestor of the Carews of Crowcombe. (See Burke's *Commoners*, vol. i. p. 266.

The eldest son having disobliged his mother, that lady settled seventeen manors upon her younger sons, entailing the lands upon them and the issue of their bodies, substituting for want thereof, the one to be the heir of the other, and "in witness whereof (she says in her conveyance) to each of these deeds five times indented, I have set my seal; and because my seal is to many unknown, have procured the seal of the mayor of the city of Exeter to be also adjoyned."

† Carew, in his survey of Cornwall, calls this gentleman "Dr. Carew, one of the ancientest masters in chancery, in which calling, after his younger years, spent

John,
Anthony, } d. issueless.
Harvey,

The eldest son,

Thomas Carew, esq. of Anthony, was M.P. for Saltash, in the 5th of Elizabeth. He m. Elizabeth, daughter of Sir Richard Edgecombe, knt. of Mount Edgecombe, in the county of Devon, and was s. by his son,

Richard Carew, esq. the celebrated antiquary, and surveyor of Cornwall, sheriff of that county in the 24th Elizabeth, and M.P. for Saltash in the 27th of the same reign. Of this learned person, Anthony Wood, in his quaint style, gives the following account: "He was born at East Anthony, of an ancient and genteel family, 1555, became a gent. com. of Christ Church very young, about the time that his kinsman, George Carew, (afterwards Earl of Totness,) and William Camden, studied there; at fourteen years of age, he disputed extempore with the matchless Sir William Sidney, in the presence of the Earls of Leicester, Warwick, and other nobility, at what time they were lodged in Christ Church to receive entertainment from the muses; after he had spent three years in Oxon, he retired to the Middle Temple, where he spent three years more, and then was sent with his uncle, (Sir George Carew, as it seems,) in his embassage unto the King of Poland, whom, when he came to Dantzick, he found that he had been newly gone from thence into Sweden, whither also he went after him. After his return, and a short stay made in England, he was sent by his father into France, with Sir Henry Nevill, who was then ambassador leiger unto *King* Henry IV. He was high sheriff of Cornwall, 1586. In 1589, he was elected a member of the college of antiquaries, and about that time he made an historical survey of his native county, which was afterwards printed, he being then accounted a religious, ingenious man, learned, eloquent, liberal, stout, honest, and well skilled in several languages, and the most excellent manager of bees in Cornwall. He was intimate with the most noted scholars in his time, particularly with Sir Hen. Spelman, who in an epistle, (in his treatise, *De non temerandis Ecclesiæ*,) to him, doth not a little extoll him, for his ingenuity, virtue, and learning." Camden characterises him, as a person no less eminent for his honourable ancestors, than his own virtue and learning, who hath described and drawn this county, (Cornwall,) not in little, but at large, and whom I cannot but acknowledge to have been my chief guide through it." And again, speaking of Anthony, in Cornwall, he says, "Richard Carew, lord of it, 1607, who not only lived up to the dignity of his ancestors, but excelled them all in the ornaments of virtue." This eminent person m. Julian, daughter of John Arundel, esq. of Trerice, (and one of the heirs of her mother, Catharine Cosgwarth), by which lady he had several children. He d. 6th Nov. 1620, and was buried with his ancestors in the church of East Anthony, and there was shortly after a splendid monument erected to his memory. His eldest son and heir,†

I. Richard Carew, esq. of Anthony, was created a Baronet by *King* Charles I., 9th August, 1641. He m. first, in his father's lifetime, Bridget, daughter of John Chudleigh, esq. of Ashton, in the county of Devon, and by that lady had issue,

Alexander, his successor.
Elizabeth, m. to — Kendall.
Martha, m. to Pendarves of Pendarves.
Mary, d. unm.
Gertrude.

He m. secondly, Miss Rolle, of Heanton, and by her had two other sons, namely,

John, M.P. for Tregony, in 1641.
Thomas (Sir), of Barley, in the county of Devon, m. Elizabeth, daughter of John Cooper, esq. of Bowell, in the same county, and had several children.

Sir Richard was s. at his decease by his eldest son,

II. Sir Alexander Carew, M.P. for Cornwall in 1641. This gentleman having espoused the cause of the parliament, was accused of treason, and tried at Guildhall, in 1644, "for adhering to the king, and betraying his trust,"‡ convicted, and sentenced to death. On the Sunday ensuing, his lady presented a petition to the House of Commons, setting forth, that her husband was in a kind of distracted condition, and unfit to die, and therefore prayed he might be reprieved: whereupon a committee was sent to visit him, and report his condition, who declared him not to be distracted; that he might have time, however, to settle his estate and prepare himself for death, execution was respited for above a month, viz. till Monday, December 23, 1644, when he was brought by the lieutenant and his officers to a scaffold erected on Tower Hill, and there decapitated. He had m. Jane, daughter of Robert Rolle, esq. of Heanton, in the county of Devon, and sister of Sir Robert Rolle, knt. and had issue,

abroad to his benefit, he hath reposed himself." He again mentions him thus:—"Master George Carew, (afterwards Sir George) in his younger yeres, gathered such fruit at the universitie, the innes of court, and forrayne travel could yeeld him: upon his returne, he was first called to the bar, then supplyed the place of secretarie to the Lord Chancellour Hatton; and after his decease, performed the like office to his two successors, by special recommendation from her Majestie, who also gave him the prothonotaryship of the chancery, and in Anno 1598, sent him ambassador to the King of Poland, and other northern potentates, where through unexpected accidents, he underwent extraordinary perils, but God freed him from them, and he performed his duty in acceptable maner, and at this present the commonwealth useth his service as a master of the chancery."

† His younger son, John Carew, was a gallant soldier, and served with distinction in the Low Countries, and other parts. Having lost his right hand by a cannon ball at the siege of Ostend, in 1601, he was known amongst his friends as "one-handed Carew." He m. Alice, daughter of John Hilman, esq. of Furlong, and left issue. This branch is now extinct in the male line, but is still continued in the female by the families of Hoblyn, Peter, and Tremayne.

‡ Lord Clarendon relates, that, at the breaking out of the civil war, Plymouth was esteemed one of the most considerable towns in the west of England; that there was in it a strong castle towards the sea, with good platforms and ordnance; and, about a musket-shot from the town, there was an island with a fort in it, much stronger than the castle; and that the mayor and corporation of Plymouth seized both the castle and island, and kept them for the parliament: that, as a reward for the service thus rendered, the parliament committed the government thereof to the mayor, who was well enough instructed what respect to pay to their committee, which was appointed to reside there for his assistance, and to order the affairs in those parts. His lordship continues, "Of that committee, Sir Alexander Carew was one, a gentleman of good fortune in Cornwal, who served in parliament as knight for that county, and had, from the beginning of the parliament, concurred in all conclusions with the most violent, with as full a testimony of that zeal and fury, to which their confidence was applied, as any man. To him the custody and government of that fort and island, which was looked upon as the security of the town, was committed, and a sufficient garrison put into it. The mount commanded the castle and the town, about which a wall was cast up of earth, weak and irregular. After the battle of Stratton, and the king's forces prevailing so far over the

John, his successor.

Thomas, of Harrowbear, from whom descended

Alexander, in holy orders, who *s.* as seventh baronet.

Sir Alexander was *s.* by his elder son,

III. Sir John Carew, member in the restoration parliament for Cornwall, and again in that chosen in [illegible]. This gentleman *m.* first, Sarah, daughter of Anthony Hungerford, esq. of Farley Castle, and sister of Sir Edward Hungerford, K.B. and by her had two daughters,

Sarah, *m.* to Jonathan Rashleigh, esq. of Menabilly, in Cornwall, and left a daughter,

Sarah Rashleigh, who *m.* the Rev. Carolus Pole, rector of St. Breok, and with a younger son and daughter, had a son and heir,

Reginald Pole, who *m.* Anne, daughter of John Francis Buller, esq. of Morval, in Cornwall, and had with other children,

Reginald Pole, who inherited the estates of the Carews, and assuming their surname, was the late Right Hon. Reginald Pole Carew, of East Anthony.

Rachael, *m.* to Ambrose Manaton, esq. of Manaton, in Devonshire.

He *m.* secondly, Elizabeth, daughter of Richard Norton, esq. of Southwick, Hants, but of this marriage there was no surviving issue; and thirdly, Mary, daughter of Sir William Morrice, bart. of Werrington, in Devon, and by that lady had

Alexander,
William, } fourth and fifth baronets.

Gertrude, *m.* first, to Sir Godfrey Copley, bart. of Sprotborough, in the county of York, and secondly, to Sir Coplestone-Warwick Bampfylde, bart.; by the latter she had issue,

Sir Richard Warwick Bampfylde, bart. grandfather of George-Warwick, first Baron Poltimore.

Mary Bampfylde, *m.* first, to Sir Coventry Carew, bart. and secondly, to William Buller, esq. M.P. for Westloe.

Sir John *d.* in 1692, and was *s.* by his elder son,

IV. Sir Alexander Carew, who *d. s. p.* and was *s.* by his brother,

V. Sir William Carew, M.P. for Cornwall. This gentleman *m.* Lady Anne Coventry, only daughter and heiress of Gilbert, fourth Earl of Coventry, and dying [illegible] March, 1744, was *s.* by his only son,

VI. Sir Coventry Carew, who *m.* 1st July, 1738, his cousin, Mary, only daughter of Sir Coplestone-Warwick Bampfylde, bart. of Poltimore, but *d. s. p.* 24th March, 1748, when the Baronetcy reverted to his kinsman,

VII. The Rev. Sir Alexander Carew (refer to Sir Alexander, the second bart.) who *d.* also issueless, when the title became extinct.

The estates, including East Anthony, passed at the decease of Lady Carew, widow of Sir Coventry Carew, to John Carew, esq.* of Camerton, of the Crowcombe branch, and at his demise without male issue to the great-grandson of the third baronet (to whom refer), the Right Hon. Reginald Pole Carew, of East Anthony.

Arms—Or, three lioncels passant in pale sa. armed and langued gu.

CAREW, OF BEDDINGTON.

Created 11th Jan. 1715.—Extinct 19th Aug. 1762.

Lineage.

Sir Nicholas Throckmorton, knt. of Pauler's Perry, in Northamptonshire (fourth son of Sir George Throckmorton, of Coughton, by Catharine, his wife, daughter of Nicholas, Lord Vaux of Harrowden, see Burke's *Baronetage*), was a distinguished person at the time in which he lived, and filled successively the appointments of chief butler, chamberlain of the Exchequer, and ambassador to France and Scotland. He *m.* Anne, daughter of Sir Nicholas Carew, K.G. of Beddington, and sister and heir of Sir Francis Carew, by whom he had issue,

I. Arthur (Sir), of Pauler's Perry, knt. sheriff of Northamptonshire, who *m.* Anne, daughter of Sir Thomas Lucas, of Colchester, and had four daughters, his co-heirs, viz.

Mary, *m.* in 1608, to Thomas, Baron Wotton.

Anne, *m.* in 1614, to Sir Peter Temple, bart. of Stowe.

Elizabeth, *m.* in 1617, to Richard, Lord Dacre.

Catherine, died unmarried.

II. Nicholas, of whom presently.

I. Elizabeth, *m.* to Sir Walter Raleigh.

The younger son,

Sir Nicholas Throckmorton, knt. of Beddington, in Surrey, inherited the estate and assumed the surname of his maternal ancestors, Carew. He *m.* Mary, eldest daughter of Sir George More, knt. of Loseley, and was *s.* by his son,

Sir Francis Carew, of Beddington, who *m.* Susan, daughter of Sir William Romney, and dying 9th April, 1649, left a son and successor,

---

[illegible] that Bristol was taken by them, and Exeter closely [illegible], Sir Alexander Carew began to think, his island and fort would hardly secure his estate in Cornwal, and understood the law so well, (for he had had a good education [illegible] know, that the side he had chosen would be no [illegible] the better, than it should continue the stronger; [illegible] having originally followed no other motives than of [illegible] and interest, resolved now to redeem his [illegible], and found means to correspond with some of his [illegible] friends and neighbours in Cornwal, and by them to [illegible] a direct overture to surrender that fort and island to the king, upon an assurance of his Majesty's pardon, and a full remission of his offences. Sir John Berkley, [illegible] then lay before Exeter, was the next supreme officer [illegible] to entertain such a treaty, and he instantly, by the same conveyance, returned him as ample assurance [illegible] own conditions as could be; with advice, that he [illegible] not upon defect of forms (which upon his engagement should be supplied with all possible expedition to [illegible] own satisfaction) defer the consummating the work, [illegible] hereafter possibly might not be in his power to effect. But he was so sottishly and dangerously wary of his own security, (having neither courage enough to obey his conscience, nor wicked enough to be prosperous against it,) that he would not proceed till he was sufficiently assured that his pardon was passed the great seal of England; before which time, though all imaginable haste was made, by the treachery of a servant whom he trusted, his treaty and design were discovered to the mayor and the rest of the committee: and according to the diligence used by that party in cases of such concernment, he was suddenly, and without resistance, surprised in his fort, and carried prisoner into Plymouth, and from thence by sea sent to London, when he was condemned by a court-martial, and executed as above related."

* John Carew, esq. of Camerton and East Anthony, left two daughters,

Mary, *m.* to George Henry Warrington, esq. of Pentrepant, the present G. H. Carew, esq. of Crowcombe.

Elizabeth.

Sir Nicholas Carew, of Beddington, who m. Susan, dau. of Sir Justinian Isham, and had, with other issue,

Francis (Sir), his heir.

Philippa, m. Richard Gee, esq. of Orpington, in Kent, and had a son,

Richard Gee, of Orpington, who m. Elizabeth, daughter and heir of John Holt, esq. and died in 1791, leaving issue,

1. William Gee, of Beddington.
2. Richard Gee, of Beddington.
3. Philippa Gee, d. unm.

Sir Nicholas d. in 1687-8, and was s. by his son,

Sir Francis Carew, of Beddington, baptized 12th September, 1663, who m. Ann, daughter of William Boteler, and dying in 1689, was s. by his son,

I. Nicholas Carew, esq. of Beddington, b. 6th February, 1686-7, M.P. for Haslemere, and subsequently knight of the shire for Surrey, who was created a Baronet 11th June, 1715. He m. Anne, daughter of Nicholas Hacket, esq. of Bucks, and had one son and one daughter, viz.

Nicholas-Hacket, his heir.

Anne, m. first, to Thomas Fountayne, esq. of Melton, in Yorkshire; and secondly, to Joshua Ward, esq. of the Inner Temple.

Sir Nicholas died in March, 1726-7 (his widow, who wedded, secondly, in 1728, William Chetwynd, esq. M.P. died in 1746), and was s. by his only son,

II. Sir Nicholas-Hacket Carew, of Beddington, who m. in April, 1741, the daughter of John Martin, esq. of Overbury, in Gloucestershire, M.P. for Tewkesbury, but dying without male issue 19th August, 1762, he devised his estates, first to his daughter Catharine, who d. unmarried in 1769, and subsequently to different relations; they ultimately devolved on Richard Gee, esq. (grandson of Richard Gee, esq. of Orpington, by Philippa, daughter of Nicholas Carew, esq. of Beddington). Mr. Gee assumed the surname and arms of Carew, but d. unmarried in 1816, bequeathing the property to his brother William's widow, Mrs. Anne Paston Gee, who died in 1828, and by her will devised Beddington, &c. to Admiral Sir Benjamin Hallowell, who assumed the surname of Carew and died in 1836, when he was s. by his son, the present Captain Carew, R.N. of Beddington.

Arms—Or, three lioncels passant in pale sa.

CARLETON, OF HOLCOMBE.

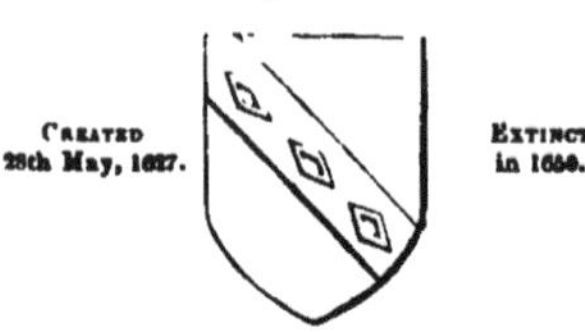

Lineage.

I. Sir John Carleton, of Holcombe, in Oxfordshire, created a Baronet in 1627, was eldest son and heir of George Carleton, esq. of Holcombe, by Elizabeth, his wife, daughter and co-heir of Sir John Brockett, of Brockett Hall, Herts, and inherited in 1631, under the will of his uncle, Sir Dudley Carleton, Viscount Dorchester, that nobleman's estate at Brightwell, in Oxfordshire. He m. in 1625, Anne, daughter of Sir R. Houghton, knt. of Houghton, in Lancashire, and relict of Sir John Cotton, of Lanwade, in Cambridgeshire, by whom he had one son and two daughters, viz.

George, his heir.

Anne, b. at Cheeveley, 29th October, 1627, m. in 1647, George Garth, esq. of Morden, in Surrey, and had issue. She d. in 1655, and was buried at Morden.

Catharine, b. at Cheeveley, in 1630, m. in 16[illegible] to John Stone, esq. and d. at Crawley, in Be[illegible]fordshire, in 1668, leaving with other issue, a son and evantual heir,

John Stone, esq. of Brightwell, who d. without issue in 1732, the last of his family, bequeathing his estates to Mary Stone, his widow, for life, with remainder to his cousin and heir,

Francis Lowe, esq. by whose great-grandson,

William-Francis Lowndes-St[illegible] esq. of Brightwell Park, in Ox[illegible]shire, they are now possessed. See Burke's *Commoners*, vol. iii. p. [illegible]

Sir John Carleton d. in London, in November, 16[illegible] and was buried at Brightwell. His widow surv[illegible] until 17th May, 1671, and was interred at Lanwa[illegible] the burial place of the Cotton family. Sir John's [illegible] son,

II. Sir George Carleton, of Holcombe, d. unmarried in 1650, seised of the manors of Brightwell [illegible] wallis, and Holcombe, in the county of Oxford a[illegible] administration was granted in February, 1651, to [illegible] two sisters, as co-heirs, but a fine was levied [illegible] George Garth, and Anne, his wife, John Stone, a[illegible] Catharine, his wife, and a recovery suffered of the estates, and by a subsequent deed in the same year between the same parties, John Stone agreed to p[illegible] off certain rent charges, &c. and also the sum [illegible] £5400 to George Garth, esq. which was accord[illegible] paid, whereby the said George Garth released [illegible] the estates to John Stone, and Catharine, his wife, and their heirs for ever. Those estates are at present enjoyed by William-Francis Lowndes-Stone, esq. of Brightwell Park.

At Sir George Carleton's decease, in 1650, the Baronetcy became extinct.

Arms—Arg. on a bend sa. three mascles of the fi[illegible]

CARPENTIER, OF FRANCE.

Created 9th Oct. 1656.—Extinct, date unknown.

Lineage.

In 1656, a Baronetcy of England was conferre[illegible]

I. Sir Arthur Marigni Carpentier, but [illegible] gentleman, who was of French extraction, and [illegible] descendants, no particulars have ever been obtained.

CARR, OF SLEAFORD.

Lineage.

I. Sir Edward Carr, of Sleaford, in Lincoln[illegible] who was created a Baronet 29th June, 1611, m. [illegible]

Katherine, daughter of Charles Bolle, esq. of Haugh, which lady *d. s. p.*, and secondly, Anne, daughter of Sir Richard Dyer, knt. of Staughton, in the county of Huntingdon, by whom he left at his decease in 1619, a son,

II. SIR ROBERT CARR, of Sleaford, who *m.* Mary, daughter and co-heir of Sir Richard Gargrave, knt. of Nostell, in the county of York, and dying 14th Aug. 1667, was *s.* by his son,

III. SIR ROBERT CARR, of Sleaford, who *m.* Elizabeth, daughter of Sir John Bennet, sister of Henry, Lord Arlington, and was *s.* at his decease, in November, 1682, by his son,

IV. SIR EDWARD CARR, of Sleaford, at whose decease *s. p.* 1683, aged twenty-one, the BARONETCY became EXTINCT.

Arms—Gu. on a chev. or, three etoiles sa.

CARTERET, OF METESCHES.

CREATED 9th May, 1645.

EXTINCT 1776.

Lineage.

REGINALD DE CARTERET, son of Sir Philip de Carteret, Lord of St. Owen, preserved, by his prudence and valour, the island of Jersey from falling into the hands of the French in the year 1374, when Bertrand du Guesclin, constable of France, famous for his many victories over the English, passed suddenly from Bretagne into Jersey, with an army of ten thousand men, wherein were the Duke of Bourbon, and the flower of the French chivalry. At that time this Reginald de Carteret secured Mount Orgueil Castle, and defended it so bravely, that after many violent assaults the constable withdrew his forces, leaving many of his best soldiers dead under the walls. For this great achievement, Reginald and his seven sons were all knighted by *King* EDWARD III. in one day. From this gallant personage we pass to his descendant,

SIR PHILIP CARTERET, who undertook, in the reign of ELIZABETH, to plant such a colony in the island of Sark, as should keep out the French, and he accordingly enlarged the settlement, and thereby improved his own estate. He *m.* Rachael, daughter and heir of Sir George Paulet, son and heir of Lord Thomas Paulet, of Cossington, in the county of Somerset, second son of William, Marquess of Winchester, and had, with other issue,

- PHILIP (Sir), his successor, who *m.* Anne, daughter of Sir Francis Dowse, knt. of Wallop, in the county of Southampton, and was *s.* by his eldest son,
  - PHILIP, in the seigniory of St. Owen. This gentleman was created a BARONET in 1670, as SIR PHILIP CARTERET, of St. Owen, in Jersey. He *m.* Anne Dumasque, and dying in 1672, was *s.* by his son,
    - PHILIP, second baronet, who *m.* Elizabeth, daughter of Sir Edward Carteret, and dying in 1693, was *s.* by his son,
      - CHARLES (Sir), third baronet, who was one of the gentlemen of the privy chamber to *Queen* ANNE, and high bailiff of the island of Jersey. Sir Charles *d.* in 1715, when the BARONETCY EXPIRED, but his estates passed to Lord Carteret.
- HELIER, of whom presently.
- Rachael, *m.* first, to — Beaver, esq. of the island of Jersey, and secondly, to — De Vic, esq.
- Judith, *m.* to Sir Brian Johnson, of Buckinghamshire.

The second son,

HELIER CARTERET, esq. deputy governor of Jersey, *m.* Elizabeth Dumasque, and had, with other children,

I. SIR GEORGE CARTERET, a naval officer of high reputation, who, through the influence of the Duke of Buckingham, was appointed in the 2nd of *King* CHARLES I. joint governor of Jersey, and at the breaking out of the civil war, held the office of comptroller of the navy. Sir George was, however, so much esteemed by all parties, that when the parliament passed the ordinance for the Earl of Warwick to command the fleet, then fully and entirely at their disposal, they likewise resolved that Captain Carteret should be vice-admiral: but he declined the appointment at the express command of the king. Upon which Lord Clarendon observes, "his interest and reputation in the navy was so great, and his diligence and dexterity in command so eminent, that it was generally believed he would, against whatsoever the Earl of Warwick could have done, have preserved the major part of the fleet in their duty to the king." Having thus retired from the navy, he withdrew with his family to Jersey; but subsequently returned to aid the projects of the royalists, when he was created by *King* CHARLES a BARONET, 9th May, 1645. He again, however, went back to his government in Jersey, and there, in the ruin of the royal cause, afforded an asylum to the Prince of Wales, (who appointed him his vice-chamberlain,) Mr. Hyde, afterwards Lord Clarendon, and other refugees of distinction. After this he defended the island of Jersey in the most gallant manner against the parliamentarians, and ultimately only surrendered upon receiving the command of *King* CHARLES II. so to do. Elizabeth Castle, in the island of Jersey, under Sir George Carteret, was the last fortress that lowered the royal banner. At the restoration, Sir George formed one of the immediate train of the restored monarch in his triumphant entry into London; and the next day he was sworn of the privy-council, and declared VICE-CHAMBERLAIN. He was afterwards returned to parliament by the corporation of Portsmouth. Sir George *m.* Elizabeth, daughter of Sir Philip Carteret, knt. of St. Owen, and had issue,

- PHILIP (Sir), who had eminently distinguished himself during the civil wars, and was governor of Mount Orgueil Castle, when it was invested by the parliamentary forces in 1651. Sir Philip *m.* Jemima, daughter of Edward Montagu, first Earl of Sandwich, vice-admiral of England, and had issue,
  - GEORGE, who *s.* his grandfather.
  - Philip, captain of marines. Lost at sea in 1693.
  - Edward, M.P. joint post-master-general, *m.* Bridget, daughter of Sir Thomas Exton, judge of the high court of admiralty, and *d.* in 1739, leaving issue.

  Sir Philip Carteret being with his father-in-law, Lord Sandwich, in the great naval engagement off Solebay, 28th May, 1672, was blown up with that gallant officer in the Royal James.
- James, captain R.N. in the reign of *King* CHARLES II.
- George, *d.* unm. in 1656.

Anne, m. to Sir Nicholas Slaning, of the county of Devon, K.B.

Caroline, m. to Sir Thomas Scot, of Scot's Hall, Kent.

Louisa-Margaretta, m. to Sir Robert Atkins, of Saperton, in the county of Gloucester.

Sir George d. 13th January, 1679, and was s. by his grandson,

II. Sir George Carteret, second baronet, who was elevated to the peerage on the 19th October, 1681, as Baron Carteret, of Hawnes, with remainder, default of male issue, to his brothers, and their heirs male. This nobleman, when only eight years of age, was m. to Lady Grace Granville, youngest daughter of John, Earl of Bath, and co-heiress of her nephew, William-Henry, last Earl of Bath of that family; a marriage agreed upon by his grandfather, Sir George Carteret, and the Earl of Bath, to cement the friendship which had long subsisted between them. By this lady his lordship had issue, John, his successor, with another son, Philip, and a daughter, Jemima, who both d. unmarried. His lordship, who was a zealous supporter of the revolution, d. at the early age of twenty-six, in 1695. His widow, Lady Carteret, having succeeded as co-heiress to the great Bath estates, upon the decease of her nephew, William-Henry Granville, Earl of Bath, in 1711 (when that dignity became extinct), was created on the 1st January, 1714, *Viscountess Carteret*, and Countess Granville, with remainder of the viscounty, default of male issue in her son, John, Lord Carteret, to the uncle of that nobleman, Edward Carteret, esq. and his male heirs. Her ladyship d. in 1744, and was s. by her only surviving son,

III. Sir John Carteret, second Lord Carteret, as Earl Granville. His lordship was appointed one of the lords of the bedchamber at the accession of *King* George I., and constituted in 1716 lord-lieutenant and custos rotulorum of the county of Devon. In 1719 he was accredited ambassador extraordinary to the court of Sweden. In 1721 he was declared principal secretary of state, and in 1724 constituted lord lieutenant of Ireland, which high office he retained for the six following years. He was thrice one of the lords justices during the occasional absence of the king, and a knight of the most noble order of the garter. His lordship m. first, 17th October, 1710, Frances, only daughter of Sir Robert Worsley, bart. and grand-daughter maternally of Thomas Thynne, Viscount Weymouth, by whom he had surviving issue,

Robert, his successor.

Grace, m. to Lionel, Earl of Dorset.

Louisa, m. to Thomas Thynne, Viscount Weymouth, and had issue,

Thomas, Viscount Weymouth, created Marquess of Bath, d. in 1784, and left

Thomas, present Marquess of Bath, and other issue.

Henry-Frederick, having inherited the Carteret estates, under the will of his grandfather, Earl of Granville, after the decease of his uncle, assumed the surname and arms of Carteret, and was created in 1784, Baron Carteret, of Hawnes, with remainder to the younger sons of his brother, the Marquess of Bath. His lordship d. in 1826, and the barony passed according to the limitation to his nephew, Lord George Thynne, present Lord Carteret.

Georgiana-Carolina, m. first, to the Hon. John Spencer, and secondly, to William, Earl Cowper.

Frances, m. to John, Marquess of Tweedale.

The earl espoused, secondly, Lady Sophia Fermor, daughter of Thomas, Earl of Pomfret, and had an only daughter,

Sophia, who m. in 1765, William Petty, second Earl of Shelburne, afterwards Marquess of Lansdown, by whom she had an only son,

John, second Marquess of Lansdown, half brother of Henry, present marquess.

His lordship d. 2nd January, 1763, and was s. by his son,

IV. Sir Robert Carteret, third Lord Carteret, and second Earl Granville. His lordship d. without issue in 1776, when the Baronetcy, with the Barony of Carteret, Earldom of Granville, and Viscounty of Carteret, became extinct.

Arms—Gules, four fusils in fesse ar. for Carteret.

CASTLETON, OF ST. EDMUNDSBURY.

Created 9th Aug. 1641. Extinct 17th Nov. 1[illegible]

Lineage.

William Castilton, of the county of Lincoln, was father of another

William Castilton, who was of Ditton, in Surrey. His son,

Robert Castilton, of Ditton, m. first, Elizabeth Gilbert, of Clare, in Suffolk, but by her had no issue. He m. secondly, a daughter of — Clement, of [illegible] and had William, John, Francis, Judith, Sarah, and Elizabeth. The eldest son,

William Castleton, was of Edmundsbury, in Suffolk, and in the 14th of James I. possessed the manors of Clopton, otherwise Clopton Hall, in Woolpit, and Rattlesden, and several other lands there. He m. Anne, daughter of William Hill, of Bury, and was s. by his son,

I. William Castleton, esq. of Edmundsbury, who was created a Baronet by *King* Charles I. 9th August 1641. He m. Mrs. Bacon, widow of — Bacon, esq. of Hesset, in Suffolk, and daughter of — Mason, esq. of the same county, and had issue,

John, his successor.

William, m. Miss Sidney, and had two sons, viz.

William, d. s. p.

Charles, in holy orders, who inherited as sixth baronet.

Anne, m. to John Jermy, esq. of Gunton, in Norfolk.

Elizabeth, m. to John Southby, esq. of Bury, in Suffolk.

Sarah.

Sir William was s. by his elder son,

II. Sir John Castleton, whose seats were Shipdam in Norfolk, and Sturston, in Suffolk. He m. Margaret, daughter and heir of Robert Morse, esq.* of the latter place, by which marriage he acquired it, and by her had issue,

John, his successor.

* By Margaret, his wife, daughter of Henry Bedingfeld, esq.

George, } *d. s. p.*
Charles, }
Robert, fourth baronet.
Philip, fifth baronet.

Sarah, *m.* to Sir Henry Bacon, bart. of Heringflete, in Suffolk.
Margaret, *m.* to Thomas Baispool, esq.
Elizabeth, *m.* to the Rev. Edward Bosworth.

Sir John was *s.* by his eldest son,

III. Sir John Castleton, who *m.* Bridget, daughter of Thomas Read, esq. of Bardwell, in Suffolk, but dying issueless in 1705, was *s.* by his brother,

IV. Sir Robert Castleton, who *d.* unm. and was *s.* by his brother,

V. Sir Philip Castleton. This gentleman *m.* Miss Clarke, daughter of Osborne Clarke, gent. and had one son and two daughters, all of whom predeceased him, issueless. At his decease the baronetcy reverted to his kinsman (refer to the first baronet),

VI. The Rev. Sir Charles Castleton, rector of Gillingham, in Norfolk, who *m.* in 1693, Elizabeth, second daughter of Mr. Edward Taverner, of St. Olaves Abbey, in Heringfleet, county of Suffolk, and had issue,

Charles, }
John, } seventh, eighth, and ninth baronets.
William, }
Edward, in holy orders, eleventh baronet.

Sarah.
Elizabeth, *m.* to the Rev. Robert Leman, rector of Kettlebaston, in Suffolk.
Anne.

The eldest son,

VII. Sir Charles Castleton, who *d.* unm. 22nd October, 1749, and was *s.* by his brother,

VIII. The Rev. Sir John Castleton, rector of Gorstone, in Suffolk, and afterwards of Hopton, in Essex, who *d. s. p.* 7th November, 1777, and was *s.* by his brother,

IX. Sir William Castleton, who dying (at Hingham, in Norfolk,) 16th January, 1788, aged eighty-seven, was *s.* by his son,

X. Sir John Castleton, who *d. s. p.* 11th June, 17[illegible], when the title reverted to his uncle,

XI. The Rev. Sir Edward Castleton, rector of Thornham with Holme, in the county of Norfolk, who *d.* in 1794, aged eighty-seven, and was *s.* by his son,

XII. Sir Edward Castleton, who resided at Lynn, in Norfolk, and being reduced in circumstances, did not assume the title. He *d. s. p.* 17th November, 1810, when the Baronetcy became extinct.

Arms—Az. on a bend or, three snakes of the field.

CHALONER, OF GUISBOROUGH.

Created 30th July, 1620. | Extinct about 1640.

Lineage.

Sir Thomas Chaloner, of Steeple Clayton, in Bucks, and of Guisboro', in Yorkshire, son of Sir Thomas Chaloner, of London, and the descendant of an ancient Welsh family, *m.* first, Elizabeth, daughter of William Fleetwood, sergeant-at-law and recorder of London, and had by her, who *d.* in 1603,

I. William, his heir.
II. Edward, D. D. chaplain to Charles I. *m.* Elizabeth, daughter of Dr. Hoveden, prebendary of Canterbury, and dying at Oxford in 1625, left issue. In his descendant the representation of the Chalouer family is at present vested.
III. Thomas, *d. s. p.*
IV. James, *m.* Ursula, sister of Sir W. Fairfax, of Steeton, and *d.* in 1659, leaving issue,

I. Mary, *m.* to Sir Edward Fisher.

Sir Thomas wedded, secondly, Judith, daughter of William Blount, of London, and by her, who *d.* in 1615, had several children. He *d.* himself in 1613, and was *s.* by his son,

I. Sir William Chaloner, of Guisborough, who was created a Baronet in 1620, but dying *s. p.* in 1640, the title became extinct.

Arms—Sa. a chev. between three cherubim or.

CHAMBERLAYNE, OF WICKHAM.

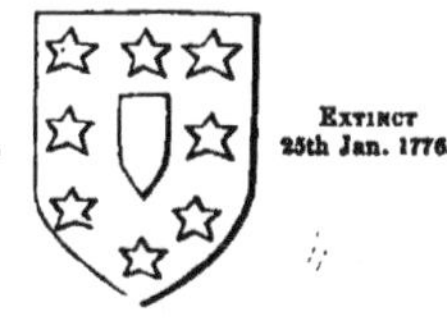

Created 4th Feb. 1642. | Extinct 25th Jan. 1776.

Lineage.

This family is stated to have sprung from the Counts of Tankerville, in Normandy.

William, Count of Tankerville, came into England with the Conqueror; but returned to the dukedom, leaving behind him his kinsman,

John de Tankerville, who was chamberlain to King Henry I. and father of

Richard, chamberlain to King Stephen, who from his office assumed his surname, and bore for arms first and fourth, gules, an escutcheon, argent, in an orle of eight mullets, or; second and third, gules, a chevron, between three escallops, or, which his descendants afterwards bore. His son,

William Chamberlayne, Lord of North Riston, was chamberlain to King Henry II. and for having made prisoner Robert de Bellemont, Earl of Leicester, had permission in 1174, from the king, to quarter that nobleman's arms with his own. He *m.* the daughter of Clifton, and left a son,

Robert Chamberlayne, father of

Sir Richard Chamberlayne, who *m.* Jane, daughter and heir of John Gatesden, and was succeeded by his son,

Sir Robert Chamberlayne, who married a daughter of Griffith, of Northamptonshire, and left a son and heir,

Sir John Chamberlayne, who *m.* Jane, daughter and heir of John Mortein, son and heir of Sir John Mortein, by the heir of Ekney, and was succeeded by his son,

Sir Richard Chamberlayne, who m. Jane, daughter of Sir John Reyns, of Clifton Reyns, knt. and had, with several other children,

m. Richard (Sir), who settled at Sherborne, in Oxfordshire, where his posterity continued until the time of James I.* when

John Chamberlayne, esq. the last male descendant died, leaving two daughters, his co-heirs, namely,

Mary, m. first, to Sir Thomas Gage, bart. of Firle, and secondly, to Sir William Goring, bart. of Burton, both in Sussex.

——, m. to Lord Abergavenny.

John.

The younger son,

John Chamberlayne, esq. of Hopton, in the county of Derby, married Alice Bensted, and left a son and heir,

Thomas Chamberlayne, esq. who m. a daughter of Knifton, and was father of

John Chamberlayne, esq. who m. — Elton, and had a son and heir,

John Chamberlayne, esq. who m. Agnes Keynes, and was s. by his son,

William Chamberlayne, esq. who m. Elizabeth Fleming, of Dartmouth, and had issue,

Thomas (Sir), of Presbury, a diplomatist in the reigns of Henry VIII. Edward VI. *Queen* Mary, and *Queen* Elizabeth. This gentleman m. first, Anne Vander-Zenney, of the Low Countries; secondly, Elizabeth, daughter of Sir John Ludington, and relict of — Machine: from this marriage descended the Chamberlaynes of Maugersbury, and the Rev. Doctor Thomas Chamberlayne, D.D. who was Dean of Bristol in the time of George II. Sir Thomas Chamberlayne wedded, thirdly, Anne Kirkeet, half sister to Anthony Monk, of Devonshire, grandfather to the Duke of Albemarle, from whom descended the Chamberlaynes of Oddington.

William.

The younger son,

William Chamberlayne, esq. settled in Ireland, and was father of

Sir Thomas Chamberlayne, knt. an eminent lawyer, chief justice of Chester, from which he was promoted, in 1616, to be one of the judges of the Court of King's Bench. He retired from the latter high judicial seat in 1622, and was permitted to resume his former office, in which he died. He m. Elizabeth, daughter of Sir George Fermor, knt. of Easton Neston, in the county of Northampton, and widow of Sir William Stafford, knt. of Blatherwick, in the same county, and by her had

Thomas, his heir.

George, of Wardington, in the county of Oxford, m. Anne, daughter of Sir Richard Saltinstall, knt. of South Okingdon, Essex, and had issue. The eventual heiress of the Chamberlaynes of Wardington,

Elizabeth, m. Wenman Coke, esq. of Holkham.

The eldest son,

i. Thomas Chamberlayne, esq. of Wickham, in the county of Oxford, was created a Baronet by *King* Charles I. 4th February, 1642. He m. a daughter of the knightly family of the Aclands,† in the county of Devon, and dying in 1671, was succeeded by his elder son,

ii. Sir Thomas Chamberlayne, who m. Margaret, daughter of Edmund Prideaux, esq. of the Inner Temple, and had two daughters, his co-heirs, viz.

i. Catherine, m. first, to Richard, Viscount Wenman.

ii. Penelope, m. to Sir Robert Dashwood, bart. of Northbrooke, in Oxfordshire.

He d. in 1682, and leaving no male issue, the baronetcy devolved upon his brother,

iii. Sir James Chamberlayne, who m. Margaret, daughter of — Goodwin, gent. of Bodicote, in the county of Oxford, and had issue,

James, his successor.

Henry.

Thomas.

He died in October, 1699, and was succeeded by his eldest son,

iv. Sir James Chamberlayne, lieutenant colonel in the horse-guards, m. Miss Walker, whose father was clerk of the House of Commons, and dying without male issue 23rd December, 1776, was succeeded by his brother,

v. Sir Henry Chamberlayne, with whom the Baronetcy expired 25th January, 1776.

Arms—Gu. an inescutcheon arg. between eight mullets in orle or.

CHAPLIN, OF LONDON.

Created 19th Sept. 1715.

Extinct 23rd May, 1730.

Lineage.

i. Sir Robert Chaplin, descended from Sir Francis Chaplin, knt. alderman of London, living in the time of Charles II. represented the borough of Great Grimsby in parliament, and was created a Baronet in 1715. Engaging in the South Sea scheme in 1720, Sir Robert became a director of the company, and was involved in the losses of that calamitous enterprise. He d. without male issue (one of his daughters m. the Hon. Mr. Bateman, younger brother to Viscount Bateman), and was s. by (the son of his eldest brother Porter Chaplin,) his nephew,

ii. Sir John Chaplin, on whom the title was limited. This gentleman married a widow lady named Morris, but dying issueless 23rd May, 1730, aged nineteen, the Baronetcy became extinct.

Arms—Erm. on a chief vert, three griphons' heads erased or.

---

* Francis Chamberlayne, esq. who represented New Shoreham in parliament, and Richard Chamberlayne, esq. of Princethorpe, in Warwickshire, descended from this branch of the family.

† So says Collins, but Le Neve enquires, whether he did not marry Anne, daughter of Richard Chamberlayne, esq. of Temple House, in the county of Warwick?

CHAPMAN, OF LONDON.

CREATED 27th June, 1720

EXTINCT about 1784.

Lineage.

Sir John Chapman, knt. son of Jasper Chapman, of Rushbury, in Shropshire, was an eminent merchant and alderman of London, of which city he served as lord mayor in 1688, and proclaimed in the February of that year *King* William and *Queen* Mary. Sir John dying 7th May, 1737, left, with two daughters, the elder, the wife of Sir Oliver Ayshcomb, bart. of Lyfford, in Berkshire; the younger, Bethia, died unmarried; a son and successor,

I. Sir William Chapman, who was knighted in October, 1714, and created a Baronet in June, 1720. He *m.* Elizabeth, dau. of Thomas Webb, alias Wood, esq. of Kensington, and had two sons, John and William. Sir William *d.* 7th May, 1737, and was *s.* by his son,

II. Sir John Chapman, of Cockenheath, in Hertfordshire, M.P. for Taunton, who *m.* in November, 1736, Rachel, dau. and co-heir of James Edmonson, esq. but dying *s. p.* 29th January, 1781, was *s.* by his brother,

III. Sir William Chapman, who died issueless about 1784, when the Baronetcy became extinct.

Arms—Party per chev. arg. and gu. a crescent counterchanged.

CHARDIN, OF THE INNER TEMPLE, LONDON.

CREATED 28th May, 1720.

EXTINCT 26th April, 1755.

Lineage.

Sir John Chardin, a gentleman of French extraction, well known for his travels into Persia and the eastern countries, emigrated to England in consequence of the persecutions to which those professing the Protestant religion were exposed in his native country, and received from *King* Charles II. in 1680, the honor of knighthood. Sir John died 25th December, 1712, leaving a son, John, his heir, and other issue, of whom one daughter, Julia, *m.* Sir Christopher Musgrave, bart. of Hartley Castle, in Westmoreland; and another *m.* a Mr. St. Leger, by whom she had a daughter, the wife of John Ded, esq. The son and heir,

I. Sir John Chardin, of the Inner Temple, London, was created a Baronet in 1720, but dying *s. p.* in 1755, aged sixty-eight, the Baronetcy became extinct.

Arms—Arg. a chev. between two roses in chief gu. and a dove in base az.

CHARLETON, OF HESLEYSIDE.

CREATED 6th March, 1645.

EXTINCT (date unknown).

Lineage.

William Charleton, esq. of Hesleyside, in Northumberland, left two sons, namely,

- Edward, his heir.
- William, who *m.* first, Jane, daughter of William Swinburne, esq. of Capheaton, by whom he had an only daughter, a nun; and secondly, Elizabeth, daughter of Sir Edward Musgrave, bart. by whom he had a son,
  - William, of York and Long Lea, who purchased the whole of Hesleyside from the heirs of Sir Edward Charleton, bart. He married that gentleman's daughter and co-heir Dorothy, and was father of
    - William Charleton, esq. of Hesleyside, who married a daughter and co-heir of Roger Crofts, of East Appleton, and was *s.* by his son,
    - Edward Charleton, esq. of Hesleyside, father, by Teresa, his wife, dau. of Sir John Swinburne, bart. of Capheaton, of
    - William Charleton, esq. of Hesleyside, who *m.* Margaret, daughter of John Fenwicke, esq. by Mary, his wife, daughter of John Thornton, esq. of Netherwitton, and by her, who died 12th March, 1833, aged 75, had a son and successor,
    - William-John Charleton, esq. of Hesleyside, *b.* in 1782, sheriff of Northumberland in 1837, *m.* Catherine-Henrietta, daughter of Francis Cholmeley, esq. of Bransby, and has five sons and two daughters.

The elder son,

I. Sir Edward Charleton, of Hesleyside, in Northumberland, who was created a Baronet in 1645, *m.* Mary, daughter and co-heir of Sir Edward Widdrington, bart. of Cartington, and had three daughters, his co-heirs; of whom one, Dorothy, *m.* William Charleton, esq. her cousin; another *m.* — Talbot, esq.; and a third, Catherine, became the wife of Sir Nicholas Sherburne, of Stonyhurst. At Sir Edward's decease the title expired.

Arms—Or, a lion rampant gu. (Powys,

CHARLTON, OF LUDFORD.

Created 12th May, 1686.—Extinct 3rd Dec. 1784.

Lineage.

I. Sir Job Charlton, of Ludford, in the county of Hereford (representative of a branch of the ancient house of Charlton of Appley, see Burke's *Commoners*, vol. i. p. 27), was appointed chief justice of Chester, and nominated one of the judges of the Common Pleas *temp.* Charles II. In the 2nd of James II. he was advanced to the dignity of a Baronet, and was speaker of the House of Commons. He m. first, Dorothy, daughter and heiress of William Blunden, esq. of Bishop's Castle, by whom he had

- FRANCIS, his successor.
- Jane, m. to Thomas Hanmer, esq. of the Fenns, in Flintshire, and had two sons, William and Job, and a daughter, m. to Admiral Cornwall, of Berington.
- Dorothy, m. to Sir Edward Leighton, bart. of Wattlesborough.
- Mary, m. to — Barrell, esq. of Essex.

Sir Job m. secondly, Lettice, daughter of Walter Waring, esq. of Oldbury, and had further issue,

- Gilbert, who m. Anne, daughter and co-heir of Harvey Staunton, esq. of Staunton, in Nottinghamshire, and had, with other issue, a daughter, Anne, who m. Richard Brough, esq. and was grandmother of Elizabeth Brough, married to the Rev. Dr. Aspinshaw, who has assumed the surname of Staunton, and is the present DR. STAUNTON, of Staunton. (See BURKE'S *Commoners*, vol. i. p. 526.)
- Emma, m. first, to Thomas Cornwallis, esq. of Abermarles; and secondly, to Dr. J. Robinson, lord bishop of London.

Sir Job Charlton was s. at his decease, 27th May, 1697, by his eldest son,

II. SIR FRANCIS CHARLTON, who m. first, Dorothy, daughter and co-heir of the Rev. Mr. Bromwych, by whom he had a son, BLUNDEL, his successor; and secondly, Miss Cam, by whom he left two sons and a daughter, Emma, m. to John Lloyd, esq. of Aston, in Shropshire. Sir Francis d. 21st April, 1729, and was s. by his son,

III. SIR BLUNDEL CHARLTON, who m. Mary, sister of Lord Foley, and had issue,

- FRANCIS (Sir), his successor.
- Robert-Job, in holy orders, rector of Brampton, in the county of Hereford, and vicar of Kidderminster, Worcestershire, d. before his brother, unmarried.
- Emma, d. unmarried.
- ELIZABETH, m. to Edmund Lechmere,* esq. of Hanley Castle, in the county of Worcester, knight in parliament for that shire in 1734, and had issue,
  - NICHOLAS LECHMERE, of Hanley Castle, b. in 1733, who succeeded to the Charlton estates upon the demise of his uncle, Sir Francis Charlton, in 1784, and assumed that additional surname. He espoused Susanna, daughter of Jesson Case, esq. of Powyck, and had issue,
    1. EDMUND, present possessor.
    2. Francis, b. in 1790.
    3. Emma, d. in 1809.

    Mr. Lechmere-Charlton was s. at his decease by his elder son,
    - EDMUND LECHMERE-CHARLTON, esq. now representative of the two families of Lechmere and Charlton.

Sir Blundel died in December, 1742, and was s. by his son,

IV. SIR FRANCIS CHARLTON, of Ludford, a gentleman of the privy chamber, who died unmarried 3rd December, 1784, when the BARONETCY became EXTINCT; the estates devolving on his nephew, NICHOLAS LECHMERE, esq. of Hanley Castle.

Arms—As CHARLTON, OF HESLEYSIDE.

CHAYTOR, OF CROFT HALL.

CREATED 29th June, 1671.

EXTINCT in 1720.

Lineage.

I. SIR WILLIAM CHAYTOR, of Croft (son of Nicholas Chaytor, esq. lieutenant-colonel in the royal service, by Ann, his wife, dau. and co-heir of William Lambton, esq. of Houghtonfield, in Durham, and great-grandson of Christopher Chaytor, esq. of Butterby, by Elizabeth, sister and sole heir of Richard Clervaux, esq. of Croft), was created a BARONET 28th June, 1671. He m. Peregrina, dau. of Sir Joseph Cradock, knt. of Richmond, but dying s. p. s. in 1720, the BARONETCY became EXTINCT. The estates devolved on Sir William's nephew,

HENRY CHAYTOR, esq. who then became "of Croft." He was direct ancestor of the present

SIR WILLIAM CHAYTOR, of Croft, who was created a BARONET in 1831.

Arms—Party per bend dancettée arg. and az. three cinquefoils, two in chief and one in base, counter changed.

CHEERE, OF WESTMINSTER.

CREATED 18th July, 1766.—EXTINCT in March, 1808.

Lineage.

I. SIR HENRY CHEERE, of Westminster, the statuary, received the honor of knighthood in 1760, on presenting a congratulatory address to his majesty on his accession to the throne, and was advanced to the dignity of a BARONET 18th July, 1766. He m. Helen, daughter of Sauvignion Randall, esq. and dying in 1781, was s. by his son,

II. THE REV. SIR WILLIAM CHEERE, who d. s. p. in 1808, when the title became EXTINCT.

Arms—Quarterly; erminois and gu. a label of five points az.

CHERNOCKE, OF HULCOTT.

CREATED 21st May, 1661.

EXTINCT in 17[illegible].

Lineage.

ROBERT CHERNOCKE, esq. of the Lancashire family, married first, Frances, daughter of — Ackworth, esq. of Tuddington, in Bedfordshire, and settled in the county. By this lady he had several children, of whom were RICHARD, his successor, and Florence, the wife of Siworth Pettes, of Boughton-

* Mr. Lechmere was representative of the ancient family of that name, for an account of which, see PAYNE[illegible], of Allensmore, in BURKE'S *Commoners*, vol. i. p. 148.

mder-Blene, in Kent. He married a second time, and had other issue. He died in 1547, and was buried at Hulcott, where a monument to his memory, thus inscribed, was erected: "Robert Chernocke, esquier, father of Richard Chernocke, esq. here enterred, did descende of an anciente house, called Chernocke Hall, in Lancashire: he had, by two wives of worshippefull parentage, ten children; six by one, by the other four. He was the first that planted this familye in this countye: he left his estate to his son RICHARD, departing this life, about sixty years of age, *anno Domini* 1547." His son and heir, the said

RICHARD CHERNOCKE, esq. who was three times sheriff of the county of Bedford, viz. in the 26th, 28th, and 33rd of ELIZABETH, m. first, Mary, daughter of Sir George Puttenam, knt. of Sherfeld, in the county of Southampton, and by her had several children. His second wife was Audrey, daughter of William Frodsham, of Elton, but that lady *d. s. p.* This gentleman re-edified the parish church of Hulcote at his own expense, as well as his mansion-house there. He d. 14th August, 1615, at the age of eighty-four, was buried in the chancel of the church, which himself had built, under a monument erected in memory of his wife and children, and was *s.* by his eldest son,

JOHN CHERNOCKE, esq. of Hulcote, who m. Elizabeth, daughter of Sir John Arundell, knt. of Lanherne, and dying in 1641, was *s.* by his eldest son,

SIR ROBERT CHERNOCKE, knt. of Hulcote, who m. Agnes, fourth daughter of Oliver, Lord St. John of Bletsho, and sister of the first Earl of Bolingbroke, and dying 20th July, 1679, was *s.* by his eldest son,*

I. SIR JOHN CHERNOCKE, OF HULCOTE, BARONET, so created, in the lifetime of his father, by *King* CHARLES II 21st May, 1661. He m. Audrey, daughter of Sir William Villiers, bart. of Brookesby, in the county of Leicester, eldest brother of the first Duke of Buckingham, and dying in March, 1680, was *s.* by his only son,

II. SIR VILLIERS CHERNOCKE, who m. Anne, daughter of John Pynsent, esq. of Comb, in Surrey, prothonotary of the Court of Common Pleas, and had issue,

- PYNSENT, his successor.
- St. John, Robert, Villiers, } all *d.* unmarried.
- Mary, m. first, to the Rev. Mr. Cheyney, rector of Perton Hall, in the county of Bedford; and secondly, to the Rev. J. Littlejohn, rector of Hulcote, and vicar of Salford, in the same county.
- Adria.
- Elizabeth, *d.* unmarried.
- Anne, m. to the Rev. William Bunbury, rector of Great Catworth, in Huntingdonshire, and had issue.
- Honor.

Sir Villiers, who represented the county of Bedford in parliament, died in November, 1694, and was *s.* by his eldest son,

III. SIR PYNSENT CHERNOCKE, high sheriff of the county of Bedford in 1703, and knight of the same shire in the parliaments which assembled at Westminster in the 4th and 12th of *Queen* ANNE. He m. Helen, daughter and co-heir of William Boteler, esq. of Biddenham, in Bedfordshire, and had issue,

- BOTELER, his successor.
- VILLIERS, fellow of New College, Oxford.
- Anne, *d.* unmarried.
- Helen, m. to Edward Hervey, esq. of Chiltern, in Bucks, and had two sons,
  - EDWARD HERVEY, in holy orders.
  - Pynsent Hervey, captain R.N. *d. s. p.*
  - Helen Hervey, m. to the Rev. Joseph Bayle, of Bishop's Waltham, Hants, but had no issue.
- Penelope, m. first, to Robert Abbott, esq. of Steppingley Park, in the county of Bedford, by whom she had one child. Mr. Abbott *d.* in February, 1730-1, and his widow m. Captain Hervey.
- Elizabeth, m. to — Chauncey, esq. of Little Court, Herts, *d.* without issue.

Sir Pynsent was compelled to alienate the estate of Tingriff, to defray the expenses he had incurred in contesting the county of Bedford with the Russell family. He *d.* 2nd September, 1734, and was *s.* by his elder son,

IV. SIR BOTELER CHERNOCKE, M.P. for the borough of Bedford in 1740. This gentleman *d.* unmarried about the year 1756, and was *s.* by his brother,

V. SIR VILLIERS CHERNOCKE, who resided at Twyford, in Hampshire. He m. Miss Sophia Harris, but dying without issue in 1779, the BARONETCY EXPIRED, while the Bedfordshire estates passed to (the elder son of his sister Helen) his nephew,

THE REV. EDWARD HERVEY, of Hulcote, who m. Mary, daughter of the celebrated Browne Willis, esq.† of Whaddon Hall, Bucks, and had issue,

- CHARLOTTE HERVEY, m. in 1779, to the Rev. Edward Orlebar Smith, and had issue,
  - CHARLES-HERVEY SMITH, her heir.
  - Edward-Orlebar Smith, in holy orders, rector of Hulcote, m. in May, 1822, his cousin, Julia, youngest daughter of the Rev. Thomas Willis, and sister of John Willis Fleming, esq. of Stoneham Park, Hants.
  - Boteler-Chernocke Smith, of Trinity Hall, Cambridge, m. in 1823, Sarah, daughter of Dr. Whitby, M.D. of Warren House, Ashby-de-la-Zouch, and has issue,
    1. Boteler.
    2. Chernocke.
    3. Charlotte.
    4. Sarah.
    5. Julia.
  - Charlotte-Hervey Smith.
  - Jane-Maria Smith.
  - Eliza-Diana Smith.
  - Anna-Penelope Smith.
- MARY HERVEY, ELIZA HERVEY, } *d. s. p.*
- BARBARA HERVEY, m. to the Rev. B. Watkin, of Lockridge House, Wilts, and survived him, but *d. s. p.*

Mr. Hervey dying without male issue, a portion of the estates reverted to Mrs. Elizabeth Chauncey, only surviving daughter of Sir Pynsent Chernocke, who divided it amongst her great nieces, Barbara Hervey, first cousin to the deceased Mr. Hervey, and the four daughters of that gentleman. Barbara devised her share to William Mountague, esq. and the remainder eventually centred in the issue of CHARLOTTE, wife of the Rev. Edward Orlebar Smith. Her eldest son, CHARLES-HERVEY SMITH, esq. is now "of Apsley House," in the county of Bedford, formerly one of the estates of the Chernockes.

Arms—Arg. on a bend sa. three cross crosslets of the first.

* He had several children, but none of the younger ones left issue except Robert, who was father of Francis Chernocke, esq. of Wedgenock Park, in Warwickshire.

† By Catherine, his wife, only child and heiress of Daniel Eliot, esq. of Port Eliot.

CHESTER, OF CHICHLEY.

CREATED 23rd Mar. 1619.

EXTINCT 17th May, 1769.

Lineage.

The family was of ancient standing in the county of Gloucester, and so early as the time of HENRY VI.

ROBERT CHESTRE was of such note, that in the 23rd of that monarch's reign he had a license, with others, to found a gild or fraternity to the praise and honour of the Trinity, in the town of Stow St. Edward, in the said county, to endure for ever: to consist of a warden or master and as many persons as should think fit to be of the fraternity; which warden or master, with the majority of the fraternity, and their successors, are empowered to choose annually a warden, on the eve of Trinity, for the government of the same: also, that they be one body corporate, have a common seal, purchase lands, &c.: and likewise are empowered to erect a chantry, and purchase lands of the value of £10 per annum for the maintenance of a chaplain, to be appointed by the said Robert Chestre and others, who should pray at the altar of the holy Trinity, in the parish of Stow St. Edward aforesaid, for the welfare of the king and Margaret, his queen, and for the souls of their progenitors, and for the welfare of Sir Ralph Boteler, knt. Lord Sudley, treasurer of England, Sir John Beauchamp, of Powick, knt. and for the warden of the said society. This Robert Chestre was father of three sons, viz.

WILLIAM.

Richard, an alderman of the city of London, who, in the 10th of EDWARD IV. was one of the executors of his brother William. His wife's name was Alice, who survived him, as appears by her last testament, bearing date the last of August, 1504 (20 HENRY VII.), wherein she desires to be buried in St. Buttolph, without Aldgate, near her late husband, Richard Chestre. She lived after his death among the nuns at the Minories, and bequeaths her black hood of profession to Mrs. Slaland, sister at St. Catherine's; constitutes Thomas Bullisdon (who had married Joan, her daughter,) executor; and styling herself Dame Alice Chestre, widow, late the wife of Richard Chestre, citizen and skinner of London, and alderman and sheriff thereof, revokes all other wills.

Henry, of Bristol, merchant, who makes his will 3rd February, 1470 (11 EDWARD IV.), bequeaths his body to be buried in the church of All Saints, in that city, and constitutes Alice, his wife, his executrix, who made her will the 10th December, 1485, wherein she desires her body to be buried in All Saints, Bristol, near her husband, Henry Chestre, and constitutes executor her son,

John Chestre, of Bristol, merchant, which John made his will 22nd December, 14[illegible] He was *s.* by his son,

William Chestre, alias Chester, an alderman of Bristol, whose testament bears date 2nd September, 1538. This William left sons, one of whom, THOMAS, it is conjectured, was the Thomas Chester who purchased Amsbury, in Gloucestershire, in the time of ELIZABETH, and founded the family of that place.

The eldest son,

WILLIAM CHESTRE, who was likewise citizen and skinner of London, and merchant of the staple at Calais, had a grant, in the 7th of EDWARD IV. of the arms and crest afterwards borne by his descendants, under the seal of William Hawkslow, clarencieux king of arms, dated 22nd May. He was possessed of much wealth, and was a person of great piety, as the charities enumerated in his will evince. That instrument bears date 5th May, 1476, soon after which he died, for it was proved 27th September following. By one clause, he gives Agnes Chestre, his wife, his lands, rents, plate, and household goods, as long as she lives a widow; but if she marry, to have only 300 marks, with his plate and household goods, but none of his lands, which he wills, after her decease or marriage, to John Chestre, his son, except his rents in London and in Sussex, which he desires his executors to sell, and dispose of the money for his soul, and his father and mother's souls. He constitutes Agnes, his wife and Richard Chestre, his brother, his executors. The said Agnes, whose maiden name was Hill, died in the [illegible] of RICHARD III. and her last will bears date [illegible] June, 1484 (the probate whereof is on the 13th July following). Their son and heir,

JOHN CHESTRE, writes himself citizen and draper of London in his last testament, and died in May, 1[illegible] He appears to have married Joan, widow of — [illegible] and to have had, with a daughter Alice, two sons, NICHOLAS and WILLIAM, between whom and his wife he divides all his goods and chattels, his wife one moiety, and his sons the other; which bequest he makes the larger, on condition "she never to marry, as she had said unto him;" and constitutes her sole executrix. The line of the elder son, Nicholas, failing, the representation and fortune eventually devolved upon

SIR WILLIAM CHESTER, knt. son of John, the younger son. This William was bred to his father's occupation, a draper, and thereby considerably augmented his patrimony. Living in great reputation, he was elected one of the sheriffs of London in 1544, 2nd PHILIP and MARY. He had been knighted before, and was a great benefactor to the city, in the time of EDWARD VI. for, following the charitable example of that prince, Sir William Chester, knt. and alderman, and John Calthorp, citizen and draper, at their own expense, made the brick walls, and way on the back side, which lead from the said hospital to the hospital of St. Bartholomew; they also covered and vaulted the town ditch from Aldersgate to Newgate, which before was very noisome and contagious to the said hospital. He was lord mayor in 1560, 2nd ELIZABETH, and was returned to parliament by the city in 1[illegible] He became afterwards so strictly religious, that for a considerable time before his death, he retired from all business, entered himself a fellow commoner at Cambridge, lived there some years, made a great proficiency in the course of the university, and was reputed a learned man. Sir William *m.* first, Elizabeth, daughter of Thomas Lovett, of Astwell, in Northamptonshire,* and had issue,

* By Elizabeth, his wife, daughter and heir of John Boteler, esq. of Woodhall, in the county of Hertford.

i. WILLIAM, his heir.

ii. Thomas, who was Bishop of Elphin, in Ireland, *anno* 1580, *m.* one of the daughters of Sir James Clavering, knt. of Axwell, in the county of Northumberland, but *d.* without issue, in June, 1584.

iii. John,
iv. Daniel,
v. Francis, } all *d.* issueless.

i. Frances, *m.* to Francis Robinson, of London.

ii. Jane, *m.* to Richard, brother of Sir Thomas Offley, knt.

iii. Emma, *m.* to John Gardiner,
iv. Susan, *m.* to John Trott, } of London.

He *m.* secondly, Joan, daughter of John Turner, of London, and widow of Alderman William Beswick, but had no other issue. At what precise time he died does not appear, but he was buried with his wives in the church of St. Edmund, Lombard Street, he having in his lifetime erected a fair monument against the north side of the chancel, in the wall of that church. His eldest son,

WILLIAM CHESTER, esq. *m.* first, in the lifetime of his father, Anne, daughter of John Fryer, gent. of London, and by her, who *d.* in 1567, had an only surviving child, Elizabeth, wife of Thomas Heton, elder brother of Martin Heton, Bishop of Ely. He *m.* secondly, Judith, dau. and co-heir of Anthony Cave, esq. of Chichley,* in the county of Bucks, and thereby acquired that manor. By this lady he left, at his decease in 1567, an only son,

i. ANTHONY CHESTER, esq. of Chichley, who attended *Queen* ELIZABETH, at Tilbury camp, and commanded a troop of horse, to oppose the Spanish invasion. He was constituted sheriff of Bucks, in the forty fourth year of that queen's reign, and created a BARONET by JAMES I. 23rd March, 1619. Sir Anthony *m.* first, Elizabeth, daughter of Sir Henry Butler, of Woodhall, in the county of Hertford, and by that lady, who *d.* 5th April, 1629, had issue,

ANTHONY, his heir.

William, baptized 27th April, 1595, of Gray's Inn, married twice, and left three daughters, his co-heirs.

Henry (Sir), baptized 11th May, 1598, of Tilsworth, in the county of Bedford, sheriff in the 12th of CHARLES I. and made a knight of the Bath at the coronation of *King* CHARLES II. Sir Henry *m.* first, Judith Bankworth, daughter of Mr. Bankworth, of Bow Lane, London, and sister of Dr. Bankworth, and by her had a son, Robert, who died at the age of eighteen. He *m.* secondly, Mary, daughter of Thomas Wood, esq. of Hackney, and sister of Sir Henry Wood, knt. and of Thomas Wood, Bishop of Lichfield and Coventry: she was widow of Mr. Alderman Samuel Cranmer, of London. He had no issue by this lady; and, in consequence, his estates devolved at his decease upon his elder brother.

John, baptized 7th June, 1601, *m.* Catherine, dau. of Mr. Ashton, and *d. s. p.*

Robert, baptized in September, 1606, died unmarried.

Mary, *m.* to Sir Robert Bell, knt. of Beaupree Hall, Norfolk.

Elizabeth, *m.* no less than five husbands, all gentlemen of good estates.

Judith,
Anne,
Dorothy, } *d.* young and unmarried.

He *m.* secondly, 5th September, 1631, Mary, daughter of John Ellis, esq. of Kiddal, in the county of York, and had by her (who *m.* secondly, Samuel Lodington, esq.) another son, Robert, who *d.* in 1633, at the age of twelve. Sir Anthony, who was again sheriff of Bucks in the 4th of CHARLES I. *d.* in 1635, aged seventy, and was buried at Chichley on the 3rd December in that year. He was *s.* by his eldest son,

ii. SIR ANTHONY CHESTER, baptized 23rd March, 1593. This gentleman was a loyal and zealous subject of *King* CHARLES I. At the breaking out of the rebellion he served in the royal army, and for contributing very largely to the cause, had his estate sequestered and his mansion at Chichley rendered uninhabitable. He behaved himself with singular bravery at Naseby and in other engagements, which forced him to fly into Holland, and to remain there until composition was effected for his life, liberty, and lands, with the usurping powers. Sir Anthony *m.* Elizabeth, daughter of Sir John Peyton, knt. of Dodington, in Cambridgeshire, and by that lady (who survived him many years, dying his widow at the advanced age of eighty-nine, 3rd July, 1692,) had issue,

Henry, who died unmarried in his father's lifetime.

ANTHONY, his successor.

Peyton, gentleman of the bedchamber to Henry, Duke of Gloucester, *d.* unmarried.

William, a West India merchant, who amassed a large fortune in trade. He *m.* Sarah, daughter of Major Thomas Healmes, of the island of Barbadoes, and had four sons, who all died issueless, and two daughters, namely, DOROTHY, *m.* to Mr. Butler, of Barbadoes, and ELIZABETH, the wife of — Nanfan, esq. of the county of Worcester.

John, *d.* unmarried.

Alice, *m.* to John Millicent, esq. of Bergham, in Cambridgeshire.

Dorothy, *m.* to Colonel John Fisher, of Wisbich.

Frances, *m.* to Samuel Wiseman, esq. of Barbadoes.

Diana, *d.* unmarried.

Elizabeth, *m.* to William Ryley, esq. barrister-at-law, and keeper of the records in the Tower.

Ruperra, *m.* to Edward Coney, esq. of South Luffenham, in the county of Rutland, son of Sir Sutton Coney, knt. of Basinthorp, in Lincolnshire.

Sir Anthony *d.* in 1651, and was buried at Chichley 15th February. He was *s.* by his eldest son,

---

* The manor of CHICHLEY, part of the possessions of the dissolved priory of Tickford, became the estate of Cardinal Wolsey, in the 18th of HENRY VIII, and on the forfeiture of that prelate reverted to the Crown, and it remained so invested until the last year of HENRY's reign, when it was granted to

ANTHONY CAVE, esq. a younger son of the Caves of Stanford, in Northamptonshire, who *m.* Eliza, daughter of Thomas Lovet, esq. of Astwell, in the same county, and by that lady, (who *m.* secondly, John Newdigate, esq. of Harefield, Middlesex, and thirdly, Richard Weston, one of the judges of the king's bench,) he left four daughters, his co-heirs, viz.

JUDITH, *m.* to WILLIAM CHESTER, esq. and had the manor of CHICHLEY.

ANNE, *m.* to GRIFFITH HAMPDEN, esq. of Hampden, Bucks.

MARTHA, *m.* to JOHN NEWDIGATE, esq. of Arbury, Warwickshire.

MARY, *m.* to SIR JEROME WESTON, knt. son and heir of Judge Weston, and was mother of SIR RICHARD WESTON, knt. lord treasurer of England, created Earl of Portland in 1633, which dignity became EXTINCT in 1688.

III. SIR ANTHONY CHESTER, who m. 21st May, 1657, Mary, daughter of Samuel Cranmer, esq. an alderman of London,* by whom (who d. his widow, 12th May, 1710,) he had issue,

- Anthony, baptized in 1663, d. unmarried in May, 1665.
- JOHN, his successor.
- Henry, baptized 29th September, 1668, of Hadon, in the county of Northampton, m. Theodosia, daughter and heir of Thomas Tower, esq. of Haddenham, in the Isle of Ely, and left a son,
  - ANTHONY, in holy orders, succeeded as ninth baronet.
- William, d. unmarried.
- Thomas, b. 12th March, 1674, m. Elizabeth, daughter of Daniel Wingfield, esq. of London, merchant, and had a son and two daughters, viz.
  - John.
  - Mary, m. to — Horton, esq. of Yorkshire.
  - Anne.
- Cæsar, d. unmarried.
- Robert, m. Elizabeth, daughter of Mr. Henry Allen, merchant, and d. s. p.
- Mary, m. to Francis Duncombe, esq. of Broughton, in the county of Bucks.
- Elizabeth, m. to Charles-Nicholas Eyre, esq. one of the gentlemen of the privy chamber and cupbearer to *Queen* MARY, and had an only son,
  - Charles-Chester Eyre.
- Henrietta, d. young.
- Diana, m. to the Rev. Mr. Remington, rector of Hunnanby, in Yorkshire.
- Catherine, m. to Sir Henry Cambell, bart. of Clayhall, Essex.
- Judith, m. to Robert Oneby, esq. of the Inner Temple, barrister-at-law, and of Barwel, in the county of Leicester.
- Dorothy, m. to John Wilson, esq. of Thorp, also in Leicestershire.
- Alice, d. unmarried.
- Penelope, m. to the Rev. Thomas Allen, rector of Loughborough.

Sir Anthony d. 15th February, 1697-8, in the sixty-fifth year of his age, and was s. by his eldest surviving son,

IV. SIR JOHN CHESTER, b. in 1666, m. first, Anne, eldest daughter and co-heir of William Wollaston, esq. of Shenton, in the county of Leicester, and by that lady, who d. 3rd October, 1704, had issue,

- WILLIAM, his successor, b. 5th September, 1687.
- Thomas, b. 31st March, 1689, lieutenant-colonel in the army, cast away near the coast of Ireland, and d. unmarried.
- JOHN, sixth baronet.
- Francis, m. Berthia, daughter and co-heir of Thomas Wood, esq. of Kensington, and one of the co-heirs of Sir Henry Wood, knt. one of the clerks of the board of green cloth to CHARLES II. By her he had a son,
  - FRANCIS, who inherited as eighth baronet.
- Mary, Rebecca, } d. unmarried.
- Catherine, m. in 1718, John Toller, esq. of Billingborough, in the county of Lincoln, serjeant-at-law, and had three daughters.
- Elizabeth.
- Anne, m. to — Snead, esq. of the county of Buckingham.
- Penelope, m. to Richard Smith, esq. of Padbur[illegible] Bucks.

He m. secondly (April, 1714), Frances, widow of [illegible] Charles Skrimshire, knt. of Norbury Manor, in Sta[illegible]fordshire, only child of Sir William Noel, bart. [illegible] Kirkby, in the county of Leicester, by Frances [illegible] second wife), daughter of Humble, Lord Ward, but h[illegible] no other issue. This gentleman beautified and rep[illegible] the church at Chichley, having wholly rebuilt [illegible] chancel and paved it with marble. He likewise [illegible] a vault for the future sepulture of his family. He d. 9th February, 1726, and was s. by his eldest son,

V. SIR WILLIAM CHESTER, who m. Penelope, daughter of George Hewett, esq. of Stretton, in the [illegible] of Leicester, and had six daughters. He d. 21st [illegible] 1726, and was s. in the title and chief part of [illegible] estate by his next surviving brother,

VI. SIR JOHN-CHESTER, M.P. for the county of B[illegible]ford. This gentleman m. in 1718, Frances, daug[illegible] of Sir Edward Bagot, bart. of Blithfield, in the [illegible] of Stafford, and had issue,

- CHARLES-BAGOT, his successor.
- Anthony.
- Frances.

Sir John d. in 1747, and was s. by his son,

VII. SIR CHARLES-BAGOT CHESTER, at whose [illegible] s. p. 25th May, 1755, the manor of Chichley, [illegible] devolved by will on his cousin, Charles Bag[illegible] younger brother of William, first Lord Bag[illegible] that gentleman assumed in consequence, by [illegible] parliament, the surname and arms of CHESTE[illegible] son is the present CHARLES CHESTER, esq. of Ch[illegible] Sir Charles-Bagot Chester was s. in the Baronet[illegible] his cousin,

VIII. SIR FRANCIS CHESTER, who also died [illegible] at Chelsea in October, 1766, and was s. by his [illegible]man,

IX. THE REV. SIR ANTHONY CHESTER, rector of [illegible] Haddon, who m. Elizabeth Birt, but died with[illegible] 17th May, 1769, aged sixty-two, when the Ba[illegible] became EXTINCT. His widow survived until [illegible] 1808.

Arms—Party per pale arg. and sa. a chev. [illegible] between three rams' heads erased counterchang[illegible]

CHILD, OF SURAT.

CREATED 4th Feb. 1684-5. EXTINCT in [illegible]

Lineage.

JOHN CHILD, of London, gentleman, m. first, Frances, daughter of Francis Goodyer, of Hereford, and had, with two daughters, the elder married to [illegible] Ward, the younger to Mr. Thomas Mitchel, [illegible] Bombay, and merchants there, an only son,

I. JOHN CHILD, esq., who being general of all [illegible] English forces, by sea and land, in the northern part of India, and president of the honourable company[illegible]

* And sister of Sir Cæsar Cranmer, knt. of Ashwood, Bucks.

council at Surat, was created a BARONET, 4th February, 1684. He m. Mary, daughter of John Shackstone, esq. deputy governor of Bombay, and had two sons,

CÆSAR, his successor.
John, d. of the small-pox, unmarried, in 1718.

Sir John continued to reside in India, until his decease at Bombay, about the year 1690. He was s. by his son,

II. SIR CÆSAR CHILD, who m. in 1698, Hester, daughter of John Evance, esq. of London, and niece of Sir Stephen Evance, knt. and goldsmith, and by that lady had issue,

CÆSAR, his successor.
Stephen, John, } d. unm.
Hester, m. in 1716, to John Tyssen, esq., and d. in 1723.
Susanna, m. in 1721, to William Cleland, esq.
Anne, m. in 1724, to James Collet, esq.
Elizabeth, m. to William Cleland, esq. of Tapley Hall, Devon.
Frances, d. unmarried.

Sir Cæsar d. of the small-pox, 7th March, 1724, and was s. by his eldest son,

III. SIR CÆSAR CHILD, at whose decease, s. p. in 1753, the BARONETCY became EXTINCT.

Arms—Vert, two bars engr. between three leopards' heads or.

CHOLMLEY, OF WHITBY.

CREATED 10th Aug. 1641.

EXTINCT 9th Jan. 1688.

Lineage.

This was a branch of the ancient Cheshire stock of Cholmondeley, springing from,

ROBERT, younger son of Hugh de Cholmondeley, deputy sergeant of Cheshire, *temp.* EDWARD I. and II.

RICHARD CHOLMLEY, great grandson of Robert, was appointed *temp.* HENRY VII. lieutenant governor of Berwick, and made subsequently governor of Hull. In 1513, he and his brother Roger commanded the garrison of that town, the king's tenants at Hatfield, and others, under the Earl of Surrey at Flodden, and for their gallantry on that memorable occasion, received the honour of knighthood, as well as the thanks of their sovereign. Sir Richard dying without legitimate issue, was s. by his brother,

SIR ROGER CHOLMLEY, knt. of Kinthorp, in Yorkshire, who m. in 1512, Katharine, daughter of Sir Marmaduke Constable, knt. of Flamborough, and left, with other issue, a daughter, Ann, m. first, to Sir John Gascoigne, knt. and secondly, to Henry Nevill, fifth Earl of Westmorland (his lordship's second wife), and a son,

SIR RICHARD CHOLMLEY, knt. of Roxby, who purchased in 1541, a lease for twenty-one years, of the abbey lands in the neighbourhood of Whitby, and subsequently obtained a grant of all the possessions of the monastery thereof. This gentleman inheriting the martial spirit of his ancestors, joined the expedition under the Earl of Hertford, against the Scotch, and so gallantly distinguished himself, that, after the burning of Edinburgh, he was knighted at Leith, 11th May, 1544. He m. first, Margaret, daughter of Lord Conyers, and had by her,

I. FRANCIS, his heir.
II. Roger, III. Richard, } who m. two sisters, the daughters of a gentleman named Dallrivers. From Roger descended the CHOLMLEYS of BRANSBY.
I. Margaret, m. James Strangways, esq. Lord of Sneton.
II. Jane, m. to Ralph Salvin, esq. of Newbiggin.
III. Elizabeth, m. to Sir — Beckwith, of Handale Abbey.

He m. secondly, Lady Katharine Clifford, one of the most celebrated beauties of the age, daughter of Henry, first Earl of Cumberland, and widow of John, Lord Scrope, of Bolton, by whom he had,

HENRY, successor to his brother Francis.
Katharine, m. to a gentleman named Dutton.

"Sir Richard," says the Historian of Whitby, "loved pomp, and generally had fifty or sixty servants about his house; nor would he ever go up to London without a retinue of thirty or forty men. He was bred a soldier and delighted much in feats of war, being tall in stature and strongly made. His hair and eyes were black, and his complexion so swarthy, that he was frequently called 'the Black Knight of the North.'" His eldest son,

SIR FRANCIS CHOLMLEY, of Whitby, married about 1570, Jane Bulmer, but dying issueless in 1579, was, under the entail in his father's will, s. by his youngest brother,

SIR HENRY CHOLMLEY, knt. of Whitby and Roxby, who m. about 1579, Margaret, daughter of Sir William Babthorpe, knt. and had issue,

RICHARD (Sir), his heir.
Henry.
John.
Barbary, m. to Thomas Lord Falconberg.
Dorothy, m. to Nicholas Bushell, esq. of Whitby.
Hilda, m. to Toby Wright, esq.
Margaret, m. to Timothy Conyers, esq.
Mary, m. to the Hon. Henry Fairfax, son of Lord Fairfax, of Denton.
Susanna, m. to Richard Theakston, esq.
Annabella, m. to Henry Wickham, chaplain to CHARLES I.

Sir Henry d. in 1614, and was s. by his son,

SIR RICHARD CHOLMLEY, knt. of Whitby, high sheriff of Yorkshire in 1624, and M. P. for Scarborough in 1620. He m. first, Susanna, daughter of John Legard, esq. and by her, who died in 1611, had issue,

HUGH (Sir), his heir.
Henry (Sir) a lawyer of distinction, m. Katharine, daughter of Robert Stapylton, esq. of Wighill, and relict of Sir George Twisden, bart. of Burley.
Margaret, m. to Sir William Strickland, knt.
Ursula, m. to George Trotter, esq.

He m. secondly, in 1613, Margaret, sister of Sir William Cobb, knt. of Adderbury, in Oxford, and had by her,

Richard (Sir), of Gromont, knt. colonel in the service of CHARLES I. and a gallant adherent, during the civil wars of that unhappy prince. He was eminently distinguished at the taking of Exeter, some time after, having been appointed commander-in-chief of all the forces which besieged Lyme, he received a wound before that town, of which he died. This gallant cavalier m. Margaret, daughter of Lord Pawlett, and relict of Dennis Rolle, esq. of Brickton, in Devon, and left two daughters.

William.

Sir Richard d. 23rd September, 1631, and was s. by his son,

I. Sir Hugh Cholmley, knt. of Whitby, b. 22nd July, 1600, M. P. for Scarborough, who was created a Baronet in 1641. On the outbreaking of the civil war, Sir Hugh enrolled himself under the royal banner, and was appointed governor of Scarborough Castle, a general in the northern parts of England, a colonel of dragoons, and judge of all marine affairs in every port on the Yorkshire coast, between the Tees and Bridlington. In Scarborough he continued his residence until the parliament had obtained possession of every place in Yorkshire, except the castles of Pontefract and Scarborough, when an armed force being sent down to besiege these two places, Sir Hugh made a gallant defence for more than twelve months: he disputed every inch of ground with the besiegers, and bravely repulsed all their assaults. Furthermore, on the fall of the castle, when the whole was reduced almost to a heap of ruins, and Sir John Meldrum, who commanded the siege, sent proposals to him mixed with menaces, he resolutely withstood the assault, slew Sir John, and beat off his troops with great loss. During the whole siege, Lady Cholmley continued with her husband in the castle, where she was of great service by attending the sick and wounded. Finally the place being surrendered on honourable terms in 1645, Sir Hugh went into exile, his estate was sequestered, his mansion at Whitby converted into a garrison, and every thing valuable plundered. He remained abroad until 1649, when his brother, Sir Henry Cholmley, finding means to pacify the parliament, he was again permitted to return to England, and on certain conditions once more suffered to enter into the possession of his estate.

He m. Elizabeth, daughter of Sir William Twisden, bart. and had issue,

William, his heir.

Hugh.

Ann, m. to Richard Stephens, esq.

Elizabeth, d. unm.

Sir Hugh Cholmley, d. 30th November, 1657, and was s. by his son,

II. Sir William Cholmley, of Whitby, b. in December, 1625, who m. first, 1654, Katherine Hotham, of Fyling Dales, which lady d. s. p. in June, 1655, and secondly, in April, 1657, Elizabeth, daughter of Sir John Saville, bart. of Methley, by whom (who m. secondly, Sir Nicholas Strode, bart.) he had issue,

Hugh, his heir.

Elizabeth, m. to Sir Edward Dering, bart. of Surrenden, in Kent.

Katharine, d. young.

Margaret, m. to William Turner, esq. of Kirkleatham.

Sir William d. in October, 1663, and was s. by his son,

III. Sir Hugh Cholmley, of Whitby, who died in minority, in June, 1665, and was s. by his uncle,

IV. Sir Hugh Cholmley, of Whitby, who was appointed by Charles II. governor of Tangier, in Africa, where he resided many years, and had the direction of building the mole there. He m. in February, 1666, Lady Ann Compton, eldest daughter of Spencer, Earl of Northampton, and had an only surviving child,

Mary, b. in 1667, who m. Nathaniel Cholmley, esq. of London, and had issue,

1. Hugh, b. in August, 1684, M. P. for Hedon, high sheriff of Yorkshire in 1724, and surveyor-general of his majesty's crown lands, m. in March, 1716, Catherine, only daughter and eventual heir of Sir John Wentworth, bart. of Elmsall and Howsham and dying 25th May, 1755, aged seventy-one, left with other issue, a son and successor,

Nathaniel Cholmley, esq. of Whitby and Howsham, M. P. who m. first, 1750, Catherine, daughter of Sir Rowland Winn, bart. of Nostel, and had by her two daughters,

1. Catherine, heiress to her father, m. in 1774, to Henry Hopkins Fane, esq. who assumed the surname of Cholmley, and d. in 1809, leaving, besides seven daughters, a son, George Cholmley, esq. of Whitby.

2. Mary, m. to Abraham Grimes, esq.

Mr. Nathaniel Cholmley, m. secondly, Henrietta-Catherine, daughter of Stephen Croft, esq. of Stillington, and thirdly, Anne-Jesse, third daughter of Leonard Smeldt, esq. of Langton. By the second wife he had,

3. Henrietta, m. to Sir William Strickland, bart.

4. Anne-Elizabeth, m. to Constantine-John, Lord Mulgrave, and left a daughter, the Hon. Ann-Elizabeth Cholmley Phipps, who m. lt.-gen. Sir John Murray, bt.

2. John, b. 1686, colonel under the Duke of Marlborough, d. at Whitby in 1724.

1. Ann, d. young.

Sir Hugh d. at Whitby, 9th January, 1688, when the Baronetcy expired. His estates centered in his daughter and heiress, Mary.

Arms—Gu. two helmets in chief arg. and a garb in base or.

CHOLMONDELEY, OF CHOLMONDELEY.

Created 29th June, 1611.—Extinct 2nd Oct. 1659.

Lineage.

I. Robert Cholmondeley, esq. of Cholmondeley, in Cheshire, (son of Sir Hugh Cholmondeley, knt. and eldest brother of Thomas Cholmondeley, esq. of Vale Royal, ancestor of Lord Delamere,) was created a Baronet, 29th June, 1611, and in 1628, advanced to the peerage of Ireland, as Viscount Cholmondeley of Kells. His lordship was likewise enrolled amongst the peers of England, as Baron Cholmondeley, of Wiche and Mulbank, and further advanced to the Earldom of Leinster. He m. Catherine, daughter of John, Lord Stanhope, of Harrington, but d. s. p. 2nd October, 1659, when all his honours, including the Baronetcy, became extinct; but his estates reverted to his nephew, Robert Cholmondeley, esq. created Viscount Cholmondeley, of Kells, in 1661. His lordship's descendant and representative is George Horatio, present Marquis of Cholmondeley.

Arms—Gu. two helmets in chief, ppr. garnished or, in base a garb of the last.

CHUDLEIGH, OF ASHTON.

CREATED 1st August, 1622.

EXTINCT 1st August 1745.

Lineage.

This family was of long continuance in Devonshire, and flourished for several generations, at Broad Cleft, in that county, frequently serving the office of sheriff, in the reigns of RICHARD II., HENRY VI., and HENRY VII. ASHTON, in the same county, anciently called ASSERISTON, and ASHERISTON, came with other lands to the Chudleighs, so early as the beginning of the fourteenth century, by the intermarriage of

JOHN CHUDLEIGH, with Thomasine, daughter of Richard, son of Sir Richard Prous, knt. when they were conveyed by deed (dated in 1320), from "Richard Prous, and Margaret, his wife, to John Chudleigh and his heirs." From John and Thomasine descended

SIR JAMES CHUDLEIGH, knt. of Ashton, who m. Jane, daughter and heir of Sir John De, knt. and was s. by his son,

JAMES CHUDLEIGH, esq. of Ashton, who m. Margaret, daughter of William, Lord Stourton, of which marriage the beginning of the covenant runs thus: "That James Chudleigh, shall marry Margaret, daughter to William, Lord Stourton, who giveth him an hundred Marks, anno, 15 EDWARD IV. 1476." His son and heir,

WILLIAM CHUDLEIGH, esq. of Ashton, m. Joan, daughter of Sir William Hody, knt. of Dorsetshire, and had a son,

SIR RICHARD CHUDLEIGH, knt.* who m. Mary, daughter of Sir Nicholas Wadham, knt. of Merifield, in the county of Somerset, and was s. by his son,

CHRISTOPHER CHUDLEIGH, esq. of Ashton. This gentleman m. Christiana, daughter of William Stretchley, esq. of Stretchley, in the county of Devon, and thus added considerably to his paternal fortune. He left a son and heir,

JOHN CHUDLEIGH, esq. of Ashton, "who," according to Prince, "was of a right martial, bold, and adventurous spirit; for, living in the reign of *Queen* ELIZABETH, the famous actions of Drake, Cavendish, &c. so employed his thoughts, that he had a noble emulation in him, to equal, if not excel the bravest heroes, and their noblest exploits, not at land, where is the least danger, but at sea." He did not live, however, to accomplish his generous designs, but died young, in the Streights of Magellan, leaving, by his wife, daughter of George Speke, esq. of White Lackington, in the county of Somerset, two sons and two daughters, viz.

- GEORGE, his heir.
- John (Sir), who received the honour of knighthood from *King* CHARLES I. 22nd September, 1625.
- Alice, m. to Sir William Langham, knt. of Cottesbrooke.
- Bridget, m. to Sir Richard Carew, bart. of East Anthony.

The elder son,

I. GEORGE CHUDLEIGH, esq., of Ashton, in the county of Devon, was created a BARONET by *King* JAMES I. 1st August, 1622. At the time of his father's decease, Sir George was a minor of three or four years of age, "but," says an old writer, "by his careful and prudent Trustees, and his own virtuous disposition, had his youth well educated, and his person excellently adorned, with all the accomplishments requisite to a fine gentleman; so that, having been abroad for the most exquisite breeding that age could yield, he retired home, well improved, and fixed his habitation at his seat at Ashton. Here, his demeanour was so courteous and obliging, and withal, so discreet and prudent, that he lived in great esteem and reputation among his neighbours, and was looked upon as an ornament to his country." Sir George Chudleigh was elected to the parliament which met at Westminster in 1640, and at first opposed the court, but afterward both himself and his son took up arms for the king, and he published a declaration in 1643, in vindication of his doing so. He m. Mary, daughter of Sir William Strode, knt. of Newnham, in the county of Devon, and had issue,

- I. GEORGE, his successor.
- II. Thomas, m. Miss Vaughan, and had a son,
  - Thomas, who was envoy to Holland *temp.* CHARLES II. He m. Elizabeth, daughter of — Cole, esq. of Oxfordshire.
- III. James, colonel in the parliament's army but after falling into the hands of the royalists at the battle of Stratton,† turned over to the king. He fell at Dartmouth when the town and castle surrendered to Sir Thomas Fairfax. Lord Clarendon vindicates his defection, and in mentioning the manner of his death, calls him "a gallant young gentleman, who received a shot with a musquet, in the body, at the siege of Dartmouth, of which he died within a few days, and was a wonderful loss to the king's service." He was unmarried.
- IV. ———, m. to — Rolle, esq. of Devonshire.
- V. ———, m to — Ashford, esq. of Ashford.
- VI. ———, m. first, to Clifford, of Ugbrook, in Devonshire, and secondly, to Cole, esq. of Oxfordshire.

Sir George died in 1657. Prince says, "when the royal cause sunk, this family, as well as others, paid dear for their loyalty." He was s. by his eldest surviving son,

II. SIR GEORGE CHUDLEIGH, who m. Elizabeth, daughter of Hugh Fortescue, esq. of Fillegh, in the county of Devon, and had issue,

- John, d. unm.
- GEORGE, his heir
- Hugh, of Westminster, m. Susan, daughter of Sir Richard Strode, knt. of Newenham, and sister and heir of John Strode, esq. of Chalmington, in Dorsetshire, by whom he left a son,
  - GEORGE, of Chalmington, who m. Isabella Garniere, of Westminster, and dying in 1739, left issue,
    - JOHN, who s. as sixth baronet.
    - Susannah, m. to the Rev. Nathan Haines, D. D. and had *inter alios*, a son, HUGH-CHUDLEIGH HAINES, esq.
    - Anne-George, m. to the Rev. Samuel Strong.

* This Sir Richard Chudleigh, is the gentleman whose case is so well known amongst lawyers, and is reported by Lord Coke, under "The case of perpetuities, or, Chudleigh's Case."

† The Earl of Stamford attributed the loss of this battle to the treachery of Col. James Chudleigh.

Elizabeth, *m.* to — Hunt, of Chudleigh, in the county of Devon.
Grace, *m.* to Thomas Gibbon, of Exeter.
Jane, *m.* to Roger Strode, esq. of Devon.
Dorothy, *m.* to Charles Ford, esq. of Exeter.

He *d.* in 1691, and was *s.* by his son,

III. SIR GEORGE CHUDLEIGH, who *m.* Mary,* daughter of Richard Lee, of Winslade, in Devonshire, and by her (who *d.* in 1710), had with other issue,

GEORGE, his successor.
Thomas, colonel in the army, who left by Harriet his wife, a son and daughter,
THOMAS, who inherited as fifth Baronet.
ELIZABETH, *b.* in 1720, *m.* first, 4th August, 1744, to Augustus John, Earl of Bristol, and secondly, in 1769, to Evelyn, Duke of Kingston.†

He *d.* in 1719, and was *s.* by his son,

IV. SIR GEORGE CHUDLEIGH. This gentleman *m.* Frances, daughter and co-heir of Sir William Davie, bart. of Creedy, in the county of Devon, and had three daughters, his co-heirs, viz.

I. MARY, *m.* to Humphry Prideaux, esq. of Place.
II. FRANCES, *m.* to Sir John Chichester, bart.
III. MARGARET, *m.* to Sir Henry Oxenden, bart.

He *d.* 10th October, 1738, and was *s.* by his nephew,

V. SIR THOMAS CHUDLEIGH, an officer in the army, who *d.* unm. at Aix-la-Chapelle, in June, 1741, and was buried 12th July following, at Chelsea. He was *s.* by his cousin,

VI. SIR JOHN CHUDLEIGH, who was of Chalmington, in the county of Dorset. This gentleman was killed at Ostend, 1st August, 1745, and dying unmarried, the BARONETCY became EXTINCT. His sisters became his heirs, and from them the estate of Chalmington passed to their nephew, Hugh Chudleigh Haines, esq. by whom it was sold, in 1799, to WILLIAM BOWER, esq. of Dorchester.

Arms—Erm. three lioncels rampt. gu.

CHUTE, OF HAUXFALL PLACE.

CREATED 17th Sept. 1684. EXTINCT 4th Feb. 1721.

Lineage.

I. SIR GEORGE CHUTE, son of Sir George Chute, knt. of Surrenden, in Kent, grandson of Edward Chute, esq. of Surrenden, high sheriff of Kent, 11 CHARLES I. and a lineal descendant of Philip Chute, of Appledore, in the same county, standard bearer to HENRY VIII. who obtained, in recompence for his gallant services at the siege of Boulogne, an augmentation to his armorial ensigns, was seated at Hauxfall Place, in Kent, and was created a BARONET in 1684. He died, without issue, in 1721, when the title became EXTINCT. The manor of Surrenden he devised to Edward Austen, esq. of Tenterden, afterwards a baronet, who subsequently sold it to Thomas Best, esq. of Chatham.

Arms—Gu. semée of mullets or, three swords in fess arg. pomelled gold.

*** The senior branch of the Chute family, (of which was CHALLONER CHUTE, speaker of the House of Commons to Richard Cromwell's parliament,) was seated at the Vine, in Hampshire, and preserved a male descent until 1776, the period of the decease of John Chute, esq., when the property devolved on Thomas Lobb, esq. (great grandson, through his mother, of Challoner Chute, esq. of the Vine,) and from his son, the Rev. Thomas Vere Chute, the estates have passed to their present proprietor, WILLIAM L... WIGGETT CHUTE, esq. of the Vine and Pickenham Hall.

CLARGES, OF ST. MARTIN'S IN THE FIELDS.

CREATED 30th Oct. 1674. EXTINCT 17th Feb. 1[illegible]

Lineage.

This family originally from DE GLARGES, in the Province of Hanault, was founded in England in the time of EDWARD IV. by

JOHN DE GLARGES, whose only son,

JOHN DE GLARGES, was father of

ROBERT DE GLARGES, who is stated to have lived and died in the University of Cambridge. He had two sons, JOHN, his heir, Robert, who died unmarried and three daughters.

The elder son,

JOHN DE GLARGES, or Clarges, *m.* Anne Leaver, and had issue,

THOMAS (Sir), his successor.
ANNE, *m.* to General Monk, afterwards DUKE OF ALBEMARLE, and had an only son,
CHRISTOPHER MONK, second Duke of Albemarle.‡

He was *s.* by his son,

---

* This lady published several poems and a volume of essays.

† This is the well-known Duchess of Kingston, found guilty by the House of Lords of bigamy.

‡ The following singular statement was made in a trial of an action of trespass, between William Sherwin, plaintiff, and Sir Walter Clarges, bart. and others, defendants, at the bar of the King's Bench, at Westminster, 15th November, 1700:—

"The plaintiff, as heir and representative of Thomas Monk, esq. elder brother of George, Duke of Albemarle, claimed the manor of Sutton, in the county of York, and other lands, as heir at law to the said duke, against the defendant, devisee under the will of Duke Christopher, who died issueless in 1688. Upon this trial it appeared that Anne, the wife of George, Duke of Albemarle, was daughter of John Clarges, a farrier in Savoy, and farrier to Col. Monk. In 1632, she was married at the church of St. Lawrence Pountney, to Thomas Ratford, son of Thomas Ratford, late a farrier's servant to Prince CHARLES, and resident in the Mews. She had a daughter born in 1634, who *d.* in 1638; her husband and she lived at the Three Spanish Gipsies, in the New Exchange, and sold wash balls, powder, gloves, and such things, and

Sir Thomas Clarges, knt.* whose successful proceedings to restore Charles II. through his brother-in-law Monk, are curiously detailed by the chronicler, Sir Richard Baker. He m. Mary, third daughter of George, and sister and co-heir of Edward Procter, esq. of Norwell-Woodhouse, Notts, and dying at his house in Piccadilly, 4th October, 1695, was s. by his only child,

I. Sir Walter Clarges, bart. who had been so created by *King* Charles II. 30th October, 1674. He m. first, Jane, daughter of Sir Dawes Wymondsell, knt. of Putney,† and had a daughter, Jane, m. to Anthony Hammond, esq. of Somersham, in Huntingdonshire, M. P. for the borough of Huntingdon, *temp.* Queen Anne. Sir Walter wedded, secondly, Jane, daughter of the Honourable James Herbert, of Kingsey, Bucks, and granddaughter of Philip, Earl of Pembroke, and by that lady had, Thomas, his successor, and other issue.‡ He m. thirdly, Elizabeth, relict of Sir Dawes Wymondsell, knt. of Putney, and second daughter and co-heir of Sir James Gould, an alderman of London, and by her had

- Robert, M. P. for Reading in the last parliament of *Queen* Anne.
- Walter, m. Lady Elizabeth Shirley, eldest daughter of Robert, first Earl Ferrers.
- Peter.
- George.
- Gould.
- Christopher.
- Leonard, an officer in the army.
- ———, m. to Robert Snell, esq. of the Temple.
- ———, m. to — Shelley, esq. of Gloucestershire.

Sir Walter represented the City of Westminster in parliament in the reigns of *King* William and *Queen* Anne. He d. in March, 1705-6, and was s. by his eldest son,

II. Sir Thomas Clarges, M.P. for Lostwithiel, in Cornwall, who married Barbara, youngest daughter and co-heir of John, Viscount Fitzharding, and had issue,

- Thomas, b. in 1721, who m. ———, daughter and co-heir of John, Viscount Barrington, and dying v. p. left a son,
  - Thomas, successor to his grandfather.
- Barbara, m. to George Wright, esq. M.P. for Leicester, grandson of Sir Nathan Wright.

Sir Thomas d. 19th February, 1759, and was s. by his grandson,

III. Sir Thomas Clarges, who m. Miss Skrine, and d. 27th July, 1783, and was s. by his son,

IV. Sir Thomas Clarges, at whose decease unmarried in 1834 the title became extinct. "By will, he left the bulk of his fortune, consisting of landed property worth £10,000 a year, to Major Hare, a distant kinsman, and £100 a year to the eldest son of his near relative, Sir Dudley St. Leger Hill."§

Arms—Barry of ten arg. and az. on a canton sa. an Indian ram's head couped of the first, armed with four horns or.

CLARKE, OF SNAILWELL.

Created 25th July, 1698.

Extinct 23rd May, 1806.

Lineage.

John Clarke, esq. of Bocking, in Essex, descended from a Kentish family, was father of

John Clarke, esq. of Bury, who died about 1681, leaving a daughter, the wife of Thomas Barnardiston, esq. of Hackney, in Middlesex, and a son,

I. Samuel Clarke, esq. of Snailwell, in the county of Cambridge, who was created a Baronet by *King* William III. 25th July, 1698. He m. Mary, daughter of Major Robert Thompson, of Newington Green, in the county of Middlesex, and had issue,

- Robert, his successor.
- Samuel, d. unm.
- Frances, m. to Thomas Lucke, esq. barrister-at-law, and d. 1st November, 1718.
- Margaret, m. to the Rev. Mr. Malabar.
- Mary, d. unm.

He d. 8th March, 1719, and was s. by his son,

II. Sir Robert Clarke, M. P. for the county of Cambridge. This gentleman m. Mary, only surviving daughter of Arthur Barnardiston, esq. and granddaughter of Sir Nathaniel Barnardiston, of Barnardiston, in the county of Suffolk, and by her, who d. in January, 1732-3, had issue,

- Samuel, his successor, b. 21st May, 1712.
- Robert, successor to his brother, b. 22nd Jan. 1714.
- Arthur, who inherited as sixth Baronet, b. 5th February, 1715.
- John, b. 15th May, 1717.
- Mary, b. 15th April, 1720. }
- Anne, b. 4th February, 1724. } one of whom m. Benj. Lane, esq. of Hampstead.
- Jane, b. 7th April, 1727. }

Sir Robert d. in Nov. 1746, and was s. by his eldest son,

III. Sir Samuel Clarke, who d. unmarried, 10th November, 1758, and was s. by his brother,

IV. Sir Robert Clarke, who m. Elizabeth Littel, and dying 18th August, 1770, was s. by his son,

V. Sir John Clarke, who d. young and unmarried, 8th November, 1782, when the title reverted to his uncle,

VI. Sir Arthur Clarke, at whose decease in 1806, the Baronetcy became extinct. The manor of Snailwell was sold by Sir Samuel Clarke, to the grandfather of the Hon. Thomas Brand, of whom it was purchased by the late John Tharp, esq. of Chippenham.

Arms—Or, on a bend engrailed az. a mullet arg.

---

she taught girls plain work. About 1647, she being sempstress to Monk, used to carry him linen. In 1648, her father and mother died; in 1649, she and her husband fell out, and parted; but no certificate from any parish register appears reciting his burial. In 1652, she was married in the church of St. George, Southwark, to General George Monk, and in the following year, was delivered of a son, Christopher, 'who was suckled by Honour Mills, who sold apples, herbs, oysters,' which son Christopher succeeded his father as second duke."

* The pedigree as far as this gentleman and the Duchess of Albemarle, is by Corneille de Montigny, de Glarges, Chevalier de l'ordre St. Michael, Seigneur de Estemones, en la Province d'Hanault, chief du nom et famille de Montigny de Glarges, 4th February, 1675, and was entered in the Earl Marshall's book, in the College of Arms, 7th February, 1675. Le Neve's MSS. vol. iii. p. 198. There are certainly though too few descents for such a period of time.

† By Jane, his wife, only daughter of Sir Robert Coke, knt. of Hyneham, in the county of Gloucester.

‡ One of his daughters was wife of — Tancred, esq. master of the buck hounds to *King* William, and another of — Howell, esq.

§ Gentleman's Magazine.

CLERE, OF ORMESBY.

CREATED 27th Feb. 1620. EXTINCT 22nd Aug. 1622.

Lineage.

The family of Clere was established in England by one of the companions in arms of the CONQUEROR, and remained for centuries, maintaining the highest position in the county of Norfolk.

SIR ROBERT CLERE, knt. of Ormesby,* representative of this ancient line at the close of the fifteenth century, famed for his great wealth and manly courage, served as sheriff of Norfolk in 1501, and was present at the celebrated interview between HENRY VIII. and the French King, 7th of June, 1520. He m. first Anne, daughter of Sir William Hopton, knt. by whom he had a son, William, who *d. s. p.* and secondly, Alice, daughter of Sir William Boleyn, knt. of Blickling and aunt of the ill-fated Queen, ANNA BOLEYN, by whom he had issue,

- I. JOHN, his heir.
- II. Richard.
- III. Thomas, buried at Lambeth in 1545. An epitaph by Henry Howard, Earl of Northampton, perpetuates his memory.
- I. Elizabeth, *m.* to Sir Robert Peyton, knt. of Iselham.
- II. Anne, a nun at Denny.
- III. Dorothy, *m.* to Robert Cotton.
- IV. Audrey *m.* to William Jenney.

Sir Robert, *d.* 10th August, 1529, and by his will, dated nine days previously, directs above all things, that if any persons could prove that he had hindered them, or against conscience wronged them, in their goods or substance, that his executors, on such proof, should make them restitution. His eldest son and heir,

SIR JOHN CLERE, of Ormesby, knt. was treasurer, in 1540, of the king's army in France, and in 1557, having been constituted vice-admiral, was sent to sea with a fleet under his command, to alarm the northern coasts of Scotland. He landed at Kirkwall, but the Scots suddenly attacking him, he and eighty of his men were either killed or drowned. Sir John *m.* Anne, daughter of Sir Thomas Tirrell, knt. of Gipping, in Suffolk, and had issue,

- I. Robert, slain at Musselburgh.
- II. Thomas, *d.* at Florence.
- III. EDWARD, the heir.
- I. Elizabeth, *m.* first, Walter Heronden, esq. and secondly, to Francis Trevor, esq. of Tacolneston.
- II. Margaret, *m.* to William Haddon, esq.

The only surviving son,

EDWARD CLERE, esq. of Ormesby and Blickling, M. P. for Thetford, 1556, and for Grampound in 15[illegible] and 1563, who served as sheriff of Norfolk in 15[illegible] *m.* Frances, daughter and heir of Sir Richard Fulmerston, knt. and had three sons, viz.

- I. EDWARD (Sir), his heir.
- II. Francis (Sir), *m.* Elizabeth Wroth, and *d. s. p.*
- III. Gilbert, *d. unm.*

Edward Clere was buried at Blickling, under a most curious altar tomb, placed between the chancel and Boleyn's Chapel; his effigies which laid upon it long since passed away, but there remained the arms and matches of his family from the CONQUEST, to the time that his son and heir, Sir Edward Clere, and his mother, Frances, erected the tomb. The said son and heir

SIR EDWARD CLERE, of Ormesby, was knighted at Norwich, by Queen ELIZABETH, in her royal progress and served as sheriff of Norfolk in 1586. He m. first, Margaret, daughter of William Yaxley, esq. of Yaxley, in Suffolk, by whom he had a son,

HENRY.

He *m.* secondly, Agnes, daughter of Robert Crane, esq. of Chilton, and widow of Sir Christopher Heydon of Baconsthorp, and by her had another son, Robert, who *d.* young. Sir Edward affecting much splendour and maintaining a vast retinue, became involved in embarrassment, and was forced to sell a considerable portion of his estate. (The manor of Blickling was purchased by Sir Henry Hobart, knt. attorney general. He *d.* in London, 8th June, 1606, and was there interred with great solemnity, 14th August following, being succeeded by his son,

I. SIR HENRY CLERE, of Ormesby, who was knighted by JAMES I. at the Charter House, 11th May, 1603, and created a BARONET 27th February, 1620. He m. Muriel, daughter of Sir Edmund Mundeford, knt. of Feltwell, in Norfolk, and had an only child.

ABIGAIL, *m.* to John Cromwell, esq. of London, second son of Sir Oliver Cromwell, knt. of Hinchenbrooke.

Sir Henry died 21st August, 1622, and with him the BARONETCY EXPIRED.†

Arms—Arg. on a fess az. three eagles displayed or.

CLERKE, OF LAUNDE ABBEY.

CREATED 18th June, 1661. EXTINCT 10th April, [illegible]

Lineage.

This family was long seated at Willoughby, in the county of Warwick, of which was, one RICHARD [illegible]

---

* The estate of Ormesby was acquired in the thirteenth century, by the marriage of Nicholas de Clere with Annable, daughter and heir of Sir William de Ormesby, knt.

† A branch of the family settled in Ireland, and continued eminent in that part of the kingdom, until it eventually terminated in an heiress,

MARY CLERE, only daughter of John Clere, esq. of Kilbury, who m. 28th June, 1734, Sir William Parsons, bart. of Birr Castle, M. P. for the King's County, and had, with other issue,

LAURENCE PARSONS, who inherited the baronetcy from his father, and the barony of Oxmantown, with the Earldom of Rosse, from his uncle, and is the present (1837) EARL OF ROSSE.

...ND, *alias* CLERKE, styled esquire, 23 HENRY VI. who hen held the whole manor of Willoughby, by lease, of he guardian and brethren of the hospital of St. John, without the East Gate at Oxford, founded by HENRY II.; we find further, that William Wainflete, Bishop f Winchester, having, 26 HENRY VI., commenced the oundation of Magdalen College, in Oxford, on the ite of the said hospital, did, in the 35th of the same eign, obtain from the said master and brethren, the rant of this lordship of Willoughby, whereunto it as ever since continued, being possessed by the president and fellows thereof at the present time; yet as constantly leased out to the descendants of the aid Richard Clerke, persons of fair estate in that ounty, of which family was

HENRY CLERKE, who had two sons,

- EDWARD, his heir.
- Hierome, father of John Clerke, of Gilsborough, Northamptonshire, barrister-at-law, and bencher of Lincoln's Inn, in 1648.

The elder son,

EDWARD CLERKE, had issue,

- WILLIAM, his heir.
- Henry, of Rochester, serjeant-at-law.
- Samuel, D. D. of Kingsthorpe, Northamptonshire, chaplain in ordinary to *King* JAMES I. and to *King* CHARLES I. He *m.* Margaret, daughter of William Peyto, esq. of Chesterton, in the county of Warwick.

The eldest son,

WILLIAM CLERKE, esq. of Willoughby, had by his wife, Agnes, three sons, viz.

- Richard.
- ROBERT.
- John (Sir), who in HENRY the VIII.'s time, having taken the Duke of Longvile prisoner, at the battle of Spurs, was for that signal service rewarded by the king with an honorary addition to his arms, viz. "Sinister, a canton, azure, with a demi ram, salient, argent, two fleur de luces, or, in chief, and over all, a baton, trunked," as appeareth on his monument, at Thame, in Oxfordshire, which arms, "argent on a bend, gules, between three pellets, as many swans, proper," were borne by the Clerkes above mentioned, and continued to Sir John Clerke's descendants, who resided at Weston, by Thame, and at Crewton, in Northamptonshire.

The second son,

ROBERT CLERKE, esq. of Willoughby, *m.* Elizabeth, daughter of Clark, of the Ware, and had issue,

- HENRY, from whom descended the Clerkes of Kingsthorpe, in Northamptonshire, of Ulcombe, in Kent, and of Willoughby, in Warwickshire.
- William.
- Clement.

The youngest son,

CLEMENT CLERKE, esq. *b.* in 1546, *m.* Mary, daughter of Thomas Clerke, esq. of Willoughby, and had two sons,

- GEORGE.
- Thomas.

The elder,

SIR GEORGE CLERKE, was of Watford, in Northamptonshire, and having served the office of sheriff for London, received the honour of knighthood. He *m.* Barbara, daughter of Robert Palmer, esq. of Hill, in the county of Bedford, and had issue,

- GEORGE, of Watford, who *m.* Mary, daughter of Philip Holman, esq. of Warkworth, Northamptonshire, and left issue.
- Robert, of Long Buckley, in Northamptonshire, barrister at-law, *m.* Frances, daughter of John Cotes, esq. of Woodcote, in Shropshire, and had issue.
- CLEMENT.
- Elizabeth, *m.* to John Walcot, esq. of Walcot, Salop.
- Mary, *m.* to Sir Robert Atkyns, K. B. chief baron of the Exchequer.
- Barbara, *m.* to Sir Wadham Wyndham, knt. one of the justices of the King's Bench.
- Sarah, *m.* to Thomas Kinnersley, esq. of Loxley, in Staffordshire.
- Dorcas, *m.* to John Cotes, esq. of Woodcote, Salop.

Sir George *d.* in 1648. His youngest son,

I. CLEMENT CLERKE, esq. of Launde Abbey, in the county of Leicester, was created a BARONET by *King* CHARLES II., 18th June, 1661. He *m.* Catherine, daughter of George Talbot, esq. of Ridge, in Shropshire, and had issue,

- I. TALBOT, his successor.
- II. Clement, deputy governor of the Isle of Wight, died unmarried.
- III. George, who *m.* Dorothy, daughter of — Pearse, esq. of Oakfield, Berks, and had a son and daughter, viz.
  - TALBOT, who inherited as sixth BARONET.
  - Dorothy, *m.* to Philip Jennings, esq. of Duddleston, in Shropshire, nephew to Admiral Sir John Jennings, knt. governor of Greenwich Hospital.
- IV. Thomas, *d.* unmarried.

Sir Clement was *s.* by his eldest son,

II. SIR TALBOT CLERKE, who *m.* Hannah, daughter of .... and dying in 1706, was *s.* by his eldest son,

III. SIR CLEMENT CLERKE, who *d.* unmarried about the year 1715, and was *s.* by his brother,

IV. SIR TALBOT CLERKE, who *m.* Barbara, daughter and co-heir of Thomas Gladin, esq. of Durrent Hall, in the county of Derby, by whom, (who *m.* secondly, John Monk Morgan, esq. of Monmouthshire,) he had, with a daughter, an only son, his successor, at his decease, 16th February, 1723.

V. SIR TALBOT CLERKE, at whose decease, in minority and unmarried, 20th November, 1732, the Baronetcy devolved upon his cousin, (refer to GEORGE, third son of the first Baronet),

VI. SIR TALBOT CLERKE, who *m.* Lucy, daughter of the Rev. Mr. Rogers, of Painswick, in the county of Gloucester, but dying *s. p.* 10th July, 1758, the BARONETCY became EXTINCT.

Arms—Arg. on a bend gu. between three pellets, as many swans ppr.

CLERKE, OF DUDDLESTONE.

CREATED 26th Oct. 1774.—EXTINCT 22nd April, 1788.

Lineage.

I. SIR PHILIP JENNINGS CLERKE, of Duddlestone, in Salop, was created a BARONET in 1774, but having no child, the title expired with him, in 1788.

Arms—See CLERKE, of Launde Abbey.

CLIFTON, OF CLIFTON.

CREATED 4th March, 1660. EXTINCT 13th Nov. 1694.

Lineage.

The very ancient family of CLIFTON has been, for a long series of generations, seated in the county of Lancaster, and its male representative, Thomas Clifton, esq. still resides at Lytham, in that shire. (See BURKE'S *Commoners*, vol. ii. p. 55.) The chief of the house at the commencement of the seventeenth century,

I. SIR THOMAS CLIFTON, of Westby and Clifton, *b.* 7th July, 1628, was created a BARONET, 4th March, 1660. He *m.* first, Bridget, daughter of Sir George Heneage, of Hainton, in Lincolnshire, by whom he had several children, who all died young, except

MARY, who *m.* Thomas, sixth Lord Petre. From this marriage lineally descends William-Francis-Henry, present LORD PETRE.

Sir Thomas wedded secondly, Bridget, daughter of Sir Edward Hussey, knt. of Honington, and had by her one son and one daughter, viz.

THOMAS, *b.* in 1669, and *d. v. p.* issueless, in 1688.
BRIDGET, *m.* to Sir Francis Andrews, of Denton.

Sir Thomas Clifton and Lord Molyneux, with several other Catholic gentlemen of rank, were accused of high treason in 1689, but all acquitted. He died 13th November, 1694, when the BARONETCY EXPIRED; but the family estates devolved on his nephew, THOMAS CLIFTON, esq. ancestor of the present THOMAS CLIFTON, esq. of Clifton and Lytham.

Arms—Sa. on a bend arg. three mullets gu.

CLOSE.

CREATED 12th Dec. 1812. EXTINCT April, 1813.

Lineage.

The family of CLOSE, originally from Yorkshire, has been for several generations, most respectably settled in Ireland.

MAXWELL CLOSE, esq. (great grandson of the first settler) succeeded his grandmother, Lady Maxwell, who died in 1756, in the possession of Elm Park, in the county of Armagh. He *m.* in 1748, Mary, eldest daughter of Captain Robert Maxwell, of Fellows Hall, brother of John, Lord Farnham, and dying in 1793, left, *inter alios*, three sons,

SAMUEL, his heir, of Elm Park, in holy orders, father of the present MAXWELL CLOSE, esq. of Drumbanagher, in the county of Armagh. (See BURKE'S *Commoners*, vol. iii. p. 367.)
Robert, *d.* unm.
BARRY, of whom we have to treat.

The third son,

I. SIR BARRY CLOSE, a very distinguished officer in the service of the East India Company, in which he attained the rank of major-general, was created a BARONET 12th December, 1812, but dying unmarried in April following, the title became EXTINCT.

Arms—Az. on a chev. arg. between three mullets or two bugle horns ppr. stringed gu. with a stirrup [illegible] in the centre also ppr.

COBB, OF ADDERBURY.

CREATED 9th Dec. 1662. EXTINCT 29th March, 17[illegible]

Lineage.

WILLIAM COBB, esq. of Adderbury, in the county of Oxford, (descended from a family seated at Sandringham, in Norfolk,) living about the time of Queen ELIZABETH and JAMES I.; *m.* Alice, daughter of [illegible] Wild, esq. of Oldham, in Lancashire, and had a large family, of which only one son and two daughters survived himself, namely,

WILLIAM (Sir), his heir.
Catherine, *m.* to Sir George Russell, knt. of the county of Bedford.
Margaret, *m.* to Sir Richard Cholmeley, knt. of Whitby, in Yorkshire.

He died in 1598. His wife survived him, and dying 23rd October, 1627, was buried in the chancel of Adderbury Church.* Mr. Cobb was *s.* by his son,

SIR WILLIAM COBB, knt. who *m.* Susan, daughter and co-heir of Noah Floyd, esq. of the county of Gloucester, by whom, who *d.* in 1639, he had [illegible] children, but few only attained maturity; of them were,

THOMAS, his heir.

* The inscription on his tomb was as follows:

Here lyeth buryed ye boddy of Alice Cobb, Widow, sometime wife of William Cobb, esq. descended from ye ancient family of ye Cobbs, of Sandringham, in the County of Norfolk, by whom she was ye mother of 16 Children, 7 Sons, and 9 Daughters, all of which she lived to see buryed [illegible] onely, ye right worshipful Sir William Cobb, [illegible] her onely Son, and Dame Catherine, who married Sir George Russell, of Bedfordshire, knt. and Dame Margaret, who married to Sir Richard Cholmeley, of Yorkshire, knt. She lived a Maid 19 Years, a Wife 26 Years, and after her Husband's Death, who deceased in October, Anno 1598. She lived a Widow 30 Years, having performed the part both of a constant loveing Wife, and a Kind and carefull Mother, resting now with the Almighty, whome her greatest care was ever to serve and feare. She dyed ye 23rd of October, A. Dni 1627.

James, buried at Chelsea.
Arthur.
Francis.
Winifred, m. to Captain Steward Walker.
Alice, m. to Major Croker, of Hook Norton, in Oxfordshire.
Susanna, m. the Honourable Richard Fiennes, fourth son of Lord Say and Sele.

He d. in 1658, was buried at Adderbury, 16th March, in that year, and s. by his eldest surviving son,

I. Thomas Cobb, esq. of Adderbury, who was created a Baronet by King Charles II., 9th December, 1662. Sir Thomas m. first, Catherine, second daughter of Sir Richard Onslow,* knt. of West Clandon, Surrey, which lady died issueless. He m. secondly, Christian, daughter of Sir Edward Bisshopp,† bart. of Parham, and by her had issue,

William, d. unm. } before their father.
Thomas, d. unm. }
Edward, successor to his father.
John, D.D. Warden of New College, Oxford, m. Sarah, daughter of Sir Hugh Stukely, bart. of Hinton, Hants, but d. s. p. in 1725; his widow m. the next year, St. John, esq. of Farley, and surviving him, she m. thirdly, Captain Francis Townsend.
George, successor to his brother Edward.

Sir Thomas d. in February, 1699, and was s. by his eldest surviving son,

II. Sir Edward Cobb, who d. unmarried in 1744, and was s. by his brother,

III. Sir George Cobb, who m. Anne, daughter and co-heir of Joseph Langton, esq. of Newton Park, in the county of Somerset, and acquired thereby that estate. She was widow of Robert Langton, esq. of Bristington, eldest son of Sir Thomas Langton, knt. of Bristol. Sir George had issue,

Charles, d. young.
Anne.
Christian, who m. Paul Methuen, esq. of Corsham, in Wiltshire, M.P., and was grandmother of the present,
Paul Methuen, esq. of Corsham, M. P.

Sir George Cobb falling accidentally, 29th March, 1762, into a moat, at the seat of John Blagrave, esq. near Reading, was drowned, at the advanced age of ninety, when the Baronetcy became extinct.

Arms—Sa. a chev. arg. between three dolphins naiant embowed or, a chief of the last.

COCKS, OF DUMBLATON.

Created 7th April, 1661.

Extinct 4th April, 1765.

Lineage.

The first of this family, a branch of that of Cocks Hall, in Kent, whom we find in Gloucestershire, was Thomas Cocks, esq. of Bishop's Cleve, in that county, living in the time of Henry VIII. who m. Elizabeth Holland, of a Lancashire family, and had, with other issue,

Thomas, who had one son,
Sir John Cocks, knt. whose issue failing, his estate, the manor of Northley, and other lands, passed to
Henry Stafford, grandson of Elizabeth Cocks.
Richard, of whom presently.
Charles, bencher of the Middle Temple, who d. in 1654, and left his property (including the manor of Dumbleton, which he had inherited from his sister Dorothy,) to his nephew, Sir Richard Cocks.
Anne, m. to — Barnsly, esq. of Barnsly Hall, in the county of Worcester.
Dorothy, m. first, to Edmund Hutchyngs, esq. of Dumbleton, and secondly, to Sir Charles Percy.
Elizabeth, m. to — Stafford, esq. Her grandson, Henry Stafford, inherited Northley, as stated above.

The second son,

Richard Cocks, esq. of Castleditch, in the county of Hereford, m. Judith, daughter and co-heir of John Elliott, of the City of London, and had two sons, Thomas, his heir, (ancestor of the Lord Somers,) and

I. Richard Cocks, esq. of Dumbleton, in the county of Gloucester, who inherited the real and personal property of his uncle, Charles Cocks, esq. of the Middle Temple, and was created a Baronet by King Charles II. 7th April, 1661. He m. Susannah, daughter of Ambrose Elton, esq.‡ of the Hasle, in the county of Hereford, and had issue,

Richard, who m. Mary, daughter of Sir Robert Cooke, of Highnam, in the county of Gloucester, (by Dorothy, his wife, daughter of Sir Miles Fleetwood,) and dying in his father's lifetime, 1669, left three sons,
Richard, successor to his grandfather.
Robert, third Baronet.
Charles.
Dorothy.
Mary.
Susanna, m. first, Roger Thompson, of the City of London, merchant, and secondly, Sir Edward Fust, bart. of Hill, in the county of Gloucester.
Jane.
Charles, d. unm.
John, m. Anne, eldest daughter of Walter Savage, esq. of Broadway, in the county of Worcester, but had no issue.
Judith, d. unm.
Elizabeth, m. to Sir John Fust, bart. of Hill, in the county of Gloucester.

Sir Richard, who was sheriff of Gloucestershire in 1669, d. in September, 1684, and was s. by his grandson,

II. Sir Richard Cocks, who m. first, Frances, daughter of Richard Nevil, esq. of Billingbear, in the county of Berks, and secondly, Mary, daughter of William Bethell, esq. of Swindon, in Yorkshire, but had no issue. Sir Richard was knight of the Shire for the county of Gloucester, for three successive parliaments, in the reign of King William, and sheriff

* Grandfather of the first Lord Onslow.
† By his wife, Lady Mary Tufton, daughter of Nicholas, Earl of Thanet.

‡ By Anne, his wife, daughter of Sir Edward Aston, of Tixall, in the county of Stafford, sister of Walter, Lord Aston.

in 1692. He *d.* in October, 1726, and was *s.* by his brother,

III. *The Rev.* SIR ROBERT COCKS, D. D. Rector of Bladon, cum Woodstock and Rollright, in the county of Oxford. This gentleman *m.* Mrs. Anne Fulks, of Oxford, and had several sons, who all died issueless, except ROBERT, the fourth son, who inherited the title and estates, and five daughters. He *d.* 9th February, 1735-6, and was *s.* by his son,

IV. SIR ROBERT COCKS, who *m.* Elizabeth, second daughter of James Cholmeley, esq. of Easton, in the county of Lincoln, but dying without surviving issue, 4th April, 1765, the BARONETCY became EXTINCT; the manor of Dumbleton devolving on John Cocks, esq. of Castleditch, father of Charles, the great LORD SOMERS.

Arms—Sa. a chev. between three attires of a stag, fixed to the scalp arg.

COGHILL, OF RICHINGS.

CREATED 24th March, 1781.

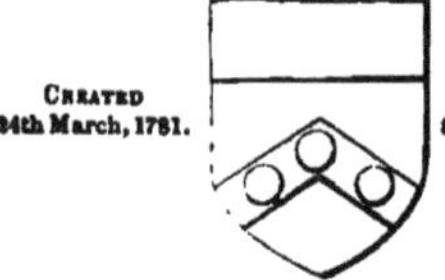

EXTINCT 8th March, 1790.

Lineage.

I. MAJOR JOHN MAYNE, of Richings, in Buckinghamshire, (an estate he purchased from the Duke of Northumberland, and which was afterwards sold to the Right Hon. John Sullivan,) *m.* Hester, only daughter and heir of James Coghill, LL.D. register of the Prerogative Court, and relict of Charles Moore, Earl of Charleville, and assuming in consequence, the surname and arms of COGHILL, was created a BARONET in 1781. He died, however, without issue in 1790, when the title became EXTINCT. Sir John's widow, the countess of Charleville, bequeathed her property, at her decease, to her cousin,

JOHN CRAMER, esq. who assumed the surname of COGHILL, and was created a BARONET. His son is the present SIR JOSIAH COGHILL, bart. of Coghill.

Arms—Gu. on a chev. arg. three pellets, a chief sa.

COKE, OF LONGFORD.

CREATED 30th Dec. 1641.

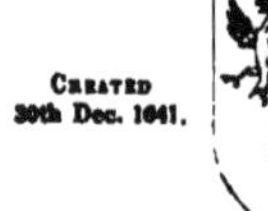

EXTINCT 26th Aug. 1727.

Lineage.

This family sprang from

SIR THOMAS COKE, knt. of Munteby, Lord of Duddington, Pouldin, &c. who had three sons,

THOMAS (Sir), a knight banneret, who died, before his father, leaving a son,

THOMAS, *d.* unm.

Peter.

JOHN.

The youngest son,

JOHN COKE, esq. of Whitwell, continued the line, and was living in the 36th EDWARD III. (1362). His son and heir,

JOHN COKE, esq. of Crostwick, was father of two sons, William, who *d. s. p.* and

ROBERT COKE, esq. of Ryston, who *m.* Agnes, daughter and heir of Roger Crispin, esq. of Happersburgh, and was *s.* by his son,

JOHN COKE, esq. of Ryston, who *m.* Alice, daughter and co-heir of William Folcard, Lord of Sparham, in Norfolk, and had two sons, John, who died without issue, and

ROBERT COKE, esq. of Sparham, who *m.* Anne, daughter of — Woodhouse, of Norfolk, and was *s.* by his son,

ROBERT COKE, esq. of Mileham, in Norfolk, living 35 HENRY VIII. He *m.* Winifred, daughter and co-heir of William Knightley, esq. of Morgrave-Knightley, in Norfolk, and by her, (who *d.* in January, 1569, left at his decease, in 1561, a son and heir, afterward the great law luminary,

SIR EDWARD COKE, knt. successively LORD CHIEF JUSTICE of both Benches, and a privy counsellor in the reign of JAMES *the First.** He *m.* first, Bridget, daughter and co-heir of John Paston, esq. and by that lady, had issue,

I. Edmund, who *d. s. p.*

II. Robert (Sir), married Theophila, only daughter of Thomas, Lord Berkeley, but died without issue, 19th July, 1653, and was buried at Epsom.

III. Arthur, *m.* Elizabeth, daughter and heir of Sir George Walgrave, knt. of Hitcham, in Norfolk, and died at St. Edmundsbury, 6th December, 1629, leaving four daughters, his co-heirs.

IV. John, of Holkham, in Norfolk, married Meriel, daughter and heir of Anthony Wheatley, esq. and had several children; but the estates eventually devolved upon the youngest son,

John, who dying unmarried, the estate of Holkham fell to the heirs of Henry Coke, of Thurrington.

V. Henry, of Thurrington, in the county of Suffolk, *m.* Margaret, daughter and heir of Richard Lovelace, esq. of Kingsdown, in Kent, and was *s.* by his eldest son,

Richard, who married Mary, daughter of Sir John Rous, bart. and left an only son,

ROBERT COKE, of Thurrington, who at the decease of his cousin, inherited Holkham; and from him derived through the female line, the present

THOMAS WILLIAM COKE, esq. of Holkham.

VI. CLEMENT, of whom presently.

I. Anne, *m.* to Ralph Sadler, esq. son and heir of Sir Ralph Sadler, knt.

II. Bridget, *m.* to William Skinner, esq. son and heir of Sir Vincent Skinner.

Sir Edward Coke, *m.* secondly, Lady Elizabeth Cecil, daughter of Thomas, Earl of Exeter, and of that lady

* See BURKE'S *Commoners*, vol. I. p. 3. COKE, of Holkham.

riage were two daughters, Elizabeth, who died unmarried, and Frances, wife of John Villiers, Viscount Purbeck. The chief justice died at Stoke Pogis, 3rd September, 1633, in the eighty-third year of his age, and was buried at Tittleshell, in Norfolk. His youngest son,

CLEMENT COKE, esq. m. Sarah, daughter and heir of Alexander Reddish, esq. of Reddish, in Lancashire, (by the daughter and co-heir of Sir Robert Langley, of Agecroft, in the same county,) and acquired thereby the estate of Longford, in the county of Derby. He died in May, 1619, and was succeeded by his elder son,

I. EDWARD COKE, esq. of Longford, who was created a BARONET 30th December, 1641. Sir Edward m. Catherine, daughter and co-heir of Sir William Dyer, knt. of Great Stoughton, in the county of Huntingdon, and had issue,

ROBERT, his successor.
EDWARD, heir to his brother.
Catherine, m. to Cornelius Clarke, esq. of Norton.
Anne, d. unm.
Theophila, m. to — Bullock, esq.

He was s. by his elder son,

II. SIR ROBERT COKE, M. P. for the county of Derby, in the 1st of JAMES II. He m. Sarah, daughter and co-heir of — Barker, esq. of Abrightlee, in Salop, but dying without issue, in January, 1687, was s. by his brother,

III. SIR EDWARD COKE, who d. unmarried, 25th August, 1727, when the BARONETCY became EXTINCT, and the estates passed to the deceased's kinsman,

EDWARD COKE, esq. second son of Edward Coke, esq. of Holkham, and brother of Thomas Coke, created LORD LOVELL in 1728. He died unmarried in 1733, and was s. by his brother,

ROBERT COKE, esq. of Longford, vice chamberlain to Queen ANNE, who died without issue, and the Derbyshire estates then united with those of Norfolk.

Arms—Party per pale gu. and az. three eagles displayed arg.

COLBRAND, OF BOREHAM.

CREATED 21st Dec. 1621.

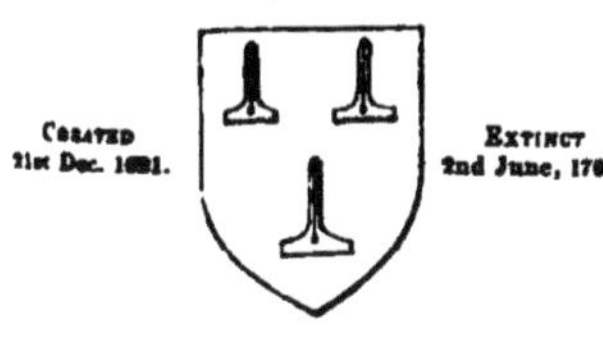

EXTINCT 2nd June, 1709.

Lineage.

JAMES COLBRAND, esq. of Chichester, the lineal descendant of John Colebrand, of Boreham, in the 46 EDWARD III., died 43 ELIZABETH, leaving by Martha, his wife, daughter of Lord St. John, of Bletsoe, a son and successor,

I. SIR JOHN COLBRAND, of Boreham, in Sussex, who was created a BARONET 21st December, 1621. He m. first, Ann Wilson, and had by her a daughter, Walsingham, unmarried in 1634, and a son, JAMES, his heir. He m. secondly, Sarah Needham, of Derbyshire, by whom, who wedded secondly, Humphrey Newton, esq. of Axmouth, in Devon, he had four sons and five daughters, viz. Thomas, John, Henry, ROBERT (fifth Baronet), Sara, Frances, Bridget, Martha, and Jane. Sir John died in 1627, and was succeeded by his son,

II. SIR JAMES COLBRAND, of Boreham, living in 1634, who m. Margaret, daughter of Richard Amhurst, sergeant-at-law, by Margaret, his wife, daughter of Sir Thomas Palmer, bart. of Wingham, and was s. by his son,

III. SIR RICHARD COLBRAND, of Boreham, colonel in the royal army, slain in the civil wars. He d. unm. and was s. by his brother,

IV. SIR CHARLES COLBRAND, at whose decease, unmarried, of the small-pox, in 1672, the Baronetcy reverted to his uncle of the half-blood,

V. SIR ROBERT COLBRAND, son of Sir John Colbrand, first Baronet, by his second wife. He m. Mary, daughter of Thomas Southland, esq. of Lee, in Kent, but dying s. p. 2nd June, 1709, the title became EXTINCT.

Arms—Az. three levels with their plummets, or.

COLBY, OF KENSINGTON.

CREATED 21st June, 1720.

EXTINCT 23rd Sept. 1729.

Lineage.

JOHN COLBY, esq. of Brundyche, in Suffolk, m. Alice, daughter and heir of John Brewse, esq. of Hardwick, third son of Sir Thomas Brewse, knt. and left a son and successor,

THOMAS COLBY, esq. of Beccles, in Suffolk, who m. first, Beatrice, daughter of Thomas Felton, esq. of Playford, in that county, and secondly, Ursula, daughter of Edward Read, of Norwich, relict of Sir John Brend, knt. By the former he left a son and successor,

THOMAS COLBY, esq. of Beccles, who m. Amy, daughter of Thomas Brampton, esq. of Letton, in Norfolk, and had with other issue, a son,

PHILIP COLBY, esq. of Kensington, in Middlesex, who m. Elizabeth, second daughter and co-heir of William Flewellin,* esq. alderman of London, and left an only surviving son,

I. SIR THOMAS COLBY, of Kensington, one of the commissioners of his Majesty's navy, and M. P. for Rochester, who was created a BARONET 21st June, 1720. He d. unm. 23rd September, 1729, when the title became EXTINCT; his property devolving on the family of BULLOCK,* of Shipdham, in Norfolk.

Arms—Az. a chev. between three escallops or, within a bordure engr. of the last.

* Mr. Alderman Flewellin's eldest daughter and co-heir, Mary, m. THOMAS BULLOCK, esq. of Shipdham, ancestor of the late Rev. COLBY BULLOCK. (See BURKE's *Commoners*, vol. iv. p. 129.)

COLE, OF BRANCEPETH.

Created 4th March, 1640.

Extinct before 1727.

Lineage.

I. Sir Nicholas Cole, of Brancepeth, in Durham, who was created a Baronet, 4th March, 1640, *m.* Mary, daughter of Sir Thomas Liddell, bart. of Ravensworth, and was *s.* by his son,

II. Sir Ralph Cole, of Brancepeth, who *m.* first, Miss Windham, and secondly, Katherine, daughter of Sir Henry Foulis, bart. of Ingleby manor, in Yorkshire. Sir Ralph died in 1660, and having survived his son Nicholas, was *s.* by that gentleman's son,

III. Sir Nicholas Cole, of Brancepeth, who *m.* Anne, daughter of Collier Campbell, but dying *s. p.* 1710-11, was *s.* by his brother,

IV. Sir Mark Cole, of Brancepeth, at whose decease the title became extinct. Brancepeth Castle is now the property of the Russell family.

Arms—Arg. a fesse eng. sa. between three scorpions reversed of the second.

COLLIER.

Created 20th Sep. 1814.—Extinct March, 1824.

Lineage.

I. Sir George Ralph Collier, K.C.B. Captain R. N. a distinguished naval officer, was created a Baronet 20th September, 1814. He *m.* Maria, daughter and co-heir of John Lyon, M. D. of Liverpool, but dying *s. p.* in March, 1824, the title became extinct.

COMPTON, OF HARTBURY.

Created 6th May, 1686.

Extinct 29th Aug. 1773.

Lineage.

The manor of Hartbury, part of the possessions of the abbey of Gloucester, was conferred upon the family of Compton at the dissolution.

William Compton, esq. of Hartbury, descended from the Comptons of Wiltshire, *m.* Jane, daughter of Sir Walter Dennis, knt. of Fairford, in the county of Gloucester, and left issue,

Walter Compton, esq. of Hartbury, who *m.* Dorothy, daughter of Sir John Highford, knt. and was *s.* by his son,

William Compton, esq. of Hartbury, who *m.* Elenor, daughter of Sir William Meux, knt. of the Isle of Wight, and was *s.* by his son,

Walter Compton, esq. of Hartbury, who *m.* Mary, daughter of Dr. Thomas Habington, esq. of Hindlip, by Mary his wife, eldest daughter of Edward Parker, Lord Morley, and was father of

I. William Compton, esq. of Hartbury, in the county of Gloucester, who was created a Baronet by *King* James II. 6th May, 1686. He *m.* Catherine, daughter of Thomas Bond, esq. of Hoxton, Middlesex, and sister of Sir Thomas Bond, bart. of Peckham, and dying about the year 1696, was *s.* by his son,

II. Sir William Compton, of Hartbury and Hindlip, who *m.* Jane, daughter and heir of — Hyde, esq. of Hurst, in the county of Berks, and by her, who *d.* in February, 1728-9, had, with two daughters, both unm. two sons, viz.

William, his successor.
Dennis.

He *d.* 5th June, 1731, and was *s.* by his elder son.

III. Sir William Compton, of Hartbury, who *m.* Miss Holder, and had issue,

William, his heir.
Walter, successor to his brother.
Jane, *m.* to John Berkeley, esq. and had two daughters (co-heirs to their mother),
Catherine Berkeley, *m.* to Robert Canning, esq. of Foxcote, in Warwickshire, and died in 1823, *s. p.*
Jane Berkeley, *m.* to Thomas Anthony, present Viscount Southwell.
Catherine, *m.* to Edward Bancroft, esq. *d. s. p.*
Helen, *m.* to J. Dalby, esq.

Sir William *d.* 3rd May, 1758, and was *s.* by his son,

IV. Sir William Compton, of Hartbury, at whose decease, without issue, in 1760, the Baronetcy passed to his brother,

V. Sir Walter Compton, of Hartbury, who *m.* Miss Sarah Mary Moseley, but dying *s. p.* 29th August, 1773, the Baronetcy expired.

The estates eventually vested in Sir Walter's nieces, the daughters of his sister, Mrs. Berkeley. Mr. Canning, of Foxcote, the husband of the elder, enjoying Hartbury; and Lord Southwell, who married the younger, possessing Hindlip.

Arms—Arg. a fesse nebule gu. on a chief of the last a helmet between two lions' heads erased, or.

CONSTABLE, OF EVERINGHAM.

Created 20th July, 1642.

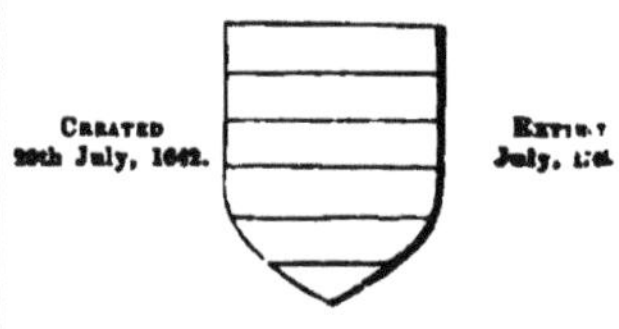

Extinct July, 1746.

Lineage.

The surname of Constable was assumed from the office of Constable of Chester, one of the high degrees constituted by Hugh Lupus, and held by this family soon after the Norman Conquest.

Robert de Lacy, younger brother of Roger, constable of Chester, and baron of Halton, enjoyed the lordship of Flamburgh, by gift of that nobleman, and was *s.* by his son,

Robert Constable, of Flamburgh, who, by Agnes his wife, was father of

William Constable, of Flamburgh, whose wife is called the Lady Julian, and who was *s.* by his son,

Sir Robert Constable, of Flamburgh, who was knighted with three hundred more at a grand festival at Whitsuntide, in the 34th year of Edward I. when the same honour was conferred by the king upon Edward, Earl of Carnarvon, his eldest son, preparatory to his expedition into Scotland. Sir Robert was living in the 13th of Edward II. and was father of

Sir Marmaduke Constable, knt. sheriff of the county of York, in the 40th and 41st of Edward III. His son and heir,

Sir William Constable, knt. of Flamburgh *m.* a daughter of the Lord Fitz Hugh, and was *s.* by his son,

Robert Constable, sheriff of Yorkshire, in the 8th, 9th, and 10th years of Richard II. who had to wife a daughter of William Skipwith, esq. and left a son and heir,

Sir Marmaduke Constable, knt. who *m.* Catherine, daughter and heir of Robert Cumberworth, esq.* and was *s.* by his eldest son,

Sir Robert Constable, who was knighted before 9th Henry VI. in which year he was sheriff of Yorkshire. He *m.* Agnes, daughter of Sir William Gascoigne, knt. and had issue,

- Robert (Sir), his heir.
- William.
- Marmaduke.
- Thomas.
- Richard.
- Elizabeth, *m.* to Robert Treyer.
- Jane, *m.* to John Welles.

He was *s.* by his eldest son,

Sir Robert Constable, knt. of Flamburgh, M. P. for the county of York, in the 17th of Edward IV. and sheriff in two years afterwards. He *m.* Agnes, daughter of Sir Roger Wentworth, of Nettlested, in Suffolk, and had issue,

- Marmaduke, his heir.
- John, dean of Lincoln.
- Philip.
- Robert, of Cliffe, sergeant-at-law.
- William, of Caythorpe and Wassand, living in 1528, represented now by
  - The Rev. Charles Constable, of Wassand, whose only daughter,
    - Mary Constable, *m.* in 1818, George, eldest son of Sir William Strickland, bart.
- Elizabeth, *m.* to Thomas Metham, esq.
- Margaret, *m.* to Sir William Ever, knt.
- Agnes, *m.* first, to Sir Gervase Clifton, knt. and secondly, to Walter Griffith, esq.
- Margery, *m.* to Sir Ralph Bigot, knt.
- Anne, *m.* to Sir William Tyrwhit, knt.
- Catherine, *m.* to Sir Ralph Ryder, knt.

He *d.* in 1488, and was *s.* by his eldest son,

Sir Marmaduke Constable, knt. of Flamburgh, in the county of York, who shared, with his four sons, in the glory of Flodden. He *m.* first, Joyce, daughter of Sir Humphry Stafford, knt. and had issue,

I. Robert (Sir), who inherited Flamburgh, and received the honour of knighthood for his signal services against the Cornish rebels in 1497; but afterwards, 28 Henry VIII., taking part in the commotions excited in Lincolnshire by John, Lord Hussey, and others, he was attainted and executed at Hull. He *m.* Jane, daughter of William Ingleby, esq. of Ripley, in the county of York, and left a son and heir,

   Marmaduke (Sir), of Nuneaton, (See Constable, of *Flamborough*) extinct Baronet.

II. Marmaduke (Sir).

III. William (Sir), of Hatfield, who *m.* the daughter and heir of John Hatfield, esq. of Hatfield, in Holderness.

IV. John (Sir), of Kinalton, in Nottinghamshire, who *m.* Jane, daughter and heir of Henry Sothill, esq. of Idle, in the county of York.

I. Eleanor, *m.* first, to John Ingleby, esq. of Ripley; and secondly, to — Berkeley, esq.

II. Agnes, *m.* to Sir Henry Oughtred, knt.

Sir Marmaduke, *m.* secondly, Margery, daughter of Henry, Lord Fitz Hugh, but by that lady had no issue. His second son,

Sir Marmaduke Constable, knt. was of Everingham, in the county of York, which estate he acquired with his wife Barbara, daughter and heir of Sir John Sothill. He was *s.* by his son,

Sir Robert Constable, knt. of Everingham, who *m.* Catherine, daughter of Sir George Manners, Lord Ros,† and had three sons,

- Marmaduke (Sir), his heir.
- Robert (Sir), of Newark.
- John, of Kikesby.

The eldest son,

Sir Marmaduke Constable, knt. *m.* Jane, daughter of William, Lord Conyers, of Hornby, and had issue,

- Robert (Sir), his successor.
- Roger, who *d. s. p.*
- Everill.

He was *s.* by his eldest son,

Sir Robert Constable, knt. of Everingham. This gentleman *m.* Margaret, daughter of Sir Robert Tyrwhit, knt. and by that lady had seven sons and four daughters, viz.

- Marmaduke, his heir.
- Robert, who *m.* Jane, daughter of Thomas Delman, esq.
- Michael.
- Roger, *m.* Mary, daughter of — Cottou, esq.
- Henry, *d. s. p.*
- William.
- Francis, *m.* the daughter of John Lengar, esq.
- Barbara, *m.* to Sir Thomas Metham, knt.
- Elizabeth, *m.* to William Langdale, esq.
- Frances, *m.* to Walter Rudston, esq. of Hayton.
- Jane, *m.* to Robert Sotheby, esq.

The eldest son,

Marmaduke Constable, esq. of Everingham, *m.* Frances, daughter of Thomas Metham, esq. of Metham, in Yorkshire, and had five sons, all of whom died issueless, except the eldest,

I. Philip Constable, esq. of Everingham, who was created a Baronet by *King* Charles I. 20th July, 1642, and was a severe sufferer in the royal cause. Sir Philip, *m.* Anne, only daughter of Sir William Roper knt. of Eltham, in Kent, and had issue,

   Marmaduke, his successor.

* By Sibil, his wife, daughter and heir of Sir William Sergers, knt.

† By Anne, his wife, daughter and sole heir of Sir Thomas St. Leger, knt. and his wife, Anne Plantagenet, Duchess of Exeter, sister of *King* Edward IV.

Philip, } both monks.
Thomas, }

Barbara, a nun, at Cambray.

Anne, *d. s. p.*

Katherine, married to Edward Sheldon, esq. of Steeple Barton, in Oxfordshire, and died 30th April, 1681.

Sir Philip lies buried at Steeple Barton Church, under a handsome monument, and this inscription:

Here lyeth the Body of S^r. Philip
Constable of Everingham in the County
of York Baronet, whose whole Estate
was confiscated by the Usurpers for
his Loyalty to K. Charles the first.
He died Febr. 25. Anno Dni 1664.
This Sr. Philip was father to Katherine
wife of Edward Sheldon of Steeple
Barton Esq; which Edward was son
of Ralph, and he a younger son of
Edward Sheldon of Beoly and he
the son and heir of Ralph Sheldon
of the said place, in com. Wigorn.
which last purchased one of the
three Mannors in Steeple Barton
of the Dorms with the house
belonging thereto (built by John
Dorm) which is now possest by
Ralph Sheldon, son and heir of
Edward Sheldon by Katherine
Constable his wife.

Sir Philip was *s.* by his eldest son,

II. SIR MARMADUKE CONSTABLE, bart. *b.* in 1619, *m.* Anne, daughter of Richard Sherborne, esq. of Stonyhurst, in Lancashire, and had (with two daughters, Anne and Elizabeth, both nuns), a son and heir,

III. SIR PHILIP-MARK CONSTABLE, bart. of Everingham, *b.* 25th April, 1651, *m.* Margaret, daughter of Sir Francis Ratcliffe, bart. of Dilston, in Northumberland, afterwards Earl of Derwentwater, and had issue,

MARMADUKE, his successor.

William, *d.* unm.

ANNE, *m.* to William, second, but eldest surviving son of Sir Thomas Haggerston, bart. of Haggerston, in Northumberland.

Catharine.

He was *s.* at his decease by his elder son,

IV. SIR MARMADUKE CONSTABLE, bart. of Everingham, who died abroad at the age of ninety, in July, 1746, and leaving no issue, the BARONETCY became EXTINCT. Everingham and the other estates devolved upon his great nephew, the grandson of his sister, Anne, WILLIAM HAGGERSTON, esq. who assumed the additional name of CONSTABLE. He *m.* Lady Winifred Maxwell, only surviving daughter and heir of John, Lord Maxwell, (who assumed the title of Earl of Nithsdale, at the decease of his father, the attainted Lord Nithsdale, in 1744, and inherited the estates, the forfeiture affecting the life interest of the attainted lord only). Mr. Haggerston-Constable had issue,

Marmaduke-William-Constable-Maxwell, esq. of Everingham and Carlaverock, who *d.* in 1819, leaving, with other issue, a son and heir, the present, WILLIAM-CONSTABLE-MAXWELL, esq. of Everingham.

William, who assumed the surname of MIDDLETON.

Charles, who assumed the surname of STANLEY.

Mary Haggerston-Constable, *m.* to John Webb Weston, esq. of Sutton Place, Surrey.

Theresa Haggerston-Constable.

(For details of the families of Constable and Maxwell, see BURKE'S *Commoners*, vol. i. p. 325.)

Arms—Barry of six or and az.

CONSTABLE, OF FLAMBOROUGH.

CREATED 29th June, 1611.—EXTINCT 15th June, 1644.

Lineage.

This was the elder branch of the house of CONSTABLE, of Everingham, extinct Baronets, to wh[ich] refer for the pedigree in full.

SIR MARMADUKE CONSTABLE, knt. of Flamborough in the county of York, *m.* first, Joyce, daughter of Sir Humphry Stafford, knt. and, by that lady, had,

ROBERT (Sir), his successor.

Marmaduke (Sir), from whom the CONSTABLES of *Everingham.*

William (Sir), of Hatfield.

John (Sir), of Kinalton.

Eleanor, *m.* first, to John Ingleby, esq. of Ripley, and secondly, to — Berkeley, esq.

Agnes, *m.* to Sir Henry Oughtred, knt.

He wedded, secondly, Margery, daughter of Henry Lord Fitzhugh, but by her had no issue. Sir Marmaduke was *s.* at his decease, by his son,

SIR ROBERT CONSTABLE, of Flamborough, who received the honour of knighthood, 17th June, 1497 (12 HENRY VII.) at the battle of Blackheath, for his valorous conduct against the Cornish rebels. He was afterwards concerned in the risings about religion in the 28th of HENRY VIII. and pardoned for the same but being in the commotion in Lincolnshire, with John, Lord Hussey, and others, occasioned by the assessment of a subsidy, was attainted and executed at Hull. He left by his wife, Jane, daughter of William Ingleby, esq. of Ripley, in the county of York, a son and heir,

SIR MARMADUKE CONSTABLE, who was high sheriff of Yorkshire, in the 1st and 24th of HENRY VIII., and served the king in his wars; was with him at the siege of Terowen, and the battle which followed, when he received the honour of knighthood, conferred upon him at Lisle, the king and court sojourning there. Advancing in the royal favour, he had a grant by letters patent, dated 20th May, 32nd HENRY VIII., under the designation of "Sir Marmaduke Constable, of London, knt. son of Sir Robert Constable of Flamborough, in Yorkshire," of the monastery and manor of Nuneaton, in Warwickshire, with all the lands in that county thereunto belonging. He was afterwards, in the first year of EDWARD VI made a knight banneret in the camp of Roquesborough by the Earl of Surry, general of the army. Sir Marmaduke resided chiefly at Nuneaton, where he died 20th April, in the 2nd year of ELIZABETH,* leaving by Elizabeth

* Sir Marmaduke lies buried on the North side of the chancel of the church of Nuneaton, under a fair tomb, whereon is the effigies of a knight in armour, lying on his back, his head resting on a pillow, his hands conjoined in prayer, and at his feet a lion couchant, with the following inscription round the verge:

Here lyeth Sir Marmaduke Constable, Knyght, which dyed the xx daye of
April, in ye yere of our Lord, M. D. and thre-
score, Sone and heyre to Sir Robert
Constable, Knyght, lord of Flam-
bourghe and Home——Spaldyng-
more, and the sayd Sir Marmaduke
hadde too wiffe, Elezabethe dowghter
to the Lord Darsse, by hur he hadde two
Sons, Robert and Marmaduke, and
viii Dawghters; the second Wyf,
Margaret Bootlir Dawghter of Wil
lm Bootlir, Gent.

his first wife, daughter of the Lord D'Arcy, two sons, Robert and Marmaduke, and eight daughters. He was s. by his elder son,

Sir Robert Constable, thirty years of age at the time of his father's death, who was knighted by the Earl of Sussex, in 1570, being with that general, in the expedition that year into Scotland to aid the young King, James VI. against the Hamilton faction. Sir Robert sold the monastery and manor of Nuneaton to Sir Ambrose Cave, in the 6th of Elizabeth. He m. first, Dorothy, daughter of Sir William Gascoigne, knt. but by that lady had no issue. He wedded, secondly, Dorothy, daughter of Sir John Widdrington, knt. and relict of Sir Roger Fenwick, knt. by whom he left a son and heir,

I. Sir William Constable, of Flamborough, in the county of York, who for his services under the Earl of Essex (A. D. 1599) in Ireland, received the honour of knighthood; being involved in the subsequent proceedings of that nobleman, he was arraigned for high treason, but remanded without trial, on a special letter from the queen, that he and others were unwarily drawn in. On the 20th March following, he had her majesty's warrant to Sir John Popham, knt. lord chief justice, to be admitted to bail. Sir William was created a Baronet by *King* James I. 29th June, 1611, and served in parliament, first for the borough of Knaresborough, and afterwards for the county of York, from the 25th of James I. to the time of his decease. He m. Dorothy, daughter of Sir Thomas Fairfax, and became a great stickler for the liberty of the subject, and being imprisoned on account of ship money, adopted a decided part against the king. He was a colonel in the parliament's army, and his name appears in the warrant for the execution of the unhappy Charles. He died during the usurpation, 15th June, 1654-5, and thus escaped personally the resentment of the restored monarch; but his lands, &c. were specially excepted, in the general pardon, granted by Charles II. as likewise all pains, penalties, and forfeitures, as though the Act of Grace had never passed. Leaving no issue, the Baronetcy, at his decease, became extinct.

Arms—Barry of six or and az.

CONWAY, OF BODRYTHAN.

Created 25th July, 1660. 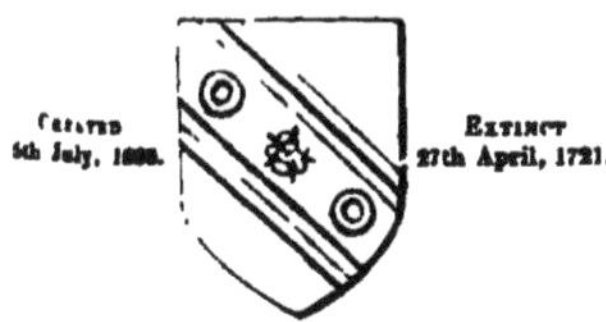 Extinct 27th April, 1721.

Lineage.

The family of Conway was established in England by Sir William Coniers, knt. one of the companions in arms of the Conqueror.

John Conway, of Bodrythan, who m. first, Ellen, daughter of Edmund Minshull, esq. and had by her a son, Hugh (Sir), treasurer of Calais. He m. secondly, ———, daughter of Edward Stanley, esq. son of Sir William Stanley, knt. of Hooton, and had by her several children, of whom

John, was ancestor of the Bodrythan family.

Edward, of Arrow, was ancestor of the Lords Conway, of Ragley. (See Burke's *Extinct Peerage*).

James, of Soughton and Ruthin: the eventual heiress of this line of the family,

Catherine Conway, m. the Rev. John Potter, rector of Badgworth, in Somersetshire, and dying in 1775, left a son,

John-Conway Conway, LL. B. of Lower Soughton, in Flintshire, who m. in 1784, Mary Elizabeth, daughter of Howel Lloyd, esq. of Hafodunos, and had one son and one daughter, viz.

Benjamin-Conway Conway.

Susanna-Benedicta.

Henry, of Perth Kinsey, whose daughter, Katherine, m. John Symond, of Dyffryn Clwyd.

The eldest son,

John Conway, esq. of Bodrythan, m. Janet, daughter of Thomas Salusbury, esq. of Llyweny, and his descendants continued at Bodrythan, untitled, until

I. Sir Henry Conway, of Bodrythan, was created a Baronet, 25th July, 1660. He m. Mary, daughter and heir of Richard Lloyd, esq. and dying about the year 1676, was s. by his son,

II. Sir John Conway, of Bodrythan, who m. first, Margaretta Maria, daughter and co-heir of John Digby, and secondly, a daughter of Richard Grenvile, esq. of Wotten Underwood, Bucks, but dying without male issue, in 1721, the title became extinct.

Arms—Sa. on a bend cottised arg. a rose gu. between two annulets of the first.

CONYERS, OF HORDEN.

Created 14th July, 1628.  Extinct 15th April, 1810.

Lineage.

Of this ancient family originally written Coigniers, styled from a place in France, was

Roger de Coigniers, who came into England towards the close of the Conqueror's reign, and was constituted by the bishop of Durham (who *d.* in 1095), constable of Durham. The next of the family, and second of the name,

Roger de Coigniers, was Lord of Howton Coigniers, and of Sokebourne, by the gift of Ranulph, of Durham, who died in 1128. The third of the same name,

Roger de Coigniers, Lord of Howton Coigniers, in the county of York, and of Sokebourne, in Durham, was living in the 24th of Henry II. His son and successor,

Robert de Coigniers, of Howton Coigniers and Sokebourne, living under Richard I. and *King* John, direct progenitor of

Sir Humphry Coigniers, knt. of Sokebourne, living in the 5th Henry III. who was father of

Sir John Coigniers, knt. who flourished in the reign of Edward I. He m. Scolastica, daughter and co-heir of Ralph de Cotam, and had two sons,

John, who had, by Elizabeth his wife, a daughter,

Elizabeth, the wife of Robert de Colvile, and mother of Sir William Colvile, knt.

He had a second wife, Christian, and by her had also a daughter,

Petronilla, who *m.* Robert Herle, and died *s. p.*

Roger.

The younger son,

Roger Coigniers, living *temp.* Edward II. had two sons, Geoffrey, who died issueless, and

Sir John Coigniers, knt. of Sokebourne, living in 1334, who *m.* Elizabeth, widow of Sir William Place, knt. and third daughter and co-heir of Sir William de Aton, by Isabel, his wife, daughter of Henry Percy, and dying in 1395, was *s.* by his son,

Robert Coigniers, of Sokebourne, who *m.* Isabel, daughter and co-heir of William Pert, esq. by Joane, his wife, daughter and co-heir of Stephen Scrope, and dying in 1433, left a daughter Johanna, *m.* to Sir Philip Dymoke, knt. of Scrivelsby, and a son,

Sir Christopher Coigniers, knt. of Sokebourne, who, by Mariora, daughter of Sir William de Eure, knt. had issue. The eldest son,

William (Sir), who *m.* Anne, daughter of Sir Ralph Bigott, knt. of Setrington, continued the main stem of the family, but it eventually failed in the direct male line, with

William Conyers, esq. of Sokebourne, who died 11th September, 1635, leaving three daughters,

Katherine.

Anne, *m.* to Francis Talbot, eleventh Earl of Shrewsbury, and had an only daughter and heir.

Mary, *m.* to John Stonor, esq. of Stonor, in Oxfordshire.

From a younger son of Sir Christopher descended

Richard Conyers, esq. (second son of Sir John Conyers, K. G. of Hornby, in Yorkshire, by Margaret his wife, daughter and co-heir of Philip, sixth Baron Darcy.) He *m.* Elizabeth, daughter and heir of Sir Robert Claxton, knt. of Horden, in the county of Durham, and obtaining that estate, became "Conyers, *of Horden.*" He was *s.* by his eldest son,

Robert Conyers, esq. of Horden, heir to his mother in 1507, who *m.* Margery, daughter of — Bamforth, of Seham, in Durham, and was *s.* by his eldest son,

Christopher Conyers, esq. of Horden, who *m.* Elizabeth, daughter of John Jackson, of Bedale, and was father of

Richard Conyers, esq. of Horden, who *m.* Isabel, daughter and co-heir of Robert Lumley, esq. of Ludworth, and was *s.* by his only surviving son,

Christopher Conyers, esq. of Horden, who *m.* first, a daughter of Cuthbert Conyers, esq. of Layton, but by her had no issue. He *m.* secondly, 4th November, 1586, Anne, daughter, of John Hedworth, knt. of Harraton, in the county of Durham, and, by that lady, had

I. John Conyers, esq. of Horden, who was created a Baronet by *King* Charles I. 14th July, 1628. He *m.* about 1606, Francis, daughter of Thomas Groves, citizen of York, and had issue,

Christopher, his heir.

John, bapt. at Easington, 26th September, 1622, *d.* 1667, leaving issue, from whom the tenth baronet derived his descent.

Robert, of Nettlesworth, died 1664.

Anne.

Elizabeth.

Troth, *d.* before 1663.

Frances, *m.* to Richard Fairlee.

Mary.

Philadelphia.

Susanna.

Timothea, *d.* 1656.

Sir John dying in 1664, was *s.* by his son,

II. Sir Christopher Conyers, of Horden, bapt. 20 March, 1621, who *m.* first, Elizabeth, daughter of William Langhorne, esq. of London, and sister of Sir William Langhorne, bart. of Charlton, in Kent, by whom (who *d.* 27th April, 1644,) he had a son,

John, his successor.

He *m.* secondly, Julia, daughter of Richard, Viscount Lumley, and relict of Alexander Jermyn, esq. of Lavington, in Sussex, and by that lady had a daughter,

Julia, *m.* first, to Sir William Blacket, bart. of Newcastle, and secondly, to Sir William Thompson, knt. one of the barons of the Exchequer.

Sir Christopher *d.* in October, 1693, and was *s.* by his son,

III. Sir John Conyers, of Horden, who inherited the estates of his uncle, Sir William Langhorn, at the decease of that gentleman, in 1714, whereby he became possessed of the seat and estate of Charlton, Kent, beside other broad and fertile lands. He *m.* [illegible] Mary Newman, and with her had the estate of [illegible] Baldwins, at Great Stoughton, in Huntingdonshire. He had issue,

Baldwyn, his successor.

Christopher, died young.

John,
Edward,
Christopher,
William, } all *d.* issueless.

Mary, *m.* to Edward Checkley, gent. of Alwalton, in the county of Huntingdon.

Sir John *d.* 14th September, 1719, aged seventy [illegible] and was buried in Great Stoughton Church. He was *s.* by his only surviving son,

IV. Sir Baldwyn Conyers, who *m.* first, Sarah, only daughter and heir of Edward Conyers, esq. of Blaston, in the county of Leicester, by whom he acquired the manor of Bradley, in that shire, but had no issue. He *m.* secondly, Margaret, eldest daughter of Henry Nevil, esq. of Holt, and by that lady had

John, who *d.* unm. 4th September, 1729.

Margaret,
Frances, } nuns.

Elizabeth.

Harriot, *m.* to Thomas Wollascot, esq. of Cav[illegible]sham, in the county of Berks.

Charlotte, *m.* to John Baptist Gastaldi, [illegible] from Genoa at the British court.

Teresa, *m.* to Charles, fifth Earl of Traquair.

Sir Baldwyn died 17th April, 1731, and was buried at Great Stoughton Church, where a marble monument was erected to the memory of himself and his son, thus inscribed:

This Monument is erected in Memory
of Sr Baldwyn Conyers, Bart. and his son, who
both lye interr'd in this Chancel.
Sr Baldwyn, dyed the 17th of April 1731
in the 51 Year of his Age.

John Conyers, Esq; his only son, died the
4th of Septr. 1729 in the 19th Year of his Age
a Young Gentleman of Fine Parts, and whose Death
Was lamented by all that Knew him

After the decease of Sir Baldwin, the manor of Horden was sold by his co-heirs to Rowland Burdon, esq. and the manor of Charlton, went by entail, first to William Langhorn Games, esq. and secondly, to the Rev. John Madryon, of the county of Essex, [illegible]

when it passed to his sister, Mrs. Weller, and from her to her daughter, m. to Sir Thomas Spencer Wilson, bart. of East Bourne, in Sussex. The baronetcy reverted to his cousin (son of John Conyers, of Chester, gent. who is stated to have been the son of John Conyers, the second son of the first baronet),

V. Sir Ralph Conyers, bapt. at Chester, 30th June, 1697, who m. Jane, daughter of Ralph Blakiston, esq. brother of Sir Nicholas Blackiston, bart. of Shieldsrow, in Durham, and had issue,

Blackiston, his successor.
Nicholas, seventh baronet.
Thomas, ninth baronet.
William, bapt. at Chester, 14th July, 1735, major of the Chatham division of marines, d. about 1800, at Rochester, in Kent, leaving a daughter, Jane, then under age.

He d. 22nd November, 1767, and was s. by his eldest son,

VI. Sir Blackiston Conyers, captain of marines, and collector of the customs at Newcastle, d. unmarried in October, 1791, and was s. by his brother,

VII. Sir Nicholas Conyers, bapt. 27th July, 1729, comptroller of customs at Glasgow, who d. in 1796, and was s. by his son,

VIII. Sir George Conyers, who d. s. p. (his widow wedded, secondly, Mr. Campbell) when the Baronetcy reverted to his uncle,

IX. Sir Thomas Conyers, bapt. 12th September, 1731, who m. Isabel, daughter of James Lambton, esq. of Whitehall, in the county of Durham, and had issue,

Jane, m. to William Hardy, of Chester Le Street.
Elizabeth, m. to Joseph Hutchinson, of Chester Le Street.
Dorothy, m. to Joseph Barker, of Sedgefield.

Sir Thomas died at Chester le Street, 15th April, 1810, when the Baronetcy became extinct.

Arms—Az. a maunch or.

COOKE, OF BROME HALL.

Created 29th June, 1663.

Extinct Jan. 1708.

Lineage.

I. Sir William Cooke, of Brome Hall, in Norfolk, who was created a Baronet in 1663, m. first, Mary, daughter of Thomas Astley, esq. of Melton Constable; and secondly, the relict of William Stuart, esq. of Barton Mills, in Suffolk. By the former he left a son and successor,

II. Sir William Cooke, of Brome Hall, who m. Jane, daughter and co-heir of William Stuart, esq. of Barton Mills, and had seven daughters, viz.

Dorothy, m. to John Herne, esq. of Amering Hall, Norfolk, d. s. p.
Jane, d. unm.
Mary, m. to Richard Freeston, esq. of Mendham, Suffolk, d. s. p.
Elizabeth, m. to Thornhagh Gurdon, esq. of Letton, in Norfolk, and had, with three daughters, a son,
Thornhagh Gurdon, esq. of Letton, grandfather of the present
Theophilus-Thornhagh Gurdon, esq. of Letton. (See Burke's *Commoners*, vol. i. p. 395.)
Bridget, m. to — Proctor, esq. of Langley, Norfolk, and left issue.
Agneta, m. to Charles Bedingfeld, esq. son of Philip Bedingfeld, esq. of Ditchingham, in Norfolk, and had issue.
Lettice, m. to John Gurdon, esq. of Assington, in Suffolk, and left issue.

Sir William Cooke died at Letton in 1708, and was buried in the parish church of Cranworth cum Letton, where a handsome monument was erected to his memory. With him the Baronetcy expired: the estates he ordered by will to be sold and the produce divided amongst his daughters.

Arms—Gu. on a fess or, three trefoils az. in chief a lion passant arg.

COOKES, OF NORGROVE.

Created 24th Dec. 1664.

Extinct about 1701.

Lineage.

The family of Cookes came into England with the Conqueror.

Edward Cookes, esq. of Bentley Pauncefoot, in the county of Worcester, son of William Cookes, of Norgrove, in the same shire, by Ann, his wife, daughter and co-heir of Humphry Jennets, esq. of that place, m. Mary, daughter of Nicholas Cotton, esq. of Hornchurch, in Essex, and niece of Richard Weston, Earl of Portland, by whom, who died 10th August, 1656, he had issue,

I. William, his heir.
II. Henry, of Barbon, in Worcestershire, m. Mary, daughter of Richard Stanley, esq. of Stoke Prior, and d. in 1678, leaving a son,
John, of London, living in 1707. He married twice, but had surviving issue only by his second wife, Elizabeth, eldest daughter of Sir William Russell, knt. alderman of London. His son,
Henry, b. 26th April, 1702, was father of
Thomas, in holy orders, rector of Notgrove, in Gloucestershire, who m. 14th February, 1765, Ann, daughter and heir of John Denham, esq. of Welling, in Kent, and had, with other issue, a son,
Denham-James-Joseph, rector of Stanford and vicar of Clifton-on-Terne, who m. Maria-Henrietta, daughter of Charles John-

stone, esq. and left, *inter alios*, a son and heir, the present THOMAS-HENRY COOKES, esq. of Bentley, M.P.

III. Edward, of Powick, living in 1683, married, with issue.

IV. Thomas, of Bidford Grange, Warwickshire, *d.* about 1670, leaving issue.

I. Ann, *m.* to Richard Amphlett, esq. of Clent, in Staffordshire.

II. Alice, *m.* to John Arris, esq. of Charingworth, Gloucestershire.

Edward Cookes died 7th April, 1637, and was *s.* by his son,

I. SIR WILLIAM COOKES, of Norgrove, who was created a BARONET 24th December, 1664, for his zeal in support of the royal cause. He *m.* first, Anne, daughter and co-heir of John Cookes, esq. which lady *d. s. p.*; and secondly, Mercie, daughter of Edward Dineley, esq. of Charlton, in Worcestershire, and sister of Sir Edward Dineley, knt. By her, who wedded secondly, Mark Dineley, esq. he had issue,

THOMAS, his heir.

William, who *m.* Mary, daughter and co-heir of Posthumus John Rea, esq. of Powyck, and *d. s. p.* 1673. His widow *m.* Basil Fielding esq. of Barnacle, Warwickshire.

Mercie, *m.* in 1672, to Henry Winford, esq. of Astley, in Worcestershire, second son of Sir John Winford, knt.

Sir William was *s.* by his son,

II. SIR THOMAS COOKES, of Bentley Pauncefoot and Norgrove, **Founder of Worcester College Oxford**. This gentleman greatly augmented, by endowing with an annual sum, the schools of Bromsgrove and Feckenham. He *m.* Lady Mary Windsor, eldest daughter of Thomas, Earl of Plymouth, but died *s. p.* about 1701, when the BARONETCY became EXTINCT.

Arms—Arg. six martlets gu. 3, 2, and 1, between two chevrons of the second.

COOPER, OF WALCOT.

CREATED 19th Feb. 1828.—EXTINCT 24th Dec. 1828.

Lineage.

I. SIR JOHN-HUTTON COOPER, born 7th December, 1765, F.R.S. and F.S.A. of Walcot, in Somersetshire, lieutenant-colonel of the 2nd regiment of Somersetshire Militia and groom of the bedchamber to his late Majesty when Duke of Clarence, was fifth son of Benjamin Cooper, esq. of Sleaford, in Lincolnshire, by Anne, his first wife, daughter and heir of Robert Caudron, esq. of Great Hale, and grandson of the Rev. Benjamin Cooper, a clergyman connected with the Collegiate Church of Southwell. Colonel Cooper was returned to parliament by the borough of Dartmouth in 1825, and in 1828 was created a BARONET. He *m.* first, in 1790, Elizabeth-Mary, daughter of Edward Ellis, esq. of Anwick; secondly, in 1797, Phillis, daughter of William Neate, esq. of London; and thirdly, in 1821, Maria-Charlotte, only daughter of Sir George Baker, bart.; but dying issueless in December, 1828, the BARONETCY EXPIRED. He left two surviving brothers, Christopher Cooper, M.D. of Doncaster, and Benjamin Cooper, esq. of Stamford.

COPE, OF BREWERNE.

CREATED 1st March, 1713.

EXTINCT 28th Dec. 1781.

Lineage.

This was a branch of the existing family of Cope of Bramshill Park, in the county of Oxford, baronets. (See BURKE's *Peerage and Baronetage*.)

ANTHONY COPE, esq. of Hanwell, was created a BARONET 29th June, 1611. He *m.* Frances, daughter of Sir Rowland Lytton, of Knebworth, Herts, and dying in 1615, was *s.* by his eldest* son,

SIR WILLIAM COPE, M.P. for the county of Oxford, who *m.* Elizabeth, daughter and heir of Sir George Chaworth, knt. of Wiverton, Notts, and had two sons viz.

JOHN, who became Sir John Cope, bart. of Hanwell, at the decease of his father in 1637, and continued that line.

JONATHAN.

The second son,

JONATHAN COPE, esq. of Ranton Abbey, in the county of Stafford, *m.* Anna, daughter of Sir Hatton Fermor, knt. of Easton Neston, in the county of Northampton, and was *s.* by his son,

JONATHAN COPE, esq. of Ranton, who *m.* Susan, daughter of Sir Thomas Fowle, knt. of London, and had issue,

JONATHAN, his heir.

William, *d.* unm.

Anthony, *m.* Anne, youngest daughter of Sir Robert Dashwood, bart. of Northbrook, but left no issue.

He was *s.* by his eldest son,

I. JONATHAN COPE, esq. of Brewerne, in the county of Oxford, who was created a BARONET by Queen ANNE 1st March, 1713. Sir Jonathan represented the borough of Banbury in the last parliament of Queen ANNE and the first of *King* GEORGE I. He married Mary, youngest daughter of Sir Robert Jenkinson, bart. of Walcot, in the county of Oxford, and had issue,

1. JONATHAN, of Orton Longueville, in Huntingdonshire, who married first, 14th September, 1741, Lady Arabella Howard, eldest daughter of Henry, fourth Earl of Carlisle, K.G. and had by her,

CHARLES, who *s.* his grandfather.

Arabella, *m.* in 1763, to John Walker Heneage, esq. of Compton Basset, Wilts.

Mr. Cope *m.* secondly, in 1752, Jane, daughter of Lieutenant-General Francis Leighton, of Wattlesborough, in Shropshire, and widow of Captain the Honorable Shaw Cathcart, and by that lady left

* From a younger son of Sir Anthony descended the Copes of Icombe, in Gloucestershire, now represented by the HOPTONS of Canon Frome.

Jonathan, who inherited as fourth baronet.

Jenny, m. in 1775, to Charles Pigott, esq. son of Robert Pigott, esq. of Chetwynd Park, Salop.

Anne, married, first, in 1780, to John Cowper, esq.; secondly, in 1796, to Wade Toby Caulfeild, esq. of the Queen's County; and thirdly, to Monsieur de Boileville, of Normandy.

Mr. Cope died before his father, 2nd November, 1763.

I. Anne, married, in 1736, to Sir Thomas Whitmore, K.B. of Apley, in Shropshire, M.P. for Bridgenorth.

II. Henrietta-Maria, m. to Valentine Knightley Chetwode, esq.

III. Mary, m. to Sir Robert Jenkinson, bart. and d. s. p. in 1765.

IV. Susanna, m. to William, fourth Viscount Chetwynd, and died in 1791, leaving issue.

Sir Jonathan d. 28th March, 1765, and was s. by his grandson,

II. Sir Charles Cope, of Brewerne, who m. in 1767, Catherine, youngest daughter of Sir Cecil Bisshopp, bart. and sister of Lord De la Zouch, by whom he had issue,

Charles, his successor.

Arabella-Diana, m. first, in 1790, to John-Frederick, third Duke of Dorset; and secondly, in 1801, to Charles, Earl Whitworth.

Catherine-Anne, m. to George, Earl of Aboyne, who succeeded, at the decease of George, fifth Duke of Gordon, in 1836, to the Marquisate of Huntly.

Sir Charles d. 14th June, 1781, and his widow wedded, in the following year, Charles, first Earl of Liverpool. He was s. by his son,

III. Sir Charles Cope, of Brewerne, who died a minor and unmarried 28th December, 1781, when his estates devolved upon his sisters as co-heirs, and the Baronetcy reverted to his uncle,

IV. Sir Jonathan Cope, of Brewerne, who m. in April, 1779, Annabella, only daughter of William Candler, esq. of Callan, in the county of Kilkenny, by Mary, his wife, daughter of William Vavasour, esq. of Weston Hall, in the county of York, and granddaughter of Henry Candler, D.D. of Callan Castle, in the county of Kilkenny, archdeacon of Ossory; by that lady he had issue,

Jonathan, in holy orders, rector of North Wraxall and Woodborough, in Wilts, and of Langridge, in Somersetshire, d. unmarried 10th March, 1814, at Reading.

Charles, d. on board the Hannibal, in Port Royal, 30th September, 1795, unmarried.

Henry Thomas, killed at Seringapatam, unmarried.

Sir Jonathan d. 30th December, 1821, when the Baronetcy became extinct. The manor of Morton Pinkeney, in Northamptonshire, which Sir Jonathan possessed, he devised by will to his wife's nephew, Edward Candler, esq.

Arms—Arg. on a chev. az. between three roses gu. stalked and leaved vert, as many fleurs-de-lys of the field.

COPLEY, OF SPROTBOROUGH.

Created 17th June, 1661. Extinct 9th April, 1709.

Lineage.

Sir William Copley, lineal descendant of Adam de Copley, slain at the siege of York in 1070, m. first, *temp.* Henry VIII. Dorothy, daughter and co-heir of Sir William Fitz-William, of Sprotborough, and had by her a son,

Philip, his heir.

He m. secondly, Margaret, daughter of Piers Savage, esq. of Hatfield, and had four sons,

Francis, of Mansfield Woodhouse, d. in 1580.

Christopher, of Wadworth, ancestor of

Lionel Copley, of Wadworth, b. in 1677, who inheriting under the will of Sir Godfrey Copley the estate of Sprotborough, voluntarily bound up that property in strict entail to his male issue only; in remainder, not to the children of his own daughters, but to the issue of Catherine Moyle, the only child of Sir Godfrey. He left issue,

Godfrey, of Sprotborough, d. s. p.

Lionel, of Sprotborough, d. s. p.

William, d. young.

Castiliana, m. to the Rev. Charles Willatts,

Mary, m. to William Parkyns, esq.

Catherine, d. young.

Anne, m. to Richard Higgins, esq. of York, and was great-grandmother of the present Godfrey Higgins, esq. of Skellow Grange and Wadworth. (See Burke's *Commoners*, vol. ii. p. 155.)

John, of Broughton, d. s. p.

Philip, rector of Sprotborough, d. s. p.

The eldest son of Sir William,

Philip Copley, esq. of Sprotborough, m. Mary, daughter of Sir Bryan Hastings, knt. and died 19th October, 1577. His descendant,

I. Godfrey Copley, esq. of Sprotborough, was created a Baronet 17th June, 1661. He m. first, Eleanor, daughter of Sir Thomas Walmesley, knt.; and secondly, Elizabeth, daughter of Sir William Stanhope, knt. Sir Godfrey died circa 1684, and was s. by his son,

II. Sir Godfrey Copley, of Sprotborough, F.R.S. who m. first, Katherine, daughter and heir of John Purcell, of Nantriba, in Montgomeryshire; and secondly, Miss Carew; and left at his decease, 9th April, 1709, an only daughter,

Catherine, who m. Joseph Moyle, esq. second son of Sir Walter Moyle, knt. of Beke, and had a son,

Joseph Moyle, who assumed, on inheriting Sprotborough, the surname of Copley, and was created a Baronet in 1778. His son is the present

Sir Joseph Copley, bart. of Sprotborough. (See Burke's *Peerage and Baronetage*.)

Sir Godfrey Copley died 9th April, 1709, when the Baronetcy expired.

Arms—Arg. a cross moline gu.

CORBET, OF STOKE.

CREATED 19th Sept. 1627.

EXTINCT 7th May, 1750.

Lineage.

This family, which Camden designates as famous at the time of the Conquest, descended from

CORBEAU, a noble Norman; which Corbeau or Corbet was father of two sons, who flourished in the reign of the CONQUEROR, namely,

> ROGER, who held of Roger de Montgomery, Earl of Shrewsbury, Huelbeck, Hundeslet, Actun, Ternley, and Prestun, all in Shropshire. He left issue,
>
> > WILLIAM CORBET, of Watlesborough, of whom hereafter.
>
> ROBERT, who held of the same great feudal proprietor, Ulistan, Rotclinghope, Branton, Udecote, Langedunin, Weymore, Rorenton, Middleton, and Meredon. He left issue,
>
> > ROBERT (Sir), Lord of Alcester, who *d. s. p.*
> >
> > SYBEL, *m.* to Henry Herbert, chamberlain to *King* HENRY I.
> >
> > ALICE, *m.* to William Botreaux.

WILLIAM CORBET, of Watlesborough, son and heir of the elder brother, left likewise two sons,

> THOMAS, his heir.
>
> Robert, of Caus Castle, whose descendant was summoned to parliament as a baron by EDWARD I. (See BURKE'S *Extinct Peerage.*)

The elder son,

THOMAS CORBET, of Watlesborough, was father of

SIR ROGER CORBET, knt. who, by his first wife, left a son and heir,

SIR RICHARD CORBET, knt. who *m.* Joan, daughter and heir of Bartholomew Turret, of Moreton, and had issue,

RICHARD CORBET, of Moreton, who gave Kynwilton to the monastery of Buildas. He was father of

SIR ROBERT CORBET, of Moreton, whose son and successor,

SIR THOMAS CORBET, of Moreton, was father of

SIR ROBERT CORBET, of Moreton, who *d.* in the 49th EDWARD III. and was *s.* by his son,

SIR ROGER CORBET, of Moreton Corbet, who *m.* Margaret, daughter and heir of Erdington, Lord of Shawbury, and dying 18 RICHARD II. was *s.* by his son,

ROBERT CORBET, esq. of Moreton Corbet, who *m.* Margaret, daughter of Sir William Malleroy, knt. and died 17 HENRY VI. leaving a son and heir,

SIR ROGER CORBET, knt. of Moreton Corbet, w[illegible] *m.* Elizabeth,* daughter and heir of Thomas He[illegible] esq. and had issue,

SIR RICHARD CORBET, knt. of Moreton Corb[illegible] gentleman *m.* Elizabeth, daughter of Walter, L[illegible] Ferrars, of Chartley, and by her (who *m.* second[illegible] Sir Thomas Leighton, of Watlesborough,) left a so[illegible] and heir,

SIR ROBERT CORBET, knt. of Moreton Corbet, wh[illegible] *m.* Elizabeth, daughter of Sir Henry Vernon, knt. [illegible] Haddon, and had two sons,

> ROGER, his heir, who *m.* Anne, daughter of A[illegible]drew, Lord Windsor, and from him descend [illegible] *extant* Corbets of Moreton.
>
> REYNOLD.

The younger son,

REYNOLD CORBET, one of the judges of the Court [illegible] Common Pleas in the time of ELIZABETH, *m.* Alic[illegible] daughter of John Gratewood, esq. and niece and co-heir of Sir Rowland Hill, and left a son and heir,

RICHARD CORBET, esq. who *m.* Anne, daughter [illegible] Lord Chancellor Bromley, and was *s.* by his eldest son,

I. JOHN CORBET, esq. of Stoke, in the county [illegible] Salop, who was created a BARONET by *King* CHARLES I. "This gentleman," says Blakeway, "was one of those five illustrious patriots worthy of the eternal gratitude of their country, who opposed the forced loan in 16[illegible] a most illegal measure of CHARLES I. while under [illegible] sway of Buckingham; which, if it had succeed[illegible] would have turned this limited monarchy into a Tur[illegible]ish despotism." He *m.* Anne, daughter of Sir [illegible] Mainwaring, knt. of Ightfield, in the county of Sa[illegible] and by her (who was known as the "good Lady [illegible]bet") had no less than ten sons and ten daughters, [illegible] whom †

> JOHN, the eldest, succeeded his father.
>
> Henry, *m.* Catherine, sister of Lord Ch[illegible]ley.
>
> Anne, *m.* Nathaniel Desborough, esq.
>
> Margaret, *m.* William Stafford, esq. of [illegible]wick, in Northamptonshire.
>
> Anne, *m.* Robert Anstruther, esq. of W[illegible], in the county of York.
>
> Frances, *m.* David Maurice, esq. of [illegible], in the county of Denbigh.
>
> Alice, *m.* Thomas Cotton, esq. of Palley, in Shropshire.
>
> Dorothy, *m.* John Selbury, esq.
>
> Menial, *m.* Sir Humphrey Briggs, bart. of [illegible]ton, in the county of Salop.
>
> Susan, *m.* George Spurstow, of Spurstow, in [illegible]shire.
>
> Grace, *m.* Sir William Pulteney, knt.

Sir John was *s.* by his eldest son,

II. SIR JOHN CORBET, who *m.* Letitia, daughter of Sir Robert Knollys, knt. of Gray's Court, in the county of Oxford, grandson of Sir Francis Knollys, [illegible] and was *s.* by his only so[illegible] [illegible]tleman *m.* The[illegible]

III. SIR JOHN CORBE[illegible] [illegible] Cambell, [illegible] phila, daughter and [illegible] Woodford, and by h[illegible]

> ROBERT, his s[illegible]
>
> Theophila.

[illegible] *m.* second[illegible] [illegible]ton, esq. [illegible]dly, Sir [illegible] two o[illegible] [illegible] his [illegible]

---

* This lady married, after Sir Roger Corb[illegible] John de Tiptoft, Earl of Worcester, and [illegible] lordship, *m.* thirdly, Sir William Stanley.

† The others, Vincent, Richard, George, [illegible]phrey, Rowland, Arthur, Robert, all die[illegible]

M.P. for Salop, one of the clerks of the Board of Green Cloth *temp.* GEORGE I. and afterwards one of the commissioners of the Customs. He *m.* Jane, dau. of Sir William Hooker, knt. lord mayor of London, and had, with other children who *d.* unmarried, two sons and a daughter, viz.

WILLIAM, his successor.
HENRY, successor to his brother.

Anne, *m.* to Thomas D'Avenant, esq. and had a son,
CORBET D'AVENANT, who assumed the surname of CORBET, and was created a BARONET in 1786. (See that title.)

He *d.* 3rd October, 1740, and was *s.* by his elder son,

V. SIR WILLIAM CORBET, who *m.* Harriot, daughter of Robert Pitt, esq. of Boconnock, and sister of the first Earl of Chatham, but dying *s. p.* 15th September, 1748, was *s.* by his brother,

VI. *The Rev.* SIR HENRY CORBET, rector of Adderley, who *d.* unmarried 7th May, 1750, when the BARONETCY became EXTINCT, and the estates devolved on his nephew, CORBET D'AVENANT, esq.

Arms—Or, a raven ppr.

CORBET, OF SPROWSTON.

CREATED 4th July, 1623.—EXTINCT in 1661.

Lineage.

JOHN CORBET, esq. living *temp.* HENRY VIII. (son of John Corbet, by Margaret Dixon, and said to be the grandson of Corbet of Moreton), *m.* Jane, daughter of Ralph Berney, of Gunton, and had issue,

MILES (Sir), his heir.

Mary, *m.* to Sir Roger Woodhouse, of Kimberley.
Elizabeth, *m.* to James Noon, gent. of Norfolk.
Bridget, *m.* to Bryan D'Arcy, of Essex.

The son,

SIR MILES CORBET, knt. *m.* first, Catherine, daughter of Sir Christopher Heydon, of Baconsthorp; and secondly, Catherine, widow of John Spilman, esq. of [illegible]burgh, and daughter of William Sanders, esq. of [illegible] in Surrey. By the former he left a son,

SIR THOMAS CORBET, knt. of Sprowston, high sheriff of Norfolk in 1622, who *m.* Ann, daughter of Edward Barret, esq. of Belhouse, in Essex, and heiress of her mother, Elizabeth, daughter and co-heir of Sir Robert [illegible], of Shrubland Hall, in Suffolk, and had issue,

JOHN (Sir), his heir.
MILES, of Lincoln's Inn, one of the registrars in Chancery. [illegible] Corbet acquired unenviable celebrity [illegible] judges of the ill-fated CHARLES I. [illegible] ted as a regicide in 1661.

Catherine, [illegible]
Anne, *m.* [illegible]
[illegible] renthain, in Suffolk.
[illegible]
[illegible] son, of Tavesham.
[illegible]

[illegible]

[illegible] owston, was created [illegible] *m.* Anne, daughter [illegible] ham, in Hertford[illegible]

[illegible] brother,

I. Elizabeth, *m.* to Robert Houghton, esq. of Ranworth.
II. Anne, *m.* to Francis Corey, esq. of Bramerton.

Sir John *d.* 19th January, 1627, aged thirty-seven, and was *s.* by his elder son,

II. SIR JOHN CORBET, of Sprowston, at whose decease unmarried the title passed to his brother,

III. SIR THOMAS CORBET, of Sprowston, living in 1661, who was a devoted royalist during the civil wars and suffered much in consequence. He sold Sprowston to Sir Thomas Adams, bart. and as he never married, the BARONETCY EXPIRED with him in 1661.

Arms—Or, a raven ppr.

CORBET, OF MORETON CORBET.

CREATED 29th Jan. 1642.—EXTINCT 6th Aug. 1688.

Lineage.

This is another branch of the very ancient family of Corbet, seated at Moreton Corbet since the commencement of the thirteenth century. For the early descent, see BURKE'S *History of the Commoners*, vol. iii. p. 189.

SIR VINCENT CORBET, knt. of Moreton Corbet, who succeeded his brother in 1606, married Frances, daughter and heir of William Humfreston, esq. of Humfreston, in Shropshire, and had issue,

ANDREW, his heir.
Robert, of Humfreston, ancestor of the CORBETS of Ynysymaengwyn, and of the Corbetts of Darnhall and Elsham, now represented by THOMAS GEORGE CORBETT, esq. one of the representatives of the northern division of Lincolnshire in parliament.

Margaret, *m.* first, to Thomas Corbet, esq. of Stanwardine; and secondly, to Sir Thomas Scriven, knt.
Mary, *m.* to Sir Richard Hussey, knt. of Albright Hussey.

Sir Vincent's elder son,

SIR ANDREW CORBET, knt. of Moreton Corbet, married Elizabeth, daughter of William Boothby, esq. and had, with nine daughters, six sons, viz.

VINCENT, his heir.
Andrew.
Robert, of Lawley.
Richard, of Shawbury, ancestor of the present SIR ANDREW-VINCENT CORBET, bart. of Moreton Corbet.
Arthur.
Henry.

Sir Andrew died in 1637, and was *s.* by his son,

I. SIR VINCENT CORBET, of Moreton Corbet, a devoted royalist, *b.* in 1617, who was created a BARONET in 1642. He *m.* Sarah, daughter of Sir Robert Monson, of Carlton, in Lincolnshire, and by her (who was raised to the peerage after her husband's decease, *for life only*, as VISCOUNTESS CORBET,) had issue,

Andrew, *d.* young.
VINCENT, his heir.
[illegible] rister-at-law, *d.* in 1678 *s. p.*
[illegible] r Thomas Estcourt, knt. of Wilt-
[illegible]
[illegible] Sir John Bolles, knt.
[illegible] ineas Fowke, M.D.

[illegible] 656, and was *s.* by his son,

II. Sir Vincent Corbet, of Moreton Corbet, born about 1642, who m. Elizabeth, daughter of Francis Thornes, esq. of Shelvocke, in Shropshire, and had issue,

Vincent, his heir.

Beatrice, baptized in 1669; m. to John Kynaston, esq. of Hordley and Albrightlee, and had a son, Corbet Kynaston, M.P. for Salop.

Sir Vincent d. 4th February, 1680, and was s. by his son,

III. Sir Vincent Corbet, of Moreton Corbet, b. in 1670, who died at Christ Church, Oxford, in the nineteenth year of his age, 6th August, 1688, when the Baronetcy became extinct.

Arms—Or, a raven ppr.

CORBET, OF STOKE AND ADDERLEY.

Created 27th June, 1786.—Extinct 31st March, 1823.

Lineage.

I. Sir Corbet Corbet, of Stoke-upon-Tern and Adderley, in Shropshire, who was created a Baronet in 1786, was son of Thomas D'Avenant, esq. of Clearbrooke, in Herefordshire, by Anne, his wife, daughter and heir of Sir Roger Corbet, bart. of Stoke, and assumed the surname of Corbet on inheriting the estates of his maternal ancestors. He m. Hester, youngest daughter of Sir Lynch Salusbury Cotton, bart. of Combermere, but dying s. p. 31st March, 1823, the Baronetcy became extinct. He devised the Adderley estate to Richard Corbet, esq. second son of Sir Andrew Corbet, bart. and his other property to the Cotton family.

Arms—Or, a raven sa.

CORBET, OF LEIGHTON.

Created 20th June, 1642.

Extinct 25th Sept. 1774.

Lineage.

I. Sir Edward Corbet, of Leighton, in the county of Montgomery, son of Thomas Corbet, esq. by the daughter and co-heir of Moreton, and a descendant of the Corbets of Caus Castle, was created a Baronet 20th June, 1642. He m. Margaret, daughter of Edward Waties, esq. of Burway, in Shropshire, and had issue,

Edward, who m. Anne, daughter of Sir Richard Newport, knt. (afterwards Lord Newport), and dying v. p. 30th May, 1653, left, with two daughters, who both d. s. p. one son,

Richard, successor to his grandfather.

Thomas.

Francis.

Richard.

Charles.

Waties, of Elton, in Herefordshire, who m. Margaret Weaver, of that place, and dying in 1689, was buried, 20th February, at Lebotwood, in Shropshire. His son,

Waties, of Elton, was father of

Richard, } both d. s. p.
Adam, }

Thomas, whose son is stated to have been

Charles, of London, bookseller, d. in 1752, leaving a son,

Charles, who claimed and assumed the Baronetcy on the death of Sir Richard.

Jane, m. to John Flint, gent.

Martha.

Anne.

Margaret, m. to John Matthews, of Trefnany.

Mary, d. young.

Sir Edward was s. by his grandson,

II. Sir Richard Corbet, of Leighton, who m. Victoria, daughter and co-heir of Sir William Uvedale, knt. of Wickham, in Hampshire, and had issue,

Uvedale, his heir.

Lucy, d. young.

Diana, m. to Thomas Roch, esq. of Shropshire.

Anne, d. in 1706.

Victoria, m. to Sir Charles Lloyd, bart. of Garth.

Sir Richard d. 1st August, 1683, and was s. by his son,

III. Sir Uvedale Corbet, of Longnor and Leighton, who m. in 1693, Mildred, daughter of James, Earl of Salisbury, and had by her (who m. secondly, Sir Charles Hotham, bart.) issue,

Richard, his heir.

Edward, d. s. p. in 1764, buried at Leebotwood.

Francis, b. 11th June, 1701. This gentleman is stated by some accounts to have died unmarried in Scotland, but others affirm that he was Dean of St. Patrick's, Dublin, and ancestor of the present Henry Corbet Singleton, esq. of Aclare, in Meath.

Robert, a colonel in the Guards, who m. the daughter of the late William Kynaston, esq. M.P. for Shrewsbury, master in chancery, and d. in 1750, s. p.

Charles-Thomas, an officer in the Guards, d. s. p.

Elizabeth, d. in 1724.

Sir Uvedale d. 15th October, 1701, and was s. by his son,

IV. Sir Richard Corbet, of Longnor and Leighton, M.P. for Shrewsbury, b. in 1696, at whose decease unmarried, 25th September, 1774, the Baronetcy is stated by some accounts to have become extinct, but it was claimed and assumed by Mr. Charles Corbet, as descended from Waties, the youngest son of the first baronet. He died in reduced circumstances in May, 1808, leaving a son, Richard, in the East India Company's service.

Arms—Or, two ravens ppr. within a bordure engrailed gu. bezantée.

CORDELL, OF LONG MELFORD.

Created 22nd June, 1660.

Extinct in May, 1704.

Lineage.

The ancient family of Cordell was seated for a considerable period in the county of Suffolk, and one ts members in the time of ELIZABETH, SIR WILLIAM CORDELL, of Long Melford, attained considerable eminence as a lawyer, filling the important office of master of the rolls. He m. Mary, daughter and heir of Richard Clopton, esq. but died without issue 17th May, 23 ELIZABETH, and was buried in the church of Long Melford, in which town he founded and endowed an alms-house. His estate at Foxley, in Norfolk, ultimately vested in his sister and heir, JOAN, who m. Richard Alington, esq. of Horseheath, in Cambridgeshire, and left two daughters and co-heirs, Mary, m. to Sir John Savage, of Clifton, in Cheshire, and Cordelia, m. to Sir John Stanhope. A male branch of the family, however, continued at Long Melford, and shortly after the Restoration was raised to the degree of BARONET in the person of

I. SIR ROBERT CORDELL, of Melford, who m. Margaret, daughter and co-heir of Sir Edmund Wright, knt. lord mayor of London, and died circa 1680, leaving a son and successor,

II. SIR JOHN CORDELL, of Melford, who m. Elizabeth, daughter of Thomas Waldegrave, esq. of Smallbridge, in Suffolk, and had issue,

JOHN, his heir.

Elizabeth, m. to Thomas King, esq. (eldest son of Robert King, esq.) killed in a duel.

Margaret, m. to Charles Firebrace, esq. only son of Sir Robert Firebrace, bart.

Sir John died circa 1690, and was s. by his son,

III. SIR JOHN CORDELL, of Melford, who m. Alionora, daughter and co-heir of John Haskinstiles, of London, merchant, but by her, who died in April, 1705, he had no issue. Sir John was killed by a fall from his horse in May, 1704, when the BARONETCY became EXTINCT. His sisters were his co-heirs.

Arms—Gu. a chev. erm. between three griffins' heads erased arg.

CORNISH, OF SHARNBROOK.

CREATED 29th Jan. 1766.

EXTINCT 30th Oct. 1770.

Lineage.

I. SIR SAMUEL CORNISH, vice-admiral of the Red, K. B. &c. was created a BARONET 29th January, 1766. He purchased from Sir Philip Boteler, bart. of Teston, in Kent, the manors of Sharnbrook, Tofte, and Temple Hills, in the county of Berks, but dying s. p. in 1770 the BARONETCY became EXTINCT. The estates devolved, under Sir Samuel's will, on his nephew, Admiral Samuel Pitchford, who assumed the surname of CORNISH.

Arms—Sa. a chev. embattled or, between three roses arg.

CORYTON, OF NEWTON.

CREATED 27th Feb. 1662.

EXTINCT in July, 1739.

Lineage.

PETER CORYTON, esq. of Coryton and Newton-Ferrars, m. Joan, daughter of John Wreye, esq. of Militon, in Cornwall, by Blanche, daughter and co-heiress of Henry Killegrewe, esq. and had issue,

WILLIAM, his successor.

John.

Mary, m. to Thomas Trefusis, esq. of Trefusis.

The elder son,

WILLIAM CORYTON, esq. of Coryton and Newton-Ferrars, was vice-warden of the stannaries of Cornwall from 1603 to 1630, one of the representatives for the county of Cornwall 21 JAMES I., and member for several other places at subsequent periods. This gentleman, the friend and partisan of HAMPDEN, PYM, and ELIOT, zealously co-operated with these eminent persons in resisting forced loans and arbitrary power. He likewise distinguished himself as a strenuous advocate for the petition of RIGHT, and was one of those who were imprisoned for having forcibly detained the speaker (Finch) in the chair. This staunch patriot espoused Elizabeth, daughter of Sir John Chichester, of Raleigh, in the county of Devon, and had a son and successor,

I. JOHN CORYTON, esq. of Coryton and Newton-Ferrars, who, having represented for several years the county of Cornwall in parliament, was created a BARONET 27th February, 1661. He m. Ann, only daughter and heiress of John Mills, esq. of Colebrooke, Devon, and had issue,

JOHN, his heir.

WILLIAM, successor to his brother.

Elizabeth, who m. William Goodall, esq. of Fowey, and was grandmother of

PETER GOODALL, esq. who inherited the estates and assumed the surname of CORYTON. His representative is the present

JOHN TILLIE CORYTON, esq. of Pentillie Castle, in Cornwall.

Anne, m. in 1665, to John Peter, esq. of Harlyn, in Cornwall, and was direct ancestor of the present

WILLIAM PETER, esq. of Harlyn and Chiverton.

Sir John Coryton d. in 1680, and was s. by his elder son,

II. SIR JOHN CORYTON, of Newton-Ferrars, in Cornwall, who m. Elizabeth, daughter and co-heir of Sir Richard Chiverton, knt. but dying without issue, was s. by his brother,

III. SIR WILLIAM CORYTON, of Newton-Ferrars, M. P. for Callington in the reigns of CHARLES II. JAMES II. WILLIAM III. and *Queen* ANNE, who m. Susanna, daughter of Sir Edward Littleton, bart. of Pillaton, in the county of Stafford, and dying in December, 1711, left, with a daughter, Susanna, who d. unmarried, a son and successor,

IV. SIR JOHN COTTON, of Newton-Ferrars, who m. Rachel, daughter of William Helyar, esq. of East Coker, in the county of Somerset, M.P. for that shire, but dying *s. p.* in July, 1739, the BARONETCY EXPIRED.

Arms—Arg. a saltire sa.

COTTINGTON, OF HANWORTH.

CREATED 16th Feb. 1623.

EXTINCT in 1653.

Lineage.

I. FRANCIS COTTINGTON, esq. fourth son of Philip Cottington, esq. of Godmanston, in the county of Somerset, having held the office of clerk of the council in the reign of *King* JAMES I. and being secretary to CHARLES, *Prince of Wales*, was created a BARONET by that monarch on the 16th February, 1623. After the accession of *King* CHARLES I. Sir Francis Cottington was constituted chancellor and under-treasurer of the Exchequer, and being accredited ambassador to the court of Madrid, for the purpose of negociating a peace, he was elevated to the peerage on the 10th July, 1631, as LORD COTTINGTON, *Baron of Hanworth*, in the county of Middlesex. His lordship was next commissioned to exercise the important office of lord-treasurer during the king's absence in Scotland, in the 9th CHARLES I. and was constituted master of the wards upon his majesty's return. During the civil wars, Lord Cottington remained faithfully attached to his royal master, and eventually went into exile with *King* CHARLES II. from which he never returned. His lordship married Anne, daughter of Sir William Meredith, knt. and widow of Sir Robert Brett, by whom he had a son and four daughters, all of whom predeceased him unmarried. He *d.* at Valladolid in 1653, when the BARONETCY, together with the BARONY OF COTTINGTON, became EXTINCT, and his estates passed to his nephew, CHARLES COTTINGTON, esq. who had his lordship's remains brought over to England and interred in Westminster Abbey, where he erected a stately monument.

Arms—Az. a fesse between three roses or.

COTTON, OF CONNINGTON.

CREATED 29th June, 1611.

EXTINCT 27th Mar. 1752.

Lineage.

This ancient family, to which the learned world has been so much indebted, all authorities agree, is descended out of Cheshire, where there are two towns of the same denomination; one in the hundred of Nantwich, the other in Broxton.

WILLIAM DE COTUN, was father of

SIMON DE COTUN, who lived in the time of EDWARD I. and left a son,

WILLIAM DE COTUN, who married first, Isabel, and secondly, Joan, and was *s.* by his son,

EDMUND DE COTUN, whose wife's christian name was Catherine. He lived in the time of EDWARD III and had two sons,

ROBERT, of Coton, near Hanbury, in Staffordshire, whose name is mentioned in deeds 30 EDWARD III. but his line terminated in heirs female about the time of HENRY V.

WILLIAM.

The younger son,

WILLIAM COTTON, married, towards the latter end of EDWARD *the Third's* reign, Agnes, daughter and heir of Walter de Ridware, of Hampstall-Ridware in the county of Stafford (by Joan, his wife, daughter and heir of Walter Walsheif, and Juliana, his wife, daughter and heir of John Basyng, of Beyleston, in Derbyshire), and thereby acquired the estate of Ridware and other broad lands, and assumed the Ridware arms, which his descendants continued to bear. He was *s.* by his son,

JOHN COTTON, of Hampstall-Ridware, who m. Isabel, daughter and heir of William Faulconer, esq. of Thurcaston, in the county of Leicester, and *s.* by his son,

SIR RICHARD COTTON, knt. of Ridware. This gentleman m. Elizabeth, sister and eventually co-heir of Sir Hugh Venables, baron of Kinderton, in Cheshire, and had two sons, viz.

JOHN, who inherited Ridware, living in the [illegible] HENRY VI. and 2nd EDWARD IV. progenitor of the Cottons, of Ridware, and the Cottons of Bould and Crackmarsh, in the county of Stafford.

WILLIAM.

The younger son,

WILLIAM COTTON, esq. fell at the battle of St. Albans, in the war of the Roses, *temp.* HENRY VI. He m. Margaret, daughter and heir of Robert de Wesenham, son of Sir Hugh de Wesenham, by Agnes, his wife, sister and heir of Bernard, son of Sir John de Brus, of Connington, in the county of Huntingdon, and of Exton in the county of Rutland. By this marriage he became possessed of those lordships the continuous seat of his posterity. His widow, m. secondly, Sir Thomas Billing, knt. lord chief justice of England, in the reign of EDWARD IV. and thirdly, Thomas Lacy, esq. of Grancestre, near Cambridge. She died 14th March, 1499, and was buried on the south side of the altar of the church of St. Margaret, Westminster, by her first husband. Weaver exhibits the graphical draughts of both their monuments. He is represented in armour with a surcoat of his arms, of the spread eagle, upon his knees at prayer, a book before him, and behind a group of fifteen children, all mature grown, whereof eight seem to be sons, and the other seven daughters, in a scroll over his head, *s. hoc. s. m.* His eldest son and heir,

THOMAS COTTON, esq. of Connington, served the office of sheriff of the counties of Cambridge and Huntingdon, in the 15th HENRY VII. He m. Eleanor, daughter of Richard Knightley, esq. of Fawsley, in Northamptonshire, and had issue,

THOMAS, his heir.
William.
George.
Anthony.
Richard.

Eleanor, m. to Robert Mulsho, esq. of Thingdon, in Northamptonshire.

Mary, m. to — Grantoft, esq. of Stanton, in the county of Huntingdon.

Margaret, a nun, at Barking, in Essex.

He d. in 1506, and was s. by his eldest son,

THOMAS COTTON, esq. of Connington, sheriff of Cambridge and Huntingdon, 4 HENRY VIII. m. Joan, daughter of John Paris, esq. of Linton, in Cambridgeshire, and had issue.

THOMAS, his heir.

Richard, in holy orders.

Eleanor, m. first, to Edward Pitcher, esq. of Trumpington, in Cambridgeshire, secondly, to – Pepys, of Cottenham, and thirdly, to Doctor Walker, M. D. of Cambridge.

He d. in the 9th of HENRY VIII. and was s. by his eldest son,

THOMAS COTTON, esq. of Connington, sheriff of Huntingdon and Cambridge, 1st EDWARD VI. m. Lucy, daughter and co-heir of Thomas Harvey, esq. of Elmstoke, in the county of Lincoln, and was s. by his eldest son,

THOMAS COTTON, esq. of Connington M. P. for the county of Huntingdon, 4 and 5 PHILIP and MARY. This gentleman m. first, Elizabeth, daughter of Francis Shirley, esq. of Staunton-Harold, in the county of Leicester,* (son of Sir Ralph Shirley, knt. and Joan, his wife, daughter of Sir Robert Sheffield, knt.) and had issue,

ROBERT, his heir.

Thomas, of Gedding Abbots, in the county of Huntingdon, m. Mary, daughter of Robert Apreece, esq. of Washingly, in the same county, and left a son and heir,

John Cotton, esq. of Gedding, who m. Frances, daughter of John Gifford, esq. of White Ladys, in the county of Stafford, and left an only daughter and heiress,

JANE COTTON, who m. Basil Fitzherbert, esq. of Norbury and Swinnerton.

Lucy, m. to — Talcarne, esq. of Ashton, in Essex.

Dorothy, m. to Maurice Baude, esq. of Somerby, in the county of Lincoln.

Johanna, m. to John Baude, esq. of the same place.

Mr. Cotton m. secondly, Dorothy, daughter of John Tamworth, esq. of Hawsted, in Leicestershire, and by that lady had,

Henry, d. unm. 11th June, 1614.

Ferdinand, } merchants.
John, }

Catherine, unm. in 1613.

Frances, second wife of Sir Edward Montagu, K. B. created BARON MONTAGU, of Boughton, and mother of

Edward Montagu, second BARON MONTAGU, whose son,

Ralph, third Baron Montagu, was created by Queen ANNE, DUKE OF MONTAGU. (See BURKE's *Extinct and Dormant Peerage*).

Rebecca, m. to William Mulsho, esq. of Thingdon, in Northamptonshire.

His eldest son and heir,

I. ROBERT COTTON, esq. of Connington, one of the most learned men of his time, was born 22nd January, 1570, at the village of Denton, in the vicinity of the family seat, and after receiving an early education of the first description, was sent to Trinity College, Cambridge. He subsequently devoted himself to literature, and the collecting of those celebrated manuscripts, which have since immortalized his name, under the designation of "THE COTTONIAN LIBRARY." He began this great work in the year 1588, when finding his residence at home not altogether adequate to the object he had in view, he came up to London, associated himself with Camden, and became a member of the Society of Antiquaries. In 1603, Mr. Cotton received the honour of knighthood from *King* JAMES I. being one of those so distinguished immediately before his majesty's coronation. "During this reign, and in the many and various difficulties arising in state points, Sir Robert was looked upon, by common suffrage, one of the best instructed therein; hence, Henry, Earl of Northampton, lord privy seal in 1606, became his familiar and perpetual friend, consulted him in what he publicly delivered, made him his confident, and found a return of wisdom and fidelity." He was, subsequently, often consulted upon public affairs, and was amongst those, who to recruit the treasury, devised the order of hereditary knights, or BARONETS, to which dignity he was himself one of the first gentlemen raised, having been created a BARONET on the 29th June, 1611. In the same reign Sir Robert was twice sent to parliament by the county of Huntingdon, and fully sustained in the senate the high reputation he had attained in literature. He d. on the 6th May, 1631, in his sixty-first year, at his house in Westminster, whence, with solemn pomp, his remains were conveyed to Connington, as appointed by his will, and interred on the south side of the church, under a fair monument, erected by the piety of his wife and son; which lady was Elizabeth, daughter and co-heir of William Brocas, esq. of Thedingworth, in the county of Leicester. His only surviving son and heir,

II. SIR THOMAS COTTON, M. P. for the county of Huntingdon, m. first, Margaret, daughter of William, Lord Howard, of Naworth, and by that lady had issue,

JOHN, his successor.

Lucy, m. to Sir Philip Wodehouse, bart. of Kimberley, in Norfolk, and had a son,

Sir Thomas Wodehouse, knt. from whom descend the Lords Wodehouse.

Lady Wodehouse d. 26th June, 1684.

Frances.

He m. secondly, Alice, daughter and sole heir of Sir John Constable, knt. of Dromondby, in the county of York, and relict of Edmund Anderson, esq. of Eyworth, and by her had,

Thomas, who d. at the age of seventeen.

Robert (Sir), of Hatley St. George, in Cambridgeshire, M. P. for that county, m. Gertrude, second daughter of Sir William Morrice, of Werington, in the county of Devon, bart. secretary of state to CHARLES II. and had an only surviving daughter and heiress,

Alice Cotton, who m. Robert Trefusis, of Trefusis, in Cornwall, ancestor of the present Lord Clinton, and conveyed the estate of Hartley St. George to her husband, from whom descending to their son, Robert Trefusis, M. P. of Trefusis, it was sold by him to Thomas Pearce, esq. a commissioner of the navy.

Philip, of Connington, aged thirty-seven in 1684, m. twice, (his first wife was Frances, daughter

* By Dorothy, his wife, daughter of Sir John Gifford, knt. of Chillington, in the county of Stafford, and widow of ... Congreve, esq.

of Sir Toby Tyrell, of Thornton, county of Berks, and widow of Sir John Hewett, bart.) but dying *s. p.* he bequeathed his estates to his nephew, Thomas, the son of his brother William.

William, of Cotton Hall, in the county of Chester, *m.* Mary, daughter of the Rev. Robert Pulleyn, of Thurleston, in Leicestershire, and had issue,

1. Thomas, of Connington, devisee of his uncle Philip, *m.* Anne, daughter and heiress of Thomas Andrews, (grandson and heir of Sir Thomas Andrews, knt. citizen of London,) by Anne, daughter and heir of Samuel Shute, esq. sheriff of London in 1681, and left an only daughter and heiress,

    FRANCIS, who *m.* DINGLEY ASCHAM, esq. and conveyed Connington and the other estates to him.

1. Mary, *m.* Jonathan Symonds, esq. of Great Ormesby, in the county of Norfolk, and had issue.
2. Alice, *m.* to William Shiers, gent. buried at Great Ormesby, 30th October, 1749.
3. Catherine.
4. Frances, married to Dr. Lewis, a physician in London.

Sir Thomas *d.* 13th May, 1662, aged sixty-eight years, and was buried in the south chancel of the church at Connington. He was *s.* by his eldest son,

III. SIR JOHN COTTON, *b.* 1621, M. P. for the borough of Huntingdon, in the reign of CHARLES II. and for the county in the time of JAMES II. He *m.* first, Dorothy, daughter and sole heir of Edmund Anderson, of Stratton and Eyworth, in the county of Bedford, and had issue,

JOHN, who *m.* Frances, daughter of Sir George Downing, bart. of East Hatley, in the county of Cambridge, and dying in the lifetime of his father, *anno* 1681, left two sons and a daughter, viz.

JOHN, successor to his grandfather.

Thomas, *m.* Frances, only daughter and heir of William Langton, esq. of Peterborough, and left an only daughter,

MARY.

Frances, *b.* 1677, *m.* to William Hanbury, esq. of Little Marcle, in Herefordshire, and had issue.*

Dorothy, *m.* to —— Dennis, esq. of Gloucestershire.

He *m.* secondly, Elizabeth, daughter of Sir Thomas Honywood, knt. of Marks Hall, Essex, and sister and heir of John Le Mott Honywood, esq. who *d.* 3rd April, 1702. By this lady he had several children, but only three to survive, viz.

ROBERT, who succeeded as fifth baronet.

Elizabeth, *m.* first, to Lyonel Walden, esq. of Huntingdon, and secondly, to — Smith, esq. of Westminster; by her first husband she had,

Lionel Walden, who *d.* unm.

Elizabeth Walden, co-heir to her brother, m. first, to Charles Pitfield, esq. and secondly to Talbot Touchet, esq. By the former she had,

Charles Pitfield, who *m.* Miss Ashley, daughter of Solomon Ashley, esq. M. P. and *d. s. p.*; his widow *m.* the Honourable Felton Hervey, youngest son of the Earl of Bristol.

Elizabeth Pitfield, *m.* to Edward Wigley, esq. of Long Whatton, in Leicestershire.

Hester Walden, co-heir to her brother, m. Humphrey Orme, esq. of Peterborough, captain in the royal navy, and had a son,

Walden Orme.

Mary Honywood, *m.* Doctor Roger Kenyon, and died *s. p.*

Sir John was *s.* by his grandson,

IV. SIR JOHN COTTON, of Connington, M. P. for the county of Huntingdon in 1711, who *m.* Elizabeth, daughter of the Honourable James Herbert, of [illegible]sey, in Oxfordshire, (younger son of Philip, Earl of Pembroke,) by Catherine, his wife, daughter of Thomas, Duke of Leeds, but dying *s. p.* 5th February, 1730-1, the baronetcy, and a portion of the estates passed to his uncle,

V. SIR ROBERT COTTON, of Gedding, in the county of Huntingdon, who *m.* first, Elizabeth, daughter of — Wigston, esq.; and secondly, Mrs. Morton. He *d.* 12th July, 1749, aged eighty, and was succeeded by his son,

VI. SIR JOHN COTTON, who *m.* Jane, daughter of Sir Robert Burdett, bart. of Bramcote, and had one son and four daughters, viz.

JOHN, died at Durham of the small-pox, 13th November, 1739.

Jane, *m.* in October, 1741, to Thomas Hart, esq. of Warfield, Berks.

Elizabeth.

Frances.

Mary.

Sir John *d.* 27th March, 1752, when the BARONETCY became EXTINCT.

Arms—Az. an eagle displayed arg.

---

* The daughters of Frances Cotton and William Hanbury were,

MARY HANBURY, *m.* to the Rev. Martin Annesley, D.D. vicar of Bucklebury, Berks, and had issue,

I. Francis Annesley.

II. Arthur Annesley, D.D. vicar of Chewton, whose son,

The Rev. Arthur Annesley, of Clifford, in Gloucestershire, *m.* Elizabeth Vere, dau. of George Booth Tyndale, esq. of Bathford, in Somersetshire, and had issue,

1. Francis, in holy orders, *b.* in 1800.
2. Arthur, *b.* 1803.
3. William, in holy orders, *b.* in 1804, *m.* Laura, daughter of Major-Gen. Jones, of Fonmore, in Glamorganshire.
4. George, who *m.* Emily, daughter of Albert Foster, esq.
5. Martin, *b.* 1811.

1. Caroline.
2. Frances.
3. Elizabeth Vere.

III. William.

IV. Martin.

V. James.

I. Mary.

II. Katherine, *m.* to the Rev. Dr. Trollop.

III. Elizabeth, *m.* to George Booth Tyndale, esq. of Bathford, in Somersetshire.

ELIZABETH HANBURY, *m.* to Thomas Neale, esq.

FRANCES HANBURY, *m.* to F. Barrel, esq.

CATHERINE HANBURY, *m.* to Velters Cornewall, esq. of Moccas Court.

COVERT, OF SLOUGHAM.

CREATED 2nd July, 1660.  EXTINCT 11th Mar. 1679.

Lineage.

The family of Covert was seated at Chaldon, in Surrey, so early as the time of HENRY II. and remained there until about the close of the fourteenth century, when the estate was sold by

WILLIAM COVERT, of Sullington, who died 25th September, 1444, leaving by Grace, his wife, daughter of John Barentyne, five sons, viz.

I. JOHN, his heir.
II. Thomas.
III. Roger.
IV. Henry.
V. William, of Hascomb, whose son,
 William, of Hascomb, m. a daughter of Richard Wasse, and had two sons and three daughters, viz.
  Giles, of Hascomb, in Surrey, d. 23rd June, 1556.
  Richard, of Hascomb, heir to his brother, m. Catherine, daughter of William Ernley, of Cookham, in Sussex, and had four sons and as many daughters; of the latter, Susan, m. Robert Coke, of Kent, and Elizabeth, m. Reginald Bray, of Shere, in Surrey.
  Agnes, m. to William Bartelott, esq. of Stopham, in Sussex.
  Mabel, m. to Richard Blake.
  Jane, m. to Hugh Gunter.

The eldest son,

JOHN COVERT, of Sullington, living 10th HENRY VII. m. Ann, daughter and heir of Thomas Vaver, gentleman usher to HENRY VIII, by Joan, his wife, daughter of Sir John Pelham, and had three sons, viz.

WILLIAM, his heir.
Thomas, of Sullington, who m. Elizabeth, daughter of John Sidney, and had, with junior issue, a son,
 RICHARD, of whom presently, as successor to his cousin.
John.

The eldest son,

WILLIAM COVERT, of Slougham, in Sussex, and of Hascomb and Wisley, in Surrey, married Ann, daughter of Sir Thomas Flemyng, and sister and co-heir of John Flemyng, and dying 20 September, 1494, left a son,

JOHN COVERT, of Slougham in Sussex, who m. Isabel, daughter and heir of John Pelham, and had three daughters, Ann, Elizabeth, and Dorothy. He d. 12th August, 1503, and was s. by his cousin,

RICHARD COVERT, of Slougham, who m. first, the daughter and heir of John Tagger; secondly, Elizabeth, daughter of George, Lord Abergavenny; thirdly, Jane, daughter of William Ashburnham; and fourthly, Blanch, daughter of John Vaughan. He d. 7th June, 1547, leaving issue,

JOHN, his heir.
George, of Slougham, who m. Elizabeth, daughter of Sir Humphrey Forster, of Aldermanston, Berks, and had, with a daughter, Ann, the wife of Francis Poole, esq. of Dicheling, in Sussex, a son,
 Humphrey, of Godstone, in Surrey, who m. Ann, daughter of John Covert, of Slougham, and had issue,
  William, of London, goldsmith.
  Humphrey, d. s. p.
  John, d. s. p.
  George, of Cuckfield, in Sussex, d. in the lifetime of his father, leaving three sons, Thomas, John, and Walter, of Woodmancote, living in 1623.
  Mary, m. to John Dodd, of Taurige.
  Agnes.
  Frances, m. to John Haselden of Haling.
Elizabeth, m. to Thomas Thrale.

The elder son,

JOHN COVERT, esq. of Slougham in Sussex, fined for his knighthood 25 HENRY VIII, m. first, Elizabeth, daughter of John Coke, of Rustington, by whom he had a son, WILLIAM; and secondly, at Twineham, in 1547, Ann, daughter of William Beard, by whom he had with three daughters, a son Edward, (father of John Covert, esq. of Abberton, in Sussex). John Covert died at the siege of Bologne in 1558, and was s. by his son,

WILLIAM COVERT, esq. who m. Benedict Herenden, and had a son and successor,

WILLIAM COVERT, esq. of Ledes Abbey, in Kent, who m. Elizabeth, sister of Sir William Steed, and dying in 1614, was s. by his son,

SIR WALTER COVERT, of Maidstone, in Kent, who m. Ann, daughter and heir of John Covert, of Slougham, and by her, who died 22nd September, 1632, left, at his decease before 1632, a son,

I. SIR JOHN COVERT, of Slougham, b. 6th June, 1620, who was created a BARONET 2nd July, 1660. This gentleman married Isabella, daughter of Sir William Leigh, knt. of Longborow, in Gloucestershire, and relict of Gervase Warmshey, of Worcester, by whom, who died in September, 1660, he had issue,

Walter, buried 30th September, 1672.
Jane, d. unm. in 1658.
Isabel, d. unm. in 1661.
MARY, m. in 1676, to Henry Goring, esq. son of Sir Henry Goring, bart. of Highden, and had a son,
 SIR HENRY GORING, third bart. of Highden, ancestor of the present SIR CHARLES FORSTER GORING, bart. of Highden, in Sussex.
ANN, who became seised of the manor, of Slougham at her father's death. She m. 26th December, 1671, to Sir James Morton, and had two sons,
 John Morton, who possessed the manor of Slougham.
 James Morton, who sold Slougham to Charles Sergison, esq.

Sir John Covert died 11th March, 1678-9, s. p. when the BARONETCY became EXTINCT.

Arms—Gu. a fesse erm. between three martlets or.

CRANE, OF CHILTON.

CREATED 21st April, 1626. EXTINCT Feb. 1642-3.

Lineage.

JOHN CRANE, who died 20 HENRY VII. was descended from an ancient and knightly family long settled in the counties of Suffolk and Norfolk. He married Agnes, daughter of John Calthorp, and left, with a daughter, Elizabeth, m. to Richard Martin of Melford, a son,

ROBERT CRANE, esq. who m. twice and dying 4 EDWARD VI. was s. by his son,

ROBERT CRANE, esq. of Stonham, living 1559 and 1565, who m. Bridget, daughter of Sir Thomas Jermyn, knt. of Rushbrooke, and had issue,

- HENRY, his heir, of Chilton, who m. twice; from his first wife he was divorced; he had a daughter Reuben, m. to Captain Harvey. His widow m. secondly, Sir W. Carew, knt.
- ROBERT.
- Martha, m. to Dudley Fortescue, esq.
- Bridget, m. first, to Francis Claxton, esq. and secondly, to John Warburton, esq.; thirdly, to Sir Christopher Heydon; and fourthly, to Sir Edward Clere.
- Ursula, m. to Henry Smith, esq. of Stanhow.
- Anne, married.
- Elizabeth, m. to Edward Wright, esq.
- Agnes, m. first, to John Smith, esq. of Halesworth, in Suffolk, who died in 1568.

The elder son,

ROBERT CRANE, esq. was father of

I. SIR ROBERT CRANE, of Chilton, in Suffolk, high sheriff in 1632, and knight of the shire in several parliaments, who was created a BARONET 21st April, 1626. He m. first, Dorothy, daughter of Sir Henry Hobart, bart. lord chief justice of the Court of Common Pleas, by whom he had no issue, and secondly, Susan, daughter of Sir Giles Alington, knt. of Horseheath, by whom who wedded secondly, Isaac Appleton, esq. of Waldingfeld, he had four daughters his co-heirs,

- MARY, m. to Sir Ralph Hare, bart.
- JANE, m. first, to Sir William Airmine, bart. and secondly, to John, Lord Belasyse.
- SUSAN, m. to Sir Edward Walpole, K.B.
- KATHERINE, m. to Edmund Bacon, esq. nephew of Sir Robert Bacon, bart.

Sir Robert died in February, 1642-3, when the BARONETCY EXPIRED.

Arms—Arg. a fess between three crosses bottonée fitchee gu.

CRANE, OF WOODRISING.

CREATED 20th March, 1642.—EXTINCT, 1645.

Lineage.

SIR FRANCIS CRANE, knt. chancellor of the order of the garter, (deriving probably from a common ancestor with the Cranes of Chilton,) purchased the lordship of Woodrising, in Norfolk, from Sir Thomas Southwell, in the early part of the seventeenth century, and seated himself there. This gentleman brought into England the manufacture of curious tapestry established at Mortlake, in Surrey. He gave five hundred pounds towards the rebuilding of St. Paul's, and added four poor knights to the number of those in Windsor Castle. He m. Mary, sister of Sir Peter de la Maire, and dying s. p. at Paris, 6th June, 1636, was s. by his brother.

I. SIR RICHARD CRANE, of Woodrising, in Norfolk, who was created a BARONET 20th March, 1642. He m. Mary, daughter of William, Lord Widdrington, but dying s. p. in 1645, the BARONETCY EXPIRED: his niece and adopted heir, Mary Bond, conveyed the manor of Woodrising to her husband, William Crane, esq. of Loughton Bucks, but in 1668, they sold the lordship to Gabriel Bedle, citizen of London.

Arms—As Crane, of Chilton.

CRAVEN, OF SPERSHOLT.

CREATED 4th June, 1661. EXTINCT 1713.

Lineage.

I. SIR ANTHONY CRAVEN, of Spersholt, in the county of Berks, (son of Thomas Craven, esq. of Apuldrewick, by Margaret, his wife, daughter of Robert Craven, esq. of the noble family of Craven,) was created a BARONET in 1661, but dying in 1670, s. p. the title EXPIRED. The manor of Spersholt has since been possessed, successively, by the families of Palmer, Ra[illegible]mond, and Gabbit.

Arms—Arg. a fess between six cross crosslets fitchee gu.

CRISPE, OF HAMMERSMITH.

CREATED 14th April, 1665. EXTINCT [illegible].

Lineage.

I. SIR NICHOLAS CRISPE, of Hammersmith, (son of Ellis Crispe, esq. of Hammersmith, by Anne, his wife, daughter of Sir George Strode, knt. of Westerham, in Kent, grandson of Sir Nicholas Crispe, knt. of London, and great grandson of Ellis Crispe, esq. of Marshfield, in Gloucestershire, alderman and sheriff of London in 1625,) who is said to have been the first inventor of the art of making bricks as now practised, was created a Baronet in 1665. This gentleman, who entered into business with a larger fortune than most retire with, was one of the farmers of the Customs, and a merchant of high consideration, trading chiefly to the coast of Guinea. On the breaking out of the civil wars, he remained firm in his allegiance, and advanced very large sums to supply the necessities of his royal master. Lloyd, indeed, gives us a very high idea of Sir Nicholas's activity and enterprise, as well as of the signal services he rendered the king: "One while," says he, "you would meet him with thousands of gold; another while, in his way to Oxford, riding in a pair of panniers, like a butter-woman going to market; at other times, he was a porter carrying on his majesty's interest in London; he was a fisherman in one place and a merchant in another. All the succours which the king had from beyond sea, came through his hands, and most of the relief he had at home was managed by his conveyance."* As a farther proof of zeal in the royal cause, Sir Nicholas raised, at his own expense, a regiment of horse, and putting himself at their head, behaved with distinguished gallantry. When the king's affairs grew desperate, he retired to France. The losses which his fortune sustained from the resentment of the parliament, may be imagined, when it is mentioned that three-fourths of a pension of 4000*l.* per annum, granted to the elector palatine, were ordered to be paid out of his and Lord Colpeper's estates. Sir Nicholas returned subsequently to England, and submitting to a composition, embarked again in trade with his usual spirit and his usual success.† He lived to see his master's son restored to the possession of his kingdoms, and after all his losses, left a very considerable fortune. About the beginning of CHARLES the First's reign, Sir Nicholas built of brick, a most magnificent mansion by the water side, at Hammersmith, at an expense, it is said, of nearly 23,000*l.* This house was plundered during the early part of the civil war, and when the army was stationed at Hammersmith, in August, 1647, Fairfax took up his quarters there, Sir Nicholas Crispe being then in France. A newspaper of September 10, (the army being then at Putney,) mentions an odd circumstance of a cook being in custody for using Lady Crispe's name to invite the general to dine with her.‡

Sir Nicholas died in 1665, and the baronetcy continued with his descendants until the demise, issueless in 1740, of his great grandson, SIR CHARLES CRISPE, bart. of Oxfordshire. The villa at Hammersmith which Sir Nicholas erected, was sold, in 1683, to Prince Rupert, who gave it to his beautiful mistress, Margaret Hughes, a much admired actress in the reign of CHARLES II. From her, it was purchased by Timothy Lannoy, esq. and from the Lannoy family passed to George Dodington, esq. afterwards Lord Melcombe, who repaired and modernized the house, giving it the name of La Trappe. His lordship devised it to Thomas Wyndham, esq. and it was subsequently the property of Mrs. Sturt, but in the year 1792, was purchased by the Margrave Brandenburgh-Anspach, and became, more recently, celebrated as the residence of CAROLINE, the Queen Consort of GEORGE IV.

Arms—Arg. on a chev. sa. five horse shoes or.

CROFTS, OF STOW.

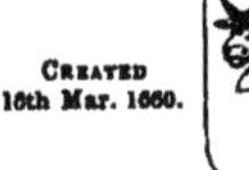

CREATED 16th Mar. 1660.

EXTINCT 1664-5.

Lineage.

The family of Crofts, in ancient times of knightly degree, flourished for several centuries at Saxham, in the county of Suffolk.

SIR JOHN CROFTS, knt. representative of the family *temp.* PHILIP and MARY, married the daughter and heir of George Sampson, esq. and had two sons, namely,

THOMAS, of Bardwell, in Suffolk, who *m.* Margaret, daughter of Sir John Copledike, and dying 38 ELIZABETH, left a son,

CHARLES, who died 14 JAMES I. leaving issue,

1. CHARLES (Sir), who *m.* first, Bridget Poley, of Badley; and secondly, Jane, daughter of Sir Rowland Litton. He died in 1663, aged eighty-three, leaving three daughters,

Bridget, *m.* to — Read, of Lincolnshire.

Elizabeth, *d.* unm.

Cicely, *m.* to Francis Brewster, esq. of Wrentham.

2. John, barrister-at-law.
3. Robert, merchant of London.

1. Elizabeth, *m.* to Robert Drury, esq. of Rougham.
2. Margaret, *m.* to John Syllett.
3. Susan, *m.* first, to Thomas Aldham, of Sapiston, in Suffolk; and secondly, to — Aldham, of the same place.

EDMUND.

Sir John's son,

EDMUND CROFTS, esq. of West Stow, in Suffolk, *m.* first, a daughter of Thomas, Lord Burgh, by whom he had one son, John, who died *s. p.* 3 ELIZABETH; and two daughters, Margaret, *m.* to John Southwell, of Barham, and Alice, who *d.* unmarried. He wedded, secondly, Elizabeth, daughter of Sir Thomas Kilson, by whom he left, at his decease 5 PHILIP and MARY, a son,

THOMAS CROFTS, esq. who *m.* Susan, daughter of John Poley, esq. of Badley, and had issue,

JOHN (Sir), his heir.
Henry.
William.
Robert, died unm.
Edmund.

Anne, *m.* to Sir Richard Gresham, knt.
Anne, *m.* to Sir Robert Barker, knt.

---

* Lloyd's Memoirs, p. 627.

† Lysons's Environs of London.

‡ Sir Nicholas placed against the north wall of the chancel, in the chapel at Hammersmith, a fine bronze bust of CHARLES I. with the following inscription: "This Effigies was erected by the special appointment of Sir Nicholas Crispe, Knt. and Baronet, as a grateful commemoration of that glorious Martyr, King CHARLES I. of blessed memory." Underneath is a pedestal of black marble, on which stands an urn, inclosing the heart of Sir Nicholas Crispe. On the pedestal is this inscription: "Within this Urne is entomb'd the heart of Sir Nicholas Crispe, Knight and Baronet, a loyal sharer in the sufferings of his late and present Majesty. He first settled the trade of gold from Guiny, and there built the castell of Cormantine. Died 26 February, 1665, aged 67."

Elizabeth, *m.* to Anthony Penning, of Kettleburg.
———, *m.* to John Grime, gent.

Thomas Crofts died 10 James I. and was *s.* by his son,
Sir John Crofts, knt. of Saxham, in Suffolk, who *m.* Mary, daughter of Sir Thomas Shirley, knt. of Sussex, and had issue,

I. Henry (Sir), knt. of Saxham, who married twice. By his first wife, Margery, he left with three daughters, one son,
   1. William, of Saxham, who was elevated to the peerage as Baron Crofts, of Saxham, 16th Charles II. His lordship *m.* first, Dorothy, daughter of Sir John Hobart, bart. of Intwood, and widow of Sir John Hele, knt.; and secondly, Elizabeth, daughter of William, Lord Spencer, but dying *s. p.* in 1677, the title became extinct.

   By his second wife, Elizabeth, Sir Henry had issue,
   2. John, D.D. who adhered to the royal cause, and suffered in consequence. After the restoration, he was promoted to the deanery of Norwich, and *d.* there in 1670.
   3. Charles.
   4. Edmund, died *s. p.*
   1. Elizabeth, *m.* to Frederick, Lord Cornwallis.
   2. Mary, *m.* to Sir Edmund Poley.
   3. Esther.

II. Anthony, of whom presently.
III. John, cupbearer to *King* Charles.
IV. Samuel.
V. Edward.

I. Anne, *m.* to Thomas, Earl of Cleveland.
II. Frances, *m.* first, to Sir John Compton, knt. who died in 1625; and secondly, to Edmund Poley, esq. of Badley.
III. Dorothy, *m.* to Sir John Burnett.
IV. Jane, *m.* to Sir Humphrey Mildmay, of Essex.
V. Mary, *m.* to Sir Christopher Abdy, knt. of London.
VI. Cicely, *m.* to — Killegrew, esq.
VII. Arabella.
VIII. Alice, *m.* to Sir Owen Smith, knt. of Norfolk.

The second son,
Anthony Crofts, esq. was father of
I. Sir John Crofts, of West Stow, in Suffolk, who was created a Baronet in 1660, but dying in 1664-5, *s. p.* the title became extinct.

Arms—Or, three bulls' heads couped sa.

CROPLEY, OF CLERKENWELL.

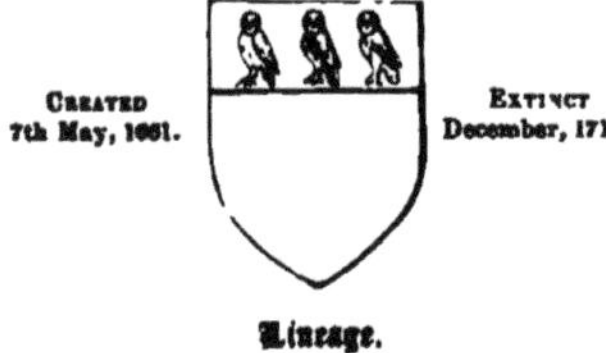

Created 7th May, 1661.

Extinct December, 1713.

Lineage.

I. Sir John Cropley, of Clerkenwell, in the county of Middlesex, who was created a Baronet in 1661, married Elizabeth, only daughter, and heir of Daniel Hollingworth, gent. of London, and was *s.* by his son,

II. Sir Edward Cropley, who *m.* Martha, daughter of Robert Wilson, of London, merchant, and dying about 1672, was *s.* by his son,

III. Sir John Cropley, at whose decease, unmarried, in December, 1713, the Baronetcy expired. Sir John had a sister *m.* to Thomas Marsh, esq. of C[illegible] foot, but he gave the greatest part of his estate to Thomas Micklethwaite, esq.

Arms—Ar. on a chief gu. three owls of the field.

CROSSE, OF WESTMINSTER.

Created 13th July, 1713.

Extinct 12th Mar. [illegible]

Lineage.

Thomas Crosse, esq. of the city of Westminster, died in 1682, leaving issue,

Thomas, his heir.
Robert, *m.* Mary, eldest daughter of Sir Thomas Feild, knt. of Stanstedbury, in the county of Hertford.
Henry, *d.* unm.
Mary, *m.* to William Martin, esq. of Netteswellbury, in Essex.
Anne, *d.* unm.

The eldest son,

I. Thomas Crosse, esq. M. P. for the city of Westminster, in the reigns of *King* William, Queen Anne, and *King* George I. was created a Baronet by Queen Anne, 13th July, 1713. He *d.* 27th May, 17[illegible], and was buried in St. Margaret's, Westminster, where a monument was erected to his memory, with the following inscription:

Within this Church lie interred the Remains
of Sir Thomas Crosse, Bart. eldest son of Thomas Crosse
of this Parish, Esq.
He was educated under Dr. Busby, and in five Parliaments had the
Honour of being chosen a Representative of the City and Liberty of Westminster.
Publick Charities of every Kind he chearfully promoted
and as liberally contributed to;
But his heart was never more open, than when he privately conveyed his
Assistance to a sick and necessitous neighbour.
Preferring the silent Testimony of his own Conscience
to the Thanks and good wishes of Multitudes.
He married Jane, Daughter of Patrick Lambe, of Stoke Poges,
in the County of Bucks, Esq; by whom he had issue two Sons,
Thomas, who died an infant, and John, who succeeded to his
Honour and Estate, and who, in dutiful commemoration of his
dear Father, and of the mutual affection, and happy friendship
that subsisted between them, hath caused this Monument to be
erected in the place, which the Vestry of this Parish unanimously
desir'd his acceptance of, as a Mark of their Esteem for
the Memory of the Deceased, and the many good Offices he
had done them.
He was born November xxix. M.D.CL.XIII.
and died May xxvii MDCCXXXVIII.
In the seventy-fourth year of his Age.

Sir Thomas was *s.* by his son,

II. Sir John Crosse, M. P. for Wotton Basset, who *d. s. p.* 12th May, 1762, when the Baronetcy became extinct.

Arms—Quarterly az. and arg. in the first and fourth quarters, a cross moline of the second.

CROWE, OF LLANHERNE.

Created 8th July, 1627.

Extinct ....

Lineage.

I. Sir Sackville Crowe, of Llanherne, in the county of Caermarthen, son of William Crowe, esq. of Sarketts, in Kent, by Anne, his wife, daughter and co-heir of John Sackville, esq. of Sussex, was created a Baronet in 1627. He married Mary, sister of John, eighth Earl of Rutland, daughter of Sir George Manners, of Haddon, by Grace, his wife, daughter of Sir Henry Pierrepont, knt. and dying in the Fleet Prison, London, in 1683, was *s.* by his son,

II. Sir Sackville Crowe, of Llanherne, who *m.* first, Anne, daughter of Sir William Rouse, bart.; and secondly, Elizabeth, daughter of William Herbert, esq. of Llanarttock, in Monmouthshire, and relict of Sir Henry Vaughan, of Derwhitt, in Caermarthenshire, but dying *s. p.* the Baronetcy became extinct.

Arms—Gu. a chevron or, between three cocks ar.

CULLEN, OF EAST SHEEN.

Created 17th June, 1661.

Extinct 15th Oct. 1730.

Lineage.

This appears to have been an ancient family of Breda, in the Duchy of Brabant, and it deduced from Arnold Van Ceulen, who was living there in the year 1300.

Richard Cullen, who came into England on the persecution of the Protestants, in the Low Countries, by the Duke d'Alva, *m.* Mrs. Thamar, of Walwyn, and was father of

Abraham Cullen, esq. who *m.* Mrs. Abigail Moone, (of a noble house in Brabant) and left a son and heir,

I. Abraham Cullen, esq. of East Sheen, in the county of Surrey, M. P. for Evesham, who was created a Baronet by *King* Charles II. 17th June, 1661. Sir Abraham *m.* Abigail, youngest daughter of John Rushout, of the city of London, merchant, and had issue,

John, his successor.
Rushout.
Abraham.

Catherine.
Eliza.
Abigail.
Hester.
Anne.
Mary.

He *d.* in 1668, and was *s.* by his eldest son,

II. Sir John Cullen, who, dying unmarried in 1677, was *s.* by his brother,

III. Sir Rushout Cullen, M. P. for the county of Cambridge from 1697 to 1710. He *m.* first, Mary, daughter of Sir John Maynard, of Isleham, in the same county, and relict of Francis Buller, esq. of Cornwall, and of William Adams, esq.* and by that lady left a daughter,

> Mary, *m.* to Sir John Dutton, bart. of Sherborne, but died *s. p.*

He *m.* secondly, Eleanor, daughter of William Jarret, of the city of London, merchant, but by her had no issue. Sir Rushout *d.* 15th October, 1730, when the Baronetcy became extinct.

Arms—Or, an eagle displayed sa.

CULPEPER, OF PRESTON HALL.

Created 17th May, 1627.

Extinct 18th May, 1723.

Lineage.

The manor of Preston, in the county of Kent, with the seat called Preston Hall, situated at a short distance from the River Medway, opposite the village of Aylesford, was possessed in very ancient times by the family of Colepeper, or Culpeper, which spread, in various branches, over the counties of Kent and Sussex, and produced warriors and statesmen of high eminence in the ages in which they flourished. The first recorded ancestor of note, Thomas de Colepeper, was a distinguished lawyer, and one of the *Recognitores Magnæ Assisæ*, or judges of the great assize, *temp. King* John; shortly after his time, the family separated into different branches, one continued at Bayhall, (*See Culpeper of Wakehurst*,) while another seated itself at Preston Hall.

Walter Colepeper, died in the last year of Edward II. seised, as appears by inquisition taken in that year, of estates in Langley, Boughton, East and West Farleigh, Yalding, Malling, Brenchley, Tunbridge, and Shipboone. By Joane, his wife, he left three sons,

> Thomas, of Preston Hall, *d. s. p.*
> Jeffry (Sir), of whom presently.
> John.

The second son,

Sir Jeffry Colepeper, of Preston Hall, succeeded his brother in that estate, and served as sheriff of Kent

* Son and heir of Sir William Adams, of Sprowston.

in the 39th and 47th of EDWARD III. His son and heir,

WILLIAM COLEPEPER, of Preston Hall, in Aylesford, was father of

SIR JOHN COLEPEPER, knt. of Oxenheath, in Kent, one of the judges of the Court of Common Pleas, in the reign of HENRY IV. By Katherine, his wife, he left a son,

SIR WILLIAM COLEPEPER, knt. of Oxenheath, who was sheriff of Kent 5th HENRY VI. and dying the following year, was interred in West Peckham Church, as was his wife Elizabeth, who died in 1460. His son and successor,

SIR JOHN COLEPEPER, knt. of Oxenheath, living *temp.* HENRY V. and HENRY VI. was father of

SIR WILLIAM COLEPEPER, knt. of Preston Hall, in Aylesford, who *m.* a daughter of Ferrers, of Groby, and had three sons,

I. RICHARD (Sir), knt. of Oxenheath, who *m.* Isabella, daughter and co-heir of Otwell Worceley, of Stamworth, and left three daughters, his co-heirs, viz.

MARGARET, *m.* to William Cotton, third son of Sir Thomas Cotton, knt. of Lanwade.

JOYCE, *m.* to Lord Edmund Howard, younger son of Thomas, Duke of Norfolk.

ELIZABETH, *m.* to Henry Barham, of Teston.

Sir Richard, who was sheriff of Kent, 11th EDWARD IV. died 2 RICHARD III. leaving his daughters his co-heirs. To the eldest, Margaret, *m.* to William Cotton, was allotted the manor of Oxenheath, but her son, Sir Thomas Cotton, knt. alienated the estate to John Chowne, of Fairlane, whose great grandson, Sir George Chowne, sold Oxenheath to Nicholas Millar, esq. by whose descendant, Leonard Bartholomew, esq. it was bequeathed to his nephew, Sir WILLIAM GEARY, bart.

II. WILLIAM, of whom presently.

III. Jeffry.

The second son,

WILLIAM COLEPEPER, esq. of Preston Hall, *m.* Margaret Pedwarden, and was father of

EDWARD COLEPEPER, esq. of Preston Hall, whose son, by Jane, his wife, daughter of — Sheldon, of Bedfordshire,

JOHN COLEPEPER, esq. of Preston Hall, living *temp.* EDWARD VI. who *m.* Jane Whetenhall, and had, with two daughters, the elder, Anne, *m.* to John Sedley, esq. of Southfleet, and the younger *m.* to Charles Blower, esq. of Silham, in the county of Rutland, a son,

THOMAS COLEPEPER, esq. of Preston Hall, who *m.* Margaret, daughter of Thomas Colepeper, esq. of Bedgbury, and had issue,

THOMAS, his heir.

Anne, *m.* to Henry, younger son of Sir Henry Crispe, knt.

Mary, *m.* to Henry Crispe, of St. John's, in Thanet.

Thomas Colepeper died in 1567, aged seventy, and was *s.* by his son,

SIR THOMAS COLEPEPER, knt. of Preston Hall, who *m.* Mary, only daughter of Thomas Pynner, of Mitcham, in Surrey, chief clerk comptroller to *Queen* ELIZABETH, and dying 12th October, 1604, left, with other issue, a son and successor,

I. SIR WILLIAM COLEPEPER, of Preston Hall, who was created a BARONET 17th May, 1627. He *m.* the eldest daughter of Sir Richard Spencer, and had an only son and heir,

II. SIR RICHARD COLEPEPER, of Preston Hall, who *m.* Margaret Reynolds, and had issue,

THOMAS, his heir.

Alicia, *m.* first, to Robert Stapley, esq. of Sussex; secondly, to Sir Thomas Taylor, bart. of Maidstone; thirdly, to Thomas Culpeper, esq. barrister-at-law; and fourthly, to John Milner, M.D. She died in 1734, *s. p.*

Sir Richard was *s.* by his only son,

III. SIR THOMAS COLEPEPER, of Preston Hall, who was sheriff of Kent 2nd *Queen* ANNE, 1704. He died *s. p.* 18th May, 1723, (when the BARONETCY EXPIRED) leaving his sister, ALICIA, then the widow of Thomas Culpeper, esq. his sole heir. That lady marrying the October following, JOHN MILNER, M.D. of [illegible], in Yorkshire, settled the manor and estate of Preston Hall on her husband and his heirs. Dr. Milner [illegible] in February, 1724, bequeathing his property to his brother, CHARLES MILNER, M. D., who resided at Preston Hall, until his demise in 1771, when he devised his estates to his nephew, the Rev. JOSEPH [illegible], who assumed the surname and arms of MILNER. They are now possessed by that gentleman's grand-nephew, CHARLES MILNER, esq. of Preston Hall.

Arms—Arg. a bend eng. gu.

CULPEPER, OF WAKEHURST.

CREATED 20th Sept. 1628.—EXTINCT 28th March, 17[illegible]

Lineage.

The family of COLEPEPER, or CULPEPER, is of ancient date in the county of Kent; before the time of EDWARD III. it was divided into chief branches, the Culpepers of Preston Hall, and the Culpepers of Bay Hall; from the latter descended those of Bedgebury, Wakehurst, Wigshill, and the Lords Colepeper of Thoresway, in the county of Lincoln. The elder has [illegible] not however been established, each claimed [illegible] all bore the same coat armour without difference, and carried it in the field of battle; at Poictiers, one Culpeper is stated to have borne in a silver shield, "a *bloody bend engrailed.*"

SIR JOHN COLEPEPER, of Bay Hall, in the parish of Pepenbury,[†] Kent, was father of

SIR THOMAS COLEPEPER, of Bay Hall, who is recorded in the Chronicles as a partisan of Thomas, Earl of Lancaster, in 1321, against *King* EDWARD II. and was executed at Winchelsea. He left a son and [illegible]

JOHN COLEPEPER, esq. of Bay Hall, who was [illegible] of Kent in the 43rd of EDWARD III. He *m.* Elizabeth, daughter and co-heir of Sir John Hardrishall, knt. of Hardrishall, in the county of Warwick, by Maud [illegible]senden, an heiress, and thereby became possessed of divers manors. He was *s.* by his son,

SIR THOMAS COLEPEPER, knt. high sheriff of Kent in the 18th RICHARD II. who *m.* Joan, daughter and co-heir of Nicholas Green, esq. of Exton, in the county of Rutland, by Jane, daughter and co-heir of John Bruce, esq. of Exton, and thereby acquired that estate. He had issue,

I. THOMAS (Sir), who inherited Exton, and had a daughter and heir,

CATHERINE COLEPEPER, marrying SIR JOHN HARRINGTON, conveyed the estate to that family, and her son and heir,

---

[*] Sir Thomas Colepeper, of Bedgebury, was governor of Winchelsea, in the time of EDWARD II.

[†] Sir Jeoffrey Colepeper, of Pepenbury, was sheriff of Kent in the reign of EDWARD I.

ROBERT HARRINGTON, esq. was great grandfather of

SIR JOHN HARRINGTON, knt. who was created BARON HARRINGTON, of Exton, in 1603. (See BURKE's *Extinct Peerage*.)

II. WALTER. } These gentlemen, with Peter Colepeper, were returned among the gentry of Kent, 12 HENRY VI.
III. Nicholas. }

The second son,

WALTER COLEPEPER, esq. who was sometime seated at Goudehurst, in Kent, but in his declining years, at Bedgebury, where he was buried in 1462, left issue,

I. JOHN (Sir), who m. Agnes, daughter and heir of John Bedgebury, esq. of Bedgebury, in Kent, and thereby acquired that estate, where he was buried in 1488. He had two sons,
   ALEXANDER (Sir), who continued the line of Bedgebury.
   Walter, from whom the Barons Colepeper, the Colepepers, of Wiggshill and Folkington, in Sussex, the Colepepers, of Hollingborn, &c.

II. Richard, m. the daughter and co-heir of Richard Wakehurst, of Wakehurst, in Sussex, but died without issue, when his property devolved upon his brother.

III. NICHOLAS.

The third son,

NICHOLAS COLEPEPER, esq. inherited the estate of his brother Richard, without issue. He m. Elizabeth, the sister of Richard's wife, and daughter and co-heir of Richard Wakehurst, of Wakehurst, and had issue, five sons, of whom the eldest,

RICHARD COLEPEPER, esq. m. Joan, daughter of Richard Nayler, of London, and was father of

JOHN COLEPEPER, Lord of Wakehurst, who m. Emma, daughter and co-heir of Sir John Ernle, knt. and had three sons, THOMAS, William, and Edward; the eldest,

THOMAS COLEPEPER, m. Phillipa, daughter of John Trecher, of Presthouse, in Suffolk, and was father of

SIR EDWARD COLEPEPER, of Wakehurst, who received the honour of knighthood from *King* JAMES I. 23rd July, 1603. He m. Elizabeth, daughter of William Fernfold, esq. of Nashin, Sussex, and had three sons viz.

I. John (Sir), who *d. s. p.* in the lifetime of his father.
II. WILLIAM.
III. Edward, m. Mary, daughter of Sir Edward Bellingham, knt. and was living in 1634.

The second son,

I. WILLIAM CULPEPER, esq. of Wakehurst, in the county of Sussex, was created a BARONET by *King* CHARLES I. 20th September, 1628. Sir William m. Jane, daughter, and eventually heir, of Sir Benjamin Pellett, knt. of Bedney, in Sussex, and had issue,

BENJAMIN, his heir.
EDWARD, successor to his brother.
William.
John.
Elizabeth, } *d.* issueless.
Jane, }
Dorothy.
Anne, m. to *Simeon* Burrell, esq. of Cuckfield, in Sussex.
Catherine.
Mary.

He was *s.* at his decease by his eldest son,

II. SIR BENJAMIN CULPEPER, of Wakehurst, who was five years of age at the visitation in 1634. He *m.* Catherine, daughter and co-heir of Goldsmith Hudson, esq. and had an only child, ELIZABETH. Dying without issue male, the baronetcy devolved, at his decease, upon his brother,

III. SIR EDWARD CULPEPER, who had a son,

BENJAMIN, who m. Judith, daughter of Sir William Wilson, bart. of Eastborne, in Sussex, and dying in the lifetime of his father, left
   WILLIAM, who *s.* his grandfather.

Sir Edward was *s.* by his grandson,

IV. SIR WILLIAM CULPEPER, of Wakehurst, who *d.* 28th March, 1740, when the BARONETCY became EXTINCT.

Arms—Arg. a bend eng. gu.

CURLL, OF SOBERTON.

CREATED 20th June, 1678.

EXTINCT 1678-9.

Lineage.

I. SIR WALTER CURLL, of Soberton, in Hampshire, (son of Dr. Walter Curll, Bishop of Rochester, and subsequently of Winchester, who died in 1647, and grandson of Curll of Hatfield, Herts,) was created a BARONET in 1678, but dying *s. p.* shortly after, the title EXPIRED.

Arms—Vert, a chev. engr. or.

CURSON, OF WATER PEERY.

CREATED 30th April, 1661.

EXTINCT 28th May, 1750.

Lineage.

This family, descended from a common ancestor with the existing noble house of Scarsdale, was very ancient, and its members were of rank from the Conquest to the time of its extinction.*

ROBERT DE CURSON, living in the time of HENRY II. m. Alice, daughter of De Somervile, and left a son,

RICHARD DE CURSON, who m. Patronel, daughter and

* About the time of *King* JOHN, lived the celebrated Cardinal Curzon of this family.

co-heir of Richard de Camvile, Baron of Creeth, and had a son,

Robert de Curzon, of Croxhall, in the county of Derby, living *temp.* Henry III. whose line terminated in an heir female,

Mary Curzon, daughter and sole heir of Sir George Curzon, knt. of Croxhall, who m. Edward Sackvile, Earl of Dorset, K. G.

This Richard conferred, in the 10th of Richard I. the town of Kedleston, in the county of Derby, upon his kinsman,

Thomas Curzon, who bore for his arms, "Vairy or and gules, on a bend sable, three popinjays, or." From which Thomas we pass to his descendant,

John Curzon, of Kedleston, living in the time of Henry IV. who m. Margaret, daughter of Sir Nicholas Montgomery, knt. and had three sons, viz.

i. Richard, Capt. of Sandgate Castle, 11 Henry VI. father of

John, commonly called John with the White Head, from whom the Lords Scarsdale.

ii. Walter, of whom presently.

iii. Henry, whose line terminated in the time of Henry VIII.

The second son,

Walter Curzon, esq. m. Isabell, daughter of Robert Saunders, esq. of Harrington, in the county of Northampton, and had issue,

Richard, his heir.

Thomas.

Gregory.

Mary, m. first, to John Power, esq. of Bletchington, in the county of Oxford, and secondly, to William Bowen, of Edgecote, Bucks.

Anne, m. to William Belson, esq. of Brill, in Buckinghamshire.

The eldest son,

Richard Curzon, esq. m. Anne, daughter of William Gifford, esq. of Cowley, Bucks, and had issue,

Vincent, his heir.

Isabel, m. to Edmond Hampden, esq. of Bailes.

Dorothy, m. to Ambrose Digby, esq. of Horton, Bucks.

Catherine, m. to Edmund Townley, esq. of Royle, in Lancashire.

He was s. by his son,

Vincent Curzon, esq. who m. Elizabeth, daughter of Roger Corbet, esq. of Morton Corbet, and was s. by his son,

Sir Francis Curzon, knt. who m. Anne, daughter of Judge Southcote, by whom he had three sons, John, Francis, and Richard, and a daughter Mary, the wife of John Barney, esq. of London. His eldest son,

Sir John Curzon, knt. m. Mary, daughter of Robert, Lord Dormer, and had issue,

Robert, who m. Lady Diana Tufton, daughter of Nicholas, Earl of Thanet, but d. s. p. in the life time of his father.

William, d. unmarried.

Thomas, of whom presently.

Elizabeth, m. to Anthony Belson, esq. of Stokenchurch, Bucks.

Frances.

The only surviving son,

i. Thomas Curson, esq. of Water Perry, in the county of Oxford, was created a Baronet by *King* Charles II. 30th April, 1661. He m. Elizabeth, daughter of William Burrow, esq. of Burrow, in Leicestershire, and dying about 1681, (his widow died in 1697,) was s. by his only surviving child,

ii. Sir John Curson, who m. first, Penelope, daughter and co-heir of William Child, esq. of the county of Worcester, and by her had

Francis, his heir.

Robert, John, William, Peter, } died unm.

Catherine, m. to — Vaughan, esq. of Courtfield.

Mary, m. to John Brinkhurst, esq. of the Moor, in the county of Bucks.

He m. secondly, Anne, daughter of Robert Dormer, esq., sister of the fourth Lord Dormer, and widow of Edmund Powell, esq. of Sandford, in Oxfordshire, but by that lady had no issue. Sir John d. in December, 1727, and was s. by his eldest son,

iii. Sir Francis Curson, who m. first, Elizabeth, daughter of Francis Knollys, esq. of Winchingdon, in Bucks, by whom he had one son, who died at the age of fourteen. He wedded, secondly, the daughter of Edmund Powell, esq. of Sandford, but dying s. p. 20th May, 1750, the title became extinct. The estate of Water Perry devolved, eventually, on Francis, present Lord Teynham, who assumed, in consequence, the surname of Curzon.

Arms—Arg. on a bend sa. three popinjays or, collared gu.

CURTIUS.

Created 2nd April, 1652.—Extinct ....

Lineage.

Sir William Curtius, resident in Sweden for Charles II. was created a Baronet in 1652, but of him or his descendants nothing further is known.

CURWEN, OF WORKINGTON.

Created 12th Mar. 1626-7.

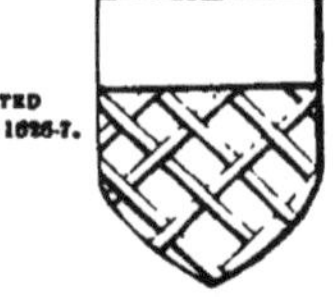

Extinct in 1664.

Lineage.

i. Sir Patrick Curwen, of Workington, representative of the very ancient family of Curwen, so long seated in the county of Cumberland, (See Burke's *Commoners*, vol. i. p. 579) represented that shire in parliament, and was created a Baronet in 1626. He m. Isabel, daughter and co-heir of George Selby, esq. of Whitehouse, in Durham, but dying, issueless in 1664, the Baronetcy expired, while the estates devolved on his brother,

Thomas Curwen, esq. at whose decease, unm. temp. Charles II. they passed to his half-brother,

Eldred Curwen, esq. of Workington, whose son Henry, dying s. p. this branch of the family became extinct, but the estates and representation reverted to his cousin,

Eldred Curwen, esq. sheriff of Cumberland temp. George II. whose grandaughter and heiress

Isabella Curwen, m. John Christian, esq.

Unerigg Hall, and was mother of the present,

Henry Curwen, esq. of Workington, in Cumberland.

Arms—Arg. fretty gu. a chief az.

CUTLER, OF LONDON.

Created 9th Nov. 1660.—Extinct 15th April, 1693.

Lineage.

I. Sir John Cutler, of London, who was created a Baronet in 1660, m. first, Elisha, daughter of Sir Thomas Tipping, knt. of Wheatfield, in Oxfordshire; by whom he had a daughter,

Elizabeth, m. to Charles Bodville Robartes, Earl of Radnor.

He m. secondly, Elizabeth, daughter and co-heir of Sir Thomas Foot, bart. of London, by whom he had another daughter, m. to Sir William Portman, bart. of Orchard Portman. Sir John died without male issue in 1693, aged eighty-five, when the title expired.

CUTTS, OF CHILDERLEY.

Created 21st June, 1660.—Extinct in 1670.

Lineage.

Sir John Cutts, knt. of Thaxted, in Essex, living temp. Henry VIII. settled at Childerley, in the county of Cambridge, before the year 1516, and served the office of sheriff of that county. He m. a daughter of Sir John Hinde, and was grandfather of

Sir John Cutts, knt. of Childerley, whose short name is said to have disgusted the Spanish Ambassador, whom Queen Elizabeth had consigned to his care: his excellency found, however, as we are told, that what his host "lacked in length of name, he made up in the largeness of his entertainment." Sir John maintained a style of living more magnificent than prudent, and was obliged, in 1599, to alienate the manor of Thaxted to Thomas Kemp, esq. His son and successor,

I. Sir John Cutts, of Childerley, the sixth of the same name in lineal descent, was created a Baronet by Charles II. a few weeks after the restoration. He died, however, unm. in 1670, when the title became extinct, but the estate of Childerley devolved on a distant relative,

John Cutts, esq. of Woodhall, in Essex, descended from Richard, brother of Sir John Cutts, the first of Childerley. He left two sons and three daughters, viz.

Richard, died unm.

John, of Childerley, in Cambridgeshire, a gallant military officer under the Duke of Marlborough, created in 1690, Baron Cutts, of Gowran. He married first, the sister of Sir George Treby; and secondly, a daughter of Sir Henry Pickering, of Whaddon, but died without issue in 1706-7, in Ireland, whither he had gone as one of the lords justices. The estate of Childerley was sold by his lordship in 1686 to Felix Calvert, esq.

Anne, m. to John Withers, esq. of the Middle Temple.

———, m. to John Acton, esq. of Basingstoke, Joanna, died unm.

D'AETH, OF KNOWLTON.

Created 16th July, 1716. Extinct in April, 1808.

Lineage.

This family was originally of Aeth, in Flanders, whence the surname, but was remotely settled at Charles Place, in Dartford.

William Death or D'Aeth, gent. of Dartford, married, in the time of Edward VI. Anne, daughter and heir of Vaughan of Erith, and had several children, of whom the third, but eldest surviving son,

Thomas D'Aeth, became his heir, and was living in 1615. This gentleman m. Joan, daughter of William Head, and was s. by his eldest son,

Thomas D'Aeth, who m. Mary, daughter of Mr. Serjeant Barton, and had three sons, Adrian, Abell, and Thomas, of whom the first and second died without issue; the third,

Thomas D'Aeth, settled in the city of London, and was an eminent merchant there. He m. Elhanna, daughter of Sir John Rolt, knt. of Milton Earnest, in the county of Bedford, and was s. by his only surviving son,

I. Thomas D'Aeth, esq. of Knowlton, in the county of Kent, who was created a Baronet on the 16th July, 1716. He m. first, Elizabeth, daughter of Admiral Sir John Narborough, knt. and sole heiress of her brother, Sir John Narborough, bart. of Knowlton. By this lady (who d. 24th June, 1721, in the thirty-ninth year of her age,) he had issue,

I. Narborough, his successor.
II. Thomas.
I. Elizabeth, m. in 1740, to the Hon. and Rev. Godfrey Dawney, one of the prebendaries of Canterbury, son of Henry, second Viscount Dawney, and d. s. p.
II. Elhanna, m. to Capt. Fitzgerald, of the French service, and d. s. p.
III. Sophia, m. in 1749, to William Champneys, esq. of Vintners, in Kent, and d. s. p. in 1772.
IV. Bethia, m. first, to Herbert Palmer, esq. of Wingham, in Kent; and secondly, to John Cosnan, esq. but d. s. p.
V. Harriet, a minor in 1735, m. Josiah Hardy, esq. consul at Cadiz, and had five daughters, viz.
    1. Harriet Hardy, m. to William Hughes, esq. of Betshanger, in Kent (his second wife), and by him, who d. in April, 1786, had issue,
        George-William Hughes, of whom hereafter as inheritor of the D'Aeth estates.
        Harriet Hughes, m. to George Leonard Austen, esq. of Sevenoaks, in Kent.
        Louisa Hughes.
        Charlotte Hughes, d. unm.
    2. Elizabeth-Sophia Hardy, m. to Edward Markland, esq. of Leeds.
    3. Priscella Hardy, m. to John Godby, esq. of Greenwich.

4. Louisa Hardy, *m.* to John Cooke, esq. captain of the Bellerophon, killed at Trafalgar.

5. Charlotte Hardy, *m.* to Lieut.-Colonel George-John Hamilton, R.A.

Sir Thomas *m.* secondly, Jane, daughter of Walter Williams, esq. of Dingeston, in Monmouthshire, and by that lady had another son, Francis, in holy orders, rector of Knowlton, *d.* unmarried in 1784. The baronet, who represented Canterbury in parliament in 1708 and Sandwich in 1714, *d.* 4th January, 1745, and was *s.* by his eldest son,

II. SIR NARBOROUGH D'AETH, of Knowlton, in the county of Kent, who *m.* Anne, daughter and heir of John Clarke, esq. of Blake Hall, in Essex, and dying 8th October, 1773 (his will, dated 15th February, 1771, was proved 24th January, 1774), was *s.* by his only son,

III. SIR NARBOROUGH D'AETH, of Knowlton, who died unmarried in April, 1808, when the BARONETCY became EXTINCT, and the estates devolved upon his cousin, GEORGE-WILLIAM HUGHES, esq. who assumed the surname and arms of D'AETH, and is now of Knowlton Court. (See BURKE's *Commoners*, vol. iii. p. 85.)

Arms—Sa. a griffin passant or, between three crescents arg.

DALISON, OF LAUGHTON.

CREATED 29th June, 1611.

EXTINCT 14th June, 1645.

Lineage.

The family of Dallison or Dalyson was one of considerable importance, and is stated to have derived from William D'Alanzon, one of the companions in arms of the CONQUEROR. The representative of the family in the sixteenth century,

WILLIAM DALYSON, esq. of Laughton, in the county of Lincoln, son of William Dallison and grandson of William Dalyson by a daughter of John Vavasour, of Spaldington, was sheriff and escheator of that county. He died 18th December, 1546, leaving by his wife, a daughter of George Wastneys, esq. of Haddon, in Notts, two sons and three daughters, viz.

I. GEORGE, his heir.

II. William, who represented the county of Lincoln in parliament in 1554, and became subsequently one of the judges of the Court of King's Bench. He *m.* Elizabeth, only daughter of Robert Dighton, esq. of Sturton Parva, in Lincolnshire, and by her, who wedded, secondly, Sir Francis Ascough, knt. left at his decease, 8th January, 1558, four sons and five daughters. Of the former, the eldest,

WILLIAM DALISON, esq. wedded, in 1574, Silvester, daughter of Robert Dean, of Halling, in Kent, and by her, who *m.* secondly, William Lambard, esq. left at his decease, 9th November, 1583, a son and successor,

SIR MAXIMILIAN DALISON, knt. of Halling, who *m.* first, Paulina, daughter of Sir Michael Sonds, knt. of Throwley, by whom he had no issue; and secondly, Mary, daughter of Sir William Spencer, knt. [illegible] Oxfordshire, by whom he was father of

WILLIAM DALISON, esq. of Halling, who *m.* Elizabeth, daughter of Sir James Oxenden, knt. of Dean, and was *s.* at his decease in May, 1642, by his son,

MAXIMILIAN DALISON, esq. of Halling, who *m.* Frances, only daughter and heir of Thomas Stanley, esq. of Hamptons, in Kent, and had issue,

THOMAS, his heir.

Charles, who died 24th February, 17[illegible] leaving by Bennett, his first wife, daughter of Henry Sheafe, of Chatham, three sons and a daughter, Bennett, *m.* in 1760, to the Rev. Josiah Morgan.

Elizabeth, *m.* to William Hodgkins, esq. of Hammersmith, in Middlesex.

Mary, *m.* to Thomas Kirrill, esq. of Hadlow, in Kent.

The elder son,

THOMAS DALISON, esq. of Hamptons, *m.* first, Susan, second daughter of Sir Thomas Style, bart. of Wateringbury; and secondly, Elizabeth, third daughter of Sir Thomas Twisden, bart. of Bradborne, but had issue only by the former, viz.

THOMAS, his heir.

Elizabeth, *b.* in 1686, *m.* John Boys, esq. of Hode Court, in Kent, and had a daughter and co-heir,

ANNE BOYS, who *m.* Rev. Osmund Beauvoir, D.D. and was mother of

ELIZABETH BOYS, who *m.* William Hammond, esq. of St. Albans Court, Kent, and their younger son,

MAXIMILIAN-DUDLEY-DIGGES HAMMOND, assumed the surname and arms of DALISON only in 1819. He *m.* in that year, Anna Maria, daughter of Sir John Shaw, bart. and has issue.

Thomas Dalison *d.* 1st July, 1726, and was *s.* by his son,

THOMAS DALISON, esq. of Manton, in Lincolnshire, and of Hamptons, in Kent, [illegible] 5th October, 1684, who *m.* first, Jane, [illegible] daughter of Richard Etherington, of [illegible]sex, by whom he had two daughters, Jane, *m.* to Sir Jeffery Amherst, K.B. and *d. s. p.*; and Mary, who died unmarried. He *m.* secondly, in 1729, Isabella, daughter of Peter Burrell, esq. of Beckenham, and had

WILLIAM, his heir.

Thomas, in holy orders, M.A. died unmarried.

Maximilian, *d. s. p.*

FRANCES-ISABELLA, *m.* in 1768, to William-Daniel Master, esq. of [illegible] in Kent, but *d. s. p.* 21st December, [illegible]

Mr. Dalison *d.* in 1741, and was *s.* by his son,

WILLIAM DALISON, esq. of Hamptons, [illegible] tenant colonel of the West Kent mil[illegible] *b.* in 1730, who died unmarried 11th January, 1800. His estates vested in his sister Mrs. Master, who bequeathed them to her cousin, Maximilian Hammond, esq. enjoining him to take the name of DALLISON, and rebuild the mansion of Hamptons.

i. ——, wife of Kiddall.
ii. ——, wife of Pierpoint.
iii. Anne, *m.* to Edward Tirwhitt, esq. of Stainfield.

The eldest son,

GEORGE DALLISON, esq. of Laughton, in Lincolnshire, living 3rd EDWARD VI. married the daughter of Robert Hopkinson, esq. of Kirmington, and had issue,

WILLIAM, his heir.

Anne, *m.* to John Wharfe.
Ellen, *m.* to — Anderson.

He *d.* in 1549, and was *s.* by his son,

WILLIAM DALLISON, esq. of Laughton, living 21st ELIZABETH, who *m.* Anne, daughter of Robert Dighton, esq. of Sturton, and had issue,

ROGER, his heir.
Maximilian (Sir), knt.
Gilbert.

Elizabeth, *m.* to John Langton, esq. of Langton, in Lincolnshire.

The eldest son,

I. SIR ROGER DALLISON, of Laughton, lieutenant-general of the Ordnance, was created a BARONET 29th June, 1611. He *m.* first, a daughter of Sir Valentine Br-wn-; and secondly, Elizabeth Tirwhitt, by the latter of whom he left a son and successor,

II. SIR THOMAS DALLISON, of Laughton, who was slain, gallantly fighting under the royal banner, at Naseby 14th June, 1645, and as he left no issue, with him the title became EXTINCT.

Arms—Gu. three crescents or, a canton erm.

DALSTON, OF DALSTON.

CREATED 15th Feb. 1640-1.

EXTINCT 7th March, 1765.

Lineage.

The family of DALSTON, one of great antiquity in the county of Cumberland, was founded by

ROBERT, second brother of Hubert de Vallibus, Lord of Gilsland in the time of the CONQUEROR, who had the BARONY OF DALSTON conferred upon him by his kinsman, Ranulph de Meschines, Earl of Chester; and his posterity possessed it, in lineal descent, until King STEPHEN gave Cumberland to DAVID, *King of Scots.* HENRY II. recovering the county, seized the barony of Dalston, and united it to the forest of Englewood, whereof it continued a member until HENRY III. in the fourteenth year of his reign, disforested Englewood, and gave or sold it to Walter Malclerk, then Bishop of Carlisle and lord treasurer, whose successors in the see of Carlisle ever afterwards enjoyed the estate. The descendants of Robert de Dalston held, however, the old mansion house, with the manor and lordship, of Dalston Parva. Of those descendants,

HENRY DE DALSTON, son of Reginald, gave Brownelston, part of his manor, to the priory of Carlisle.

JOHN DE DALSTON, son of Robert, *m.* a daughter and co-heir of Kirkhide, with whom he had the estate at Kirkhide.

THOMAS DE DALSTON had the manor of Uldale, part of the barony of Utterdale, given him by *King* HENRY VIII. as a reward for the services he had rendered at the battle of Sollom Moss. From this Thomas descended the Dalstons of Acornbank, in Westmoreland,* and

SIR JOHN DALSTON, knt. sheriff of Cumberland in the 10th JAMES I. His son and heir,

SIR GEORGE DALSTON, knt. was M.P. for Cumberland in the 16th CHARLES I. and was sheriff in the 16th of the preceding reign. This gentleman had a son, WILLIAM, and a daughter, Catherine, the wife of Sir Henry Fletcher, knt. of Hutton, in Cumberland. Sir Henry fell at Rowton Heath, near Chester, fighting for *King* CHARLES I. in 1645, and his widow, who was a lady of great courage and resolution, endured sequestration, incarceration, plunder, &c. from the rebels with a brave and masculine spirit. She lived, however, to see her daughters married into some of the first families in the county. Sir George Dalston's only son and heir,

I. SIR WILLIAM DALSTON, knt. of Dalston, in Cumberland, was created a BARONET by *King* CHARLES I. 15th February, 1640-1, in which year he was M.P. for Carlisle. "When the rebellion broke out, both he and his father behaved themselves very bravely and dutifully towards the king, and were great sufferers for the royal cause; the latter being obliged to pay £700 and Sir William £3000 to the sequestrators." Sir William resided chiefly at Heath Hall, in Yorkshire (an estate which came into the family by marriage), and died 13th January, 1683, leaving issue, by Anne, the daughter of Thomas Bolles, esq. of Osberton, in the county of Nottingham, and Dame Mary Bolles, his wife, BARONETTESS OF NOVA SCOTIA,†

GEORGE (Sir), who received the honour of knighthood, and died in the lifetime of his father. He *m.* Brown, eldest daughter of Sir William Ramsden, knt. of Byrom and Longley, in the county of York, and by that lady (who *m.* secondly, Edward Andrews, esq. of Westminster; and thirdly, Sir Richard Fisher, bart. of Islington; and died at Turnham Green, aged eighty-seven, 15th March, 1739-40,) left an only daughter and heir,

FRANCES, who *m.* first, John Jermy, esq. of Sturton Hall, in Suffolk, and secondly, Sir William Halton, bart.

JOHN (Sir), knighted at Whitehall 16th February, 1663, and eventually heir to his father.

Mary, *m.* to Thomas, second son of Thomas Gent, esq. of Moyns, in Essex.

The second, but eldest surviving son, became, at the death of his father,

* Johanna, daughter and co-heir of SIR RICHARD DALSTON, of Acorn Bank, in Westmoreland, wedded SIR THOMAS ALEN, ancestor of the present COLONEL LUKE ALEN, C.B. representative of SIR THOMAS ALEN, bart. of Waltons, and of the most ancient line of Alen, which, removing from England, where it had been settled since the period of the CONQUEST, was established in Ireland *temp.* HENRY VIII. by ARCHBISHOP ALEN. See BURKE'S *Commoners*, vol. ii. p. 363.

† This is the only lady upon whom the dignity of BARONETTESS has ever been conferred.

II. Sir John Dalston, bart. of Dalston. He m. Margaret, second daughter of Sir William Ramsden, knt. (sister to his brother's wife), and had, with one daughter, m. to Brown of Islington, two sons,

Charles, his successor.
John, a major in the army.

Sir John, who was sheriff of Cumberland in the 1st James II. was s. at his decease by his elder son,

III. Sir Charles Dalston, bart. who m. first, the daughter and co-heir of Sir Francis Blake, knt. of Whitney, in the county of Oxford, and had (with four daughters, of whom one m. Francis Fauquier, esq.) a son,

George, his heir.

He m. secondly, Anne, fourth daughter of Sir Michael Wentworth, of Woolley, and widow of Sir Lion Pilkington, bart. of Chevet. By this lady (who m. thirdly, in 1750, John Maude, esq. of Alverthorpe Hall, in Yorkshire, see Burke's *Commoners*, vol. ii. p. 86,) he had another daughter, who died young and unmarried. He was s. at his decease by his son,

IV. Sir George Dalston, bart. who m. Anne, dau. of George Huxley, esq. but dying *s. p. m.* (his only daughter married a French gentleman named Dillon) 7th March, 1765, the title became extinct. Four years before his death, Sir George sold his estate at Dalston to Monkhouse Davison, esq. after whose decease it was purchased by John Sowerby, esq.

Arms—Arg. a chevron between three daws' heads erased sa. bills or.

D'ANVERS, OF CULWORTH.

Created 21st Mar. 1642-3.

Extinct 20th Aug. 1776.

Lineage.

Richard D'Anvers, of Cothorp, in Oxfordshire, said to be descended from Roland D'Anvers, one of the companions in arms of the Conqueror, m. the daughter and heir of John de Brancestre, of Oxfordshire, and left a son and heir,

John D'Anvers, of Cothorp, who wedded, first, Alice, daughter and heir of William Verney, of Byfield, and had issue,

I. Robert (Sir), of Ipwell, who purchased the estate of Culworth. Sir Robert was king's sergeant in 1443 and justice of the Common Pleas in 1450. He m. Agnes, daughter of Richard Quatremains, of Rycot, in Oxfordshire, and dying in 1467, left three daughters, his co-heirs, viz.

Agnes, m. first, to Hugh Unton, esq.; and secondly, to Sir Walter Denys, of Gloucestershire.

Alice, m. to — Burnaby, esq. of Watford, and *d. s. p.*

Joan, m. to Henry Frowick, esq. of Gunnoldsbury, in Middlesex.

II. John, LL.D. in holy orders.

III. Richard, of whom presently.

I. Agnes, m. to Thomas Boddington.

II. Alicia, m. to Henry Tracey.

He m. secondly, Joan, daughter of William Br[illegible] esq. of Waterstoke, in Oxfordshire, and had by [illegible] who wedded, secondly, Sir Walter Mauntell, of He[illegible] ford, five sons and four daughters, viz.

I. Thomas (Sir), of Banbury, in Oxfordshire, *d. s. p.*

II. William (Sir), of Chamberhouse, in Berkshire and of Upton, in Warwickshire, one of the judges of the Court of Common Pleas temp. Henry VII. He m. Anne, daughter and heir of John Pury, esq. of Chamberhouse, and was ancestor of the Danvers of Upton and [illegible]worth.

III. Simon, *d. s. p.*

IV. Edward, *d. s. p.*

V. Henry, cofferer to Henry VII. m. Beatrix daughter of Sir Ralph Verney, and had issue.

I. Agnes, m. first, to Sir John Fray, lord chief baron; secondly, to John, Lord Wenlock, and thirdly, to Sir John Say, knt.

II. Amicia or Margaret, m. to John Langston, esq. of Caversfield, in Oxfordshire.

III. Elizabeth, m. to Thomas Poure, esq. of Bl[illegible]ingdon, Oxfordshire.

IV. Jane, m. to Richard Fowler, esq. of Buckingham, chancellor of the duchy of Lancaster.

John D'Anvers' third son,

Richard D'Anvers, esq. of Prescote, in Oxfordshire, purchased from his nieces the estate of Culworth. He m. Elizabeth, daughter of John Langston, esq. of Caversfield, Buckinghamshire, and was s. by his son,

Sir John D'Anvers, knt. of Culworth, sheriff of Northamptonshire 10th Henry VII. This gentleman m. Anne, daughter of Sir John, and sister and heir of Sir Edward Stradling, knt. of Dantsey, in W[illegible] by which marriage he acquired the estate of Dantsey and had issue,

I. Thomas, his heir, seated at Dantsey, who m. Margaret, daughter of Sir William Courtenay, knt. of Powderham Castle, and was grandfather of

Sir John Danvers, knt.* who m. Elizabeth Nevil, youngest daughter and co-heir of John, Lord Latimer, who died in 1577, and acquired by that lady (who m. secondly, Sir Edmund Carey, knt.) the castle of Danby, in Yorkshire. He had issue,

Charles (Sir), who lost his life in the insurrection of Essex temp. Elizabeth, and was attainted.

Henry, created Baron Danvers of Dantsey, in 1603, and in 1626 Earl of Danby. He was afterwards made a knight of the Garter. (See Burke's *Extinct Peerage*.)

John (Sir), of Chelsea, in Middlesex, M.P. for the university of Ox[illegible], one of the judges who sat on King Charles I. His daughters and co-heirs were

Anne, m. first, to Sir Henry Lee, bart. of Ditchley, in Oxfordshire, and secondly, to Henry Wilmot, first Earl of Rochester.

Elizabeth, m. first, to Robert [illegible]

* Knighted by Henry VII. on the marriage of *Prince* Arthur.

liers *alias* Wright, Viscount Purbeck.

Anne, wife of Sir Arthur Porter, of Newark, Gloucestershire.

Lucy, m. to Sir Henry Baynton, of Bromham, in Wiltshire.

Eleanor, m. to Thomas Walmesley, esq. of Dunkenhalgh, in the county of Lancaster, and left a son and two daughters,

Sir Thomas Walmesley, knt. of Dunkenhalgh.

Elizabeth Walmesley, wife of Richard Sherburne, esq. of Stonyhurst.

ANNE WALMESLEY, who m. first, William Middleton, esq. of Stockeld; and secondly, Sir Edward Osborn, bart.; by the latter she had

SIR THOMAS OSBORN, bart. created Duke of Leeds.

Dorothy, m. to Sir Peter Osborn, knt. of Chicksand.

Elizabeth, wife of Sir Edward Hobby, of Gloucestershire.

Katherine, wife of Sir Richard Gargrave, knt. of Nostel.

II. WILLIAM, of whom presently.

III. John, living in 1537.

I. Margaret, m. to Edward Fiennes, Lord Say and Sele.

II. Dorothy, m. to Sir Anthony Hungerford, knt. of Down Ampney.

III. Susanna, m. to Walter, Lord Hungerford.

IV. Anne, m. to Thomas Lovett, esq. of Astwell.

he second son,

WILLIAM D'ANVERS, esq. had the paternal estate of ...worth, and m. in 1523, Elizabeth, daughter of ...ard Fiennes, Baron Say and Sele, by whom he ...d issue,

JOHN, his heir.

Mary, m. to Robert Barker, esq.

Dorothy, m. to Henry Sacheverell, esq. of Sadington, in Leicestershire.

Anne, m. to George Blount, esq. of Wigginton, in Oxfordshire.

... d. 20th June, 1544, and was *s.* by his son,

JOHN D'ANVERS, esq. of Culworth, who m. Dorothy, ...ughter and co-heir of Sir William Rainsford, knt. ... Great Tew, in the county of Oxford, and had two ...ns and three daughters, viz.

I. SAMUEL, his successor.

II. Daniel, of Herley, in Oxfordshire, who m. 12th November, 1563, Susanna, daughter of — Pope, esq. of Wroxton, in Oxfordshire, and had, with other issue, a son,

William, of London, father of

Daniel, of Northampton, M.D. who m. Jane, daughter of the Rev. Thomas Knightley, of Charwelton, and dying in 1690, left issue,

Knightley, barrister-at-law, deputy-recorder of Northampton, author of "Abridgement of the Common Law," *d.* in London, January, 1740.

Jane, m. to John Rushworth, esq. of Northampton, and had, with other issue, a daughter, Alicia, wife of Charles Watkins, esq. of Daventry.

I. Temperance, m. to Anthony Dillon, esq. of Devonshire.

II. Justice.

III. Prudence.

John D'Anvers *d.* 4th August, 1556, and was *s.* by his son,

SAMUEL D'ANVERS, esq. of Culworth. This gentleman m. Anne, daughter of Leonard Piggot, esq. of Little Horwood, in Bucks, and was *s.* by his only surviving son,

SIR JOHN D'ANVERS, knt. of Culworth, baptized 10th October, 1580, who m. in 1604, Dorothy, daughter of Gabriel Pulteney, esq. of Misterton, in the county of Leicester, and had (with several daughters, of whom Margaret, m. Thomas Risley, esq. of Chetwode; Mary, m. Laurence Manley, esq. of Spratton; Susan, m. Edmund Bray, esq.; and Catherine became the wife of John Griswold, esq.) a son and successor,

I. SAMUEL D'ANVERS, esq. of Culworth, who was created a BARONET 21st March, 1642-3. He m. Lady Anne Pope, daughter and co-heir of Sir William Pope, Earl of Downe, in Ireland. Sir Samuel D'Anvers, who was sheriff of Northamptonshire the year of the martyrdom of *King* CHARLES, appeared at the assizes with his retinue in deep mourning, and was a great sufferer by his zeal in the royal cause. He died 27th January, 1683, and was *s.* by his son,

II. SIR POPE D'ANVERS, of Culworth, baptized 12th December, 1644, who m. Anne, daughter and co-heir of William Barker, esq. of Sunning, Berks, and had a large family, of which only three children survived, viz.

JOHN, his successor.

Daniel, of Eydon, m. in 1712, the daughter and co-heir of the Rev. Moses Hodges, D.D. of Sulgrave, and had two sons and a daughter, viz.

1. Barker, buried 7th September, 1741.
2. John, died unmarried in 1745.

1. MARTHA, m. at Thorpe Mandeville, 17th September, 1746, to Daniel Rich, esq. of the Temple, son of Sir Robert Rich, bart. of Sunning, Berkshire, and dying in 1753, left issue,

Daniel-Danvers Rich, colonel in the 3rd regiment of Foot Guards, died unmarried in 1783.

MARTHA RICH, } devisees of Mrs. Meriel
FRANCES RICH, } Danvers, of Culworth Manor.

Frances.

He *d.* 4th May, 1712, and was *s.* by his son,

III. SIR JOHN D'ANVERS, of Culworth. This gentleman m. first, Meriel, daughter of Sir Robert Leicester, bart. of Nether Tabley, in Cheshire, by whom (who *d.* in 1701) he had an only child,

Samuel, *b.* in 1701, *d.* unm. in 1722.

He m. secondly, Susannah, sister and co-heir of Sir Edward Nicolls, bart. but by that lady (who *d.* in 1730) had no issue. Sir John wedded, thirdly, Mary, daughter of the Rev. John Hutchins, rector of Eydon, in Northamptonshire, and by her (who *d.* in 1784) had issue,

HENRY, his successor.

Anthony, *d.* young in 1735.

MICHAEL, successor to his eldest brother.

MERIEL.

Mary, *d.* young in 1747.

Sir John *d.* 20th September, 1744, and was *s.* by his eldest surviving son,

IV. SIR HENRY D'ANVERS, of Culworth, who *d.* unmarried at the age of twenty-two, 10th August, 1753, and was *s.* by his brother,

V. SIR MICHAEL D'ANVERS, of Culworth, born 29th September, 1738, high sheriff of Northamptonshire in 1763, who died unmarried 20th August, 1776, when the

Baronetcy became extinct; the manor of Culworth devolving on his sister and heiress, Meriel Danvers, who devised it in moieties to Martha and Frances, the daughters and co-heirs of her first cousin, Daniel Rich, esq.

Arms—Gu. a chev. between three mullets of six points pierced or.

D'ANVERS, OF SWITHLAND.

Created 4th July, 1746.  Extinct 21st Sept. 1796.

Lineage.

Samuel D'Anvers, esq. *m.* Elizabeth Morewood, of Overton, in the county of Derby, an heiress, and was father of

i. Joseph D'Anvers, of Swithland, in the county of Leicester, M.P. for Boroughbridge in 1722, and subsequently for Bramber and Totness, who was created a Baronet by *King* George II. 4th July, 1746. He *m.* Frances, daughter of Thomas Babington, esq. of Rothley Temple, in Leicestershire, and dying 21st October, 1753, was *s.* by his only child,

ii. Sir John D'Anvers, bart. who *m.* Mary, daughter and heir of Joel Watson, esq. of Clapham, in Surrey. Sir John was sheriff of Leicestershire in 1755, and dying 21st September, 1796, aged seventy-three, without male issue, the Baronetcy became extinct. He left, however, an only surviving daughter and heiress,

> Elizabeth Danvers, then the wife of the Hon. Augustus-Richard Butler (second son of Brinsley, second Earl of Lanesborough), who assumed the name and arms of Danvers in addition to those of Butler. She died in 1802, leaving two sons,
>
> > George-John-Danvers Butler-Danvers, esq. now of Swithland.
> >
> > George-Augustus Butler-Danvers, *b.* in 1798.

Arms—Arg. on a bend gu. three martlets of the field.

DARCY, OF ST. OSITH'S.

Created 19th June, 1660.  Extinct in Oct. 1698.

Lineage.

John Darcy, of Tolleshunt Tregos, second son of Robert Darcy, of Danbury, ancestor of the Lords Darcy of Chiche (see Burke's *Extinct Peerage*), married Anne, daughter of Sir Thomas Tyrell, [illegible] Heron, and had a son,

Anthony Darcy, of Tolleshunt, sheriff of Es[illegible] and Hertfordshire in 1511, who *m.* Elizabeth, dau[illegible] of Christopher Wilkinson, esq. and was father of

Thomas Darcy, esq. of Tolleshunt, *b.* in 1511, [illegible]ried three wives; by the second, Anne, daughter [illegible] Sir John Munday, lord mayor of London in 15[illegible] had two sons,

> Anthony, who left only a daughter.
>
> Thomas, sheriff of Essex in 1580, who *m.* Mar[illegible]garet, daughter of Eustace Sulyard, esq [illegible] well, and dying in 1586 left issue,
>
> 1. Thomas, who *m.* Camilla, daughter [illegible]cent Guicciardime, of Florence, and [illegible] who wedded, secondly, Francis Ha[illegible] esq. of Ickworth, he left six daughters
>   - Mary, *m.* to the Hon. Christopher [illegible]vill, third son of Edward, Lord [illegible]gavenny.
>   - Elizabeth, *m.* to Sir Henry Mildmay knt. of Woodham Walter.
>   - Bridget, *m.* to Sir George Fenner [illegible]
>   - Frances, *m.* to Sir Henry Vane, [illegible] secretary of state to Charles I.
>   - Margaret, *m.* to John Browne, esq
> 2. Eustace.
> 3. John, who *d. s. p.*
>
> 1. Bridget.
> 2. Dorothy.
> 3. Margaret.
> 4. Anne.
> 5. Mary, *m.* to Richard Southwell, esq. [illegible] Woodrising, in Norfolk.
> 6. Elizabeth, *m.* to Henry Maynard, esq [illegible] Great Waltham.

By his third wife, Elizabeth, daughter of John [illegible]don, esq. and sister of Sir Christopher He[illegible] Baconsthorp, he left a son,

Brian Darcy, esq. of St. Osith and Tiptree, at [illegible] latter place he built a fine house out of the r[illegible] the priory. He served the office of sheriff of Es[illegible] 1585, and died in two years after. He *m.* Brid[illegible] daughter of John Corbet, esq. of Sprowston, in Nor[illegible] and was *s.* by his son,

John Darcy, esq. of St. Osith and Tiptree, [illegible] serjeant-at-law, who *m.* Dorothy, daughter of Thom[illegible] Audeley, esq. of Berechurch, in Essex, and had a [illegible] and heir,

Thomas Darcy, esq. of St. Osith and Tiptre[illegible] *m.* in 1621, Mary, daughter of Sir Andrew Asch[illegible] Writtle, and had by her, Mary, and a posthu[illegible] son,

i. Thomas Darcy, esq. of St. Osith and Tiptre[illegible] in 1632, who was created a Baronet 20th June [illegible] He *m.* first, Cicely, daughter of Sir Symonds [illegible] bart. by whom he had no surviving issue, [illegible]condly, Jane, daughter and heir of Robert C[illegible] by whom he had

> Thomas, his heir.
>
> Brian, *b.* in October, 1669.
>
> William.
>
> John.
>
> Elizabeth.
>
> Frances, *m.* to the Right Rev. Sir William Daw[illegible] bart. Archbishop of Canterbury.

The eldest son,

ii. Sir Thomas Darcy, at whose decease [illegible] in October, 1698, the Baronetcy expired. [illegible] passed from the Darcys to Richard Bennett, esq. [illegible] finally to the Price family.

Arms—Arg. three cinquefoils gu.

DARELL, OF WEST WOODHEY.

CREATED 12th June, 1622.

EXTINCT ....

Lineage.

WILLIAM DARELL, esq. third son* of William Darell, of Sesay, in Yorkshire, m. Elizabeth, daughter and heir of Thomas Calston, esq. of Littlecote, in Wiltshire, and thus acquired that estate. His son and successor,

SIR GEORGE DARELL, knt. of Littlecote, m. first, Margaret, daughter of John, Lord Stourton, by whom he had a daughter, Elizabeth, m. to Sir John Seymour, knt. grandfather of the Protector Somerset. Sir George m. secondly, Elizabeth, daughter of Sir Edmund Hart, knt. and dying 14 EDWARD IV. was s. by his son,

SIR EDWARD DARELL, knt. of Littlecote, who m. first, Alice, daughter of Sir Richard Crofts, knt. by whom he had a son,

> JOHN, who m. Johanna, daughter of John Fettiplace, of Slifford, and dying *v. p. temp.* HENRY VIII. left a son,
>
> EDWARD (Sir), successor to his grandfather.

Sir Edward m. secondly, Mary, daughter of John, Lord Fitzwalter, by whom he had no issue; and thirdly, Alice Fly, of Sussex, by whom he had a daughter, Katharine, m. to Francis Choke. Sir Edward died 9th March, 21 HENRY VIII. and was s. by his grandson,

SIR EDWARD DARELL, knt. of Littlecote, who m. Alice, daughter of Sir Thomas Essex, knt. of Berkshire, and had issue,

> WILLIAM, of Littlecote, living in 1587, who alienated to SIR JOHN POPHAM the estate of Littlecote, and *d. s. p.* in 1590. For the curious tradition of the supposed murder at Littlecote House, and of the consequent ruin of this branch of the family, refer to BURKE'S *History of the Commoners*, vol. ii. p. xii.
>
> THOMAS, of whom presently.
>
> Eleanor, m. to Egremund Ratcliffe.

The second son,

THOMAS DARELL, esq. of Hungerford, was father of

I. SIR JOHN DARELL, of West Woodhey, in Berkshire, who was created a BARONET in 1622. He m. first, Anne, daughter of Sir Thomas Chamberlain, knt. and secondly, Anne, daughter of William Young, esq. but dying *s. p. m.* the title became EXTINCT. West Woodhey afterwards passed to the family of Rudyerd, of whom it was purchased by the grandfather of the late Sir Robert Sloper, K.B.

Arms—Az. a lion rampant or, crowned arg.

DARNELL, OF HEYLING.

CREATED 6th Sept. 1621.

EXTINCT about 1640.

Lineage.

I. SIR THOMAS DARNELL, of Heyling, in Lincolnshire, who was created a BARONET 6th September, 1621, married Sarah, daughter of Thomas Fisher, esq. and sister of Sir Thomas Fisher, bart. of Islington, but leaving no son at his decease, which occurred about the year 1640, the title became EXTINCT.

Arms—Az. two bars between six mascles voided or, three in chief, two in fesse, one in base.

DAVERS, OF ROUGHAM.

CREATED 12th May, 1682.

EXTINCT about 1806.

Lineage.

I. ROBERT DAVERS, esq. having acquired a large fortune in Barbadoes, returned to England, and purchased Rougham, with other estates, in the county of Suffolk; and, in consideration of the sufferings of himself and his father in the royal cause, was created a BARONET by *King* CHARLES II. 12th May, 1682. Sir Robert *d.* about the year 1688, and was *s.* by his son,

II. SIR ROBERT DAVERS, bart. of Rougham, who m. the Hon. Mary Jermyn, second daughter and co-heir of THOMAS, second LORD JERMYN, and had issue,

> ROBERT, JERMYN, } third and fourth baronets.
>
> Thomas, admiral R.N. m. Catherine, daughter and heir of William Smithson, M.D. and had issue,
>
> > Thomas Smithson, *d. s. p.*
> >
> > Catharine Smithson, *d. s. p.*
> >
> > Mary Smithson.
>
> Henry, *d.* young.
>
> Mary, m. 29th October, 1765, to Clemence Corrance, esq. of Parham, M.P. for Oxford. (See BURKE'S *Commoners*, vol. iii. p. 378.)
>
> Isabella, m. to Brigadier-General Moyle.
>
> Henrietta, m. to Roger Pratt, esq. of Ryston, in the county of Norfolk, and was grandmother of the present ROGER-EDWARD PRATT, esq. of Ryston Hall.
>
> Penelope, m. to Dr. Pake.

---

* Marmaduke, the eldest son of William Darell, of Sesay, inherited the paternal estate; and John, the second son, purchased CALE HILL, in Kent, *temp.* HENRY IV.

Elizabeth, m. to John King, esq. of Norfolk.

Sir Robert, who frequently represented the county of Suffolk in parliament in the reigns of *Queen* ANNE and *King* GEORGE I. died 1st October, 1722, and was *s.* by his eldest son,

III. SIR ROBERT DAVERS, bart. auditor of the excise, who *d. s. p.* 1st June, 1723, and was *s.* by his brother,

IV. SIR JERMYN DAVERS, bart. who had been elected M.P. for St. Edmundsbury in the second parliament of *King* GEORGE I. which met 10th May, 1722, and was chosen knight of the shire for Suffolk in the first parliament of the succeeding monarch, summoned to meet 28th November, 1727. He m. Margaretta, daughter and co-heir of the Rev. Mr. Green, and had issue,

ROBERT, } *d.* unm.
HENRY, }
CHARLES, successor to his father.
Thomas, *d. s. p.*

MARY.
ELIZABETH, m. to Frederick, Earl of Bristol and Bishop of Derry, grandfather of Frederick-William, present MARQUIS OF BRISTOL.

Sir Jermyn died in February, 1743, and was *s.* by his only surviving son,

V. SIR CHARLES DAVERS, of Rougham, M.P. for St. Edmundsbury, at whose decease unmarried about 1806, the title became EXTINCT.

Arms—Arg. on a bend gu. three martlets or.

DAVIES, OF LONDON.

CREATED 11th Jan. 1685-6.—EXTINCT (date unknown).

Lineage.

I. SIR GEORGE DAVIES, consul and agent at Naples, was raised to a BARONETCY in 1685-6, but of himself or his descendants nothing further is known.

DAVY, OF GROSVENOR STREET.

CREATED 20th Oct. 1818. — EXTINCT in 1829.

Lineage.

I. SIR HUMPHREY DAVY, D.C.L. president of the Royal Society, and member of numerous literary institutions throughout Europe, having distinguished himself by his scientific researches, was, in consideration of his eminence in that walk of literature, created a BARONET on the 20th October, 1818. Sir Humphrey, who was *b.* 17th December, 1779, *m.* in 1812, Jane, daughter and co-heiress of Charles Kerr, esq. and relict of Shuckburgh A. Apreece, eldest son of Sir Thomas Apreece, bart. but dying *s. p.* at Geneva in 1829, the BARONETCY became EXTINCT.

Arms—Sa. a chev. engrailed erm. between two annulets in chief or, and in base a flame ppr. [illegible] passed by a chain of the first, issuing from a [illegible] wreath gold.

DAWES, OF PUTNEY.

CREATED 1st June, 1663. — EXTINCT 20th May, [illegible]

Lineage.

I. SIR JOHN DAWES, knt. of Putney, in the county of Surrey, son of Sir Thomas Dawes, and grandson of Sir Abraham Dawes, knt. of Putney, one of the [illegible] mers of the customs *temp.* CHARLES I. was created a BARONET by *King* CHARLES II. 1st June, 1663. He m. Christian, daughter and heir of William Lyons, esq. of Bocking, in Essex, and had issue,

I. ROBERT, his successor.
II. John, *d.* unm.
III. WILLIAM, in holy orders, Bishop of Chester, afterwards Archbishop of York, and [illegible] Archbishop of Canterbury, succeeded as third baronet.

I. Elizabeth, m. to Dr. Peter Fisher, and [illegible] 1696.

He was *s.* at his decease (his widow m. secondly Sir Anthony Dean, knt. of London,) by his eldest son,

II. SIR ROBERT DAWES, who *d.* unmarried, and was *s.* by his only surviving brother,

III. SIR WILLIAM DAWES, a churchman, who as stated above, attained its highest dignity, the [illegible] of Canterbury. He m. Frances, eldest daughter and [illegible] heir of Sir Thomas D'Arcy, bart. of Braxted [illegible] in Essex, and by her (who *d.* 22nd December, [illegible]) had surviving issue,

D'ARCY, his successor.

Elizabeth, m. to Sir William Milner, bart. [illegible] for the city of York, and was great grandmother of the present SIR WILLIAM-MORDAUNT-[illegible] MILNER, bart. of Nun-Appleton Hall, in the county of York.

His grace *d.* at the age of fifty-three, 30th April [illegible] and was *s.* by his son,

IV. SIR D'ARCY DAWES, bart. who m. in 1733 [illegible] daughter and co-heir* of Richard Roundell, [illegible] Hutton Wandsley, in the county of York, and [illegible] lady (who m. secondly, Beilby Thompson, [illegible] Escrick,†) had issue,

WILLIAM, his successor.

---

* She was only child of her father by his first wife, Frances, daughter of Sir William St. Quintin, bart. Mr. Roundell had by his second wife two other daughters, viz.

MILDRED, m. to John Bourchier, esq.

CATHERINE, m. to the Hon. Christopher Dawnay.

† By Mr. Thompson (to whom she was [illegible]) she had two sons and a daughter, viz.

Beilby Thompson, of Escrick, who *d. s. p.*
Richard Thompson, of Escrick, *d.* unm. in [illegible]
Jane Thompson, m. to Sir Robert Law[illegible] had, *inter alios*, a son, the present PA[illegible] THOMPSON, esq. of Escrick Park, M.P.

Elizabeth, m. to Edward Lascelles, esq. ancestor of the Earls of Harewood.

He d. 16th August, 1732, and was s. by his son,

Sir William Dawes, who d. unmarried 28th May, 1741, when the Baronetcy became extinct.

Arms—Arg. on a bend az. cottised gu. three swans between six pole-axes sa.

DECKER, OF LONDON.

Created ...th July, 1716. Extinct 18th Mar. 1749.

Lineage.

Matthew Decker, esq. a native, by birth, of Amsterdam, but of a Flemish commercial family, settled in the city of London as a merchant in 1702, and was created a Baronet by King George I. 20th July, 1716. He m. Henrietta, daughter of the Rev. Richard Watkins, D.D. rector of Wickford, in Warwickshire, and had issue,

Catherine.

Henrietta-Maria, m. in May, 1737, to the Hon. John Talbot, second son of Lord Chancellor Talbot, but d. s. p.

Mary, m. in December, 1738, to William Crofts, esq. of Saxham, in Suffolk.

Sir Matthew represented Bishop's Castle in parliament. He resided at Richmond, in Surrey, and his gardens were the first in England to bring the pine-apple to maturity in this climate. He d. 18th March, 1749, when the Baronetcy became extinct, and his property devolved upon his daughters as co-heirs.

Arms—Arg. a demi-buck gu. between his fore-legs an arrow erected in pale or.

DELAVAL, OF SEATON.

Created ... June, 1660. Extinct ....

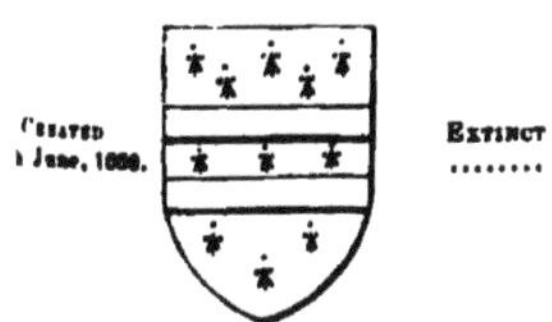

Lineage.

At the time of the general survey,

Sir Henry De la Val, knight banneret, was lord of Seaton De la Val, in the county of Northumberland, which he was s. by his son,

Sir Lewis De la Val, knight banneret, father of

Sir Guy De la Val, lord of Seaton De la Val, who was likewise proprietor of Naseby, in Northamptonshire, and held twenty knights' fees in the 13th of Henry II. He is, like his father and grandfather, a knight banneret. Sir Guy m. a daughter of Maurice de Creon, a feudal baron, and dying in the first year of *King* John, was s. by his son,

Sir William De la Val, whose son,

Sir John De la Val, was father of

Sir Gilbert De la Val, one of the barons in arms against *King* John. He held Claverdon, in Northumberland, by barony, performing the service of two knights' fees, and was s. by his son,

Sir Eustace De la Val, who held another barony in the same county. He was s. by his elder son,

Sir Robert De la Val, who m. Margaret, daughter of William De Greystock,* but dying s. p. 1 Edward I. was s. by his brother,

Sir Henry De la Val. This feudal lord had three sons, all knights, viz.

- I. Eustace (Sir), who m. Margaret, daughter of Ralph Nevil, Lord of Raby, and had a son, Robert (Sir), who d. s. p.
- II. Hugh (Sir), m. Maud, daughter and co-heir of Hugh de Bulbec, Baron of Headon, but died issueless.
- III. Henry (Sir).

The youngest son and eventual heir of his brothers,

Sir Henry De la Val, m. the Lady Helena de Molton, and was s. by his son,

Sir Hugh De la Val, father of

Sir Robert De la Val, who d. 27th Edward III. leaving three sons,

- I. William, sen. (Sir), who left a son, Henry, who d. s. p.
- II. William, jun. (Sir), who had, by gift of his father, the manor of Benwell, and was father of
  - John, whose son,
    - William, m. Mary, daughter of Sir William de Widderington, knt. but d. s. p.
- III. Robert (Sir).

The third son,

Sir Robert De la Val, was father of

Sir John De la Val, who m. first, Margaret, daughter of Sir John de Mitford, but by that lady had no issue. He wedded, secondly, Elizabeth, daughter of William Whitchester, and left an only daughter and heiress,

Elizabeth De la Val, who m. John Horsley, and obliged her husband to take the name and arms of De la Val. She had issue two sons, George, who d. s. p. 16 Henry VIII. and

Sir John De la Val, who m. Mary, daughter of Thomas Carnaby, esq. and had issue,

John (Sir), his heir.

Edward, m. a daughter of John Ogle, esq. of Ogle Castle, and left posterity.

The elder son,

Sir John De la Val, who was sheriff of Northumberland in the first year of Philip and Mary, married Anne, daughter of Ralph, Baron Ogle, and had a son and successor,

Sir John Delaval, knt. of Seaton, who was sheriff of Northumberland in the 17th and 25th years of Elizabeth. He m. Dorothy, daughter of Sir Ralph Grey, knt. of Chillingham, and was s. by his son,

---

* William, Lord of Greystock, m. Mary, eldest of the daughters and co-heirs of Robert de Merlay, a great baron of the north, by whom he acquired the ... of Morpeth, in Northumberland, and had issue,

John, his heir.

William.

Margaret, m. to Sir Robert De la Val.

Burke's *Extinct Peerage.*

DEL

SIR RALPH DELAVAL, knt. of Seaton, sheriff of Northumberland in the 2nd and 19th JAMES I. This gentleman m. Jane, daughter of Thomas Hilton, esq. and had a numerous issue. He was *s.* by his eldest son,

ROBERT DELAVAL, esq. of Seaton, who m. Barbara, daughter of Sir George Selby, knt. and was father of

I. RALPH DELAVAL, esq. of Seaton Delaval, who was created a BARONET by *King* CHARLES II. 29th June, 1660. Sir Ralph m. Lady Anne Fraser, widow of Hugh, Master of Lovat,* and daughter of Alexander Leslie, Earl of Leven, and had issue,

> ROBERT, who died 1st August, 1682, aged thirty-six, his father then being alive, and was buried in St. George's Chapel at Windsor, leaving by his wife,
>
> > RALPH, successor to his grandfather.
> >
> > JOHN, third baronet.

He was *s.* at his decease by his grandson,

II. SIR RALPH DELAVAL, of Seaton Delaval. This gentleman wedded Diana, daughter of George Booth, Lord Delamere, by which lady (who m. secondly, Sir Edward Blacket, bart. of Newby, in the county of York,) he had

> ELIZABETH, m. to William Blount, esq. of Kidmore End, and was mother of
>
> > LISTER BLOUNT, esq. of Maple Durham. (See BURKE'S *Commoners*, vol. iii. p. 168.)

He died in August, 1696, and having had no male issue, was *s.* by his brother,

III. SIR JOHN DELAVAL, who died in June, 1727, and was *s.* by his son,

IV. SIR THOMAS DELAVAL, but of himself or his descendants we have no particulars.

Arms—Erm. two bars vert.

DELAVAL, OF FORD.

CREATED 1st July, 1761.—EXTINCT 21st May, 1808.

Lineage.

FRANCIS-BLAKE DELAVAL, esq. descended from the Delavals of Seaton Delaval, in Northumberland, m. Rhoda, daughter of Robert Apreece, esq. of Washingly, in the county of Huntingdon, by Sarah, daughter and heiress of Sir Thomas Hussey, bart. and left issue at his decease in 1752,

> FRANCIS-BLAKE, who was installed a knight of the Bath in 1761. Sir Francis m. Isabella, widow of Lord Nassau Paulett, and daughter of Thomas, sixth Earl of Thanet, but *d. s. p.* in 1771.
>
> JOHN-HUSSEY.
>
> Edward-Thomas, *d.* unm.
>
> Rhoda, m. to Sir Edward Astley, bart. of Melton Constable, in the county of Norfolk.
>
> Anne, m. first, to the Hon. Sir William Stanhope, K.B.; and secondly, to Captain Morris.
>
> Sarah, m. to John Savile, first Earl of Mexborough.

The second son and eventual continuator of the family,

I. JOHN-HUSSEY DELAVAL, esq. of Ford, in the county of Northumberland, was created a BARONET 1st July, 1761, and elevated to the peerage of Ireland in 1782, as Baron Delaval, of Redford, in the county of Wicklow. His lordship was enrolled amongst the peers of Great Britain, 21st August, 1786, in the dignity of BARON DELAVAL, of Seaton Delaval, in the county of Northumberland. He m. first, Susannah, daughter of R. Robinson, esq. and widow of John Potter, esq. by which lady (who *d.* 1st October, 1783,) he had issue,

> John, *b.* in 1755, *d.* unmarried in 1775.
>
> SOPHIA-ANNE, m. to — Jadis, esq. and *d.* 26th July 1793.
>
> ELIZABETH, m. 19th May, 1781, to George, sixteenth Lord Audley, and *d.* in 1785.
>
> FRANCES, m. to John Fenton Cawthorne, esq.
>
> SARAH, m. to George, Earl of Tyrconnel, and had an only daughter (heiress of the earl),
>
> > LADY SUSANNA CARPENTER, who m. Henry, second Marquess of Waterford.

His lordship m. secondly, Miss Knight, but had no other issue. He *d.* 21st May, 1808, when the BARONETCY, with his higher honours, became EXTINCT.

Arms—Erm. two bars vert.

DELVES, OF DODINGTON.

CREATED 8th May, 1621. EXTINCT 12th Sept. 17[illegible]

Lineage.

DELVES HALL, near Uttoxeter, in the county of Stafford, was the ancient seat and residence of the family: in the 31st of EDWARD I. it was possessed by

JOHN DE DELVES, father of

RICHARD DE DELVES, of Delves Hall, living in the times of EDWARD II. and EDWARD III.; in the latter reign he was constable of Heleigh Castle, near Betley. He was *s.* by his son,

SIR JOHN DE DELVES, who, in the 29th EDWARD III. was one of the four esquires who attended James Lord Audley, Baron of Heleigh, K.G. in the French wars under EDWARD THE BLACK PRINCE, and who for their services at the battle of Poictiers, were rewarded with an annuity of five hundred marks among them, and were allowed an addition to their arms of a chevron, bearing a similitude to their captain's, Lord Audley's coat. Delves afterwards received the honour of knighthood (36 EDWARD III.), the same year had the wardship of the Duchess of Bretagne, and the year following was one of the justices of the King's Bench. Sir John de Delves founded a chantry at Hondebridge, near Chester, and endowed it, in the 43rd EDWARD III. 1369, in which year he died and was interred at Audley, in Staffordshire. He m. Isabel, daughter and co-heir of Philip de Malpas alias Egerton, but having no issue male, was *s.* by his brother,

SIR HENRY DELVES, of Delves Hall, who m. first, Catherine, daughter of Sir John Arderne, and widow of William Chetilton and Ralph Wetenal, and secondly, Margaret, daughter of William Brereton. Sir Henry had a son and heir,

> JOHN, M. P. for the county of Stafford, *temp.* [illegible]

* By whom she was mother of Hugh, tenth Lord Fraser of Lovat.

chard II., in which monarch's reign he was also sheriff, and being escheator of that county, of Salop, and of the marches of Wales, had a grant of the lordship of Walton-upon-Trent. He died the year before his father, 18th Richard II. leaving

John, successor to his grandfather.
Henry.
Hugh.

Matilda, m. to Edmund Basset, of Blore.
Ellen, m. to William de Egerton.
Beatrix, m. to Richard de Wibunbury.

Henry Delves dying 19th Richard II. was s. by his grandson,

John Delves, esq. of Delves Hall, a soldier in the French wars, sheriff of Staffordshire 11th Henry IV. died 7th Henry VI. and was s. by his eldest son,

Richard Delves, esq. who, for want of male issue, was s. by his brother,

Sir John Delves, of Delves Hall, who was sheriff of Staffordshire and comptroller of the petty customs at London, as also warden of the Mint, *temp.* Henry VI. and having been knighted, was slain at the battle of Tewkesbury, and attainted by parliament for his adherence to the house of Lancaster. He m. Ellen, daughter of Ralph Egerton, esq. of Wrinehill, and had issue,

John, who being with his father at Tewkesbury, was beheaded 11th Edward IV.; he left two daughters, Elizabeth, m. to Sir James Blunt, and Ellen, the wife of Robert Sheffield, of Butterwick.
Ralph, successor to his brother.
Richard, a priest, canon of Lichfield and rector of Warrington, where he was buried in 1529.
Henry, father of
Sir Henry, who s. his uncle Ralph, and continued the line.

Sir John was s. by his eldest son,

John Delves, esq. beheaded as stated above, and leaving no male issue, was s. by his brother,

Ralph Delves, esq. who died without issue, and was s. by his cousin,

Sir Henry Delves, of Dodington, (son of Henry Delves, and grandson of John Delves, sheriff of Staffordshire 11 Henry IV.) He was twice sheriff of Cheshire in the time of Henry VIII. was knighted, and sat in parliament for that county. He d. 6th August, 1559, was buried at Wibunbury, and s. by his son,

John Delves, esq. who m. Mary, daughter of William Sneyd, esq. of Keel, in the county of Stafford, and dying 15th June, 1571, was s. by his son,

Henry Delves, esq. who m. Frances, daughter of Thomas Stanley, esq. of Alderley, in Cheshire, and was s. at his decease, 8th October, 1606 (he was buried at Wibunbury the 10th), by

I. Sir Thomas Delves, of Dodington, in the county of Chester, b. at Alderley 14th Elizabeth, knighted 8th July, 1603, and created a Baronet by *King* James I. 8th May, 1621. He m. first, Mary, daughter of Thomas Wilbraham, esq. of Woodhey, and by that lady had Henry, his successor, and Lawrence, Richard, and Thomas, who all died issueless. Sir Thomas m. secondly, Mary, daughter of Edward Baber, esq. of Chew, in Somersetshire, and widow of Sir Roger Wilbraham, but had no other issue. He served the office of sheriff of Cheshire in 1638, and was s. at his decease by his eldest son,

II. Sir Henry Delves, bart. b. in 1589, sheriff of Cheshire in 1640, m. first, Catherine, daughter and co-heir of Sir Roger Wilbraham, one of the masters of requests to *King* James I. and by her had

Thomas, his successor.

Mary, m. to Sir Thomas Mainwaring, bart. of Peover, in the county of Chester.
Catherine, m. to Edward Glegg, esq. of Gayton, in the same county.
Grace, m. to Joshua Edisbury, esq. of Pentry yr Claud, in Derbyshire.

He m. secondly, Mary, daughter of Randal Leicester, citizen of London, but had no other issue. He d. 23rd May, 1663, and was s. by his son,

III. Sir Thomas Delves, bart. of Dodington, b. 28th August, 1630, sheriff in 1665, m. first, Elizabeth, only daughter and heir of Hall Ravenscroft, esq. of Horsham, in Sussex, and had two sons,

Thomas, his heir.
Henry.

He m. secondly, Rachel, daughter of Francis Forrester, esq. of Watling Street, Salop, without issue. Sir Thomas d. 15th May, 1713, and was s. by his elder son,

IV. Sir Thomas Delves, bart. of Dodington, b. 4th October, 1652. This gentleman m. first, Jane, daughter of Sir Richard Knightly, K.B. of Fawesley, in Northamptonshire, by whom he had one daughter,

Elizabeth, m. to Sir Brian Broughton, bart. of Broughton, in the county of Stafford, and had issue,

Sir Brian Broughton, bart. of whom hereafter as heir to his grandfather, Sir Thomas Delves.

Jane Broughton, m. to Sir Rowland Hill, bart.
Elizabeth Broughton, d. unmarried in 1725.

He m. secondly, Lady Elizabeth Booth, daughter of Henry, Earl of Warrington, which lady d. s. p. in 1697; thirdly, Elizabeth, daughter of Andrew Barker, esq. of Fairford, in Gloucestershire, and by her had

Henry, b. 18th July, 1700, and d. at Warwick, on his return from France, unmarried in April, 1725, his father being then alive.

Sir Thomas m. fourthly, Rhoda, daughter of Sir John Huband, bart. but by that lady had no issue. He d. 12th September, 1725, when the Baronetcy, through failure of male issue, became extinct, and the estates passed, under the will of the deceased baronet, to his grandson,

Sir Brian Broughton, bart. of Broughton, in the county of Stafford, who, in compliance with the injunction of that instrument, assumed the additional surname of Delves. Sir Brian was grandfather of the present

Sir John Delves-Broughton, bart. (Refer to Burke's *Peerage and Baronetage*.)

Arms—Arg. a chevron gu. fretted or, between three turves or delves sa.

DE NEUFVILLE, OF FRANKFORT.

Created 16th March, 1709.—Extinct, date unknown.

Lineage.

I. Sir Robert de Neufville, of Frankfort, in Germany, was created a Baronet in 1709, but no further particulars concerning him have ever been obtained.

DENIS, OF ST. MARY'S AND BLACKMONSTONE.

Created 28th Oct. 1767.—Extinct 12th June, 1778.

Lineage.

The Rev. Jacob Denis, born in La Rochefocault, in Angoumois, fled from France at the Revocation of the Edict of Nants, and settled at Chester, where he was ordained, and married Mrs. Martha Leach, a lady of ancient family in Lancashire, by whom he had twelve children, of whom, the youngest but one,

I. Peter Denis, esq. of Blackmonstone and St. Mary's, in Kent, adopting the naval profession, sailed round the world with Commodore Anson, and returned his first lieutenant. Soon after, being put into commission, he commanded the Centurion on the 3rd May, 1747, and began the attack, for which Lord Anson dispatched him with the news of the signal victory then achieved over the French fleet. In 1758, he commanded the Dorsetshire, and captured the Reasonable, of equal force. Participating subsequently in many hard-fought actions, this gallant officer attained the rank of vice-admiral of the red, and was created a Baronet in 1767, an honour which expired at his decease in 1778.

DENNY, OF GILLINGHAM.

Created 3rd June, 1642.

Extinct ....

Lineage.

In 1642, a Baronetcy was conferred upon

I. Sir William Denny, of Gillingham, in Norfolk, who m. Miss Catherine Young, but had no issue. Sir William died in great indigence and with him the title expired.

Arms—Gu. a saltier between 12 crosses, pattée, or.

DENTON, OF HILLESDON.

Created 12th May, 1699.

Extinct April, 1714.

Lineage.

King Edward VI. granted the manor of Hillesdon, in the county of Buckingham, to

Thomas Denton, esq. the descendant of a very ancient family, and from him it passed in direct succession to

I. Sir Edmund Denton, who was created a Baronet in 1699. This gentleman married Mary, daughter and co-heir of Anthony Rowe, esq. of Hackney, in Middlesex, but by her (who wedded, secondly, Trevor, Viscount Hillsborough,) he had no issue. He died in April, 1714, when the Baronetcy expired. The manor of Hillesdon continued in a collateral branch of the family until Elizabeth, daughter and co-heir of Alexander Denton, esq. conveyed it to her husband, George Chamberlayne, esq. whose daughter, Elizabeth Chamberlayne, inherited the estate, and married William Coke, esq. of Holkham. (See Burke's *Commoners*, vol. i. p. 6.) The manor-house was, during the civil wars, made a garrison for the king, being then the seat of Sir Alexander Denton, who suffered severely for his devoted attachment to his royal master. The garrison was surrendered in 1643, the house plundered, and Sir Alexander committed to prison, where he died broken-hearted.

Arms—Arg. two bars gu. in chief three cinquefoils of the second.

DE RAEDT, OF HOLLAND.

Created 30th May, 1660.—Extinct, unknown.

Lineage.

I. Sir Gualter de Raedt, of the Hague, was created a Baronet in 1660, but of him no information can be obtained.

DEREHAM, OF WEST DEREHAM.

Created 8th June, 1661.

Extinct 16th Jan. 1739.

Lineage.

This family derived its descent from

Herlwinus, an Anglo-Saxon, living at the time of the Norman Conquest. His son,

Geoffrey, possessed property in the parish of Dereham, in Norfolk, and thence assumed the surname of Dereham. He was *s.* by his son,

Geoffrey de Dereham, who granted, in the reign of Henry II. to Hubert Walter, then dean of York, afterwards archbishop of Canterbury, the land on which that prelate founded the abbey of West Dereham.

Elias de Dereham, was one of the executors to the will of the said archbishop, in the time of *King* John.

Thomas de Dereham, was settled at Crimplesham in the 18th of Edward III. His son or grandson, another

Thomas de Dereham, of Crimplesham, *temp.* Henry V.* m. Elizabeth, daughter and heir of Baldwin de Vere, of Denver, in Norfolk, younger brother of Robert de Vere, of Addington, of the Veres, Earls of Oxford. This lady died in the 8th of Edward IV. and had a solemn anniversary with mass, obsequies, and offerings, annually celebrated for her soul, in the parish church of Crimplesham. Their grandson,

Thomas de Dereham, esq. m. Elizabeth, daughter

* Sir Robert Dereham, knt. distinguished himself eminently in the French wars of Henry IV

of Sir John Audley, knt. of Swaffham, in Norfolk. The name of this Thomas occurs in the return of the gentry of Norfolk, made by the commissioners of Henry VI. "as Thomas de Dereham, of West Dereham." His descendant,

Thomas de Dereham, purchased from the crown, in Henry VIII. the scite of the then lately dissolved monastery, of West Dereham, and removed the residence of the family back again from Crimplesham to that place. From this Thomas we pass to

I. Thomas Dereham, esq. of Dereham Abbey, in the county of Norfolk, (son of Sir Thomas Dereham, knt.) who was created a Baronet by *King* Charles II. 8th June, 1661. He *m.* first, Elizabeth, daughter and heir of Richard Scott, esq. of Scotts Hall, Kent, but by her had no issue. He *m.* secondly, Elizabeth, eldest daughter and co-heir of Sir Richard Gargrave, knt. of Kingsley Park, in the county of York, and by that lady had

- Henry, his successor.
- Richard (Sir), heir to his brother.
- Lucy, *d.* unm.
- Penelope, *m.* first, to Thomas Keble, esq. of Newton Hall, Suffolk, and had one surviving daughter,
  - Penelope Keble, *m.* first, to Thomas Ruse, esq. and secondly, to the Rev. Robert Palmer, D.D.
- She (Penelope Dereham) *m.* secondly, John Shaw, esq. of Colchester.

Sir Thomas was *s.* at his decease by his elder son,

II. Sir Henry Dereham, bart. who *m.* one of the daughters and co-heirs of Sir John Maynard, knt. serjeant-at-law, but dying *s. p.* in 1682, was *s.* by his brother,

III. Sir Richard Dereham, bart. who *m.* Frances Villiers, daughter of Robert Wright, alias Villiers, the assumed son and heir of Sir John Villiers, Viscount Purbeck, (*refer to* Burke's *Extinct Peerage*,) and had issue,

- Thomas, his successor.
- Richard, *d.* unm.
- Elizabeth, *m.* to Sir Simeon Stuart, bart. of Hartley Mauduit, in the county of Southampton.

He *d.* in Jamaica, and was *s.* by his son,

IV. Sir Thomas Dereham, bart. who was educated at the court of Cosmo III. Grand Duke of Tuscany, and resided chiefly at Florence. He *d.* unm. at Rome, 16th January, 1738, when the Baronetcy became extinct, and his sister, Elizabeth, wife of Sir Simeon Stuart, bart. became his heir. She was great-grandmother of the present Sir Simeon-Henry Stuart, bart.

Arms—Az. a buck's head caboshed or.

DE VIC, OF GUERNSEY.

Created 3rd Sept. 1649.—Extinct ....

Lineage.

Sir Henry de Vic, of Guernsey, chancellor of the garter, was created a Baronet in 1649. He *m.* Margaret, daughter of Sir Philip Carteret, knt. of St. Owen's, in Jersey, and dying 20th November, 1672, was *s.* by his son,

II. Sir Charles de Vic, at whose decease, in early life, unm. the title became extinct.

Arms—Or, three caltraps sa. a chief of the second.

D'EWES, OF STOWLANGTOFT HALL.

Created 15th July, 1641.

Extinct 21st April, 1731.

Lineage.

Paul D'Ewes, esq. one of the six clerks in Chancery, son of Gerard D'Ewes, of Upminster, in Essex, and a lineal descendant of the ancient family of D'Ewes, Lords of Kessal, in the duchy of Guelderland, married Cecilia, only daughter and heir of Richard Symonds, esq. of Coxden, in Dorsetshire, and had issue,

- Symonds, his heir.
- Richard.
- Johanna, *m.* to Sir William Elliot, knt. of Godalming.
- Grace, *m.* to Wyseman Bokenham, esq. of Weston, in Suffolk.
- Mary, *m.* to Sir Thomas Bowes, knt. of Essex.
- Elizabeth, *m.* to Sir William Poley, knt.

Paul D'Ewes died in 1630, and was *s.* by his son,

I. Sir Symonds D'Ewes, of Stowlangtoft, born in 1602, at Coxden, the seat of his maternal grandfather. This eminent antiquary commenced at a very youthful age, even while a student at St. John's College, Cambridge, those historical studies, in which he eventually attained such distinction, and, almost at the same early period, gained the friendship and acquaintance of Cotton, Selden, Spelman, and many others of the first rank in the republic of letters. The labours of Sir Symonds have contributed not a little to illustrate the general history of Great Britain; and his most prominent work, "The Journals of all the Parliaments during the Time of Queen Elizabeth," exists as an able record of the important transactions of one of the most glorious reigns in English history. In 1639, Sir Symonds served the office of sheriff of Suffolk, having been knighted some time previously; and in the long parliament, which was summoned to meet 3rd November, 1640, was elected member for Sudbury. In 1641, he was created a Baronet by Charles I.; yet, upon the breaking out of the civil war, he adhered to the parliament, and took the solemn league and covenant in 1643. He continued to sit in the House of Commons until December, 1648, when he was turned out with others who were thought to retain some little regard for the person of the king, and the old constitution in church and state. He wedded, first, in 1626, Anne, daughter and heir of Sir William Clopton, knt., a lady of exquisite beauty, by whom he had two daughters, namely:

- Cecilia, *m.* to Sir Thomas Darcy, bart. of St. Osith's, Essex.
- Isolda, died unm.

He *m.* secondly, Elizabeth, daughter and co-heir of Sir Henry Willoughby, bart. of Risley, in Derbyshire, and by her, who *m.* secondly, Sir John Wray, had a son Willoughby, his heir. Sir Symonds died 18th April, 1650, aged forty-eight, and was *s.* by his son,

II. Sir Willoughby D'Ewes, who *m.* Priscilla daughter of Francis Clinton, esq. of Stourton, in Lincolnshire, and had issue,

Symonds, his heir.

Priscilla, *m.* to John Hastings, esq. of Hinton, in Northamptonshire.

Elizabeth, *m.* to Heigham Coke, esq. of Suckley, and had a son,

D'Ewes Coke, esq. of Suckley, great grandfather of the present D'Ewes Coke, esq. of Brookhill Hall, Derbyshire.

Sir Willoughby died 13th June, 1685, and was *s.* by his son,

III. Sir Symonds D'Ewes, who *m.* Delariviere, daughter and co-heir of Thomas, Lord Jermyn, and by her, who died in 1702, had issue,

I. Jermyn, his heir.
II. Willoughby, *d.* in 1710, aged nineteen.
III. Symonds, *d.* 1693.
IV. Thomas, *d.* 1698.

I. Delariviere, *m.* to Thomas Gage, esq. eldest son of Sir Thomas Gage, bart.

II. Mary, *m.* to George Tasburgh, esq. of Bodney, in Norfolk, by whom she had one son,

George Tasburgh, who *m.* first, in 1755, Teresa, daughter of Thomas, Viscount Gage, which lady died *s. p.* in 1773, and secondly, Barbara, daughter of Thomas Fitzherbert, esq. of Swinnerton, by whom he had no issue. Mr. Tasburgh's widow wedded, for her second husband, George Crathorne, esq. of Crathorne, and died in 1808, leaving a daughter, Mary-Anne-Rosalia Crathorne.

III. Harriott, *m.* to Thomas Havers, esq. of Thelton Hall, Norfolk, and from this marriage descends the present

Thomas Havers, esq. of Thelton Hall. (See Burke's *Commoners*, vol. i. p. 381.)

IV. Merelina, *m.* to Richard Elwes, esq.

Sir Symonds died in May, 1722, and was *s.* by his son,

IV. Sir Jermyn D'Ewes, who died unm. 21st April, 1731, when the Baronetcy became extinct.

Arms—Or, a fess vair between three quatrefoils gu.

DIGGS, OF CHILHAM CASTLE.

Lineage.

From Roger de Mildenhall, of the parish of St. Stephens, alias Nackington, living *temp.* John, lineally descended,

James Diggs, esq. of Barham, (son of John Diggs, esq. of Barham, by Joan, daughter of Sir Gervase Clifton, knt.) who *m.* first, Mildred, daughter of Sir John Fineux, chief-justice of England, and co-heir to his mother, one of the daughters and co-heirs of William Apulderfield, esq. by whom he had a son, John, of Barham. He wedded, secondly, Phillippa, daughter of John Engham, of Chart, and had another son,

Leonard Diggs, esq. of Wootton Court, in Kent, a famous mathematician, *temp.* Edward VI. and

Queen Mary, who *m.* Sarah, sister of Sir James [illegible] ford, knt. and had, beside three daughters, Mary, [illegible] of — Barber; Anne, *m.* to William Diggs, of [illegible] ington; and Sarah, *m.* to — Martin, a son and [illegible] cessor,

Thomas Diggs, esq. who *m.* Anne, daughter of [illegible] Warham St. Leger, knt. of Ulcombe, in Kent, and [illegible] her, who died in 1636, aged eighty-one, and was [illegible] at Chilham, left at his decease in 1595, with other issue, a son and successor,

Sir Dudley Diggs, knt. an eminent lawyer [illegible] master of the rolls, living in 1619, who purchased [illegible] estate of Chilham, in Kent. He *m.* Mary, [illegible] daughter and co-heir of Sir Thomas Kempe, [illegible] Olantigh, by which lady he acquired Chilham [illegible] and had, with other issue,

Thomas, his heir.
John, of Faversham.
Dudley, fellow of All Souls' College.
Edward, of Virginia in 1684.

Anne, *m.* to Anthony Hammond, esq. of St. Alban's Court, in Kent, and had four sons,

William Hammond, of St. Alban's Court, [illegible] tor of the present

William-Osmond Hammond, esq. [illegible] Alban's Court. (See Burke's *Commoners*, vol. i. p. 131.)

Dudley Hammond.

Anthony Hammond, grandfather of James Hammond, the Elegiac Poet.

Edward Hammond, died at sea.

The eldest son,

Thomas Diggs, esq. of Chilham Castle, *m.* [illegible] daughter of Sir Maurice Abbot, knt. and [illegible] 1687, having had, with six daughters, six sons, [illegible]

Maurice, his heir.
Dudley, of Gray's Inn, died *s. p.*
John, *b.* in 1642, died *s. p.*
Thomas, *b.* in 1643, died *s. p.*
Edward, *b.* in 1649, a colonel in the army, who [illegible] in 1679, Dame Frances Moore, of [illegible] died *s. p.*

Leonard, *b.* in 1651, of Chilham Castle, who [illegible] Elizabeth, daughter of Sir John Osborne [illegible] of Chicksand, and died in 1717, leaving [illegible]

John, of Chilham Castle, died in 1720, [illegible]

Thomas, a colonel in the army, who *m.* Elizabeth, daughter of John, Lord Delawarr. He sold the castle and manor of Chilham [illegible] James Colebrooke, citizen of London, [illegible] son, Robert Colebrooke, esq. sold them [illegible] Thomas Heron, esq. of Newark on Trent, and from the Herons, Chilham was [illegible] chased in 1792, by Thomas Wildman [illegible]

Elizabeth, *m.* to Adam Williamson, [illegible] general and governor of Gravesend [illegible] bury, and died in 1746, leaving a daughter [illegible]

Elizabeth Caroline Williamson, [illegible] Daniel Fox, esq. of the Sax [illegible] Office.

The eldest son,

I. Sir Maurice Diggs, of Chilham Castle, [illegible] ated a Baronet 6th March, 1665-6. He *m.* first [illegible] net, daughter of Mark Dixwell, esq. of Folkestone [illegible] Brome, in Kent, and secondly, Judith, daughter [illegible] co-heir of George Rose, esq. of Eastergate, [illegible] but dying *s. p.* in 1666, the title became extinct. [illegible] Maurice's widow wedded, secondly, Daniel [illegible] esq. of Ham Court, in Surrey.

Arms—Gu. on a cross arg. five eagles displayed [illegible]

DILLINGTON, OF KNIGHTON.

CREATED 6th Sept. 1628. EXTINCT 4th July, 1721.

Lineage.

TRISTRAM DILLINGTON, esq. of Knighton George, in the Isle of Wight, son of Anthony Dillington, esq. of the same place, left by Jane, his wife, daughter of Nicholas Martin, esq. of Achilhampton, in Dorsetshire, one son and two daughters, viz.

ROBERT, his heir.

Barbara, m. to John Bayley, esq. of London.

Ann, m. to Francis Alexander, esq.

The son and heir,

I. ROBERT DILLINGTON, esq. of Knighton George, was created a BARONET in 1628. He m. first, Mabell, daughter of Sir Humphrey Forster, knt. of Berkshire, and secondly, Catherine, sister of Richard, Lord Gorges; by the former of whom he had, *inter alios*, a son,

ROBERT, who predeceased his father, leaving with others, a son, ROBERT, successor to his grandfather, and a daughter, Mabell, m. to Sir William Meux, bart. of Kingston, in Hants.

Sir Robert died in 1664, and was *s.* by his grandson,

II. SIR ROBERT DILLINGTON, who m. first, Jane, daughter of John Freke, esq. of Shrowton, and secondly, Hannah, daughter of William Webb, citizen of London, and dying about the year 1687, was *s.* by his eldest son,

III. SIR ROBERT DILLINGTON, who died unm. in two years after his father, and was *s.* by his brother,

IV. SIR JOHN DILLINGTON, who died *s. p.* about 1712, and was *s.* by his half-brother,

V. SIR TRISTRAM DILLINGTON, major in the guards, at whose decease, issueless, in 1721, the BARONETCY became EXTINCT.

Arms—Gu. a lion saliant or.

DIXWELL, OF BROME.

CREATED [illegible]th June, 1660. EXTINCT 25th March, 1750.

Lineage.

This family was originally of Dixwell Hall, and lords of the manor of Dixwell, in the county of Hertford; they possessed that estate until the beginning of the reign of *King* RICHARD, when they exchanged it, with John, of Durham, for the manor of Great Munden, in the same county. Some considerable lapse of time afterwards,

WILLIAM DIXWELL, lineally of the same stock, having m. Margaret, daughter and heir of Adam Sampson, of Coton, in the county of Warwick, removed from Tingreth, in Bedfordshire, and settled there. He was *s.* by his son,

WILLIAM DIXWELL, esq. who m. Anne, sister and heir of Henry Mitchel, esq. of Dodford, in Northamptonshire, and left a son and heir,

JOHN DIXWELL, esq. This gentleman wedded, Mary, daughter of Humphrey Grey, esq. of Enville, in Staffordshire, and was *s.* by his son,

WILLIAM DIXWELL, esq. who m. Elizabeth, daughter of John Knight, esq. of Brookehoult, in the county of Northampton, and left a son and heir,

CHARLES DIXWELL, esq. of Coton, who m. Abigail, daughter of Henry Herdson, esq. of Stourton, in Lincolnshire, and had issue,

I. WILLIAM, who inherited Coton. (See DIXWELL, *of Cotton Hall*, Extinct Baronets.)
II. Edward.
III. Humphrey.
IV. BASIL.
V. Barbara.

He (Charles) lies buried in Churchover, in the county of Warwick, where on a large alabaster monument, fixed to the south wall, are the images of a man and his wife, kneeling at a desk between them, with four sons and one daughter; on the top, a shield on the right hand, with the arms of Dixwell, another on the left,—or, a cross, between twelve billets, sable, between four fleurs-de-lis, gules, and in the middle, quarterly, 1. The arms of Dixwell; 2. Or, a cross, between twelve billets, sa. with this inscription:

> This Monument was erected, Anno Dom. 1641, in the Memorie of Charles Dixwell, of Coton, Esq; and of Abigail, his wife; he dying in the year of our Lord, 1591; and She, in the year 1635. And of four Sons, and one Daughter that issued from them, viz: William Dixwell, Esq; Edward Dixwell, Humphry Dixwell, Sir Basil Dixwell, Knight and Baronet, and Barbara Dixwell; all whose Figures, this Work doth represent.

The youngest son,

I. SIR BASIL DIXWELL, bart. having inherited from his maternal uncle, John Herdson, considerable estates at Folkestone, and in other parts of Kent, transplanted himself into that county, and settled at Terlingham, where he continued until the year 1622, when he removed to Broome, in the same county, a manor of his, on which he had recently erected a handsome mansion house. He served the office of sheriff in the 2nd year of CHARLES I. and was created a BARONET by that monarch, 18th February, 1627. He died unm. in 1641, when the BARONETCY became EXTINCT, and his estates devolved, under his will, upon his nephew,

MARK DIXWELL, esq. son of his brother William, who m. Elizabeth, daughter of Matthew, and sister and heir of William Read, esq. of Folkestone, by which lady (who wedded, secondly, Sir Henry Oxenden, bart.) he had a son and heir,

I. BASIL DIXWELL, esq. of Brome, in the county of Kent, who was created a BARONET by *King* CHARLES II. 19th June, 1660. Sir Basil m. Dorothy, daughter and co-heir of Sir Thomas Peyton, bart. of Knowlton, and had issue,

BASIL, his successor.

ELIZABETH, one of the maids of honour to *Queen* MARY, m. to George Oxenden, LL.D. master of Trinity Hall, Cambridge, and by him, (who was third son of Sir Henry Oxenden, bart. of Dene, and died in 1764,) left two sons, Henry and George Oxenden, the elder, succeeding his uncle in 1709, became

SIR HENRY OXENDEN, fourth baronet, of Dene, in Kent, but dying *s. p.* was *s.* by his brother,

SIR GEORGE OXENDEN, fifth baronet, M.P. for Sandwich, who *m.* in 1729, Elizabeth, eldest daughter and co-heir of Edmund Dunch esq. of Little Withenham, Berks, and had two sons,

SIR HENRY OXENDEN, sixth baronet, father of SIR HENRY OXENDEN, seventh and present baronet. See BURKE'S *Peerage* and *Baronetage*.

GEORGE OXENDEN, of whom hereafter, as inheritor of the Dixwell estates.

Sir Basil was *s.* at his decease by his only son,

II. SIR BASIL DIXWELL, bart. auditor of the Excise, and governor of Dover Castle, in which latter post he continued the greater part of the reign of WILLIAM III. He was also M.P. for the town and port of Dover. In the reign of *Queen* ANNE, he was dismissed from his employments, but restored at the accession of GEORGE I. He *m.* first, Dorothy, daughter of Sir John Temple, bart. of East Sheen, Surrey; and secondly, (his first wife dying about the year 1718,) Catherine, daughter of William Longueville, esq. son of Sir Thomas Longueville, of Bradwell Abbey, Bucks, baronet of Nova Scotia, but had issue by neither. He *d.* 25th March, 1750, when the BARONETCY became EXTINCT, and the estates devolved, under his will, upon his nephew, GEORGE OXENDEN, esq. who, in consequence, assumed the name of DIXWELL; but that gentleman dying unmarried in 1753, they are now in the possession of SIR HENRY OXENDEN.

Arms—Argent, a cheveron gules, between three fleurs-de-lis.

DIXWELL, OF TIRLINGHAM.

CREATED 19th Feb. 1627-8.—EXTINCT in 1641.

Refer to DIXWELL of BROOME.

DIXWELL, OF COTON HALL.

CREATED 11th June, 1716.—EXTINCT 14th Jan. 1757.

Lineage.

This was the senior branch of the family, from which the DIXWELLS of Broome, and of Tirlingham, in Kent.

CHARLES DIXWELL, esq. of Coton Hall, in the county of Warwick, *m.* Abigail, daughter of Henry Herdson, esq. of Stourton, in Lincolnshire, and had issue,

WILLIAM, his successor.
Edward.
Humphry.
BASIL.
Barbara.

He *d.* in 1591, and was *s.* by his eldest son,

WILLIAM DIXWELL, esq. of Coton Hall, who wedded Elizabeth, daughter of Roger Brent, esq. of Pillerton, in Warwickshire, and had several children. He grandson,

BRENT DIXWELL, esq. of Coton Hall, *m.* Anne, daughter of John Sandys, esq. of Loveline, in the county of Worcester, and had issue,

WILLIAM, his successor.
John, died aged twelve, 27th March, 1701.
Elizabeth.

He *d.* 10th June, 1690; his wife in 1692. He was *s.* by his elder son,

I. WILLIAM DIXWELL, esq. of Coton Hall, high sheriff of Warwickshire, in the 3rd of GEORGE I. created a BARONET, by that monarch, 11th June, 1716. He *m.* in 1712, Mary, daughter of Sir Roger Cave, bart. of Stanford,* but that lady died 11th February, 1712-13, in less than a year after her marriage, without issue, and Sir William remained afterwards a widower. He *d.* 14th January, 1757, when the BARONETCY became EXTINCT.

Arms—See DIXWELL of BROOME.

DORMER, OF LEE GRANGE.

CREATED 23rd July, 1661.

EXTINCT in 1726.

Lineage.

PETER DORMER, esq. of Lee Grange, Bucks, younger son of Geoffrey Dormer,† esq. of West Wycombe, by Ursula, his wife, daughter and heir of Bartholomew Collingridge, died 1st April, 1555, leaving by Agnes, his first wife, daughter of Thomas Cowper, esq. of Quainton, a son and successor,

GABRIEL DORMER, esq. of Lee Grange and Purston, who *m.* Bridget, daughter of Thomas Lovett, esq. of Astwell, and by her, who wedded, secondly, James Hawtrey, esq. of Chequers, in Bucks, had a son,

PETER DORMER, esq. of Lee Grange and Purston, who *m.* in 1659, Margaret, daughter of Thomas Fleetwood, esq. of the Vache, and dying 3rd December, 1583, was *s.* by his son,

SIR FLEETWOOD DORMER, of Lee Grange and Purston, who *m.* Mary, third daughter of Sir Euseby Isham, of Braunston, and widow of Edward Ayscough, esq. of Cottesbrooke, by whom he had issue,

I. JOHN, his heir.
II. Peter.
III. Fleetwood (Sir), of Arle Court, in Gloucestershire; emigrated to Virginia.
IV. Euseby.

I. Margaret.
II. Dorothy.
III. Mary, *m.* to William Shepherd, of Rollwright.

Sir Fleetwood *d.* 1st February, 1638-9, and was *s.* by his son,

* By his second wife, Mary, sister of the Right Hon. William Bromley, speaker of the House of Commons, and secretary of state, *temp. Queen* ANNE.

† From Geoffrey Dormer's eldest son, Sir W. Dormer, descends the BARON DORMER.

John Dormer, esq. of Lee Grange and Purston, barrister-at-law, who m. Katherine, daughter and heir of Thomas Woodward, esq. of Ripple, in Worcestershire, and had issue,

i. John (Sir), his heir.
ii. Robert, who inherited Lee Grange and Purston on the demise of his nephew, Sir William, and was M.P. for Bucks. He eventually became a judge of the Court of Common Pleas. He m. Mary, daughter and co-heir of Sir Richard Blake, of London, and dying 18th September, 1726, left four daughters, his co-heirs, viz.

Mary.
Catherine.
Elizabeth, m. to John, Lord Fortescue, of Credan.
Ricarda, m. to John Packhurst, esq. of Catesby.

iii. Fleetwood, barrister-at-law, M.P. for Chipping Wycomb.

i. Mary, m. to Sir John Busby, of Addington, in Bucks.
ii. Catherine, m. to John Packhurst, esq. of Catesby, M.P.

The eldest son,

I. John Dormer, esq. of Lee Grange and Purston, was created a Baronet in 1661. He m. Susanna, daughter and co-heir of Sir Richard Brawne, of Allscott, in Gloucestershire, and dying 7th November, 1675, left, with a daughter, Susanna, wife of Francis Sheldon, esq. of Abberton, in Worcestershire, a son and successor,

II. Sir William Dormer, of Lee Grange and Purston, at whose decease, unmarried, 9th March, 1725-6, aged fifty-seven, the Baronetcy became extinct.

Arms—Az. ten billets or, 4, 3, 2, and 1; on a chief of the second a demi-lion issuant sa.

DOUGLAS, OF CASTLE DOUGLAS.

Created 7th July, 1801.

Extinct in 1869.

Lineage.

William Douglas, esq. of Newton Stuart, or Newton Douglas, in Wigtonshire, married Grisel M'Kean, and had three sons, John, James, and William. The first,

John Douglas, esq. of Newton Douglas, married Mary, daughter of James Heron, of Pennington, and had five sons and a daughter, viz.

i. William, his heir.
ii. James, of Orchardton, in Kirkcudbright and of Gretna Green, in Dumfries, m. Elizabeth, daughter of William Douglas, esq. of Worcester, and had a son William, and three daughters, Sarah, Mary, and Matilda.
iii. John, died unm.
iv. George, of New York, who m. Margaret, daughter of Peter Corrie, esq. and had issue, George, William, Elizabeth, Margaret, Harriot, and Elizabeth.
v. Samuel, of Crae and Cannick, in Kirkcudbright, merchant, m. Elizabeth, daughter of William Stephenson, esq. of London, and had an only daughter, Elizabeth.

i. Margaret, m. to David M'Haffie, merchant.

The eldest son,

I. William Douglas, esq. of Castle Douglas, in Kirkcudbright, and of Newton Douglas, in Wigtonshire, was created a Baronet in 1801, but dying unm. in 1809, the title became extinct.

Arms—Az. on a chev. or, between two lions, counter rampant arg. baronially crowned of the second in chief, and in base, a lymphad with sails furled also of the second, three mullets of the field: on a chief per pale arg. and gold, on the dexter side a human heart ensigned with a regal crown, and on the sinister a thistle leaved and seeded, all ppr.

DOWNING, OF EAST HATLEY.

Created 1st July, 1663.

Extinct in 1764.

Lineage.

Arthur Downing, esq. of Lexham, in Norfolk, (son of Geoffrey Downing, by Elizabeth, daughter of Thomas Wingfield, esq. of Dunham Magna,) m. Susan, daughter (and co-heir with her sister Anne, wife of John Wingfield, esq. of Upton,) of Thomas Calybut, esq. of Castle Acre, in Norfolk, and had a son,

Calybut Downing, esq. of Shennington, in Gloucestershire, who m. Elizabeth, daughter of Robert Wingfield, esq. of Upton, in Northamptonshire, by Elizabeth, his wife, sister of William Cecil, Lord Burghley, treasurer to *Queen* Elizabeth, and was father of

Calybut Downing, who became a commoner in Oriel College, Oxford, in 1623, and subsequently entering into holy orders, was made rector of Hickford, in Buckinghamshire, and of West Ildesley, in Berkshire; which latter he afterwards exchanged for the living of Hackney, in Middlesex. He m. Margaret, daughter and co-heir of Robert Brett, D.D. and dying in 1644, left two sons,

i. George (Sir), his heir.
ii. Henry, whose son Col. Adam Downing, was a distinguished officer in *King* William III.'s army in Ireland. His descendant and representative, is the present George Alexander Fullerton, esq. of Westwood, in Hampshire, and of Ballintoy Castle, in Ireland. (See Burke's *Commoners*, vol. iv. p. 298.)

The elder son,

I. Sir George Downing, of East Hatley, in Cambridgeshire, was created a Baronet, 1st July, 1663. This distinguished person, who acted a prominent part in the eventful period in which he lived, was sent, during the Protectorate, ambassador to the States General of Holland. He sat for several years in parliament; and after the Restoration, became secretary of the treasury, teller of the exchequer, and one of his majesty's commissioners of customs. With Sir George Downing, when secretary of the treasury, originated the important act of the 17 CHARLES II. "To make all the money that was to be raised by this bill to be applied only to those ends to which it was given, which was the carrying on of the war, and to no other purpose whatsoever, or by what authority soever." This important innovation, and one which was the origin of estimates being laid before the House of Commons, was the more necessary in that reign, as it was well known the public service was much injured by the application of money to the purposes of the pleasures of the court, instead of the interests and defence of the country. Sir George Downing was opposed violently by Lord Clarendon, who was such a slave to his narrow prepossessions, that he would rather see the dissolute excesses he abhorred derive nourishment from that revenue which had been allotted to maintain the national honour, and which, by its deficiencies thus aggravated, had caused the navy to be laid up, and the coasts to be left defenceless, than suffer them to be restrained by the only power to which thoughtless luxury would submit. In 1670, Sir George Downing proceeded again as ambassador to Holland, on the recall of Sir W. Temple, and remained there until 1672, when the war again broke out. He *m.* a lady greatly distinguished for beauty, Frances, fourth daughter of Sir William Howard, knt. of Naworth Castle, in Cumberland, and sister to the first Earl of Carlisle, and dying in 1684, left issue,

I. GEORGE (Sir), his heir.
II. William *d. s. p.*
III. Charles, comptroller of the customs, who *m.* Sarah, daughter and heir of Sir Thomas Garrard, bart. and *d.* 15th April, 1740, leaving a son,
    JACOB (Sir), who *s.* as fourth baronet.
I. Frances, *m.* to John Cotton, esq. son and heir of Sir John Cotton, bart.
II. Philadelphia, *m.* to Sir Henry Pickering, bart. of Whaddon.
III. Lucy, *m.* to Sir Richard Bulkeley, bart. of Old Baron.
IV. Mary, *m.* to Thomas Barnardiston, esq. of Bury.
V. Anne.

His eldest son,

II. SIR GEORGE DOWNING, of East Hatley, one of the tellers of the exchequer *temp.* JAMES II. *m.* Catherine, eldest daughter of James, Earl of Salisbury, by Margaret his wife, daughter of John, Earl of Rutland, and had an only son,

III. SIR GEORGE DOWNING, of East Hatley, knight of the bath, and **Founder of Downing College**, Cambridge. He *m.* Miss Forester, daughter of Sir William Forester, knt. of Watling-street, in Shropshire, and died *s. p.* in 1749. By a will dated in 1717, he devised all his property to his cousin and heir, SIR JACOB DOWNING; and in case that gentleman's line failed, he directed the foundation of a College at Cambridge, which latter event, after much litigation, took place in 1800. Sir George represented Dunwich in parliament. His aforesaid cousin and heir,

IV. SIR JACOB DOWNING *m.* a daughter of — Price, esq. but died without issue in 1764, when the BARONETCY became EXTINCT. Sir Jacob's widow wedded, secondly, Admiral Sir George Bowyer, bart.

Arms—Barry of eight arg. and vert, over all a gryphon rampant or.

DOYLE, OF THE ISLAND OF GUERNSEY.

CREATED 29th Oct. 1825.

EXTINCT 8th Aug. 1834.

Lineage.

CHARLES DOYLE, esq. of Bramblestown, in the county of Kilkenny, son of William Doyle, esq. of [illegible] in Carlow-shire, married Elizabeth, daughter of the Rev. Nicholas Milley, of Johnville, and dying in 17[illegible] left issue,

William, barrister-at-law, king's counsel, and master in chancery, in Ireland, *m.* twice, and had issue.
Charles, R.N.
Nicholas-Milley, in holy orders, had two sons, Charles, and John-Milley (Sir), lieutenant-col. in the army, late M.P. for the county of Carlow.
JOHN, of whom presently.
Welbore-Ellis, a major-general in the army, father of the present SIR FRANCIS HASTINGS DOYLE, bart.

Catherine, *m.* to the Rev. Thomas Burke.

The fourth son,

I. SIR JOHN DOYLE, G.C.B. and K.C. a general in the army, colonel of the 87th regiment, and governor of Charlemont, was created a BARONET in 182[illegible] [illegible] dying unmarried, 8th August, 1834, the title became EXTINCT.

Arms—Arg. three stags' heads erased gu. within a bordure compony or and az. on a canton az. a palm branch in bend sinister under it the word "Egypt."

D'OYLEY, OF CHISELHAMPTON.

CREATED 7th July, 1666.

EXTINCT ....

Lineage.

The founder of the family of D'OYLEY, of Chiselhampton, in the county of Oxford, came into England at the time of the Norman Conquest, and the pedigree states that the D'Oylys were Lords of Oigli, or [illegible] in Normandy, long before that event.

ROBERT D'OYLY, eldest son of the Lord de [illegible] for his good services at Hastings, was rewarded by [illegible] victorious chief with two baronies, and many [illegible] manors and lordships in England, but principally [illegible] in Oxfordshire, as appears by Domesday-Book and the abbey books of Osenay, by Oxford, and of Missenden, in Bucks. Of both which abbies the family were founders, *temp.* HENRY I. and were also great benefactors to the abbies of Abbington, Eynsham, Godston, and Thame, in England, as well as to several others in France. The family likewise built the castle and bridge at Oxford, A.D. 1071, which was then their ancient seat, and new made the walls about the same city. Robert D'Oyly was king's constable and feudal Baron of Hokenorton in Oxfordshire. He *m.* Algitha, daughter and heir of Wigotus, a noble Saxon, Lord of Wallingford, by whom he had an only daughter and heir,

MAUD D'OYLY, Lady of Wallingford, who inheriting the spirit of her ancestors, valiantly defended the *Empress* MAUD in her castle of Walingford. She *m.* first, Miles Crispin, and secondly, Brian Fitz Count, Lord of Bergavenny.

Robert and his wife Algitha, were buried in the abbey of Abington, to which, and St. Mary's Church there, they were bountiful benefactors. He was *s.* in the barony of Hocknorton by his brother,

NIGELL D'OYLY, who was king's constable, *temp.* WILLIAM *Rufus.* This Nigell came in at the Conquest with his two brothers, Robert, whom he inherited from, and GILBERT D'OYLY who had grants of lands also in Oxfordshire. He (Nigell) *m.* the Lady Agnes, and had two sons; Foulk, the younger, was buried at [illegible]ham, A.D. 1126. The elder,

ROBERT D'OYLY, succeeded his father as king's constable, and in the barony of Hocknorton. He *m.* Editha, daughter of Fory, Lord of Greystock, and had two sons and a daughter, viz.

HENRY, his successor.
GILBERT, ancestor of the D'OYLEYS of CHISELHAMPTON.

Editha, *m.* to Gilbert Basset, of Bicester, in Oxfordshire.

This Robert built the Abbey of Missenden, and richly endowed it. He likewise founded the celebrated Abbey of Osney, at the request of his wife, *anno* 1129, and gave lands to it in the 29th HENRY I. He was *s.* by his elder son,

HENRY D'OYLY, Baron of Hokenorton, and king's constable. He *m.* Margaret, daughter of Humphry Bohun, Earl of Hereford, and had issue,

HENRY, } successively Lord of Hokenorton.
ROBERT, }

MARGERY, heir to her brothers.
Maud, *m.* to Maurice de Gaunt.
Joan, *m.* to Simon Fitzwalter, Lord of Daventry.

He was *s.* by his elder son,

HENRY D'OYLY, Baron of Hokenorton, and king's constable. This feudal lord had two wives, but leaving no surviving issue, was *s.* at his decease (which occurred in Austria, in his return from Jerusalem, whither he had accompanied *King* RICHARD I.), by his brother,

ROBERT D'OYLY, Baron of Hokenorton, and king's constable, at whose decease, issueless, the estates devolved upon his eldest sister,

MARGERY D'OYLY, who *m.* Henry de Newburgh, the Earl of Warwick, and was mother of Thomas, the 6th Earl. Thus terminated the male line of the elder branch of the family of D'Oyly, but it was continued (without however the honors and estate) through Gilbert D'Oyly's (the younger brother of the first feudal [illegible]) eldest son,

ROBERT D'OYLY, who was *s.* by his son,

JOHN D'OYLY, of Wrembam, father of

ROGER D'OYLY who removed to his seat of Pus-hall, or Pushil, held under the crown, by the tenure of presenting yearly to the king a table cloth of three shillings price, or three shillings for all services. He was *s.* by his eldest son,

ROGER D'OYLY, father of

ROBERT D'OYLY, who left a son and heir,

RICHARD D'OYLY, father of

THOMAS D'OYLY, who purchased the estate of Junden in 1364. He *m.* Alicia, daughter of Atlude, of Woburn, and was *s.* by his son,

WILLIAM D'OYLY, who *m.* Isabella, daughter of — More, cousin and next heir of the Lady Cheyney, of Hinton, and had issue,

RICHARD, his successor, a learned and mortified priest.

Margaret, *m.* to John Warfield.
Isabella, *m.* to Thomas Wickham, of Swalcliffe.

He *d.* in 1424, and was *s.* by his son,

RICHARD D'OYLY, who *d.* in 1435, and was *s.* by his cousin,

WILLIAM D'OYLY, who *d.* in 1449, leaving a son and heir,

JOHN D'OYLY, a famous soldier in France. He bought Southland, and marrying Isabella, daughter and co-heir of Richard More, of Burgfield, Berks, was *s.* by his son,

THOMAS D'OYLY, who was seated at Marlow, but purchased, with his son John, CHISELHAMPTON, which continued afterwards the designation of the family. He *m.* first, Alice Curson, an heiress, and secondly, another Alice, daughter of — Hall, of Oxenbridge, in Wiltshire, and widow of Sir William Cotesmore, by her he had no issue, but by his first wife, left several sons and daughters. The eldest son and heir,

JOHN D'OYLY, esq. of Chiselhampton, in the county of Oxford, *m.* Frances, sister and co-heir of Sir Christopher Edmonds, knt. (maid of honour to *Queen* ELIZABETH) and had a numerous family. He was *s.* by his eldest son,

SIR ROBERT D'OYLY, knt. "a great courtier in the reign of *Queen* ELIZABETH," who *m.* Elizabeth, daughter of the lord keeper, Sir Nicholas Bacon, and was killed at the black assises, at Oxford, by the stench of the prisoners, together with many other persons of distinction, *anno* 1577. He *d. s. p.* and was *s.* by his brother,

JOHN D'OYLY, esq. who *m.* Ursula, sister of Sir Anthony Cope, bart. of Hanwell, and had issue,

COPE (Sir), his successor.

Margery, *m.* to George Barston, esq.
Elizabeth, *m.* first in 1597, to Francis Harvey, esq. secondly, to Sir Robert Browne, bart. and thirdly, to Sir Guy Palmes, knt.
Dorothy, *m.* in 1598, to Francis Quarles, esq. of Rumford, in Essex.
Mary, *m.* to Henry Howton, esq. of Cotharp.
Priscilla, bapt. 11th August, 1594, *m.* to Edward Goddard, esq. of Englesham, younger brother of Thomas Goddard, esq. of Swindon, in Wiltshire.

He was *s.* at his decease by his son,

SIR COPE D'OYLY, who is characterised as "a noble and renowned knight, at that time the honour of this ancient and honourable house." He *m.* Martha, daughter, of James Quarles, esq. of Rumford, and had a numerous family. Sir Cope died 4th August, 1633.* The eldest son and heir,

JOHN D'OYLY, esq. m. Mary, daughter and co-heir of Sir John Shirley, knt. of Isfield, in Sussex, and had two sons, viz.

- JOHN, his successor.
- Thomas, m. his cousin, Dorothy, daughter of John Michel, esq. of Kingston Russell, which lady m. secondly, the Rev. John Owen, D.D.

He was s. at his decease by his elder son,

I. JOHN D'OYLY, esq. of Chiselhampton, in the county of Oxford, who was created a BARONET by *King* CHARLES II. 7th July, 1666. He m. Margaret, daughter and co-heir of Sir Richard Cholmeley, knight-banneret, of Whitby Abbey, in the county of York, and had seven sons and two daughters, viz.

- Cholmeley, who *d. s. p.*
- JOHN, his heir.
- Richard, capt. of marines, killed scaling the walls of Gibraltar, *d. s. p.*
- Thomas, an officer in the Customs, m. Mrs. Fortescue, widow of Hugh Fortescue, esq. uncle of the Lord Clinton.
- Robert, col. in the army, lieut.-governor of the Tower, m. Miss Freman, sister of Ralph Freman, esq. of Hamels, M.P. for Hertfordshire.
- Shirley, in holy orders, *d. s. p.*
- Hugh, an officer, in the Customs.
- ———, m. to Samuel Wotton, esq. of Ingleborne, in Devon.
- Elizabeth, m. to the Honourable George Mordaunt.

Sir John D'Oyly, who was M.P. for Woodstock, at the revolution, and captain of the county troop, *d.* in 1709, and was *s.* by his eldest surviving son,

II. SIR JOHN D'OYLY, bart. who m. first, Susanna, daughter of Sir Thomas Put, bart. of Comb, in Devonshire, and by her had,

- THOMAS, his heir.
- JOHN, fellow of Merton College, Oxford, who s. as fourth baronet.
- Shirley.
- WILLIAM, who *s.* as fifth baronet.
- Margaret.
- Ursula, m. to Thomas Young, esq. of Newington, in Oxfordshire, and died in January, 1701, leaving a son and daughter.
- Cholmeley, m. to William James, esq. of Nass, in Gloucestershire, and has two sons and a daughter.

He wedded, secondly, Rebecca, daughter and co-heir of Goddard Carter, esq. of Alvescot, in the county of Oxford, but by that lady had no issue. He died about the year 1746, and was *s.* by his eldest son,

III. SIR THOMAS D'OYLEY, who m. Mary, daughter of Samuel Wotton, esq. of Engleborne, in the county of Devon, and had two daughters, viz.

- Susanna, m. in 1767, to Dr. William Newcome, bishop of Dromore.
- Rebecca, died in infancy.

Sir Thomas died 6th February, 1759, and was s. by his brother,

IV. SIR JOHN D'OYLY, rector of Cuxham, in Oxfordshire, who died unmarried, November, 1773, and was *s.* by his brother,

V. SIR WILLIAM D'OYLY, who m. Miss Meah, and with him the BARONETCY is stated to have become EXTINCT, but that fact is very doubtful.

Arms—Or, two bendlets az.

---

* He was buried at —— in Oxfordshire, with the following inscription to himself and his wife:

To the Glorious Memorie of that Noble knt. Sir Cope D'Oyly,
late Deputy Lieut. of Oxfordshire, and Justice of Oyer and Terminer.
Heir of the
Antient and famous Family of the D'Oyly's, of the same Countie, Founders
of the noble Abbies of Oseney and Missenden, &c.
Who put on Immortality the 4th of August, in the year of our Redemption
1633

Ask not who is buried here
Go ask the Commons, ask the Shire,
Go ask the Church, They'll tell thee who,
As well as blubber'd Eyes can do;
Go ask the Heralds, ask the Poor,
Thine Ears shall hear enough to ask no more.
Then if thine Eye bedew this sacred Urn,
Each drop a Pearl will turn
To adorn his Tomb, or if thou canst not vent,
Thou bringst more Marble to his Monument.

Sacred to the Pious Memory of that rare example of undistained Virtue,
Martha,
Wife of the said Sir Cope D'Oyly, knt. eldest daughter of James Quarles, of
Romford, Esq; who receiv'd the Crown of Glory, in the year of Grace,
1618

Wouldst thou, (Reader,) draw to life
The perfect copy of a Wife,
Read on, and then redeem from shame,
That lost, that honorable Name,
This Dust was once in Spirit a Jael,
Rebecca in Grace, in Heart an Abigail,
In Works a Dorcas, to the Church a Hannah,
And to her Spouse, Susanna.
Prudently simple, providently warie,
To the World a Martha, and to Heaven, a Marie.

They had { 5 Sons & 5 Daughters } Sons { John, James, Robert, Charles, Francis } Daughters { Martha, Maria, Dorothia, Elisa, Joanna

Dorothia married Hubertus Arnold, of Armswel, Esq.
Joanna, the youngest, John Michel, of Kingston-Russel, Esq. } both of Dorsetshire.

D'OYLY, OF KANDY.

CREATED 29th Aug. 1821.  EXTINCT 25th May, 1824.

Lineage.

THOMAS D'OYLY, D. D. (descended from Edward D'Oyly, esq. of Littlemarsh, in the parish of Stone, Bucks,) archdeacon of Lewes, in Sussex, chancellor of the diocese of Chichester, and prebendary of Ely, *m.* 6th February, 1744, Henrietta-Maria, second daughter of Robert Godfrey, esq. of London, (by Elizabeth, sister of Matthias Mawson, bishop of Ely). They both *d.* on the same day, 27th January, 1770, leaving issue three sons,

- I. MATTHIAS, of whom hereafter.
- II. Thomas, vicar of Walton-upon-Thames, and chaplain in ordinary to the king, *b.* 2nd April, 1745, *m.* March, 1772, Susanna, daughter of Barham Rushbrooke, esq. of Westowe, county of Suffolk, and *d.* October, 1816, without issue.
- III. Francis, lieut.-gen. and col. of the 67th foot, *m.* Anne, daughter of Hugh Thomas, D. D. dean of Ely, and master of Christ's College, Cambridge, and *d.* in 1803, without issue.

The eldest son,

REV. MATTHIAS D'OYLY, rector of Uckfield, in Sussex, archdeacon of Lewes, and prebendary of Ely, *b.* 3rd November, 1743, *m.* May, 1770, Mary, daughter of George Poughfer, esq. of Leicester, and *d.* November, 1816, having had issue,

- I. Thomas, D.C.L. and sergeant-at-law, *b.* 16th November, 1772, *m.* 4th January, 1820, Elizabeth, daughter of the Rev. Nicholas Simons, of Canterbury, and has one son, Thomas.
- II. JOHN, of whom presently.
- III. Francis (Sir), K.C.B. lieut.-col. in the 1st guards, slain at Waterloo, unm.
- IV. George, D.D. rector of Lambeth and of Sundridge, *b.* 31st October, 1778, *m.* 9th August, 1813, Maria-Frances, daughter of William Bruene, esq. of London, and has issue,
  - Francis, *b.* 27th November, 1815.
  - George-Henry, *b.* 27th June, 1817.
  - Henry-Thomas, *b.* 3rd April, 1819.
  - Charles-John, *b.* 31st July, 1820.
- V. Henry, capt. in the 1st guards, *b.* 21st April, 1780.
- I. Henrietta, *d.* unm. 1804.

The second son,

SIR JOHN D'OYLY, official resident at Kandy, in the island of Ceylon, *b.* 6th June, 1774, was created a BARONET in 1821, but dying unm. in three years after, the title became EXTINCT.

Arms—Or, two fleurs-de-lis in bend, sable, between as many bendlets, azure.

DRAKE, OF ASHE.

CREATED 31st Aug. 1660.  EXTINCT 21st Oct. 1733.

Lineage.

Of the old Devonshire house of Drake,* was

JOHN DRAKE, esq. who married in the time of HENRY V. Christiana, daughter and heir of John Billet, esq. of Ashe, in the county of Devon, and thereby that estate, situated in the parish of Musberry, accrued to the family, and eventually became the place of their designation, although their more usual residence was at Mount Drake, a mansion built by them in the same parish. His son and heir,

JOHN DRAKE, esq. of Otterton, *m.* Christiana, daughter and heiress of John Antage, and had a son and heir,

JOHN DRAKE, esq. of Otterton, in Devonshire, who *m.* the daughter of Crewse, of Crewse-Morchard, in the same county, and had a son and heir,

JOHN DRAKE, esq. of Otterton, who *m.* Agnes, daughter of John Kelloway, esq. and was *s.* by his son,

JOHN DRAKE, esq. of Exmouth, who *m.* Margaret, daughter of John Cole, of Rill, near that place, and had three sons and a daughter, viz.

- JOHN, his successor.
- John.
- Gilbert,† from whom the Drakes of Spratshays, in the parish of Littleham, Devon, a cadet, whereof was
  - Robert Drake, who had his education first at Oxford, and was afterwards of the Inner Temple; he obtained a considerable estate at Dale-Ditch, in the parish of East Budleigh, the greater part of which he devoted at his death, about the year 1628, to pious uses.
- Agnes, *m.* to William Pole, esq. of Shute.

He was *s.* at his decease by his eldest son,

JOHN DRAKE, esq. of Ashe, who *m.* Anne, daughter of Roger Grenville, esq. of Stowe, in Cornwall, and left at his decease, 4th October, 1558,

- BERNARD (Sir), his successor.
- Robert, of Wiscomb, in the parish of Southlegh, Devon, *m.* Elizabeth, daughter, of Humphrey Prideaux, of Thewborough, by whom, with other issue, he had Robert and Henry, the former a colonel in the Netherlands, of great esteem with the Prince of Orange and the States General, and the latter a captain in the army, both killed in the prime of life in the defence of Ostend.
- Richard, ancestor of the DRAKES of Shardeloes.

The eldest son and heir,

SIR BERNARD DRAKE, knt. of Mount Drake and Ashe,

---

* "That curious and ingenious antiquary, Sir William Pole, knt. of Shute, in his manuscripts, makes mention of Peter le Drak, that held Hernford cum Terra de la Wood, in Dertington, at half a knight's fee, 31 EDWARD I. and also to that of others of this family, who were possessed of several lands in Devonshire."

A branch of the Drakes of Ashe, settled at an early period in Ireland, and became seated at Drakerath, in the county of Meath. The present representative is CHRISTOPHER DRAKE, esq. of Roristown. (See BURKE's *Commoners*, vol. iv. p. 192.)

† From this Gilbert it is probable that the Drakes of Bystock, near Exmouth, descend.

was a very distinguished p[illegible] and "employed in several great offices at se[illegible]ing much in favour with *Queen* ELIZABETH, who conferred the honour of knighthood upon him in 1585. He *m.* Gertrude, daughter of Bartholomew Fortescue, esq. of Filleigh, in Devonshire, and dying in 1585, was *s.* by his eldest son,

JOHN DRAKE,* esq. of Mount Drake and Ashe, who *m.* Dorothy, daughter of William Button, esq. of Alton, Wilts, and dying in 1628, was *s.* by his son,

SIR JOHN DRAKE, knt. of Ashe. This gentleman *m.* Helena, second daughter of Sir John Butler, bart. created BARON BUTLER, *of Bramfield*, and co-heir of her brother William, second and last Lord Butler, of Bramfield, and had issue,

- JOHN, his heir.
- George, *d.* unm. in 1664.
- Thomas, who *d.* in Ireland in 1659.
- Henry.
- Dorothy, *m.* to William Yardley, esq.
- Mary, *d.* unm.
- Eleanora, *m.* to John Briscoe, esq. of Cumberland.
- Elizabeth, *m.* to Sir Winston Churchill, knt. of Standish, in Gloucestershire, and was mother of the great DUKE OF MARLBOROUGH.
- Gertrude, *d.* unm.
- Ivanna, *d.* unm.
- Jane, *m.* to William Yonge, esq. of Castleton, in Dorsetshire.
- Anne, *m.* to Richard Strode, esq. of Chalmington, Dorsetshire.

He *d.* in 1636, and was *s.* by his eldest son,

I. SIR JOHN DRAKE, knt. of Ashe, who was created a BARONET by *King* CHARLES II. 31st August, 1660. He *m.* first, Jane, daughter of Sir John Yonge, bart. of Culliton and Slutcomb, both in Devon, and by her had two sons,

- JOHN, his successor.
- Walter, *d.* unm. in 1674.
- Elizabeth, *m.* to Sir John Briscoe, knt. of Boughton, Northamptonshire, but *d. s. p.* in 1694.

He wedded, secondly, Dionysia, daughter of Sir Richard Strode, knt. of Newenham, in the county of Devon, and by that lady (who *d.* in 1697, and was buried at Axminster) [illegible]d

- BERNARD, heir to [illegible] half-brother.
- George.
- WILLIAM, heir to B[illegible]d in the baronetcy and his half-sister, El[illegible] in the estates.

Sir John *d.* 1669, and [illegible] his eldest son.

II. SIR JOHN DRAKE[illegible]of Ashe, who rebuilt the mansion house there, w[illegible] had been burnt down and demolished by the rebe[illegible] in the civil wars. He *d.* unmarried in 1683, and was buried at Musberry, whereupon ELIZABETH, his sister, became sole heir, and settled the estates upon her youngest half-brother, WILLIAM. Sir John was *s.* in the baronetcy by his brother of the half-blood.

III. SIR BERNARD DRAKE, bart. who *m.* Elizabeth, daughter of George Prestwood, esq. of Butterford in Devon, [illegible]elict of Hugh Stowell, esq. of Perrybere, and [illegible]ly daughter,

- E[illegible]TH, *m.* to Thomas Tothill, esq. of Bagtor.

He was *s.* at his decease by his only surviving brother,

IV. SIR WILLIAM DRAKE, bart. of Ashe, who had previously received the honour of knighthood from *King* JAMES II. This gentleman *m.* first, Judith, daughter and co-heir of William Eveleigh, esq. of Tallaton, near Ottery St. Mary, in the county of Devon, and by that lady had two sons and th[illegible] daughters, viz.

- JOHN, } WILLIAM, } 5th and 6th Baronets.
- ELIZABETH, *m.* to William Walrond, esq. of Bo[illegible] in Devon,† and was mother of
  - William Walrond, esq. of Bovey, who *m.* [illegible]rah, sister and heir of William Oke, e[illegible] Axmouth, and dying in 1762, left an [illegible] surviving child,
    - JUDITH-MARIA-WALROND, of Bovey, w[illegible] *m.* 22nd July, 1778, John Rolle, esq. Stevenstone, created in 1796, Lord R[illegible]. She *d. s. p.* 1st October, 1820.
- Judith, *d.* an infant.
- ANNE, *m.* to Thomas Prestwood, esq. of Butterford, in Devon.

He wedded, secondly, a daughter of Sir Peter Prideaux, bart. of Netherton, in Devon, but had n[illegible] issue. He was *s.* at his decease by his elder son.

V. SIR JOHN DRAKE, bart. who dying unm. 6th September, 1724, was *s.* by his brother,

VI. SIR WILLIAM DRAKE, bart. who *m.* in 1726, [illegible] daughter of William-Peere Williams, esq. M. P. [illegible] Bishops Castle, in Shropshire, but died *s. p.* 21st [illegible]ber, 1733, when the BARONETCY became EXTINCT. [illegible] manor of Musbury was purchased by the [illegible] Tucker, from Capt. William Peer Williams, [illegible] of Lady Drake. The mansion of Ash, now [illegible] as a farm house, is celebrated as the birth pla[illegible] of JOHN, DUKE OF MARLBOROUGH.

Arms—Arg. a wivern with wings displayed gu.

DRAKE, OF SHARDELOES.

CREATED [illegible] July, 1641.

EXTINCT in 16[illegible]

Lineage.

This was a branch of the DRAKES of Ashe.

JOHN DRAKE, esq. of Ashe, in the county of Devon, *m.* Anne, daughter of Roger Grenville, esq. of S[illegible] in Cornwall, and left, at his decease in 1558,

- BERNARD (Sir), from whom the baronets of Ashe.
- Robert, of Wiscomb, in Devon.
- RICHARD.

The youngest son,

RICHARD DRAKE, esq. one of the equerries to Queen ELIZABETH, *m.* Ursula, daughter of Sir William [illegible]ford, knt. and dying 11th July, 1603, was *s.* by his son,

FRANCIS DRAKE, esq. of Esher, one of the gentlemen of the privy chamber in ordinary, who wedded Joan, daughter of William Tothill, esq. of Shardeloes, Bucks, and had issue,

- WILLIAM, his heir.
- John, *d.* unm. in 1622.

* From William Drake, a [illegible]r son of this John Drake, descended the Drak[illegible]rbury, whose representative in 1822, was FRANCIS [illegible]TIO NELSON DRAKE, esq. of Wells.

† Great grandson of JAMES WA[illegible] Devonshire, through his second so[illegible] Bovey. *Refer to* BURKE'S Comm[illegible] 352.

Francis, of Walton-on-Thames, m. first, Elizabeth, daughter of Sir Alexander Denton, and secondly, Dorothy, daughter of Sir William Spring, bart. of Pakenham Hall, in Suffolk; by the latter he had a son,

WILLIAM (Sir), who inherited Shardeloes from his uncle.

Joan.

Mr. Drake d. 17th March, 1633, and was s. by his eldest son,

I. WILLIAM DRAKE, esq. of Shardeloes, in the county of Buckingham, b. in 1606. This gentleman, who was chirographer to the Court of Common Pleas, was created a BARONET 17th July, 1641. He d. unm. in 1669, when the BARONETCY became EXTINCT, and the estates devolved upon his nephew, SIR WILLIAM DRAKE, knt. ancestor of the present THOMAS TYRWHITT DRAKE, esq. of Shardeloes. (Refer to BURKE's *Commoners*, vol. i. p. 388.)

Arms—Arg. a wivern, wings displayed and tail nowed, gu.

DRAKE, OF PROSPECT.

CREATED 28th May, 1782. EXTINCT 19th Nov. 1789.

Lineage.

This was a branch of the family founded by the celebrated circumnavigator Admiral SIR FRANCIS DRAKE, so renowned in the *time* of ELIZABETH.

SIR FRANCIS DRAKE, bart. of Buckland, in the county of Devon, nephew and godson of the immortal seaman, married for his second wife, Joan, daughter of Sir William Strode, knt. and was s. by his elder son,

SIR FRANCIS DRAKE, bart. who dying s. p. was s. by his nephew,

SIR FRANCIS DRAKE, bart. M.P. for Tavistock, *temp.* CHARLES II. who was s. by his only son (by his third wife, a daughter of lord chief justice, Sir Henry Pollexfen),

SIR FRANCIS HENRY DRAKE, bart. M. P. for Tavistock, who m. Anne, daughter of Samuel Heathcote, esq. of Hursley, and had three sons and a daughter,* of whom, the youngest son,

I. FRANCIS SAMUEL DRAKE, esq. a distinguished seaman, was created a BARONET 12th April, 1782, for the gallant services he had rendered as rear-admiral, in the glorious victory achieved by admiral Rodney, in the West Indies. Sir Francis married first, Miss Elizabeth Hayman, of Kent, and secondly, Miss Onslow, daughter of George Onslow, esq. M. P. but died s. p. 19th November, 1789, when the BARONETCY became EXTINCT.

Arms—Sa. a fess wavy between the two pole stars, arctic and antarctic, arg.

DRAPER, OF SUNNINGHILL.

CREATED 9th June, 1660.—EXTINCT in Dec. 1703.

Lineage.

I. SIR THOMAS DRAPER, of Sunninghill Park, in the county of Berks, who was created a BARONET in 1660, married an heiress of the family of Carey, of Sunning Hill, but having no son, the title EXPIRED with himself in 1703. His grandson, THOMAS DRAPER BARBER, esq. eventually inherited Sunninghill, and sold it in 1769, to Jeremiah Crutchley, esq.

DRURY, OF RIDDLESWORTH.

CREATED 7th May, 1627. EXTINCT 27th April, 1712.

Lineage.

SIR ROBERT DRURY, of Egerley, Bucks, younger son of Sir Robert Drury, knt. of Hawsted, in Suffolk, died about 1575, leaving by Elizabeth, his wife, only daughter and heir of Edmund Brudenell, esq. four sons and four daughters, viz.

I. ROBERT, of Egerly, who m. Anne Bourman, and had a son, Sir Henry Drury, knt. of Egerly, and three daughters, of whom the eldest, Elisabeth, married John Banks, of Lower Shelford, Cambridgeshire.

II. WILLIAM (Sir), lord justice and governor of Ireland, m. Margaret, daughter of Thomas, Lord Wentworth, and widow of John, Lord Williams, of Thame, and dying in Dublin in 1579, left two daughters,

Jane, m. to Richard Chetwood, esq. of Oxfordshire.

Anne, m. to Robert Hartwell, esq. of Northamptonshire.

III. DRUE (Sir), of whom presently.

IV. Edmund, m. and had issue.

I. Anne, m. to Robert Woodliese, of Peterley, Bucks.

II. Margaret, m. to Henry Trenchard, esq.

III. Lucy, m. to Robert Tesh, gent.

IV. Elizabeth, m. to Rowland Hinde, of Hedsworth, Bucks.

The third son,

SIR DRUE DRURY, of Lyndsted, gentleman usher of the privy chamber to *Queen* ELIZABETH, and one of the keepers of Queen Mary, of Scotland; married first, Elizabeth,† daughter of Sir Philip Calthorpe, by Amata Boleyn, his wife, aunt to Queen Anne Boleyn, and secondly, Catherine, only daughter and heir of William Finch, esq. of Lynsted, in Kent; by the latter, he had issue,

---

* ANNE-POLLEXFEN DRAKE, who m. the celebrated defender of Gibraltar, GENERAL ELLIOT, created in 1787, LORD HEATHFIELD, now represented by SIR THOMAS-TRAYTON FULLER-ELLIOT-DRAKE, baronet. (*Refer to* BURKE's *Peerage and Baronetage*.)

† She had been married twice previously, first to Sir Henry Parker, K. B. eldest son of Henry, Lord Morley, and secondly, to Sir William Woodhouse.

I. Drue, his heir.

I. Elizabeth, *m.* to Sir Thomas Wingfield, of Letheringham.

II. Frances, *m.* to Sir Robert Botiler, of Wotton, Herts.

III. Anne, *m.* to Sir John Deane, of Maplested, Essex.

Sir Drue Drury, died in 1617, aged ninety-nine, and was *s.* by his son,

I. DRUE DRURY, esq. of Riddlesworth, in Norfolk, *b.* in 1588, who was created a BARONET in 1627. He *m.* Anne, daughter of Edward Wallgrave, esq. of Canfield, in Essex, and dying in 1632, was *s.* by his son,

II. SIR DRUE DRURY, who *m.* Susan, daughter of Isaac Jones, esq. of London, and had issue,

ROBERT, his heir.

Drue, died *s. p.*

DIANA, *m.* to Sir William Wake, bart. and from this marriage descends the present

SIR WILLIAM WAKE, bart. who inherits Riddlesworth Hall from the DRURYS.

The elder son,

III. SIR ROBERT DRURY, of Riddlesworth, married first, Elizabeth, daughter and heir of Edward Dunstan, of Waldingfield, Suffolk; secondly, Eleanor, daughter of Samuel Harsnet, esq. of Great Fransham, relict of William Marsham, esq. of Stratton, in Norfolk; and thirdly, Diana, daughter of George Vilet, of Pinkney Hall, but died *s. p.* 27th April, 1712, aged seventy-eight, when the BARONETCY became EXTINCT.

Arms—Arg. on a chief vert, a tau between two mullets pierced or.

DRURY, OF OVERSTONE.

CREATED 16th Feb. 1739.—EXTINCT 19th Jan. 1759.

Lineage.

The family which derived its surname from a place in the Duchy of Normandy, was established in England at the Conquest.

JOHN DE DRURY, son and heir of the Norman, settled at Thurston, in Suffolk, and bore for arms, "*Argent, on a chief vert, two mullets pierced or.*" He left a son,

JOHN DE DRURY, of Thurston, father of

HENRY DE DRURY, of Thurston, whose son,

JOHN DRURY, of Thurston, was father of

HENRY DRURY, of Thurston, who *m.* Havise, daughter of Richard Green, of Barkeway, and had three sons and two daughters,

JOHN, his heir.

Nigell, who was sheriff of London, 1 EDWARD I.

Roger, parson of Bradfield, in Suffolk.

Maud, *d.* unm.

Alice, *m.* to William Sweeting, esq. of Suffolk.

The eldest son and heir,

JOHN DRURY, esq. of Thurston, living *temp.* EDWARD I. *m.* Amable, daughter of Thomas Newton, and had issue, Roger, parson of Beckerton, and his heir,

NICHOLAS DRURY, esq. of Thurston. This gentleman *m.* Joane, daughter and heir of Sir Simon Saxham, knt.† by whom he had three sons, viz.

‡ ROGER (Sir), who *m.* Margery, daughter and sole heir of Sir Thomas Naunton, of Rougham, and left at his decease, in 1405, a son and [illegible]

WILLIAM (Sir), who *m.* Katherine, daughter of Sir Ottes Swynford,‖ and was ancestor of the DRURYS of Rougham.

‡ NICHOLAS, *m.* Joane, daughter of Thomas Heath, of Mildenhead, in Suffolk, and went with John of Gaunt into Spain, and thence to the Holy Land, at which time he added the golden [illegible] to his arms, which his descendants afterwards always bore.

‡ JOHN, of Wetherden, in Suffolk.

In the visitation of Cambridgeshire and Huntingdonshire, *Anno* 1684, the descents of the branch before us was entered, and thence the details following are derived.

RICHARD DRURY, citizen of London, of the Drurys of Rougham, died about the year 1606, aged forty-[illegible]. He *m.* Catherine, daughter of William Beswick, of Spelmonden and Horsmonden, in Kent, and had issue.

WILLIAM, his heir.

Etheldred, *m.* to Robert Corbet, citizen of London.

Rachel, *m*, to — Tulle, gent. of Kent.

This Richard bore for arms—argent, on a *chief* vert, a tau, between two mullets pierced, or, with an annulet for distinction, denoting his being the fifth son. His son and heir,

WILLIAM DRURY, esq. of Earith, in Huntingdonshire, was lord of the manor of Cole, in that county, about 1632. He was at the visitation in 1684, and died aged eighty-two about 1690; having had two wives, first, Mary Brown, of Stow, in Huntingdonshire, by whom he had several children, who all died in infancy; second, Catherine, daughter, and at length heir, of Richard Winde, of Earith, and by that lady he had four sons and five daughters, viz.

I. RICHARD, his heir.

II. William, of Earith, who *m.* a daughter of Mr. Garland, citizen of London, and had issue.

Garland.

William.

John.

Drue, *m.* Mary, daughter of Doctor Henley, D. D. chaplain to *Queen* ANNE, and had issue,

DRUE.

Elizabeth.

Elizabeth.

Catherine.

III. Joseph, } *d. s. p.*
IV. Winde, }

I. Catherine, *m.* to John Cholmley, of Credenhill, in Herefordshire.

II. Mary, *d.* unm.

III. Alice, *m.* to Joseph Ives, of Wittlesea, in the Isle of Ely.

IV. Susan, *m.* to Edward Young, of St. Ives, in Huntingdonshire.

V. Elizabeth, *m.* to William Wiseman, gent. of Wittlesea.

* The family of DRURY came into England at the Conquest, and at an early period separated into three distinct branches; the first seated at Rougham; the second at Wetherden; and the third at HAWSTED.

† By his wife, Agas, daughter and, after the death of her brother, heir of Sir Richard Fryssell, by his wife, Catherine, eldest daughter and co-heir (with her sister Joan, wife of Thomas Ickworth, esq. of Ickworth in Suffolk,) of Sir John Geedinge, of Geedinge, also in Suffolk.

‡ From these three brothers descended the Drurys of Rougham, Saxham, Hawsted, Egerly, Riddlesworth, [illegible]thorp, &c.

§ By Margery his wife, second daughter and co-heir of Sir Thomas Aspall, which Margery wedded, in her widowhood, Sir George Felbrigg, of Playford, in Suffolk.

‖ By his wife KATHARINE, daughter of Sir Payne Roelt, a knight of Hainault, Guienne king of arms, which lady married secondly, JOHN OF GAUNT, Duke of Lancaster.

The eldest son and heir,

RICHARD DRURY, esq. of Colne and Cambridge Town, high sheriff of the counties of Cambridge and Huntingdon in 1676, m. Priscilla, daughter and heir of Robert Glapthorne, esq. of Wittlesea, and granddaughter of George Glapthorne, esq. one of the gentlemen of the privy chamber, and providers of the army to *King* CHARLES I. and by that lady had issue,

RICHARD, his heir.
Glapthorne.
James.
Robert.
George, in holy orders, rector of Claydon, Suffolk, m. a daughter of John Clarke, esq. of Ipswich, and had a son,
GEORGE, A.M. rector of Overstone and Claydon, who m. Miss Cavell, only child of the late Rev. Richard Cavell, and dying in 1807, left (with three daughters, Elizabeth, m. to Samuel Montgomery, esq. lieutenant-colonel in the army; Miriam, m. to Samuel Duke, esq.; and Amy, m. to the Rev. William Betts;) three sons,
Thomas, admiral R. N. who left two sons both deceased.
George, succeeded his father to the advowson of Claydon and Akenham. His son George died at Bruges, leaving one son, George, and one daughter.
Richard-Vere, an officer in the army, who m. first, Frances, only daughter of Sir George Vandeput, bart. by Mary, his wife, daughter of Baron Augustus Schutz, of Shotover House, near Oxford, and had by her three sons and one daughter, viz.
1. GEORGE-VANDEPUT, who m. Charlotte-Jane, eldest daughter of Henry Thompson, esq. of Kirby Hall, Yorkshire.
2. Augustus-Vere, captain R. N. who m. Maria, daughter of Captain Smyth, brother of Sir William Smyth, bart. of Hill Hall, Essex.
3. Richard-Vere, d. at Woolwich.
4. Frances-Schutz, m. to Captain Hawkins, of the East India Company's military service, and had one son, deceased, and three daughters, two of whom still survive, and are both married in India.
He m. secondly, Susannah, daughter of the Rev. John Gibson, and granddaughter of Dr. Gibson, bishop of London, by whom he had issue,
5. Robert, now residing at Corfu.
6. Anna, m. to Captain Agnew.
7. Caroline, m. to the Rev. J. Stewart, rector of Gilston.
Elizabeth, m. to Thomas Skeeles, gent. of Bluntsham, in Huntingdonshire.
Priscilla, m. to the Rev. Robert Beaumont, rector of Witnesham, Suffolk.

He d. in 1692, and was s. by his eldest son,

RICHARD DRURY, esq. of Colne, who m. Joyce, daughter and sole heiress, at the death of her brother, of Thomas Beacon, esq. of Ilford, in Essex, and dying, aged sixty-five, 1st November, 1733, was s. by his only son,

THOMAS DRURY, esq. of Overstone, in Northamptonshire, Colne, in the county of Huntingdon; and of Ilford, in Essex, F. R. S. and M.P. for Maldon, who was created a BARONET by *King* GEORGE II. 16th February, 1739. Sir Thomas m. Martha, second daughter of Sir John Tyrell, bart. of Heron, in Essex, and had issue,

Thomas-James-Joseph, b. 4th September, 1738, d. unm. in the lifetime of his father, 1746.
MARY-ANNE, m. 15th July, 1761, to John, second Earl of Buckinghamshire, and had three daughters and co-heirs,
HENRIETTA, m. first, to Armar, Earl of Belmore, and secondly, to William, Marquis of Lothian.
CAROLINE, m. to William, second Lord Suffield.
Sophia, m. to Richard, second Earl of Mount Edgcumbe.
JOCOSA-CATHERINE, m. in 1770, to Sir Brownlow Cust, Lord Brownlow, and had an only child, Ethelred-Anne, d. unm. 1788.

Sir Thomas Drury died 20th January, 1759, when the BARONETCY EXPIRED, but his estates descended to his daughters in undivided moieties. In August, 1770, the younger of those ladies purchased from the Earl of Buckinghamshire, her late sister's moiety, and in the following October married Sir Brownlow Cust, bart. afterwards Lord Brownlow, who eventually became possessed of the whole Drury estate, in Northamptonshire, which his Lordship sold in 1791, to John Kipling, esq. one of the six clerks in Chancery.

Arms—Arg. on a chief vert, a tau between two mullets pierced or.

DRYDEN, OF CANONS ASHBY.

CREATED 16th Nov. 1619.		EXTINCT 21st March, 1770.

Lineage.

Of this family the first we find mentioned

WILLIAM DREYDEN or DRIDEN, father of

DAVID DRYDEN, esq. who m. Isabel, daughter and heir of William Nicholson, esq. of Staffehill, in Cumberland, and was s. by his son,

JOHN DRYDEN, esq. who m. Elizabeth, daughter of Sir John Cope, knt. of Canons Ashby, and had eight sons and four daughters. He d. 30th September, 1584, and was s. by his eldest son,

I. ERASMUS DRYDEN, esq. of Canons Ashby, in the county of Northampton, who took the degree of bachelor of arts in the university of Oxford 17th June, 1577, levied a fine of the manor on his father's decease, served the office of sheriff of his county in the 40th of ELIZABETH, and again in the 17th of the succeeding reign, in which he was raised to the rank of BARONET, by patent dated 16th November, 1619. Sir Erasmus m. Frances, second daughter and co-heir of William Wilkes, esq. of Hodnel, in Warwickshire, and had issue,

I. JOHN, his successor.
II. William, of Farndon, Notts, who m. first, daughter of Cave, esq. of the county of Leicester, and had a son and two daughters,
JOHN, who succeeded as fourth baronet.
Elizabeth, m. to Ambrose Mayhew, of Grimsbury.
Susanna, m. to John Spicer.
By his second wife he also had issue.

III. Erasmus, of Tichmarsh, in Northamptonshire, *m.* Mary, daughter of the Rev. Henry Pickering, D.D. and dying in 1654, had issue,

1. JOHN DRYDEN, the poet, who *m.* Lady Elizabeth Howard, daughter of Thomas, Earl of Berkshire, and had three sons,
   - Charles, unfortunately drowned at Datchet Ferry, near Windsor, died unmarried.*
   - John, resided at Rome and was in the service of the Pope. He wrote a play called "The Husband his own Cuckold."
   - ERASMUS-HENRY, who inherited as fifth baronet.

   Dryden *d.* 1st May, 1701.†
2. ERASMUS, who succeeded his nephew, and became sixth baronet.
3. Henry, *d.* at Jamaica, but left a son, Richard, living in 1708.
4. James, *m.* Elizabeth, daughter of Mr. Dunch, of London, merchant, and *d.* in 1694, leaving two daughters.
5. Agnes, *m.* to Silvester Emelyn, esq. of Stamford, Lincolnshire.
6. Rose, *m.* to Dr. Laughton, D.D. of Catworth, Huntingdonshire.
7. Martha, *m.* to Mr. Bletso, of Northampton.
8. Frances, *m.* to Mr. Joseph Sandwell, of London, merchant. She *d.* 10th October, 1736, aged nearly ninety.

I. Elizabeth, *m.* to Sir Richard Phillipps, bart. of Picton Castle.

II. Mary, *m.* to Sir Edward Hartopp, bart. of Freathby, in Leicestershire.

III. Dorothy, *m.* to Edward Salway, esq. of Stanford, in the county of Worcester, M.P. for Droitwich in 1658. (See BURKE'S *Commoners*, vol. i. p. 153.)

IV. Susan, *m.* to Sir John Pickering, bart. of Tichmarsh.

Sir Erasmus *d.* 22nd May, 1632, and was *s.* by his eldest son,

II. SIR JOHN DRYDEN, sheriff of Northamptonshire in 1634, and elected its knight to serve in parliament in 1640, *m.* first, Priscilla, daughter of James Quarles, esq. of Rumford, in Essex; and secondly, Anne, daughter of Henry Parvis, esq. of Ruckholts, in the same county; but those ladies died both without issue. Sir John *m.* thirdly, Honor, daughter of Sir Robert Bevile, knt. of Chesterton, in the county of Huntingdon, and had by her,

I. ROBERT, his successor.

II. John, of Chesterton, M.P. for the county of Huntingdon *temp.* WILLIAM III. and *d.* unm. in January, 1707.

III. Erasmus, who lived a bachelor at Canons Ashby.

IV. Richard, *d.* unm. in the twenty-fourth year of his age.

V. Bevile, *d.* unm.

VI. Benjamin, a citizen of London, *d.* issueless.

I. Frances, *m.* to Ralph Sneyd, esq. eldest son of William Sneyd, esq. of Keel Hall, Staffordshire.

II. Anne, *m.* to Walter Pigot, esq. of Chetwynd, Salop, and had a son,

Robert Pigot, M.P. for the county of Huntingdon, who inherited the estate of Chesterton from his uncles.

Sir John *d.* about the year 1658, and was *s.* by his eldest son,

III. SIR ROBERT DRYDEN, who died unmarried in the seventy-sixth year of his age, having outlived all his brothers, 19th August, 1708, and was buried on the 30th of the same month in the church of Canons Ashby. He left his estate at Canons Ashby to Edward Dryden, the second son of Erasmus Dryden, of Tichmarsh, but the Baronetcy devolved upon his cousin (refer to William, second son of the first baronet).

IV. SIR JOHN DRYDEN, of Faradon, Notts, who *m.* Elizabeth, daughter of Mr. Lock, of Northamptonshire, and had issue,

- John, killed by a fall from his horse in his father's lifetime, *d.* unm.
- Honor, *m.* to Mr. Joseph Bateman, a surgeon in London.
- Elizabeth, *d.* unm.

He was *s.* at his decease by his cousin,

V. SIR ERASMUS-HENRY DRYDEN (only surviving son of THE POET), who died unmarried in 1711, when the Baronetcy devolved upon his uncle,

VI. SIR ERASMUS DRYDEN, who *m.* Elizabeth, daughter of Mr. Edward Martyn, of the city of Westminster, and had issue,

EDWARD, who, at the decease of Sir Robert Dryden in 1708, inherited the estate of Canons Ashby, *m.* Elizabeth, daughter of Edward Allen, son of Sir Thomas Allen, knt. a Turkey merchant, of London, and dying before his father 3rd November, 1717, left issue,

1. JOHN, successor to his grandfather.
2. Robert.
3. Erasmus, in holy orders, rector of Hampstead, Berks, *m.* in 1747, Miss Blagrave and *d. s. p.*
4. Edward, of Oporto, merchant.
5. Bevile, of Ore, in Berkshire, *m.* Mary, daughter of — Dubber, esq. of Cirencester in the county of Gloucester, and had four daughters, viz.
   - ELIZABETH, heir to her uncle.
   - Maria, *m.* to William Ramsay, esq. of Inveresk, and died in 1820, leaving, with three daughters, a son, John Turner Ramsay, esq. of Tusmore, in Oxfordshire.
   - Philippa, *m.* to Thomas Steele, esq.
   - Anne, *d.* unm.
6. Elizabeth.
7. Mary, *m.* to Allen Puleston, esq.
8. Anne.

Elizabeth, *m.* to Richard Martyn, D.D. prebendary of Westminster.

Mary, *m.* to John Shaw, esq. of the Board of Green Cloth.

He *d.* 3rd November, 1718, aged eighty-two, and was *s.* by his grandson,

VII. SIR JOHN DRYDEN, of Canons Ashby, who *m.* first, Frances, daughter and heir of Thomas Ingram, esq. of Barraby, in the county of York; and secondly, Elizabeth, daughter of John Roper, esq. of Berkhamstead, Herts, but dying *s. p.* 21st March, 1770, the BARONETCY EXPIRED; the estates devolved upon Sir John's niece,

---

* CHARLES DRYDEN was usher of the palace to his Holiness CLEMENT XI., and, upon his return to England, left his brother John to officiate in his stead, and was drowned in swimming across the Thames, near Windsor, in 1704. He wrote several pieces, and translated the Sixth Satire of Juvenal.

† And was buried in Westminster Abbey, where the Duke of Buckingham ordered a noble and [illegible] monument to be erected to his memory.

ELIZABETH DRYDEN, who m. in 1781, John Turner, esq. brother of Sir Gregory Page Turner. This gentleman assumed the surname of DRYDEN only in 1791, and was created a BARONET in 1795. Their grandson is the present REV. SIR JOHN DRYDEN, of Canons Ashby.

Arms—Az. a lion rampant, and in chief a sphere between two estoiles, or.

Note.—In Canons Ashby, says Mr. Bridges (Hist. of Northamptonshire), there is one room of thirty feet long upon twenty feet wide, which is reported to be rafted, floored and wainscoted with the timber of a single oak which grew in that lordship.

DUCIE, OF LONDON.

CREATED 28th Nov. 1629. EXTINCT in May, 1703.

Lineage.

I. SIR ROBERT DUCIE, knt. sheriff of London in 1620, was created a BARONET 28th November, 1629, and was lord mayor in 1631. He m. Elizabeth, daughter of Alderman Richard Pyott, and had issue,

RICHARD, his successor.
WILLIAM.
Hugh (Sir), K.B. who had two sons,
WILLIAM, } fourth and fifth baronets.
ROBERT, }
Robert, whose only daughter,
ELIZABETH DUCIE, heir of her uncle, Lord Downe, m. Edward Moreton, esq. of Moreton, in Staffordshire, and was mother of Matthew-Ducie Moreton, created in 1720 Lord Ducie. (See BURKE's *Peerage and Baronetage*.)

Sir Robert Ducie accumulated immense wealth in trade. He was banker to *King* CHARLES I., and notwithstanding losing eighty thousand pounds by his loyalty, died, it was said, worth more than four hundred thousand pounds. He was *s.* at his decease, about the year 1634, by his eldest son,

II. SIR RICHARD DUCIE, bart. who died unmarried in 1656, and was *s.* by his brother,

III. SIR WILLIAM DUCIE, bart. who was made a knight of the Bath at the coronation of *King* CHARLES II. and raised to the peerage of Ireland as VISCOUNT DOWNE. He m. Frances, daughter of Francis, Lord Seymour, of Trowbridge, but died without issue 9th September, 1679, when his estates devolved upon his niece, ELIZABETH DUCIE (from whom the *extant* LORDS DUCIE), and he was *s.* in the Baronetcy by his nephew,

IV. SIR WILLIAM DUCIE, bart. who *d. s. p.* and was *s.* by his brother,

V. SIR ROBERT DUCIE, bart. who died unmarried in May 1703, when the BARONETCY became EXTINCT.

Arms—Or, a fesse vair between three cinquefoils

DUCK, OF HASWELL-ON-THE-HILL.

CREATED 19th Mar. 1687. EXTINCT 26th Aug. 1691.

Lineage.

I. SIR JOHN DUCK, of Haswell-on-the-Hill, created a BARONET in 1687, was the wealthiest burgess on the civic annals of the city of Durham. His birth, parentage, &c. remain in impenetrable obscurity. He was bred a butcher, under John Heslop, in defiance of the whole craft, in whose books there still exists a *gentle* reprimand to Heslop "to forbear to set John Ducke on worke in the trade of a butcher on paine of 39*s.* 11*d.*" John Duck, however, was born to greatness, and grew rich in despite of the butchers, and married the daughter of his benefactor.* He built a splendid mansion in Silver Street, Durham, and endowed an hospital at Lumley, in the palatinate. In the former, a pannel still remains recording his happy rise to fortune. The baronet, then *humble Duck, cast out* by the butchers, stands near a bridge in an attitude of despondency, and in the air a raven is seen bearing in his bill a piece of money, which, according to tradition, fell at his feet, and which, "being put out to use," was the nucleus on which he wound a splendid fortune. On the right is a view of the mansion house in Silver Street, and on the left the hospital at Lumley. He died without issue, and was buried in St. Margaret's 31st August, 1691, where his wife, "pia, prudens, felix," lies buried beside him. Sir John's large property seems to have gone to Lady Duck's nieces, viz. Elizabeth Heslop, who married George Tweddell, alderman of Durham; and Jane Heslop, who married, first, James Nicholson, of Durham, cordwainer (father of James Nicholson, esq. of West Rainton, in the county palatine, M. P. for the city of Durham in 1708, who died in 1727, leaving three daughters and co-heirs, viz. Jane, *m.* to Thomas, Earl of Strathmore, grandfather to the present earl; Anne, who *m.* the Hon. Patrick Lyon, brother to the earl; and Mary, who died a spinster); and secondly, Richard Wharton, attorney-at-law. Sir John Duck mentions in his will, Anne, the daughter and only child of his late brother, Robert Duck, who died before 1691, but appears to have been uncertain of her existence; "if she be alive" are the words used.

At the demise of Sir John Duck the BARONETCY became EXTINCT.

Arms—A fess between three buckles.

DUDDLESTONE, OF BRISTOL.

CREATED 11th Jan. 1691-2.—EXTINCT (date unknown).

Lineage.

I. SIR JOHN DUDDLESTON, a merchant at Bristol, was the first who invited to his house *Prince* GEORGE

* Viz. Anne, daughter of John Heslop, of the city of Durham, butcher: she died 14th December, 1695, aged

of Denmark on his highness's visit to that city, and he was in consequence knighted, and subsequently created a BARONET.* Sir John lost in the great storm at sea, November, 1704, more than twenty thousand pounds, and was thereby greatly reduced. His grandson and heir,

II. SIR JOHN DUDDLESTON, held an humble appointment in the Customs at Bristol, and in the year 1727 was living in a very low condition. Of himself or his descendants (if any) nothing further is known.

DUDLEY, OF CLAPTON.

CREATED 1st Aug. 1660.

EXTINCT 15th June, 1764.

Lineage.

This family claimed descent from the PAGANELLS, who were Lords of Dudley soon after the Conquest. Their heir female, HAWYSE PAGANELL, married JOHN DE SOMERIE, and conveyed to her husband the lordship and castle of Dudley, which passed again with a co-heir of that family, MARGARET DE SOMERIE, to the family of Sutton on her marriage with

JOHN DE SUTTON, who thus obtained Dudley Castle, and his son and heir,

JOHN DE SUTTON, was summoned to parliament as Baron Sutton of Dudley in 1342. A descendant of his,

JOHN SUTTON, assumed the name of DUDLEY,† and from him is stated to have derived

THOMAS DE DUDLEY, who settled at Clapton, in the county of Northumberland, and was one of the lords of Clapton Manor. His grandson,

—— DE DUDLEY, married, in 1395, AGNES HOTOT, the eventual heiress of the ancient family of Hotot, and from that marriage lineally descended

I. WILLIAM DUDLEY, esq. of Clapton, in Northamptonshire, who was created a BARONET 1st August, 1660. Sir William m. first, a daughter of M. de Pl[illegible] secondly, Jane, daughter of Sir Roger Smith, knt. of Edmondthorp, in the county of Leicester, but these ladies both died issueless. He wedded, thirdly, Mary, daughter and heir of Sir Paul Pindar, knt. of Lo[illegible], and by her had

MATTHEW, his successor.

William, in holy orders, rector of Clapton, died unmarried in May, 1726.

Mary, m. to Sir John Robinson, bart.

He *d.* in 1670, and was *s.* by his elder son,

II. SIR MATTHEW DUDLEY, bart. who m. Lady Mary O'Bryen, youngest daughter of Henry, Earl of Thomond, and had surviving issue,

WILLIAM, his heir.

Sarah-Henrietta.

Sir Matthew was several times returned to parliament, and at one period represented the county of Huntingdon. He was appointed a commissioner of the Customs in 1706, and turned out in 1712, but was reinstated by *King* GEORGE I. and died in office 13th April, 1721. He was *s.* by his son,

III. SIR WILLIAM DUDLEY, bart. who m. Elizabeth, daughter and sole heir of Sir Richard Kennedy, bart. of the kingdom of Ireland, and had three sons and a daughter, O'Bryen, William, John, and Elizabeth, who all predeceased him, young and unmarried. He *d.* at York 15th June, 1764, aged sixty-three, when the BARONETCY became EXTINCT.

Arms—Az. a chevron or, between three lions' heads erased arg.

Crest—On a ducal crown or, a woman's head with a helmet thereon, hair dishevelled, throat-latch [illegible] ppr.

Note.—The occasion of obtaining this crest is thus mentioned in a manuscript written in 1390 by a [illegible] who was parson of Clapton:—"The father of Agnes HOTOT, the great heiress who married Dudley, having a dispute with one Ringsdale about the title to a piece of land, they agreed to meet on the disputed ground

---

* Prince George of Denmark, the husband of *Queen* ANNE, in passing through Bristol, went to the Exchange, accompanied by one gentleman only, and remained there until the merchants had pretty generally withdrawn, none of whom had sufficient resolution to speak to him. At length a person of the name of John Duddlestone, a bodice maker, mustered the necessary courage, and going up to the prince, inquired if he were not the husband of *Queen* ANNE? Having learned that this was the case, Duddlestone said he had observed with much concern that none of the merchants had invited the prince home to dinner; but this was not for want of love to the queen or to him, but because they did not consider themselves prepared to receive so great a man. He added that he was ashamed to think of his royal highness dining at an inn, and therefore entreated that he would go home and dine with him, and bring the gentleman along with him, informing him that he had a good piece of beef and a plum pudding, with ale of his dame's own brewing. The prince admired the loyalty of the man, and though he had ordered dinner at the White Lion, he accompanied the bodice maker home. Duddlestone called his wife, who was up stairs, desiring her to put on a clean apron and come down, for the queen's husband and another gentleman were come to dine with them. She immediately came down with her clean blue apron, and was immediately saluted by the prince. In the course of dinner, the prince invited his host to town and to bring his wife with him, at the same time giving him a card to facilitate his introduction at court. A few months after, Duddlestone, with his wife behind him on horseback, [illegible] for London, where they soon found the prince, and [illegible] by him introduced to the queen. Her majesty [illegible] them most graciously, and invited them to an [illegible] ing dinner, informing them that they must have [illegible] clothes for the occasion. They were allowed [illegible] for themselves, when they both selected purple [illegible] such as the prince then had on. The dresses [illegible] pared, and they were introduced by the queen [illegible] the most loyal persons in Bristol, and the only [illegible] that city who had invited the prince, her husband [illegible] their house. After the entertainment was over, [illegible] desired Duddlestone to kneel, laid a sword on [illegible] and, to use Lady Duddlestone's own words, said [illegible] "Ston up, Sir Jan." He was then offered [illegible] place under government; but he would not accept [illegible] informing the queen that he had £50 out at [illegible] he apprehended that the number of people he [illegible] court must be very expensive. The queen [illegible] Duddlestone a present of her gold watch from [illegible] which her ladyship considered so great an ornament [illegible] she never went to market without having it [illegible] over her blue apron.—*Percy Anecdotes.*

† This JOHN (SUTTON) DUDLEY was father of [illegible] DUDLEY, the notorious minister of HENRY VII [illegible] cestor of the Dudleys, Earls of Warwick. (Burke's *Extinct Peerage*.)

and decide the affair by combat. Hotot on the day appointed was laid up with the gout, but his daughter Agnes, rather than the land should be lost, armed herself cap-a-pee, and mounting her father's steed, went and encountered RINGSDALE, whom, after a stubborn contest, she unhorsed; and when he was on the ground, she loosened her throat-latch, lifted up her helmet, and let down her hair about her shoulders, thus discovering her sex." In commemoration of this exploit the crest was adopted and ever afterwards used.

DUDLEY, OF KILSCORAN HOUSE.

CREATED 17th April, 1813.—EXTINCT 1st Feb. 1824.

Lineage.

I. SIR HENRY BATE-DUDLEY, who was created a BARONET in 1813, derived from a respectable family settled in Worcestershire and Staffordshire as early as the reign of CHARLES I. He was born at Fenny ...mpton, 25th August, 1745. His father, the REV. HENRY BATE, held for many years the living of St. Nicholas, Worcester; and being afterwards presented to the rectory of North Farmbridge, in Essex, removed with his family into that county, and took up his abode at Chelmsford. In this latter benefice his son Henry, who took holy orders, succeeded him at his death; but the emoluments of the living being but trifling, he turned his thoughts towards the public press, and established the "Morning Post" newspaper. A few years afterwards, in 1780, he originated the "Morning Herald," to which he devoted much of his time; commencing also about the same time the "Courier de l'Europe," a journal printed in the French language, and the "English Chronicle." At this period he was the intimate associate of most of the wits of the day, and was a contributor to the "Probationary Odes," the "Rolliad," and other works of a similar class. In ...1, the advowson of the valuable rectory of Bradwell-juxta Mare was purchased in trust for him, subject to the life of the Rev. George Pawson; in consequence of which, he is said to have expended during the lifetime of that incumbent upwards of £28,000 in repairs, embankments, plantations, &c. for the benefit of the living. In 1784 he assumed the name of Dudley, in compliance with the will of a relation belonging to that family. Mr. Pawson dying in 1797, Mr. Dudley presented himself to the vacant benefice, but doubts having arisen in the mind of the Bishop of London as to the legality of the transaction, his lordship refused institution, and a compromise was at length effected by the proposed substitution of the Rev. Richard Birch, brother-in-law of the patron. This arrangement was, however, made too late; inasmuch as the delay had caused a lapse of the living to the crown, which bestowed it on the Rev. Mr. Gamble, chaplain-general of the army. The case was thought a hard one, and a petition signed by the Lord Braybrooke, the Lord Lieutenant of Essex, and most of the magistrates and gentry of the county, was forwarded to ministers, enumerating the services of Mr. Dudley in his capacity of a magistrate, under very trying circumstances, for which he had been publicly thanked by Lord Kenyon ... on the circuit. A favourable answer was returned, and in 1804 he was presented to the living of ...ran, barony of Forth, Ireland, to which was ... added the chancellorship of the diocese of Ferns. ..., the Duke of Bedford, then lord-lieutenant of Ireland, gave him the rectory of Kilglass, in the county of ...rford, which he retained until 1812, when he resigned all his Irish preferment for the living of ...ingham, in Cambridgeshire; his relation, Mr. Birch, having been in the meantime instituted to the long-disputed rectory of Bradwell on the decease of Mr. Gamble. Shortly after, Mr. Dudley obtained a Baronetcy; and in 1816, the dignity of a prebend in Ely Cathedral, which he retained till the day of his death, 1st February, 1824.

Of a comprehensive mind and active habits, Sir Henry distinguished himself on many occasions as a useful magistrate; while his literary abilities were manifested in the composition of a variety of dramatic pieces, some of which still maintain their footing on the stage. Among these are "The Flitch of Bacon," written for the purpose of introducing his friend Shield to the public as a composer; "The Woodman;" "The Rival Candidates;" "The Blackamoor Washed White," (at the representation of which, party spirit ran so high as to produce a serious conflict, in which swords were drawn, &c. among the audience); "The Travellers in Switzerland;" and lastly, a short but popular piece, brought out about thirty years since under the title of "At Home." To his discriminating patronage the country is mainly indebted for discovering and fostering the talents of Gainsborough the painter; and he is said to have been one of the first to appreciate those of Mrs. Siddons, whom he introduced to Garrick. His person was handsome and athletic; while, in his earlier years, the warmth of his temperament betrayed him, notwithstanding his cloth, into several quarrels. The cause of two of these rencontres (with Messrs. Fitzgerald and Miles) is said to have been Mrs. Hartley, *an actress*, celebrated for her beauty, who, singularly enough, after the lapse of half a century, died on the very same day with her quondam champion. A third, of more equivocal character, fought with Mr. Stoney Bowes, made a great noise at the time. Sir Henry, at the time of his decease, was a magistrate for seven English counties and four in Ireland. He *m.* Mary, daughter of James White, esq. of Berra, in Somersetshire, but had no issue: the BARONETCY EXPIRED with him.

DUKE, OF BENHALL.

CREATED 16th July, 1661. — EXTINCT 25th Aug. 1732.

Lineage.

ROGER DUKE was sheriff of London in the 2nd, 4th, and 5th of RICHARD I., and his son,

PETER DUKE, served the same office in the 10th of *King* JOHN. This Peter was father of

ROGER DUKE, who was sheriff of London in the 11th of HENRY III. and mayor in the 12th, 13th, 14th, and 15th of the same reign. His son,

WALTER DUKE, of Brampton *temp.* EDWARD III., did his homage at Framlingham Castle, 2nd RICHARD II. to William Ufford, Earl of Suffolk, then Lord of Framlingham Manor, for his lands in Shadingfield, holden of the said manor by one knight's fee. He was *s.* by his son,

ROGER DUKE, whose son,

ROBERT DUKE, held the lands in Shadingfield 11th HENRY VI. His son and heir,

John Duke, of Brampton, m. Joan, daughter and heir of Spark, of Astacton, in Norfolk, and of Ickesall, in Suffolk, and was s. by his son,

Thomas Duke, esq. of Brampton, who m. first, the daughter and heir of Woodwell, and by her had an only daughter, the wife of Normanville. He wedded, secondly, Margaret, daughter and heir of Henry Baynard, esq. of Speckshall, in Suffolk, and by that lady had

- William, his heir.
- John, *d. s. p.*
- Robert, m. Elizabeth, daughter of Sir Nicholas Wren, and *d. s. p.*
- Thomas, a priest.

He was *s.* by his eldest son,

William Duke, esq. who paid (23rd Henry VIII.) twenty shillings aid to the Lord of Framlingham Manor. He m. Thomasine, daughter of Sir Edmund Jenny, of Knottishall, Suffolk, and was *s.* by his son,

George Duke, esq. of Brampton, who was buried at Frenshall; and by Anne, daughter of Sir Thomas Blenerhasset, knt. of Frenshall, left two sons, viz.

- Edward, his heir.
- George, of Honington, m. Elizabeth, daughter and co-heir of Austin Curtis, of the same place, and had issue,
  - George, of Wandsworth, who, for services done to *King* Charles I. and *King* Charles II., had an augmentation to his arms, viz. "*On an escutcheon azure, a fleur-de-lys crowned or;*" with an alteration of his crest. He m. Catherine, daughter of Richard Braham, of Wandsworth, and had, with other issue,
    - Edward, of Middlesex, doctor of physic, who m. Elizabeth, daughter of Robert Tollemache, of Helmingham, Suffolk, and heir of her brother Ptolemy, by which lady he left a son,
      - Tollemache Duke, of Bentley, who m. a daughter of Sir Lewis Palmer, bart. of Carleton, Leicestershire, and had a son,
        - Tollemache, who *d.* young.
        - Elizabeth.
    - Elizabeth.

The elder son and heir,

Edward Duke, esq. of Brampton and Shadingfield, in the county of Suffolk, m. Dorothy, daughter of Sir Ambrose Jermyn, knt. of Rusbrook, in Suffolk, and had issue. This gentleman purchased Benhall, and dying in 1598, was *s.* by his son,

Ambrose Duke, esq. of Benhall, who wedded Elizabeth, daughter and co-heir of Bartholomew Calthorp, esq. of Suffolk, and by her (who *d.* in 1611) left at his decease in 1610 a son and heir,

I. Sir Edward Duke, of Benhall, in the county of Suffolk, who, having first received the honour of knighthood, was created a Baronet by *King* Charles II. 16th July, 1661. He m. Ellen, daughter and co-heir of John Panton, esq. of Brunslip, in the county of Denbigh, and had no less than twenty-nine children, of whom survived,

- John, his successor.
- Robert, who *d.* unm.
- Elizabeth, m. to Nathaniel Bacon, esq. of Friston.
- Alathea, m. first, to Offley Jenny, esq. of Knodishall, in Suffolk, by whom she left an only surviving child, Robert Jenny, of Leisten. She wedded, secondly, Ralph Snelling, esq. of [illegible]ford; and thirdly, William Foster, esq. [illegible] Madesford.

Sir Edward, who was of Benhall, Brampton, [illegible] Worlingham, *d.* about the year 1671, and was [illegible] his elder surviving son,

II. Sir John Duke, bart. M. P. for Oxford [illegible] William III. who m. Elizabeth, daughter of Edw[illegible] Duke, M.D. and had issue,

- Edward, his successor.
- Elizabeth, *d.* young.
- Jane, m. to John Bream, esq. of Campsey Ash [illegible] Suffolk.
- Anne, m. to Thomas Tyrrell, esq. of Gippin, in the same county.
- Arabella, m. to Maurice Shelton, esq. of Barn[illegible]ham, in Suffolk.

He *d.* about the year 1705, and was *s.* by his son.

III. Sir Edward Duke, bart. who m. Mary, [illegible]ter and sole heir of Thomas Rudge, esq. of the [illegible] of Stafford, and had issue,

- Edward, who *d.* young.
- Elizabeth, also *d.* young.

Sir Edward died without surviving issue 25th Au[illegible] 1732, when the Baronetcy became extinct.

Arms—Az. a chev. between three birds close [illegible] membered gu.

DUNCAN, OF MARY-LE-BONE.

Created 14th Aug. 1764.

Ext[illegible] in Sept. [illegible]

Lineage.

This was a branch of the family of Du[illegible] Lundie, immortalized by the celebrated A[illegible] Duncan, "of Camperdown."

Alexander Duncan, esq. of Lundie, in the [illegible] of Angus, m. Isabella, daughter of Sir Peter M[illegible] bart. of Aughterlyne, and had issue,

- Alexander, his heir, grandfather of Ad[illegible]can, who fought and won the great nava[illegible] off Camperdown, 11th October, 179[illegible], [illegible] created, in consequence, Baron Dun[illegible] Lundie, and Viscount Duncan, of [illegible]down. His son is now Earl of Camp[illegible] (Refer to Burke's *Peerage and Baronetage*.)
- William.

The younger son,

I. William Duncan, M.D. physician-extra[illegible] to the king, was created a Baronet 14th August [illegible] Sir William m. Lady Mary Tufton, eldest daug[illegible] Sackville, Earl of Thanet, but died without [illegible] September, 1774, when the Baronetcy became [illegible]tinct.

Arms—Gu. two roses in chief and a bugle-h[illegible] base arg. strung and garnished az.

DUNCUMB, OF TANGLEY PARK.

CREATED 4th Feb. 1661-2.

EXTINCT in Aug. 1706.

Lineage.

WILLIAM DUNCUMB, of Ivingho Aston, in the county of Bucks, married Mary, daughter and sole heir of Richard Reynes, esq. of Clifton-Reynes, in the same shire, and had issue,

ROGER.

Thomas, of Much Brickhill, Bucks, who m. Isabella, daughter of Thomas Saunders, esq. of Agmondesham, and was ancestor of the Duncombes of Brickhill, an estate now enjoyed by PHILIP-DUNCOMBE PAUNCEFORT-DUNCOMBE, esq. of Great Brickhill. (See BURKE'S *Commoners*, vol. ii. p. 74.)

Elizabeth, m. to William Dreyner, of Cranbrook.

The elder son,

ROGER DUNCUMB, esq. of Littington, in Bedfordshire, living in 1565, married Cecily, daughter of Edmund Conquest, esq. of Houghton Conquest, and had a son,

GEORGE DUNCUMB, esq. of Weston in Albury, Surrey, who m. Judith, daughter of John Caryll, esq. of Tangley, in the same county, and had issue,

I. JOHN, b. 24th March, 1604; m. in 1626, Mary, daughter of Sir Edward Onslow, and had two sons and three daughters, viz.
  1. George, b. in 1628, who m. Elizabeth, daughter of Robert Holt, esq. of Warwickshire, but d. s. p.
  2. Roger, of Weston, who d. in 1676, having had by Anne, his wife, daughter of William Pell, of London,
    George, of Weston, d. s. p. about 1654.
    Roger, d. s. p.
    Henry, who m. first, Olive, daughter of John Child, of Guildford; and secondly, Charity, daughter of Dr. Duncumb. He d. in 1669, leaving a daughter,
      MARY, m. to Charles Eversfield, esq. of Denne, in Sussex.
    William, m. Susannah, daughter of Thomas Doyley, and d. s. p. in 1691.
  3. Dorothy, m. to Vincent Randyll, esq. of Chilworth.
  4. Judith.
  5. Elizabeth.

II. GEORGE, of whom presently.
III. Roger.
IV. Edward.
V. William, d. s. p.
VI. Anthony, m. Jane, daughter of Edward Bray, esq. of Shere.
VII. Thomas, d. s. p.
VIII. Richard, m. Judith, daughter of Thomas Farnaby, esq. and d. s. p.

  I. Letitia, m. to Robert Woodroffe, esq. of Poyle.
  II. Mary, m. to Daniel Caldwell, esq.
  III. Elizabeth, m. to Thomas Merry, esq.

George Duncumb died 21st March, 1646. His second son,

GEORGE DUNCUMB, of Shalford, married Charity, daughter of John Muscott, of London, and by her, who died in 1677, had issue,

I. JOHN, who m. Jane, daughter and co-heir of John Stynt, of London, and had two sons, namely,
  GEORGE, who m. Martha, daughter of Sir John Peyton, and died 24th May, 1719, having had issue,
    1. GEORGE, b. in 1676, who m. Anne, daughter of Sir Henry Pollexfen, chief justice of the Common Pleas, and dying before his father, in 1706, left an only child,
      MARY, m. first, to John Butler; and secondly to Richard Uthwatt.
    2. HESTER, m. to Robert Woodroffe, esq. of Poyle, and had issue.
    3. MARTHA, m. to Nathaniel Sturt, esq. and had issue two sons, who d. s. p. and a daughter, Frances, m. to John Chatfield, esq.
  Stynt, who m. Elizabeth, sister of Sir Richard Heath, of Clandon, and d. in 1690, leaving a son,
    John, of Wribbenhall, Worcestershire, who m. Elizabeth, daughter of William Wood, of Birmingham, and had, with other issue,
      George, of Kidderminster, whose daughter, Sarah, m. Mr. Cox, of London, and was mother of Dr. Joseph Cox, M.D.
      Joseph, whose daughter and heir, Elizabeth, m. S. F. Perkins, esq. barrister.
      Mary, m. to John Ingram, esq. of Bewdley, and was mother of Lady Winnington.
II. FRANCIS, of whom presently.
III. Thomas, rector of Shere, who m. Ursula Lamb, of Oxford, and was father of
  George, rector of Shere, who m. Anne, daughter of Sir Richard Heath, of Clandon, and dying in 1743, left issue,
    1. Thomas, rector of Shere, who m. Lucretia, daughter of Robert Pountney, of Kensington, and d. in 1764, leaving issue,
      Thomas, rector of Shere, who m. Ann Holland, and died in 1804, leaving
        Thomas, rector of Shere.
        John, m. Ann Webb, of Herefordshire, and had issue.
        William, captain R.N.
        George.
        Edward.
        Lucy, m. to — Street.
        Catharine.
        Ann.
      Robert, rector of Prince William's parish, in Carolina, m. Elizabeth, daughter of — Gibbs, of Towcester, and d. in 1765.
      Lucretia, m. to James Culcheth, of Daventry.

2. Ann, m. to Edward Bray, esq. of Shere, in Surrey, and had issue.
3. Catherine, m. to the Rev. William Martin, rector of Rusper, in Sussex, and had issue.

IV. Henry.
V. William, rector of Ashted.
VI. Richard.
VII. Anthony, d. in 1709.

I. Charity, m. to William Street, esq. of Shalford.
II. Mary, m. to Henry Pollexfen, esq.

The second son,

I. FRANCIS DUNCOMB, esq. of Tangley Park, was created a BARONET in 1661. He married Hester, daughter and co-heir of John Stynt, esq. and relict of John Caryll, esq. and by her, who died in 1675, left at his decease, 4th November, 1670, with five daughters, one son,

II. SIR WILLIAM DUNCOMB, who m. Anne, daughter of Sir Ralph Bassh, K.B. knt. of Stanstedbury, Herts, but d. s. p. in 1706, when the title became EXTINCT.

Arms—Per chev. eng. gu. and arg. three talbots' heads erased, counterchanged.

DUTRY, OF LONDON.

CREATED 19th June, 1716.

EXTINCT 20th Oct. 1728.

Lineage.

I. DENNIS DUTRY, esq. a merchant of London and one of the directors of the East India Company, was created a BARONET by *King* GEORGE I. 19th June, 1716. Sir Dennis was of a family of consideration in Brabant, where his great-grandfather is stated to have been one of the prime ministers at the court of the Governante of the Netherlands, the Duchess of Parma. Sir Dennis m. Mary, daughter of Hillary Reneu, an eminent and wealthy merchant, but died without issue 20th October, 1728, when the BARONETCY became EXTINCT. His widow m. Gervase Vanneck.

Arms—Az. a stirrup between three stars or.

DUTTON, OF SHERBORNE.

CREATED 22nd June, 1678.

EXTINCT 1st Feb. 1743.

Lineage.

The family of DUTTON is one of the most ancient in the palatinate of Chester.

ODARD, kinsman of Hugh Lupus, Earl of Chester, was rewarded at the CONQUEST with the manor of Dutton, and thence the surname of his descendants. Of those,

SIR HUGH DUTTON, of Dutton, was father of another

SIR HUGH DUTTON, knt. who m. Jane, daughter of Sir Robert Holland, and left a son and heir,

SIR THOMAS DUTTON, knt. of Dutton, sheriff of Chester in 1268, who m. Eleanor, daughter of Sir Pierce Thornton, knt. and was father of

EDMUND DUTTON, esq. who was s. by his son,

SIR PETER DUTTON, knt. whose brother,

HUGH DUTTON, esq. m. Petronilla, daughter and heir of Ralph Vernon, of Hatton, in Cheshire, and left a son,

JOHN DUTTON, esq. who m. Margaret, daughter of Sir William Atherton, and was father of

SIR PIERS DUTTON, of Dutton, who built in 1539 the New Hall at Dutton. He m. Isabell, daughter and co-heir of Robert Grosvenor, of Hulme. His successor,

RICHARD DUTTON, esq. was grandfather of

WILLIAM DUTTON, esq. who m. Agnes, daughter of John Conway, of Flintshire. His younger son,

THOMAS DUTTON, esq. purchased the manor of Sherborne, in the county of Dorset, from Sir Christopher Alleyn, and died in 1581. He m. first, Mary, daughter of Robert Taylor; secondly, Anne, daughter of Stephen Kyrton, alderman of London, and widow of Sir Thomas Wythers; he had a third wife, whose name is not mentioned. His son and heir,

WILLIAM DUTTON, esq. of Sherborne, served the office of sheriff for the county of Gloucester in 15[illegible] and 1601. He m. Anne, daughter of Sir Ambrose Nicholas, knt. lord mayor of London, by whom (who m. secondly, Sir Paul Tracey,) he had seven sons and seven daughters. He d. in 1618, and was s. by his eldest son,

JOHN DUTTON, esq. of Sherborne, M.P. for the county of Gloucester. Of this gentleman, Anthony Wood says, "He was one of the knights for that county (Gloucester) to sit in the said parliament, [illegible], but being frighted thence by the tumults that came up to the parliament doors, as other royalists were, he conveyed himself privately to Oxford, and sate there. He was a learned and prudent man, and as one of the richest, so one of the meekest men in England. He was active in making the defence and drawing up the articles of Oxon when the garrison was to be surrendered to the parliament; for which, and his steady loyalty, he was afterwards forced to pay a round sum in Goldsmith's Hall, London." He m. first, Elizabeth, daughter of Sir Henry Baynton, of the county of Wilts, and had two daughters, his co-heirs, viz.

ELIZABETH, m. to George Colt, esq.

LUCY, m. to Thomas Pope, Earl of Downe, in Ireland, and was mother of

LADY ELIZABETH POPE, sole heir of her father, who m. first, Sir Francis Henry Lee, of Ditchley; and secondly, Robert, third Earl of Lindsey. (See BURKE'S *Peerage*.)

He wedded, secondly, Anne, daughter of Dr. John King, Bishop of London, but by that lady, who survived him and m. Sir Richard Howe, had no other issue. He d. in 1656, when Sherborne and other large estates devolved upon his nephew,

WILLIAM DUTTON, who thus became "of Sherborne." He was elder son of Sir Ralph Dutton, gentleman of the privy-chamber-extraordinary to King CHARLES I. and sheriff of Gloucestershire in 16[illegible], by Mary, his wife, daughter of Sir William Duncomb.

knt. of London.* He *m.* Mary, daughter of John, Viscount Scudamore, and widow of Thomas Russell, esq. of Worcestershire, but leaving no issue at his decease (his son John having predeceased him in 1664), was *s.* by his brother,

I. Ralph Dutton, esq. of Sherborne, M.P. for the county of Gloucester, who was created a Baronet by King Charles II. 22nd June, 1678. He *m.* first, Grisel, daughter of Sir Edward Poole, of Kemble, in the county of Wilts, and by that lady had one daughter, *m.* to William Green, esq. of London. Sir Ralph wedded, secondly, Mary, only daughter of Peter Barwick, M.D. to Charles II. and by her had issue,

John, his heir.
Ralph, *d. s. p.*
Anne, *m.* to James Naper, esq. of Loughcrew, in the county of Meath, and had issue,
James-Lennox Naper.
William Naper, *d.* unm.
Anne Naper, *m.* to Dillon Pollard, esq. of Castle Pollard, in the county of Westmeath.
Mary, *m.* to Sir Thomas Reade, bart. of Shipton Court, in the county of Oxford, and was mother of Sir John Reade, fourth baronet, of Shipton Court, grandfather of the present Sir John Chandos Reade.

He *d.* about the year 1721, and was *s.* by his elder son,

II. Sir John Dutton, bart. who *m.* first, Mary, daughter of Sir Rushout Cullen, bart. of Upton, in the county of Warwick; and secondly, Mary, daughter of Francis Keck, esq. of Great Tew, in the county of Oxford, but died issueless 1st February, 1743, when the Baronetcy became extinct; while the estates passed, under Sir John Dutton's will, to his nephew,

James-Lennox Naper, esq. of Loughcrew, with an injunction to assume the name and arms of Dutton, which he complied with. He *m.* first, a daughter of General Ingoldsby, and by her had an only child, John, who *d.* unmarried in 1771. He wedded, secondly, Jane, daughter of Christopher Bond, esq. of Newland, in Gloucestershire, and by that lady had, with younger children,

James Dutton, who inherited the English estates, and was "of Sherborne," from which he took the title of Baron Sherborne when elevated to the peerage in 1784. (Refer to Burke's *Peerage and Baronetage.*)

William Dutton, who, upon inheriting the Irish estates, resumed the original surname of Naper, and became "Naper of Loughcrew." (Refer to Burke's *Commoners*, vol. ii. p. 689.)

Arms—Quarterly, arg. and gu.; in the second and third quarters a fret or.

DYCER, OF UPHALL.

Created 18th March, 1660-1.—Extinct circa 1676.

Lineage.

I. Robert Dycer, esq. of Uphall, Herts, was created a Baronet 18th March, 1660-1. He *m.* Dorothy, dau. of William Styles, esq. of Emingston, in Suffolk, and dying 26th August, 1667, aged seventy-two, was *s.* by his son,

II. Sir Robert Dycer, who *m.* Judith, daughter of Richard Gulstone, esq. of Herts, and had an only daughter,

Dorothy, *m.* to William Harvey, esq. M.P. and was great grandmother of the late Sir Eliab Harvey, G.C.B. of Rolls Park, Essex. (See Burke's *Commoners*, vol. ii. p. 434.)

Sir Robert *d.* about 1676, when the Baronetcy expired.

DYER, OF STOUGHTON.

Created 8th June, 1627. Extinct in 1670.

Lineage.

The family of Dyer was one of considerable antiquity and influence.

Sir Richard Dyer, knt. one of the gentlemen of the privy chamber to James I. son of Laurence Dyer, esq. and grandnephew and heir of Sir James Dyer, knt. chief-justice of the Court of Common Pleas, married Maria, daughter of Sir William Fitzwilliams, knt. some time lord deputy of Ireland, and by her, who *d.* in 1601, he left at his decease in 1605, with other issue, a daughter, Anne, *m.* to Sir Edward Carre, knt. and a son,

Sir William Dyer, knt. of Great Stoughton, in the county of Huntingdon, living in 1613, who *m.* Catherine, daughter and co-heir of John Doyley, of Merton, in Oxfordshire, and had issue,

Ludovick.
Richard.
Doyley.
Anne.
Catherine, *m.* to Sir Edward Coke, bart.

The eldest son,

I. Ludovick Dyer, esq. of Great Stoughton, *b.* in 1605, was created a Baronet 8th June, 1627. He *m.* Elizabeth, daughter of Sir Henry Yelverton, knt. but dying without surviving issue in 1670, the title became extinct.

Arms—Sa. three goats passant arg. attired or.

EARLE, OF CRAGLETHORPE.

Created 2nd July, 1629. Extinct 13th Aug. 1697.

Lineage.

I. Sir Richard Earle, of Craglethorpe, in Lincolnshire, who was created a Baronet in 1629, married

---

* Sir Ralph Dutton's estate was sequestered in the great rebellion, and he was forced himself to fly beyond sea; but being beaten back by adverse winds in his passage from Leith to France, he was cast on Barat Island, and died there in 1646.

Frances, daughter of Sir Edward Hartop, bart. of Buckminster, in the county of Leicester, and was *s.* at his decease by his grandson,

II. Sir Richard Earle, son and heir of John Earle, esq. who died *v. p.* This gentleman, having never married, was *s.* at his demise by his uncle,

III. Sir Richard Earle, who *m.* Ellena, daughter of William Welby, esq. of Denton, in Lincolnshire, and by that lady, who wedded, secondly, Edward Payne, esq. of Hough, left at his demise, which occurred about the year 1684, a son and successor,

IV. Sir Richard Earle, at whose demise unmarried 13th August, 1697, aged twenty-four, the Baronetcy became extinct.

Arms—Gu. a fess between three sheldrakes arg.

EAST, OF HALL PLACE.

Created 5th June, 1766.

Extinct 11th Dec. 1828.

Lineage.

This family was one of note for a considerable time in the city of London.

Gilbert East, of the parish of St. Botolph without Bishopsgate, was father of

William East, esq. of the Middle Temple, admitted 14th March, 1675, who *m.* Elizabeth, only daughter of Jeremy Gough, citizen of London, and had by her (who was buried 22nd November, 1748, at Witham, in Essex,) two sons and one surviving daughter (three other daughters died infants), viz.

- William, his successor.
- Gilbert, of the Middle Temple, admitted 22nd March, 1716. He was clerk of the assize for the northern circuit, and lord of the manor of Wenham, in Suffolk. He *d.* unm.
- Martha, *m.* to Sir Philip Parker-a-Morley, bart. and died 30th March, 1758, leaving two daughters,
  - Martha Parker, *m.* to John-Thynne Howe, second Lord Chedworth.
  - Elizabeth Parker, *m.* to James Plunket, esq.

He *d.* 4th March, 1726, and was buried at Witham, in Essex, in the church of which place, on the north side of the chancel, was erected a fine monument of white and grey marble, with a long Latin inscription to the memory of himself, his wife, and children. He was *s.* by his elder son,

William East, esq. of the Middle Temple (admitted 23rd February, 1713). This gentleman was of Hall Place, in the parish of Hurley, in the county of Berks, and of Kennington, in Surrey. He *m.* Anne, only daughter of Sir George Cooke, knt. of Harefield, in Middlesex, chief prothonotary of the Court of Common Pleas, and by that lady (who *d.* 1st April, 1762,) had issue,

- William, his heir.
- Anne, *m.* to Henry Norris, esq. of Hempsted, in Kent, son of Admiral Sir John Norris, knt.
- Elizabeth, *m.* to Sir Capil Molineux, bart. of Castle Dillon, in Ireland.

Mr. East was *s.* at his decease by his son,

I. William East, esq. of Hall Place, in the county of Berks, *b.* 27th February, 1737-8, who was created a Baronet 5th June, 1766. Sir William *m.* 29th June, 1763, at Olveston, in the county of Gloucester, Hannah, second daughter of Henry Casmajor, esq. of Tokington, in that county, and had issue,

- Gilbert, his successor, admitted of the Middle Temple.
- Augustus-Henry, *b.* 24th August, 1766, *m.* 22nd December, 1792, Caroline-Anne, eldest daughter of George Vansittart, esq.
- Mary, *b.* 24th September, 1765.

He wedded, secondly, 29th July, 1769, Miss Jackson, and had another daughter,

- Mary, who *m.* Sir William Clayton, bart. M.P. for Great Marlow, and their second son is the present East George Clayton East, esq. of Hall Place.

Sir William *d.* 12th October, 1819, aged eighty-three, and was *s.* by his son,

II. Sir Gilbert East, bart. *b.* 17th April, 1764; *m.* Eleanor-Mary, eldest daughter of William Jolliffe, esq. but *d. s. p.* 11th December, 1828, when the Baronetcy became extinct. His widow *m.* 31st March, 1834, the Hon. John-Craven Westenra, son of Lord Rossmore.

Arms—Sa. a cheveron between three horses' heads erased arg.

EDWARDS, OF YORK.

Created 7th Dec. 1691.

Extinct 16th Mar. 176[illegible]

Lineage.

William Edwards, esq. of an ancient Welsh family settled in Yorkshire, where he possessed about an hundred pounds a-year, and served as lieutenant colonel in the civil wars under *King* Charles, wherein he lost his life, and his lands fell into the hands of sequestrators. He *m.* the sister (or aunt) of Sir Solomon Swale, of Swale Dale, in the county of York, but does not appear to have had issue. His brother,

Sir James Edwards, knt. was lord mayor of London in 1679, and lent *King* Charles II. thirty thousand pounds while that prince was in exile at Breda, which debt was honourably discharged after the restoration, when he received the honour of knighthood. He *d. s. p.* 13th February, 1690, was buried at Guildhall Chapel, London, and *s.* by his nephew,

I. James Edwards, esq. who was created a Baronet 7th December, 1691. Sir James was of Reedham Hall, in Norfolk, of which county he was sheriff in 1[illegible]; he was also gentleman of the privy-chamber to the king. He *m.* first, a daughter of Mr. Alderman Wright, of York, and had

- James, his successor.

He wedded, secondly, Miss Howell, of Hackney, and by that lady had

- Nathaniel, in holy orders, heir to his brother
- Meriel.

Sarah.
Catherine.
Jane.

Sir James dying in March, 1702, was *s.* by his elder son,

II. Sir James Edwards, bart. F.R.S. who *m.* in 1718, Mary, only daughter and heir of Matthew Kirby, D.D. of Walton-upon-Thames, by whom (who *d.* 31st October, 1739,) he had no issue. He *d.* in 1744, and was *s.* by his half-brother,

III. Sir Nathaniel Edwards, bart. *clerk*, vicar of Weybridge, in Surrey, who died unm. 10th March, 1764, when the Baronetcy became extinct.

Arms—Erm. a lion rampant guardant az. a canton or.

ELDRED, OF SAXHAM MAGNA.

Created 29th Jan. 1641-2.

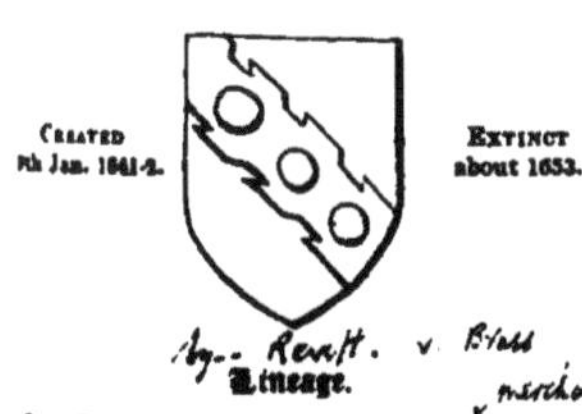

Extinct about 1653.

Lineage.

John Eldred, esq. of Saxham, in Suffolk, (descended from a very ancient family which claimed Saxon origin) had issue, four sons and two daughters, viz.

I. Revet, his heir.
II. John.
III. Joseph, fellow of New College, Oxon, *d. s. p.*
IV. Henry, *d. s. p.*

I. Catherine, *m.* to Sir Samuel Tryon, bart.
II. Anne, *m.* to Sir Robert Henley, knt.

The eldest son,

I. Sir Revet Eldred, of Saxham Magna, in Suffolk, was created a Baronet in 1641-2. He *m.* Anne, dau. and co-heir of John Blakey, or Blackwell, gent. of Hampshire, but by her, who wedded, secondly, Mr. Thomas Arnold, of London, had no issue. He died about 1653, and with him the Baronetcy expired.

Arms—Or, on a bend raguly sa. three besants.

ELLIOTT, OF PEEBLES.

Created 25th July, 1778.—Extinct 7th Nov. 1786.

Lineage.

John Elliott, M. D. physician to the Prince of Wales, was created a Baronet in 1778, but dying unmarried at Brocket Hall, Herts, 7th November, 1786, the title became extinct.

ELLYS, OF WYHAM.

Created 30th June, 1660.

Extinct 14th Jan. 1742.

Lineage.

The name of Ellys is of old standing in the county of Lincoln, of which the parish church of Great Paunton bore evidence, that ancient structure having been erected by Anthony Ellys, esq. who had married a lady of the family of Ascough, as appeared by his and her arms, and the inscription on the tower of the church.

A younger branch of the family had formerly settled in Bedfordshire, and possessed the lordship of Norhill there, but that branch is long extinct.

Sir Thomas Ellis, who received the honour of knighthood from Queen Elizabeth, was great grandfather* of

I. Thomas Ellys, esq. of Wyham, in the county of Lincoln, who was created a Baronet 30th June, 1660, for his eminent services to the house of Stewart. Sir Thomas *m.* Anne, daughter of Sir John Stanhope, of Elvestan, and niece of Philip, first Earl of Chesterfield, by whom he had issue,

William, his successor.
John, who *d.* at the age of twenty-four, unm. and lies buried in the Temple Church.
Jane, *m.* to — Strode, esq. of Barrington, in the county of Somerset, and had a son,
William Strode.

Sir Thomas was *s.* at his decease by his son,

II. Sir William Ellys, bart. who inherited likewise a considerable estate from his uncle, Sir William Ellys, an eminent lawyer in the reign of Charles I. afterwards, *temp.* Charles II. attorney-general, and one of the judges of the Court of Common Pleas. The baronet *m.* Isabella, daughter of the Right Honourable Richard Hampden, sometime chancellor of the exchequer, and grandaughter of the celebrated John Hampden; by her he had five sons and five daughters, of whom only one son and two daughters married, viz.

Richard, eldest son and heir.
Anne, *m.* to Edward Check, esq. of Pergo.
Isabella, *m.* to Richard Hampden.

Sir William *d.* 6th October, 1727, aged seventy-four, and was *s.* by his eldest son,

III. Sir Richard Ellys, bart. who *m.* first, Elizabeth, elder daughter and co-heir of Sir Edward Hussey, bart. of Honington, in the county of Lincoln, and secondly, Sarah, daughter and co-heir of George Gould, esq. of Ivor, in Buckinghamshire, but had no issue. He *d.* 14th January, 1742, when the Baronetcy became extinct.

Arms—Gules, on a fesse, argent, between three crescents, or, as many eschallops, azure.

* Of his daughters,
Dorothy Ellis, *m.* William Ashurst, esq. of Ashurst, in Lancashire.
Frances Ellis, *m.* William Savile, esq. of Oxton, in Nottinghamshire.

ELWES, OF STOKE.

CREATED 22nd June, 1660. 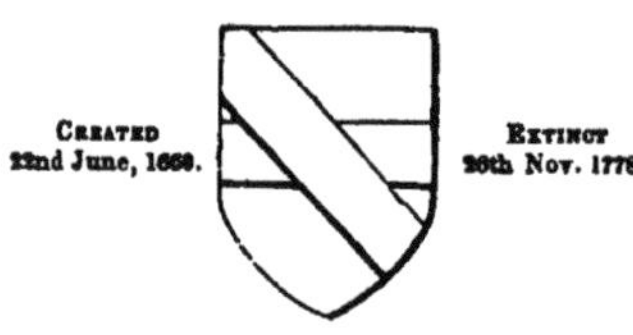 EXTINCT 26th Nov. 1778.

Lineage.

The first of this family upon record,

WILLIAM HELWISH, or ELWES, was of Askham, in the county of York. He *m.* the daughter of — Livesey, of Lancashire, and had issue,

EDWARD, of Askham.

John, of Worlaby, in Lincolnshire, whose son, SIR GERVASE ELWAIES, was lieutenant of the Tower, at the time Sir Thomas Overburie died in custody there, and was executed for being privy to his death, 1 JAMES I. (for details see BURKE'S *Commoners*, vol. ii. p. 464.)

Thomas, of Hubblethorpe, in Lincolnshire.

GEOFFREY, of whom presently.

Mary, *m.* to a merchant of London.

Elizabeth, *m.* to — Burgh.

The youngest son,

GEOFFREY ELWES, an alderman of the city of London, married Elizabeth, daughter of Robert Gabbott, and heir of her brother, Robert Gabbot, a merchant, in London, and by her, who *d.* in 1625, had, with other issue,

JEREMY, his heir, who continued the chief line, which is now represented by ROBERT-CARY ELWES, esq. of Great Billing, in Northamptonshire.

JOHN (third son).

JOHN ELWES, the third son of alderman Geoffrey Elwes, was a citizen of London, and like his father attained the aldermanic gown. He was living in 1634, and marrying Elizabeth, daughter of Roger Hebbs, of Weybridge, in Surrey, was *s.* by his son,

SIR GERVASE ELWES, knt. of Woodford, in Essex, who *m.* Frances, second daughter of Sir Robert Lee, knt. of Billeslee, in the county of Warwick, and by that lady (who wedded secondly, Sir Richard Everard, bart. of Much Waltham,) had issue,

GERVASE, his heir.

Robert, *d.* unm.

Jeremy, of London, merchant, *m.* Miss Lee, of London, and had,

Jeremy.

Catherine, *m.* to Mr. Soame, of London.

——— *m.* to Dr. Pagitt, of Doctors' Commons.

John (Sir), of Grove House, Fulham, *m.* Elizabeth, daughter and co-heir of Walter Raleigh, esq. of East Horsley, Surrey, and had a son,

WILLIAM, who inherited as third baronet.

Mary, *m.* to Thomas Plomer, esq.

Sir Gervase was *s.* by his eldest son,

I. GERVASE ELWES, esq. of Stoke College, in the county of Suffolk, who was created a BARONET, by *King* CHARLES II. 22nd June, 1660. Sir Gervase m. Amy, daughter of Dr. Trigge, of Highworth, in W[illegible]shire, and had issue,

I. Trigge, who *d.* in his father's lifetime.

II. GERVASE *m.* Isabella, daughter of Sir Thomas Hervey, knt. of Ickworth, and sister of the first Earl of Bristol, and dying before his father, left at his decease,

HARVEY, successor to his grandfather.

Amy, *m.* to Robert Meggot, esq. an eminent brewer in the borough of Southwark, grandson of Sir George Meggot, and had issue,

JOHN MEGGOT, who assumed, in 1751, the surname of ELWES, and inherited the estates of his uncle, SIR HARVEY ELWES.

ANNE MEGGOT, *m.* to John Timms, esq. and by him had a son,

RICHARD TIMMS, lieut.-colonel royal horse guards, father of

JOHN TIMMS, who eventually inherited the estates of this branch of the family of ELWES.

III. Richard.

IV. John, captain in the army.

I. Amy, *m.* to Sir John Robinson, knt. of Denston Hall, Suffolk.

II. Frances, *m.* to Ralph Bromsall, esq.

III. Elizabeth,
IV. Rebecca,
V. Anne, } *d.* unm.

Sir Gervase represented the county of *Suffolk* in parliament, and dying in May, 1706, was *s.* by his grandson,

II. SIR HERVEY ELWES, bart. M.P. for Sudbury, *temp. Queen* ANNE. This gentleman, who was of most parsimonious habits, died unmarried, 18th September, 1763, bequeathing his large estates to his nephew JOHN MEGGOT, esq. who had previously assumed the additional surname of ELWES, and afterwards as "ELWES THE MISER," became so notorious by habits the most penurious, generosity the most disinterested, and integrity the most rigid.* The baronetcy, at the decease of Sir Harvey, devolved upon his cousin,

III. SIR WILLIAM ELWES, bart. who resided in Love Lane, Isleworth, upon a very limited income, and was buried there, 26th November, 1778. He appears to have left three sons,

HENRY.

William,
Thomas, } These gentlemen proved their father's will in 1779, after which there is no other clue to any of the name.

If these sons were legitimate, the eldest would have succeeded to the BARONETCY at the death of his father. At the decease of their mother, called Dame Johanna Elwes, formerly Bobulia, none of her kin appear to have taken out letters of administration to her effects.

Arms—Or, a bend gules, surmounted by a fess azure.

---

* ELWES *the Miser*, lived to an advanced age, beyond four score, and died 26th November, 1789. His chief residence, prior to the decease of his uncle, was at his own seat at Marcham; here he had two illegitimate sons, who inherited his great personal property, amounting to several hundred thousand pounds; his landed property fell to his great nephew, JOHN TIMMS, esq. who assumed the name of ELWES, and *d.* at Stoke, 5th February, 1824.

ELWILL, OF EXETER.

Created
th Aug. 1709.

Extinct
1st March, 1778.

Lineage.

i. Sir John Elwill, knt. of Exeter, (whose mother s heiress of Pole, of Exeter,) was created a Baro-t by *Queen* Anne, 26th August, 1709. He *m.* first, ances, daughter of Sir John Bampfylde, bart. of tkimore, in the county of Devon, but by that lady d no issue. Sir John *m.* secondly, Miss Leigh, ughter and heir of — Leigh, esq. of Egham, and d, (with two daughters, the elder married to Mr. ader, of London, the younger to captain Emmerly,) o sons. He *d.* 25th April, 1717, and was *s.* by his ler son,

ii. Sir John Elwill, bart. who *m.* Miss Style, ughter and heir of Humphrey Style, esq. of Lang-y, in Kent, but had no issue. He died 10th Septem-r, 1727, (his widow *m.* secondly, in 1730, Mr. Henry rtlet), and was *s.* by his brother,

iii. Sir Edmund Elwill, bart. who filled for seve-l years the office of comptroller of Excise. He *m.* ne, daughter of William Speke, esq. of Beauchamp, Somersetshire, and dying 2nd February, 1740, was by his only son,

iv. Sir John Elwill, bart. who wedded Selina, dow of Arthur, Earl of Ranelagh, and daughter of ter Bathurst, esq. of Clarendon Park, Wilts, by the dy Selina Shirley, his wife, daughter of Robert, st Earl Ferrers, and had an only daughter,

> Selina-Mary, *m.* first to Felton-Lionel Hervey, esq. and secondly, to the Right Honourable Sir William-Henry Fremantle, K.G.H. By her first husband she was grandmother of the present Sir Frederic H. Bathurst Hervey, bart.

died the 1st of March, 1778, and leaving no male ue, the Baronetcy became extinct.

Arms—Ermine, on a chevron ingrailed, between ee eagles displayed gules, three annulets or.

NGLEFIELD, OF WOTTON BASSET.

Created
h Nov. 1612.

Extinct
21st March, 1822.

Lineage.

The ancient family, according to Camden, was sur-ned from the town of Englefield, or Englesfeld, in rkshire, of which place they are stated to have been proprietors, in the second year of *King* Egbert, A.D. 803. In several pedigrees

Hasculfus de Englefyld, is first mentioned, as Lord of Englefyld, about the time of Canute, afterwards in the fourth year of Harold *Harefoot*, and again in the reign of Hardicanute. He died *temp.* Edward *the Confessor*. This Hasculf purchased a hide of land, in Englefeld, of Hasculf de Pinkeny, to which deed Hely Englefeld, son to another Hasculf Englefeld, was witness.

Guy de Englefyld, son and heir of Hasculf, lived in the time of William *the Conqueror*, and was father of

Hely de Englefeld, living *temp.* William *Rufus*, who had two sons, William and Peter: the elder,

William de Englefeld, gave the parsonage of Englefeld, to the abbey of Reading, Joseph being then abbot in the reign of Henry I. as appears by his deed, *sans date*, sealed with his seal, which deed recites that he gave the said parsonage to the said Joseph, and the convent there, and their successors, in consideration that his ancestors, in time past, had done so, long before his days. This gift of the Church of Englefeld, soon after is mentioned in a charter of *King* Henry II. wherein he confirms the several donations to the Abbot of Reading, but without notice of the donor's name. This William had three sons,

> William (Sir), who *d. s. p.*
> Alan (Sir).
> Thomas.

The second son,

Sir Alan de Englefeld, was father of

William de Englefeld, who was living in the time of Richard I. and was *s.* by his son,

John Englefeld, of Englefeld, father of

Sir William Englefeld, presumed to be the person mentioned with Geoffrey de Leuknore, in an inquisition to enquire about lands, given by *King* John to Margery de Lacy, to found the priory of Acornbury, in the county of Hertford, and by the name of William de Englefeld, is recorded as one of the justices itinerant for the counties of Sussex, Southampton, and Wilts, *anno* 1255, 39 Henry III.; and for Norfolk and Suffolk, 41 Henry III. 1262, for Bedford, Essex, Hertford, and Kent; and 47 Henry III. 1263, for Southampton and Wilts. Sir William's son and heir,

Sir John de Englefeld died in the 4th of Edward I. 1276. He was likewise Lord of Shiplake, Ascott, &c. His son and successor,

Sir William de Englefeld, died in France, in the reign of Edward I. having had issue Roger (Sir), Andrew, and William. The eldest,

Sir Roger de Englefeld, was returned one of the knights for Berkshire, in the parliament 6th Edward II. 1312, and dying 36th Edward III. 1362, left by Joan, his wife, a daughter, Alice, the wife of Mortely, and two sons, Philip (Sir), and William, the elder of whom,

Sir Philip de Englefeld, enjoyed the ancient inheritance, and died 3 Richard II. 1380; by Joan his wife he had three sons,

> i. John (Sir), knight of the shire for Berks, 21st Richard II. He had posterity to the third generation, but the line expiring without male issue, the estate devolved upon the descendants of his next brother.
> ii. Philip.
> iii. Nicholas, of Ricot, in the county of Oxford, comptroller of the household to Richard II. *m.* Jane, daughter and heir of John Clark, of Lanynton-Gernon, and *d.* 1st April, 1415, as appears by his epitaph in Ashdon Church,

Essex.* He left two daughters, his co-heirs, viz.

CICELY, m. to William Fowler.

SIBIL, m. to Richard Quatermains, and Ricote passed to that family, from whom it eventually went to the Norris's, created Baron Norris of Rycote, and eventually centred in the Earls of Abingdon.

The second son,

PHILIP ENGLEFELD, esq. m. Alice, daughter and heir of Walter Rossale, and sister and heir of Sir John Rossale, knt. and thereby acquired the Isle of Rossel, Udlington, Eton, and Yeagden, in the county of Salop. He had issue,

PHILIP, his successor.

ROBERT.

The elder son,

PHILIP ENGLEFELD, esq. of Englefeld, served the office of sheriff of Berkshire in 1439, and died in nine years after, without issue, and was s. by his brother,

ROBERT ENGLEFELD, esq. of Englefeld, who d. in 1473, and was s. by his grandson,

SIR THOMAS ENGLEFELD, of Englefeld, (son of John Englefeld, by Joan, daughter of John Milborn,) who received the honour of knighthood on the marriage of *Prince* ARTHUR, son of HENRY VII. In 1496, he was elected speaker of the House of Commons, and in 1505, was made judge or justice of Chester, which office he held until his death and was speaker of the first parliament called by HENRY VIII. He m. Margery, daughter of Sir Richard Danvers, knt. of Prescot, and had, with other issue,

Richard, who d. without issue.

THOMAS, successor to his father.

Elizabeth, m. to Robert White, esq.

Joan, m. to Henry Lenham, esq.

Anne, m. to William Delabere, esq.

Margaret, m. to John Lyngen, esq.

He was s. by his son,

SIR THOMAS ENGLEFELD, of Englefeld, who was sheriff of the counties of Berks and Oxford in 1520, and having been educated at the Middle Temple, was the next year autumnal reader, and called to the dignity of the coif by letters patent, dated 3rd December, 1524. He had £100 per annum granted to him for life, and three years after was constituted one of the justices of the Court of Common Pleas, having received the honour of knighthood. He m. Elizabeth, daughter of Sir Robert Throckmorton, knt. of Coughton, and had issue,

FRANCIS (Sir), his successor.

JOHN, heir to his brother.

Thomas.

Anne, m. to Humphrey Coningsby, esq. ancestor of the Earls of Coningsby.

Susan, m. to Humphrey Burdet, esq.

Margaret, m. first to George Carew, esq. and secondly, to Sir Edward Saunders, knt. lord chief baron of the Exchequer, *temp.* ELIZABETH.

He died in 1537, and was s. by his eldest son,

SIR FRANCIS ENGLEFELD, of Englefeld, who was sheriff of the counties of Berks and Oxford, at the death of HENRY VIII. and first year of Edward VI. and received the honour of knighthood 22nd February, 1547. He was one of the chief officers in the *Princess* MARY's family, and one of those sent by the protector and council to prohibit the hearing and celebrating mass in her highness's house; but refusing to deliver such orders, and submitting rather to any punishment, he was committed for several months to prison, with Sir Robert Rochester, Sir Walgrave, and Dr. Francis Mallet, the princess's chaplain. Upon *Queen* MARY's accession to the throne, he was, in consideration of his faithful services, sworn of the privy council, appointed master of the wards, and had from the crown, the manor and park of Fullbrook, in the county of Warwick, to hold *in capite*, being part of the forfeited lands of the attainted John Dudley, Duke of Northumberland. He sate in parliament, in the same reign, for the county of Berks; but on Elizabeth's accession, he was obliged, with Sir Thomas Gage, Sir Thomas Shelley, and others, to depart the kingdom. In the 6th of ELIZABETH, he was indicted in the King's Bench for high treason committed at Nemures, in *partibus transmarinis*, and outlawed. He was subsequently attainted and convicted of high treason, at the parliament, 29th October, 29 ELIZABETH, and all his manors, lands, and vast possessions were declared forfeited to the queen; but Sir Francis having by indenture of the 18th of the same reign, settled his manor and estate of Englefeld on Francis, his nephew, with power, notwithstanding, of revoking his grant, if he, during his natural life, should deliver or tender to his nephew a gold ring; with intent to make void the uses of his said settlement, various disputes and points of law arose, whether the said manor and estate of Englefield were forfeited to the queen; but the case, after procrastinated discussion, not appearing clear, the queen, in the ensuing parliament, 35 ELIZABETH, had a special act passed to confirm the attainder, and to establish the forfeiture to herself, her heirs, and assigns; enacting that the queen should take the advantage of revocating an assurance, with a condition made by him upon the tender of a ring of gold to his nephew, &c.; and the queen in consequence tendering by R. Broughton and H. [illegible] the ring to Englefield, the nephew, seized and confiscated the said manors and estate, and many other possessions. By this arbitrary stretch of power, the manor and estate of Englefeld, which had been upwards of 780 years in the family, were alienated and transferred to the crown. Sir Francis retired to Valladolid, in Spain, where he was a bountiful benefactor to the English College, and being worn out with persecution and years, died, and was buried there, about the year 1592. He m. Catherine, daughter and heir of Sir Thomas Fettiplace, of Compton Beauchamp in the Vale of Berks; but having no issue, the representation of the family devolved upon his brother,

JOHN ENGLEFELD, esq. Lord of Wotton Basset in Wiltshire, who m. Margaret, daughter of Sir Edward Fitton, knt. lord president of Connaught, of Gawsworth, in Cheshire,† and dying 1st April, 1567, was s. by his only child,

I. FRANCIS ENGLEFIELD, esq. of Wotton Basset in the county of Wilts, as well as Englefield, in Berks, who was created a BARONET by *King* JAMES I [illegible] November, 1612. Sir Francis m. a daughter of the Honourable Anthony Brown, eldest son of Anthony, first Viscount Montague, and had issue,

I. Thomas, m. Mary, daughter of William W[illegible]cot, esq. of Shenfield, Berkshire, but died before his father, *s. p.*

II. FRANCIS (Sir), heir to his father.

III. THOMAS, who s. as fourth baronet.

---

* Here lyth Nicholas Inglefield Esquyr, sometime Controler of the Hous to King Rychard II. who died the first of April, in the Yere of Grase, M.CCCC.XV. whos Soul, Jesu Perdon. Amen, Amen, Amen.

† By Mary, his wife, daughter of Sir G[illegible]bottle, knt. of Horton, and Jane, his wife, daughter of Henry Willoughby, knt. of Risley, in the county of Derby.

IV. John, *d.* before his father, unm.

V. Anthony, of White-Knights, near Reading, *m.* Susan, daughter of — Ryley, esq. of Oxford, by whom, who *d.* 2nd June, 1664, and was buried in the middle of the north chancel of Sunning Church, Berks, he had a son and heir,

Anthony, who *m.* Alice, daughter of Thomas Stokes, esq. of London, and had a numerous family.* He was *s.* by his eldest surviving son,

Henry, of White-Knights, who *m.* Catherine, daughter of Benjamin Poole, esq. of London, and had with other issue,†

HENRY, who *s.* as sixth baronet.

VI. William, who left at his decease in 1662, a daughter and heir, the wife of — Fettiplace, esq.

VII. Henry, *m.* first, Elizabeth, daughter of — Pickford, of Cornwall, but by her had no issue; secondly, Elizabeth, daughter of Sir Walter Blount, bart. of Sodington, by whom he had,

Henry, *d.* unm.

Elizabeth, *m.* to Sir William Kennedy, of Ireland.

Mary, *m.* to Thomas Havers, esq. of Thelton, in Norfolk.

Catherine.

He wedded, thirdly, Anne, daughter of John Huband, esq. of Ipsley, in the county of Warwick, but by that lady had no issue.

I. Dorothy, *m.* to Sir Edward Morgan, bart. of Llantarnam, in Monmouthshire.

II. Mary, *m.* to Christopher, fourth Lord Teynham.

III. Margaret, *m.* first, to Hatton Berners, esq. of Whittlebury, in the county of Northampton, and secondly, to Sir William Bradshaigh, knt.

Sir Francis lived until 1631, as appears by a beautiful monument in the north chapel of Englefield Church, against the north wall, adorned with the portraitures of a knight in armour, and his lady, both kneeling at desk; behind him kneel four sons, and behind her one daughter, in praying postures; on the side of the desk, the arms of Englefield, impaling Browne; under the monument, there is a brass plate on a stone thus engraved:

Here lyeth interr'd
The Body of Sir Francis Englefield, Baronet,
(Only Child of John Englefield, Esq; and Margaret,
His Wife,) who married Jane, eldest Daughter to
Anthony Browne,
Eldest Son of Anthony, Viscount Mountagu,
By whom he had issue ten Children, viz.
Thomas, Dorothy, Francis, Thomas, John,
Anthony, William, Mary, Margaret,
And Henry; of which,
Thomas, the elder, Dorothy, and John,
Died before their Father.
He dyed
The 26th of Octb.
Anno Dom. 1631.
Being 60 Years, 3 Months, and 27 Days old.

Sir Francis was *s.* by his eldest surviving son,

II. SIR FRANCIS ENGLEFIELD, bart. who had received the honour of knighthood from *King* JAMES I. 19th August, 1622. He *m.* Winifred, daughter and co-heir of William Brooksby, esq. of Sholeby, in the county of Leicester, and had issue,

FRANCIS, his heir.

Helen, *m.* to Sir Charles Waldegrave, bart. and was mother of

HENRY, first BARON WALDEGRAVE.

Mary, *m.* to Sir George Browne, K.B.

Catherine, *m.* to William Turvile, esq. of Aston Flamvile, in the county of Leicester.

Sir Francis *d.* 1st May, 1666,‡ and was *s.* by his son,

III. SIR FRANCIS ENGLEFIELD, bart. who *m.* Lady Honoria O'Bryen, daughter of Henry, Earl of Thomond, but had no issue; his lady surviving him, married secondly, Sir Robert Howard, knt. sixth son of Thomas, first Earl of Berkshire. The baronet was *s.* in his title and estates by his uncle,

IV. SIR THOMAS ENGLEFIELD, bart. who *m.* first, Mary, daughter of Sir Henry Winchcomb, bart. but by that lady had no issue. He wedded, secondly, Mary, daughter of George Huntley, esq. of the county of Gloucester, and had

CHARLES, his successor.

Anne, *d.* unm. in 1678.

Philadelphia, *m.* to Henry Fossan, gent.

Elizabeth, who also married.

Sir Thomas was *s.* at his decease by his son,

V. SIR CHARLES ENGLEFIELD, bart. who *m.* Susan, natural daughter of John, Lord Culpeper, and had issue, THOMAS and Charlotte, who both died young. He *d.* 21st April, 1728, and was *s.* by his cousin (refer to issue of Anthony, of White Knights, fifth son of the first baronet),

VI. SIR HENRY ENGLEFIELD, bart. who *m.* first in 1742, Mary, daughter of Thomas Berkeley, esq. of Spetchley, in the county of Worcester, by whom he had no surviving issue. He wedded, secondly, in 1751, Catharine, daughter of Sir Charles Bucke, bart. of Hanby Grange, in the county of Lincoln, and by that lady had

HENRY-CHARLES, his heir.

Francis.

Francis-Michael.

Ethelinda-Catherine.

Teresa-Anne.

He *d.* 25th May, 1780, and was *s.* by his eldest son,

VII. SIR HENRY-CHARLES ENGLEFIELD, bart. who *d.* 21st March, 1822, when the title became EXTINCT.

Arms—Az. a griffin passant and a chief or.

---

* There were ten sons and seven daughters. The former all died unmarried, except HENRY, the fourth son, who succeeded his father. Of the daughters, Martha, *m.* Walter Blount, esq. of Maple Durham; Elizabeth, *m.* William, son of Sir John Dorrington, knt. of Sussex; and Mary, *m.* Sir William Swinburne, bart. of Capheaton. The others were either nuns or died unmarried.

† The younger children of this Henry and Catherine (who survived his widow, and *m.* Edward Webb, esq. of Gray's Inn, London), were

Charles, } *d.* unm.
Francis, }

Catherine, *d.* young.

Theresa.

Martha.

Mary, *m.* to Francis Smith Carrington, esq. of Wotton Hall, in Warwickshire.

Elizabeth. Anne.

‡ Sir Francis was obliged to obtain the following letter from *King* CHARLES I. to protect him from the pains and penalties of recusancy:

CHARLES REX,

WHEREAS our trusty and well beloved Sir Francis Englefield, Knight and Baronet, being a recusant, is thereby subject to our laws and statutes in that case provided: these are to signify our royal will and pleasure, that no person or persons shall, at any time hereafter, sue, prosecute, or implead, either by way of indictment, information, or otherwise, against the said Sir Francis, for being a recusant, or convicted by virtue of any of our laws or statutes against Popish recusants, till we shall signify our pleasure to the contrary. Given under our signet, at our palace of Westminster, Decemb. the 6th, in the 10th year of our reign.

ENYON, OF FLORE.

CREATED in 1642.

EXTINCT in 1642.

Lineage.

JAMES ENYON, esq. of Honingham, Warwickshire, who purchased the manor of Flore, in Northamptonshire, died 25th September, 1623, leaving by Constance his wife, a son and successor,

JAMES ENYON, esq. of Flore, who m. Dorothy, eldest daughter of Thomas Coxe, esq. of Bishops Itchington, in Warwickshire, and by her, who m. secondly, John Wyrley, esq. of Dodford, and died in 1678, aged eighty-three, had, with two daughters, Constance, m. in 1631, to Robert Wilmer, esq. of Sywell, and Alice, m. to Hannibal Horsey, esq. of Honingham, a son,

I. JAMES ENYON, esq. of Flore, who was created a BARONET in 1642. He m. Jane, daughter of Sir Adam Newton, bart. of Charlton, in Kent, and had issue,

- DOROTHY, m. to Thomas Stanley, esq. son and heir of Sir Thomas Stanley, of Cumberlow Green, Herts.
- CONSTANCE, m. to Richard Minshull, eldest surviving son of Richard, Lord Minshull.
- CATHERINE, m. first to Sir George Buswell, bart. of Clipston, and secondly, to Sir John Garrard, bart. of Lamer; by the latter she left a daughter and heir,
  - JANE GARRARD, m. to Montagu Drake, esq. of Shardeloes.

Sir James Enyon, before the expiration of the year in which he was created a baronet, fell in a duel with Sir Nicholas Crispe. Both parties were volunteers in the royal cause, and the dispute arose at their quarters in Gloucestershire. The fatal result made an indelible impression on the mind of the survivor, who ever after wore mourning, except in the field of battle, when he cherished the hope of being united to his friend by a fortunate bullet; and through life, hallowed every return of the melancholy anniversary, by closing his chamber in darkness, and devoting himself to fasting and prayer. Sir James Enyon dying without male issue, the title expired with him. The manor of Flore, after passing through many families, is now the property of that of PACK.

Arms—Arg. a chev. between three ravens sa.

ERNLE, OF ETCHILHAMPTON.

CREATED 2nd Feb. 1661.

EXTINCT 30th Dec. 1787.

Lineage.

MICHAEL ERNLE, esq. of Bourton, lineally descended from Richard de Ernle of Ernle, living *temp.* HENRY III. served as sheriff of Wiltshire 22nd ELIZABETH. He m. first Mary, only daughter and heir of R... Finnamore, esq. of Whetham House, in the parish of Calne, Wilts, and by her had two sons and two daughters,

- JOHN (Sir), knt. of Whetham, ancestor of the ERNLES of WHETHAM, in Wiltshire, now represented by Major-General JAMES KYRLE-M... of Much Marcle, in Herefordshire, and of Whetham in Wiltshire. (See BURKE'S Commoners, vol. iii. p. 615.)
- Richard.
- Mary, m. to William Blacker, esq. of New Sarum.
- Cecilia, m. to William Daniel, esq.

Michael Ernle wedded, secondly, Susan, eldest daughter and co-heir of Sir Walter Hungerford, knt. of Farley Castle, in Somersetshire, eldest son of Walter, Lord Hungerford, and by her, who m. secondly, Sir Carew Reynolds, knt. was father of

EDWARD ERNLE, esq. of Etchilhampton, in Wiltshire, baptized at Calne 4th December, 1567, who m. Gertrude, daughter of John St. Lowe, esq. of Knighton, in the same county, and by her, who d. 21st April, 1662, had two sons, viz.

- WALTER (Sir), his heir.
- Michael, of Brimslade, in Wiltshire, who m. Mary, daughter of William Wither, esq. of Manydown, in Hants, and was father of
  - EDWARD, of Brimslade Park, who died ... February, 1734, aged sixty-three, having issue,
    - MICHAEL, who assumed the baronetcy on the demise of Sir John Ernle, the ... baronet.
    - EDWARD, successor to his brother.
    - John, fellow of New College, d. 1737, aged twenty-five.
    - Frances, d. unm.
    - Another daughter, m. to William J..., esq. of Ramsbury Manor, Wilts, and ... two daughters and co-heirs,
      - ELIZABETH, m. to William Langham, esq.
      - ELEANOR, m. to Francis Burdett, esq.

Mr. Ernle d. 30th November, 1656, was buried at Bishop's Cannings, and s. by his son,

I. SIR WALTER ERNLE, of Etchilhampton, who was created a BARONET 2nd February, 1660-1. He m. Martha, daughter of Edward Tooker, esq. of Maddington, and sister and co-heir of Sir Giles Tooker, bart. and had by her (who was buried at Maddington 16th Nov. 1683) two sons and a daughter, viz.

1. EDWARD, b. 17th October, 1649; m. Anne, daughter of Edward Ashe, esq. of Heytesbury, in Wiltshire, and dying v. p. 21st June, 16.., left issue,
   - WALTER, successor to his grandfather
   - EDWARD, heir to his brother.
   - Michael, buried at Bishop's Cannings ... November, 1674.
   - Elizabeth, m. to Thomas Shatterden, esq. who took the surname of DRAX, and secondly, to John Colleton, esq. By the former she left a son,
     - HENRY DRAX, esq. of Ellerton Abbey, who m. Elizabeth, only surviving daughter and heir of SIR EDWARD ERNLE, bart.

II. Walter, of Conock, in Wiltshire, high sheriff of that county in 1716; m. Mary, sister and co-heir of Anthony Hungerford, esq. of the Leigh near Cricklade, and dying 27th January, 1720-1, left issue,

1. WALTER (Sir), of Conock, who inherited the BARONETCY on the demise of his cousin, Sir Edward Ernle, bart. of Maddington, third baronet. Sir Walter *d. s. p.* 16th July, 1732, aged fifty-six.
2. JOHN (Sir), of Conock, successor to his brother as fifth baronet.

1. Gertrude, *m.* to Isaac Warriner, esq. and *d.* 21st December, 1700, and was mother of Gifford Warriner, esq. who *m.* his cousin, Elizabeth Ernle.

1. Susan, baptized 24th November, 1665, *m.* at Maddington 14th September, 1685, to William Whitaker, esq. of Motcomb, in Dorsetshire.

Sir Walter *d.* 25th July, 1682, was buried at Bishop's Cannings, and *s.* by his grandson,

II. SIR WALTER ERNLE, who *d.* in minority in 1690, and was *s.* by his brother,

III. SIR EDWARD ERNLE, who *m.* FRANCES, only daughter and heir of General the *Rt. Hon.* THOMAS ERLE, of Charborough, member of the privy council *temp. Queen* ANNE and GEORGE I. and had an only daughter and heir,

ELIZABETH, who *m.* Henry Drax, esq. of Ellerton Abbey, in Yorkshire, and was great grandmother of the present Mrs. SAWBRIDGE ERLE-DRAX, of Charborough Park, in Dorsetshire.

Sir Edward Ernle *d.* 31st January, 1728-9, and was *s.* in the baronetcy by his cousin,

IV. SIR WALTER ERNLE, at whose decease *s. p.* 16th July, 1732, aged fifty-six, the title passed to his brother,

V. THE REV. SIR JOHN ERNLE, rector of All Cannings, Wilts, who *m.* Elizabeth, daughter of John Smith, esq. of Alton, and *d.* 20th March, 1734, leaving an only surviving daughter and heir,

ELIZABETH, *b.* 20th April, 1716, who *m.* Gifford Warriner, esq. and *d.* 17th November, 1757, leaving a son and successor,

GIFFORD WARRINER, esq. of Conock, who *m.* Elizabeth, daughter of Gabriel Hutfield, esq. of Hays, in Kent, and *d.* 30th January, 1820, aged seventy-four, leaving two sons,

Gifford Warriner.

ERNLE WARRINER, of Conock Manor House, Wilts, *m.* Susan, second daughter of the Rev. John Amyet, of South Brent in Devon, and has issue.

Sir John died 20th March, 1734, when the baronetcy was assumed by his kinsman,*

VI. SIR MICHAEL ERNLE, of Brimslade Park, who died unm. 16th February, 1771, aged sixty-seven, and was *s.* by his brother,

VII. THE REV. SIR EDWARD ERNLE, rector of Avington, Berks, who *d.* 26th December, 1787, aged seventy-five, the last male heir of this family.

Arms—Arg. on a bend sa. three eagles displayed or.

ESSEX, OF BEWCOT.

CREATED 25th Nov. 1612. EXTINCT ....

Lineage.

The family of Essex, one of remote antiquity, was originally settled in the county from which it derived its surname, but acquired considerable property in Berks, *temp.* HENRY VIII. partly by inheritance from the Rogerses, of Benham, and partly by purchase.

THOMAS ESSEX, esq. of Bewcot, in Berkshire, son and heir of Sir Thomas Essex, knt. of the same place, married Joan, daughter of Thomas Harrison, esq. and had, with a daughter, Joan, wife of William Anderson, esq. a son and successor,

I. WILLIAM ESSEX, esq. of Bewcot, in Berkshire, who was created a BARONET in 1612. He *m.* Jane, eldest daughter of Sir Walter Harcourt, of Stanton Harcourt, Oxfordshire, and had a son,

CHARLES, colonel in the parliamentary service.

Sir William having subsequently dissipated his ample inheritance, accepted the command of a company of foot, under the parliament, in the regiment commanded by his son Colonel Charles Essex, and was taken prisoner at the battle of Edgehill, in which his son was slain. Sir William died soon after, *s. p.* and the BARONETCY EXPIRED.

Arms—Arg. an orle gu.

ESTCOURT, OF NEWTON.

CREATED 17th Mar. 1626-7. EXTINCT about 1684.

Lineage.

I. SIR GILES ESTCOURT, of Newton, in Wiltshire, created a BARONET 17th March, 1626-7, married Anne, daughter of Sir Robert Mordaunt, bart. of Little Massingham, in Norfolk, and was father of

II. SIR GILES ESTCOURT, slain in Italy. He died unm. and was *s.* by his brother,

III. SIR WILLIAM ESTCOURT, who was killed at the Globe Tavern, London, by Henry St. John, esq. about 1684, and as he never married, the title EXPIRED with him.

Arms—Erm. on a chief indented gu. three etoiles or.

* There must have been a special limitation in the patent, or the title could not have descended to the Brimslade branch, which derived from the *brother* of the first baronet.

ETHERINGTON, OF KINGSTON-UPON HULL.

CREATED 22nd Nov. 1775.

EXTINCT 16th Aug. 1819.

Lineage.

HENRY ETHERINGTON, esq. descended from the Etheringtons of Great Driffield, in the county of York, was a merchant of opulence, at Kingston-upon-Hull, and m. Miss Jane Porter, by whom he had surviving issue,

HENRY, his heir.

Jane, d. unm.

Margaret, m. to John Mons, esq. of Walsingham, in Durham.

He was s. at his decease by his son,

I. HENRY ETHERINGTON, esq. of Kingston-upon-Hull, who was created a BARONET 22nd November, 1775. Sir Henry m. Maria-Constantia, daughter of Sir Thomas Cane, bart. but dying s. p. 16th August, 1819, the title became EXTINCT.

Arms—Per pale, argent and sable, three lions rampant counterchanged, two and two.

EVELYN, OF GODSTONE.

CREATED 29th May, 1660.

EXTINCT in 1671.

Lineage.

The family of Evelyn came, according to the earliest accounts, from Evelyn, in Shropshire, and removed thence to Harrow on the Hill, Middlesex, *temp.* HENRY IV. In 1579,

GEORGE EVELYN, esq. of Long Ditton, (who first brought the art of making gunpowder to perfection in England) purchased Wotton, in Surrey. He m. first, Rose, daughter and heir of Thomas Williams, esq. nephew of Sir John Williams, knt. by whom he had ten sons and six daughters, of whom,

THOMAS (Sir), was of Long Ditton.

JOHN (Sir), was of Godstone.

GEORGE, was of Everley and West Dene. The daughter and heiress of Sir John Evelyn, knt. of West Dene, m. Robert Pierrepoint, esq. of Thoresby, and was mother of Evelyn, Duke of Kingston.

He wedded, secondly, Joan Stint, and had by her six sons and two daughters, of whom he left surviving at

his decease in 1603, a daughter, Catherine, m. to Thomas Stoughton, esq. of Stoughton, and one son.

RICHARD, of Wotton, ancestor of the EVELYNS of Wotton, and of John Evelyn, esq. the elegant author of "Silvia."

The second son of George Evelyn, by his first wife,

SIR JOHN EVELYN, knt. of Godstone and Marden, M. P. took part with the parliament against the king, and was a distinguished actor in the unhappy events of the disastrous period in which he lived. He m. Elizabeth, daughter and heir of William Stevens, and had issue,

JOHN, his heir.

Elizabeth, m. to Edward Engham.

Frances, m. to Francis Clerk.

Margaret, m. to John Saunders.

Ann, m. to John Hartopp.

Jane, m. to Sir Anthony Benn.

Susan.

Sarah.

Sir John Evelyn was s. by his son,

SIR JOHN EVELYN, of Godstone, knt. who m. in 1618, Thomasine, daughter and co-heir of William Heynes, esq. of Chesington, and by her (who was buried at Godstone in 1643) had issue,

I. JOHN, his heir.

II. George, of Nutfield, who died in 1699, leaving by Margaret, his first wife, with several daughters, two sons,

1. George, b. in 1678, of Nutfield and Rookesnest, who m. Mary, daughter of Thomas Garth, esq. and by her, who wedded, secondly, Charles Boone, esq. left at his decease in 1724, three daughters, viz.

Ann, m. first to Thomas Gregg, and secondly to Daniel Boone, esq.

Elizabeth, m. to Peter Bathurst, esq. of Clarendon Park.

Mary, died unm. 1744.

2. Edward, b. in 1681, of Felbridge, in Surrey, who m. Julia, daughter of the Duke of Ormond, and dying in 1751, left with a daughter, Julia, m. to James Sayer, esq. a son,

JAMES, of Felbridge, who m. first in 1734 Annabella, daughter of Thomas Medley, esq. of Buxted, and secondly in 1761, Jane, widow of Francis Fane, esq. and a daughter of Sir Richard Cust. He died, leaving by his first wife, two daughters and co-heirs, viz.

Ann, d. unm. in 1791.

Julia-Annabella, m. to Sir George Augustus Shuckburgh, bart. who assumed the surname of EVELYN, and had an only daughter,

Julia, m. to the Hon. Charles C. Jenkinson, now Earl of Liverpool, and died in 1814, leaving three daughters.

George Evelyn, of Nutfield, left by Frances, his second wife, a son,

William, of St. Clere, in Kent, who m. first, Frances, daughter and heir of William Glanville, esq. and assumed the surname of GLANVILLE. By her he had a daughter

FRANCES, m. to Admiral Edward Boscawen, and had issue,

George-Evelyn, third Viscount Falmouth.

Frances, m. to Admiral John Leveson Gower.
Elizabeth, m. to Henry, fifth Duke of Beaufort.

He m. secondly, Bridget, daughter of — Raymond, esq. and had issue,

William, of St. Clere, M.P. for Hythe, whose daughter and heiress, Frances, m. Alexander Hume, esq. who took the name of Evelyn.
George-Raymond, who m. Jane-Elizabeth, Countess of Rothes, and by her ladyship, who wedded secondly, Sir Lucas Pepys, bart. had a son,
George-William, tenth Earl of Rothes.
A daughter m. to — Langton, esq. of Somerset.
Sarah, m. to Charles Price, esq.
A daughter.

i. Jane, b. in 1631, m. to Sir William Leach, of Squerries, in Kent.
ii. Elizabeth, m. to Edward Hales, esq.

The eldest son,

i. Sir John Evelyn, knt. of Godstone, b. 12th March, 1632-3, was created a Baronet in 1660. He m. first, Mary, daughter of George Farmer, esq. one of the prothonotaries of the Common Pleas, and secondly, Ann, daughter of Sir John Glynn, of Henley Park, serjeant-at-law, but had no issue. Sir John, by great extravagance, wasted his estate, and after his decease, the property of Marden was sold to Sir Robert Clayton, knt. He died in 1671, when the Baronetcy expired, but the representation of this branch of the ancient family of Evelyn, together with the manor of Godstone, devolved on his brother, George Evelyn, esq. of Nutfield.

Arms—Az. a griffin passant and a chief or.

EVELYN, OF LONG DITTON.

Created 17th Feb. 1682-3.—Extinct 3rd May, 1692.

Lineage.

Thomas Evelyn, esq. of Long Ditton, in Surrey, eldest son of George Evelyn, esq. of Wotton, by Rose Williams, his first wife, married 1st December, 1577, Francisca Moore, and had issue, to marry,

Thomas (Sir), his heir.

Jane, m. 1604-5, to John Bodley.
Elizabeth, m. to Henry Constantine.
Dorothy, m. to James Dockeris.
Frances, m. to Edward Ventris.
Rose, m. to Thomas Keitley, citizen of London.

His son and successor,

Sir Thomas Evelyn, knt. of Long Ditton, baptized ... August, 1587, married Anna, daughter and heir of Hugh Gold, and dying in 1659, was s. by his son,

i. Sir Edward Evelyn, of Long Ditton, born 25th January, 1625-6, who was created a Baronet in 1682-3. He m. Mary Balam, and by her, who was buried 10th July, 1696, had issue to survive infancy,

Ann, b. in 1661, m. 1682, to William Hill, esq. of Teddington, Middlesex.
Mary, b. in 1662, m. 1685, to William Glynn, esq.
Penelope, b. in 1672, m. 1690, to Sir Joseph Alston, bart.

Sir Edward died 3rd May, 1692, when the Baronetcy became extinct. The manor of Long Ditton, which descended to the Alstons, was sold, previously to 1721, by Evelyn Alston, esq. to Sir Peter King, afterwards Lord King.

Arms—As Evelyn of Godstone.

EVERARD, OF MUCH WALTHAM.

Created 29th Jan. 1628-9.  Extinct in 1745.

Lineage.

Ralph Everard, living in the reign of Henry III. and of Edward I. was father of

Walter Everard, living *temp.* Edward II. and Edward III. who left a son,

William Everard, of Marshbury, in Essex, whose son and heir was living there in the reigns of Richard II. and Henry IV.; he (the son) had two sons, both baptised, John; of whom

John Everard, the elder, was of Newarks, in Good-Estre, and Marchbury. He left a son and heir,

Thomas Everard, of Waltham-Magna, who m. the daughter and co-heir of John Cornish, of Langleys, in Much Waltham, and county of Essex, and had six sons and three daughters. He was living in the reign of Henry VII. and was s. by his fourth son,

Richard Everard, esq. in the manor of Langles, in Much Waltham. He m. first, Elizabeth, daughter of Richard Stephens, gent. and had, with three daughters, an only son, Richard. He m. secondly, Agnes-Upcher, relict of Thomas Wood, and by her had another daughter. He possessed the manor of Langleys, and the manor of Havering, in Felsted, and several lands and tenements, in Little Raine, Little Dunmore, Good-Estre, High-Estre, with lands and tenements in Great Waltham. He d. 29th December, 1561, and was s. by his grandson, (on whom and his heirs, by will dated 19th December, 1561, he settled the manors of Langleys and Havering,)

Richard Everard, esq. of Langles, (son of Richard Everard, by Mary, his wife, daughter of Thomas Wood, of Raine Parva.) This gentleman m. Clementia, daughter of John Wiseman, esq. of Great Canfield, and had issue,

Anthony (Sir), his heir.
Matthew, d. s. p.
Hugh, heir to Much Waltham at the decease of his eldest brother.
John, of Great Badon.
Mary, m. to John Wiseman, esq.

This Richard and his wife lived together fifty-three years. She died in September, 1611, and he the 25th July, 1617; both lie buried in Waltham Church. He was s. by his eldest son,

Sir Anthony Everard, who received the honour of knighthood 23rd July, 1603, before the coronation of *King* James I. He m. first, Anne, daughter of Sir Thomas Bernardiston, knt. of Ketton, in Suffolk, by whom he left an only daughter and heir,

Anne, m. to Sir William Maynard, bart. of Little Easton, afterwards created Lord Maynard, (refer to Burke's *Peerage and Baronetage*,) and carried lands in Fox-heath, and several other parishes, with the lordship of Sandon, out of the family.

Sir Anthony m. secondly, Anne, daughter of Sir Anthony Felton, K. B. of Playford, in Suffolk, but by that lady had no issue. He d. in 1614, was buried at Waltham, and succeeded by his brother,

Hugh Everard, esq. of Much Waltham, who was sheriff of Essex in 1626. He m. Mary, daughter of Thomas Brand, otherwise Bond, gent. and dying in 1637, (his wife died the same year, and both were buried in Waltham Church) was s. by his only son,

I. Richard Everard, esq. of Much Waltham, in the county of Essex, who was created a Baronet by *King* Charles I. 29th January, 1628-9. Sir Richard m. first, Joan, daughter of Sir Francis Barrington, bart. and had issue,

- Richard, his heir.
- Barrington.
- Robert, d. issueless.
- Hugh, fellow of Emmanuel College, Cambridge.
- Winifred, m. to Sir William Luckyn, bart.

He wedded, secondly, Frances, daughter of Sir Robert Lee, of Billesley, in the county of Warwick, relict of Sir Gervase Elwes, knt. of Woodford, in Essex, but by her had no issue. He was s. at his decease by his eldest son,

II. Sir Richard Everard, bart. who was sheriff of Essex in the 20th of Charles I. He m. first, Elizabeth, daughter of Sir Henry Gibbs, of Falkland, in Scotland, knight of the bed chamber to *King* James I. and by her had,

- Richard d. unm.
- Hugh, his heir.
- Jane, d. young.

Sir Richard m. secondly, Jane, daughter of Sir John Finnet, master of the ceremonies to James I. and Charles I. He d. in August, 1694, aged seventy, and was s. by his son,

III. Sir Hugh Everard, bart. a military man, who in his early life had distinguished himself in Flanders. He m. Mary, daughter of John Brown, M.D. of Salisbury, and had

- Richard, his successor.
- Hugh, drowned in the great storm in 1703. He was lieutenant of the Restoration.
- Morton, killed on board the Hampshire, commanded by Lord Maynard.
- Elizabeth, m. to the Rev. Mr. O'Burne, vicar of Thaxted, in Essex.
- Frances, d. unm.

Sir Hugh was receiver general of the land tax, and justice of the peace for the county of Essex. He d. in January, 1705-6, aged fifty-one, was buried at Waltham, and s. by his son,

IV. Sir Richard Everard, bart. who m. Susanna, daughter, and co-heir of Richard Kidder, D.D. bishop of Bath and Wells, (his lordship was killed at his palace in Wells, by the great storm in November, 1703,) and had issue,

- Richard, his heir.
- Hugh, heir to his brother.
- Susanna, m. in Virginia, to Mr. White, a considerable merchant and planter there.

Sir Richard was governor of North Carolina, under the lord proprietors, and after his return to England, d. in Red Lion Street, London, 17th February, 1732-3. His widow d. 12th September, 1739. He was s. by his elder son,

V. Sir Richard Everard, bart. who d. unm. [illegible] March, 1741-2, and was s. by his brother,

VI. Sir Hugh Everard, bart. who went out to Georgia and m. there; but dying issueless in 1745, the Baronetcy became extinct.

Arms—Argent, a fesse wavy, between three estoiles, gules.

EYLES, OF LONDON.

Created 1st Dec. 1714.

Extinct 1st Nov. 17[illegible].

Lineage.

Sir John Eyles, of an ancient Wiltshire family, received the honour of knighthood from *King* James II. in the last year of that prince's reign. Sir John was then lord mayor of London, and vacated the civic chair on the arrival of the Prince of Orange. He m. Miss Cowper, daughter of a citizen of London, and had issue,

- I. ——, his heir.
- II. Francis, who died at Earnshill, in the county of Somerset, in December, 1735, and left his estate to his nephew, Francis Eyles, esq. M.P. for Devizes.
- I. Sarah, m. to Joseph Haskin Styles, esq. of London.
- II. Mary, m. to Sir John Smyth, bart. of Isleworth.
- III. Elizabeth, m. in 1716, to James Montagu, esq. of Lackham.

Sir John resided at South Broom Hall, in the county of Wilts. His brother,

I. Francis Eyles, esq. an eminent merchant and alderman of London, and many years one of the directors of the East India Company, was created a Baronet by *King* George I. 1st December, 1714. He m. Elizabeth, daughter of Mr. Ayley, of London, merchant, and by that lady, who d. 6th April, 1735, had issue,

- I. James, who d. unm.
- II. John, his heir.
- III. Edward, d. unm.
- IV. Joseph (Sir), sheriff of London in 1724, alderman in 1738, M.P. *temp.* George I. and George II. first for the borough of Southwark, and afterwards for Devizes. Sir Joseph m. Sarah, daughter of Alderman Sir Jeffrey Jeffreys, knt. and died 8th February, 17[illegible], leaving one son and two daughters.
- I. Elizabeth, m. to Sir Thomas Clark, knt. of Brickendonbury, in the county of Herts.
- II. Frances, m. to Nicholas, second son of Sir Jeffrey Jeffreys, knt.
- III. Mary, m. to William Richardson, esq. of Somerset, in the county of Londonderry.

Sir Francis died in June, 1716, and was s. by his eldest son,

II. Sir John Eyles, sub-governor of the South Sea Company, member in the last parliament of Queen Anne and in the first and second of *King* George [illegible]

for Chippenham, and in the first of GEORGE II. for the city of London. He was, first, alderman of Vintry Ward, and lord mayor in 1727, and was afterwards alderman of Bridge Ward Without, being then father of the city. Sir John was appointed postmaster-general in 1739. He m. his cousin, Mary, daughter of Joseph Haskin Styles, esq. of London, and by her, who d. in November, 1735, had issue,

FRANCIS, his heir.

Mary, m. to William Bumstead, esq. of Upton, in Warwickshire.

Sir John d. 11th March, 1745, and was s. by his son,

III. SIR FRANCIS HASKIN-EYLES-STYLES, who assumed the additional surname of Haskin-Styles upon inheriting the estate of his uncle, Benjamin Haskin-Styles, esq. He m. Sibella, daughter of Philip Egerton, D.D. rector of Ashbury, in Cheshire, and dying 26th January, 1762, was s. by his son,

IV. SIR JOHN HASKIN-EYLES, bart. who d. s. p. 1st November, 1768, when the BARONETCY became EXTINCT.

Arms—Arg. a fesse engrailed sa. in chief three fleurs-de-lis of the second.

FALKINER, OF ABBOTSTOWN.

CREATED 21st Dec. 1812.

EXTINCT in 1815.

Lineage.

DANIEL FALKINER, esq. of Dublin, merchant, had, with one daughter, Hannah, m. to — Travers, esq. three sons, viz.

I. JOHN, of Dublin, father, by Mary, his wife, of three daughters, his co-heirs, viz.

Elizabeth, m. to Freeman Rogers, esq.

Rebecca, m. to William Gibson, esq.

Sarah, m. to — Taylor, esq.

II. DANIEL, of whom presently.

III. Caleb, of Cork, merchant, who m. Mary Riggs, and was great-grandfather of the present SIR RIGGS FALKINER, bart. of Anne Mount, in the county of Cork.

The second son,

DANIEL FALKINER, esq. lord mayor of Dublin, married a daughter of George Spence, esq. and was father of

FREDERICK FALKINER, esq. of Abbotstown, in the county of Dublin, who m. Elizabeth, daughter of ... Hamilton, esq. of Bailiborough, in the county of Cavan, and dying in 1785, left, with other issue, a daughter, Anne, m. to Benjamin Geale, esq. of Mount ..., in the county of Kilkenny (see BURKE'S *Commoners*, vol. iii. p. 290), and a son,

I. FREDERICK-JOHN FALKINER, esq. of Abbotstown, M.P. for the county of Dublin, who was created a BARONET 21st December, 1812. He m. Anne-Frances, daughter and co-heir of Sackville Gardiner, esq. but dying s. p. in 1815, the title became EXTINCT.

Arms—Or, three falcons close ppr. belled gu.

FANSHAWE.

CREATED 2nd Sept. 1650.

EXTINCT about 1695.

Lineage.

THOMAS FANSHAWE, esq. of Dronfield, in Derbyshire, and of Ware Park, in the county of Hertford, son and heir of John Fanshawe, of Fanshawe Gate, succeeded to the office of king's remembrancer of the Exchequer on the death of his uncle in 1568, served as a baron of the Cinque Ports for Rye in the parliament of the 13th *Queen* ELIZABETH, and was burgess for Arundel in several subsequent parliaments. He m. first, Mary or Alice, daughter of Anthony Bourchier, esq. of Gloucestershire, and had by her a son,

HENRY, his heir.

He wedded, secondly, Jane, daughter of Thomas Smythe, esq. of Ostenhanger, in Kent, by whom he had issue,

THOMAS (Sir), knt. of Jenkins, in Essex, clerk of the crown and surveyor-general to JAMES I. He m. Anne, daughter of — Babington, esq. of the county of Leicester, and had a son,

THOMAS (Sir), knt. who m. for his first wife, the daughter and heir of Sir Edward Heath, of Cotesmore, in Rutlandshire.

William, of Parslows, in Essex, auditor of the duchy of Lancaster, m. Katherine, second daughter of Sir John Wolstenholme, knt. and had issue.

Alice, m. to Sir Christopher Hatton, K.B. son and heir of Lord Chancellor Hatton.

Catharine, m. to John Bullock, esq. of Darley and Norton, in Derbyshire.

Margaret, m. to Sir Benjamin Ayloffe, bart.

Mary, m. to Thomas Hardwicke, esq. of Leeds.

Elizabeth, d. unm.

Thomas Fanshawe died in March, 1600-1, and was s. by his son,

SIR HENRY FANSHAWE, knt. of Ware Park, remembrancer of the Exchequer, M.P. for Westbury and Boroughbridge. This gentleman married Elizabeth, sixth daughter of Thomas Smythe, esq. of Ostenhanger, and had by her, who died in 1631,

I. THOMAS (Sir), made a knight of the Bath at the coronation of CHARLES I. and raised to the peerage of Ireland by CHARLES II. as VISCOUNT FANSHAWE, of Donamore, in 1661. His lordship m. first, Anne, daughter of Sir Giles Alington, of Horseheath, in Cambridgeshire; and secondly, Elizabeth, daughter of Sir William Cockaine, knt. which lady m. secondly, Sir Thomas Rich, bart. By his first wife, Lord Fanshawe left at his decease, in 1665, three sons and four daughters, viz.

1. THOMAS, second Viscount Fanshawe, K.B. who m. first, Catharine, daughter and heir of Knighton Ferrers, esq. of Beyford, in Herts; and secondly, Sarah,

daughter of Sir John Evelyn, knt. of West Dene, and widow of Sir John Wray; by this lady his lordship left at his decease in 1674 a son and a daughter, viz.

Evelyn, third Viscount Fanshawe, who died at Aleppo, in Turkey, 10th October, 1687, aged nineteen.

Katharine.

The second Viscount Fanshawe conveyed the manor and estate of Ware to Sir Thomas Byde, knt.

2. Charles, fourth Viscount Fanshawe, *d. s. p.* in 1710.
3. Simon, fifth Viscount Fanshawe, *d. s. p.* in 1716.

1. Anne.
2. Katharine.
3. Abigail.
4. Elizabeth, *m.* to Sir Thomas Fanshawe, of Jenkins.

II. Simon (Sir), knt. baptized 23rd April, 1604; *m.* Katharine, second daughter and co-heir of Sir William Walter, knt. of Wimbledon, in Surrey, and widow of Knighton Ferrers, esq.
III. Walter, baptized 1st September, 1605.
IV. Richard, of whom presently.
V. Henry, killed in the Low Countries.

I. Alice, *m.* to Sir Capel Bedell, of Hammerton, in Huntingdonshire.
II. Mary, *m.* to William Newce, of Great Hadham, Herts.
III. Joan, *m.* first, to William, third son of Sir Oliver Boteler, bart. of Teston; and secondly, to Sir Philip Warwick, knt.
IV. Elizabeth.
V. Anne.

The fourth son,

I. Sir Richard Fanshawe, knt. baptized 12th June, 1608, M.P. for the university of Cambridge, was created a Baronet 2nd September, 1650. He *m.* 18th May, 1644, Anne, eldest daughter of Sir John Harrison, knt. of Balls, in Herts, and had, with several other children, who all died young and unmarried, a daughter, Margaret, *m.* to Vincent Grantham, esq. of Goltho', Lincolnshire; and a son and successor,

II. Sir Richard Fanshawe, born at Madrid 6th August, 1665, deaf and dumb, who died unmarried about 1695, when the title became extinct.

Arms—Or, a chev. between three fleurs-de-lis sa.

FARINGTON, OF CHICHESTER.

Created 17th Dec. 1697.

Extinct 7th Aug. 1719.

Lineage.

Thomas Farington, esq. descended from a younger brother of Farington of Farington, in Lancashire, was alderman of Chichester and three times mayor. He died in 1572, leaving by Joan, his wife, a son,

John Farington, esq. alderman of Chichester who *m.* first, Anne, daughter of John Diggens, esq. M.P. and by her, who died in 1583, had issue,

Thomas, his heir.
John, of Chichester.

Elizabeth, *m.* in 1614, to William Crewe.

He wedded, secondly, a lady named Jane, who *d.* in 1621, and had a daughter,

Joan, *m.* to John Comber, esq. of Shermanbury in Sussex.

The elder son,

Thomas Farington, esq. was alderman of Chichester in 1634, and one of the commissioners of the peace of that city. He *m.* Miss Dorothy Payne, of the same place, and had issue,

John (Sir), his heir.

Ann, *m.* to Daniel Broad, of Newport, Isle of Wight.
Eliza, *m.* to George Taylor, of Chichester.

Mr. Alderman Farington *d.* in 1653, aged eighty-one and was *s.* by his son,

Sir John Farington, of Gray's Inn, aged about twenty-five in 1634, who *m.* Ann, daughter of John May, esq. of Rawmere, in Sussex, brother of Sir Humphrey May, knt. and by her, who died in 1680, had issue,

Richard, his heir.
Thomas, *d.* unm. in 1697.
John.

Frances, *m.* first, to Sir Charles Goring; and secondly, to Henry Edmonds, esq. of Yapton. She *d. s. p.*
Ann, *m.* to William Vinall, of Deptford.
Grisel, *m.* to Barnham Dobell, M.D. of Chichester.
Dorothy.
Awdrey.

Sir John died in 1685, and was *s.* by his son,

I. Richard Farington, esq. of Chichester, who was created a Baronet 17th December, 1697. He *m.* Elizabeth, only daughter and heir of John Peachey, esq. of Ertham, and had issue,

John, who *m.* Elizabeth, daughter of Sir Thomas Miller, bart. and *d. s. p.* in the lifetime of his father.
Thomas, predeceased his father.
Richard, *d.* in infancy.

Sir Richard *d.* 7th August, 1719, and, as he survived all his sons, the Baronetcy expired with him.

Arms—Arg. a chev. gu. between three leopards' heads sa.

FELLOWS, OF CARSHALTON.

Created 20th Jan. 1718-19.—Extinct 26th July 1724.

Lineage.

I. John Fellows, esq. sub-governor of the South Sea Company, purchased for £3,800 from Dr. Radcliffe that gentleman's house at Carshalton, in Surrey, and was created a Baronet in 1718-19. He died 26th July, 1724, aged fifty-three, and, as he had no issue, with him the Baronetcy expired. His residence at Carshalton subsequently belonged to Lord Chancellor Hardwicke, and after him to the Hon. Thomas Walpole, from whom it was purchased by John Hodsdon Durand, esq. who sold it to David Mitchell, esq.

FELTON, OF PLAYFORD.

CREATED 20th July, 1620.  EXTINCT 18th Nov. 1719.

Lineage.

The ancient family of Felton, previously seated at Shotley, in Suffolk, removed to Playford, in the same county, on acquiring that estate in marriage with the heiress of Sampson.

ROBERT FELTON, esq. of Shotley, son of John Felton, by the heiress of Alcott, married Margery, daughter and heir of Thomas Sampson, esq. of Playford, and had a son,

THOMAS FELTON, esq. of Playford, living 4 HENRY VIII. who m. Cecilia, daughter of Thomas Seckford, esq. and was father of

THOMAS FELTON, esq. of Playford, who m. Mary, daughter of Sir Richard Cavendish knt. of Trimley, in Suffolk, by a daughter of Sir William Brandon, knt. and left at his decease, 20 ELIZABETH, one son and three daughters, viz.

ANTHONY, his heir.
Beatrix, m. to Thomas Colby, esq. of Beccles.
Frances, m. to John Cotton, esq. of Essex.
Cicely, m. to Richard Preston, esq. of Mendham.

The son and heir,

SIR ANTHONY FELTON, K. B. of Playford, high sheriff of Suffolk in 1597, m. Elizabeth, daughter of Henry, Lord Grey, and was s. by his son,

I. HENRY FELTON, esq. of Playford, who was created a BARONET 20th July, 1620. He m. Dorothy, daughter of Sir Bassingborne Gawdy, knt. and had a son,

II. SIR HENRY FELTON, of Playford, who m. Susannah, daughter of Sir Lionel Talmach, bart. of Helmingham, and had issue,

I. ADAM, } successive baronets.
II. THOMAS, }
III. COMPTON, }
IV. Robert, captain in the army, d. s. p.
V. Henry, D.D. rector of Long Melford, in Suffolk, m. Lady Isabella May, and had one son,
Henry, who died young.
I. Susan, m. first, to Thomas Herbert, esq. and secondly to Francis, Lord Howard of Effingham.
II. Dorothy, m. first to Allaxton; and secondly to Sir John Poley, knt. of Boxted.
III. Elizabeth, d. unm.

Sir Henry Felton died in 1690, and was s. by his son,

III. SIR ADAM FELTON, of Playford, who m. Elizabeth, daughter of Sir George Reresby, of Thrybergh, in Yorkshire, widow, first, of Sir Francis Foljambe, bart.; secondly, of Edward Horner, esq.; and thirdly, of William, Viscount Castlemaine. By this lady he had no issue, and dying in February, 1696, was s. by his brother,

IV. SIR THOMAS FELTON, of Playford, comptroller of the queen's household, who m. Lady Elizabeth Howard, daughter and co-heir of James, Lord Howard de Walden and Earl of Suffolk, and had an only daughter and heir,

ELIZABETH, m. to JOHN HERVEY, esq. of Ickworth, who was created EARL OF BRISTOL in 1714, and from this marriage descend
FREDERICK-WILLIAM, present MARQUESS OF BRISTOL, and CHARLES, LORD HOWARD DE WALDEN.

Sir Thomas died 2nd March, 1708, and was s. by his brother,

V. SIR COMPTON FELTON, who m. Frances, daughter of Mr. Finch of Playford, and had an only daughter and heir,

ELIZABETH, m. to John Platers, esq. of Worlingham.

Sir Compton d. 18th November, 1719, aged sixty-nine, and with him the BARONETCY EXPIRED.

Arms—Gu. two lions passant in pale erm. crowned or.

FENWICK, OF FENWICK AND WALLINGTON.

CREATED 9th June, 1628.  EXTINCT 27th Jan. 1697.

Lineage.

DE FENWYKE, Lord of the Castell and Tower of Fenwyke, and lord of the manor in the parish of Stamfordham, Northumberland, living *temp.* HENRY I. and STEPHEN, was father of

SIR ROBERT DE FENWYKE, knt. Lord of the Castell and Tower of Fenwyke, *temp.* HENRY II. and RICHARD I. whose son and successor,

SIR ROBERT DE FENWYKE, knt. Lord of Fenwyke and the two Matfens,* living in the reign of JOHN,

* West Matfen passed from the Fenwicke family about the year 1660, when it was sold to Mr. Dagleish, or Douglas of Newcastle, from whom it came to the Blackett family, and the present Sir Edward Blackett, bart. has rebuilt Matfen Hall. Mr. Fenwicke, who sold Matfen, d. 29th December, 1744, aged eighty-four, leaving issue, by his wife, who d. 2nd October, 1708, aged forty four, two sons and two daughters. Of the sons, the elder,

JOHN FENWICKE, esq. of Morpeth, m. about 1720, Catherine, second daughter and co-heir of John Wilkinson, esq. of Morpeth, and Barbara, his wife, daughter and heir of William Wilson, esq. of Longframlington, and by her, who was born 27th December, 1697, and d. 20th January, 1773, aged seventy-six, left at his decease, 21st ... 1750, two sons; the younger, William, of the ... House, d. s. p. The elder,

JOHN FENWICKE, esq. M.D. of Morpeth, b. 8th March, 1722, m. Mary, youngest daughter of John Thornton, esq. of Netherwitton, son and heir of Nicholas Thornton, esq. of Netherwitton Castle, Northumberland, by his wife, Anne, second daughter of Sir John Swinburne, bart. of Capheaton Castle, in the same county, and his wife, Isabel, sole daughter and heiress of Henry Lawson, esq. of Brough Hall, in the county of York, by Catherine, daughter and co-heiress of Sir William Fenwicke, knt. of Meldon. After her father was slain at Melton Mowbray, in the service of CHARLES II. her mother re-married Sir Francis Radclyff, bart. who was created Earl of Derwentwater, by JAMES II. By Mary, his wife, who died 9th November, 1773, Mr. Fenwick left at his decease, 23rd December, 1783, aged sixty-one, two sons and three daughters, viz.

I. JAMES, his heir.

had three sons, Adam, William, and Thomas. The third,

Sir Thomas de Fenwyke, knt. Lord of Fenwyke and Capheaton, sold the latter to Alan de Swinburne, in 1274, by deed, sealed with his coat of arms, "Per fesse gu. and arg. six martlets counterchanged." His son,

Sir Thomas de Fenwyke, Lord of Fenwyke, knighted by Edward I. in 1286, was father, *inter alios*, of

Alan de Fenwyke, who *m.* the daughter and heir of Barrett, of Walker, and was *s.* by his son,

Sir John de Fenwyke, knt. Lord of Fenwyke, sheriff of Northumberland in 1399. He *m.* Elizabeth, daughter and co heir of Sir Alan Heaton, knt. of Heaton Castle, and had two sons,

Allan (Sir), knt. Lord of Fenwyke, a prisoner with his brother John in Scotland at the period of his father's demise. He left a son,

Henry (Sir), knt. of Fenwyke, at whose decease, without male issue, Fenwyke went to his cousin, John Fenwicke, of Newburn and Wallington, while the lands of Heaton were divided between his six daughters and co-heirs.

John (Sir), knt. of whose line we have to treat.

The second son,

Sir John de Fenwicke, knt. a warrior of the martial reign of Henry V. served that monarch with distinction in his French wars, and obtained in recompense, from his royal master, the lordship of Troubleville, in Normandy, and permission to bear for his motto, "A tous jours loyal." His son and heir,

John Fenwicke, esq. of Newburn, *m.* first, Mary, youngest daughter and co-heir of William del Strother, of Kirkharle, by Joan, his wife, only daughter of Robert de Wallington, Lord of Wallington, and had issue,

John, of Newburn, father by Isabella, his wife, of

Ralph, who had two sons: the elder, William, died *s. p.*; the other was found by an inquest, 7th March, 1501, to be "fatuus et idiota."

William, of whom presently.

Robert, of Chibburne, from whom the Fenwickes of Kenton and Butterby.

John Fenwicke *m.* secondly, Elizabeth, sister of Sir Roger Widdrington, knt. and had other children, from whom derived the Fenwickes of Stanton, Nunnykirk, Harbottle, Brinkburne, East Heddon, Greenleighton, and Langshaws. The second son of the first marriage,

William Fenwicke, esq. of Fenwycke, *m.* Joan, daughter and co-heir of Thomas Musgrave, of Ryall, and dying before 3rd July, 1485, was *s.* by his son,

John Fenwicke, esq. of Wallington and Ryal, found to be next heir of Henry Fenwicke in 1501, and as such, had Fenwicke Tower, &c. awarded to him in 1598. He *m.* Margery, daughter of John Harbottle, and had two sons: John, his heir; and Roger, of Bitchfield. The elder,

John Fenwicke, esq. Lord of Fenwicke and Wallington, *m.* Joan Clavering, and was *s.* by his son.

Sir Roger Fenwicke, knt. Lord of Fenwicke and Wallington, who *m.* Dorothy, daughter of Sir John Widdrington, of Widdrington, and had a son,

Sir William Fenwicke, knt. of Wallington, born about the year 1550, whose wardship and marriage the queen granted November 3, 1560, to William [illegible], esq. and on May 19, 1571, being then of full age, he had especial living of the lands of which his father died seized at the Redeswire skirmish, 9th July, [illegible]

> "Proud Wallington was wounded sair,
> Albeit he was a Fenwicke feirs."

Sir William had lands demised to him by the crown [illegible] James I. The family estate according to the survey [illegible] Northumberland in 10 Elizabeth, consisted of the manor and castle of Fenwicke, the villa and manor of Wallington (where he resided), Walker, Cambo, [illegible] Herterton Hall, Catcherside, half of Ryall, Greenleighton, Gunnerton, and Hawick, with lands in east Matfen, also of the villa Eshenden, of Wittom [illegible] Hawick. His will, dated 3rd December, 1612, proved at York 13th March, 1613, directs his body to be buried at Stannerton, and gives to his second son, William, the lordship of Meldon, &c. &c. Sir William *m.* first, Grace, daughter* and co-heir of Sir John Forster, knt. of Edderstone, Lord Warden of the middle marches, and had issue, John. He *m.* secondly Margaret, daughter of William Selby, esq. of Newcastle, and had issue,

i. William (Sir), knt. of Meldon.
ii. Roger, of Shortflah, from whom were the Fenwickes of Bywell.

i. Elizabeth, *m.* Sir Caudius Forster, of Bamburgh castle, created a Baronet 7th March, [illegible]
ii. Dorothy. iii. Anne. iv. Margaret. v. [illegible]

The son by the first marriage,

i. Sir John Fenwicke, knt. of Wallington, was thirty-five years old 14th September, 1614, when the inquest after the death of his father was taken, and from whom he inherited Fenwicke, East Matfen, Wallington, Camboe, Walker, Eshington, Gunnerton, Ryal, Liverthope, and Harewood; two [illegible] in Fenwicke, two in Catcherside, one in Greenleighton, two in Longwitton, two in Hawkwell and Bruston, all which he had special living, 12th February, [illegible] John Forster, his grandfather, 22nd April, 1602, settled upon him the manor and capital messuage of Hexham with lands and tenements there, and Anick Grange, Payfield or Priorthornes, Dotland Park, Hexham

---

ii. John-Ralph, of the city of Durham, who *m.* Dorothy, eldest daughter and co-heir of Robert Spearman, esq. of Old Acres, in the county of Durham, but had no issue.

i. Catherine.
ii. Margaret, *m.* William Charlton, esq. of Hesleyside, and *d.* 12th March, 1832, leaving one only child, the present William John Charlton, esq.
iii. Mary, *m.* to General De Martenne, of the French army, and has issue, William de Martenne.

The eldest son,

James Fenwicke, esq. of Longwitton Hall, in the parish of Hartburn, Northumberland, *b.* 15th October, 1759, *m.* Jane, only child and heiress of John Manners, esq. of Longframlington, in the county of Northumberland, the last of the Longframlington branch of the noble house of Etal, now represented by the Duke of Rutland, and *d.* at Longwitton Hall, 3rd February, 1837, aged seventy-eight, having had issue,

i. John Manners, of Longframlington, Northumberland, *b.* 16th May, 1796.
ii. William, major in the 23rd Royal Welsh Fusileers, *b.* 14th August, 1797, and *d.* at [illegible] 11th September, 1837, aged forty.
iii. James-Thomas, M D. of Blackett Street, Newcastle-upon-Tyne, *b.* 13th June, 1799.
iv. Edward, *b.* 7th October, 1800.
v. Thornton, *b.* 2nd April, 1803.
vi. Thomas, *d.* 7th May, 1823.
vii. Manners, *b.* 24th July, 1806.

i. Jane, *b.* 22nd September, 1803, *m.* 17th February 1835, to Henry Montonnier Hawkins, esq. of Gaer and Tredunnock, in the county of Monmouth, and *d.* at Ross, in Herefordshire, [illegible] December, 1835, leaving an only daughter, Jane-Henrietta Hawkins.

* Eleanor, another sister, *m.* Sir Francis Russel, [illegible] son of the Earl of Bedford.

Vills, the tithes of Hexham, Acumbe, Anicke, Sandhoe Wall, and Fallowfield. In 1618 he purchased Rothley, of Lord Eure, and in 1632 the regality of Hexham, with its long train of manors. He was in parliament for Cockermouth and for the county of Northumberland, 21 JAMES I. and 1, 12, 13, 15, and 16 CHARLES I. which last named king, in 1628, created him a baronet. As a member of the House of Commons in the long parliament, his loyalty was so conspicuous as to procure him the honour of being put into the band of brave men, who, on January 22, 1643, were discharged and disabled for sitting and being any longer members of the House during that parliament, for deserting the service of the house, and being in the king's quarters, and adhering to that party. He died about 1658. Sir John had issue by his first wife, Catherine, daughter of Sir Henry Slingsby, knt. of Scriam in the west Riding of Yorkshire, three children, John Fenwicke, esq. a colonel of a regiment of dragoons, m. Mary, daughter of George Selby, knt. of Whitehaven, near K[illegible], in the county of Dublin, and was slain in the battle of Marston Moor July 2, 1644, *d. s. p.* Catherine and Elizabeth. Sir John m. 2ndly, Grace, dau. of Thomas Lorain, esq. of Kirkharle, and had issue,

I. WILLIAM (Sir), knt. his heir. II. Allan.

I. Grace, m. to Peter Venables, esq. son and heir of Peter Venables, baron of Kinderton.

The eldest son,

I. SIR WILLIAM FENWICKE, of Wallington, aged [illegible] five in 1666, who was returned in 1643, to the long parliament in the room of his father, then discharged from it, and became a stanch supporter of the Commonwealth. He died in 1676, and left by Jane, his [illegible] daughter of Henry Stapleton, esq. of Wighill, Yorkshire, a son and heir,

III. SIR JOHN FENWICKE, of Fenwicke and Walling[illegible] a member of the healing parliament 25th April, [illegible], and of the successive parliaments of CHARLES II. and JAMES II. He, Sir John, possessed considerable [illegible]nt, and was romantically attached to the House of Stuart, but his "moral character," as a supporter of [illegible] in his trial observed, "was none of the best." [illegible] alienated the estates of a long line of ancestry, was attainted of high treason, and beheaded; but he [illegible] splendid traits in his character, and good men [illegible] his death on account of the harsh and unconsti[illegible] measure by which it was accomplished. Af[illegible] great fire of London in 1666, he built the great [illegible] Christ's Hospital, in which the boys dine and [illegible]. His restless spirit had led him, in the year [illegible] to assist in concerting plans for the restoration [illegible] King JAMES II. but in 1696, finding that govern[illegible] was acquainted with his proceedings, he set out [illegible] France, but was apprehended at New Romney, in [illegible], committed to the tower, and indicted at the Old [illegible] on the oaths of George Porter, esq. and Cor[illegible] Goodman, gent. on the 28th of May of that year, [illegible] "compassing and imagining the death and de[illegible]struction of the king, and adhering to his enemies," [illegible] finding his case a bad one, he and his friends, by [illegible] plans and suggestions, got his trial put off till [illegible] had succeeded by golden persuasions in removing [illegible] Goodman out of the country. There was therefore now [illegible] one witness against him, and as parliament had [illegible] before passed a law "That no person should be [illegible] or attainted of high treason, when corruption of [illegible] is incurred, but by the oath of two lawful wit[illegible]nesses, unless the party confess, stand mute," &c. he [illegible] began to rely on the uniform practice of the [illegible] to judge by law or precedent, and to hope that [illegible] against him would be stayed. He was [illegible] too to try the experiment of softening Wil[illegible] heart, by a full disclosure of his own and his [illegible] guilt in a written account of their plans and proceedings. Besides the persons immediately engaged with him in "the plot," Admiral Russell, Lord Marlborough, the Duke of Shrewsbury, Lords Godolphin and Both, Sir Ralph Delaval, and others, all eminently known and believed to be in the interest of the government, and none but which were in some post of trust and employment in it, were accused in his informations, "of correspondencies and intrigues carried on with the court of St. Germain, and though this account is known now to be true in every particular, it neither gained William's favour, nor served the design of Fenwicke. William indeed is said to have entertained a personal enmity against Fenwicke, for some expressions reflecting on his conduct, when he served in the army in Holland. On the 6th of November, 1696, the king laid these informations before the House of Commons, which brought in a bill of attainder against him, summoned him to its bar, and endeavoured to draw further confession from him, which he steadily declined to do, alleging that he had made a full disclosure to the king. The bill was supported and opposed with great zeal and ability. Powerful arguments were advanced to justify parliament in proceeding to judgment upon bills of attainder, contrary to the rules and maxims of Westminster Hall. On the opposite side it was shewn that parliament could not consistently move an enactment contrary to the salutary law it had passed in the last session, that no one should be convicted of treason but on the oath of two witnesses. But the stern spirit that ruled the land in William's day was a stranger to mercy: Sir John was condemned by a law made on purpose to stain the scaffold with his blood, made after the crime was done for which he was accused by a guilty oppressor, a proceeding "which cannot be too much condemned as a breach of the most sacred and unalterable rules of justice," which will stand as a lasting reproach upon the persons who commenced and supported it.* The ayes for the act were 189, noes 156, majority 33. In the House of Lords the majority was only seven, and forty peers, seven of whom were bishops, entered their protest against it. One act of mercy was allowed to Sir John, he was not dragged through the street to be hanged at Tyburn as the law required, but the king in consideration it is supposed of the high rank of Lady Fenwicke, by his writ of 18th January, 1697, omitted all execution of the act of forfeiture except beheading him on Tower Hill, which was done on the 27th of that month. He met his fate with great firmness and composure in the fifty-second year of his age. His body was buried near the altar of St. Martin's church, near those of his three sons, Charles, who died *s. p.* of the small-pox, aged sixteen, William died, aged six years, Howard died, aged one and a-half, all buried in St. Martins, London. His only daughter and eldest child, Jane Fenwicke, was buried in St. Nicholas, Newcastle. Sir John's wife was Lady Mary Howard, eldest daughter of Charles, Earl of Carlisle. This faithful and amiable lady exerted herself with the most devoted zeal and tenderness to save the life of her husband. She endeavoured with the agency of one Chancy to get the two witnesses to withdraw, and succeeded with Goodman, but the upright Captain Porter after taking a bribe of £300, made a discovery to government. She also requested to be a sharer with him in his confinement, which he would not permit, because "he knew it would kill her." The following inscription is on a monument in the Howard aisle, in York Cathedral. "This monumental pillar is erected and dedicated by the Right Honourable the Lady Mary Fenwicke, eldest daughter to Charles Howard, Earl of Carlisle, as a testimony of respect to the memory of Sir John Fen-

* Hodgson's Northumberland.

wicke, bart. of Fenwicke Castle, in the county of Northumberland, her deceased husband, by whom she had four children, one daughter and three sons. Jane, her eldest, died very young, and was buried in a vault in the parish church of St. Nicholas, Newcastle-upon-Tyne; Charles, William, and Howard, her three sons, do all lie with their father in the parish church of St. Martin-in-the-Fields, London, where he was interred 28th January, 1696, aged fifty-two. Lady Fenwicke died 27th October, 1708, aged fifty.

Arms—Per fesse gu. and arg. six martlets counterchanged.

FERMOR, OF WELCHES.

CREATED 4th May, 1725.

EXTINCT 2 th Oct. 1784.

Lineage.

The family of Fermor came originally out of France in the reign of EDWARD III. and branches of it continued to a recent period in Picardy, where probably the name may yet be found. In the Visitation of Sussex, a

JOHN FERMOR is the first mentioned, and he was possibly the Frenchman who settled in that county in the latter end of EDWARD's reign. His son and heir,

WALTER FERMOR, married Margery Lee, an heiress, and was father of

JOHN FERMOR, father of another
JOHN FERMOR, whose son,
JOHN FERMOR, was *s.* by his son and heir,
WILLIAM FERMOR, father of

ALEXANDER FERMOR, esq. of Welches, in the county of Sussex, who *m.* Elizabeth, daughter of William Fowle, esq. of Riverhall, in the same county, and was *s.* by his eldest son,

WILLIAM FERMOR, esq. of Welches, who was residing there in the 17th of ELIZABETH. He *m.* first, Miss Fulwar, but by her had no issue; secondly, Elizabeth or Anne, daughter of George Scott, esq. of Congherst, in Kent, and by that lady had,

William, who *m.* Alice, daughter of — Williams, esq. of the city of London, but *d. s. p.*
Anne, *m.* to Alexander Elliot, esq. of Biblesham, in the county of Sussex.

He *m.* thirdly, Margaret, daughter of William Squire, esq. of the city of London, and had

ALEXANDER, his heir.
Bridget, *m.* first, John Olive, esq. of Hastings, and had issue, Richard, Judith, and Margaret. She wedded, secondly, the Rev. Thomas Higginson and by him had a son, Alexander.

He was *s.* by his only surviving son,

ALEXANDER FERMOR, esq. of Welches, living in 1634. This gentleman, distinguished for his loyalty to *King* CHARLES I. raised an independent company of soldiers for the service of that prince during the civil war, and for that act of fidelity subsequently suffered a long and close imprisonment at Lewes, in Sussex. He *m.* first Mary, eldest daughter of Anthony Fowle, esq. of Rotherfield, in the same county, and had issue,

WILLIAM, his heir.
Henry, *m.* Mary, daughter of — Elsteck, of Seaford, in Sussex, and had a son, who *d.* young.
Anthony, *d.* unm.
Elizabeth, *m.* to Walter Lapp, gent.
Margaret. Mary.

He was *s.* by his eldest son,

WILLIAM FERMOR, esq. of Welches, who was nine years of age in 1634, and we find him in [illegible] a barrister-at-law. He *m.* first, Mary, daughter of Robert Pickering, esq. of the county of Sussex, and had a son, Alexander, who died young. He wedded, secondly, Margaret, daughter of Peter Buck, esq. of Rochester, and by her had a son,

William, who *m.* Elizabeth Shorthose, and had a dau. Mary, the wife of Charles Bere, esq. of Devon.

He wedded, thirdly, Martha, daughter of Tristram Thomas, gent. of Kent, and had issue,

HENRY, his heir.
James, *m.* Mrs. Luck, but *d. s. p.*
Charles, *m.* a dau. of Sir Theop. Jones, but *d. s. p.*
John, colonel in the army and M. P. for Malmesbury, *d.* unm. in December, 1722.

The eldest son and heir,

I. HENRY FERMOR, esq. of Welches, in the county of Sussex, was created a BARONET by *King* GEORGE I. 4th May, 1725, with special remainder to Charles Eversfield, junior, esq. of Denn, in the same county. Sir Henry *m.* first, Dorothy, daughter of John Thornycroft, esq. and sister of Sir John Thornycroft, bart. by whom he had a son and two daughters, who all died young. He *m.* secondly, Mary, daughter of William Thomas, esq. of Folkington, in Sussex, sister of Sir William Thomas, bart. and relict, first, of John Eversfield, esq. of Horsham, in Sussex; secondly, of Sir Thomas Beckford, of London, merchant; and thirdly, of Corbett Hene, gent. of St. Martin's-in-the-Fields. By this lady he had no issue. He *d.* at Sevenoaks, in Kent, 3rd June, 1734, and was *s.* according to the limitation, by

II. SIR CHARLES EVERSFIELD, bart. (son and heir of Charles Eversfield, esq. M.P.* of Denn, in the county of Sussex), who *d. s. p.* 26th October, 1784, when the BARONETCY became EXTINCT, and the estates centred in the descendants of his sisters, and are now enjoyed by CHARLES-GILBERT EVERSFIELD, esq. of Denne Place, the baronet's great-grandnephew.

Arms—Gu. a cheveron vairy arg. and az. between three lions rampant or.

---

* NICHOLAS EVERSFIELD, esq. of Grove, near Hastings, high sheriff of Sussex in 1619 (son of Thomas Eversfield, esq. sheriff in 1599), *m.* Dorothy, daughter of Edward Goring, esq. of Okehurst, in the same county, and was great grandfather of the above

CHARLES EVERSFIELD, esq. of Denne Place, who *m.* Mary, daughter and co-heir of Henry Duncombe, esq. of Weston, in the county of Surrey, by whom (who was buried at Horsham) he had issue,

CHARLES EVERSFIELD, who inherited the Baronetcy conferred upon SIR HENRY FERMOR.
OLIVE EVERSFIELD, who *d.* at the age of ninety in 1803, and was *s.* by her nephew,

WILLIAM MARKWICK, esq. who assumed in consequence the name of EVERSFIELD.

MARY EVERSFIELD, *m.* at East Bourne, [illegible] June, 1735, to JAMES MARKWICK, esq. of C[illegible]field, in Sussex, and had a son,

WILLIAM MARKWICK, who assumed the surname of Eversfield under the will of his aunt Olive. He died 8th April [illegible] leaving issue,

JAMES EVERSFIELD, (father of the present Charles-Gilbert Eversfield, esq.) Charles, and Sophia, wife of Rev. [illegible] Bligh, esq.

FERRERS, OF SKELLINGTHORPE.

CREATED 19th Dec. 1628.

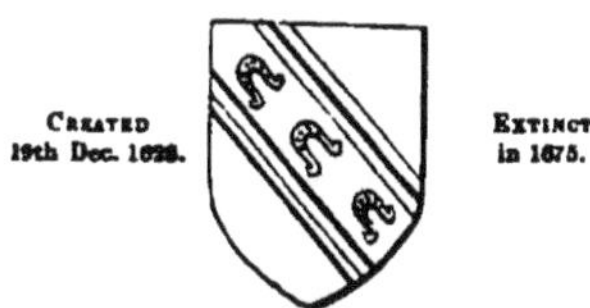

EXTINCT in 1675.

Lineage.

I. SIR HENRY FERRERS, of Skellingthorpe, in Lincolnshire, who was created a BARONET in 1628, married Anne, daughter of James Scudamore, esq. and dying in 1663, was *s.* by his son,

II. SIR HENRY FERRERS, who died without issue in 1675, aged forty-five, when the BARONETCY became EXTINCT.

Arms—Arg. on a bend gu. cottised sa. three horse shoes of the first.

FETHERSTON, OF BLACKESWARE.

CREATED 4th Dec. 1660.

EXTINCT 17th Oct. 1746.

Lineage.

CUTHBERT FETHERSTONE (of the ancient stock of the Fetherstones of Hetherye Clough, in the parish of Stanhope, in the county of Durham), the founder of this branch of the family, died in 1615, and was buried in St. Dunstan's-in-the-West, London, where a monument in the wall of the south aisle was thus inscribed:

Memoriæ sacrum
Hic jacet Cutbertus Fetherstone, Generos. nuper Oyesarius & Proclamator Dom. Regis, in Curia hospitii Regis coram ipso rege ubicunque fuerat in Anglia.

Functus est hoc munere, ann. 35. obiit 10 Decembris, 1615, aetatis 78.

Quem saepe transiit casus, aliquando invenit.

Under the above is another monument, with the following inscription:

Before this pew door, next to the body of the above-named Cuthbert Fetherstone, lyeth his beloved wife, Katherine Fetherstone. Who as they piously lived in wedlocke forty odde yeeres together, so at their deaths they desired to be interred together; not doubting, at the general Resurrection, through Christ's Merits, to rise together, and for ever in Heaven to live together.

Obiit Novemb. 1622, aetatis 85.

And this in part they do attaine,
Who by their Deaths new Lives doe gaine.

Corpus moritur per poenam, resurgit per gloriam.
Anima moritur per culpam, resurgit per gratiam.

This Cuthbert had issue by his above-mentioned wife Katherine, three sons and a daughter, viz.

- Ralph, who *d. s. p.* in 1631.
- HENRY.
- Edward, of Lincoln's Inn, died unmarried.
- Mary, *m.* to Francis Hutton, in the retinue of Count Gondemar, and had an only daughter, CATHARINE HUTTON, who *m.* George Thomason, of Westham, the learned collector of the "Royal Pamphlets" in the British Museum, and had, with other issue, a son, the REV. GEORGE THOMASON, rector of Halston, and a daughter, KATHERINE, who *m.* William Stonestreet, of Westham, in Sussex, and was ancestor of the present REV. GEORGE-STONESTREET GRIFFIN-STONESTREET, LL.B. of Stondon Hall, Essex.

The second son,

HENRY FETHERSTON, of London, living in 1635, *m.* first, Mary, daughter of Mr. Gaynes Newman, but that lady died issueless. He wedded, secondly, Katherine, daughter of Michael Heneage, esq. keeper of the records in the Tower of London, and by her had

- HENEAGE, his heir.
- Grace, *m.* to William Barker, esq. who fined for alderman of London.

He was *s.* at his decease by his son,

I. HENEAGE FETHERSTON, esq. who purchased from John King, gent. the estate of Blackesware, in the county of Herts, and was created a BARONET by *King* CHARLES II. 4th December, 1660. Sir Heneage *m.* Mary, daughter of Sir Thomas Bennet, bart. of Babraham, in Cambridgeshire, and had a numerous family. One of the daughters married Henry Bertie, esq. of Chesterton, in Oxfordshire, and the eldest surviving son,

II. SIR HENRY FETHERSTONE, succeeded his father 23rd October, 1711. This gentleman married Anna-Maria, daughter and heir of James Williamson, esq. of London, merchant, but *d. s. p.* 17th October, 1746, aged 100, when the BARONETCY EXPIRED. Blackesware was sold by the Fetherstones to Sir Thomas Leventhorpe, bart. from whom it passed to Sir Thomas Clutterbuck, knt. and from the Clutterbucks it came to the Plumers, being now possessed by ROBERT PLUMER WARD, esq. of Gilston.

Arms—Gu. on a chev. between three ostrich feathers arg. a pellet.

FETTIPLACE, OF CHILDREY.

CREATED 30th Mar. 1661.

EXTINCT 8th April, 1743.

Lineage.

The first FETTIPLACE in England, was gentleman usher to WILLIAM *the Conqueror*, and came in with that monarch.

JOHN FETEPLACE, descended from the Norman usher, living in the time of HENRY VI. was grandfather of

WILLIAM FETEPLACE, who conferred a considerable estate upon Queen's College, Oxford, and founded a free-school at Childrey, in Berks, in the church of which place he was buried, under the following inscription:

Here under this lyeth the bodies of
William Feteplace, esq; and Elizabeth, his
Wife, founder of this Chauntrey, founded
in the Honour of the blessed Trinity, our
Lady, and Sent Kateryn; which Elizabeth
deceased, the 14th day of January, the yeare
of our Lord 1516. and the said William
deceased, the —— day of —— in the yeare of
our Lord God 15—— On whose Sowles,
and all Christian Sowles, Jhesu have Mercy.*

The family removed its residence about the middle of the sixteenth century, from Childrey, in Berks, to Swinbrook, in Oxfordshire, retaining however both seats.

I. John Fettiplace, esq. of Childrey, in the county of Berks, in consideration of his services and sufferings in the cause of *King* Charles I. was created a Baronet soon after the restoration, by patent dated 30th March, 1661. Sir John *m.* first, Anne, daughter of Sir Francis Wenman, of Carswell, in the county of Oxford, and had issue,

Edmund, Charles, Lorenzo, George, } who all succeeded to the baronetcy.

Anne, *m.* to James Pitts, esq. of Kyre, in the county of Worcester, and survived him thirty years, during which period she lived a widow, conspicuous for piety and benevolence. She founded and endowed almshouses at Kyre, for poor widows, with an allowance for a chaplain; and a free school at Swinbrook, for the education of poor children, with an allowance to the school-master for ever.

Arabella, *m.* to Sir Rowland Lacy, knt. of Pudlicot, in the county of Oxford.

Diana, *m.* to Robert Bushel, esq. of Cleve Pryer, in Worcestershire, and their son inherited the estates and assumed the surname of Fettiplace. He was father of

Charles Fettiplace, esq. of Childrey.

Mary, *d.* unm.

Sophia, *m.* to Francis Broderick, esq. of Langford, in Berks, and *d.* 6th October, 1700.

Sir John *m.* secondly, Susan, daughter of Thomas Cook, esq. of Staunton, in Worcestershire, and relict of Laurence Bathurst, esq. of Lechlade, in the county of Gloucester, but by that lady (who *m.* thirdly, Sir John Cutler, knt.) had no issue. He was *s.* at his decease by his eldest son,

II. Sir Edmund Fettiplace, bart. who *d.* unm. about the year 1707, and was *s.* by his brother,

III. Sir Charles Fettiplace, bart. who *d.* unm. about the year 1714, and was *s.* by his brother,

IV. Sir Lorenzo Fettiplace, bart. at whose decease unm. 10th February, 1726, the baronetcy devolved upon his only surviving brother,

V. Sir George Fettiplace, bart. who died unm. 8th April, 1743, when the title became extinct, and the estates devolved on his nephew, Mr. Bushel.

Arms—Gules, two cheverons, argent.

FIREBRACE, OF LONDON.

Created 28th July, 1698.

Extinct 28th Mar. 1759.

Lineage.

This family was presumed to have been Norman, and to have derived its surname from the French words *Fier-à-bras*, strong of arm, but at what period it came into England is not ascertained.

In the visitation of Leicestershire, *anno.* 1682, the pedigree begins with

Robert Firebrace, gent. of the town and borough of Derby, who died in 1645, having had issue by his wife, Susanna, daughter of John Hierome, of London, merchant, six sons, and one daughter, viz.

Robert, who *d.* unm.

Bryan, *d. s. p.*

Samuel, John, } died unm.

Benjamin, *d. s. p.*

Henry,

Rebecca, *m.* to Thomas Moseley, esq. of Loughborough, in the county of Leicester.

The youngest son,

Henry Firebrace, esq. *b.* 2nd October, 16[illegible], of Stoke-Golding, in the county of Leicester, was the clerk of the kitchen to *King* Charles *the First*, and adhered with great fidelity to that unhappy prince. When his majesty was confined in Carisbrook Castle, Mr. Firebrace engaged with Mr. Barrow, Mr. T[illegible], and Mr. Cresset, to effect his deliverance, and for that purpose a vessel was provided, horses procured, and every other matter arranged, but the project proved abortive. The particulars of the affair is related at great length in the life of Dr. Barwick. "Mr. Firebrace had the honour, it seems, to be known to the king, by several services he had done him in the time of the treaty at Uxbridge, at Oxford, and other places, and being at Newcastle, when the Scots delivered his majesty to the English, and new servants were put about him, by his majesty's direction he applied to some of the commissioners, and prevailed to be admitted to that post; in which attending his majesty in his confinement, he found means to concert with him several methods of escape. One, he says, was, that his majesty should come out of his bedchamber window, which having found wide enough for his head, his majesty concluded would not be too narrow for his body, and therefore rejected his proposal of making it a little wider for fear that should occasion a discovery. Mr. Worseley, (the late Sir Edward,) Mr. Richard Osborne, and Mr. John Newland, of Newport, were all engaged in the secret, and very faithful, the two former waiting on horseback beyond the counterscarp, with a good horse, &c. for his majesty, to carry him to Newland's boat that was ready, and Mr. Firebrace prepared to receive him, as he was to let himself down by a cord from the window, and conduct him across

* In the east window of this chapel, are the pictures of men in armour, having on their surcoats the arms of Fettiplace, which seem of great antiquity. The family has long flourished in divers parts of the county of Berks, as at North Denchworth, Maidencot, &c. and we find a Sir Philip Fettiplace, lord of the manor of North Denchworth, so early as the reign of Edward I., he bore for his arms, "in a field, two cheverons," as appears by a seal made use of by him in the time of that monarch.

the court, (no sentinel being in the way,) to the great wall of the castle, and thence let him down by a stick on a long cord. The signal given, his majesty put himself forward but then too late found himself mistaken, he sticking fast between his breast and shoulders, and not able to get forward or backward, but that at the instant before he endeavoured to get out, he mistrusted, and tied a piece of his cord to a bar of the window within, by means whereof he forced himself back. This attempt thus failing, Mr. Firebrace sent for files and aquafortis from London, to make the passages more easy, and to help in other designs which he proposed, but while they were thus concerting new plans for the escape, Hammond was directed from above to have a careful eye on those about the king which occasioned Mr. Firebrace, and others to be dismissed; and in Mr. Firebrace's absence, the other attempt, of which Lord Clarendon gives account, and confounds it with this, was as fruitlessly made."

This Henry Firebrace, who afterwards received the honour of knighthood, was appointed by *King* CHARLES II. chief clerk of the kitchen, clerk comptroller supernumerary of his majesty's household, and assistant to his majesty's officers of the green cloth. He *m.* first, Elizabeth, daughter of Thomas Davell, of Stoke Golding, and had issue by her,

- HENRY, D.D. fellow of Trinity College, Cambridge, aged thirty-two in 1682.
- BASIL, aged twenty-nine, 1682, of whom presently.
- John, *d.* an infant.
- George.
- Susanna, *m.* to Thomas Hall, esq. of Elymore Hall, Durham.

Sir Henry *m.* secondly, Alice, daughter of Richard Bagnall, of Reading, and widow of John Bucknall, [illegible] of Creeke, in Northamptonshire, but by that lady left no issue. He *d.* 27th January, 1690, aged [illegible]enty two, and was interred in Stoke Golding church, in Leicestershire. His second son,

I. SIR BASIL FIREBRACE, was a merchant of the city of London, and having served the office of sheriff in [illegible], received the honour of knighthood. He was created a BARONET by *King* WILLIAM III. 28th July, [illegible] Sir Basil *m.* Elizabeth, daughter of Thomas H[illegible]gh, of London, merchant, and had issue,

- CHARLES, his successor, *b.* in 1679.
- George, *b.* in 1681.
- HESTER, *b.* in 1676, *m.* to Basil Fielding, fourth EARL OF DENBIGH, and was mother of
  - WILLIAM, fifth earl.

[illegible] 7th May, 1724, and was *s.* by his elder son,

II. SIR CHARLES FIREBRACE, bart. who *m.* Margaret, [illegible]ter and co-heir of Sir John Cordell, bart. of Long [illegible]ford, in Suffolk, and dying 2nd August, 1727, was [illegible] only son,

III. SIR CORDELL FIREBRACE, bart. M.P. for the [illegible] of Suffolk, *temp.* GEORGE II. who *m.* in Octo[illegible] [illegible], Bridget, relict of Edward Evers, esq. of Ips[illegible] and third daughter of Philip Bacon, esq. of the [illegible] place, (second son of Sir Nicholas Bacon, K.B. [illegible] Shrubland Hall, Suffolk,) but died without issue, [illegible] March, 1759, when the BARONETCY became EX[illegible], and the estates passed to the Earls of Denbigh. [illegible] Cordell's widow married for her third husband in [illegible]2, William Campbell, esq. brother to John, third [illegible] of Argyle, and died in 1782.

*** A branch of the Firebrace family settled in the [illegible] Indies. William Newton Firebrace, esq. a member of the Hon. Court of Criminal and Civil Justice at [illegible]. He *d.* in 1821, leaving three sons and one daughter, William, capt. 38th regiment; Samuel, LL.D. [illegible] at British Guiana; James; and Elizabeth-Ann.

Arms—Azure, on a bend, or, three crescents, sable, between two roses, argent, seeded, or, bearded, vert.

FISHER, OF PACKINGTON MAGNA.

CREATED 7th Dec. 1622.

EXTINCT in 1739.

Lineage.

The first of this name that settled in Warwickshire, was

JOHN FISHER, lord of the manor of Packington Magna, in that county, descended from an ancient family at Dottel, in Shropshire. He was gentleman pensioner to the *Kings* HENRY VIII. and EDWARD VI. and the *Queens* MARY and ELIZABETH, and in the fifth of the last, served the office of sheriff for Warwickshire, for which county he was in the commission of the peace from the beginning of MARY's reign, to the time of his decease, 13th of ELIZABETH. His wife was Katherine, daughter of Sir Thomas Digby, knt. of Olney, Bucks, and widow of Simon Wheeler of Kenilworth. By her he had two sons, Thomas the younger died in Ireland, unm. the elder,

SIR CLEMENT FISHER, succeeded to his father's estate. Having been made treasurer by Robert, Earl of Leicester, for the expedition into the Netherlands in 1585, he subsequently received the honour of knighthood from *King* JAMES I. Sir Clement *m.* Mary, daughter of Francis Repington, esq. of Amington, in the county of Stafford, and had issue,

- ROBERT (Sir), his heir, who received the honour of knighthood, in his father's lifetime.
- Anne, *m.* first, to Sir Thomas Dilke, of Maxtock, in the county of Warwick, and secondly, to Sir Harvey Bagott, bart. of Blithfield, in Staffordshire.
- Lettice, *m.* to Sir Robert Throckmorton of Haseley, in the county of Warwick.
- Mary, *m.* to Sir Edward Littleton, of Pillaton Hall, in Staffordshire.

Sir Clement *d.* in 1619, was buried at Packington, and *s.* by his son,

I. SIR ROBERT FISHER, knt. of Packington, in the county of Warwick, who was created a BARONET by *King* JAMES I. 7th December, 1622. He *m.* Elizabeth, daughter of Sir Anthony Teringham, knt. of Teringham Court, in the county of Northampton, and had issue,

- I. CLEMENT, his heir.
- II. Thomas, *m.* Dorothy, daughter of James Lacon, esq. of West Copies, in the county of Salop, and died before his elder brother, (he was buried at Packington in 1681,) having had issue,
  1. CLEMENT, who *s.* his uncle as third BARONET.
  2. Thomas, *d.* an infant.
  3. Francis, *m.* Mary, daughter of Sir Arthur Caley, of Newland, in Warwickshire, and relict of Sir Samuel Marrow, bart. but *d. s. p.* in 1701, and was buried at Packington.
  4. Thomas, *d.* at sea, unm.
  5. ROBERT, who *s.* as fourth baronet.
  1. Lettice, *m.* first, to Sir Charles Lee, knt. and secondly, to the bishop of Worcester.

2. Jane, *m.* to Thomas Byrch, esq. of Leacroft, in Staffordshire, son of Edward Byrch, serjeant-at law.
3. Dorothy, *m.* to Griffin May, esq. a captain in the army.
4. Elizabeth, *m.* to John Jennens, second son of Humphry Jennens, esq.
5. Mary, *m.* to Edward Bedingfeld, esq. brother of Sir Henry Bedingfeld, bart.

III. Francis, *m.* Margaret, daughter of Sir Edward Littleton, bart. of Pillaton Hall, and relict of Sir George Brown, knt. of Radford, in the county of Warwick, but *d. s. p.* 27th March, 1692.

I. Lettice, *m.* to Sir Richard Shilton, knt. of West Bromwich, in the county of Stafford.

II. Catherine, *m.* to Thomas Whitwick, son of John Whitwick, serjeant-at-law.

He *d.* 29th March, 1647, was buried at Packington, and *s.* by his eldest son,

II. SIR CLEMENT FISHER, bart. who *m.* Jane, daughter of John Lane, esq. of Bentley, in the county of Stafford, the lady so celebrated for assisting in the escape of CHARLES II. after the unfortunate battle of Worcester, for which eminent service she obtained, after the restoration, a pension of one-thousand a year for life. Sir Clement and his father Sir Robert, were severe sufferers in person and property by their loyalty to the Stewarts. Sir Clement *d. s. p.* 15th April, 1683, and his distinguished wife 9th September, 1689; both were buried at Packington. He was *s.* by his nephew,

III. SIR CLEMENT FISHER, bart. who *m.* Anne, daughter of Humphrey Jennens, esq. of the county of Warwick, and by that lady (who *d.* 17th January, 1707,) had an only daughter and heiress,

MARY, *m.* to Heneage Finch, second Earl of Aylesford, and was grandmother of the present (fifth) Earl. She conveyed the manor of Packington to the family of her husband.

Sir Clement was *s.* in the title by his only surviving brother,

IV. SIR ROBERT FISHER, bart. who *m.* Anne, daughter of Jaques Wiseman, of London, gent. but died without issue about the year 1739, when the BARONETCY became EXTINCT.

Arms—Argent, a chevron vaire between three demilions rampant, gules.

*** Packington, the seat of this family, now in the possession of the Earl of Aylesford, five miles from Coventry, and six from Coleshill, in Warwickshire, was erected from the foundation by Sir Clement Fisher, the third baronet, father of the Countess of Aylesford, and adorned with gardens, statues, canals, &c.

FISHER, OF ST. GILES.

CREATED 19th July, 1627. EXTINCT 7th Oct. 1707.

Lineage.

I. SIR THOMAS FISHER, of St. Giles, in the county of Middlesex, who was created a BARONET in 1627, *m.* Sarah daughter and co-heir of Sir Thomas Fowler bart. of Islington, and had issue,

THOMAS, his heir.
John, died young.
RICHARD, who succeeded as fourth baronet.
Sarah, *m.* to Sir Henry Ducie, K.B.
Susan.
URSULA, *m.* to Sir William Halton, bart. of Sanford, in Essex,

Sir Thomas died 22nd May, 1636, and was *s.* by his eldest son,

II. SIR THOMAS FISHER, who *m.* Jane, daughter of Sir John Prescot, knt. of Hoxne, in Suffolk, and by her, who wedded, secondly, William Maynard, esq. second son of Lord Maynard, left at his decease in September, 1670, a son and successor,

III. SIR THOMAS FISHER, who died unm. in April 1671, aged eighteen, and was *s.* by his uncle,

IV. SIR RICHARD FISHER, who *m.* first, Anne Legh of St. John's Close, and secondly, Browne, eldest daughter of Sir William Ramsden, knt. of Longley, in Yorkshire, and relict of Sir George Dalston, knt. but as he died issueless, 7th October, 1707, the BARONETCY became EXTINCT. His sister and eventual heir, Ursula, conveyed the manor of Berners (inherited from the Fowlers,) to the HALTON family, and it continued in their possession until 1754, when it was devised by Sir William Halton, bart. (grandson of Ursula Fisher to the family of TUFNELL.

Arms—Or, three demi-lions ramp. and a chief indented gu.

FITTON, OF GAWSWORTH.

CREATED 2nd Oct. 1617.

EXTINCT August, 1643.

Lineage.

SIR EDWARD FITTON, knt. representative of the Gawsworth branch of the ancient Cheshire family of Fitton, *temp.* HENRY VIII. served as sheriff for the palatinate 35th of that reign. He *m.* Mary, daughter and co-heir of Guicciard Harbottle, of Northumberland, and had issue,

EDWARD (Sir), his heir.
Thomas, of Siddington, *d.* 20th April, 1590, m. Anne, daughter of Peter Warburton, and had two daughters,
  Frances, *m.* to John Wills, of Staffordshire.
  Margaret, *m.* to Robert Hyde, of Norbury.
Francis, *m.* 1588, Catherine, Countess Dowager of Northumberland, and *d. s. p.*
Anthony, died in Ireland.
George.
John.
Jane, *m.* to Kynaston, of Oteley.
———, *m.* to Sir Francis Inglefield.
———, *m.* to Sir Richard Leveson, of Trentham.
Katherine, *m.* to John Mere, esq. of Mere.

Sir Edward died 17th February, 2 EDWARD VI. and was *s.* by his son,

SIR EDWARD FITTON, knt. of Gawsworth, lord president of Connaught and Thomond, and treasurer of

Ireland, who m. in 1530, Anne, daughter of Sir Peter Warburton, knt. of Arley, in Cheshire, and had issue,

Edward (Sir), his heir.

Alexander, settled in Ireland. On his son,

William, of Awne, in Ireland, Sir Edward Fitton, settled the estate as heir male. He m. Eva, daughter of Sir Edward Trevor, of Brynkynallt, and had two sons, viz.

Alexander, who was seized of the Gawsworth estate, which Charles, Lord Brandon, recovered from him in 1663 and 1664. This Alexander became eventually chancellor of Ireland, and was created Baron Fitton, Lord Gawsworth, by James II. after his abdication. He m. the daughter of Thomas Jolly, esq. of Cofton, and had issue.

Edward, supposed to have *d. s. p.*

John, *d. s. p.*

Richard, *d. s. p.*

Margaret, m. to Sir Randle Mainwaring, knt. of Peover.

Mary, m. to William Tatton, esq. of Withenshaw.

Sir Edward died 3rd July, 1579, and was *s.* by his son,

Sir Edward Fitton, knt. of Gawsworth, president of Munster, who m. Alice, daughter and sole heir of John Holcroft, esq. of Holcroft, in Lancashire, and had by her, who *d.* in 1626, two sons and two daughters, viz.

Edward, his heir.

Richard, *d. s. p.*

Mary, maid of honour to *Queen* Elizabeth, m. first to Captain Lougher, and secondly, to Captain Polwhele.

Alice, m. to Sir John Newdigate, of Arbury, Warwickshire.

Sir Edward died at Gawsworth, in 1606, and was *s.* by his son,

I. Edward Fitton, esq. of Gawsworth, born 3rd December, 1572, who was created a Baronet in 1617. He m. Anne, daughter and co-heir of James Barret, of South Wales, and had

Edward, his heir.

Penelope, m. to Sir Charles Gerrard, knt. of Hassel, in Lancashire, and had a son,

Charles Gerrard, Lord Brandon, and Earl of Macclesfield, who recovered the Gawsworth estate from Alexander Fitton.

Mary, m. to Geffry Minshull, of Stoke.

Frances, m. to Henry Mainwaring, esq. of Carincham.

Alice, m. to Sir John Meyrick, of Monkton.

Anne, m. first to Sir John Brereton, knt. of Brereton, and secondly, to Sir Gilbert Gerrard, knt.

Lettice, m. to John Cole, esq. of Shropshire.

Jane, m. to Thomas Minshull, esq. of Erdeswick, in Cheshire.

Sir Edward *d.* 10th May, 1619, and was *s.* by his son,

II. Sir Edward Fitton, of Gawsworth, bapt. 1603, sheriff of Cheshire in 1653, who m. first, 1622, Jane, daughter of Sir John Trevor, knt. of Plas Teg, in Denbighshire, and secondly, Felicia, sister of Ralph Sneyd, esq. of Keel, which lady married secondly, Sir Charles Adderley, knt. Sir Edward Fitton, who was a distinguished officer in the royal service, died shortly after the taking of Bristol in 1643, without surviving issue, when the Baronetcy became extinct. After the decease of Sir Edward, a violent dispute arose between Charles, Lord Brandon, and Alexander Fitton, esq. for the inheritance of the estates, and a very curious tract was published in 1663, giving a narrative of the proceedings that ensued. From that statement it appears that Sir Edward Fitton resolved, in 1641, to revive the ancient entail of the Gawsworth estate, and settled the same by indenture on William Fitton, his heir male kinsman. The said settlement is said to be confirmed by deed poll dated 3rd April, 18 Charles I. by Sir Edward Fitton. This narrative further asserts that when importuned by divers people, and also immediately before his death, he said he would rather settle his estate on Ned Fitton, the bonny beggar, (a man who kept beggars from his gate) than any one of his sisters' children. Nevertheless, a will was brought forward by Lord Gerard, nineteen years after Sir Edward Fitton's death, and after the most singular species of litigation, his lordship succeeded in obtaining possession of the property. From his son the second Earl of Macclesfield, Gawsworth passed to Lady Mohun, daughter and heiress of his sister, and co-heiress, with Charlotte Mainwaring. Having subsequently vested, under Lord Mohun's will, in his second wife, Elizabeth Lawrence, it passed to Anne Griffiths, issue of the said Elizabeth by a first marriage, and was sold by the trustees of her marriage settlement to her husband, the Rt. Hon. William Stanhope, from whom it has descended to Charles, present Earl of Harrington.

Arms—Arg. on a bend az. three garbs or.

FLEETWOOD, OF CALDWICK.

Created 29th June, 1611.

Extinct in Jan. 1780, or 3rd Dec. 1802.

Lineage.

This family, which had been seated many ages in Lancashire, removed into the county of Stafford in the beginning of the sixteenth century.

John Fleetwood, lord of the manor of Plumpton-Parva, in the county of Lancaster, was father of a daughter, Anne, the wife of John Ethalston, of Ribleston, and of a son and heir,

Henry Fleetwood, living in the 3rd Henry VI. whose son and successor,

Edward Fleetwood, living in the 13th Edward IV. m. Elizabeth, daughter of Roger Holland, esq. and was father of

William Fleetwood, esq. of Hesketh, in the county of Lancaster, who m. Helen, daughter of Robert Standish, esq. and had issue,

I. John, his successor.

II. Thomas, of the Vache, in Bucks, held the office of master of the mint. He m. first, Barbara ——, an heiress, and by her had

Everard, M.P. who m. Joan Cheney, and left issue.

Margaret, m. to Peter Dormer, esq. and was mother of

Sir Fleetwood Dormer, knt. of Shipton Lee, Bucks.

Thomas Fleetwood married, secondly, Bridget, daughter of Sir John Spring, knt. of Lavenham, Suffolk, and by that lady (who wedded, secondly, Sir Robert Wingfield, knt. of Letheringham, in the same county), had

George (Sir), of the Vache, in Chalfont St. Giles's, Bucks, m. Catherine, daughter of Sir Henry Denny (by his wife, Honora, daughter of Lord Grey of Wilton), and sister of Sir Edward Denny, created Earl of Norwich (see BURKE's *Extinct Peerage*). By this lady Sir George Fleetwood had a numerous issue.*

William (Sir), of Cranford, in Middlesex, receiver of the Court of Wards.†

James, bishop of Worcester.

Edward.

Michael.

Henry, of Longby, Bucks.

Edmund, ancestor of the Fleetwoods of Rossall, now represented by PETER HESKETH FLEETWOOD, esq. of Rossall, M.P.

Bridget, *m.* to Sir William Smith, of Hill Hall.

Joyce, *m.* first to Sir Hewit Osborne, knt. and secondly, to Sir Peter Freetiville.

III. Robert, was father of

SIR WILLIAM FLEETWOOD, knt. an eminent lawyer of the Middle Temple, recorder of London, and serjeant-at-law in the time of ELIZABETH. "He was a learned man, and a good antiquary, but of a marvellous merry and pleasant conceit." He purchased an estate at Missenden, in Bucks, and dying in 1593, left two sons and two daughters, viz.

1. SIR WILLIAM FLEETWOOD, of Missenden, from whom descended the Fleetwoods of that place. Missenden was on the expiration of Sir William's male descendants, conveyed by heirs female, to the families of Ansell and Goostrey. After the decease of Thomas Goostrey, esq. it was purchased in 1767, by J. Oldham Oldham, esq.

2. SIR THOMAS FLEETWOOD, attorney general to *Prince* HENRY, eldest son of JAMES I.

1. Cordelia Fleetwood, *m.* to Sir David Foulis, bart. of Ingleby, in the county of York.

2. Elizabeth Fleetwood, *m.* to Sir Thomas Chaloner, knt. tutor to *Prince* HENRY.

IV. Edmund, a monk at Sion, in Middlesex.

I. Agnes, *m.* to John Jellibrand, esq. of Chorley, in Lancashire.

II. Janet, *m.* to John Blackledge, esq. of Leyland, in Lancashire.

The eldest son and heir,

JOHN FLEETWOOD, esq. of Penwortham, near Preston, in Lancashire, *m.* Jane, daughter and co-heir of Thomas Langton, esq. baron of Walton and lord of the fee and manor of Newton, and thus became possessed of that lordship: he had issue three sons and several daughters, and was *s.* by his eldest son,

---

* Of the seventh son, James, Anthony Wood gives the following details:

JAMES FLEETWOOD, his seventh son, was admitted scholar of King's College, Cambridge, in 1622; afterwards he became chaplain to Dr. Wright, Bishop of Lichfield, by whom he was preferred to the vicarage of Prees, in Shropshire, and soon after collated to the prebendship of Eccleshall, belonging to the church of Lichfield, but before he was admitted or installed the Rebellion broke out. Afterwards, being forced for his loyalty to forsake his preferment, he betook himself to the wars, and became chaplain to the regiment of John, Earl of Rivers, and in the quality of a chaplain he continued to the end of the wars. In 1642 he was, by the king's special command, honoured with the degree of doctor of divinity for the service he did him at Edge Hill fight, and soon after was made chaplain to Charles, Prince of Wales, and rector of Sutton Colfield, in the county of Warwick. After the wars were ceased, and he ejected thence, he became tutor to three earls, viz. to the Earl of Lichfield, Earl of Kildare, and Earl of Stirling; afterwards, to two dukes, namely, to Esme, Duke of Richmond and Lenox, with whom he travelled into France (where he died), and to Charles, who succeeded him in the dukedom. After the restoration of *King* CHARLES II. he was the first that was sworn chaplain in ordinary to him, was made provost of King's College, Cambridge, in June, 1660, and about that time rector of Anstey, in Hertfordshire, and of Denham, in Bucks. In July, 1675, he was appointed Bishop of Worcester, and *d.* 17th July, 1683, aged eighty-one, and was buried in Worcester Cathedral, over whose grave is a marble monument, with the following epitaph of his own making:

M. S.

Epitaphium hoc vivus vidensque scripsi.
Ponant quorum intererit.

Ego Ja. Fleetwood, S. T. P. Cathed. Wigorn. Episcopus nonagesimus, miserrimus Peccatorum. Hic jaceo qui dignissimus in æternum jacerem, sed Misericordia Domini gratiam consecutus sum,

Quo mihi nobilitas fucata? Hoc glorior unum,
Quod Christus de carne mea est. Proinde.
Nemo me lacrymis decoret, me vindice Christo
Incolumen renovet patefacti fossa Sepulchri
Mox Coeli tentabo vias, Christumque supernè
Vivus Carne mea viventem in Carne videbo. Vixi. Dixi.

Johannes Fleetwood, Archidiaconus Wigorniensis, Filius prædicti Præsulis natu minimus, Epigraphen hanc poni curavit. In Memoriam Reverendi admodum Patris, qui vitam cum morte mutavit Julii 17, Ætatis suæ octagesimo primo Anno Consecrationis 8vo salutis humanæ reparatæ, anno 1683.

† Sir William Fleetwood, of Cranford, receiver of the Court of Wards, *m.* Joan, sister to the Lord Clifton, by whom he had three sons: Miles, the elder, was receiver of the Court of Wards, and George, the third, went to Sweden, was a famous general there, and created a baron; he was father of Gustavus, Baron Fleetwood of Sweden. The second son,

Sir William Fleetwood, cupbearer to JAMES I. and Charles I. comptroller of Woodstock. He married two wives; by the first he had

Sir Miles Fleetwood, knt. of Ardwinkle, in Northamptonshire.

Colonel William Fleetwood.

By the second, Miss Harvey, he had several other sons, of whom the eldest,

CHARLES FLEETWOOD, commonly called Lord FLEETWOOD, was general and commander-in-chief to RICHARD CROMWELL, the Protector, and had for his first wife, the widow of General Ireton, Oliver Cromwell's daughter, but had no [illegible] Fleetwood, Clarendon says, "was a weak man, but very popular with all the praying part of the army; a man, whom the parliament would have trusted, if they had not resolved to have no general, being as confident of his fidelity to them as any man's, and Lambert knew well how to govern him, as Cromwell had done Fairfax, and then in like manner lay him aside; and when intelligence was brought of any murmur among the soldiers, by which a revolt might ensue, he was desired to go amongst them, to [illegible] them, he would fall on his knees to prayers, could hardly be prevailed on to go to them; when he was amongst them, and in the [illegible] any discourse, he would invite them all to [illegible] and put himself on his knees before them; when some of his friends importuned him to appear more vigorous in the charge he had, without which they must all be destroyed, they could get no other answer from him, than 'God had [illegible] his face, and would not hear him:' so [illegible] ceased to wonder why Lambert had [illegible] him to the office of general, and had been [illegible] with the second command himself."

General Fleetwood's daughter, Elizabeth, married Sir John Hartopp, M.P. and was [illegible] the present Sir Edmund Cradock Hartopp, [illegible] Freathby.

THOMAS FLEETWOOD, esq. who m. Mary, daughter of Sir Richard Shirburne, knt. of Shirburne, in the county of Lancaster (and Maud, his wife, daughter of Sir Richard Bold, of Bold, knt. by Margery, his wife, daughter of Sir Thomas Butler, knt. of Beausey, both in Lancashire), and left two sons,

RICHARD, his heir.

William, m. Dorothy, daughter of Sir Edward Cokaine, knt. of Ashborne, in the county of Derby.

He was s. by his elder son,

I. RICHARD FLEETWOOD, esq. of Calwich, in the county of Stafford (the first of the family who resided), who was created a BARONET, by *King* JAMES I. 29th June, 1611. Sir Richard m. Anne, daughter of Sir John Pershall, bart. of Horsley, in the same county, and had issue,

THOMAS, his successor.

Richard, *d. s. p.*

William, living in 1663.

Robert, m. a daughter of Mr. Colman, of Canth, in Staffordshire.

Henry, m. Agatha, daughter of Thomas Gifford, esq. of Plardick, in the county of Stafford, and d. in 1689; his widow d. in 1692.

Mary, *d. s. p.*

Elizabeth, m. to — Broughton, esq.

Dorothy, m. to — Barnesfield, esq.

He was s. at his decease by his eldest son,

II. SIR THOMAS FLEETWOOD, bart. who m. Gertrude, daughter of Rowland Eyre, esq. of Hassop, in the county of Derby, and had issue,

I. RICHARD, his heir.

II. Thomas, m. first, Elizabeth, daughter of — Coyney, esq. and had a son, THOMAS, who succeeded his uncle as fourth baronet. He m. secondly, and had two other sons, William, who *d.* a bachelor, and JOHN, who inherited as fifth baronet.

III. Rowland, of Prestwood, in the county of Stafford, who *d. s. p.* and left his estate to his nephew, Sir John Fleetwood.

IV. William, who m. Mrs. Piget, widow of — Piget, esq. of Shropshire.

I. Anne, m. to Edward Tildesley, esq. of the Lodge, in the county of Lancaster.

Sir Thomas was s. by his eldest son,

III. SIR RICHARD FLEETWOOD, bart. who m. Anne, daughter of Sir Edward Golding, bart. of Colston Basset, in the county of Nottingham, and had three sons and five daughters,

Thomas, who m. the daughter and heir of Christopher Bannister, esq. of Bank, in the county of Lancaster, and dying in the lifetime of his father, left an only daughter, Elizabeth who became the wife of THOMAS LEGH, esq. younger brother of Peter Legh, esq. of Lyme, in Cheshire. (See BURKE's *Commoners*, vol. ii. p. 633.)

Rowland, } Edward, } predeceased their father unm.

Sir Richard surviving his sons, was s. at his decease by his nephew,

IV. SIR THOMAS FLEETWOOD, bart. This gentleman m. Magdalen, daughter of Thomas Berrington, esq. of ... Hall, in Salop, and dying without issue in December, 1739, was interred at New Church, in Cheshire, and s. by his half brother,

V. SIR JOHN FLEETWOOD, bart. who m. Philippa, sister of William Berrington, esq. of Shrewsbury, and dying in 1741, was s. by his son,

VI. SIR THOMAS FLEETWOOD, bart. who died unm. in January, 1780, when the title is supposed to have become EXTINCT, although it was assumed by a Thomas Fleetwood, who *d. s. p.* in 1802. The estate of Calwich Abbey was sold by the Fleetwoods to BERNARD GRANVILLE, esq. great-grandson of the celebrated Sir Bevil Granville.

Arms—Per pale nebulée az. and or, six martlets counterchanged.

FLEMING, OF BROMPTON PARK.

CREATED 22nd April, 1763

EXTINCT 6th Nov. 1763.

Lineage.

I. JOHN FLEMING, esq. of Brompton Park, in the county of Middlesex, was created a BARONET 22nd April, 1763. Sir John m. Jane, daughter of William Coleman, esq. of Garnhay, in the county of Devon, but dying without issue, 6th November, 1763, the BARONETCY became EXTINCT.

Arms—Arg. a chevron gu. within a double treasure flory counterflory of the last.

FLETCHER, OF HUTTON.

CREATED 19th Feb. 1640-1.

EXTINCT 19th May, 1712.

Lineage.

HENRY FLETCHER, esq. of Cockermouth, son of William Fletcher, who had augmented the family estates by commercial pursuits, was a person of so much importance, as he entertained Mary Queen of Scots with great magnificence, in her journey from Workington to Carlisle in 1568, and presented her majesty with robes of velvet. He married, and had, with three daughters, seven sons, viz.

I. WILLIAM, who purchased MORESBY, was ancestor of the FLETCHERS of that place, which branch became extinct in the eighteenth century, at the demise of Thomas Fletcher, esq.

II. Lancelot, from whom descended the FLETCHERS of Tallantire, who became extinct in the male line at the death of Henry Fletcher, esq. The manor of Tallantire was given by that gentleman to his daughter, Anne, who m. Matthias Partis, a merchant at Newcastle-upon-Tyne. In 1776 the estate was purchased of Henry Hopper, devisee of Fletcher Partis, esq. by William Browne, esq.

III. James, *d. s. p.*

IV. John, *d. s. p.*

V. Henry, *d. s. p.*

VI. THOMAS, of whose line we have to treat.

VII. Robert.

The sixth * son,

Thomas Fletcher, esq. of Cockermouth, married Jane, daughter and heir of — Bullen, and had, besides daughters, five sons, namely,

i. Richard (Sir), his heir.
ii. Thomas, a merchant in London.
iii. Philip, ancestor of Henry Fletcher, esq. of Clea Hall, in Cumberland, who was created a Baronet in 1782, and was grandfather of the present Sir Henry Fletcher, bart.
iv. Launcelot.
v. Henry.

The eldest son,

Sir Richard Fletcher, knt. of Cockermouth, acquiring considerable wealth by commerce, purchased Hutton and other large estates in Cumberland. Sir Richard served as sheriff for that county 14 James I. He m. first, a daughter of — Richmond, by whom he had three children, who all died unmarried; and, secondly, Barbara, daughter of Henry Crackenthorpe, esq. of Newbiggen, and by that lady had

Henry, his heir.
Bridget, m. to John Patrickson, esq. of Calder Abbey.
Isabel, m. to Richard Lowther, esq. of Ingleton, in Yorkshire: and secondly, to Sir John Ashton, bart. of Whalley Abbey.
Mary, m. to Sir John Lowther, bart. of Lowther.
Catherine, m. to Thomas Lister, esq. of Gisborne, in Yorkshire.
Winifred, m. first, to George Braithwaite, esq. of Warcop, in Westmoreland; secondly, to Sir Richard Dacre, knt.; and thirdly, to Christopher Lister, esq. of Thornton.

Sir Richard was s. by his son,

i. Henry Fletcher, esq. of Hutton, in Cumberland, who served twice as sheriff of that county *temp.* Charles I. and was created a Baronet in 1640. This gentleman m. Catherine, daughter of Sir George Dalston, bart. of Dalston, and by her (who wedded, secondly, Dr. Thomas Smith, afterwards Bishop of Carlisle), had issue,

Richard, who predeceased his father, unm.
George, heir to his father.
Henry, died young.
Barbara, m. to Sir Daniel Fleming, of Rydal.
Frances, m. to William Fletcher, esq. of Moresby.
Bridget, m. to Christopher Dalston, esq. of Acornbank.

At the commencement of the civil contentions of the reign of the unhappy Charles I. Sir Henry Fletcher raised, chiefly at his own expense, a regiment for the royal service, and fell fighting at the skirmish of Rawton Heath in 1645: when he was s. by his only surviving son,

ii. Sir George Fletcher, of Hutton, M.P. for Cumberland, who m. first, Alice, daughter of Hugh, Earl of Coleraine, and had by her one son and three daughters, viz.

Henry, his heir.
Lucy, m. to Francis Bowes, esq. son of Sir Thomas Bowes.
Catherine, m. to Lionel Vane, esq. of Long Newton, in Durham, and had issue,
George Vane, whose only son,
The Rev. Henry Vane, was created a Baronet in 1782. He m. Frances, daughter and heir of John Tempest, esq. of Sherburn, and had an only son,
Sir Henry Vane-Tempest, bart. whose daughter and heiress,
Frances-Anne, m. Charles William Marquess of Londonderry.
Henry Vane, who assumed the surname of Fletcher. He died unmarried in 1761.
Walter Vane, who inherited Hutton, the estate of his maternal ancestors, and assumed the additional surname of Fletcher. His son,
Lionel Wright Fletcher Vane, esq. of Hutton, was created a Baronet in 1786, and was grandfather of the present Sir Francis Fletcher Vane, bart.
Lionel Vane, m. and had issue.
Mary Vane, m. to John Spearman, esq. of Sedgefield.
Alice, died unmarried.

Sir George m. secondly, Mary, daughter of James Johnston, Earl of Hartfell, and relict of Sir George Graham, bart. and had by her

George, a military officer, *d. s. p.*
Thomas, a merchant in London, *d. s. p.*
Susanna, died unm.
Mary, died unm.

Sir George Fletcher died 23rd July, 1700, aged [illegible] seven, and was *s.* by her son,

iii. Sir Henry Fletcher, of Hutton, who [illegible] after having settled his estates upon a distant relative Thomas Fletcher, esq. of Moresby, to Douay, in France, where he shortly after (19th May, 1712) died in a convent of English monks, and lies buried in a magnificent chapel there, which he built for the community at his own expense. With him the Baronetcy expired. At his demise, his sisters, as heirs at law, prosecuted their title to the whole estate, but after much litigation, it was agreed that Thomas Fletcher, esq. of Moresby should enjoy the demesne and lordship of Hutton for his life; and if he died without issue, then Henry Fletcher Vane, esq. should inherit the whole property. Mr. Fletcher, of Moresby, did die *s. p.* and the estates passed to the Vane family.

Arms—Arg. a cross engr. sa. between four [illegible] of the second, each charged with a pheon of the [illegible]

FOLEY, OF HALSTEAD.

Created 1st July, 1767. Extinct 7th March, 1782.

Lineage.

Richard Foley, esq. of Stourbridge, in the county of Worcester, an eminent iron master, who amassed an immense fortune, had, by his first wife, an only son, Richard, of Langford, in Staffordshire, whose male line became extinct; and by the second, Anne, daughter of William Brindley, esq. of Hyde, in the latter county, five sons and four daughters: the sons were,

i. Edward, who m. and d. issueless.
ii. Thomas.

* By some accounts he is styled *eldest* son.

III. Robert, from whom the Foleys of Stourbridge.
IV. Samuel, father of three sons,
1. Samuel, Bishop of Down and Connor, in Ireland.
2. John, M.D. of Cheshire.
3. Solomon, in holy orders, D.D.
V. John, a Turkey merchant, *d.* unmarried.

The eldest surviving son,

THOMAS FOLEY, esq. of Whitley Court, in the county of Worcester, *m.* Anne, daughter of John Browne, esq. of Spelmanden, in Kent; by the addition of whose great fortune to his paternal inheritance, he left, at his decease a very large estate in several counties: he had three sons, viz.

I. THOMAS, his heir, M.P. for the county of Surrey, father of
THOMAS FOLEY, esq. M.P. for Worcestershire, who was created BARON FOLEY, of Kidderminster, in 1711, and was *s.* in 1732-3, by his son,
THOMAS, second baron, who *d.* unm. in 1766, when the barony expired.
II. Paul, of Stoke Edith Court, in the county of Hereford, chosen speaker of the House of Commons, 14th March, 1694-5. His grandson,
THOMAS FOLEY, esq. of Whitley Court, was created Baron Foley, of Kidderminster, in 1756. (See BURKE'S *Peerage and Baronetage*).
III. PHILIP.

The third son,

PHILIP FOLEY, esq. of Prestwood, in the county of Stafford, M.P. *m.* Penelope, daughter of William Paget, fifth Lord Paget, and had two sons,

I. PAUL, of Prestwood, who *m.* Elizabeth, daughter of William Turton, esq. of Ulderwas, in Staffordshire, son and heir of Judge Turton, and had, with three daughters, Frances, *d.* unmarried; Elizabeth, wife of Walter Noel, esq. of Hilcot; and Penelope, of John Howard, esq. of Lichfield, an only son,
WILLIAM, who *m.* Anna-Maria Bromwich, by whom he left
WILLIAM, who *d.* unmarried.
ELIZABETH, *m.* to Thomas Hodyetts, esq. of Shettend, in the county of Stafford, and left one daughter, who *d.* issueless.
II. ROBERT.

The second son,

ROBERT FOLEY, esq. *m.* Mary, daughter of the Rev. Ralph Machland, and had issue,

I. THOMAS, *m.* Mary, daughter of Admiral St. Loo, and *d.* in January, 1779.
II. Philip, rector of Shelsley, in Worcestershire, *m.* Anne, only daughter of John Titmarsh, esq. of Barrington, in Cambridgeshire.
III. Edward, *d.* unm.
IV. ROBERT-RALPH.
V. Harry Thomas, rector of Holt, in Worcestershire.
I. Penelope, *m.* to the Rev. H. Whitmore, rector of Stockton, Salop.

The fourth son,

I. ROBERT RALPH FOLEY, esq. of Halstead Place, in Kent, was created a BARONET 1st July, 1767. Sir Robert *m.* Dorothy, only daughter of Thomas Hinchliffe, esq. of Bilcliffe, in Yorkshire, but dying *s. p.* in March, 1782, the BARONETCY EXPIRED.

Arms—Argent, a fesse, engrailed, between three cinquefoils, within a bordure, sable.

FOLJAMBE, OF WALTON.

CREATED 24th July, 1622. EXTINCT 17th Dec. 1640.

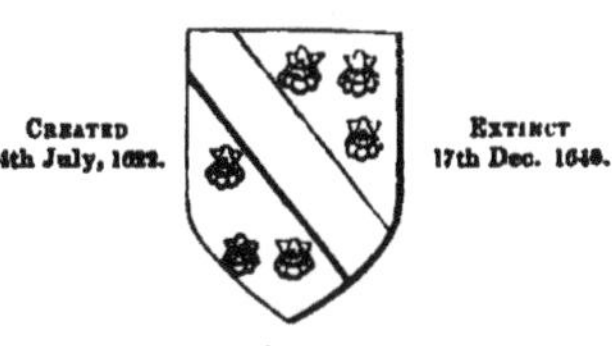

Lineage.

The family of FOLJAMBE has been seated from a very remote period in the county of Derby, and so early as the reign of HENRY III. Sir Thomas Foljambe appears, with other knights, as witness to several charters. Through a race of persons of principal account in the northern part of Derbyshire, we arrive at

HENRY FOLJAMBE, esq. of Walton, near Chesterfield, who *m.* Benedicta, daughter of Sir William Vernon, knt. and had two sons,

GODFREY, his heir.
Roger, of Linacre Hall, who *m.* Ellen, daughter of John Coke, esq. and was ancestor of the present
GEORGE SAVILE FOLJAMBE, esq. of Osberton, in the county of Nottingham, and of Aldwark, in Yorkshire. (See BURKE'S *Commoners*, vol. iv.)

The elder son,

SIR GODFREY FOLJAMBE, knt. of Walton, in Derbyshire, representative of the ancient house of Foljambe, *temp.* HENRY VIII. was sheriff of the county of Derby twice in that reign. He *m.* Catherine, daughter of Sir John Leake, and had a son and successor,

SIR JAMES FOLJAMBE, knt. of Walton, in Derbyshire, and of Aldwark, in the West Riding of the county of York, who was sheriff of Derbyshire 2 and 3 of PHILIP and MARY. He *m.* first, Alice, daughter and co-heir of Thomas Fitz-William, esq. of Aldwark, slain at Flodden in 1513, and had issue,

GODFREY (Sir), knt. of Walton, who *m.* Troth, daughter of Sir William Tyrwhit, of Kettleby, and by her, who wedded, secondly, Sir William Mallory, left at his decease, 22nd December, 1584, an only child,
GODFREY, of Walton, *b.* 21st November, 1558, sheriff of Derbyshire 31 ELIZABETH, *d. s. p.*
George, of Brimmington, in Derbyshire, *b.* 21st June, 1538, whose only daughter and heir, Troth, is said to have been married to Sir Edward Bellingham, of New Timber, in Sussex.
James, twin with George.
Frances, *m.* to John Thorn, or Thomas.
Cecily, *m.* to George Greenhalgh, of Teversal.
Mary, *m.* to Vincent Fearne, or Harris.

Sir James married, secondly, Constance, daughter of Sir Edward Littleton, knt. of Pillaton, and had by her,

FRANCIS, of whom presently.
Barbara, *m.* to Thomas Fletcher, esq. of Staffordshire.
Anne.
Jane.
Catherine.
Grace, *m.* to Henry Morgan.

Sir James Foljambe died 26th September, 1558, and lies buried at Chesterfield, where a monument is erected to his memory. His son by his second wife,

Francis Foljambe, esq. of Aldwark, m. Frances, daughter of Thomas Burdett, esq. of Birthwaite, and relict of Francis Wortley, esq. of Wortley, by whom he left at his decease, in 1606, a son,

I. Francis Foljambe, esq. of Walton and Aldwark, sheriff of Derbyshire in 1633, who was created a Baronet in 1622. This gentleman advanced the family in honours, but he weakened it by his extravagance. In the family history he is described as "a man of a profuse temper and excessive hospitality." He sold Walton and several other estates. Sir Francis m. first, Elizabeth, daughter of Sir William Wray, of Glentworth, by whom he had an only daughter and heir,

> Frances, m. first to Sir Christopher Wray, and secondly, to John Troutbeck, M.D. She died issueless.

He wedded secondly, Elizabeth, daughter of Sir George Reresby, but by her, (who m. secondly, Edward Horner, esq. of Mells, thirdly, Sir William Monson, Viscount Castlemaine, and fourthly, Sir Adam Felton, bart. of Playford,) had no issue. He died at Bath, 17th December, 1640, when the Baronetcy became extinct.

Arms—Sa. a bend between six escallops, or.

FORSTER, OF ALDERMASTON.

Created 20th May, 1620.

Extinct in Dec. 1711.

Lineage.

The family of Forster, or Foster, is of great antiquity in the county of Northumberland, and from Thomas Forster, a younger son of Anthony Forster, by Thomasine, daughter of Sir Edward Bray, descended the branch of the Forsters long seated at Aldermaston, in the county of Berks.

The son or grandson of this Thomas married the daughter and heir of Harpden, of Harpden, in the county of Oxon, and from him descended

Humphry Forster, of Harpden, who married Alice, the daughter of Thomas Nonor, of Nonor, in the county of Oxon, by whom he had issue,

Sir Humphry Forster, knt. of Harpden, who m. Alice, daughter and co-heir of Sir Stephen Popham,* knt. and dying in 1500, left issue,

Sir George Forster, K.B. of Aldermaston in the county of Berks,† jure uxoris, sheriff of Berks, in 1516, married Elizabeth, daughter and heir of John Delamere, of Aldermaston, eldest son of Sir Thomas Delamere, knt.‡ and by her, who died 7th December, 1526, left at his decease, in 1533, a son and heir,

Sir Humphry Forster, knt. of Aldermaston, sheriff, 1532 and 45, married Elizabeth, daughter of William, Lord Sandys, of the Vine, and had issue,

> William.
>
> Elizabeth, m. George Covert, of Sussex.
>
> Anne, m. Edward Bryansdon.
>
> Margaret, m. Anthony Elmes, of Bowlneday, in the county of Oxon.

Sir Humphry died in 1555, and was succeeded by his son,

William Forster, of Aldermaston, sheriff of Berks, 1567, m. first, Jane, daughter of Sir Anthony Hungerford, knt. of Down Ampney,§ in the county of Gloucester, of whom he left at his decease, 10th January, 1574, a son and successor,

Sir Humphry Forster, knt. of Aldermaston, sheriff of Berks, 1579 and 1592, m. Margaret, daughter of John Barrett, of Stanford Dingley, in the county of Berks, and had issue,

> William.
>
> Thomas, bapt. 1579.
>
> Richard, bapt. 1580.
>
> Matthew, bapt. 1584.
>
> Roger, bapt. 1586.
>
> Daniel, bapt. 1588, m. Margaret, daughter of — Elmes, of Bowlneday, in the county of Oxon, relict of Richard Spire.
>
> Mabel, bapt. 1580, m. Sir Robert Dillington, of Knighton, Isle of Wight, and had issue.
>
> Jane, bapt. 1581, m. Cuthbert Bacon, of Hants.
>
> Mary, bapt. 1596.

Sir Humphry died in 1601, and was succeeded by his son,

Sir William Forster, of Aldermaston, K.B bapt. 1575, sheriff of Berks, 1607, m. 1594, Mary, daughter of Sir Mark Stewart, of the Isle of Ely, and by her, who died in 1661, had issue,

> Humphry, his heir.
>
> Mary, m. first, Sir Edward Stafford, of Bradfield, in the county of Berks, and had issue; secondly, Thomas Hamlyn Bursuivant, third Sir Thomas Mainwaring; and thirdly, the celebrated antiquary, Elias Ashmole.

Sir William died in 1618, and was succeeded by his son,

1. Sir Humphry Forster, knt. of Aldermaston, sheriff of Berks 1619, who was created a Baronet in 16..

* Sir Stephen Popham, and Sir John Popham the chief justice, were descended from the same common ancestor in the time of Henry III. Sir Stephen was sheriff of Hants in the 6th and 19th of Henry VI. He left four daughters his co-heirs. His grandfather married Sibill, the second daughter and co-heir of Laurence St. Martin, by Sibilla, daughter and heir of Sir John Lorty, which coats of arms are in consequence introduced in the windows at Aldermaston, as is also the coat of Zouche, of Dean, in consequence of another ancestor having married the daughter and heir of Olivia de Zouch. (Vide p. 196, vol. ii. Burke's *Commoners*.)

† Anthony Forster, of Cumnor in Berks, so celebrated in the history of Leicester and Amy Robsart, was, as his monumental inscription shows, no relation to this family.

‡ The descent of the Aldermaston property has never been distinctly traced, but there would appear to have been four generations of Richards, beginning with Richard the grantee, *temp.* Henry I. and terminating in a daughter and heir, married to a Delamere, perhaps Sir Peter Delamere, and father or grandfather of Sir Thomas Delamere, knight of the holy sepulchre, and sheriff of Berks in 1472. He died in 1490, and being buried at St. Bridget's Sion, left by Elizabeth, his wife, a granddaughter and heir Elizabeth, the wife of Sir George Forster. He had also a younger son, George, to whose son, John Delamere, Elizabeth Forster was in 1507 proved heir.

§ Her mother was Jane, daughter of Sir Edward Darrell, of Littlecote. She remarried Sir Edward Hungerford, of Farley, son of Walter, Lord Hungerford.

He married Anne, daughter of Sir William Kingsmill, knt. of Sidmanton, in the county of Hants, and by her, who died 12th October, 1673, had issue,

Humphry, died *s. p.*

William his heir who *d. v. p.* in 1669. He *m.* Elizabeth, daughter of Sir John Tyrrell, of Heron, in Essex, and had issue,

Humphry, successor to his grandfather.
William, *d.* 1677, aged twenty-five.
John, killed in a duel, 1683, aged twenty-five.

Anne, *d.* 12th January, 1664.
Elizabeth, *m.* William Pert, of Essex, and secondly, Henry Kelsey, and had issue by her first husband,

Elizabeth Pert, who married first, William Forster, of Bamborough Castle, in Northumberland, but had no issue; and secondly, William, third Lord Stawell, by whom (who died in 1742) he had issue,

William, bapt. 7th October, 1712, in London, died 1740, *s. p.*

Charlotte, bapt. 31st March, 1709, in Soho Square, *m.* first, Ruishe Hasell, a major in the army; and after his death, Ralph Congreve, esq. of Congreve, in the county of Stafford. She died 7th July, 1763, *s. p.* when the property passed, by bequest, to the family of her last husband, Mr. Congreve, and the representation of the Forsters became vested in the heirs of Margaret Pratt and Sophia Halstead.

Lady Stawell died in 1748.

Edward, *d. s. p.*
John, died 1674, *s. p.*
George, bapt. 1630.
Charles, bapt. 1631, *d.* 1698.
Philip, bapt. 1634, *d. s. p.*
Stewart, *m.* first, Miss Wilde, and had issue,

Stewart, of the Phoenix frigate, *d. s. p.* before 1687.

Humphry, of Yardly Bury, in the county of Herts, *d. s. p.* before 1693.

He *m.* secondly, Elizabeth, daughter of Lord Henry Paulett, of Amport, but by her had no issue. He died 1689, aged forty-five.

Frances, bapt. 1609.
Anne, bapt. 1619, *d.* 16th May, 1636.
Mary, *d.* 9th September, 1636.
Bridget, *d.* 29th May, 1637.
Margery, bapt. 1623.
Margaret, bapt. 1626, *m.* Sir George Pratt, knt. of Coleshill, in the county of Berks, and had issue.
Sophia, bapt. 1622, *m.* Laurence Halstead, esq. and had issue.

Sir Humphry died in 1663, aged sixty-eight, and was succeeded by his grandson,

II. Sir Humphry Forster, bart. of Aldermaston, sheriff of Berks, 1704, who *m.* Judith, daughter and co-heir of Sir Humphrey Winch, bart. of Haines, in the county of Bedford, and by her (who *d.* 1729) had issue,

Humphry, *d.* 1682.
William, *d.* 1683, aged seven.
Rebecca, *d.* 1676, aged two.

Sir Humphry died in 1711, when the Baronetcy became extinct, and his estates eventually devolved on his niece, Lady Stawell.

Arms—Sa. a chev. engrailed between three arrows arg.

FORSTER, OF BAMBOROUGH.

Created 7th Mar. 1619-20.

Extinct about 1623.

Lineage.

I. Sir Claudius Forster, of Bamborough Castle, in Northumberland, who was created a Baronet in 1619-20, married Elizabeth, daughter of Sir William Fenwick, knt. but died *s. p.* about 1623, when the title became extinct.

Arms—Arg. a chev. vert between three bugle horns sa.

FORSTER, OF EAST GREENWICH.

Created 11th July, 1661.—Extinct ....

Lineage.

I. Sir Reginald Forster, of East Greenwich in Kent, who devoted himself zealously to the royal cause during the civil wars, and expended a large fortune in the service of his unhappy master, was rewarded by a Baronetcy shortly after the restoration. He *m.* Blandina, daughter of John Acton, goldsmith, of London, and dying circa 1684, was *s.* by his son,

II. Sir Reginald Forster, who married first, Miss Nash, of Greenwich, an heiress, and secondly, a Warwickshire lady, also an heiress, but died without male issue, at Stratford on Avon, subsequently to the year 1695, when the Baronetcy became extinct.

FORSTER, OF STOKESLY.

Created 18th Sept. 1649.—Extinct before 1714.

Lineage.

I. Richard Forster, esq. of Stokesly, in the county of York, who was raised to the degree of Baronet in 1649, married Joan Midleton, of Leighton, in Lancashire, and left at his decease, 17th January, 1661, a son and successor,

II. Sir Richard Forster, of Stokesly, who *m.* Clare, daughter of Anthony Meynell, of North Kilvington, in Yorkshire, and left (with a daughter, Mary, *m.* to Collingwood, of Hetton-in-the-Hole, in the county of Durham) a son,

III. Sir Richard Forster, of Stokesly, at whose decease, unm. before 1714, the Baronetcy became extinct.

FORTESCUE, OF FALLAPIT.

CREATED 31st Mar. 1664.

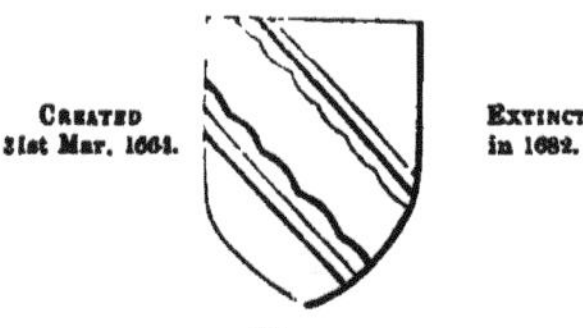

EXTINCT in 1682.

Lineage.

This was a branch of the ancient stock of Fortescue of Devon, established by SIR RICHARD LE FORTE, one of the companions in arms of the Conqueror. See BURKE's *History of the Commoners*, vol. ii. p. 541.

LEWIS FORTESCUE, esq. (youngest son of John Fortescue, esq. of Spirelston, and lineal descendant of William Fortescue, of Winston, the common ancestor of all the branches of the family) having been bred to the bar, was successively one of the readers of the Middle Temple, sergeant-at-law, and a baron of the exchequer. He was raised to the bench about the close of HENRY VIIIth's reign. He *m.* ELIZABETH, daughter and heiress of JOHN FORTESCUE, esq. of FALLAPIT, by whom he acquired that estate, and had a son and successor,

JOHN FORTESCUE, esq. of Fallapit, *b.* in 1525, *m.* Honoria, daughter of Edmund Speccott, esq. of Thornbury, and by her (who *d.* in 1606, aged seventy-eight) left at his decease, in 1595, a son and successor,

EDMUND FORTESCUE, esq. of Fallapit, *b.* in 1552, who *m.* Mary, daughter of Henry Champernowne, esq. of Modbury, and sister of Sir Richard Champernowne, knt. by whom (who *d.* in 1611) he had issue (to survive infancy) viz.

I. JOHN, his heir.
II. Francis, *b.* in 1587.
III. Nicholas, *b.* in 1596.

I. Honor, *b.* in 1583, *m.* to Humphrey Prideaux, esq. of Soldon, in the county of Devon. (See BURKE's *Commoners*, vol. i. p. 204.)
II. Elizabeth, born in 1584, married to John Nycholls, esq.

Edmund Fortescue, who was sheriff for the county of Devon in 1623, *d.* in 1624, and was *s.* by his eldest son,

JOHN FORTESCUE, esq. of Fallapit, who *m.* Sarah, daughter of Sir Edmund Prideaux, bart. of Netherton, by whom (who *d.* in 1628, aged forty-four) he had issue,

I. EDMUND, his successor.
II. John, *b.* in 1614.
III. Thomas, *b.* in 1615.
IV. PETER, *b.* in 1617, who *m.* Elizabeth, daughter of John Bastard, esq. of Gerston, in Devon, and had issue,

Peter, John, Peter, } who all *d.* young.
EDMUND, successor to his cousin, and continuator of the line at Fallapit, of whom hereafter.

Sarah, *d.* young

V. George, who *d.* in 1671, aged fifty-one.

I. Maria, *b.* in 1611, who *m.* Richard Wise, of Totnese.
II. Bridget, *b.* in 1619.

John Fortescue died in 1649, aged sixty-three, and was *s.* by his son,

SIR EDMUND FORTESCUE, knt. of Fallapit, *b.* in 1610, of whom Prince, in his Worthies of Devon, makes the following mention: "This gentleman having served *King* CHARLES I. with great courage, cost, and fidelity, as a justice of the peace, high sheriff of the county, and a brave commander in the wars, making as honourable articles for the surrender of Charles Fort, at Salcombe, Devon, whereof he was governor, as could be demanded; upon the fall of that king and his cause, fled beyond sea, and died in Holland." He was interred at Delph, where there was a monument erected to his memory. He *m.* Jane Southcote, of Mohun-Ottery, and by that lady (who died in 1643) had

John, *d.* in infancy.
EDMUND, heir.

Jane, who *d.* in 1641.
Catherine, *m.* to Thomas Glanville, esq.
Maria, *m.* to George Southcote, esq. of Buckland.

Sir Edmund was *s.* at his decease by his son,

SIR EDMUND FORTESCUE, knt. of Fallapit, who was created a BARONET 31st March, 1664. This gentleman *m.* Margery, daughter of Henry, fifth Lord Sandys, of the Vine, and left (with two daughters, Jane, married to William Coleman, esq. and Sarah, who died unmarried, in 1685, aged twenty-one) a son and successor,

SIR SANDYS FORTESCUE, bart. of Fallapit, *b.* in 16[illegible] who *m.* Elizabeth, daughter of Sir John Lenthall, knt. of Basingsleigh, and having no son, but one only daughter, Elizabeth, the title became EXTINCT at his decease in 1682, and the estates passed to (the son of his grand uncle, Peter) his cousin,

EDMUND FORTESCUE, esq. who *m.* Mary, daughter of Sampson Wyse, esq. of Dittisham, and by her, who died in 1722, had issue,

I. MARY, *m.* to the Right Hon. William Fortescue, of Buckland Filleigh, master of the rolls, and dying in 1710, aged twenty one, left an only daughter and heir,

MARY, *m.* to John Spooner, esq. but died without surviving issue, when Fallapit reverted to her aunt.

II. ELIZABETH, *d.* in 1768, aged seventy-three.
III. SARAH, *d.* in 1703, aged five.
IV. DOROTHY, *m.* to Thomas Bury, esq. son of Sir Thomas Bury, knt. of Exeter, and dying in 1733, aged thirty four, left (with a younger daughter, Dorothy Bury, who died unm. in 1792, aged sixty-two,) an elder daughter,

CATHERINE BURY, *m.* to the Rev. NATHANIEL WELLS, rector of East Allington, in Devon, and had (with [illegible] younger sons, and six daughters, see BURKE's *Commoners*, vol. ii. p. 543

EDMUND WELLS, who inherited FALLAPIT from his great aunt, Elizabeth Fortescue, and assumed the surname and arms of FORTESCUE. His grandson is the present WILLIAM BLUNDELL FORTESCUE, esq. of Fallapit.

V. GRACE, *d.* unm. in 1743-4.

Arms—Az. a bend engr. arg. cotised or.

FORTESCUE, OF WOOD.

CREATED 20th Jan. 1666-7.—EXTINCT in 1686.

Lineage.

This was another branch of the great house of FORTESCUE, descended from SIR HENRY FORTESCUE, chief justice of the Court of Common Pleas, in Ireland, by Joan, his first wife, heiress of Wood, in Devonshire. The male line of the original Fortescues, of Wood, failed, and the representation and estate were conveyed by a female heir, ELIZABETH FORTESCUE, to her husband LEWIS FORTESCUE, esq. of Preston, representative of another branch of the family. His direct descendant,

I. PETER FORTESCUE, esq. of Wood, was created a BARONET in 1666-7. He married first, Bridget, daughter of Sir John Eliot, of Port Eliot, in Cornwall; and secondly, Amy, daughter of Peter Courtenay, esq. of St. Michael, in the same county, and relict of Sir Peter Courtenay, knt. but as he left no male issue at his decease in 1686, the BARONETCY became EXTINCT.

Arms.—As FORTESCUE OF FALLAPIT.

FOWELL, OF FOWELLSCOMBE.

CREATED [illegible] April, 1661.

EXTINCT in Nov. 1692.

Lineage.

This Anglo-Saxon family, traced on proofs for nine [illegible] in the Visitation of 1620, is of very great [illegible], and is considered to have existed at Fowellscombe, in the parish of Ugborough, Devon, previously [to] the Conquest. (See BURKE'S *Commoners*, vol. iv.)

[illegible] DE FOGHIL, or DE FOGHILL, son and heir of [illegible] stated to have derived his descent from [illegible] by the daughter and heiress of Coome, lived [in] the thirteenth century, and m. the daughter and [heiress] of TREVAZE, of Trevaze, in Cornwall, which [illegible] remained with their descendants until the di[vision] of the estates of the elder branch of the family, [in] 1692, between the sisters of the last baronet. Their [great]-great-grandson and heir (through daughters and [heiresses] of WALLRONDE, HALLVELL, and ——, of [illegible], all in Devon), was

[illegible] FOUHEL, esq. of Foubelscombe, M.P. for [illegible] 33 HENRY VI. (1435.) He married Elinor, [eldest] daughter, by his wife, Margaret, eldest daughter [and] sole heir of William Stighul, of Devon of Sir [illegible] Reynell, knt. Lord of Trumpington and Badlingham, in Cambridgeshire, and of Malston, in Devon, ancestor of the Reynells, of that place, and of Ogwell, and of the Reynells, baronets. (See BURKE'S *Peerage and Baronetage*, and *Commoners*, vol. iv.) This William Foubel, M.P. for Totness, died 23rd March, 1507, and his wife, Elinor, the 9th of April, the same year, and as appears by inscription on a brass plate in their vault, were interred in the Fowell aisle of the church of Ugborough. Their son and heir,

SIR RICHARD FOWHIL, knt. of Fowhilscombe, m. first, Blanch, daughter and co-heir of Hayes of Devon; and secondly, Elizabeth, daughter of Sir Richard Edgcombe, knt. sheriff of Devon in 1487. By the former he had issue,

THOMAS, his heir, and

JOANE, married, first, to Sir Philip Courtenay, knt. of Loughter, second son of Sir Philip Courtenay, knt. of Molland, both in Devon, and had by him an only daughter,

Elizabeth Courtenay, married to Sir William Strode, knt. of Newenham Park, in Devon, ancestor, by her, of the present Strodes of Newenham.

She wedded, secondly, Humphrey Prideaux, esq. of Thoughborough and Adeston, in Devon, ancestor, by her of the present Sir Edmund Prideaux, bart. of Netherton, in that county. (See BURKE'S *Peerage and Baronetage*.)

The son and heir,

THOMAS FOWHILL, of Fowhillscombe, married Maria, eldest daughter, by his wife, Joane, daughter and co-heir of Richard Whitley, esq. of Efford, of Richard Halse, esq. of Kenedon, both in Devon, and dying in 1544, was s. by his son and heir,*

RICHARD FOWHILL, esq. of Fowhillscombe, who m. 27th January, 1541, Grace, second daughter, by his wife, Jane, daughter of Nicholas Dillon, esq. of Chimwell, in Devon, of John Somaster, esq. of Paynsford, in that county, and had issue three sons and one daughter,

I. ARTHUR, his heir.

II. William, of Blackhall and Diptford Down, in the adjoining parishes of North Huish and Diptford, b. at Fowellscombe in 1556, and m. Agnes, eldest daughter, by Anne, daughter of John Bligh, esq. of Bodmin, in Cornwall, of William Achym, esq. of Plenynth, or Plynt, in that county. His grandson and heir,

RICHARD FOWELL, of Blackhall and Diptford, m. in 1655, Elizabeth, eldest daughter of Sir Thomas Hele, bart. of Fleet Damarell, in Devon, M.P. sheriff of Devon, 1636, and co-heir of her brothers, Sir Samuel and Sir Henry Hele, barts.; on the death of the latter of whom, in 1677, s. p. that title (for which see that family, page 251), expired. Their son and heir,

WILLIAM FOWELL, esq. of Black Hall and Diptford, born at Blackhall in 1659, became, at the decease of Sir John Fowell, the third baronet, in 1692, heir male of the family. He died in April, 1714, aged fifty-five, leaving issue by his wife, Susannah, daughter of John Smyth, esq. of Tavistock, in Devon,

* This Thomas Fowhill, of Fowhillscombe, m. secondly, [illegible] daughter of — Bevyll, of Cornwall, by whom he [illegible] sons, Thomas, Robert, and William, one of [whom, it] is considered, originated the London branch of [the family], a descendant of which is supposed to have been JOSEPH FOWELL, esq. of London, the successful Russia merchant, whose only daughter and heiress, Sarah, m. Isaac Buxton, esq. and was grandmother of JOHN FOWELL BUXTON, esq. late M.P. for Weymouth, the philanthropic advocate of slave emancipation.

1. JOHN, his heir, *b.* in 1683, continuator of the Black Hall branch.*

2. Richard, M.A. fellow of Exeter College, Oxon, rector of Hilperton, and vicar of Corsham, in Wilts, *b.* at Black Hall, in October, 1695, *m.* in November, 1723, Anne, daughter of James Harris, esq. of the Close, in Salisbury, of the noble family of Harris, now Earls of Malmesbury, and died in 1750, aged fifty-five, leaving issue, of whom

  JOHN-POWELL, his son and heir, fellow of Exeter College, Oxon, D.D. rector of Bishopsbourne, &c. in Kent, and co-chaplain with Bishop Porteus to Secker, Archbishop of Canterbury, left issue, by his wife, Susannah, daughter of Thomas Alkin, esq. of Canterbury, an only daughter and heir,

    ULIANA-MARGARET-FOWELL, born at Bishopsbourne, 27th June, 1778, *m.* 23rd April, 1796, John Charles Tufnell, esq. of Bath, a major in the army, and lieutenant-colonel of the Middlesex militia, second son of George Foster Tufnell, esq. of Islington, in the county of Middlesex, by his wife, Mary, daughter of John Parhill, esq. (see BURKE'S *Commoners*) and has, with other issue, a son,

      JOHN-CHARLES-FOWELL TUFNELL, in holy orders, *m.* and has issue.

1. Elizabeth, *b.* in February, 1693, *m.* 1716, Arthur Hele, esq. of Stert, in Devon, eldest son and heir, by his wife, Margaret, dau. of J. Prows[illegible], esq. of Moore, in Devon, of Solomon Hele, esq. of Stert, and had issue.

III. John, barrister-at-law, town-clerk of Plymouth, *b.* at Fowellscombe in 1557, *m.* Anne, daughter, by his wife, Agnes, one of the three daughters and co-heirs of John Servington, esq. of Tavistock, in Devon, of John Croker, esq. of Lyneham, in that county, and had issue three sons, of whom

  EDMOND, eldest son and heir, M.P. for Tavistock, 1640 and 1658-9, and for Plymouth 1672, was ancestor, by his wife, Elizabeth daughter of Sir Anthony Barker, of Sunning, in Berkshire, knt. M.P. for that place, of the Fowells of Stoke Damarel, in Devon, and of Harewood and Letchiry, in Cornwall.

I. Elizabeth, *m.* Edward Harris, esq. of Cornworthy Priory, in Devon, and had issue, Sir Thomas Harris, knt. serjeant-at-law, M.P. for Callington, Bossiney, and Truro, *temp.* Queen ELIZABETH, and father, by his wife, *Elizabeth*, daughter of Henry Pomeroye, esq. of Devon, of Sir Edward Harris, knt. of Cornworthy Priory, chief justice of Munster, in Ireland.

ARTHUR FOWELL, esq. of Fowellscombe, *b.* in 154[illegible], married 13th September, 1574, Maria, only daughter by his wife Agnes, daughter of John Southcote, esq. of Bovey Tracey, in Devon, of Richard Reynell, esq. of East Ogwell, in that county, M.P. for Ashburton, and sheriff of Devon, 1585, lineal descendant and heir of the above named Sir Walter Reynell, knt. [illegible] of Trumpington, and by her, who survived him [illegible] married secondly, Sir Edmond Prideaux, bart. of Netherton, in Devon, had issue,

1. Richard, *b.* March, 1580, *d.* January, 158[illegible]

---

* Fowell of Black Hall.

JOHN FOWELL, esq. of Black Hall and Diptford, *b.* in 1683, *m.* 21st October, 1729, Elizabeth, only surviving child and heir of John Newton, esq. of Crabaton Court, in Devon, and dying in November, 1756, aged seventy-five, was *s.* by his son and heir,

JOHN FOWELL, esq. of Black Hall and Diptford, *b.* at Blackhall, 30th October, 1735, who *m.* 28th February, 1763, Mary, eldest surviving daughter, and eventual senior co-heir, by his wife, the daughter and heiress of Warwick, of James Digby, esq. of Red Hall, in the county of Lincoln, heir male of the North Luffenham branch of the noble family of Digby (see BURKE'S *Peerage* and *Commoners*, vol. iv.), and was *s.* at his decease, in 1820, aged eighty-seven, by his son and heir,

THE REV. JOHN DIGBY FOWELL, in holy orders, of Black Hall and Diptford, rector of Torbrian, in Devon, *b.* at Black Hall, 20th January, 1765. He *m.* 24th July, 1793, Sarah, second daughter and co-heir, by his wife, Isabella, daughter and co-heir of Kirkham, of Peter Knowling, esq. of Washbourne House, in Devon (whose sister, Mary, *m.* Miles Sandys, esq. of West Lyvingston, in Devon, and was mother of the present Sir Edwyn Baynton Sandys, bart.), and *d.* in 1829, aged sixty-four, leaving surviving issue,

JOHN-DIGBY, born at Black Hall, 29th January, 1796, *m.* 12th August, 1819, Frances, only daughter of Samuel Cumming, esq. of Totness, in Devon.

Francis Kirkham, *b.* at Black Hall, 18th July, 1798, *m.* in 1830, Anne, second daughter, by Elizabeth, fourth daughter of Charles Coxwell, esq. of Ablington House, in the county of Gloucester, of Richard Estcourt Cresswell, esq. of Pinkney Park and Bibury, in that county, formerly M.P. for Cirencester.

William-Newton, *b.* at Black Hall, 5th June, 180[illegible], a lieutenant R. N.

Henrietta-Digby, *b.* at Black Hall, *m.* Richard Samuel Sprye, a captain in the Indian army, Madras Presidency, and in 1833, deputy judge-advocate general of its Northern Division,‡ second surviving son, by Anne, his wife, daughter of Samp[illegible] Crapp, esq. of Trevollard House, in Cornwall, [illegible] the Rev. John Sprye, vicar of Ugborough, in Devon, (see BURKE'S *Commoners*, vol. iv. [illegible]) has surviving issue, of five sons and five daughters [illegible]

  Reynell-Richard-Hele-Powell Sprye.
  Courtenay-Edward-Hele-Powell Sprye.

  Henrietta-Anne-Hele Powell Sprye.
  Isabella-Mary-Hele-Powell Sprye.
  Frances-Helen-Hele-Powell Sprye.
  Sarah-Emily-Hele-Powell Sprye.

Isabella-Georgiana, *b.* at Black Hall, *m.* Samuel Crapp, esq. of Boulogne-sur-Mer, in the kingdom of France, banker, only surviving child and heir of Benjamin Crapp, esq. of Plymouth, in Devon.

Sarah-Knowling, *b.* at Black Hall, *d.* at the [illegible] Ugborough, in October, 1829, unm. and buried [illegible] that church, in the Sprye vault.

---

‡ Captain Sprye has been many years collecting materials for a history of the parliamentary families of [illegible] native county, Devon, at the interesting period of [illegible] Civil War and Commonwealth; and to his cordial [illegible] work is considerably indebted for valuable assistance [illegible] Devonshire families.

II. ARTHUR, of Fowellscombe, *b.* August, 1582, drowned accidentally at his uncle's, Sir Richard Reynell, of Ford, in Devon, in 1612, aged thirty, unmarried.

III. EDMOND, heir to his brother.

I. Grace, *m.* first, Richard Barrett, esq. of Tregarthine, in Cornwall, by whom she had issue, two daughters his co-heirs, and secondly, Sir Richard Carnsew, knt. of Carnsew, in that county, the friend of Carew the Cornish historian.

The third son,

I. SIR EDMOND FOWELL, knt. of Fowellscombe, heir to his brother, Arthur, was born there in 1593, knighted at the Palace of Greenwich, 3rd November, 1619, and elected M.P. for Ashburton in the long parliament, and for the county of Devon in 1656. He was also one of the parliamentary committee and deputy lieutenants for that shire, and president of the committee for sequestration. He was created a BARONET 30th April, 1661. He *m.* in 1614, Margaret, eldest daughter, by his wife Catherine, only daughter of Henry, Lord Norreys of Rycote, of Sir Anthony Paulett, knt. of Hinton St. George, captain of the guard to *Queen* ELIZABETH, and sister of John, first Baron Paulett, of Hinton, ancestor of the Earls Paulett. By her Sir Edmond had surviving issue, two sons and five daughters,

I. JOHN, his heir.

II. Edmond, of Panquit, in the adjoining parish of Modbury, *b.* at Fowellscombe in 1637, *m.* in 1659, Elizabeth, daughter by his wife Bridget, sixth daughter (by Bridget, daughter of Sir Thomas Burdet, bart.) of Thomas Erisley, esq. only son of Sir George Erisley, bart. of Drakelow, in the county of Derby, and Susan, his wife, daughter of Sir Humphry Ferrers, knt. of Thomas Brome, esq. of Ewithington, in the county of Hereford, and *d.* in 1681, aged forty-three, having had issue two daughters, Bridget and Elizabeth.

I. Maria, *b.* at Fowellscombe in 1615.

II. Elizabeth, *b.* there in 1622, *m.* 2nd January, 1656, to Richard Cabell, esq. of Brooke, in Devon, sheriff of the county in 1664, son and heir of Richard Cabell, esq. of Brooke, and his wife Maria, daughter of George Prestwood, esq. of Whitcombe, in Devon, by his wife, the daughter of Sir Nicholas Martyn, knt. of Oxton, in that shire, M.P. for the county of Devon, in the long parliament, in whose daughter's house, in Watlin Street, London, the five members were concealed when *King* CHARLES followed them into the city. They had issue, which terminated in an heiress, who carried Brooke in marriage to the family of Fownes, of Stapleton, in Dorset. (See BURKE's *Commoners*, vol. i.)

III. Grace, *b.* at Fowellscombe in 1627, *m.* 29th September, 1653, to Edmond Williams, esq. of Stowford, in Devon, descendant and heir of Thomas Williams, esq. thereof, speaker of the House of Commons in the reign of ELIZABETH, and had a son and heir,

John Williams, esq. of Stowford, who *m.* his kinswoman, daughter of Arthur Champernowne, esq. of Dartington House, in Devon, by his wife Margaret, second surviving daughter of Sir John Fowell, second baronet.

IV. Anne, *b.* at Fowellscombe in 1629.

V. Florence, *b.* there in 1634, *m.* Servington Savery, esq. of Shilston, in Devon, son and heir of Christopher Savery, esq. of Shilston, a colonel of foot on the parliamentary side, and father of Christopher Savery, esq. thereof, sheriff of Devon in 1693, and lieutenant-colonel of the militia.

Sir Edmond Fowell *d.* in October, 1674, aged eighty-one. He made a settlement of his estates and property on the marriage of his eldest son and heir; but when on his death bed, his sons being reduced to two in number, the youngest of them having only daughters, and the eldest only one surviving son, Sir Edmond strictly enjoined them to settle Fowellscombe Park and other manors and lands, on the heir male, William Fowell, of Black Hall. He was *s.* by his son,

II. SIR JOHN FOWELL, of Fowellscombe, born there in 1623, colonel of a regiment of foot in the service of the Parliament, governor of Totness,* mentioned in the letters of Fairfax to the parliament, after the taking of Dartmouth, and M.P. for Ashburton in 1658. He *m.* Elizabeth, daughter, by his wife Elizabeth, eldest daughter of Sir John Rayney, bart, of Sir John Chichester, of Raleigh, in Devon, knt. and bart. and had issue that survived him,

I. JOHN, his heir.

I. Elizabeth, *m.* in 1691, George Parker, esq. of Boringdon, in Devon, ancestor of the Earl of Morley, Viscount Boringdon, and *d.* in October, 1697, leaving issue a son,

Edmund Parker, esq. who attained his age in 1712, but was killed in the lifetime of his father, by a fall from his horse, while riding on the banks of the Lara, near Boringdon. He *d. s. p.*

II. Margaret, *m.* to Arthur Champernowne, esq. of Dartington House, in Devon, ancestor, by her, of the present Henry Champernowne, esq. of Dartington. (See BURKE's *Commoners*, vol. ii. p. 273.)

Sir John Fowell *d.* in 1676, aged sixty-two. In his will, dated 2nd June that year, he makes reference to the dying injunction of his father, to preserve Fowellscombe Park and estates in the male line of the family, and adds, "to which enjoinment of my said dear deceased father, I readily yield all dutiful obedience." He was *s.* by his son,

III. SIR JOHN FOWELL, of Fowellscombe, *b.* in 1665, M. P. for Totness, 1688, to his death, and one of the 151 members of the celebrated convention who voted against making the Prince of Orange king, but for declaring the Princess queen. He *d.* in 1692, aged twenty-seven, unm. when the BARONETCY became EXTINCT, and the heir maleship of the family devolved on the before named

WILLIAM FOWELL, esq. of Black Hall and Diptford, to whom this Sir John Fowell, in reference to the dying command of his grandfather, Sir Edmond, and the will of his father, Sir John, gave by his will, dated 4th November, 1691, Fowellscombe, with *all* his lands and possessions, making him his sole heir and executor. Owing, however, to the omission by the person who drew up the instrument and superintended its execution, of one of the three required attesting signatures, the intentions of the testator, and of his predecessors, were defeated, and the will set aside, by Parker and Champernowne, the husbands of his sisters, notwithstanding these had fortunes indepen-

* A very fine portrait of this Sir John Fowell, bart in full armour, by Sir Godfrey Kneller, is amongst the family paintings, in possession of the present John Digby Fowell.

dently secured to them by their father, from *other* lands. By them Fowellscombe Park, with all the manors and estates not appropriated by the second baronet to their fortunes, were held in coparcenary until August, 1712, when a partition was made by George Parker, his wife, Elizabeth, being dead, and their son and heir apparent, Edmund Parker; and Margaret Champernowne, at that time a widow. Under this agreement, the manors and estates of Harburtonford and Ludbrooke, &c. which included Higher and Lower Whichcombe, were allotted to the Parkers; and Fowellscombe Park, Boulterscombe, and other lands, to Mrs. Champernowne, who removed from Dartington House to Fowellscombe, and there died, 13th March, 1729. By her will, dated 3rd January preceding, she gave £2000 to Arthur, the eldest son of her eldest son; £800 to her daughter, who had married her relative, John Williams, esq. of Stowford, and other legacies; after which she devised all her freehold manors and estates in Devon and Cornwall, including Fowellscombe Park, to her younger son, Henry. He also made it his residence, and died in 1757, without issue, when his nephew and heir, Arthur Champernowne, of Dartington House, heir also of his grandmother, Margaret Fowell, sold Fowellscombe to Mr. George Herbert, of Plymouth, by deed dated 9th January, 1759. His son and heir, George, banker of Plymouth, sold it on 13th March, 1784, to Mr. Thomas King, of Plymouth, who dying unm. 13th January, 1792, left it to his three brothers, John, Richard, and Robert. John *d.* also unm. 26th January, 1795, intestate, when his share devolved to Richard, as heir-at-law: to him his brother Robert released his third, thereby enabling Richard, who *d.* 19th January, 1811, *s. p.* to entail the mansion and estates on his nephew. John, the eldest son of Robert, and his three brothers. This John King, esq. is the present owner; but he has not resided in the county of Devon for several years past, and during that period Fowellscombe, a battlemented mansion of Elizabethan date, originally erected in the form of the roman initial of the family name, has remained uninhabited. The park was in greater part divided off for tillage after its purchase by Mr. Herbert.

Arms—Argent, a chev. sa. on chief gu. three mullets pierced of the first.

FOWLER, OF HARNAGE GRANGE.

CREATED 1st Nov. 1704. EXTINCT 1st March, 1773.

Lineage.

This family was of great antiquity before the reign of RICHARD I., when in that warlike prince's expedition to the Holy Land

SIR RICHARD FOWLER, of Foxley, in the county of Bucks, serving as a commanding officer against the Infidel, *anno* 1190, maintained at his own expense a certain number of British bowmen, all his own tenants, to serve in the wars; and by his extraordinary vigilance having saved the Christian camp from a nocturnal surprise, received the honour of knighthood in the field from his royal master, who caused t[illegible] crest which he then bore—a head and [illegible] changed for the vigilant owl. From Sir Richard [illegible]scended

JOHN FOWLER, esq. of Foxley, who m. the [illegible] of Loveday, and was *s.* by his son,

HENRY FOWLER, esq. of Foxley, who m. the [illegible] and heir of John Barton, and left a son and heir

SIR WILLIAM FOWLER, knt. of Ricote, in the [illegible] of Oxford. This gentleman m. Cecilia, only dau[illegible] and heir of Sir Nicholas Inglefield, knt. and had issue,

- RICHARD, his heir.
- Thomas.
- Cecilia, m. to Thomas Rooke, esq. of [illegible] Bucks.

He was *s.* by his elder son,

SIR RICHARD FOWLER, who was knighted by [illegible]WARD IV. and made chancellor of the duchy of [illegible]caster. He m. Jane, daughter of John Danvers [illegible] of Colthorp, in the county of Oxford, and was [illegible] his elder son,

SIR RICHARD FOWLER, knt. who m. Eliz[illegible] daughter of Thomas Windsor, and sister of [illegible] Lord Windsor, but dying without issue, was [illegible] brother,

THOMAS FOWLER, esquire of the body to EDW[illegible] He married Margery Coleville, and was *s.* by [illegible] son,

ROGER FOWLER, esq. of Broomhill, in the coun[illegible] Stafford. This gentleman m. Isabella, daughter [illegible] co-heir of William Lee, of Morpeth, treasurer of [illegible]wick, and had issue,

I. ROWLAND, his heir, who m. the daughter [illegible] Bradshaw of Presteign, in the county of Radnor, and had two sons,
   1. GEORGE, } who both married, but d[illegible]
   2. Brian, } issueless.

II. Brian, of St. Thomas, in the county of Staff[illegible] m. Jane, daughter and heir of John [illegible] esq. of Bettisfield, in the county of F[illegible] left, with other issue, a son and heir.
   Walter, of St. Thomas, who m. Mary daughter of Ralph of Beoly, in the co[illegible] Worcester, and from him descended [illegible] Fowlers of St. Thomas's.

III. WILLIAM.

IV. James, m. Margaret Morton, of W[illegible] in the county of Stafford, and left issue [illegible] which descend the FOWLERS OF P[illegible]. (See BURKE's *Commoners*, vol. iv.)

V. Johanna.

VI. Alicia.

The third son,

WILLIAM FOWLER, esq. of Harnage Grange, [illegible] county of Salop, m. Mary, daughter of John [illegible] M.D. and had issue,

- RICHARD, his heir.
- Peter.
- Thomas.
- Margaret, m. to Thomas Vaughan, esq. of Pr[illegible] in the county of Carnarvon.
- Alicia.
- Mary.
- Elizabeth.

The eldest son,

RICHARD FOWLER, esq. of Harnage Grange [illegible] Mary, daughter of Sir Edward Littleton, knt. [illegible] [illegible]ton Hall, in the county of Stafford, and was [illegible] his eldest son,

WILLIAM FOWLER, esq. of Harnage Grange [illegible] Anna, daughter of Richard Perks, esq. of [illegible]

bury, in the county of Stafford, and had eight sons and a daughter. He was *s.* by the eldest son,

RICHARD FOWLER, esq. of Harnage Grange, who *m.* the Hon. Margaret Newport, daughter of Richard, first Baron Newport, of High Ercall, by Rachael, his wife, daughter of John Leveson, esq. of Haling, and sister and co-heir of Sir Richard Leveson, K.B. of Trentham, in the county of Stafford. By this lady Mr. Fowler had a numerous family. He was *s.* by his eldest son,

FRANCIS-LEVESON FOWLER, esq. of Harnage Grange. This gentleman *m.* Anne, daughter of Peter Venables, esq. baron of Kinderton, by whom he had a son, Richard, who died young, and a daughter,

FRANCES, who, on the death of her brother, became sole heiress. She *m.* first, Thomas Needham, sixth Viscount Kilmorey, and was mother of Robert, seventh viscount. Her ladyship *m.* secondly, in 1690, Theophilus, seventh Earl of Huntingdon; and thirdly, the Chevalier de Legonday, colonel of horse, one of the French prisoners taken with Count Tallard at the battle of Hockstedt.

Mr. Fowler dying without male issue, the representation of the family devolved upon his brother,

I. WILLIAM FOWLER, esq. of Harnage Grange, in the county of Salop, who was created a BARONET by Queen ANNE, 1st November, 1704. Sir William *m.* Mary, daughter of Sir Robert Cotton, bart. of Combermere, in Cheshire, and had issue,

RICHARD, his heir.
William, who *d.* young.
Anne.
Mary, *m.* to John Dickens, esq. of Layton.
Esther.
Elizabeth.

Sir William *d.* about the year 1717, and was *s.* by his son,

II. SIR RICHARD FOWLER, bart. who *m.* Sarah, daughter of William Sloane, esq. of Portsmouth, and niece of Sir Hans Sloane, bart. by whom (who *m.* secondly, Francis Annesley, of the Inner Temple, son of Francis, Viscount Valentia,) he had issue,

WILLIAM, his heir.
Richard-Sloane, *d. s. p.*
HANS, who inherited as fifth baronet.
SARAH, *m.* to Colonel Hodges, of the Guards. Of this lady hereafter as heir of her brother Sir Hans.

He *d.* before 1727, and was *s.* by his eldest son,

III. SIR WILLIAM FOWLER, bart. who *m.* in 1728-9, a daughter of Brigadier-General Newton, and by her (who *d.* at Shrewsbury, 19th March, 1736,) had issue,

WILLIAM, his heir.
Lucy, *m.* to Mr. John Jones, of London, distiller.
Letitia, *m.* to Launcelot Baugh, gent. of Lentuardine.
Harriet, *m.* to Joseph Hughes, esq. of the Auditor's Office.

He was *s.* at his decease by his son,

IV. SIR WILLIAM FOWLER, bart. cornet of Dragoons, who *d.* unmarried in Germany, *anno* 1760, and devised his estate in possession to his sisters; the Baronetcy reverted to his uncle,

V. SIR HANS FOWLER, bart. who, under the entail of his brother Sir William's will, was entitled to the other part of the estate on the death of his mother. He *m.* Miss Dibbs, of Dedington, in Oxfordshire, but *d.* without issue, 1st March, 1773, when the BARONETCY became EXTINCT, and the Welsh estates of Abbey-cwm-hir, &c. devolved upon his sister,

SARAH HODGES, wife of Colonel Hodges, of the Guards, by whom she had issue,

1 THOMAS HODGES, esq. of Abbey-cwm-hir, who assumed the name of FOWLER. He *m.* in 1803, Lucy, relict of Thomas Humphrey Lowe, esq. of Bromsgrove, elder daughter and co-heir of Thomas Hill, esq. of Court of Hill, M.P., and left an only daughter and heiress,

SARAH-GEORGIANA FOWLER, who *m.* the Rev. John Durand Baker, B.A. and is the present representative of the family. (Refer to BURKE's *Commoners*, vol. ii. p. 375.)

2. Sarah Hodges, who *m.* Colonel Hastings, of the Guards, father of the late Earl of Huntingdon.

Arms—Az. a cheveron arg. charged with three crosses formée sa. between three lions passant guardant or.

FOWLER, OF ISLINGTON.

CREATED 21st May, 1628.		EXTINCT in 1656.

Lineage.

In 1548, the manor of Berners or Barnersbury, Islington, Middlesex, was the property of THOMAS FOWLER, gent. and passed from him in direct descent to

I. SIR THOMAS FOWLER, knt. of Islington (son of Sir Thomas Fowler, knt.), who was created a BARONET in 1628. He *m.* Elizabeth, daughter and heir of William Pierson, esq. of the Inner Temple, and had issue,

John, who *m.* Sarah, daughter of John Fowler, esq. but *d. v. p.* and *s. p.*
SARAH, *m.* to Sir Thomas Fisher, bart.
JANE, *m.* to Richard Corbet, esq.
ELIZABETH, *m.* to Gerard Gore, esq.
MARTHA, *d.* unm.

Sir Thomas Fowler *d.* in 1656, when the title became EXTINCT.

Arms—Az. on a cheveron arg. between three herons or, as many crosses formée gu.

FRANCKLYN, OF MOOR PARK.

CREATED 16th Oct. 1660.	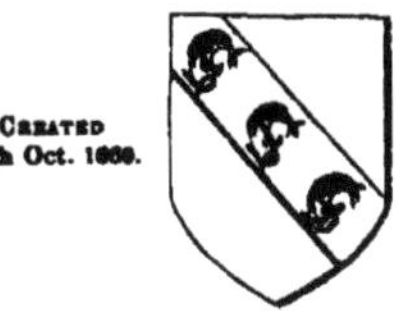	EXTINCT 5th Oct. 1728.

Lineage.

This family was anciently of Skipton, in Craven, in the county of York.

SIR JOHN FRANCKLYN, knt. of Willesden, in Middlesex, M.P. for that county, *m.* Elizabeth, daughter of

George Purefoy, esq. of Madeley, Berks, and was *s.* by his son,

I. Sir Richard Francklyn, knt. of Moor Park, in the county of Hertford, who was created a Baronet by *King* Charles II. 16th October, 1660. He *m.* first, Elizabeth, daughter and co-heir of Sir Thomas Cheeke, knt. of Pyrgo, in Essex, and by her had three sons and a daughter, viz.

Richard, his heir.
Thomas, successor to his brother.
Robert, died at King's College, Cambridge, unmarried.

Essex, died young.

Sir Richard *m.* secondly, Eleanora, daughter of Sir Samuel Tryon, bart. of Halstead, in Essex, and sister and heir of Sir Samuel Tryon, bart. and by that lady had three daughters, namely,

Eleanora, *m.* to Charles May, esq. son and heir of Sir Algernon May, knt. and *d. s. p.*
Elizabeth, *m.* to Dr. Richard Willis, Bishop of Winchester, and *d. s. p.*
Essex.

Sir Richard, who represented the county of Hertford in parliament, died about the year 1685, and was *s.* by his eldest son,

II. Sir Richard Francklyn, bart. who *m.* Lady Anne Rich, eldest daughter of Thomas, third Earl of Warwick,* and widow of Thomas Barrington, esq. but dying without male issue in 1695, was *s.* by his brother,

III. Sir Thomas Francklyn, bart. This gentleman *m.* Mary, daughter of Ralph Hawtrey, esq. of Rislip, in Middlesex, and widow of Christopher Clitherow, esq. of Pinners, in the same county, but dying 5th October, 1728, aged seventy-two, without issue, the Baronetcy became extinct.

Arms—Arg. on a bend az. three dolphins naiant of the first.

FREER, OF WATER EYTON.

Created 11th July, 1620.—Extinct about 1630.

Lineage.

I. Edward Freer, esq. of Water Eyton, in Oxfordshire, was created a Baronet in 1620. Sir Edward *m.* Mary, daughter of John Stafford, esq. of Blatherwyck, in Northamptonshire, but *d. s. p.* about 1630, when the title expired.

FREKE, OF WEST BILNEY.

Created 4th June, 1712.

Extinct 13th April, 1764.

Lineage.

This family descended from

Francis Freke, esq. "a person of good repute in Somersetshire," whose son,

Robert Freke, esq. was for many years auditor of the Treasury in the reigns of Henry VIII. and Queen Elizabeth, and died worth a plum, an immense fortune in those times. He left three sons and seven daughters, viz.

I. Sir Thomas Freke, knt. of Ewern Courtney, in Dorsetshire, "a person of considerable note, great trust, and authority in the county of Dorset *temp.* Elizabeth and James I. He *m.* Elizabeth, only daughter and heir of John Taylor, alderman of London, and had, with other issue,

John, of Ewern Courtney, who married twice and had issue.
Ralph, of Hannington, in Wiltshire, ancestor of the Frekes of that place.

II. John, of Hilton.
III. William.

I. Mary, *m.* to William Hodges.
II. Frances, *m.* to John Culliford, of Encomb.
III. Susanna.
IV. Margaret, *m.* to Sir Robert Meller.
V. Elizabeth, *m.* to Thomas Beale.
VI. Ann.
VII. Jean.

The youngest son,

William Freke, esq. who was of Sarson, in Hampshire, *m.* Anne, daughter of Arthur Swaine, esq. and removed with his son Arthur into Ireland, which

Arthur Freke, esq. lived near the city of Cork, and marrying Dorothy, daughter of Sir Piercy Smyth, of Youghall, had a son,

Piercy Freke, esq. who enjoyed a fair estate in the county of Cork, and coming into England, *m.* his kinswoman, Elizabeth, daughter of Ralph Freke, esq. with whom he had a considerable fortune, and purchased the estate of Bilney, in Norfolk, whereat he was *s.* by his son,

I. Ralph Freke, esq. who was created a Baronet by *Queen* Anne, 4th June, 1712. Sir Ralph *m.* Elizabeth, daughter of Sir John Meade, bart. and had issue,

Piercy, his successor.
Ralph, who *d.* at Richmond in 1727 unm.
John-Redmond, successor to his brother Piercy.

Grace, eventually sole heiress of the family, who *m.* in 1741, the Hon. John Evans, second son of George, Lord Carbery, and left, with other issue, a son,

John Evans, esq. who assumed, in compliance with the testamentary injunction of his maternal uncle, the additional surname of Freke, and was created a Baronet in 1768. Sir John Evans-Freke's eldest son is the present John, Lord Carbery.

Sir Ralph died about the year 1718, and was *s.* by his eldest son,

II. Sir Piercy Freke, bart. member in the parliament of Ireland for Baltimore, who *d.* unmarried at Dublin 10th April, 1728, and was *s.* by his brother,

III. Sir John-Redmond Freke, bart. who *m.* Elizabeth Brodrick, but *d. s. p.* 13th April, 1764, when the Baronetcy became extinct.

Arms—Sa. two bars or, in chief three mullets of the same.

* By his second wife, Anne, daughter of Sir Thomas Cheeke, of Pyrgo.

FRYER, OF LONDON.

CREATED 13th Dec. 1714.—EXTINCT 11th Sept. 1726.

Lineage.

I. JOHN FRYER, esq. alderman of London, who was created a BARONET in 1714, married Isabella, daughter of Sir Francis Gerard, bart. but by her, who wedded, secondly, Henry, first Viscount Palmerston, had no issue. Sir John died 11th September, 1726, when the title became EXTINCT.

FULLER, OF THE INNER TEMPLE.

CREATED 1st Aug. 1687.—EXTINCT in 1709.

Lineage.

I. JAMES CHAPMAN FULLER, esq. of the Inner Temple, who was created a BARONET in 1687, m. first, Frances, daughter of John Fincham, esq. of Upwell; and secondly, Emma, daughter of Richard Hoe, esq. of the county of Norfolk, and relict of Sir Edward Wintour, but had no issue. Sir James died in the Fleet Prison in 1709, and the BARONETCY EXPIRED with him.

FURNESE, OF WALDERSHARE.

CREATED 27th June, 1707.

EXTINCT in 1735.

Lineage.

I. SIR HENRY FURNESE, knt. of Waldershare,* in Kent, an alderman of the city of London, was created a BARONET by *Queen* ANNE, 27th June, 1707. He m. first, Anne, daughter of Robert Brough, esq. and had by that lady an only child,

ROBERT, his heir.

Sir Henry wedded, secondly, Matilda, daughter of Sir Robert Vernon, and widow of Anthony Balam, esq. and by her had a daughter,

Matilda, m. to Richard, Lord Edgcumbe.

He d. 3rd November, 1712 (having represented the borough of Sandwich in several parliaments), and was s. by his son,

II. SIR ROBERT FURNESE, bart. M.P. for Bramber in [illegible] and for New Romney in 1714, m. first, Anne, daughter of Anthony Balam, esq. by whom he had a daughter,

ANNE, m. to the Hon. John St. John, who became Viscount St. John.

He wedded, secondly, Lady Arabella Watson, daughter of Lewis, first Earl of Rockingham, and by her had

HENRY, his successor.

CATHERINE, m. first, in 1736, to Lewis, second Earl of Rockingham; and secondly, in 1751, to Francis, Earl of Guildford. She *d. s. p.*

Sir Robert m. thirdly, Lady Selina Shirley, daughter of Robert, first Earl Ferrars, and by that lady, who *d.* in 1779, had a daughter,

SELINA, m. to Sir Edward Dering, (sixth) bart. of Surrenden-Dering, in Kent, and was mother of SIR EDWARD DERING, the seventh baronet.

The baronet *d.* 7th March, 1733, and was *s.* by his son,

III. SIR HENRY FURNESE, bart. who died unmarried in 1735, aged nineteen, when the BARONETCY became EXTINCT; the estates vesting in his three sisters in equal shares and proportions. The manor of Waldershare became eventually the property of the eldest, Catherine, Countess of Rockingham, who, having no issue, devised it to her second husband, Francis, Earl of Guildford.

Arms—Arg. a talbot sejant and border sa.

FUST, OF HILL.

CREATED 21st Aug. 1662.

EXTINCT 15th April, 1779.

Lineage.

This family was of great antiquity, and in remote times united with houses of high distinction: it produced many persons of eminence, amongst whom may be enumerated JOHN FUST, of the city of Mentz, in Germany, who about the year 1430, invented the art of printing, RICHARD FUST, who flourished in the reign of EDWARD IV. and THOMAS FUST, who suffered martyrdom in 1555, having been burnt to death, at a stake in the market-place at Ware.

EDWARD FUST, of the city of London, m. about the year 1564, Jane Singleton, and had issue,

RICHARD, his heir.

Edward, *b.* 8th October, 1569, *d.* unm.

Samuel, a merchant at Bristol, *d.* there unm.

Julian, *b.* 2nd November, 1566, m. first, to Sir Thomas Hackett, knt. master of the Court of Wards, *temp.* JAMES I. and secondly, to Sir Randolph Crew, knt. chief justice of the Common Pleas in the same reign.

Jane, *d.* unmarried.

Barbara, *b.* 12th October, 1573, m. to Francis Chaloner, of Lindfield and Kenwalls, in Sussex.

Elizabeth, *b.* 31st January, 1577, m. to Henry Fleetwood, esq. of Longby, Bucks.

Anne, *d.* unm.

The eldest son,

RICHARD FUST, esq. purchased in the time of *Queen* ELIZABETH, the manor of Hill or Hull, in the county

* This manor Sir Henry Furnese purchased *temp.* WILLIAM and MARY, and rebuilt the mansion after a design, it is said, of Inigo Jones.

of Gloucester. He *m.* first Anne, daughter of Robert John Hide, esq. of Ingarstone, in Essex, and Addisham, in Kent; and secondly, Catherine, daughter of Giles Hambler, of Ghent. By the former he had issue,

EDWARD, his heir.
Richard, *d.* unm.

Jane, *b.* 26th January, 1663, *m.* to the Rev. Richard Astley, rector of Melton Constable.
Julian, *b.* 15th January, 1664, *m.* to James Poe, esq. of Swindon Hall, in the county of York, and left an only daughter,
ANNE POE, *m.* to Sir Thomas Jenner, knt. recorder of London, and one of the judges of the Common Pleas, *temp.* JAMES II. and WILLIAM III.
Anne, *d.* unm.

He was *s.* by his eldest son,

I. EDWARD FUST, esq. of Hill, in the county of Gloucester, who for his fidelity to the house of Stewart in its extremity, was created a BARONET by *King* CHARLES II. 21st August, 1662. Sir Edward *m.* Bridget, daughter of Sir Thomas Denton, knt. of Hillersdon, Bucks, and had issue,

Edward, *d.* unm.
Richard, *b.* 27th January, 1632, *d.* unm.
Poultney, *b.* in February, 1635, *d.* unm.
JOHN, his heir, *b.* 5th December, 1637.
Richard, *b.* 23rd October, 1664, bred a merchant, *d.* unm.

Elianor, *m.* to George Bennet, esq. of Bath.
Margaret, *m.* first, to Ralph Ironsides, M. D. brother of Dr. Gilbert Ironsides, Bishop of Bristol in 1670, and, secondly, to Preke, esq. of Dorsetshire.

Sir Edward *d.* 6th April, 1674, and was *s.* by his eldest surviving son,

II. SIR JOHN FUST, sheriff of Gloucestershire in 1675. He *m.* Elizabeth, daughter of Sir Richard Cocks, bart. of Dumbleton, in the same county, and dying 12th February, 1698, was buried in a vault adjoining Hill Church, and *s.* by his only surviving child,

III. SIR EDWARD FUST. This gentleman married four wives: first, Anne-Mary, daughter of Thomas Stephens, esq. of Lipiat, in the county of Gloucester, and by her had a daughter, Elizabeth, who *m.* Thomas Warner, esq. of Packenhull, in the same county. His second wife was Elizabeth, daughter and heir of William Mohun, esq. of Portishead, in the county of Somerset, and by her had, to survive infancy, one son,

EDWARD, his heir.

He wedded, thirdly, Catherine, daughter of Francis Mohun, esq. of Fleet, in Dorsetshire, and had by that lady,

FRANCIS, heir to his half brother.
Catherine, *b.* 4th January, 1703-4.

His fourth wife was Susanna, daughter of Richard Cocks, esq. sister of Sir Richard Cocks, bart. of Dumbleton, and widow of Roger Thompson, of London, merchant; by her he had three children, John, Richard, and Edward, who all died in infancy. He *d.* 5th August, 1713, and was *s.* by his elder surviving son,

IV. SIR EDWARD FUST, high sheriff of Gloucestershire in 1717, who *m.* Dorothy, daughter of the above-mentioned Roger Thomson, of London, and had four children, who all died young. He died 27th February, 1727-8 (his widow *m.* Gilbert Maximilian Mohun, esq. of Fleet), and was *s.* by his half brother,

V. SIR FRANCIS FUST, who *m.* 28th September, 1724, Fanny, daughter of Nicholas Tooker, of the city of Bristol, merchant, and had surviving issue,

JOHN, his heir, *b.* 26th August, 1725.
Gilbert-Maximilian, *b.* 5th January, 1727.
Denton, *b.* 6th October, 1736.

Fanny-Francelia, *b.* 16th March, 1729-30.
Julian, *b.* 10th April, 1740.

Sir Francis *d.* 26th June, 1769, and was *s.* by his brother,

VI. SIR JOHN FUST, who died at the age of fifty-four 15th April, 1779, without issue, and his brothers having, similarly, predeceased him, the BARONETCY became EXTINCT.

Arms—Argent, on a chevron between three forest bills' heads, dimidiated per pale sable, as many mullets of the field pierced.

FYTCHE, OF ELTHAM.

CREATED 7th Sept. 1688. EXTINCT 13th June, 17[illegible].

Lineage.

I. SIR THOMAS FYTCHE, of Eltham and Mount Mascall, in Kent, descended from the ancient family of Fytche, in Essex, having been knighted by King CHARLES II. was created a BARONET in the following reign, 7th September, 1688. He *m.* Anne, only daughter and heir of Richard Comport, esq. of Eltham, and dying 16th September, 1688, was *s.* by his son,

II. SIR COMPORT FYTCHE, bart. who *m.* [illegible] daughter of Sir Lumley Robinson, bart. of Kentwell Hall, in the county of Suffolk, and dying [illegible] December, 1720, was *s.* by his son,

III. SIR WILLIAM FYTCHE, bart. who *d.* a minor, unm. 13th June, 1736, when the BARONETCY became EXTINCT.

Arms—Vert, a chevron between three leopards' faces or.

GALBRAITH, OF SHANWALLY.

CREATED 30th Jan. 1813. EXTINCT 30th April, [illegible]

Lineage.

SAMUEL GALBRAITH, esq. of Dundaff's Fort [illegible] county of Donegal, *m.* Jane, daughter of John [illegible], esq. and had issue,

JAMES GALBRAITH, esq. of Londonderry, who *m.* Elizabeth, daughter of John Whitehill, esq. of Cagh[illegible], in the county of Londonderry, and had a son.

I. SIR JAMES GALBRAITH, who was created a BARONET in 1813. He m. Rebecca-Dorothea, daughter and co-heir of John Hamilton, esq. of Castlefin (by Jane Hamilton, of Brown Hall, in the county of Donegal), and had issue,

I. JANE, m. 4th November, 1830, to Captain Charles-George Stanhope, son of the late Rear Admiral Stanhope.
II. Letitia-Elizabeth.
III. Angel-Isabella.
IV. Harriet.
V. Isabella.

Sir James died at Wells, in Somersetshire, 30th April, 1827, when the BARONETCY became EXTINCT.

Arms—Per pale, az. and gules, three bears' heads ar. muzzled, sable, in the centre point a trefoil, slipped arg.

GANS, OF THE NETHERLANDS.

CREATED 29th June, 1682.—EXTINCT ......

Lineage.

I. SIR CORNELIUS GANS, of the Netherlands, was created a BARONET, 1682, with remainder to one Stephen Groulart; but of the dignity nothing further is known.

GARDINER, OF ROCHE COURT.

CREATED 11th Dec. 1660. EXTINCT 30th Oct. 1779.

Lineage.

ROBERT GARDINER, esq. (descended from the Gardiners of Wigan, in Lancashire,) m. Mary, sister of Sir William Palmer, and was s. by his son,

I. SIR WILLIAM GARDINER, K. B. of Roche Court, in the county of Southampton, who was made a Knight of the Bath at the coronation of *King* CHARLES II. and created a BARONET in the same year, 24th December, 1660. He m. Anne, daughter and heir of Robert Brocas, esq.* of Beaurepaire, in Hampshire, and had two sons, namely,

BROCAS, his heir.
Bernard, D. D. warden of All Souls College, Oxford, who m. Grace, daughter and co-heir of Sir Sebastian Smythe, knt. of Cuddesdon, in Oxfordshire, and their only surviving child,
GRACE, m. in 1742, Robert Whalley, M. D. of Oxford, and had issue,
JOHN WHALLEY, of Tackley, in Oxfordshire, who inherited the estates of Sir William Gardiner.
JAMES WHALLEY, successor to his brother.
Thomas-William Whalley.
Grace Whalley, m. to Sir William Henry Ashhurst, knt. judge of the King's Bench.

Sir William dying in 1691, was s. by his eldest son,

II. SIR BROCAS GARDINER, who m. Alicia, daughter of Sir John Kelynge, knt. son of the Lord Chief Justice Kelynge, and had issue,

WILLIAM, his successor.
FRANCES, who married.
Catherine, m. to Edward Kay, gent. of Hatton Garden.

Sir Brocas was made one of the commissioners of the Stamp Office in the reign of *Queen* ANNE, and continued in that post until his death, 13th January, 1739-40, being then nearly eighty years of age. He was s. by his son,

III. SIR WILLIAM GARDINER, who d. unm. 30th October, 1779, when the BARONETCY became EXTINCT. His estates passed to his cousin, John Whalley, esq. of Tackley, in Oxfordshire, who assumed, in compliance with the testamentary injunction of his predecessor, the name and arms of GARDINER, and was created a BARONET in 1783. He died s. p. in 1797, and was s. in the title (which was thus limited) by his next brother, Sir James Whalley Smythe Gardiner, bart. whose son is the present Sir James W. S. Gardiner, bart. of Roche Court.

Arms—Or, on a chevron gu. between three gryphons' heads erased az. two lions counterpassant or.

GARRARD, OF LAMER.

CREATED 16th Feb. 1621-2. EXTINCT 1st July, 1767.

Lineage.

The name of this family was originally ATTEGARE, and they were seated in the county of Kent.

ALLURED ATTEGARE, of Buckland, in that county, was father of

SIR SIMON ATTEGARE, knt. of Buckland, in Sittingborne, Kent, whose son,

STEPHEN ATTEGARE, assumed the surname of GARRARD. His great-grandson,

WILLIAM GARRARD, of Sittingborne, was father of

JOHN GARRARD, who bore for arms, "*Argent, on a fesse sable a lion passant of the first.*" His son,

SIR WILLIAM GARRARD, knt. was of Dorney, in Bucks. He was a citizen of London, and LORD MAYOR in 1555. Sir William m. Isabel, daughter and co-heir of Julius Nethermill, esq. of Coventry, and had issue,

I. WILLIAM (Sir), his heir.
II. George, m. Margaret, daughter of George D'Acres, esq. of Cheshunt, Herts, and had

* Descended from SIR BERNARD BROCAS, knt. who came into England with the CONQUEROR, under whom he was a great commander, and obtained for his services lands to the amount of £400 per annum, situated in the county of Hants, where he erected a mansion house, and called it Beaurepaire, from a place in France, whereof his ancestors were lords. He encompassed the mansion with a large moat, dug by his soldiers.

George, who *d. s. p.*

Anne, *m.* to Sir Dudley Carlton, vice-chamberlain to *King* CHARLES I. created Viscount Dorchester, and had a son, Henry, who *d.* young.

Frances, *m.* to Sir Richard Harrison, knt. of Hurst, Berkshire.

III. JOHN (Sir), heir to his elder brother.

IV. Peter.

I. Anne, *m.* to Sir George Barne, knt. lord mayor of London, and had issue. (See BURKE's *Commoners*, vol. i. page 139.)

Sir William died in 1571. In St. Magnus's Church, near London Bridge, was erected a fair monument to his memory, thus inscribed:

> Sir William Garrard, Haberdasher, Mayor, 1555, a grave, sober, wise, and discreet Citizen, equal with the best, and inferior to none of our time, deceased 1571, in the parish of St. Christopher, but was buried in this Church of St. Magnus, as in the Parish where he was born.

His eldest son and heir,

SIR WILLIAM GARRARD, knt. of Dorney, *m.* Elizabeth, daughter of Sir Thomas Roe, knt. lord mayor of London, and his wife, Mary, daughter of Sir John Gresham, knt. of the same city, and had, with seven sons, who all predeceased him unmarried, the following daughters,

MARY, *m.* to Kedderminster.
ANNE, *m.* to Hynde.
ELIZABETH, unm.
JUDITH, *m.* to Gresham.
JANE, unm.
MARTHA, *m.* to Palmer.
KATHERINE, unm.

He *d.* 17th November, 1607, was buried in Dorney Church, where a fine monument recorded his memory, and leaving no male issue, the representation of the family devolved upon his brother,

SIR JOHN GARRARD, knt. sheriff of London in 1592, and lord mayor in 1601. He *m.* Jane, daughter of Mr. Richard Partridge, citizen of London, and died 7th May, 1625, leaving two sons and six daughters, and was buried in St. Magnus Church, "where on a fair monument, in the south isle of the chancel is this incription for him and his lady:"

> Here lieth interred the Bodies of Sir John Gerrard, Knt. and Dame Jane, his wife, who was Daughter to Richard Partridge, Citizen and Haberdasher of London, by whom he had 13 Children; five whereof died young. They lived comfortably together, 43 years.
>
> He was Lord-Mayor of London, in the year 1601. She departed this Life, the 24 Jan. 1616; and he left this world, the 7 of May, 1625, being 79 years old; leaving only 2 Sons, and six Daughters behind him.
>
> This Monument was erected at the Charges of Benedict Gerrard, Gent. his youngest son, 1629.

Their surviving children were,

JOHN (Sir).
Benedict.
Anne, *m.* to Sir John Read, of Wranghill, in the county of Lincoln.
Elizabeth.
Ursula, *m.* to Francis Hamby, esq. of Lincolnshire.
——, *m.* to Sir George Sams.
——, *m.* to — Lindley, esq.
——, *m.* to — Robinson, esq. of Totness.

The eldest son and heir,

I. SIR JOHN GARRARD, knt. of Lamar, in the county of Herts, was advanced to a BARONETCY by *King* JAMES I. 16th February, 1621-2. He married first, in 1611, Elizabeth, eldest daughter of Sir Edward Barkham, knt. lord mayor of London in 16[illegible], by whom he had six sons and eight daughters. She died 17th April, 1632, and lies buried in the north aisle of the church of Whethampstead, in the county of Hertford: upon a handsome marble monument (whereon are placed two marble figures, at full length, of Sir John Garrard, and Dame Elizabeth, his wife), is an inscription setting forth her many virtues, age, marriage, &c. Of their surviving children were,

JOHN, successor to his father.

Jane, the wife of Sir Justinian Isham.

Sir John wedded, secondly, Elizabeth, relict of Sir Moulton Lambard, knt. of Sevenoaks, Kent, but by that lady had no issue. He *d.* about the year 16[illegible] and was *s.* by his eldest son,

II. SIR JOHN GARRARD, bart. who *m.* Jane, daughter of Sir Moulton Lambard, knt. and died in 1685, leaving issue,

JOHN, his successor.
SAMUEL, heir to his brother.
Nethermill.
Edward.
Elizabeth, *m.* first, to Sir Nicholas Gould, [illegible] and, secondly, to Thomas Neale, esq.
Jane, *m.* to Sir Thomas Spencer, bart. of Yarnton, in the county of Oxford.
——, *m.* to Anthony Farringdon, esq. serjeant-at-law.
Rachael, *m.* to Richard Emerton, esq. of Hackney end, in the county of Hertford.

He died in 1686, and was *s.* by his eldest son,

III. SIR JOHN GARRARD, who *m.* Katharine, daughter and co-heir of Sir James Enyon, knt. of F[illegible] in the county of Northampton, and relict of Sir George Boswell, bart. of Clipston, by whom he left at his decease, 13th January, 1700, an only daughter and heiress,

JANE GARRARD, who *m.* Montague Drake, esq. of Shardeloes, M.P. and *d.* in 1724, leaving a daughter, Mary Drake, the wife of Sir Edward Everard, bart. and a son and heir,

MONTAGUE-GARRARD DRAKE, esq. of Shardeloes, M.P. for the county of Bucks, in 17[illegible] *m.* Isabella, daughter and heir of Thomas Marshall, esq. and dying in 1728, was *s.* by his eldest surviving son,

WILLIAM DRAKE, esq. LL.D. M.P. who *m.* in 1746-7, Elizabeth, daughter of John Raworth, esq. and dying [illegible] left several sons, of whom the [illegible] son,

CHARLES DRAKE, inherited the estates of his cousin, Sir Benet GARRARD, bart. in 1767.

Sir John leaving no male issue, the baronetcy devolved upon his brother,

IV. SIR SAMUEL GARRARD, LORD MAYOR of London in 1710, and M.P. for several years for the borough of Agmondesham. He *m.* first, Elizabeth, daughter of George Poyner, esq. of Coddicote-Bury in the county of Herts, but by that lady had no issue. He *m.* secondly, Jane, daughter of Thomas Benet, esq. of Salthorp, Wilts, by whom he left three sons, viz.

SAMUEL, his successor.
THOMAS, barrister-at-law, and common serjeant of the city of London, *m.* in March, 172[illegible], Margaret, only daughter of Robert Cox, esq. of Hatton Garden, M.P. for the city of Bath. He *d. s. p.* in 1758.
BENET, successor to his elder brother.

Sir Samuel *d.* senior alderman of London, and president of Bridewell and Bethlehem hospitals, 10th March, 1724. He was *s.* by his eldest son,

V. SIR SAMUEL GARRARD, bart. who *d.* unm. 1st December, 1761, and was *s.* by his only surviving brother,

VI. SIR BENET GARRARD, bart. M.P. for Agmondesham. This gentleman died also unm. 1st July, 1767, when the BARONETCY became EXTINCT, and the manor and estate of LAMER devolved, under Sir Benet's will, upon his cousin,

CHARLES DRAKE, esq. (refer to descendants of JANE GARRARD, only child and heiress of the third Baronet). This gentleman assumed the additional surname of GARRARD. He *m.* Anne, 4th daughter of Miles Barne, esq. of Sotterley, and dying in July, 1817, was *s.* by his only son, the present CHARLES-BENET DRAKE GARRARD, esq. of Lamer.

Arms—Arg. on a fesse sable a lion passant of the first.

GARRARD, OF LANGFORD.

CREATED 10th Aug. 1662.

EXTINCT 12th Mar. 1728.

Lineage.

THOMAS GARRARD, an opulent citizen of London, who served the office of sheriff, died in 1632, and was *s.* in his estate by his son,

I. SIR JACOB GARRARD, of Langford, in the county of Norfolk, an alderman of the city of London, who received the honor of knighthood in 1641 (having served the office of sheriff in 1636), and was created a BARONET 16th August, 1662. Sir Jacob was a merchant of great wealth, and, says an old writer, "a gentleman of exemplary probity, religiously practising in all his transactions, that excellent maxim, of *doing as he would be done unto*, of extensive charity to the poor, both by large legacies in money, and by twelve acres marsh land, called Oxleas, in the parish of Westham, Essex, appropriated for ever, many years before his decease, *for the binding out of four apprentices, three of the parish of West, and one of the parish of East Ham*; also three pounds issuing out thereof, to buy coals for the poor of Gracechurch street, *London*, and the overplus to other pious uses: he gave likewise £10 per annum, *for ever, for a lecture* in the parish church of Needham Market, in Suffolk." *Sir Jacob* was zealously attached to *King* CHARLES I. and for his services to that unhappy monarch was prosecuted as a delinquent, and tried for his life, but acquitted for want of evidence. In thankful remembrance of which event he appointed a sermon to be preached yearly on the anniversary of the day of his deliverance, being the 9th of January, if it happen on a Sunday, or else the next ensuing Sunday, at the parish church of Westham, by some orthodox divine, bestowing £1 on the preacher, 6*s.* 8*d.* on the reader, 2*s.* 4*d.* on the clerk, and 2*s.* on the sexton, and directing fifty poor to participate in his charity on that day. He *m.* Mary, daughter of Ambrose Jennings, of London, gent. and had four surviving children, viz.

THOMAS, his successor.

Jacob, } both *m.* but *d. s. p.*
Isaac, }

Mary, *m.* to Richard Berney, esq. of Reedham, in Norfolk.

He *d.* about the year 1666, and was *s.* by his eldest son,

II. SIR THOMAS GARRARD, bart. who *m.* Sarah, daughter and heir of Nicholas Beaumont, esq. of Peason Hall, in Suffolk, and had issue,

JACOB, who *m.* Abigail, daughter of Sir John Holland, bart. of Quiddenham, in Norfolk, and dying in the lifetime of his father, left two daughters,

ALATHEA, *m.* to Sir Francis Bickley, bart. of Attleburgh, in Norfolk.

SARAH, *m.* to Charles Downing, esq. comptroller of the customs in the port of London.

NICHOLAS, heir to the baronetcy at the decease of his brother.

A daughter, *m.* to Samuel Kerridge, esq. of Shelley Hall, Suffolk.

Sir Thomas *d.* about the year 1690, and was *s.* by his only surviving son,

III. SIR NICHOLAS GARRARD, bart. who *m.* Cecilia, only daughter of Sir Edwyn Stede, knt. of Stede Hill, in Kent, and had no male issue. He *d.* 12th March, 1728, when the BARONETCY became EXTINCT.

Arms—Az. two lions rampant guardant combatant arg.

GAWDY, OF WEST HERLING.

CREATED 13th July, 1663.

EXTINCT 10th Oct. 1723.

Lineage.

The family of GAWDY is stated to have derived from Sir Brews Gawdey, a French knight, taken prisoner in 1352, who was naturalized, and settled in Suffolk. His descendant,

THOMAS GAWDEY, esq. of Harleston, serjeant-at-law, left by Anne, his wife, daughter and co-heir of John Bassingbourne, esq. of Woodhall, Herts, a son,

SIR BASSINGBOURNE GAWDY, died seised of West Herling, &c. in Norfolk, 25th January, 1589, leaving by Anne, his wife, daughter and heir of John Wootton, esq. of Tuddenham, two sons, namely,

BASSINGBOURNE, his heir.

Philip (Sir), knt. who *m.* Bridget Strongman, and had a son, Francis, who died *s. p.* and five daughters, the youngest of whom was born in 1614.

The elder son,

SIR BASSINGBOURNE GAWDIE, knt. of West Herling, who served the office of sheriff for Norfolk, in 1573, 1593, and 1601, married, first, Anne, daughter and heir of Sir Charles Framlingham, knt. of Crow's Hall, in Debenham, by Dorothy, his wife, daughter of Sir Clement Heigham, knt. and had by her two sons, viz.

FRAMLINGHAM, his heir.
CHARLES (Sir), knt. of Crow's Hall, in Suffolk, whose son was created a BARONET in 1661. (See GAWDY, OF CROW'S HALL.)

Sir Bassingbourne married, secondly, Dorothy, daughter of Sir Nicholas Bacon, of Redgrave, and by her, who m. secondly, Sir Henry Felton, bart. of Playford, and died in 1652, had two sons and two daughters, who all died *s. p.* Sir Bassingbourne died in 1606, and was *s.* by his son,

FRAMLINGHAM GAWDY, esq. of West Herling, *b.* 8th August, 1589, sheriff of Norfolk in 1627, who *m.* Lettice, daughter and co-heir of Sir Robert Knowles, knt. and had issue by her, who was buried at West Herling, 3rd December, 1630, six sons and two daughters, viz.

I. WILLIAM, his heir.
II. Framlingham.
III. Bassingbourne, *b.* in 1614.
IV. Thomas, *b.* in 1617, who died unm.
V. Charles, *b.* in 1618.
VI. Robert, *b.* in 1620.

I. Lettice.
II. Anne.

Framlingham Gawdy died in 1654, and was *s.* by his eldest son,

I. WILLIAM GAWDY, esq. of West Herling, who was created a BARONET in 1663. Sir William *m.* Elizabeth, daughter and heir of John Duffield, gent. of East Wretham, in Norfolk, and by her, who died in 1653, had issue,

Bassingbourne, who died unm. at London, of the small-pox, and was buried in the Temple in 1660.
JOHN, successor to his father.
William, died unm.
Framlingham, of Bury.

Anne, died unmarried.

Sir William died in 1666, and was *s.* by his son,

II. SIR JOHN GAWDY, of West Herling, *b.* 4th October, 1639. This gentleman, who was deaf and dumb, possessed considerable ability, and attained no small degree of celebrity as a painter. He *m.* Anne, daughter of Sir Robert de Grey, knt. of Martin, and had one son and one daughter, viz.

BASSINGBOURNE, his heir.
Anne, who *m.* Oliver Le Neve, esq. of Great Wichingham, and had issue,
Oliver Le Neve, who *d. s. p.* in 1696.
ISABELLA LE NEVE.
ANNE LE NEVE, *m.* to John Rogers, of Stanford, licentiate in physic.
HENRIETTA LE NEVE, *m.* to Edward Le Neve, esq. citizen of London.

Sir John died in 1699, and was *s.* by his son,

III. SIR BASSINGBOURNE GAWDY, of West Herling, at whose decease unmarried, in 1723, the BARONETCY became EXTINCT; Sir Bassingbourne's three nieces, the daughters of his sister, Mrs. Le Neve, being his heirs. Those ladies joined, and conveyed the whole estate to Joshua Draper, esq. who sold it to Richard Gipps, esq.

Arms—Vert, a tortoise passant arg.

GAWDY, OF CROW'S HALL.

CREATED 20th April, 1661.—EXTINCT.......

Lineage.

SIR CHARLES GAWDY, knt. of Crow's Hall, in Suffolk, *b.* in 1591, second son of Sir Bassingbourne Gawdy, knt. of West Herling, married Judith, daughter of Sir William Waldegrave, of Smallbridge, and had a son,

I. CHARLES GAWDY, esq. of Crow's Hall, who was created a BARONET in 1661. He *m.* Vere, daughter and co-heir of Sir Edward Cook, knt. of Gedding Hall, Essex, and had issue,

I. CHARLES, his heir.
II. Francis, died *s. p.*
III. Edmund, living in 1695.
IV. Bassingbourne, *d. s. p.*
V. Henry, *d. s. p.*

I. Anne, *m.* to Wentworth Garneys, esq. of Boyland Hall, Norfolk.

The eldest son,

II. SIR CHARLES GAWDY, of Crow's Hall, married Mary, daughter of George, Earl of Desmond, and had issue. With his son, the THIRD BARONET, the title expired.

Arms—As GAWDY, OF WEST HERLING.

GELL, OF HOPTON.

CREATED 29th Jan. 1641-2.

EXTINCT 14th July [illegible]

Lineage.

The GELLS were seated at Hopton, in Derbyshire, so early as the reign of EDWARD III. and the first recorded ancestor, Ralph Gell, is supposed to have married the heiress of Hopton. During the civil wars the then chief of the family,

I. SIR JOHN GELL,* of Hopton, attained considerable eminence as a parliamentary leader; captured the city of Lichfield, and rendered very important services to his party in his native county. A [illegible] narrative of the services he performed, written by himself, for the purpose of refuting, as it appears, certain charges brought against him after the [illegible] dents got into power, gives a full and interesting account of his actions, which tended, in several ways, to the destruction of the royal cause in Derbyshire; indeed Lord Clarendon observes that, after a [illegible] there was in that county no visible party for the king; the whole shire being under the power of John Gell. Subsequently to the termination of the war, Sir John was much dissatisfied with the treatment he received from the parliament, and [illegible]

* THOMAS GELL, esq. younger brother of Sir John, was a barrister of the Inner Temple, of extensive practice, recorder of the borough of Derby, and representative thereof in the last parliament of CHARLES I. [illegible] gentleman of distinguished abilities, and held [illegible] lieutenant-colonel in his brother's regiment.

incurred the hostility of the ruling powers to so great an extent, that he was sentenced by the high court of justice to be imprisoned for life and his estates to be confiscated; but two years afterwards he procured his pardon. He was created a BARONET in 1641-2. Sir John m. first, Elizabeth, daughter of Sir Percival Willoughby, of Wollaton, in the county of Nottingham, and secondly, Mary, daughter of Sir Francis Radcliffe, of Ordsall, in Lancashire, and widow of John Stanhope, esq. of Elvaston. By the latter he had no issue, but by the former he left at his decease, in November 1761, (with four daughters, Millicent, m. Richard Radcliffe, esq. of Manchester; Elizabeth, m. to Henry Wigsall, esq.; Bridget, m. to John Wigley, esq.; and Eleanor, m. to Anthony Alsop, esq.) a son and successor,

II. SIR JOHN GELL, of Hopton, who m. Katherine, daughter of John Packer, esq. of Denington Castle, in the county of Berks, and had issue,

PHILIP, his heir.

CATHERINE, who m. William Eyre, esq. of Highlow, in Derbyshire, and their second son,

JOHN EYRE, esq. inheriting Hopton, assumed the surname of GELL. He m. Isabella, daughter and co-heir of William Jessop, esq. of Broom Hall, and had (with several daughters, one of whom, Anne, was wife of Hugo Meynel, esq.) two sons. The younger, Admiral John Gell, d. unm. The elder,

PHILIP GELL, esq. of Hopton, m. Dorothy, daughter and co-heir of William Milnes, esq. of Aldercar Park, and by her, who wedded, secondly, Thomas Blore, esq. F.S.A. left at his decease, in August, 1795, a daughter, Mary, and two sons, viz.

PHILIP GELL, esq. of Hopton, who m. Georgiana-Anne, youngest daughter of Nicholas Nicholas, esq. of Boys Court, in Kent, and had issue.

SIR WILLIAM GELL, knt. M.A. F.R.S. F.S.A., &c. the celebrated classical antiquary, who died 4th February, 1836, aged fifty-nine.

Sir John Gell died about 1689, and was s. by his son,

III. SIR PHILIP GELL, of Hopton, who m. Elizabeth, daughter of Sir John Fagg, bart. of Wiston, in Sussex, but died without issue 14th July, 1719, when the BARONETCY EXPIRED; the estates devolving, under Sir Philip's will, on his nephew JOHN EYRE, esq. who assumed the surname of GELL, and by his descendant they are still possessed.

Arms—Per bend az. and or, three mullets of six points in bend, pierced and counterchanged.

GERARD, OF HARROW-ON-THE-HILL.

CREATED 2 April, 1620. EXTINCT ....

Lineage.

JAMES GERARD, esq. second son of William Gerard, of Ince, in Lancashire, by Elizabeth, his wife, daughter of Sir John Byron, knt. married Margaret, daughter of John Holcroft, esq. of Holcroft, and had two sons, viz.

GILBERT, a distinguished lawyer, master of the rolls, *temp. Queen* ELIZABETH, who erected the stately mansion of Gerards Bromley, in the county of Stafford, and was ancestor of the Gerards, Lords Gerard, of Bromley, the Earls of Macclesfield, and the Gerards, of Fiskerton.

WILLIAM.

The younger son,

WILLIAM GERARD, esq. of Flamberds, in the parish of Harrow-on-the-Hill, Middlesex, m. Dorothy, daughter of John Ratcliff, esq. of Langley, and dying 15th April, 1583, was s. by his son,

I. GILBERT GERARD, esq. of Flamberds, who was created a BARONET in 1620, and represented Middlesex in parliament. He m. Mary, daughter of Sir Francis Barrington, bart. and had issue,

FRANCIS, his heir.
Gilbert (Sir).
Thomas.
John.
Mary, d. unm.
Winifred, m. to Tristram Conyers, esq. sergeant-at-law.
Katherine, m. to Sir Charles Pym, bart.
———, m. to Sir John Heydon.

The eldest son,

II. SIR FRANCIS GERARD, of Flamberds, married Isabel, daughter of Sir Thomas Cheek, knt. and had three sons, successively baronets. The eldest,

III. SIR CHARLES GERARD, of Flamberds, M.P. for Middlesex, wedded Honora, daughter of Charles, Lord Seymour, of Trowbridge, and had an only daughter and heir,

ELIZABETH, m. first, to Warwick Lake, esq. by whom she was grandmother of Gerard, LORD LAKE; and secondly, to Miles Stapleton, esq.

Sir Charles died in 1701, and was s. by his brother,

III. SIR FRANCIS GERARD, of Flamberds, who dying in August, 1704, was s. by his brother,

IV. SIR CHEEK GERARD, of Flamberds, at whose decease unm. in February, 1715, the BARONETCY became EXTINCT. The estate of Flamberds devolved on Elizabeth, daughter and heir of Sir Charles Gerard, the third baronet, and in 1767, was sold by Sir Thomas Stapleton, bart. Gerard Lake, esq. and others, to Francis Herne, esq.

Arms—A saltire gu.

GERARD, OF FISKERTON.

CREATED 17th Nov. 1666.—EXTINCT ....

Lineage.

GILBERT GERARD, esq. grandson of William Gerard, of Ince, having attained eminence in the profession of the law, was chosen autumn reader by the benchers of Gray's Inn, and the next year appointed, with Nicholas Bacon, joint treasurer of the society. In some time after, when the Princess ELIZABETH was brought before the council, Mr. Gerard advocated her cause so ably, that he was committed to the Tower, where he remained during the rest of *Queen* MARY's reign. Upon the accession of ELIZABETH, he was released and constituted attorney-general. He afterwards received the honour of knighthood, and was appointed master of the rolls, when he had held the attorney-generalship no less than three-and-twenty years. This Sir Gilbert erected a stately mansion in the county of Stafford, where he resided, called Gerard's Bromley. He *m.* Anne, daughter of William Ratcliffe, esq. of Wimersley, in Lancashire, and had issue,

- Thomas, created in 1603, Baron Gerard, of Gerard's Bromley.
- Ratcliffe, of whom presently.
- Frances, *m.* to Sir Richard Molineux, bart.
- Margaret, *m.* to Peter Leigh, esq.
- Catherine, *m.* to Sir Richard Hoghton, bart.

Sir Gilbert died in 1592. His second son,

Ratcliffe Gerard, esq. of Hatsall, in Lancashire, *m.* Elizabeth, daughter and heir of Sir Charles Somerset, K.B. fifth son, of Henry, Earl of Worcester, and had issue,

- Charles (Sir), knt. a distinguished royalist commander, created Baron Gerard, of Brandon in 1645, and Earl of Macclesfield in 1679. (See Burke's *Extinct Peerage.*)
- Thomas, *d. s. p.*
- Ratcliffe, of whom presently.
- Gerard (Sir), governor of Worcester, *d. s. p.*

The third son,

Ratcliffe Gerard, esq. married Jennet, daughter of Edward Barret, of Pembrokeshire, and was father of

I. Gilbert Gerard, esq. of Fiskerton, in Lincolnshire, was created a Baronet 17th November, 1666. He *m.* first, Mary, daughter of Sir John Brereton, knt. by whom he had no issue, and secondly, Mary, daughter and co-heir of Dr. John Cosins, bishop of Durham, by whom he left a daughter, Charlotte, *m.* to John Barcroft, esq. and a son,

II. Sir Gilbert Cosins Gerard, of Fiskerton, married first, Mary, daughter and heiress of Charles Berkeley, Earl of Falmouth, from whom he was divorced in 1684, and secondly, Lady Morland, but had no issue by either. The title became extinct at his decease.

Arms—As Gerard of Harrow.

GERMAINE, OF WESTMINSTER.

Created 25th Mar. 1698.

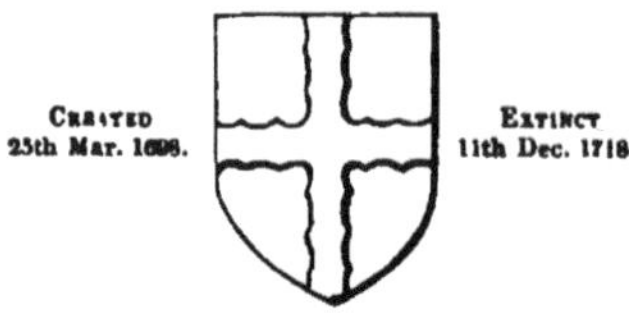

Extinct 11th Dec. 1718.

Lineage.

I. Sir John Germaine, knt. of Westminster, in Middlesex, who was created a Baronet in 1698, married first, Mary, daughter and heir of Henry, Earl of Peterborough, and relict of Henry, Duke of Norfolk, by whom he had no issue, and secondly, Elizabeth, daughter of Charles, Earl Berkeley, by whom he had three children, James, John, and Elizabeth, who all died in their infancy. Lady Mary Germaine, Sir John's first wife, inherited the barony of Mordaunt, of Turvey, and the manor of Drayton, in Northamptonshire. She died in 1705, and left her whole property to Sir John Germaine, who bequeathed it at his decease in 1718, to his second wife, Lady Elizabeth Germaine, and under that lady's will it devolved on Lord George Sackville, (second son of Lionel, first, Duke of Dorset,) who assumed by act of parliament the surname of Germaine. His lordship, the celebrated Lord George Germaine, was created in 1782, Viscount Sackville. His son is Charles, present Duke of Dorset.

Arms—Az. a cross engr. or.

GIDEON, OF SPALDING.

Created 21st May, 1759.

Extinct 25th Dec. 18[illegible]

Lineage.

Sampson Gideon, esq. of Spalding, in Lincolnshire, a gentleman of large estate, paternal and personal, *m.* Jane, daughter of Charles Ermell, esq. and dying [illegible] October, 1762, left issue,

- Sampson, his successor.
- Susanna, *d.* unm.
- Elizabeth, *m.* in 1757, to William-Hall, [illegible] Viscount Gage, and had an only son who [illegible] an infant.

His son and heir,

I. Sampson Gideon, esq. of Spalding, in Lincolnshire, and Belvedere, in Kent, was created a Baronet 21st May, 1759. He *m.* 6th December, [illegible] Maria-Marou, daughter of the Right Hon. Sir Eardly Wilmot, lord chief justice of the Court of Common Pleas, and by that lady, who *d.* 1st Mar. 1794, had issue,

- Sampson-Eardley, William, } both in the army, and both predeceased their father.
- Maria-Marou, *b.* 22nd November, 1767, *m.* [illegible] September, 1794, to George-William, Lord Saye and Sele, and *d.* 5th September, 1834, leaving a son and daughter. (See Burke's *Peerage and Baronetage.*)
- Charlotte, *b.* in 1768, *m.* 22nd September [illegible] to Culling Smith, esq. who succeeded his brother in 1812, and became Sir Culling Smith, bart. Her ladyship died 15th September, 18[illegible] leaving with two daughters, the present Sir Culling Eardley Smith, bart.
- Selina, *b.* in 1772, *m.* 25th June, 17[illegible] Walbanke-Childers, esq. of Cantley, in the county of York, and had with younger children the present John Walbanke-Childers, of Cantley. (Refer to Burke's *Commoners*, vol. [illegible] 229.)

Sir Sampson Gideon was raised to the peerage of Ireland in October, 1789, as Baron Eardley, of Spalding. He died at the age of eighty, 25th December [illegible] when, his sons having predeceased him, the barony and Baronetcy became extinct. His lordship's possessions devolved upon his daughters as co-heirs [illegible] beautiful seat of Belvedere, in Kent, falling to the eldest, the late Viscountess Saye and Sele. Lord Saye and Sele assumed in March, 1825, by sign manual, on behalf of himself and his issue, in compliance with a proviso, in an indenture of settlement made by his father-in-law, the surname and arms of Eardley, in addition to, and before those which his lordship then [illegible]

Lord Eardley enjoyed a very large fortune, but his generosity was as extended, and he was benevolent as he was rich.

Arms—Party per cheveron, vert and or; in a chief, a rose or, between two fleurs-de-lis argent; in base, a lion rampant, reguardant, azure.

GIFFORD, OF BURSTALL.

CREATED 21st Nov. 1660.

EXTINCT 6th June, 1736.

Lineage.

THOMAS GIFFORD, esq. of Burton, in Wiltshire, son of Morris Gifford, of Rodenhurst, in the same county, and grandson of Edward Gifford, gent. of Rodenhurst, had two sons, JOHN, of Boreham, in Essex, and George, of Mount Deverell, in Wilts. The elder,

JOHN GIFFORD, esq. of Boreham, married Mary, daughter of William Hanham, esq. of Purston Dell, in Dorsetshire, and had five sons, namely,

WILLIAM, who m. Mrs. Johnson, of Somersetshire.
JOHN, of whom presently.
Thomas, died *s. p.*
Christopher, settled in Ireland.
Botevile.

The second son,

JOHN GIFFORD, M.D. of London, married Catherine, daughter of John Legat, of Hornchurch, in Essex, by Margaret, his wife, daughter of Thomas Reding, of Pinner, in Middlesex, and had issue,

JOHN, twenty-nine years of age in 1634, *d. s. p.*
THOMAS, successor to his father.

Margaret.
Mary.

The only surviving son,

THOMAS GIFFORD, esq. marrying Anne, daughter and heir of Gregory Brooksby, esq. of Burstall, in Leicestershire, acquired with her that estate, and had issue,

I. HENRY, his heir.
II. Thomas.
III. Gregory.
IV. Morris.
V. William.

I. Katherine, m. to Robert Guldeford, esq. of Hempsted.
II. Mary, m. to George Nevill, Lord Abergavenny.

The eldest son,

I. HENRY GIFFORD, esq. of Burstall, in Leicestershire, was created a BARONET in 1660. He m. Mary, daughter of Baynham Vaughan, esq. of Ruerden, in Leicestershire, and dying about 1665, left with three daughters, Anne, Mary, and Elizabeth, a son and successor,

II. SIR JOHN GIFFORD, of Burstall, who was resident in 1695, in France; but died *s. p.* in Golden Square, London, 6th June, 1736, when the title became EXTINCT.

Arms—Gu. three lions passant arg.

GLEANE, OF HARDWICKE.

CREATED 6th Mar. 1665-6.

EXTINCT 16th June, 1745.

Lineage.

SIR PETER GLEANE, an eminent merchant of the city of Norwich, was mayor of that city in the year 1615, and received the honour of knighthood from *King* JAMES I. He m. Maud, daughter of Robert Suckling, esq. of Norwich, and was grandfather of

I. PETER GLEANE, esq. of Hardwicke, (son of Thomas Gleane, esq. by his wife, daughter and co-heir of Thomas Brewse, esq. who was created a BARONET by *King* CHARLES II. 6th March, 1665-6. Sir Peter represented the city of Norwich in parliament, and afterwards (*anno* 1678) the county of Norfolk. He m. Penelope, daughter and co-heir of Sir Edward Rodney, knt. of Rodney Stoke, in the county of Somerset, and dying about the year 1694, was *s.* by his elder son,

II. SIR THOMAS GLEANE, bart. This gentleman ruined his estate by the profuseness of his extravagance. He m. twice, first, Miss Mapes, daughter of Captain Mapes, of Rollesby, in Norfolk, and secondly, Miss Chamberlayne, but dying *s. p.* was *s.* by his brother,

III. SIR PETER GLEANE, bart. a proctor of the court of Canterbury, who m. first, a daughter of Doctor Peters, of that city, by whom he had two sons and two daughters, one of whom m. Mr. Edgecomb, of St. Clement's Danes, Middlesex. He wedded, secondly, Mrs. Manger, but had no other issue. Sir Peter was *s.* at his decease by his son,

IV. SIR PETER GLEANE, bart. who m. Johanna Skinner, but died *s. p.* aged forty-nine, 16th June, 1745, when the BARONETCY became EXTINCT.

Arms—Ermine, on a chief sable, three lions rampant, argent.

GODOLPHIN, OF GODOLPHIN.

CREATED 29th April, 1661.

EXTINCT 27th Aug. 1716.

Lineage.

This family derived its surname from GODOLPHIN, anciently written Godolghan, in Cornwall, which word in Cornish signifies a white eagle, and that emblem became the device on the shield of the family.

JOHN DE GODOLPHIN was living at the time of the Norman Conquest, and amongst other feudal possessions, was lord of the manor of Godolphin, where he resided. His lineal descendant,

John Godolphin, esq. of Godolphin, was sheriff of Cornwall in the 19th and 23rd of Henry VII. and joint steward, with Sir Robert Willoughby, Lord Brooke, of the mines in Cornwall and Devonshire. His elder son and successor,

William Godolphin, esq. of Godolphin, m. Margaret, daughter and co-heir of John Glinne, esq. of Moreval and Lowewater, and was s. by his elder son,

Sir William Godolphin, knt. an eminent person in the time of Henry VIII. who received for his services the honour of knighthood, and was constituted warden of the stanneries. Sir William lived to an advanced age, and was several times elected knight of the shire for Cornwall, in the reign of Henry VIII. and Edward VI. He was thrice sheriff in the former reign, once in the latter, and again in the reign of Elizabeth; and he attained beside a high military reputation, particularly at the siege of Boulogne. Crew, in the survey of Cornwall, says, "He demeaned himself very valiantly beyond seas, as appeared by the scars he brought home, no less to the beautifying of his fame, than the disfiguring of his face." Sir William m. Blanch, daughter of Robert Langden, esq. and had three daughters,

- Margaret, m. to Sir Robert Verney.
- Grace, m. to Sir John Sydenham, of Brimpton, Somersetshire.
- Anne, m. to Sir John Arundel, of Talvern, in Cornwall.

Sir William left no male issue, and the representation of the family devolved, at his decease, upon his nephew,

Sir Francis Godolphin, knt. M.P. for Cornwall, in the 31st of Elizabeth, and colonel of a regiment of twelve companies, armed with four hundred and seventy pikes, four hundred and ninety muskets, and two hundred and forty calivers. He m. Margaret, daughter of John Killigrew, esq. of Arwenick, in Cornwall, and was s. by his eldest son,

Sir William Godolphin, knt. member for Cornwall in the first parliament of James I. who m. Thomasin, daughter of Thomas Sidney, esq. of Wrighton, in Norfolk, and had issue,

- Francis, his heir.
- Sidney, a very accomplished person, and a poet of some celebrity, fell fighting for the king in the civil wars, at the battle of Chagford, and was buried at Okehampton, 10th February, 1642.
- William, colonel of a regiment, and a gallant officer in the service of *King* Charles.
- Penelope, m. to Charles Berkeley, Viscount Fitzhardinge.

Sir William d. in 1613, and was s. by his eldest son,

Sir Francis Godolphin, K.B. M.P. for St. Ives before the breaking out of the rebellion. After which he retired to his estate in Cornwall, secured the Isle of Scilly for the king, and raised a regiment of foot, the command of which was given to his brother, Colonel William Godolphin. He was created a knight of the bath at the coronation of *King* Charles II. Sir Francis m. Dorothy, second daughter of Sir Charles Berkeley, knt. of Yarlington, in the county of Somerset, and had a numerous family. His eldest son and heir,*

I. William Godolphin, esq. of Godolphin, was created a Baronet 29th April, 1661. Sir William lived in retirement, and dying unm. 17th August, 1710, bequeathed his estates to his nephew, Francis, second Earl of Godolphin, (see Burke's *Extinct Peerage*, Godolphin, Earls of Godolphin) and the Baronetcy became extinct.

Arms—Gules, an eagle with two heads displayed, between three fleurs-de-lis, argent.

GOLDING, OF COLSTON BASSETT.

Created 27th Sep. 1642.

Extinct about 1716.

Lineage.

I. Edward Golding, esq. of Colston Bassett, in the county of Nottingham, who was created a Baronet in 1642, married Eleanor, daughter of John Throckmorton, esq. of Coughton, in the county of Warwick, and had issue, of which the eldest son, John, was a Capuchin friar at Rouen. Sir Edward also entered himself a friar of that holy community, and died at Rouen, when the title devolved on his second son,

II. Sir Charles Golding, of Colston Bassett, who m. Mary, daughter of James Ravenscroft, esq. of Alkmundbury, in the county of Huntingdon, and dying in 1667, was s. by his son,

III. Sir Edward Golding, who m. the daughter and heir of John Wyldman, esq. of Burton, in Leicestershire, but had no issue. He died about 1716, when the Baronetcy expired.

GOODERE, OF BURHOPE.

Created 5th Dec. 1707.

Extinct about 1776.

Lineage.

John Goodere, esq. of Burhope, in the county of Hereford, son of Francis Goodere, esq. of Hereford, and grandson of Thomas Goodere, esq. of Leyntall Stocks, in the same shire, acted some time as deputy-governor of Bombay, and was living in 1683. He m. Anne, daughter of John Morgan, of Kent, and had issue,

- Edward, his heir.
- Jeremy, who d. unm. in the East Indies.
- Elizabeth, m. to Charles Somerset, esq. of Canon Pion, in Herefordshire, third son of Lord John Somerset.

The elder son,

I. Edward Goodere, esq. of Burhope, M.P. for Evesham and afterwards for the county of Hereford, was created a Baronet in 1707. He m. Eleanor, only daughter and heir of Sir Edward Dinely, knt. of Charleton, in Worcestershire, by Frances, his wife, daughter of Lewis Watson, Lord Rockingham, and had issue,

* Sir Francis's third son was the Lord Treasurer Godolphin, and his fourth son, Dr. Henry Godolphin, dean of St. Paul's, and provost of Eton. The latter is now represented by Mrs. Ormsby-Gore, of Porkington, in Shropshire.

John, his heir.

Samuel.

Eleanor, who m. Samuel Foote, esq. of Truro, in Cornwall, some time M.P. for Tiverton, and had issue,

Edward Foote.

John Foote, who assumed the surname of Dinely, as heir to his uncle.

Samuel Foote, the celebrated dramatic writer.

Eleanor Foote.

Sir Edward died 29th March, 1739, and was s. by his son,

II. Sir John-Dinely Goodere, of Burhope and Charleton, who assumed the surname of Dinely as heir to his maternal ancestors. He m. Mary, daughter and heir of Mr. Lawford, of Stapleton, near Bristol, and had an only son, who died before his father unmarried. Sir John having for a series of years lived on bad terms with his younger brother Samuel, threatened to disinherit him in favour of his sister's son, John Foote,* esq. of Truro, and cut off the entail of the property before his son's death. This circumstance so alarmed Captain Goodere, that he formed the horrid resolution of murdering his brother, and executed his dreadful purpose 17th January, 1741. On the day of the murder, a friend at Bristol, who knew the mortal antipathy that existed between the brothers, invited them both to dinner in the hope of reconciling them, and they had parted in the evening in seeming amity. Captain Goodere had, however, watched his opportunity, and taken measures to ensure the perpetration of the horrid deed. Several of his crew, placed by the captain's orders in the street near College Green, seized Sir John as he passed, and under pretence that he was disordered in his senses, hurried him by violence to the ship, where the unfortunate gentleman was strangled by two sailors, named White and Mahony, Captain Samuel Goodere himself standing sentinel at the door while the crime was committed. Suffice it to add, that the murder was immediately discovered, and the captain,

III. Sir Samuel Goodere, who of course had succeeded as third baronet, was tried, with his two accomplices, at Bristol, 20th March following, found guilty, and executed on the 15th April. This wretched man (who was captain of the Ruby man-of-war, and had distinguished himself in his gallant profession at the capture of St. Sebastian, Ferrol, and St. Antonio,) m. Miss Elizabeth Watts, of Monmouthshire, and had issue,

Edward-Dinely, } successive baronets.
John-Dinely, }

Anne, m. to John Williams, of Monmouthshire, and d. s. p.

Elizabeth, } d. unm.
Mary, }

The elder son,

IV. Sir Edward-Dinely Goodere, died a lunatic in March, 1761, and never having married, was s. by his brother,

V. Sir John-Dinely Goodere, at whose decease unmarried the Baronetcy became extinct.

Arms—Gu. a fesse between two chevrons vaire.

GORDON, OF NEWARK-UPON-TRENT.

Created 22nd Aug. 1764.

Extinct 9th May, 1831.

Lineage.

I. Sir Samuel Gordon, knt. descended from Sir John Gordon, knt. of Lochinvar, through his youngest son, William Gordon, of Cricklaw, was created a Baronet on the 21st August, 1764, having been previously knighted, when high sheriff of the county of Nottingham, in 1760. Sir Samuel married Miss Elizabeth Bradford, niece and heiress of Sir Matthew Jenison, by whom he left, with a daughter, Eleanor, a son,

II. Sir Jenison-William Gordon, of Newark-upon-Trent, in the county of Nottingham, who m. in 1781, Harriet-Frances-Charlotte, daughter of the Hon. Edward Finch-Hatton, and granddaughter of Daniel, Earl of Winchelsea, by whom (who d. in 1821) he had no issue. He d. 9th May, 1831, when the Baronetcy became extinct; the estates devolving on the Earl of Winchelsea.

Arms—Az. three boars' heads erased or.

GORGES, OF LANGFORD.

Created 25th Nov. 1612.

Extinct in Sept. 1712.

Lineage.

This family by paternal extraction was of the surname of Russell, of the same lineage as the Dukes of Bedford, and derive the name of Gorges from a maternal ancestor.

Ivo de Gorges, the first of the name to be met with, is witness to a charter, *temp.* Henry I. which Geva, daughter of Hugh Lupus, Earl of Chester, made to the priory of Canewell, in the county of Stafford, and contemporaneous with him was

Patrick de Gaurges, who gave half a carve of land in Kirby Mesperton to the abbey of St. Mary at York, mentioned in a confirmation charter of *King* Henry II. After him came

* John Foote, esq. became heir to his uncle, Sir John Dinely-Goodere, and assumed the surname of Dinely; Dame Mary Dinely-Goodere, the widow of Sir John, surviving her husband, and holding the Charleton estate [illegible], married, secondly, William Rayner, a printer in White Friars, London, who, being thus in possession, partly by his marriage and partly by purchase from Mr. Foote-Dinely, became seised of the whole in fee, and sold Charleton to Joseph Biddle, esq. of Evesham, from whose executors it was purchased in 1774 by Messrs. Beesley, Socket, Lilly, and Bevington, of Worcester, in partnership.

RALPH DE GORGES, who flourished in the time of HENRY III. He was governor of the castles of Sherburne and Exeter, and had a military summons to the war in Wales in the 54th of the same king's reign. He attended *Prince* EDWARD to the Holy Land, and died in two years after. His son,

RALPH DE GORGES, was marshal of the king's army in Gascony, 21 EDWARD I. and the next year continuing in those parts, was made prisoner and carried to Paris. He does not appear, however, to have been detained long in captivity, for we find him within a brief period again engaged in active service both in France and Scotland; and, in consideration of his services, he was summoned to parliament as a BARON 4th March, 1309. He died seised of the manor of Wraxhall, *inter alia*, 17 EDWARD II. and was *s.* by his son,

RALPH DE GORGES, who *d. s. p.* and was *s.* by his sister,

ELEANOR DE GORGES, who *m.* Sir Theobald Russel,* son of Sir William Russel, of Kingston Russel, in the county of Dorset, and had issue,

SIR THEOBALD RUSSELL, of whom presently.
Sir Ralph Russell, of Kingston Russell, who left issue,
Sir Maurice Russell, of Kingston Russell.

The elder son,

SIR THEOBALD RUSSELL, assumed his maternal surname GORGES, and also adopted the armorial bearings of the family, which occasioned a dispute, 21 EDWARD III. between him and Warburton of Cheshire; and that gentleman establishing his right to the arms in the Court of the Earl Marshal, Henry, Earl of Lancaster, GORGES had assigned to him "a chevron gules on the losengy or and azure," which his posterity bore for some time, until they assumed again their ancient and hereditary coat, viz. "*arg. a gurges or whirlpool, az.*" Sir Theobald was sheriff of the counties of Dorset and Somerset 35 EDWARD III. and served in parliament with Maurice de Bruine as knight of the shire for the county of Southampton 50 EDWARD III. having their writ of expenses for £15. 12*s.* for thirty-nine days' attendance. He died 4 RICHARD II. seised of the manor of Wraxhall, leaving by Mary, his wife, daughter of Thomas Beauchamp, of Hatch, four sons; three of whom died issueless, and the line was carried on by the fourth,

SIR THOMAS GORGES, who *d.* 5 HENRY IV. and was *s.* by his son,

JOHN GORGES, of Wraxhall, who *d.* 2 HENRY V. and was *s.* by his brother,

SIR THEOBALD GORGES, knight banneret, who in the reign of HENRY VI. was lieutenant of Normandy under Richard, Duke of York, then Regent of France, and had a salary from the crown for his government and maintenance. He *m.* first, Joane, daughter of — Hanchford, and by her had issue,

WALTER, who died in the lifetime of his father, leaving a son,
EDWARD, heir to his grandfather.
Elizabeth, *m.* to Thomas Grenvile.
Jane, *m.* to John Hatch, of Dillon, in Devonshire.

He *m.* secondly, Joane, daughter of John Beauchamp, of Lillesdon, and had another son, Richard, to whom he gave lands in Sturminster and Hasington. Sir Theobald *d.* 9 EDWARD IV. and was *s.* by his grandson,

SIR EDWARD GORGES, who received the honour of knighthood at the creation of ARTHUR, *Prince of Wales*, son of HENRY VII. He *m.* Lady Anne Howard, daughter of John, Duke of Norfolk, and had, with three daughters, five sons, viz.

I. EDWARD (Sir), his heir.
II. Edmund, who married the daughter of Sir John Walsh, of Gloucestershire, and left posterity.
III. William, *m.* Winifred, daughter of Richard Badock, and had issue.
IV. Thomas.
V. Nicholas.

The eldest son,

SIR EDWARD GORGES, knt. who *m.* first, a daughter of — Newton, by whom he had a son, Edward, ancestor of the branch of the family seated at Wraxall. He *m.* secondly, Mary, daughter of Sir Anthony Poynts, by his wife, the daughter and heir of Sir William Hudfield, and of that marriage were two daughters, Elizabeth and Frances, and four other sons, namely,

William (Sir), who *m.* the daughter of Rudeckshud, and *d.* in 1516.
Arthur (Sir), who *m.* Lady Elizabeth Clinton, daughter of Henry, Earl of Lincoln.
Ferdinand (Sir), captain of the castle of Plymouth, died in 1397, leaving a son,
John, who *m.* Lady Frances Clinton, daughter of Thomas, Earl of Clinton.
THOMAS (Sir).

The youngest son,

SIR THOMAS GORGES, knt. who was of Langford, in the county of Wilts, *m.* Helena, daughter of George Wolgargus Swavenburg, a Swede, widow of William Parr, Marquess of Northampton, and had, with two daughters, Elizabeth and Frances, four sons, viz.

EDWARD (Sir), his heir.
Theobald (Sir), who *m.* the daughter of Henry Hole, of Saperton, in the county of Somerset.
Tillot (Sir).
Robert (Sir), of Redlinch, in the county of Somerset, *m.* Mary, daughter and heir of William Harding, of Swerey, and had four sons,

Sir Thomas *d.* in 1610, and was *s.* by his eldest son,

I. SIR EDWARD GORGES, who received the honour of knighthood from *King* JAMES I. 9th April, 1603, having met his majesty in the county of Northumberland as he passed the English border, and was created a BARONET by the same prince 25th November, 1612. He was afterwards made a peer of Ireland, as Baron Gorges, of Dundalk, in the county of Louth. He *m.* first, Katherine, daughter of Sir Robert Osborne, knt. of Kelmash, in Northamptonshire, and relict of Edward Haselwood, esq. of Maidwell, by whom he had a son, Thomas, who predeceased him. He wedded, secondly, Jane, daughter of — Thruxton, and widow of Sir John Levingstone, and by her left a son and successor,

II. SIR RICHARD GORGES, second Lord Gorges of Dundalk, who *m.* Bridget, daughter of Richard Kingsmill, esq. of Sidmanton, in the county of Southampton, but died without surviving issue, when all his honours, including the BARONETCY, EXPIRED.

Arms—Arg. a whirlpool az.

* SIR THEOBALD RUSSELL *m.* a second wife, Eleanor, daughter of John de la Tour, of Berwick, in the county of Dorset, and from that marriage sprang the NOBLE house of RUSSELL.

GORING, OF BURTON.

CREATED 16th May, 1621.

EXTINCT 29th Feb. 1724.

Lineage.

The family of GORING derives its surname from a rape in the hundred of Arundel.

SIR WILLIAM GORING, knt. gentleman of the privy chamber to EDWARD VI. lineally descended from John, Lord of Goring *temp.* EDWARD I. *m.* Elizabeth, daughter and co-heir of John Covert, esq. of Slougham, in Sussex, and had issue,

- HENRY, his heir.
- George, of Oving Dean, who *m.* Maria, eldest daughter and co-heir of William Everard, esq. and had a son,
  - GEORGE, whose son GEORGE was elevated to the peerage as BARON GORING and EARL OF NORWICH, dignities which ceased with his only son and successor, Charles, second earl, in 1672. (See BURKE's *Extinct Peerage*.)
- Robert, living *temp.* EDWARD VI. who *m.* Mary, daughter of Thomas Olney.
- Ann, *m.* first, to Sir George De la Lyne; and secondly, to Thomas Browne.
- Elinor, *m.* to John Fenner, of Crawley, and was mother of Sir Edward Fenner, one of the judges of the Court of King's Bench.

The eldest son,

SIR HENRY GORING, knt. of Burton, in Sussex, *m.* Dorothy, second daughter and co-heir of William Everard, esq. of Sussex, and had issue,

- WILLIAM (Sir), his heir.
- Edward, of Wappingthorn and Oakhurst, ancestor of the present
  - SIR CHARLES FORSTER GORING, bart. of Highden, in Sussex.
- Barbara, *m.* to R. Ernley, esq.
- Elizabeth, *m.* to Thomas Selwyn, esq. of Huston, in Sussex.
- Mary, *m.* to Anthony Dering, esq.

Sir Henry died in 1594, and was *s.* by his son,

SIR WILLIAM GORING, knt. of Burton, who left at his decease in 1601, by Anne, his wife, daughter of Robert Burbage, of Hayes, in Middlesex, a son,

SIR HENRY GORING, knt. of Burton, who *m.* Elinor, daughter of Sir William Kingsmill, of Hampshire, and dying in 1626, was *s.* by his son,

I. WILLIAM GORING, esq. of Burton, who was created a BARONET 16th May, 1621. He *m.* Eleanor or Bridget, daughter of Sir Edward Francis, knt. and was *s.* by his son,

II. SIR HENRY GORING, of Burton, who *m.* Mary, daughter and co-heir of George Chamberlaine, esq. of Sherborne Castle, in Oxfordshire, and relict of Sir Thomas Gage, bart. of Firle, in Sussex, by whom, who died in 1694, he had issue,

- WILLIAM, his heir.
- ANN, *m.* to Richard Biddulph, esq. of Biddulph, in Staffordshire, and was ancestor of the BIDDULPHS OF BURTON.

Sir Henry died in May, 1683, and was *s.* by his son,

III. SIR WILLIAM GORING, of Burton, who *m.* Dorothy, daughter of Edmund Plowden, esq. of Plowden, in Shropshire, and relict of Philip Draycot, esq. but had no issue. He died 29th February, 1724, aged sixty-five, when the title became EXTINCT; his sister Ann, *m.* to RICHARD BIDDULPH, esq. being his heir.

Arms—Arg. a chev. between three annulets gu.

GOSTWICK, OF WILLINGTON.

CREATED 25th Nov. 1612.

EXTINCT in 1766?

Lineage.

WILLIAM DE GOSTWICK, Lord of Willington, in the county of Bedford, *anno* 1209, 9 HENRY III. was father of

HUGO DE GOSTWICK, of Willington *temp.* EDWARD I. from whom, after six generations,* sprang

SIR JOHN GOSTWICK, of Willington, living in the time of HENRY VI.† who was grandfather of

SIR JOHN GOSTWICK, treasurer of the first fruits and rents to *King* HENRY VIII. and afterwards master of the horse to the same prince. This gentleman *m.* Margaret, daughter of Oliver, Lord St. John, and was *s.* by his son,

JOHN GOSTWICK, esq. who *m.* Elizabeth, daughter of Sir William Petre, knt. of Ingerstone, in Essex, and dying in 1541, was *s.* by his son,

WILLIAM GOSTWICK, esq. of Willington, who *m.* Martha, daughter of Sir Humphrey Ratcliffe, knt. of Elnestow, in Sussex, and co-heir of her brother, Edward Ratcliffe, sixth Earl of Sussex. He was *s.* by his son,

I. WILLIAM GOSTWICK, esq. of Willington, sheriff of the county of Bedford 37 ELIZABETH, who was created a BARONET by *King* JAMES I. 25th November, 1612. Sir William *m.* Jane, daughter and heir of Henry Owen, esq. of Wotton, in Bedfordshire, and had several children. A noble tomb was erected to his memory in the middle of a chapel in the church of Willington (the burying-place of the family), the image of a knight in armour in full proportion lying thereon, and on the north side of the tomb this inscription:

* In BARNES's EDWARD III. mention is made of William Gostwick, who was taken prisoner in 1373, 47th of the reign, with several English knights and esquires, by the French, near Soissons, after having fought valiantly.

† John Gostwyck and William Gostwyck were farmers of the fishery of the river Ouse and of the coney-warren of Wellington in the 12th of HENRY VII. as appears by an original account of the manor, then belonging to Thomas Howard, Earl of Surrey.

Here lyeth the body of Sir William Gostwyke, Bart. who had to wife Jane Owen, the Daughter of Henry Owen, Esq; by whom he had issue seven Sons, and four Daughters. He, with a most christian Resolution, and assured Hope of a joyful Resurrection, departed this Life the 19th of September, 1615, in the 50th Year of his Age: the Lady Jane Gostwyke, his Widow, to perform her last Duty and Love to the sacred Memory of her dear Husband, at her own Cost and Charge, caused this Monument to be erected.

On the south side of the same tomb:

Ask who lies here, and do not weep,
He is not dead, he doth but sleep;
This stony Register is for his Bones,
His Fame is more perpetual than these stones:
And his own Goodness with himself being gone,
Shall live when earthly Monuments are none.

His eldest son and heir,

II. SIR EDWARD GOSTWICK, received the honour of knighthood at Whitehall in 1607; he inherited the Baronetcy in five years afterwards. He *m.* Anne, daughter of John Wentworth, esq. of Gosfield, in the county of Essex, and had issue,

- EDWARD, his heir, born deaf and dumb.
- Thomas, married Elizabeth, daughter of Mynheer Dorislaus, ambassador from Holland to OLIVER CROMWELL, and *d. s. p.*
- William, of Cople, in the county of Bedford, born deaf and dumb, and *d.* in 1696, *m.* Joane, daughter of Mr. Anthony Wharton, of St. Sepulchre's, London, and had three sons, who all *d.* young, and two daughters, namely, Mary, who died young, and Anne, the wife of Mr. Eames, of Northill, in Bedfordshire.
- Elizabeth, *m.* to Francis Reading, of Willington.
- Mary, *m.* first, to William Spencer, esq. of Cople, in Bedfordshire; and secondly, to Sir Clement Armiger, knt. of Cople.
- Frances, *m.* to the Hon. Francis Mordaunt, third son of Henry, fourth Lord Mordaunt, of Turvey.
- Anne, *m.* to — Thorne, esq.
- Jane, *m.* to — Oliver, esq. of St. Neots, in the county of Huntingdon.

Sir Edward *d.* 20th September, 1630, and was *s.* by his eldest son,

III. SIR EDWARD GOSTWICK, bart. This gentleman, as stated above, was born deaf and dumb. He *m.* Mary, daughter of Sir William Lytton, knt. of Knebworth, in the county of Hertford, and had five sons and two daughters, all of whom died unmarried except the second son, his successor at his decease,

IV. SIR WILLIAM GOSTWICK, M.P. for the county of Bedford from the 10th of *King* WILLIAM to the 12th of *Queen* ANNE, who *m.* Mary, daughter of Sir William Boteler, of Walton Woodhall, in the county of Hertford, K.B. and had issue,

- JOHN, his heir, who died in the lifetime of his father, leaving by his wife, Martha, daughter of Anthony Hammond, esq. of Cambridge,
  - WILLIAM, successor to his grandfather.
  - John, who held a place in the Customs at Boston, in Lincolnshire, *m.* Mary, eldest daughter of Robert Bell, esq. of Bedford, and widow of — Throckmorton, esq. of the county of Buckingham, but *d. s. p.*
- Anne, *m.* to Edward Nelthorpe, esq. second son of Sir Goddard Nelthorpe, bart.

Sir William wasted his estate, and died in the parish of St. Martin-in-the-Fields, London, in 1723. He was *s.* by his grandson,

V. SIR WILLIAM GOSTWICK, bart. who resided at North Tawton, in the county of Devon. He was an officer in the army, and *m.* Loveday, daughter of Edward Gostwicke, and sister and heir of Edward Gostwicke, of North Tawton, mercer, but died without issue in 1766. Sir William was the last who bore the title, but whether the BARONETCY became then EXTINCT is not ascertained. In his will dated in 1766 Sir William bequeathed his property to his kinswoman Loveday Gostwicke, whom he afterwards married, and Dame Loveday in her will, 1766, makes her nephew, Edward Gostwicke, residuary legatee.

Arms—Arg. a bend gu. between six Cornish choughs ppr. on a chief az. three mullets or.

GOULD, OF LONDON.

CREATED 13th June, 1660.—EXTINCT in 1664.

Lineage.

I. NICHOLAS GOULD, esq. of London, who was created a BARONET in 1660, married Elizabeth, daughter of Sir John Garrard, bart. of Lamer, in Herts. and [illegible] her, who wedded, secondly, Thomas Neale, esq. [illegible] no son. He died in 1664, and with him the BARONETCY EXPIRED.

GREEN, OF MITCHAM.

CREATED 2nd Nov. 1664.—EXTINCT about 16[illegible].

Lineage.

I. WILLIAM GREEN, esq. of Mitcham, in Surrey, [illegible] created a BARONET in 1664, but as he left no issue, the title EXPIRED at his decease about 16[illegible].

GREEN, OF SAMPFORD.

CREATED 26th July, 1660.  EXTINCT in Dec. 16[illegible]

Lineage.

The family of GREEN held formerly considerable possessions in the county of Essex. The estate at Sampford was acquired by the marriage of

WILLIAM GREENE, esq. (second son of John Greene, esq. by Agnes, his wife, daughter of John Dale [illegible] of Widdington Hall), with Margaret, daughter of William Bateman, esq. sheriff of the counties of [illegible] and Herts from the 19th to the 22nd of R[illegible] William Greene died 11th January, 14[illegible], his widow in 1495, leaving two sons, JOHN, and [illegible] parson of Little Sampford, and two daughters, the elder *m.* to Fitz-Geffrey, and the younger to [illegible] Basset, of Bradwell. The elder son,

SIR JOHN GREENE, knt. of Sampford, who married three wives, and died in 1530, left a son and successor,

SIR EDWARD GREENE, knt. of Sampford who possessed also the manors of Twys, Bloys, and [illegible] in Essex. He *m.* first, Margery, daughter of [illegible]

Allington; and secondly, Margaret Curson. His eldest son by his first wife,

ROOKE GREENE, esq. of Sampford, married Elianor, daughter of William Fitch, esq. of Little Canfield Hall, and had by her four sons and eight daughters. He died 9th April, 1602, and was *s.* by his eldest son,

WILLIAM GREENE, esq. of Sampford, who *m.* Catharine, daughter of Nicholas Timperley, esq. of Hintlesham Hall, Suffolk, and had four sons and four daughters. The eldest of the former,

JOHN GREENE, esq. of Sampford, *b.* 14th September, 1575, wedded Frances, daughter of Sir John Russel, of Strensham, in Worcestershire, and had issue, EDWARD, Francis, John, William, Rooke, and Catharine. The eldest son,

I. EDWARD GREENE, esq. of Sampford, was created a BARONET 26th July, 1660. He married three wives, but left no male issue at his decease in December, 1676, when the title EXPIRED. Sir Edward, by his extravagancy and love of gambling, entirely ruined his estate, and his large inheritance passed from his family. The manor of Sampford was alienated to Sir William Halton, bart. and those of Grassals and Blois to Randall Wilmer, esq. of Helmesley, in Yorkshire. Of his two daughters and co-heirs, the elder, ANN, married William Gossip, esq. of Thorparch, who sold Grassals and Blois to Richard Salwey, esq. of Woodford; and the younger, MARY, wedded Joshua Field, esq. of Heaton.

Arms—Party per fess sa. and arg. a lion rampant crowned counterchanged.

GREEN, OF MARASS.

CREATED 27th June, 1786.

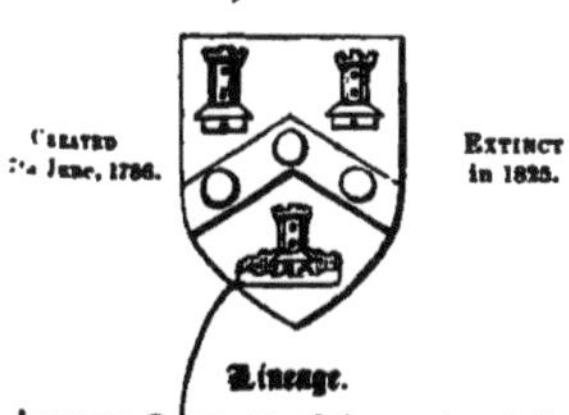

EXTINCT in 1825.

Lineage.

BAINBRIDGE GREEN, esq. of the county palatine of Durham, *m.* Miss Helen Smith, of Aberdeen, and had an only surviving child,

I. WILLIAM GREEN, esq. a general officer in the army and chief engineer at Gibraltar, who was created a BARONET 27th June, 1786. Sir William *m.* 26th February, 1754, Miriam, daughter of Lieut.-Colonel Justly Watson, of the Engineers, and grandaughter of Colonel Jonas Watson, who commanded the detachment of the Royal Artillery at the siege of Carthagena and was killed there. By that lady (who *d.* ... June, 1782,) he had issue,

JUSTLY-WATSON, his heir.

William-Smith, *b.* 13th January, 1761; *d.* 8th September, 1763.

Miriam, *m.* to Major Oliver Nicholls, and had
- William-Jasper Nicholls.
- Oliver Nicholls.
- Justly-Watson Nicholls.
- Miriam Nicholls.
- Helen Nicholls.
- Mary Nicholls.
- Charlotte Nicholls.

Helen-Mary, *m.* to Charles Holloway, esq.

Susanna.

Louisa-Anne.

Charlotte.

Sir William was some time commander-in-chief of the forces in the Island of Malta. He *d.* in February, 1811, and was *s.* by his son,

II. SIR JUSTLY-WATSON GREEN, bart. born at Newfoundland 8th October, 1755, and died unmarried in 1825, when the BARONETCY became EXTINCT.

Arms—Party per cheveron, in chief vert, two castles arg. in base a castle surrounded by a fortification ppr. over all a cheveron or, charged with three torteauxes.

GREEN, OF MILNROW.

CREATED 5th Dec. 1805.

EXTINCT 12th July, 1831.

Lineage.

CHRISTOPHER GREEN, esq. an officer in the army, slain at the battle of Minden, *m.* Britannia, daughter of Charles Hamilton, esq. of Monaghan, in Ireland, and had issue,

Nicholas, an officer in the 37th regiment, died in 1769.

CHARLES, of whom presently.

Christopher, who *m.* Miss Anne Fortnum.

Anne, *m.* to Thomas-David Boswell, esq. of Auchinleck, N. B. and had issue.

The second son,

I. SIR CHARLES GREEN, knt. a general officer in the army and colonel of the 87th regiment, received the honour of knighthood in 1803, and was created a BARONET 5th December, 1805. Sir Charles resided at Milnrow, in the county of York. He died unmarried 12th July, 1831, when the BARONETCY became EXTINCT.

Arms—Or, three leopards passant ppr. on a chief sa. a demi-griffin segreant erm. holding a key erect gold, between two cinquefoils of the fourth.

GRESHAM, OF LIMPSFIELD.

CREATED 31st July, 1660.

EXTINCT 20th Oct. 1801.

Lineage.

Of this ancient family the first upon record is EDWARD GRESHAM, father of

JOHN GRESHAM, of Gresham, in Norfolk, living *temp.* EDWARD III. and RICHARD II. whose son,

JOHN GRESHAM, of Holt, in the same county, *m.* first, Mary, daughter of William Rookwood, by whom he had three sons and a daughter, who all died young. He *m.* secondly, Margaret, daughter of William Bilingford, of Blackford in Norfolk, and was *s.* by his son,

JOHN GRESHAM, of Holt, who *m.* Alice, daughter of Alexander Blyth, esq. and heir of her brothers, John, and Ralph Blyth, and had three sons, viz.

I. WILLIAM.
II. RICHARD (Sir).
III. JOHN (Sir), of Titsey, in Norfolk, of whom hereafter, as continuator of the family.

The second son,

SIR RICHARD GRESHAM, knt. was sheriff of London, in 1531, and lord mayor in 1537. He was twice married, but appears to have had issue only by his first wife, Audrey, daughter of William Lyne, of London, viz.

I. JOHN (Sir), who *m.* Frances, daughter and heir of Sir Henry Thwaites, knt. of Lound on the Wolds, in the county of York, and left an only daughter his heir,

ELIZABETH GRESHAM, who *m.* Sir Henry Neville, knt. of Billingbere, in Berkshire, brother of Edward, Lord Abergavenny, and from this marriage descended the Lords Braybrook. (Refer to BURKE'S *Peerage and Baronetage.*)

II. THOMAS (Sir).
III. William.

I. CHRISTIAN, *m.* to Sir John Thynne, ancestor of the Marquesses of Bath. This lady inherited the estates of her brother, Sir Thomas Gresham.

Sir Richard died 20th February, 1548, and was buried in St. Laurence Jury. His second son,

SIR THOMAS GRESHAM, knt. having become one of the most opulent merchants and eminent citizens of London, immortalized himself by founding the great mart, since so celebrated all over the world as the Royal Exchange. The ground upon which the structure is erected, was given by the city to Sir Thomas, and on the 7th June, 1566, he laid the foundation stone, accompanied by several aldermen, who each put down a piece of gold, which the workmen took up; the building was pursued with so much diligence, that it was completed in the November of the next year, and *Queen* ELIZABETH caused it to be proclaimed by herald and sound of trumpet, THE ROYAL EXCHANGE. Beside his public endowments, this enterprising citizen erected a magnificent structure, called Osterley House, in the county of Middlesex, (which afterwards came into the family of Child, and is now the property of the Earl of Jersey,*) where he entertained *Queen* ELIZABETH in the most sumptuous style. The queen on her arrival happening to offer an opinion that the court would be improved, were it separated in the centre by a wall; Sir Thomas, in the night time, sent for workmen to London, and before the morning dawn, two courts acknowledged the superior judgment of her majesty. "It is questioned, (says an old authority) whether the queen next day, was more contented with the conformity to her fancy, or more pleased with the surprise and sudden performance thereof, whilst her courtiers disported themselves with their several expressions, some avowing it was no wonder he should so change a building, who could build a change." Sir Thomas *m.* Anne, daughter of William Fernley, esq. of Creting, in Suffolk, and relict of — Read, esq. by whom he had a son, Richard, who died before him, 1564, and lies buried at St. Helen's, Bishopsgate.† Sir Thomas Gresham *d.* 21st November, 1579, and was buried under a large stately monument, in the parish church of Great St. Helen's, London.‡ Sir Thomas dying without mak[illegible]

---

* His lordship *m.* Lady Sarah Sophia Fane, eldest daughter of John, tenth Earl of Westmorland, by ANNE, daughter and sole heir of Robert Child, esq. of Osterley Park.

† Sir Thomas Gresham left a natural daughter, Anne, *m.* to Sir Nathaniel Bacon, K.B. of Stifkey, in Norfolk, and left three daughters, viz.

ANNE BACON, *m.* to Sir Roger Townshend, of Rainham, ancestor of the Lords Townshend.
ELIZABETH BACON, *m.* to Sir Thomas Knyvet, of Aswelthorp, in Norfolk.
WINIFRED BACON, *m.* to Sir Robert Gawdy, of Claxton, in Norfolk.

‡ The will of Sir Thomas Gresham contains the following instructions regarding the disposition of the rents of the Royal Exchange:

"Concerning the buildings in London, called the Royal Exchange, and all pawns, and shops, cellars, vaults, messuages, tenements, and other whatsoever myne hereditaments, parcell, or adjoyning to the said Royal Exchange; I will and dispose, that after expiration, and determination of the particular uses, estates and interest for life, and intayle thereof, limited in the said indenture, bearing date the 20th of May: I will and dispose, that one moiety thereof shall remain, and the use thereof shall be unto the major and commonalty, and citizens of London, by whatever especial name or addition the same corporation is made or known, and to their successors, for term of fifty years then next ensuing, upon trust or confidence, and the intent that they do perform the payments and other intents in these presents hereafter limited, thereof to be done and performed. And the other moiety of the said buildings, called the Royal Exchange, pauns, &c. shall remain, and the use thereof shall be to the wardens and commonalities of the mysterie of the mercers of the City of London: (viz.) to the corporate body and corporation of the Company of Mercers, in London, by whatsoever especial name or addition the same corporation is made or known, and to their successors, for term of fifty years ensuing, upon trust and confidence, and to the intent that they do perform the payments and other intents, in these presents hereafter lymited, thereof by them to be done and performed. And I will and dispose, that after such time as the [illegible] moiety of the said Royal Exchange, and other premises, &c. shall come to the said Major and Corporation of the said City; and from thence, so long as they and their successors shall by any means or title, have, hold, or enjoy the same, they and their successors, every year shall give and distribute, to and for the sustentation, maintenance, and finding four persons, from tyme to tyme, to be chosen, nominated and appointed by the same major and commonaltie, and citizens and their successors, meete to read the lectures of divinity, astronomy, music and geomatry, within my own dwelling house, in the Parish of St. Helen's, in Bishopsgate Street, and St. Peter's, the Poor, in the City of London, (the [illegible] whereof hereafter in this my last will, is by me [illegible] and disposed unto the said major and commonaltie, and citizens of the said city,) the summe of two hundred pounds of lawful money of England, in manner and [illegible] following, (viz.) to every of the said readers, for the [illegible] being, the sum of fifty pounds, of lawful money of England, yearly, for their salaries and stipends, [illegible] for four sufficiently learned, to read the said lectures [illegible] said stipends and sallaries, and every of them, to be [illegible] at two usual terms in the year, yearly, (that is to say, the feasts of the Annunciation of St. Mary, the V[illegible] and St. Michael, the Archangel, by even portions [illegible] paid.

"And farther, that the said mayor and commonaltie, and citizens of the said city, and their successors, from [illegible] forth, and so long, &c. shall give and distribute the [illegible] of fifty-three pounds, six shillings, and eight pence [illegible] yearly, in manner and form following, (viz.) unto [illegible] almes houses in the said parish of St. Peter's the [illegible] to every of them the said almes-houses, the [illegible]

issue, his elder brother, Sir John, leaving a daughter only, and his younger brother, William, dying issueless, the representation reverted to the family of his uncle,

Sir John Gresham, knt. of Titsey, in the county of Norfolk, sheriff of London in 1537, and lord mayor in 1547. This gentleman m. first, Mary, daughter and co-heir of Thomas Ipswell, of London, by whom he had (with several other children)

- William, his heir.
- John, of Fulham, m. Elizabeth, daughter and heir of Edward Dormer, esq. and was ancestor of the Greshams, of Fulham, and of Albury, and Haslemere, in Surrey.

He m. secondly, Catherine, daughter of — Sampson, and relict of Edward Dormer, esq. Sir John d. in 1556, and Stowe, gives the following account of his pompous funeral :—"Sir John Gresham, knt. mercer, merchant of the staple, and merchant adventurer, late mayor and alderman of this city, was buried with a standard, and a penon of arms, and a coat armour of damask, and four penons of arms, besides an helmet, a target, and a sword, mantles, and the crest, a goodly hearse of wax, and ten dozen of pensils, and twelve dozen of escotcheons. He gave an hundred black gowns of fine cloth unto poor men and women: he had four dozen of great staff torches, and a dozen of great long torches; he gave, moreover, an hundred of fine black gowns, two, unto the present maior, and the old maior, likewise other to Sir Rowland Hill, and to Sir Andrew Judd, and to the chamberlain, to Mr Blackwell, and to Mr. Common-hunt, and his men, to the porter that belonged to the staple, and to all his farmers, and his tenants. The church, and streets, were all hung with black, and arms in great store, and on the morrow, three goodly masses were sung: one of the trinity, another of our ladie, and the third, of requiem. Then a sermon was preached, by Mr Harpsfield, archdeacon of Canterbury, and after, all the company came home to as great a dinner as had been seen, for a fish day, for all that came; for nothing was lacking." Sir John was buried in St. Michael Basishaw Church, London, under a marble tomb in the fourth isle of the choir. He was s. by his eldest son,

William Gresham, esq. of Titsey, in Surrey, who m. Beatrix, daughter of Thomas Guybon, esq. of Lynn, in Norfolk, by whom he had issue,

- William (Sir), his heir.
- Thomas (Sir), who succeeded his brother.

He d. in 1576, and was s. by his elder son,

Sir William Gresham, of Titsey, who was heir male of his cousin, Sir Thomas Gresham, founder of the Royal Exchange, at the decease of that eminent person in 1579. He m. a daughter of — Finch, esq. and having a daughter only, Elizabeth, who died unmarried, was s. at his decease by his brother,

Sir Thomas Gresham, knt. of Titsey, who m. Mary, daughter of John Lennard, esq. of Knowl, in Kent, and relict of — Walsingham, esq. and had issue,

- John (Sir), his heir.
- Edward (Sir), heir to his brother.
- Thomas, who m. Miss Frances Strickland, and had a son, Leonard.

Sir Thomas was s. by his eldest son,

Sir John Gresham, knt. of Titsey, who m. Elizabeth, daughter of Sir Thomas Bisshopp, bart. of Parham, and dying s. p. in 1643, was s. by his brother,

Sir Edward Gresham, knt. of Titsey, in Surrey, This gentleman m. first, Mary Clark, and had a son,

- Thomas, who m. a daughter of Lady Bridges, and left a daughter and heir,
  - Jane Gresham, who m. John, son of Charles Lloyd, esq. of the county of Montgomery, and had a son,
    - Samuel Lloyd, of Lincoln's Inn, living in 1695.

He wedded, secondly, Mary, daughter of Edward Campion, esq. of Putney, and relict of Mr. Wright, by whom he had

- Marmaduke.
- Elizabeth, m. to Sir Anthony Oldfield, bart. of Spalding, in Lincolnshire.

Sir Edward's son by his second wife,

I. Marmaduke Gresham, esq. of Limpsfield, in the county of Surrey, was created a Baronet by *King* Charles II. 31st July, 1660. He served in parliament for East Grinstead, in that year, and m. Alice, daughter of Dr. Richard Corbet, bishop of Norwich, by whom (who died in 1682) he had issue,

- Edward, his successor.
- Marmaduke, } *d. s. p.*
- John, }
- Charles, who inherited as third baronet.
- William, *d. s. p.*
- Elizabeth, } *d.* unm.
- Alice, }
- Mary, m. to Dr. Thorpe, and *d. s. p.*

Sir Marmaduke *d.* at a great age, in 1696, and was *s.* by his son,

II. Sir Edward Gresham, who married Martha, daughter of Sir John Maynard, knt. serjeant-at-law, of Gunnersbury, in Middlesex, and had an only daughter Elizabeth, who *d.* unm. He *d.* about the year 1709, and was *s.* by his brother,

III. Sir Charles Gresham, F.R.S. *b.* 31st May, 1660, m. Miss Godfrey, and had issue,

- Marmaduke, his successor.
- Edward.
- Charles, m. and survived his wife, without issue.
- Mary.
- Elizabeth.
- Mary, m. to William, only son of William Hoskyns, esq. of Barrow Green, in Surrey.
- Anne.
- Beatrix, m. to Mr. Nathaniel Edwards, of Lombard Street.

He *d.* 4th April, 1718, and was *s.* by his eldest son,

IV. Sir Marmaduke Gresham, who married Anne, daughter of William Hoskyns, esq. of Barrow Green, Surrey, and had issue,

- Charles, his successor.
- John, successor to his brother.
- Anne.

Sir Marmaduke *d.* at Bath, aged forty-one, 2nd January, 1741-2, and was *s.* by his elder son,

---

[illegible] marks, thirteen shillings, and four pence, to be paid [illegible] usual terms in the year," &c. &c.

[illegible] Anne, the widow of Sir Thomas, had by the gift [illegible] husband, in the several counties of Norfolk, Suffolk, [illegible], York, Durham, Derby, Cambridge, Somerset, [illegible], London, Middlesex, of clear yearly value, in fee [illegible] £1139 12s. 2¼d., beside divers lands, tenements, [illegible] London and Sussex, for the term of her natural [illegible] £1037 14s. 4d. in all £2609 5s. 6¾d., beside all Sir Thomas gave and assured in marriage, with Anne, his base daughter, to Nathaniel Bacon, esq. in fee tail, the manors of Hemesley, with the parsonage there, in the county of Norfolk, and the manors of Marston and Langham, with the two sheep pastures there, in the same county, and also the manor of Combes, with the appurtenances, in Suffolk, the whole of the yearly value of £280 15s.

v. Sir Charles Gresham, who *d.* unm. about the year 1751, and was *s.* by his brother,

vi. Sir John Gresham, who *m.* Henrietta Maria, eldest daughter of Sir Kenrick Clayton, bart. and had an only daughter and heiress,

Catherine Gresham, who *m.* in 1804, William Leveson-Gower, esq. second son of Admiral the Hon. John Leveson-Gower, and grandson of John, first Earl Gower, by whom she has issue,

William Leveson-Gower, *b.* in 1806.
Catherine Leveson-Gower.
Frances-Elizabeth Leveson-Gower.

Sir John *d.* 20th October, 1801, when the Baronetcy became extinct.

Arms—Argent, a chevron ermines between three mullets pierced, sable.

GREY, OF CHILLINGHAM.

Created 15th June, 1619.

Extinct 29th June, 1706.

Lineage.

Sir Thomas Grey, knt. of Berwyke, in Northumberland, *m.* Jane, daughter of John, Lord Mowbray, and had issue,

i. John (Sir), a person of high military reputation, *temp.* Henry V. In the second year of that monarch's reign, he was with the king before Caen, and behaved so valiantly, that in requital of his services, he had a grant of the castle and lordship of Tilye, in Northumberland, then forfeited by Sir William Harcourt, an adherent of the king's enemies; the next year (6th Henry V.) we find him again distinguished in the French wars, and rewarded with the Earldom of Tankerville, in Normandy, to hold by homage and delivery of a bassinet or helmet at the castle of Roan, on the feast of St. George, yearly. This gallant person at length fell at the battle of Baugy Bridge, in fording a river near the castle of Beaufort, with the Duke of Clarence and divers others of the English nobility. (For his descendants the Earls of Tankerville, in Normandy, and Lord Grey, of Powis, in England, refer to Burke's *Extinct and Dormant Peerage.*)
ii. Thomas (Sir).
iii. Henry (Sir), of Kettringham, in Suffolk.
iv. William, lord bishop of London.

i. Maud, *m.* to Sir Henry Ogle, knt.

From the second son,

Sir Thomas Grey, knt. of Heton, descended

Ralph Grey, esq. of Chillingham, who *m.* Isabel, daughter and heir of Sir Thomas Grey, of Horton, and was *s.* by his son,

i. William Grey, esq. of Chillingham, in Northumberland, who was created a Baronet 15th June, 1619, and elevated to the peerage as Baron Grey, of Werke, 11th February, 1624. He *m.* Anne, daughter and coheir of Sir John Wentworth, of Gosfield, in Essex and had issue,

Ralph, his heir.
Elizabeth, died in 1668.
Katherine, *m.* first to Sir Edward Mosley, bart. of Hough, in Lancashire, and Rolleston, in the county of Stafford, and secondly, to Charles, eldest son of Dudley, Lord North, which Charles was summoned to parliament, as Lord North and Grey, of Rolleston. Her ladyship *m.* thirdly, Colonel Russell.

In the year 1643, when the Lord Keeper Lyttleton deserted the House of Lords, and carried the great seal to the king at Oxford, Lord Grey was elected speaker at Westminster. He *d.* in 1674, and was *s.* by his son,

ii. Sir Ralph Grey, bart. and second Lord Grey of Werke, who *m.* Catherine, daughter of Sir Edward Forde, knt. of Hartling, in Sussex, and widow of Alexander, eldest son of John, Lord Colepeper, and had issue,

Forde, his heir.
Ralph, successor to his brother.
Charles.

Catherine, *m.* to Richard Neville, esq. and had

Grey Neville, who *m.* Elizabeth, daughter of Sir John Boteler, and *d. s. p.* in 1723.
Henry Neville, who assumed the surname of Grey, and died *s. p.* in 1740. His widow, Elizabeth, married John Wallop, Earl of Portsmouth.
Catherine Neville, *m.* to Richard Aldworth, esq. of Stanlake, in the county of Oxford, and *d.* in 1740, leaving a son,

Richard Aldworth, who assumed the surname and arms of Neville, and was father of

Richard Aldworth Neville, second Lord Braybrook.

His lordship *d.* 15th June, 1675, and was *s.* by his eldest son,

iii. Sir Forde Grey, bart. third Lord Grey, of Werke. This nobleman was a chief adherent of the Duke of Monmouth, and commanded the horse at Sedgemoor. He is accused, though, of playing the part of a double traitor, and the loss of the battle was attributed to his treachery; certain it is, that he made terms for himself, and preserved his life by bearing testimony against his associates. After the revolution he was in favour with *King* William, and was created Earl of Tankerville. He married Mary, daughter of George, Lord Berkeley, and had an only daughter,

Mary-Grey, who *m.* Charles Bennet, second Lord Ossulston, in whom the Earldom of Tankerville was revived, and in whose descendants it still continues.

His lordship *d.* in 1701, when the Earldom of Tankerville expired; but his other honours devolved upon his brother,

iv. Sir Ralph Grey, bart. fourth Lord Grey, of Werke. This nobleman attended *King* William in most of his campaigns, and was made governor of Barbadoes in 1698. He *d.* unmarried 29th June, 1706, when the barony and Baronetcy became extinct. He devised a considerable estate to his cousin, William, Lord North and Grey, son of Charles, Lord Grey, of Rolleston.

Arms—Gules, a lion rampant within a bordure, engrailed argent.

GRIFFITH, OF BURTON-AGNES.

CREATED ... June, 1627.  EXTINCT in 1656.

Lineage.

I. HENRY GRIFFITH, esq. of Burton Agnes, in the ...nty of York, representative of an ancient family in ...t shire, was created a BARONET in 1627. He m. ...ary, daughter and co-heir of Sir Henry Willoughby, ...rt. of Risley, in Derbyshire, and had issue,

HENRY, his heir.

FRANCES, sole heiress, who m. Sir Matthew Boynton, bart. of Boynton and Barmston, and from this marriage descends the present

SIR FRANCIS BOYNTON, bart. who now resides at Burton Agnes.

...e son and heir,

II. SIR HENRY GRIFFITH, married Margaret, daugh...r, and eventual heiress, of Sir Francis Wortley, ...rt. but had no issue to survive him. He died in ...4, and the BARONETCY became EXTINCT.

GRIMSTON, OF BRADFIELD.

CREATED ...th Nov. 1612.  EXTINCT October, 1700.

Lineage.

...e Right Honourable

... EDWARD GRIMSTON, knt. M.P. for Ipswich, *temp.* ...ELIZABETH, and comptroller of Calais in that reign, and ...viously in the time of EDWARD VI. when he was ...pointed to the office (*anno* 1552*), died at the ad...vanced age of ninety-eight, and was *s.* by his son,

... EDWARD GRIMSTON, esq. of Bradfield, in the county ...Essex, M.P. for the borough of Eye, in the 31st of ...ELIZABETH, m. Joan, daughter and co-heir of Thomas ..., esq. of Lavenham, in Suffolk, and granddaugh...ter maternally, of John Harbottle, esq. of Crosfield, in ...same county, and was *s.* at his decease in 1610, by ...eldest son,

I. SIR HARBOTTLE GRIMSTON, knt. of Bradfield, in ...county of Essex, who was created a BARONET 25th ...ovember, 1612. This gentleman served the office of sheriff of Essex, in 1614, and represented the county in three parliaments, *temp.* CHARLES I. He m. Elizabeth, daughter of Ralph Coppenger, esq. of Stoke, in Kent, and had five sons, Edward, *d. s. p.*; HARBOTTLE; Henry; Thomas; and William. He *d.* in 1648, and was *s.* by his son,

II. SIR HARBOTTLE GRIMSTON, bart. who represented Colchester in parliament, *temp.* CHARLES I. He was bred to the bar, and took an active part against the king's government, so long as he could do so constitutionally, but after the murder of the unfortunate CHARLES, (from whose mock trial until his execution, Sir Harbottle was kept a close prisoner) he lived in retirement, until the restoration of the monarchy, when (25th April, 1660) he was elected speaker of the House of Commons which accomplished that desired event. Sir Harbottle *m.* first, Mary, daughter of Sir George Croke, knt. one of the justices of the Common Pleas, and had (with five other sons, who all died before him)

SAMUEL his heir.

MARY, m. to SIR CAPEL LUCKYN, bart. of Messing Hall, and had *inter alios*,

SIR WILLIAM LUCKYN, bart. who m. Mary, daughter of Mr. Alderman Sherrington, of London, and had

HARBOTTLE LUCKYN, who *s.* his father as fourth baronet.

WILLIAM LUCKYN, who became fifth baronet at the decease of his brother in 1736. This gentleman inherited the estates of his great uncle, Sir Samuel Grimston.

ELIZABETH, married to Sir George Grubham Howe, bart. of Cold Barwick, Wilts, and was mother of

SIR JAMES HOWE, bart. who *d. s. p.* in 1735.

He m. secondly, Anne, eldest daughter and eventually heiress of Sir Nathaniel Bacon, K.B. and widow of Sir Thomas Meautys, but by that lady had no surviving issue. Sir Harbottle, who was sworn of the privy council, and constituted master of the rolls, died aged eighty-two, in January, 1683-4, and was *s.* by his son,

III. SIR SAMUEL GRIMSTON, bart. M.P. for St. Albans, *temp.* CHARLES II. and WILLIAM III. who m. first, lady Elizabeth Finch, eldest daughter of Heneage, Earl of Nottingham, lord chancellor of England, and had an only daughter,

ELIZABETH, GRIMSTON, m. to William Savile, second Marquess of Halifax, and had an only daughter,

LADY ANNE SAVILE, who m. Charles, third Earl of Aylesbury, and had issue,

Robert, Lord Bruce, who *d. s. p.*

Mary, m. in 1728, to Henry Brydges, Duke of Chandos.

Elizabeth, m. to the Honourable Bezy Bathurst, and *d. s. p.*

He m. secondly, Lady Anne Tufton, youngest daughter of John, second Earl of Thanet, by whom he had no issue. He *d.* in October, 1700, when the BARONETCY became EXTINCT, and the estates devolved, under Sir Samuel's will, upon his great nephew,

WILLIAM LUCKYN, esq. M.P. for St. Albans, who assumed the surname of GRIMSTON, and was elevated to the peerage 29th May, 1719, as VISCOUNT GRIMSTON. His lordship, at the decease of his elder brother, Sir Harbottle Luckyn, bart. of

* ... the beginning of 1558, Calais being taken by the ... ...use, Sir Edward Grimston, the comptroller, ...ngst the prisoners, and was closely confined in ... ...le, from which prison he effected his escape in two years after, by cutting out one of the window bars with a file, and letting himself down by a rope, conveyed to him by his servant, with whom he changed clothes.

Messing Hall, succeeded to that baronetcy. He was great grandson of

JAMES-WALTER, fourth Viscount Grimston, and first Earl of Verulam. (See BURKE's *Peerage and Baronetage.*)

Arms—Argent, on a fesse sa. three mullets of six points or, pierced gules.

GUISE, OF ELMORE.

CREATED 10th July, 1661.

EXTINCT 6th April, 1783.

Lineage.

SIR WILLIAM GYSE, a younger brother of an illustrious Norman family, following the fortunes of *Duke* WILLIAM, came into England at the conquest, and obtained as his portion of the spoil, Aspley-Guise, with several other lordships, in the counties of Bedford and Buckingham. Sir William bore for arms, "ermine a cheveronel, gules." From this gallant person descended,

ANSELME DE GYSE, who *m.* in HENRY II.'s time, Magotta, daughter of Hubert de Burgh, the great EARL OF KENT, and thus acquired the manor and royalty of ELMORE, in the county of Gloucester. He then assumed, (according to the custom of the age,) the arms of the said Earl, "gules seven losenges vary three, three and one," with the addition of a "canton or, charged with a mullet pierced, sable;" from Anselme lineally descended,

SIR WILLIAM GUISE, of Elmore, who was made a knight of the Bath, 5th HENRY VII. when the prince himself received the honour. He *m.* Mary, daughter of William Ratsey of Colemore, and had a son,

JOHN GUISE, esq. who *m.* a daughter of Richard Pauncefort, esq. of Hasfield, and was *s.* by his son,

SIR WILLIAM GUISE, knt. of Elmore, high sheriff of Gloucestershire, in the 6th of JAMES I. who *m.* Miss Ken, eldest daughter and co-heir* of Christopher Ken, esq. of Ken, in the county of Somerset, and was *s.* by his only son,

WILLIAM GUISE, esq. of Elmore, sheriff, of Gloucestershire, in 1647. This gentleman *m.* Cecilia, daughter of John Dennis, esq. of Pucklechurch, and had issue,

I. CHRISTOPHER, his heir.
II. John, *m.* to Hester, daughter of Major Stratford.
III. William, died unm.
IV. Henry, from whom descend the *extant* baronets, "GUISE *of Highnam*," in the county of Gloucester. (Refer to BURKE's *Peerage and Baronetage.*)

I. Elizabeth, *m.* to Thomas Horton, esq. of Coomend.
II. Eleanor, *m.* first, to Lawrence Washington, esq. of Garesden, Wilts, and had by him, an only daughter,

ELIZABETH WASHINGTON, (heir of her father,) who *m.* Robert, first Earl Ferrers.

She *m.* secondly, Sir William Pargiter, of Greetworth, in the county of Northampton, by whom she had a daughter,

ELEANOR GREETWORTH, who *m.* first, Sir Henry Deering, knt. by whom she had no issue, and secondly, Charles Howe, esq. and had by him a daughter and heir,

LEONORA-MARIA HOWE, who *m.* Peter Bathurst esq. of Clarendon Park, Wilts.

III. Frances, *m.* to John Codrington, esq. of Codrington, in the county of Gloucester.

Mr. Guise was *s.* at his decease by his eldest son,

I. CHRISTOPHER GUISE, esq. of Elmore, in the county of Gloucester, who was created a BARONET by King CHARLES II. 10th July, 1661. Sir Christopher *m.* first, Elizabeth, daughter of Sir Laurence Washington, knt. of Garsden, in Wilts, but by that lady had no issue. He *m.* secondly, Rachel Corsellis, of a noble Italian family, and was *s.* at his decease by his only son,

II. SIR JOHN GUISE, bart. M.P. for the county of Gloucester, *temp.* CHARLES II. and WILLIAM III. He *m.* Elizabeth, second daughter of John Grubham Howe, esq. of Lagnor,† Notts, and had issue,

JOHN, his heir.

Anne, *m.* to Edward Blount, esq. of Blagdon, Devon.

Rachel, *m.* to Sir Roger Bradshaigh, of Haigh in Lancashire.

He *d.* 19th November, 1695, and was *s.* by his son,

III. SIR JOHN GUISE, bart. M.P. for the county of Gloucester, who *m.* first, Elizabeth, daughter of Sir Nathaniel Napier, bart. of Critchell, in the county of Dorset, and had by her a son, JOHN, his heir. He wedded, secondly, Anne, daughter and co-heir of Sir Francis Russell, bart. of Strensham, Worcestershire, and relict of Sir Henry Every, bart. but had no other issue. Sir John *d.* 16th November, 1732, and was *s.* by his son,

IV. SIR JOHN GUISE, bart. M.P. for Ailesbury, and col. in the guards. He *m.* a daughter of — Saunders, esq. of Buckinghamshire, and dying about the year 1769, left, with a daughter, Jane, *m.* to Shute Barrington, Bishop of Durham, a son,

V. SIR WILLIAM GUISE, bart. who *d. s. p.* 6th April, 1783, when the BARONETCY became EXTINCT.

Arms—Gu. seven lozenges vairy three, three and one.

GULDEFORD, OF HEMSTED.

CREATED 4th Feb. 1685.

EXTINCT ....

Lineage.

The Guldefords, eminent alike for the public services they rendered to the state, and the noble alliances they formed, appear to have been settled in Kent soon after the Conquest.

* The youngest daughter, ELIZABETH KEN, *m.* JOHN, first LORD POULETT, *of Hinton St. George*, ancestor of the Earls of Poulett.

† In right of his wife, Annabella, natural daughter and co-heir of Emanuel Scrope, Earl of Sunderland, and Lord Scrope, of Bolton.

WILLIAM GULDEFORD, (descended from William de ...uldeford of Hemsted, sheriff of Kent 11 RICHARD II.) ... Joan, daughter and heir of John Halden, of Halden, ...d was grandfather of

SIR JOHN GULDEFORD, who was comptroller of the ...yal household in the reign of EDWARD IV. Subse...ently espousing the cause of the Earl of Richmond, ...th he and his son were attainted in parliament, RICHARD III. but on the accession of HENRY VII. ...r John had the attainder reversed, and was con...tuted of the privy council. He died in 1493, and ...s buried in the Cathedral of Canterbury. His son ...d heir,

SIR RICHARD GULDEFORD, having fled on the attain...r, returned with the Earl of Richmond, and received ...e honour of knighthood at Milford Haven. After the ...rl's accession to the throne, he continued to enjoy ...e royal favour, he was sworn of the privy council, ...stituted master of the ordnance, and made a knight ...neret for his services against the Cornish rebels at ...ackheath. In the 9th of the same reign, Sir Richard ...pt his shrievalty for Kent at his seat of Halden, and that year had the knighthood of the garter conferred ...on him. He was afterwards comptroller of the ...usehold. He *m.* twice; by his first wife he had issue,

- I. EDWARD (Sir), knt. marshal of Calais, lord warden of the Cinque Ports, constable of Dover Castle, and master of the ordnance. He *m.* Eleanor, daughter of Thomas, Lord Delawarr, and had issue,
  - RICHARD (Sir), knt. who *d.* in Spain, *s. p.*
  - JANE, heiress of her brother, *m.* to John Dudley, Duke of Northumberland, and had issue,
    - Henry, *d.* at the siege of Bologne.
    - John, *d. v. p.* unm.
    - AMBROSE, EARL OF WARWICK.
    - GULDEFORD, who *m.* the unfortunate LADY JANE GREY, and was attainted and beheaded.
    - ROBERT, Earl of Leicester.
    - Henry, slain at St. Quinton.
    - Charles, died young.
    - Mary, *m.* to Sir Henry Sidney, K.G.
    - Catherine, *m.* to Henry, Earl of Huntingdon.
- II. GEORGE, of whom presently.

- I. Elizabeth, *m.* first, to Thomas Isley; secondly, to William Stafford; and thirdly, to Richard Shirley.
- ... Philippa, *m.* to Sir John Gage, K.G.
- Mary, *m.* to Christopher, son and heir of Thomas Kempe.
- ... Fridesweda, *m.* to Sir Matthew Browne, knt.

...ichard wedded, secondly, Joane, sister of Nicho... Lord Vaux, and had by her two sons, viz.

- ... HENRY (Sir), K.G. a person of considerable celebrity, who for his services against the Moors in the reduction of Grenada, received the honour of knighthood from King Ferdinand of Spain, and an augmentation to his paternal coat of arms of "a pomegranate slipped upon a canton," being the ensigns of that regained province. In his own country, Sir Henry had the office of bearer of the royal standard granted to him for life, was created a knight banneret, and constituted master of the horse. He *m.* twice, but died without issue 23 HENRY VIII.
- ... Nicholas.

...ichard's second son,

... GULDEFORD, esq. was of Hemsted, in Kent, ...ept his shrievalty there, 16 HENRY VIII. He *m.* Elizabeth, daughter and heir of Sir Robert Mortimer, of Mortimer's Hall, in Essex, by Isabella his wife, daughter of John Howard, Duke of Norfolk, and had issue,

- JOHN (Sir), his heir.
- Mary, *m.* to Owen West.
- Anne, *m.* first, to Walter Wadland, and secondly, to Richard Lyne, of Sussex.

The son and heir,

SIR JOHN GULDEFORD, knt. of Hemsted, sheriff of Kent 6 EDWARD VI. *m.* first, Barbara, daughter of Thomas, Lord Delawarr, and had by her three sons and four daughters, viz.

- I. THOMAS, his heir.
- II. George.
- III. Henry.

- I. Anne, *m.* to Walter Mayney, esq. of Biddenden.
- II. Eliza, *m.* to William Cromer, esq. of Tunstall.
- III. Mary, *m.* to George Herlackenden, esq. of Woodchurch.
- IV. Dorothy, *m.* to Sir Thomas Walsingham, esq. of Scadbury.

Sir John *m.* secondly, Mary, daughter of William Fitz William, of Northamptonshire, and relict of John Shelley, of Sussex, by whom he had a son, Richard, who died in 1586. Sir John was *s.* by his eldest son,

SIR THOMAS GULDEFORD, knt. of Hemsted, who had the honour of entertaining *Queen* ELIZABETH at his mansion, on her majesty's progress into Kent, 10th August, 1575. He *m.* Elizabeth, daughter of John Shelley, esq. of Michel Grove, and had issue,

- I. HENRY (Sir), his heir.

- I. Mary, *m.* to John, son and heir of Sir Richard Baker, knt. of Sisinghurst.
- II. Elizabeth, *m.* to Thomas Gage, esq. of Firle.
- III. Eleanor.
- IV. Barbara, *m.* to Sir Thomas Heneage, knt. of Lincolnshire.

Sir Thomas was *s.* by his son,

SIR HENRY GULDEFORD, knt. of Hemsted, who *m.* Lady Elizabeth Somerset, daughter of Edward, Earl of Worcester, and had a son,

EDWARD GULDEFORD, esq. of Hemsted, who *m.* Catherine, daughter of the Hon. Thomas Petre, third son of John, first Lord Petre, and had issue,

- EDWARD, his heir.
- Thomas.
- Joseph, living in 1712.

- Elizabeth, *m.* to John Brook, esq. of Maidley, in Shropshire.
- Catherine, *m.* to Thomas Bodenham, esq. of Rotherwas.
- Mary, *m.* to Sir Samuel Tuke.

The eldest son,

EDWARD GULDEFORD, esq. of Hemsted, *m.* Anne, daughter of Sir Robert Throckmorton, bart. of Coughton, and dying in 1678, was *s.* by his son,

I. ROBERT GULDEFORD, esq. of Hemsted, who was created a BARONET 1 JAMES II. He *m.* Clare, daughter and co-heir of Anthony Monson, esq. of Northorp, in Lincolnshire, but left no issue at his decease, when the BARONETCY became EXTINCT. The manor of Hemsted was sold about 1718, to Admiral Sir John Norris, from whose grandson, John Norris, esq. it was purchased, in 1780, by THOMAS HALLET HODGES, esq. high sheriff of Kent in 1786.

Arms—Or, a saltier between four martlets sa. a canton of Granada for augmentation.

HAL

GURNEY, OF LONDON.

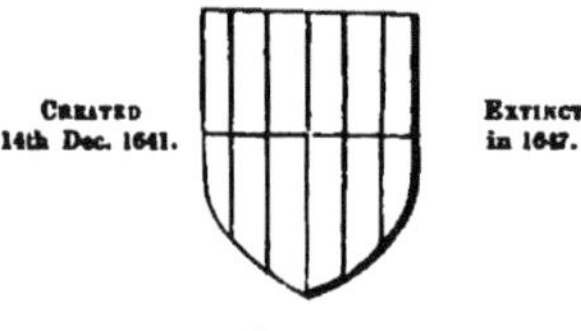

CREATED 14th Dec. 1641. EXTINCT in 1647.

Lineage.

I. SIR RICHARD GURNEY, alias GURNARD, knt. distinguished alike for his courage, loyalty, and sufferings, served the office of lord mayor of London in 1641, and was in that year created a BARONET by *King* CHARLES I.

"The House of Commons," we quote Maitland, "not forgetting the great offence committed against them by Sir Richard Gurney, the lord mayor, in causing his majesty's commission of array to be proclaimed in divers parts of the city, preferred several articles of impeachment against him; for which he was, by the sentence of the peers, not only degraded from the office of mayoralty, but likewise for ever rendered incapable of bearing any office and receiving any further honour, and also to remain a prisoner in the Tower of London during the pleasure of the House of Lords." Sir Richard did not long survive these misfortunes, but died a prisoner in 1647, when the BARONETCY became EXTINCT. He had been twice married, first to Elizabeth, daughter of Henry Sandford, esq. of Birchington, in the Isle of Thanet, and secondly, to Mrs. Elizabeth South, a widow, daughter of Richard Gosson, of London, goldsmith.

HALES, OF WOODCHURCH.

CREATED 29th June, 1611. EXTINCT in Aug. 1669.

Lineage.

The town of HALES, in Norfolk, is presumed to have originated the surname before us. ROGER DE HALYS, in the 19th HENRY II. gave a tenement which he possessed in that place to the Abbey of Baungey; and another ROGER DE HALYS was returned, 18 EDWARD I. by the sheriff of Norfolk, as a knight or freeman, on the jury in a cause between the King, the Bishop of Norwich, and Robert Tateshale.*

By what means the family came into Kent does not appear. Philipot, in his survey of that county, states that their habitation in Halden was called from them, *Hales Place*, "from whence (saith he) as from their fountain, the several streams of the Hales that in divided rivulets have spread themselves over the whole country, did originally break forth."

NICHOLAS DE HALES, of Hales Place, was father of

SIR ROBERT DE HALES, knight, prior of the hospital of Jerusalem, and admiral of the North Seas of England, *temp.* EDWARD III. and constituted treasurer in the 4 RICHARD II. "in which year he had the hard fate in the beginning of the insurrection under Wat Tyler to be dragged from his habitation, and suffer death on Tower Hill, and his house at Hybury, built like another paradise, was utterly destroyed in that popular fury, as the chronicles testifie." His brother and heir,

SIR NICHOLAS DE HALES, knt. was father of

THOMAS DE HALES, of Hales Place, who had three sons, viz.

- JOHN, his heir.
- THOMAS, from whom the Hales of Coventry, in Warwickshire.
- HENRY, whose son, George, was of Ledenham, in Kent, and was father of Edward Hales, of Rumford, in Essex.

The eldest son and heir,

JOHN HALES, of Hales Place, was *s.* by his son,

HENRY HALES, of Hales Place, who *m.* Julian, daughter and heir of Richard Capel, esq. of Lon[illegible] in Tenterden, and had two sons, viz.

- THOMAS, father of SIR CHRISTOPHER HALES, a celebrated lawyer, attorney-general and afterwards master of the Rolls in the reign of HENRY VIII. *m.* Elizabeth, daughter of John Caunton, an alderman of London, and *d.* in 1541, leaving three daughters, his co-heirs,
  - ELIZABETH, *m.* to Sir George Sydenham, [illegible]
  - MARGARET, *m.* first, to — West; secondly, to — Dodman, and thirdly, to William [illegible]den, of Kent.
  - Mary, *m.* first, to — Culpeper, and secondly, to, — Arundel.
- JOHN.

The second son,

JOHN HALES, had a son and heir,

JOHN HALES, who was a BARON OF THE EXCHEQUER, and was seated at Dungeon, near Canterbury, which estate he purchased from Roger Brent, esq. *temp.* HENRY VIII. and was residing there when he visited Kent, in the 30th of that reign. He was acting steward for the Abbey of St. Augustine, at Canterbury, jointly with Sir Henry Guildford, knt. comptroller of the king's house, and afterwards of Thomas Howard, Duke of Norfolk. He *m.* Isabel, daughter and co-heir of Stephen Harris,† and had issue,

1. JAMES (Sir) his heir, like his father, a lawyer of eminence, serjeant-at-law, *temp.* HENRY VIII. and one of the justices of the Common Pleas in the reign of EDWARD VI. Sir James was the only judge who refused to subscribe the king's will for disinheriting the Ladies Mary and Elizabeth, as against both law and conscience; yet in the next reign he was

* This latter Roger is supposed to have been the SIR ROGER DE HALYS, knt. whose daughter, Alice, captivated by her beauty, THOMAS, *of Brotherton*, son of *King* EDWARD I. and becoming his wife, was mother of MARGARET PLANTAGENET, sole heir of her father, who was created DUCHESS OF NORFOLK.

† Hasted calls her Harvey.

committed to prison,* and so severely treated by his keeper, that he made an attempt upon his own life: he was released soon after, but in so settled a melancholy, that he drowned himself near his house in Kent, anno 1555. His wife was the daughter and heir of Thomas Hales, esq. of Henley-upon-Thames, and by her he left issue two sons and a daughter.†

- II. THOMAS, of Thanington, in Kent, from whom the Hales of Beaksbourne.
- III. EDWARD.
- IV. William, of Nackington.
- I. Mildred, m. to John Honywood, esq. of Seen, in Kent.

[illegible] third son of Baron Hales,

EDWARD HALES, esq. of Tenterden, m. Margaret, [illegible]ughter of John Honywood, esq. of Seen, and had [illegible].

- I. John, who m. Mary, daughter and co-heir of Robert Horne, Bishop of Winchester, but d. s. p.
- II. Edward of Chelham, m. first, Mary, daughter and heir of Stephen Ford, of Tenterden, and secondly, Martha, daughter of Thomas Hales, but d. s. p.
- III. WILLIAM, heir to his father and brothers.
- I. Jane, m. to Sir Thomas Honywood, knt. of Elmsted, in Kent.
- II. Elizabeth, m. to William Austen, esq. of Tenterden.

[illegible] third son, and eventual heir of his father and [illegible],

WILLIAM HALES, esq. of Tenterden, m. Elizabeth, [illegible]ghter of Paul Johnson, esq. of Fordwich, in Kent, [illegible] had issue,

EDWARD (Sir), his heir.

Mary, m. to Simon Smith, esq. of Boughton-Monchelsey, in Kent.

Elizabeth, m. to Robert Kenrick, esq. of King's Sutton, in Northamptonshire.

[illegible] s. at his decease by his son,

SIR EDWARD HALES, knt. who m. first, Deborah, [illegible]ghter and heir of Martin Harlackenden, esq. of [illegible], in Kent, by which event he acquired [illegible]siderable estate. Sir Edward was created a BARONET, 29th June, 1611. He served in several parliaments, and being zealously devoted to the liberty of the subject, took part in the rebellion against *King* CHARLES I. He died in September, 1654, aged seventy-eight, and was buried at Tunstall, under a noble monument, with the effigies cut in full proportion. He m. secondly, Martha, daughter of Sir Matthew Carew, knt. and relict of Sir John Cromer, knt. of Tunstall, in Kent, and by this marriage added another fine estate to his family, but by his second wife had no issue: by the first he had

- I. JOHN (Sir), m. Christian, daughter and co-heir of Sir James Cromer, knt. of Tunstal, and dying in the lifetime of his father, left an only child,

  EDWARD, successor to his grandfather.
- II. Edward, of Chelston, in Kent, m. a daughter of John Evelyn, esq. of Deptford, and left a son, Edward.
- III. Samuel, m. Martha Horenden, and had a son and daughter, Christian, m. to J. Hugessen.
- IV. Thomas, d. s. p.

Sir Edward was s. by his grandson,

II. SIR EDWARD HALES, bart. of Woodchurch, who in his younger years, risked life and fortune, in endeavouring to rescue *King* CHARLES I. from his imprisonment in the Isle of Wight, of which enterprise Clarendon gives the following details:—" Mr. L'Estrange [the famous Sir Roger] had a great friendship with a young gentleman, Mr. Hales, who lived in Kent, and was married to a lady of a noble birth and fortune, he being heir to one of the greatest fortunes in that country, but was to expect the inheritance from an old severe grandfather, who, for the present, kept the young couple from running into any excess; the mother of the lady being of as sour and strict a nature as the grandfather, and both of them so much of the parliament party, that they were not willing any part of their estates should be hazarded for the king. At the house of this Mr. Hales, Mr. L'Estrange was, when, by the communication which that part of Kent always hath with the ships which lie in the Downs, the report first did arise, that the fleet would presently declare for the king; and those seamen who came on shore, talked as if the city of London would join with them. This drew

---

* [illegible]YPE, in his *Memorials Ecclesiastical*, says, "[illegible] Hales, knt. of Kent, a pious and good man, [illegible] and able judge, under *King* HENRY and *King* [illegible], was made a prisoner in the King's Bench, by [illegible] of Winchester, Lord Chancellor; and thence [illegible] the Counter, in Bread Street, and from [illegible] the Fleet; here, one Foster, a gentleman of [illegible], laboured to persuade him to embrace the [illegible] doctrine, by his argument; *That the error was* [illegible] *danger, but the truth full of peril.* When it [illegible] that Hales was inclinable to relent, Day, [illegible] Chichester, and Portman, a judge, came to [illegible] being then the month of April, 1554,) and did [illegible] deal with him, that they overcame him at [illegible] his having lain three weeks in that prison of [illegible]. But the trouble that arose in his conscience [illegible] he had done, filled him with great terror, and [illegible] him with sorrow; so that he attempted, in [illegible] of his servant, to kill himself with his pen-[illegible] being ill, and lying sobbing and sighing, [illegible] down his servant upon an errand, and in the [illegible] wounded himself in divers places of his [illegible] his servant came in on the sudden, and at that [illegible] his death. But after his recantation, [illegible] home unto his own country and habita-[illegible] with grief and despair, he drowned him-[illegible] shallow pond near his own house, which is [illegible] this day." —The family of Beaksbourne denied, [illegible] that he so destroyed himself, and said, "That [illegible] retiring to his seat at Thanington, near Canterbury, amused himself with the pleasures of a country life, and crossing the river over a narrow bridge, as he was walking in his meadows, fell in accidentally, and was drowned, aged eighty-five."

† The elder son and heir of SIR JAMES HALES,

HUMPHREY HALES, esq. of the Dungeon, m. the daughter and heir of Robert Atwater, of Royton, near Lenham, and had issue,

JAMES (Sir), his heir.

Humphrey, who was York herald, left two sons,

John, of Lenham, who m. Margaret, daughter of George Took, of Beer, and was father of Anthony and Humphry.

Samuel, m. Elizabeth, daughter of Edward Hammond, esq. of St. Albans Court, Kent.

Abigail, m. to Anthony Sampson, of Notts.

The elder son,

SIR JAMES HALES, knt. of Dungeon, m. Alice, daughter of Sir Thomas Kemp, knt. and one of the heirs of her mother, Cecilia, eldest daughter of Sir Thomas Cheyney, knt. and was s. by his son,

CHEYNEY HALES, esq. of Dungeon, who d. 18th March, 1596, leaving by Mary, his wife, daughter of Richard Hardres, of Hardres (who outlived him, and m. in her widowhood William Ashenden, and again becoming a widow, m. thirdly, George Waller, esq.) a son and heir,

SIR JAMES HALES, knt. of Dungeon, living in 1619.

many gentlemen of the country, who wished well, to visit the ships, and they returned more confirmed of the truth of what they had heard. Good fellowship was a vice spread everywhere; and this young great heir, who had been always bred among his neighbours, affected that which they were best pleased with; and so his house was a rendezvous for those who delighted in the exercise, and who every day brought him the news of the good inclinations of the fleet for the king; and all men's mouths were full of the general hatred the whole kingdom had against the parliament as well as the army. In this posture of affairs, Mr. L'Estrange easily induced Mr. Hales to put himself at the head of his own county, that was willing to be led by him; and his lady, who was full of zeal for the king, joining with him, the young gentleman resolved to do something for his majesty's service, at a juncture when the Scots were ready to march into England, and most parts of the kingdom ready to rise; but being not enough conversant in the affairs of the world, he referred himself and the whole business to be governed by Mr. L'Estrange, who was believed by his discourse to be an able soldier. Accordingly letters were sent to particular gentlemen, and warrants to the constables of hundreds, requiring 'In his majesty's name, all persons to appear at a time and place appointed, to advise together, and lay hold on such opportunities as should be offered for relieving the king, and delivering him out of prison.' And meeting accordingly, they unanimously elected Mr. Hales for their general: a good body of horse and foot was in consequence drawn together at Maidstone, Mr. Hales having taken up, on his own security, nearly EIGHTY THOUSAND POUNDS to defray the expense; and they were so strong, that the commander of the parliament forces, sent to suppress them, wrote word that he durst not advance. On the news of this commotion (the first in the kingdom), the Earl of Norwich was dispatched to Kent, to command as general. Upon the news of another general being sent, Mr. Hales retired, with his friend, Mr. L'Estrange, to Holland, and lived beyond seas, on account of the great debts he had contracted in the king's service."—The lady alluded to in the above narrative, as Sir Edward's wife, was the Hon. Anne Wotton, youngest daughter and co-heir* of Thomas, second Lord Wotton of Marley, by his wife, Mary, daughter and co-heir of Sir Arthur Throckmorton, of Paulers Perry, in Northamptonshire. Sir Edward had issue,

EDWARD, his successor.
John, of the Inner Temple, } all died unm.
Charles,
Thomas,

He died in France, and was *s.* by his eldest son,

III. SIR EDWARD HALES, bart. This gentleman enjoyed the favour of *King* JAMES II. under which prince he had a regiment of foot, was of the privy council, and one of the lords of the Admiralty, deputy governor of the Cinque Ports, and lieutenant-general of the Tower. Sir Edward had an action brought against him by Arthur Godden, his coachman, for the penalty of £500, for neglecting to take the oaths of supremacy and allegiance, within three months after he had his regiment, grounded upon the act of the 25th CHARLES II. and was convicted at Rochester assizes for the same; but moving it into the King's Bench, pleaded the king's dispensing power, and had judgment given for him,† eleven of the judges being of opinion that the king might dispense in that case. At the Revolution he was confined for a year and a half in the Tower: on his release he went to France, and in consideration of his services was created by the abdicated monarch Earl of Tenterden,‡ with remainder[illegible] tations to his brothers, John and Charles. Sir Edward *m.* Frances, daughter of Sir Francis Windebank, knt. of Oxfordshire, and by her, who *d.* in [illegible] had issue,

Edward, who fell at the Boyne, unm.
JOHN, successor to the baronetcy.
Charles, } lived to man's estate, and all *d.* unm.
Robert,
James,

Anne, *d.* unm.
Mary, *m.* to — Bauwens, esq. judge of the Admiralty at Ostend.
Frances, *m.* to Peter, 4th Earl of Fingall.
Jane, } *d.* unmarried.
Elisabeth,
Catherine,
Clare, *m.* to Mr. Hussey, of the kingdom of Ireland.

---

* Lord Wotton died in 1730 (when the barony became extinct), leaving four daughters, his co-heirs, viz.

1. KATHERINE, who *m.* Henry, Lord Stanhope, and was mother of Philip, second Earl of Chesterfield, and secondly, John Poliander Kirkhoven, Lord of Hempfleet, in Holland, by whom she had a son, Charles-Henry Kirkhoven, created BARON WOTTON, *of Wotton.* Her ladyship, after the death of her first husband, was created by CHARLES II. COUNTESS OF CHESTERFIELD, for life.
2. HESTHER, *m.* to Baptist, Viscount Camden.
3. MARGARET, *m.* to Sir John Tufton, knt.
4. ANNE, *m.* to Sir Edward Hales, knt.

† This memorable case was argued by Sir Edward Northey, for the plaintiff, and Sir Thomas Powis, for the defendant; the Lord Chief Justice Herbert delivered the opinions of the twelve judges.

‡ Abstract from the Patent of Creation:

"James the Second, by the grace of God, &c.

"To our Archbishops, Dukes, &c.—Whereas it is a kingly act, and a singular testimony of our benevolence, to enoble those persons we find worthy of our favour, as well that others may see how grateful the faithful duty of our subjects is to Us, as that they themselves may be encouraged to endeavour at great matters. Whereas, therefore, the fidelity of our well beloved and most faithful counsellor, Sir Edward Hales, of Hackington, otherwise St. Stephens, in our county of Kent, have been by various changes abundantly known [illegible] likewise bring to our minds the ancient nobility [illegible] family, as well on the father's as mother's side [illegible] especially the great merit of Robert Hales, [illegible] Lord High Treasurer of our kingdom of England [illegible] the Prior of the Hospital, who upon account of [illegible] prudent advise which he gave to our predecessor [illegible] Richard the Second, had, on a popular sedition [illegible] fury of the mob, his head struck off; and his [illegible] great-grandfather, who in a rebellion, by reason [illegible] fidelity towards the most serene kings, our father [illegible] brother of happy memory; besides what they [illegible] suffered by the loss of liberties and legal [illegible] and his great-grandfather, Sir Edward Hales, of T[illegible] in the county of Kent, baronet, suffered five [illegible] prisonment in the Tower of London; and his father [illegible] Edward Hales, of Tunstal, aforesaid, suffered ban[illegible] and confiscation of goods. His mother sprang from [illegible] ancient Earls of Hereford, and from the sister of St. Edward the Confessor; and finally, the said Sir Edward Hales, by his wise administration of many [illegible] for his fidelity to us and the Catholic church, [illegible] great fortitude suffered by the present rebellion, &c. [illegible]

"His eldest son, Edward, in the mean time, [illegible] by the brightness of his wit, the politeness of [illegible] ners, the greatness of his mind, very dear [illegible] killed in Ireland, at the battle of the Boyne, [illegible] courageously fighting against the enemy, &c. &c.

"Know ye therefore." &c. &c.

He died in France in 1695, was buried in the church of St. Sulpice, in Paris, and *s.* by his eldest surviving son,

II. Sir John Hales, bart. who *m.* first, Helen, daughter of Sir Richard Bealing, of Ireland, secretary to the queen dowager of Charles II. and had issue,

John, who *d.* in infancy.

Edward, who *m.* Mrs. Bulstrode, widow of Captain Bulstrode, and grandaughter of Sir Richard Bulstrode, by whom, dying before his father, he left

Edward, who *s.* his grandfather.

Frances, *m.* to George Henry Lee, second Earl of Lichfield, of that family.

He *m.* secondly, Helen, daughter of Dudley Bagnel, esq. of Newry, and by that lady (who *d.* in 1737) had three sons,

James, an officer in the emperor's service, killed in Italy, in 1735.

Alexander.

Philip.

Sir John *d.* in 1744, and was *s.* by his grandson.

III. Sir Edward Hales, bart. who wedded, first, Barbara-Mabella, daughter and heir of John Webb, esq. elder son of Sir John Webb, bart. of Oldstock, and had by that lady, who *d.* in 1770, surviving issue,

Edward, his heir.

Anne, a nun.

Barbara, *m.* to M. Jouchere, a French officer, and survived his widow.

Mary, *m.* to M. Demorlaincourt, a French officer.

He *m.* secondly, in 1790, Mrs. Palmer, but by her had no issue. Sir Edward *d.* in August, 1802, and was *s.* by his son,

IV. Sir Edward Hales, who *m.* in 1789, Lucy, second daughter of Henry Darell, esq. of Colehill, but dying issueless, 15th March, 1829, the Baronetcy became extinct.

Arms—Gules, three arrows or, feathered and bearded argent.

HALES, OF BEAKSBOURNE.

Created 12th July, 1660.—Extinct 12th April, 1824.

Lineage.

This was a branch from the same stock as the Hales of Woodchurch.

Thomas Hales, one of the barons of the Exchequer, temp. Henry VIII. was seated at Dungeon, near Canterbury, and marrying Isabell, dau. and co-heir of Stephen Harris, left issue,

I. James (Sir), his heir.

II. Thomas, of Thanington.

III. Edward, from whom the Hales of Woodchurch.

IV. William, of Nackington.

I. Mildred, *m.* to John Honywood, esq. of Seen, in Kent.

The second son,

Thomas Hales, esq. of Thanington, *m.* Jane, only daughter and heir of Clement Holloway, esq. and was *s.* by his son,

Sir Charles Hales, knt. of Thanington, who *m.* Anne, dau. of Robert Honywood, esq.* of Charing, in Kent, and was *s.* by his eldest son,

Thomas Hales, esq. who *m.* Anne, daughter of Sir Thomas Payton, bart. of Knowlton, in Kent, and had issue,

Robert, his heir.

Samuel, of New Windsor, Berks, *m.* Frances, daughter of Sir Robert Bennet, knt. of Windsor, and had issue.

Stephen.

Mary, *m.* to Andrew Plumpton, esq. of New Windsor.

He was *s.* by his eldest son,

I. Robert Hales, esq. of Beaksbourne, in Kent, who was created a Baronet by *King* Charles II. 12th July, 1660. Sir Robert *m.* Catherine, daughter and co-heir of Sir William Ashcomb, knt. of Allvescot, in Oxfordshire, and had issue,

I. Thomas, his heir, who *m.* Mary, daughter and heir of Richard Wood, esq. of Abbot's Langley, Herts, and dying in the lifetime of his father, left

1. Thomas, successor to his grandfather.
2. Charles.
3. Robert, one of the clerks of the privy council, *m.* Sarah, daughter and heir of William Andrews, esq. and relict of Colonel Hallett, and had two daughters,

   Sarah, *m.* first, to the Rev. Mr. Johnson, and secondly, to the Rev. Mr. Negus.

   Jessica, *m.* first, to — Clerk, of Swaffham, and secondly, to — Hudson. She *d.* in 1768.

4. William, *m.* Mary, daughter and co-heir of John Gillon, gent. of the Isle of Thanet, and had issue,
5. Stephen, B.D. F.R.S.† vicar of Teddington, Middlesex, and rector of Farrington, Hants, *m.* Mary, daughter and co-heir of Dr. Henry Newce, of Much Hadham, Herts.

1. Mary, *m.* the Hon. Robert Booth, D.D. dean of Bristol, and archdeacon of Durham.‡
2. Anne, *m.* to Samuel Milles, esq. of Herne, in Kent.

---

* The wife of this gentleman, Mary Honywood, had at her decease no less than 367 persons, all living, directly descended from her, viz. 16 children,
114 grand-children.
228 great-grandchildren.
9 great-great-grandchildren.

† Dr. Hales acquired high reputation by his researches and works upon natural and experimental philosophy.

‡ The Dean was youngest son of Sir George Booth, first Baron Delamere, of Dunham Massie, in the county of Chester, in 1661 (see Burke's *Extinct Peerage*). Mrs. Hales was his second wife, and by her he had five sons and three daughters, viz.

1. Robert Booth, who *d.* unm. in 1733.
2. George Booth, in holy orders, *d.* unm. in 1725.
3. Edward Booth, *d.* unm.
4. Nathaniel Booth, succeeded as fourth Lord Delamere, and with him, in 1770, the barony expired.
5. William, *d.* young.

1. Mary Booth, *d.* unm.
2. Elizabeth Booth, *m.* to Charles Thrupple, esq. of the city of London.
3. Vere Booth, *m.* to George Tyndale, esq. of Bathford, in Somersetshire.

His first wife was Anne, daughter of Sir Robert Booth, chief justice of the court of Common Pleas in Ireland, and by her he had a son, Henry, who *d. s. p.* The dean *d.* in 1730, and his widow in 1732.

3. Elizabeth, *m.* to the Rev. John Metcalfe, vicar of Sunbury.

II. William, *m.* Mary, daughter and co-heir of Samuel Bland, esq. of London, one of the gentlemen of the band of pensioners, and had a son,

Robert, *m.* first, Martha, daughter of Mr. Wickham, of Falmouth, merchant, and had by her

Robert, *b.* 28th June, 1712.

Joseph, *b.* 19th July, 1714.

He (Robert, *Sen.*) *m.* secondly, Jane Green, and, by that lady, had another son, Edward, and four daughters, Jane, Anne, Mary, and Elizabeth.

Sir Edward was *s.* at his decease by his grandson,

II. Sir Thomas Hales, bart. M.P. for the county of Kent, *temp. King* William and *Queen* Anne, *m.* Mary, daughter of Sir Charles Pym, bart. of Brymore, in Somersetshire (and sister and sole heir of Sir Charles Pym), and had, with other issue (who *d. s. p.*)

Thomas, his heir.

Mary, *m.* to Sir Brooke Bridges, bart. of Goodneston.

Catherine, *m.* to Edward Cook, esq. of Canterbury.

Anne.

Elizabeth, *m.* first, to Benjamin Lethieuillier, esq. of East Sheen, Surrey, and secondly, to Charles Pyott, esq. of St. Martin's, near Canterbury.

Sir Thomas acquired the estate of Brymore with his wife, and took up his abode there. He *d.* 7th January, 1748, and was *s.* by his son,

III. Sir Thomas Hales, bart. This gentleman was clerk of the board of Green Cloth, and sate in parliament *temp.* George I. and George II. He *m.* Mary, daughter of Sir Robert Marsham, bart. of the Mote, near Maidstone, father of the first Lord Romney, and by her (who *d.* 4th August, 1769), had issue,

I. Thomas-Pym, his heir.

II. Charles, captain 3rd regiment of Foot Guards.

III. Robert.

IV. John.

V. George.

VI. Philip, who succeeded his eldest brother in the baronetcy.

I. Mary, *m.* to the Right Rev. Dr. Charles Moss, Bishop of Bath and Wells.

II. Catherine.

III. Elizabeth.

IV. Anne, *m.* first, to Anthony Duncombe, Lord Feversham (his third wife), and secondly, to William, first Earl of Radnor.

V. Margaretta, *m.* in 1769, to Samuel Pechell, esq. of Richmond, in Surrey, one of the masters in Chancery.

VI. Harriet.

VII. Caroline.

Sir Thomas *d.* 6th October, 1762, and was *s.* by his eldest son,

IV. Sir Thomas-Pym Hales, bart. M.P. for Dover, and afterwards for Downton, Wilts, *m.* Mary, daughter and heir of Gervas Heyward, esq. of Sandwich, in Kent, and relict of George Cousmaker, esq. of Staple, in the same county, and had five daughters, viz.

I. Mary-Anne, *b.* in 1765.

II. Jane, *b.* in 1766, *m.* in July, 1795, to the Rev. Henry Bridges, son of Sir Brook Bridges, bart.

III. Elizabeth, *b.* in 1769, *m.* to John Calcraft, esq. of Remston, in Dorsetshire.

IV. Harriet, *b.* in 1770.

V. Caroline, *b.* in 1772, *m.* in 1796, to Colonel the Hon. John William Gore, second son of Arthur-Saunders, second Earl of Arran, and has issue. (See Burke's *Peerage and Baronetage.*)

Sir Thomas-Pym, *d.* 18th March, 1773, and was *s.* by his only surviving brother,

V. Sir Philip Hales, bart. one of the grooms of his majesty's bedchamber, *m.* in 1795, Elizabeth, daughter and heir of Thomas Smith, esq. of [illegible]worth, Notts, and had a daughter,

Elizabeth Hales.

He *d.* 12th April, 1824, and leaving no male issue, the Baronetcy became extinct.

Arms—As Hales, of Woodchurch.

HALES, OF COVENTRY.

Created 28th Aug. 1660.—Extinct before 1812.

Lineage.

Thomas Hales, second son of Thomas de Hales, of Hales Place (see Hales of Woodchurch, *Extinct Baronets*), was father of

James Hales, whose son,

John Hales, had a son and heir,

Thomas Hales, alderman of Canterbury, who *m.* a daughter of Trefie of Cornwall, and had four sons, viz.

I. Christopher, his heir.

II. John,* clerk of the hanaper *temp.* Henry VIII. Dugdale, in his *Antiquities of Warwickshire*, mentions that "St. John's Hospital in Coventry was, by letters patent dated 23rd July, 37 Henry VIII. with all the lands and possessions thereunto belonging, granted un[illegible]

* Of this eminent man Anthony Wood thus speaks: "He was commonly called Club-foot Hales, because in his younger days he had got that deformity by a wound from his own dagger at the bottom of his foot. This person being very much addicted to letters from his childhood, was sent to the university, and having a happy memory, accompanied with incredible industry, became admirably well skilled in the Latin, Greek, and Hebrew tongues, and at length in the municipal laws and in antiquities, which made him admired by all ingenious men of his time. In the reign of Henry VIII. he was clerk of the hamper (hannaper) for several years, and obtained a fair estate in Warwickshire and elsewhere upon the dissolution of monasteries and chauntries; founded a free-school at Coventry, and for the use of the youth to be taught there, did write *Introductiones ad Grammaticam*, partly in English and partly in Latin. He wrote also *Highway to Nobility*; and translated into English *Precepts for the Preservation of Health.* When Queen Mary came to the crown, he fled beyond sea as voluntary exile, and settling at Frankfort, in Germany, we find him a zealous man for the uniting of the exiles there in [illegible]. When Queen Elizabeth succeeded he returned, and the first thing that made him then to be noted was an oration to Queen Elizabeth at her first entrance to her reign, [illegible] was not spoken, but delivered in writing to her by a nobleman. He also wrote a little book in favour of the house of Suffolk, especially of the children of Edward Seymour, Earl of Hertford, eldest son of Edward, Duke of Somerset, who was married to the Lady Katherine Grey, daughter of Henry, Duke of Suffolk (of near alliance in blood to the queen), the effect of which was to derive the title of the crown of England, in case Queen Elizabeth should die without issue, to the house of Suffolk. This marriage, notwithstanding the Archbishop of Canterbury did by his sentence pronounce unlawful [illegible]

John Hales, gent. and his heirs; which John, being an active man in those days, and clerk of the hamper (an office then of no small benefit), and having accumulated a great estate in monastery and chantry lands, resolved to erect a lasting monument to his memory (for he had neither child nor wife), and thereupon designing the foundation of a free-school here, and that the king should have the honour thereof (for which respect he had no little favour in his purchases as I have credibly heard), obtained license for the amortizing of lands thereto of CC marks p. ann. value. This John Hales bought also the Whitefryers, in Coventry, of Sir Ralph Sadler, knt. He *d.* 5th Cal. January, 1572; and by will appointed Hales Place, alias Whitefryers, in Coventry, to be sold. He was buried in the church of St. Peter's the Poor, in Broad Street, London, as his epitaph, on a fair ancient plate in the wall, in Stow's Survey imports. But notwithstanding the before-specified appointment, the estate was not sold, for John Hales, esq. descended from Christopher, his eldest brother, enjoyed it."

II. Bartholomew, of Snitterfield, *m.* Mary, daughter and heir of George Harpur, esq. and was father of

Sir Bartholomew Hales, knt. of Snitterfield, who *m.* Katherine, daughter of Sir Thomas Griesley, of Drakelow, in the county of Derby, relict of Francis Dethick, esq. of Newhall (she married for her third husband, Henry Gibbs, esq.) and by that lady had an only daughter, Elizabeth, who died before her father. He *d.* in 1619.

IV. Stephen, of Newland, in the county of Warwick, *m.* Anne, daughter of Richard Morrison, of Bucks, and was father of

Sir Charles Hales, knt. of Newland, one of the king's council at York, who *d.* 2nd February, 1618, leaving issue by Elizabeth, daughter of Walter Fish, of London,

Stephen Hales, heir to his cousin, Sir Bartholomew, *m.* Abigail, daughter of William Walter, esq. of Wimbledon, in Surrey, and had a son,

Sir Stephen Hales, K. B. who *d. s. p.* in 1668, and was buried at Snitterfield, in Warwickshire.

... first son and heir (of Alderman Hales), ... Stephen Hales, esq. was *s.* by his son, ... Hales, esq. of Whitefriers, in Coventry, who ... heir to his uncle John Hales, clerk of the hanaper, inherited his large estates. His son and heir,

Christopher Hales, esq. of Whitefriers, had three sons; the second was a Turkey merchant in London, the third was of Lincoln, and the eldest,

I. John Hales, esq. of Coventry, having succeeded his father, was created a Baronet by *King* Charles II. 28th August, 1660. Sir John *m.* Anne, daughter of Mr. Alderman Johnson, of London, and had issue,

Christopher, his heir.
Edward, successor to his brother.

Dorothy, *m.* to Michael Rutter, esq. of Burton-on-the-Hill, in the county of Gloucester.
———, *m.* to Mr. Eyre, of Lincoln.

He *d.* in 1677, and was *s.* by his elder son,

II. Sir Christopher Hales, M.P. for Coventry *temp. King* William and *Queen* Anne. He died unmarried 19th January, 1717, and was *s.* by his brother,

III. Sir Edward Hales. This gentleman, after the death of his brother, procured an act of parliament for the sale of the estate of the Whitefriers in Coventry to discharge Sir Christopher's debts. It was purchased by John, Duke of Montagu, who conveyed it in 1722 to Samuel Hill, esq. of Shenston Park, in Staffordshire; the mansion-house was sold to two tradesmen in Coventry. Sir Edward *m.* Elizabeth, daughter of — Thorpe, esq. of St. Martin's-in-the-Fields, Middlesex, and died 7th September, 1720, leaving issue,

Christopher, his heir.
Edward, *m.* in January, 1735-6, Susannah, daughter of Charles Bertie, esq. of Uffington, in the county of Lincoln.
John.
Anne.*
Catherine.*
Elizabeth.*

He was *s.* by his eldest son,

IV. Sir Christopher Hales, who *m.* in September, 1736, Harrison, daughter of Benjamin Columbine, esq. of Moreley, in the county of Antrim, in Ireland, and had a son and heir, John, and a daughter, Elizabeth. He died at Hammersmith 8th May, 1776, and was *s.* by his son,

V. Sir John Hales, who *m.* Anne, daughter and heir of John Scott, esq. of North End, and had three sons and five daughters. He died 15th March, 1802, and was *s.* by his son,

VI. Sir John-Scott Hales, of the 90th regiment, who died at Lisbon 22nd February, 1803, and was *s.* by his brother,

VII. Sir Samuel Hales, who also died unmarried 2nd January, 1805, and was *s.* by his brother,

VIII. Sir Christopher Hales, who *d. s. p.* before 1812, when the Baronetcy was extinct.

Arms—Gu. three arrows or, feathered arg.

... Hales, who was esteemed a man very opinionate, though otherwise very learned, did maintain in the ... that *their sole consent did legitimate their con-*... Which pamphlet flying abroad, came straight ... the court; whereupon the queen and the nobles ... offended, the author was quickly discovered ... imprisoned in the Tower of London. Soon ... Nicholas Bacon, then lord keeper, was presumed ... a finger in it, for which he had like to have ... office, if Sir Anthony Browne, who had been ... justice of the Common Pleas in Queen Mary's ... have accepted of it, which her majesty of... him, and the Earl of Leicester earnestly exhorted ... take it, but he refused it, for that he was of a dif... religion from the state: and so Sir Nicholas ... remained in his place, at the great instance of Sir ... Cecil (afterwards lord treasurer), who though ... be privy to the said book, yet was the matter so wisely laid upon Hales and Bacon, that Sir William was kept free, and thereby had more authority and grace to procure the others pardon, as he did. Soon after, John Lesley, Bishop of Ross, a great creature of Mary, Queen of Scots, did answer that book, for which he got the good-will of many, of others not. As for our author Hales, he gave way to fate on the 5th of the Kalends of January, in fifteen hundred, seventy and two. He died without issue, so that his estate, which chiefly lay in Warwickshire, of which his principal house in Coventry, called Hales Place, otherwise the White-fryers, was part, went to John, son of his brother Christopher Hales (some time also an exile at Frankfort), whose posterity doth remain there."

* One of these ladies became the wife of Mr. Taylor, of London, but which is not known.

HALFORD, OF WISTOW.

CREATED 18th Dec. 1641.

EXTINCT 21st July, 1780.

Lineage.

RICHARD HALFORD, esq. of Clipstone, in Northamptonshire, was father of

EDWARD HALFORD, esq. of Langham, in the county of Rutland, and Welham, in the county of Leicester, who *m.* Dionesia, daughter of — Bury, esq. of Rutland, and was *s.* by his son,

I. RICHARD HALFORD,* esq. of Wistow, in Leicestershire, high sheriff of that county 19 JAMES I. who was created a BARONET 18th December, 1641. Sir Richard *m.* first, Isabella, daughter of George Bowman, esq. of Medbourne, in the same county, and had two sons and two daughters, viz.

I. ANDREW, his heir, of Kilby. This gentleman married thrice, and had by his first wife,†

THOMAS, successor to his grandfather.
Richard, } *d.* unm.
Andrew, }
Elizabeth.
Joan, *m.* to Andrew Freeman.
Mary.

Mr. Halford (as well as his father) was a devoted adherent of CHARLES I. in the civil war, and raised and maintained for the service of his majesty a body of men at his own charge in the county of Leicester; with those, amongst other duties, he made a party of rebels prisoner, amongst whom was one Flude, high constable of Guthlaxton hundred, and carried them to the king's camp, where they were all tried and hanged. He was afterwards himself condemned by the Protector for the murder of these men, and his life cost him no less a sum than thirty thousand pounds. He died in the lifetime of his father, 1657, aged fifty-four, and was buried at Wistow.

II. George, of Turlangton, in Leicestershire, *d. s. p.*

I. Joan, *m.* first, to — Bowman; and secondly, to Francis St. John.

II. Mary, *m.* to Samuel Luddington, esq.

Sir Richard was so remarkable for his loyalty to the king, that his majesty made Wistow the place of his retirement when in Leicestershire, where the baronet not only hospitably entertained his royal guest, but supplied him with large sums of money. Sir Richard was several times plundered, and at last compounded for his estate for £2000. He *d.* in 1658, aged seventy-eight, and was *s.* by his grandson,

II. SIR THOMAS HALFORD, bart. who *m.* Selina, eldest daughter of William Welby, esq. of Denton, in the county of Lincoln, and had a numerous family. He died in 1619, and was *s.* by his eldest son,

HAL

III. SIR THOMAS HALFORD, bart. M.P. for the county of Leicester *temp.* CHARLES II. who died unmarried in 1689, and was *s.* by his brother,

IV. SIR WILLIAM HALFORD, bart. who *m.* Judith, daughter of Thomas Boothby, esq. of Tooley Park, in the county of Leicester, but died without issue in 1695, was buried at Wistow, and *s.* by his brother,

V. SIR RICHARD HALFORD, bart. in holy orders, who *m.* Mary, daughter of the Rev. William Cotton, rector of Broughton-Asley, in the county of Leicester, and had issue,

WILLIAM, his successor.
Thomas, *m.* Elizabeth, daughter of Thomas Palmer, esq. of Leicester, and had four sons, the youngest of whom,
CHARLES, succeeded as seventh baronet.
Charles, fellow of New College, Oxford.
Welby, *d.* unm.
Benjamin.
Mary, *d.* in 1742.
Rebecca, *d.* in 1728.
ELIZABETH, who *m.* John Smalley, esq. alderman of Leicester, and their daughter,
HESTER SMALLEY, marrying James Vaughan, M.D. had issue,
HENRY VAUGHAN, who succeeding to the Halford estates, assumed that surname and is the present SIR HENRY HALFORD, bart.
JOHN VAUGHAN (Sir), knt. one of the barons of the Exchequer.
PETER VAUGHAN, D.D. dean of Chester, *d.* in 1826.
CHARLES VAUGHAN (Sir), knt. envoy extraordinary to the United States.
EDWARD VAUGHAN.
Almenia-Selina Vaughan.

Sir William enlarged the possessions of the family by purchasing the manor of Kebworth-Harcourt. He *d.* in 1727, was buried at Wistow, and *s.* by his eldest son,

VI. SIR WILLIAM HALFORD, bart. who preferred a claim to the office of great pannater at the coronation of GEORGE II. He died unmarried in 1768, and was *s.* by his nephew,

VII. SIR CHARLES HALFORD, bart. who *m.* Sarah, daughter of Edward Farnham, esq. of Quenby House, in the county of Leicester, but dying *s. p.* 21st July, 1780, the BARONETCY became EXTINCT. The estates Sir Charles bequeathed, after the demise of his widow, Sarah, Lady Halford (who *m.* in July, 1783, Basil, sixth Earl of Denbigh), to his cousin, HENRY VAUGHAN, M.D. who was created a BARONET 27th September, 1809, and assuming the surname of HALFORD at the decease of the lady above-mentioned, which event occurred 2nd October, 1814, is now (1837) Sir HENRY HALFORD, bart. (See BURKE's *Peerage and Baronetage.*)

Arms—Arg. a greyhound passant sa. on a chief az. three fleurs-de-lis or.

HALFORD, OF WELHAM.

CREATED 27th June, 1706.—EXTINCT .....

Lineage.

The representative of the ancient family of HALFORD of Welham, Leicestershire,

* From a son or brother of Sir Richard Halford, the first baronet of Wistow, the present RICHARD HALFORD, esq. of Paddock House, near Canterbury, claims to be descended.

† His second wife was Mary, daughter and co-heir of Humphrey Hasket, esq. of Creeton, in the county of Lincoln; and the third, Mary, daughter and co-heir of William Nichols, esq. of Halsted, Essex, and widow of Richard Orton, esq. of Lea Grange.

I. Sir William Halford, knt. b. in 1663 (son and heir of Sir William Halford, knt. by Elizabeth, his wife, daughter of Sir John Pretyman, bart. and grandson of William Halford, esq. by Mary, his wife, daughter of Sir Henry Atkyns, knt. of Clapham), was created a Baronet in 1706. He m. Lady Frances Cecil, daughter of James, third Earl of Salisbury, and dying in March, 1708-9, was s. by his son,

II. Sir James Halford, of Welham, living in 1712, with whom the Baronetcy is supposed to have expired. The estate of Welham eventually became by purchase the property of Francis Edwards, esq.

Arms—As Halford of Wistow.

HALTON, OF SAMFORD.

Created 10th Sept. 1642.

Extinct 9th Feb. 1823.

Lineage.

John Halton, of Swansea, a gentleman of Cambridgeshire, was living in the 12th Henry VI. 1433. His descendant (presumed only),

Robert Halton, esq. serjeant-at-law, married Joan, daughter and heir of John Drayner, of Hoxton, and had issue,

- I. Roger, his heir.
- II. William (Sir), of the Middle Temple, and of Great Abington, Cambridgeshire, knt. who d. unmarried, and was buried in Great Abington Church.*
- III. Robert.
- I. Frances, m. to Thomas Massingberd, esq. of Braytoft, and had, with other issue,
  - Henry Massingberd, esq. of Gunby.
  - Sir Drayner Massingberd, ancestor of the Massingberds of South Ormsby. (See Burke's *Commoners*, vol. i. and iii.)

The third son,

Robert Halton, esq. who was of Sabridgeworth, in Hertfordshire, m. first, Heather, daughter of William Booth, esq. and had five sons, Roger, Thomas, William, Robert, and John. His second wife was Mrs. [illegible], a widow, but by her had no issue. The third son,

I. William Halton, esq, executor and heir of his uncle Sir William, purchased the estate of Little Samford Hall, in Essex, from Sir William Green, bart. and paid his ingress fine 16 Charles I. He was created a Baronet 10th September, 1642. Sir William m. first, Mary, daughter of Sir Edward Altham, knt. of Marks Hall, in the county of Essex, and by her (who d. 29th December, 1644, aged twenty-six,) had

William, his heir.

Mary, died unmarried.

He m. secondly, Ursula, daughter of Sir Thomas Fisher, bart. of Islington, and by that lady (who m. secondly, Matthew Meriton, esq. of London, merchant) had two sons,

- Thomas, of whom hereafter.
- Richard, m. Mary, daughter of George Johnson, gent. and dying in 1703, left (with two daughters, Ursula and Susan,) a son,
  - George, who m. Hannah, eldest daughter of Mr. Fenwick Lambert, of London, and dying 7th May, 1729, was buried in London. He left three sons,
    - Thomas, who s. as fifth baronet.
    - William, } d. unm.
    - George, } d. unm.

Sir William died about the year 1662, and was s. by his eldest son,

II. Sir William Halton, bart. who dying unmarried 4th March, 1675, was buried at Latton, in Essex, and s. by his half-brother,

III. Sir Thomas Halton, bart. who m. Elizabeth, daughter of John Cressener, esq. of London, by whom (who d. 26th August, 1716,) he had several children; of which all died unmarried except

William, his heir.

Mary, m. to James Nicholl, esq. of the Court Lodge, in Sussex. She d. 29th May, 1739, and was buried at Munfeild.

Sir Thomas died 6th September, 1726, was buried at Islington, and s. by his son,

IV. Sir William Halton, bart. who m. Frances, daughter of Sir George Dalston, knt. eldest son and heir of Sir George Dalston, knt. of Heath Hall, in the county of York, (she was widow of John Jermy, esq. of Starton Hall, in Suffolk,) but dying s. p. 12th February, 1754, the Baronetcy reverted to his cousin (refer to Richard, youngest son of the first baronet),

V. Sir Thomas Halton, bart. who m. Mary Burton, of London, and dying in 1766, was s. by his son,

VI. Sir William Halton, bart. This gentleman m. Mary, daughter of Michael Garner, esq. of King's Ripon, Huntingdonshire, but died without male issue 9th February, 1823, when the Baronetcy became extinct. His only daughter,

Mary, m. John Haughton James, esq. of Haughton Hall, in the Island of Jamaica, and had a numerous family, of which the eldest son, Philip Haughton James, esq. is now representative of the Haltons.

Arms—Party per pale az. and gu. a lion rampant arg.

HAMILTON, OF LONDON.

Created 11th May, 1642.—Extinct before 1726.

Lineage.

In 1642 a Baronetcy was conferred on

I. John Hamilton, esq. of London, but of him or his descendants we have no information: the title did not exist in 1726.

---

* There is a monument in the north chancel wall, whereon is a cumbent statue in armour, and a lion at his feet, with this inscription:

> Here under this Monument lyeth interred the
> body of Sir William Halton, Knight, who in
> Faith and much patience changed this life for
> a better, upon the 20th of November, in the year
> of our Lord 1639, being near upon the age of 70 years.

HANMER, OF HANMER.

CREATED 8th July, 1620.  EXTINCT, 5th May, 1746.

Lineage.

This family, genealogists deduced from a person of great power, and of knightly degree, namely,

SIR THOMAS MACKFEL, whose son,

SIR JOHN MACKFEL, assumed the surname of HANMER in the time of Edward I. from the town of Hanmer, in the county of Flint, where he resided, and which constituted part of his great possessions. He was constable of Carnarvon castle in the same reign, and is said to have married Hawes, daughter and heir of Enion ap Griffith, ap Gwinwinwin, Lord of Powis, a descendant from Bleddwyn ap Kynwyn, Prince of Wales. By this lady he had three sons, OWEN, surnamed Goch, from his being *red*, who succeeded to the lordship of Hanmer in 2nd EDWARD II., and dying issueless, divided his lands between his brothers, David and Philip. The latter at length becoming sole heir, was

PHILIP HANMER, of Hanmer. He m. Agnes, daughter and heir of David ap Rice, ap Evans, ap Jones, and had issue,

- DAVID, his heir.
- James.
- Margaret, m. to Morgan Goch ap Griffith.
- Mirannoy, m. to Gruffe ap Howell, de Overton.

The elder son and heir,

SIR DAVID HANMER, knt. of Hanmer, being a person learned in the laws, was constituted, for his fidelity to the English nation, one of the justices of the King's Bench, 20th February, 1383, 6th RICHARD II., when he had the honour of knighthood conferred upon him. Sir David m. Angharad, daughter of Lhyvelin Dhu ap Griffith, ap Jorworth Voell, and had issue,

- GRIFFITH, who m. Gwervill, daughter of Tudor ap Grono, of Anglesey, and left an only daughter,
  - ANGHARAD, m. to John Puleston, esq. of Emral.
- JENKIN or JOHN.
- Margaret, m. the famous OWEN, surnamed GLYNDOWER, and had several sons and daughters.

The second son,

SIR JENKIN or JOHN HANMER, or HANNEMERE (as the name was then written), m. first, Margaret, daughter and heir of David, son and heir of Blethwyn Vychan, of Ockenholt, lineally descended from Edwyn, Lord of Tregangle, alias Englefield. By this lady he acquired lands, and a mansion house called Llwyn Derwn, in Tregangle, and had a son, GRIFFITH. He m. secondly, Eve, daughter of David ap Grono, ap Jorwith, by whom he had three other sons, viz.

- John, of Halton, whose grandson,
  - Sir Edward Hanmer, m. Margaret, daughter of Sir Thomas Salisbury, knt. but died without issue, when his sister,
  - Jane Hanmer, became his heir. She m. Sir Roger Puleston, knt. of Emral.
- EDWARD, of the Fens, in the county of Flint, from whom lineally descends the present SIR JOHN HANMER, bart. of Hanmer.
- Richard, of Bettisfield, from whom the Hanmers of Bettisfield and Burbridge descended.

This Sir Jenkin or John Hanmer was slain in the battle of Shrewsbury, in the time of Henry IV. He had previously divided his property between his sons GRIFFITH, and EDWARD of the Fens. The elder,

GRIFFITH HANMER, of Hanmer, m. Eleanor, daughter of Sir Peers Dutton, knt. and had issue,

- RICHARD, his heir.
- Elizabeth, m. to Ellis Eyton, of Eyton.
- Alice, m. to David Lloyd.
- Margaret, m. to David Eyton.
- Janet, m. to William ap Rys, of Togingle.
- Maud, m. to Lewes Yalle.

He was *s.* by his son,

RICHARD HANMER, esq. of Hanmer, who m. Margaret, daughter of Sir Roger Kynaston, knt. of Hordley, in the county of Salop, and had five sons. Thomas, his heir, John, Christopher, David, and Humphrey, and three daughters, viz.

- Ermine, m. to Sir Edward Puleston, knt.
- Dorothy, m. to Edward Brereton, esq. of Borasham.
- Eleanor, m. to Richard Wicherley, esq. of Wicherley.

His eldest son and heir,*

SIR THOMAS HANMER, of Hanmer, received the honour of knighthood at Bullogne from HENRY VIII. and departed this life 10th February, 1543. He m. Jane, daughter of Sir Randolph Brereton, knt. of Malpas, and had five sons, THOMAS (Sir), his heir, Randle, John, Richard, and Humphrey, with as many daughters, viz.

- Eleanor, m. to William Hanmer, esq. of the Fens, who by his last testament, bearing date [illegible] January, 1570, the probat whereof is on the [illegible] April following, bequeaths his body to be buried in the chancel on the north side of the church of Hanmer.
- Elizabeth, m. to John Conway, esq.
- Margaret, m. to David Bird, esq.
- Catherine, m. to Peter Puleston, esq.
- Mary, m. to Roger Kynaston, esq.

He was *s.* by his eldest son,

SIR THOMAS HANMER, who was made a knight by the king's royal mandate, 22nd February, 1st EDWARD VI. He m. Catherine, daughter and heir of Dav[illegible] son of Thomas Salter, esq. of Oswestre, in the county of Salop, and had, with a daughter, Margaret, m. first, to Roger Puleston, esq. of Emral, and, secondly, to John Puleston, esq. of Lleway Knottey, four sons, John, Thomas, William, and Randle, whereof the eldest,

JOHN HANMER, esq. of Hanmer, was M.P. for the borough of Flint in the 13th ELIZABETH. He m. Jane, daughter of Sir John Salusbury, knt. of Llewenny, in the county of Denbigh, and was *s.* by his eldest son,

SIR THOMAS HANMER, knt. of Hanmer, who attended the Earl of Denbigh into France, in the 27th of ELIZABETH, when the nobleman was deputed by her majesty to invest HENRY III. with the Garter. He was afterwards, 35th ELIZABETH, elected knight to serve

---

* Cousin-german to this Richard was Sir Edward Hanmer, knighted in Scotland in the reign of HENRY VII for his valiant behaviour in the army, under the command of the Earl of Surrey.

in parliament for the county of Flint, and when *King* James ascended the throne, he was honored with knighthood at Whitehall, 23rd July, 1603, previous to the king's coronation. In the 15th of that reign he was appointed, among others, of the council to William, Lord Compton, president of the marches of Wales, and departed this life 16th April, 1619. He *m.* first, Lady Anne Talbot, daughter of John, Earl of Shrewsbury, by whom he had an only daughter, Catherine, who *d.* an infant. Sir Thomas *m.* secondly, Catherine, daughter of Sir Thomas Mostyn, knt. and by that lady had

- John, his heir.
- Thomas, who *m.* the widow of — Charlton, esq. of Apley, and *d. s. p.*
- Roger.
- Anne, *m.* to Humphrey Dymoke, esq. of Willington.
- Ursula, *d.* unm.
- Margaret, *m.* to Roger Ellis, esq. of Alrey, in the county of Flint.

Sir Thomas was *s.* by his eldest son,

I. John Hanmer, esq. of Hanmer, who was created a Baronet by *King* James I. 8th July, 1620, and was elected knight of the shire for Flint in the three years afterwards. Sir John *m.* Dorothy, daughter and coheir of Sir Richard Trevor, knt. of Trewallyn, in the county of Denbigh, and had issue,

- Thomas, his successor.
- John, captain in the army, slain in action, and *d. s. p.*
- David, *d. s. p.*
- Mary, *m.* to Sir Edward Lister, knt. of Rowton, in Shropshire.
- Catherine, *m.* to Edward Kynaston, esq. of Ottley, in the same county.

Sir John, who was generally esteemed, died much lamented in the flower of his age, *anno* 1624, and was *s.* by his eldest son,

II. Sir Thomas Hanmer, bart. who *m.* first, Elizabeth,* daughter of Sir Thomas Baker, and sister and heir of Thomas Baker, esq. of Whittingham, in Suffolk. By this lady he had a son and daughter, viz.

- John, his successor.
- Trevor, *m.* to Sir John Warner, knt. of Parham, in Suffolk.

Sir Thomas *m.* secondly, Susan, dau. of Sir William Hervey, knt. of Ickworth, also in Suffolk,† and aunt of John Hervey, first Earl of Bristol, by her he had

- William, who *m.* Peregrine, daughter of Sir Henry North, bart. and sister and co-heir of Sir Henry North, bart. of Mildenhall in Suffolk, to whom he (Sir Henry) gave his whole estate. By this lady Mr. William Hammer had an only son,
  - Thomas, who succeeded as fourth Baronet.
- Thomas (Sir), barrister-at law, knighted by *King* Charles II. and made solicitor to *Queen* Catherine, *d.* young and unm.
- Susanna, *m.* to Sir Henry Bunbury, bart. of Stanny Hall, in the county of Chester, and had, with other issue,
  - Sir Charles Bunbury, } fourth and fifth ba-
  - Sir William Bunbury, } ronets of Stanny.

  The latter inherited the estate of Mildenhall on the decrease of his cousin Sir Thomas Hammer in 1746.

——, *m.* to Robert Booth, esq. of Chester, and *d. s. p.*

Sir Thomas, who represented the county of Flint in parliament, died in that honorable station in 1678, and was *s.* by his eldest son,

III. Sir John Hanmer, bart. a major general in the army, M. P. for the county of Flint *temp.* Charles II., and for the town of Flint in the reigns of James II. and William III. He *m.* Mary, daughter and heir of Joseph Alston, esq. of Netherhall, in Suffolk, but had no issue. Sir John, who served with great honour as commander of a regiment on the side of William, at the battle of the Boyne, died in the year 1701, and was *s.* by his nephew (of the half blood),

IV. Sir Thomas Hanmer, bart. *b.* in 1676. This gentleman was returned to parliament, at the accession of *Queen* Anne, for the county of Flint; elected, in 1707, by the county of Suffolk, and placed in the speaker's chair in 1712. In reference to that event is the following couplet of Dr. Johnson:

> Illustrious age! how bright thy glories shone,
> When Hanmer fill'd the chair, and Anne the throne.

Sir Thomas was distinguished in the literary as the political world, and a splendid edition of Shakspeare's plays, published by the university of Oxford, to which he presented the MS., testify to his refined judgment and critical acumen. He *m.* first, in 1698, Isabella, Dowager Duchess of Grafton, widow of Henry, first Duke of Grafton, only daughter and heir of Henry Bennet, Earl of Arlington; and, secondly, Elizabeth, only daughter and heir of Thomas Folkes, esq. of Barton, in Suffolk, but had no issue. Sir Thomas *d.* 5th May, 1746, when the Baronetcy became extinct. The estate of Mildenhall, in Suffolk, devolved upon his cousin and heir-at-law, Sir William Bunbury, bart. and the estate of Hanmer passed to the heir male, and is now possessed by Sir John Hanmer, bart.

Arms—Arg. two lions passant guardant az. armed and langued gu.

HARBY, OF ALDENHAM.

Created 17th July, 1660. Extinct in July, 1674.

Lineage.

William Harby, gent. of Ashby, in Northamptonshire, son of Nicholas Harby, of the county of Cambridge, married Emma, daughter of William Wilmore, of Ashby, and had issue,

- I. Thomas, his heir.
- II. William.
- III. John, of London, merchant, *m.* first, Anne, daughter of Richard Downes, of London, and secondly, Ann, daughter of Sir Richard Saltonstall.
- IV. Erasmus.

* One of the maids of honour to Anne, queen consort of Charles I.
† By Susan, daughter of Sir Robert Jermyn, knt. of Rushbrook, in Suffolk.

v. Edward.

i. Isabel, m. to William Atkyns, esq. of Thydmyngton, in Worcestershire.

ii. Margaret.

The eldest son,

Thomas Harby, esq. of Adston, or Aveston, in Northamptonshire, married, first, Alice, daughter of John Fox, gent. of Bearford, in Oxfordshire; secondly, Margaret Malyn, of London, widow of John Marsh, gent. of London, and thirdly, Katharine, daughter of Clement Throckmorton, esq. of Hasely, in Warwickshire, third son of Sir George Throckmorton, knt. of Coughton. By his last wife, Thomas Harby had issue,

Francis, of Adston, who m. Elizabeth, daughter of John D'Oyley, esq. of Chiselhampton, and died in July, 1607.

Clement, of London, m. first, Sarah, daughter and co-heir of Ferdinando Poynts, esq.; and secondly, a daughter of Robert Barker, printer to the king, and had issue.

Job, of whom presently.

Emma, m. to Robert Charlton, merchant, of London, and d. 24th June, 1622.

Katharine, m. to Daniel Oxenbridge, M.D.

Anne, m. to Jeremiah Dole, of Over Dunsborne, in Gloucestershire.

Mary, m. to John Sherborow, of London.

Susan.

The third son,

i. Sir Job Harby, knt. of London, merchant, one of the commissioners of the customs, purchased the manor and estate of Aldenham, in Hertfordshire, from Lucius Cary, Viscount Falkland, in 1642, and was created a Baronet in 1660. He m. Elizabeth, daughter of Sir Richard Wiche, of London, and had issue,

Erasmus, his heir.

Elizabeth, m. in 1638, to Sir Edmund Hoskins, of East Grinsted, in Surrey, sergeant-at-law.

Anne, d. 1669.

Rebecca.

Susan, m. to Roger Pocock, of London, merchant.

Sir Job died in 1663, and was s. by his son,

ii. Sir Erasmus Harby, of Aldenham, who m. Lady Frances Fane, daughter of Mildmay, second Earl of Westmoreland, but left no issue at his decease in 1674, when the title became extinct. The manor and estate of Aldenham Sir Erasmus sold to Denzil Holles, Lord Holles, of Ifield.

Arms—Gu. a fesse dancettée erm. between ten billets arg.

HARDRES, OF HARDRES.

Created 3rd June, 1642. Extinct 31st Aug. 1764.

Lineage.

This ancient family came from Ardres in Picardy, although it is uncertain whether their advent was before or after the Norman conquest.

"The manor of Hardres, in Kent (saith Philpot) had long had owners of its own name. We read of them in Doomsday Book, where 'tis said Robertus de Hardres held half a plow land in Lissinge, 20 Wil. I. He was ancestor of Philip de Hardres, who was one of the Recognitores Magnæ Assisæ, in King John's reign; his son, of the same name, was a man of great eminency under King Henry III., and married Grace, daughter and heir of Stephen de Herengod, who settled on him the manor of Elmstede, and other lands.

Dart, in his Antiquities of Canterbury, speaking of the same family, says, "They have been of ancient continuance in this county ever since the Conquest, at which time Robert de Hardres held lands at Hardres; a descendant was a great benefactor to the convent at Canterbury. Philip de Hardres was a person of note in King John's reign. William de Ardres was member of parliament for Canterbury 1, 2, and 7 Edward II., as was his father under Henry III. Edmund and Thomas Hardres are in the list of gentry of the county, *temp.* Henry VI."

Sir Robert Hardres, knt. (son and heir of Philip who lived in the time of Henry III.), was living *temp.* Edward I. He m. Margaret, dau. of Sir Richard Estangrove, knt. of Kent, and was s. by his son,

Sir Robert Hardres, knt. who m. Jane, daughter of Thomas Boughton, esq. of Kent, and left a son and heir,

Henry Hardres, whose son and heir, by Joan, daughter of John Stephens, esq.

Philip Hardres, esq. m. Grace, daughter and co-heir of Stephen Heringwood, esq. and was s. by his son,

George Hardres, esq. living in 1485, who m. the daughter and coheir of William Lucy, esq. and had a son and heir,

James Hardres, esq. This gentleman m. Ann, daughter of Robert Hill, and relict of James Aucher, esq. and dying in 1490, was s. by his son,

Christopher Hardres, esq. who m. Dorothy, daughter of Sir John Paston, knt. and was s. at his decease, in 1536, by his son,

Thomas Hardres, esq. who died in 1556, leaving by Mary, daughter of Edward Oxenden, esq. a son and heir,

Richard Hardres, esq. high sheriff of Kent in the 30th Elizabeth, who espoused Mary, daughter of Sir Thomas Wroth, knt. of Durance, in Middlesex, and was s. by his son,

Sir Thomas Hardres, knt. who m. Eleanor, daughter and sole heir of Henry Thoresby, esq. of Thoresby, in the county of York, one of the masters in chancery, and had issue,

Richard (Sir), his heir.

Thoresby, who left issue.

Peter, D.D. who had the canonry of the tenth prebend in the cathedral of Canterbury, and was deprived in the great rebellion, but restored at the restoration.

Thomas (Sir), of Gray's Inn, serjeant-at-law, author of a volume of reports of cases adjudged in the Exchequer from the year 1655 to 21 Charles II. He left issue by his wife Philadelphia. His descendant,

John Hardres, esq. of St. George's, Canterbury, was M.P. for that city *temp.* Anne and George I.

Anne.

In Hardres church is a fair monument to Sir Thomas Hardres, and Eleanor his wife, who brought a great estate into the family. He was s. by his eldest son,

i. Sir Richard Hardres, knt. of Hardres, who was created a Baronet by King Charles I. 3rd June 1642. He m. Anne, daughter of Thomas Godfrey, esq.

of Lydd, in Kent, and was *s.* at his decease by his eldest son,

II. Sir Peter Hardres, bart. who *m.* Phoebe, daughter of Edward Barry, esq. of Lydd, and dying about 1675, was *s.* by his son,

III. Sir Thomas Hardres, bart. who *m.* Ursula, daughter of Sir William Rooke, knt. and dying, aged twenty-eight, 23rd February, 1688, was *s.* by his son,

IV. Sir William Hardres, bart. This gentleman was elected knight of the shire for Kent in 1710. He sat for Dover in 1714, and for the city of Canterbury in the first parliament of George II. He *m.* Elizabeth, daughter of Richard Thomas, esq. of Lamberhurst, in Kent, and widow of William Disher, of London, merchant, by whom he had issue,

William, his successor.
Elizabeth, *m.* to the Rev. David Jones.

Sir William died at Hardres Court, of the gout in his stomach, 8th July, 1736. He was interred with his ancestors in the parish church of Upper Hardres, and *s.* by his son,

V. Sir William Hardres, bart. who *m.* Frances, daughter and coheir of John Corbet, esq. of Bourn Place, but dying issueless, aged forty-six, 31st August, 1764, when the Baronetcy became extinct. He devised the manor of Hardres, &c. to his widow, in fee, at whose demise intestate, in 1783, it became vested in her heirs, who were the Rev. Charles Beckingham, A.M. (son of her sister Katherine); Elizabeth, her sister, widow of the Rev. Thomas Denward; Ignatius Geoghegan, esq. (son of her sister Antonia), and William Hougham, jun. esq. (an only son of her sister Hannah.)

Arms—Gules, a lion rampant, ermine, debruised, with a cheveron or, (denoting the tenure of the manor of Hardres, by knight's service, of the castle of Tunbridge, in Kent, the ancient seigniory of Gloucester, who bore three such cheverons on the same field.)

Note—At the seat of the family, Hardres Court, in the parish of Great Hardres, in Kent, were, according to tradition, the gates of Bullogne, which were given by Henry VIII. to a member of the family who had attended the king at the siege.

HARE, OF STOW BARDOLPH.

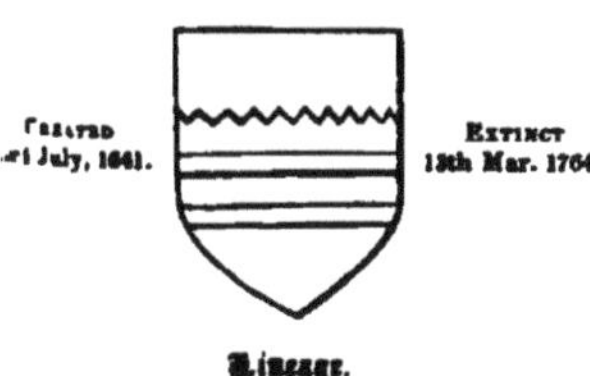

Lineage.

The family of Hare *claimed* to be a scion of the house of Harecourt or Harcourt, in Lorrain, who were counts of Normandy.

Sir John Hare, knt. *m.* Elizabeth, daughter of Sir John de Ashton, and left a son and heir,

William Hare, esq. who *m.* Anne, daughter of Sir Thomas Mydelton, knt. of Mydelton Hall, in Lancashire, and was *s.* by his son,

John Hare, esq. who *m.* Agnes, daughter of Sir John Shirley, knt. of Whiston, in Sussex, and left a son and heir,

Sir Thomas Hare, knt. who *m.* Julian Hussey, of Lincolnshire, and was *s.* by his son,

Nicholas Hare, esq. father, by Elizabeth, daughter of Sir Thomas de Walingham, knt. of

Richard Hare, esq. who *m.* Elizabeth, daughter of John Seckford, esq. of Suffolk, and left a son and heir,

John Hare, esq. who *m.* Jane Neville, and was *s.* by his son,

Thomas Hare, esq. This gentleman *m.* Joyce, daughter of John Hyde, esq. of Norbury, and was father of

John Hare, esq. who *m.* Catherine, daughter of Richard de Aunderson, and was *s.* by his son,

Nicholas Hare, esq. father of

John Hare, esq. who *m.* Elizabeth, daughter of — Fortescue, esq. and had two sons, namely,

I. Nicholas (Sir), of Brusyard, in Suffolk, *m.* Catherine, daughter and co-heir of Sir John Bassingbourn, knt. of Woodhall, in Hertfordshire, and had issue,
   1. Michael, *m.* first, Elizabeth, daughter of Henry Hobart, esq. of Hales Hall, in Norfolk, and secondly, Mary, fourth daughter of Sir Thomas Brudenell, of Dean, in the county of Northampton.
   2. Robert, clerk of the Pells, } *d. s. p.*
   3. William, }
   1. Anne, *m.* to Thomas Rous, esq. of Henham, in Suffolk.
   2. Audrey, *m.* to Thomas Tymperley, esq. of Hintlesham, in the same county.
   3. Thomasine, *d. unm.*

   Sir Nicholas Hare was twice chosen speaker of the House of Commons, in the reign of Henry VIII. and was master of requests and chief justice of Chester. He was sworn of the privy council, master of the rolls, and afterwards lord keeper of the great seal, *temp.* Mary. The estates of Sir Nicholas, his sons dying without issue, devolved upon his brother.*

II. John.

The second son,

John Hare, esq. having eventually inherited the estates of his brother, Sir Nicholas, became "of Stow-Bardolph." The name of this gentleman's wife is not mentioned, but it appears he was father of ten children, viz.

I. Nicholas, a bencher of the Inner Temple. This gentleman rebuilt, in 1589, the mansion house at Stow Bardolph, at an outlay of £40,000. He also built a very spacious dormitory adjoining to the chancel of Stow-Bardolph church, for depositing the remains of himself and family. He *d.* in 1591, *s. p.* leaving his estate to his next brother.

* Sir Nicholas purchased, in the year 1553, the liberty or franchise of the whole hundred of Clackclose, which comprises Stow-Bardolph, and thirty one towns all adjoining, to which his descendants, as lords paramount, have, in virtue of that office, the execution of all writs whatever; hold a court, in the nature of sheriff's turn, and a court every three weeks for the trial of actions, &c. in the hundred. In the patent is an express prohibition to the county sheriff and his officers, to enter into the hundred to do any act of authority, on any pretence or occasion whatsoever, except in default of the lord paramount's bailiff. This is a very ancient franchise, having been granted by *King* Edgar to the abbey of Ramsey, where it remained, until Henry VIII. at the dissolution of the monasteries, granted it to Lord North, who sold it to Sir Nicholas Hare.

II. Ralph, also a bencher of the Inner Temple, *d.* without issue in 1601, and was *s.* by his next brother.

III. Richard, of whom presently.

IV. Rowland, *d. s. p.*

V. Edmond, *d. s. p.*

VI. Hugh, a bencher of the Inner Temple, and master of the court of Wards, died without issue, and left by his will, dated 25th December, 1619, above £20,000, to be equally divided between his two nephews, John Hare, grandson of his brother Richard, and Hugh Hare, son of his brother John: he left beside several legacies to his other relations and friends.

VII. Thomas, *d.* issueless.

VIII. John,* *m.* first, Lucia, daughter of — Barlow, esq. by whom he had no issue; secondly, Margaret, daughter of John Crouch, esq. of Cornbury, in Hertfordshire, and by that lady (who after his decease became the third Countess of Henry, first Earl of Manchester), had two sons, Nicholas, who *d. s. p.* and

Hugh Hare, created Lord Coleraine, 3rd August, 1625, *m.* Lucia, daughter of Henry, first Earl of Manchester.

I. Elizabeth.

II. Margaret.

The third son,

Richard Hare, esq. inherited the estates on the demise of his elder brothers, and became of Stow-Bardolph. He *m.* Elizabeth, daughter of Richard Barnes, esq. and by her (who *m.* secondly, George Rotheram, esq. and thirdly, Sir George Perient, knt. and died 2nd December, 1656), had two sons, Ralph (Sir), and Richard. The elder,

Sir Ralph Hare, was created a knight of the Bath at the coronation of *King* James I. 1603. He *m.* first, Mary, daughter of Sir Edward Holmden, knt. and by her had one son,

John, his heir.

Sir Ralph *m.* secondly, Anne, daughter of John Crouch, esq. of Cornbury, by whom (who *m.* secondly, Edward, Lord Montagu of Boughton) he had no issue. Sir Ralph was very remarkable for his extensive charity to the poor. In 1603 he erected a row of six houses at Stow-Bardolph, for the reception of six poor persons, who were born in the parish, or had resided constantly there, for ten years at least, and endowed the said houses with lands to a considerable value, to be a maintenance for the poor inhabitants thereof for ever. He gave in his lifetime by deed, bearing date 30th April, 1623, to St. John's College, Cambridge, the glebe, tithes, &c. of the impropriate rectory of Marham, in Norfolk, with the advowsons of the vicarage, which his grandfather, John Hare, had purchased from Henry VIII. at the dissolution of the monasteries, to be employed in erecting a spacious library, and afterwards in maintaining thirty poor scholars in that college for ever. He died in August, 1623, and was *s.* by his only son,

Sir John Hare, knt. who was distinguished in the lifetime of his father, having had the honour of knighthood conferred upon him at Newmarket, 4th December, 1617. He *m.* Elizabeth, only daughter of Thomas, Lord Coventry, lord keeper of the great seal, *temp.* Charles I. and had issue,

I. Ralph, his heir.

II. John, of Bromsthorp, in Norfolk, *m.* Susan, daughter and co-heir of John Walpole, esq. of Bromsthorp, and left

John Hare, Richmond herald, who *d.* in 1720.

Elizabeth Hare, *m.* to Philip Bedingfield, esq. of Bromsthorp.

Anne Hare, *d.* in 1734.

III. Hugh, *d.* unm.

IV. Nicholas, *m.* Catherine, daughter of William Gery, esq. of Bushmead, in the county of Bedford, and had a son,

Ralph Hare, of Harpham, *m.* Anne, daughter of Sir John Willis, bart. of Fen Ditton in Cambridgeshire, and dying in September, 1728, left

1. Thomas, of Harpham, who *d.* in 1736, leaving by Mary, daughter of Joseph Sharpe, esq. a son, Hugh, and a daughter, Anne.
2. Ralph, of Bennet College, Cambridge.
3. John, LL.B. rector of Harpham and Wilby.
1. Mary, *m.* to Thomas Lobb, esq. of Great Cressingham.
2. Anne, }
3. Susan, } *d.* unm.
4. Elizabeth, *m.* to John Dethick, esq. of Wareham, in Norfolk.

V. Thomas, *d.* unm.

I. Elizabeth, *m.* first, to Woolley Leigh, esq. of Addington, in Surrey, and, secondly, to Sir John Lowther, of Ackworth, in Yorkshire.

II. Anne, *m.* to Sir John Sydenham, bart. of Brimpton, in the county of Somerset.

III. Mary, *m.* to Thomas Savage, esq. of Elmley Castle, in Worcestershire.

IV. Susan, *m.* to Thomas Barrow, esq.

V. Sarah, *m.* to John Earle, esq. of Heydon in Norfolk.

VI. Margaret, *m.* to John Corrance, esq. of Rendlesham, in Sussex. (See Burke's *Commoners*, vol. iii. p. 371.)

Sir John was *s.* by his eldest son,

I. Ralph Hare, esq. of Stow Bardolph, in the county of Norfolk, who was created a Baronet by *King* Charles I. 23rd July, 1641. Sir Ralph *m.* first, Mary, daughter and co-heir of Sir Robert Crane, bart. of Chilton, in Suffolk, by whom he had seven children, of whom Thomas, his successor, alone survived infancy. He *m.* secondly, Vere, daughter of Sir Roger Townshend, bart.† of Raynham, in Norfolk, but by her had no issue. He espoused, thirdly, Elizabeth, daughter of — Chapman, esq. of Suffolk, and by that lady left a posthumous son, John, who died in infancy. Sir Ralph, who represented the county of Norfolk in parliament, *d.* in February, 1671-2, and was *s.* by his son,

II. Sir Thomas Hare, bart. who *m.* Elizabeth, sister of Sir Robert Dashwood, bart. of Northbrook, in the county of Oxford, and had issue,

I. Ralph, his successor.

II. Thomas, successor to his brother.

III. George, major of Dragoons, succeeded as fifth baronet.

IV. Richard, *d.* in infancy.

I. Elizabeth, *m.* to Sir Thomas Robinson, bart. of Worlingham, in Suffolk.

II. Mary, *m.* to Thomas Leigh, of London, a Turkey merchant, and had a son,

* From this John Hare descended the Hares of Docking Hall, Norfolk, an estate now possessed by Humphrey John Hare, esq.

† By Mary, second daughter and co-heir of Horatio, Lord Vere of Tilbury.

Thomas Leigh, esq. of Iver, in the county of Bucks, whose son and heir,

THOMAS LEIGH, esq. assumed the name of HARE, and was created a BARONET in 1818.

iii. Susan.

iv. Margaret, d. unm.

v. Sarah.

Sir Thomas soon after he came of age, was elected knight of the shire for the county of Norfolk, and dying 1st January, 1693, was buried in the dormitory, adjoining to the chancel, in Stow Bardolph Church, with this inscription on a noble monument, with his figure in a cumbent posture:

In Memory of Sr. Thos. Hare, Bart. who
departed this Life the 1st day of January, 1693, aged
.. years, and left a lady and 4 Sons and 5 Daughters.
The Glorious Sun which sets at Night,
Appears Next Morn as clear and bright;
The Gaudy Deckings of the Earth,
Do every Spring receive new Birth;
But Life when fled has no return,
In Vain we sigh, in Vain we Mourn;
Yet does the Turtle justly grieve her fate,
When she is left behind without her Mate,
Not less does she who raised this Tomb,
And wishes here to have a Room;
With that dear He who underneath does lye,
Who was the Treasure of her Heart and pleasure of
her Eye.

He was s. by his eldest son,

III. SIR RALPH HARE, bart. who m. Susan, daughter and co-heir of Walter Norborne, esq. of Calne, in Wiltshire, but dying 22nd September, 1732, aged fifty one, without issue, was s. by his brother,

IV. SIR THOMAS HARE, bart. who wedded Rosamond, daughter of Charles Newby, esq. of Hooton, in the county of York, and had two daughters, Elizabeth and Mary. He d. 21st February, 1760, aged seventy-..., and was s. by his brother,

V. SIR GEORGE HARE, bart. who died unm. aged seventy three, 18th March, 1764, when the BARONETCY became EXTINCT, and his sisters became his co-heirs. Of these, MARY, the second, married, as stated above, Thomas Leigh, esq. of London, and had a son,

THOMAS LEIGH, esq. of Iver, in the county of Bucks, who m. Anne, daughter of Dr. Robert Clavering, Bishop of Peterborough, and had with two daughters, Anne, the wife of Robert Williams, esq. and Mary, of Thomas Trewern, esq., a son and heir,

THOMAS LEIGH, esq. of Stow Hall, in Norfolk, who assumed the surname of HARE, and was created a BARONET, 14th December, 1818. Sir Thomas was father of the present SIR THOMAS HARE, bart. of Stow Hall.

Arms—Gules, two bars and a chief indented or.

HARLAND, OF SUTTON HALL.

CREATED 23rd Oct. 1808.

EXTINCT 20th Feb. 1810.

Lineage.

... HOAR, esq. of Middleton St. George, in Durham, keeper of the regalia of England in the Tower of London, son of William Hoar, esq. (who inherited an estate in the county of Middlesex,) married, 1st January, 1750, Frances, daughter of William Sleigh, esq. of Stockton-upon-Tees, and had issue,

WILLIAM, barrister-at-law, who assumed the surname of HARLAND, and died in December, 1834. His only son and heir is the present

WILLIAM CHARLES HARLAND, esq. of Sutton Hall, in the county of York. (See BURKE's *Commoners*, vol. iii. p. 194.)

George, of Twyford Lodge, Hants.

CHARLES, of whom presently.

Thomas, admiral royal navy, who m. in 1788, Katherine Dorothy, daughter of Peregrine Bertie, esq. of Low Layton, Essex, and assumed the surname of BERTIE.

Mary, m. to Richard Mark Dickens, esq. colonel of the 34th regiment.

Frances.

The third son,

1. CHARLES HOAR, esq. marrying at Easingwold, in 1802, Anne, only daughter and heiress of Philip Harland, esq. of Sutton Hall, in Yorkshire, and widow of the Rev. Henry Goodricke, assumed the surname and arms of HARLAND. He was created a BARONET in 1808, but left no issue at his decease in 1810, when the BARONETCY EXPIRED. His widow, the heiress of Sutton Hall, survived until the 24th June, 1826, when she was succeeded by the nephew of her husband, the present WILLIAM CHARLES HARLAND, esq. of Sutton Hall, M.P. for Durham.

Arms—Arg. on a bend between two cottises three stags' heads cabossed az.

HARRIES, OF TONG CASTLE.

CREATED 12th April, 1623

EXTINCT ....

Lineage.

JOHN HARRIES, esq. of Cruckton, in Shropshire, descended from John Harries, of Cruckton, who was living in 1463, married, and had four sons, namely,

THOMAS, of whom presently.

Rowland, of Ludlow.

Arthur, of Prescot, near Baschurch, whose grandson,

THOMAS HARRIES, esq. of Weston Lizard, succeeded to Cruckton, and served as sheriff of Shropshire in 1730. His descendant,

THOMAS HARRIES, esq. of Cruckton, sheriff of Shropshire in 1802, married Barbara Mary Anne, daughter and co-heir of John Smitheman, esq. of Little Wenlock.

Richard, of Cruckton, which, as youngest son, he inherited, according to the custom of the manor of Pontesbury; his descendants became extinct in the third generation.

The eldest son,

I. SIR THOMAS HARRIES, knt. an eminent lawyer, made serjeant-at-law, 1589, purchased Tong Castle, in

Shropshire, from Sir Edward Stanley, and was created a BARONET in 1623. Sir Thomas m. Eleanor, daughter of Roger Gifford, M.D. of London, physician to *Queen* ELIZABETH, and had a daughter and eventual heiress,

ELIZABETH, who married William Pierrepoint, of Thoresby, second son of Robert, first Earl of Kingston, and was grandmother of

EVELYN, first DUKE OF KINGSTON, whose son, EVELYN, last Duke of Kingston, sold the estate and castle of Tong to GEORGE DURANT, esq.

As Sir Thomas Harries left no male issue, the title EXPIRED at his decease.

Arms—Barry of eight erm. and az. over all three annulets or.

HARRIS, OF BOREATTON.

CREATED 22nd Dec. 1622.

EXTINCT in 1685.

Lineage.

I. THOMAS HARRIS, esq. of Boreatton, in Shropshire, master in Chancery, son of Roger Harris, draper, of Shrewsbury, and grandson of William Harris, yeoman, of Wheathill, in the parish of Condover, was created a BARONET in 1622: an elevation which rather shocked the feelings of the age, for, at its first institution the baronetcy was confined to men of descent, and Captain Simon Leeke impleaded Sir Thomas Harris in the court of Chivalry, as unworthy of the distinction. Nevertheless he transmitted the honour to his son and heir,

II. SIR PAUL HARRIS, of Boreatton, who succeeded his father in 1629, and served the office of sheriff of Shropshire in 1637. At the breaking out of the civil war, he remained firm in his allegiance, and was an active commissioner of array. "He sent out warrants," says Gough, "requiring and commanding all men, both householders with their sons and servants, and sojourners and others, within the hundred of Pimhill, that were between the age of sixteen and sixty, to appear, on a certain day, upon Myddle Hill. I was then about eight or nine years old, and went to see this great show; and there I saw a multitude of men; and upon the highest bank of the hill I saw one Robert More standing, with a paper in his hand, and three or four soldiers' pikes stuck upright in the ground by him, and there he made proclamation, that if any person would serve the king as a soldier in the wars, he should have fourteen groats a week for his pay. Sir Paul was a person," adds our rustic historian, "not well beloved by the ancient gentry of the county, for, being as they termed him, but a buck of the second head; yet being a baronet, and a proud, imperious person, he took place of those of ancient knight's degree: neither was he beloved by the common people." He died in 1644, and was *s.* by his son,

III. SIR THOMAS HARRIS, of Boreatton, who also devoted himself to the royal cause, and compounded for his estate in the sum of £1542. In the year 1655 he was implicated in the general rising then concerted against the government of Cromwell: the seizure of Shrewsbury was that branch of the enterprise for which he undertook, but it was frustrated by the indiscretion of one of those engaged, Ralph Kynaston of Maesbrook. "This gentleman," says Blakeway, "publickly enlisted troopers on the 7th March, 1655, and the forces were to have been mustered in Boreatton Park, on the 9th at night: however, on the morning of that day, the governor of Shrewsbury, Humphrey Mackworth, receiving intelligence of the design, instantly impressed the best horses in the town, marched to Boreatton, and seized the insurgents, with their ammunition, which consisted in part of bullets made from the lead on the roof of that mansion. It is difficult to say how Sir Thomas escaped with his life, but he survived to the Restoration." Sir Thomas m. Mary, daughter of Thomas Mytton, esq. of Halston, in Shropshire, but dying *s. p.* was *s.* by his brother,

IV. SIR GEORGE HARRIS, who *d.* issueless, and was *s.* by his brother,

V. SIR PAUL HARRIS, who also left no child, and was *s.* by his uncle,

VI. SIR ROGER HARRIS, who died in 1685, when the BARONETCY became EXTINCT. The estate of Boreatton was purchased after the Restoration by THOMAS HUNT, esq. of Shrewsbury.

Arms—Or, three hedgehogs two and one az.

HARRIS, OF HAYNE.

CREATED 1st Dec. 1673.

EXTINCT about [illegible].

Lineage.

JOHN HARRIS, a younger son of the Harrises of Radford, was father (by his wife, the heiress of Stone of Stone) of

WILLIAM HARRIS, who wedded Thomasine, daughter and heiress of Walter Hayne, of Hayne, and was *s.* by his son,

JOHN HARRIS, esq. of Stone, a lawyer of high reputation, who was chosen in 1536, autumnal reader at Lincoln's Inn, and called in 1540, to the degree of serjeant-at-law. He was subsequently a King's serjeant and recorder of the city of Exeter. "The eminency," says Prince, in his Worthies of Devon, "of this great lawyer in his profession, we may infer from that considerable estate he acquired, and left to his family. For to his own fair inheritance he added, the hundred, manor, and advowson of Lifton, near adjoining to Hayne, which he purchased from the Lord Neville, Earl of Westmoreland." Serjeant Harris, m. the daughter of Michael Kelly, esq. of Ratcliffe, in Devonshire, and had issue,

WILLIAM, his heir.
John.
Oliver.
Anthony.
Arthur.
Alice, m. to John Wise, esq. of Sydenham.

Wilmoty, *m.* to John Trevillian, esq. of Nettlecombe.

The eldest son,

WILLIAM HARRIS, esq. of Hayne, *m.* Mary, daughter of Sir Fulk Grevill, knt. of Beauchamp's Court, in Warwickshire, and had, with four daughters, a son and successor,

ARTHUR HARRIS, esq. of Hayne, and of Kenegie, of which latter estate he became possessed before the year 1600. This gentleman espoused Margaret, daughter and heiress of John Davils, esq. of Totely, in Devon, and had issue,

I. JOHN, his successor.
II. ARTHUR, father of

CHRISTOPHER, who inherited the estates at the decease of his cousin, SIR ARTHUR HARRIS, bart.

Mr. Harris, who is mentioned by Carew as one of the resident magistrates of Devonshire in his time, and commanding a provincial regiment belonging to Mounts Bay, died in 1628, and was interred in the north aisle of Gurval Church, where a fine monument was erected to his memory. He was *s.* by his son,

JOHN HARRIS, esq. of Hayne and Kenegie, who wedded, first, Florence, daughter of Sir John Windham, but by her had no issue. He espoused, secondly, Cordelia, eldest daughter of Sir John Mohun, of Boconnoc, created in 1628, Lord Mohun, of Oakhampton (see BURKE's *Extinct and Dormant Peerage*), by whom he had an only son and successor,

ARTHUR HARRIS, esq. of Hayne and Kenegie, who was created a BARONET in 1673. Sir Arthur *m.* Theophila, daughter of John Turnor, serjeant-at-law, but died without issue about 1686, when the title became EXTINCT, and the estates passed to his cousin,

CHRISTOPHER HARRIS, esq. who *m.* Elizabeth, daughter of William Martin, esq. of Linderidge, and was *s.* by his son,

WILLIAM HARRIS, esq. of Hayne, M.P. for St. Ives, 2nd WILLIAM and MARY, and for Oakhampton, *temp.* Queen ANNE. He served as sheriff of Devon in 1703, and died in six years after, leaving issue,

1. CHRISTOPHER, of Hayne, M.P. *d. s. p.* in 1718.
2. JOHN, of Hayne, master of the household to GEORGE II. and GEORGE III. died *s. p.* 1767.
3. William, whose son,

CHRISTOPHER, of Hayne, succeeded his uncle. He married Penelope, daughter of the Rev. Isaac Donnithorne, of St. Agnes, in Cornwall, and had two daughters,

PENELOPE.
ELIZABETH, married to her cousin, Isaac Donnithorne, esq. who assumed the surname of HARRIS, and has issue.

1. Jane, married to William Arundel, esq. of Trengwainton and Menedarva, both in Cornwall, and was mother of

WILLIAM ARUNDEL, esq. of Trengwainton, ancestor of the present

WILLIAM ARUNDEL HARRIS ARUNDEL, esq. of Lifton Park, Devon.

Arms—Sa. three crescents within a bordure arg.

HAR

HARTOPP, OF FREATHBY.

CREATED 3rd Dec. 1619.	EXTINCT 13th Jan. 1762.

Lineage.

The first of this family upon record is

RALPH HARTOPP, who was living in the reign of RICHARD II. A.D. 1377, and from him proceeded,

JOHN HARTOPP, of Burton-Lazers, in the county of Leicester, who wedded Jane, daughter of William Englebeard, or Englebert, and was grandfather of

THOMAS HARTOPP, of Burton-Lazers, who *m.* Elbert daughter of John Allen, and had issue,

I. WILLIAM, his heir.
II. Valantine, of Burton-Lazers, who *d.* in 1633, leaving by Ann, his wife, daughter and heir of William Goodman, (with three daughters,) a son and heir,

Sir William Hartopp, who was knighted at Ashby-de-la-Zouch, 2nd September, 1617, and dying in 1622, was *s.* by his son,

Sir Thomas Hartop, knt. of Burton-Lazers, *b.* in 1600, who *m.* Dorothy, daughter of Sir Thomas Bendish, bart. and had issue. (See BURKE's *Commoners*, vol. iii. p. 402.)

III. Richard, of the Middle Temple, *d. s. p.*
IV. Joan, *m.* to Octavian Fisher, esq. of Trekingham, in Lincolnshire.

The eldest son,

WILLIAM HARTOPP, esq. *m.* Eleanor Adcock, and dying 2nd September, 1586, left four sons, viz.

I. Thomas, *b.* in 1570, *d.* issueless.
II. EDWARD, his heir.
III. Valentine, of Little Dalby.
IV. GEORGE, from whom descend the HARTOPPS, of Dalby, in Leicestershire, now represented by EDWARD BOURCHIER HARTOPP, esq. of Dalby House. Refer to BURKE's *Commoners*, vol. iii. p. 401.

The eldest surviving son,

I. EDWARD HARTOPP, esq. served in his youth, under the Earl of Leicester, in the Low Countries, *temp.* ELIZABETH, and after his return, was sheriff of Leicestershire 15 JAMES I. when he resided at Buckminster, but afterwards removed to Freathby, in the same county, where he possessed a good estate, and was created a BARONET 3rd December, 1619. Sir Edward *m.* Mary, daughter of Sir Erasmus Dryden, bart. of Canons Ashby, in Northamptonshire, and had issue,

EDWARD, his heir.
Richard, *d. s. p.*
Frances, *m.* to Sir Richard Earle, bart. of Craglethorpe, in Lincolnshire.
Anne, *m.* to Thomas White, esq. of Cotgrave, Notts.
Elizabeth, *m.* to Montague Cholmley, esq. of Easton, in the county of Lincoln.

Sir Edward represented the county of Leicester, in the reign of CHARLES I. He *d.* in 1652, and was *s.* by his elder son,

II. SIR EDWARD HARTOPP, bart. of Freathby, *b.* in

1668, who *m.* Mary, daughter of Sir John Cook, knt. of Melburn, in the county of Derby, one of the principal secretaries of the state to *King* CHARLES I. and had issue,

JOHN, his heir.

Mary, *m.* to Smith Fleetwood, esq. of Stoke Newington, in Middlesex.

Sir Edward, who raised a regiment for the service of the Parliament, *d.* in 1658, and was *s.* by his son,

III. SIR JOHN HARTOPP, bart. M.P. for the county of Leicester, in three parliaments, *temp.* CHARLES II. This gentleman *m.* Elizabeth, daughter of Charles Fleetwood,* the celebrated parliamentary general, and son-in-law of Cromwell, and had several children, of whom,

JOHN, the only surviving of four sons, succeeded him.

Frances, *m.* to Sir Nathaniel Gould, knt. of Stoke Newington, and had a daughter,

Mary Gould, *m.* to Sir Francis St. John, bart. of Thorp, in Northamptonshire.

Elizabeth, *m.* to Thomas Cook, esq. of Stoke Newington, some time governor of the Bank.

Sir John *d.* 1st April, 1722, aged eighty-five, and was *s.* by his son,

IV. SIR JOHN HARTOPP, bart. who *m.* first in 1716, Sarah, daughter of Sir Joseph Wolfe, knt. an alderman of the city of London, and had two daughters,

I. ANNE HARTOPP, who *m.* Joseph Hurlock, esq. of Fort Marlborough, governor of Bencoolen, and afterwards one of the directors of the East India Company, by whom she had an only child,

ANNE HURLOCK, eventually heir and representative of the HARTOPPS.

II. ELIZABETH HARTOPP, *m.* to Timothy Dallowe, M.D. but died without issue.

Sir John married secondly, Miss Sarah Marsh, but had no other issue. He died at Bath, 13th January, 1762, aged eighty-two, when the BARONETCY became EXTINCT. The estates eventually centred in his granddaughter,

ANNE HURLOCK, who at the decease of her kinswoman, Mrs. Jane Fleetwood, succeeded, by bequest, to the Fleetwood property, in the county of Norfolk likewise. She *m.* in 1777, Edmund Bunney, esq. (son of Joseph Bunney, esq. of Newark, by Mary, daughter of Edmund Cradock, esq.) who assumed by sign manual, the surnames of CRADOCK and HARTOPP, and being created a BARONET in 1796, became SIR EDMUND CRADOCK-HARTOPP. (See BURKE'S *Peerage and Baronetage.*)

Arms—Sa. a chevron ermine between three otters passant, argent.

HASTINGS, OF REDLINCH.

CREATED 7th May, 1667.—EXTINCT about 1668.

Lineage.

I. RICHARD HASTINGS, esq. of Redlinch, in the county of Somerset, was created a BARONET in 1667. He *m.* Margaret, daughter of Sir Robert Poynts, of Iron Acton, in Gloucestershire, but by her, who wedded, secondly, Samuel Gorges, esq. of Wraxall, in the county of Somerset, had no issue. He *d.* about a year after his creation, and with him the BARONETCY EXPIRED.

HATTON, OF LONG STANTON.

CREATED 5th July, 1641.

EXTINCT 19th Sept. 1812.

Lineage.

The family of HATTON was anciently of great repute in the county palatine of Chester.

WOLFRID, or WOLFAITH, brother of Nigel, Baron of Halton, was Lord of Halton, in Cheshire, by the gift of HUGH LUPUS. He was grandfather of

SIR ADAM HATTON, knt. of Hatton, whose descendant, (ninth in the line from Wolfrid)

HUGH HATTON, of Hatton, *m.* Mary, daughter of Sir John Ardern, knt. and left two sons, viz.

I. JOHN, his heir, who had an only daughter and heir,

MAUD HATTON, who *m.* Ralph Vernon, and her son,

ROBERT VERNON, inherited Hatton.

II. HUGH.

The second son,

HUGH HATTON, *m.* Margaret, daughter and heir of Jeffery de Brayne, and we pass from him to his descendant, (fifteenth from Wolfrid)

PETER HATTON, esq. who *m.* Margaret, daughter and co-heir of Sir George Bostock, knt. of Moulton, in the county of Chester, and had issue,

I. RICHARD, his heir, ancestor of the Hattons of Alderton, in Shropshire.

II. Peter, from whom the Hattons, of Kirsty Brehen, in the same county.

III. HENRY, of whom presently.

IV. Robert, ancestor of the Hattons, of Norley in Cheshire, and of London.

V. John, from whom the branches of Marsh [illegible]

VI. Ralph, founder of the Hattons, of Wavertham

VII. Adam, from whom the Hattons, of Northw[illegible] and Sutton, in Surrey.

VIII. Simon, ancestor of the branch of Stanton [illegible] in Cheshire.

IX. Hugh, *d. s. p.*

The third son,

HENRY HATTON, esq. *m.* Elizabeth, daughter and heir of William Holdenby, esq. of Holdenby, in the county of Northampton, and had two sons, John and Richard. The elder,

JOHN HATTON, esq. *m.* Joan, daughter of John S[illegible]by, esq. of Kent, and had issue,

I. WILLIAM, of Holdenby, who *m.* Alice, daughter of Laurence Saunders, esq. of Harrington in Northamptonshire, and had three sons, viz.

1. Francis, *d.* young.
2. Thomas, *d. s. p.*
3. CHRISTOPHER (Sir), who attained an eminence in the reign of ELIZABETH

* By his first wife, Frances, daughter and heir of Thomas Smith, esq. of Winston, in Norfolk.

He inherited Holdenby, and erected a splendid residence there.* Sir Christopher was first noticed by the queen at a mask at court, for the comeliness of his person, and his grace in dancing; and he subsequently, although not bred a lawyer, attained the high station of LORD CHANCELLOR, was sworn of the privy council, and made a knight of the garter, his instalment taking place 23rd May, 1588.† He *d.* unm. in 1591.

II. JOHN, of whom hereafter.
III. Christopher.

I. DOROTHY, *m.* to John Newport, esq. of Harrougham, in the county of Warwick, and had a son,

SIR WILLIAM NEWPORT, who changed his name to HATTON, on inheriting the property of his uncle, the lord chancellor. He *m.* Elizabeth, daughter and heir of Sir Francis Gawdy, knt. chief justice of the Common Pleas, and had an only daughter,

FRANCES HATTON, *m.* to Robert Rich, second Earl of Warwick.

Sir William dying thus without male issue, the chancellor's estates passed, under his will, to John Hatton, esq.

The second son,

JOHN HATTON, esq. of Gravesend, in Kent, *m.* Joan, daughter of War, or Ware, esq. of Sussex, and had two sons, WILLIAM, of Gravesend, and

JOHN HATTON, esq. of Stanton, in Cambridgeshire, living in 1579, who *m.* Jane, daughter of Robert Shute, one of the barons of the exchequer, and one of the justices of the Common Pleas, and by her had three sons, viz.

I. CHRISTOPHER (Sir), of Kirby, in the county of Northampton, made knight of the Bath, at the coronation of JAMES I. This gentleman inherited, on the failure of the male issue in Sir William (Newport) Hatton, the great estates of the Lord Chancellor Hatton. He *m.* Alice, daughter of Thomas Fenshaw, esq. of Ware Park, and dying in 1619, was *s.* by his son,

SIR CHRISTOPHER HATTON, made a knight of the Bath at the coronation of CHARLES I. and distinguished himself afterwards by his zeal in the royal cause, was created, in 1643, BARON HATTON, *of Kirby*. His elder son and heir,

CHRISTOPHER, second Lord Hatton, of Kirby, was created in 1682, VISCOUNT HATTON, of Gretton. His lordship *d.* in 1706, and was *s.* by his son, by his third wife, Elizabeth, daughter and co-heir of Sir William Haslewood, of Maidwell, Northamptonshire,

WILLIAM, second Viscount Hatton, who *d.* unm. in 1762, when the honours became extinct.‡ (See BURKE's *Extinct Peerage*.)

II. Robert.
III. THOMAS.

The youngest son,

I. THOMAS HATTON, esq. of Long Stanton, in the county of Cambridge, was created a BARONET by *King* CHARLES I. 5th July, 1641. Sir Thomas, *m.* Mary, daughter of Sir Giles Allington, knt. of Horseheath, in the same county, and had issue,

THOMAS, his heir.
John, *d. s. p.*
CHRISTOPHER, who succeeded as fifth BARONET.
Mary.
Elizabeth, *m.* to Sir William Boteler, knt. of Kinton, Bedfordshire.
Jane.

He *d.* 23rd September, 1658, aged seventy-five, and was *s.* by his eldest son,

II. SIR THOMAS HATTON, bart. who *m.* Bridget, daughter of Sir William Goring, bart. of Burton, in Sussex, and had issue,

CHRISTOPHER, his successor.
THOMAS, successor to his brother.
Mary, *m.* to John Pocklington, esq. of Huntingdon.
Elizabeth, *m.* to Thomas Day, esq. of Qui, in Cambridgeshire.
Rebecca, *m.* to — Crayker, esq. of London.
Dorothy, *m.* to Tirrel Dalton, esq. of Fulborne, in Cambridgeshire.

He was *s.* by his eldest son,

III. SIR CHRISTOPHER HATTON, bart. who *d.* young and was *s.* by his brother,

IV. SIR THOMAS HATTON, bart. who also *d.* young, when the baronetcy reverted to his uncle,

V. SIR CHRISTOPHER HATTON, bart. This gentleman *m.* Elizabeth, daughter of Thomas Buck, esq. of Westwick, in Cambridgeshire, and had several sons and one daughter, of whom all predeceased him except THOMAS and JOHN, his successors, and William, who *m.* Susanna, daughter of Mr. Hinton, and had a son Christopher, in holy orders, rector of Gorton, in Cambridgeshire, the daughter died soon after him unmarried. He *d.* in October, 1720, and was *s.* by his elder surviving son,

VI. SIR THOMAS HATTON, bart. who *m.* first, Elizabeth, daughter and heir of Cooper Orlebar, esq. of Hinwick, in the county of Bedford, but that lady dying 5th May, 1732, aged forty-four, he married soon after, Henrietta, daughter of Sir James Astry, knt. of Woodend, in the parish of Arlington, in the county of Bedford,§ but leaving no issue, was *s.* by his brother,

---

* Camden, in the "Britannia," speaking of Holdenby house, says it was a stately and truly magnificent piece of building, erected by Sir Christopher Hatton, privy councillor to QUEEN ELIZABETH, lord chancellor of England, and knight of the garter, upon the lands and inheritance of his great grandmother, heir of the ancient family of the Holdenbies; for the greatest and last monument of his youth, as himself afterwards was wont to say.

† SIR CHRISTOPHER HATTON died a bachelor, 20th November, 1591, having adopted Sir William Newport, his nephew, who changed his name to Hatton, but in default of issue male by him, the estates were then settled on his godson, CHRISTOPHER HATTON, son and heir of John HATTON, his next kinsman in the male line.

‡ CHRISTOPHER, the second baron and first viscount, had, by his first wife, Lady Cecilia Tufton, daughter of the Earl of Thanet, an only daughter,

ANNE HATTON, who *m.* Daniel Finch, second Earl of Nottingham, and sixth Earl of Winchelsea, and had with other issue,

The Honourable EDWARD FINCH, who assumed the additional surname of HATTON, upon inheriting the estates of his uncle, of the half-blood, William, last Viscount Hatton. The grandson of this Edward,

GEORGE-FINCH-HATTON, esq. inherited, in 1826, the Earldoms of Winchelsea and Nottingham.

§ By Anne, his wife, second daughter of Sir Thomas Penyston, bart. of Cornwell, in Oxfordshire.

VII. SIR JOHN HATTON, bart. who m. Mary, daughter of Thomas Hawkes, gent. and widow of Mr. William Hitch, by whom he had one son and three daughters. He *d.* 1st July, 1740, and was *s.* by his son,

VIII. SIR THOMAS HATTON, bart. who m. Harriet, daughter of Dingley Ascham, esq. of Connington, in Cambridgeshire, and dying 7th November, 1787, was *s.* by his son,

IX. SIR JOHN HATTON, bart. who m. in 1798, Miss Bridgman, daughter of Mr. Bridgman, an American refugee, but dying *s. p.* about the year 1811, was *s.* by his brother,

X. SIR THOMAS-DINGLEY HATTON, bart. who died in consequence of a fall from his curricle, 19th September, 1812, and being unm. the BARONETCY became EXTINCT.

Arms—Az. a chevron between three garbs or, with a mullet for distinction.

HAWKESWORTH, OF HAWKESWORTH.

CREATED 6th Dec. 1678.

EXTINCT 17th March, 1735.

Lineage.

The family of HAWKESWORTH was seated in Yorkshire at a very remote period. Its representative in the commencement of the seventeenth century,

SIR RICHARD HAWKESWORTH, knt. of Hawkesworth, m. first, Anne, daughter of Thomas Wentworth, esq. of North Elmsal, by whom he had a daughter,

Katherine, m. first, to William Lister, esq.; and secondly, to Sir John Bright, bart.

Sir Richard wedded, secondly, Mary, daughter of Sir Henry Goodrick, knt. and had by her one son and one daughter, viz.

WALTER, his heir.

Jane, m. Francis Braildon, esq. of Braildon, and their daughter and heir,

Mary Braildon, m. Bradwardin Tindall, esq. and had a daughter and heir,

Lucy, the wife of Edward Thomson, esq. of Marsden.

Sir Richard *d.* 11th February, 1657, and was *s.* by his son,

WALTER HAWKESWORTH, esq. of Hawkesworth, living in 1666, who m. Alice, daughter of Sir William Brownlow, bart. and had a son and successor,

I. WALTER HAWKESWORTH, esq. of Hawkesworth, who was created a BARONET 6th December, 1678. This gentleman m. Anne, daughter of Sir Robert Markham, bart. of Sedgebrook, in Lincolnshire, and was *s.* by his son,

II. SIR WALTER HAWKESWORTH, of Hawkesworth, who m. Judith, eldest daughter and co-heir of John, only son of Sir William Aiscough, knt. of Osgodby, in Lincolnshire, and had to survive him an only daughter and heir,

FRANCES, who m. Thomas Ramsden, esq. and had, with a daughter, Judith, wife of Richard Beaumont, esq. of Whitley, a son,

WALTER RAMSDEN, who assumed, in compliance with the will of his grandfather, the surname and arms of HAWKESWORTH. He m. Frances-Elizabeth, daughter of Joseph Hall, esq. of Skelton Castle, and dying 17th October, 1760, left issue a daughter, Frances, m. to Legendre Starkie, esq. of Huntroyd, and a son and successor,

WALTER RAMSDEN-BEAUMONT-HAWKESWORTH, esq. of Hawkesworth, who assumed the surname of FAWKES pursuant to the testamentary injunction of Francis Fawkes, esq. of Farnley. He m. Amelia, eldest daughter of James Farrer, esq. and had issue. His eldest son and heir is the present

WALTER RAMSDEN-FAWKES, esq. of Farnley, in Yorkshire.

Sir Walter Hawkesworth *d.* 17th March, 1735, when the BARONETCY became EXTINCT.

Arms—Sa. three falcons close ppr.

HAWKINS, OF TREWITHAN.

CREATED 28th July, 1791.

EXTINCT 6th April, 1829.

Lineage.

THOMAS HAWKINS, esq. of Managnasie, in Cornwall, m. and had by Audrey, his wife, several children; the eldest of whom,

JOHN HAWKINS, esq. was of St. Erth, in Cornwall, and m. Loveday, daughter of George Trenhayle, gent. living in 1676, by whom he had issue,

I. THOMAS, his heir.

II. George, vicar of Sithney, in Cornwall, m. Anne Kempe, and by her had

George, *d. s. p.*

Anne, m. to Alexander Trevethan, of Edstone.

III. Reginald, D.D. master of Pembroke Hall, Cambridge, *d. s. p.*

IV. Francis, m. Constance Angrove, and had a son and daughter, viz.

John, who m. Elizabeth, daughter of Henry Hawkins, of St. Austle, in Cornwall, and had two sons,

Francis, *d. s. p.*

John, m. Catherine Thomas, of Trewren.

Frances, m. to the Rev. William Robinson, vicar of Helston and Wendron.

I. Audrey, m. to John Alexander.

II. Mary, m. to John Eathorne.

III. Anne, m. to Thomas Lakey.

The eldest son and heir,

THOMAS HAWKINS, esq. of Trewinnard, in the parish of St. Erth, in Cornwall, m. first, Florence, daughter of James Pread, of Trevethow, and by that lady had a daughter, Florence, m. to John Williams, of Helston, merchant. He m. secondly, Anne, daughter, and at length co-heir, of Christopher Bellot, esq. of [illegible] in Cornwall, and dying in 1716, was *s.* by his only surviving son,

Christopher Hawkins, esq. of Trewinnard, who m. Mary, daughter of Philip Hawkins, esq. of Pennans, by whom he had Jane, wife of Sir Richard Vyvyan, bart. of Trelowarren, and a son, his successor,

Thomas Hawkins, esq. of Trewithan, in Cornwall, M.P. for Grampound, who wedded Anne, daughter of James Heywood, esq. of London, and had issue,

Philip, *d. s. p.*
Christopher, his heir.
Thomas, *d. s. p.*
John, m. Hester, daughter of Humphrey Sibthorpe, esq. M.P. for the city of Lincoln, and has issue.
Mary, m. to Lieutenant-Colonel Charles Trelawney Brereton, son of General Harry Trelawney, and had issue.

Mr. Hawkins died 1st December, 1770, aged forty-two. His second son,

I. Christopher Hawkins, esq. F.R.S. and F.S.A. of Trewithan and Trewinnard, both in Cornwall, born in 1758, M.P. for St. Michael's, who was created a Baronet 28th July, 1791. Sir Christopher died unmarried 6th April, 1829, when the Baronetcy expired.

Arms—Per saltire or and arg. on a saltire sa. five fleurs-de-lis of the first, all within a bordure gobony or and sa.

HAWLEY, OF BUCKLAND.

Created 14th March, 1643. Extinct 26th Aug. 1774.

Lineage.

I. Francis Hawley, esq. of Buckland House, in the county of Somerset, descended from Francis Hawley, esq. M.P. for Corfe Castle, in Dorsetshire, *temp.* Elizabeth, raised a troop of horse in 1642 for the royal cause, and in consideration of that and many other services rendered to the unhappy Charles, was created a Baronet by his majesty 14th March, 1643, and further advanced to the peerage of Ireland, as Lord Hawley, Baron of Donamore, in July, 1646. He had a son,

Francis, who m. Gertrude, daughter of Richard Gethins, esq. of the county of Cork, and predeceasing his father, left issue,
Francis, successor to his grandfather.
Richard, who m. Jane, daughter of Mr. Harbin, of Somersetshire, and had issue,
Richard.
Elizabeth.
Mary.
Catharine, second wife of Robert Napier, esq. of Punknoll, in Dorsetshire.

Lord Hawley died 22nd December, 1684, aged seventy-six, and was *s.* by his grandson,

II. Sir Francis Hawley, second Lord Hawley, M.P. for Bramber, in Sussex, in 1713 and 1715, who m. Lady Elizabeth Ramsay, only daughter of William, Earl of Dalhousie, and by her, who died in February 1712, had issue,

Francis, his heir.
William, appointed, in 1721, page of honour to George, *Prince of Wales*; m. in 1725, Anne, daughter of Atkins, of Gravesend, in Kent.
Rachel.
Elizabeth.
Gertrude.

Lord Hawley died at Bath 30th May, 1743, and was *s.* by his son,

III. Sir Francis Hawley, third Lord Hawley, lieutenant-governor of Antigua, who m. Margaret, daughter of Thomas Tyrrel, esq. of London, but *d. s. p.* 26th August, 1772, when the Baronetcy expired.

Arms—Vert, a saltire engrailed arg.

HELE, OF FLEET.

Created 28th May, 1627. Extinct in April, 1677.

Lineage.

Of this very ancient family, fruitful as the county of Devon is known to have been in distinguished houses, it may with truth be stated, that it was one of the most eminent, the most widely spread, and the most affluent which even that quarter of England could boast of. Every printed history of Devon, whether Pole, Risdon, Prince, or Polwhele, abundantly testifies the fact; while Westcott, Chapell, and other collectors, whose works have not yet been published, strengthen those accounts; still more fully confirmed by the different herald's visitations of Devonshire and Cornwall, preserved in the College of Arms, and in the Harleian MSS. Heale, Heal, or Hele, a manor in the parish of Bradninch, in the Hundred of Harridge, in the North of Devon, was, from the earliest time of which any record exists, and, as is presumed, from long before the Conquest, in the possession of the family, which had its dwelling there, and gave it name.

The herald's visitations commence with

Sir Roger de la Heale, Lord of Heale, in the reign of Henry III. fifth in descent from whom, through several knights named Roger and Nicholas, was

William de la Heale, who left issue two sons,

I. Nicholas.
II. Roger, who became heir male of the family on the death of Nicholas.

Nicholas de la Hele, son and heir, died in the first year of *King* Henry V. leaving issue by his wife, Alice, cousin and heir of William de Percehay, of Comb Flory, an only daughter, Alice Hele, who married William Prannceys, esq. of Brixham, in Devon, who, in right of his wife, became Lord of Hele, and succeeded to Comb Flory, where his descendants continued seated, matching, as they descended, with various western knightly families, as Ashforde of Ashforde, Courtenay of Powderham, Barckley, Wyndham of Orghard, Chichester, and others.

Roger Heale, second son of William de Heale, and heir male on the death of his brother Nicholas, lived *temp. King* Henry IV. having served in the Scotch wars, and been there taken prisoner. His son and heir,

William Heale, settled at Hele, called for distinction *South* Hele, in the parish of Cornwood, in the South of Devon, and had issue by his wife, Joan, daughter of Simon Cole, esq. of Slade, in that county, five sons and one daughter,

i. John, of South Heale, who left issue,

Walter Heal, of South Heal, who *m.* Jane, daughter of Thomas Fortescue, esq. of Wymeston, in Devon, by whom he had numerous sons and daughters, of whom,

John Hele, esq. of Hele, eldest son and heir, *m.* Alice, daughter and heir of Richard Brooking, esq. of Holberton, in Devon, and was living *s. p.* at the time of the visitation in 1620.

ii. Hugh, of Cornwood, ancestor of the Heles of that place, and of Diptford, in Devon, whose representative, Jacob Bickford Hele, esq. of Stert, in the latter parish, great-great-great-grandson through daughters of Upton of Lupton, Prowse of Moore, Fowell of Black Hall, and Bartlett of Exeter, all in Devon, of John Hele, esq. of Diptford, at the time of the herald's visitation, died in July, 1835, aged seventy-eight, unmarried; and was presumed to have been the last male heir of this ancient family. He was interred on the 12th July, with his ancestors in the church of Diptford; and it is a remarkable fact, that there was but just sufficient room left in the vault for his coffin.

iii. Nicholas, of whose line we have to treat.

iv. Baldwin.

v. William.

i. Joan, *m.* to John Stert, esq. of Devon.

The third son,

Nicholas Hele, esq. also of South Hele, *m.* first, Dyonisia, daughter of Walter Woodley, esq. of Tidbourne St. Mary, in Devon, by whom he had two sons and one daughter,

i. William, of Bridge Revell, or Bridgwell, in Cornwall, who *d. s. p.**

ii. John, of Holberton, in Devon, who *m.* Elizabeth, daughter of Thomas Pollexfen, esq. of Kitley, in that county,† and had, with nine daughters, one son,

Walter, of Gnaton, in Holberton, who *m.* Elizabeth, daughter of William Strode, esq. of Newnham Park, in Devon, lineal descendant and heir of William Strode, esq. of Newnham, who *m.* Elizabeth, sole child and heir, by his wife, Joan, daughter of Richard Fowell, of Fowellscomb, of Sir Philip Courtenay, knt. of Loughtor, in Devon,‡ great-grandson of Sir Philip Courtenay, of Powderham Castle, sixth son of Hugh Courtenay, second Earl of Devon, by his wife Margaret de Bohun, daughter of Humphrey, Earl of Hereford and Essex, and the Princess Elizabeth, daughter of *King* Edward I. By her he had issue,

1. Sampson, of Gnaton, high sherif of Devon, 19th *King* James I. 1621. He *m.* Joan, eldest daughter of Sir John Glanville, knt. of Killworthy, in Devon, lord chief justice of the Common Pleas, (for account of whom and of his sons, see Prince's *Worthies*, and Fowells of Black Hall, in Burke's *Commoners*, vol. iv. for his representatives), and had issue.§

1. Judith, *m.* to Gilbert Yarde, esq. of Bradley, in Devon.
2. Jane, *d.* unm.
3. Joan, *m.* to Thomas Fowndes, esq. of Plymouth.
4. Frances, *m.* to John Snelling, esq. of Chaddlewood, in Devon.
5. Isabel, } *d.* unm.
6. Agnes, }
7. Elizabeth, }
8. Susan, *m.* to Thomas Isaac, esq. of Postillow or Polslow, in the parish

* Branches of the family from other sons settled early in Cornwall, and there flourished. In 1400, John Heale, of St. Ives, in that county, granted lands for ever to John Hicks: and John Heale was at an early date returned M.P. for St. Ives, while Nicholas Hele was M.P. for Liskeard in 1620, in 1623, and again in 1625. Among the Cornish branches of the family, was the one seated at Bennetts, the last of which, George John Hele, esq. was sheriff of Cornwall in 1628; Lucy Hele, his heiress, married, in 1670, or 1674, Francis Basset, esq. of Tehidy, in Cornwall, the great grandfather of the late Lord De Dunstanville, father of Frances, the present Baroness Basset, (see Burke's *Peerage*,) who inherited, with her, large possessions including the manor of Penlean.

† Now the seat, by descent, of Edmond Pollexfen Bastard, esq. formerly M.P. for the county of Devon. (See Burke's *Commoners*.)

‡ He was second and youngest son by Elizabeth, the daughter and heir of Hingeston, of Sir Philip Courtenay, knt. of Molland, in Devon, and had two sisters,

i. Elizabeth, who *m.* her kinsman, Edward Courtenay, Earl of Devon, by whom she had William Courtenay, Earl of Devon, who *m.* the Princess Katherine, daughter of King Edward IV. and had issue, Henry Courtenay, Marquis of Exeter, father of Edward, the second and last marquis, who died unm. at Padua; and

ii. Margaret, who *m.* as shown above, Sir John Champernowne, knt. of Modbury Castle, by whom she was ancestor of Sir Henry Champernowne, knt. whose daughter Bridget, was the wife of Thomas Hele, esq. of Fleet, father of the first baronet.

§ Sampson Hele's children were,

Mathew, of Holwell, in Devon, *b.* 1616, high sheriff of that county at the Restoration, 1660, when it is said the branches of his family were so numerous and all of such good estate within the county, that he assembled a grand jury, representing the heads thereof, and seldom under twenty, *all of his name and blood*, gentlemen of estate and quality: which made the judge observe, when he heard Hele, of Wisdom, esq. called—a gentill seat in the parish of Cornwood—'that he thought they must be all descended from Wisdom, in that they had acquired such considerable fortunes.'" He left issue a son and heir,

Mathew, of Holwell, who died *s. p.* 1674, and was succeeded by his uncle, Sampson.

John, *d. s. p.*

Sampson, heir to his nephew Mathew, *b.* in 1621 and high sheriff of Devon 4th William and Mary 1691, whose son,

Sampson, died *v. p.* in 1685, leaving by his wife Dorothy, daughter of Sir Francis Drake, bart. of Buckland, also descended from Fowell, of Fowellscomb, through Strode and Courtenay, a son and successor,

Roger, of Holwell, who *m.* Juliana, daughter of Thomas Prestwood, esq. of Butcombe, in Devon, and had by her, who married secondly, Sir Thomas Pett, bart. two daughters, his co-heirs,

of Heavytree, in the county of Devon.

I. Joane, m. first, to John Cholwich, esq. of Rowden, in Devon; and secondly, to John Browninge.

Nicholas Hele, of South Hele, m. secondly, Margery, daughter of Richard Downe, esq. of Holdsworthy, in Devon (for which family see PRINCE's *Worthies*), and had issue by her,

III. THOMAS, of whom presently.

IV. Hugh, of Newton Ferrers, in Devon, who m. Cicely, daughter and heir of Nicholas or William Cole, esq. of Painton, in Devon, and had one son and three daughters.

V. Walter, of Brixton, in Devon, who m. Joane, daughter of Thomas Maynard, esq. of Brixton, and had issue two sons, Elize and Nicholas; the elder of whom, having lost his only son, left his estate to charitable uses, particulars of which are recorded in PRINCE's *Worthies*.

VI. John (Sir), knt. of Wembury, in Devon, serjeant-at-law, of whom PRINCE observes "that he was a most eminent person in his profession, of any other in his days, of his rank, belonging to the long robe; an evident proof and demonstration whereof is the vast wealth and riches he acquired (with God's blessing) by his own industry, which in buildings, lands, and monies, amounted to above an hundred thousand pounds, a good part of which he bestowed in charity to the poor. He purchased a fair estate in the parish of Wembury, about four miles east of Plymouth, where he built a most noble house, beyond any other in those days in all this country, and equal to the best now; a sightly seat for show, for receipt spacious, for cost sumptuous, for situation salubrious; near the sea, upon an advanced ground, having a delightsome prospect both of sea and land; round which lay a noble park, well stocked with fallow deer, whose reflection, as they were grazing, might be seen in the marble clavels, through the casements, of the chamber chimneys." Sir John Hele m. Margaret, daughter and co-heir of Ellis Warwick, esq. of Batsborow, and dying 4th June, 1608, left issue (beside three sons who *d. s. p.* named Ellys, Benjamin, and Thomas,) six sons and one daughter, viz.

1. WARWICK (Sir), knt. of Wembury, high sheriff of Devon 17 *King* JAMES I. who m. first, Mary, eldest daughter of John Halse, esq. of Kenidon, in Devon, and relict of William Hawkins, esq.* of Plymouth, (for both of which families see also PRINCE's *Worthies*;) and secondly, Margaret, daughter of Sir William Courtenay, knt. of Powderham Castle, but *d. s. p.* in January, 1625. His lady afterwards married Sir John Chudleigh, and dying 17th July, 1628, was buried at Richmond, in Surrey.
2. John, *d. s. p.*
3. Francis (Sir), knt. who m. Jane, daughter of Rogers of Cannington, in Somersetshire, and left, with one daughter, a son,
   John, whose only daughter and heir m. Sir Edward Hungerford, K. B. who sold the estate of Wembury to George, Duke of Albemarle; from whose son, Christopher, Duke of Albemarle, it was purchased in 1686 by John Pollexfen, esq. of Plymouth, merchant; his son, John Pollexfen, esq. bequeathed it, with other estates, in 1744, to Dame Frances Chudleigh, at whose demise they devolved on her daughters and coheirs. (See CHUDLEIGH Baronetcy.) The manor of Wembury was allotted, on partition, to Elizabeth Chudleigh, who sold it in 1757 to William Molesworth, esq. whose heiress brought it to Lord Camden; and from him Wembury was purchased in 1803 by Thomas Lockyer, esq. of Plymouth.
4. Nicholas, m. Dorothy Stradling, of Bristol, and had two daughters.

JULIANA, m. first, in 1725, Peregrine, third Duke of Leeds, by whom she had no issue; and secondly, 7th Oct. 1732, Charles, second Earl of Portmore, K. T. by whom she had issue. (See BURKE's *Peerage*.)

CHARITY, m. to the Right Hon. George Treby, of Plympton, in Devon, son of Sir George Treby, lord chief justice of the Common Pleas, and had issue, a son, George, who *d. s. p.* and three daughters, viz.

CHARITY TREBY, who married Paul Henry Ourry, esq. commissioner of the Navy, and had issue,

PAUL TREBY OURRY, who assumed in 1785 the name and arms of TREBY.

Charity Ourry, m. to Montague-Edmond Parker, esq. of Whiteway (next brother of John, first Lord Boringdon, father of John, present Earl Morley, (see BURKE's *Peerage*,) by whom she was grandmother of MONTAGUE EDMOND PARKER, esq. of Whiteway, M.P. for South Devon. (See BURKE's *Commoners*, vol. II page 455.)

Caroline Ourry, m. to Sir William Molesworth, bart. of Pencarrow, in Cornwall, by whom she was grandmother of the present SIR WILLIAM MOLESWORTH, bart.

DOROTHY TREBY, who m. Edward Drewe, esq. (see PRINCE's *Worthies*), and had a son and daughter, viz.

Edward Drewe, deceased.

Dorothea-Juliana Drewe, m. to Arthur Kelly, esq. of Kelly, in Devon. (See BURKE's *Commoners*.)

ANNE TREBY, who m. Benjamin Hayes, esq. and had a son and heir,

Treby Hele Hayes, esq. of Dellamore, in Devon.

Walter.

Alice, died in infancy.
Elizabeth, born in 1614.
Joan.
Sarah.

* She had issue by her first husband Hawkins, who was descendant and heir of the great admiral, daughters and coheiresses; of whom Frances Hawkins m. John Newton, esq. of Crabaton Court, in Devon, whose descendant and heir, John Newton, of Crabaton Court, left an only surviving child, Elizabeth Newton, who m. 21st October, 1729, John Powell, esq. of Black Hall. (See BURKE's *Commoners*, vol. IV)

5. Walter, *m.* Honor, daughter of Thomas Maynard, esq. of Sherford, in Devon, and relict of John Fortescue, esq. of Spridleston, in that county, and had issue, at the time of visitation, a son,
   Warwick.
6. George, *m.* Lucy, daughter of John Ellacott, esq. of Exeter, and had issue, at that time, one son and one daughter,
   Warwick.
   Margaret.
7. Philippa, *m.* to Sir Reginald Mohun, knt. and bart. of Hall Bodinneck and Boconnock, in Cornwall, and had issue, at that time, one son and one daughter,
   John Mohun, Lord Mohun, of Okehampton.
   Elizabeth Mohun.

VII. William.

II. Thomasin, *m.* to John Luxton.
III. Elizabeth.

The eldest son of Nicholas Hele, of South Hele, by his second wife, Margery Downe, to whom we have now to confine ourselves, was

THOMAS HELE, esq. of Exeter and of Fleet Damarell, in the parish of Holberton, in the county of Devon, which he purchased, being then, as it is now, one of the most beautiful seats and estates in the county,* high sheriff of the shire 43 *Queen* ELIZABETH, 1601. He married Julian, daughter of John Smyth, esq. of Exeter, and had by her three sons and two daughters,

I. THOMAS, his heir.
II. Nicholas, who appears to have *d. s. p.* and whose will, dated 19th February, 1652, was proved 22nd March, 1654.
III. Lewis, of Babcombe, in Devon, who *d.* 7th January, 1657, having issue two sons and one daughter,
   1. Warwick, of Babcombe, high sheriff of Devon 17 JAMES I. 1619, married Grace, daughter of Thomas Gilbert, esq. of Babcombe, by whom (who died 27th January, 1668, aged fifty-four,) he had issue a son, who succeeded him on his death in December, 1643,
      Thomas, of Babcombe, living in 1671.
   2. Lewis, living in 1652.
   1. Susan, living in 1634, having had issue.

I. Joan, *m.* to Robert Rolle, esq. of Heanton, in Devon, and *d.* in 1634, having had issue.
II. Grace.

The eldest son and heir,

THOMAS HELE, esq. of Fleet, high sheriff of Devon 16 JAMES I. 1618, *m.* Bridget, daughter (by Catherine, eldest daughter of Sir Richard Edgcombe, knt. of Mount Edgcombe, high sheriff of Devon 35 HENRY VIII. and 1 *Queen* MARY, the builder of Mount Edgcombe House and ancestor of the earls thereof,) of Sir Henry Champernowne, knt. of Modbury Castle or Court,† in Devon, and had six sons and four daughters, viz.

I. Samuel, born about 1590, and *d. s. p.*
II. THOMAS (Sir), his heir.
III. Nicholas, of London, and of Chigwell or Chey nell, in Essex, who died before 31st January. 1636, *s. p.*
IV. Henry, living in 1634, not twenty-seven years of age, and *d. s. p.*
V. Francis, *d. s. p.*
VI. Richard, named in the will of Sir Samuel Hele, of Fleet, the second baronet, and *d.* in 1673, leaving issue by his wife, Mary, daughter of Richard Hillersden, esq. of Membland, in Devon, who *d.* in February, 1667, a son and heir,
   Richard, of whom hereafter, as inheritor of Fleet, agreeably to the entail of his cousin, Sir Samuel, after the death of Sir Henry, the third baronet, in 1677.

I. Penelopy, *m.* to Christopher Blackhall, esq. of Totness, in Devon, his second wife.
II. Dulcibella, *m.* first, to Sir Samuel Cosworth, knt. of Cosworth, in Cornwall, by whom she had issue, beside a daughter, Bridget, five sons, of whom Edward, Samuel, and John died young, and Robert and Nicholas were successively heirs to the estate, and dying without issue, cut off the entailed property of their family from their cousin, John Cosworth, whereby Bridget became sole heiress and carried the Cosworth lands, in marriage to *her* cousin, Henry Minors, esq. of St. Enodor, who had a daughter, Ann Minors, *m.* to Francis Vivian, esq. of Trevan, in that county whose only child, Mary Vivian, married her kinsman, Sir Richard Vivian, of Trelowarren, bart. to whom she carried the accumulated estates of Vivian, Cosworth, and Minors, re uniting, by her marriage, the two branches of the Vivian family, after a separation of at least three centuries. Dulcibella Hele *m.* secondly, Roskymer Courtenay, esq. of Probus, in that county, fifth son, by Catherine, daughter and co-heir of William Roskymer, of Peter Courtenay, esq. of Lanrake, in the county of Cornwall.
III. Bridget, *m.* to William Pendarvis, esq. of Roscarrow, in Cornwall.
IV. Elizabeth, *m.* to Richard Luckyn, esq. of Dov Hall, in the county of Essex.
V. Honor, unmarried in 1634.

Sir Thomas Hele *d.* in November, 1634, on the 1[illegible] of which month he was buried in the church of Holberton. He was succeeded by his second son,

I. SIR THOMAS HELE, knt. of Fleet, high sheriff Devon, who was created a BARONET by *King* CHARLES 28th May, 1627, the 3rd year of his reign, being the first baronetcy conferred by him on a Devonshire family, and the eighth elevation to the same rank gentry of that county from the institution of the order in 1611. He was a member for Okehampton, with Sir Edward Wise, K.B. of the celebrated parliament 1640, and among those who, adhering to the sovereign gave attendance at Oxford, in January, 1643. [illegible] served the royal cause also actively in the field, [illegible]

---

* Fleet, one of the finest seats and estates in the county of Devon, about two miles from Modbury, was possessed by the Heles, and continued in their family until the year 1716, when, issue male in that family failing, it became the property of James Bulteel, esq. to whom it was devised by will of Richard Hele, who *d.* in 1709, in the event of his only son dying, as he did, *s. p.* The mansion is finely situated on an eminence on the western side of the river Erme, and part of it, shewing that it was originally built in the shape of the initial of Hele, is very ancient; but many alterations were made by the last proprietor, who erected an extensive and elegant front towards the north, which commands a delightful prospect over the valley through which the river winds, with Ermington Church, and in the distance the celebrated hills on [illegible] moor called the East and West Beacons. Another part of the view includes a fine wood, together with the church and western extremity of the town of Modbury.—Vide RISDON'S *Devon*, and BRITTON'S *Beauties of England and Wales.*

† See note ‡, ante.

articularly at the siege of Plymouth, from 15th September, 1643, to 25th December following; during which period he was one of the chief commanders of his majesty's forces. For thus acting against the parliament, he was made to pay, beside a fine, a composition for his estate of £280 per annum. He m. twice: first, Penelopy, daughter and co-heir of Emorbe Simson, esq. of Wigborow, in the county of Somerset, by whom he had an only son,

I. Thomas, of Wigborow, who m. Amy, daughter of Thomas Luttrell, esq. of Dunster Castle, in Somerset, by his wife, Jane, daughter of Sir Francis Popham, of Littlecot (see Burke's *Commoners*), but died at Wigborow, *v. p.* 13th November, 1665, *s. p.* devising that estate, by will, to his wife for life, with remainder to his brother Henry. His widow re-married George Reynell, esq. (See Burke's *Commoners*).

Sir Thomas Hele's second wife was Elizabeth, daughter of Carson, of Oxfordshire, by whom, who died in [illegible], and was buried in Holberton Church, 14th March in that year, he had two sons (to survive him) and two daughters, viz.

I. Samuel (Sir), heir to his father.

II. Henry (Sir), heir to his brother.

I. Elizabeth, m. at Ermington, in October, 1655, Richard Fowell, esq. of Black Hall and Diptford Down, in Devon, (see Burke's *Commoners*, vol. iv.) and by him, who *d. v. p.* in September, 1669, aged forty, and was buried in Diptford Church. Elizabeth Hele, who *d.* in November, 1690, and was there buried on the 13th of that month, had a son and heir,

William Fowell, of Black Hall and Diptford Down, who on the death, in 1692, of Sir John Fowell, of Fowellscomb, third baronet of that family, M.P. for Totness, unm. became heir male of his family, (see Fowell Baronetcy,) and on the death in April, 1677, *s. p.* of Sir Henry Hele, of Fleet, third baronet, representatives of the Heles, baronets. He was ancestor, through daughters and heiresses of Smyth of Tavistock, Newton of Crabaton Court, in Devon, and Digby of Red Hall, in Lincoln, of the late

John Digby Fowell, of Black Hall and Diptford Down, who *d.* in 1829, leaving by his wife, Sarah, second daughter and co-heir, by Henrietta Kirkham, daughter and co-heiress of a branch of the Kirkhams of Blackdon and Pynhoe, in Devon, of Peter Knowling, esq. of Washbourne House, in that county,* surviving issue three sons and three daughters,

1. John-Digby Fowell, *b.* at Black Hall, 20th January, 1796, *m.* 12th August, 1819, Frances, only daughter of Samuel Cumming, esq. of Totness, of the family of Cumming, *of Coulter*, baronets.

2. Francis-Kirkham Fowell, *b.* at Blackhall, 16th July, 1798, *m.* in 1820, Anne, second daughter, by his wife, Elizabeth, fourth daughter of Charles Coxwell, esq. of Ablington House, in the county of Gloucester, of Richard Estcourt Cresswell, esq. of Pinkney Park and Bibery, in that county, formerly M.P. for Cirencester.

3. William-Newton Fowell, *b.* there, 5th June, 1803, a lieutenant R.N. unm.

1. Henrietta-Digby Fowell, *b.* there, *m.* to Richard Samuel Sprye, a captain in the Indian army, Madras presidency, second surviving son, by Anne, his wife, daughter of Sampson Crapp, of Trevollard House, in the county of Cornwall, of the Rev. John Sprye, vicar of Ugborough, in Devon, (see Burke's *Commoners*, vol. iv.) and has surviving issue five sons and five daughters,

Reynell-Richard-Hele-Fowell Sprye.

Courtenay-Edward-Hele-Fowell Sprye.

Henrietta-Anne-Hele-Fowell Sprye.

Isabella-Mary-Hele-Fowell Sprye.

Frances-Helen-Hele-Fowell Sprye.

Sarah-Emily-Hele-Fowell Sprye.

2. Isabella-Georgina Fowell, born there, *m.* 17th August, 1819, to Samuel Crapp, esq. of Plymouth, as yet *s. p.*

3. Sarah-Knowling Fowell, *b.* there, *d.* in October, 1829, aged twenty, unm.

II. Honor Hele, bapt. 25th March, 1639, *m.* first, 1st January, 1661, to Gregory Huckmore, esq. of Buckland Baron, in Devon; and secondly, Sir Richard Bonithorn, knt. of Carclew, in Cornwall, whose wife she was in 1683, and *d.* in 1710, aged seventy-six, leaving an only daughter and heiress,

Jane Bonithorn, *m.* to Samuel Kemp, esq. of Penryn, in Cornwall.

Sir Thomas Hele *d.* in November, 1670, intestate, and was buried in the church of Holberton, on the 16th of that month, and was succeeded by his sixth son,

II. Sir Samuel Hele, of Fleet, who *m.* 28th April, 1668, at St. Martin's in the Fields, London, Mary, daughter of Anthony Hungerford, esq. of Farley Castle, and sister of Sir Edward Hungerford, K.B. thereof, by whom, who *d.* 1672, and was buried in Holberton Church, 18th January in that year, he had an only daughter,

Jane, *m.* to Sir Arthur Shene, bart. only son of Sir James Shene, knt. who was created a Baronet 7th February, 1662, but *d. s. p.* Her husband, who survived her, *d.* 24th June, 1725.

Sir Samuel died in February, 1672, and was buried in Holberton Church. By his will, dated 4th March, 1671, and proved 4th January, 1675, he entailed Fleet House and estates on the male line of his family, viz. after his brother, on his cousin, Richard Hele, before named, with remainder to Thomas Hele, of Babcombe, who was named executor, but died before probate, and others. He was succeeded by his only remaining brother,

III. Sir Henry Hele, of Fleet, *b.* about 1664, *m.* at

* See Sandys' *Baronetcy* and Burke's *Peerage*.

St. Germans, in the county of Cornwall, 13th July, 1676, Susan, daughter of John Eliot, esq. of Port Eliot, of the family of the Barons Eliot and Earls of St. Germans; but *d.* in April, 1677, *s. p.* when the BARONETCY became EXTINCT, its representation devolving upon his nephew, William Fowell, esq. of Black Hall, but Fleet and its estates passed, under the will of Sir Samuel, to the heir male,

RICHARD HELE, before named, in holy orders, and rector of St. Helen's, in Cornwall, who removing to Fleet, died there, 29th July, 1682, leaving issue by his wife, Judith, daughter of George Carey, D.D. of Clovelly, in the county of Devon, Dean of Exeter,* who *d.* in May, 1704, one son and one daughter,

RICHARD.

Ann, *m.* to J. Woolcombe, esq. of Pilton, in the county of Devon, but *d. s. p.*

The son, Richard Hele, esq. of Fleet, M.P. for West Looe in 1702, *d.* in December, 1709, leaving issue an only child,

JAMES MODYFORD HELE, who *d.* a minor in London, in August, 1716, the last of the male line of Fleet, when Fleet and its estates passed, as a mark of private friendship, under the will of his father, who had inherited it solely from the wish of the second baronet, that it should continue in the *name*, as well as blood of the family, from the right heirs of the original purchaser as well as of the baronets, the Fowells of Black Hall,† to James Bulteel, esq. of Membland, in the county of Devon, an entire stranger in blood, whose grandson and heir is the present John Bulteel, esq. of Fleet, whose eldest son and heir apparent, John Crocker Bulteel, esq. of Lyneham, in Devon, formerly M.P. for the south of that county, *m.* Lady Elizabeth Grey, third daughter of Earl Grey, K.G. and has issue. (See BURKE's *Peerage.*)

Arms—Ar. five lozenges in pale erm. the centre one charged with a leopard's face or.

HENDLEY, OF CUCKFIELD.

CREATED 8th April, 1661.

EXTINCT about 1675.

Lineage.

GERVASE HENDLEY, of Coursehorne, in Kent (where his ancestors were seated prior to 1334), *m.* Elizabeth, daughter of Walter Roberts, and had a son,

SIR WALTER HENDLEY, knt. of Coursehorne, *m.* first, a daughter of John Hales, one of the barons of the Exchequer, by whom he had a son, THOMAS, his heir, and Elizabeth, widow of William Coke, of London. He *m.* secondly, Elizabeth Bellingham, of Sussex, by whom he had a son, John, of Wales. Sir Walter was *s.* by his son,

THOMAS HENDLEY, esq. of Coursehorne, who *m.* first, Anne, daughter and heir of Henry Bowyer, esq. of Cuckfield, in Sussex, by Elizabeth, his wife, daughter and heir of Thomas Vaux, clerk comptroller of Henry the Eighth's Hospital, and had issue,

THOMAS, his heir.

Francis.

Margery, *m.* to Francis Handbury, of Lymington

He *m.* secondly, Mary, daughter of Walter Roberts, esq. of Glassenbury, and had by her three sons. His son and heir by his first wife,

SIR THOMAS HENDLEY, knt. of Coursehorne, high sheriff of Kent, was living in 1619. He *m.* Elizabeth, daughter of John Wilford, esq. of Enfield, and had with several daughters, one of whom, Ann, *m.* in 1629, Thomas Taylor, of Godmersham, four sons, viz.

Bowyer, aged twenty in 1619.

Thomas, aged nine in 1619.

WALTER, of whom presently.

John, *b.* in 1617, who *m.* Priscilla, daughter of Thomas Fludd, esq. of Gore Court, and was ancestor of the HENDLEYS of Gore Court, in Kent.

Sir Thomas Hendley's son or grandson,

I. WALTER HENDLEY, esq. of Cuckfield, in Sussex, was created a BARONET in 1661. He *m.* Frances, daughter and co-heir of Sir Thomas Springett, bart. of the Broyle, in Sussex, but died without male issue about 1675, when the title became EXTINCT.

Arms—Paly, bendy, gu. and az. eight martlets in orle or.

HENE, OF WINKFIELD.

CREATED 1st Oct. 1642.—EXTINCT after 169[illegible]

Lineage.

The manor of Folijohn, in Winkfield, Berks, was granted in 1630 to

I. HENRY HENNE, esq. who was created a BARONET in 1642. He *m.* Dorothy, daughter of Henry Stapleford, esq. of Paul's Walden, Herts, and dying in 1668, was *s.* by his son,

II. SIR HENRY HENE, of Winkfield, who *m.* Mary, daughter of Sir John Corbett, bart. of Adderley, in Shropshire, and had issue,

RICHARD, his heir.

PENELOPE, co-heir to her brother, who sold a moiety of the estate, in 1735, to Mr. [illegible] from whom it was, in 1744, purchased by L[illegible] Henry Beauclerk.

* Her sister, Dorothy Cary, *m.* Thomas Harris, esq. of the Close of Salisbury, ancestor of the Earl of Malmesbury.

† No family has been more unfortunate in the loss of property to which they were heirs at law, or bequeathed to them by will, than the Black-Hall Fowells. In addition to the loss of Fleet, as here shewn, in order that it might go to the heirs male, the last of which kin left it to a stranger, they lost Fowellscomb, to which they *were* the heirs male, and which was bequeathed to them orally or by will by the three last owners of it of their family, owing to some informality in the will of Sir John Fowell, the last baronet, whereon that seat and estates went to the families of Parker, of Boringdon, and Champernoune, of Dartington, into which the sisters of the baronet married. (See that title.) While, again, at a still more recent period *the whole* of the large property of the late James Digby, esq. of Red Hall, the last heir male of the North Luffenham branch of the house of Digby, passed, contrary to every expectation of the family, by will made very shortly before Mr. D[illegible] decease in 1811, from his nephew and heir-at-law, the late John Digby Fowell, of Black-Hall, to Mr. D[illegible] *younger* sister, Henrietta, Mrs. Pauncefort, whose [illegible] surviving child, Philip Duncombe Pauncefort Duncombe, esq. of Brick Hill Manor, in the county of Bucks, succeeded to it on her death intestate. (See DUNCOMBE family, BURKE's *Commoners.*)

Alice, co-heir to her brother, m. to James Dewhurst, esq. who sold her moiety of the estate, in 1749, also to Lord Henry Beauclerk.

The son and heir,

III. Sir Richard Henn, of Winkfield, died unmarried in the early part of the last century, when the Baronetcy expired.

HENLEY, OF HENLEY.

Created 30th June, 1660.

Extinct about 1740.

Lineage.

Robert Henley, esq. of Henley, in the county of Somerset, high sheriff in 1613, was grandfather of

Sir Robert Henley, knt. bencher of the Temple, and master of the King's Bench, who m. first, Mrs. Brett, and by her had a son, ancestor of the Henleys of Grange, in Hampshire. He m. secondly, Anne, second daughter of John Eldred, esq. of Saxham, in Suffolk, and had by that lady three sons, Andrew, ... and Robert. Sir Robert died in the possession of an estate worth £4000 a-year. His eldest son by the second wife,

I. Andrew Henley, esq. of Henley, was created a Baronet by *King* Charles II. Sir Andrew m. Mary, daughter of Sir John Gayer, knt. of London, and had issue,

Robert, his heir.
Andrew, successor to his brother.

Catherine, m. to Carleton Whitelocke, esq.
Mary.

He died about 1675, and was succeeded by his elder son,

II. Sir Robert Henley, M.P. for Andover in 1681. This gentleman died unmarried about 1689, leaving the estate £30,000 in debt, and was succeeded by his brother,

III. Sir Andrew Henley, who continuing the extravagant course of his brother, soon run out and sold the estate. He m. a daughter of Mr. Ball, of Yeatly, in Hampshire, and had (with two daughters) his successor,

IV. Sir Robert Henley, who appears to have been in comparatively humble circumstances. It is stated that he first went with the queen's letter to sea, and was afterwards customer in the port of Sandwich. He m. Mrs. Bowles, of Camberwell, but died without issue about the year 1740, when the Baronetcy became extinct.

Arms—Az. a lion rampant arg. crowned or, a border of the second, semée of torteauxes.

HERBERT, OF RED CASTLE.

Created 16th Nov. 1622.

Extinct 8th March, 1748.

Lineage.

The Hon. Sir Edward Herbert, knt. of Red Castle, in the county of Montgomery (afterwards called Powis Castle), second son of William, first Earl of Pembroke, m. Mary, only daughter and heir of Thomas Stanley, esq. of Stenden, in Hertfordshire, master of the Mint in 1570, and was s. by his eldest son,

Sir William Herbert, K.B. so created at the coronation of *King* James I. who was elevated to the peerage in 1629, as Baron Powis, of Powis Castle. He m. Eleanor, daughter of Henry Percy, Earl of Northumberland, and had (with two daughters) a son and heir,

I. Percy Herbert, of Red Castle, who, in the lifetime of his father, and before that gentleman was raised to the peerage, was created a Baronet 16th November, 1622. Sir Percy m. Elizabeth, daughter of Sir William Craven, knt. alderman of London, and had issue,

William, his successor.

Mary, m. to George, Lord Talbot, eldest son of John, Earl of Shrewsbury.

He inherited the barony of Powis on the decease of his father in 1656, and dying in 1666, was s. by his son,

II. Sir William Herbert, third Lord Powis, who was created, in 1674, Earl of Powis, and on the accession of *King* James II. Viscount Montgomery and Marquess of Powis. His lordship, following the fortunes of his royal master, withdrew into France at the Revolution, and was subsequently created Marquess of Montgomery and Duke of Powis.* He was afterwards outlawed for not returning within a limited time and submitting to the new government. He m. Lady Elizabeth Somerset, daughter of Edward, Marquess of Somerset, and dying at St. Germains, 2nd June, 1696, was s. by his only son,

III. Sir William Herbert, who was restored to the honours enjoyed by his father prior to the Revolution, and was thus fourth Lord Powis, and second Earl and Marquess. His lordship m. Mary, daughter and co-heir of Sir Thomas Preston, bart. of Furness, in Lancashire, and had two sons, viz.

William, his heir.
Edward, m. Henrietta, daughter of James, first Earl Waldegrave, and dying in 1734, left by that lady (who m. secondly, Mr. Beard, the comedian,) a posthumous child,

Barbara Herbert, who m. first, Henry-Arthur Herbert, created Baron Herbert, of Chirbury, in 1743.

The marquess died in 1745, and was s. by his elder son,

IV. Sir William Herbert, third Marquess of Powis,

* These latter honours were of course never acknowledged in England.

who died unmarried 8th March, 1748, when all his honours, including the BARONETCY, became EXTINCT; and his estates devolved, under his lordship's will, upon the husband of his niece, Henry-Arthur, Lord Herbert of Chirbury.*

Arms—Party per pale az. and gu. three lions rampant arg. a crescent for difference.

HERBERT, OF BROMFIELD.

CREATED in 1660.—EXTINCT in 1669.

Lineage.

FRANCIS HERBERT, esq. of Dolgiog, in Montgomeryshire, son of Matthew Herbert, esq. (uncle to the celebrated Lord Herbert of Chirbury), by Margaret, sister of Francis Foxe, of Bromfield, in Salop, had two sons, namely,

- I. MATTHEW, his heir.
- II. Francis, of Oakley Park, whose son,
  - RICHARD, of Oakley Park, a magistrate and deputy-lieutenant for Salop, married Florentia, daughter of Richard, second Lord Herbert of Chirbury, and had
    - FRANCIS, whose son,
      - HENRY-ARTHUR HERBERT, esq. was created Baron Herbert of Chirbury, 21st December, 1743, and in three years after advanced to the EARLDOM OF POWIS, having espoused Barbara, niece of William Herbert, last Marquess of Powis. His lordship's son and successor, the second Earl of Powis, dying *s. p.* in 1801, the honours became *extinct*, while the estates passed to his sister, LADY HENRIETTA-ANTONIA HERBERT, wife of Edward, Lord Clive.
    - George, who *m.* in 1693, Martha, daughter of John Newton, of Heightley, and relict of Richard Owen, and had a son,
      - FRANCIS, M.P. for Montgomery, who *m.* Mary, daughter of Rowland Baugh, esq. by Mary, his wife, daughter and co-heir of Thomas, Lord Folliott, and had George, Henry, and Mary, who *m.* Captain Frederick Cornewall, of Diddlebury, and was mother of the late Bishop of Worcester.

The elder son of Francis Herbert of Dolgiog,

I. MATTHEW HERBERT, esq. of Bromfield, in Shropshire, high sheriff thereof in 1655, was created a BARONET in 1660. He *m.* Mary, daughter of Sir Thomas Lucy, of Charlecote, in Warwickshire, but *d. s. p.* in 1669, when the BARONETCY became EXTINCT.

Arms—As HERBERT OF RED CASTLE.

HERBERT, OF TINTERNE.

CREATED 3rd July, 1660.—EXTINCT ....

Lineage.

I. THOMAS HERBERT, esq. of Tinterne, in the county of Monmouth, created a BARONET at the Restoration, *m.* first, Lucy, daughter of Sir Walter Alexander, knt.; and secondly, Elizabeth, daughter of Sir Gervase Cutler, knt. and relict of Henry Edmunds, esq. of Yorkshire. Sir Thomas was *s.* at his demise by his son.

II. SIR HENRY HERBERT, who fixed his residence in Yorkshire, and married Anne, daughter of Sir Thomas Harrison, knt. of Allerthorpe, in that county. Sir Henry appears to have died without issue, and the BARONETCY is supposed to have EXPIRED with him.

Arms—As HERBERT OF RED CASTLE.

HERON, OF CHIPCHASE.

CREATED 20th Nov. 1662.

EXTINCT 27th May, 1801.

Lineage.

This family, anciently written HAIRUN, HEYRON and HEIRUN, was long of eminence in the county of Northumberland. One of its members, William Heron, who had license to castellate his house at Ford, was summoned to parliament as a baron in the reign of EDWARD III. and another, Sir Richard Heron, was similarly dignified by RICHARD II. (See BURKE's *Extinct Peerage*.)

SIR JOHN HAIRUN, one of the soldiers of the CONQUEROR, possessed Ford, with a very good estate, and acquired Chipchase by marriage with the daughter and heir of its Saxon lord, Sir William Chipches, of Chipches Castle. From Sir John we pass to his lineal descendant,

I. CUTHBERT HERON, esq. of Chipchase Castle, in the county of Northumberland, who was created a BARONET by *King* CHARLES II. 20th November, 1662. Sir Cuthbert *m.* first, Elizabeth, third daughter of Sir Richard Graham, bart. of Netherby, and had with five daughters, three sons, namely,

- I. CUTHBERT, his heir, who *m.* Elizabeth, daughter of Sir John Mallory, knt. of Studley, in the county of York, and dying in the lifetime of his father, left an only child, his heir
  - ELIZABETH HERON, living in 1688, *m.* to Ralph Jennison, esq. of Walworth.
- II. JOHN, successor to the baronetcy.
- III. CHARLES, heir to his brother.

Sir Cuthbert *m.* secondly, Miss Thompson, daughter of George Thomson, esq. of Yorkshire, and by that lady had another son,

- IV. CUTHBERT, who *m.* Catherine, daughter of Richard Myddleton, esq. of Offerton, in Durham and dying in 1738, left a son,
  - THOMAS, who succeeded as fifth baronet.
- I. Dorothy.
- II. Mary.
- III. Henrietta.
- IV. Elizabeth, *m.* to — Fenwick, esq. of Northumberland.
- V. Catherine, *m.* to Mr. Smith, of Southampton.

He was *s.* at his decease, in 1688, by his eldest surviving son,

II. SIR JOHN HERON, who *m.* Anne, daughter of

---

* Refer to BURKE's *Extinct and Dormant Peerage*.

John Heron, esq. of Brampton, in Huntingdonshire, and left an only daughter and heir,

HENRIETTA HERON, m. to Mr. Huxley, of London.

His wife, who survived him, died 29th October, 1713, and was buried in the Abbey Church of Bath. He was s. at his decease, about the year 1693, by his brother,

III. SIR CHARLES HERON, who m. Catherine, daughter of Sir William Poultney, knt. of St. James's Street, Middlesex, and had one son, Harry, and three daughters, of whom two died young, and the third, Catherine, m. Mr. Panton, of Banff, in Scotland. He was s. at his decease by his son,

IV. SIR HARRY HERON,* an officer in the Guards, who m. Elizabeth Coventry, but dying without issue in 1749, was s. by (the only surviving son of Cuthbert Heron, esq. his uncle by the half-blood), his cousin,

V. SIR THOMAS HERON, who inherited the estates and assumed the surname of his maternal uncle, Francis Myddleton, esq. of Offerton. He m. first, Margaret, daughter of Ralph Finlay, esq. of Carrickfergus, and secondly, Elizabeth, daughter of Alexander Arbuthnot, esq. of Portree, in Scotland. By the former, who died in 1753, he had an only daughter,

> MARY, who sold the estate of Grinkle Park to her cousin, Robert Wharton Myddleton, esq. She m. Captain Baron, of Alnwick, and had two daughters, viz.
>
> > Elizabeth Baron, who died in 1796, aged sixteen.
> >
> > MARY BARON, m. to George Lynn, esq. of Southwick House, in the county of Northampton.

Sir Thomas dying thus without male issue, 27th May, 1801, the estate of Bowlby, &c. passed to his cousin, Robert Wharton, esq.† of Old Park, in the county of Durham, who assumed the surname and arms of MYDDLETON. At the decease of Sir Thomas the BARONETCY is said to have become EXTINCT, but has been assumed by Cuthbert Heron, esq. of Newcastle-upon-Tyne.

Arms—Azure, three herons arg.

HERVEY, OF KIDBROOKE.

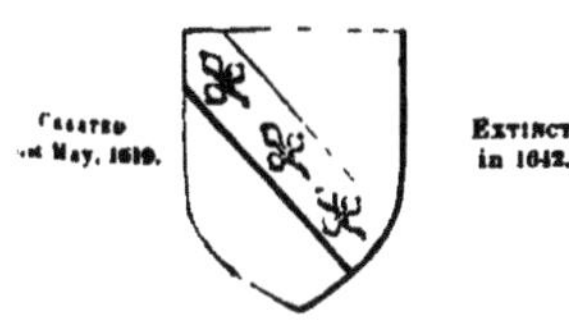

CREATED 31st May, 1619. EXTINCT in 1642.

Lineage.

SIR NICHOLAS HERVEY, of the privy chamber to King HENRY VIII. and ambassador from that monarch to the emperor's court at Ghent, left by his second wife, Bridget, daughter and heir of Sir John Wiltshire, of Stone Castle, in Kent, and widow of Sir Richard Wingfield, two sons, the elder of whom,

HENRY HERVEY, esq. was father of

I. SIR WILLIAM HERVEY, of Kidbrooke, in Kent, who acquired high military reputation in the reigns of ELIZABETH, JAMES I. and CHARLES I. He first signalized himself against the Armada, having boarded one of the galleons, and killed the captain, Hugh Monçade, with his own hand; he was afterwards knighted and employed in Ireland, where continuing his eminent career, he was created a BARONET 31st May, 1619, and the next year raised to the peerage of that kingdom, as Baron Hervey of Ross, in the county of Wexford. He was subsequently made a peer of England, in the dignity of Baron Hervey, of Kidbrooke. He m. first, Mary, relict of Henry, Earl of Southampton, and daughter of Anthony, Viscount Montacute, and secondly, Cordelia, daughter and co-heir of Brian Anslow, esq. of Lewisham, in Kent. He had three sons, William, killed in Germany, John, died in Ireland, and Henry, who died young, beside an only daughter and eventual heir,

> ELIZABETH HERVEY, who m. John Hervey, esq. of Ickworth, and *d. s. p.* Mr. Hervey's estates devolved upon his brother, Sir Thomas Hervey, knt. whose eldest son,
>
> > John Hervey, became Earl of Bristol.

His lordship outliving his sons, died in 1642, when all his honours, including the BARONETCY, became EXTINCT.

Arms—Gules, on a bend arg. three trefoils slipped vert.

HEWET, OF HEADLY HALL.

CREATED 11th Oct. 1621. EXTINCT 7th June, 1822.

Lineage.

ROBERT HEWET, esq. a gentleman of ancient extraction,‡ possessed a considerable estate at Killamarch, in Derbyshire, *temp.* HENRY VIII.§ and had two sons, Robert, who *d. s. p.* and his successor,

WILLIAM HEWET, esq. who *d.* in 1599, aged seventy-seven, and was buried in St. Paul's Cathedral, London: he left four sons, JOHN, his heir, Solomon, Thomas, and William; from the three last sprung the families of Hewet, of Pishobury, Herts, the

---

* About the year 1737 Sir Harry Heron is stated to have mortgaged Chipchase Castle and estate to Archibald Reed, of Bellingham, whose only son, John, left the property to his daughter, who m. Christopher Soulsby, esq. who took the surname of Reed.

† Mr. Wharton was son of Thomas Wharton, esq. M.D. of Old Park, the friend and correspondent of Gray the poet, and grandson of Robert Wharton, esq. of Old Park, by Mary, his wife, daughter of Richard Myddleton, esq. of Offerton, and sister of Catharine, the mother of Sir Thomas Heron, bart. (see BURKE's *Commoners*, vol. i. 171).

‡ There was a SIR WALTER HEWET, who made a distinguished figure in EDWARD III.'s wars in France.

§ Of the same family was SIR WILLIAM HEWET, lord mayor of London, 1559, but whether brother to this Robert is not certain; of him we find the following circumstance related in STOW's Survey of London:

" Sir William Hewet, clothworker, mayor, 1559, son of Edmund Hewet. He *d.* 6th February, 1566. His wife was the daughter of Leveson, of Kent. This mayor was a merchant possest of a great estate valued at £6000 per annum, and was said to have had three sons, and one daughter; to which daughter this mischance happened (the father then living upon London bridge). The maid

who died unmarried 8th March, 1748, when all his honours, including the BARONETCY, became EXTINCT; and his estates devolved, under his lordship's will, upon the husband of his niece, Henry-Arthur, Lord Herbert of Chirbury.*

Arms—Party per pale az. and gu. three lions rampant arg. a crescent for difference.

HERBERT, OF BROMFIELD.

CREATED in 1660.—EXTINCT in 1669.

Lineage.

FRANCIS HERBERT, esq. of Dolgiog, in Montgomeryshire, son of Matthew Herbert, esq. (uncle to the celebrated Lord Herbert of Chirbury), by Margaret, sister of Francis Foxe, of Bromfield, in Salop, had two sons, namely,

- I. MATTHEW, his heir.
- II. Francis, of Oakley Park, whose son,
  - RICHARD, of Oakley Park, a magistrate and deputy-lieutenant for Salop, married Florentia, daughter of Richard, second Lord Herbert of Chirbury, and had
    - FRANCIS, whose son,
      - HENRY-ARTHUR HERBERT, esq. was created Baron Herbert of Chirbury, 21st December, 1743, and in three years after advanced to the EARLDOM OF POWIS, having espoused Barbara, niece of William Herbert, last Marquess of Powis. His lordship's son and successor, the second Earl of Powis, dying *s. p.* in 1801, the honours became *extinct*, while the estates passed to his sister, LADY HENRIETTA-ANTONIA HERBERT, wife of Edward, Lord Clive.
    - George, who *m.* in 1693, Martha, daughter of John Newton, of Heightley, and relict of Richard Owen, and had a son,
      - FRANCIS, M.P. for Montgomery, who *m.* Mary, daughter of Rowland Baugh, esq. by Mary, his wife, daughter and co-heir of Thomas, Lord Folliott, and had George, Henry, and Mary, who *m.* Captain Frederick Cornewall, of Diddlebury, and was mother of the late Bishop of Worcester.

The elder son of Francis Herbert of Dolgiog,

I. MATTHEW HERBERT, esq. of Bromfield, in Shropshire, high sheriff thereof in 1655, was created a BARONET in 1660. He *m.* Mary, daughter of Sir Thomas Lucy, of Charlecote, in Warwickshire, but *d. s. p.* in 1669, when the BARONETCY became EXTINCT.

Arms—As HERBERT OF RED CASTLE.

HERBERT, OF TINTERNE.

CREATED 3rd July, 1660.—EXTINCT ....

Lineage.

I. THOMAS HERBERT, esq. of Tinterne, in the county of Monmouth, created a BARONET at the Restoration, *m.* first, Lucy, daughter of Sir Walter Alexander, knt.; and secondly, Elizabeth, daughter of Sir Gervase Cutler, knt. and relict of Henry Edmunds, esq. of Yorkshire. Sir Thomas was *s.* at his demise by his son.

II. SIR HENRY HERBERT, who fixed his residence in Yorkshire, and married Anne, daughter of Sir Thomas Harrison, knt. of Allerthorpe, in that county. Sir Henry appears to have died without issue, and the BARONETCY is supposed to have EXPIRED with him.

Arms—As HERBERT OF RED CASTLE.

HERON, OF CHIPCHASE.

CREATED 20th Nov. 1662. EXTINCT 27th May, 1801.

Lineage.

This family, anciently written HAIRUN, HEYRUN, and HEIRUN, was long of eminence in the county of Northumberland. One of its members, William Heron, who had license to castellate his house at Ford, was summoned to parliament as a baron in the time of EDWARD III. and another, Sir Richard Heron, was similarly dignified by RICHARD II. (See BURKE's *Extinct Peerage*.)

SIR JOHN HAIRUN, one of the soldiers of the CONQUEROR, possessed Ford, with a very good estate, and acquired Chipchase by marriage with the daughter and heir of its Saxon lord, Sir William Chipches, of Chipches Castle. From Sir John we pass to his lineal descendant,

I. CUTHBERT HERON, esq. of Chipchase Castle, in the county of Northumberland, who was created a BARONET by *King* CHARLES II. 20th November, 1662. Sir Cuthbert *m.* first, Elizabeth, third daughter of Sir Richard Graham, bart. of Netherby, and had, with five daughters, three sons, namely,

- I. CUTHBERT, his heir, who *m.* Elizabeth, daughter of Sir John Mallory, knt. of Studley, in the county of York, and dying in the lifetime of his father, left an only child, his heir.
  - ELIZABETH HERON, living in 1693, *m.* to Ralph Jennison, esq. of Walworth.
- II. JOHN, successor to the baronetcy.
- III. CHARLES, heir to his brother.

Sir Cuthbert *m.* secondly, Miss Thompson, daughter of George Thomson, esq. of Yorkshire, and by that lady had another son,

- IV. CUTHBERT, who *m.* Catherine, daughter of Richard Myddleton, esq. of Offerton, in Durham, and dying in 1738, left a son,
  - THOMAS, who succeeded as fifth baronet.
- I. Dorothy.
- II. Mary.
- III. Henrietta.
- IV. Elizabeth, *m.* to — Fenwick, esq. of Northumberland.
- V. Catherine, *m.* to Mr. Smith, of Southampton.

He was *s.* at his decease, in 1688, by his eldest surviving son,

II. SIR JOHN HERON, who *m.* Anne, daughter

* Refer to BURKE's *Extinct and Dormant Peerage*.

a numerous family, five sons and six daughters. The eldest son,

I. SIR THOMAS HEWETT, knt. purchased the manor and estate of Pishobury, in Hertfordshire, and served the office of sheriff for that county in 1638 and 1660, in which latter year he was created a BARONET. He m. first, Frances, daughter of Sir John Hobart, bart. of Blickling, lord chief justice of the Common Pleas, and by her, who died 21st May, 1632, had a daughter,

Dorothy, m. 2nd April, 1666, to Sir William Beversham, of Holbrook Hall, Suffolk.

Sir Thomas m. secondly, about 1633, Margaret, eldest daughter of Sir William Lytton, knt. of Knebworth, and relict of Thomas Hillersdon, esq. by whom, who died in 1669, he had issue,

GEORGE, his heir.

Elizabeth, m. to Sir Richard Anderson, bart. of Penley.

Margaret, m. to Sir Edward Farmer, knt. of Canons.

Anne, m. to Sir John Rivers, bart. of Chafford.

Arabella, m. to Sir William Wiseman, bart. of Canfield.

Mary, m. to Sir Charles Crofts Reade, knt. of Bardwell, in Suffolk.

Jane, m. to Charles Staples, esq. of Westminster.

Sir Thomas d. 4th August, 1662, aged fifty-seven, and was s. by his son,

II. SIR GEORGE HEWETT, of Pishobury, who was raised to the peerage of Ireland, in 1689, as Baron of James Town, in the county of Longford, and Viscount Hewett, of Gowran, in the county of Kilkenny, but died unmarried, 2nd December following, aged forty-seven, when all his honours, including the BARONETCY, became EXTINCT. From him the *Manor* of Pishobury passed to his sister, Lady Reade, who sold it to Ralph Freman, esq. of Hamels, from whose ... Philip, Earl of Hardwicke, it was purchased in ...23, by Rowland Alston, esq. of Harold House, Bedfordshire. The *Estate* of Pishobury was devised by Lord Hewett to his sister, Lady Wiseman, who conveyed it, in 1701, to William Gardiner, esq. whose granddaughter, Rose, brought it in marriage to Jeremiah Milles, esq.

Arms—Gu. a chev. engr. between three owls close ...

HEYMAN, OF SOMERFIELD.

CREATED ... Aug. 1641.

EXTINCT 20th Nov. 1808.

Lineage.

The family of HEYMAN, an ancient Kentish one, ... honours and estates in the counties of Kent and ... and in the city of London, centuries gone by. ... its members were conspicuous for their extensive benevolence.*

RALPH HEYMAN, esq. was possessed of a good estate in the reign of HENRY VII. He purchased the manor of Harenge, in Kent, from Sir Francis Willoughby, which his son,

PETER HEYMAN, esq. settled upon his son Peter. In the 25 HENRY VIII. Otterpole, in Kent, was purchased by Peter Heyman, esq. from Thomas Wombwell, esq. of Northfleet.

Somerfield estate, in the parish of Sellinge, in Kent, belonged to William Tilde, esq. who died leaving one daughter, ELIZABETH TILDE, his heir, who became the wife of

PETER HEYMAN, esq. about the middle of HENRY VIII. 1527. By this lady he had issue,

RALPH, his heir.

William, m. Elizabeth, daughter of Sir Reginald Scot, knt. and had a son, Thomas.

Mary, m. to Paul Johnson, esq. of Fordwich.

Catherine, m. to William Hamon, esq. of Acris.

Margaret, m. first, to John Poynet, esq. and secondly, to John Hill.

Mildred, m. to Thomas Corbet, of London.

Anne, m. to Robert Cutts, of London.

Emeline, d. unm.

He m. secondly, Mary, daughter of William Tirrell, esq. of Beeches, in Essex, and by her left an only daughter,

Jane, heir to her mother, m. John Honywood, esq. of Elmsted, in Kent, and had an only daughter,

Catherine Honywood, who m. Sir Edward Scot, knt. of Scotts Hall, in that county.

This Peter Heyman was one of the gentlemen of the bedchamber to EDWARD VI. and had a grant from that monarch, of Claverty, in Kent. He d. in August, 1550, and was s. by his eldest son,

RALPH HEYMAN, esq. of Somerfield, living in 1577, m. Anne, daughter of William Naunton, esq. of Suffolk, and had issue,

HENRY, his heir.

William, who gave a perpetual exhibition for the education of youths at the King's School at Canterbury, and at Trinity College, Cambridge.

Elizabeth, m. to Sir Thomas Scott, knt. of Scott's Hall.

Mary, m. to John Boade, esq. of Feversham.

Anne, m. to Adam Sprackling, esq. of Fordwich.

Elizabeth, m. to Thomas Tournay, esq. of New Buildings.

Margaret, m. to William Hales, esq. of Hepington.

Rebecca.

He d. in 1601, and was s. by his elder son,

HENRY HEYMAN, esq. of Somerfield, who m. Rebecca, daughter and co-heir of Dr. Robert Horne, bishop of Winchester, by whom he had four sons and three daughters, of the latter, Elizabeth, m. Sir Peter Godfrey, knt. of Lyd, in Kent. He d. in 1613, and was s. by his eldest son,

SIR PETER HEYMAN, knt. who m. first, Sarah, daughter and co-heir of Peter Collet, of London, merchant, and had by her,

HENRY, his heir, born at Selling, in Kent, 20th November, 1610.

Sarah, m. to Laurence Rooke, esq. of Monksnorton, in Kent.

He m. secondly, Mary, daughter and co-heir of Randolph Wolley, of London, merchant, by whom he had

* Tenterden free school, in Kent, was founded by a ... ten nearly four hundred years ago, and an estate of ... hundred pounds a year, in divers parts of Kent, was left by another branch of the family for charitable uses for ever.

Hewets, of Shire Oakes, Notts, and the Hewets, of Stretton, in Leicestershire. The eldest son,

JOHN HEWET, esq. survived his father but three years, dying in 1602. He *m.* Elizabeth, daughter of Sir Robert Hampson, knt. alderman of London, by whom (who *m.* secondly, Sir Gilbert Wakering, and thirdly, Sir Robert Bevile, K. B.) he had

JOHN, his heir.

Catherine, *m.* in 1617, to George Byng, esq. of Wrotham.

He was *s.* by his son,

I. JOHN HEWET, esq. of Headly Hall, in the county of York, who was created a BARONET by *King* JAMES I. 11th October, 1621. Sir John *m.* Catherine, daughter of Sir Robert Bevile, K. B. of Chesterton, in Huntingdonshire, and co-heir of her brother, Sir Robert Bevile, jun. K. B. who *d.* in 1640, and by that lady had issue,

- I. JOHN, his successor.
- II. Robert.

- I. Elizabeth.
- II. Catherine, *m.* to Robert Cheek, esq. of Purgo, in Essex.
- III. Frances.
- IV. Anne.
- V. Grace, *m.* to Sir Thomas Brograve, bart. of Hamels, Herts.

Sir John *d.* in 1657, aged fifty-nine, after he had seated his family at Waresby, in Huntingdonshire; and by his services and sufferings in the troublesome times acquired high reputation for loyalty. He was *s.* by his elder son,

II. SIR JOHN HEWET, who *m.* Frances, daughter of Sir Toby Tyrrell, bart. of Thornton, Bucks, by whom (who survived him, and *m.* secondly, Philip Cotton, esq. of Conington, in Cambridgeshire) he had a numerous family, viz.

- I. JOHN, his successor.
- II. Tyrrell, rector of Scotter, in Lincolnshire, *m.* but *d. s. p.*
- III. Robert, *d.* unm.
- IV. Thomas, *d.* young.
- V. Benjamin, *d.* unm.
- VI. Charles.
- VII. William, of St. Neots, who left three sons,
  1. WILLIAM, who *s.* as fourth baronet.
  2. TYRRELL, who succeeded his nephew, and became sixth baronet.
  3. Thomas.
- VIII. James, lieutenant of the Carlisle man-of-war, blown up at sea.
- IX. Thomas, M.D. *m.* Mrs. Pinkney, and left a son and daughter,
  - Thomas, of Clare Hall, in holy orders.
  - Anne.
- X. Toby.
- XI. Benjamin.

- I. Hester, *m.* to Ulysses Blount, esq. seventh son of Sir Henry Blount, knt. of Tittenhanger, Herts.
- II. Frances, *m.* to Henry Scrope, esq. of St. Neots, Huntingdonshire, but had no issue.
- III. Theodora.
- IV. Edith, *m.* to William Dove, esq. of Upton, Northamptonshire.
- V. Catherine.
- VI. Arabella.
- VII. Elizabeth, *m.* to — Broke, esq. of Nacton, in Suffolk, M.P. for Ipswich.

Sir John *d.* 30th September, 1684, and was *s.* by his eldest son,

III. SIR JOHN HEWET, sheriff of the counties of Cambridge and Huntingdon 2 JAMES II. *m.* first, Anne, daughter of Francis Stokes, esq.* of Tiderton, Wilts. and had two sons, who both died issueless, and two daughters, of which Anne, the elder, *m.* John Hagar, esq. of Bourn, in Cambridgeshire, and had a son, Hewet Hagar. Sir John wedded, secondly, Eleanor, eldest daughter of Sir John Osborne, bart. of Chicksands, in the county of Bedford, but had no child by that lady. Dying thus without male issue, the baronetcy devolved upon his nephew,

IV. SIR WILLIAM HEWET, captain R.N. who married Elizabeth, daughter of Mr. Levemore, of Gosport, and had three sons, WILLIAM, his heir, Levemore, and Herbert, with a daughter, Elizabeth. He *d.* in 17[illegible], and was *s.* by his eldest son,

V. SIR WILLIAM HEWET, captain R.N. lost before Pondicherry in the Duc d'Aquitaine, of which ship he was in command, 1st January, 1761: with Sir William perished his brother Levemore, and Herbert having died some years before, the baronetcy reverted to his uncle,

VI. SIR TYRREL HEWET, who married Miss Gedding, daughter of Mr. Robert Gedding, of the Post Office, and had two sons, BYNG and THOMAS. He *d.* 1[illegible] February, 1770, and was *s.* by the elder.

VII. SIR BYNG HEWET, who went to India in the Company's service in the year 1768, and was killed there about the year 1770. He was *s.* dying *s. p.* by his brother,

VIII. Sir THOMAS HEWET, who *m.* Mary, daughter of Mr. Tebbutt, of Sudbury, in the county of Northampton, but *d. s. p.* 7th June, 1822, when the BARONETCY became EXTINCT.

Arms—Gules, a chevron engrailed between three owls close arg.

HEWETT, OF PISHOBURY.

CREATED 19th July, 1660.—EXTINCT 2nd Dec. 1[illegible].

Lineage.

SIR WILLIAM HEWETT, knt. who died in the parish of St. Martin in the Fields, London, in 1637, *m.* Elizabeth, daughter of Richard Wiseman, esq. and he

---

playing with her, out of a window over the river Thames, by chance dropt her in, almost beyond expectation of being saved. A young gentleman, named Osborne, then apprentice to Sir William, the father (which Osborne was one of the ancestors of the Duke of Leeds in a direct line), at this calamitous accident, immediately leap'd in bravely, and saved the child. In memory of which deliverance, and in gratitude, her father afterwards bestowed her in marriage on the said Mr. Osborne, with a very great dowry, whereof the late estate of Sir Thomas Fenshaw, in the parish of Barkin, in Essex, was a part; as the late Duke of Leeds, himself, told the Rev. Mr. John Hewyt, from whom I have this relation; and together with that estate in Essex, several other lands in the parishes of Harthel, and Wallis or Wales, in Yorkshire, now in the possession of the said most noble family; also, that several persons of quality courted the said young lady; and particularly the Earl of Shrewsbury. But Sir William was pleased to say, Osborne saved her, and Osborne should enjoy her. The late Duke of Leeds and the present family, preserve the picture of Sir William, in his habit of lord mayor, at Kiveton House, Yorkshire, to this day, valuing it at £300."

* Son of Christopher Stokes, esq. of Tiderton, whose wife was sister to the Lord Chancellor Hyde, Earl of Clarendon.

a numerous family, five sons and six daughters. The eldest son,

I. Sir Thomas Hewett, knt. purchased the manor and estate of Pishobury, in Hertfordshire, and served the office of sheriff for that county in 1638 and 1660, in which latter year he was created a Baronet. He m. first, Frances, daughter of Sir John Hobart, bart. of Blickling, lord chief justice of the Common Pleas, and by her, who died 21st May, 1632, had a daughter,

Dorothy, m. 2nd April, 1666, to Sir William Beversham, of Holbrook Hall, Suffolk.

Sir Thomas m. secondly, about 1633, Margaret, eldest daughter of Sir William Lytton, knt. of Knebworth, and relict of Thomas Hillersdon, esq. by whom, who died in 1669, he had issue,

George, his heir.

Elizabeth, m. to Sir Richard Anderson, bart. of Penley.

Margaret, m. to Sir Edward Farmer, knt. of Canons.

Anne, m. to Sir John Rivers, bart. of Chafford.

Arabella, m. to Sir William Wiseman, bart. of Canfield.

Mary, m. to Sir Charles Crofts Reade, knt. of Bardwell, in Suffolk.

Jane, m. to Charles Staples, esq. of Westminster.

Sir Thomas d. 4th August, 1662, aged fifty-seven, and was s. by his son,

Sir George Hewett, of Pishobury, who was raised to the peerage of Ireland, in 1689, as Baron of St. James Town, in the county of Longford, and Viscount Hewett, of Gowran, in the county of Kilkenny, but died unmarried, 2nd December following, aged forty-seven, when all his honours, including the Baronetcy, became extinct. From him the *Manor* of Pishobury passed to his sister, Lady Reade, who sold it to Ralph Freman, esq. of Hamels, from whose son, Philip, Earl of Hardwicke, it was purchased in 1683, by Rowland Alston, esq. of Harold House, Bedfordshire. The *Estate* of Pishobury was devised by Lord Hewett to his sister, Lady Wiseman, who conveyed it, in 1701, to William Gardiner, esq. whose granddaughter, Rose, brought it in marriage to Jeremiah Milles, esq.

Arms—Gu. a chev. engr. between three owls close arg.

HEYMAN, OF SOMERFIELD.

Created 12th Aug. 1641. Extinct 20th Nov. 1808.

Lineage.

The family of Heyman, an ancient Kentish one, held honours and estates in the counties of Kent and Sussex, and in the city of London, centuries gone by, and its members were conspicuous for their extensive benevolence.*

Ralph Heyman, esq. was possessed of a good estate in the reign of Henry VII. He purchased the manor of Harenge, in Kent, from Sir Francis Willoughby, which his son,

Peter Heyman, esq. settled upon his son Peter. In the 25 Henry VIII. Otterpole, in Kent, was purchased by Peter Heyman, esq. from Thomas Wombwell, esq. of Northfleet.

Somerfield estate, in the parish of Sellinge, in Kent, belonged to William Tilde, esq. who died leaving one daughter, Elizabeth Tilde, his heir, who became the wife of

Peter Heyman, esq. about the middle of Henry VIII. 1527. By this lady he had issue,

Ralph, his heir.

William, m. Elizabeth, daughter of Sir Reginald Scot, knt. and had a son, Thomas.

Mary, m. to Paul Johnson, esq. of Fordwich.

Catherine, m. to William Hamon, esq. of Acris.

Margaret, m. first, to John Poynet, esq. and secondly, to John Hill.

Mildred, m. to Thomas Corbet, of London.

Anne, m. to Robert Cutts, of London.

Emeline, d. unm.

He m. secondly, Mary, daughter of William Tirrell, esq. of Beeches, in Essex, and by her left an only daughter,

Jane, heir to her mother, m. John Honywood, esq. of Elmsted, in Kent, and had an only daughter,

Catherine Honywood, who m. Sir Edward Scot, knt. of Scotts Hall, in that county.

This Peter Heyman was one of the gentlemen of the bedchamber to Edward VI. and had a grant from that monarch, of Claverty, in Kent. He d. in August, 1550, and was s. by his eldest son,

Ralph Heyman, esq. of Somerfield, living in 1577, m. Anne, daughter of William Naunton, esq. of Suffolk, and had issue,

Henry, his heir.

William, who gave a perpetual exhibition for the education of youths at the King's School at Canterbury, and at Trinity College, Cambridge.

Elizabeth, m. to Sir Thomas Scott, knt. of Scott's Hall.

Mary, m. to John Boade, esq. of Feversham.

Anne, m. to Adam Sprackling, esq. of Fordwich.

Elizabeth, m. to Thomas Tournay, esq. of New Buildings.

Margaret, m. to William Hales, esq. of Hepington.

Rebecca.

He d. in 1601, and was s. by his elder son,

Henry Heyman, esq. of Somerfield, who m. Rebecca, daughter and co-heir of Dr. Robert Horne, bishop of Winchester, by whom he had four sons and three daughters, of the latter, Elizabeth, m. Sir Peter Godfrey, knt. of Lyd, in Kent. He d. in 1613, and was s. by his eldest son,

Sir Peter Heyman, knt. who m. first, Sarah, daughter and co-heir of Peter Collet, of London, merchant, and had by her,

Henry, his heir, born at Selling, in Kent, 20th November, 1610.

Sarah, m. to Laurence Rooke, esq. of Monksnorton, in Kent.

He m. secondly, Mary, daughter and co-heir of Randolph Wolley, of London, merchant, by whom he had

* Tenterden free school, in Kent, was founded by a member of this family nearly four hundred years ago, and an estate of several hundred pounds a year, in divers parts of Kent, was left by another branch of the family for charitable uses for ever.

three sons and three daughters. On Peter, his second son, he settled Harenge, in Kent. Sir Peter represented the borough of Hythe in several parliaments, during the reigns of JAMES I. and CHARLES I. His eldest son and heir,

I. HENRY HEYMAN, esq. of Somerfield, in Kent, was created a BARONET by *King* CHARLES I. 12th August, 1641. Sir Henry *m.* Mary, daughter and heir of Daniel Holford, esq. of Westurreck, in Essex, and had issue,

- PETER, his successor, *b.* in Blackfriars, London, 10th July, 1642.
- Henry, *b.* at Selling, 24th May, 1646, } *d.* unm.
- Robert, *b.* at Selling, 6th July, 1647, } *d.* unm.
- Mary, *b.* in Blackfriars, 28th April, 1643, *m.* to Sir Richard Sandys, of Northborne, in Kent, (who was killed by his own fowling-piece in going over a hedge) and had a son,
  - RICHARD SANDYS, esq. who was created a BARONET in 1684, but *d.* without male issue in 1726.
- Anne, *b.* in Blackfriars, 19th May, 1644, *d.* unm.

He *d.* at Somerfield in 1658, and was *s.* by his eldest son,

II. SIR PETER HEYMAN, who *m.* Mary, daughter of Mr. Rich, of Clapham, and had two surviving sons, viz.

- BARTHOLOMEW, his heir.
- Peter, in holy orders, rector of Headcorn, in Kent, and one of the ten vicars of the diocese of Canterbury, *m.* Catherine, daughter of Mr. Thomas Tilden of that city, a civilian, by whom he had several children. The eldest son and heir,
  - Henry, of Stroud, *m.* Elizabeth, daughter of Hatch Underwood, and left a daughter and an only son,
    - HENRY-PIX, in holy orders, who *s.* as fifth baronet.
    - A daughter, *m.* to — Baker, of Hawkhurst.

Sir Peter *d.* at Canterbury, 5th October, 1723, and was buried in the parish church of St. Alphage, in that city, where his wife was also interred. He was *s.* by his elder son,

III. SIR BARTHOLOMEW HEYMAN. This gentleman had his sight impaired in his youth by an accident with gunpowder, which rendered him unfit for the army, to which it was intended to bring him up, and the family having suffered in their fortune to a great extent in the troublesome times of CHARLES I. and CHARLES II. he was made one of the poor knights of Windsor some years before his decease. He *m.* Elizabeth, daughter of Thomas Nelson, of Sandwich, in Kent, merchant, and dying 9th June, 1742, was *s.* by his only child,

IV. SIR PETER HEYMAN, who was in the navy, and *m.* at the age of seventeen, Miss Kempe, daughter and sole heiress of — Kempe, esq. of Plymouth, and had three children, who as well as his wife predeceased him. He *d.* at the age of seventy, in July, 1790,* when the Baronetcy devolved upon his cousin, (refer to Peter, second son of the second baronet.)

V. SIR HENRY-PIX HEYMAN, in holy orders, rector in 1797 of Fressingfield, Suffolk, *d. s. p.* 20th November, 1808, when the BARONETCY became EXTINCT.

Arms—Argent, on a chevron engrailed azure, three cinquefoils or, between three martlets sable.

HICKMAN, OF GAINSBOROUGH.

CREATED 16th Nov. 1643.

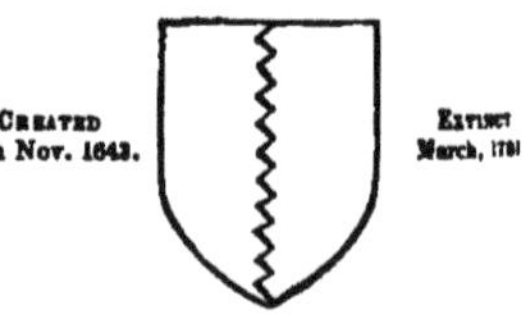

EXTINCT March, 1781.

Lineage.

The first of this family upon record is

ROBERT FITZ HICKMAN, lord of the manors of Bloxham and Wickham, in the county of Oxford, 56 HENRY III. 1272. He had two sons, JOHN and WILLIAM. JOHN, the elder was knighted, and according to the custom of those times, was surnamed de Bloxham. He (Sir John) served in parliament for Oxfordshire, 12th and 15th of EDWARD II. but dying without issue, his brother,

WILLIAM HICKMAN, inherited the estate: which William is mentioned in deeds dated 2 EDWARD III. *anno* 1327, and was father of SIR ROGER and John, both surnamed de Bloxham. Sir Roger was a chief commander in the French wars of EDWARD III. [illegible] died without issue, when the estates devolved upon the younger son,

JOHN HICKMAN, living in 1377, from whom we pass to his lineal descendant,

WALTER HICKMAN, esq. of Woodford, in Essex, who made his will 29th October, 1540, and was *s.* by his son,

ANTHONY HICKMAN, esq. of Woodford, who *m.* Eve, daughter of Sir William Lock, knt.† and co-heir of [illegible]

---

* Sir Peter Heyman was reduced so much in circumstances as to be obliged to appeal to the public for relief, and the following advertisement was issued by him in 1783:—

"Under the patronage of several noble personages of the first distinction.—For the benefit of an English Baronet, at Pasquallí's Great Rooms, Tottenham Street, Tottenham Court Road, on Thursday the 22nd of May instant, at noon, will be a Grand Concert of Vocal and Instrumental Music, by the most capital Performers: with refreshments.—Tickets 10*s.* 6*d.* each."

"Sir Peter Heyman, of Windsor, baronet, for whose benefit the concert is to be, is descended from a very ancient family that came to England with the Norman conqueror in 1066; several of which were in parliament, and held places of honour and trust under the crown. His lady is descended from a baronet, and a family equally ancient and respectable. As his family inheritance was dissipated by his grandfather, he only succeeded to the dignity (a creation so early as 1641), which he hath enjoyed near forty years; and it being unaccompanied with any property, is the cause he now suffers real distress, which is rendered more poignant and severe by his age and infirmities. And this concert, which is countenanced by several of the first distinction, is intended as the means of rescuing him and his lady from their present distress. He earnestly intreats your kind notice and protection on this very useful occasion, which he will ever most gratefully remember. You will be attended to-morrow by a friend of Sir Peter Heyman, with a list of the subscribers, and more tickets should you be disposed to give it support.—20th May, 1783."

† In the 25th of HENRY VIII. 1534, when the pope issued his bull against the King of England and his kingdom, and posted it up at Dunkirk, this William Lock went over and took it down; for which act Henry gave him £100 per annum, land of inheritance, made him one of the gentlemen of his privy chamber, did him other honours, and knighted him.

I. CHRISTOPHER, his heir, who *m.* Esther, daughter of Mr. Alderman William Dobson, of Hull, and dying in the lifetime of his father, 1st January, 1684-5, left issue,

1. ROBERT, successor to his grandfather.
2. Christopher, *d. s. p.*
3. William, M.A. rector of Rowley, East Riding county of York, *m.* a daughter of Mr. Crofts, of Stillington, and had (with four daughters, who all *d.* unm.) an only son,

   ROBERT, who *s.* as third baronet.

4. Henry, *m.* Miss Davison, daughter of Mr. Davison, of Blakiston, in Durham, and had two sons, who both *d.* young. He *d.* 22nd September, 1723.

II. Robert, *m.* Anne, daughter of — Hammerton, esq. of Auckborough, in Lincolnshire, and relict of Edmund Monckton, esq. and had one son, who *d.* unmarried, and a daughter,

Jane, *m.* to John Legard, esq. of Anlaby.

III. Anne, *d.* unm.

Sir Robert *m.* secondly, Jane, daughter and sole heir of Christopher Constable, esq. of Hatfield, in the county of York, relict of John Lister, esq. of Linton, but had no other issue. He *d.* in March, 1685, and was *s.* by his grandson,

II. SIR ROBERT HILDYARD, of Winestead, near Pattrington, in the county of York, M.P. for Heydon, in Yorkshire, *temp. King* WILLIAM and *Queen* ANNE. This gentleman dying unmarried 30th November, 1729, was *s.* by his nephew,

III. SIR ROBERT HILDYARD, M.P. for Great Bedwyn, in Lincolnshire, *temp.* GEORGE II., *m.* in 1738, Maria-Catherina, only child of Henry D'Arcy, esq. of Sedbury, in Yorkshire, and had issue,

ROBERT D'ARCY, his heir.

Anne-Catharine, *m.* to James White, esq.

He *d.* 1st February, 1781, and was *s.* by his son,

IV. SIR ROBERT-D'ARCY HILDYARD, high sheriff of the county of York in 1783, who *m.* Mary, daughter of Sir Edward Dering, bart. of Surrenden-Dering, but *d. s. p.* 6th November, 1814, when the BARONETCY EXPIRED.

Arms—Azure, three mullets or.

Crest—Originally a rein-deer ppr. but afterwards a cock sable, beaked, legged, and wattled, gules.

Note—The latter crest was granted to the family for their behaviour at the battle of Towton, within nine miles of York, between the houses of York and Lancaster, wherein Sir Robert Hildyard, father of Robert of Ribblesdale, alias Hildyard, was slain, commanding under the banner of Lancaster.

HOBY, OF BISHAM.

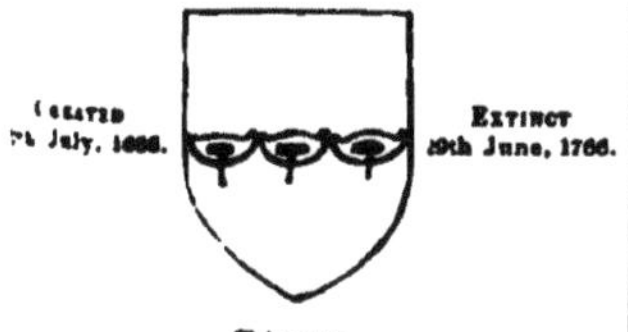

CREATED 2nd July, 1666. EXTINCT 29th June, 1766.

Lineage.

WILLIAM HOBY, esq. (son of Gwalter Hoby, of Radnor) married two wives, by the first he was father of

PHILIP (Sir), of Bisham, in the county of Berks, of the privy council to *King* HENRY VIII., who *m.* Elizabeth, daughter of Sir Walter Stoner, knt. but *d. s. p.* in 1558, having made his half-brother,

THOMAS (Sir), his heir.

By the second, Catherine, daughter and sole heir of John Forden, he had three other sons, William, SIR THOMAS, and Richard. This William took Sir John Oldcastle, Lord Cobham, prisoner, and for that service had a grant from the crown of the lordship of Brangarth. The second son of the second marriage having been adopted by his half-brother Sir Philip, became, at the decease of that gentleman,

SIR THOMAS HOBY, knt. of Bisham, in the county of Berks, and was afterwards, 1566, sent ambassador to the French court. He *m.* Elizabeth, daughter of Sir Anthony Cook, knt. of Gidea Hall, in Essex, and had two sons,

EDWARD, his heir.

Thomas-Posthumous, *m.* the daughter of Arthur Dakens, esq. of Hackness, in the county of York.

He died in his embassy at Paris, 1566, and was buried at Bisham, where in a chapel, built on the south side of the chancel, and against the south wall, was erected from the ground a very fair raised monument, whereon were two knights in complete armour, their heads resting upon their helmets. The inscription, a long Latin epitaph, was written by Lady Hoby, a lady distinguished for learning. Sir Thomas was *s.* by his elder son,

SIR EDWARD HOBY, knt. whom Camden calls "that famous and worthy knight, a person to whom I owe very particular respect, and whose more than ordinary obligations are, and always will be, so much the subject of my thoughts, that I can never possibly forget them." He *m.* first, Margaret, dau. of Henry Cary, first Lord Hunsdon, K.G. but by her had no issue. Sir Edward espoused, secondly, Anne —, and thirdly, a daughter of Upton. By the last lady he had a son and heir,

PEREGRINE HOBY, esq. who *m.* Catherine, daughter of Sir William Dodington, knt. of Breamor, Hants, and had issue,

EDWARD, his heir.

JOHN.

Thomas.

Philip, who *m.* Elizabeth, daughter of Sir Timothy Tyrrell, knt. of Shotover.

Mary, *m.* to William Fleetwood, esq. of Great Missenden, Bucks.

He *d.* in May, 1678, and was *s.* by his son,

I. EDWARD HOBY, esq. of Bisham, in the county of Berks, who was created a BARONET by *King* CHARLES II. 12th July, 1666. Sir Edward *m.* Elizabeth, daughter and co-heir of Francis Styles, esq. of Little Missenden, in the same county, and had two daughters, Elizabeth and Catherine. He *d.* 12th September, 1675, and was *s.* under the limitation by his brother,

II. SIR JOHN HOBY, of Bisham, who *m.* Mary, daughter and heir of Thomas Long, esq. of Wiltshire, and had two sons, John, who predeceased him, and THOMAS, his successor. He *d.* in May, 1702, and was *s.* by his son,

III. SIR THOMAS HOBY, who *m.* Elizabeth, daughter of Sir John Mill, bart.* and dying 25th July, 1730, was *s.* by his eldest son,

* By Margaret his wife, daughter of Thomas Grey, esq. of Wolbesting, Sussex.

IV. SIR THOMAS HOBY, M.P. for Great Marlow, who *d.* unmarried 1st June, 1744, and was *s.* by his brother,

V. SIR PHILIP HOBY, in holy orders, dean of Ardfert, who died unmarried 29th June, 1766, when the BARONETCY became EXTINCT. Sir Philip devised his estates to his cousin, SIR JOHN MILL, bart. who assumed in consequence the surname of HOBY, and from that gentleman's widow Bisham Abbey was purchased by George Vansittart, esq.

Arms—Arg. three spindles in fesse gules, threaded or.

HODGES, OF MIDDLESEX.

CREATED 31st March, 1697.—EXTINCT 1st April, 1722.

Lineage.

I. SIR WILLIAM HODGES, of Cadiz, in Spain, and of Middlesex, was created a BARONET in 1697. He *m.* Sarah, daughter and co-heir of Joseph Hall, of London, merchant, and dying 31st July, 1714, was *s.* by his son,

II. SIR JOSEPH HODGES, F.R.S. who dissipated the whole of his estate; resided for a period in France and Spain, and finally died in London, unm. 1st April, 1722, when the title became EXTINCT.

HOLLAND, OF QUIDDENHAM.

CREATED 15th June, 1629.  EXTINCT 17th Feb. 1729.

Lineage.

JOHN HOLLAND, esq. of Harleston, in the county of Norfolk, was eldest son of Bryan Holland, esq. of Lea Hall, in Glossop, Derbyshire, and father of another

BRYAN HOLLAND, esq. who married Catherine, daughter and co-heir of Peter Paine, esq. and left a son,

JOHN HOLLAND, esq. of Wortwell, in Norfolk, father of

SIR THOMAS HOLLAND, knt. of Quiddenham, in the same county, who *m.* Mary, daughter of Sir Thomas Knyvet, and had two sons, JOHN and Edward. He was *s.* by the elder,

I. JOHN HOLLAND, esq. of Quiddenham, who was created a BARONET by *King* CHARLES I. 15th June, 1629. Sir John *m.* Alathea, daughter and co-heir of John Panton, esq. of Bruinshop, in the county of Denbigh, and widow of William, Lord Sandys, of the Vine, and had issue,

THOMAS, his heir, who dying in the lifetime of his father, left a son,

JOHN, successor to his grandfather.

Abigail, *m.* to Jacob, eldest son of Sir Thomas Garrard, bart. of Norfolk, and had two daughters,

Alathea Garrard, } co-heirs to their father
Sarah Garrard, } who predeceased Sir Thomas.

Sir John, who reached the very advanced age of ninety-eight, *d.* 19th January, 1701, and was *s.* by his grandson,

II. SIR JOHN HOLLAND, who *m.* Lady Rebecca Paston, younger daughter and co-heir of William Paston, second and last Earl of Yarmouth of that family, and had a son and two daughters, viz.

WILLIAM, his successor.

Isabella-Diana.

Charlotte.

Sir John, who was comptroller of the household, and of the privy council to *Queen* ANNE, *d.* about the year 1724, and was *s.* by his son,

III. SIR WILLIAM HOLLAND, who married Mary, daughter of Arthur Upton, merchant, but died without issue, 17th February, 1729, when the BARONETCY EXPIRED.

Arms—Azure, semée of fleurs-de-lis, a lion rampant guardant argent.

HOLLAND, OF WITTENHAM.

CREATED 27th Nov. 1800.—EXTINCT 15th Oct. 1811.

Lineage.

GILES DANCE, of Hoxton, in the parish of St. Leonard, Shoreditch, died 8th July, 1751, and left a son,

GEORGE DANCE, esq. architect to the city of London, who *m.* Elizabeth, daughter of Mr. Gould, of Hackney, and dying 11th February, 1768, at the age of seventy-five, left issue,

I. James, who *m.* Miss Hooper, and had

Nathaniel.

Sarah.

II. Giles.

III. NATHANIEL.

IV. William.

V. George, professor of architecture in the Royal Academy, and architect to the city of London, *b.* in March, 1740-1, *m.* Mary, daughter of Thomas Gurnell, of Ealing, Middlesex, and had

Thomas, in holy orders, of Salisbury, *b.* [illegible] April, 1773.

I. Hester, living in 1800, widow of Nathaniel Smith, esq. of Bloomsbury, one of the directors of the East India Company. She was *m.* 4th December, 1764.

The third son,

I. NATHANIEL DANCE, esq. lord of the manor of Wittenham, Berks, M.P. for East Grinstead, took the additional surname of HOLLAND, by sign manual, and was created a BARONET 27th November, 1800. Sir Nathaniel Dance-Holland *m.* Harriet, daughter of Sir Cecil Bisshopp, bart. and widow of Thomas Dummer, esq. of Cranbury, Hants, and of Thomas Chamberlaine, esq. but *d. s. p.* 15th October, 1811, when the BARONETCY EXPIRED.

Arms—Per pale, azure and gules, a lion rampant regardant, ermine, between eight fleurs-de-lis, alternate, argent and or.

I. Christopher, his heir, who m. Esther, daughter of Mr. Alderman William Dobson, of Hull, and dying in the lifetime of his father, 1st January, 1684-5, left issue,

1. Robert, successor to his grandfather.
2. Christopher, *d. s. p.*
3. William, M.A. rector of Rowley, East Riding county of York, *m.* a daughter of Mr. Crofts, of Stillington, and had (with four daughters, who all *d.* unm.) an only son,

   Robert, who *s.* as third baronet.
4. Henry, *m.* Miss Davison, daughter of Mr. Davison, of Blakiston, in Durham, and had two sons, who both *d.* young. He *d.* 22nd September, 1723.

II. Robert, *m.* Anne, daughter of — Hammerton, esq. of Auckborough, in Lincolnshire, and relict of Edmund Monckton, esq. and had one son, who *d.* unmarried, and a daughter,

   Jane, *m.* to John Legard, esq. of Anlaby.

III. Anne, *d.* unm.

Sir Robert *m.* secondly, Jane, daughter and sole heir of Christopher Constable, esq. of Hatfield, in the county of York, relict of John Lister, esq. of Linton, but had no other issue. He *d.* in March, 1685, and was *s.* by his grandson,

II. Sir Robert Hildyard, of Winestead, near Patrington, in the county of York, M.P. for Heydon, in Yorkshire, *temp.* *King* William and *Queen* Anne. This gentleman dying unmarried 30th November, 1729, was *s.* by his nephew,

III. Sir Robert Hildyard, M.P. for Great Bedwyn, in Lincolnshire, *temp.* George II., *m.* in 1738, Maria-Catherina, only child of Henry D'Arcy, esq. of Sedbury, in Yorkshire, and had issue,

Robert D'Arcy, his heir.

Anne-Catharine, *m.* to James White, esq.

He *d.* 1st February, 1781, and was *s.* by his son,

IV. Sir Robert-D'Arcy Hildyard, high sheriff of the county of York in 1783, who *m.* Mary, daughter of Sir Edward Dering, bart. of Surrenden-Dering, but *d. s. p.* 6th November, 1814, when the Baronetcy expired.

Arms—Azure, three mullets or.

Crest—Originally a rein-deer ppr. but afterwards a cock sable, beaked, legged, and wattled, gules.

Note—The latter crest was granted to the family for their behaviour at the battle of Towton, within nine miles of York, between the houses of York and Lancaster, wherein Sir Robert Hildyard, father of Robert Riddesdale, alias Hildyard, was slain, commanding under the banner of Lancaster.

HOBY, OF BISHAM.

Created 13th July, 1666. Extinct 29th June, 1766.

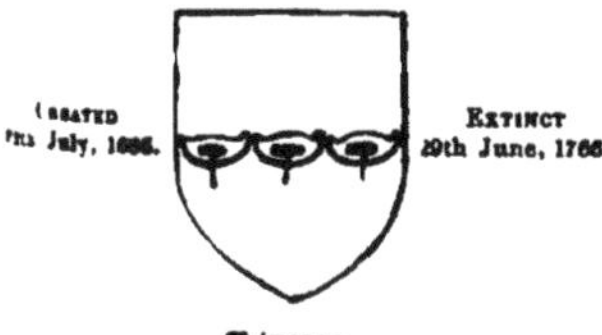

Lineage.

William Hoby, esq. (son of Gwalter Hoby, of Rad-[illegible] married two wives, by the first he was father of

Philip (Sir), of Bisham, in the county of Berks, of the privy council to *King* Henry VIII., who *m.* Elizabeth, daughter of Sir Walter Stoner, knt. but *d. s. p.* in 1558, having made his half-brother,

Thomas (Sir), his heir.

By the second, Catherine, daughter and sole heir of John Forden, he had three other sons, William, Sir Thomas, and Richard. This William took Sir John Oldcastle, Lord Cobham, prisoner, and for that service had a grant from the crown of the lordship of Brangarth. The second son of the second marriage having been adopted by his half-brother Sir Philip, became, at the decease of that gentleman,

Sir Thomas Hoby, knt. of Bisham, in the county of Berks, and was afterwards, 1566, sent ambassador to the French court. He *m.* Elizabeth, daughter of Sir Anthony Cook, knt. of Gidea Hall, in Essex, and had two sons,

Edward, his heir.

Thomas-Posthumous, *m.* the daughter of Arthur Dakens, esq. of Hackness, in the county of York.

He died in his embassy at Paris, 1566, and was buried at Bisham, where in a chapel, built on the south side of the chancel, and against the south wall, was erected from the ground a very fair raised monument, whereon were two knights in complete armour, their heads resting upon their helmets. The inscription, a long Latin epitaph, was written by Lady Hoby, a lady distinguished for learning. Sir Thomas was *s.* by his elder son,

Sir Edward Hoby, knt. whom Camden calls "that famous and worthy knight, a person to whom I owe very particular respect, and whose more than ordinary obligations are, and always will be, so much the subject of my thoughts, that I can never possibly forget them." He *m.* first, Margaret, dau. of Henry Cary, first Lord Hunsdon, K.G. but by her had no issue. Sir Edward espoused, secondly, Anne —, and thirdly, a daughter of Upton. By the last lady he had a son and heir,

Peregrine Hoby, esq. who *m.* Catherine, daughter of Sir William Dodington, knt. of Breamor, Hants, and had issue,

Edward, his heir.

John.

Thomas.

Philip, who *m.* Elizabeth, daughter of Sir Timothy Tyrrell, knt. of Shotover.

Mary, *m.* to William Fleetwood, esq. of Great Missenden, Bucks.

He *d.* in May, 1678, and was *s.* by his son,

I. Edward Hoby, esq. of Bisham, in the county of Berks, who was created a Baronet by *King* Charles II. 12th July, 1666. Sir Edward *m.* Elizabeth, daughter and co-heir of Francis Styles, esq. of Little Missenden, in the same county, and had two daughters, Elizabeth and Catherine. He *d.* 12th September, 1675, and was *s.* under the limitation by his brother,

II. Sir John Hoby, of Bisham, who *m.* Mary, daughter and heir of Thomas Long, esq. of Wiltshire, and had two sons, John, who predeceased him, and Thomas, his successor. He *d.* in May, 1702, and was *s.* by his son,

III. Sir Thomas Hoby, who *m.* Elizabeth, daughter of Sir John Mill, bart.* and dying 25th July, 1730, was *s.* by his eldest son,

* By Margaret his wife, daughter of Thomas Grey, esq. of Wolbesting, Sussex.

IV. Sir Thomas Hoby, M.P. for Great Marlow, who *d.* unmarried 1st June, 1744, and was *s.* by his brother,

V. Sir Philip Hoby, in holy orders, dean of Ardfert, who died unmarried 29th June, 1766, when the Baronetcy became extinct. Sir Philip devised his estates to his cousin, Sir John Mill, bart. who assumed in consequence the surname of Hoby, and from that gentleman's widow Bisham Abbey was purchased by George Vansittart, esq.

Arms—Arg. three spindles in fesse gules, threaded or.

HODGES, OF MIDDLESEX.

Alathea Garrard, } co-heirs to their father,
Sarah Garrard, } who predeceased Sir Thomas.

Sir John, who reached the very advanced age of ninety-eight, *d.* 19th January, 1701, and was *s.* by his grandson,

II. Sir John Holland, who *m.* Lady Rebecca Paston, younger daughter and co-heir of William Paston second and last Earl of Yarmouth of that family, and had a son and two daughters, viz.

William, his successor.
Isabella-Diana.
Charlotte.

Sir John, who was comptroller of the household, and of the privy council to *Queen Anne*, *d.* about the year 1724, and was *s.* by his son,

Qy 1, 8 Holt – arg on bend engr sa Gr … Grotholmest
2. arg 3 boars sa bones in mouth — Castell
3. az a chev or betw 3 castles arg — Mancetter
4. Vair arg & sa bend gu — Erdington
5 Arg 3 bottles gu — Asheldon
6 Erm dance gu — Bagot
7 arg 2 chev az label gu
son th. of Robt & Eliz co-h. Jordayne
Wm Holt 1582 & Kath Dormer d & h Jno Dormer by h. of Sutton
1, 4 Dormer 2 Chubbs 3 arg lion gu
or … Sutton … (Lee 1574)

HOLLES, OF WINTERBOURNE.

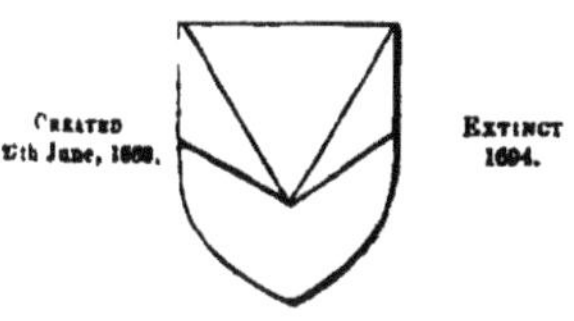

CREATED 27th June, 1660. EXTINCT 1694.

Lineage.

SIR WILLIAM HOLLES, alderman of London, and lord mayor in 1540, acquired immense wealth in trade, and was founder of the family, which has since in its different branches attained so much eminence. He had three sons,

Thomas (Sir), who squandered his estate, and died in prison.
WILLIAM.
Francis, *d. s. p.*

The second son,

WILLIAM HOLLES, esq. inherited the manor of Houghton, in Nottinghamshire, and settled there. He m. Anne, daughter and co-heir of John Dansell, esq. of Dansell, in Cornwall, and was *s.* at his decease by his grandson,

JOHN HOLLES, esq. of Houghton (son of Dansell Holles, by Anne, sister of John Sheffield, Lord Sheffield). This gentleman was raised to the peerage in 1616, by *King* JAMES I.* as Baron Houghton, and made Earl of Clare in 1624. He *m.* Anne, daughter of Sir Thomas Stanhope, of Shelford, Notts, and had ... sons, JOHN, second Earl of Clare (see BURKE's *Extinct Peerage*), and

DANSELL HOLLES, who *m.* first, Dorothy, only daughter and heir of Sir Francis Ashley, of Dorchester, and by that lady had one surviving son, FRANCIS. He *m.* secondly, Jane, eldest daughter and co-heir of Sir John Shirley, of Isville, in Sussex, and thirdly, Esther, second daughter and co-heir of Gideon de Lou, lord of the manor of Columbiers, in Normandy, but had no other issue. Mr. Holles, who opposed the court in the time of CHARLES I. assisted in bringing about the Restoration, and was elevated to the peerage 20th April, 1661, as Baron Holles, of Ifield, in the county of Sussex.† His lordship *d.* 17th February, 1679-80, and was *s.* by his son,

SIR FRANCIS HOLLES, BARONET, of Winterbourn ..., in the county of Dorset, who had been so created 27th *June*, 1660, as second Lord Holles. His lordship *m.* first, Lucy, youngest daughter of Sir Robert Carr, bart. of Sleaford, in the county of Lincoln, by whom he had two daughters, who both died young. He wedded, secondly, Anne, eldest daughter and co-heir of Sir Francis Pile, bart. of Compton Beauchamp, Berks, and had an only son, his successor at his decease, 1st March, 1689-90,

SIR DANSELL HOLLES, third Lord Holles of Ifield, who died unmarried in the nineteenth year of his age, in 1694, when his honors, including the BARONETCY, became EXTINCT. His lordship's estates devolved upon his kinsman and heir-at-law,

John Holles, Duke of Newcastle, whose only daughter and heiress,

Lady Henrietta-Cavendish Holles, *m.* in 1713, Edward, Lord Harley, son and heir of Robert, Earl of Oxford, and had an only surviving child,

Lady Margaret-Cavendish Harley, who wedded William Bentinck, second Duke of Portland.

Arms—Erm. two piles in point, sa.

HOLMAN, OF BANBURY.

CREATED 1st June, 1663.—EXTINCT about 1700.

Lineage.

I. JOHN HOLMAN, esq. of Banbury, in Oxfordshire, who was created a BARONET in 1663, *m.* Jane, daughter of Samuel Forbes, of Kew, but died without male issue about 1700, when the title became EXTINCT.

HOLTE, OF ASTON.

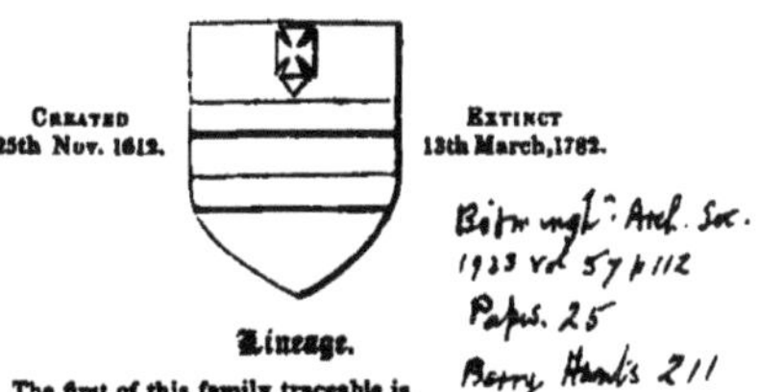

CREATED 25th Nov. 1612. EXTINCT 13th March, 1782.

Lineage.

The first of this family traceable is

SIR HUGH HOLTE, who *m.* Matilda, daughter of Sir Henry de Erdington, Lord of Erdington, and left a son and heir,

JOHN ATTE HOLTE, who *m.* *temp.* EDWARD II. Alice de Castello, daughter and at length sole heir of Sir George de Castello, and was *s.* by his son,

SIMON DEL HOLTE, who left by his wife, Albreda de Bermingham, two sons, JOHN and Walter. The elder,

JOHN ATTE HOLTE, called senior, in respect that his son was living at the same time, 21 EDWARD III. He had also two sons, JOHN and Walter: the first of whom,

JOHN ATTE HOLTE, purchased the manor of Dudston in the 38th of the same reign for forty marks from John de Grimesarwe, and Maud de Grimesarwe in two years afterwards conveyed the manor of ASTON to the said John Atte Holte, denominated of Bermingham, as her charter, dated at Aston on Sunday next before the feast of St. Agapite the Martyr, testifies. He *m.* Eleanor, daughter and co-heir of William Durvassal, of Spernall, but dying childless, the estates passed to his uncle,

WALTER HOLTE, of Aston, escheator for the counties of Warwick and Leicester, *temp.* EDWARD III. and RICHARD I. who *m.* Margery, daughter of Sir William Baget, knt. of Bagington, and was *s.* by his eldest son,

JOHN HOLTE, styled of Yardley, whose son and heir,

---

* ... through the Duke of Buckingham, to whom he paid £10,000 in the first instance, and £5000 subsequently for the ...

† ... details of this high spirited nobleman, see BURKE's *Extinct Peerage*.

IV. SIR THOMAS HOBY, M.P. for Great Marlow, who *d.* unmarried 1st June, 1744, and was *s.* by his brother,

V. SIR PHILIP HOBY, in holy orders, dean of Ardfert, who died unmarried 29th June, 1766, when the BARONETCY became EXTINCT. Sir Philip devised his estates to his cousin, SIR JOHN MILL, bart. who assumed in consequence the surname of HOBY, and from that gentleman's widow Bisham Abbey was purchased by George Vansittart, esq.

Arms—Arg. three spindles in fesse gules, threaded or.

HODGES, OF MIDDLESEX.

CREATED 31st March, 1697.—EXTINCT 1st April, 1722.

Lineage.

I. SIR WILLIAM HODGES, of Cadiz, in Spain, and of Middlesex, was created a BARONET in 1697. He *m.* Sarah, daughter and co-heir of Joseph Hall, of London, merchant, and dying 31st July, 1714, was *s.* by his son,

II. SIR JOSEPH HODGES, F.R.S. who dissipated the whole of his estate; resided for a period in France and Spain, and finally died in London, unm. 1st April, 1722, when the title became EXTINCT.

HOLLAND, OF QUIDDENHAM.

CREATED 15th June, 1629.  EXTINCT 17th Feb. 1729.

Lineage.

JOHN HOLLAND, esq. of Harleston, in the county of Norfolk, was eldest son of Bryan Holland, esq. of Lea Hall, in Glossop, Derbyshire, and father of another

BRYAN HOLLAND, esq. who married Catherine, daughter and co-heir of Peter Paine, esq. and left a son,

JOHN HOLLAND, esq. of Wortwell, in Norfolk, father of

SIR THOMAS HOLLAND, knt. of Quiddenham, in the same county, who *m.* Mary, daughter of Sir Thomas Knyvet, and had two sons, JOHN and Edward. He was *s.* by the elder,

I. JOHN HOLLAND, esq. of Quiddenham, who was created a BARONET by *King* CHARLES I. 15th June, 1629. Sir John *m.* Alathea, daughter and co-heir of John Panton, esq. of Bruinshop, in the county of Denbigh, and widow of William, Lord Sandys, of the Vine, and had issue,

THOMAS, his heir, who dying in the lifetime of his father, left a son,

JOHN, successor to his grandfather.

Abigail, *m.* to Jacob, eldest son of Sir Thomas Garrard, bart. of Norfolk, and had two daughters,

Alathea Garrard, } co-heirs to their father,
Sarah Garrard, } who predeceased Sir Thomas.

Sir John, who reached the very advanced age of ninety-eight, *d.* 19th January, 1701, and was *s.* by his grandson,

II. SIR JOHN HOLLAND, who *m.* Lady Rebecca Paston, younger daughter and co-heir of William Paston, second and last Earl of Yarmouth of that family, and had a son and two daughters, viz.

WILLIAM, his successor.

Isabella-Diana.

Charlotte.

Sir John, who was comptroller of the household, and of the privy council to *Queen* ANNE, *d.* about the year 1724, and was *s.* by his son,

III. SIR WILLIAM HOLLAND, who married Mary, daughter of Arthur Upton, merchant, but died without issue, 17th February, 1729, when the BARONETCY EXPIRED.

Arms—Azure, semée of fleurs-de-lis, a lion rampant guardant argent.

HOLLAND, OF WITTENHAM.

CREATED 27th Nov. 1800.—EXTINCT 15th Oct. 1811

Lineage.

GILES DANCE, of Hoxton, in the parish of St. Leonard, Shoreditch, died 8th July, 1751, and left a son,

GEORGE DANCE, esq. architect to the city of London, who *m.* Elizabeth, daughter of Mr. Gould, of Hackney, and dying 11th February, 1768, at the age of seventy-five, left issue,

I. James, who *m.* Miss Hooper, and had

Nathaniel.

Sarah.

II. Giles.

III. NATHANIEL.

IV. William.

V. George, professor of architecture in the Royal Academy, and architect to the city of London, *b.* in March, 1740-1, *m.* Mary, daughter of Thomas Gurnell, of Ealing, Middlesex, and had

Thomas, in holy orders, of Salisbury, *b.* [illegible] April, 1773.

I. Hester, living in 1800, widow of Nathaniel Smith, esq. of Bloomsbury, one of the directors of the East India Company. She was [illegible] 4th December, 1764.

The third son,

I. NATHANIEL DANCE, esq. lord of the manor of Wittenham, Berks, M.P. for East Grinstead, took the additional surname of HOLLAND, by sign manual, and was created a BARONET 27th November, 1800. Sir Nathaniel Dance-Holland *m.* Harriet, daughter of Sir Cecil Bisshopp, bart. and widow of Thomas Dummer, esq. of Cranbury, Hants, and of Thomas Chamberlaine, esq. but *d. s. p.* 15th October, 1811, when the BARONETCY EXPIRED.

Arms—Per pale, azure and gules, a lion rampant regardant, ermine, between eight fleurs-de-lis, alternate, argent and or.

HOLLES, OF WINTERBOURNE.

CREATED 27th June, 1660. EXTINCT 1694.

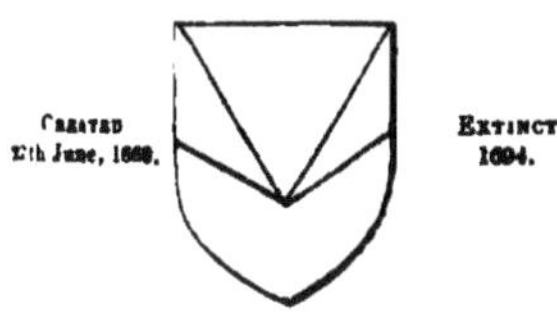

Lineage.

SIR WILLIAM HOLLES, alderman of London, and lord mayor in 1540, acquired immense wealth in trade, and was founder of the family, which has since in its different branches attained so much eminence. He had three sons,

Thomas (Sir), who squandered his estate, and died in prison.
WILLIAM.
Francis, *d. s. p.*

The second son,

WILLIAM HOLLES, esq. inherited the manor of Houghton, in Nottinghamshire, and settled there. He m. Anne, daughter and co-heir of John Dansell, esq. of Dansell, in Cornwall, and was *s.* at his decease by his grandson,

JOHN HOLLES, esq. of Houghton (son of Dansell Holles, by Anne, sister of John Sheffield, Lord Sheffield). This gentleman was raised to the peerage in 1616, by *King* JAMES I.* as Baron Houghton, and made Earl of Clare in 1624. He m. Anne, daughter of Sir Thomas Stanhope, of Shelford, Notts, and had two sons, JOHN, second Earl of Clare (see BURKE'S *Extinct Peerage*), and

DANZELL HOLLES, who m. first, Dorothy, only daughter and heir of Sir Francis Ashley, of Dorchester, and by that lady had one surviving son, FRANCIS. He m. secondly, Jane, eldest daughter and co-heir of Sir John Shirley, of Isville, in Sussex, and thirdly, Esther, second daughter and co-heir of Gideon de Lou, lord of the manor of Columbiers, in Normandy, but had no other issue. Mr. Holles, who opposed the court in the time of CHARLES I. assisted in bringing about the Restoration, and was elevated to the peerage 20th April, 1661, as Baron Holles, of Ifield, in the county of Sussex.† His lordship *d.* 17th February, 1679-80, and was *s.* by his son,

SIR FRANCIS HOLLES, BARONET, of Winterbourn St. Martin, in the county of Dorset, who had been so created 27th June, 1660, as second Lord Holles. His lordship m. first, Lucy, youngest daughter of Sir Robert Carr, bart. of Sleaford, in the county of Lincoln, by whom he had two daughters, who both died young. He wedded, secondly, Anne, eldest daughter and co-heir of Sir Francis Pile, bart. of Compton Beauchamp, Berks, and had an only son, his successor at his decease 1st March, 1689-90,

SIR DANZELL HOLLES, third Lord Holles of Ifield, who died unmarried in the nineteenth year of his age, in 1694, when his honors, including the BARONETCY, became EXTINCT. His lordship's estates devolved upon his kinsman and heir-at-law,

John Holles, Duke of Newcastle, whose only daughter and heiress,

Lady Henrietta-Cavendish Holles, *m.* in 1713, Edward, Lord Harley, son and heir of Robert, Earl of Oxford, and had an only surviving child,

Lady Margaret-Cavendish Harley, who wedded William Bentinck, second Duke of Portland.

Arms—Erm. two piles in point, sa.

HOLMAN, OF BANBURY.

CREATED 1st June, 1663.—EXTINCT about 1700.

Lineage.

I. JOHN HOLMAN, esq. of Banbury, in Oxfordshire, who was created a BARONET in 1663, *m.* Jane, daughter of Samuel Forbes, of Kew, but died without male issue about 1700, when the title became EXTINCT.

HOLTE, OF ASTON.

CREATED 25th Nov. 1612. EXTINCT 13th March, 1782.

Lineage.

The first of this family traceable is

SIR HUGH HOLTE, who *m.* Matilda, daughter of Sir Henry de Erdington, Lord of Erdington, and left a son and heir,

JOHN ATTE HOLTE, who *m. temp.* EDWARD II. Alice de Castello, daughter and at length sole heir of Sir George de Castello, and was *s.* by his son,

SIMON DEL HOLTE, who left by his wife, Albreda de Bermingham, two sons, JOHN and Walter. The elder,

JOHN ATTE HOLTE, called senior, in respect that his son was living at the same time, 21 EDWARD III. He had also two sons, JOHN and Walter: the first of whom,

JOHN ATTE HOLTE, purchased the manor of Dudston in the 38th of the same reign for forty marks from John de Grimesarwe, and Maud de Grimesarwe in two years afterwards conveyed the manor of ASTON to the said John Atte Holte, denominated of Bermingham, as her charter, dated at Aston on Sunday next before the feast of St. Agapite the Martyr, testifies. He *m.* Eleanor, daughter and co-heir of William Durvassal, of Spernall, but dying childless, the estates passed to his uncle,

WALTER HOLTE, of Aston, eschaetor for the counties of Warwick and Leicester, *temp.* EDWARD III. and RICHARD I. who *m.* Margery, daughter of Sir William Bagot, knt. of Bagington, and was *s.* by his eldest son,

JOHN HOLTE, styled of Yardley, whose son and heir,

---

* Through the Duke of Buckingham, to whom he paid £10,000 in the first instance, and £5000 subsequently for the [illegible]

† For details of this high spirited nobleman, see BURKE'S *Extinct Peerage.*

died *s. p.* 25th May, 1764; and he married secondly, Mary-Bathea, daughter of the Rev. John Woolin, rector of Emley, in Yorkshire, by whom he had four sons and four daughters. The eldest son,

Thomas, of Howroyde, *m.* in 1789, Lady Mary Gordon, daughter of George, third Earl of Aberdeen, and was father of two sons, the Rev. Joshua-Thomas Horton, of Howroyde, and Colonel George-William Horton, and of one daughter, Mary, *m.* to F. B. Hacket, esq. (See Burke's *Commoners*, vol. i. p. 288.)

Mary, Anne, Jane, } died unmarried.

Susannah, *m.* 24th March, 1742, to George Lloyd, esq. of Hulme, near Manchester, and had issue. His grandson, William-Horton Lloyd, esq. was named after his grand-uncle, Sir William Horton. (See Burke's *Commoners*, vol. i. p. 244.)

Sarah.

He *d.* 18th March, 1757, at Manchester, was buried at Oldham, and *s.* by his eldest son,

I. William Horton, esq. of Chaderton, in the county of Lancaster, who was created a Baronet 14th January, 1764, being at the time sheriff of Lancashire. Sir William *m.* in 1751, Susannah, daughter and heir of Francis Watts, esq. of Barnes Hall, in Yorkshire, and had three sons, viz.

Watts, his successor.

Thomas, in holy orders, successor to his brother.

William, *b.* 21st October, 1767, lieutenant-colonel 2nd Lancashire Militia; *d.* 15th April, 1816.

He died 25th February, 1774, and was succeeded by his eldest son,

II. Sir Watts Horton, *b.* 17th November, 1753; *m.* 3rd June, 1778, Harriet, daughter of James, Lord Stanley, eldest son of Edward, eleventh Earl of Derby, and by that lady, who died at Bath in 1830, had an only child,

Harriet-Susanna-Anne, *b.* 4th January, 1790; *m.* in 1813, to Charles Rees, esq. younger brother of John Rees, esq. of Killymaenllwyd, in Carmarthenshire; and *d.* 29th December, 1827, leaving issue.

He died 15th November, 1811, and having no male issue, was *s.* by his next brother,

III. Sir Thomas Horton, *b.* 21st July, 1758, in holy orders, vicar of Badsworth; *m.* in 1779, Elisabeth, daughter of James, Lord Stanley, eldest son of Edward, eleventh Earl of Derby, and had by her (who *d.* in 1796) an only child,

Charlotte, *m.* to George Pollard, esq. of Stannery Hall, Halifax, Yorkshire, and had issue,

George-Thomas Pollard, *m.* 31st August, 1835, Clara, eldest daughter of James Royds, esq. of Woodlands, Cheshire.

Elizabeth Pollard.

Henrietta Pollard, *m.* 30th October, 1830, to Robert Bell, esq. of Sculcoates, Hull.

Fanny Pollard, *d.* unmarried 14th February, 1832.

Sir Thomas died 2nd March, 1831, when the Baronetcy became extinct.

Arms—Gu. a lion rampant arg. charged on the breast with a boar's head couped close az. within a bordure engrailed arg.

HOWE, OF COLD BARWICK.

Created 20th June, 1660. | Extinct 19th Jan. 1735.

Lineage.

Henry Howe, living *temp.* Henry VIII. left a son

John Howe, esq. of Hunspell de la Heise, in the county of Somerset, who *d.* in 1574, and was *s.* by his son,

John Howe, esq. who *m.* Jane, daughter of Nicholas Grubham, esq. of Bishop's Lydiard, in Somersetshire, and the sister of Sir Richard Grubham, of Wishford, Wilts, who had a grant, in 14 James I. of a part of the Subpœna Office. By this lady he had issue,

John, from whom descended the Howes, of Compton, in Gloucestershire.

George (Sir).

The second son,

Sir George Howe, knt. inherited, with his brother considerable personal and real estates from his uncle Sir Richard Grubham, and was of Cold Barwick, in the county of Wilts. Attached with great firmness to the monarchy, he supplied the king with large sums of money, during the troubles *temp.* Charles I. was knighted, and represented the borough of Hindon in parliament. He *m.* Dorothy, daughter of Humphrey Clarke, alias Woodchurch, esq. of Woodchurch, in Kent, and had issue,

George Grubham, his heir.

John, *m.* a daughter of Strode, and settled at Somerton, in Somersetshire.

Margaret-Grubham, *m.* to John Still, esq. of Shaftesbury.

He was *s.* by his elder son,

I. George-Grubham Howe, esq. of Cold Barwick, M.P. for Hindon, who was created a Baronet 20th June, 1660. Sir George *m.* in 1650, Elizabeth, daughter of Sir Harbottle Grimston, bart. of Bradfield Hall, in Essex, speaker of the House of Commons at the Restoration, and afterwards master of the Rolls. By her he had many children, but all died young except five, namely,

James, his successor.

Dorothy, *m.* to Henry Lee, esq. of Dungeon, near Canterbury.

Anne, *m.* to John Lisle, esq. of Moyles Court, Hants.

Elizabeth, *m.* to Robert Hovenden, esq. of Frid...

Margaret, *m.* to Sir George Rooke, vice-admiral of England, *temp.* Queen Anne.

Sir George *d.* 26th September, 1676, and was *s.* by his son,

II. Sir James Howe, who *m.* first, Elizabeth, daughter of Edward Nutt, esq. of Nackington, in Kent, which lady dying 8th September, 1691, he wedded secondly, Elizabeth, daughter and co-heir of — Stratford, esq. of Halling, in Gloucestershire, but *d.* *s. p.* 19th January, 1735, aged sixty-six, when the Baronetcy expired.

Arms—Or, a fesse between three wolves' heads couped sable langued ppr.; a crescent for difference

HOWE, OF COMPTON.

CREATED 22nd Sept. 1660. EXTINCT 12th July, 1814.

Lineage.

HENRY HOWE, living in the time of HENRY VIII. ad two sons, JOHN and Thomas, and a daughter, arried to John Walsh. The elder son,

JOHN HOWE, esq. was possessed of the manor of Hunpell de la Heies, in the county of Somerset, and of ands, &c. in the counties of Devon, Essex, and city l London. He d. 27th May, 1574, and was s. by his n,

JOHN HOWE, esq. who was eighteen years old at e father's decease, and marrying Jane, daughter of icholas Grubham, of Bishop's Lydiard, in Somersetire, and sister of Sir Richard Grubham, of Wishrd, in Wilts, lord of the manor of Compton Abdale, the county of Gloucester, became seated at Bishop's ydiard, and had issue three sons and a daughter, s

JOHN, his heir.
George (Sir), ancestor of the extinct baronets Howe, of Cold Barwick.
Lawrence.

Elizabeth, m. to John Bainton, esq.

e eldest son and heir,

I. JOHN HOWE, esq. acquired the manor of Compn, in Gloucestershire (of which county he was erif in 1650), by the gift of his uncle, Sir Richard rubham, with Wishford, and other estates in the unty of Wilts, and was created a BARONET, 22nd ptember, 1660. He m. Bridget, daughter of Thomas h, esq. of North Cerney, in the former county, e of the masters in Chancery, and had issue,

I. RICHARD-GRUBHAM, his heir.

II. JOHN-GRUBHAM, M.P. for the county of Gloucester, who acquired Langar* in Nottinghamshire, where he fixed his abode, by marrying Annabella, one of the illegitimate daughters and co-heirs of Emanual Scrope, Earl of Sunderland, by which lady, who by patent of CHARLES II. dated 1st June, 1663, was raised to the rank of an earl's daughter, he had issue (her ladyship d. 21st March, 1703),

1. SCROPE, b. in November, 1648, represented the county of Nottingham in parliament, temp. CHARLES II. WILLIAM III. and Queen ANNE, and was raised to the peerage of Ireland in 1701, as Baron of Clenawly, and Viscount Howe. His lordship m. first, in 1674, Lady Anne Manners, daughter of John, eighth Duke of Rutland, by whom he had two daughters,

Annabella, m. to — Golding, esq.
Margaret, m. to Captain Mugg.

He m. secondly, Juliana, daughter of William, Lord Allington, and had by her, with two daughters, his successor,

EMANUEL, second Viscount, who s. as fourth baronet.

2. John-Grubham, of Stowell, in Gloucestershire, who was created, in 1741, Lord Chedworth, (refer to BURKE's *Extinct Peerage*).
3. Charles, of Gritworth, Notts, whose only daughter and heir m. Peter Bathurst, esq. of Clarendon Park, Wilts.
4. Emanuel-Scrope, groom of the bedchamber to *King* WILLIAM.

1. Bridget, m. to Sir John Bennet, K.B. created Lord Ossulston.
2. Annabella, d. unm.
3. Elizabeth, m. to Sir John Guise, bart.
4. Diana, m. to Sir Francis Molyneux, bart.
5. Mary.

III. Thomas (Sir) m. Hesther, daughter of Sir William Mainwaring, but left no issue,

Sir John was s. at his decease by his eldest son,

II. SIR RICHARD HOWE, who m. Anne, daughter of Dr. John King, Bishop of London, and relict of John Dutton, esq. of Sherborne, in the county of Gloucester, and dying in 1703, was s. by his only son,

III. SIR RICHARD HOWE, M.P. for the county of Wilts, who m. 12th August, 1673, Mary, daughter of Sir Henry Frederick Thynne, bart. of Kempsford, but died s. p. 3rd July, 1730, when his estates and baronetcy passed to his cousin,

IV. SIR SCROPE HOWE, second Viscount Howe, in the peerage of Ireland (refer to John-Grubham, second son of the first baronet), who m. 25th April, 1719, Maria-Sophia-Charlotte, eldest daughter of the Baron Kilmansegge,† master of the horse to GEORGE I. and had issue,

GEORGE-AUGUSTUS, his heir.
RICHARD, R.N. successor to his elder brother.
John, d. in 1769.
WILLIAM, colonel 46th regiment, M.P. for Nottingham, served with high reputation in the American war, succeeded his brother Richard.
Thomas, d. in 1771.

Caroline, m. to John Howe, of Hanslop, Bucks.
Charlotte, m. to Robert Fettiplace, esq. of Swinbrook, in Oxfordshire.
Juliana, d. in March, 1863.
Mary, m. to Sir William Augustus Pitt, K.B.

His lordship d. 29th March, 1735, and was s. by his eldest son,

---

* The manor of Langar, formerly the inheritance of Tiptofts, passed from them to the family of Scrope e marriage of Roger, Lord Scrope of Bolton, with garet, eldest of the three daughters and co-heirs of bert, Lord Tiptoft, whose descendant, Thomas, Lord pe, K. G. m. in 1584, Philadelphia, second daughter Henry Cary, first Lord Hunsdon, by whom he had son, Emanual, Lord Scrope of Bolton, created in , Earl of Sunderland, who having no issue by his , Lady Elizabeth Manners, daughter of John, Earl of and, settled his estate upon his natural children by Martha Jones, of whom his only son, John, dying unm. his three daughters became his co-heirs, namely,

MARY, m. first, to Henry Cary, son of the Earl of Monmouth, and secondly, to Charles, first Duke of Bolton.
ANNABELLA, m. to John Grubham Howe, esq.
ELIZABETH, m. to Thomas Savage, Earl Rivers.

† By his wife, Sophia-Charlotte, daughter of Count Platen of the Empire, created Countess of Leinster, in Ireland, and Countess of Darlington, in England.

v. Sir George-Augustus Howe, 3rd Viscount Howe, M.P. for Nottingham, from 1747 to 1754, a brigadier-general in the army, and an officer of high reputation, slain at Ticonderoga, in North America, 5th July, 1758.* Dying a bachelor, he was *s.* by his brother,

vi. Sir Richard Howe, fourth Viscount (the celebrated Admiral Howe), who for his eminent professional services was created a peer of Great Britain in 1782, as Viscount Howe, and advanced in 1788, being at the same time created Baron Howe, of Langar, with reversion of the barony to his female issue, primogenitively. His lordship was elected a knight of the Garter in 1797. He *m.* in 1758, Mary, daughter of Chiverton Hartopp, esq. of Welby, in Nottinghamshire, and had three daughters, viz.

Sophia-Charlotte, who inherited the barony of Howe, of Langar.

Maria-Juliana, *d.* unm.

Louisa-Catherine, *m.* first, to John-Dennis, Marquess of Sligo, and secondly, to Sir William Scott, afterwards Lord Stowell, and *d.* in 1817.

The Earl *d.* 5th August, 1799, when the honours obtained by himself, in remainder to his male issue, expired. The barony devolved upon his eldest daughter, and the Irish peerage, with the baronetcy, passed to his brother,

vii. Sir William Howe, K.B. fifth Viscount Howe, a general officer in the army, and chief in command of the forces in America, from the return of General Gage in 1775, to 1778. He *m.* Frances, fourth daughter of the Right Hon. Thomas Conolly, of Castletown, in Kildare, but died without issue, 12th July, 1814, when his honours, including the Baronetcy, became extinct.

Arms—Or, a fesse between three wolves' heads erased sa.

HUBAND, OF IPSLEY.

Created 2nd Feb. 1660-1. Extinct 10th Nov. 1730.

Lineage.

This family was founded by

Hugh Hubald, who held Ipsley of Osbernus at the Norman invasion. His descendant, another

Hugh Hubald, held lands in the same place, *temp.* Henry II. His son,

Sir Henry Hubald or Hubant, was taxed for one knight's fee in Ipsley, 20 Henry III. This Sir Henry was in commission for goal delivery for Warwick in the 45th of the same reign, and in the 29th was one of those who held Kenilworth Castle against the king, for which his manor of Ipsley and his other lands were seised; but the treason being purged by the *Dictum de Kenilworth*, he was again a commissioner for goal delivery at Warwick, in the 53rd, 54th, and 56th of the same Henry. His son and heir,

Sir John Hubald, of Ipsley, *m.* Margaret, daughter of Sir William Lucie, knt. of Charlecote, and had issue, John, who served in the wars in Britanny, William, in those of Gascoign; Thomas, Robert, and Geffrey. In 15 Edward II. Sir John Hubald was employed with divers persons of quality upon the king's service in Wales, and in the 18th of the same reign was in the commission to inquire what persons were seised of lands in Warwickshire, from the yearly value of £5 to £1000, and to certify the same. The next year (19 Edward III.) he had a military summons to attend the king in the French wars, and was in the commission of array for Warwickshire, for providing archers. He was *s.* at his decease by his eldest son,

Sir John Hubald, who, in the 29 Edward III. was one of the knights of the shire in the parliament held at Westminster. To him succeeded

Thomas Hubald, a commissioner, 2 Richard II. for assessing a subsidy for Warwickshire. He was father of

Richard Hubald, who is ranked amongst the persons of note in Warwickshire, 12 Henry VI. He made oath for observance of certain articles concluded in the parliament then holden, and bore for his arms "Sable, three leopards' faces." After him was

Thomas Huband, living 29 Edward IV. and

Richard Huband, who flourished in the time of Henry VII. and marrying Anne, daughter of Thomas Burdet, of Arrow, was father of

John Huband, esq. living 21 Henry VIII. who was *s.* by

Nicholas Huband, esq. who *d.* 7 Edward VI. From him descended

John Huband, esq. of Ipsley, in the county of Warwick, a person in great favour with Robert, Earl of Leicester, who constituted him constable of Kenilworth. He *m.* Mary, youngest daughter of Sir George Throckmorton, knt. and *d. s. p.* 1583. His brother and heir,

Ralph Huband, esq. dying in 1605, left a son,

John Huband, esq. of Ipsley, living in 1642, who *m.* the daughter of Sir Henry Poole, knt. of Oaksey, in Wilts, and was *s.* by his son,

Ralph Huband, esq. lord of Ipsley, who *m.* Anne, daughter of Gervase Tevery, esq. of Stapleford, Notts, and had three sons, John, Tevery, and Ralph, who was a gentleman commoner of Queen's College, Oxford, and dying 23rd July, 1670, was buried at St. Peter's Church, in that city. Ralph was *s.* by his eldest son,

i. John Huband, esq. of Ipsley, who was created Baronet by King Charles II. 2nd February, 1660. Sir John *m.* Jane, daughter of Lord Charles Pawlet, of Dowles, Hants, and had (with two daughters, Jane and Martha) a son and heir at his decease, in 1710,

ii. Sir John Huband, who *m.* Rhoda, eldest daught

* Upon the death of this gallant officer being known in England, the following address to the Electors of Nottingham was written by his mother, which, considered as coming from the mother of three eminently distinguished officers, made a strong sensation:

"To the Gentlemen, &c. of the Town and County of Nottingham.

"As Lord Howe is now absent upon the public service, and Lieutenant-Colonel Howe is with his regiment at Louisbourgh, it rests upon me to beg the favour of your votes and interests, that Lieutenant-Colonel Howe may supply the place of his late brother as your representative in parliament.

"Permit me, therefore, to implore the protection of every one of you, as the mother of him whose life has been lost in the service of his country.

"Charlotte Howe."

ter of Sir Thomas Broughton, bart. of Broughton, in the county of Stafford, and had issue,

John, his successor.
Rhoda, m. to Sir Thomas Delves, bart. of Dodington, in Cheshire.
Mary.
Jane.

He d. 24th June, 1716-17, and was s. by his son,

III. Sir John Humand, who died a minor and unm. aged seventeen, 10th November, 1730, when the Baronetcy became extinct.

Arms—Sable, three leopards' faces jessant fleurs-de-lis argent.

HUMBLE, OF LONDON.

Created 21st June, 1660. Extinct 6th Feb. 1745.

Lineage.

William Humble, of Humbleton, in the county of York, was father of

William Humble, of London, of the fraternity of the Holy Ghost, whose son,

Thomas Humble, of London, stationer, m. Agnes, daughter of Mr. Johnson, and left a son,

George Humble, of London, stationer, and deputy of Langborn Ward in 1633, m. Agnes, daughter of Mr. John Moody, and had a numerous family. His eldest son,

I. William Humble, esq. of London, b. in 1612, in consideration of £20,000 which he furnished to *King Charles* II. in his majesty's exile, was created a Baronet 21st June, 1660. Sir William m. Eliza, daughter of John Allanson, gent. and had issue,

George, his heir, m. Mary, daughter of Sir John Nulls, knt. of London, and dying in the lifetime of his father, left

William, George, John, } second, third, and fourth baronets.
Thomas.
Mary, m. to Christopher Tilson, esq.
Anne, m. to Samuel King, esq.

William, created a baronet, see Humble, *of Kensington.*

Jane, m. to Basil Moor, esq. of Gubbins, in Hertfordshire.

Elizabeth, m. to Dr. Bradly, prebend of York.

Diana, m. to Mr. Atkins, son of John Atkins, of Yorkshire.

He d. 20th December, 1686, and was s. by his grandson,

II. Sir William Humble, who d. unm. aged twenty, February, 1687, and was s. by his brother,

III. Sir George Humble, who was killed in a quarrel at the Blue Posts Tavern, in March, 1702-3, and was s. by his brother,

IV. Sir John Humble, who m. Sarah, daughter and co-heir of Andrew Lant, esq. of Thorpe Underwood, in the county of Northampton, and had surviving issue,

William, his heir.
Mary.

He d. 7th February, 1723, and was s. by his son,

V. Sir William Humble, who m. the Hon. Elizabeth Vane, daughter of Gilbert, second Lord Barnard, and dying in November, 1742, was s. by his son,

VI. Sir John Humble, who d. at school, at Felstead, aged six, 6th February, 1745, when the Baronetcy expired.

Arms—Sa. a buck trippant or, a chief indented of the last.

HUMBLE, OF KENSINGTON.

Created 16th March, 1687.—Extinct 12th Aug. 1705.

Lineage.

I. William Humble, esq. of Kensington, in the county of Middlesex, second son of Sir William Humble, bart. of London, was created a Baronet 16th March, 1687. He m. first, Frances, daughter of Sir Anthony Hasilrigge, bart.; and secondly, Mary, daughter of Fisher, of Isleworth, but dying s. p. 12th August, 1705, the Baronetcy expired.

Arms—See Humble of London.

HUMPHREYS, OF LONDON.

Created 30th Nov. 1714. Extinct 14th June, 1737.

Lineage.

I. Sir William Humphreys, knt. an alderman of the city of London, served the office of sheriff in 1704, when *Queen* Anne conferred upon him the honour of knighthood, and was lord mayor in the first year of George I. when having had the honour of entertaining the king and queen at Guildhall, he was in consequence created a Baronet 30th November, 1714. Sir William m. first, Margaret, daughter of William Wintour, esq. of Dymock, in the county of Gloucester, and granddaughter of Sir William Maxey, of Bradwell Hall, Essex, and had by her an only surviving child,

Orlando, his heir.

He m. secondly, Ellen, relict of Robert Lancashire, of London, merchant, but had no other issue. Sir William who sate in parliament for Marlborough, d. in October, 1735, and was s. by his son,

II. Sir Orlando Humphreys, who m. Ellen, daughter and co-heir of the above mentioned Robert Lancashire, by whom he left no male issue at his decease, 14th June, 1737, when the Baronetcy became extinct.

Arms—Sable, three nags' heads erased, argent.

HUNGATE, OF SAXTON.

CREATED 15th Aug. 1642.

EXTINCT 3rd Dec. 1749.

Lineage.

Drake, in his antiquities of York, states that "the ancient family of the Hungates seem to derive their name from Hungate, in the city of York. They were possessed of North Dalton, Bornby, Hayton, Saxton, Sherborn, Cowick, &c.

WILLIAM HUNGATE, of Bornby, (the first of the family in the visitation) was father of

WILLIAM HUNGATE, esq. of Bornby, who *m.* Margery, daughter of Sir Anthony Ughtred, knt. of Kexby, and had two sons, William and Leonard. The elder,

WILLIAM HUNGATE, esq. *m.* Oliva, daughter of William Sally, or Sauley, of Saxton, in the county of York, and had three sons, WILLIAM, Robert, and Edward. The eldest son and heir,

WILLIAM HUNGATE, esq. *m.* Alice, daughter of Sir Thomas Gower, knt. of Stitenham, in Yorkshire, and had eight sons,* and two daughters. Of the sons, WILLIAM was the eldest, and succeeded his father; the daughters were Alice, who *m.* R. Angier, esq. and Anne, the wife of Oliver Rither, esq.

WILLIAM HUNGATE, esq. (the eldest son and heir) of North Dalton, *m.* Audrey, daughter of John Saltmarsh, esq. of Saltmarsh, and was *s.* by his eldest son,

WILLIAM HUNGATE, esq. of Saxton, living in 1553, who *m.* Anne, daughter of Thomas Stillington, esq. of Acaster, and had issue,

- WILLIAM, his heir.
- Robert, barrister-at-law, founded a school at Sherebourn, in the county of York. He *d.* 25th July, 1619.
- Ralph.
- Edmund, *m.* Jane, daughter of Richard Bell, esq. barrister-at-law, died in 1614, and was buried in St. Cuthbert's Church.

- Anne, *m.* to John Anlaby, esq.
- Margery, *m.* to William Power, esq.
- Isabel, *m.* to Leon. Foster, esq.
- Jane, *m.* to Nicholas, second son of Sir William Fairfax, knt. of Walton,
- Catherine, *m.* to Christopher Babthorp, esq.

The eldest son and heir,

WILLIAM HUNGATE, esq. of Saxton, *m.* Margaret, daughter and co-heir of Roger Sotheby, esq. of Pocklington, in Yorkshire, and grandaughter maternally, of Sir William Constable, knt. of Hatfield, and had issue,

- WILLIAM (Sir), of Saxton, who *m.* Elizabeth, daughter of William Middleton, esq. of Leighton, and *d. s. p.* in December, 1634.
- PHILIP.
- Thomas.
- Roger.
- Robert.

The second son,

I. PHILIP HUNGATE, esq. of Saxton, was created a BARONET by *King* CHARLES I. 15th August, 1642. He *m.* Dorothy, daughter of Roger Leigh, M.D. of Hatt[illegible] in the county of York, and widow of Andrew Y[illegible] esq. of Browne, by whom he had issue,

- FRANCIS, col. in the army, *temp.* CHARLES I. [illegible] at Chester, 1645, left by his wife, Jean, daughter of Robert Middleton, esq. of Leighton, in Lan[illegible]shire (co-heir of her brother Francis),
  - FRANCIS, successor to his grandfather.
  - William, col. in Lord Dunbar's regiment.
  - Mary, *m.* to John Fairfax, esq. of Gilling
- Col. Francis Hungate's widow, Jean, *m.* Walter Hammond, esq. of Scarthingwell, in the county of York.
- Elizabeth, *m.* to Gilbert Stapleton, esq. of Carlton in the county of York.
- Mary, *m.* first to Sir Marmaduke Grimston, knt. and secondly to Sir Henry Browne, knt. Kiddington.
- Catherine, *m.* first to Marmaduke Cholmley, esq. of Bransby, in the county of York, and secondly to Sir William Howard, knt.

Sir Philip was *s.* by his grandson,

II. SIR FRANCIS HUNGATE, who *m.* Margaret, fourth daughter of Charles Smith, Viscount Carrington, and had issue,

- PHILIP, his heir.
- Francis, M.D.
- Roger.
- William.

- Margaret.
- Elizabeth.

He was *s.* by his eldest son,

III. SIR PHILIP HUNGATE, who *m.* Elizabeth, daughter of William, Lord Monson, by whom (who *m.* secondly, Lewis Smith, esq. of Wotton, in Warwickshire) he left three sons,

FRANCIS, PHILIP, CHARLES, } successive baronets.

The eldest son and heir,

IV. SIR FRANCIS HUNGATE, *m.* Elizabeth, daughter of William Weld, esq. of Lulworth Castle, [illegible] Nicholas Fairfax, esq. of Gilling, and had one surviving daughter,

- MARY, who *m.* Sir Edward Gascoigne, of Parlington.

He *d.* 26th July, 1710, and was *s.* by his brother,

V. SIR PHILIP HUNGATE, who *m.* Elizabeth, daughter of Mr. Cotton, but dying *s. p.* was *s.* by his brother,

VI. SIR CHARLES HUNGATE, who *d.* a bachelor [illegible] unm. 3rd December, 1749, when the BARONETCY became EXTINCT.

Arms—Gules, a chevron engrailed between three talbots sejant, argent.

---

* From Robert, the fourth son, lineally descended

William Hungate, of Middlesex, Thomas Hungate, of York, John Hungate, of London, } sons of Thomas Hungate, of Haverhill, Suffolk, and Mary, his wife, daughter of Mr. Webb, of Clare, in that county.

HUSSEY, OF HONINGTON.

CREATED 29th June, 1161.

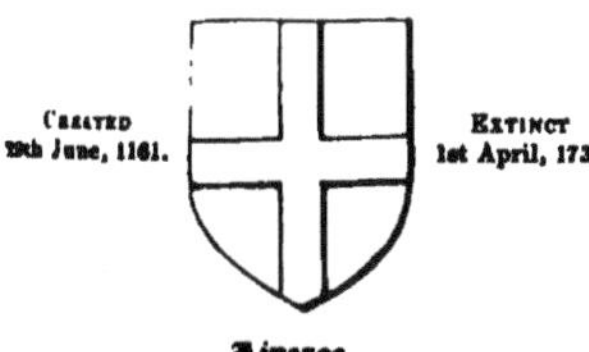

EXTINCT 1st April, 1734.

Lineage.

SIR WILLIAM HUSSEY, knt. lord chief justice of the King's Bench, *temp.* EDWARD IV. m. Elizabeth, daughter of Thomas Berkeley, esq. of Wymondham, and had issue,

- I. JOHN, his heir, summoned to parliament by HENRY VIII. as Baron Hussey, of Sleford, in the county of Lincoln. (See BURKE's *Extinct Peerage.*)
- II. ROBERT (Sir).
- III. William, ancestor of the Husseys of Yorkshire.
- I. Elizabeth, m. to Richard Grey, Earl of Kent, but *d. s. p.*
- II. Mary, m. to William, Lord Willoughby.

The second son,

SIR ROBERT HUSSEY, knt. was of Halton, in Lincolnshire, and served the office of sheriff in the 34th HENRY VIII. His son and heir,

SIR CHARLES HUSSEY, of Honington, received the honour of knighthood from *Queen* ELIZABETH, and was sheriff of Lincolnshire in the 33rd of her majesty's reign. He m. Ellen, daughter of Lord Chief Baron Birch, and had two sons,

- EDWARD (Sir), his heir.
- Charles (Sir).

The elder son,

I. SIR EDWARD HUSSEY, knt. of Honington, in the county of Lincoln, was created a BARONET by *King* JAMES I. 29th June, 1611. He was sheriff of Lincolnshire in the 16th of that reign, and again in the 12th of CHARLES, and served in parliament in 1640. Sir Edward was a great sufferer in the civil wars, and so obnoxious to the usurped authorities, that in the propositions at Uxbridge, 1644, he was one of those to be removed from his majesty's councils. He m. Elizabeth, daughter of George Anton, and niece and heir of Thomas Taylor, esq. of Doddington Pigot, in Lincolnshire, and had issue,

- I. THOMAS, his heir, m. Rhoda, daughter and co-heir of Thomas Chapman, esq. of London, and dying in the lifetime of his father, left
  - 1. THOMAS, successor to his grandfather.
  - 2. William (Sir), ambassador from *King* WILLIAM III. to the Port, m. Mary, daughter of Sir John Buckworth, bart. and *d. s. p.*
  - 1. Rhoda, m. to John Amcoats, esq. of Astrop, in Lincolnshire.
  - 2. Jane.
  - 3. Mary, m. to Thomas Ball, esq. of Minehead.
- II. John, capt. royal army, slain at Gainsborough.
- III. CHARLES, of Caythorp, in the county of Lincoln, created a BARONET by *King* CHARLES II. 21st July, 1661. His son,
  - SIR EDWARD HUSSEY inherited the Honington baronetcy in 1706.
- IV. Edward, *d.* issueless.
- I. Jane, m. to Sir Thomas Williamson, bart.
- II. Mary, m. to Sir Robert Bolles, bart.
- III. Rebecca, m. to Sir Robert Markham, of Sedgbrook, in Lincolnshire.
- IV. Bridget, m. to Sir Thomas Clifton, bart. of Lytham.
- V. Anne, m. to Charles Pelham, esq. of Brocklesby, in Lincolnshire.

Sir Edward died about the year 1648, and was *s.* by his grandson,

II. SIR THOMAS HUSSEY, M.P. for the county of Lincoln, *temp.* WILLIAM III. who m. Sarah, daughter of Sir John Langham, bart. and left two surviving daughters, his co-heirs, viz.

- ELIZABETH HUSSEY, m. to Sir Richard Ellys, bart. and *d. s. p.*
- SARAH HUSSEY, m. to Robert Apreece, esq. of Washingley, in the county of Huntingdon, and from this marriage lineally descends the present (1837) SIR THOMAS GEORGE APREECE, bart. of Washingley. (Refer to BURKE's *Peerage and Baronetage.*)

He *d.* in December, 1706, when the baronetcy passed to his cousin,

III. SIR EDWARD HUSSEY, second baronet of Caythorp, in the county of Lincoln. This gentleman m. first, Charlotte, only child of Daniel Brevint, D.D. dean of Lincoln, by whom he had several children, but only two survived him, viz.

- Charlotte, m. Thomas Pochin, esq. of Barkby, in Leicestershire, and their daughter, Charlotte Pochin, m. to CHARLES-JAMES PACKE, esq. of Prestwold Hall, eventually inherited the estates of her grandfather, Sir Edward Hussey, bart. and conveyed them to the PACKE family. (See BURKE's *Commoners*, vol. i. p. 156.)
- Sarah.

He m. secondly, Elizabeth, daughter of Sir Henry Davie, bart. and by her had two sons,

HENRY, EDWARD, } fourth and fifth baronets.

Sir Edward *d.* 16th February, 1725, and was *s.* by his elder son,

IV. SIR HENRY HUSSEY, third baronet of Caythorp, who *d. s. p.* 14th February, 1730, and was *s.* by his brother,

V. SIR EDWARD HUSSEY, fourth baronet of Caythorp. This gentleman died issueless, 1st April, 1734, when the BARONETCY of Honington, and the BARONETCY of Caythorp, both EXPIRED.

Arms—Quarterly, first and fourth or, a cross vert, second and third barry of six, ermine and gules.

HUSSEY, OF CAYTHORPE.

CREATED 21st July, 1661.—EXTINCT 1st April, 1734.

Lineage.

I. CHARLES HUSSEY, esq. of Caythorpe, in the county of Lincoln, second son of Sir Edward Hussey, bart. of Honington, was created a BARONET by *King* CHARLES II. 21st July, 1661. Sir Charles m. Elizabeth, daughter of Sir William Brownlowe, bart. of Humby, in Lincolnshire, and dying in 1664, was *s.* by his elder son,

II. SIR CHARLES HUSSEY, who *d.* unm. about the year 1680, and was *s.* by his brother,

III. SIR EDWARD HUSSEY, of Caythorpe, who at the

decease of his cousin, Sir Thomas Hussey, of Honington, without male issue, in 1706, succeeded to the older baronetcy, and carried on the main branch of his house. (Refer to Hussey *of Honington*.)

Arms—Same as Hussey of Honington.

INGLEBY, OF RIPLEY.

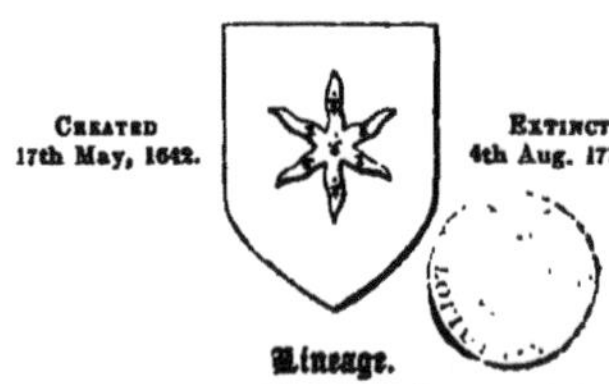

Created 17th May, 1642.

Extinct 4th Aug. 1772.

Lineage.

This family, according to Camden, flourished with great antiquity and reputation at Ripley, a market town in the West Riding of the county of York.

Sir Thomas Inglesy, knt. one of the justices of the court of Common Pleas, *m.* Catherine Ripley, and had issue, Thomas, his heir, Henry, prebend of South Cave, 12 Richard II. John, William, David, and Alice. The eldest son,

Thomas Inglesy, esq. who was knight of the shire of York, 23 Edward III. *m.* Eleanor, daughter and heir of William Mowbray, esq. of Kirtlington,* and had two sons, William, who died issueless, and

John Inglesy, esq. living *temp.* Henry IV. who continued the line. He was founder of the monastery of Mount Grace. He *m.* Ellen, daughter and heir of Sir Bryan Rocliffe, knt. of Rocliffe, and had issue,

Thomas, his heir.

Catherine, *m.* to Walter Pedwardine, esq. of Lincolnshire.

Jannet, *m.* to John Holme, esq. of Holdernesse.

Isabel, *m.* to Thomas de la River, esq. of Bransby.

He was *s.* by his son,

Thomas Inglesy, esq. who *m.* Ellen, daughter of John Holme, esq. and left, with a daughter, Elizabeth, the wife of Thomas Beckwith, esq. of Clint, a son and heir,

Sir William Inglesy, knt. who wedded Joan, daughter of Sir Bryan Stapleton, knight of the Garter, and had (with two daughters, Agnes, *m.* to John Sothil, esq. of Everingham, and Katherine, *m.* to William Arthington, esq. of Arthington,) a son and heir,

John Inglesy, esq. who *m.* Margery,† daughter of Sir James Strangeways, knt. and was *s.* by his son,

Sir William Inglesy, of Ripley, who *m.* Catherine, daughter of Thomas Stillington, esq. and had issue,

John, his heir.

Jane, *m.* to Sir Robert Constable, knt.

Anne, *m.* first, to Richard Goldsborough, esq. secondly, to Robert Warcup, esq. and thirdly, to Thomas Wriothesley, Garter king of arms.

The son and heir,

John Inglesy, esq. of Ripley, *m.* Eleanor, daughter of Sir Marmaduke Constable, knt. of Flamborough, and dying in 1502, was *s.* by his only surviving son,

Sir William Inglesy, knt. of Ripley, who *m.* Cecily, daughter of Sir George Talboys, and by her (who wedded, secondly, John Torney, esq.) had issue,

William (Sir), his heir.

John, of Lawkland, ancestor of Sir Charles Ingleby, knt. one of the judges, *temp.* James II.

George, *d. s. p.*

Frances, *m.* to James Pulleine, esq. ancestor of the Pulleines of Carleton and Crake Hall.

Elizabeth, *m.* to Mr. Richard Maltus.

He was *s.* by his eldest son,

Sir William Inglesy, knt. of Ripley, who was treasurer of Berwick, and *d.* in 1578-9, having had issue, by Anne, daughter of Sir William Mallory, of Studley, in the county of York, five sons and five daughters, viz.

i. William (Sir), high sheriff of Yorkshire in the 7 Elizabeth, *m.* first, Anne, daughter and heir of T. Thwaites, esq. and secondly, Anne, daughter of Anthony Smithyes, esq. of Brantingham, but *d. s. p.*

ii. David, *m.* Lady Anne Nevill, youngest daughter of Charles, sixth Earl of Westmoreland, and left three daughters, viz.

Mary, *m.* to Sir Peter Middleton, knt.

Frances, *m.* to Sir Robert Hodshon, knt.

Ursula, *m.* to Robert Widdrington, esq.

iii. Francis, *d.* young.

iv. Sampson.

v. John, *m.* Catherine, daughter of Sir William Babthrop, knt. of Babthrop, and relict of George Vavasor, esq. of Spaldington, and left a daughter,

Catharine, *m.* to Marmaduke Frank, esq. of Knighton, in the county of York.

i. Jane, *m.* to George Winter, esq. of Coldwell, in Worcestershire.

ii. Grace, *m.* to William Birnard, esq. of Knaresborough.

iii. Isabel, *m.* to Thomas Markinfeld, esq.

iv. Elizabeth, *m.* to Peter Yorke, esq.

v. Catharine, *m.* to Sir William Arthington, knt. of Arthington, and had a son,

Cyril Arthington.

The fifth son,

Sampson Inglesy, esq. *m.* Elizabeth, daughter of Sir John Yorke, knt. and had issue,

William, his heir.

Anne, *m.* to Francis Swale, esq.

Catherine.

Mary, *m.* to Francis Appleby, esq. of Lartington.

Jane.

Elizabeth, a nun at Ghent.

He was *s.* by his son,

i. Sir William Inglesy, knt. of Ripley, who was created a Baronet by *King* Charles I. 17th May, 1642. He *m.* Anne, daughter of Sir James Bellingham, knt. of Levens, in Westmoreland, and dying in 1657-8, aged seventy-one, was *s.* by his son,

ii. Sir William Inglesy, *b.* in 1621, who *m.* Margaret, eldest daughter of John Savile, esq. of Methley, in the county of York, and had issue,

i. John, his successor.

i. Margaret, *m.* to Mark, eldest son of Sir Robert Shaftoe, knt. recorder of Newcastle.

ii. Anne, *m.* to John, son of Sir John Arderne, knt. of Harden, in Cheshire.

---

* By Margaret, daughter and heir of John Chaumont, esq. of Colton, in the ainsty of York.

† She *m.* secondly, Richard Lord Wells.

‡ By Anne, his wife, daughter of Henry Howard, Earl of Surrey, and sister of Thomas, Duke of Norfolk.

III. Elizabeth, *d.* in 1678.
IV. Mary, living unm. in 1741.
V. Katharine, *d.* in 1701.

He *d.* in November, 1682, aged sixty-one, and was *s.* by his son,

III. SIR JOHN INGLEBY, who *m.* Mary, daughter of Mr. Johnson, and had surviving issue, JOHN, his heir, and Margaret. He *d.* 25th January, 1742, and was *s.* by his son,

IV. SIR JOHN INGLEBY, who *d.* 14th July, 1772, without legitimate issue, when the BARONETCY became EXTINCT.

Note.—The last baronet, Sir John Ingleby, left an illegitimate son,

JOHN INGILBY, esq. who inheriting the estates, was of Ripley, and was created a BARONET in 1781. He *m.* in 1780, Elizabeth, daughter and sole heir of Wharton Amcotts, esq. of Kettlethorpe, in Lincolnshire, and was father of the present (1837)

SIR WILLIAM AMCOTTS-INGILBY, bart. of Kettlethorpe Park and Ripley Castle, (refer to BURKE'S *Peerage and Baronetage*).

Arms—Sa. a star of six rays arg.

INGOLDSBY, OF LETHENBOROUGH

CREATED 30th Aug. 1661.

EXTINCT 25th April, 1726.

Lineage.

The family of Ingoldsby was of ancient standing in the county of Lincoln, and derived in direct descent from Sir Roger Ingoldsby, Lord of Ingoldsby, in that ... anno 1230.

... RICHARD INGOLDSBY, of Lethenborough, in the county of Buckingham, knt. was found, by an inquisition taken at the demise of his father, Francis Ingoldsby, esq. in 1634, to be his eldest son and heir. He *m.* Elizabeth, daughter of William Palmer, esq. of ...addeston, Bucks, and had issue,

RICHARD, his heir.
Dorothy, bapt. 12th July, 1582, *m.* first, 28th May, 1602, to Sir Christopher Pigot, knt. of Doddershall, and secondly, to Maximilian Petty, esq.
Agnes, *m.* to Richard Sergeant, esq. of Dinton, Bucks.
Martha, *m.* to John Pessey, esq.

Richard, who was sheriff of Bucks 3 JAMES I. ... in 1635, and was *s.* by his son,

SIR RICHARD INGOLDSBY, of Lethenborough, knighted by JAMES I. 22nd October, 1617, when that monarch ... Hinchinbrooke, the seat of Sir Richard's ...-in-law, Sir Oliver Cromwell, K. B. He *m.* Elizabeth, daughter of Sir Oliver, and by her, who *d.* ... May, 1666, had issue,

FRANCIS, baptized 14th August, 1614, *d.* at Lethenborough. In the parliaments called by the Protector in 1654 and 1656, he represented the county of Buckingham, but at the Restoration, gaining the royal favour, he was placed on the list of those on whom it was intended to have conferred the knighthood of the Royal Oak. Subsequently, however, by a course of extravagance, he dissipated his fortune, sold Lethenborough House to Mr. Robinson, his steward, and after mortgaging as far as he could his whole estates, went to London about the year 1673, and in 1679 was admitted a pensioner at the Charter House, where he died 1st October, 1681. By Lettice, his wife, daughter of Crawley Norton, esq. of Offleys, Herts, he had issue,

1. Francis-Richard, bapt. 23rd April, 1652.
2. Edward, *d.* young.

1. Ellen.
2. Ann.
3. Lettice.
4. Martha.
5. Elizabeth.

II. RICHARD (Sir) K. B. the celebrated parliamentary general. This distinguished person was one of the commissioners of the high court of justice for the trial of his sovereign, signed the warrant for his execution, was one of the chief confidants of Oliver Cromwell, governor of Oxford Castle, and one of the lords of the upper house. When he found the cause of his cousin Richard desperate, he strenuously exerted himself in promoting the restoration of the exiled monarch, and so effectually recommended himself to his favour, that he not only procured his pardon, being the only one of the regicides who had a free one, but was made a knight of the Bath. He *m.* Anne, daughter of Sir George Croke, one of the judges of the court of King's Bench, and widow of Thomas Lee, esq. of Hartwell, and dying in 1685, left, with a daughter, Jane, the wife of Thomas Marriot, esq. of Ascot, in Gloucestershire, a son and successor,

RICHARD, who *m.* Mary, only daughter of William Colmore, esq. of Warwick, and died 14th April, 1703, leaving issue,

THOMAS, of Waldridge, *b.* in 1688, sheriff of Bucks 7 GEORGE I. and M.P. for Aylesbury, who had issue,

RICHARD,* of Waldridge, M.P. for Aylesbury, who died *s. p.*
MARTHA, *m.* in 1762, to George, late Marquess of Winchester.

Richard, living in 1713.
Frances, unm. in 1713.
Henrietta, living in 1713.
Letitia, died in 1711.

III. OLIVER (Sir), knt. *b.* in 1619, a parliamentary officer, slain at Pendennis.
IV. JOHN, *b.* in 1621, who is stated to have been also engaged on the parliamentary side, and to have died at sea.
V. HENRY, of whom we have to treat.
VI. GEORGE (Sir), killed in the Dutch wars.
VII. THOMAS, a captain in his brother Richard's regiment.
VIII. WILLIAM, *b.* in 1627.

I. Elizabeth, died unm.
II. Sarah, died unm.
III. Ann, *b.* in 1621, *m.* to Sir Edward Chaloner, knt.

* In some pedigrees of the family, Richard is stated to have had a brother Thomas, brigadier-general in the army, ... died in 1737, leaving a daughter, *m.* to JAMES LENOX NAPER, esq. of Loughcrew.

IV. Mary, *b.* in 1629, *m.* to Major Read, who was wounded at the siege of Bristol, in 1645.

The fifth son,

I. Sir Henry Ingoldsby, born in 1622, held at first a commission in the royal army, but subsequently deserting his ill-fated master, became a colonel in the service of the parliament. He went afterwards to Ireland, and was there most useful to his party, but Lord Clarendon records that he performed acts of barbarity in that oppressed kingdom utterly revolting to humanity. Sir Henry was returned to parliament by the counties of Kerry, Limerick, and Clare, in 1654, 1656, and 1659. Like his brother Richard, he was equally zealous in paving the way for future favour with the exiled monarch, whose restoration he foresaw; with this view he hastened from Ireland, where he had a command, took possession of Windsor Castle, then in the hands of the republicans, and garrisoned it for the parliament, who appeared to be favourably disposed towards the restoration of the monarchy. For this service he was created a Baronet by Charles II. 30th August, 1660, having already obtained a similar dignity from the Protector Cromwell, in 1658. He died in Ireland in 1701, one of the oldest officers in the army, and left by Anne, his wife, daughter of Sir Hardress Waller, a son and successor,

II. Sir George Ingoldsby, who *m.* Mary, daughter of Sir Peter Stanley, bart. and had, with a daughter, Ann, married to Sir Francis Blundel, bart. a son and successor,

III. Sir William Ingoldsby, who *m.* Theophila, daughter of Sir Kingswill Lucy, bart. of Broxbourne, Herts, and had a daughter, Anne. Sir William *d.* 25th April, 1726, when the Baronetcy became extinct.

Arms—Erm. a saltire engr. sa.

INNES, OF LOCHALSH.

Created 28th April, 1819. Extinct 16th Aug. 1831.

Lineage.

The Rev. Berould Innes (descended from the stock of the ducal house of Roxburghe) was chanter of the diocese of Moray, and minister of the parish of Alvess, in that county. He *m.* Jean, daughter of Colin Falconer, Bishop of Moray, and had issue,

- James, in holy orders, church of Scotland.
- William, *m.* and had issue.
- Hugh, an episcopal clergyman.
- Joan, *m.* to John Gilzean, of Coltfield.

The eldest son,

The Rev. James Innes, *m.* Catherine, daughter of Hugh Falconer, esq. of Inverness, and had, with a daughter, Jean, wife of Captain Mackenzie, of the Scotch brigade, a son and heir,

The Rev. Hugh Innes, *b.* 30th July, 1727, *m.* Jean, daughter of Thomas Graham, esq. and dying in 1765, left an only son,

I. Hugh Innes, esq. of Lochalsh, in the county of Ross, and Coxton, in Moray, M.P. who was created a Baronet 28th April, 1819. Sir Hugh *d.* unm. 16th August, 1831, when the Baronetcy expired.

Arms—Quarterly, first and fourth, arg. three stars of six rays az. for Innes; second and third, or a chief sa. three escallops of the field, for Graham.

JACKSON, OF HICKLETON.

Created 31st Dec. 1660. Extinct in 17[illegible]

Lineage.

Of this family, one of good note in the county of York, was

John Jackson, of Edderthorp, near Darfield, in that county, who *m.* Ellen, daughter of John W[illegible]son, of Bolton, and dying in February, 1[illegible], aged sixty-four, left no less than seven sons and seven daughters. The eldest son,

Sir John Jackson, knt. of Nottingley, in Yorkshire, who was educated in the study of the law at Lincoln's Inn, was attorney to the council established in the North, in the commission of the peace for the West Riding, 32 Elizabeth. In 4 James I. he was constituted autumnal reader in that inn of court, and 13th of the same reign treasurer. He received the honour of knighthood, and married Elizabeth, daughter of Sir John Savile, of Methley, knt. one of the barons of the Exchequer, and had issue,

- John, his heir.
- Henry, barrister-at-law, clerk of assize for the northern circuit, *m.* a daughter of Sir George Snigg, one of the barons of the Exchequer, but left no issue.
- Francis, of Hooton Paynell, in Yorkshire, barrister-at-law.
- Jane, *m.* to Sir Francis Thornhaugh, knt. of Fenton, in Yorkshire.
- Elizabeth, *m.* first, to Robert Williamson, esq. [illegible] Walkingham, Notts, and secondly, to Sir R[illegible] Hutton, knt. of Hooton Paynel, in the county of York.
- Lucy, *m.* to Henry Tindall, esq. of Brotherton, Yorkshire.

He was *s.* by his eldest son,

Sir John Jackson, knt. of Hickleton, who, [illegible] Charles I. was treasurer for the maimed soldiers, and served several times in parliament for the borough of Pontefract. He *m.* first, Elizabeth, daughter of John Thornhaugh, of Fenton, Notts, by whom he had no issue, and secondly, Fiennes, daughter of Sir Thomas Waller, governor of Dover Castle, and dying 2nd July, 1637, was *s.* by his elder son,

I. John Jackson, esq. of Hickleton, in the county of York, who was created a Baronet by King Charles II. 31st December, 1660. Sir John *m.* [illegible] Catherine, daughter of George Booth, esq. of Dunham Massey, by whom, who *d.* in 16[illegible], he had one son and three daughters, viz.

- John, his successor,
- Fiennes, *m.* to Nicholas Mauleverer, esq. of [illegible]well.

Vere, m. to John Adams, esq. son of Sir William Adams, of Owston.

Catherine, living in 1679.

He m. 2ndly, his cousin, Lucy, daughter of Henry Tindall, esq. of Brotherton, and relict of Sir William Jopson, of Heath Hall, and by her had a son,

BRADWARDINE, successor to his brother.

Sir John was s. at his decease by his elder son,

II. SIR JOHN JACKSON, who died unm. 6th February, 1679, aged twenty-seven, having sold his estates to pay his debts. He was s. by his brother, of the half blood,

III. SIR BRADWARDINE JACKSON, one of the commissioners of the land tax, 6 ANNE. This gentleman was living unm. in 1727, but the period of his decease and of the EXTINCTION of the BARONETCY has not been ascertained.

Hickleton was purchased from the Jacksons by Sir Michael Wentworth, knt. of Woolley.

Arms—Gu. a fess between three sheldrakes arg.

JACOB, OF BROMLEY.

CREATED 11th Jan. 1665.

EXTINCT 4th Nov. 1790.

Lineage.

WILLIAM JACOB, of Horseheath, in the county of Cambridge, died 23rd HENRY VIII. leaving a son,

RICHARD JACOB, of Horseheath and Gamlingay, in the same county, who m. Winifrid, daughter of William Chambers, of Royston, and was s. by his son,

ROBERT JACOB, esq. of Gamlingay, who m. Catherine, daughter and heir of William Abraham, of London, merchant, and left a son,

ABRAHAM JACOB, esq. of Gamlingay, who m. Mary, daughter of Francis Rogers, of Dartford, and had (with other issue),

JOHN (Sir), his heir.

Robert, who by his second wife, Margaret, daughter of Alexander Packer, esq. of King's Charleton, in Gloucestershire, had

James.

Alexander, a Turkey merchant in London, m. the Hon. Elizabeth Brydges, daughter of Henry, eighth Lord Chandos. She survived her husband, and m. secondly, the Rev. Thomas Dawson, D.D. vicar of Windsor.

John, m. to Elizabeth Halliday, and had issue.

Ellen, m. to Henry Rott, esq.

Mary, m. to George Bury, esq.

Elizabeth, m. to Thomas Wilmer, esq.

Barbara, m. to Robert Seylliard, esq.

He d. 6th May, 1629, and was s. by his eldest son,

I. SIR JOHN JACOB, of Bromley, in Essex, who was knighted by *King* CHARLES I. in 1633, being one of the farmers of the Customs in the port of London, and in the enjoyment of a clear estate of £2000 per annum, for adhering to the king, his lands were sequestered, and his personal property considerably reduced by the loans he made at different times to his royal master. Lloyd, in his memoirs of eminent persons who suffered for their allegiance, thus mentions him: "We must not separate Sir Nicholas Crisp from the worshipful Sir John Jacob, his partner, both in the farming of the Custom House, and his sufferings; a man ever forward to assist his majesty, saying, What! shall I keep my estate, and see the king want wherewithal to protect it? If it please God to bless the king, though I gave him all I had I can be no loser; if not, though I keep all I can be no saver; and to relieve the clergy, valuing more their prayers and God's blessing than his own estate, employing under him only those honest cavaliers that suffered with him."

In consideration of his loyalty, so zealous and so generous, Sir John was created a BARONET by *King* CHARLES II. 11th January, 1665. On the restoration his estate was restored to him, he was made a commissioner of the Customs, and again became one of the farmers thereof. He m. first, Elizabeth, daughter of John, grandson of Sir Leonard Halliday, knt. lord mayor of London, and by her had two sons, Abraham and Henry, who both died before him issueless, and a daughter, Susanna, the wife of Sir Richard Wingfield, bart. of Letheringham, in Suffolk. Sir John m. secondly, Alice, daughter of Thomas Clowes, of London, and relict of John Eaglesfield, also of London, merchant, by whom he had

JOHN, his heir.

Francis, *d. s. p.*

Robert, killed in Scotland, *d. s. p.*

Alice, m. to Henry West, esq. of Wooham Court, in Sussex.

Mary, m. to Walter, son and heir of Sir Arnold Beams, knt. of Bridge Court, in Kent.

Helen, m. to John, son of Sir John Hebdon.

He wedded, thirdly, Elizabeth, eldest daughter and co-heir of Sir John Ashburnam, knt. by whom he had a daughter, Margaret, m. to — Muschamp, esq. of Row Barnes, in Surrey. Sir John died in February or March, 1666, his funeral sermon was preached in the latter month. He left to the parish of Gamlingay £40 per annum for maintaining ten poor people in an almshouse which he had finished in his lifetime. His widow m. Sir William Wogan, knt. serjeant-at-law, and d. in 1697. He was s. by his eldest son,

II. SIR JOHN JACOB, who m. the Hon. Catherine Allington, daughter of William, Lord Allington, and dying in 1675, was s. by his son,

III. SIR JOHN JACOB, who went early into the army (almost all his father's estate being seized upon by the creditors of his grandfather, for money he had borrowed for *King* CHARLES I. which was never repaid by the crown), and served for seventeen years in the reigns of JAMES II. and WILLIAM III. in the latter as colonel of an old regiment of foot, which commission he resigned in favour of his brother-in-law, James, Earl of Barrymore. Sir John was at the battle of the Boyne, sieges of Cork and Kingsale, and was severely wounded at Killicranky. King William, who had a high esteem for him, constituted him colonel of Hastings's regiment. He m. Lady Dorothy Barry, daughter of Richard, Earl of Barrymore, and had issue,

HILDEBRAND, his heir, who m. Muriel, daughter of Sir John Bland, bart. of Kippax Park, in Yorkshire, and dying 3rd June, 1739, his father then living, left an only son,

HILDEBRAND, successor to his grandfather.

CATHERINE, b. in 1695, m. to Abraham Oakes, LL. D. rector of Long Melford, and was grandmother of the present (1837) SIR HENRY-THOMAS OAKES, bart. (see BURKE's *Peerage and Baronetage*.)

ELIZABETH, b. in 1696.

DOROTHY, *b.* in 1703, *m.* to Captain Morley, of Halstead, in Essex.

Sir John *d.* 31st March, 1740, and was *s.* by his grandson,

IV. SIR HILDEBRAND JACOB, who *d. s. p.* 4th November, 1790, when the BARONETCY EXPIRED.

Arms—Arg. a chevron gu. between three tigers' heads erased ppr.

JACQUES, OF MIDDLESEX.

CREATED 2nd Sept. 1628.

EXTINCT in 1650.

Lineage.

I. Sir JOHN JACQUES, one of his majesty's gentlemen pensioners, was created a BARONET by *King* CHARLES I. but as he had no issue, the title EXPIRED at his decease in 1650.

Arms—Arg. on a fesse sa. three escallops or.

JAMES, OF CRESHALL.

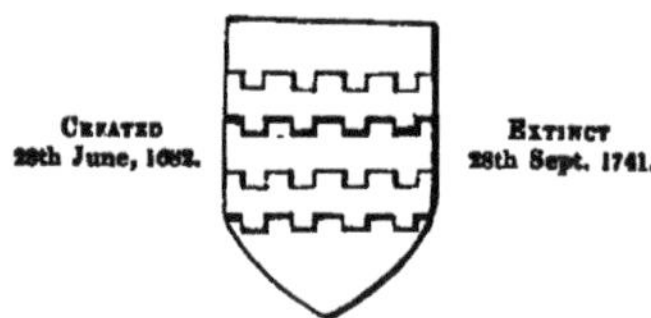

CREATED 28th June, 1682.

EXTINCT 28th Sept. 1741.

Lineage.

The JAMES's were originally, says Philpot, called *Haestrecht*, from a lordship of that name near Utrecht, of which they were proprietors.

ROGER, son of JACOB VAN HAESTRECHT, came into England *temp.* HENRY VIII. and being known after the Dutch manner by the name of ROGER JACOB, that name finally settled in JAMES, and he was called Roger James. He *m.* Sarah, daughter and heir of Henry Morskin, esq. of London, and had issue,

I. ROGER JAMES, of Upminster, in Essex, father of SIR ROGER JAMES, of Rygate, who left a daughter,
   ELIZABETH JAMES.
II. Arnold James, of London, *m.* Mary, daughter of John Vanhulst, of that city.
III. William James, who purchased *temp.* ELIZABETH the manor of Ightham Court, and was ancestor of the branch of the family seated there, now represented by DEMETRIUS GREVIS JAMES, esq. of Ightham Court, sheriff of Kent in 1833. (See BURKE'S *Commoners*, vol. i. p. 397.)
IV. Thomas James.
V. RICHARD JAMES.
VI. John James, of Grove Manor, who *m.* Susanna, daughter and co-heir of Peter Vandewall, of Antwerp, and had issue.
VII. George James, of Malendine, near Rochester, *m.* Audrey, daughter of John Smith, esq. and had issue.

The fifth son,

RICHARD JAMES, esq. *m.* Gertrude, daughter of John Smyth, and had, with other issue,

JOHN (Sir), his heir.
EMLIN, *m.* to Mr. James Cane, citizen and vintner of London, and had a son,
   JAMES CANE, of whom presently as heir of his uncle.

He was *s.* by his eldest son,

SIR JOHN JAMES, of Crishall, in Essex, who purchased that estate in May, 1649, from John Pra[illegible]dock, esq. and was knighted in 1655. He built Crishall Hall, and dying a bachelor 15th February, 16[illegible] a stately monument was raised to his memory by his nephew James Cane, to whom he devised his estates on the condition of taking his name, who having complied with the injunction, inherited as

I. CANE JAMES, esq. of Crishall, and was created a BARONET by *King* CHARLES II. 28th June, 1682. He Cane *m.* first, Susan, daughter of Sir Peter Seame, bart. of Haidon, in Essex, but by that lady had no issue. She died five months after her marriage, 12th September, 1680, aged seventeen, and was buried under a marble monument at Haidon church. He *m.* secondly, Anne, daughter and co-heir of Francis Philipps, esq. of the Inner Temple, and of Kemps[illegible] Park, Middlesex, by whom he had issue,

JOHN, his heir.
Philip, a Hamburgh merchant, died at Schie[illegible] in Holland, and was buried there.
Francis, *d. s. p.*
George, *d.* young.
Catherine, } *d.* young.
Elizabeth, }

He *d.* 19th May, 1736, aged eighty, and was *s.* by his eldest son,

II. SIR JOHN JAMES, who *d.* unmarried, aged forty-seven, 28th September, 1741, and was buried at Crishall, when the BARONETCY became EXTINCT. Sir John left his estates by will to charitable uses, but the bequest being contrary to the statute of George II. HAESTRECT JAMES, the heir male and head of the family, after a long Chancery suit, obtained possession. His only child, Elizabeth, married William James, esq. of Ightham, and their son, Richard, dying *s. p.* in 1667, left his estates to his cousin, the present DEMETRIUS GREVIS JAMES, esq.

Arms—Quarterly, first and fourth, arg. two [illegible] crenelle or counter-embattled gu.; second and third, arg. three ferdemolins bar-ways, sa.

JAMES, OF ELTHAM.

CREATED 27th Aug. 1778.

EXTINCT 16th Nov. 17[illegible]

Lineage.

I. WILLIAM JAMES, esq. of Park Farm Place, [illegible] Kent, was created a BARONET in 1778. He *m.* Anne[illegible] elder daughter and co-heir of Edmond Goddard, esq. of Hartham, in Wiltshire, eldest son of the Rev. Thomas Goddard, A.M. canon of Windsor, and by her, who died 9th August, 1769, had one son and one daughter, viz.

Edward-William, his heir.

Elizabeth-Anne, who m. in 1783, Thomas Boothby Parkyns, esq. who was created Baron Rancliffe in 1795, and had issue,

George-Augustus-Henry-Anne, present Lord Rancliffe.

Elizabeth-Anne, m. to Sir Richard Levinge, bart.

Henrietta-Elizabeth, m. to Sir William Rumbold, bart.

Maria-Charlotte, m. first, to the Marquess de Choiseul; and secondly, to the Prince de Polignac, ex-minister of Charles X. of France.

Sir William died in December, 1783, and was s. by his only son,

II. Sir Edward-William James, of Eltham, who d. unmarried 16th November, 1792, when the Baronetcy became extinct.

Arms—Az. on a chevron, between three lions passant guardant or, ducally crowned of the last, three grenades sa. fired ppr.

JANSSEN, OF WIMBLEDON.

Created 11th Mar. 1714.

Extinct 8th April, 1777.

Lineage.

This family was originally of Guelderland, and descended from the

Baron de Heez, who in the troubles of the Netherlands headed a party of those who opposed the Duke of Alva, and was constituted by his associates Governor of Brussels. He was in some years afterwards made prisoner by the Duke of Parma, and beheaded, and all his estate was confiscated. His family being thus dispersed, his youngest son,

Theodore Janssen de Heez, sought an asylum in France, and living there to an advanced age, left a large fortune and numerous issue. His eldest son,

Abraham Janssen, was father of

I. Sir Theodore Janssen, who removing into England in 1680, with a considerable estate, was naturalized, and in the reign of *King* William received the honour of knighthood. Having during that monarch and the reign of *Queen* Anne given ample proofs, on several occasions, of his zeal for the interest of Great Britain, particularly regarding its commercial relations with France, when that subject was pending in parliament, after the treaty of Utrecht, he was created a Baronet at the especial request of the Elector of Hanover (afterwards George I.), 11th March, 1714. In the same year he was elected to parliament by the borough of Yarmouth. Sir Theodore m. Williamsa, daughter of Sir Robert Henley, of the Grange, in Hampshire, and by that lady (who d. in September, 1731) he had issue,

I. Abraham, }
II. Henry, } successive Baronets.
III. Stephen-Theodore, }
IV. William, m. a daughter of James Gaultier, esq. which lady d. in January, 1737-8.
V. Robert.

I. Henrietta.
II. Barbara, m. to Thomas Bladen, esq. M.P.
III. Mary, m. 20th July, 1730, to Charles Calvert, sixth Lord Baltimore, and was mother of Frederick, seventh lord.

Sir Theodore realized by forty years success in trade a very large fortune, but in the year 1720, having the misfortune of being a South Sea director, he was involved in the common calamity of his colleagues, although his innocence was deemed to have been established by the fact of his being a loser, not a gainer, by their proceedings. He d. in September, 1748, aged ninety years, and was s. by his eldest son,

II. Sir Abraham Janssen, who d. 19th November, 1765, and was s. by his next brother,

III. Sir Henry Janssen, who d. unmarried at Paris, 21st February, 1766, and was s. by his brother,

IV. Sir Stephen-Theodore Janssen, lord mayor of London, and afterwards chamberlain of the same city. He m. Catherine, daughter of Colonel Soulegre, of the island of Antigua, but d. 8th April, 1777, without male issue, when the Baronetcy expired.

Arms—Quarterly, first, arg. two bundles of reeds, vert; second, party per fesse, or and az. two swans naiant, ppr.; third, per fesse, or and az. one swan naiant, as in the second quarter; fourth, arg. one bundle of reeds, as in the first quarter.

JASON, OF BROAD SOMERFORD.

Created 5th Sept. 1661.

Extinct 5th May, 1738.

Lineage.

I. Robert Jason, esq. of Broad Somerford, in the county of Wilts, was created a Baronet 5th September, 1661. Sir Robert m. Miss Rowe, daughter of Sir — Rowe, knt. of Shacklewell, in Middlesex, by whom (who m. secondly, Sir Christopher Aires; and thirdly, David Warren, esq.) he had issue,

Robert, his heir.

Henry, who had

Robert, who succeeded as fourth baronet.

Samuel, an officer in the army, died unmarried.

Sarah, married to John Cox, of London, and had issue.

Sir Robert died about the year 1675, and was s. by his elder son,

II. Sir Robert Jason, who m. Anne, daughter of George Dacres, esq. of Cheshunt, Herts, and had, with a daughter, Anne, the wife of Thomas Partington, of London, a son, and successor at his decease about 1687,

III. Sir George Jason, who dying unmarried about the year 1697, was s. by his cousin,

IV. Sir Robert Jason, who m. Anne, daughter of Captain David Warren (by the relict of the first baronet), and had two sons and five daughters, viz.

Warren, his successor.
Robert, sixth baronet.

Anne.
Frances.
Catherine.
Celia.
Joan.

He d. in 1723, and was s. by his elder son,

V. Sir Warren Jason, who died unmarried 12th November, 1728, and was s. by his brother,

VI. Sir Robert Jason, who m. Miss Collins, but dying issueless 5th May, 1738, the Baronetcy became extinct.

Arms—Az. a toison (or golden fleece) or, within a double tressure counterflory of the second.

JEBB, OF TRENT PLACE.

Created 4th Sept. 1778.

Extinct 4th July, 1787.

Lineage.

Samuel Jebb, M.D. a native of Nottingham, practised as a physician with great success at Stratford, in Essex, and became eminent by several learned works; among others "The History of the Life and Reign of Mary Queen of Scots." He married a relation of the celebrated apothecary, Mr. Dillingham, of Red Lion Square, and dying 9th March, 1772, left, with other issue, a son,

I. Richard Jebb, M.D. b. at Stratford in 1729, who followed his father's profession and became so esteemed a practitioner, that when the Duke of Gloucester fell dangerously ill in Italy, he was requested to go thither to attend the health of that prince, and his conduct on that occasion gave so much satisfaction that he was called abroad a second time in 1777. About the same period he was made physician-extraordinary to the king; and in 1780 appointed physician-in-ordinary to the Prince of Wales. He not only held those offices about the royal family, but was for several years one of the physicians chiefly employed by them. Upon the death of Sir Edward Wilmot in 1786, he was constituted physician-in-ordinary to his majesty, but did not survive the appointment many months; for being in attendance on two of the princesses who were affected with the measles, he was suddenly attacked with a fever in their apartments at Windsor, to which he fell a victim, after a few days' illness, 4th July, 1787, in the fifty-eighth year of his age. He had been created a Baronet in 1778; but, as he never married, the title expired with him.

Sir Richard Jebb's father,

Dr. Samuel Jebb, had three brothers,

I. Richard, who settled in Drohgeda and became a merchant there. His only son

John, alderman of Drogheda, had by his second wife, Alicia Forster, two sons, namely,

1. Richard (named after his second cousin, Sir Richard Jebb, bart. M.D. who left him his br…. Adopting the legal profession, Mr. Jebb attained great eminence at the bar, and was constituted in 1818 one of the judges of the Court of King's Bench in Ireland. He m. Jane Louisa, eldest daughter of John Finlay, esq. M.P. for the county of Dublin, and died in 1834, leaving issue.

2. John, D.D. the late celebrated Bishop of Limerick, born 27th September, 1773; died unmarried 9th December, 1833.

II. Joshua, alderman of Chesterfield, grandfather of Joshua Jebb, esq. of Walton, and of Richard Jebb, esq. of Tapton Grove, both in Derbyshire.

III. John, D.D. dean of Cashel, father of the learned John Jebb, M.D. F.R.S.

Arms—Quarterly, vert and or; in the first quarter a falcon close arg. belled of the second; in the fourth a hawk's lure of the third.

JEFFREYS, OF BULSTRODE.

Created 17th Nov. 1681.

Extinct 9th May, 1702.

Lineage.

I. George Jeffreys,* so notorious as the venal, brutal, and sanguinary "Judge Jeffreys," was created a Baronet 17th November, 1681, and raised to the peerage in the dignity of Baron Jeffreys, of Wem, in the county of Salop, in 1685. He was a younger son of John Jeffreys, esq. of Acton, in Denbighshire, by Margaret, daughter of Sir Thomas Ireland, knt. of Bewsey, in Lancashire. He m. first, Mary, daughter of Thomas Nesham, M.A. and had by her

John, his heir.

Margaret, m. to Sir Thomas Stringer, of Durrants, in Middlesex.

Sarah, m. to Captain Harmage, of the Marines.

He wedded, secondly, Anne, daughter of Sir Thomas Bloodworth, knt. and widow of Sir John Jones, of Furman, in Gloucestershire. On the landing of the

* For more ample details of this infamous person, refer to Burke's *Extinct and Dormant Peerage.*

† A branch of the family still continues in Shropshire, represented by William Egerton Jeffreys, esq. of Tilley Park, near Wem.

Prince of Orange, Jeffreys attempted to leave the kingdom in disguise, and for that purpose was on board a Newcastle collier, which was to convey him to Hamburgh, when he was discovered and brought before the lords of the council, who committed him to the Tower, where he died in 1689. He was *s.* by his son,

II. SIR JOHN JEFFREYS, second Lord Jeffreys of Wem, who *m.* Lady Charlotte Herbert, daughter and heir of Philip, Earl of Pembroke, and had an only surviving daughter,

> HENRIETTA-LOUISA, who *m.* Thomas, first Earl of Pomfert, and was great-grandmother of the present (1837) earl.

He *d.* 9th May, 1702, when his honours, including the BARONETCY, became EXTINCT.

Arms—Arg. a lion rampant, a canton sa.

JENKINSON, OF WALTON.

CREATED 17th Dec. 1685.

EXTINCT 28th June, 1739.

Lineage.

RICHARD JENKINSON, merchant, *m.* Frances, daughter of Thomas Bennet, gent. of Derbyshire, and left a son,

I. PAUL JENKINSON, esq. of Walton, in the county of Derby, who was created a BARONET by *King* JAMES II. 17th December, 1685. Sir Paul *m.* Barbara, third daughter of John Cotes, esq. of Woodcote, in Shropshire, and had surviving issue,

> PAUL, his heir.
> JONATHAN, successor to his brother.
>
> Lettice.
> Mary.

He died in 1714, and was *s.* by his elder son,

II. SIR PAUL JENKINSON, who *m.* Katherine, daughter and co-heir of John Revel, esq. of Ogston, in Derbyshire, by whom (who wedded, secondly, William Woodyeare, esq. of Crookhill, near Doncaster,) he left an only surviving daughter,

> ELIZABETH, who became possessed of the estate of Walton, and gave it to her mother, who bestowed it on her second husband, by whose heir, John Woodyeare, esq. it was sold in 1813 to SIR THOMAS WINDSOR HUNLOKE, bart.

He dying thus without male issue, 14th January, 1721-2, he was *s.* by his brother,

III. SIR JONATHAN JENKINSON. This gentleman *m.* Mary, second daughter of Sir Robert Clerke, of Watford, in Northamptonshire, but died without male issue, 28th June, 1739, when the BARONETCY EXPIRED.

Arms—Az. two barrulets in fesse or, in chief three [illegible] ppr.

JENOURE, OF MUCH DUNMOW.

CREATED 30th July, 1628.

EXTINCT 15th Aug. 1755.

Lineage.

In the Visitation for Essex, 1634,

WILLIAM JENOURE, of Stonham Aspall, in Suffolk, is the first mentioned of this family, and lived about the time of EDWARD IV. He *m.* Catherine Whitnige, of Branham, in the same county, and was *s.* by his eldest surviving son,

JOHN JENOURE, prothonotary of the Court of Common Pleas, who *m.* the daughter of John Fincham, esq. and died in 1542, aged seventy-six; his widow died in five years after, and both were buried in the church of Dunmow; they had issue,

> RICHARD, who married the daughter of Anthony Catesby, esq. of Whiston, in Northamptonshire, and dying in the lifetime of his father, left by her (who *m.* secondly, Sir Richard Wiston, knt. of Roxwell, in Essex,)
>
> > ANDREW, heir to his grandfather.
> > Anthony, *m.* Jane, daughter of John Zouche.*
> >
> > Brathe, *m.* to William Argent, gent.
> > Jane, *m.* to John Walters, of Laventhorpe.
> > Mary, *m.* to William Tiffin, of Wakes.
>
> Dorothy, *m.* to — French, esq. of Shelford, in Cambridgeshire.
>
> Elizabeth, *m.* first, to Thomas Bokenham, esq. of Levermore, in Suffolk; and secondly, to Richard Mitchell, esq. of Codington.

John Jenoure was *s.* by his grandson,

ANDREW JENOURE, esq. who *m.* Grysogona, daughter and heir of Thomas Smith, esq. of Camden, in the county of Gloucester, and relict of Edward Smith, esq. by whom he had a daughter, Grysogona, wife of William Glascock, of Dunmow, and a son and heir,

I. KENELM JENOURE, esq. of Much Dunmow, in the county of Essex, who was created a BARONET by *King* CHARLES I. 30th July, 1628. Sir Kenelme *m.* Jane, daughter of Sir Robert Clarke, knt.† one of the barons of the Exchequer, and had issue,

> ANDREW, his successor.
> Henry.
> Robert, *m.* Rose Berrington, and left issue.
> William.
>
> Grysogona, *m.* to Sir John Prescot, knt. of Radwinter.
>
> Susan, *m.* to Christopher Gore, of London, merchant.
>
> Anne, *m.* to Sir Richard Hatton, knt. of Thames Ditton, in Surrey.

He died about 1629, and was succeeded by his eldest son,

II. SIR ANDREW JENOURE, who *m.* first, Margaret, daughter of Richard Smith, esq. of Strexton, in the

* And Alice, his wife, daughter and heir of Richard Goring, esq. of Cranby, in Surrey.
† By his wife, the sister of Henry Maynard, esq.

county of Northampton, but by that lady had no issue. He wedded, secondly, Mary, daughter of Sir John Bramston, K.B. of Skeens, and had by her

- Andrew, who m. Sarah, daughter of Robert Milborn, esq. of Markshall, in Essex, and dying in the lifetime of his father, left a son,
  - Maynard, successor to his grandfather.
- William, m. Anne, daughter of Sir Henry Clark, knt. of Essex.
- Richard.
- Edward.
- Margaret, m. to Dr. Gurdon, a civilian, who died 7th December, 1675, and was buried in Great St. Helen's, London.
- Susan, m. first, to — Wall; and secondly, to — Legett.
- Anne, m. to Robert Privian, esq. of Hornchurch, Essex.

Sir Andrew was succeeded at his decease by his grandson,

III. Sir Maynard Jenoure, who m. Elizabeth, only daughter of Sir John Marshall, knt. of Sculpens, Essex,* and had issue,

- John, his heir.
- Maynard, an officer in the army, *d. s. p.*
- Joseph, m. Elizabeth, daughter of John Sandford, esq. of Bishop's Stortford, in Essex.
- Mary, m. to James, son of Lord Bellenden.

He was *s.* by his son,

IV. Sir John Jenoure. This gentleman m. Joan, only daughter and heir of Richard Day, gent. of Northweld, in Essex, and dying 17th April, 1739, was *s.* by his elder son,

V. Sir Richard-Day Jenoure, who died without issue in March, 1744, and was succeeded by his brother,

VI. Sir John Jenoure, captain in the Guards, who died issueless 15th August, 1755, when the Baronetcy expired.

Arms—Az. a cross patonce between four fleurs-de-lis or.

JONES, OF RAMSBURY MANOR.

Created 27th May, 1774.—Extinct 3rd May, 1791.

Lineage.

William Jones, esq. of Ramsbury Manor, in the county of Wilts, married the sister and eventual heiress of the Rev. Sir Edward Ernle, bart. of Brimslade, and had, with a son who died without issue, two daughters, viz.

- Elizabeth, who married William Langham, esq. younger brother of Sir James Langham, seventh baronet, of Cottesbrook.
- Eleanor, who married Francis Burdett, esq. and was mother of the present (1837)
  - Sir Francis Burdett, bart. of Foremark, who eventually inherited Ramsbury Manor.

The husband of Mr. Jones's elder daughter, assuming the name and arms of Jones, became

I. William Jones, esq. of Ramsbury Manor, and was created a Baronet in 1774. He died, however, without issue in 1791, when the title became extinct.

JONES, OF ALBEMARLIS.

Created 25th July, 1643. — Extinct ....

Lineage.

I. Henry Jones, esq. of Albemarlis, in the county of Caermarthen, was created a Baronet by King Charles I. in 1643. He m. Elizabeth, daughter of Sir John Salisbury, knt. and relict of John Salisbury, esq. of Rugg, by whom he left no male issue at his decease, when the Baronetcy expired.

Arms—Arg. on a cross raguled az. five bezants between four pheons gu.

JUXON, OF ALBOURNE.

Created 28th Dec. 1660. — Extinct 3rd Feb. 17[illegible]

Lineage.

William Juxon, the pious and loyal Bishop of London, the son of Richard Juxon, of Chichester, in Sussex, was born in 1582, and educated, upon the foundation, at Merchant Taylor's School, from whence he was elected a fellow of St. John's College, Oxford, in 1598. Entering into holy orders, he became very popular as a preacher; and having risen high in royal favour, was chosen to succeed Laud in the see of London. In less than two years after, his lordship was appointed lord high treasurer of England; but he was not made for the times in which he lived, and when he saw the storm approaching which was to overturn the whole edifice of church and state, he resigned his office 17th May, 1641, shortly after the execution of Strafford. In the unhappy scenes which followed—the trial and death of Charles—the good bishop attended his ill-fated master with the most zealous devotion. The words of exhortation which he addressed to the royal martyr on the scaffold are too well known to be more than alluded to here. It was remarked by the regicides that the king, the moment before he stretched out his neck to the executioner, addressed to Juxon, in a very earnest accent, the single word "Remember." Great mysteries were consequently supposed to be concealed under that expression, and the generals vehemently insisted that the prelate should inform them of the king's meaning. Juxon

* By Dorothy, his wife, daughter and co-heir of John Mead, esq. of Sculpens.

replied that his majesty having frequently charged him to inculcate on his son the forgiveness of his murderers, had taken this opportunity in the last moments of his life, when his commands he supposed would be regarded as sacred and inviolable, to reiterate that desire; and that his mild spirit thus terminated its present course by an act of benevolence to his greatest enemies. Some months after, when the commonwealth was established, Juxon was deprived of his bishopric, and retired to his private estate, the manor of Little Compton, in Gloucestershire, where he continued until consecrated Archbishop of Canterbury at the Restoration. His grace did not long survive that happy event, but died 4th June, 1663, in his eighty-first year, leaving his nephew,

I. Sir William Juxon, his heir. This gentleman served the office of sheriff of Gloucestershire in 1676, and was created a Baronet in 1660, being styled "of Albourne, in Sussex." He m. Elizabeth, daughter of Sir John Walter, bart. of Saresden, in Oxfordshire, and was *s.* by his son,

II. Sir William Juxon, who m. in 1726, Susannah, daughter of John Marriott, esq. of Suffolk, but by her (who wedded, secondly, Charles, Viscount Fane,) had no issue. He died 3rd February, 1740, aged seventy-nine, and with him the title expired.

Arms—Or, a cross gu. between four blackamoors' heads couped ppr.

KAYE, OF WOODESHAM, OR WOODSOME.

Created 4th Feb. 1641-2.

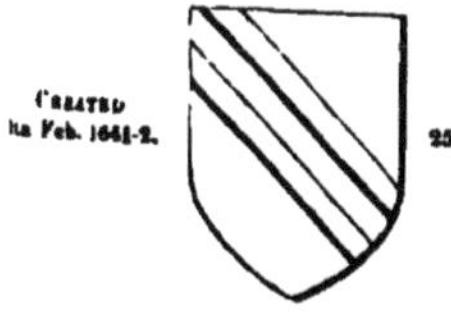

Extinct 25th Dec. 1810.

Lineage.

Sir John Kaye, knt. living at the time of the Conquest, married the daughter and heiress of Sir John Woodesham, of Woodesham, in the county of York, and had two sons, John (Sir), his heir, and Richard, who went into Lancashire, and marrying the heiress of Crompton of Crompton, was founder of the Keays of that county. The elder son,

Sir John Kaye, knt. of Woodesham, m. the daughter and heiress of Sir John Copley, and was *s.* by his son,

Sir Robert Keay, knt. who m. the daughter and heir of Mallet of Upton Mallet, and from him we pass, through a line of eminent persons,* to his lineal descendant,

Sir William Keay, knt. of Woodesham, who m. the daughter of Gaston of Sedbuer, and was *s.* by his son,

John Keay, esq. of Woodesham, who, by the daughter of Harley of Harley, left a son and heir,

Robert Keay, esq. who married the daughter of Plumpton of Plumpton, and was succeeded by his son,

Arthur Keay, esq. living in the time of Henry VIII. who m. Beatrice, daughter of Matthew Wentworth, esq. of Bretton, in Yorkshire, and left a son and heir,

John Keay, esq. living in 1585, who, by Dorothy, daughter of Robert Maleverer, esq. of Wothersome, in Yorkshire, had a son and successor,

Robert Keaye, esq. living in 1612, who married Anne, daughter of John Flower, esq. of Whitwell, in the county of Rutland, and was succeeded by his son,

John Kaye, esq. of Woodsome, who m. Anne, daughter of Sir John Ferne, knt. secretary to the council in the north *temp.* Charles I. and dying in 1641, left a daughter, Elizabeth, the wife of Ralph Asheton, esq. of Middleton, in Lancashire, and a son and heir,

I. John Kaye, esq. of Woodsome, in the county of York, who was created a Baronet by *King* Charles I. 4th February, 1641. He was colonel of horse in his majesty's service, and suffered during the troubles in person and property, but survived to witness the Restoration. Sir John m. first, Margaret, daughter and co-heir of Thomas Moseley, esq. alderman and lord mayor of York,† by whom he had two sons and a daughter, viz.

John, his heir.
Robert, } *d.* unm.
Margaret, } *d.* unm.

He m. secondly, Elizabeth, daughter of Sir Ferdinando Leigh, of Middleton, and relict of Francis Burdett, esq. of Birthwaite, in Yorkshire, by whom he had four sons, who all died issueless, and five daughters, who all died unmarried. His third wife was Catharine, daughter of Sir William St. Quintin, bart. of Harpham, and relict of Michael Wentworth, esq. of Woolley, but by her he had no issue. She survived him, and married after his decease Henry Sandys, esq. of Downe, in Kent; and after that gentleman's decease, she became the wife (her fourth husband) of Hugh, Earl of Eglinton. Sir John *d.* 25th July, 1662, and was *s.* by his son,

II. Sir John Kaye, M.P. for the county of York, who m. Anne, daughter of William Lister, esq. of Thornton, in Craven, sister and heir of Christopher Lister, esq. and by her had issue,

Arthur, his successor.

George, m. Dorothy, daughter and heir of Robert Savile, esq. of Bryan Royd, in Yorkshire, and had issue,

- John, who *s.* as fourth baronet.
- Robert, merchant at Leeds, *d.* unm.
- George, *d.* young.
- Catherine, m. to Nicholas Roberts, esq. of Hexham.

Anne, married to Sir Bryan Stapylton, bart. of Myton.

He *d.* in 1706, and was *s.* by his son,

III. Sir Arthur Kaye, M.P. for the county of York, m. Anne, daughter and co-heir of Sir Samuel

* Who intermarried with the heiresses of Bendon of ... (in Lincolnshire), of Bradfeld, of Malbank, of ... of Grimston Garth, &c. &c.

† By Elizabeth, his wife, daughter and co-heir of Thomas Trigot, esq. of South Kirby, in Yorkshire.

Marow, bart. of Berkswell, in the county of Warwick,* and left an only daughter,

> Elizabeth Kaye, who m. first, George, Viscount Lewisham, eldest son of William, first Earl of Dartmouth (who died before his father), and was mother of William, second earl. She conveyed the estate of Woodesome to her husband's family. She m. secondly, Francis, Lord North and Guildford, and by him was grandmother of Francis, present (1837) Earl of Guildford.

He died 10th July, 1726, when the Baronetcy devolved upon his nephew,

iv. Sir John Lister-Kaye, of Grange, M.P. for the city in 1734, elected alderman thereof in 1735, and served the office of lord mayor in 1737. He m. first, Ellen, daughter of John Wilkinson, esq. of Greenhead, near Huddersfield, and had a son, John, his successor. Sir John m. secondly, in 1730, Dorothy, daughter of Richard Richardson, M.D. of North Bierley, in the West Riding, by Dorothy, his wife, daughter of Henry Currer, esq. of Kildwick, and had four sons; of whom one only, Richard, in holy orders, who eventually succeeded his half-brother, survived; and two daughters, Dorothy, the wife of Robert Chaloner, esq. of Bishop Auckland; and Lister, of Christopher Miles, esq. He died 27th December, 1789, and was succeeded by his son,

v. Sir John Lister-Kaye, bart. who served the office of sheriff for Yorkshire in 1761, and died unmarried 27th December, 1789, leaving his estates to John Lister-Kaye, of whom hereafter; while the Baronetcy devolved upon his brother,

vi. The Very Rev. Sir Richard Kaye, Dean of Lincoln, who m. Mrs. Mainwaring, relict of Thomas Mainwaring, esq. of Goltho, in Lincolnshire, and daughter of William Fenton, esq. of Glassho, near Leeds, but died without issue 25th December, 1810, when the Baronetcy expired.

> The estates, at the demise of the fifth baronet, passed, as stated above, under his will, to
>
> John Lister-Kaye, esq. who thus became of Denby Grange, in the county of York, and as such was created a Baronet 18th October, 1800. His son is the present (1837)
>
> Sir John Lister-Kaye, bart. of Denby Grange.

Arms—Quarterly; first and fourth, arg. two bendlets sa. for Kaye; second and third, erm. on a fesse sa. three mullets or, for Lister.

KEATE, OF THE HOO.

Created 12th June, 1660. Extinct 6th March, 1757.

Lineage.

William Keate, of Hagborne, in Berkshire, left five sons, viz.

- i. John, of Chetington, Berks.
- ii. Ralph.
- iii. Edward, of Locking, Berks.
- iv. George.
- v. Hugh, of Hagborne.

The second son,

Ralph Keate, of Whaddon, in Wiltshire, m. Anne, daughter of John Clarke, esq. of Ardington, in Berkshire, and had with other issue,

Gilbert Keate, esq. of London who m. first, Joan, daughter of Nicholas Turbervile, esq. of Crediton, in Devon, and secondly, Elizabeth, daughter of William Armstrong, esq. of Remston, Notts, and by her had another son,

i. Jonathan Keate, esq. of the Hoo, in the county of Hertford, which estate he acquired with his first wife, Susannah,† daughter of William, and sister and heir of Thomas Hoo, of the Hoo, and Kimpton, both in Hertfordshire. Mr. Keate was created a Baronet by *King* Charles II. 12th June, 1660. Sir Jonathan was sheriff of the county of Hertford, 17 Charles II and knight of the same shire in parliament, in the 30th of the same reign. By his first wife he had issue

> Gilbert-Hoo, his heir.
> Jonathan, Susan, Elizabeth, } all *d. s. p.*

He m. secondly, Susanna, daughter of John Orlebar, citizen of London,‡ but by her had no issue. He d. 17th September, 1700, and was s. by his son,

ii. Sir Gilbert-Hoo Keate, who had, by Elizabeth his wife,

> Henry-Hoo, his successor.
> Jonathan, an ensign in the guards, *d. s. p.*

---

* By Mary, daughter and co-heir of Sir Arthur Cayley, knt. of Newland, in the county of Warwick.

† Doctor Kidder, afterwards bishop of Bath and Wells, speaks thus of this lady, in the sermon he preached at her funeral, 19th June, 1673, at Kempton: "Her extraction was honourable, in a direct line from the Lord Hastings and Hoo, of whose family she was heir general, and the sole inheritrix of those ancient possessions that remained to the barony; the lord, her ancestor, being a person of that renown, that in those fatal quarrels between the Houses of York and Lancaster, and when those quarrels were at the height, he was pitched upon to treat and mediate between the two parties."

‡ He was the youngest son of John Orlebar, of Harrold, in the county of Bedford. (See Burke's *Commoners*, vol. i. p. 246.)

§ He was buried in Kimpton Church, in Hertfordshire where, on the chapel south wall, is a monument, with arms of Keate and Hoo, and this inscription:

> Here lie interred the Remains of Sir Jonathan Keate, of the Hoo, Bart. who built that fine Seat of the Family; he died Sept. 17, 1700, aged 67.
> Of Dame Susanna Keate, his first wife, who was the only daughter and Heiress of the Hon. William Hoo, Esq. She died 1673, æt. 34.
> Of Sir Gilbert Hoo Keate, Bart: Son and Heir of Sir Jonathan, and the said Dame Susanna. He died April 13, 1705, aged 44.
> Of Mrs. Mary Keate, sister of Sir Gilbert-Hoo. She died unmarried, Jan. 5, 1705, aged 48.
> Of Dame Susanna, second wife and Relict of Sir Jonathan, her only Husband. She was Daughter of Mr. John Orlebar (an eminent Citizen of London, of a good Family, in the County of Bedford) ob. Jan. 13, 1719.

William, D.D. vicar of Kimpton, successor to his elder brother.

He d. 13th April, 1705, and was s. by his eldest son,

III. Sir Henry-Hoo Keate, who d. unmarried, and was s. by his brother,

IV. Sir William Keate, D.D. who d. 6th March, 1757, aged seventy-two, without issue, when the Baronetcy expired. His predecessor, Sir Henry-Hoo Keate, conveyed in 1732 the whole of his estates to Mrs. Margaret Brand, from whom they have descended to Lord Dacre.

Arms—Argent, three cat-a-mountains passant in pale ...

KEMEYS, OF KEVANMABLEY.

Created ... May, 1642.

Extinct 29th Jan. 1735.

Lineage.

The house of Kemeys, originally *de Camois, Camoes, de Camys*, is of Norman extraction, and its founder in England appears on the Battle Abbey roll. The family acquired large possessions in the counties of Surrey and Sussex, and so early as 1258, Ralph de Camois was a territorial baron. His son of the same name had summons to parliament in the 49th Henry III. and his descendants sate as barons until the decease, issueless, 5 Henry VI. of Hugh de Camois, who left his sisters his co-heirs.*

A branch of the family which had located in Pembrokeshire, enjoyed large possessions there, and as lords of Camoes and St. Dogmaels, exercised authority little short of regal. In the conquest of Monmouthshire and Glamorganshire, the Camays were distinguished and rewarded with grants of "Kemey's Commander," and "Kemey's Inferior."

Edward Kemeys, son of Edward Kemeys, who was at the conquest of Upper Gwent, married Nest, daughter and heir of Andrew de Began, and thus acquired the lordship of Began, which for centuries after was the principal seat of his descendants. His great-great-great-grandson,

Ievan Kemeys, of Began, m. Crisley, daughter of Morgan ap Llewellen, and had issue,

Ievan, his successor.

Margaret, m. to Ievan ap Morgan. Her grandson,

Morgan Williams, living in the time of Henry VIII. m. the sister of Thomas Cromwell, Earl of Essex, and had a son,

Sir Richard Williams, who assumed the surname of Cromwell, and was great-grandfather of

Oliver Cromwell, the protector.

He was s. by his son,

Ievan Kemeys, of Began, from whom lineally descended

David Kemeys, esq. of Kevanmably, in the county of Glamorgan, who m. Katherine, daughter of Sir William Bawdripp, and was s. by his son,

Rhys Kemeys, esq. of Llanvary, who married a daughter of the Rev. William Aubrey, D.D. and left a son,

I. Nicholas Kemeys, esq. of Kevanmably, in the county of Glamorgan, who was created a Baronet by Charles I. 13th May, 1642. He was colonel of a regiment of horse, and on the outbreaking of the rebellion, was constituted by the king, governor of Chepstow Castle, and defended that fortress, soon after, gallantly and successfully against a superior force under the command of Cromwell in person; who was replaced in the siege by Colonel Ewer, against whom Sir Nicholas and his son continued to hold out, and to make frequent and brilliant sortees, till at length, worn down with fatigue, the garrison suffered a breach to be effected, when the governor and forty of his men died sword in hand, defending the castle to the last. Sir Nicholas m. Jane, daughter of Sir Rowland Williams, knt. of Llangibby, and was s. by his son and heir, his brave companion in arms,

II. Sir Charles Kemeys, M.P. for Glamorganshire, who m. first, Blanch, daughter of Sir Lewis Mansel, bart. but by her had no issue. He wedded, secondly, Margaret, daughter of Sir George Whitmore, lord mayor of London in 1631-2, and dying about the year 1658, was s. by his son,

III. Sir Charles Kemeys, M.P. for Monmouth. This gentleman m. Mary, daughter of Philip Wharton, fourth Baron Wharton, and widow of Edward Thomas, esq. of Wenvoe, in the county of Glamorgan, and had issue,

Charles, his heir.

Jane, m. to Sir John Tynte, bart. of Halsewell, in the county of Somerset, and had issue,

Sir Charles Kemeys-Tynte, bart. of Halsewell, d. s. p.

Jane Tynte, who m. Major Hassell, and had an only daughter and heir,

Jane Hassell, who wedded Colonel Johnstone, and was mother of the present Colonel Kemeys-Tynte.

He died in December, 1702, and was succeeded by his son,

IV. Sir Charles Kemeys, knight of the shire for Monmouth in the last parliament of *Queen Anne*, and for Glamorgan in the two succeeding parliaments. Sir Charles experienced on his travels much attention from George I. and frequently joined the private circle of the elector. On his highness subsequently ascending the throne of England, he was pleased to ask, why his old acquaintance, Sir Charles Kemeys, had not paid his respects at court, and commanding him to repair to St. James's, sent him a message, to the purport, that the King of England hoped Sir Charles Kemeys recollected the number of pipes he had smoked with the Elector of Hanover in Germany. Sir Charles who had retired from parliament, and was a stanch jacobite, replied, that he should be proud to pay his duty at St. James's to the Elector of Hanover, but that

---

* ...

Margaret de Camois, m. to Ralph Radermilde.

Eleanor, m. to Roger Lewknor.

Between the descendants of whom the Barony of Camois continues in abeyance. Burke's *Extinct and Dormant Peerage*.

he had never had the honour of smoking a pipe with the King of England. Sir Charles *d.* unm. 29th June, 1735, when the BARONETCY EXPIRED, and his extensive estates devolved upon his nephew, SIR CHARLES KEMEYS-TYNTE, bart. and are now enjoyed by Sir Charles's grandnephew, the present Colonel KEMEYS-TYNTE, of Kevanmably and Halsewell.

Arms—Vert on a chevron argent, three barbed arrow heads sa.

KEMPE, OF PENTLOW.

CREATED 5th Feb. 1626-7.

EXTINCT about 1667.

Lineage.

GEORGE KEMPE, esq. of Pentlow, in Essex, sixth son of William Kempe, esq. of Spains Hall, in the same county, *d.* 22nd March, 1606, leaving, by Margaret Appulderfield, his wife, five sons,

- JOHN, his heir.
- Charles, of Walthamstow.
- William.
- George.
- Christopher, whose eldest son, Thomas, was of Spains Hall, in Finchingfield, and that estate continued with his male descendants until the decease of JOHN KEMPE, esq. who bequeathed it to his sister, MARY, *m.* in 1727, to Sir Swinnerton Dyer, bart. and by the Dyer family it was sold, in 1760, to Samuel Ruggles, esq.

The eldest son,

JOHN KEMPE, esq. of Pentlow, *m.* Eleanor, daughter of John Drewe, esq. of Devonshire, one of the exigencies of the Court of Common Pleas, and had, *inter alios*, two sons,

- George, his heir.
- John, bapt. 13th May, 1604, who *m.* a sister of Sir Robert Brooke, and had a son,
  - JOHN, successor to his uncle.

Mr. Kempe, died 7th January, 1609, aged forty-eight, and was *s.* by his son,

I. GEORGE KEMPE, esq. of Pentlow, bapt. 12th November, 1602, who was created a BARONET 5th February, 1626. He *m.* Miss Brooke, and had by her two daughters, one of whom married Sir John Winter. He died about the year 1667, and as he had no son, the title became EXTINCT. His estate at Pentlow he settled on his nephew,

JOHN KEMPE, esq. who *m.* Catherine, daughter of Robert Flower, gent. of Boreley, and widow of Ralph Redman, gent. and had by her three daughters,

Lucy, } both died unm.
Mary, }

Barbara, *m.* to Francis Danyell, esq. of Bulmer.

Arms—Arg. a chev. engr. gu. between three stars azure.

KENRICK, OF WHITLEY.

CREATED 29th March, 1679.

EXTINCT about 16[illegible]

Lineage.

I. WILLIAM KENRICK, esq. of Whitley, in Berkshire, who was created a BARONET in 1679, *m.* Grace, daughter and heir of Peter Kibblewhite, esq. of Swindon, Wiltshire, and dying about the year 1686, aged [illegible] three, was *s.* by his son,

II. SIR WILLIAM KENRICK, of Whitley, who married Mary House, of Reading, and had no male issue [illegible] died about the year 1699, and the BARONETCY became EXTINCT.

Arms—Erm. a lion rampant sa.

KEYT, OF EBRINGTON.

CREATED 22nd Dec. 1660.

EXTINCT 6th July, 17[illegible]

Lineage.

WILLIAM KEYT, esq. of Ebrington, in the county of Gloucester, with whom the pedigree begins, *m.* [illegible] Eglantine, daughter of Edmund Riley, esq. of C[illegible] in the same county, and by her had two sons and [illegible] daughters, viz.

- JOHN, his successor.
- William, *d.* unm. 29th March, 1662, aged [illegible]ven, and was buried at Ebrington.
- Anne, *m.* to Mr. John Andrews, of Asthall [illegible] county of Oxford.
- Elizabeth, *m.* to Mr. Glover.

He wedded, secondly, Eleanor, daughter and [illegible] of John Salmon, gent. of Nottingham, and widow of [illegible] Thomas Porter, of Mickleton, but had no other [illegible] Mr. Keyt was high sheriff of the county of W[illegible] and " rich in good works, as well as in worldly [illegible] being not only charitable to the poor in his [illegible] but also at his death; he ordered the milk of two [illegible] to be given every year, from the 10th May, to [illegible] of November, unto the poor of Ebrington for [illegible] He died on the Ides, that is, on the 13th October [illegible] according to his epitaph, but by the parish register [illegible] was buried on the 12th of that month, in the [illegible] eighth year of his age. He was *s.* by his elder son

JOHN KEYT, esq. who *m.* first, Jane, daughter of [illegible] Thomas Porter, of Mickleton, and secondly, Ma[illegible] daughter of Mr. William Harrison, of C[illegible] the county of Worcester, and widow of Mr. B[illegible]

King's Coughton, in Warwickshire. By the latter he had no issue; by the former he had

- John, his heir.
- Francis, m. Alice, daughter of Sir William Spencer, bart. of Yarnton, in the county of Oxford, and had two daughters, viz.
  - Elizabeth, m. to Capt. Theophilus Nichols.
  - Alice, m. to Richard Dighton, esq. of Clifford Chambers, in the county of Gloucester.

  Francis, and his wife were buried at Mickleton.
- Hastings, baptised 5th April, 1621. This gentleman who served as a captain in the royal army under Sir Jacob Astley, fell at Stow, 21st March, 1645.
- Farmer, d. young.
- Thomas, baptised 27th October, 1622, m. Mary, daughter of Walter Dayrell, esq. of Abingdon, and relict of John Morris, Hebrew professor and canon of Christchurch, Oxford, but had no issue. Thomas and his wife were both buried at Ebrington. He d. 5th January, 1701, aged eighty. She 9th November, 1661.
- Samuel, d. young.
- Jane, bapt. 14th May, 1609, m. to Capt. Thomas Wells, and died in Ireland.
- Elizabeth, m. 20th May, 1630, to George Hyde, esq. of Blagrove, Berks.
- Anne, m. to John Hobday, esq. of Thornton, in the county of Warwick, and had issue.
- Eglantine, baptised 18th December, 1614, m. to Thomas Clopton, esq. of Clopton, in the county of Warwick, by whom she had two sons,
  - Sir John Clopton, knt.
  - Thomas Clopton, who d. unm.

"John Keyt, (says his biographer) was in the worst of times a true son of the Church of England, and a loyal subject to his prince; he was a justice of the peace, and high sheriff, first of Worcestershire, and afterwards of Gloucestershire; a lover of hospitality, but a hater of intemperance; very just in paying tradesmen and workmen, and very charitable to his poor neighbours. It pleased God to translate him to a better world, on the 25th April, in the year of our Lord 1660, and in the seventy-sixth year of his age, and he lies buried in the chancel of Ebrington." He was s. by his eldest son,

I. John Keyt, esq. of Ebrington, who having raised a regiment at his own expense for the service of *King* Charles I. was created a Baronet by Charles II. 22nd December, 1660. Sir John m. Margaret, daughter and heir of William Tayler, esq. of Bricksworth, in Northamptonshire, and had issue,

- William, his heir, born at Ragley, in the county of Warwick.
- Thomas, bapt. 2nd May, 1641, d. 21st July, 1660.
- Francis, d. 16th July, 1698.
- Elizabeth, m. to Sir John Talbot, knt.
- Margaret, m. 17th December, 1668, to Sir John Packington, bart.

Sir John d. 26th August, 1662; Lady Keyt, 28th June, 1669. He was s. by his son,

II. Sir William Keyt, who m. Elizabeth, daughter and eventually sole heir of the Honourable Francis Coventry, second son, by his second wife, of the Lord-Keeper Coventry, and had issue,

- William, his heir, who m. 19th September, 1687, his cousin, Agnes, daughter of Sir John Clopton, knt. of Clopton, by Barbara, only daughter and heir of Sir Edward Walker, knt. garter king of arms, and had a numerous family, of whom were,
  - William, successor to his grandfather.
  - John, b. 24th September, 1695.
  - Hastings, b. 9th May, 1700.
  - Elizabeth, m. 27th December, 1712, to Thomas-Charles, Viscount Tracey.
  - Margaret, m. to James Huggeford, esq. of Dicson, in the county of Gloucester.
  - Agnes, b. thirty-five weeks after the death of her father.

  Mr. Keyt d. 31st October, 1702.*
- Margaret, m. 13th October, 1702, to Thomas Noble, esq. of Leicester, and d. 7th March, 1710, leaving a son, William Noble.
- Dorothy, m. to Gilbert, fourth Earl of Coventry, and had an only daughter,
  - Lady Anne Coventry, who m. Sir William Carew, bart. of Anthony.

Sir William d. 26th November, 1702, and was s. by his grandson,

III. Sir William Keyt, who m. 23rd November, 1710, the Hon. Anne Tracy, daughter of William, fourth Viscount Tracy, (by his second wife, Jane, sister of Thomas, Lord Leigh) and had issue,

- Thomas-Charles, his successor.
- John, d. unm.
- Robert, successor to his elder brother.
- Agnes.
- Elizabeth.

Sir William, who served in the last parliament of *King* George I. and in the first of George II. for the town of Warwick, died at Norton, in the county of Gloucester, in September, 1741,† and was s. by his eldest son,

---

* Mr. Keyt's death having occurred before his father's, Queen Anne conferred the dignity of a baronet's wife and one, upon his widow and children, by the following warrant:

Anne, R.

Anne, by the Grace of God, Queen of England, Scotland, France, and Ireland, defender of the Faith, &c. To our right trusty, and right well-beloved cousin and counsellor Charles, Earl of Carlisle, Earl Marshal of England, during the minority of our right trusty, and right entirely beloved cousin, Thomas, Duke of Norfolk,) greeting. Whereas, we are humbly informed, that William Keyt, the eldest son to Sir William Keyt, late of Ebrington, in the county of Gloucester, Bart. dying a few weeks before his father, the widow and younger children of the said William Keyt, cannot, by the ordinary rules of honour, enjoy the title, place, and precedency, which would otherwise have been justly due to her and them, in case the said William Keyt, had survived his father: we therefore, for divers good causes and considerations, us especially moving, are graciously pleased to ordain, that Agnes Keyt, John Keyt, Hastings Keyt, Elizabeth Keyt, Margaret Keyt, and Agnes Keyt, the relict and younger children of the said William Keyt, shall from henceforward have, hold, and enjoy, the same title, pre-eminence, place, and precedence, respectively, as if the said William Keyt had survived his father, and been actually possessed of the dignity of a Baronet. And our will and pleasure is, that you, our Earl Marshal, to whom the cognizance of matters of this nature properly belongs, do see this our order observed and kept, by our several officers of arms, and cause these presents to be registered in the College of Arms; and for so doing, this shall be your warrant. Given at our Castle, at Windsor, the 5th day of June, 1704, in the third year of our reign. By her Majesty's command. C. Hedges.

† "This Sir William Keyt, who was burned to death, is supposed to have been a lunatic, and to have set his house on fire himself; for Thomas Whitstone, a servant, held him in his arms, and would have saved him, but he would not permit it." Fosbrooke's *Gloucestershire.*

iv. Sir Thomas-Charles Kett, who d. issueless, 24th July, 1755, and was s. by his only surviving brother,

v. Sir Robert Kett, of Middleham, in the county of York, who d. s. p. 6th July, 1784, when the Baronetcy became extinct. The estate at Ebrington, in Gloucestershire, had been sold soon after the third baronet's decease, to Sir Dudley Rider.

Arms—Azure, a chevron between three kites' heads erased, or.

KILLEGREW, OF ARWENNICK.

Created 22nd Dec. 1660.  Extinct 8th Jan. 1704.

Lineage.

Sir Henry Killigrew, knt. (descended from a very ancient family settled in Cornwall from a very remote period, for so early as the time of Richard II. Killigrew of Killigrew acquired the estate of Arwenick in marriage with the heiress thereof) followed the court for advancement in the time of Elizabeth, "according," says Hale, "to the constant genius of his family." He m. Catherine, daughter of Sir Anthony Cooke, knt. of Giddy Hall, in Essex, and had by her two daughters; of whom one m. Sir Nicholas Lower, knt. of Clifton, in Cornwall, and d. s. p. 6th June, 1638; and the other wedded, first, Sir Jonathan Trelawney, knt.; and secondly, Sir Thomas Reynell, knt. of Ogwell. The male line of the family was continued by

i. William Killigrew, esq. of Arwenick, in Cornwall, who was created a Baronet in 1660, with remainder to his brother. Sir William died unmarried in 1665, after having wasted the whole of his paternal estate, and alienated the barton and manor of Arwenick to his brother,

Sir Peter Killigrew, knt. This gentleman was commonly known as Sir Peter the Post, from his great diligence in conveying messages to Charles I. during the civil war. He had an only son,

ii. Sir Peter Killigrew, of Arwenick, who succeeded his uncle as second baronet, and m. Frances, daughter of Sir Roger Twisden, of East Peckham, Kent, by whom he had one son and two daughters, viz.

George, who was killed by a Captain Walter Vincent at a tavern in Penryn. His antagonist did not long survive, though acquitted at the trial at Launceston; he took the affair so much to heart that he sunk under the affliction. Mr. Killigrew m. Anne, daughter of Sir John St. Aubyn, bart. and left an only daughter, who m. Mr. Dunbar, an Irish gentleman.

———, m. to Richard Erisey, esq. of Erisey, in Cornwall, and had a daughter and eventual heiress, who wedded John West, esq. and their only child,

Frances West, became ultimately the representative of the families of West, Erisey, and Killigrew. She m. the Hon. Charles Berkeley, brother of the last Lord Berkeley of Stratton, and had an only child,

Sophia, m. to Lord Wodehouse.

Anne, m. to Martin Lyster, esq. of Staffordshire, who assumed the surname of Killigrew.

Sir Peter, at the untimely decease of his son, settled his estates on Martin Lyster, esq. and Anne, his wife, on condition that they should assume the name and arms of Killigrew, with remainder to the family of Erisey, and died, shortly after making this settlement, 8th January, 1704, when the title became extinct.

Arms—Arg. an eagle displayed sa. a border of the second bezantée.

KINGSMILL, OF SIDMANTON.

Created 24th Nov. 1800.  Extinct 4th May, 1823.

Lineage.

John Kingsmill, one of the judges of the Court of Common Pleas, son of Richard Kingsmill, of Barkham, Berks, m. Joan, daughter of Sir John Gifford, knt. of Ishill, and dying in 1504, left a son,

Sir John Kingsmill, knt. of Sidmanton, Hants, who m. Constance, daughter of John Goring, esq. of Burton, in Sussex, and had four sons, viz.

i. William (Sir), his heir.

ii. George (Sir), one of the justices of the Common Pleas, m. Sarah, Lady Hastings, daughter of Sir James Harington.

iii. Richard (Sir), surveyor of the Court of Wards, d. in 1600; m. first, Alicia, sister and heiress of Richard Fauconer, esq. of Hoursbourne, Hants, relict of Thomas Wroughton, of Overton; and secondly, Elizabeth, daughter of Alderman David Woodroff, of London, and relict of the Rev. George Stonehouse.

iv. Thomas.

The eldest son,

Sir William Kingsmill, knt. m. Bridget, daughter of George Raleigh, and was s. by his son,

Sir William Kingsmill, knt. who d. in 1600 [illegible] m. Anne, daughter of William Wilkes, esq. of Middleton Cheney, in the county of Northampton, and left a son and heir,

Sir Henry Kingsmill, knt. who m. Bridget, daughter and co-heir of John White, esq. of Southwick, Hants, and dying in 1625, was s. by his son,

Sir William Kingsmill, knt. who m. Anne, daughter of Sir Anthony Haslewood, knt. of Maidwell, in the county of Northampton, and had issue,

William (Sir), his heir.

Bridget.

Anne, m. to Heneage, fourth Earl of Winchilsea. This lady attained some celebrity as a poetess. She d. s. p.

Sir William was s. by his son,

Sir William Kingsmill, knt. who m. first, Frances, daughter of Mr. Alderman Colwel, of London, and by her had three sons and a daughter, viz.

William, died unmarried in 1766.

Henry, died unmarried in 1710

Thomas, died young.

FRANCES, *b.* in 1682; *m.* Hugh Corry, esq. of Newton, in the county of Down, and had a daughter,

ELIZABETH, who *m.* Robert Bice, esq. of Sidmanton, admiral of the Blue.

He married a second time, and had two other daughters, Rebecca, who died young, and Penelope, wife of John Waterman, esq. of Barkham, Berks. Sir William *d.* in 1698, and his sons all dying unmarried, the representation of the family eventually devolved upon his granddaughter, ELIZABETH, the wife of Admiral Bice. The admiral, in consequence, assumed, by act of parliament in 1766, the surname and arms of Kingsmill, and thus became

I. ROBERT KINGSMILL, esq. of Sidmanton, in the county of Southampton. He was M.P. for Tregony, and in his professional capacity had the command-in-chief of his majesty's ships and vessels on the coast of Ireland. He was created a BARONET 24th November, 1800, with special remainder to his brother EDWARD* and the heirs male of his body, and dying issueless 23rd November, 1805, when he had attained the rank of admiral of the White, was *s.* by his nephew,

II. SIR ROBERT KINGSMILL, who *m.* Elizabeth daughter of Charles Newman, esq. of Calcutta, and had issue, a daughter, Eliza-Catherine. He *d.* 4th May, 1823, and leaving no male heir, the BARONETCY EXPIRED.

Arms—Arg. semée of cross crosslets sa. a chevron erm. between three fers-de-moline of the second, a chief of the third.

KNELLER, OF WHITTON.

CREATED 24th May, 1715.—EXTINCT 19th Oct. 1723.

Lineage.

I. SIR GODFREY KNELLER, the celebrated painter, was born at Lubeck about 1648, when his father was surveyor-general of the mines, and inspector of Count Mansfeldt's revenues. For a long continuance of years Kneller stood at the head of his profession, but he has left behind him few *good* pictures. According to his own doctrine, he did as much and no more than was necessary to pass current among his employers. "History painters," he said, "make the dead live, and don't begin to live till they are dead; I paint the living, and they make me live." He died in October, 1723, and was buried at his seat at Whitton, in Middlesex, but a monument was erected to him in Westminster Abbey, executed by Rysbrach, and inscribed with these lines of Pope, more beautiful than just:

"Kneller, by heaven and not a master taught,
Whose art was Nature, and whose pictures thought;
When now two ages he had snatch'd from fate,
Whate'er was beauteous and whate'er was great,
Rests crown'd with princes' honours, poets' bays,
Due to his merit, and brave thirst of praise.
Living, great Nature fear'd he might outvie
Her works; and dying, fears herself may die."

Sir Godfrey *m.* Susannah, sister of William Crawley, esq. captain R.N. but left no legitimate issue at his decease 19th October, 1723, aged seventy-eight, when the BARONETCY, which had been conferred on him in 1715, EXPIRED.

KNIGHTLEY, OF OFFCHURCH.

CREATED 30th Aug. 1660.

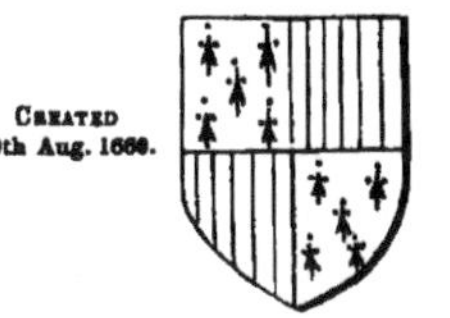

EXTINCT in 1668.

Lineage.

EDWARD KNIGHTLEY, esq. younger brother of Sir Richard Knightley, of Fawsley, in the county of Northampton, was of Offchurch, in the county of Warwick, *temp.* ELIZABETH. He *m.* three wives, and had by the second, Elizabeth, daughter of Sir William Lenthall, of Latchford, in Oxfordshire, a son and successor,

RICHARD KNIGHTLEY, esq. of Offchurch, who *m.* Ann, daughter of Sir John Pettus, and was *s.* by his son,

I. JOHN KNIGHTLEY, esq. of Offchurch, created a BARONET 30th August, 1660. He *m.* Bridget, daughter of Sir Lewis Lewknor, of Sussex. His son and successor,

II. SIR JOHN KNIGHTLEY, of Offchurch, a magistrate and deputy-lieutenant of the county of Warwick, in which shire he possessed great influence, *d. s. p.* and bequeathed the manor and estate of Offchurch to his kinsman, JOHN WIGHTWICK, esq. who assumed the surname of Knightley, and marrying Mary, daughter of Sir Samuel Marow, bart. had issue.

Arms—Quarterly; first and fourth, erm.; second and third, paly of six or and gu.

KNIVETON, OF MERCASTON.

CREATED 29th June, 1611.

EXTINCT about 1706.

Lineage.

NICHOLAS DE KNIVETON, of Mercaston, in the county of Derby, *d.* 46 EDWARD III. leaving by Joan, his wife, Nicholas Kniveton, of Underwood, and

---

* CHARLES BICE, esq. of Castle Chichester, *m.* Jane, sister of — Robinson, esq. of Newtown Ardes, in the co. of Down, and dying in 1746, left issue,

ROBERT, created a BARONET, as above, with remainder to his brother.

EDWARD, of Belfast, principal surveyor of his majesty's revenue at that port, assumed, like his brother, the surname and arms of KINGSMILL, by sign manual, in December, 1787, *m.* Catherine, daughter of George Spaight, of Carrickfergus, and had issue,

ROBERT, who inherited the Baronetcy from his uncle.

Margaret, *m.* to Cutland Skinner, esq. captain in the 70th Foot, *d. s. p.*

Prudentia, *m.* to George Bateson, esq. captain in the Guards.

Dorothy.

Thomas de Kniveton, of Mercaston, living 14 Richard II. who m. Margaret, daughter of — Curson, and widow of — Okeover, and dying 25 Henry VI. was s. by his son,

John Kniveton, of Mercaston, living 25 Henry VI. who *d. s. p.*; his brother,

Nicholas Kniveton, became his heir; which Nicholas was sheriff of the counties of Nottingham and Derby 5 Henry VII. and by Joan, his wife, he left a son and heir,

Nicholas Kniveton, who was one of the esquires of the body to *King* Henry VII. He was twice married; by his first wife, Joan Maliverer, he left a son,

John Kniveton, esq. of Mercaston, who m. Joan, daughter of Sir Nicholas Montgomery, knt. of Cubley, and had two sons,

- John, who was denominated of Harteshome and Underwood, and dying in the lifetime of his father, left by Anne, his wife, daughter of Thomas Dethick, esq. of Newball, in the county of Derby,
  - Thomas, heir to his grandfather.
- Nicholas.

He was s. by his grandson,

Thomas Kniveton, esq. of Mercaston, who m. Joan, eldest daughter of Ralph Leech, esq. of Chatsworth, in the county of Derby, and had issue,

- William, his heir.
- George, died in his passage to Ireland.
- Saintlow, a celebrated antiquary.
- Elizabeth, m. to William Kniveton, esq. of Bradley.
- Margaret, m. to Gabriel Armstrong, esq. of Nottinghamshire.
- Jane, m. to Griffin Harmead, esq. of Northumberland.
- Anne, m. to George Sutton, esq. of Over Haddon, in the county of Derby.
- Mary, m. to Sir George Chaworth, knt. of Annesley, Notts.

He was s. by his eldest son,

i. William Kniveton, esq. of Mercaston, high sheriff for Derbyshire 29 Elizabeth, and knight of the shire 1 James I. who was created a Baronet 29th June, 1611, and served again as sheriff for the county of Derby in the 12th year of *King* James's reign. He m. Matilda, daughter and sole heir of John Rollesly, esq. of Rollesly, and had issue,

- Gilbert (Sir), his heir, who was knighted at Greenwich 29th May, 1605.
- Rollesly.
- William.
- Elizabeth, m. to Thomas Kniveton, esq. of Mogington.
- Margaret, m. to — Davenport, esq. of Henbury.
- Joan, m. to the Rev. Mr. Greves, rector of Brailesford.

Sir William died about the year 1631-2, and was s. by his eldest son,

ii. Sir Gilbert Kniveton, sheriff of Derbyshire 21 James I. m. first, Mary, daughter and co-heir of Andrew Grey, esq. of the county of Hertford, and had issue,

Andrew, } successive baronets.
Thomas, }

He m. secondly, Frances, daughter of Sir Robert Dudley, bart. Sir Gilbert was s. at his decease by his elder son,

iii. Sir Andrew Kniveton, who *d. s. p.* about the year 1670, and was s. by his brother,

iv. Sir Thomas Kniveton, one of the gentlemen pensioners to *King* Charles II. and *King* James II. died without issue about 1706, when the Baronetcy expired.

Arms—Gu. a chevron vair arg. and sa.

KNOLLYS, OF GROVE PLACE.

Created 6th May 1642.—Extinct in 1648.

Lineage.

i. Henry Knollys, esq. of Grove Place, Hants. was created a Baronet in 1642, but died unmarried in six years after, when the title expired.

KNOLLYS, OF THAME.

Created 1st April, 1754. Extinct 29th June, 1772.

Lineage.

This family was founded by

Sir Robert Knollys, K.G. the celebrated general in the martial times of Edward III. the companion in arms of the Black Prince, and the most renowned warrior of his day. In 1 Richard II. Sir Robert was governor of the castle of Brest, and in the 3rd of the same reign he went with Thomas Plantagenet (of Woodstock), Earl of Buckingham, to assist the Duke of Brittany against the French, when they marched quite through France without resistance. The next year, on the outbreak of Jack Straw's insurrection he led the citizens of London against the rebels, and thus terminated, at an advanced age, his military career. Independently of those high deeds which rendered his name famous all over the world, Sir Robert left other noble memorials behind him. He erected a stately bridge over the river Medway, near Rochester, known as Rochester Bridge. He enlarged the house of Friers Carmelites, commonly called White Friers, in the city of London, and he founded a college at Pontefract, in Yorkshire, where his wife the Lady Constance, was born, endowing it with an estate of £180. per annum. He died at the manor of Sconethorp, in Norfolk, full of honour and wealth being at least ninety years of age, 15th August, 1407, and was buried with his lady in the church of the White Friers. He left issue, a daughter, Emma, the wife of Anthony Babington, and a son and heir,

Thomas Knollys, who was seated at North Mymms, in Hertfordshire, and had two sons,

- Robert, whose daughter married Henry Ferdwick, of Weley, and her daughter conveyed the estate in marriage to John Coningsby.
- Thomas.

From the younger son,

Thomas Knollys, descended

Robert Knollys, who m. Margaret D'Oyley, and was father of

Robert Knollys, gentleman of the privy chamber to *King* Henry VIII. who had from that monarch a lease for a certain number of years of the manor of Rotherfield Grey, called Greys, in the county of Oxford. He m. Lettice, daughter of Sir Thomas Penyston, Lord of Haurage and Marshal, in Bucks, and by her (who m. secondly, Sir Robert Lee, of Quarrendon, Bucks, and thirdly, Sir Thomas Tresham, lord prior of St. John,) had a daughter, Jane, m. to Sir Richard Wingfield, of Kimbelton Castle, and a son and heir.

Sir Francis Knollys, upon whom Henry VIII. conferred the lordship of Rotherfield Grey, in fee, and made him one of the gentlemen pensioners. He was afterwards high in favour with *Queen* Elizabeth, was sworn of her majesty's privy council, constituted vice-chamberlain of the household, and employed on several important negociations abroad. In the 29th of Elizabeth he was appointed one of the judges to sit in judgment on the unhappy Queen of Scotland, and was subsequently made treasurer of the household, and installed a knight of the Garter. He *m.* Catherine, daughter of William Carey, esquire of the body to Henry VIII. by his wife, Lady Mary Boleyne, sister of *Queen* Anne Boleyne, and had issue, viz.

i. Henry, member in the first parliament of *Queen* Elizabeth, for the borough of Reading, *m.* Margaret, daughter and heiress of Sir Ambrose Cave, chancellor of the duchy of Lancaster, and dying in the lifetime of his father, left two daughters,

  Elizabeth, *m.* to Sir John Willoughby, of Risley, in the county of Derby.

  Lettice, *m.* to William, Lord Paget.

ii. William (Sir), treasurer of the household to James I. and raised to the peerage by that monarch as Baron Knollys and Viscount Wallingford, and made by Charles I. Earl of Banbury. (Refer to Burke's *Extinct and Dormant Peerage*, for details of this nobleman, and the litigation that ensued regarding the succession to his honours.)

iii. Robert (Sir), K. B. left by his wife, Joan Higham,

  Sir Robert Knollys, *m.* Joanna, daughter of Sir John Wolstenholme, and had (with a younger son, William, and three daughters: the eldest *m.* to Sir John Corbet, of Stoke, in Shropshire; the second, to Egerton, of Staffordshire; the third, to Holmby, of Yorkshire,) a son and heir,

    Robert Knollys, who *m.* Mary Saunders, of Menogwell, in Oxfordshire, and left a son,

      Robert, M.P. for the county of Oxford, with whom this branch expired.

iv. Richard, whose son,

  Francis, *m.* first the daughter of Sir Charles Wiseman, and secondly, Alice, daughter of Sir William Beecher, of Middlesex, by whom he left one daughter and two sons. He *d.* 4th August, 1640.

v. Francis (Sir), of whom presently.

vi. Thomas (Sir), commander in the Low Countries, under Maurice, Prince of Orange, *m.* Odelia de Morada, daughter of John de Morada, Marquess of Bergen, and left a daughter,

  Penelope, *m.* to William Le Hunt.

vii. Lettice, *m.* first, to Walter Devereux, Earl of Essex, and was mother of

  Robert, *Earl of Essex*, the ill-fated favourite of *Queen* Elizabeth.

  She *m.* secondly, Robert Dudley, Earl of Leicester, and thirdly, Sir Christopher Blount. This lady lived to see the grandchildren of her grandchildren.

viii. Anne, *m.* to Thomas, Lord de la War.

ix. Cecilia, maid of honour to *Queen* Elizabeth, married Sir Thomas Leighton, of Feckenham, Wilts.

iv. Catherine, *m.* first, to Gerard Fitzgerald, Lord Ophaly, son and heir of the Earl of Kildare, and secondly, to Sir Philip Boteler, of Watton Woodhall.

The fifth son,

Sir Francis Knollys, knt. inherited under his father's will the manor of Battel, and other estates in the vicinity of Reading, and was styled of Reading Abbey. He represented the city of Oxford in parliament, and afterwards the county of Berks. He *m.* Lettice, daughter of John Barret, esq. of Hanham, in Gloucestershire, and was *s.* by his son,

Sir Francis Knollys, knt. who *m.* Ellen, daughter and heir of Richard Milles, esq. of Lower Winchendon, Bucks, and left a son and heir,

Richard Knollys, esq. who *m.* Mary Bellingham, of Everingham, in Sussex, sister and heir of Henry Bellingham, and was *s.* by his son,

Francis Knollys, esq. who *m.* Anne, daughter and co-heir of — Bateman, esq. of Berkshire, and had, with a daughter, Elizabeth, wife of Sir Francis Curson, of Waterferry, in Oxfordshire, a son and heir,

Francis Knollys, esq. M.P. for Reading, who *m.* Elizabeth, youngest daughter and co-heir of John Striblehill, esq. of Thame, in the county of Oxford, and dying, of the small-pox, in 1701, was *s.* by his son,

Francis Knollys, esq. of Thame, M.P. for the city of Oxford, died a bachelor, 24th June, 1754, and was *s.* by his brother,

Richard Knollys, esq. who *m.* first, Elizabeth, daughter and co-heir of Humphrey Thayer, esq. secondly, Hannah, daughter of Theophilus Salivey, esq. of Woodford, and thirdly, Anne, daughter of John Taylor, esq. By the two last he had no issue, by the first, an only son,

i. Francis Knollys, esq. of Thame, in the county of Oxford, who was created a Baronet 1st April, 1754. Sir Francis was sheriff of Oxfordshire in 1757, and was elected to parliament for Reading in 1761. He *m.* in 1756, Mary, daughter and heiress of Sir Robert Kendall Carter, of Kempston, in the county of Bedford, third son of John Kendall, esq. of Basingbourn Hall, in Essex, but dying without issue 29th June, 1772, the Baronetcy expired.

Arms—Quarterly, first and fourth, az. crusuly of crosslets, a cross moline voided or; second and third, gules a chevron arg. charged with three roses of the first.

KNYVETT, OF BUCKENHAM.

Created 22nd May, 1611.

Extinct about 1690.

Lineage.

Camden makes this name a corruption of *Dunevit*, and Leland derives it from *Dunevit*, a town in Cornwall, on the river Tamar. The family claimed Danish extraction.

Othomarus de Knyvet, lord of the castle and borough of Launceston, is stated to have been ousted of his possessions at the Conquest, for having taken up arms against the Conqueror, but intermarrying with Emme, daughter of William Dammartin, a Norman, obtained restoration. From Othomarus, after four descents, sprang

SIR JOHN DE KNEVIT, Lord of Southwick, who was great-grandfather of another

SIR JOHN KNEVIT, whose son and heir,

RICHARD KNEVIT, m. Joan, daughter and co-heir of Sir Richard Wourch, knt. and was father of

SIR JOHN KNEVIT, knt. barrister-at-law, who attained the coif in 31 EDWARD III.; was made one of the justices of the King's Bench in two years after; chief justice, 39th of the same reign; and was constituted LORD CHANCELLOR OF ENGLAND in the 49th of the same king. He m. Eleanor, elder daughter of Ralph Basset, second Lord Basset of Welledon,* and his eldest son and heir,

JOHN KNEVIT, was found by inquisition, 10 HENRY IV. to be co-heir with Sir John de Aylesbury to the family of Basset, on the extinction of the heirs male, (refer to BURKE's *Extinct and Dormant Peerage.*) He served as one of the knights in parliament for Huntingdonshire 21 RICHARD II. and by Joan, his wife, daughter of Sir John Botetort, of Mendlesham, in Suffolk, left, with two daughters, an only son,

SIR JOHN KNEVIT, knt. who m. Elizabeth, daughter of Sir Constantine de Clifton, second Baron Clifton, and eventually co-heir of her noble family. By this marriage he acquired a fair inheritance, including the castle of Buckenham, in Norfolk. Sir John served the office of sheriff for that county and Suffolk, 15 RICHARD II. and it is presumed was buried at Buckenham, where were many ancient monuments of the Knevits, recognised by their armorial ensigns, the inscriptions being entirely worn out. His only son and heir,

SIR JOHN KNEVIT, knt. in whom or his representatives the BARONY OF CLIFTON became vested, on the demise of his uncle, Sir John de Clifton, third baron. Sir John Knevit m. first, Alice, daughter of Reginald, Lord Grey of Ruthyn, and had a son,

EDMUND, his heir.

He m. secondly, Joan, daughter of Humphrey Stafford, Duke of Buckingham, and widow of William, Viscount Beaumont, and by her had another son,

Edward (Sir), who was sheriff for the counties of Norfolk and Suffolk, 31 HENRY VIII.

He d. 7 HENRY VII. and was s. by his elder son,

SIR EDMUND KNEVIT, knt. of Buckenham, who m. Eleanor, sister of Sir James Tyrell, knt. and had a daughter, Anne, wife of Sir George St. Leger, and five sons, of whom

THOMAS, (the eldest) succeeded to the estate.

EDMUND, who was serjeant porter to *King* HENRY VIII. m. JANE BOURCHIER, only surviving daughter of Sir John Bourchier, second BARON BERNERS, and acquired thereby the manor of Ashwellthorpe, in Norfolk. By this great heiress† he had three sons, and three daughters, viz.

1. JOHN KNYVET, of Plumstead, in Norfolk, who d. before his mother, leaving a son and heir,

SIR THOMAS KNYVET, through whose descendant

ELIZABETH KNYVET, wife of his grandfather, HENRY WILSON, esq. of Didlington,

ROBERT WILSON, esq. was summoned to parliament in 1832, as LORD BERNERS.

2. William, ancestor of the KNYVETTS, of Fundenhall, in Norfolk, who continued to reside there. One of their descendants, marrying against the consent of his father, removed to London, and from that time to the day of his death, was an entire stranger to his family and connections in Norfolk. He was father of the late Mr. Knyvett, organist and composer to GEORGE III. who purchased an estate at Sonning, near Reading, in Berkshire, now the residence of his eldest son, CHARLES KNYVETT, esq.
3. Edmund.

1. Rose, wife of Oliver Reymes.
2. Alice, wife of Oliver Spiers.
3. Christian, wife of Thomas Foster.

The eldest son,

SIR THOMAS KNYVET, of Buckenham, was made knight of the Bath at the coronation of HENRY VIII 23rd June, 1509, and subsequently constituted master of the horse to the same monarch. He m. Muriel, widow of John Grey, Viscount Lisle, and daughter of Thomas, Duke of Norfolk, and had issue,

I. EDMUND (Sir), his heir.
II. Ferdinando.
III. Henry (Sir), knighted by *Queen* ELIZABETH in 1574. He m. Anne, daughter and heir of Sir Christopher Pickering, and thence descended the brothers,

1. Sir HENRY KNYVETT, knt. of Carleton, in Wiltshire, who left two daughters, his co-heirs, viz.

KATHERINE KNYVETT, who m. first the Hon. Richard Rich, by whom she had no issue, and secondly Thomas Howard, first Earl of Suffolk, and the estate of Carleton, or Charleton, passed to her second son, the Hon. Thomas Howard, who was created Earl of Berkshire. (Refer to BURKE's *Peerage and Baronetage.*)

ELIZABETH KNYVETT, m. to Thomas, third Lord Lincoln, ancestor of the (extant) Dukes of Newcastle.

2. SIR THOMAS KNYVETT, who was of the bedchamber to *Queen* ELIZABETH, and afterwards of council to *Queen* Anne, consort of JAMES I. to which king he became one of the gentlemen of the privy council, and was entrusted to discover the gunpowder plot, which he happily effected. Sir Thomas was summoned

---

* His younger daughter,

JOANE BASSET, m. Sir John de Aylesbury, and had a son,

SIR JOHN DE AYLESBURY, who was declared co-heir with John Knevit to the Basset estates.

† She was interred in the church of Ashwellthorp, under the following inscription:

JANE KNYVET resteth here, the only Heir by Right
Of the LORD BERNERS, that Sir John Bourchier hight
Twenty years and three a Wydoo's Life she ledd,
Alwayes Keeping Howse, where Rich and Pore were fedd;
Gentill, most quyet, voyd of Debate and Stryf;
Ever doying Good. Lo! thus she ledd her life.
Even to the Grave, where Erth on Erth doth ly.
On whos Soul, God grant of his abundant Mercy.
The xviii of February, MDLXI.

parliament in 1607, as BARON KNYVETT, of Escrick, but *d. s. p.* in 1622, when the title became EXTINCT; his fortune devolved upon his niece, KATHERINE, whose son, by the Earl of Suffolk, Sir Edward Howard, was created Baron Howard, of Escrick.

I. Catherine, *m.* first to Sir William Farmer, knt. of Barkam, in Norfolk, and secondly to Nicholas Mynne, esq.

II. Anne, *m.* to — Thoresby, esq.

The eldest son and heir of Sir Thomas Knyvett and Muriel, Viscountess Lisle,

SIR EDMUND KNYVETT, knt. of Buckenham, represented the county of Norfolk in parliament, with Nicholas L'Estrange, in the 1st of EDWARD VI. He m. Anne, daughter of Sir Thomas Shellon, knt. and was *s.* by his eldest son,

SIR THOMAS KNYVETT, of Buckenham, who received the honour of knighthood, at the Charter House, from King JAMES I. 11th May, 1603. He was *s.* by his son,

I. PHILIP KNYVETT, esq. of Buckenham, in the county of Norfolk, who was created a BARONET at the institution of the order, 22nd May, 1611. Sir Philip m. Katherine, daughter and heir of Charles Ford, esq. of Butley Abbey, in Suffolk, and dying about the year 1634-5, was *s.* by his son,

II. SIR ROBERT KNYVETT, who *m.* first, Elizabeth, daughter of William Ludley, esq. of Middleham, in the county of York; secondly, Dorothy, daughter of William Thornborough, esq. of Salstead, in Westmoreland, and thirdly, Philippa, daughter of Thomas Russell, of Barsham, in Norfolk, gent. but died issueless about the year 1699, when the BARONETCY became EXTINCT. The castle and estate of Buckenham were alienated by Sir Philip Knyvett.

Arms—Argent a bend sable, a bordure engrailed of the last.

KYRLE, OF MUCH MARCLE.

Lineage.

In the oldest writings relative to the KYRLES, the name is variously written *Crul*, *Crull*, and *Crulle*; afterwards *Cyll* and sometimes *Curl*, until it was at length spelt universally KYRLE.

WALTER KYRLE, of the Hill, living in 1469, married and had two sons,

I. WALTER, of the Hill, whose only daughter and heiress, Alice, wedded Christopher Clarke, esq. and was represented by the late Mrs. Jane Clarke, whose heir is the present KINGSMILL EVANS, esq. of the Hill. (See BURKE's *Commoners*, vol. ii. p. 242).

II. JAMES, of whose descendants we are about to treat.

This

JAMES KYRLE* inherited Walford Court,† and was father of

THOMAS KYRLE, living about the year 1500, who *m.* Johan, daughter and heir of Hugh Abrahall, esq. by Alice, his wife, daughter of John Rudhall, esq. of Rudhall, and had, with four daughters (one of whom, Bridget, *m.* Roger Pye, esq. of Mynde, see BURKE's *Commoners*, vol. i. p. 350), nine sons,

I. WALTER, of Walford Court, who *m.* Joan, daughter of Richard Warncombe, esq. and had with several other sons, who *d. s. p.* a son and successor,

ROBERT KYRLE, esq. of Walford Court, high sheriff of Herefordshire, who *m.* Jane, daughter of E. Evans, alias Bithell, esq. and had with four daughters, (one of whom, Penelope, married Roger Hereford, esq. of Priors Court,) two sons, namely,

1. JAMES, his heir.
2. Walter, of Ross, barrister-at-law and justice of the peace, *m.* Alice, daughter and sole heir of John Mallet, of Berkeley, in the county of Gloucester, and dying in February, 1650, left two sons, viz.

JOHN, "**The Man of Ross,**" born at the Whitehouse Dymock, in May, 1637, *d.* at Ross, *s. p.* 7th November, 1724.

Walter, living in 1683.

Robert Kyrle was *s.* by his elder son,

JAMES KYRLE, esq. of Walford Court, justice of the peace and high sheriff for Herefordshire. He *m.* Anne, daughter of Robert Waller, esq. of Beaconsfield, in Bucks, by Anne, his wife, sister of JOHN HAMPDEN, the patriot, and by her, who *d.* 19th September, 1642, had, with four daughters, seven sons, viz.

1. ROBERT, his heir.
2. James, } all *d. s. p.*
3. John,
4. William,
5. Richard (Sir), knt. of the kingdom of Ireland, living in 1683, married two wives, and had issue by both.
6. Edward, *d.* unm.
7. Thomas, *m.* in Ireland, and had a son, Vandervort, who was devisee of "THE MAN OF ROSS."

James Kyrle died 1st February, 1646, and was succeeded by his eldest son,

ROBERT KYRLE, esq. of Walford Court. Inheriting the republican principles of his mother's connections, he was a distinguished military officer under CROMWELL, holding the commission of captain of troopers, and is styled "a stony hearted Rebell," in the narrative of the plundering of Master Swift's house at Goodrich. He married,

* There were many families in various parts of England, about the middle of the sixteenth century, possessing names ... each nearly approaching those of Kyrle, who ... probably connected with this family.

† Walford Court, or Manor House, still exists. From ... here Captain Kyrle is reported by tradition to have bombarded Goodrich Castle, which, from the relative position of the two places, is not improbable. The estate passed, as hereafter shewn, from the Kyrles to the Gwillyms, and was sold by them to John Clarke, esq. of the Hill, about the year 1727. It is now, under the will of the late Mrs. Clarke, the property of K. Evans, esq.

first, Mildred, daughter of Sir William Maxey, of Bradwell Hall, Essex, and secondly, Elizabeth, daughter of John Brayn, gent. of Little Dean, in Gloucestershire. By the latter, who *d.* 5th September, 1668, he had issue,

1. James, aged sixteen in 1663, *d.* before June, 1689.

1. Mary, *m.* to — Yates, of Bristol.
2. Elizabeth, *m.* to William Gwillym, esq. of Langston, in Herefordshire, and died 12th December, 1714, leaving a son, Robert.

Robert Kyrle *d.* in 1669, aged fifty-one, and was buried in the family chapel in Walford Church, on the 2nd October, in that year.

II. William, of Blayson, whose only daughter and heiress, Joan, *m.* John Aylway.

III. Charles, who *m.* Joane, daughter of William Pigot, esq. and had issue.

IV. THOMAS, ancestor of the KYRLES, of Much Marcle.

V. Hugh, *d.* in London, unm.

VI. John, *d. s. p.*

VII. James, who *m.* a daughter of — Morgan of Newent.

VIII. Richard, in holy orders, afterwards Sir Richard, vicar of Walford; upon the resignation of which, he became vicar of Much Marcle and Foy. This Sir Richard drew up a pedigree of his family from its earliest establishment in Herefordshire to the year 1662, on which document the present account is founded.

IX. Anthony, a justice of the peace, whose daughter Sarah, became the wife of William Scudamore, esq. of Bellingham.

The fourth son,

THOMAS KYRLE, esq. Lord of the manor of Much Marcle, in the county of Hereford, in the commission of the peace for that shire, and for Worcestershire, *m.* Frances, daughter and heir of John Knotsford, esq. of Malvern, and left a son and successor,

JOHN KYRLE, esq. of Much Marcle, justice of the peace, and twice high sheriff for Herefordshire, who was created a BARONET 17th May, 1627. He *m.* Sybill, daughter and heir of Philip Scudamore, esq. and had issue,

I. FRANCIS, high sheriff of Herefordshire, who *m.* Hester, daughter of Sir Paul Tracy, bart. of Stanway, in the county of Gloucester, and dying *v. p.* in 1649, left

1. JOHN, successor to his grandfather.
2. Richard, *d. s. p.*
3. Giles, *d. s. p.*

1. Elizabeth, *m.* to Robert Holmes, esq. of Netherton, in Gloucestershire.
2. Dorothy, *m.* first, to John Abrahall, esq. and secondly, to Sir Bennet Hoskyns.
3. Anne, *m.* to — Lechmere, of Fownhope.
4. Hester, *m.* to — Prior, of Pillith, in Radnorshire.

II. Thomas, of Gray's Inn, *d. s. p.*

I. Joane, *m.* to John Nourse, esq.

II. Sibill, *m.* to Thomas Capell, of How Capell, in Herefordshire.

Sir John Kyrle, *d.* in 1650, and was *s.* at his decease by his grandson,

SIR JOHN KYRLE, bart. of Much Marcle, who *m.* 16th December, 1647, Rebecca Vincent, and by her, who wedded, secondly, John Booth, esq. of Letton, had issue,

VINCENTIA, *b.* 2nd October, 1651, who *m.* 6th December, 1674, Sir John Ernle, knt. of Burytown in Wiltshire, son of Sir John Ernle, knt. chancellor of the exchequer, and had issue,

JOHN KYRLE ERNLE, esq. of Whetham and Much Marcle, who *m.* Constantia, [illegible] daughter of Sir Thomas Rolt, knt. of [illegible]comb, Herts, and dying in October, [illegible] left an only daughter and heir,

CONSTANTIA ERNLE, who *m.* in 1741, Thomas, Viscount Dupplin, afterwards [illegible] of Kinnoul, and had an only [illegible] Thomas John Ernle Hay, *b.* 13th August 1742, who *d.* 14th October, 1743. [illegible] countess herself died in 1753, and [illegible] interred at Calne on the 7th July, leaving no issue. She settled her estates upon the next heir and sole representative of her ancestors (the son of her [illegible] cousin, Elizabeth),

JAMES MONEY, esq. of Pitsford.

HESTER ERNLE, *b.* 8th February, 1673-4, [illegible] William Washbourne, esq. son and heir [illegible] parent of Wm. Washbourne, esq. of Pytch[illegible] in Northamptonshire, and left, beside [illegible] other children who all died without issue [illegible] daughter,

ELIZABETH WASHBOURNE, who *m.* in [illegible] Francis Money, esq. of Wellingborough and died 2nd March, 1726, leaving an only son,

JAMES MONEY, esq. of Pitsford [illegible] Northamptonshire, [illegible] army, who *m.* Eugenia, daughter and heir of George Stoughton [illegible] of St. John's, Warwick, and [illegible] grandfather of the present

JAMES KYRLE-MONEY, esq. a major-gen. in the army, of Much Marcle, in Herefordshire [illegible] Whetham, in Wiltshire, and Pitsford, in Northamptonshire. (See BURKE'S *Commoners*, vol. iii. p. 615.)

HESTER, *m.* to William Wintour, esq. of [illegible]

ELIZABETH, *m.* to John Midlebrooke, esq.

SIBILL, *m.* to Giles Wintour, esq.

Sir John Kyrle, who was M.P. for Herefordshire [illegible] the period of his decease, died 4th January, [illegible] aged sixty, when the BARONETCY became EXTINCT.

Arms—Vert, a chev. between three fleurs-de-lis [illegible]

LADE, OF WARBLETON.

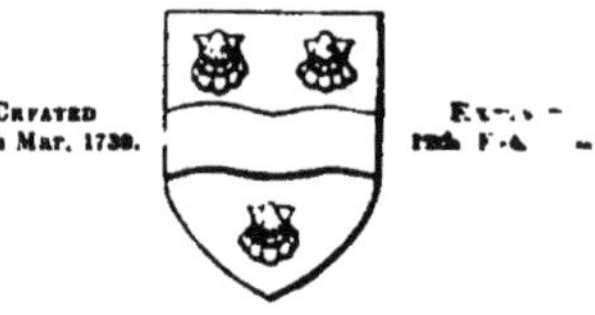

Lineage.

THOMAS LADE, of Barham, in Kent, died [illegible] 1601, leaving by his wife, Elizabeth, sister and [illegible] Thomas Mumbray, of Sutton, a daughter, [illegible]

wife of William Nethersole, of Wimingwould, in the same county, a son and heir,

VINCENT LADE, of Barham, gent. who *m.* in 1575, a daughter of Vincent Denne, esq. of Denhill, in Kent, and dying 27th August, 1625, left four sons, viz.

I. ROBERT, his heir of Gray's Inn, barrister and recorder of Canterbury, to whom Sir William Segar, garter, confirmed the arms of the family viz. "argent, a fesse wavy, between three escallops sable." CREST, "on a wreath a panther's head guardant;" quartering Mumbray, "Gules, a lion rampant, argent, collared and chained, sable." He married in 1619, Mary, daughter of William Lovelace, of the Friars, in Canterbury, and was ancestor of the Lades of Canterbury and Barham.

II. THOMAS.

III. John, } *d. s. p.*
IV. Vincent, }

V. William.

The second son,

THOMAS LADE, died five years before his father, but having *m.* Margaret, daughter of William Denwood, of Ebbsfleet, in Kent, left three sons and four daughters,

VINCENT, *m.* Elizabeth, daughter of Mr. Knowler, of Canterbury, and left issue.

THOMAS.

John, of Adsam, in Kent, *m.* Hannah, daughter of Walter Cloak, of Winchop, near Canterbury, and left four daughters, viz.

MARY, *m.* to — Denne, of Canterbury.

SARAH, *m.* to William Cullen.

ANNE, *m.* to John Roberts, gent. of Warbleton.

MARGARET, *d.* unm.

Elizabeth, *d.* unm.

Margaret, *d.* unm.

Ann, *m.* to John Roberts, esq. of Warbleton.

The second son,

THOMAS LADE, of Warbleton, in Sussex, *m.* Mary, daughter of John Nutt, of Mayers, in Sussex, gent. by whom he had issue.

I. VINCENT, of Warbleton, married and had one son and four daughters, viz.

VINCENT, *d. s. p.*

ANNE, *m.* first to Thomas Wandell, of Southwark, druggist, and secondly to William Nutt, gent. of Marshalls, Sussex.

ELIZABETH, *m.* to John Whitborne, of Jamaica, and had three sons,

Lade Whitborne, *d. s. p.*

Charles Whitborne.

JOHN WHITBORNE, of whom hereafter.

MARY, *m.* to John Price, of Richmond, in Surrey.

PHILADELPHIA, *m.* to John Inskipp, esq. of Uckfield, in Sussex, and had a son,

JOHN INSKIPP, who eventually inherited the estates of the family.

II. Thomas, *d.* unm.

III. JOHN, of whom presently.

I. Anne.

II. Catherine, *m.* to Mr. Hugh Offley, of Posingworth, Sussex.

Thomas Lade, *d.* in December, 1668. His youngest son,

JOHN LADE, esq. was an eminent brewer in the borough of Southwark, and amassed a considerable fortune. He represented the borough in parliament, temp. QUEEN ANNE and *King* GEORGE I. and was created a BARONET by GEORGE II. 11th March, 1730, with remainder, in default of male issue, to his nephew, JOHN WHITBORNE, who had previously assumed the name of LADE. Sir John *d.* a bachelor, 30th July, 1740, and was *s.* by his nephew aforesaid,

II. SIR JOHN LADE, who died unm. 12th February, 1747, when the BARONETCY EXPIRED; but the greater part of his fortune devolved, under his will, upon his cousin,

JOHN INSKIPP, esq. who assumed the surname of LADE, and was created a BARONET in 1758. His only son and heir is the present (1837)

SIR JOHN LADE, bart. Refer to BURKE'S *Peerage and Baronetage*.

Arms—Argent a fesse wavy between three escallops sable.

LANE, OF TULSKE.

CREATED 11th Feb. 1660-1.

EXTINCT 2nd Aug. 1724.

Lineage.

I. RICHARD LANE, esq. of Tulske, in the county of Roscommon, was created a BARONET in 1660-1. He *m.* first, Mabell, daughter and heir of Gerald Fitzgerald, esq. of Clonbolg and Rathaman; and secondly, Mary, daughter of Thomas Leicester, esq. By the former, he left at his decease, 5th October, 1668, a son and successor,

II. SIR GEORGE LANE, an eminent politician, who filled the office of secretary of state for Ireland, and was raised to the peerage of that kingdom by the title of Viscount Lanesborough, of the county of Longford. His lordship married, first, Dorcas, daughter of Sir Anthony Brabazon, knt. and secondly, Frances, daughter of Richard, Earl of Dorset. His son and successor,

III. SIR JAMES LANE, second Viscount Lanesborough, married Mary, daughter of Sir Charles Compton, knt. but died without issue, 2nd August, 1724, when all his honours, including the BARONETCY, became EXTINCT, and the estates devolved on his sister and heiress,

THE HON. FRANCES LANE, (daughter of George, Lord Lanesborough, by Lady Frances Sackville, daughter of Richard, fifth Earl of Dorset,) who *m.* in 1691, Henry Fox, esq. and had, with several daughters, three sons,

GEORGE FOX, M.P. for the city of York, who assumed the additional surname of LANE, and was created BARON BINGLEY, of Bingley. He died without surviving issue in 1772.

JAMES FOX, who inherited the Surrey estates of his grandmother, Lady Lanesborough, and died *s. p.* in 1753.

SACKVILLE FOX, grandfather of the present

GEORGE LANE FOX, esq. of Bramham Park, Yorkshire, M.P. for Beverley. (See BURKE'S *Commoners*, vol. ii. p. 493.)

Arms—Arg. a lion rampt. gu. within a border sa. on a canton of the first, a harp and crown or.

LANGHORNE, OF LONDON.

CREATED 28th Aug. 1668.

EXTINCT 26th Feb. 1714.

Lineage.

I. WILLIAM LANGHORNE, esq. of London, an East India merchant, (son of William Langhorne, esq.) purchased from the executors of Lord Downe, the manor and estate of Charlton, in Kent, and was created a BARONET in 1668. He m. first, Grace, daughter of John, Earl of Rutland, and relict of Patrick, Viscount Chaworth, which lady died *s. p.* in 1700. Sir William wedded, secondly, Mary Aston, but by her, who m. after his decease, George Jones, esq. of Twickenham, had no child. He died 26th February, 1714, when the BARONETCY EXPIRED. His estate at Charlton was inherited by (the son of his sister Elizabeth, Lady Conyers,) his nephew,

SIR JOHN CONYERS, bart. of Horden, and remained with his descendants until the death of Sir Baldwin Conyers, bart. in 1731, when the manor of Charlton went by entail, first to William Langhorne Games, esq. who died without male issue, when it passed to the Rev. John Maryon, of the county of Essex. That gentleman left it by will to his niece, Margaretta-Maria, who m. first, John Badger Weller, esq. of Hornechurch, and secondly, John Jones, esq.; by the former she had a daughter, Jane, married to SIR THOMAS SPENCER WILSON, bart. of Eastbourne. This lady was grandmother of the present (1837) SIR THOMAS MARYON WILSON, who through her enjoys the manor and estate of Charlton.

Arms—Sa. a cross arg. on a chief of the second, three bugle horns sa. stringed gu.

LANGLEY, OF HIGHAM GOBION.

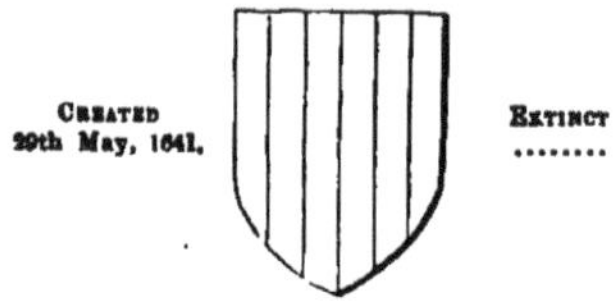

CREATED 29th May, 1641.

EXTINCT ....

Lineage.

WILLIAM LANGLEY, of Langley, in the bishoprick of Durham, had two sons, viz.

HENRY, his heir.

Thomas, lord chancellor of England, bishop of Durham, and a cardinal, 1417. Bishop Goodwin, says, "he was consecrated bishop of Durham, 1406, at which time, he gave over his chancellorship, but eleven years after, it was laid upon him again; after which he continued in that place about six years; in the mean space, viz. 6th June, 1411, he was made cardinal, together with Robert Halam, bishop of Salisbury. This man bestowed the sum of £499. 6s. 7d. in repairing of that gallery in the west end of his church which was first built by Hugh Pudsey, his predecessor; he also founded two schools in the Place Green, one for grammar, another for musick; thirty-one years he continued bishop here, and dying 1437, was buried, as I am informed, in the gallery, and lieth entombed before the altar there, under the table of the consistory."

The elder son,

HENRY LANGLEY, esq. of Dalton, in the West Riding of the county of York, married the daughter of Kaye of Woodsome, in the same county, by whom he had two sons, namely, Thomas, of Rathorp Hall, ancestor of the Langleys of that place, and

ROBERT LANGLEY, esq. of Langley, father of

GEORGE LANGLEY, who had two sons, viz.

ROBERT, who had an only daughter and heiress.

WILLIAM.

The second son,

WILLIAM LANGLEY, esq. left a son and heir,

GEORGE LANGLEY, esq. of Stainton, in Yorkshire, who m. Jane, daughter of John Hall, of Sherbourn, in the same county and had, (with a daughter the wife of William Forster, of Erdswick,) three sons, viz.

WILLIAM, his heir.

Matthew, married but left no issue.

John, *d. s. p.*

The eldest son,

I. WILLIAM LANGLEY, esq. of Stainton, in the county of York, and of Higham Gobion, in the county of Bedford, was created a BARONET by *King* CHARLES I. 29th May, 1641. He m. Elizabeth daughter of Roger Lambley, esq. and sister of Richard, Viscount Lumley, and had issue,

William, *d.* unm. in his father's lifetime, 1634.

ROGER, heir to his father.

Dorothy, m. to William Bristow, esq. of the county of Somerset.

Sir William died in Holborn, and was buried at St. Andrew's Church in 1651. He was *s.* by his son.

II. SIR ROGER LANGLEY, of Sheriff Hutton Park, in the county of York. This gentleman, who was thirty eight years of age in 1665, m. first, Mary, daughter of Thomas Keighley, esq. of Hertingfordbury, Herts, and had

I. WILLIAM, his heir, who m. Isabella, daughter of Sir John Griffith, knt. of Erith, in Kent, and dying in the lifetime of his father, anno 1696, left by her, (who m. secondly, Thomas Barnes, esq. of East Winch, in Norfolk,)

1. ROGER, successor to his grandfather.
2. William, of Elwick, m. Margaret, daughter of — Sutton, esq. of Barbadoes, and widow of Abraham Jaggard, by whom he left a daughter and heir,

   ISABELLA, m. in 1734, to William Fitzpatrick, esq. of High Barnes, in Durham. (See BURKE's *Commoners*, vol iii. p. 15.)

3. THOMAS, who *s.* as fourth baronet.
4. Haldanby, m. Mary, daughter of Charles Peck, esq. of Gildersley, in Derbyshire, and dying 30th May, 1728, left three sons, viz.

   Gilbert, m. Miss Brown, *d. s. p.*

   HALDANBY, who inherited as fifth baronet.

   James.

II. Richard, } all died issueless.
III. Roger,
IV. Thomas,

I. Mary, m. to Mr. Prescot, of Essex.
II. Rose, m. to Peter Priaux, of London, merchant.
III. Elizabeth, } d. unm.
IV. Frances,

He m. secondly, Barbara, daughter and co-heir of Mr. Serjeant Chapman, of Foxton, in Leicestershire, but by her had no issue. His third wife was Sarah, daughter of John Neale, esq. of Malden Ashe, in Essex, by whom he had

William, who d. young.
John, major in the army, m. a daughter of — De la Hay, esq. of Westminster.
David, killed in an engagement in the West Indies, 1706.
Mary, } d. unm.
Sarah,

Sir Roger was foreman of the jury on the trial of the seven bishops, and was a commissioner of the prize office in the reign of *King* WILLIAM. He d. in 1698, having sold the manor of Higham Gobion to Arabella, Countess of Kent) and was s. by his grandson,

III. SIR ROGER LANGLEY, who m. Mary, daughter of Stanislaus Browne, esq. of Eastbourne, in Sussex, and had an only child, Charles, who died an infant. Sir Roger d. in 1716, and was s. by his brother,

IV. SIR THOMAS LANGLEY. This gentleman m. the second daughter of Captain Robert Edgeworth, of Longwood, in the county of Meath, and had two sons, Tyrell and John, who predeceased him, unm. and three daughters. He d. 1st December, 1762, aged ninety-eight, and was s. by his nephew,

V. SIR HALDANBY LANGLEY, who is stated to have left a son and heir,

VI. SIR HENRY LANGLEY, at whose decease, if such a person inherited rightly, the BARONETCY EXPIRED.

Arms—Paly of six, argent and vert.

LAROCHE, OF OVER.

CREATED 17th Aug. 1776.

EXTINCT in, or about 1805.

Lineage.

PETER CROTHAIRE, of the province of Bordeaux, came into England in the train of GEORGE, PRINCE OF DENMARK, and at the desire of his master, assumed the surname of LAROCHE.* He had three sons and a daughter,

JOHN LAROCHE, his heir.
James Laroche, alderman and merchant of Bristol—died there—will dated 8th February, 1770, proved 21st November following, m. Clementia, daughter of Louis Cassamajor, of Bristol, but had no issue.
Peter Laroche, who d. young.
Eleanor Laroche, d. at Bristol, unm. about 1798, aged ninety-six, will dated 9th August, 1797, codicil, 8th November following, proved 16th November, 1798.

The eldest son,

JOHN LAROCHE, esq. b. in 1700, M.P. for Bodmin, from his maturity to his decease; m. Elizabeth, daughter of Isaac Garnier, of Westminster, an eminent apothecary, and had issue,

John, of Haleburton, b. May, 1732, major East Devon militia, m. a French lady, but d. s. p.
Henry, of Totness, in Devon, d. in 1802.
JAMES.
Elizabeth, m. to John Fulford, esq. of Great Fulford, in Devonshire, d. s. p. in 1791.
Catherine, m. to Charles Berners, esq. of Wolverston Park, in Suffolk, d. 1800, and left issue,
Charles Berners.
James Berners, banker in London.
Henry Berners, m. a daughter of John Jarratt, esq. of Jamaica.
William Berners, who m. another daughter of John Jarratt, esq.
Maria Berners, m. Herbert Jarratt, esq.
Frances.
Susan.

Mr. Laroche officiated as esquire to John, Lord Delawar, on his lordship's installation as a knight of the bath, in 1725. His third son,

I. JAMES LAROCHE, esq. of Over, in Almondsbury, in the county of Gloucester, b. in 1734, M.P. for Bodmin, was created a BARONET 17th August, 1776. Sir James m. in December, 1764, Elizabeth-Rachel-Anne, daughter and heiress of William Yeamans, esq. of Antigua, and widow of Mr. Archibald, by whom, who d. 27th January, 1781, he had no issue. He d. about the year 1805, when the BARONETCY became EXTINCT.

Arms—Quarterly; first and fourth or, a raven ppr. second and third argent, on a mount vert, an eagle close looking at the sun in his glory in the canton.

LAWDAY, OF EXETER.

CREATED 9th Nov. 1642.

EXTINCT about 1648.

Lineage.

I. SIR RICHARD LAWDAY, of Exeter, who was created a BARONET in 1642, lost his life in the king's service during the civil wars. Mr. William Lawday, sometime of Bath, in Somersetshire, living in 1822, claimed to be the immediate male representative of the baronet, but the title has lain dormant (if it did not then become extinct) since the decease of Sir Richard.

Arms—Party per saltier gu. and sa. a griffin segreant or.

* He had a brother who assumed likewise the name of LAROCHE.

LAWRENCE, OF IVER.

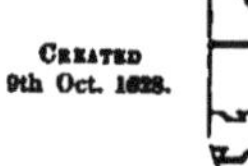

CREATED 9th Oct. 1628. EXTINCT April, 1714.

Lineage.

SIR ROBERT LAWRENCE, knt. who married Margaret Holden, of Lancashire, had four sons, of whom the eldest, Sir Robert, was ancestor of the Lawrences of Standish, Crick Grange, and Sevenhampton; * and the second

THOMAS LAWRENCE, was father of

ARTHUR LAWRENCE, esq. who was seated at Priors Court, in Gloucestershire. He was ancestor of

I. JOHN LAWRENCE, esq. of Delaford in Iver, Bucks, and of Chelsea, Middlesex, who was created a BARONET in 1628. He m. Grisel, daughter and co-heir of Jarvis Gibbon, esq. of Benenden, in Kent, and dying in November, 1638, was *s.* by his son,

II. SIR JOHN LAWRENCE, of Chelsea, father of

III. SIR THOMAS LAWRENCE, who m. a daughter of Mr. English, but had no issue. Sir Thomas spent all his estate, and about the year 1700, emigrated to Maryland. "Sir Thomas Lawrence, bart." who was buried at Chelsea, in April, 1714, is presumed to be this gentleman.

Arms—Arg. a cross raguly gu. on a chief of the second a lion passant guardant or.

LAWRENCE, OF ST. IVES.

CREATED 17th January, 1748.—EXTINCT in 1756.

Lineage.

I. SIR EDWARD LAWRENCE, knt. of St. Ives, in the county of Huntingdon, was created a BARONET in 1748, with remainder to his nephew, Isaac Wollaston, esq. of Loseby, and dying *s. p.* in 1749, was succeeded by that gentleman. (See WOLLASTON OF LOSEBY.)

Arms—As LAWRENCE OF IVER.

LAWSON, OF BROUGH HALL.

CREATED 6th July, 1665. EXTINCT 1834.

Lineage.

The Lawsons, from whom this family sprung, were for several generations seated at Burwell, and afterwards at Alindell, in Northumberland.

WILLIAM LAWSON, esq. of Cramlington, in that county, was father of

JAMES LAWSON, esq. of Cramlington, who, in the time of HENRY VIII. was an eminent merchant at Newcastle-upon-Tyne. He m. Alice, daughter of Mr Bertram, of Bentley, and was *s.* by his son,

EDMUND LAWSON, esq. who m. Margery, daughter and heir of Ralph Swinnow, esq. of Rock Castle, in Northumberland, and left a son and heir,

SIR RALPH LAWSON, who received the honour of knighthood from *King* JAMES I. He m. Elizabeth, daughter and sole heir of Roger Brough, esq. of Brough Hall, near Catterick, in the county of York, and living to a great age, left (with two daughters, Jane, wife of Thomas Rokeby, esq. of Mortham, and Alice, of Thomas Inglebby, esq. of Lawkland) three sons, of whom the eldest,

ROGER LAWSON, esq. was seated at Heaton, near Newcastle-upon-Tyne, which place was afterwards sold, and died in London, in the lifetime of his father. He m. Dorothy, daughter of Sir Henry Constable, knt. of Burton Constable, in the county of York, and had a numerous issue. His wife died in [illegible], at St. Anthony's, near Newcastle, which then belonged to the family, and was subsequently sold or lost by sequestration. His eldest surviving son,

HENRY LAWSON, esq. of Brough Hall, m. Anne, daughter of Robert Hodgson, esq. of Hebburne, in the county of Durham, and had, with other issue,

- Roger, who *d.* young.
- HENRY, m. Catherine, eldest daughter and co-heir of Sir William Fenwick, of Meldon, in Northumberland, and falling at the battle of Melton Mowbray, 1644, fighting for the king, left an only daughter,
  - ISABELLA, m. to Sir John Swinburne, bart. of Capheaton.

  His widow m. Sir Francis Ratcliffe, afterwards Earl of Derwentwater.
- JOHN.

The third son,

I. JOHN LAWSON, esq. captain of horse in the service of the king (CHARLES I.), inherited Brough Hall, but did not long enjoy the possession, until the estate fell under sequestration, and afterwards, in the year [illegible], was, pursuant to two acts of parliament relating to the sale of forfeited estates, sold, and Captain Lawson himself condemned to banishment. In consideration of these his great sufferings, he was created a BARONET by *King* CHARLES II. 6th July, 1665. Sir John m. Catherine, third daughter of Sir William Howard, of Naworth Castle, in Cumberland, sister of Charles, first Earl of Carlisle, and had issue,

- John, *d.* at Calais, returning from his travels.
- HENRY, heir to his father.
- Charles, captain of horse in the Duke of Monmouth's regiment, killed in Germany.
- William, a priest.
- Philip, m. Lady Anna-Maria Knollys, daughter of Nicholas, Earl of Banbury, and relict of Walter Littleton, esq. but *d. s. p.* in [illegible]. His widow m. Colonel Harvey, of Leicestershire.
- Thomas, a priest.

Catherine, Mary, Anne, Elizabeth, Frances. } These ladies embraced a [illegible] life at Ghent.

* The male line of the Sevenhampton branch, continued for many generations, until the demise of [illegible] Walter Lawrence, esq. His only child, MARY, married, 1797, WILLIAM MORRIS, esq. and was mother of the [illegible] WALTER LAWRENCE LAWRENCE, esq. of Sandywell Park, near Cheltenham.

Sir John was s. by his eldest surviving son,

II. SIR HENRY LAWSON, of Brough Hall, who m. Elizabeth, daughter of Robert Knightley, esq. of Offchurch, in the county of Warwick, and had issue,

JOHN, his heir.

Anne, m. to William Witham, esq. of Cliffe, in Yorkshire.

Elizabeth, m. to Stephen Tempest, esq. of Boughton, in the same county.

Sir Henry d. in 1725, and was s. by his son,

III. SIR HENRY LAWSON, who m. Mary, eldest daughter of Sir John Shelley, bart. of Michelgrove, by whom he left issue,

HENRY, his heir.

Thomas, a priest, living in 1800.

John, m. Elizabeth, daughter of Thomas William Selby, esq. of Biddleston, in Northumberland, and had issue,

Thomas, a priest.

John, of York, M.D. m. Clarinda, eldest daughter of John Fallan, esq. of Cloona, in the county of Roscommon, and widow of William Bermingham, esq.

Henry, a priest.

Elizabeth, m. to John Webbe Weston, esq. of Sutton Place, Surrey, and d. in 1791, leaving a large family.

Mr. John Lawson d. in London in 1791, aged sixty-nine.

Mary, } nuns at Bruges, where they died, the Bridget, } former in 1783, the latter in 1787.

Sir John d. 19th October, 1739, aged fifty, and was s. by his eldest son,

IV. SIR HENRY LAWSON. This gentleman m. Anastasia, youngest daughter of Thomas Maire, esq. of Lartington Hall, in Yorkshire, and of Hardwick, near the sea, in Durham,* and by her, who d. 8th November, 1764, had issue,

JOHN, his successor.

HENRY, b. 25th December, 1750. This gentleman inherited under the will of his uncle, John Maire, esq. the estates of that family, to enjoy the same so long as the title and property of his own family remained in his elder brother, but should he succeed to those, the estates of the Maire family were then to devolve upon his sister Catherine. In consequence of this bequest he assumed, in 1771, by sign manual, the surname of MAIRE.

Mary, b. 26th July, 1742, a nun at Bruges.

Catherine, b. 9th August, 1747, m. in 1772, to John Silvertop, esq. of Minster-acres, in Northumberland, and had issue,

George Silvertop, heir to his father, and present proprietor of Minster-acres. (See BURKE's *Commoners*, vol. iii. p. 301.)

John Silvertop, d. young.

Henry-Thomas-Maire Silvertop, who inherited eventually the Maire estates. He m. Eliza, daughter of Thomas Witham, esq. and niece and heiress of William Witham, esq. of Cliffe, and assumed, in consequence, the surname of Witham. He is the present (1837) Henry Witham, esq. of Lartington Hall. (Refer to BURKE's *Commoners*.)

Charles Silvertop, colonel in the Spanish service.

Mary Silvertop.

Henry d. in October, 1781, aged sixty-nine, and was interred in the family aisle of the church at Catterick, where a handsome monument was erected to his memory by his son and successor,

V. SIR JOHN LAWSON, who m. first, 1st August, 1768, Elizabeth, youngest daughter of William Scarisbrick, esq. of Scarisbrick, in Lancashire, and by that lady, who d. 10th June, 1801, had two surviving children, viz.

ANASTASIA, m. in 1789, to Thomas Strickland, esq. of Sizergh, in Westmoreland, and had issue. (See BURKE's *Commoners*.)

ELIZABETH, m. 5th June, 1789, to John Wright, esq. of Kelvedon Hall, in Essex, and had issue.

He m. secondly, Monica, daughter of Miles Stapleton, esq. of Dreux, in the county of York, and died 27th June, 1811, aged sixty-seven: leaving thus no male issue, the title and estate devolved upon his brother, HENRY MAIRE, esq. who, according to the stipulations of his uncle, John Maire's will, was obliged to transfer the Maire estate to his sister, Mrs. Silvertop. He therefore resumed his own name, and inherited his paternal title and estates as

VI. SIR HENRY LAWSON, of Brough Hall. He m. in 1773, Monica, youngest daughter of Nicholas Stapleton, esq. of Carlton, in Yorkshire, and became a widower without issue, 8th January, 1800. Sir Henry m. secondly, Catherine, only daughter of Henry Fermer, esq. of Worcester, but died s. p. in 1834, when the BARONETCY became EXTINCT. His estates were inherited by his nephew, WILLIAM WRIGHT, esq. who assumed the surname of LAWSON.

Arms—Arg. a chevron between three martlets, sa.

LAWSON, OF ISELL.

CREATED 31st Mar. 1688. 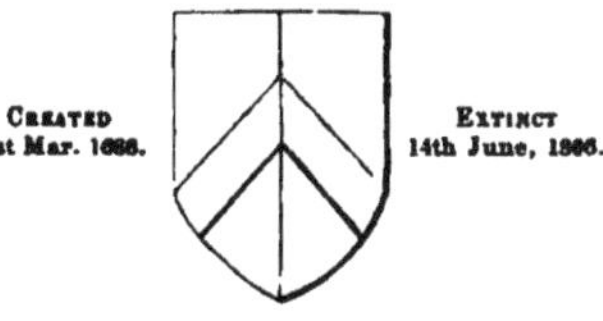 EXTINCT 14th June, 1806.

Lineage.

The patriarch of this family,

JOHN LAWSON, lived in the time of HENRY III. and was then Lord of Fawlesgrave, in the county of York. He was father of another

JOHN LAWSON, living in the 13th of the same reign, who m. Julian, daughter of — Covell, and was s. by his son,

THOMAS LAWSON, who flourished *temp.* EDWARD I. and by the daughter of — Chancie, left a son and heir,

ROBERT LAWSON, a liege subject of EDWARD II. whose wife, the daughter of Harbet, was mother of his successor,

RICHARD LAWSON, who m. Anne Conyers, was living in the 8th of EDWARD III. and was s. in his estate by his son,

THOMAS LAWSON, living in the 24th of the same reign, who by Jane, daughter of Sir William Boynton, knt. was father of

ROGER LAWSON, who m. Anne Etton. He was

* By Mary, his wife, daughter of Richard Fermor, esq. of Tusmore, in Oxfordshire.

alive 9th HENRY IV. and was *s.* at his decease by his son,

JOHN LAWSON, living 4th HENRY VI. husband of Jacquina Northrop, and father of

THOMAS LAWSON, living in the 22nd of the same reign, who took to wife the daughter of Threlkeld, and left a son and heir,

JOHN LAWSON, who flourished *temp.* EDWARD IV. and marrying the daughter of Hilton, was father of

WILLIAM LAWSON, living 20th HENRY VII. *m.* the daughter of George Hedworth, and was *s.* by his son,

THOMAS LAWSON, who was alive 27th HENRY VIII. and having married the daughter of Sir — Dorrell, knt. had issue,

I. GEORGE, of Little Usworth, in the county of Durham, who *m.* Mabella, daughter and heir of Sir Reginald Carnaby, knt. and had, with three daughters, Dorothea, Elizabeth, and Mabella, four sons, viz.

1. THOMAS, who sold Little Usworth to Sir Wilfrid Lawson, and *d.* unm.

2. Edward, who *m.* Mary, daughter of John Copley, esq. of Skelbrooke, and had

Wilfrid, who *m.* Mary, daughter of Joseph Watkinson, and had a daughter,

Elizabeth, *m.* to Richard Wilton, esq. of Wakefield.

John, a merchant in Denmark.

Godfrey, mayor of Leeds in 1669: he *m.* Elizabeth, daughter of Joseph Watkinson, and *d.* in 1709, leaving a son, George, who *d. s. p.* and two daughters, Mary, *m.* to Ralph Lowther, esq. and Elizabeth, *m.* to John Trotter, esq. of Skelton Castle.

3. Robert, *m.* and *d. s. p.*

4. Ralph.

II. Wilfrid (Sir), *m.* first, the daughter of — Redmade, or Redman, and secondly, a daughter of Leigh, of Isel,* but *d. s. p.* bequeathing his estate to his nephew William, son of his younger brother.

III. GILFRID.

I. Barbara, *m.* to Thomas Whitehead.

II. Elizabeth, *m.* to William Lee.

III. Ursula.

The youngest son,

GILFRID LAWSON, esq. living *temp.* ELIZABETH, *m.* the daughter of Seamer, and had a son,

WILLIAM LAWSON, esq. living in the 40th of the same reign, and heir to his uncle, Sir Wilfrid Lawson, knt. He *m.* the daughter of Bewley, and was *s.* by his son,

I. WILFRID LAWSON, esq. of Isell, in Cumberland, who was created a BARONET by *King* JAMES II. 31st March, 1688. Sir Wilfrid *m.* Jane, daughter of Sir Edward Musgrave, of Hayton Castle, Baronet of Nova Scotia, and had issue,

I. WILLIAM, his heir, *m.* Milcha, daughter of Sir William Strickland, bart. of Boynton, in the county of York, and had

WILFRID, successor to his grandfather.

Jane.

Frances, *d.* unm. in 1694.

II. Wilfrid, of Brayton, in Cumberland, *m.* Sarah daughter and co-heir of — James, esq. [illegible] Washington, and left issue,

GILFRID, M. P. for Cumberland temp. QUEEN ANNE, GEORGE I. and GEORGE II. who *s.* as sixth BARONET.

ALFRED, successor to his brother as seventh BARONET.

III. Edward, *m.* Mary, daughter of — Briscoe, esq. of Grenhoe, in Cumberland, and *d. s. p.* in 1694.

IV. George, *d. s. p.*

V. Henry, *m.* Mary, daughter of — Taylor, esq. and had a son,

Wilfrid, aged sixteen in 1694.

Jane, *m.* to William Benson, esq. of Broughton, in Cumberland.

Mary.

I. Elizabeth, *m.* to John Stapleton, esq. of Warter in Yorkshire.

II. Judith, *m.* to Miles Pennington, esq. of Seaton in Cumberland.

III. Katherine, *m.* to Andrew Hudleston, esq. of Hutton-John, in Cumberland.

IV. Jane, *m.* to Robert Constable, of Cliffe, in Yorkshire.

V. Frances, *m.* to Henry Tolson, esq. of Woodhall in Cumberland.

VI. Mary, *m.* to Christopher Richmond, esq. of Catterlane.

VII. Isabel, *m.* to D'Arcy Curwen, esq. of [illegible] Park.

VIII. Winifrid, *m.* to John Swinburne, of [illegible]waite.

Sir Wilfrid represented the county of Cumberland in parliament at the Restoration, and the year following served for Cockermouth, and dying in 1688, was *s.* by his grandson,

II. SIR WILFRID LAWSON, M.P. for Cockermouth 2nd WILLIAM and MARY, *m.* Elizabeth, only daughter and heir of George Preston, esq. of Holker, in Lancashire,† and had issue,

WILFRID, his successor, *b.* in 1696.

William, *d.* unm.

John, an officer in the army on the Irish establishment, lost his life at a review in Dublin, by a ball aimed at another officer, and *d. s. p.*

---

* THORESBY marries Sir Wilfrid Lawson to the daughter of Redman, and Le Neve says he married a daughter of Leigh, of Isell, the widow of Thomas Leigh, of Isell. The fact is, probably, that he had two wives, and so we have assumed. He was buried in Isell church, under the following inscription:

Hic jacet ille cinis, qui modo Lawson erat.

Even such is Time, which takes in trust
Our youth and joys, and all we have;
And pays us but with age and dust,
Within the dark and silent grave.
When we have wander'd all our ways,
Shuts up the story of our days:
And from which earth, and grave, and dust,
The Lord will raise me up I trust.

Wilfridus Lawson miles obiit 16 die Apr. anno etatis suæ 87, ann. eque salutis 1632.

† By Mary Lowther, only sister of John, Viscount Lonsdale.

Elizabeth, killed by a fall from her horse while riding in Castle Howard Park, Yorkshire, *d.* unm.

Jane, } *d.* unm.
Mary, }

Sir Wilfrid *d.* in 1704, leaving a character of the highest probity behind him. Amongst other remarkable traits of nice conscientious feeling, was his relinquishing the impropriate tithes of Isell to the living for ever; which he did with so much exactness, that with the profits he had received himself to that time, he bought a piece of land, which he settled likewise on the living. He acted somewhat similarly towards government regarding his estate, which finding undertaxed, he computed the difference, and left £600 to be paid to make up the loss to the state. *Queen* ANNE gave the money back, however, to his family. He was *s.* by his eldest son,

III. SIR WILFRID LAWSON, F.R.S. one of the grooms of the bedchamber to *King* GEORGE I. and M.P. for Cumberland *temp.* GEORGE I. and GEORGE II. He *m.* Elizabeth-Lucy, daughter of Lieutenant-general Harry Mordaunt, and niece of Charles, third Earl of Peterborough, by whom he left two sons and two daughters, viz.

WILFRID, } fourth and fifth baronets.
MORDAUNT, }

Elizabeth.

Charlotte.

He *d.* 13th July, 1737, and was *s.* by his elder son,

IV. SIR WILFRID LAWSON, who *d.* 2nd May, 1739, aged seven years, and was *s.* by his brother,

V. SIR MORDAUNT LAWSON, who *d.* 8th August, 1743, aged ten, and was *s.* by his cousin, (refer to second son of the first baronet,)

VI. SIR GILFRID LAWSON, who *d.* 23rd August, 1749, *s. p.* and was *s.* by his brother,

VII. SIR ALFRED LAWSON, who *d.* 14th February, 1752, and was *s.* by his son,

VIII. SIR WILFRID LAWSON. This gentleman served the office of sheriff of Cumberland in 1756, and was elected knight of the shire in 1761. He *d.* 1st December, in the following year, and was *s.* by his brother,

IX. SIR GILFRID LAWSON, who *m.* Emilia, daughter of John Lovict, esq. by whom (who *d.* 20th May, 1769) he had a daughter, Emilia, who *d.* unmarried in 1796, and a son, his successor, in 1794,

X. SIR WILFRID LAWSON, who *m.* Anne, daughter of John Hartley, esq. of Whitehaven, but died issueless 14th June, 1806, when the BARONETCY EXPIRED. Sir Wilfrid bequeathed his estates to the nephew of his wife,

THOMAS WYBERGH, esq. (second son of Thomas Wybergh, esq. of Clifton Hall, Westmoreland, and Isabella Hartley, Lady Lawson's sister) who assumed in consequence the surname and arms of LAWSON. He *d. s. p.* in 1812, and was *s.* by his brother, who, having taken the name and arms likewise of Lawson, on inheriting became

WILFRID LAWSON, esq. of Brayton House, and Isell, in Cumberland, and having been created a BARONET in 1831, is now (1837) SIR WILFRID LAWSON. (Refer to BURKE's *Peerage and Baronetage.*)

Arms—*Per* pale, arg. and sa. a chevron counterchanged.

LEAR, OF LONDON.

LEAR, OF LINDRIDGE.

First Patent { CREATED 2nd July, 1660. EXTINCT about 1684.

Second Patent { CREATED 2nd August, 1683. EXTINCT before 1740.

Lineage.

I. PETER LEAR, esq. who acquired a considerable fortune in Barbadoes, was on his return from the island created a BARONET, 2nd July, 1660, but dying issueless about the year 1684, the title under that patent became EXTINCT, but he had previously obtained another patent, dated 2nd August, 1683, with special remainder to his nephews, and was succeeded accordingly by the elder, as

II. SIR THOMAS LEAR, of Lindridge, in the county of Devon. He represented Ashburton in parliament 13 WILLIAM III. and 1st of *Queen* ANNE, and *m.* Isabella, daughter of Sir William Courtenay, knt. of Powderham Castle, but dying *s. p.* in December, 1705, was *s.* by his brother,

III. SIR JOHN LEAR, who *m.* the daughter of Christopher Wolston, gent. of Devon, and had an only child,

MARY LEAR, who *m.* Sir Thomas Tipping, bart.

Sir John *d.* sometime before 1740, when the BARONETCY EXPIRED.

Arms—Ar. a fesse ragule, between three unicorns' heads erased or.

LEE, OF QUARENDON.

CREATED 29th June, 1611. EXTINCT 1776.

Lineage.

BENEDICT LEE, esq. younger son of John Lee,* esq. of Lee Hall, in Cheshire, acquired the estate of Quarendon, in Bucks, and changed his arms to "Argent, a fesse between three crescents sa." He *m.* Elizabeth, daughter and co-heir of William Sanders, esq. of Oxfordshire, and had issue,

* From Thomas, the eldest son of this John Lee, descended the family of Lee of Lee, and Darnhall, now represented by JOHN TOWNSHEND, esq. of Hem and Trevallyn, in Denbighshire. (See BURKE's *Commoners*, vol. iii. 118.)

i. Robert (Sir), of Burston, Buckinghamshire, whose grandson,

Sir Henry Lee, K.G. *temp.* Elizabeth, died *s. p.* and his cousin, Henry Lee, became his heir.

ii. Benedict.

iii. Roger, of Pickthorn.

iv. John, ancestor of the Lees, of Binfield, Bucks.

The second son,

Benedict Lee, esq. of Hulcote, married Elizabeth, daughter of Robert Cheney, esq. of Chesham Boyes, in Bucks, and was *s.* by his son,

Sir Robert Lee, father of

i. Sir Henry Lee, who was declared heir to his cousin, Sir Henry Lee, K.G. and thus became "of Quarendon." He received the honour of knighthood from *King* James I. and was created a Baronet 29th June, 1611. Sir Henry *m.* Eleanor, daughter of Sir Richard Wortley, of Wortley, in the county of York, and dying about the year 1631, was *s.* by his son,

ii. Sir Francis Henry Lee, of Quarendon, Berks, and Ditchley, in Oxfordshire, *m.* Anne, daughter of Sir John St. John, of Lidiard Tregose, in the county of Wilts, bart. and dying about the year 1641, was *s.* by his son,

iii. Sir Henry Lee, who *m.* Anne, daughter of Sir John Danvers, of Cornbury, in the county of Oxford, and sister and heir of John Danvers, esq. but having daughters only was *s.* at his decease by his brother,

iv. Sir Francis Henry Lee, of Ditchley, who *m.* Lady Elizabeth Pope, daughter and heir of Thomas, Earl of Downe, in Ireland, by whom (who married, secondly, Robert, third Earl of Lindsey), he had a son and successor,

v. Sir Edward Henry Lee, who was raised to the peerage in 1674, as Baron of Spellesbury, Viscount Quarendon, and Earl of Lichfield. He *m.* Lady Charlotte Fitzroy, natural daughter of *King* Charles II. by Barbara Villiers, Duchess of Cleveland, and had issue,

Edward, *d.* unm.
James, *m.* Sarah, daughter of John Bagshaw, and *d.* in 1711.
Charles, *d.* unm.
George-Henry, successor to his father.
Fitzroy-Henry, *d. s. p.* in 1720.
Robert, who *s.* his nephew.

Charlotte, *m.* to Benedict Calvert, Lord Baltimore.
Anne.
Barbara, *m.* first, to Colonel Lee, and secondly, to Sir George Browne, bart.; by the latter she had a daughter,

Barbara Browne, heir of her father, who *m.* Sir Edward Mostyn, bart. of Talacre.

His lordship, who refused to swear allegiance to the new government at the Revolution, *d.* 14th July, 1716, and was *s.* by his son,

vi. Sir George-Henry Lee, second Earl of Lichfield, who *m.* Frances, daughter of Sir John Hales, of St. Stephens, Tunstall, and Woodchurch, in Kent, and had issue,

George Henry, his successor,
James, *d.* in 1742.
Charles-Henry, *d.* in 1740.

Charlotte, *m.* to Henry, eleventh Viscount Dillon.
Mary, *m.* to Cosmo Neville, esq.
Frances, *d.* unm.
Harriot, *m.* to John, Lord Bellew.
Anne, *m.* to Hugh, fifth Lord Clifford of Chudleigh.

His lordship *d.* 15th February, 1742-3, and was *s.* by his son,

LEE

vii. Sir George Henry Lee, third Earl of Lichfield, chancellor of the university of Oxford, capt. of the band of gentlemen pensioners, and custos brevium of the court of Common Pleas. He *m.* Dina, only daughter and heir of Sir Thomas Frankland, bart. but dying *s. p.* in 1775, was *s.* by his uncle,

viii. Sir Robert Lee, fourth Earl of Lichfield, previously M.P. for the city of Oxford. He *m.* Catherine, daughter of Sir John Stonehouse, of Radley, Berks, but died issueless, in 1776, when all his honours, including the Baronetcy, expired. The estates devolved upon his niece, Charlotte, Viscountess Dillon. Her grandson, Henry Augustus, thirteenth Viscount Dillon, assumed the additional surname and arms of Lee, which are borne by his son and successor, Charles-Henry Dillon-Lee, present [illegible] Viscount Dillon.

The manor of Quarendon was sold by the late Lord Dillon, in 1802, to James Dupré, esq. of Wilton Park.

Arms—Arg. a fesse between three crescents [illegible]

LEE, OF HARTWELL.

Created 16th Aug. 1660. | Extinct in 18[illegible].

Lineage.

This family, supposed to have been a [illegible] branch of the Leghs of Cheshire, settled in B[illegible] the beginning of Henry IV.'s reign.

William Lee, of Moreton, in the parish of [illegible] died in 1486; fourth in descent from him,

Sir Thomas Lee, knt. of Moreton, married E[illegible] daughter and eventually heiress of Michael [illegible]den, esq. of Hartwell, and had no less than twenty-four children. His eldest son and heir,

Thomas Lee, esq. possessed Moreton and Hartwell. He was sheriff of Bucks, 4 Charles I. and married Jane, daughter of Sir George Throckmorton, knt. of Fulbrook, was *s.* at his decease, in 1642, by his son,

Thomas Lee, esq. of Moreton and Hartwell, who married about 1632, Elizabeth, daughter of Sir [illegible] Croke, knt. one of the justices of the King's Bench, by whom (who *m.* secondly, Sir Richard [illegible] K.B.) he had three sons, Thomas, William, George, and a daughter, Mary, the wife of Sir William Morley, knt. of Barecourt. He was *s.* by his eldest son,

i. Thomas Lee, esq. of Hartwell, in the county of Bucks, who was created a Baronet 16th August, 1660. "He was (says Browne Willis, who drew the pedigree of the family) a gentleman of great accomplishments, and at the Restoration, and for several years afterwards, as long as he lived, was returned to serve in parliament, and was much admired for his elegant speeches in the House of Commons [illegible] he was a leader in the debates." He married [illegible] daughter and heir of Sir John Davis, knt. of [illegible]borne, Berks, and by her (who *d.* in 1709) had [illegible]

Thomas, his successor.
John, a captain in the army.
Lyonel.

Mary.
Frances.
Jane.
Anne, *m.* first, to Richard Winkworth, esq. of Maudlins, in Ireland, and secondly, to Captain Nasback.
Martha, *m.* to John Padmore, esq.
Elizabeth, *m.* to Colonel Richard Beck.

He *d.* in February, 1699, and was *s.* by his eldest son,

II. SIR THOMAS LEE, M.P. who *m.* Alice, daughter and heir of Thomas Hopkins, esq. of London, merchant, and had issue,

I. THOMAS, his successor.
II. WILLIAM (Sir), lord chief justice of England, and a privy councillor, *m.* first, Anne, daughter of Mr. Goodwin, of Bury, and had a son,
  WILLIAM, who *m.* Philadelphia, daughter of Sir John Dyke, bart. and dying in 1778, left (with four daughters, Philadelphia; Harriet, wife of John Piott, esq. merchant of London; Louisa, and Sophia), a son,
    WILLIAM, who, in pursuance of the will of Mr. Antonie, of Colworth, in Bedfordshire, took the name of ANTONIE.
  Sir William Lee married secondly, Margaret, relict of Mr. Melmoth, and daughter of Roger Drake, esq. but by that lady had no issue.
III. John, colonel in the Guards, *m.* first, a daughter of Sir Thomas Hardy, knt. and secondly, Mary, daughter of — Browne, esq. of Arlsey, in Bedfordshire; by the latter (who wedded secondly, Colonel Schutz), he had
  Thomas, of Hampton Court, equerry to the Duke of Gloucester.
  John, an ensign in the Foot Guards.
  Colonel Lee *d.* in 1760.
IV. George (Sir), LL.D. a privy councillor, one of the lords of the Admiralty, and treasurer to her royal highness the Princess Dowager of Wales, *m.* Judith, daughter of Humphrey Morice, esq. but dying without issue, 18th December, 1758, left his fortune to his nephew, Sir William Lee, bart.
I. Sarah, *d.* in 1693.

Sir Thomas was *s.* at his decease by his eldest son,

III. SIR THOMAS LEE, M.P. for the county of Bucks, *m.* Elizabeth, daughter and heir of Thomas Sandys, and had issue,

WILLIAM, his heir.
Thomas.
Anne, *m.* to George Vernon, esq. created, in 1762, Lord Vernon, of Kinderton.

He *d.* in December, 1749, and was *s.* by his son,

IV. SIR WILLIAM LEE. This gentleman devoted himself to the improvement of his seat at Hartwell, displaying great taste in his manner of planting and laying out the grounds, and his additions to the mansion-house, the east and south fronts of which he rebuilt; he also rebuilt the parish church, to which his uncles contributed, viz. the Chief Justice £1000, and Sir George Lee £500. He was distinguished by his benevolent attentions to the poor, and having studied the science of medicine, was their gratuitous physician. Sir William *m.* in 1763, Lady Elizabeth Harcourt, daughter of Simon, Earl of Harcourt, and had issue,

WILLIAM, *b.* in 1764, } successive baronets.
GEORGE, *b.* in 1767, }

He *d.* 6th July, 1799, and was *s.* by his elder son,

V. SIR WILLIAM LEE, who adopting a military life, became lieutenant-colonel of the 16th Light Dragoons, in which he served several campaigns in Germany. Exchanging into the 25th Light Dragoons, he went in May, 1800, to join that regiment in Madras, and died there, 7th February, 1801: dying unm. he was *s.* by his brother,

VI. SIR GEORGE LEE, in holy orders, rector of Hartwell, and vicar of Stowe, who *d.* unm. in 1827, when the BARONETCY EXPIRED.

Arms—Az. two bars or, a bend cheque or, and gules.

LEE, OF LANGLEY.

CREATED 3rd May, 1620.

EXTINCT April, 1660.

Lineage.

I. HUMPHREY LEE, esq. of Langley and Acton Burnell, in Shropshire, son of Richard Lee, esq. of Langley, by Eleanor, his wife, daughter of Walter Wrottesley, esq. of Wrottesley, was fourth in descent from Richard Lee, esq. sheriff of the county in 1479, and representative of one of the oldest families in England. In 1620 he was created a BARONET, being the first Shropshire gentleman who received that honour. He *m.* Margaret, daughter of Richard Corbett, esq. of Stoke, one of the judges of the court of King's Bench, and had issue,

RICHARD, his heir.
Margaret, *m.* to Sir Francis Kynaston, knt. of Oteley, in Salop.
Cecilia.
Alice.
Mary.

Sir Humphrey was succeeded by his son,

II. SIR RICHARD LEE, of Langley and Acton Burnell, M.P. for Salop, who suffered much in the royal cause, and had to compound for his estate in the sum of £3719. He *m.* Elizabeth, daughter of Sir Edward Allen, knt. alderman of London, and left at his decease, in April, 1660, issue, to survive him, two daughters, his co-heirs, viz.

RACHAEL, *m.* to Ralph Cleaton, esq. second son of Ralph Cleaton, of Oneley, in Salop; she obtained for her inheritance Lea Hall and the other estates of her ancestors in that neighbourhood, and transmitted them to her descendant in the third generation,
  RICHARD CLEATON, who had two daughters,
    ALATHEA, *m.* to James Apperley, M.D.
    JANE, *m.* to Watkin Williams Wynne, esq. of Voclas, in Denbighshire, whose daughters married, the one the Hon. Charles Finch, and the other, Thomas Assheton Smith, esq. of Tedworth, Hants. Lea Hall and the other estates were sold to Sir Thomas Tyrwhitt Jones, bart.
MARY, *m.* to Edward Smythe, esq. who was created a BARONET, ancestor of the present
  SIR EDWARD SMYTH, bart. of Acton Burnell and Langley.

At the death of Sir Richard Lee the BARONETCY became EXTINCT.

Arms—Gu. a fess componée or and az. between eight billets, four in chief and four in base, arg.

*** A branch of this ancient family, that of Lee of Coton Hall, in Shropshire, which separated at a very early period from the parent stock, still preserves a male succession. (See BURKE'S *Commoners*.)

LEICESTER, OF TABLEY.

CREATED 10th Aug. 1660.

EXTINCT 5th Aug. 1742.

Lineage.

The LEICESTERS, (or LEYCESTERS, as formerly written,) are of great antiquity in the county of Chester, and enjoyed lands there so early as the time of *King* JOHN.

SIR NICHOLAS DE LEICESTER, knt. who *d.* in 1295, *m.* Margaret, daughter of Geffery Dutton,* and acquired thereby the village, manors, and mansion of Nether-Tabley, Wethall, &c. His son and heir,

ROGER LEICESTER, resided at Wethall, and had a grant from Sir John de Grey, son of Reginald de Grey, justice of Chester, of a third part of Over Tabley, cum Ludlow, which places were given to the said Sir John by William de Tabley, Lord of Tabley and Knutsford. This Roger died about the year 1340, and was *s.* by his son,

NICHOLAS LEICESTER, who died in the same year, leaving by his wife, Mary, daughter of William Mobberley, of Mobberley, co-heir of her mother, Maud, and half sister of Sir Ralph Mobberley,

- JOHN, his heir.
- Ralph, who *m.* Joan, daughter and heir of Robert Toft, of Toft, in Cheshire, and died *temp.* RICHARD II. He was ancestor of the LEYCESTERS of Toft Hall, now represented by RALPH LEYCESTER, esq. of Toft Hall; of the LEYCESTERS of Poole, whose heiress, Mary, married Sir Henry Delves, bart.; and of the present GEORGE HANMER LEYCESTER, esq. of White Place, near Maidenhead, Berkshire.

The elder son and heir,

JOHN LEICESTER, served in the French wars in 1373 and 1380, under JOHN *of Gaunt*, and erected the manor hall of Nether Tabley, 4 RICHARD II. He married the next year, Joan, daughter of Robert Touchet, of Nether Whetley, and dying in 1398, was *s.* by his son,

WILLIAM LEICESTER, who is the first of the family styled "de Tabley," but this may be in consequence of the statute of additions, passed in 1 HENRY V.; for, previously to the enactment of that law, few [illegible] written of any place or with the title of [illegible] Certain it is, that this William lived at his [illegible] house of Nether Tabley, which continues to the present time the seat of his descendants. He [illegible] wives, but left issue only by one, Agnes, sister [illegible] Piers Dutton, viz. JOHN, Lawrence, and Jeffery. He *d.* in 1428, and was *s.* by the eldest,

JOHN LEICESTER, esq. of Nether Tabley, who [illegible] 1422, Elizabeth, daughter of Hammon Massey, [illegible] Rixton, in Lancashire, and had six sons, JOHN [illegible] heir; Hammon, parson of Mobberly; Randle; Nicholas; Henry; and William. He *d.* in 1468, and was [illegible] by his eldest son,

JOHN LEICESTER, esq. of Tabley, who *m.* in 14[illegible] Margery, daughter of John Legh, esq. of High Le[illegible] in Westhall, and dying in 1496, was *s.* by his eldest son,

THOMAS LEICESTER, esq. of Nether Tabley, who *m.* Margaret, sixth daughter and co-heir of Robert Grosvenor, esq. of Houlme, near Peover, and so acquir[illegible] a moiety of Nether and Little Peover, and one-thir[illegible] of Over Alderley, with lands in Allostock and [illegible] by this lady he had a son, JOHN, his heir. After [illegible] decease, he married three other wives, by the first [illegible] whom he had two other sons. He *d.* in 1526 and was *s.* by his eldest son,

JOHN LEICESTER, esq. of Tabley. This gentleman *m.* first, in 1479, Lucy, daughter of John Ratcliff [illegible] Ratcliffe, in Lancashire, and had a son, Wal[illegible] who wedded Anne, daughter of Richard S[illegible] Bradwell, in Staffordshire, but died issueless. He (John) *m.* secondly, in 1490, Alice, daughter of [illegible] Henshaw, esq. of Milne House, by Chelford, and by that lady had issue,

- PETER, his heir.
- Richard.
- James, ancestor of the Leicesters of Hal[illegible]
- Laurence.
- Isabel, *m.* to John Ogle, esq. of Ro[illegible]y.

He *d.* in 1543, and was *s.* by his eldest son,

PETER LEICESTER, esq. of Tabley, who married [illegible] daughter of Sir John Holford, of Holford, and [illegible] PETER, his heir; ADAM; William, from whom [illegible] Leicesters of Legh, in Staffordshire; Al[illegible] *m.* [illegible] Geoffery Brereton; and Margaret, *m.* to Richard [illegible] kenhead. He *d.* 8th April, 1577, was buried at [illegible] worth on the 11th, and *s.* by his eldest son.

PETER LEICESTER, esq. of Tabley. This gent[illegible] *m.* Elizabeth, daughter and sole heir of Edward [illegible] wich, esq. of Colwich, in Staffordshire, and died [illegible] July, 1581, leaving three daughters, Alice, *m.* to [illegible] George Leycester, of Toft; Elizabeth, *m.* to [illegible] Legh, esq. of East Hall, in High Legh; and Katherine *m.* to John Ireland, esq. of Hutt; when he was [illegible] his brother,

ADAM LEICESTER, esq. of Tabley, who *m.* [illegible] daughter of Peter Shakerly, esq. of Houlme, [illegible] widow of Thomas Holford, and dying 17th Jan[illegible] was *s.* by his son,

PETER LEICESTER, esq. of Tabley, who *d.* 7th Ma[illegible] 1647, aged fifty-nine, and was buried at Budworth. [illegible] *m.* Elizabeth, daughter of Sir Randle Mainwaring of Over Peover, and had issue,

- PETER, his heir.
- Philip, fellow of Brasenose College, *d.* unm. [illegible]

---

* Jeffery Dutton (writes Sir Peter Leicester, the historian of Cheshire), son of Adam de Dutton, gave Nether Tabley to his daughter Margaret, and her heirs, about the end of the reign of HENRY III. This Margaret first married Robert de Denbigh, and had no issue. Afterwards she married Nicholas de Leicester, by whom she had issue, and to whose succeeding progeny the manor of Nether Tabley still belongeth. He was afterwards [illegible] Sir Nicholas Leicester, knt. so styled in [illegible] seneschal to Henry Lacy, Earl of Lincoln, [illegible] Cheshire. His son Roger's son and heir, [illegible] in 1340, and his son, John Leicester, who served in [illegible] wars of France, under John of Gaunt, in 1373 and [illegible] built the old manor hall of Nether Tabley

Thomas, *b.* in 1620; *d.* unm. in 1652.
Adam, captain in the army.

The eldest son and heir,

I. PETER LEICESTER, esq. of Tabley, *b.* 10th August, 1600, the celebrated antiquary, and historian of Cheshire, who was created a BARONET 10th August, 1660. Sir Peter *m.* 6th November, 1642, Elizabeth, third daughter of Gilbert, second Lord Gerard, of Gerard's Bromley, in Staffordshire, and dying 11th October, 1678, was *s.* by his son,

II. SIR ROBERT LEICESTER, *b.* 11th September, 1643, married 6th June, 1667, Meriel, daughter and heir of Francis Watson, esq. of Church Aston, in Salop, and had surviving issue,

FRANCIS, his successor.

Meriel, *m.* to John Danvers, esq. who after her decease, succeeding his father, became Sir John Danvers, bart.

He *d.* 7th July, 1684, and was *s.* by his son,

III. SIR FRANCIS LEICESTER, *b.* 30th July, 1674, M.P. for Newton, in the county of Lancaster, who *m.* Frances, daughter and sole heir of Joshua Wilson, esq. of Colton, in Yorkshire, and widow of Bryan Thornhill, esq. by whom he had one daughter. He *d.* 5th August, 1742, when the BARONETCY became EXTINCT. His only child and heiress,

MERIEL LEICESTER, *b.* 25th November, 1705, *m.* first, in 1723, Fleetwood Legh, esq. of Bank, and by him who *d.* in 1725, had a daughter,

Anne-Meriel Legh, who *m.* Peter Brooke, esq. of Mere, and *d. s. p.*

She wedded, secondly, Sir John Byrne, bart. of Timogue, in the Queen's County, and was *s.* by her son,

SIR PETER BYRNE, who assumed the name of LEICESTER, and was father of

SIR JOHN FLEMING LEICESTER, created BARON DE TABLEY in 1826. (Refer to BURKE'S *Peerage and Baronetage.*)

Arms—Az. a fesse gu. between three fleurs-de-lis or.

LEIGH, OF STONELEIGH.

CREATED 29th June, 1611.

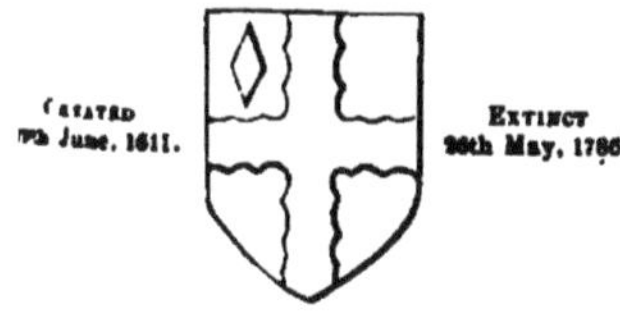

EXTINCT 26th May, 1786.

Lineage.

This was a branch of the great Cheshire family of Legh, founded by

SIR THOMAS LEIGH, knt. lord mayor of London in 1558, first great-grandson of Sir Peter Leigh, knight-banneret, who fell at Agincourt in 1415. Sir Thomas was brought up by Sir Rowland Hill, an opulent merchant and alderman of the same city, and obtained the hand of his favourite niece, Alice Barker, otherwise Coverdale, in marriage, and with her the greater part of his wealth. Sir Thomas received the honour of knighthood during his mayoralty, and dying 17th November, [illegible], was buried in Mercers' Chapel, London. His widow survived him two-and-thirty years; she resided at Stoneleigh, and lived to see her children's children to the fourth generation. She was interred in 1603 at that place, where she had founded an hospital for five poor men and five poor women, all to be unmarried, and to be nominated after her decease by her third son, Sir Thomas Leigh, of Stoneleigh, and his heirs for ever. She had issue by Sir Thomas Leigh,

I. ROWLAND, who was largely provided for at Longborough, in Gloucestershire, by Sir Rowland Hill. From him descended the Leighs of Longborough and Adlestrop, now represented by CHANDOS LEIGH, esq. of Stoneleigh.
II. Richard, *d.* in 1570 *s. p.*
III. THOMAS.
IV. William, of Newnham Regis, in the county of Warwick. (See LEIGH OF NEWNHAM.)

I. Mary, *m.* first, to Richard Cobbe, esq.; and secondly, to Robert Andrews, esq. of London.
II. Alice, *m.* to Thomas Connye, esq. of Basingthorpe, in Lincolnshire.
III. Katherine, *m.* to Edward Barber, serjeant-at-law.
IV. Winifred, *m.* to Sir George Bond, knt. of London.

Sir Thomas's third son,

I. SIR THOMAS LEIGH, of Stoneleigh, in the county of Warwick, received the honour of knighthood from *Queen* ELIZABETH, and was made a BARONET on the institution of the order, 29th June, 1611. He *m.* Catherine, fourth daughter of Sir John Spencer, knt. of Wormleighton, in Warwickshire, and had issue,

JOHN (Sir), *m.* first, Ursula, daughter of Sir Christopher Hoddesdon, knt. lord of the manor of Leighton, in Bedfordshire, and had a son,

THOMAS, heir to his grandfather.

Sir John Leigh *m.* secondly, Anne, eldest daughter of Sir John Cope, bart. of Hanwell, in Oxfordshire, but by her had no issue. He *d.* before his father.

Thomas (Sir), Fernando, } *d. s. p.*

Alice, *m.* to Sir Robert Dudley, knt. She was created Duchess of Dudley for life.

He died 1st February, 1625, and was *s.* by his grandson,

II. SIR THOMAS LEIGH, M.P. for the county of Warwick *temp.* CHARLES I. who, for his zeal in the royal cause, was created in 1643 Baron Leigh, of Stoneleigh. He *m.* Mary, daughter and co-heir of Sir Thomas Egerton, eldest son of the Lord Chancellor Egerton, and had issue,

I. THOMAS (Sir), his heir, who *m.* first, Anne, daughter and sole heir of Richard Bingham, esq. of Lambeth, in Surrey, and had a daughter, Anne, who died young. He *m.* secondly, Jane, daughter of Patrick Fitzmaurice, Lord Kerry, and dying before his father, left

THOMAS, successor to his grandfather.

Honora, *m.* first, to Sir William Egerton; and secondly, to Hugh, Lord Willoughby, of Parham.

Mary, *m.* to Arden Bagot, esq. of Pipe Hall, in the county of Warwick.

Jane, *m.* to William, Viscount Tracy.

II. Charles, of Leighton, who surviving his own children, left his estate to his grandnephew, the Hon. Charles Leigh.

I. Elizabeth, *m.* to John, Lord Tracy.
II. Vere, *m.* to Sir Justinian Isham, bart.
III. Ursula, *m.* to Sir William Bromley, K.B.

His lordship *d.* 22nd February, 1671, and was *s.* by his grandson,

III. SIR THOMAS LEIGH, second Lord Leigh, who *m.*

first, Elizabeth, daughter and heir of Sir Richard Brown, knt. of Shingleton, in Kent, but by her had no issue. He wedded, secondly, the Hon. Eleanor Watson, eldest daughter of Edward, second Lord Rockingham, and granddaughter, maternally, of the unfortunate Earl of Strafford, and by her had

- Edward, his successor.
- Charles, who inherited the estates of his great-uncle, the Hon. Charles Leigh, of Leighton. He *m.* Lady Barbara Lumley, but *d. s. p.* in 1749.
- Anne, *d.* unm. in 1734.
- Eleanor, *m.* to Thomas Verney, esq. and *d.* in 1756.

He *d.* in 1710, and was *s.* by his elder son,

IV. Sir Edward Leigh, third Lord Leigh, who *m.* Mary, daughter and heir of Thomas Holbech, esq. of Fillongley, in the county of Warwick, and heir, through her mother, of Bernard Paulet, esq. by whom he had issue,

- Edward, who *d.* in the lifetime of his father, *anno* 1737.
- Thomas, successor to his father.
- Mary, Eleanor, Anne, } *d.* unm.

His lordship *d.* in March, 1737, and was *s.* by his son,

V. Sir Thomas Leigh, fourth Lord Leigh, who *m.* first, Maria-Rebecca, daughter of the Hon. John Craven, and sister of William, fifth Lord Craven, by whom he had

- Edward, his successor.
- Mary.

He *m.* secondly, Catherine, daughter of Rowland Berkeley, esq. of Cotheridge, in Worcestershire, and had another daughter,

- Anne, *m.* to Andrew Hacket, esq. and died of the small-pox.

His lordship *d.* 30th November, 1749, and was *s.* by his son,

VI. Sir Edward Leigh, fifth Lord Leigh, who died unmarried 26th May, 1786, when all his honours, including the Baronetcy, are presumed to have become extinct. Stoneleigh, at the decease of his lordship, devolved upon his only surviving sister,

The Hon. Mary Leigh; and at her death, 2nd July, 1806, it came to the Rev. Thomas Leigh; and from him passed to his nephew, James-Henry Leigh, esq. of Addlestrop, father of the present (1837)

Chandos Leigh, esq. of Stoneleigh. (Refer to Burke's *Commoners*, vol. iii. p. 223.)

Arms—Gu. a cross ingrailed arg. a lozenge in the dexter chief of the second.

LEIGH, OF NEWNHAM.

Created 24th Dec. 1618.—Extinct 21st Dec. 1653.

Lineage.

William Leigh, esq. of Newnham Regis, in the county of Warwick, fourth son of Sir Thomas Leigh, lord mayor of London at the decease of *Queen* Mary, *m.* Frances, daughter of Sir James Harrington, of Exton, in the county of Rutland, and was *s.* by his son,

Sir Francis Leigh, K. B. who *m.* the Hon. Mary, daughter of Sir Thomas Egerton, Viscount Brackley, Lord Chancellor of England, and left a son and heir,

I. Francis Leigh, esq. of Newnham, who was created a Baronet 24th December, 1618, and raised to the peerage ten years after as Baron Dunsmore. His lordship having subsequently distinguished himself in the cause of royalty during the civil war, was created Earl of Chichester in 1644. He *m.* first, Susan, daughter and heir of Richard Northan, esq. but by her had no issue. He wedded, secondly, Audrey, daughter and co-heir of Sir John Butler, Baron Butler, of Bramfield, and widow of Sir Francis Anderson, and by that lady had

- Elizabeth, *m.* to Thomas Wriothesley, fourth Earl of Southampton.
- Mary, *m.* to George Villiers, Viscount Grandison in the peerage of Ireland.

His lordship *d.* 21st December, 1653, when the earldom of Chichester devolved, according to a special limitation in the patent, upon his son-in-law, Thomas, fourth Earl of Southampton, and the barony of Dunsmore, with the Baronetcy, became extinct.

Arms—As Leigh of Stoneleigh.

LEKE, OF SUTTON.

Created 22nd May, 1611.

Extinct in 1736.

Lineage.

I. Sir Francis Leke, knt. of Sutton,* in the county of Derby, being a gentleman of ancient family and ample fortune, was created a Baronet on the institution of the order, 22nd May, 1611. In thirteen years after he was raised to the peerage, as Baron Deincourt, of Sutton; and taking an active part in favour of the king during the civil war, was made Earl of Scarsdale in 1645. He *m.* Anne, daughter of Sir Edward Carey, knt. of Berkhampstead, in the county of Hertford, and had issue,

- Francis, slain in France.
- Nicholas, his heir.
- Edward, Charles, } fell fighting under the royal standard.
- Anne, *m.* to Henry Hildyard, esq. of Winstead and East Horsley, in Surrey.
- Catherine, *m.* to Cuthbert Morley, esq.
- Elizabeth, Muriel, } *d.* unm.
- Frances, *m.* to Viscount Gormanston.
- Penelope, *m.* to Charles, Lord Lucas.

His lordship felt the execution of his royal master Charles I. so deeply, that he clothed himself in sack

---

* This manor was acquired by the marriage of Richard de Grey (son of William de Grey, of Sandford and Sandiacre, a younger son of Henry de Grey, of Thurrock,) with Lucy, daughter and heir of Robert de Hareston, Lord of Sutton in the Dale; which, with divers other lordships, by issue male failing, came by a female branch to the Hilarys, who took the name of Grey; by a female heir of which line, married to Sir John Leke in the reign of Henry IV. the same came to this family. Burke's *Extinct Peerage*.

cloth, and causing his grave to be dug some years before his death, laid himself therein every Friday for divine meditation and prayer. He *d.* in 1655, and was *s.* by his son,

II. SIR NICHOLAS LEKE, second Earl of Scarsdale, who married Lady Frances Rich, daughter of Robert, second Earl of Warwick, and had issue,

- ROBERT, his successor.
- Richard, *m.* Mary, daughter of Sir John Molyneux, bart. and had
  - NICHOLAS, successor to his uncle.
  - Robert, *d.* young.
  - Frances.
  - Lucy.
- Mary.

His lordship *d.* in 1680, and was *s.* by his elder son,

III. SIR ROBERT LEKE, third Earl of Scarsdale, who wedded Mary, daughter and co-heir of Sir John Lewis, of Ledstone, in the county of York, but had no surviving issue. His lordship, *temp.* JAMES II. was lord-lieutenant of Derbyshire, colonel of horse, and groom of the stole to *Prince* GEORGE *of Denmark*. He died in 1707, and was *s.* by his nephew,

IV. SIR NICHOLAS LEKE, fourth Earl of Scarsdale, who died unmarried in 1736, when all his honours, including the BARONETCY, became EXTINCT.

Arms—Arg. on a saltier engrailed sa. nine annulets or.

LEKE, OF NEWARK-UPON-TRENT.

CREATED 15th Dec. 1663.—EXTINCT about 1682.

Lineage.

I. SIR FRANCIS LEKE, of Newark-upon-Trent, in the county of Nottingham, governor of the Block House at Gravesend, was created a BARONET 15th December, 1663. He married Frances, daughter of Sir William Thorold, knt. but died without male issue about 1682, when the BARONETCY became EXTINCT.

Arms—As LEKE OF SUTTON.

LEMAN, OF NORTHAW.

CREATED 3d Mar. 1664-5.

EXTINCT in 1762.

Lineage.

The first upon record of this family,

JOHN LEMAN, of Gillingham, in Norfolk, and of Beccles, in Suffolk, left two sons and two daughters, viz.

- WILLIAM, his heir.
- JOHN (Sir), sheriff of London in 1606 and lord mayor in 1616. Sir John Leman acquired an estate of £4000 per annum. He bought the manor of Warboys, in Huntingdonshire, from Sir Oliver Cromwell. He also purchased lands in Framlingham and other parts of Suffolk, and left a great portion of his property to his nephew, William Leman, esq. He *d.* 26th March, 1632, and was buried in St. Michael's, Crooked Lane, London, on the south side of the chancel.
- Margaret, *m.* to — Collin.
- Anne, *m.* to Richard Barber, of Shadbrooke, Suffolk.

The elder son,

WILLIAM LEMAN, esq. of Beccles, *m.* Alice, daughter of — Bourne, of Norwich, and had five sons,

I. JOHN, of Beccles and Otley, ancestor of the Lemans of Charsfield, Winhaston, Weston, and Parham.

II. Robert, of Ipswich, buried in St. Stephen's Church there, left two daughters, his co-heirs,
- MARY, *m.* to Richard Bennet, esq. of Kew, in Surrey, brother of Sir Richard Bennet, bart. of Babraham, in Cambridgeshire, and had a daughter,
  - MARY BENNET, *m.* to Sir Henry Capel, K.B. created BARON CAPEL, of Tewkesbury, and *d. s. p.*
- ALICE, *m.* first, to Thomas Barker, esq. of Fresingfield, in Suffolk; and secondly, to Charles Goring, second Earl of Norwich, but *d.* issueless.

III. Thomas, of Gillingham, who *m.* Margaret, dau. of John Smith, esq. of Laxfield, in Suffolk, and had a son and two daughters,
- John, of Bruens Hall, in Suffolk, who *m.* Anne, daughter of Thomas Weld, esq. of Windham, in Norfolk, and left issue.
- Margaret, *m.* to Thomas Smith, gent. of Walsoken, in Norfolk.
- Alice, *m.* to John Parker, of Wickham Market, in Suffolk.

IV. WILLIAM, of whom presently.

V. Philip, of Thames Ditton, in Surrey.

The fourth son,

WILLIAM LEMAN, of London, woollen draper, and heir to the chief part of his uncle, Alderman Sir John Leman's wealth, purchased the manor of Northaw, in Hertfordshire, from William Sidley, esq. In 1634 he served the office of sheriff for that county, and was elected to parliament by the borough of Hertford in 1645. He *m.* Rebecca, daughter and co-heir of Edward Prescot, of Thoby, in Essex, and of London, salter, by whom he had issue,

I. WILLIAM, his heir.

II. John, *m.* Elizabeth, daughter of Mr. Haley, of Edgeworthbury, in Middlesex, and had two daughters,
- Elizabeth.
- Anne.

III. Thomas, of London, draper, *m.* Mary, daughter of Mr. Hickford, of London, and had
- Hickford, aged nineteen in 1695.
- Robert, aged eighteen in 1695, a student at Trinity College, Cambridge.
- Rebecca.

IV. Edward, of Fenchurch Street, London, merchant, in 1695, *m.* Mary, daughter of Sir Thomas Holt, knt. serjeant-at-law, and had
- Edward, aged nine in 1695.
- Susanna-Maria.

V. James, *d.* unm.

VI. Philip, in holy orders, rector of Warboys, in Huntingdonshire, *m.* Catherine, daughter of Richard Carter, gent. of Colne, in the same county, and had issue.

VII. Tanfeild, barrister-at-law, died 16th January, 1704.

I. Rebecca, *m.* to Tanfeild Vachel, esq. of Coley, in Berkshire.

II. Ellen, *m.* to James Wainwright, of London

III. Martha, *m.* to Richard Harrison, gent. of Hadley, in Hertfordshire.
IV. Mary, *m.* to Thomas Overman, gent. of Southwark.
V. Priscilla, *d.* unm.
VI. Elizabeth, *m.* to James Winstanley, of London.
VII. Alice, *m.* to John Jennings, gent. of London.
VIII. Anne, *d.* unm.

The eldest son and heir,

I. WILLIAM LEMAN, esq. of Northaw, was created a BARONET by *King* CHARLES II. 3rd March, 1664-5. Sir William was high sheriff of Hertfordshire 28 CHARLES II. and representative in parliament for Hertford 2 WILLIAM and MARY, 1690. He *m.* in 1655, Mary, daughter of Sir Lewis Mansell, bart. of Margam, in Glamorganshire,* and had issue,

MANSELL, who died in his father's lifetime, 13th March, 1687, leaving by Lucy, daughter of Richard Aley, esq. alderman of London,
WILLIAM, heir to his grandfather.
Lucy, died in 1745.
Robert.
Mary, *m.* to Peter Pheasant, esq. of Upwood, in Huntingdonshire.
Rebecca, *d.* in 1695.
Elizabeth, *m.* to Henry, son of Alderman Aley.
Lucy, *m.* to John Wolf, of London, merchant.
Theodosia, *m.* to Lewis Newnham, esq. of London and Sussex.
Sarah, *m.* in 1697, to Sir George Hutchins, who had been one of the commissioners of the great seal, and died in 1700.

He died at his house at Northaw 18th July, 1701, and was *s.* by his grandson,

II. SIR WILLIAM LEMAN, who *m.* Anna-Margaretta, one of the daughters of Colonel Brett by the Countess of Macclesfield,† and *d. s. p.* 22nd December, 1741. He was *s.* by his cousin,

III. SIR TANFEILD LEMAN, who *d.* in Southwark *anno* 1762, when the BARONETCY is presumed to have EXPIRED. The estate of Northaw passed, on the death of Lucy, sister of the second baronet, to her cousin, Richard Aley, esq.; and after being enjoyed by John Granger, esq. and William Strode, esq. was sold to Patrick Thompson, esq. of Turnham Green, Middlesex.

Arms—Az. a fesse between three dolphins naiant embowed arg.

LENNARD, OF WEST WICKHAM.

CREATED 15th Aug. 1642. EXTINCT 8th Oct. 1727.

Lineage.

GEORGE LENNARD, esq. was father of

JOHN LENNARD, esq. of Chepsted, who *m.* Anne, daughter and heir of John Bird, of Middlesex, and had a son and heir,

JOHN LENNARD, esq. of Chevening, in Kent, who, by Catherine, daughter of Thomas Weston, of Chepsted, had issue,

JOHN LENNARD, esq. of Knol and Chevening, who was custos brevium in the reign of ELIZABETH, and purchased from Sir William Heydon, knt. the manor of West Wickham, Kent. He *m.* Elizabeth, daughter of William Harman, of Crayford, and had three sons

I. SAMPSON, who *m.* MARGARET FIENES, sister and heir of George Fienes, tenth Lord Dacre, and thus acquired the estate of Herstmonceux, in Sussex. On the death of her brother, Mrs. Lennard claimed the barony of Dacre, and her claim being admitted in 1604, she became BARONESS DACRE. They had issue,
HENRY LENNARD, twelfth Lord Dacre. His great-grandson,
THOMAS LENNARD, fifteenth Lord Dacre, was created in 1674 Earl of Sussex, but dying without male issue in 1741 that dignity expired, and the barony of Dacre devolved eventually upon his daughter,
LADY ANNE BARRET LENNARD. (See BURKE'S *Peerage.*)
II. Timothy, whose line failed.
III. SAMUEL (Sir).

The youngest son,

SIR SAMUEL LENNARD, knt. of West Wickham, in Kent, *b.* in 1553; *m.* Elizabeth, daughter of Sir Stephen Slany, knt. alderman of London; and was *s.* in 1618 by his son,

I. STEPHEN LENNARD, esq. of West Wickham, who was created a BARONET 15th August, 1642. Sir Stephen *m.* first, Catherine, daughter of Richard Hale, esq. of Clatry, in Essex, and by her had a daughter,

Elizabeth, *m.* to John Holmden, esq. of Surrey.

He *m.* secondly, Anne, daughter of Sir Morton Lambert, of Greenwich, by whom he had a son, Samuel, who *d.* young. He wedded, thirdly, Anne, daughter of Sir John Oglander, knt. and by that lady had

STEPHEN, his successor.
Francis, *d.* unm.
Christian, *m.* to Sir Thomas Stanley, bart. Alderley, in Cheshire.

Sir Stephen was *s.* at his decease by his son,

II. SIR STEPHEN LENNARD, M.P. for Kent temp. Queen ANNE, who *m.* Elizabeth, daughter of Delalynd Hussey, esq. of Thomson, in Dorsetshire, and had issue,

SAMUEL, his successor.
ANNE, *m.* to Nicholas Carew, esq. of Beddington, in Surrey.
ELIZABETH, *m.* to Sir John Leigh, knt. of Addington, in Surrey.
DOROTHY, *d.* unm.

He *d.* 15th December, 1709, and was succeeded by his son,

III. SIR SAMUEL LENNARD, lieutenant-colonel of the 2nd troop of Horse Guards and M.P. for Hythe, who died unmarried 8th October, 1727, when the BARONETCY EXPIRED. West Wickham is now the property and residence of SIR CHARLES-FRANCIS FARNABY, bart.

Arms—Or, on a fesse gu. three fleurs-de-lis of the first, a crescent for difference.

* By his third wife, Lady Elizabeth Montague, daughter of Henry, Earl of Manchester.

† First wife of Charles Gerard, second Earl of Macclesfield, from whom he separated; she was daughter of Sir Richard Mason, knt. of Shropshire.

L'ESTRANGE, OF HUNSTANTON.

CREATED 1st June, 1629.

EXTINCT 2nd Sept. 1760.

Lineage.

The first mention we find of this family is by Sir William Dugdale, thus: "At a great just or turnament held at Castle Peverel, in the Peak of Derbyshire, where, among divers other persons of note, [illegible], Prince of Wales, and a son of the King of Scots, were present; there were also two sons of the Duke of Brettaign, and that the youngest of them, [illegible], was called Guy L'Estrange, from whom the several families of the L'Estranges do descend."

HAMON L'ESTRANGE, who obtained, *temp.* EDWARD [illegible] Hunstanton,* in Norfolk, by gift of his brother, John L'Estrange, sixth Baron Strange, of Knockyn, [illegible] Margaret, daughter of Ralph Vernon, and was *s.* by his son,

HAMON L'ESTRANGE, of Hunstanton, who *m.* Catharine, daughter and heir of John, Lord Camois, and [ha]d issue,

SIR JOHN L'ESTRANGE, knt. who *m.* Eleanor, daughter and heir of Sir Richard Walkefare, knt. and dying [illegible], was *s.* by his son,

JOHN L'ESTRANGE, esq. who espoused Alice, daughter and heir of Nicholas Beaumont, and was *s.* by his [illegible]

HENRY L'ESTRANGE, esq. who *m.* Catherine, daughter of Roger Drury, esq. of Halsted, in Suffolk, and dying in 1485, was *s.* by his son,

SIR ROGER L'ESTRANGE, of Hunstanton, esquire of the body to HENRY VII. who *m.* Anne, daughter of Sir Christopher Heydon, knt. and dying *s. p.* in 1506, was *s.* by his brother,

SIR ROBERT L'ESTRANGE, of Hunstanton, who *m.* [illegible], daughter and co-heir of Thomas, son of Sir Thomas L'Estrange, of Wellisborn, in Warwickshire, and [illegible] who *m.* secondly, Sir Edward Knyvet,) left [at his] decease in 1511 a son and successor,

SIR THOMAS L'ESTRANGE, high sheriff of Norfolk in [illegible], who *m.* Anne, daughter of Nicholas, Lord Vaux, [and] had sixteen children; of whom NICHOLAS, the [eld]est, succeeded at Hunstanton; and RICHARD, settling in Ireland, was ancestor of the L'ESTRANGES of [Moys]town, in the King's County, now represented by [HENRY] PAISLEY L'ESTRANGE, esq. of Moystown, lieutenant colonel of the King's County militia. Sir Thomas L'Estrange died *temp.* HENRY VIII. and was *s.* by his son,

SIR NICHOLAS L'ESTRANGE, of Hunstanton, knighted in Ireland, *m.* Ellen, daughter of Sir William Fitzwilliam, of Milton, in Northamptonshire, and dying in 1579, was *s.* by his son,

HAMON L'ESTRANGE, esq. who left by his wife, Elizabeth, daughter and heir of Sir Hugh Hastings, knt. of Gressinhall† and Elsing, in Norfolk, a son and heir,

SIR NICHOLAS L'ESTRANGE, knt. M.P. for Norfolk 1 EDWARD VI. who married two wives: by the second, Anne, daughter of Sir William Paston, of Paston, relict of Sir George Chaworth, he had no issue; but by the first, Mary, daughter of Sir Robert Bell, knt. of Beaupre Hall, in Norfolk, lord chief baron of the Exchequer, was father of

SIR HAMON L'ESTRANGE, knt. of Hunstanton, who *m.* Alice, daughter and co-heir of Richard Stubbe, esq.‡ of Sedgeford, in Norfolk, and had (with a daughter, Elizabeth, the wife of Sir William Spring, of Pakenham,) three sons, viz.

I. NICHOLAS, his successor.
II. Hamon, of Pakenham, in Suffolk, left issue.
III. ROGER (Sir), who became so celebrated. He was born about the year 1617, and having in 1644 obtained a commission from *King* CHARLES I. for reducing Lynn, in Norfolk, then in possession of the parliament; the design was discovered to Colonel Walton, the governor, and L'Estrange made prisoner. He was immediately after tried by a court martial at Guildhall, in London, and condemned to death as a spy, but was reprieved, and continued in Newgate for several years. At length, with his keeper's privity, he made his escape, and got beyond sea with much difficulty. In 1653 he returned to England upon the dissolution of the Long Parliament, and advertised the council, then sitting at Whitehall, "that finding himself within the act of indemnity, he thought it convenient to give them notice thereof." He was subsequently, after a good deal of trouble, fully discharged on giving two thousand pounds bail. Lord Clarendon calls him "a man of good wit, and a fancy very luxuriant, and of an enterprising nature." After the Restoration he wrote many books, pamphlets, and papers, and his observations made a considerable impression. He was afterwards knighted, and served in the parliament called by *King* JAMES II. in 1685, for Winchester. He was continued licenser of the press until *King* WILLIAM'S accession, when he experienced some annoyance, being considered a disaffected person. He went to his grave, however, in peace, although he had survived his intellect. Of his works Mr. Winstanley says, "those who shall consider the number and greatness of his books, will admire he should ever write so many; and those who have read them, considering the style and method they are written in, will more admire he should write so well." He *d.* 11th December, 1704,§ in the eighty-eighth year of

---

* CAMDEN, speaking of Hunstanton, says: "It is the [illegible] where *King* EDMUND resided near a whole year, [illegible] learning to get by heart *David's Psalms* in the Saxon [illegible]. The very book was religiously preserved by [illegible] of St. Edmund'sbury till the dissolution of [illegible]. But neither is the place to be omitted [illegible] account, that it has been the seat of the famous [illegible] L'Estrange, knights, ever since John, Baron Strange of Knockyn, bestowed it upon his younger [illegible] Hamon, which was in the reign of EDWARD II."

† [illegible] Elizabeth, daughter and co-heir of Hugh Hast[ings], Gressenhall came to Hamon L'Estrange; and by Anne, the other daughter and co-heir, Elsing to William Brown, brother of Anthony, first Viscount Montagu, her husband.

‡ The other daughter and co-heir of Richard Stubbe, DIONISIA, *m.* Sir William Yelverton, bart. of Rougham, in Norfolk.

§ STOW, in his Survey, says: "Upon the middle pillar on the north side of St. Giles's in the Fields, Middlesex, is this inscription:

Sir Roger L'Estrange, knt. born the 17 Dec. 1616,
Dyed 11 Dec. 1704."

his age, leaving no issue by Anne, his wife, daughter of Sir Thomas Doleman, knt.

Sir Hamon *d.* in 1654; Alice, his wife, in 1656. He was *s.* by his eldest son,

I. Nicholas L'Estrange, esq. of Hunstanton, who was created a Baronet by *King* Charles I. 1st June, 1629. Sir Nicholas married Anne, daughter of Sir Edward Lewkenor, knt. of Denham, in Suffolk, and had issue,

- I. Nicholas, his heir.
- II. John, of Gressinhall, *m.* Dorothy, daughter of Hamon L'Estrange, esq. of Barton Mere, in Suffolk, and left issue.
- III. Roger, of Hoo, in Norfolk, who had three wives. He *d.* in October, 1706, aged sixty-three, and was buried at Hoo, leaving issue only by his second wife, Susan, daughter and co-heir of Francis Laud, gent. of Thuxton, viz.
  - Lewkenor.
  - Roger.
  - John.
  - Hellen.
- IV. Edward, of Horsted, in Suffolk, left issue.
- V. William, of Mileham, in the same county.
- VI. Thomas, rector of Brisley, in Norfolk.
- VII. Charles.

He *d.* in 1656, his widow in 1663, and was *s.* by his eldest son,

II. Sir Nicholas L'Estrange, who *m.* first, Mary, daughter of John Coke, esq. of Holkham, in Norfolk, and had one surviving son,

Nicholas, his successor.

He *m.* secondly, Elizabeth, daughter of Sir Justinian Isham, bart. of Lamport, in Northamptonshire, and by that lady had

Charles, *d.* unm.
Thomas, *m.* a daughter of — Dunwell, esq.

Elizabeth, *m.* to Robert Tash, esq.
Jane, *m.* to William Barnesly, esq. of the Inner Temple, and *d.* 22nd November, 1734.

Sir Nicholas died in 1669, and was succeeded by his eldest son,

III. Sir Nicholas L'Estrange, who *m.* Anne, dau. of Sir Thomas Wodehouse, knt. of Kimberley Hall, in Norfolk, and had three sons and two daughters, viz.

Hamon, who *d.* unm. on his travels.
Thomas, } Henry, } fourth and fifth baronets.

Armine, *m.* to Nicholas Styleman, esq. of Snettisham, in Norfolk.
Lucy, *m.* in 1721, to Sir Jacob Astley, bart. of Melton Constable, and was mother of Sir Edward Astley, bart. She *d.* 25th July, 1739.

Sir Nicholas *d.* in 1725, his widow in 1727; he was *s.* by his son,

IV. Sir Thomas L'Estrange. This gentleman *m.* Anne, daughter and at length sole heir of Sir Christopher Calthorpe, K.B. of East Barsham, in Norfolk, but died without issue in 1751, and was *s.* by his brother,

V. Sir Henry L'Estrange, who *m.* Mary, daughter of the Right Hon. Roger North, of Rougham, but died issueless 2nd September, 1760, when the Baronetcy expired.

Arms—Gu. two lioncels passant guardant arg. Anciently, over all a bend az. for difference.

LEVENTHORPE, OF SHINGEY HALL

Created 30th May, 1622.

Extinct 30th Aug. [illegible]

Lineage.

I. Sir John Leventhorpe, knt. of Sawbridgeworth, Herts (son of Edward Leventhorpe, esq. of Shingey Hall, in the same county, by Mary, his wife, [illegible] daughter of Sir Henry Parker, and lineally descended from John Leventhorpe, esq. who, coming from Leventhorpe Hall, in Yorkshire, settled in the county of Hertford and represented that shire in parliament), served as sheriff of Herts in 1607, and was created a Baronet 30th May, 1622. He *m.* Joan, eldest daughter of Sir John Brograve, knt. of Hamells, attorney general of the duchy of Lancaster, and by her, who died in 1628, had issue six sons and seven daughters. Of the latter, the eldest, Joan, *m.* Sir Edward [illegible] of Mark Hall, Essex; and the second, Bridget, became the wife of Sir John Fowle, of Kent. Of the sons, the eldest surviving,

II. Sir Thomas Leventhorpe, succeeded as second baronet upon the demise of his father 25th September, 1625. This gentleman *m.* Dorothy, daughter of Sir Giles Alington, knt. of Horseheath, in Cambridgeshire, and by her (who *m.* secondly, [illegible] of Hertfordshire,) had issue,

John, } Thomas, } successive baronets.

Dorothy, *d.* in 1639.
Bridget, *b.* in 1627.
Joan, *m.* 26th June, 1682, to Charles Caesar, esq. of Much Hadham.

Sir Thomas died 30th April, 1636, and was *s.* by his son,

III. Sir John Leventhorpe, baptised 30th July [illegible] at whose decease, unmarried, of the small-pox, 25th November, 1649, the Baronetcy devolved on his brother,

IV. Sir Thomas Leventhorpe, born 30th November, 1635, who *m.* 2nd January, 1654-5, Mary, daughter of Sir Capel Bedell, bart. of Hamerton, in Huntingdonshire, and by her (who died in London [illegible] 1683) had an only daughter and heir,

Mary, *m.* 15th June, 1672, to John Coke, esq. of Melbourne, in Derbyshire, and had issue.

Sir Thomas was killed by a kick from a horse at Elvaston, in Derbyshire, 27th July, 1679, and was *s.* by his uncle,

V. The Rev. Sir Charles Leventhorpe, rector of White Roding, in Essex, baptised 13th September, 1594, at whose decease unmarried 30th August, [illegible] the Baronetcy became extinct. The manor of Shingey Hall was sold by Sir Thomas's grandson, Thomas Coke, esq. to Ralph Freman, esq. of Hamels, from whom it was purchased by Edward Gardiner, esq.

Arms—Arg. a bend gobonée gu. and sa.

LEWIS, OF LLANGORSE.

Created 14th September, 1627.—Extinct in 1672.

Lineage.

Lodowick Lewis, descended from Lewis of Ffrwdgrech, became, in right of his wife, one of the daughters and co-heirs of William Watkins, esq. possessed of the Llangorse estate, in the county of Brecon. His son and successor,

I. William Lewis, esq. of Llangorse, M.P. for Breconshire in 1660, was created a Baronet 14th September, 1627, and resided principally at Borden, in Hants. He *d.* in 1672 (when the Baronetcy became extinct), having had an only son,

Lodowick, who *d. v. p.* leaving three daughters, from one of whom, Elizabeth, sprang

Lewis Pryse, esq. who inherited the Gogerddan estate, and was father of

Margaret Pryse, the wife of Edward Loveden Loveden, esq. of Buscot Park, Berks, who, in conjunction with his son, the present Pryse Pryse, esq. of Gogerddan, sold in 1806 the greatest part of the Llangorse property.

LEWYS, OF LEDSTON.

Created 15th Oct. 1660. Extinct in 1671.

Lineage.

John Lewys, esq. of Marre, barrister-at-law, recorder of Doncaster, &c. son of Robert Lewys, of Marre, the descendant of an ancient Welsh family, married Mary, daughter of Lionel Reresby, esq. of Thrybergh, and dying 17th October, 31 Elizabeth, left a son,

Thomas, of Marre, treasurer for lame soldiers in the West Riding of Yorkshire, *m.* Jane, daughter of Edmond Munday, esq. and left at his decease 20 James I.

Thomas, *d. s. p.* His widow, Elizabeth, daughter and co-heir of Thomas Talbot, esq. of Bashall, *m.* secondly, Theobald, Viscount Bourke, of Mayo.

Francis, *d. s. p.*

Mary, *m.* to Thomas, son of Sir William Chaytor.

Richard, of whom presently.

Margaret, *m.* to J. Mauleverer, esq.

[illegible]en, *m.* to John Ramsden, esq.

[illegible]h, *m.* to Timothy Bright, esq.

Mary, *m.* to Richard Horsfall, esq.

The second son,

Richard Lewys, esq. married Jane, eldest daughter and co-heir of Gervase Brinsley, esq. of Brinsley, and dying in 1661, left, with other issue, a son,

I. Sir John Lewys, of Ledston, who was created a Baronet in 1660. He *m.* Sarah, third daughter and co-heir of Sir Thomas Foot, lord mayor of London in 1649, and by her, who wedded, secondly, Denzil Onslow, esq. had two daughters, his co-heirs, viz.

Elizabeth, *m.* to Theophilus, Earl of Huntingdon.

Mary, *m.* to Robert, Lord Deincourt, son and heir of Nicholas, Earl of Scarsdale.

Sir John died in 1671, when the Baronetcy became extinct.

Arms—Sa. a chev. between three trefoils or.

LEY, OF WESTBURY.

Created 20th July, 1619. Extinct in 1679.

Lineage.

I. Sir James Ley, knt. a younger son of Henry Ley, esq. of Treffont Ewias, in the county of Wilts, having attained great eminence at the bar, was made serjeant-at-law, 1 James I. and the next year constituted chief justice of the Court of King's Bench in Ireland. In fifteen years afterwards, residing then at Westbury, in Wiltshire, he was created a Baronet 20th July, 1619, having some time previously received the honour of knighthood. In 1622 he was appointed lord treasurer, and the same year created Baron Ley. On the accession of Charles I. his lordship was made Earl of Marlborough, and soon after appointed president of the council. He *m.* first, Mary, daughter of John Pettey, esq. of Stoke Talmage, in the county of Oxford, and had issue,

Henry, his heir.

James, *d.* in 1618 unm.

William, successor to his nephew.

Elizabeth, *m.* to Morice Carant, esq. of Tooner, in Somersetshire.

Anne, *m.* to Sir Walter Long, of Draycot, Wilts, M.P. for Wilts.

Mary, *m.* to Richard Erisey, esq. of Erisey, in Cornwall.

Dionysia, *m.* to John Harington, esq. of Somersetshire.

Margaret, *m.* to — Hobson, esq. of Hertfordshire.

Esther, *m.* to Arthur Fuller, esq. of Bradfield, in the county of Hertford.

Martha, *d.* unm.

Phœbe, *m.* to — Biggs, esq. of Sturst, Berks.

His lordship *m.* secondly, Mary, widow of Sir William Bower, knt.; and thirdly, Jane, daughter of John, Lord Butler, of Bramfield, but had no other issue. He* died in 1628, and was *s.* by his eldest son,

II. Sir Henry Ley, second Earl of Marlborough, who *m.* Mary, daughter of Sir Arthur Capel, knt. of

* His lordship was esteemed a person of great talents and integrity, and left behind him several learned works in law and history.

Hadham, in Hertfordshire, by whom he had a daughter, Elizabeth, who *d.* unmarried, and a son, his successor at his decease about the year 1638,

III. SIR JAMES LEY, third Earl of Marlborough. This nobleman, a naval officer and eminent mathematician and navigator, was constituted lord admiral of all his majesty's ships at Dartmouth and parts adjacent. In 1662 he was employed in the American plantations; but in 1665, commanding "that huge ship, called the Old James, in that great fight at sea with the Dutch upon the 23rd June, was there slain by a cannon-bullet." He died unmarried, and the honours reverted on his lordship's decease to his uncle,

IV. SIR WILLIAM LEY, fourth Earl of Marlborough, who *m.* Margaret, daughter of Sir William Hewyt, knt. of Beccles, in Norfolk, but died issueless in 1679, when all his honours, including the BARONETCY, EXPIRED.

Arms—Arg. a chevron between three seals' heads couped sa.

LIPPINCOTT, OF STOKE BISHOP.

CREATED 7th Sept. 1778.

EXTINCT 23rd Aug. 1829.

Lineage.

GEORGE LIPPINCOTT, esq. of Sydbury, in Devonshire, was father of

THOMAS LIPPINCOTT, esq. bapt. 1st February, 1572, of Pynhill, in the parish of Sydbury aforesaid, who *m.* 15th July, 1605, Elizabeth ———, and had issue,

- THOMAS, of Culmstock, in Devon, who *m.* Dorothy Baker, and had a numerous family.
- HENRY, of whom presently.
- John, *m.* Mary Bartlett.
- Walter, bapt. at Sydbury, 22nd August, 1619, buried May, 1682. He left issue.

The second son,

HENRY LIPPINCOTT, esq. of Almshayne, in the county of Devon, bapt. at Sydbury, 7th January, 1613, *m.* about the year 1670, Rebecca, daughter of — Mills, of Uffculm, and was *s.* by his only surviving son,

HENRY LIPPINCOTT, esq. who *m.* Mary, daughter of Timothy Peperell, of Culmstock, and by her, who *d.* in 1752, had issue,

- HENRY, his heir.
- Rebecca, bapt. 13th September, 1733.
- Elizabeth, bapt. 6th June, 1735, *d.* in 1762.

He *d.* in 1745, and was *s.* by his son,

I. HENRY LIPPINCOTT, esq. of Stoke Bishop, in the county of Gloucester, a merchant at Bristol, and sheriff of that city in 1769, who was created a BARONET 7th September, 1778. Sir Henry *m.* Catherine, daughter and heir of Charles Jefferies, esq. (by Anne his wife, only daughter of Sir William Cann, bart. and eventually heiress of her brother Sir Robert Cann, and had an only child,

II. SIR HENRY CANN LIPPINCOTT, who *d.* issueless. 23rd August, 1829, when the BARONETCY EXPIRED.

Arms—Quarterly; first and fourth, per fesse, counter embattled, gules and sable, three talbots statant, guardant argent, two and one; second and third sa. a chevron argent, between three mermaids, ppr. crined and combed or.

LITTLETON, OF PILLATON HALL.

CREATED 28th June, 1627.

EXTINCT 18th May, 1812.

Lineage.

By an ancient pedigree in the College of Arms it appears that the family of LITTLETON, or LYTTLETON, was settled at Frankley, in Worcestershire, about 1235,* when it is recorded that

THOMAS DE LYTTLETON, *m.* Emma de Frankley, an heiress, lady of the manor of Frankley, but whether he was a stranger in the county, or resided in the town of South Lyttleton, in the Vale of Evesham, as there is reason to think he did, is a matter of doubt; they had an only daughter, EMMA, who *m.* first, Augerus de Tatlington, of Tredington, in the same county, and secondly, Nicholas Whetamstede. She was a benefactress to the Abbey of Halesowen, in Shropshire, and *d.* in 1298. Thomas Lyttleton *m.* secondly, Asceline, daughter and heir of William Fitz Warin, esq. of Upton, one of the justices itinerant and judge of the Common Pleas, 12 HENRY II. and next year sheriff of Worcestershire, by that lady he had three sons, EDMUND, THOMAS, and John. The eldest,

EDMUND DE LYTTLETON, *m.* Lucia de Boys, but having no issue, was *s.* by his brother,

THOMAS DE LYTTLETON, who resided at his manor of Coulesdon, in Upper Snodsbury, and had lands at Newenton, (vulgo Naunton Beauchamp) in the county of Worcester. In the 9th EDWARD II. he was elected knight of the shire for Worcester. He *m.* Lucia de Bois, or Atwood, of a considerable family at Wolverley, in that county, and was *s.* by his son,

THOMAS DE LYTTLETON, who *m.* Julian, daughter of Robert de Somery, and had two sons, John, the younger, was appointed commissioner of array, with other, the chief gentlemen of the county of Worcester, 1 HENRY IV. on a rumour of foreign invasion. He *m.* Beatrix Preschevel, of a noble family in the county of Warwick, by whom he had an only daughter, the wife of Jeffery Frere, esq. The elder son,

THOMAS DE LUTTELTON,† recovered, by a writ of right, the manor of Frankley, on failure of issue of his cousin, Thomas de Tatlington. He was esquire of the body to HENRY IV. and HENRY V. and had an an-

* SELDEN was possessed of two grants of lands to the monastery of Evesham, in 7 HENRY II. 1161, to both of which John de Lyttleton was witness. This is the most ancient that the name of Lyttelton is to be met with, and as the land so given, was at Lench, near South-Lyttelton, it is probable, this John was ancestor to Lyttelton of Frankley.

† Thomas thus spelled the name, and sealed with the chevron between three escallops, as used by his posterity.

pensions granted him by both kings out of the fee farm rents of Worcester, *pro bono et gratuito servicio*, as expressed in the grants. He took to wife, Maud, daughter and heir of Richard Quartermain, of a large estate at Ricote and North Weston, in Oxfordshire, by Joan his wife, daughter and heir of Grey, of Rotherfield, and had an only daughter and heiress,

ELIZABETH, who *m.* THOMAS WESTCOTE, esq. but previously to her marriage, insisted that her husband should take the name of LYTTLETON.

He (Thomas) *d.* about the year 1431. Maud, his wife, surviving him, holding Frankley in dower or jointure, married secondly, John Massey, esq. His son-in-law,

THOMAS WESTCOTE, alias LYTTLETON, was escheator of Worcestershire, 29th HENRY VI. and died in that reign, leaving by the heiress of Littleton, who wedded, secondly, Thomas Hewster, esq. of Lichfield, (with four daughters, of whom Anne, *m.* Thomas Porter, esq. of Barston, in Warwickshire) four sons, viz.

- I. THOMAS, his heir.
- II. Nicholas, } who both retained their paternal surname of WESTCOTE, though often solicited by their mother to call themselves LYTTLETON: she once expostulating with them, whether they thought better of themselves than their elder brother, they answered, that he had a fair estate to alter his name, and if they might share with him, they would do the like. NICHOLAS *m.* Agnes, daughter and heir of Edmund Vernon, of Staffordshire, and was ancestor of the Westcotes of that county. GUY wedded Greenevill, of Gloucestershire, and from him the Westcotes of Devon and Somerset.
- III. Guy, }
- IV. Edmund, *d.* unm.

The eldest son and heir,

SIR THOMAS LYTTLETON, K B. became one of the great law luminaries of his country, and is immortalized by one work alone, his celebrated "TREATISE ON TENURES."* In 1454, he was called to the degree of serjeant-at-law, and afterward appointed steward of the Marshalsea of the king's household; the next year he was constituted king's serjeant, and rode justice of the assize in the northern circuit. On the accession of EDWARD IV. he sued a general pardon, which was granted to him, and in the 6th year of that prince's reign, he was appointed one of the judges of the Court of Common Pleas, when he had a grant of 110 marks out of the customs of London, Bristol, and Hull, and moreover 106s. 11½d. for a robe and furs, and 6s. 6d. for a summer robe. In the 15th of *King* EDWARD, he was made a Knight of the Bath, with the Prince of Wales, and several persons of the highest distinction. Sir Thomas *m.* Joan, daughter and co-heir of William Burley, esq. of Broomscroft Castle, in Shropshire, and relict of Sir Philip Chetwynd, knt. of Ingestry, Staffordshire, (with whom he acquired large possessions) and had three sons,

- I. WILLIAM (Sir), of Frankley, from whom the LORDS LYTTELTON, refer to BURKE's *Peerage*.
- II. RICHARD, of whom presently.
- III. Thomas, of Spechley, near Worcester, ancestor of the Lord Keeper Lyttelton, *temp.* CHARLES I. and of Sir William Lyttelton, speaker of the House of Commons in the reign of WILLIAM III. (See LITTLETON OF STOKE MILBURGH.)

This celebrated judge made his last will 22nd August, 1481, and died the next day, at his seat at Frankley, in a great and good old age. His widow survived him twenty-four years, and died 22nd March, 1505, nearly fourscore, leaving a great estate, which came by her father and mother,† to her eldest son, Sir William. The second son,

RICHARD LITTLETON, esq. to whom his father gave a moiety of the manor of Baxterley, in Warwickshire, *m.* Alice, daughter and heir of William Winesbury, esq. of Pillaton Hall, in the county of Stafford, and had issue,

- Richard, *d. s. p.*
- EDWARD (Sir), his heir.
- Ellen, *m.* first to John Cotes, esq. of Woodcote, in Shropshire, and secondly to William Basset, esq. of Blore, in the county of Stafford.
- Margaret, *m.* first to William Humphry Pigot, esq. of Salop, and secondly to — Clifton, esq. of Derbyshire.
- Anne, *m.* to Thomas Middlemore, esq. of Edgbaston, in the county of Warwick.

He (Richard) *d.* 9th HENRY VIII. and was *s.* by his son,

SIR EDWARD LITTLETON, knt. of Pillaton Hall, who had a grant from HENRY VIII. of the office of constable and keeper of the castle of Stafford, and keeper of his parks, and bailiff of his manor of Parebriggs, in the county of Stafford, for life. He was sheriff of Staffordshire 15 and 31 HENRY VIII. and 4 EDWARD VI. He *m.* first, Hellen, daughter of Humphrey Swinnerton, esq. of Swinnerton, in the county of Stafford, and by her had seven sons, the six eldest died without issue, the seventh, EDWARD, succeeded as heir, beside two daughters, Barbara, wife of Henry Gower, esq. of Worcestershire, and afterwards of John Folliot, esq. of Pirton; and Constance, wife of Sir James Fuljambe, knt. Sir Edward *m.* secondly, Isabel, relict of — Wood, and daughter of Richard Hill, sister and heir of Robert Hill, esq. of Hounhill, in the county of Stafford, (she *m.* secondly, Ralph Egerton, esq. of Wrinehill) but by that lady had no issue. He died 10th October, 1558, and was *s.* by his son,

SIR EDWARD LITTLETON, knt. sheriff of Staffordshire, 5 ELIZABETH who *m.* Alice, daughter of Francis Cockayne, esq. of Ashburne, in Derbyshire, and had issue,

- I. EDWARD (Sir), his heir.
- II. Thomas, *m.* Cassandra, daughter of Thomas Lane, esq. of Bentley, in the county of Stafford, and left issue.
- III. Francis, of Melsho, in the county of Salop, *m.* Gertrude, daughter of Thomas Sutton, of Overhaddon, in the county of York, and left issue.
- IV. Walter, of Eccleshall, in the county of Stafford, *m.* Alice, daughter of John Comberford, esq. of the same county.
- V. John, *d. s. p.*
- VI. James, *m.* Mercy, daughter of John Stone, esq. of London, relict of William Bowyer, esq. and left issue.
- VII. Devereux, *m.* Jane, daughter of George Allen, esq. of Woodhouse, in the county of Derby, and left issue.

- I. Jane, *m.* to John Lane, esq. of Bentley.

---

* Which was commented upon by Sir Edward Coke, and which is so much studied by gentlemen of the profession. The celebrity and usefulness of the work have survived to our own time; and notwithstanding the progressive accession of statutes and reports, the large alterations both in the knowledge and practice of the law, and accumulation of publications, Lyttleton, with Coke's commentary, will ever continue to demand the attention and applause of our ablest advocates.

† The daughter and heir of Grendon, of Grendon.

II. Constance, *m.* to Thomas Holt, esq. of Gristlehurst, in Lancashire.
III. Mary, *m.* to Walter Vernon, esq. of Hounhill, in Staffordshire.
IV. Grace, *m.* first to Francis Harnage, esq. of Belsardine, in the county of Salop, and secondly, to Silvanus Lacon, esq. of the same county.
V. Margaret, *m.* to Sir John Repington, knt. of Amington, in the county of Warwick.

Sir Edward *d.* 19th July, 1574, and was *s.* by his eldest son,

SIR EDWARD LITTLETON, knt. sheriff of Staffordshire 25th and 35th of ELIZABETH, M.P. for the county of Stafford, in the 39th of the same reign, *m.* Margaret, daughter and co-heir of Sir William Devereux, knt. youngest son of Walter, Viscount Hereford, and had issue,

I. EDWARD (Sir), his successor.
II. Thomas, *m.* Elizabeth, daughter and heir of Adam Morton, esq. of Wilbrighton, in the county of Stafford.

I. Mary, *m.* to Richard Fowler, esq. of King's Harnage, Salop.
II. Anne, *m.* to Humphrey Salwey, esq. of Stanford, in Worcestershire.
III. Jane, *m.* to Richard Knightley, esq. of Fawesley, in the county of Northampton.
IV. Ellen, *m.* to William Babington, esq. of Curborough, in the county of Stafford.
V. Margaret, *m.* to John Skinner, esq. of Cofton, in Worcestershire.
VI. Lettice, *m.* to John Fulnethy, archdeacon of Stafford.
VII. Constance, *m.* to Richard Hill, gent. of London.

Sir Edward was *s.* at his decease by his son,

SIR EDWARD LITTLETON, M.P. for Staffordshire, 21 JAMES I. and sheriff 24th of the same reign, *m.* Mary, daughter of Sir Clement Fisher, knt. of Packington, in the county of Warwick, and had issue,

EDWARD, his heir.
Fisher, *m.* Anne, daughter of John Baynton, esq. of Wiltshire.
Walter (Sir), chancellor of the diocese of Lichfield and Coventry, *m.* Priscilla, daughter of Sir Lewis Pemberton, knt. of Rushden, in Northamptonshire, and had four sons, viz.

Walter, of Lichfield, *m.* a daughter of William Talbot, esq. of Sturton Castle, Staffordshire, and left issue.
Edward, *m.* a daughter of — Mullins, but *d. s. p.*
Fisher, LL.D. *m.* Elizabeth, daughter of Pincebeck, of London, and widow of Skegnes, and *d.* in March, 1696-7.
Henry, merchant of London, *d. s. p.*

William, *m.* the daughter and heir of John Webster, of Amsterdam, merchant.

Lettice, *m.* first, to William Washbourne, esq. of Washbourne, and secondly, to John Clent, esq. of Knightwick, both in Worcestershire.

Mary, *m.* to Euseby Shuckburgh, esq. of Naseby, in Northamptonshire.

Margaret, *m.* first, to Sir George Browne, knt. of Radford, in Warwickshire, and secondly, to Sir Robert, Fisher, bart of Packington.
Anne, *m.* to Sir Thomas Holte, bart. of Aston.

Sir Edward *d.* in July, 1629,* and was *s.* by his eldest son,

I. EDWARD LITTLETON, esq. of Pillaton Hall, in the county of Stafford, who was created a BARONET by *King* CHARLES I. 28th June, 1627. Sir Edward *m.* Hester, daughter of Sir William Courtern, knt. of London, and by her (who *m.* secondly, Thomas Thorne, esq. of Shelvock, in Shropshire,) had issue,

William, who *d. v. p.*
EDWARD, his heir.
James, *d. s. p.*

Anne, *m.* to — Cole, esq. of Shrewsbury.
Margaret, *m.* to Robert Napier, esq. eldest son of Sir Robert Napier, of Luton Hoo, in the county of Bedford.

Sir Edward was a zealous royalist, and had to pay £1347 for composition for his estate. He was *s.* by his son,

II. SIR EDWARD LITTLETON, who *m.* first Mary, daughter of Sir Walter Wrotesley, bart. of Wrotesley, and had

I. EDWARD, who died in the lifetime of his father, 24th January, 1704, leaving by his wife, Susannah, daughter of Sir Theophilus Biddulph bart. (which lady *d.* 25th August, 1722.)

1. EDWARD, successor to his grandfather.
2. Theophilus, *d.* unm.
3. Fisher, barrister-at-law, died in 17[illegible]. He had *m.* Frances, elder daughter and co-heir of James Whitehall, esq. of Pipe Ridware, in Staffordshire, and had two sons and a daughter, viz.

EDWARD, fourth baronet.
Fisher, barrister-at-law, *m.* Mary, only daughter and heir of Thomas Seav[illegible] esq. of Northreps, in Norfolk, but had no issue.
FRANCES, *m.* to MORETON WALHOUSE, esq. of Hatherton, in the county of Stafford.

1. Susan, *m.* to Sir John Coryton, bart.
2. Mary, *m.* to Edward Arblaster, esq. of Longdon, in Staffordshire.
3. Elizabeth, *m.* to Humphry Hodgetts, esq.
4. Catherine, *m.* to John Floyer, esq. son of Sir John Floyer, M.D. of Lichfield
5. Jane, *m.* to John Eggington, esq. of [illegible]baston, in Staffordshire.

II. Walter, major in the army, *m.* Lady Anne Knollys, daughter of Nicholas, Earl of Banbury. He fell in a duel and left no issue

I. Elizabeth, *m.* to Walter Chetwynd, esq. of Ingestree, in Staffordshire, and had issue
II. Hester, *m.* to Humphrey Persehouse, esq. of Reynolds Hall, in Staffordshire.

Sir Edward *m.* secondly, Joyce, daughter of his cousin Littleton, of Teddesley Hay, and by that lady had

---

* In the chancel of Penkrich Church, against the north wall, is a very noble monument of variegated marble, whereon are the effigies of two knights and their ladies, under two arches, one above the other, the arms in great measure broken off; the names of the children, with their effigies, were about the tomb; but the latter are entirely defaced. Underneath is a Latin epitaph, and over one of the knights is the following inscription, in letters of gold:

Reader, 'twas thought enough, upon the Tomb
Of the Great Captain, th' Enemy of Rome,
To write no more, but (Here lies Hannibal
Let this suffice thee then, instead of all
Here Lye two Knights, the Father and the Son
Sir Edward, and Sir Edward Littleton.

† The other daughter and co heir married Mr. J. Parker of the Court of Common Pleas.

Devereux, who *d.* unm. at his seat at Tamworth, 7th June, 1747.

Walter, *d.* unm.

Henry, deputy governor of Cork, left no issue.

Fisher, barrister-at-law, succeeded to the estate of his eldest brother.

William, capt. R.N. left a son,

Edward, who inherited the property of his uncle Fisher. He *m.* his cousin, Joyce, eldest daughter of Stanford Wolferstan, esq. of Statfold, and *d. s. p.*

Adam, killed in a duel, *d.* unm.

———, *m.* — Dilke, esq. of Maxtoke Castle, in Warwickshire.

Sarah, *m.* to Stanfold Wolferstan, esq. of Statfold.

He *d.* about 1709, and was *s.* by his grandson,

III. SIR EDWARD LITTLETON. This gentleman *m.* Mary, only daughter of Sir Richard Hoare, knt. lord mayor of the city of London, and one of its representatives in parliament, *temp.* *Queen* ANNE, but died *s. p.* 2nd January, 1742, and was *s.* by his nephew,

IV. SIR EDWARD LITTLETON, who *m.* Frances, eldest daughter of Christopher Horton,* esq. of Catton, in the county of Derby, but *d.* issueless 18th May, 1812, when the BARONETCY EXPIRED. Sir Edward had removed the seat of the family from Pillaton Hall, to Teddesley, in the same county. His estates devolved upon his grand-nephew,

EDWARD JOHN WALHOUSE, esq. who assumed the surname and arms of LITTLETON. He was raised to the peerage in 1835, and is now (1837) BARON HATHERTON, *of Hatherton*, in the county of Stafford.

Arms—Argent, a chevron between three escallops sa.

LITTLETON, OF STOKE MILBURGH.

CREATED 14th Oct. 1642.—EXTINCT in Jan. 1710.

Lineage.

SIR THOMAS LYTTELTON, K.B. of Frankley, the celebrated author of the "Treatise on Tenures," *m.* Joan, widow of Sir Philip Chetwynd, of Ingestrie, in Staffordshire, and daughter and co-heir of Sir William Burley, of Bromscroft Castle, in the county of Salop, and dying 23rd August, 1481, left issue,

WILLIAM, ancestor of the LORDS LYTTLETON, of Frankley.

RICHARD, ancestor of the LITTLETONS, of Pillaton and Teddesley.

THOMAS, of whose line we have to treat.

The youngest son,

THOMAS LITTLETON, was seated at Spetchley, in Worcestershire. He *m.* Anne, daughter and heir of John Botreaux, esq. of Botreaux Castle, in Cornwall, and from this marriage descended SIR EDMUND LYTTLETON, of Mounslow, lord keeper of the great seal, Lord Lyttleton of Mounslow; and

ADAM LITTLETON, esq. of Stoke Milburgh, in Shropshire, created a BARONET 14th October, 1642. He *m.* Awdrey, daughter and eventual heir of Thomas Poynts, esq. of North Skynden, in Essex, and dying about the year 1647, left a son,

II. SIR THOMAS LITTLETON, who *m.* his cousin, Anne, daughter and heir of Edmund Lord Littleton, of Mounslow, lord keeper of the great seal, and dying in April, 1681, was *s.* by his son,

III. SIR THOMAS LITTLETON, speaker of the House of Commons, *temp.* WILLIAM III. who *m.* Ann, daughter of Benjamin Baun, esq. of Westcoate, in Gloucestershire, but died without issue in January, 1710, when the BARONETCY became EXTINCT.

Arms—Arg. a chevron between three escallop shells sa.

LIVESEY, OF EAST CHURCH.

CREATED 11th July, 1627.

ATTAINTED in 1660.

Lineage.

The family of Livesey was originally of Livesey, in the county of Lancaster, a scion of which

EDMUND LIVESEY, of Parva Markham, in Nottinghamshire, left by his wife, a daughter of Nevil, two sons, Henry, whose only daughter and heir, *m.* — Roken; and

ALEXANDER LIVESEY, who *m.* Anne, Fleshwell, of Slaby, in Derbyshire, and was father of

ROBERT LIVESEY, esq. of Streatham, in Surrey, who served as sheriff of Sussex and Surrey in 1592, and 1602. He *m.* first, Amy, daughter of John Brooke, of London, and had by her, an only daughter, Martha, *m.* to Sir Edward Peyton, bart. He wedded, secondly, Elizabeth, daughter of Maurice Berkeley, esq. of Wymondham, in Leicestershire, and by her, who *m.* after Mr. Livesey's decease, Robert Pakenham, had three sons, viz.

Edward, whose son Robert was living abroad in 1619.

William, *d. s. p.*

GABRIEL, of whom we have to treat.

The third son,

GABRIEL LIVESEY, esq. of Hollingbourne, in Kent, inherited, by bequest, from Henry Richards, the manor and estate of Minster, in the same county, and served the office of sheriff in 1618. By Anne, his second wife, daughter of Sir Michael Sondes, knt. of Throwley, he left at his decease, 18th March, 1622, an only son,

I. SIR MICHAEL LIVESEY, of East Church, in Kent,

---

* CHRISTOPHER HORTON, esq. *m.* Frances, only daughter and heir of Sir Eusebius Buswell, bart. of Cadeby, in the county of Leicester, and had issue,

CHRISTOPHER, *m.* Lady Anne Luttrell, second daughter of Simon, Earl of Carhampton, and had one son, who died an infant. His widow *m.* H. R. H. HENRY-FREDERICK, DUKE OF CUMBERLAND, youngest son of *King* GEORGE II. but had no issue by His Royal Highness.

EUSEBIUS, *m.* Phœbe, daughter of Davies Davenport, esq. of Capesthorne, in Cheshire: his eldest daughter ANNE, *m.* Robert-John, eldest son of the late Sir Robert Wilmot, bart. who having taken the name of Horton, is the present *Rt. Hon.* SIR ROBERT-JOHN WILMOT-HORTON, bart.

Frances, *m.* to Sir Edward Littleton, as above.

Elizabeth, *m.* to George, third Lord Carberry.

who was created a BARONET in 1627. Sir Michael, siding with the parliament in the troubled times in which he lived, acted as one of the king's judges, and signed the death warrant of the ill-fated CHARLES. He died before the Restoration, nevertheless immediately after that event, an act of parliament passed, for his attainder and the forfeiture of all his lands, which were granted to James, Duke of York. The BARONETCY was of course EXTINGUISHED.

Arms—Arg. a lion rampt. gu. between three trefoils vert.

LLOYD, OF YALE.

CREATED 21st June, 1647.

EXTINCT 1st April, 1700.

Lineage.

EVAN LLOYD, esq. of Yale, in Denbighshire, (described in the inscription on his monument in Llanarmon Church, North Wales, as " one of the deputy lieutenants, custos rotulorum, and justice of the peace in Denbighshire, a captain-general in the service of his majesty *King* CHARLES, in Ireland, son and heir of Sir John Lloyd, knight banneret, and grandson of Sir Evan Lloyd, knight banneret, the twelfth of his race lineally descended from Ynyr of Yale, and the tenth of his house of the name of Lloyd;") married Mary, daughter and co-heir of Sir Richard Trevor, knt. and had issue,

- JOHN, his heir.
- Roger, *m.* Miss Nightingale, and had issue.
- Trevor, a captain in the army of CHARLES I. who *m.* in 1639, Miss Medhop, an heiress, by whom he acquired estates in the King's County, and in the county of Tipperary. From this Trevor Lloyd descend the LLOYDS of Gloster, in the former county, now represented by HARDRESS LLOYD, esq. of Gloster. (See BURKE'S *Commoners*, vol. ii. p. 550.)
- Catharine, *m.* to John Lewis, esq. of Presaddfed.
- Mary, *m.* to William Parry, esq. of Pontygof.
- Magdalen, *m.* to Robert Humphreys, esq. of Bodlewyddan.

Evan Lloyd, in the words of the monumental inscription alluded to above, " departed this life on the 17th April, in the year of our Lord, 1637, at Presaddfyd, in the Isle of Anglesea, and his body, by order of Mary, his wife, was brought away thence, and interred in the sepulchre of his fathers at Llanarmon, in Yale." His eldest son,

JOHN LLOYD, esq. of Yale, a magistrate and deputy-lieutenant for the county of Denbigh, married, first, Margaret, daughter of Sir Bevis Thelwall, knt. and secondly, Eleanor, daughter of Sir William Jones, knt. of Castellmarch, one of the judges of the King's Bench, and widow of John Price, esq. of Rhiwlas. By his first wife, John Lloyd had a son and heir,

I. SIR EVAN LLOYD, of Yale, who was created a BARONET 21st June, 1647. He wedded Anne, daughter of Sir Charles Williams, knt. of Llangibby, and dying in October, 1663, was *s.* by his son,

II. SIR EVAN LLOYD, of Yale, who *m.* Mary, daughter and co-heir of Rees Tanat, esq. and had an o[illegible] daughter and heir,

- MARGARET, who *m.* Richard Vaughan, esq. of C[illegible]sygedol, and was mother of
  - CATHERINE VAUGHAN, who *m.* the Rev. Hu[illegible] Wynn, D. D. prebendary of Salisbury, a[illegible] left a daughter,
    - MARGARET WYNN, heir to her uncle, Wi[illegible]liam Vaughan, esq. This lady *m.* S[illegible] Roger Mostyn, bart. of Mostyn, and [illegible] five daughters.

Sir Evan Lloyd died 6th April, 1700, when the BA[illegible]NETCY EXPIRED.

Arms—Quarterly; first and fourth, paly [illegible] arg. and gu.; second, az. a lion rampant arg.; [illegible] erm. a lion rampant az. crowned or.

LLOYD, OF GARTH.

CREATED 10th May, 1661.

EXTINCT Nov. [illegible]

Lineage.

HUMPHRY LLOYD, esq. of Lear, married Gwe[illegible] daughter of Thomas ap Rees, of Newtown, and [illegible] father of

DAVID LLOYD, esq. of Moyle y Garth, in Montgomeryshire, who *m.* Elizabeth, eldest daughter of [illegible] Vaughan, esq. of Llwydyarth, and was *s.* by his son,

I. CHARLES LLOYD, of Garth, who was created a BARONET by *King* CHARLES II. 10th May, 16[illegible] Charles *m.* Elizabeth, daughter of John Bow[illegible] of Whitley, in the county of Warwick, and [illegible] issue,

- CHARLES, his successor.
- Edward, *m.* a daughter of John Penryn, [illegible] Dythur, in Montgomeryshire.
- John, *d. s. p.*
- Elizabeth.
- Susan.
- Hester.

He *d.* about the year 1678, and was *s.* by his [illegible] son,

II. SIR CHARLES LLOYD, who wedded Catherine, daughter of John Huxley, esq. of Wirehall, [illegible]dlesex, and had, with four daughters, Catherine, [illegible]rah, Anne, and Elizabeth, an only son, his successor at his decease, about the year 1692,

III. SIR CHARLES LLOYD, who *m.* first, [illegible] daughter of Sir Richard Corbet, bart. of Longnor, [illegible] Shropshire, by whom he had no surviving issue. [illegible] wedded, secondly, Jane, daughter of Sir Edw[illegible] Leighton, bart. of Watlesborough, in Salop, and [illegible] of Thomas Jones, esq. of Shrewsbury, by whom [illegible] *d.* in June, 1734) he had a son, Charles, who [illegible] less, and a daughter,

- VICTORIA.

He *d.* in November, 1743, when the BARONETCY EXPIRED.

Arms—Sable, three nags' heads erased arg.

LLOYD, OF MITFIELD.

Created 1st April, 1708.  Extinct 1750.

Lineage.

David ap Llewellin Llwyd, m. Lenky, daughter of John Lloyd, of Llwy David, and had a son,

Llewellin Llwyd, esq. of Castlehowell, who m. Margaret, daughter of Thomas ap Watkins, of Noyadd, in Llanarth, and was s. by his son,

Hugh Llewellin Llwyd, esq. of Lhanlhyr, high sheriff of Cardiganshire, 9th Elizabeth. This gentleman m. Joane, daughter and co-heir of Griffith Henry, esq. and had four sons, viz.

- i. Morgan.
- ii. Griffith, LL.D. D.D. principal of Jesus College, Oxford, to which he was a benefactor.
- iii. Thomas.
- iv. Richard, A.M.

The third son,

Thomas Lloyd, esq. precentor and treasurer of St. David's, to which church he was a considerable benefactor, m. Frances, daughter of Marmaduke Middleton, esq. (sister of Middleton, Bishop of St. David's,) and was s. by his son,

Sir Marmaduke Lloyd, knt. of Maes y Vellin, or Milfield, in the county of Cardigan, an eminent lawyer, who was appointed chief justice of the great sessions for the several counties of Radnor, Brecon, and Glamorgan, and one of the judges before the president of his majesty's council in the marches of Wales. He m. Mary, daughter of John Stedman, esq. of Strataflorida, by whom he had a daughter, Anne, the wife of Nicholas Williams, esq. of Edwinsford, in the county of Carmarthen, and a son and heir,

Sir Francis Lloyd, knt. comptroller of the household to *King* Charles I. who endured much in the cause of his royal master during the civil war. He m. first, Lady Mary Vaughan, daughter of John, Earl of Carbery, but by her had no surviving issue. He wedded, secondly, Bridget, daughter of Richard Leigh, esq. of Carmarthen, and had

- Lucius, *d. s. p.*
- Charles, his heir.
- Frances.

Sir Francis, who was also one of the gentlemen of the privy chamber to Charles II. was *s.* at his decease by his only surviving son,

i. Sir Charles Lloyd, of Milfield, in the county of Cardigan, who was knighted by *King* William III. and created a Baronet by *Queen* Anne 1st April, 1708. Sir Charles m. first, Jane, daughter and heir of Morgan Lloyd, esq. of Greengrove, in the same county, by whom he had two daughters,

- Jane, m. to William Glover, esq. of Carmarthen.
- Eleanor, *d.* unm.

He wedded, secondly, Francis, daughter of Sir Francis Cornwallis, knt. of Abermaries, in Carmarthenshire, and by her had

- Charles-Cornwallis, his successor.
- Lucius-Christianus, heir to his brother.
- Emma, *m.* to Doctor Foy, a physician at Carmarthen.
- Elizabeth.
- Frances.

Sir Charles *d.* 28th December, 1723, and was *s.* by his son,

ii. Sir Charles-Cornwallis Lloyd, who *m.* Mrs. Jennings, of Somersetshire, but *d. s. p.* 25th February, 1729, and was *s.* by his brother,

iii. Sir Lucius Christianus Lloyd, who *m.* Anne, daughter of Walter Lloyd, esq. of Peterwell, in the county of Cardigan, the king's attorney-general for Wales, and M.P. for Cardigan, but died issueless in 1750, when the Baronetcy became extinct.

Arms—Sable, a spear's head (its point imbrued with blood) between three scaling ladders arg.

LLOYD, OF WOKING.

Created 28th Feb. 1661-2.  Extinct in 1674.

Lineage.

i. John Lloyd, esq. of Woking, in Surrey, the descendant of an ancient Welsh family, seated at The Forest, in Caermarthenshire, was created a Baronet in 1661-2. He *m.* Beatrix, daughter of Francis, Viscount Valentia, and widow of James Zouch, esq. of Woking, and dying 1st January, 1663, was *s.* by his son,

ii. Sir John Lloyd, who resided at The Forest. He *m.* Mary, daughter of Matthew Smallwood, LL.D. Dean of Lichfield, *d.* in 1674, when the Baronetcy became extinct. His sister and heir,

- Beatrice, married Sir John Barlow, bart. of Slebetch, and had two daughters,
  - Beatrice, *m.* first, to Sir Anthony Rudd, bart. and secondly, to Griffith Lloyd, esq.
  - Ann, died unm.

Arms—Gu. a lion rampant within a bordure dancettè arg.

LLOYD, OF PETERWELL.

Created 26th Jan. 1763.—Extinct 19th Aug. 1769.

Lineage.

i. Herbert Lloyd, esq. of Peterwell, in the county of Cardigan, son of Walter Lloyd, esq. of Voelallt, by his wife, daughter and heir of Daniel Evans, esq. of Peterwell, was created a Baronet in 1763. He *m.* Beatrix, sister of Dr. Powell, of Nantees, but died without issue, 19th August, 1769, when the Baronetcy became extinct. Sir Herbert's nephew, John Adams, esq. of Whitland, spent the whole property, and the estate was consequently sold to Albany Wallis, esq.

LONG, OF WHADDON.

CREATED 26th Mar. 1661.

EXTINCT 21st May, 1710.

Lineage.

HENRY LONGE, esq. of Whaddon,* in the county of Wilts, fourth son of Henry Long, of Trowbridge, who died in 1535, *m.* Mary, daughter of Thomas Horton, esq. of Iford, grandson of Sir Roger Horton, of Catton, in Derbyshire, and dying in 1558, was *s.* at Whaddon, by his second son,

HENRY LONGE, esq. of Whaddon, who married Mary, daughter of Robert May, esq. of Broughton Gifford, and dying in 1611, was succeeded by his eldest son,

HENRY LONGE, esq. of Whaddon, who *m.* Rebecca, daughter of Christopher Bailey, esq. and (by her, who *m.* secondly, Henry Sherfield, esq. M.P. for Sarum, in 1623 and 1628,) had issue,

I. Henry, *d.* young.
II. WALTER, his heir.
III. Robert, of Stanton Prior, in Somersetshire, married Alice, daughter of Thomas Coward, esq. of Witton, Wilts, and relict of John Harrington, esq. of Kelston, in the same county. He died in 1698, aged ninety-one, having had issue,

  Henry, admitted of Lincoln's Inn, in 1657.

  Mary, married to George Stedman, esq. of Midsome Norton, in Somersetshire; and secondly, to Thomas Bere, esq. of Huntsham, in Devon, and died in 1702, leaving issue.

IV. Thomas, colonel in the army.

I. Mary.
II. Rebecca.
III. Mary, *m.* to Timothy Wade, of London, merchant.
IV. Martha, *m.* to Roger Knight, esq. of Greenham, Berks.

Mr. Longe *d.* in 1612, and was *s.* by his eldest surviving son,

I. WALTER LONG, esq. of Whaddon. This gentleman, who was sheriff of Wilts, and member for Bath, 1627, being closely connected in politics with the Puritan party, became a zealous parliamentarian, and was one of the seven members sent to the Tower by CHARLES in 1628. On the outbreak of the civil war, he raised a troop of horse, and leading it in a charge at Edgehill, had his horse shot under him. In 1647 he incurred the displeasure of the army and its chief, and fled with Holles and others into France, "because," says Holles, "the princes of the Philistines loved them not." He then joined CHARLES II [illegible] on the Restoration was created a BARONET 26th Mar[illegible] 1661. Sir Walter *m.* first, Mary, daughter of Jo[illegible] Cocks, and by her had issue,

  WALTER, his heir, baptised in 1627, at Wha[illegible]
  Henry, baptised in the same year, and at the same place, *d. s. p.*
  Robert, of Lincoln's Inn, *d. s. p.*

  Mary, *d. s. p.*
  REBECCA, married to Sir Philip Parker, bart [illegible] Erwaston, in the county of Suffolk, and [illegible] issue,

    SIR PHILIP PARKER, bart who married Ma[illegible] daughter of Samuel Fortrey, esq. of B[illegible] Fen, in Cambridgeshire, and had a [illegible]

      PHILIP PARKER, his successor.

      CATHERINE, married to Sir John Per[illegible] val, created Viscount Perceval, a[illegible] of the Earl of Egmont. (See B[illegible] *Peerage.*)

      MARY, married to Daniel Dering[illegible] grandson of Sir Edward Dering, [illegible] of Kent.

    Walter Parker, *d.* unm.
    CALTHORPE, heir to his uncle, Sir Walter

    Walter Parker Long, *d.* unm.
    Rebecca-Parker, } *d.* unm.
    Mary-Parker, }

Sir Walter *m.* secondly, Elizabeth, daughter of [illegible] Cotes, esq. of Woodcote, in Shropshire, but [illegible] other issue. He *d.* in 1672, and was *s.* by his [illegible] son,

II. SIR WALTER LONG, who died unm. 21st Ma[illegible] 1711, aged eighty-four, when the BARONETCY EXP[illegible] Sir Walter bequeathed his estates to his nephew [illegible] thorpe Parker, who assumed the surname of Lo[illegible] and thus became

  CALTHORPE LONG, esq. of Whaddon. He m[illegible] nysia, daughter of John Harrington, [illegible] Kelston, in Somersetshire, but died *s. p.* a[illegible] seventy two, in 1729, and was succeeded by his nephew,

    SIR PHILIP PARKER A MORLEY, bart. who [illegible] the surname of LONG, but died without male issue in 1741, when the estate [illegible] Whaddon passed to Thomas Long, esq. [illegible] Rowden.†

Arms—Sa. semée of cross crosslets, a lion rampant arg.

LONG, OF WESTMINSTER.

CREATED 1st Sept. 1662.—EXTINCT 14th Sept. [illegible]

Lineage.

This family was of good note and antiquity [illegible] county of Wilts, where they acquired the est[illegible] Draycot Cerne, by the intermarriage of

JOHN LONG (younger son of Robert Long or [illegible] M.P. for Wilts in 1433, by Alice, daughter a[illegible] of Reginald Popham) with Margaret, daughter [illegible]

* Supposed to descend from the parent stock of the LONGES of Wraxall, (refer to BURKE's *Commoners*, vol. iv. page 65.)

† Descended from Edward Longe, of Monk[illegible] third son of Henry Longe, of Whaddon, by Mary [illegible] ter of Thomas Horton, esq. (refer to BURKE's *Commoners*, vol. iv. page 67.)

Edward Wayte, knt. "by the heyre of Cerne, lord of the manor of Draycot."* They had issue,

Thomas (Sir), his heir.
Richard (Sir).
William.

The eldest son,

Sir Thomas Long, of Draycot-Cerne, inherited Wraxhall, in the same county, from his uncle, Henry Long, in 1490. Sir Thomas m. Mary, daughter of Sir George Darel, of Littlecot, in the same county, and had issue,

i. Henry (Sir), his heir.
ii. Richard (Sir), of Shengay and Hardwick, in the county of Cambridge, m. Margaret, daughter and heir of John Donnington, esq. and relict of Sir Thomas Kitson, of Hengrave, in Suffolk, by whom (who m. secondly, John Bourchier, Earl of Bath) he had
  Henry, b. in 1534.
  Catherine, m. to Edward Fisher, esq. of Ickington, in Warwickshire.
  Jane.
  Mary.
  Sir Richard d. in 1545, and was s. by his son, Henry Long, esq. of Shengay, who d. in 1573, and left an only daughter,
    Elizabeth, m. to William Lord Russell of Thornhaugh.
iii. Thomas, a priest.
iv. Robert, of Mawditt, Wilts.
v. John.
vi. William.
vii. Edward.

i. Joan, m. to Edward Mylle, esq.

Sir Thomas, who was sheriff of Wilts in 1501, and among the "great compaignye of noblemen" who served under Edward, Duke of Buckingham, against Perkin Warbeck, d. in 1510, and was s. by his eldest son,

Sir Henry Long, of Wraxhall and Draycot, sheriff of Wilts in 1512 26 37 and 42, and for Somersetshire in 1536. M.P. for Wilts in 1552-3. Sir Henry was one of the retinue of Henry VIII. at the field of the cloth of gold, and was knighted for making a gallant charge at Terrouenne, in sight of Henry, when he received the grant of a new crest, viz. a lion's head with a hand in its mouth. He married, first, Frideswide, daughter of Sir John Hungerford, knt. of Down Ampney, in Wilts, and by her had two daughters to survive, viz.

Elizabeth, married to Michael Quinton, of Bubton, Wilts, and had issue.
Jane, m. to Thomas Leversedge, of Frome Selwood, in Somersetshire.

Sir Henry m. secondly, Eleanor, daughter of Richard Wrottesley, of Wrottesley, in the county of Stafford, and relict of Edmund Leversedge, esq. of Frome Selwood, and by that lady had

Robert, his heir.
Benedict.
Edmund, of Kelwayes, in Wiltshire, m. Susan, daughter of Nicholas Snell, esq. M.P. for Wilts, and had Henry, Cecily, and Alice.
Anthony, of Ashley, in Wilts, m. Alice, daughter of William Butler, esq. of Badmington, in Gloucestershire, and dying in 1578, was s. by his son,
  Henry Long, esq. of Ashley, whose son,
    Anthony Long, esq. of Walcot, near Bath, was father of
      Nathaniel, of London, merchant, who d. in 1714, leaving issue.
Richard, of Lineham (for his issue, see Burke's *Commoners*, vol. iii. page 214.)
Margery, m. to Robert Hungerford, esq. of Cadenham.
Thomasine.
Cicely, m. to Francis Stradling, esq.

Sir Henry d. in 1556, and was s. by his eldest son,

Sir Robert Long, of Wraxhall and Draycot, b. in 1517, sheriff of Wilts in 1575, esquire of the body to *King* Henry VIII. and gentleman pensioner to the same prince, whom he served at the winning of Bulloigne. He married Barbara, daughter of Sir Edward Carne, knt. of Wenny, in Glamorganshire, and dying in 1581, was s. by his son,

Sir Walter Long, of Wraxhall and Draycot, sheriff in 1602, M.P. for Wilts in 1592, m. first, Mary, eldest daughter of Sir Thomas Packington, of Westwood, Worcestershire, and had by her a son, John, ancestor of the Longs of Wraxhall. (See Burke's *Commoners*, vol. iii. page 214). Sir Walter wedded, secondly, Catherine, daughter of Sir John Thynne, knt. of Longleat, Wilts, and had by that lady, with several daughters, four sons, viz.

i. Walter (Sir), of Draycot Cerne, m. first, Lady Anne Ley, second daughter of James, Earl of Marlborough, and had a son,
  James, heir to his uncle Robert.
  Sir Walter m. secondly, Elizabeth, daughter of George Master, esq. of Cirencester, and by her had a son, Walter, of Marlborough, captain in the service of Charles I. d. s. p. in 1673.
ii. Thomas, who had a son slain at Tangiers.
iii. Henry, slain at the Isle of Rhé, in 1672.
iv. Robert.

The youngest son,

i. Robert Long, esq. of Westminster, having been secretary to *King* Charles II. in his majesty's exile, was sworn of the privy council at the Restoration, and made auditor of the exchequer. He was created a Baronet by his royal master, 1st September, 1662, with remainder to his nephew, James, and the heirs male of his body. Sir Robert died a bachelor, 13th July, 1673, and the baronetcy devolved, according to the limitation, upon his nephew,

ii. Sir James Long, of Draycot-Cerne, who commanded a troop of horse, in the civil war, for *King* Charles I. He m. Dorothy, daughter of Sir Edward Leech, of Shipley, in Derbyshire, and had issue,

James, his heir, who died in his father's lifetime. He m. first, Susan, daughter of Colonel Giles Strangwayes, of Melbury, in Dorsetshire, one of the privy council *temp.* Charles II. and had three sons,

Robert, }
Giles, } successive baronets.
James, }

---

* He was son of Sir Robert Long, by Alicia de Seymour, heiress of North Bradley, niece and heir of Reginald de Bradley, (the grant of Bradley was from [illegible] the Norman, by the name of Reginald de Bradmlete *hospite nostro*.) Sir Robert was son of Rogerus de Lang, by the daughter and heir of St. Maur, by whom he obtained many great manors and extensive estates. His mother was Zouch, also a great heiress. His Rogerus) father married Berkeley of Beverston, an heiress too.

He m. secondly, Mrs. Mary Kightley, and by her had a daughter,

Mary, m. to Colonel Butler, of Ireland.

Margaret, m. to Sir Richard Mason, knt.

Dorothy, m. to Sir Henry Heron, K.B. of Cressy Hall, in the county of Lincoln.

Sir James d. in February, 1691-2, and was s. by his grandson,

III. SIR ROBERT LONG, who d. of the small-pox, four days after his grandfather, and was s. by his brother,

IV. SIR GILES LONG, who d. unm. about the year 1698, and was s. by his brother,

V. SIR JAMES LONG, M.P. for the county of Wilts, *temp.* Queen ANNE, m. the Hon. Henrietta Greville, daughter of Fulke, Lord Brooke, and dying 16th March, 1729, was s. by his elder son,

VI. SIR ROBERT LONG, M.P. for Wotton Basset, m. May, 1735, Lady Emma Child, daughter of Richard, Earl of Tilney,* of Wanstead, in Essex, and Tilney Hall, Hants, and heir of her brother, John, second earl. By her ladyship, who d. 8th March, 1758, Sir Robert had issue,

JAMES, his heir, who assumed the additional surname of TILNEY.

Robert, d. in 1739.

Richard, d. young.

Charles, of Grittleton, Wilts, m. Hannah, daughter of Thomas Phipps, esq. of Heywood, in the same county, by whom (who m. secondly, James Dawkins, esq.) he had a daughter,

Emma, m. to William Scrope, esq. of Castle Combe, and her only child, EMMA SCROPE, m. George Poulett Thomson, esq. who assumed the name of Scrope.

Dorothy.

Emma.

Sir Robert d. 10th February, 1767, and was s. by his eldest son,

VII. SIR JAMES TILNEY-LONG, b. in 1736, M.P. for Wilts, married first, Harriett, fourth daughter of Jacob Bouverie, Viscount Folkestone, but by that lady, who d. 13th November, 1777, had no issue. He m. secondly, Lady Catherine Sidney Windsor, daughter of Other Lewis, fourth Earl of Plymouth, and by her ladyship, who d. in 1823, had

JAMES, his heir.

CATHARINE, heir to her brother.

Dorothy.

Emma.

He d. 28th November, 1794, and was s. by his son,

VIII. SIR JAMES TILNEY-LONG, who d. 14th September, 1805, aged eleven, the last known male descendant of the Longs of Wraxall and Draycot, when the BARONETCY EXPIRED, while the immense estates, real and personal, amounting to £25,000 a-year, and nearly £300,000 devolved upon his eldest sister,

CATHERINE TILNEY-LONG, b. in 1789, who m. the Hon. William Wellesley-Pole, only son of William, Lord Maryborough, and dying in 1825 left two sons and a daughter, viz.

WILLIAM-RICHARD-ARTHUR TILNEY LONG WELLESLEY, b. in 1813, now of Draycot, in the county of Wilts.

James-Fitzroy-Henry Tilney-Long-Wellesley, b. in 1815.

Victoria-Catharine-Mary Tilney-Long-Wellesley.

Arms—Sable, semée of cross-crosslets, a lion rampant arg.

LORT, OF STACKPOOLE COURT.

CREATED 15th July, 1662. EXTINCT 19th Sept. 1698.

Lineage.

I. ROGER LORT, esq. of Stackpoole Court, in the county of Pembroke, who was created a BARONET 15th July, 1662, m. first, Hester, sister of Arthur Annesley, Earl of Anglesea; and secondly, Anne, daughter of Humphrey Wyndham, esq. of Dunraven Castle in the county of Glamorgan. Sir Roger died about the year 1664 (his widow wedded secondly Sir Edward Mansel), and was s. by his son,

II. SIR JOHN LORT, of Stackpoole Court, who m. Lady Susan Holles, fourth daughter of John, second Earl of Clare, by Elizabeth his wife, daughter and co-heir of the celebrated General Sir Horace Vere, Lord Vere of Tilbury, and had issue,

GILBERT, his heir.

ELIZABETH, m. to Sir Alexander Campbell, son of Sir Hugh Campbell, of Cawdor Castle, in the county of Nairn, and had a son,

JOHN CAMPBELL, esq. of Cawdor, who inherited the estates of his maternal ancestors the Lorts of Stackpoole Court. He m. the eldest daughter and co-heir of Lewis Pryse, esq. of Gogerddan, and his great grandson is the present

JOHN-FREDERICK CAMPBELL, EARL CAWDOR. (See BURKE'S *Peerage*.)

Sir John died about 1673, and was s. by his son

III. SIR GILBERT LORT, who died unmarried 19th September, 1698, aged twenty-eight, when the BARONETCY became EXTINCT. The estates passed to the Campbells of Cawdor, and are now enjoyed by Earl Cawdor.

Arms—Gu. a cross, or.

---

* SIR RICHARD CHILD, bart. of Wanstead, in Essex, was created by GEORGE I. Baron Newton and Viscount Castlemain, in the peerage of Ireland, and by GEORGE II. Earl of Tilney. His lordship m. Dorothy, only surviving daughter and heir of John Glynne, esq. of Henley Park, in Surrey, by his wife, Dorothy, daughter of Francis Tilney, esq. of Rotherwick, in the county of Southampton. In 1734 an act of parliament passed, enabling his lordship's eldest son, JOHN, and his heirs to bear the surname of TILNEY, in consequence of an estate of £7000 a year, which devolved upon the Countess of Tilney, as heir of Anne, Lady Craven. The earl had issue,

JOHN, Viscount Castlemain.

Josiah, m. in 1754, Henrietta, daughter of R. Knight, Lord Luxborough, afterwards Earl of Catherton, d. s. p.

EMMA, m. in 1735, to SIR ROBERT LONG, bart.

Dorothy.

His lordship was s. by his elder son,

JOHN, second Earl of Tilney, who d. s. p. when all his honours EXPIRED, and his great fortune passed to his nephew, Sir James Tilney-Long, eldest son of his sister Lady Emma Long.

LOVETT, OF LISCOMBE HOUSE.

CREATED 23rd Oct. 1781.

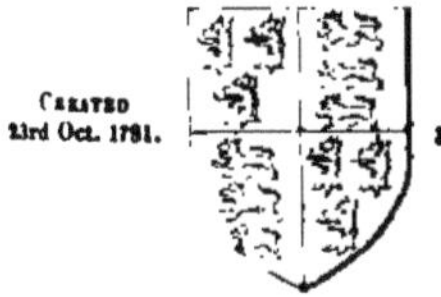

EXTINCT 30th Jan. 1812.

Lineage.

The family of LOUETH, LOUETH, DE LUVIET, DE LUVET, LOVET or LOVETT, as the name is variously written in Domesday, is of Norman extraction.

RICHARDUS DE LOUET,* de Normania, was living at the time of the Conquest, and was accompanied into England by his two sons, WILLIAM and Robert, from the latter descended the Lovets of Worcestershire.

WILLIAM LOVETT, the eldest son, held considerable estates in the counties of Bedford, Berks, Leicester, and Northampton, *in capite*, by grant from the Conqueror. He was also appointed master of the wolf hounds, in consequence of which, he took for his arms *argent, three wolves passant, in pale, sable*. He made Northamptonshire his chief residence, as did his descendants for several generations, until their removal to Liscombe, in Buckinghamshire, which subsequently continued their abode for five hundred years. This William, besides being represented as a man in high favour with the king for his military talents, is said to have been one of the strongest and stoutest men of the day, of which many feats are still recorded. He married a French lady, at whose death he was so deeply affected, that taking her remains over to Normandy to be buried, he retired himself into an adjacent monastery, and every day until the day of his death, payed a visit to her tomb, and on that day caused himself to be carried and laid upon the grave, where he expired. In his family this was long a nursery story, and gave rise to a nursery song. He lived to a great age, and was *s.* by his son,

WILLIAM LOVETT, whose great-great grandson,

SIR ROBERT LOVETT, knt. of Rushton and Newton, in the county of Warwick, left a daughter, Alicia, *m.* to William de Wever, of Cester Over, in the same county, and two sons, Robert and John. To the younger,

JOHN LOVETT, he gave his estate at Newton, with the manor of Dodisthorp, near Peterborough, where he erected (by license from the Bishop of Lincoln), in consequence of the badness of the roads, a chantry chapel for the use of his family. This John purchased Cester Over from his nephew, Robert de Waver, and dying without issue, left all his estates to his great nephew (the grandson of his brother, and eldest son of Sir Richard Lovett, of Newton),

ROBERT LOVETT, who settled at Liscombe, in Buckinghamshire, of which, with Hollingdon and Soulbury, he levied a fine in 1304. These lordships remained in the family to the time that the male line became extinct, a period exceeding five centuries. He *m.* Sarah, daughter and heiress of Sir Nicholas De Turville, of Helmeden, in Northamptonshire, and was *s.* by his son,

THOMAS LOVETT, who, upon making the king's son a knight in 1347, accounted for these manors with his other lordships, amounting to twenty-three knight's fees, and one half and one eighth. By his wife, Clementia, he had issue,

- WILLIAM, his heir.
- Richard, to whom he gave the manor of Welford in whose descendants it remained until it passed to the Temple family, by the intermarriage of JOCOSA, daughter and co-heir of WILLIAM LOVETT, esq. of Welford, with Richard Temple, esq. of Temple Hall, in the county of Leicester.
- Nicholas, who got from his father the lordship of Richton. He *m.* the sister and co-heir of Richard Lions, of Oakley, which, from him, took the name of Lovett's manor, in Oakley. This branch of the family became extinct in the third generation.
- Maud, *m.* De Arches.

He was *s.* by his eldest son,

WILLIAM LOVETT, of Liscombe, who presented to Soulbury in 1376 and 1391. In 1359, he had inherited the estates of his great uncle, John Lovett, of Newton, but being an improvident person, he soon dissipated those, with a great part of his paternal property. In 1366, he conveyed the manor of Overbury to his sister, Maud de Arches; and in 1386, he sold to William Purefoy and his heirs (after the death of his mother Clementia, then the wife of John Parount), his lands at Cester Over, in Warwickshire; and having disposed of estates of large amount to several other people, he died in 1392, and was *s.* by his son,

ROGER LOVETT, of Liscombe, who presented to Soulbury in 1435. In 1418, he appears again in possession of the manor of Helmeden, which he settled upon his son JOHN, who *m.* Margaret de Ingleton. John died soon after, in the lifetime of his father, leaving a son,

SIMON LOVETT, successor to his grandfather, who presented to Soulbury in 1467. This Simon left three sons, viz.

- I. John, *d. s. p.*
- II. WILLIAM, of Liscombe.
- III. Thomas, of Astwell, in the county of Northampton, which house and estates, with others of great value in that county, as well as in the counties of Oxford and Gloucester, he acquired by his marriage with Joan, daughter and co-heir of Thomas Billinge, esq. son and heir of Sir Thomas Billinge, knt. chief justice of the Common Pleas.†

He was *s.* by his elder surviving son,

---

* This Richardus de Louet, who was one of the few accompanied the Conqueror into England without receiving pay for his services, returned to die in his own country, and his tomb may be seen to this day in the cathedral at Rouen.

† This THOMAS LOVETT, of Astwell, served the office of sheriff for Northamptonshire in 1482, and dying in ..., was *s.* by his son,

THOMAS LOVETT, esq. of Astwell, who *m.* Anne, sister and sole heir of Richard Drayton, of Strixton, in Northamptonshire, was sheriff in 1491, and died in 1502, leaving a son, then seventeen years of age,

THOMAS LOVETT, esq. of Astwell, who *m.* first, Elizabeth, daughter of John Butler, esq. of Woodhall, in the county of Bedford, and had issue,

- THOMAS, his heir.
- Elizabeth, *m.* to Alderman Sir William Chester, knt. of the city of London.
- Amye, *m.* to James Bury, esq. of Hampton Poyle, in Oxfordshire.
- Margaret, *m.* to Thomas Foxley, esq. of Blakesley, in Northamptonshire.
- Constance, *m.* to John Matthew, esq. of Bradden, in the same county.
- Anne, *m.* first, to John Heneage, esq. of Pendeston,

WILLIAM LOVETT, esq. of Liscombe, who was *s.* by his son,

ROGER LOVETT, esq. living in 1491, and *s.* at his decease by his brother,

THOMAS LOVETT, esq. of Liscombe, who *m.* a daughter of Neville of Gothurst (son and heir of Sir Robert Neville, by Joan, daughter and heir of Sir John Nowers, of Gothurst), and sister of Michael Neville, whose daughter and heiress, Mary, *m.* Thomas Mulshoe, and was grandmother of Mary Mulshoe, who *m.* Sir Everard Digby, and thus conveyed the Gothurst estate to that family. They had issue,

John, *d. s. p.*
RICHARD, the heir.
William, *m.* Anne, daughter and heir of Edward Cope, esq. of Spraton.
Robert, alderman of Nottingham, *m.* Miss Bonner of the same place, and had issue.

The second son,

RICHARD LOVETT, esq. of Liscombe, *m.* Alice, daughter of Thomas Martin, of London, and had a daughter Alice, wife of John Taylor, of the same city, with a son and heir,

LAURENCE LOVETT, esq. of Liscombe, who *m.* Elizabeth, daughter, and (on the death of her niece, Rawson Williams (only child of her only surviving brother, Nicholas Williams, of Burfield), without issue), coheiress of Sir Reginald Williams, of Burfield, in the county of Berks (elder brother of John, Lord Williams of Thame, and) son of Sir John Williams, of Thame Park (the maternal representative of the ancient family of Perceval, Lords of Corevill, in Somersetshire, a branch of the baronial house of Lovel and Holland), by Elizabeth, his wife, daughter and coheiress of Richard More, esq. of Burfield, by Elizabeth, daughter and heiress of William Brocas, esq. of Southampton, and was *s.* at his decease by his only surviving child,

FRANCIS LOVETT, esq. of Liscombe, who *m.* Anne, daughter of Augustine Crispe, esq. of Boughton, in Northamptonshire, and left a son and heir,

SIR ROBERT LOVETT, of Liscombe, sheriff of Bucks in 1608, and *d.* in 1643. He *m.* first, Susan, daughter of Richard Brookes, esq. and sole heir of her maternal grandfather, Richard Pate, of Matson, in Gloucestershire; she was the widow of Sir Ambrose Willoughby. By this lady he had two daughters,

I. Frances, *m.* to John Gareaway, nephew and heir of Sir William Gareaway, knt.
II. Susan, *m.* to Francis Saunders, esq. of Dinton, Bucks.

He *m.* secondly, Anne, daughter of Richard Saunders, esq. of Dinton, by Elizabeth, his wife, daughter of Blount, of Blountshall, in the county of Leicester, and by her had issue,

I. ROBERT, his heir.
II. EDWARD, successor to his brother.
III. CHRISTOPHER, who, at the time of the Restoration, was settled in Turkey as a merchant, but removed, in 1669, to Dublin, of which city he became sheriff and lord mayor. He *m.* Frances O'More,* and had issue,
  1. CHRISTOPHER, who inherited the Liscombe and other estates of the family from his cousin ROBERT.
  2. JOHN (Colonel), heir to his brother.
  3. Edward, *m.* Miss Cuffe, of the Queen's County, and had a daughter, Clotilda, who *d.* unm. and a son,
     John, who *m.* Amelia, daughter of Jonas Wheeler, esq. and had
       John, captain of horse, died unmarried.
       Amelia, *m.* to Sir Gilfrid Lawson, bart.
  1. Anne, *m.* first, to William Tighe, esq. of Rutland, in the county of Carlow; and secondly, to Thomas Coote, one of the judges of the court of King's Bench, in Ireland.
  2. Frances, *m.* to Major-general Pearce, of Norfolk.
  3. Mary, *m.* to Medhop Lloyd, esq. of Lemagh, in the King's County, ancestor of the Lloyds of Gloster, in the same county. (See BURKE's *Commoners*, vol. ii. p. 550.)
  4. Rebecca, *m.* to Jonathan Ashe, esq. of Ashe Grove, in Tipperary.
IV. Laurence, of Eythorp, left two daughters,
  SARAH, *m.* to the Rev. William Butterfield.
  SUSANNAH, *m.* first, to — Horton, esq., and, secondly, to Colonel JOHN LOVETT, and by the latter had issue,
    ROBERT LOVETT.
    Christopher Lovett, of Dublin, who *m.* Mrs. Wellington, daughter of — Cooke, and had issue.

I. Elizabeth, *m.* to John Combes, esq.
II. Anne, *m.* first, Edward Bourchier, fourth Earl of Bath, but by his lordship (she was his second wife) had no issue. She wedded secondly, Baptist Noel, third Viscount Campden, and had by him one still-born child only.
III. Dorothy, *m.* to John Herne, esq.

---

in Lincolnshire; and secondly, to William Palmer, esq. of Carlton.
Bridget, *m.* to Gabriel Dormer, esq. of Lee Grange.

He *m.* secondly, Jane, daughter and co-heir of John Pinchpole, esq. of London, and by her had a son George, who *d.* unmarried. He was sheriff of Northamptonshire in 1506, and dying in 1543, was *s.* by his son,

THOMAS LOVETT, esq. of Astwell, who *m.* Anne, daughter of Sir John Danvers, of Dantesey, in Wilts, and had issue,

THOMAS, his heir.
John, *d.* unm.

Anne, *m.* to Robert Leeson, esq.
Elizabeth, *m.* first, to Anthony Cave, esq. of Chichley, Bucks; secondly, John Newdegate, esq. of Harefield, M.P. for Middlesex in 1571; and thirdly, Mr. Justice Weston.
——, *m.* first, to Thomas Barker, esq. and, secondly, to Thomas Duncombe, esq. of Whitechurch, Bucks.

He served the office of sheriff in 1553, and 1561. He was *s.* at his decease by his son,

THOMAS LOVETT, esq. of Astwell, who *m.* Elizabeth, daughter of Richard Fermor, esq. of Easton Neston, and by her (who *m.* secondly, William Grey, esq. of Dagnam land, in Essex) left a daughter, his heir, viz.

Jane, *m.* to John Shirley, esq. of Staunton Harold, in the county of Leicester, ancestor of the Earls Ferrers, and conveyed to her husband Astwell, and the greater portion of the estates in Oxford, Gloucester and Northampton.

Note—There was formerly in the great hall at Astwell, a table thirty-three feet long, three feet broad, and [illegible] inches deep, all of one plank of oak.

* Frances O'More was daughter and heiress of R[illegible] O'More, the descendant and representative of the [illegible] family of the O'Mores, Princes of Leix, whose [illegible] estates had been forfeited in the reign of ELIZABETH.

IV. Mary, *m.* to the Rev. John Downe, D.D.
V. Sarah, *m.* to Robert Herne, esq.
VI. Rebecca.
VII. Penelope.
VIII. Arabella, *m.* to Charles Playdell, esq.

The eldest son and heir,

ROBERT LOVETT, esq. of Liscombe, was sheriff of Buckinghamshire in 1664, and died in 1609, aged seventy-four. He *m.* first, Penelope, daughter and heir of Thomas Aylet, esq. of Howells, in Essex, and had issue,

ROBERT, who *m.* Theodosia, daughter of Sir John Halsey, knt. but *d. s. p.* in the lifetime of his father.

LETTICE, *m.* to Thomas Pigott, esq. of Doddeshall, Bucks, but *d.* issueless.

PENELOPE, *m.* to Edward Bate, esq. of Maid's Morton, Bucks, and had a daughter, who *m.* first, Clifton Packe, esq. of Prestwould, in Leicestershire, and had a daughter, Penelope Packe,* *m.* to Richard Verney, afterwards Lord Willoughby de Broke. Mrs. Packe *m.* secondly, Colonel James Pentlebury, of the artillery.

Robert dying without surviving male issue, was *s.* by his brother,

EDWARD LOVETT, esq. of Corfe, in the county of Devon, who *m.* Joan, daughter and heir of James Searle, esq. of Tostock, and had two daughters, Penelope, wife of Sir Henry Northcote, bart. and Joan, of Hatch, esq. with a son and heir,

ROBERT LOVETT, esq. of Liscombe and Corfe, who *d.* unm. and was *s.* by his first cousin,

CHRISTOPHER LOVETT, esq. eldest son of Christopher Lovett, lord mayor of Dublin, but this gentleman dying unm. was *s.* by his brother,

JOHN LOVETT, esq. of Liscombe and Corfe, who *m.* first, Susannah, widow of — Horton, esq. and daughter and co-heiress of Laurence Lovett, esq. of Eythorp, and had issue,

ROBERT, his heir.
Christopher, of Dublin, who *m.* Mrs. Wellington, and had issue.

Colonel Lovett *m.* secondly, the Hon. Mary Verney,† daughter of Ralph Verney, Viscount Fermanagh, of Middle Claydon, Bucks, and had further issue,

III. Verney, M.P. for Wendover. This gentleman was major in the 39th Foot, when that regiment went to India, the first of his majesty's regiments which served there. He *d.* unm. and was buried at Soulbury.
IV. John, captain R.N. a distinguished officer, *d.* unmarried.

I. Mary, *d.* young.
II. Elizabeth, *d.* unm.

Colonel John Lovett died in 1710, and was succeeded by his eldest son by his first wife (Susannah, widow of Horton, and daughter of Laurence Lovett, of Eythorp),

ROBERT LOVETT, esq. of Liscombe, in Bucks, and of Kingswell, in the county of Tipperary, who served the office of sheriff of the King's County, and married Sarah, daughter of Jonathan Ashe, esq. of Ashe Grove, in Tipperary, by whom he had surviving issue,

Robert, who *d.* unm.
JONATHAN, heir to his father.
William, captain 1st regiment of horse, *d.* unmarried.

Susannah, *m.* to Jonathan Darby, esq. of Leap Castle, in the King's County.
Mary, *d.* young.
Lettice, *m.* to Damer Darby, esq. younger brother of Jonathan, and died, leaving an only daughter.

He was *s.* by his son,

JONATHAN LOVETT, esq. of Liscombe, in Bucks, and Kingswell, in the county of Tipperary, of which latter he served the office of sheriff. He *m.* Eleanor, daughter of Daniel Munsergh, esq. of Macrony, in the county of Cork, and had issue,

I. JONATHAN, his heir.
II. Robert, *d.* young.
III. Verney, inherited the Irish property, and was of Kingswell. He was in holy orders, D.D. and chaplain to the Prince of Wales. He *m.*

---

* This lady died in her eighteenth year, 31st August, and the following lines compose her epitaph:

Underneath this stone doth lie
As much virtue as could die;
Which when alive did vigour give
To as much beauty as could live.

† In a pocket book of this lady's the following memorandum was found some years since. "Soon after my marriage, I rode over to see Liscombe, the ancient seat of my husband's family, being only about twelve miles from my father's. Mr. Lovett, to whom it belongs, not living in it, allowed Mr. Sandby, a very respectable man, the clergyman of the parish, to live in the house, who received us with great politeness. The house is old and very gloomy, surrounded with high walls and trees, but it has a venerable appearance. You go through a great gateway into a court, round which the house and chapel are built. The windows, all of which have more the look of a monastery than a mansion. Mr. Sandby, to whom I made the remark, assured me I must not judge from appearances, for though it might have a gloomy outside, there were more joyful hearts within than in any house in the county, for there were more marriages in Liscombe chapel than in any three churches in the neighbourhood. From the court you enter a great hall, which is a large room, and is entirely hung round with old armour. The gentleman assured me they were particularly curious, and endeavoured to explain to me their different uses; but I begged to be excused, as I could not attend murdering men. "Well, madam," says Mr. Sandby, "I will shew you something more in your way presently." From thence we proceeded through a variety of long passages and little rooms, for except the hall and the drawing room over it, which is a large and very handsome room, they are all small, but from their numbers must have held a very large family; as Mr. Sandby assured me, of all sizes, there were more than fifty. But what with the old tapestry, and the dark gilt leather furniture, and black oak, (for I believe this family considered paint as great an abomination in their house as they would on the faces of their wives and daughters,) I never saw any place more calculated to induce one to change this world for another. We came at last to the nursery, and Mr. Sandby directed my attention to a something in a great old frame over the chimney, but which, being in the old black letter, like a church Bible, I could not read a word of. "That, madam," says he, "is the nursery song of this family, founded on the two characters of the warrior and the lover, which tradition represents as eminently united in William Lovett, the founder of this house.

The song is as follows:

May my child be as stout,
May my child be as strong,
And my brave boy live also as long,
As Willy of Normandy.

From the nursery we proceeded to a little closet with a thousand locks. Mr. Sandby shewed us a chest full of papers and parchments, which, he said, were the different grants and appointments for some centuries of this family; and in my lifetime I never saw anything more beautifully illumined than some of them were. He said the chest contained as curious a collection of letters as were in the possession of any private family in the kingdom. He said the letters were in general from some of the first people in the court of JAMES I. and CHARLES I.

Frances-Mary, daughter and co-heiress of Henry Gervais,* of Lismore, D. D. archdeacon of Cashel, and had three sons and three daughters, viz.

JONATHAN-HENRY, who went to India, a writer in the Company's service, and was ambassador and resident, at one time, at the court of Persia. He died unmarried.
William, R. N. *d.* unm.
HENRY-WILLIAM, who inherited Kingswell, on the death of his father; and Soulbury and the estates in Ireland (devised in 1770, by Verney Lovett, to the late baronet), on the death of Sir Jonathan.

Elizabeth, *m.* to Colonel Cameron.
Melesina-Henrietta, *m.* to the Rev. Mr. Woodward, son of the Bishop of Cloyne.
Frances-Mary, *m.* to John Ashton Yates, esq. of Dingle Head, Lancashire, and Bryanstone Square, M. P. for the county of Carlow.

I. Mary, *m.* to Richard Weekes, esq. of Limerick, and survived his widow, without issue.
II. Eleanor, *m.* to Jonathan Darby, esq. of Leap Castle, in the King's County.
III. Jane, *m.* to John Bennet, one of the judges of the King's Bench, in Ireland, and *d.* leaving issue.
IV. Elizabeth, *d.* young.
V. Susanna, *m.* to William Henn, esq. master in chancery in Ireland, son of William Henn, one of the judges of the King's Bench.
IV. Elizabeth, *m.* to John Pigott, esq. of Capard, in the Queen's County.

The eldest son and heir,

I. SIR JONATHAN LOVETT, of Liscombe, in the county of Buckingham, was created a BARONET† 23rd October, 1781. Upon the death of his uncle Verney in 1770 he succeeded to the Irish estates, so that in him centred the remnant of the estates of the Lovett family in both kingdoms. In the year 1772 he enclosed the common field of Soulbury and Hollingdon, and expended large sums of money in the reparation of the old house at Liscombe, which, from the non-residence of the family for nearly a century, had fallen into decay. He m. Sarah, daughter of Jonathan Darby, esq. of Leap Castle, in the King's County, and had issue,

ROBERT-TURVILLE-JONATHAN, died in 1807.

Elizabeth.
Letitia.
Arabella, died unmarried.

He died 12th January, 1812, when the BARONETCY EXPIRED, and the paternal estates, Liscombe, &c. devolved upon his daughter as co-heirs, whilst the estates at Soulbury and in Ireland, devised by Verney Lovett in 1770, passed to his nephew, HENRY WILLIAM LOVETT, esq. now heir male of this ancient family.

Arms—Quarterly; first and fourth, sa. three wolves' heads or, for LOVETT of Normandy; second and third, arg. three wolves passant, in pale sa. for LOVETT of England.

---

to Sir Robert Lovett; who, from them, appears to have been a man of distinguished abilities, as the letters are upon very important subjects, and those of CHARLES I. allude particularly to the times. One, the contents of which I wished my father to be informed of (I begged to take an account in writing): it was from the secretary of state, Sir Edward Nicholas, in the year 1642. He writes to Sir Robert Lovett as his old friend, wishing him to come to London, as he can assure him he will not have any difficulty to obtain what he long ago should have been in possession of. "I asked," said Mr. Sandby, "the late Mr. Lovett, my patron, what that alluded to. He said, his father had told him, that upon the first creation of baronets, he had been promised to have been one. Why he had been omitted he could never learn, but that he attributes it to a disagreement he once had with Lord Salisbury upon some militia business; but of this he was not certain. However, thinking himself very ill used, he retired into the country, and never went to court again. That upon hearing from Sir Edward Nicholas, he wrote to thank him, but declined the honour on account of the largeness of his family, and that from the declining state of his health, he was unequal to undertake the journey, and which was really the case, for he died soon after. My patron, one of the best of men, never made any application for what I told him, many times, I thought he had such good pretensions. But his answer was always, I do not love obligations, and a refusal I should consider an insult; let things remain therefore as they are." Mrs. Lovett, in continuation, proceeds; "My father was so pleased with the account I gave him, that in a few days after, he went to Liscombe himself. Upon his return, he said he was highly entertained; that they were some of the most interesting letters he had ever read, and put many things in a different point of view from what he had before seen them in; that he had not time to go through the tenth part of them, but that he had promised to spend two or three days with Mr. Sandby to look over them all. I do not remember his ever mentioning whether he did so or not. Happening by accident, many years after, to find the above memorandum, and Mr. Lovett, to whom Liscombe then belonged, being in England, (for the family have long resided in Ireland,) I took the first opportunity of inquiring after my old friends the arms and papers at Liscombe, but sorry am I to record their fate. He said upon the death of his elder brother, who died a few months before he was of age, his mother had ordered some new furniture, which ha[illegible] put into the house (as he intended residing there [illegible] sold; but that by some unfortunate mistake, the [illegible] had sold the whole, old and new, and that a trace was [illegible] remaining. That a blacksmith, who had purchased [illegible] of the old armour, declared he believed it had been made by the devil, for that he could make no use of it. [illegible] an equal degree of inattention, the papers were [illegible] that the chest was left open, and that the only [illegible] could ever receive of them was, that the children [illegible] made kites of the letters, and that the tailor of the parish told him he had cut up many of the parchments for measures, and he believed others had done the same; [illegible] there were very pretty pictures at the tops of them (alluding to the illumined letters,) which he had given his child. To the public probably the loss is not [illegible] teresting, but to the family it is irreparable.

* This gentleman's grandmother, Madame St. Ge[illegible] on the revocation of the edict of Nantes fled to Ir[illegible] with her youthful son, afterwards the celebrated [illegible] Gervais, who, on account of his great wit and ta[illegible] Dean Swift used to say was the only person he was af[illegible] of in company.

† The origin of the creation of the title is thus rela[illegible] —In the summer of the year 1781, the Earl of Ches[illegible] field having been some time absent from court, was [illegible] by *King* GEORGE III. where he had been so long [illegible] a visit to Mr. Lovett, of Buckinghamshire," said the [illegible] "Ah!" said the king, "is that Lovett of Liscombe [illegible] they are of the genuine old Norman breed; how happens it that they are not baronets? would he accept the [illegible] Go tell him," continued the king, "that if he'll accept it's much at his service; they have ever been staunch [illegible] the crown at a pinch." The communication was [illegible] ingly made, and the baronetage accepted; and Sir Jonathan, on going to court, was not less gratified than [illegible] nished at the cordial reception he met with, his [illegible] not only shewing a perfect knowledge of his descent [illegible] of the loyalty of the family, but likewise making particular inquiries as to the contents of the curious [illegible] mentioned in the note below, as having been at Lis[illegible] At a later period Sir Jonathan, who possessed great influence in the county of Bucks, was offered a pe[illegible] but having lost his only surviving son, he declined [illegible] honour.

LOWTHER, OF WHITEHAVEN.

Created 11th June, 1642.

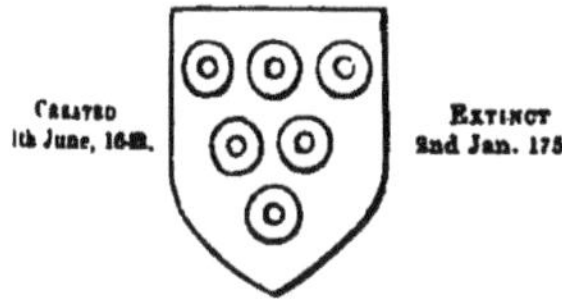

Extinct 2nd Jan. 1755.

Lineage.

The family of Lowther is of great antiquity in the county of Westmorland. The name is local, and has been written Loder, Louder, Loader, Louthery, and Lowther, from the town and manor of Lowther.* The manor was part of the great barony of Appleby, and its lords held it in cornage (a sort of military tenure) from the Viponts and Cliffords.

Sir Gervasius de Louther, knt. lived *temp.* Henry III., and his great-grandson,

Sir Hugh de Louther, knt. was attorney-general to Edward I. and returned one of the knights for Westmoreland to the parliament held at Lincoln in the 29th of the same reign. He *m.* a daughter of Peter de Fiiliol, of Cumberland, and had two sons, Hugh (Sir), and Thomas, one of the justices of the King's Bench 5 Edward III. The elder,

Sir Hugh de Louther, knt. having taken up arms with Thomas, Earl of Lancaster, and others against Piers Gaveston *temp.* Edward II. and being concerned in the death of the said Gaveston, had the king's pardon, according to a special provision, in the parliament held at Westminster 15th October, 1313, wherein it was enacted that none should be called to account for the said offence. In 17 Edward II. he was one of the knights of the shire for Cumberland, and the next year was a commissioner of array for the same county on the occasion of a menaced invasion by the French king, as he was again in the Edward III. for the counties of Westmoreland and Cumberland. In the 14th of that reign he served for Westmoreland in the parliament held at Westminster. The next year he was again returned, with Peter de Tilliol, for Cumberland to the parliament held at Woodstock, and they had a writ for £19. 12*s.* to be levied on the county, for their expenses in attending there nine days. He was sheriff of Cumberland 26, 27, and 28 Edward III. In the 23rd of the same reign he served again as one of the knights for Cumberland, in which year a complaint was made by Sir William Ramsell, of Scotland, that being taken prisoner at the battle of Durham by John de Standish, whom he had paid for his redemption, was delivered to Sir Hugh de Louthre, knt. to be conveyed safely from his enemies, who in consideration of a falcon he presented to him, undertook to conduct him and entertain him at his house for three weeks. After which he delivered him to John, son and heir of Thomas de Louthre, his kinsman, to convey him out of the king's dominions; but the said John and Thomas carried him to strange places under close confinement, until he agreed to pay the said John de Louthre and Thomas a fine of 230 marks; whereupon the king commissioned Henry de Piercy, Ralph de Nevill, and Thomas de Lucy, to inquire into the fact. He departed this life about the 46th of the same Edward, and was *s.* by his son,

Sir John de Louther, knt. who was returned to parliament by the county of Westmoreland 50 Edward III. and 2 Richard II. He was *s.* by his elder son,†

Sir Robert de Louther, knt. M.P. for Cumberland 15 and 17 Richard II. 2, 5, and 8 Henry IV. and 2 Henry V. In the 6th of the last reign he was sheriff of the same county. He *d.* in 1430, was buried in the parish church of Louther, and *s.* by his son,

Sir Hugh de Louther, knt. who, in the lifetime of his father, served under Henry V. in the wars of France, and was one of the heroes of Agincourt. In the 4th, 9th, and 27th, Sir Hugh represented Cumberland in parliament, and was sheriff in the 18th and 34th of the same reign. He *m.* Anne, daughter of John de Darentwater, of Cumberland, and was *s.* by his son,

Sir Hugh Louther, who *m.* Mabel, daughter and heir of Sir William Lancaster, of Stockbridge, and was father of

Sir Hugh Louther, who *m.* Anne, daughter of Lancelot Thirkeld, knt. and was *s.* by his son,

Sir Hugh Louther, who was made a knight of the Bath 17th November, 1501, on the marriage of *Prince* Arthur, eldest son of Henry VII. He *m.* Dorothy, daughter of Henry, Lord Clifford, and had a son and heir,

Sir John Lowther, knt. sheriff of Cumberland 7 and 24 Henry VIII. In 4 Edward VI. he *m.* Lucy, daughter of Sir Thomas Curwen, of Workington, in Cumberland; and was *s.* by his eldest son,

Sir Richard Lowther, knt. sheriff of Cumberland 8 and 30 Elizabeth. He was likewise lord warden of the West Marches, and thrice commissioner in the great affairs between England and Scotland. When Mary, Queen of Scots, sought safety in England, and arrived at Cumberland 17th May, 1568, *Queen* Elizabeth sent orders to Sir Richard Lowther to convey her majesty to Carlisle; but he subsequently incurred Elizabeth's displeasure by permitting the Duke of Norfolk to visit the royal captive. He *d.* aged seventy-seven, in the year 1607, and was *s.* by his eldest son (by Frances, his wife, daughter of John Middleton, esq.)

Sir Christopher Lowther, *b.* 8th September, 1577, who received the honour of knighthood from *King* James I. at Newcastle, whither Sir Christopher attended his majesty with "a gallant companie" from the Scottish border, 13th April, 1603. He *m.* first, Eleanor, daughter of William Musgrave, esq. of Hayton, in Cumberland, and had by that lady, with daughters, eight sons, viz.

I. John, his heir.

II. Gerard (Sir), of St. Michael's, Dublin, chief justice of the Common Pleas in Ireland, and afterwards (1654) lord chancellor of that kingdom. He *m.* first, Anne, daughter of Sir Ralph Bulmer, and relict of — Welbury, esq.; secondly, Anne, daughter of Sir Laurence Parsons; and thirdly, Margaret, daughter of Sir John King; but died issueless.

---

* That is, lower than the hills that surround, as that part of the county is called the bottom of Westmoreland.

† His younger son, William de Louther, obtained the king's license, 14 Richard II. with Sir Thomas Swinburne and Sir John Etton, knts. William Selveyn, Henry Van-Croy-pole, and Simon Ward, to challenge certain persons of the kingdom of Scotland to perform and exercise feats of arms; and thereupon the king appointed John, Lord Roos, to fix a camp and to be judge in the said exercise. In 2 Henry IV. this William de Louther was sheriff of Cumberland, and afterwards in the 7th, 8th, and 9th years of the same reign.

III. Richard.
IV. Christopher.
V. William.
VI. Launcelot (Sir), of Youngston, in Kildare, one of the barons of the Exchequer, and a privy councillor in Ireland.
VII. Robert, from whom descended the branch of Marske, in Yorkshire.
VIII. George.

Sir Christopher *m.* secondly, Mary, daughter of Thomas Wilson, dean of Durham (secretary of state to *Queen* ELIZABETH), and relict of Burdett of Bramcote, in the county of Warwick. He was *s.* at his decease by his eldest son,

SIR JOHN LOWTHER, knt. M.P. for Westmoreland *temp.* JAMES I. and CHARLES I. He was knighted by the latter king, and was of his majesty's council for the government of the northern parts. He *d.* 15th September, 1637, leaving by his wife, Eleanor, daughter of William Fleming, esq. of Rydale, three sons and two daughters, viz.

I. JOHN, created a Baronet of Nova Scotia in 1640, and was *s.* in 1675 by his grandson,

SIR JOHN LOWTHER, who was raised to the peerage in 1696 as VISCOUNT LONSDALE, which dignity expired with HENRY, the third viscount, in 1750, when the estates devolved upon

SIR JAMES LOWTHER, who was created Earl of Lonsdale, in 1784, to himself and the heirs of his body; but having no issue, his lordship obtained a new patent in 1797, creating him VISCOUNT LOWTHER, with special remainder, which conferred the inheritance upon

SIR WILLIAM LOWTHER, of Swillington, present (1837) EARL OF LONSDALE. (Refer to BURKE's *Peerage and Baronetage*.)

II. CHRISTOPHER.
III. WILLIAM, of Swillington, ancestor of the present EARL OF LONSDALE.

I. Agnes, *m.* to Roger Kirkby, esq.
II. Frances, *m.* to John Dodsworth, esq.

The second son,

I. CHRISTOPHER LOWTHER, esq. of Whitehaven, in Cumberland, was created a BARONET by *King* CHARLES I. 11th June, 1642. Sir Christopher *m.* Frances, daughter and heir of Christopher Lancaster, esq. of Stockbridge, in Westmoreland, and had by her (who *m.* secondly, John Lamplugh, esq. of Lamplugh, in Cumberland,) a daughter, Frances, married to Richard Lamplugh, esq. of Ribton, and a son, his successor in 1644,

II. SIR JOHN LOWTHER, M.P. for Cumberland from 32 CHARLES II. to 12 WILLIAM III. and was one of the commissioners of the Admiralty in the latter reign. He *m.* Jane, daughter of Woolley Leigh, esq. of Addington, in Surrey, and had issue,

CHRISTOPHER, } successive baronets.
JAMES, }

Jane, *d.* unmarried 27th February, 1730-1.

He *d.* in January, 1705-6, and was *s.* by his elder son,

III. SIR CHRISTOPHER LOWTHER, who died issueless 2nd October, 1731, and was *s.* by his brother,

IV. SIR JAMES LOWTHER, F.R.S. M.P. for Cumberland *temp. Queen* ANNE, GEORGE I. and GEORGE II. He *d.* unmarried 2nd January, 1755, when the BARONETCY EXPIRED.

Arms—Or, six annulets, three, two, and one, sa.

LOW

LOWTHER, OF SWILLINGTON.

CREATED 6th Jan. 1714-15.—EXTINCT 22nd Dec. 17[illegible]

Lineage.

SIR WILLIAM LOWTHER, knt. of Leeds, youngest [illegible] of Sir John Lowther, knt. of Lowther, and Eleanor Fleming, his wife (refer to LOWTHER OF WHITEHAVEN) purchased the maner of Swillington, in the county of York, of George, Lord Darcey and Conyers, and was possessed of Great Preston and Garforth, in the same county. He was one of the council in the north, and M. P. for Pontefract from 1661 to 1678. He *m.* J[illegible] daughter of William Busfeild, of Leeds, merchant, and had issue,

WILLIAM, his heir.
Richard, in holy orders, rector of Swillington, [illegible] in 1702, leaving by Margaret, his wife, daughter of John Adams, esq. of Rowcliffe, in Yorkshire, two sons,
John.
Richard, rector of Swillington, chaplain to the Prince of Orange, and minister of the English church at Rotterdam, who dying in [illegible]cember, 1756, left
WILLIAM.
Mary, *m.* to Mr. Vevers.
Elizabeth, *m.* to Mr. Robson.
Jane, *m.* to Sir Francis Bland, bart. of Kippax,
Eleanor, *m.* to Richard Harrison, esq. of Cave,
Mary, *m.* to William Ellis, esq. of Kidwell,
Frances, *m.* to Richard Beaumont, esq. of Whitley.
Agnes, *m.* to William Dawson, esq.
Dorothy, *m.* to Robert Baynes, esq. of Knostrop,

Sir William, who was a commissioner of the [illegible] and burgess in parliament for Pontefract [illegible] CHARLES II. died, aged eighty, in February, 16[illegible] was *s.* by his son,

SIR WILLIAM LOWTHER, knt. of Great Preston [illegible]riff of Yorkshire in 1681, and M.P. for Pont[illegible] He was born in August, 1639, and died 7th De[illegible] 1705, having had issue, by Catherine, daughter [illegible] Thomas Harrison, esq. of Dancer's Hill, Herts [illegible] Cave, in Yorkshire, five sons and two daughters,

WILLIAM, his heir.
Richard, of Leeds, merchant, *m.* first, Chr[illegible] daughter of Sir Christopher Wandesford [illegible] of Kirklington, in the county of York, and [se]condly, Mary, daughter of Sir Robert F[illegible] and had by the latter three daughters, M[illegible] Catherine, and Elizabeth.
Robert, of Calverley.
CHRISTOPHER, sole executor to his father, [illegible] left him an estate at Little Preston, in the c[ounty] of York. He *m.* Elizabeth, daughter of [illegible] Maude, esq. of Alverstborp, Wakefield, and [illegible]croft. (See BURKE's *Commoners*, vol. ii. [illegible] He died in 1718, leaving
WILLIAM, of Little Preston, rector of [Swil]lington and prebendary of York, of w[hom] hereafter as heir to Sir William Low[ther] the second baronet.
Martha, *m.* to George Thompson, esq. [illegible] and had issue a son, George W[illegible] Thompson.

Catherine, m. to Henry, son and heir of Henry Slingsby, esq. master of the Mint.
Mary, m. to John Stanhope, esq. of Horsforth, in the county of York.

The eldest son,

I. WILLIAM LOWTHER, esq. of Swillington, high sheriff of Yorkshire in 1697 and M.P. for Pontefract in the reigns of WILLIAM III. Queen ANNE, and GEORGE I. was created a BARONET 6th January, 1714-15. Sir William m. Amabella, daughter of Banaster, third Lord Maynard, and had issue,

WILLIAM, his successor.
Henry, of Newcastle upon-Tyne, M.D. d. in 1743.
John, governor of Surat, d. s. p.
Amabella, } d. unm.
Jane, }

He d. 6th March, 1629, and was s. by his eldest son,

II. SIR WILLIAM LOWTHER, M.P. for Pontefract, m. first, in 1719, Diana, daughter of Thomas Condon, esq. of the county of York, which lady died issueless in 1736, and Sir William m. secondly, Catherine, eldest daughter of Sir William Ramsden, bart. but died s. p. 22nd December, 1763, when the BARONETCY became EXTINCT. Sir William bequeathed the estate of Swillington to his cousin,

THE REV. WILLIAM LOWTHER, of Little Preston, rector of Swillington and prebendary of York, who, being created a BARONET 22nd August, 1764, became SIR WILLIAM LOWTHER, of Swillington. He m. Anne, daughter of the Rev. Charles Zouch, vicar of Sandal, in the county of York, and had two sons,

WILLIAM, who inherited the barony and viscounty of Lowther on the decease of James, Earl of Lonsdale, in 1802, and was afterwards himself created EARL OF LONSDALE. (See BURKE's Peerage.)
JOHN, of Swillington, created a BARONET in 1824.

Arms—Or, six annulets, three, two, and one, sa.

LOWTHER, OF MARSKE.

CREATED 15th June, 1697.—EXTINCT 3rd Feb. 1753.

Lineage.

ROBERT LOWTHER, esq. seventh son of Sir Christopher Lowther, knt. and Eleanor Musgrave, his wife (see LOWTHER OF WHITEHAVEN), m. first, a daughter of Butler, and secondly, Elizabeth, daughter of William Holcroft, esq. of Lancashire, by whom he had two sons. John, the younger, was a merchant at Dantzic, and marrying Mary, daughter of Colonel John Lowther, left issue. The elder son and heir,

ANTHONY LOWTHER, esq. of Marske, in the county of York, M.P. for Appleby in 1678-9, m. Margaret, daughter of Sir William Penn, knt. admiral to *King* CHARLES II. and was s. by his eldest surviving son,

I. WILLIAM LOWTHER, esq. of Marske, who was created a BARONET by *King* WILLIAM III. 15th June, 1697. Sir William m. Catherine, daughter and heir of Thomas Preston, esq. of Holker, in Lancashire, (see BURKE's *Commoners*, vol. i. p. 479,) and had issue,

THOMAS, his successor.
Preston.
Catherine.
Margaret.

He d. in April, 1704, and was s. by his elder son,

II. SIR THOMAS LOWTHER, M.P. for Lancaster, who m. July, 1723, Lady Elizabeth Cavendish, daughter of William, second Duke of Devonshire, and dying 2 March, 1745, was s. by his son,

III. SIR WILLIAM LOWTHER, who d. unmarried in 1753, when the BARONETCY became EXTINCT. He devised Holker and the rest of the estates he had inherited from the Prestons to his cousin, Lord George Cavendish.

Arms—Or, six annulets, three, two, and one, sa.

LUCAS, OF FENTON.

CREATED 20th May, 1644.

EXTINCT about 1668.

Lineage.

In 1644 a BARONETCY was conferred on

I. SIR GERVAS LUCAS, of Fenton, in Lincolnshire, descended from an ancient family in that county. During the civil conflicts of the unhappy times in which he lived, Sir Gervas adhered with devoted attachment to the royal cause, and was governor of Belvoir Castle for *King* CHARLES. He died unmarried about 1668, and with him the BARONETCY EXPIRED.

Arms—Arg. a chevron gu. between three ogresses, on a chief az. a moor cock of the field between two cross crosslets fitchée or.

LUCY, OF BROXBURNE.

CREATED 11th Mar. 1617-8.

EXTINCT 19th Nov. 1759.

Lineage.

For the early descent of the LUCYS refer to BURKE's *History of the Commoners*, vol. iii. p. 97.

SIR THOMAS LUCY, knt. of Charlecote, in the county of Warwick, only son and heir of Sir Thomas Lucy, immortalized by Shakspeare as JUSTICE SHALLOW, m. first, Dorothy, daughter of Nicholas Arnold, esq. and by her had a son, Thomas, who d. young, and a daughter, Joyce, wife of Sir William Cook, knt. of Highnam. Sir Thomas m. secondly, Constance, daughter and heir of Sir Richard Kingsmill, knt. of High Clere, Hants, and had a large family; of whom, THOMAS, the eldest son, inherited Charlecote and carried on the principal line of the family; while the second son,

I. SIR RICHARD LUCY, acquiring, by intermarriage with Elizabeth, daughter and co-heir of Sir Henry Cock, of Broxburne, Herts, and relict of the Hon. Robert West, the estate of Broxburne, settled there. He received the honour of knighthood in 1617, and was created a BARONET 11th March, 1617-18. Sir Richard m. secondly, Rebecca, daughter and co heir of Thomas Chapman, esq. of Wormley, Herts. By his first wife he had a daughter, Constantia, m. to Henry, Lord Colerain, and an only son, his successor at his decease 6th April, 1667,

II. Sir Kingsmill Lucy, F.R.S. of Facombe, Hants, m. Lady Theophila Berkeley, daughter of George, Earl of Berkeley, and by her ladyship (who m. secondly, Robert Nelson, esq. of London,) had a son and two daughters, viz.

- Berkeley, his heir.
- Theophila, m. to Sir William Ingoldsby, bart.
- Mary, d. unm.

He died about the year 1678, and was s. by his son,

III. Sir Berkeley Lucy, F.R.S. who m. Catherine, daughter of Charles Cotton, esq. of Beresford, in the county of Stafford, and by her (who d. in June, 1740,) had an only surviving daughter and heiress,

- Mary Lucy, m. to the Hon. Charles Compton, youngest son of George, fourth Earl of Northampton, and had issue,
  - Charles Compton, } seventh and eighth Earls
  - Spencer Compton, } of Northampton.
  - Mary Compton, m. first, to Richard Haddock, esq. R.N.; and secondly, to Arthur Scott, esq. R.N.
  - Jane Compton, m. to George, first Lord Rodney.
  - Catherine Compton, m. to John, Earl of Egmont; she was created Baroness Arden.
  - Elizabeth Compton, m. to the Hon. Henry Drummond, son of William, fourth Viscount Strathallan, and d. in 1819.

Sir Berkeley d. 19th November, 1759, when the Baronetcy expired.

Arms—Gu. three luces (or pikes) hauriant arg.

LUMLEY, OF BRADFIELD.

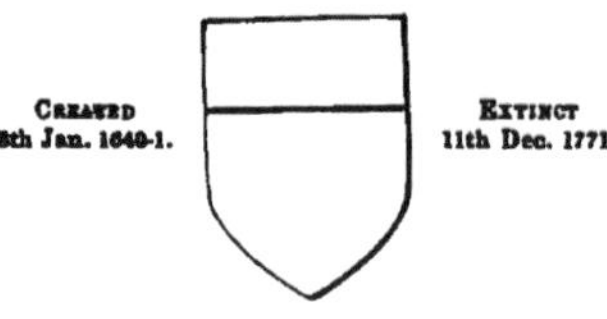

Created 8th Jan. 1640-1. Extinct 11th Dec. 1771.

Lineage.

Dominigo Lomely, an Italian by birth, and of the bedchamber to Henry VIII. commanded a troop of horse and maintained them at his own expense at Boulogne for the use of the king. His son,

James Lomelin or Lumley, was a merchant of London, and died at the advanced age of eighty-eight in 1592, when he was s. by his son,

Sir Martyn Lumley, knt. sheriff of London in 1614, and lord mayor in 1623. He died in 1634, and was magnificently interred at Great St. Helens; the funeral directed by Sir Henry St. George, Sir William Le Neve, and others of the heralds. By his will, dated 1st September, 1631, he gave to the churchwardens of St. Helens and their successors for ever an annuity or rent-charge of £20, to be issuing out of his messuage or tenement in the parish of St. John the Evangelist, London, upon trust, for establishing a lecture or sermon for ever to be preached in that parish church on Thursday evening weekly from Michaelmas to Lady-Day, and the said churchwardens to pay the same to a goodly divine for preaching the said lecture; he bequeathed also £4 per annum for the use of the poor of the said parish. He m. Mary Witham, and was s. by his son,

I. Martyn Lumley, esq. of Bradfield Magna, in the county of Essex, knight of that shire in the Long Parliament, who was created a Baronet by Charles I. 8th January, 1640-1. Sir Martyn m. first, Jane, daughter and heir of John Meredith, esq. of Denbighshire, and by her had an only daughter, Prudence, wife of Sir Roger Mostyn, bart. of Mostyn, in the county of Flint. He m. secondly, Mary, daughter of Alderman Edward Alleyn, of London, and by that lady had a son, his successor in 1651,

II. Sir Martyn Lumley, who m. Anne, daughter of Sir John Langham, bart. of Cottesbrooke, and dying in August, 1702 (his wife d. in 1692), was s. by his only son,

III. Sir Martyn Lumley, who wedded, first, Elizabeth, daughter of Sir Jonathan Dawes, knt. alderman of London, and had an only surviving child, Anne, wife of Sir Stephen Anderson. He m. secondly, Elizabeth, daughter of Richard Chamberlayn, esq. of Gray's Inn, and by her had

- James, his successor.
- Elizabeth, m. to the Right Rev. Dr. Cecil, Bishop of Bangor, and survived his widow.

Sir Martyn m. thirdly, Elizabeth, daughter of Clement Rawlinson, gent. of Sanscate, in Lancashire. He d. 12th January, 1710, and was s. by his son,

IV. Sir James Lumley, who died unmarried 11th December, 1771, when the Baronetcy became extinct.

Arms—Or, a chief gu. (same as the city of Naples).

LUMSDEN, OF AUCHINDOIR.

Created 9th Aug. 1821.—Extinct 15th Dec. 1821.

Lineage.

In 1821 a Baronetcy was conferred on

I. Sir Harry Nivan Lumsden, of Auchindoir, co. Aberdeenshire, but he survived the creation but four months. He d. s. p. and the title of course expired.

LYDE, OF AYOT ST. LAWRENCE.

Created 13th Oct. 1772. Extinct 22nd July, 1791.

Lineage.

Cornelius Lyde, esq. of Stanton Wick, in Somersetshire, b. 2nd March, 1640-1 (son of William Lyde of Week, and grandson of another William Lyde, who was born in 1576), m. 16th May, 1661, Mary Bak... and by her, who d. 8th June, 1715, had issue,

- James, of Stanton Wick and of the city of Bristol, merchant, baptized 6th June, 1671; m. Martha, daughter of Michael Pope, also of Bristol and d. 12th March, 1731.
- John, baptized 26th January, 1673-4; died abt. 1728.
- Samuel, of London, M.D. m. Anna-Regina, daughter of the burgomaster of Leyden, in Holland and d. s. p.

Stephen, baptised 9th June, 1681, colonel of militia in Virginia, and representative in the House of Burgesses in that colony for King William County. He *d. s. p.* leaving a widow, who *m.* — Taylor, esq.

Lyonel, of whom presently.

Cornelius, baptized 20th January, 1686-7, who purchased the estate of Ayot St. Lawrence, in the county of Hertford. He *m.* first, in 1716, Mary, daughter of John Peck, which lady *d. s. p.* in 1718; and secondly, 30th November, 1727, Rachel, daughter of Cornelius Wittenom, esq. of London, by whom, who *d.* in 1782, aged eighty-four, he left at his decease, 11th July, 1747, two daughters, his co-heirs; the elder of whom,

Rachel, married her cousin, Sir Lyonel Lyde, bart.

Susanna.

Mr. Lyde *d.* 25th July, 1717, and was buried at Chew Magna, in Somersetshire. His fifth son,

Lyonel Lyde, esq. baptized 28th February, 1682, was mayor of the city of Bristol. He married two wives; by the first, whom he married in Virginia, he had a son,

Cornelius, a representative for King William County and colonel of a regiment in Virginia. His son,

Lyonel, was blown up in an engagement at sea in his passage to England in 1747.

By his second wife, who was an heiress and died 24th February, 1729-30, Mr. Lyde had issue,

Lyonel, of whom presently.

Samuel, born at Bristol 5th February, 1729-30, who *m.* Anne, daughter of John Lewis, gent. of Richmond, and left an only surviving child,

Rachel, *m.* to the Rev. James Wiggett, of Crudwick, in Wiltshire.

Anna-Maria, *b.* in 1721, who *m.* Chauncy Poole, esq. of Bristol, and had issue,

Nicholas Poole, who *m.* Martha, daughter of Cornelius Denne, of Cheapside, London, and *d. s. p.*

Lyonel Poole, of Shirehampton, in the county of Gloucester, who assumed the surname and arms of Lyde, as heir to his uncle Sir Lyonel. He *d. s. p.*

Anna-Maria Poole, *m.* to Levy Ames, esq. mayor of Bristol in 1789, who assumed the surname of Lyde, and had issue several sons and daughters.

Mr. Lyde died in 1744, and was buried at Bristol. His elder son by his second marriage,

I. Lyonel Lyde, esq. of Ayot St. Lawrence, born at Bristol 9th May, 1724, was created a Baronet 13th [illegible]ber, 1772. He *m.* in 1747, Rachel, daughter and co-heir of his uncle Cornelius Lyde, esq. of Ayot, but *d. s. p.* 22nd July, 1791, when the title became extinct. The manor of Ayot St. Lawrence passed by will to his nephew, Lyonel Poole, esq. of Shirehampton, and from him to the family of Ames.

Arms—Az. an eagle displayed double-headed erm.

MACKINTOSH, OF MACKINTOSH.

Created 30th Dec. 1812.

Extinct 21st Jan. 1820.

Lineage.

The family of Mackintosh, of that ilk, lineally descends from Shaw, second son of Duncan M'Duff, third Earl of Fife, and great-grandchild to Duncan M'Duff who slew Macbeth. This Shaw, being sent by Malcolm IV. in the year 1163, to repress a rebellion in Morayland, which he effected in a most signal manner, was rewarded with the constabulary of the castle of Inverness; and from his residence among the people of the country who spoke the Gaelic only, was called Mac-in-tosh-ick, that is to say, Thomas, son or the principal and first man in dignity in the shire. He thus became the first of the name, and the progenitor of a long line of chiefs.

I. Æneas Mackintosh, of Mackintosh, the twenty-third laird, was created a Baronet in 1812. He *m.* Margaret, daughter of Sir Ludovick Grant, bart. of Dalvey, in the county of Moray; but *d. s. p.* 21st January, 1820, when the title became extinct. The present chief of this ancient and distinguished clan is Alexander Mackintosh, twenty-sixth laird of Mackintosh. (See Burke's *Commoners*, vol. iv.)

Arms—Quarterly: first or, a lion rampant gu.; second arg. a dexter arm couped fesseways, holding up a heart gu.; third az. a boar's head or; fourth or, a galley, her sails furled and oars in saltier sa. flags gu.

MACKWORTH, OF NORMANTON.

Created 4th June, 1619.

Extinct in 1803.

Lineage.

Mackworth, in the county of Derby, gave name to this ancient family, which had been seated there for several generations.* The chief of the line, who first settled in Rutlandshire, was

Thomas Mackworth, of Mackworth, in Derbyshire, who by intermarriage with Alice Basings, sister and

* A member of the family was amongst the victors at the battle of Poictiers, as one of the esquires in immediate attendance upon James, Lord Audley, K.G. John [illegible], Lord Audley, son-in-law, and eventually heir of the said James, granted, in consideration that John and James Mackworth were valiant men, and for the services rendered by them and their ancestors to the Audley family, a part of the arms of Audley, viz. party per pale indented, sable and ermine, a chevron, gules, fretté or, to be borne by the Mackworths and their descendants. In witness to which grant he put his seal of arms, viz. *Quarterly; first and fourth, frette, and second and third, ermine*, a chevron, circumscribed, *Sigillum Johannis D'Audley*, at his manor of Marketon, 1st August, 1404.

heir of Sir John de Basings,* acquired a fair inheritance in that county, but principally the towns and manors of Normanton, Empingham, and Hardwick, which first place, thence forward, became the seat of the family. This Thomas was *s.* by his son,

Henry Mackworth, of Normanton, who was sheriff of Rutland 18 Edward IV. and had two sons,

John, his heir, who predeceased him, leaving a son,
George, who inherited.

Thomas, ancestor of the Mackworths of Betton, now represented by Sir Digby Mackworth, bart. and of the Mackworths who took the name of Praed.

He was *s.* by his grandson,

George Mackworth, sheriff of Rutland 12 Henry VII. and 14, 22, and 26 Henry VIII. He *m.* Anne, daughter of Geffrey Sherard, esq. of Stapleford, and had a son, his successor in 1536,

Francis Mackworth, esq. of Normanton, who *m.* Ellen, one of the eight daughters of Humphry Hercy, esq. of Grove, in Nottinghamshire,† and co-heir of her brother Sir John Hercy, knt. (who *d. s. p.* 12 Elizabeth). This Francis was sheriff of Rutlandshire in the 30th and 35th of Henry VIII. and 3rd of *Queen* Mary. He *d.* in 1557, and was *s.* by his son,

George Mackworth, esq. who was thrice sheriff of Rutland *temp.* Elizabeth. He *m.* first, Grace, daughter of Ralph Rokeby, esq. serjeant-at-law; and secondly, Anne, daughter of Edmund Hall, esq. of Gretford: and was *s.* by his son,

I. Thomas Mackworth, esq. of Normanton, in the county of Rutland, sheriff in the 41 Elizabeth and 7 James I. who was created a Baronet 4th June, 1619. Sir Thomas *m.* Elizabeth, daughter and heir of Henry Hall, esq. of Gretford, in Lincolnshire, and sole heir of her mother, one of the daughters and co-heirs of Francis Neale, esq. of Tugby, in the same county, and had four sons, viz. Henry, his heir; Francis (Sir), *d.* unm.; Peregrine, *m.* the widow of Alexander Moor, esq. of Grantham, barrister-at-law, but had no issue; Neale, *d.* unm. Sir Thomas *d.* in March, 1625-6, and was *s.* by his eldest son,

II. Sir Henry Mackworth, who rebuilt the manor house at Normanton, and having married Mary, daughter of Robert Hopton, esq. of Witham, and sister and co-heir of Ralph, Lord Hopton,‡ had issue,

I. Thomas, his successor.
II. Robert, *m.* first in 1625, Elizabeth, daughter of John Hatcher, esq. of Empingham, and had,
  Robert, of Huntingdon, *m.* Mary, daughter of William Dowse, of the same place, merchant, and dying in 1733, left
    Thomas, who inherited as fifth baronet.
    Elizabeth, *m.* to Lewis Smith, esq. of Great Gedding.
  He (Robert sen.) *m.* secondly, Margaret, eldest daughter of Edward Corbet, esq. and had by her, a son who *d.* young, and a daughter Mary, the wife of Piercy Butler, esq.
III. Henry, *m.* Dorothy Hall, of Gretford, in Lincolnshire, and had two sons, viz.
  1. Henry, *m.* Katherine Roberts, of Empingham, and had Henry, sixth baronet.
  2. Thomas, killed in a duel.
IV. Edward, a merchant, *d. s. p.*
V. Gustavus, *m.* Dorothy, widow of Thomas, Lord Grey, of Groby, mother of Thomas, second Earl of Stamford, and daughter and co-heir of Edward Bourchier, fourth Earl Bath, by whom he had issue.
I. Margaret, *m.* to Philip Young, esq. of Keniton, in Shropshire.
II. Jane, *m.* to Hugh Underwood, esq. of Wittlesea, in the Isle of Wight.

Sir Henry *d.* in Aug. 1640, and was *s.* by his eldest son,

III. Sir Thomas Mackworth, M.P. for the county of Rutland, from the 31st of Charles II. to the time of his death. He *m.* first, Dorothy, daughter of Captain George Darell, of Cale Hill, in Kent, and by her had issue,

Thomas, who died in his father's lifetime.
Dorothy, *m.* to John Wingfield, esq. of Tickencote, in the county of Rutland, (refer to Burke's *Commoners*, vol. ii. p. 476.)
Utrechia, *d.* unm.

Sir Thomas wedded, secondly, Anne, daughter of Humphrey Mackworth, esq. of Betton, in Salop, and by her had to survive,

Thomas, successor to his father.
Jane, *m.* to Abraham Rys, gent. of Lincolnshire, and survived his widow, issueless.

He *d.* in November, 1694, and was *s.* by his son,

IV. Sir Thomas Mackworth, M.P. for the county of Rutland, in the room of his father, and re-elected to the 1st and 4th of *Queen* Anne, and two last parliaments of George I. He *d.* unm. in March, 1743, when his grandnephew (the grandson of his half-sister, Dorothy) the Rev. John Wingfield, of Trickencote, became his heir in blood, and the Baronetcy devolved upon his cousin and heir-at-law (refer to Robert, second son of the second baronet),

V. Sir Thomas Mackworth, an apothecary at Huntingdon, and alderman of that borough. He *m.* first, Elizabeth, daughter of John Maule, esq. and had by her four daughters,

Mary, *m.* to the Rev. Charles Nailour, of New Ross, in Ireland, and had issue.
Elizabeth, *m.* to James Robinson, of Ely.
Sally, *m.* to Leonard Fausett, of Lincoln.
Sukey, *m.* to John Wilkinson, of Wisbeach.

Sir Thomas *m.* secondly, Mary, relict of the Rev. Wm. Waller, of Great Stoughton, in Huntingdonshire, and daughter of the Rev. Leonard Reresby, of Thrybergh, in the county of York, but by her had no issue. He *d.* 17th October, 1769, and was *s.* by his cousin, (refer to Henry, third son of the second baronet,)

VI. Sir Henry Mackworth, who *m.* Elizabeth, daughter of the Rev. Edward Lamb, rector of Acle, in Norfolk, and dying 14th Jan. 1774, was *s.* by his son,

VII. Sir Henry Mackworth, one of the almsmen upon the poor knights' charity, in the Charter House

---

* Sir John de Basings, son of John, son of Thomas, by Margaret, his wife, daughter and heir of Thomas de Normanville, son of Ralph, son of Thomas de Normanville, who died *temp.* Henry III., whose ancestors, soon after the Conquest, were Lords of Normanton, and were also seated at Kenerton, in the hundred of Blackborne, in Kent, until their male issue failing, both that estate and this in Rutland, went with an heiress to the Basings, a family of great note and antiquity, descended from Adam de Basing, lord mayor of London in 1251, whose habitation in the city, occupied the place where Blackwell-hall was erected; from him the street and ward adjoining were denominated Basing's-hall Street, and Basing's-hall Ward.

† By Elizabeth, daughter of Sir John Digby, knt. of Ketteley.

‡ Sir Ralph Hopton, K.B. was created in 1643, in consequence of a victory he had then achieved over the parliamentarians, at Stratton, in Cornwall, Lord Hopton, *of Stratton*, with remainder, default of male issue, upon his uncle, Sir Arthur Hopton, knt. who having predeceased his lordship, the barony expired, and his estates devolved upon his sisters, as co-heirs, viz.

I. Rachel, *m.* to — Morgan, esq.
II. Mary, *m.* first to — Hartop, and secondly to Sir Henry Mackworth.
III. Catherine, *m.* to John Windham, esq.
IV. Margaret, *m.* to Sir Baynham Throgmorton, bart.

Burke's *Extinct Peerage.*

London, where he died issueless in 1663, when the Baronetcy expired.

Arms—Party per pale, indented, sable and ermine, a chevron gules, fretté or.

MACPHERSON, OF CALCUTTA.

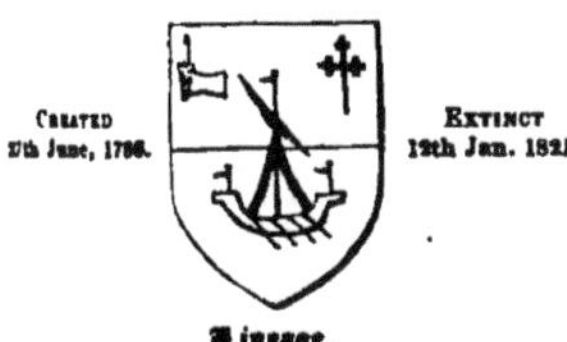

Created 27th June, 1786. Extinct 12th Jan. 1821.

Lineage.

John Macpherson, esq. younger son of Dr. John Macpherson, D.D. an eminent Scottish divine, by a daughter of Macleod, of Bemire, having been appointed a member of the supreme council of Bengal, in 1780, and governor-general on the return of Warren Hastings to England, in 1784, received, eventually, the unanimous thanks of the court of directors, for his conduct in India, and was created a Baronet 27th January, 1786. Sir John returned to Britain in 1787, and sate in parliament afterwards for the borough of Horsham. He *d.* unm. 12th January, 1821, when the Baronetcy became extinct.

His elder and only brother, *The Rev.*

Martin Macpherson, *m.* Miss Mary Mackinnon, of Corrychatican. This gentleman is mentioned thus by Dr. Johnson, in his Tour to the Hebrides: "The house was filled with company, among whom Mr. Macpherson and his sister,* distinguished themselves by their politeness and accomplishments. By him we were invited to Ostig."

Arms—Party per fesse or and azure, a lymphad or galley, her sails furled, her oars in action, of the first. In the dexter chief point a hand couped, grasping a dagger, point upwards, gules; and in the sinister chief point, a cross crosslet fitchée of the last.

MADDOX, OF WORMLEY.

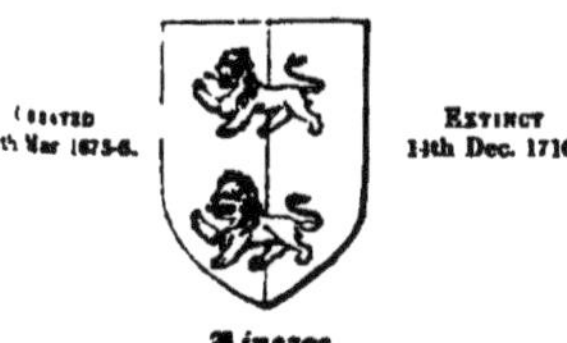

Created 11th Mar 1675-6. Extinct 14th Dec. 1716.

Lineage.

Benjamin Maddox, esq. of Wormley, Herts, was created a Baronet 11th March, 1675-6. He *m.* Dorothy, daughter of Sir William Glascock, knt. but had no son. He *d.* 14th December, 1716, when the Baronetcy expired.

Arms—Per pale az. and gu. two lions passant in pale or.

MAINWARING, OF OVER PEOVER.

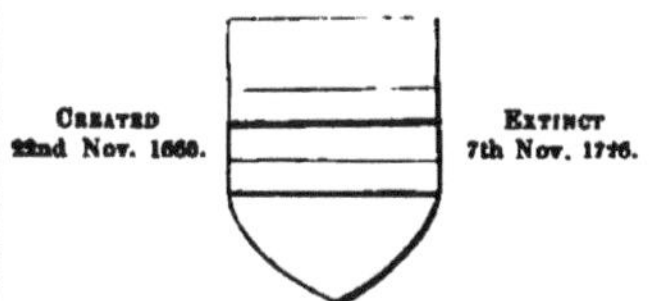

Created 22nd Nov. 1660. Extinct 7th Nov. 1726.

Lineage.

Ranulphus, a noble Norman in the train of William *the Conqueror*, one of the soldiers of fortune, who acquired as their share of the spoil, the county of Chester, had, for his immediate division, fifteen lordships there, amongst which was Peuer (afterwards *Over-Peover*). His son and heir,

Richard de Masnilwaren, was father of

Roger de Masnilwaring, who gave Plumley, to the Abbey, of St. Werburge, in Chester, when he made his son, Wido, a monk there; his other sons, William and Randle, being witnesses, which grant, with many others, Richard, Earl of Chester confirmed in 1119, 19 Henry I. His great-grandson, (the descendant of his son William),

Sir Ralph de Masnilwaring, knt. justice of Chester, *temp.* Richard I. *m.* Amicia, daughter † of Hugh Keveliok, Earl of Chester, and left a son and heir,

Roger Manwaring, of Warmincham, in Cheshire, who conferred by deed upon his younger son, William, *temp.* Henry III. the estate of Over Peover, which

William Manwaring, fixed in consequence, his habitation there. He had several children, and was *s.* by his eldest son,

William Manwaring, of Over Peover, living in 1296.

William Manwaring, of Over Peover, (son of Roger Manwaring and Christian de Birtles,) living in 19 Edward II. *m.* Mary, daughter of Henry Davenport, and was *s.* by his elder son,

William Manwaring, of Over Peover, who *m.* first Joan, daughter and heir of William Praers, of Baddiley, near Nantwich, and had a son, William, his heir. He wedded, secondly, Elizabeth, daughter of Nicholas Leycester, and sister of John Leycester, of Nether Tabley, by whom he had

John, } both Lords of Over Peover.
Randle, }
Thomas, }
Alan, } living in the 38th of Edward III.
Richard, }
Emma, *m.* to Richard Winnington, son and heir of Sir Richard Winnington.

---

* Isabel Macpherson.

† Dugdale considers this lady to be a legitimate daughter of the Earl of Chester, but Sir Peter Leicester, in his Antiquities, totally denies the fact. "I cannot but mislike (he says) the boldness and ignorance of that herald, who gave to Mainwaring (late of Peover) the elder, the quartering of the Earl of Chester's arms; for if he ought of right to quarter that coat, then must he be descended from a co-heir to the Earl of Chester, but he was not; for the co-heirs of Earl Hugh married four of the greatest peers in the kingdom." Upon this question of legitimacy, a paper war ensued between Sir Peter Leicester and Sir Thomas Mainwaring, and the matter was finally referred to the judges, of whose decision Wood thus records:—"At an assise held at Chester in 1675, the controversy was decided by the justices itinerant, who, as I have heard, adjudged the right to Mainwaring."

heir of Sir John de Basings,* acquired a fair inheritance in that county, but principally the towns and manors of Normanton, Empingham, and Hardwick, which first place, thence forward, became the seat of the family. This Thomas was *s.* by his son,

Henry Mackworth, of Normanton, who was sheriff of Rutland 18 Edward IV. and had two sons,

John, his heir, who predeceased him, leaving a son, George, who inherited.

Thomas, ancestor of the Mackworths of Betton, now represented by Sir Digby Mackworth, bart. and of the Mackworths who took the name of Praed.

He was *s.* by his grandson,

George Mackworth, sheriff of Rutland 12 Henry VII. and 14, 22, and 26 Henry VIII. He *m.* Anne, daughter of Geffrey Sherard, esq. of Stapleford, and had a son, his successor in 1536,

Francis Mackworth, esq. of Normanton, who *m.* Ellen, one of the eight daughters of Humphry Hercy, esq. of Grove, in Nottinghamshire,† and co-heir of her brother Sir John Hercy, knt. (who *d. s. p.* 12 Elizabeth). This Francis was sheriff of Rutlandshire in the 30th and 35th of Henry VIII. and 3rd of *Queen* Mary. He *d.* in 1557, and was *s.* by his son,

George Mackworth, esq. who was thrice sheriff of Rutland *temp.* Elizabeth. He *m.* first, Grace, daughter of Ralph Rokeby, esq. serjeant-at-law; and secondly, Anne, daughter of Edmund Hall, esq. of Gretford; and was *s.* by his son,

I. Thomas Mackworth, esq. of Normanton, in the county of Rutland, sheriff in the 41 Elizabeth and 7 James I. who was created a Baronet 4th June, 1619. Sir Thomas *m.* Elizabeth, daughter and heir of Henry Hall, esq. of Gretford, in Lincolnshire, and sole heir of her mother, one of the daughters and co-heirs of Francis Neale, esq. of Tugby, in the same county, and had four sons, viz. Henry, his heir; Francis (Sir), *d.* unm.; Peregrine, *m.* the widow of Alexander Moor, esq. of Grantham, barrister-at-law, but had no issue; Neale, *d.* unm. Sir Thomas *d.* in March, 1625-6, and was *s.* by his eldest son,

II. Sir Henry Mackworth, who rebuilt the manor house at Normanton, and having married Mary, daughter of Robert Hopton, esq. of Witham, and sister and co-heir of Ralph, Lord Hopton,‡ had issue,

i. Thomas, his successor.

ii. Robert, *m.* first in 1625, Elizabeth, daughter of John Hatcher, esq. of Empingham, and had,

Robert, of Huntingdon, *m.* Mary, daughter of William Dowse, of the same place, merchant, and dying in 1733, left

Thomas, who inherited as fifth baronet.

Elizabeth, *m.* to Lewis Smith, esq. of Great Gedding.

He (Robert sen.) *m.* secondly, Margaret, eldest daughter of Edward Corbet, esq. and had by her, a son who *d.* young, and a daughter Mary, the wife of Piercy Butler, esq.

iii. Henry, *m.* Dorothy Hall, of Gretford, in Lincolnshire, and had two sons, viz.

1. Henry, *m.* Katherine Roberts, of Empingham, and had Henry, sixth baronet.

2. Thomas, killed in a duel.

iv. Edward, a merchant, *d. s. p.*

v. Gustavus, *m.* Dorothy, widow of Thomas, Lord Grey, of Groby, mother of Thomas, second Earl of Stamford, and daughter and co-heir of Edward Bourchier, fourth Earl Bath, by whom he had issue.

i. Margaret, *m.* to Philip Young, esq. of Keniton, in Shropshire.

ii. Jane, *m.* to Hugh Underwood, esq. of Wittlesea, in the Isle of Wight.

Sir Henry *d.* in Aug. 1640, and was *s.* by his eldest son,

III. Sir Thomas Mackworth, M.P. for the county of Rutland, from the 31st of Charles II. to the time of his death. He *m.* first, Dorothy, daughter of Captain George Darell, of Cale Hill, in Kent, and by her had issue,

Thomas, who died in his father's lifetime.

Dorothy, *m.* to John Wingfield, esq. of Tickencote, in the county of Rutland, (refer to Burke's *Commoners*, vol. ii. p. 476.)

Utrechia, *d.* unm.

Sir Thomas wedded, secondly, Anne, daughter of Humphrey Mackworth, esq. of Betton, in Salop, and by her had to survive,

Thomas, successor to his father.

Jane, *m.* to Abraham Rys, gent. of Lincolnshire, and survived his widow, issueless.

He *d.* in November, 1694, and was *s.* by his son,

IV. Sir Thomas Mackworth, M.P. for the county of Rutland, in the room of his father, and re-elected in the 1st and 4th of *Queen* Anne, and two last parliaments of George I. He *d.* unm. in March, 1745, when his grandnephew (the grandson of his half sister, Dorothy) the Rev. John Wingfield, of Trickencote, became his heir in blood, and the Baronetcy devolved upon his cousin and heir-at-law (refer to Robert, second son of the second baronet),

V. Sir Thomas Mackworth, an apothecary at Huntingdon, and alderman of that borough. He *m.* first, Elizabeth, daughter of John Maule, esq. and had by her four daughters,

Mary, *m.* to the Rev. Charles Nailour, of New Ross, in Ireland, and had issue.

Elizabeth, *m.* to James Robinson, of Ely.

Sally, *m.* to Leonard Fausett, of Lincoln.

Sukey, *m.* to John Wilkinson, of Wisbeach.

Sir Thomas *m.* secondly, Mary, relict of the Rev. Mr. Waller, of Great Stoughton, in Huntingdonshire, and daughter of the Rev. Leonard Reresby, of Thribert, in the county of York, but by her had no issue. He *d.* 17th October, 1769, and was *s.* by his cousin, (refer to Henry, third son of the second baronet.)

VI. Sir Henry Mackworth, who *m.* Elizabeth, daughter of the Rev. Edward Lamb, rector of Acle, in Norfolk, and dying 14th Jan. 1774, was *s.* by his son,

VII. Sir Henry Mackworth, one of the almsmen upon the poor knights' charity, in the Charter House

---

* Sir John de Basings, son of John, son of Thomas, by Margaret, his wife, daughter and heir of Thomas de Normanville, son of Ralph, son of Thomas de Normanville, who died *temp.* Henry III., whose ancestors, soon after the Conquest, were Lords of Normanton, and were also seated at Kenerton, in the hundred of Blackborne, in Kent, until their male issue failing, both that estate and this in Rutland, went with an heiress to the Basings, a family of great note and antiquity, descended from Adam de Basing, lord mayor of London in 1251, whose habitation in the city, occupied the place where Blackwell-hall was erected; from him the street and ward adjoining were denominated Basing's-hall Street, and Basing's-hall Ward.

† By Elizabeth, daughter of Sir John Digby, knt. of Ketteley.

‡ Sir Ralph Hopton, K.B. was created in 1643 in consequence of a victory he had then achieved over the parliamentarians, at Stratton, in Cornwall, Lord Hopton, *of Stratton*, with remainder, default of male issue, upon his uncle, Sir Arthur Hopton, knt. who having predeceased his lordship, the barony expired, and his estates devolved upon his sisters, as co-heirs, viz.

i. Rachel, *m.* to — Morgan, esq.

ii. Mary, *m.* first to — Hartop, and secondly to Sir Henry Mackworth.

iii. Catherine, *m.* to John Windham, esq.

iv. Margaret, *m.* to Sir Baynham Throgmorton, bart.

Burke's *Extinct Peerage*.

…nadon, where he died issueless in 1863, when the Baronetcy expired.

Arms—Party per pale, indented, sable and ermine, a chevron gules, fretté or.

MACPHERSON, OF CALCUTTA.

Created …th June, 1786.  Extinct 12th Jan. 1821.

Lineage.

John Macpherson, esq. younger son of Dr. John Macpherson, D.D. an eminent Scottish divine, by a daughter of Macleod, of Bemire, having been appointed member of the supreme council of Bengal, in 1780, and governor-general on the return of Warren Hastings to England, in 1784, received, eventually, the unanimous thanks of the court of directors, for his conduct in India, and was created a Baronet 27th January, 1786. Sir John returned to Britain in 1787, and sate in parliament afterwards for the borough of Horsham. He d. unm. 12th January, 1821, when the Baronetcy became extinct.

His elder and only brother, *The Rev.*

Martin Macpherson, m. Miss Mary Mackinnon, of Corrychatican. This gentleman is mentioned thus by Dr. Johnson, in his Tour to the Hebrides: "The house was filled with company, among whom Mr. Macpherson and his sister,* distinguished themselves by their politeness and accomplishments. By him we were invited to Osteg."

Arms—Party per fesse or and azure, a lymphad or galley, her sails furled, her oars in action, of the first. In the dexter chief point a hand couped, grasping a dagger, point upwards, gules; and in the sinister chief point, a cross crosslet fitchée of the last.

MADDOX, OF WORMLEY.

Created 11th Mar. 1675-6.  Extinct 18th Dec. 1716.

Lineage.

Benjamin Maddox, esq. of Wormley, Herts, was created a Baronet 11th March, 1675-6. He m. Dorothy, daughter of Sir William Glascock, knt. but had no son. He d. 14th December, 1716, when the Baronetcy expired.

Arms—Per pale az. and gu. two lions passant in pale or.

MAINWARING, OF OVER PEOVER.

Created 22nd Nov. 1660. 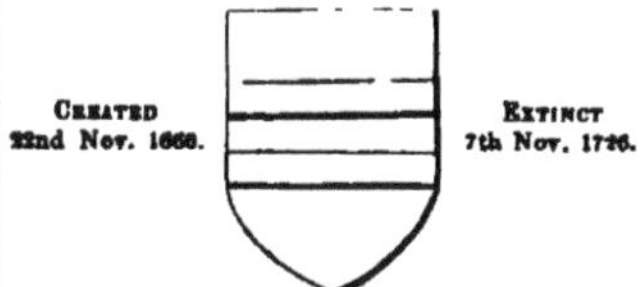 Extinct 7th Nov. 1726.

Lineage.

Ranulphus, a noble Norman in the train of William *the Conqueror*, one of the soldiers of fortune, who acquired as their share of the spoil, the county of Chester, had, for his immediate division, fifteen lordships there, amongst which was Peure (afterwards *Over-Peover*). His son and heir,

Richard de Masnilwaren, was father of

Roger de Masnilwaring, who gave Plumley, to the Abbey, of St. Werburge, in Chester, when he made his son, Wido, a monk there; his other sons, William and Randle, being witnesses, which grant, with many others, Richard, Earl of Chester confirmed in 1119, 19 Henry I. His great-grandson, (the descendant of his son William),

Sir Ralph de Masnilwaring, knt. justice of Chester, *temp.* Richard I. m. Amicia, daughter† of Hugh Keveliok, Earl of Chester, and left a son and heir,

Roger Manwaring, of Warmincham, in Cheshire, who conferred by deed upon his younger son, William, *temp.* Henry III. the estate of Over Peover, which

William Manwaring, fixed in consequence, his habitation there. He had several children, and was s. by his eldest son,

William Manwaring, of Over Peover, living in 1296.

William Manwaring, of Over Peover, (son of Roger Manwaring and Christian de Birtles,) living in 19 Edward II. m. Mary, daughter of Henry Davenport, and was s. by his elder son,

William Manwaring, of Over Peover, who m. first Joan, daughter and heir of William Praers, of Baddiley, near Nantwich, and had a son, William, his heir. He wedded, secondly, Elizabeth, daughter of Nicholas Leycester, and sister of John Leycester, of Nether Tabley, by whom he had

John, }
Randle, } both Lords of Over Peover.

Thomas, }
Alan, } living in the 39th of Edward III.
Richard, }

Emma, m. to Richard Winnington, son and heir of Sir Richard Winnington.

---

* Isabel Macpherson.

† Dugdale considers this lady to be a legitimate daughter of the Earl of Chester, but Sir Peter Leicester, in his Antiquities, totally denies the fact. "I cannot but mislike (he says) the boldness and ignorance of that herald, who gave to Mainwaring (late of Peover) the elder, the quartering of the Earl of Chester's arms; for if he ought of right to quarter that coat, then must he be descended from a co-heir to the Earl of Chester, but he was not; for the co-heirs of Earl Hugh married four of the greatest peers in the kingdom." Upon this question of legitimacy, a paper was ensued between Sir Peter Leicester and Sir Thomas Mainwaring, and the matter was finally referred to the judges, of whose decision Wood thus records:—"At an assise held at Chester in 1675, the controversy was decided by the justices itinerant, who, as I have heard, adjudged the right to Mainwaring."

Ellen, *m.* to Ralph, grandson of Richard Vernon, of Shibrook in Cheshire.

Joan, *m.* to William Legh, of Baggiley.

This William, who was styled, "William Manwaring the elder," 33 EDWARD III.* died in 1364, (Elizabeth, his widow, was living in 1405,) and was *s.* by his eldest son,

WILLIAM MANWARING, of Over Peover, who wedded, first, (in 1366,) Catherine, daughter of John Belgrave, of Belgrave, in Cheshire, and secondly, Clementia Cotton, but had no issue. In the 17th of RICHARD II. his seal bore the arms of the family without distinction, viz. "arg. two barrs gu." inscribed about *S. Willielmi Maynwaring.* For at that period, the elder house of Warmincham was extinct, and devolved to a daughter. He made his will in 1394, wherein, amongst other matters, he bequeaths his body to be buried in Aghton Church, and his picture in alabaster to cover his tomb in the said church; giving to the said church, a part of Christ's cross, which the wife of Randle Manwaring, his half-brother, had in her custody, shut up in wax: to the chapel of Over Peover, he gave *Unam togam de blueto ut fiat inde vestimentum ibidem.* He left also a competent salary for a chaplain to celebrate masses for his soul in the chapel of St. Mary, in Aghton Church, for seven years. He *d.* in 1399, and was *s.* by his half-brother,

JOHN MANWARING, of Over Peover, who *m.* about 13 RICHARD II. Margaret, daughter and heir of Sir John Stafford, of Wigham, and widow of Sir John Warren, of Pointon, in Cheshire, but had no issue by her.† The king granted to this John, all the lands and goods of Sir Hugh Browe, which the said Hugh had forfeited by his rebellion, dated 18 Augusti, 4 HENRY IV. He (John) waited on the prince, afterwards HENRY V. and he was made sheriff of Cheshire (*quamdiu nobis placuerit*) 18th September, 4 HENRY IV. and continued in office 5th and 6th of the same king, in which writ, the Earl of Chester calls him, *armigerum suum.* He had also an annual pension from HENRY IV. of twenty marks, and was constituted, with Matthew Del Mere, and Thomas Meyshawe, judges of the gaol delivery at Chester, *hâc vice, nono die Aprilis*, 5 HENRY IV. He *d.* in 1410, and was *s.* by his brother,

RANDLE MANWARING, esq. of Over Peover, who *m.* Margery, widow of Richard Buckley, of Chedill, in Cheshire, and daughter of Hugh Venables, Baron of Kinderton, and had issue,

JOHN (Sir), his heir.

William, from whom descended the Manwarings of Ightfeild, in Shropshire.‡

Ralph, from whom the Manwarings of Kermincham, in Cheshire. Their representative at the close of the seventeenth century,

ROGER MANWARING, esq. of Kermincham, baptised in 1673; *m.* first, Elizabeth, daughter of Joshua Ratcliffe, esq. of Todmorden, and had by her a son and heir,

I. JAMES, who *d. v. p.* leaving by Margaret, his wife, daughter of Swettenham, esq. of Swettenham, a son,

ROGER, who *d. s. p.*

He *m.* secondly, Frances, daughter of — Potts, of Moston, and dying in 1728, left by her,

II. JOHN, of Kermincham, whose child, Elizabeth, *m.* John Parnell, esq. of Sandbach.

III. Frances, *m.* to John Uniacke, esq. of Cottage, in Youghall, in the county of Cork, and had issue,

1. JOHN-MANWARING Uniacke, who *m.* Mary, daughter of the Rev. Dixie Blundell, D.D. and had issue.

2. Catherine Uniacke, *m.* in 1778 John-Robert Parker, esq. of Green Park, in the county of Cork, and their third son Roger Manwaring Parker assumed, in 1809, the surname and arms of Manwaring by desire of his great-aunt, Mrs. Jones.

3. Francis Uniacke, *m.* to Henry Turner, esq. of Kensington Place, Bath.

IV. Mary, *m.* to Richard Jones, esq. and *d. s. p.* in 1806.

V. Catherine, *m.* first, in 1761, to Daniel Herring, esq. of Bath; and secondly, in 1778, to Thomas Lowfield, esq. also of Bath.

---

* "He sealed with his coat of arms, most usually, three bars, with a lion passant, in chief, inscribed about the seal, *Sigill. Willielmi De Maynwaringe;* which coat of arms he gave in distinction from Manwaring, of Warmincham, out of which family his ancestor branched. For Roger Manwaring, of Warmincham, in the reign of HENRY III. sealed with six barrulets; whose son and heir, Sir Thomas Manwaring, of Warmincham, used only two barrs in his seal; as I (Sir Peter Leicester) have seen on their seals. And after the male line of Manwaring, of Warmincham, failed, then did the heir of Manwaring, of Over Peover, assume the two barrs only, in the reign of RICHARD II. as next heir male, leaving off his coat of three barrs, with a lion in chief."

† He had a bastard son, by Margery Winnington, called Peter Manwaring.

‡ "A descendant of this branch was (though a younger son) Dr. Roger Manwaring, who was born at Stretton, in Shropshire, and educated in the university of Oxford. He was some time vicar of St. Giles's in the Fields, and chaplain to K. Charles 1st, before whom, preaching three sermons, entitled *Religion and Allegiance*, he was called in question for it by parliament, charged with endeavouring to destroy the king and kingdom by his divinity, and sentenced to be imprisoned, was fined £1000, and ordered to make his submission, and was disabled to have or enjoy any preferment, or office. However, the king soon after pardoned him, and gave him the rich living of Stanford Rivers, in Essex, in 1633, made [illegible] dean of Worcester, and two years after nominated [illegible] to the bishopric of St. David's; in 1640 his troubles were revived in parliament, and tho' the old grudge lay [illegible] the bottom of the prosecution, yet the new crimes [illegible] popish innovations, conversing with papists, and be[illegible] sociable and jovial, were trumped up against him, [illegible] which he was (as Lloyd, in his memoirs expresses [illegible]) apprehended suddenly, confined severely, fined hea[vily] plundered violently, and persecuted from place to [place] continually, insomuch, that for the two last years of [his] life, not a week passed over his head without a mess[age] or an injury; which he desired God not to remem[ber] against his adversaries, and adjured all his friends [to] forget.' Under these his troubles he had nothing left [but] a small temporal estate to support him, and died at Ca[r]marthen, July 16, (A. Wood says, July 1) 1653. He [was] of a pious life and conversation, and very charitable [as] appears particularly, by one of the three great de[signs] which he had in pursuit, namely, the redeeming of [cap]tives; and though he laboured under a very severe [cha]racter, with the Puritans, (and not without reason, [if the] accusation against him was true, of straining the [pre]rogative in the matter of raising money without the c[onsent] of parliament;) yet by the Royalists, he was esteem[ed] worthy of the great function which he bore, being a [per]son of great zeal for the Church of England."

WALKER's *Sufferings of the Cler[gy]*

Elizabeth, m. to Ralph Egerton, esq. of Wryne Hill, in Staffordshire.

Cicily, m. to Thomas Fowleshurst, esq. of Crew, in Cheshire.

Joan, m. in 1411, to John, son and heir of Ralph Davenport, esq. of Davenport, in Cheshire.

Ellen, m. to Thomas Fitton, esq. of Gawseworth, in the same county.

Agnes, affianced to William Bromley, esq. of Badington, in Cheshire, son of Sir John Bromley, but died before marriage.

Margaret, m. first in 1436, to William Bromley, the affianced husband of her deceased sister. She outlived him, and m. secondly, Sir John Needham, of Crannach, *Justiciarius de banco*, and judge of Chester, 1 Edward IV.

his Randle, commonly called Honkyn Manwaring, the language of those times, died in 1546, and was by his eldest son,*

Sir John Manwaring, knt. of Over Peover, who m. first in 1411, Margaret, daughter of John Delves, sen. of Dodington, in Cheshire, and had a son and two daughters, viz.

William, his heir, m. in 1443, Ellen, daughter of Sir John Butler, knt. of Bewsey, in Lancashire, and dying in his father's lifetime, left a son,

John, successor to his grandfather.

Elizabeth, m. in 1436, to Piers Warburton, son and heir of Sir Geoffrey de Warburton, of Arley.

Margaret, m. to Hamnet, son and heir of John Ashley, esq. of Ashley.

Sir John had a second wife, called Joan. He d. about the end of Edward IV.'s reign, and was s. by his grandson,

John Manwaring, esq. of Over Peover, who m. ...ud, daughter of Robert Legh, esq. of Adlington, and had issue,

John (Sir), his heir.

Robert.

Maud, m. in 1496, to Thomas Starkey, esq. of Wrenbury, in Cheshire.

Joan, m. in 1512, to Sir Thomas Ashton, of Ashton *super* Mersey, in the same county.

He d. ...th July, 1495, and was s. by his elder son,

Sir John Manwaring, of Over Peover, knighted in France in 1513. He m. Catherine Honford, sister of William Honford, esq. of Honford, in Cheshire, and had issue,

Randle (Sir), his heir.

Edmund, John, Piers, — *d. s. p.*

Philip, successor to his eldest brother.

Edward, from whom descend the Mainwarings of Whitmore, in Staffordshire; of Bromborough, in Cheshire; and of Oteley, in Shropshire. (See Burke's *Commoners*, vols. iii. and iv.)

Robert, ancestor of the Manwarings of Merton Sands, in Cheshire. About the middle of the seventeenth century, Charles Manwaring, esq. sold Merton Sands to Thomas Fleetwood, esq. and from the Fleetwoods the estate passed to the Cholmondeleys of Vale Royal.

Thomas.

George.

Henry.

Margaret.

Catherine, m. in 1531, to William, son of Humphrey Newton, esq. of Pownall.

Sir John was sheriff of Flintshire in 1514, and died the next year, at the age of forty-five. He was s. by his eldest son,

Sir Randle Manwaring, knt. of Over Peover. This gentleman, m. Elizabeth, daughter of Sir Randle Brereton, of Malpas, and widow of Richard Cholmondeley, esq. of Cholmondeley, in Cheshire, and had three daughters, viz.

I. Margaret, m. to Sir Arthur Manwaring, knt. of Ightfeild,† in Shropshire.

II. Elizabeth, m. first, to Peter Shakerley, esq. of Houlm, in Allostock, Cheshire; and secondly, in 1561, to Christopher Holford, esq. of Holford.

III. Catherine, m. to John Davenport, esq. of Henbury, in Cheshire.

Sir Randle m. secondly, in 1551, Elizabeth, daughter of Sir Ralph Leycester, of Toft, but by that lady, who wedded, secondly, Sir Edmund Trafford, of Trafford, had no other issue. He d. 6th September, 1557, and in default of male issue, was s. by his brother,

Philip Manwaring, esq. of Over Peover, who m. Anne, daughter of Sir Ralph Leycester, of Toft, and had issue,

Randle (Sir), his heir.

Edmund, of Ranmore, near Nantwich.

Elizabeth, *d. s. p.*

He d. 11th April, 1573, and was s. by his elder son,

Sir Randle Manwaring, knt. of Over Peover, who m. first, Margaret, daughter of Sir Edward Fitton, of Gawseworth, in Cheshire, sometime treasurer of Ireland in the time of Elizabeth, and had issue,

Randle (Sir), his heir.

Edmund, LL.D. chancellor of Chester, 1643, father of Sir William Mainwaring, killed at the siege of Chester.

---

* Beside his legitimate children, he had a bastard son ...Emma Farrington, called Hugh Manwaring, from ...m the Manwarings of Croxton, near Middlewich; ... Thomas Manwaring of North Road, another bastard ... and Randle, another, with three bastard daughters. ... last male heir of the Croxton branch, James Mainwaring, esq. left three daughters, the eldest of whom married Michael Oldfield, esq. and their son, Mainwaring Oldfield, esq. sold the manor of Croxton to Roger ...braham, esq. of Dorfold.

† Her grandson, Arthur Maynwaring, esq. born at ...field in 1668, was a person of considerable note immediately before and after the revolution. At first he espoused the cause of James, and wrote in favour of it, ... his introduction to the Duke of Somerset, and the ... of Dorset, and Buckingham, wrought a complete change in his political views. He studied the law until ...-five or twenty-six years of age, about which time ...father died, and left him a good estate, but very much encumbered. Upon the conclusion of the peace of Ryswick he went to Paris, and on his return was made one of the commissioners of the Customs, he was admitted a member of the Kit-Cat Club, and was looked upon as one of the chief ornaments and supports of it by his pleasantry and wit. In the beginning of *Queen* Anne's reign, the Lord Treasurer Godolphin, engaged Mr. Scone to retire from the auditorship of the imposts, his lordship paying several thousand pounds as an equivalent, and bestowed the office upon Mr. Maynwaring. In the parliament of 1705, he was burgess for Preston, in Lancashire. He had a considerable share in the publication called the Medley, and was author of several other pieces. He sold Ightfield to Lord Kilmorey, and died at St. Albans 13th November, 1712, having some time before his death made his will, in which he left Mrs. Oldfield, the celebrated actress, his executrix, by whom he had a son, Arthur Maynwaring, and divided his estate pretty equally between him, and Mrs. Oldfield, and his sister; he was buried at Chertsey, in Surrey, where his father and grandfather lay, and where they had formerly an estate and seat. Sir Richard Steele dedicated to him the first volume of the Tatler.

Thomas, D.D. parson of Weldon, Northamptonshire, living in 1634.

Philip (Sir), secretary of Ireland, under the lieutenantcy of the Earl of Strafford, died unm. 2nd August, 1661, at London.

Anne, *m.* at Great Budworth, 31st August, 1591, to Lawrence, son and heir of Sir Thomas Smith, of Hough, in Cheshire.

Catherine, *m.* to Sir Edward Stanley, of Bickerstaff, in Lancashire.

Elizabeth, *m.* in 1611, to Peter Leycester, esq. of Nether Tabley.

Eleanor, *d.* unm.

Sir Randle *m.* secondly, Catherine, widow of William Brereton, esq. of Honford, in Cheshire, and daughter of Roger Hurleston, of Chester. This gentleman rebuilt the hall, at Over Peover in 1586. He was sheriff of Cheshire in 1605, and dying 27th May, 1612, was *s.* by his eldest son,

SIR RANDLE MANWARING, (the younger) knt. who was sheriff of Limerick, in Ireland, in 1605, the year his father served the office for Cheshire, for which county he was himself sheriff in 1619, and mayor of Chester at the same time. He *m.* Jane, daughter of Sir Thomas Smith, of Hough, and had issue,

PHILIP, his heir.

George, of Marthall, living in 1666, *m.* Elizabeth, daughter of Robert Tatton, esq. of Withenshaw, and relict of John Lathom, esq. of Winslow, in Cheshire.

Elizabeth, *m.* first, to Robert Ravenscroft, esq. of Bretton, and had issue. She *m.* secondly, Sir Francis Gamul, knt. of Chester, but by him had no children, she survived both her husbands, and died at Chester, 13th August, 1661.

Anne, *m.* to Robert Brierwood, esq. of Chester, barrister-at-law, afterwards Sir Robert Brierwood, knt. judge of three shires in Wales.

Margaret, *m.* to Henry, son and heir of Henry Birkenhead, of Backford, prothonotary of Chester, but had no surviving issue. She died at Chester, 25th July, 1661.

Sir Randle *d.* 12th January, 1632, and was *s.* by his elder son,

PHILIP MANWARING, esq. of Over Peover, captain of the light horse of Chester, and sheriff of Cheshire, in 1639. He *m.* in 1622, Ellen, daughter of Edward Minshull, esq. of Stoke, near Nantwich, and had issue,

Randle, who *d. s. p.* before his father.

THOMAS, his heir.

Edward, living in 1666, *m.* Frances, daughter of Peter Holbrooke, esq. of Newbrook, in Cheshire.

He *d.* 10th December, 1647. Ellen, his widow, built in 1648, a neat chapel of stone, on the north side of the chancel of Over Peover Church, with two fine monuments for herself and her husband, and "a fair vault under the said chapel for burial." The elder surviving son and heir,

I. THOMAS MAINWARING, esq. of Over Peover, high sheriff of Cheshire in 1657, and one of the knights of the shire, with Sir George Booth, (afterwards Lord Delamere,) in the restoration parliament, was created a BARONET by *King* CHARLES II. 22nd November, 1660. Sir Thomas *m.* 26th May, 1642, Mary, daughter of Sir Henry Delves, bart. of Doddington, and had six sons and six daughters, who all died unmarried, except

JOHN, his heir.

Elizabeth, *m.* to Peter, son and heir of Sir Geffery Shakerley, knt. of Shakerley and Hulme, but *d. s. p.*

Anne *m.* to Robert Alport, esq. of Overton, and had a daughter,

Jane Alport, *m.* to John Lacon, esq. of West Copies, in Shropshire.

Sir Thomas *d.* 28th June, 1689, and was *s.* by his son,

II. SIR JOHN MAINWARING, *b.* 9th May, 1656; who *m.* 28th September, 1676, Elizabeth, eldest daughter of Roger Whitley, esq. of Peel, in Cheshire, and had with other issue,

THOMAS, his heir.

Roger, *m.* Elizabeth, daughter and heir of Middleton, of Shipton, in Yorkshire, but *d. s. p.* [illegible] 1707.

Henry, *b.* 3rd August, 1686; *m.* 28th July, [illegible] Diana, only daughter of William Blackett, esq. deceased, oldest son of Sir Edward Blackett, bart. of Newby, but died before his brother Thomas, leaving his wife *enciente*, who after the death of her brother-in-law, Sir Thomas Mainwaring, gave birth to a son,

HENRY, who inherited the baronetcy.

Mrs. Henry Mainwaring, wedded, secondly, the Rev. Thomas Wetenhal, rector of Walthamstow, in Essex, and by him had a son,

THOMAS WETENHAL, *b.* 21st December, [illegible]

Sir John who was for many years member for Chester, deputy lieutenant and captain of light horse, *d.* [illegible] November, 1702, and was *s.* by his son,

III. SIR THOMAS MAINWARING, born at Pe[illegible] August, 1681, *m.* 29th March, 1724-5, Martha, [illegible] daughter and co-heir of William Lloyd, esq. of Halston, in Flintshire, but by her (who *m.* secondly Edward Mainwaring, esq. of Whitmore,) he had no issue. He *d.* 20th September, 1726, and was *s.* by his nephew,

IV. SIR HENRY MAINWARING, who was born a baronet, and the thirtieth male representative of his [illegible] He received the earlier part of his education under the celebrated Mr. Dongworth, at Durham School, whence, in February, 1742-3, he was admitted of Lincoln College, Oxford, where he obtained the degree of M.A. In 1750, he went abroad and made the tour of Italy, and on his return served as captain in the [illegible] Cheshire, and was afterwards (1764) promoted to the majority of the same regiment. He *d.* unm. [illegible] 1797, when the BARONETCY EXPIRED, but the estates Sir Henry bequeathed to his uterine brother,

THOMAS WETENHAL, esq. who assumed in consequence the surname and arms of MAINWARING. He *m.* in 1781, Catherine, youngest daughter of William Watkins, esq. of Nantwich, and had, with other issue, his son and heir,

HENRY MAINWARING, esq. who was created a BARONET in 1804, and is now SIR HENRY MAINWARING, of Over Peover.

Arms—Argent, two bars, gules.

MANN, OF LINTON.

CREATED 3rd March, 1755.

EXTINCT 2nd April [illegible]

Lineage.

EDWARD MANN, of Ipswich, in the county of Suffolk, comptroller of the customs there, married [illegible] Dyer, and left a son,

EDWARD MANN, of Ipswich, who wedded [illegible]

daughter of Mannock of Stoke Nayland, in Suffolk, and had a son,

Thomas Mann, of the Inner Temple, usher of the Rolls, who m. Elizabeth, daughter of William Alston, gent. of Marlesford, in Suffolk, and had five sons and four daughters. His eldest son,

Robert Mann, esq. of London, and afterwards of Linton, in Kent, m. Eleanor, daughter and heir of Christopher Guise, esq. of Abbot's Court, in Gloucestershire, and had issue,

- I. Edward-Louisa, his heir.
- II. Horatio (Sir), heir to his brother.
- III. Galfridus, of Egerton, in Kent, M.P. for Maidstone, m. Sarah, daughter of John Gregory, esq. of the city of London, and had one surviving son and four daughters, viz.
  - 1. Horatio, who s. his uncle Sir Horatio.
  - 1. Alice, b. 31st May, 1739; m. to — Apthorpe, esq.
  - 2. Sarah, b. in 1740; d. unm.
  - 3. Catharine, b. in 1742; m. to the Hon. and Right Rev. James Cornwallis, Bishop of Lichfield and Coventry, who, at the decease of his nephew in 1813, became fourth Earl Cornwallis.
  - 4. Eleanor, m. to Thomas Powis, esq.
- I. Eleanor, m. to Sir John Toriano, knt. of London, merchant.
- II. Mary, m. to Benjamin Hatley Foote, esq. of Malling Abbey, in the county of Kent, and had issue,
  - George-Talbot-Hatley Foote, of Malling Abbey, d. in 1821.
  - John Foote, banker in London, m. Eleanor, daughter of Jos. Martin, esq. and had issue. (See Burke's *Commoners*, vol. i. p. 272.)
- III. Catharine, m. to the Rev. Francis Hender Foote, who d. in 1773, and had issue (refer as above).

Mr Mann d. in 1752, and was s. by his eldest son,

Edward-Louisa Mann, esq. of Linton, who d. unm. [illegible] December, 1755, and was s. by his brother,

Sir Horatio Mann, K.B. and Baronet; the latter dignity conferred 3rd March, 1755, with remainder, in default of the heirs of his body, to his brother Galfridus and the heirs male of that gentleman. Sir Horatio was accredited, in 1740, envoy-extraordinary and minister-plenipotentiary at the court of Florence. He died in that city, at an advanced age, 6th November, 1786, where he had resided forty-six years, and was s. by his nephew (the only son of Galfridus),

II. Sir Horatio Mann, M.P. for Sandwich, who had previously succeeded to his father's estates. In January, 1774, he acted as proxy at the installation of his uncle Sir Horatio as knight of the Bath, and receiving on the occasion the honour of knighthood himself, was afterwards called Sir Horace Mann for distinction. He m. in 1765, Lady Lucy Noel, daughter of Baptist, fourth Earl of Gainsborough, and had three daughters,

- Lucy, m. in 1786, to James Mann, esq. of Egerton Lodge, near Lenham.
- Emily, m. in 1792, to Robert Heron, esq. now Sir Robert Heron, bart.
- Harriet, m. 28th July, 1801, to Colonel Rochford, of Ireland.

He d. 2nd April, 1814, when the Baronetcy expired.

Arms—Sa. on a fesse counterembattled, between three goats passant arg. as many ogresses.

MANNOCK, OF GIFFORD'S HALL.

Created 1st June, 1627.

Extinct 3rd June, 1787.

Lineage.

This family is stated to have come originally from Denmark, and to have flourished in England under her Danish kings.

Robert Mannock, living at Stoke-juxta-Neyland, in Suffolk, in the time of Edward III. was father of

William Mannock, whose son,

John Mannock, left a son and heir,

Philip Mannock, who purchased Gifford's Hall 6 Henry VI. His grandson,

John Mannock, esq. of Gifford's Hall, in Stoke-by-Newland, in the county of Suffolk, left a son and successor,

George Mannock, esq. who m. Catherine, daughter of Thomas Waldgrave, esq. of Smallbridge, and dying 22nd August, 1541, was s. by his eldest son,

William Mannock, esq. who m. Audrie, daughter of John Allington, esq. of Westley, in Cambridgeshire, and had several sons. He d. 8th July, 6 Philip and Mary. The inquisition, taken the following September, sets forth that he died 8th July post, seised of the manors of Holton Hall, Raymes, Giffords, and Chamberlains, in Stoke Newland, and that Francis, his son and heir, is five years old. The said son,

Francis Mannock, esq. m. Mary, daughter of William Fitch, esq. of Little Canfield, in Essex, and died 2nd November, 1590, leaving, with several daughters, an only son,

William Mannock, esq. thirty-four years of age at his father's death. He m. Etheldred, daughter of Ferdinando Parys, esq. of Linton, in Cambridgeshire, and d. 15th March, 15 James I. He was s. by his eldest son,

I. Francis Mannock, esq. of Gifford's Hall, in Suffolk, who was created a Baronet by King Charles I. 1st June, 1627. Sir Francis m. Dorothy, daughter of William Saunders, esq. of Blofield, in Norfolk, and had three sons, Francis, William, and John, with a daughter, Anne, the wife of Valentine Saunders, esq. of Blofield. He d. 26th November, 1634, and was s. by his eldest son,

II. Sir Francis Mannock, who m. in 1636, Mary, eldest daughter of Sir George Heneage, knt. of Hainton, in the county of Lincoln, and had issue,

- William, his heir.
- Francis.
- John.
- Thomas, of Great Bromley Hall, Essex, who m. Mary, daughter of Sir Cecil Bisshopp, bart. of Parham, but d. s. p.
- Mary, m. to John Petre, esq. of Fidlers, in Essex, son of the Hon. John Petre, fourth son of the second Lord Petre, and is now represented by the Cannings of Foxcote.
- Catherine, m. to John Newport, esq. of Pelham, in Hertfordshire.
- Anne, m. to Sir Daniel Arthur, of London, merchant.
- Bridget, m. to Robert Strickland, esq.

Audrey, *m.* to Peter Lynch, esq.

Sir Francis *d.* 26th April, 1686, and was *s.* by his eldest son,

III. SIR WILLIAM MANNOCK, who *m.* Ursula, daughter of HENRY NEVIL *alias* SMITH, esq. of Holt, in the county of Leicester, and had issue,

- FRANCIS, his successor.
- William.
- John.
- Ursula.
- Anne.
- Etheldred, *m.* to Henry Timperley, esq. of Hinclesham Hall, in Suffolk.
- Elizabeth.
- Faith.

Sir William *d.* 26th January, 1713-14, and was *s.* by his eldest son,

IV. SIR FRANCIS MANNOCK. This gentleman married Frances, daughter and heir of George Yates, esq. of North Waltham, in the county of Southampton, and had issue,

- WILLIAM, his successor.
- FRANCIS, inherited as seventh baronet.
- THOMAS, who *s.* his brother Francis, and was eighth baronet.
- GEORGE, ninth baronet.
- Ursula, *m.* to James Nihell, esq.
- Etheldred.
- Mary.
- Anne.

He *d.* 27th August, 1758 (his widow 18th May, 1761), and was *s.* by his eldest son,

V. SIR WILLIAM MANNOCK, who *m.* first, Teresa, daughter of Anthony Wright, esq. of Whaleside, in Essex (a banker in Covent Garden), but by that lady had no issue. He wedded, secondly, Elizabeth, daughter and co-heir of Robert Allwyn, esq. of Treford, in Sussex, by whom he had a daughter, Mary, who died an infant, and a son, WILLIAM-ANTHONY, *b.* 28th May, 1759. He *d.* 16th March, 1764, and was *s.* by his son,

VI. SIR WILLIAM-ANTHONY MANNOCK, who *d.* unm. 24th March, 1776, and was *s.* by his uncle,

VII. SIR FRANCIS MANNOCK, who *m.* Elizabeth, daughter of Thomas Stonor, esq. of Watling Park, in the county of Oxford, but dying issueless 17th September, 1778, was *s.* by his brother,

VIII. SIR THOMAS MANNOCK, who wedded, first, Mary, daughter of George-Brownlow Doughty, esq. of Snarford Hall, in the county of Lincoln; and secondly, Anastasia, daughter of Mark Browne, esq. of Eastbourne, in Sussex, but *d. s. p.* 2nd September, 1781, and was *s.* by his brother,

IX. SIR GEORGE MANNOCK, who was killed by the overturning of the Dover mail, 3rd June, 1787, and dying issueless, the BARONETCY EXPIRED.

Arms—Sa. a cross flory arg.

MANSEL, OF MARGAM.

CREATED 22nd May, 1611.

EXTINCT 29th Nov. 1750.

Lineage.

PHILIP DE MANSEL, stated to have come into England with the CONQUEROR, *m.* a lady named Mountsorrell, and had several children. From his eldest son and heir,

HENRY MANSEL, descended

SIR JOHN MANSEL, knt. who figured in a most distinguished manner in the reign of HENRY III. He was at one time chancellor of London, and provost of Beverley, afterwards treasurer of York, and finally lord chancellor to the king. He was frequently employed upon the most important foreign missions to the pope, to the King of Castile, and to the Scotch. But one circumstance alone establishes his great influence; in the 46th of HENRY III. there being some apprehension of his stirring up strife between the king and his peers, HENRY wrote to the pope and cardinals that he was innocent. He *m.* Joan, daughter of Simon Beauchamp, of Bedford, and had a son and heir,

SIR THOMAS MANSEL, knight banneret, who, according to Hollinshed, was taken prisoner, 46 HENRY III. at Northampton. His son,

HENRY MANSEL, settled, *temp.* EDWARD I. in Glamorganshire, and was father of

SIR WALTER MANSEL, knt. who held of King EDWARD I. *in capite*, the manor of Missenden, in the county of Bucks. He was buried at St. Botolph's Church, in London, and was great-grandfather, or great-great-grandfather of

RICHARD MANSEL, esq. of Missenden, who *m.* Lucy, daughter and sole heir of Philip Scurlage, Lord of Scurlage Castle, in the county of Glamorgan, and was *s.* by his son,

SIR HUGH MANSEL, knt. whose wife was Elizabeth, daughter and heir of Sir John Penrys, knt. lord of Oxwick and other large territories in Glamorganshire, all of which accrued to Sir Hugh, and by the lady was father of

RICHARD MANSEL, esq. of Oxwick, who *m.* Elizabeth, daughter of Hamon Turbervile, of Penline, in Glamorganshire, and was *s.* by his son,

JOHN MANSEL, esq. of Oxwick, whose son and heir,

PHILIP MANSEL, esq. fell in the war of the Roses, and was attainted. He *m.* Mary, daughter of Griffith ap Nicholas, esq. of Newton, in the county of Caermarthen, and had a son and heir,

JENKIN MANSEL, esq. who procured a repeal of his father's attainder and a restoration in blood and estate. He *m.* Edith, daughter and co-heir of Sir George Kynaston, knt. of Kent, and had issue,

- RICE, his heir.
- Hugh, *m.* Jane, daughter and co-heir of Richard Owgan, of Kent, and left a son,
  - Robert, groom of the bedchamber to King HENRY VIII.
- Philip, *m.* Anne, daughter of William Dawndecourt.
- Alice, *m.* to John Drew, of Bristol.
- Anne, *m.* to David ap Rees Wynn, of St. Cothen.
- Jane, *m.* to John Wynn ap Jenkin ap Richard.
- Elizabeth, *m.* to Christopher Flemyng.

The eldest son and heir,

SIR RICE MANSEL, received the honour of knighthood before the 27th of HENRY VIII. in which year he was sent with a supply of soldiers into Ireland to assist the lord deputy in suppressing a rebellion raised in that kingdom by the Earl of Kildare. In the same year he had a grant for life of the chamberlainship of Chester, and in a few years after a grant of the site of the monastery of Margam, in the county of Glamorgan, and the royalty of the Avon water, to him and his heirs. He *m.* first, Eleanor, daughter and sole heir of James Basset, esq. of Beaupre, but by her left no surviving issue. He wedded, secondly, Anne, daughter of Sir Giles Bruges, knt. of Coberley, in the county of Gloucester, and by her had three sons, viz.

all died in his lifetime, and two daughters, whereof only two survived; namely, Catherine, wife of William Basset, esq. of Beaupre; and Elizabeth, of William Morgan, esq. of Lantarnam, in the county of Monmouth. He *m.* thirdly, Cicely, daughter of William Dabridgecourt, and had

- Edward, his successor.
- Anthony, *m.* to Elizabeth, daughter of John Basset, esq. of Lanthrithed.
- Mary, *m.* to Sir Thomas Southwell, knt. of Uprising, in Norfolk.

His last will and testament bears date 10th December, 1568, and the probate thereof 10th May, 1569. He was *s.* by his son,

Sir Edward Mansel, who had received the honour of knighthood in 1572, was chamberlain of Chester, and a man of great honour, integrity, and courage, distinguishing himself in many services during the reign of Elizabeth. He *m.* Lady Jane Somerset, youngest daughter of Henry, Earl of Worcester, by whom (who *d.* 16th October, 1597,) he had issue,

- Thomas, his heir.
- Francis, who was created a Baronet, and was founder of the branch of Trimsaran.
- Robert (Sir), knighted by the Earl of Essex for his valour in the capture of the town of Calais in 1596, and having signalized himself in several encounters, was made vice-admiral of the fleet by *King* James I. in which station he was continued by Charles I. and lived to a very old age, much esteemed for his great integrity, personal courage, and experience in maritime affairs.
- Philip, died, leaving a son,
  - Thomas.
- Elizabeth, *m.* to Sir Walter Rice, knt. of Newton, in Carmarthenshire, and had issue.
- Cecil, *m.* to Rowland Williams, esq. of Llangiby, in the county of Monmouth, and had issue.
- Mary, *m.* to Christopher Turberville, esq. of Pennlyne, and had issue.
- Anne, *m.* to Edward Carne, esq. of Nashe, and had issue.

Sir Edward was *s.* by his eldest son,

I. Thomas Mansel, esq. of Margam, in Glamorganshire, was created a Baronet 22nd May, 1611. Sir Thomas *m.* first, Mary, daughter of Lewis, second Lord Mordaunt; and secondly, Jane, daughter of Thomas Pole, esq. By the latter he had a daughter, Mary, wife of Edward Stradling, esq. and by the former he had three sons.* Sir Thomas *d.* 20th December, 1631, and was *s.* by his son,

II. Sir Lewis Mansel, who wedded, first, Lady Katherine Sydney, daughter of Robert, first Earl of Leicester, and aunt of Algernon Sydney, but by that lady had no issue. He *m.* secondly, Katherine, daughter of Sir Edward Lewis, of Van, in the county of Glamorgan, by whom he had two daughters, Jane, *m.* to Abraham Wogan, esq. and Blanche, *m.* to Sir Charles Kemeys, knt. He *m.* thirdly, Lady Elizabeth Montague, daughter of Henry, Earl of Manchester, by whom (who wedded, secondly, Sir Edward Sebright,) he had issue,

- Edward, his heir.
- Henry.
- Elizabeth, *m.* to Sir William Wiseman, bart. of Rivenhall.
- Mary, *m.* to William Leman, esq. of Northaw.

He *d.* about the year 1638, and was *s.* by his elder son,

III. Sir Edward Mansel, who *m.* Martha, daughter of Edward Carne, esq. of Wenny, in the county of Glamorgan, and had issue, viz.

- Edward, *d.* unm.
- Thomas, heir to his father.
- Martha, *m.* to Thomas Morgan, esq. of Tredegar.
- Elizabeth, *m.* to Sir Edward Stradling, bart. of St. Donats.

Sir Edward *d.* 17th November, 1706, aged seventy, and was *s.* by his only surviving son,

IV. Sir Thomas Mansel, who was comptroller of the household to *Queen* Anne, one of her majesty's privy council, one of the commissioners of the Treasury, one of the tellers of the Exchequer, and raised to the peerage, in 1711, as Baron Mansell, of Margam. He *m.* Martha, daughter and heir of Francis Millington, esq. of the city of London, merchant, by whom he had issue,

- I. Robert, his heir, who *m.* Anne, daughter and co-heir of the celebrated Admiral Sir Cloudesley Shovel, knt. and dying before his father, 29th April, 1723, left with a daughter, a son, viz.
  - Thomas, successor to his grandfather.
- II. Christopher, } sixth and seventh baronets and
- III. Bussy, } third and fourth barons.
- I. Martha.
- II. Elizabeth.
- III. Mary, *m.* to John Ivory Talbot, esq. of Laycock, in Wiltshire, and the descendant of this marriage is the present Christopher Rice Mansel Talbot, esq. of Margam, M.P.

His lordship *d.* 10th December, 1723, and was *s.* by his grandson,

V. Sir Thomas Mansell, second Lord Mansell. This nobleman *d.* unmarried in 1723, when his honours reverted to his uncle,

VI. Sir Christopher Mansell, third Lord Mansell, who *d.* unmarried 29th January, 1744, and was *s.* by his brother,

VII. Sir Bussy Mansell, fourth Lord Mansell, who *m.* first, Lady Betty Hervey, daughter of John, Earl of Bristol, but by her ladyship had no issue. He *m.* secondly, Lady Barbara Blacket, widow of Sir Walter Blacket, bart. and daughter of William, second Earl of Jersey, by whom he had an only daughter and heiress,

- Louisa-Barbara Mansell, who *m.* George, second Lord Vernon, by whom she had one daughter to survive infancy,
  - The Hon. Louisa Vernon, who died in 1786 unmarried.
- Lady Vernon died in the same year.

His lordship *d.* 29th November, 1750, when all his honours, including the Baronetcy, expired.

Arms—Arg. a chevron between three manches sa.

MANSEL, OF TRIMSAREN.

Created 22nd Feb. 1696-7.—Extinct 6th April, 1798.

Lineage.

Sir Francis Mansel, bart. so created in 1621-2 (second son of Sir Edward Mansel, knt. of Margam, in Glamorganshire), *m.* first, Catherine, daughter and heir of Henry Morgan, esq. of Muddlescombe, in the county of Carmarthen, and thus acquiring that estate, was designated therefrom. By this lady he had issue,

* The Mansells, of Plassy, in the county of Limerick, claim to derive from the second of these sons, and if that claim be established in law, the Baronetcy of Mansel, of Margam, would not be extinct, but centre in the Irish branch.

ANTHONY, who fell at Newby, under the royal standard, leaving a son,

SIR EDWARD MANSEL, second baronet, of Muddlescome.

Francis, principal of Jesus' College, Oxford, died in 1665.

Richard, m. Catherine, daughter and heir of Rees Morgan, esq. of Ischoed, and left a son,

SIR RICHARD MANSEL, third baronet, of Muddlescombe, ancestor of the present (1837)

SIR JOHN-BELL-WILLIAM MANSEL, ninth baronet, of Muddlescombe. (See BURKE'S *Peerage and Baronetage*.)

Sir Francis m. secondly, Dorothy, daughter of Alban Stepney, esq. of Prendergast, and by her had

JOHN.

Edward, captain in the army, left a son, Rawleigh, who married Frances, widow of Henry Mansel, and daughter and heir of Sir John Stepney, second baronet, of Prendergast, in Pembrokeshire.

Rawleigh.

Catherine, m. to Sir John Stepney, first baronet, of Prendergast.

Cicely, m. to George Jones, esq. of Abercothy, in the county of Carmarthen.

The eldest son of the second marriage,

JOHN MANSEL, esq. m. Mary, eldest daughter of Sir Henry Vaughan, knt. of Derwidd, (and relict of Charles Philips, esq. of Lewes Lodge, in Carmarthenshire, at nine years of age; so that she was maid, wife, and widow the day her husband died), and left a son and heir,

HENRY MANSEL, esq. who m. Frances,* only daughter and heir of Sir John Stepney, second baronet, of Prendergast, in the county of Pembroke, and was s. by his son,

I. EDWARD MANSEL, esq. This gentleman married Dorothey, daughter of Philip, and sister of Edward Vaughan, esq. of Trimsaran, in Carmarthenshire, who at his death in 1683, bequeathed to her his whole estate, and Mr. Mansel, on being created a BARONET, 22nd February, 1696, was designated "Sir Edward Mansel, of Trimsaran." He had several children, and dying 19th February, 1720, was s. by his eldest son,

II. SIR EDWARD MANSEL, of Trimsaren, who m. first, Anne, daughter of Thomas Price, esq. of Gorth-Lloyn, in the county of Carmarthen, but by that lady (who d. 1st November, 1731) had no issue. He married, secondly, in 1740, Mrs. Bayley, of the Vineyard, near Hereford, and dying in 1754, was s. by his son,

III. SIR EDWARD-VAUGHAN MANSEL, who m. Mary, daughter of Joseph Shewen, and dying about the year 1780, was s. by his son,

IV. SIR EDWARD-JOSEPH-SHEWEN MANSEL, who died unmarried 6th April, 1798, when the BARONETCY EXPIRED.

Arms—Arg. a chevron between three maunches sa.

MAPLES, OF STOW.

CREATED 30th May, 1627.—EXTINCT in 1634-5.

Lineage.

In 1627, a Baronetcy was conferred on

I. THOMAS MAPLES, esq. of Stow, in the county of Huntingdon, but as he died without male issue in 1634-5, the title became EXTINCT.

MARKHAM, OF SEDGEBROOKE.

CREATED 15th Aug. 1642.

EXTINCT in 1779.

Lineage.

MARKHAM, a village in Nottinghamshire, Camden observes, gave name to the Markhams, "a family very famous heretofore both in antiquity and valour," of which was

SIR ALEXANDER DE MARKHAM, constable of the Castle of Nottingham, in the time of HENRY III. He was father of

ALEXANDER DE MARKHAM, whose grandson,

JOHN DE MARKHAM, was an eminent lawyer in the reigns of EDWARD II. and EDWARD III. He m. Joan, daughter of Sir Nicholas Bothomsell, knt. and was father of

ROBERT DE MARKHAM, serjeant-at-law, who married a daughter of Sir John Caunton, knt. of Caunton, and had a son,

SIR JOHN MARKHAM, knt. one of the justices of the Common Pleas from 20th RICHARD II. to the 9th of HENRY IV. This learned person m. first, Elizabeth, daughter of Sir John de Cressy, knt. and coheir of her brother, Sir Hugh de Cressy, who d. s. p. temp. HENRY IV.; by this lady the judge acquired great possessions in Lincolnshire, and by the partition of the property made at Retford, 10 HENRY IV. the manors of Risegate, Braytoft, and Exton, in that county, fell to his posterity. He had issue,

ROBERT (Sir), who m. Elizabeth, daughter and heir of Sir Nicholas Burdon, knt. and was ancestor of the Markhams, of Cotham and Allerton, Notts, of which family was the Right Rev. William Markham, Archbishop of York. (See BURKE'S *Commoners*, vol. ii. page 283.)

Sir John m. secondly, Millicent, daughter and co-heir of Sir John Bekeringe, knt. relict of Sir Nicholas Burdon, knt. and had another son,

JOHN (Sir).

The judge died in 1409, and was interred in West or Little Markham Church, Notts. His son by his second wife,

SIR JOHN MARKHAM, knt. an eminent lawyer, was appointed lord chief justice of the King's Bench, in HENRY VI. and his patents renewed on the accession of EDWARD IV. Of this learned and eminent man the following details are given by Fuller:

"John Markham was born at Markham, in Nottinghamshire, descended of an ancient and worthy family. He employed his youth in the study of the municipal law of this realm, wherein he attained in such eminency, that *King* EDWARD IV. knighted him, and made him lord chief justice of the King's Bench, in the place of Sir John Fortescue, that learned and upright judge, who fled away with *King* HENRY VI. Yet Fortescue was not missed, because Markham

* This lady m. secondly, Captain Edward Mansel.

† KATHERINE CRESSY, the other co-heir, m. Sir John Clifton, knt.

ucceeded him; for though these two judges did severally lean to the sides of Lancaster and York, yet oth sat upright in matters of judicature.

"We will instance and insist on one memorable ct of our judge, which, though single in itself, was iurall in the concernings thereof.

"*King* EDWARD IV. having married into the family f the Woodvills (gentlemen of more antiquity than ealth, and of higher spirits than fortunes) thought fit for his own honour to bestow honour on them: ut he could not so easily provide them of wealth as tles. For honour he could derive from himself, like ght from a candle, without any diminishing of his wn lustre; whereas wealth flowing from him, as ater from a fountain, made the spring the shallower, herefore he resolved to cut down some prime subrts, and to engraft the queen's kindred into these states, which otherwise like suckers must feed on e stock of his own exchequer.

"There was at this time, one Sir Thomas Cook, late rd mayor of London and knight of the Bath, one ho had well lick'd his fingers under *Queen* MARGARET, hose wardroper he was, and customer of Hampton) man of great estate. It was agreed that he should accused of high treason, and a commission of oyer nd terminer granted forth to the Lord Mayor, the uke of Clarence, the Earl of Warwick, the Lord ivers, Sir John Markham, Sir John Fogg, to try m in Guild-Hall: and the king by private instrucons to the judge appeared so farre, that Cook, though was not, must be found guilty, and if the law ere too short, the judge must stretch it to the purose. The fault laid to his charge was, for lending oneys to *Queen* MARGARET, wife to *King* HENRY VI.; e proof was the confession of one Hawkins, who ing rack'd in the Tower, had confessed so much. e councel for the king hanging as much weight on e smallest wire, as it would hold, aggravated each rticular, and by their rhetoricall flashes blew the ult up to a great height. Sir Thomas Cook pleaded r himself, that Hawkins indeed upon a season came him, and requested him to lend one thousand rks upon good security. But he desired first to w for whom the money should be: and underanding it was for *Queen* MARGARET, denied to lend money, though at last the said Hawkins deended so low, as to require but one hundred pounds, departed without any penny lent to him.

Judge Markham, in a grave speech, did recapitu[illegible], and collate the material points on either [illegible] ing that the proof reached not the charge [illegible] treason, and misprision of treason was the [illegible] it could amount to; and intimated to the jury, tender in matter of life, and discharge good [illegible]. The jury being wise men (whose appre[illegible] could make up a whole sentence of every [illegible] of the judge) saw it behoved them to draw up [illegible] into as narrow a compass as might be, lest it [illegible] their own case; for they lived in a troublesome [illegible], wherein the cards were so shuffled, that two [illegible] were turn'd up trump at once, which amazed [illegible] how to play their games. Whereupon they ac[illegible] the prisoner of high treason, and found him [illegible] as the judge directed. Yet it cost Sir Thomas [illegible], before he could get his liberty, eight hundred [illegible] to the queen, and eight thousand pounds to [illegible], a sum in that age more sounding like the [illegible] of a prince, than the fine of a subject. Be[illegible], the Lord Rivers (the queen's father) had, during [illegible] imprisonment, despoiled his houses, one in the [illegible] other in the country, of plate and furniture, [illegible] he never received a penny recompence. [illegible] righted him of the wrongs men did him by [illegible] the remnant of his estate to him, and his [illegible] erity, which still flourish at Giddy Hall.

"As for Sir John Markham, the king's displeasure fell so heavy on him, that he was outed of his place, and Sir Thomas Billing put in his room, though the one lost that office with more honour than the other got it; and gloried in this, that though the king could make him no judge, he could not make him no upright judge. He lived privately the rest of his days, having (besides the estate got by his practice) fair lands by Margaret, his wife, daughter and co-heir of Sir John Leke, of Cotham, in Nottinghamshire, whose mother, Joan, was daughter and heir of Sir John Talbot, of Swannington, in Leicestershire."

Sir John Markham left a son and heir,

THOMAS MARKHAM, lord of Sedgebroke, in Nottinghamshire, who *m.* Catherine, daughter and co-heir of William Hartshorne, esq. and was *s.* by his son,

JOHN MARKHAM, esq. who *m.* Eleanor, daughter of Sir John Turbervile, knt. and was father of

RICHARD MARKHAM, esq. living in 1562, who by Anne, daughter of George Heveningham, esq. had a numerous progeny. His eldest son and heir,

JOHN MARKHAM, esq. living *temp.* ELIZABETH, *m.* Mary, daughter of Gervase Lee, esq. of Southwell, Notts, and was *s.* by his son,

SIR JOHN MARKHAM, knt. who *m.* a daughter of Sir Peter Warburton, knt. of Arley, in Cheshire, and had

SIR ANTHONY MARKHAM, knt. who married Bridget, daughter of Sir James Harrington, bart. and had four sons, viz.

- I. JOHN, who *m.* the daughter of Sir Thomas Tirringham, knt. of Tirringham, Bucks, by whom he had two sons, who both died young.
- II. ROBERT.
- III. Henry, } *d. s. p.*
- IV. Francis, } *d. s. p.*

The second but eldest surviving son, and eventual heir,

I. ROBERT MARKHAM, esq. of Sedgebrooke, in the county of Nottingham, was created a BARONET by *King* CHARLES I. 15th August, 1642. Sir Robert *m.* first, Rebecca, daughter of — Eyre, esq. of Derbyshire, but by her had no issue. He wedded, secondly, Rebecca, daughter of Sir Edward Hussey, bart. of Honington, in Lincolnshire, and by that lady had two sons and seven daughters, viz.

- I. ROBERT, his heir.
- II. Anthony, colonel in the Guards, *m.* Catherine, daughter of Sir William Whorwood, knt. of Stourton Castle, in Staffordshire, and by her (who *m.* secondly, Sir Harry Cambell, bart. of Clay Hall, in Essex) he had
  - 1. Thomas, *m.* Frances, daughter of Andrew Convenent, M.D. and left issue,
    - JAMES-JOHN, fourth baronet.
    - Mary, *m.* to Mr. Dambourges.
  - 2. Walter, *d.* unm.
  - 1. Mary, *d.* unm.
  - 2. Rebecca, married to Captain Rolle, of the Guards, and left a son.
  - 3. Anne, *m.* to Mr. Morein, a surgeon.
- I. Rebecca, *m.* to Reginald Heber, esq. of Marton, in Yorkshire, and had issue.
- II. Elizabeth, *m.* to Charles Bull, esq. of Skipton, in Craven.
- III. Frances, *m.* to Christopher Broughton, esq. of Longdon, in Staffordshire.
- IV. Anne, *m.* to Sir Walter Hawksworth, bart.
- V. Catherine, *m.* to Christopher Villiers, esq. of Gostoke, Notts.
- VI. Jane, } *d.* unm.
- VII. Diana, } *d.* unm.

Sir Robert was *s.* at his decease by his eldest son,

II. Sir Robert Markham, who wedded Mary, daughter and co-heir of Sir Thomas Widdrington, knt. serjeant-at-law, of Sherburn Grange, in Northumberland, and had issue,

George, his successor.
Robert, *d.* young.

Ursula, *m.* first, Altham Annesley, Lord Altham in the peerage of Ireland; and secondly, Samuel Ogle, esq. By the latter she left

George Ogle, *m.* Frances, eldest daughter of Sir Thomas Twisden, bart.
Robert Ogle, captain of horse, in Ireland.
Thomas Ogle.

Sir Robert *d.* 11th August, 1690, and was *s.* by his son,

III. Sir George Markham, F.R.S. who *d.* unm. 9th June, 1736, bequeathing his estate to the Rev. Doctor Bernard Wilson, prebendary of Worcester, and rector of Newark-upon-Trent. The baronetcy devolved upon his cousin (refer to Anthony, second son of the first baronet).

IV. Sir James-John Markham, who *m.* 31st August, 1735, Sarah, daughter of — Clive, esq. but died without issue, in 1779, when the Baronetcy became extinct.

Arms—Az. on a chief or, a demi-lion rampant issuing gu.

MAROW, OF BERKSWELL.

Created 16th July, 1679. Extinct before 1714.

Lineage.

William Marow, son of Stephen Marowe, of Stevenhithe, in Middlesex, was lord mayor of London 35 Henry VI. He *m.* Catherine, daughter and coheir of John Rich, citizen of London, and had, with two daughters, Johanna, wife of William Clopton, esq. and Catherine, of Sir Robert Throckmorton, knt. of Coughton, two sons, Thomas, serjeant-at-law, who died 21 Henry VII. and

William Marow, living 22 Edward IV. who *m.* Joanna, daughter of William Chedworth, alderman of London, and had, beside two daughters, Elizabeth, *m.* to George Medley, and Catherine, to Ralph Daniel, a son and heir,

Thomas Marow, esq. who *m.* first, a daughter of Baldwin Dowse, of Balshall; and secondly, Catherine, daughter of Roger Wigston, esq. of Wolston, in Warwickshire. By the former he left at his decease, in 1536, two sons, Edward Marow, of Elmedon, and

Thomas Marow, of Hoxton, in Middlesex. To this gentleman and Alice, his wife, only daughter and heir of Richard Harregong, the manor of Berkswell, in the county of Warwick, which had reverted to the crown on the attainder of John, Duke of Northumberland, was granted in 3 and 4 Philip and Mary. Thomas Marow *d.* 3 Elizabeth, and was *s.* by his son,

MAR

Samuel Marow, esq. of Berkswell, who *m.* Margaret, daughter of Sir John Littleton, knt. of Frank[illegible] in Worcestershire, and dying in 1610, was succeeded by his son,

Sir Edward Marow, knt. of Berkswell, who wed[illegible] Ursula, daughter of Richard Fiennes, Lord Say [illegible] Sele, and dying in 1632, left with other issue, a [illegible] and successor,

Samuel Marow, esq. of Berkswell, who *m.* [illegible] daughter of Gerard Whorwood, esq. of Sturton Cast[illegible] in Staffordshire, and had one son, Edward, his [illegible] and two daughters, Anne and Ursula. He died [illegible] 1635, and was *s.* by his son,

Edward Marow, esq. of Berkswell, who *m.* [illegible] daughter of Sir Thomas Grantham, of Goltho[illegible], in Lincolnshire, and was father of

I. Samuel Marow, esq. of Berkswell, who was created a Baronet 16th July, 1679. He *m.* Mar[illegible], daughter and heir of Sir Arthur Cayley, knt. of [illegible]land, in Warwickshire, and left, at his decease, when the Baronetcy became extinct, five daughters, his co-heirs, namely,

Anne, *m.* to Sir Arthur Kaye, bart. of W[illegible] in Yorkshire.
Elizabeth.
Ursula, *m.* to Robert Wilmot, esq. of O[illegible].
Mary, *m.* to John Knightley, esq. of Offchurch.
Arabella.

Arms—Az. a fesse engr. between three women's heads, couped at the shoulders arg. hair dishevelled [illegible]

MARWOOD, OF LITTLE BUSHBY.

Created 31st Dec. 1660. Extinct 23rd Feb [illegible]

Lineage.

James Marwood, esq. of Nunthorp, in the [illegible] of York, the first of this family upon record, m[illegible] a daughter of James Cleasby, of Cleasby, in the same county, and had two sons, William, who *d. s. p.* [illegible] his heir,

Henry Marwood, esq. of Little Busby, [illegible] Yorkshire, who *d.* in 1639, leaving by Anne, his [illegible] the daughter of John Constable, esq. of [illegible] in the same county, three sons and two daughters, viz.

George, his heir.
William, of Stubby, in the county of Lincoln.
Francis, citizen of London.

Anne, *m.* to Giles Wetherell, esq. of [illegible] Durham.
Barbara, *m.* to Josias Matthews, esq. grandson of the Most Rev. Toby Matthews, D.D. Archbishop of York.

The eldest son,

I. George Marwood, esq. of *Little* [illegible] created a Baronet by *King* Charles II. [illegible] ber, 1660. Sir George *m.* Frances, daughter of [illegible] Walter Bethell, knt. of Alne, in the county of [illegible] and had issue,

Henry, his successor.

George, a Hambrough merchant, had two sons, viz.

Samuel, } third and fourth baronets.
William, }

Walter.

Barbara, m. to Sir Thomas Keblethayt, knt. of Norton, in Yorkshire.

Frances, m. to Richard Weston, esq. of Gray's Inn.

Anne, m. to William Metcalf, esq. of Alletton, Yorkshire.

He d. 19th February, 1679, aged seventy-eight, and was s. by his son,

II. Sir Henry Marwood, sheriff of Yorkshire, in 1675 who m. first, Margaret, fourth daughter of Conyers, second Lord D'Arcy, and sister of Conyers, first Earl of Holderness, and had two daughters only. He m. secondly, Dorothy, second daughter of Allen Bellingham, esq. of Levens, in Westmoreland, and had

George, who m. Constance, second daughter and co-heir of Sir Thomas Spencer, bart. of Yarnton, in the county of York, but d. s. p. in the lifetime of his father.

Sir Henry wedded, thirdly, Martha, daughter of Sir Thomas Wentworth, knt. of Empsall, in Yorkshire, widow of Thomas Wombwell, esq. of Wombwell. He d. at the advanced age of ninety, 1st November, 1725, when the estates fell to his daughters, as co-heirs, and the Baronetcy devolved upon his nephew,

III. Sir Samuel Marwood, who m. Miss Peirson, of Stokesley, but d. issueless, aged sixty-seven, in October, 1739, and was s. by his brother,

IV. Sir William Marwood. This gentleman died s. p. 23rd February, 1740, when the Baronetcy expired.

Arms—Gu. a chevron erm. between three goats' heads erased arg.

MASHAM, OF HIGH LEVER.

Created 20th Dec. 1621.  Extinct 14th June, 1776.

Lineage.

Sir William Masham, of High-Lever, in the county of Essex, created a Baronet on the 20th December, 1621, m. Winifred, daughter of Sir Francis Barrington, bart. of Barrington Hall, son of Sir Thomas Barrington, by Winifred, his wife, widow of Sir Thomas Hastings, and second daughter and co-heir of Henry Pole, Lord Montagu, (attainted and beheaded in 1539,) son and heir of Sir Richard Pole, by his wife, Margaret, Countess of Salisbury, daughter, and eventually co-heir of George Plantagenet, Duke of Clarence, younger brother of *King* Edward IV. By this marriage the family of Masham allied itself with the noblest blood in the realm. Sir William died about 1656, and was s. by his grandson,

II. Sir William Masham, of High Lever, (eldest son of William Masham, esq. by Elizabeth his wife, daughter of Sir John Trevor, knt.) He died unm. about 1663, and was s. by his brother,

III. Sir Francis Masham, who m. first, Mary, daughter of Sir William Scot, bart. Marquis de La Mezansene, in France, by whom he had eight sons and one daughter, one son of whom only survived him. He m. secondly, Damaris, daughter of Ralph Cudworth, D.D. and had by her a son, Francis Cudworth, accomptant general to the High Court of Chancery. Sir Francis died 7th February, 1723, and was s. by his son,

IV. Sir Samuel Masham, who m. Abigail, daughter of Francis Hill, esq. a Turkey merchant, and sister of General John Hill. This lady was nearly related to the celebrated Sarah, Duchess of Marlborough, and was introduced by her grace, whom she eventually supplanted, to the notice of *Queen* Anne. Sir Samuel, who was an eighth son, was originally a page to the queen, whilst Princess of Denmark, and also one of the equerries, and gentlemen of the bed-chamber to Prince George. Upon the discomfiture of the Marlborough party, and the establishment of his wife as the reigning favourite, he was elevated to the peerage 31st December, 1711, as Baron Masham, *of Otes, in the county of Essex:* and having had a grant in reversion of the office of remembrancer of the exchequer, succeeded to that post on the death of Lord Fanshaw in 1716. His lordship had issue,

George, who died s. p. in the lifetime of his father.

Samuel, successor to the title.

Francis, died s. p. in the lifetime of his father.

Anne, m. to Henry Hoare, esq. and had issue,

Susannah, m. first to Charles, Viscount Dungarvon, and secondly to Thomas, first Earl of Aylesbury.

Anne, m. to Sir Richard Hoare, bart.

Elizabeth, d. unmarried in 1794.

Lord Masham died in 1758, and was s. by his only surviving son,

Samuel Masham, second baron. This nobleman m. first, Harriet, daughter of Salway Winnington, esq. of Stanford Court, in the county of Worcester, by whom (who d. in 1761,) he had no issue. He espoused, secondly, Miss Dives, one of the maids of honour to the dowager Princess of Wales, but had no issue. His lordship, who filled several public employments, died in 1776, when the Baronetcy, together with the Barony of Masham, became extinct.

Arms—Or, a fesse humette gu. between two lions passant sa.

MASSINGBERD, OF BRAYTOFT HALL.

Created 22nd Aug. 1660.  Extinct 8th Dec. 1723.

Lineage.

This family, whose name has been written Masyngberd, Massingbergh, and Massingberd, is traced to the time of Edward I. when its patriarch,

LAMBERT MASSINGBERD, resided at Sutterton. His great-grandson,

THOMAS MASSYNGBERD, living in 1434, m. Juliana, daughter and co-heir of Thomas, son and heir of Gilbert Bernak,* and was s. by his son and heir,

ROBERT MASSYNGBERDE, esq. who m. Agnes, daughter and sole heir of Robert Halliday, of Burgh, and had two sons,

- I. RICHARD, his heir.
- II. Thomas, m. Elizabeth, daughter and co-heir of Sir Thomas Hoo, created Lord Hoo, of Hastings, and made a knight of the garter.

He d. in the 38th of HENRY VI. and was s. by his elder son,

RICHARD MASSYNGBERDE, esq. who m. Maud, daughter of Thomas Kyme, esq. and was s. by his eldest son,

SIR THOMAS MASSYNGBERDE, knt. who marrying JOAN, younger daughter, but the heiress of John Braytoft, of Braytoft Hall,† fixed his abode there. He had issue,

- I. AUGUSTIN, who purchased, in 1538, the manors belonging to Sir John Markham, in Braytoft, and elsewhere, m. Margaret, daughter of Robert Elrington, esq. of Hoxton, in Middlesex, and dying in the lifetime of his father, *anno* 1549, left,
  - 1. THOMAS, heir to his grandfather.
  - 2. William, whose grandson,
    - John, an eminent merchant of London, and treasurer of the East India Company, left at his decease, in 1653, two daughters, his heirs, viz.
      - ELIZABETH, m. to George, first Lord Berkeley.
      - MARY, m. to Robert, third Earl of Lindsey.
  - 3. Christopher, who was appointed in 1548, clerk of the council within the town of Calais for life.
  - 4. John, m. Dorothy, relict of Ralph Quadring, esq. and eldest daughter of Sir Robert Hussey, knt. of Linwood, and left, with two daughters, a son,
    - Augustin, of Sutterton.
  - 1. Grace, m. to Stephen Spackman, esq.
  - 2. Anne, m. first to Christopher Forcet, esq. of Billesby, and secondly to Christopher Somercotes, esq. of Somercotes.
  - 3. Ursula, m. to John Davy, esq.
  - 4. Edith, m. to Augustin Caundest, esq. and d. in 1560.
  - 5. Elizabeth, buried at Braytoft, 18th October, 1588.
- II. Oswaladd, prior of Kilmainham, and principal of the Order of St. John of Jerusalem, at its dissolution by *Queen* ELIZABETH.
- III. Alan, died unm.
- IV. Martin, m. Ursula Elrington, and left issue.
- I. Edith, m. to Richard Lytler, of Tathwell.
- II. Cecily, m. to Thomas Moore.

Sir Thomas having survived his wife, became, *temp.* HENRY VIII. a knight of St. John of Jerusalem, and added the second escutcheon to the family arms. He was s. at his decease, 25th May, 1552, by his grandson,

THOMAS MASSINGBERD, esq. of Braytoft Hall, M.P. for Calais, in the 6th of EDWARD VI. who m. first, Alice, daughter and sole heir of Richard Bevercoats, esq. of Newark, and by her had, THOMAS, his heir, with other children. He wedded, secondly, Dorothy, daughter and heir of Richard Ballard, gent. of Orby, and by that lady had another son and three daughters. He d. in 1584, and was s. by his son,

THOMAS MASSINGBERD, esq. who m. Frances, daughter of Sir George Fitz Williams, knt. of Maplethorpe, and dying at Gunby, 11th September, 1620, was s. by his eldest son,

THOMAS MASSINGBERD, esq. of Braytoft Hall and Gunby, both in the county of Lincoln, barrister-at-law. This gentleman m. Frances, daughter of Robert Halton, esq. of Clee, serjeant-at-law, by Joan his wife, daughter of John Draner, esq. of Hoxton, and had issue,

- I. HENRY, his heir.
- II. Draner (Sir), the Parliamentary commander, who raised a troop of horse in the early part of the civil war,‡ but afterwards went abroad and received the royal pardon. He inherited from the Draners, Henxworth, in Hertfordshire, and purchasing the lordship of Ormsby, in Lincolnshire, was ancestor of the MASSINGBERDS of Ormsby, refer to BURKE'S *Commoners*, vol. i. p. 661. The male representation of the family now centres in this branch.
- I. Frances, m. first to John Day, esq. of Sausthorpe, and secondly to Thomas Pitcher, esq. of Trumpington, in Cambridgeshire.
- II. Elizabeth, m. to John Booth, esq.
- III. Susannah, married first, in 1625, to Richard Cater, esq. (killed by a fall from his horse, 10th July, 1631,) and secondly, in 163[illegible], to Richard Godney, esq. of Swaby.
- IV. Alice, m. to Thomas Day, esq. of Sausethorpe.
- V. Margaret, m. to Leonard Purley, gent. of Firsthorp.

Mr. Massingberd died suddenly on his way to church 5th November, 1636, was buried at Gunby, and s. by his son,

I. HENRY MASSINGBERD, esq. of Braytoft Hall and Gunby, b. in 1609. This gentleman was admitted fellow commoner of Christ College, Cambridge, [illegible] April, 1627, whence he removed to the Inner Temple and entered a student there, 17th June, 1629. In 1658 CROMWELL created him a BARONET, and the patent is now in the possession of Thomas Massingberd, esq. of Candlesby House;§ the historians of the family have studiously omitted to notice its existence, and Wotton Dale asserts, that Sir Henry had "maintained an inviolable allegiance to his lawful sovereign." There is some reason to believe that he did not then assume the title. Soon after the Restoration, Sir Henry was re-created a BARONET 22nd August, 1660. He m. first, Elizabeth, youngest daughter of William Lyster, esq. of Rippingale and Colby, and had issue,

---

* Second son of Sir Hugh Bernak, of Bernak Hall, in the county of Lincoln, by Maud his wife, eldest daughter and co-heir of Sir William Woodthorpe, knt. of Woodthorpe.

† His eldest daughter, AGNES BRAYTOFT, was prioress of the nunnery, of Crabhouse, in Norfolk.

‡ Sir Draner's banner represented a knight on horseback, with the motto "Deus, oculi nostri defixi sunt in Te, sic Pacem quærimus."

§ The preamble to the patent sets forth that the honour is conferred "as well for his faithfulness and good affection to us and his country, as for his descent, patrimony, ample estate, and ingenious education, every way answerable, who out of a liberal mind hath undertaken to maintain thirty foot souldiers in our dominion of Ireland, for three whole years." The patent bears the initial of Oliver's christian name, encircling a good likeness of him, in a robe of ermine.

Henry, *d.* unm. in 1666, aged twenty-five.

John, *d.* unm. in 1671.

Frances, *m.* first to George Saunderson, esq. of Thoresby, and secondly to Timothy Hildyard, esq.

Elizabeth, *m.* to Sir Nicholas Stoughton, bart. of Stoke, in Surrey.

Sir Henry wedded, secondly, Anne, relict of Nicholas Stoughton, esq. of Stoke, and daughter and sole heir of William Evans, esq. of London, and by that lady had,

William, his heir.

He *m.* thirdly, Elizabeth Rayner, of Yorkshire. He *d.* in September, 1680, aged seventy-one, and was *s.* by his son,

II. Sir William Massingberd, of Gunby, who *m.* 11th July, 1673, Elizabeth, daughter of Richard Wynne, esq. of London, and had a son and daughter, viz.

William, his successor.

Elizabeth, *m.* to Thomas Meux, esq. son of Henry Meux, esq. of Stoughton manor.

He *d.* about the year 1719, aged seventy, and was *s.* by his son,

III. Sir William Massingberd, of Gunby, M.P. for Lincolnshire, *b.* in 1677. This gentleman died unm. 9th September, 1723, when the Baronetcy expired. Sir William devised his estates to his sister,

Elizabeth Meux, who had by her husband, Thomas Meux, esq. above mentioned, two sons; from the younger, Henry Meux, descends the present (1837) Sir Henry Meux, bart. of Theobalds: the elder,

William Meux, esq. having inherited the property of his mother, became of Gunby, and assumed the surname and arms of Massingberd.* He *d.* in 1780, and was *s.* by his grandson,

Henry Massingberd, of Gunby, who *m.* Miss Elizabeth Hoare, and *d.* about the year 1787, leaving an only daughter and heir,

Anne Massingberd, who *m.* Peregrine Langton, esq. second son of Bennet Langton, esq. of Langton, in Lincolnshire, which Peregrine assumed the name of Massingberd. Their son and heir is the present (1837)

Rev. Algernon-Langton Massingberd, of Gunby and Bratoft, in the county of Lincoln. (See Burke's *Commoners*, vol. iii. p. 104.)

Arms—Azure, three quaterfoils, two and one, and in chief a boar passant or charged on the shoulder with a cross patée gules.

MATTHEWS, OF GOBIONS.

Created 15th June, 1662.—Extinct in 1708.

Lineage.

Samuel Matthews, of Gobions, in Essex, the first of his family there seated, was according to his contemporary, Mr. Symonds, "living near Romford, and being a forward lad, waiting for employment at the court got to be under clerk to Sir Thomas Mewtys, clerk of the privy council: in which employment he took to his wife the heiress of a citizen worth £4000, and that set him up in the world. He was a parliamentary officer, and died in 1658." His son and heir,

I. Philip Matthews, esq. of Gobions, in Essex, was created a Baronet 15th June, 1662. He *m.* Anne, daughter of Sir Thomas Wolstonholme, bart. of Forty Hill, in Enfield, and by her, who died 20th March, 1735, aged eighty-nine, had issue,

John, his heir.

Dorothy, died unm.

Elizabeth, *m.* to Thomas Dawson, D.D. and had issue.

Sir Philip died in 1685, and was *s.* by his son,

II. Sir John Matthews, colonel in the Foot Guards, who was slain at the battle of Oudenarde, and as he died *s. p.* the Baronetcy became extinct. The estate of Gobions was sold by the Matthews family to William Curwen, and from his son, John Curwen, esq. it was purchased by Sir Philip Hall, of Upton, sheriff of Essex in 1727.

MAULIVERER, OF ALLERTON-MAULIVERER.

Created 4th Aug. 1641.

Extinct March, 1713.

Lineage.

Sir Thomas Mauliverer, knt. of Allerton Mauliverer, representative, at the commencement of the 16th century, of that ancient family, married Elizabeth, daughter of John de la River, esq. and had issue,

I. Richard (Sir), knt. father, by Jane his wife, daughter of Sir Robert Plompton, of Sir Thomas Mauliverer, knighted at Flodden, who *m.* Elenor, daughter of Sir Henry Oughtred, and had an only daughter and heir,

Jane, *m.* first to Sir Henry Wharton; secondly to Robert, Lord Ogle; and thirdly to Sir Richard Mauliverer.

II. Thomas.

III. Francis.

IV. George.

V. Gilbert, of whom presently.

I. Mary, *m.* to Edward Copley, esq.

II. Bridget, *m.* to John Vavasour, esq.

The fifth son,

Gilbert Mauliverer, esq. married Elizabeth Royden, of Denbighshire, and left, with two daughters, Anne, *m.* to William Lusher, and Frances to Henry Battle, a son and successor,

Sir Richard Mauliverer, knt. high sheriff of Yorkshire, 31 Elizabeth, who *m.* first, Jane, Lady Ogle, daughter and heir of his cousin, Sir Thomas

* Sir William Massingberd did not by his will require his nephew to take his name, but bequeathed a genealogical History of his family, by Robert Dale, esq. Suffolk herald, to his cousin, Burrell Massingberd, esq. of Ormsby, son and heir of Sir Drayner Massingberd.

Mauliverer, and secondly, Katherine, daughter of Sir Ralph Bourchier. By the latter (who *m.* secondly, Sir Richard Trevor,) he left a son and successor,

I. THOMAS MAULIVERER, esq. of Allerton Mauliverer, who was created a BARONET in 1641. This baronet sat on the trial, and affixed his signature to the death warrant of *King* CHARLES. He *m.* first, Mary, daughter of Sir Richard Hutton, lord chief justice of the Common Pleas, by whom he had no child, and secondly, Mary, daughter of Sir Thomas Wilbraham, knt. by whom he left, at his decease in 1655, with two daughters, Grace, *m.* to Thomas Scott, and Elizabeth to Richard Beverley, a son,

II. SIR RICHARD MAULIVERER, gentleman of the privy chamber, who *m.* Ann, daughter of Sir Henry Clerk, bart. and had issue,

THOMAS, } successive baronets.
RICHARD, }
William.
Charles, drowned when a boy at York.
Henry.
Judith.
Mary.

The eldest son,

III. SIR THOMAS MAULIVERER, *m.* Katherine, daughter and heir of Sir Miles Stapleton, knt. but by her, who wedded, secondly, John Hopton, esq. had no issue. He *d.* about 1687, and was *s.* by his brother,

IV. SIR RICHARD MAULIVERER, who *m.* Barbara, daughter of Sir Thomas Slingsby, bart. of Scriven, and had a son, RICHARD, his heir. His widow wedded, secondly, John, Lord Arundel, of Trerice, and thirdly, Thomas, Earl of Pembroke and Montgomery. Sir Richard died *circa* 1689, and was *s.* by his son,

V. SIR RICHARD MAULIVERER, at whose decease unmarried, in March, 1713, the title became EXTINCT.

Arms—Gu. three greyhounds courant in pale arg. collared or.

MAWBEY, OF BOTLEYS.

CREATED 30th July, 1765.

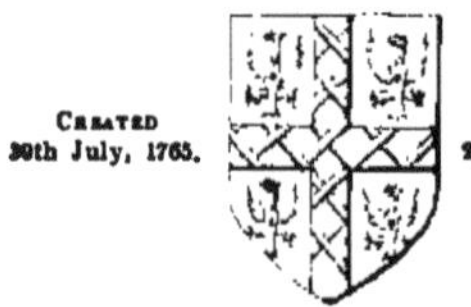

EXTINCT 28th Aug. 1817.

Lineage.

The name of this family has been written, MAWTEBY, MAULTBY, MAUTEBY, MAWBIE, MAWBY, and MAWBEY. The designation was assumed from the village of Mawtby, in Norfolk, of which the founders of the family were early enfeoffed by the crown.

SIMON DE MAUTEBY, had an interest therein in the 10th of RICHARD I. when he was tenant, and Lambert Fitz Otho petent, in a fine of sixteen acres of land. He was great grandfather of

SIR WALTER DE MAUTEBY, who had a grant in 1248, of free warren in Mauteby, and was lord thereof in the 34th and 41st years of HENRY III. He married Christian, daughter and co-heir of Sir Piers de Bassingham, sub collector and accountant in the 15th of *King* JOHN, and was *s.* by his son,

SIR WALTER DE MAUTEBY, father of

SIR ROBERT DE MAUTEBY, who by the finding of a jury was established, Lord of Mauteby in the 20th of EDWARD I. 1292, and his name occurs again as lord in 1700. He was *s.* by his son,

SIR JOHN DE MAUTEBY, Lord of Mauteby in 1316, in 1330, and in 1336. He married Avelina de Grenon, of Sparham, in Norfolk, with whom he had Mauteby's manor in that town. The said Avelina (called in the 9th of EDWARD II. Avelina de Mauteby,) was returned lady of the said manor. He was, in the 6th year of EDWARD I, Lord of Bassingham, West Becham, and Matlask, and was *s.* by his son,

SIR ROBERT DE MAUTEBY, who was lord of these manors in 1347, and left at his decease a son and heir,

SIR JOHN DE MAUTEBY, who was Lord of Mauteby, Bassingham, West Becham, Matlask, Mauteby's manor, in Sparham, Mawtby's manor, in Winterton, with lands held of the Abbot of St. Bennet. His eldest son,

SIR JOHN DE MAUTEBY, died *v. p.* was feoffee of the manors of Lanwades, in Uleston, Peek Hall, in Titleshall, in Norfolk, and sealed with a plain cross. He was buried in 1374, before the altar of St. Mary's, in the church of Preton St. Edmund, in Suffolk, where he resided. He left an only daughter and heir,

ALIANORA DE MAUTEBY, who *m.* Sir William Calthorpe, who thereupon quartered the arms of Mauteby with his own.

Sir John *d.* 30th October, 1403, and was *s.* by his eldest surviving son,

SIR ROBERT DE MAUTEBY, who settled his estates in 1413. By his wife Eleanora (who *m.* after his decease, Thomas Chambers, esq.) he had several sons, of whom the eldest,

JOHN DE MAUTEBY, inherited the estates at the decease of his father. He *m.* Margaret Berney, daughter of John Berney, esq. of Reedham, in the county of Norfolk, and left an only daughter,

MARGARET DE MAUTEBY, who succeeded to the great estate of the family, under the settlement made by her grandfather. She *m.* John Paston, esq. son and heir of Sir William Paston, the judge, and from her descended, in a direct line,

SIR ROBERT PASTON, created a baronet in 1641, and afterwards a peer in 1673, as Viscount Yarmouth. He was made Earl of Yarmouth in 1679.

The fifth son,

THOMAS DE MAUTEBY, esq. was of Sparham, in Norfolk, and was great-great-grandfather of

RICHARD MAUTBEY, esq. of the same place, but who resided at Kilworth, in Leicestershire. He *m.* Margaret Spencer, and had three sons,

WILLIAM, his heir.
Richard, *m.* Jane Bird, and had two sons and a daughter.
Robert, baptised at Kilworth, 12th May, 1561, *m.* 5th July, 1582, Alicia Coleman, and had a son
George, who *m.* Dorothy, the only daughter of his uncle Richard.

The eldest son,

WILLIAM MAUTBEY, esq. *m.* at South Kilworth, 3rd January, 1580, Agnes Carey, and dying in 1641, had issue,

1. JOHN, baptised at Kilworth, 10th January, 1583, *m.* Agnes, daughter of William Chamberlayne, esq. of Leicester, and had two sons,
   Roger, *d.* unm.
   Erasmus, an active partisan of the parliament, *temp.* CHARLES I. killed at Kenilworth

way Down, a volunteer in Sir Arthur Heselrigge's regiment.

II. RICHARD.

III. Thomas, baptized at Kilworth, 22nd March, 1594, married Eleanor Cartwright, and had a son,

William, b. in 1655, progenitor of the Mawbeys of South Kilworth.

The second son,

RICHARD MAWBEY, esq. b. in 1588, m. Elizabeth, daughter of — Shuckburgh, esq. of Naseby, in the county of Northampton, and was s. by his son,

ERASMUS MAWBEY, esq. baptized at South Kilworth, 7th March, 1616, m. first, Mary, daughter of Robert Wright, by whom he had seven sons, Robert, Richard, Erasmus, Thomas, John, Francis, and WILLIAM. He m. secondly, Elizabeth Slee, of Tickenhall, in the county of Derby, and by her had five other sons and two daughters. He d. in 1694. The youngest son of the first marriage,

WILLIAM MAWBEY, b. at Shenton, 31st January, 1659, was settled at Raunston, and buried there 12th December, 1733. He m. Anne, daughter of Mr. John Walker, of Swannington, in the county of Leicester, and left an only son,

JOHN MAWBEY, who m. first, Martha, eldest daughter of Thomas Pratt, of Raunston, and had by her, who d. in 1737, surviving issue,

JOHN, m. first, Mary, daughter of Mr. Jonathan Darling, of Raunston, and secondly, Anne, daughter of Mr. William Fielding; by the former he had a daughter, Elizabeth, who survived but two months; by the latter another daughter, Maria, who d. in her eighth year of the small-pox. He was in partnership with his brother, Sir Joseph Mawbey, in an extensive malt distillery and vinegar manufactory, at Vauxhall, and died 2nd March, 1798.

JOSEPH.

Anne, m. to Mr. John Cooper, of Burbage, in the county of Leicester.

Mary, m. to Mr. William Alcock, of Raunston, and had,

Joseph Alcock, of the treasury.
William Alcock.
John Alcock, of the Temple.
Thomas Alcock, an officer in the East India Company's service, at Bengal.
Maria Alcock.

He (John sen.) m. secondly, Mrs. Shepherd of Rawnston, but had no other issue. He d. in 1754. The youngest son,

I. JOSEPH MAWBEY, esq. having been taken into partnership by his uncle, Joseph Pratt, esq. of Vauxhall, in an extensive malt distillery and vinegar manufactory, (which Joseph d. in 1754, leaving him a considerable fortune,) and having m. Elizabeth, the only surviving daughter, and eventual heir of his cousin, Richard Pratt, esq. of Vauxhall, amassed great wealth, and rose to rank and distinction. In 1757, he served the office of sheriff for Surrey; in 1761, he was returned to parliament by the borough of Southwark, and was created a BARONET 30th July, 1765, as Sir Joseph Mawbey, of Botleys, in the county of Surrey. At the general election in 1774, Sir Joseph stood a contested election for the county of Surrey, but was defeated; the next year, however, one of his successful opponents, Sir Francis Vincent, having died, he was returned by a large majority against the son of his deceased rival and Mr. Norton. He was subsequently twice returned for the same county in 1780 and 1784. Amidst the occupation of extensive commercial pursuits,* and the duties of a legislator and a magistrate, Sir Joseph cultivated a love of study, and having, when a school-boy, written many poetical pieces, he afterwards relaxed at intervals in the same way, and was for several years a regular correspondent of the magazines. By his lady he had issue,

JOSEPH, his heir.

Catherine, m. 14th August, 1792, to Thomas Lynch Goleborn, esq. of Jamaica.

Mary.

Emily.

Sir Joseph d.† 16th June, 1798, and was succeeded by his son,

II. SIR JOSEPH MAWBEY, who m. 9th August, 1796, Charlotte-Caroline-Maria, only daughter, by his first wife, of Thomas Henchman, esq. of Littleton, in the county of Middlesex, and had two daughters. He d. 28th August, 1817, when having had no male issue, the BARONETCY EXPIRED.

Arms—Or, a cross, gules, fretty, or, between four eagles displayed azure, each charged with a bezant on the breast.

* The works carried on by Sir Joseph and his brother, paid more than £600,000. per annum, to government in [illegible].

† Lady Mawbey d. at Botleys, 19th August, 1790, and was buried in the family vault, in Chertsey chancel, 26th of the same month. A monument to her memory is erected against the wall of the chancel, on which is the following inscription, written by Sir Joseph:

Dame Elizabeth Mawbey,
Wife of Sir Joseph Mawbey, Bart.
Of Botleys, in this Parish,
After sustaining a long and painful illness,
with the greatest fortitude and resignation,
Died on the 19th of August, 1790,
In the 46th year of her age.

"Why weep for me," the blameless woman said,
"We all must die, and I am not afraid;
No good to me affords or sigh, or tear,
I have done no wrong, and therefore cannot fear;
Good works and truth shall cheer life's parting scene,
For virtue only makes the mind serene."
Yes, we must part! the conflict now is o'er,
And husband, children, friends, in vain deplore!
But ah! blest Saint! to all around impart
Thy settled goodness, thy unerring heart,
Which bade thee shine, in ev'ry state of life,
As Daughter, Maiden, Parent, Friend, and Wife.

MAYNARD, OF ESTAINES PARVA.

CREATED 29th June, 1611.

EXTINCT 30th June, 1775.

Lineage.

SIR HENRY MAYNARD, knt. (grandson of John Maynard, esq. M.P. for St. Albans) purchased Estaines, in the county of Essex, and was subsequently designated therefrom. He was secretary to Burghley; represented the county of Essex in parliament in the time of ELIZABETH; and was sheriff in the last year of her majesty's reign. Sir Henry m. Susan, daughter and co-heir of Thomas Pearson, esq. and had with other issue,

- I. WILLIAM, his successor.
- II. John (Sir), K.B. of Tooting, in Surrey, M.P. for Lostwithiel in 1640. He was impeached in 1647 of high treason, expelled the House of Commons, and committed prisoner to the Tower. He d. in 1658, leaving a son,
  - Sir John Maynard, K.B. who d. in 1665, leaving an only daughter and heir,
    - Mary Maynard, who m. first, William Adams, esq.; secondly, Sir Rushout Cullen, bart.; and thirdly, Francis Buller, esq. of Shillingham, in Cornwall.
- III. Charles, auditor of the Exchequer, *temp.* CHARLES II. father of
  - Sir William Maynard, bart. from whom
    - HENRY MAYNARD, present (1837) VISCOUNT MAYNARD, descends.

Sir Henry d. in 1610, and was s. by his eldest son,

I. SIR HENRY MAYNARD, of Estaines Parva, who received the honour of knighthood in 1608, was created a BARONET 29th June, 1611, and elevated to the peerage of Ireland, in 1620, as Lord Maynard of Wicklow. He was created a peer of England in eight years afterwards, by the title of Baron Maynard, of Estaines. He married first, Frances, daughter of William, Lord Cavendish; and secondly, Anne, daughter and heir of Sir Anthony Everard, knt. of Langleys, in Essex, and dying in 1640, was s. by his only son (of the second marriage),

II. SIR WILLIAM MAYNARD, second Lord Maynard, a privy councillor, and comptroller of the household, *temp.* CHARLES II. and JAMES II. His lordship m. first, Dorothy, daughter and sole heir of Sir Robert Banaster, knt. of Passingham, in the county of Northampton, and had two surviving sons, BANASTER, his successor, and William. He m. secondly, Lady Margaret Murray, daughter of James, Earl of Dysert, and had another son and a daughter. He d. in 16[illegible], and was s. by his son,

III. SIR BANASTER MAYNARD, third Lord Maynard, who m. Lady Elizabeth Grey, only daughter of Henry, tenth Earl of Kent, by whom he had a large family. His lordship d. 4th March, 1717-18, aged seventy-[illegible] and was s. by his third, but eldest surviving son,

IV. SIR HENRY MAYNARD, fourth Lord Maynard, who d. unm. 7th December, 1742, and was s. by his brother,

V. SIR GREY MAYNARD, fifth Lord Maynard, who also d. unm. 27th April, 1745, and was s. by his brother,

VI. SIR CHARLES MAYNARD, fifth Lord Maynard, who was created, in 1766, Baron Maynard, of Much Easton, and Viscount Maynard, of Easton Lodge, both in the county of Essex, in reversion, default of his own male issue, to his kinsman, Sir William Maynard, bart. of Waltons, in the same, the descendant of Charles Maynard, auditor of the exchequer, *temp.* CHARLES II. youngest son of Sir Henry Maynard, Burghley's secretary. Sir Charles d. unm. at the advanced age of eighty-five, 30th June, 1775, when the recently created peerage descended according to the limitation (refer to BURKE'S *Peerage and Baronetage*) while all his other honours, including the BARONETAGE, became EXTINCT.

Arms—Ar. a chevron az. between three sinister hands, couped at the wrist gu.

MAYNE, OF MARSTON-MORTAINE.

CREATED 22nd April, 1763.

EXTINCT in 1794.

Lineage.

I. WILLIAM MAYNE, esq. eldest son, by his [illegible] wife,* of William Mayne, esq.† of Powis-Logie, Clackmannanshire (see BURKE'S *Commoners*, [illegible] page 170), was created a BARONET, 22nd April 1763, as Sir William Mayne, of Marston-Mortaine, in the county of Bedford, was sworn of the privy council in Ireland, in March, 1766, and created a peer of Ireland as Baron Newhaven, in 1776. He m. in 17[illegible] the Hon. Frances Allen, daughter of Joshua, [illegible] Viscount Allen, and co-heir of her brother, John, the [illegible] viscount, by whom he acquired a considerable estate, and had one son, who died in infancy. His lordship d. in 1794, when his honours, including the BARONETAGE, EXPIRED.

Arms—Arg. a chevron gu. voided, of the [illegible] between two pheons in chief sa. a fleur-de-lis [illegible] within a bordure engrailed of the last.

---

* Helen Galbraith, of the Balgair family, granddaughter of Sir Philip Musgrave, bart.

† James Mayne, esq. of St. Ninians, second son of William Mayne, esq. of Powis, by Eupham Christie, his first wife, left an only daughter, Euphemia, m. first, to James Henderson, esq. of Westerton; and [illegible] James Alexander, esq. provost of Stirling. [illegible] the second marriage, EDWARD ALEXANDER, [illegible] to Powis in 1808, upon the demise of his [illegible] Mayne, esq.

MAYNEY, OF LINTON.

CREATED 9th June, 1641.

EXTINCT in 1706.

Lineage.

John Mayney, esq. of Biddenden, in Kent (de-scended from a very ancient family established at the Conquest, of which was the celebrated Sir Walter de Mayney, of the reign of Edward III.) left, by Let-tice his wife, two sons, John, his heir, and Walter, of Staplehurst, sheriff of Kent 13 Elizabeth. The elder,

John Mayney, esq. was of Biddenden, and served as sheriff in 1566, in which year he died, leaving by Margaret, his wife, daughter and heir of Ralph John-son, of Tisehurst, two sons, Anthony and Walter. The former,

Anthony Mayney, esq. of Biddenden, wedded Bridget, daughter of William Tanfield, esq. of North-amptonshire, and was father of

Sir Anthony Mayney, knt. who sold his estate at Biddenden to Sir Edward Henden, one of the barons of the Exchequer *temp.* Charles I. and purchased Linton, in Kent. His son and heir,

Walter Mayney, esq. of Linton, was father of

I. Sir John Mayney, knt. of Linton, who was created a Baronet in 1641. During the civil wars, Sir John was one of the most devoted adherents of royalty, and in the cause of his ill-fated master, spent all his estate. Linton he sold to Sir Francis Withens, and it even-tually became the property of the Manns. Sir John m. Mary, daughter of Sir Peter Ricaut, of Aylesford, knt. and died about the year 1676, leaving a son and successor,

II. Sir Anthony Mayney, who died unm. in 1706, when the Baronetcy became extinct. This unfortu-nate gentleman, male heir of one of the most eminent British families, and son of a gallant cavalier who had sacrificed a great estate in the service of his king, is stated to have died of actual want, his brother, borne down by indigence, having previously, in 16— committed suicide.

Arms—Party per pale arg. and sa. three chevronels between as many cinquefoils counterchanged.

MERCES, OF FRANCE.

CREATED in 1660.

Lineage.

Monsieur Anthony de Merces, was created a Baronet in 1660, but of him, or his descendants, nothing further is known. Those may possibly still exist in France, and this Baronetcy not be extinct.

MEREDITH, OF STANSLEY.

CREATED 13th Aug. 1622.

EXTINCT 3rd Jan. 1739.

Lineage.

This, an ancient family of the principality of Wales, traced its descent from Ednyfed Gwernowy, a chief-tain of North Wales, and head of one of the fifteen tribes.

Rowland Meredith, of Alington, who assumed the surname since borne by his descendants, married Elizabeth, daughter of Edward Brereton, of Bors-sham, and was *s.* by his son,

John Meredith, of Alington, who *m.* Catherine, daughter of John ap Iolyn ap Madoc, and had two sons, John, continuator of the line of Alington, and

Richard Meredith, seated at Pentrebychan, in Denbighshire, who *m.* Jane, daughter and heir of Morgan ap David ap Robert, and had issue,

William (Sir),

Hugh, whose descendant, Henry Warter-Mere-dith, esq. is still resident at Pentrebychan Hall. (Refer to Burke's *Commoners*, vol. iii. p. 425.)

The elder son,

Sir William Meredith, of Stansley, in the county of Denbigh, and of Leeds Abbey, in Kent, who was treasurer and paymaster of the army, *temp.* Eliza-beth and James, *m.* Jane, daughter of Sir Thomas Palmer, bart. of Wingham, by whom (who wedded, secondly, John, Earl of Carbury) he had issue,

William, his heir.

Anne, *m.* first, to Sir Robert Brett; and secondly, to Francis, Lord Cottington.

Jane, *m.* to Sir Peter Wyche.

He was *s.* at his decease by his son,

I. William Meredith, esq. of Stansley, who was created a Baronet, 13th August, 1622. Sir William *m.* Susanna daughter of Francis Barker, esq. of Lon-don, and had issue,

Richard, his heir,

Roger, one of the masters in Chancery, *m.* Anne, daughter of Sir Brocket Spencer, bart. of Offley, Herts, but died *s. p.*

Elizabeth, *m.* to Sir Henry Oxenden, of Dean, in Kent.

He *m.* secondly, Mrs. Aynscombe, relict of Thomas Aynscombe, esq. and sister of Sir Henry Goring, bart. but by her had no other children. He *d.* 10th April, 1675, and was *s.* by his son,

II. Sir Richard Meredith, who married Susanna, daughter of Philip Skippen, esq. of Tobsham, in Nor-folk, the noted parliamentary commander, as Major-general Skippen, and had, with five daughters, who all *d.* unm. six sons, viz.

William, third baronet.

Henry, a colonel in the army, who *m.* 12th April, 1709, Mary, daughter and heir of Walter At-wood, gent. of Hackney, and had an only daughter,

Susanna, died unm.

Richard, fourth baronet.

Thomas, was knight of the shire for Kent, 12 William III. and *d. s. p.*

Philip, *d.* unm. before his father.

Roger, *s.* as fifth baronet.

He was *s.* by his eldest son,

III. Sir William Meredith, who died unm. about 1682, and was *s.* by his brother,

IV. Sir Richard Meredith, who also died unm. in August, 1723, and was *s.* by his youngest brother,

V. Sir Roger Meredith, of Leeds Abbey, in Kent, M.P. for that county, 1727, who *m.* Mary, daughter of Francis Tyssen, esq. of Shacklewell, and widow of Samuel Gott, esq. but *d. s. p.* 3rd January, 1739, when the Baronetcy expired. The estate of Leeds Abbey passed, under Sir Roger's will, to his niece, Susanna Meredith, and was eventually sold in 1765, to John Calcraft, esq. of Ingress.

Arms—Az. a lion rampant or.

MEUX, OF KINGSTON.

Created 11th Dec. 1641.

Extinct 6th Mar. 1705-6.

Lineage.

Lodovick Meux, esq. *m.* Alice, daughter and heir of William Drew, esq. of Kingston, in the Isle of Wight,* and had issue,

Thomas, his heir.

Henry, *m.* Elizabeth, sister of John Savage, esq. and left a daughter,

Jane Meux, *m.* to Matthew Fulwer, esq.

Ralph, *m.* and left a daughter,

Agnes Meux, *m.* to John Mole, esq.

The eldest son and heir,

Thomas Meux, esq. of Kingston, left a son and heir,

Sir William Meux, knt. of Kingston, who *m.* Jane, daughter of Richard Cooke, esq. of Rustington, in Sussex, and had issue,

William, who died in France.

Richard.

John, *m.* Jane, daughter of Sir Thomas Blennerhasset, knt.

The second son, and eventual heir,

Richard Meux, esq. of Kingston, married Dorothy, daughter of Thomas Cooke, esq. of Harbridge and Somerley, in Hampshire, and had three sons and two daughters, viz.

William, his heir.

Thomas, of Bishopstown, Wilts, *m.* first, Eleanor, widow of — Young, esq.; secondly, Mrs. Hiles, second sister of Anthony Lisley; and thirdly, another (the third) sister of Anthony Lisley.

John, *m.* in 1582, a daughter of Hill of Bishopstown.

Elizabeth, *m.* to William Bethell, gent. of H[illegible] near Winchester.

Jane, *m.* to John Worsley, esq. of Apuldercombe.

The eldest son and heir,

William Meux, esq. of Kingston, married Eleanor, daughter of Sir Henry Strangways, knt. and had issue,

John (Sir), his heir.

Anne, *m.* to Edward White, esq. of Winchelsea.

Eleanor, *m.* to William Okeden, esq. of Ell[illegible]ham, in the county of Southampton.

He was *s.* by his son,

Sir John Meux, knt. of Kingston, who *m.* Cecilie, daughter of Sir William Button, knt. of Alton, Wilts, and had issue,

William (Sir), his heir.

Bartholomew, of Lealand, in the Isle of Wight, buried at Kingston, 19th December, 1638. [illegible] in his will (proved 23rd June, 1639), of Brix[illegible] in the Isle of Wight, *m.* Radcliffe, daughter of William Gerard, esq. of Harrow-on-the-Hill, and from this marriage descended

Sir Henry Meux, bart. of Theobald's Park, Herts, the eminent London brewer. Refer to Burke's *Peerage and Baronetage*.

Eleanor, *m.* to William Compton, esq. of Hartbury, in the county of Gloucester.

Mary, *m.* to William Higford, esq. of Dixon, in the county of Gloucester.

This Sir John Meux entered his pedigree at the Visitation of Hants, in 1622. He was *s.* at his decease by his elder son,

Sir William Meux, knt. of Kingston, l[illegible] 1641, who *m.* first, Winifred, daughter of Sir Francis Barrington, bart. of Barrington Hall, in the county of Essex, and had issue,

John, his heir.

Cecilie, of Swaffham, in Cambridgeshire, *d.* unm. in 1697.

Jane, *m.* to — Meade, esq. of Lofts, in Essex.

Sir William was *s.* by his son,

I. John Meux, esq. of Kingston, in the Isle of Wight, who was created a Baronet 11th December, 1641. Sir John *m.* Elizabeth, daughter of Sir Robert Worsley, bart. of Apuldercombe, by whom (who *d.* in 1652) he had issue,

William, his heir.

Henry, *d.* unm. in 1701, buried 1st January, 1702, at Kingston.

John, *d.* in 1649.

Anne, of Westminster, *d.* unm. in 1725.

Elizabeth, *d.* unm. before her sister.

He *d.* in February, 1657, and was *s.* by his son,

II. Sir William Meux, who *m.* first, Mabel, daughter of Sir Robert Dillington, bart. of Knighton, in the Isle of Wight, and by that lady had four children, who all died young. He wedded, secondly, E[illegible], daughter of George Browne, esq. of Buckland, in Surrey, and by her had

William, his successor.

Henry, aged three years in 1694, *d.* unm.

Elizabeth, *m.* 2nd May, 1710, to Sir John Miller[illegible]

---

* Jordan de Kingston, lord of Kingston, in the Isle of Wight, was father of

Sir John Kingston, of Kingston, whose only daughter and eventual heiress,

Eleanor Kingston, *m.* William Drew, and left a son and heir,

John Drew, of Kingston, grandfather of the [illegible] mentioned above,

Alice Drew, as marrying Lodowick Meux.

bart. of Froyle, in the county of Hants, and left an only daughter and heir,

ELIZABETH MILLER, who married Sir Edward Worsley, of Gatcombe, in the Isle of Wight.

JANE, of St. Margaret's, in the city of Westminster, *d.* unm.; will dated 17th June, 1747, proved 23rd April, 1750.

ANNE, of St. Margaret's, in the city of Westminster, *d.* unm. and was buried there. Will dated 13th July, 1732, and proved by her sister Jane, sole executrix, 20th December, 1742.

Sir William made his will in 1693, it was proved 11th May, 1697, and he was *s.* by his son,

III. SIR WILLIAM MEUX, who died unmarried, aged twenty-one, 6th March, 1705-6, when the BARONETCY became EXTINCT, and the property devolved upon his sisters as CO-HEIRS.

Arms—Paly of six or and az. on a chief gu. three crosses pattée of the first.

MEYERS.

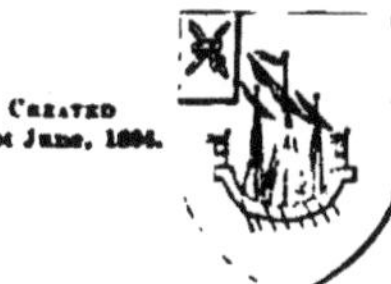

CREATED 21st June, 1804. EXTINCT 16th May, 1811.

Lineage.

CHRISTOPHER MEYERS, esq. of Monkstown, in the county of Dublin, formerly of Cumberland, *m.* Jane Graham, and by whom (who *d.* in 1800), he had issue,

Graham, *b.* about 1743, *d.* in 1801, leaving issue three daughters.

John, *m.* Miss Johnson, and left a son,

Christopher, captain 16th Light Dragoons, *m.* a daughter of James M'Evers, esq. of New York.

James, captain 15th Foot.

WILLIAM.

Mary.

The youngest son,

I. WILLIAM MEYERS, esq. *b.* at Whitehaven, 1st ... 1750-1, who attained the rank of lieutenant-general in the army, with the colonelcy of the 2nd West India regiment, was created a BARONET 21st June, 1804. He had been previously commander-in-chief of the Leeward Islands. Sir William *m.* in ... 1779, Elizabeth, daughter of James M'Evers, of New York, and had issue,

WILLIAM JAMES, his successor, *b.* in Park Street, Dublin, 27th November, 1783.

Eliza, *m.* at Cork, in 1801, to Captain William Erskine, of the 16th Foot.

The general died 29th July, 1805, and was *s.* by his son,

II. SIR WILLIAM-JAMES MEYERS, a lieutenant-colonel in the army, who died in consequence of wounds received at the battle of Albuera, 16th May, 1811, and being unmarried, the BARONETCY EXPIRED.

Arms—Arg. a lymphad with her sails furled, a flag at head and stern gu. a double-tongued pendant at each top of the last, on a canton gu. a baton sinister or, surmounted by a sword arg. hilt or, in saltire, over both a mural crown arg.

MIDDELTON, OF RUTHYN.

CREATED 22nd Oct. 1622. UNASSUMED.

Lineage.

The family of Middleton or Myddelton is said to have descended from Poyth Vlaydd, lord of Penlyn, in Merionethshire, whose descendant, Riride, married Cicely, sister and heir of Sir Alexander Middleton, of Middleton, in Shropshire, and was father of Riride, whose great-grandson,

DAVID MYDDELTON, of Gwaynenog, in Denbighshire, receiver of North Wales *temp.* EDWARD IV. *m.* Ellen, daughter of Sir John Done, knt. of Utkington, in Cheshire, and had, with other issue,

ROGER MYDDELTON, of Gwaynenog, ancestor of the MYDDELTONS of Gwaynenog,*

and

FULKE MYDDELTON, esq. who *m.* Margaret, daughter of Thomas Smith, alderman of Chester, and had, with other issue,

RICHARD MYDDELTON, esq. of Denbigh, who married Jane, daughter of Hugh Dryhurst, of the same place, by Lucy, his wife, daughter of Robert Greensdyke, and had several children; of whom,

THOMAS (the eldest surviving son) was ancestor of the MIDDLETONS OF CHIRKE,

and

I. HUGH MIDDELTON (the sixth son), of Ruthyn, in Denbighshire, was a citizen and goldsmith of London. This public spirited man rendered his name ever honoured and respected, as the projector of an undertaking arduous in the extreme, deemed for many years impracticable, which has proved fraught with the most essential benefit to the inhabitants of London. An act of parliament was obtained, through the advice of Middelton, for the purpose of drawing a trench from the springs near Ware, in Hertfordshire, to the metropolis, which then suffered from an insufficient supply of water; but the difficulties of the project appeared so great that the corporation declined to embark in it: whereupon Mr. Middelton, with a spirit equal to the importance of the undertaking, begun the work at his own risk and charge on the 20th February, 1608. Its progress, it is probable, was attended with greater difficulties than he had foreseen, and his pecuniary resources failed long before it was completed. The body corporate of London still refused to lend any

* The late REV. ROBERT MYDDELTON, D.D. of Gwaynenog, *m.* Mary, only child of James Ogilvie, esq. and left ... said successor, the present ROBERT MYDDELTON, esq. of Gwaynenog, *b.* 23rd September, 1795, who *m.* 8th ... 1823, Louisa, second daughter of the late Sir George-William Farmer, bart. and has a son, ROBERT.

assistance, and the works which had been effected by four years' arduous labour, were on the point of being abandoned, when the enterprising projector applied to *King* James, who covenanted, in consideration that a moiety of the shares were made over to him, to advance money for the completion of the undertaking. It now went on without interruption; and on the 29th September, 1613, the water was let into the basin at the place now called the New River Head at Islington.

The following account of the ceremony upon the occasion was published at the time: "A troop of labourers, to the number of sixty and upwards, all in green caps alike, bearing in their hands the symbols of their several employments in so great a business, marching, with drums before them, twice or thrice round the cestern, orderly present themselves before the mount; and after their departure, the speech (being forty-eight lines in verse) was said, ending thus:

> "Now for the fruits then; flow forth pretious spring,
> So long and dearly sought for, and now bring
> Comfort to all that love thee, loudly sing,
> And with thy chrystal murmurs strucke together,
> Bid all thy true well-wishers welcome hither.

"At which words the flood-gate opens, and the stream is let into the cestern, drums and trumpets giving it triumphant welcome; and for the close of this their honourable entertainment a peal of chambers."

One of the most difficult parts of the work still remained to be accomplished—the conveyance of the water to the various quarters of the metropolis. The expense attending this was very great, and a considerable time elapsed before the water came into general use; so that the shares became of small value, the annual dividends for many years being under £5. The general establishment of the plan, however, together with the incalculable advantages deriveable from it, which were at length universally acknowledged, have, in the course of a century and a half, so raised the shares as to increase the annual income nearly a hundred fold. The property of the New River was, by a partition made soon after the commencement of the undertaking, divided into seventy-two shares. Thirty-six of these, called "the Adventurer's Shares," were originally vested in Sir Hugh Middelton, and the remaining moiety were enjoyed by the crown until alienated. Like many other public benefactors, Sir Hugh derived himself no advantage from his enterprizing exertions; on the contrary, the outlay so impoverished him that he was under the necessity of engaging in the business of a civil engineer. In 1622 he was created a Baronet, and died in 1631. By his will, dated 21st November, 1631, he bequeathed to each of his children by name, except John and Hugh, his two eldest sons (who died before the making of his will), and William, his third son, and Jane, the wife of Dr. Chamberlen (to whom he had before given their full portions), a pecuniary legacy, and also devised to each of them, after the decease of his wife, one share in the New River water. He devised another share to the then Court of Assistants of the Goldsmiths' Company, London, and their successors, upon trust, to dispose of the profits every half-year, after the death of his wife, in weekly portions of twelve-pence a-piece to the poor of the Company of Goldsmiths, at the discretion of the wardens and assistants, and "especial to such poor men of my name, kindred, or country, as are or shall be free of the said company." And for the better declaration of what parts were meant to be devised, he added, that the one-half of the water was divided into thirty-six parts or shares, "thirteen of which parts or shares are to myself belonging, and are in the name of myself, and other feoffees in trust to my use, and the profits by me received, and therefore my meaning is, that the six several parts or shares hereby devised and given are six of the parts or shares of my said thirteen parts, and no other." He died in the month after the making of this will, and was interred, agreeably to his desire, in the parish church of St. Matthew, London. He *m.* Elizabeth, daughter and sole heir of John Olmstead, esq. of Ingateston, in Essex, and had issue five sons and four daughters, viz.

I. John, } both *d. v. p. s. p.*
II. Hugh, }
III. William, successor to his father.
IV. Henry, baptized in the parish church of St. Matthew, London, 14th June, 1607, and appears to have died before 1678, leaving two sons,
    William, supposed to have died *s. p.*
    Henry, *b.* about the year 1662, bound apprentice to Robert Andrews, surgeon, in Crutched Friars, 17th January, 1676, became an inhabitant of the parish of St. Olave, Hart Street, 25th December, 1684, and died at an advanced age. He had been twice married, and left issue,
        Starkey, *b.* 3rd April, 1688, who practised physic in London, and had a son, Henry, also a medical man in London, who *d. s. p.* 9th September, 1759; and a daughter, who was living in 1792, the widow of Dr. John [illegible] Reading.
        Henry, baptized 30th July, 1690, and died at West Ham, in Essex, 30th November, 1726, leaving a son, Starkey,* and a daughter, Anna-Maria, living in 1792, wife of William Grampree.
V. Simon, who had four sons, viz. Simon who died at Constantinople in January, 17[illegible], Hugh, Benjamin, and Hezekiah; and [illegible] daughters, Sarah, Hannah, Anne, Elizabeth, and Rebecca. By his will, dated 15th J[illegible] 1678, Simon, after reciting that he was [illegible] of eighteen 36th shares and a half of the New River water, viz. seventeen 36th shares of the king's moiety, and one 36th share of the adventurer's moiety, devised to his executors one 36th share of the king's moiety, "charged with a proportionable part of the fee-farm rent due and payable for the same to the king's majesty, and with one hundred pounds per annum to Henry Middleton deceased and his heirs." He gives to his eldest surviving son Hugh, his house at Hackney, and to all his younger children seven 36th shares of the king's moiety. Of this Hugh, the son of Simon, more hereafter.

I. Jane, *m.* to Peter Chamberlen, M.D. of London, and was grandmother of

* This Starkey Middleton was born at West Ham, 7th June, 1719; was married at St. Luke's, Middlesex, 2nd March, 1741; and died at Hoxton in September, 1769, leaving four children, viz.

I. Joseph, who *d.* in 1787, leaving Susannah, Mary, Elizabeth, and Joseph.
II. Elizabeth, who *m.* a Mr. Smith, and had a [illegible] Henry Smith.
III. Jabez, who had three children, Elizabeth, [illegible] and Jane.
IV. Martha, living unmarried in 1792.

HUGH CHAMBERLEN, M.D. of Alderton Hall, who m. first, Mary, daughter and sole heir of Nathaniel Bacon, esq. of Friston Hall, Suffolk; and secondly, Mary, Lady Crewe, daughter of Sir Willoughby Aston, bart. of Aston, in Cheshire. By the former he left three daughters, his co-heirs,

MARY, d. unm.

ANNA-MARIA, m. to the Right Hon. Edward Hopkyns. (See BURKE's *Commoners*, vol. iv. p. 122.)

CHARLOTTE, m. to Richard Luther, esq. of Myles's, in Essex, and left issue,

JOHN LUTHER, of Myles's, in Essex, M.P. for that county, *d. s. p.*

CHARLOTTE, m. to Henry Fane, esq. of Wormsley, and was grandmother of the present JOHN FANE, esq. of Wormsley.

REBECCA, m. to John Taylor, esq. of the Circus, Bath, and of Grosvenor Place, London, and was grandmother of JOHN TAYLOR-GORDON, M.D. (See BURKE's *Commoners*, vol. iv. p. 7.)

II. Hester, m. to Richard Price, esq.

III. Elizabeth.

IV. Ann.

...r Hugh's eldest surviving son and successor,

II. SIR WILLIAM MIDDELTON, m. Eleanor, daughter of Sir Thomas Harris, bart. of Shrewsbury, and had issue,

HUGH, his heir.

Elizabeth, who had four New River shares. She m. John Greene, of Enfield, clerk to the New River Company; and dying in childbed, December, 1675, in her forty-third year, was buried in the north aisle of Enfield Church, where a monument was erected to her memory. She left two sons, Giles and William, and two daughters, Elizabeth and Catharine, one of whom married Mr. North, a brewer. The younger son,

WILLIAM GREENE, esq. m. Jane, daughter of Hamey Burwell, of Enfield, merchant, and by her, who *d.* in 1767, had an only daughter and heiress,

JANE GREENE, who m. the Rev. Richard Ellicombe, A. B. of Balliol College, Oxford, who recovered, in right of his wife, after a lawsuit, four New River shares. He died in 1778 (his widow survived until 1786), leaving issue, Richard-Amey Burwell, who *d. s. p.*; WILLIAM, of whom presently; Hugh Myddelton; and Jane. The second son,

THE REV. WILLIAM ELLICOMBE, A.B. curate of Exmouth, *b.* in 1745; wedded, in 1773, Hannah, daughter of Thomas Rous, esq. of Exeter; and was father of the present

REV. HENRY-THOMAS ELLACOMBE, vicar of Bitton, in Gloucestershire.

...William was *s.* at his decease by his son,

III. SIR HUGH MIDDELTON, who appears to have *d. s. p.* in 1675, when the BARONETCY ceased to be ...med, but it *certainly* was not then EXTINCT, nor, ...all probability, has it since expired.

Arms—Arg. on a pile vert, three wolves' or griffins' ...ds erased of the field.

MIDDELTON, OF HACKNEY.

CREATED 6th Dec. 1681.—EXTINCT (date unknown).

Lineage.

SIMON MIDDELTON, of Hurst Hill, Edmonton, Middlesex, youngest son of Sir Hugh Middelton, bart. the projector of the New River, married four wives; by the first he had no issue; by the second, Mary, daughter of John Soame, esq. of Burnham Market, in Norfolk, he had two sons and four daughters, viz.

HUGH, of whom presently.

Simon, *d.* unm.

Mary, m. Edm. Soame, of London, eighth son of Sir William Soame, knt. of Thurlow, in Suffolk.

Sarah, m. to Robert, Earl of Oxford and Mortimer.

Hannah, m. John Matthew, merchant, of London.

Anne, m. to Bennet Swayne, merchant, of London.

By his third wife, Elizabeth Smithesby, Simon Middelton had two sons and two daughters, viz.

Benjamin. Ezekiah, *d.* unm.

Elizabeth, m. to John Lane, of London, merchant.

Rebecca, m. to William Barnham, esq. mayor of Norwich, and was mother of a daughter, Sarah, the wife of Charles Wood, esq. of London.

Simon Middelton's fourth wife was Mrs. Mary Ellis, widow, daughter of Sir Samuel Luke, knt. of Bedfordshire, who survived him, and wedded for her third husband Mr. Barrington, of London and Hoxton, and after his decease Mr. Blackerby. Simon Middelton was *s.* by his eldest son,

I. HUGH MIDDELTON, esq. of Hackney, in Middlesex, who was created a BARONET in 1681. He m. Dorothy, daughter of Sir William Oglander, bart. of Nunwell, in the Isle of Wight, and by her, from whom he was divorced by act of parliament, had an only daughter,

DOROTHY, m. to Henry Berkeley, esq. of the Middle Temple, and *d.* in 1735.

Sir Hugh spent all his estate, and died in obscurity about the commencement of the eighteenth century, when the BARONETCY became EXTINCT. Hugh Middelton, who resided in the parish of Kemberton, Shropshire, under the assumed name of William Raymond, and died 10th March, 1702, is supposed to have been Sir Hugh, the baronet.

Arms—As MIDDELTON OF RUTHYN.

MIDDLETON, OF CHIRKE.

CREATED 4th July, 1660.  EXTINCT 5th Jan. 1718.

Lineage.

SIR THOMAS MIDDLETON, knt. eldest son of Richard Middleton, esq. governor of Denbigh Castle, *temp.* EDWARD VI. MARY, and ELIZABETH, by Jane, his wife, daughter of Hugh Dryhurst, esq. was sheriff and alderman of London, and filled the civic chair in 1613. He was a munificent benefactor to the Goldsmith's Company. His son and heir,

SIR THOMAS MYDDELTON, knt. of Chirk Castle, died in 1666, having had three sons, namely,

I. Thomas, his heir. II. Robert.
III. Richard, who had two sons, Robert and John.
The eldest son,

I. Thomas Myddelton, esq. of Chirk Castle, in Denbighshire, was created a Baronet in 1660. He *m.* first, Mary, daughter of Thomas Cholmondeley, esq. of Vale Royal, in Cheshire; and secondly, Jane, daughter of John Trevor, esq. of Denbighshire. He died in July, 1663, aged thirty-nine, and was *s.* by his son,

II. Sir Thomas Myddelton, of Chirk Castle, who *m.* first, Elisabeth, daughter and co-heir of Sir Thomas Wilbraham, of Woodhey; and secondly, Charlotta, daughter of Sir Orlando Bridgman, bart. He *d.* 5th February, 1683, leaving an only daughter and heir,

Charlotte, *m.* first, to Edward, Earl of Warwick; and secondly, to the Right Hon. Joseph Addison.

Sir Thomas was *s.* by his brother,

III. Sir Richard Myddelton, of Chirke Castle, who *d.* in June, 1716, leaving with a daughter, Mary, who *d.* unm. a son,

IV. Sir William Myddelton, at whose decease unmarried 5th January, 1718, aged twenty-four, the Baronetcy became extinct. The estate of Chirk Castle, together with the lordships of Chirk, Chirklands, and Ruthen, followed the entail to

Robert Myddelton, esq. of Llysfasi, son of Richard, the third son of Sir Thomas Myddelton, knt. of Chirk Castle, who *d.* in 1666. His brother,

John Myddelton, esq. died in 1747, and was *s.* by his son,

Richard Myddelton, esq. of Chirk Castle, who died in 1795, leaving a son and successor,

Richard Myddelton, esq. at whose decease unm. in 1796, Chirk Castle devolved on his eldest sister, Charlotte (the present possessor) who *m.* Robert Biddulph, esq. and has issue.

Arms—Arg. on a bend vert, three wolves' or griffins' heads erased of the field.

MIDDLETON, OF LEIGHTON HALL.

Created 24th June, 1642.

Extinct 27th Feb. 1673.

Lineage.

This is a junior branch of the ancient knightly family of Middleton, of Middleton Hall, in Westmoreland; the first of whom on record is

Thomas Middleton, of Middleton Hall, in the reign of Edward III. His son and heir,

John Middleton, of Middleton, *m.* a daughter of John Medcalf, and had issue,

I. Thomas, *s.* to Middleton Hall, and ancestor of John Middleton, esq. of Middleton, *temp.* Charles II. who left two daughters, his co-heirs: Bridget, *m.* to Joshua Hebblethwaite, of Dent; and Mary, *m.* to James Cragg, of Dent.

II. John. III. Jeffrey, of whom presently.

I. Jacomia, or Jacobina, *m.* to Richard Preston, esq. of Preston Patrick, and had issue.

The third son,

Sir Jeffrey Middleton, knt. was father of

Sir Robert Middleton, of Leighton Hall, in the county of Lancaster, who in the reign of Richard III. *m.* Ann, daughter and sole heir of Roger de Betham, of Betham, and thereby brought a great addition of fortune to his family. They had issue,

Thomas Middleton, esq. of Leighton, who *m.* Joan, daughter of Sir Thomas Strickland, and dying 8 Henry VIII. left issue,

Gervase Middleton, esq. who *m.* — Kirtham, of Northamptonshire, and dying 1 Edward VI. was *s.* by his son,

George Middleton, esq. of Leighton, *b.* in 15[illegible], who *m.* first, a daughter of Sir Marmaduke Tunstal, of Thurland Castle, and had two daughters; and secondly, Margaret, daughter of Sir Christopher Metcalf, knt. of Nappa, by Lady Elizabeth Clifford, daughter of Henry, Earl of Cumberland, by Margaret, daughter of Henry Algernon, fifth Earl of Northumberland, by whom he had three sons and three daughters. He was *s.* by his eldest son,

Thomas Middleton, esq. of Leighton Hall, who *m.* Katharine, sister to Sir Richard Hoghton, bart. of Hoghton Tower, and had, with eight daughters, three sons, viz.

George, his heir.

Thomas, who *d. s. p.*

Robert, who *m.* Jane, daughter and coheir of Thomas Kitson, gent. of Warton, where his posterity remained until very recently, but in very reduced circumstances.*

The eldest son,

I. George Middleton, esq. of Leighton Hall, was a brave and active partizan of Charles I. in whose army, besides liberally contributing to the expenses of the war, he served as colonel; for which, on the decline of the king's affairs, he was compelled to compound for his estate. He was knighted by the [illegible] at Durham, 26th June, 1642, and was created a Baronet by patent bearing date the day following. After the Restoration he served the office of high sheriff of Lancashire two years successively, viz. 14 and 1[illegible] Charles II. He *m.* first, Frances, daughter and [illegible] of Richard Rigg, esq. of Little Strickland, and had a son, Geoffrey, who died young, and a daughter,

Mary, who became sole heiress; she *m.* Somerford Oldfield, esq. of Somerford, in Cheshire, and had issue,

George-Somerford Oldfield, esq. who [illegible] the death of Ann, Lady Middleton, [illegible] at Leighton. He *m.* Lady Clarke, and [illegible] two surviving daughters, viz.

I. ——, *m.* to Albert Hodgson, esq. who [illegible] Leighton as his wife's portion. This gentleman unfortunately engaged in the rebellion in 1715, was taken [illegible] Preston, and long detained in pr[illegible]. His estate being confiscated, remained in the hands of government till 17[illegible], when it was put up to auction, and [illegible] chased by a confidential friend, who, on certain conditions, restored it to Mr. Hodgson, who resided there till 17[illegible]. He left two daughters, his co-heirs.

Ann, *m.* to George, younger son of Charles Townley, esq. of Town[illegible], who rebuilt Leighton Hall

* One of his grandsons, Robert Middleton, was a mariner, and died in 1699, leaving a large family. He had a sister, Margaret, who *m.* Thomas Booker, gent. and was mother of Robert Booker, of Broughton, whose only child, Margaret, *m.* Robert, son of Richard Preston, esq. of Cockerham.

residéd there many years, but having no issue, devised it to his nephew, the late J. Townley, esq. who sold it for £28,000 to Mr. Warwick, a banker.

Mary, m. in 1737, to Ralph Standish, esq. of Standish and Borwick, but *d. s. p.*

2. ———, m. to — Fletcher, of Hutton, but had no issue.

Sir George m. secondly, Ann, daughter of George Preston, esq. of Holker Hall, in Lancashire, but by her had only one son,

Thomas, who died young.

Dying 27th February, 1673, aged seventy-three, he was buried at Warton, and the BARONETCY became EXTINCT; Ann, his widow, surviving him, was interred near him 12th April, 1765. The ancient hall at Leighton, once so celebrated for its hospitality, has long been removed; and in the place of the old residence of the Middletons, appears the long line of a modern front, consisting of a centre and two wings. This has, moreover, been coated by a facing of polished limestone, extremely dazzling and oppressive to the eye in sunshine. The massy oak and beech woods, too, the former of great antiquity, and the herd of fallow deer which adorned the park, have also long since disappeared.

Arms—Arg. a saltire engrailed sa. a mullet for difference.

MILDMAY, OF MOULSHAM.

CREATED [illegible] June, 1611.

EXTINCT 13th Feb. 1625-6.

Lineage.

This family, the name originally spelt without the [illegible] "y," deduced from

HUGO MILDME, living in 1147. His son,

SIR ROBERT MILDME, who flourished in the reign of HENRY III. had two sons, HERBERT MILDME and

[illegible] MILDME, of Hambleton, in Lancashire, living [illegible]. His descendant in the sixth degree,

SIR ROBERT MILDME, m. Matilda, daughter and heir [illegible] Le Rous, and left a son and heir,

THOMAS MILDME, who m. Margaret, daughter of [illegible] Cornish, of Great Waltham, in Essex, and was [illegible] by his son,

WALTER MILDME, of Writtle, in Essex, who left by [illegible] wife the daughter of Everard of Great Waltham, [illegible] and heir,

[illegible] THOMAS MILDME, one of the auditors of the Court of Augmentations in the time of HENRY VIII. [illegible] purchased the manor of Moulsham, in Essex. [illegible] m. Agnes, daughter of — Reade, esq. and had [illegible]

I. THOMAS, his heir.

II. William, of Springfield Barnes, ancestor of SIR WILLIAM MILDMAY, created a BARONET in [illegible].

III. John, of Cretingham, in Suffolk, from whom descended

Robert Mildmay, of Tarling, in Essex, whose line is now extinct.

IV. WALTER, of Apelthorpe, in Northamptonshire, KNIGHT OF THE GARTER, principal councillor, chancellor, and treasurer to *Queen* ELIZABETH, *d.* 11th May, 1589; *m.* a sister of the Secretary Sir Francis Walsingham, and left two sons,

1. SIR ANTHONY MILDMAY, knt. of Apelthorpe, ambassador to the court of France in 1596; *d.* 11th September, 1617; *m.* Grace, daughter and co-heir of Sir Henry Sherington, of Lacock, in Wiltshire, and had an only daughter and heiress,

MARY MILDMAY, who *m.* Francis Fane, first Earl of Westmoreland.

2. Sir Humphrey Mildmay, knt. of Danbury Place, Essex, *m.* Mary, daughter of Henry Capel, esq. of Hadham, Herts, and had two sons,

John, of Danbury, killed at Newbury. He had no issue.

HENRY (Sir), master of the Jewel Office *temp.* JAMES I. and CHARLES I. *m.* Anne, daughter and co-heir of Sir Leonard Haliday, knt. alderman of London, and his line terminated with his great-grandaughter,

LETITIA MILDMAY, who *m.* Humphrey Mildmay, esq.

I. Johanna, *m.* to Christopher Peyton, esq.

II. Thomazine, *m.* to Anthony Bencher, esq.

The eldest son and heir,

THOMAS MILDMAY, esq. of Moulsham Hall and Bishops' Hall, in Essex, one of the auditors of the Court of Augmentations, *m.* Avicia, daughter of William Gunson, esq. of London, and dying in October, 1567, was *s.* by his son,

SIR THOMAS MILDMAY, knt. of Moulsham, who *m.* Lady Frances Ratcliffe, only daughter, by his second wife, of Henry Ratcliffe, LORD FITZWALTER and Earl of Sussex, and had, with other issue,

THOMAS, his heir.

HENRY (Sir), of Woodham Walter, in Essex, died in 1654. On the death of his brother, Sir Henry became representative of the family. His grandson,

BENJAMIN MILDMAY, was summoned to parliament in the BARONY OF FITZWALTER 10th February, 1669. (Refer to BURKE's *Extinct Peerage*.)

Anthony, carver to *King* CHARLES I. and his constant and faithful attendant during his majesty's imprisonment. Mr. Anthony Mildmay and Mr. Herbert were authorised to inter the king.

Anne, *m.* to Sir Roger Appleton, bart.

Sir Thomas died 26th July, 1608, and was *s.* by his eldest son,

I. SIR THOMAS MILDMAY, knt. of Moulsham, who was created a BARONET 29th June, 1611. He *m.* first, Elizabeth, daughter of Sir John Puckering, keeper of the great seal; and secondly, Anne, daughter of John Savile, esq.; but died *s. p.* 13th February, 1625-6, when the BARONETCY EXPIRED, while the estate passed to his brother and heir, Sir Henry Mildmay, of Woodham Walter.

Arms—Arg. three lions rampant az. armed and langued gu.

MILDMAY, OF MOULSHAM.

CREATED 5th Feb. 1765.—EXTINCT 8th Aug. 1771.

Lineage.

WILLIAM MILDMAY, esq. second son of Sir Thomas Mildme, auditor of the Court of Augmentations *temp.* HENRY VIII. received a grant of Coggleshall Abbey, in Springfield Barnes, from EDWARD VI. in 1548. He *m.* Elizabeth, daughter of John Paschall, esq. of Great Baddow, and died 13th February, 1570-1, leaving a son and heir,

SIR THOMAS MILDMAY, knt. of Springfield Barnes, who *m.* Alicia, daughter of Adam Winthorpe, esq. of Grotton, in Suffolk, and had issue,

- I. WILLIAM, his heir, who *m.* Margaret, daughter of Sir George Hervey, of Marks, near Rumford, constable of the Tower, and died in the lifetime of his father, leaving
  1. THOMAS, successor to his grandfather.
  2. CAREW-HERVEY, of Marks.*
- II. Henry (Sir), of Graces, died in 1639, and was *s.* by his son,
  - Henry Mildmay, esq. M.P. for Essex *temp.* CHARLES II. and WILLIAM and MARY, *m.* Mary, sister of Benjamin Mildmay, Lord Fitzwalter, and had five daughters, his co-heirs, viz.
    - MARY,† *m.* to Charles Goodwin, esq. of Rovant, in Sussex.
    - ANNE,† *m.* to Sir Draner Massingberd, of Ormsby.
    - LUCY,† *m.* to Thomas Gardiner, esq. of Tolebury, in Essex.
    - ELIZABETH,† *m.* to Edmund Waterson, esq. of London.
    - FRANCES,† *m.* to Christopher Fowler, esq. of London.
    - KATHERINE,† *m.* to Colonel Thomas Townshend.
- III. Walter, of Portlands, in Great Baddow.

Sir Thomas *d.* 15th December, 1612, and was *s.* by his grandson,

SIR THOMAS MILDMAY, knt of Barnes, who married a daughter of John Ernle, esq. of Whetham, in Wiltshire, and left an only son and heir,

WILLIAM MILDMAY, esq. of Barnes, who *m.* Sibilla, daughter of Sir Thomas Palmer, bart. of Wingham, in Kent, and left a son and heir,

WILLIAM MILDMAY, esq. chief of Surat, in the [illegible] service of the East India Company, who *m.* Sa[illegible] Wilcox. This gentleman became heir and repre[illegible]tative of the elder branch of the family at the dec[illegible] *s. p.* in 1625, of Sir Thomas Mildmay, bart. of M[illegible]sham. He was *s.* by his son,

I. WILLIAM MILDMAY, esq. of Moulsham Hall, [illegible] the county of Essex, who was created a BARONET [illegible] February, 1765. He *m.* Anne, daughter of Hum[illegible] Mildmay, esq. but *d. s. p.* 8th August, 1771, whe[illegible] BARONETCY EXPIRED, while the estates and repr[illegible]tation devolved upon

CAREW-HERVEY MILDMAY, esq. of Shawford H[illegible], Hants, Hayle Grove, Somersetshire, and [illegible] Hall, Essex, who bequeathed his estate [illegible] to his grandniece, JANE MILDMAY, the wi[illegible] SIR HENRY PAULET ST. JOHN, bart. [illegible] the present SIR HENRY-CAREW ST. JOHN MIL[illegible]MAY, bart.

Arms—As preceding article.

MILL, OF CAMOIS COURT.

CREATED 31st Dec. 1619.

EXTINCT [illegible]th Feb[illegible]

Lineage.

The surname of this family was originally [illegible] Atte-Mill, Atte-Mull, and Mull, but finally settle[illegible] in MILL.

JOHN MILL, of Grantham, in Sussex, *m.* [illegible] in the reign of HENRY VIII. Catherine, daughter [illegible] heir of Sir Roger Lewcknor,‡ of Camois Court, [illegible] same county, and was *s.* by his only son,

LEWKNOR MILL, esq. of Camois Court, who *m.* [illegible] daughter of John Crook, esq. of Southampton [illegible] *s.* by his eldest son,

I. JOHN MILL, esq. of Camois Court, who was [illegible]ated a BARONET 31st December, 1619. He *m.* [illegible] Elizabeth, daughter of Sir George Moore, knt. [illegible]ley, but by that lady had no issue. He [illegible]

---

* CAREW-HERVEY MILDMAY, esq. of Marks, in the county of Essex, *m.* Dorothy, daughter of Sir Gilbert Gerrard, of Harrow-on-the-Hill, in Middlesex, and was *s.* by his son,

FRANCIS-HERVEY MILDMAY, esq. who *m.* Mary, daughter of Matthew Honeywood, esq. of Charing, in Kent, and had issue,

CAREW, his heir.

George, *m.* Elizabeth Benham, and left a daughter, Elizabeth, who *m.* Henry Eaton, esq. of Raynham, in Essex.

The elder son,

CAREW MILDMAY, esq. sheriff of Essex in 1713, *m.* Anne, daughter of Richard Barret Lennard, esq. of Bellhouse, in that county, and had issue,

CAREW-HERVEY, his heir.

Humphrey, *m.* Letitia, daughter and heir of Haliday Mildmay, grandson of Sir Henry Mildmay, master of the Jewel Office *temp.* JAMES I. and CHARLES I. and had a daughter, Anne, wife of Sir William Mildmay, bart. and a son, CAREW.

Anne, *m.* to Thomas Savile, esq.

He was *s.* by his elder son,

CAREW-HERVEY MILDMAY, esq. of Shawford House, Hants, Hayle Grove, Somersetshire, and Mars[illegible] Essex, who married twice; but died without [illegible] the advanced age of ninety-six, in 1780, bequea[illegible] whole fortune to his grandniece, Jane, Lady S[illegible] eldest daughter and co-heir of his nephew,

CAREW MILDMAY, esq. of Shawford House [illegible] gentleman *m.* Jane, daughter of William Pescod, esq. [illegible] left three daughters, his co-heirs, viz.

JANE MILDMAY, who *m.* Sir Henry Paule[illegible] and inherited the estates of her great-[illegible] which occasion her husband assumed [illegible] surname and arms of MILDMAY. Her son [illegible] is the present (1837)

SIR HENRY-CAREW ST. JOHN MILDMAY [illegible] (See BURKE'S *Peerage and Baronet*[illegible])

ANNE MILDMAY, *m.* to John Clerk, esq [illegible] they.

LETITIA MILDMAY, *m.* to George William R[illegible] esq. of Lamstone, Hants.

† The Barony of Fitzwalter is in abeyance [illegible] the descendants of these ladies.

‡ THOMAS DE CAMOIS, summoned to pa[illegible] RICHARD II. and HENRY V. [illegible]

condly, Anne, daughter of Sir Thomas Fleming, lord chief justice of England, and had, with other children,

i. John (Sir), of Newton Berry, in the county of Southampton, made a knight banneret by *King* Charles I. slain at Oxford in the lifetime of his father. He *m.* Philadelphia, daughter of Sir Henry Knollys, of Grove Place, Hants, comptroller of the household to Charles I. and by her (who *m.* secondly, Christopher, Lord Teynham,) left an only son,

John, successor to his grandfather.

ii. Thomas, *m.* Catherine, daughter and sole heir of Andrew Mundy, esq. of Nutshelling, and acquired thereby that estate.

iii. Richard, of Oxford, *d.* unm.

iv. Lewknor, of Partford, Wilts, *d.* unm.

v. Edward, of Eling, in the county of Southampton, *m.* Jane, daughter of Thomas Burgess, esq. of Byson, in the same county.

Sir John represented the borough of Southampton in several parliaments, and was *s.* at his decease by his grandson,

II. Sir John Mill, who *m.* Margaret, daughter of Colonel Henry Sandys, of Mottisfont, and sister and co-heir of Edwyn, eighth and last Lord Sandys, of the vine, and dying in 1670, was *s.* by his only son,

III. Sir John Mill, high sheriff of the county of Southampton in 1685, who *m.* Margaret, daughter and heir of Thomas Grey, esq. of Woolbeding, in Sussex, and had issue,

John, } Richard, } fourth and fifth baronets.

Mary, *d.* unm.

Margaret, *m.* to Robert Knollys, esq. of Grove Place.

Elizabeth, *m.* to Sir Thomas Hoby, bart. of Somerby, in the county of Southampton, and of Bisham, Berks.

Philadelphia.

Sir John, who inherited the estates of his uncle, Edwyn, Lord Sandys, was *s.* at his decease by his elder son,

IV. Sir John Mill, who dying unmarried in 1681, was *s.* by his brother,

V. Sir Richard Mill, high sheriff of Southampton [illegible], and M.P. for Midhurst, *m.* Margaret, eldest sister of Robert Knollys, esq. of Grove Place, Hants, and had issue,

Richard, } John, } Henry, } Charles, } all baronets in succession.

Margaret.

Philadelphia.

Elizabeth.

Mary.

Martha, *m.* to William Dodsworth, esq.

Sir Richard *d.* 16th May, 1760, and was *s.* by his eldest son,

VI. Sir Richard Mill, M.P. for Southampton, who *m.* in 17[illegible], Dorothy, daughter and heir of Richard [illegible], esq. of Redcliff, in the county of Somerset, by Henrietta, his wife, daughter of Charles Yate, esq. and had two daughters,

Henrietta, *d.* unm.

Sophia, who inherited from the Yate family the estate of Arlingham Court, in Gloucestershire. She *m.* the Chevalier Del Caiua, a Neapolitan nobleman.

He *d.* 17th March, 1770, and the Baronetcy devolved upon his next brother,

VII. Sir John Mill-Hoby (having assumed the additional name in compliance with the will of his cousin, Sir Philip Hoby, bart.), *b.* in 1719, *m.* Miss Elizabeth Comyn, but *d. s. p.* in 1790, when he was *s.* by his brother,

VIII. Sir Henry Mill, in holy orders, rector of Woolbeding and Kingston Bowsey, died without issue in November, 1781, and was *s.* by his only surviving brother,

IX. Sir Charles Mill, LL.B. in holy orders, *b.* in 1722; *d.* 10th July, 1792, leaving by Mary, his wife, one son and one daughter, viz.

Charles, his heir.

Mary, *m.* first, to Captain Stephen L. Popham; and secondly, to John Barker, of Wareham, in Dorset. By the latter she left a son,

The Rev. John Barker.

Sir Charles was *s.* by his son,

X. Sir Charles Mill, who *m.* in 1800, Selina, eldest daughter of Sir John Morshead, bart. of Trenant Park, in Cornwall, but died without issue 26th February, 1835, when the Baronetcy expired, while the estates passed to (the son of his only sister, Mary, by her second husband, John Barker, esq. of Wareham, in Dorsetshire,) his nephew,

The Rev. John Barker, who assumed the surname and arms of Mill in 1835, and being subsequently created a Baronet, is now (1838)

Sir John Barker-Mill, bart. of Mottisfont, in Hampshire.

Arms—Party per fesse arg. and sa. a pale counterchanged, and three bears salient, two and one, of the second, muzzled and chained or.

MILLER, OF OXENHOATH.

Created 13th Oct. 1660.

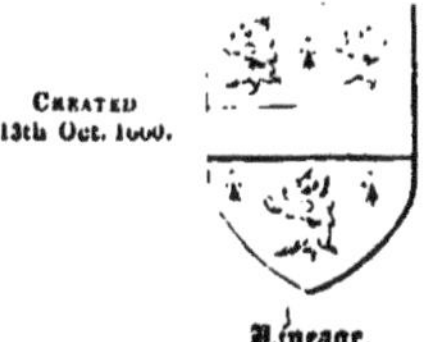

Extinct in 1714.

Lineage.

Nicholas Miller, esq. of Horsnells Crouch, in Wrotham, Kent, sheriff of that county 8 Charles I. purchased from Sir George Chowne, knt. of Fairlane, the manor of Oxenhoath, in the parish of West Peckham. He *m.* Jane, daughter of John Polley, esq. of

---

[illegible] daughter and heir of William de Louches, and [illegible]

[illegible] ard, who died before his father, leaving issue, [illegible] h, who *s.* to the Barony of Camois. [illegible] garet, *m.* to Ralph Radmilde. [illegible] ano, *m.* to Roger Lewknor, from whom descended

Sir Roger Lewknor, of Camois Court, whose daughter and heir,

Catherine Lewknor, *m.* as above, John Mill, esq.

Lord Camois *d.* in 1421, and was *s.* by his grandson,

Hugh de Camois, second lord, at whose decease *s. p.* 5 Henry VI. the estates devolved upon his sisters as co-heirs, and the barony of Camois fell into abeyance amongst them, and so continues with their descendants.

Burke's *Extinct Peerage.*

Preston, in Kent, and by her, who died 6th January, 1640, had issue,

JAMES, *d. s. p.*

NICHOLAS, heir to his father.

Matthew, of Buckland, in Surrey.

Elizabeth, *m.* to Sir Robert Kempe, of Finchenfield, Essex.

Margaret, *m.* to John Boys, esq. son of Sir Edward Boys, of Nonington.

Jane, *m.* to William James, esq. of Ightham.

Mary, *m.* to Edmund Alleyn, esq. son and heir of Sir Edward Alleyn, bart.

Nicholas Miller *d.* 8th August, 1640, aged seventy-four, and was *s.* by his son,

SIR NICHOLAS MILLER, knt. of Oxenhoath in Kent, who *m.* Anne, daughter of William Style, esq. of Langley, in Beckenham, and had, with four daughters, Jane, Anne, Elizabeth, and Margaret, four sons, viz.

HUMPHREY, his heir.

Nicholas, to whom his grandfather, Nicholas Miller, bequeathed his family seat of Crouch, in Wrotham, and other estates. He *m.* Margaret, daughter of John Polhill, gent. of Offord, and *d.* 7th February, 1693, leaving a numerous family. The estates of Crouch and Wingfield continued for some years with his descendants, until conveyed by an heiress to the Mandys of Derbyshire, by whom they were sold, in 1756, to Sarah, Viscountess Falkland, and from that noble family they passed to Francis Motley Austen, esq. of Wilmington.

John.

Charles.

Sir Nicholas *d.* 20th February, 1658, aged sixty-six, and was *s.* by his son,

I. HUMPHREY MILLER, esq. of Oxenhoath, who was created a BARONET in 1660, and served as sheriff of Kent in 1666. He died in August, 1709, leaving by Mary, his wife, daughter of Sir John Borlace, of Stratton Arely, Bucks, a daughter, ELIZABETH, of whom presently, and a son and successor,

II. SIR BORLACE MILLER, of Oxenhoath, who *m.* Susannah, daughter of Thomas Medley, esq. of Buxted, in Sussex, but died without issue in 1714, when the BARONETCY became EXTINCT; the estate of Oxenhoath descended to his sister and heir,

ELIZABETH, wife of Leonard Bartholomew, esq. of Rochester; she died 2nd May, 1720, leaving a son and successor,

PHILIP BARTHOLOMEW, esq. of Oxenhoath, who *m.* first, in 1711, the only daughter and heir of John Knowe, gent. of Ford, and by her, who died in 1722, had two sons, viz.

LEONARD, his heir.

John-Knowe, *d. s. p.*

He *m.* secondly, Mary, youngest daughter of Alexander Thomas, esq. of Lamberhurst, by whom, who died in 1775, he had an only daughter,

Mary, who *m.* in 1748, Francis Geary, esq. admiral R.N. and had issue.

Mr. Bartholomew died 9th January, 1730, and was *s.* by his son,

LEONARD BARTHOLOMEW, esq. of Oxenhoath, who died without issue 26th April, 1757, and bequeathed his estates to his nephew, WILLIAM GEARY, esq. who succeeded subsequently to the Baronetcy conferred on his father, and died 6th August, 1825, leaving a son and successor, the present SIR WILLIAM RICHARD POWLETT GEARY, bart. of Oxenhoath.

Arms—Erm. a fess gu. between three griffins' heads erased az.

MITCHELL, OF WESTSHORE, N. B.

CREATED 19th June, 1724.

EXTINCT 5th April, 1[illegible]

Lineage.

The MITCHELLS, an old Scottish race, were of [illegible]sideration in the reign of JAMES VI. who for [illegible] loyalty and good services granted to

WILLIAM MITCHELL (son of John Mitchell), an[d] his heirs for ever, a charter of the lands of Ba[illegible] in the county of Stirling, with all the usual privileg[es]. That the said William's predecessors were very an[]cient proprietors of these lands is implied by [the] words in the charter: *Dilecto nostro Willielmo M[it]chell, veteri nativo possessori*; in the same [he is] styled, *Vir honorabilis, Willielmus Mitchell, de [Ban]deth*, and the witnesses thereto are James, Earl [of] Arran, and Patrick, Lord Bishop of St. Andrews. The charter was dated at Holyrood House, 8th February, 1584. The descendant of this William,

JOHN MITCHELL, of Bandeth, in holy orders, ha[d a] grant from CHARLES I. of the archdeaconry of T[ing]wall, in Zeatland. He *m.* Margaret, eldest daughter of Robert Forrester, of Queenshaugh, and had a son,

JOHN MITCHELL, esq. who wedded Jean [illegible] daughter and heir of Andrew Umpray, esq. of [illegible] and had, with several daughters, four sons, viz.

JOHN, his heir.

James, of Girleston, *m.* first, Lillias Dunbar, and had one son, John, who died young, and a daughter, Grizel, the wife of John Scott, esq. [of] Gibleston. He *m.* secondly, Barbara, daughter of Sinclair of House, and by her had a daughter, Elizabeth, *m.* to Magnus Henderson, [of] Gardie.

Charles, of Pittadied, who wedded, first, Jane Blackwood, sister of Sir Robert Blackwood, knt. but by her had no issue. He *m.* secondly, Margaret, daughter of Sir Henry W[illegible] of Pitrivie, and had one son and three daughters.

Andrew, an apothecary in London.

The eldest son,

I. JOHN MITCHELL, esq. of Westshore, in Zetland, was created a BARONET by *King* GEORGE I. 19th J[une], 1724. Sir John *m.* Margaret, eldest daughter of Francis Murray, esq. and had surviving issue,

ANDREW, his heir.

Francis.

John-Charles.

Elizabeth, *m.* to Thomas Gifford, esq. of Busta.

Jean, *m.* to Charles Neven, esq. of W[illegible] and *d. s. p.*

Barbara, *m.* to Alexander Sinclair, jun. of B[illegible]

Sir John *d.* in June, 1739, and was *s.* by his son,

II. SIR ANDREW MICHALL, one of the faculty of advocates in Scotland. He *m.* first, Jane, daughter of Charles Mitchell, of Pittedie; and secondly, [illegible] daughter of Sir John Elphinstone, of Logie, [and] dying 29th June, 1764, was *s.* by the eldest son of his first marriage,

III. SIR JOHN MITCHELL, who m. Elizabeth, daughter and heir of John Bruce Stewart, esq. of Symbister, but died s. p. 5th April, 1783, when the BARONETCY EXPIRED.

Arms—Sa. a fesse between three mascles or, within a bordure chequy of the second and first.

MODYFORD, OF LONDON.

CREATED 19th Feb. 1660-1.

EXTINCT in 1673.

Lineage.

I. SIR JAMES MODYFORD, of London and Chiswick, lieutenant-governor of Jamaica, was created a BARONET in 1660-1. He m. Elizabeth, daughter and eventually sole heir of Sir Nicholas Slanning, knt. of Maristow, in Devon, the celebrated cavalier commander during the civil war, but had no male issue to survive him. He died, and was buried at St. Andrew's, Jamaica, 13th January, 1675, when the BARONETCY became EXTINCT. The estate of Maristow, &c. passed with Sir James's daughter,

GRACE, in marriage to Peter Heywood, esq. Their grandson and heir,

JAMES MODYFORD HEYWOOD, esq. of Maristow, died in 1798, leaving four daughters, his co-heirs, who sold Maristow, with the manors of Bickleigh, Buckland, &c. to Sir Manasseh-Masseh Lopes, bart.

Arms—Erm. on a bend az. a mullet arg. between two garbs or.

MODYFORD, OF LINCOLN'S INN.

CREATED 1st March, 1663-4.—EXTINCT in 1703.

Lineage.

I. SIR THOMAS MODYFORD, brother of Sir James Modyford, and also governor of Jamaica, was created a BARONET in 1663-4. He m. Elizabeth, daughter of Lewis Palmer, esq. of Devonshire, and dying in Jamaica 2nd September, 1679, was s. by his son,

II. SIR THOMAS MODYFORD, who survived his father little more than a month, dying 19th October, 1679, and was s. by his brother,

III. SIR CHARLES MODYFORD, who resided at Angels, in Jamaica. He m. Mary, daughter and co-heir of Sir Thomas Norton, bart. and dying in that island about 1686, was s. by his son,

IV. SIR NORTON MODYFORD, who m. Miss Guy, of Barbadoes, but dying s. p. about 1690, was s. by his brother,

V. SIR THOMAS MODYFORD, who resided at St. Jago de la Vega, in Jamaica. He m. first, a daughter of John Hathersale, merchant, of London; and secondly, Jane, daughter and heir of Sir William Beeston, knt. governor of Jamaica; but d. s. p. m. in 1703, when the title became EXTINCT. His widow married Charles Long, esq. of Longueville, in Jamaica.

Arms—As MODYFORD OF LONDON.

MOHUN, OF BOCONNOC.

CREATED 25th Nov. 1612.

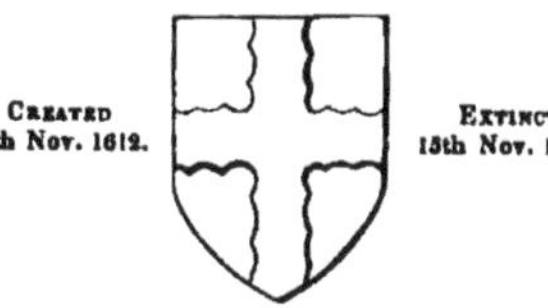

EXTINCT 15th Nov. 1712.

Lineage.

The family of MOHUN came in at the Conquest, when

SIR WILLIAM DE MOHUN, having at the head of forty-seven stout knights rendered good service at the battle of Hastings, acquired the castle of Dunster, with fifty manors in Somersetshire, beside many other lordships in Wilts, in Devonshire, and Warwickshire. Seventh in lineal descent from Sir William was

JOHN DE MOHUN, who had summons to parliament as BARON MOHUN, of Dunster, in the time of EDWARD I. and was s. at his decease by his grandson,

JOHN DE MOHUN, second Lord Mohun of Dunster, who left at his decease three daughters, his co-heirs, amongst whom the barony of Mohun of Dunster fell into abeyance.

But from a younger son of John, the first baron, namely,

REGINALD DE MOHUN, descended

I. REGINALD MOHUN, esq. of Boconnoc, in Cornwall, who was created a BARONET by *King* JAMES I. 25th November, 1612. Sir Reginald m. Philippa, daughter of Sir John Hele,* knt. of Wembury, in Devon, by Margaret, his wife, daughter and co-heir of Ellis Warwick, esq. of Batsborow, and had issue,

JOHN, his heir.

Elizabeth.

He was s. at his decease by his son,

II. SIR JOHN MOHUN, who was advanced to the peerage by letters patent, dated 15th April, 1628, as Baron Mohun, of Oakhampton, in the county of Devon. During the civil war his lordship was one of the chief cavalier commanders in Cornwall and the West of England, and did good service to the royal cause. He m. Cordelia, daughter of Sir John Stanhope, of Shelford, Notts, and widow of Sir Roger Aston, by whom he had issue,

JOHN, his successor.

WARWICK, heir to his brother.

Charles, slain at Dartmouth, fighting under the royal standard.

Cordelia, m. to John Harris, esq. of Hayne, in Devonshire.

Theophila, m. to James Campbell, esq. son of Mr. Alderman Campbell, of London.

Philadelphia.

* See family of Hele, p. 254.

His lordship died in 1644, and was succeeded by his eldest son,

III. Sir John Mohun, second Lord Mohun, who *d.* unm. and was *s.* by his brother,

IV. Sir Warwick Mohun, third Lord Mohun, who *m.* Catherine, daughter of Welles of the county of Southampton, and dying in 1665, was *s.* by his son,

V. Sir Charles Mohun, fourth Lord Mohun, who *m.* Lady Philippa Annesley, daughter of Arthur, first Earl of Anglesey, and had with a daughter, Elisabeth, who *d.* unm. in 1709, a son and successor at his decease, before 1682,

VI. Sir Charles Mohun, fifth Lord Mohun. This nobleman was of so vehement and violent a temperature, that he incurred twice the imputation of murder, was twice tried for that most heinous crime, but both times acquitted. His career, however, terminated violently. "Men of blood shall not live out half their lives." Having had a dispute with the Duke of Hamilton, regarding the estates bequeathed to him by the uncle of his first wife, Charles, second Earl of Macclesfield, he challenged that nobleman, and a desperate rencounter ensued, in which both the combatants lost their lives; Lord Mohun, by the hand of his antagonist; the Duke of Hamilton, by the treachery of Lord Mohun's second, General Macartney, who was tried for the offence, 18th June, 1710, in the court of King's Bench, and acquitted of the murder, but convicted of manslaughter. Lord Mohun's death occurred 15th November, 1712. He *m.* first, Charlotte, daughter of — Mainwaring, esq. by his wife, Lady Charlotte Gerard, sister of Charles, second Earl of Macclesfield; and secondly, Elisabeth, daughter of Doctor Thomas Lawrence, and widow of Colonel Griffith, but having no issue, his honours, including the Baronetcy, expired with him.

Arms—Or, a cross ingrailed sa.

MOLYNEUX, OF TEVERSAL.

Created 29th June, 1611.

Extinct 9th June, 1812.

Lineage.

Amongst the Norman nobles who entered England with the Conqueror, in 1066,

William de Molines appears to have been one of the most distinguished, as well from the Battle Abbey roll, wherein his name standeth the eighteenth [illegible] order as from the old chronicles of the duchy, where [illegible] "he is set down and placed as a most especial [illegible] chief man in nearness and singular credit" with [illegible] royal master. To this William Roger de Poytiers,† who was then possessed of all that tract of land [illegible] Lancashire between the rivers Ribble and Mersey, [illegible] gift of the crown, gave among other lands the [illegible] of Sephton, Thorneton, Kerdon, ten carucates [illegible] half of land, at the service of half a knight's [illegible] whereof he, William, made Sephton his chief [illegible] and was *s.* at his decease by his son,

Vivian de Molines,‡ whose son and heir,

Adam de Molines, Dominus de Sefton, *m.* [illegible] only daughter and heir of Benedict de Garnet [illegible] of Speke, in Lancashire, and from him we pass several generations, each highly eminent,§ to

Sir Richard Molyneux, who eminently distinguished himself in the wars of France, was at [illegible] battle of Azincourt, and received the honour of knighthood in the reign of Henry V. He was in [illegible] also with Henry VI. who by letters patent conferred upon him, his sons, and their heirs, the chief [illegible]ship of the royal forests and parks in West [illegible]shire, the stewardship of Salford, and the [illegible] constable of Liverpool. He was slain at Blore H[eath] with the Lord Audley, in 1459. Sir Richard *m.* [illegible] Joan, daughter and heir of Sir Gilbert Haydock [illegible] and relict of Sir Peter Legh, of Lyme, and by [illegible] had several sons, of whom Richard, the eldest, was ancestor of the Earls of Sefton and Sir T[illegible] the second of the family before us. He [illegible] secondly, Helen, daughter of Radcliffe of Ra[illegible] Tower, and relict of Sir William Harrington, [illegible] that lady had two daughters, Anne, wife of [illegible] Nevil, of Leversedge, and Margaret, of Sir [illegible] Leigh, knt. of Bradley.

The second son,

Sir Thomas Molyneux, of Haughton, in [illegible]hamshire, was of the privy council to Henry [illegible] and behaving valiantly in the expedition into [illegible]land, *anno* 1482, was made a knight banneret [illegible] Richard, Duke of Gloucester, at Berwick [illegible] same year he built the church and [illegible] Hawton, and died in 1492. He *m.* first, Elizabeth, daughter of Sir Robert Markham, knt. of [illegible] Notts, by whom he had a son, Robert, his heir [illegible] a daughter, Elizabeth, who *m.* first, John Bacar[illegible] and secondly, Stephen Hatfield, esq. of [illegible] Sir Thomas *m.* secondly, Catherine, daughter of [illegible] Cotton, esq. of Redware, in Staffordshire, and [illegible] of Thomas Poutrell, esq. of Hallam, in the county [of] Derby, and had by her

> Edmund (Sir), K.B. one of the justices [illegible] Common Pleas in 1550, and died in 15[illegible] Edmund *m.* Jane, daughter of John Ch[illegible] esq. of Chesham-boys, Bucks, and had [illegible]
>
> John, of Thorp, *m.* Anne, daughter of [illegible]

---

† Called by the Conqueror, his familiar in arms, and styled "de Poytiers," because his wife was a Potaine, or native of the province of Poytiers: he was son of Roger, Count Mountgomerie, Arundel, and Shrewsburie, by Mabel, sister and heir of Arnald, Count of Bellesmayne, in Normandy.

‡ Other accounts differ from this, and say, that William, and Vivian de Moulines, his brother, were in the first expedition of the army sent by William the Conqueror, under the conduct of Roger de Poytiers, and that the said Roger gave the lordship of Sephton, &c. to Vivian de Molines and his posterity, shortly after the entrance of the Normans, which coincides with other authorities. Camden, in his Britannia, speaking of Lirpole (Liverpool) observes, "The name is not to be met with in old writings; but only that Roger de Poictiers, [illegible] lord of the honour of Lancaster, built a castle [illegible] government whereof was enjoyed for a long time [illegible] noble family of the Molyneux, knights (and [illegible] Molyneux), whose chief seat is hard by, at S[illegible] which the said Roger de Poictiers bestowed upon [illegible] de Molyneux, a little after the coming of the [illegible] for all the land between the Rebell and the M[illegible] longed to the said Roger, as appears by Domesday."

§ Sir Thomas Molyneux was constable [illegible] "a man of great power, authority, and [illegible] in Lancashire and Cheshire," *temp.* Richard [illegible]

Sir William Molyneux distinguished [illegible] battle of Navarre, in Spain, under Edward [illegible] *Prince*, and was made a knight banneret [illegible]

Lascelles, esq. of Gatford, Notts, and had two sons.*

Thomas, m. Jane, daughter of Sir Richard Molyneux, knt. of Sefton.

Edmund.

Anthony.

Margaret, m. to Francis Fleetwood, esq.

Dorothy, m. to Robert Purslow, esq.

Anthony, D.D. rector of Sefton and Walton, in Lancashire, and Tring, in Hertfordshire, d. in 1558, leaving two daughters,

Ellen, m. first, to John Bond, esq. of Coventry; and secondly, to Laurence Ireland, esq. of Lidiat.

Margaret, m. to Sir Hugh Willoughby, knt. of Risley, in the county of Derby.

Sir Thomas was s. by his eldest son,

Robert Molineux, esq. of Hawton, who m. Dorothy, daughter of Thomas Poutrell, esq. of West Hallam, in Derbyshire, and was s. by his eldest surviving son,

Richard Molineux, esq. who m. Margaret, daughter of Edmund Bussy, esq. of Hather, in Lincolnshire, and had a daughter, Mary, the wife of Daniel Disney, esq. of Norton Disney, and a son and heir,

Francis Molineux, esq. who m. Elizabeth, daughter and co-heir of Thomas, son of Roger Greenhalgh, esq. of Teversal, in Nottinghamshire, by whom he acquired the manor of Teversal. He was high sheriff of Notts, 24 Elizabeth, and was s. at his decease by his eldest son,

Thomas Molineux, esq. who m. Alice, daughter and co-heir of Thomas Cranmer, esq. of Aslacton, in Nottinghamshire (great nephew of the archbishop), and by that lady (who wedded, secondly, Sir John Thorold, knt. of Cawnton) had two sons, John and Thomas, and a daughter, the wife of Sir Anthony Thorold, knt. of Marston, in Lincolnshire. He d. in [illegible]7, and was s. by his elder son,

I. John Molyneux, esq. of Teversal, in the county of Nottingham, who was created a Baronet 29th June, 1611. He had a grant from *Queen* Elizabeth, of the lordships of Carleton, Kingston, and Carleton-[illegible], which were the possessions of Thomas, Lord Darcy: these lands his descendants sold to Sir Gervase Clifton, bart. Sir John Molineux lived in great splendour, but beyond his income, which compelled him to mortgage the manor of Hawton to Sir John Leke, and it became afterwards the inheritance of the Earls of Scarsdale of that family. He was sheriff of Nottinghamshire in the 7th and 9th of James I. He m. first, Isabel, daughter of John Markham, esq. of Sedgebrook, in Lincolnshire, and by her had

Francis, his successor.

Thomas, d. s. p.

Mary, m. to Michael Fawkes, esq. of Farnley, in Yorkshire.

Elizabeth, m. to Gilbert Gregory, esq. of Barnby Dun, in the same county.

Sir John wedded, secondly, Anne, daughter of Sir James Harrington, of Ridlington, in Rutlandshire, and widow of Sir Thomas Foljambe, knt. of Walton, in the county of Derby, by whom he had a son,

Roger, a colonel in the army, m. Jane, eldest daughter and co-heir of Sir Robert Monson, of Carleton, in Lincolnshire.

He was s. at his decease by his eldest son,

II. Sir Francis Molyneux, who m. Theodosia, daughter of Sir Edward Heron, K.B. of Cressy Hall, in the county of Lincoln, and had issue,

I. John, his heir.

II. Francis, of Mansfield, Notts, who m. Grace, daughter of Conyers, Lord D'Arcy, widow of John Best, esq. of Middleton, in the county of York, and had two sons,

1. Darcy, who m. Elizabeth, daughter of Mr. Basset, of Doncaster, and left

William.

John.

2. Francis, m. Mary, daughter of Charles Tancred, esq. of Whixley, in Yorkshire, and had four daughters.

I. Elizabeth, m. to Hugh Cartwright, esq. of Hexgrave, Notts.

II. Theodosia, m. to Edward Bunny, esq. of Newland, in Yorkshire.

III. Anne.

IV. Isabel.

Sir Francis d. 12th October, 1674, and was s. by his elder son,

III. Sir John Molyneux, b. in 1623, who m. Lucy, daughter of Alexander Rigby, esq. of Middleton, in Lancashire, one of the barons of the Exchequer, and widow of Robert Hesketh, esq. of Rufford, in the same county, by whom he had issue,

Francis, his successor.

John, d. unm.

Thomas, a Turkey merchant, afterwards of Preston, in Lancashire, m. Mary, daughter of Gilbert Mundy, esq. of Allestree, in the county of Derby, and dying 25th May, 1727, left an only son,

Rigby, who m. a daughter of Oliver Marton, esq. of Lancaster, and had an only daughter,

Mary, who m. first, John Bushell, M.D.; and secondly, Captain Griffiths.

Mary, m. to the Hon. Richard Leke, and was mother of Nicholas Leke, fourth Earl of Scarsdale.

Elizabeth, m. to Edmund Jodrell, esq. of Erdaley, in Cheshire.

Sir John was s. at his decease, in 1691, by his eldest son,

IV. Sir Francis Molyneux, M.P. for the county of Nottingham, *temp. Queen* Anne, who m. Diana, daughter of John Howe, esq. of Langar Castle, and sister of Scroop, Viscount Howe, and had issue,

John, d. before his father.

Francis, verdurer of Sherwood forest, died in October, 1733, before his father, leaving by his wife, Mary, daughter and co-heir of — Brewer, esq. two daughters,

Diana.

Mary.

Scroop, d. before his father.

Charles, } fifth and sixth baronets.
William, }

Annabella, m. to John Plumptre, esq. of Nottingham.

Lucy, m. to Charles Croke Lisle, esq. of Moyle's Court.

Diana.

He d. 12th March, 1742, aged eighty-seven, and was s. by his eldest surviving son,

---

* Namely,

1. Edmund Molineux, of Thorpe, who m. first, the daughter of John Hearle, esq. and had a daughter, Anne, who died unm. He m. secondly, Bridget, daughter and co-heir of Robert Sapcote, esq. and by her had

Sir John Molineux, knt. of Thorpe.

Edmund Molineux.

Richard Molineux.

2. Rutland Molineux, of Woodcotes, who m. Mary, daughter and heir of Cuthbert Bevercotes, of Bevercotes, Notts.

v. Sir Charles Molyneux, who served as sheriff of the county of Nottingham, and *d.* unm. 28th July, 1764. He was *s.* by his brother,

vi. Sir William Molyneux, one of the verdurers of Sherwood forest. He *m.* Anne, daughter and heir of William Challand, esq. of Wellow, Notts, and had issue,

- Francis (Sir), his heir.
- Anne.
- Juliana, *m.* to Henry Howard, esq. of Glossop, in the county of Derby, and had issue,
  - Bernard Howard, who *s.* as twelfth Duke of Norfolk, in 1815.
  - Henry-Thomas Howard, who assumed the additional name of Molyneux, in 1812.
  - Edward-Charles Howard, *m.* Miss Elizabeth Maycock, and left issue, at his decease, in 1816.
  - Mary Howard, *m.* to Robert-Edward, tenth Lord Petre.
  - Juliana-Barbara Howard, married to Robert-Edward, ninth Lord Petre.

Sir William *d.* in 1781, and was *s.* by his son,

vii. Sir Francis Molyneux, who had been previously knighted, and appointed gentleman usher of the black rod. He *d. s. p.* 9th June, 1812, when the Baronetcy expired, and the estates passed to his nephew,

Henry-Thomas Howard, esq. who assumed thereupon the additional surname of Molyneux, and in 1817, that of Howard, still in addition to "Howard-Molyneux," in which year he was granted the rank and precedency of a duke's younger son. Lord Henry Howard, having conformed to the established church, officiated as deputy earl-marshal for his elder brother, the Duke of Norfolk. He *m.* 12th September, 1801, Elizabeth, daughter of Edward Long, esq. and dying 17th June, 1824, left by that lady (who died his widow, 24th May, 1834), one son and four daughters, viz.

- Henry, *b.* 25th July, 1802.
- Henrietta-Anne, *m.* in 1830, to the Earl of Carnarvon.
- Isabella-Catherine, *m.* in 1829, to Viscount Andover.
- Charlotte-Juliana-Jane, *m.* in 1831, to James Wentworth Buller, esq. M.P. of Downes, in Devonshire.
- Juliana-Barbara, *m.* in 1831, to Sir John Ogilvie, bart.

Arms—Az. a cross moline quarter pierced or.

MONINS, OF WALDERSHARE.

Created 29th June, 1611. Extinct in 1678.

Lineage.

John Monins, or Monyn, (descended from Sir Simon de Monyn, knt. of the castle of Mayon, in Normandy, who attended William the Conqueror in his expedition to England,) acquired the manor of Waldershare in Kent, *temp.* Henry VI. partly by purchase from the family of Goldwell, and partly by marriage with the daughter and heir of Colby, who inherited the estate in right of his wife, the heiress of Thomas Maimes. John Monins fixed, in consequence, his residence there, and erected a new mansion about a mile south eastward from the ancient house of the Maimes. He left, with three daughters, married to Finneys, Crayford, and Evering, three sons, of whom the eldest,

Robert Monins, of Waldershare, living *temp.* Richard III. married a daughter and co-heir of Crawford, and had by her two sons and three daughters, of whom the youngest, Alice, was mother of Matthew Parker, archbishop of Canterbury. The elder son Richard, who wedded the daughter and co-heir of Petyt, mayor of Dover in 1509, *d. s. p.* the younger

John Monins, of Swanton, compounded 25th Henry VII. for 10 marks, to be excused being made a knight of the bath, at the creation of Henry, Prince of Wales. By Battel Anstyve, of Cambridge, his wife, he had two daughters, one *m.* to — Bedingfeld, and two sons, namely,

- Edward, his heir.
- John, lieutenant of Dover Castle, from whom descended the families of Monins of Dover and Canterbury.

The elder son,

Edward Monins, esq. of Waldershare, who procured his lands to be disgavelled, *temp.* Edward [illegible] married Parnel, daughter and heir of Anthony Lovrick, esq. of Herne, and had, by her, four daughters, *m.* to Brook, Engeham, Lane, and Hammond, of St. Albans Court,* and a son and successor,

Richard Monins, esq. of Saltwood Castle, who [illegible] 3 Elizabeth, leaving by Katherine, his wife, daughter of Thomas Alefe, of Coleshill, several children. The eldest son,

John Monins, esq. of Swanton, died without issue in 1566, and was *s.* by his brother,

Sir Edward Monins, knt. of Waldershare, who *m.* Elizabeth, daughter of Thomas Lovelace, esq. and had issue,

- William, his heir.
- Elizabeth, *m.* to Sir Henry Crispe.
- Priscella, *m.* to John Chamberlaine, esq.
- Frances, *m.* to — Darcy.
- Mary, *m.* to Robert Hart.

Sir Edward died in 1602, and was *s.* by his son

i. Sir William Monins, knt. of Waldershare, who was created a Baronet 29th June, 1611. He married twice, but had issue only by his second wife, [illegible] daughter of Roger Twisden, esq. of Roydon, several children, namely,

- Edward, his heir.
- Thomas, successor to his brother.
- John, who *m.* Mary, daughter and heir of W. Lee Hamon, and had two sons,
  - Edward, buried at Eythorne in 1687
  - William, of Shepperdswell.
  - Jane.
- William, died unm.
- Anne, *m.* to Sir Richard Beteman, bart.
- Jane, *m.* first to Sir Timothy Thornhill, knt. secondly to Mathews, thirdly to Swift, and fourthly to Sir Thomas Peyton, knt. of Knowlton.

Sir William died 24th February, 1642, and was *s.* by his son,

ii. Sir Edward Monins, of Waldershare, high sheriff

---

* Alice, daughter of Edward Monins, was second wife of Thomas Hammond, esq. of St. Albans Court, Kent. (See Burke's *Commoners*, vol. i. p. 130.)

riff of Kent 21 Charles I. He m. Elizabeth, daughter of Sir Thomas Style, of Wateringbury, and by her, who died in 1703, had five daughters, viz.

Susan, m. in 1673, to Peregrine Bertie, second son of Montague, Earl of Lindsey, and left two daughters, her co-heirs, (who sold Waldershare to Sir Henry Furnese,)

Mary, m. first to Anthony Henley, esq. of the Grange, Hants, and secondly to the Hon. Henry Bertie, third son of James, Earl of Abingdon. By the former she was mother of

Robert Henley, Earl of Northington, lord high chancellor.

Bridget, m. to John, first Earl Poulet.

Jane, m. to Sir John Knatchbull, bart.

Elizabeth, m. to John, son of Sir Anthony Perceval, knt.

Anne, m. first to Sir Roger Pratt, knt. of Norfolk, and secondly to Sigismund Trafford, esq.

Frances.

Sir Edward died in 1663, and was s. by his brother,

III. Sir Thomas Monins, who m. Elizabeth, daughter of James Darell, esq. of Calehill, in Kent, and relict of Robert Bromfield, esq. of Tilmanstone, but died s. p. in 1678, aged seventy-three, when the Baronetcy became extinct.

Arms—Gu. three crescents or.

MONNOUX, OF WOTTON.

Created 4th Dec. 1660. Extinct 3rd Feb. 1814.

Lineage.

In the book of Chauntries of Essex, in Walthamstow, is the following entry, without date: "Lands and tenements there put in feoffment by George Monox, gent. for the maintenance of a priest to sing mass in the church there, during the term of twenty years. And one Sir John Hugeson, clerk, of the age of forty years, and of good conversation, literate and teacheth a school there, ys now incumbent thereof. The said town of Walthamstow, is a great town, and having yn it to the number of three hundred and fifty housely people. The said incumbent celebrateth in the said church of Walthamstow, £7. yerely valew of the same, doth amount to the som of £6. 13s. 4d. Plate absolute none, goods and chattels none."

Le Neve begins the pedigree with

John Monox, of Stanford, in Worcestershire, who left a son and heir,

Richard Monox, who was father of two sons, namely, George (Sir), and Richard. The elder,

Sir George Monox, knt. had a grant from Henry VIII. of the manor of Gowers and Buckerells, in Chinford, in Essex, but those lands were purchased back from him by the king. He was sheriff of London in 1509, and lord mayor in 1515. He purchased the manor of Gonalston, Notts, from Sir William Pierpont, knt. and his arms* were painted on the wall in Gonalston Church. Sir George died 9th February, 1543, without issue, and his estates went to the heirs of his nephew, Richard, which

Richard Monox left two sons, Thomas and Humphrey. The elder, his heir,

Thomas Monox, died 4th December, 20th Henry VIII. as appears by the Inquisition, dated 27th October, in the next year, seised of lands in London; the manor of Bozunes, in Wotton, Bedfordshire; Gonalston, in Notts, &c. and was s. by his son,

George Monnoux, esq. who was eight years old 30th Henry VIII.† He m. the Hon. Elizabeth Mordaunt, eldest daughter of John, second Lord Mordaunt, and was s. by his son,

Humphrey Monnoux, esq. of Wotton, in the county of Bedford, who m. Anne, daughter of Edward Waldgrave, esq. of Lawford, in Essex, and left a son and heir,

Lewis Monnoux, esq. of Wotton. This gentleman m. first, Elizabeth, daughter of Thomas Walsh, esq. of Walderne, in Sussex, and secondly, Jane, daughter of Henry Birch, esq. of Oldcomb, in Somersetshire; by the latter he had no issue; by the former he left a son and heir,

I. Humphrey Monnoux, esq. of Wotton, in the county of Bedford, who was created a Baronet 4th December, 1660. Sir Humphrey m. Mary, daughter of Sir Thomas Wodehouse, bart. of Kimberley, in Norfolk, and had three sons and a daughter, viz.

I. Humphrey, his heir.

II. Lewis, of Sandy, in Bedfordshire, m. Lucy, daughter of Edmund Wodehouse, esq. of East Lexham, in Norfolk, and had issue,

1. Humphrey, who m. Mary, daughter of Thomas Savage, esq. of Elmley Castle, Worcestershire,‡ and had

Philip, who inherited as fifth baronet.

2. Lewis, in holy orders, rector of Sandy, in Bedfordshire, m. Miss Edwards, and had several children.

III. Philip, d. s. p.

I. Blanch, m. to Benjamin St. John, esq. of Cole Orton, in Leicestershire.

He was s. at his decease by his eldest son,

II. Sir Humphrey Monnoux, who m. Alice, daughter of Sir Thomas Cotton, bart. of Connington, in Huntingdonshire, and had surviving issue,

Philip, his successor.

Alice, m. to Sir John Cope, bart.

Frances, m. first to Sir Edward Gould, knt. of Highgate, Middlesex, and secondly to John Venables, esq. of Woodcote, Hants.

Sir Humphrey d. in July, 1685, and was s. by his son,

III. Sir Philip Monnoux. This gentleman m. Dorothy, eldest daughter of William Harvey, esq. of Chigwell, in Essex, and dying 25th December, 1707, aged twenty-nine, was s. by his only son,

IV. Sir Humphrey Monnoux, M.P. for Tavistock,

* Argent, on a chevron sable, between three oak leaves, vert three plates, (Bezants) on a chief gules, a bird between two anchors of the first.

† This gentleman had granted to him by Harvey, clarencieux, 10th June 1561, by the designation of George Monoux, of Walthamstow, nephew and heir of Sir George Monoux, knt. a confirmation of the coat of his said uncle, which was first granted by Wriothesley, Garter, and Benott, clarencieux.

‡ By Elizabeth his wife, of Thomas Coventry, Earl of Coventry, and daughter of Richard Graham, esq.

and afterwards for Stockbridge, who died issueless, 3rd December, 1757, when the BARONETCY reverted to his cousin, (refer to Lewis, second son of the first baronet,)

v. SIR PHILIP MONNOUX, major in the Bedfordshire militia, who served the office of sheriff for that county in 1763. He m. Elizabeth, daughter of Ambrose Riddell, esq. of Eversholt, and had, with five daughters,* one son,

PHILIP, his successor.

He d. at the age of sixty-six, 17th April, 1805, and was s. by his son,

vi. SIR PHILIP MONNOUX, who d. unm. 27th February, 1809, and was s. by his kinsman,

vii. SIR PHILIP MONNOUX, in holy orders, who died issueless, 3rd February, 1814, when the BARONETCY EXPIRED.

Arms—Argent, on a chevron sable, three besants between as many oak leaves, vert.

MONTGOMERY, OF MAGBIE HILL.

CREATED 28th May, 1774.

EXTINCT 9th July, 1831.

Lineage.

In the year 1371,

HUGH DE EGLINTOUN, obtained a charter of the lands of Giffeyn, from ROBERT II. as they had previously fallen by forfeiture to the crown of Scotland,† and those, with other great possessions, passed with his heiress to her husband,

JOHN DE MONTGOMERY, of Eaglesham, who was s. by his son,

JOHN DE MONTGOMERY, of Eglintoun, Ardrossan, &c. who is stated by Douglas, to have bestowed that fine estate upon his second son,

ROBERT DE MONTGOMERY, who lived in the reigns of JAMES I. and JAMES II. (inter 1424 and 1460) and who marrying Janet, daughter of Alexander Murray, of Touch Adam, was s. by his son,

SIR ADAM MONTGOMERY, of Griffen, who had two sons, between whom he divided his lands, namely, ADAM and John. The elder,

ADAM MONTGOMERY, designated of Griffen, and living in the times of JAMES V. and *Queen* MARY, was succeeded there by his eldest son, ADAM, while his second son,

TROILUS MONTGOMERY, became founder of the family of Macbeth, or Magbie Hill. He m. Janet, daughter of Sir Hugh Montgomery, of Braidstane, and was s. by his elder son,

WILLIAM MONTGOMERY, Laird of Macbeth Hill, in the county of Peebles, who died s. p. and was s. by his brother,

ANDREW MONTGOMERY, b. in 1598, who m. a daughter of Galbraith, of Kilcroich, and had three sons, ROBERT, his heir; Adam, killed at the battle of Worcester, in 1651; and William, who went to Poland, and died issueless. The eldest son,

ROBERT MONTGOMERY, succeeded his father in Macbeth Hill. He m. a daughter of Sir James Lockhart, of Lee, and had, with two daughters, one the wife of John Rowat, the other of J. Hamilton, of Newton, three sons, viz.

WILLIAM, his heir.

James, d. s. p.

Hugh, who married and had three sons.

He was s. by his eldest son,

WILLIAM MONTGOMERY, of Macbeth Hill, who m. Miss Peter, only daughter and heiress of John Peter, of Whitesiead, and had two sons, WILLIAM, his heir, and James, who d. s. p. with four daughters, married respectively to Alexander Macleod, William Thyne, James Ure, of Shirgarton, and Capt. Robert Tetler. The elder son,

WILLIAM MONTGOMERY, of Macbeth Hill, m. a daughter of John Hooks, of Gaunt, and was s. by his eldest son,

WILLIAM MONTGOMERY, of Macbeth, or Magbie Hill, who m. Barbara, daughter of Robert Rutherford, esq. of Bowland, and had two sons,

I. WILLIAM, his heir.

II. James, of Stanhope, lord chief baron of the Exchequer, in Scotland, M.P. for Peebleshire, created a Baronet in 1801. (Refer to BURKE's *Peerage and Baronetage*.)

He d. in 1768, in the eighty-sixth year of his age, and was s. by his elder son,

I. WILLIAM MONTGOMERY, esq. of Magbie Hill, in the county of Peebles, who was created a BARONET 28th May, 1774. Sir William m. first, Hannah, daughter and co-heir of Alexander Tomkins, esq. of the county of Londonderry, and by that lady had issue,

William Styre, an officer in the army, who died of wounds received in battle, in America, at the age of nineteen.

ELIZABETH, m. 3rd July, 1773, to Luke Gardiner, Viscount Mountjoy, in Ireland, and dying 7th November, 1783, left, with other issue,

CHARLES-JOHN, second Lord Mountjoy, who was created Earl of Blessington, and died in 1829, (when his honours expired) leaving two daughters,

HARRIET-ANNE-FRANCES, m. in 1827, to Count Alfred D'Orsay.

Mary.

BARBARA, m. in 1774, to the Right Hon. John Beresford, (his second wife).

ANNE, m. to George, first Marquess Townshend (his lordship's second wife).

He wedded, secondly, in 1761, Anne, daughter of Henry Watt, esq. of Mount Lewis, in Ireland, and had two other sons and three daughters, viz.

GEORGE, his heir.

Robert, col. 9th regiment of foot, killed in a duel by Capt. Macnamara, 6th April, 1803.

JEAN, m. to William Reynell, esq. of Castle Reynell, in Westmeath.

HARRIET, m. to George Byng, esq. of Wrotham Park, M.P. for Middlesex.

---

* Of these daughters, one m. first, Sir John Payne, and secondly, Col. Buckworth, and another, Frances, became the wife of the Hon. Samuel Henry Ongley.

† "It seems probable, that Griffen, immediately previous to the grant of it, by ROBERT the 2nd, to Hugh de Eglintoun, had been the property of the king himself, who had acquired it, while steward, from his grandfather Robert Bruce, or from his uncle David the 2nd; having fallen to the crown by forfeiture, during the contest with the Baliol party. This seems to be the only way to account for Griffen being designed in Kyle Stewart, which, to the present day, it is still held to be—though locally situated in Cunninghame." ROBERTSON's *Ayrshire Families*.

Amilia, m. in 1795, to Charles-Cobbe Beresford, esq.

Sir William died 25th December, 1788, aged seventy-one, and was *s.* by his son,

II. Sir George Montgomery, who *d. s. p.* 9th July, 1831, when the Baronetcy expired.

Arms—Quarterly; first and fourth, three fleurs-de-lis, or; second and third, three annulets or, stoned azure; over all, dividing the quarters, a cross waved or.

MOODY, OF GARESDON.

Created 11th Mar. 1621-2.

Extinct about 1662.

Lineage.

I. Henry Moody, esq. of Garesdon, in Wiltshire, who was created a Baronet in 1621-2, married Deborah, daughter of Walter Dunch, esq. of Avebury, in the same county, and dying about 1632, was *s.* by his son,

II. Sir Henry Moody, who sold the estate of Garesdon, and settled in New England, where he is presumed to have died *s. p.* in 1662. If he did, the Baronetcy then became extinct.

Arms—Vert, a fesse engr. arg. surmounted of another gu. between three harpies of the second crined or.

MOOR, OF MAYDS MORTON.

Created 26th July, 1665.—Extinct ....

Lineage.

I. George Moor, esq. of Mayds Morton, in Buckinghamshire, was created a Baronet 26th July, 1665. He m. first, Elizabeth, daughter of Edward Hungerford, esq. of Cadenham, Wilts, and secondly, Frances, daughter and co-heir of Henry Sandford, esq. of Bobbing, in Kent. He died, however, without male issue, and the Baronetcy became extinct.

MOORE, OF FAWLEY.

Created 21 May, 1627.

Extinct 10th April, 1807.

Lineage.

Of this ancient family, the first mentioned, Francis Moore, was father of

Roger Moore, who m. Elizabeth, daughter of — Hall, of Bradford, and had issue,

Richard Moore, who by his wife, Elizabeth, daughter of William Brocas, esq. of Beaupre, Hants, had two sons,

Richard, his heir.

George, m. Isabella Gore, and had a son,

Edward, whose son and heir,

Edward, of the county of Wilts, m. Eleanor, daughter of Reynolds, of Trowbridge, and had a son,

John Moore, of Ewell, who m. Agnes, daughter of Henry Bartlet, and left issue.

The elder son,

Richard Moore, esq. of Burfield, in the county of Berks, m. Catherine Ariott, and had issue,

John, who inherited Burfield, and was twenty-two years of age at the decease of his father, m. Elizabeth Wittingstall, and left an only daughter and heiress,

Elizabeth Moore, m. to John Mahew, esq.

Elizabeth, m. to Sir John Williams, of Thame, in the county of Oxford, and had issue,

Sir Reginald Williams, who left an only daughter and heir,

Elizabeth, m. to Laurence Lovett, esq. of Liscombe, Bucks.

John Williams, who was created by *Queen* Mary, Lord Williams, of Thame. (See Burke's *Extinct Peerage*.)

Isabella, m. to John D'Oyley, esq.

Christian, m. to Henry Wilkins, esq.

Matilda, m. to Robert Lechingham, esq. of Buckinghamshire.

Alice, m. to John Ralphe, esq.

Anne.

Beside these children, Richard Moore is stated to have had a younger son, named after himself, viz.

Richard Moore, who was father of

William Moore, esq. who m. a daughter of Hildesly, of Hildesly, and left a son and heir,

Edward Moore, esq. who died in the first year of Elizabeth, leaving by Elizabeth his wife, daughter and heir of Hall, of Tilehurst, in Berks,

Sir Francis Moore, knt. an eminent person in the time of Elizabeth, of whom the following details are given by Anthony Wood. "He was born at East Hildersly, or Ilderley, near Wantage, in Berks, educated in Grammar learning at Reading, entered a Commoner in St. John's College, Oxford, 1574, or thereabouts, continued there till near Batchelor's Standing, and then he retired to the Middle Temple, where after severe encounters had with the crabbed parts of the municipal laws, he became a Barrister, and noted for his great proficiency in his profession, and integrity in his dealings. In the latter end of Queen Elizabeth, and beginning of King James, he was several times elected a Burgess, to sit in Parliament, in which he was a frequent speaker; afterwards he was Counsellor, and Under Steward for several years to the University of Oxford; the members of which conferred upon him the degree of Master of Arts, in 1612. Two years after, he was made Serjeant-at-law, and in 1616, March 17, received the honor of Knighthood at Theobalds, from his Majesty, King James I. After his death some of his Works were published, which bear these titles,

Cases collected and reported from the original in French, that then (1663) remained in the hands of

Sir Jeffrey Palmer, Attorney General to King Charles the 2nd, which is the same, as I take it, written fairly with the Author's hand in fol. that was lately in the library of Arthur, Earl of Anglesey.

His learned reading 4 James 1st, in the Middle Temple Hall, concerning Charitable Uses, abridged by himself. London, 1676, fol. published by George Duke, of the Inner Temple, Esq.

Our Author, F. Moore, was a member of that parliament, as it seems, wherein the Statute concerning Charitable Uses was made, and was, as 'tis farther added, the penner thereof. At length paying the last debt to nature on the 20th November, 1621, aged 63, was buried in a Vault under the Church at Great Fawley, near to Wantage, before mentioned, in which Vault his posterity (who are Baronets, living in that parish) have been since, and are hitherto interred, as I have been instructed by his grandson, Sir Henry Moore, Bart." So far Anthony Wood—further may be stated that Sir Francis *m.* Anne, daughter of William Twitty, esq. of Boreham, in Essex, and had issue,

- I. Francis, *d.* at Lyons, unm.
- II. HENRY, aged twenty-one in 1617.
- III. William, *m.* to Mrs. Blount, and left a son,
  - Francis, who *m.* Mary, daughter of Edward Cary, esq. of Torr Abbey.

- I. Margaret, *m.* to Sir Jeffrey Palmer, knt. attorney-general to *King* CHARLES II.
- II. Anne, *m.* to John Jerningham, esq. eldest son of Sir Henry Jerningham, first baronet of Cossy Hall, in Norfolk, and was mother of Sir Henry Jerningham, the second baronet.
- III. Elizabeth, *m.* to Sir Richard Blount, of Maple Durham, in the county of Oxford.
- IV. Dorothy, *d.* unm.

The eldest surviving son and heir,

HENRY MOORE, esq. of Fawley, in the county of Berks, was created a BARONET 21st May, 1627. He *m.* Elizabeth, daughter of William Beverley, esq. of Kenoe, in the county of Bedford, and had issue,

- HENRY, his successor.
- St. John (Sir), who *m.* Miss Pooley, and had several children, who all *d. s. p.*

- Anne, *m.* to Sir Matthew Hale, knt. lord chief justice of England.
- Elizabeth, *m.* to Sir Seymour Pile, bart. of Oxford, in Wilts.
- Frances, *m.* to Gabriel Pile, esq. of Okemarsh, in Berkshire.
- Margaret, *m.* to William Duckett, esq.

Sir Henry *d.* about the year 1635, and was *s.* by his eldest son,

II. SIR HENRY MOORE, who wedded, first, Judith, daughter of Mr. Alderman Campbell, of London, and by her had one daughter, Judith, who *d.* young. He *m.* secondly, Mary, daughter of William Hitchcock, esq. of Knitely, in the county of Bucks, by whom he had

- FRANCIS, who *m.* Frances, daughter and sole heir of Alexander Jermin, esq. of Cordington, in Sussex, and left, at his decease in his father's lifetime,
  - RICHARD, successor to his grandfather.
  - Henry, twin with his elder brother, *d.* unm. 8th June, 1734.
  - Francis.
  - Catherine, Anne, Dorothy, Mary, } *d.* unm.
- William, *m.* Anne, daughter of Henry Wells, esq. of Brambridge, Hants.

He *d.* about 1690, and was *s.* by his grandson,

III. SIR RICHARD MOORE, who *m.* Anastasia, daughter and co-heir * of John Aylward, esq. of London, and had eight sons and six daughters, viz.

- I. Francis, *d.* an infant.
- II. RICHARD, his successor.
- III. JOHN, heir to his brother.
- IV. Francis, *d.* young.
- V. James, } *d. s. p.*
- VI. Henry, } *d. s. p.*
- VII. THOMAS, heir to his brother John.
- VIII. William.

- I. Frances, *m.* to Richard Harcourt, of Lon[illegible] merchant, and *d. s. p.*
- II. Mary.
- III. Helena.
- IV. Anastasia.
- V. Elizabeth.
- VI. Anne.

He *d.* 10th December, 1737, and was *s.* by his eldest surviving son,

IV. SIR RICHARD MOORE, who *d.* unm. 12th [illegible] 1738, and was *s.* by his brother,

V. SIR JOHN MOORE, who sold the manor of Fa[illegible] in 1765, to the Vansittarts, from whom it was purchased in 1778, by Bartholomew Tipping, esq. [illegible] niece and heir, Mary-Anne, *m.* the Rev. Philip [illegible]ton. Sir John *d. s. p.* 25th August, 1790, and was *s.* by his brother,

VI. SIR THOMAS MOORE, who *d.* issueless [illegible] 1807, when the BARONETCY EXPIRED.

Arms—Argent, a moor cock, sable, combed and wattled, gules.

MOORE, OF JAMAICA.

CREATED 28th Jan. 1764.—EXTINCT 16th Jan. [illegible]

Lineage.

JOHN MOORE, settled in the reign of CHARLES [illegible] at Barbadoes, and was possessed of considerable property in that island, with which he removed to Jamaica, and fixing there, married Elizabeth, daughter of Colonel Smart, and had two sons and two daughters. The elder son, John, died without issue. The younger,

SAMUEL MOORE, esq. *m.* Elizabeth Lowe, sister and co-heir of Samuel Lowe, esq. of Goadby, in the county of Leicester, and left an only surviving son and heir,

I. HENRY MOORE, esq. who was constituted lieutenant-governor of Jamaica, and was commander-in-chief there for several years. On his return he was created a BARONET 28th January, 1764, and in [illegible] July of the following year, appointed governor of the province of New York, where he resided until [his] death. Sir Henry *m.* Catharina-Maria, eldest dau[ghter] [illegible]

* MARY AYLWARD, the other co-heir, *m.* Charles Howard, son of the Honourable Charles Howard, son of Henry Frederick, Earl of Arundel, and was mother of Charles, tenth Duke of Norfolk.

…er of Samuel Long, esq. of Longville, in the island of Jamaica, and had issue,

JOHN-HENRY, his heir.
Susanna-Jane.

He d. 11th September, 1769, and was s. by his son,

II. SIR JOHN-HENRY MOORE, who died without issue, 6th January, 1780, when the BARONETCY became EXTINCT.

MOORE.

CREATED …th March, 1766. EXTINCT 2nd Feb. 1779.

Lineage.

HENRY, third EARL OF DROGHEDA, who m. in 1675, …ary, daughter of Sir John Cole, bart. of Newland, near Dublin, died in 1714, leaving with other issue,

CHARLES, Lord Moore, who died v. p. in 1714, leaving two sons,

HENRY, fourth Earl of Drogheda, who d. s. p.
EDWARD, fifth Earl of Drogheda, ancestor of the present peer.

Arthur, d. s. p.
HENRY, of whom we have to treat.
John, d. in 1716.
William, of Moor Hall, in the county of Louth.
Robert, } who both married.
Capel, }

…e third son,

THE HON. AND REV. HENRY MOORE, rector of Mal…s, in Cheshire, m. Catherine, daughter of Sir Thomas …atchbull, bart. of Mersham Hatch, in Kent, and …dow of Sir George Rooke, vice-admiral of England, …d had issue,

THOMAS, D.D. who m. Elizabeth, daughter and co-heir of Sir Thomas Hare, bart. and d. s. p.
JOHN, of whom presently.
Mary, m. to Poulter Forrester, D.D. prebendary of St. Paul's, and archdeacon of Lincoln. She died s. p. in 1789.

… younger son,

I. SIR JOHN MOORE, K.B. rear-admiral of the Red, … created a BARONET 4th March, 1766. He m. Pe…lope, daughter of William Matthew, captain-general and governor-in-chief of the Leeward Islands, and … four daughters,

CATHERINE, m. to Sir Charles Warwick Bampfylde, bart.
PENELOPE, m. to Ralph, second son of Ralph Sneyd, esq. of Keel.
ANNE.
…LIA-MARIA.

… John Moore died without male issue in 1779, …en the BARONETCY became EXTINCT.

…rms—Az. on a chief indented or, three mullets …ed gu.

MORDEN, OF WRICKLESMARSH.

CREATED 20th Sept. 1688. EXTINCT 6th Sept. 1708.

Lineage.

I. SIR JOHN MORDEN, of Wricklesmarsh, in Kent, amassed a large fortune at Aleppo, as a Turkey merchant, and was created a BARONET in 1688. He m. Susan, daughter of Joseph Brand, esq. of Edwardstone, in Suffolk, but died s. p. in 1708, when the title EXPIRED. Several years previous to his death, he erected, at Blackheath, a college, not far from his own residence, for the support of decayed merchants, for whose relief there had previously existed no institution of the kind; and by his will endowed it with an estate to the value of £1300 a year. The pensioners have coals, candles, and medical attendance provided for them, and a small annuity allowed. After Lady Morden's decease in 1721, the manor of Wricklesmarsh was sold to Sir Gregory Page, bart. of Greenwich, and from his eventual heir, Sir Gregory Turner Page, bart. it was purchased by John Cator, esq. of Beckenham.

Arms—Arg. a fleur-de-lis gu.

MORE, OF MORE HALL.

CREATED 22nd Nov. 1675. EXTINCT 21st May, 1810.

Lineage.

The family of MORE, or DE LA MORE, was in possession of More Hall, and Bank Hall, both in the county palatine of Lancaster, for a long series of generations. Amongst its members was

SIR WILLIAM DE LA MORE, who was made a knight banneret by EDWARD the Black Prince, at the battle of Poictiers. He was a very considerable man in that time, and wrote the life and death of EDWARD II. and EDWARD III. which is used by Barnes and other historians of those periods.

SIR JOHN DE LA MORE, was member for Cumberland 6th of HENRY IV. His descendant,

JOHN MORE, esq. of Bank Hall, m. Eleanor, youngest daughter of Sir Richard Molineux, knt. of Sephton, in Lancashire, and from this marriage lineally derived,

COL. JOHN MORE, of More Hall, who defended Liverpool against CHARLES I. He married a daughter of Rigby, and left a son and heir,

I. EDWARD MORE, esq. of More Hall, who was to

have been created a Baronet in the year 1660, but the *Recepi* was not signed until March 1, 1661-2, nor the patent finally passed, under the great seal, before 22nd November, 1675. Sir Edward *m.* first, a daughter of Sir William Fenwick, of Meldon, in Northumberland, and by that lady had Cleave, his successor, and Thomas, who *d. s. p.* He *m.* secondly, a daughter of Sir Thomas Bloodworth, and had a daughter Matilda, the wife of Thomas Whitloe, gent. of Bootle, in Lancashire. He was *s.* by his son,

II. Sir Cleave More, M.P. for Bramber in 1708, *m.* Anne, daughter and heir of Joseph Edmonds, esq. of Cumberlow, in Hertfordshire, and dying 23rd March, 1729-30, was *s.* by his only son,

III. Sir Joseph-Edmonds More, who *m.* a daughter of — Newnam, esq. of Lincoln's Inn Fields, and had issue,

Joseph-Edmonds, his successor.
Cleave, *m.* in July, 1741, Miss Storer.
Thomas.

Anne, *m.* in 1734, to Henry Popple, esq. under treasurer to *Queen* Caroline.
Sophia, *m.* in March, 1740-1, to Mr. John Beck, of Watford, in Hertfordshire.

He *d.* 29th March, 1741, and was *s.* by his eldest son,

IV. Sir Joseph-Edmonds More, who *m.* in 1736, Henrietta-Maria, daughter of William Morris, esq. of Farnam, near Faringdon, in the county of Berks, and dying 29th March, 1741, was *s.* by his only son,

V. Sir William More. This gentleman left an only daughter and heir,

Elizabeth, *m.* in 1795, to Charles Browning, esq. of Horton Lodge, Surrey.

Sir William *d.* 21st May, 1810, when the Baronetcy expired.

Arms—Quarterly; first and fourth, argent, three greyhounds courant, in pale, sable, collared, or; second and third, argent, ten trefoils, slipped; 4, 3, 2, 1, vert.

MORE, OF LOSELEY.

Created 18th May, 1612. Extinct 24th July, 1684.

Lineage.

The Mores of Loseley, in Surrey, came originally from Derbyshire.

Sir Christopher More, knt. king's remembrancer in the Exchequer, who purchased the manor of Loseley, was sheriff of Surrey and Sussex in the 24th and 31st of Henry VIII. He *m.* first, Margaret, daughter and heir of Walter Mudge, esq. and secondly, Constance, daughter of Richard Sackville, esq. of Buckhurst. By the latter, who wedded, secondly, William Heneage, he had no issue, but by the former he had a numerous family, viz.

William, his heir.

Margaret, *m.* to Thomas Fiennes, brother of the Lord Dacre.
Elizabeth, *m.* to John Wintershull, of Wintershull.
Ann, *m.* to John Scarlett.
Bridget, *m.* to Compton, of the Isle of Guernsey.
Eleanor, *m.* to William Heneage, of Milton.

Sir Christopher died 10th August, 1549, and was [illegible] his son,

Sir William More, of Loseley, *b.* 30th January, 1519-20, M.P. for Guildford, and subsequently for Surrey, who received the honour of knighthood from the Earl of Leicester, in Lord Lincoln's garden, at [illegible] the Queen being present. He *m.* first, Margaret, daughter and co-heir of Ralph Daniel, esq. of Swaffham, Norfolk, and secondly, Mabel, daughter of [illegible] Dingley, esq. of Wolverton, in the Isle of Wight. [illegible] had issue only by the first, viz.

George, his heir.

Elizabeth, *m.* first to Richard Polsted, esq. of Albury, in Surrey, secondly to Sir John Wolley, knt. of Pirford, and thirdly, to Sir Thomas Egerton, afterwards Lord Ellesmere.
Anne, *m.* to Sir George Manwaring, knt. of Ightfield, in Shropshire.

Sir William died 20th July, 1600, and was *s.* by his son,

Sir George More, knt. of Loseley, *b.* 28th November, 1553, sheriff of Surrey and Sussex in 15[illegible], had a grant from the crown, 42 Elizabeth, of the lordship and hundred of Godalming. In the beginning of the next reign, he was appointed treasurer to Henry, Prince of Wales, and in 1606, had the honour of entertaining the king at Loseley. In 16[illegible] his majesty conferred on him the chancellorship of the garter, and in 1615, appointed him lieutenant of the Tower of London, in the room of Sir Gervase Elwes. Sir George More represented Guildford, and afterwards the county of Surrey, in several parliaments. He *m.* Ann, daughter and co-heir of Sir Adrian [illegible]ings, knt. and widow of — Knight, esq. of St. [illegible] Hants, by whom (who died 19th November, [illegible]) he had issue,

I. Robert, his heir.
II. William, *b.* 1585.
III. George, *b.* 1587.
IV. John, *b.* 1589.

I. Mary, *b.* in 1582, *m.* 17th January, [illegible] Sir Nicholas Throckmorton Carew, knt. of Bedington, in Surrey.
II. Margaret, *b.* 1583, *m.* to Thomas Grymes, [illegible]
III. Anne, *b.* 1584, *m.* in 1602, to John Donne, afterwards dean of St. Pauls.
IV. Elizabeth, *b.* in 1586, *m.* to John [illegible] (afterwards Sir John, bart.), of C[illegible]
V. Frances, *b.* in 1590, *m.* to Sir John Oglander, knt. of Nunwell.

Sir George died 16th October, 1632. His eldest son,

Sir Robert More, knt. of Loseley, *b.* 21st [illegible] 1581, M.P. for Surrey, who *m.* Frances, daughter of Samson Lennard, esq. by Margaret, his wife, Baroness Dacre, and had (with other issue who *d. s. p.*)

Poynings, his heir.
Nicholas, rector of Fecham, in Surrey, who m. Susan, daughter of Richard Saunders, and [illegible] 22nd December, 1684, left issue,

Robert, of Loseley, who died *s. p.* in 16[illegible]
Elizabeth, *d.* unm. 13th February, 16[illegible]
Margaret, eventual heiress of Loseley, who *m.* Sir Thomas Molyneux, knt. and [illegible] 14th September, 1704, leaving with daughters, a son and heir,

Sir More Molyneux, knt. of Loseley [illegible]

who m. 1st March, 1721-2, Cassandra, sister and co-heir of Francis Cornwallis, esq. of Abermarles, in Caermarthenshire, and had issue.

Robert, major in the army, whose daughter Frances, m. John Latton, esq. of Esher Place, Surrey.

Anne, m. to James Gresham, esq.

Sir Robert died 2nd February, 1725-6, and was s. by his son,

I. Sir Poynings More, knt. of Loseley, M.P. for Haslemere, and also for Guildford, who was created a Baronet 18th May, 1642. He m. Elizabeth, daughter of Sir William Fytche, knt. of Canfield Hall and Woodham Walters, in Essex, and by her, who wedded, secondly, Christopher Rous, esq. of Suffolk, and d. in 1666, he left, at his decease, 11th April, 1649, a son and successor,

II. Sir William More, of Loseley, M.P. for Haslemere, and sheriff of Surrey 21 Charles II. He m. Mary, daughter and heir of Sir Walter Hendley, bart. of Cuckfield, in Sussex, but died without issue 24th July, 1684, in the forty-first year of his age, when the Baronetcy became extinct. The estates reverted to Sir William's uncle, the Rev. Nicholas More, and were conveyed, in marriage, by his daughter and eventual heiress, Margaret, to the family of Molyneux.

Arms—Az. on a cross arg. five martlets sa.

MORGAN, OF LLANGATTOCK.

Created 1st Feb. 1660-1.

Extinct 29th April, 1767.

Lineage.

Bledrin ap Cadivor Vaur, lord of Elvest, who is reputed to have borne for his arms, "Arg. three bulls' heads caboshed sa. armed or," died in 1119, and was buried at Llangattock, in Monmouthshire. He m. Clydwen, daughter of Gryffyd ap Cydrich, and was ancestor of the Morgans of Tredegar, and Llantarnam and of Lewis Morgan, esq. of Llangattock, whose son and heir,

I. Thomas Morgan, esq. of Llangattock, in the county of Monmouth, who was created a Baronet 1st February, 1660-1, for his great zeal in promoting the Restoration. He had distinguished himself, when Colonel Morgan, as one of the most successful parliamentary leaders in the west of England; during the Protectorate he was promoted to the rank of major-general, and commanded the British auxiliary force which gained the battle of Dunkirk against the Spaniards. He became subsequently general of horse under Monk, and so high in the confidence of his commander, that Monk declared, the November preceding the return of the king, "that the presence and usefulness of Major-General Morgan, in Scotland, was so serviceable to him, that he looked upon his single person as a counterpoise to those hundred and fifty officers who had left the service or had been cashiered." He was subsequently appointed by the King, at the especial recommendation of Monk, then Earl of Albemarle, governor of Jersey, whilst his brother, Sir Henry Morgan (far better known as Captain Morgan, *the Buccaneer*), was made governor of Jamaica. Sir Thomas Morgan is mentioned at great length by Falle, in the introduction to his History of Jersey, who thus concludes: "Of this brave man, I shall only add, in commendation of his great vigilance, and care of his charge, that he never allowed himself to be long absent from it, and would sit whole days on the carriage of a cannon, hastening and encouraging the workmen employed in the new fortifications of Elizabeth Castle, which were carried on under his order and inspection. Though he fell not in battle, he may be said to have died in the bed of honour, by dying on his post, i.e. in the island, after he had put it in a better state of defence, and every way on a better military foot than it ever had been before." Sir Thomas m. De la Riviere, daughter and eventual heiress of Richard Cholmondley, esq. of Brame Hall, in the county of York, and dying 13th April, 1679, aged seventy-three, was s. by his eldest son,

II. Sir John Morgan, of Kinnersley Castle, M.P. for the county of Hereford, *temp.* Charles II. governor of Chester, and colonel of the Welsh Fusileers. He m. Hester, daughter and co-heir of James Price, esq. of Pilleth, in the county of Radnor, and had issue,

Thomas, his heir.

Hester, m. to John Walsham, esq. of Knill Court, in the county of Hereford, and left issue. Her representative is the present Sir John James Walsham, bart. of Knill Court.

Delarivière, d. unm.

Annabetta, m. to Thomas Clutton, esq. of Pensax, in Worcestershire, and left issue.

Sir John was s. at his decease by his only son,

III. Sir Thomas Morgan, of Kinnersley Castle, M.P. for Herefordshire, *temp.* Queen Anne, m. Anne, only child of John Roydhouse, esq. of St. Martin's-in-the-Fields, Middlesex, and dying 14th December, 1716, was s. by his only child,

IV. Sir John Morgan, M.P. for the city of Hereford, who m. Miss Jacobsen, daughter of Sir Jacob Jacobsen, but died issueless, 29th April, 1767, when the Baronetcy expired. The chief estate, that of Kinnersley Castle, was entailed on various relations of the last baronet, and became eventually the property of Colonel Clutton, of Pensax, by whom it was sold.

Arms—Arg. three bulls' heads caboshed sa.

MORGAN, OF LLANTARNAM.

Created 12th May, 1642.

Extinct in 1681.

Lineage.

Llewellin ap Ivor, lord of St. Clere, lineally descended from Kidiver Vawr, lord of Kilsaint, married Angharad, daughter and heir of Sir Morgan Meredith, knt. lord of Tredegar, and was father of

Morgan ap Llewellin, lord of St. Clere and Tredegar, who m. Maud, daughter of Rhys ap Gronwy, lord of Kybor, and had two sons, viz.

Llewellyn, of Tredegar, ancestor of the Morgans of Tredegar.

Philip.

The second son,

PHILIP MORGAN, esq. of Langston, acquired that estate in marriage with the daughter and heir of Sir John Norris, knt. of Penlline Castle. He was direct ancestor* of

WILLIAM MORGAN, esq. sheriff for Monmouthshire in 1567, and M.P. in 1571, who was the first proprietor of Llantarnam. He m. Elizabeth, daughter of Sir Rees Mansel, knt. of Margam, and was s. by his son,

EDWARD MORGAN, esq. of Llantarnam and Penrice, M.P. for Monmouthshire in 1586, who m. Elizabeth, daughter and heir of Hugh Smith, esq. of Long Ashton, in Somersetshire, and had a son and successor,

WILLIAM MORGAN, esq. of Llantarnam, who m. the Lady Frances Somerset, daughter of Edward, Earl of Worcester, and was father of

I. SIR EDWARD MORGAN, of Llantarnam, who was created a BARONET in 1642. He m. Mary, daughter of Sir Francis Englefield, bart. of Wotton Basset, in Wiltshire, and was s. at his decease, 24th June, 1653, by his son,

II. SIR EDWARD MORGAN, of Llantarnam, living in 1661, who m. Frances, daughter of Thomas Morgan, esq. of Mangham, and was s. by his son,

III. SIR EDWARD MORGAN, of Llantarnam, who m. for his second wife, Mary, daughter of Humphrey Baskerville, esq. of Pontrilas, in the county of Hereford, and by that lady, who wedded, secondly, John Grubham Howe, esq. father of the first Lord Chedworth, had two daughters,

ANNE, who died unm. bequeathing her moiety of the inheritance to John Howe, esq. who had married her mother, Lady Morgan.

FRANCES, m. Edmund Bray, esq. eldest son of Sir Edmund Reginald Bray, of Barrington Park, Gloucestershire, and had issue,

REGINALD MORGAN BRAY, died unmarried 6th April, 1741.

MARY BRAY, who wedded John Blewitt, esq. of London, and dying in 1756, had issue,

EDMUND BLEWITT, esq. d. unm.

EDWARD BLEWITT, esq. who m. Miss Courcy, and by her, who wedded secondly, John Macnamara, esq. left at his decease in 1766, two sons, JOHN, who d. s. p. and

EDWARD BLEWITT, esq. who m. in 1796, Amelia, daughter and co-heir of James Duberley, esq. of Ensham Hall, Oxfordshire, and had issue,

EDWARD BLEWITT, esq.

REGINALD-JAMES BLEWITT, esq. of Llantarnam Abbey, M.P. for the Monmouthshire boroughs.

Edmund Blewitt, b. in January 1800; d. in 1831, leaving by Mary Prothero, his wife, an only daughter, Amelia Rees.

Frances-Mary-Ann Blewitt, m. to Richard Brinsley Dowling, esq. barrister-at-law, and has an only daughter, Florence-Blewitt.

Reginald, d. unm. 1761.

Frances Blewitt, m. to Joseph Newton, esq. and had a daughter, Mary, now living.

Catharine Blewitt, m. to William Dunham, esq. of Mangersbury, in Gloucestershire, and had a daughter Catharine, who m. Col. Kingsmill Evans, and was mother of the present KINGSMILL EVANS, esq. of the Hill Court, Herefordshire. (See BURKE's *Commoners*, vol. ii. p. 20.)

FRANCES BRAY, who m. Thomas Fettyplace, esq. and had issue, Frances, wife of Richard Gorges, esq. of the Eye, Herefordshire; Mary, m. first, to B. Shaw, esq. and secondly, to William Kemeys, esq.; and Arabella, m. to John Webb, esq. father of the present Colonel Webb, of Adwell.

Sir Edward died in 1681, at an early age, when, at the death of his uncle James, who is said to have succeeded to the title, the BARONETCY became EXTINCT.

Arms—Arg. a griffin segreant sa.

MORICE, OF WERRINGTON.

CREATED 20th April, 1661. EXTINCT 27th Jan. [illegible]

Lineage.

IEVAN MORICE,† fellow of All Soul's College, Oxford, doctor of laws and chancellor of Exeter, [illegible] the descendant of an ancient Welsh family, m. [illegible] daughter of John Castle, of Ashbury, in Devon, and left a son and heir,

SIR WILLIAM MORICE, knt. who was born [illegible] parish of St. Martin, in the city of Exeter, m. [illegible]

---

* The intervening descent was as follows:

Philip Morgan, esq. of Langston = Gwenllian, daughter and heir of Sir John Norris, of Penlline Castle, Glamorganshire.

Jenkin ap Philip, of Langston = Cicely, daughter of Sir John Welsh, knt.

Morgan ap Jenkin,‡ of Langston = Elizabeth, daughter of Sir Roger Vaughan.

Sir Thomas Morgan, knt. of Pencoed = Joan, daughter and heir of John Gwillim Herbert, of [illegible]

John Morgan, esq. of Caerleon, second son = Ely, daughter of Lewes ap Richard Gwynn, esq. of the [illegible]

William Morgan, first of Llantarnam.

† The MORRICES of Betshanger, in Kent, descend from Captain William Morys, eldest brother of [illegible] ancestor of the Werrington family. (See BURKE's *Commoners*, vol. iii. p. 232.)

‡ By his third wife, Morgan ap Jenkin had a son, John Morgan, esq. of Tredunnock, in Monmouthshire, ancestor of the MORGANS of TREDUNNOCK, now represented by Mrs. JANE HAWKINS.

MOR

vember, 1662. "His father, Dr. Morice, dying an. 1665, left this his son, not full four years old, and a widow, very rich, who became the third wife of Sir Nicholas Prideaux, of Soulden, in the parish of Holdsworthy, a pretty market town lying near the borders of Cornwall." Lady Prideaux attended with great zeal to the education of her son, and under her guidance he became a person distinguished in his time for learning and accomplishments. He resided with her at Churston, in West Putford, a small parish to the west of Bytheford, where he most sedulously followed his studies, and her ladyship, until her decease in October, 1647, had the entire direction of his affairs. Soon after his return home, he was married to one of the grandaughters of his step-father. In 1645, he was elected to the Long Parliament, by the county of Devon, without solicitation on his part, but did not take his seat. In 1651, he was appointed sheriff for Devonshire, having the year before settled at Werrington, in that county, which he had purchased from Sir Francis Drake, and being an intimate friend of General Monk's, was subsequently employed in the restoration* of the exiled monarch. In March, 1759, through the influence of Monk, he was made colonel of foot, and constituted governor of Plymouth, and he attended the general to Dover, in 1660, to receive the restored monarch, when he received the honour of knighthood, and at Canterbury was sworn one of the principal secretaries of state, and of his majesty's privy council. He held the seals of office until 1668, when he resigned, and retired into private life. He m. as stated above, Elizabeth, dau. of Humphrey Prideaux, esq. of Soulden, in Devonshire, and had issue,

William (Sir), his heir.

John, a Turkey merchant, father of

John Morice, esq. M.P. for Cornwall, *temp.* George I. who m. Elizabeth, daughter of Sir Jeffry Jeffreys, knt. alderman of London, and died 13th February, 1734-5. He had one son and five daughters, of which all were dead in 1741, except one daughter, the wife of Jeffry Jeffreys, esq. of the Priory.

Humphrey, a Hamburgh merchant, who *m.* a daughter of — Trollope, esq. of Lincolnshire, and had a son,

Humphrey Morice, M.P. for Grampound, and sub-governor of the Bank, *temp.* George I. and George II.

Nicholas, *d.* unm.

Thomasine, *m.* to Sir Walter Moyle, knt. of Bake, in Cornwall.

Gertrude, *m.* to Sir Robert Cotton, knt. of Hatley St. George, in Cambridgeshire, and had a daughter,

Alice Cotton, *m.* to Samuel Trefusis, esq. of Trefusis.

Elizabeth.

Anne, *m.* to Sir John Pole, bart. of Shute.

Sir William *d.* 12th December, 1676, and was *s.* by his eldest son,

Sir William Morice, bart. of Werrington, who had been a Baronet so created by *King* Charles II. 20th April, 1661. This gentleman *m.* first, Gertrude, daughter of Sir John Bampfylde, bart. of Poltimore, and by that lady had issue,

William, *m.* Anne, daughter and co-heir of Richard Lower, M.D. and *d.* in his father's lifetime, *s. p.*

Mary, *m.* to Sir John Carew, bart. of Anthony, in Cornwall.

Gertrude, *m.* to Sir Walter Young, bart. of Culliton, in Devonshire.

He *m.* secondly, a daughter of Richard Reynell, esq. of Ogwell, in Devonshire, by whom (who *d.* before her husband) he had an only son, his successor at his decease, about the year 1690,

II. Sir Nicholas Morice, M.P. for Newport, *temp. Queen* Anne, *King* George I. and *King* George II. *m.* Lady Catherine Herbert, eldest daughter of Thomas, Earl of Pembroke, and by her ladyship, who *d.* in 1710, had issue,

William, his successor.

Catherine, *m.* in 1725, to Sir John St. Aubyn, bart. and *d.* 16th June, 1740, leaving issue,

John St. Aubyn, who *s.* his father, and was fourth baronet.

Barbara St. Aubyn, *m.* to Sir John Molesworth, bart. M.P. for Cornwall.

Barbara, *m.* in 1728, to Sir John Molesworth, bart. of Pencarrow, and died 17th May, 1735, leaving a son,

Sir John Molesworth, M.P. who *m.* his cousin, Barbara St. Aubyn.

He *d.* 27th January, 1725-6, and was *s.* by his son,

III. Sir William Morice, M.P. for Newport, and afterwards for Launceston, *m.* first in September, 1731, Lady Lucy Wharton, daughter of Thomas, Marquess of Wharton. Her ladyship died 2nd February, 1738-9. Sir William *m.* secondly, Anne, daughter of Thomas Bury, esq. of Bury-narber, in Devonshire, but had no issue. He *d.* 24th January, 1750, when the Baronetcy expired, while his large estates devolved upon the families of St. Aubyn and Molesworth. Werrington is now, by purchase, the property of the Duke of Northumberland.

Arms—Gules, a lion rampant, regardant, or.

MORLAND, OF SULHAMSTEAD BANISTER.

Created 18th July, 1660.—Extinct in Nov. 1716.

Lineage.

I. Samuel Morland, a man of considerable celebrity at the period in which he lived, was son of the Rev. Thomas Morland, rector of Sulhamstead, in Berkshire, and born about 1625, as we learn from one of his works, dated 1695, wherein he says he had then passed the seventieth year of his age. He received his education at Winchester school, and Magdalen College, Cambridge. In 1653, he went to Sweden, in the famous embassy of Bulstrode Whitelock, and became subsequently assistant to secretary Thurloe. In a few months after he was sent by Cromwell to the Duke of Savoy, to remonstrate against the persecution of the Waldenses, and published on his return, a "History of the Evangelical Churches of the Valley Piedmont." As an ingenious mechanic, however, the

* "This Sir William was one of the chief instruments [of] the Restoration, for though General Monk had the [pow]er to execute, yet Sir William's head conducted that [a]ffair. Indeed the publishers of Lord Clarendon's [History], have tacitly, though unjustly deprived him of the [share] he had in that memorable scene, and have accumu[lated] honours on another western family that were only [...] in. For proof of his merit in that transaction, nothing can be stronger than the king's giving him the seals at Canterbury, on his return to London, so great and speedy an honour, could only be the reward of the greatest services, and which both the king and Lord Clarendon, had before equally acknowledged by letters under their own hands from Breda."

See the Letters in Thurloe's Collection.

reputation of Sir Samuel Morland stands highest, and amongst his inventions are enumerated the speaking trumpet, the fire engine, a capstan for heaving anchors, and the STEAM ENGINE: others claim this great discovery, but the proofs in favour of Morland are extremely convincing.

In 1675, Sir Samuel (who had been created a BARONET in 1660,) obtained a lease of Vauxhall House, made it his residence, and considerably improved the premises, every part of which showed the inventive genius of the proprietor; the side table in the dining room was supplied with a large fountain, and the glasses stood under little streams of water. His coach had a movable kitchen with clockwork machinery, with which he could make soup, broil steaks, or roast a joint of meat. About 1684, he purchased a house at Hammersmith, near the waterside, and all his letters we have seen in the Lambeth Library, or British Museum, are thence dated. He gave a pump and well, adjoining to his house, for the use of the public, which benefaction was thus recorded upon a tablet fixed in the wall: "Sir Samuel Morland's well, the use of which he freely gives to all persons, hoping that none who shall come after him, will adventure to incur God's displeasure, by denying a cup of cold water (provided at another's cost and not their own) to either neighbour, stranger, passenger, or poor thirsty beggar, July 8, 1695." This pump has been removed, but the stone tablet was preserved in the garden of the house, afterwards known by the name of Walbrough House.

Sir Samuel married four wives; the first was a French lady, Susanne de Milleville, daughter of Daniel de Milleville, Baron of Boessey; the second, Carola, daughter of Sir Roger Harsnet, knt.; and the third, Anne, daughter of George Feilding, esq. After her death, he was entrapped into a fourth marriage, with a woman who pretended to be an heiress of £20,000. This, he himself stated, proved his ruin. Of abandoned character, she probably impaired his property by extravagance, and though he obtained a divorce from her in 1688, the rest of his history is but a melancholy detail of disappointments and distress. In 1689, he wrote a long letter to Archbishop Tenison, giving an account of his life, and concluding with a declaration that his only wish was to retire and spend his life in "Christian solitude," for which he begs the archbishop's "helping hand to have his condition truly represented to his majesty." He died in January, 1696, and was *s.* by his son,

II. SIR SAMUEL MORLAND, at whose decease *s. p.* in November, 1716, the BARONETCY became EXTINCT.

MORRISON, OF CASHIOBURY.

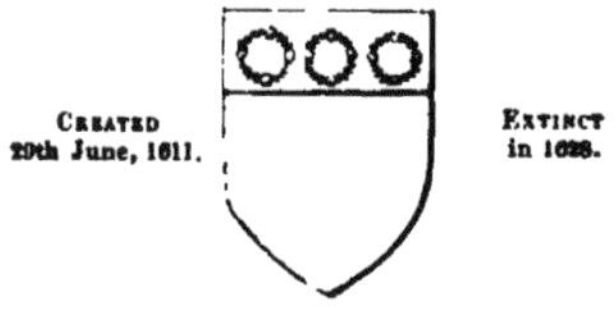

CREATED 29th June, 1611. EXTINCT in 1628.

Lineage.

WILLIAM MORTSINE, or MORISON, of this family, possessed lands at Chardwell, in the county of York, about the reign of HENRY VI. which descended to his son, of his own name,

WILLIAM MORTSINE, or MORISON, who *m.* Elizabeth, daughter of Roger Lee, of Preston, in Yorkshire, and had a son and heir,

THOMAS MORTSINE, of Chardwell, and afterwards of the county of Hertford, who marrying a daughter of Thomas Merry, of Hatfield, in that county, had, with a daughter, the wife of Stephen Hales, of Coventry, two sons, viz.

RICHARD (Sir), his heir.

Fines, fellow of Peter House, in Oxford, who after taking a master's degree, and studying the civil law, obtained a license in 1589, at the age of twenty-three, of the master and fellows of the house to travel, and leaving the university he embarked in 1591, and spent the following seven years abroad; returning in 1598, he became secretary to Sir Charles Blount, lord deputy of Ireland. He died in 1614, and his travels were published in 1617, (London) entitled "An Itinerary, containing ten years travels through the twelve dominions of Germany, Bohmerland, Switzerland, Netherland, Denmark, Poland, England, Scotland, and Ireland, divided into three parts."

The elder son,

SIR RICHARD MORTSINE, or MORISON, spent, with his brother, several years in the university of Oxford, took a degree in arts, afterwards travelled, and became distinguished amongst the most accomplished men of his time. In 1537, he was a prebendary of Yetminster Secunda, in the church of Salisbury, and being at length recommended to HENRY VIII. as a person of worth and ability, he was accredited ambassador to the Emperor Charles V. as he was again, by Edward VI. He received the honour of knighthood in [illegible], and died at Strasburgh, 17th March, 1556. Sir Richard was the author of many works, was esteemed a learned man, encouraged learning, and was liberal to several scholars of note. He realised by his own exertions a fair estate, comprising the manor of Whitesbury, or Whichbury, in Wilts and Hants; the manor of East Chinolk, in Somersetshire; and the manor Cashiobury, where he had commenced the erection of a mansion house. He *m.* Bridget, eldest daughter of John, Lord Hussey, of Sleford,* and by that lady (who *m.* secondly, Henry, Earl of Rutland, and thirdly, Francis, Earl of Bedford,) had issue,

CHARLES (Sir), his heir.

Elizabeth, *m.* first, to William, eldest son of Henry, Lord Norreys; and secondly, to Henry Clinton, Earl of Lincoln.

Mary, *m.* to Bartholomew Hales, esq. of Chesfield.

Jane-Sibilla, *m.* first to Edward, Lord Russel, son of the second Earl of Bedford. His lordship d. in the lifetime of his father issueless, and her ladyship *m.* secondly, Arthur, Lord Grey of Wilton.

Sir Richard was *s.* by his son,

SIR CHARLES MORRISON, of Cashiobury, in the county of Hertford, who received the honour of knighthood from *Queen* ELIZABETH. This gentleman finished the mansion at Cashiobury, a stately structure in the midst of a park, with beautiful gardens and fine walks. He *m.* Dorothea, daughter of Nicholas Clarke, esq. and had issue,

CHARLES (Sir), his heir.

Bridget, *m.* to Robert Ratcliffe, sixth Earl of Sussex. (Refer to BURKE's *Extinct Peerage.*)

* Beheaded and attainted in 1537.

Sir Charles *d.* in 1599, and was interred in Watford Church, on the south side of a chapel (in the chancel) which he had built, where a noble monument was erected to his memory. He was *s.* by his son,

II. SIR CHARLES MORRISON, who was made a Knight of the Bath at the coronation of *King* JAMES I. and created a BARONET 29th June, 1611. He *m.* the Hon. Mary Hicks,* daughter and co-heir of Baptist, Viscount Campden, and left an only surviving child,

ELIZABETH, who *m.* Arthur, Lord Capel, and was mother of

Arthur Capel, first EARL OF ESSEX.

Sir Charles *d.* in 1628, and was interred in Watford Church, where a sumptuous monument was raised to the memory of himself and his wife, with their effigies curiously wrought in marble thereon, as also the effigies of two sons, who died young, and of his daughter, the Lady Capel. The BARONETCY EXPIRED with Sir Charles, and his estates passed to the noble house of Capel. Cashiobury has ever since been the chief seat of the EARLS OF ESSEX.

Arms—Or, on a chief gules, three chaplets gold.

MORTON, OF MILBOURNE ST. ANDREW.

CREATED 26 Mar. 1618-9. EXTINCT in 1698.

Lineage.

The family of MORTON, derived its surname from Morton, (anciently written MARTON,) a hamlet, in the parish of Harworth, in the confines of Nottinghamshire, at the utmost boundary whereof, near to Bawtry Town, in Yorkshire, an hospital was founded by the Mortons, and a chapel wherein they were buried in consequence of which they were styled indifferently *Bautrey*, or *Morton*.

The first we meet with is

WILLIAM DE MORTON, whose son,

PETER DE MORTON, gave to the monks of Blithe, one toft of land in Marten, with all appurtenances, of timber in his wood, to make them lodging and for firing: as likewise a toft in the same town, and free multure in the mill thereunto belonging, on condition that they would receive him into their society "when God should give it into his heart." To Peter succeeded,

NICHOLAS DE MORTON, whose wife, Agnes having survived him, did fealty in her widowhood to the prior of Blythe the Friday next after the Ascension of our Lord, 1289, in the name of ROGER, her son, then under age, for two bovats of land in Marton, which the said Roger claimed to hold of the said prior, and acknowledging to owe 4*s.* per annum, and gave for relief eight shillings. The said,

ROGER DE MARTON, was father of

THOMAS DE MARTON, whose son, and heir,

SIR ROBERT DE MORTON, knt. of Bautre, served in parliament for the county of Nottingham, in the 35th 39th 40th and 43rd of EDWARD III. in the last mentioned year he is called a knight, and in seven years afterwards he was constituted escheator of the counties of Nottingham and Derby, as he was again in the 1st of RICHARD II. He was returned to parliament twice subsequently for Nottinghamshire, in the 3rd and 17th of the last named king. Sir Robert was *s.* by his son,

CHARLES MORTON, of Morton, who had two sons, viz.

ROBERT, from whom after six generations, descended

ANTHONY MORTON, esq. of Morton, who wasted the estate in the reign of ELIZABETH, and his son,

ROBERT MORETON, sold Harewerth to Mr. William Saunderson,

WILLIAM.

The younger son,

WILLIAM MORETON, esq. settled at Milbourne St. Andrew, in the county of Dorset, and had two sons,

RICHARD, his heir.

William, of Cerne, in Dorsetshire, M.P. for Shaftsbury, *temp.* HENRY VI. as was his grandson,

Robert, in the 17th of EDWARD IV. from him descended the Mortons, of London, whereof

SIR ALBERT MORTON, was secretary of state, *temp.* JAMES I.

The elder son and heir,

RICHARD MORETON, esq. of Milbourne St. Andrew, *temp.* HENRY VI. was father of five sons, viz.

I. JOHN the celebrated CARDINAL MORTON, archbishop of Canterbury, and lord chancellor of England, *temp.* HENRY VII. of whom ANTHONY WOOD, states, "that he was a wise and eloquent man, but in his nature harsh and haughty—that he was much accepted by the King, but envy'd by the Nobility, and hated by the people. He won the King's mind with Secrecy and Diligence, chiefly because he was his old servant in his less fortunes, and for that also he was in his affections, not without an inveterate Malice against the House of York, under which he had been in trouble." This eminent man died at the advanced age of ninety, in September, 1500, and was buried in the Cathedral Church, at Canterbury.

II. Thomas, archdeacon of Ely.

III. RICHARD.

IV. William, who had a son Thomas.

V. Rowland (Sir), of Thwining, in Gloucestershire, from whom the Moretons of Herefordshire descended. He had issue,

Robert, bishop of Worcester, 3rd HENRY VII. elected.

Thomas, of Lechlade, in the county of Gloucester, whose grandson,

Sir Anthony Morton, of the same place left two daughters, his co-heirs, Elizabeth, wife of Sir George West, and —, wife of Ralph Johnson, of London.

The third son,

RICHARD MORTON, esq. sheriff of Dorset and Somerset, 22 EDWARD IV. *m.* Elizabeth, daughter of Richard Turberville, of Bere Regis, in the county of Dorset, and by her, (who *m.* secondly, Coker, of Mapouder,) left a son,

JOHN MORTON, esq. of Sturminster Marshall, in the

* She *m.* secondly, Sir John Cooper, bart. of Wimbourne St. Giles; and thirdly, Sir Richard Alford, knt.

county of Dorset, who m. Lucy, daughter of Thomas Hussey, esq. and had issue,

THOMAS, his heir.

Isabel, m. to George Anketil, of Almer.
Elizabeth, a nun.
Lucy, m. first to Thomas Hody, of Stawel, and secondly to Thomas Francis, of Cranborne.
Frances, m. to William Hody, of Hamson.
Edith, m. first to — Smith, and secondly to Thomas Chimney.

He died in 1521, and was s. by his son,

THOMAS MORTON, esq. of Milbourne St. Andrew, who married Warbrugh, third daughter and co-heir of Sir George Delalind, and left,

I. GEORGE, his heir.
II. Thomas, ancestor of the Henbury line.

I. Lucy, m. to Thomas Mompesson, esq. of Little Bartington.
II. Cicely, m. to John Champneys, esq. of Orchardleigh, in Somersetshire.
III. Mary, m. to Augustin Laurence, of Sherford.
IV. Bridget, m. to Thomas Basket, of Divelish.
V. Margaret, m. to George Lovell.

He d. in 1591, and was s. by his son,

GEORGE MORTON, esq. who, by his wife, daughter of Francis, of Combe Flory, was father of

SIR GEORGE MORTON, of Milbourne, St. Andrew, who, with several others, received the honour of knighthood, at the Tower, 1603, preceding the coronation of *King* JAMES I. He m. Joan, daughter of — Holloway, of Walton, (some accounts make her wife to his father,) in Somersetshire, and had three sons, GEORGE, William, and John, with a daughter, Elena, m. to Thomas Hussey. Sir George was s. by his eldest son,

I. GEORGE MORTON, esq. of Melbourne St. Andrew, in the county of Dorset, who was created a BARONET 1st March, 1618-19, and represented the county in parliament 1 CHARLES I. during the trouble of whose reign he was a faithful royalist. Sir George m. Catharine, daughter of Sir Arthur Hopton, of Witham, in Somersetshire, and dying in 1661, was s. by his son,

II. SIR JOHN MORTON, of Milbourne St. Andrew, who married three wives. By the first, Eleanor, who died in 1671, he had an only daughter,

ANNE, who m. Edmund Pleydel, esq. of Midgehall, Wilts, M.P. for Wootton Bassett, and dying in 1726, left surviving issue,

EDMUND MORTON PLEYDELL, who m. Deborah, daughter of William Kuffen, esq. and died in March, 1754, leaving issue.
Nevile Morton Pleydell, of Shitterton, who m. Betty, daughter of Charles Brune, of Plumber, and had with other issue, a daughter, Jane, m. to Humphrey Prideaux, esq.
Thomas Morton Pleydell, d. s. p. 1773.
Henrietta, m. to Walter Hardiman, esq. of Wilts.
Arethusa, m. to G. Ryves, esq. of Ranston.
Cornelia, m. to the Rev. Timothy Collins, canon of Wells.

Sir John Morton's second wife, was Anne, daughter of Sir Francis Wortley, of Wortley, and the third, Elizabeth, daughter of Benjamin Culm, D.D. by Deborah, daughter of Sir Charles Pleydel, but by neither had he any issue to survive him. He died in 1698, aged seventy-one, when the BARONETCY EXPIRED. The estates were inherited by the Pleydells.

Arms—Quarterly; gu. and erm. in the first and fourth a goat's head erased, arg. attired or.

MOSLEY, OF HOUGH.

CREATED 20th July, 1640.

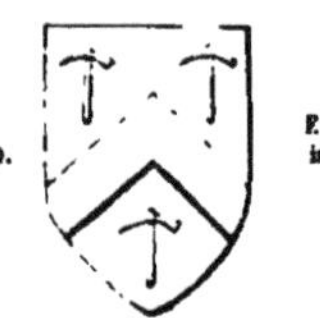

EXTINCT in [illegible]

Lineage.

The family of MOSLEY was founded by
JENKIN MOSLEY, of Hough End, whose son
JAMES MOSLEY, was father of
EDWARD MOSLEY, of Hough End, who m. [illegible] daughter of Alexander Elcock, of Hilgate, in Chesh[illegible] and had three sons,

I. NICHOLAS (Sir), his heir.
II. ANTHONY, of Ancoats, who m. Alice, dau[illegible] of Richard Webster, esq. of Manchest[illegible] and dying in 1670, was s. by his son,

OSWALD, of Ancoats, m. Anne, dau[illegible] and co heir of Ralph Lowe, esq. [illegible] End, in the county of Chester, and [illegible] in 1630, left

NICHOLAS, of Ancoats.
EDWARD (Sir), of Hulme, in the [illegible] of Lancaster, who inherited the [illegible] of Sir Edward Mosley, bart. [illegible]

III. OSWALD, of Garret.

The eldest son,

SIR NICHOLAS MOSLEY, knt. was lord [illegible] London in 1599. He m. Margaret, daught[illegible] Whitbroke, of Bridgenorth, in Salop, and [illegible] sons,

ROWLAND, his heir.
Edward (Sir), attorney-general for the [illegible] Lancaster, d. s. p.

Sir Nicholas d. at the advanced age of [illegible] 12th December, 1612, and was s. by his elder [illegible]

ROWLAND MOSLEY, esq. who m. first, [illegible] ter of Humphry Hoghton, of Manchester, and [illegible] daughter,

Margaret, m. to William Whitmore, esq. [illegible] in Shropshire, and left a daughter,

ANNE WHITMORE, heir to her father [illegible] Sir Richard Sawyer, knt.

He wedded, secondly, Anne, daughter and [illegible] Richard Sutton, esq. of Sutton, in Cheshire [illegible] with another daughter Anne, a son and he[illegible]

I. EDWARD MOSLEY, esq. of Hough, in the [illegible] of Stafford, who was created a BARONET [illegible] 1640. He m. Mary, daughter of Sir Gerv[illegible] knt. (and heir of her mother, Elizabeth, [illegible] and heir of Sir John Bentley, knt. of Bre[illegible] in Derbyshire), by whom he had issue,

EDWARD, his successor.

Mary, m. to Joseph Maynard, esq. of [illegible] bury, in Middlesex, son and heir of [illegible] Maynard, knt. serjeant at-law, one of [illegible] missioners of the great seal, *temp.* [illegible] III. and had two daughters (co-heirs [illegible] father),

ELIZABETH MAYNARD, m. to Sir Henry [illegible] bart. and had with other issue,

SIR JOHN HOBART, bart. created [illegible] bart, and Earl of Buckingham[illegible]

MARY MAYNARD, m. to Henry Grey, Earl of Stamford.

Anne, d. unm.

Sir Edward d. in 1657, and was s. by his son,

II. SIR EDWARD MOSLEY, who married Katherine, younger daughter of William Grey, first Lord Grey of Werke, but died without issue in 1665, when the BARONETCY became EXTINCT, and the estates devolved upon SIR EDWARD MOSLEY, knt. of Hulme, in Lancashire. Rolleston passed in jointure to Sir Edward's widow, whose second husband, Charles, eldest son of Dudley, Lord North, was summoned to parliament as Baron North and Grey of Rolleston. Her ladyship m. thirdly, Colonel Russell.

Arms—Quarterly; first and fourth, sa. a chevron between three battle-axes arg.; second and third, or a fesse between three eaglets displayed sa.

MOSLEY, OF ROLLESTON.

CREATED 18th June, 1720.—EXTINCT 22nd Sept. 1779.

Lineage.

ANTHONY MOSLEY, esq. of Ancoats, in the county of Lancaster, brother of Sir Nicholas Mosley, knt. lord mayor of London, in 1599, m. Alice, daughter of Richard Webster, of Manchester, gent. and left a son and heir,

OSWALD MOSLEY, esq. of Ancoats, who m. Anne, daughter and co-heir of Ralph Lowe, esq. of Mile End, in Cheshire, and had issue,

- I. NICHOLAS, his heir.
- II. Edward (Sir), of Hulme, in the county of Lancaster, who inherited the estates of Sir Edward Mosley, bart. in 1665, with the exception of Rolleston, which devolved in jointure upon the baronet's widow. Sir Edward Mosley, knt. of Hulme, married Muriel, daughter of Richard Saltingstal, esq. of Huntroyd, in the county of York, and left an only daughter, his heir,
    - ANNE MOSLEY, who m. Sir John Bland, knt. of Kippax Park. ((See BURKE's *Commoners*, vol. iii. page 326.)
- III. Oswald.
- IV. Samuel.
- V. Francis, fellow of the collegiate church of Manchester, and rector of Wimslow, in Cheshire, m. Catherine Davenport, and had
    - 1. Francis, in holy orders, rector of Rolleston.
    - 1. Anne, m. to Richard Whitworth, esq. of Adbaston, and was mother of Lord Whitworth, a peer of Ireland, who d. in 1725, when the dignity expired; from her second son descended Charles, Lord Whitworth, a peer of England, who died in 1825, when the dignity likewise became extinct.
    - 2. Catherine, m. to Joseph Hooper, of Manchester, gent. and was mother of
        - Francis Hooper, D. D.
- Anne, m. to Humphry Booth, esq. of Salford, and was mother of
    - Sir Robert Booth, knt. lord chief justice of the Common Pleas in Ireland.
- Margaret, m. to John Anger, esq.
- Mary, m. to John Crowther, citizen of London; her daughter became the wife of Thomas Butterworth, gent. of Manchester, and left two daughters: Susan Butterworth, married to Sir Henry Hoghton, bart. of Hoghton Tower, and Anne Butterworth, the wife of Daniel Bayley, of Manchester, gent.

Mr. Mosley was s. by his eldest son,

NICHOLAS MOSLEY, esq. of Ancoats, who m. Jane, daughter of John Lever, esq. of Alkrington, in Lancashire, and was s. by his son,

OSWALD MOSLEY, esq. of Ancoats, in Lancashire, and Rolleston, in the county of Stafford, who married Mary, daughter of Joseph Yates, esq. of Stanley House, near Blackburn, and dying at an advanced age, in 1726, left issue, of whom,

- OSWALD, inherited the estates.
- NICHOLAS, of St. Paul's, Shadwell, Middlesex, who d. in 1697, m. Elizabeth, daughter of Mr. Cooke, and left a son,
    - NICHOLAS MOSLEY, esq. of Manchester, who m. Elizabeth, daughter of William Parker, esq. of Derby, and dying in 1733, was s. by his son,
        - JOHN-PARKER MOSLEY, who inherited the estates of his cousin, the REV. SIR JOHN MOSLEY, bart. of Rolleston.

Mr. Mosley d. in 1726, and was s. by his son,

I. OSWALD MOSLEY, esq. who possessed the estate and manor of Rolleston, in Staffordshire, with the perpetual advowson of the rectory of Rolleston, and the estate of Ancoats, with the manor of Manchester. He was sheriff of Staffordshire in 1715, and created a BARONET by GEORGE I. 18th June, 1720. Sir Oswald m. Elizabeth, daughter of John Thornhaugh, esq. of Fenton, Notts, and had issue,

- OSWALD, his heir.
- JOHN, successor to his brother.
- Elizabeth, m. to Humphrey Trafford, esq. of Trafford, and d. s. p.

Sir Oswald d. 9th June, 1751, and was s. by his elder son,

II. SIR OSWALD MOSLEY, who d. unm. 26th February, 1757, and was s. by his brother,

III. SIR JOHN MOSLEY, in holy orders, who d. unm. 22nd September, 1779, when the BARONETCY EXPIRED, and the estates devolved upon his cousin,

- JOHN-PARKER MOSLEY, who then became of Rolleston, and was created a BARONET 24th March, 1781. He d. 29th September, 1798, and was s. by his grandson, the present (1837)
    - SIR OSWALD MOSLEY, bart. of Ancoats and Rolleston.

Arms—As preceding article.

MOSTYN, OF MOSTYN.

CREATED 3rd Aug. 1660. — EXTINCT 17th April, 1831.

Lineage.

The MOSTONS, as the name was originally written, of Flintshire, sprang from Tudor Trevor, Lord of

Bromfield, Chirk, Maelor, Whittington, and Oswaldstree, and for centuries have held high station amongst the leading men of the principality.

RICHARD, the son of Howell ap Jevan Vychan, m. Catherine, daughter of Sir Thomas Salisbury, and had, with five daughters, two sons,

THOMAS, } who assumed the name of MOSTON, from PIERCE, } the seat of the family, by the advice and direction of Richard Lee, Bishop of Lichfield, then (*temp.* HENRY VIII.) lord president of Wales.

The younger son, Pierce, purchased TALACRE, and from him the *extant* baronets Mostyn, of Talacre, descend. The elder son,

WILLIAM MOSTON, esq. of Moston,* was chief of the family in the time of ELIZABETH, and was directed, under her majesty's commission, dated in the 9th of her reign, with others of the principal gentlemen of North Wales, to hold an Eisteddfa, or session of the poets, musicians, and bards, at Caerwis (the last convened by royal authority), in which commission it is set forth that his ancestors had the right to bestow the silver harp on the person judged the most worthy by the commissioners. He married Margaret, daughter of Robert Powell, esq. of Park, and had three sons and two daughters, of whom the eldest son and heir,

SIR THOMAS MOSTYN, knt. of Mostyn, alone left issue. He m. Ursula, daughter and heir of William Goodman, esq.† and had three sons and two daughters, viz.

I. William, died in the Temple, unm.
II. ROGER, his heir.
III. Thomas, m. Anne, daughter and heir of William Hughes, Bishop of St. Asaph, and from him descended the Mostyns, of Rhyd, in Flintshire.

I. Margaret, m. to Pierce Griffith, esq. of Penrhyn, in Carnarvonshire.
II. Catherine, m. to Sir Thomas Hanmer, knt. of Hanmer.

Sir Thomas was appointed in the beginning of *King* JAMES I. one of his majesty's council for the principality of Wales and the Marches. He was *s.* at his decease by his elder surviving son,

SIR ROGER MOSTYN, knt. who married Mary, eldest daughter of Sir John Wynne, of Gwyder, bart.‡ and had issue,

I. THOMAS (Sir), of Kilken, died before his father, leaving by Elizabeth, his wife, daughter of Sir John Whitlock, knt. chief justice, two sons,
   ROGER (Sir), heir to his grandfather.
   Thomas, from whom the Mostyns of Kilken [illegible].
II. John, M.P. for Anglesey 21 JAMES I. and afterwards for the borough of Flint. He d. [illegible] at his seat, Maesmynnan, leaving his property to his elder brother.
III. William, in holy orders, archdeacon of Bangor, m. twice, and left issue.§
IV. Richard, captain in the army, died of wounds received at his landing in the Isle of Rhé [illegible] the force sent to relieve Rochelle, unm.
V. Robert, m. Margaret, daughter and heir of Henry Conway, esq. of Nant, in Flintshire.
VI. Edward, } both died young.
VII. Pierce, }
VIII. Roger, married Elizabeth, daughter and heir of Hugh Pugh, esq. of Dole y Cerrig[illegible], Montgomeryshire.

I. Sydney, m. to Sir Richard Grosvenor, bart. of Eaton, in Cheshire.
II. Catherine, m. to Colonel the Hon. R[illegible] Bulkeley, son and heir of Thomas, Viscount Bulkeley.

Sir Roger was succeeded at his decease by his grandson,

I. SIR ROGER MOSTYN, knt. of Mostyn, who took up arms for *King* CHARLES I. and having his majesty's commission, raised and maintained three hundred men at his own expense for the service: with this corps he took the castle of Hawarden, and entered at its head the city of Chester, then besieged by the parliamentarians. He likewise repaired the castle of Flint at his own charge, and was appointed governor thereof. In this fortress he sustained a long siege, enduring the greatest hardships, and surrendered at last only under the especial order of the king. He thus expended above sixty thousand pounds, and had his mansion house at Mostyn so dilapidated and spoiled, that he was obliged to live for several years at a farm-house, in the vicinity, after he had obtained his discharge from Conway Castle, [illegible]

---

* IEVAN VYCHAN, the lineal predecessor of this William, married in the reign of RICHARD II. Angharad, daughter and heir of Howell ap Tudor ap Ithel Vychan, of Moston, and thus that estate became part of the possessions of the family.

† By Margaret, his wife, daughter of Sir William Brereton, knt. of Brereton.

‡ By his wife, Sidney, daughter of Sir William Gerrard, lord chancellor of Ireland, in 1576.

§ PENNANT, in his History of Whiteford and Holywell, gives a plate of the monument of the wife of this William Mostyn, with the following account and inscription:

"The first (of the monuments) has the figure of a man and woman kneeling on opposite sides of a desk. Three sons are behind the man, and two daughters behind the woman, in the same attitudes. They are most neatly engraven on a tablet of white marble, and the whole included in a very neat frame. The inscription gives their brief tale:

'Neere to this lieth the body of Elizabeth Mostyn, one of the coheiresses of Richard Aldersey, of the city of Chester, gent. wife of William Mostyn, Arch. Bang. and rector of Chryselton. By whom he had issue three sonnes and two daughters. She departed this life the 10th of April, Ann. Dni. 1647.'

"Two of the sons were heads of families, viz. Mostyns, of Brinwyn, in Montgomeryshire, and Mostyns, of Segroit, in Denbighshire."—So far for Pennant, but [illegible] says nothing of the third son,

RICHARD MOSTYN, who was a wholesale linen-draper in London, and acquired a handsome fortune, m. Mary, daughter of John Soame, and [illegible] daughter of Sir William Soame, knt. and had [illegible] daughters, viz.

ANNE, *b.* in 1683, m. about 1708, to Thomas [illegible]ton, esq. of Chaderton, and was [illegible] William Horton, bart.

SYDNEY, m. to Richard Marriett, esq. of [illegible] in Warwickshire, and had issue,

Richard Marriet, who *d.* unm. in 17[illegible].

SIDNEY MARRIET, heir to her brother, [illegible] m. John Lowe, esq. and had two daughters, who *d.* young women. Mr. Lowe [illegible] Aldacot to James West, of the [illegible] and purchased Locko, near De[illegible] was sheriff of the county in 17[illegible]. [illegible] Lowe died at Derby, in 17[illegible], [illegible] survived her husband many years [illegible] the property of the Marriets [illegible] brother, Richard Lowe, a [illegible] in Covent Garden, who was sheriff [illegible]byshire in 1792.

JANE, *d.* unm. at Chaderton, in 17[illegible].

SUSANNA, *b.* in 1694, *d.* unm. at Derby [illegible] aged ninety-six.

...e suffered imprisonment. On the restoration of the ...oyal family, Sir Roger was created a BARONET 3rd ...ugust, 1660. He m. first, Prudence, daughter of Sir ...artyn Lumley, bart. of Barfield, in Essex, by whom ...e had two sons and two daughters,

Thomas, } d. young.
John, }

Jane, the wife, first, of Roger Paleston, esq. of Emeral, in Flintshire, and afterwards of Sir John Trevor, knt. master of the Rolls.

Mary, who m. William Salisbury, esq. of Rug, in the county of Monmouth.

...ir Roger m. secondly, Mary, eldest daughter of Tho...as, Viscount Bulkeley, and by that lady had, with ...ther issue, who all died young,

Thomas, his heir.

Roger, lived to manhood, and died unm.

Richard, of Penbeddw, M.A. of Christ Church, Oxford, married Charlotta-Theophila, daughter and co-heir of John Digby, esq. of Gothurst, Bucks (son and heir of Sir Kenelm Digby), and had two daughters,

BRIDGET, m. to Lytton Lytton, esq. of Knebworth, Herts, and died without issue in 1710.

CHARLOTTE, married to Richard Williams, esq. youngest son of Sir William Williams, bart.

...r Roger* m. thirdly, Lumley, daughter of Coetmor, ...Coetmor, in Carnarvonshire, but had no other ...ue. He died in 1726, and was succeeded by his ...dest son,

II. SIR THOMAS MOSTYN, M.P. for Carnarvon, who ... Bridget, only daughter and heir of Darcy Savage, ... of Leighton, in the county of Chester,† and ac...ired by her the manors of Beeston, Peckforton, ...ghton, Great Neston, and Thornton, all in Che...re. He had issue seven sons and four daughters, ...o all died young, except

ROGER, his heir.

Thomas, m. Margaret, eldest daughter and heir of William Mostyn, esq. of Rhyd, in the county of Flint, but died without issue 21st December, 1727. He served in parliament for the borough of Flint.

John, M.A. of Christ Church, Oxford, d. unm. 24th December, 1738.

Thomas was s. by his eldest son,

III. SIR ROGER MOSTYN, M.P. for the county of ...ster, and afterwards for Flintshire, from 1701 to ... He was appointed by *Queen* ANNE paymaster of the Marines, and by *King* GEORGE I. one of the tellers of the Exchequer. Sir Roger m. Lady Essex Finch, daughter of Daniel, second Earl of Nottingham, and had issue,

THOMAS, his successor.

Savage.

Roger.

Essex, m. to Robert, second Duke of Roxburghe.

Anne.

Mary-Bridget.

Charlotte.

Elizabeth.

Sir Roger d. 5th May, 1739, and was s. by his eldest son,

IV. SIR THOMAS MOSTYN, M.P. for the county of Flint. This gentleman m. Sarah, daughter and co-heir of Robert Western, esq. of London,‡ by whom (who d. 29th May, 1740), he had surviving issue,

ROGER, his successor.

Thomas.

Ann, m. 1777, to Thomas Pennant, esq. of Downing and Bychton, in the county of Flint, the celebrated naturalist and traveller.

Frances.

He died 24th March, 1758, and was succeeded by his son,

V. SIR ROGER MOSTYN, who m. 12th May, 1776, Margaret, daughter and heir of the Rev. Hugh Wynne, LL.D. prebendary of Salisbury,§ and by her (who d. 14th October, 1792), he had issue,

THOMAS, his heir.

Essex, d. unm.

Charlotte, m. to Sir Thomas-Swymmer Mostyn-Champneys, bart. but has no issue.

ELIZABETH, married to Sir Edward Pryce Lloyd, bart. now Lord Mostyn, and has a son and heir,

THOMAS-EDWARD LLOYD, who assumed the name and arms of MOSTYN.

Anna-Maria, m. to Sir Robert Williames Vaughan, bart. and has issue,

Robert Williames Vaughan, esq.

Catherine.

Mary-Bridget.

Sir Roger, who was member for Flintshire in eight parliaments, d. 26th July, 1796, and was s. by his son,

VI. SIR THOMAS MOSTYN, M.P. for the county of Flint, sheriff for Carnarvonshire in 1794, died unmarried 7th April, 1831, aged forty-four, when the

---

...ir Roger and Pyers Pennant, of Bychton, seem to ... been companions, from the P. S. to the following ... epistle:

"Mostyn, 1761.

"DEAR PYERS,

I hope you will excuse me for asking for the four ...nds you owe me for the pair of oxen; for I want the ... to make up twenty pounds, to send my son to ... next week.

"I am, dear Pyers, yours, &c.
"ROGER MOSTYN.

P. S. How does your head do this morning?—mine ... confoundedly."

... this time money was so scarce, that four pounds ... a pair of oxen, and the baronet was thought very ... in sending his heir apparent to the university with ... pounds in his purse.

...h, whose sister was Sir Roger's mother, speaks ... in the following terms, notwithstanding their ... were so widely different: "Then the parliament forces (in 1643) took in Mostyn House, belonging to Colonel Mostyn, the governor of Flint; and in Mostyn four pieces of ordnance and some arms. This Colonel Moystyn is my sister's son, a gentleman of good parts and mettle, of a very ancient family, large possessions, and great interest in the country, so that in twelve hours he raised fifteen hundred men for the king, and was well beloved there, living very nobly."

† Only son of *The Hon.* THOMAS SAVAGE (second son of Thomas, Viscount Savage), by Elizabeth, his wife, daughter and co-heir of William Whitmore, esq. of Leighton, by Margaret, daughter of Sir Hugh, and sister and heir of Sir George Beeston, of Beeston, in the same county.

‡ By Anne, his wife, eldest daughter and co-heir of Sir Richard Shirley, bart. of Preston, in Sussex.

§ By Catharine, his wife, sister of William Vaughan, esq. of Corsygedol, in Merionethshire, and heiress of Robert Wynne, esq. of Bodygallen, in Carnarvonshire

Baronetcy expired, and the principal part of the estates devolved, under Sir Thomas's will, upon his nephew,

The Hon. Edward Lloyd, who assumed, in compliance with the will of his uncle, by sign manual, in May, 1831, the additional surname and arms of Mostyn. He is also presumptive heir to the entailed estates of the family, now possessed by Lady Mostyn-Champneys, eldest surviving daughter of the late Sir Roger Mostyn.

Arms—Per bend sinister erm. and ermines, a lion rampant or.

MOTTET, OF LIEGE.

Created 16th Nov. 1660.

Lineage.

I. Giles Mottet, of Liege, in Flanders, was created a Baronet of England after the restoration of Charles II.; but of him or his descendants (if there were any) we have no account.

MOYER, OF PETSEY HALL.

Created 25th Mar. 1701.

Extinct 27th April, 1716.

Lineage.

Samuel Moyer, merchant, had two sons, viz.

Samuel, his heir.

Lawrence, of Low Leyton, merchant, who married Martha, daughter of William Boothby, esq. of Tottenham High Cross, and had issue,

Benjamin, of Petsey Hall, heir to his uncle.

John, who m. Frances, daughter of Edward Brewster, esq.

Martha, m. to Thomas Thorpe, esq.

Lydia, m. to Peter Hartop, esq.

Catharine.

The elder son,

I. Sir Samuel Moyer, of Petsey Hall, Essex, an opulent Turkey merchant, son of Samuel Moyer, also a merchant, served as sheriff of the county in 1696, and was created a Baronet in 1701. He m. Rebecca, daughter of Alderman Sir William Jolliffe, and had issue,

Mary, m. to Charles Le Barre, of Northamptonshire.

Elizabeth, m. to — Jennings, esq.

Sir Samuel died in 1716, when the Baronetcy became extinct.

Arms—Arg. two chevronels gu.

NAPIER, OF LUTON-HOO.

Created 25th Nov. 1612.

Extinct in 17[illegible].

Lineage.

The family of Naper or Napier claims descent from the ancient Scottish Earls of Lennox, raised to the dignity by Malcolm III. about the year 1057, and the claim is sustained by a certificate of Sir Archibald Naper, knt. of Merchistoun, deputy-treasurer of Scotland, and of the privy council to *King* Charles [illegible] enrolled in the college of arms by Sir William Segar, knt. garter.*

Alexander Napier (called for distinction Sa[illegible]) son of Sir Alexander Napier, and brother of Sir Archibald, came into England *temp.* Henry VIII and settled at Exeter. He m. Anne, daughter of Edward Birchley, of Hertfordshire, and had issue,

I. John, who m. Jean, daughter of — Webb, and had an only daughter and heir,

Anne Napier, who m. Matthew Sadler, of Basingstoke.

II. Robert (Sir).

III. Richard, rector of Linford, Bucks.

The second son,

I. Sir Robert Napier, purchased the manor of Luton-Hoo, in Bedfordshire.† He was knighted by *King* James I. in his majesty's progress, anno [illegible] and further advanced, by the same monarch, to a Baronetcy 25th November, 1612. Sir Robert m. first, Miss Stapers; and secondly, Margaret, daughter of Richard Barnes, citizen and mercer of London, but by those ladies had no issue. He wedded, thirdly, Mary, daughter of John Robinson, merchant, and by her had

Robert (Sir), his heir.

Richard (Sir), of Linford, m. first, Anne, daughter of Sir Thomas Tyrringham, knt. of Tyrringham, in Bucks, and had

Robert, M.D. } both *d.* unm.
Richard, a merchant, }

He married, secondly, Mary, daughter of Thomas Vinor, esq. lord mayor of London in 16[illegible], and by her had

Thomas, of Brockhill, Middlesex.

Mary, *d.* unm.

Alexander, m. Elizabeth, daughter of Lewis Cokayn, esq. of Cokayn-Hatley, in the county of Bedford, and had a son,

Lewis, of Woodstock, in Oxfordshire, who m. the daughter of the Rev. John Griffith, [illegible] reader at the Temple.

Mary, m. to Sir Thomas Middleton, knt. of Chirk Castle, in the county of Denbigh.

Christian, m. to Sir Thomas Eversfield, kt. [illegible] Den, in Sussex.

* The certificate is set forth in Burke's *History of the Commoners*, vol. ii. p. 630.

† A fine seat, with a park, in the parish of Luton, anciently belonging to the family of Hoo.

Sarah, *m.* to Sir Walter Leach, knt. of Chadleigh, in Devonshire.

Margaret, *m.* to Thomas Mytton, esq. of Halston, in Shropshire, the celebrated parliamentary general *temp.* CHARLES I.

Sir Robert *d.* in April, 1637, and was *s.* by his eldest son,

II. SIR ROBERT NAPIER, who had received the honour of knighthood from *King* JAMES I. at Whitehall, 30th April, 1623. He *m.* first, Frances, daughter of Sir William Thornhurst, knt. of Agincourt, in Kent,‡ and by that lady had an only son,

ROBERT, his heir, who *m.* Margaret, daughter of Sir Edward Littleton, bart. of Pillaton Hall, in Staffordshire, and dying in the lifetime of his father, left a son,

ROBERT, who *s.* his grandfather.

He *m.* secondly, Lady Penelope Egerton, daughter of John, first Earl of Bridgewater, and had two other sons and a daughter, viz.

JOHN, of whom presently, as heir to his nephew.

Alexander, of Hatton Garden, London, *m.* Mary, daughter and heir of Richard Mason, esq. of Worldham, Hants, and had issue,

Robert, *d.* unm.

Penelope, *d.* unm.

Jane.

Elizabeth.

Frances, *m.* first, to Sir Edward Barkham, bart. of Southacre, in Norfolk; and secondly, to Lord Richardson, Baron of Cramond, in Scotland.

Sir Robert settled his estate on JOHN and ALEXANDER, the sons of his second marriage, and surrendered his patent of honour, to the intent that the said dignity should be granted to himself, with remainder to the said John and Alexander; but dying in 1660, before the new grant passed the seals, the honour in being devolved upon his grandson,

III. SIR ROBERT NAPIER, who died unmarried in 1673, when the BARONETCY of 1612 EXPIRED, but he was *s.* in the representation of the family by his uncle of the half-blood,

IV. SIR JOHN NAPIER, who had been created a BARONET 4th March, 1660-1, with the precedency of 25th November, 1612.* Sir John represented the county of Bedford in the reign of CHARLES II. but having afterwards the misfortune to fall twice from his horse, became so crazed that a commission of lunacy was awarded against him. His wife was Elizabeth, daughter of Sir Theophilus Biddulph, bart. of West Combe, in Kent, and by her he had issue,

John, *d.* unm.

THEOPHILUS, his heir.

Archibald, *m.* Mrs. Angier, and left

JOHN, who *s.* his uncle as sixth baronet.

Elizabeth, *d.* unm.

Edward, } *d.* unm.
Alexander, }

Susan, *m.* to John Highlord, esq. of Harrow.

FRANCES, heir to Luton-Hoo under the will of her nephew.

He *d.* in August, 1711, and was *s.* by his eldest surviving son,

V. SIR THEOPHILUS NAPIER, who *m.* Elizabeth, daughter of John Rotherum, esq. of Much Waltham, in Essex, but *d. s. p.* about the year 1719. His widow *m.* secondly, Thomas, Lord Howard of Effingham; and surviving him, *m.* thirdly, Sir Conyers D'Arcy, K.B. Sir Theophilus was *s.* by his nephew,

VI. SIR JOHN NAPIER, who died unmarried in 1747, when the BARONETCY became EXTINCT. Sir John bequeathed LUTON-HOO to his aunt,

MRS. FRANCES NAPIER, who devised it to Francis Herne, esq. by whom the estate was sold, in 1763, to John, Earl of Bute.

Arms—Arg. a saltier engrailed, between four roses gu.

NAPIER, OF MIDDLE MARSH HALL.

CREATED 25th June, 1641.—EXTINCT 25th Jan. 1765.

Lineage.

JOHN NAPIER, a younger son of Sir Alexander Napier, knt. of Merchistoun, came into England *temp.* HENRY VII. and settled at Swyre, in the county of Dorset. He *m.* Anne, daughter of John Russel, of Berwick, and had

I. EDWARD, of Swyre, in Dorset, and of Holywell, in Oxfordshire, who *m.* a daughter of Sir John Peyto, of Wavesham, in the latter county, and left issue.

II. Nicholas, of Tintinhull, in Somersetshire.

III. JAMES.

The third son,

JAMES NAPIER, esq. of Baglake or Puncknoll, in the county of Dorset, *m.* a lady named Hilliard, and had three sons, viz.

JOHN, of Baglake.

WILLIAM, of Puncknoll.

ROBERT (Sir).

The youngest son,

SIR ROBERT NAPIER, an eminent lawyer, was constituted, in 1593, lord chief baron of the Exchequer in Ireland, when he received the honour of knighthood from *Queen* ELIZABETH; in the thirty-fourth year of which sovereign's reign he purchased the estate of Middle Marsh, in the county of Dorset, and served as high sheriff in 1606. Sir Robert *m.* first, Catherine, daughter of John Warham, esq. and by that lady had a daughter, Anne, the wife of Sir John Ryves, of Damory Court. He *m.* secondly, Magdalen, daughter of Sir Anthony Denton, of Oxfordshire, by whom (who *d.* in 1635) he had a son, his heir at his decease 20th September, 1615,

SIR NATHANIEL NAPIER, who was knighted by *King* JAMES I. at Newmarket in 1617, and subsequently served as sheriff and member of parliament for the county of Dorset. Sir Nathaniel was included in an instrument recorded in the Heralds' College, as of the blood of the Napers or Napiers of Merchistoun. He *m.* Elizabeth, daughter and heir of John Gerard, esq. of Hyde, in the Isle of Purbeck, and had issue,

GERARD, his heir.

Robert, of Puncknoll, *d.* in 1686, leaving issue.

John, *d. s. p.*

James, of Loughcrew, in the county of Meath, ancestor of the present JAMES-LENOX-WILLIAM NAPER, esq. of Loughcrew. (See BURKE's *Commoners*, vol. ii. p. 630.)

---

‡ By his wife, ANNE, daughter and co-heir of the Hon. Charles Lyte Howard, only son of Thomas, Viscount Bindon, by his second wife, Gertrude, daughter of Sir William Lyte, of Billesdon, Somersetshire.

* This might be deemed a revival of the old patent, but that it was granted several years before that had expired. We have, however, continued the enumeration of the successors as though it were, and call Sir John the fourth, whereas, strictly speaking, he was the first of his own creation. He obtained the estates from his father, and was the fourth representative of the first baronet of the original creation.

Nathaniel, left issue.
Henry.

Magdalen, *m.* to — Clarke, esq. of Hampshire.
Elizabeth, *m.* to Humphrey Walrond, esq. of Sea.

Sir Nathaniel erected the mansion at More Critchell, which was destroyed by fire. His wife *d.* 7th October, 1624; himself 6th September, 1635, when he was *s.* by his eldest son,

I. GERARD NAPIER, esq. of Middle Marsh Hall, in the county of Dorset, who was created a BARONET 25th June, 1641. Sir Gerard distinguished himself in arms for the royal cause during the civil war, and lost more than £10,000 by his loyalty. His estates in the counties of Dorset and Kent were sequestered in 1645, and he was disqualified from representing Melcombe. During the exile of *King* CHARLES II. he transmitted to his majesty 500 broad pieces by Sir Gilbert Taylor, who detained the money, and was arrested for it by Sir Gerard after the Restoration; but Sir Gilbert acknowledging the receipt, was, through the king's mediation, forgiven; and Sir Gerard was ordered a number of deer annually from the New Forest without fee. Notwithstanding the persecution and heavy losses he endured, Sir Gerard still augmented his paternal property. He had the honour of entertaining the king and queen at More Critchell, when the court removed to Salisbury from the plague in 1665. He *m.* Margaret, daughter and co-heir of John Colles, esq.* of Barton, in the county of Somerset, and had one surviving son, NATHANIEL, and two daughters, Elizabeth and Mary. He *d.* 14th May, 1673, and was *s.* by his son,

II. SIR NATHANIEL NAPIER, who *m.* first, in 1656, Blanch, daughter of Sir Hugh Wyndham, knt. of Sylton, in the county of Dorset, and by that lady (who *d.* in 1695) he had issue,

Wyndham, *d.* unmarried at the age of twenty.
Gerard, *m.* Elizabeth, daughter and heir of Jacob Lucy, esq. an alderman of the city of London, with whom he had a large fortune. Both died in 1689, leaving no issue.
Lenox, *d.* in 1689 unmarried, in the twenty-fourth year of his age.
NATHANIEL, who *s.* to the estate and title.

Elizabeth, *m.* to Sir John Guise, bart. of Rendcomb, in the county of Gloucester.

He *m.* secondly, in 1697, Miss Susanna Guise, but had no other issue. Sir Nathaniel sat in parliament for several years, representing at different times the county of Dorset and the boroughs of Poole and Corfe Castle. "He was (says an old author) a gay, ingenious gentleman, well versed in several languages, and understood very well architecture and painting; he has left behind him several pieces of his own drawing, besides many others of good value, which he had collected on his travels." He *d.* in January, 1708, and was *s.* by his only surviving son,

III. SIR NATHANIEL NAPIER, M.P. for the county of Dorchester *temp. King* WILLIAM and *Queen* ANNE. He *m.* first, Jane, daughter of Sir Robert Worseley, bart. of Appuldercombe, in the Isle of Wight, but by that lady had no issue. He wedded, secondly, Catherine, younger daughter of William, second Lord Allington, and co-heir of her brother Giles, third lord, and by her had

WILLIAM, his heir.
GERARD, successor to his brother.
Wyndham.

DIANA, *m.* to Humphry Sturt, esq. of Horton, in Dorsetshire, and *d.* 1st February, 1739-40, leaving, with other issue,
HUMPHRY STURT, who inherited the estates of the Napiers at the decease of Sir Gerard, the sixth baronet.
Catherine, *d.* unm.
Blanch, *d.* young.

He *d.* 24th February, 1728, and was *s.* by his eldest son,

IV. SIR WILLIAM NAPIER, who *d.* unmarried 27th January, 1753, and was *s.* by his brother,

V. SIR GERARD NAPIER, who *m.* Bridget, daughter of Edward Phelips, esq. of Montacute, in the county of Somerset, and dying 25th October, 1759, was *s.* by his son,

VI. SIR GERARD NAPIER, who *m.* Elizabeth, daughter of Sir John Oglander, bart. of Nunwell, in the Isle of Wight, but dying 25th January, 1765, aged twenty-six, the BARONETCY EXPIRED. His widow *m.* James Webb, esq. and *d.* 16th October, 1814. The estates devolved upon his cousin,

HUMPHRY STURT, esq. of Horton, M.P. for Dorsetshire.

Arms—As NAPIER OF LUTON-HOO.

NAPIER, OF PUNCKNOLL.

CREATED 25th Feb. 1681.—EXTINCT in 1743.

Lineage.

ROBERT NAPIER, esq. of Puncknoll, second son of Sir Nathaniel Napier, of More Critchell, by Elizabeth, his wife, daughter and heir of John Gerard, esq. was master of the Hanaper Office in the reigns of CHARLES I. and CHARLES II. and had many employments at court after the Restoration. He *m.* first, Anna, daughter of Allan Corrance, esq. of Wykin, in Suffolk, secondly, Catherine, sister of Lord Hawley; and thirdly, Mary, daughter of Sir Thomas Evelyn, bart. of Long Ditton, and relict of Edmond Ironside, esq. By the first he left, at his decease in 1686, a daughter, Anne, *m.* to John Fry, of Yarty, in Devonshire, son of the regicide John Fry, and a son,

I. SIR ROBERT NAPIER, knt. of Puncknoll, master of the Hanaper Office, who served in the convention and other succeeding parliaments for the boroughs of Weymouth, Melcombe Regis, and Dorchester, and was created a BARONET 25th February, 1681. He *m.* Sophia, daughter of Charles Evelyn, esq. of Godstone, in Surrey, and dying 31st October, 1700, was *s.* by his son,

II. SIR CHARLES NAPIER, of Puncknoll, who *m.* Melony, daughter of Arthur Alibone, esq. and had issue. Sir Charles sold the estate at Puncknoll to William Clutterbuck, esq. and from the Clutterbucks it has descended to the Fromes, by whose representative, the REV. GEORGE-CLUTTERBUCK FROME, A.M. it is now possessed. He died in 1743, but whether the BARONETCY then EXPIRED, or a son of Sir Charles survived to inherit, we have not ascertained.

Arms—As NAPIER OF MORE CRITCHELL.

* JOHN COLLES left three daughters, his co-heirs, namely,
MARGARET, *m.* to Sir Gerard Napier, bart.
ELIZABETH, *m.* first, to Herbert Dodington, esq.; and secondly, to the Hon. John Coventry, second son of the Lord Keeper Coventry.
ANNE, *m.* to Sir William Portman, bart.

NARBOROUGH, OF KNOWLTON.

CREATED 15th Nov. 1688.—EXTINCT 22nd Oct. 1707.

Lineage.

SIR JOHN NARBOROUGH, knt. of Knowlton, in the county of Kent, an admiral in the royal navy, m. Elizabeth, daughter of John Hill, esq. a commissioner in the navy, and by that lady (who m. secondly, Rear-Admiral Sir Cloudesley Shovel, who was cast away on the rocks of Scilly 22nd October, 1707,) had issue,

JOHN, his heir.
James.
ELIZABETH, m. about 1714, to Sir Thomas D'Aeth, bart. of North Cray, and had, with other issue,
SIR NARBOROUGH D'AETH, bart.
Harriet, married Josiah Hardy, esq. consul at Cadiz, and had five daughters, of whom the eldest, Harriet, became the second wife of William Hughes, esq. and was mother of the present GEORGE-WILLIAM HUGHES-D'AETH, esq. of Knowlton Court.

Sir John was s. by his elder son,

I. JOHN NARBOROUGH, esq. of Knowlton, who was created a BARONET 15th November, 1688, with remainder to his brother, default his own male line; but both were lost with their step-father, Sir Cloudesley Shovel, on the rocks of Scilly, 22nd October, 1707, when the BARONETCY became EXTINCT; the estates passing to their sister ELIZABETH, who m., as stated above, Sir Thomas D'Aeth.

NEVILE, OF GROVE.

CREATED ..th Feb. 1674-5. EXTINCT in 1686.

Lineage.

This was an offshoot from the once great and potent ..ily of NEVILE, Lords of Raby, who became subsequently Earls of Westmorland, and whose line may ..duced from Saxon times.

..ALPH DE NEVILL was summoned to parliament .. BARON from 8th June, 1294, to 18th February, 31, in which latter year he died, and was s. by his .. surviving son,

RALPH DE NAVILL, second baron, summoned to parliament from 20th November, 1330, to 20th January, .. His lordship m. Alice, daughter and co-heir of ..h de Audley, and had JOHN (Sir), his heir, the ..lord, with five younger sons. The fourth son, .. ROBERT NAVILE, of Eldon, was lineal ancestor (for the intermediate links refer to BURKE's Commoners, vol. ii. p. 8,) of

..NEVILE, esq. who m. Barbara, sister and co-heir of Sir John Hercy, of Grove, in the county of Nottingham, and fifth daughter of Sir Humphrey Hercy, by Elizabeth, his wife, daughter of Sir John Digby, of Ketelby, and had issue,

JOHN, his heir.
GEORGE, of Thorney, in the county of Nottingham, ancestor of the present
CHRISTOPHER NEVILE, esq. of Thorney. (See BURKE's *Commoners*, vol. ii. p. 8.)
Dionysius, ancestor of the Neviles of Badsworth.

The eldest son,

JOHN NEVILE, esq. of Grove, m. Gertrude, daughter of Richard Whalley, esq. and was s. by his son,

HERCY NEVILE, esq. of Grove, who married Bridget, daughter of — Saville, esq. of Lupset, and had (with a daughter, Barbara, m. first, to Thomas Pate, esq.; secondly, to John Babington, esq. of Rampton; and thirdly, to Anthony Eyre, esq. of Loughton, in Yorkshire,) a son and successor,

GILBERT NEVILE, of Grove, who m. Margaret, daughter of Sir Thomas Bland, of Kippax Park, Yorkshire, and had two sons, EDWARD, his heir; and Anthony, a major in the royal army during the civil wars, who died 24th February, 1688, aged sixty-nine. The elder son,

EDWARD NEVILE, esq. of Grove, m. Maria Scott, of Camberwell, and had, with two daughters, Catherine, who died unmarried in 1683, and Anne, m. to John Millington, esq. barrister-at-law, a son and heir,

I. EDWARD NEVILE, esq. of Grove, who was created a BARONET in 1674. This gentleman, who represented Retford in parliament, m. Elizabeth, sister of Robert Holt, esq. of Warwickshire, and widow of — Kidderminster, esq. but d. s. p. in 1686, when the title EXPIRED.

Arms—Gu. a saltire arg.

NEWDIGATE, OF ARBURY.

CREATED 24th July, 1677. EXTINCT 2nd Dec. 1806.

Lineage.

This family, variously written in old charters and upon ancient monuments, NIWUDGATE, NIWODEGATE, &c.* assumed their surname from, or gave the name to, Newdigate, a town in the hundred of Reigate and county of Surrey, of which, with the manors and lands thereunto pertaining, they were lords and proprietors from time immemorial until the reign of CHARLES I.

JOHN DE NIWUDEGATE, living *temp.* King JOHN, left, by his wife Agnes, three sons, RICHARD, William and Robert. To the eldest,

RICHARD DE NIWUDEGATE, it appears, by an old deed, one William Young granted, for homage and service, half a yard of land; and by another dateless charter, of William Tassardus, he held the same lands in the parish of Niudigate as his father did. He m. Alicia, daughter of Walter de Horley, as is evident by a deed of William de Longo Ponte, whereby the said William grants to him all that land which Walter de

* The name came, in all probability, at first from Saxony, and was derived from the city of Nieuweide, upon th.. ..er.

Horleia conferred upon him with Alice, his daughter, in free marriage. He had three sons, JOHN, William, and Peter, and was *s.* by the eldest,

JOHN DE NYWDEGATE, living in the time of HENRY III. who was *s.* by his son,

WILLIAM DE NYWDEGATE, who added to the estate several lands situated in the parishes of Newdegate and Charlewode, which he acquired by grants from Henry Kymer and William Egloff. He was living 17 EDWARD I. for in that year Thomas de la Lynde assigned to him his wood in Lynde; after which, Gilbert Wytecrofte, of the parish of Cherlewode, granted to him all his land called the Berland, in the parish of Newdigate. His son and heir,

SIR HENRY DE NEWDEGATE, knt. living *temp.* EDWARD I. *m.* Catherine, daughter and co-heir of Sir Nicholas Malmains, knt.† and was *s.* by his elder son,

JOHN DE NEWDEGATE, who *d. s. p.* and was *s.* by his brother,

WILLIAM DE NEWDEGATE, who flourished *temp.* EDWARD II. He *m.* the daughter and heiress of John Echingham, and had four sons, JOHN, Richard, Robert, and William. The eldest,

JOHN DE NEWDEGATE, wedded, in the beginning of EDWARD III.'s reign, a lady named Agnes, of what family is not recorded, and had three sons, viz.

I. WILLIAM, who inherited, at the decease of his father, the manor and lands of Newdegate, was sheriff of Surrey and Sussex 25 EDWARD III. and several times member of parliament for the former county. He *m.* Amicia ——, and *d.* about 1 RICHARD II. leaving a son and heir,

JOHN NEWDEGATE, of Newdegate, in whose male descendants the estate continued vested until the year 1612, when

THOMAS NEWDEGATE, of Newdegate, Cherlewode, and Horlee, in the county of Surrey, and of Rowesparr, in Sussex, died, leaving by Mary, his wife, (who *m.* secondly, Henry Darell, esq.) two daughters, his co-heirs, viz.

MARY, *m.* to William Steper.

ANNE, *m.* to William Smithyman.

II. JOHN.

III. Thomas, to whom his father, by deed dated 7 EDWARD III. granted his tenements in Hullond for life, remainder to his brother John for life, remainder to William and his heirs.

The second son,

SIR JOHN NEWDEGATE, having served in the wars of EDWARD III. in France, received the honour of knighthood, and had a fleur-de-lis granted to him for a crest. He *m.* Joanna, daughter and co heir of William de Swanland, by whom he acquired the manor of HAREFIELD, in Middlesex, and had a son and heir, JOHN. She married, after the decease of Sir John, Edward Salle, and outlived him. Sir John de Newdegate was *s.* by his son,

v. Lysons 1800 p215

JOHN NEWDEGATE, esq. of Harefield, living in the reigns of HENRY V. and HENRY VI. He *m.* first, Elizabeth, daughter of Walter Knoll, esq. of Crawley, and Margaret, his wife, to whom, by deed of entail dated 7 HENRY V. the manor of Downe, in the hundred of Godalming, Surrey, is devised for her life; remainder to Elizabeth, her daughter, for life also; remainder to William Newdegate, son of the said Elizabeth, and his heirs. By her he had two sons, WILLIAM and Thomas. He *m.* secondly, Catharine, daughter and heir of Roger Chambers, and had a daughter, Margaret, wife of — Castlemain. He was *s.* at his decease by his elder son,

WILLIAM NEWDEGATE, esq. of Harefield, who wedded Editha, daughter of John Bowett, esq. of Surrey, and left at his decease, 36 HENRY VI. a son and heir,

JOHN NEWDEGATE, esq. lord of Harefield, in Middlesex, and of Crawley, in Surrey. He *m.* Elizabeth, daughter of Thomas Young, one of the justices of the Common Pleas, and heir of her brother, Thomas Young, esq. of Bristol, and was *s.* by his son,

JOHN NEWDEGATE, esq. of Harefield, one of the king's serjeants, learned in the law, who *m.* Amphelicia, daughter and heir of John Nevill, esq. of Sutton, in Lincolnshire, and had, with several daughters,

JOHN, his heir.

Silvester, Duncan, } knights of St. John.

Sebastian, who, upon the death of his wife in 1524, became a Carthusian monk, and suffered 27 HENRY VIII. for opposing the king's supremacy.

Mr. Serjeant Newdegate was *s.* at his decease by his eldest son,

JOHN NEWDEGATE, esq. of Harefield, *b.* 6 HENRY VII.; *m.* Anne, daughter and heir of Nicholas Hylton, esq. of Cambridge; and dying in 1545, was *s.* by his eldest son,

JOHN NEWDEGATE, esq. of Harefield, M.P. for Middlesex in 1571, 1573, and 1574. This gentleman *m.* first, Mary, daughter of Sir Robert Cheney, knt. of Chesham Boys, in Buckinghamshire, by whom he had a son, JOHN. He wedded, secondly, Elizabeth, daughter of Thomas Lovett, esq. of Astwell, in the county of Northampton, and relict of Anthony Cave, esq. He was *s.* by his son,

JOHN NEWDEGATE, esq. who exchanged, in 1586, the manor and lands of Harefield, with Sir Edmond Anderson, knt. chief justice of the Common Pleas, for the estate of Arbury, in the county of Warwick, where Sir Edmond had recently erected a quadrangular stone mansion upon the site of the dissolved priory of Erdbury, which he had obtained from the heirs of Charles Brandon, Duke of Suffolk, the grantee at the time of the dissolution. Mr. Newdegate *m.* first, Martha, daughter and heir of Anthony Cave, esq. of Chicheley, in Bucks, by whom he had JOHN, his heir, with five younger sons and three daughters. He *m.* secondly, Mary Smith, and by her had a son, Henry, of Hampton, to whom he gave the manor of Little Asted, in Surrey. He wedded, thirdly, Winifred Wells, of Staffordshire, and dying in 1592, was *s.* by his eldest son,

SIR JOHN NEWDEGATE, knt. of Arbury, in the county of Warwick, and of Brackenbury, in Middlesex, *b.* in 1570; *m.* Anne, eldest daughter of Sir Edward Fitton, knt. of Gawsworth, in Cheshire; and dying 12th April, 1610, left a son and heir,

JOHN NEWDIGATE, esq. of Arbury, *b.* in 1600. This gentleman wrote the name with an i, which alteration was subsequently adopted. He *d. s. p.* in 1642, and was *s.* by his brother,

I. RICHARD NEWDIGATE, esq. serjeant-at-law, constituted in 1654 one of the three judges then appointed. Mr. Justice Newdigate incurred the displeasure of CROMWELL by laying it down at the York assizes, where he presided at the trials for high treason of the Earls of Bellasis and Dumfries, &c. that there was [illegible]

† The daughters and co-heirs of Sir Nicholas Malmains were the above CATHERINE, and

BEATRIX, *m.* to Otho de Grandison, brother to the Lord Grandison.

PETRONILLA, *m.* to Sir Thomas St. Omer.

ELIZABETH.

JOAN.

...w making it treason to levy war against a lord protector; for this he was dismissed, but reinstated and constituted chief justice of the upper bench in 1659. On the Restoration he was created a BARONET by King CHARLES II. 24th July, 1677, and remitted the fees usually paid on such an occasion for the patent. He m. in 1631, Juliana, daughter of Sir Francis Leigh, K.B. and had surviving issue,

RICHARD, his heir.

Robert, of Hillingdon, m. first, Frances, daughter of Thomas Harrison, esq.; and secondly, Juliana, daughter of Robert Beale, esq.

Thomas, of Lewes, in Sussex, and of Hawton, Notts, left two sons, Richard, of the Inner Temple, d. in 1745, and John, of the Six Clerks' Office, d. in 1740.

Anne, m. to German Pole, esq. of Radborn, in Derbyshire.

Mary, m. to Sir George Parker, bart. of Willington, in Sussex.

...r Edmond Anderson, with whom the judge's grandfather had exchanged the manors of Harefield and Moor Hall, conveyed those estates to Alicia, Countess Dowager of Derby, and of her ladyship's heirs Sir Richard Newdigate purchased back, in 1674, the ancient patrimony of his family. He also added to his possessions the castle and manor of Astley and the manor of St. John's, both in Warwickshire. He d. in 1678, and was s. by his eldest son,

II. SIR RICHARD NEWDIGATE, M.P. for the county of Warwick in 1681 and 1685, who m. first, Mary, daughter of Sir Edward Bagot, bart. of Blithfield, in the county of Stafford, and had issue,

I. RICHARD, his heir.

II. Francis, b. in 1684, settled at Nottingham, m. Millicent, daughter of German Pole, esq. of Radbourn, and had

Francis, of Kirkhallam, m. his cousin, Elizabeth, daughter of German Pole, esq. but d. s. p.

Millicent, m. to Christopher Parker, esq. of Salford Priors, in Warwickshire, and had, with four daughters, three sons, viz.

1. Robert Parker.
2. Francis Parker, of Kirkhallam, who assumed, under the will of his uncle, the surname and arms of NEWDIGATE. He m. Frances, daughter of Ralph Sneyd, esq. of Keel, and had a son,

FRANCIS NEWDIGATE, of Kirkhallam, who m. Lady Barbara Legge.

3. Charles Parker, of Harefield, m. Jane, daughter of Sir John Anstruther, bart. and died 24th April, 1795, leaving

FRANCIS PARKER, of Arbury, who assumed the surname of NEWDIGATE on inheriting the estate of Hallam from Mr. Newdigate, of Bath.

CHARLES-NEWDIGATE PARKER, of whom hereafter.

III. Amphelis, d. unm.

IV. Mary, m. to William Stephens, esq. of Barton, in the Isle of Wight.

... Francis, m. to Sir Charles Sedley, bart. of Chartley, in Kent.

... Anne, m. to John Venables, esq. of Woodcote, in Hants.

V. Jane, m. to Samuel Boys, esq. of Hawkhurst, in Kent.

VI. Juliana, m. to Robert Glegg, esq. of Gayton, in Cheshire.

VII. Elizabeth, m. to Abraham Meur, esq.

Sir Richard m. secondly (his first wife dying in 1692), Miss Henrietta Wigginton, but by her (who wedded, secondly, Sir Francis Windham, bart. of Trent,) had no issue. He d. 4th January, 1710, and was s. by his elder son,

III. SIR RICHARD NEWDIGATE, of Harefield and Arbury, b. in 1668; m. first, in 1694, Sarah, daughter of Sir Cecil Bisshopp, bart. of Parham, but by her had no issue. He wedded, secondly, Elizabeth, daughter of Sir Roger Twisden, bart. of Bradburne, in Kent, and had to survive youth,

EDWARD, ROGER, } fourth and fifth baronets.

Elizabeth, m. to the Hon. John Chichester, only brother of the Earl of Donegal.

Mary, m. to Charles Palmer, esq. of Ladbrooke, and had issue.

Juliana, m. to John Ludford, esq. of Ansley Hall, and had issue.

Sir Richard d. in 1727, aged fifty-nine, and was s. by his eldest son,

IV. SIR EDWARD NEWDIGATE, who died a minor in 1734, and was s. by his brother,

V. SIR ROGER NEWDIGATE, b. in 1719, M.P. for the county of Middlesex in 1742; m. first, Sophia, daughter of Edward Conyers, esq. of Copped Hall, in Essex; and secondly, in 1776, Hester, daughter of Edward Mundy, esq. of Shipley, in Derbyshire, but d. s. p. 23rd November, 1806, when the BARONETCY became EXTINCT. At Sir Roger's decease, the Warwickshire estate devolved on the grandson of Sir Roger's first cousin, Millicent Newdigate (refer to second baronet), FRANCIS PARKER, esq. who had previously taken the name of NEWDIGATE for his life only; while the Middlesex property passed to another grandson of the said Millicent Newdigate, CHARLES-NEWDIGATE PARKER, esq. who assumed, in consequence, the surname and arms of NEWDEGATE* only. This gentleman m. in 1815, Maria, daughter of Ayscough Boucherett, esq. of Willingham, in the county of Lincoln, and dying 23rd April, 1833, left an only son and successor, the present

CHARLES-NEWDIGATE NEWDEGATE, esq. of Harefield, Arbury, and Astley Castle.

Arms—Gu. three lions' gambs erased arg.

NEWMAN, OF FIFEHEAD-MAGDALEN.

CREATED 20th Dec. 1699.

EXTINCT 4th June, 1747.

Lineage.

By a certificate under the hand of HUMPHREY NEWMAN, gentleman, it appears that at the dissolution of the monasteries, the Newmans were lessees, under the Abbots of St. Augustin, in Bristol, of the manors

* Sir Roger made it a point that his heir should spell the name Newdegate, as anciently written.

and demesnes of Fifehead-Magdalen, Dorset, and that there were distinct branches of the family seated at Queen's Camel, Wincanton, and other places in Somersetshire.

Robert Newman, who lived and died at Fifehead Farm, and was buried in the chancel there, as directed by his will, dated in 1556, left four sons, of whom the youngest,

Thomas Newman, of Fifeild, in Dorsetshire, was father of another

Thomas Newman, esq. who *m.* Ellen, daughter of Richard Mayo, esq. and dying 21st October, 1649, was *s.* by his eldest son,

Richard Newman, esq. who *m.* first, Elizabeth, daughter of Giles Symonds, esq. and had a daughter, Anne, the wife of Robert White, esq. of Dorsetshire. He *m.* secondly, Elizabeth, daughter and co-heir of Christopher Perry, esq. of Kenn, in Somersetshire, and died 10th July, 1664, when he was *s.* by his son,

Richard Newman, esq. who wedded Anne, eldest daughter of Sir Charles Harbord, surveyor-general to *Kings* Charles I. and Charles II. and had issue,

- Richard, his heir.
- Francis-Hollis, of North Cadbury, in Somersetshire, *b.* in 1671, *m.* Ellinor, daughter of Thomas Monpesson, esq. of Brewham.
- Elizabeth, *m.* to Thomas Warre, esq. of Swell, in Somersetshire.
- Anne-Christian, *m.* to Sir William Honeywood, bart.

He *d.* 24th September, 1695, and was succeeded by his son,

Richard Newman, esq. of Evercreech Park, in the county of Somerset, who *m.* in 1675, Grace, daughter and co-heir of Henry Edmonds, esq. of Preston Hall, in Northamptonshire, and had issue,

- Richard, his heir.
- Anne, *m.* to Ashburnham Toll, esq. of Graywell, Hants, and had,
  1. Edmund Toll, who *d.* in 1774, leaving one son and two daughters, viz.
     - Ashburnham Toll, *d.* unm. 5th January, 1800.
     - Mary Toll, *m.* to John Bulley, of Reading, surgeon.
     - Jane Toll, *m.* to John Aldridge, of Lincoln's Inn, gent.
  2. Ashburnham Toll, of Preston Deanery, in the county of Northampton, attorney-at-law, married Mary, daughter of Lieutenant-colonel Geary, of the 10th Dragoons, and dying 25th May, 1771, leaving
     - Charles Toll, of Preston Deanery, *b.* in 1739, who assumed, in 1775, the surname and arms of Newman, *m.* in 1765, Hester, daughter of John Langham, esq. of Cottesbroke, and had issue,
       - James, captain R.N. lost at sea, 24th December, 1811.
       - Charles, surgeon R. N.
       - Frances.
       - Maria, *m.* to James Payne, esq. of Hardingstone, in Northamptonshire.
     - Ashburnham-Philip Toll, in holy orders, of whom hereafter.
     - Richard-Newman Toll, M.D.
     - Anne Toll, *d.* in 1824, unm.
     - Mary Toll, *m.* to Mr. Pitman, of Odyham, solicitor.
  3. Charles Toll.
  4. Frederick Toll, father of the Rev. John Toll, of King's Clear, *d. s. p.*

Mr. Newman *d.* in June, 1682, and was *s.* by his son

I. Richard Newman, esq. of Fifehead-Magdalen, in the county of Dorset, Evercreech Park, in Somersetshire, and Preston Hall, in the county of Northampton, who was created a Baronet 20th December, 1699. Sir Richard *m.* Frances, daughter and co-heir of Sir Thomas Samwell, bart. of Upton, and had issue,

- Samwell, his successor.
- Elizabeth, Mrs. Kitchen, *d. s. p.*
- Barbara, died unm. in 1763.
- Frances, heir to her brother.

He *d.* 30th December, 1721, and was *s.* by his son,

II. Sir Samwell Newman, who *d.* unm. 4th June, 1747, when the Baronetcy expired, and his estates devolved upon his sisters, the survivor of whom,

Frances Newman, became eventually sole heiress. She died unmarried 25th August, 1775, and bequeathed a considerable portion of her estates to Sir James Langham, bart. of Cottesbroke. Her heirs were her cousins,

- Charles Toll, of Preston Deanery, who assumed the surname of Newman, and his brother,
- Ashburnham-Philip Toll, in holy orders, of Thornbury Park, a prebendary of York, who assumed the surname and arms of Newman. He *d. s. p.* in 1802, and was *s.* by his brother,
- Richard-Newman Toll, M.D. who assumed, in 1802, the surname of Newman. His son is the present (1837)
  - Henry-Wenman Newman, esq. of Thornbury Park, in the county of Gloucester. (Refer to Burke's *Commoners*, vol. i. p. 111.)

Arms—Quarterly; sa. and arg. in the first and fourth, three mullets of the second, in the centre an inescutcheon gu. charged with a portcullis imperially crowned or, being an augmentation granted by the king to Colonel Newman, for his conduct at the battle of Worcester.

NEWTON, OF BARRS COURT.

Created 16th Aug. 1660.

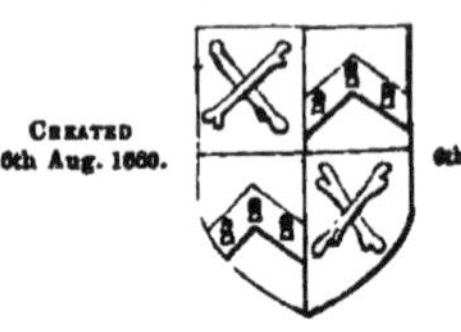

Extinct 6th April, 174

Lineage.

This family derived from

Howell ap Grono, Lord of Newton in Re... whose son,

Cradock ap Howell ap Grono, was father of

Sir William Cradock, who *m.* Jane, daughter of Sir Matthew Wogan, and lies buried at Newton. His lineal descendant,

Sir Richard Cradock, chief justice of England, changed his name to Newton, and marrying Emma, daughter and co-heir of Sir Thomas Perret, of Le...ton, had issue,

John (Sir), his heir, who *m.* Isabel, daughter and heir of Sir John Chedder.

Thomas (Sir).

The younger son,

SIR THOMAS NEWTON, *m. temp.* EDWARD IV. Joan, daughter and heir of Sir John Barr, of Barrs Court, and acquired that, the manor of Bitton, and other estates. His son and heir,

JOHN NEWTON, esq. of Barrs Court, in the county of Gloucester, *m.* Margaret, daughter of Sir Edmund Gage, of Wraxwell, in the county of Somerset, and left a son and heir,

SIR JOHN NEWTON, who *m.* Margaret, daughter of Sir Anthony Points, and was father of

SIR HENRY NEWTON, who by Catherine, his wife, daughter of Sir Thomas Paston, left a son and heir,

SIR THEODORE NEWTON, lord of Bitton in 1608, who *m.* Penelope, daughter of Sir John Rodney, of Rodney's Stoke, in the county of Somerset, and was *s.* by his son,

I. JOHN NEWTON, esq. of Barrs Court, who was created a BARONET by *King* CHARLES II. 16th August, 1660, with remainder, default his own male issue, to JOHN, son of Thomas Newton, esq. of Gunwarley, in Lincolnshire. Sir John *m.* Grace Stone, but died issueless in 1661, leaving his estate to his successor, according to limitation in the patent of baronetcy,

II. SIR JOHN NEWTON, *b.* 9th June, 1626, who *m.* Mary, daughter of Sir Gervase Eyre, knt. of Rampton, Notts, and had a numerous family, of which

Gervase, *d. s. p.*

JOHN, succeeded to the title.

Elizabeth, *m.* to Francis Stringer, esq. of Sutton-upon-Lound, Notts.

Mary, *m.* — Marwood, esq. of Laughton, in Lincolnshire.

Jane, *m.* William Sacheverell, esq. of Morley, in Derbyshire.

Lucy, *m.* to — Screop, esq. of Louth, in Lincolnshire.

Hester, *m.* to Colonel Seymour.

Frances, *m.* to — Winfield, esq. of Eggington, in Derbyshire.

He *d.* 31st May, 1699, aged seventy-three, and was *s.* by his son,

III. SIR JOHN NEWTON, who *m.* first, Abigail, daughter of William Heveringham, esq. of Heveringham, in Suffolk, and had a daughter Cary, who *m.* Edward Coke, esq. of Holkham, and was mother of Thomas Coke, created Earl of Leicester in 1744, and great-grandmother of Thomas William Coke, esq. of Holkham, raised to the same dignity in 1837. Sir John Newton *m.* secondly, Susannah, sister and co-heir of Sir Michael Wharton, knt. of Beverley, in Yorkshire, and relict of Sir John Bright, of Badsworth, and by that lady had a daughter *m.* to John Archer, and a son, viz.

MICHAEL (Sir), his heir, made a knight of the Bath in 1725. He inherited a large estate at the death of his uncle, Sir Michael Wharton.

He *d.* aged eighty-five, 12th February, 1734, and was *s.* by his son,

IV. SIR MICHAEL NEWTON, K. B. who married Lady Margaret Coningsby, daughter of Thomas, Earl of Coningsby (by his second wife, Frances, daughter and heir of Richard, Earl of Ranelagh). Her ladyship was created in the lifetime of her father (1716) Baroness and Viscountess Coningsby, of Hampton Court, and after his decease, inheriting his lordship's English peerage (see BURKE's *Extinct Peerage*), became COUNTESS OF CONINGSBY. By this lady Sir Michael had an only child, JOHN, who died an infant. Her ladyship, who outlived her husband several years, *d.* in 1761, when all her honours expired. Sir Michael Newton *d.* 6th April, 1743, when the BARONETCY became EXTINCT.

Arms—Quarterly; first and fourth, sa. two shin bones saltirewise, the sinister surmounted of the dexter arg.; second and third, arg. on a chevron az. three garbs or.

NEWTON, OF CHARLTON.

CREATED 2nd April, 1629.

EXTINCT 22nd Jan. 1700.

Lineage.

I. ADAM NEWTON, installed dean of Durham, 27th September, 1606, was chosen by *King* JAMES I. to be tutor to his son, *Prince* HENRY, and treasurer to his highness's revenue, and created a BARONET, as SIR ADAM NEWTON, of Charlton, in the county of Kent, which manor was conferred by grant from the crown, and upon which he erected a noble mansion, and designed to have rebuilt the parish church; but departing this life, 13th January, 1629, "he left (observes PHILPOT, in his *Villary Cantiarium*) to Sir David Cunningham, knt. and bart. late cofferer to *Prince* CHARLES, Mr. Newton, his brother, and Mr. Peter Newton, gentleman usher to *King* CHARLES, who have most amply discharged the trust, and in a manner new built a great part thereof, and erected the steeple new from the ground, and furnished it with a new ring of bells, decorating the said church without and within, that it surpasses most in the shire." Sir Adam *m.* Dorothy, daughter of Sir John Puckering, knt. lord keeper of the great seal, *temp.* ELIZABETH, and was *s.* by his elder son,

II. SIR WILLIAM NEWTON, of Charlton, who died unm. and was *s.* by his brother,

III. SIR HENRY NEWTON, who inherited by deed of settlement the estates of his uncle, SIR THOMAS PUCKERING, bart. on the decease of that gentleman's only surviving child, JANE PUCKERING, and assumed in consequence the surname of Puckering, taking up his abode at the Priory, in Warwickshire, the seat of his said uncle. Sir Henry espoused the royal cause in the civil wars, and was at the battle of Edge Hill. He was chosen by the town of Warwick, member in the convention parliament which restored CHARLES II.; and was afterwards representative for the same place in the Long Parliament. He was deputy lieutenant for Warwickshire, and was appointed by patent, by *King* CHARLES II. paymaster-general of the forces. "His good housekeeping and liberality to the poor, who scarcely ever went away unfed from his gates, gained him the general love and esteem of his neighbours, and he was distinguished throughout the kingdom for being a generous benefactor to the poor cavaliers, whose services were not rewarded by *King* CHARLES II." He *d.* 22nd January, 1700, at the advanced age of eighty-three, leaving no surviving issue by his wife, Elizabeth, daughter of Thomas Murray, esq. when the BARONETCY became EXTINCT. Sir Henry's estate devolved, by his own settlement, upon his wife's niece, Jane daughter and co-heir of Henry Murray, esq. groom of the bedchamber to Charles II. widow of Sir John Bowyer, bart. of Knippersley, in the county of Stafford for her life, remainder to Vincent Grantham, esq. of Goltho, in Lincolnshire.

Arms—Az. two ostrich's feathers in saltier arg. between three boars' heads of the same langued gu. tusked or.

NEWTON, OF LONDON.

Created 25th Jan. 1660-1.—Extinct about 1670.

Lineage.

I. Sir Robert Newton, citizen of London, was created a Baronet in 1660-1. He m. Elizabeth, daughter and co-heir of Francis Longston, esq. of London, but left no male issue at his decease, which occurred about 1670, when the title became extinct.

NICOLLS, OF HARDWICK.

Created 1641.

Extinct 1717.

Lineage.

The name of this family was spelt at different periods, Nycol, Nicoll, Nicolls, Nicholls, and Nicholl. The arms, "sa. three pheons arg." were borne by William Nicoll, of Hardwick, Northamptonshire, who was born in the reign of Edward IV. and died at the advanced age of ninety-six. His grandson, Francis Nicolls, esq. of Hardwick, had a confirmation of these arms, with the addition of "a canton arg." The exact same coat armour was also used by the Nicholls, of Llantwitt Major,* in Glamorganshire, and by the Nicholls of Cornwall, who derived probably from a common ancestor with the Northamptonshire family, but which branch is the senior it is difficult to ascertain.

Thomas Nicolls, esq. serjeant-at-law, (son of William Nicolls, who was buried in Hardwicke Church, in 1575, aged ninety-six,) purchased, *temp.* Elizabeth from Wiston Brown a third part of the manor of Hardwicke, Northamptonshire. He m. Anne, daughter of John Pell, esq. of Eltington, and had issue,

> Francis, of Hardwicke, *b.* in 1557, governor of Tilbury Fort, in 1588, who m. Anne, daughter of David Seymour, esq. and was father of
>
> > Francis, of whom presently as heir to his uncle.
>
> Augustine.
>
> William, of Tilton, in Leicestershire.

The second son,

Sir Augustine Nicolls, knt. of Faxton, which he acquired from Anthony Morgan, esq. was born at Ecton, in Northamptonshire. Adopting the legal profession, he entered himself at the Middle Temple, and was reader in the last year of Elizabeth. During her majesty's reign he obtained the coif, and by James I. was made king's serjeant. He eventually became one of the judges of the court of Common Pleas. He m. Mary, widow of Edward Bagshaw, esq. but had no issue. Sir Augustine died in 1616, while on the northern circuit, at Kendall, in Westmoreland, and, Fuller informs us, that a monument was there erected to his memory. By the inquisition taken after his decease, the manor of Faxton with its appurtenances devolved on his nephew and heir,

I. Francis Nicolls, esq. of Hardwicke, in Northamptonshire, M.P. for that county in 1627, and [illegible] sheriff in 1631, who was created a Baronet in [illegible] He m. Mary, daughter of Edward Bagshaw, esq. and had with a daughter, Mary, a son and successor,

II. Sir Edward Nicolls, of Hardwicke and Faxton who m. first, Judith, daughter of Sir Rowland [illegible] John, knt. by whom he had seven daughters, and secondly, Jane, daughter of Sir Stephen Soame, of Haydon, in Essex, by whom he had a son and two daughters, namely,

> Edward, his heir.
>
> Anne, *d.* 17th April, 1676.
>
> Susanna, m. to Sir John Danvers.
>
> Jane, m. first, to John Rainsford, esq.; and secondly, to — Kemeey, esq.

Sir Edward died 28th February, 1682, and was [illegible] by his son,

III. Sir Edward Nicolls, of Hardwicke and Faxton, at whose decease *s. p.* in 1717, the Baronetcy became extinct; the estates devolving on his two sisters, Lady Danvers and Mrs. Kemeey. By his will Sir Edward settled lands in Hardwick and other places for augmenting the eight following livings: All Saints in Northampton, Oundle, Kettering, [illegible]well, Hardwick, Moulsom, Grainsborough, and Spratton with £30 each yearly.

Arms—Sa. three pheons arg.

NOEL, OF BROOK.

Created 29th June, 1611.

Extinct 6th Apr. [illegible]

Lineage.

Robert Noel, lord of Ellenhall, and other [illegible] lands, *temp.* Henry I. acquired, by grant from [illegible]rence, prior of Coventry, and the monks of that [illegible] the greater part of Gainsborough, in the county [illegible] Warwick. In the reign of Henry II. he found[ed the] priory of Raunton, or Ronton, near Ellenhall [his] chief seat, for canons regular of St. Augustine [and] had two sons,

* From the Nicholls, of Llantwitt Major, descend the Nicholls of Monmouthshire, now represented by W[illegible] Hawkins, of the Gaer, in the parish of Tredunnock; and the Nicholls of Ham, of Dimlands, and of Merth[illegible] (See Burke's *Commoners.*)

THOMAS, sheriff of Staffordshire, *temp.* HENRY II. and RICHARD I. *m.* Margaret, eldest daughter of Gay le Strange, Lord of Knockyn, and co-heir of her brother, Ralph le Strange, by whom he left two daughters, viz.

- ALICE NOEL, *m.* to William de Harcourt, lord of Stanton Harcourt, in the county of Warwick, and had Ellenhall, and other estates as her moiety of her father's property. (See BURKE'S *Commoners*, vol. ii. p. 221.)
- JANE NOEL, *m.* to William de Dunston, and had for her share Ronton, &c.

PHILIP.

The younger son,

PHILIP NOEL, of Hilcote, in the county of Stafford, which estate he had from his father, left a son and heir,

ROBERT NOEL, of Hilcote, who *m.* Joan, daughter of Sir John Acton, knt. and hence descended in a direct line,

JAMES NOEL, esq. of Hilcote, who was appointed by act of parliament, 5 HENRY VIII. one of the justices of the peace for assessing and collecting the pole tax. He *m.* a daughter of Richard Pole, esq. of Langley, in the county of Derby, and was *s.* at Hilcote by his eldest son, while a younger son,

ANDREW NOEL, esq. became the founder of a distinct branch. At the dissolution of the monasteries, he had a grant of the manor and scite of the late preceptory of Dalby-upon-Wold, in Leicestershire, which had belonged to the knights of St. John, and of the manor of Parybarre, in the county of Stafford. He served as sheriff of Rutland, 28 HENRY VIII. again in the reign of EDWARD VI. and afterwards in the time of MARY. He *m.* first, Elizabeth, daughter and heir of John Hopton, esq. of Hopton, in Shropshire, and widow of Sir John Perient, by whom he had ANDREW, his heir, with other children. He wedded secondly, Dorothy, daughter of Richard Conyers, esq. of Wakerley, in the county of Northampton, widow of Roger Flower, esq. and by that lady had a son, JOHN, from whom the NOELS of *Kirby Mallory*. He was *s.* at his decease by his eldest son,

SIR ANDREW NOEL, knt. of Dalby, in the county of Leicester, a person of great note in the days of good Queen Bess, living in such magnificence as to vie with the nobility of the largest fortune. Fuller says, "that for person, parentage, grace, gesture, valour, and many other excellent parts, (amongst which skill in music), Sir Andrew Noel was of the first rank in the court." He was knighted by the queen, and became a favourite but the expenses consequent on his mode of living, forced him to alienate Dalby, on which his royal mistress is said to have made the following couplet.

"The word of denial, and letter of fifty,
Is that gentleman's name who will never be thrifty."

Sir Andrew was thrice sheriff of Rutland, and knight of the shire in several parliaments. He *m.* Mabel, sixth daughter of Sir James Harrington, knt. sister of John, Lord Harrington, of Exton, and had issue,

- EDWARD, (Sir), his heir.
- Charles, *d.* unm. in 1619.
- Arthur.
- Alexander, of Whitwell.
- Lucy, *m.* to William, Lord Eure.
- Theodosia, *m.* to Sir Edward Cecil, afterwards Lord Wimbledon.
- Elizabeth, *m.* to George, Earl of Castlehaven, in Ireland.

Sir Andrew *d.* at his seat, Brook, 9th October, 1607, and was *s.* by his eldest son,

I. SIR EDWARD NOEL, knt. of Brook, in the county of Rutland, who was created a BARONET, 29th June, 1611, and advanced to the peerage as Baron Noel, of Ridlington, 23rd March, 1616-17. He *m.* Julien, eldest daughter and co-heir of Sir Baptist Hicks, bart. who was subsequently, 5th May, 1628, created Baron Hicks, of Ilmington, and Viscount Camden, with remainder to his son-in-law, Lord Noel, and dying in the October of the following, those honours so descended. Lord Noel had issue,

- BAPTIST, his heir.
- Henry, *m.* Mary, daughter of Henry Perry, esq. of London, and *d. s. p.* His widow *m.* Sir William Fermor, bart. of Easton Neston, in the county of Northampton, and was grandmother of the first Earl of Pomfret.
- Anne.
- Penelope, *m.* to Viscount Chaworth.
- Eleanor.
- Mary, *m.* to Sir Erasmus de la Fountain, of Kirby Bellers, in the county of Leicester.

His lordship *d.* 10th March, 1643, and was *s.* by his eldest son,

II. SIR BAPTIST NOEL, second Lord Noel, and third Viscount Campden. This nobleman following his father, raised troops for the royal cause, and took an active part in the war. He was in consequence compelled to pay to the sequestrators £9000 composition for his estate, and an annuity of £150. His princely residence, at Campden, was burnt down by the royal army to prevent its becoming a garrison to the parliamentarians. On the restoration, his lordship was constituted lord-lieutenant of the county of Rutland. He *m.* first, Lady Anne Fielding, daughter of the Earl of Denbigh, but by her ladyship had no surviving issue. He *m.* secondly, Anne, daughter of Sir Robert Lovett, of Liscombe, Bucks, Countess Dowager of Bath, and again had no surviving child. His lordship *m.* thirdly, Hester, daughter and co-heir of Thomas, Lord Wotton, and had, by that lady,

- EDWARD, his successor, who was created in 1681, Baron Noel, with remainder, default of male issue, to his brothers.
- Henry, of North Luffenham, in the county of Rutland, *m.* Elizabeth, daughter and heir of Sir William Wale, and left an only daughter and heir,
  - JULIANA NOEL, who *m.* Charles Boyle, Earl of Burlington.
- Mary, *m.* to James, Earl of Northampton.
- Juliana, *m.* to William, Lord Allington.
- Elizabeth, *m.* to Charles, Earl Berkeley.

Lord Camden *m.* fourthly, Lady Elizabeth Bertie, daughter of Montagu, second Earl of Lindsey, and had four other children, viz.

- BAPTIST, of Luffenham, M. P. for the county of Rutland, *m.* Susannah, daughter and heir of Sir Thomas Fanshaw, and left an only son,
  - BAPTIST, who eventually inherited the honours of the family.
- John, *m.* Elizabeth, daughter of Bennet, Lord Sherrard, and had issue,
  - John, M. P. for Northamptonshire, *d.* unm.
  - Thomas, *m.* Elizabeth, widow of Baptist Noel, fourth Earl of Gainsborough.
  - Bennet, *m.* Miss Adam.
  - Elizabeth, *d.* unm.
  - Bridget, *m.* to David, Lord Milsington.
  - Alice.
- Catherine, *m.* to John, tenth Earl of Rutland.
- Martha-Penelope, *m.* to — Dormer, esq.

His lordship *d.* 29th October, 1682, and was *s.* by his eldest son,

III. SIR EDWARD NOEL, third Lord Noel, and fourth

Viscount Campden, who was created in 1682, Earl of Gainsborough, with remainder, default his own male issue, to his brothers. He *m.* first, Lady Elizabeth Wriothesley, daughter and co-heir of Thomas, fourth Earl of Southampton, by whom he acquired the lordship of Tichfield, and had issue,

- WRIOTHESLEY-BAPTIST, his heir.
- Frances, *m.* to Simon, Lord Digby, and died in 1684.
- Jane, *m.* to William, Lord Digby, brother of Simon.
- Elizabeth, *m.* to Richard Norton, esq. of the county of Southampton.
- Juliana, *d.* unm.

His lordship *m.* secondly, Mary, daughter of James, son of Philip, Earl of Pembroke, and widow of Sir Robert Worseley, bart. He *d.* in 1689, and was *s.* by his son,

IV. SIR WRIOTHESLEY-BAPTIST NOEL, fourth Lord Noel, fifth Viscount Campden, and second Earl of Gainsborough. His lordship *m.* Catherine, daughter of Fulke Greville, fifth Lord Brook, and left two daughters, his co-heirs, viz.

- Elizabeth, *m.* in 1704 to Henry, first Duke of Portland.
- Rachel, *m.* in 1705-6, to Henry, second Duke of Beaufort.

He *d.* 21st September, 1690, when all his honours devolved upon his kinsman, (refer to issue of Sir Baptist, second baronet, and third Viscount Campden,)

V. SIR BAPTIST NOEL, of Luffenham, in the county of Rutland, third Earl of Gainsborough, who *m.* Lady Dorothy Manners, daughter of John, Duke of Rutland, and had issue,

- BAPTIST, his successor.
- John, *d.* in 1718.
- James, M. P. for Rutlandshire, *d.* unm. in 1752.
- Susan, *m.* to Anthony, fourth Earl of Shaftesbury.
- Catherine.
- Mary, *d.* in 1718.

His lordship *d.* 16th April, 1714, and was *s.* by his eldest son,

VI. SIR BAPTIST NOEL, fourth Earl of Gainsborough. His lordship *m.* Elizabeth, daughter of William Chapman, esq. by whom (who *m.* secondly, Thomas Noel, esq.) he had issue,

- BAPTIST, his successor.
- HENRY, heir to his brother.
- Charles, *d.* young.
- Elizabeth.
- JANE, *m.* to Gerard-Anne Edwards, esq. of Welham Grove, and had a son,
  - GERARD EDWARDS, of whom presently, as heir to the estates of his uncle, HENRY, eighth baronet, and sixth Earl of Gainsborough.
- Juliana, *m.* to George Evans, Lord Carbery, and *d.* in 1760.
- Penelope, *d.* young.
- Anne.
- Lucy, *m.* to Sir Horatio Mann, K. B.
- Mary.
- Susanna.
- Sophia, *m.* to Christopher Nevile, esq. and had a son, CHRISTOPHER NEVILE, esq. who assumed his maternal surname, and is the present CHRISTOPHER NOEL, esq. of Wellingore, near Lincoln.

He *d.* 21st March, 1751, and was *s.* by his eldest son,

VII. SIR BAPTIST NOEL, fifth Earl of Gainsborough, who *d.* a minor, on his travels, at Geneva, in 1759, unm. and was *s.* by his brother,

VIII. SIR HENRY NOEL, sixth Earl of Gainsborough, who *d.* unm. 8th April, 1798, when all his honours, including the BARONETCY, became EXTINCT. His estates devolved upon (the son of his sister Jane) his nephew,

GERARD EDWARDS, esq. of Welham Grove, who thereupon assumed the surname and arms of NOEL, and having inherited a baronetcy, in 1813, is the present (1837)

SIR GERARD NOEL, bart. of Exton Park, in the county of Rutland.

Arms—Or, fretty gules, a canton ermine.

NOEL, OF KIRKBY MALLORY.

CREATED 4th July, 1660.—EXTINCT 17th April, 1823.

Lineage.

ANDREW NOEL, esq. a younger son of James N[illegible] esq. of Hilcote, acquired by grant from the crown *temp.* HENRY VIII. the manor and scite of the preceptory of Dalby-upon-Wold, in the county of Leicester, and settled there. He *m.* first, Elizabeth, daughter and heir of William Hopton, esq. of Hopton in Salop, and relict of Sir John Pengent, knt. by whom he had a son, SIR ANDREW NOEL, of Dalby, ancestor of the Earls of Gainsborough; and two daughters, Lucy, *m.* to William Lord Evers, and Theodosia, *m.* to Cecil Viscount Wentworth. His second wife was Dorothy, daughter of Reginald Conyers, esq. of W[illegible]ley, in Northamptonshire, and widow of Roger F[illegible]er, esq. by her he left another son,

JOHN NOEL, esq. of Whellesburgh, who *m.* A[illegible] daughter and heir of John Fowler, esq. of W[illegible]burgh, by Barbara, daughter and co-heir of Thomas Harvey, esq. of Elmsthorpe, and was father of

WILLIAM NOEL, esq. of Kirkby Mallory, sheriff of Leicestershire in 1604, and of Warwickshire in [illegible]. He *m.* Frances, eldest daughter and co-heir of [illegible] Fulwood, esq. of Frere Hall, in the county of Warwick, and had issue,

- WILLIAM, his heir.
- VERE, successor to his brother.
- Edward, rector of Sibbesdon, aged eleven in [illegible] *m.* Elizabeth, daughter of the Rev. John [illegible]grave, rector of Broughton Astley, and had [illegible]
- Henry, of Pickering Grange, barrister-at-law [illegible] *s. p.* in 1694.
- Andrew, of Congeston, who left an only dau[illegible] and heir.
- Elizabeth, *m.* first, to Ralph Adderley, esq. [illegible]rewas, in Staffordshire, by whom she had [illegible] Sir Charles Adderley, knt. of Hams Hall [illegible] secondly, to Ralph Floyer, esq. of Hints.
- Anne, *m.* to Thomas Grey, esq. of Langley.
- Frances *m.* to Henry Kendal, esq. of Smythe[illegible] in Derbyshire.
- Eleanor, *m.* to John Stafford, esq. of H[illegible]
- Catharine, *m.* to Richard Corbet, esq. of Sa[illegible] Grace.

William Noel died in 1641, and was *s.* by his son,

WILLIAM NOEL, esq. of Kirkby Mallory, aged [illegible] in 1719; who *m.* Frances, daughter and co-heir [illegible] chard Creswell, esq. serjeant-at law, of E[illegible] the Vale, but dying *s. p.* in 1651, was succeeded [illegible] brother,

I. VERE NOEL, esq. of Kirby Mallery, in the [illegible] of Leicester, aged eleven in 1619, who was [illegible] BARONET 4th July, 1660. Sir Vere *m.* Elizabeth [illegible]ter of Sir Wolston Dixie, knt. of Bosworth, and [illegible] in 1670, was *s.* by his son,

II. SIR WILLIAM NOEL, who *m.* first, Mary [illegible]

daughter of John, Lord Lovelace, by ANNE, BARONESS WENTWORTH, and had issue,

THOMAS, his successor.

JOHN, heir to his brother.

Sir William m. secondly, Frances, third daughter of Humble, Lord Ward, and had by her a daughter,

Frances, aged about nine in 1681, m. first, to Sir Charles Skymsher, knt. of Norbury Manor; and secondly, to Sir John Chester, bart. of Chichley.

Sir William d. 13th April, 1665, aged thirty-three, and was s. by his son,

III. SIR THOMAS NOEL, of Kirkby Malory, who m. in 1681, Anne, daughter of William Whitlock, esq. of Phillis Court, Oxfordshire, but dying s. p. in 1688, was s. by his brother,

IV. SIR JOHN NOEL, of Kirkby Malory, who m. Mary, daughter and co-heir of Sir John Clobery, knt. of Winchester, and by her, who d. in 1751, had issue,

CLOBERY, his heir.

William, b. 19th March, 1695, an eminent lawyer, who sat for several years in parliament for the boroughs of Stamford and West Looe, and became, eventually, one of the judges of the court of Common Pleas. He m. Elizabeth, daughter of Sir Thomas Trollope, bart. of Casewick, in the county of Lincoln, and d. 8th December, 1762, having had issue,

Mary, m. to Thomas Hill, esq. of Tern, in Shropshire, and had a son, Noel Hill, created in 1784, BARON BERWICK, of Attingham.

Anne, d. unm.

Frances, m. to Bennet, Earl of Harborough, and had a daughter, Frances, m. to Major-Gen. Morgan.

Elizabeth.

Anne, m. to Francis Mundy, esq. of Osbaston.

Sir John d. 1st July, 1697, and was s. by his son,

V. SIR CLOBERY NOEL, M.P. of Kirkby Malory, sheriff of Leicestershire in 1718, who m. Elizabeth, daughter of Thomas Rowney, esq. of Oxford, and by her who d. 24th June, 1743, aged forty-nine, had issue,

EDWARD, his heir.

Clobery, in holy orders, M. A. b. 31st July, 1716, d. s. p. in 1763.

Thomas, captain, R. N. b. 26th September, 1717, d. 5th June, 1756, of wounds received in the action off Minorca, under Admiral Byng.

John, in holy orders, rector of Steeple Aston, in Oxfordshire, and vicar of Aston, in Warwickshire, d. s. p.

Rowney, b. 26th July, 1726, rector of Elmsthorpe and Kirkby Malory, D. D. and dean of Salisbury, m. Maria, daughter of Thomas Boothby Skrimsher, esq. of Tooley Park, and d. s. p. 6th July, 1786.

Mary.

Sir Clobery d. 30th July, 1733, aged thirty-nine, and was s. by his son,

VI. SIR EDWARD NOEL, of Kirkby Malory, who became BARON WENTWORTH upon the demise of his cousin, Martha Lovelace, Lady Wentworth, in 1745. His lordship m. Judeth, daughter and heir of William Lamb, esq. of Farndish, in the county of Northampton, and had issue,

THOMAS, his successor.

Judeth, m. to Sir Ralph Milbanke, bart. This lady and her husband assumed the additional surname of "NOEL" upon the decease of her brother, Thomas, Viscount Wentworth. She d. in 1822, leaving an only daughter and heiress, (Sir Ralph d. in 1825,)

ANNA ISABELLA, b. 17th May, 1792, m. 2nd January, 1815, to the celebrated poet, *George*, LORD BYRON, and has an only child,

ADA BYRON, m. in 1835, to Peter, present Lord King.

Elizabeth, m. in 1777, to James-Bland Burgess, esq. (afterwards Sir James Lamb, bart.) but died s. p. in 1779.

Sophia-Susanna, m. in 1777, to Nathaniel, Lord Scarsdale, and dying 1782, left issue,

NATHANIEL CURZON, Baron Scarsdale.

William Curzon, killed at Waterloo.

Sophia-Caroline Curzon, m. in 1800, to Robert, Viscount Tamworth, who d. in 1824, issueless.

His lordship was advanced, by letters patent, dated 4th May, 1762, to the dignity of Viscount WENTWORTH, *of Wellesborough, in the county of Leicester*, and dying in 1774, was s. by his son,

VII. THOMAS NOEL, second Viscount Wentworth, and ninth successor to the Barony of Wentworth. His lordship died s. p. in 1815, when the VISCOUNTY became EXTINCT, but the BARONY OF WENTWORTH fell into ABEYANCE between his lordship's sister, JUDETH, *Lady Milbanke*, and his nephew, the *Honourable* NATHANIEL CURZON, as it still continues between Lady Milbanke's only child,

ANNA-ISABELLA, Dowager LADY BYRON,

and

Lord Scarsdale.

Arms—As NOEL, OF BROOK.

NORREYS, OF SPEKE.

CREATED 3rd Dec. 1606.

EXTINCT ....

Lineage.

THOMAS NORREYS, esq. of Speke, in Lancashire, the representative of a highly distinguished family, married Lettice, daughter and heir of Thomas Norreys, esq. and had issue,

WILLIAM (Sir), his heir.

Edmund, of Fifield, in Berkshire, ancestor of the Fifield branch of the family, now EXTINCT.

Nicholas, of Tarleton, ancestor of the late HENRY NORRIS, esq. of Davyhulme Hall, whose only daughter and heir, MARY, m. in 1809, ROBERT JOSIAS JACKSON HARRIS, esq. who assumed, in consequence, the surname and arms of NORREYS. (See BURKE'S *Commoners*, vol. i. p. 310.)

The eldest son,

SIR WILLIAM NORREYS, knt. of Speke, married Catherine, daughter of Sir Henry Bold, of Bold Hall, and from Sir William, the manor of Speke passed to his line of descendant,

THOMAS NORREYS, esq. of Speke, b. in 1618, who m. Catherine, daughter of Sir Henry Garraway, knt. and died in 1700, leaving issue,

I. THOMAS, his heir, of Speke, M.P. for Liverpool, *temp.* WILLIAM III. who m. Miss Aston, daughter of Sir William Aston, bart. and left an only daughter and heir,

MARY, who conveyed Speke to her husband,

Lord Sydney Beauclerk. She had an only child,

Topham Beauclerk, esq. whose son, Charles George Beauclerk, esq. sold the estate of Speke in 1797, to Richard Watt, esq.

II. William, of whom presently.

III. Edward, M.D. of Chester, M.P. for Liverpool, *d.* in 1726, leaving two daughters,

Catherine, *m.* to Ralph Leycester, esq. of Toft.

Susanna, *m.* to — Warburton, esq.

The second son,

I. Sir William Norreys, M.P. for Liverpool, ambassador to the Great Mogul, was created a Baronet in 1698. He *m.* Elizabeth, daughter and heir of Robert Read, esq. of Bristol, relict, first, of Isaac Meynell, of Lombard Street, London, and secondly of Nicholas Pollexfen, esq. also of London, but had no issue. At Sir William's decease the Baronetcy expired.

Arms—Quarterly; arg. and gu.; in the second and third quarters, a fret or, over all a fesse az.

NORTH, OF MILDENHALL.

Created 14th June, 1660.

Extinct 6th July, 1695.

Lineage.

Sir Henry North, knt. of Mildenhall, in Suffolk, younger son of Roger, second Lord North, served in the wars of the low countries, *temp.* Elizabeth, and received the honour of knighthood from the Earl of Leicester. He *m.* Mary, daughter and co-heir of Richard Knevit, esq. and had issue,

Roger, his heir.

Henry, of Laxfield, in Suffolk, left, by Sarah Jennor, his wife, two sons, Henry and Edward.

Elizabeth.

Mary.

Dorothy.

Sir Henry *d.* in 1620, aged sixty-four, and was *s.* by his son,

Sir Roger North, knt. of Mildenhall, *b.* 18th February, 1577, who *m.* first, Elizabeth, daughter and coheir of Sir John Gilbert, knt. of Great Finborow, Suffolk; and secondly, Thomasine, daughter of Thomas Clence, esq. of Holbrook. The latter *d. s. p.* but by the former, (who *d.* 29th November, 1612), he had two sons and a daughter,

Henry, his heir.

Dudley.

Mary, *m.* to Colonel Thomas Blagge, of Hollinger, governor of Wallingford Castle, and had five daughters his co-heirs. The youngest, Margaret, so often mentioned in Evelyn's Memoirs, *m.* Sydney Godolphin, the celebrated Earl of Godolphin; and the eldest, Henrietta-Maria, became the wife of Sir Thomas Yarburgh, knt. of Snaith, in Yorkshire.

Sir Roger *d.* 17th June, 1651, and was *s.* by his son,

I. Sir Henry North, of Mildenhall, who was created a baronet 14th June, 1660. He *m.* Sarah, daughter of John Rayney, esq. of West Malling, in Kent, and by her, who *d.* 1st July, 1670, had issue,

Henry, his heir.

Thomasine, *m.* to Thomas Holland, esq. son and heir of Sir John Holland, bart. of Quiddenham, Norfolk, and *d.* 28th September, [illegible], in the 28th year of her age.

Peregrina, *m.* to William Hanmer, esq. and was mother of

Sir Thomas Hanmer, bart. speaker of the House of Commons, who resided at Mildenhall, which estate passed at Sir Thomas's decease, in 1746, to his nephew, Sir William Bunbury, bart. of Stanny Hall, by whose grandson, Sir Henry Edward Bunbury, bart. it is now (1837) enjoyed.

Dudleia, *m.* to Sir Thomas Cullum, bart. of Hawstead.

Sir Henry North died 5th July, 1695, when the Baronetcy expired.

Arms—Az. a lion passant or, between three fleurs-de-lis arg.

NORTON, OF ROTHERFIELD.

Created 23rd May, 1622.

Extinct in [illegible].

Lineage.

Richard Norton, living 10 Henry VII. the representative of a very ancient and eminent Hampshire family, *m.* Elizabeth, daughter and heir of [illegible] William Rotherfield, by Elizabeth, his wife, daughter and co-heir of William Dawtry, esq. and thus acquired the estate of Rotherfield, from which his descendants were designated. He was *s.* by his son,

John Norton, esq. of Rotherfield, Hants, who *m.* Anne, daughter of Sir George Puttenham, of Sherfield, in the same county, and had four sons, Richard, his heir; Thomas, of Nutley; John, of [illegible]; and Marmaduke, of Hateley. The eldest,

Sir Richard Norton, knt. of Rotherfield, *m.* first, Elizabeth, daughter and heir of William [illegible] Wymering, by Anne, his wife, sister and heir of [illegible] mond Mountpesson, of Batington, Wilts. and had issue,

John, his heir.

Mary, *m.* to Sir Henry Uvedall, knt.

Sir Richard *m.* secondly, Catherine, daughter of John Kingsmill, esq. and had by her a daughter, [illegible], wife of Sir Henry Whitehead, knt. and a son,

Daniel, (Sir), a stanch parliamentarian, who signalised himself in behalf of the Commons [illegible] the civil wars. He *m.* Honora, daughter and co-heir of John White, esq. of Southwick, [illegible] riff of Hants in 1588, grandson of John White, esquire of the body to Henry VIII. who obtained on the departure of the Canons, a grant from

his royal master, of the priory of Southwicke.
Sir Daniel Norton had a son and successor,

Daniel, of Southwick, whose son,

Richard Norton, esq. of Southwick, m. the Hon. Elizabeth Fiennes, dau. of Lord Saye, and had a son, Richard,[*] the last heir male of the family, and a daughter, who m. Richard Whitehead, esq. of Norman Court, Hants, and left an only daughter and heir,

Mary, m. in 1717, to Alexander Thistlethwayte, esq. of Winterslow, Wilts, and their son, Francis Thistlethwayte, esq. of Norman Court, recovered as heir-at-law after his uncle, Mr. Norton's decease, the Southwick estate, which had been bequeathed, in an extraordinary will, to government. He *d. s. p.* and was *s.* by his brother, the Rev. Thomas Thistlethwayte, D.D. of Southwick, who *m.* Selina, daughter of Peter Bathurst, esq. of Clarendon Park, Wilts, and was father of Robert Thistlethwayte, esq. of Southwick, M. P. for Hants during twenty years. His son and heir is the present Thomas Thistlethwayte, esq. of Southwick. (See Burke's *Commoners*, vol. iii. p. 473.)

Sir Richard died in 1592, and was *s.* by his eldest son,

John Norton, esq. of Ernshott, father by Joane Cole of

I. Sir Richard Norton, knt. of Rotherfield, who was created a baronet 23rd May, 1622. He *m.* Mabell, daughter of Mr. Alderman Henry Beecher, or Becker, of London, and had an only daughter and heiress,

Elizabeth, who *m.* Francis Paulet, esq. of Amport, grandson of William, fourth Marquis of Winchester, and had a son and heir,

Norton Paulet, esq. of Amport, whose son, George Paulet, esq. of Amport, succeeded as twelfth Marquis of Winchester, and was father of the present peer.

Sir Richard died in 1652, and the Baronetcy expired.

Arms—Vert, a lion rampant, or.

NORTON, OF COVENTRY.

Created 23rd July, 1661.—Extinct in 1691.

Lineage.

Simon Norton, esq. of Coventry, son of John Norton, of Allesley, in Warwickshire, and a descendant of the Nortons, of Yorkshire, *d.* in 1641, leaving by Prudence Jesson, his wife, three sons, John, of Allesley, Thomas, of Coventry; and Simon, who *m.* Mary, daughter of Sir Henry Hastings. The second son,

I. Thomas Norton, esq. of Coventry, was created a Baronet in 1661. He *m.* Anne, daughter of John Jermy, esq. of Hutton Hall, in Suffolk, and had issue,

Mary, *m.* to Sir Charles Modyford, bart.

Anne, *m.* to William Russell, esq. of Cambridgeshire.

Frances.

Elizabeth, *m.* to William Norton, esq. of Southwick.

Sir Thomas died in 1691, when the Baronetcy became extinct.

NORWICH, OF BRAMPTON.

Created 24th July, 1641. — Extinct January, 1742.

Lineage.

Simon de Norwich, *m.* Margaret, heir of Holt-Hetol Gifford, and thus acquired the manor of Brampton, Rowell, &c. His grandson, another

Simon de Norwich, *m.* Alice, only daughter and heir of Richard Christian, of Harborough, by whom he obtained large estates in the counties of Leicester and Northampton. He was *s.* by his posthumous son,

Simon Norwich, who was found to be cousin and heir to Sir Richard Holt. He *m.* Isabel, daughter of Richard Tunstall, and had issue. The sixth in lineal descent from him,

I. Sir John Norwich, knt. of Brampton, in the county of Northampton, who was created a Baronet by *King* Charles I. 24th July, 1641. He married first, Anne, daughter of Sir Roger Smith, knt. of Edmondthorp, in Leicestershire, and had issue,

Roger, his heir.

John, *d.* in Smyrna.

Erasmus, *m.* and left a family.

Simon, *d.* in Ireland.

Anne, *m.* to George Tresham, esq. of Newton, in Northamptonshire.

Mary, *m.* to Walter Kirkham, esq. of Fineshade, in the same county.

Judith, *m.* to — Atkins, esq.

He married secondly, Mary, daughter of Sir Henry Atkins, of Cheshunt, and dying in October, 1661, was *s.* by his eldest son,

II. Sir Roger Norwich, M. P. for Northamptonshire, *temp.* Charles II. He was a deputy lieutenant and verderor of the forest; but in the reign of James II. not coinciding in the measures of the court, he retired. He married Catherine, daughter of Sir Hatton Fermor, knt. of Easton, widow of Sir John Shuckburgh, bart. of Shuckburgh, in Warwickshire, and by that lady had,

Erasmus, his heir.

Catherine, *m.* to Edward Lloyd, esq. of Edgworth, in Middlesex, cupbearer to *King* William, and captain of horse.

Mary, *m.* to John Hicks, esq. of Trevetick, in Cornwall.

Arabella, *m.* to Thomas Smith, esq. of Trowlsworth, in Leicestershire, younger brother of the Lord Chief Baron Smith, of Scotland.

Sir Roger *d.* in September, 1691, and was *s.* by his son,

III. Sir Erasmus Norwich, who *m.* first, Lady Anabella Savage, younger daughter of Thomas, third Earl of Rivers, but by her ladyship had no issue. He *m.* secondly, June, daughter and heir of William Adams, esq. (son and heir of Sir William Adams, bart. but who died before his father,) and heir of her uncle, Sir

---

[*] This gentleman bequeathed by a most extraordinary will his great landed and personal property to the parliament of Great Britain, in trust, for the use "of the poor, hungry, thirsty, naked, strangers, sick, wounded, and prisoners, to the end of the world." This singular disposition, however, was set aside, and the estates eventually devolved on the Thistlethwaytes.

Charles Adams, bart. by this lady he left at his decease in August, 1739, a son,

IV. SIR WILLIAM NORWICH, who died unm. in 1742, when the BARONETCY EXPIRED.

The manor of Brampton appears to have been sold by one of the Norwich family to the Dyves. From Sir Lewis Dyve it was purchased by Sir Christopher Hatton, and is now possessed by Earl Spencer.

Arms—Party per pale, gules, and azure, a lion rampant, ermine.

OAKES.

CREATED 2nd Nov. 1813. EXTINCT 9th Sept. 1822.

Lineage.

HILDEBRAND OAKES, esq. a lieutenant-colonel in the army, m. Sarah, daughter of Henry Cornelissan, esq. of Braxted Lodge, in Sussex, and dying in 1797, was s. by his eldest son,

I. SIR HILDEBRAND OAKES, G. C. B. a lieutenant general in the army, and some time commander-in-chief of the island of Malta, who was created a BARONET 2nd November, 1813. Sir Hildebrand having no issue, obtained a second patent 1st June, 1815, re-creating him, with remainder to his brother, HENRY OAKES, esq. and that gentleman's male issue. He d. 9th September, 1822, when the first BARONETCY EXPIRED, and the second passed according to the limitation. (Refer to BURKE's *Peerage and Baronetage*.)

Arms—Arg. on a chevron engrailed sa. between three sprigs of oak fructed ppr. a cross of eight points of the field; on a canton gu. a mullet of eight points within an increscent of the first.

OCHTERLONY.

CREATED 7th March, 1816. EXTINCT 15th July, 1825.

Lineage.

ALEXANDER OCHTERLONY, Laird of Pitforthy, in the county of Angus, b. 16th September, 1695, m. 1st November, 1721, Elizabeth, daughter of David Tyrie, of Dunnydeer, in Aberdeenshire, and had issue,

- GILBERT, of Newtown Mill and Pitforthy, m. 25th September, 1745, Maria, daughter of William Smith, professor of philosophy at Aberdeen, but died without issue 6th February, 1786.
- DAVID, of whom presently.
- James, died in the Isle of Man 8th March, 1769, leaving a daughter, Elizabeth, wife of Alexander Fairweather, of Brechin, and afterwards of Philadelphia.
- Alexander, lieutenant of the *Juno*, killed by accident at Quiberon Bay, unm. in 1769.
- Charles, died in Bengal, 1755.
- Elizabeth, died unm. in 1782.
- Jane, m. 18th September, 1748, to John Lyon, esq of Forgandenny and Castle Lyon, North Britain, and died in April, 1775, leaving issue. (See BURKE's *Commoners*, vol. iv.)

The second son,

DAVID OCHTERLONY, of Boston, New England, b. 30th October, 1723, m. Catharine,* daughter of Andrew Tyler, esq. of that place, by Marian, his wife, sister of Sir William Pepperell, bart. and had DAVID, his heir, Gilbert, d. in 1763; Alexander, d. in 1803, and Catherine d. in 1762. He d. in 1765, and was s. by his son,

I. DAVID OCHTERLONY, esq. of Boston, in New England (where he was born 12th February, 1758), who having attained the rank of major-general in the East Indies, with the coloneley of the 20th Native Infantry, distinguished himself in the command of the Indian army in the war with Nepaul, when his services received the unanimous thanks of parliament, and he was further honoured by being created a BARONET 7th March, 1816. Sir David was recreated 8th December, 1822, extending the limitation to CHARLES METCALFE OCHTERLONY, esq. of Delhi. He died unmarried 15th July, 1825, when the first BARONETCY became EXTINCT, and the other descended according to the patent. (Refer to BURKE's *Peerage and Baronetage*.)

Arms—Az. a lion rampant arg. holding in his paws a trident erect gold, and charged on the shoulder with a key, the wards upwards, of the field; a chief embattled or, thereon two banners in saltire, the one of the Mahratta states vert, inscribed *Delhi*; the other of the states of *Nepaul*; the staves broken and encircled by a wreath of laurel ppr.

OLDFIELD, OF SPALDING.

CREATED 6th Aug. 1660. EXTINCT about 1706.

Lineage.

In 1660, a Baronetcy was conferred upon

I. ANTHONY OLDFIELD, esq. of Spalding, in Lincolnshire. He m. first, a daughter of Sir Edward Gresham, knt. of Lingfield, in Surrey, and secondly, Jane, daughter of Parke, of Fleto, in the county of Lincoln. Sir Anthony died about the year 1680, and was s. by his son,

II. SIR JOHN OLDFIELD, of Spalding, who m. Margaret, daughter of Sir Simon Degge, knt. but died without male issue about 1706, when the BARONETCY EXPIRED. One of his daughters and co-heirs, Elizabeth, married John Wingfield, esq. of Tickencote, in Rutlandshire, and was great-grandmother of the present JOHN WINGFIELD, esq. of Tickencote. (See BURKE's *Commoners*, vol. ii. p. 462.)

Arms—Or, on a pile vert, three garbs of the field

* She m. secondly, Sir Isaac Heard, garter king of arms.

O'NEILL, OF UPPER CLANEBOYS.

CREATED 13th Nov. 1643.

EXTINCT ....

Lineage.

This was a branch from the Milesian stack from which the extant noble family of O'NEILL claims descent, the ROYAL HOUSE OF ULSTER.

HUGH BOY O'NEILL, from whom the territories called the Clanaboys, in the counties of Down and Antrim, received their name, grandson of HUGH MEITH, King of Ulster in 1122, recovered those lands from the English (which had been wrested from his family at the invasion *temp.* HENRY II.), and his descendants enjoyed them until the reign of JAMES I. when a portion was conquered by force of arms from the O'Neills, more purchased by *King* JAMES from them and some part left in their possession, which has descended to the O'NEILLS of Shane Castle. *King* JAMES, when he instituted the order of Baronets, had chiefly in view the subduing the clan O'Neill in Ulster, and the Ulster hand—the red hand of O'Neill—was given as a badge to the order.

I. BRYAN O'NEILL, in consideration of his gallant services at the battle of Edge Hill, was created a BARONET by *King* CHARLES I. 13th November, 1643. Sir Bryan *m.* Jane Finch, of the family of the Earl of Nottingham, and dying in 1680, was *s.* by his son,

II. SIR BRYAN O'NEILL, one of the judges of the Court of King's Bench in Ireland *temp.* JAMES II. who *m.* Mary Plunket, sister of Christopher, tenth Lord Dunsany, and dying in 1694, was *s.* by his son,

III. SIR HENRY O'NEILL. This gentleman *m.* first, Mary, daughter of Mark Bagot, esq. of Mountarran, in the county of Carlow, by whom he had an only son,

RANDALL, his heir.

He *m.* secondly, Rose, daughter of Captain James Paterson, and by that lady had two other sons,

Brabazon.
Henry.

He was *s.* at his decease by his eldest son,

IV. SIR RANDALL O'NEILL, who *m.* Mrs. Margaret Graham; and thus terminates any recorded account of the family. The BARONETCY is presumed to be EXTINCT, but a person who called himself

SIR FRANCIS O'NEILL, the sixth baronet, lived a very poor man on the estate of the late Lord Netterville at Douth, near Drogheda, from whom he rented a small farm at one-fourth of its value; but, even unable to pay that, he was dispossessed. This unfortunate descendant of royalty had the patent of baronetcy in his possession, but whether he was in the line of descent does not appear. Baronetcies have been frequently assumed in Ireland by parties who had no claim whatsoever, but being collateral relations of a deceased and extinct baronet, may have discovered the patent amongst his papers. One of the sons of Sir Francis was employed, about twenty-five years ago, at a small inn near Duleek, in the capacity of "boots and ostler"—*sic transit gloria mundi.*

Arms—Arg. two lions rampant combatant gu. and supporting a sinister hand couped at the wrist gu.; in chief three mullets of the second; in base a salmon naiant ppr.

ORBY, OF CROYLAND.

CREATED 9th Oct. 1658.

EXTINCT 7th Feb. 1724.

Lineage.

I. THOMAS ORBY, esq. of Croyland Abbey, in Lincolnshire, servant to the queen mother, was created a BARONET in 1658. He *m.* Katherine Guernier, of France, and dying in 1691, was *s.* by his son,

II. SIR CHARLES ORBY, of Croyland Abbey, who *m.* Anne, daughter of Richard Swinglehurst, gent. of London, and relict of Thomas Winter, esq. governor of Massalapatam, in the East Indies, and dying in 1716, was *s.* by his son,

III. SIR THOMAS ORBY, of Croyland Abbey, who *m.* Lady Charlotte Mainwaring, daughter of Charles Gerard, Earl of Macclesfield, and had an only daughter and heir,

Elizabeth, who *m.* first, Lord John Hay, second son of John, second Marquess of Tweeddale; and secondly, General Robert Hunter, governor of Jamaica. By the latter she was ancestor of the ORBY HUNTERS, of Croyland Abbey.

Sir Thomas died in 1724, and with him the title EXPIRED.

Arms—Erm. three chevrons gu. on a canton of the second a lion passant guardant or.

ORMSBY, OF CLOGHANS.

CREATED 29th Dec. 1812.

EXTINCT 9th Aug. 1833.

Lineage.

I. CHARLES-MONTAGUE ORMSBY, esq. *b.* 23rd April, 1767, barrister-at-law and king's counsel, son of Captain Ormsby, of the 45th regiment, and grandson of Charles Ormsby, esq. of Cloghans, in the county of Mayo, received the honour of knighthood in 1806, and was created a BARONET 29th December, 1812. Sir Charles *m.* in 1794, Elizabeth, daughter of Thomas Kingsbury, esq. and left two sons. He *d.* 3rd March, 1818, and was *s.* by the elder,

II. SIR JAMES ORMSBY, *b.* 27th February, 1796, who *d. s. p.* in 1822, and was *s.* by his brother,

III. Sir Thomas Ormsby, *b.* 26th May, 1797; *m.* in 1824, Mary, only daughter of Francis Slater Rebow, esq. of Wivenhoe Park, in the county of Essex, a major-general in the army; but died without issue 9th August, 1833, when the Baronetcy expired. His widow *m.* secondly, John Gurdon, esq.* who assumed the surname of Rebow in 1835. The representation of the family devolved, at Sir Thomas's decease, on his uncle, Stephen Ormsby, esq. brother of the first baronet. Sir Charles Ormsby had two other brothers, William and James, both deceased, who have left children, and two sisters, Mrs. Carey and Mrs. Corneille.

Arms—Gu. a bend between six crosses crosslet or.

OSBALDESTON, OF CHADLINGTON.

Created 25th June, 1664. Extinct 7th April, 1749.

Lineage.

This was a branch of the ancient family of Osbaldeston, of Osbaldeston, in Lancashire.

Sir John Osbaldeston, who was knighted at the battle of Poitou, acquired a large accession of property by marrying Joan, only daughter and heir of Roger Coghull, esq. of Chadlington, in Oxfordshire. He thus acquired, about 5 Henry VI. Chadlington, Shepenhul, and other manors in that county. The descendants of the said Sir John bore the arms of that heiress; viz. "quarterly argent and sable, four leopards' heads counterchanged." His son and heir,

John Osbaldeston, is mentioned in an indenture, dated 2nd June, 35th Henry VI. to consent to the sale of Underwood, in the forest of Whichwood. He was father of

Thomas Osbaldeston, whose son,

John Osbaldeston, was sheriff of Oxfordshire and Berkshire 12 Henry VIII. and was *s.* by his son,

Richard Osbaldeston, whose son and heir,

John Osbaldeston, was father of

Arthur Osbaldeston, esq. of Chadlington, in the county of Oxford, who *m.* Frances, daughter of Thomas Kettlby, of Stepel, in Shropshire, and was *s.* by his son,

Hercules Osbaldeston, esq. of Chadlington, who married thrice; the male issue of his first and second wife failed; by the third, Judith, daughter of Thomas Emeley, of Helingdon, he left at his decease in 1635,

John Osbaldeston, esq. of Chadlington, who *m.* Joan, daughter of Sir Edward Littleton, knt. of Henley, in Salop, and had several children; of whom his eldest son and heir,

I. Littleton Osbaldeston, esq. of Chadlington, was created a Baronet by *King* Charles II. 25th June, 1664. Sir Littleton *m.* Catherine, daughter of Thomas Browker, esq. of Sundridge, in Kent, and had issue,

- Lacy, his successor.
- John.
- Charles.
- Joanna-Maria.

The baronet, who represented Woodstock in 1678, died about the year 1692, and was *s.* by his eldest son,

II. Sir Lacy Osbaldeston, who married Elizabeth, daughter and heir of William Blagrave, esq. of W[illegible]hill, in the county of Oxford, and had issue,

- Richard, } successive baronets.
- William, }
- Charles, }
- Catherine.
- Diana.

He was *s.* at his decease by his eldest son,

III. Sir Richard Osbaldeston, who dying young and unm. about the year 1701, was *s.* by his brother,

IV. Sir William Osbaldeston, who *m.* Catherine, eldest daughter of Richard, Viscount Wenman, of Thame, and widow of the Hon. Robert Bertie, son of the Earl of Abingdon, by whom he had one son and three daughters, who all predeceased him but one daughter,

Catherine.

He *d.* 18th September, 1726, and was *s.* by his brother,

V. Sir Charles Osbaldeston, who married, but died issueless 7th April, 1749, when the Baronetcy expired.

Arms—Arg. a mascle sa. between three ogresses or pellets.

OUGHTON, OF TETCHBROOK.

Created 27th Aug. 1718. Extinct 4th Sept. 17[illegible]

Lineage.

Robert Oughton (grandson of John Oughton who settled at Old Fillongley, in Warwickshire, about the year 1400) purchased the Parks of New Fillongley, where his descendants continued afterwards [illegible]. His great-great-grandson,

Thomas Oughton, esq. married Anne, eldest daughter and co-heir of William Riplingham, esq. of Great Harborough, in Warwickshire, and thereby acquired a great accession of fortune. He was *s.* by his son,

Adolphus Oughton, esq. who *m.* Martha, daughter of Alexander Prescott, esq. of Thoby Abbey, in [illegible] and had a son and successor,

Adolphus Oughton, esq. who *m.* Mary, daughter of Richard Samwell, esq. of Upton, in Northamptonshire, by Frances, his wife, daughter of Thomas, Viscount Wenman, and was *s.* by his son,

I. Adolphus Oughton, esq. of Tetchbrook, in Warwickshire, M.P. for Coventry, who was created a Baronet 27th August, 1718, on his being appointed to represent his royal highness the Duke of York, as his proxy, at his instalment as knight of the Garter at Windsor. He *m.* his cousin, Frances, relict of Sir Edward Bagot, bart. of Blithfield, in Staffordshire, and daughter and heir of Sir Thomas Wagstaffe, [illegible] *d. s. p.* 4th September, 1736, when the Baronetcy expired.

Arms—Party per pale gu. and sa. a lion rampant [illegible]

* Second son of Theophilus Thornhagh Gurdon, esq. of Letton, in Norfolk. (See Burke's Commoners, vol. [illegible] p. [illegible])

PAGE, OF GREENWICH.

CREATED 3rd Dec. 1714.

EXTINCT 4th Aug. 1775.

Lineage.

GREGORY PAGE, esq. descended from a good family in Hampshire, was a considerable merchant in London and a director of the East India Company. His eldest son,

I. GREGORY PAGE, esq. of Greenwich, was created a BARONET by *King* GEORGE I. 3rd December, 1714. Sir Gregory, like his father, was an eminent merchant, and for many years an East India director. He served in parliament for New Shoreham *temp. Queen* ANNE and *King* GEORGE I. He *m.* Mary, daughter of Thomas Trotman, citizen of London, and had issue,

GREGORY, his heir.

Thomas, of Battlesdon, in the county of Bedford, *m.* Julian, sister of Viscount Howe, but died issueless.

MARY, *m.* to SIR EDWARD TURNER, bart. of Amersden, in the county of Oxford, and was mother of

SIR EDWARD TURNER, *b.* in 1719, who *m.* in 1739, Cassandra, eldest daughter of William Leigh, esq. of Adlestrop, and had with two daughters, two sons,

SIR GREGORY TURNER, who inherited the estates of the PAGES, and was father of the present SIR GREGORY OSBORNE PAGE TURNER, bart. of Ambrosden.

John Turner, who assumed the surname of DRYDEN, and was created a BARONET.

Sophia, *m.* to Lewis Way, esq. of Richmond, in Surrey, and *d.* 2nd January, 1735-6.

Sir Gregory *d.* 25th May, 1720, and was *s.* by his elder son,

II. SIR GREGORY PAGE, of Wricklemarsh, in Kent, who *m.* Mrs. Martha Kenward, but had no issue. He died at the advanced age of ninety, 4th August, 1775, when the BARONETCY EXPIRED. Sir Gregory's property devolved upon his great-nephew,

SIR GREGORY TURNER, bart. who assumed, in consequence, the additional surname and arms of PAGE. His son is the present (1837)

SIR GREGORY-PAGE TURNER, bart. (Refer to BURKE'S *Peerage and Baronetage.*)

Arms—Az. a fesse indented between three martlets

PAKINGTON, OF AILSBURY.

CREATED 22nd June, 1620.

EXTINCT 6th Jan. 1830.

Lineage.

The antiquity of this family was beyond dispute: it is manifest from the foundation of the monastery at Kenilworth, that it flourished in the time of HENRY I. and it appears to have assumed the surname from one of the Pakingtons, in Staffordshire, Warwickshire, or Leicestershire, for in each of those counties we meet with lordships, so designated, the proprietors of which wrote themselves anciently de Pakington.*

ROBERT PAKINGTON, living in the reign of HENRY IV. was father of

JOHN PAKINGTON, recited in an office found before Robert Russel, escheator of the county of Warwick, 14 HENRY VI. He left a son of his own name,

JOHN PAKINGTON, esq. who *m.* Elizabeth, daughter and heir of Thomas Washbourne, esq. of Stanford, in the county of Worcester, and had three sons, namely,

I. JOHN, of the Inner Temple, constituted chirographer of the Common Pleas in the 24th of HENRY VII. during life, and being learned in the law was elected, 11 HENRY VIII. Lent reader, and in the 20th of the same reign, treasurer of the society of the Inner Temple, in which year he had a grant from the king, "that he the said John Pakington, for the time to come, shall have full liberty, during his life, to wear his hat in his presence, and his successors, or of any other persons whatsoever, and not to be uncovered on any occasion or cause whatsoever, against his will and good liking, also that he shall not be appointed, called, or compelled to take the order of knighthood, or degree, state, or order, of a baron of the Exchequer, serjeant-at-law, or any office or encumbrance thereto relating." In 1532, he was called to be serjeant-at-law, for which the king gave him a special discharge for taking the said degree, and having been appointed a justice of North Wales, was in 1535, commissioned to conclude and compound all forfeitures, offences, fines, and sums of money due to the king, or his father HENRY VII. In 1542, he had a patent for justice of Brecknock, Glamorgan, and Radnor, in South Wales, during life, having a grant of all the manors belonging to the monastery of Westwood, in the county of Worcester, and soon after received the honour of knighthood. The many other honours conferred upon him are too nu-

* PAGINGTON, afterwards PAKINGTON, Staffordshire, within two miles of Tame, was held of the bishop, by Orbel, in the 20th year of William the Conqueror; in HENRY III.'s time, by Robert de Pakington; and in the 1st of EDWARD I. David de Pakington held it of the same by the fourth part of a knight's fee. Richard de Pakington married one of the sisters and co-heirs of Robert de Kasly, Lord of Freseley, in Warwickshire, who lived *temp.* HENRY II., and the late baronets had in their possession two ancient deeds, without date, judged to be at least four centuries and a half old; one of Robert Wittington, clerk, signed and sealed in the presence of Peter Wyke, Hugh Pakington, and Alexander Abbetot, knights, the other attested by Richard Spechell and Hugh Pakington, knights.

merous to be recorded here. At the time of his death, 1560, he was seized of thirty-one manors, and of other lands that he had purchased of seventy different persons, as appears by a large book concerning his estate, which was preserved amongst the family testimonials.* Sir John Pakington's wife was Anne, widow of Tychbourne, and of the family of Rolle.† She *d.* 22nd August, 1563. His fortune was divided between his daughters,

URSULA, *m.* to Sir John Scudamore, knt.
BRIDGET, *m.* to Sir John Lyttleton, knt. of Frankley.

and his two younger brothers, Robert and Humphrey.

II. ROBERT.

III. Humphrey, a merchant of London, who had the manor of Chadesley Corbet settled upon him, by his brother Sir John, and left an only son,

John, of Harvington, in Worcestershire, who *m.* Elizabeth Newport, and had a son and heir,

Humphrey Pakington, esq. of Chaddesley Corbet, who *m.* Abigail Sacheverell, and left two daughters, his co-heirs, viz.

MARY, *m.* to Sir John Yate, bart.
Anne, *m.* to Sir Henry Audley, knt.

The second son,

ROBERT PAKINGTON, esq. was one of the members of parliament for the city of London, *temp.* HENRY VIII. and was barbarously murdered in the street, in 1537.‡ He *m.* Catherine, one of the co-heirs of Sir John Baldwin, lord chief justice of the Common Pleas, and his wife, daughter of William Dormer, esq. of Wycombe, Bucks, (by this alliance the manor of Ailsbury, with other considerable lands came into the family,) and had issue,

THOMAS, his heir.

Elizabeth, *m.* to John Lane, esq. and afterwards Alderman Sir Richard Mallory, knt. of London.
Anne, *m.* to Richard Cupper, esq. of Glympton, in the county of Oxford.
Margaret, *m.* first to Benedict Lee, esq. of Burston, in Bucks, and secondly, to Sir Thomas Scot, of Yorkshire.

The son and heir,

SIR THOMAS PAKINGTON, was in ward to the lord privy seal, in the 37th HENRY VIII. when Catherine, his mother, then twenty-three years of age, was found one of the co-heirs of Sir John Baldwin, (who *d.* 22nd December, in the same year). He received the honour of knighthood from *Queen* MARY, and on the death of his uncle, the said Sir John Baldwin, succeeded to a great estate. He was sheriff of Worcestershire in the 3rd of ELIZABETH, and dying 2nd June, 1571, at Bath Place, Holborn, was conveyed in great pomp to Ailsbury, the officers of the college of arms attending, and buried in the parish church there. His wife, who survived him, and *m.* secondly, Thomas Tashmarsh, esq. was the daughter of Sir Thomas Kitson, knt. of Hengrave, in Suffolk, and by her had surviving issue,

JOHN (Sir), his heir.

Mary, *m.* to Sir Walter Long, knt. of Wraxall and Draycot, in Wiltshire, M.P. for that county.
Catherine, *m.* first, to John Davis, esq. of the same county; secondly, to Sir Jasper Moore; and thirdly, to Sir — Mompesson, of Teddington.
Margaret, *m.* to Thomas Litchfield, esq.

He was *s.* by his son,

SIR JOHN PAKINGTON, K.B. one of the privy council and an especial favourite of *Queen* ELIZABETH. The queen first took notice of Sir John in her progress to Worcester, when she invited him to attend her court, where he lived at his own expense, in great splendour and reputation, with an equipage not inferior to some of the highest officers, although he had no greater honour than Knight of the Bath, which was conferred upon him in the lifetime of his father. He was remarkable for his stature and comely person, and had distinguished himself so much by his manly exercises, that he was called "Lusty Pakington." Having by his expensive life contracted great debts, he took the wise resolution of retiring into the country, and said he would feed on bread and verjuice until he had made up his extravagancies; which coming to the royal ear, the queen gave him a grant of a gentleman's estate in Suffolk, worth eight or nine hundred pounds a year, besides goods and chattels, which had escheated to the crown, but after he had been in the country to take possession, he could not behold the miseries of the distressed family without remorse and compassion; and the melancholy spectacle of the unhappy mother and her children, wrought so effectually upon his fine feelings, that he repaired to court immediately, and humbly besought the queen to excuse him from enriching himself by such means, and did not leave the presence until he had obtained his request, which involved the restoration of the property to the rightful owner. Soon after this he left the court, but not before he had liquidated all his debts: and then, with great reputation and honour, he commenced his journey into the country, being handsomely attended by servants and tenants to the number of sixty, well mounted and appointed, who came purposely from his estates to pay him this compliment, and waited at the court gates while he was taking leave of the queen. After his settlement in the country, ELIZABETH granted him, for sixty years, (in the 25th of her reign,) for his good and faithful services, several lordships, manors, and lands, which had fallen to the crown, in no less than seventeen counties. He was also constituted lieutenant and custos rotulorum of Worcestershire, and appointed bow bearer of Malvern Chase, one of the best in England, which he retained until he had finished his noble park at Hampton Lovet, and then, that chase being at too great a distance from his dwelling, he obtained the queen's leave to dispose of it. He was in ELIZABETH's favour to the end, as appears as well from other evidence as from a grant she made him for eight years, (in the 40th year of her reign, he paying into the Exchequer £40 per annum,) that no one should import into the kingdom, or make any starch, but by his permission. By his affability and obliging deportment, he acquired the good opinion of his equals and inferiors; and by his courage and resolution, on occasions requiring the

* LELAND takes notice that he resided at a very goodly new house of brick, called Hampton Court, six miles from Worcester, which lordship was purchased from the Lord Mountjoy.

† Another authority states, that Sir John Pakington, knt. *m.* Anne, daughter of Henry Dacres, late sheriff of London, and widow of Robert Fairthwayte, of London, merchant taylor, and that she was buried at St. Buttolph's, 22nd August, 1563, but does not mention her as widow of Tychbourne; by her will, however, she bequeaths to her son, Nicholas Tychbourne, and his children, the greater part of her estate, plate, jewels, &c.

‡ STOW, vol. i. p. 29, says, "ROBERT PAKINGTON, mercer, slain with a gun, as he was going to morrow mass from his house in Cheape, to St. Thomas of Acars, in the year 1536; the murderer was never discovered, but by his own confession, made when he came to the gallows, at Banbury, to be hanged for felony."

exercise of those attributes, he became formidable to persons in power; a memorable instance of this occurred when he executed the office of sheriff for his county. The Lord Chief Baron Periam, having committed a gentleman at the assizes, Sir John sitting in his sheriff's seat, called to him to stay, telling the judge he would answer for his forthcoming; neither could he be dissuaded, by all the menaces he received from the bench, from adhering to this resolution, boldly alleging in his defence, that the gentleman was his prisoner, and he, as sheriff, was accountable for him. Sir John Pakington *m.* the daughter of Mr. Humphry Smith, of Cheapside, Queen Elizabeth's silkman, of an ancient family in Leicestershire. The lady was the widow of Benedict Barnham, esq. an alderman of London, "who left her very rich, and that consideration, together with her youth and beauty, made it impossible for her to escape the addresses even of the greatest persons about the court; but Sir John was the only happy man who knew how to gain her, being recommended by his worthy friend, Mr. William Seabright, town clerk of London, who had purchased the manor of Besford, in Worcestershire. This lady had by her first husband four daughters, which were very young when they lost their father, and therefore needed a faithful friend to manage and improve their fortunes, in which capacity Sir John acquitted himself so honourably, that they had ten thousand pounds each for portion, an immense sum in those days.* Sir John Pakington had issue, one son and two daughters, viz.

JOHN, his heir.

Anne, *m.* first to Sir Humphrey Ferrers, knt. of Tamworth, and secondly, to Philip, first Earl of Chesterfield.

Mary, *m.* to Sir Robert Brooke, of Nacton, in Suffolk, master of the ceremonies to *King* JAMES I.

This great man who lived to see his children's children, departed this life at his house at Westwood,† in the seventy-seventh year of his age, in January, 1625. His widow married thirdly, Lord Kilmurry, and fourthly, Thomas, Earl of Kelly.‡ His son and heir,

I. SIR JOHN PAKINGTON, bart. of Ailesbury, in the county of Bucks, created 22nd June, 1620, *m.* Frances, daughter of Sir John Ferrers, knt. of Tamworth, and by that lady, who *m.* secondly, Alexander Lesley, Earl of Leven, had, with a daughter, who *m.* first, Colonel Washington, and secondly Samuel Sandys, esq. of Ombersley, in the county of Worcester, an only son, JOHN. Sir John resided at Ailesbury, and was elected to parliament by that borough, in the 21st of JAMES I. but died at the early age of twenty-four, in October, 1624, previously to his father, and was *s.* by his son,

II. SIR JOHN PAKINGTON, who at the decease of his grandfather, inherited the estates of the family, and resided subsequently at Westwood. He was then in his fifth year, and under the guardianship of Lord Coventry, the then lord keeper, "by whose vigilant care of his education, both by travel and other advantages, he became a most accomplished gentleman." He was elected one of the knights for Worcestershire, in the 15th CHARLES I. and when the rebellion broke out, was member for Ailesbury; and having on all occasions given proofs both of his fidelity to the crown, and the rights of the subject, was entrusted by the king, in 1642, with a commission for arraying men for his service in Worcestershire, on account of which he was taken prisoner, committed to the Tower, and fined £5000: had his estate sequestered, his house in Buckinghamshire (one of the best in that county) levelled with the ground, and such great wastes committed in his woods, that an estimate of the loss, still remaining in the hand writing of his lady, amounts to £20,348. His seal in the loyal cause never swerved, for notwithstanding the had suffered so much for his loyalty, he had the courage to join *King* CHARLES II. with a troop of horse, at the battle of Worcester, and was taken prisoner there, yet was so popular, that when afterwards tried for his life, not one witness could be procured to swear against him; he was consequently acquitted and set at liberty, but was afterwards fined £7670, and compelled for the said fine, to convey the market house, the tolls, the court leet, and certain grounds called Heydon Hill, parcel of the estate at Ailesbury, to Thomas Scot, (who was one of the king's judges,) and other trustees, for the use of the town, which they kept until after the Restoration, when, by a special act of parliament, the said conveyances were made void. Sir John *m.* Dorothy, one of the daughters of his guardian, Thomas, Lord Coventry, and had with two daughters, the elder *m.* to Anthony Eyre,

---

* These ladies were married, the eldest to Lord Audley, the second, ALICE, to Sir Francis Bacon, the celebrated philosopher, created Viscount St. Alban's; the third to Sir John Soames, and the youngest to Sir William Constable.

† After he had finished his stately structure at Westwood, Sir John invited the Earl of Northampton, lord president, and his countess, to a house warming; and as his lordship was a jovial companion, a train of above ... knights and gentlemen accompanied him, who staid ... some time, and at their departure, acknowledged they had met with so kind a reception, *that they did not know whether they had possessed the place, or the place them.* The delightful situation of his mansion was what ... had never before seen; the house standing in the middle of a wood, cut into twelve large ridings and at a good distance, one riding through all of them, the whole surrounded by a park of six or seven miles, with, at the further end, facing the house, an artificial lake of 122 acres. ... most splendid entertainment was given, however, to ... I. and his queen, at Ailsbury, when his majesty honored him with a visit, after his arrival from Scotland, before his coronation: upon this occasion he set no ... expense, thinking it a disparagement to be outdone by any fellow subject, when such an opportunity offered, and the king and court that they had never met with a more noble reception.

‡ LLOYD, in his lives of the statesmen and favourites of England, since the Reformation, thus speaks of Sir John Pakington: "His handsome features look the most, and his neat parts the wisest at. He could smile ladies to his service, and argue statesmen to his design, with equal ease. His reason was powerful, his beauty more. Never was a brave soul more bravely seated; nature bestowed great parts on him, education polished him to an admirable frame of prudence and virtue. Queen Elizabeth called him her Temperance, and Leicester his Modesty. It is a question to this day, whether his resolution took the soldiers, his prudence the politicians, his compliance the favourites, his complaisance the courtiers, his piety the clergy, his integrity and condescension the people, or his knowledge the learned, most. This new court star was a nine days' wonder, engaging all eyes, until it set satisfied with its own glory. He came to court, he said, as Solomon did, to see its vanity, and retired as he did, to repent it. It was he who said first, what Bishop Sanderson urged afterwards, *That a sound faith was the best divinity, a good conscience the best law, and temperance the best physic.* Sir John Pakington in *Queen* ELIZABETH's time was virtuous and modest, and Sir John Pakington, in *King* CHARLES's time, loyal and valiant; the one did well, the other suffered so. Greenham was his favourite, Hammond his, the one had a competent estate and was contented, the other hath a large one and is noble; this suppresseth factions in the kingdom, the other composed them in the court, and was called by courtiers Moderation. Westmoreland tempted his fidelity, and Norfolk his steadfastness; but he died in his bed an honest and a happy man."

esq. of Rampton, Notts; the younger, to William Godfrey, esq. of Lincolnshire, an only son, his successor, at his decease, 13th January, 1680.*

III. SIR JOHN PAKINGTON, M.P. for Worcestershire, *temp. King* CHARLES II. and *King* JAMES II. who *m.* Margaret, daughter of Sir John Keyt, bart. of Ebrington, in Gloucestershire, and died in March, 1688, when he was *s.* by his only child,

IV. SIR JOHN PAKINGTON. This gentleman was a strenuous asserter of the rights and liberties of the country, and in the year 1702, preferred that remarkable complaint to the House of Commons, against William, Lord Bishop of Worcester, and Mr. Lloyd his son, for interfering in the election of the county of Worcester, by sending threatening letters to the clergy and freeholders, and aspersing his conduct in parliament.† Sir John was constantly elected one of the knights for Worcestershire in every parliament, from his first being chosen, at nineteen years of age, (except one, when he voluntarily declined it,) to his death, notwithstanding the powerful opposition generally made against him. He *m.* first, Frances, eldest daughter of Sir Henry Parker, bart. of Hunnington, in the county of Warwick, by whom he had two sons, John and Thomas, who both died young and unmarried, and two daughters, viz.

- Margaret.
- Frances, *m.* to Thomas-Charles, Viscount Tracy, of Ireland.

Sir John *m.* secondly, Hester, daughter and sole heir of Sir Herbert Perrot, knt. of Haroldstone, in the county of Pembroke, and by that lady had a son, HERBERT-PERROT, his successor. He *d.* 13th August, 1727, was interred with his ancestors at Hampton-Lovet, and *s.* by his son,

V. SIR HERBERT-PERROT PAKINGTON, M.P. for the county of Worcester, who *m.* in 1721, Elizabeth, daughter of John Conyers, esq. of Walthamstow, in Essex, and had issue,

- JOHN, } sixth and seventh baronets.
- HERBERT-PERROT, } sixth and seventh baronets.
- Hester.
- Cecilia.

He *d.* 24th September, 1748, at Leyden, and was *s.* by his elder son,

VI. SIR JOHN PAKINGTON, who *m.* in 1761, Mary, daughter of Henry Bray, esq. of Bromyard, in Herefordshire, but died *s. p.* 30th November, 1762, when he was *s.* by his brother,

VII. SIR HERBERT-PERROT PAKINGTON, who *m.* in 1759, Elizabeth, daughter of Cæsar Hawkins, esq. and relict of Herbert Wylde, esq. of Ludlow, in the county of Salop, and by that lady (who *d.* 23rd February, 1812,) had issue,

- JOHN, his successor.
- Thomas, *d. s. p.*
- ELIZABETH, *m.* to William Russell, esq. of Powick, in the county of Worcester, and dying in May, 1813, left a son,
  - JOHN SOMERSET RUSSELL, who assumed the surname of PAKINGTON on the death of the eighth baronet.
- Dorothy, deceased.
- ANNE.
- Louisa, deceased.

Sir Herbert *d.* at Bath in 1795, and was *s.* by his son,

VIII. SIR JOHN PAKINGTON, D.C.L. born in 1760, who died *s. p.* 6th January, 1830, when the title became EXTINCT. The estates descended to JOHN SOMERSET RUSSELL, esq. (son of Elizabeth, Sir John Pakington's eldest sister), and to Anne Pakington, Sir John's younger sister, as joint heirs at law. Mr Russell has assumed the surname of PACKINGTON.

Arms—Party per chev. sa. and arg. in chief three mullets or, in base as many garbs gu.

PALGRAVE, OF NORWOOD BARNINGHAM.

CREATED 24th June, 1641.

EXTINCT 3rd Nov. 1732.

Lineage.

JOHN DE PALGRAVE, of Palgrave, in Norfolk, m. Sibill, daughter of William de Hetherset, of Hetherset, in the same county, and left a son and heir,

JOHN PALGRAVE, esq. who *m.* Mary, daughter of Sir William Yelverton, knt. of Rougham, and was *s.* by his son,

HENRY PALGRAVE, esq. who by his wife, Anne, daughter of John Glemham, esq. of Glemham, in Suffolk, was father of

GEORGE PALGRAVE, esq. of Palgrave, one of the gentlemen of Norfolk, in the list returned by the commissioners 12 HENRY VI. from whom lineally descended

---

* His accomplished wife died 13th May, in the year preceding. Her ladyship who was esteemed one of the most learned of her sex at the time, is the reputed author of the well known treatise, *The Whole Duty of Man.*

† The House of Commons after hearing evidence,

Resolved, *nem. con.*

That Sir John Pakington has fully made out the charge which he exhibited against the Lord Bishop of Worcester.

Resolved, *nem. con.*

That Sir John Pakington has fully made out the charge against Mr. Lloyd, the said Lord Bishop's son.

Resolved,

That it appears to this House, that the proceedings of William, Lord Bishop of Worcester, his son, and his agents, in order to the hindering of the election of a member for the county of Worcester, has been malicious, unchristian, and arbitrary, in high violation of the liberties and privileges of the Commons of England.

Resolved,

That an humble address be presented to her majesty that she will be graciously pleased to remove William, Lord Bishop of Worcester, from being her almoner.

Ordered,

That Mr. Attorney General do prosecute Mr. Lloyd, the Lord Bishop of Worcester's son, for his said offence, after his privilege of the Lower House of Convocation is out.

Veneris 20 die Novembris, 1702.

Mr. Comptroller reported to the House, that their resolution and address to her majesty for removing William, Lord Bishop of Worcester, from being lord almoner to her majesty, had been presented to her majesty, and that her majesty was pleased to give this most gracious answer: "I am very sorry that there is occasion for this address against the Bishop of Worcester, I will order and direct that he shall no longer continue to supply the place of almoner, but I will put another in his room to perform that office."

...n Palgrave, esq. of Norwood Barningham, county of Norfolk, who was created a Baronet ...arles I. 24th June, 1641. Sir John m. first, ...eth, daughter of John Jermy, esq. of Gunton, in ...e county, and had issue,

...gustine, his heir.

...hn.

...isabeth.

...secondly, Anne, daughter of Sir William de ...of Martin, also in Norfolk, and widow of Cot... ...scoign, esq. of Islington, in Middlesex, and by ...ady had

...lliam.

...ement.

...rsula, who m. — Smith, and was mother of

Samuel Smith, of Colkirk, whose four daughters, (Catherine, wife of Thomas Bendish, esq.; Ursula, of Offley, of Derbyshire; Theodosia, wife of Samuel Sparrow, gent. of Lanham; and Lucy, wife first of Pett, of Debenham, and secondly of Jonas Rolph, of Lyme,) were co-heirs to Sir Richard Palgrave, the last baronet.

...hn was s. by his eldest son,

Sir Augustine Palgrave, who m. first, Barbara, ...ter of Cotton Gascoign, esq. of Islington, and ...dly, Katherine, daughter of Sir William Spring, ...elict of — Lawrence, esq. of Brockdish, Herts, ...y those ladies had no issue. He m. thirdly, Miss ..., eldest daughter of Sir Richard Grubham Howe, of Wishford, Wilts, and by her had surviving ...,

...ichard, his heir.

...lizabeth.

...rith.

...as s. at his decease by his son,

Sir Richard Palgrave, who d. unm. 3rd No...er, 1732, when the Baronetcy expired: at his ..., the lordship of Northwood Berningham, by a ... in Chancery, was ordered to be sold, by his ..., who were the four daughters of Samuel Smith, ...ate of Colkirk, in Norfolk, who was son of Ur..., daughter of Sir John Palgrave, the first baronet.

...rms—Azure a lion rampant, guardant, argent.

PARKER, OF ARWARTON.

Created ... July, 1661.

Extinct 20th Jan. 1740.

Lineage.

...ir William Parker, standard-bearer and privy ...ncillor to Richard III. m. Alice Lovel, only ...ughter and heir of Henry Lovel, Lord Morley,* ...d left a son and heir,

Sir Henry Parker, who was summoned to parliament as Baron Morley, from 15th April, 1523, to 28th October, 1555. He m. Alice, daughter of Sir John St. John, of Bletsho, in the county of Bedford, and had an only son (who predeceased him),

Sir Henry Parker, K.B. so created at the coronation of *Queen* Anne Boleyne. He m. first, Grace, daughter of John Newport, esq. and by that lady had (with two daughters) a son,

Henry, who became Lord Morley at the decease of his grandfather, in 1555. His grandson, William Parker, Lord Monteagle and Morley, was the nobleman to whom the remarkable letter was addressed, which led to the discovery of the Gunpowder plot. (See Burke's *Peerage and Baronetage.*)

Sir Henry m. secondly, Elizabeth, daughter and heir of Sir Philip Calthorp, knt. of Erwarton, in Suffolk,† and by her had a son,

Sir Philip Parker, of Erwarton, who was sheriff of Suffolk in 1578, and in that year received the honour of knighthood from *Queen* Elizabeth, in her progress through the county. He married Catherine, daughter of Sir John Goodwin, of Winchendon, Bucks, and had surviving issue,

Calthorpe, his heir.

Catherine, m. to Sir William Cornwallis.

He was s. by his son,

Sir Calthorpe Parker, who was knighted by *King* James I. before his coronation. He m. Mercy, daughter of Sir Stephen Soame, and left a son and heir,

Sir Philip Parker, knighted 19th November, 1624, who represented the county of Suffolk in 1640. Sir Philip m. Dorothy, daughter and heir of Sir Robert Gawdy, of Claxton, in Norfolk,‡ and had issue,

Philip, his heir.

Calthorpe, Robert, } d. unm.

Winifrid, m. to Sir John Barker, bart. of Trimley, in Suffolk.

Dorothy, Mary, } d. unm.

Mercy, married first, to William Guibbon, esq. of Thursford; and secondly, to Edmond Wodehouse, esq. of East Lexham, in Norfolk.

Sir Philip was s. by his eldest son,

I. Philip Parker, esq. of Arwarton, in the county of Suffolk, who was created a Baronet 16th July, 1661. He m. first, Rebecca, daughter of Sir Walter Long, bart. of Whaddon, and by her had issue,

Philip, his heir.

Calthorpe, who inherited the estates of his maternal uncle, Sir Walter Long, bart. of Whaddon, and assumed the surname of Long. He resided at Whaddon after the decease of his uncle in 1710; but dying without issue, those estates passed, under the will of the said Sir Walter, to Calthorpe's nephew, Sir Philip Parker a Morley, bart.

Walter, d. unm.

Rebecca, Mary, Anne, } d. unm.

---

* ...hich Henry was son and heir of

Sir William Lovel, by Alianore Morley, his wife, the daughter and heir of Robert Morley, Lord Morley. Sir William, in right of the said Alianore, was himself summoned to parliament as Lord Morley, his father-in-law being then dead.

† By Amata, his wife, daughter of Sir William Boleyne, and aunt to *Queen* Anne Boleyne. The estate of Erwarton or Arwarton came to the Calthorpes by the intermarriage of Sir Oliver Calthorpe with Isabel, sister and heir of Sir Bartholomew Bacon, of Erwarton.

‡ By Winifrid, his wife, daughter and co-heir of Sir Nathaniel Bacon, knt. of Hiveky, in Norfolk.

Sir Philip *m.* secondly, Hanah, daughter and heir of Philip Bacon, esq. of Wolverstone, in Suffolk, relict of Sir Thomas Bedingfeld, and by her had two other daughters, Anne and Dorothy, who both *d.* unm. He *d.* about the year 1690, and was *s.* by his eldest son,

II. Sir Philip Parker, who *m.* Mary, daughter of Samuel Fortrey, esq. of Byall-Fen, in Cambridgeshire, and had issue,

Philip, his successor.

Catherine, *m.* to Sir John Perceval, who was created Viscount Perceval, of the kingdom of Ireland, in 1715, and Earl of Egmont in 1733. (Refer to Burke's *Peerage and Baronetage.*)

Mary, *m.* to Daniel Dering, esq. grandson of Sir Edward Dering, bart. of Surenden Dering.

He *d.* about 1700, and was *s.* by his son,

III. Sir Philip Parker, M.P. *temp.* George I. and George II. for Harwich, who inherited Whaddon and the estates of the Longs, on the decease of his uncle, Calthorpe Long, esq. issueless, and assumed the additional surnames of A Morley-Long. He *m.* Martha, daughter of William East, esq. of the Middle Temple, and had two daughters,

Martha, *m.* to John Thynne Howe, second Lord Chedworth, but *d. s. p.*

Elizabeth, *m.* to James Plunkett, esq.

Catharine.

Sir Philip Parker-a-Morley-Long, who was the last heir male of the old Lords Morley, died 20th June, 1740-1, when the Baronetcy expired. Whaddon and the property attached to it passed, under the will of Sir Walter Long, bart. to Thomas Long, esq. of Rowden (refer to Burke's *Commoners*, vol. iv. page 67), and his own estates to his daughters as co-heirs.

Arms—Arg. a lion passant gu. between two bars sa. thereon three bezants, two and one, in chief as many bucks' heads caboshed of the second.

PARKER, OF RATTON.

Created 22nd May, 1674.

Extinct 19th April, 1750.

Lineage.

The family of Parker was of great antiquity in the county of Sussex, and its progenitor, Geffrey Parker, of Bexley, is mentioned in deeds 12 Edward I.

John Parker, esq. of Ratton, representative of the family in the early part of the sixteenth century, was deputy to George Boleyn, Lord Rochford, warden of the Cinque Ports. He *m.* first, Jane, daughter of Richard Sackville, esq. of Buckhurst, and had by her a son and daughter, viz.

Thomas, his heir.

Elizabeth, *m.* to Sir Edward Gage, knt. of Firle, in Sussex.

He *m.* secondly, Jane, daughter of William Farnfield, of Sussex, and had two sons, namely,

Thomas, of East Bourne, who married Elizabeth, daughter and co-heir of Thomas Selwyn, esq. of Friston, and had a son, Selwyn, and other issue.

Edward, whose daughter, Elizabeth, *m.* Henry Palmer, esq. younger son of Sir Thomas Palmer, knt.

The eldest son,

Thomas Parker, esq. of Ratton, in Sussex, married Eleanor, daughter of William Waller, esq. of Groombridge, in Kent, and had two sons,

Nicholas (Sir), knt. his heir.

John (Sir), knt. colonel of foot 1 James I. and captain of Pendennis Castle, in Cornwall, by patent during life. He died 15th October, 1617, aged seventy, unmarried.

Thomas Parker died 16th April, 1580, and was *s.* by his son,

Sir Nicholas Parker, knt. of Ratton, who *m.* first, Jane, daughter of Sir William Courtenay, knt. of Powderham, in Devon; secondly, Elizabeth, daughter of John Baker, esq.; and thirdly, Catherine, daughter of Sir John Temple, bart. of Stow, Bucks. The two former died *s. p.* but by the last he had issue,

I. Thomas, his heir.

II. John, *d. s. p.*

III. Robert, *d. v. p.* unm.

IV. Nicholas.

V. Henry, *d.* unm.

I. Anne, *m.* first, to Adrian Moore, esq. of Odyar, Hants; and secondly, to Sir John Smith, knt.

II. Mary, died unm.

Sir Nicholas died 9th March, 1619, aged seventy-three, and was *s.* by his son,

Sir Thomas Parker, knt. of Ratton, who *m.* Philadelphia, daughter of Henry Lennard, Baron Dacre of the South, and had issue,

George, his heir.

Grace, *m.* to Sir William Campion, knt. of Combwell, in Kent.

Philadelphia, *m.* to Samuel Boys, esq. of Hawkhurst, in Kent.

Rachel, *m.* to William Gee, esq. of Bishop's Burton, in Yorkshire.

Catherine, *m.* to Sir Thomas Nutt, knt. of Mays in Sussex, and died 2nd May, 1700, leaving two daughters: Philadelphia, married to Sir Thomas Dyke, bart. and Catherine, married to Anthony Bramston, esq. of Skreens.

Anne, *m.* first, to John Shirley, esq. of Isfield, in Sussex; and secondly, to Francis Barham, esq.

Margaret, *m.* to Thomas, Earl of Berkshire.

Sir Thomas died 31st May, 1663, aged sixty-eight and was *s.* by his son,

George Parker, esq. of Ratton, who *m.* Mary, daughter of Sir Richard Newdegate, bart. of Arbury, Warwickshire, serjeant-at-law, and had issue,

Robert, his heir.

Richard, of Hedsor, Bucks, who *m.* Sarah, daughter and co-heir of Robert Chilcot, esq. of Isleworth, in Middlesex, and had a son, Jeffery, and three daughters: Julianna, *m.* to Cecil Bowyer, esq.; Anne, *d.* unm.; and Elizabeth, *m.* to William Bowyer, esq.

Mr. Parker died 12th July, 1673, aged fifty-three, and was *s.* by his son,

I. Robert Parker, esq. of Ratton, who was created a Baronet 22nd May, 1674. He *m.* Sarah, daughter of George Chute, esq. of Bristo Causeway, in Surrey, and had issue,

George, his heir.

Robert, who *d. s. p.* in the East Indies.
Thomas, died abroad *s. p.*
William, barrister-at-law, *d.* unmarried 1st January, 1727.
German, who *d.* unmarried.

Lucy, *d.* young.
Philadelphia, *m.* to Colonel Piper, of Essex.

Sir Robert *d.* 30th November, 1691, aged thirty-seven, and was *s.* by his son,

II. Sir George Parker, of Ratton, who *m.* Mary, daughter of Sir Walter Bagot, bart. of Blithfield, in Staffordshire, and had issue,

Walter, his heir.
Thomas, died an ensign in the Guards.
Nicholas, died unmarried, aged twenty-three, in 1734.

Sarah, *m.* to Thomas Luxford, esq. of Laming, in Sussex.
Anne.
Jane.
Philadelphia, *m.* to Nathaniel Trayton, esq. of Lewes.

Sir George died 18th June, 1726, and was succeeded by his son,

III. Sir Walter Parker, of Ratton, at whose decease unmarried 19th April, 1750, the Baronetcy became extinct. The Chalvington property passed to the Fullers, Thomas Fuller, esq. fourth son of Thomas Fuller, esq. of Rose Hill and Waldron, Sussex, having married Eleanor, daughter of John Lidgiter, esq. which lady was heiress both to the Traytons and Parkers.

Arms—Az. frettée and a fess or.

PARSONS, OF LANGLEY.

Created 9th April, 1661.

Extinct in 1812.

Lineage.

Ralph Parsons, of Northamptonshire, the first of the family upon record, was father of

John Parsons, esq. of Boveny, in the county of Bucks, who *m.* the daughter of — Cutler, and left a son,

Sir John Parsons, knt. of Boveny, who *m.* Elizabeth, daughter and sole heir of Sir John Kidderminster, of Langley,* and was *s.* by his son,

I. William Parsons, esq. of Langley, in the county of Bucks, who was created a Baronet 9th April, 1661. He *m.* Elizabeth, daughter and heir of Sir Lawrence Parsons, knt. and had, with two daughters, two sons, viz. Colonel Parsons, who *m.* the daughter of Sir John Barker, and *d. s. p.* and an elder, his successor, about the year 1664,†

II. Sir John Parsons, who *m.* Catherine, daughter of Sir Clifford Clifton, knt. and co-heir of her brother, Sir William Clifton, of Clifton, in the county of Nottingham, bart. and was *s.* by his only son,

III. Sir William Parsons, who *m.* first, Frances, daughter of Henry Dutton, esq. and had issue,

John, fellow of Merton College, Oxford, died in his father's lifetime.
William, lieutenant in Colonel Cholmondeley's regiment of Foot, *m.* Mary, daughter of John Frampton, esq. of the Exchequer, and had issue,
Mark, who succeeded his grandfather.
Grace, to whom her maternal aunt, the Duchess of Northumberland, left a considerable fortune.

Sir William *m.* secondly, Isabella, fifth daughter and co-heir of James Holt, esq. of Castleton, in Lancashire, and relict of Delaval Dutton, esq. but had no other issue. He *d.* about 1760, and was *s.* by his grandson,

IV. Sir Mark Parsons, who *d.* unm. in 1812, when the Baronetcy became extinct.

Arms—Arg. a chevron between three holly leaves erect vert.

PASTON, OF OXNEAD.

Created 8th June, 1642.

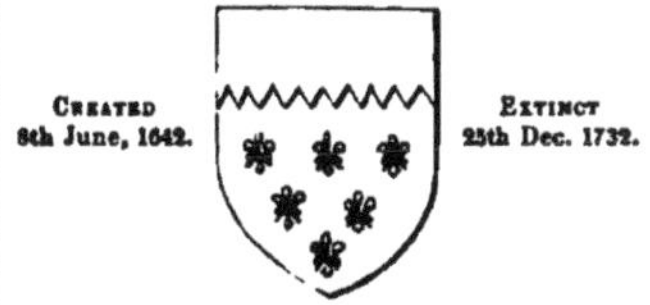

Extinct 25th Dec. 1732.

Lineage.

The ancient and "worshipful" family of Paston settled in England, according to many creditable writers, immediately after the Conquest; and Wolstan, the first recorded ancestor, is stated to have had a grant of lands at Paston, in Norfolk, whence he derived his surname.

Sir William Paston, knt. born at Paston, son and heir of Clement Paston, by Beatrix, his wife, daughter and heir of John de Somerton, adopted the legal profession, and was one of the judges of the court of Common Pleas *temp.* Henry VI. He married Agnes, daughter and co-heir of Sir Edmund Berry, knt. and had issue,

John, his heir.
Edmund, who was retained in 1474, by Richard, Duke of Gloucester, constable and admiral of England, to serve him with the king, in his voyage over sea, for a whole year, with three archers, well horsed, armed, and arraied.
Walter.
William (Sir), knt. a devoted adherent of the Lancastrian cause, *m.* Anne, daughter and co-heir of Edmund Beaufort, Duke of Somerset, and had two daughters,

* By Mary, his wife, daughter of Sir William Gerrard, of Dorney, knt.

† The executors of Sir William Parsons, the first baronet, sold Langley, in 1669, to Henry Seymour, esq. From the Seymours it passed by sale to Lord Masham, and from his lordship was purchased, in 1736, by the Duke of Marlborough, whose successor sold the park and manor to Sir Robert-Bateson Harvey, bart.

Anne, *m.* to Sir Gilbert Talbot.
Elizabeth, *m.* to Sir John Savill.

Elizabeth, *m.* to Robert, son of Robert, Lord Poynings.
Anne, *m.* to William Yelverton, esq.
Margery, *m.* to Richard Colle, esq.

Sir William, commonly known as "the good judge," died in London, 14th August, 1444, aged sixty-six, and was buried in our Lady's chapel at the east end of the cathedral church of Norwich. His eldest son and successor,

JOHN PASTON, esq. of Oxnead, in Norfolk, aged twenty-three at his father's decease, *m.* Margaret, daughter and heir of Sir John de Mauteby, and dying in 1466, was succeeded by his son,

SIR JOHN PASTON, knt. who served with distinction in the French wars, and was deputed to conduct the king, EDWARD's, sister into France, on her marriage with Charles, Duke of Burgundy. He died 15th November, 19 EDWARD IV. *s. p.* and was *s.* by his brother and namesake,

SIR JOHN PASTON, *junior*, who was made a knight banneret for his conduct at the battle of Stoke, and was one of those appointed to receive the Princess Catherine of Spain, wife of Prince Arthur, on her landing at Plymouth. He *m.* Margery, daughter of Sir Thomas Brews, of Hinton Hall, and had issue,

WILLIAM, his heir.
Philip, who married Anne, daughter and heir of Robert Guggs, of Sparham, and relict of John Blakeney, esq.

Elizabeth, *m.* first, to William Clere, esq. of Ormesby; and secondly, to Sir John Fineux, lord chief justice.

Sir John died in 1503, and was succeeded by his son,

SIR WILLIAM PASTON, knt. of Oxnead, an eminent barrister-at-law, who lived to a great age, and died in 1554, having had, by Bridget, his wife, daughter of Sir Henry Heydon, knt. of Baconsthorp, in Norfolk, five sons and seven daughters, viz.

ERASMUS, who predeceased his father, in 1538, leaving by Mary, his wife, daughter of Sir Thomas Wyndham, of Felbrigge, a son,
WILLIAM, successor to his grandfather.
Henry.
John, of Huntingfield Hall, Suffolk, who married Anne Moulton, and had two daughters, his co-heirs, viz.
Bridget, *m.* to Lord-chief-justice Coke.
Elizabeth, *m.* to Ambrose Jermyn, esq.
Clement, of Oxnead, born at Paston Hall, a naval officer of the reign of HENRY VIII. In an engagement with the French, he took their admiral, the Baron de St. Blankheare, and retained him prisoner at Castor, until ransomed by 7000 crowns. "Henry VIII. called this Clement *his champion*; the Duke of Somerset stiled him, *his souldier*; Queen Mary, *her seaman*; and Queen Elizabeth, *her father*." He died *s. p.* in 1599.
Thomas (Sir), knighted at Bologne, being then one of the gentlemen of the king's privy chamber. He *m.* Anne, daughter and co-heir of Sir John Leigh, of Addington, in Surrey, and was ancestor of the PASTONS of Berningham Winter, in Norfolk.

Eleanor, *m.* to Thomas, Earl of Rutland.
Anne, *m.* to Sir Thomas Tindale, of Hockwold.
Elizabeth, *m.* to Sir Francis Leak, of Derbyshire.
Margery, a nun.
Mary, *m.* to Sir John Chaworth, of Notts.
Margaret.
Bridget, *m.* to — Carre, esq.

Sir William was *s.* by his grandson,

SIR WILLIAM PASTON, knt. of Paston, who married Frances, daughter of Sir Thomas Clere, of Stokesby, and dying 20th October, 1610, left, with a daughter, Anne, *m.* first, to Sir George Chaworth; and secondly, to Sir Nicholas L'Estrange, a son and successor,

CHRISTOPHER PASTON, esq. of Paston, who married Anne, daughter of Philip Audley, esq. of Pagrave, in Norfolk, and was *s.* by his son,

SIR EDMUND PASTON, knt. of Paston, who *m.* Catherine, daughter of Sir Thomas Knevet, of Ashwellthorp, and by her, who died in 1628, left at his decease, in 1632, aged forty-eight, a son and successor,

I. SIR WILLIAM PASTON, of Paston and Oxnead, high sheriff of Norfolk in 1636, who was created a BARONET 8th June, 1642. He *m.* first, Lady Catherine Bertie, daughter of Robert, Earl of Lindsey; and secondly, the sister of Sir William Hewet. He died 22nd February, 1662, leaving by his first wife a son and successor,

II. SIR ROBERT PASTON, of Oxnead and Paston, who having devoted his fortune and energies to the royal cause, during the civil wars, was elevated to the peerage by *King* CHARLES II. 19th August, 1673, as *Baron Paston, of Paston*, and VISCOUNT YARMOUTH, both in the county of Norfolk. His lordship *m.* Rebecca, daughter of Sir Jasper Clayton, knt. of London, and had issue,

WILLIAM, his successor.
Robert, *m.* Anne, daughter and co-heir of Philip Harbord, esq. of Besthorp, in Norfolk.
Jasper, *m.* Lady Fairborn, widow of Sir Palmes Fairborn.
Thomas, a colonel in the army, drowned in [illegible], leaving by his wife, Dorothy, daughter of Edward Darcy, esq.
Robert, captain R. N.
Rebecca, married to Admiral Sir Stafford Fairborn.
Margaret, *m.* to Hieronimo Alberto di Conti, a German.

The viscount was advanced to the EARLDOM OF YARMOUTH, 30th July, 1679. He was esteemed a man of refined taste and learning, and dying in 1683, was *s.* by his eldest son,

III. SIR WILLIAM PASTON, second Earl of Yarmouth. This nobleman espoused, first, Charlotte-Jemima-Maria, natural daughter of *King* CHARLES II. by the Viscountess Shannon, wife of Francis Boyle, Viscount Shannon, and daughter of Sir William Killigrew, and had issue,

CHARLES, Lord Paston, a brigadier in the army, who predeceased his father.
William, a captain in the royal navy, died before his father.

Charlotte, *m.* first, to Thomas Herne, esq. of Haveringland, in Norfolk; and secondly, Major Weldon.
Rebecca, *m.* to Sir John Holland, of Quidenham, bart.

His lordship *m.* secondly, Elizabeth, daughter of Lord North, and widow of Sir Robert Wiseman, but by that lady had no issue. He *d.* in 1732, leaving no male issue, and as the male line of his brothers had previously ceased, the BARONETCY, together with the superior honours, became EXTINCT.

Arms—Arg. six fleurs-de-lis, three, two, and one sa. a chief indented or.

PATE, OF SYSONBY.

CREATED 28th Oct. 1643.

EXTINCT in 1652.

Lineage.

HENRY PATE, of Eye Kettleby, son of Edward Pate,* of the same place, was aged forty in 1507. He had three sons, of whom the second,

I. JOHN PATE, esq. of Sisonby, in Leicestershire, was created a BARONET in 1643. He m. first, Elizabeth, daughter of Sir William Skipwith, of Cotes; and secondly, Lettice, eldest daughter of Sir Thomas Dilke, of Maxstoke Castle, Warwickshire. By the former, who died 17th August, 1626, aged thirty-seven, he had issue,

ABIGAIL, m. Sir Thomas Smith, bart. of Hatherton, in Cheshire, and dying 25th October, 1691, aged sixty-seven, left an only daughter and heir,

FRANCES-PATE SMITH, b. 2nd November, 1663; m. to Richard Lister, esq. of Thorpe Ernald, in Leicestershire, and had issue,

JOHN-PATE LISTER.

Abigail Lister, m. to Henry Browne, esq. of Shelbroke, Yorkshire.

FRANCES, m. to Charles, fourth son of Charles Lord Carrington, and d. in 1693.

Sir John Pate d. in 1652, aged sixty-seven, when the BARONETCY became EXTINCT.

Arms—Arg. three text R's sa.

PAUL, OF RODBOROUGH.

CREATED 3rd Sept. 1762.

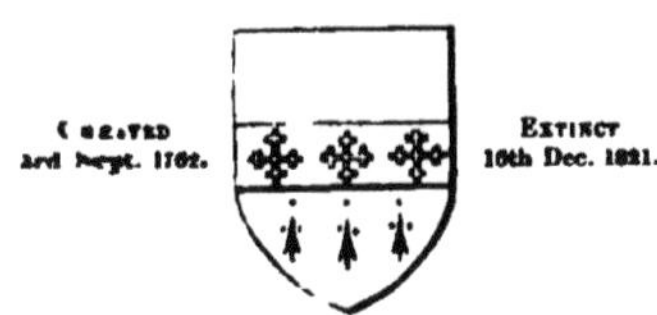

EXTINCT 16th Dec. 1821.

Lineage.

THE REV. ONESIPHORUS PAUL, of Warnborough, in the county of Wilts, had two sons, NICHOLAS, his heir, George, who d. unm. and a daughter, Elizabeth, wife of the Rev. Thomas Prance, minister of Easingwould, in Yorkshire. The elder son,

NICHOLAS PAUL, esq. m. Elizabeth, daughter of Thomas Dean, of Woodchester, in Gloucestershire, and had two sons, viz.

I. DEAN, of Stroud, who m. first, Elizabeth, daughter of William Andrews, esq. of Stonehouse, in the county of Gloucester, who died 4th August, 1741. He m. secondly, Anne Gastrell, daughter of John Selfe, of Cirencester, who d. 7th September, 1746; and thirdly, Margaret, daughter of Philip Hampton, of Westbury, which lady d. 11th May, 1764: by the first and third he had no family; by the second he had one son,

JOHN PAUL, M.D. of Salisbury, who married Frances, youngest daughter of Robert Snow, esq. of Hendon, in the county of Middlesex, and of London, banker,† and had issue,

JOHN-DEAN PAUL, b. in 1775, of London, banker, in whom the Baronetcy was revived.

Mr. Dean Paul, of Stroud, d. 11th March, 1764, and with his three wives lies buried at Woodchester.

II. Onesiphorus.

The second son,

I. SIR ONESIPHORUS PAUL, resided at Woodchester, where he was extensively engaged in the manufacture of the fine woollen cloths, for which that neighbourhood is distinguished, and which owe much of their unrivalled excellence to his ingenious and spirited improvements. In August, 1750, he had the honour to receive and entertain at his house his royal highness Frederick Prince of Wales; in 1760 he was sheriff of Gloucestershire: and on presenting an address from the county to *King* GEORGE III. on his accession to the throne, received the honour of knighthood. He was created a BARONET 3rd September, 1762, as "Sir Onesiphorus Paul, of Rodborough, in the county of Gloucester." He married first, Jane, daughter of Francis Blackburn, esq. of Richmond, in the county of York, and by her, who d. 26th May, 1748, had issue,

GEORGE-ONESIPHORUS, his successor.

Jane, m. to Thomas Pettat, esq. of Stanley Park, in the county of Gloucester, and died s. p. in 1810.

Elizabeth, m. to George Snow, esq. of Dorsetshire (eldest son of Robert Snow, of Hendon, aforesaid), and died 7th January, 1772, leaving

Robert Snow, major in the Royal Westminster regiment of Middlesex Militia.

Jane Snow, m. to Colonel James Clitherow, of Boston House, Middlesex.

Valentinia Snow, d. an infant.

He m. secondly, Catherine, daughter and co-heir of Francis Freeman, esq. of Norton Male-reward, in Somersetshire, but by that lady, who d. 20th October, 1766, had no surviving issue. The baronet m. thirdly, Sarah, daughter of John Peach, esq. of Woodchester, widow of John Turner, of Kingstanley, in Gloucestershire, but by her, who d. in April, 1801, had no issue. Sir Onesiphorus d. 21st September, 1774, aged sixty-nine, and was s. by his son,

II. SIR GEORGE-ONESIPHORUS PAUL, high sheriff for Gloucestershire in 1780, who d. s. p. in 1820, when the BARONETCY became EXTINCT. His cousin, John Dean Paul, esq. elder son of Doctor Paul, of Salisbury, inherited Rodborough, and being created a BARONET 3rd September, 1821, is the present (1837) SIR JOHN

---

* Edward Pate's younger brother,

JOHN PATE, of Brin, in Essex, m. Ellen, daughter of Thomas Saltmarsh, of Epping, and had issue,

EDWARD, of Brin, who m. Anne, daughter of William Blount, esq. of Osbaston, and was ancestor of Mr. William Pate, "the learned woollen draper," distinguished by Swift and the other wits of *Queen* ANNE's reign.

Thomas, who m. Mary, daughter of Neville, of Grove, Notts, and had a son, Edmund.

† By Valentine, his wife, daughter of George Paul LL. D. vicar-general and king's advocate in the Commons.

DEAN PAUL, of Rodborough. (Refer to BURKE's *Peerage and Baronetage*.)

Arms—Arg. on a fesse az. three crosslets or, in base three ermine spots.

PAYLER, OF THORALBY.

CREATED 28th June, 1642.  EXTINCT in 1706.

Lineage.

I. EDWARD PAYLER, esq. of Thoralby, in the county of York, who was created a BARONET in 1642, married Anne, daughter of William Watkinson, esq. and dying about 1649, was *s.* by his grandson (the son of his son Watkinson),

II. SIR WATKINSON PAYLER, of Thoralby, who *m.* Alathea, daughter of Sir Thomas Norcliffe, knt. of Langton, but died without surviving issue in 1706, when the BARONETCY EXPIRED.

*** THOMAS TURNER, of Kent, assumed the surname of PAYLER some time after Sir Watkinson's death. He had, with a daughter, Margaret, wife of the Rev. Edward Taylor, of Bifrons, a son, the late THOMAS-WATKINSON PAYLER, esq. of Heden.

Arms—Gu. on a bend or, between three lions passant guardant arg. as many mullets of six points pierced sa.

PELSANT, OF CLIPSTON.

CREATED 5th Mar. 1713-14.  EXTINCT ....

Lineage.

EUSEBIUS PELSANT, esq. son and heir of Eusebius Pelsant, esquire of the body to CHARLES I. of Cadeby, in the county of Leicester, by Anne, his second wife, sister of Sir George Buswell, bart. of Clipston, in Northamptonshire, inherited that estate and assumed the surname of BUSWELL. He *m.* Frances, only daughter of Sir Richard Wingfield, of Tickencote, and had three sons, EUSEBIUS, George, and Wingfield. The eldest,

I. EUSEBIUS BUSWELL, esq. of Clipston, was created a BARONET in 1713-14. He *m.* first, Hester, second daughter of Sir Charles Skymsher, knt. of Norbury Manor, in Staffordshire; and secondly, Honor, daughter of Ralph Sneyd, esq. of Keel, in the same county. By the latter he had a daughter, Frances. He died without male issue, when the BARONETCY became EXTINCT.

Arms—Arg. five lozenges in fesse between three bears' heads erased gu. muzzled or.

PENEYSTONE, OF LEIGH.

CREATED 25th Nov. 1612.  EXTINCT 24th Dec. 1705.

Lineage.

This family claimed descent from

SIR THOMAS DE PENYSTON, knt. of Truro, in Cornwall, living in the time of the Conqueror, who had three sons,

JOHN (Sir),
Thomas,
William,
} witnesses to the foundation charter of the nunnery of Kirklees, in Yorkshire, made by Reineus Flandrensis.

From the eldest son,

SIR JOHN DE PENYSTON, knt. descended, in the fourth degree,

SIR GILES PENYSTON, knt. who built Penystone, in the county of York, and enjoyed great possessions in Cornwall by Isabel, his wife. His son and heir,

SIR GEOFFERY PENYSTON, knt. living at Penystone, *temp.* HENRY III. was grandfather of

SIR EDMUND PENYSTON, who *m.* Beatrix, daughter and heir of Sir Geoffery Fauconberg, and possessed the manor of Beaconsfield, in Buckinghamshire, *temp.* EDWARD II. He was *s.* by his son,

SIR WALTER PENYSTON, who *m.* Dorothy, daughter of Sir Humphrey Ingleby, knt.; but we pass through a long line of descendants, all of whom formed distinguished alliances, to

THOMAS PENESTONE, of Beaconsfield, who *m.* Elizabeth, daughter of Humphrey Ashfield, of Heythrop, and had several sons and daughters who left posterity. THOMAS, the eldest son, died in his lifetime, and left issue by Mary, his wife, daughter and co-heir of John Somer, esq. of Newland, in Kent, an only son,

I. SIR THOMAS PENESTONE, who succeeding to his mother's inheritance, beame seated at Leigh, in Sussex; and having received the honour of knighthood was created a BARONET 25th November, 1612. He *m.* first, Anne, fourth daughter of Sir William Stonehouse; and secondly, Martha, fourth daughter of Sir Thomas Temple, bart. of Stowe; but by those ladies had no surviving issue. Sir Thomas *m.* thirdly, Elizabeth, daughter and sole heir of Sir Thomas Waller, of Halstead, in Kent, widow of Sir William Pope, and by her had two daughters; the elder, Elizabeth, *m.* to John Hastings, esq. of Dalisford, in Worcestershire; the younger, to Sir James Astry, knt. master in chancery; and two sons, John, who *d.* in 1622, and an elder, his successor at his decease *circa* 1644,

II. SIR THOMAS PENEYSTONE, of Cornwell, in the county of Oxford, who *m.* Elizabeth, only daughter and heir of Sir Cornelius Fairmedow, knt. of London, and had issue,

THOMAS,
FAIRMEDOW,
} third and fourth baronets.
Charles, *d.* unm.

He died about the year 1674, and was *s.* by his eldest son,

III. SIR THOMAS PENEYSTONE, who died unmarried in 1679, and was *s.* by his brother,

IV. Sir Fairmedow Pennystone, who m. first, Elizabeth, daughter of Sir Compton Read, bart. of Shipton, in the county of Oxford; and secondly, Mary, daughter of — Powney, esq. of Old Windsor, Berks, and widow of Sir William Paul, knt. of Braywick, in the same county, but d. s. p. 24th December, 1765, when the Baronetcy expired.

Arms—Arg. three Cornish choughs ppr

PENNYMAN, OF MARSKE.

Created 6th May, 1628.  Extinct 22nd Aug. 1643.

Lineage.

James Pennyman, esq. of Ormsby, in the county of York, from whose eldest son and heir, Colonel Sir James Pennyman, knt. of Ormsby, created a baronet in 1663-4, the *extant* baronets of Ormsby derive (see Burke's *Peerage and Baronetage*), had an illegitimate son

William Pennyman, one of the masters in chancery, father of

I. William Pennyman, esq. of Marske, in the county of York, who was created a Baronet 6th May, 1628. Sir William was a zealous supporter of the royal cause, and in high favour with the king, who made him governor of Oxford and colonel of a regiment of foot. He m. Anne, daughter and heir of William Atherton, esq. but died issueless 22nd August, 1643, and was buried in Christ Church Cathedral, Oxford, when the Baronetcy became extinct.

Arms—Gu. a chev. erm. between three half-spears, their staves, or, headed arg.

PEPPERELL, OF MASSACHUSETTS.

Created 15th Nov. 1746.  Extinct 6th July, 1759.

Lineage.

William Pepperell, descended from a Cornish family, but a native by birth of New England, his grandfather having settled there, was bred a merchant, and attained high reputation and wealth in the mercantile world; but his private affairs, although numerous and weighty, not entirely engrossing his attention, he devoted the remainder of his time to the service of the public. He was early in life chosen to represent his town in the great and general court, and sooner than customary had a seat at the board as one of his majesty's council, to which post of honour he was ever afterwards elected until the time of his decease. He was also a colonel in the militia of New England, and so highly did he stand in public estimation, that when the project was formed by the New England government for the reduction of Louisbourgh, he was made choice of and commissioned by the governors of the several provinces to command the troops upon the important occasion. It was the united voice of the province "that his appointment to the chief command gave them great satisfaction and hopes;" and those hopes were not disappointed, for Louisbourgh, after sustaining a siege of forty-nine days, surrendered to the arms of Lieutenant-General Pepperell, with the fortresses and territory thereunto belonging, thus crowning the expedition with triumph. For this signal service he was created a Baronet 15th November, 1746, "as Sir William Pepperell, of the province of Massachusetts, in North America," and had a grant of arms conferred upon him at the same time to perpetuate the memory of the event. Sir William m. Mary, daughter of Samuel Hirst, esq. of Boston, in New England, and died, aged sixty-three, 22nd August, 1759, leaving an only daughter and heir,

- Elizabeth, who m. Nathaniel Sparhawk, merchant, of New England, and had issue,
  - Nathaniel Sparhawk, whose son was recently residing in America.
  - William Sparhawk, who succeeded to the property of his maternal grandfather, and took the name of Pepperell.
  - Samuel Sparhawk.
  - Andrew Sparhawk.
  - Mary Sparhawk, m. to Charles Jervis, M.D. of Boston.

At the decease of Sir William, the Baronetcy expired.

Arms—Arg. a chevron gu. between three pine-cones vert, with the augmentation of a canton of the second, charged with a fleur-de-lis of the first.

PEPPERELL, OF BOSTON, IN THE PROVINCE OF MASSACHUSETTS.

Created 9th Nov. 1774.—Extinct 18th Dec. 1816.

Lineage.

I. William Sparhawk, esq. son of Nathaniel Sparhawk, of New England, merchant, by Elizabeth Pepperell, only daughter and heir of Lieutenant-General Sir William Pepperell, bart. having become heir to his grandfather at the decease of that distinguished officer in 1759, assumed the surname of Pepperell, and was created a Baronet 9th November, 1774. He m. 12th November, 1767, Elizabeth, daughter of the Hon. Isaac Royall, of his majesty's council in Massachusetts' Bay, and had issue,

- William-Royall, b. 5th July, 1775; d. 27th September, 1798.
- Elizabeth-Royall, m. the Rev. Henry Hutton, M.A. rector of Beaumont, in Essex, and survives his widow with four sons and six daughters.
- Mary, m. to William Congreve, esq. of Congreve, in Staffordshire, and of Aldermaston, in Berkshire.
- Harriet, relict of Sir Charles Thomas Palmer, bart. of Wanlip Hall, in Leicestershire.

Sir William d. 18th December, 1816, when the Baronetcy expired, and his daughters became his heirs. The American estates were confiscated during the war of the Independence.

Arms—As Pepperell of Massachusetts.

PESHALL, OF HORSLEY.

CREATED 25th Nov. 1612.  DORMANT since Feb. 1712.

Lineage.

RICHARD DE PESHALL, son of Sir Richard Peshall by Alice Swinnerton, his wife, was a knight and a person of great power in Staffordshire, having been high sheriff, an office in those days of great authority, 7 EDWARD III. and from the 11th to the 15th of the same king. He *m.* Margaret, daughter and heir of Hugh, lord of Knighton, and thus added that manor to his possessions. He was *s.* by his son,

SIR ADAM DE PESHALL, who was sheriff 15 EDWARD III. and made a similar accession to his estate by marriage with two heiresses, the daughters of John Weston, lord of Weston Lisard, in the county of Salop, and John de Caverswall, of Bishop's Offley. By the former he had a son and heir,

SIR ADAM DE PESHALL, of Weston Lisard, whose grandson and heir, another

SIR ADAM PESHALL, left two daughters, his co-heirs, viz.

MARGARET PESHALL, who *m.* Sir Richard Mytton, and conveyed to him the estate of Weston Lisard. (Refer to BURKE'S *Commoners*, vol. ii. p. 518.)

JOHANNA PESHALL, *m.* to W. de Birmingham.

By the latter he had a son,

SIR RICHARD DE PESHALL, who acquired a considerable fortune with his wife, Johanna, daughter and heir of Reginald Chetwynde, of Chetwynde, and left a son and heir,

SIR THOMAS PESHALL, knt. living 4 RICHARD II. who, by his first wife, Philippa, had two sons,

RICHARD, } who *m. temp.* HENRY IV. two sisters,
NICHOLAS, } the daughters of Hugh Malpas, of Checkley,* and thus brought great estates into the family. RICHARD, the elder son, left two daughters, *m.* in the time of HENRY VII.; the elder, Isabella, to SIR THOMAS GROSVENOR; and the younger, Jocosa, to W. PIGOTT, of Cheshire. Of NICHOLAS, more presently.

Sir Thomas, by his second wife, Alice, daughter of Roger Knightley, of Knightly, in Staffordshire, left a son,

HUMPHRY, of Over Tayne, father of

Richard, who *m.* Alice, daughter of Robert Knightly, esq. of Gowsell, and had a son,

Humprey, father of

HUGH PESHALL, who, by his wife, Isabella, daughter and heir of John Stanley, of Pipe, left three daughters, his co-heirs, viz.

CATHERINE, *m.* to Sir John Blount, knt. of Kinlett, in Salop.

ISABELLA, *m.* to Richard Fane, of Tonbridge, in Kent.

JOCOSA, *m.* to Humphrey Walrych, of Dudmaston, in Salop.

The second son of the first marriage,

NICHOLAS PESHALL, by Helen, his wife, daughter and co-heir of Hugh Malpas, left a son and heir,

HUGH PESHALL, esq. the first of the family who resided at Horsley, in the county of Stafford. He was sheriff 4 HENRY VII. and by Julian, his wife, daughter of Sir Robert Corbet of Morton Corbet, had a son and heir,

HUMPHREY PESHALL, esq. of Horsley, who *m.* Helen, daughter of Humphrey Swinnerton, esq. of Swinnerton Castle, and widow of Henry Delves, esq. and had issue,

JOHN, of Checkley.

RICHARD, whose son,

HENRY, *d. s. p.*

William, from whom descended

John Peshall, of Naples.

The eldest son and continuator of the family,

JOHN PESHALL, esq. of Checkley, *m.* Hellena, daughter of John Harcourt, esq. of Ranton, in the county of Stafford, and left a son and heir,

RICHARD PESHALL, esq. who *m.* Isabel, daughter and heir of Thomas Rolleston, esq. of Derbyshire, and had seven sons and two daughters. The eldest son,

THOMAS PESHALL, esq. succeeding to the family estates, resided at Horsley. He *m.* Joanna, daughter of Sir Edmund Fettiplace, of Berkshire, and was *s.* by his son,

I. JOHN PESHALL, esq. of Horsley, in Staffordshire, who was created a BARONET by *King* JAMES I. 25th November, 1612, and in four years afterwards was sheriff of the county. He *m.* Anne, daughter of Ralph Sheldon, esq. of Beoly, in the county of Worcester, and had issue,

THOMAS, his heir, *b.* in 1596, who *m.* Bridget, daughter of Sir William Stafford, knt. of Blatherwick, and dying in the lifetime of his father, left

JOHN, successor to his grandfather.

Bridget, *m.* to George, son of William Massey, esq.

Anne, *m.* to Christopher Hawley, esq.

Elizabeth, *m.* to Sir Robert Bosvile, of Bianno[illegible]

Lettice, *m.* to John Barber, gent. of Flashbrook

Humphrey, ancestor of the PESHALLS of Halne [illegible] whose representative the Baronetcy of Horsley is said to have passed at the decease of Sir Thomas Peshall in 1712.

Ralph.

William (Sir), *m.* first, Mary, daughter of Richard Thimelby, esq.; and secondly, Frances, daughter of Walter, Lord Aston.

John, *m.* Bridget, daughter of Robert Knightley, esq. of Warwickshire.

Anne, *m.* to Sir Richard Fleetwood, bart.

Elizabeth, *m.* to William Scot, esq. of Sussex

Dorothy, *m.* to William Stanford, esq. of Perry hall.

Jane, *m.* to Richard Colvert, esq. of Corkeram.

Katherine, *m.* to James Pool, esq. of Wirhall

Margaret, *m.* to Richard Brent, esq.

Frances, *m.* to John Stanford, esq. of Sayford

Sir John *d.* 13th January, 1646, and was *s.* by his grandson,

---

* HUGH MALPAS, of Checkley, *m.* the daughter and heir of

ADAM DE PRAYERS, who *m.* Helen, daughter and heir of

RICHARD BLACKENHALL, of Blackenhall, in Cheshire, who married the daughter and heir of

HUGH WISTASTON, who was possessed of Checkley by his father's marriage, with the daughter and heir of ROBERT PRAYERS

II. Sir John Peshall, who m. in 1669, Frances, daughter of Colonel Thomas Legh, of Adlington, in Cheshire, and dying in 1701, was s. by his son,

III Sir Thomas Peshall. This gentleman m. Miss Medcalf, and had a son,

John, who m. Charlotte, daughter of Thomas, Lord Colepeper, and died before his father in 1706, leaving two daughters, his co-heirs, viz.

Frances, m. to Thomas Ireland, esq. of the county of Salop, and had a son.

Arabella, baptized in 1702, m. to John, third Earl of Breadalbane.

Sir Thomas d. in February, 1712, and since that time the Baronetcy has lain dormant.

Arms—A cross forme flourette sa. on a canton gu. a wolf's head of the first.

PETTUS, OF RACKHEATH.

Created 23rd Sept. 1641.

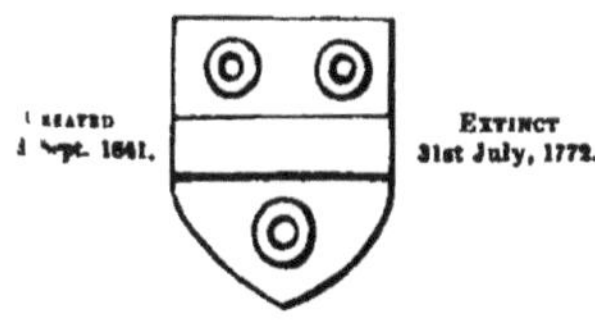

Extinct 31st July, 1772.

Lineage.

Thomas Pettus, an opulent citizen of Norwich, who was buried in St. Edmund's Church, Lombard Street, London, was father of

John Pettus, of the city of Norwich, gent. who m. ... Dethick, widow of Simon Dethick, esq. and left a son and heir,

Thomas Pettus, esq. mayor of Norwich in 1591, who m. Christian, daughter of Simon Dethick, esq. of Norwich, and had issue,

John (Sir), his heir.

Thomas, mayor of Norwich in 1614, died in 1620, leaving by Cecily, his wife, daughter of William King, of Hempstead, in Norfolk,

William, of London, who m. Mary, daughter of Sir Peter Gleane, knt. of Norwich, and had a numerous progeny.

Alexander, who left issue.

William, *d. s. p.*

Elizabeth, m. to Augustine Whale, gent. of Norwich.

Cecily, m. to Humphrey Camden, of London.

Anne, m. to Mr. Alderman, Robert Debny, of Norwich.

The eldest son,

Sir John Pettus, knt. m. Bridget, daughter and heir of Augustine Curtis, esq. of Honnington, in Suffolk, and had one son and four daughters, viz.

Augustine, his heir.

Anne, m. to Robert Knightly, esq. of Offchurch, in the county of Warwick.

Christian, m. to Sir Peter Saltingstall, knt. of Barkway, in the county of Hertford.

Bridget, m. to Martin Sidley, esq. of Morley, in Norfolk.

Elizabeth, *d. s. p.*

John, who left a benefaction to the preachers of the Cathedral Church at Norwich, which is commemorated by an annual sermon, *d.* 9th April, 1613, and was s. by his son,

Sir Augustine Pettus, who, like his father, received the honour of knighthood. He m. first, Mary, daughter of Henry Vylett, esq. of Lynn, and had a son,

Thomas, his heir.

Sir Augustine m. secondly, Abigail, daughter of Sir Arthur Heveningham, knt. of Heveningham, in Suffolk, and by that lady had two other sons, viz.

Thomas, (bearing the same name as his half-brother,) m. Anne, daughter of Calibut Walpole, esq. of Houghton, which lady surviving him, m. secondly, Sir Henry Hungate, knt. of Bradenham, in Norfolk.

John.

The eldest son,

I. Thomas Pettus, esq. of Rackheath, in the county of Norfolk, for his zeal and fidelity to the royal cause, was created a Baronet by *King* Charles I. 23rd September, 1641. Sir Thomas m. first, Elizabeth, daughter of Sir Thomas Knyvet, knt. of Ashwellthorpe, in Norfolk, and had issue,

Thomas, his heir.

Augustine, *d. s. p.*

John, successor to his elder brother.

His first wife dying in 1653, Sir Thomas m. secondly, Anne, daughter of Arthur Everard, esq. of Stow Park, Suffolk, who surviving him, m. secondly, Edward Warner, esq. of Parham, in the same county. Sir Thomas *d.* 21st November, 1654, and was s. by his eldest son,

II. Sir Thomas Pettus, who m. Elizabeth, daughter of Walter Overbury, esq. of Barton, in Warwickshire, and had one son, who died in minority, and a daughter,

Elizabeth, his sole heir, who m. Rowland Okeover, esq. of Okeover, in Derbyshire.

Sir Thomas was sheriff of Norfolk in 1664. He *d.* in 1671, and was s. by his brother,

III. Sir John Pettus, F.R.S. who m. Mary, daughter and co-heir of Nicholas Burwell, esq. of Gray's Inn, and niece of Sir John Burwell, knt. of Rougham, in Suffolk, by whom he had issue,

Horatio, his heir.

John.

Robert.

Charles.

Frances, m. to the Rev. Mr. Faucett, rector of Castor, near Norwich.

Sir John, who was cupbearer to *King* Charles II. *King* James II. and *King* William, and one of the commissioners of appeals, died 25th October, 1698, aged fifty-eight, and was s. by his eldest son,

IV. Sir Horatio Pettus. This gentleman m. Elizabeth, youngest daughter of Sir Thomas Meers, knt. of Kirton, in the county of Lincoln, and had issue,

Thomas, who died in the twenty-first year of his age, in 1723, unm.

John, his successor.

Horatio, sixth baronet.

Mary, m. to Leonard Batchelor, esq. of Norwich.

Anna-Maria.

He *d.* 9th March, 1731, and was s. by his eldest surviving son,

V. Sir John Pettus, who m. Rebecca, daughter of Edmund Prideaux, esq. of Prideaux Place, in Cornwall, and granddaughter of Dr. Humphrey Prideaux, dean of Norwich, but died without male issue in May, 1743, and was s. by his brother,

VI. Sir Horatio Pettus, who *d. s. p.* 31st July, 1772, when the Baronetcy expired.

Arms—Gules, a fesse argent between three annulets or.

PEY

PEYTON, OF ISLEHAM.

Lineage.

The PEYTONS, Camden observes, have had a common progenitor with the UFFORDS, who became Earls of Suffolk,* the founder of both being William Mallet, a Norman baron, who was sheriff of Yorkshire in the 3rd of WILLIAM I. and obtained grants of sundry lordships and manors from the crown, amongst which were Sibton and Peyton Hall, which he possessed at the time of the survey. "Iselham (says the same author) formerly belonged to the Bernards, which came to the family of the Peytons by marriage. Which knightly family of Peyton, flowed out of the same male stock, when the Uffords, Earls of Suffolk, descended; albeit they assumed the surname of Peyton, according to the use of that age, from their manor of Peyton Hall, in Boxford, in the county of Suffolk."

The first of the family by the name of PEYTON upon record, was

REGINALD DE PEYTON, second son of Walter, Lord of Sibton, younger brother of Mallet, sheriff of Yorkshire. This Reginald held the lordships of Peyton Hall, in Ramshold and Boxford, in Suffolk, of Hugh de Bigod; he was sewer to Roger Bigod, Earl of Norfolk, and gave lands to the monks of Thetford, to pray for the soul of Hugh Bigod. He had two sons, WILLIAM, who held certain lands in Boxford, of the fee of the abbey of St. Edmundsbury, as appears by charter of his nephew John, and

JOHN DE PEYTON, to whom *King* STEPHEN and his cousin-german, William de Cassineto, Lord of Horsford, granted all his lands in Peyton, to hold, as his ancestors before held the same. This John had four sons, viz.

I. JOHN (Sir), the elder.
II. Robert, who was lord justice of Ireland, *temp.* HENRY III. and EDWARD I. He was Lord of Ufford, in Suffolk, and assumed the surname of Ufford therefrom.
III. Peter, Lord of Peyton Hall, who held lands in Ramshot and Peyton, in the time of *King* JOHN. He was father of
    Robert, who was *s.* by his son,
        Sir John de Peyton, knt. whose male line seemed to fail, *temp.* EDWARD III.
IV. John, the younger, who sold to John his eldest brother, all the lands which he had in Boxford, of the fee of the abbey of St. Edmond's and Stoke Neyland, which their father, John de Peyton, and William, their uncle, formerly possessed.

The eldest son,

SIR JOHN DE PEYTON, succeeded his father, and was Lord of Peyton Hall, in Boxford, while he possessed lands beside in Stoke Neyland, in Suffolk. He flourished under HENRY III. as appears by a catalogue of knights in that reign. His wife was Matilda de Buriis,† by her he had three sons and one daughter, viz.

JOHN, his heir.
William.
James.

Agnes.

His eldest son,

SIR JOHN DE PEYTON, knt. who served in the parliament held at Westminster, 29th EDWARD I. as one of the knights of the shire for Suffolk, soon after which he died. He had three wives, Agnes, Agnes, and Clementia, and was *s.* by his son,

SIR ROBERT DE PEYTON, who in many of his evidences is styled Chevalier and Monsieur. He had two wives: first, the Lady Christiana de Apleton, widow of William de Apleton, and heir to lands in Haswell and Boxford, who died 19th EDWARD II. leaving no children, and was buried at Stoke Neyland, with great pomp, the funeral expenses being thus set down: "fifty quarter of wheat £4. 10*s.* one hogshead of wine £53. 4*s.* four muttons 5*s.* each, eight bacon hogs 24*s.* ten calves," &c. His second wife was Joan de Marney, of the noble family of the Marneys of Layor Marney, in Essex, by whom there was issue,

JOHN (Sir), his heir.
William, from whom there was a release to his father, Robert, dated 13 EDWARD III.
John, jun. to whom William Castelayne, John le Rikell, &c. granted the manor of Beedles at Waldingfield, 5 EDWARD III.

The eldest son,

SIR JOHN DE PEYTON, *m.* Margaret, daughter and co-heir of Sir John Gernon, knt. of Lees, in Essex, Lord of Wicken, in Cambridgeshire, and of Bakewell, in the county of Derby, and in her right possessed the manor of Wicken, as in the 17th RICHARD II. he jointly, with her, held part of the manor of Estthorpe, by the service of one knight's fee. He *d.* in RICHARD's reign, his wife in the 2nd of HENRY V. Their son and heir,

JOHN DE PEYTON, esq. wedded Joan, daughter and heir of Sir Hammon Sutton, of Wicksho, in the county of Suffolk, and thus that estate came into the family. By her (who *m.* secondly, Sir Roger Drury) he had

JOHN, his heir.
Thomas.
Robert.

Margery, *m.* to Thomas Daubeny, esq of Sharrington, in Norfolk.

He died about the 5th of HENRY IV. and was *s.* by his son,

JOHN DE PEYTON, then in minority. He *m.* Grace, daughter of John Burgoyne, esq. of Drayton, in the county of Cambridge, and had issue,

* Of this family, says Sir William Dugdale, which afterwards arrived to great honour, I have not seen any thing memorable, until the 53rd of HENRY II. when Robert, a younger son of John de Peyton, of Peyton, in Suffolk, assuming his surname from the lordship of Ufford, in that county, became
ROBERT DE UFFORD, his son,
SIR ROBERT DE UFFORD, was summoned to parliament as a baron in 1308, and his son and successor,
ROBERT DE UFFORD, second baron, was created EARL OF SUFFOLK in 1337. The earldom expired in 1382. The BARONY is still in abeyance. BURKE's *Extinct and Dormant Peerage.*

† LE NEVE calls her Matilda, sister and heir of Symond de Notelle.

JOHN, his heir.
THOMAS.

Anne, m. to Jeffry Lockton, esq.

He died in the flower of his age, the 6th October, 4 HENRY V. and was s. by his elder son,

JOHN DE PEYTON, who died a minor, 20th October, 11 HENRY VI. and was s. by his brother,

THOMAS DE PEYTON, then seventeen years of age, and seised of the manor of Esthorp. His mother, Grace, dying the 6th May, he was found her heir to the manor of Messing, which was held of the crown, as of the honour of Keynes, by the service of one knight's fee, also of the manor of Binchall, and the castle. Upon the feast of All Saints, 18 HENRY VI. his age was proved at Cambridge, viz. twenty-two years, at which time it was sworn by John Welford, that he was born and baptized at Dry-Drayton, in that county, A. D. 1418, many agreeing in the verdict, among whom Robert Chapman alleged, that the day on which he was born being the feast of St. Valentine, there was a great storm; one knew it by the great wind; another broke his leg by a fall from his horse; another, for that his wife was buried; another, for then his lease was burnt; another, for then his daughter Margaret was burnt; another fell from a tree and broke his arm, as the several jurors deposed upon their oaths. This Thomas was sheriff of Cambridge and Huntingdon, 21st and 31st of HENRY VI. and about the 17th of EDWARD IV. he began to build the church at Iselham, agreeing then with John Waltham, alias Sudbury, free-mason for the same. In the chancel of which church he lies interred, having a monument erected there to his memory. He m. first, Margaret, daughter and co-heir of Sir John Bernard, knt. of Iselham, by that lady he acquired the estate of Iselham, and had issue,

THOMAS, who m. Joan, daughter of Calthorpe, of Norfolk, and thus acquired the manor of Calthorpe, with other lands in that county. He died before his father, leaving

ROBERT (Sir), heir to his grandfather.
John.
Edward.

Elizabeth, m. to Edward Langley, esq. of Knowlton, in Kent.
Jane, m. to John Langley, esq. of Lowleworth, in Cambridgeshire.
Anne, m. to John Ashby, esq. of Harefield, in Middlesex.
Dorothy.

His widow, Joan, m. William Mauleverer, esq.

Margaret.
Grace.

He m. secondly, Margaret, daughter and co-heir of Sir Hugh Francis, of Giffords, in the county of Suffolk, widow of Thomas Garnish, esq. of Kenton, in the same shire, and by her had two other sons, namely,

Christopher, who had great possessions in Wickhambrook and Bury. In the 12th of HENRY VII. he was sheriff of the counties of Cambridge and Huntingdon. He m. a daughter of Leonard Hide, esq. of Hide Hall, in Hertfordshire, but died in the 15th HENRY VII. without issue.*

Francis, of St. Edmundsbury, heir was also of Coggeshall, in Essex. He m. Elizabeth, daughter of Reginald Brook, esq. of Aspall-stoneham, in Suffolk, and had two sons, Edmund, the younger, who was customer of Calais, left no issue. The elder son,

Christopher, of St. Edmundsbury, m. Jane, daughter of Thomas Mildmay, esq. and had issue.†

Thomas Peyton d. 30th July, 1484, and was s. by his grandson,

SIR ROBERT PEYTON, of Iselham, who was sheriff of the counties of Cambridge and Huntingdon, in the 14th HENRY VII. He m. Elizabeth, daughter of Sir Robert Clere, of Ormesby, in Norfolk, and had issue,

ROBERT (Sir), his heir.
John (Sir), m. Dorothy, daughter of Sir John Tyndall, K.B. of Hockwould, in Kent, and from him descended the PEYTONS of Knowlton and Dodington.

Margaret, m. to Francis Jenney, esq. of Knotshall, in Suffolk.
Elizabeth, m. to Sir William Wigston, knt. of Wolston, in Warwickshire.

He d. in the 9th of HENRY VIII. and was s. by his elder son,

SIR ROBERT PEYTON, knt. who was sheriff of the counties of Cambridge and Huntingdon in 17th and 27th HENRY VIII. and accompanied that king to the siege of Balleyne. He was again sheriff in the 1st of *Queen* MARY. He m. Frances, daughter and heir of Francis Hassylden, esq. of Little Chesterford, in Essex, and of Steeple Marden, in Cambridgeshire, and in her right acquired these estates, with other lands in the county of Rutland. By this lady (who founded the famous hospital at Iselham) he had six sons and two daughters, viz.

I. ROBERT (Sir), his heir.
II. William.
III. Richard, of Little Chesterfield, in Essex, m. Mary, daughter of Leonard Hyde, esq. of

* This CHRISTOPHER and his wife were buried in Iselham church, on the roof whereof was cut in wood,

'Pray for the good Prosperity of Christopher Peyton, and Elizabeth his Wife, and for the Soul of Thomas Peyton, esq; and Margaret his Wife; Father and Mother of the said Christopher Peyton: and for the Souls of all the Posterity of the said Christopher Peyton.'

† Three sons, namely,

I. THOMAS, of St. Edmundsbury, customer of Plymouth, who by Lady Cecilia Bourchier, daughter of John, second Earl of Bath, left a son,

Sir Henry Peyton, "who followed long the wars in the Low Countries, and was knighted by JAMES I. He m. Lady Mary Rogers, widow of Andrew Rogers, esq. of Brianston, in Dorsetshire, and daughter of Edward Seymour, Duke of Somerset.

II. Christopher (Sir), knighted by JAMES I. was auditor of Ireland. He m. Anne, daughter of William Palmer, esq. of Warwickshire, and left three daughters, his co-heirs, viz.

ELIZABETH PEYTON, m. to Richard Cooke, of St. Edmundsbury.
CECILY, m. to Henry Rookwood, esq. of Ewsham.
THOMAZIN, m. first to Captain Baptist Castillion, of the bedchamber to *Queen* ELIZABETH, and secondly to Robert Pigott, esq. of Desart, in Ireland.

III. Henry, of London, m. Mary, daughter of William Pickering, also of London, and left posterity.

Hyde Hall, in Hertfordshire.* She outlived him, and *m.* secondly, Sir John Carey, Lord of Hunsdon.

IV. Christopher.

V. Edward.

VI. John.

I. Catherine, *m.* to — Williams, esq. of the county of Oxford.

II. Elizabeth, *m.* to Thomas Wrenne, esq. of Hinton, in the Isle of Ely.

Sir Robert *d.* 1st August, 1550, and was *s.* by his eldest son,

SIR ROBERT PEYTON, who was M.P. for Cambridgeshire in the 4th and 5th of *Queen* MARY, and sheriff of the united counties of Cambridge and Huntingdon, in the 9th of ELIZABETH. He received the honour of knighthood from JAMES I. at Royston, in November, 1606. Sir Robert *m.* Elizabeth, daughter of the LORD CHANCELLOR RICH, and aunt of Robert, Earl of Warwick, and had issue,

Robert, who *d.* unm.

JOHN, his heir.

Richard, *d. s. p.*

Mary, *m.* first, to Robert Balam, esq. of Wolsoken, in Norfolk, and secondly, to Sir Richard Cox, of Braham, in the Isle of Ely.

Frances, *m.* to John Hagar, esq. of Bourne Castle, in Cambridgeshire.

Winifride, *m.* first to — Osborne, esq. barrister-at-law; secondly to — Harefleet, esq. of Kent; and thirdly, John Hornbye, esq. of Lincolnshire.

He was *s.* by his eldest surviving son,

I. SIR JOHN PEYTON, of Iselham, in the county of Cambridge, who received the honour of knighthood from *King* JAMES I. He was sheriff of Cambridge and Huntingdon, in the 35th of ELIZABETH, when he was knight of the shire for the last, as he was again in the 1st of JAMES the *First*, and the next year sheriff a second time. In the 9th year of the same monarch, he was created a BARONET, 22nd May, 1611, on the institution of the order. Sir John *m.* Alice, daughter of Sir Edward Osborne, lord mayor of London in 1585, and had issue,

EDWARD (Sir), his heir.

John, *d. s. p.*

Robert, fellow of Queen's College, Cambridge.

Roger.

William, of Warlingworth, *m.* Tabitha, daughter of Henry Payne, esq. of Walthamstow, and left two sons, John and William.

Thomas, slain at Burse, in Holland.

Anne, *m.* to Sir Robert Bacon, bart. of Riborough, in Norfolk, third son of Sir Nicholas Bacon, bart. of Redgrave.

Alice, *m.* to Sir John, son and heir of Sir John Peyton, of Dodington.

Elizabeth, *m.* to Sir Anthony Irby, knt. of Boston in Lincolnshire.

Mary, *m.* to Sir Roger Meers, knt. of Hoghton, in Lincolnshire.

Frances, } *d.* unm.
Susan, }

He *d.* about the year 1617, and was *s.* by his eldest son,

II. SIR EDWARD PEYTON, who was knighted at Whitehall, 4th February, 1610, and during the life-time of his father was denominated "of Great Bradley, in Suffolk." He served in parliament from 18th of JAMES I. to the 3rd of CHARLES I. as one of the knights of the shire for the county of Cambridge, and was custos rotulorum thereof, which office he was deprived of by the influence of the Duke of Buckingham. "Whereat he was so much disgusted, that he first drew his pen against the court, and writ several pamphlets with great acrimony against CHARLES I. and the royalists." He subsequently sided with the presbyterians in the great rebellion, and so impoverished himself in the cause, that he was obliged to sell Iselham, and drawing his son into joining him, sold the whole estate with the reserve only of annuities during both their lives. Sir Edward *m.* first, Matilda, daughter of Robert Livesay, esq. of Tooting, in Surrey, by whom he had

JOHN, his heir.

Edward, in holy orders, had three sons, Edward, Robert, and Henry.

Robert.

Amy, *m.* to Henry Lawrence, esq. of St. Ives, in Huntingdonshire, and of St. Margaret's, in the county of Hertford.

He *m.* secondly, Jane, daughter of Sir James Calthorp, knt. of Crockthorpe, in Norfolk, (widow of Sir Henry Thomelthorpe, knt.) and by that lady had one son.

Thomas, who *m.* Elizabeth, daughter of Sir William Yelverton, of Rougham, in Norfolk, and dying in 1683, left four sons,

William, of Dublin, *m.* Frances, daughter and co-heir of Sir Herbert Lunsford, knt. by whom he had no male issue. He *d.* in 1[illegible]

Robert, of Virginia.

Charles, of Grimston, in Norfolk, *m.* Elizabeth, daughter of William Bladwell of Swanington, in the same county, and had six sons, viz.

1. YELVERTON, capt. R. N. who inherited as fifth baronet.

2. Bladwell, *m.* Mary, daughter of William Probart, esq. of Court Evanwenge, in Radnorshire, and had (with two daughters)

CHARLES, who inherited as sixth baronet.

---

* Of this RICHARD, we have the following account from his epitaph in Iselham Church.

Here under lyeth a Worthy Esquire that, Richard Peyton hight,
An honest Gentleman, and thyrd Son to Robert Peyton, Knyght.
In Gray's-Inn, Student of the Lawe, where he a Reader was;
He feared God, and loved hys Word, in truth hys life did pass:
In practising of Justice, loe, was hys whole Delyght;
He never wronged any one to whom he might do Right.
Whom he esteemed an honest Fryend, who he might stand in stead,
He never left to do hym Good wyth Words, with Purse, and Deed.
Fourteen Years Space he marry'd was unto a beautiful Wyfe,
By Parent named Mary Hyde, they lived devoyd of Stryfe,
The Earth hym bear twice twenty Years, and vyrtuously he lyved,
A vyrtuous Lyfe he dyd embrace, and vyrtuously he dyed,
Anno Domini, 1574.
The thyrtieth Day of April, Year seventy and four,
A thousand fyve hundred being put to that more.

William, of Grimston, *m.* Alice, daughter of William Robotham, esq. and *d. s. p.*.
4. Charles. *d. s. p.*
5. Colby, *d. s. p.*
6. JOHN, a citizen of London, *m.* first, Dorothy, daughter of James Altham, esq. of Marks Hall, in Essex, and had by her a son,

JOHN, who *s.* as seventh baronet.

He *m.* secondly, Susan, daughter of Peter Calvert, esq. of Hunsdon, in Hertfordshire, and had another son,

YELVERTON, who inherited as eighth baronet.

Thomas, *m.* Miss Roberts, niece of Sir John Roberts, bart. of Bromley.

Sir Edward *m.* thirdly, Dorothy, daughter of Mr. Edward Ball, of Stockwell, and by her had two other sons,

Edward, of Surinam, merchant, who *d.* in 1675. He *m.* Mary, daughter of Mr. Mulfin, an Italian merchant, and left an only daughter, his heir,

Angiola, *m.* to M. Francis Ceffis, of Venice.

Joseph, *m.* Mary, daughter and co-heir of Marmaduke Vincent, esq. of Great Smeaton, in the county of York, and had a son,

Vincent, *b.* in 1685.

This baronet died in April, 1657, and was *s.* by his eldest son,

III. SIR JOHN PEYTON, who *m.* first, a daughter of Sir Edward Bellingham, but by her had no issue. He *m.* secondly, Miss Hobart, and had three sons and a daughter, viz.

Edward, who *d.* young.
JOHN, his successor.
Thomas, captain in the guards, and favourite of *King* CHARLES II. *d.* unm.

Martha, *m.* to George Duncombe, esq. of Shalford, in Surrey.

He *d.* in 1666, and was *s.* by his son,

IV. SIR JOHN PEYTON, who served his king and country in several military stations; for presently after the Restoration, he went with the Earl of Rutherford to Tangier, under whom he served until his lordship's death, and then returning into England, he rode in the guards in the Lord Oxford's regiment, from which, through the influence of the Duke of Leeds, his kinsman, to be a lieutenant in Sir John [illegible]ner's company, in the Duke of Buckingham's regiment. He went into Ireland with this regiment in 1678, and continuing to reside there, after the revolution, he was appointed by *Queen* ANNE, governor of Ross Castle, in Kerry. He *m.* first the daughter of Mr. Newman, and widow of Kana O'Hara; secondly, a daughter of — Lloyd, esq. of Morton Hall, in Wales, and widow of Richard Barry; and thirdly, Mrs. Rebecca Williams, of Liverpool, widow of the Rev. Mr. Tomlinson, but died *s. p.* at Dublin, 23rd March, 1721, when the baronetcy devolved upon his cousin, (refer to issue of the second baronet,)

V. SIR YELVERTON PEYTON, captain R. N. who *m.* [illegible], daughter of Mr. Philip Facy, of Plymouth, but *d.* issueless, 10th October, 1748, and was *s.* by his nephew,

VI. SIR CHARLES PEYTON, who *m.* Ruth, daughter of Mr. Box, of Hammersmith, but *d. s. p.* 6th November, 1760, and was *s.* by his cousin (refer to issue of the second baronet),

VII. SIR JOHN PEYTON,* who died in 1772, without issue, and was *s.* by his half-brother,

VIII. SIR YELVERTON PEYTON, who *m.* the daughter of Thomas Bayly, of Arley, in the county of Warwick, and widow of Felix Calvert, esq. but died *s. p.* 18th October, 1815, when the BARONETCY is presumed to have EXPIRED.

Arms—Sable, a cross engrailed or.

PEYTON, OF KNOWLTON.

CREATED 29th June, 1611.—EXTINCT in Feb. 1683.

Lineage.

This was a branch of the ancient family of Peyton of Iselham, in the county of Cambridge.

SIR ROBERT PEYTON, of Iselham, *m.* Elizabeth, daughter of Sir Robert Clere, knt. of Ormesby, in Norfolk, and had two sons, ROBERT (Sir), who succeeded to, and carried on the line of, Iselham; and

SIR JOHN PEYTON, knt. to whom his father gave the manor of Calthorpe, in Bumeham, St. Martin's, and Knowlton, in Kent. He *m.* Dorothy, daughter of Sir John Tindall, K.B. and had issue,

THOMAS (Sir), his heir.
John (Sir), governor of the Tower, from whom the PEYTONS of Doddington.
Elizabeth, *m.* to Thomas Moyns, esq.
Frances, *m.* to — Engham, esq. of Goodneston.

He was *s.* by his elder son,

SIR THOMAS PEYTON, of Knowlton, who *m.* Anne, daughter of Sir Martin Calthorpe, knt. lord mayor of London, and had issue,

SAMUEL (Sir), his heir.
Alice, *m.* to Robert Darell, esq. of Cale Hill, in Kent.
Mary, *m.* to Sir Francis Clarke, knt. of Merton Abbey.
Anne, *m.* to Thomas Hales, esq. eldest son of Sir Charles Hales, knt.
Elizabeth, *m.* to Sir Robert Banester, knt.

He *d.* in 1611, and was *s.* by his son,

I. SIR SAMUEL PEYTON, knt. of Knowlton, in Kent, who was created a BARONET 29th June, 1611. He *m.* Mary, eldest daughter and co-heir of Sir Roger Ashton, knt. and had (by her, who wedded, secondly, in 1626, Edward Cholmeley, esq.) three sons and three daughters, viz.

THOMAS, his heir.
Samuel, *d. s. p.*
Edward, who left a son, killed in Flanders.
Anne, *m.* to Henry Oxendon, esq. of Herne.
Elizabeth.
Margaret, *m.* to Thomas Osborn, esq.

He *d.* in 1623, and was *s.* by his eldest son,

II. SIR THOMAS PEYTON, of Knowlton, who *m.* first, a daughter of Sir Peter Osborne; secondly, Cecilia, widow of Sir William Swan, knt.; and thirdly, Jane, daughter of Sir William Monins, bart. By his second wife he had issue,

Thomas, who *d. s. p.* in 1667.
DOROTHY, *m.* to Sir Basil Dixwell, bart.
CATHERINE, *m.* to Sir Thomas Longueville, bart.

---

* If ROBERT PEYTON, of Virginia, left male descendants, as it is reported, this gentleman succeeded wrongfully, Robert being the elder brother of his grandfather, Charles Peyton, of Grimston, and the second son of Thomas Peyton, only son of the second baronet, by his second wife.

Elizabeth, *m.* to William Longueville, esq. of the Inner Temple.

Esther, *m.* to Thomas Sandys, esq.

Sir Thomas, who was a member of the first parliament after the Restoration and a prise commissioner, had a grant of £2000 per annum in the coal farm. He died in February, 1683, when the Baronetcy expired. The manor of Knowlton devolved on his daughters as co-heirs, who joined with their trustees in the sale to Sir John Narborough, bart.

Arms—Sa. a cross engrailed or.

PEYTON, OF DODDINGTON.

Created 10th Dec. 1660.—Extinct 25th Dec. 1660.

Lineage.

Sir Robert Peyton, knt. of Iselham, in Cambridgeshire, *m.* Elizabeth, daughter of Sir Robert Clere, knt. of Ormesby, in Norfolk, and had two sons, Robert (Sir), his heir, and

Sir John Peyton, knt. of Knowlton, in Kent, who *m.* Dorothy, daughter of Sir John Tindall, K.B. and had likewise two sons, Thomas (Sir), his heir, and

Sir John Peyton, knt. of Doddington, in the county of Cambridge, governor of the Tower *temp.* Elizabeth, and of the queen's privy council; afterwards in the reign of James I. governor of the islands of Jersey and Guernsey, in which office he succeeded Sir Walter Raleigh. "Sir John Peyton," in the words of an old writer, "was educated after the politest manner of the age he lived in, by serving in the wars of Flanders under the most able and experienced soldiers and politicians of that time." Amidst the sunshine of a court and the affluence of a large fortune, his conduct was so regular and temperate that his life was prolonged to the age of ninety-nine years, in so much health and vigour that he is said to have rode back hunting three or four days before his death. He *m.* Dorothy, daughter and heir of Edward Beaupre, esq. of Outwell, in Norfolk, widow of Sir Robert Bell, one of the barons of the Exchequer, and was *s.* at his decease by his only son,

Sir John Peyton, knt. who *m.* Alice, second daughter of Sir John Peyton, bart. of Iselham, and had three sons and six daughters, viz.

- Robert, his heir.
- Algernon, in holy orders, heir to his brother.
- Henry, who, in the rebellion, taking up arms in the royal cause, was unfortunately killed by his own soldiers at Banbury, having forgotten the pass-word.
- Elizabeth, *m.* to Sir Anthony Chester, of Chichley, Bucks.
- Anne, *m.* to — Lowe, esq.
- Dorothy, *m.* to Laurence Oxburgh, esq. of Emneth, in Norfolk.
- Frances, *m.* to Francis Fortescue, esq. barrister-at-law, solicitor to *Queen* Mary, consort of Charles I.
- Susanna, *m.* to John Riches, esq. of Tring Hall, in Norfolk, and *d.* in 1706, aged ninety.
- Anne, *m.* to — Brent, esq. of Worcestershire.

He was *s.* at his decease by his eldest son,

Robert Peyton, esq. who *m.* Elizabeth, daughter of Sir Richard Anderson, knt. of Penley, in Hertfordshire, but *d. s. p.* 1658, when he was *s.* by his brother,

Algernon Peyton, D.D. rector of Doddington, in the Isle of Ely, who *m.* Elizabeth, daughter of J[illegible] Cook, esq. of Chissel, in Essex, and had issue,

- John, his heir.
- Algernon, of Peyton Hall, created a Baronet in 1666-7.
- Henry, who embraced a military life, and was made a brigadier, and governor of Galway, in Ireland, by *Queen* Anne. He *d.* unm. in 17[illegible]
- Dorothy, *d.* young.
- Elizabeth, *m.* to Gregory Parlet, esq. of Dow[illegible] in Norfolk.
- Alice, *m.* first, to the Rev. John Nelson, LL.D prebendary of Ely; and secondly, to J[illegible] Cremer, gent. of Norfolk. She *d.* in 1717.

Doctor Peyton was *s.* by his eldest son,

I. John Peyton, esq. of Doddington, in the county of Cambridge, who was created a Baronet 10th December, 1660, but died unm. 25th December following; when the Baronetcy expired, and the estates devolved upon his next brother, Sir Algernon Peyton, bart.

Arms—Sa. a cross engrailed or, with a crescent for difference.

PEYTON.

Created 21st March, 1666-7.—Extinct 29th June, 17[illegible]

Lineage.

I. Sir Algernon Peyton, Baronet, (second son of the Rev. Doctor Peyton, D.D.) so created 21st March 1666-7, succeeded to the estates and representation of the family on the decease issueless, in 1660, of his elder brother, Sir John Peyton, bart. of Doddington. Sir Algernon *m.* Frances, daughter and heir of Sir Robert Sewster, knt. of Ravely, in the county of Huntingdon, by whom (who *m.* secondly, C[illegible] Skelton,) he had issue,

- Sewster, his successor.
- Anne, *m.* to Philip Bell, esq. of Walling[illegible] in Norfolk.
- Algerina, *m.* to George Dashwood, esq. of Pe[illegible] Hall, in Suffolk, a colonel in the army [illegible] George Dashwood, of London), and had a son,
  - George Dashwood.

Sir Algernon was *s.* by his son,

II. Sir Sewster Peyton, master of the buck [illegible] *temp. Queen* Anne, who *m.* Anne, second daughter of George Dashwood, esq. of London, and had issue[*]

- Thomas, his heir.
- Henry, died of a fever, unmarried, [illegible] September, 1741.
- Anne, *m.* to Richard Dashwood, esq. of [illegible] Cley, in Norfolk.
- Margaret, *m.* to her cousin, George Dashwood, esq. (son of her aunt, Algerina Peyton, [illegible] George Dashwood), and had a son,
  - Henry Dashwood.
- Henrietta, *d.* young.

Sir Sewster *d.* 28th December, 1717, and was *s.* by his son,

III. Sir Thomas Peyton, who *m.* in 17[illegible] [illegible] Skevington, only daughter of Thomas Skevington, esq. of Skevington, in Leicestershire, and heir of her brother, Thomas Skevington, esq. but died without issue aged seventy, 29th June, 1771, when the Baronetcy expired. The estates devolved, under the will of Sir Thomas, upon his nephew,

---

* Sister of Sir Robert Dashwood, bart. of Northbrook, in Oxfordshire; to Robert Dashwood, esq. [illegible] Norfolk; and to Colonel George Dashwood, the husband of Sir Sewster Peyton's sister.

Henry Dashwood, esq. who assumed, in consequence, the surname and arms of Peyton. He was created a Baronet in 1776, and his son and successor is the present (1837)

Sir Henry Peyton, bart. of Doddington. (See Burke's *Peerage and Baronetage*.)

Arms—Sa. a cross engrailed or, with a crescent for difference.

PHELIPS, OF BARRINGTON.

Created 16th Feb. 1619-20.

Extinct about 1690.

Lineage.

"All I can learn (says Collins) of this gentleman (the first baronet) is that he was son and heir of Thomas Phillips, second son of Thomas Phillips, of Montacute, in the county of Somerset, whose father, Richard Phillips, was of the county of Dorset; which Thomas, of Montacute, is probably the same Thomas Phelyps who was constituted (31 Henry VIII.) chief builder and supervisor of the buildings in the town and marches of Calais." He,

Thomas Phelips, or Phylyps, had by his wife, the daughter of Smith of the county of Somerset,

- John, whose descendants were of Corfe, in the county of Dorset. The heiress of this branch, Jane Phelips, m. the Rev. Sir James Hanham, bart.
- Thomas.
- Richard.
- Edward (Sir), elected serjeant-at-law 45 Elizabeth, and made king's serjeant 1 James I. knighted at Whitehall 23rd July, 1603, before the coronation of the king; and having served in several parliaments, was chosen speaker in the first parliament of James I. wherein he represented the county of Somerset; he was afterwards appointed master of the Rolls. Sir Edward left a son,
  - Sir Robert Phelips, knt. M.P. for the county of Somerset 21 James I. and 1 and 3 Charles I. His son and heir,
    - Edward Phelips, of Montacute, in Somersetshire, *b.* in 1613, represented that county in the Long Parliament. He was ancestor of the Phelips of Montacute, and the present Charles Phelips, esq. of Briggins Park, Hants. (See Burke's *Commoners*, vol. iii.)

The second son,

Thomas Phelips, was father of

I. Sir Thomas Phelips, knt. of Barrington, in the county of Somerset, who was created a Baronet 16th February, 1619-20. He *m.* Cherity, daughter and co-heir of William Waller, esq. of Oldstoke, in the county of Southampton, by whom, who *m.* secondly, William, Viscount Ogle, he left at his decease, in 1627, a son,

II. Sir James Phelips, who *m.* Elizabeth, daughter of Sir Richard Tichborne, bart. and was *s.* at his decease, in 1653, by his son,

III. Sir James Phelips, who *d. s. p.* in Ireland, about the year 1690, when the Baronetcy became extinct.

Arms—Arg. a chevron between three roses gu. seeds and leaves ppr.

PICKERING, OF WHADDON.

Created 2nd Jan. 1660-1.

Extinct in 1705.

Lineage.

I. Henry Pickering, esq. purchased of the Tempests the manor and estate of Whaddon, in Cambridgeshire, in 1648, and being thence designated, was created a Baronet in 1660-1. He was succeeded at his decease by his son,

II. Sir Henry Pickering, of Whaddon, at whose decease, without male issue, in 1705, the title became extinct. Sir Henry's widow sold the manor of Whaddon, in 1716, to Edward, Lord Harley, of whom it was purchased by Lord Chancellor Hardwicke.

Arms—Erm. a lion rampt. az. armed gu. crowned or.

PILE, OF COMPTON-BEAUCHAMP.

Created 12th Sept. 1628.

Extinct 4th May, 1761.

Lineage.

This family enjoyed extensive estates in the county of Berks for several centuries, and frequently received the honour of knighthood. The last of these knights,

Sir Gabriel Pile, or Pyle, married one of the daughters of Sir Peter Welch, some time cofferer to *King* James I. and was *s.* by his eldest son,

I. Francis Pile, esq. of Compton-Beauchamp, in Berkshire, was created a Baronet by *King* Charles for his services to the crown, 12th September, 1628. Sir Francis *m.* Elizabeth, daughter of Sir Francis Popham, knt. of Littlecott, in the county of Wilts, and had (with three daughters) three sons, viz.

- Francis, his successor.
- Seymour, of Axford, Wilts, who succeeded his brother in the baronetcy.
- Gabriel, of Okemarsh, Berks, *m.* Frances, third daughter of Sir Henry Moore, bart. of Fawley.

He *d.* 1st November, 1635, was buried at Collinborn Kingston, in Wilts, and *s.* by his eldest son,

II. Sir Francis Pile, who *m.* first, Mary, daughter of Samuel Dunch, esq. of Pusey, in Berks, and by that lady had a son, Francis, who *d.* young. He *m.* secondly, Miss Still, only daughter of the Right Rev.

John Still, Bishop of Bath and Wells, and had three daughters, his co-heirs, viz.

I. Anne, m. to Francis, second Lord Holles, of Ifield, and was mother of

Danzill Holles, third Lord Holles, with whom the title expired in 1694.

II. Elizabeth, m. to Sir Thomas Strickland, bart. of Boynton, in Yorkshire.

III. ———, m. — Richards, esq. of Yaverland, in the Isle of Wight.

Sir Francis d. about 1649, when the baronetcy devolved upon his brother,

III. Sir Seymour Pile, of Axford, in Wiltshire, who m. Elizabeth, second daughter of Sir Henry Moore, bart. of Fawley, in Berkshire, and was s. at his decease by his elder son,

IV. Sir Francis Pile, who m. Frances, daughter of Sir Bulstrode Whitlocke, knt. of Chilton, Berks, by whom he had two sons and two daughters. He was s. by his elder son,

V. Sir Seymour Pile, who m. Jane, only daughter of John Lawford, esq. of Stapleton, in Gloucestershire, by whom (who d. in July, 1726,) he had a daughter and a son and successor,

VI. Sir Francis-Seymour Pile, of North Stoneham and Somerley, Hants, who m. Anne, daughter and co-heir of Sir Ambrose Crowley, knt. of Greenwich, and relict of Richard Fleming, esq. but died without issue 4th May, 1761, when the Baronetcy expired.

From the Piles, the estate of Compton Beauchamp, in Beauchamp, in Berkshire, passed by marriage, about the year 1670, to the family of Richards, of Yaverland, in the Isle of Wight. Mr. Richards, the last heir male of this family, bequeathed it, in case his daughter died s. p. to Mr. Wright, of Oxford, maternal grandfather of John Atkyns Wright, esq. of Compton Beauchamp, formerly M.P. for Oxford.

Arms—Arg. a cross between four nails gu.

PINDAR, OF IDENSHAW.

Created 22nd Dec. 1662.

Extinct in 1704-5.

Lineage.

I. Peter Pindar, esq. collector of the Chester customs, son of Reginald Pindar, of Southwell, in Northamptonshire, purchased from John Hurleston, esq. his brother-in-law, the manor of Idenshaw, in Cheshire, and was created a Baronet in 1662. He m. first, Judith, daughter and co-heir of Jeffry Walkenden, esq. of the Inner Temple; and secondly, Dorothy, daughter of John Hurleston, esq. of Pickton, and was s. by his son,

II. Sir Thomas Pindar, of Idenshaw, who m. Anne, daughter and heir of Robert Wynne, esq. of Flintshire, and was father of

III. Sir Paul Pindar, of Idenshaw, at whose decease unmarried in 1704-5, the Baronetcy became extinct.

Arms—(Disallowed by Sir William Dugdale in the visitation of 1663)—Arg. three lions' heads az. crowned or.

PLAYTERS, OF SOTTERLEY.

Created 13th Aug. 1623.

Extinct 23rd Sept. [illegible]

Lineage.

This family has been "of good antiquity" in the counties of Norfolk and Suffolk, as fully established by old deeds and records appertaining thereto.

Thomas Playters, esq. of Thorndon, in Suffolk, was father of

Thomas Playters, esq. of Thorndon and Sotterley, who died 21st September, 1479. He held [illegible] manor and advowson, in Norfolk, Sotterley, and Ug-shall manor, in Suffolk; and lies buried in Sotterley church. By Anne, his wife, sister of Roger Denny, esq. of Tatington, also in Suffolk, he left a son and heir,

William Playters, esq. who was living in [illegible]. He married Jane, daughter of Sir Edmund Jenny, knt. of Knotshall, in Suffolk, and had five sons, four of whom died unm. and he was s. at his decease, 11th November, 1512, by the fifth,

Christopher Playters, esq. living in [illegible], who d. in 1547, seized of Sotterley, Ugshall, and Brisen[illegible] manors, in Suffolk. He married first, Dorothy, sister and co-heir of William Aslack, esq. of Carrow, in Norfolk, by whom he had one son, Thomas; and secondly, Anne, daughter of William Read, esq. of Beccles, in Suffolk, by whom he had several other children. His eldest son and heir,

Thomas Playters, esq. who married Elizabeth, daughter of Sir Thomas Jermyn, knt. of Rushbrook, in Suffolk, and dying 9th September, 1571, was s. by his son,

William Playters, esq. of Sotterley, who held the manor of Eloghe, Ugshall manor and advowson, Sotterley manor and advowson, with lands in divers towns in Suffolk, half the manor of Berrys, also Holkham, in Norfolk, the manor of Scotts, in Essex, &c. He married first, Thomasine, daughter of George Duke, esq. of Frense; secondly, Elizabeth, daughter of Thomas Timperley, esq. of Hintlesham, in Suffolk; thirdly, Thomasine, daughter and co-heir of Edm[illegible] Tirrell, esq. of Beeches, in Essex; and fourthly, Mary, daughter and co heir of William Drake, esq. [illegible] Hardly, in Norfolk; two of those ladies left no [illegible] issue; the issue of the fourth failed after two descents; the second was mother of the son and heir,

I. Sir Thomas Playters, of Sotterley, high sheriff of Suffolk in 1605, who was knighted at Newmarket 19th October, 1603, and created a Baronet 13th August, 1623. He married first, Anne, daughter of Sir William Swan, knt. of Southfleet, in Kent, and had surviving issue,

William, his heir.

Frances, m. to Hamond Bosown, esq. of [illegible]set, in Norfolk.

Sir Thomas married secondly, Anne, daughter of Sir Anthony Browne, knt. of Elsinge, in Norfolk, and by that lady had

Thomas, m. Mary, daughter of Sir Augustine Palgrave, knt. of Norwood Berningham, in [illegible]

folk, and *d. s. p.* His widow *m.* Thomas Well, esq.

Lyonel, rector of Ugshall, who succeeded as fourth baronet.

Anthony, } *d. s. p.*
Roger, }

John, *m.* Camilla, daughter of Thomas Browne, esq. of Elsinge.

Elizabeth, *m.* to Sir Stephen Soame, knt. of Haidon Hall, in Essex.

Judith, *m.* to Richard Moseley, esq.

Lidia, *m.* to Henry Warner, esq. of Mildenhall, in Suffolk.

Parnel, *m.* to John Harbonne, esq. of Barsham.

——, *m.* to Edward Barnwell, esq. of Hylamn.

Anne, *m.* to George Gent, esq. of Moyns.

Sir Thomas died in June, 1683, and was *s.* by his eldest son,

II. Sir William Playters, who was deputy lieutenant and vice admiral of the county of Suffolk, and colonel of a regiment, until turned out by the rebellious parliament, as recorded upon his tomb. He *m.* Frances, daughter and heir of Christopher Le Grys, esq. of Billingford, in Norfolk, by whom (who *d.* 6th September, 1659,) he had an only son, his successor,

III. Sir Thomas Playters, high sheriff of Suffolk in 1646 who was made colonel of a regiment of Curassiers, five hundred strong, by commission, dated at Oxford, 29th July, 19 Charles I. he was also admiral of six English ships. He married Rebecca, daughter and co-heir of Thomas Chapman, esq. of Wormley, in Hertfordshire, but had no issue. He died at Messina, in Sicily, *anno* 1651, aged thirty-five, (his widow *m.* secondly, Richard Lacy, esq.; and thirdly, Sir Rowland Lytton, knt. of Knebworth,) when the baronetcy reverted to his uncle of the half blood,

IV. Sir Lyonel Playters, rector of Ugshall, in Suffolk. Walker, in his sufferings of the Clergy, relates many acts of persecution and plunder inflicted upon this gentleman, whom he describes as a meek and peaceable temper, during the rebellion. He lived, however, to see the restoration of the monarchy, and to be re-established in his own estates. He married Elizabeth, daughter of John Warner, gent. of Bran-don, in Norfolk, and by her, who died in September, 1660 had issue,

John, } fifth and sixth baronets.
Lyonel, }

Elizabeth, *m.* to Thomas Edgar, esq. of Glemham, in Suffolk.

Anne, } *d.* unm.
Lydia, }

He *d.* in 1679, and was *s.* by his elder son,

V. Sir John Playters, who *m.* first, Jane, daughter of Thomas Read, esq. of Berdwell, in Suffolk, but by that lady he had no issue. He *m.* secondly, Isabel, daughter and sole heir of Thomas Hall, of London, merchant, and had a son and daughter, who both died young. He was *s.* at his decease by his brother,

VI. Sir Lyonel Playters. This gentleman *m.* Martha, daughter of Talmash Castel, esq. of Raveningham, in Norfolk, and had issue,

John, his successor.

Richard, *d.* at sea, unm.

Lyonel, *m.* one of the daughters and co-heirs of Dr. Gould, a physician, and *d.* in January, 1722-3, at Sotterley, leaving issue.

Thomas, *d.* unm.

Caroline, *m.* to John Norris, gent. of Witton, in Norfolk.

Anne.

He *d.* in 1699, and was *s.* by his eldest son,

VII. Sir John Playters, who *m.* Elizabeth, daughter of John Felton, esq. of Worlingham, in Suffolk, and niece of Sir John Feltoun, bart. and had several children, of whom, however, only two survived to maturity, viz.

John, his heir, who *m.* first, Anne-Caroline, dau. and heir of John Turner, esq. and by her had issue,

John, successor to his grandfather.

Charles, heir to his brother.

Elizabeth, *m.* in 1758, to John Norris, esq. of Winchingham, in Norfolk.

Mr. Playters, who *d.* before his father, *m.* secondly, Elizabeth, daughter of Joshua Lewis, esq. of Great Farringdon, Berks, and had another son,

William-John, who succeeded as tenth baronet.

Mary.

Sir John *d.* 11th December, 1768, and was *s.* by his grandson,

VIII. Sir John Playters, who *d.* unm. at Ingatestone, in Essex, 26th May, 1791, and was *s.* by his brother,

IX. Sir Charles Playters, who was sometime of East Bergholt, in Essex, and died at Hainford, in Norfolk, unm. in 1806. He was *s.* by his half-brother,

X. Sir William John Playters, who resided at Yelverton, in Norfolk. He *m.* first, in 1782, Miss Patena Clarke, who *d. s. p.* 14th August, 1825, when he *m.* secondly, Miss Anne Wright. Sir William *d.* aged seventy-five, 23rd September, 1832, and the Baronetcy expired.

Arms—Bendy wavy of six, argent and azure.

Note—A correspondent of the Gentleman's Magazine states, that Sir William John Playters, the last baronet, left an illegitimate daughter,

Elizabeth Wright, who *m.* Robert Moore, esq. an officer in the army, and to whom Sir William devised his estates in Norfolk. Lieutenant George-Charles-Degen Lewis, great grandson of Joshua Lewis, whose daughter was mother of Sir William Playters, entered a caveat to the will, but withdrew it.

PLEYDELL, OF COLESHILL.

Created 15th June, 1732.

Extinct 14th Oct. 1768.

Lineage.

William Pleydell, esq. of Coleshill, in the county of Berks, *b.* about the year 1425, *d.* in 1495, seized of lands in Berkshire and the adjoining counties. He was interred in the church of Coleshill, with his wife, Isabella, under the directions of his will, dated 6th November, 1494, and registered in the prerogative office. His son and heir,

Thomas Pleydell, esq. *d.* in 1527, possessed of a considerable estate, (the appraisement of his moveables only, made 9th October, 1527, amounting to £363. 7*s.* a large sum for those times,) and was interred, with Agnes, his wife, in a chapel, (which, for that purpose, he had caused to be erected on the south side of the church of Coleshill,) called in his will, "the new chapel of the salutation of our blessed ladie," and, by him, amongst other donations, endowed with ten marks yearly to a priest, to sing and pray for his soul, and the souls of his family. The probate to his will, is under the seals of Thomas, Cardinal Wolsey, Archbishop of York and Legate; and William Warham, Archbishop of Canterbury. He had (with two daughters, Rose, wife of Ambrose Champneys, esq. of Frome Selwood, and Elizabeth,) a son and successor,

WILLIAM PLEYDELL, esq. of Coleshill, who *m.* Agnes, daughter and co-heir of Robert Reason, esq. of Corf Castle, in the county of Dorset, by whom he had,

I. TOBIAS, his heir, *m.* Eleonora, daughter of John Yate, of Buckland, Berks, and was seised of the manor, town and hundred of Farringdon, in that county, which he had purchased of Sir Francis Englefield, and the said John Yate, where he and his wife lie interred under a handsome monument, in the chancel. He *d.* 18th October, 1583.

II. GABRIEL, of Midgehill, Wilts. His grandson,

SIR CHARLES PLEYDELL, of Midgehill knighted in 1620, *d.* in 1642; leaving by his second wife, Jane, daughter of Sir John St. John, of Lydiard Tregoze, and widow of Robert Atty, esq. a son,

OLIVER, whose son and heir,

EDMUND, M.P. for Wotton Basset, Wilts, *m.* Anne, daughter and sole heir of Sir John Morton, of Milbourne St. Andrew, in the county of Dorset, bart. and was father of

EDMUND MORTON PLEYDELL, esq. of Milbourne, M.P. for the county of Dorset, who *m.* Deborah, daughter of William Kuffen, esq. and died in 1754, leaving issue.

III. THOMAS, of Shrivenham.

IV. JOHN, of Westcot, in Berkshire, father of

ROBERT PLEYDELL, who, in 1621, was seised of the manors of Amney Crucis, Amney Mary, and Amney Peter, in the county of Gloucester, with those of Wescot and Irley, in Berkshire. He *d.* in 1642, and those estates descended successively to his son, grandson, and great grandson, all of Amney Crucis, and all named Robert; the son *d.* about 1675; the grandson *m.* Sarah, daughter of Philip Sheppard, of Hampton, in Gloucestershire; the great grandson *d.* in 1719, unm. leaving two sisters; the elder *d.* unm. when the younger,

CHARLOTTE-LOUISA PLEYDELL, became sole heir. This lady *m.* 10th August, 1724, the honourable John Dawnay, eldest son of Henry, second Viscount Downe, and by him, who predeceased his father, had two sons, viz.

HENRY-PLEYDELL DAWNEY, who, succeeding his grandfather, in 1741, became third VISCOUNT DOWNE.

JOHN DAWNEY, who succeeded his brother as fourth VISCOUNT DOWNE. This nobleman's elder son,

JOHN-CHRISTOPHER, was the fifth viscount, but *d. s. p.* and the second,

HENRY, is the sixth and present (1837) VISCOUNT DOWNE. (See BURKE's *Peerage and Baronetage.*)

The third son,

THOMAS PLEYDELL, esq. received from his father the manor of the Abbot of Cirencester, in Shrivenham, in Berkshire, and several lands in Dunsborn and Amney, in the county of Gloucester, at which last place he was interred, in 1685. He had two sons, viz.

JOHN, his heir.

Edward, of Crickdale, in Wiltshire, whose great grandson and successor, (after his son and grandson bearing the same christian name,

Edward Pleydell, of Crickland, M.P. for that borough, *m.* Annabella, daughter of the Right Honourable Sir John Ernle, of Whetham, in the same county, chancellor of the exchequer in the reigns of CHARLES II. JAMES II. and WILLIAM and MARY, and left an only son,

Edward Pleydell, of Crickland, Berkshire

The elder son,

JOHN PLEYDELL, esq. of Shrivenham, in Berkshire, *m.* Anne, daughter of Oliver Ashcomb, esq. of Lyford, in the same county, and dying 2nd August, 1623, was *s.* by his son,

OLIVER PLEYDELL, esq. who *d.* in 1690, seised of the paternal estate above mentioned, and of several others in the counties of Berks, Gloucester, and Wilts. He had two sons (the younger died unm., and several daughters, of the latter, Martha, *m.* Sir Robert Brooke, bart. of Nacton, and Mary was the wife of Thomas Goddard, esq. of Swindon.* His son and heir,

THOMAS PLEYDELL, esq. of Shrivenham, *m.* 16th February, 1666, MARY, only daughter of Sir George Pratt, bart.† and eventually sole heir of her brother, SIR HENRY PRATT, OF COLESHILL, and had an only son, THOMAS, his heir. Mr. Pleydell *d.* in 1679, and Mary, his widow, carried into other families part of the estate which had descended to her from her grandfather, Sir Henry Pratt, but the residue vested absolutely in her mother, Dame Margaret Pratt, at some part of which, comprising the manors of Coleshill, Coxwell, Magna, and Coxwell Parva, in the county of Berks; she died seised in 1698, together with the family seat of Coleshill, which she herself had procured to be built, in 1650, by Inigo Jones. Her grandson and heir,

THOMAS PLEYDELL, esq. of Coleshill, *m.* first, in 1691, Jane, daughter of Sir Nicholas Stuart, bart. of Hartley Mauduit, in the county of Southampton, and had an only child,

MARK-STUART, his heir.

He *m.* secondly, Rachel, daughter of Michael Ernle, esq. of Brimslade Park, Wiltshire, and by her had

Thomas-Forster, who *d.* unm. in 1731.

Mr. Pleydell *d.* 2nd February, 1727, and was *s.* by his elder son,

I. MARK-STUART PLEYDELL, esq. of Coleshill, in the county of Berks, who was created a BARONET by King GEORGE II. 15th June, 1732. Sir Mark inherited the estates of this branch of his own family, and those specified above of the family of Pratt. He *m.* 14th

---

* She was mother of RICHARD and PLEYDELL GODDARD, successively of Swindon, see BURKE's *Commoners*, vol. iv. p. 326.

† By Margaret, his wife, daughter of Sir Humphrey Forster, bart. son of Sir William Forster, made a knight of the Bath 25th July, 1603, by Mary, his wife, one of the maids of honour to QUEEN ELIZABETH, daughter of Sir Mark Stuart, knt. of Stntney, in Cambridgeshire.

January, 1719, Mary, daughter and sole heir of Robert Steuart, son of John Steuart, esq. of Ascoy, in Bute, and had an only daughter,

HARRIET PLEYDELL, who m. 14th January, 1747-8, William, first EARL OF RADNOR, (his lordship's first wife,) and had an only child,
JACOB, Viscount Folkstone, who, succeeding his father in 1765, became second Earl of Radnor, (refer to BURKE'S *Peerage and Baronetage*.)

Sir Mark Stuart Pleydell *d.* 14th October, 1768, aged seventy-five, when the BARONETCY EXPIRED; he devised his estates to his grandson, Lord Folkstone, and to other members of the family of Radnor, in remainder, directing that each inheritor, should, on his accession, adopt the surname of PLEYDELL-BOUVERIE.

Arms—Argent, a bend, gules, guttee of the field, between two plovers, of the second, a chief, cheque, or and sable, with the distinction of the second house.

PLOMER, OF THE INNER TEMPLE.

CREATED 6th Jan. 1660-1.

EXTINCT 20th April, 1697.

Lineage.

WILLIAM PLOMER, citizen of London, who died 15th March, 1607, left by his wife, a daughter of Robert de la Free, three sons, viz.

I. JOHN, of London, who m. Audrey, daughter of John Page, esq. of Harrow, Middlesex, and dying in 1666, left, by her, who wedded, secondly, Sir Robert Bennett, of Windsor, a daughter, Elizabeth, wife of Walter Vaughan, of Moccas, and a son,
JOHN PLUMER, esq. of New Windsor, Berks, who m. Anne, daughter of Philip Gerrard, esq. and was *s.* by his son,
JOHN PLUMER, esq. of Blakesware, Herts, sheriff 1 WILLIAM and MARY, m. in 1678, Mary, eldest daughter of William Hale, esq. of King's Walden, and dying in 1719, left issue,
WALTER, M.P. died in 1746.
WILLIAM, of whom presently.
Richard, M.P. died in 1750.

Anne, m. James Hamilton, Lord Paisley, afterwards seventh Earl of Abercorn, and had
James, eighth Earl of Abercorn.
John, great-grandfather of James, present Marquess of Abercorn.
George, in holy orders, a canon of Windsor, whose daughter, Jane, m. first, William Plumer, esq. of Gilston Park; secondly, Richard John Lewin, esq. R. N.; and thirdly, Robert Ward, esq. who assumed the surname of Plumer, and is the present Robert Plumer Ward, esq. of Gilston Park. (See BURKE'S *Commoners*, vol. i. p. 71.)

Catherine, wife of Thomas Byde, esq.

The second son,
WILLIAM PLUMER, esq. of Blakesware, M.P. for Herts, m. in 1731, Elizabeth, daughter of Thomas Byde, esq. of Ware Park, and dying in 1767, was *s.* by his son,
WILLIAM PLUMER, esq. M. P. for Herts, who m. first, Frances Dorothy, daughter of Lucius, fifth Lord Falkland; and secondly, his cousin, Jane, daughter of the Hon. and Rev. George Hamilton, D. D. but *d. s. p.* in 1822, having devised his estates to his widow, who conveyed them to her last husband, ROBERT WARD, esq.

II. Edmund, of London, *d.* 14th August, 1624.
III. THOMAS.

The third son,
THOMAS PLOMER, esq. m. a daughter of Mr. Alderman Elwais, of London, and dying at Mitcham, in Surrey, in 1630, was *s.* by his son,
I. WALTER PLOMER, esq. of the Inner Temple, who was created a BARONET in 1660-1. He died unm. 20th April, 1697, aged seventy-seven, when the title became EXTINCT.

Arms—Per chev. flory and counterflory arg. and sa. three martlets counterchanged.

POLE.

CREATED 12th Sept. 1801.

EXTINCT 6th Sept. 1830.

Lineage.

This was a branch of the family of POLE, of Shute, in the county of Devon.

SIR JOHN POLE, third baronet, of Shute,* m. Anne, youngest daughter of Sir William Morrice, knt. of Werrington, in the county of Devon, one of the principal secretaries of state to *King* CHARLES II. and had surviving issue,

WILLIAM (Sir), who, at the decease of his father, 13th March, 1707, became fourth baronet of Shute.
John, an officer in the army, *d.* unm. in 1710.
CAROLUS, of whom presently.

Ureth, m. to Sir John Trevelyan, bart.

The youngest son,
CAROLUS POLE, in holy orders, was rector of St. Breock, in Cornwall, and sometime proctor in convocation for the clergy of the diocese of Exon. He m. Sarah, eldest daughter of Jonathan Rashleigh, esq. of Menabilly, in the same county, by Sarah, elder daughter, by his first wife, of Sir John Carew, bart. of Anthony, and was *s.* by his elder son,

* The BARONETCY of Shute being still extant, refer to BURKE'S *Peerage and Baronetage*, for the earlier descents.

Reginald Pole, esq. of Stoke Damarele, in the county of Devon, who *m.* Anne, second daughter of John Francis Buller, esq. of Morval, in Cornwall, and had issue,

- I. Reginald, who inherited the estates of the Carew family, and assuming the additional surname and arms of Carew, became (having been sworn of the privy council) the *Right Hon.* Reginald Pole Carew, of Anthony, (see Burke's *Commoners*, vol. i. p. 559.)
- II. Charles-Morice.
- III. Edward.
- I. Anne, *m.* to Charles, first Lord Somers.
- II. Sarah, *m.* to Henry-Hippisley Coxe, esq. and *d. s. p.*

The second son,

I. Sir Charles-Morrice Pole, K.C.B. and admiral of the red, of Aldenham Abbey, Herts, was created a Baronet 12th September, 1801. He *m.* 8th June, 1792, Henrietta, daughter of John Goddard, esq. of Woodford Hall, in the county of Essex, and niece of Henry Hope, esq. of Amsterdam, and by that lady had two daughters, viz.

- Henrietta-Maria-Sarah, *m.* in August, 1821, to William Stuart, esq. only son of Dr. William Stuart, Archbishop of Armagh, and grandson of John, Earl of Bute.
- Anna-Maria.

Sir Charles died 6th September, 1830, when the Baronetcy expired.

Arms—Az. a lion rampant, argent, within an orle of nine fleurs-de-lis, or, a crescent for difference.

POLLARD, OF KING'S NYMPTON.

Created 31st May, 1627.

Extinct in 1693.

Lineage.

Sir Lewis Pollard, knt. (son of Robert Pollard, second son of John Pollard, of Way), born in 1465, entering at the Middle Temple, devoted himself to the study of the law, with so much success, that in 20 James I. he was called to the degree of serjeant, and in 1515 constituted one of the judges of the Common Pleas. "In this honourable office," says Prince, "he continued for many years, until age and the consequent infirmities thereof, sued out his quietus est." The same author thus continues: "This high and great trust of a judge (an higher than which is hardly found upon earth, the lives and livelyhoods of men being therein concern'd) Sir Lewis Pollard executed with great faithfulness and expectation; the fragrant odour whereof perfumes his memory unto this day." Sir Lewis acquired by his profession a considerable fortune, and purchased the estate of King's Nympton, in Devon, where he erected a stately mansion, and enclosed a large park. He married Agnes, daughter of Thomas Hext, esq. of Kingston, in the parish of Staverton, and had by her eleven sons and as many daughters. Four of the sons attained the honour of knighthood, Sir Hugh, Sir John, Sir Richard, [illegible] Sir George, who "won his title by his stout [illegible] of Bulloin in France;" all the others, especially [illegible] archdeacon of Barnstaple and canon of Exeter [illegible] well advanced. The daughters intermarried with [illegible] first families in the county; the eldest becoming [illegible] wife of Sir Hugh Stukely, of Affton; the second [illegible] Sir Hugh Courtenay, of Powderham; the third [illegible] Sir Hugh Pawlet, of Stamford Peveril; and the [illegible] of Sir John Crocker, of Lineham.

The judge's son,

Sir Hugh Pollard, knt. of King's Nympton [illegible] Elizabeth, daughter and heir of John Vallet[illegible] esq. [illegible] St. Laurence Clist, in Devon, and was *s.* by his [illegible]

Sir Lewis Pollard, knt. of King's Nympton, [illegible] eminent lawyer, who was Lent reader of the [illegible] Temple 1 Edward VI. and recorder of the city [illegible] Exeter 2nd of the same reign. He subsequently [illegible] tained the coif of serjeant. His son and successor,

Sir Hugh Pollard, knt. of King's Nympton, was father of

I. Lewis Pollard, esq. of King's Nympton, who was created a Baronet 31st May, 1627. He married Margaret, daughter of Sir Henry Berkeley, knt. and was *s.* by his son,

II. Sir Hugh Pollard, of King's Nympton. "[illegible] Hugh," says Prince, "was a gentleman of [illegible] mind, that no way degenerated from his ancestors, being magnificently hospitable to all persons who came to his house, either occasionally or by invitation. [illegible] the time of our late unhappy wars, he adhered [illegible] cording to the obligations of honour and conscience, to the interest of oppressed royalty; and both [illegible] purse and person endeavoured to support the [illegible] cause of his dear parents, his mother the church [illegible] his father the king. He was content to hazard [illegible] for their sakes, and to stand or fall with them. [illegible] the late civil wars he served his majesty in the [illegible] and became governor of Dartmouth (a port of [illegible] importance), in his own country, when garrisoned for the king; and afterward, in time of peace, served his son, *King* Charles II. of gracious memory [illegible] court, being made by him comptroller of his household. When the garrison of Dartmouth was attacked by the parliamentarians, this gentleman, the governor, with many other honourable persons of the [illegible] then there, made at first a resolute and vigorous [illegible]fence; and at length, the place not being [illegible] surrendered upon good articles, when most of the commanders returned to their own houses. [illegible] time after this, when the best cause and the [illegible] fell by the sins of all and the hands of [illegible] Hugh Pollard, able to yield distressed [illegible] farther service for the present, retired to his house at Nympton Regis, where he spent the [illegible] his fortunes in hospitality among his friends [illegible] neighbours; on which a witty poet in his time [illegible] rhymed:

> ——at Nimton Regis
> Where th'one drinks and t'other pledges."

Sir Hugh married, first, Bridget, Countess Dowager [illegible] Berkshire, daughter of Edward, seventeenth Earl [illegible] Oxford, and had an only daughter. He sold King's Nympton to Sir Arthur Northcote, bart. and from the Northcotes it was purchased by James Buller [illegible] Sir Hugh Pollard died in 1667, and was *s.* by his brother,

III. Sir Amyas Pollard, who inherited but very little, if any, of the ancient estate. He died [illegible] after 1693, and with him the Baronetcy became extinct.

Arms—Arg. a chev. sa. between three escallops [illegible]

POOLE, OF POOLE.

Visit: Devon 1620

JOHN, his heir, *temp.* ELIZABETH, m. Mary, daughter of Sir Rowland Stanley, knt. of Hooton, and dying in his father's lifetime, left

~~his grandfather.~~ ...er of Thomas

102. c

Hanl...

widow of Jno Borye

Rich = Margery d of Sir Borye

Geo = Thomasin d of Coffestone

Rich = Mary d Kes molsford
of Langley 1620

...he eldest son,

J... POOLE, esq. of Poole, living in 1566, m. first, ... daughter of Sir John Pitton, knt. of Gawsworth, in Cheshire, but by that lady had no issue. He wedded secondly, Catherine, daughter of George Minshull, esq. of Minshull, and had

... baronet 25th October, 1677, with remainder, default of his own male issue, to his brother William, and his issue male. Sir James m. first, Anne, daughter of Thomas Eyre, esq. of Hassop, in Derbyshire, and by her had

Reginald Pole, esq. of Stoke Damarele, in the county of Devon, who m. Anne, second daughter of John Francis Buller, esq. of Morval, in Cornwall, and had issue,

1. Reginald, Car

I
II

I

The
I.
of th
Bar
1792
Woo
Hen
had

Sir
roni

Ar
nine

P

C
31st

Sir
secon
enter
study
James
in 161
Pleas
contin
quent
The
great
found
being
with
odour
Sir L
fortune, and purchased the estate of King's in Devon, where he erected a stately mansion, and enclosed a large park. He married Agnes, daughter of Thomas Hext, esq. of Kingston, in the parish of Staverton, and had by her eleven sons and as many daughters. Four of the sons attained the honour of knighthood, Sir Hugh, Sir John, Sir Richard, and Sir George, who "won his title by his stout defence of Bulloin in France;" all the others, especially

little, if any, of the ancient estate. He died soon after 1693, and with him the Baronetcy became extinct.

Arms—Arg. a chev. sa. between three escallops

POOLE, OF POOLE.

CREATED ...th Oct. 1677.

EXTINCT 25th May, 1821.

Lineage.

This very ancient family, the stem of many eminent branches, took its surname from the lordship of Poole, in Wirrall hundred, in Cheshire, where, as Camden observes, they had lived honorably, and in a flourishing condition many years. Their patriarch,

ROBERT PULL, *alias* POOLE, *alias* DE LA POOLE, Lord of Barretspoole, 8 EDWARD I. *m.* Elizabeth, daughter of Hugh de Raby, his great-grandson, another

ROBERT DE PULL, *m.* the daughter and heir of Thomas de Capenhurst, and was *s.* by his son,

SIR JOHN DE PULL, knt. living in 3 RICHARD II. 8 HENRY IV. and 3 HENRY V. who was father of

THOMAS POOLE, of Poole, who *m.* by dispensation 1425, Elizabeth, daughter of Sir William Stanley, knt. of Hooton, and was *s.* by his son,

THOMAS POOLE, of Poole, in Wirrall, living 7 HENRY VI. who, by a daughter of Mainwaring, had a son and heir,

THOMAS POOLE, esq. who *m.* Matilda, daughter of Edward Fitton, of Gawsworth, in Cheshire, and had issue,

- THOMAS, *d. v. p.* and *s. p.* 23 HENRY VII.
- John, *d.* issueless.
- Randle, a priest.
- WILLIAM, (Sir).
- Margaret, *m.* to Thomas Gilbert Scarisbrick, esq.
- Elizabeth, *m.* to John Minshull.
- Blanch, *m.* to — Bunbury, of Staney.
- Margery, *m.* to — Bellington, of Chester.
- Mabel, *m.* to Richard Standish, esq.
- Mary, *m.* to John Whitmore, esq.

The fourth son,

SIR WILLIAM POOLE, of Poole, was made sheriff of Cheshire, *durante bene placito*, in 16 HENRY VIII. He had to wife, Margaret, daughter of Thomas Hough, esq. of Leighton, and, by that lady, had a daughter, Matilde, *m.* first, to Sir Thomas Grosvenor, knt. and secondly, to Robert Fletcher, and a son and heir,

THOMAS POOLE, esq. of Poole, who *m.* Mary, daughter of Sir John Talbot, knt. of Grafton, and had issue,

- JOHN, his heir.
- Ranulp, *m.* Eleanor, daughter of Sir Henry Delves, knt. but left no issue.
- Thomas, *m.* Elizabeth, daughter of Lawrence Rope, esq. of Stapeley.
- Barnabas.
- Margaret, *m.* to George Vernon, esq. of Richmond.
- Elizabeth, *m.* to John Butler, esq. of Dunstable.
- Frances.

The eldest son,

JOHN POOLE, esq. of Poole, living in 1566, *m.* first, Susan, daughter of Sir John Fitton, knt. of Gawsworth, in Cheshire, but by that lady had no issue. He wedded secondly, Catherine, daughter of George Minshull, esq. of Minshull, and had

JOHN, his heir, *temp.* ELIZABETH, *m.* Mary, daughter of Sir Rowland Stanley, knt. of Hooton, and dying in his father's lifetime, left

- JOHN, heir to his grandfather.
- Francis, *m.* Elizabeth, daughter of Thomas Frogge, esq. of Minshull.
- Henry.
- Mary.
- Eleanor, *m.* to John Bowes, esq.

William.

Rowland.

Reginald, *m.* Cecily, daughter of the Rev. Matthew Wood, vicar of Webbenbury, and had issue.

Maude, *m.* to John Culcheth, of Culcheth.

Margaret, *m.* to James Skrymshire, esq. of Norbury Manor, in the county of Stafford.

Bridget, or Bryttain, *m.* to Sir Thomas Stuart, knt. of Ely.

He *d.* 5th December, 1616, and was *s.* by his grandson,

JOHN POOLE, esq. of Poole. This gentleman *m.* Dorothy, daughter of Thomas Tyldesley, esq. of Morleys, in Lancashire, and dying in May, 1641, was *s.* by his elder son,

JAMES POOLE, esq. of Poole, *b.* in 1603; who *m.* first, Catherine, daughter of Sir John Talbot, knt. of Grafton, in the county of Worcester; and secondly, Catherine, daughter of Sir John Pershall, bart. of Horsley, in the county of Stafford. By the latter he had a daughter, Margaret, who died unm. He died himself of wounds received at the siege of Chester in 1643, and was buried at Namptwich, in Cheshire. Leaving no male issue, he was *s.* by his brother,

THOMAS POOLE, esq. This gentleman *m.* first, Dorothy, daughter of John ap Meredith Vychan, esq. of Merionethshire, and had by her a son JAMES, his heir. He wedded secondly, Ellen, daughter of Francis Draycott, esq. but by that lady (who *m.* after his decease Sir Edward Mostyn, bart. of Talacre) he had no issue. He was *s.* by his son,

JAMES POOLE, esq. of Poole, who *m.* Mary, sister of Sir Edward Mostyn, bart. of Talacre, by her (who *m.* secondly, Sir William Gerard, bart.) had three sons,

Benjamin, of London, who *d.* in January, 1656, leaving by Margaret, his wife, daughter of Anthony Lowther, esq. of Cleveland, a daughter and heir, who *m.* John Nicol, esq. of Minchenden, in Middlesex, and was mother of a daughter and heiress, *m.* to James, Duke of Chandos.

JAMES, his heir.

WILLIAM, *m.* Mrs. Hesketh, of Birchley, in Lancashire, and had issue,

WILLIAM, receiver general of the Stamp Office, *m.* first, Grace, sister of Thomas Pelham, esq. of Stanmer Place, Sussex; and secondly, Dorothea, daughter of the Rev. Daniel Walter, vicar of Cuckfield, in Sussex, and prebendary of Chichester. By the latter he had, with two daughters, Henrietta, and Grace, wife of Thomas Sanden, M.D. of Chichester, a son,

HENRY, who inherited the baronetcy in 1804.

Edward, M. D.

The second son,

I. JAMES POOLE, esq. of Poole, who was created a baronet 25th October, 1677, with remainder, default of his own male issue, to his brother William, and his issue male. Sir James *m.* first, Anne, daughter of Thomas Eyre, esq. of Hassop, in Derbyshire, and by her had

James, who *m.* Meliora, daughter of — Gumbleton, esq. of Kent, but *d.* issueless before his father, 8th October, 1706.

Francis, heir to his father.

Anne, *m.* to Robert Molineux, esq. of Mosborough, in Lancashire.

The baronet *m.* secondly, Anne, daughter of — Kirkham, esq. relict of Sir Thomas Estcourt, knt. of Pinkney, in Wilts, a master in chancery, and by that lady (who *d.* in March, 1698) had three other sons,

William, Thomas, } died young.

Rowland, *m.* Bridget, daughter of Richard Hudleston, esq. of Milom Castle, in Cumberland, and had three daughters,

Bridget.
Anne.
Elizabeth.

Sir James *m.* thirdly, Frances, daughter and co-heir of Major-general Randolph Egerton, of Betley, in Staffordshire, and widow of Sir John Corbet, bart. of Stoke, but by her had no issue. He was *s.* by his elder surviving son,

II. Sir Francis Poole, M.P. for Lewes in 1743, who *m.* Frances, daughter of Henry Pelham, esq. of Lewes, in Sussex, and niece of Lord Pelham, by whom he had two sons and a daughter, viz.

Henry, Ferdinand, } third and fourth baronets.

Frances, *m.* 6th October, 1767, to Henry, second Viscount Palmerston, but died within two years (1st June, 1769) without male issue.*

He *d.* 16th February, 1763, and was *s.* by his elder son,

III. Sir Henry Poole, commissioner of excise, who *d. s. p.* 8th July, 1767, and was *s.* by his brother,

IV. Sir Ferdinand Poole, sheriff of Sussex in 1789; *m.* in 1772, Miss White, daughter of Thomas White, esq. of Horsham and had no male issue. He *d.* 8th June, 1804, when default of this line, male, the Baronetcy reverted to the grandson, of William Poole, esq. brother of the first baronet, to whom it was limited,

V. Sir Henry Poole, who *m.* Charlotte, daughter and co-heir of Jonathan Burward, esq. of Woodbridge, in Suffolk, and had issue,

Henry, died in early youth.
Henrietta.
Charlotte-Elizabeth, *m.* to Robert Willis Blencowe, eldest son of Robert Blencowe, esq. of Hayes End, Middlesex.

He *d.* 25th May, 1821, aged seventy-seven, when the Baronetcy expired.

Arms—Azure, seme of fleur-de-lis, or, a lion rampant, argent.

POPE, OF WILCOTE.

Created 29th June, 1611.

Extinct 18th May, 1668.

Lineage.

William Pope, gent. of Dedington, in Oxfordshire, who died in 1523, had, by Margaret, his wife, two sons and one daughter, viz.

Thomas, (Sir), *b.* at Dedington about the year 1508, the celebrated **Founder of Trinity College**, Oxford. He filled, during the reigns of Henry VIII. and *Queen* Mary, several high official appointments, and from Edward VI. received a grant of the manor of Tittenhanger, Herts. He *d.* in 1559, *s. p.*

John, of whom presently.

Alice, *m.* to Edward Love, esq. of Eynsore, in Oxfordshire, and was mother of

Frances Love, who *m.* William Blount, esq. of Osbaston, and had a son,

Sir Thomas-Pope Blount, knt. who eventually inherited the manor of Tittenhanger. (See Blount's *Baronetcy*.)

The second son,

John Pope, esq. of Wroxton, who died in 1583, *m.* first, Anne Stavely, of Bygnell, and had, by her, a daughter, *m.* in 1573 to Edward Blount, esq. of Burton-on-Trent. He *m.* secondly, a daughter of Sir John Brockett, knt. of Brockett Hall, Herts, by whom he

---

* Epitaph in Ramsay church, Hants.

In the vault beneath are deposited the remains of Frances,
Viscountess Palmerston,
Daughter of Sir Francis Poole, bart.
She was married to Henry, Viscount Palmerston, Oct. 6,
1767, and died in childbed, June 1, 1769.
With the nobler virtues that elevate our nature,
She possessed the softer talents that adorn it.
Pious, humble, benevolent, candid, and sincere,
She followed the dictates of humanity. And her heart
was warm with all its best affections.
Her sense was strong, her judgment accurate, her
wit engaging, and her taste refined.
While the elegance of her form, the graces of her manners,
and the natural propriety that ever accompanied
her words and actions, made her virtues doubly attracting,
and taught her equally to command respect and love.
Such she lived, and such she died, calm, and resigned to
the dispensation of Heaven, leaving friends
to deplore her loss, and cherish the dear remembrance of
that worth they honoured living, and lament in death
To the memory of the best of wives,
the best of friends,
He, for whom she joined those tender names,
dedicates this marble.

had, with six daughters, a son, WILLIAM, (Sir), his heir; and thirdly, a daughter of Sir Edmund Wyndham, by whom he had no issue. His only son,

I. SIR WILLIAM POPE, b. at Wroxton in 1573, was made a knight of the Bath in 1603, and created a BARONET in 1611, being then styled of Wilcote. In 1629, he was raised to the peerage of Ireland, as Baron of Belturbet, and EARL of DOWNE. His lordship m. in 1595, Anne, daughter of Sir Owen Hopton, lieutenant of the Tower of London, and relict of Henry, Lord Wentworth, of Nettlested, and had, with a daughter who died unm. two sons, namely,

> WILLIAM (Sir), knt. b. at Wroxton in 1596, who m. Elizabeth, eldest daughter of Sir Thomas Watson, knt. of Halstead, in Kent, and by her, who wedded secondly, Sir Thomas Peneystone, bart. of Cornwell, in Oxfordshire, left at his decease, v. p. in 1624, with two daughters, three sons,
>
> > THOMAS, successor to his grandfather.
> > John, b. in 1623. } Mr. Warton, inadvertently, puts the supposition that one of these was grandfather of Alexander Pope, the poet. From the circumstance that their brother Thomas, second Earl of Downe, was successor to the title by his uncle, it is clear that these two gentlemen must have died without legitimate male issue.
> > William, b. in 1624. }
>
> THOMAS, who succeeded his nephew as third earl.

The Earl of Downe died 2nd July, 1631, and was buried at Wroxton, under an alabaster monument of costly workmanship, made by the famous Nicholas Stone, on which appear the recumbent figures of himself and his wife, large as life. His grandson and successor,

II. SIR THOMAS POPE, second Earl of Downe, b. at Cogges in 1622, an active royalist during the civil war, who m. Lucy, daughter of John Dutton, esq. of Sherborne, and had an only daughter and heir,

> ELIZABETH, m. first, to Sir Francis Henry Lee, bart. of Quarenden, Bucks; and secondly, to Robert, Earl of Lindsey.

His lordship died at Oxford, 28th December, 1660, and was s. by his uncle,

III. SIR THOMAS POPE, third Earl of Downe, b. at Wroxton in 1598, who had been knighted at Woodstock in 1625. He married in 1636 Beata, daughter of Sir Henry Poole, of Saperton, in Gloucestershire, and had issue to survive him,

> THOMAS, his heir.
>
> ANNE, b. in 1637, m. to Sir Edward Boughton, bart. of Lawford, but d. s. p.
>
> BEATA, b. in 1639, m. in 1668, to Sir William Soames, bart. of Thurlowe, in Suffolk, but died s. p.
>
> FRANCES, b. in 1647, m. in 1671, to Sir Francis North, the celebrated Lord Keeper, and died in 1678, leaving issue.*
>
> FINETTA, m. in 1674, to Robert Hyde, esq. son of Alexander Hyde, Bishop of Salisbury.

His lordship died 11th January, 1667, was buried at Wroxton, and succeeded by his son,

IV. SIR THOMAS POPE, fourth Earl of Downe, who survived his father little more than four months, and died 18th May, 1668, when all his honours, including the BARONETCY, EXPIRED; his sisters being his co-heirs. Wroxton is now the seat of the EARL OF GUILFORD, the descendant of the third.

Arms—Per pale or and az. on a chev. between three griffins' heads erased four fleurs-de-lis all counterchanged.

PORTMAN, OF ORCHARD.

CREATED 25th Nov. 1612.

EXTINCT in 1690.

Lineage.

So early as the reign of EDWARD I. the Portmans appear to have been persons of distinction in the county of Somerset; at that period

THOMAS PORTMAN flourished, and bore a coat armour, which he derived from his grandfather, the same ever afterwards borne by the family. His lineal descendant,

WILLIAM PORTMAN, settled at Taunton, in the time of HENRY IV. and was a liberal benefactor to the priory there, where he was buried. His son and heir,

WILLIAM PORTMAN, m. Christian, daughter and heir of William Orchard, of Orchard, and was s. by his son,

JOHN PORTMAN, esq. who d. in 1521, leaving a son and heir,

SIR WILLIAM PORTMAN, knt. an eminent lawyer *temp.* HENRY VIII. who became one of the judges of the Common Pleas, and afterwards lord chief justice of England. His lordship died in 1555, and was interred in St. Dunstan's church, London, where a monument was erected to his memory. He was s. by his son,

SIR HENRY PORTMAN, knt. of Orchard-Portman,

* This match, we are informed by Roger North's life, was produced by that of her sister, with Mr. Soame, whose seat, at Thurlowe, was about four miles from the residence of the North family, at Catlage. For, on that event, the grave Countess of Downe, as the custom was, attended the new married couple to their habitation, and made some stay there, during which time the visits of joy were made; and amongst the rest, the family from Catlage made their appearance; and the countess and her daughters, in due time, made their return, which happened to be when Sir Francis North was there. His mother laid her eyes upon the eldest unmarried daughter, and when they were gone, turned about and said, "Upon my life this lady would make a good wife for my son Frank." In short, at the next visit, by the consent of her son, she went to the countess, who consented that Sir Francis should make his advances. Her fortune was then £14,000. The marriage took place, and there were great feastings and jollities in the neighbourhood. It was a cavalier country, and the Popes eminent sufferers for their loyalty in the late wars; and his lordship having the like character, and being known to be an obliging, as well as a flourishing loyalist, there was scarce a family which did not shew all respect imaginable to the new married folks, by visits, invitations, and festival rejoicing. So that it was about three weeks before Sir Francis could clear himself of these well intended importunities.... But after he had enjoyed all possible happiness with his wife for about three years, it was not a little curtailed by the bitterness poured into his cup by her sickness, which began about 1674, and at last brought her to her grave. He took a house for her at Hammersmith, for the advantage of better air, but at length the distemper proceeded from bad to worse; and he went down with her to Wroxton, where she died, 15th November, 1678.

who *m.* Jane, daughter of Thomas Michell, esq. and dying in 1599, was *s.* by his son,

I. John Portman, esq. of Orchard Portman, who was created a Baronet 25th November, 1612. Sir John *m.* Anne, daughter of Sir Henry Gifford, knt. and had issue,

Henry, heir to his father.
John, heir to his brother.
Hugh (Sir).
William, who *s.* as fourth baronet.

Joan, *m.* to George Speke, esq. of Whitelackington, and had an only daughter,

Philippa Speke, who *m.* Edward Berkeley, esq. of Pylle, and left a son,

Edward Berkeley, esq. of Pylle, who *m.* Elizabeth, daughter of John Ryves, esq. and had, (with another son, who died *s. p.*)

William Berkeley, of whom hereafter, as heir to the Portmans.

Anne, *m.* to Sir Edward Seymour, of Bury Pomeroy Castle, in the county of Devon, and had issue: from her eldest son, Edward Seymour, the Dukes of Somerset derive; and to the fifth,

Henry Seymour, we shall have to revert presently.

Elizabeth, *m.* to John Blunt, esq. of Holcombe.
Grace, *d.* unm.

Sir John *d.* 4th December, 1612, and was *s.* by his eldest son,

II. Sir Henry Portman, who *m.* Lady Anne Stanley, daughter of William, Earl of Derby, but died issueless in February, 1624, when he was *s.* by his brother,

III. Sir John Portman, who *d.* unm. in 1632, and was *s.* by his only surviving brother,

IV. Sir William Portman, who *m.* Anne, daughter and co-heir of John Colles, esq. of Barton, in the county of Somerset, by Elizabeth, daughter and sole heir of Humphrey Wyndham, esq. of Wiveliscombe. He *d.* in 1645, and was *s.* by his son,

V. Sir William Portman, F.R.S. who was made a knight of the Bath by *King* Charles II. He married first, Elizabeth, daughter and heir of Sir John Cutler, bart.; secondly, Elizabeth, daughter of Thomas Southcote, esq. of Buckland All Saints, in the county of Devon; and thirdly, Mary, daughter and heir of Sir John Holman, knt. but had no issue. He died in 1690, when the Baronetcy expired. Sir William devised Orchard Portman, with other estates to a large amount, to his cousin,

Henry Seymour, esq. who assumed in consequence the surname of Portman. He married first, Penelope, daughter of Sir William Haslewood, of Maidwell; and secondly, Meliora, daughter of William Fitch, esq. of High Hall, Dorsetshire, but died without issue, when the property devolved, by further limitation, upon another cousin of the last baronet's,

William Berkeley, esq. who then assumed the surname of Portman only. He married Anne, daughter of Sir Edward Seymour, of Bury Pomeroy, and was *s.* at his decease by his elder son,

Henry-William-Berkeley Portman, esq. of Orchard Portman, the great-grandfather of

Edward-Berkeley Portman, created Lord Portman in 1837. (See Burke's *Peerage and Baronetage.*)

Arms—Or, a fleur-de-lis az.

POTTS, OF MANNINGTON.

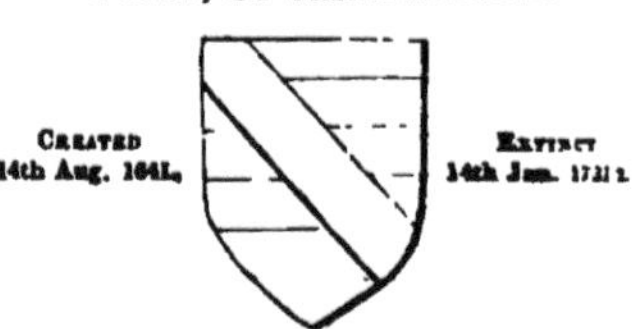

Lineage.

This family, originally of the counties of Chester and Lancaster, removed into Norfolk in the sixteenth century.

John Pot, son of Roger, and grandson of Sir William Pot, had a grant of arms in the year 1583. He was of Lincoln's Inn, and married Catherine, daughter of Sir Philip Boteler, knt. of Wood Hall, Herts, whose son and heir,

John Potts, esq. of Lincoln's Inn, *m.* Anne, daughter and co-heir of John Dodge, esq. of Mannington, by whom (who survived him and died in 164[illegible]) he left two sons, viz.

John, his heir.

Charles, a bencher of the Middle Temple, died at an advanced age, leaving by Anne, his wife, daughter of Nathaniel Wright, of London, merchant, an only daughter,

Anne, *m.* to Sir William Villers, knt. of Bedford Row, in the county of Middlesex.

The elder son,

I. Sir John Potts, knt. of Mannington, in the county of Norfolk, was created a Baronet 14th August, 1641. Sir John was elected to parliament for his native county in 1640, and was one of the [illegible] members who was restored, and accounted one of the number which brought in *King* Charles II. [illegible] "He was obliged," says an old writer, in the time of the Court of Wards, "to marry a daughter of Goodsill, esq. a favourite at court, with a small fortune;" by her he had three daughters, one of whom *m.* James Scambler, esq. of Woollerton, in Norfolk. Sir John *m.* secondly, Ursula, daughter of Sir Henry Willoughby, knt. of Risley, in the county of Derby, and widow of — Spelman, esq. of Narborough, in Norfolk. By that lady he had (with a daughter married to Beddingfeild of Ditchingham) three sons, viz.

John, his heir.

Francis, who *d.* on his travels, and was buried at Naples, leaving a daughter and heir, Anne, *m.* to Sir William Villiers, bart.

Charles, deputy-governor of Windsor Castle, *d.* *s. p.*

Ursula, *m.* to Philip Bedingfeild, esq. of Ditchingham.

He *d.* in 1673, and was *s.* by his son,

II. Sir John Potts, who *m.* first, Susan, daughter of Sir John Heveningham, knt. of Heveningham, in Norfolk, and had issue,

Roger, his heir.

Ursula, } *d.* unm.
Elizabeth, }

He wedded, secondly, Elizabeth, daughter of [illegible] Samuel Browne, of Bedfordshire, one of the judges of the court of Common Pleas, but had no other children. He was *s.* by his son,

III. Sir Roger Potts. This gentleman m. Mary, daughter and heir of William Davy, esq. of Great Ellingham, in Norfolk, by whom he left, with four other daughters, who d. unm.

Algernon, } fourth and fifth baronets.
Charles, }

Susan, m. to Matthew Long, esq. of Dunston, in Norfolk.

He d. aged seventy, 14th October, 1711, and was s. by his son,

IV. Sir Algernon Potts, who m. Frances, daughter and co-heir of — Calibut, of Saham-Tony, and relict of Thomas Crane, of Norwich, merchant, but d. s. p. 16th September, 1716, and was s. by his brother,

V. Sir Charles Potts, merchant of London, who m. first, Elizabeth, only sister of William Newman, esq. of Baconsthorp, in Norfolk; and secondly, Mary, daughter of Thomas Smith, of London, merchant. He died, however, without issue, aged fifty-six, 14th January, 1731-2, when the Baronetcy became extinct. His widow survived until 1736, and after her death the manor of Mannington was sold to the Hon. Horatio Walpole.

Arms—Az. two bars, and over all a bend or.

POWELL, OF EWHURST.

Created 10th May, 1661.

Extinct 5th July, 1742.

Lineage.

John ap Howell, esq. of Ednor, in the county of Salop, m. Rose, sister of William Crowder, esq. of Knighton, in Radnorshire, and was father of

Meredith Powell, esq. of Brampton-Ralf, in the county of Somerset, who m. Alice, daughter of John Rudhm, of Culhampton, Devon, and left a son and heir,

I. Nathaniel Powell, esq. of Ewhurst, in Sussex, and Boughton Monchensy, in Kent, who was created a Baronet by *King* Charles II. 10th May, 1661. Sir Nathaniel m. Sarah, daughter of William Muddle, esq. of Ewhurst, and had issue,

Nathaniel, his heir, who received the honour of knighthood.

Mary, m. to John Buck, esq.
Anne, m. to John Green, esq.
Katherine, m. to Thomas Gunston, esq.
Dammaris, m. to Charles Fowkes, esq.

The baronet, who purchased the manor of King's-north, in Kent, from Sir John Baker, in the time of Charles I. d. in March, 1674-5, and was s. by his son,

II. Sir Nathaniel Powell, who m. first, Elizabeth, daughter of Sir Robert Barnham, bart. of Boughton-Monchensy, and had, with a daughter, two sons, viz.

Barnham, his heir, who died in the lifetime of his father, leaving by his wife, Elizabeth, daughter of James Clitherow, esq. of Boston House, Middlesex, three sons, namely,

Nathaniel, successor to his grandfather.

James, d. unm.
Christopher, heir to his elder brother.

Nathaniel, who left no issue.

He m. secondly, Frances, daughter of Sir Philip Stapleton, knt. of Wighill, in the county of York, and by that lady had three other sons. The two younger d. s. p.; the eldest,

Leonard, m. Margaret, daughter of Sir Francis Lawley, bart. of Canall, in the county of Stafford, by whom (who surviving him, m. secondly, Sir Nathan Wright, bart. of Southall, Middlesex,) he left two sons and a daughter.

Sir Nathaniel died about the year 1707, and was s. by his grandson,

III. Sir Nathaniel Powell, who d. unm. in 1708, and was s. by his only surviving brother,

IV. Sir Christopher Powell, M. P. for Kent in 1734, who m. in 1728, Miss Newington, but died without issue, 5th July, 1742, when the Baronetcy expired. The trustees of his widow sold his estate at Boughton Monchensie to Mr. John Briscoe, of London, who alienated it, in 1771, to Willshire Emmett, esq. high sheriff of Kent in 1774.

Arms—First and fourth, gu. a lion rampant regardant or; second and third, arg. three boars' heads couped sa.

POWELL, OF BIRKENHEAD.

Created 29th Jan. 1629.

Extinct date unknown.

Lineage.

Thomas Powell, esq. married, *temp. Queen* Elizabeth, Alice, eldest daughter and co-heir of Ralph Worseley, esq. of Chester, grantee of the dissolved priory of Birkenhead, Cheshire, and thus acquired that estate. He was s. by his son,

Thomas Powell, esq. of Horsley, in Denbighshire, and of Birkenhead, Cheshire, who m. Dorothy, daughter of Morris Wynne, esq. of Gwydir, and was father of

I. Thomas Powell, esq. of Horsley and Birkenhead, who was created a Baronet in 1629. He m. Katherine, daughter of Sir John Egerton, of Egerton and Oulton, in Cheshire, by Margaret, his wife, daughter of Sir Rowland Stanley, knt. of Hooton, and by her (who was born in 1584,) had one son and one daughter, viz.

John, who m. Margaret, daughter of Edward Puleston, esq. of Allington, and dying v. p. December, 1642, left with a daughter, Catherine, wife of Rossendale of Wrexham, a son,

Thomas, successor to his grandfather.

Frances, m. first, to Edward Norreys, esq. of Speke, in Lancashire; and secondly, to John Edwards, esq. of Hansty.

Sir Thomas was s. by his grandson,

II. Sir Thomas Powell, of Horsley and Birkenhead, b. in 1631, who married first, Mary, daughter of William Conway, esq. of Bodryddan, in Carnarvonshire, and had by her a son,

Thomas, of Horsley, who *m.* twice, and had issue. He died *v. p.* before 1694.

Sir Thomas *m.* secondly, Jane, daughter of Robert Ravenscroft, esq. of Bretton, in Flintshire, and by her had two daughters,

Elizabeth, *m.* to Thomas Eaton, esq.

Margaret.

In 1694, Sir Thomas was living, but appears to have died not long after, when it is presumed that the Baronetcy became extinct. The estate of Birkenhead was sold to John Cleiveland, esq. M.P. for Liverpool in 1710, whose daughter and eventual heiress, Alice Cleiveland, *m.* first, Francis Price, esq. of Bryn-y-pys, in Flintshire; and secondly, Thomas Lloyd, esq. of Gwernhayled.

Arms—Sa. an escutcheon between three roses arg.

POWELL, OF PENGETHLY.

First Patent { Created 18th Jan. 1621-2. Extinct in 1653.

Second Patent { Created 23rd Jan. 1660-1. Extinct in 1680-1.

Lineage.

i. Edward Powell, esq. of Pengethly, in the county of Hereford, one of the masters of the requests, son and heir of Edmund Powell, esq. of Fulham, in Middlesex, and of Pengethly, was created a Baronet 18th January, 1621-2. He *m.* Mary, daughter of Sir Peter Vanlore, knt. but died without issue at his manor of Munster House, Middlesex, in 1653, when the title became extinct. He bequeathed his estates to his nephew,

i. William Hinson, of Pengethly, who assumed the surname and arms of Powell, and was created a Baronet 23rd January, 1660-1. He *m.* first, Mary, daughter and heir of John Pearle, esq. of Aconbury, in Herefordshire, and relict of Sir John Brydges, bart. of Wilton Castle; and secondly, Katherine, daughter of Dr. Richard Zouch, judge of the Admiralty, but died without male issue in 1680-1, when the second creation also became extinct. Sir William left an only daughter and heir,

Mary, who *m.* Sir John Williams, bart. of Eltham, in Kent, and their youngest daughter and co-heir,

Penelope Williams, marrying Thomas Symonds, esq. of Sugwass, in Herefordshire, conveyed Pengethly to her husband. Their great grandson is the present

Thomas-Powell Symonds, esq. of Pengethly, *b.* in December, 1788, who *m.* in 1816, Elizabeth, youngest daughter of Abraham-Holden Turner, esq. of Hendon, and has two sons,

Thomas-Powell, *b.* in 1817.

William-Turville, *b.* in 1818.

Arms—Az. a chev. between three suns or, within a bordure erm.

POWELL, OF BROADWAY.

Created 19th Jan. 1698.—Extinct 21st March, 1721.

Lineage.

i. Thomas Powell, esq. of Broadway, in Caermarthenshire, was created a Baronet in 1698. He *m.* the daughter and heir of Sir James Herbert, knt. of Colebrook, in Monmouthshire, and dying 28th August, 1720, was *s.* by his son,

ii. Sir Herbert Powell, at whose decease unm. 21st March, 1721, the title became extinct.

PRATT, OF COLESHILL.

Created 28th July, 1641.—Extinct in 1673-4.

Lineage.

i. Henry Pratt, esq. alderman of London, purchased in 1626 the manor and estate of Coleshill, in the county of Berks, and was created a Baronet in 1641. He *m.* Mary, daughter of Thomas Adams, esq. of Wisbech, and dying 6th April, 1647, was buried in the parish church of Coleshill, where a handsome monument was erected to his memory. His son and successor,

ii. Sir George Pratt, of Coleshill, *m.* Margaret, daughter of Sir Humphrey Foster, of Aldermaston, Berks, and had issue,

Henry, his heir.

Mary, *m.* to Thomas Pleydell, esq. of Shrivenham.

Sir George dying about 1673, was *s.* by his son,

iii. Sir Henry Pratt, of Coleshill, at whose decease in 1673-4, the title became extinct. The estate passed to the family of Pleydell.

PRESTON, OF THE MANOR OF FURNESS.

Created 1st April, 1644.

Extinct about 17.4

Lineage.

This ancient family was seated at Preston Richard and Preston Patrick, in the county of Westmorland, from time immemorial; but the first of the family upon record was,

Richard de Preston, who was possessed of those lordships *temp.* Henry II. His successor,

Sir Richard de Preston, was witness to several grants of lands in Lancashire by Sir John le Fleming with Sir William de Furness and others: he was also witness to a grant and confirmation of lands in Preston, Holme, and Hutton, by William de Lancaster the third to Patric, grandson of Gospatric, *temp.* Henry III. His son and heir,

Richard de Preston, was one of the jurors on the

inquisition post mortem of William de Lindesay 11 Edward I. He was succeeded by

Sir Richard de Preston, who was one of the jurors in a cause between the King and the Abbot and Convent of St. Mary's, York, concerning the advowson of the two churches at Appleby, A.D. 1291.

Richard de Preston, his son and heir, was witness, A.D. 1333, to a release of lands, at Old Hutton, by Gilbert de Culwen to Thomas, son of Patric de Culwen. By Annabella, his wife, who survived him, he had issue,

Sir Richard de Preston, who represented the county of Westmoreland in parliament 17 Edward III. His son,

Sir Richard de Preston, had likewise the honour of being knight of the shire for Westmoreland 27 Edward III. his father being then still living. In the year 1366, he obtained a license to impark five hundred acres of land. His successor,

Sir John de Preston, of Preston Richard and Preston Patrick, was M.P. for Westmoreland, 36, 39, and 46 Edward III. He had issue,

I. Richard.
II. John.

Sir Richard de Preston, the elder son, leaving daughters only at his decease, the manor of Preston Richard passed from the Preston family through these ladies, whilst the Preston Patrick estate devolved upon his brother,

Sir John de Preston, who was one of the judges of the court of Common Pleas in the reigns of Henry IV. and Henry V. and retired from the bench in 1427, in consequence of his great age and infirmity. He left issue,

I. John, a priest, who had a grant in 2 Henry V. of the church of Sandal from the prior of St. Pancras.
II. Richard, the heir.
I. ——, a daughter, married to Thomas de Ros, of Kendal Castle, whence maternally descended *Queen* Katherine Parr.

Richard Preston, esq. of Preston Patrick and Under Levins Halls, in the county of Westmoreland, son and heir, *m.* Jacobina, daughter of John Middleton, esq. of Middleton Hall; and 30 Henry VI. he and his said wife obtained from the archdeacon of Richmond a license to have an oratory within the manors of Preston and Levins. His son,

Thomas Preston, esq. of Preston Patrick and Under Levins Halls, *m.* a daughter of — Redmayne, esq. of Twistleton, and had issue,

I. John, his successor.
II. Lawrence, whose son, Henry, left one daughter and heiress, Ann, wife of William, first Lord Paget, K.G.
I. Helen, who espoused Thomas Stanley, Lord Monteagle, K.B.

John Preston, esq. of Preston Patrick and Under Levins Halls, son and heir, *m.* Margaret, daughter of Sir Richard Redmayne, of Harewood Castle, Yorkshire, and Over Levins Hall,* Westmoreland, and by her had issue,

Sir Thomas Preston, of Preston Patrick and Under Levins Halls, in Westmoreland, and Furness Abbey and Holkar Park, Lancashire, who soon after the dissolution of the monasteries purchased from the trustees of the crown the site of the abbey of Furness, with other large estates, in value amounting to upwards of £3000 a year. He wedded Ann, daughter of William Thornburgh, esq. of Hampsfield, in Lancashire, which lady was, through the families of Musgrave, Fitzwilliam, Plantagenet, and De Warren, fifteenth in descent from *King* William *the Conqueror*. By her he had issue,

I. John, the heir, born 1511.
II. Christopher, from whom descended the Prestons of Holker.†

* This romantic seat, so much admired for the beauty of its park and gardens (which latter are preserved in the old style), passed from the Redmaynes to the Bellinghams, and from them to the Grahams, and then to the Suffolk family, and is now possessed in right of his marriage by the Hon. Colonel Fulk-Greville Howard, brother to Lord Templetown.

† Christopher Preston, esq. of Holker Hall, *m.* first, Margaret Southworth, and had issue,

I. John, his heir.
II. Thomas, who *m.* the Lady Wandesworth, of Kirklington, but died *s. p.*
I. Ann, *m.* to Charles Laton, esq. of Sexey, in Cleveland, but died *s. p.*

He *m.* secondly, — Jephson, and had one daughter,

II. Elizabeth, *m.* first, to Thomas Tildesley, esq. of Morley, by whom she had two sons, one of whom was the renowned
Sir Thomas Tildesley, the celebrated loyalist, who lost his life at Wigan Lane.
She *m.* secondly, Thomas Latham, esq. of Parbold; and thirdly, Thomas Westby, esq. of Mowbreck, and had issue by each husband.

Christopher Preston died 27th May, 1594, and was buried at Cartmel Church.

John Preston, esq. of Holker, his son and heir, *m.* Margaret, daughter and heiress of William Benson, esq. of Hugill, which lady brought to her husband a moiety of the manor of Preston Richard, which had been carried out of the Preston family by heiresses, *temp.* Henry IV.; by her he had one son, George, his only child. Mr. Preston died 11th September, 1597, and was buried at Cartmel. His widow *m.* secondly, Thomas Farington, esq. of Werden, in the county of Lancaster.

George Preston, esq. of Holker, son and heir, was a great benefactor to the stately church of Cartmel. He also made an appointment for the apprenticing the sons of poor people in Cartmel, and a foundation for fitting several scholars for St. John's College, Oxford. He *m.* first, Elizabeth, sister to Sir Ralph Ashton, of Great Lever, bart. by whom he had

I. Thomas, his heir.
II. Christopher, who died *s. p.*
I. Frances, who *m.* Robert Duckenfield, esq. of Duckenfield, in Cheshire, and had with other issue,
Robert Duckenfield, esq. born 1619, the famous colonel in the service of the parliament, ancestor to the baronet family of Duckenfield.

Mr. Preston *m.* secondly, Margaret, daughter of Sir Thomas Strickland, of Sysergh Castle, in Westmoreland, knight of the Bath, and had further issue,

III. George, who died *s. p.*
II. Ann, *m.* Sir George Middleton, of Leighton, knt. and bart. one of the most distinguished loyalists *temp.* Charles I. He *d.* in 1673, and she, who was his second wife without issue, *d.* at Leighton Hall, 12th April, 1705.
III. Elizabeth, *m.* first, John Sayer, esq. of Yarm; secondly, Nathaniel West, esq. of Borwick Hall (grandson of Thomas Lord De la War); and thirdly, to George Leybourne, esq. of Cunswick Park. By her second husband she had
A daughter, *m.* to Robert Plumpton, esq. of Yorkshire.
IV. Frances, *m.* to Francis Biddulph, esq. of Biddulph.

Mr. Preston *d.* in April, 1640, and was buried at Cartmel, and was succeeded by

Thomas Preston, esq. of Holker, his son and heir. He was deputy lieutenant of Lancashire, and high sheriff in 1664. In early life he (with his kinsmen, the Prestons of the Manor and of Cockerham) taking up arms for the king greatly damaged his estate; but after the Restoration he was one of those gentlemen in Lancashire whom Charles II. for their loyalty had selected for the order of the Royal Oak, had it been instituted, his estate being then valued at £2000 per annum. He *m.* Katharine

III. George, who died *s. p.*

I. Ann, *m.* to William Banastre, esq. of Basington, in Bolland.

II. Ellen, *m.* first, Sir James Leybourne, of Cunswick Park, in Westmoreland (by whom she had Elizabeth, wife, first, of Thomas, Lord Dacre, of Gillesland; secondly, of Thomas Howard, fourth Duke of Norfolk, K.G.); and secondly, William Stanley, third Lord Monteagle (by whom she had Elizabeth, mother to William, Lord Morley and Monteagle, the discoverer of the Gunpowder plot).

III. Jane, *m.* to William Lamplough, esq. of Dovenby Hall, in Cumberland.

IV. Dorothy, *m.* William Travers, esq. of Nateby Hall, in Lancashire.

V. Elizabeth, *m.* Robert Canceñeld, esq. of Robert Hall, in Lancashire.

VI. Catharine, *m.* Sir Thomas Carus, one of the judges of the court of Queen's Bench, *temp.* ELIZABETH (and was mother of Mary Carus, who married Henry Kighley, esq. and had issue, Ann, wife of William Cavendish, first Earl of Devonshire, whence the Duke of Devonshire, and also the Earl of Burlington, who possesses the vast estates of the Prestons of Holker, in Lancashire, which were devised to his great uncle, Lord George Cavendish, by Sir William Lowther, bart. of Holker, the maternal representative of that family).

Sir Thomas died in 1523, and was succeeded by his eldest son,

JOHN PRESTON, esq. of Preston Patrick and Under Levins Halls, and also of the manor and abbey of Furness, who making Furness his principal residence, his family were thenceforth termed "Prestons of the Manor." He was sheriff of Lancashire in 1569. He married* Margaret, daughter to Sir Thomas Curwen, of Werkington, in Cumberland, by Agnes, daughter to Sir Walter Strickland, of Sysergh Castle, and by her had issue,

I. THOMAS, his heir.

II. Nicholas, a lawyer, *d. s. p.*

III. THOMAS, who having married Margaret, daughter and heiress of Roger Fytche, of Elel, in Cockerham, thenceforth became seated there. They had issue,

1. WILLIAM.
2. Nicholas.
3. John.
4. Roger.†
5. Thomas.
6. Christopher.

Mr. Preston died in December, 1596, and was succeeded by his eldest son,

WILLIAM PRESTON, of Cockerham, who died in May, 1623, leaving issue by his wife, who died in June, 1612, a son,

WILLIAM PRESTON, of Cockerham, who upon the breaking out of the civil wars taking up arms for *King* CHARLES I. thereby greatly incumbered his estate: his name was included in the list of loyalists whose estates were declared to be forfeited to the parliament by an act passed 18th November, 1652. He married first, 24th July, 1618, Clement, daughter of — Braide; and secondly, 9th May, 1642, Elizabeth Denys, and was succeeded by his only surviving son by his first marriage,

WILLIAM PRESTON, of Cockerham, born January, 1632, died in April, 1665, leaving

daughter to Sir Gilbert Hoghton, bart. of Hoghton Tower, and by her had

I. George, who *m.* Mary Lowther, only sister to John, Lord Viscount Lonsdale, but he died *s. p.* leaving
   Elizabeth, his only child, who *m.* Sir Wilfrid Lawson, bart. of Isell.

II. THOMAS, who became heir.

I. Margaret, who *m.* Edward Ogle, esq. of Whiston, in the county of Lancaster (son of Cuthbert Ogle, esq. by Elizabeth Harrington, his wife, and grandson of Henry Ogle, esq. by Elizabeth Whitby, his wife). She died 5th October, 1675, leaving issue,

1. Cuthbert Ogle, named in remainder to a considerable portion of the Holker estate (after Katharine Lady Lowther) by his uncle, Thomas Preston. He was born in 1673, and was living in 1696.

1. Katharine, living in 1696.
2. Elizabeth Ogle.

Mr. Preston died at Holker, 9th January, 1678, and was succeeded by

THOMAS PRESTON, esq. of Holker, his only surviving son. He was born in 1646. When his kinsman, Sir Thomas Preston, bart. settled the manor of Furness upon the Jesuits, his indignation was so strongly excited, that he endeavoured by all means in his power to persuade the Prestons of Cockerham (who were Sir Thomas's heirs male) to prosecute the suit against them; but they being advised that even if the suit should terminate favourably, it would be forfeited to the crown, and being greatly impoverished by the exertions they had made only a few years before in the royal cause, and having little interest at court, abandoned all idea of it; whereupon he undertook it, and after some years and enormous expense, succeeded in proving that it was forfeited to the crown, upon which it was immediately seized: but Mr. Preston having considerable interest, and his services having been properly represented, he obtained from the crown a long lease of the whole estate upon most advantageous terms. He subsequently represented Lancaster in parliament. He *m.* first, Mary, daughter of George Dodding, esq. of Conishead Priory, but by her had no issue; and secondly, Elizabeth, daughter to Sir Roger Bradshaigh, bart. of Haigh (a lady of unequalled prudence) by whom he had

Katharine Preston, sole heiress, who *m.* Sir William Lowther, bart. of Marske, and conveyed to him all the large property in Lancashire of the Preston family.

Mr. Preston *d.* in London, 31st January, 1696, but was buried at Cartmel. His lady surviving him, died 29th February, 1732, and was likewise buried there, where there are numerous splendid monuments of the family.

* He had a second wife, Dorothy, daughter of — Lupton, esq. of Dalemaine, in Cumberland, and relict of Richard Redmayne, esq. of Over Levins, Westmoreland, and Harewood Castle, Yorkshire, but had no issue by her.

† This Roger Preston seated himself at Up-Ottery, in Devonshire. He *m.* Alice, daughter of William Purfe, of Membury, in that county, and had issue,

I. Roger.

II. Henry, of Up-Ottery, living in 1620. He m. Miss Martin, and had (with two daughters) three sons,

1. Christopher, born about 1590.
2. Henry.
3. William.

There is no further mention of this branch made in the Visitations; but even if it does not now exist, it may have continued in the male line nearly a century beyond this period, as the late Robert Preston, esq. distinctly remembered having been told by his father that his father and mother (Richard Preston and Mary Hesketh) had shortly after their marriage been on a visit to their relations, the Prestons of Devonshire.

by Alice, his first wife, who died in February, 1678 (with other issue),

RICHARD PRESTON, of Cockerham, born 17th September, 1661, who, partly in consequence of the incumbrances created by the loyalty of his grandfather to *King* CHARLES, and partly in consequence of his own extravagance, was forced to alienate nearly all his property. He died in 1721, aged sixty years, having had (surviving) issue by Dorothy, his first wife, daughter and co-heir of Robert Dennis, esq.

1. JOHN, who succeeded to the wreck of the Cockerham estate, which he sold, and purchasing from the heirs of Sir Thomas Preston, and also acquiring by marriage estates in Preston Patrick,* Leasgill, and Heversham, he thenceforth wholly resided in Westmoreland. He left (surviving male) issue,

   William, D.D. Lord Bishop of Ferns, who died in 1789, aged sixty.

   Thomas, whose only son,

      John Preston, of Leasgill, died 28th June, 1816, without male issue.

By his second, Mary, daughter and co-heir of Henry Hastings, of Dublin, a branch of the noble house of Huntingdon, who surviving him forty-four years, died 7th March, 1765 (with three daughters), an only surviving son,

2. Robert, born 29th May, 1713, died 18th March, 1788, leaving by Margaret, his wife, only child of Robert Boucher, of Broughton, gent. who died in July, 1802, with other issue,

   ROBERT, of the Lower House, now called Firgrove, West Derby, Lancashire, who *m.* Miss Janet Wilkinson, and *d.* 19th November, 1833, having had issue, with three daughters, an only surviving son,

      Robert, born 28th April, 1793, who *m.* Ellen-Sarah, daughter of Peter Berthon, esq. and by her (who *m.* secondly, William-Robert Preston, esq. of Aigburth) had issue, with two daughters, one son,

         Robert-Berthon Preston, a minor, now living.

   Richard, of Liverpool, who *m.* first, Miss Collins; and secondly, Isabella, daughter of Mr. Edward Rushton, of Liverpool, and died 1st November, 1830, leaving issue.

   William, of Birchfield, afterwards of Fairview, Toxteth Park, and Liverpool, who died 16th May, 1828, leaving (with a younger son and two daughters)

      William-Robert, *b.* 22nd June, 1808, *m.* as above-mentioned, Ellen-Sarah, relict of Robert Preston, jun. esq. and has issue.

i. Margaret, *m.* to Roger Kirkby, esq. of Kirkby, in Lancashire.

The eldest son,

THOMAS PRESTON, esq. of Preston Patrick and Under Levins Halls, and also of the manor and abbey of Furness, succeeded his father, and served the office of sheriff of Lancashire in 1565. He married Margaret, daughter of John Westby, esq. of Moubreck, and dying 14th June, 1604, was buried at Heversham, being succeeded by

JOHN PRESTON, esq. his only child, who *m.* Elizabeth, daughter and co-heir of Richard Holland, esq. of Denton, in Lancashire, and by her had issue,

i. Thomas, *d.* young.
ii. JOHN, his heir, born 1617.

i. Ann, *d.* young.
ii. Margaret, *m.* Sir Francis Howard, of Corby Castle, second son of Lord William Howard, of Naworth Castle, and had issue,
   Thomas Howard, slain at Atherton Moor.
   Elizabeth, *m.* Edward Standish, esq. of Standish.
iii. Agnes, *m.* Christoper Anderson, esq. of Lostock.
iv. Frances, *m.* Francis Downes, esq. of Wardley Hall.

Mr. Preston's will bears date September, 1612, and he died shortly afterwards, being succeeded by his only surviving son,

i. JOHN PRESTON, esq. of Preston Patrick and Under Levins Halls, in Westmoreland, and of the Manor and Abbey of Furness, in Lancashire, who upon the breaking out of the civil wars, took part with the king, and rendered that unfortunate monarch such efficient service that he was in return created a BARONET 1st April, 1644, by the style of Sir John Preston, "of the Manor of Furness." He did not, however, long enjoy his dignity, being slain at the head of a regiment raised at his own expense in an engagement with the parliamentary troops, A.D. 1645. He married, in 1637, Jane, daughter and sole heir of Thomas Morgan, esq. of Heyford Hall, in Northamptonshire, and Weston-sub-Weathley, in Warwickshire, and by her, who brought him a vast estate, he had issue,

i. JOHN, second baronet.
ii. THOMAS, third baronet.

i. Ann, *m.* Sir William Gerard, bart. of Bryn and Garswood.
ii. Elizabeth, *m.* William, eleventh Lord Stourton.

The elder son,

ii. SIR JOHN PRESTON, bart. dying unm. in April, 1663, was succeeded by his brother,

iii. SIR THOMAS PRESTON, of the Manor and Abbey of Furness, in Lancashire, Preston Patrick and Under Levins Halls, in Westmoreland, and Heyford Hall, in Northamptonshire, who thus became third baronet. Sir Thomas had been a Catholic priest, but on succeeding to the title he obtained a dispensation from the Pope, and married the Hon. Mary Molyneux, daughter of Caryll, third Viscount Molyneux, by whom he had issue,

* A portion of the estate acquired by him at Preston Patrick has since been sold by his representatives, and another portion is now in the possession of Richard Rushton Preston, esq.

I. Francis, died young.

I. Mary, who *m.* William, Marquis of Powis.
II. Ann, who *m.* Hugh, second Lord Clifford, of Chudleigh.

Lady Preston died 6th June, 1673, and Sir Thomas being now a widower, was persuaded to return to his former functions; whereupon he settled his Westmoreland and Northamptonshire estates upon his daughters, and the estate of the Manor and Abbey of Furness upon the Jesuits; upon the legality of this grant a trial arose, and the estate was adjudged to be forfeited to the crown, which immediately seized upon it, but granted a long lease of the abbey to the Prestons of Holker, who had been mainly instrumental in bringing to light the illegal settlement made by Sir Thomas Preston. Sir Thomas, after making this disposition of his property, went over to Flanders, and entering a monastery there, spent the remainder of his days, and died about the year 1710, and with him EXPIRED the BARONETCY of "Preston of the Manor."

Arms—Arg. two bars gu. on a canton of the last a cinquefoil or.

PRESTWICH, OF HOLM.

CREATED 25th April, 1644.—EXTINCT in 1689.

Lineage.

I. THOMAS PRESTWICH, esq. of Holm, in Lancashire, the descendant of an ancient Lancastrian family, was created a BARONET in 1644, but died without male issue in 1689, when the title became EXTINCT, though it was assumed by the subsequent proprietors of Holm.

PRICE, OF THE ISLAND OF JAMAICA.

CREATED 7th Oct. 1768.

EXTINCT ....

Lineage.

FRANCIS PRICE, the first of this family upon record, went out to Jamaica a captain in the army, under Penn and Venables, in 1655, and settling there, *m.* the rich widow of Colonel Rose, and left at his decease three sons and a daughter, of whom

CHARLES PRICE, esq. being the adopted heir of his maternal half brother, Thomas Rose, esq. became possessed by will of "Rose Hall," in St. Thomas's in the Vale, and other considerable estates in Jamaica. He *m.* Sarah, daughter of Philip Edmunds, esq. also of that island, and had issue,

CHARLES, his heir.
Thomas, who *m.* Miss Anne Moor, but died without issue.
JOHN, whose grandson, ROSE PRICE, esq. was created a BARONET in 1815, and was *s.* by his son, the present SIR CHARLES DUTTON PRICE, bart. of Trengwainton. (See BURKE's *Peerage and Baronetage.*)

The eldest son,

I. CHARLES PRICE, esq. of Rose Hall, obtained the name of "the Patriot," for the numerous acts of public munificence he performed for a series of years in Jamaica,* his native country. He filled, for a lengthened period, the chair of the honourable house of Assembly, and was created a BARONET 7th October, 1768. He died in 1772, leaving by Mary Sharpe, his wife, three sons and a daughter, viz.

CHARLES, his heir.
John, who *d.* and was buried at Lincoln.
ROSE, successor to his brother.

Sarah, *m.* to a gentleman named Archbold.

The eldest son,

II. SIR CHARLES PRICE, of Rose Hall, also succeeded his father as speaker of the house of Assembly. He *m.* Elisabeth, daughter of John Guy, esq. of Berkshire House, in Jamaica, and widow of John Woodcock, esq. but died *s. p.* 18th October, 1788, when he was *s.* by his brother,

III. SIR ROSE PRICE, of Rose Hall, at whose decease *s. p.* the BARONETCY became EXTINCT.

Arms—Sa. a chev. erminois between three spear-heads, embued at the points, ppr.

PRINGLE, OF LONDON.

CREATED 5th June, 1766.

EXTINCT 18th Jan. 1782.

Lineage.

The Pringles are of very ancient descent, and still possess considerable influence in North Britain. The chief families of the name are the PRINGLES of Whytbank (now represented by ALEXANDER PRINGLE, esq. M.P. for Selkirkshire), the PRINGLES of Clifton (now represented by ROBERT PRINGLE, esq.), and the PRINGLES of Stitchel.

I. JOHN PRINGLE, M.D. of Pall Mall, physician to the army, *temp.* GEORGE II. (youngest son of Sir John Pringle, bart. of Stitchel House, in the county of Roxburgh, *vide* BURKE's *Peerage and Baronetage*), was created BARONET 5th June, 1766. Sir John *m.* in 1752, Charlotte, second daughter of Dr. Oliver, an eminent physician at Bath, but died without issue 18th January, 1782. Sir John Pringle was appointed one of the physicians to *King* GEORGE III. At his decease the BARONETCY became EXTINCT.

Arms—Azure, three escalops argent, with a mullet for distinction.

* At his own and considerable expense, Sir Charles Price laid out the beautiful road from Spanish town into St. Thomas's in the Vale; it is called "the sixteen mile walk," and is quite a bowling-green road for the [illegible] carriages, waggons, &c. Sir Charles was indeed fit for a wider sphere of action than Jamaica.

PROBY, OF ELTON.

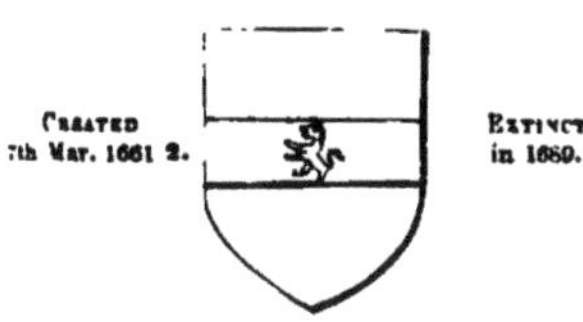

Lineage.

Sir Heneage Proby, of Elton, in Huntingdonshire, eldest son of Sir Peter Proby, lord mayor of London in 1622,) represented the borough of Agmondesham for many years, and was sheriff of Bucks. He m. Ellen, daughter of Edward Allen, esq. of Finchley, in Middlesex, and dying 10th February, 1667, left issue two daughters, Elizabeth and Helen, and three sons, Thomas, John, and Heneage. The eldest,

Thomas Proby, esq. of Elton, M.P. for Agmondesham, and subsequently in 1661, for Huntingdonshire, who was created a Baronet in 1661-2. He m. Frances, daughter of Sir Thomas Cotton, bart. of Connington, in Huntingdonshire, and had issue,

Thomas, who *d.* unm. on his travels.

Alice, *b.* in 1673, who *m.* the Hon. Thomas Watson Wentworth, M.P. and had an only child,

Thomas Watson Wentworth, first Earl of Malton and Marquess of Rockingham. (See Burke's *Extinct Peerage*.)

Frances, } *d.* unm.
Elizabeth, }

Sir Thomas *d.* in 1689, when the Baronetcy expired. Elton passed to his brother,

John Proby, esq. M.P. for Huntingdonshire, at whose decease issueless, that estate was inherited by his cousin,

William Proby, esq. some time governor of Fort St. George, in the East Indies (son of Charles Proby, esq. third son of Sir Peter Proby, the lord mayor). His descendant is the present Earl of Carysfort.

Arms—Erm. on a fesse gu. a lion passant or.

PRYCE, OF NEWTOWN.

Lineage.

This old Welch family traced a long and honourable descent, passing over the early parts of which, we shall begin with

David ap Eynion, of New Town, in the county of Montgomery, who m. Mathevis, daughter of Meredyth ap Llewelyn, of Llynwen, and was *s.* by his eldest son,

David Lloyd, who *m.* Gwenllian, daughter of Owen ap Griffith, ap Eynion, Lord of Towyn, and had an only son,

Rees David Lloyd, esquire of the body to *King* Edward IV. who fell at "Banbury fight," 1469. His wife was Margaret, daughter and heir of Evan ap Owen, of Neuadd Wen, in Powis, and by her had two sons, Thomas and Meredith Pryce, (or ap Rice,) and two daughters, Gwenllian, wife of Edward ap Howel, and Catherine, *m.* to Rees Lloyd ap Rhydderch.

Thomas Pryce, esq. of New Town, the elder son, *m.* first, Florence, daughter of Howel Clun, esq. of Clun, and had by her, four sons and two daughters, viz.

Matthew, his heir.

Oliver, ancestor of the Bolviers, of Neuaddwen, in Powis.

Richard, *d. s. p.*

John, from whom the Prices of Pennarth, in Ynfrin-Llanwair.

Gwen, *m.* to Humphrey Lloyd, esq. of Llai, near Poole,

Margaret, *m.* to Meredith David Vaughan, esq. of the Lloynwent.

He *m.* secondly, Gwen, daughter of Meredith Morgan, and had another son and daughter, namely, William and Catherine, wife of Owen ap Howel Goch, ancestor to the Owens of Machynleth. He was *s.* by his eldest son,

Matthew Pryce, esq. who *m.* first, Jane, daughter of Llen Vaughan, ap Sir David Gam, and had a daughter, Catherine, the wife of Thomas Tannat, esq. of Abdar Tannat. He *m.* secondly, Joice, daughter of Evan Gwyn James, esq. of the Monachty, in Radnorshire, and by that lady had two sons and four daughters, viz.

I. John, his heir.

II. Arthur, of Vainor, who *m.* first Lady Bridget, Bourchier, youngest daughter of John, fourth Earl of Bath, and by her ladyship had a son,

Edward, who *m.* Margaret, daughter of Dr. Nicholas Robinson, bishop of Bangor, by whom he had (with two younger sons, Thomas and Edward, who *d. s. p.* and a daughter, Jane, the wife of Thomas Fox, esq.) a son and heir,

Arthur, of Yaysnor, who *m.* Mary, daughter of Owen Vaughan, esq. of Llwydyarth, in Powis, and left an only daughter and heiress,

Bridget Price, who *m.* Sir George Devereux, of Sheldon Hall, Warshire, and was grandmother of the ninth Viscount Hereford.

Arthur Price, of Vainor, *m.* secondly, Jane, sister of Sir Randolph Brereton, knt. of Malpas, and by her had another son, John, who *m.* Margaret, daughter of Thomas Vaughan, esq. of Llynwent.

I. Elizabeth, *m.* to Edward Herbert, esq. ancestor of the Lords Herbert, of Cherbury.

II. Margaret, *m.* to Hugh Howel Edenhope, esq. of Shadwell.

III. Joyce, *m.* to Owen Blayney, esq. of Gregunog.

IV. Catherine, *d. s. p.*

His elder son and heir,

John Pryce, esq. of Newtown, *m.* Elizabeth, daughter of Rees Morris, esq. of Abberbachaso, and had issue,

Edward, his heir.

Matthew, *m.* Catherine, daughter and co-heir of

Lewis Gwin, esq. of Llanidloes, by whom he had one son and six daughters, viz.

John, of Park.*

Richard, } *d.* issueless.
Arthur, }

Bridget, *m.* to Lewis Blaney, esq. of Gregynog.
Mary, *m.* to Thomas Powell, esq. of Nantgwilt.
Margaret, *m.* to David Lloyd, esq. of Crynfrin, in Cardiganshire.
Joyce, *m.* to James Matthews, esq. of Trefnaney.

The eldest son and heir,

EDWARD PRYCE, esq. of Newtown, *m.* Julian, daughter of John Vaughan, esq. of Llwydyarth, in Powis, and had with a daughter, Jane, *m.* to William Robinson, esq. of Gwersilt, in Denbighshire, a son and heir,

I. JOHN PRYCE, esq. of Newtown, who was created a BARONET by *King* CHARLES I. Sir John *m.* Catherine, daughter of Sir Richard Pryse, knt. of Gogerddan, in the county of Cardigan, and had issue,

EDWARD, an officer in the royal army, *temp.* CHARLES I. distinguished by his valour in several actions, was killed in endeavouring to appease a tumult, and *d.* unmarried in his father's lifetime.
MATTHEW, successor to his father.
Mary, *d.* unm.
Elizabeth, *m.* Edward Clun, esq. of Clun.

Sir John was *s.* by his only surviving son,

II. SIR MATTHEW PRYCE, who *m.* Jane, daughter of Henry Vaughan, esq. of Kilkenain, in Cardiganshire, and had issue,

JOHN, his heir.
VAUGHAN, successor to his brother.
Edward.
Jane, *m.* to Richard Mostyn, esq. of Dolycosttay.
Anne.

He *d.* about 1674, and was *s.* by his eldest son,

III. SIR JOHN PRYCE. This gentleman *m.* Anna-Maria, daughter of Sir Edmund Warcup, knt. of English, in the county of Oxford, and had surviving issue,

ANNA-MARIA.
ELIZABETH.
PENELOPE.
JULIANA, *m.* to William Davie, esq. of Orleigh, in Devonshire.

Having thus no male issue, the baronetcy, at his decease, devolved upon his brother,

IV. SIR VAUGHAN PRYCE, who *m.* Anne, daughter of Sir John Powell, knt. of Broadway, in Carmarthenshire, one of the justices of the Court of King's Bench, and had issue,

JOHN, his heir.
Arthur.
Matthew, }
Edward, } all died *s. p.*
Vaughan, }
Mary, *d.* unm.

He *d.* about 1720, and was *s.* by his eldest son,

V. SIR JOHN PRYCE, who *m.* first, Elizabeth, daughter and heir of Sir Thomas Powell, bart. and by her (who *d.* 22nd April, 1731,) had

JOHN-POWELL, his successor.
Anna-Elizabeth.
Diana.

He *m.* secondly, Mary, eldest daughter of John Morris, of Wern Goch, in Montgomeryshire, and by that lady, (who *d.* 3rd August, 1739,) had two daughters,

Mary.
Elizabeth.

The baronet wedded, thirdly, Eleanor, relict of Roger Jones, esq. of Buckland, in the county of Brecon. He *d.* in October, 1748, and was *s.* by his only son,

VI. SIR JOHN-POWELL PRYCE, who *m.* Elizabeth, daughter and heir of Richard Manley, esq. of Carleigh Court, in Berkshire, and dying 4th July, 1776, was *s.* by his son,

VII. SIR EDWARD-MANLEY PRYCE, who *m.* the daughter of Mr. Flinn, of Norfolk Street, in the Strand, but died without legitimate issue, 28th June, 1791, when the BARONETCY EXPIRED.

Arms—Gules, a lion rampant, reguardant, or.

PRYSE, OF GOGERDDAN.

CREATED 9th Aug. 1641.

EXTINCT 1694.

Lineage.

This very old Welch family traces its descent from a remote era.†

SIR RICHARD PRYSE, knt. of Gogerddan, in the county of Cardigan, *m.* Gwenllian, daughter and sole heir of Thomas Pryse, of Aberbychan, in Montgomeryshire, and dying 6th February, 1622, was *s.* by his elder son,

SIR JOHN PRYSE, knt. of Gogerddan and Aberbychan, who *m.* Mary, daughter of Sir Henry Bromley, of Shadron Castle, in Shropshire, and was *s.* by his elder son,

I. RICHARD PRYSE, esq. of Gogerddan, who was created a BARONET 9th August, 1641. Sir Richard *m.* first, Hester, daughter of Sir Hugh Middleton, bart. and secondly, Mary, relict of Sir Anthony Vandycke. By the former he had issue,

RICHARD, his heir.
THOMAS, successor to his brother.
Carbery, *m.* Hester, daughter of Sir Bulstrode Whitlock, knt. and left a son,
CARBERY, who inherited as fourth baronet.

Sir Richard *d.* about the year 1651, and was *s.* by his eldest son,

II. SIR RICHARD PRYSE, who *d. s. p.* and was *s.* by his brother,

III. SIR THOMAS PRYSE, who *d.* issueless in May, 1682, and was *s.* by his nephew,

---

* This gentleman, JOHN PRYCE, esq. of Park, *m.* Mary, daughter of William Reed, esq. of Castle Bromshill, in Herefordshire, and had issue,

MATTHEW, his heir.
John, }
William, } *d. s. p.*
Catherine, *m.* to Hugh Matthews, esq. of Llanvairwaterden.
Mary, *m.* to John Reynolds, esq. of Garthmill.
Bridget, *m.* to John Edwards, esq. of Meliaygreeg.
Dorothy, *m.* to Lodowick Lewis, esq. of Dolegwernant.

The only surviving son,

MATTHEW PRYCE, esq. *m.* Hesther, daughter of John Thelwall, esq. of Bathefoin Park, but *d. s. p.*

† For the pedigree at large from the eleventh century refer to BURKE'S *Commoners*, vol. iii. p. 486.

IV. SIR CARBERY PRYSE. In 1690, during the life of his gentleman, mines were discovered on the estate of Gogerddan, of such immense value, as to obtain the designation of "the Welch Potosi." Sir Carbery in consequence procured an act of parliament to enable him to form a company, and commenced working, but was opposed by the Society of Minors Royal, and a lawsuit ensued. Pending which, the baronet and his partners, amongst whom were several noblemen, obtained another act of parliament, 1693, empowering all the subjects of the crown of England, to enjoy and work their own mines, in England and Wales, notwithstanding they might contain gold and silver, provided the king, and those who might claim under him, might have the ore, paying the proprietors for it upon the bank, within thirty days after raising, and before its separation from the lead. Sir Carbery himself is stated to have conveyed the news of the passing of this bill from London (having relays of horses) to Escairhir within forty-eight hours. Sir Carbery died *s. p.* about the year 1696, unm. when the BARONETCY EXPIRED, while the estates passed, eventually to his kinsman,

THOMAS PRYSE, esq. M.P. for Cardigan in 1743, son of John Pryse, of Glanmeryn, and devolved at his decease *s. p.* upon his cousin,

LEWIS PRYSE, esq. son of Walter Pryse, of Painswick, in Gloucestershire, which Lewis *m.* Margaret, daughter and co-heir of Edward Ryves, esq. of Woodstock, and had issue,

Lewis, who *d.* unm. in 1776.

MARGARET, *m.* to Edward-Loveden Loveden, esq. of Buscot, Berks, and had a son,

PRYSE LOVEDEN.

Mr. Pryse *d.* 12th March, 1798, and his daughter having predeceased him, (1784,) the estates devolved upon his grandson, who having assumed the name and arms of Pryse, is the present (1837)

PRYSE PRYSE, esq. of Gogerddan, M.P.

Arms—Or, a lion rampant, regardant, sa.

PUCKERING, OF WESTON.

CREATED 15th Nov. 1612.

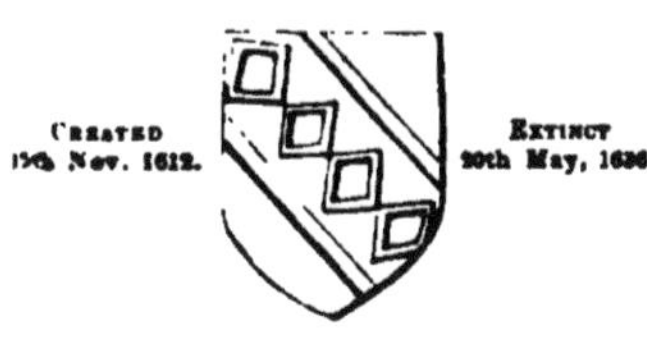

EXTINCT 20th May, 1636.

Lineage.

WILLIAM PUCKERING, of Flamborough, in the county of York, was father of

SIR JOHN PUCKERING, knt. an eminent lawyer in the reign of ELIZABETH, successively one of the governors of Lincoln's Inn, serjeant-at-law, and speaker of the House of Commons. In the 28th of the same reign, he received the honour of knighthood, and was made queen's serjeant, and in four years afterwards, the great seal was committed to his custody. He *m.* Anne, daughter of George Chowne, esq. of Kent, and left at his decease, 38th ELIZABETH, a son and heir,

I. THOMAS PUCKERING, esq. of Weston, in Hertfordshire, (an estate his father had by grant from the crown,) who was created a BARONET in the 10th year of *King* JAMES I. (25th November, 1612,) and afterwards resided at the Priory near Warwick. He *m.* Elizabeth, daughter of Sir John Morley, of Glynne, in Sussex, but having no surviving issue, the BARONETCY EXPIRED, at his decease, 20th March, 1636, while the priory and other estates devolved upon his nephew,

SIR HENRY NEWTON, bart. who then assumed the surname of PUCKERING.

Arms—Sable, a bend fusille, cotised argent.

PUREFOY, OF WADLEY.

CREATED 4th Dec. 1662.

EXTINCT in 1691.

Lineage.

The family of Purefoy, one of considerable antiquity, was seated at Misterton, in Leicestershire, so early as 1277.

PHILIP PUREFOY, of Misterton, living in 1344, *m.* Margaret, daughter and sole heir of Simon Shireford, of Shireford, in Warwickshire, and had two sons,

I. THOMAS, of the Middle Temple, who purchased the manor of Drayton, in the county of Leicester, about the year 1397. He *m.* Katharine, daughter and heir of Whellesburgh, of Fenny Drayton, and was great-great-grandfather of

THOMAS PUREFOY, esq. of Drayton, who *d.* in 1542, leaving by Margery, his wife, daughter of Sir Ralph Fitzherbert, of Norbury, four sons and five daughters, viz.

1. RALPH, of Drayton, whose grandson, GEORGE PUREFOY, esq. of Drayton, *d.* in 1593, leaving an only daughter and heir, JOYCE, wife of Edward Purefoy, esq. of Shalleston.
2. Michael, of Caldecote, Warwickshire, eschenator for that county *temp.* PHILIP and MARY, who married Joyce, daughter and co-heir of John Hardwick, of Lindley, and was ancestor* of the PUREFOYS of *Caldecote*,† *Barwell*, *Wolvershill*,‡ &c.
3. Hugh.
4. Anthony, slain at Oxford.
1. Joyce, *m.* to John Ruding, esq. of Ardbury, in Warwickshire.
2. Isabella, } nuns.
3. Dorothy, }
4. Joan, wife of John Staresmore.
5. Elizabeth, wife of Thomas Cawarden,

* Several of his descendants settled in Ireland.

† COLONEL WILLIAM PUREFOY, of Caldecote, the parliamentarian and regicide, died 8th September, 1659, having had two daughters, of whom the elder *m.* George Abbott, esq. M.P. Colonel Purefoy was great-grandson of Michael Purefoy, the eschenator.

‡ The last William Purefoy, esq. of Wolvershill, had a brother, George, of Hinckley, who died in 1722, leaving, with a son, George, who died in 1742, two daughters, Mary, wife of Joseph Harper, esq. of Hinckley, and Anne, of John Strong Rasor, gent.

esq. of Mavesyn Ridware, Staffordshire.

II. WILLIAM.

The second son,

WILLIAM PUREFOY, esq. of Shireford, living in 1396, *m.* Margaret, daughter of Sir William Chetwynd, of Ingestre, and had a son,

WILLIAM PUREFOY, who acquired, in marriage, the manor of Shalleston with Margery, daughter and heir of Adam Ayott, esq. of Shalleston, Bucks. His great-great-grandson,

NICHOLAS PUREFOY, esq. of Shalleston, sold the estate of Shireford. He wedded, first, Alice, daughter of Thomas Denton, esq. of Besils Lee, Berks, by whom he had a son, EDWARD, his heir; secondly, Clemence Lidiate, by whom he had another son, Simon; and thirdly, Catherine, daughter of Richard Brayfield, of Bucks, by whom he had, with other issue, a daughter, Isabella, wife of Thomas Goodwin, afterwards Bishop of Bath and Wells. Nicholas Purefoy died in 1547, and was *s.* by his son,

EDWARD PUREFOY, esq. of Shalleston, *b.* 13th June, 1494, who *m.* Anne, daughter of Richard Fettiplace, esq. of Basilsleigh, Berks, and dying 1st June, 1558, left, with other issue, John, of Shalleston, and

WILLIAM PUREFOY, esq. of Holingborne, in Kent, *b.* 1st March, 1524, who *m.* first, Beatrix Strelley, widow, daughter and heir of Thomas de Chilshurst, by whom he had two sons,

- John, M.A. canon of Christchurch, Oxford, rector of Flore, in Northamptonshire, &c. *d. s. p.* in 1601.
- Thomas, who *m.* Blendina, daughter of Thomas Godwin, Bishop of Bath and Wells, and had a daughter and heir, Marmion.

He *m.* secondly, Cecily, daughter of John Goodwin, of Winchendon, Bucks, by whom he had several sons; and thirdly, Mary, daughter of William Boys, esq. of Fredvile. His eldest son by his second wife,

EDWARD PUREFOY, esq. of Shalleston, *m.* Joyce, daughter and heir of George Purefoy, esq. of Drayton, and dying 15th March, 1594, was *s.* by his son,

GEORGE PUREFOY, esq. of Drayton, in Leicestershire, and of Wadley, Berks, who *m.* first, Mary, daughter and heir of Sir Valentine Knightley, and had by her, who died in 1617, three sons and five daughters,

- GEORGE, his heir.
- Edward, } *d. s. p.*
- Valentine, }
- Elizabeth, *m.* to Sir John Firebrace, knt.
- Joyce.
- Jane, *m.* to Sir Thomas Hales, bart. of Coventry.
- Lucy, *m.* to George Grey, of Kingston Mabreward, Dorset.
- Anne, *m.* to Edward Fleetwood, of Penwortham, Lancashire.

He *m.* secondly, Dorothy, sister of Edward, Lord Denny; and thirdly, Jane, daughter of Francis Roberts, esq. of Willesdon, Middlesex, widow of Sir Thomas Glover, of Hayes. Mr. Purefoy *d.* 13th May, 1628, aged forty-five, and was *s.* by his son,

GEORGE PUREFOY, esq. of Wadley, *b.* 11th January, 1605, named as one of the knights of the Royal Oak, his estate being valued at £3000 a-year. He *m.* first, 28th February, 1626, Anne, eldest daughter and co-heir of Sir Thomas Glover, knt.; and secondly, Anne, daughter and co-heir of Sir Francis Darcy, knt. of Brentford. The last lady *d. s. p.*; but by the former Mr. Purefoy had, with other issue,

- GEORGE, his heir.
- Knightley, of Shalleston, Bucks, who *m.* Mary, second daughter and co-heir of Henry Sandford, esq. of Kent, and died 13th January, 1691, leaving a son,
  - Henry, of Shalleston, *b.* 10th July, 1664, who *m.* Elizabeth, daughter of Leonard Fish, esq. and had two sons,
    - Henry, of Shalleston, *b.* in 1698, high sheriff of Bucks in 1749. He died 29th April, 1762, the last male heir of the family. Under his will, Shalleston passed to his cousin, the Rev. George Huddleston Purefoy-Jervoise.
    - Fish, died before 1758.
- Mary, *m.* Thomas Jervoise, esq. of Herriard, Hants, M.P. for Southampton, and had a son and heir,
  - THOMAS JERVOISE, esq. of Herriard, M.P. who married twice; by his first wife he had a son, Thomas, who died unmarried, and a daughter, Elizabeth, married to Sir Daniel O'Carroll; by his second wife he had, with a daughter, Mary-Elizabeth, *m.* to Samuel Clarke,* esq. of West Bromwich, a son,
  - RICHARD JERVOISE, esq. of Britford, Wilts, who *m.* in 1733, Anne, daughter and heir of Tristram Huddleston, esq. of Croydon, and had, with other issue who died unmarried, a son,
  - THE REV. GEORGE-HUDDLESTON JERVOISE, of Herriard, M.A. who inherited Shalleston, and assumed the surname of PUREFOY. He *m.* Mary, second daughter and co-heir of the Rev. Wright Hawes, and had [illegible] and other children.

Mr. Purefoy died 28th March, 1661, and was *s.* by his son,

GEORGE PUREFOY, esq. of Wadley, who *m.* Catharine, daughter and co-heir of Sir Henry Willoughby, bart. of Risley, and relict of Sir James Bellingham, bart. of Levins, and dying at Herriard, Hants, about 16[illegible] left, *inter alios*, a daughter, ANNE, eventual heiress, and a son,

I. HENRY PUREFOY, esq. of Wadley, baptised 14th August, 1656, who was created a BARONET in 16[illegible]; but as he *d. s. p.* 19th August, 1686, the title became EXTINCT.

Arms—Az. three stirrups or.

PUTT, OF COMBE.

CREATED 20th July, 1666. EXTINCT 5th May, 17[illegible].

Lineage.

I. THOMAS PUTT, esq. of Combe Gillisham, in the county of Devon, (grandson of Nicholas Putt, who purchased that manor and estate from Sir Henry Beaumont, of Leicestershire, in 1615,) was cre-

* The eldest son of this marriage, Jervoise Clarke, esq. M. P. of Idsworth Park, Hants, assumed the surname of JERVOISE, and was father of the REV. SAMUEL-JERVOISE CLARKE-JERVOISE, created a Baronet in 1813.

BARONET in 1666. He m. Ursula, daughter and co-heir of Sir Richard Cholmondeleigh, knt. of Grosmont, in Yorkshire, and had issue,

- THOMAS, his heir.
- Margaret, m. to Robert, sixth Earl of Roscommon.
- ———, m. to Charles Gorsuch, esq.
- Susanna, m. to Sir John D'Oyley, bart. of Chiselhampton.

Sir Thomas d. about the year 1687, and was succeeded by his son,

II. SIR THOMAS POTT, of Combe, who married Margaret, daughter of Sir George Trevilian, bart. of Nettlecomb, in Somersetshire, but died without issue 5th May, 1721, when the title became EXTINCT. The manor and seat passed, under Sir Thomas's will, to his cousin, RAYMUNDO POTT, esq. the male heir of the family.

Arms—Arg. in a mascle sa. a lion rampt. of the first.

PYE, OF HONE.

CREATED 13th Jan. 1664-5. EXTINCT 23rd May, 1734.

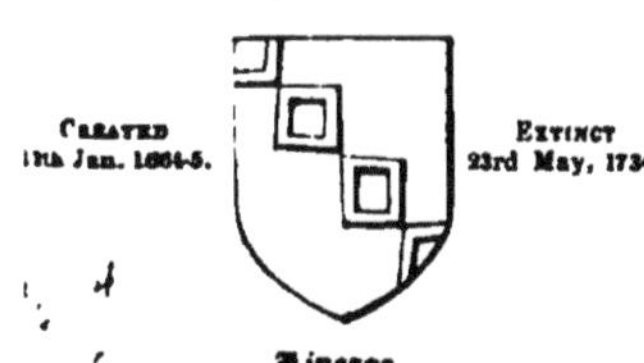

Lineage.

WILLIAM PYE, esq. of the Mynde, in Herefordshire,* d. 20th August, 1611, leaving the following five sons,

I. WALTER (Sir), of the Mynde, attorney-general to the Court of Wards, *temp.* CHARLES I. from which monarch he received the honour of knighthood, 29th June, 1649. His son and heir,

SIR WALTER PYE, of the Mynde, m. in 1628, Elizabeth, daughter of John Saunders, esq. of Denton, and had two sons and a daughter, WILLIAM, Robert, and Catherine, who all adhering to the church of Rome, and their allegiance to the STUARTS, disposed of Kilpec Castle, the ancient residence of the family, and retired to the continent.

II. ROBERT.
III. John.
IV. William.
V. Thomas.

The second son,

SIR ROBERT PYE, knt. was auditor of the receipt of the Exchequer to JAMES I. and CHARLES I. Sir Robert purchased of the Untons, the manor and estate of Faringdon, in Berks, and during the civil wars, garrisoned his mansion there for the king, when it was stoutly besieged by his son, Sir Robert Pye. He m. Mary, second daughter and co-heir of John Croker, esq. of Baltisford, in the county of Gloucester, and left at his decease in 1662, (with four daughters) three sons, viz.

I. ROBERT (Sir), his heir, who became of Faringdon, at the decease of his father. This gentleman espoused the republican cause, and in the rebellion, was colonel of horse in General Fairfax's regiment. Under the protectorate, he was twice returned to parliament for Buckinghamshire, but afterwards distinguished himself by zeal for the restoration of CHARLES II. He m. Anne, daughter of the celebrated JOHN HAMPDEN. His great great-grandson and representative was the late

HENRY JAMES PYE, esq. of Farringdon, the POET LAUREATE, who m. twice; by his first wife he had two daughters, Mary, m. to Capt. Jones, and Matilda, m. to S. J. Arnold, esq. and by his second wife, one son and one daughter, viz.

HENRY-JOHN.
Jane-Anne, m. to Francis Willington, esq.

II. John.
III. Thomas, a Turkey merchant.

The second son,

I. JOHN PYE, esq. of Hone, in the county of Derby, was created a BARONET 13th January, 1664-5. Sir John m. Rebecca, daughter of Nicholas Raynton, esq. of Enfield, in Middlesex, and had issue,

CHARLES, his heir.
Elizabeth, m. to Thomas Severne, esq. of Wallop Hall, Salop, gentleman of the bedchamber to *King* WILLIAM III. and left a son,

GENERAL SEVERNE.

Anne, m. to Charles Watkins, esq. of Aynho, in the county of Northampton, and had a son and heir,

RICHARD WATKINS, clerk, rector of Clifton, who m. Miss Meysey, and had issue,

1. CHARLES, who assumed the surname of Meysey, on succeeding to the estate of Shakenhurst, in Worcestershire, he *d. s. p.*
2. RICHARD, in holy orders, rector of Rock, in Worcestershire, left a son, CHARLES.
3. JOHN, in holy orders, devisee for life of his nephew, Charles.

He *d.* about 1697, and was *s.* by his son,

II. SIR CHARLES PYE, who m. first, Philippa, daughter of Sir John Hobart, bart. of Blickling, in Norfolk, but by that lady had no surviving issue. He wedded, secondly, Anne, daughter of Richard Stevens, esq. of Eastington, in Gloucestershire, and had,

RICHARD, his heir.
ROBERT, successor to his brother.
Rebecca, died unm. in 1748.
Philippa, *d.* unm. in 1769.
MARY, who became eventually heir and representative of the family.

Sir Charles purchased the estates of Clifton and Houghton, in Staffordshire. He *d.* 12th February, 1721, and was *s.* by his elder son,

III. SIR RICHARD PYE, who died unm. 22nd November, 1724, and was *s.* by his brother,

IV. SIR ROBERT PYE, clerk, F.R.S. who also died a bachelor 23rd May, 1734, when the BARONETCY EXPIRED. The estates devolved eventually upon the last surviving sister of Sir Robert,

MARY PYE, who died unmarried in 1774, devising them to her first cousin, GENERAL SEVERNE, for life, remainder to her first cousin, (once removed,) the REV. RICHARD WATKINS. General Severne inherited on her decease, and died himself in 1787, aged eighty-nine, when the property came to the WATKINS'S. CHARLES WATKINS,

* For his predecessors, vide BURKE'S *Commoners*, vol. i. p. 350.

son and heir of the devisee, Richard, died *s. p.* in 1812, having cut off the entail, and settled the property for life on his uncle, the Rev. John Watkins, with remainder to Henry John Pye, esq. son and heir of the Poet Laureate. On the death of Mr. Watkins, Mr. Pye succeeded accordingly, and is now the representative of the family. (See Burke's *Commoners*, vol. i. p. 351.)

Arms—Erm. a bend fusilly gules.

PYE, OF LEKHAMPSTED.

Created 27th April, 1641.—Extinct in 1672-3.

Lineage.

I. Edmund Pye, esq. of Lekhamsted and Bradenham, in the county of Bucks, was created a Baronet 27th April, 1641: he died, however, without male issue in 1672-3, when the title became extinct. Sir Edmund left by Catherine, his wife, two daughters, his co-heirs, viz.

Margery, *m.* John, Lord Lovelace, and had a daughter and heir,

Martha, Baroness Wentworth, who *m.* Sir Henry Johnson, and *d. s. p.* in 1745, when Bradenham, with other estates, passed to Viscount Wentworth, who sold that property in 1787 to John Hicks, esq.

Elizabeth, *m.* to the Hon. Charles West, eldest son of Charles, fifth Lord Delawarr, but *d. s. p.* The Lekhamsted estate was inherited by Mrs. West, but at her decease it became the property of her niece, Martha, Lady Wentworth, from whom it passed to the Rev. Henry Beauclerk, son of Lord Henry Beauclerk.

Arms—~~As Pye, of Faringdon.~~

PYM, OF BRYMMORE.

Created 14th July, 1663.

Extinct in 1687-8.

Lineage.

Philip Pym, esq. of Brymmore, in the county of Somerset, who *d.* in 12 *King* Edward IV., 1471, *m.* Joan, daughter of John, and sister and heir of Peter Tryvit, and was *s.* by his son,

Roger Pym, esq. of Brymmore, who married Joan, daughter of Richard Gilbert, esq. of Wollavington (by Eleanor, his wife, second daughter and co-heir of William Doddisham, esq.) and heir of her brother, Richard Gilbert, by whom he had a son and heir,

Alexander Pym, esq. of Brymmore, who *m.* Thomasine, daughter of Steynings of Rencote, and was *s.* by his son,

Reginald Pym, esq. of Brymmore, who wedded Maria, daughter of Thomas D'Abridgecourt, esq.* and had two sons, the younger of whom *m.* a daughter of Tillye. The elder,

Erasmus Pym, esq. succeeded his father. He *m.* Catharine, daughter of Edward Bampfylde, esq. of Poltimore, in Devonshire, and had issue,

Alexander, his heir.
William.

Mary, *m.* to Edward Arthur, son of Thomas Arthur, esq. of Clopton, in Somersetshire.

Brydget, *m.* to Henry Mallins, esq. of the county of Dorset.

The son and heir,

Alexander Pym, esq. who *m.* first, Elizabeth, daughter of John Conyan, esq. of London, and by that lady had a daughter,

Catharine, living in 1583, *m.* William Cholmley, of Highgate.

He *m.* secondly, Philippa, daughter of Humphery Coles, esq. of Burton, in the county of Somerset (by his wife, Elizabeth, daughter of Sir Richard Lambert, knt. lord mayor of London), and by her† had

John, his heir.

Jane, *b.* in 1581, *m.* Robert, second son of Sir Anthony Rouse, knt. of Halton.‡

He was *s.* by his only son,

John Pym, esq. of Brymmore, in the county of Somerset, *b.* in 1584, M.P. of Tavistock, in Devonshire, one of the most celebrated actors in the eventful drama which terminated in the decapitation of Charles I. He was educated at Pembroke College, Oxford, whence he removed to one of the Inns of Court, and was called to the bar. His subsequent career, his determined resistance to what he deemed the unconstitutional proceedings of the court, and his devoted adherence to the interests of the parliament, are so well known as to need no comment here. Pym *m.* Anne, daughter of John Hook, esq. of Bramshot, and had issue,

Alexander, *d.* a bachelor.
Edward, his heir.

Philippa, *m.* to Thomas Symons, esq. of Whittleford, in Cambridgeshire, and had issue,

John Symons.
Thomas Symons.
Robert Symons.

Anne Symons.
Priscilla Symons.
Lucy Symons.
Philippa Symons.
Mary Symons.

Dorothy, *m.* at St. Mary's, Westminster, 1st January, 1640, to Sir Francis Drake, bart.

* Son and heir of Sir Thomas D'Abridgecourt, knt. by Alicia, his wife, daughter of Sir Thomas Delamare, knt.

† She survived her husband, Pym, and remarried Sir Anthony Rouse, of Halton, in Cornwall, knighted in 1603, who died in 1620, leaving by her two daughters, namely,

Philippa Rouse, *m.* to Humphrey Nicholes, of Penrose.

Dorothy Rouse, *m.* to John Upton, of Lupton, in Devonshire.

‡ By his wife, Elizabeth, daughter of Thomas Southcot, and co-heir of her mother, Grace, daughter of John and sister and heir of Nicholas Barnehouse, of Marsh, in the county of Devon, by his wife, Margaret, daughter and heir of Nicholas Kirkham, which John Barnehouse was son of John Barnehouse and Jane, his wife, daughter of John Pope, son of Edward Barnehouse, of Kingston, in Devonshire, by Joan, daughter and heir of J— Brightriston.

Buckland Monachorum, in the county of Devon, M.P. for Newport, in Cornwall, in 1640, and colonel of a regiment of horse for the parliament, called the Plymouth regiment. They died without issue, administration to Sir Francis's property granted 31st May, 1662. His will dated 20th April of the preceding year, and proved 9th April, 1662.

Katherine, unm. in 1643.

Pym's only surviving son,

I. CHARLES PYM, esq. of Brymmore, in the county of Somerset, who was created a BARONET 14th July, 1663. He was a parliament man, in the parliament of 1640, and in the Pensioners' parliament. He m. Katherine, daughter of Sir Gilbert Gerrard, bart. of Harrow-on-the-Hill, in the county of Middlesex, by whom he had a son and daughter, viz.

CHARLES, his heir.

MARY, m. to Sir Thomas Hales, bart. of Beaksbourne, in Kent.

Sir Charles died about the year 1672, and was s. by his son,

II. SIR CHARLES PYM, who was killed in a rencounter at a tavern in 1667-8, and as he d. unm. the BARONETCY EXPIRED, while the estates devolved upon his sister. (Refer to HALES *of Beaksbourne, extinct baronets.*)

Arms—Sa. a bull's head couped arg. enclosed in a wreath or and az.

PYNSENT, OF ERTHFONT.

CREATED 13th Sept. 1687.

EXTINCT in 1781.

Lineage.

JOHN PYNSENT was father of

JOHN PYNSENT, of Chudleigh, in the county of Devon, who m. Joan, daughter of William Downham, of Abhampton, in the same county, and had issue,

I. JOHN, of Carleton-Corlieu, in the county of Leicester, one of the prothonotaries of the court of Common Pleas, m. Mary, daughter of Simon Clifford, esq. of Boscomb, in Wilts, and had three daughters,

GRISELL, m. to John St. Barbe, esq. of Broadlands, Hants, and had issue.

ELIZABETH, m. to Sir John Bolles, bart. of Scampton, in Lincolnshire, and d. s. p.

ANNE, m. to Sir Villiers Chernocke, bart. of Hulcote.

He d. 29th August, 1628, and was buried in Croydon Church, Surrey.*

II. Humphry, d. s. p.

III. WILLIAM.

IV. Robert, m. Anne, daughter of Stephen Bettenham, gent. of Bromley, in Kent, and died issueless.

I. Elizabeth, m. to Thomas Washer, esq. of Henoke, in Devon.

II. Grace, m. to William Tottle, esq. of Bovey, in the same county.

III. Eleanor, d. unm.

The third son,

WILLIAM PYNSENT, esq. m. Anne, daughter and co-heir of John Lancelott, citizen of London, by whom (who survived him, and m. secondly, the Rev. Richard Knightsbridge, rector of Streatham, in Surrey), he had a daughter, Anne, who died young, and an only son,

I. WILLIAM PYNSENT, esq. of Erthfont, in Wiltshire (heir male of his uncle the prothonotary), who was created a BARONET by *King* JAMES II., 13th September, 1687. Sir William m. Patience, daughter of Mr. Alderman John Bond, of London, and had issue,

WILLIAM, his heir.
Lancelot.
John.
Robert, deputy clerk of the crown, died of the gout in the stomach, 19th September, 1738.

Patience.
Anne.
Elizabeth.

Sir William, who was sheriff of Wilts, in 1694, died about the year 1719, and was s. by his eldest son,

II. SIR WILLIAM PYNSENT, who married Mary, widow of Edmund Star, esq. of New Court, and daughter and co-heir of Thomas Jennings, esq. of Burton, in Shropshire, and had issue,

WILLIAM, his successor.

Mary.
Leonoria.

He d. 15th June, 1754, and was s. by his son,

III. SIR WILLIAM PYNSENT, who d. s. p. 8th January, 1765, and was s. by his cousin,

IV. SIR ROBERT PYNSENT, in holy orders, at whose decease s. p. in 1781, the title became EXTINCT.

Arms—Gu. a chevron ingrailed between three mullets arg.

* Where, on the north wall was placed a black marble slab, supported by two black marble Corinthian pillars; above appear the arms—"Gules, on a chevron, engrailed, three stars, argent,"—underneath:

Here lyes the Body of John Pynsent, Esq; one of the Prothonotaries of his Majesty's Court of Common-Pleas, who departed this Life, the 29th of August, 1628.

The meanest part of him is only told,
In this Inscription, as this Tombe doth hold,
His worser part, and both these early may,
In length of time, consume and wear away;
His Virtue doth more lasting Honours give,
Virtue, and Virtuous Soule for ever live;
This doth embalme our Dead beyonde the art,
Proud Ægypt used of old, his head and Heart,
Prudence and Pietie enriched, his Hand,
Justice and Charity, did still command;
He was the Churches and Poore Man's Friend,
Wealth got by Law, the Gospel taught to spend.
From hence he learn't that what is sent before,
Of our Estates, doth make us rich farr more,
Than what we leave, and therefore did he send,
Great Portions wekely, thus he did commend,
His Faith by Workes, in Heaven did Treasure lay,
Which to possess his Soule is called away;
Here only is reserved his precious Dust,
Untill the Resurrection of the Just."

RADCLYFFE, OF DERWENTWATER.

CREATED 31st Jan. 1620.

EXTINCT 24th Feb. 1716.

Lineage.

I. FRANCIS RADCLYFFE, esq. of Derwentwater,* in the county of Cumberland, was created a BARONET 31st June, 1620. He m. Isabel, daughter of Sir Ralph Grey, knt. of Chillingham, in Northumberland, and was s. by his son,

II. SIR EDWARD RADCLYFFE, who m. Elizabeth, daughter and heir of Thomas Barton, esq. of Wenby, in the county of York, and was s. by his son,

III. SIR FRANCIS RADCLYFFE, who was raised to the peerage by *King* JAMES II., in 1688, as Baron Tyndale, Viscount Radcliffe and Langley, and Earl of Derwentwater. He m. Catharine, daughter and heir of Sir William Fenwick, of Meldon, in Northumberland, and had issue,

- FRANCIS, his successor.
- Edward, d. unm.
- Thomas, an officer in the army.
- William.
- Arthur.
- Anne, m. to Sir William Constable, knt. of Flamborough, in Yorkshire.
- Catherine.
- Elizabeth.
- Mary.

His lordship d. in 1696, and was s. by his eldest son,

IV. SIR FRANCIS RADCLYFFE, second Earl of Derwentwater, who m. Mary Tudor, natural daughter of *King* CHARLES II. by Mrs. Davis, and had issue,

- JAMES, his heir.
- Francis, d. s. p.
- Charles,† who m. Charlotte Maria Livingston, COUNTESS OF NEWBURGH, in her own right, and had with other issue,
  - JAMES-BARTHOLOMEW, third Earl of Newburgh.
  - Mary, m. in 1755, to Francis Eyre, esq. of Walworth Castle, in Northamptonshire, and had a son,
    - Francis Eyre, who inherited as sixth EARL OF NEWBURGH.
- Mary-Tudor.

He d. 29th April, 1705, and was s. by his eldest son,

V. SIR JAMES RADCLIFFE, third Earl of Derwentwater. This nobleman, with his brother Charles, joining in the effort made in 1715 to place the Chevalier St. George upon the throne, was made prisoner, sent to the Tower, and soon afterwards found guilty of high treason. In pursuance of which conviction he was beheaded upon Tower Hill, 24th February, 1716, when all his honours, including the BARONETCY, fell under the ATTAINDER. His lordship m. Anna-Maria, daughter of Sir John Webb, bart. and had issue,

- JOHN, *Viscount Radcliffe*, d. in 1731.
- Mary, m. to Robert-James, eighth Lord Petre.

Arms—Ar. a bend engrailed sa.

RAYNEY, OF WROTHAM.

CREATED 22nd Jan. 1641-2.

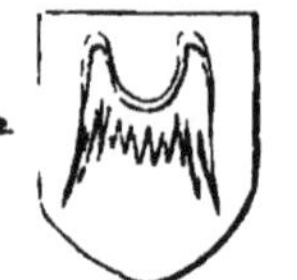

EXTINCT in 1721.

Lineage.

WILLIAM RAYNEY (lineally descended from John Reignie, who held the manors of Edgeford, Devon, and Smithley, in Yorkshire, so early as the reign of EDWARD III.) died 21st HENRY VII., leaving by his wife, the daughter and heir of Hall, a son,

JOHN RAYNEY, of Smethley, who m. the daughter and co-heir of Sir Robert Hopton, or Hexton of Su[illegible] lington, and had two sons, viz.

- ROGER, his heir.
- Henry, of Perrymore, in Yorkshire, who purchased from John Byron, esq. in 1569, the estate of Tyers Hill, in the same county. He m. in 1569, Alice Porter, and had two sons, GERVAS RAYNEY, esq. of Perrymore, and
  - FRANCIS RAYNEY, esq. of Tyers Hill, who m. 5th November, 1589, Margaret, daughter of James Green, esq. of Brierley, and was s. by his son,
  - JOHN RAYNEY, gent. of Tyers Hill, who m. first, in 1612, Anne, daughter of William Wentworth, of South Kirkby; and secondly Isabel, daughter of Nathaniel Eyre, of Bramley; by the former he left, with three daughters, Isabel, m. to John Carrington

---

* Beyond Hay Castle, in Cumberland, the river Derwent falls into the ocean, which rising in Barrodale (a vale surrounded with crooked hills), runs among the mountains called Derwent Fells; wherein at Newlands, and some other places, some rich veins of copper (not without a mixture of gold and silver), were found; about which there was a memorable trial, between Queen Elizabeth and Thomas Percy, Earl of Northumberland, the lord of the manor; but in virtue of the royal prerogative (there being veins of gold and silver), it was determined in favour of the queen. Through these mountains the Derwent spreads itself into a spacious lake, wherein are three islands: one the seat of the family of Ratcliffe, knt. *temp.* HENRY V. who m. Margaret, daughter and heir of Sir John de Derwentwater, knt.; another inhabited by miners; and the third, supposed to be that wherein Bede mentions St. Herbert to have led a hermit's life.—BANKS.

† CHARLES RADCLIFFE, implicated with his brother in the treason of 1715, was made prisoner at Preston the 14th November in that year, and being transferred to London, was condemned to death, but effected his escape from Newgate, and retired into France. On the death of his nephew, John Viscount Ratcliffe, he assumed the title of Earl of Derwentwater. Still adhering to the fortunes of the Stewarts, he embarked, with his son, to join CHARLES-EDWARD, in 1745; but being made prisoner, he was committed to the Tower, and beheaded under his former sentence, 8th December, 1746.

Jane, m. to Robert Arnold; and Mary, to Mr. Chapman, a son and successor,

HENRY RAYNEY, of Tyers Hill, b. in 1614, who married Priscilla, daughter of William Wordsworth, and dying in 1692, left issue,

FRANCIS, his heir.

HENRY, of London, b. in 1661, successor to his brother.

Thomas, alderman of Doncaster, m. in 1715, Frances, daughter of Mr. Alderman John Payram, of the same place, and had issue,

Henry, d. s. p. in 1731.

THOMAS, successor to his uncle.

Frances, m. in 1740, to William Seaton, of Doncaster, and d. s. p.

PRISCILLA (of whom presently), m. to Nathaniel Pearson, esq.

Mary.

Catherine, married to John Ellis, gent. of Woolley.

Elizabeth, m. to Christopher Dowson, of Arthington.

The eldest son,

THE REV. FRANCIS RAYNEY, M.A. of Tyers Hill, b. in 1651, d. unm. 28th November, 1697, and was s. by his brother,

HENRY RAYNEY, of London, who m. Frances, daughter of Thomas Wright, esq. of Sandy Downham, Suffolk, and had a daughter, Elizabeth, m. to Robert Wright, of London. Henry Rayney d. in 1740, leaving Tyers Hill to his nephew,

THOMAS RAYNEY, esq. at whose decease issueless in 1748, it passed to his sister,

PRISCILLA RAYNEY, who m. 27th October, 1743, Nathaniel Pearson, esq. of Doncaster, and dying in 1751, left two daughters and co-heirs,

MARY PEARSON, who m. 18th January, 1777, Freeman Bower, esq. of Killerby Hall, and died in 1794, leaving issue,

HENRY BOWER, esq. F.S.A. of Doncaster.

Frances-Mary Bower, m. to the Rev. Henry Watkins, of Barnborough, and had issue.

Henrietta-Priscilla Bower, married to James Jackson, esq. and had issue.

Wilhelmina-Elizabeth Bower.

FRANCES PEARSON, who married in 1784, George Pearson, M.D. F.R.S. of George Street, Hanover Square, and had two daughters,

FRANCES-PRISCILLA, m. to Sir John Dodson, D.C.L. and has issue.

Mary-Anne.

Upon the demise of Dr. Pearson, 9th November, 1828, Tyers Hill devolved, by his will, upon Sir John Dodson.

...he elder son of John Rayney, of Smethley,

R..ger RAYNEY, esq. of Smethley, aged thirty-five, Philip and MARY, m. Elizabeth, daughter of John ...hornhill, esq. of Pixby, and had, with a daughter, ...len, wife of Thomas Cutler, esq. of Stainborough, ...son and successor,

JOHN RAYNEY, esq. merchant and alderman of ...ondon, a most bountiful benefactor to the township ...W...rsborough, Yorkshire. This gentleman acquired ...est Malling, in Kent, by grant from JAMES I. and ...rchased Wrotham Place, in the same county, where ...seated himself. He m. Susan, daughter of Walter ...ann, esq. of Kingston, and had issue,

JOHN, his heir.

Elizabeth, m. to John Acton, esq. of Ipswich.

Ann, m. to John Smith, esq.

Sarah, m. to Sir Henry North, bart. of Mildenhall, Suffolk.

Susan, d. young.

Alderman Rayney died 21st May, 1633, and was s. by his son,

I. JOHN RAYNEY, esq. of Wrotham and West Malling, in Kent, who received the honour of knighthood at the coronation of CHARLES I. and was created a BARONET 22nd January, 1641. He m. Catherine, daughter of Thomas Style, esq. of London, and had four sons and three daughters: John; Thomas; Richard; William; Susannah, m. to William Selby, esq. of Ightham; Elizabeth, m. to Sir John Chichester, bart.; and Martha, m. to Nathaniel Bonnel, of London, merchant. He m. secondly, Frances, daughter of Edward Gibbes, esq. of Warwickshire, and had by her a son, EDWARD, who had issue. Sir John Rayney, who served as sheriff of Kent in 1615, died 3rd March, 1660, and was s. by his son,

II. SIR JOHN RAYNEY, of Wrotham and West Malling, who m. Mary, daughter of Jeremy Blackman, esq. of Southwark, and dying about 1680, was s. by his son,

III. SIR JOHN RAYNEY, of Wrotham and West Malling, b. in 1660, who m. first, Vere, daughter and coheir of Sir Thomas Beaumont, bart. of Gracedieu, in Leicestershire, and had by her

JOHN BEAUMONT, his heir.

THOMAS, successor to his brother.

Vere, d. s. p. m.

Mary.

Sir John m. secondly, Jane, eldest daughter and coheir of Thomas Manley, esq. of Rochester, which lady died in 1700; and thirdly, Jane, daughter of Sir Demetrius James, knt. of Ightham, in Kent, by whom, who died in 1714, he had two daughters,

Catherine, m. to Edward Bettenson, esq.

Hellena, d. unm. 8th September, 1736.

Sir John Rayney died in February, 1704-5, and was s. by his son,

IV. SIR JOHN BEAUMONT RAYNEY, lieutenant-colonel in the army, who died unm. in 1716, and was s. by his brother,

V. SIR THOMAS RAYNEY, at whose decease without issue in 1721, aged thirty-one, the BARONETCY became EXTINCT.

Soon after the decease of Sir John Rayney, the third baronet, Wrotham Place was sold to the Stephensons, and from them purchased in 1725, by Captain Nicholas Haddock. The manor of West Malling Sir John conveyed, about the time of the Restoration, to Isaac Honywood, esq.

Arms—Gu. two wings in lure erm.

READE, OF BROCKET.

CREATED 16 Mar. 1541-2.  EXTINCT 22nd Feb. 1711-2.

Lineage.

SIR THOMAS READE, of Barton, in Berkshire, m. Mary, fifth daughter and co-heir of Sir John Brocket, knt. and, acquiring with her Brocket Hall, with a considerable estate in Hertfordshire, served as sheriff of that county in 1618. He had issue,

Thomas, who succeeded at Barton. He married Mary, daughter of Sir Thomas Cornwall, of Burford, in Salop, and had, with other issue, two sons,

Compton, of Barton, in Berkshire, and of Shipton Court, Oxfordshire, who was created a Baronet in 1660. His representative is the present

Sir John Chandos Reade, bart. of Shipton Court.

Edward, who had the estate of Ipsden, granted to him by his father in 1637. He was ancestor of the present

John Reade, esq. of Ipsden House, Oxfordshire.

Richard.
John, of whom presently.

Mary, m. to Sir Robert Dormer, knt. of Bucks.
Elizabeth.
Frances.

The third son,

I. John Reade, esq. who inherited Brocket Hall, Herts, was created a Baronet 16th March, 1641-2, and served as sheriff of the county in 1655. He m. Susan, daughter of Sir Thomas Style, bart. of Wateringbury, in Kent, and by her, who d. in 1657, left at his decease in 1693-4, a daughter, Mary, m. to Sir John Bucknall, knt. of Oxhey, Herts, and a son and successor,

II. Sir James Reade, of Brocket Hall, bapt. 10th March, 1654-5, sheriff of Herts in 1693, who m. Love, daughter and co-heir of Robert Dring, esq. of Isleworth, in Middlesex, and by her, who d. 9th November, 1731, aged seventy-six, had issue,

John, his heir.

Dorothea, m. Robert Dashwood, esq. son and heir apparent of Sir Robert Dashwood, bart. of Northbrooke, and had a son,

Sir James Dashwood, bart. M.P. for Oxfordshire, grandfather of the present

Sir George Dashwood, bart. of Kirklington. (See Burke's *Peerage and Baronetage*.)

Anne, m. to Robert Myddleton, esq. of Chirk Castle, Denbighshire.

Love, m. 6th August, 1719, to Thomas Winnington, esq. of Stanford.

Mary.

Susan, died under age unm.

Sir James died 16th October, 1701, and was s. by his son,

III. Sir John Reade, of Brocket Hall, who died without issue, at Rome, 22nd February, 1711-12, aged twenty-two, when the title became extinct,* and his sisters became his co-heirs. Upon partition, the estate of Brocket fell to the share of Love, m. in 1719, to Thomas Winnington, esq. and was subsequently sold to Matthew Lambe, esq. grandfather of the present Viscount Melbourne.

Arms—Gu. a saltire between four garbs or.

REEVE, OF THWAITE.

Created 22nd Jan. 1662-3.—Extinct about 1688.

Lineage.

I. George Reeve, esq. of Thwaite, in Suffolk, [illegible] created a Baronet in 1662-3. He m. the daughter and co-heir of Robert Crane, esq. of Chilton, in the same county, and dying about 1679, was s. by his son,

II. Sir Robert Reeve, of Thwaite, who m. Margaret, sister of Sir Richard Onslow, bart. of West Clandon, in Surrey, but died without male issue about the year 1688, when the title became extinct.

RERESBY, OF THRYBERGH.

Created 16th May, 1642. Extinct 12th Aug. [illegible]

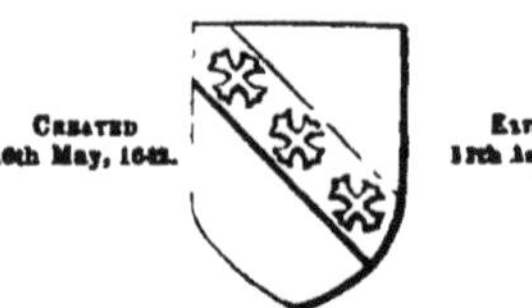

Lineage.

The family of Reresby, or Reveresby, was seated at Thribergh, in the county of York, or in the parts bordering from the time of the Conquest.

Sir Adam Reresby, knt. m. Anne, daughter of Sir Andrew Beke, knt. and had issue,

Alexander, his successor.

Annabella, m. to Sir William Ormesby, knt. of Ormesby.

Elizabeth, married to Sir William Green, knt. of Newby.

Cassandra, m. to Philip Blensby.

Jane, m. to Robert Cumberworth.

Anne, m. to Sir John Somercotes, knt.

His son and heir,

Alexander Reresby, m. Amarilla Ondrebie [illegible] had, with two daughters, Ursula, the wife of Sir Adam Thrusknoy, knt.; and Mary, of John [illegible] Noblethorp, in Lincolnshire, a son and heir.

Isidore Reresby, who m. Amicia, daughter and co-heir of D'Eyncourt, and co-heir of Serlo de [illegible]ley, by whom he acquired the manor of Pinxton [illegible] had issue,

Ralph, his heir.

Eleanor, m. to John Wickersley, esq.

Mary, m. to Thomas Bakewich, esq.

Jane, m. to Peter Frechville, esq. of Staveley, in the county of Derby.

His son,

Ralph Reresby, was lord of the manor of Ash[illegible] in Derbyshire, and knight for that shire [illegible] II. with William Russell. He exchanged [illegible] Ashover, with Sir Robert Willoughby, and m. Margery, daughter of Ralph, and sister and heir of [illegible] Normanville, lord of Thribergh. His son and heir

---

* In 1810, the Rev. William Reade, rector of Tom-grang, in Cornwall, claiming to be descended from [illegible] Reade, the first baronet, assumed the title; and his son, as the eldest son of a baronet, received the honour of knighthood.

Sir Adam Reresby, knt. lord of Thribergh, in the county of York, and of Ashover, in Derbyshire, had a daughter, Elizabeth, m. first, to Oakover, of Oakover, in Staffordshire; secondly, to Lowe, of Denbigh, in Derbyshire; thirdly, to Hallam, of Hallam; and fourthly, to Thomas Powtrell, of West Hallam, and a son and heir,

Ralph Reresby, esq. who married Dorothy, daughter of Thomas Bradborne, esq. of Bradborne, and had issue,

- Thomas (Sir), his heir.
- Christian, m. to John Bentley, esq.
- Bridget, m. to William Bensford, esq.

He was s. by his son,

Sir Thomas Reresby, knt. who wedded Cecily, daughter and co-heir of Richard Gothain, esq. of Brimsforth, in the county of York, and had a son and three daughters, viz.

- Thomas (Sir), his successor.
- Anne, married to Thomas Barry, esq. of Teversal, Notts.
- Mary, a nun at Cotham.
- Jane, d. unm.

His son and heir,

Sir Thomas Reresby, knt. who m. Lucia, daughter of John Sheffield, esq. and had, with several sons, two daughters, Isabella, wife of William Wentworth, esq. of Wentworth Woodhouse; and Judith, of Richard Symmes, esq. of Barnsley. He was s. by his eldest son,

Sir Thomas Reresby, knt. who died in 1439, leaving by Maud, daughter of Sir John Nevil, of Chete,* a son and heir,

Ralph Reresby, esq. who m. Agnes, daughter of Sir John Stapleton, knt. of Wighill, in the county of York, and dying 1st June, 1466, was succeeded by his son,

Ralph Reresby, esq. who d. in 1530. He m. Margaret, daughter of Sir Richard Fitzwilliams, knt. of Aldwarke, and had five daughters,† with a son and heir,

Thomas Reresby, esq. of Thribergh, whose will was proved in 1543. He married Elizabeth, daughter of [illegible] Pulnetby, esq. of Pulnetby, in the county of Lincoln, and had, with younger sons,

- Lionel, his heir.
- Ellen, m. to Roger Vavasor, esq. of Dennaby.
- Elizabeth, m. to Robert Lowe of Denbigh.
- Jane, m. to Thomas Gascoigne, esq.

He was s. by his son,

Lionel Reresby, esq. who left by his wife, Anne, daughter of Robert Swift, esq. of Rotherham, six sons and seven daughters,

- Thomas, his successor.
- Ralph.
- William.
- Leonel, m. Jane, daughter of Thomas Hardwicke, esq. and had a daughter, Edith, m. to Francis Tindal, esq. of Brotherton.
- Godfrey.‡
- Arnold, married Thomasine, daughter of Thomas Whalley, esq. of Sibthorpe, Notts.
- Margaret, m. to Ralph Bower, esq. of Betsworth.
- Anne, m. first, to Thomas Eyre, of Highlow; secondly, to Thomas Hardwicke; and thirdly, to Edward Holme, esq. of Paul Holme.
- Ellen, m. to Marmaduke Tyrwhitt, esq.
- Elizabeth, m. to Thomas or Francis Copledyke, esq. of Harrington, in the county of Lincoln.
- Barbara, m. to Thomas Pilkington, esq. of Bradley.
- Mary, m. to John Lewes, esq.
- Jane, m. to Gervase Wastneys, esq. of Headon, Notts.
- Edith, m. to George Markham, esq. of Etton.

The eldest son,

Thomas Reresby, esq. of Tribergh, living in 1584, m. Margaret, daughter of Thomas Babington, esq. of Dethick, in the county of Derby, by whom he had (with younger sons‡ and four daughters, the latter married thus: Anne, to Thomas Trigot, esq. of South Kirby; Edith, to Michael Cookson, of Wadworth; Mary, to Sir Richard Harper, knt. of Little Over, in the county of Derby; and Margaret to Elland), a son and heir,

Sir Thomas Reresby, knt. of Tribergh, justice of the peace for the West Riding, 40 and 41 Elizabeth, m. in 1588, Mary, daughter of Sir John Monson, knt. of South Carlton, in Lincolnshire, and dying in 1619, left

- George (Sir), his successor.
- Gilbert, died in Ireland, leaving by his wife, Anne, daughter of Sir John Skinner, knt. an only daughter, his heir,
  - Mary, m. to Sir John Fortescue, knt.
- Edward, } d. unm.
- Adam, }
- Jane, m. to Sir John Shelley, bart. of Michelgrove.
- Elizabeth, m. to Sir John Campbell.
- Mary, m. to Robert Stuart, esq.
- Bridget, m. to Neal Scot, gent.

His son and heir,

Sir George Reresby, knt. m. Elizabeth, daughter and co-heir of John Tamworth, esq. of Sherville Court, and had surviving issue,

- John (Sir), his heir.
- George.
- Tamworth (Sir), of Sherville.
- Elizabeth, m. first, to Sir Francis Foljamb, bart. of Aldwark, in the county of York; secondly, to Edward Horner, esq. son of Sir John Horner, knt. of Mells, in Somersetshire; thirdly, to William Monson, Viscount Castlemaine, in Ireland;§ and fourthly, to Sir Adam Felton, bart. of Playford, in Suffolk.

Sir George d. 3rd February, 1628, and was s. by his eldest son,

I. Sir John Reresby, knt. of Thribergh, in the county of York, governor of Hull, who was created a

---

* Others call her daughter of Bosvile of Chete.

† Viz. Elizabeth, the eldest, m. first, to John Bosvile, [illegible] of Newhall; and secondly, to Eyre, of Holme: the second, m. to Rere, of Belton, in Lincolnshire; the third, [illegible]ington, of Barnby; the fourth, Agnes, to Robert [illegible]rsby, of Mansfeld; and the fifth, to John Baxter, of [illegible].

‡ From Godfrey descended Leonard Reresby, of Ecclesfield, whose daughter, Mary, m. in 1692, to William [illegible]well, esq. of Sheffield.

§ This William Monson, who was second son of Sir Thomas Monson, bart. master falconer to James I. was created by Charles I. Viscount Castlemain, in the peerage of Ireland; but being instrumental in the death of his royal master, he was degraded in 1661, and sentenced with Sir Henry Mildmay and Mr. Robert Wallop, to be drawn on a sledge, with a rope about his neck, from the Tower to Tyburn, and back again, to remain a prisoner for life.

BARONET by *King* CHARLES I. 16th May, 1642. He *m.* Frances, daughter of Edmund Yarburgh, esq. of Balne Hall, in the county of York, and by her, who wedded, secondly, James Moyser, esq. had issue,

JOHN, his successor.
Tamworth.
Edmund, *b.* in 1636, *d.* unm.
Gervace, *b.* in 1640, a merchant in Spain.
Yarburgh, rector of Holme, in Spalding Moore.
Bridget, *m.* to Mr. Burgh.
Elizabeth, *d.* young.

He *d.* in April, 1646, and was *s.* by his eldest son,

II. SIR JOHN RERESBY, of Thribergh, governor of York, whose memoirs of his own life and times are well known, who *m.* Frances, daughter of William Brown, esq. of York, and had (with two daughters, one married to John Lacy, esq.; the other, first, to Mr. Smith, and secondly, to Mr. Tilly, warden of the Fleet), five sons, viz.

WILLIAM, his heir.
Tamworth, a major in Colonel Stanwix's regiment, *d. s. p.*
George, } *d.* unm.
John, }
LEONARD, successor to his brother William.

He *d.* in May, 1689, and was *s.* by his eldest son,

III. SIR WILLIAM RERESBY. This gentleman afforded a melancholy contrast to the high reputation of his distinguished father. "In 1705 (says Hunter) he had sold Thribergh and the estates connected with it. He was alive in 1727, when Wotton's account of the Baronets was published. In that work he is said to be reduced to a low condition. Brooke was informed that he was tapster of the Fleet prison. This is not improbable, for his tastes and habits appear to have been of the lowest order. I have seen one sad evidence. He died in great obscurity, a melancholy instance how low pursuits and base pleasures may sully the noblest name, and waste an estate gathered with labour, and preserved by care a race of distinguished ancestors. Gaming was amongst his follies, and particularly that lowest specimen of the folly, the fights of game cocks. The tradition at Thrybergh is (for his name is not quite forgotten), that the estate of Dennaby was staked and lost on a single main." This profligate person died fortunately unmarried, when the BARONETCY, probably nothing more remained, devolved upon his brother,

IV. SIR LEONARD RERESBY, who *d.* unm. 11th August, 1748, when the BARONETCY EXPIRED.

The estate of THRYBERGH was sold by SIR WILLIAM RERESBY to JOHN SAVILE, esq. of Methley, in the same county, and devolved upon that gentleman's grandaughter,

ELIZABETH SAVILE, who *m.* the Hon. John Finch, second son of Heneage, Earl of Aylesford, and was *s.* by her son,

SAVILE Finch, esq. of Thrybergh, M.P. who had no issue, and having full power over the estates, left them to his wife, Judith, daughter of John Fullerton, esq. That lady lived for twenty years after her husband's death at Thrybergh, and at her decease in 1803, bequeathed it to her own family, the FULLERTONS.

Arms—Gu. on a bend arg. three crosses patonce sable.

RICH, OF SUNNING.

CREATED 20th Mar. 1660-1.

EXTINCT 6th April, 1803.

Lineage.

WILLIAM RICH, of Minty, in the county of Gloucester, *m.* a daughter of John Packer, of Cheltenham, and was father of

THOMAS RICH, an alderman of the city of Gloucester, *anno* 1600, who, beside what paternal estate he inherited, was seized of the manor of Astwood Court, in Worcestershire. He *m.* Anne, daughter of Thomas Machyn, of Gloucester, and had, with a daughter, Anne, *m.* first to Toby Clements, of Gloucester, and secondly to John Hanbury, esq. of Feckenham, in Worcestershire, a son and heir,

I. THOMAS RICH, esq. of Sunning, in the county of Berks, who, as a Turkey merchant, amassed a large fortune, and attained a high character for benevolence and public spirit. He supplied his unhappy sovereign while in exile, with considerable sums of money, and with equal liberality contributed to the support of the oppressed clergy at home. At his decease, he left £16,000 in public charities. On the Restoration, he was created a BARONET by the restored monarch, by patent dated 20th March, 1660-1. Sir Thomas married first, Barbara, daughter of Gilbert Morewood, esq. of Seale, in the county of Leicester and by her had a son, Gilbert, who *d. s. p.* He *m.* secondly, Elizabeth, daughter of William Cockayn, esq. an alderman of London, and had

WILLIAM, his heir.
Mary, *m.* to Sir Robert Gayer, K.B.

Sir Thomas *d.* 15th October, 1667, aged sixty-six, and was *s.* by his son,

II. SIR WILLIAM RICH, who represented the city of Gloucester in parliament in 1698. He *m.* Lady Anne Bruce, daughter of Robert, Earl of Aylesbury, and was *s.* at his decease in 1711, by his only son,

III. SIR ROBERT RICH, who *m.* Mary, daughter of Sir William Walter, bart. of Sarsden, in Oxfordshire, by his wife, the Lady Mary Tufton, daughter of the Earl of Thanet, and had (with two daughters, one the wife of Captain Wilson of the guards, and the other of Walter Knight, esq. of Ruscomb, Berks.) five sons, viz.

WILLIAM, his successor.
Thomas, of Bombay, living in 1741.
Charles.
James.
Daniel, of the Temple.

He *d.* 9th November, 1724,* and was *s.* by his eldest son,

IV. SIR WILLIAM RICH, who *m.* Elizabeth, daughter of William Royall, esq. of Minstead, Hants, and had issue,

THOMAS, his heir.

* His lady survived him and was living at Sunning in 1741.

le d. 17th July, 1762, aged seventy, and was s. by his ...

v. SIR THOMAS RICH, vice-admiral R. N. m. Anne, daughter and co-heir of Richard Willis, esq. of Digswell, Herts, but died without legitimate issue, 6th April, 1803, when the BARONETCY EXPIRED.

Arms—Or, on a saltire, raguled, gules, five crosses, fitchy, of the first.

RICH, OF LONDON.

CREATED 4th Jan. 1675-6. EXTINCT 19th May, 1785.

Lineage.

The RICH's were originally of Hampshire, where

JOHN LE RICH, of Rich's Place, flourished about the reign of EDWARD II. His son and heir,

ROBERT LE RICH, was living *temp.* EDWARD III. and was father of

JOHN LE RICH, of Rich's Place, who was alive in the 13th of HENRY IV. and had two sons, RICHARD and William. The elder,

RICHARD RICH, was a mercer in the city of London, and one of the sheriffs thereof in 1441. He was a person of note in his time, and distinguished by some charitable foundations. He made his will in 1463, and bequeathed his body to be buried in the chapel of St. ...ry, within the church of St. Lawrence, *in veteri ...* He appointed Catherine, his daughter, and ...mas, his son, Robert Lane, chaplain, William Ma...er, John Walden, and Thomas Urswick, (the husbands of his daughters,) to be clothed, the day of his funeral, in black cloth, and that all the sons of his ... daughters, and one servant of Marewe, Waldon, ... Urswick, and all his own servants in London, be clothed in black cloth; and that the aforesaid Thomas ...wick, have for himself, and his wife, and all his children, to the buying of this vesture, forty shillings. ...side his daughters, this substantial citizen had two sons, viz.

I. JOHN, died in his father's lifetime, leaving a son,

JOHN, citizen and mercer of London, father of

THOMAS, who m. one of the daughters and co-heirs of Sir Edward Shaw, knt. lord mayor of London, and had a son and heir,

RICHARD RICH, esq. of Weld or Burntwood, in Essex, who m. Rachael, daughter of Thomas Newborough, esq. of Berkley, in Somersetshire, and had two sons, Robert, the younger, was a master in Chancery, 1620. The elder,

EDWARD RICH, esq. of Horndon, died in 1599, leaving by Joan, daughter and heir of Edward Sanders, of London, a son and heir,

ROBERT RICH, of Stondon, in Essex, who m. Elizabeth, daughter of Sir Thomas Dutton, knt. and was s. by his son,

NATHANIEL RICH, of Stondon, who m. first, Elizabeth, daughter of Sir Edmund Hampden, of Hampden, and secondly, Anne, dau. of John, Earl of Ancram, by the latter he had two sons,

1. NATHANIEL, receiver of the king's taxes in 1694, who m. Mary, daughter of Matthew Rud, and had several children.
2. ROBERT, of whom hereafter as successor to SIR CHARLES RICH, bart.

II. THOMAS.

The younger son,

THOMAS RICH, m. Elizabeth, daughter of one Meyne, of London, and had a son,

RICHARD RICH, who wedded Joan, daughter of — Dingley, and by her was father of

RICHARD RICH, a successful and intriguing lawyer in the time of HENRY VIII. who by pliancy, profligacy, and, it is said, perjury,* made his way to the honours and emoluments of his profession, and became LORD CHANCELLOR OF ENGLAND, when he was raised to the peerage, *anno* 1547, as LORD RICH. He m. Elizabeth, sister of William Jenks, of London, grocer, and dying in 1568, was s. by his eldest son,

ROBERT RICH, second Lord Rich, who m. Elizabeth, daughter and heir of George Baldry, esq. son and

---

* When solicitor-general, he was sent by the king, (HENRY VIII.) with Sir Richard Southwell and Mr. ... to take away Sir Thomas More's books, then ... in the Tower for refusing the oath of succession ... supremacy. Mr. Rich pretending friendship to him, ... protesting he had no commission to talk with him ... the affairs of the supremacy, put a case to him, ... if it were enacted by parliament, that Richard ... should be king, and that it should be treason in any ... deny it, what offence were it to contravene that ... Sir Thomas More answered, he should offend if he ... so, because he was bound by the act; but that this ... a case of little moment. Whereupon Sir Thomas ... he would propose a higher case; Suppose it were ... by parliament, that God should not be God, whe... were not an offence to say it according to the act. Rich replied, yes; but said withal, I will propose a middle case; the king, you know, is constituted supreme head of the church, why should not you, Master More, accept him for such, as you would me, if I were made king? More rejoined, the case is not the same; because, said he, a parliament can make a king, and depose him, and that every parliament man may give his consent thereto, but that a subject cannot be bound so in the case of supremacy. Rich swearing to this pretended conversation with the ex-chancellor, on the trial of that eminent man, was a great means of his condemnation. When he gave evidence in open court, Sir Thomas More exclaimed, "If I were a man, my lords, that had no regard to my oath, I had no occasion to be here as a criminal; and if this oath, Mr. Rich, you have taken be true, then I pray I may never see God's face; which were it otherwise, is an imprecation I would not be guilty of to gain the whole world."

heir of Sir Thomas Baldry, knt. an alderman of London, and had, with daughters, three sons, viz.

- Richard, *d. s. p.* in the lifetime of his father, leaving Katherine, daughter and co-heir of Sir Henry Knevit, knt. his widow.
- Robert, who became third Lord Rich, and from whom descended the subsequent Earls of Warwick and Holland of that family, (refer to Burke's *Extinct and Dormant Peerage.*)
- Edwin (Sir).

The third son,

Sir Edwin Rich, knt. of Mulbarton, in Norfolk, which manor he purchased from William Gresham, esq. in the 42nd of Elizabeth, *m.* Honora, daughter of Charles Worlick, esq. and had issue,

- Robert, who *m.* Elizabeth, daughter of Sir Adam Felton, of Playford, and *d. s. p.*
- Edwin (Sir), of Lincoln's Inn, who in 1675, gave £200 towards the repair of the roads between Wymondham and Attleburgh, in Norfolk, whereupon, by order of sessions, the justices ordered a pillar to be erected by the road side, in remembrance of the gift. He *m.* Jane, daughter of — Reeve, esq. and relict of Sir John Suckling, knt. and *d. s. p.* 16th November, 1675.
- Richard, *d. s. p.*
- Charles.
- Frances, *m.* to Nathaniel Acton, esq.
- Margaret.
- Honora.

The youngest son,

I. Charles Rich, esq. inherited the estate of Mulberton, on the decease of his brothers issueless. He was created a Baronet, as "Sir Charles Rich, of London," 24th January, 1675-6, with remainder to Robert Rich, esq. of Stondon, in Essex, second son of Nathaniel Rich, by Elizabeth Hampden, his wife. Sir Charles *m.* Elizabeth, daughter of Mr. Cholmondeley, and had two daughters, his co-heirs, viz.

- Elizabeth, *m.* to Peter Cevill, a French gentleman.
- Mary, *m.* to Robert Rich, esq. to whom the baronetcy was limited.

He *d.* 16th May, 1677, aged fifty-nine, and was *s.* by his son-in-law,

II. Sir Robert Rich, of Rosehall, in Suffolk, one of the lords of the Admiralty, and M.P. for Dunwich, *temp.* William III. By his wife, Mary, daughter and co-heir of his predecessor, he had, with several daughters, four sons, viz.

- Charles, } third and fourth baronets.
- Robert, }
- Nathaniel.
- Cholmondeley.

Sir Robert *d.* 1st October, 1699, and was *s.* by his eldest son,

III. Sir Charles Rich, who *d. s. p.* and was *s.* by his brother,

IV. Sir Robert Rich, a field mashal in the army, colonel of the 4th dragoons, and governor of Chelsea Hospital. He represented Dunwich in parliament, in the first parliament of George I. and sate afterwards for Beeralston and St. Ives. He *m.* one of the daughters and co-heirs of Col. Griffin, one of the clerks of the board of green cloth to *Queen* Anne, and had issue,

- Robert, his successor.
- George, *d.* unm.
- Elizabeth, *m.* to George, first Lord Lyttelton, (his lordship's second wife).
- Mary, *d.* unm.

He *d.* 1st February, 1768, and was *s.* by his elder son,

V. Sir Robert Rich, of Rosehall, Suffolk, who in 1756, was appointed governor of Londonderry and Culmore Fort, in Ireland, and in 1760, made a lieutenant-general. He *m.* Mary, sister of Peter, first Earl of Ludlow, and had an only daughter,

- Mary-Frances, who *m.* 4th January, 1794, the Rev. Charles Bostock, LL.D. of Shirley House, Hants.

Sir Robert *d.* 19th May, 1785, when, in default of male issue, the Baronetcy expired. The estate devolved upon Sir Robert's only daughter, whose husband assumed in consequence the surname and arms of Rich, and being created a Baronet in 1791, became Sir Charles Rich, of Shirley House, in the county of Hants. (See Burke's *Peerage and Baronetage*

Arms—Gules, a chevron between three crosses botoné, or.

RICHARDS, OF BRAMBLETYE HOUSE

Created 22nd Feb. 1683-4.

Supposed to be Dormant.

Lineage.

This family was founded by

John Richards, who came into England with the Queen Mother of Charles II. from Thoulouse, and had a numerous issue. His youngest son,

I. Sir James Richards, of Brambletye House, in the county of Suffolk, was first knighted by Charles II. for saving several men of war, and was created a Baronet by the same prince, 22nd February, 1683-4. He *m.* first, Mrs. Anne Popely, of Redhouse, in Bristol, and by her had two sons,

- John, his successor.
- Arthur.
- Elisabeth.

Sir James *m.* secondly, Beatrice Herrera, a Spanish lady, and by her had,

- Joseph, } third and fourth baronets.
- Philip, }
- James.
- Lewis.
- Clara.

He *d.* about the year 1705, and was *s.* by his eldest son,

II. Sir John Richards, a colonel in the Spanish service, and afterwards a merchant at Cadiz. He *d.* unm. and was *s.* by his half-brother,

III. Sir Joseph Richards, who *d.* unm. 2nd June, 1738, and was *s.* by his brother,

IV. Sir Philip Richards, a general officer in the Spanish service, who *m.* the eldest daughter of the Duke de Montemar, commander-in-chief of the Spanish forces sent into Italy in 1735. Of this Baronet and his descendants, nothing further is known.

Arms—Argent, a chevron, and in base a lion rampant, azure.

RIDGEWAY, OF TORRINGTON.

CREATED 25th Nov. 1612.

EXTINCT 7th Mar. 1713-14.

Lineage.

This family, anciently written RIDGEWAY, *alias* 'acock (alluding to which the old bearing of arms was three peacocks' heads erased), had been in Devonshire from a very early period, as manifested by the ollections of Sir William Pole, the best antiquary of hat county. The name may be presumed to have een local, there being two places so called in the hire,—one near Plymouth, the other in the parish of 'alcomb, near Honiton.

The first who advanced the family was

STEPHEN RIDGEWAY, who was one of the stewards f the city of Exeter 6 EDWARD IV. 1466, and mayor hereof 7 HENRY VII.; son or grandson to whom, in ll probability, was

JOHN RIDGEWAY, esq. who purchased from the I. hune of Dunster the manor of Tor, in the county f Devon, and was elected one of the representatives f the city of Exeter in the two first parliaments alled by *Queen* MARY. He *m.* Elizabeth, daughter f John Wentford, and was *s.* by his son,

THOMAS RIDGEWAY, esq. who purchased, in 1599, rom Sir Edward Seymour the scite of the Abbey of r. in Devon. He *m.* Mary, daughter of Thomas 'athwaite, esq. and co-heir of her mother, Grace, aughter and heir of John Barnhouse, esq. of Marsh, Devonshire, and by her had a son and heir,

I. SIR THOMAS RIDGEWAY, who was employed in reland in a military capacity *temp.* ELIZABETH, and lanted the first Protestant colony in that kingdom. le was high sheriff of Devonshire in 1600, and reeived the honour of knighthood. At the accession of ing JAMES to the throne of England he was elected ne of the knights of the shire for the county of Devon the first parliament called by that prince, who connued to employ him in some of the highest places of ust and command in Ireland, and had him sworn the privy council. He was advanced to the dignity BARONET 25th November, 1612; created a peer of e kingdom of Ireland in 1616, as Baron of Gallenidgeway; and advanced in 1622 to the earldom of ondonderry. He *m.* Cicely, sister and co-heir of enry Mackwilliam (the lady was maid of honour to ueen ELIZABETH), and had issue,

ROBERT, his heir.
Edward.
Macwilliam.

Marie, *d.* young.
Cassandra, *m.* to Sir Francis Willoughby, knt.

is lordship was *s.* by his eldest son,

II. SIR ROBERT RIDGEWAY, second Earl of Londonerry, who *m.* Elizabeth, daughter and heir of Sir 'n Weston, knt. of Lichfield, and was succeeded his son,

III. SIR WESTON RIDGEWAY, third Earl of Londonerry, who *m.* Martha, daughter of Sir Richard Temple, bart. and left, with several daughters, two sons, ROBERT and Thomas. The eldest son,

IV. SIR ROBERT RIDGEWAY, fourth Earl of Londonderry, *m.* Lucy, daughter of Sir William Jopson, bart. and had two daughters, his co-heirs, viz.

LUCY, *m.* to Arthur, fourth Earl of Donegal, and *d. s. p.* 16th July, 1736.
FRANCES, *m.* to Thomas Pitt, esq. M.P. for Wilton, who was created Earl of Londonderry.

His lordship died 7th March, 1713-14, when all his honours, including the BARONETCY, became EXTINCT. Tor Mohun, the old Ridgeway estate in Devon, was sold, about 1768, by the Earl of Donegal to Sir Robert Palk, bart. The scite of the Abbey of Tor was purchased from the first Earl of Londonderry, in 1653, by John Stawell, esq. of Indiho, from whom Sir George Cary, knt. purchased it in 1662.

Arms—Sa. a pair of wings conjoined and elevated arg.

ROBARTES, OF TRURO.

CREATED 3rd July, 1621.

EXTINCT 1764.

Lineage.

RICHARD ROBARTES, of Truro, in Cornwall, where he resided in the enjoyment of a considerable fortune in the time of HENRY VIII. *m.* Anne, daughter of — Jeffery, of St Breage, and had, with several daughters, two sons, viz.

JOHN, his heir.
Richard, father of
Sir Josias Robartes, knt. whose son,
Sir Francis Robartes, knt. died siezed of the manor of Bodmin, leaving a son and heir,
HUGH ROBARTES, with whom this branch expired, its estates reverting to the elder.

The elder son,

JOHN ROBARTES, esq. inherited a very ample estate, and dying in 1614, left, by Philippa, daughter of John Gavrigan, esq. of Gavrigan, in Cornwall, an only son,

SIR ROBERT ROBARTES, of Truro, who was sheriff of Cornwall in the time of his father, and received the honour of knighthood from *King* JAMES I. at Whitehall, in 1616. He was created a BARONET 3rd July, 1621, and in four years after, (1625) through the influence of the favourite Buckingham, to whom it is recorded that he paid ten thousand pounds, he was raised to the peerage as Baron Robartes, of Truro. He *m.* Frances, daughter and co-heir of John Hender, esq. of Botreaux Castle, in Cornwall, and had issue,

JOHN, his heir.

Mary, *m.* to William Rous, esq. of Halton, in Cornwall.
Jane, *m.* to Charles, Lord Lambert.

He *d.* in 1634, and was *s.* by his son,

II. SIR JOHN ROBARTES, second Lord Robartes. This nobleman took an active part against the king in the civil war, and had a command in Essex's army, at the battle of Edge Hill. He was afterwards governor of Plymouth, and lord lieutenant of the county of Devon. He retired, however, and lived in privacy at Lanhydrock, during the usurpation of Cromwell. In the end promoting the Restoration, he was favourably received by CHARLES, by whom his name was restored to the privy council, and in 1660, he was constituted lord lieutenant of Ireland. In 1679, he was created Viscount Bodmin and Earl of Radnor. His lordship m. first, Lady Lucy Rich, daughter of Robert, EARL OF WARWICK, and had issue,

- I. ROBERT, Viscount Bodmin, a man of eminent ability, who d. about the year 1681, at the court of Denmark, where he was ambassador. He m. Sarah, daughter and heir of John Bodvile, esq. of Bodvile Castle, in Carnarvonshire, and left issue,
  - 1. CHARLES-BODVILE, successor to his grandfather.
  - 2. Russell, one of the tellers of the Exchequer, m. Lady Mary Booth, daughter of Henry, Earl of Warrington, and had
    - HENRY, who succeeded as third Earl of Radnor.
    - MARY, m. to Thomas Hunt, esq. of Mollington Hall, in the county of Chester, and had two sons,
      - 1. THOMAS HUNT, of Mollington Hall, who m. Mary, daughter of Peter Bold, esq. of Bold Hall, and left a daughter,
        - ANNA-MARIA-HUNT, of whom hereafter as heiress of the Radnor estates.
      - 2. GEORGE HUNT, who s. to the property of HENRY, third Earl of Radnor.
      - 1. Isabella, m. to Col. Leigh, of Adlington.
      - 2. Sarah, d. unm.
      - 3. Lucy, m. to the Hon. George Booth, second son of George, first Lord Delamere.
      - 4. Essex, d. unm.
- II. Hender, M.P. for Bodmin, d. unm.
- III. John, d. young.

He m. secondly, Isabella, daughter of Sir John Smith, knt. and had nine other children, viz.

- IV. Francis, who sate in parliament in the times of CHARLES II., JAMES II., WILLIAM III., and *Queen* ANNE. He was distinguished in literature and science, and was vice-president of the Royal Society. He m. Lady Anne Boscawen, relict of Sir Hugh Boscawen, esq. and daughter of Wentworth, seventeenth Earl of Kildare, and had
  - 1. JOHN, who became fourth EARL OF RADNOR.
  - 2. Francis, m. Mary, daughter of William Wallis, esq. of Groveby, Wilts, and died in 1734, leaving an only son,
    - John.

  Mr. Francis Robartes, sen. d. at Chelsea in February, 1717-18.
- V. Henry, m. Miss Frances Coryton, and d. s. p.
- VI. Warwick.
- VII. Charles, d. unm.
- I. Isabella, m. first in 1669, to John, Lord Moore, afterwards second Earl of Drogheda, and secondly to Daniel Wycherly, esq. of Shropshire.
- II. Diana, d. unm.
- III. Araminta, m. to the Right Rev. Bishop H[illegible]kins.
- IV. Olimpia.
- V. Essex, m. to John Speccot, esq. of Penh[illegible], Cornwall.

Lord Radnor is characterised as "a stanch presbyterian, sour, and cynical; just in his administr[illegible] but vicious under the semblance of virtue. [illegible] above any of his quality; but stiff, obstinate, [illegible] and jealous, and every way intracticable." He [illegible] 1685, and was s. by his grandson,

III. SIR CHARLES-BODVILE ROBARTES, second [illegible] of Radnor. This nobleman was called to the pr[illegible] council by *King* WILLIAM III. and appointed [illegible] lieutenant and custos rotulorum of Cornwall, [illegible] warden of the Stanneries, and high sheriff [illegible] duchy. In the reign of GEORGE I. he was made [illegible]surer of the chamber, constable of Carnarvon Cas[illegible] and re-sworn of the privy council. He m. E[illegible] daughter and heir of Sir John Cutler, knt. [illegible] city of London, with whom he acquired the [illegible] of Wimpole, in Cambridgeshire, which he so[illegible] Lord Hardwicke. He died s. p. in 1723, and [illegible] by his nephew,

IV. SIR HENRY ROBARTES, third Earl of Radnor who d. unm. at Paris in 1741, and was s. in [illegible]nours by his cousin,

V. SIR JOHN ROBARTES, fourth Earl of Radnor who d. unm. in 1764, when all the honours, including [illegible] BARONETCY, became EXTINCT.

On the decease of HENRY, third earl and [illegible] baronet, the estates devolved upon that [illegible] man's nephew,

GEORGE HUNT, esq. of Lanhydrock, [illegible] wall, who d. s. p. and was s. by his [illegible]

ANNA-MARIA HUNT, who m. 15th [illegible]ber, 1804, the Hon. Charles [illegible] Agar, youngest son of John, [illegible] count Clifden, by whom, (who [illegible] June, 1811,) she had a son and [illegible].

THOMAS-JAMES AGAR, who assumed [illegible] additional surname of R[illegible] and is now (1837) of Lanh[illegible] (See BURKE'S *Commoners*, vol. [illegible] p. 316.)

Arms—Az. three estoiles of six points, and [illegible] waved or.

ROBERTS, OF GLASSENBURY

Lineage.

This family was said to have derived from a [illegible]man of Scotland, one

WILLIAM ROOKHERST, who came into England [illegible] settled at Goodhurst, in Kent, in the third [illegible] the reign of HENRY I. He assumed afterwards [illegible]

surname of ROBERTS;* and having purchased certain lands in Goudhurst, called Winchet Hill, he there built a mansion, calling it Rookherst, after his own name. Here his descendants continued for 274 years, until the reign of RICHARD II. when

STEPHEN ROOBERTES marrying the daughter and heir of William Tyllye, esq. to whom the manor and lands of Glassenbury belonged, was, in her right, possessed thereof, and built "a fair sumptuous house" on the hill of Glassenbury, which came by lineal descent to

WALTER ROBERTHE, esq. who, in the year 1472, caused the same to be pulled down, and the next year erected, at the charge of eighteen hundred pounds, another moated house in the valley of Glassenbury and parish of Cranebrook, which ever afterwards continued the abode of the family.† This Walter became possessed of the whole estate by the death of his brother Stephen, who died without issue. He was a person much famed for his eminent qualifications and hospitality, as also for adhering to the Lancastrian interest, by which he became a great sufferer during the rule of RICHARD III. Having concealed Sir John Guldeford in his house at Glassenbury, where that person was seized by Sir Edward Stanley and Sir John Savage, he was attainted of treason, his lands seized, and forced himself to abscond until the accession of HENRY VII. when he was restored to his possessions. In the 4th of that reign he had a grant from the crown to impark six hundred acres of land and one thousand acres of wood in Cranebrook, Gowdehurst, and Ticehurst, in the counties of Kent and Sussex; as also that he and his heirs should have free warren in all his lands and woods, and fishing in his waters, in the parishes aforesaid, with all liberties and franchisements in such cases granted. He was sheriff of the county of Kent in the same year, and having lived under six kings, HENRY VI. EDWARD IV. EDWARD V. RICHARD III. HENRY VII. and HENRY VIII. departed this life at more than eighty years of age, A.D. 1522. This Walter m. first, 23rd October, 1463, Margaret, daughter and heir of John Penn, esq. of Penn's Place, Herts; secondly (his first wife dying 4th May, 14[illegible]), Isabel, daughter of Sir John Culpeper, knt. and thirdly, Alice, daughter of Richard Naylor, esq. and widow of Lord Abergavenny: by those ladies he had no less than thirty children.‡ His son and heir,

THOMAS ROBERTES, esq. of Glassenbury, was sheriff of Kent 25 HENRY VIII. He m. Elizabeth, daughter of James Frammingham, esq. of Suffolk, and had issue,

WALTER, his heir.
Thomas, who died in 1567.
John, ancestor of the Roberts of *Bornell Ticehurst*, and Stone House, Warbleton, Sussex.
Mary, m. to Thomas Cheney, of Woodley.
Jane, m. first, to Richard Burston; and secondly, to Richard Love.

Dying in 1537, he was s. by his son,

WALTER ROBERTES, esq. of Glassenbury, who married Frances, daughter of Mr. Alderman John Maynard, of London (which lady was born when the *Emperor* CHARLES V. visited England, and had the honour to have his imperial majesty for her godfather); by her he had issue,

THOMAS (Sir), his heir.
Edmund, m. Judith, third daughter of William Bird, esq. of the city of London, and widow of Thomas Blunt. He died 12th September, 1625, leaving issue.
Alexander, of Therp, near Egham, in Surrey. This gentleman was a great traveller. He m. a daughter of Thomas Culwich, esq. of London, and dying in 1640, left issue.

The eldest son and heir,

I. SIR THOMAS ROBERTS, of Glassenbury, who was knighted by *King* JAMES I. at Whitehall, before his coronation, 23rd July, 1603, and was created a BARONET 3rd July, 1620. He m. Frances, daughter of Martyn James, esq. of Smarden, in Kent, and had issue,

WALTER (Sir), his successor.
Thomas, John, William, } all d. unm.
Frances, m. first, to John Hooper, esq. of Stockberry; and secondly, to Henry Crisp, esq.
Elizabeth, m. to Sir Alexander Culpeper, knt. of Bedgbury.
Anne, m. to Thomas Crisp, esq. of Goudhurst.

Sir Thomas is described as "hospitable without excess, and charitable without ostentation." It is farther stated, that "in all other respects he shewed himself a prudent and judicious gentleman, a lover of his country, and a good Christian; he valued the memory of his ancestors, and bore in his mind their good actions, as well as the care they had taken in preserving the estate entire for many generations; whereupon, in the year 1599, he caused an inscription to be set up in the church of Cranebrook, containing a memorial of his family, that his posterity, having it always before their eyes, might be induced to imitate their example, and preserve the credit and repute his forefathers had lived in." He d. 21st February, 1627, and was s. by his son,

II. SIR WALTER ROBERTS, who was knighted by *King* JAMES at Greenwich 7th May, 1624. This gentleman augmented his estate by marrying Margaret, daughter and heir of George Roberts, esq. of Brenchley, in Kent, and had five sons and three daughters, but none of them survived him. His eldest son,

THOMAS, m. Elizabeth, daughter and heir of Sir Matthew Howland, knt. and dying 23rd January, 1636, left two sons, viz.

HOWLAND, who succeeded his grandfather as third baronet.
Walter, who assumed the name of HOWLAND on inheriting the estate of Bristow Causey, in Surrey, from his mother's family. He m. Elizabeth, daughter of — Nutting, esq. of Cambridge, but leaving no issue, his possessions devolved upon his nephew, Sir Thomas Roberts.

Sir Walter was s. at his decease by his grandson,

III. SIR HOWLAND ROBERTS, who m. Bridget, daughter of Sir Robert Jocelyn, knt. of Hyde Hall, in Hertfordshire, and had issue,

* The name was at different times written ROOBERTES, [illegible], ROBERD, ROBERT, ROBERTHE, and ROBERTS.

† There were successively from WILLIAM ROOKHERST, alias ROBERTS, thirteen esquires of the name and progeny who dwelt in the parishes of Goudherst and Cranebrook to the year 1599, when Thomas Roberts, esq. of Glassenbury, erected a plain monument of black marble in the chancel of the church of Cranebrook, with an inscription thereon setting forth the descent of his family as here related.

‡ Of whom the following, mentioned in his will, survived to maturity: THOMAS, his eldest son, Clement, John, William, George, Edmund, and Martin; Elizabeth Hendley, Mary St.-Nicholas, Joan Horden, Elizabeth Tukke, Joan Leed, Dorothy St.-Nicholas. On those and their heirs male he entails his estates, remainder to William Ashburnham, of Ashburnham, and his heirs male.

Thomas, his heir.

Jocelyn, *b.* 29th October, 1659; *m.* Hannah, second daughter of Joseph Harris, citizen and merchant taylor, of London, and left three daughters, viz.

1. Bridget, *m.* to Edmund Farrington, a Turkey merchant.
2. Hannah, *m.* to Mr. Langton, of London, goldsmith.
3. Rebecca, *d.* unm.

Bridget, *b.* in 1657; *m.* 5th October, 1675, to Edmund Trench, of London.

Elizabeth, *b.* in 1661, *d.* young.

Dorothy, *b.* in 1662, after the decease of her father; *m.* to John Spence, esq. of Malling, in Sussex.

Sir Howland *d.* in November, 1661, aged twenty-seven, and was *s.* by his elder son,

iv. Sir Thomas Roberts, *b.* 2nd December, 1658, who was returned knight for the county of Kent in 1691, and again 7 William III. He *m.* 31st May, 1683, Jane, daughter and co-heir of Sir John Beale, bart. of Farningham, in Kent, and had issue,

Thomas, his successor.

Walter, heir to his brother.

Jane, *b.* 5th April, 1684; *m.* Samuel Trench, of London; and *d. s. p.* 20th October, 1706.

Bridget, *b.* 1st December, 1686; *m.* to Edmund Trench, of London; and *d.* 9th June, 1720, leaving a son,

Edmund Trench, who *d.* in 1725.

Sir Thomas *d.* 20th November, 1706, in the forty-eighth year of his age, and was *s.* by his son,

v. Sir Thomas Roberts, *b.* 27th June, 1689. This gentleman *m.* in 1714, Elizabeth, only daughter and heir of Samuel Newbery, citizen of London, but died *s. p.* 5th January, 1729-30 (his lady died 30th July, 1727), and was *s.* by his brother,

vi. Sir Walter Roberts, who *m.* in 1726, Elizabeth, only daughter and heir of William Slaughter, esq. of Rochester, and had by her, who died 15th July, 1744, two daughters, viz.

Elizabeth, who died in 1743, aged sixteen.

Jane, *m.* in 1752, to George, third Duke of St. Albans, and *d. s. p.* in December, 1778.

Sir Walter died 7th July, 1745, when the Baronetcy expired. The manor of Glassenbury was devised to Sir Thomas Roberts, bart. of Ireland.

Arms—Az. on a chevron arg. three mullets sa.

ROBERTS, OF WILLESDON.

Created 8th Nov. 1661.

Extinct in 1700.

Lineage.

Edmund Roberts, esq. of Willesdon, in Middlesex, who died in 1585, left by Katharine, his first wife, sister of Sir Robert Chester, knt. three sons and three daughters, viz.

Francis, his heir.

Thomas, of Leicester, who *m.* Anne, daughter of Thomas Burnaby, of Watford, in Northamptonshire, and had issue.

Edmund, *d.* unm.

Katherine, *m.* to Ciampenti Haliano, an Italian.

Elizabeth, *m.* to Mr. Windoner, proctor of civil law.

Mary, *d.* unm.

The eldest son,

Francis Roberts, esq. of Willesdon, *m.* Mary, eldest daughter and co-heir of John Barne, second son of Sir George Barne, knt. lord mayor of London, and had issue,

Barne, who *m.* Mary, daughter of Sir William Glover, knt. alderman of London, and dying *v. p.* 30th January, 1616, left issue,

Barne, *b.* in 1605, *d.* at Eton College.

William, successor to his grandfather.

Anne, *m.* to Dr. King, M.D. of St. Albans and was mother of Sir John King, knt.

Robert, rector of Hinksworth, Herts, *d.* 11th May 1636.

Frances, *m.* to Richard Franklyn, esq. and was mother of Sir John Franklyn, knt. M.P. for Middlesex in four parliaments.

Jane, *m.* first, to Sir Thomas Glover, knt. of London; and secondly, to George Purefoy, esq.

Elizabeth, *m.* to Sir J. Saunders.

Francis Roberts died in 1631, and was *s.* by his grandson,

i. William Roberts, esq. of Willesdon, *b.* in [illegible], who, during the civil conflicts of the reign of Charles I. sided with the parliament, and was one of the commissioners appointed to try the ill-fated monarch. By Cromwell he was called to the upper house in 165[illegible] and after the restoration created a Baronet. By Eleanor, his first wife, daughter and heir of Robert Atye, esq. of Kilbourne, in Middlesex, Sir William had issue,

William, his heir.

Thomas, baptized 6th July, 1645, who had two sons and five daughters, namely,

William, who *s.* as fourth baronet.

Thomas, *d.* unm.

Judith, who was married.

Eleanor, wife of the Rev. T. Knight, curate of Willesdon.

Mary, *m.* to the Rev. William Hawkins, vicar of Willesdon.

Elizabeth, *m.* to Thomas Lander, of London.

Sarah, *m.* to Mr. Pattinson.

Francis, baptized 29th November, 1646.

Richard, baptized 9th April, 1648.

Mary, *m.* 27th June, 1649, to Thomas Harr[illegible], esq. of South Mimms.

Anne, *m.* to John Nelthorpe, esq. of Willesdon.

Jane, *m.* to Samuel Gibbs, esq. of Stoke Neyland, Suffolk.

Frances, baptized 6th March, 1635-6.

Elizabeth, baptized 22nd September, 1639.

Eleanor, *m.* 16th November, 1654, to Luke Carwell, esq.

Sir William *d.* in September, 1662, and was *s.* by his son,

ii. Sir William Roberts, of Willesdon, baptized 24th June, 1638, who died 9th March, 1687, leaving a son and successor,

iii. Sir William Roberts, of Willesdon, at whose decease unmarried 18th May, 1698, aged thirty-[illegible] the title passed to his cousin,

iv. Sir William Roberts, of Willesdon, who m. Elizabeth, daughter of Francis, Lord Howard of

Effingham, but *d. s. p.* in 1709, when the Baronetcy expired. His widow *m.* secondly, William Hutchinson, who was of Willesdon during his wife's life.

Arms—Arg. six pheons sa. on a chief of the second a greyhound current of the first, gorged or.

ROBERTS, OF BOW.

Created 2nd Feb. 1690-1.—Extinct 14th Dec. 1693.

Lineage.

I. John Roberts, esq. of Bow, in Essex, was created a Baronet in 1690-1. He *m.* first, Mary, daughter of William Amy, merchant, of Exeter; and secondly, Deborah, daughter of Mr. Powell, merchant, of Bristol, and widow of Mr. Buffett, of London, silkman; but died without issue 14th December, 1693, when the title became extinct.

ROBERTSON, OF HOLLAND.

Created 20th Feb. 1677.

Extinct 18th Jan. 1835.

Lineage.

I. Alexander Robertson, esq. (a descendant of the ancient family of Robertson, of Strowan, see Burke's *Commoners*,) was created a Baronet of England 20th February, 1677. He subsequently settled in Holland, acquired a considerable fortune there, and assumed the name of Colyear. Sir Alexander was *s.* at his decease by his elder son,

II. Sir David Colyear, a military officer of high reputation, who distinguished himself in 1674, as commander of the Scots' regiment in the pay of the United States of Holland, and afterwards under the banner of the Prince of Orange, in the years 1689 and 1690, in Ireland. Sir David was elevated to the peerage of Scotland 1st June, 1699, by the title of *Lord Portmore and Blackness*; and created 13th April, 1703, *Baron Colyear*, *Viscount Milsington*, and Earl of Portmore. The earl *m.* Katharine, only child of Sir Charles Sidley, bart. of Southfield, in the county of Kent, (mistress to *King* James II. by whom she had an only surviving daughter, Lady Catherine-Darnley, who *m.* first, James, Earl of Anglesey; and secondly, John Sheffield, Duke of Buckingham and Normanby,) who had been created 20th January, 1685, Baroness of Darlington and Countess of Dorchester, for life, with a pension of £5000 a year on the Irish establishment. His lordship *d.* in 1729, and was *s.* by his only surviving son,

III. Sir Charles Colyear, second earl, K.T. His lordship, *m.* in 1732, Juliana, daughter of Roger Hale, esq. and relict of Peregrine, third Duke of Leeds, and dying in 1785, left issue,

- William-Charles, his heir.
- Juliana, *m.* Henry Dawkins, esq. of Sandlynch, and their son and heir, James Dawkins, esq. has assumed the surname of Colyear.

The son and successor,

IV. Sir William-Charles Colyear, third earl, *m.* in 1770, Mary, second daughter of John, eighth Earl of Rothes, by whom he left issue,

- Thomas-Charles, the present earl.
- William, lieutenant colonel in the army, and equerry to the Duke of Cumberland, died *s. p.*
- Catherine-Caroline, *m.* 9th October, 1810, to Joseph Brecknell, esq.

His lordship *d.* in 1823, and was *s.* by his son,

V. Sir Thomas-Charles Colyear, fourth Earl of Portmore, who *m.* first, 26th May, 1793, Lady Mary-Elizabeth Bertie, only child of Brownlow, fifth Duke of Ancaster, by whom, who died in 1797, he had a son,

- Brownlow-Charles, who inherited the great personal property of his grandfather, the Duke of Ancaster, at the decease of that nobleman in 1809, but died at Rome, in 1819, of wounds received from a banditti.

The earl wedded, secondly, 6th September, 1828, Frances, youngest daughter of William Murrells, esq. His lordship *d.* 18th January, 1835, when all his honours including the Baronetcy, became extinct.

Creations—Baronet, 20th February, 1677. Baron, 1st June, 1699. Earl, &c. 13th April, 1703.

Arms—Gu. on a chevron between three wolves' heads, truncated and erased ar. as many oak-trees, eradicated, ppr. fructed or.

ROBINSON, OF NEWBY.

Created 30th July, 1660.

Extinct 6th Feb. 1689.

Lineage.

William Robinson, an eminent Hamburgh merchant, who resided several years at Hamburgh, Lubeck, and other Hans town, settling at York in *Queen* Elizabeth's reign, was twice lord mayor of that city, and twice represented it in parliament. He *m.* first, the daughter of John Redman, of Fulworth, in Yorkshire, and had a son, William, his heir. He *m.* secondly, the daughter of Thomas Harrison, of York, and by her had another son, Thomas. Between these two sons he fairly divided his property at his decease in 1616, aged ninety-four, leaving to the city of York £80 and a silver bowl doubly gilt, and to the Company of Merchants of the same city £40. The younger son, Thomas, inherited the estates in Richmond, but he *d. s. p.* in 1625, when the whole fortune centred in the elder son,

William Robinson, esq. This gentleman served the office of sheriff for the city of York in 1607. He was elected alderman in 1616, and lord mayor in three years after. He *m.* Margaret, daughter of Sir Henry Jenkins, knt. of Grimstone, and dying about 1626, was *s.* by his son,

Sir William Robinson, M.P. for the city of York, who was knighted by *King* Charles I. at Edinburgh in 1633, and was sheriff of Yorkshire in 1639. He *m.* first, Mary, daughter and co-heir of Sir William Bamburgh, bart. of Housam, in the county of York, and by her had a son, William, who *d. s. p.* He *m.* secondly, Frances, daughter of Sir Thomas Metcalfe, knt. of Nappa, and by that lady had two sons and three daughters, viz.

METCALFE, his heir.

Thomas, who *m.* Elizabeth, daughter of Charles Tancred, esq. of Arden, in Yorkshire, and had issue,

WILLIAM, heir to the estates of his uncle Metcalfe.

Tancred, of London, M.D. who lived to an advanced age, and had one son.

Elizabeth.

Margaret.

Elizabeth, *m.* to Philip Rycot, merchant.

Margaret, *m.* to William Weddell, esq. of Erswick, in the county of York.

Frances, *m.* to Robert Bell, esq. of Overton, also in Yorkshire.

Sir William *d.* in 1658, and was *s.* by his elder son,

I. METCALFE ROBINSON, esq. of Newby, in the county of York, who was created a BARONET 30th July, 1660. He *m.* Margaret, daughter of Sir William D'Arcy, of Witton Castle, in the county of Durham, but left no issue. Sir Metcalfe represented the city of York in three parliaments, *temp.* CHARLES II. He *d.* 6th February, 1688-9, and was interred at Topcliffe, in Yorkshire; where, towards the east end of the north aisle of that church, is a handsome monument, railed in, with Sir Metcalfe Robinson's bust, encircled with a curious garland and ornamented with the trophies of war. At his decease the BARONETCY EXPIRED, while the estates devolved upon his nephew,

WILLIAM ROBINSON, esq. who was created a BARONET in 1689. From this Sir William Robinson lineally descend the EARLS DE GREY and OF RIPON. (Refer to BURKE'S *Peerage and Baronetage.*)

Arms—Vert, a chevron between three bucks standing at gaze or.

ROBINSON, OF KENTWELL HALL, IN LONG MELFORD.

CREATED 26th Jan. 1681-2.

EXTINCT 21st April, 1743.

Lineage.

I. SIR THOMAS ROBINSON, knt. prothonotary of the Court of Common Pleas, was created a BARONET by *King* CHARLES II. 20th January, 1681-2. He *m.* Jane, daughter of Lumley Dew, esq. of Bishop's Upton, in the county of Hereford, and had several children. Sir Thomas lost his life, 12th August, 1683, by leaping from his chamber-window in the Middle Temple to avoid the fury of a fire, and was *s.* by his then only surviving child,

II. SIR LUMLEY ROBINSON, who *m.* Anne, daughter and heir of John Laurence, esq. of Westminster, by whom (who *m.* secondly, Sir William Foulis, bart. of Ingleby, in the county of York,) he had

THOMAS, his successor.

Anne, *m.* to Sir Comport Fitch, knt.

He *d.* aged thirty-six, 6th June, 1684, was buried in Westminster Abbey, and *s.* by his son,

III. SIR THOMAS ROBINSON, who *m.* Elizabeth, daughter of Sir Thomas Hare, bart. of Stow Bardolph, in Norfolk, but *d. s. p.* 21st April, 1743, when the BARONETCY EXPIRED.

Arms—Vert, on a chevron between three bucks trippant or, three cinquefoils gu.

RODES, OF BARLBOROUGH.

CREATED 14th Aug. 1641.

EXTINCT in Oct. 1743.

Lineage.

The family of RODES is one of great antiquity, having flourished for several centuries in the counties of Nottingham, Lincoln, York, and Derby, successively. Its patriarch,

GERARD DE RODES, a baron, the capital seat of whose barony was Horn Castle,* in Lincolnshire, lived in the reigns of HENRY II. RICHARD I. JOHN, and HENRY III. from all of whom he received great favours, and by *King* JOHN was employed as an ambassador. His lineal descendant,

WILLIAM RODES, of Thorp *juxta* Rotheram, in the county of York, *m.* Anne, daughter and heir of John Cachehorse, esq. of Stavely Woodthorpe, in the county of Derby, and was father of

JOHN RODES, esq. of Stavely Woodthorpe, who was his son,

JOHN RODES, esq. was father of

ROBERT RODES, esq. who *m.* Elizabeth Wasse, and left a son and heir,

JOHN RODES, esq. of Stavely Woodthorpe, who *m.* Attelina, daughter of Thomas Hewitt, esq. of Wales, in Yorkshire. He was sheriff of Derbyshire, and was *s.* at his decease by his son,

FRANCIS RODES, esq. of Stavely Woodthorpe, was one of the judges of the Common Pleas in the time of ELIZABETH. This learned person erected Barlborough Hall in 1583, but died at Stavely Woodthorpe a few years after its completion. He *m.* first, Elizabeth, daughter of Brian Sandford, esq. of Thorpe Salvine, in Yorkshire, and by that lady had

JOHN (Sir), his heir.

Peter, of Hickleton.

* As we find in CAMDEN that the barony of Horn Castle was a soke or seigniory of thirteen lordships, Gerard de Rodes was consequently a "greater baron," and as ambassador he attained a still higher rank; his absence in that capacity will account for his name not occurring on the roll of Magna Charta. BURKE's *Commoners.*

He m. secondly, Mary, daughter of Francis Charlton, esq. of Appley, in Shropshire, and by her had

Godfrey (Sir), of Great Houghton, knighted in 1615, who married four wives, and left, with other issue, Elizabeth, the third wife and widow of the ill-fated Earl of Strafford, and a son and heir,

Sir Edward Rodes, knt. of Great Houghton, whose male line terminated with

William Rodes, esq. of Great Houghton, who died unmarried in 1740, leaving his two sisters his co-heirs, namely,

Mary, d. unm. in 1789.

Martha, m. to Hans Busk, esq. of Leeds, and had, with other issue who died issueless,

Rachael Busk, who m. Richard Slater Milnes, esq. of Fryston.

Frances, m. to Sir Richard Tempest, knt.

Judith, m. to Jonas Waterhouse, esq.

Bridget, d. unm.

The judge's eldest son,

Sir John Rodes, who was knighted at the Tower [illegible]th March, 1603, served as sheriff of Derbyshire 36 Elizabeth. He sold Stavely Woodthorpe to the Duke of Portland, and resided entirely at Barlborough. He m. first, Anne, daughter of George Benson, esq. of the county of Westmoreland, but by her had no issue; secondly, Dorothy, daughter of George Savile, esq. of Thornhill, by whom he had one son,

John, of Horbury, who is said to have been disinherited by his father. There is the strongest presumptive evidence that this John Rodes was the founder of the Devonshire family of Rodes of Bellair, now represented by George-Ambrose Rhodes, esq. of Bellair and Shapwick. (See Burke's *Commoners*, vol. iii. p. 566.)

Sir John m. thirdly, Frances, daughter of Marmaduke Constable, esq. of Holdernesse, and relict of Henry [illegible]k, esq. and by that lady had

Francis, his heir, the elder son having been disinherited.

Henry, d. young.

Lennox, m. to Sir Marmaduke Langdale.

Catherine, m. to Sir John Hotham, bart.

He d. in 1639, and was s. by his son,

I. Francis Rodes, esq. of Barlborough, in the county of Derby, who received the honour of knighthood at Whitehall 9th August, 1641, and was created a Baronet on the 14th of the same month. Sir Francis m. Elizabeth, daughter and sole heir of Sir George Las-[illegible], knt. of Sturton and Gateford, Notts, and by her (who m. secondly, Allan Lockhart, esq. and d. in 1666,) had issue,

Francis, his successor.

Peter, a divine, slain at Winfield Manor.

Clifton, of Sturton, who m. first, Lettice, daughter of Sir Gervase Clifton, bart. of Clifton, by whom he had a son, Gervase, who died an infant. He m. secondly, Elizabeth, daughter of John Scrimshire, esq. of Cottgrave, Notts, and had

John, who d. s. p.

Anne, m. to Dr. Witringham, rector of Retford, Notts.

John, of Sturton, m. Elizabeth, daughter of Simon Jessop, esq. of Colton, in Staffordshire, and had

John, m. Mary, daughter of William Tigh, citizen of London, and left issue.

Francis, } went to America.
Charles, }

Anne, m. to Mr. Harrison.

Peter, } left no issue.
George, }

Sir Francis d. in 1645, and was s. by his eldest son,

II. Sir Francis Rodes, who m. Anne, daughter of Sir Gervase Clifton, bart. of Clifton, and had, with a daughter, Frances, the wife of William Hussey, esq. a son and successor at his decease 3rd May, 1651,

III. Sir Francis Rodes. This gentleman wedded Martha, daughter of William Thornton, esq. of Grantham, in the county of Lincoln, and had one son and two daughters, viz.

John, his heir.

Frances, m. to Gilbert Heathcote, M.D. of Cutthorp, in Derbyshire, and had issue,

I. Cornelius Heathcote, M.D. who m. Elizabeth Middlebrooke, of Thorn, in Yorkshire, and had

Gilbert Heathcote, of whom presently as heir to his great-uncle, Sir John Rodes.

John Heathcote, who died aged twenty-eight, leaving by Milicent Saterthwaite, his wife,

1. Cornelius Heathcote, heir to his uncle Gilbert.

2. John Heathcote, d. unm.

1. Elizabeth Heathcote, m. to the Rev. Philip Acklom Reaston, rector of Barlborough, and had a son,

Cornelius-Heathcote Reaston, who succeeded his uncle, Cornelius Heathcote, in the estates of Rodes.

2. Mary Heathcote, m. first, to Miers; and secondly, to Capt. Massey.

I. Martha Heathcote, m. to Benjamin Bartlett, esq. of Bradford.

II. Elizabeth Heathcote, m. to Peter Acklom, esq. of Hornsey.

Anne, m. to William Thonton, esq. of Bloxham.

Sir Francis d. in March, 1675, and was s. by his only son,

IV. Sir John Rodes, who d. unmarried in October, 1743, when the Baronetcy expired, and the estates devolved upon his great-nephew, Gilbert Heathcote, who assuming the name of Rodes, became

Gilbert Rodes, esq. of Barlborough.* He d. unmarried in 1768, and was s. by his nephew,

Cornelius Heathcote, who also assumed the name of Rodes, and also died a bachelor, at the age of seventy, 6th March, 1825, when the estates passed to his nephew,

The Rev. Cornelius-Heathcote Reaston, who assumed the surname of Rodes, and is now (1837) of Barlborough.

Arms—Arg. two cottises erm. and in a bend a lion passant gu. between two acorns az.

---

* "Barlborough Hall," says Pilkington, "is a handsome mansion of the age of Queen Elizabeth, having been built in her reign by Francis Rodes, one of the justices of the Common Pleas." The principal front of this house retains its original appearance, having projecting bows terminating in octagonal embattled turrets and large transom windows.

ROKEBY, OF SKIERS.

CREATED 29th Jan. 1660-1.

EXTINCT in July, 1678.

Lineage.

"A celebrity has recently been given (we quote the learned historian of Yorkshire, the Rev. Joseph Hunter,) to the romantic beauties of 'Rokeby,' by Sir Walter Scott. Few persons visit the neighbourhood without observing with what extreme accuracy of observation and felicity of expression the bard has described the passage through the glen:

> A stern and lone, yet lovely road,
> As e'er the foot of minstrel trode;

or view 'Egliston's grey ruins,' or 'Rokeby's turrets high,' without feeling that the charm of poetry is thrown over them."

The poet has touched upon the historical interest which belongs to Rokeby and Mortham, and has given what professes to be a pedigree of their ancient lords, but it was no part of *his* plan to enter *critically* into their history. We shall endeavour to do so more minutely, and present the reader with more definite information on the antiquity, the character, and eminent services of the family who held for many centuries this now classic spot.

At the period of the Conquest, all the territory abutting on the Tees, at their northern border, was granted to Alan, Earl of Bretagne, and formed his English Earldom of Richmond. These broad lands were partioned among the junior members of his family and his followers, and in the distribution, Rokeby became part of the possessions of the Fitz Alans, a northern baronial house, whose chief seat was at Bedale. But their interest at Rokeby was scarcely more than nominal for, beneath them, was a subinfeudation, in favour of a family which, residing on the lands of Rokeby, was usually described as "De Rokeby," and eventually assumed that name as a personal appellative.

Tradition asserts that the family had been seated on these lands in Saxon times, but it first appeared prominent in public affairs in the person of THOMAS DE ROKEBY, whose rise in royal favour is circumstantially related by Froissart. "In the 1st year of the reign of EDWARD III." says the old Chronicler, "the Scots, under the command of the Earl of Moray and Sir James Douglas, ravaged the country as far as Newcastle. Edward was in those parts with a more powerful army, and an engagement was expected and wished for, when the Scotch army suddenly disappeared, and no information could be gained respecting the route they had taken. The young king caused it to be proclaimed throughout the host, that whoever should bring certain intelligence where the Scotch army were, should have one hundred pounds a year in land, and be made a knight by the king himself. Immediately fifteen or sixteen knights and esquires passed the river with much danger, ascended the mountains, and then separated, each taking different routes. On the fourth day, Rokeby, who was one of them, gave the king exact information where the Scotch army lay." "This," continues Hunter, "is not a legendary story invented by some family annalist or doating chronicler of public affairs, the veracity of the narrative being here supported by the most authentic records of the realm; and it is a gratifying fact that we are so often enabled to prove circumstances in our old Chronicles, (which on a first view have an air of romance and fable,) by fiscal documents, where least of all anything imaginatory is to be found. In the Patent Rolls, 1 EDWARD III. m. 7, is a grant to Thomas de Rokeby of £100, to be taken annually from the Exchequer 'till £100 lands shall be provided for him, in which the service is described nearly as it is related by Froissart, and in the same rolls, 3 EDWARD III. m. 7. is a grant to him in fee of the manor of Paulinesgray, in Kent, with lands in the North which had lately belonged to Michael and Andrew de Harcla, forfeited, in release of his £100 annuity from the Exchequer. Sir Thomas Rokeby subsequently held commands against the Scots, was twice high sheriff of Yorkshire, and became (12 and 13 EDWARD III. governor of the castles of Berwick, Edinburgh, and Stirling. In 1346, he pre-eminently distinguished himself at the battle of Neville's Cross, and was one of the few magnates present at that engagement to whom the letter of thanks was addressed, of which a copy is to be found in the Fœdera. In 1349, he went to Ireland as lord justice, and held that appointment until 1355, when Maurice Fitz Thomas, Earl of Desmond, succeeded him. The administration of Sir Thomas Rokeby, in Ireland, is famous for the attempt he made to abolish the custom of *coigne and livery*, a species of arbitrary purveyance for the persons in authority there, and a tradition has been handed down attested by Hollinshead, that being once censured for using wooden dishes and cups, as not befitting his degree, Sir Thomas replied, that he would rather drink out of such cups and pay gold and silver, than drink out of gold and silver and make wooden payments. In the latter transactions of his life, Sir Thomas appears with the addition, "the Uncle," to his name, and another Sir Thomas Rokeby occurs, styled "the Nephew." He seems to have participated in the triumph of Neville's Cross, and to have accompanied the elder Rokeby to Ireland. A third SIR THOMAS ROKEBY, was high sheriff of Yorkshire, 8th HENRY IV. and during the year of his shrievalty, the Earl of Northumberland made his last attempt to dethrone *King* HENRY. Sir Thomas collecting the posse comitatus, met the earl at Bramham Moore, and a conflict ensued in which Nothumberland and the Lord Bardolph were slain. The next Rokebys, distinguished in state affairs, were WILLIAM ROKEBY, lord chancellor of Ireland and Archbishop of Dublin, who died in 1521, and Sir Richard Rokeby, his younger brother, comptroller to Cardinal Wolsey. The archbishop was interred in a sepulchral chapel built by himself at Sandal Parva in Yorkshire, and his tomb still remains. While the eminent churchman was running the race of high preferment, the eldest branch of the family remained quietly on the hereditary patrimony of Rokeby and Mortham. In the reign of HENRY VII. the head of the house was another

SIR THOMAS ROKEBY, who had three sons; the two younger were the ancestors of families of the name resident at Marske and Staningford. The eldest son,

RALPH ROKEBY, esq. of Mortham, who succeeded to the paternal inheritance, was living in the reigns of HENRY VII. and HENRY VIII. The era of the "Hunting" of the Felon Sow of Rokeby, which may be seen in the notes to the poem of Rokeby, refers to the time of this Ralph, and the Mrs. Rokeby mentioned in it, is supposed to be his wife, Margaret, eldest daughter and co-heir of Robert Danby, esq. of Yafforth, and a cousin and co-heir of Sir Richard Conyers. By this lady he had issue,

Thomas, his heir.
John, D.C.L. a learned divine and civilian.
Richard, a soldier under Lord Scroop, of Bolton, whose standard he is said to have borne at Flodden. He *m.* a daughter of Ellerker, of Risby, and had a son Thomas, a military officer, who *d. s. p.*
Ralph, of Skiers, an eminent lawyer, made serjeant-at-law 6 EDWARD VI. He *m.* Dorothy, daughter of Thomas Danby, esq. and had issue,

1. William, of Skiers, in Yorkshire, in the commission of the peace, *m.* Mary, daughter and heir of John Rokeby, esq. of Kirk Sandal, and had issue,
   Thomas, whose only daughter and heir Grace, *m.* Conyers, Lord Darcy and Earl of Holdernesse.
   William, a soldier in the French wars.
   Ralph, who left two daughters, Mabel, wife of Colonel Gabriel Savile; and Priscilla, of Captain Musgrave.
   Robert, slain in France.
   Dorothy, *m.* to William Rokeby, esq. of Hotham.
2. Ralph, who left behind him a MS. history of the ancient family of which he was a member. He *m.* first, Douglas, daughter of William Ferne, esq. of Doncaster, by whom he had no child, and secondly, Joan, daughter of John Portington, esq. of Portington, by whom he had a daughter,
   ANN, *m.* to Sir John Hotham, of Scarborough.
3. George, who *m.* first, Joan, second daughter and co-heir of Henry Rokeby, esq. of Kirk Sandall, and secondly, Elizabeth Ferne, widow of Anthony Rothwood, by both of whom he had issue.
4. John, who *m.* Margery, daughter of Thomas Westby, esq. of Ranfield, and had, with two daughters, Margaret and Faith, one son,
   Thomas, who *m.* Mrs. Smith, of Beverley, and was father of Sir Thomas Rokeby, knt. Marshall de Camp in France.

1. Grace, *m.* to George Mackworth, esq. of Empringham, and *d. s. p.*
2. Frances, *m.* to the Rev. John Latham.
3. Jane, *m.* to Robert Byard, gent.
4. Mary, *m.* to William Puleston, esq.
5. Margery, *m.* to William Headley.

The eldest son,

THOMAS ROKEBY, esq. of Mortham is described by Ralph Rokeby, the historian of the family, as "a plain man as might be, whose words came always from his heart without faining, a trusty friend, a forward gentleman in the field, and a great housekeeper, whereby he reigned so in the heart and good will of his countrymen, that his son and heir, Christopher Rokeby, being assaulted at a quarterly race by Christopher Nevile, brother to the mighty Earl of Westmoreland,) whom the earl had sent thither with two men to kill him, was both defended and guarded from the violence of adversaries, and was able so to have rebounded the blows given him by them, that should have spilt the best blood in their bodies, of his part had been willing, for there not a gentleman in the field but cried a Rokeby!' but the good old Thomas, being then in the commission of the peace, commanded and entreated peace, (as he said,) it grieves me to see him bleed that bleeds, yet keep the peace." Thomas Rokeby, *m.* a daughter of Robert Constable, of Cliff, in Yorkshire, and had, with a daughter *m.* to Wycliffe, of Wycliffe, four sons,

I. CHRISTOPHER, of Mortham, who *m.* Margaret, daughter of Sir Roger Lascelles, of Brackenburgh, and had, with daughters, two sons. The younger, Roger, *d. s. p.* the elder,
   JOHN, of Mortham, appears by the visitation of Yorkshire, 1584, to have been then in prison in the Fleet, "religionis causâ." He *m.* a daughter of the ancient family of Thweng, and was succeeded by his son, who bore the favourite family name of
   THOMAS, and was knighted. Of his descendants little more than their names are recorded. It would, otherwise have been gratifying to have known something of the personal habits and actions of those in whose time the chief line of the ancient family of Rokeby fell to decay, and especially of Sir Thomas Rokeby himself, whose necessities must have been great, (it may be presumed) when he disposed of the domain at Rokeby. The purchaser was William Robinson, esq. and it remained with the Robinsons until sold to the father of the present proprietor, JOHN B. S. MORRITT, esq.
II. Ralph, master of St. Katherine's, and one of the masters of requests to *Queen* ELIZABETH.
III. THOMAS, of whose line we have to treat.
IV. Anthony.

The third son,

THOMAS ROKEBY, esq. is thus described by Ralph Rokeby, the historian of the family, to whom we have already referred. "Thomas Rokeby I will mention with reverence, for he beareth about him continually an arre and ensign of valour and honourable service done to his country; for being at Norram Chase, lieutenant to his brother, Christopher, he had a spear broken in his face; after, in the chase, he dismounted himself to mount his captain, who had his horse slain under him, where exposing himself to all danger for his brother's deliverance, he was taken prisoner when others fled." Thomas Rokeby married Katherine Leigh, and had issue,

WILLIAM, his heir.
Ralph.
Elizabeth, *m.* to Richard Vincent, of Frisby.
Susan, *m.* to William Cartwright, of Normanby.

The elder son,

WILLIAM ROKEBY, esq. of Hotham, in Yorkshire, aged twenty-eight in 1584, *m.* Dorothy, daughter of William Rokeby, esq. of Skiers, and had four sons and one daughter, viz.

I. WILLIAM, his heir.
II. Alexander, who *m.* Susan, daughter of Gervase Bosville, esq. of Edlington, and had issue,
   William, of Sandall, living in 1661.
   Alexander, who died at Trinity College, Cambridge, aged about seventeen.
III. Thomas, of Barnby (slain at Dunbar in 1650), *m.* Elizabeth, sister of Sir William Bury, of Grantham, in Lincolnshire, and had, with six daughters, five sons, viz.
   William, of Ackworth Park, whose male issue became extinct in 1766, by the death of his son, Thomas, in that year.
   Thomas (Sir), knt. sometime fellow of Catherine Hall, Cambridge, and afterwards of Gray's Inn, who became one of the judges of the Court of King's Bench. To this gentleman, who *d. s. p.*, there is a sumptuous monument in the chapel of Archbishop Rokeby, at Sandal.
   John, *d. s. p.*
   Joseph, who left (beside two daughters, the

elder, Elizabeth, m. to John Buxton, esq. and the younger, to Richard Wyndlow, esq. of York,) an only son,

Joseph, of New Building and Sandal, in the county of York, in whom vested the representation of the family from 1706 to 1741, in which year he d. s. p.

Benjamin, who m. Rebecca, only daughter and heir of Thomas Langham, esq. of Arthingworth, in Northamptonshire, by whom he acquired that estate, and had an only son,

Langham Rokeby, esq. of Arthingworth, who m. Catherine, daughter of Major Morgan, and was s. by his son,

Thomas Rokeby, esq. of Arthingworth, who m. in 1743, Elizabeth, only daughter and heir of Col. John Scott, of Galashiels, and dying 8th September, 1796, left, with four daughters, of whom the second, Catherine, m. Joseph Jekyll, esq. of Bath, a son and successor,

The Rev. Langham Rokeby, of Arthingworth, who m. in 1780, Maria Isabella, daughter of Somerset Davies, esq. of Wigmore Hall, Herefordshire, and d. 26th December, 1826, having had issue,

Langham, his heir.

Henry-Ralph, b. in 1788, rector of Arthingworth, m. in 1827, Caroline, youngest daughter of the Rev. George Boulton, of Oxendon, and has issue.

Anna-Maria-Isabella, d. unm.

Charlotte Jane, d. in 1803.

The elder son, the present,

Langham Rokeby, esq. of Arthingworth, b. in 1784; lieut.-col. of the Northamptonshire Militia, is now representative of the ancient house of Rokeby.

IV. Philip, who m. Jane, daughter of William Godfrey, esq. of Thunnock, in Lincolnshire, and had issue,

1. Joseph.
2. Philip.
3. Nathaniel.
1. Catherine.

I. Mary, m. to Christopher Legard, esq. of Anlaby.

The eldest son,

I. William Rokeby, esq. of Skiers, in Yorkshire, was created a Baronet 29th January, 1660-1. He m. Frances, daughter of Sir William Hickman, knt. of Gainsborough, in Lincolnshire, and had with three daughters, Elizabeth, Mildred (wife of William Sandford, esq. of Askham), and Bridget (m. to Alexander Montgomery, esq. of Welton), two sons, viz.

Alexander, who m. Margaret, daughter of John Coke, esq. of Holkham, in Norfolk, and dying v. p. left an only son,

William, successor to his grandfather.

Willoughby, successor to his nephew, as third baronet.

Sir William was s. by his grandson,

II. Sir William Rokeby, of Skiers, aged nine in 1665, who m. Dorothy, daughter and heir of Edward Darcy, esq. but dying s. p. in April, 1676, was s. by his uncle,

III. Sir Willoughby Rokeby, of Skiers, at whose decease in the July of the same year, the Baronetcy became extinct. The representation of the family now vests in Langham Rokeby, esq. of Arthingworth.

Arms—Arg. a chev. sa. between three rooks ppr.

BAYNTUN-ROLT, OF SPYE PARK.

Created 9th July, 1762.

Extinct 19th Aug. 1816.

Lineage.

Sidney, in his Treatise on Government, affirms that, in antiquity of possession and name, few of the nobility equal the family of Bayntun. From a very curious pedigree preserved in the Museum, it appears that, in the time of Henry II. the Bayntuns were knights of St. John of Jerusalem. Sir Henry Bayntun was knight-marshal to the king, an office of high authority in those days, and his second son, Henry, a knight of St. John, was slain in Bretagne in 1291. *Temp.* Henry IV. Sir Henry Bayntun taking part with the Earl of Northumberland, was beheaded at Berwick; and in 1471, Sir Robert Bayntun fought against the king at Tewkesbury, was made prisoner, and attainted. The Bayntuns were long settled at Falston, in Wiltshire; but upon the demise of Richard Beauchamp, Lord St. Amand,

John Bayntun, esq. (son of the attainted Sir Robert Bayntun), who was his cousin and heir, removed to Bromham, anciently the seat of the Roches. This John Bayntun, who was restored in blood 19 Henry VII. m. Jane, daughter of Thomas Digges, esq. of Chilham, in Kent, and had issue,

Edward, his heir.
Richard.
John.
Thomas.

Eleanor, married to Richard Hill, esq. of Mitchell Dean.
Elizabeth, a nun at Laycock.
Margaret.
Margery, m. to Knighton, of Sussex.

He died 31st October, 1516, was buried in Bromham Church, and s. by his son,

Sir Edward Bayntun, knt. of Bromham, who rose high in favour with Henry VIII. and was vice-chamberlain to three of his queens. By King Henry, Sir Edward was deputed to use his private friendship with Cardinal Pole, his cousin, to bring over the prelate to his majesty's views, but all his endeavours proved unavailing. He attended his royal master in his expeditions to France, and is supposed to have died there. He m. first, Elizabeth, daughter of Sir John Sulliard, knt. chief justice of the Common Pleas, and had by her

Andrew, who m. Philippa Brulet, and had an only daughter, Anne, wife of William Aston.
Edward (Sir), heir to his father.

Anne, m. first, to Henry Poole; and secondly, to Edward Fabian.
Bridget, m. to Sir James Stumpe, of Malmesbury.
Jane, m. to Sir William St. Looe.
Ursula, m. first, to Thoresby, of Norfolk; and secondly, to Erasmus Spelman.

Sir Edward m. secondly, Isabel, sister of Sir John Alley, of Stockwell, in Surrey, and had by that lady, who survived him, two sons and a daughter, viz.

Henry, who *m.* a daughter of Sir Richard Cavendish, of Nottingham, and had issue,

James.

Edward, *d.* in Ireland *s. p.*

Ferdinand, of Sarum, living in 1623, who *m.* Jane, daughter of John Weare, *alias* Browne, of Calne.

Elizabeth.

Francis.

Ann, *d.* young.

Sir Edward *d.* in 1545, and was *s.* by his son,

SIR EDWARD BAYNTUN, knt. of Bromham, who died in 1593, leaving by Agnes, his wife, daughter of Griffith Rice, of Carew Castle, in Pembrokeshire (son of Sir Rice ap Thomas, knight of the Garter *temp.* HENRY VII.), a daughter, Anne, *m.* to Sir William Eyre, knt. of Wilts, and a son and successor,

SIR HENRY BAYNTUN, knt. of Bromham, who *m.* Lucy, daughter of Sir John Danvers, knt. of Dantsey, in Wiltshire, and *d.* 24th September, 1616, leaving, besides a daughter, Elizabeth, *m.* in 1619, to John Dutton, esq. of Sherborne, a son,

SIR EDWARD BAYNTUN, knt. of Bromham, baptised at Bremhill 5th September, 1593, who *m.* first, Elizabeth, daughter of Sir Henry Maynard, of Eston, in Essex, and by her, who *d.* 30th March, 1635, had, with other issue,

EDWARD (Sir), his heir.

Henry, baptised 14th November, 1621, who *m.* Joan, daughter of Trimnell, of Bremhill, and had a son,

Edward, who married his cousin Lucy, third daughter of his uncle, Sir Edward Bayntun.

Anne, baptised 21st November, 1622; *m.* in 1640, to Hugh Rogers, esq.*

Sir Edward wedded, secondly, Mary Bowell, and had issue,

Robert, who *d.* unm.

Nicholas, who *m.* a daughter of Sir — Osbaldeston, of Chadlington, and had issue.

Anne, *d.* young.

Sir Edward *d.* in 1657, and was *s.* by his son,

SIR EDWARD BAYNTUN, of Bromham, baptised 2nd December, 1618, who took an active part in the troubled times in which he lived, and acted as commissioner of the parliament, residing in the Scots army. At the Restoration he was created knight of the Bath. He *m.* Stuarta, daughter of Sir Thomas Thynne, and sister of Thomas Thynne, esq. of Longleat, by whom he had issue,

HENRY, his heir.

Thomas, of Little Chalfield, in Wiltshire, married and had issue. His daughter Rachel was mother of the Duke of Kingston.

Lucy, *m.* to her cousin, Edward Bayntun, esq. and had issue.

Sir Edward died suddenly 20th July, 1679, and was *s.* by his son,

HENRY BAYNTUN, esq. of Bromham, baptised 17th November, 1664, who *m.* Anne, eldest daughter and co-heir of John Wilmot, Earl of Rochester, by his wife, the heiress of the ancient family of Mallet of Enmore, and by her, who wedded, secondly, the Hon. Francis Greville, father of Francis, Lord Brooke, had issue,

JOHN, his heir.

ANNE, successor to her brother.

Mr. Bayntun *d.* in 1691, and was *s.* by his son,

JOHN BAYNTUN, esq. of Bromham, who *m.* Catharine Fromricker, but dying *s. p.* in 1716, was *s.* by his sister,

ANNE BAYNTUN, who *m.* first, Edward Rolt, esq. M.P. of Sacombe Park, Herts, son and heir of Sir Thomas Rolt, knt. and by him, who died in December, 1722, had issue,

Thomas Rolt, of Sacombe, who *m.* Ann, daughter of Felix Calvert, esq. of Nine Ashes, in Hunsdon, and died in 1754, leaving a son and two daughters, viz.

Thomas, killed at St. Cass in 1758.

Cecilia-Ethelred, *d.* unm. in 1761.

Mary, *m.* to Timothy Caswall, esq. LL.D. and had a son, GEORGE CASWALL, esq. of Sacomb

EDWARD ROLT, successor to the Bayntun estate.

John Rolt, rector of Bromham and Yatesbury, in Wiltshire, married and had issue.

Henry Rolt, } *d.* unm.
Wilmot Rolt, }

James Rolt, living in 1761.

Elizabeth Rolt, *m.* to Brigadier-General John Prideaux, son of Sir John Prideaux, bart. and had issue.

Anna-Maria Rolt, *d.* unm. in 1723.

She wedded, secondly, James, Lord Somerville, and by his lordship had

James Somerville.

Hugh Somerville.

Ann Somerville, *m.* to George Burgis, esq. commissioner of excise.

The heiress of the Bayntuns *d.* in 1734, and was *s.* by her second son,

I. EDWARD ROLT, esq. of Spye Park, Wilts, M.P. for Chippenham, groom of the bedchamber to the Prince of Wales, and finally surveyor of the duchy of Cornwall. He assumed the additional surname of Bayntun, and was created a BARONET in 1762, as Sir Edward Bayntun-Rolt, of Spye Park. He *m.* Mary Poynter, of Herriard, Hants, and had issue,

ANDREW, his heir.

Constantia, *m.* to Richard Foster, esq.

Sir Edward died in January, 1800, and was *s.* by his only son,

II. SIR ANDREW BAYNTUN-ROLT, of Spye Park, who *m.* first, in 1777, Lady Mary-Alicia Coventry, eldest surviving daughter of George-William, sixth Earl of Coventry; and secondly, Anna-Maria Maude. He *d.* 12th August, 1816, when the BARONETCY became EXTINCT, but the estates devolved on Sir Andrew's only daughter and heiress (by his first wife),

MARIA-BARBARA, *m.* in 1797, to the Rev. John Starky, D.D. rector of Charlinch, Somersetshire, and had, with many younger children, a son and successor, the present

JOHN-EDWARD-ANDREW STARKY, esq. of Bromham, Wilts, *b.* 8th March, 1799, who *m.* 17th April, 1833, Charlotte, fifth daughter of William Wyndham, esq. of Dinton, Wilts, and has issue.

Arms—Sa. a bend lozengy arg. for BAYNTUN, quarterly with arg. a bend sa. charged with three dolphins embowed of the first, for ROLT.

ROTHWELL, OF EWERBY AND STAPLEFORD.

CREATED 16th Aug. 1661.—EXTINCT in 1694.

Lineage.

I. RICHARD ROTHWELL, esq. of Ewerby and Stapleford, in Lincolnshire, was created a BARONET in 1661, but died without male issue in 1694, when the title became EXTINCT.

ROUSE, OF ROUSE LENCH.

Lineage.

The family of Rouse appears to have been established in England by one of the companions in arms of the CONQUEROR, and the name of its patriarch is to be found on the roll of Battle Abbey. In 1641 a BARONETCY was conferred on

I. THOMAS ROUSE, esq. of Rouse Lench, in Worcestershire, son and heir of Sir John Rouse, knt. of the same place, who died in 1645, by Esther, his wife, daughter of Sir Thomas Temple, of Warwickshire. Sir Thomas *m.* first, Jane, daughter of Sir John Ferrers, of Tamworth Castle, in that shire, by whom he had a son,

EDWARD, his heir.

His second wife was Frances, daughter of David Murray, esq. and by her he had

FRANCIS, successor to his half-brother.
THOMAS, who *s.* as fourth baronet.

Elizabeth, *d.* in 1729.

Sir Thomas married a third time, but by that marriage had no issue. He died 26th May, 1676, and was *s.* by his son,

II. SIR EDWARD ROUSE, of Rouse Lench, who married Elizabeth, daughter of John Lisle, esq. of Moxhull, in Warwickshire, but died without issue 5th November, 1677, when he was succeeded by his half-brother,

III. SIR FRANCIS ROUSE, of Rouse Lench, who *m.* Frances, daughter of Thomas Archer, esq. of Umberslade, in Warwickshire, but by her (who wedded, secondly, John Chaplin, esq. of Tathwell, in Lincolnshire,) had no issue. He *d.* 31st July, 1687, and was *s.* by his brother,

IV. SIR THOMAS ROUSE, of Rouse Lench, who *m.* Anne, daughter of Charles Hooker, esq. and had two sons, who died in their infancy. Sir Thomas died himself in 1721, aged fifty-seven, when the BARONETCY became EXTINCT, and his estate passed to his only surviving sister,

ELIZABETH, at whose decease unmarried in 1729,

THOMAS PHILLIPS, esq. inherited, and assumed the surname of ROUSE only. He served as sheriff of Worcestershire in 1733, and died unmarried in 1768, bequeathing his property to

CHARLES-WILLIAM BOUGHTON, who took the name of ROUSE. His son, the present proprietor of Rouse Lench, is

SIR WILLIAM-EDWARD ROUSE-BOUGHTON, bart. of Lawford.

Arms—Sa. two bars engrailed arg.

RUDD, OF ABERGLASSNEY.

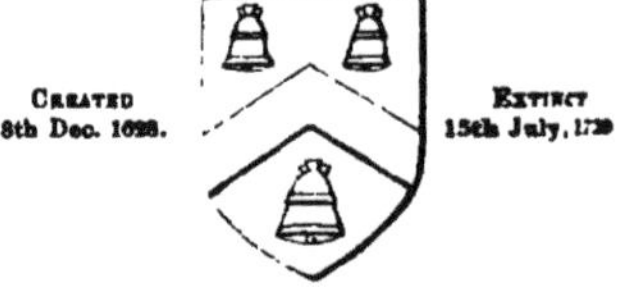

Lineage.

The first of the name of RUDD who settled in the county of Carmarthen,

ANTHONY RUDD, Bishop of St. David's, purchased a good estate there, and erected a handsome seat in the parish of Langathen, which he called Aberglassney. The learned prelate was of the ancient family of Rudd of Yorkshire; he was some time fellow of Trinity College, Cambridge, and was advanced to the see of St. David's in 1593. He *m.* Anne Dalton, and had two sons,

Anthony, who married, but *d. s. p.*
RICE.

The bishop *d.* 7th March, 1614, and was interred in a vault in the church of Langathen. His only surviving son and heir,

I. RICE RUDD, esq. of Aberglassney, in the county of Carmarthen, was created a BARONET 8th December, 1628. Sir Rice *m.* first, Jane, daughter of Thomas ap Rice, esq. of Richeston, in the county of Pembroke, and had three sons, viz.

ANTHONY, who *m.* Judith, daughter and sole heir of Thomas Rudd, esq. of Higham Ferrars, in the county of Northampton, and dying before his father, left a son,
RICE, successor to his grandfather.
Urian.
THOMAS, whose son,
ANTHONY, inherited as third baronet.

He *m.* secondly, Elizabeth, sister of Sir John Aubrey, of Llantrithyd, but by that lady had no issue. He *d.* in May, 1664, and was *s.* by his grandson,

II. SIR RICE RUDD, who was elected knight for the county of Carmarthen in 1660, and continued its representative until his decease in July, 1701. He *m.* Dorothy, sister of Sir Francis Cornwallis, knt. of Abermarles, in the same shire, but dying *s. p.* was *s.* by his cousin,

III. SIR ANTHONY RUDD, who *m.* first, Magdalen daughter of Sir Henry Jones, knt. of Abermarles, and secondly, Beatrice, daughter of Sir John Barlow, bart. of Slebetch, in the county of Pembroke, and heir of her mother, Beatrice, elder daughter of Sir John Lloyd, bart. of Forrest, in Carmarthenshire. By the former he had no issue; by the latter (who *m.* secondly, Griffith Lloyd, esq.) he had two sons and a daughter, viz.

JOHN, his heir.
Anthony, *d. s. p.*

Anne, *m.* to Richard Gwynne, esq. of Tallaris, in Carmarthenshire.

Sir Anthony was *s.* by his elder son,

IV. SIR JOHN RUDD, who died issueless 15th July, 1739, when the BARONETCY EXPIRED.

Arms—Ar. a chevron erm. between three bells arg.

RUDSTON, OF HAYTON.

CREATED 29th Aug. 1642.

EXTINCT

Lineage.

SIR JOHN RUDSTON, knt. lord of the manor of Hayton, in the east riding of the county of York, living temp. King JOHN, left a son and successor,

WALTER RUDSTON, of Hayton, who married Oswyn, daughter of Stephen Shalleros, and was s. by his son,

JOHN RUDSTON, of Hayton, who m. a daughter of Thomas Wilberforce, and left a son and heir,

GREGORY RUDSTON, of Hayton, from whom we pass to his lineal descendant towards the close of the fifteenth century,

MATTHEW RUDSTON, esq. of Hayton, who married a daughter of Thomas Studham, esq. of Pocklington, and had issue,

WALTER, his heir.

John (Sir), lord mayor of London in 1528, who left a son and heir,

Robert Rudston, who purchased from Sir Thomas Wyatt the manor of Boughton Monchensie, in Kent. His second son and eventual heir,

Belnap Rudston, of Boughton Monchensie, dying s. p. devised his estate, by will dated in 1613, to Sir Francis Barnham, knt. and it is now in the possession of that gentleman's representative,

THOMAS RYDER, esq. of Boughton.

Anne, m. to William Wensley, esq. of Brians Burton.

The elder son,

WALTER RUDSTON, esq. was great-grandfather of

WALTER RUDSTON, esq. who inherited Hayton at the decease of his father in 1618. He m. Frances, daughter of Marmaduke Constable, esq. and sister of Sir Marmaduke Constable, bart. of Everingham, by whom he had, with other issue,

I. WALTER, his heir.

II. William, who m. Hester, daughter of Francis Savile, esq. of Barnesley, and left a daughter,

HESTER, who m. William Calverley, esq. and had a son,

CHARLES CALVERLEY, who m. Catherine Mitchell, and left a son,

WILLIAM CALVERLEY, whose son and heir,

RUDSTON CALVERLEY, inherited eventually the Rudston estates.

The eldest son and heir,

I. WALTER RUDSTON, esq. of Hayton, in the county of York, was created a BARONET by King CHARLES I. 29th August, 1642, and had the honour of entertaining his majesty at Hayton on the king's march to demand the possession of Hull from Sir John Hotham, the parliamentary general. Sir Walter adhering to the fortunes of his royal master, suffered confiscation and other persecutions. He m. Margaret, daughter of Sir Thomas Dawney, bart. of Cowick, through whose exertions the property was restored at last to his son, and had issue,

THOMAS, his heir.

Walter.

Faith.

Barbara.

Margaret.

Elizabeth.

He died about 1655, and was s. by his elder son,

II. SIR THOMAS RUDSTON, baptized 8th August, 1639, m. Katherine, daughter and co-heir of George Mountayne, esq. of Westow, in Yorkshire, and had issue,

THOMAS, his heir.

Walter, d. s. p.

ELIZABETH, heir to her elder brother.

He died about the year 1682, and was s. by his elder son,

III. SIR THOMAS RUDSTON, at whose decease the BARONETCY became EXTINCT, and the estates devolved upon his sister,

ELIZABETH RUDSTON, of Hayton, who m. Henry Cutler, esq. eldest son of Sir Gervais Cutler, knt. of Stainborough Hall (now Wentworth Castle), in the West Riding, but had no issue. Mrs. Cutler survived her husband, and at her decease devised her property at Hayton and elsewhere to her cousin and heir general,

RUDSTON CALVERLEY, esq. who assumed, in consequence, the surname and arms of RUDSTON. He m. in 1761, Anne, daughter of William Stockdale, esq. and dying in 1806, was s. by his eldest son,

The Rev. Thomas-Cutler Rudston-Read, now of Hayton. (Refer to BURKE's *Commoners*, vol. iv. p. 362.)

Arms—Arg. three bulls' heads erased.

RUSSELL, OF CHIPPENHAM.

CREATED 19th Jan. 1628-9.

EXTINCT 25th April, 1804.

Lineage.

The first member of this family recorded is

THOMAS RUSSELL, of Yaverland, in the Isle of Wight, who held the manors and advowsons of Yaverland and Wathe, the manor of Rouburgh, in the Isle of Wight, and Carisbroke Castle, *in capite*, and died 16 HENRY VI.

I. SIR WILLIAM RUSSELL, knt. of Chippenham, in the county of Cambridge (son of William Russell, esq. of Surrey, and grandson of Maurice Russell, of Yaverland), having been many years treasurer of the navy, was created a BARONET by King CHARLES I. 19th January, 1628-9. Sir William m. first, Elizabeth, daughter of Sir Francis Cherry, knt. but by that lady had no issue. He wedded, secondly, Elizabeth, daughter of Thomas Gerard, esq. of Burnell, in Cambridgeshire, and had seven sons and three daughters, viz.

I. FRANCIS, his heir.

II. William (Sir), some time of St. Edmund's Bury, commonly called the black Sir William, and styled the cream of the Russells, on account of his loyalty. He *m.* Anne Bendish, an heiress, but left no issue.

III. Gerard, of Fordham, in Suffolk, *m.* first, Mary, daughter of — Cherry, esq. of Surrey, and had three sons; Gerard and John, the two younger, died issueless; the eldest,

WILLIAM, of Fordham, *m.* Elizabeth, daughter of HENRY CROMWELL, son of the PROTECTOR, and had, with other issue,

FRANCIS, baptized at Fordham Abbey 19th January, 1691, and buried in the city of London. He married, and left to survive childhood,

THOMAS, a military officer, *b.* 27th February, 1724, who had two children, a son and daughter, viz.

WILLIAM RUSSELL, who died abroad. This gentleman, if he had survived Sir George Russell, bart. of Chippenham, would have succeeded to that ancient title.

REBECCA RUSSELL, who *m.* first, James Harley, esq. but by that gentleman had no issue. She *m.* secondly, William Dyer, esq. of Ilford, a magistrate and deputy-lieutenant for the county of Essex, and by him (who *d.* 17th January, 1824,) left at her decease 17th January, 1832, three sons and two daughters, viz.

WILLIAM-ANDREW DYER, of Harley Street, London.

Charles-Adams Dyer, of Canewdon Hall, Essex.

Thomas-John Dyer, of the Hon. East India Company's service.

Mary-Eliza Dyer.

Louisa Dyer.

Mr. Gerard Russell *m.* secondly, a daughter of — Lloyd, esq. and by her had one daughter,

Mabell, *m.* to Richard Russell, esq.

IV. Edward, buried at Chippenham 10th July, 1647.

V. Robert, buried at Chippenham 17th February, 1640.

VI. John, baptized 31st January, 1623, and died an infant.

VII. John, baptized 29th November, 1624, *d. s. p.*

I. Elizabeth, *m.* first, to Edward Lewknor, esq. of Denham, in Suffolk, and had a daughter,

Mary Lewknor, *m.* to Horatio, first Viscount Townshend.

Mrs. Lewknor having survived her first husband, wedded, secondly, John Gauden, D.D. afterwards Bishop of Worcester.

II. Anne, *m.* to John Bodvile, of Bodvile Castle, in Carnarvonshire, and had a daughter,

Sarah Bodvile, *m.* to John, Viscount Bodmyn, son of the Earl of Radnor. The viscount dying in the lifetime of his father, his widow was raised by patent to the rank of an earl's wife.

III. Sarah, *m.* to Sir Thomas Chichley, knt. of Wimpole, in Cambridgeshire.

Sir William *m.* thirdly, Elizabeth, daughter and [illegible] heir of Michael Smallpage, gent. of Chichester, and relict of John Wheatly, esq. of Catesfield, in Sussex, by this lady he had two other sons, namely,

VIII. William, baptized 7th December, 1621, [illegible] young.

IX. WILLIAM (Sir), of Langherne, in Carmarthenshire, created a BARONET in 1660. (See RUSSELL OF LANGHERNE.)

He was *s.* by his eldest son,

II. SIR FRANCIS RUSSELL, who *m.* at Chippenham, 19th September, 1631, Catherine, daughter and heir of John Wheatley, esq. of Catesfield, by Elizabeth Smallpage (which Elizabeth, as stated above, married for her second husband Sir William Russell), by which lady he had issue,

I. JOHN, his successor.

II. Robert, *b.* 21st October, 1644, of Mildenhall, Suffolk, *m.* the daughter and co-heir of Thomas Soame, esq. of Thurlow, a captain of [illegible] in the service of *King* CHARLES I.

III. Gerard, *b.* 2nd January, 1645, a Hamburgh merchant, *m.* Miss Younker, of Hamburgh.

IV. Killephet, *b.* in 1647, *d.* in 1650.

V. Killephet, *b.* 11th March, 1652, left a son, Francis, who *d.* an infant.

VI. Edward, baptized at Chippenham 12th October, 1654.

I. Elizabeth, *m.* to HENRY CROMWELL, lord deputy of Ireland, younger son of the PROTECTOR, and had issue,

OLIVER CROMWELL, his heir, *d. s. p.*

HENRY CROMWELL, of Spinney Abbey, ancestor of the Cromwells of Cheshunt Park. (See BURKE'S *Commoners*, vol. i. p. [illegible])

ELIZABETH CROMWELL, *m.* to William Russell, esq. of Fordham.

II. Sarah, *d.* an infant in 1637.

III. Sarah, baptized 24th August, 1639; *m.* first, to — Reynolds, esq. of Cambridgeshire; and secondly, to Henry, Earl of Thomond.

IV. Catharine, baptized 23rd December, 1641, *m.* — Sheers, of Hertfordshire.

V. Frances, baptized 15th November, 1649, *m.* to John Hagar, esq. of Bourn, in Cambridgeshire.

VI. Anne, *m.* to Henry Underwood, esq. of Whittlesey, in the Isle of Ely.

Sir Francis was *s.* at his decease by his eldest son,

III. SIR JOHN RUSSELL, baptized at Chippenham [illegible] October, 1640; *m.* ELIZABETH, daughter of the PROTECTOR CROMWELL, and widow of Robert Rich, esq. son of Robert, third Earl of Warwick, and had issue,

I. WILLIAM, his heir.

II. Rich, captain in *King* WILLIAM'S Guards, *m.* Mabell, daughter of Gerard Russell, esq. of Fordham, and *d. s. p.*

III. John, *b.* 14th October, 1670, governor of Fort William, Bengal; *m.* first, Rebecca, sister of Sir Charles Eyre, of Kew; and secondly, Johanna, widow of Colonel Rivett. By the latter he had one daughter, who died young.

* By this marriage the estate of Checkers came into the family. The lady was daughter and heir of Serjeant Thurbane by his second wife, the sister of Lord Cutt. The serjeant's first wife, with whom he acquired the estate, but by whom he had no issue, was one of the [illegible] daughters and co-heiresses of Sir Robert [illegible] of Checkers, to whom it descended, through the Haw[illegible] from Sir Ralph de Checkers.

by the former he left at his decease, 5th December, 1735, a son and three daughters, viz.

Charles, an officer of rank in the army,* m. in 1737, Mary-Johanna-Cutts, daughter of the aforesaid Colonel Rivett, and had issue,

John, who inherited as eighth baronet.
Mary, bedchamber-woman to the *Princess* Amelia, *d.* unm.

Frances, bedchamber-woman to H.R.H. the *Princess* Amelia, *m.* to John Rivett, esq. of Checkers, and *d. s. p.*
Mary, *m.* to — Holmes, esq. and *d. s. p.*
Elizabeth, *m.* to Samuel Greenhill, esq. of Swincombe, in the county of Oxford, and had a son,

John-Russell Greenhill, LL.D. of whom hereafter.

I. Christian, buried at Chippenham 28th August, 1680.
II. Elizabeth, *m.* to Sir Thomas Frankland, bart. of Thirkelby, in the county of York, and was great-great-grandmother of the present

Sir Robert Frankland Russell, bart. of Thirkelby.

Sir John was *s.* by his eldest son,

IV. Sir William Russell, who *m.* Miss Gore, of Ireland, and had two sons and a daughter, namely,

William, his heir.
Francis, successor to his brother.
Mary, *d.* unm. in December, 1735.

Sir William having spent the remainder of a considerable fortune in raising troops at the Revolution, sold his estate at Chippenham, and dying in September, 1707, was *s.* by his elder son,

V. Sir William Russell, who died in Ireland *s. p.* in May, 1738, and was *s.* by his brother,

VI. Sir Francis Russell, one of the council at Fort William, in Bengal, who *m.* in 1725, Miss Gee, and was *s.* by his only son,

VII. Sir William Russell, lieutenant in the 1st regiment of Foot Guards, who *d.* unmarried in 1783, and was *s.* by his kinsman (refer to John, third son of the third baronet),

VIII. Sir John Russell, of Checkers, in the county of Bucks, *b.* 31st October, 1741. This gentleman was a student of Christ Church, Oxford, and barrister-at-law. He *m.* Catherine, daughter of General George Cary, second son of Viscount Falkland, and had two sons,

John, his successor.
George, heir to his brother.

Sir John *d.* in 1783, and was *s.* by his elder son,

IX. Sir John Russell, who *d.* unmarried in 1802, and was *s.* by his brother,

X. Sir George Russell, who died without issue 12th April, 1804, when the Baronetcy expired, and the estate of Checquers devolved upon his aunt,

Mary Russell, bedchamber-woman to H. R. H. the *Princess* Amelia, at whose decease unmarried the property of the Russells passed to her cousin,

The Rev. John-Russell Greenhill, LL.D. (Refer to Russell of Checquers Court.)

*** The Baronetcy of Chippenham would have devolved, at the decease of Sir George Russell, upon the Fordham Abbey branch, which descended from Gerard Russell, of Fordham, the third son of Sir William, the first baronet, if a male heir of that line had then appeared; but William Russell, of Fordham, the last male, who was residing abroad, died issueless; whether before or after Sir George is not ascertained. His only sister,

Rebecca Russell, married, as stated above, for her second husband, William Dyer, esq. of Ilford, in Essex, and left, with other issue, a son and heir,

William-Andrew Dyer, esq. of Harley Street, in the county of Middlesex, who now represents the Fordham branch, and through that the Baronets of Chippenham.

Arms—Arg. a lion rampant gu. on a chief sa. three roses of the first.

RUSSELL, OF LANGHERNE.

Created 8th Nov. 1660.—Extinct about 1714.

Lineage.

I. Sir William Russell, knt. of Langherne, in the county of Carmarthen, youngest son of Sir William Russell, bart. of Chippenham, was created a Baronet 8th November, 1660, and was commonly called the white Sir William. He *m.* Hesther, daughter of Sir Thomas Rouse, bart. of Rouse Lench, and had an only daughter, his heir,

Mary Russell, *m.* first, to Hugh-Calverley Cotton, esq. elder son of Sir Robert Cotton, bart. of Combermere, by whom (who died before his father) she had an only child,

Catherine Cotton, *m.* to Thomas Lewis, esq. of St. Pierre.

Mrs. Cotton *m.* secondly, Lord Arthur Somerset, son of the Duke of Beaufort.

Sir William *d.* about the year 1714, when the Baronetcy expired.

Arms—As Russell of Chippenham.

RUSSELL, OF CHECQUERS COURT.

Created 15th Sept. 1831.—Extinct in 1837.

Lineage.

The Rev. Samuel Greenhill, of Swincombe, in the county of Oxford, *m.* Elizabeth, youngest daughter of John Russell, esq. governor of Fort William, Bengal, youngest son of Sir John Russell, third bart. of Chippenham, and left a son and heir,

John-Russell Greenhill, LL.D. of Cottisford House, in the county of Oxford, who, on the decease of his cousin, Mary Russell (see Russell of Chippenham), inherited the estate of Checkers or Checquers, in the county of Bucks. He *m.* Elizabeth, only child of M. Noble, esq. of the county of Durham, and had an only son,

I. Robert Greenhill, esq. of Checquers Court, in Buckinghamshire, who assumed, by sign manual, in 1815, the surname and arms of Russell, and was created a Baronet 15th September, 1831. Sir Robert Greenhill-Russell was bred to the bar, and represented the borough of Thirsk for some time in parliament. He died unmarried in 1837, when the Baro-

* He was appointed a major in the 2nd regiment of Foot Guards, with the rank of colonel, in 1745; and colonel of the 34th Foot in 1751. He commanded the 1st battalion of Foot Guards at the battle of Fontenoy.

NENCY EXPIRED, and the estate devolved, under his will, upon his kinsman,

SIR ROBERT FRANKLAND, bart. of Thirkelby, who has since assumed the additional name of RUSSELL.*

Arms—As RUSSELL OF CHIPPENHAM.

RUSSELL, OF STRENSHAM.

CREATED 12th Mar. 1626-7.

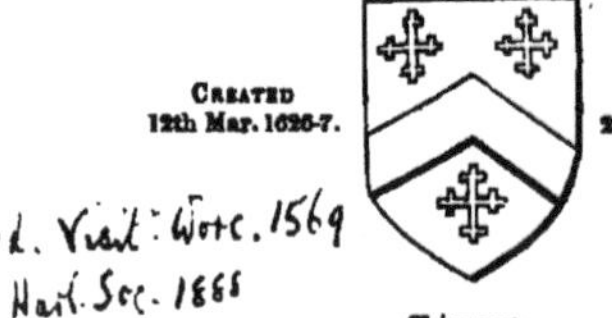

EXTINCT 24th Jan. 1705.

Lineage.

The Russells of Strensham, in Worcestershire, established in England at the Conquest, were possessed of Strensham so far back as the close of the thirteenth century, for at that period, SIR JAMES RUSSELL, lord of Strensham, presented to the living; a date which agrees with the inscription on the monument of Sir Francis Russell, buried in 1705, which states that the Russells had flourished in Strensham about 460 years. By the marriage of Sir William Russell, knt. with Agnes, daughter and co-heir of Thomas Hodington, the Russells inherited half the lands of Cassey and Cookesey. In the civil war,

I. SIR WILLIAM RUSSELL,† of Strensham (who was created a BARONET in 1626-7), acted a conspicuous part in support of the royal cause, and devoted a considerable portion of his fortune to the service of the king; yet, notwithstanding that diminution, his estate was valued at £3000 a-year when the order of the Royal Oak was projected. "In the propositions (we quote Dr. Nash's Worcestershire) offered by Mr. Henry Washington, governor of Worcester, for the surrender of that town to Mr. Edward Whalley, commander of the parliament forces, who lay at Mr. Fleet's, of Hollow, in the year 1646, the thirty-first article was, that the several garrisons of Worcester, Evesham, Strensham, Hartlebury, and Madresfield, should be disgarrisoned, and the Bishop of Worcester, Sir William Russell, and Colonel Lygon, be restored to the possession of their houses and estates. In the treaty negotiated soon after concerning the surrender of Worcester between Mr. Washington and Major-General Raynesborough, it was insisted upon by the latter that Sir William Russell should be exempted from the benefit of the treaty. This caused a long delay: Sir William was much pressed to escape in disguise, which he refused, saying he would willingly surrender himself for the public good, he had but a life to lose, and it could not be better spent. Upon his resolute refusal to escape or stop the treaty any longer, the noblemen and gentlemen, thinking themselves bound in honour, signed a letter to Sir Thomas Fairfax, desiring that Sir William Russell might have the benefit of the treaty, and that he could not by any other means so much oblige the county. Sir Thomas replied that Sir William Russell should be used as a gentleman and be prisoner to Major-General Raynesborough. He afterwards compounded with the parliament committee for £1800 and £50 a-year settled upon his estate."

Sir William m. Frances, daughter of Sir Thomas Reade, of Barton, in Berkshire, and had, with other issue,

FRANCIS, his heir.

Mary, m. first, to Wingfield, Earl of Ardglass; and secondly, to Charles Cotton, the poet.

Sir William d. in 1669, and was buried at Strensham, with this inscription, "Corpus Gulielmi Russell baronetti manerii de Strensham dom. hic in spe quiescit. Vir fuit ingenio natalibus suis digno, egregia erga regem temporibus iniquissimis fide, nec capitis periculo nec magna rei familiaris jactura unquam concussus." Sir William was s. by his son,

II. SIR FRANCIS RUSSELL, of Strensham, who m. Anne, daughter of Sir Rowland Lytton, knt. of Knebworth, in Herts, and had three daughters, his co-heirs,

ANNE, m. first, to Sir Harry Every, bart. of Eggington, in Derbyshire; secondly, to Richard Lygon, esq. of Beauchamp's Court, Worcestershire; and thirdly, to Sir John Guise, bart. of Rendcombe, in Gloucestershire; but d. s. p. 22nd February, 1734.

MARY, m. to Thomas Jones, esq. of Shropshire.

ELIZABETH, lady of the manor of Strensham, who m. William Dansey, esq. of Brinsop, in the county of Hereford, and had a daughter,

CATHERINE DANSEY, lady of the manor of Strensham, who m. John Ravenhill, esq. of the county of Hereford, and had an only daughter and heir,

---

* ELIZABETH RUSSELL, youngest daughter of Sir John Russell, third bart. of Chippenham, married Sir Thomas Frankland, bart. of Thirkelby, in the county of York, and was great-great-grandmother of Sir Robert Frankland, the devisee of Sir Robert Greenhill-Russell, whose grandmother, Elizabeth Russell, daughter of Governor Russell, was niece of the said Elizabeth.

† Sir John Russell, knt. of Strensham, son of Robert Russell, and representative of the family at the middle of the sixteenth century, died 15th August, 1556. = Edith, daughter of Sir Thomas Umpton, died 8th October 1562.

Sir Thomas Russell, knt. 1560, married secondly, Margaret, daughter of William Lygon, esq. = Frances, daughter and heir of Sir Roger Chomley.

Sir John Russell, *temp.* ELIZABETH = Elizabeth, daughter of Ralph Sheldon.

Sir Thomas Russell, knt. died 1632 = Elizabeth, daughter of Sir William Spencer.

- Sir William Russell, first baronet.
- Elizabeth, m. to John Hornyhold, esq. of Blakemore Park.
- Margaret, m. to John Winter, esq. of Hodington.
- Anne, m. to John Cocks, esq. of Crowle.

458.c (107.[illegible])

Russel Visit 1584 [illegible] 102 d. 458.a.

2 [illegible]

3. [illegible] 33

4 [illegible] 3 [illegible] or

5 [illegible]

6 [illegible]

7 [illegible]

8 [illegible]

11 [illegible] art. delete

12 arg on [illegible]

13 " " " [illegible]

14 " " " [illegible]

15 [illegible]

[illegible]

[illegible] Visit 1569 [illegible]

[illegible]

NETCY EXPIRED, and the estate devolved, under his will, upon his kinsman,

SIR ROBERT FRANKLAND, bart. of Thirkelby, who has since assumed the additional name of Russell.*

possession of their houses and estates. In the treaty negotiated soon after concerning the surrender of Worcester between Mr. Washington and Major-General Raynesborough, it was insisted upon by the [illegible]

Sir William Russell, first baronet.

Elizabeth, m. to John Hornyhold, esq. of Blakemore Park.

Margaret, m. to John Winter, esq. of Hodington.

Anne, m. to [illegible] Cocks, [illegible]

NETCY EXPIRED, and the estate devolved, under his will, upon his kinsman,

SIR ROBERT FRANKLAND, bart. of Thirkelby, who has since assumed the additional name of RUS-SELL. [illegible]

possession of their houses and estates. In the treaty negotiated soon after concerning the surrender of Worcester between Mr. Washington and Major General Raynesborough, it was insisted upon by the latter that Mr. William Russell should be [illegible]

Frances Ravenhill, who m. first, Richard Nash, D.D. of Clerkenleap, in Worcestershire; and secondly, to Charles Trubshaw Withers, esq. of Sansomfields, near Worcester.

Francis Russell died 24th January, 1705, aged ...y-eight, when the Baronetcy became extinct, ...was buried on the 2nd February following at ...ensham, under a large marble monument, with ...figure of a widow weeping over her husband, and ...inscription: "M. S. Francisci Russell, baronetti, illustri majorum stirpe oriundi, qui per 400 plus ...us annos amplissimarum in hac vicinia ditionum ...dium dominus erat, quas ipse ornavit, et in melius movit, ingenio felicissimo propensissimâque omnibenefaciendi voluntate, nominis et patriæ decus ...rem duxit Annam, filiam Rowlandi Lytton, militis, Knebworth, in agro Hertfordiensi, cum quâ per ...nnos vitam egit, affectu mortuo et verè conjugali, ...ue gratam. Hæc autem, ægre jam superstes, ...nto optimo monumentum hoc extrui voluit; suas ...m cum ejus exuviis hic reponi cupiens, plena fide ...ue lætæ resurrectionis obtinendæ. Ex illâ tres ...epit filias, quas superstites reliquit, Annam, Ma..., et Elizabetham. Ipse mortem obiit, 24 Jan. ... 1705, æt. suæ 68."

...r Francis's estates were equally divided between three daughters. Two shares were soon re-united ...the death of one of the sisters; the third, after ...ing through different proprietors, was purchased ...775 by Dr. Treadway Nash, brother of Dr. Richard ...h, who acquired the other two portions in mar...e with Frances Ravenhill, lady of the manor of ...nsham.

...rms—Arg. a chevron between three cross crosslets

SABINE, OF ION HOUSE.

Created ... Mar. 1671. Extinct in 1705.

Lineage.

John Sabine, esq. eldest son* of John Sabine, ... of Patricksbourne, in Kent, who died in 1656, ...ed the only daughter and heir of William Al... esq. (who had purchased Ion House, in the ... of Upper Gravenhurst, Bedfordshire, from Wil... Whitbread, esq. in 1639,) and being described of ... House, was created a Baronet in 1671. He died ... without issue in 1705, when the title became ... The estate at Gravenhurst he had sold to ... Hinde, esq. from whose family the Duke of ... bought it in 1724.

...s—Arg. an escallop sa. on a chief of the last, ...mullets pierced of the first.

SADLEIR, OF TEMPLE DINSLEY.

Created 3rd Dec. 1661. Extinct in 1706.

Lineage.

Sir Ralph Sadleir, knt. the distinguished statesman of Henry *the Eighth's*, of Edward *the Sixth's*, and *Queen* Elizabeth's reign, m. Margaret Mitchell, a laundress in the family of his first patron, the Earl of Essex, and had several children; but it being discovered that Margaret's former husband, Matthew Barré, was alive, although supposed to have died abroad, the issue of Sir Ralph and Margaret were obliged to be legitimised by act of parliament. Those children were

I. Thomas (Sir), of Standon, sheriff of Hertfordshire 29 and 37 Elizabeth. (See Burke's *Commoners*, vol. ii. p. 561.)

II. Edward.

III. Henry, of Everley, in the county of Wilts.

I. Anne, m. to Sir George Horsey, knt. of Diggswell, in Hertfordshire.

II. Mary, m. to Thomas Bowles, esq. of Wallington, in the same county.

III. Jane, m. to Edward Bashe, esq. of Stanstedbury, also in Hertfordshire.

IV. Dorothy, m. to Edward Elrington, esq. of Borstall, in Essex.

Sir Ralph Sadleir was of the privy council more than forty years, and during the greater part of that time one of the knights of the shire for the county of Hertford. He died at Standon 30th March, 1587, in the eightieth year of his age, leaving behind him twenty-two manors, several parsonages, and other great estates in the counties of Hertford, Gloucester, Warwick, Buckingham, and Worcester; of which, he had settled the manor of Temple Dinsley, in Herts, upon his second son,

Edward Sadleir, esq. who m. Anne, daughter and co-heir of Sir Richard Leigh, knt. of Sopwell,† near St. Albans, and dying in the lifetime of his father, 26 Elizabeth, left issue,

Leigh, his heir.

Richard, who inherited Sopwell, m. Joyce, daughter of Robert Honywood, esq. of Charing, in Kent, and had (with issue from whom descended the Sadleirs of Sopwell Hall, in the county of Tipperary,) a son and heir,

Robert, of Sopwell, Herts, who left an only daughter and heir,

Ellen Sadleir, of Sopwell, who m. in 1662, Thomas Saunders, esq. of Beechwood, and by him (who sold the estate of Sopwell to Sir Harbottle Grimston) she had an only daughter and heiress,

* ... younger brother, Philip Sabine, of Patricksbourne, m. Mary, daughter and heir of Richard Chilborne, ... Sir Charles Chilborne, serjeant-at-law, and had ... son, Chilborne Sabine, esq. of Patricksbourne.

† Henry VIII. granted to Sir Richard Leigh, knt. in the thirtieth year of his reign, the site of the priory of Sopwell, in the county of Hertford.

Anne Saunders, *m.* first, to Sir Edward Sebright, bart.; and secondly, to Charles Lyttleton, esq.
Edward, of Lotsford.
Thomas, *d.* unm.
Ellen, *d.* in 1600.

He was *s.* by his eldest son,

Leigh Sadleir, esq. of Temple Dinsley, who *m.* Elizabeth, daughter of — Pascall, esq. of Preston, in Essex, and dying 30 Elizabeth, was *s.* by his only son,

Thomas-Leigh Sadleir, esq. of Temple Dinsley, in the county of Hertford, and Aspley Guise, in Bedfordshire. This gentleman wedded Frances, daughter of Francis Berrie, esq. of Beckering Park, in Bedfordshire, and had, with several daughters, six sons, viz.

Thomas, *d.* unm.
Edwin, heir to his father.
Ralph, who inherited Aspley Guise, *d.* unm.
Leigh, who *m.* Mary, daughter of George Haddon, esq. of Kingham, in Oxfordshire, and left a son and heir,
George, of Aspley Guise, who had a son and heir,
George, who died in returning from the East Indies in 1752, *s. p.*
Edward, *d.* unm.
William, who became of Aspley Guise, and is now represented by the Rev. Henry-Riddell Moody, rector of Chartham, in Kent.

He was *s.* by his eldest surviving son,

i. Edwin Sadleir, esq. of Temple Dinsley, in the county of Hertford, who was created a Baronet 3rd December, 1661. Sir Edwin *m.* Elizabeth, eldest daughter of Sir Walter Walker, knt. LL.D. and had surviving issue,

Edwin, his heir.
Mary, *m.* to Edward, eldest son of Edward Brereton, esq. of Burhas, in the county of Denbigh.

He *d.* in July, 1672, and was *s.* by his son,

ii. Sir Edwin Sadleir, who *m.* Mary, daughter and co-heir of John Lorymer, citizen and apothecary of London, and widow of William Croon, M.D. but had no issue. Sir Edwin sold the estate of Temple Dinsley to Benedict Ithell, esq. who was sheriff of Herts 1 George II. from whose family it passed by will to the Harwoods, and from them to the Dartons. Sir Edwin *d.* 14th July, 1719, in the fifty-eighth year of his age, when the Baronetcy expired.

Arms—Or, a lion rampant, party per fesse az. and gu.

ST. BARBE, OF BROADLANDS.

Created 30th Dec. 1663.

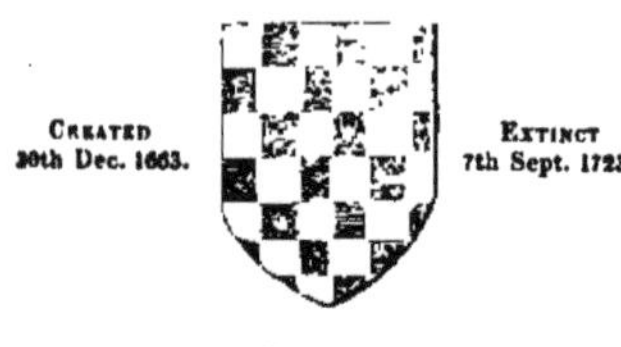

Extinct 7th Sept. 1723.

Lineage.

The St. Barbes came into England at the time of the Conquest, and the name appears on the roll of Battel Abbey.

Robert de St. Barbe (the Norman) was, according to an ancient charter of the abbey of Glastonbury, progenitor of

Robert St. Barbe, of South Brent, in Somersetshire, whose grandson,

Richard St. Barbe, of South Brent, was living *temp.* Edward I. His grandson,

John St. Barbe, of South Brent, *m.* Margaret, daughter of Sir Hugh Langland or Longlande, by Margaret, sister and co-heir of Sir Simon Furneaux, and by her (who wedded, secondly, Sir Richard Acton, knt.) had issue,

Richard, his heir.
Isabella, *m.* to Sir William Stradling, esq. of St. Donats, in Glamorganshire.
Joan, *m. temp.* Henry V. to Ralph Durborough.

The son and heir,

Richard St. Barbe, inherited through his mother the estate of Ashington, in the county of Somerset, and from him we pass to his great-grandson,

Richard St. Barbe, esq. of Ashington, who married Margery, daughter of Humphrey Grey, esq. of Withybrook, in the county of Warwick, and had issue,

Henry, his heir.
Thomas, who married and had issue.*
Anthony, *d. s. p.*
John, *d. s. p.*
William, ancestor of the St. Barbes of Lymington. (See Burke's *Commoners*, vol. ii. p. 46

The eldest son,

Henry St. Barbe, esq. of Ashington, *m.* Eleanor, daughter of Edward Lewknor, esq. of Trotton, in Sussex, and had a large family. He was buried at Ashington in 1567 (his interment being the first entry in the parish register), and his eldest son, John, died *s. p.* in 1570; in consequence, therefore, the second son,

Edward St. Barbe, esq. became of Ashington, and was sheriff of Somersetshire in 1580. He *m.* Frances, daughter and heir of William Fleming, esq. of Broadlands, in Hampshire, and had issue,

Henry, his heir.
Grace, *m.* to Sir Simeon Steward, knt. of Stuntney, in Cambridgeshire.
Ursula, *d.* unm.
Frances, *m.* to William Paulet, esq. of Paulton.
Jane, *m.* to Edward Tyringham, son of Sir Anthony Tyringham, of Tyringham.

He *d.* in 1592, and was *s.* by his son,

Henry St. Barbe, esq. of Ashington and Broadlands, who *m.* Amy, daughter of Edward Rogers, esq. of Cannington, in Somersetshire, by Katharine his wife, daughter of Chief Justice Sir John Popham, and had issue,

John, his heir.
Henry, *d.* in 1634, } *s. p.*
George, *d.* in 1635, }
Francis, slain at the battle of Newburgh in 164[illegible]
Catherine, *m.* to Sir William Pole, knt. of Shute, and had a daughter,
Jane Pole, who *m.* Edward Sydenham, esq. of Combe, and her grandson,
Humphrey Sydenham, became eventually heir of this branch of the St. Barbes.

He was *s.* by his eldest son,

John St. Barbe, esq. of Ashington and Broadlands.

* His granddaughter, Ursula St. Barbe, *m.* Sir William Usher, clerk of the council to *Queen* Elizabeth, and her only daughter, Mary Usher, becoming the wife of Henry Colley, esq. was great-grandmother of the Marquess Wellesley, the Duke of Wellington, &c.

…e of the knights for Hampshire in 1634, m. Grissell, daughter and heir of John Pynsent, esq. prothonotary of the Common Pleas, and dying in 1658, was s. by his eldest son (his three younger sons, Henry, Francis, and Edward, died issueless),

I. JOHN ST. BARBE, esq. of Broadlands, in the county of Hants, and Ashington, in Somersetshire, who was created a BARONET 30th December, 1663. Sir John m. first, Honour, daughter of Colonel Richard Norton, of Southwick; and secondly, Alice, daughter of the Hon. Richard Fiennes, and widow of John Horn, esq. of Winchester, but died issueless 7th September, 1723, when the BARONETCY became EXTINCT. Sir John St. Barbe was buried at Ashington, and his monument there sets forth "that he possessed those amiable qualities which birth, education, travel, greatness of spirit, and goodness of heart produce." He devised his estates to his cousin, HUMPHREY SYDENHAM, esq.

Arms—Checquy arg. and sa.

ST. GEORGE, OF CARRICKDRUMRUSK.

CREATED 5th Sept. 1660.

EXTINCT 18th Aug. 1735.

Lineage.

SIR GEORGE ST. GEORGE, of Carrickdrumrusk, in the county of Leitrim, (second son of Sir Richard St. George, knt. clarencieux king of arms, and elder brother of Capt. Richard St. George, ancestor of the St. George's, of Woodsgift, in the county of Kilkenny,) m. Catherine, daughter of Gifford, governor of the King's and Queen's Counties, *temp.* ELIZABETH, and had issue,

OLIVER, his heir.
George (Sir), knt. of Dunmore, in the county of Galway, who m. Elizabeth, daughter of Sir Robert Hannay, bart. and had issue,

Richard, whose daughter, Mary, m. James Mansergh, esq. and had a son Richard St. George Mansergh, who left issue, Richard James Mansergh and Steppey Mansergh, who both assumed the surname of St. George.
George, d. unm.

Jane, m. to St. George Ashe, bishop of Clogher.
Catharine, m. to Charles Crowe, bishop of Cloyne.
Elizabeth.
Lettice.
Emilia.

Lettice, m. to Arthur Dillon, esq. of Lismullen, in Meath.
Mary, m. to Lord Coote, of Collooney.
Elizabeth, d. young.
Ann, m. to Sir Henry Brooke, knt. of Donegal.
Eleanor, m. to Sir Arthur Gore, bart.
Sarah, m. to Sir Thomas Newcomen, bart.

Sir George St. George was murdered at Sir John Moore's house at Croghan, in the King's County. His son and successor,

I. SIR OLIVER ST. GEORGE, knt. of Carrickdrumrusk, was appointed one of the commissioners for settling the affairs of Ireland, 12 CHARLES II. and was created a BARONET for his good services, at the Restoration. He m. Olivia, daughter of Michael Beresford, esq. of Coleraine, and dying in 1696, was s. by his son,

II. SIR GEORGE ST. GEORGE, who represented the borough of Carrick in parliament in 1704, and in 1715, was raised to the peerage of Ireland, as BARON ST. GEORGE, of Hatley St. George, in the county of Roscommon. His lordship was of the privy council to GEORGE I. and GEORGE II. and was made vice-admiral of Connaught in 1727. He m. Margaret, daughter of John, Viscount Massareene, and dying in 1735, his honours, including the BARONETCY, became EXTINCT. He left two daughters,

I. MARY, b. 10th August, 1693, m. 20th December, 1714, John Usher, esq. M.P. for Carrick, and subsequently vice-admiral of Connaught, and had issue,

ST. GEORGE USHER, esq. M. P. who was created BARON ST. GEORGE, of Hatley St. George, in 1763. His lordship married 18th July, 1752, Elizabeth, daughter and heir of Christopher Dominick, esq. of Dublin, and left at his decease in 1770, an only child,

EMILIA-OLIVIA, married in 1775, to William-Robert, second Duke of Leinster.

Judith Usher, m. to George Lowther, esq. of the county of Meath.

II. OLIVIA, married to Christopher French, esq. of Tyrone, in the county of Galway.

Arms—Arg. a chief az. over all a lion rampant gu. ducally crowned or, armed and langued of the second.

ST. JOHN, OF LONGTHORPE.

CREATED 10th Sept. 1715.

EXTINCT in Sept. 1756.

Lineage.

OLIVER ST. JOHN, esq. who was created by *Queen* ELIZABETH, in the first year of her reign, LORD ST. JOHN, of Bletshoe, m. Anne, daughter and heir of John Fisher, esq. and had, with four daughters, four sons, viz.

I. JOHN, second Lord St. John of Bletshoe, who m. Catherine, daughter of Sir William Dormer, knt. of Ethorpe, in the county of Bucks, and left an only daughter and heiress,

ANNE ST. JOHN, who m. William, Lord Howard, son of Charles, Earl of Nottingham.

II. OLIVER, who succeeded his brother, and became

third Lord St. John of Bletshoe: from him descended the extinct Earls of Bolingbroke and the present (1837) Lord St. John of Bletshoe.

III. Thomas.

IV. Francis.

The third son,

The Hon. Thomas St. John, was father of

Oliver St. John, esq. of Cayshoe, in the county of Bedford, who *m.* Sarah, daughter of Edward Buckley, esq. of Odell, in the same county, and had two sons, Oliver, his heir, and John, who *d.* unmarried, with a daughter, Elizabeth. He was succeeded by his elder son,

Oliver St. John, esq. of Longthorpe, in the county of Northampton, who was of Lincoln's Inn, afterwards constituted solicitor-general by *King* Charles I. and finally made lord chief justice of the Court of Common Pleas. He married first, Johanna, only daughter and heir of Sir John Altham, knt. of Latton, in Essex, and by her had two sons and two daughters, viz.

Francis, his heir.
William, *d.* unm.

Johanna, *m.* to Sir Walter St. John, bart. of Lydiard Tregose.
Catherine, *m.* to Henry St. John, esq. of Tandragee, in Ireland, brother of Sir Walter.

The judge *m.* secondly, Elizabeth, daughter of Henry Cromwell, esq. of Upwood, in the county of Huntingdon, and had another son and daughter, viz.

Oliver, who *m.* Elizabeth, daughter of — Hammond, esq. of Kent.

Elizabeth, *m.* to Sir John Bernard, bart. of Brampton, in Huntingdonshire.

He *m.* thirdly, Mrs. Cockcraft, the widow of a London citizen, but had no other issue. His eldest son,

Francis St. John, esq. of Emanuel College, Cambridge, and afterwards of Lincoln's Inn, *m.* first, Mary, only daughter and heir of Dionysius Wakeringe, esq. of Kelvedon, in Essex, and by that lady had one son, Oliver, who died unmarried on his travels in France. He wedded, secondly, Mary, eldest daughter of Dannett Foorth, an alderman of London, and by her had issue,

Francis, his heir.
William, *d.* young.
Oliver, *d.* unm.
Walter, a merchant in London.

Johanna, *d.* young.
Mary, *m.* to Samuel Browne, esq. of Arlesey, in the county of Bedford.
Elizabeth.

Mr. St. John, who served for Peterborough in several parliaments, was *s.* at his decease by his eldest surviving son,

I. Francis St. John, esq. of Longthorpe, in the county of Northampton, who was created a Baronet 10th September, 1715. Sir Francis *m.* Mary, eldest daughter of Sir Nathaniel Gould, knt. and had two daughters, viz.

Frances.
Mary, *m.* to Sir John Bernard, bart. of Brampton.

Sir Francis was sheriff of Northamptonshire in the first year of *King* George I. He *d.* in September, 1756, when the Baronetcy expired.

Arms—Arg. on a chief gu. two mullets pierced or.

ST. PAULE, OF SNARFORD.

Created 29th June, 1611.

Extinct in 1614.

Lineage.

Thomas de St. Paule having married, about the time of Edward III. the daughter and heir of John de Snarford, of Snarford, in the county of Lincoln, became proprietor of that estate, which he made his principal residence, although he was possessed previously of Byron, in Yorkshire, which came to him by lineal descent from Bryan de St. Paule, who lived under *King* Stephen. He was *s.* by his son,

William St. Paule, esq. of Snarford, whose great grandson,

George St. Paule, esq. was father of

John St. Paule, esq. of Snarford, who died without issue, and was *s.* by his brother,

Thomas St. Paule, esq. of Snarford, who had issue,

George, his heir.

Faith, *m.* to Sir Edward Tyrwhitt, bart. of Stainfield.

He was *s.* at his decease by his son,

I. George St. Paule, esq. of Snarford, who was created a Baronet 29th June, 1611. Sir George *m.* Frances, daughter of Sir William Wray, knt. by whom (who wedded, secondly, Robert Rich, Earl of Warwick,) he had no issue. He *d.* in 1614, when the Baronetcy expired, and the estate devolved upon his sister Faith, Lady Tyrwhitt.

Arms—Arg. a lion rampant double queued gu. crowned or.

ST. QUINTIN, OF HARPHAM.

Created 8th Mar. 1641-2.

Extinct 22nd July, 1795.

Lineage.

This family is said to have been denominated from St. Quintin, the capital of Lower Picardy, in France.

Sir Herbert St. Quintin, one of the companions in arms of the Norman, acquired at the Conquest as his division of the spoil, the manor of Skipsey, with the borough of Woodshall and Brandsburton, in Mapleton, sixteen oxgangs of land in Killing, the manor of Houlbridge, with the Fen and the Marsh, from the bank to the sea-dyke, and Carltown, in the county of Nottingham. Sir Herbert was father of

Oliver St. Quintin, whose eldest son, Sir Robert, in the time of William *Rufus*, was one of the twelve knights, who with Robert Fitshamon, divided certain lands in Wales which they had acquired by conquest there. He built a castle on those lands, and called it St. Quintin Castle.* Oliver's second son,

Sir Herbert St. Quintin, left a son and successor,

Amatellus St. Quintin, feudal baron of St. Quintin, who m. *anno* 1169, Catharine, daughter of Sir John Freshmarsh, knt. and had two sons,

John (Sir), of Brandsburton and Skipsey, who m. in the time of *King* John, *anno* 1209, the daughter of Randle de Maschines, but had no issue.

Herbert (Sir).

The younger son,

Sir Herbert St. Quintin, by the death of his brother issueless, baron of St. Quintin and lord of Brandsburton, m. Anne, second daughter and co-heir of Roger d'Estoteville, and had, with other sons, who d. issueless,

William (Sir), lord of St. Quintin, m. Beatrix, daughter of Saire, Lord Sutton of Holderness, and from him descended the Barons St. Quintin.

Alexander (Sir).

Margery, m. to Sir William Rochfort, knt.

Agnes, m. to Sir Foulke Constable, knt.

The youngest son,

Sir Alexander St. Quintin, obtained from his mother, in the time of Edward II. the lordship of Harpham, in the east riding of Yorkshire. He m. Margaret, daughter of Sir William Dealbano Justinian, and was s. by his eldest son,

Sir William St. Quintin, who wedded Joan, daughter of Sir John Routhe, and was father of

Sir William St. Quintin, who m. the daughter of Sir John Hesterton, and had two sons, Galfrid, his heir, and John, who *d. s. p.* and a daughter, Constance, wife of Sir William Rochford, knt. His eldest son and heir,

Sir Galfrid St. Quintin, m. Alice, daughter of Sir William Ross, of Ingramthorp, and had two sons: the younger, Thomas, m. the daughter of Sir Simon Northrop, knt. and *d. s. p.* The elder,

Sir Galfrid St. Quintin, succeeded his father, and m. in 1326, the daughter of Sir Robert Constable, knt. of Flamborough, and left an only son,

Sir William St. Quintin, who m. in 1353, the daughter of Sir Marmaduke Thwenge, and was s. by his eldest son,

Sir Thomas St. Quintin, living in 1370, who m. Agnes, daughter and heir of Robert Warrine, in whose right he was lord of Newbriggon, and had certain lands in Pickeringhathe. His eldest son,

Thomas St. Quintin, living in 1399, m. Elizabeth, daughter of Nicholas Gascoigne, and was father of

Anthony St. Quintin, who m. Elizabeth, daughter of Sir William Franks, of Grimsby, and had a numerous progeny. His second son,

William St. Quintin, who had succeeded his elder brother, was living in 1422. He m. the daughter of Herrington, and was father of

Sir John St. Quintin, who m. in 1422, the daughter of Thomas Hohne, of Panelholme, and was s. by his son,

John St. Quintin, who wedded Eleanor, daughter of Edmund Thwaites, and had four sons,

I. John, his heir.

II. Edmond, master of the hospital of St. Sepulchre's, in the parish of Preston, in Holderness, at the time of its dissolution.

III. Herbert, } *d.* unm.
IV. Walter, }

The eldest son and heir,

John St. Quintin, living in 1485, m. Margery, daughter of Sir Robert Constable, of Flamborough, and was s. by his son,

Sir William St. Quintin, who m. in 1509, Dorothy, daughter of Sir Bryan Hastings, and was s. by his eldest son,

Gabriel St. Quintin, esq. who married in 1558, the daughter of Sir George Griffith, knt. of Wichmore, in the county of Stafford, and of Agnes Burton, in Yorkshire, and was s. by his son,

George St. Quintin, esq. living in 1584, who m. a daughter of William Creke, esq. of Cottingham, in the county of York, and had issue,

William, *b.* in 1579, his heir.

Herbert, m. Etevill, second sister and co-heir of Robert Lacy, esq. of Folkton, in the county of York, but had no issue.

Gabriel.

Alice, }
Dorothy, } *d.* young.
Mary, }

He was s. by his eldest son,

I. William St. Quintin, esq. of Harpham, in the county of York, who was created a Baronet by *King* Charles I. 8th March, 1641-2. Sir William m. Mary, eldest daughter and co-heir of John Lacy, esq. of Folkton, and had issue,

Henry, his heir.

William, of Hayton, m. Margaret, daughter of Thomas Wood, esq. of Thorpe juxta Rudstown, in Yorkshire.

Thomas, of Flamborough, m. Anne, second daughter of Thomas Wood, esq. of Thorp, in the county of York.

Dorothy, married to Sir William Cayley, bart. of Brompton, in the county of York.

Catherine, m. first, to Michael Wentworth, esq. eldest son of Sir George Wentworth, knt. of Woolley; secondly, to Sir John Kaye, bart. of Woodsome; thirdly, to Henry Sandys, esq.; and fourthly, to the Earl of Eglintoun.

Frances, m. to Francis Lascelles, esq. of Stank, in the county of York, ancestor of the Earls of Harewood.

Sir William *d.* about the year 1651, in the seventieth year of his age, soon after the assizes of York, when he officiated as high sheriff. He was buried at Harpham, and his sons erected a handsome monument to his memory. He was s. by the eldest son,

II. Sir Henry Quintin, who m. Mary, daughter of Henry Stapleton, esq. of Wighill, in the county of

---

* In 1134, Adelina, or Alice St. Quintin, with the consent of her son, Sir Robert St. Quintin, founded a priory for nuns of the Cistercian order, in a place which she held near Appleton, in Yorkshire, and called it Nun Appleton. It was commended to the patronage of St. Mary, and St. John, the apostle and evangelist. This land lay on each side of the river Wharf, partly essarted, and partly not, which was confirmed by Thomas à Becket, Archbishop of Canterbury, and Osbert, Archdeacon of York, was one of the witnesses to the foundation charter, made by Alice de St. Quintin, widow of Robert, son of Fulco, before she was married again to Eustace de Merch.

York, and had (with six younger sons, who all died unm.)

WILLIAM, his heir, who m. Elizabeth, youngest daughter of Sir William Strickland, bart. of Boynton, and dying in the lifetime of his father, left

WILLIAM, who succeeded his grandfather.

George, Walter, } d. unm.

Hugh, married Catherine, eldest daughter of Matthew Chitty, esq. and had two sons and a daughter, viz.

WILLIAM, who inherited as fourth BARONET.

Matthew Chitty.

Catherine, d. young.

Frances, married to Thomas Roundell, esq. of Hutton.

Margaret, m. to Charles Hublethwayte, esq. of Norton.

Mary, m. to James Hustler, esq.

Catherine, d. young.

Mary, m. to Mr. Aldride, of Beverley.

Deborah, m. to Major Burch, of London.

He was s. at his decease by his grandson,

III. SIR WILLIAM ST. QUINTIN. This gentleman represented the borough of Kingston-upon-Hull in parliament in the reigns of *King* WILLIAM, *Queen* ANNE, and *King* GEORGE I. and was a commissioner of the customs, until the act passed disqualifying that commission from sitting in parliament, when he resigned his place, and continued a member of the House of Commons until his death. After resigning the commissionership he was twice appointed one of the lords of the treasury, and afterwards vice-treasurer and receiver-general of Ireland, which post he retained during the remainder of his life. He died "universally lamented by all who knew him, for his great abilities, probity, and love of his country, 30th June, 1723, unmarried, in the sixty-third year of his age," when he was s. by his nephew,

IV. SIR WILLIAM ST. QUINTIN, M.P. for Thirsk, in the county of York, and sheriff in 1733. He m. Rebecca, daughter of Sir John Thompson, knt. lord mayor of London, and by that lady, who d. in October, 1757, had issue,

WILLIAM, his heir.

CATHERINE, m. to Christopher Griffith, esq. of Padworth, in the county of Berks.

MARY, m. to George Darby, esq. of Newton, in Hampshire, captain R.N. and had a son,

WILLIAM THOMAS DARBY, esq. of Sunbury, in Middlesex, who assumed in 1795, the surname and arms of ST. QUINTIN, upon inheriting the estates of Scampston, in Yorkshire. He m. Arabella Bridget, daughter of Thomas Calcraft, esq. by Cecil Ann, his wife, sister of the late John Walker Heneage, esq. of Compton Basset, Wilts, and d. leaving issue.

He d. in 1771, and was s. by his son,

V. SIR WILLIAM ST. QUINTIN, who m. Charlotte, only daughter of Henry Fane, esq. of Wormsley,* in the county of Oxford, by his first wife, Charlotte, only daughter of Nicholas Rowe, the poet, but by that lady, who d. 17th April, 1762, had no issue. Sir William d. 22nd July, 1795, when the BARONETCY EXPIRED.

Arms—Or, a chevron gu. and a chief vaire.

SALUSBURY, OF LLEWENNY.

CREATED 10th Nov. 1619.

EXTINCT 23rd May, 1684.

Lineage.

THOMAS SALUSBURY, the descendant of an ancient Welsh family, had the honour of knighthood conferred upon him by HENRY VII. at the Bridge Foot, upon that monarch's entry into London, after the battle of Blackheath, where Sir Thomas Salusbury had distinguished himself against the Cornish rebels. He m. Joan, daughter of Sir William Vaughan, chamberlain of North Wales, and had issue,

ROGER, his heir.

John, of Denbigh.

Fulco, dean of St. Asaph.

Thomas, ancestor of the Salisburys of Dolbelidan, Denbighshire, of whom was Henry Salisbury, an eminent physician and critic.

Margaret, m. to Edward Hanmer.

Sir Thomas lived to a great age, and was s. at his decease by his son,

SIR ROGER SALUSBURY, knt. of Llewenny, father of

SIR JOHN SALUSBURY, knt. of Llewenny, chancellor and chamberlain of Denbighshire, and M.P. for that county *temp.* HENRY VIII. and MARY. He was made one of the knights of the Carpet by royal mandate, 1 EDWARD VI. He m. Jane, daughter and co-heir of David Middleton, esq. alderman of West Chester, and had, with two daughters, Jane and Elizabeth, six sons, viz.

JOHN, his heir, who m. Catharine, daughter and heir of Tudor ap Robert, and died v. p. leaving two sons,

Thomas, who was executed in 1586 for participation in the conspiracy to deliver Mary Queen of Scots from imprisonment. He left an only daughter,

Margaret, m. to William Norris, esq. of Speke.

JOHN, successor to his grandfather.

George, who m. Mary, daughter of Thomas Grosvenor, esq. of Eaton.

Thomas, who married Elena, daughter of Richard Lloyd, esq. of Rossendale.

Hugh, who m. Anne, daughter of Sir George Stradling, knt.

Roger, D. C. L. of Jesus College, Oxford, who m. Katherine, second daughter of Sir Richard Clough, knt. of Plâs Clough, in Denbighshire, and acquired with her the curious mansion of Bachegraig, which Sir Richard had erected in the Dutch style of architecture, near Denbigh. His great-grandson,

THOMAS SALUSBURY, esq. of Bachegraig, colonel in the army, m. Anne, daughter and heir of Thomas Perceval, esq. of North Wes

* Whose elder brother, Thomas Fane, inherited in 1762, the EARLDOM of WESTMORELAND.

ton, in Somersetshire, and relict of Evan Lloyd, esq. by whom he had, with a daughter, Elizabeth, two sons,

THOMAS, of Bachegraig, who married his cousin, Lucy, daughter and co-heir of John Salusbury, esq. and died in 1714, leaving two sons, viz.

1. JOHN, of Bachegraig, *b.* in 1710, who *m.* a daughter of Sir Robert Cotton, bart. and had a daughter,

HESTER LYNCH SALUSBURY, of Bachegraig, married, first, to Henry Thrale, esq.; and secondly, to Gabriel Piozzi, esq. This lady was the friend and correspondent of Dr. Johnson. The estate of Bachegraig she left from her grandson and heir, Captain Mostyn, R. N. to the present Sir John Piozzi Salusbury, knt. of Brynbella.

2. NORFOLK, of Plas y werd, Denbighshire, ancestor of the SALUSBURYS of Llanwern, in Monmouthshire. (See BURKE's *Peerage and Baronetage.*)

Robert, who *m.* Margaret, daughter of Edward Stanby, of Enlow.

Sir John died 18th March, 1578, and was *s.* by his grandson,

SIR JOHN SALUSBURY, knt. of Llewenny, surnamed *the Strong*, who represented the county of Denbigh in parliament 43 ELIZABETH. He *m.* Ursula, daughter of Henry Stanley, Earl of Derby, and had four sons and three daughters. He died in 1613, and was *s.* by the eldest son,

I. HENRY SALUSBURY, esq. of Llewenny, in Denbighshire, who was created a BARONET 18th November, [illegible]. He *m.* first, Hester, daughter of Sir Thomas Myddleton, knt. of Chirk Castle, by whom he had issue, Thomas, John, Ursula, and Elizabeth; and secondly, Elizabeth, daughter of Sir John Vaughan, Lord Carbery, by whom he had a daughter, Anne, wife of the Hon. Arthur Stanhope, son of Philip, first Earl of Chesterfield. Sir Henry died 2nd August, 1632, and was *s.* by his son,

II. SIR THOMAS SALUSBURY, of Llewenny, the celebrated poet, D.C.L. and M.P. for Denbighshire. He *m.* Hester, daughter of Sir Edward Tyrrell, bart. of Thornton, Bucks, and dying in 1743, was *s.* by his only son,

III. SIR JOHN SALUSBURY, of Llewenny, member for Denbigh in all the parliaments of CHARLES II. He *m.* Jane, daughter of Edward Williams, esq. of Wigg. but died *s. p.* 23rd May, 1684, when the BARONETCY became EXTINCT. His estates devolved upon his sister and heiress,

HESTER, *m.* to Sir Robert Cotton, bart. of Combermere, in Cheshire, M.P. for that county. The great-great-grandson of this marriage is the present

Stapleton Cotton, VISCOUNT COMBERMERE (see BURKE's *Peerage and Baronetage*).

Arms Gu. a lion rampant arg. crowned or between three crescents of the last.

SAMWELL, OF UPTON.

CREATED 22nd Dec. 1675.

EXTINCT 18th Oct. 1789.

Lineage.

JAMES SAMWELL, esq. (of the Samwells of Cornwall) was father of

JOHN SAMWELL, esq. whose second son,

RICHARD SAMWELL, esq. of Cotsford, married Amy, daughter of Thomas Gifford, of Twyford, in Bucks, was father of

FRANCIS SAMWELL, esq. who removed from Cotsford, in Oxfordshire, and settled first at Northampton, and afterwards at Rothersthorp. He was auditor to *King* HENRY VIII. and *m.* Mary, sister of the Rev. William Bill, D.D. of Ashwell, in Hertfordshire, almoner to *Queen* ELIZABETH. His son and heir,

SIR WILLIAM SAMWELL, was auditor to *Queen* ELIZABETH, and received the honour of knighthood at the coronation of *King* JAMES I. He married Jane, daughter of Sir Henry Skipwith, knt. of Keythorp, in the county of Leicester, and had issue,

I. RICHARD (Sir), his heir.

II. Arthur, of Morton Murrell, in the county of Warwick, *m.* Mary, daughter of Sir Stephen Harvey, K.B. and *d.* in 1667, leaving two daughters,

MARY.

ANNE, *m.* to Francis Bagshaw, esq. of Culworth.

III. Robert, *d.* unm.

IV. Anthony, of Dean's Yard, Westminster, *m.* Anne, daughter of — Heynes, of Chessington, in Surrey, and had, with a daughter, Elizabeth, wife of Robert Coke, esq. of Trusley, in Derbyshire, a son and heir,

William Samwell, esq. of Deans Yard, and of Watton, in Norfolk, who *m.* Anne, daughter of Sir Denner Strutt, bart. of Little Warley, in Essex, and had an only daughter,

ANNE SAMWELL, who married William Henry Fleming, esq. and conveyed to him the manor of Watton. She *d.* 29th April, 1728.

Mr. Samwell *d.* in 1676, and his widow was afterwards married to John, third son of Sir Philip Wodehouse, bart. of Kimberley, in Norfolk, whom she also survived, and *d.* 19th August, 1720.

I. Frances, *d.* unm.

II. Jane, *m.* to Sir Sapcote Harrington, knt. of Exton, in Rutlandshire, and was mother of the celebrated

JAMES HARRINGTON, author of "The Commonwealth of Oceana."*

* This work was seized in the press by CROMWELL, but released through the medium of Mrs. Claypole, Oliver's favourite daughter, at whose suggestion it was dedicated to him on its publication in 1656. It is said, when Oliver perused it, he declared "that the gentleman had wrote it very well, but must not think to cheat him out of his power and authority; for what he had won by the sword he would not suffer himself to be deprived of by the pen."

Sir William was *s.* by his eldest surviving son,

SIR RICHARD SAMWELL, knt. of Upton and Gayton, both in the county of Northampton, who *m.* Mary, daughter of Sir Richard Verney, knt. of Compton, in Warwickshire, and had issue,

Richard, his heir.

Francis, *m.* Rebecca, daughter of Robert Selsby, esq. of Duston, in the county of Northampton, and had issue.

Jane, *m.* to Sir Edward Rossiter, knt. of Somerby, in the county of Lincoln.

He *d.* in 1668. His son and heir,

RICHARD SAMWELL, esq. of Upton, who wedded Frances, eldest daughter and co-heir of Thomas, Viscount Wenman, of Tuam, and had surviving issue,

THOMAS, his heir.

Margaret, *m.* to Thomas Catesby, esq. of Ecton, in Northamptonshire.

Penelope, *m.* to Sir William Yorke, knt. of Lessingham, in Lincolnshire.

Elizabeth, *d.* unm.

Agnes, *m.* to Robert Codrington, esq. of Codrington, in Gloucestershire.

Frances, *m.* to Sir Thomas Wagstaff, of Tachebrooke, in Warwickshire, and had a daughter,

FRANCES WAGSTAFF, *m.* first, to Sir Edward Bagot, bart. of Blithfield; and secondly, to Sir Adolphus Oughton, bart.

Mary, *m.* first, to Adolphus Oughton, esq. and was mother of

Sir Adolphus Oughton, bart. who married his cousin, Frances, widow of Sir Edward Bagot, bart. and *d. s. p.*

She *m.* secondly, Roger Pope, esq.

Mr. Samwell was *s.* by his son,

I. THOMAS SAMWELL, esq. of Upton, in the county of Northampton, M.P. for that shire, who was created a BARONET 22nd December, 1675. Sir Thomas *m.* first, Elizabeth, daughter and heir of George Gooday, esq. of Bower Hall, in Essex, and by that lady had two surviving daughters, viz.

ELIZABETH, *m.* to Sir John Langham, bart. of Cottesbrooke Park, in Northamptonshire.

FRANCES, *m.* to Sir Richard Newman, bart. of Fifehead-Magdalen, in the county of Dorset.

He wedded, secondly, Anne, daughter and heir of Sir John Godschalk, knt. of Atherston-upon-Stower, in Warwickshire, and by her had, with a daughter, Finetta, who *d.* young, an only son, his successor, at his decease in February, 1693,

II. SIR THOMAS SAMWELL, M.P. for Coventry, baptized 14th April, 1687, who *m.* first, Millicent, daughter of the Rev. Thomas Fuller, D.D. rector of Hatfield, Herts, by whom he had issue,

THOMAS, his successor.

Millicent, *d.* unm.

Frances, *m.* in 1749, to John Ashe, esq. of Langley Burrell, Wilts, and *d. s. p.*

Anne, *m.* to Timothy Stoughton, esq. of Allesley, in Warwickshire, and *d. s. p.*

Mary, *m.* to the Rev. Stephen Langham, fourth son of Sir John Langham, bart. and had four daughters, of whom the three youngest died unm. The eldest, Millicent, married William Drought, esq. and left one son and two daughters.

Sir Thomas *m.* secondly, Mary, daughter of Sir Gilbert Clarke, knt. of Chilcot, in the county of Derby, and relict of William Ives, esq. of Bradden, in Northamptonshire, and by that lady had

WENMAN, who inherited as fourth BARONET.

CATHERINE, *m.* in 1734, to Thomas-Atherton Watson, esq. of Bedlington, in Northumberland, and by him (who *d.* in 1793) left at her decease in 1790,

THOMAS-SAMWELL WATSON, of whom presently, as heir of his uncle, Sir Wenman Samwell.

WILLIAM-LANGHAM WATSON.

Atherton Watson.

Camilla-Matilda Watson.

Charlotte-Felicia Watson, *m.* in 1798, to the Rev. Benjamin Tinley, B.D. of Whissendine, in Rutlandshire, and was left a widow, with a family, in 1804.

Sir Thomas *d.* 16th November, 1757, and was *s.* by his elder son,

III. SIR THOMAS SAMWELL, *b.* 28th February, 1710, *d.* a bachelor, 3rd December, 1779, and was *s.* by his half brother,

IV. SIR WENMAN SAMWELL, *b.* in 1728, *m.* Elizabeth, daughter of Thomas Smith, esq. of East Haddon, but died issueless 18th October, 1789, when the BARONETCY EXPIRED, and the estates devolved upon his nephew,

THOMAS SAMWELL WATSON, esq. who in consequence assumed the additional surname and arms of SAMWELL. He *d. s. p.* in 1831, and was *s.* by his brother,

WENMAN-LANGHAM WATSON, who in like manner assumed the surname and arms of SAMWELL, and is the present

WENMAN-LANGHAM WATSON-SAMWELL, esq. of Upton (refer to BURKE's *Commoners*, vol. I. page 446).

Arms—Arg. two squirrels sejant addorsed.

SANDERSON, OF COMBE, IN GREENWICH.

CREATED 19th July, 1720.

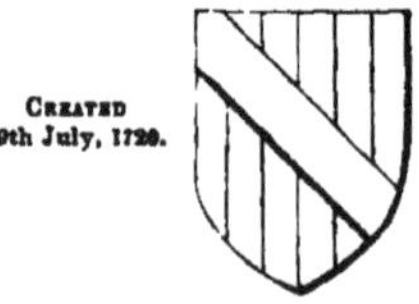

EXTINCT 30th Oct. 1760.

Lineage.

WILLIAM SANDERSON, esq. whose father was killed in the service of CHARLES I. was after the Restoration an officer in the Dutch wars, and lost his life by an accidental fall in action, *anno* 1664-5. He *m.* Elizabeth, daughter of — Smith, of Old Buckenham, in Norfolk, and left a son,

RALPH SANDERSON, esq. who was made a captain in the West Indies, by Sir John Harman, and was captain of several ships in the Dutch wars. He married Ephrim, daughter of — Garrett, esq. of Norfolk, and dying in 1690, was *s.* by his only son,

I. SIR WILLIAM SANDERSON, who had the honour of knighthood conferred upon him by King GEORGE I on board the Peregrine yacht, under the royal standard at Gravesend, before his majesty landed on coming to England to assume the crown, and was created a BARONET by the same monarch 19th July, 1720. He *m.* first, Drury, daughter and co-heir of Sir William Wray, bart. of Ashby, in the county of Lincoln, and had issue,

Ralph, } both naval officers, *d.* in the lifetime of
Edward, } their father, *s. p.*

WILLIAM, his heir.

Tufton, *m.* first, to Captain Barrie; and secondly, to Alexander Horton, esq. of the Grove, Bucks.

He married secondly, Elizabeth, daughter of Samuel Howe, esq. judge of the Admiralty, relict of Simon Degge, esq. of Derby, but by her had no child. Sir William, who was gentleman usher of the black rod, *d.* 17th May, 1727, and was *s.* by his only surviving son,

II. SIR WILLIAM SANDERSON, gentleman usher of the black rod. This gentleman *m.* first, Mary, daughter of Captain Richard Cook, of Greenwich, and by her had a daughter,

Mary.

He wedded secondly, Mrs. Bignel, who *d. s. p.* 20th January, 1728-9. His third wife, whom he *m.* in June, 1730, was Charlotte, daughter of Sir Richard Gough, knt. of Chelsea, and by that lady left at his decease, 10th January, 1754, an only son, his successor,

III. SIR WILLIAM SANDERSON, who died aged fifteen, 29th October, 1760, when the BARONETCY became EXTINCT.

Arms—Paly of six, arg. and az. a bend sa.

SANDERSON, OF LONDON.

CREATED 6th Dec. 1794.—EXTINCT 23rd June, 1798.

Lineage.

I. JAMES SANDERSON, esq. of London, who was created a BARONET in 1794, *m.* first, Elizabeth, daughter of John Judd, esq. of Chelmsford; and secondly, Elizabeth, daughter of Alderman Thomas Skinner, of London, but died without male issue, in 1798, when the title became EXTINCT.

SANDFORD, OF HOWGILL.

CREATED 12th Aug. 1641.

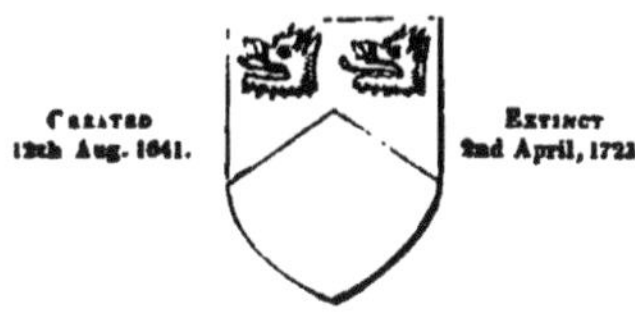

EXTINCT 2nd April, 1723.

Lineage.

RICHARD SANDFORD, esq. younger son of Sir Thomas Sandford, knt. of Askham, in Westmoreland, by Anne, his wife, daughter and co-heir of Anthony Crackenthorp, esq. of Howgill, in the same county, inherited that estate from his mother, and founded the Sandfords of Howgill. He *m.* Anne, daughter of John Warriner, esq. of Helsington, and had eighteen children, of whom the eldest,

SIR THOMAS SANDFORD, knt. of Howgill Castle, died without issue, and was *s.* by his brother,

SIR RICHARD SANDFORD, knt. of Howgill Castle, who *m.* Anne, widow of Pennington of Seaton, and daughter of Henry Crackenthorpe, of Newbiggin, by whom he had a son and successor,

I. THOMAS SANDFORD, esq. of Howgill Castle, who was created a BARONET 12th August, 1641. He married Bridget, daughter of Sir George Dalston, knt. of Dalston, and had issue, RICHARD, George, William, Anne, Elizabeth, and Catharine. The eldest son,

II. SIR RICHARD SANDFORD, of Howgill Castle, *m.* Mary, daughter of Sir Francis Bowes, knt. of Thornton, in the county of Durham, and had issue,

RICHARD, his heir.

MARY, *m.* to Robert Honywood, esq. of Marks Hall, Essex, and was mother of

GENERAL PHILIP HONYWOOD, of Howgill Castle.

Sir Richard was murdered in the White Fryars, London, 8th September, 1675, by Henry Symbal and William Jones, who were executed shortly after. Sir Richard's son and successor,

III. SIR RICHARD SANDFORD, of Howgill Castle, said to have been born the hour of his father's decease, died unmarried 2nd April, 1723, when the BARONETCY became EXTINCT. The estates passed to his sister.

Arms—Per chev. sa. and erm. in chief two boars' heads couped or.

SANDYS, OF WILBERTON.

CREATED 25th Nov. 1613.

EXTINCT in 1644.

Lineage.

ROBERT SANDYS, of St. Bees, in Cumberland, 1399 *temp.* HENRY IV. was father of

JOHN SANDYS, of Furness-fells, in Lancashire, whose son and heir,

WILLIAM SANDYS, of Furnese-fells, was father of

WILLIAM SANDYS, of Hawkeshead, who *m.* Margaret, daughter and heir of William Rawson, of Yorkshire, and left a son and heir,

WILLIAM SANDYS, father of

GEORGE SANDYS, citizen of London, who *m.* Margaret, daughter of John Dixon, of the same city, and was father of*

EDWYN SANDYS, an eminent divine in the time of ELIZABETH, and in succession (1559) Bishop of Worcester, (1569) Bishop of London, and (1567) Archbishop of York. Doctor Sandys was educated at Cambridge, and was vice-chancellor of the university at the decease of EDWARD VI. when, by order of the Duke of Northumberland, he preached against Queen MARY, and defended the right of Lady Jane Grey; for this line of conduct he was imprisoned a year, but then received a pardon. He retired subsequently into Germany, and openly professing the reformed re-

* From his fifth son, MYLES, descended the Lords Sandys of the Vine, and the present SIR EDWIN BAYNTUN-SANDYS, bart.; and from his sixth son, Anthony, derives the present MYLES SANDYS, esq. of Graythwaite Hall, Lancashire.

ligion, remained abroad until the accession of ELIZABETH, by whom he was preferred in the manner stated above. He died in 1588, leaving behind a high reputation for learning, probity, and other Christian virtues. His grace m. Cecilia, daughter of Thomas Wilford, esq. of Cranbrook, in Kent, and had issue,

- I. SAMUEL (Sir), his heir, of Ombersley, in the county of Worcester, high sheriff in 1619, ancestor of the LORDS SANDYS, of Ombersley. (See BURKE's *Extinct and Dormant Peerage*.)
- II. EDWIN (Sir), ancestor of the Sandys of Northborne Court.
- III. MILES (Sir).
- IV. GEORGE, a traveller and poet, died in 1643.

The third son,

I. SIR MYLES SANDYS, of Wilberton, in the county of Cambridge, received the honour of knighthood from *King* JAMES I. and was created a BARONET 25th November, 1612. He m. Elizabeth, daughter of Edward Cook, gent. of North Cray, and had seven sons and a daughter, who all died issueless. Sir Miles represented his native county in parliament 3 CHARLES I. and dying in 1644, was s. by his eldest son,

II. SIR MYLES SANDYS, who had received the honour of knighthood in the lifetime of his father. He m. Elizabeth, daughter and heir of Thomas Park, esq. of Wisbeach, in the Isle of Ely, but died without issue in 1644, when the BARONETCY EXPIRED.

Arms—Or, a fesse wavy between three crosses crosslet fitché gu.

SANDYS, OF NORTHBORNE.

CREATED 15th Dec. 1684.—EXTINCT 2nd May, 1726.

Lineage.

SIR EDWIN SANDYS, second son of Dr. Edwin Sandys, Archbishop of York, received the honour of knighthood from *King* JAMES I. and was distinguished as a politician in that king's and in the subsequent reign. "He was (says an old writer) a leading man in all parliamentary affairs, well versed in business, and an excellent patriot to his country; in defence of which, by speaking too boldly, he, with Selden, was committed into custody 16th June, 1621, and not delivered thence till the 18th July following, which was voted by the House of Commons a great breach [illegible] their privileges. He was treasurer to the undertakers for the western plantations, which he effectually advanced, was a person of great judgment, and, as [illegible] author saith, *ingenio et gravitate morum insignis*. He wrote while he was at Paris, *anno* 1629, [illegible] Speculum, or a View or Survey of the State of Religion in the Western Part of the World. H[illegible] £1500 to the university of Oxford for the endowment of a metaphysic lecture; and departing this life [illegible] year 1629, was buried in the church of Northbourne in Kent, where he had a seat and fair estate." [illegible] Edwin m. first, Margaret, daughter of John Ever[illegible], esq. of Devonshire, and by that lady had a daughter,

- Elizabeth, m. to Sir Thomas Wilsford, knt. [illegible] Heding, in Kent.

He wedded, secondly, Anne, daughter of Th[illegible] Southcott, esq.; thirdly, Elizabeth, daughter of [illegible]mas Nevinson, esq. of Eastrey: by the former [illegible] a daughter, Anne; by the latter, no issue. [illegible] fourthly, Catharine, daughter of Sir Richard B[illegible]ley, knt. of Anglesey, and by her (who d. [illegible]) had, with other issue,

- EDWIN, his heir, a colonel in the parliame[illegible] army.
- Richard, who purchased Downehall, [illegible] was, like his brother, a colonel in the par[illegible]ment's army. He m. Hester, daughter of [illegible] Aucher, second son of Anthony Aucher, esq. [illegible] Bourne, in the same county.*

The elder son,

EDWIN SANDYS, esq. of Northbourne Court, a [illegible] in the parliament's army, received a mortal [illegible] the battle of Worcester, and died in 1642, leaving [illegible] Catherine, daughter and at length heir of [illegible] Champneys, esq. of Hall Place, Kent, a son and [illegible]

SIR RICHARD SANDYS, knt. of Northbourne C[illegible] who m. Mary, daughter of Sir Henry Heyman, [illegible] and being accidentally killed by his fowling pie[illegible] passing over a hedge, *anno* 1669, was s. by his [illegible]

I. RICHARD SANDYS, esq. of Northbourne C[illegible] who was created a BARONET 15th December [illegible] Sir Richard m. first, Miss Ward, daughter an[illegible] of Prebendary Ward, of Salisbury; and second[illegible] Mary, daughter and co-heir of Sir Francis Rolle [illegible] of Bicton, in the county of Devon, and left daughters only at his decease 2nd May, 1726, when the BA[illegible]

---

* His son,

EDWIN SANDWYS, was father of

JORDAN SANDYS, esq. of Downehall, captain in the royal navy, buried at Downe 9th January, 1734, left by his wife, Deborah, daughter of George St. Quintin, of London, merchant, a son and heir,

HENRY SANDYS, esq. of Downehall, who m. Priscilla, eldest surviving daughter and co-heir of Sir Richard Sandys, bart. of Northborne Court, and acquired thereby the estate of Northborne: he left at his decease in 1726 a son and heir,

RICHARD SANDYS, esq. of Northborne Court and Canterbury, justice of the peace for the county of Kent, m. Susan-Crayford, daughter of James Taylor, of London, merchant, and by her, who d. in 1777, had issue,

- RICHARD, in holy orders, his heir.
- Edwin-Humphry, m. first, Sarah, daughter of Sir William Fagg, bart. but by her, who d. in 1782, had no issue to survive infancy. He m. secondly, Helen, daughter and heir of Edward-Lord Chick, esq. and had by that lady
  - EDWIN, in holy orders, rector of Upper Hardress, in Kent, b. in 1785; m. in 1816, Mary-Lilias, daughter of William Lumsdaine, esq. of Edinburgh, and has issue.
  - Charles, of Canterbury, b. in 1786; m. in 1815, Miss Sedley-Frances Burdett, and has issue.
  - George, b. in 1791, lieutenant in the royal [illegible] d. at sea in 1812 unm.
  - James, b. in 1794, lieutenant in the roya[illegible] drowned at sea in 1815 unm.
  - John, in holy orders, b. in 1799.
  - Mary.
  - Sarah, d. in 1813 unm.

The elder son and heir,

RICHARD SANDYS, in holy orders, m. first, C[illegible] daughter of William Hougham, esq. and had by h[illegible]

- RICHARD-EDWIN, lieutenant in the royal [illegible] killed in action off Copenhagen 2nd April, [illegible] d. unm.
- CATHERINA, co-heir of her brother, m. in [illegible] J[illegible] Chesshyre, esq. captain in the royal navy.

Mr. Sandys m. secondly, Lady Frances-Alicia [illegible] widow of William Aslong, and daughter of Charle[illegible] Earl of Tankerville, by whom (who wedded, thirdly, Rev. Edward Beckingham Benson, rector of D[illegible]) had another daughter,

- ALICIA-ARABELLA, co-heir of her half-brother, m. [illegible] 1804, to Francis Cockburn, esq. son of the late [illegible] James Cockburn, bart. of Langton.

The Rev. Richard Sandys d. in 1782.

[...]ACY EXPIRED. Of those daughters, ANNE, the youngest surviving, m. Charles Pyott, esq. of St. Martin's, near Canterbury, and d. in 1789; PRISCILLA, the eldest surviving, m. Henry Sandys, esq. of Downe Hall, and conveyed to him the estate of Northbourne Court, which passed to their son and heir,

RICHARD SANDYS, esq. of Northbourne Court, whose granddaughters became eventually coheirs of the line, namely,

CATHARINA SANDYS, wife of Captain John Chesshyre, R.N.

ALICIA-ARABELLA SANDYS, wife of Francis Cockburn, esq. son of Sir James Cockburn, bart. of Langton.

Arms—As SANDYS OF WILBERTON.

SAS-VAN-BOSCH, OF HOLLAND.

CREATED 22nd Oct. 1680.—EXTINCT, unascertained.

Lineage.

I. SIR GELEBRAND SAS-VAN-BOSCH, secretary to the Admiralty at Rotterdam, was created a BARONET 22nd October, 1680, but of him or of his descendants, being residents and natives of Holland, nothing further has been ascertained.

SAUNDERSON, OF SAXBY.

CREATED 25th Nov. 1612. EXTINCT in 1723.

Lineage.

ALEXANDER DE BIDDIC, living in 1333, and descended in a direct line from Robert de Biddic, who flourished in the time of the *Empress* MAUD, m. Jane, daughter of Richard Chancellor, of Brafferton, and had issue; of whom were

ROBERT OF THOMAS DE BIDDIC, *alias* SAUNDERSON, who m. and left a son and heir,

ROBERT SAUNDERSON, whose great-granddaughter,

JANE SAUNDERSON, carried Biddic to the family of her husband, SIR ROBERT HILTON, bart. of Hilton;

and

JAMES SAUNDERSON, who was buried at Washington in RICHARD II. *anno* 1387, leaving by Margaret, his wife, daughter of Sir Walter Hilton, knt. of Eskdale, a son and heir,

ALEXANDER SAUNDERSON, who m. Maria, daughter of John Falton, esq. and was s. by his son,

ROBERT SAUNDERSON, who wedded Elizabeth, daughter of Thomas Staveley, of Stanhope, and was father of

JAMES SAUNDERSON, of Tickhill, in the county of York, who had four sons,

WILLIAM, his heir.

Nicholas, of Erby and Gowk Hill Hall, Yorkshire, ancestor of the Saundersons of Stirrup, Sheffield, Blythe, Serleby Hall, &c. &c. Of the Blythe branch was Robert Saunderson, D.D. Bishop of Lincoln.

John, of Midhope, ancestor of the Saundersons of Pawhill, Midhope, Maltby, Thurlestane, &c.

Robert, of the Ewes, near Sandbeck, married and had issue.

The eldest son,

WILLIAM SAUNDERSON, of Tickhill, in the county of York, whose son, by Jane Lamplugh, his wife,

WILLIAM SAUNDERSON, of Tickhill, called in some accounts Henry, m. Jane, daughter of Lambton, of Lambton, and had issue,

Robert, whose two daughters, Alice and Margaret, *d. s. p.*

NICHOLAS, of whom presently.

Margaret, m. to Hewett.

Alice, m. to Christopher Eyre, esq. of Highlow Padley, in the county of Derby, and had issue.

The second son,

NICHOLAS SAUNDERSON, of Revesby, married Agnes, daughter of William London, and had, with two daughters, Dorothy, wife of Robert Trigott, and Maria, of John Kaym, several sons, of whom the youngest,

ROBERT SAUNDERSON, esq. purchased the estate of Saxby, in Lincolnshire, and erected the mansion of Fillingham. He *d.* 2nd November, 1583, aged sixty-three, leaving by Catharine,* his wife, daughter of Vincent Grantham, esq. of St. Catharine's, Lincoln, with three daughters (of whom the eldest, Ann, m. Sir John Staingate, knt.), three sons, viz.

NICHOLAS (Sir), his heir.

Robert, *d. s. p.*

Thomas, of Gainsborough, in Lincolnshire; admitted of Lincoln's Inn in 1591; will dated 4th March, 1640, was proved in the Prerogative Court of Canterbury 3rd December, 1642: the preface to that document is curious for the mass of proverbial and other moral and religious remarks. He m. first, Jane, daughter of Denzil Holles, esq. by whom he had a son,

Robert, living in 1642, the father of several children.

He m. secondly, Dorcas, daughter of Sir Julius Cæsar, chancellor of the Exchequer; and thirdly, Dorothea, daughter of Richard Maddison, esq.

The eldest son,

I. NICHOLAS SAUNDERSON, esq. of Saxby, in Lincolnshire, M.P. for Gainsborough and afterwards for Lincoln, aged twenty-one at the death of his father, was created a BARONET 25th November, 1612, and raised to the peerage of Ireland, as Viscount Castleton, in 1628. His lordship m. Mildred, daughter and heir of John Eltoft, esq. of Boston, and had issue,

NICHOLAS, his heir.

William (Sir), knt. m. Jane, daughter of Sir John Cooper, of Dorsetshire, and *d.* in 1642.

George, of Thoresby Abbey Grange, Lincolnshire, who m. first, Elizabeth, daughter and sole heir of Thomas Bostock, of London; and secondly, Susannah, daughter of Sir George Fitzwilliam, of Mabblethorpe.

Robert, who had lands from his father at Friskney.

Frances, m. first, to Edward Coppledike, esq. of Startington, in Lincolnshire; and secondly, to Sir Edward Waldegrave.

* She m. secondly, William Rokeby, esq. of Skiers.

Anne, *m.* to Sir Philip Tyrwhitt, bart. of Stainfield, Lincolnshire.

Margaret, *m.* to Sir Peregrine Bertie.

Lord Castleton died about 1630, and was succeeded by his son,

II. SIR NICHOLAS SAUNDERSON, second Viscount Castleton, whose will, dated 2nd March, 1639, was proved in the Prerogative Court of Canterbury 1st January, 1641. His lordship *m.* Frances, daughter of Sir George Manners, knt. of Haddon, and had issue,

- NICHOLAS, his heir.
- PEREGRINE, successor to his brother.
- GEORGE, who inherited as fifth viscount.
- Rutland, Francis, Charles, } all living in 1652.
- Mildred, *m.* 3rd July, 1651, to Thomas, Viscount Falconberg.
- Grace, *d.* unm.

His lordship was *s.* by his eldest son,

III. SIR NICHOLAS SAUNDERSON, third Viscount Castleton, fifteen years old at his father's decease. He died intestate without issue, and was succeeded by his brother,

IV. SIR PEREGRINE SAUNDERSON, fourth Viscount Castleton, whose will was dated 4th November, 1649, and administration granted to his next brother,

V. SIR GEORGE SAUNDERSON, fifth Viscount Castleton, who *m.* first, Grace, daughter of Henry Bellasis, son and heir of Thomas, Lord Fauconberg; and secondly, Sarah, daughter of Sir John Evelyn, of West Dean, relict of Sir John Wray, of Glentworth, and of Thomas, Viscount Fanshawe. By the former his lordship had issue,

- NICHOLAS, whose will, dated 7th November, 1691, was proved 6th March, 1692. He *m.* Elizabeth, daughter and heir of Sir John Wray, of Glentworth, and had an only son,
  - WRAY, who *m.* Mary, daughter of Lewis Watson, Earl of Rockingham, and died in the lifetime of his grandfather *s. p.*
- Hugh, *d.* 18th January, 1655.
- Charles, *d.* 20th May, 1684.
- Samuel, *d.* young.
- John, of Glentworth, George, } both *d. s. p.*
- Thomas, whose will was proved 18th July, 1767.
- JAMES, heir to his father.

His lordship died at Sandbeck 27th May, 1714, and was *s.* by his only surviving son,

VI. SIR JAMES SAUNDERSON, sixth Viscount Castleton, who was created a peer of England in 1714, as BARON SAUNDERSON, of Saxby. In 1716 he was made Viscount Castleton, of Sandbeck, in Yorkshire, and in 1720 advanced to the EARLDOM OF CASTLETON. His lordship *d. s. p.* in 1723, when the BARONETCY and all his other honours became EXTINCT. His great estate he bequeathed to his cousin on the mother's side, Thomas Lumley, third Earl of Scarborough, who thereupon assumed, by act of parliament, the additional surname of "SAUNDERSON."*

Arms—Paly of six arg. and az. a bend sa.

SAVAGE, OF ROCK SAVAGE.

CREATED 29th June, 1611.

EXTINCT in 1728.

Lineage.

Of this family, whose chief abode for many generations had been at the castle of Frodsham, in Cheshire, and occasionally at another house more recently erected at Clifton, on the opposite side of the river called ROCK SAVAGE, was

SIR JOHN SAVAGE, a good and faithful ally of the Earl of Richmond, and one of the brave soldiers who placed that prince upon the throne as HENRY VII. Sir John was subsequently in the wars of France, and fell at the siege of Boloine. His son and heir,

SIR JOHN SAVAGE, knt. *m.* Lady Elizabeth Somerset, daughter of Charles, first Earl of Worcester, and was *s.* by his son,

SIR JOHN SAVAGE, knt. who *m.* Lady Elizabeth Manners, daughter of Thomas, first Earl of Rutland, and had two sons, JOHN and Thomas. The younger,

I. SIR THOMAS SAVAGE, knt. of Rock Savage, in the county of Chester, was created a BARONET (being the nineteenth from the institution of the order) 29th June, 1611. He *m.* Mary, daughter and co-heir of Richard Allington, esq. and left at his decease in 1615, with two daughters, Elizabeth, wife, first, of Thomas Manwaring, and secondly, of Sir Ralph Done, and Grace, wife of Sir Richard Wilbraham, bart. of Woodhey, several sons, of whom the eldest,

II. SIR THOMAS SAVAGE, of Rock Savage, who was raised to the peerage as Viscount Savage 6th November, 1626. He *m.* Elizabeth, eldest daughter and co-heir of Thomas, Lord Darcy, afterwards Viscount Colchester and Earl Rivers, and had issue,

- JOHN, his heir.
- Thomas, who *m.* Bridget, widow of Sir Edward Somerset, and daughter and heir of William Whitmore, esq. of Leighton, by Margaret, his wife, sister and heir of Sir George Beeston, of Beeston, in Cheshire. From this marriage descended the Savages of Beeston, in Cheshire.
- Francis.
- Charles, whose daughter, Mary, married Jeremy Thoresby, of Leeds.
- Jane, *m.* to John Pawlet, Lord St. John, afterwards Marquess of Winchester.
- Dorothy, *m.* to Charles, Lord Andover.
- Elizabeth, *m.* to Sir John Thimbelby, of Irnham, Lincolnshire.

---

* Robert Saunderson, of Alford, in Lincolnshire, who died in 1741, aged sixty-seven, bore the arms of the Saundersons of Saxby, but his connexion with that family has not yet been exactly ascertained. He left two daughters, his co-heirs, viz.

ELIZABETH, *m.* to William Gonville, esq. of Alford, and had an only daughter,

FRANCES GONVILLE, *m.* in 1786, to Boardman Bromhead, esq. of Thurlby Hall, Lincolnshire, and was mother of SIR GONVILLE BROMHEAD, bart. of Thurlby Hall.

BRIDGET, *m.* to Charles Beaty, gent. of Louth, and had three daughters,

MARY BEATY, *m.* to A. Pearson, esq.

ELIZABETH BEATY, *m.* to John Waterhouse, esq. of Wellhead, Halifax, in Yorkshire, and had issue.

FRANCES BEATY, *m.* to John Shaw, esq. of London, and had an only daughter and heir, Elizabeth, *m.* to Benjamin Bond, esq.

Anne, m. to Robert Brudenell, Earl of Cardigan.
Katharine, a nun at Dunkirk.
Henrietta-Maria, m. to Ralph Sheldon, esq. of Beoley.

His lordship, who was chancellor of the Queen's Court at Westminster, died in London in 1635, and was s. by his son,

III. Sir Thomas Savage, second Viscount Savage, of Rock Savage, who succeeded to the Earldom of Rivers in 1639. His lordship m. first, Catharine, daughter of William Parker, Lord Morley and Mountegle, by whom he had issue,

Thomas, his heir.
John, d. s. p.
Richard, who m. Alice, widow of John Barnston, esq. of Churton, and daughter and heir of Thomas Trafford, esq. of Bridge Trafford, and had a son,

John, of whom presently as inheritor of the family honours.

Elizabeth, m. to William, Lord Petre.
Jane, m. first, to Lord Chandos; secondly, to Sir William Sidley; and thirdly, to George Pitt, esq. of Strathfieldsay, Hants. Her grandson by the last, George Pitt, esq. was created Baron Rivers in 1776.
Mary, m. to Henry Killigrew, esq. groom of the bedchamber to James, Duke of York.
Catharine, m. to Sir Charles Sidley.

Lord Rivers m. secondly, Mary, daughter of Thomas Ogle, esq. and had by her a son, Peter. His lordship d. in 1654, and was s. by his son;

IV. Sir Thomas Savage, Earl Rivers, who m. first, Elizabeth, illegitimate daughter of Emanuel, Earl of Sunderland; and secondly, Arabella, daughter of Robert Bertie, Earl of Lindsey. The latter d. s. p. but by the former his lordship had issue,

Thomas, Viscount Colchester, who predeceased his father, having had by Charlotte-Maria, his wife, daughter of Charles, Earl of Derby, an only daughter, Charlotte-Catherine, who d. s. p.
Richard, successor to his father.

Elizabeth, d. s. p.
Annabella, m. to Sir Erasmus Norwich.

Lord Rivers d. in 1694, and was s. by his son,

V. Sir Richard Savage, Earl Rivers, who married Penelope, daughter and heir of Roger Downes, esq. of Wardley, in Lancashire, and had by her an only daughter,

Elizabeth, m. to James Barry, Earl of Barrymore, and had an only daughter,

Lady Penelope Barry, m. to James, second son of George, Earl of Cholmondeley, but d. s. p.

His lordship* d. in 1714, and was s. by his cousin,

VI. John Savage, a Catholic priest, who never assumed the honours. He died, of course unmarried, in 1728, when the Baronetcy, as well as the superior titles, became extinct.

After the decease of this the last male heir of the family, the estates, under a settlement made by Richard, Earl Rivers, passed to Lady Penelope Cholmondeley, that nobleman's granddaughter. Her ladyship died issueless in 1786, when Clifton and her other estates devolved on her husband's great-nephew, George-James, Earl of Cholmondeley, who was afterwards created Earl of Rocksavage and Marquess of Cholmondeley.

Arms—Arg. six lioncels sa. three, two, and one.

SAVILE, OF THORNHILL.

Created 29th June, 1611.

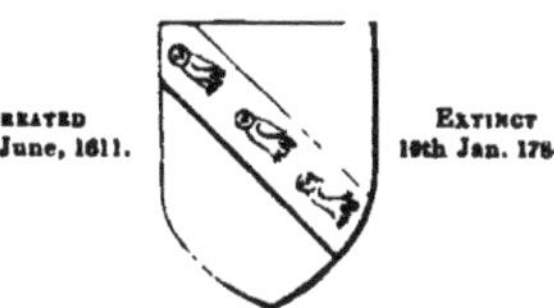

Extinct 10th Jan. 1784.

Lineage.

The Saviles came originally from the province of Anjou, in France, but they have been settled in different parts of Yorkshire for several centuries. The first of the name upon record is

Sir John Savile, of Savile Hall, who married the daughter of Sir Simon de Rockley. His great grandson,

Thomas Savile, of Newstead, in the county of York, m. the daughter and heir of Sir Richard Tankersley, knt. and had issue,

John (Sir), his heir.
Henry, who m. about the year 1300, Ellen, daughter and heir of Thomas Copley, of Copley, in Yorkshire, and was ancestor of the Saviles of Copley and the Saviles of Methley.

The elder son,

Sir John Savile, knt. m. the daughter and heir of — Rochdale, esq. and left a son,

John Savile, who m. the daughter of Sir Robert Latham, knt. and was father of

Sir John Savile, knt. who m. Jane, daughter of Matthew de Bosco, *alias* Wood, and had a son and heir,

John Savile, who m. Margaret, daughter and coheir of Henry Rishworth, and was s. by his son,

Sir John Savile, knt. who was sheriff of Yorkshire 3 and 11 Richard II. and twice returned to parliament by the same county, in the 7th and 8th of the same king. He m. Isabel, daughter and heir of Thomas Eland, esq. of Eland, also in Yorkshire, and had two sons,

John (Sir), his heir, who m. Isabel, daughter of Robert Ratcliffe, esq. and had issue,

John (Sir), who m. Isabel, daughter of Sir William Fitzwilliams, knt. but d. s. p.

Isabel, heir of her brother, m. to Thomas D'Arcy, son of Lord D'Arcy.

Henry.

The younger son and eventual heir male,

Henry Savile, esq. m. Elizabeth, daughter and sole heir of Simon Thornhill, esq. of Thornhill, in the county of York,† and by that alliance he acquired the manor of Thornhill and other extensive estates. He left a son and heir,

* His lordship left two illegitimate children: by Mrs. Colydon, a daughter, Betsy Savage, who had a fortune of £40,000, and married Frederick, Earl of Rochford; and by the Countess of Macclesfield, a son, Richard Savage, the celebrated and unfortunate poet.

† Son and heir of Sir Bryan Thornhill, knt. a person of great note in the time of Edward III. having served in several parliaments as knight of the shire; he was descended from Jordan de Thornhill.

Sir Thomas Savile, knt. of Thornhill, one of the gentry of the county of York returned by the commissioners 12 Henry VI. and knight of the shire in the 20th of the same king. He m. Margaret, daughter of Sir Thomas Pilkington, knt. and was s. by his son,

Sir John Savile, knt. of Thornhill, who was twice sheriff of Yorkshire, 33 Henry VI. and 1 Edward I. and knight of the shire in the 29th of the former king. He m. Alice, daughter of Sir William Gascoigne, knt. of Gawthorp, in the same county, and had three sons, viz.

- I. John (Sir), whose grandson,
  - Sir Henry Savile, was made a knight of the Bath at the coronation of *Queen* Anne Boleyn. He m. Elizabeth, daughter of Thomas Sothill, esq. of Sothill, and had issue,*
    - Edward, who married the daughter of Sir Richard Leigh, knt. of St. Albans, and died issueless in 1562.
    - Dorothy, m. to John Kay, esq. of Woodsome, in Yorkshire.
- II. William, *d. s. p.*
- III. Thomas.

The youngest son,

Thomas Savile, esq. of Lupset, m. Margaret, daughter of Thomas Balforth, esq. and had issue,

- John, his heir.
- Thomas, of Grantham.
- George, of Wakefield.

The eldest son,

John Savile, esq. m. Anne, daughter of William Wyatt, esq. and was s. by his only son,

Henry Savile, esq. of Lupset, who m. Joan, daughter and heir of William Vernon, esq. of Barrowby, in the county of Lincoln, and widow of Sir Richard Bosom, knt. by whom he had issue,

- I. George, his heir.
- II. Francis, m. Catherine, daughter and co-heir of William, Lord Conyers.
- III. Cordell, m. Mary, daughter and heir of William Welbeck, esq. of Sutton, Notts.
- I. Bridget, m. to Henry Nevil, esq. of Grove, Notts.

Mr. Savile was sheriff of Yorkshire 9 Elizabeth, receiver-general for the same county, and one of the honourable council established in the north. He was s. by his eldest son,

I. Sir George Savile, knt. of Thornhill, in the county of York, who was created a Baronet by *King* James I. 29th June, 1611, and was sheriff of Yorkshire in two years after. He m. first, Lady Mary Talbot, daughter of George, sixth Earl of Shrewsbury, and by her ladyship had an only son,

- George (Sir), who died before his father in 1618, leaving by Anne, his second wife,† the daughter of Sir W. Wentworth, bart. of Wentworth Woodhouse, two sons,
  - George, heir to his grandfather.
  - William, successor to his brother.

Sir George m. secondly, Elizabeth, daughter of Sir Edward Ayscough, knt. of South-Kelsey, in Lincolnshire, and widow of George Savile, esq. of Wakefield, and by her had

- John (Sir), of Lupset, in Yorkshire, who m. first, Elizabeth, daughter of John Armitage, esq. of Kirklees, and by her had an only daughter, the wife of William Hirstler, of Cleveland. He m. secondly, Anne, daughter of Sir John Soame, knt. by whom he had one son and two daughters, viz.
  - John, of Lupset, who inherited as sixth baronet.
  - Mary, m. to — Jennison, esq. of Newcastle.
  - Anne, m. to John Harris, esq. of London.
- Richard, *d. s. p.*
- Henry, of Bowling, in Yorkshire, m. Anne, daughter of Robert Crewse, of London, merchant and had (with three daughters, Elizabeth, m. to Count Montfelto; Anne, to Sir Robert Ferrers, and Mary;) an only surviving son,
  - John, in holy orders, rector of Thornhill, who left by his second wife (he had no issue by the first), Barbara, daughter of Thomas Jennison, esq. of Newcastle-upon-Tyne,
    - George, who s. as seventh baronet.
    - Anne, m. to Sir Nicholas Cole, bart. of Brancepeth, in Durham.
    - Gertrude.
- Mary, m. to John Archer, esq. of Gray's Inn.

Sir George was s. by his grandson,

II. Sir George Savile, who died unmarried in his minority, and was s. by his brother,

III. Sir William Savile, who m. Anne, daughter of Thomas, Lord Coventry, lord keeper, a lady remarkable for her zeal and attachment to the royal cause, from the support of which no difficulties nor dangers, nor even the fear of death itself, could deter her. By her ladyship he had issue,

- George, his successor.
- Henry, vice chamberlain to *King* Charles II. and M.P. for Newark, *d. s. p.*
- Anne, m. to Thomas, Earl of Plymouth.
- Margaret.

He *d.* 24th January, 1643, and was s. by his eldest son,

IV. Sir George Savile, who, in consideration of his father's and his own eminent services in the civil wars, was advanced to the peerage by Charles II. (in 1668) as Viscount Halifax, and afterwards created Earl and Marquess of Halifax. His lordship m. first, Lady Dorothy Spencer, daughter of Henry, Earl of Sunderland, by whom he had

- Henry, who *d. s. p.* in his father's lifetime.
- William, Lord Savile, heir to his father.
- George, who fell at the siege of Buda, in 1686, and died unmarried.
- Anne, m. to John, Lord Vaughan.

He m. secondly, Gertrude, daughter of the Hon. William Pierrepoint, of Thoresby, second son of Robert, first Earl of Kingston, and by her had another daughter,

- Elizabeth, m. to Philip, Earl of Chesterfield.

Lord Halifax was lord privy seal and some time president of the council *temp.* Charles I. and Burnet describes him "as a man of great and ready wit; full of life and very pleasant, but much turned to satire; his imagination was too hard for his judgment, and a severe jest took more with him than all arguments whatever. He let his wit run much on matters of religion, which got him the reputation of a confirmed atheist; but he denied the charge." He died in 1695, and was s. by his eldest surviving son,

* Sir Henry Savile had a bastard son by Margaret Barkston,
  Sir Robert Savile, from whom descended the Saviles, Earls of Sussex. (See Burke's *Extinct Peerage*

† By his first wife, Sarah, daughter and co-heir of John Rede, esq. of Cotesbrooke, in Northamptonshire, he had no issue.

v. Sir William Savile, second Marquess of Halifax, who m. first, Elizabeth, daughter of Sir Samuel Grimston, bart. by whom he had a daughter,

Lady Anne Savile, who m. Charles, third Earl of Ailesbury.

He m. secondly, Lady Mary Finch, daughter of Daniel, Earl of Nottingham, by Lady Essex Rich, daughter and co-heir of Richard, Earl of Warwick and Holland, and by her ladyship had two sons and a daughter who died young, with two other daughters to survive, viz.

Lady Dorothy Savile, m. to Richard Boyle, third Earl of Burlington.

Lady Mary Savile, m. in 1722, to Sackvile Tufton, esq. who inherited in 1729 the earldom of Thanet as seventh earl.

His lordship d. 31st August, 1700,* when his honours in the peerage became *extinct*, his daughters inherited his estates as co-heirs, and the Baronetcy reverted to (refer to John Savile, eldest son by his second wife of the first baronet,) his kinsman,

vi. Sir John Savile, of Lupset, in the county of York, who died unmarried in 1704, when his sisters became his co-heirs, and the Baronetcy devolved upon his cousin (refer to Henry Savile, third son of the first baronet by his second wife),

vii. Sir George Savile, of Rufford, in Nottinghamshire, F.R.S. M.P. for the county of York in the first parliament of George II. He married in 1722, Mary, daughter of John Pratt, esq. of the city of Dublin (by Honoretta, daughter of Sir John Brooke, bart. of Ellenthorpe, in Yorkshire), and had issue,

George, his successor.

Arabella, m. to — Hewett, esq. and d. in September, 1767.

Barbara, m. in 1752, to Richard, fourth Earl of Scarborough, and was grandmother of the present (1837) earl.

He d. 16th September, 1743, and was s. by his son,

viii. Sir George Savile, F.R.S. vice-president of the Society of Arts and Sciences, M.P. for the county of York, and colonel of the 1st battalion of West Riding militia. This gentleman died unmarried in his fifty-eighth year, 10th January, 1784, when his only surviving sister, Barbara, Countess of Scarborough, became his heir, and the Baronetcy expired.

Arms—Arg. on a bend sa. three owls engrailed of the field.

SAVILE, OF METHLEY.

Created 29th June, 1611.—Extinct 23rd June, 1632.

Lineage.

This was a branch from the same stock as the family of Savile of Thornhill.

Thomas Savile, of Newsted, grandson of Sir John Savile, of Savile Hall, in the county of York, m. the daughter and heiress of Sir Richard Tankersley, knt. and had two sons, John (Sir), from whom the Saviles of Thornhill, and

Henry Savile, esq. who, about the year 1300, m. Ellen, daughter and heir of Thomas Copley, of Copley, in the county of York, and thus acquired that estate, a fine having been levied thereon 4 Henry IV. He had issue,

i. John, his heir, from whom the extinct Baronets of Copley.

ii. Thomas.

iii. Nicholas.

The second son,

Thomas Savile, m. Anne, daughter of John Stansfeild, of Stansfield, and had four sons, viz.

John, of Hullingridge, married Alice, daughter of Ralph Lister, of Halifax.

Thomas, who m. Elizabeth, Lady Waterton, of Walton, but had no issue.

Henry.

Nicholas.

The youngest son,

Nicholas Savile, esq. of New Hall, m. Margaret, daughter of William Wilkinson, and had Thomas, ancestor of the Saviles of Wellborne, with an elder son and heir,

John Savile, esq. of Newhall, who m. Margery, daughter of John Gleadhill, and had four sons and four daughters, viz.

Nicholas, m. Jennet, daughter of Thomas Foxcroft, esq. and left issue.

John, m. Elizabeth, daughter of — Trigot, esq. of South Kirby.

Henry, of whom presently.

Thomas, m. Jennet, daughter of Nicholas Boothroyd, and from him descended the Saviles of Watergate, near Halifax.

Agnes, m. to Thomas Harrison, of Woodhouse.

Alice, m. to Robert Holt, esq. of Stubley, in Lancashire.

Jane, m. to Thomas Gleadhill, of Barksland.

Elizabeth, m. to John Blythe, esq. of Quarnby.

The third son,

Henry Savile, esq. seated himself at Bradley, near Halifax, and marrying Ellen, daughter of Robert Ramsden, esq. had three sons,

i. John (Sir), his heir.

ii. Henry (Sir), a person of note in the times of Elizabeth and James I.: to the former he was tutor for the Greek tongue, and from the latter he received the honour of knighthood, at Windsor, 21st September, 1604. He was born in 1549, and entered the university of Oxford in 1561, where he took the degree of bachelor of arts in 1565, and afterwards grew famous as a Greek scholar and mathematician. Through *Queen* Elizabeth's influence he was elected warden of Merton College, and in 1596, provost of Eton. He was subsequently employed by her majesty as resident in the Low Countries. On the accession of James I. he still retained the royal favour, and received the honour of knighthood, as stated above. His only son, Henry, dying soon after, leaving him no hope of founding a family, he devoted much of his wealth to publishing books. He collected the best copies of St. Chrysostom, and employed learned men to transcribe, and annotate them, which he fairly set forth at his own cost, computed at £8000, in a superb edition; but the papists at Paris (writes an old author) had their emissaries in England, who surreptitiously procured this knight's learned labours, and sent them over weekly by the post into France, sheet by sheet as here they passed the press; and *Fronto Duceus*, a French cardinal, printed them, as received out of England, only joyning thereunto a Latin translation, and some

* His widow m. John, first Duke of Roxburghe, and was mother of Robert, the second duke.

other inconsiderable additions, inasmuch that there were two editions of St. Chrysostom at the same time." Sir Henry, whose learned reputation spread abroad as well as at home, died at Eton College, 19th February, 1621, and was buried in the chapel there, under a black marble, and the university of Oxford erected in Merton College a sumptuous monument to his memory. Elizabeth, his daughter and sole heir, m. Sir John Sidley, bart. of Ailesford, in Kent.

III. John, student in the university of Oxford, where he was elected proctor, in 1529, but d. unm.

The eldest son,

Sir John Savile, of Bradley Hall, was a learned judge, and one of the barons of the Exchequer in the time of *Queen* Elizabeth and James I. He married first, Jane, daughter of Richard Garth, esq. of Morden, in Surrey, and by her had

Henry, his heir.

Elizabeth, married to Sir John Jackson, knt. of Hickleton.

Jane, m. to Sir Henry Godrich, knt. of Ribston.

Sir John m. secondly, Elizabeth, eldest daughter of Thomas Wentworth, of North Elmsall, and relict of Richard Tempest, esq. of Bowling, and by her had a son,

John.

The judge m. thirdly, Dorothy, daughter of the Lord Wentworth of the South, and widow of Sir William Widmerpool, knt. and of Sir Martin Forbisher, knt. of Altofts. His fourth wife was Margery, daughter of Ambrose Peate, citizen of London, and widow of Sir Jerome Weston: by those latter ladies he had no issue. His eldest son and heir,

I. Sir Henry Savile, of Methley, in the county of York, received the honour of knighthood at the coronation of *King* James I. and was created a Baronet 29th June, 1611. Sir Henry was several times vice-president of the council of the North, deputy lieutenant, colonel of a militia regiment, and one of the knights of the shire for the county of York. He m. Mary, daughter and co-heir of John Dent, citizen of London, by whom, who survived him, and re-married Sir William Sheffield, knt. he had, with several children who all died young, a son, John, who died just as he had attained maturity, in France, during the lifetime of his father. Sir Henry died 23rd June, 1632, in the fifty-third year of his age, when the Baronetcy expired, and the estates devolved upon his half brother,

John Savile, esq. ancestor of the Earls of Mexborough. (See Burke's *Peerage and Baronetage*.)

Arms—As Savile of Thornhill.

SAVILE, OF COPLEY.

Created 24th July, 1662.—Extinct in 1689.

Lineage.

Henry Savile married about the year 1300 Ellen, daughter and heir of Thomas Copley, of Copley, in the county of York, and acquired that estate, a fine having been levied thereon 4 Henry IV. He had three sons, John, his heir, Thomas, ancestor of the Saviles of Methley, now represented by the Ear[illegible] Mexborough, and Nicholas. From the eldest son [illegible]

John Savile, esq. of Copley, lineally descended

I. John Savile, esq. of Copley, who was created [illegible] Baronet 24th July, 1662. He m. Mary, daughter [illegible] Clement Paston, esq. of Barningham, in Norfolk, [illegible] left by her an only daughter and heir,

Elizabeth-Mary, m. to Lord Thomas Howard.

Sir John died in 1689, when the Baronetcy bec[illegible] extinct.

Arms—As Savile of Thornhill.

SCLATER, OF CAMBRIDGE.

Created 25th July, 1666.

Extinct 10th Dec. 16[illegible]

Lineage.

I. Thomas Sclater, esq. of Catley Park, in [illegible] county of Cambridge, who acquired by purchase [illegible] siderable estates in that shire, and served the [illegible] sheriff in 1686, was created a Baronet in 16[illegible] [illegible] m. Susan, daughter of Mr. Freeston, of Norw[illegible] relict, first, of Mr. Cotton, and secondly, of Dr [illegible] ber, D.D. of Trinity College, Cambridge, but had no issue. He died 10th December, 1684, when the Baronetcy became extinct. The estates, Sir Thomas [illegible] queathed to his great nephew, Thomas Sclater [illegible] a student at Trinity College. That gentleman* [illegible] wards assumed the additional surname of Bacon [illegible] was at the time of his death, in 1736, M.P. for [illegible] bridge. In 1768, Thomas Sclater King, esq. to whose family the estates had been devised by Mr Bacon sold them to Lord Montfort, from whom they were purchased, three years after, by Dr. Keene, Bishop of Ely.

Arms—Arg. a saltier az.

SCROPE, OF COCKERINGTON.

Created 16th Jan. 1666-7.

Extinct in 16[illegible]

Lineage.

This was a branch of the ancient and [illegible] family of Scrope, of Bolton.

Sir Richard le Scrope, first Lord Scrope, [illegible] ton, was summoned to parliament [illegible]

---

* He m. Elizabeth, sister of Peter Standley, esq. of Paxton Place, Hants, which lady died in 1726, and was interred at Linton, under a handsome monument designed by Wilton.

ring the reigns of EDWARD III. and RICHARD II. He was renowned in arms, and received the honour of knighthood from the former monarch at the battle of Durham, where the Scotch sustained a defeat in 1346, and he was present the same year at the siege of Calais. "Without attempting to follow this nobleman through all his martial exploits, which, however, stand recorded by these eye-witnesses, the several royal, noble, and knightly deponents in the celebrated controversy sustained by him with Sir Richard Grosvenor, for the right of bearing his family coat of arms, it is enough to say, that between 1346 and 1385, a period of forty years, there was scarcely a battle of note in England, France, or Scotland, where the English forces were engaged, in which Scrope did not gain honour. But as a statesman he was still more distinguished. He was lord high treasurer to EDWARD III. and twice lord chancellor of England in the reign of RICHARD II. by both which sovereigns he was entrusted with many other employments of honour and confidence. Walsingham states him to have been remarkable for his extraordinary wisdom and integrity, and records his firmness in refusing to put the great seal," as chancellor, to the profuse grants made by RICHARD II. to his favourites. When, RICHARD, incensed by this, sent messenger after messenger to Scrope, "desiring him forthwith to return the great seal," he refused to deliver it to any other person than to the king himself.* Lord Scrope erected the stately castle of Bolton, in Richmondshire, and died full of honours at the age of seventy-three, in 1403, temp. HENRY IV. By Blanch, daughter of Sir William de la Pole, he had four sons, viz.

- WILLIAM, (Sir), K.G. created Earl of Wiltshire, beheaded in 1399, his father then living.
- ROGER, successor to his father.
- Richard, Archbishop of York, beheaded *temp.* HENRY IV.
- STEPHEN (Sir), Lord of Bentley, in Yorkshire, and of Castle Combe, in Wilts, ancestor of the present (1838) William Scrope, esq. of Castle Combe, and of Cockerington, in Lincolnshire. (Refer to BURKE's *Commoners*, vol. iii. p. 693.)

William, Earl of Wiltshire, dying before his father, the barony of Scrope devolved upon the second son,

ROGER, second Lord Scrope, of Bolton, from whom we pass to

HENRY, sixth Lord Scrope, who married the Lady Elizabeth Percy, daughter of Henry, Earl of Northumberland, and had two sons, HENRY, his heir, seventh lord, and

JOHN SCROPE, of Spennithorne, in the county of York, and of Hambledon, Bucks. This gentleman *m.* Phillis, daughter of Ralph Rokeby, esq. of Rokeby and Morton, in the same county, and had with other issue,

- HENRY, of Spennithorne and Danby, *m.* Margaret, daughter and heir of Simon Conyers, esq. of Danby, and thus sprang the SCROPES of Danby.
- RALPH (fourth son).

The fourth son,

RALPH SCROPE, esq. of Hambledon, Bucks, *m.* Elizabeth, daughter of William, Lord Windsor, and relict, first, of Henry Sandys, and secondly, of Sir George Powlett, knt. By that lady he had three sons, viz.

- I. ADRIAN (Sir), his heir.
- II. Ralph, father of
  - Henry Scrope, who *m.* Anne, daughter and heir of Sir John South, of South Summercotes, and left a son,
    - John, *b.* in 1632.
- III. Richard, *d. s. p.*

He was *s.* by his eldest son,

SIR ADRIAN SCROPE, knt. of Cockerington, in the county of Lincoln, who *m.* Ursula, daughter of Sir John Clifton, of Barrington, in the county of Somerset (by Anne, youngest daughter of Thomas Stanley, second Lord Monteagle,) and had issue,

- GERVASE (Sir), his successor.
- Adrian, believed to be the regicide, Col. Adrian Scrope, whose signature is on the death warrant of *King* CHARLES.
- Edwyn.
- Robert.
- William.
- John.
- Elizabeth.
- Jane.

Sir Adrian died 10th December, 1623, and was buried at Cockerington. His monument is in Cockerington Church, in white marble of excellent Italian workmanship. The knight's full size figure reclines at length on an altar tomb, represented in armour leaning on one arm, full of spirit and dignity. On a tablet adjoining is carved his coat of arms, crest, &c. with two falcons as supporters, and the following inscription. "The thrice noble Sir Adrian Scrope, knt. deceased the 10th December, 1623."

"Tombes are but dull log-bookes, they onely keep,
Their names alive who in their wombes do sleep,
But, who would pen the virtues of this Knight,
A story not an epitaph must write."

He was *s.* by his eldest son,

SIR GERVASE SCROPE, knt. high sheriff of Lincoln in 1634, *m.* Catherine, daughter of John Hungerford, esq. of Hungerford, in the county of Wilts, and had two sons, viz.

- ADRIAN (Sir), his heir.
- St. Leger, who left Carr, and other issue.

He *d.* in 1667, and was *s.* by his elder son,

SIR ADRIAN SCROPE, of Cockerington, K.B. who *m.* Mary, daughter of Sir John Carr, and had issue,

- CARR, his heir.
- Gervase, *d.* in the lifetime of his father, *s. p.*
- ROBERT, heir to his elder brother.

Sir Adrian was buried at Cockerington in 1667, and *s.* by his eldest son,

I. SIR CARR SCROPE, of Cockerington, M.A. of Wadham College, Oxford, who was created a BARONET, 16th January, 1667-8. Sir Carr was one of those literary men about the court of CHARLES II. whom Pope calls, "The Mob of Gentlemen, who write with ease." He made several translations from Ovid, Virgil, and Horace, with some love songs and lampoons, to be found in the volumes of Dryden's Miscellanies. His name occurs frequently among the wits and poetasters of that day, and he appears to have been, in love as well as verse, a rival of Rochester, who addresses a bitter lampoon to him. (See ROCHESTER's *Works.*) He *d.* unm. in 1680, when the BARONETCY EXPIRED, and the estates devolved upon his only surviving brother,

ROBERT SCROPE, esq. of Cockerington, who *m.* Lucy, daughter of Sir John Newton, of Ganwarby, and had issue,

- GEORGE, his heir.
- Catherine, *d.* young.
- Elizabeth, *m.* to William Pownall, esq. and *d. s. p.* in 1717.
- Lucy, *d.* unm. in 1719.

Mr. Scrope *d.* in 1718, and was *s.* by his son,

* BURKE's *Commoners.*

George Scrope, esq. of Cockerington, who m. first, Elizabeth, daughter of Richard Cresswell, esq. of Sedbury, in the county of Salop, and by that lady had,

Adrian, who *d.* aged ten, in 1730.
Gervase, heir to his father.
Carr, capt. R.N. *d. s. p.* in 1762.
Frederick-James, heir to his brother.

Elizabeth, *m.* to Lancelot Lee, esq. and *d. s. p.* in 1751.

Mary, *m.* first to Francis, Earl of Deloraine, by whom she had no issue, and secondly, Thomas Vivian, esq. recorder of Lincoln. By that gentleman she had an only daughter,

Mary Vivian, *m.* to John Peart, esq. who assumed the name of Scrope.

He *m.* secondly, Frances, fourth daughter and co-heir of Thomas Lister, esq. of Coleby, in the county of Lincoln, and by her had another son,

Thomas, who *s.* his half-brother, Frederick-James.

George Scrope *d.* in July, 1741, was buried in Lincoln Cathedral, and *s.* by his eldest surviving son,

Gervase Scrope, esq. of Eastcot Park, Middlesex, and Cockerington, Lincolnshire, who *d.* unm. aged sixty-five, in 1776, and was *s.* by his brother,

Frederick-James Scrope, esq. who entailed the estates upon the Scropes of Castle Combe, on the failure of his own line. He *d.* unm. aged sixty-two, in 1780, and was *s.* by his half-brother,

Thomas Scrope, esq. of Coleby and Cockerington, who *m.* Eliza-Maria, daughter of William Clay, esq. but had no issue. He *d.* in 1792, aged sixty-nine, and his widow *m.* in 1794, Gen. Albemarle Bertie, who became ninth Earl of Lindsey on the decease of the Duke of Ancaster in 1809. At Mr. Scrope's death the estates devolved upon his niece Mary Vivian and her husband, John Peart, who in consequence assumed the name of Scrope; but that lady dying *s. p.* in 1795, the estates of North and South Cockerington passed then in virtue of the entail created by Feederick-James Scrope, to

William Scrope, esq. of Castle Combe, in the county of Wilts. (Refer to Burke's *Commoners*, vol. iii. p. 693.)

Arms—Azure a bend or.

SCUDAMORE, OF HOLME LACY.

Created 1st June, 1629.

Extinct 2nd Dec. 1716.

Lineage.

The Scudamores, one of the most eminent families in the West of England, was established at a remote era, in Herefordshire.

The name is variously written in records *de Eskidmore*, *Esquidmore*, *Escuedmore*, *Schidemore*, and *Skydmore*. That the family was anciently of plentiful estate and good esteem, appears evident from their early benefactions to the Abbey of Dore, and other religious houses.

Ralph de Eskidemore gave some of his demesne lands to the Abbey of Dore, which

Walter de Eskidemore augmented in the 14th of *King* Stephen. His son,

Walter de Eskidemore is mentioned in the time of Henry II. In lineal descent from him comes

Sir Godfrey de Scudamore, knt. who in the 4th of Henry III. was one of the four knights returned for the county of Wilts, who, by order of parliament, were to enquire into all transgressions and injuries committed as well by justices, sheriffs, bailiffs, or other persons; the inquisitions so made, to be sealed with their own seals, and the seals of the jurors, to be delivered in their own proper persons to the king's counsel, at Westminster, eight days after Michaelmas. In the 48th of the same monarch, he was appointed by the king, conservator of the peace for the county of Wilts. He was *s.* by his son,

Sir Peter de Scudamore, knt. who was likewise of great power, as appears by a writ directed to him, in the 15th Edward I. to put the statute of Winton in execution, and preserve the peace. He had no issue, and was *s.* by his brother,

Sir Walter de Scudamore, who was summoned amongst the knights to attend Edward I. in his expedition against the Scots, having been knighted in the 34th of that monarch, when the king to augment the splendour of his projected enterprise, "begirt Edward, Earl of Carnarvon, his eldest son, with the military belt, and the young prince immediately after, conferred the same honour at the high altar in Westminster Abbey, on nearly three hundred gentlemen, sons of earls, barons, and knights;" he sealed with a cross patee fitchee, as appears from a charter of his to Dore Abbey. His son and heir,

Sir Peter de Scudamore, who flourished in the beginning of Edward III.'s reign, had two sons, Walter and Thomas. The younger son,

Thomas de Scudamore, married the eldest daughter and heir of Clara de Ewyas, by Ivan Whelan, her husband, upon which he assumed the arms of the stirrups and the surname of Ewyas. Their son and heir,

Philip de Escudamore, *alias* de Ewyas, was *s.* by his son,

Sir John Scudamore, knt. of Ewyas and Holme-Lacy, who was escheator of Herefordshire, Gloucestershire, and the Marches of Wales, in the 12th Richard II. and was constituted in the 20th of the same reign, constable of Goderick Castle, during the minority of the Lord Talbot. He *m.* Alice, daughter, and one of the co-heirs, of Owen Glendower, and left a son,

Philip Scudamore, esq. father, by Agnes, his wife, daughter and co-heir of John Huntercombe, of

George Scudamore, esq. who *m.* a daughter of the old family of Brughill, and was *s.* by his son,

Philip Scudamore, esq. who wedded one of the daughters and heirs of Osborne, of London, and had a son and heir,

William Scudamore, esq. of Holme Lacy, who *m.* Alice, daughter of Sir Richard Mynors, and was *s.* by his son,

John Scudamore, esq. of Holme Lacy, who *m.* Sybell, daughter of Watkyn Vaughan, of Hergest, and in the 22nd Henry VIII. being styled by the king, *Generosorum Hostiariorum Cameræ suæ*, was constituted steward of the lordships of Usk, Caerleon, and Crillocke, in Wales, and constable of Uske Castle, for life, after the demise or surrender of William V[illegible] gan, esq. He had a grant likewise in the 31st of the same reign, of the site of Dore Abbey, Herefordshire, to him and his heirs. This John and his wife have this inscription (praying them that passeth, of their charity, to say for their souls a *pater noster* and an ave) round their noble alabaster monument in the church of Holme Lacy:

> "Here Lythe JOHN SCUDAMOR Esquir, sometyme one of The foure gentyllmen USHERS unto our late Soverange Lord King HENRY the eighte, and afterwarde admytted one of The Esquirs for his highnes body, and SIBEL his Wyef, and JOHN deceased, in The yere Of our Lorde God a Thousand Five hundred ——"

He had issue,

- William, who m. Ursula, daughter and co-heir of Sir John Pakington, knt. of Hampton Lovet, and had four sons and a daughter, Jane, m. to Thomas Scudamore, esq.
- Richard.
- Philip, who m. Joan, relict of Walter Kyrle, esq. and had a daughter, Sybell.
- John, married and had issue.
- Katherine, m. to Richard Monington, esq.
- Joan, m. first, to Walter Guillim; and secondly, to Charles Herbert.
- Jane, m. first, to John Warncomb; and secondly, to Sir Walter Devereux, knt.
- Elizabeth, m. to Humphrey Baskerville, esq.
- Sybell, m. first, to Thomas Daunsey, esq. of Brinsop; and secondly, to John De la Bere.

John Scudamore was s. by his grandson, (son of William, who predeceased his father, and Ursula, his wife, daughter and co-heir of Sir John Pakington, knt. of Hampton Lovet,)

SIR JOHN SCUDAMORE, who was gentleman usher to Queen ELIZABETH, received the honour of knighthood and was elected by the county of Hereford in five successive parliaments during that reign. He married first, Eleanor, daughter of Sir James Croft, and had issue,

- JAMES (Sir), who was knighted for his valour at the siege of Calais, and in the 1st of JAMES I. served in parliament for Herefordshire. Sir James married Anne, daughter of Sir Thomas Throckmorton, and dying before his father, he left issue,
  - JOHN, successor to his grandfather.
  - MARY, m. to SIR GILES BRYDGES, of Wilton Castle.*
- Alice.
- Ursula, wife of Alexander Walwyn, esq. of Old-court.

Sir John Scudamore, the "Sir Scudamore of Spencer's Fairy Queen," was s. by his grandson,

I. JOHN SCUDAMORE, esq. of Holme Lacy, who was created a BARONET 1st June, 1620, and in eight years afterwards raised to the peerage of Ireland, as Baron Dromore and Viscount Scudamore, of Sligo. He m. Elizabeth, only daughter and heir of Sir Arthur Porter, knt. and dying in 1671, was s. by his grandson,

II. SIR JOHN SCUDAMORE, second Viscount Scudamore, (only son of James, only surviving son of the first Viscount, who died before his father). This nobleman m. Frances, daughter of John, Earl of Exeter, and dying 22nd July, 1697, was s. by his son,

III. SIR JAMES SCUDAMORE, third Viscount Scudamore, who m. Frances, only daughter and heir of Simon, Lord Digby, and died 2nd December, 1716, aged thiry-two, leaving an only daughter, when all his honours, including the BARONETCY EXPIRED. His lordship's daughter and heir,

- *The Honourable* FRANCES SCUDAMORE, b. in 1711, m. first, Henry Somerset, Duke of Beaufort, and secondly, Charles Fitzroy Scudamore, esq. By the latter she left an only child,
  - FRANCES SCUDAMORE, of Holme Lacy, who m. Charles, Duke of Norfolk, but died issueless in 1820, when the estates devolved partly upon SIR EDWIN FRANCIS STANHOPE, bart. and DANIEL H. BURR, esq.† (See notes at foot.)

Arms—Gu. three stirrups leathered and buckled or.

SCUDAMORE, OF BALLINGHAM.

CREATED 23rd July, 1644.—EXTINCT ....

Lineage.

I. JOHN SCUDAMORE, esq. of Ballingham, in the county of Hereford, who was created a BARONET in 1644, m. Penelope, daughter of Sir James Scudamore, knt. of Holme Lacy, in the same shire, and was s. by his son,

II. SIR JOHN SCUDAMORE, of Ballingham, who married a daughter of Sir George Graham, of Norton, in Yorkshire, and dying without male issue 22nd August, 1684, was s. by his brother,

III. SIR BARNABY SCUDAMORE, of Ballingham, who m. Sarah, daughter of John Row, merchant of Bristol, and relict of William Harris, of London, but died without male issue, when the BARONETCY became EXTINCT.

Arms—As SCUDAMORE, OF HOLME LACY.

---

* MARY SCUDAMORE's grandson, by SIR GILES BRYDGES,

SIR JOHN BRYDGES, bart. of Wilton Castle, inherited the BARONY OF CHANDOS, as eighth baron, in 1676. He d. in 1714, and was succeeded by by his son,

JAMES, ninth Baron Chandos, who was created, in 1714, Earl of Caernarvon, and in 1719, Duke of Chandos. His grace m. Mary, only surviving daughter of Sir Thomas Lake, of Cannons, in Middlesex, and had two surviving sons,

JOHN, Marquess of Caernarvon, who d. before his father, leaving two daughters, his co-heirs, viz.

1. CATHERINE, m. first, to Captain Lyon, of the Horse Guards, and secondly to EDWIN-FRANCIS STANHOPE, esq. By the latter she had a son,

HENRY-EDWIN STANHOPE, admiral of the blue, created a BARONET in 1807, d. in 1814, leaving a son and heir,

SIR EDWIN-FRANCIS STANHOPE, bart. who inherited Home Lacy at the decease of the Duchess of Norfolk.

2. Jane, m. to James Brydges, esq. of Pinner.

HENRY, who became Marquess of Caernarvon, at the decease of his brother.

† HENRY HIGFORD, clerk, descended from John Higford, esq. of Dixton, in Gloucestershire, who married a Miss Scudamore, of Holme Lacy, died in 1793, devising his property to his nieces, Mrs. Parsons and Mrs. Davis, both of Chepstow. The daughter and heir of the latter,

MARY DAVIS, was second wife of Lieut.-General Daniel Burr, of the East India civil service, and mother of the present DANIEL HIGFORD DAVALL BURR, esq. M. P. of Gayton, in Herefordshire, who enjoys a portion of the Scudamore estates.

SELBY, OF WHITEHOUSE.

CREATED 3rd March, 1664.

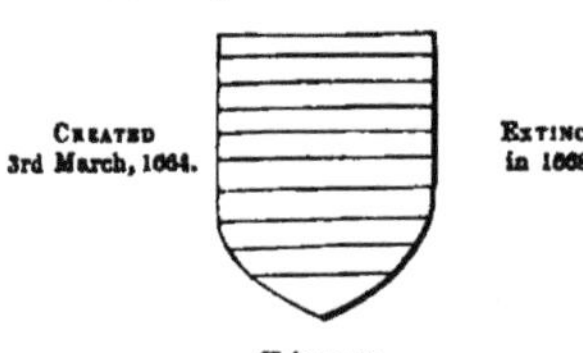

EXTINCT in 1668.

Lineage.

WILLIAM SELBY, esq. (son of George Selby, alderman of Newcastle, and grandson of William Selby, merchant adventurer of that place) served as sheriff of that corporation in 1564, and was mayor in 1573. He *m.* Elizabeth, daughter and heir of Gerard Fenwick, of Newcastle, and had with other issue,

GEORGE (Sir), knt. sheriff of Newcastle in 1594, and mayor in 1600, 1606, 1611, and 1622. This Sir George Selby had the honour of entertaining *King* JAMES on his various progresses Northwards, and thence was distinguished by the title of "the king's host." He *m.* Margaret, daughter of Sir John Selby, knt. of Twisell, and dying 30th March, 1625, aged sixty-eight, left issue,

Margaret, *m.* to Sir William Belasyse, knt.
Elizabeth, *m.* to Sir John Delaval, knt.
Barbara, *m.* to Robert Delaval, esq.
Isabel, *m.* to Sir Patricius Curwen, bart. of Workington.
Dorothy, *m.* to Sir William Darcy, of Wilton Castle.
Mary, *m.* to John Fenwick, eldest son of Sir John Fenwick, of Wallington.

WILLIAM, of whom presently.
Isabel.
Mary.
Margaret, second wife of Sir William Fenwick, knt. of Wallington.
Jane, *m.* to William Wray, esq. of Beamish, in Durham.
Elizabeth, *m.* to William Simpson, esq. of Newcastle.
Eleanor.
Barbara.
Grace.

The second son,

SIR WILLIAM SELBY, knt. of Winlaton, in Durham, and of Bolam, in Northumberland, *m.* Elizabeth, daughter and heir of William Widdrington, esq. younger son of Sir John Widdrington, knt. of Widdrington, and had issue,

William, who was slain in a duel in White Hall, Dyke Nook, 4th December, 1636, by John Trollop, of Thornley. He had no issue.
GEORGE, successor to his father.
John, *d.* unm.
Thomas, who *m.* Dorothy, third daughter and co-heir of John Swinburne, esq. of Black Heddon, in Northumberland, by Mary, his wife, sister and co-heir of Robert Collingwood, esq. of Eslington.

Sir William died in 1649, and was *s.* by his son,

I. SIR GEORGE SELBY, of Whitehouse and Winlaton, both in the county of Durham, who was created a BARONET 3rd March, 1664. He *m.* Mary, daughter of Richard, Viscount Molyneux, and had issue,

I. GEORGE, his heir.
I. Frances, *m.* to Sir Piers Mostyn, of Talacre, and *d.* in 1719.
II. Clare, buried 1st October, 1660.
III. Mary, living in 1668.
IV. Charlotte, living in 1668.
V. Julia, living in 1668.
VI. Elizabeth, living in 1668.

Sir George died in September, 1668, and was *s.* by his son,

II. GEORGE SELBY, who died an infant within an hour after his father when the BARONETCY became EXTINCT.

Arms—Barry or and sa.

SEYMOUR, OF LANGLEY.

CREATED 4th July, 1681.

EXTINCT in 1714.

Lineage.

SIR EDWARD SEYMOUR, of Bury Pomeroy, in the county of Devon, created a BARONET 29th June, 1611, *m.* Elizabeth, daughter of Sir Arthur Champernoun, knt. of Dartington, in the same county, and dying in 1613, was *s.* by his eldest son,

SIR EDWARD SEYMOUR, bart. of Bury Pomeroy, who *m.* Dorothy, daughter of Sir Henry Killigrew, knt. of Laroch, in Cornwall, and had a large family. EDWARD, the eldest son, inherited the title, and from him descend the present Duke of Somerset, and the Marquess of Hertford. The second son,

HENRY SEYMOUR, esq. born in 1612, was in his youth page of honour to *King* CHARLES I. and on the out break of the civil war, went with the Marquess of Hertford into Somersetshire, and was with his lordship at Sherburn, when with only two troops of horse and 400 foot, he withstood the whole force of the Earl of Bedford, consisting of above 7000 foot beside horse and artillery, and the Marquess sending the Earl of Bedford a challenge, Mr. Seymour was chosen to be the bearer. When all was lost, he went with his royal master abroad, and was entrusted with the last letter and message that the prince sent to his father, which delivering the 27th of the same month, in the evening of the day that CHARLES was sentenced to death, his sorrow is stated to have been unbounded. He kissed the king, clasped his legs, and mourned aloud. To him the king imparted his last communication to the prince. In the year 1660, he was elected to the restoration parliament, by the borough of East Loe, and he continued afterwards to represent the same place until his decease. He was appointed a groom of the bedchamber, comptroller of the Customs, and clerk of the hanaper. Mr. Seymour came to reside at Langley, in Bucks, in the year 1666, renting the house and park from the trustees of Sir William Parsons, then deceased, and about the year 1669, purchased the said estate, and got a grant from the king of the manor of Langley, under a reserved rent of £43. 8*s.* 10*d.* per annum. At this seat he lived in retirement the latter part of his life, in the general esteem of all who knew him, as a gentleman of great honour, generosity, affability, and charity. He [illegible] nd endowed, in his lifetime, an alms house, at Langley, for six poor decayed people; and by his last will and testament, gave £400 to put out poor boys apprentices, beside other charitable legacies to particular persons. He m. first, Elizabeth, daughter of Sir Joseph Killigrew, knt. widow of William Basset, esq. of Claverton, in the county of Somerset, but by that lady, who died in 1671, had no issue. His second wife was Ursula, daughter of Sir Robert Austen, bart. of Bexley, in Kent, and widow of George Stowel, esq. of Cotherston, in the same county. By her he had, with a daughter, an only son,

Henry, b. 20th October, 1674, who at seven years of age, his father being then living, was created a Baronet by *King* Charles I. 4th July, 1681, with remainder to his said father and the heirs male of the body of that gentleman.

Mr. Seymour died, aged seventy-four, 9th March, 1686, and was s. by his son,

I. Sir Henry Seymour, of Langley, who was elected to parliament on returning from his travels, 10th William III. for East Loe, and he represented the same borough in six other parliaments. In 1710, he was prevailed upon to offer himself for the county of Bucks, and stood a severe contest, losing his election by twenty votes only. He died unm. at London, in 1714, when the Baronetcy expired. His personal property fell to his sister, while the estate devolved upon Sir Edward Seymour, bart. of Bury Pomeroy.

Arms—Gules, two wings conjoined in lure, or.

SHERARD, OF LOPETHORPE.

Created 29th May, 1674. | Extinct 23th Nov. 1748.

Lineage.

Robert Sherard, lord of the manor of Stapleford, Henry IV. in the county of Leicester, in right of his wife, Agnes, daughter and heir of Sir Lawrence Hawberk, knt. was father of

Lawrence Sherard, of Stapleford, who was sheriff of Rutlandshire, in the 16th of Henry VI. and of Leicestershire, in the 21st of the same reign. He m. Elizabeth, daughter and heir of John Woodford, grandson and heir of Sir Robert Woodford, of Sproxton, also in Leicestershire, and had issue,

i. Robert, of Stapleford, *d. s. p.*
ii. Geoffrey.
iii. Christopher, of London, } *d. s. p.*
iv. William, of Saxby, 29 Henry VI. } *d. s. p.*

The second son,

Geoffrey Sherard, esq. on the death of his elder brother, became heir and representative of the family. He was sheriff of Rutland in 1468, 1480, and 1484, and in 35 Henry VI. Joyce, daughter of Thomas Ashby, esq. of Lowsby, in Leicestershire, by whom he had two sons, viz.

Thomas, of Stapleford,* ancestor of the Earls of Harborough.
Robert.

The younger son,

Robert Sherard, esq. of Lopthorp, in the county of Lincoln, had a son and daughter, viz.

Rowland, his heir.
Rose, m. to William Thorold, esq. of Lincolnshire.

He was s. by his son,

Rowland Sherard, esq. who m. Jane, daughter of Austin Porter, esq. of Belton, in Lincolnshire, and dying 9th October, 1592, was succeeded by his eldest son,

Sir William Sherard, knt. living in 1634, aged then about eighty. He m. first, Frances, daughter of John Harrington, esq. of Wytham, in Lincolnshire, and had a son, John, his heir. His second wife, was Bridget, daughter of Sir Kenelm Digby, of Stoke Dry, in Rutlandshire, and by her had William, Kenelm, and Rowland. He was s. by his eldest son,

John Sherard, esq. of Lopthorp. This gentleman m. first, Rose, daughter of Francis Sherard, esq. sister of the first Lord Sherard, and by her had an only daughter, Anne, who is supposed to have died s. p. He m. secondly, Elizabeth, daughter of Richard Brownlow, esq. of Belton, and by that lady, who d. 6th February, 1658, had

Richard, his heir.
Mary, m. to George Middlemore, of London, merchant.
Frances, m. to Roger Smith, of Withcock, in the county of Rutland.
Audrie, m. Humphrey Brooke, M.D. of London.

He was s. by his only son,

Richard Sherard, esq. who m. Margaret, daughter of Lumley Dewe, esq. of Bishop Upton, in the county of Hereford, by whom he had three sons and three daughters, viz.

John, his heir.
Richard, heir to his elder brother.
Brownlow, heir to Richard.
Alice, m. to Sir John Brownlow, bart. of Belton, in the county of Lincoln, and had four daughters, viz.
  Elizabeth, m. to John, Earl of Exeter.
  Alice, m. to Francis, Lord Guildford.
  Jane, m. to Peregrine, Duke of Ancaster.
  Eleanor, m. to Sir John Brownlow, of Bruton, in the county of Somerset, created Viscount Tyrconnel, in Ireland, 14th May, 1718, and d. s. p.
Mary.
Elizabeth, m. to Peter Whitcomb, esq. of Braxted, in Essex.

He d. 12th September, 1668, and was s. by his eldest son,

I. John Sherard, esq. of Lopthorp, in the county of Lincoln, who was created a Baronet 29th May, 1674, with remainder to his brothers, and the heirs male of their bodies. Sir John was sheriff of his county in 1711, and died unm. 1st January, 1724, aged sixty three. He was buried in the chancel of North Wytham Church, under a handsome monument, and s. by his brother.

* Burton, in his Leicestershire, speaking of Stapleford, s. s. "In this town, (of a long time,) hath been the ancient family of Sherard, who beareth argent, a chevron, gules, between three torteauxes; which house yet here continueth at this day; and in the church are the arms of Sherard, Sherard and Hawberk, Sherard and Woodford, Sherard and Asby," &c.

II. Sir Richard Sherard, who died also unm. 14th June, 1730, and was buried with his family in North Wytham Church, where a monument was erected to his memory with an inscription, concluding with these lines

Honour'd where known, endearing where allied;
Much lov'd he liv'd, and much lamented died.

He was *s.* by his only surviving brother,

III. Sir Brownlow Sherard, who wedded Dame Mary Anderson, relict of Sir Richard Anderson, bart. of Penley, in the county of Hertford,* and daughter of the Right Hon. John Methuen, Lord Chancellor of Ireland. By her he had an only son, Brownlow, his successor. He *d.* 30th January, 1736, aged sixty, and was interred in the family vault in North Wytham Church,† and was *s.* by his son,

IV. Sir Brownlow Sherard, of Lopthorp Hall, in Lincolnshire, and Newton Hall, Essex, who *m.* 16th July, 1738, Mary, eldest daughter of Col. the Hon. Thomas Sydney, of Ranworth, in Norfolk, and grand-daughter of Thomas, Earl of Leicester, but died without issue, when the Baronetcy expired.

Arms—Argent, a chevron, gules, between three torteauxes.

SHERBURNE, OF STONYHURST.

Created 4th Feb. 1685.

Extinct 14th Dec. 1717.

Lineage.

The family of Sherburne was of great antiquity and distinction in the county of Lancaster, and possessed Stonyhurst from the time of the early Plantagenets. Under Edward I. Sir Robert Sherburn was seneschall of Wiswall and Blackburnshire, and in the martial reign of the third Edward, Sir John Sherburn, attending his royal master in his French wars, served at the siege of Calais. His direct descendant,

Hugh Sherburne, esq. son of Sir Richard Sherburne, of Stonyhurst, by Johanna, his wife, daughter of Henry Langton, of Walton, founded the chantry at Mitton, in Lancashire. He *m.* Anne, daughter of Sir Thomas Talbot, of Bashall, and had issue,

- Thomas, his heir.
- Robert.
- Grace, *m.* to Roger Nowell, 3 Henry VIII.
- Anne, *m.* to John Talbot, of Salisbury.
- Jane, *m.* to Ralph Cliderow, of Awkeley.
- Ellen, *m.* to John Brockholes, esq. of Claughton.

Hugh Sherburne died 19 Henry VIII. and was *s.* by his son,

Thomas Sherburne, esq. of Stonyhurst, who *m.* Jane, daughter of Sir John Townley, of Townley, and dying 28 Henry VIII. left issue,

- Richard, his heir.
- John, who *m.* Katherine, daughter of Evan Browne, and co-heir to her brother James Browne, with whom he acquired the estate of Ribleton.
- Robert, a lawyer, reader to the Hon. Society of Gray's Inn, who *m.* Dorothy, daughter and co-heir of Thomas Catteral, of Little Mitton, and thus acquired that property.
- Grace, *m.* to Roger Sherburne, esq. of Wolfhouse.

The eldest son,

Richard Sherburne, esq. of Stonyhurst, who died 26th July, 1594, *m.* first, Matilda, daughter of Richard Bold, esq. of Bold, and had by her,

- Richard, who *m.* first, Katherine, daughter of Charles, Lord Sturton, secondly, Anne, daughter of Henry Kighley, and thirdly, Anne, daughter of Holden, of Chaighley. He died before the 2nd April, 1628.
- Thomas, died young.
- Hugh, *m.* a sister of Sir Roger Dyneley.
- Margaret, *m.* to Lord Townley, of Barnside.
- Dorothy, *m.* to Thomas Fleetwood, esq. of Calver.
- Mary, *m.* to John Edwards, esq. of Checke.

Richard Sherburne *m.* secondly, Dame Isabel Wood, and had by her (with three daughters, Grace, wife of William Hoghton, of Grimsargh; Jane, *m.* to John Southworth, esq. of Samlesbury; and Isabel,) one son,

Richard Sherburne, esq. of Dunnow, near Slaidburn, who *m.* Dorothy, daughter of Richard Ashton, esq. of Downham, and had issue,

- Henry, who *m.* Anne, daughter of Francis, Lord Dacre, and died without surviving issue, in 1612.
- Richard, successor to his father.
- Katherine, *m.* to William Pennington, esq. of Muncaster.

The only surviving son,

Richard Sherburne, esq. of Stonyhurst, aged thirty-seven, 4 Charles I. *m.* first, Elizabeth, daughter of Sir Richard Molyneux, of Sefton, by whom he had a daughter, Elizabeth, who died young, and secondly, Elizabeth, daughter of Thomas Walmesley, esq. of Dunkenhalgh, by whom he left at his decease, 11th February, 1667, a daughter, Anne, wife of Sir Marmaduke Constable, bart. of Everingham, and a son,

Richard Sherburne, esq. of Stonyhurst who *m.* Isabel, daughter of John Ingleby, esq. of Lawkland, and had issue,

- Nicholas, his heir.
- Richard, of Wrigglesworth, who *m.* Anne, daughter of John Causefield, esq. and *d. s. p.* 6th April, 1690.
- Elizabeth, *m.* to William, son and heir of Sir John Weld, knt. of Lulworth, in Dorsetshire, and had issue.

Richard Sherburne died 16th August, 1689, and was *s.* by his son,

---

* She was previously widow of Humphrey Simpson, esq.

† A handsome marble monument was erected to his memory, with an inscription, concluding in verse thus:

To shun the follies, vices, cares of life,
And private peace prefer to public strife;
To taste below the sweets of heav'nly rest,
Gives us on earth th' enjoyments of the blest.
Thus thought the man, whom virtuous actions gave
Ease in the world, and refuge in the grave;
Who would not wish to be like him retir'd,
And find in death, what he in life desir'd.

I. Nicholas Sherburne, esq. of Stonyhurst, who was created a Baronet 4th February, 1685. He m. Catherine, daughter and co-heir of Sir Edward Charlton, bart. of Hesleyside, in Northumberland, and had issue,

Richard-Francis, b. in 1693, died in 1702.

Maria-Winifred Francisca, m. to Thomas, eighth Duke of Norfolk.

Sir Nicholas died 14th December, 1717, when the Baronetcy expired. The estates devolving on his only surviving daughter the Duchess of Norfolk. Her grace d. without issue in 1754, and was succeeded in the possessions of the Sherburnes by the children of her aunt Elizabeth, wife of William Weld, esq. of Lulworth, and they are still enjoyed by the Weld family. (See Burke's *Commoners*, vol. i.) In 1794, the stately mansion of Stonyhurst, was fixed upon as the seat of an English Catholic College, the heads of which having been driven from their establishment at Liege, by the proscriptions of the French Revolution, were induced, in consequence of the judicious mitigation of the penal enactments in England against Catholic seminaries, to seek an asylum in their native country. A long lease was accordingly obtained of the house and of the college farm, on moderate terms, from the late Thomas Weld, esq. and the old baronial hall of the Sherburnes, with its towers and park-like grounds, converted into a seat of learning.

Arms—Arg. a lion rampant guardant vert.

SHIERS, OF SLYFIELD.

Created 16th Oct. 1684.

Extinct 18th July, 1685.

Lineage.

Robert Shiers, esq. of Slyfield House, in Great Bookham, Surrey, son and heir of George Shiers, esq. of London, who purchased Slyfield in 1614, died 29th July, 1668, leaving by Elizabeth, his wife, six children. The eldest son and successor,

I. George Shiers, esq. of Slyfield House, was created a Baronet 15th October, 1684. He m. Elizabeth, daughter and heir of Edmund Dickenson, M.D. of St. Martin's Lane, London, but had no issue. He died 18th July, 1685, aged twenty-five, when the title became extinct. Sir George bequeathed £30 a year to the poor of Great Bookham, and £20 a year to those of Fetcham. The residue of his estates he gave to his mother, Elizabeth, who died 14th August, 1700, having been a most liberal benefactress to the poor, to whom, as her monumental inscription states, she administered medicine with a skill equal to that of the most experienced physician. In 1693, Mrs. Shiers settled the estate of Slyfield and the manor farm of Tollingtons, with lands in Herts, on herself for life, with remainder to the Rev. Hugh Shortrudge and the heirs of his body, remainder to herself in fee, with power to revoke and appoint new uses. She subsequently made a will, and devised her estates to charitable uses, of which Exeter College, Oxford, was to have a considerable part. In consequence of informality in the document, Dr. Shortrudge set the will aside, but fulfilled the testator's injunctions, by vesting it in trustees for the same purpose as she did.

Arms—Or, on a bend az. between a lion rampant in chief sa. and three oak leaves in base ppr. as many escallops of the field.

SHIRLEY, OF PRESTON.

Created 6th March, 1665.

Extinct in 1705.

Lineage.

I. Anthony Shirley, esq. of Preston, in Sussex, who was created a Baronet in 1665, was son of Thomas Shirley, esq. by Elizabeth, his wife, daughter of Drew Stapley, esq. of London, grandson of Thomas Shirley, esq. of Preston, and great-grandson of Anthony Shirley, who was second son of William Shirley, esq. of Wistenston, and lineally derived from the Shirleys of Staunton Harold. The baronet m. Anne, daughter of Sir Richard Onslow, knt. of West Clandon, in Surrey, and dying about 1683, left with a daughter, Elizabeth, a son,

II. Sir Richard Shirley, of Preston, b. about 1654, who m. Judith, sister of Sir James Bateman, knt. and had by her, who wedded, secondly, Sir Henry Hatsell, Richard, his heir; Anthony; Anne, wife of Thomas Western, of Rivenhall; Judith; and Mary. Sir Richard d. in 1692, and was s. by his son,

III. Sir Richard Shirley, of Preston, at whose decease unm. in 1705, the Baronetcy became extinct, his sisters being his co-heirs.

Arms—Paly of six or and az. a canton erm.

SHIRLEY, OF OAT HALL.

Created 27th June, 1786.—Extinct 26th Feb. 1815.

Lineage.

William Shirley, esq. son of William Shirley, who died in 1701, by Elizabeth, his wife, daughter of John Goodman, derived (it is stated) his descent from the Shirleys of Wistenston. He m. Elizabeth, daughter of Francis Baker, of London, and had issue,

William, killed in America in 1755.
John, died at Oswego.
Thomas, of whom presently.
Ralph, died young.

Elizabeth, m. to Eliakim Hutchinson, esq.
Frances, m. to William Bolland, of London.
Judith.
Harriet, m. to Robert Temple.
Maria, m. to John Erving, of Boston, New England.

The third son,

I. Thomas Shirley, esq. b. at Boston, New England, a major-general in the army, and governor of the Leeward Islands, was created a Baronet in 1786. He m.

Anne, eldest daughter of Thomas Western, esq. of Rivenhall, Essex, by Margaret, his wife, sister and co-heir of Sir Richard Shirley, bart. of Preston, and by her, who *d.* in 1777, left at his decease in March, 1800, an only surviving son,

II. Sir William Warden Shirley, of Oat Hall, Wivelsfield, Sussex, who *d.* without issue 26th February, 1815, when the Baronetcy became extinct.

Arms—As Shirley of Preston.

SIDLEY, OF AILESFORD.

Created 20th June, 1611.

Extinct 20th Aug. 1701.

Lineage.

This family (of very great antiquity in the county of Kent) was anciently seated at Romney Marsh, where there are lands now called Sidley's and Sidley's Marsh; they built afterwards, *temp.* Edward III. a mansion house at Scadbury, in Southfleet, in the same county. Philpot, in his Villare Cantiarum, takes notice that their arms were in the old hall there, and the date 1337.

John Sidley, or Sedley, (as the name has been frequently written) auditor of the Exchequer to *King* Henry VII. lord of the manor of Southfleet, and also of Mortimer,* in Kent, *m.* first, Elizabeth, daughter and co-heir of Roger Jenks, of London; secondly, Elizabeth, daughter of John Cotton, esq. of Hampstall-Ridware, in the county of Stafford; and thirdly, Agnes, daughter and heir of John Wyborne, esq. of Hakewell, in Kent, but left issue by the second only, viz.

- William, his heir.
- Martin, of Morley, in Norfolk, *m.* the daughter and heir of Mountney, of Mountnesing, in Essex.

The elder son,

William Sidley, esq. of Scadbury, sheriff of Kent in 1597, *m.* Anne, daughter and heir of Roger Grove, or Greene, of London, and had issue,

- John, his heir.
- Robert, *m.* Elizabeth, daughter of George Darrell, esq. of Calehill.
- Nicholas, *m.* Jane, daughter and heir of William Isaac, esq. and was father of
  - Sir Isaac Sidley, bart. of Great Chart.
- Frances, *m.* to Thomas Hyde, esq.
- Elizabeth, *m.* to John Culpeper, esq. of Wigsell, in Kent.

He was *s.* by his eldest son,

John Sidley, esq. of Southfleet, who was high sheriff of Kent 8 Elizabeth. He *m.* Anne, daughter of John Culpeper, esq. of Ailesford, in the same county, and had issue,

- William, his heir.
- John, *d. s. p.*
- Richard, lord of the manor of Northall, or Northaw, in Hertfordshire, *temp.* James I. which estate he purchased from Lord Russell. He *m.* Elizabeth, daughter of John Darrell, esq. of Calehill, founder's kin at All Souls College, Oxford, and left a son and heir,
  - William Sidley, who married first, Anne, daughter and co-heir of Henry Botler, esq. of London, and that lady dying in 1647, he *m.* secondly, Mary, daughter of Sir Robert Honeywood, of Pett, in Charing, Kent.† By the former he had issue,
    - Anne Sidley, who *m.* John Nourse, esq. of Woodeaton, in Oxfordshire, and *d.* 30th August, 1669, leaving
      - Martha Nourse, *m.* to Robert Pitt, M.D. of Blandford, Dorsetshire, and her daughter,
        - Martha Pitt, *m.* Sir George Brydges Skipwith, bart.
      - Elizabeth Nourse, *m.* to Charles Harris, esq. barrister-at-law, and her daughter,
        - Elizabeth Harris, *m.* James Bourchier, LL.D. king's professor of law at Oxford, and had issue,
          - Thomas Bourchier.
          - Elizabeth Bourchier, *m.* to Joseph Smith, LL.D. of Oxford, and had issue,
            - Harris Smith, admitted to Winchester College, as founder's kin, about the year 1772, in right of his descent from John Sidley, and his wife, Anne Culpeper.
            - Mary Smith, married to George Anson Nutt, esq.
      - Susanna Nourse, *m.* to Dr. Thomas Craddock, rector of Slimbridge, Gloucestershire.
      - Mary Nourse, *m.* to Dutton Seaman, esq. of Rotherby, in Leicestershire. Her only son, Dutton Seaman, was comptroller of the city of London.

---

* Philpot says that this manor went from the Mortimers to the Englefields of Berks, and continued with them until the end of Henry VII. when it was alienated to John Sidley.

† By Mary, his wife, daughter and co-heir of Robert Waters, of Lenham, in Kent. Of this lady it is recorded, that at his decease she had no less than 367 lawful descendants then living: 16 of her own body (by her only husband, Honywood), 114 grand-children, 228 in the third generation, and 9 in the fourth. See Ward's lives of the Professors of Gresham College, under the account of Sir John Croke, whose son, William, *m.* Dorothy, one of her daughters. The following singular story is related of the same remarkable woman: falling at one time in a low desponding state of mind, she was impressed with the idea that she should be damned; and exclaiming, in a paroxysm of the malady, "I shall be damned as sure as that glass is broken." She flung thrice with violence a glass which she happened to have in her hand on a marble slab, by which she was standing, but the glass rebounded each time, and did not break. The story adds, that the circumstance wrought a complete cure, and had more effect in composing her mind than the reasoning of all the great divines whom she had consulted; she is painted in the act of flinging the glass, according to the story. She died at Markeshall, in Essex, 11th May, 1620, in the ninety-third year of her age, and forty-fourth of her widowhood, and was buried at Lenham, the place of her birth.

Mr. Sidley purchased a moiety of the estate of Nurstede, and was succeeded at his decease by his eldest son,

I. WILLIAM SIDLEY, esq. of Aylesford, who purchased the other moiety of Nurstede, and was created a BARONET 29th June, 1611. Sir William m. Elizabeth, daughter and co-heir of Stephen Darrell, esq. of Spelmander in Kent (widow of Henry, Lord Abergavenny). He was founder of the Sidleian lecture of natural philosophy at Oxford, in 1621, and he resided at the Friars at Rilesford, "the fair habitation," saith Doctor Holland, in his additions to Camden, "of Sir William Sidley, painfully and expensively studious of the common good of his country, as both his endowed house for the poor, and the bridge there, with the common voice do testify." He was s. by his son,

II. SIR JOHN SIDLEY, sheriff of Kent, 19 JAMES I. who m. Elizabeth, daughter and heir of the celebrated Sir Henry Savile, founder of the astronomy professorship at Oxford (was warden of Merton College, in that university, and provost of Eton), and had issue,

HENRY, his heir.
WILLIAM, successor to his brother.
CHARLES, who inherited as fifth baronet.

He died 13th August, 1638, and was succeeded by his eldest son,

III. SIR HENRY SIDLEY, who d. unm. in 1641, and was s. by his brother,

IV. SIR WILLIAM SIDLEY. Of this gentleman, Anthony Wood states, "that when he was a young man, he lived very high in London, with his friend, Robert Dormer, esq. of Rousham, in Oxfordshire (whose wife was Anne, one of the daughters of Sir Charles Cotterell, master of the ceremonies), and they endeavoured who should outvie each other in gallantry and in splendid coaches." He m. Lady Jane Savage, daughter of John, Earl Rivers, and relict of George, Lord Chandos, but by her ladyship (who m. after his decease George Pitt, esq. of Strathfieldsay) had no issue. He died in 1656, and was succeeded by his brother,

V. SIR CHARLES SIDLEY, b. in 1639, distinguished for his wit and gallantry. As a critic, too, he was so much admired, that he became a kind of oracle among the poets, and no performance was approved or condemned until Sir Charles Sedley had given judgment. King Charles used to say, that nature had given him a patent to be Apollo's viceroy. After a long course of profligacy and extravagance, Sir Charles began to apply himself to politics, and sat in several parliaments for the borough of Romney. He took an active part in promoting the Revolution, which at first excited astonishment, as he had received many favours from JAMES II. but those had been cancelled by an intrigue which the monarch carried on with his daughter, afterwards created COUNTESS OF DORCHESTER. This elevation by no means gratified Sir Charles, and on being asked why he appeared so warm for the revolution, he is stated to have replied, "from a principle of gratitude, for since his majesty has made my daughter a countess, it is fit I should do all I can to make his daughter a queen." He married Catherine, third daughter of John, Earl Rivers, and had by her an only daughter,

CATHERINE, mistress to JAMES II. by whom she was created COUNTESS OF DORCHESTER for life. After the dissolution of her connexion with the king, she married Sir David Colyear, Earl of Portmore.

Sir Charles married secondly, (whilst his first wife was living,) Catherine Ayscough, of Yorkshire, by whom he had a son, SIR CHARLES SIDLEY, knt. who d. s. p. leaving by Frances, his wife, third daughter of Sir Richard Newdigate, a son, CHARLES, created a BARONET in 1702. Sir Charles Sidley d. 20th August, 1701, when the title became EXTINCT.

Arms—Az. a fessy wavy between three goats' heads erased arg.

SIDLEY, OF SOUTHFLEET.

CREATED 10th July, 1702.—EXTINCT in 1781.

Lineage.

I. SIR CHARLES SIDLEY, of Southfleet, was knighted 12th March, 1688, and created a BARONET by *Queen* ANNE, 10th July, 1702. He m. the daughter and heir of — Collinge, esq. of Nuthall, Notts, and by her, who d. 20th April, 1738, had issue,

CHARLES, his heir.

ELIZABETH, m. in November, 1730, Sir Robert Burdett, bart. of Bramcote, and was grandmother of the present (1838) SIR FRANCIS BURDETT.

Amongst other legacies, Sir Charles left £400 to a schoolmaster at Wymondham and Southfleet, and £100 each to Merton and Magdalen Colleges, Oxford. He d. in 1727, and was s. by his son,

II. SIR CHARLES SIDLEY, who m. in 1718, Elizabeth, daughter of William Frith, esq. and acquired thereby the manors of Hayford and Harleigh. This gentleman exchanged his family estate of South and Northfleet, with the Rev. Thomas Sanderson, for the estate of Kirkby Beler, in Leicestershire. He sate in parliament for the town of Nottingham, in 1747, and dying 23rd August, 1778, left an only daughter and heir, Elizabeth-Rebecca-Anne, m. to Henry, third Lord Vernon. At Sir Charles's decease, the BARONETCY became EXTINCT.

Arms—As SIDLEY OF AILESFORD.

SIDLEY, OF GREAT CHART.

CREATED 14th Sept. 1621.—EXTINCT ......

Lineage.

WILLIAM SIDLEY, esq. of Southfleet, sheriff of Kent in 1597, m. Anne, daughter of Roger Grove, of London, and had three sons, viz.

JOHN (Sir), from whom the Baronets of Ailesford.
Robert, m. Elizabeth, daughter of George Darrell, esq. of Calehill.
Nicholas.

The youngest son,

NICHOLAS SIDLEY, esq. m. Jane, daughter of William Isaac, esq. and left a son and heir,

I. SIR ISAAC SIDLEY, of Great Chart, in Kent, who received the honour of knighthood, and was created a BARONET 14th September, 1621. He m. Miss Holditch, daughter and heir of — Holditch, esq. of Ranworth and Foulden, in Norfolk, and left at his decease, about 1627 (with two daughters, one the wife of Robert Houghton, esq. of Shelton, in Norfolk, the other, Elizabeth, the wife of Sir Thomas Wiseman, knt. of Riven Hall, in Essex), a son and heir,

II. SIR JOHN SIDLEY. This gentleman having sold the estates of Ranworth and Foulden, purchased St. Cleres from Robert Moulton, esq. "who (says Philpot) hath upon the old foundation erected that magnificent pile, which for grandeur, elegance, and majestick aspect it carries to public view, surrenders a priority but to few structures in the county." He m. Mary, daughter of — Bradshaw, and had issue,

Isaac, his heir.
John, successor to his nephew.
Elisabeth, m. to John Gilborne, gent.
——, m. to — Vane, esq.

Sir John d. in November, 1673, and was s. by his elder son,

III. Sir Isaac Sidley, who married twice; by his first wife he had a daughter, who m. first, Sir Charles Houghton, knt. of Kent; and secondly, Sir George Prettyman, bart. of Lodington, in Leicestershire. Sir Isaac Sidley m. secondly, Cecily, daughter of — Marsh, esq. and by her (who m. secondly, Leonard Peckham, esq. of Yaldham) left, with two daughters, Mary, m. to George Tomlyn, of St. Cleres, and Frances, an only son, his successor,

IV. Sir Charles Sidley, who d. unm. in October, 1702, and was s. by his uncle,

V. Sir John Sidley, who m. Mary, daughter of — Nichols, of Keirising, in Kent, and by her, who d. in 1701, had issue,

George, his successor.

He was s. by his son,

VI. Sir George Sidley, who was seated near Lewes, in Sussex. He had with a daughter, two sons, viz.

George, his successor.
Charles, heir to his brother.

He was s. by his eldest son,

VII. Sir George Sidley, who d. unm. and was s. by his brother,

VIII. Sir Charles Sidley, at whose decease, without male issue, the Baronetcy became extinct.

Arms—As Sidley of Ailesford.

SILVESTER, OF YARDLEY.

First Patent { Created 20th May, 1815. Extinct 30th March, 1822.

Second Patent { Created 11th Feb. 1822. Extinct in Sept. 1828.

Lineage.

Daniel Silvester, a distinguished advocate in the parliament of Bourdeaux, in France, m. Susanna Bernardine, and by her (who d. in London, 1722) had issue,

I. Peter, M.D. physician to *King* William III. and commissioner of the sick and hurt, died 16th September, 1718.
II. Francis-Jason.

The second son,

Francis-Jason Silvester, who resided on his estate near Bourdeaux, m. 1713, Catherine Berbineau, and by her (who d. 13th November, 1763) had issue,

Sir John Silvester, M.D. physician to the army in the Low Countries, 1744, knighted 1774. He m. 1739, Catherine-Aletta-Everardina, daughter of Colonel Daulnis, of the Dutch service, and d. 2nd November, 1789, leaving issue by her (who d. 20th March, 1773) one son and one daughter, viz.

John, his heir.
Mary-Rachael, b. 1741, m. April, 1772, Philip Carteret, esq. rear-admiral R. N. and d. May, 1815, having had issue by him (who d. July, 1796) one son and two daughters, viz.
Philip Carteret.
Elizabeth-Mary, m. 10th March, 1818, to William Symonds, esq.
Caroline Carteret, m. to Cole St. George, esq.

Sir John Silvester's son and heir,

I. John Silvester, esq. was born September, 1745, bred to the bar, and elected in 1803, recorder of the city of London, which office he continued to fill till his death. He m. December, 1793, Harriet, daughter of the Rev. Owen Davies, of Southampton, and widow of the Rev. John-Miles Speed, of Eling, Hants. He was created a Baronet 20th May, 1815, and 11th February, 1822, had a second patent with remainder, in default of issue male of his body, to his nephew, Philip Carteret, esq. Sir John d. without issue, 30th March, 1822, when the first creation expired, but in the second he was succeeded, pursuant to the limitation of the patent, by his nephew,

II. Sir Philip Carteret, C.B. captain R.N. who assumed in consequence the additional surname and arms of Silvester. He died s. p. in 1828, when the second patent also became extinct.

Arms—Arg. a sea-lion ducally crowned az.

SIMEON, OF CHILWORTH.

Created 18th Oct. 1677. Extinct 22nd Dec. 17—.

Lineage.

John Simeon, esq. of Baldwin's Brightwell, in the county of Oxford, which seat had been the abode of his ancestors for some generations before, m. Anne daughter and coheir of Anthony Mollins, esq. and had (with three daughters*) two surviving sons, viz.

George, } who both received the honour of knighthood.
John, }

He d. 15th James I. possessed (beside several other estates) of the manor of Baldwin's Brightwell, Mimsgrove, Brittwell prior, Chilworth, and Stoke Talmage as appears by the Inquisition, *post mortem*, taken at Watlington, 28th May, 16 James I. He was s. by his elder son,

Sir George Simeon, knt. who m. Mary, daughter of the Hon. George Vaux, eldest son (by his second wife) of William, third Lord Vaux of Harrowden, and sister and co-heir of William, 5th lord, and by that lady had two daughters, namely,

Anne, who is presumed to have died unm.

* The eldest daughter married Edmond Plowden, esq. of Shiplake; the second, Edward Gascoigne, esq.; and the third, Ralph Ireland, esq.

ELIZABETH, married to Edmund Butler, Viscount Mountgarrett.†

He *m.* secondly, Margaret, daughter of Sir Richard Molyneux, bart. of Sefton, in the county of Lancaster, and was *s.* at his decease by the youngest, and only surviving son, of five,

I. JAMES SIMEON, esq. of Chilworth, in the county of Oxford, who was created a BARONET by *King* CHARLES II. 18th October, 1677. Sir James married Bridget, daughter, and at length sole heir of Walter Heveningham, esq. of Aston, in the county of Stafford, and had issue,

EDWARD, his successor.
James, *d.* abroad, in May, 1714.
MARGARET, *m.* to Humphrey Weld, esq. of Lulworth Castle, in the county of Dorset, and had, with two elder sons, who died before their father, and two daughters (see BURKE'S *Commoners*, vol. i. page 196),
EDWARD, who inherited Lulworth Castle, and continued the family.
THOMAS, who assumed the surname of SIMEON.

Sir James *d.* about 1709, and was *s.* by his son,

II. SIR EDWARD SIMEON, who *d.* unm. 22nd December, aged eighty-seven, when the BARONETCY EXPIRED, and the estates devolved upon his nephew,

THOMAS WELD, who in consequence assumed the surname of SIMEON. He *m.* Mary, daughter of Thomas Fitzherbert, esq. of Swinnerton, and had an only child,
MARY SIMEON, who took the veil at Bruges.

Arms—Party per pale sable and or, a pale counterchanged, upon every one of the first a trefoil of the second. Le Neve blazons the arms borne by Sir James Simeon thus: Per fesse, or and sable, a pale counterchanged, and three trefoils slipped ppr.; and states, that Edmund Symons, of Pyrton, in the county of Oxford, bore, Per fesse, or and sable, a pale and three trefoils counterchanged: referring to Visit. Oxon. c. 29, fo. 78.

SKEFFINGTON, OF FISHERWICK.

CREATED 8th May, 1627.

EXTINCT 25th Feb. 1816.

Lineage.

The very ancient family of Skeffington derived its name from the village of Skeffington, in the county of Leicester, where it was seated at a very early period.

SIR WILLIAM SKEFFINGTON, knt. was appointed by *King* HENRY VIII. in 1529, his majesty's commissioner to Ireland, where he arrived in the August of that year, with instructions to find out means to restrain the exactions of the soldiers, to call a parliament, and to provide that the possessions of the clergy might be subject to bear their part of the public expense. Sir William was, subsequently, a very distinguished political personage in Ireland, and *d.* in the government of that kingdom, as lord deputy, in December, 1535. His great-grandson,

JOHN SKEFFINGTON, esq. of Fisherwick, in the county of Stafford, *m.* Alice, seventh daughter of Sir Thomas Cave, bart. of Stamford, in Northamptonshire, and had a son and successor,

I. SIR WILLIAM SKEFFINGTON, knt. of Fisherwick, sheriff of Staffordshire, 43 ELIZABETH and 21 JAMES I. who was created a BARONET in 1627. He *m.* Elizabeth, daughter of Richard Dering, esq. and had issue,

JOHN, his heir.
RICHARD, successor to his nephew.
Elizabeth, *m.* to Michael Biddulph, esq. of Elmhurst, in Staffordshire, and was mother of Sir Theophilus Biddulph, bart.
Cicely, *m.* to Edward Mytton, esq. of Weston, in Staffordshire.
Mary, *m.* to Richard Pyott, esq. of Strethay, in Staffordshire.
Hesther, *m.* to Sir William Bowyer, knt.
Lettice, *m.* to John Bayly, esq. of Hoddesdon, Herts.
Alice, *m.* to Alexander Walthall, esq. of Wistaston, in Cheshire, and had a son, Richard, his heir, ancestor of the present JAMES WALTHALL HAMMOND, esq. of Wistaston, and several daughters, of whom the second, Mary, *m.* Robert Weever, esq. of Poole, in Cheshire, and was mother of Mary Weever, the wife of John Minshull, esq.* sheriff of Chester in 1702.

Sir William was *s.* at his decease by his son,

II. SIR JOHN SKEFFINGTON, of Fisherwick, sheriff of Staffordshire in 1638, who *m.* Cicely, sister and co-heir of Sir John Skeffington, of Skeffington, and had a son,

III. SIR WILLIAM SKEFFINGTON, of Fisherwick, who died unm. soon after his father, and was *s.* by his uncle,

IV. SIR RICHARD SKEFFINGTON, of Fisherwick, who *m.* Anne, youngest daughter of Sir John Newdigate, knt. of Arbury, in the county of Warwick, and had issue,

JOHN, his heir.
Richard, } who *d.* unm.
William, }
Anne, *d.* unm.
Mary, *m.* to William Bunbury, esq.
Elizabeth, *m.* to William Ferrar, esq. of Dromore.

---

† The descendant of this lady, GEORGE MOSTYN, esq. has recently petitioned parliament, claiming through her the BARONY OF VAUX OF HARROWDEN. (See BURKE'S *Peerage*, Appendix, "Peerages before Parliament.")

* This JOHN MINSHULL, esq. sheriff of Chester in 1702, and mayor in 1711, (who was son of Randal Minshull, and grandson of another Randal Minshull, by Elizabeth, his wife, daughter of William Leycester, esq. mayor of Chester in 1669,) descended from the Minshulls, of Cheshire, an ancient and ennobled family allied to the chief houses of the palatinate, the Vernons, the Breretons, the Cholmondeleys, the Fittons, the Egertons, &c. By Mary Weever, his wife, he left at his decease, in 1729, a son,

ALEXANDER MINSHULL, esq. of the Inner Temple, who m. Sarah Alvarez, and died in 1740, leaving a son,

JOHN MINSHULL, esq. clerk of the Nisi Prius and marshal of the court of King's Bench, who died in 1785, and was *s.* by his son,

JOHN MINSHULL, esq. who died at Highgate in 1822, leaving by Mary, his wife, daughter of Captain Thomas Staunton, two daughters, viz.

ANN, *m.* to Lynde Walter, esq. of Boston, North America, and has, with three daughters, one son, Lynde Minshull Walter.
MARY, *m.* to Dominick Mazzinghi, esq. and has one son, Thomas-John, of the Inner Temple, and two daughters, Juliet-Mary, wife of the Rev. J. W. Worthington, and Cassandra-Ann.

Sir Richard *d.* in 1647, and was *s.* by his son,

v. Sir John Skeffington, of Fisherwick, who *m.* Mary, only daughter and heiress of Sir John Clotworthy, a very active personage in promoting the restoration of *King* Charles II. who was elevated to the peerage of Ireland, 21st November, 1660, as *Baron of Loughneagh*, and Viscount Massareene, with remainder, in default of male issue, to his son-in-law, the said Sir John Skeffington, and his issue male, by his said wife, in default of which, to the heirs general of his lordship. Sir John Skeffington inherited accordingly in 1665, and became second Viscount Massareene. By the heiress of Clotworthy he had issue,

- Clotworthy, his heir.
- Mary, *m.* to Sir Charles Houghton, bart.
- Margaret, *m.* to Sir George St. George.
- Frances.

His lordship died in 1695, and was succeeded by his only son,

vi. Sir Clotworthy Skeffington, third Viscount Massareene, who *m.* Rachael, daughter of Sir Edward Hungerford, K. B. of Farley Castle, in Somersetshire, and by her, who died 2nd February, 1731, had issue,

- Clotworthy, his heir.
- Hale, *d.* unm.
- John, of Darvock, in Antrim, *d.* unm. in 1741.
- Jane, *m.* to Sir Hans Hamilton, bart.
- Rachael, *m.* first, to Randal, fourth Earl of Antrim; and secondly, to Robert Hawkins Macgill, esq. of Gill Hall, in Downshire.
- Frances-Diana, *d.* unm.
- Mary, *m.* to Edward Smyth, Bishop of Downe and Connor.

This nobleman *d.* in 1713, and was *s.* by his son,

vii. Sir Clotworthy Skeffington, fourth Viscount Massareene, who *m.* in 1713, Catharine, eldest daughter of Arthur, fourth Earl of Donegal, and had issue,

- Clotworthy, his heir.
- Arthur, captain in the army, *d. s. p.* in 1747.
- John, rector of Clonmarney.
- Hungerford, M.P. for Antrim.
- Hugh, a dragoon officer.
- Catharine, *m.* to Arthur Mohun, Viscount Doneraile.
- Rachael.

His lordship dying in 1738, was *s.* by his eldest son,

viii. Sir Clotworthy Skeffington, fifth Viscount Massareene, who was created 16th July, 1756, Earl of Massareene. His lordship *m.* first, in 1738, Anne, eldest daughter of the Rev. Richard Daniel, Dean of Down, by whom he had no issue; and secondly, in 1754, Elizabeth, only daughter of Henry Eyre, esq. of Rowter, in the county of Derby, by whom he had several children, viz.

- i. Clotworthy.
- ii. Henry.
- iii. William, *d. s. p.* 1814.
- iv. John, *d. s. p.*
- v. Chichester, fourth earl.
- vi. Alexander, *d. s. p.*

- i. Elizabeth, *m.* to Robert, first Earl of Leitrim.
- ii. Catharine, *m.* to Francis, first Earl of Llandaff.

He *d.* in 1757, and was *s.* by his eldest son,

ix. Sir Clotworthy Skeffington, second Earl of Massareene. This nobleman *m.* twice, but dying without issue in 1805, the family honours devolved upon his brother,

x. Sir Henry Skeffington, third Earl of Massareene, who *d.* unm. 12th June, 1811, when the peerage descended to his brother,

xi. Sir Chichester Skeffington, fourth Earl of Massareene. This nobleman married Harriet, elder daughter of Robert, first Earl of Roden, by whom he had issue an only daughter, Harriet, to whom descended, at his lordship's decease, in 1816, the Viscounty of Massareene and the Baroness of Loughneagh, while the earldom and Baronetcy expired. Her ladyship *m.* in 1810, Thomas-Henry, Viscount Ferrard, and died in 1831, leaving, with other issue, a son, John Skeffington, present Viscount Massareene.

Arms—Ar. three bulls' heads erased sa. armed or for Skeffington.

SKIPWITH, OF NEWBOLD HALL.

Created 25th Oct. 1670.

Extinct in 17[illegible].

Lineage.

This family, originally written Schypwyc, and hence nominated from a town and lordship so called in the East Riding of York, descends from

Robert de Estoteville, Baron of Cottingham, in the time of the Conqueror, of whom and his descendants, the feudal lords of Cottingham, Dugdale treats at great length in the Baronage. His son,

Robert de Estoteville, acquired a great inheritance with his wife, Erneburga, daughter and heir of Hugh, son of Baldrick, a great Saxon thane, and among other lands, had the lordship of Schypwic, or Skipwic. He left three sons,

- Robert, his heir, from whom the territorial lords of Cottingham, whose male line terminated in the 17th of Henry III.
- Osmund, who *d.* at Joppa, in Palestine, was ancestor of the Estotevilles, of Grensing Hall.
- Patrick, of Skipwith.

The youngest son,

Patrick de Estoteville, having by gift of his father, the lordship of Skipwith, his descendants took their name therefrom, in accordance with the custom of the age. He *m.* Beatrix, daughter and heir of Sir Pagan de Langtun, and was *s.* by his son,

Jeffery de Schypwith, who *m.* Mariana, daughter and heir of William de Manlthorp, and had two sons, Reginald and Gerard. The elder, Reginald, was hostage for the Lord Scales, in the barons' wars, 9th of John. His son and heir,

Sir William de Skipwith, Lord of Skipwith, was living *temp.* Henry III. and marrying Alice, daughter of Sir John Thorp, and heir of Sir William Thorp, knts. became possessed of a great estate in Lincolnshire, and was the last of the family who resided at Skipwith. His son and heir,

Sir John de Skipwith, living at Thorp, was sometimes styled de Thorp; he likewise possessed the manor of Beakby, in right of his mother, and having married Isabel, daughter and heir of Sir Robert de Arches, knt. of Wrauby, in the same county, had also possession of that estate. He was *s.* by his son,

John de Skipwith, who resided at Beakby, and augmented his patrimony by marriage with Margaret ughter and co-heir of Herbert de Flinton, of Yorkhire,* by whom he had a son and heir,

William de Skipwith, who married Margaret, ughter of Ralph Fitz Simon, Lord of Ormsby, in e county of Lincoln, and sister and sole heir of imon Fitz Ralph, whereby he became possessed of at inheritance, which was the possession of Sir alph Fitz Simon, knt. who in several charters was rmed *nobilis*, and had obtained the estate and manor y his wife, the daughter and heir of Ormsby, of rmsby; from this marriage with Margaret Fitz Simon proceeded three sons,

- John, eldest son and heir, *d. s. p.* 10 Edward III. the same year which his father died.
- William (Sir).
- Ralph (Sir), from whom descended the Skipwiths, of Heburgh, in Lincolnshire, who held lands in Southliston, Kernington, Heighburgh, Alesby, and Laseby, in the time of Henry IV.

Sir William Skipwith, the second son, succeeded is elder brother, in the estate, a few months after e father died. Sir William was bred to the bar, and ttained great eminence. He was first chosen one of e king's serjeants, and in the 33rd of Edward III. nstituted one of the judges of the King's Bench. three years afterwards, he was sworn in lord chief ron of the Exchequer, and he continued in that gh judicial station until the 40th year of the same ing, the time of his decease. His lordship married bee, only daughter and heir of Sir William de Hilft, Lord of Ingoldmells,† and had issue,

- William (Sir), his heir.
- John, heir to his elder brother.
- Patrick.
- Stephen.
- Alice, m. to Robert, fourth Lord Willoughby de Eresby.
- Margaret, m. to William Vavasor, esq.

he eldest son,

Sir William Skipwith, pursuing the learned prossion of his father, was constituted one of the justes of the King's Bench in the 50th of Edward III. d his patent was renewed in the 1st of Richard II. hen he was senior judge of that court, and deported mself therein so uprightly, that his name is handed wn by our historians with the highest honour. On e accession of Richard, he obtained free warren in l his demesnes at Ormesby, Ingoldmells, Carleton, ovenham, and Bekeby; and in the 11th year of the me reign, had at his own request, a quietus from his ire of justice.‡ "The Collar of Esses," (says an old riter,) "now worn by the judges, first introduced om the initial letters of Sanctus Simon Simplicius, an uncorrupted justicier in the primitive times, well suited this Sir William Skipwith, who died full of honour, without issue male, leaving only one daughter, married to George, Lord Monboucher, whereupon the bulk of his estate descended to his brother and heir."

John Skipwith, esq. of Ormesby, high sheriff of Lincolnshire, 18 Richard II. and one of the knights in parliament for the same county, *temp.* Henry V. He m. Alice, daughter of Sir Frederick Tilney, knt. of Tilney, in the county of Norfolk, and had three sons, viz.

- William, d. in his father's lifetime issueless.
- Thomas (Sir), his heir.
- Patrick, from whom the Skipwiths of Utterby, in the county of Lincoln, and from a younger son of that line sprang the Skipwiths of Snore, in Norfolk.

He was *s.* at his decease, 9 Henry V. by his elder surviving son,

Sir Thomas Skipwith, who distinguished himself in the French wars, and was knighted in France by Henry V. He m. Margaret, daughter of John, Lord Willoughby de Eresby, and died before the 19th of Henry VI. for in that year, his son and heir,

Sir William Skipwith, was in possession of the estates. The records in the Tower, style this William, son of the said Thomas, and state that he was seized by inheritance of Skipwith and Menthorp, in the county of York; South Ormesby, Kettleby, Walmesgare, Calthorp, Covenham, Garnethorp, Wargholme, Laseby, Caldale, and Somercose, in the county of Lincoln. He was knighted in France, *temp.* Henry VI. and was sheriff of Lincolnshire in the 37th of that king's reign. In the 1st of Edward IV. he was constituted seneschal of the dominion or demesne of Borewell, in the same county: in a charter to Richard III. he is mentioned as possessed of Ingoldmells, and the advowson of the church of St. Peter. He m. first, Joan, daughter of Sir Robert Mortimer, knt. but by that lady had no issue. He wedded, secondly, Agnes, daughter of Sir John Constable, knt. of Burton Constable, and widow of Sir — St. Quintin, and had by her,

- John (Sir), his heir.
- Alice, m. to Sir John Markham, knt.

He died in the 1st of Henry VII. and was *s.* by his son,

Sir John Skipwith, who was made a knight banneret for his services against the Cornish rebels, being with the king at the battle of Blackheath. He m. Catherine, daughter of Richard Fitz Williams, esq. of Wadsworth, and had issue,

* By a daughter and co-heir of Walter de la Lynde, of Laseby, in the county of Lincoln, and of Balbrook, Suffolk, son of Sir John de la Lynde, knt. seneschal the city of London, in the time of Henry III.

† By Alice, his wife, sister and sole heir of Ralph de er, Lord of Calthorp and Covenham, in the county of ncoln. Sir William de Hiltoft was son of another William, by Agnes, daughter of Thomas, and one of sisters and co-heirs of William de Mumby, a family ended from the house of Willoughby. Sir William de Willoughby, having two sons, by his wife, ice Beke, heir of the feudal lords of Eresby. The der, Robert, inherited the barony on the decease of his cle, Anthony Beke, bishop of Durham, and was summoned to parliament as Lord Willoughby de Eresby. The unger, Thomas de Willoughby, m. Margaret, sister d co-heir of Alan de Mumby, and took the name; his n William, dying without issue, the estates passed to r William Hiltoft, the husband of his daughter Agnes.

‡ Knighton, in his Chronicle, says, that notwithstanding the threats of the Duke of Ireland, Sir William pretended indisposition, and did not attend the council at Nottingham, when all the judges were summoned to meet there, in order to subscribe to several questions, whereby they might take occasion to work the death of the Duke of Gloucester; this judge wisely foreseeing the event, got his quietus, and his brethren, who were all so overawed, that they gave their opinions illegally, and were afterwards all of them arrested on the bench at the desire of the parliament, being charged with over-ruling the actions and determinations of the lords, by their advice and directions, upon assurance that all was done according to law; yet afterwards had given the king a contrary judgment at Nottingham, and had delivered as their opinion, that the actions of the said parliament was illegall and trayterous. On this charge they were all (except Sir William Skipwith) condemned by the Lords Temporal, with assent of the king, to be drawn and hanged as traytors, their heirs disinherited, and their lands, &c. forfeited; but this sentence, as to their lives, was respited.

WILLIAM (Sir), his successor.
Catherine, m. to Sir Thomas Heneage, knt. of Hampton, in the county of Lincoln.
Mary, m. to George Fitz Williams, esq. of Mablethorp.
Elizabeth, m. first to Anthony Riggs, esq. and secondly to Matthew Thimelby, esq.
Margaret, m. to Richard Yarborough, esq.

He was s. by his only son,

SIR WILLIAM SKIPWITH, knt. who was sheriff of Lincolnshire in the 18th of HENRY VIII. He m. first, Elizabeth, daughter of Sir William Tyrwhit, knt. of Kettleby, in the same county, and by that lady had

WILLIAM (Sir), his heir.
Lionel, ancestor of the Skipwiths, of Calthorp.
John, of Walmsgare, whose son Lionel, *d. s. p.*
George, of Cotes or Cottenham.

Elizabeth, m. to Thomas Clifford, esq. of Brakenburgh, in the county of Lincoln.
Anne, m. 36 HENRY VIII. to William Hatcliffe, esq. of Hatcliffe.
Bridget, one of the maids of honour to *Queen* ELIZABETH, m. to — Cave, esq. of Leicestershire.
Eleanor, m. to Richard Bolles, esq.

Sir William m. secondly, Alice, daughter and heir of Sir Lionel Dymoke, of Scrivelsby, in the county of Lincoln, and by her acquired a considerable estate, and left an only child,

HENRY, ancestor of the SKIPWITHS of Prestwould. (Refer to BURKE's *Peerage and Baronetage.*)

He was s. by his eldest son,

SIR WILLIAM SKIPWITH, of Ormesby, &c. who received the honour of knighthood for his services at the battle of Muscleborough, 1st of EDWARD VI. In the 6th of the same reign he was returned to parliament by the county of Lincoln, and was sheriff, in the 4th of *Queen* ELIZABETH. Sir William m. first, Elizabeth, only daughter and heir of Sir Richard Page, knt. of Beechwood, in the county of Hertford, of the privy council to *King* HENRY VIII. and by that lady had one son and six daughters, viz.

RICHARD (Sir), his heir.

Frances, m. first to Francis Constable, esq. of Burstwick, in Yorkshire, and secondly to Ralph Ellerker, knt. of Risby, in the same county.
Anne, m. to Francis Kersey, esq.
Mabilla, m. to Thomas Skipwith, esq. of Utterby, in Lincolnshire.
Elizabeth, m. to Thomas Portington, esq. of Portington.
Mary, m. to George Metham, esq.
Margaret, m. to John Try, esq. of Hardwick, in the county of Gloucester.

He m. secondly, Anne, daughter of John Tothby, esq. of Tothby, in Lincolnshire, and by her had a son,

EDWARD, of Benisthorp, progenitor of the SKIPWITHS, of Grantham, and of Methringham.

Sir William d. in 1587, was buried with his ancestors in the chancel of the church, at Ormesby, 7th March, in that year, and s. by his eldest son,

SIR RICHARD SKIPWITH, knt. of Ormesby, who m. Mary, daughter of Sir Ralph Chamberlain, knt. of Gidding, in Suffolk, and had issue,

WILLIAM, his heir.
EDWARD, heir to his brother.
HENRY, whose line eventually carried on the family.

Catherine, m. to Charles Ayscough, esq.
Susan, m. to William Skipwith, esq. of Utterby.

He was s. by his eldest son,

WILLIAM SKIPWITH, esq. of Ormesby, who m. first Anne, relict of Sir Robert Constable, knt. but by her had no issue. He m. secondly, Anne, daughter of Thomas Portington, esq. of Portington, in the county of York, but having no male issue to survive, was s. by his brother,

EDWARD SKIPWITH, esq. who m. Christian, daughter of Robert Ask, esq. of Aughton, in the county of York, but his posterity becoming likewise extinct, the representative of the family eventually devolved upon the line of his brother, HENRY, which

HENRY SKIPWITH, having adopted the profession of arms, attained high renown as a military officer. He was bred in the Netherlands, under the famous General Lord Willoughby, and afterwards went captain into Ireland, where he distinguished himself at the sieges of Blackwater and Kinsale. He m. Margaret, daughter of Richard Fulwar, esq. of Copwood, in Sussex, and left at his decease, 7th March, 1629-30, an only son,

WILLIAM SKIPWITH, esq. who m. Elizabeth, daughter and co-heir of Richard Redding, esq. of Harrow-on-the-Hill, and was s. by his son,

I. FULWAR SKIPWITH, esq. of Newbold Hall, in the county of Warwick, who was created a BARONET by *King* CHARLES II. 25th October, 1670. Sir Fulwar m. first, Dorothy, daughter of Thomas Parker, esq. of Anglesey Abbey, in the county of Cambridge, and had issue,

HUMBERSTON, his heir, m. Elizabeth, daughter of Sir George Cony, knt. and dying in the lifetime of his father, left a son and daughter, viz.

FULWAR, successor to his grandfather.
ELIZABETH, m. to William, second Lord Craven.

Fulwar.
Elizabeth.

He m. secondly, Elizabeth, daughter of Edward Skipwith, esq. of Grantham, and relict of Sir George Cony, knt. but had no other issue. Sir Fulwar d. about 1678, and was s. by his grandson,

II. SIR FULWAR SKIPWITH, M.P. for the city of Coventry, in 1713. He m. Mary, daughter of Sir Francis Dashwood, bart. of Wickham, Bucks, and had issue,

FRANCIS, his successor.
Fulwar-Humberston.
George, *d.* in 1729, aged eleven.

Elizabeth.
Mary.

He died at Bath, 13th May, 1728, and was succeeded by his son,

III. SIR FRANCIS SKIPWITH, who married in 1734, Ursula, youngest daughter of Thomas Cartwright, esq. of Aynho, in the county of Northampton, and had issue,

THOMAS GEORGE, his heir.
Francis-William.
Fulwar, *d.* in 1747.

He *d.* 6th December, 1778, and was *s.* by his eldest son,

IV. SIR THOMAS GEORGE SKIPWITH, who m. Selina, daughter of George Ferrers, esq. grandson of Robert, first Earl Ferrers, but died without issue, in 1790, when the BARONETCY is presumed to have become EXTINCT.

Arms—Argent, three bars, gules, a greyhound in chief, sable, collared, or.

SKIPWITH, OF METHERINGHAM.

CREATED 27th July, 1678.—EXTINCT 4th June, 1756.

Lineage.

SIR WILLIAM SKIPWITH, of Ormesby, in the county of Lincoln, knight banneret, married, for his second wife, Anne, daughter of John Tothby, esq. of Tothby, in the same county, and by that lady left an only son,

EDWARD SKIPWITH, esq. of Benisthorpe, who m. Mary, daughter of Richard Hansard, esq. of Bickersthorp, in Lincolnshire, and had, with a daughter, Elizabeth, wife of Richard Osney, esq. of Louth, in the same county, a son and heir,

EDWARD SKIPWITH, esq. of Gosberton and Grantham, who married Elizabeth, daughter of Sir John Hather, knt. of Coteby, in Lincolnshire, and had issue,

EDWARD, who m. Alice, daughter of Marmaduke Prickett, esq. and had a son,

EDWARD, who *d. s. p.*

THOMAS (Sir).

John, *d. s. p.*

Charles, m. to Martha, daughter and heir of John Fleming, esq. but *d. s. p.*

William, m. Dorothy, daughter of Anthony Hawkridge, esq. but left no issue.

Henry, *d. unm.*

Elizabeth, m. first to Sir George Cony, knt. and secondly to Sir Fulwar Skipwith, bart.

————, m. to Sir Edward Bashe, knt.

————, *d. unm.*

Mary, m. to — Buck, esq. of Lincolnshire.

he second but eldest surviving son and heir,

I. SIR THOMAS SKIPWITH, knt. of Metheringham, in Lincolnshire, serjeant-at-law, was created a BARONET by King CHARLES II. 27th July, 1678. He m. first, Elizabeth, daughter and heir of Ralph Lathom, esq. of Upminster, in Essex, and by her had

THOMAS, his successor.

Susan, m. to Sir John Williams, bart. of Minster Court, in the Isle of Thanet.

He married secondly, Elizabeth, daughter of Sir John ..., knt. of London, and widow of Edward Maddison, esq. but had no other issue. Sir Thomas was knighted at Whitehall, 29th May, 1673, subsequently, as stated above, created a baronet. He died at his house in Lincoln's Inn Fields, in June, 1694, and was *s.* by his son,

II. SIR THOMAS SKIPWITH, who married Margaret, daughter and co-heir of George, Lord Chandos, and widow of William Brownlowe, esq. of Humby, in the county of Lincoln, and had issue,

GEORGE BRIDGES, his heir.

Lucy.

He died in June, 1710, and was succeeded by his son,

III. SIR GEORGE-BRIDGES SKIPWITH, who married Martha, daughter and heir of Robert Pitt, M.D. but died issueless 4th June, 1756, when the BARONETCY EXPIRED.

Arms—As SKIPWITH OF NEWBOLD HALL.

SLANNING, OF MARISTOW.

CREATED 19th Jan. 1662-3.

EXTINCT 21st Nov. 1700.

Lineage.

The Slannings, an old Devon family, acquired the estate of Ley, in the parish of Shaugh, by a marriage with the heiress of Nicholas AtLey. They were afterwards of Bickleigh and Maristow.

NICHOLAS SLANNING, esq. (of Ley, son of William Slanning, by Jane, his wife, daughter and heir of William Horston, and grandson of Nicholas Slanning, who married the heiress of AtLey), left by Elizabeth, his wife, daughter of Thomas Maynard, of Sherfford, in Devon, four sons,

NICHOLAS, of Ley, whose only child, Agnes, m. Edward Marler, of Crayford, in Kent, and had daughters, his co-heirs, of whom Margaret wedded her cousin, Gamaliel Slanning, of Hele.

William, who m. Wilmot, daughter of Baldwin Yate, and had issue.

JOHN, of whom presently.

Thomas.

The third son,

JOHN SLANNING, esq. m. Jane, daughter of William Crewse, esq. of Morchard, in Devon, and had two sons, Nicholas and John. The elder,

NICHOLAS SLANNING, esq. of Hele, in Devon, married Margaret, daughter of Henry Champernoune, esq. of Modbury, in the same county, and had issue,

GAMALIEL, his heir.

Nicholas, living in 1620, of Ley, *d. s. p.*

Elizabeth, m. to Christopher Blackhall, of Totness, and *d. s. p.*

The elder son,

GAMALIEL SLANNING, esq. of Hele, m. his cousin, Margaret, daughter and co-heir of Edward Marler, esq. of Crayford, in Kent, and left at his decease a daughter, Elizabeth, aged twelve in 1620, m. to Sir John Seymour, bart. of Berry, in Devon, and a son,

SIR NICHOLAS SLANNING, knt. of Maristow and Bickleigh, in Devon, aged nine in 1620, recorder of Plympton and M.P. for that borough 15 CHARLES I. and for Penryn in the following year. At the breaking out of the civil war, Sir Nicholas was appointed governor of Pendinnis Castle, and soon distinguished himself in the royal cause. He was so active a soldier and so sound a counsellor as to be considered one of the Devon and Cornish commanders who formed "the four wheels of Charles's wain;" and who, to the great injury of the sovereign's success, were severally killed about the same period at the battles of Stratton and Lansdowne and the siege of Bristol; in all of which Sir Nicholas Slanning bore a very conspicuous part, "advancing" at Lansdowne, 5th July, 1643, "from hedge to hedge at the head of his men, in the mouths of muskets and cannons, insomuch they thought him immortal, as indeed he was that day;" while at the siege of Bristol, 26th of the same month, "his courage and resolution carrying him on a little too far as he made a brave assault upon the town, he was unfortunately slain, to the great grief of all the army, in the twenty-eighth year of his age," when was written the ode in which the four friends and commanders were thus mentioned:

"The four wheels of Charles's wain,
Granville, Godolphin, Trevanion, Slanning, slain."

Clarendon, in recording the storming and reduction of Bristol, says, "here both Slanning and Trevannion fell, the life and soul of the Cornish regiments; both young, neither of them above eight-and-twenty, of entire friendship to each other and to Sir Bevill Granville, whose body was not yet buried;" and declares his death to have had "the royal sacrifice of his sovereign's very particular sorrow."

Sir Nicholas Slanning *m.* Gertrude, daughter of Sir James Bagge, knt. of Saltram, in Devon, by Grace, his wife, second daughter of John Fortescue, esq. of Buckland Filleigh, and had issue,

- NICHOLAS, his heir.
- Margaret, *m.* to Sir John Molesworth, bart. of Pencarrow, and *d. s. p.*
- Elizabeth, *m.* to Sir James Modyford, bart. of London, governor of Jamaica, and had, with other issue, a daughter, Grace, who wedded Peter Heywood, esq. and was grandmother of James Modyford Heywood, esq. of Maristow, who died in 1798, leaving four daughters, his co-heirs, who sold Maristow, with the manors of Bickleigh, Buckland, &c. to Sir Manasseh Masseh Lopes, bart.

Sir Nicholas was *s.* by his son,

I. SIR NICHOLAS SLANNING, K.B. F.R.S. standard-bearer to the band of gentlemen pensioners, and cup-bearer to the queen, who was created a BARONET 19th January, 1662-3. He *m.* first, Anne, daughter of Sir George Carteret, bart. of St. Owen's, Jersey; secondly, Mary, daughter of Sir Andrew Henley, bart. of Henley, Somersetshire; thirdly, Mary, daughter and co-heir of James Jenkin, esq. of Treseny, in Cornwall; and fourthly, a daughter of Edmond Parker, esq. of Bovingdon. He left issue only by the second, a son and successor,

II. SIR ANDREW SLANNING, of Maristow, aged twenty in 1694, who *m.* Elizabeth, daughter and co-heir of — Hele, esq. of South Tawton, in Devon, but had no issue. He died 21st November, 1700, in consequence of a wound received in a scuffle at the Rose Tavern, Covent Garden, three days previously. The title EXPIRED with him, but his extensive possessions passed to the heirs of Elizabeth, his aunt, wife of Sir James Modyford, bart.

Arms—Arg. two pallets engrailed gu. over all on a bend az. three griphons' heads erased or.

SLINGSBY, OF SCRIVEN.

CREATED 23rd Oct. 1628. EXTINCT in 1630.

Lineage.

JOHN SLINGSBY, esq. of Scriven, in Yorkshire, representative of a very ancient family in that county, *m.* Margery, daughter of Simon Pooley, esq. of Badley, in Suffolk, and *d.* in 1513, leaving, with other issue,

- THOMAS, of Scriven, his heir, ancestor of the present SIR CHARLES SLINGSBY, bart. of Scriven. (See BURKE's *Peerage and Baronetage*.)
- SIMON.

The youngest son,

SIMON SLINGSBY, esq. was father of

PETER SLINGSBY, esq. whose son,

I. SIR ANTHONY SLINGSBY, was created a BARONET 23rd October, 1628, being at the time governor of Zutphen, in Holland. He *d. s. p.* in 1630, when the title became EXTINCT.

Arms—Gu. a chev. between two leopards' heads in chief and a bugle-horn in base, arg.

SLINGSBY, OF BIFRONS.

CREATED 19th Oct. 1657.—EXTINCT ....

Lineage.

SIR GUILFORD SLINGSBY, knt. comptroller to the navy to *King* JAMES I. eighth son of Francis Slingsby, esq. of Scriven, by Mary, his wife, only sister of Thomas Percy, Earl of Northumberland (see BURKE's *Peerage and Baronetage*), *m.* Margaret, daughter of William Water, esq. alderman of York, and had, with other issue, a son,

I. SIR ARTHUR SLINGSBY, of Bifrons, in Kent, who received the honour of knighthood at Brussels 24th June, 1657, and was created a BARONET, by letters patent dated at Bruges, 9th October following. He *m.* a Flemish lady, and had two sons and two daughters,

- CHARLES.
- PETER.
- Anne-Charlotte.
- Mary, *b.* subsequent to the date of his will in 1664.

Sir Arthur *d.* in 1665, and was *s.* by his son,

II. SIR CHARLES SLINGSBY, of Bifrons, who in [illegible] was, together with his brother, beyond seas, as appears by the will of his uncle, Francis Slingsby, of St. Martin's in the Fields, proved the ensuing year at the Prerogative Office. Sir Charles sold Bifrons* in [illegible] Since that year no further particulars have been obtained of the BARONETCY, which is presumed to be EXTINCT.

Arms—As SLINGSBY OF SCRIVEN.

SLINGSBY, OF NEWCELLS.

CREATED 16th March, 1660-1.—EXTINCT in 1661 !

Lineage.

I. ROBERT SLINGSBY, esq. of Newcells, in Herts, supposed to have been second son of Sir Guilford Slingsby, knt. and elder brother of Sir Arthur Slingsby, bart. of Bifrons, was created a BARONET 16th March, 1660-1. He *m.* first, Elizabeth, daughter and heir of Robert Brooke, esq. of Newcells; and secondly, Elizabeth, daughter of Sir Edward Radclyffe, knt. of Dilston, in Northumberland, and widow of Sir William Fenwick, bart. of Meldon; but *d. s. p.* before the close of the year in which he had been created, when the BARONETCY became EXTINCT.

Arms—As SLINGSBY OF SCRIVEN.

* Bifrons became subsequently for many generations the residence of the Taylor family.

SLOANE, OF CHELSEA.

CREATED 3rd April, 1716. EXTINCT 11th Jan. 1753.

Lineage.

ALEXANDER SLOANE, of Killileagh or White's Castle, in the county of Down, in the kingdom of Ireland, receiver-general to the Lord Claneboy of the taxes of that county, wherein he resided before and after the civil war, m. Sarah, daughter of the Rev. Dr. Hicks, of Winchester, chaplain to Archbishop Laud, and had issue,

I. JAMES, of the Inner Temple, barrister-at-law, some time M.P. for Thetford, in Norfolk, died 5th November, 1704, and was buried in the Temple Church.* He left by Mary Rumbold, his wife, daughter of the keeper of the wardrobe to CHARLES II. one son, Joseph, who *d. s. p.*

II. Alexander, } both died issueless.
III. Henry, }

IV. William, of Chelsea, *b.* at Killyleagh in 1658, *m.* Jane, daughter of Alexander Hamilton, esq. of Killileagh, in the county of Down, and had one son and one daughter,

William, of Chelsea, and of Stoneham, Hants, living in 1741, *m.* first, Barret, daughter of Dacres-Leonard Barret, esq. of Belhouse, in Essex; secondly, Hesther, daughter of Sir Gilbert Heathcote, knt. an alderman of London; but by neither of those ladies had issue. He wedded, thirdly, Elizabeth, only daughter of John Fuller, esq. of Rose Hill, Sussex, and had three daughters.

Sarah, *m.* first, to Sir Richard Fowler, bart. of Harnage Grange, Shropshire; and secondly, to Francis Annesley, esq. of the Temple; by the former she left, with other issue, a son, SIR HANS FOWLER, bart. and a daughter, Sarah Fowler, wife of Colonel Hodges, of the Guards, whose son Thomas assumed the surname of FOWLER, and *d.* in 1820, leaving an only daughter.

V. John, } *d.* issueless.
VI. Robert, }
VII. HANS.

The youngest son,

I. HANS SLOANE, M.D. of Chelsea, *b.* at Killyleagh 16th April, 1660, having attained great celebrity in his profession, and presided several years over the College of Physicians, was created a BARONET by *King* GEORGE 3rd April, 1716. Sir Hans *m.* Elizabeth, relict of Fulk Rose, esq. of Jamaica, and daughter and co-heir of John Langley, esq. an alderman of London (by Elizabeth, his wife, daughter and co-heir of Richard Middleton, also an alderman of London): by that lady (who died 27th September, 1724, and was buried at Chelsea,) he had two surviving daughters, his co-heirs, viz.

SARAH, *m.* to George Stanley, esq. son of George Stanley, esq. of Poultons, in the county of Southampton, and left one son and two daughters,

HANS STANLEY (the Right Hon.), a lord of the Admiralty from 1757 to 1763, and in 1765 ambassador-extraordinary to the Empress of Russia. He *d.* 13th January, 1780, having bequeathed his moiety of the manor of Chelsea to his sisters, with a reversion to Lord Cadogan.

Anne Stanley, *m.* to Welbore Ellis, afterward Lord Mendip.

Sarah Stanley, *m.* to Christopher D'Oyley, esq. M.P.

ELIZABETH, *m.* to Charles, second Lord Cadogan, and was grandmother of the present (1838) EARL OF CADOGAN.

Sir Hans Sloane, who was chosen president of the Royal Society at the vacancy caused by the decease of Sir Isaac Newton, 20th March, 1727, *d.* 11th January, 1753, and was interred in seven days after in the churchyard of Chelsea in the same vault with his deceased wife, under a handsome monument erected by his daughters. As he left no male issue, the BARONETCY EXPIRED with him. The manor of Chelsea, which Sir Hans purchased in 1712 from William, Lord Cheyne, second Viscount Newhaven, descended to his two daughters as co-heirs.

Arms—Gu. a sword in pale, point downwards, blade arg. hilt or, between two boars' heads couped at the neck of the third; on a chief erm. a lion passant of the first between two mascles sa.

SMITH, OF CRANTOCK.

CREATED 27th Sept. 1642. EXTINCT in 1661.

Lineage.

I. JOHN SMITH, esq. of Crantock, in Cornwall, a merchant in London, who bore the arms, and is presumed to have been of the family of Smith of Tregonnick, was created a BARONET in 1642, but as he died without male issue (he left two daughters), the title became EXTINCT in 1661.

Arms—Az. a saltire between four martlets arg.

---

* Under a stone bearing the following inscription:—

Jacobus Sloane,
de Interiori Templo, Armiger,
Subtus jacet,
ob. 5 Novembris, 1704,
Ætatis 49.

Neque altra arget importanus Cliens,
Patronum, dum in vivis, vigilantissimum.

SMITH, OF HATHERTON.

CREATED 16th Aug. 1660.

EXTINCT in 1706.

Lineage.

SIR THOMAS SMITH, knt. of Hough, in Cheshire, who died 1st July, 1538, left by Katherine, his wife, daughter of Sir Andrew Brereton, of Brereton, with other issue, two daughters, Ursula, m. to Sir Rowland Stanley, of Hooton, and Bridget, to Robert Fulleshurst, and a son,

SIR LAURENCE SMITH, of Hough, knighted at Leith in 1544, who was sheriff of Cheshire in 1553, and mayor of Chester in 1558, 1563, and 1570. He m. first, Anne, daughter of Thomas Fulleshurst, esq. of Crue; and secondly, 20th January, 1560-1, Jane, daughter of Sir Piers Warburton, of Arley, and widow of Sir William Brereton, knt. of Brereton. By the former he had issue,

Laurence, sheriff of Cheshire in 1567, *d. s. p.*
THOMAS.
Edward.

Eleanor, m. to Thomas Cowper, esq. of Chester.
Mary, m. 16th January, 1562, to John Hurleston, esq. of Picton.

Sir Laurence *d.* 23rd August, 1582, aged sixty-six, and was *s.* by his son,

SIR THOMAS SMITH, knt. of Hatherton, in Cheshire, mayor of Chester in 1596, and sheriff of Cheshire in 1600, who m. Anne, daughter of Sir William Brereton, of Brereton, and had, with a daughter, Jane, wife of Sir Randle Mainwaring, the younger, of Over Peover, a son and successor,

LAURENCE SMITH, esq. of Hatherton, who m. Anne, daughter of Sir Randle Mainwaring, of Over Peover, and had two sons, THOMAS, his heir; and Stephen, gentleman usher to the Marquess of Ormond in Ireland, where he died in 1665, leaving issue. The elder,

SIR THOMAS SMITH, knt. of Hatherton, mayor of Chester in 1622, and sheriff of Cheshire in 1623, married Mary, daughter of Sir Hugh Smith, knt. of Long Ashton, in Somersetshire, and had twenty-two children. The eldest daughter, Mary, m. first, George, son of Thomas Cotton, esq. of Combermere; and secondly, Sir Robert Holt, bart. of Aston. The elder son,

I. THOMAS SMITH, esq. of Hatherton, was created a BARONET in 1660. He m. Abigail, daughter and co-heir of Sir John Pate, bart. of Sisonby, in Leicestershire, and had issue,

FRANCES-PATE, *b.* 2nd November, 1663, married to Richard Lister, esq. of Sisonby, and had a son, John Pate Lister, esq. and a daughter, Abigail, m. to Henry Browne, esq. of Shelbroke, in Yorkshire.

Sir Thomas *d.* 22nd May, 1675, and was succeeded by his nephew,

II. SIR THOMAS SMITH (son of his brother, Laurence Smith, of Bow, Middlesex, to whom the title was limited). This Sir Thomas died without male issue in 1706, when the BARONETCY EXPIRED.

The manor of Hatherton was sold by the representatives of Sir Thomas Smith, the first baronet, about the year 1700, to Mr. Salmon, from whose grandson, the Rev. Matthew Salmon, it was purchased in 1784 by Charles Bate, esq. of Nantwich. This gentleman died in 1814, bequeathing the manor of Hatherton to his wife, Joan Bate, for life, and after her death to her nephew, Mr. Matthew Mare, of Basford.

Arms—Az. two bars wavy erm. on a chief or, a demi lion rampant sa.

SMITH, OF EDMONTHORPE.

CREATED 20th Mar. 1660-1.

EXTINCT 15th Feb. 17[illegible].

Lineage.

The original name of this family was HERIS, but in the reign of HENRY VII. William Heris, of Withcock, in Leicestershire, assumed the name and arms of SMITH.

ERASMUS SMITH, esq. of Somerby, third son of John Smith, of Withcock, purchased the manor of Husband's Bosworth, Leicestershire, in 1565. He m. first, a lady named Bydd; and secondly, Margery, daughter of William Cecil, Lord Burleigh, and relict of Roger Cave. By the former he left a son,

SIR ROGER SMITH, of Husband's Bosworth and of Edmonthorpe, in Leicestershire, knighted at Whitehall in 1635. He m. first, Jane, daughter of Sir Edward Heron, serjeant-at-law, and had by her (who *d.* in 1599) a son,

EDWARD, who predeceased his father in 16[illegible], leaving by Elizabeth, his wife, daughter of Sir Edward Heron, K.B. of Creasy Hall, a son,
EDWARD, successor to his grandfather.

Sir Roger m. secondly, Anna, daughter of Thomas Goodman, esq. of London, and by her (who *d.* in 16[illegible], aged sixty-six,) had issue,

ERASMUS, of Weald Hall, Essex, living in 16[illegible], aged seventy-three, who m. Mary, daughter of Hugh Hare, Lord Coleraine, and had, with three daughters, six sons, who all *d. s. p.* excepting the fourth,

HUGH, of Weald Hall, high sheriff of Essex 11 GEORGE II. who m. Dorothy, daughter of Dacre-Barret Lennard, esq. of Belhouse and *d.* in 1745, aged seventy-three, leaving two daughters,

DOROTHY, m. to the Hon. John Barry.
LUCY, m. to James, *Lord Strange*, eldest son of Edward, fifth Earl of Derby.

Roger, who m. Anna, daughter of Thomas Cotton, esq. of Laughton, and died in London about 16[illegible], leaving several children, of whom the eldest was Roger Smith, of Frolesworth.

Anna, m. to Sir John Norwich, bart. of Brampton.
Mary, m. to Sir William Dudley, bart.

Sir Roger Smith died in 1655, aged eighty-four, and was *s.* by his grandson,

I. EDWARD SMITH, esq. of Edmonthorpe, high sheriff of Leicestershire in 1666, was created a BARONET in 1661. He m. first, Constantia, daughter of Sir William Spencer, bart. of Yarnton, Oxfordshire; secondly, Frances, daughter of Sir George Marwood, of Busby, in Yorkshire, and relict of Sir Richard Weston: and thirdly, Bridget, widow of Richard Baylis, of Woodford, Essex. By the two last he had no child; but by the first he had four sons and a daughter, viz.

EDWARD, his heir.
William, died at sea in 1677.
Henry, who died in 1698.
Erasmus, d. s. p.

Constantia, m. to Thomas Smith, esq. of Snitterton.

Sir Edward d. 6th September, 1707, and was s. by his son,

II. SIR EDWARD SMITH, of Edmonthorpe, who married Olivia, daughter and heir of Thomas Pepys, esq. of Merton Abbey, Surrey, but died without surviving issue 15th February, 1721, when the title became EXTINCT. He devised his estate at Edmonthorpe to his cousin, Edward Smith, esq. M.P. for Leicestershire, descended from Roger Smith, of Frolesworth. He d. in 1762 s. p. the last of the family at Edmonthorpe, which was sold after his death to William Pochin, esq. of Barkby.

Arms—Gu. on a chev. or, between three besants as many crosses pattée fitchée sa.

SMITH, OF LONG ASHTON.

CREATED 16th May, 1661.

EXTINCT in 1741.

Lineage.

JOHN SMYTH, of Aylberton, in the county of Gloucester, living in the time of HENRY VI. had issue a son and heir,

ROBERT SMITH, whose great grandson,

JOHN SMITH, was father of two sons, viz.

HUGH, who m. the daughter of Arthur Beckhaw, and left a daughter,

ELIZABETH, m. to William Morgan, esq. of Llantarnan Abbey, in the county of Monmouth.

MATTHEW.

The younger son,

MATTHEW SMITH, esq. m. Jane, daughter and co-heir of John Tyther, esq. and left a son and heir,

SIR HUGH SMITH, knt. of Long Ashton, in the county of Somerset, who m. Elizabeth, daughter of Sir Thomas Gorges, knt. of Langford, in the county of Wilts,* (sister of Lord Gorges), and had issue,

THOMAS, his heir.

Helen, m. to Sir Francis Rogers, knt. of Cannington, in the county of Somerset.
Mary, m. to Sir Thomas Smith, bart. of Hatherton, in Cheshire.

He was s. by his son,

THOMAS SMITH, esq. of Long Ashton, who m. Florence, daughter of John, Lord Poulet, of Hinton St. George, in Somersetshire, and by that lady (who survived him and m. secondly, Thomas Pigott, esq. of Ireland,) left a son and heir,

I. HUGH SMITH, esq. of Long Ashton, who was created a BARONET by King CHARLES II. 16th May, 1661. Sir Hugh m. Elizabeth, daughter of John Ashburnham, esq. of Ashburnham, and was s. by his only son,

II. SIR JOHN SMITH, who m. one of the daughters and co-heirs of Sir Samuel Astry, knt. of Henbury, in Gloucestershire, clerk of the crown in chancery, and had two sons and five daughters, viz.

I. JOHN, his successor.
II. Hugh, d. unm. in 1735.

I. ———, m. to Thomas Coster, esq. some time M.P. for Bristol.
II. ARABELLA, m. to Edward Gore, esq. of Somersetshire, ancestor of the family of GORE-LANGTON, of Newton Park. (See BURKE's *Commoners*, vol. i. p. 145.)
III. ———, m. to Gerard Smith, gent. of Bristol.
IV. FLORENCE, m. first, to John Pigott, esq. by whom she had no issue; and secondly, to JARRIT SMYTH, esq. of the city of Bristol.
V. ———, d. unm.

He died about the year 1726, and was s. by his elder son,

III. SIR JOHN SMITH, who married in 1728-9, Miss Pym, daughter of Mr. Pym, of Oxford, but died without issue in 1741, when the BARONETCY EXPIRED, and the estates passed to his sister FLORENCE, whose second husband,

JARRIT SMYTH, esq. M.P. for Bristol in 1756 and 1761, was created a BARONET, as "SIR JARRIT SMYTH, of Long Ashton," in January, 1763. Their great-grandson is the present (1837)

SIR JOHN SMYTH, bart. of Long Ashton.

Arms—Gu. on a chev. arg. between three cinquefoils of the second, three leopards' faces sa.

SMITH, OF ISLEWORTH.

CREATED 20th April, 1694.

EXTINCT 11th Oct. 1760.

Lineage.

JAMES SMITH, esq. of Hammersmith, an alderman of London, m. first, Mary, daughter of Mr. Allen, of London, and by her had issue,

* By Helen, his wife, daughter of Wolfangus Snavenburgh, of Sweden, and relict of William Parr, Marquess of Northampton.

RICHARD, *d. s. p.*

James, married first, Elizabeth Stanton; and secondly, Mary, daughter of William Goddard, of London.

Anne, *m.* first, to Adrian Dent, of London; and secondly, to Andrew Harbyn, of Parendon Magna, in Essex.

He *m.* secondly, Sarah, daughter of Robert Cotton, esq. of West Barge Holt, in Essex, by whom he had no less than fifteen children, of whom

JOHN received the honour of knighthood, and of him presently.

Sarah, *m.* Bud Wase, esq. of Datchet, Bucks.
Elizabeth, *m.* Henry Street, esq. of London.
Mary, *m.* Abraham Otgar, of London, merchant.

Several of his children lie buried in Hammersmith Church, where a very noble monument was erected to his memory, of black and white marble. The eldest son of the second marriage,

SIR JOHN SMITH, knt. alderman of the city of London, and sheriff in 1669, *m.* first, Anne, daughter of William Wase, esq. of Dalchet, in Bucks, and had a son,

James, who *m.* Sarah Burrell, and died without issue.

He *m.* secondly, Jane, daughter and sole heir of Robert Deane, esq. of Yorkshire, and by that lady left three sons and two daughters, viz.

JOHN, his successor.
Robert, *d.* in minority unm.
Charles, of Isleworth, *m.* Anne, daughter of William Williamson, esq. of Westminster, serjeant-at-arms, and had five daughters, namely,

ANNE, *m.* in July, 1739, to Legh Masters, esq. M.P. for Newton, in Lancashire.
SARAH, *d.* unm.
REBECCA, *m.* to — Orchard, esq. of Devonshire.
DEANE.
ELIZABETH, *m.* in June, 1738, to Henry Hawley, esq. of Brentford, in Middlesex, and *d. s. p.* in 1740.

Sarah, } *d.* unm.
Jane, }

Sir John *d.* in 1670, and was *s.* by the eldest son of his second marriage,

I. JOHN SMITH, esq. of Isleworth, who having advanced several sums of money towards carrying on the war with France, was created a BARONET (6 WILLIAM and MARY) 20th April, 1694, and was one of the gentlemen of the privy chamber to *King* WILLIAM and to *Queen* ANNE. Sir John *m.* 22nd September, 1691, Mary, second daughter of Sir John Eyles, knt. an alderman of London, and by that lady (who died in December, 1724,) left two sons and two daughters, viz.

JOHN, his successor.
James, *d. s. p.*
MARY.
ELIZABETH.

He *d.* 16th August, 1726, and was succeeded by his elder son,

II. SIR JOHN SMITH, who *d.* unm. 11th October, 1760, when the BARONETCY EXPIRED.

Arms—Quarterly: 1st and 4th, az. a lion rampant or, on a chief arg. a mullet gu. between two torteauxes; 2nd and 3rd, gu. two chevronels within a bordure arg.

SMITH, OF PICKERING, UPPER CANADA, AND OF PRESTON, NORTHUMBERLAND.

CREATED 30th Aug. 1821.

EXTINCT 9th May, 1837.

Lineage.

I. DAVID-WILLIAM SMITH, esq. only child of the late Colonel John Smith, who died in 1795 in the command of Fort Niagara, North America, by Anne, his wife, daughter of William Waylen, esq. of Rowde Hill and Devizes, Wilts, entered at an early period his father's regiment, and attained the rank of captain. Afterwards, having settled in Canada, he was called to the bar in that colony, with precedence as deputy judge advocate, filled several high official appointments, and was finally speaker of the House of Assembly. For these public services he obtained his patent of creation 30th August, 1821. "The consummate ability (we quote a recent writer in the Gentleman's Magazine) with which for a long period he administered the affairs of the Duke of Northumberland, is well known, and the kindness and warm-hearted generosity of his character, united with the manners of a high-minded English gentleman, endeared him to all who had the honour of his acquaintance, and will cause him to be long remembered in the neighbourhood of Alnwick, where his death has caused a blank which will not be readily filled."

Sir David Smith, who was born 4th September, 1764, *m.* first, 3rd November, 1788, Anne, eldest daughter of the late John O'Reilly, esq. of Ballykilcrist (now Anne's-ville), in the county of Longford, by whom (who died 5th November, 1798,) he had issue,

DAVID-WILLIAM, R.N. born 6th June, 1794, killed by a shot from a French battery when on board the Spartan frigate, 11th May, 1811.

MARY-ELIZABETH, *m.* in 1814, to Charles Tylee, esq. and has issue,

Robert Tylee.
David Tylee, an officer in the army.

Mary Tylee.
Anne Tylee.
Sarah Tylee.

SARAH.
ANNE.

He wedded, secondly, 11th April, 1823, Mary, youngest daughter of the late John Tylee, esq. of Devizes, and had by that lady, who survives, one daughter,

HANNAH.

Sir David died 9th May, 1837, when the BARONETCY became EXTINCT.

Arms—Per pale gu. and az. on a chev. or, between three cinquefoils arg. as many leopards' faces az. on a chief of the third a beaver passant ppr.

SMYTH, OF REDCLIFFE.

CREATED 10th May, 1661. EXTINCT 20th June, 1732.

Lineage.

I. WILLIAM SMYTH, esq. of Redcliffe, in the county of Bucks, governor of Hillersdon, in that county, and a stanch royalist, was created a BARONET by *King* CHARLES II. soon after the Restoration, 10th May, 1661. Sir William m. first, Margaret, daughter of Sir Alexander Denton, knt. by whom he left no male issue. He wedded, secondly, a daughter of Sir Nathaniel Hobart, one of the masters in Chancery, and by her had two sons, WILLIAM, who died unmarried in his father's lifetime, and THOMAS. He was a member of the Long Parliament, and dying at a very advanced age in 1696, was succeeded by his only surviving son,

II. SIR THOMAS SMYTH, who *d.* unm. 20th June, 1732, when the BARONETCY EXPIRED.

Arms—Sa. on a chevron, between six crosses pattée fitchee arg. three fleurs-de-lis az.

SMYTH, OF ISFIELD.

CREATED 2nd Dec. 1714. EXTINCT 2nd Oct. 1811.

Lineage.

SIR ROBERT SMYTH, bart. of Upton, in the county of Essex, had by his first wife, Judith, daughter of Nicholas Walmesley, esq. of Dunkenhalgh, with other issue, ROBERT, his successor, from whom the present baronet of Upton.

SIR JAMES SMYTH (the second son), who was knighted by *King* CHARLES II. and was lord mayor of London in the first year of *King* JAMES II. He m. first, Mary, daughter of Sir William Peak, knt. lord mayor of London, but by that lady had no issue. His second wife was Elizabeth, daughter and co-heir of Arthur Shirley, esq. of Isfield, by whom he had an only son, JAMES. He m. thirdly, Philadelphia, daughter of Sir William Wilson, bart. of Eastborne, in Sussex, without issue. He *d.* aged seventy-three, 9th December, 1706, and was *s.* by his son,

I. JAMES SMYTH, esq. of Isfield, in Sussex, who was created a BARONET 2nd December, 1714. Sir James married Mirabella, daughter and co-heir of Sir Robert Legard, knt. one of the masters in Chancery, and dying 20th February, 1716-17, was succeeded by his only son,

II. SIR ROBERT SMYTH, who married Lady Louisa-Caroline-Isabella Hervey, second daughter of John, Earl of Bristol, by whom (who *d.* 11th May, 1770,) he had issue,

HERVEY, his successor.

ANNA-MIRABELLA-HENRIETTA, *m.* in 1761, to William-Beale Brand, esq. of Polsted Hall, in Suffolk.

He died 10th December, 1773, and was succeeded by his son,

III. SIR HERVEY SMYTH, *b.* in 1734. This gentleman was aide-de-camp to General Wolfe at the siege of Quebec, and afterwards colonel in the Foot Guards. He *d.* unm. 2nd October, 1811, when the BARONETCY EXPIRED.

Arms—Az. two bars, unde, erm. on a chief or, a demi-lion issuant sa.

SNOWE, OF SALESBURY.

CREATED 25th June, 1679. EXTINCT 16th Oct. 1702.

Lineage.

I. JEREMY SNOWE, esq. of Salesbury, Herts, was created a BARONET in 1679. He *m.* Rebecca, daughter of Thomas Ward, of London, merchant, but died without issue 16th October, 1702, when the title became EXTINCT.

Arms—On a fess, between two others wavy, counter-wavy, a lion passant.

SOAME, OF THURLOW.

CREATED 5th Feb. 1684. EXTINCT 7th Sept. 1798.

Lineage.

THOMAS SOAME, of Botley, or Betley, in Norfolk, gent. was father of

THOMAS SOAME, gent. of Betley, who married first, Anne, daughter and heir of Francis Knighton, esq. of Little Bradley, in Suffolk, and widow of Richard Le Hunt, of Hunts Hall, in Bradley, Suffolk, and had by her,

THOMAS, of Bradley, in Suffolk, and Bentley, in Norfolk, *m.* Elizabeth, daughter of Robert Allington, esq. of Horseheath, in the county of

Cambridge, son and heir of Sir Giles Allington, knt. by whom he had RICHARD, who *d. s. p.* and other issue.
STEPHEN (Sir).
Robert, D.D. *d. s. p.*

Mary, married to Richard Farington, sheriff of London.

He *m.* secondly, a daughter of Carew, and by that lady had a daughter, Margaret, *m.* to William Brooke, esq. of Mendlesham, in Suffolk. He *d.* 16th April, 11th ELIZABETH. The inquisition, dated 2nd August, in the same year, says, he died seised of lands in Little Bradley, Little Thurlow, (called by several names,) and two tenements, 100 acres of land and pasture, 12 of wood, in Betley, in North Elmham, Bylney, Great Bittering, and Gressinghall, in Norfolk, held of the Lord Cromwell's manor of Elmham. He died at Betley, 16th April, then last past, and Thomas, of Little Bradley, was found his son and heir, twenty-six years old." His second son,

SIR STEPHEN SOAME, was of Betley, in Norfolk, and of London, of which city he was sheriff in 1589, and lord mayor in 1598. He purchased the manor of Brickendon, in the county of Hertford, and several other estates, and married Anne, daughter of William Stone, esq. of Segenhoe, in the county of Bedford, by whom he had six sons and five daughters, viz.

I. WILLIAM, his heir.
II. STEPHEN (Sir), of Heydon, in Essex, high sheriff of that county in the 19th of JAMES I. This gentleman had the manor of Berkesdon, in Hertfordshire, by gift of his father. He *m.* Elizabeth, daughter of Sir Thomas Playters, bart. of Sotterley, in Suffolk, and had issue,

1. PETER, lord of the manor of Berkesdon, of whom hereafter.
2. John, } *d. s. p.*
3. Stephen, }

1. Anne, *m.* to Sir Gabriel How, knt. of Wotton-under-Edge.
2. Jane, *m.* to Sir John Hoskins.
3. Mary, *m.* to Edward Pettiplace, esq. of Kingston, in Berks.
4. Jane, *m.* to Sir Edward Nicholl, knt. of Faxton, in the county of Northampton.

III. Thomas (Sir), of Throcking, in Hertfordshire, sheriff of London in 1635, alderman in 1640, when he received the honor of knighthood. In that year he was elected to parliament by the city where he manifested his loyalty to the crown, and was in consequence one of the members secluded from the house. Sir Thomas *m.* Joane, daughter of William Freman, esq. of Aspeden, in Hertfordshire, and had three sons, who all died young, and three daughters, viz.

1. ANNE, *m.* to Sir Thomas Abdy, bart. of Felix Hall.
2. ELIZABETH, *m.* to John Garneys, esq. of Boyland Hall, Norfolk.
3. MARY, *m.* to Abraham Clerk, esq. of London.

Sir Thomas repaired the tower of Throcking Church, and raised it with brick. He *d.* [illegible] January, 1670, aged eighty-eight, and was buried in the chancel of that church.

IV Nicholas, *d.* young.
V. John, of Burnham, in Norfolk, *m.* Mary, eldest daughter of Thomas Perient, esq. of Birch in Essex, and had issue, but his children all *d. s. p.* his widow *m.* Sir Thomas Glemham, knt. of Suffolk.
VI. Matthew, *d.* unm.

I. Mercy, *m.* to Sir Calthorpe Parker, knt. of Erwarton, in Suffolk.
II. Mary, *d.* an infant.
III. Anne, *m.* to Sir John Wentworth, knt. of Somerly, in Suffolk.
IV. Judith, *m.* to Sir Francis Anderson, knt. of Eyworth, in Bedfordshire.
V. Jane, *m.* to Sir Nathaniel Barnardiston, knt. of Keddington, in Suffolk.

Sir Stephen *d.* 23rd May, 1619, aged seventy-five, was buried in Little Thurlow,* and succeeded by his eldest son,

SIR WILLIAM SOAME, knt. who was sheriff of Suffolk in the 8th of CHARLES I. This gentleman *m.* first, Bridget, fourth daughter and co-heir of Benedict Barnham, esq. an alderman of London, and by that lady had issue,

I. STEPHEN, of Little Thurlowe, who *m.* first, Mary, eldest daughter and co-heir of Sir John Dyeham, knt. of Borstall, Bucks, and widow of Lawrence Banaster, esq. by whom he had

Stephen, *d. s. p.*
WILLIAM (Sir), successor to his grandfather

* Under the following inscription:

Consecrated
to the Memory
of the Right Worshipfull Sr. Stephen
Soame, Kt. Lord Mayor of the Citie of
London, in the year of our Lord, 1593, and Mayor
of the Staple there, almost 20 yeares, who was the
second Son of Thomas Soame, of Botely, alias Betely,
in the County of Norfolcke, Gentleman, and Anne, his Wife,
Daughter and Heir of Francis Knighton, of Little Bradley,
in the County of Suffolcke, Esquyer, and the Widowe of Richard
Lehunt, of the said Towne, and County, Gentleman. The said Sir Stephen,
in his life-time re-edified and newly glazed the great North Window of
the Cathedrall Church of St. Paul, in London. Newly settled and
adorned at
his own charge, the roof of Grocer's Hall, in that City, gave to the
same Company £10 to be bestowed weekly in Bread upon the poor prisoners of the Counter in the Poultry of London, for ever. In this Towne of
Little Thurlow, erected and buylt a Free-School, with £20 maintenance
for a Master, and £10 for the Usher there, yearly for ever, where he
erected and endowed an almshouse besides for 9 poor People, with maintenance for ever, the maintenance of both places to be paid by annuity,
forth of the Mannour of Carleton, in Cambridgeshire. He departed this
life May 23, being Trinity Sunday, 1619, at the age of threescore and fifteene yeares, at his Mansion house, by him formerly buylt in this
Parish of Little Therlowe.

Penelope, *m.* to Thomas Stone, esq. of Risden, in Hertfordshire.

Mary, *m.* to Miles Sandys, esq. of Missenden, Bucks.

He *m.* secondly, Anne, daughter and co-heir of Ambrose Coppinger, D.D. relict of Isaac Crane, esq. of Lavenham, in Suffolk, but by that lady (who wedded secondly, Sir Thomas Reeve, bart. of Thwait, in the same county) had no issue. He died before his father.

II. William (Sir), of Haughley, in Suffolk, knt. *m.* Catherine, daughter and co-heir of William Wilson, of London, merchant, by whom he had

John, *b.* in 1656.
Thomas.
Catherine.
Bridget.
Anne.

III. Thomas, *m.* Anne-Cecil, daughter of Sir Edward Chester, knt. of Ceckenhatch, Herts.

IV. John, *m.* Margaret, daughter of Osias Churchman, of London.

V. Matthew, *d.* young.

VI. Barnham, *m.* Anne Newport, of London.

VII. Bartholomew, of London, woollen draper, and of Little Thurlow, by gift of his nephew, Sir William Soame, bart. *m.* Susan, daughter of Richard Hutchinson, of London, merchant, and had issue,

William.
Bartholomew.
Thomas, *d.* young.
Edmund.
Richard, *m.* Mary, daughter of Benjamin Brownsmith, of London.
Catherine, *m.* to Isaac Stackhouse, of London.
Susan.
Mary.

VIII. Edmund, *m.* Mary, daughter of Simon Myddleton, of London, and sister of Sir Hugh Myddleton.

Sir William's second wife was named Smith, but he does not appear to have had any other issue. He *d.* in 1655, and was *s.* by his grandson,

I. Sir William Soame, knt. of Little Thurlow, in the county of Suffolk, who was sheriff of Suffolk in the time of Charles II. and advanced to a Baronetcy by that monarch, 5th February, 1684-5, with remainder, in default of male heirs of his own body, to Peter Soame, esq. of Heydon, in Essex, eldest son and heir of Sir Stephen Soame, knt. and the heirs male of his body. Sir William *m.* first, Lady Beata Pope, daughter of Thomas, Earl of Down, in Ireland, and secondly, Mary, daughter of Sir Gabriel Howe, of Gloucestershire, but died without issue at Malta, in his embassy to Turkey. Sir William bequeathed Little Thurlow to his uncle, Bartholomew, and was succeeded under the especial limitation in the patent, by his kinsman,

II. Sir Peter Soame, of Heydon, in Essex. This gentleman preferred a claim at the coronation of James II. to hold the bason and ewer for a moiety of the manor of Heydon, and the towel for the other moiety, and that he might be admitted in person, or by a proper deputy, to perform the office, and to have all the fees belonging to that service. He *m.* Susanna, youngest daughter of Ralph Freman, esq. of Aspoden Hall, in Hertfordshire, and had issue,

Peter, his successor.

Freman, *m.* the daughter of Mr. Gray, a Spanish merchant.

Susan, *m.* to Sir Cane James, bart. of Creshall, in Essex, who *d.* 23rd December, 1680.

Elizabeth.

He *d.* about the year 1697, and was *s.* by his elder son,

III. Sir Peter Soame, who *m.* Joane, daughter and heir of George Chute, esq. of Stockwell, in Surrey,* and had issue,

Peter, his heir.
Susan.
Anne.
Jane.

Sir Peter *d.* of the small-pox in 1709, and was *s.* by his son,

IV. Sir Peter Soame, one of the gentlemen of his majesty's privy chamber. He *m.* Miss Philipps, daughter of Governor Philipps, of Stanwell, in Middlesex, by whom he had a son, Peter, who *d.* 20th April, 1757. Sir Peter *d.* 7th September, 1798, when the Baronetcy became extinct. He bequeathed his estate to

Sir Buckworth Buckworth-Herne, bart. who assumed, in accordance with his testamentary injunction, the additional surname and arms of Soame, by sign manual, 12th December, 1806. (Refer to Burke's *Peerage and Baronetage*.)

Arms—Gules, a chevron between three mallets, or.

SOUTHCOTT, OF BLIGHBOROUGH.

Created 24th Jan. 1661-2.

Extinct before 1691.

Lineage.

I. George Southcott, esq. of Blighborough, in the county of Lincoln, was created a Baronet 24th June, 1661-2. He *m.* Katherine, daughter and heir of John Elliott, esq. of Essex, and by her, who wedded, secondly, Nicholas Fairfax, esq. he left at his decease in December, 1664, a son and successor,

II. Sir George Southcott, of Blighborough, who died unmarried before 1691: the Baronetcy expired with him.

Arms—Arg. a chev. gu. between three martlets sa.

SPEELMAN, OF HOLLAND.

Created 9th Sept. 1686.—Extinct ....

Lineage.

In 1686, a Baronetcy was conferred on

I. Cornelius Speelman, general to the states of Holland, but nothing beyond the creation of the title has been ascertained.

* By Joan, his wife, daughter of Sir Walter St. John, of Battersea.

SPEKE, OF HASILBURY.

CREATED 13th June, 1660. EXTINCT 14th Jan. 1682.

Lineage.

I. HUGH SPEKE, esq. of Hasilbury, in Wiltshire (a descendant of the ancient family of Speke of Somersetshire, now represented by WILLIAM SPEKE, esq. of Jordans, see BURKE'S *Commoners*, vol. iv.), was created a BARONET 12th June, 1660. He *m.* Anne, daughter and heir of John Mayne, esq. of Staplehurst, and relict of Mr. Croke, from whom she had been divorced. By her he left at his decease, 15th July, 1661, a son and successor,

II. SIR GEORGE SPEKE, of Hasilbury, who wedded Rachel, daughter of Sir William Wyndham, of Orchard Wyndham, in Somersetshire, but died without issue 14th January, 1682, when the BARONETCY became EXTINCT.

Arms—Arg. two bars az. over all an eagle displayed with two necks gu. armed or.

SPENCER, OF YARNTON.

CREATED 29th June, 1611. EXTINCT in 1771.

Lineage.

This was a branch issuing from the stock of the noble houses of Marlborough and Spencer.

From an illustrious line of progenitors arose,

WILLIAM SPENCER, esq. of Redburn, in the county of Warwick, *anno*, 1 HENRY VII. (an estate forfeited to the crown, by the attainder of William Catesby, esq.) who married Elizabeth, sister of Sir Richard Empson, knt. and had, with a daughter Jane, two sons, JOHN and Thomas. The elder,

SIR JOHN SPENCER, knt. denominated of Snitterfield, in Warwickshire, which estate he acquired with his wife, Isabel, daughter and co-heir of Walter Graunt, esq. purchased in the 22nd of HENRY VII. the great lordship of Wormleighton, in the same county, and soon after began the structure of a fair manor house there, in which, when inquisitions were taken concerning wastes and inclosures of lands, in the 9th and 10th of HENRY VIII. he was certified to have his residence, with sixty persons of his family; being a good benefactor to the church. He was knighted by *King* HENRY VIII. and by his last will and testament, it appears that he was possessed of a very great estate, was a noble housekeeper, had a great reverence for the clergy, was very liberal to his poor neighbours, as also bountiful to his tenants and servants. He *d.* 14th April, 1522, and was *s.* by his son,

SIR WILLIAM SPENCER, who received the honour of knighthood from HENRY VIII. at York Place, (now called Whitehall,) in 1529, the parliament then sitting; in two years after, he was sheriff of Northamptonshire, and died during his shrievalty. Sir William married Susan, daughter of Sir Richard Knightley, knt. of Fawsley, in the county of Northampton, and had issue,

- JOHN (Sir), his heir.
- Isabel, *m.* to Sir John Cotton, knt. of Landwade, in Cambridgeshire.
- Jane, *m.* to Sir Richard Bruges, knt. of Shefford, Berks.
- Dorothy, *m.* to Thomas Spencer, esq. of Everton, in Northamptonshire.
- Anne, *m.* to Sir John Goodwin, knt. of Winchington, Bucks, and *d. s. p.*
- Maria, *m.* to Thomas Boles, esq. of Walington, in Hertfordshire.

Sir William *d.* 22nd June, 1532, and was *s.* by his son,

SIR JOHN SPENCER, knt. sheriff of Northamptonshire in the 5th of EDWARD VI. and was knight of the same shire in parliament, in the 4th and 5th of WILLIAM and MARY. He was again sheriff in the 13th of ELIZABETH, and in two years after, was appointed by writ, (with other justices of the county, "of prime quality,") a commissioner to enquire after such persons as transgressed the law made in the 1st of ELIZABETH, entitled, "an Act for the uniformity of the Common Prayer, and Service in the Church, and Administration of the Sacraments." Sir John was a great economist, yet kept a plentiful establishment, and enjoins by his last will and testament, hospitality to be kept in his houses at Althorp and Wormleighton, by his heir after his decease, as he had done. He was fond of a country life, an encourager of industry, and a practical husbandman. At his decease he had numerous flocks of sheep and other cattle in the grounds and parks of Althorp and Wormleighton. He married Catherine, daughter of Sir Thomas Kitson, knt. of Hengrave, in Suffolk, and left great estates to his four sons, who were heads of so many families. These sons and their sisters were,

- JOHN (Sir), from whom the Dukes of Marlborough and Earls of Spencer.
- Thomas, who built a fine house at Claverdon, in the county of Warwick, and for his hospitality is called, by Sir William Dugdale, the Mirror of that county. He *m.* Mary, eldest daughter of Henry Cheeke, esq. and had an only child,
  - ALICE, *m.* to Sir Thomas Lucy, knt. of Charlecote.

  He *d.* in 1580, and having thus no male issue settled the manor of Claverdon and other lands upon his great-nephew, Sir William Spencer, bart. of Yarnton.
- WILLIAM (Sir), of whom presently.
- Richard (Sir), of Offley, in the county of Hertford, from whom the Spencers of that county descended.
- Margaret, *m.* first to Giles Allington, esq. of Horseheath, in the county of Cambridge, and secondly to Edward Eldrington, esq.
- Elizabeth, *m.* to George, second Lord Hunsdon, K.G.
- Catherine, *m.* to Sir Thomas Leigh, knt. of Stoneleigh.
- Mary, *m.* to Sir Edward Aston, knt. of Tixall.
- Anne, *m.* first to William Stanley, third Lord Monteagle, (his lordship's second wife,) secondly

to Henry, Lord Compton, and thirdly to Robert Sackville, son and heir of Thomas, Lord Buckhurst.

Alice, *m.* first to Fernando, Earl of Derby, and secondly to the Lord Keeper, Sir Thomas Egerton.

r John Spencer *d.* 8th November, 1586, and was *s.* his eldest son. His third son,

Sir WILLIAM SPENCER, who possessed a fine estate Yarnton, in the county of Oxford, received the ho-ur of knighthood from *Queen* ELIZABETH, in 1592, d marrying Margaret, daughter of Francis Bowyer, q. of the county of Middlesex, had issue,

THOMAS, his heir.

George.

Elizabeth, *m.* to Sir Thomas Russell, knt. of Strensham.

Catherine, *m.* to Sir Henry Montagu, ancestor of the Dukes of Manchester.

Mary, *m.* to Sir Maximilian Dalyson, knt. of Haling, in Kent.

Alice, *m.* to Sir Thomas Colvile, knt. of Newton, in Cambridgeshire.

Margaret, *m.* to Sir John Woodward, knt. of Evesham.

e *d.* 18th December, 1609, and lies buried with his ly under a curious altar-monument, raised against e north wall, near the east window of the south ancel of the church of Yarnton, in Oxfordshire: it composed of different sorts of marble, and adorned ith arms of war, battle-axes, swords, carbines, standrds, sheafs of arrows, &c. On the tomb, under an rch, lies the figure of a knight on his back, completely rmed, (excepting his head-piece,) and his lady on the ft in the habit of the times. His head rests on a riffin's head, (his crest,) hers on a pillow, with their ands in a devout posture. The arch is supported by ur pillars of the Corinthian order, and at the top, etween two pyramids, is a shield of the quarterings f arms belonging to the family, viz. seven coats. On e side of the tomb is a tablet, and two men kneeling n cushions on the right side thereof, as also four men on the left. Another tablet under the arch, xhibits the inscription in gilt letters. Sir William as *s* by his son,

I. SIR THOMAS SPENCER, knt. of Yarnton, who was eated a BARONET by *King* JAMES I. 29th June, 1611, nd afterwards knighted at Whitehall by the same onarch. He married Margaret, daughter of Richard ranthwait, esq. serjeant-at-law, by whom (who wedd, secondly, Richard Butler, Viscount Montgarret,) e had issue,

WILLIAM, his successor.

Thomas, } *d. s. p.*
John, }

Richard, *m.* to Mrs. Anne Wagstaffe, and had two sons and two daughters, viz.

THOMAS, who succeeded as fourth baronet.

Charles, of Lyons Hall, in the county of Hereford, *m.* Anne, daughter of Francis Pember, esq. of Elston, in that county, and was grandfather of

CHARLES, who succeeded as seventh BARONET.

Mary, *m.* to — Richards, esq.

Gertrude, married first to John Crump, esq. of Lugwardine, in the county of Hereford, and secondly to Essex Sherborne, esq. of Pembridge.

Edward, *d.* a bachelor.

Alice.

Anne.

Margaret.

Catherine.

Sir Thomas, who was famous in his time for his great hospitality, rebuilt the tower at the west end of Yarnton Church, as also a noble mansion house near the old one. He *d.* 16th August, 1622, and was *s.* by his eldest son,

II. SIR WILLIAM SPENCER, who, as his father had been, was knighted after he had become a baronet, by *King* CHARLES I. at Oxford, 27th August, 1629. He succeeded to the estate of his great-uncle, Thomas Spencer, esq. of Claverdon, in the county of Warwick, and thereby possessed a very great inheritance. Sir William married Constance, eldest daughter of Sir Thomas Lucy, knt. of Charlecote, and by that lady (who *m.* secondly, Sir Edward Smith, knt.) had

THOMAS, his successor.

Constance, *m.* to Sir Edward Smith, bart. of Edmonthorpe.

Alice, *m.* to Francis Keyt, esq. of Mickleton, in the county of Gloucester.

He was *s.* at his decease by his son,

III. SIR THOMAS SPENCER, who married Jane, daughter of Sir John Gerrard, bart. of Lamer, Herts, and had nine children, of whom survived to maturity,

William, who predeceased his father, dying at the age of twenty-six, unm.

JANE, *m.* to Robert Spencer, Viscount Teiviot, in Scotland.

CONSTANCE, *m.* to George Marwood, esq. only son of Sir Henry Marwood, bart. of Little Busby, in Yorkshire.

ELIZABETH, *m.* first to Sir Samuel Gerard, knt. of Brafferton, in the county of York, and secondly to Francis Basset, esq. of Tehidy, Cornwall.

CATHERINE, *m.* first to John Dormer, esq. of Ascot, in Oxfordshire, and secondly to Lieut.-Gen. the Hon. Harry Mordaunt, brother of Charles, third Earl of Peterborough.

Sir Thomas died 6th March, 1684-5, and was buried with his ancestors at Yarnton, under a noble and curious monument of white mable, erected to his memory, against the north wall of the south chancel. It represents the statues of seven persons, in full proportion and dresses of the time. His own figure stands on a pedestal, with his lady's on his right hand; the figure of his son is placed on his left. On her right hand sits a daughter lamenting, and under her another daughter. On the son's left hand is also a daughter, and under her another, all weeping. Under Sir Thomas Spencer is a tablet bearing the inscription. On the right side of the tablet, under the statue of the first daughter, is another, kneeling, her hand reposed on a skull; and beneath her is another, praying, laying her hand on an hour glass; lower there is another daughter. Over all is a shield of the arms and quarterings of the family. Sir Thomas leaving no more issue, his daughters became his co-heirs, and the BARONETCY devolved upon his cousin, (refer to Richard, fourth son of the first baronet,)

IV. SIR THOMAS SPENCER, of Eardington, in the county of Salop, who married Elizabeth, daughter of Ancor Palmer, esq. of Bricklehampton, in Worcestershire, and by that lady had seven sons and six daughters, of whom all died unm. except

HENRY, his successor.

WILLIAM, heir to his brother.

Ursula, *m.* to Mr. Hugh Philips, of London.

He *d.* about the year 1722, and was *s.* by his eldest surviving son,

V. SIR HENRY SPENCER, who *d. s. p.* at Stratford-upon-Avon, in 1726, and was *s.* by his youngest brother,

VI. SIR WILLIAM SPENCER, who married Elizabeth, daughter of Thomas Dee, gent. of Bridgenorth, but died without male issue, when the BARONETCY passed to his cousin, (refer to Richard, fourth son of the first baronet,)

VII. SIR CHARLES SPENCER, who was a minor in 1741, at whose decease the title became EXTINCT.

Arms—Quarterly, argent and gules, in the second and third quarter, a fret or; over all, a bend sable, three escallops argent.

SPENCER, OF OFFLEY.

CREATED 4th March, 1626.—EXTINCT Sept. 1633.

Lineage.

SIR RICHARD SPENCER, knt. fourth son of Sir John Spencer, knt. of Althorpe, by Katharine, his wife, daughter of Sir Thomas Kitson, knt. inherited from his father the manors of Offley and Cockernhoo, Herts. He married Helen, fourth daughter and co-heir of Sir John Brocket, knt. of Brocket Hall, and had issue,

- JOHN, his heir.
- BROCKET, created a baronet in 1642. (See next article.)
- Elizabeth, *m.* to Sir William Colepeper, bart. of Aylesford.
- Anne, *m.* to Sir John Boteler, K.B.
- Alice, *m.* to Sir John Jennings, K.B.

Sir Richard died in November, 1624, and was *s.* by his eldest son,

I. JOHN SPENCER, esq. of Offley, who was created a BARONET in 1626. He married Mary, daughter of Sir Henry Anderson, bart. of Penley, and had an only daughter,

- ALICE, *m.* to Sir James Atham, of Mark Hall, Essex, and had an only daughter and heir, Mary Altham, who *m.* Sir John Tufton, but *d. s. p.*

Sir John *d.* in September, 1633, when the BARONETCY became EXTINCT.

Arms—As SPENCER, OF YARNTON.

SPENCER, OF OFFLEY.

CREATED 20th Sept. 1642.—EXTINCT 16th Nov. 1712.

Lineage.

I. BROCKET SPENCER, esq. only brother and heir male of Sir John Spencer, bart. inherited Offley at that gentleman's decease, and was created a BARONET in 1642. He married Susanna, daughter of Sir Nicholas Carew, of Beddington, in Surrey, and had by her, who *d.* 9th May, 1692, with other issue,

- RICHARD, his heir.
- JOHN, successor to his nephew.
- Elizabeth, *m.* 2nd November, 1677, to Sir Humphrey Gore, knt. of Gilston, by whom she had an only daughter and heir,
  - ELIZABETH GORE, *m.* in 1714, to Sir Henry Penrice, knt. LL.D. judge of the Admiralty Court, and had issue,
    - Spencer Penrice, *d.* unm.
    - ANNA-MARIA PENRICE, *m.* in 1751, to Sir Thomas Salusbury, knt. LL.D. and *d. s. p.* 7th March, 1750.
- Susanna, *m.* to Abraham Nelson, esq.
- Anne, *m.* to Roger Meredith, esq.
- Alice, *m.* to Granado Pigott, esq. of Abingt[illegible] Pigott.

Sir Brocket *d.* 3rd July, 1668, and was *s.* by his son.

II. SIR RICHARD SPENCER, of Offley, who married 23rd July, 1672, Mary, daughter of Sir John Muster[illegible] knt. of Colwick, Notts, and by her (who married secondly, Sir Ralph Radcliffe, knt. of Hitchen,) he left at his decease, in February, 1687-8, a son and successor,

III. SIR JOHN SPENCER, of Offley, bapt. 27th February, 1677-8, at whose decease unm. 6th August, 16[illegible], the title reverted to his uncle,

IV. SIR JOHN SPENCER, of Offley, who *d. s. p.* 16th November, 1712, aged sixty-seven, when the BARONETCY became EXTINCT. The manor of Offley became vested in his four sisters, who all *d. s. p.* save the eldest, Lady Gore, whose granddaughter, Anna-Maria Penrice, conveyed it to her husband, Sir Thomas Salusbury.

Arms—As SPENCER, OF YARNTON.

SPRIGNELL, OF COPPENTHORP.

CREATED 14th Aug. 1641.

EXTINCT in Aug. 169[illegible]

Lineage.

I. RICHARD SPRIGNELL, esq. of Coppenthorp, in the county of York, who was created a BARONET in 1641, *m.* Anne, daughter of Mr. Gideon Delaune, of London, apothecary, and died about the year 1659, leaving a son and successor,

II. SIR ROBERT SPRIGNELL, of Coppenthorp, who *m.* Anne, daughter of Sir Michael Livesey, bart. of East Church, Kent, but dying without issue in 1680, was *s.* by his brother,

III. SIR WILLIAM SPRIGNELL, of Coppenthorp, at whose decease unmarried in August, 1691, the BARONETCY became EXTINCT.

Arms—Gu. two bars gemelles or, in chief a lion passant guardant of the second.

SPRING, OF PACKENHAM.

CREATED 11th Aug. 1641.

EXTINCT 17th Aug. 17[illegible]

Lineage.

This family, an old one of the county of Suffolk, is first traced in the records of public charity. In the church of Lavenham, in that county was erected a statue of brass to the memory of

Thomas Spring, (son of Thomas and Agnes Spring, f Lavenham, deceased 18 Henry VI. 1440,) who, as he inscription on his monument states, built the ves- ry of that church, where he lies interred. He *d.* 7th eptember, 1486, and left by Margaret, his wife, two ons and a daughter, viz.

Thomas, his heir.
James, slain in a fight between Lavenham, and Brent-Elly, in 1493.

Cecilia, *m.* to Robert Sexton, gent. of Lavenham.

le was *s.* by his elder son,

Thomas Spring, of Lavenham, who *m.* first, Alice, aughter of Thomas Appleton, esq. of Waldingfield, nd by her had

John (Sir), his heir.
Robert, *m.* Anne, daughter of Thomas Eden, esq. of Lavenham, which lady surviving him, *m.* secondly, Sir Philip Paris, knt.

Anne, *m.* to Sir Thomas Jermyn, knt. of Rushbrooke, in Suffolk.
Rose, *m.* to — Gibbon, esq. of Lynn Regis, in Norfolk.

e *m.* secondly, Anne, daughter of — King, esq. of xford. Mr. Spring, who was an opulent clothier, . in 1510, and was *s.* by his elder son,

Sir John Spring, who received the honor of knight- ood from *King* Henry VII. He *m.* Dorothy, daugh- r of Sir William Waldegrave, knt. of Smallbridge, Suffolk, and had, with two daughters, Frances, *m.* Edmund Wright, esq. of Little Buckenham, in Nor- lk, and Bridget, *m.* first to Thomas Fleetwood, esq. d secondly to Sir Robert Wingfield, knt. of Lethe- ngham, a son and successor, at his decease 1 Edward VI.

Sir William Spring, of Pakenham, who received e honor of knighthood from *Queen* Elizabeth. He . first, Anne, fourth daughter of Sir Thomas Kitson, nt. of Hengrave, and secondly, Susan, daughter of r Ambrose Jermyn, knt. of Rushbrooke. He *d.* in e year 1599, leaving one son and three daughters, z.

John, his heir.

Margaret, *d.* unm.
Anne, *m.* to Thomas Hynson, esq.
Dorothy, *m.* to Edmond Jermyn, esq.

s son and successor,

John Spring, esq. of Pakenham, *m.* Mary, daughter of r John Trelawny, knt. of Trelawny, in Cornwall, whom (who *m.* secondly, Sir Robert Gardiner, knt.) left at his decease in 1601, an only son,

Sir William Spring, who was knighted by *King* mes I. He *m.* the daughter of Sir William Smith, Mounthall, *alias* High Hall, in Essex, and had issue,

William, his heir.

Anne, *m.* to Sir Thomas Gaudy, knt. of Gaudy Hall, Norfolk.
Bridget, *m.* to John Hobart, esq. of Langley, in the same county.
Frances, *d.* young.
Elizabeth, *m.* to John Sidley, esq. of Morley, also in Norfolk.
Dorothy, *m.* to Thomas Drake, gent. of London.

was *s.* by his son,

i. Sir William Spring, of Pakenham, who was ighted by *King* Charles I. and afterwards created Baronet by the same monarch, 11th August, 1641. e *m.* Elizabeth, daughter of Sir Hammond L'Estrange, t. and had issue,

William, his successor,

Thomas, *d.* unm.
John, *d.* young.
Elizabeth, *d.* unm.
Catherine, *m.* first to Capt. Laurence, and secondly to John Palgrave, esq. of Norfolk.
Dorothy, *m.* to Sir Christopher Calthorpe, K. B. of East Barsham, in Norfolk.

He *d.* about the year 1655, and was *s.* by his son,

ii. Sir William Spring, who *m.* first, Mary, daughter of Sir Dudley North, K. B. but had no issue by that lady. He *m.* secondly Sarah, daughter of Sir Robert Cordell, bart. of Melford Hall, in Suffolk, and had

Thomas, his successor.
John, who succeeded as fifth Baronet.

Sarah, *m.* to John Macky, esq.

Sir William *d.* circa 1684, and was *s.* by his elder son,

iii. Sir Thomas Spring, who *m.* Merilina, fifth daughter and co-heir of Thomas, Lord Jermyn, by whom (who *m.* secondly, Sir William Gage,) he had surviving issue,

William, his heir.
Merilina, *m.* to Thomas Disciplence, esq. of Bury St. Edmunds, a justice of the peace for the county of Suffolk, and had two daughters,

Merelina, who *m.* Michael Lebeup, esq. and had a son,

Michael Lebeup, esq. who *m.* Mary, daughter of George Waddington, esq. of Bury, and had issue,

Michael Lebeup.
Mary Lebeup.
Merelina Lebeup.

Delariviere, *m.* to John Godbold, esq.

Mary, *m.* to the Rev. John Symonds, rector of Horringeth, and had issue,

John Symonds, LL.D. recorder of Bury, appointed professor of modern history at Cambridge, 1771, living in 1802, at his villa, called St. Edmunds Hill, an estate which he inherited from his maternal grandmother, the Hon. Merelina Jermyn.
Thomas Symmonds, capt. R.N. *d.* in 1792. He *m.* first, Mary Noble, and secondly, Elizabeth Mallet, by the latter he had

Jermyn.
Thomas.

Mariana, *m.* to John Benjafield, esq. and had a son,

Frederick Benjafield.

Elizabeth, *m.* to the Rev. Mr. Higham.

Delariviere Symmonds, *m.* to the Rev. Mr. Casburn, and had issue.
Anna-Maria Symmonds, *d. s. p.*

Henrietta, *d.* unm. in 1733.
Delariviere, *d.* unm. in 1733.

Sir Thomas *d.* about 1710, and was *s.* by his son,

iv. Sir William Spring, who *d.* unm. in March, 1736-7, and was *s.* by his uncle,

v. Sir John Spring, who *m.* Elizabeth, daughter of Mr. Nightingale, and had issue,

John, *m.* to Miss Cordell, and *d.* before his father *s. p.*

Charles, James, Sarah, Mary, } *d.* before their father.

He *d.* 17th August, 1769, aged seventy, when the Baronetcy expired.

*** A younger son of the Springs of Lavenham, settled in Ireland, and was ancestor of the present Right Honourable Thomas Spring Rice, M. P. chancellor of the exchequer.

Arms—Arg. a chevron between three mascles gu.

SPRINGETT, OF BROYLE PLACE.

Lineage.

HERBERT SPRINGETT, of Lewes, in Sussex, son of Thomas Springett, by Margaret, his wife, daughter of Edmund Roberts, of Hawkhurst, in Kent, had a grant of arms 21st November, 1612. He married Anne Stempe, and had issue,

- THOMAS, his heir.
- Herbert, of Ringmer, who died 21st May, 1621, aged sixty-five, leaving by Katherine Partridge, his wife, two sons and a daughter, viz.
  - WILLIAM (Sir), knt. who died in 1643.
  - Herbert.
  - Catherine.
- Elizabeth, *m.* to Simon Stone, esq. of the Middle Temple, barrister-at-law.

The elder son,

SIR THOMAS SPRINGETT, knt. of Broyle Place, in Sussex, *m.* Mary, daughter of John Bellingham, esq. of Erringham, and had issue,

- HERBERT, his heir.
- Thomas, *b.* in 1617.
- Anthony, *b.* in 1620, whose son Anthony, *m.* in 1658, Dorothy Moore, of Wivelsfield, and died 8th April, 1689, leaving two sons, namely,
  - Anthony, rector of Plumpton and Westmeston, who died in 1735, aged seventy-three.
  - William, of Plumpton, who died in 1732, aged sixty-seven.
- Mary, *m.* to Thomas Southland, esq. of Ickham, in Kent.
- Ann, *b.* in 1616.
- Frances, *m.* to Walter Hendley, esq. of Cuckfield,

Sir Thomas died 17th September, 1639, aged fifty-one, and was *s.* by his son,

I. HERBERT SPRINGETT, esq. of Broyle Place, who was created a BARONET in 1660-1. He *m.* Barbara, eldest daughter of Sir William Campion, knt. of Combwell, in Kent, by Elizabeth, his wife, eldest daughter and co-heir of Sir William Stone, knt. of London, and by her, who died in 1696, aged eighty-five, had issue,

- MARY, *m.* to Sir John Stapley, bart. of Patcham, and died in 1708, aged seventy-four, leaving issue.
- ELIZABETH, *m.* to John Whalley, esq. of Ringmer.
- CHARITY, died unm.

Sir Herbert died 5th January, 1662, when the BARONETCY became EXTINCT.

Arms—Per fesse undée arg. and gu. a fesse wavy between three crescents counterchanged.

STANDISH, OF DUXBURY.

Lineage.

The Standishes of Duxbury, a family of antiquity and note, derived from a common ancestor with the Standishes of Standish, viz.

RALPH STANDISH (son of Thurston de Standish, living in 1221), who had two sons,

- JORDAN, heir to his father, living in 1271, ancestor of the Standishes of Standish, now represented by CHARLES STRICKLAND-STANDISH, esq. M.P. of Standish. (See BURKE'S *Commoners*, vol. [illegible] p. 64.)
- HUGH, from whom the Standishes of Duxbury

The second son,

HUGH STANDISH, *m.* (34 EDWARD I.) Alice, daughter of Sir Richard Molyneux, of Sefton, in Lancashire and had two sons, William Standish, who died young, and

RICHARD STANDISH, of Duxbury, living 9 EDWARD III.; he was father of two sons, Hugh and John. The elder,

HUGH STANDISH, of Duxbury, wedded, in 1369, his kinswoman, Alice, daughter of Henry Standish, of Standish, and had three sons and a daughter, viz. William, Alexander, Christopher, and Clemence. The only son to survive youth,

CHRISTOPHER STANDISH, of Duxbury, *m.* (9 RICHARD II.) Margaret, daughter of Sir Thomas Fleming, and had issue,

- RALPH, who *m.* (7 HENRY V.) Joan, daughter of Sir Thomas Gerrard, knt. but *d. s. p.*
- ROWLAND (Sir), who received the honour of knighthood 19 HENRY VI. He brought the relics of St. Lawrance from Normandy to Chorley Church. He *d. s. p.*
- JAMES, continuator of the family.

This

JAMES STANDISH, of Duxbury, living 6 EDWARD IV. left by Alice, his wife, a son and successor,

CHRISTOPHER STANDISH, esq. of Duxbury, who m. Elizabeth, daughter of William Bradshaigh, esq. of Haigh, and was *s.* by his son,

JAMES STANDISH, esq. of Duxbury, father, by Alice his wife, of

CHRISTOPHER STANDISH, esq. of Duxbury, whose son,

SIR CHRISTOPHER STANDISH, of Duxbury, was knighted by RICHARD III. He married and had issue, THOMAS, James, Hugh, Alexander, Rowland, Anne and Maud, wife of William Bradshaigh, esq. of Haigh. The eldest son,

THOMAS STANDISH, esq. of Duxbury, *m.* in [illegible], Catharine, eldest daughter of Sir Alexander Standish, of Standish (knighted at Hutton Field in 1482), by Sibilla, his wife, daughter of Henry Bold, esq. of Bold, in Lancashire, and had a son and successor.

James Standish, esq. of Duxbury, who m. first, Elizabeth, daughter of Evan Hadock; and secondly, Elizabeth, daughter of John Butler, esq. of Rawcliffe. He was s. by his son,

Thomas Standish, esq. of Duxbury, who m. Margaret, daughter of Sir Thomas Hoghton, of Hoghton Tower, in Lancashire, and was s. by his son,

Alexander Standish, esq. of Duxbury, father, by Margaret, his wife, daughter of Sir Ralph Assheton, bart. of Whaley Abbey, of several children. The eldest son,

Thomas Standish, esq. of Duxbury, m. first, Anne, elder daughter of Sir Thomas Wingfield, knt. of Letheringham, in Suffolk, and had by her Thomas, Alexander, Richard, Anne, and Ratclyffe. He m. secondly, Anne, daughter of Christopher Whittingham, esq. of Suffolk, by whom he had Ralph, Gilbert, Henry, Catherine, Margaret, and Dorothy. Mr. Standish was at his decease by his eldest son,

Thomas Standish, esq. of Duxbury, who m. Elizabeth, daughter of Thomas Vaux, esq. of Dotchet, and had a daughter who died young at Exford. Mr. Standish was slain at Manchester by the parliamentarians, and leaving no issue, was s. by his next brother,

Alexander Standish, esq. of Duxbury, who m. first, Alice, daughter of William Farington, esq. of Shawe Hall, Lancashire, and relict of Banister of Bank; and secondly, Margaret, relict of Colonel Clifton. He d. however, without issue, and was s. by his brother,

Richard Standish, esq. of Duxbury, who m. Elizabeth, daughter of Piers Legh, esq. of Lyme (eldest son of Sir Peter Legh, M.P. for Cheshire 43 Elizabeth), by Anne, his wife, daughter of Sir John Saville, of Howley, in the county of York, and had issue, Richard, his heir, Peter, Alexander, Ralph, John, Hugh, Elizabeth, Anne, and Frances. The eldest son,

I. Richard Standish, esq. of Duxbury, was created a Baronet 8th February, 1676-7. He m. Margaret, daughter of Thomas Holcroft, esq. of Holcroft, in Lancashire, and had by her (who wedded, secondly, Sir Thomas Stanley, bart. of Bickerstaff, and d. in October, 1735, aged nearly a hundred,) three sons and three daughters, Thomas, his heir, Peter, Charles, Elizabeth, Margaret, and Frances. The eldest son,

II. Sir Thomas Standish, of Duxbury, m. Jane, daughter of Charles Turnor, esq. of Cleveland, in Yorkshire, and had, with several other children, a son,

Thomas, who m. Catherine, widow of John Smith, esq. of Heath, in Yorkshire, and daughter and co-heir of Robert Frank, esq. of Pontefract, recorder and M.P. for that town. By her he left at his decease v. p. an only surviving child,

Frank, successor to his grandfather.

Sir Thomas Standish died in December, 1756, and was s. by his grandson,

III. Sir Frank Standish, of Duxbury, at whose decease s. p. 18th May, 1812, the Baronetcy became extinct, and the estates devolved on his cousin,

Frank Hall, esq. only son of the late Anthony Hall, esq. by Miss Charlotte Rey,* his wife, and grandson of Mr. Hall by Margaret, his wife, daughter of Sir Thomas Standish, the second baronet, and relict of William Wombwell, esq. Mr. Frank Hall assumed the surname of Standish, and is the present proprietor of Duxbury.

Arms—Az. three standishes arg.

STANLEY, OF GRANGE GORMAN.

Created 13th April, 1699. Extinct 30th Nov. 1744.

Lineage.

Stephen Stanley, esq. of Grange Gorman, in the county of Dublin, married Margaret, only daughter of Sir William Tichborne, knt. by Judith, his wife, daughter and co-heir of John Bisse, esq. lord chancellor of Ireland, and was father of

I. John Stanley, esq. of Grange Gorman, who was secretary to the Earls of Dorset and Sunderland, when lord chamberlain of the household. He was afterwards warden of the Mint, and again secretary to the Earls of Jersey and Kent, as lord chamberlain. He was made a Baronet of Ireland, and afterwards created a Baronet of England by *King* William III. 13th April, 1699. Sir John was for many years one of the commissioners of the Customs. He married Anne, daughter of Bernard Granville, esq. and niece of John, Earl of Bath, but had no issue. His lady died 1st March, 1729-30, and himself 30th November, 1744, when the Baronetcy became extinct.

Arms—Argent, on a bend azure, three bucks' heads caboshed, or, with a mural crown in a sinister chief, or.

STAPLEY, OF PATCHAM.

Created 28th July, 1660. Extinct in 1701.

Lineage.

The Stapleys of Sussex derived, according to Edmund Knight, Norroy, from the Stapleys of Cheshire.

I. John Stapley, esq. of Patcham, in Sussex, son and heir of Anthony Stapley, esq. of Patcham, by Ann, his wife, sister of George, Lord Goring, and grandson of Anthony Stapley, esq. of Framfeild, was created a Baronet in 1660, by Charles II. at the Restoration. He married Mary, eldest daughter and co-heir of Sir Herbert Springett, bart. of Broyle Place, and by her, who died in 1708, aged seventy-four, had issue,

Herbert, who m. Alice, daughter of Sir Richard Culpeper, knt. but predeceased his father, s. p.

Philadelphia, m. to Peter Courthorpe, esq. of Danny, in Sussex.

* This lady m. after her first husband Mr. Hall's decease, Sir William Purves-Hume-Campbell, bart.

Elizabeth, *m.* to John Briggs, LL.D. of Chichester.

Mary, *m.* to Walter Dobell, esq. of Street, in Sussex.

Barbara, *m.* to William Hay, esq. of Glyndbourne, in Sussex, M.P. for Seaford.

Sir John Stapley died in 1701, aged seventy-three, when the Baronetcy became extinct.

Arms—Arg. on a fesse engr. ermines between three harts two dragons' heads erased, or.

STAPYLTON, OF MYTON.

Created 22nd June, 1660.

Extinct 2nd Jan. 1817.

Lineage.

This family is of great note and antiquity, several of its ancestors having been in the earliest times summoned amongst the barons to parliament, and being honoured with the Garter at, and soon after the institution of that noble order. The name is derived from Stapilton, on the river Teys, in the bishoprick of Durham, and it is to be frequently found in old records, conferring benefactions upon the different religious establishments in the county of York.*

Sir Miles de Stapleton, having distinguished himself in the wars of Gascony and Scotland, was summoned to parliament as a Baron, 6 Edward II. His son,

Sir Miles de Stapleton, *m.* Sibil, daughter and co-heir of John de Bella Aqua, or Beaulieu, and added no small advantage to his house, enjoying thereby, *inter alia*, the manor of Carleton, in the county of York, which was part of her inheritance. He *d.* in 1314. His son, another

Sir Miles de Stapleton, *m.* Elizabeth, daughter and sole heir of John de Richmond, who brought the manor of Kirkby-Fleatham into the family, and had three sons,

- Nicholas, summoned to parliament as a Baron in 1342. (See Burke's *Extinct Peerage*.)
- Miles (Sir), *m.* Cicely, daughter of Sir Robert Ufford, from whom proceeded
  - Sir Miles Stapleton, one of the knights of the Garter at the institution of the order.
- Gilbert.

The third son,

Gilbert Stapleton, *m.* Agnes, eldest daughter and co-heir of Bryan Fitz Alan, Baron of Bedale, the heir-general of Hagget, and had issue,

Sir Bryan Stapleton, knt. of Carleton, living 49 Edward III. and one of the knights of the Garter, *temp.* Richard II. This gallant knight is said to have slain a saracen, in open battle, in the presence of the Kings of England, France, and Scotland. He inherited a great estate in his mother's right, and having to wife Alice, daughter of Sir John St. Philibert, knt. left a son and heir,

Sir Bryan Stapleton, who *m.* Elizabeth, daughter and heir of Sir William Aldborow, knt. and had two sons,

- Bryan (Sir), called junior, in reference to his father, ancestor of the Stapletons of Carleton.
- Miles (Sir).

The younger son,

Sir Miles Stapleton, knt. *m.* Joan, widow of William Brechnells, and daughter and co-heir of Sir George Uffiet, of Wighill, in the aynsty of York, in whose right he was seized of Wighill, Easdike, Swanland, with lands upon Hull banks, and in other places. He was *s.* by his son,

Sir John Stapleton, knt. who married Margaret, daughter of Norton, of Norton Conyers, and was father of

Sir William Stapleton, knt. who *m.* Margaret, daughter of Sir James Pickering, knt. and was *s.* by his son,

Sir Bryan Stapleton, knt. of Wighill, who *m.* Jane, daughter of Sir Lancelot Thirkeld, knt. and had seven sons, Christopher, his heir, Bryan, Lancelot, Miles, William, Richard, and Robert, with four daughters, namely,

- Elizabeth, *m.* to Robert Saltmarsh, esq.
- Jane, married to Robert Conyers, esq. of Hutton Paynel.
- Eleanor, *m.* to Sir Thomas Wharton, summoned to parliament, in 1545, as Baron Wharton.
- Margaret, *m.* to John Copley, esq. of Hotham.

The eldest son and heir,

Christopher Stapleton, esq. of Wighill, who *m.* first, Alice, daughter of William Ask, esq. of Ask, and by her had issue,

- Bryan, his heir.
- Robert (Sir), heir to his brother.
- Anne, *m.* to John Ireton, esq. of Ireton.
- Isabel, *m.* to John Lampleugh, esq.
- ——, *m.* to Henry Hamilton, esq.

He *m.* secondly, Margaret, daughter of Sir John Nevile, knt. of Leversedge, in the county of York, but had no additional family. He was *s.* at his decease by his elder son,

Bryan Stapleton, esq. who *d. s. p.* and was *s.* by his brother,

Sir Robert Stapleton, who *m.* Elizabeth, daughter of Sir William Mallory, knt. of Studley, in the county of York, by whom (who *m.* secondly, Marmaduke Slyngesby, esq.) he had

- Robert (Sir), his successor.
- Elizabeth, *m.* to Bryan Hammond, esq. of Scathingwell.
- Bridget, *m.* to John Norton, esq.

He was *s.* by his son,

Sir Robert Stapleton, who was sheriff of York...

---

* A.D. 1159, *i. e.* about 6 Henry II. Robert de Stapleton is amongst the witnesses to a charter of Henry de Lascy, baron of Pontefract, wherein the said Henry confirms to that church, and the monks of Pontefract, with other matters, the church of Dardington, with the chapel of Stapilton.

And the same Robert, *anno* 33 Henry II. was a benefactor to the priory of Monks-Bretton, in the county of York, and gave them *terram de Chudecerda*, as recited in a confirmation charter to that priory made by Pope Urban III. A.D. 1186.

In 17 John, Nicholas de Stapilton was governor of Midleham Castle, the same doubtless who is called son of Gaffry de Stapilton, in a charter of the same, dated 12 Henry III. unto the abbey of Jorvaulx, confirming their possessions, and specifying therein a ... land, in Mersk, with the appertenances, and another ... in Barton, as the gift of the said Nicholas to those ...

shire, 23 Elizabeth, and received the judges "with seven score men, in suitable liveries." He lived in great hospitality and esteem: an author, who seems not over favourable to his memory (Sir John Harrington) describes him as a man well spoken, properly seen in languages, had scarce an equal, and next to Sir Philip Sidney, no superior in England. Sir Robert *m.* first, Catherine, daughter of Sir Marmaduke Constable, of Everingham, knt. by whom he had

Henry, who succeeded his father at Wighill. This line* terminated in an heiress,

Martha Stapleton, who *m.* in 1783, General the Hon. Granville Anson Chetwynd, who assumed in consequence the additional surname and arms of Stapylton.

Philip.

Jane, *m.* to Christopher Wyvill, esq.

Dorothy.

Sir Robert *m.* secondly, Olive, daughter and co-heir of Sir Henry Sherrington, knt. of Lacock, in Wiltshire (widow of John Talbot, esq. of Salwarp), and by that lady had

Bryan.

Robert.

Edward.

Olive, *m.* to Sir Robert Dyneley, knt. of Bramhope, in Yorkshire.

Ursula, *m.* to Sir Robert Baynard, knt. of Lackham.

Mary.

Grace.

The elder son of the second marriage,

Bryan Stapylton, esq. who was receiver-general to *King* Charles I. settled himself at Myton, near Boroughbridge, in the county of York. He *m.* Frances, daughter of Sir Henry Slingsby, knt. of Scriven, and had issue,

Henry, his heir.

Robert.

Miles, *m.* Elizabeth, daughter of Mr. Hynde, of London, and was ancestor of the Stapyltons, of Norton, in Durham. (Refer to Burke's *Commoners*, vol. ii. page 210.)

Oliva, *m.* first, to Sir William Vavasor, bart. of Copmanthorp, in the county of York, major-general to the King of Sweden, killed at the siege of Copenhagen, in 1658. She *m.* secondly, John Hutton, esq. of Maske, in the same county.

Ursula, *m.* to Thomas Pepys, esq. of Hatchambarnes, in Surrey.

He was *s.* by his eldest son,

I. Henry Stapylton, esq. of Myton, who was created a Baronet by *King* Charles II. 22nd June, 1660. Sir Henry married the Hon. Elizabeth D'Arcy, second daughter of Conyers, Lord D'Arcy, afterwards created Earl of Holdernesse, and had, with a daughter, Grace, the wife of Thomas Robinson, esq. of Holmby, a son and successor, at his decease, in 1679,

II. Sir Bryan Stapylton, who *m.* Anne, daughter of Sir John Kaye, bart. of Woodsome, in the county of York, and had surviving issue,

John, his successor.

Anne.

He *d.* 23rd November, 1727, and was *s.* by his son,

III. Sir John Stapylton, who wedded Mary, daughter and heir of Francis Sandys, esq. of Scroby, in the county of Nottingham, and had, with daughters,† seven sons, viz.

Miles, }
Bryan, } who all succeeded to the baronetcy.
John, }
Martin, }
Christopher.
Francis.
Henry.

Sir John was nominated a candidate for the county of York, but died before the election came on, 24th October, 1733, when he was *s.* in his title and estates by his eldest son,

IV. Sir Miles Stapylton, M.P. for the county of York. This gentleman *m.* in 1738, Anne, daughter of Edward Waller, esq. of Hall-Barn, Bucks, by whom (who *d.* 13th November, 1791,) he had an only child,

Anne, who *d.* unm. 9th June 1770.

He *d.* 14th May, 1752, and was *s.* by his brother,

V. Sir Bryan Stapylton, who *d.* unm. 27th June, 1772, and was *s.* by his brother,

VI. Sir John Stapylton, a naval officer, who *d.* unm. in 1785, and was *s.* by his brother,

VII. Sir Martin Stapylton, in holy orders. This gentleman *m.* Leeky, daughter of Mr. Love, a merchant of Bristol, and had issue,

Francis-Samuel, } *d.* in the lifetime of their father,
Henry, } unm.
Martin, eventually heir.

Anne, *m.* in 1770, to the Rev. John Bree, rector of Markstay, in Essex, and had issue,

Martin Bree, of whom hereafter, as heir to his uncle, Sir Martin Stapylton.

John Bree, of Keswick, deceased.

Robert-Francis Bree, in holy orders, of Sydenham, in Kent.

Anne Bree, *d.* unm.

Sir Martin *d.* 21st January, 1801, and was *s.* by his only surviving son,

VIII. Sir Martin Stapylton, who *d.* issueless, 2nd January, 1817, when the Baronetcy became extinct, and the estates devolved upon his nephew, Martin Bree, esq. who in consequence assumed the surname and arms of Stapylton, and is the present (1838)

Martin Stapylton, esq. of Myton.

Arms—Arg. a lion rampant sa.

STAPYLTON, OF CARLTON.

Created 20th March, 1661-2.—Extinct in 1707.

Lineage.

Gilbert Stapylton, esq. of Carlton, in Yorkshire, son and heir of Richard Stapylton, esq. by Elizabeth, his wife, daughter of Sir Henry Pierrepoint, and representative of the ancient family of Stapylton‡ in the middle of the seventeenth century, *m.* first, Katherine, daughter of W. Hungate, esq. by whom he had no surviving issue; and secondly, Ellen, daughter of Sir

* A younger branch of which was

Sir Philip Stapleton, who purchased Warter in the Woulds, in the east riding, and was one of the five members of parliament demanded by *King* Charles I. when his majesty went to the House of Commons for that purpose.

† One of those ladies *m.* Henry Waller, esq. M.P. for Wycombe, Bucks.

‡ For a detailed pedigree, refer to Whitaker's *History of Leeds*.

John Gascoigne, by whom he had a daughter, ANNE, married to RALPH ERRINGTON, esq. and a son and successor,

I. MILES STAPYLTON, esq. of Carlton, *b.* in 1631, who was created a BARONET in 1661-2. He *m.* first, Elizabeth, daughter of Robert, Earl of Lindesay; and secondly, Miss Longueville; but died without issue in 1707, when the title became EXTINCT: the estates descended to the Erringtons.

Arms—As STAPYLTON OF MYTON.

STEPHENS, OF ST. FAITH'S.

CREATED 13th Mar. 1795.

EXTINCT 20th Nov. 1809.

Lineage.

This was an old Gloucestershire family, and very frequently during the seventeenth century gave sheriffs to that county.

HENRY STEPHENS, of Frocester, in Gloucestershire, *m.* the daughter and co-heir of Edward Lugg, of the county of Hereford, and by her (who *d.* in 1552) had several children, of whom the eldest son,

EDWARD STEPHENS, esq. purchased the manor of Eastington, in the same county, from Henry, Lord Stafford, in 1573. He *m.* Jane, daughter of Richard Fowler, gent. of Stonehouse, also in Gloucestershire, and had issue,

RICHARD, of Eastington, executor to his father, in 1587, *m.* one of the daughters of Edward St. Loe, esq. of Knighton, in Wiltshire, and left issue.
James, of Eastington, *m.* Catherine, daughter of Richard Browning, of Coley, in Gloucestershire, and had issue. He died 19th February, 1599.
THOMAS.

He *d.* 22nd October, 1587. His third son,

THOMAS STEPHENS, esq. of Over Lipiate, in Gloucestershire, attorney-general to *Prince* HENRY and CHARLES I. sometime reader of the Middle Temple, *d.* 26th April, 1613, aged fifty-five. He *m.* Elizabeth, daughter and heir of John Stone, of Over Lipiate, and had issue,

EDWARD, of Little Sodbury, in Gloucestershire, *b.* in 1590, *d.* about 1670. He married Anne, daughter of Sir Thomas Crewe, knt. of Stene, in Northamptonshire, and had issue.
Thomas, of Over Lipiate, bencher of the Middle Temple, living in 1613, *d.* in 1679, married four wives, and left issue.
NATHANIAL.

The youngest son,

NATHANIAL STEPHENS, esq. of Horton and Cherington, both in Gloucestershire, *m.* Elizabeth, daughter and eventually heir of Robert Tiringham, esq. of Weston-upon-Favell, in Northamptonshire, and Barby, in Leicestershire, and had two sons, viz.

EDWARD, of Alderley, Horton, and Cherington, and of the Middle Temple, barrister-at-law, baptised 25th July, 1633. He *m.* Mary, daughter of John Raynsford, esq. of Staverton, in Northamptonshire, and Walshamcote, in the county of Warwick, and had issue.
TYRINGHAM.

The younger son,

TYRINGHAM STEPHENS, in holy orders, archdeacon of the diocese of Leicester, *b.* 16th May, 1635, married first, Isabel, fourth daughter of George Rayson, esq. of Leicester, by whom (who *d.* about 1665) he had one surviving daughter, Elizabeth. He *m.* secondly, Millicent, fourth daughter of William Inge, esq. of Thorpe Constantine, in Staffordshire,* and by that lady had

TYRINGHAM, *d.* in 1710, aged thirty-eight,
Walter,
Thomas, an officer in the army,
NATHANIEL, in holy orders.
Richard, *m.* but *d. s. p.* in 1745.
Jane, *m.* to Thomas Foxon, esq.

The fourth son,

The Rev. NATHANIEL STEPHENS, was rector of Alphamstone, in Essex, *b.* in 1679, *m.* Ellis, daughter of Philip Deane, of Harwich, gent. by whom (who *d.* in 1762) he had issue,

TYRINGHAM, a commissioner of the Victualling Office, *b.* in 1713, *d.* unm. in 1766.
Nathaniel, captain R. N. *b.* in 1721, died unm. in 1747.
PHILIP.
Grace, *d.* unm. in 1783.
Millicent, *b.* in 1715, *m.* to William Howe, gent. of Mislethorne, in Essex, and had issue,

William Howe, captain R. N. died unm. in 1760.
Tyringham Howe, post captain R. N. *m.* but *d. s. p.* in 1783.
Nathaniel Howe, *d.* young.
Philip Howe, captain of Marines, *m.* Miss Mary-Anne Tongue, of Gibraltar, both living in 1795.
Stephens Howe, aid-de-camp to the king, and lieutenant-colonel 63rd regiment, *b.* 1st March, 1759, M.P. for Yarmouth, *d.* unm. 9th July, 1796.
Millicent Howe, *m.* first, to Thomas Wilkinson, esq. captain R. N.; and secondly, to Gabriel Mathias, esq. of Scotland-yard, in the county of Middlesex.
Grace Howe, living unm. in 1795.

The youngest son,

I. PHILIP STEPHENS, esq. *b.* 11th October, 1725, of St. Faith's and Horseford, in Norfolk, and of Fulham, in Middlesex, was created a BARONET 17th March, 1795, with remainder to his nephew, Colonel Stephens Howe. Sir Philip was first secretary to, and afterwards, one of the lords of the Admiralty. He represented the borough of Sandwich in parliament. He died unm. 20th November, 1809, and his nephew, Colonel Stephens Howe, having predeceased him, the BARONETCY EXPIRED.

Arms—Per chevron, az. and arg. in chief two falcons rising or.

* By Elizabeth, his wife, daughter and heiress of Thomas Tunsted, esq. of Tunsted, in Derbyshire.

STEPNEY, OF PRENDERGAST.

CREATED 24th Nov. 1621.  EXTINCT 12th Sept. 1825.

Lineage.

The origin of this family is deduced from

HENRY STEPNEY, esq. of Aldenham, in Hertfordshire,* who was s. by his son,

RALPH STEPNEY, esq. of St. Alban's, lord of Aldenham, who was interred in Aldenham Church 3rd December, 1548. He left, by the daughter and heir of Cressy, a son and successor,

WILLIAM STEPNEY, esq. lord of Aldenham, whose son and heir,

THOMAS STEPNEY, esq. m. the daughter and heir of John Wynde or Wyld, esq. of Ramsey, in the county of Huntingdon, and had two sons, viz.

ROBERT, whose son and successor,

POOL STEPNEY, sold the lordship of Aldenham to Sir Edward Cary, knt. father of Lord Falkland.

ALBAN.

The younger son,

ALBAN STEPNEY, esq. who was registrar of the diocese of St. David's, m. Margaret, daughter and co-heir of Thomas Catharn, esq. of Prendergast, in the county of Pembroke, but by that lady had no issue. He m. secondly, Mary, daughter and co-heir of William Philipps, esq. of Picton Castle, and had by her

JOHN, his heir.

Philip, barrister-at-law, d. s. p.

Thomas (Sir), who is characterized as "a great courtier." He m. first, Mrs. Wallop, a widow, the daughter of — Fisher, esq. of Hants, but that lady brought him no children. Sir Thomas m. secondly, Mary, eldest daughter and co-heir of Sir Bernard Whetstone, knt. of Woodford, in Essex, and by her had Bernard and other issue.†

Dorothy, m. to Sir Francis Mansell, bart. of Muddlescombe.

Joan, m. to John Philipps, esq. of Nash, in Pembrokeshire.

Alban Stepney acquired a very plentiful estate by his two matrimonial alliances. He was s. at his decease by his eldest son,

I. JOHN STEPNEY, esq. of Prendergast, in Pembrokeshire, who was created a BARONET by *King* JAMES I. 24th November, 1621. Sir John m. Catherine, daughter of Sir Francis Mansell, bart. of Muddlescombe, in Carmarthenshire, and had issue,

JOHN, his heir.

Alban, d. aged twenty-one, unm.

Thomas, m. Price, daughter and co-heir of Sir Henry Jones, bart. of Albemarles, and had

JOHN, who inherited as third baronet.

Charles, m. a daughter of Sir Richard Pryse, bart. of Gogarthan (she was the widow of Vaughan of Llanelthy), and had three sons and a daughter, viz.

Richard, m. Miss Tancred, and d. s. p.

Charles, paymaster of Waller's Marine Regiment, d. s. p. of wounds received at Cork in 1690.

Alban, d. at sea s. p.

Jane, m. to M. Bloysdon, of Dresden.

Jane, m. to Thomas Vaughan, esq. of Penteparke, in the county of Carmarthen.

Dorothy, m. to Richard Bloome, esq. of Aberguilly, in the same county.

Martha, m. to William Bladwell, esq. of Swannington, in Norfolk.

Frances.

The first baronet d. in August, 1634, and was s. by his eldest son,

II. SIR JOHN STEPNEY, who m. Magdalen, daughter and co-heir of Sir Henry Jones, bart. of Albemarles, in Carmarthenshire, and had an only daughter and heir,

FRANCES STEPNEY, who m. first, Henry Mansell, esq. of Llanelthy; and secondly, Captain Edward Mansell.

Sir John leaving thus at his decease no male issue, the Baronetcy, with a portion of the estate, devolved upon his nephew,

III. SIR JOHN STEPNEY, who m. Justina, daughter and heir of Sir Anthony Vandyke, the celebrated painter,‡ and was s. by his only son,

---

* CHAUNCY, in his Antiquities of Hertfordshire, says, the manor of Aldenham coming to the crown upon the dissolution, *King* HENRY VIII. granted it, with the advowson, to HENRY STEPNEY, who died leaving issue RALPH STEPNEY, who held it of *King* EDWARD VI. *in capite*.

† GEORGE STEPNEY, an English poet and statesman, who was born in London in 1663, is supposed to be a son of this Sir Thomas Stepney. He received his education at Westminster School, and was removed thence to Trinity College, Cambridge, in 1682, where, being of the same standing with Charles Montagu, afterwards Earl of Halifax, a strict friendship grew up between them. To this fortunate incident was owing all the preferment Stepney afterwards enjoyed, who is supposed not to have had parts to have reached any distinction without the powerful protection of Halifax. When Stepney set out in life he appears to have been attached to the Tory interest, for one of his first poems was an address to James II. upon his majesty's accession. Upon the Revolution he was nominated to several foreign embassies, and was very successful in his negotiations. He died at Chelsea in 1706, and was buried at Westminster Abbey, where a fine monument was erected to his memory with a pompous inscription.

‡ SIR ANTHONY VANDYKE's children, according to his pedigree, stood in proximity to the throne, which is thus explained by Burnet in speaking of the Gowry conspiracy:

"One thing which none of the historians have taken notice of, and might have induced the Earl of Gowry to have wished to put King James out of the way; for upon the king's death, he stood next to the succession to the crown of England; for King Henry the Seventh's daughter, that was married to King James the Fourth, did, after his death, marry Dowglass, Earl of Angus; but they could not agree; so a precontract was proved against him, upon which, by a sentence from Rome, the marriage was voided, with a clause in favour of the issue, since born under a marriage *de facto* and *bona fide*: Lady Margaret Dowglas was the child so provided for. I did peruse the original bull, confirming the divorce: after that, the queen dowager married one Francis Steward, and had by him a son, called Lord Methuen by King James the Fifth. In the patent he is called *Frater noster uterinus*. He had only a daughter, who was mother or grandmother to the Earl of Gowry; so that by this, he might be glad to put the king out of the way, that so he might stand next to the succession of the crown of England. He had a brother, then a child, who when he grew up, and found he could not carry the name of Ruthen, which, by an act made after this conspiracy, none might carry, he went and lived beyond sea, and it was given out that he had the philosopher's stone. He had two sons, who died without issue, and one daughter, married to Sir Anthony Vandike, the famous picture drawer."

IV. SIR THOMAS STEPNEY, M.P. for the county of Carmarthen, who *m.* Margaret, sister and co-heir of Walter Vaughan, esq. of Llanelthy, and dying 24th February, 1744, was *s.* by his son,

V. SIR JOHN STEPNEY, who *m.* Eleanor, daughter and heir of John Lloyd, esq. of Buckleethwen, in Carmarthenshire, by whom (who died in 1733) he had one son and three daughters, viz.

- THOMAS, his heir.
- Margaret, *d.* unm.
- Mary, *m.* to John Allen, esq. of Dale, in Pembrokeshire.
- Justina, *m.* to Thomas Popkin, esq. of Forest, in the county of Glamorgan.

He *d.* in 1748, and was *s.* by his son,

VI. SIR THOMAS STEPNEY. This gentleman married Eleanor, only daughter and heir of Thomas Lloyd, esq. of Danyralt, in the county of Carmarthen, and by that lady (who *d.* in June, 1795,) had issue,

- JOHN, his heir.
- THOMAS, successor to his brother.
- Margaretta-Eleanor, *d.* unm.
- Elizabeth-Bridgetta, *b.* in 1749, *m.* Joseph Gulston, esq. of Ealing Grove, Middlesex, and *d.* in 1779, leaving an only daughter.
- Justina-Maria, *m.* first, to Francis Head, esq. of St. Andrew's Hall, Norfolk; and secondly, to Colonel Cowel, of the Coldstream Guards. By her first husband she had a daughter, the widow of the Rev. George Herbert, and by her second, two sons.

Sir Thomas *d.* 7th October, 1772, and was *s.* by his elder son,

VII. SIR JOHN STEPNEY, M.P. for the borough of Monmouth, envoy-extraordinary in 1775 at the court of Dresden, and at Berlin in 1782. Sir John died at Vienna in October, 1811, unmarried, and was *s.* by his brother,

VIII. SIR THOMAS STEPNEY, who married 8th June, 1813, Catherine, relict of Russell Manners, esq. and daughter of the Rev. Dr. Pollock, of Grittleton, Wilts, but *d. s. p.* 12th September, 1825, when the BARONETCY became EXTINCT. His widow, Lady Stepney, survives, and is the authoress of several works of fiction.

Arms—Gu. a fess checky or and az. between three owls arg.

STONHOUSE, OF AMBERDEN HALL.

CREATED 11th June, 1641.

EXTINCT 13th April, 1695.

Lineage.

I. JAMES STONHOUSE, esq. of Amberden Hall, Essex, son of Sir James Stonhouse, by Anne, his wife, daughter of Sir Humphrey Weld, and grandson of George Stonhouse, esq. of Radley, Berks, was created a BARONET in 1641. His son and successor,

II. SIR JAMES STONHOUSE, of Amberden Hall, married Miss Blewet, of Holcombe, in Devon, and was *s.* by his elder son,

III. SIR BLEWET STONHOUSE, who died unmarried and was *s.* by his brother,

IV. SIR GEORGE STONHOUSE, of Amberden Hall, who *m.* Miss Hamilton, and left a son and successor,

V. SIR JOHN STONHOUSE, who *m.* Elizabeth, daughter of George Cole, esq. of Buckish, in Devon, and [illegible] Enstone, in Oxfordshire, and had issue,

- GEORGE, his heir.
- ELIZABETH, *m.* to Thomas Jervoise, esq. of Herriard, Hants, and conveyed to him the [illegible] of Amberden Hall, which was sold to Thomas Sclater Bacon, esq.

Sir John was *s.* by his son,

VI. SIR GEORGE STONHOUSE, of Amberden Hall, at whose decease in minority, 13th April, 1695, the BARONETCY became EXTINCT.

Arms—Arg. on a fess sa. between three hawks volant, az. a leopard's face between two mullets or.

STOUGHTON, OF STOUGHTON.

CREATED 29th Jan. 1660-1.

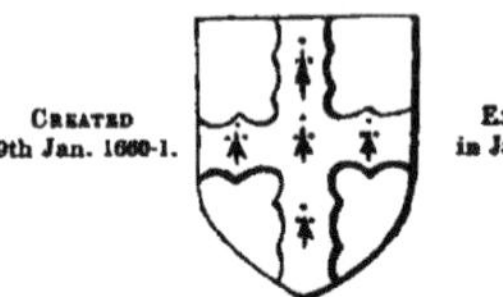

EXTINCT in Jan. [illegible]

Lineage.

This family derived its name from STOCHE or STOKE, in Surrey, and "TUN," the Saxon word for "inclosure." In the time of STEPHEN, Godwin de Stoc [illegible] resided at Stoctun, and in the 3rd of EDWARD III HENRY DE STOCTUN had royal licence to empark there 160 acres of land. In the early part of the 16th century, the family became divided into two branches. The younger seating itself at St. John's, Warwick, a large and ancient mansion, originally the hospital of St. John the Baptist, remained there for a series of years, maintaining a leading position in the county, until the male line expired with George Stoughton, esq. of St. John's, who left an elder daughter and heiress, Eugenia, who *m.* JAMES MONEY, esq. of Pitsford, in Northamptonshire, and of Much Marcle, in Herefordshire, and thus the representation of the Stoughtons of St. John's has merged in the MONEYS. The elder branch continued at Stoughton, in Surrey, and its chief at the middle of the 17th century,

I. NICHOLAS STOUGHTON, esq. of Stoughton, son of Anthony Stoughton, and grandson of Sir Laurence Stoughton, knt. was created a BARONET 29th January, 1660-1. He *m.* in 1662, Elizabeth, daughter of Sir Henry Massingberd, bart. of Braytoft, in Lincolnshire, and dying 30th June, 1686, left (with several daughters, of whom Frances, *m.* Charles Ventris, esq. and Henrietta became the wife of Philip Neve, serjeant at law) a son and successor,

II. SIR LAWRENCE STOUGHTON, of Stoughton, who *m.* Mary,* daughter of John Burnaby, of Leadenhall, brewer, but died without issue, in January, 1692, when the BARONETCY became EXTINCT. At Sir L. [illegible]

* She *m.* secondly, Watkinson Payler, esq.; and thirdly, Thomas Turnoer, esq. barrister at-law.

ence's decease, the mansion called Stoughton Place, situated on a delightful eminence near the middle of the manor, was pulled down, the site is now a plough-[illegible] field of about six acres, with part of the ancient moats remaining, and is known by the name of the Stoughton Gardens." In the church of Stoke, at the east end of the north aisle, is the Stoughton chapel. There are many ancient monuments to the family, with quaint and interesting descriptions.

Arms—Az. a cross engrailed ermine.

STRADLING, OF ST. DONATS'.

CREATED 21st May, 1611.

EXTINCT 27th Sept. 1738.

Lineage.

"This ancient and knightly family (says Collins) is extracted from the eastern people called *Easterlings* or *Oesterlings*, who dwelt near the Baltic Sea."

SIR WILLIAM DE ESTERLING, the first that came into England, was one of the twelve knights who accompanied Robert Fitz-Hammon,* Earl of Gloucester, to the aid of Justin ap Gorgant, King of Glamorgan, against Prince Rese, about the year 1090, *temp.* WILLIAM *Rufus*; and the said Robert Fitz-Hammon, on the death of Rese, turning his forces against Justin, and conquering his whole dominion, divided it amongst his followers. For his share of the spoil, Esterling had the manor and castle of St. Donats, which afterwards continued the chief seat of his descendants. His son and heir,

SIR JOHN ESTERLING, *m.* Matilda, daughter and heir of Sir Robert Corbet, knt. and was father of

SIR MORRIS ESTERLING, who *m.* Cicely, daughter and heir of Picot de Say, and was *s.* by his son (the first who abbreviated the name),

SIR ROBERT STRADLING, knt. who married Howise, heiress of St. Donats Castle, daughter of Sir Hugh [illegible]ron, knt. and their great-great-grandson,

SIR PETER STRADLING, knt. having married Johan, daughter and sole heir of Thomas Hawey, acquired in the time of EDWARD I. the manors of Hawey and [illegible]lfreyands, in the county of Somerset, with Compton Hawey, in Dorsetshire. He was *s.* by his son,

SIR EDWARD STRADLING, knt. of St. Donats, who married Eleanor, daughter of Sir Gilbert Stradling, [illegible] by some accounts, Strongbow, and heir of her mother, a daughter of Richard Garnon, of whose inheritance he possessed two manors in Oxfordshire. He was *s.* by his son,

SIR EDWARD STRADLING, who was returned by the county of Somerset to the parliament held at Westminster 17 EDWARD III. and had £12 allowance for forty nine days' expenses, "coming, stay, and returning." He *m.* Gwenlian, sister and heir of Sir Charles, and daughter of Sir Roger Berkrolls,† and thereby acquired the lordship of East Orchard, in the county of Glamorgan. He *d.* 9 HENRY IV. and was *s.* by his son,

SIR WILLIAM STRADLING, who performed a pilgrimage to Jerusalem, and was there made a knight of the Holy Sepulchre. He *m.* Isabel, daughter and heir of Sir John St. Barbe, knt. and was *s.* by his son,

SIR EDWARD STRADLING, who accompanied his father to the Holy Sepulchre, and was also made, with him, knight of that order, about the beginning of the reign of *King* HENRY VI. He *m.* Jane, daughter of Henry Beaufort, (son of John of Gaunt,) afterwards made Cardinal of St. Eusebius, Bishop of Winchester, and Lord Chancellor of England. He left a son and heir,

SIR HENRY STRADLING, who, in his passage from St. Donats to his seat in Somersetshire, was made prisoner by Colin Dolphin, a pirate of Britany, and his ransom was rated so highly—2200 marks—that he was compelled to sell for its liquidation his two manors in Oxfordshire, the castle and manor of Rogerstown, called in Welch Tre-Gwilym, together with the lordship of Sutton, in Monmouthshire. He went afterwards, according to the devotion of those times, and visited the Holy Sepulchre and other revered antiquities in Palestine, where he likewise received the order of knighthood of the Sepulchre; but in returning, died in the Isle of Cyprus, being under twenty-six years of age, and was buried in the city of Famagusta, leaving a son and heir,

THOMAS STRADLING, esq. for whom the following cenotaphial memorial was erected in the chapel of St. Donats':

"Here lyeth Thomas Stradling, Esq. son to Sir Harry Stradling, Knt. and Elizabeth, his wife (the daughter of William Thomas, of Ragland, in the county of Monmouth‡), who dy'd at Cardife, in teh Monastery of Preaching-Fryers, the 8th day of September, in the year of our Lord 1480; whose Bones, after the Dissolution of the said Monastery, Sir Thomas Stradling, Knt. his Grand-son, caus'd to be taken up and carry'd to St. Donats, and bury'd by his Son the 4th of June, 1537; and afterwards Sir Edward Stradling, Knt. the 5th of that Name, translated the said Bones out of the Chancel into the Chapel annex'd to the said Chancel, in the year of our Lord 1573; after whose Death, his Wife was marry'd to Sir Rees ap Thomas, Knight of the Garter, and dy'd at Picton, in the County of Pembroke, the 5th day of February, in the year of our Lord 1535, and was bury'd at Carmarthen, in the Church of the Monastery of Preaching-Fryers, with the said Sir Rees ap Thomas, her husband."

This Thomas Stradling, by Janet, his wife, daughter of Thomas Mathew, esq. of Radyr, in Glamorganshire, had issue two sons, viz.

EDWARD (Sir), who *m.* Elizabeth, daughter of Sir Thomas Arundel, knt. of Lanheyron, in Cornwall, and dying *v. p.* left issue,

I. THOMAS, successor to his grandfather.

II. Robert, who *m.* Denis, daughter of Watkin Loughor, esq. of Tythegstone, in Glamorganshire, and left a son, who *d. s. p.* and seven daughters, his co-heirs, of whom the eldest,

ELIZABETH, *m.* to Thomas Turberville,

* Sir Robert Fitz Hamon stiled himself thus,—"Sir [illegible] Fitzhomon, by the Grace of God, Prince of Glamorgan, Earle of Corbaile, Baron of Thorigny and Granville, Lord of Gloucester, Bristow, Tewksbury, and Cardiff, Conqueror of Wales, neare Kinsman unto the King, General of his arms in France." He was son of Lord Hamon Dentatus, sixth Earl of Corbaile, in Normandy, descended from Rollo, Duke of Normandy.

† By his wife, one of the co heirs of Payn de Turberville, lord of Castle Coity.

‡ And sister of the whole blood to William Herbert, first Earl of Pembroke.

esq. of Llantwitt Major, descended from Sir Payn de Turberville, knt. of Coity Castle, one of Fitzhammons, and had a son and heir,

EDMOND TURBERVILLE, esq. of Llantwitt Major, who m. Catherine, daughter and heir of Watkin Thomas John Watkin, esq. and had an only child and heir,

CECIL, m. to Iltyd Nicholl, esq. and was ancestor of the NICHOLLS of Monmouthshire, of the Nicholls of the Ham, now represented by ILTYD NICHOLL, esq. of the Nicholls of Dimlands, of the Nicholls of Merthymawr, &c.

III. Edward, m. to the daughter and heir of Robert Raglon, of Llantwitt Major.

IV. John, in holy orders.

I. Jane, m. to Alexander Popham, esq. of Somersetshire.

II. Catherine, m. to Sir Thomas Palmer, of Sussex.

HENRY, who m. the daughter and heir of Thomas Jubb, esq. a learned lawyer, and had a son,

FRANCIS, who resided at St. George's, near Bristol. He m. Mary, daughter of Bartholomew Mitchel, esq. and left a son,

JOHN (Sir), of whom hereafter as heir to Sir Edward Stradling.

Jane, m. to Sir William Griffyth, of Caernarvonshire.

He was s. by his grandson,

SIR THOMAS STRADLING, knt. who m. Catherine, daughter of Sir Thomas Gamage, knt. of Coity, and left a son and heir,

SIR EDWARD STRADLING, knt. of whom the following details are given by Anthony Wood: "Sir Edward Stradling was educated in the University of Oxford; but before he took a degree, travell'd into various Countries; spent some Time at Rome, return'd an accomplish'd gentleman; and retiring to his Inheritance, which was large, built a firm Structure on that Foundation of Literature he had laid at Oxford, and elsewhere. In 1575, or the year after, he receiv'd the Honour of Knighthood, became a very useful Man in his Country, and was at the Charge of such Herculean Works for the publick good, that no Man, in his Time, went beyond him, for his singular knowledge in the British Language and Antiquities, for his eminent Encouragement of Learning, and learned Men, and for his great Expence and indefatigable Industry, in collecting together several Ancient Manuscripts of Learning and Antiquity; all which, with other Books, were reduc'd into a well-order'd Library at St. Donats, to the great Credit and Renown of the Family. He writ a Welsh Grammar mostly in Latin. He wrote also the Conquest of the Lordship of Glamorgan, or Morganive, with other pieces; and having marry'd Agnes, daughter to Sir Edward Gage, of Firle, in Sussex, paid his last debt to Nature, 15th May, 1609, without Issue, aged Eighty years or more, and was bury'd in a Chapel he himself had built (dedicated to the Virgin Mary), joining to the Parish-Church of St. Donats." Sir Edward devised his estate to his next kinsman,

I. SIR JOHN STRADLING, who was educated at Oxford, and took a degree in arts, as a member of Magdalen Hall in 1583, "being then accounted a Miracle for his forwardness in Learning and Pregnancy of Parts." He was knighted by *King* JAMES I. 15th May, 1608, being then denominated of the county of Salop; and the next year, having inherited the estates and representation of the family, he settled at St. Donats; and was created a BARONET 21st May, 1611, "at which time he was esteem'd a most wise and learned person. In the year 1620 he was high sheriff of the county of Glamorgan, "and being involved in secular affairs and the service of his country, was taken off writing till the latter part of *King* JAMES I. at which time he published *Beati Pacifici*, printed in 1623, and *Divine Poems*, in seven several classes, written to *King* CHARLES I." He m. Elizabeth, daughter of Edward, son of Sir Edward Gage, of Firle, and had issue,

EDWARD, his heir.

Thomas, lieutenant-colonel under his elder brother at Edge Hill, *d. s. p.*

John, a captain in the expedition to the Isle of Rhee under the Duke of Buckingham, where he was slain.

Harry (Sir), knighted by *King* CHARLES I. He was captain of a man-of-war, but after the parliament, in the time of the rebellion, had got all the king's ships into their power, he resigned his post. Being in Pembroke Castle when it was surrendered by Poyer and Laugharne, he was banished to Ireland, and died at Cork, where he was interred. Lord Clarendon says that he and Kettleby were the only captains the parliament could not corrupt.

Edmund, *d.* young.

Francis, captain of foot in Ireland *temp.* CHARLES I. where he died before the rebellion.

Donat, *d.* young.

George, D.D. dean of Gloucester.

Jane, m. to William Thomas, esq. of Wenvoe.

Elizabeth, m. to — Jennings, esq. of Essex.

Frances, *d.* unm.

Sir John died 9th September, 1637, and was s. by his eldest son,

II. SIR EDWARD STRADLING, of St. Donats. This gentleman was colonel of foot in the service of the king at the battle of Edge Hill, where he was made prisoner and carried to Warwick Castle. After his release he repaired to Oxford, and dying in that city in June, 1644, was buried in the chapel of Jesus College. He m. Mary, daughter of Sir Thomas Mansel, bart. of Margam, and had issue,

EDWARD, his successor.

John, major-general in the service of King CHARLES I. made prisoner at St. Fagans, and was conveyed to Windsor Castle, where he died.

Thomas (Sir), colonel of foot *temp.* CHARLES I. knighted by *King* JAMES II. and made captain of the Foot Guards and serjeant porter. He died at Merthymawr, and was buried in the parish church.

Mansel.

Jane, m. to Thomas Carne, esq. of Nash, in Glamorganshire.

Dorothy, m. to Henry Hill, esq. of East Orchard.

Joan, m. to David Mathews, esq. of Llandaff.

Anne.

Elizabeth, m. first, to Edward Turberville, esq. of Sutton; and secondly, to Lewis Thomas, esq.

Sir Edward was s. by his eldest son,

III. SIR EDWARD STRADLING. This gentleman, who, like his father and uncles, was a zealous royalist, brought a troop of horse to the assistance of the king at Newbury, and after the loss of that day retired to Oxford, where he died of a consumption. He m. Catherine, daughter of Sir Hugh Perry, an alderman ondon, and by her (who *m.* secondly, Bushy Mansel, sq. of Britton Ferry,) had a son and two daughters, iz.

Edward (Sir), his heir, who was knighted by Charles II.
Catherine, *m.* to Sir William Waller, knt.
Jane, *m.* to George Bowen, esq. of Kettlehill, in the county of Glamorgan.

le was *s.* by his son,

iv. Sir Edward Stradling, who married Elizabeth, aughter of Anthony Hungerford, esq. of Farley Cas-e, in the county of Somerset, and had surviving issue wo sons, viz.

Edward, his successor.
Thomas, died at sea.

le died 5th September, 1685, and was succeeded by is son,

v. Sir Edward Stradling, who was in possession f St. Donats, the ancient inheritance of the family, ith the manors and lordships of Sully Berkrolls and st Orchard, two other donations of Robert Fitz-lamon to Sir Reynald de Sully and Sir Lawrence erkrolls, two of the twelve knights which had ac-ompanied him into England. Sir Edward married lisabeth, daughter of Sir Edward Mansel, bart. of argam, and sister of Lord Mansel, and had issue,

Edward, *b.* 26th March, 1699, *d. s. p.*
Thomas, *b.* 24th July, 1710, heir to his father.

ir Edward *d.* 5th April, 1735, and was *s.* by his son,

vi. Sir Thomas Stradling, who *d.* unmarried at lontpellier 27th April, 1738, aged twenty-eight, when he Baronetcy expired.

The estate of St. Donats Castle was bequeathed to he Drakes of Shardeloes, and is now possessed by homas Tyrwhitt Drake, esq. Merthymawr and lonknash passed to Hugh Bowen, esq. and Penlline, amphey, and Cwm Hawey to Bussey Mansel, esq.

Arms—Paly of six arg. and az. on a bend gu. three inquefoils or.

STRUTT, OF LITTLE WARLEY HALL.

Created 5th Mar. 1641. Extinct in 1648.

Lineage.

In 1340, when a charter of freedom was obtained by he Helvetic Confederacy,

Godfried Strutz de Hinkelred, of Under Walden, hief of the Swiss Auxiliaries, received the honour of nighthood, but in subsequent dissensions being upon he less fortunate side, was obliged to seek an asylum n England, where it appears he took up his perma-ent abode, and from him descended

i. Sir Denner Strutt, knt.* of Little Warley Hall, in the county of Essex, who was created a Baronet in 1641. Sir Denner *m.* first, Dorothy, daughter of Francis Stasmore, esq. M.P.; secondly, Elizabeth, daughter of Sir Thomas Wodehouse, of Kimberley, in the county of Norfolk; thirdly, Mary, daughter and heir of Thomas Chapman, esq. of London; and fourthly, Elizabeth Cuss.† By his second wife, he left two daughters, his co-heirs,

Blanch, *m.* to Thomas Bennet, esq. of Wiltshire, a relation of Lord Ossulston, and had by her, Denner, Thomas, Andrew, and John.
Anne, *m.* to William Samwell, esq. of Watton, Norfolk.

During the civil war, he adhered with devotion to the royal cause, and was slain at Colchester, prior to the surrender of that town to the parliamentary forces, 27th August, 1648.‡ At Sir Denner's decease, his estate at Warley fell into the possession of Gen. Desborough, and the Baronetcy became extinct, while the representation of the family devolved upon his brother,

The Rev. Mr. Strutt, the clergyman of Faulkbourne, in Essex, ancestor of the present Col. Joseph Holden Strutt, of Terling Place, Essex, who sat for more than forty years in successive parliaments. He *m.* Lady Charlotte Mary Gertrude Fitzgerald, Baroness Rayleigh, daughter of James, Duke of Leinster, and has, with two daughters, one son, John James, present Lord Rayleigh.

Arms—Sa. a chev. arg. between three crosses crosslet fitchee or.

STUKELEY, OF HINTON.

Created 9th June, 1627.

Extinct in 1719.

Lineage.

Hugh Stewkley or Stukeley, of Marsh, in Somersetshire (son of Peter Stukeley, of Marsh, and grandson of George Stewkley, of Marsh, by Joan, his wife, daughter of Sir James Luttrell, knt. of Dunster), married Elizabeth, daughter of Richard Chamberlayne, esq. alderman of London, and had issue,

Thomas (Sir), his heir.
George-Luttrell, who *m.* Elizabeth, daughter of Sir Humphrey Drewell, knt. and *d. s. p.*
Joan, *m.* to George Luttrell, esq. of Dunster, in Somersetshire, high sheriff of that county in 1593, and was ancestor of the Luttrells of Dunster Castle, now represented by John Fownes-Luttrell, esq.
Susan, *m.* to Sir Henry Drewry, knt. of Hewgley, Bucks.

---

* Sir Denner's sister, Amy, wedded William Dawtrey, [illegible] of Moore House, whose joint representatives are, [illegible] Fane, esq. of Wormesley, and John Taylor-[illegible], M.D.

† This lady *m.* secondly, William Ward, esq. of Little [illegible]ghton, Northamptonshire.

‡ There still remains in the church of Little Warley, one of the most beautiful monuments in the county of Essex, erected to the memory of Sir Denner Strutt, knt. and bart.

Ursula, *m.* to Henry St. John, esq. of Farley.
Margaret, *d.* unm.

The elder son and heir,

Sir Thomas Stukeley, knt. of Marsh, in Somersetshire, and Hinton, Hants, living in 1623, *m.* Elizabeth, daughter and co-heir of John Goodwin, esq. of Over Wichingdon, Bucks, son and heir of Sir John Goodwin, and left, with other issue, a son and successor,

I. Hugh Stukeley, esq. of Hinton, who was created a Baronet 9th June, 1627. He *m.* Sarah, daughter and co-heir of Ambrose Dauntsey, esq. of Lavington, Wilts, and dying about 1642, was *s.* by his son,

II. Sir Hugh Stukeley, of Hinton, who *m.* first, Catherine, daughter and heir of Sir John Trott, bart. of Laverstoke, Hants; and secondly, Mary, daughter of John Young, esq.; but dying without male issue in 1719, the title became extinct.

Arms—Chequy arg. and sa. a fess gu. within a bordure az.

STYCH, OF NEWBURY.

Created 8th Oct. 1687.

Extinct 11th May, 1725.

Lineage.

I. William Stych, esq. of Newbury, in Essex, was created a Baronet in 1687, with remainder, in default of male issue, to his brother. He married Margaret, daughter of Sir Thomas Longueville, bart. of Wolverton, Bucks, and dying about 1699, was *s.* by his brother,

II. Sir Richard Stych, of Newbury, at whose decease 11th May, 1725, the title became extinct.

Arms—Sa. three garbs or, two and one.

STYDOLF, OF NORBURY.

Created 24th Dec. 1660.

Extinct in 1676-7.

Lineage.

John Stydolf, born in 1534, son and heir apparent of Thomas Stydolf, by Joan Dawtrey, his wife, and the descendant of an ancient family seated at Stidulfe's Place, in Kent, before the time of Edward III. married twice. By his first wife, Ann, daughter and heir of John Hawley, esq. he had two sons, Thomas, his heir, and William, of Hedley. The latter was esquire of the body to Charles I. and had a son, Sigismund. The former,

Thomas Stydolf, of Norbury, in Surrey, married Elizabeth, daughter and heir of Thomas Hussey, esq. of Lincolnshire, and dying in 1604, was succeeded by his son,

Sir Francis Stydolf, knt. of Norbury, who m. Mary daughter of Sir James Altham, baron of the Exchequer, and left issue,

Richard, his heir.
Jane, *m.* first, to Henry Yates, esq.; secondly, to Sir Henry Onslow; and thirdly, to John Amherst, esq.

Sir Francis died 12th March, 1655, aged seventy-five, and was *s.* by his son,

I. Richard Stydolf, esq. of Norbury, who was created a Baronet 4th December, 1660. He married Elizabeth, daughter of Sir George Stonehouse, and by her (who wedded, secondly, Lord Byron, and died in 1703,) he had two daughters, his co-heirs, viz.

Frances, *m.* to Jacob, Lord Astley, and *d. s. p.* 1692.
Margaret, *m.* to Thomas Tryon, esq. and dying before 1705, left two sons,
James Tryon, of Bullwick, Northamptonshire, father of two sons, Charles and James. The elder,
Charles Tryon, esq. of Bullwick, whose son,
Charles Tryon, esq. of Norbury, m. Mary, daughter of Robert, Earl Ferrers, and had issue,
Charles.
——, D.D. *d.* in 1771.
Robert.
William, lieutenant-governor of New York, *d.* in 1788.
Mary.
Samuel Tryon, whose son,
John Tryon, of Colley Weston, *m.* Sarah Burton, and had a daughter,
Elizabeth, wife of Richard Dickson Skrine, esq. of Cobham.

Sir Richard died 13th February, 1676-7, when the Baronetcy became extinct.

Arms—Arg. on a chief sa. two wolves' heads erased or.

STYLE, OF LANGLEY, IN BECKINGHAM.

Created 20th May, 1627.

Extinct 10th Nov. [illegible]

Lineage.

Sir Humphrey Style, knt. of Langley, in Kent, sheriff 35 Henry VIII. son of John Style, a distinguished diplomatist, by Elizabeth, his wife, daughter and co-heir of Sir Guy Wolstan, of London, *m.* first, Bridget, daughter of Sir Thomas Baldrey, knt. and had three sons,

Edmund, his heir.
Oliver, sheriff of London *temp.* James I. He

purchased the manor of Wateringbury, in Kent, and was ancestor of the present

Sir Thomas-Charles Style, bart. of Wateringbury. (See Burke's *Peerage and Baronetage*.)

Nicholas (Sir), knt. alderman of London. He m. Gertrude, daughter of Edward Bright, of London, and dying 16th November, 1615, left issue,

Humphrey, of Westerham.

Mary, m. to Simon Lawrence, of London, merchant.

Sir Humphrey m. secondly, Elizabeth, daughter of George Peniset, esq. and had by her (who m. secondly, Christopher Mead, esq.) one daughter, Mary. He d. 7th April, 1557, and was s. by his eldest son,

Edmund Style, esq. of Langley, b. 27th March, 1538, who m. Mary, daughter of John Berney, esq. of Reedham, in Norfolk, and had two sons,

William, his heir.

Edmund, who m. Catharine, daughter of John Scot, esq. of Halden, and had a son, John, and a daughter, Mary.

The elder son,

William Style, esq. of Langley, m. first, Anne, daughter of John Eversfield, esq. of Den, in Sussex, and had by her a son and a daughter,

Humphrey, his heir.

Anne, m. Sir Nicholas Miller, knt. of Oxenheath.

He m. secondly, Mary, daughter of Sir Robert Clarke, knt. one of the barons of the Exchequer, by whom he had, with three daughters, Mary, Elizabeth, and Margaret, eight sons, namely,

I. William, barrister-at-law, who inherited Langley upon the demise of his half-brother, Sir Humphrey. He wedded Elizabeth, daughter and heir of William, son of John Duleing, esq. alderman of Rochester, and d. in December, 1699, aged eighty, having had issue,

William, d. s. p. in his father's lifetime.

Humphrey, of Langley, whose only daughter and heir, Elizabeth, m. first, to Sir John Elwill, bart. of Exeter; and secondly, to Henry Bartlett.

Mary. Esther.

II. George.

III. Richard.

IV. Robert.

V. Edmund.

VI. Michael.

VII. Thomas, LL.D.

VIII. Francis.

The eldest son,

I. Sir Humphrey Style, knt. of Langley, gentleman of the privy chamber to James I. and cupbearer to Charles I. was created a Baronet 20th May, 1627. He married Elizabeth, daughter and heir of Robert Perrshall, esq. of Lincoln's Inn, and widow of Sir Robert Bosvill, knt. of Eynsford, but had no issue. He died 10th November, 1659, when the Baronetcy became extinct.

Arms—Sa. a fesse or, fretted of the field, between three fleurs-de-lys gold, with a border of the second.

SUDBURY, OF ELDON.

Created 25th June, 1685.—Extinct 27th March, 1691.

Lineage.

I. John Sudbury, esq. of Eldon, in Durham, who was created a Baronet 25th June, 1685, m. Bridget, daughter of Sir Thomas Exton, knt. LL.D. but d. without male issue, 27th March, 1691, when the title became extinct.

SUTTON, OF MOULSEY.

Created 5th March, 1806.—Extinct 6th Nov. 1813.

Lineage.

Thomas Sutton, esq. of Moulsey, in Surrey, who d. in 1789, m. Jane, daughter of Sir Thomas Hankey, knt. alderman of London, by Sarah, his wife, eldest daughter of the celebrated Sir John Barnard, M.P. and had issue,

John (Sir), K.C.B. admiral R.N. m. in 1797, his cousin, the Hon. Frances Hotham, eldest daughter of Beaumont, second Lord Hotham, by Susannah, his wife, daughter of Sir Thomas Hankey, and d. 8th August, 1825.

Thomas (Sir), of whom presently.

The second son,

I. Thomas Sutton, esq. of Moulsey, in Surrey, was created a Baronet 5th March, 1806. He m. Lucy, daughter of Thomas Ashton Smith, esq. and had two daughters,

Lucy, m. to Colonel Sir George Berkeley.

Caroline-Mary-Selina, m. to an Italian nobleman.

Sir Thomas died 6th November, 1813, when the title became extinct.

SWALE, OF SWALE.

Created 21st June, 1660.

Extinct ....

Lineage.

"This family (says Le Neve) derive their descent from Alured, son of John Swale; which John married Alice, the sister of Walter, son of Gilbert de Gaunt, a noble baron, and had the manor of West Grenton, in Swaledale, given to Alured, his nephew; Sir Solomon Swale affirming, in 1692, that he had the original deed in Yorkshire, at his house of South Stainley. This John Swale is witness to several deeds of Walter de Gaunt to the priory of Bridlington, and concerning Alured, this note out of the Pipe rolls, which is under Sir William Dugdale's hand; Ex magno rotulo pipæ de anno tertio regis Henrici secundi anno scilt. ab incarnatione Domini 1157. Evericsire Bertramus de Bulmer, reddit compotum de firma comitatus, &c. nova placita et novæ conventiones Aluredus de Sualedale et homines sui reddunt compotum de 8° libris."

The descendant of Alured,

William Swale, m. Isabel, daughter and heir of John Mundy, and was father of another

William Swale, who m. Joan, daughter and coheir of Jeffery Applegarth, of Kilton. His son and heir,

George Swale, m. Joan, daughter of John Vavasor, esq. of Weston, and from this marriage, after three generations, sprang

John Swale, esq. who m. Anne, daughter of John Slingsby, esq. of Scriven, and was s. by his son,

Thomas Swale, esq. who left by his wife, Cicely, daughter of John Pulleyn, esq. of Killing Hall, a son and heir,

Solomon Swale, esq. who *m.* Dorothy, daughter of Christopher Wyvil, esq. of Burton Constable, and had a son and successor,

Francis Swale, esq. of South Stainley, in the county of York, who *m.* Anne, daughter of Sampson Ingleby, esq. (a younger son of Sir William Ingleby, knt. of Ripley), and had issue,

- Solomon, his heir.
- Thomas, *d.* unm.
- John, married two wives, but had no issue. He was engaged in the service of Charles I.
- Charles, major of foot, in the king's service at Oxford when the city surrendered to the parliamentarians. He retired to France, and died in the service of the French king.
- Robert, captain of horse under *King* Charles I. and *King* Charles II. He married and had a son, John. He *d.* at Malaga.

Francis Swale had several daughters beside. He died 26th December, 1629, and was *s.* by his eldest son,

I. Solomon Swale, esq. of Swale Hall and South Stainley, both in the county of York, who was created a Baronet 21st June, 1660. Sir Solomon represented Aldborough in the parliament that voted the restoration of Charles II. and served the office of sheriff for his native county in 1675. He *m.* first, Mary, daughter of Robert Porey, esq. of Poreys, in Norfolk; and secondly, Anne, daughter of Charles Tancred, esq. of Whixley, in Yorkshire: by the latter he had no issue; by the former he had

- John, William, } who predeceased their father unmarried.
- Henry, his successor.
- Robert, M.D. married Isabel, daughter of Thomas Mitchell, of London, and left two sons, Robert and William.
- Solomon, Godfrey, Aldred, } all died unmarried.
- Anne, married to John Winchcomb, esq. of Gray's Inn.

Sir Solomon died, aged seventy, 4th December, 1678, and was *s.* by his eldest surviving son,

II. Sir Henry Swale, *b.* in 1630, married Dorothy, daughter of Ralph Crathorne, esq. of Crathorne, in the county of York, and had four sons and three daughters, viz.

- Solomon, his successor.
- Henry, a merchant at Malaga, *m.* Rose-Lunetia, daughter of Mr. Colomo, a merchant of the same place, and left two sons,
  - Sebastian-Fabian-Enrique, who inherited as fourth baronet.
  - Enrique-Antonio, who married at Malaga and had one daughter.
- Francis, John, } *d.* unm.
- Margaret, *m.* to Laurence, son of George Witham, esq. of Cliffe, in the county of York.
- Dorothy, Anne, } *d.* unm.

He *d.* 19th January, 1682-3, and was *s.* by his eldest son,

III. Sir Solomon Swale, who died unmarried, aged sixty-eight, 30th December, 1733, and was interred with his grandmother near the altar in Paddington Church, Middlesex. The Baronetcy devolved upon his nephew,

IV. Sir Sebastian-Fabian-Enrique Swale, who *m.* Elizabeth, daughter of Mr. Smith, of Poole, and had three daughters, viz.

- Elizabeth-Easter.*
- Frances-Theotrora.
- Dorothy-Fabiana.

Sir Sebastian *d.* without male issue, when the Baronetcy became extinct.

Arms—Az. a bend nebulé arg.

SWAN, OF SOUTHFLEET.

Created 1st March, 1666.

Extinct 7th April, 1712.

Lineage.

"The family of Swan," says Hasted, "wrote themselves *gentlemen* so early as the reign of Richard II."

I. Sir William Swan, of Hook Place, in Southfleet, Kent (son of Sir Thomas Swan, of Southfleet, knighted at Theobald's 11th January, 1630, and grandson of Sir William Swan, living *temp.* James I.), was created a Baronet in 1666. He *m.* Hesther, daughter of Sir John Ogle, knt. of Pinchbeck, in the county of Lincoln, and dying in 1680, was *s.* by his son,

II. Sir William Swan, of Hook Place, in Southfleet, who sold that seat, with the estate, to the family of Harrington. By Judith, his wife, he had no child, and at his decease, 7th April, 1712, the Baronetcy became extinct.

Arms—Az. a chevron erm. between three swans ppr.

SYDENHAM, OF BRIMPTON.

Created 28th July, 1641.

Extinct 10th Oct. 1739.

Lineage.

This family derived its surname from a place near Bridgewater, in Somersetshire, its ancient seat.

John de Sydenham, living 9 Henry III. *m.* the heiress of Kitsford, in the same county, and had two sons, William and Richard. The elder,

William de Sydenham, married Joan, daughter of William de Gothayre, and had issue,

---

* So called from being born on Easter Monday.

Roger.

Simon, m. Marsilla, daughter of John Hillary, of Badyalton, and had, with two daughters, Margery, wife of John de Radyngton and Christina, an only son,

Simon, whose son,

Hugh, living *temp.* Richard II. married Joan, heir of William Polleswell or de Poulesbill, of that place, in Somersetshire, and had, with a daughter, Mary, the wife of Roger Bolton, of Bolterscombe, a son,

Robert, ancestor of the Sydenhams of Combe, as at foot.*

William, *d. s. p.*

The eldest son,

Roger de Sydenham, was of Sydenham and Kitsford in 15 Edward III. and had two sons, John, the elder of whom had no male issue, but left an only daughter and heir, who conveyed the estate of Sydenham to the Caves, and from them it passed to the Percivals, ancestors of the Earls of Egmont. The younger son,

Richard de Sydenham, settled himself at Combe-Sydenham, in the western part of Somersetshire. He was constituted a judge of the Common Pleas in 1 Richard II. He m. Joan, daughter and co-heir of Robert Delingrige, of Bromfield,† and had issue,

Henry, his heir.

Simon, a churchman, first Archdeacon of Sarum and Berks, then Dean of Sarum, and eventually, 6 Henry VI. made Bishop of Chichester. He was sent by *King* Henry ambassador to the Emperor of Germany, and presented him with a golden cup.

Joan, m. to Thomas Bratton, of Bratton, in Somersetshire.

The eldest son,

Henry de Sydenham, m. Margery, daughter and co-heir of John Whitton, of Whitton, in Somersetshire, and had two sons, both called John, and living in 9 Henry V. John, the younger, was of Orchard, in Somersetshire.‡ The elder,

John Sydenham succeeded his father. He married Emillia Hussey, an heiress, and was *s.* by his son,

John Sydenham, esq. knight of the shire for Somerset, who married Joan, daughter and heir of John Sturton, esq. of Brimpton, and had issue,

i. Walter, his heir.

ii. Alexander, m. the widow of Popham, and had

1. John, of Leigh, who had two sons,

John, *d. s. p.*

Alexander, whose only daughter and heir, Elizabeth, was the second wife of Sir John Points, of Iron Acton.

2. Silvester, whose daughter and heir married Winter.

3. John, of Chelworthy.§

iii. Richard, of Aller, in Somersetshire.‖

---

* The early descents of the Sydenhams, as given in Hutchins' Dorset, differ materially from this deduction.

† By the daughter and co-heir of Walter Delalynde, grandson of the famous Thomas Delalynde, who slew the white hart in the forest, since called White Hart Forest.

‡ He m. Margaret, daughter and co-heir of Richard Popham, of Alfacton, in the same county, and was *s.* by his son,

John Sydenham, of Orchard, who m. the daughter and heir of John Gambon, of Merton, whose son and heir,

John Sydenham, esq. of Orchard, m. Elizabeth, daughter of Sir William Hody, knt. whose daughter,

Alionora, or Elizabeth Sydenham, m. Sir John Wyndham, knt. and conveyed to the Wyndhams the seat of Orchard, thenceforward called Orchard-Wyndham, and afterwards part of the possessions of the Earls of Egremont.

Who, by the daughter and heir of Herne, left a son and heir,

George Sydenham, esq. of Chelworthy, who m. Mary, daughter of Thomas Warre, esq. of Hestercombe, and was *s.* by his son,

Richard Sydenham, esq. of Chelworthy, who m. Elizabeth, daughter of — Hall, esq. of Henwick, in Worcestershire, and had (with four daughters, Mary, Elizabeth, Ursula, and Catherine), five sons, viz.

Henry, his heir.

Hopton, in holy orders.

Edward (Sir), who was knight-marshal of the king's host, during the civil wars.

Francis (Sir).

Richard.

The eldest son,

Henry Sydenham, esq. of Chelworthy, m. Elizabeth, daughter of Humphrey Walrond, esq. of Sea, in Somersetshire, and was *s.* by his son,

Sir Humphrey Sydenham, knt. of Chelworthy, who left several daughters, his co-heirs, of whom Anne m. Roger Sydenham, esq. of Lee; another was mother of Sir Sydenham Fowke, of Suffolk; and another, of Sydenham Bergh, rector of Brimpton.

Married Jane, daughter of — Cambray, of the county of Denbigh, and had four sons,

Christopher.

William, m. Agnes, daughter of — Worth, of Washfield, and left a son,

John Sydenham, of Langford, in Somersetshire, who m. Katherine, daughter of Thomas Newton, and left a son,

Nicholas, sheriff of Somersetshire, *temp.* Elizabeth.

Thomas, of Winford Eagle, in the county of Dorset, m. Alice, daughter of William Stevens, and had, with a daughter, Elizabeth, wife of Elias Holcombe, of Devonshire, a son,

Thomas, who m. Joan, daughter of William Speke, of Dolish, in Somersetshire, and left a son,

Richard, who wedded Johanna, daughter of Moor, of Moorhayes, in Devonshire, and was *s.* by his son,

Thomas, who m. Elizabeth, daughter of Sir Thomas Fulford, knt. and had a son and heir,

William, who wedded Johanna, daughter of Sir John Jeffery, of Coltherston, in Dorsetshire, and had issue,

William, colonel in the civil wars, and governor of the Isle of Wight.

Thomas, M.D. celebrated for his works.

Francis, killed in the civil war, 1644.

Mary, m. to Richard Lee, esq. of Wingland.

Elizabeth, m. to Roger Sydenham, esq. of Skilgate.

Martha, m. to William Laurence, of Wraxhall.

The eldest son,

Colonel William Sydenham, m. Grace, daughter of John Trenchard, esq. of Warmwell, Dorsetshire, and had

William.

Thomas.

John, *d.* 1708.

Mary, m. to Walter Thornhall, of Weymouth.

Frances, m. to Robert Thornhull, esq. of Wolland.

The eldest son,

William Sydenham, m. Martha, daughter of John Michel, esq. but *d.* without surviving issue in 1718.

IV. Walter, the younger, to whom his eldest brother, Walter, grants the manor and advowson of Ashbrittle, in tail male, to revert in failure to his own.

V. Henry.

VI. George, who was archdeacon of Salisbury, and chaplain to HENRY VII. and HENRY VIII. He was buried at Salisbury in 1523.

I. Joan, *m.* to John St. Barbe, esq. of Ashington.

II. Alice, *m.* to John Buller, esq. of Cillsdon.

He was *s.* by his eldest son,

WALTER SYDENHAM, esq. of Brimpton, who *m.* Margaret, daughter of Sir Robert Harcourt, knt. and had, with a daughter, Dorothy, wife of Laurence Courtenay, esq. of Enthie, in Cornwall, a son and successor,

JOHN SYDENHAM, esq. of Brimpton, who *m.* first, Elizabeth, daughter of Sir Humphrey Audley, knt; and secondly, a daughter of Arundel, of Lanherne. By the former he had two sons, namely,

JOHN (Sir), his heir.

Thomas, of Whetstow.*

He was *s.* by his elder son,

SIR JOHN SYDENHAM, knt. of Brimpton, who *m.* Giles, daughter of Sir Giles Brydges, knt. and sister of the first Lord Chandos, by whom he had issue,

JOHN (Sir), his heir.

George (Sir), of Combe Sydenham, *m.* Elizabeth, daughter and co-heir of Sir Christopher Hales, knt. and had an only daughter,

ELIZABETH SYDENHAM, *m.* first, to the famous Sir Francis Drake; and secondly, to William Courtenay, esq. of Powderham.

John, of Hatch Bishop, in Somersetshire.

Elizabeth, *m.* to Richard Bampfield, esq. of Poltimore, in Devonshire.

Anne, *m.* to Alexander Sydenham, esq. of Luxborough.

Mary, *m.* to John Fits, esq. of Fitsford, in Devonshire.

The eldest son,

SIR JOHN SYDENHAM, knt. *m.* first, Grace, daughter and co-heir of Sir William Godolphin, knt. of Godolphin, in Cornwall; and secondly, Mary Blunt: by the former he had a daughter, Ursula, wife of Points, of Acton Points, in Gloucestershire, and a son, his successor,

SIR JOHN SYDENHAM, knt. of Brimpton, who *m.* first, Mary, daughter and co-heir of John Buckland, esq. of Westharptree, in Somersetshire (who after his death married the Lord Grey); and secondly, Mary, daughter of Sir Thomas Guilford, knt. By the former he had, with a daughter, Frances, wife of Edward Paston, esq. of Horton, in Gloucestershire, three sons, viz.

George, died in the lifetime of his father, *s. p. anno* 1615.

JOHN, heir to his father.

Ralph (Sir), M.P. in 1641, followed the king to Oxford, was after the Restoration made master of the Charter House, and died in 1671. He *m.* the widow of Sir Arthur Chichester, knt. and had one son,

John, who *m.* Jane, daughter and co-heir of Alexander Portrey, esq. and had surviving issue, John, and a daughter, the wife of John Bowdage, esq. of Devon.

Sir John Sydenham was served as sheriff for Nottingham, and died in 1625, when he was *s.* by his elder surviving son,

JOHN SYDENHAM, esq. who *m.* Alice, daughter of William Hoby, esq. of Hales, in Gloucestershire, and sister and heir of Sir William Hoby, knt. and had issue,

JOHN, his heir.

George, a major in the king's army, who died in 1664-5. He *m.* first, Susan, daughter and co-heir of John Sydenham, esq. of Combe, and by that lady had a son, George, who *d.* an infant. He *m.* secondly, Elizabeth, daughter of — Gilbert, esq. of South Hams, in Devonshire, and had a daughter, Susan, who *d.* unm. in [illegible]

Mary.

Katherine.

The elder son and heir,

I. JOHN SYDENHAM, esq. of Brimpton, in the county of Somerset, was created a BARONET 28th July, 1641. Sir John *m.* in 1638, Anne, second daughter of Sir John Hare, of Stow Bardolph, in Norfolk, and dying in 1642, was *s.* by his son,

II. SIR JOHN-POSTHUMUS SYDENHAM, M.P. for the county of Somerset, *temp.* CHARLES II. This gentleman *m.* first, Elizabeth, daughter of John, Lord Poulett, but by her had no surviving issue. He married secondly, Lady Mary Herbert, daughter of Philip, Earl of Pembroke and Montgomery, and had by her ladyship,

John, who predeceased his father.

PHILIP, successor.

Mary, *d.* unm. in 1686.

He *d.* in 1696, aged fifty-four, and was *s.* by his only surviving son,

III. SIR PHILIP SYDENHAM, M.P. for the county of Somerset, who *d.* unmarried 10th October, 1739, aged sixty-three, when the BARONETCY EXPIRED.

Several estates of the family were sold by Sir John Posthumus Sydenham, the second, and by Sir Philip, the third baronet. Brimpton, however, continued in the family, devolving on Humphrey Sydenham, esq. of Combe, who *d.* 12th August, 1757. It was afterwards purchased by Mr. Fane, and is now the property of the Earl of Westmoreland.

Arms—Arg. three rams sa.

* THOMAS SYDENHAM, the second son, who settled at Whetstow, in the parish of Lawrence-Lydiard, in Somersetshire, *m.* Elizabeth, daughter of William Cross, of Charlynch, in the same county, and had issue,

THOMAS, his heir.

Simon, *m.* the daughter of — Cape.

Christopher.

The eldest son,

THOMAS SYDENHAM, esq. *m.* Dorothy, daughter of David Sellick, of Moorbath, in Devonshire, and had issue,

WALTER, his heir.

Thomas, who had two sons, Thomas and John.

John, of Moorbath, who *m.* Anne, daughter of John Byam, D.D and had surviving issue,

Walter, *m.* Agnes Combe, of Willand, and had issue.

William, *m.* and had several children.

Sarah.

George, of Poole, in Moorbath, *m.* Mary [illegible], of Bampton, and had three sons,

George, of New England.

Thomas.

Walter.

Margaret, *m.* to Isaac Mauduit, esq. of Exeter.

Elizabeth, *m.* first, to John Parsons, esq. of D[illegible]ton; and secondly, to George Peppin, esq.

Katherine, *m.* to — Melhuish.

Grace, *m.* to — Chorley.

The eldest son,

WALTER SYDENHAM, esq. *m.* Jane, daughter of [illegible] Fulford, and had three sons, WALTER, George, and Thomas, and one daughter, Jane, wife of Farthing, of Nettlecombe. The eldest son,

WALTER SYDENHAM, esq. of Whetstow, *m.* the daughter of Farthing, of Nettlecombe.

Sydenham of Combe.

Robert de Sydenham (son of Hugh Sydenham and ran Polleswell), m. Alice, co-heir of Roger Helyer, rd of Choburgle, and left two sons, Robert, the ther of another Robert, who *d. s. p.* 15 Henry VI. nd

John Sydenham, of Indecote, who m. Agnes, co-eir of Choboroughe, or Chubworth, and had two ns, both called John. The *younger* John and his ife, Alianor, had an annuity out of the manor of rborough, 13 Edward IV. The elder,

John Sydenham, marrying the heiress of Collyn Culmstock, in Devonshire, removed from Baddlen thither. He left three sons, Edward, his heir, homas, barrister-at-law, of the Temple, and John, ctor of Brushford, in Somersetshire. The eldest n,

Edward Sydenham, marrying Joan, daughter and eir of Walter Combe, of Combe, removed thither. le had issue,

John.

George, of Exter, from whom descended

Roger Sydenham, of Lee, in Somersetshire, who marrying a sister of the famous Dr. Thomas Sydenham, left a son,

Roger, who by Anne, daughter and co-heir of Sir Humphrey Sydenham, knt. of Chelworthy, left three sons, John-Roger, Philip, and Thomas.

he elder son,

John Sydenham, esq. of Combe, m. Elizabeth, ughter and co-heir of John Frank, of Allerbutler, Somersetshire, and had issue,

John, his heir.

Thomas, of Sterte, m. Radigunde Glass, and had two sons, John and Thomas.

Johanna, m. to William Huyshe, esq. of Doniforde.

Radigove.

Elizabeth, m. to Humphrey Cruse, esq.

e *d.* in 1561, and was *s.* by his elder son,

John Sydenham, esq. who married first, Elizabeth, ughter of Sir Hugh Pollard, and had a daughter, ho *d.* young. He m. secondly, Mary, daughter of cholas Ashford, esq. of Ashford, in Devonshire, and y that lady had

Humphrey, his successor.

Amos.

Thomas.

George, m. in 1593, Abignell, daughter of Samford of Ninehead.

Agnes.

Jane.

Margaret, m. in 1567, to William Champneys, esq.

Elizabeth, Joan, Anne, I reale, } *d.* unm.

Susan, m. to Martin Samford, esq. of Ninehead.

e *d.* in 1596, and was *s.* by his eldest son,

Humphrey Sydenham, esq. of Combe, who m. rst, Jane, daughter of John Champneys, esq. of arnscombe, and by her had

I. John, his successor, m. Margery, daughter of Sir Anthony Poulet, and sister of John, Lord Poulet, by whom he had four surviving daughters, viz.

Anne, married to Captain Thomas Tyllesley, governor of Surinam.

Margaret, m. to the Rev. Thomas Slater, of Currymallet.

Susan, m. to Major George Sydenham, brother of Sir John Sydenham, bart. of Brimpton.

Elizabeth, m. to Thomas Collford, esq. of Bromfield, in Somersetshire.

II. Roger, of the Middle Temple, m. Joan Catford, a widow.

III. Humphrey, in holy orders, continuator of the family.

IV. William, m. Margaret, daughter of — Cudmore, and *d.* in 1669, *s. p.*

V. Hugh, *d.* unm.

I. Mary, *d.* unm.

II. Penelope, m. to John Walrond, esq. of Bradfield.

He m. secondly, Jane, widow of — Godolphin, esq. of Treveneigh, in Cornwall, and by her had three other sons, George, Gavregan, and Nicholas. His eldest son, John, succeeded him, but his male line failing, the representation devolved upon

Humphrey Sydenham, *Clerk*, styled for his eloquence *Silver Tongue* Sydenham. He was rector of Pockington and Oldcombe, in Somersetshire, and marrying Mary, daughter of William Cox, esq. of Crookhern, in the same county, had two sons and a daughter, viz.

Humphrey, his heir.

Edward, *d.* young in 1637.

Anne, m. to Francis Thomas, esq.

He was *s.* by his only surviving son,

Humphrey Sydenham, esq. of Combe, who married Jane, daughter and co-heir of Sir William Pole, knt. of Shute,* eldest son of Sir John Pole, bart. and had issue,

William, who predeceased him unm.

Humphrey, his heir.

John, of Dulverton, m. first, Margaret, daughter of William Butler, esq. of Oldacre, in Durham; and secondly, Margaret, daughter of — Galard.

Jane, m. to John Williams, eldest son of John Williams, esq. of Herringston, in Dorsetshire.

Mr. Sydenham was *s.* by his elder surviving son,

Humphrey Sydenham, esq. who m. first, Elizabeth, daughter of George Peppin, esq. of Dulverton, and by her had three sons and one surviving daughter, viz.

Humphrey, his successor.

George.

Philip, who *d.* young.

Elizabeth, m. to Laurence Jackson, B.D. of Ardleigh, in Essex.

He married secondly, Katherine, daughter of William Floyer, esq. of Berne, in Dorsetshire, and had another son, Floyer. He *d.* in 1710, and was *s.* by his eldest son,

Humphrey Sydenham, esq. of Coombe, devisee of Sir John St. Barbe, bart. This gentleman wedded Grace, daughter of Richard Hill, esq. of the Priory, in Devonshire, and was *s.* by his only son,

St. Barbe Sydenham, esq. of Coombe, who married Ellery, daughter of Sydenham Williams, esq. of Herringston, in Dorsetshire, and left an only child,

Catherine Sydenham, m. in 1761, Lewis-Dimoke Grosvenor Tregonwell, esq. of Anderson, in Dorsetshire, and had a son, the present (1837)

St. Barbe Tregonwell, esq. of Anderson.

The estate of Combe is now possessed by the Rev. John Sydenham.

* By Catherine, his wife, daughter of Henry St. Barbe, esq. of Ashington and Broadlands.

SYLYARD, OF DELAWARE.

CREATED 18th June, 1661.

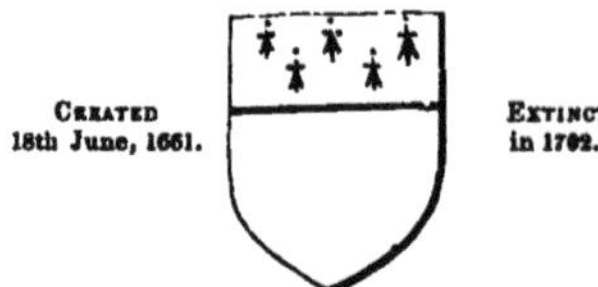

EXTINCT in 1702.

Lineage.

From

JOHN SEYLIARD, of Seyliard in Hever, Kent (who acquired, *temp.* HENRY IV. the estate of Delaware, in the same county, in marriage with Elenora, only daughter and heir of William Paulin, esq.), lineally descended,

I. JOHN SYLYARD, esq. of Delaware, who was created a BARONET 18th June, 1661. He died about 1670, leaving by Mary Glover, his wife, a son and successor,

II. SIR THOMAS SYLYAYD, of Delaware, who *m.* first, Frances, daughter of Sir Francis Wyatt, knt. of Bexley; and secondly, Margaret, daughter of Philip, Lord Wharton, and relict of Major Dunch, of Pusey, Berks. He died in 1692, and was *s.* by his son,

III. SIR THOMAS SYLYARD, of Delaware, who alienated that estate about the year 1700 to Henry Streatfeild, esq. of Chidingstone. Sir Thomas *m.* Elizabeth, daughter and heir of Sir Sandys Fortescue, of Fallapit, in the county of Devon, and dying in 1701, left a son and successor,

IV. SIR THOMAS SYLYARD, at whose decease in infancy the following year the title became EXTINCT.

Arms—Az. a chief erm.

SYMONS, OF THE MYNDE.

CREATED 23rd May, 1774.

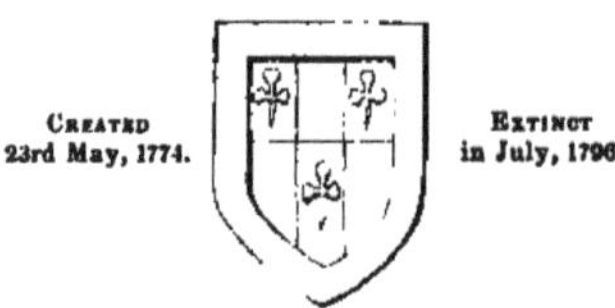

EXTINCT in July, 1796.

Lineage.

RICHARD SYMONS, citizen of London, who purchased the Mynde estate, in Herefordshire, about the year 1740, had one son, JOHN, and two daughters, ELIZABETH and ANNA SOPHIA, upon whom he entailed the estate in strict settlement directing that each person who inherited should adopt the surname and arms of Symons. John and Elizabeth (*m.* to Mr. Justice Clive) both died *s. p.* The other daughter,

ANNA SOPHIA SYMONS, wedded Richard Peers, citizen of London, and had issue,

RICHARD PEERS, her heir.

Elizabeth Peers, *m.* Sir Charles Blunt, bart. of London, and had, with other issue, a son, the present SIR CHARLES WILLIAM BLUNT, bart.

The only son,

I. RICHARD PEERS, esq. who inherited the Mynde estate, and assumed the surname of SYMONS, was created a BARONET 23rd May, 1774; but died unm. in 1796, when the title became EXTINCT. The property devolved at Sir Richard's decease upon THOMAS RAYMOND, esq. grandson of Ann (youngest sister of Richard Symons, the testator), by her husband, Philip Hampton, esq. of Boseley, in Gloucestershire, and son of Mary (daughter of Philip and Ann Hampton), who *m.* William Raymond, esq. of Thornbury,

THOMAS RAYMOND, upon succeeding to the estate in 1796, assumed the surname and arms of Symons. He *m.* Mary Chapman, and left sons, THOMAS-HAMPTON, Richard Harcourt, Charles-Frederick-Raymond, and Mary Ann Jane. He died in 1818, and was *s.* by his son,

THOMAS HAMPTON SYMONS, of the Mynde Park, who *m.* Elizabeth, second daughter of the Rev. Dr. Hannington, prebendary of Hereford, and died 22nd January, 1831, leaving issue,

THOMAS-GEORGE SYMONS, now of the Mynde Park, *b.* 25th October, 18[illegible].

Henry-Longden Symons, *b.* 24th September, 1829.

Elizabeth-Fanny.

Ellen-Jane.

Mary-Anne-Brookland.

Arms—Per fesse sa. and arg. a pale counterchanged three trefoils slipped or, two and one, within a bordure all counterchanged.

TARLETON.

CREATED 6th Nov. 1818.

EXTINCT in Jan. 18[illegible].

Lineage.

EDWARD TARLETON, of Church Hill, Liverpool, descended from the old Lancashire family of Tarleton of Aigburth, an alderman of that borough, and mayor in 1682, *m.* Anne, daughter of Henry Coles, an alderman also of Liverpool, and mayor in 1661, and had issue. He *d.* in 1690, and his grandson (it is presumed)

JOHN TARLETON, born in 1719, an alderman of Liverpool, and mayor in 1764, repurchased the old family seat of Aigburth. He *m.* 25th June, 17[illegible], Jane, eldest daughter of Bannastre Parker, esq. and by her, who *d.* 23rd May, 1797, had issue,

I. WILLIAM, who *d.* 9th June, 1778.

II. THOMAS, *b.* 6th July, 1753, *m.* Mary, daughter of Lawrence Robinson, esq. of Clitheroe, in Lancashire.

III. BANNASTRE.

IV. John, of Finch House, in Lancashire, *b.* [illegible] October, 1755, *m.* 26th October, 1790, Isabella, second daughter and co-heir of James Collingwood, esq. of Unthank, in Northumberland, and had a son,

John-Collingwood, *b.* 23rd October, 1792, of Collingwood Hall, Northumberland.

v. Layton, b. 5th September, 1763, mayor of Liverpool in 1792, m. 25th April, 1795, Jemima, eldest daughter and co-heir of Thomas Robinson, M.D. of Liverpool, but by her (who d. 4th December, 1796, had no issue.

i. Bridget, m. 23rd October, 1781, to Edward Falkner, esq. and had issue.

he third son,

i Banastre Tarleton, esq. b. 21st August, 1754, general officer in the army, colonel of the 21st ight Dragoons, and a grand cross of the Bath, was vated a Baronet 6th November, 1818. General arleton represented his native town some time in arliament. He married 17th December, 1798, Susanrcilla, natural daughter of Robert Bertie, fourth uke of Ancaster, but died in January, 1833, without sue, when the Baronetcy expired.

Arms—Gules, a chevron erminois between three nquefoils or.

TAYLOR, OF PARK HOUSE.

Created ...th Jan. 1664.

Extinct in 1720.

Lineage.

John Taylor, of Shadockhurst, in the county of ..., the descendant of an ancient family in that unty (see Burke's *Commoners*, vol. iv. p. 237), Thomasine, daughter of John Isaac, of Sevington, d by her, who d. in 1551, had issue,

William, his heir, of Romney, m. Mary, daughter of Richard Taylor, and d. in 1571. His only son,

John Taylor, of Thurnham, married Anne, daughter and heir of Henry Brockhill, of Allington, and left two sons,

Brockhill, living in Ireland in 1619, had two daughters, his co-heirs, viz.

Elizabeth Taylor, m. to Humphrey Perrott.

Jane Taylor.

Thomas, of Ballyhaise, in the county of Cavan, living in 1619, who had a son, Brockhill, who died 1636, leaving a daughter, Mary, married to Thomas Newburgh, of Ballyhaise.

Barbara.

Thomassine, m. to John Davy, of Udymere, Sussex.

Mary.

John.

Joane, d. unm. 1573.

Margaret, m. to Giles Collins, gent. of Hythe.

Alice, m. to John Stringer, gent. of Old Romney, and left an only daughter, Susan, m. in 1601, to Sir Edward Scott, K.B. of Scottshall, and had issue.

Elizabeth.

..n Taylor d. in 1551. His younger son,

John Taylor, esq. lord of the manor of Shadochurst, m. first, Elizabeth, daughter of Philip Chute, esq. of Bethersden, and by that lady had surviving issue,

George, of Criels Court, who removed into Sussex. He married in 1591, Joane, daughter of Richard Burrow, esq. of Boughton, who died in 1602, leaving two sons, John and William, who both died issueless, and a daughter, Elizabeth, b. in 1602.

Matthew, ancestor of the branch of the family which settled in America, and which is now represented by Major Pringle Taylor, of Pennington House, in the county of Hants. (See Burke's *Commoners*, vol. iv. p. 237.)

Susan, b. in 1560, m. to Godwin Freebody, of Sussex.

Philippa, } d. unm.
Eve, }

He m. secondly, Bridget, daughter of Richard Buck, of Rye, and had four other children, viz.

Thomas.

John, of Momfords, m. Anne, daughter and coheir of William Austen, esq. of Goodhurst, by whom (who d. in 1623) he had

John, of Winchelsea, who married Elizabeth, daughter of the Rev. Henry Amy, of Hawkins, in the county of Kent.

John, d. s. p.

Anne, m. to William Whitfield, of Patricksbourne, gent.

Elizabeth, m. to Thomas Roberts, esq. nephew of Sir Thomas Roberts, bart.

Anne, d. s. p.

Mary, m. to Walter Bustian, son of Wigan Bustian, of Shorne.

Mary, m. to Robert White, of Waltham, in Kent.

Elizabeth, m. to Thomas Broadnax, of Godmersham, in the same county, and had issue.

The elder son of the second marriage,

Thomas Taylor, esq. of Wilsborow, lord of the manor of Shadochurst in 1595, m. Agnes, daughter of Thomas Miller, esq. of Northfleet, and dying in 1611, left issue,

Thomas, his heir.

Jane, m. to John Chapman, gent. of Aythorne.

Maria, or Moravia, m. to Thomas Waller, of Penshurst, gent.

His only son,

Thomas Taylor, esq. of Wilsborow, of the king's body in ordinary, lord of the manor of Shadochurst, b. in 1595, m. first, Catherine, daughter of Sir Thomas Honywood, knt. of Elmested, and by her, who died in 1625, had

John, of Wilsborow, b. in 1622, d. s. p. in 1642.

Elizabeth, m. to Norton Halke, gent. of Bircholt.

Mary, m. to Henry Johnson.

Katherine, m. to Boys Owen, gent.

He married secondly, Anne, daughter of Sir Thomas Hendley, knt. of Corshorne, in Kent, and died in 1631. By his second wife he left a son,

i. Thomas Taylor, esq. of Gray's Inn, London, and of Park House, in Maidstone, in Kent, lord of the manor of Shadochurst, b. in 1630, who was created a Baronet 18th January, 1664-5. Sir Thomas m. Elizabeth, daughter and sole heir of George Hall, esq. of Maidstone, and by her (who wedded secondly, Percy Goring, esq. fourth son of Sir William Goring, bart. of Cockham and Burton, in the county of Sussex, and d. in 1696) had surviving issue,

Thomas, his heir.

Elizabeth, b. in 1656.

He *d.* in 1665, and was *s.* by his son,

II. SIR THOMAS TAYLOR, *b.* 19th August, 1657, who *m.* Alicia, sister and heir of Sir Thomas Culpeper, of Preston Hall, Aylesford, in Kent, and by her (who wedded secondly, Thomas Colepepyr, esq. of the Middle Temple, and thirdly, John Milner, esq. he left at his decease, in 1696, a son and successor,

III. SIR THOMAS TAYLOR, *b.* in 1693, who *d.* unm. in 1720, when the BARONETCY became EXTINCT.

Arms—Arg. on a chief sa. two boars' heads couped of the field.

TAYLOR, OF LYSSON HALL, IN JAMAICA.

CREATED 1st. Sept. 1778.

EXTINCT 18th May, 1815.

Lineage.

I. JOHN TAYLOR, esq. F.R.S. of Lysson Hall, in the Island of Jamaica, was created a BARONET, 1st September, 1778. Sir John *m.* Elizabeth-Gooden, daughter and heir of Philip Houghton, esq. of the same island, and dying in 1788, was *s.* by his son,

II. SIR SIMON-RICHARD-BRISSETT TAYLOR, who died *s. p.* 18th May, 1815, when the BARONETCY EXPIRED.

Arms—Arg. a saltire sa. between two human hearts in chief and in base, and two cinquefoils vert in the other quarters.

TEMPEST, OF STELLA.

CREATED 23rd Dec. 1622.

EXTINCT 31st May, 1742.

Lineage.

The family of Tempest has been seated for centuries in the counties of York and Durham, and many of its members held places of great trust upon the Scottish border, in the time of the EDWARDS and the HENRYS.

ROGER TEMPEST, lord of the manor of Bracewell, Yorkshire, *temp.* HENRY I. was witness to several charters cited in the Monasticon. His son,

RICHARD TEMPEST, of Bracewell, living 18th STEPHEN was father of

ROGER TEMPEST, of Bracewell, who paid half a mark into the treasury, *temp.* HENRY II. He was *s.* by his son,

RICHARD TEMPEST, of Bracewell, who in the reign of HENRY III. gave the advowson of that place to the monks of Kirkstall. His son,

JOHN TEMPEST, of Bracewell, was father of

SIR ROGER TEMPEST, knt. of Bracewell, who *m.* in the reign of EDWARD I. Alice, daughter and heir of Walter de Waddington, Lord of Waddington, and was *s.* by his son,

RICHARD TEMPEST, of Bracewell, who died in 12[illegible] leaving two sons, JOHN, his heir; and Richard (Sir), knt. governor of Berwick-upon-Tweed. The elder,

JOHN TEMPEST, of Bracewell and Waddington joined the confederacy under Thomas Plantagenet, Earl of Lancaster, that subverted Piers Gaveston's Power. He *m.* Mary, daughter of Sir Hugh Clitheroe, knt. and had issue,

- JOHN (Sir), knt. of Bracewell, ancestor of the TEMPESTS of Bracewell, of Tong, and of Broughton, all in Yorkshire.
- RICHARD (Sir), knt. of whose descendants we have to treat.

The younger son,

SIR RICHARD TEMPEST, knt. *m.* Isabel, only daughter and heir of Sir John Grass, knt. of Studley, and relict of Sir Hugh Clitheroe, by whom he had a son

SIR WILLIAM TEMPEST, knt. of Studley, M.P. for the county of York, 2 HENRY IV. He *m.* Eleanor, daughter and heir of Sir William Washington, knt. of Washington, and by her, who died in 1451, had two sons, namely,

- WILLIAM, of Studley, who died in 1444, leaving two daughters, his co-heirs, namely,
  - ISABELLA, *m.* to Richard Norton, esq. of Norton Conyers, Yorkshire.
  - DIONYSIA, *m.* to William Mallorie, esq. to whom she conveyed the manor of Studley. From this marriage descends the present MRS. LAWRENCE, of Studley.
- ROWLAND (Sir), of whom we have to treat.

The second son,

SIR ROWLAND TEMPEST, knt. acquired by gift of Sir Robert Umfraville, the estate of Holmside, and in the 18th HENRY VI. obtained lands from his brother, Sir William Tempest, of Studley. He *m.* Isabella, daughter and co-heir of Sir William Elmdon, knt. by Elizabeth, his wife, sister and co-heir of Gilbert Umfraville, and was father of

ROBERT TEMPEST, esq.* who *m.* Anne, daughter of Lambton, of Lambton, in the county of Durham, and was *s.* by his son,

NICHOLAS TEMPEST, esq. who *m.* Agnes, daughter of John Marley, of Gibside, and dying in 15[illegible], left a son,

THOMAS TEMPEST, esq. who *m.* Elizabeth, daughter of Rowland Place, esq. of Halnaby, in the county of York, and was father of

I. NICHOLAS TEMPEST, esq. of Stella, in the county of Durham, who was created a BARONET in 1622. He *m.* Isabel, daughter of Robert Lambton, esq. of Lambton, and had issue,

- THOMAS, his heir.
- William, } who both *d. s. p.*
- Henry, }
- Isabel, *m.* to Sir Bertram Bulmer.
- Elizabeth, *m.* to Christopher Athye, esq.
- Jane, *m.* to Thomas Chaytor, esq. of Butterby, in the county of Durham, ancestor of the present Sir William Chaytor, bart. of Croft.
- Margaret, *m.* to Gilbert Errington, esq.

* From Robert Tempest, who *m.* the daughter of Lambton, also descended the TEMPESTS, of Holmeside, [illegible] brook, Brancepeth, Wynyard, &c.

Sir Nicholas died 26th March, 1626, aged seventy-three, and was *s.* by his son,

II. Sir Thomas Tempest, of Stella, who *m.* Troth, daughter of Sir Richard Tempest, knt. of Bracewell and Bolling, by Elizabeth, his wife, daughter of Sir Francis Rodes, knt. one of the judges of the Common Pleas, and had issue,

Richard, his heir.
Nicholas, of Halliwell, who *m.* Margaret, daughter of William Swinburne, esq. of Capheaton, in Northumberland, and had an only daughter,
Troth, *m.* to John Witham, esq. of Cliffe.
Thomas, who *m.* Jane, daughter of Sir Jordan Metham, knt. of Metham, in Yorkshire, and had three sons,
Thomas, *d. s. p.*
Richard, *d. s. p.*
Nicholas, who *s.* his cousin, Sir Francis Tempest, as sixth baronet.
Isabel, *m.* to John Swinburne, esq. of Capheaton, in Northumberland.
Troth, *m.* to John Kennet, esq. of Coxhow, in Durham.
Catherine, *m.* to Bryan Salvin, esq. of Butterby, son of Gerard Salvin, esq. of Croxdale, in the county of Durham.
Mary, *m.* to John, son and heir of Sir Nicholas Thornton, knt. of Witton, in Northumberland.

Sir Thomas died in August, 1641, and was *s.* by his son,

III. Sir Richard Tempest, of Stella, col. of a regiment of horse in the service of Charles I. He *m.* Sarah, daughter of Sir Thomas Cambell, knt. lord mayor of London, and dying in 1662, was *s.* by his son,

IV. Sir Thomas Tempest, of Stella, who *m.* Alice, second daughter and co-heir of William Hodgson, esq. of Hebburn, in the county of Durham, by Margaret, his wife, daughter of Sir Thomas Haggerston, bart. of Haggerston, and had issue,

Francis, his heir.
Jane, *m.* to William, Lord Widdrington.
Troth, died young.

Sir Thomas died in 1692, aged fifty, and was *s.* by his son,

V. Sir Francis Tempest, of Stella, who died unm. in 1698, when the estates devolved on his sister, Lady Widdrington, and the title passed to his cousin,

VI. Sir Nicholas Tempest, then in an impoverished condition, who was allowed an annuity of £240, by Lord Widdrington. He *m.* Anne, daughter of Mr. [illegible], but died *s. p.* 31st May, 1742, aged seventy-eight, when the Baronetcy became extinct.

Arms—Arg. a bend engr. between six martlets sa.

TEMPEST, OF TONG.

Created 25th May, 1664.—Extinct 29th Jan. 1819.

Lineage.

The Tempests were of rank in the county of York at a very remote era, and during the sway of the Plantagenets, were frequently entrusted with high commands upon the Scottish border. The pedigree is so amply set forth under Tempest of Broughton, at page 474, and Plumbe-Tempest, page 286, in the first volume of Burke's *History of the Commoners*, that for the early descents we shall refer to that work, and commence the family before us, with the person who acquired Tong Hall, by which designation his descendant was eventually raised to a baronetcy.

Henry Tempest, esq. eighth son of Sir Richard Tempest, knt. of Bracewell, in the county of York, by Rosamond, daughter and heir of Tristram Bolling, esq. of Bolling Hall, in the same county, married Ellinor, daughter and heir of Christopher Mirfield, esq. of Tong Hall, also in Yorkshire,* and thereby acquired the lordship of Tong. He *d.* in 1591, and was *s.* by his son,

Richard Tempest, esq. of Tong Hall, who married Elizabeth, daughter and co-heir of Thomas Savile, esq. of Overthorpe, and dying in 1607, was succeeded by his son,

Richard Tempest, esq. of Tong Hall, who married Alice, daughter of William Mauliverer, esq. of Arncliffe, and was *s.* in 1612, by his son,

John Tempest, esq. of Tong Hall. This gentleman married Katherine, daughter of Robert Duckinfield, esq. of Duckinfield, in the county palatine of Chester, and left at his decease in 1623, a son and heir,

Henry Tempest, esq. of Tong Hall, elected M.P. for the county of York in 1654 and 1656. He married Mary, daughter of Nicholas Bushall, esq. of Bagdall Hall, and dying in 1657, was *s.* by his son,

I. John Tempest, esq. of Tong Hall, who was created a Baronet 25th May, 1664. He married Henrietta-Catharina, daughter and heir of Sir Henry Cholmley, knt. of Newton Grange, in the county of York, and had issue,

Henry, of Newton Grange, in right of his mother, at the decease of that lady in 1680, *m.* Alathea, daughter of Sir Henry Thompson, of Marston, in Yorkshire, and had two daughters, who both died unm. He *d.* in 1683, before his father.
George, who became heir at the decease of his brother.
Catherine, *d.* unm.
Henrietta, *m.* to Ferdinando Latus, esq.

Sir John Tempest, who at the decease of Richard Tempest, esq. of Bracewell, without male issue, in 1657, became chief of the family, was *s.* at his decease by his only surviving son,

II. Sir George Tempest, who married Anne, daughter and heir of Edward Frank, esq. of Campsal, in the county of York, and by that lady (who *d.* in 1746) had three sons, namely,

Henry, his heir.
Nicholas, *m.* Miss Galley, of Newcastle, but *d. s. p.* in 1756.
John, of Nottingham, capt. in Churchill's dragoons, *m.* Elizabeth, fourth daughter of William Scrimshire, esq. of Cotgrave, Notts, and had issue,
John, major in the horse guards, *d.* unm. in 1786.

---

* Richard de Tong held the manor of Tong in 1194 of Hugh Nevile, of Brearley, as lord of the fee, and it [illegible] in his family until the reign of Henry VI. [illegible]
Hugh de Tong, left an only daughter and heiress,
Margaret de Tong, who conveyed the lordship of Tong to her husband, Robert, son and heir of William Mirfield, esq. of Howley Hall, in the county of York. The great-grandson of this marriage,
Christopher Mirfield, esq. of Tong Hall, *m.* Elizabeth, daughter of Arthur Pilkington, esq. of Bradley, and left at his decease, in 1557, an only daughter and heiress,
Ellinor Mirfield, who *m.* Henry Tempest. Burke's *Commoners*.

Elizabeth, of whom hereafter.

Anne, m. to the Rev. Nathan Haines, D.D. vicar of St. Mary's Nottingham, and died in 1811, leaving an only child,

Nathan-Tempest Haines, who d. at Lambeth in 1837, s. p.

Henrietta, d. unm. in 1823.

Sir George died in 1745, and was succeeded by his eldest son,

III. Sir Henry Tempest, who married Maria, eldest daughter of Francis Holmes, esq. of Wegston, in the county of Leicester, and dying 3rd November, 1753, was s. by his only son,

IV. Sir Henry Tempest, who married Sarah-Pritchard, only child of Henry Lambert, esq. of Hope End, in Herefordshire, and thus acquired that estate. Sir Henry d. 29th January, 1819, when the Baronetcy expired. The estate of Tong, with the representation of the family devolved upon his cousin,

Elizabeth Tempest, who wedded Thomas Plumbe, son and heir of William Plumbe, esq. of Wavertree Hall, and of Aughton, both in the county of Lancaster, and had a numerous family, of whom, her eldest son and heir, having assumed the additional surname and arms of Temple, is the present (1838)

John Plumbe-Tempest, esq. of Tong Hall, Yorkshire, and of Aughton, in Lancashire, colonel of the first royal Lancashire militia.

Arms—As Tempest of Stella.

TEMPLE, OF SHEEN.

Created 31st Jan. 1665-6.

Extinct in Jan. 1699.

Lineage.

I. Sir William Temple, (elder brother of Sir John Temple, speaker of the Irish House of Commons, ancestor of the Viscounts Palmerston,) had a reversionary grant, after his father's decease, of the Mastership of the Rolls. He was created a Baronet 31st January, 1665, and sworn of the privy council. Sir William established a very high reputation for learning and abilities, and his writings on various subjects are greatly esteemed. He m. Dorothy, second daughter of Sir Peter Osborn, and had an only son,

Peter, who married a French lady, and left two daughters,

Elizabeth, m. to John Temple, esq. of Moor Park.

Dorothy, m. to Nicholas Bacon, esq. of Shrubland Hall.

Sir William Temple d. in January, 1699, when the title became extinct.

Arms—Arg. two bars sa. each charged with three martlets or.

TENCH, OF LOW LEYTON.

Created 8th Aug. 1715.

Extinct 2nd June, 1737.

Lineage.

I. Fisher Tench, esq. of Low Leyton, in Essex, only surviving son of Nathaniel Tench, esq. of Low Leyton, who died 2nd April, 1710, aged seventy-eight, served the office of sheriff of Essex in 1712, and was created a Baronet 8th August, 1715. He married Elizabeth, daughter of Robert Bird, esq. and had issue,

Nathaniel, his heir.

Jane, married to Adam Soresby, esq. of Chesterfield, in Derbyshire, but died s. p. 16th May, 1752.

Sir Fisher d. 31st October, 1736, aged sixty-three, and was s. by his son,

II. Sir Nathaniel Tench, of Low Leyton, at whose decease unm. 2nd June, 1737, aged forty, the Baronetcy became extinct.

Arms—Arg. on a chev. between three lions' heads erased, gu. a cross crosslet or.

THOMAS, OF MITCHELSTOWN.

Created 3rd March, 1641-2.—Extinct ....

Lineage.

I. Edward Thomas, esq. of Mitchelstown, in the county of Glamorgan, was created a Baronet 3rd March, 1641-2. He m. Susan, daughter of Sir Thomas Morgan, knt. of Ruperra, and dying in 1673, was s. by his son,

II. Sir Edward Thomas, of whom, or of his descendants (if he had any) we have not ascertained any particulars.

THOMAS, OF FOLKINGTON.

Created 23rd July, 1660.

Extinct 13th Nov. 1703.

Lineage.

I. William Thomas, esq. of Folkington, in Sussex, married Barbara, daughter and heir of Sir Herbert Springett, bart. of the Broyle, in Sussex, and was created a Baronet in 1660. He died, however, without issue in 1706, aged sixty-five, when the title expired.

Arms—Sa. a chev. and canton erm.

THOMPSON, OF HAVERSHAM.

CREATED 19th Dec. 1673.  EXTINCT 11th April, 1745.

Lineage.

I. JOHN THOMPSON, esq. of Haversham, in the county of Bucks, son of Maurice Thompson, esq. of Haversham, and descended from Maurice Thompson, esq. of 'heston, Herts, was created a BARONET 12th December, 1673. Sir John was a leading member of the House of Commons, and having devoted himself zealously in the promotion of the Revolution, was raised o the peerage as BARON HAVERSHAM, in 1696. He married first, Lady Frances Annesley, daughter of Arthur, first Earl of Anglesey, and widow of John Wyndham, esq. of Fellbrigge, by whom he had issue,

MAURICE, his successor.
George, *d. s. p.*
Helena, *m.* to the Rev. Thomas Gregory, rector of Toddington, Bedfordshire, and had a son,
John Wentworth Nazianzen Gregory, who *m.* Frances, daughter of Capt. Allen, R.N. and had an only daughter and heir,
Frances-Annesley Gregory, *m.* to Robert Austen, esq. of Shalford, in Surrey, and was mother of the present Sir Henry Edmund Austen, of Shalford.
Elizabeth, *m.* to Joseph Granger, esq.
Mary, *m.* to Arthur Annesley, fifth Earl of Anglesey.
Frances, *m.* to Thomas Armstrong, esq. a captain in the army, sixth son of Edmund Armstrong, esq. of Stonestown, in the King's County, and had issue.
Martha, *m.* to Sir John Every, bart.
Catherine, *m.* to Mr. White.
Dorothy, *m.* to Capt. Beckford.
Altharina, *m.* to Mr. Priaux.

His lordship married secondly, Martha Grahme, a widow lady, but had no other issue. He *d.* 22nd May, 1709, and was *s.* by his elder son,

II. SIR MAURICE THOMPSON, second Lord Haversham,* colonel in the guards, and officer of distinction, *m.* first, Elizabeth, daughter and heir of John Smith, esq. of Hertfordshire, and by her had two daughters, namely,

I. ELIZABETH, *m.* 19th May, 1724, to John Carter, esq. of Weston Colvile, in Cambridgeshire, and had issue,
JOHN CARTER-POLLARD, who died at Paris, *s. p.* in 1806.
Anne Sophia, who *d.* unm. in June, 1797.
ELIZABETH, who *m.* General Hall, of Wratting Park, Cambridgeshire, colonel of the 3rd regiment of foot, and died at her house of Weston Colvile, 24th January, 1814, aged eighty-two, leaving issue,
JOHN HALL, esq. of Weston Colvile, who by his marriage with Miss Haylock, of Dullingham, has no issue.
Elizabeth-Anne Hall, who wedded John Morse, esq. of Sprowston Hall, Norfolk, and has issue,
John-Hall Morse, living *s. p.*
Elizabeth-Anne-Ella Morse, *m.* to Simon Digby, esq. of Osbertstown, descended from the ennobled branch of the great house of Digby, and has issue. (See BURKE's *Commoners*, vol. iv.)

II. ANNE, *m.* to Richard Reynolds, esq. son of Dr. Richard Reynolds, bishop of Lincoln, and *d. s. p.* in 1737.

His lordship married secondly, Elizabeth, widow of William Green, esq. and sister of Richard Annesley, fifth Earl of Anglesey, but by her had no issue. He *d.* 11th April, 1745, when his honours, BARONY and BARONETCY EXPIRED.

Arms—Or, on a fesse dancetté az. three estoiles arg. on a canton of the second, the sun in glory, ppr.

THORNHILL, OF OLLANTIGH AND BARBADOES.

CREATED 14th Dec. 1682.  EXTINCT ....

Lineage.

I. SIR TIMOTHY THORNHILL, of Barbadoes, descended from the Thornhills of Ollantigh, in Kent, a family long settled in that country, was created a BARONET 14th December, 1682, but as he had no issue by his wife, Miss Barrett, the title EXPIRED with him.

Arms—Gu. two bars gemelles, arg. a bend of the last, on a chief of the second, a tower arg.

THORNHURST, OF AGNES COURT.

CREATED 12th Nov. 1622.  EXTINCT 16th Dec. 1627.

Lineage.

In the 23rd year of HENRY VIII. Stephen Thornhurst was possessed of leasehold property at Aghne, or Agnes Court, Kent, which passed to his descendant,

I. GIFFORD THORNHURST, esq. of Agnes Court, who was created a BARONET in 1622. He married Susan, daughter of Sir Alexander Temple, knt. but died without male issue, 16th December, 1627, when the title became EXTINCT.

Arms—Erm. on a chief gu. two leopards' heads arg.

---

* In early life, his lordship was one of the pages to Sophia, Electress of Hanover. He subsequently served as a volunteer in *King* WILLIAM's army, and for his singular gallantry at the siege of Namur, was rewarded by a company in the guards. At a late period, he declined the offer, made him by Sir Robert Walpole, to continue the peerage in the female line, not choosing to vote against the whig principles of his family.

THORNICROFT, OF MILCOMBE.

CREATED 12th Aug. 1701. EXTINCT 23rd June, 1743.

Lineage.

This was a younger branch of the family of THORNYCROFT, of Thornycroft, in Macclesfield Hundred, in Cheshire.

JOHN THORNYCROFT, esq. barrister-at-law, second brother of Edward Thornycroft, esq. of Thornycroft, d. 25th September, 1687, aged seventy-one, leaving by Dorothy, his wife, daughter of Sir John Howel, knt. a son and heir,

I. JOHN THORNICROFT, esq. of Milcombe, in the county of Oxford, who was created a BARONET 12th August, 1701.* He married Elizabeth, daughter and heir of Josiah Key, gent. of Milcombe, and had issue,

- JOHN, his heir, b. in 1691.
- ELIZABETH, m. to Roger-Peter Handasyd, esq. of Gains, in the county of Huntingdon, M.P. for the town of the same name, brigadier-general in the army, and colonel of a regiment of foot.
- Dorothy, d. unm.

Sir John d. 8th December, 1725, and was s. by his son,

II. SIR JOHN THORNICROFT, who married Terceira, daughter of Andrew Bonnell, merchant, but d. without issue, 23rd June, 1743, aged fifty-two, when the BARONETCY EXPIRED.

Arms—Vert, a mascle or, between four cross crosslets argent.

THOROLD, OF HARMESTON.

CREATED 9th Sept. 1709. EXTINCT 1st Jan. 1738.

Lineage.

The family of THOROLD, which the present SIR JOHN CHARLES THOROLD, bart. of Marston, in the county of Lincoln, represents in the senior branch, is one of great antiquity in that county, and has had at different times four baronetcies conferred upon it, of which one alone remains, three others having become extinct.

SIR RICHARD THOROLD, knt. of Selby,† in the county of York, living 42 EDWARD III. married Joan, daughter and heir of Robert de Hough, of Marston, in the county of Lincoln, (son of Alexander de Hough, by Maud, daughter of Michael, and sister and co-heir of Robert de Marston,) and was s. by his son,

JOHN THOROLD, of Selby, and of Marston, living 1 RICHARD II. who married the daughter of William Morfield, and left a son and heir,

RICHARD THOROLD, of Marston, living 16 HENRY VI. who by Isabel, daughter of Ralph Birnand, of Knaresborough, in the county of York, had a son and heir,

WILLIAM THOROLD, living 13th EDWARD IV. married Joan, daughter and heir of William Brerehaugh, of Selby, and by her (who re-married 22 EDWARD IV. Ralph Malhome,) had a son,

JOHN THOROLD, of Marston, and of Westburgh, living 12 HENRY VII. married Alice, daughter of Thomas Staunton, esq. of Staunton, in the county of Nottingham, and issue,

- WILLIAM, his heir.
- Jane, m. first to Robert Winter, esq. of Swineshed, and secondly to Richard Arnold, esq. of Colby, both in Lincolnshire.

His son and heir,

WILLIAM THOROLD, Lord of Marston and Blankney, in the county of Lincoln, was sheriff of that county in the 5th and 6th of PHILIP and MARY, and part of the first of *Queen* ELIZABETH, and died 28th November, 1569. He married first, Dorothy, daughter of Thomas Leeke, esq. of Hallom, in the county of Nottingham, and by that lady had

- ANTHONY (Sir), his heir, ancestor of the THOROLDS of Marston, now represented by SIR JOHN CHARLES THOROLD, bart.
- WILLIAM.
- RICHARD, of Morton, in the county of *Lincoln*.
- Alice, m. first to Thomas Pell, esq. of Barleston, and secondly to — Porter, of Siston, in Lincolnshire.

He married secondly, Margaret, daughter of Sir Robert Hussey, knt. of Halton, in Lincolnshire, and widow of Henry Sutton, esq. of Wallenger, in the same county. By her he had two other sons, viz.

- Edmond (Sir), of the High Hall, in Hough, who m. Eleanor, eldest daughter and co-heir of William Audley,‡ gent. of the Hough, in the county of Lincoln, and his line terminated with
  - Sir William Thorold, of Hough, knighted by *King* CHARLES II. who m. Anne, daughter of Sir Charles Dallison, knt. serjeant-at-law, and d. s. p. in 1666.

---

* SIR JOHN THORNYCROFT, soon after his creation, delivered the following petition to the lords of the Treasury, whereby he obtained a privy seal pursuant to his request.

To the Rt. Hon. the Lords Commissioners of his Majesty's Treasury.

The humble Petition of Sir John Thornicroft, of Milcomb, in the county of Oxon, Bart.

Sheweth,

That his Majesty having been graciously pleased to confer the dignity of a Baronet of this Kingdom upon your Petitioner, and the heirs male of his body, by letters patent dated 12th day of August, last past; and there being the sum of one thousand ninety-five pounds payable to his Majesty, in respect of that dignity,

Your Petitioner humbly prays your Lordships, that a privy seal may be granted to him, in order to his being discharged from the said sum of one thousand ninety-five pounds, as is usual in the like cases, and your Petitioner shall ever pray, &c.

† This SIR RICHARD THOROLD, in an old parchment pedigree of the family, drawn up in or about 1648, is made to be the first who bore for his arms, "Sable, three goats salient, argent;" before Sir Richard, the coat was, "Barry of six, argent and sable, on a canton sable, a martlet or."

‡ By Jane, his wife, daughter and sole heir of Alexander Haugh, esq. of the Haugh.

Robert, of the Low Hall, in Hough, m. Agnes, second daughter and co-heir of William Audley, of Hough, which lady married secondly, Augustine Earle, esq. of Straglethorpe.

e second son of the first marriage,

William Thorold, obtained from his father, about : time of Edward IV. the lands of Harmeston, in) county of Lincoln. He was also of the city of adon, where he married Margaret, daughter and ir of Mr. Baldock, citizen of London, and had two ns,

William, m. Rose, daughter of Rowland Sherrard, esq. of Lobthorpe, in the county of Lincoln, but *d. s. p.*

Thomas, who continued the line.

e younger son,

Thomas Thorold, esq. of Harmeston, married first, becca, daughter of Thomas Green, of the city of ndon, and by her had one surviving son, Charles. : married secondly, Prudence, daughter of Mathew :dell, also of London, and had Matthew and Elizath. The son and heir,

Charles Thorold, esq. of Harmeston and the city London, of which city he was chosen sheriff, and ed for alderman. He married first, Anne, daughter William Wheat, esq. of Glympton, in Oxfordshire, d had one son, Thomas, who died at Smyrna, unarried. He married secondly, Anne, daughter of r. George Clarke, of the city of London, and by that ly had surviving issue,

Charles (Sir), received the honour of knighthood 5th April, 1704, and in 1706 served the office of sheriff for London. He was likewise alderman of cordwainers ward, where he died 1st April, 1709, unm. and was buried with his father at St. Andrews Undershaft.

George (Sir).

Samuel, who *s.* his brother George.

e second son of the second marriage,

i. Sir George Thorold, of Harmeston, received e honour of knighthood 16th May, 1708, and on Midmmer-day, 1710, was elected sheriff of London, hav- previously succeeded his brother as alderman. He s created a Baronet by Queen Anne, 9th September, 1709, with remainder, default of male issue, to his other, Samuel. Sir George was Lord Mayor in the morable year 1720. He married Elizabeth, daughr of Sir James Rushout, bart. of Northwick, in the unty of Worcester, but died *s. p.* 29th October, 1722, hen the baronetcy devolved, according to the limitan, upon his brother,

ii. Sir Samuel Thorold, who *d.* issueless, 1st of nuary, 1738, when the title became extinct.

Arms—Sable, three salient goats argent.

THOROLD, OF HARMESTON.

Created 24th May, 1741.—Extinct in 1764.

Lineage.

This was a branch of the family of Thorold, of Marsn.

William Thorold, Lord of Marston and Blankney, it by his first wife, Dorothy, daughter of Thomas -ke, esq. of Hallom, Notts, three sons, viz.

Anthony (Sir), his heir.

William, of Harmeston, whose line ceased with Sir Samuel Thorold, bart. of Harmeston, in 1738.

Richard, of Morton.

The third son,

Richard Thorold, esq. of Morton, in the county of Lincoln, a captain in the low countries, m. first, Jane, only daughter of Robert Coney, esq. of Morton, and secondly, Elisabeth, daughter of Richard Coney, esq. of Bassingthorpe, in the same county. By the latter he had no issue, by the former he had,

i. John, his heir.

ii. Thomas, rector of Cathorp, in Lincolnshire, living in 1634, m. Elizabeth, daughter of Lion Ellis, of the city of London, and sister of Sir William Ellis, knt. by whom he had two sons and three daughters, viz.

1. Timothy, M.D. of Fulbeck, m. Elizabeth, daughter of Gabriel Savile, of Newton, in the county of Lincoln, and had issue,
   - William, *d.* unm. in 1663.
   - Elizabeth, m. to — Thornhill, } co-heirs.
   - Margaret, } co-heirs.
   - Mary, m. to Anthony Williams, gent. of Swarby, } co-heirs.
2. William.

1. Jane, m. to William Thompson, esq of Wroxham, in the county of Lincoln.
2. Anne, m. to Thomas Savile, esq. of Newton.
3. Elizabeth, m. first to — Longlands, of Carlthorpe, and secondly to Thomas Tunstal.

iii. Edmund, marshal of the Exchequer, m. Mary, daughter of John Reeve, of London, and had issue,

1. Nathaniel, marshal of the Exchequer.
2. Richard.
3. Simon, of London.

1. Elizabeth, m. to the Rev. William Burgh, D.D. rector of St. Michael, Cornhill.

iv. Daniel.

He *d.* in 1609, and was *s.* by his eldest son,

John Thorold, esq. of Morton, who m. first, Elizabeth, daughter and heir of John Burgh, esq. of Saltfleetby, in the county of Lincoln, by whom he had

Nathaniel, of Grantham.

Joseph, } *d. s. p.*
William, } *d. s. p.*

Elizabeth, m. to Walter Brockett, esq. of Brockett Hall, in the county of Hertford.

Anne.

He m. secondly, Jane, daughter of Edward Ellis, esq. of Chesterton, in Cambridgeshire, and had Edmund, of Friston, in Lincolnshire, Anne, the wife of — Walsall, and other daughters. His eldest son,

Nathaniel Thorold, esq. of Grantham, in the county of Lincoln, and of Gray's Inn, in Middlesex, m. Anne, daughter of George Lascels, esq. of Elston, Notts, and had two sons,

Richard, his heir, who m. Dorothy, daughter of Mr. Wort, citizen of London, and by her (who remarried Mr. Perkins,) left at his decease, in 1665, a son,

Nathaniel, of Grantham, living in 1667.

Eubulus, *b.* in 1627.

He *d.* in 1665. His younger son,

Eubulus Thorold, esq. married first, Elizabeth, daughter of Doctor Barbor, of Lincoln, by whom he had no issue. He married secondly, Mary, daughter of — Hodgskin, of Barston, in the same county, and by that lady left a son,

John Thorold, esq. who married Anne, daughter of John Alcock, gent. of the county of Lincoln, and left a son,

I. NATHANIEL THOROLD, esq. who it would appear inherited the estate of Harmeston, at the decease of his kinsman, Sir Samuel Thorold, in 1738, and was created a BARONET 24th March, 1741. Sir Nathaniel *d.* unm. at Naples, in August, 1764, when the BARONETCY EXPIRED.

Arms—As THOROLD OF HARMESTON.

THOROLD, OF THE HAUGH.

CREATED 14th June, 1644.—EXTINCT 2nd Dec. 1706.

Lineage.

WILLIAM THOROLD, lord of the manor of Marston and Blankney, in the county of Lincoln, married for his second wife, Margaret, daughter of Sir Robert Hussey, knt. of Halton, and by her had two sons, EDWARD (Sir), of the High Hall, and ROBERT, of the Low Hall. The younger,

ROBERT THOROLD, esq. of the Low Hall, in the county of Lincoln, married Agnes, second daughter and heir of William Audley, esq. of the Haugh,* by whom (who married secondly, Augustine Earle, esq. of Straglethorpe,) he had a son and heir,

ANTHONY THOROLD, esq. of the Haugh, who married Catherine, daughter of Edward Haselwood, esq. of Maidwell, in Northamptonshire, and was *s.* by his son,

I. ROBERT THOROLD, esq. of the Haugh, who was created a BARONET 14th June, 1644. Sir Robert married first, Anne, daughter of Henry, and sister of Sir Henry Carvil, knt. of St. Mary's, in Norfolk, but by that lady had no issue. He wedded, secondly, the Honourable Katherine Roper, daughter of Christopher, Lord Teynham, and was *s.* by his son,

II. SIR ROBERT THOROLD, who married Catherine, daughter of Sir Henry Knollys, of Grove Place, Hants, and dying about 1695, was *s.* by his son,

III. SIR ROBERT THOROLD, who *d. s. p.* 30th November, 1706, when the BARONETCY EXPIRED.

Arms—As THOROLD OF HARMESTON.

THROCKMORTON, OF TORTWORTH.

CREATED 29th June, 1611. EXTINCT June, 1682.

Lineage.

THROCKEMERTONA, THROCKMORTON, or the ROCKMOOR TOWN, from whence the family of Throckmorton obtained its name, is situated in the vale of Evesham, in the parish of Fladbury, anciently written Flandenburgh, in Pershire hundred, county of Worcester, a manor containing two hamlets, Hull, *alias* Hill, and Moor.

JOHN THROCKMORTON, was lord of the said manor, about sixty years after the Conquest, A. D. 112[illegible], which leaves little room to doubt that the family possessed it, at the entrance of the Normans, or long before, the etymology of the name being either British or Saxon; from this John we pass to his descendant, another

JOHN THROCKMORTON, Lord of Throckmorton, in 13 EDWARD III. *anno* 1339, who had in marriage Agnes or Anne, daughter and heir of Sir Richard Abberbury, of Abberbury, in the county of Oxford, and was *s.* by his son,

THOMAS THROCKMORTON, who was of the retinue of Thomas Beauchamp, Earl of Warwick, in 20 RICHARD II. was escheator of Worcestershire in 3 HENRY IV. and in the 6th of the same king, constable of Elmley Castle. He *m.* Agnes Besford, an heiress, and left a son and heir,

JOHN THROCKMORTON, who made a distinguished figure in the times of HENRY V. and HENRY VI. in the latter reign he bore the title of Under Treasurer of England. He made his will at London, 12th April, 23 HENRY VI. which date it bears, and bequeathed his body to be buried in the parish church of St. John the Baptist, at Fladbury, appointing that his executors should provide a marble stone, of such largeness as might cover as well the graves of his father and mother as his own, and his wife's, in case she should determine to repose there. Of this testament he appoints Rauf Boleter, Lord Sudley, then Treasurer of England, his overseer. He died in the same year, as appears by the probate, leaving Eleanor, his wife, surviving, who was daughter and co-heir of Sir Guy de Spineto, Lord of Coughton, in the county of Warwick:† by this lady he had issue,

- THOMAS, his heir, ancestor of the present Sir CHARLES THROCKMORTON, bart. of Coughton Court.
- JOHN.
- Eleanor, *m.* to Richard Knightly, esq. of Fawsley, in the county of Northampton.
- Maud, *m.* to Sir Thomas Greene, of Norton, in the same county.
- Margaret, *m.* to John Rous, esq.
- Agnes, *m.* to John Winslow, esq.
- Elizabeth, *m.* to Robert Russell, esq.

The younger son,

JOHN THROCKMORTON, esq. became proprietor of a fair estate in Gloucestershire, by marriage with Isabel, daughter and co-heir of Edward Bruges, esq. of Lane, in that county, and dying in 1436, was *s.* by his son,

JOHN THROCKMORTON, esq. who *m.* first, Anne, daughter of Thomas Scargill; and secondly, a daughter of — Nanfan. By the first wife he had a son,

CHRISTOPHER THROCKMORTON, esq. who was sheriff of Gloucestershire in 5 HENRY VII. He *m.* a daughter of Sir John Harley, of Herefordshire, and was *s.* by his eldest son,

WILLIAM THROCKMORTON, esq. sheriff of Gloucestershire in 21 HENRY VIII. *m.* Margaret, daughter and co-heir of Sir David Matthew, knt. of Rayder, and thus acquired the manor of Totworth. He had three sons and three daughters, from Anthony, the second son, descended the Throckmortons, of Cheston, in Hertfordshire. The eldest son and heir,

SIR THOMAS THROCKMORTON, knt. was sheriff of Gloucestershire in 5 PHILIP and MARY, and resid[illegible]

* By Jane, his wife, daughter and sole heir of Alexander Haugh, esq. of the Haugh.

† Whose father, WILLIAM, held notable employments, in Warwickshire, in *temp.* EDWARD II. and was grandson of another,

WILLIAM DE SPINETO, who *m.* Idonea, daughter of Sir Simon de Cocton, knt. the lineal heir male of Ralph, and of William de Cocton, lord of the manor of Coughton, before the reign of HENRY II.

Cess Court, in that county. He m. Margaret, one of the six daughters and co-heirs of Thomas Whittington, esq. of Pauntley. He d. in 1586, leaving two sons and two daughters, one the wife of Sir John Tracey, knt. of Toddington. His elder son and heir, Sir Thomas Throckmorton, knt. sheriff of Gloucestershire 39 and 43 Elizabeth, and died in 1607. He married two wives, Elizabeth, daughter of Sir Richard Berkeley, and a daughter of Sir Edward Rogers; by the former he left a son and heir,

I. Sir William Throckmorton, of Totworth, in the county of Gloucester, who was knighted by *King* James I. and created a Baronet by the same prince, 1st June, 1611. He m. first, Cicely, daughter and co-heir of Thomas Baynham, esq. of Clowerwall, in Gloucestershire, with whom he had that manor, and had, with other issue,

Baynham, his successor.
Nicholas, (Sir), whose son,
William, inherited as fourth baronet.

He m. secondly, Miss Alice Morgan; and thirdly, Miss Sarah Hale. Sir William was s. at his decease by his son,

II. Sir Baynham Throckmorton, who made his residence at Clowerwall. He m. Margaret, daughter of Robert Hopton, esq. and sister and co-heir of Ralph, Lord Hopton. He d. 28th May, 1664, and was s. by his son,

III. Sir Baynham Throckmorton, who m. first, Mary, daughter and heir of Giles Garton, esq. of Billinghurst, in Sussex, by whom he had a daughter, m. to Captain Grimshaw. Sir Baynham m. secondly, Catharine, daughter of Piers Edgecumbe, esq. of Mount Edgecumbe, in Devonshire, and had another daughter, Katherine, m. to Thomas Wyld, esq. M. P. for the city of Worcester, and a commissioner of the revenue in Ireland. Sir Baynham was s. in the title by his cousin,

IV. Sir William Throckmorton, who fell in a duel in June, 1682, and as he d. s. p. the Baronetcy became extinct.

Arms—Gules, on a chevron argent, three bars gemels sa.

TICHBORNE, OF BEAULIEU.

Created 12th July, 1697.

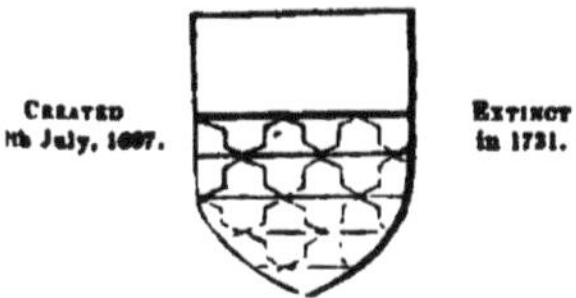

Extinct in 1731.

Lineage.

This branch of the ancient family of Tichborne, of Tichborne, of which the senior line exists, in the person of Sir Henry-Joseph Tichborne, bart. of Tichborne Park, Hants, (see Burke's *Peerage* and *Baronetage*), was founded by

Sir Henry Tichborne, knt. fourth son of Sir Benjamin Tichborne, first baronet, of Tichborne, an eminent soldier, distinguished in Ireland *temp.* James I. and his ill fated son, Charles. Sir Henry was born in 1581, and acquired his military education in the Low countries. *King* James gave him the command of an independent company of foot, in Ireland, and constituted him governor of the Castle of Lifford, after which the same king conferred upon him the honour of knighthood, at his late father's seat, at Tichborne, 29th August, 1623. He was colonel of a regiment of foot, at the breaking out of the rebellion in Ireland of 1641, and being then esteemed the best officer in that kingdom, was appointed with his own regiment of 1000 men, Sir Thomas Lucas's troops of horse, to secure the town of Drogheda, and to be governor thereof. Sir Henry arrived at Drogheda on the 4th November, 1641, and subsequently defended the place with great bravery and success. He afterwards obtained several advantages over the rebels, and, on the 12th May, 1642, was appointed one of the lords justices of Ireland, in the room of Sir William Parsons. Of his appointment to this high office, Lord Clarendon says, "Sir Harry Tichborne, being a man of so excellent a fame, that though the parliament was heartily angry at the removal of the other, and knew this would never be brought to serve their turn, yet they had nothing to object against him." Sir Henry continued one of the lords justices, until the Marquiss of Ormonde was sworn lord lieutenant, and was afterwards appointed by the king, field marshal of the forces in Ireland; which honourable post he held till his death, A. D. 1667, when he was buried at Drogheda, with his wife, Jane, daughter of Sir Robert Newcomen, bart. who lived with him many years, and died about 1664. They had five sons and three daughters, viz.

Benjamin, captain of horse, in the service of Charles I. killed by the rebels in the twenty-first year of his age.
William, heir to his father.
Richard, major of horse, *temp.* Charles II. and James II. d. unm.
Henry, } d. unm.
Samuel, }
Dorcas, m. to William Toxteth, esq. of Drogheda, a native of Lancashire.
Amphilis, m. to Richard Broughton, esq. major of the foot guards in Ireland, *temp.* Charles II.
Elizabeth, m. to Roger West, esq. of the Rock, in the county of Wicklow.

The eldest surviving son,

Sir William Tichborne, of Beaulieu, in the county of Louth, in Ireland, received the honour of knighthood from *King* Charles II. He m. Judith, daughter and co-heir of John Bysse, esq. lord chief baron of the exchequer in Ireland, and had, with a daughter, Margaret, married to Stephen Stanley, esq. of Grange Gorman, in the county of Dublin, six sons, viz.

Henry, his heir.
Benjamin, killed in the thirty-ninth year of his age, at the battle of Hockstet, anno 1704. He m. Elizabeth, daughter of Major Edward Gibbs, of the city of Gloucester, and left three daughters, whereof Judith m. first, Charles, Earl of Sunderland; and secondly, Sir Robert Sutton, K. B.
William, captain in the sea service, *temp.* William III. was cast away off Plymouth in 1692, aged twenty-three, and d. unm.
John, colonel of his majesty's forces, and governor of Athlowe.
Richard, M. A. of Trinity College, Dublin, and sometime of Magdalen, Oxford, d. unm. in 1692, aged twenty-one.
Bysse, captain of foot, lost his life in the defence of Gibraltar, anno 1704.

He was s. by his eldest son,

I. Sir Henry Tichborne, of Beaulieu, in the county of Louth, b. in 1663, who for his services in the revolution was knighted by *King* William in 1694, and created a Baronet 12th July, 1697. Sir Henry was ennobled by *King* George I. who advanced him to the peerage of Ireland, as Baron Ferrard, of Beaulieu, 26th September, 1715. He *m.* Arabella, daughter of Sir Robert Cotton, of Combermere, in the county of Chester, and had issue,

Henry, *b.* 20th April, 1694; *m.* Mary, daughter and heir of John Fowke, esq. of Atherdee, and coming to England in the year 1769, was unfortunately cast away in the bay of Liverpool, leaving his wife *enceinte*, who was delivered of a daughter, Elizabeth, who *d.* young.

William, *m.* Charlotte-Amelia, second daughter of Robert, Viscount Molesworth, but *d. s. p.*

Salisbury, *m.* to William Aston ... of Louth.

His lordship *d.* in 1731, when his h... and Baronetage became extinct.

Arms—Vaire, a chief, or.

TIPPING, OF WHEA...

Created 24th Mar. 1697-8.

Lineage.

I. Thomas Tipping, esq. of Wheatfi... shire, who was created a Baronet in ... Anne, daughter of Thomas Cheek, es... Essex, by Letitia, his wife, elder dau... length sole heir, of the Hon. Edward ... Earl of Bedford, and had issue,

Thomas, his heir.

Letitia, *m.* to Samuel, Lord Sandys, ...

Catherine, *m.* to Thomas, Lord A... berslade.

Sir Thomas died 1st July, 1718, and was ...

II. Sir Thomas Tipping, of Wheatfie... ried Mary, daughter and heir of Sir Joh... but *d. s. p.* 20th February, 1725, when th... became extinct.

Arms—Or, on a bend eng. vert three p... field.

TOLLEMACHE, OF HELMIN...

Created 22nd May, 1611. F... 9th M...

Lineage.

"Notwithstanding," says Collins, "Hugh Talmashe, who subscribed, about the reign of *King* Stephen, to the charter, *sans date*, of John de St. John made to Eve, the first Abbess of Godstow, in the county of Oxford, is the first of the family I meet with; yet without doubt, it has flourished from the time of the Conquest; and in Doomsday-book, Tedmag (as the name was then spelt) is said to possess lands."

Hugh de Talmashe, above mentioned, or another of the same name, took upon him in his old age, the habit of a monk, at Gloucester, and gave to the monastery a moiety of his town of Hampton, which

Peter de Talmashe, his son, confirmed in the time of Hamlin, the abbot; from Peter ...

... Jermyn, knt. of Rushbrook ... Suffolk.

I. Sir Lionel Tollemache, of Helmingham, high sheriff of Suffolk in 6 and 14 James I. was created a Baronet 22nd May, 1611. He *m.* Catherine, daughter ...

ter of Henry, second Lord Cromwell, and grand-daughter of John, Marquis of Winchester, and was *s.* by his son,

II. Sir Lionel Tollemache, who had received the honour of knighthood in the lifetime of his father, and represented the borough of Orford in parliament, in 18 James I. and 3 Charles I. He *m.* Elizabeth, daughter of John, Lord Stanhope, of Harrington, and had issue,

I. Lionel, his heir.

I. Elizabeth, *m.* to William, Lord Allington.

II. Catherine, *m.* to Sir Charles Mordant, bart.

III. Susannah, *m.* to Sir Henry Felton, bart.

IV. Anne, *m.* to Sir Robert Broke, of Nacton.

V. Jane, *m.* to Thomas Cholmondeley, esq. of Vale Royal.

VI. Bridget, *m.* to Sir Nicholas Bacon, knt. of Shrubland.

He *d.* 6th September, 1640, and was *s.* by his son,

III. Sir Lionel Tollemache, who *m.* Lady Elizabeth Murray, elder daughter and heir of William, first Earl of Dysart, who, upon the decease of that nobleman, became Countess of Dysart, and obtained from Charles II. in 1670, a confirmation of the dignity, with the privilege of nominating any one of her children, whom she pleased, her heir. Her ladyship, after the decease of Sir Lionel, *m.* John, Duke of Lauderdale, but had no child by the duke. Sir Lionel had issue,

Lionel, *Lord Huntingtower*, heir to his father and mother.

Thomas, a distinguished military officer, died of a wound received in action, anno 1694.

William, R. N.

Elizabeth, *m.* to Archibald, first Duke of Argyll, and *d.* in 1735.

Catherine, *m.* first, to James, Lord Down; and secondly, to John, fifteenth Earl of Sutherland.

Sir Lionel *d.* in 1669, and was *s.* by his eldest son,

IV. Sir Lionel Tollemache, Lord Huntingtower, who, at the decease of his mother, the Duchess of Lauderdale in 1697, became Earl of Dysart. He *m.* Grace, daughter and co-heir of Sir Thomas Wilbraham, bart. of Woodhey, in Cheshire, and had issue,

Lionel, Lord Huntingtower, who *m.* Miss Cavendish, and *d.* in 1712, leaving

Lionel, successor to his grandfather.

Henrietta, *m.* to John Clutterbuck, esq. of Mill Green, Essex.

Elizabeth, *m.* to Sir Robert Cotton, bart. and *d. s. p.*

Catherine, *m.* to John, Marquess of Carnarvon.

He *d.* 3rd February, 1726, and was *s.* by his grandson,

V. Sir Lionel Tollemache, third Earl of Dysart, K.T. who *m.* in 1729, Lady Grace Carteret, and had issue, for which refer to Burke's *Peerage* and *Baronetage*. He *d.* 10th March, 1770, and was *s.* by his eldest surviving son,

VI. Sir Lionel Tollemache, fourth Earl of Dysart, who *m.* first, Charlotte, illegitimate daughter of Sir Edward Walpole; and secondly, Magdelena, daughter of David Lewis, esq. of Malvern Hall, in the county of Warwick, but *d. s. p.* 22nd February, 1799, when the honours devolved upon his brother,

VII. Sir Wilbraham Tollemache, fifth Earl of Dysart. His lordship *m.* Anna-Maria, another daughter of the above mentioned David Lewis, but *d.* 9th March, 1821, without issue, when the Baronetcy expired, but his higher honours and estates devolved upon his only surviving sister,

Lady Louisa Manners, widow of John Manners, esq. of Grantham Grange, who then became Countess of Dysart, refer to Burke's *Peerage and Baronetage*.

Arms—Argent a fret, sa.

TOOKER, OF MADDINGTON.

Created 1st July, 1664. Extinct 17th March, 1675.

Lineage.

Charles Tooker, esq. of Maddington, in Wiltshire, son of John Tooker, and grandson of William Tooker, of Maddington, *m.* Maud Nipperhead, and had three sons,

Giles, his heir.

Thomas, who *m.* Alice, daughter of Nicholas Snow, esq. of Winterborne Stoke, Wilts, and had issue.

Charles, of Lincoln's Inn, and of Abingdon, Berks, married and had issue.

The eldest son,

Giles Tooker, esq. of Lincoln's Inn, and of Sarum, *m.* Elizabeth, daughter of Thomas Eyre, esq. of that place, and had two sons and a daughter, Edward; William; and Elizabeth, *m.* to William Chafin, esq. He *d.* in November, 1623, and was *s.* by his son,

Edward Tooker, esq. of Maddington and New Sarum, who *m.* Mary, fourth daughter of Sir John Hungerford, knt. of Doun Ampney, Gloucestershire, and relict of William Platt, esq. and had issue,

Giles, his heir.

Martha, *m.* to Sir Walter Ernle, of Echilhampton, Wilts.

Philippa, *m.* to Sir Thomas Gore, knt. of Barrow, in Somersetshire.

Edward Tooker *d.* in 1658, aged eighty-six, and was *s.* by his son,

I. Giles Tooker, esq. of Maddington, who was created a Baronet in 1664, but died without issue 17th March, 1675, when the title expired; his sisters were his co-heirs.

Arms—Vert on a bend engr. arg. three hearts, gu.

TOPP, OF TORMARTON.

Created 25th July, 1668. Extinct ....

Lineage.

John Topp, esq. of Stockton, Wilts, son of Thomas Topp, left with a daughter, Mary, wife of William Colbourne, gent. two sons,

John, of Stockton, who died in 1635. He was an-was ennobled by *King* George I. who advanced him to the peerage of Ireland, as Baron Ferrard, of Beaulieu, 26th September, 1715. He *m.* Arabella, daughter of Sir Robert Cotton, of Combermere, in the county of Chester, and had issue,

Henry, *b.* 20th April, 1684; *m.* Mary, daughter and heir of John Fowke, esq. of Atherdee, and coming to England in the year 1709, was unfortunately cast away in the bay of Liverpool, leaving his wife *enceinte*, who was delivered of a daughter, Elizabeth, who *d.* young.

William, *m.* Charlotte-Amelia, second daughter of Robert, Viscount Molesworth, but *d. s. p.*

Salisbury, *m.* to William Aston, esq. of the county of Louth.

His lordship *d.* in 1731, when his honours, the barony and Baronetage became extinct.

Arms—Vaire, a chief, or.

TIPPING, OF WHEATFIELD.

Created 24th Mar. 1697-8.

Extinct 20th Feb. 1725.

Lineage.

i. Thomas Tipping, esq. of Wheatfield, in Oxfordshire, who was created a Baronet in 1697-8, married Anne, daughter of Thomas Cheek, esq. of Pirgo, in Essex, by Letitia, his wife, elder daughter, and at length sole heir, of the Hon. Edward Russell, fourth Earl of Bedford, and had issue,

Thomas, his heir.

Letitia, *m.* to Samuel, Lord Sandys, of Ombersley.

Catherine, *m.* to Thomas, Lord Archer, of Umberslade.

Sir Thomas died 1st July, 1718, and was *s.* by his son,

ii. Sir Thomas Tipping, of Wheatfield, who married Mary, daughter and heir of Sir John Lear, bart. but *d. s. p.* 20th February, 1725, when the Baronetcy became extinct.

Arms—Or, on a bend sng. vert three pheons of the field.

TOLLEMACHE, OF HELMINGHAM.

Created 22nd May, 1611.

Extinct 9th March, 1821.

Lineage.

"Notwithstanding," says Collins, "Hugh Talmashe, who subscribed, about the reign of *King* Stephen, to the charter, *sans date*, of John de St. John made to Eve, the first Abbess of Godstow, in the county of Oxford, is the first of the family I meet with; yet without doubt, it has flourished from the time of the Conquest; and in Doomsday-book, Tow mag (as the name was then spelt) is said to possess lands."

Hugh de Talmashe, above mentioned, or another of the same name, took upon him in his old age, the habit of a monk, at Gloucester, and gave to the monastery a moiety of his town of Hampton, which

Peter de Talmashe, his son, confirmed in the time of Hamlin, the abbot; from Peter we pass to

Hugh de Talmashe, who, in 25 Edward I. [illegible] of the crown the manor of Bentley, and a part of the village of Aketon, in the county of Suffolk [illegible] knights' service.

William de Talmashe, was summoned amongst the knights of the counties of Norfolk and Suffolk, to attend the king at Berwick-upon-Tweed, with horse and arms for an expedition into Scotland.

Sir Peter Talmashe, was foreman of the jury [illegible] the case of John Hasting's claim of the stewardship [illegible] the liberty of St. Edmundsbury, in Suffolk, which was tried by inquisition, before the eschaetor, at the [illegible] of St. Edmunds, 30 Edward I.

John Talmashe held, in the time of Edward II. the said manor of Bentley from the crown by knight's service: at the same time, Catherine Talmashe, presumed to be his mother, held half a knight's fee in Bentley, *in capite*. From this John, who took the black cross, and whose arms were placed in York Minster, descended

Sir Lionel Tollemache, of Bentley, who flourished in the times of Henry VI. and Edward IV. He *m.* Anne, daughter and heir of Helmingham, of Helmingham, and thus acquired that inheritance, which became after the chief seat of his descendants. He was *s.* by his son,

John Tollemache, esq. who *m.* the daughter and heir of Roger Louth, of Sewtrey, in the county of Huntingdon, and had five sons and five daughters. He was *s.* by his eldest son,

Lionel Tollemache, esq. who was sheriff of Norfolk and Suffolk, in 4 Henry VIII. and in the [illegible] year of the same king, Richard Downes aliened to him the mansion, site, and precinct of the late dissolved monastery of Dognashe, with the manors of Dognashe and Charles, and divers other lands. In 36 Henry's the king granted him the manor of [illegible]den, with the rectory thereof, likewise the manor and rectory of Le Church Hey, and the manors of [illegible]hall, Wyllowe, and Overhall. He *m.* Edith, daughter and heir of — Joice, esq. of Creke Hall, in Helmingham, and dying before 7 Edward VI. was *s.* by his son,

Sir Lionel Tollemache, of Helmingham, who acquired large estates by purchase in the reign of Elizabeth. From which monarch he received the honour of knighthood, and the further honour of a royal visit to, and sojourn for four days, at Helmingham; during the queen's stay, she stood sponsor to her host's son and heir, and presented her lute on the occasion to his lady; the royal gift is still preserved in the family. Lady Tollemache was Dorothy, the daughter of Sir Richard Wentworth, of [illegible]. Sir Lionel *d.* 18 Elizabeth, and was *s.* by his son,

Sir Lionel Tollemache, knt. who was sheriff of Norfolk and Suffolk, in 34 Elizabeth. He *m.* [illegible] daughter of Sir Ambrose Jermyn, knt. of Rushbrook, in Suffolk.

i. Sir Lionel Tollemache, of Helmingham, [illegible] sheriff of Suffolk in 6 and 14 James I. was created a Baronet 22nd May, 1611. He *m.* Catherine, daughter

...er of Henry, second Lord Cromwell, and grand-daughter of John, Marquis of Winchester, and was s. by his son,

II. SIR LIONEL TOLLEMACHE, who had received the honour of knighthood in the lifetime of his father, and represented the borough of Orford in parliament, in 1 JAMES I. and 3 CHARLES I. He m. Elizabeth, daughter of John, Lord Stanhope, of Harrington, and had issue,

I. LIONEL, his heir.

I. Elizabeth, m. to William, Lord Allington.
II. Catherine, m. to Sir Charles Mordant, bart.
III. Susannah, m. to Sir Henry Felton, bart.
IV. Anne, m. to Sir Robert Broke, of Nacton.
V. Jane, m. to Thomas Cholmondeley, esq. of Vale Royal.
VI. Bridget, m. to Sir Nicholas Bacon, knt. of Shrubland.

He d. 6th September, 1640, and was s. by his son,

III. SIR LIONEL TOLLEMACHE, who m. Lady Elizabeth Murray, elder daughter and heir of William, first Earl of Dysart, who, upon the decease of that nobleman, became COUNTESS OF DYSART, and obtained from CHARLES II. in 1670, a confirmation of the dignity, with the privilege of nominating any one of her children, whom she pleased, her heir. ...

LADY LOUISA MANNERS, widow of John Manners, esq. of Grantham Grange, who then became COUNTESS OF DYSART, refer to BURKE'S *Peerage and Baronetage*.

Arms—Argent a fret, sa.

TOOKER, OF MADDINGTON.

CREATED 1st July, 1664.

EXTINCT 17th March, 1675.

Lineage.

CHARLES TOOKER, esq. of Maddington, in Wiltshire, son of John Tooker, and grandson of William Tooker, of Maddington, m. Maud Nipperhead, and had three ...

... heir.
... o m. Alice, daughter of Nicholas Snow, ... nterborne Stoke, Wilts, and had issue.
... Lincoln's Inn, and of Abingdon, Berks, ... nd had issue.

..., esq. of Lincoln's Inn, and of Sarum, ... daughter of Thomas Eyre, esq. of that ... two sons and a daughter, EDWARD; ... Elizabeth, m. to William Chafin, esq. ... ber, 1623, and was s. by his son,
... ER, esq. of Maddington and New Sa... ry, fourth daughter of Sir John Hun... Doun Ampney, Gloucestershire, and ... Platt, esq. and had issue,
... eir.
... to Sir Walter Ernle, of Echilhamp...
... to Sir Thomas Gore, knt. of Barrow, ... tshire.
... d. in 1666, aged eighty-six, and was

... ER, esq. of Maddington, who was cre... in 1664, but died without issue 17th ... n the title expired; his sisters were

... a bend engr. arg. three hearts, gu.

..., OF TORMARTON.

EXTINCT ....

Lineage.

... of Stockton, Wilts, son of Thomas ... daughter, Mary, wife of William ... wo sons,
... ton, who died in 1635. He was su...

cestor of the Topps, of Stockton, whose eventual heiress,

Susan Everard, (only daughter and heir of Robert Everard, esq. of Stowey, by Susan, daughter and heir of Edward Topp, esq. of Stockton,) m. Robert Everard Balch, esq. of St. Audries, Somersetshire, who sold Stockton to the father of Harry Biggs, esq. the present proprietor.

Alexander, who m. Elizabeth, eldest daughter of Thomas Lingen, esq. of Whitton, in Shropshire, and had a son,

Lingen, of Whitton, sheriff of Salop, 1679, ancestor of Topps, of Whitton.

Deriving from the same source as the Topps of Stockton, was

i. Francis Topp, esq. of Tormarton, in Gloucestershire, who was created a Baronet 25th July, 1668. He d. in 1676, leaving by Elizabeth, his wife, a son and successor,

ii. Sir John Topp, of Tormarton, who m. Barbara, daughter of Sir Walter St. John, bart. of Lydyard, Wilts, but died without male issue, when the Baronetcy became extinct.* Tormarton was inherited by Sir John Topp's daughter, St. John, m. first, to John Hungerford, esq. and secondly, to Thomas Peach, esq.

Arms—Arg. on a canton gu. a gauntlet clasped or.

TRACY, OF STANWAY.

Created 29th June, 1611.

Extinct in 1677.

Lineage.

The surname of Tracy accrued to this family from a maternal ancestor, descended from the Tracys, Lords of Barnstaple, in the county of Devon, who came in with the Conqueror, and were styled from the town of Traci, in Normandy.

Harold, according to Dugdale, the son of Ralph, Earl of Hereford, but by other authorities an illegitimate son of *King* Harold, possessed at the general survey, numerous lordships in England, amongst which were Sudley, and Todington, in the county of Gloucester, with the Castle of Ewyas, and other lands in Herefordshire, secured, doubtless, by his intermarriage with Maud, daughter of Hugh Lupus, Earl of Chester. This Harold had two sons,

John, his heir.

Robert, who had the Castle of Ewyas, and assumed therefrom the surname of Ewyas.

The elder son assuming his surname from Sudley, the chief seat which he inherited, became

John de Sudley. He m. the daughter and heir of Traci, feudal Lord of Barnstaple, and had issue,

Ralph, his successor, for whose descendants refer to Burke's *Extinct Peerage*.

William, who adopted his mother's name of Tracy.

The younger son,

William de Tracy,† lived in the reign of Henry II. and held lands of his brother, Ralph de Sudley, by one knight's fee, which was probably the manor of Todington, for it appears by Doomsday Book, that it was held by the Lord Sudley, of the manor of Sudley; and in the reign of Edward I. the Tracys are expressly said to be possessed of it, and this William, in a deed of Otwell, Lord of Sudley, son and heir of the said Ralph, is called his uncle; but that this is the same Sir William Tracy, who was concerned in the assassination of Thomas a Becket, does not appear, although Fuller, in his Worthies, makes the assassin to be Sir William Tracy, of Todington, whom he describes as "a man of high birth, state, of stomach, a favourite of the king's, and his daily attendant;" but, says Collins, "I am not of his opinion, and 'tis evident there were others of the same name living at the time." The son of this William,

Sir Oliver Tracy, is mentioned amongst the knights of Gloucestershire, that paid scutage in the second of *King* John, his son,

Sir William Tracy, is recorded among the knights of the same county, in the 17th Edward I. and with Ralph de Sudley, his kinsman, is stated to have had a command in the Scottish war. He left a son and heir,

Sir William Tracy, of Todington, who was in ward to Laurence Tresham, 27th Edward I. at which time he is certified to hold £40. lands. In the beginning of the reign of Edward II. he was at the tournament at Dunstable, as appears by an old drawing of a knight in armour, bearing a standard with the arms of the family. In the 17th of Edward II. he was jointly with John Bermansel, high sheriff of Gloucestershire, which office in those times was of great authority. He left a daughter, Margery, wife of John Archer, of Umberslade, and a son and heir,

Henry Tracy, whose son, another

Henry Tracy, was father of

Thomas Tracy, whose son and heir,

Sir John Tracy, was sheriff of Gloucestershire for five years in succession, beginning in 1363, 38 Edward III. He was knight of the same shire in the parliaments held at Westminster, in the 33, 37, 46, and [illegible] Edward III. and again sheriff in 1366. He left a son,

Henry Tracy, father of

John Tracy, of Todington, high sheriff in 1379, who left issue,

William Tracy, of Todington, high sheriff in [illegible]. His son and heir,

William Tracy, m. Alice, daughter and co-heir of Guy de la Spine. He was high sheriff 5 Henry V. and "one of those persons of quality in the county of Gloucester, who bearing ancient arms from his ancestors, and holding by tenure, had summons in the [illegible] Henry V. to serve the king in person for defence of the realm." He was s. by his son,

William Tracy, sheriff in the 22nd and 23rd Henry VI. who left his estate to a son of his own name, a fourth

William Tracy, who was sheriff in 1449, and commissioner to array soldiers in the same county (Gloucestershire,) in seven years afterwards. He m. Margery, daughter of Sir John Pauncefoot, and had two sons, Henry and Richard. The elder,

Henry Tracy, m. Alice, one of the daughters and

* Of this family was William Richard Topp, esq. captain 14th regiment. He m. Mary-Elizabeth, daughter and co-heir of Bowyer Leftwich Wynn, esq. and had issue. The elder of his two daughters, Elizabeth-Mary, m. 1st February, 1820, John Branston Freer, [illegible] Stratford-upon-Avon.

† This William and his posterity differenced their coat armour from the elder house of Sudley, by an escallop shell between the two bendlets.

co-heirs of Thomas Baldington, esq. of Adderbury, in the county of Oxford, and had three sons, WILLIAM, Richard, and Ralph, a monk. The eldest,

SIR WILLIAM TRACY, of Todington, was sheriff of Gloucestershire, in the 5th HENRY VIII. *anno* 1512. He was a gentleman of excellent parts and sound learning, and is memorable for being one of the first who embraced the reformed religion in England, as appears by his last will dated 22nd HENRY VIII. which was condemned in the Bishop of London's Court, after his decease, and an order sent to Parker, chancellor of Worcester, to raise his body; but he too officiously burning the corpse, the recorder only warranting him to raise the body according to the law of the church, he was afterwards fined £400, and turned out of the chancellorship. The will being rather of a curious nature and characteristic of the times, we insert an abstract from it at foot.* Sir William, *m.* Margaret, daughter of Sir Thomas Throckmorton, of Corse Court, in Gloucestershire, and had, with two daughters, three sons, viz.

WILLIAM, of Todington, ancestor of the VISCOUNTS TRACY, of *Ruthcoole, in Ireland*, whose heiress, the daughter of the eighth Viscount, *m.* CHARLES HANBURY, esq. who assumed the additional surname of TRACY.

The peerage is claimed by JAMES TRACY, esq. and the case is now before the House of Lords.

RICHARD.

Robert. *d. s. p.*

The second son,

RICHARD TRACY, esq. obtained from his father the manor of STANWAY, in the county of Gloucester, part of the lands of the Abbey of Tewksbury, which came to him by grant from the crown. "This Richard," says an old writer, "was well educated, and wrote learnedly of his father's faith several Treatises in the English tongue, and that most remarkable one, entitled *Preparations for the Cross*, written experimentally, having suffered much in his estate for his father's reputed heretical will: he also wrote *prophetically, anno* 1550, (few years before the beginning of Queen MARY,) another Treatise, *To teach one to die*, which is annexed to his '*Preparation to the Cross*,' which was reprinted, and falsely ascribed by the editor, to be composed by John Friths, being one of the three that was found in the belly of a cod brought into the market to be sold at Cambridge, A.D. 1626, wrapped about with canvas, very probably what that voracious fish plundered out of the pocket of some shipwrecked seaman." In the 2nd of ELIZABETH, he was sheriff of Gloucestershire, and having married Barbara, daughter of Thomas Lucy, esq. of Charlecote, had with three daughters, three sons, PAUL, Nathaniel, and Samuel. He was *s.* by the eldest,

I. PAUL TRACY, esq. of Stanway, in the county of Gloucester, high sheriff in the 20th of ELIZABETH, who was created a BARONET by *King* JAMES I. 29th June, 1611. Sir Paul *m.* Anne, daughter of Ralph Shakerley, esq. and had ten sons, and as many daughters, of whom

RICHARD (Sir), the eldest, succeeded his father.

Anne, *m.* Edward Hall, esq. of the county of Worcester.

Lucy, *m.* Ray Aylworth, esq. of Aylworth, in the county of Gloucester.

Alice.

Hesther, *m.* Francis, eldest son of John Kyrle, esq. of Much Marcle, in Herefordshire, and had a son,

Sir John Kyrle, (see KYRLE.)

Elizabeth.

Susan, *m.* to William Price, esq. of Winchester.

Barbara.

Margaret.

He *d.* about 1626, and was *s.* by his eldest son,

II. SIR RICHARD TRACY, who had received the honour of knighthood, in the lifetime of his father, and was sheriff of Gloucestershire, in the 4th of *Queen* MARY. He *m.* Anne, daughter of Sir Thomas Coningsby, of Hampton, in the county of Hereford, and had three sons, HUMPHREY, RICHARD, and JOHN. He *d.* about the year 1637, and was *s.* by the eldest,

III. SIR HUMPHREY TRACY, sheriff of Gloucestershire, in the 15th CHARLES I. who suffered severely for his loyalty during the rebellion, having had to pay to sequestrators £1600, for composition for his estate. He *d.* without issue in 1651, and was *s.* by his brother,

IV. SIR RICHARD TRACY, who likewise died *s. p.* and was *s.* about 1666, by his only surviving brother,

V. SIR JOHN TRACY, who *d.* issueless in 1677, when the BARONETCY EXPIRED. Sir John Tracy devised Stanway and his other estates to the *Honourable* FERDINANDO TRACY, second son of John, third Viscount Tracy, the descendant of WILLIAM TRACY, esq. of Todington, elder brother of RICHARD TRACY, esq. of Stanway, Sir John's grandfather; which Ferdinando *m.* the daughter of Sir Anthony Keck, knt. and was *s.* by his son,

JOHN TRACY, esq. of Stanway, who *m.* Anne, daughter of Sir Robert Atkins, lord chief baron of the Exchequer, and had four sons: Robert Tracy; John Tracy Keck; Anthony Tracy, (who

---

* "**In the name of God Amen.**" I William Tracy, of Todington, in the County of Gloucester, make my Testament and last Will, as hereafter followeth:

First and before all things I commit my self to God, and to his Mercy, believing, without any doubt or Mistrust, that by his Grace, and the Merits of JESUS CHRIST, and by the virtue of his Passion and Resurrection, I have, and shall have, Remission of all my Sins, and Resurrection of Body and Soul, according as it is written: "I believe that my Redeemer liveth, and that at the last day, I shall rise out of the Earth, and in my Flesh shall see my Saviour." This my hope is laid up in my bosom.

And touching the Wealth of my Soul, the Faith that I have taken and rehears'd, is sufficient, (as I suppose) without any other Man's Works or Merits. My Ground and Belief that there is but one God, and one Mediator between God and Man, which is JESUS CHRIST; so that I accept none in Heaven or in Earth, to be Mediator between me and God, but only JESUS CHRIST; all others to be but as Petitioners in receiving of Grace, but none able to give Influence of Grace; and therefore will I bestow no part of my goods for that Intent, that any man shall say or do to help my soul, for therein I trust only to the promises of Christ, "He that believeth, and is baptiz'd, shall be sav'd; and he that believeth not, shall be damned."

As touching the burying of my body, it availeth me not whatsoever be done thereto; for St. Augustine saith, *De Cura agenda pro Mortuis*, that the Funeral Pomps are rather the Solace of them that live, than the Wealth and Comfort of them that are dead, and therefore I remit it only to the discretion of my Executors.

And touching the distribution of my temporal Goods, my purpose is, by the Grace of God, to bestow them to be accepted as the Fruits of Faith; so that I do not suppose that my Merit shall be by the Good bestowing of them, but my Merit is the Faith of JESUS CHRIST only, by whom such Works are good; according to the words of our Lord: "I was hungry, and thou gavest me Meat, &c." And it followeth, "That ye have done to the least of my Brethren; ye have done it to me:" and ever we should consider the true saying, "That a good Work maketh not a good man, but a good man maketh a good work; for Faith maketh a man both good and righteous, for a righteous man liveth by Faith, and whatsoever springeth not of Faith, is Sin."

For my Temporal Goods, &c.

m. Lady Susan Hamilton, sister of James, Duke of Hamilton); and Thomas Tracy. The male line of this branch has become EXTINCT, and the property of Stanway is in the possession of the Earl of Wemyss, the grandson of Anthony Tracy.

Arms—Or, two bends, gules, in the chief point an escallop, sable.

TRESHAM, OF RUSHTON.

CREATED 29th June, 1611.

EXTINCT in 1650-1.

Lineage.

THOMAS TRESHAM, of Sywell, in the county of Northampton, m. the daughter and heir of Rempston, and was father of

SIR WILLIAM TRESHAM, knt. attorney-general to *King* HENRY V. who m. a daughter of William Vaux, of Harrowden, in Northamptonshire, and had two sons,

- THOMAS, his heir.
- Henry, of Newton, in Northamptonshire, which estate he acquired with Alice, his wife, daughter and co-heir of Sir Edward Mulsho, and was ancestor of the Treshams of Newton, of which line was Sir Thomas Tresham, knt. high sheriff of Northamptonshire, in the 8th of JAMES I.

He was *s.* by his elder son,

SIR THOMAS TRESHAM, who was comptroller of the household to *King* HENRY VI. and settled himself at Rushton, in Northamptonshire. He m. Margaret, daughter of the Lord Zouch, and was *s.* by his son,

JOHN TRESHAM, esq. of Livedon and Rushton, who m. Elizabeth, only daughter and heir of James Harrington, esq. of Hornby and Wolfage, and was *s.* by his son,

SIR THOMAS TRESHAM, who was high sheriff of Northamptonshire, in 16 and 31 HENRY VIII. and received the honour of knighthood in the interim. He m. the Honourable Mary Parr, youngest daughter and co-heir of William, Lord Parr, of Horton, and had issue,

- JOHN, who died in his father's lifetime, leaving by Eleanor, his wife, daughter of Anthony Catesby, esq. of Wishton, two sons and two daughters, viz.
  - THOMAS (Sir), heir to his grandfather.
  - William, whose son,
    - THOMAS (Sir), succeeded his uncle, Sir Thomas Tresham.
  - Muriel, m. to William, third Lord Vaux, of Harrowdon, (his second wife). See BURKE'S *Extinct Peerage.*)
  - ——, m. to George Walton, esq.

He was *s.* by his grandson,

SIR THOMAS TRESHAM, of Rushton, a gentleman of great influence in his county, who having zealously promoted the pretensions of *Queen* MARY to the throne, and assisted in proclaiming her majesty, was constituted high sheriff of Northamptonshire, in the 3rd and fourth years of her reign, and was constituted prior of the re-erected order of St. John of Jerusalem. As he died without issue, his lands descended to his nephew,

SIR THOMAS TRESHAM, who received the honour of knighthood from *Queen* ELIZABETH, on the 13th July, 1575, at Kenilworth, and is thus spoken of by Fuller. "Hard to say, whether greater his delight or skill in buildings, tho' more fortunate in beginning, than fortunate in finishing his fabrics, amongst which the market-house at Rothwell, adorned with the arms of the gentry of the county of Northampton, was highly commendable, who was zealous in the Romish Perswasion, which afterwards cost him a long confinement in Wisbich Castle." He married Muriel, daughter of Sir Robert Throckmorton, knt. of Coughton, in the county of Warwick, and had issue,

- FRANCIS (Sir).
- LEWIS, heir to his brother.
- William, m. the daughter of Reed, of Cotesbrook, in Northamptonshire.
- Frances, m. to Edward, Lord Stourton.
- Elizabeth, m. to William, Lord Monteagle.
- Catherine, m. to John Webb, esq. of Oldstock
- Mary, m. to Thomas, Lord Brudenell.
- Anne, m. to William Fletcher, esq. of Sussex.
- Bridget, m. to Edward Parham, esq. of Somersetshire.

The eldest son and heir,

SIR FRANCIS TRESHAM, knt. being involved in the gunpowder plot, was attainted of high treason. He m. Anne, daughter of Sir John Tufton, and had issue,

- Lucy.
- Elizabeth, married to Sir George Heneage, knt. of Lincolnshire.

He was *s.* by his brother,

I. SIR LEWIS TRESHAM, knt. of Rushton, who was created a BARONET 29th June, 1611. He married Mary, daughter and heir of Alderman John Moore, of London, and dying in 1639, was *s.* by his son,

II. SIR WILLIAM TRESHAM, who married Frances, daughter of Sir John Gage, bart. of Firle, in Sussex, but *d.* without issue in 1650-1, when the BARONETCY became EXTINCT.

Arms—Party per saltire, sable and or, in chief, and in base, each three trefoils slipped, 2, 1, and 1, 2.

TREVOR, OF ENFIELD.

CREATED 11th Aug. 1641.

EXTINCT 5th Feb. 1676.

Lineage.

SIR THOMAS TREVOR, fifth son of John Trevor, esq. of Trevallin, in Denbighshire, ancestor of the Viscounts Hampden (see BURKE'S *Extinct Peerage*), was born on the 6th July, 1586; a day memorable in his family for six successive principal branches who had their birth thereon. Adopting the legal profession, he attained considerable eminence at the bar, and after passing through the usual gradations of office, was eventually constituted chief baron of the Exchequer. His lordship wedded Prudence, daughter of Henry Boteler, esq.; and secondly, Frances, daughter and heir of Daniel Blennerhassett, esq. of Norfolk. By the former, who died in 1614, he left at his decease, December, 1656, an only son,

I. Thomas Trevor, esq. of Enfield, in Middlesex, who was created a Baronet in 1641, and made a knight of the Bath at the coronation of Charles II. He m. first, Anne, daughter of Robert Jennor, esq. of London; and secondly, Mary, daughter of Samuel Fortrey, esq. of Kew, but died without issue, 5th February, 1676, when the title became extinct.

Arms—Party per bend sinister, erm. and erminois, a lion rampant or.

TROTT, OF LEVERSTOKE.

Created 12th Oct. 1660.—Extinct 14th July, 1672.

Lineage.

I. John Trott, esq. of Leverstoke, in Hampshire, who was created a Baronet 12th October, 1660, married Elizabeth, daughter and co-heir of Sir Edmund Wright, lord mayor of London, and had by her, who wedded, secondly, Lord James Russell, sixth son of William, Duke of Bedford, an only daughter and heir,

Catherine, married to Sir Hugh Stukely, bart. of Hinton, Hants.

Sir John Trott died 14th July, 1672, and as he left no male issue, the Baronetcy became extinct.

TRYON, OF LAYER MARNEY.

Created 28th Mar. 1620.  Extinct 24th April, 1724.

Lineage.

The first of this family that came into England, was Peter Tryon, who fled from the persecution of the Duke of Alva. His family had long flourished in the Low Countries, and was so opulent, that the emigrant brought with him the very large sum, in those days, of sixty thousand pounds sterling. His wife's name was Mary, she died 3rd January, 1618, and was interred by her husband in the church of St. Christopher's, near the Royal Exchange. By that lady he had issue,

Moses, of London, who left an only daughter, who m. Mr. Huckeley, of Edmonton, in Middlesex.

Samuel, heir to his father.

Mary, m. to Sir Sebastian Harvey, knt. lord mayor of London in 1618, (the year Sir Walter Raleigh was beheaded,) and had an only daughter, (heir to Sir Sebastian).

Mary Harvey, m. to Sir Francis Popham, knt.

Hester, m. to Sir William Courteen, bart. of London.

He was s. by his second son,

I. Sir Samuel Tryon, who received the honour of knighthood from King James I. at Newmarket, 25th April, 1615, and was created a Baronet 28th March, 1620. He m. Elizabeth, daughter of John Eldred, citizen of London, and departing this life, 8th March, 1626, was buried in the vault belonging to the family, in the chancel of Halsted Church, Essex. The first estate Sir Samuel had in that county, was the manor of Layer Marney, which he purchased from Peter Tuke, esq. He afterwards bought the lordship of Halsted from Sir Thomas Gardiner knt. and pulling down the old building, erected a neat structure in its stead, called Boys Hall. He lived and died in Halsted. His widow afterwards married Sir Edward Wortley, knt.* He was s. by his son,

II. Sir Samuel Tryon, but ten years and ten months old at the decease of his father, and afterwards in ward to his mother's second husband, Sir Edward Wortley, who is stated to have wasted his estate, and to have induced Sir Samuel, when young, to marry his niece, Eleanor, daughter of Sir Henry Lee, of Quarendon. By this lady he had,

Samuel, his heir.

Alianora, m. to Sir Richard Franklyn, bart. of Moor Park, Herts.

His first wife dying, the baronet married secondly, Susan, daughter of John Harvey, esq. of Newton, in Suffolk. This lady, who was remarkable for personal beauty, married after the decease of Sir Samuel, Timothy Thornbury, gent. of London, and died in the Michaelmas after the great frost. She had issue by Sir Samuel,

Samuel-John, successor to his half-brother.

John, Moses, Anne, } all died young.

The baronet died in 1665, and was s. by his eldest son,

III. Sir Samuel Tryon, who died unm. about the year 1671, when his sister, Alianora, became his heir, and the baronetcy devolved upon his half-brother,

IV. Sir Samuel-John Tryon, who m. Mary, daughter of Robert Bowndo, of Chelmsford, draper, and had two daughters, his co-heirs, viz.

Mary, m. to Thomas Davy, gent. of Shipdam, in the county of Norfolk.

Susan.

He d. 24th April, 1724, when the Baronetcy became extinct.

Arms—Az. a fesse battelee between six estoiles or.

TUFTON, OF THE MOTE.

Created 24th Dec. 1641.  Extinct 11th Oct. 1685.

Lineage.

I. Sir Humphrey Tufton, knt. next brother of Nicholas, first Earl of Thanet, purchased *temp.* Charles I. the Mote, near Maidstone, Kent, and

* Sir Richard Wortley, knt. of Wortley, in the county of York, left issue,

Francis (Sir), knt. and baronet, his heir.

Edward (Sir), mentioned above.

Eleanor, m. to Sir Henry Lee, bart. of Quarendon, and had a daughter, Eleanor Lee, m. to Sir Samuel Tryon, bart.

being thence designated was created a BARONET in 1641. He m. Margaret, eldest daughter and co-heir of Herbert Morley, esq. of Glynd, in Sussex, and had issue,

- I. Humphry, who died unm. 3rd August, 1641.
- II. JOHN (Sir), knt. heir to his father.
- III. Charles.
- IV. Francis.
- V. Henry, of Gray's Inn, *d.* unm.

- I. Christian, *d.* unm.
- II. Olimpia, *m.* to Sir William Wray, bart. of Ashby, in Lincolnshire.
- III. Cecilia, *d.* unm.

Sir Humphrey died at his seat, Bobbing Place, in October, 1659, aged seventy-six, and was *s.* by his son,

II. SIR JOHN TUFTON, of the Mote, who *m.* first, Margaret, third daughter and co-heir of Thomas, Lord Wotton; and secondly, Mary, daughter and heir of Sir James Altham, K.B. of Markhall, Essex, but died without issue, 14th October, 1685, aged sixty-two, when the BARONETCY became EXTINCT. The estate of the Mote Sir John bequeathed to his niece, Tufton Wray, and by that lady it was alienated to Sir John Marsham, bart. by whose representative, the Earl of Romney, it is still possessed.

Arms—Sa. an eagle displayed erm. within a bordure arg.

TUKE, OF CRESSING TEMPLE.

CREATED 31st Mar. 1663-4.

EXTINCT 10th Aug. 1690.

Lineage.

I. SAMUEL TUKE, esq. of Cressing Temple, in Essex, descended from an ancient family in that county, was created a BARONET 31st March, 1663-4. He *m.* Mary, daughter of Edward Guldeford, esq. of Hemsted, Kent, and was *s.* by his son,

II. SIR SAMUEL TUKE, a gentleman of poetic attainments. He served as a colonel in the royal army, and suffered much in consequence. Sir Samuel wedded Mary, daughter of Edward Sheldon, esq. of Ditchford, in Warwickshire, and dying 26th January, 1673, was *s.* by his son,

III. SIR CHARLES TUKE, who died of wounds received at the battle of the Boyne, 10th August, 1690. He never married, and with him the BARONETCY EXPIRED.

Arms—Per fesse indented az. and gu. three lions passant or.

TULPE, OF AMSTERDAM.

CREATED 23rd April, 1675.—EXTINCT, unascertained.

Lineage.

In 1675 a BARONETCY was conferred on

I. RICHARD TULPE, of Amsterdam, but we have ascertained no particulars beyond the fact and date of the creation.

TURNER, OF WARHAM.

CREATED 27th April, 1727.

EXTINCT in 1780.

Lineage.

The family of Turner was seated for a considerable period in the county of Norfolk.

CHARLES TURNER, esq. of Wessenham, left by Elizabeth, his wife, two sons, Sir John Turner, knt. M.P. for Lynn, who *d. s. p.* in 1711, and

WILLIAM TURNER, esq. who married and had three sons, CHARLES, his heir; William, who died *s. p.*; and JOHN, who succeeded as second baronet. The eldest,

I. CHARLES TURNER, esq. of Warham, in Norfolk, M.P. for Lynn, from the Revolution until his death, was a commissioner of trade, and a lord of the Admiralty, *temp.* *Queen* ANNE, and a commissioner of the Treasury, in the reign of GEORGE II. In 1727 he was created a BARONET, with reversion, in default of male issue, to his brothers and their male issue. He married first, in 1689, Mary, daughter of Robert Walpole, esq. of Houghton, in Norfolk, and sister of Sir Robert Walpole, K.G. the celebrated minister, by whom he had issue,

- JOHN, who died in his father's lifetime, leaving three daughters, viz.
  - Maria.
  - Anne-Carolina, *m.* to John Playters, esq. son and heir of Sir John Playters, bart.
  - Dorothy-Walpole.
- Anne, *m.* to the Rev. Maurice Suckling, D.D. prebendary of Westminster, and had issue,
  - Maurice Suckling, capt. R.N. M.P. the early patron of Nelson, and a highly distinguished and gallant seaman. He *d. s. p.*
  - William Suckling, *d. s. p.*
  - Catherine Suckling, *m.* in 1749, to the Rev. Edmund Nelson, M.A. and was mother of
    - HORATIO NELSON, Viscount Nelson, the hero of Trafalgar.
- Elizabeth, *m.* to John Fowle, esq. of Brome, in Norfolk, one of the commissioners of Excise.

Sir Charles married secondly, Mary, daughter of Sir William Blois, knt. of Cockfield Hall, Suffolk, and relict of Sir Neville Catlyn, knt. of Kirby Kane, by whom, who died 30th August, 1738, he had no issue. Sir Charles *d.* 24th November, 1738, and was *s.* according to the limitation of the patent, by his only surviving brother,

II. SIR JOHN TURNER, M.P. for Lynn, *temp.* Queen ANNE, who married Miss Allen, and dying 7th January, 1739, was *s.* by his only son,

III. SIR JOHN TURNER, M.P. for Lynn, who married Frances, daughter and co-heir of John Neale, esq. of Allesley, in Warwickshire, M.P. and had two daughters, his co-heirs, viz.

- ANNE, *m.* to Robert Hales, esq. and died in 1822, leaving with junior issue, a son and heir, JOHN TURNER HALES, esq. of Suffolk.
- FANNY, *m.* to Sir Martin Browne Folkes, bart. of Hillington, and died in 1813, leaving an only

son, the present SIR WILLIAM BROWNE FOLKES, bart. of Hillington.

r John Turner died in 1780, when the BARONETCY came EXTINCT. The estate at Warham was sold by s daughters and co-heirs.

Arms—Sa. a chev. erm. between three fer de moses, or, on a chief arg. a lion passant gu.

TURNER, OF KIRKLEATHAM.

CREATED 8th May, 1782.

EXTINCT 1st Feb. 1810.

Lineage.

I. CHARLES TURNER, esq. of Kirkleatham, in Yorkshire, who represented the city of York in every arliament from 1768 until his death, was created a ARONET in 1782. He *m.* first, Elizabeth, daughter f William Wombwell, esq. of Wombwell; and seondly, Mary, daughter of James Shuttleworth, esq. f Forcet, which latter lady survived him, and *m.* econdly, Sir Thomas Gascoigne, bart. Sir Charles . 26th October, 1783, aged fifty-seven, and was *s.* by is son,

II. SIR CHARLES TURNER, at whose decease issueless, st February, 1810, aged thirty-eight, the title became XTINCT.

Arms—Arg. on a cross sa. five fers de moline of the eld.

TWISTLETON, OF BARLEY.

CREATED 2nd April, 1629.

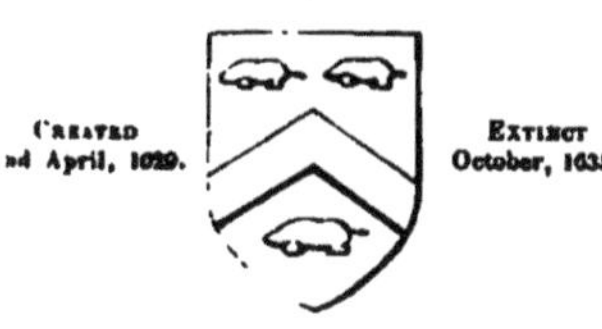

EXTINCT October, 1635.

Lineage.

I. GEORGE TWISTLETON, esq. of Barley, in Yorkshire, representative of the Twistleton family, was reated a BARONET in 1629. He married Catherine, aughter of Henry Stapylton, esq. of Wighill, but by r (who married secondly, Sir Henry Cholmeley, nt.) had no issue. He *d.* in October, 1635, when the tle became EXTINCT. The estates reverted to his ncle,

JOHN TWISTLETON, esq. of Drax, in Yorkshire, and Horseman's Place, in Kent, ancestor of the present LORD SAYE AND SELE. (See BURKE'S *Peerage and Baronetage*.)

Arms—Arg. a chev. between three moles sa.

TYNTE, OF HALSEWELL.

CREATED 7th June, 1674.

EXTINCT 25th Aug. 1785.

Lineage.

The representative of the Tyntes at the close of the sixteenth century,

EDWARD TYNTE, esq. of Wrexhall, in the county of Somerset, living in 1565, married and had two sons, EDWARD, his heir; and ROBERT (Sir), knt. who settled in Ireland in 1645, and who was ancestor of the baronets of the name, resident in that part of the kingdom. The elder son,

EDWARD TYNTE, esq. of Wrexhall, was father of

EDWARD TYNTE, esq. who purchased from his brother-in-law, John Aishe, esq. the manor of Chelvey, in the county of Somerset. He espoused Anne, daughter of Sir Edward Gorges, knt. of Wrexhall, in the same shire, and had JOHN, Robert, Hugh, Dorothy, and Florence. He *d.* in 1629, and was *s.* by his eldest son,

JOHN TYNTE, esq. of Chelvey, M.P. for Bridgewater in 1661, a devoted adherent of Royalty during the civil wars, and named in the list of gentlemen of large estates, intended to have been created knights of the Royal Oak. He *m.* Jane, daughter and heiress of Hugh Halsewell,* of Halsewell, in the county of Somerset, son of Sir Nicholas Halsewell, and thus acquired the estate which has since been the chief residence of the family. By the heiress of Halsewell, he left a son and successor,

I. HALSEWELL TYNTE, esq. of Halsewell, who was created a BARONET 7th June, 1673, in consideration of his father's distinguished services, and represented the town of Bridgewater in parliament in 1678. He *m.* Grace, daughter and co-heir of Robert Fortescue, esq. of Filleigh, in the county of Devon, by Grace, his wife, daughter of the gallant Sir Beville Granville, knt. of Stow, and had issue,

- HALSEWELL, of New College, Oxford, who predeceased his father unm.
- FORTESCUE, who *m.* the daughter of — Giffard, esq. of Cannington, but *d. v. p. s. p.* His widow wedded, secondly, Hopton Wyndham, esq. and thirdly, — Codrington, esq. of Gloucestershire.
- JOHN, successor to his father.
- Robert, had an only daughter, who *d.* young.
- Grace, *m.* to Arthur Tremaine, esq. of Sydenham, in Devonshire. (See BURKE'S *Commoners*, vol. i. p. 195).

Sir Halsewell *d.* in 1702, and was *s.* by his eldest surviving son,

II. SIR JOHN TYNTE, of Halsewell, who married Jane, eldest daughter of SIR CHARLES KEMEYS, bart. of Keyanmably, in Glamorganshire, by Mary, his wife, daughter of Philip Lord Wharton, and had three sons and a daughter, viz.

* The family of Halsewell, or De Halsewell, one of remote antiquity, possessed the estate now enjoyed by their representative, Colonel Kemeys Tynte, immediately after the Conquest.

HALSEWELL,
JOHN,
CHARLES-KEMEYS, } successive barts.

JANE, m. in 1737 to Major HASSELL, of the Royal Horse Guards, Blue, son of John Hassell, esq. by Anne, his wife, daughter and heir of Thomas St. Quintin, esq. son of Sir William Quintin, bart. and had an only daughter and heiress,

JANE HASSELL, of whom presently, as inheritor of the estates of the families of KEMEYS and TYNTE.

Sir John d. in March, 1710, and was s. by his eldest son,

III. SIR HALSEWELL TYNTE, of Halsewell, who was returned to parliament by the borough of Bridgewater, 1 GEORGE II. He m. Mary, daughter and heiress of John Watter, esq. of Brecon, and by her, who wedded, secondly, in 1736, Pawlet St. John, esq. of Dogmersfield, had two daughters, who both died young. Sir Halsewell died in November, 1730, and was succeeded by his brother,

IV. SIR JOHN TYNTE, of Halsewell, in holy orders, rector of Goathurst, in Somersetshire, at whose decease unm. in August, 1740, the estates and representation of the family devolved on his brother,

V. SIR CHARLES-KEMEYS TYNTE, of Halsewell, LL.D. who represented the county in seven parliaments, and was colonel of the second battalion of Somerset militia. Sir Charles became, at the decease of his uncle, Sir Charles Kemeys, bart. of Kevanmably, representative of that very ancient family, and inherited their large estates in the counties of Glamorgan, Brecon, and Monmouth. He m. in March, 1737-8, Anne, daughter and co-heir of the Rev. Dr. Busby, rector of Addington, in Bucks, but dying without issue, in 1785, the BARONETCY became EXTINCT, and his possessions vested in his niece,

JANE HASSELL, who married Colonel Johnstone, of the 1st regiment of Foot Guards, groom of the bedchamber, and comptroller and master of the household to his Royal Highness, George, Prince of Wales, (afterwards GEORGE IV.) who assumed, by royal license, the surnames of KEMEYS-TYNTE. Colonel Kemeys Tynte d. in 1807, and his widow in 1825, leaving with two daughters both unm. an only son, the present CHARLES-KEMEYS KEMEYS-TYNTE, esq. of Halsewell House, in Somersetshire, and of Kevenmably, in Glamorganshire.

Arms—Gu. a lion couchant between six cross crosslets arg.

TYRRELL, OF SPRINGFIELD.

CREATED 22nd Oct. 1666.

EXTINCT 5th Jan. 1766.

Lineage.

The family of TIRRELL is one of great note and antiquity, and for more than six hundred years its chief, in a direct line, enjoyed the honour of knighthood.

SIR WALTER TIRRELL, held at the general survey from the Conqueror, the lordship of Langham, in Essex. This is the knight to whom, whether truly or falsely, the death of WILLIAM *Rufus*, has been attributed by our historians. His son,

SIR HENRY TIRRELL, was father of,

SIR RICHARD TIRRELL, whose son,

SIR EDWARD TIRRELL, had issue,

SIR GEOFREY TIRRELL, father of,

SIR LIONEL TIRRELL, whose son,

SIR EDWARD TIRRELL, m. Maud, or Anne Burgate, a Suffolk heiress, and left a son and heir,

SIR HUGH TIRRELL, of Great Thorndon, in Essex, living in the time of EDWARD III. He was governor of Carisbroke Castle, which he defended against the French in 1378, 1 RICHARD II. He m. Joan, daughter and co-heir of James Flamberd, and had a son,

SIR JAMES TIRRELL, who m. Margaret, daughter and heir of Sir William Heron, knt. of Heron, and was s. by his son,

SIR WALTER TIRRELL, of Heron, who m. Jane, daughter and co-heir of Sir William Swynford, knt. of Essex, and was s. by his son,

SIR THOMAS TIRRELL, who m. first, Alice, daughter of — D'Adelcigh, but by her had no issue. He wedded secondly, Eleanora, daughter of John Flamberd, by whom he had,

SIR JOHN TYRRELL, sheriff of Essex and Hertfordshire, in 1423. He served in France, and was appointed by HENRY III. captain of the carpenters of the new works, at Calais, to be paid 12d. a day wages. He was afterwards treasurer of the household to HENRY VI. He m. Alice, daughter and co-heir of Sir William Coggeshall, knt. of Little Stamford Hall, in Essex,* by whom (who m. secondly, John Langham, esq. son and heir of Sir William Langham, knt. of Pantfield, in Essex, and d. in 1422) he had, with other issue,

THOMAS, (Sir), his heir.

William, of Gipping, in Suffolk, father of James, who was captain of Guisnes, in France, *temp.* HENRY VII.

William, jun. of Beeches, in Essex.

The eldest son,

SIR THOMAS TIRRELL, of Heron, who m. Anne, dau. of Sir William Marney, knt. of Layer Marney, in Essex, and had four sons and two daughters, viz.

WILLIAM, (Sir), his heir.

Thomas, (Sir), of South Okingdon, in Essex and Thornton, in Bucks, from whom the Tyrrells of *Thornton*, extinct baronets.

Humphrey, of Worsly.

Robert, (Sir), of Thorndon, super montem, in Essex.

Anne, m. to John D'Arcy, esq. of Tolleshunt.

Elizabeth, m. first, to Robert D'Arcy, esq. of Danbury, in Essex; and secondly, to Richard Hawte.

His eldest son,

SIR WILLIAM TIRRELL, knt. m. Eleanora, daughter of Sir Robert D'Arcy, knt. of Walden, and left a son and heir,

SIR THOMAS TIRRELL, of Heron, knight banneret. This gentleman m. Beatrix, daughter of John Cokaine, esq. of Derbyshire, and was s. by his son,

SIR THOMAS TIRRELL, knt. who m. Constance, daughter of John Blount, Lord Mountjoy, and had THOMAS, (Sir), his heir, Henry, (Sir), William, Sir, who was a knight of Rhodes, George, Charles, Sir Robert, and others. The eldest son,

* By Antiocha, his wife, daughter of the famous Sir John Hawkwood, knt. of Essex.

536.6

102.h

F. E. HOWARD,
ARCHITECT.

24, POLSTEAD ROAD,
OXFORD.

ber 1st 1927.

My dear Lamborn

I have measured up the plan

of the church a or sixteen more photographs

I gathered from the Tyrrells lived at

Gipping until r se had existed until

a short while a the materials sold.

I took down ent the photos.

N.E. buttress o
S.E. " " ing a bend.

S Buttress of c order engrailed, a martlet quefoils

Chimney stack.
E.1. A bend inde nce, impaling 3 cinquefoils.
I think this is e cottises are not
properly carved. to this.
N.1. Tyrrell im es.
2 Tyrrell imp end - Carminow
3 Arundel, qua

Ins

Tyr Filii p'd'ti Jacob

Tyr (con)sortis sue

bn! - letters in brackets conjectural

it has a marble top and the frontal

is ery fine red velvet with gold lace

an raph.

. buttress, which I read as

" oes not make sense. The motto as

g ndards is " Tout pour le mieulx"

of Thorp in the window, the crest

o ks feathers, which suggests some

p ell badge.

M. L. A. scroll. I cannot make out

w ed for. It occurs again in the window.

w ar letters, but T does not occur in

t

s sincerely,

F. E. Howard

Sir Thomas Tirrell, knt. m. Anne, daughter of r William Browne, lord mayor of London, and by r (who m. secondly, Sir William Petre, knt.) had only daughter, Catherine, m. to Sir Richard Ba-r, knt. of Sisinhurst, in Kent. He d. 3rd April, Henry VIII. and was s. by his brother,

Sir Henry Tirrell, knt. who held of the queen the nor of Heron, of her honour of Maundeville, by e service of one knight's fee, and the other manors Montfrith, Tingoods, and Poddesbroke, in Essex, r half a knight's fee, which, with Fouchers, were ld of the honour of Maundeville, since in the duchy Lancaster. Sir Henry m. Thomasine, daughter of illiam Gounston, esq. of London, and dying 30 Eli-zabeth, was s. by his eldest son,

Sir Thomas Tyrrell, knt. of Heron, who m. Mary, ughter of Sir John Sulyard, knt. of Wethersden, in ffolk, and dying in four years after inheriting, as s. by his eldest son,

Sir John Tyrrell, knt. who m. first, Elizabeth, ughter of Sir John Croke, lord chief justice of the ng's Bench; and secondly, Jocosa, daughter of John aker, esq. of Sisinhurst, in Kent, but having no ue, was s. at his decease by his brother,

Sir Thomas Tirrell, knt. This gentleman m. Mar-ret, daughter of John Filioll, esq. of Old Hall, in sex, and had two sons, viz.

John, (Sir), his successor.

Thomas, of Butlesbury, in Essex, m. Elizabeth, daughter of Thomas Steward, esq. of Chelmsford, and had a son,

John, of Billericay, also in Essex, living in 1695, m. Mary, daughter of Giles Alleyn, esq. of Hasley Hall, in the same county.*

he elder son and heir,

Sir John Tirrell, m. first, Elizabeth, daughter of orge Evelyn, esq. one of the six clerks in chancery, d by her had a daughter, Elizabeth, m. to Hum-hry Forster, eldest son of Sir Humphry Forster, bart. Aldermaston, Berks. He wedded secondly, Mar-t, daughter of Sir Laurence Washington, knt. of reden, Wilts, by whom (who d. 17th December, 39, aged ninety) he had

Laurence, d. s. p.

John, his heir.

Thomas, Charles, } d. s. p.

Martha, m. to Sir Benjamin Ayloffe, bart. of Braxted, Essex.

ir John, who suffered severely for his loyalty,† d. rd April, 1675, aged eighty-two, and was s. by his randson, the son and heir of

Sir John Tyrrell, esq. of Springfield-Barney, in he county of Essex, who was created a Baronet, 2nd October, 1666. Sir John married first, Lettice, aughter of Thomas Coppen, esq. of Mircatsal, in Herts, by whom he had a son, Charles, his heir; he m. secondly, Anne, widow of Richard Yeand, of London, merchant, which lady died issueless, 24th April, 1664. Sir John m. thirdly, Elizabeth, daughter of Alderman John Allen, of London, by whom (who married secondly, Sir Thomas Stamp, knt. alderman and lord mayor of London) he had no issue. Sir John d. in the lifetime of his father, 30th March, 1673, and was s. by his son,

II. Sir Charles Tyrrell, who inherited the estates of the family at the decease of his grandfather. He m. Martha, daughter and heiress of Charles Mildmay, esq. of Woodham Mortimer Hall, in Essex, by whom, who d. in 1690, he had, with a daughter, the wife of Colonel Wyndham, of Earisham, an only son, his successor, at his decease, 3rd February, 1714, (aged fifty-four),

III. Sir John Tyrrell, who m. first, Mary, daughter of Sir James Dolliff, knt. of Mitcham, in Surrey, and had by her,

Mary.

Martha, m. to Sir Thomas Drury, bart. of Overstone in Northamptonshire.

Anne.

Elizabeth.

He married secondly, Miss Cotton, eldest daughter of John Cotton, esq. of the Middle Temple, and of East Barnet, in Middlesex, by whom he had three sons. He d. 21st June, 1729, and was s. by the eldest,

IV. Sir Charles Tyrrell, who d. 27th July, 1735, aged eleven, and was s. by his brother,

V. Sir John Tyrrell, who m. Miss Crispe, daughter and heir of Thomas Crispe, esq. of Perbold, in Lancashire, but died s. p. m. 5th January, 1766, when the title became extinct.

Arms—Argent, two cheveronels, azure, within a bordure, engrailed, gules.

TYRRELL, OF THORNTON.

Created { *First Patent*, 31st Oct. 1627. *Second Patent*, 19th Feb. 1638.
Extinct 20th Jan. 1749.

Lineage.

This was a branch from the same stock as the Tyrrells of Springfield.

Sir Thomas Tyrrell, knight banneret, second son of Sir Thomas Tirrell, of Heron, m. Elizabeth, daughter and co-heir of Sir Humphry Le Bruin, of South Okendon, and had issue. Sir Thomas was master of the horse to Katharine, queen consort of Henry VIII. He was s. by his son,

Sir William Tyrrell, of South Okendon, who m. Elizabeth, daughter of Sir Thomas Bodley, knt. founder of the Bodleian library, at Oxford, and left a son and heir,

---

He was s. by his son,
John Tyrrell, esq. of Billericay, who m. Mary, daughter of William Marlow, esq. and was s. by his son,
John Tyrrell, esq. of Hatfield Peverell, in Essex, whose son and heir,
John Tyrrell, esq. of Boreham House, was created a Baronet in 1809, refer to Burke's *Peerage and Baronetage*.

* In East-Horndon church were several defaced monuments of the Tyrrells, and in the south chapel is a grave-stone, ith an inscription to this Sir John Tirrell, viz.

Ἐπ' αὐτόν
Semel decimatus,
Bis carceratus,
Ter sequestratus,
Tacet quoties spoliatus,
Hic jacet inhumatus.
Johannes, Tyrrell,
Eques Auratus.
Obiit die Martis, Aprilis 3o. A Dom. 1675, ætat. 82

Humphrey Tyrrell, esq. who m. Jane, daughter and heir of Robert Ingleton, esq. of Thornton, in Bucks, who brought, it is stated, thirty manors into the family, including Thornton. He was s. by his son,

George Tyrrell, esq. of Thornton, who d. in 1571, leaving issue, by Eleanor, daughter of Sir Edward Montagu, knt. lord chief justice of England,

Sir Edward Tyrrell, knt. of Thornton, who m. first, Mary, daughter of Benedict Lee, esq. of Huncote, in Bucks, and by her had, with two daughters, of whom Mary m. William Trye, esq. of Hardwick, Gloucestershire, an only son,

- Edward, his heir.

He m. secondly, Margaret, daughter of Thomas Aston, esq. of Aston, in Cheshire, and widow of T. Egerton, esq. of Walgrave, by whom he had

- Timothy, (Sir), of Oakley.‡
- John, captain of foot, killed at the battle of Newport, in Flanders, s. p.
- Thomas, (Sir), of Hanslape, and Castle Thrup, Bucks, a colonel in the parliamentary army, judge of the common pleas, and one of the commissioners of the great seal to Oliver Cromwell, who, by his wife, a daughter of — Saunders, of Bucks, left two sons,
  - Thomas, m. Hester, daughter of Sir Edward Tyrrell, of Thornton, bart. (relict of Sir Peter la Mare, and of Sir Thomas Salisbury, bart.) by whom he had a daughter,
    - Frances, m. to John Blower, gent. of Wood-Norton, in Norfolk.
  - Peter, (Sir), of Hanslape, created a Baronet 20th July, 1665.
  - Elizabeth, m. to William Lane, esq. of Hanslape.
  - Theodosia, m. to Francis Brereton, esq. of Cheshire.
- Penelope, m. to Capt. Gardiner.
- Frances, m. to Sir Edward Broughton, knt. of Marstwell, in Flintshire.
- Theodosia, m. to Edward West, esq. of Marsworth, Bucks.
- Philippa, m. to John Nourse, esq. of Woodeaton, in the county of Oxford.

TYR

- Bridget, m. to Sir William Saunderson, knt.

George Tyrrell, d. in 1751, and was s. by his eldest son,

I. Edward Tyrrell, esq. of Thornton, who was created a Baronet 31st May, 1627. Sir Edward m. first, Elizabeth, daughter of Sir William Kingsmill, knt. of Sidmanton, Hants, and had issue,

- Robert, who was disinherited, but still inherited the baronetcy, d. unm.
- Toby, successor to his father, under a new patent.
- Francis.
- Hester, m. first, to Sir Peter la Mare, knt. of L[illegible]don; secondly, to Sir Thomas Salisbury, bart. and thirdly, to Thomas, eldest son of Sir Thomas Tyrrell, of Haslape.
- Elizabeth, m. to Edmund Saunders, esq. of [illegible]worth, in the county of Northampton.

He m. secondly, Elizabeth, daughter of Sir Edward Watson, of Rockingham Castle, and widow of [illegible] John Needham, of Lichborough, both in Northamptonshire, but had no other issue. Sir Edward Tyrrell attempted to remove his eldest son from succession to the baronetcy, by surrendering the patent to the crown, in 1638, and obtaining a new one dated [illegible] February, in that year, with precedency of the former, altering the succession to his second and third sons, passing entirely over the eldest; but in the Viscount Purbeck's case, it was laid down, that a dignity cannot be surrendered to the crown, to the prejudice of the next heir, for it is annexed to the blood, and nothing but a deficiency or corruption of the blood can hinder the descent. And the House of Lords in that case resolved and adjudged, "That no fine now levied, nor at any time hereafter to be levied to the king, can bar such title of honour, or the right of any person claiming such title under him that levied, or shall levy such fine." On the death, therefore, of Sir Edward Tyrrell, in June, 1656, there were actually two baronetcies of the same precedency, the first patent inherited by the eldest son, the last by the second; the eldest son,

II. Sir Robert Tyrrell, d. unm. when both titles merged in his brother,

III. Sir Toby Tyrrell, who m. first, Edith, daughter of Sir Francis Windebank, knt. by whom he had a daughter,

---

‡ Sir Timothy Tyrrell, of Oakley, in Bucks, master of the buck hounds to *King* Charles I. and *Prince* Henry, m. Eleanor, daughter of Sir William Kingsmill, knt. of Sidmanton, Hants, and had issue,

- Timothy, (Sir), his heir.
- William, killed in the civil wars, at Chester, in 1644.
- Henry, ranger of Whaddon Chase, Bucks, m. a daughter of St. John Thompson, esq. of Crawley, in Bedfordshire, and had two daughters,
  - Catharine, m. to Henry Edlyn, esq. of Whaddon Chase.
  - Eleanor.
- Charles, d. unm. in 1694.
- Eleanor, m. first to Sir Peter Temple, knt, of Stanton, Bucks, and secondly to Richard Greenville, esq. of Wotton.
- Bridget, d. unm.
- Mary, m. to Sir Walter Pye, knt, of the Mynde, in Herefordshire.

The eldest son,

Sir Timothy Tyrrell, of Oakley, in Bucks, and Shotover, in the county of Oxford, was of the privy chamber to *King* Charles I. and rated by the sequestrators at £750 composition for his estate. He held the rank of colonel in the royal army, was governor of Cardiff, and general of the ordnance under Lord Gerard. He m. Elizabeth, only daughter and heir of the most Rev. Dr. James Usher, archbishop of Armagh, and had issue,

- James, his heir.
- Charles, d. in Ireland, unm.
- John, captain of a man-of-war, d. in 1692.
- Usher, settled in Jamaica, and m. a daughter of [illegible] Tromp.
- Elizabeth, m. to Philip, fourth son of Peregrine [illegible]by, esq. of Bisham, Berks.
- Mary, m. to Henry Cavendish, esq. of D[illegible], in Derbyshire.
- Penelope, m. to Sir James Russell, knt. of the I[illegible] of Nevis.
- Eleanora, m. to Charles, second surviving son of Sir Charles Blount, of Titenhanger.
- Bridget, m. to Samuel Byrch, esq. of Whit[illegible], Herts.

He was s. by his eldest son,

James Tyrrell, esq. of Oakley, b. in May, 1642, who was bred to the bar, but did not pursue the pr[illegible]. He m. Mary, daughter and heir of Sir Michael H[illegible]son, knt. of Fladbury, in the county of Worcester. [illegible] was a literary man, author of a General History of England, down to the time of *King* William III. [illegible] volumes, and other works. He left, with a daughter, Mary, wife of John Aldworth, a son and heir,

James Tyrrell, esq. of Shotover, M.P. a lieutenant-general in the army. One of the grooms of the bedchamber to the Prince of Wales, and governor of Gra[illegible] and Tilbury Fort. General Tyrrell devised the [illegible] Shotover to the family of Schutz, in whose possession [illegible] has since continued.

Frances, m. first, to Sir John Hewett, bart.; and secondly, to Philip Cotton, esq. of Connington, in Cambridgeshire.

He m. secondly, Lucy, daughter of Sir Thomas Barrington, bart. of Barrington Hall, in Essex, and by that lady had, with three daughters, three sons,

Thomas, his successor.
Timothy, d. s. p.
Francis.

Sir Toby d. in 1671, and was s. by his eldest son,

IV. Sir Thomas Tyrrell, who m. Frances, daughter of Sir Henry Blount, knt. of Tittenhanger, and had six sons and four daughters, the eldest of the latter, Hester, m. John Sheppard, esq. of Littlecote. Sir Thomas d. 14th October, 1705, and was s. by his eldest son,

V. Sir Harry Tyrrell, who m. Hester, eldest daughter of Charles Blount, esq. of Blount's Hall, Staffordshire, at length, heir of her brother, Charles Blount, esq. by whom he had issue,

Thomas, Harry, Charles, } successive Baronets.

Frances, m. to Thomas Vernon, esq. of Bristol, barrister-at-law.
Penelope, m. to Charles Bentley, esq.

Sir Harry d. 6th November, 1708, and was s. by his eldest son,

VI. Sir Thomas Tyrrell, who d. unm. in 1719, and was s. by his brother,

VII. Sir Harry Tyrrell, who d. a bachelor, 9th November, 1720, and was s. by his brother,

VIII. Sir Charles Tyrrell, who m. at Geneva, in 1726, Jane-Elizabeth, only daughter of Mons. John Sellon, merchant, of that city, by whom he had one surviving daughter and heiress,

Hester-Maria, m. to the Rev. William Cotton, D. C. L. of Crakemarsh Hall, in Staffordshire, and had an only daughter and heiress,

Elizabeth Cotton, m. to Thomas Sheppard, esq. of Littlecote, who was created a Baronet in 1809, see Burke's *Peerage and Baronetage*.

He d. 20th January, 1749, when the Baronetcy expired, and the estates devolved upon his daughter, whose grandson and representative is the present Sir Thomas Sheppard, bart.

Arms—See Tyrrell, of Springfield.

TYRRELL, OF HANSLAPE.

Created 20th July, 1665.—Extinct May, 1714.

Lineage.

I. Peter Tyrrell, esq. of Hanslape, in the county of Bucks, younger son of Sir Thomas Tyrrell, judge of the common pleas, and one of the commissioners of the great seal, to Oliver Cromwell, was created a Baronet 20th July, 1665. Sir Peter m. Anne, daughter of Carew Raleigh, esq. and granddaughter of Sir Walter Raleigh, and was s. by his son,

II. Sir Thomas Tyrrell, who m. Miss Dorothy Eyre, and had issue,

Eyre, who d. an infant, 3rd January, 1698, and was buried at Castlethrup.
Harriett, m. to Francis-Martin-May Mann, esq. of Kidlington, in Oxfordshire.

Sir Thomas d. in May, 1714, when the Baronetcy expired.

Arms—See Tyrrell, of Springfield.

TYRWHITT, OF STAINFIELD.

Created 20th June, 1611.

Extinct 22nd Aug. 1760.

Lineage.

Collier, in his historical dictionary, says, "The Tyrwhitts are considerably ancient, as appears by their being high sheriffs of Lincolnshire 22 Edward IV, and of Yorkshire, 14 Henry VI." And Philips* describes them as "a family of great honour and antiquity in the county of Lincoln, descended from Robert Tirwhitt, an eminent lawyer in the reigns of *Kings* Henry IV. and V. He was first called to the degree of a serjeant, and then constituted one of the justices of the court of Common Pleas, out of which court he was removed to the King's Bench." Camden speaking of Kettleby, calls it, "The seat of the famous family of the Tirwhitts, knights, who now reside at Stanfield."

Sir William Tyrwhitt, knt. of Ketilby, in the county of Lincoln, thrice sheriff of that county, viz. 22 Edward IV. 16 Henry VII. and 8 Henry VIII. m. Anne, daughter of Sir Robert Constable, knt. of Flamborough, in the county of York, and had issue,

Robert, his heir.
Philip (Sir), knight banneret, living 23 Henry VIII.
Agnes, m. to Thomas, Lord Burgh, K.G.
Elizabeth, m. to Sir William Skipwith, knt. of Ormesby, in Lincolnshire.

He d. in 1522, and was s. by his son,

Sir Robert Tyrwhitt, of Ketilby, who was knighted when sheriff of Lincolnshire in 15 Henry VIII. By his wife, Maud, daughter of Sir Robert Talboys, of Goulton, he had issue,

William (Sir), his heir, ancestor of the Tyrwhitts of Ketilby and of Cameringham; of the late learned Thomas Tyrwhitt, A.M.; of Sir Thomas Tyrwhitt, gentleman usher of the black rod; of Sir Thomas Tyrwhitt Jones, created a baronet in 1808; and of the Tyrwhitts of Nantyr. (See Burke's *Commoners*, vol. i. p. 563.)
Robert (Sir) of Leighton Bromeswould, one of the ecclesiastic commissioners for Lincolnshire, *temp.* Henry VIII. He had an only daughter and heir, Catherine, who m. Sir Henry D'Arcy, knt. and died before her father.
Philip.
Anne, m. to — Bolles, esq. of Hough.
Agnes, m. to William, son and heir of Sir William Hansard, knt.

* In his list of families raised to honour and wealth by the profession of the law.

Elizabeth, m. to William Monson, esq. of South Carleton.

Catherine, m. to John, son and heir of Sir Richard Thimelby, knt.

Margaret, m. to Matthew St. Paul, esq. of Snarford.

Maud, m. to George Portington, esq. of Sawcliff, in the county of Lincoln.

Sir Robert, who was grantee of Cameringham and Stainfield, erected at the latter the mansion house which afterwards became the designation of the branch of which we are more immediately about to treat. He was vice admiral of England, and a knight banneret. His youngest son,

PHILIP TYRWHITT, esq. who was seated at Barton-upon-Humber, in the county of Lincoln, m. Margaret, daughter and co-heir of Edward Barnaby, esq. and was s. by his son,

EDWARD TYRWHITT, esq. who settled himself at Stanfield, and marrying Anne, daughter of William Dallyson, esq. of Loughton, in Lincolnshire, and sister of Sir William Dallyson, one of the judges of the court of King's Bench, had two sons, PHILIP (Sir), and Roger. The elder,

I. SIR PHILIP TYRWHITT, succeeded to the estate at Stainfield, and with his eldest son, Edward, waited upon *King* JAMES I. at Belvoir Castle, when his majesty reposed there in his way from Scotland to take possession of the crown, and had the honour of knighthood conferred upon himself and his said son. He was afterwards created a BARONET 29th June, 1611. Sir Philip m. Martha, daughter of Sir Anthony Thorold, knt. of Marston, and dying 5th February, 1624, was s. by his son,

II. SIR EDWARD TYRWHITT, of Stanfield, knt. and bart. who m. first, Faith, daughter of Thomas, and sister and heir of Sir George St. Paul, bart. of Snarford, by whom he had issue,

PHILIP, his successor.

Edward.

Martha, m. to Sir William Helwish, knt.

Mary, m. to Charles Pelham, esq. of Manton, in the county of Lincoln.

Elizabeth, m. to Gervase Elways, esq. of Gainsborough, second son of Sir Gervase Elways, knt. of Worlaby, in Lincolnshire.

He m. secondly, Elizabeth, daughter of George Chute, esq. of Bethersden, in Kent, and by her had another son, Edward, and two daughters, Mary and Anne. Sir Edward was s. by his eldest son,

III. SIR PHILIP TYRWHITT. This gentleman was a great sufferer for his fidelity to *King* CHARLES I. and paid £3488. 15s. composition for his estate to the sequestrators. He m. Anne, second daughter of Nicholas, Viscount Castleton, and had issue,

PHILIP, his heir.

Edward, } *d. s. p.*
William, }

Nicholas, m. a daughter of Sir Thomas Grantham, knt. and had three sons, who all died without issue.

Faith, m. to George, eldest son of Sir George Heneage, knt. of Hainton, in Lincolnshire.

Frances, m. to Anthony Monson, esq. of Northrop, in Lincolnshire.

He d. about the year 1667, and was s. by his eldest son,

IV. SIR PHILIP TYRWHITT, who married Penelope, daughter of Sir Erasmus de la Fountain, knt. of Kirby Bellers, in the county of Lincoln, and had, out of twelve children, but one son and one daughter to reach maturity, namely,

JOHN, his heir.

——, m. to Sir Edward Southcot, knt. of Witham.

He d. about 1688, and was s. by his son,

V. SIR JOHN TYRWHITT, M.P. for the city of Lincoln, *temp.* GEORGE I. and GEORGE II. He m. first, Elizabeth, daughter and co-heir of Francis Phillips, esq. of Kempton Park, Middlesex, by whom he had two surviving daughters, viz.

Penelope, m. to George Short, esq. of Keal, in Lincolnshire.

Anne, m. to Car Brackenbury, esq. and had a son, James Brackenbury.

He married secondly, Mary, daughter of Sir William Drake, knt. of Shardeloes, in Bucks, and by her (who d. in 1738) had twelve children, of whom one son and four daughters survived to maturity, namely,

JOHN DE-LA FOUNTAIN, his heir.

Mary.

Juliana.

Frances.

Sarah, m. to Samuel Waddington, esq. and had a daughter, Margaretta Waddington, m. in 17[illegible] to Marmaduke Cradock, esq. and had, with [illegible] daughters, two sons, viz.

Joseph Cradock.

Charles Cradock, of the firm of Baldwin and Cradock, of London, booksellers and publishers.

He d. in November, 1741, and was s. by his son,

VI. SIR JOHN-DE-LA FOUNTAIN TYRWHITT, M.P. for the city of Lincoln, who d. unm. 22nd August, 17[illegible] when the BARONETCY EXPIRED. In 1776, his kinsman Thomas Drake, esq. of Shardeloes, assumed the additional surname of TYRWHITT, upon inheriting the estates under the will of Sir John-de-la-Fountain Tyrwhitt (refer to BURKE's *Commoners*, vol. i. page 560).

Arms—Gu. three tyrwhitts, or lapwings, or.

VALCKENBURGH, OF MIDDLEING.

CREATED 20th July, 1642.—EXTINCT date unknown.

Lineage.

I. MATTHEW VALCKENBURGH, designated "of Middleing in Yorkshire," was created a BARONET in 1642. He died about 1650, leaving by Isabella, his wife, a son and successor,

II. SIR JOHN ANTHONY VALCKENBURGH, aged twenty-one in 1664. We have been unable to obtain any information respecting the baronetcy or family since that date.

VANACKER, OF LONDON.

CREATED 31st Jan. 1700.

EXTINCT 4th Oct. 17[illegible]

Lineage.

JOHN VANACKER, of London, merchant of foreign extraction, died before 1645, leaving a daughter, Prudence, m. to James Butler, of London, and a son,

NICHOLAS VANACKER, esq. lord of the manor of

rith, in Kent, who left two sons and two daughters, iz.

Francis, lord of the manor of Erith, who *d. s. p.* 13th December, 1686, aged thirty-eight.
James, died unm.
Nicholas, of whom presently.
John, of London, an eminent Turkey merchant.
Susanna, *m.* to Sir William Hedges, knt.
Judith, *m.* to Sir Jeremy Sambrooke, knt. and by him, who *d.* at his seat, Bushill, Middlesex, 27th April, 1705, had issue,

Sir Samuel Sambrooke, bart. of whom presently.
Sir Jeremy Sambrooke, of Gubbins, Herts.
John Sambrooke, *m.* Elizabeth, daughter of Sir William Forester, and *d.* at Bath, 19th May, 1734.
Mary Sambrooke, *d.* unm.
Susanna Sambrooke, *m.* to John Freeman, esq. of Fawley Court.
Judith Sambrooke.
Elizabeth Sambrooke.
Catherine Sambrooke, *m.* to Sir William Strickland, bart.
Hannah Sambrooke, *m.* to John Gore, esq.

The third son,

I. Nicholas Vanacker, esq. a Turkey merchant, was created a Baronet in 1700, with limitation, in default of male issue; first, to his brother, John, and then to his brother-in-law, Sir Jeremy Sambrooke. Sir Nicholas died in 1703, without issue, and was *s.* by his brother,

II. Sir John Vanacker, who died *s. p.* in 1710, and was *s.* by his nephew,

III. Sir Samuel Vanacker Sambrooke, who *m.* Elizabeth, daughter of Sir Nathan Wright, knt. lord keeper of the great seal, and had issue,

Jeremy, his heir.
Elizabeth, married to Charles Wake-Jones, esq. of Waltham Abbey, Essex, who died *s. p.* 22nd March, 1739-40.
Judith, *m.* to John Crawley, esq. of Bedfordshire, M.P. for Marlborough.
Susan.

Sir Samuel *d.* 27th December, 1714, and was *s.* by his son,

IV. Sir Jeremy Sambrooke, M.P. for Bedford, who died unm. at Bushill, near Enfield, 5th July, 1740, and was *s.* by his uncle,

V. Sir Jeremy Sambrooke, at whose decease unmarried, 4th October, 1754, the Baronetcy became extinct.

Arms—Quarterly; 1st and 4th, az. three salmons naiant in pale arg.; 2nd and 3rd, or on a bend gu. three cinquefoils arg.

VAN COULSTER, OF AMSTERDAM.

Created 28th February, 1644-5.—Extinct about 1665.

Lineage.

In 1644-5, a Baronetcy was conferred on

I. Joseph Van Coulster, a native of Holland, who resided at Fulham, in Middlesex, but it expired not long after, at the decease of Sir Joseph without issue.

VANDEPUT, OF TWICKENHAM.

Created 7th Nov. 1723.

Extinct 17th June, 1784.

Lineage.

Henry Vandeput, esq. of the city of Antwerp, sprung from an ancient stock in the Netherlands,* fled thence, with several other wealthy families in 1568 (11 Elizabeth) to escape the persecution of the Duke of Alva, bringing with him a considerable fortune. His son was

Giles Vandeput, who died 24th March, 1646, having married Sarah, daughter and heiress of John Jaupin, esq. with whom he acquired a large estate. His son,

Sir Peter Vandeput, knt. born in 1611, died in 1669. He *m.* Jane, daughter of Theoderick Hoste, of London, merchant. She died in 1672, and was buried in the church of St. Margaret Pattens, London, where Sir Peter's remains were also deposited. They left issue seven children, of whom only two outlived their parents, namely, Jane Vandeput, who *m.* Sir Edward Smyth, bart. of Hill Hall, Theydon, Essex, by whom she had issue, and

Sir Peter Vandeput, knt. son and heir, born in 1651, who *m.* Margaret, daughter of Sir John Buckworth, knt. of West Sheen, in Richmond, Surrey. She died 14th August, 1731; Sir Peter in April, 1708, and was buried with his ancestors at St. Margaret Pattens. His funeral sermon, in which he bears a very high character, was preached by Dr. Brady, minister of Richmond, and afterwards printed. He had held the shrievalty of London in 1684, by commission, jointly with Sir William Gosselin, which is the only instance of the kind in history. They left, with seventeen other children,

1. Peter, his heir.
1. Mary, *m.* to Sir Peter Jackson, knt. a Turkey merchant, of London, and died his widow 14th August, 1731, leaving issue,

   1. Philip.
   2. Peter.
   3. John.
   4. Edward.
   5. George.
   1. Jane, *m.* to Anthony Corbet.
   2. Margaret.
   3. Dorothy.
   4. Mary, *m.* to Roger Morris, esq. and had with other issue, a son,

      Col. Roger Morris, who *m.* in 1758, Mary, daughter of Frederick Philipse, esq. of New York, and had, *inter alios*, a son,

      Capt. Henry Gage Morris, R.N. who *m.* Rebecca-Newenham Millerd, third daughter of the Rev. Francis Orpen, and has several

* Several branches of the family still remain in the Low Countries.

children. His eldest son is the Rev. Francis Orpen Morris. (See Burke's *Commoners*, vol. iv.)

ii. Hester.
iii. Jane, *b.* in 1679.
iv. Elizabeth, *b.* in 1683.

The son and heir,

Peter Vandeput, esq. was created a Baronet 7th November, 1723. He *m.* in 1727, Frances, daughter of Sir George Mathews, knt. of Southwark. She *d.* 1st March, 1764, and Sir Peter 25th August, 1748, at Mentz, in Germany, leaving issue several children, of whom only one son survived, viz.

ii. Sir George Vandeput, born in 1729, who had the remarkable contest with Lord Trentham for the city of Westminster, in 1750. He *m.* first, Frances, daughter of Baron Augustus Schutz, of Shotover House, near Oxford, and had by her (who died at Chelmsford, in Essex, May, 1771,) one son, *b.* 14th September, 1754, who *d.* an infant, and one daughter,

Frances, *b.* in 1750, who married Richard Vere Drury, esq. an officer in the army, youngest son of the Rev. George Drury, rector of Claydon and Akenham, in Suffolk, and had issue,

George Vandeput Drury, of the East India Company's civil service, *b.* at Claydon rectory, in 1777; *m.* Charlotte, eldest daughter of Henry Thompson, esq. of Kirby Hall, near Boroughbridge, Yorkshire.

Augustus Vere Drury, captain R. N. born in 1778.

Richard Vere Drury, died at Woolwich.

Frances Schutz Drury, *m.* to Captain Hawkins, and died in India.

Sir George *m.* secondly, 19th August, 1772, Philadelphia, youngest daughter of Lieutenant-colonel Geary, of Long Melford, in Suffolk, but by her (who died 3rd July, 1806) had no legitimate issue. Sir George died at Kensington, 17th June, 1784, when the Baronetcy became extinct.

Arms—Arg. three dolphins hauriant az.

⁂ Sir George Vandeput, the last baronet, left, by different mothers, two illegitimate children, a daughter, Philadelphia, *m.* in 1779, to Charles Smyth, esq. brother of Sir William Smyth, bart. of Hill Hall, Essex; and a son, George Vandeput, admiral in the R. N. who appears to have assumed the title of baronet. He died on the Halifax station in 1800, leaving an illegitimate son, George, who also at one time called himself a Baronet.

VANDER-BRANDE, OF CLEVERSKIRKE.

Created 9th June, 1699.—Extinct date unknown.

Lineage.

i. Sir John Peter Vander-Brande, of Cleverskirke, in Holland, burgomaster of Middleburg, representative for Zealand at the States General, and ambassador to William III. was created a Baronet in 1699. He died in 1713, leaving a son,

ii. Sir Cornelius Vander-Brande, who was consul in Flanders, and executor to his father's will: but we have obtained no further particulars of himself or his descendants.

VANE, OF LONG NEWTON.

Created 13th July, 1782.  Extinct 1st Aug. 1813.

Lineage.

This family descended from

Howell ap Vane, of Monmouth, whose direct line comes down to

Sir Henry Vane, who received the honour of knighthood at the battle of Poictiers. He *m.* Grace, daughter and heir of Sir Stephen de la Leke, knt. and had a son and heir,

John Vane, who *m.* Isabel, co-heir of Martin St. Owen, and was *s.* by his son,

Richard Vane, who had by his wife, Elizabeth, daughter of Peter Trafford, esq. two sons, Henry, the *elder*, and

Henry Vane, the younger, who *m.* Isabel, daughter and co-heir of Henry Persall, esq. and had three sons, Henry, Humphrey, and John. The youngest,

John Fane, esq. of Tunbridge, in Kent, made his will 16th April, 1488 (proved 3rd June following), by which it appears that he wrote his own name and that of his father, Fane. He *m.* Isabel, daughter of John Darell, esq. and had with other issue,

Richard, of Badshill, ancestor of the Earls of Westmoreland.

John.

Thomas, whose natural son, Thomas, married his niece, Mary Fane.

The second son,

John Fane, esq. of Hadloe, in Kent, living in 1533, *m.* Joan, daughter and co-heir of Sir Edward Hawte, of Hawte, by whom he had

Henry, his heir.

Richard, *m.* and had issue.

Mary, *m.* to Thomas Fane, natural son of her uncle.

Dorothy, *m.* to Thomas Whitenhall, esq. of East Peckham.

Anne, *m.* to John Abeech, esq. of Shropshire.

Alice, *m.* to Thomas Colley.

He was *s.* by his eldest son,

Henry Fane, esq. of Hadloe, who was involved in Wyatt's insurrection, and committed to the Tower, but pardoned in consideration of his youth. He *m.* Elizabeth, daughter of Henry White, esq. of Christchurch, Hants, and widow of Sir John Godsalve, knt. and dying 22 Elizabeth, was *s.* by his son,

Henry Fane, esq. of Hadloe, who *m.* first, Mary, only daughter and heir of Thomas Fane, esq. of Burton, but by that lady had no issue. He *m.* secondly, Margaret, daughter of Roger Twisden, esq. of East Peckham, by whom he had

Henry (Sir), his heir.

Ralph, one of the gentlemen pensioners to James I died in the Low Countries.

Eleanor.

Elizabeth, *m.* to William Towes, esq.

Margaret, *m.* first, to Richard Cutts, esq., and secondly, to Sir Thomas Merton.

He was *s.* by his elder son, who resuming the ancient name of the family, was

SIR HENRY VANE, of Raby Castle, in the county of Durham. This gentleman took a leading part in state affairs in the times of JAMES I. and CHARLES I.: in the former reign he filled the office of cofferer to the Prince of Wales; and in the latter, after enjoying other high stations, was appointed principal secretary of state for life, and sworn of the privy council. His subsequent disgrace may be attributed to his hostility to the ill-fated Strafford, against whom, it is stated, he was irritated, by that celebrated person's taking the title of Baron Raby, of Raby Castle, an estate then belonging to Sir Henry Vane. Sir Henry *m.* Frances, daughter and co-heir of Thomas Darcy, esq. of Tolleshunt Darcy, in Essex, and had issue,

- HENRY (Sir), of Fairlawn, in Kent, the well known SIR HARRY VANE of the civil wars, beheaded *temp.* CHARLES II. 24th June, 1662. He was ancestor of the DUKE OF CLEVELAND.
- William.
- GEORGE (Sir).
- Edward, *d.* young.
- Walter (Sir), of Troycliffe and Shipborne.
- Charles, of Chipwell, in Durham.

The third son,

SIR GEORGE VANE, received the honour of knighthood 22nd November, 1640. He *m.* Elizabeth, only daughter and heir of Sir Lionel Maddison, knt. of Rogerley, and Newcastle-upon-Tyne, and had, with other issue,

- LIONEL, his heir.
- George, of Richmond, in Yorkshire, *m.* Hester, daughter of Guy Carleton, Bishop of Chichester, and *d.* about 1734.
- Frances, *m.* to Humphry Mitford, esq. of Mitford, in Northumberland.

He was *s.* by his eldest surviving son,

LIONEL VANE, esq. of Long Newton, in the county of Durham, *b.* in 1647, *m.* Catharine, daughter of Sir George Fletcher, bart. of Hutton, in Cumberland, by whom he had, with a daughter, Mary, *m.* to John Spearman, esq. of Sedgefield, in Durham, four sons, viz.

- GEORGE, his heir.
- Henry, of Hutton, in Cumberland, who took the name of FLETCHER, on the death of Thomas Fletcher, of Moresby, and died unm. in 1761, aged seventy-two.
- Walter, who took the name of FLETCHER, on his brother's decease, and succeeded to the HUTTON ESTATES. His grandson,
  - LIONEL-WRIGHT FLETCHER-VANE, esq. of Hutton Hall, was created a BARONET in 1786. (See BURKE's *Peerage and Baronetage.*)
- Lionel, secretary to Frederick, Prince of Wales, married and had issue.

The eldest son and heir,

GEORGE VANE, esq. *m.* Miss Anne Bachon, and left a son,

I. HENRY VANE, in holy orders, prebendary of Durham, of Long Newton, who was created a BARONET 13th July, 1782. Sir Henry *m.* Frances, daughter and heiress of John Tempest, esq. of Sherburne, in the county of Durham, M.P. by whom (who *d.* in January, 1796) he left at his decease, 7th June, 1794, a son and heir,

II. SIR HENRY VANE-TEMPEST (having assumed the latter surname by act of parliament), who *m.* Anne-Catherine M'Donnell, Countess of Antrim, in her own right, and by her ladyship, who *d.* 30th June, 1834, had an only daughter,

FRANCES-ANNE-EMILY, *b.* in January, 1800.

Sir Henry *d.* 1st August, 1813, when the BARONETCY EXPIRED, while his large estates devolved upon his daughter,

LADY FRANCES-ANNE-EMILY VANE, who married Charles-William, Marquess of Londonderry, and has, with other issue,

GEORGE-HENRY-ROBERT-CHARLES, *Viscount Seaham*, *b.* 26th April, 1821 (refer to BURKE's *Peerage and Baronetage*).

Arms—Or, three gauntlets az. a canton gu.

VANLORE, OF TYLEHURST.

CREATED 3rd Oct. 1628.—EXTINCT in 1644-5.

Lineage.

I. PETER VANLORE, a native of Utrecht, who is supposed to have had a temporary interest in the manor of Tylehurst, Berks, by some alliance with the Kendrick family, was created a BARONET, being designated of that place, in 1628. He *m.* Susan, daughter of Lawrence Becks, of Antwerp, but *d.* without male issue in 1644-5, when the title became EXTINCT.

VAN TROMP, OF HOLLAND.

CREATED 25th March, 1674-5.—EXTINCT date unknown.

Lineage.

I. CORNELIUS MARTIN VAN TROMP, (son of Martin Herbertson Van Tromp, the celebrated Dutch admiral and competitor of Blake), became himself pre-eminently distinguished in the naval annals of his country, and sustained many hard fought battles against the English. He was one of the commanders in the sea fight of Solebay, in which Obdam was blown up, and the Dutch fleet defeated; but Van Tromp, by a masterly retreat, contributed to lessen the advantage of the victors. For many years after, his name appears conspicuous in history, and in 1677 he succeeded his famous rival, De Ruyter, as lieutenant-admiral-general of the United Provinces. Shortly before, during the peace of 1674-5, he had made a visit to London, and been created a BARONET by CHARLES II. He died 29th May, 1691, just as he was about to assume the command of a fleet destined to act against France. His remains were interred in the splendid tomb of his father, at Delft. Since his decease we have no particulars of the BARONETCY.

VAVASOR, OF HASLEWOOD.

CREATED 24th Oct. 1628.

EXTINCT 20th Jan. 1826.

Lineage.

The narrative of this ancient family, which derived its surname from the high office of KING'S VAL-

VAVASOUR, which in early times it enjoyed, is so full and minute in BURKE's *History of the Commoners*, and the *Peerage and Baronetage* of the same author, that for the early descents we shall refer to those works.

I. SIR THOMAS VAVASOR, knt. of Haslewood,* in the county of York, was created a BARONET 24th April, 1628. He married Ursula, daughter of Walter Giffard, esq. of Chillington, in Staffordshire, and had issue,

- WALTER, his heir.
- William, major in the service of *King* CHARLES I. *d.* unm.
- Thomas, slain at Marston Moor.
- John, *d.* unm.
- Peter, M.D. of York, *m.* Elizabeth, daughter of Philip Langdale, esq. of Langthorpe, and had two sons,
  - WALTER, 4th BARONET.
  - Peter, whose son,
    - WALTER, *s.* as fifth BARONET.
- Mary, a nun. In Trinity Church, Coventry, on a brass plate is the following inscription: "Here lyeth the body of Mrs. Mary Vavasor, eldest daughter of Sir Thomas Vavasor, knt. and bart. late knight marshal of the king's household, who deceased this life, 24th December, 1631.
- Frances, *m.* to Alphonso Thwenge, esq. of Kilton Castle, in Yorkshire.

Sir Thomas was *s.* by his eldest son,

II. SIR WALTER VAVASOR, a zealous supporter of the royal cause, who raised a regiment of horse and headed it, for the service of *King* CHARLES I. He *m.* Ursula, daughter of Thomas, first Viscount Fauconberg, and was *s.* at his decease by his only surviving child,

III. SIR WALTER VAVASOR, who *m.* Jane, daughter of Sir Jordan Crossland, knt. but *d.* without issue, 16th February, 1712-13, when he was *s.* by (the elder son of Dr. Peter Vavasor, of York) his cousin,

IV. SIR WALTER VAVASOR, who *d.* unm. in May, 1740, aged eighty, and was *s.* by his nephew,

V. SIR WALTER VAVASOR, who *m.* first, Elizabeth, daughter of Peter Vavasor, esq. of Willitoft, in the county of York, by whom he had a daughter, who died young. He *m.* secondly, Dorothy, daughter of Marmaduke, fourth Lord Langdale, and by that lady had,

- WALTER, } THOMAS, } sixth and seventh BARONETS.
- Peter, a general officer in the Austrian service, *m.* the Countess de Paisburg, but *d. s. p.* in 1818.

Sir Walter *d.* 13th April, 1766, and was *s.* by his eldest son,

VI. SIR WATER VAVASOR, who *m.* in 1797, Jane, only daughter and heir of William Langdale, esq. of Langthorp, but *d. s. p.* 3rd November, 1802, when he was *s.* by his brother,

VII. SIR THOMAS VAVASOR, who *d.* unm. 20th January, 1826, when the BARONETCY became EXTINCT. Sir Thomas devised the estates to his cousin,

The *Honourable* EDWARD-MARMADUKE STOURTON, who in consequence, assumed the surname of VAVASOR, only, and being created a BARONET, in 1828, is now

SIR EDWARD-MARMADUKE VAVASOR, of Haslewood, refer to BURKE's *Peerage and Baronetage.*

Arms—Or, a fesse, dancettee, sable.

VAVASOUR, OF KILLINGTHORPE.

CREATED 22nd June, 1631.—EXTINCT about 1665.

Lineage.

I. CHARLES VAVASOUR, esq. of Killingthorpe, in the county of Lincoln, a descendant of the ancient Vavasour family, was created a BARONET, with the precedency of 29th June, 1611. He died, however, unm. about 1665, when the title became EXTINCT.

Arms—As VAVASOUR, of HASLEWOOD.

VAVASOR, OF COPMANTHORPE.

CREATED 17th July, 1643.—EXTINCT 19th Feb. 16[illegible]

Lineage.

I. WILLIAM VAVASOR, esq. of Copmanthorpe, in Yorkshire, lineally descended from Henry, younger son of John Vavasour, esq. of Weston, by Margaret, daughter of Sir Peter Middleton, knt. of Stockeld, was created a BARONET in 1643. He *m.* first, a Danish lady; and secondly, Oliva, daughter of Bryan Stapleton, esq. of Myton, but had no male issue. Sir William, who was a major-general to the King of Sweden, was slain at the siege of Copenhagen, in 1658, when the BARONETCY became EXTINCT. Lady Vavasor wedded secondly, Richard Topham, esq.

Arms—As VAVASOUR OF HASLEWOOD.

VERNEY, OF MIDDLE CLAYDON.

CREATED 16th Mar. 1660-1. EXTINCT 31st March, 17[illegible]

Lineage.

SIR RALPH VERNEY, was father of

JOHN VERNEY, esq. who, in 1433, was returned one of the gentry of the county of Bucks, by the commissioners of HENRY VI. He *m.* Margaret, daughter and heir of Francis Iwardby, esq. of Quanton, in the county, and had issue,

- RALPH, (Sir), his heir.
- John, (Sir), of Penley, who, in 21 EDWARD IV. was sheriff of the counties of Bedford and Bucks, and in 14 HENRY VII. of Essex and Hertfordshire.
- Eleanor, *m.* to Sir Edward Greville.
- Catherine, *m.* to Sir John Conway, knight banneret, of Arrow, in Warwickshire.
- Margaret, *m.* to Sir Edward Raleigh, knt. of Farnborough, in the same county.

* HASLEWOOD had been the seat of the family from the time of HENRY III. Sir William le Vavasor had license from EDWARD I. to castellate the mansion, of which his father, Sir John le Vavasor, had been previously lord. From Haslewood may be seen the cathedrals of York and Lincoln, although sixty miles asunder. Here is a [illegible] quarry of stone, from which the stately church of [illegible] was built, by the bounty of the Vavasors, and the monasteries of Holden, Selby, and Beverley, with Tharnton College, in Lincolnshire, and many others.

He was *s.* by his eldest son,

SIR RALPH VERNEY, of Penley and Middle Claydon, sheriff for Bedford and Bucks in 3, 16, and 32 HENRY VIII. who *m.* Elizabeth, second daughter of Edmund, Lord Braye, and co-heir of her brother, John, last Lord Braye, who *d. s. p.* in 1557, and by that lady had issue,

- EDWARD, his heir.
- John, *d. s. p.*
- EDMUND, (Sir), inheritor of the estates after his elder brother.
- Francis.
- Ralph.
- Urian.
- Richard, (Sir), sheriff of the counties of Leicester and Warwick, in 21 HENRY VIII. and 4 ELIZABETH, ancestor of the Lords Willoughby de Broke.
- Anne, *m.* to Sir Nicholas Points, of Acton, in the county of Gloucester.
- Jane, *m.* to Sir Francis Hynde, of Madingley, in Cambridgeshire.

The two elder sons dying issueless, the estates eventually devolved upon the third,

SIR EDMUND VERNEY, of Middle Claydon, Bucks, who received the honour of knighthood, and was sheriff of Bedfordshire in 14 ELIZABETH, and for Hertfordshire in 19 and 31 of the same reign. He *m.* first, Frances, daughter of John Hastings, esq. of Elford, in Oxfordshire, by whom he had no issue; secondly, Audrey, daughter of William Gardiner, esq. of Fulmere, Bucks, (widow of Sir Peter Carew), and by that lady had,

- SIR FRANCIS VERNEY, of Penley, who *m.* Ursula, daughter and co-heir of William St. Barbe, esq. but *d.* abroad, without issue, having sold the estate of Penley.
- EDMUND.

Sir Edward *m.* thirdly, Mary, daughter of John Blackney, esq. of Sparrowham. Sir Edmund's son,

SIR EDMUND VERNEY, marshal and standard bearer to *King* CHARLES I. fell at the battle of Edgehill, 23rd October, 1642. As it was Sir Edward's duty to carry the royal standard in time of war, he attended the king in that capacity, in 1639, in the expedition against the Scots; and also at Nottingham in the unhappy difference between the king and parliament; and then declared, "that by the grace of God, they that would wrest that standard from his hand, must first wrest his soul from his body." Accordingly, at the battle of Edgehill, he charged with it amongst the thickest of the enemy, to encourage the soldiers to follow him, and being surrounded, was offered his life, if he would surrender the standard, but he rejected the offer, and fell with great honour. He *m.* Margaret, eldest daughter of Sir Thomas Denton, knt. of Hillesden, Bucks, and had with six daughters, six sons, viz.

- RALPH, his heir.
- Thomas, *d.* in 1707, aged ninety-two.
- Edmund, (Sir), who being deputy governor of Drogheda, and colonel of a regiment of horse, was killed 11th September, 1649, in the storming of that town by Cromwell, *s. p.*
- Henry, a colonel also in the king's service, died unm.
- John, *d. s. p.*
- Richard, *d. s. p.*

The eldest son,

I. RALPH VERNEY, esq. of Middle Claydon, member of the restoration parliament, was created a BARONET by CHARLES II. 16th March, 1660-1. Sir Ralph *m.* Mary, daughter and heir of John Blacknall, esq. of Waseing and Abingdon, in the county of Bucks, by whom he had three daughters, who all died young, and three sons, viz.

- Edmund, who *d.* before his father, leaving a daughter,
  - MARY, *m.* to John Kelynge, esq.
- JOHN, heir to his father.
- Ralph, *d.* in infancy.

Sir Ralph was *s.* by his elder surviving son,

II. SIR JOHN VERNEY, M. P. for the county of Bucks in 1710 and 1713, who was raised to the peerage of Ireland by *Queen* ANNE, as Baron Verney, of Belturbet, and Viscount Fermanagh. His lordship *m.* first, Elizabeth, daughter of Ralph Palmer, esq. of Little Chelsea; secondly, Mary, daughter of Sir Francis Lawley, bart. of Spoonhill, in Shropshire; and thirdly, Elizabeth, daughter of Daniel Baker, esq. alderman of London. By the first he had issue,

- RALPH, his heir.
- Elizabeth, *d.* unm.
- Mary, *m.* to Colonel John Lovett, of Dublin, all her issue *d.* unm.
- MARGARET, *m.* to Sir Thomas Cave, bart. of Stanford Hall, in the county of Leicester. Her great grandaughter and representative (1838),
  - SARAH CAVE, *m.* Henry Otway, esq. of Castle Otway, in the county of Tipperary, whose widow she survives, with issue. She assumed, in 1818, the additional name of Cave, and as Mrs. Otway-Cave, claims the BARONY of BRAYE, as the descendant of ELIZABETH BRAYE, one of the co-heirs to that dignity.

The Viscount *d.* 23rd June, 1717, and was *s.* by his son,

III. SIR RALPH VERNEY, second Viscount Fermanagh, who was created by *King* GEORGE II. in 1742, Earl Verney. He *m.* Catherine, eldest daughter and co-heir of Henry Paschal, esq. of Baddow Hall, in Essex, by whom (who *d.* 26th November, 1748) he had issue,

- John, who *m.* in 1736, Mary,* daughter of Josias Nicholson, esq. but died before his father, 3rd June, 1737, leaving his wife *enciente*. She was afterwards delivered of a daughter,
  - MARY, created in 1792, BARONESS FERMANAGH. Her ladyship *d.* unm. 15th November, 1810, having bequeathed her estates to her half-sister, Mrs. Wright.
- RALPH, his heir.
- Elizabeth, *m.* to Bennet, Earl of Harborough, and had several children, who all died infants.
- Catherine, *d.* unm. in 1750.

The Earl *d.* 4th October, 1752, and was *s.* by his son,

IV. SIR RALPH VERNEY, second Earl Verney, F.R.S. who *m.* 11th September, 1740, Mary, daughter of Henry Herring, esq. a merchant of London, and director of the bank, but died issueless, 31st March, 1791, when all his honours, including the BARONETCY, EXPIRED.

Arms—Az. on a cross arg. five mullets pierced gu.

---

* She *m.* secondly, Richard Calvert, esq. and had with two sons, who both died *s. p.* a daughter, Catherine (*m.* to the Rev. Robert Wright), who eventually inherited the estates of Mary, Lady Fermanagh, and assumed the surname of VERNEY. She died *s. p.* in 1827, and was *s.* in her estates by her cousin, SIR HARRY CALVERT, bart. who has also taken the name of VERNEY.

VERNON, OF HODNET.

CREATED 22nd July, 1660.

EXTINCT in 1723.

Lineage.

HUMPHREY VERNON, third son of Sir Henry Vernon, K. B. of Haddon, in Derbyshire, by his wife, Lady Anne Talbot, daughter of John, third Earl of Shrewsbury, married in 1493, Alice, styled "The Ladye of Hodnet," eldest daughter and heiress of Sir John Ludlow, K. B. by Lady Elizabeth Grey, his wife, daughter of Richard, Earl of Powis, and acquired, with her, the estate of Hodnet, in Shropshire. Humphrey Vernon and Alice, his wife,† lived there after the death of Sir John Ludlow, in 1495, and were succeeded, in 1542, by their son,

GEORGE VERNON, esq. of Hodnet, who *m.* Elizabeth, daughter of Thomas Pigot, esq. of Chetwynd, and was interred at Hodnet, in 1553. His eldest son, Richard, dying a minor, he was *s.* by his second son,

JOHN VERNON, esq. of Hodnet, who being but seven years old at his father's death, was under the guardianship of George, Earl of Huntingdon, and Richard, Viscount Hereford. John Vernon was the acknowledged co-heir of his cousin, Henry, Earl of Powis, and one of the claimants of the barony of Powis, undecided at his death. He succeeded in recovering some of the estates of that deceased nobleman. He *m.* under age, in 1564, Elizabeth, daughter of Sir Richard Devereux, knt. by Lady Dorothy Hastings, his wife, daughter of George, Earl of Huntingdon, and had fourteen children, several of whom *d.* young. His fourth daughter, Elizabeth, *m.* to Henry, Earl of Southampton, was grandmother of Lady Rachael Wriothesley, wife of William, Lord Russell, and mother to the first Earl of Bedford. John Vernon died in 1592, was buried at Hodnet, and succeeded by his son,

SIR ROBERT VERNON, of Hodnet, *b.* in 1577, created K. B. by *Queen* ELIZABETH, and made comptroller of her majesty's household. He *m.* Mary, daughter of Sir Robert Needham, of Shavington, sister to the first Viscount Kilmorey, and dying in 1625, was *s.* by his son,

I. HENRY VERNON, esq. of Hodnet, *b.* in 1606, who was created a BARONET in 1660. During the civil wars, his devotion to the royal cause drew down upon him the hostility of the adverse party in an especial degree, but he survived to see the Restoration. He *m.* in 1636, Elizabeth, daughter and heir of Sir Richard White, knt. of the Friers, in Anglesey, and had issue,

THOMAS, his heir.

Elizabeth, who *m.* in 1675, Robert Cholmondeley, eldest son of Thomas Cholmondeley, of Vale Royal, in Cheshire, and died in 1685, leaving an only daughter,

ELIZABETH CHOLMONDELEY, who *m.* John Atherton, esq. of Atherton and Bewsey, in Lancashire, and was mother of

ELIZABETH ATHERTON, *m.* in 1752, to THOMAS HEBER, esq. of Marton, in Yorkshire, and had issue,

RICHARD HEBER, *d. s. p. m.* in 1766.

REGINALD HEBER, father of the late RICHARD HEBER, esq. of Hodnet, one of the most accomplished scholars of his time; of Reginald Heber, the pious Bishop of Calcutta; of Thomas Cuthbert Heber, the deceased rector of Marton; and of Mary Heber, present possessor of Hodnet, wife of the Rev. Charles Cowper Cholmondeley.

Sir Henry died in 1676, and was succeeded by his son,

II. SIR THOMAS VERNON, of Hodnet, who *d.* in 1684 leaving, by Mary, his wife, daughter of George Kirk, esq. a son and successor,

III. SIR RICHARD VERNON, of Hodnet, *b.* in 167– who died in 1723, at the court of Augustus, King of Poland, where he had been accredited as envoy extraordinary by GEORGE I. With him the BARONETCY EXPIRED. He dissipated a large portion of his paternal estates, several of which he sold, but that of Hodnet passed to his sisters, Diana and Henrietta, who both died unm. and in 1752 the estate, manor and advowson of Hodnet, descended through ELIZABETH, only daughter of the first baronet, Sir Henry Vernon, to the family of HEBER.

Arms—Arg. a fret sa.

VILLIERS, OF BROOKSBY.

CREATED 19th July, 1619.

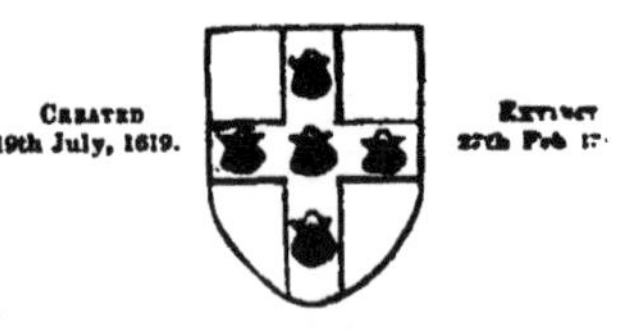

EXTINCT 27th Feb. 17–

Lineage.

The family of VILLERS came in at the Conquest and were eminent under the PLANTAGENETS.

SIR JOHN DE VILLIERS, of Brokesby, who bore for his coat armour in the time of HENRY III. "five escallops upon the cross of St. George," had a son,

SIR JOHN DE VILLERS, served in the wars of EDWARD II. and EDWARD III. His son and heir,

GEOFFREY DE VILLERS, succeeded to the estate of Brooksby, in the county of Leicester, 20 EDWARD III. and in the 26th of the same reign was one of the knights of the shire for the county of Leicester in the parliament held at Westminster. His son,

JOHN DE VILLERS, married first, Joan, one of the sisters and co-heirs of Simon Pakeman, of Kirby, in the county of Leicester, by whom he had Richard, John, Alexander, and Beatrix, the wife of Bagot. He *m.* secondly, Margaret, who was living 13 RICHARD II. at which time, viz. on the Sunday before the Feast of the Nativity of St. John, his son and heir,

† Their second son, Thomas, was ancestor of the present Lord Vernon, and their daughter, Catherine, *m.* John P–, esq. of Radborne, Derbyshire.

JOHN DE VILLERS, died seised of the manor of Brookaby and half a pound of pepper rent of assise issuing out of one virgate in Brooksby, which rent was parcel of the said manor. He *m.* Joan, daughter of William Meering, and died on the Feast of St. Catharine, 4 HENRY V. leaving his son and heir,

JOHN DE VILLERS, then twelve years old. This John died in ward to the king, and was succeeded by his brother,

WILLIAM DE VILLERS, who married Joan, sister and co-heir of John Beler, esq. and had, with other issue,

JOHN, who died in his father's lifetime, leaving by Elizabeth, his wife, daughter of John Southill, esq. of Everingham, in the county of York, a daughter, Elizabeth, and four sons, viz.

JOHN, heir to his grandfather.

Thomas, who made his will 6 HENRY VII. and *d. s. p.*

Christopher, of Burstal, sheriff of the counties of Leicester and Warwick 22 HENRY VIII. *d. s. p.* 5th August, in the 29th year of the same king, seised of the manors of Kilby, Cowdon Magna, and lands in Harborough, having settled in trustees the said manors, after his own life, upon his younger nephews, George and Thomas, and their heirs male for ever, as also the manor of Howby upon them and their brother William by a similar entail.

William, in holy orders.

Bartholomew, *m.* Margaret, daughter and co-heir of Wystonstyn, and lieth buried at Wyssendine, in the county of Rutland.

He *d.* 20 EDWARD IV. and was *s.* by his grandson,

SIR JOHN VILLIERS, of Brokesby, who was sheriff of Leicestershire and Warwickshire 6, 10, and 15 HENRY VII. and afterwards knighted at the marriage of *Prince* ARTHUR, the king's son. He *m.* Agnes, daughter of John Digby, esq. of Coleshill, in the county of Warwick, and had a daughter, Winifrid (to whom her father gave lands for life), with eight sons, viz.

JOHN (Sir), his heir.

GEORGE, THOMAS, WILLIAM, } successive lords of Brokesby.

Edward, who died possessed of lands at Flore and Howthorp, in the county of Northampton, 26th June, 5 HENRY VIII.; from him sprang the Villiers of Howthorp and those of Dowsby and Graby.

Leonard, Bartholomew, } *d. s. p.*

Anthony, of Cotness, in the county of York, died possessed of that manor 1 EDWARD VI.

He *d.* 2nd September, 22 HENRY VII. and was *s.* by his eldest son,

SIR JOHN VILLIERS, knt. of Brokesby, sheriff of Leicestershire and Warwickshire 23 and 29 HENRY VIII. This gentleman, in the 30th year of the same king, was found cousin and next heir to his uncle Christopher aforesaid, in the manor of Bourstal, being then aged fifty and upwards. He *d.* 9th December, 38 HENRY VIII. seised of the manors of Brokesby and Howby, and the advowsons of those churches, having, by a fine levied 22nd of the same reign, between Alexander Villers and Richard Holme, *querents*, the said Sir John and Dorothy, his daughter and heir apparent by Elizabeth, his wife, daughter of John Wingar), *deforcients*, settled the said manors and rent in Brokesby, Howby, and Sevelby, on himself in tail male; and, in default, to his brothers, GEORGE, THOMAS, WILLIAM, and LEONARD. He died seised also of lands and tenements in Rotherby, Tursington, &c. Dorothy, his daughter, the wife of Francis Brown, gent. being found heir to them, and aged twenty-eight years and upwards. The other lands devolved under the settlement upon his next brother,

GEORGE VILLIERS, esq. of Brokesby and Howby, who was also seised of the manor of Siwolby in fee tail, and of the manor of Burstal upon the death of John Villers, *alias* Twyford. This George left issue, by Joane, his wife, daughter of John Harrington, of Bagworth, RICHARD, his son and heir, aged three years, died a minor; and a daughter, ELIZABETH, heir to her brother, wife of Sir Edward Waterhouse, who also died without issue; so that the estates passed to the next brother mentioned in the entail,

THOMAS VILLIERS, esq. who left but one daughter, DOROTHY, the wife of William Smith, esq. of Leicestershire, when again, under the entail, the lands passed to the male heir, Thomas's next brother,

WILLIAM VILLIERS, esq. of Brokesby, who *m.* Colletta, daughter and heir of Richard Clarke, esq. of Huntingdonshire (widow of Richard Beaumont, esq. of Coleorton, in the county of Leicester), and dying 1st November, 5 and 6 PHILIP and MARY, was *s.* by his son,

SIR GEORGE VILLIERS, knt. of Brokesby, sheriff of Leicestershire 33 ELIZABETH, *m.* first, Audrey, daughter and heir of William Sanders, esq. of Harrington, in the county of Northampton, and by her, who died 29 ELIZABETH, had issue,

WILLIAM (Sir), his heir.

Edward (Sir), president of Munster, from whom the Earls of Jersey and Clarendon derive.

Elizabeth, *m.* to John, Lord Butler, of Bramfield.

Anne, *m.* to Sir William Washington, knt. of Pakington, in the county of Lincoln.

Frances.

He *m.* secondly, Mary, daughter of Anthony Beaumont, esq. of Glenfield, in the county of Leicester, which lady having survived her first husband,* was created Countess of Buckingham for life; by her he had

JOHN, created BARON VILLIERS *of Stoke* and VISCOUNT PURBECK.†

GEORGE, the celebrated favourite of JAMES I. and CHARLES I. created DUKE OF BUCKINGHAM.†

CHRISTOPHER, created EARL OF ANGLESEY.†

Susan, *m.* to William Fielding, Earl of Denbigh.

Sir George *d.* 4th January, 1605, having entailed Brokesby, Howby, Godby Marward, and the Grange of Godby, upon the issue of his first marriage; and all the tythes of herbage, grain, and hay, and all other tythes arising in Cadwel and Wikeham, in the county of Leicester, upon the children of the second. His eldest son,

I. SIR WILLIAM VILLIERS, of Brooksby, in the county of Leicester, sheriff of that shire 6 JAMES I. received the honour of knighthood from that monarch, and was afterwards created a BARONET, 19th July, 1619. He *m.* first, Anne, daughter of Sir Edward Griffin, knt. of Dingley, by whom he had no male issue; secondly, Anne, daughter of Richard Fiennes, Lord Say and Sele, which lady died issueless; and thirdly, Rebecca, daughter of Robert Roper, of Heanor, in the county of Derby. He *d.* 12th June, 1629, and was *s.* by his only son,

* Her ladyship *m.* secondly, Sir William Rayner; and thirdly, Sir Thomas Compton, K. B.

† For details, refer to BURKE'S *Extinct Peerage*.

II. Sir George Villiers, who m. Penelope, daughter and co-heir of Sir John Denham, knt. of Blechington, in the county of Oxford, and had

William, his heir.

Penelope, m. to Sir William Jesson, of Newhouse, in the county of Warwick, and had two daughters, viz.

Penelope Jesson, m. to George Hewet, esq. of Stretton, in the county of Leicester.

Anne Jesson, m. to Sir James Robinson, bart. and was great-great-grandmother of the present

Sir George-Stamp Robinson, bart.

He died about the year 1682, and was succeeded by his son,

III. Sir William Villiers, M.P. for the county of Leicester, who m. Anne, daughter and heir of Charles Potts, esq. but died without issue 27th February, 1711, aged sixty-seven, when the Baronetcy expired. Sir William sold the manor of Brooksby to the Lord Keeper Sir Nathan Wright. To his other possessions his sister's daughters became his heirs.

Arms—Arg. on a cross gu. five escallops or.

VINER, OF LONDON.

Created 18th June, 1661.

Extinct

Lineage.

I. Sir Thomas Viner, descended of a Gloucestershire family, filled the civic chair of the city of London in 1653, and was created a Baronet in 1660. He m. first, Anne, daughter of Richard Parsons, merchant; secondly, Honor, sister of Sir William Humble, bart.; and thirdly, Alice Robinson, widow of Mr. Alderman John Perrin, of London. Sir Thomas died 11th May, 1665, aged seventy-seven, and was s. by his son,

II. Sir George Viner, who m. Abigail, daughter and co-heir of Sir John Lawrence, knt. alderman of London, and dying in 1673, was s. by his son,

III. Sir Thomas Viner, at whose decease, under age, the title became extinct.

Arms—Az. a bend or, on a chief arg. a saltier engrailed gu. between two Cornish choughs ppr.

VINER, OF LONDON.

Created 10th May, 1666.—Extinct 1688.

Lineage.

I. Sir Robert Viner, lord mayor of London in 1675, was created a Baronet 10th May, 1666. He m. twice: his last wife, was Mary, daughter of John Whitchurch, esq. of Walton, Berks, and relict of Sir Thomas Hyde, bart. of Albury, Herts, but died without issue in 1688, when the title became extinct.

Arms—As preceding article.

VITUS, OF LIMERICK.

Created 29th June, 1677.—Extinct (unknown)

Lineage.

I. Sir Ignatius Vitus, otherwise White, of Limerick, a count of the Holy Roman Empire, was created a Baronet in 1677, with remainder to his nephew Ignatius Maximilian Vitus, alias White, who obtained the title of Marquis D'Abbeville from James II. He m. first, a lady whose christian name was Mary; and secondly, a daughter of Patrick Fitz-Thomas, lord of Kerry, but of Sir Ignatius or of the subsequent destination of the Baronetcy we have not been able to ascertain further.

WALKER, OF BUSHEY HALL.

Created 28th Jan. 1679.

Extinct after 1692.

Lineage.

Sir Walter Walker, knt. of Bushey Hall, Herts and of Stretham, in the Isle of Ely, LL.D. a lawyer of considerable eminence, and advocate to Katharine, queen consort of Charles II. was born at Barton-under-Needwood, in the county of Stafford, where it is conjectured he was interred, and to which parish he bequeathed a benevolent memento. He m. Mary daughter of — Lynne, of Southwick, in Northamptonshire, and had issue,

George (Sir), his heir.

William, who m. Mary, daughter of — Price, of Newtown, in Montgomeryshire, and had an only son,

Nathaniel, of Middlesex, who m. Elizabeth-Jane, daughter of Peter Pytot, esq. and was father of

Nathaniel, a major in the army, who m. Henrietta, daughter and heiress of Captain John Bagster, R. N. of the Isle of Wight, and dying at Hampton Court Palace in May, 1829, left issue,

George-Townshend, the present Lieutenant-General Sir George Townshend Walker, bart. G.C.B. (See Burke's *Peerage and Baronetage.*)

Frederick, of Bushey, Herts, a colonel in the army, m. and has issue. (See Burke's *Commoners*, vol. . p. 312.)

Charles-Montagu, of Hampton Court, captain R.N. m. and has issue.

Mary, m. to Stawell Chudleigh, esq. of Furze Place Farm, Hants.

Harriet-Louisa, m. to James Grierson, esq.

Elizabeth, married to Sir Edwin Sadleir, bart of Temple Dinsley.

Mary, m. first, to Henry Beaufoy, esq.; and secondly, to Arthur Weltden, esq.

Martha, died unm.

he elder son,

i. Sir George Walker, of Bushey Hall, Herts, was nighted at Whitehall, 22nd November, 1676, and reated a Baronet 26th January, 1679. He m. Suannah, daughter and co-heir of John Byne, esq. of owdell, in Sussex, and had issue,

Walter, his heir.

Elizabeth, under age in 1680, m. to Brown, of Horsemonden, in Kent.

Susannah, who also married.

Byne, m. to John Spence, esq. of South Malling, Sussex, and of Lebury Manor, Herts, and dying in 1721, aged thirty-nine, left issue,

Luke Spence, a magistrate for Sussex, who m. Henrietta, daughter of Sir Thomas Frederick, knt. and had a son,

Henry Spence, b. 26th February, 1747-8, who m. Philippa, daughter of Robert Butts, Bishop of Ely, and had issue,

Augustus-Frederick, b. in 1772, d. s. p.

Henry-Hume, b. in 1775, m. Miss Lowry, and has issue.

Harriet, m. to the Rev. R. Hare.

Mary-Ann, m. to the Comte de Burbell.

Henry Spence, d. s. p.

Byne Spence, married Thomas Beale, esq. of Shropshire, and had issue, Thomas-Henry, and Byne, wife of John Oakley, esq.

ir George Walker, having wasted his large property, ied in the King's Bench prison in 1690, and was uried at St. George the Martyr's. His estate of Bushey Hall became, by purchase, the property of Sir Robert Marsham. Sir George's only son,

ii. Sir Walter Walker, who inherited his mother's state, died unm. in his minority, when the title beame extinct.

Arms—Or, on a pile az. three gal traps of the first.

WALTER, OF SARESDEN.

Created 16th Aug. 1641. Extinct 20th Nov. 1731.

Lineage.

Edward Walter, of Ludlow, in the county of Salop, a Welch judge, d. 29th January, 1592, leaving by Mary, his wife, daughter of Thomas Hackluit, esq. of Eyton,

Sir John Walter, knt. who was of Brasennose College, Oxford, afterwards of the Inner Temple, and eventually lord chief baron of the Exchequer. He m. first, Margaret, daughter of William Offley, esq. of London, and had issue,

William, his heir.

Edward.

David, of Godstow, made groom of the bedchamber and lieutenant-general of the ordnance *temp.* Charles II. for his loyalty and valour during the civil war, m. Elizabeth, daughter and eventual heir of Paul, Viscount Bayning, and widow of Francis Lennard, Lord Dacre (this lady was created Countess of Sheppy for life), but died without issue in 1679.

John.

Mary, m. to Sir John Cope, bart.

Elizabeth, m. to Sir Francis Burdett, bart.

Catherine.

Margaret.

Sir John m. secondly, Anne, daughter of William Wytham, esq. of Ledstone, in Yorkshire, and relict of Sir Thomas Bigges, of Lenchwike, in the county of Worcester, but had no other issue. He d. 18th November, 1630, and was s. by his eldest son,

i. William Walter, esq. of Saresden, in the county of Oxford, who was created a Baronet by King Charles I. Sir William m. Elizabeth, daughter of Thomas Lucas, esq. of St. John's, near Colchester, and dying 23rd March, 1674, was s. by his son,

ii. Sir William Walter, who m. first, Lady Mary Bruce, daughter of Robert, Earl of Ailesbury; and secondly, Lady Mary Tufton, daughter of John, Earl of Thanet; by the latter he had

William, b. in 1671, died unm. aged twenty-one.

John, his heir.

Robert, heir to his brother.

Mary, m. to Sir Robert Rich, bart. of Sunning, in Berkshire.

He d. 5th March, 1693, and was s. by his son,

iii. Sir John Walter, M.P. for Oxford, clerk of the green cloth, m. Elizabeth, daughter of Sir Thomas Vernon, knt. by whom (who m. secondly, Viscount Harcourt,) he had no issue. He d. 11th June, 1722, and was s. by his brother,

iv. Sir Robert Walter, who m. Elizabeth, daughter of Henry Brydges, D.D. archdeacon of Rochester, and niece of James, Duke of Chandos, but died 28th November, 1731, without issue, when the Baronetcy became extinct.

Arms—Az. a fesse dancettè or, between three eagles displayed arg.

WANDESFORD, OF KIRKLINGTON.

Created 5th Aug. 1662. Extinct 12th Jan. 1784.

Lineage.

This family was of great antiquity in the county of York.

Galfridus de Wandesford, of Alnwick, was grandfather of

John de Wandesford, of Westwick, who dying in 1395, left three sons, John, Roger, and Geoffrey. The eldest,

John de Wandesford, born about the year 1370, succeeded at Kirklington, where his posterity subsequently flourished. He had issue,

John, his heir.

Thomas, an alderman of London, who d. in 1448, leaving a son, William, who d. s. p.

The elder son and heir,

John de Wandesford, died in 1463. He had seven sons and three daughters, viz.

Christopher, his heir.

Thomas, d. s. p.

Richard.

John.
George, archdeacon of Richmond, in Yorkshire.
Bryan, left no issue.
Elizabeth, m. to — Mancaly, of Sinninghurst.
Jane, m. to Thomas Lesonby.
Isabel, m. to Thomas Hetterby.

The eldest son,

CHRISTOPHER WANDESFORD, esq. of Kirklington, m. Sibel, daughter of John Thwaites, esq. and had issue,
THOMAS, his successor.
John.
Roger.
Christopher.
Anne.
Eleanor, m. to William Rees, esq. of Nottingham, lord of Laxton.
Jane, m. to Sir William Norton.

He was s. by his eldest son,

THOMAS WANDESFORD, esq. of Kirklington, who m. Margaret, daughter of Sir Henry Pudsey, and had four sons and two daughters, viz.
CHRISTOPHER, his heir.
William, of Woodel, in the county of Bedford.
Michael, whose grandson,
Sir Rowland Wandesford, knt. of Pickhay, in Yorkshire, was attorney of the Court of Wards and Liveries in 1637. His daughter,
Elizabeth, m. Philip, fourth Lord Wharton, and their only daughter,
ELIZABETH WHARTON, married Robert Bertie, third Earl of Lindsey.
John, rector of Kirklington.
Ellen, m. to Ambrose Lancaster, esq. of Westmoreland.
Elizabeth, m. to Ralph Claxton, esq. of the county of Durham.

The eldest son,

CHRISTOPHER WANDESFORD, esq. living *temp.* EDWARD IV. and HENRY VII. m. Anne, daughter of John Norton, esq. of Norton, and had
FRANCIS, his heir.
Christopher, who had issue.

The elder son,

FRANCIS WANDESFORD, esq. who m. Jane, second daughter and co-heir of John Fulthorp, esq. of Hipswell, and had by her
CHRISTOPHER (Sir).
John, died without issue.
Jane.

He was s. by his elder son,

SIR CHRISTOPHER WANDESFORD, who was knighted and served as sheriff of Yorkshire in 1578. He m. Elizabeth, daughter of Sir George Bowes, of Streatham, and was s. by his eldest son,

SIR GEORGE WANDESFORD, b. 20th May, 1573; knighted by *King* JAMES I.; and d. in 1610. He m. Catharine, daughter of — Hansby, esq. of Beverley, and had issue,
CHRISTOPHER, his successor.
John, M.P. in 1639.
William, citizen and merchant taylor of London, to whom and his heirs his eldest brother, 20th June, 1637, gave £20 per annum, issuing out of the manor of Castlecomer, and payable upon Strongbow's tomb in Christ Church, Dublin. In 1639 he was member in the Irish parliament for Ballynekill, in the Queen's County.
Nicholas, M.P. for Thomastown in the parliament of Ireland.
Michael, in holy orders, successively dean of Limerick and Derry.
Anne, m. to Mauger Norton, esq. of St. Nicholas, near Richmond, Yorkshire.
Mary.

The eldest son,

CHRISTOPHER WANDESFORD, esq. being upon the habits of intimacy and friendship with Sir Thomas Wentworth, Earl of Strafford, accompanied that eminent and ill-fated nobleman into Ireland when he was constituted chief governor of that kingdom. He was appointed in 1633 master of the rolls, at the same time being sworn of the privy council; of the [illegible] he had soon after a grant by patent for life. He was one of the lords justices in 1636 and 1639, and was appointed 1st April, 1640, lord deputy; but the fate of his friend Lord Strafford had so deep an effect upon him, that he died 3rd December, in that year. He m. first, the daughter of William and sister of Sir [illegible] Ramsden, knt. of Byrom, in Yorkshire, but by that lady had no issue. He wedded, secondly, Alice, daughter of Sir Hewet Osborne, of Kniveton, in the same county, and had issue,
GEORGE, his heir.
CHRISTOPHER, successor to his brother.
John.
Alice.
Catherine, m. to Sir Thomas Danby, knt. of Farnley, near Leeds, and died in childbed of her fifteenth child, aged thirty.

He was s. by his eldest son,

GEORGE WANDESFORD, esq. M.P. for Clogher in 1639, d. s. p. and was s. by his brother,

I. CHRISTOPHER WANDESFORD, esq. of Kirklington, in the county of York, who was created a Bart. 5th August, 1662. He m. Eleanor, daughter of Sir John Lowther, bart. of Lowther Hall, in the county of Westmoreland, and had issue,
CHRISTOPHER, his heir.
George, who had issue.
Charles, d. s. p.
Mary.
Eleanor, m. to Amias Bushe, esq. of Kilfane, in the county of Kilkenny.
Catherine, m. to Sir Richard Pyne, chief justice of the King's Bench, and d. in 1731, aged [illegible] four.
Frances, m. to Robert Maude, esq. of Ripon, in Yorkshire, and Kilkenny; d. 5th January [illegible].
Alice.
Christian, m. to Richard Lowther, merchant of Leeds, second son of Sir William Lowther, knt. of Swillington.

Sir Christopher, who was member of parliament for Rippon, d. in February, 1686, and was s. by his eldest son,

II. SIR CHRISTOPHER WANDESFORD, who was attainted by *King* JAMES's parliament in 1689, and had his estate sequestered; but on the Revolution he was sworn of the privy council by *King* WILLIAM and again in 1702 by *Queen* ANNE, who advanced him to the peerage of Ireland in 1706, as Baron Wandesford and Viscount Castlecomer. He m. Elizabeth, daughter of George Montagu, esq. of Horton, in Northamptonshire, and by that lady (who died 12th November 1731,) had issue,
CHRISTOPHER, his successor.
GEORGE, of whom hereafter as heir to his nephew.
John, in holy orders, rector of Kirklington and Catterick, d. in March, 1747-8.
Richard, d. unm.
Henrietta, m. to William Maynard, esq. of Curryglass, in the county of Cork, M.P. and died 28th April, 1736.

His lordship d. in London 15th September, 1707, and was s. by his eldest son,

III. SIR CHRISTOPHER WANDESFORD, second Viscount Castlecomer, member in the British parliament in [illegible] for Morpeth and in 1714 for Rippon. In the lear he was sworn of the privy council to *King* George I. and the next year appointed governor of the county of Kilkenny. In 1717 he was constituted secretary-at-war, and died 22nd June, 1719, leaving by his wife, Frances, second daughter of Thomas, Lord Pelham, and sister to Thomas, Duke of Newcastle, an only child,

IV. SIR CHRISTOPHER WANDESFORD, third Viscount Castlecomer, *b.* in 1717, who *d.* in London of the small-pox unmarried 8th May, 1736, and was *s.* by his uncle,

V. SIR GEORGE WANDESFORD, fourth Viscount Castlecomer, who *m.* Susannah, daughter of the Rev. Mr. Griffyth, of Cork, by whom he had several children, which but three survived, viz.

- JOHN, his heir.
- Susannah, *m.* to Thomas Newenham, esq. of Coolmore, in the county of Cork.
- Elizabeth.

He *d.* 25th June, 1751, and was *s.* by his son,

VI. SIR JOHN WANDESFORD, fifth Viscount Castlecomer, who took his seat in the Irish House of Lords in 1751, and was created in 1758 Earl of Wandesford. He *m.* 11th August, 1750, Agnes-Elizabeth, daughter and heir of John Southwell, esq. of Enniscouch, in the county of Limerick, and had issue,

- JOHN, *Viscount Castlecomer*, *b.* 23rd April, 1753, died before the earl.
- ANNE, *m.* 26th February, 1769, to John Butler, esq. of Carryricken, to whom the EARLDOM OF ORMONDE was restored by the House of Lords in Ireland in 1791.

His lordship *d.* 12th January, 1784, and his son having predeceased him, all his honours, including the BARONETCY, became EXTINCT, and the estates devolved upon his only daughter, then

LADY ANNE BUTLER. (Refer to BURKE's *Peerage and Baronetage*.)

Arms—Or, a lion rampant az.

WARBURTON, OF ARLEY.

CREATED 27th June, 1660.

EXTINCT 13th May, 1813.

Lineage.

SIR JOHN WARBURTON,* of Warburton and Arley, both in the county of Chester, one of the knights of the body to *King* HENRY VIII. Seneschal of Halton, and sheriff of Chester by patent under the great seal, for life, *m.* Jane, daughter of Sir William Stanley, knt. and was *s.* by his son,

SIR PIERS WARBURTON, knt. who *m.* Elizabeth, daughter and heir of Richard Winnington, esq. of Winnington, in Shropshire, and was *s.* in 4 EDWARD VI. by his son,

SIR JOHN WARBURTON, knt. who *m.* Mary, daughter of Sir William Brereton, of Brereton, in Cheshire, and dying in 1572, was *s.* by his eldest son,

SIR PETER WARBURTON, knt. an eminent lawyer in the time of ELIZABETH, and one of the justices of the Common Pleas. He *m.* Mary, daughter of Sir John Holcroft, knt. and having daughters only, the representation of the family devolved upon the grandson of his brother, George Warburton, esq. of the Lodge, his great nephew,

PETER WARBURTON, esq. of the Lodge, and of Arley, who married Eleanor, daughter of Robert, Viscount Kilmorey, but dying without issue, 1st August, 1641, was *s.* by his brother,

I. GEORGE WARBURTON, esq. of Arley, in the county of Chester, who was created a BARONET 27th June, 1660. Sir George married first, Elizabeth, daughter of Sir Thomas Myddleton, knt. of Chirk Castle, in Denbighshire, and had issue,

- PETER, his heir.
- George, who left issue.
- Eleanor, *m.* to Sir Francis Edwards, bart. of Shrewsbury.
- Hester, *m.* to Edward Domville, esq. of Lymme, in Cheshire.
- Mary, *m.* to William Grantham, esq. of Bury, in Lincolnshire.
- Catherine.

He married secondly, Diana, daughter of Sir Edward Bisshopp, bart. of Parham, in Sussex, and by her had,

- Thomas, of Winnington, in Cheshire, who had several children. His male line terminated with his son,
  - General Hugh Warburton, whose only daughter *m.* Richard Pennant, M.D. of Liverpool.
- Robert.
- John.
- Cecil.
- Penelope, *m.* to Sir John Mordaunt, bart.
- Catherine, *m.* to Humphrey Trafford, esq. of Trafford.

Sir George *d.* 18th May, 1676, and was *s.* by his eldest son,

II. SIR PETER WARBURTON, who *m.* Martha, daughter and heir of Thomas Dockwra, esq. of Puckeridge, Herts, and had issue,

- GEORGE, his heir.
- Thomas, of Turner's Hall, Herts, who wedded, first, Rebecca, daughter and co-heir of George Stourton, esq. of Pirton, in Bedfordshire, and by that lady had a daughter,
  - Martha, *m.* to Isaac Eles, citizen of London.

  He *m.* secondly, Anne, daughter of William Dockwra, esq. of London, and had by her,
  - PETER, fourth baronet.
  - Anne, wife of Thomas Sloughter, esq. high sheriff of Cheshire in 1755. Their only son,
    - THOMAS SLOUGHTER, captain 16th Light Dragoons, left, by Sarah, his wife, an only child,
      - ANNE-WARBURTON SLOUGHTER, married first, to the Rev. Thomas Coupland, of the Priory, Chester; and secondly, to William Owen, esq. K.C. of Glansevern, in Montgomeryshire. That highly respected gentleman died deeply lamented in 1837, leaving to his widow the whole of his estates, including the beautiful seat of Glansevern.
- Peter, captain in the army.
- Martha, *m.* to — Fouks, esq. of London.
- Anne, *m.* to Richard Dockwra, esq.
- Arabella.

He was *s.* by his son,

III. SIR GEORGE WARBURTON, who *m.* Diana, daughter of William, second Lord Allington, by whom he had one surviving child,

* For his predecessors refer to BURKE's *Commoners*, vol. ii. p. 1.

DIANA, *m.* in 1734, to Sir Richard Grosvenor, bart. of Eaton, but *d. s. p.* in 1730.

Sir George, who represented the county of Chester in several parliaments in the time of *Queen* ANNE, and *King* GEORGE I. *d.* 29th June, 1742, and was *s.* by his nephew,

IV. SIR PETER WARBURTON, who wedded in 1745, Lady Elizabeth Stanley, eldest daughter of Edward, Earl of Derby, and had issue,

PETER, his heir.
Elizabeth, Anne, Margaret, } *d. unm.*
Harriot, *m.* to John-Rowlls Leigh, esq. of Prestbury, and had
Charles Leigh, *d. s. p.*
ELIZABETH-ESTER-LEIGH, *m.* to Thomas Delves Broughton, esq.
EMMA, *m.* first, to James Croxton, esq. of Norley Bank, in Cheshire, by whom, who *d.* in 1792, she had a daughter,
EMMA CROXTON, who *m.* in 1803, the Rev. Rowland Egerton, B. A. who assumed in consequence, the additional surname of WARBURTON. By Mr. Egerton Warburton she had, with several younger children,
ROWLAND-EYLES EGERTON-WARBURTON, of whom hereafter.
Mrs. Croxton, outliving her first husband, married secondly, Mr. John Hunt, and had another daughter,

Sir Peter *d.* 18th March, 1774, and was *s.* by his son,

V. SIR PETER WARBURTON, who *m.* in 1754, Alice, daughter of the Rev. John Parker, of Astle, in the county of Chester, but had no issue. He *d.* 13th May, 1813, when the BARONETCY EXPIRED, and the estates, by Sir Peter's will, to his great nephew,

ROWLAND-EYLES EGERTON-WARBURTON, esq. now (1838) of ARLEY.

Arms—Arg. a chevron, between three cormorants sable, in the chief point a cross crosslet, of the last.

WARD, OF BEXLEY.

CREATED 19th Dec. 1660.

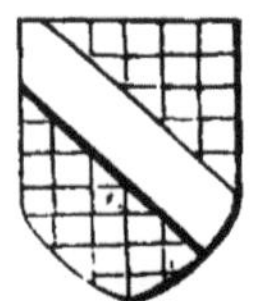

EXTINCT about 1770.

Lineage.

JOHN WARD, who possessed the manor of Kirby-Bedon, in Norfolk, in 1363; *m.* the daughter of John de Boscoe, and from him descended

ROBERT WARD, esq. of Kirby, who wedded the daughter of Sir Giles Capel, of London, knt. and had a son and heir,

HENRY WARD, esq. of Postwick, who *m.* the daughter of William Ugge, esq. of Peckthorpe, and had several children. The eldest son,

EDWARD WARD, esq. of Bexley, in Norfolk, *m.* Anne, daughter of John Havers, esq. of Winfarthing, [illegible] sister of Thomas Havers, esq. of Thelton Hall, [illegible] whom he had eight children.* He was *s.* by his eldest son,

THOMAS WARD, esq. of Bexley, who *m.* [illegible] daughter of Thomas Godsalve, esq. of Buckenham, in Norfolk, and was *s.* by his son,

THOMAS WARD, esq. who *m.* Anne, daughter of William Pert, esq. of Essex, and left a son and heir,

I. SIR EDWARD WARD, knt. of Bexley, who was twice sheriff of Norfolk, and was created a BARONET by CHARLES II. 19th December, 1660. He married first, the daughter of — Catlyn, esq. and secondly Elizabeth, daughter and heir of John Harbourne, esq. of Mundham, and granddaughter of William Harbourne, who was sent ambassador from QUEEN ELIZABETH to the Grand Seignior: by the latter he had issue, and dying about 1684, was *s.* by his son,

II. SIR EDWARD WARD, who *m.* Jane, daughter of William Rant, M.D. of London, and died about [illegible] when he was *s.* by his eldest son,

III. SIR THOMAS WARD, who *d. unm.* in [illegible], and was *s.* by his brother,

IV. SIR EDWARD WARD, who married Barbara, [illegible] and co-heir of Leonard Gooch, esq. of Earsham, Norfolk, and was *s.* by his son,

V. SIR EDWARD WARD, who *m.* Susan, daughter and heir of William Randall, of Yarmouth, merchant, and had issue,

EDWARD, his successor.
RANDALL, heir to his brother.
Susan.

He died 2nd March, 1737, and was *s.* by his son,

VI. SIR EDWARD WARD, who died unmarried, aged twenty-one, 7th April, 1742, and was *s.* by his brother,

VII. SIR RANDALL WARD, who *m.* Miss Randall, and died 8th May, 1762, leaving a son and successor,

VIII. SIR EDWARD WARD, who *d. s. p.* about the year 1770, when the BARONETCY EXPIRED.

Arms—Cheque, or and azure, a bend, ermine.

WARNER, OF PARHAM.

CREATED 16th July, 1660.

EXT[illegible]

Lineage.

I. JOHN WARNER, esq. of Parham, in Suffolk, son of Francis Warner, esq. of Parham, by Elizabeth [illegible] wife, daughter of Sir John Rous, knt. of Henham, [illegible] a lineal descendant of the ancient family of Warner, of Warner's Hall, in Great Waltham, Essex, was created a BARONET in 1660. He *m.* Trevor, daughter of Sir Thomas Hanmer, bart. of Hanmer, and had [illegible] daughters, who both took the veil. At Sir John's [illegible] cease the title became EXTINCT.

Arms—Or, a bend engr. between six roses g

---

* The youngest son,

SIR WILLIAM WARD, was a wealthy goldsmith in London, and jeweller to the queen of CHARLES I. He left a son and heir,

SIR HUMBLE WARD, who was knighted at Oxford in 1643, and having Frances, granddaughter and heir of Edward Sutton, Lord Dudley, was created BARON WARD, of Birmingham; from his son [illegible] descended the Lords Dudley and Ward, &c.

WARRE, OF HESTERCOMBE.

CREATED 2nd June, 1673.

EXTINCT 1st Dec. 1718.

Lineage.

SIR FRANCIS WARRE, esq. of Hestercombe, in the parish of Kingston, in the county of Somerset, created a BART. in 1673, was only son of Sir John Warre, knt. M. P. for the county of Somerset, who died in 1669, by Unton,* daughter of Sir Francis Hawley, of Buckland-Sororum, bart. (afterwards Baron Hawley, in the kingdom of Ireland; descended by his mother and grandmother from the Portmans, of Orchard-Portman, and the Lords Poulet of Hinton St. George.) Sir Francis Warre, in his early years was a captain in the Duke of Monmouth's own regiment, but upon his marriage he retired: he was also colonel of the Taunton regiment, vice-admiral of Somersetshire and the port of Bristol, a deputy lieutenant, in the commission of the peace, and M. P. for the boroughs of Bridgewater and Taunton in various parliaments to the year 1716. He twice married: first, Anne, daughter and heir of Robert Cuffe, esq. of Creech St. Michael, by whom he had one son, who served as a captain of dragoons, and died at Ghent, in Flanders, in the thirty-third year of his age; and secondly, Margaret, daughter of John Harbin, merchant of London, of a family of that name near Yeovil, in the county of Somerset, by whom he had

William, who died an infant.

MARGARET.

Sir Francis died 1st December, 1718, and was buried with his ancestors in the family vault at Kingston. He was heir to Kentisbere, Meriet, Atwood, Percesaye, Clavile, Combe, Chipleigh, St. Barbe, and Cuffe, whose arms he quartered with his own. At his decease the BARONETCY became EXTINCT; but Hestercombe and the other estates of which he died seized devolved upon his only surviving child and heiress,

MARGARET WARRE, who married John Bampfylde, younger and only brother of Sir Coplestone Warwick Bampfylde, of Poltimore, in the county of Devon, bart. The first wife of John Bampfylde, esq. was Elizabeth, daughter of — Basset, esq. of Heanton Court, in the county of Devon, by whom he had no issue. He was representative in parliament first for the county of Devon, which he gave up to his nephew, Sir Richard Warwick Bampfylde, bart. when he came of age, and after that for the city of Exeter. He was born 8th April, 1690, and died 17th September, 1750, and is buried at Kingston. By his second wife, Margaret, the heiress of Hestercombe, he had issue,

COPLESTONE WARRE BAMPFYLDE, who succeeded to the Hestercombe estates: of whom presently.

Elizabeth, who *d.* unm.

Margaretta, who married, as second wife, 31st December, 1753, George Tyndale,† esq. of Bathford, in the county of Somerset, lineally descended from the feudal Barons de Tyndale, in South Tyne-dale, in the county of Northumberland (see BURKE's *Commoners*), and died in December, 1792, leaving issue,

JOHN, who pursuant to the will of his maternal uncle, Coplestone Warre Bampfylde, esq. became possessed of the Hestercombe and other estates, and assumed the name of WARRE after that of Tyndale (vide infra).

Thomas Bampfylde, esq. of Withiel-Flory, in the county of Somerset, an officer in the 14th regiment of foot. He *m.* Anne, daughter of the Rev. John Dennis, a minor canon of Oxford, by whom he had issue three daughters, vis.

Anna-Margaretta, married to the Rev. Charles Taylor, and has issue.

Louisa-Vere, *m.* to George Coppy, esq. formerly of Demerara, and late of Taunton, and has issue.

Georgiana Maria, *m.* Charles Corfield, esq. of Knowle House, near Taunton, and has issue.

Thomas Bampfylde Tyndale died 17th September, 1807.

Margaretta, *m.* to Charles Hill, esq. late of Clifton, Bristol, who died and has an only child and heiress,

Caroline, *m.* to Arthur Chichester, esq. of the county of Devon, and has issue.

Elizabeth, twin sister to John. She died unmarried.

Charlotte, *m.* to Thomas Eagles, esq. late of Bristol, and has issue,

Edward.

John, in holy orders.

George Tyndale, esq. of Bathford, died in 1771, and was buried at Bathford.

COPLESTONE WARRE BAMPFYLDE, only son of Margaret, the heiress of Hestercombe, *m.* Mary, second daughter of Edward Knight, esq. of Woolverley, in the county of Worcester, but had no issue. He was for many years colonel of the Somersetshire militia, and in the commission of the peace. He died 29th August, 1791, and bequeathed Hestercombe and his other estates to his nephew and heir-at-law, John Tyndale, on condition of his assuming the name of WARRE. This

JOHN TYNDALE WARRE, eldest son of George Tyndale, esq. aforesaid, by his second wife, Margaretta Bampfylde, was possessed of Hestercombe upon the death of his uncle, and took the name of WARRE. He was born in 1756, and married 10th January, 1789, Elizabeth, only child and heiress of John Farell, esq. late of Bristol, by whom he had an only daughter and heiress, ELIZABETH-

---

* This lady had been married before to John Malet, of Enmore, by whom she had issue an only daughter and heir, Elizabeth, *m.* to John Wilmot, Earl of Rochester.

† His first wife was Vere, third daughter of the Hon. and Rev. Robert Booth, S.T.P. dean of Bristol, fifth son of George, Lord Delamer; from which lady, who *d.* 31st May, 1753, and is buried at Bathford, is descended George Booth Tyndale, esq. of Hayling, in the county of Southampton, the present head of the Tyndales (see BURKE's *Commoners*).

Maria Tyndale. He was high sheriff for the county of Somerset in 1796, in the commission of the peace, a deputy-lieutenant, and lieutenant-colonel of the Somersetshire yeomanry. He died in 1819, and was succeeded by his only child,

Elizabeth-Maria Tyndale Warre, now of Hestercombe.

Arms—Gu. two wings in pale arg.; over all, on a bend az. a crescent of the second.

WARREN, OF LITTLE MARLOW.

Created 1st June, 1775.

Extinct in 1822.

Lineage.

This family was anciently settled in Cornwall, but after the purchase of Little Marlow and Medmenham manors, Buckinghamshire became its abode.

John Burlacy, of Cornwall, was father of

Walter Burlacy, of St. Newbrine in the same county, who *m.* the daughter and heir of Oats or Oak, of Treludra, and had three sons, viz.

- Nicholas, who had a son,
  - John, from whom descended,
    - Humphrey Burlace, created by James II. after his abdication, Lord Burlace, and *d. s. p.*
- Edward, of whom presently.
- Walter, of Stithney, ancestor of Doctor Borlace, the historian of Cornwall, &c.

The second son,

Edward Borlace, esq. *m.* first, the third daughter of Sir Michael Dormer, knt. but that lady died issueless. He wedded, secondly, Miss Jane Hudleston, and by her had two sons, namely,

- Edward, who *m.* a daughter of William Bury, of Culnsberg, in Oxfordshire, and had a daughter,
  - Catharine, bapt. 14th October, 1568.

  He was buried at Little Marlow, 22nd August, 1588.
- William, *m.* Mary, daughter of — English, of Flask, and *d.* in July, 1608.

He *m.* thirdly, Parnell, daughter of Chief Justice Sir John Baldwin, knt. by whom, who outlived him and *m.* secondly, Thomas Ramsay, of Hitcham, he had a third son,

John Borlace, esq. of Marlow, who was sheriff 9 Elizabeth, member for the county of Bucks 28th of the same reign, and sheriff again in two years after. He *m.* Anne, daughter and co-heir of Sir Richard Litton, by whom (who *d.* in January, 1621,) he had

- William (Sir), his heir.
- Elizabeth, *m.* to Samuel Backhouse, esq. of Swallowfield, Berks, and left a daughter, Anne Backhouse, bapt. 2nd February, 1582.
- Dorothy, bapt. 25th June, 1564, *m.* to G. Typpynge, gent.

He *d.* in May, 1593, and was *s.* by his son,

Sir William Borlace, knt. sheriff 43 Elizabeth, M.P. for Alesbury, 1 James I. and for Wycombe, 12 James and 3rd Charles. He *m.* Mary, daughter of Nicholas Backhouse, esq. of London, and by her who *d.* in July, 1625, had issue,

- William (Sir), his successor.
- John, M.P. for Marlow, 15 and 16 Charles I. *s. p.*
- Henry, M.P. for Aylesbury, 18th James I. and Marlow, 21st of the same reign, *d. s. p.*

The eldest son,

Sir William Borlace, knt. was of Marlow and Bockmer. He *m.* Amy, daughter of Sir F. Popham of Littlecot, in Wiltshire, and had issue.

- John, his heir.
- William, M.P. for Marlow, 12 and 13 Charles II. was buried 1st November, 1665, left three daughters,
  - Henrietta, *m.* to Sir Richard Astley, bart.
  - Anne, *m.* to Lieut.-gen. Webb.
  - Alicia, *m.* to John Wallop, esq.
- Henry.
- Anne, *m.* to Richard Grenville, esq. ancestor of the Duke of Buckingham, and *d.* 30th January, 1646.
- Mary, *d.* unm. and was buried 27th February, 1637.

He was *s.* by his eldest son,

Sir John Borlace, who was created a Baronet in May, 1642. This gentleman was a conspicuous member of the administration of Ireland, and was for some time one of the lords justices of that kingdom. He was afterwards, during the civil war, voted a delinquent, and compounded for his estate by paying £9400. He *d.* in August, 1672, and was *s.* by his son,

Sir John Borlace, who died in 1689, when the Baronetcy expired, leaving an only child and heiress,

Anne Borlace, who *m.* Arthur Warren, esq. of Stapleford, in Nottinghamshire, and had issue.

- Borlace Warren, her heir.
- Arnold Warren, baptized 17th Oct. 1678.
- Arthur Warren, baptized 14th Nov. 1681.
- Charles Warren, baptized 8th June, 1683.
- John Warren, baptized 29th July, 1690.
- Baldwin Warren, baptized 15th March, 1691.
- James Warren, buried at Little Marlow in March 1774, aged eighty-nine.
- Anne Warren, *m.* to Charles, Viscount Cobham.

The eldest son,

Borlace Warren, esq. of Little Marlow, had by Anne, his wife, five sons, viz.

- Arthur who *d.* in 1768.
- Arnold, *d.* in 1767.
- Charles.
- John-Borlace.
- James.
- Catherine.
- Dorothy.
- Mary.
- Anne, *m.* to her cousin, Charles, Viscount Cobham, and *d.* in 1754.

The fourth son,

1. Sir John-Borlace Warren, G.C.B. an admiral in the royal navy, distinguished for his high professional abilities and valour, was created a Baronet 1st June, 1775. He was afterwards sworn of the privy council, and accredited ambassador extraordinary and plenipotentiary to the court of Russia. He married Caroline, daughter of General Sir John Clavering, K.C.B. and had (with a son, killed at the landing at

he Bristol troops in Egypt) an only surviving daughter and heir,

FRANCIS-MARY, m. to George Charles, fourth Lord Vernon, and was mother of the present (1838) Lord.

Sir John was M.P. for Marlow in 1774 and 1780, and subsequently for Nottingham. He d. in 1822, when the BARONETCY became EXTINCT.

Arms—Quarterly; first and fourth, cheque or, and azure, on a canton gules, a lion rampant for WARREN; second and third, ermine, on a bend, sable, two arms issuing from the clouds, rending a horse shoe, all ppr. for BORLACE.

WASTNEYS, OF HEADON.

CREATED 18th Dec. 1622.

EXTINCT 17th Dec. 1742.

Lineage.

The first person in the pedigree of this family,

SIR HARDULF GASTENEYS, knt. had two wives, Rehilda and Bertreia, and was father of

SIR ROBERT GASTENEYS, knt. whose son and heir,

SIR PHILIP GASTENEYS, m. Amphelis, daughter and co-heir of Sir Robert Morley, and left a son and successor,

SIR WILLIAM GASTENEYS, father of another

SIR WILLIAM GASTENEYS, who had two sons, both of the same name, viz.*

WILLIAM (Sir), the elder, had free warren in Brasinburgh and Carleby, in the county of Lincoln; Garthrop, in Leicestershire; and Colton, in Staffordshire, 46 HENRY III. His wife's name was Constance, and by her he left a son and heir,

JOHN (Sir), who m. Isabella, daughter of German Hay, of Acton, in the county of York, and had two sons,

WILLIAM (Sir), and John, rector of the church of Cranweys, who was living 19 EDWARD III. The elder,

WILLIAM (Sir), m. the daughter of Sir John Brett, of Norfolk, and was s. by his son,

THOMAS (Sir), living 18 EDWARD III. who m. Johanna, daughter of John Toly, of Wymondham, and left a daughter, his heir,

THOMASINE, who m. Sir Nicholas Gresley, knt. of Drakelow, in Derbyshire, and conveyed Colton and other lands, in Staffordshire, to the Gresleys.

WILLIAM (Sir), the younger.

The second son, known as

SIR WILLIAM GASTNEIS, the younger, conferred his land in Diedburgh, in the county of Leicester, upon his son,

EDMOND GASTNEIS, who purchased the manor of Totwick, in the county of York, from Sir John Horbury, knt. in the 26th of EDWARD I. and had a charter of warren from the crown, in the said manor, with the advowson of the church. His eldest son,

SIR HARDOLPH DE WASTNEIS, knt. was summoned in the 9th of EDWARD III. with others, to a council in the West Riding of the county of York. He m. twice, but leaving no issue, was s. by his brother,

SIR EDMOND DE WASTNEIS, knt. great-grandfather of

JOHN WASTNEIS, Lord of Headon, in Nottinghamshire, who was returned amongst the gentry of that county, 12 HENRY VI. His son and heir,

ROBERT WASTNEIS, held in Headon and Ousthrop, in the county of Nottinghamshire, two knights' fees, about the time of EDWARD IV. He m. Elizabeth, daughter of Thomas Nelson, of Yorkshire, merchant of the staple, and was s. by his son,

GEORGE WASTNEIS, esq. who m. Elizabeth, daughter of William Blithe. His eldest son,

GEORGE WASTNEIS, esq. m. Anne, daughter of Richard Basset, esq. of Fledborough, and was s. by his son,

GEORGE WASTNEIS, esq. who m. Mary Melford, and left a son and heir,

GEORGE WASTNEIS, esq. of Headon, in the county of Nottingham, living in 1575, who m. Jane, daughter of Lionel Reresby, esq. of Thribergh, in the county of York, and was s. by his son,

I. HARDOLPH WASTNEIS, esq. of Headon, who was created a BARONET by JAMES I. 18th December, 1622. He served as sheriff for the county of Nottingham, 11 CHARLES I. Sir Hardolph m. Jane, daughter of Gervase Eyre, esq. of Keveton, in the county of York, and had issue,

HARDOLPH, his successor.

John, of Todwick, in the county of York, m. a daughter of — Ireland, of Lancashire, and had three sons and a daughter, viz.

Hardolph, who m. Mary, daughter of Col. William Sandys, of Askham, Notts, but d. issueless.

EDWARD, third BARONET.

Daniel, d. s. p.

Jane.

George, a gallant cavalier officer, *temp.* CHARLES I. who lost his life in the service.

Anne, m. to John Rayner, esq. of East Drayton, in the county of Nottingham.

Mary, Isabel, Rosamunda, } d. unm.

Martha, m. to Richard Tye, esq. of East Retford, in the county of Nottingham.

Jane, m. to John Kirke, esq. of Eaton, in the same county.

He d. in May, 1640, and was s. by his eldest son,

II. SIR HARDOLPH WASTNEYS, steward of East Retford, in the county of Nottingham, who m. Anne, daughter of Sir Thomas Chichely, knt. of Wimpole, in the county of Cambridge, but dying without issue, in 1672, was s. by his nephew,

III. SIR EDMUND WASTNEYS, who m. Catherine,

---

* In the memorandums of BURWASH, bishop of Lincoln, is mentioned, that in 1334, the French king, CHARLES *the Fair*, threatening to invade England, EDWARD II. appoints Sir Robert de Herry and Sir William Wastneys, knts. to raise the array in the parts of Lindsey, and therewith defend the coasts; and the said Bishop Burwash was to tender them the usual oaths.

daughter and co-heir of Col. William Sandys, of Askham, Notts, and great grandaughter of Edwin Sandys, archbishop of York, and had issue,

HARDOLPH, his heir.

Catherine, m. to Edward Hutchinson, esq. a capt. in the army, second son of Samuel Hutchinson, esq. of Boston, and had an only daughter and heiress,

CATHERINE HUTCHINSON, m. first in 1728, to John Bury, esq. of Nottingham, and secondly to Robert Sutton, esq. of Scafton. By the former she left an only daughter and heir,

JUDITH-LAETITIA BURY, m. in 1755, at Headon, to Anthony Eyre, esq. of Grove, Notts.

Sir Edmund d. 12th March, 1678, and was s. by his son,

IV. SIR HARDOLPH WASTNEYS, who m. Judith, daughter and heir of Col. Richard Johnson, of Bilsby, in the county of Lincoln, but died 17th December, 1742, when the BARONETCY EXPIRED, and the estates centred eventually in the family of EYRE, of Grove. (Refer to BURKE's *Commoners*, vol. iv. p. 233.)

Arms—Sable, a lion rampant, double queued, argent, collared, gules.

WATSON, OF ROCKINGHAM CASTLE.

CREATED 18th Dec. 1621.

EXTINCT 1st July, 1782.

Lineage.

EDWARD WATSON, esq. of Rockingham Castle, in the county of Northampton, married Dorothy, daughter of the lord chief justice, Sir Edward Montagu, knt. and left a son and heir,

SIR EDWARD WATSON, of Rockingham Castle, who was sheriff of Northamptonshire in the 34th of ELIZABETH, and received the honour of knighthood in 1603. He married Anne, daughter of Kenelm Digby, esq. of Dry Stoke, and dying in 1616, was s. by his eldest son,

I. LEWIS WATSON, esq. of Rockingham Castle, who was created a BARONET 18th December, 1621. Sir Lewis was sheriff of Northamptonshire in the 9th of CHARLES I. and having zealously adhered to the king in the civil war, was raised to the peerage, as Baron Rockingham, in 1645. He married first, the Honourable Catherine Bertie, daughter of Peregrine, Lord Willoughby de Eresby, but by her ladyship had no surviving issue. His second wife was Eleanor, daughter of Sir George Manners, knt. of Haddon, in the county of Derby, and by her he had, with three daughters, an only son, his successor, at his decease, 29th January, 1652.

II. SIR EDWARD WATSON, second Lord Rockingham, who married Lady Anne Wentworth, daughter of Sir Thomas Wentworth, the eminent but unfortunate Earl of Strafford, and co-heir of her brother, William, second Earl, (refer to BURKE's *Extinct Peerage*,) and dying in 1691, was s. by his eldest son,

III. SIR LEWIS WATSON, third Lord Rockingham, who married Catherine, daughter and heir of George Sondes, Earl of Feversham, and was in consequence created Viscount Sondes, of Lees Court, in Kent, and Earl of Rockingham. He d. 19th March, 1724 and was s. by his grandson,

IV. SIR LEWIS WATSON, second Earl of Rockingham, who married Anne, daughter of Sir Henry Furnese, bart. of Waldershare, but dying s. p. in 1745 was s. by his brother,

V. SIR THOMAS WATSON, third Earl of Rockingham, who died unm. 26th February, 1746, when all his honours, save the Barony and BARONETCY, became extinct, but those devolved upon his cousin,

VI. SIR THOMAS WATSON-WENTWORTH, (the name assumed under the will of William Wentworth, second Earl of Strafford, who devised Sir Thomas estates upon that condition,) was created in 1728 [illegible] of Malton, &c. and in 1746, Marquess of Rockingham. He married Lady Mary Finch, fourth daughter of Daniel, Earl of Winchelsea and Nottingham, and had issue,

CHARLES, his successor.

ANNE, m. in 1744, to William, Earl Fitz William, and was grandmother of the present earl.

MARY, m. in 1746, to John Milbanke, esq. son of Sir Ralph Milbanke, bart.

HENRIETTA-ALICIA, m. to Mr. Sturgeon.

He d. 14th December, 1750, and was s. by his son,

VII. SIR CHARLES WATSON-WENTWORTH, second Marquess of Rockingham, K.G. an eminent statesman and PRIME MINISTER, at one time, in the reign of GEORGE III. His lordship married Mary, daughter and heir of Thomas Bright, esq. of Badsworth, in the county of York, but died s. p. 1st July, 1782, when his honours, including the BARONETCY, became EXTINCT, while the principal part of the Wentworth estates devolved upon his nephew, William, late Earl Fitzwilliam.

Arms—Ar. on a chevron engrailed azure, between three martlets sa. as many crescents, or.

Note.—For details of these noblemen, refer to BURKE's *Extinct Peerage*.

WENMAN, OF CASWELL.

CREATED 29th Nov. 1662.

EXTINCT [illegible]th Mar. [illegible]

Lineage.

FRANCIS WENMAN, esq. of Caswell, in the county of Oxford, went into Ireland in the time of ELIZABETH, and dying there, left a son and heir,

SIR FRANCIS WENMAN, knt. who was member for Oxfordshire, in 1640. He married Anne, third daughter of Sir Samuel Sandys, knt. of Ombersley, in the county of Worcester, and had issue,

FRANCIS, his heir.

Anne, m. to Sir John Fettiplace, bart. of Coln[illegible]drey, in Berks.

He was s. by his son,

I. FRANCIS WENMAN, esq. of Caswell, in the county of Oxford, who was created a BARONET 29th Novem r, 1669. Sir Francis married MARY, only daughter f Thomas Wenman, esq. and niece of Richard, first iscount Wenman,* and of PHILIP, third Viscount by hom he had several children, of whom, one son lone survived, his successor, at his decease,

II. SIR RICHARD WENMAN, who inherited the digni- s of Baron Wenman, of Kilmainham, and Viscount enman, of Tuam, on the decease of his great-uncle, hilip, third Viscount, under an especial entail of ose dignities. He m. Catherine, eldest daughter nd co-heir of Sir Thomas Chamberlayne, bart. of ham and Northbrooke, in Oxfordshire, and by at lady (who m. secondly, in 1698, James, first Earl Abingdon, and thirdly, Francis Wroughton, esq. of esket, Wilts,) had issue,

- RICHARD, his heir.
- Catherine, m. first to the Honourable Robert Bertie, of Benham, in Berkshire, fourth son of the Earl of Abingdon, and secondly to Sir William Osbaldiston, of Chadlington, and Nethercote, in Oxfordshire.

le d. about the year 1691, and was s. by his son,

III. SIR RICHARD WENMAN, fifth Viscount Wenman, ho married Susanna, daughter of Seymour Wroughton, esq. sister of his mother's third husband, and had wo sons, PHILIP and Richard. He d. at Thame ark, 28th November, 1729, and was s. by the elder,

IV. SIR PHILIP WENMAN, sixth Viscount Wenman, . 23rd November, 1719, M.P. for the city of Oxford, rom 1749 to 1754, and was afterwards knight for xfordshire. He married Sophia, eldest daughter nd co-heir of James Herbert, esq. of Tythorpe, in hat county, and had surviving issue,

- PHILIP, his heir.
- Sophia, b. in 1743, m. to William Humphrey Wykeham, esq. of Swalcliffe.

le d. 16th August, 1760, and was s. by his son,

V. SIR PHILIP WENMAN, seventh Viscount Wenman, who married 7th July, 1766, Lady Eleanor Bertie, daughter of Willoughby, Earl of Abingdon, but died issueless, 26th March, 1800, when all his honours, including the BARONETCY, EXPIRED: the estates devolved upon his only surviving sister,

- SOPHIA, wife of William Humphrey Wykeham, esq. and from her passed in succession to her grandaughter,
  - SOPHIA-ELIZABETH WYKEHAM, created BARONESS WENMAN in 1834. (Refer to BURKE's *Commoners*, vol. i. p. 419, and BURKE's *Peerage*.)

Arms—Party per pale, gules and azure, a cross patonée or.

WENTWORTH, OF WENTWORTH WOODHOUSE.

CREATED 20th June, 1611.

EXTINCT 7th Aug. 1799.

Lineage.

*** For the early descents and more ample details of this ancient family, refer to BURKE's *Extinct and Dormant Peerage*, and to BURKE's *History of the Commoners*.

I. WILLIAM WENTWORTH, esq. of Wentworth Woodhouse, Gawthorpe, &c. in Yorkshire, sheriff of that

---

* DESCENT OF THE VISCOUNTS WENMAN.

HENRY WAINMAN, m. Emmotte, daughter and heir of mpkin Hervey, of the county of Hereford, and had sue,

- RICHARD, his heir.
- John, who left a son and two daughters, Alice and Elizabeth, wife of Laurence Fermor, esq. of Oxfordshire.

le d. in the reign of EDWARD IV. His elder son,

RICHARD WENMAN, m. Anne, daughter of John Bush, f Gloucestershire, and was s. by his eldest son,

THOMAS WENMAN, esq. who m. Ursula, daughter and eir of Thomas Gifford, esq. of Twyford, in the county of ucks, and was s. by his eldest son,

SIR RICHARD WENMAN, knt. sheriff of Oxfordshire in e 5th of ELIZABETH, m. ISABEL, daughter and co-heir f John Williams, Lord Williams of Thame,† and had, ith a daughter, m. to Tasburgh, two sons, viz.

- RICHARD (Sir), his heir.
- Thomas (Sir), of Dublin, who in 1628, was made governor of the fort erected at Cork, and on the 7th June, 1729, provost marshal of the province of Munster. He d. in 1637, leaving his wife Margaret, Lady Aungier, his executrix and residuary legatee, willing the chief part of his estate to his nephew, Philip.

e elder son,

SIR RICHARD WENMAN, who succeeded at Thame Park, which came into the family with his mother, was sheriff of Oxfordshire in the 13th of ELIZABETH. He m. Jane, daughter of William, Lord Delawarr, and had issue,

- RICHARD (Sir), his heir.
- PHILIP, of whom hereafter.
- THOMAS, whose only daughter,
  - MARY, m. FRANCIS WENMAN, esq. of Caswell.
- Penelope, m. to Sir John Dynham.

The eldest son,

SIR RICHARD WENMAN, knt. who was sheriff of Oxfordshire in 1627, received the honour of knighthood, and was afterwards created a peer of Ireland, as Baron Wenman, of Kilmainham, and Viscount Wenman, of Tuam. His lordship zealously promoted the royal cause during the civil war, and at his house, Dr. Seth Ward, afterwards Bishop of Salisbury, found an asylum, when persecuted for his fidelity to the king. The Viscount m. Agnes, eldest daughter of Sir George Fermor, of Easton Neston, in Northamptonshire, and had, with a daughter, Elizabeth, the wife of Greville Verney, esq. a son and successor,

THOMAS, second Viscount Wenman, who was one of the adventurers in Ireland, when the kingdom was reduced by the English parliament; and subscribing £600, had allotted to him 617 acres, plantation measure, or one thousand statute measure, in the Barony of Garrycastle and King's County. He left at his decease but two daughters, viz.

- FRANCES, m. to Richard Samwell, esq. of Upton, in Northamptonshire.
- PENELOPE, m. to Sir Thomas Cave, bart. of Stanford, in the same county.

He was s. under a limitation in the patent, by his uncle,

PHILIP, third Viscount Wenman, who after the death of his only son, (by Barbara, his wife, eldest daughter of Sir Edward Villiers,) issueless, procured from *King* CHARLES II. in 1683, a new entail of the honours on his next heir male, SIR RICHARD WENMAN, bart. of Caswell.

---

† On the death of Lord Williams in 1559, the BARONY WILLIAMS, *of Thame*, created by summons, 2nd April, 54, fell into abeyance between his two surviving daughters, viz.

- ISABEL, m. to Sir Richard Wenman, knt.
- MARGERY, m. to Sir Henry Norris, and conveying to her husband the manor of Ryeote, he was summoned to parliament in 1572, as Baron Norris, of Ryeote

county in the last year of Elizabeth, was created a Baronet by *King* James I. 20th June, 1611. He *m.* Anne, daughter and heir of Sir Robert Atkins, knt. of Stowell, in the county of Gloucester, and dying in 1614, was *s.* by his eldest son,

II. Sir Thomas Wentworth, the eminent though unfortunate statesman, so well known in history as the Earl of Strafford, to which honour, with minor dignities and the Garter, he was raised in 1640. He *m.* first, Lady Margaret Clifford, daughter of Francis, Earl of Cumberland, and secondly, Lady Arabella Holles, daughter of John, Earl of Clare, by the former he had no issue. By the latter he had,

- William, his successor.
- Anne, *m.* to Edward Watson, Earl of Rockingham.
- Arabella, *m.* to Justin M'Carthy, son of the Earl of Clancarty.

His lordship was beheaded on Tower Hill, 12th May, 1641. His son and heir, having on the restoration of the monarchy been restored in blood and to all his father's honours, became

III. Sir William Wentworth, Earl of Strafford, &c. He *m.* first, Lady Henrietta-Maria Stanley, daughter of James, Earl of Derby, and secondly, Henrietta, daughter of Frederick Charles de Roys de le Rochefoucauld, generalissimo of the forces of the King of Denmark, but *d.* without issue, 16th October, 1665, when the greater part of his estates passed to his nephew, the Honourable Thomas Watson, and all his honours expired except the Barony of Raby, and the Baronetcy, which devolved upon his cousin,

IV. Sir Thomas Wentworth, third Baron Raby of Raby Castle, who *m.* Anne, daughter and heir of Sir Henry Johnson, of Bradenham, Bucks, and had issue,

- William, his heir.
- Anne, *m.* to the Right Honourable William Conolly, and had issue,
  - Thomas Conolly, a privy councillor in Ireland, *d. s. p.*
  - Anne Conolly, *m.* to George Byng, esq. M.P. and was mother of lieutenant-gen. Sir John Byng, created Baron Strafford.
  - Harriet Conolly, *m.* to the Rt. Hon. John Staples, M.P. and was grandmother of
    - Edward Michael Pakenham, esq. who assumed the name of Conolly, and is the present Col. Conolly, of Castletown, M. P.
  - Frances Conolly, *m.* to William, Viscount Howe, K.B. and *d. s. p.*
  - Caroline Conolly, *m.* to John, Earl of Buckinghamshire, then lord lieutenant of Ireland and left an only daughter,
    - Emily, Marchioness of Londonderry.
- Lucy, *m.* to Field Marshal Sir George Howard, K. B.
- Henrietta, *m.* in 1743 to Henry Vernon, esq. of Hilton Park, and had with several daughters, two sons, of whom the elder,
  - Henry Vernon, esq. of Hilton, *m.* first, Miss Graham, of Armagh, by whom he had a son, the present Henry-Charles-Edward Vernon-Graham, esq. of Hilton Park; and secondly, Miss Fisher, of Acton, by whom he had another son, the present Frederick-William-Thomas Vernon-Wentworth, esq. of Wentworth Castle.

His lordship, who was created Earl of Strafford, &c. and made a knight of the garter, *d.* 15th November, 1730, and was *s.* by his son,

V. Sir William Wentworth, Earl of Strafford, who *m.* Lady Anne Campbell, daughter of John, Duke of Argyll, but died *s. p.* 29th March, 1791, when he was *s.* by his cousin,

VI. Sir Frederick-Thomas Wentworth, Earl of Strafford, &c. He *m.* Eliza, daughter of Thomas Gould, esq. of Milbourne, in the county of Dorset, but died *s. p.* 7th August, 1799, when all his honours, including the Baronetcy, expired.

Arms—Sable, a chevron between three leopards' heads or.

WENTWORTH, OF BRETTON.

Created 27th Sept. 1664.—Extinct 10th July, 17[illegible]

Lineage.

From the ancient Yorkshire family of Wentworth of Wentworth Woodhouse, sprang

I. Sir Thomas Wentworth, of Bretton, in the county of York, a distinguished and gallant cavalier who was knighted by *King* Charles II. and created a Baronet by the same prince, 27th September, 1664, with remainder to his brother. He *m.* Grace, only daughter and heir of Francis Popeley, esq. of Woolley Moorhouse (who wedded secondly, Alexander, Earl of Eglintoun), but dying without issue, 5th December 1675, was *s.* by his said brother,

II. Sir Matthew Wentworth who married first, Judith, daughter of Cotton Horn, gent.; secondly, Judith, daughter of Thomas Rhodes, of Flockton, [illegible] of Samuel Thorpe, of Hopton; and thirdly, Anne, dau. of William Osbaldeston, esq. of Hummanby. By his second wife, he left at his decease 1st August, 167[illegible], a son and heir.

III. Sir Matthew Wentworth, who wedded Elizabeth, daughter of William Osbaldeston, esq. of Hunmanby, and had three sons and three daughters, viz.

- Matthew, who *d.* young, in 1692.
- William, his heir.
- Thomas, a brigadier-general in the army, and colonel of a regiment of foot, *m.* in 1720, Elizabeth, daughter and co-heir of Robert Lord, of London, gent. but died without issue.
- Grace, *m.* to Thomas Staines, esq. of Sewerby and Newby.
- Anne, *m.* to Thomas Hassell, esq. of Thorp [illegible] Yorkshire.
- Elizabeth.

Sir Matthew *d.* in 1705-6, and was *s.* by his elder surviving son,

IV. Sir William Wentworth, deputy lieutenant of the West Riding, captain of a troop of train bands, and M. P. for the borough of Malton. He *m.* Diana, daughter of Sir William Blacket, bart. of Wallington in Northumberland, by whom he had, with four sons who all died unmarried,

- I. Thomas, his heir.
- I. Diana, married to Godfrey Bosvile, esq. of Gunthwaite, and had issue,
  - William Bosvile, esq. of Gunthwaite, who devised his estates to his nephew, Godfrey Macdonald, afterwards third Lord Macdonald, who assumed in consequence the additional surname of Bosvile.
  - Thomas-Blacket Bosvile, captain in the Coldstream Guards, slain at Lincelle.
  - Elizabeth-Diana Bosvile, who *m.* Alexander, first Lord Macdonald, and had a numerous family, of which the elder

daughter, Diana, *m.* the Right Hon. Sir John Sinclair, bart. (his second wife.) See Burke's *Peerage and Baronetage*.
Julia Bosvile, *m.* to William Ward, Viscount Dudley.

ii. Elizabeth, *m.* to James Watson, M.D. of Springhead.
iii. Julia, *m.* in 1760, to the Rev. Dr. John De Chaire, rector of Rissington.
iv. Arabella, died unm.

he son and heir,

v. Sir Thomas Wentworth, was sheriff of York-
ire, in 1765. This gentleman inheriting the valuable ntailed estates, royalties, &c. of the Blacket family, sumed their surname in addition to his own. He ied 11th July, 1792, when the Baronetcy became xtinct. He settled his immense property, which, cluding mines, amounted then to more than £40,000 year, as follows:—The Yorkshire, with the greater art of the estates in Northumberland, on his eldest aughter, Mrs. Beaumont, and her sisters, Mrs. Lee, ife of William Lee, esq. of the Grove, and Miss ouisa Wentworth (afterwards Mrs. Stackpole), in ccession, and their issue male (the two younger dies enjoying a rent charge of £3000 per annum), ith remaindership to Sir John Sinclair, bart. and s heirs by his second wife, Diana, eldest daughter f Alexander, first Lord Macdonald. The Gunneston states he left to his nephew, William Bosvile, esq. of unthwaite, which property has since devolved on ord Macdonald.

Arms—As Wentworth of Woodhouse.

WENTWORTH, OF NORTH ELMSAL.

Created 28th July, 1692.—Extinct 3rd Dec. 1741.

Lineage.

The Wentworths of North Elmsal, a scion of the reat house of Wentworth of the north, acquired the state whence they were designated, by the marriage *temp.* Edward III. of

John Wentworth, with Alice, daughter and heir f John Bisset. The son of this alliance,

John Wentworth, of North Elmsal, living in 1412, Agnes, sister and co-heir of Sir William Droneid, of West Bretton, and had issue,

i. John, his heir.
ii. Roger, living 1413 and 1449, of Nettlested, in Suffolk, ancestor of the Wentworths of Nettlested, and the Wentworths of Gosfield.
iii. Thomas, of Doncaster, whose will is dated 1449.
iv. Richard, ancestor of the Wentworths of Bretton.

he eldest son,

John Wentworth, of North Elmsal, *m.* a dau. f Beaumont, of Whitley, and was *s.* by his son,

John Wentworth, of North Elmsal, father, by lizabeth, his wife, daughter of William Calverley, sq. of Calverley, of a daughter, Jane, *m.* to William oldthorpe, of Goldthorpe, and of a son,

Thomas Wentworth, of North Elmsal, whose will ated 14 Henry VIII. directs that he shall be buried t South Kirkby, and that a priest shall sing in the hapel of St. Mary Magdalene, at North Elmsal, for he souls of himself, his wife, father, and mother, and f Walter Hawksworth, his son-in-law. The will harges the estate with the payment of certain sums o the younger children. These sums the heir was o pay, and the father adds this terrible clause: "If e perform not the will, I beseech God that the malediction and curse of the Fader in hevyn and myne, as far as God hath given me power, may descend and light upon his blood for ever." He *m.* Jane, daughter of Oliver Mirfield, of Howley, and was *s.* by his son,

Sir John Wentworth, knt. of North Elmsal, whose will, dated 31st January, 1541, was proved 20th August, 1544. He *m.* first, Anne, daughter of Thomas Crake, esq. of Beverley, and had a son, John, his heir, and a daughter, Jane, wife of Robert Trigott, of South Kirkby. Sir John wedded, secondly, Jane, daughter of Roger Appleton, esq. of Dartford, in Kent, and by her, who *m.* secondly, Sir Thomas Gargrave, had issue,

Thomas, of Howley, in Yorkshire, and of Ashby, in Lincolnshire, *m.* Elizabeth, daughter of Sir Christopher Danby, of Thorpe, and had issue.
Christopher, of Sheffield.
Hector, living 1561 and 1579.
Elizabeth, *m.* to Francis Haldenby, esq. of Haldenby.
Frances, *m.* to Thomas Wombwell, esq.
Bridget, *m.* to Nicholas Hague, esq.

Sir John was *s.* by his eldest son,

John Wentworth, esq. of North Elmsal, who *m.* first, Anne, daughter of Sir Brian Hastings, of Fenwick; and secondly, Anne Pickering. By the former he left, with two daughters, Ann, wife of Thomas Sandys, and Elizabeth, of William Fletcher, a son and successor,

Thomas Wentworth, esq. of North Elmsal, whose will was proved 14th September, 1590. He *m.* Ann, daughter of Sir William Calverley, of Calverley, and had, *inter alios*, a daughter, Elizabeth, *m.* first, to Richard Tempest; and secondly, Sir John Savile, of Methley, and a son and successor,

Thomas Wentworth, esq. of North Elmsal, who *m.* a daughter of Richard Goodricke, esq. of Ribstone, and had issue,

Thomas (Sir), his heir.
Darcy, of Brodsworth.
William, } *d. s. p.*
John, }
Catherine, *m.* to Sir Rowland Wandesford of Pickhill, and had an only daughter and heir, Elizabeth, *m.* to Philip, Lord Wharton.
Ann, *m.* to Sir Richard Hawksworth, of Hawksworth.

Thomas Wentworth died in 1632-3, and was *s.* by his son,

Sir Thomas Wentworth, knt. of North Elmsal, aged twenty-two in 1612, who *m.* first, Mary, daughter of Sir William Bamborough, of Howsham, in Yorkshire; and secondly, Martha, daughter of Sir Thomas Hayes, lord mayor of London. By the latter he had two daughters: Martha, wife, first of Thomas Wombwell, esq. of Wombwell, and secondly, of Sir Henry Marwood; and Mary, wife of Sir William Middleton, of Belsay Castle. By his first wife Sir Thomas left at his decease in 1650, an only son and successor,

Thomas Wentworth, esq. of North Elmsal, aged twenty in 1630, who *m.* Agnes, daughter of Sir Henry Bellingham, bart. of Levens, and by her, who died 17th June, 1668, had issue,

John, his heir.
Henry, of Brodsworth, whose son,
John, eventually inherited North Elmsal.
Dorothy, *m.* to Edward, eldest son of Sir Thomas Gower, of Sittenham.

He *d.* 10th May, 1653, and was *s.* by his son,

Sir John Wentworth, of North Elmsal, knighted at Whitehall, 8th May, 1667. He married Catherine, daughter of Sir Thomas Norcliffe, of Langton, and widow of Christopher Lister, esq. and by her, who *m.* thirdly, Heneage Finch, Earl of Winchelsea, left at his decease, 4th June, 1671, aged twenty-six, a son and heir,

Thomas Wentworth, of North Elmsal, bapt. 26th February, 1669-70, who died in minority, 8th August, 1689, and was *s.* by his cousin,

i. John Wentworth, esq. of Brodsworth and North Elmsal, who was created a Baronet in 1692. He *m.* first, Mary, daughter of Sir John Lowther, bart. of Lowther, and by her, who *d.* 16th April, 1706, aged thirty, had an only daughter,

> Catherine, heir to her brother, *m.* to Hugh Cholmley, esq. of Whitby Abbey, and from this marriage descends the present
>
> George Cholmley, esq. of Whitby.

Sir John wedded secondly, Lady Elisabeth Cavendish, daughter of William, second Duke of Devonshire, and had by her an only son, Butler-Cavendish. He died 25th April, 1720, aged forty-seven, and was *s.* by his son,

ii. Sir Butler Cavendish Wentworth, of North Elmsal, who *m.* Bridget, daughter of Sir Ralph Milbanke, bart. of Halnaby, but died without issue, 3rd December, 1741, aged thirty-one, when the Baronetcy became extinct. Sir Butler's widow wedded John Murray, esq. and died in 1774.

Arms—As Wentworth of Woodhouse.

WENTWORTH, OF GOSFIELD.

Created 29th June, 1611.

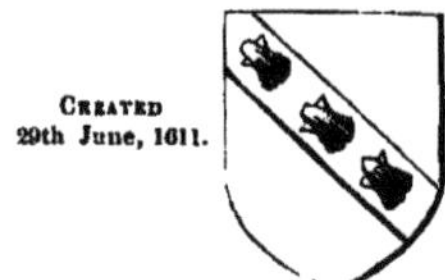

Extinct October, 1631.

Lineage.

Henry Wentworth, esq. second son of Sir Roger Wentworth, of Nettlested, in Suffolk, and the first of the family that settled in Essex, was ancestor of the Wentworths of that county, and those of Oxfordshire, Berkshire, and Bucks. He died 22nd March, 1482, and was *s.* by his son,

Sir Roger Wentworth, of Codham Hall, sheriff of Essex and Herts in 1499, who married Anne, only daughter and heir of Humfrey Tyrell, esq. of Little Warley, third son of Sir John Tyrell, of Herons. By her he acquired, with other extensive possessions, the estate of Gosfield, in Essex, and had several children. He died 9th August, 1539; his wife had predeceased him in 1534; and both lie interred under a sumptuous monument in the chancel of Gosfield church. Their eldest son and heir,

Sir John Wentworth, knt. of Gosfield, *b.* in 1494, *m.* Anne, daughter of John Bettenham, esq. of Pluckley, in Kent, and dying 15th September, 1567, was *s.* by his only child,

Anne Lady Maltravers, then a widow. She married thrice: first, Sir Hugh Rich, second son of Lord Chancellor Rich; secondly, Henry Fitzalan, Lord Maltraver; and thirdly, William Deane, esq. but had no issue. Her laydyship died 5th December, 1580, and in accordance with her desire, was buried in the church of Gosfield, within the tomb of her first husband, having ordered six hundred marks to be bestowed at her funeral. At her demise, the great inheritance of the family passed to (the son of her uncle Henry,) her cousin,

John Wentworth, esq. of Little Horkaley, b. [illegible] 1540, who was knighted. By Elizabeth, his wife, daughter of Christopher St. Lawrence, Baron of H[illegible] he left at his decease, 13th April, 1588, a son and successor,

John Wentworth, esq. of Gosfield, *b.* in 1564, who *m.* Cicely, daughter of Edward Unton, esq. and dec. 10th February, 1613, leaving a son and successor,

i. Sir John Wentworth, knt. of Gosfield, cre[illegible] a Baronet in 1611. He *m.* Catharine, daughter of [illegible] Moyle Finch, and had a son who died young, [illegible] four daughters, of whom the survivors were,

> Cecily, *m.* to Sir William Grey, of Chillingham, Baron Grey of Werk.
>
> Lucy, *m.* to Thomas Wentworth, Earl of Cleveland, and had an only daughter, Cathar[illegible] wife of William Spencer, esq. of Cople, in [illegible]fordshire.

Sir John died in October, 1631, when the Baronetcy became extinct.

Arms—Gu. on a bend arg. three escallops az.

WERDEN.

Created 28th Nov. 1672.

Extinct 13th Feb. [illegible]

Lineage.

Roger Werden, of Leyland, in the county of Lancaster, *m.* a daughter of Farringdon, of Farringdon, in the same county, and by her had issue,

Richard Werden, of Leyland and Chester, who [illegible] Lettice Blacklake, of Leyland, and had by her a son,

Thomas Werden, who *m.* Jennett, daughter of J[illegible] Clayton, of Farringdon, and was father of

Richard Werden, esq. of Chester. He *m.* [illegible] daughter and co-heir of John Banistre, esq. of Ches[illegible] (of the ancient family of Banistre, who came from Normandy with William *the Conqueror*, and possessed the manor of Preston, in the county of Lancaster, of which Robert Banistre was lord t[illegible] Richard I.) Richard Werden had issue by her,

> Edward, who *m.* Elizabeth, daughter of Ju[illegible] Peter Palmer, of Ireland, and *d.* without issue.
>
> Thomas, *d. s. p.*
>
> John, who succeeded his father.
>
> Richard, George, William, } *d. s. p.*
>
> Alice, *m.* Charles Felton, esq. of Chester.
>
> Dorothy, *m.* Hugh Williamson, esq.
>
> Ellen, accidentally drowned.
>
> Mary, *m.* — Bennett, esq.
>
> Anne, *d.* unm.

The third son,

John Werden, succeeded to the estates, and Katherine, daughter of Edward Dutton, since governor of Barbadoes, living in 1680, who died in [illegible]

Street, 22nd September, 1703, leaving two daughters. John Werden d. 7th June, 1646; by Katherine, his wife, he had issue,

Robert, of whom presently.

Katherine, m. Cary Dillon, afterwards Earl of Roscommon, in Ireland, who died at Chester in 1689, and left issue,

Robert, Earl of Roscommon.

Anne, relict of Sir Thomas Nugent, of Ireland.

The only son,

Robert Werden, in the old papers it is stated, "did eminently distinguish himself in behalf of *King* Charles I. and the royal family, both with life and fortune, the latter of which he very much impaired thereby. He sometime served as a member of parliament, and was colonel of a troop or regiment of horse. He was declared a traitor to the usurper and the realm of England, and a proclamation was issued out for apprehending him." In consequence of this proclamation, "and a price being set upon his head, together with those of Crew and Cotton, &c. &c. being all staunch royalists," he emigrated with his family and joined Charles II. and his brother James on the continent, with whom he continued till the Restoration, "having left," (as a descendant of his writes) "his estates and property to all the violence of the parliamentary forces. I have myself seen the marks where the soldiers of Cromwell played 'nine pins' in the drawing of his mansion-house at Chester." On his return with the Royal family at the Restoration, he obtained again possession of his estates. After which at different times "he held several posts of high honour and trust;" amongst others, he was major general of the land forces to *King* James II. in 1688, and treasurer to *Queen* Mary. (De Roy. Hist. Old and N. Test.) He m. first, Jane Backham; and secondly, Margaret Towse, grandaughter to Sergeant Towse, of Essex, who died *s. p.* By his first wife he had three sons and one daughter,

John, his heir.

Robert, captain of the Henrietta, third rate; slain in action against the Dutch, 28th May, 1673, at the battle of Solebay.

William, *d. s. p.* very young.

Katharine, m. Richard Watts, esq. of Muchmunden, in the county of Hertford, and had issue,

Richard Watts, died young.

Katherine Watts, m. Lord Charles Murray, second son of the Marquis of Athole, and afterwards created Earl of Dunmore, in Scotland, and had issue seven sons and three daughters.

The eldest son,

I. Sir John Werden, succeeded to the estates of his father, Robert Werden, of Leyland, Lancashire, and Cholmeaton, in the county of Chester, 23rd January, 1690. He was, by Charles II. made a baron of the Exchequer at Chester, secretary to the embassy under the Earl of Sandwich to the courts of Spain and Portugal, envoy extraordinary from the same king in 1669 to the court of Sweden, secretary to his royal highness James Duke of York (as lord high admiral of England, &c.), and commissioner of his majesty's navy. He was sometime M.P. for Ryegate, in Surrey. In the year 1672 he was created a Baronet by *King* Charles. In "1684 he was made a commissioner of the customs, and upon the abdication of *King* James II. he managed alone that important post in the customs for some time to the general satisfaction, in which he continued most of *King* William's reign. Upon *Queen* Anne's accession to the throne he was put into commission again, and she was pleased as a further mark of her esteem and favour for him, through a grateful sense of his own and his family's past services, to declare that he should continue in that commission, if he pleased, as long as she reigned, which he did." He married twice; first, Lucy, daughter and heiress of Dr. Osbourne, which lady died *s. p.*; and secondly, Mary, daughter of William Osbourne, of Kenniford, Devon, by whom, who died of small-pox 22nd August, 1683, Sir John left at his decease in October, 1716, an only son,

II. Sir John Werden, bart. of Leyland and Cholmeaton, who succeeded to his father's estates and title, born 28th April, 1683, m. first, Elizabeth, daughter of Robert Breton, esq. of Norton, in the county of Northampton, and sister to Nicholas Breton, 9th July, 1704, and by her had issue an only daughter,

Lucy, m. 13th December, 1722, to Charles, Duke of St. Albans, and had issue, Lord George Beauclerk, *b.* 25th June, 1730, died young unm. and Lady Diana Beauclerk, who m. Shute Barrington, afterwards Bishop of Durham, but *d. s. p.*

Sir John Werden m. secondly, Judith, daughter of John Eyre, esq. of Maidford, in the county of Northampton, but she died in May, 1726, without issue. He m. thirdly, Miss Verney, who had no child; and fourthly, Susanna, daughter and co-heiress of John Staveley, esq. by his wife Frances, grandchild of Sir Walter Hawksworth, of the county of York, and by her had one daughter,

Susanna Werden, co-heiress with her only half-sister, the Duchess of St. Albans; she m. Edward Bayntun, esq. of the Coldstream Guards, afterwards appointed to the consulate of Tripoli, which office he quitted on becoming his majesty's consul-general at Algiers, where he died 1st November, 1777; she died 25th August, 1819. They had a large family, but only three lived to grow up, viz.

Werden-George-Edward-Bayntun, eldest son, a captain in the army, served in America, in the 23rd regiment of Welsh Fusileers. He subsequently held a captain's commission in the 2nd Foot or Queen's Own regiment. He died unm. in 1793.

Henry-William, the present Admiral Sir Henry-William Bayntun, of Rettenden Hall, Essex.

Annica-Susan, m. 10th June, 1802, to the Rev. Edward Goddard, of Cliffe House, in the county of Wilts.

Sir John died 13th February, 1758, without male issue, when the Baronetcy became extinct.

Arms—Gu. on a bend arg. three leopards' faces of the first.

WESTCOMBE.

Created 23rd Mar. 1699.

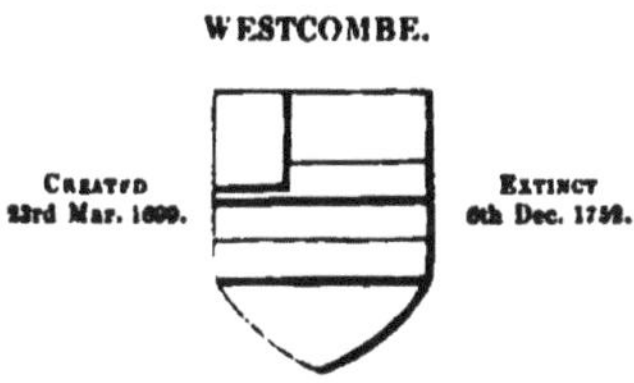

Extinct 6th Dec. 1752.

Lineage.

I. Martin Westcombe, esq. consul and agent at Cadiz, *temp. King* William III. and for a long time residing in Spain, was created a BARONET 29th March, 1699. He had issue,

ANTHONY, his heir.

Mary, m. to Colonel Bernard Granville, of Buckland, ancestor of the present COURT GRANVILLE, esq. of Calwich Abbey, in Staffordshire. Mrs. Granville d. in 1747, and was buried in Gloucester Cathedral.

The son and successor,

II. SIR ANTHONY WESTCOMBE, was deputy commissary-general, deputy judge-advocate, and commissary of the musters at Minorca. He m. in 1736, Miss Calmady, an heiress, but d. without issue 6th December, 1752, when the BARONETCY EXPIRED.

Arms—Sable, two bars or, and a canton ermine.

WHARTON, OF KIRBY KENDALL.

CREATED 19th Dec. 1677.

EXTINCT

Lineage.

I. GEORGE WHARTON, esq. treasurer and paymaster of the ordnance, *temp.* CHARLES II. was created a BARONET 19th December, 1677. Sir George was the son of George Wharton, a substantial yeoman in Strickland, near Kendall, who left at his decease an estate of forty or fifty pounds, and his son, an infant, under the guardianship of his two brothers, William and Cuthbert, who brought him up a scholar, and sent him to Oxford in the reign of CHARLES I. where he continued until he commenced master of arts. But being loyally disposed, and concluding that a time of civil war was not the most propitious to literary pursuits, he adopted the profession of arms. Leaving Oxford, he sold his lands, with the produce raised a troop of horse, and presented himself at its head to *King* CHARLES I. His majesty received him graciously, and placed him and his troop in the regiment of Sir Jacob Astley, where he continued until the regiment was routed and most of it cut to pieces at Stow, in Gloucestershire, the Colonel being made prisoner, and Wharton escaping severely wounded. He for some time afterwards remained concealed in the houses of the royalists, and set himself to compile an Almanac, called in those times, WHARTONS' *Loyal Almanac*, and much esteemed by the king's friends for foretelling things relating to the restoration, and exposing the practices of the party then in the ascendants, to whom Wharton became so obnoxious, that a reward of £500. was offered for taking him. He passed however for some time undiscovered disguised as a Spaniard, under the name of Capt. Naworth, (the letters of Wharton transposed) but was at length captured and committed to Windsor Castle, where he remained some time a prisoner. After the restoration he received the official employments mentioned above, and was created a BARONET. He m. Miss Anne Butler, and had issue,

George, a capt. in the army, died before his father.
POLYCARPUS, his heir.
Richard, an engineer.
William, capt. in the army.
Dorothy, m. to Mr. Henry Nelthorp, a banker.
Jane, m. to Mr. Sewell Wharton, druggist.
Anne.

He d. 12th August, 1681, aged sixty-seven, and was s. by his eldest surviving son,

II. SIR POLYCARPUS WHARTON, who m. Philadelphia, daughter of Justinian, and niece of Sir Edward Sherburne, knt. but died without surviving issue, when the BARONETCY became EXTINCT.

Arms—Sable, a maunch arg. a canton or.

WHEATE, OF GLYMPTON.

CREATED 2nd May, 1696.

EXTINCT 14th July, 18..

Lineage.

THOMAS WHEATE, of Walsall, in the county of Stafford, was father of

WILLIAM WHEATE, esq. of Coventry, who married Anne, daughter of Abraham Quiney, of Stratford-upon-Avon, and relict of Richard Bailey, of Lichfield, by whom he had a son and heir,

WILLIAM WHEATE, esq. of Glympton, in the county of Oxford, living in 1634, who m. Elizabeth, eldest daughter of Thomas Stone, of London, and had surviving issue,

THOMAS, his heir.
Anne, m. to Charles Thoreld, esq. of Harmston in Lincolnshire, and of London, merchant, who fined for Alderman.

He was s. by his son,

THOMAS WHEATE, esq. who m. Frances, daughter of Sir Robert Jenkinson, knt. of Walcot, in Oxfordshire, and was s. by his only son,

I. THOMAS WHEATE, esq. of Glympton, M.P. for Woodstock, who was created a BARONET 2nd May, 1696. Sir Thomas m. Anne, daughter and co-heir of George Sawbridge, esq. of London, and had issue,

THOMAS, his heir.
GEORGE, successor to his brother.
Frances, m. to *Sir Francis Page*, knt. one of the judges of the King's Bench, who d. in 1730.
Anne.

He d. 25th August, 1721, and was s. by his elder son,

II. SIR THOMAS WHEATE, M.P. for Woodstock, who m. Mary, daughter and co-heir of Thomas Gould, esq. of Oak End, Bucks, but dying s. p. in May, 1746, was s. by his brother,

III. SIR GEORGE WHEATE, barrister-at-law, and recorder of Banbury, who m. in 1742, Avice, daughter of Sir Jacob Ackworth, knt. surveyor of the Navy, and had issue,

GEORGE, his successor.
JACOB, heir to his brother.
JOHN-THOMAS, in holy orders, sixth baronet.
Esther-Henrietta.
ANNE, m. to Benjamin Barnet, esq. of London, banker, living in 1784.

Sir George d. 4th June, 1752, and was s. by his eldest son,

IV. SIR GEORGE WHEATE, lieutenant Royal Art..

lery, who *d.* unm. 26th January, 1760, and was *s.* by his brother,

v. Sir Jacob Wheate, commander of his majesty's ship Cerberus, who *m.* Maria, daughter of David Shaw, esq. of New York, but died *s. p.* in 1783, and was *s.* by his only surviving brother,

vi. Sir John-Thomas Wheate, in holy orders, who *d.* unm. 14th July, 1816, when the Baronetcy expired.

Arms—Vert, a fesse dancettée or, three garbs in chief of the last.

WHITMORE, OF APLEY.

Created 28th June, 1641.

Extinct 1699.

Lineage.

For a full account of the early ancestry of this ancient family, refer to Burke's *Commoners*, vol. ii. p. 480.

William Whitmore, esq. of London, merchant, *m.* Anne, daughter of Alderman William Bond, of that city, and by her, who *d.* 9th October, 1615, had issue,

- William (Sir), his heir.
- Thomas, *d. s. p.*
- George (Sir), knt. of Balmes, in Hackney parish, Middlesex, a devoted royalist, and consequently persecuted during the civil wars. The republican newspaper, entitled "Certain Information," for the 30th January, 1643, relates that Sir George Whitmore, alderman, and others, were carried by sea to Yarmouth, because they would not contribute monies for the *defence of the king and parliament*, as dethroning the sovereign was then called. Sir George was sheriff of London in 1621, and lord mayor in 1631-2. He died 12th December, 1654, leaving by Mary, his wife, daughter and heiress of Reginald Copcott, esq. a son and daughter, viz.
    - William, of Balmes, who is characterised by Roger North, in his life of Lord Guildford, as "an humoursome old gentleman," and a curious anecdote is told by the same writer touching his resistance to the payment of tithes. His son,
        - William Whitmore, esq. of Balmes, espoused Frances, daughter and co-heir of Sir Thomas Whitmore, K. B. of Bridgnorth, but *d. s. p.* After the extinction of the branch at Balmes, their house degenerated into a cake shop, under the name, and well known, as Sir George Whitmore's.
    - Elizabeth, who *m.* Sir John Weld, knt. of Willey, and dying before 1677, left a daughter,
        - Anne Weld, who wedded Richard Whitmore, esq. of Low Slaughter, and her descendants became heirs of the body to Sir John Weld, on the death of that gentleman's great-grandson, George Forester, esq. *s. p.* in 1811.
- Elizabeth, *m.* to Sir William Craven, bart.
- Anne, *m.* to Francis Baber, esq. of Chute, in Somersetshire.
- Margaret, *m.* to Sir R. Grubham, knt.
- Mary, *m.* to Sir Charles Montague, knt. brother to the Earl of Manchester.
- Frances, *m.* to Sir John Weld, of Arnolds, Middlesex, father of the purchaser of Lulworth.
- Jane, *m.* to N. Still, esq.

William Whitmore, of London, died 8th August, 1593, and was *s.* by his son,

Sir William Whitmore, knt. of London, *b.* 4th November, 1572, who purchased and entailed the estate of Apley, in the county of Salop; for which shire he was high sheriff in 1620. Sir William wedded first, Margaret, daughter of Rowland Moseley, of Hough, in Lancashire, and by her, who *d.* 31st January, 1606, had one son and a daughter, viz.

- George, who *d. s. p.*
- Anne, *m.* to Sir Edmund Sawyer, and *d.* in 1666.

He espoused secondly, Dorothy, daughter of John Weld, esq. of London, by whom, who *d.* in 1626, he had issue,

- Thomas (Sir), his heir.
- William, *d.* young.
- Richard, of Lower Slaughter, in the county of Gloucester, in 1667, *m.* Catherine, daughter and co-heir of Robert Deards, esq, of London, and by her, who *d.* 30th November, 1673, left at his decease, 30th August, 1667, a son,
    - Richard, of Low Slaughter, who *m.* Anne, daughter of Sir John Weld, of Willey, and dying before 1694, left
        - William, of Low Slaughter, of whom presently, as inheritor of Apley.
        - Anne, who *m.* to Walter Jones, esq. of Chastleton, and died in 1738, leaving a son,
            - Henry Jones, esq. of Chastleton, who *m.* Elizabeth, daughter of — Hancock, esq. and was *s.* at his decease, in 1761, by his son,
                - Arthur Jones, esq. of Chastleton, the last male heir of the Jones' family, who *d.* 21st November, 1828, and bequeathed the Chastleton estate to his kinsman, John Henry Whitmore, esq. on condition of his taking the name and arms of Jones.

To Sir William Whitmore and his brother, their learned countryman and relative, Thomas Gataker, inscribed a sermon, entitled "Jacob's Thankfulness," preached before the Worshipful Company of Haberdashers," in which he calls these Whitmores "the two principals now left of the family." Sir William *d.* in December, 1648, and was *s.* by his son,

i. Sir Thomas Whitmore, of Apley, in Shropshire, *b.* 20th November, 1612, who was created a Baronet 28th June, 1641. He *m.* Elizabeth, daughter and heir of Alderman Sir William Acton, knt. and by that lady, who died in 1666, had issue,

- William (Sir), his heir.
- Thomas (Sir), of Bridgnorth and Buddwas, who *m.* Frances, daughter of Sir William Brook, *alias* Cobham, a lady distinguished for great beauty, by whom, who *d.* in 1699, he had three daughters, viz.
    - Elizabeth, who *d.* unm. in 1667.
    - Dorothy, *m.* to Jonathan Langley, esq. of the Abbey, Shropshire, and *d.* in 1668.
    - Frances, *m.* first, to her cousin, William Whitmore, esq. of Balmes; and secondly, to

Sir Richard Middleton, of Chirk Castle, where she died in 1694.

Anne, *m.* to Sir Francis Lawley, bart.

Elizabeth, *m.* to John Bennet, esq. of Abingdon, Cambridgeshire.

Dorothy, *m.* to Sir Eliab Harvey, knt. of Chigwell.

Sir Thomas *d.* in 1653, and was *s.* by his eldest son,

II. SIR WILLIAM WHITMORE, of Apley, *b.* 8th April, 1637, who wedded Mary, daughter of Eliab Harvey, esq. of London, but died without issue in 1690, when the BARONETCY EXPIRED, while the estates passed to his kinsman,

WILLIAM WHITMORE, esq. of Low Slaughter, M.P. for Bridgenorth, who then became of APLEY. His representative is the present THOMAS WHITMORE, esq. of Apley.

Arms—Vert, fretty or.

WIDDRINGTON, OF WIDDRINGTON.

CREATED 9th July, 1642.

FORFEITED in 1715.

Lineage.

I. WILLIAM WIDDRINGTON, esq. of Widdrington, in the county of Northumberland, the representative and descendant of an old Northumbrian family, was created a BARONET 9th July, 1642, and the next year created Baron Widdrington, of Blankney, in the county of Lincoln. He was a zealous royalist, and raised a considerable force in support of the cause, at the head of which he fell, in the fight at Wigan Lane in 1651, when the Earl of Derby was defeated by Colonel Lilburne. His lordship *m.* Mary, daughter and heiress of Sir Anthony Thorold, knt. of Blankney, and had issue,

I. WILLIAM, his heir.

II. Edward, captain of horse, killed at the battle of the Boyne. Captain Widdrington married Dorothy, elder daughter and co-heir of Sir Thomas Horsley, knt. of Horsley, in Northumberland, and was *s.* by his only son,

EDWARD WIDDRINGTON, esq. of Felton, *b.* in 1656, who *m.* Elizabeth, daughter of Caryl, third Viscount Molyneux, who left, at his decease, in 1705, with two daughters, Theresa, wife of Sir William Wheeler, bart. and Bridget, an only son,

EDWARD-HORSLEY WIDDRINGTON, who *m.* Elizabeth, daughter of Humphrey Weld, esq. of Lulworth, and left an only daughter and heiress,

ELIZABETH WIDDRINGTON, who *m.* Thomas Riddell, esq. of Swinburne Castle, and conveyed to him the estate of Felton. She is now represented by her great-grandson,

THOMAS RIDDELL, esq. of Felton Park and Swinburne Castle, both in Northumberland.

III. Ralph, served in the Dutch wars, and lost his sight.

IV. Anthony, *d.* a bachelor.

V. Roger, killed at the siege of Maestricht.

I. Mary, *m.* to Francis Crane, esq. of Woodrising, Norfolk.

II. Jane, *m.* to Sir Charles Stanley, K.B.

Lord Widdrington fell 3rd September, 1651, and was *s.* by his eldest son,

II. SIR WILLIAM WIDDRINGTON, second Baron Widdrington, who *m.* Elizabeth, daughter of Sir Peregrine Bertie, knt. of Eveden, in the county of Lincoln, and had issue,

WILLIAM, his heir.

Henry, whose will was proved in 1720.

Roger, of Blankney, *d.* in 1715.

Edward, whose will was proved in 1688.

Mary, *m.* to Richard Forster.

Elizabeth, } nuns.
Dorothy, }

Anne, *m.* in 1659, to John Clavering, esq. of Callaly, in the county of Northumberland.

Catherine, *m.* to Edward Southcote, esq. of Ebtheborough.

He *d.* in 1676, and was *s.* by his eldest son.

III. SIR WILLIAM WIDDRINGTON, third Lord Widdrington, who *m.* Alathea, daughter and heiress of Charles, Viscount Fairfax, and had issue,

WILLIAM, his successor.

Charles, supposed to have died in 1756.

Peregrine, *m.* Mary, Duchess of Norfolk, but died *s. p.*

Mary, *m.* to Richard Towneley, esq. of Towneley.

Elizabeth, *m.* to Marmaduke, fourth Lord Langdale.

His lordship *d.* in 1695, and was *s.* by his eldest son.

II. SIR WILLIAM WIDDRINGTON, 4th Lord Widdrington, who *m.* first, Jane, daughter and heir of Sir Thomas Tempest, bart. of Stella, in the palatinate of Durham, and by that lady had issue,

HENRY-FRANCIS, *b.* in 1700, and *d. s. p.* in 1774.

William-Tempest, *d. s. p.*

Alathea, a nun.

Mary, *b.* in 1712, *m.* to Rowland Eyre, esq. of Hassop, Derbyshire.

His lordship *m.* secondly, Catharine Graham, but had no other issue. Lord Widdrington and his brothers having joined in the rising of 1715, in favour of the Stuarts, were all made prisoners at Preston, and afterwards tried and convicted of high treason, 7th July, 1716, but were included in a subsequent royal pardon. His HONOURS, however, fell under the ATTAINDER. He *d.* in 1743.

Arms—Quarterly; arg. and gu. a bend sa.

WIDDRINGTON, OF CARTINGTON.

CREATED 8th August, 1642.—EXTINCT

Lineage.

I. SIR EDWARD WIDDRINGTON, of Cartington, in Northumberland, a baronet of Nova Scotia, sprung from Roger Widdrington, of Cartington and Harbottle, who was third son of Edward Widdrington, of Swinburne, and younger brother of Sir Henry Widdrington, knt. ancestor of the Lords Widdrington, obtained a patent of an ENGLISH BARONETCY in 1642. He *m.* a daughter of Charleton, of Healeyside, but *d.* without male issue, when the title became EXTINCT. Mary, his daughter and co-heir, *m.* Sir Edward Charleton, bart. of Healeyside.

Arms—As preceding article.

WILBRAHAM, OF WOODHEY.

CREATED 5 Mar. 1620-1. EXTINCT August, 1692.

Lineage.

SIR RICHARD DE WILBURGHAM, m. first, Margery, daughter and co-heir of Warin Vernon, Baron of Shipbrook, and had, with a son who d. s. p. two daughters, the wives of Lostock and Winnington, who became heirs to their mother. He married secondly, Letitia, second daughter and co-heir of Sir William Venables, of Wyminchem. He d. in 2 EDWARD I. and was s. by the son of the latter lady,

WILLIAM DE WILBURGHAM, whose great-great-grandson,

THOMAS DE WILBURGHAM, of Radnor, m. Margaret, daughter and heiress of John Golborne, lord of Woodhey, in the county of Chester, and thus acquired that estate. He had issue,

- THOMAS, his heir.
- Randulph, from whom the WILBRAHAMS of Delamere, Dorfold, Rode, &c. derive. (Refer to BURKE's *Commoners*, vol. i. page 315.)
- William.
- Richard.
- John.

The eldest son and heir,

THOMAS WILBRAHAM, esq. succeeded to the manors of Radnor and Woodhey, and marrying *temp.* HENRY VI. Margaret, daughter of Thomas de Swettenham, was s. at his decease, 7 HENRY VII. by his eldest son,

WILLIAM WILBRAHAM, esq. of Woodhey, who m. Helena, daughter of Philip Egerton, esq. of Egerton, and was s. by his elder son,

THOMAS WILBRAHAM, esq. of Woodhey, who m. Margaret, daughter of Sir John Mainwaring, of Peover, but dying s. p. in 1558, was s. by his brother,

RICHARD WILBRAHAM, esq. master of the jewel house and of the revels to *Queen* MARY, and M.P. for Chester, m. Dorothy, daughter of Richard Grosvenor, esq. of Eaton, and was s. by his son,

THOMAS WILBRAHAM, esq. of Woodhey, who married Frances, daughter of Sir Hugh Cholmondeley, knt. of Cholmondeley, and had, with two daughters, Dorothy, wife of John Done, esq. and Mary, of Sir Thomas Delves, bart. an only son,

I. SIR RICHARD WILBRAHAM, of Woodhey, born in 1579, who was knighted by *King* JAMES I. and afterwards created a BARONET, 5th March, 1620-1. He m. Grace, daughter of Thomas, first Viscount Savage, and had issue,

- THOMAS, his heir.
- Richard.
- William, d. s. p.
- ——, m. to Venables, of Kinderton.
- Elizabeth, m. to Sir Humphrey Briggs, knt. and bart.

He d. in 1643, and was s. by his eldest son,

II. SIR THOMAS WILBRAHAM, who m. Elizabeth, daughter and co-heir of Sir Roger Wilbraham, knt. one of the masters of request to JAMES I. and had issue,

- THOMAS, his heir.
- Ralph, of Newbottle, m. Christiana, daughter of Edward Leigh, esq. of Bagulegh, and left an only daughter,
  - ELIZABETH, who m. Sackville Tufton, esq.
- Elizabeth, m. to Mutton Davies, esq. of Gwasaney, in Flintshire.

Sir Thomas, who distinguished himself in the royal cause during the great rebellion, d. 31st October, 1660, and was s. by his son,

III. SIR THOMAS WILBRAHAM, who m. Elizabeth, daughter and heir of Edward Mitton, esq. of Weston-under-Lyziard, in the county of Stafford, and had issue,

- ELIZABETH, m. to Sir Thomas Myddleton, bart. of Chirk Castle.
- GRACE, m. to Lionel, Earl of Dysart.
- Mary, m. to Richard, Earl of Bradford.

Sir Thomas d. in August, 1692, and thus having had no male issue, the BARONETCY EXPIRED, while his estates devolved upon his daughters as co-heirs.

Arms—Arg. three bendlets wavy az. The more modern arms are "az. two bars arg."

WILDE.

CREATED 13th Sept. 1660. EXTINCT

Lineage.

I. SIR WILLIAM WILDE, recorder of London, and afterwards *temp.* CHARLES II. one of the judges of the court of King's Bench, was created a BARONET in 1660, in which year he represented the city of London in parliament. He m. three wives, and had issue by the two last. Sir William died 23rd November, 1679, aged sixty-eight, and was buried in the Temple Church, having settled his property of Goldston, Kent, in tail male in the issue of his third wife, Frances, remainder to his own right heirs. By his second marriage he had a son, FELIX, his heir, and by the last another son,

- William, who left three daughters and co-heirs, viz.
  - FRANCES, m. to William Brandon, esq.
  - MARGARET, m. to John Masters, esq. and had two daughters,
    - Elizabeth Masters, m. first, to James Hall, esq.; and secondly, to Mr. Thomas Jull.
    - Margaret Masters, m. to Simon Turner, of Dover, and had a son, John, of Ash.
  - ELIZABETH, m. to Thomas Herenden, esq. of Eltham, and had two daughters and co-heirs,
    - Anna Herenden, m. to William Shapter.
    - Maria Herenden, m. to William Cowley.

Sir William's son and successor,

II. SIR FELIX WILDE, who married first, Eleanor, daughter of Sir Thomas Twysden, bart. of Bradbourn, in Kent; and secondly, Mary, daughter of Sir Thomas Style, bart. of Wateringbury, in the same county, but died without male issue, when the Baronetcy became extinct. His daughter,

Anne, m. John Cockman, M. D. and had an only child,

Eleanor Cockman, m. to Nicholas Toke, esq. of Godenton, in Kent.

Arms—Arg. a chev. and chief sa. the latter charged with three mullets or.

WILLIAMS, OF VAYNOL.

Created 15th June, 1622.

Extinct about 1693.

Lineage.

I. William Williams, esq. of Vaynol, in Carmarthenshire (sprung from Thomas Williams, of Vaynol, younger son of William Williams, of Cochwillan, ancestor of the present Sir R. B. Williams-Bulkeley, bart. of Penryn), was created a Baronet in 1622. He m. first, Ellen, daughter of William Williams, esq. of Cochwillan; and secondly, Dorothy, daughter of Edward Dymock, esq. of Willington, in Flintshire; and left a son and successor,

II. Sir Thomas Williams, of Vaynol, who m. Katherine, daughter of Robert Wynne, esq. and was father of

III. Sir William Williams, who m. first, Margaret, daughter of John Wynne, esq. of Mell; and secondly, Margaret, daughter and heir of Griffith Jones, esq. of Castle March. He was s. by his son,

IV. Sir Griffith Williams, who m. Penelope, daughter of Thomas, first Viscount Bulkeley, and died about the year 1663, leaving a son and heir,

V. Sir Thomas Williams, at whose decease in minority the Baronetcy devolved on his brother,

VI. Sir William Williams, who m. Ellen, daughter of Robert, second Viscount Bulkeley, but *d. s. p.* about 1693, when the title became extinct.

Arms—Gu. a chev. erm. between three Saxon heads couped ppr.

WILLIAMS, OF MARNHULL.

Created 19th April, 1642.

Extinct in 1644.

Lineage.

The family of Williams of Marnhull is presumed to have been a branch of the old Dorsetshire line of Williams, of Herringstone.

I. Edmond Williams, esq. of Marnhull, in Dorsetshire, son of John Williams, of London, citizen and goldsmith, was created a Baronet in 1642. He m. Mary, daughter of Sir John Beaumont, bart. of Gracedieu, in Leicestershire, but by her, who wedded secondly, John Tasburgh, esq. he left no issue at his decease in 1644, when the title became extinct. By his will, dated in the preceding year, he gave the manor of Marnhull to Mary his wife, by whom it was sold to Sir Thomas Barker and George Reeve, and from them purchased in 1651, by George Hussey, esq.

Arms—Vert, three eagles displayed in fesse or.

WILLIAMS, OF MINSTER.

Created 22nd April, 1642.—Extinct.

Lineage.

I. John Williams, citizen and goldsmith of London, brother of Sir Edmund Williams, of Marnhull, acquired considerable property at Minster, in Thanet, Kent, and was created a Baronet in 1642. His son and successor,

II. Sir John Williams, of Minster, married Susan, daughter of Sir Thomas Skipwith, bart. of Metheringham, and had an only daughter and heir,

Mary, m. first in June, 1696, to Charles, Lord Shelburne, who *d. s. p.*; secondly, Lieut.-Gen. Henry Conyngham, of Slane; and thirdly, Robert Dalway, esq. Col. of Dragoons. She died in December, 1710, and was buried at St. Mary's, Dublin. By her second husband she had several children, and in their descendants the Minster property centered.

Arms—As Williams of Marnhull.

WILLIAMS, OF LLANGIBBY.

Created 14th May, 1642.

Extinct in Dec. 175[illegible]

Lineage.

Caradoc Vreichvras, or Cradoc Fraich Fras (which means Cradoc with the strong arm), lord of Gloucester in right of his father, was grandson of Brychan Brecheiniog, prince and lord of Brecknock, a contemporary with King Arthur, who lived about the year [illegible], one of the knights of his Round Table and lord keeper of "y Castell Dolorus," or the Dolorous Tower. Cradoc was lord of Brecon after the death of all the sons of Brychan, his grandfather: he was also lord of Fferregg, or Fferlex, which lies between the Severn and Wye; he obtained it by conquest, previous to his coming into Wales. The surname of Fraich Fras is now known in English as Armstrong and Strongitharm. Cradoc was son of Llir Merini, or Molwynoca, lord of Gloucester, by Gwen, or Gwenllian, daughter of Brychan Brecheiniog. His ensign upon his shield in the field of battle was, "Sa. a chev. between three spear-heads, points imbrued gu. Cradoc had six sons by his

WILBRAHAM, OF WOODHEY.

Created
, Mar. 1620-1.

Extinct
August, 1692.

Lineage.

Sir Richard de Wilburgham, m. first, Margery, ughter and co heir of Warin Vernon, Baron of arpbrook, and had, with a son who d. s. p. two ughters, the wives of Lostock and Winnington, who came heirs to their mother. He married secondly, rtitia, second daughter and co-heir of Sir William nables, of Wymincham. He d. in 2 Edward I. d was s. by the son of the latter lady,

William de Wilburgham, whose great-great-grandn,

Thomas de Wilburgham, of Radnor, m. Margaret, ughter and heiress of John Golborne, lord of Woodey, in the county of Chester, and thus acquired that tate. He had issue,

- Thomas, his heir.
- Randulph, from whom the Wilbrahams of Delamere, Dorfold, Rode, &c. derive. (Refer to Burke's *Commoners*, vol. i. page 315.)
- William.
- Richard.
- John.

he eldest son and heir,

Thomas Wilbraham, esq. succeeded to the manors f Radnor and Woodhey, and marrying *temp.* Henr VI. Margaret, daughter of Thomas de Swettenham, as s. at his decease, 7 Henry VII. by his eldest n,

William Wilbraham, esq. of Woodhey, who m. lelena, daughter of Philip Egerton, esq. of Egerton, nd was s. by his elder son,

Thomas Wilbraham, esq. of Woodhey, who m. Margaret, daughter of Sir John Mainwaring, of Peoer, but dying s. p. in 1558, was s. by his brother,

Richard Wilbraham, esq. master of the jewel ouse and of the revels to *Queen* Mary, and M.P. or Chester, m. Dorothy, daughter of Richard Grosveor, esq. of Eaton, and was s. by his son,

Thomas Wilbraham, esq. of Woodhey, who married 'rances, daughter of Sir Hugh Cholmondeley, knt. of 'holmondeley, and had, with two daughters, Dorothy, ife of John Done, esq. and Mary, of Sir Thomas Delves, bart. an only son,

i. Sir Richard Wilbraham, of Woodhey, born in 579, who was knighted by *King* James I. and afterwards created a Baronet, 5th March, 1620-1. He m. race, daughter of Thomas, first Viscount Savage, nd had issue,

- Thomas, his heir.
- Richard.
- William, d. s. p.
- ——, m. to Venables, of Kinderton.
- Elizabeth, m. to Sir Humphrey Briggs, knt. and bart.

He d. in 1643, and was s. by his eldest son,

ii. Sir Thomas Wilbraham, who m. Elizabeth, laughter and co-heir of Sir Roger Wilbraham, knt. one of the masters of request to James I. and had issue,

- Thomas, his heir.
- Ralph, of Newbottle, m. Christiana, daughter of Edward Leigh, esq. of Bagulegh, and left an only daughter,
  - Elizabeth, who m. Sackville Tufton, esq.
- Elizabeth, m. to Mutton Davies, esq. of Gwasaney, in Flintshire.

Sir Thomas, who distinguished himself in the royal cause during the great rebellion, d. 31st October, 1660, and was s. by his son,

iii. Sir Thomas Wilbraham, who m. Elizabeth, daughter and heir of Edward Mitton, esq. of Weston-under-Lyziard, in the county of Stafford, and had issue,

- Elizabeth, m. to Sir Thomas Myddleton, bart. of Chirk Castle.
- Grace, m. to Lionel, Earl of Dysart.
- Mary, m. to Richard, Earl of Bradford.

Sir Thomas d. in August, 1692, and thus having had no male issue, the Baronetcy expired, while his estates devolved upon his daughters as co-heirs.

Arms—Arg. three bendlets wavy az. The more modern arms are "az. two bars arg."

WILDE.

Created
13th Sept. 1660.

Extinct

Lineage.

i. Sir William Wilde, recorder of London, and afterwards *temp.* Charles II. one of the judges of the court of King's Bench, was created a Baronet in 1660, in which year he represented the city of London in parliament. He m. three wives, and had issue by the two last. Sir William died 23rd November, 1679, aged sixty-eight, and was buried in the Temple Church, having settled his property of Goldston, Kent, in tail male in the issue of his third wife, Frances, remainder to his own right heirs. By his second marriage he had a son, Felix, his heir, and by the last another son,

- William, who left three daughters and co-heirs, viz.
  - Frances, m. to William Brandon, esq.
  - Margaret, m. to John Masters, esq. and had two daughters,
    - Elizabeth Masters, m. first, to James Hall, esq.; and secondly, to Mr. Thomas Jull.
    - Margaret Masters, m. to Simon Turner, of Dover, and had a son, John, of Ash.
  - Elizabeth, m. to Thomas Herenden, esq. of Eltham, and had two daughters and co-heirs,
    - Anna Herenden, m. to William Shaper.
    - Maria Herenden, m. to William Cowley.

Sir William's son and successor,

ii. Sir Felix Wilde, who married first, Eleanor, daughter of Sir Thomas Twysden, bart. of Bradbourn, in Kent; and secondly, Mary, daughter of Sir Thomas Style, bart. of Wateringbury, in the same county, but died without male issue, when the BARONETCY became EXTINCT. His daughter,

ANNE, m. John Cockman, M. D. and had an only child,

ELEANOR COCKMAN, m. to NICHOLAS TOKE, esq. of Godenton, in Kent.

Arms—Arg. a chev. and chief sa. the latter charged with three mullets or.

WILLIAMS, OF VAYNOL.

CREATED 15th June, 1622.

EXTINCT about 1693.

Lineage.

I. WILLIAM WILLIAMS, esq. of Vaynol, in Carmarthenshire (sprung from Thomas Williams, of Vaynol, younger son of William Williams, of Cochwillan, ancestor of the present SIR R. B. WILLIAMS-BULKELEY, bart. of Penryn), was created a BARONET in 1622. He m. first, Ellen, daughter of William Williams, esq. of Cochwillan; and secondly, Dorothy, daughter of Edward Dymock, esq. of Willington, in Flintshire; and left a son and successor,

II. SIR THOMAS WILLIAMS, of Vaynol, who m. Katherine, daughter of Robert Wynne, esq. and was father of

III. SIR WILLIAM WILLIAMS, who m. first, Margaret, daughter of John Wynne, esq. of Mell; and secondly, Margaret, daughter and heir of Griffith Jones, esq. of Castle March. He was *s.* by his son,

IV. SIR GRIFFITH WILLIAMS, who m. Penelope, daughter of Thomas, first Viscount Bulkeley, and died about the year 1663, leaving a son and heir,

V. SIR THOMAS WILLIAMS, at whose decease in minority the Baronetcy devolved on his brother,

VI. SIR WILLIAM WILLIAMS, who m. Ellen, daughter of Robert, second Viscount Bulkeley, but *d. s. p.* about 1693, when the title became EXTINCT.

Arms—Gu. a chev. erm. between three Saxon heads couped ppr.

WILLIAMS, OF MARNHULL.

CREATED 19th April, 1642.

EXTINCT in 1644.

Lineage.

The family of Williams of Marnhull is presumed to have been a branch of the old Dorsetshire line of Williams, of Herringstone.

I. EDMOND WILLIAMS, esq. of Marnhull, in Dorsetshire, son of John Williams, of London, citizen and goldsmith, was created a BARONET in 1642. He m. Mary, daughter of Sir John Beaumont, bart. of Grace-dieu, in Leicestershire, but by her, who wedded, secondly, John Tasburgh, esq. he left no issue at his decease in 1644, when the title became EXTINCT. By his will, dated in the preceding year, he gave the manor of Marnhull to Mary his wife, by whom it was sold to Sir Thomas Barker and George Reeve, and from them purchased in 1651, by George Hussey, esq.

Arms—Vert, three eagles displayed in fesse or.

WILLIAMS, OF MINSTER.

CREATED 22nd April, 1642.—EXTINCT.

Lineage.

I. JOHN WILLIAMS, citizen and goldsmith of London, brother of Sir Edmund Williams, of Marnhull, acquired considerable property at Minster, in Thanet, Kent, and was created a BARONET in 1642. He was s. by his son and successor,

II. SIR JOHN WILLIAMS, of Minster, married Susan, daughter of Sir Thomas Skipwith, bart. of Metheringham, and had an only daughter and heir,

MARY, m. first in June, 1690, to Charles, Lord Shelburne, who *d. s. p.*; secondly, Lieut. Gen. Henry Conyngham, of Slane; and thirdly, Robert Dalway, esq. Col. of Dragoons. She d. in December, 1710, and was buried at St. Mary's, Dublin. By her second husband she had several children, and in their descendants the Minster property centered.

Arms—As WILLIAMS OF MARNHULL.

WILLIAMS, OF LLANGIBBY.

CREATED 14th May, 1642.

EXTINCT in Dec. 17[illegible]

Lineage.

CARADOG VREICHVRAS, or Cradoc Fraich Fras (which means Cradoc with the strong arm), lord of Glamorgan in right of his father, was grandson of Brychan Brycheiniog, prince and lord of Brecknock, a contemporary with King Arthur, who lived about the year [illegible] one of the knights of his Round Table and lord [illegible] "y Castell Dolorus," or the Dolorous Tower [illegible] was lord of Brecon after the death of all the [illegible] Brychan, his grandfather: he was also lord of [illegible]regg, or Pferiex, which lies between the Severn and Wye; he obtained it by conquest, previous to his [illegible] into Wales. The surname of Fraich Fras is now known in English as Armstrong and Strongarm. Cradoc was son of Llir Merini, or Meirwyn, [illegible] Gloucester, by Gwen, or Gwenllian, daughter of Brychan Brecheiniog. His ensign upon his shield [illegible] field of battle was, "Sa. a chev. between three [illegible] heads, points imbrued gu. Cradoc had six sons [illegible]

Thomas, who *d.* in the lifetime of his father, 8th February, 1669, unmarried.

David, *m.* Mrs. Knight, relict of Dr. Knight, a physician of Shrewsbury, but died *s. p.*

Matthew, *m.* Elizabeth, daughter of Mr. Thomas Gilbert, of London, mercer, and had issue,

Gilbert, of Rose Hall, Herts, who *s.* as eighth Baronet.

Matthew, *d.* unm. at Jamaica.

Elizabeth, *m.* to the Rev. Mr. Cholmley, of Hereford.

Eleanor.

Francis, *m.* to Mr. John Castle, of London.

Sir Henry *d.* about the year 1652, and was *s.* by his eldest son,

II. Sir Henry Williams, who *m.* a daughter of Sir Walter Pye, of the Mynde, Herts, and was *s.* by his eldest son,

III. Sir Henry Williams, who *m.* Miss Whitchurch, and had two daughters, his co-heirs, of whom Elizabeth *m.* Sir Edward Williams, knt. second son of Sir Thomas Williams, bart. of Eltham, and conveyed the estate of Gwernevet, to her husband. At the decease of Sir Henry the baronetcy passed to his brother.

IV. Sir Walter Williams, who died without issue,* and was *s.* by his cousin,

V. Sir Gilbert Williams, of Rose Hall, Herts, in holy orders, vicar of Islington, Middlesex, and of Sarrat, Herefordshire, who *m.* Dorothy, daughter of William Wankford, esq. of Rickmansworth, and had issue,

David, his heir.

Matthew.

Gilbert.

William.

He *d.* in 1768, and was *s.* by his eldest son,

VI. Sir David Williams, *b.* 13th May, 1736, who *m.* Rebecca, daughter of Dr. Rowland, a physician at Aylesbury, and left with a daughter, Rebecca, a son and successor,

VII. Sir David Williams, of Rose Hall, Herts, bapt. 27th April, 1765, who *m.* Sophia, daughter of Mr. Stanley, a commissioner of the customs, and had an only daughter and heir,

Sophia Charlotte, of Rose Hall, Herts, *m.* to Thomas Tyringham Bernard, esq. of Winchendon, Bucks, and *d.* 15th May, 1837.

Sir David *d.* in 1798, when the Baronetcy became extinct.

Arms—Argent, a chevron, between three cocks, gules, on a chief sable, three spears' heads, argent sanguinated.

WILLIAMS, OF ELTHAM.

Created 22nd Nov. 1674.

Extinct in 1804.

Lineage.

Descended from the ancient family of Williams, of Tallyn, in Brecon,

I. Thomas Williams, M.D. of Eltham, in Kent, first and chymical physician to Charles II. and James II. was created a Baronet 22nd November, 1674. Sir Thomas served in several parliaments for Weobley, in Herefordshire. He *m.* first, a daughter of Sir Edmund Sawyer, of Woodbine, and by her, had issue,

John (Sir), who with his next brother received the honour of knighthood, in the lifetime of his father.

Edward (Sir), M.P. for the county of Brecon, for forty years, *m.* Elizabeth, daughter and co-heir of Sir Henry Williams, bart. of *Guernevet* by whom he acquired that estate, and had issue,

Henry, *m.* Mary, daughter of John Walbeoffe, esq. of Lauham Lach, in the county of Brecon, but *d. s. p.* in 1723. His widow *m.* Sir Humphrey Howarth, knt. and *d.* in 1742.

Thomas, LL.D. *d.* in 1730, without issue.

Edward, *d.* with issue, in 1715.

David, heir to his uncle.

Abigail, *m.* to the Rev. Thomas Price.

Mary, *m.* first to Samuel Watkins, of Llanigon, and secondly to the Rev. Henry Allen.

Sir Edward, *d.* in 1721.

James, prebendary of St. Pauls, *d.* in 1727.

Thomas, *d.* about the year 1709.

Sir Thomas *m.* secondly, a daughter of Cawarden, of Cawarden Green, in Herefordshire. He *d.* in 1714, and was *s.* by his eldest son,

II. Sir John Williams, M.P. for the county of Hereford, who *m.* Mary, only daughter and heiress of Sir William Powell, bart. of Pengethley, and had issue,

Susanna, *m.* to Henry Cornwall, of Bredwardine Castle, in Herefordshire, and had two sons, viz.

Velters Cornwall, M.P. for the county of Hereford, represented now by Sir Velters Cornwall, bart. (Refer to Burke's *Peerage and Baronetage.*)

James Cornwall, M.P. for Weobley.

Mary Cornwall, *m.* to the Hon. Henry Berkeley.

Penelope, *m.* to Thomas Symonds, esq. of Sugwass, in Herefordshire, and was great grandmother of the present Thomas Powell Symonds, esq. of Pengethly.

Sir John *d.* 17th June, 1723, when the Baronetcy devolved upon his nephew,

III. Sir David Williams, who *m.* Susannah, daughter of Thomas Witherstone, esq. of the Lodge, in the county of Hereford, by whom (who *m.* secondly, the Rev. Thomas Johnstone, of Herefordshire,) he had issue,

Henry, his successor.

Edward, heir to his brother.

Elizabeth.

Susannah.

He *d.* 9th February, 1740, and was *s.* by his elder son,

IV. Sir Henry Williams, who *d.* unm. 15th August, 1741, aged eighteen, and was *s.* by his brother,

V. Sir Edward Williams, who *m.* first, Mary, daughter and co-heir of Isaac Leheup, esq. and secondly, Mary, daughter of John Riley, esq. of St. James's Place. By the former, he had one son and one daughter, viz.

* Some accounts derive the Williamses, of Rose Hall, Herts, from Thomas, the brother of the first baronet, and assert that the baronetcy expired with Sir Walter.

June, 1643, and left with another son and four daughters, a successor,

Sir Edward Williams, knt. of Llangibby Castle, in the county of Monmouth, who married first, [illegible], daughter of Sir Edward Morgan, bart. of Llantarnam, in Monmouthshire, and had, with other issue, a daughter Anne, wife of Sir [illegible] Kemeys, bart. and a son and heir,

Sir Charles Williams, knt. of Llangibby, who m. first, a daughter of Sir William Morgan, knt. of Tredegar, in the county of Monmouth, but by her had no issue. He wedded, secondly, Anne, daughter of Sir John Trevor, knt. of Plas Teg, in the county of Flint, by whom he had

- Trevor, his heir.
- Edward, lieut.-col. in the army, who m. Elizabeth, daughter of William Bowen, of Gurrey, in Herefordshire, and had issue.
- Margaret, m. to Sir George Probert, of Pantglas, in Monmouthshire.
- Anne, m. to Sir Evan Lloyd, bart. of Yale, in the county of Denbigh.

Sir Charles d. in 1641, and was s. by his elder son,

I. Trevor Williams, esq. of Llangibby, who in consideration of the eminent services in the cause of Charles I. was created a Baronet 14th Sept. 1642. Sir Trevor m. Elizabeth, daughter and sole heir of Thomas Morgan, esq. of Machen and Tredegar, in Monmouthshire, by Rachel, his wife, sister and coheir of Ralph Lord Hopton, and had issue,

- Trevor, m. Mary, daughter of Humphrey Wyndham, esq. of Dunraven, in Glamorganshire, but died before his father, issueless.
- John, successor to his father.
- Hopton, heir to his brother.
- Thomas, who m. first, Delarivers, daughter of Sir Thomas Morgan, general of horse, and widow of Thomas Lewis, esq. of St. Pierre, in Monmouthshire, and had two sons,
  - John, heir to his uncle, Hopton.
  - Charles, d. unm.

  By his second wife he had another son,
  - Leonard, heir to his brother John.
- Rachel, m. to Henry Morgan, esq. of Bonnewyth, in Monmouthshire.
- Anne, m. to Roger Williams, esq. of Kevenheligh, in the same county.
- Margaret.
- Frances, m. to Sir William Boothby, bart. of Broadlow Ash, in the county of Derby.
- Mary, m. to — Wilcox, esq.
- Blanch.

Sir Trevor who sat in parliament for Monmouthshire, at the time of the Revolution, d. aged sixty-nine, in December, 1692, and was s. by his eldest surviving son,

II. Sir John Williams, lord of the manors of Ewyas Lacy, Waterslow, and Trecraillon, and proprietor of other lands in the county of Hereford; lord of the manor of Cairwent, in Monmouthshire, which last estate he obtained an act of parliament to sell, *temp.* William III. for the discharge of debts contracted in the public service. He married first, Anne, daughter and co-heir of Humphrey Baskerville, esq. of Pontryllas, in Herefordshire, and secondly, Anne, daughter of Philip, Earl of Pembroke, but died without issue in November, 1704, and was s. by his brother,

III. Sir Hopton Williams, M.P. for Monmouthshire *temp.* Queen Anne, who, by Mary, his wife, had two sons, who died unmarried, with a daughter, the wife of Capt. Webb. He d. in November, 1723, aged sixty, and was s. by his nephew,

IV. Sir John Williams, who m. Temperance, daughter of — Bowyer, and widow of — William[s], [of] Monmouthshire, by whom he had three daughters,

I. Laura, m. to William Addams, esq. who assumed the additional surname of Williams, and had a son and heir,

William Addams-Williams, esq. of Llangibby Castle, who m. Caroline, daughter of Samuel Marsh, esq. of [illegible], formerly M.P. for Chippenham, and was s. by his son, the present

William Addams-Williams, esq. of Llangibby Castle, M.P. for the county of Monmouth, who m. 17th August, 18[illegible], Louisa, eldest daughter of the Rev. [illegible] Vassall, D.D. of the Hom, in Gloucestershire, and has issue,

- William, b. 20th March, 18[illegible].
- Louisa-Caroline.
- Caroline-Frances.
- Augusta Maria-Marsh.

II. Mary, m. to — Herbert, esq.

III. Delarivers, d. unm.

Sir John d. 11th March, 1738, and was succeeded by his half-brother,

V. Sir Leonard Williams, who d. s. p. at [illegible], Monmouthshire, in December, 1758, when the Baronetcy became EXTINCT.

Arms—Gyronny of eight ermine and sable, a lion rampant or.

WILLIAMS, OF GWERNEVET.

Created 4th May, 1644. Extinct [illegible]

Lineage.

Sir David Williams, knt. of Gwernevet, in the county of Brecon, one of the judges of the Court of King's Bench, m. first, Margaret, daughter and heir of Sir David Gam, knt. of Aberbran, in the same county, and secondly, Dorothy Latton, widow. He had issue,

- Henry (Sir), his heir.
- Thomas, of Corndon, in Gloucestershire, and Cockthrop, in the county of Oxford, died in the year 1636, aged fifty-four, leaving by [illegible] his wife, daughter of James Hawkins, esq. of Washburne, several children.
- Roger, of the Gare, in Breconshire, left issue.
- Robert, of Cabalva, in Radnorshire, whose line terminated in a daughter and heiress,
  - Elizabeth, m. to Sir Philip Boteler, bart. of Teston, in Kent.

The eldest son and heir,

I. Sir Henry Williams, knt. of Gwernevet, was created a Baronet by King Charles I. on 4th May, 1644. He m. Eleanor, daughter of Eustace Whitney, esq. of Whitney, in the county of Hereford, and had issue,

- Henry, his heir.
- David, of Corndon, in the county of Gloucester, m. a daughter of Sir Matthew Carew, knt. and had

Thomas, who *d.* in the lifetime of his father, 8th February, 1660, unmarried.
David, *m.* Mrs. Knight, relict of Dr. Knight, a physician of Shrewsbury, but died *s. p.*
MATTHEW, *m.* Elisabeth, daughter of Mr. Thomas Gilbert, of London, mercer, and had issue,
GILBERT, of Rose Hall, Herts, who *s.* as eighth BARONET.
Matthew, *d.* unm. at Jamaica.
Elizabeth, *m.* to the Rev. Mr. Cholmley, of Hereford.
Eleanor.
Francis, *m.* to Mr. John Castle, of London.

Sir Henry *d.* about the year 1652, and was *s.* by his eldest son,

II. SIR HENRY WILLIAMS, who *m.* a daughter of Sir Walter Pye, of the Mynde, Herts, and was *s.* by his eldest son,

III. SIR HENRY WILLIAMS, who *m.* Miss Whitchurch, and had two daughters, his co-heirs, of whom ELIZABETH *m.* Sir Edward Williams, knt. second son of Sir Thomas Williams, bart. of Eltham, and conveyed the estate of Gwernevet, to her husband. At the decease of Sir Henry the baronetcy passed to his brother.

IV. SIR WALTER WILLIAMS, who died without issue,* and was *s.* by his cousin,

V. SIR GILBERT WILLIAMS, of Rose Hall, Herts, in holy orders, vicar of Islington, Middlesex, and of Sarrat, Herefordshire, who *m.* Dorothy, daughter of William Wankford, esq. of Rickmansworth, and had issue,

DAVID, his heir.
Matthew.
Gilbert.
William.

He *d.* in 1768, and was *s.* by his eldest son,

VI. SIR DAVID WILLIAMS, *b.* 13th May, 1736, who *m.* Rebecca, daughter of Dr. Rowland, a physician at Aylesbury, and left with a daughter, Rebecca, a son and successor,

VII. SIR DAVID WILLIAMS, of Rose Hall, Herts, bapt. 27th April, 1765, who *m.* Sophia, daughter of Mr. Stanley, a commissioner of the customs, and had an only daughter and heir,

SOPHIA CHARLOTTE, of Rose Hall, Herts, *m.* to Thomas Tyringham Bernard, esq. of Winchendon, Bucks, and *d.* 15th May, 1847.

Sir David *d.* in 1798, when the BARONETCY became EXTINCT.

Arms—Argent, a chevron, between three cocks, gules, on a chief sable, three spears' heads, argent sanguinated.

WILLIAMS, OF ELTHAM.

CREATED 2nd Nov. 1674.

EXTINCT in 1804.

Lineage.

Descended from the ancient family of Williams, of Tallyn, in Brecon,

I. THOMAS WILLIAMS, M.D. of Eltham, in Kent, first and chymical physician to CHARLES II. and JAMES II. was created a BARONET 2nd November, 1674. Sir Thomas served in several parliaments for Weobley, in Herefordshire. He *m.* first, a daughter of Sir Edmund Sawyer, of Woodbine, and by her, had issue,

JOHN (Sir), who with his next brother received the honour of knighthood, in the lifetime of his father.
Edward (Sir), M.P. for the county of Brecon, for forty years, *m.* ELIZABETH, daughter and co-heir of SIR HENRY WILLIAMS, bart. of *Guernevet* by whom he acquired that estate, and had issue,
Henry, *m.* Mary, daughter of John Walbeoffe, esq. of Lauham Lach, in the county of Brecon, but *d. s. p.* in 1723. His widow *m.* Sir Humphrey Howarth, knt. and *d.* in 1742.
Thomas, LL.D. *d.* in 1720, without issue.
Edward, *d.* with issue, in 1715.
DAVID, heir to his uncle.
Abigail, *m.* to the Rev. Thomas Price.
Mary, *m.* first to Samuel Watkins, of Llanigon, and secondly to the Rev. Henry Allen.
Sir Edward, *d.* in 1721.
James, prebendary of St. Pauls, *d.* in 1727.
Thomas, *d.* about the year 1708.

Sir Thomas *m.* secondly, a daughter of Cawarden, of Cawarden Green, in Herefordshire. He *d.* in 1714, and was *s.* by his eldest son,

II. SIR JOHN WILLIAMS, M.P. for the county of Hereford, who *m.* Mary, only daughter and heiress of Sir William Powell, bart. of Pengethley, and had issue,

SUSANNA, *m.* to Henry Cornwall, of Bredwardine Castle, in Herefordshire, and had two sons, viz.
VELTERS CORNWALL, M.P. for the county of Hereford, represented now by SIR VELTERS CORNWALL, bart. (Refer to BURKE's *Peerage and Baronetage*.)
James Cornwall, M.P. for Weobley.
Mary Cornwall, *m.* to the Hon. Henry Berkeley.
PENELOPE, *m.* to Thomas Symonds, esq. of Sugwass, in Herefordshire, and was great grandmother of the present THOMAS POWELL SYMONDS, esq. of Pengethly.

Sir John *d.* 17th June, 1723, when the Baronetcy devolved upon his nephew,

III. SIR DAVID WILLIAMS, who *m.* Susannah, daughter of Thomas Witherstone, esq. of the Lodge, in the county of Hereford, by whom (who *m.* secondly, the Rev. Thomas Johnstone, of Herefordshire,) he had issue,

HENRY, his successor.
EDWARD, heir to his brother.
Elisabeth.
Susannah.

He *d.* 9th February, 1740, and was *s.* by his elder son,

IV. SIR HENRY WILLIAMS, who *d.* unm. 15th August, 1741, aged eighteen, and was *s.* by his brother,

V. SIR EDWARD WILLIAMS, who *m.* first, Mary, daughter and co-heir of Isaac Leheup, esq. and secondly, Mary, daughter of John Riley, esq. of St. James's Place. By the former, he had one son and one daughter, viz.

* Some accounts derive the Williamses, of Rose Hall, Herts, from Thomas, the brother of the first baronet, and assert that the baronetcy expired with Sir Walter.

WILLYS, OF FEN DITTON.

CREATED 15th Dec. 1641.  EXTINCT 14th April, 1732.

Lineage.

THOMAS WILLYS, of Eyhall, in Cambridgeshire, son of another Thomas Willys, of the same place, m. Joan, daughter of Martin Fowkes, of Westley and Burwell, and had two sons and one daughter. Of the former, the elder,

THOMAS WILLYS, of Eyhall, and Rouses Place, m. Elizabeth, daughter of John Hasell, of Botsham, in Cambridgeshire, and dying 9th February, 1625, aged sixty-seven, left a son, and successor,

RICHARD WILLYS, esq. of Horningsey and Fen Ditton, Cambridgeshire, who m. Joan, daughter and heir of William Henmarsh, esq. of Balles, and had issue,

- THOMAS, his heir.
- RICHARD, created a BARONET in 1646, see that title.
- William, col. of horse in the royal army, during the civil war, m. the daughter of Sir John Offley, knt. of Madeley Manor, Staffordshire, but died s. p. 9th August, 1676, aged sixty-one.
- Elizabeth, m. to Sir William Man, knt. of Canterbury.

Richard Willys died 16th October, 1628, and was s. by his son,

I. THOMAS WILLYS, esq. of Fen Ditton, in Cambridgeshire, who was created a BARONET 15th December, 1641. He m. Anne, eldest daughter and co-heir of Sir John Wild, knt. of Canterbury, and by her, who died 29th October, 1685, aged seventy-five, had issue,

- JOHN, his heir.
- Richard, gentleman pensioner to CHARLES II. d. unm.
- William, of London, a Hamburgh merchant, who was buried at Fen Ditton, 9th August, 1706. He m. first, Frances, daughter of John Ayshford, esq. of Ayshford, in Devon, by whom, who died 3rd September, 1676, aged thirty-three, he had a son and daughter, William and Elizabeth, who both died young. He wedded secondly, Mary, daughter of Mr. Gore, merchant of London, and widow of George Evelyn, esq. by whom he had issue,
    - THOMAS, who succeeded as fifth baronet.
    - WILLIAM, successor to his brother.
    - Anne, m. to Mr. Michell, of Wilts.
    - Mary, m. to William Gore, esq.
    - Jane, m. to Henry Hal.
    - Frances, m. to Humphrey Pudner.
    - Hesther, m. to James Spilman.
    - Dorothy, m. to Samuel Enys, esq. of Enys, in Cornwall.
- Robert, who m. Mary, daughter of Thomas Stagg, of London, and relict of William Llewellin, of Melborn, in Cambridgeshire, by whom he left at his decease, 19th November, 1692, an only child, John.
- Henry, died young 18th January, 1632.
- Anne, m. to Anthony Fisher, esq. of Wisbeach, in the Isle of Ely.
- Elizabeth, m. to Edward Nutt, esq. of Neckinton near Canterbury.
- Jane, m. to Nicholas Repps, D.D. of Marsham, Norfolk.
- Mary.
- Hesther.
- Frances.
- Ellen.

Sir Thomas died 17th November, 1701, in the ninetieth year of his age, and was s. by his son,

II. SIR JOHN WILLYS, of Fen Ditton, who m. Mary, daughter of Thomas Savage, esq. of Elmley Castle, Worcestershire, and had issue,

- THOMAS, his heir.
- John, died young.
- Anne, m. to Ralph Hare, of Hargham, Norfolk.
- Mary, m. to Edward Snag, of Marston, Bedfordshire.
- Elizabeth, died young.

Sir John was buried at Fen Ditton, 9th August, 1701, aged sixty-eight, and succeeded by his son,

III. SIR THOMAS WILLYS, of Fen Ditton, who m. Miss Frances Rix, and had two sons, of whom the elder died in early youth, and lies buried at Great Crassingham, in Norfolk. Sir Thomas died himself of the small-pox, 17th June, 1705, and was s. by his only surviving son,

IV. SIR THOMAS WILLYS, of Fen Ditton, at whose decease unm. 1725, aged about twenty, the title devolved on his cousin,

V. SIR THOMAS WILLYS, of Fen Ditton, who also d. unm. in 1726, and was s. by his brother,

VI. SIR WILLIAM WILLYS, of Fen Ditton, at whose decease unm. 14th April, 1732, the BARONETCY became EXTINCT. The estate of Fen Ditton, was purchased after Sir William's decease in 1733, by Sarah, Duchess of Marlborough, for her grandaughter, Lady Mary Godolphin, and was part of her marriage portion. Her husband Thomas, Duke of Leeds, having procured an act of parliament for the purpose, sold it in 1749, to Thomas Panton, esq. of Newmarket.

Arms—Party per fess gu. and arg. three lions rampant counterchanged a bordure erm.

WILLYS.

CREATED 11th June, 1646.—EXTINCT in 1701.

Lineage.

I. SIR RICHARD WILLYS, knt. next brother of Sir Thomas Willys, first baronet of Fen Ditton, was colonel of a regiment of horse, colonel-general of the counties of Lincoln, Nottingham, and Rutland, and governor of the town and castle of Newark, for King CHARLES I. by whom he was created a BARONET in 1646. He m. Alice, daughter and sole-heir of Thomas Fox, M.D. of Waltham Abbey, in Essex and had issue,

- THOMAS FOX, his heir.
- Alice, d. unm.
- ANNE FOX, m. to Davenport, esq.

Sir Richard died in 1690, was buried at Fen Ditton, 5th February, and s. by his son,

II. SIR THOMAS FOX WILLYS, at whose decease unm. in 1701, aged eighty-nine, the BARONETCY became EXTINCT.

Arms—As WILLYS, OF FEN DITTON.

ay, 1763, Anne, daughter of Claudius Fonnereau, .D. of Christchurch Park, but died unm. 2nd Feruary, 1784, when the BARONETCY EXPIRED.

The estate of the Friars, Chichester, passed to the aronet's sister, Mrs. Fonnereau, but the bulk of the anded property went by entail to the male descendnt of Peer Williams, the lawyer, and thus vested in dmiral Peer Williams Freeman, in whose grandson, illiam Peer Williams Freeman, esq. of Fawley ourt, Oxfordshire, it now vests.

Arms—Gules, a wolf coming out of his den in a ck, ppr.

WILLOUGHBY, OF RISLEY.

CREATED th June, 1611.

EXTINCT in 1649.

Lineage.

This family originally surnamed BUGG, was seated Nottinghamshire for several generations, and asmed the name of WILLOUGHBY from their estate in at county.

RALPH BUGG, had two sons, RICHARD and RALPH, the younger, Ralph, *King* HENRY III. granted in e 50th year of his reign, the manor of Bingham, om which, Ralph's son and heir, RICHARD, assumed e surname of BINGHAM, and was knighted. The der son,

RICHARD BUGG, having the lordship of Willoughby, gave name to his son and heir,

SIR RICHARD WILLOUGHBY, who bought the manor f Wollaton from Sir Roger de Mortein, in the 11th DWARD II. and augmented his patrimony considerbly by other purchases, amongst which was a third art of the manor of RISLEY, in the county of Derby. le *d.* 19 EDWARD II. and was *s.* by his son,

SIR ROBERT WILLOUGHBY, one of the judges in the eign of EDWARD III. who by his first wife, Isabel, aughter of Sir Roger de Mortein, had several sons, ho all died without issue, "so that Risley (says horoton) came to Hugh Willoughby, clerk, who died HENRY IV. and is ancestor of the Willoughbys of isley," but "I rather think them (writes Collins) escended from *Sir* Henry Willoughby, knight banneret, who was possessed of Wollaton, by lineal deent from the said Sir Richard, was knight of the ody to *King* HENRY VIII. and died 20th May, 1528, s I am informed from the inscription on his monuent at Wollaton, in an arch between the south isle nd the chancel, whereon is the effigies of a knight in rmour, with two wives by his side, and underneath wo sons in armour, and two daughters in the dress of e times." He,

SIR HENRY WILLOUGHBY, had two sons, HENRY r, of Wollaton, and

WILLIAM WILLOUGHBY, who died in his father's fetime, leaving by Helena, his wife, daughter and o-heir of Sir John Egerton, of Wrine Hill, in the ounty of Chester, a son and heir,

SIR HUGH WILLOUGHBY, knt. of Risley, in the ounty of Derby, "whom I take (says Collins) to be the famous navigator (for he was of this family) who was sent out with three ships in the reign of *King* EDWARD VI. A.D. 1553, to discover Cathaa, and other Northern parts. He sailed in May, and having spent much time about the Northern Islands, subject to Denmark, where he found no commodity but dried fish and train oil, was forced about the middle of September, to put into a harbour at Lapland, called Arzina, where they could find no inhabitants, and thinking to winter there, was froze to death. However, Richard Chancellor, who commanded the second ship in the expedition, having lost Sir Hugh, made his way for Wardhouse, in Norway, the appointed place if parted by storms, and after seven days stay, proceeded on his voyage, so fortunately, that within a few days he arrived on the coasts of Muscovy, where he was friendly received by the natives, and John Basilowitz the great duke or czar, with whom he settled a trade and was the first discoverer of Russia." Sir Hugh Willoughby left issue by Johanna, his wife, daughter of Sir Nicholas Strelly, knt. a son and heir,

1. HENRY WILLOUGHBY, esq. of Risley, who was created a BARONET by *King* JAMES I. 29th June, 1611. Sir Henry married first, Elizabeth, daughter of Sir Henry Knolles, knt. of Greys, in the county of Oxford, and secondly, Lettice, daughter and co-heir of Sir Francis Darcy, knt. but dying without male issue in 1649, the BARONETCY became EXTINCT. His only daughter and heiress,

> ANNE WILLOUGHBY, *m.* first Sir Thomas Aston, bart. of Aston, in the county of Chester, and had by him, SIR WILLOUGHBY ASTON, and other children. She survived her first husband, and *m.* secondly, the Hon. Antichel Grey.

Arms—Or, two bars gules charged with three water budgets, argent.

WILLOUGHBY, OF SELSTON.

CREATED 4th Aug. 1660.—EXTINCT 10th Feb. 1670.

Lineage.

SIR WILLIAM WILLOUGHBY, knt. of Aston, in Oxfordshire, second son of William Willoughby, esq. of Normanton, died in 1615, leaving by his wife, a daughter of — Young, with other issue, a son and successor,

SIR ROTHERHAM WILLOUGHBY, knt. who *m.* Anne, daughter of Sir Richard Wortley, knt. of Wortley, in Yorkshire, and had by her, who wedded, secondly, Sir George Morton, a son and successor,

WILLIAM WILLOUGHBY, esq. who *m.* Elizabeth, daughter and co-heir of Timothy Pusey, esq. of Selston, in the county of Nottingham, and had issue,

> WILLIAM, his heir.
> Mary, *m.* to Beaumont Dixie, esq.

Mr. Willoughby died in 1630, and was succeeded by his son,

1. WILLIAM WILLOUGHBY, esq. of Selston, Notts, who was created a BARONET in 1660. He *m.* Margaret, daughter and heir of George, son and heir of Sir Maurice Abbott, knt. but died without surviving issue, 10th February, 1670, when the title became EXTINCT. He devised the lordship of South Muskham, Notts, to the learned FRANCIS WILLOUGHBY, of Wollaton.

Arms—As WILLOUGHBY OF RISLEY.

I. Thomas Winford, esq. second prothonotary of the Court of Common Pleas, was created a Baronet 3rd July, 1702, with limitation to the heirs male of the body of his elder brother. Sir Thomas m. Sarah, daughter and heir of Michael Pearce, of Drury Lane, apothecary, but by her, who died 17th September, 1735, and was buried at Hillingdon, Middlesex, had no issue. He was succeeded at his decease, under the reversion in the patent, by his nephew,

II. Sir Thomas Winford, of Glashampton and Norgrove, who m. first, Beata, daughter of Sir Henry Parker, bart. of Honington, in Warwickshire, and secondly, Elizabeth, eldest daughter of Mr. Wilmot, of Bromesgrove, in the county of Worcester, but died *s. p.* 19th January, 1743-4, when the Baronetcy became extinct.

Arms—Argent a chev. between three quarterfoils pierced sa.

WINGFIELD, OF GOODWINS.

Created 17th May, 1627.

Extinct, date unknown.

Lineage.

Sir Robert Wingfield, of Letheringham, in Suffolk, M.P. for that county in the 6th Henry VI. was then chief of the great house of Wingfield. He m. Elizabeth, daughter and co-heir of Sir Robert Gousell, by the Lady Elizabeth Fitzalan, his wife, sister and co-heir of Thomas, eleventh Earl of Arundel, and had issue,

- I. John, his heir.
- II. Robert, M.P. for Herts in 1450, and comptroller of the king's household.
- III. Richard, died *s. p.* before 1509.
- IV. Thomas (Sir), died *s. p.*
- V. William, died *s. p.*
- VI. Henry (Sir), knt. of Orford, in Suffolk, ancestor of the Wingfields of Tickencote, in Rutlandshire, now (1838) represented by John Wingfield, esq. (See Burke's *Commoners*, vol. ii. p. 476.)
- I. Elizabeth, married to Sir William Brandon, knt. and their grandson was Charles Brandon, Duke of Suffolk, the brother-in-law of Henry VIII.
- II. Catharine, m. to John Bonvyle.

The eldest son,

Sir John Wingfield, of Letheringham, served as sheriff of Norfolk and Suffolk, in the 23rd Henry VI. and again in the 12th of the following reign. In 1461, he was made a knight of the bath, at the Tower of London, and 1477, was joined in commission with the Bishop of Bath and Wells, and others, to treat with the ambassadors of France, at Amiens. Sir John married Elizabeth, daughter of Sir John Fitz Lewis, knt. of West Horndon, in Essex, and had no less than twelve sons and three daughters: from the fourth son descended the Wingfields of Dunham Magna; from the ninth son, the Viscounts Powerscourt; from the eleventh son, the Wingfields of Kimbolton; and from the twelfth son, the Wingfields of Brantham, Norton, &c. Sir John Wingfield died in 1481, and was *s.* by his eldest son,

Sir John Wingfield, of Letheringham, sheriff of Norfolk and Suffolk in 1483, and again in 1492-3. He married Anne, daughter of John Touchet, Lord Audley, and left a son and successor,

Sir Anthony Wingfield, of Letheringham, esquire of the body to the king, who was knighted by his royal master, Henry VIII. for his conduct at Terouenne and Tournay, made subsequently comptroller of the household, and installed at Windsor, a knight of the garter, 8th May, 1541. He was likewise constituted vice-chamberlain of the household, and captain of the guards. In the will of *King* Henry, he was a legatee to the amount of £200, was nominated one of the executors, and assigned of the council to Edward VI. Sir Anthony wedded Elizabeth, eldest daughter of Sir George de Vere, knt. and sister and co-heir of John, thirteenth Earl of Oxford, by whom he left at his decease,

- Robert (Sir), his heir.
- Charles, of Tempill, in the county of Lincoln, m. Elizabeth, daughter of Thomas Rich, esq. of Weald, in Essex, and had three sons, Henry, Anthony, and William.
- Anthony, of St. John's, Middlesex, gentleman usher to *Queen* Elizabeth, m. first, Margaret, widow of John Gosnold, and daughter of Thomas Blenerhasset, by whom he had two daughters, Ursula, wife of Edward Harrington, of Ely; and Margaret, of Francis Grey, of Gr..ton. He wedded, secondly, Elizabeth, daughter and co-heir of Ralph Leche, esq. of D..rbyshire. He *d.* in 1593. His widow m. secondly, George Pollard, esq.
- Henry.
- Richard.
- Elizabeth, m. to William Naunton, esq.
- Mary, m. first to Arthur Rushe; secondly to Anthony Rooke; and thirdly to Thomas Darcy.
- Margaret, m. to Francis Stone, esq. of Wavenham in Suffolk.

Sir Anthony *d.* 6 Edward VI. and was *s.* by his eldest son,

Sir Robert Wingfield, knt. of Letheringham, M.P. for Suffolk, who had by his first wife, Cecily, second daughter of Thomas, Lord Wentworth, three sons and two daughters, viz.

- Anthony (Sir), who inherited Letheringham but died without issue, when it devolved upon his youngest and only surviving brother.
- Robert, *d. s. p. m.*
- Thomas, who inherited Letheringham, at the decease of his brother.
- Mary, m. to Sir Henry Warner, knt. of Mildenhall.
- Frances, m. to William Barrowe, esq.

The youngest son,

Sir Thomas Wingfield, knt. eventually "of Letheringham," m. first, Radclyffe, daughter of Sir Gilbert Gerrard, knt. master of the rolls, and by that lady, had one daughter. He espoused, secondly, Elizabeth, daughter of Sir Drue Drury, knt. of Riddlesworth, and dying in 1609, left, with two daughters, Anne, m. to Thomas Standish, esq. of Duxbury and Cicely, m. to William Blois, esq. of Grundisburgh, a son,

I. Anthony Wingfield, esq. of Goodwins, in Suffolk, who was created a Baronet, 17th May, 1627 le m. Anne, daughter of Sir John Deane, knt. and lying in 1658, was s. by his son,

II. SIR RICHARD WINGFIELD, of Letheringham and Easton, who m. first, Susanna, daughter of Sir John Jacob, bart. and had a son, ROBERT. He wedded, secondly, a daughter of Sir John Wintour, knt. of Sidney, in the county of Gloucester, and had another son, HENRY. The elder son,

III. SIR ROBERT WINGFIELD, living, a minor, in 1742, died unmarried and was succeeded by his half-brother,

IV. SIR HENRY WINGFIELD, who wedded the Lady Eleanor Touchet, daughter of Mervyn, Earl of Castlehaven, and was s. by his elder son,

V. SIR HENRY WINGFIELD. This gentleman sold Letheringham, and followed the fortunes of *King James II*. Dying s. p. in 1712, he was s. by his brother,

VI. SIR MERVYN WINGFIELD, living in 1727, who espoused Mary, daughter of Theobald Dalton, esq. of Grenan, in the county of Westmeath, and left an only daughter,

MARY WINGFIELD, who m. Francis Dillon, esq. of Proudstown, in the county of Meath, who was created a BARON of the Holy Roman Empire, in 1767, and by him had three sons to survive,

JOHN TALBOT DILLON, BARON DILLON.
Francis Dillon, lieutenant-general in the German service, created a BARON of the Empire, had issue.
William-Mervyn Dillon, m. Sophia, daughter of Chevalier Austin Parke Goddard, of Brampton, in Kent, and had JOHN-JOSEPH, and Henrietta-Sophia.

Arms—Arg. on a bend gu. cottised sa. three pair of wings, conjoined of the field.

WINTOUR, OF HODINGTON.

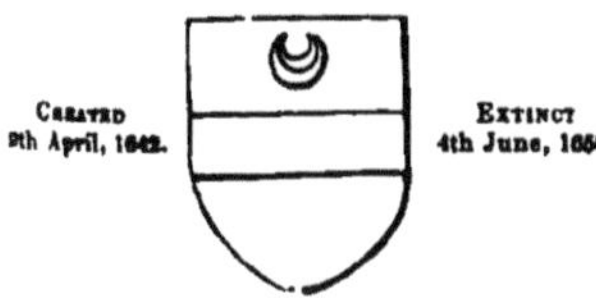

CREATED 29th April, 1642. EXTINCT 4th June, 1658.

Lineage.

The Wintors settled at Wych, in Worcestershire, temp. EDWARD II. and there continued until Roger Wintour, in the reign of HENRY VI. married the coheiress of Hodington and Cassey. From that alliance sprang, "after divers marriages with many antient and honourable families,"

I. SIR GEORGE WINTOUR, of Hodington, in Worcestershire, who was created a BARONET in 1642. He m. first, the Lady Frances Talbot, daughter of John, Earl of Shrewsbury; secondly, Mary, daughter of Charles, Lord Carrington; and thirdly, Mary, daughter and coheir of Sir George Kempe, bart. of Pentlow Hall, Essex, but died without issue, 4th June, 1658, when the title became EXTINCT. Sir George bequeathed his estate to Francis, Earl of Shrewsbury, and his brother Gilbert Talbot.

Arms—Sa. a fess, and crescent in chief erm.

WINTRINGHAM, OF DOVER STREET, ST. GEORGE'S, HANOVER SQUARE.

CREATED 7th Nov. 1774. EXTINCT 10th Jan. 1794.

Lineage.

I. CLIFTON WINTRINGHAM, M.D. fellow of the Royal College of Physicians, in London and Paris, F. R. S. and physician in ordinary to the king, was son of Clifton Wintringham, M.D. of York, who died 12th March, 1748; and obtained a BARONETCY in 1774, the dignity being limited to Gervase, son of Sir Gervase Clifton, bart. Sir Clifton Wintringham died without issue in 1794, (having survived Mr. Gervase Clifton,) and the BARONETCY then became EXTINCT. Sir Clifton published "An edition of Dr. Mead's Præcepta Medica," a work entitled, "De Morbis quibusdam Commentarii," &c.

Arms—Arg. six lions ramp. az. 3. 2. and 1.

WISEMAN, OF RIVENHALL.

CREATED 15th June, 1660. EXTINCT in 1692.

Lineage.

The family of WISEMAN appears to have existed in the county of Essex since the time of EDWARD IV. and to have been in possession of Much Canfield Park, in that county, which was obtained by purchase, in the reign of EDWARD VI. by John Wiseman, esq. who had been one of the auditors to HENRY VIII. and knighted at the battle of Spurs. The title of baronet was conferred on two of its branches, and many honourable posts under the crown were enjoyed by its descendants.

I. WILLIAM WISEMAN, esq. of Rivenhall, in Essex, son and heir of Sir Thomas Wiseman, knt. of Rivenhall, by Elizabeth, his wife, daughter of Sir Isaac Sidley, bart. (lineally descended from John Wiseman, elder brother of Thomas Wiseman, of Gaybarlands, in Chelmsford, ancestor of the present SIR WILLIAM SALTONSTALL WISEMAN, bart. of Canfield Hall,) was created a BARONET in 1660. He married Elizabeth, daughter of Sir Lewis Mansel, bart. of Margam, and had an only daughter and heir,

ELIZABETH, m. first to John Le Mott Honywood, esq. of Marks Hall, Essex, and secondly to Sir Isaac Rebow, knt. of Colchester.

Sir William died in 1692, when the title became EXTINCT. The estate of Rivenhall was sold to Thomas Western, esq.

Arms—Sa. a chev. erm. between three cronels arg.

I. Thomas Winford, esq. second prothonotary of the Court of Common Pleas, was created a Baronet 3rd July, 1702, with limitation to the heirs male of the body of his elder brother. Sir Thomas m. Sarah, daughter and heir of Michael Pearce, of Drury Lane, apothecary, but by her, who died 17th September, 1735, and was buried at Hillingdon, Middlesex, had no issue. He was succeeded at his decease, under the reversion in the patent, by his nephew,

II. Sir Thomas Winford, of Glashampton and Norgrove, who m. first, Beata, daughter of Sir Henry Parker, bart. of Honington, in Warwickshire, and secondly, Elizabeth, eldest daughter of Mr. Wilmot, of Bromesgrove, in the county of Worcester, but died *s. p.* 19th January, 1743-4, when the Baronetcy became extinct.

Arms—Argent a chev. between three quarterfoils pierced sa.

WINGFIELD, OF GOODWINS.

Created 17th May, 1627.

Extinct, date unknown.

Lineage.

Sir Robert Wingfield, of Letheringham, in Suffolk, M.P. for that county in the 6th Henry VI. was then chief of the great house of Wingfield. He m. Elizabeth, daughter and co-heir of Sir Robert Gousell, by the Lady Elizabeth Fitzalan, his wife, sister and co-heir of Thomas, eleventh Earl of Arundel, and had issue,

I. John, his heir.
II. Robert, M.P. for Herts in 1450, and comptroller of the king's household.
III. Richard, died *s. p.* before 1509.
IV. Thomas (Sir), died *s. p.*
V. William, died *s. p.*
VI. Henry (Sir), knt. of Orford, in Suffolk, ancestor of the Wingfields of Tickencote, in Rutlandshire, now (1838) represented by John Wingfield, esq. (See Burke's *Commoners*, vol. ii. p. 476.)

I. Elizabeth, married to Sir William Brandon, knt. and their grandson was Charles Brandon, Duke of Suffolk, the brother-in-law of Henry VIII.
II. Catharine, m. to John Bonvyle.

The eldest son,

Sir John Wingfield, of Letheringham, served as sheriff of Norfolk and Suffolk, in the 23rd Henry VI. and again in the 12th of the following reign. In 1461, he was made a knight of the bath, at the Tower of London, and 1477, was joined in commission with the Bishop of Bath and Wells, and others, to treat with the ambassadors of France, at Amiens. Sir John married Elizabeth, daughter of Sir John Fitz Lewis, knt. of West Horndon, in Essex, and had no less than twelve sons and three daughters: from the fourth son descended the Wingfields of Dunham; from the ninth son, the Viscounts Powerscourt; from the eleventh son, the Wingfields of Kimbolton; and from the twelfth son, the Wingfields of Brantham, Norton, &c. Sir John Wingfield died in 1481, and was *s.* by his eldest son,

Sir John Wingfield, of Letheringham, sheriff of Norfolk and Suffolk in 1483, and again in [illegible]. He married Anne, daughter of John Touchet, Lord Audley, and left a son and successor,

Sir Anthony Wingfield, of Letheringham, esquire of the body to the king, who was knighted by his royal master, Henry VIII. for his conduct at Terouenne and Tournay, made subsequently [illegible] of the household, and installed at Windsor a knight of the garter, 8th May, 1541. He was likewise constituted vice-chamberlain of the household, and [illegible] of the guards. In the will of King Henry, he was a legatee to the amount of £200, was nominated one of the executors, and assigned of the council to Edward VI. Sir Anthony wedded Elizabeth, eldest daughter of Sir George de Vere, knt. and sister and co-heir of John, thirteenth Earl of Oxford, by whom he left at his decease,

Robert (Sir), his heir.
Charles, of Tempsill, in the county of [illegible], m. Elizabeth, daughter of Thomas Rich, esq. of [illegible] Weald, in Essex, and had three sons, Henry, Anthony, and William.
Anthony, of St. John's, Middlesex, gentleman usher to Queen Elizabeth, m. first, Mary, widow of John Gosnold, and daughter of Thomas Blenerhasset, by whom he had two daughters, Ursula, wife of Edward [illegible] of Ely; and Margaret, of Francis Gr[illegible]ton. He wedded, secondly, Elizabeth, dau. and co-heir of Ralph Leche, esq. of D[illegible]. He *d.* in 1593. His widow m. secondly, [illegible] Pollard, esq.
Henry.
Richard.

Elizabeth, m. to William Naunton, esq.
Mary, m. first to Arthur Rushe; secondly to Anthony Rooke; and thirdly to Thomas D[illegible].
Margaret, m. to Francis Stone, esq. of [illegible], in Suffolk.

Sir Anthony *d.* 6 Edward VI. and was *s.* by his eldest son,

Sir Robert Wingfield, knt. of Letheringham, M.P. for Suffolk, who had by his first wife, [illegible], second daughter of Thomas, Lord Wentworth, three sons and two daughters, viz.

Anthony (Sir), who inherited Letheringham, but died without issue, when it devolved upon his youngest and only surviving brother.
Robert, *d. s. p. m.*
Thomas, who inherited Letheringham, at the decease of his brother.

Mary, m. to Sir Henry Warner, knt. of Mildenhall.
Frances, m. to William Barrowe, esq.

The youngest son,

Sir Thomas Wingfield, knt. eventually "of Letheringham," m. first, Radclyffe, daughter of Sir Gilbert Gerrard, knt. master of the rolls, and by that lady, had one daughter. He espoused, secondly, Elizabeth, daughter of Sir Drue Drury, knt. of Ri[illegible]worth, and dying in 1609, left, with two daughters, Anne, m. to Thomas Standish, esq. of Duxbury, and Cicely, m. to William Blois, esq. of Grundisburgh, a son,

I. Anthony Wingfield, esq. of Goodwins, in Suffolk, who was created a Baronet, 17th May, 1627

m. Anne, daughter of Sir John Deane, knt. and ng in 1636, was s. by his son,

: Sir Richard Wingfield, of Letheringham and ston, who m. first, Susanna, daughter of Sir John ob, bart. and had a son, Robert. He wedded, ondly, a daughter of Sir John Wintour, knt. of ney, in the county of Gloucester, and had another . Henry. The elder son,

II. Sir Robert Wingfield, living, a minor, in 2, died unmarried and was succeeded by his half-ther,

v. Sir Henry Wingfield, who wedded the Lady anor Touchet, daughter of Mervyn, Earl of Castle-en, and was s. by his elder son,

. Sir Henry Wingfield. This gentleman sold theringham, and followed the fortunes of *King* es II. Dying s. p. in 1712, he was s. by his bro-r,

VI. Sir Mervyn Wingfield, living in 1727, who oused Mary, daughter of Theobald Dalton, esq. of nan, in the county of Westmeath, and left an ly daughter,

Mary Wingfield, who m. Francis Dillon, esq. of Poudstown, in the county of Meath, who was created a Baron of the Holy Roman Empire, in 1767, and by him had three sons to survive,

John Talbot Dillon, Baron Dillon.
Francis Dillon, lieutenant-general in the German service, created a Baron of the Empire, had issue.
William-Mervyn Dillon, m. Sophia, daughter of Chevalier Austin Parke Goddard, of Brampton, in Kent, and had John-Joseph, and Henrietta-Sophia.

Arms—Arg. on a bend gu. cottised sa. three pair of ngs, conjoined of the field.

WINTOUR, OF HODINGTON.

Created th April, 1642.

Extinct 4th June, 1658.

Lineage.

The Wintours settled at Wych, in Worcestershire, *temp.* Edward II. and there continued until Roger intour, in the reign of Henry VI. married the co-ress of Hodington and Cassey. From that alliance rang, "after divers marriages with many antient nd honourable families."

I. Sir George Wintour, of Hodington, in Worcestershire, who was created a Baronet in 1642. He m. rst, the Lady Frances Talbot, daughter of John, Earl f Shrewsbury; secondly, Mary, daughter of Charles, ord Carrington; and thirdly, Mary, daughter and co-eir of Sir George Kempe, bart. of Pentlow Hall, Es-x, but died without issue, 4th June, 1658, when the tle became extinct. Sir George bequeathed his state to Francis, Earl of Shrewsbury, and his brother ilbert Talbot.

Arms—Sa. a fess, and crescent in chief erm.

WINTRINGHAM, OF DOVER STREET, ST. GEORGE'S, HANOVER SQUARE.

Created 7th Nov. 1774.

Extinct 10th Jan. 1794.

Lineage.

I. Clifton Wintringham, M.D. fellow of the Royal College of Physicians, in London and Paris, F.R.S. and physician in ordinary to the king, was son of Clifton Wintringham, M.D. of York, who died 12th March, 1748; and obtained a Baronetcy in 1774, the dignity being limited to Gervase, son of Sir Gervase Clifton, bart. Sir Clifton Wintringham died without issue in 1794, (having survived Mr. Gervase Clifton,) and the Baronetcy then became extinct. Sir Clifton published "An edition of Dr. Mead's Præcepta Medica," a work entitled, "De Morbis quibusdam Commentarii," &c.

Arms—Arg. six lions ramp. az. 3. 2. and 1.

WISEMAN, OF RIVENHALL

Created 15th June, 1660.

Extinct in 1692.

Lineage.

The family of Wiseman appears to have existed in the county of Essex since the time of Edward IV. and to have been in possession of Much Canfield Park, in that county, which was obtained by purchase, in the reign of Edward VI. by John Wiseman, esq. who had been one of the auditors to Henry VIII. and knighted at the battle of Spurs. The title of baronet was conferred on two of its branches, and many honourable posts under the crown were enjoyed by its descendants.

I. William Wiseman, esq. of Rivenhall, in Essex, son and heir of Sir Thomas Wiseman, knt. of Rivenhall, by Elizabeth, his wife, daughter of Sir Isaac Sidley, bart. (lineally descended from John Wiseman, elder brother of Thomas Wiseman, of Gaybarlands, in Chelmsford, ancestor of the present Sir William Saltonstall Wiseman, bart. of Canfield Hall,) was created a Baronet in 1660. He married Elizabeth, daughter of Sir Lewis Mansel, bart. of Margam, and had an only daughter and heir,

Elizabeth, m. first to John Le Mott Honywood, esq. of Marks Hall, Essex, and secondly to Sir Isaac Rebow, knt. of Colchester.

Sir William died in 1692, when the title became extinct. The estate of Rivenhall was sold to Thomas Western, esq.

Arms—Sa. a chev. erm. between three cronels arg.

W[illegible], OF THUNDERSLEY.

Created [illegible] Dec. [illegible].—Extinct [illegible]

Lineage.

[illegible] W[illegible], esq. of Thundersley, in Essex, a descendant of the ancient [illegible] family of the name, two other branches of which attained similar distinction, was created a Baronet in [illegible] but as he died without issue, the title became extinct.

Arms—As W[illegible] of [illegible].

WITTEWRONG, OF STANTONBURY.

Created 2nd May, 1662. Extinct 13th Jan. [illegible].

Lineage.

Jacques Wittewronge, born in the city of Ghent in [illegible] of an honourable stock, was forced to quit his native country in consequence of the persecutions to which, as a protestant, he was exposed, and in 1564, sought an asylum in England, with his wife and two young children. He had received a very liberal education, speaking the German, French, Spanish, Italian, and Latin tongues, and "having made shipwreck of his outward estate to preserve his inward peace," settled at London in the employment of a public notary, making malt, with the small pittance of his property which he had, as it were, snatched out of the fire, to live comfortable till his death, which happened in [illegible]. He had eight children, four sons and four daughters, Jacob, Abraham, Marcus, William, Christian, Sarah, Mary, and Susanna, who all, with the exception of Jacob and Abraham, whose daughter wedded Mr. Pagget, died without issue. The eldest son,

Jacob Wittewronge, born at Ghent, 15th January, 1558, was sent in 1574, to Magdalen College, Oxford, and studied there under the particular care of Dr. Humphreys, president of the college. He subsequently settled in London, and entering into partnership with Mr. Matthew Custon, a brewer, of that city, realized considerable wealth. He married first, Susanna, daughter and heir of Bernard Tileman, a German, by whom he had no male issue, and secondly, Anna,* youngest daughter and co-heir of Monsieur Garrard Vanacker, of Antwerp, merchant, by whom he had an only son, John. In 1619, Mr. Wittewrong retired into the country, to a house he had purchased at Westham, in Essex, and was there buried, as is thus mentioned by Mr. Strype in his additions to Stow's Surveys: "On the pavement under a fair marble stone, is buried James Wittewrongle, the son of James Wittewrongle, a Fleming, a singular friend to the ministers of the city, a Mecænas of studious youth, a favourer of piety and learning." His only son,

I. Sir John Wittewrong, knighted by Charles I. in 1640 and created a Baronet in 1662, purchased the manor of Stantonbury, in Bucks, of Sir John Temple, in [illegible] and [illegible] a handsome mansion. [illegible] of [illegible] in [illegible] [illegible] of the [illegible]. Sir John m. first, Mary, daughter of Sir Thomas Myddleton, knt. [illegible] in [illegible], by whom he had an only [illegible] [illegible]. Secondly, Elizabeth, daughter of [illegible] Meautys, esq. of [illegible]; and thirdly, Katherine Thompson, [illegible]. By his second wife, he had issue,

James, d. s. p.

Jacob, of Rothamsted, Herts, [illegible] and recorder of St. Albans, who m. first [illegible], daughter of Thomas [illegible], of Hillingdon, in Middlesex; secondly [illegible], daughter of Mr. [illegible], of St. [illegible]; and thirdly, Susan, daughter of Sir [illegible], of Bruntingthorpe, and widow of William [illegible], esq. of [illegible], Herts. He [illegible] [illegible] first wife,

Jacob, m. Elizabeth, only daughter of [illegible] [illegible], esq. of [illegible], Herts, and [illegible] a son,

Jacob, who m. Anne, daughter of [illegible] Bennet, and had issue.

William, died s. p.

Catherine, m. to Edward Lloyd, esq. of [illegible]shire.

Anne, m. to Robert Sebright, esq. of Croxton.

Bethia, m. to Samuel Gibbs, esq. of [illegible], in Suffolk.

Sir John died at Rothamsted, Herts, in [illegible], aged seventy-five, having a high character for [illegible], justice, and charity, and was s. by his son,

II. Sir John Wittewrong, of Stantonbury, [illegible] married first, Clare, daughter of Sir Joseph [illegible], bart. of Chelsea, in Middlesex, and by her, who d. 13th October, 1680, had an only daughter Mary [illegible] Mr. Crompton of London. He m. secondly, [illegible] Martha Sebrook, niece of Alderman Backwell, by whom he had four sons,

John, his heir.

Edward, killed at Namur.

Thomas, who m. in Barbadoes, and died at sea.

James, lieutenant in the fleet.

Martha, m. to Thomas Saunders, esq. of [illegible]worth, Northamptonshire.

Sir John died about 1700, and was s. by his son,

III. Sir John Wittewrong, of Stantonbury, M.P. for Aylesbury, and afterwards for Chipping Wycombe, and colonel in the army. He m. Mary, daughter of Mr. Samuel White, merchant of London, and had issue,

John, his heir.

George.

William.

Samuel.

Mary.

Martha, m. to John Guasley, esq. second son of John Guasley, esq. of Isleworth, in Middlesex, muster master general of the forces.

Lucia.

Susanna.

Sir John died 30th January, 1721-2, and was s. by his son,

IV. Sir John Wittewrong, captain in [illegible]

---

* She married, secondly, Sir Thomas Middleton, lord mayor of London.

Maurice Nassau's regiment, who died unmarried 27th March, 1743-4, and was *s.* by his brother,

V. Sir William Wittewrong, governor of the poor knights of Windsor, who died in January, 1761, leaving a successor,

VI. Sir John Wittewrong, at whose decease unm. 13th January, 1771, the Baronetcy became extinct.

Arms—Bendy of six arg. and gu. on a chief az. a fess or bar indented or.

WOLFF, OF CAMS HALL.

Created 16th Oct. 1766.—Extinct 3rd Feb. 1837.

Lineage.

I. Jacob Wolff, esq. (son of Baron Godfrey Wolff, of Moscow,) a native himself of the Russian empire, and, by creation of Francis the First, Emperor of Germany, a Baron of the Holy Roman Empire, having been naturalized in England, was created a Baronet 9th October, 1766. Sir Jacob *m.* in the December following, Ann, only daughter of the Right Hon. Edward Weston, secretary of state in Ireland, second son of the Right Rev. Dr. Stephen Weston, bishop of Exeter in 1724, by whom he had

James-William-Weston, present baronet.

Lucy, *m.* first to Major Parslow, and secondly to Major Ditcher.

Sir Jacob died in 1809, and was *s.* by his son,

II. Sir James-William-Weston Wolff, *b.* 24th November, 1778, who *m.* 4th January, 1800, Frances, daughter of Joseph Adkins, esq. of Lincolnshire, but died without issue, 3rd February, 1837, when the Baronetcy became extinct.

Arms, Crest, &c. as described in the German patent, viz. A shield, erect, divided in four quarters; in the centre of which, an escocheon, with the arms following; vert, a wolf, passant, ppr. and in chief, three fleurs-de-lis ar. the arms of Van Wolf. In the first quarter of the achievement or, an eagle, displayed, sa. ducally crowned gu. In the second quarter az. an armed arm issuing out of the clouds from the sinister, grasping a sword, in the attitude of striking, ppr. In the third quarter, ar. a naked arm issuing out of the clouds from the sinister holding a palm branch, ppr. And, lastly, in the fourth quarter, or, a triangle sa. Over the arms an imperial baron's coronet, with five pearls, placed on a circle of gold, surmounted with three full-faced helmets, ppr. thereon as many crests; viz. on the centre helmet a demi-wolf, salient, ppr. issuing out of a ducal coronet or; on the dexter helmet, a ducal coronet or, thereon a fleur-de-lis or, between two imperial eagles' wings, displayed, tawney; on the sinister helmet a ducal coronet or, thereon an eagle, displayed, sa. ducally crowned gu.

WOLLASTON, OF LOSEBY.

Created 7th Jan. 1748.

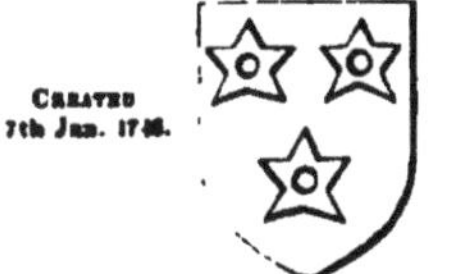

Extinct in 1756.

Lineage.

Henry Wollaston, esq. of Perton, in Staffordshire, descended from an ancient family long seated in that county, *m.* a lady, named Elliott, and had three sons, viz.

I. Richard, of London, *d. s. p.*

II. Henry, alderman of London, ancestor of the Wollastons of Shenton, in Leicestershire, now represented by Frederick William Wollaston, esq. of Shenton, formerly colonel of the 22nd Light Dragoons.

III. Edward.

The third son,

Edward Wollaston, esq. of Perton, *m.* Elizabeth, daughter of William Wollaston, esq. of Trescott Grange, and had two sons: the elder, Sir John Wollaston, knt. filled the civic chair of the city of London in 1644. The younger,

Henry Wollaston, esq. citizen of London in 1669, was father of

Richard Wollaston, esq. of Wormley, *b.* in 1635, who purchased the manor of Loseby, in Leicestershire, and died in 1691, leaving two sons, namely,

I. Josiah, his heir.

II. John, who *m.* Hannah Horton, and dying in 1692, left issue, Richard, M.P. for Whitchurch; John; Jeremiah; and Jonathan.

The elder son,

Josiah Wollaston, esq. *b.* in 1652, *m.* Elizabeth, sister of Sir Edward Lawrence, bart. of St. Ives, in the county of Huntingdon, and dying in 1689, left a son,

Isaac Wollaston, esq. *b.* in 1673, of Loseby, who *m.* his cousin, Sarah Lawrence, and dying in 1736, left a son and successor,

I. Sir Isaac Wollaston, of Loseby, who succeeded to the Baronetcy, which had been conferred, with the special remainder, on his uncle, Sir Edward Lawrence, of St. Ives. He *m.* Sarah Rowland, of the Isle of Wight, and dying 21st December, 1756, left issue,

Isaac Lawrence, his heir.

Sarah, who had the St. Ives estate and those on the Isle of Ely.* She *m.* Taylor White, esq. and was grandmother of the present Sir Thomas Woollaston White, bart.

Anne, who had the Loseby estate. She *m.* in 1772, Sir Thomas Folke, knt. and had one son and one daughter, Augustus Frederick, and Henry Anne, so named after the Duke and Duchess of Cumberland.

Sir Isaac Wollaston's only son,

II. Sir Isaac Lawrence Wollaston, of Loseby, *d.* an infant in 1756, when the title became extinct.

Arms—Arg. three mullets sa. pierced of the field.

WOLRICH, OF DUDMASTON.

Created 4th Aug. 1641

Extinct 5th June, 1723.

Lineage.

The family of Wolrich took its rise in the county of Chester, where Wulfric, its founder, was living in

* These estates were sold to the Earl of Hardwicke.

i. Mary.

ii. Anne, *m.* 6th January, 1760, Peter Thellusson, esq. of Plaistow, in the county of Kent, and of Broadsworth, in the county of York, by whom she was mother of Peter-Isaac, first Lord Rendlesham.

The eldest son,

i. Sir Ralph Woodford, of Carleby, in Lincolnshire, British resident at the Hans Towns, and minister-extraordinary to the court of Denmark, was created a Baronet 21st June, 1791. He *m.* Gertrude Reesen, a co-heiress, and had issue,

Ralph-James, second baronet.

Elizabeth, *m.* 14th June, 1801, to John Hammet, esq. eldest son of Sir Benjamin Hammet, knt. M.P. for Taunton, by Louisa, his wife, daughter of Sir James Esdaile.

Sir Ralph *d.* 26th August, 1810, and was *s.* by his only son,

ii. Sir Ralph-James Woodford, *b.* in 1784, governor of the Island of Trinidad, at whose decease unm. 17th May, 1828, the Baronetcy became extinct.

Arms—Sable, three leopards' heads, reversed, gules, swallowing as many fleurs-de-lis, argent.

WORSLEY, OF APPULDERCOMBE.

Created 29th June, 1611.

Extinct 10th Jan. 1825.

Lineage.

The family of Worsley (or De Workesley, as it was anciently written), derives from Sir Elias de Workesley, lord of the manor of Workesley, near Manchester, at the period of the Conquest. He is mentioned in an old chronicle as attending Robert, Duke of Normandy, in his expedition for the recovery of the Holy Land, and tradition affirms that he was buried at Rhodes. From this remote era, the Worsleys continued to hold large possessions in Lancashire, until the year 1377, when Elizabeth, daughter of Geoffrey Workesley, being found by an inquisition to have been born out of marriage, the lordship came to Sir John Massey, who had married the sister of Sir Geoffrey, but the estate was again taken possession of by Robert Worsley; and Thomas Brereton, esq. of Cheshire, who married the daughter and heiress of Sir John Massey, recovered it from Robert Worsley by a suit in Chancery. Worsley became, afterwards, by purchase, the property of Lord Chancellor Egerton, and from him it descended to the great Duke of Bridgewater, who made the canal from the mill in the township of Worsley, over the river Irwell, at Barton Bridge, to convey coals from his mines to Manchester. The Worsleys of Hovingham Hall, in Yorkshire,* who diverged from the parent stock, about the year 1307, still possess quit and chief rents over the townships of Worsley, Bedford, Astley, &c. in Lancashire. (See Burke's *Commoners*, vol. iv. Another branch of the family continued lords of Worsley Hall, in that county, until the 3rd Henry VIII (1512) when

Sir James Worsley, knt. of Worsley Hall, son of Hugh Worsley, esq. of Worsley, by Anne, his wife, daughter of Ralph Standish, of Standish, married the heiress of Appuldercombe, in the Isle of Wight, viz. Anne, daughter and co-heir of Sir John Leigh, or Ly of Leigh, in Dorset, by Agnes, his wife, daughter and co-heir of John Hacket, esq. of Knighton. Sir James, who was captain of the Isle of Wight, died in 153-, leaving two sons,

i. Richard, governor of the Isle of Wight, who *m.* Ursula, second daughter of Henry St. Barbe, esq. of Ashington, in Somersetshire and had two sons, John and George, who were both blown up with gunpowder at Appuldercombe, 6th September, 1557. Richard Worsley died 12th April, 1565. His widow wedded, secondly, Sir Francis Walsingham the famous secretary of state.

ii. John, of whose line we have to treat.

The second son,

John Worsley, esq. of Appuldercombe, in the Isle of Wight, *m.* Jane, daughter of Richard Meux, esq. of Kingston, son of Sir William Meux, knt. and dying in 1580, left a son and successor,

Thomas Worsley, esq. of Appuldercombe, born in 1563, educated and brought up under the celebrated Sir Francis Walsingham. He *m.* in 1585, Barbara daughter of William St. John, esq. of Farley, Hants and had issue,

i. Richard, his heir.

ii. Thomas, *b.* in 1587.

iii. John, *b.* in 1589, was of Gatcombe, in the Isle of Wight. He *m.* Cicely, daughter of Sir Edward Richards, knt. of Yaverland, and had a son,

Sir Edward Worsley, knt. of Gatcombe a firm and devoted royalist, who attempted at the greatest personal hazard, the deliverance of Charles from his imprisonment in the Isle of Wight. He *m.* Jane Barker, and had a son and successor,

John Worsley, esq. of Gatcombe, *b.* in 165-, who wedded Anne Urry, of Freshwater, in the Isle of Wight, and had two sons, namely,

Edward, his heir.

David, of Stenbery, whose son, The Rev. Francis Worsley, rector of Chale, *m.* Anne, daughter of Henry Roberts, esq. of Standen, and died in 1808, leaving with several daughters, seven sons, James, in holy orders, vicar of Thorley; Henry, a major general in the army; David, *d.* unm.; Francis, who also *d.* unm.; Robert, of Edinburgh; Charles-Cornwall Seymour, of Newport; and Thomas, of Liverpool.

John Worsley *d.* in 1727, and was *s.* by his son,

Edward Worsley, esq. of Gatcombe, who *m.* in 1708, Miss Jane Leigh, of Idlecombe and was *s.* by his son,

* Now represented by William Worsley, esq. of Hovingham Hall, a magistrate and deputy lieutenant for the North Riding of Yorkshire.

the times in which he lived, suffered so severely in property, he lost considerably more than a hundred thousand pounds, and his son Henry, and his brother-in law, Sir Thomas Dallison, both fell fighting under the royal banner. To compensate in some degree for this devotion to his family, CHARLES II. at the Restoration, re-appointed Sir John farmer of the Customs, and restored to him a patent of collector outward in the port of London, from which he had been sequestered during the usurpation. He likewise made him a BARONET. Sir John married Anne, sister of Sir Thomas Dallison, of Laughton, in Lincolnshire, and had issue,

- I. JOHN, who m. Dorothy, daughter and co-heir of Horatio, Lord Vere, of Tilbury, but predeceased his father without issue. He lies buried at Stanmore, under a stately monument of white marble.
- II. Henry, slain at Marston Moor, ex parte regis, he was unm.
- III. THOMAS, successor to his father.
- IV. Edward, d. unm.
- V. Christopher, d. unm.
- VI. Charles, d. unm.
- VII. Robert, d. unm.

- I. Anne, m. to Sandford Neville, esq. of Chevet, in Yorkshire.
- II. Elizabeth, m. to Richard Hutton, esq. of Goldsborough, Yorkshire.

Sir John d. in 1670, was buried at Stanmore, near his father, and s. by his eldest surviving son,

II. SIR THOMAS WOLSTENHOLME, who m. Elizabeth, daughter of Phineas Andrews, esq. of Denton Court, Kent, and had five sons and six daughters viz.

- I. JOHN, his heir.
- II. THOMAS, who s. as sixth baronet.
- III. Edward, died young.
- IV. Henry, who m. Mary, daughter of Stephen Jermin, esq. of Tottenham, Middlesex, but left no male issue.
- V. William, lieut. of the Tyger prize man-of-war, and capt. of the first regiment of guards under Col. How. He d. unm.

- I. Anne, m. to Sir Philip Matthews, bart. of Great Gobions.
- II. Elizabeth, died young.
- III. Mary, d. young.
- IV. Catherine, m. to Sir Henry Bathurst, knt. son of Alderman Bathurst, of Edmonton.
- V. Mildred, d. young.
- VI. Hester, m. to Thomas Hall, esq. of Islington, son of Thomas Hall, esq. first secondary in the king's remembrancer office, and had a son, Thomas, and a daughter, Mary, wife of Capt. Plukenet, of the first regiment of guards.

Sir Thomas d. in 1691, was buried in St. Margaret's, Westminster, and s. by his eldest son,

III. SIR JOHN WOLSTENHOLME, M.P. for Middlesex, temp. WILLIAM III. and Queen ANNE. He m. first, Mary, daughter and sole-heir of Nicholas Rainton, esq. of Forty Hall, in Enfield, Middlesex, and secondly Temperance, daughter of Lord Crew, and relict of Sir Rowland Alston, bart. of Odell, but had issue only by the former, viz.

- I. NICHOLAS, his heir.
- II. John, d. in the East Indies, unm.
- III. Harvey, capt. 1st regiment of guards, d. unm. in 1712.
- IV. WILLIAM, who succeeded as fifth BARONET.

- I. Mary, d. unm.
- II. Elizabeth, d. unm.
- III. Rebecca, m. to Michael Harvey, esq. of Combe, in Surrey, M.P. for Milbourne Port.
- IV. Catherine, d. unm.

Sir John d. in 1708, was buried at Enfield, and s. by his son,

IV. SIR NICHOLAS WOLSTENHOLME, who m. Grace, daughter of Sir Edward Waldo, knt. of Pinner, in Middlesex, but by her, who m. the Right Hon. William Ferdinando Carey, Lord Hunsdon, and died 9th May, 1729, aged forty-six, had no issue. He died 19th February, 1716, and was s. by his brother,

V. SIR WILLIAM WOLSTENHOLME, who m. Elizabeth, daughter of Mr. Benjamin Wheeler, and had

- ELIZABETH.
- MARY, m. to Eliab Breton, esq. of Notton, in Northamptonshire, nephew of Michael Harvey, esq. of Combe, in Surrey.

Sir William died 31st January, 1723, was buried at Enfield, and s. by his uncle,

VI. SIR THOMAS WOLSTENHOLME, who m. Miss Mary Hatton, and had with three daughters, the eldest m. to Captain White, four sons,

- Henry, who d. at Barcelona, in the Colchester man-of-war, unm.
- Thomas, d. unm.
- FRANCIS, successor to his father.
- Edmund, d. young.

Sir Thomas d. in September, 1738, and was s. by his only surviving son,

VII. SIR FRANCIS WOLSTENHOLME, at whose decease the title is stated to have become EXTINCT.

Arms—Az. a lion passant guardant between three pheons or.

WOODFORD, OF CARLEBY.

CREATED 28th July, 1791. EXTINCT 1..th May, 1828.

Lineage.

MATTHEW WOODFORD, of New Sarum, had with a daughter, Mary, wife of Robert Pellican, a son, MATTHEW WOODFORD, a minor in 1684, afterwards subdean and prebendary of Chichester. He m. Anne, daughter of John Sherer, esq. of Chichester, by whom he had a son,

MATTHEW WOODFORD, esq. of Southampton, who m. Mary, daughter and co-heiress of John Brideoak, by whom he had three sons and two daughters, viz.

- I. RALPH (Sir), first baronet.
- II. Matthew, D.D. prebendary of Winchester.
- III. John, a colonel in the army, m. first, Mary Emperor, of the county of Norfolk, by whom he had three sons; two d. young, and Emperor, a captain in the guards; and secondly, Susan, daughter of Cosmo, Duke of Gordon, relict of John Fane, ninth Earl of Westmoreland, by whom he had two sons, Alexander and John-George.

Sir Thomas *d.* 23rd September, 1768, and was *s.* by his son,

VII. SIR RICHARD WORSLEY, of Appuldercombe, *b.* 17th March, 1751, M.P. for Newport, and clerk of his majesty's privy council. He *m.* in 1775, Seymour Dorothy, daughter and co-heir of Sir John Fleming, bart. of Brompton Park, Middlesex, and had a son and daughter who both died unmarried. Sir Richard died himself 5th August, 1805, leaving his niece his heiress, and was succeeded in the baronetcy by his kinsman,

VIII. THE REV. SIR HENRY-WORSLEY HOLMES, LL.D. *b.* in December, 1775, who *m.* Elizabeth Troughear, eldest daughter of Leonard, Lord Holmes, and widow of Edward Meux Worsley, esq. of Gatcombe, and had by her, who died in January, 1832, two sons and a daughter, viz.

LEONARD-THOMAS, his heir.

Richard Fleming, M.P. for Newport, *b.* in 1791, *d. s. p.* 26th July, 1814.

Margaret.

Sir Henry died 7th April, 1811, and was *s.* by his son,

IX. SIR LEONARD-THOMAS-WORSLEY HOLMES, *b.* 16th July, 1787, M.P. for Newport, who *m.* 5th June, 1813, Anne Redstone, daughter of John Delgarno, esq. of Newport, and niece of Leonard, Lord Holmes, and had issue,

ELIZABETH, *m.* 3rd October, 1833, to the Hon. William Henry Ashe A'Court, M.P. for the Isle of Wight, son of Lord Heytesbury, and that gentleman has assumed in consequence the additional surname of HOLMES.

ANNE-EMILY.

Sir Leonard *d.* 10th January, 1825, when the title became EXTINCT.

Arms--Arg. a chev. between three falcons close sa. The arms for Worsley anciently were arg. a chief gu.

WORTLEY, OF WORTLEY.

CREATED 29th June, 1611.

EXTINCT 11th Mar. 1665.

Lineage.

SIR THOMAS WORTLEY, of Wortley, in Yorkshire, son of Nicholas Wortley, by Isabel, his wife, daughter and heir of William Tunstall, of Thurland, and representative of the ancient family of Wortley, was a distinguished personage in the times in which he lived, and knight of the body to four successive sovereigns EDWARD IV., RICHARD III., HENRY VII., and HENRY VIII. "And also (we quote the old illuminated pedigree of Wortley) Sir Thomas did serve them with great credite in their wares, having great government in this commonwealthe, being as it may appeare in great trust with the said kinges; for as yet ther remaineth a great number of letters in the house of Wortley, which were sent by the aforesaid kinges to the said Sir Thomas, sealled with their private signates; the which letters were for the execusion of theire lawes, musters, collections, and commissions, with other and divers services of great truste and credit, as the only man in these parts. And also had of the said princes gyft the stewardship of Midleton Castell, withall thinges thereunto belonginge, with the puttinge in of all the officers into the said Castell. And also he had and was steward of Kimberworth with all the commodytes therunto belonginge...... Nowe to speake of his recreation. First he was most given to showtinge in the long bowe, and many of his men were cuninge archiers, and in them he had muche delite. Also he had muche delite in huntinge that he did builde in the middest in his forest at Wharnclife, a house or lodge, at which house he did lye at, for the most part of the grease tyme; and the worshipfull of the countrye did ther resorte unto him havinge ther with hime pastime and good cheare. Many tymes he would go into the Forest of the Peake and set up ther his tent with great provision of vitailes, having in his company many worshipfull persons with his owne familye and would remaine ther iii weeks or more huntinge and makinge other worthy pastimes unto his companye.

"The said Sir Thomas had such a kinde and breed of hounds, and their cuninge in huntinge it was such that the fame of them went into Scotland, so that the kinge of Scots did write his letters desieringe him to have some of his houndes; at the which request he did send him x copple, with his own huntsman, which did remain ther ii whole yeares. Thus I leave to speak of the worthy fame of this knight, omittinge many thinges worthy to be spoken off."

This doughty knight *m.* first, in 1463, Catherine, daughter of William Fitz William, of Sprotborough, by whom he had a son, Nicholas, who *d. s. p.* and a daughter, Isabel, wife of John Talbot. He wedded secondly, Joan, daughter and heir of William Balderston, and widow first of Thomas Langton, and secondly of Sir John Pilkington, by which lady, whom he divorced, he had no child. He *m.* thirdly, Elizabeth, daughter of Sir Richard Fitz William, of Alder Park, and widow of John Fitz William, esq. of Sprotborough, by whom he left at his decease in 1514, (being buried at Hemsworth,) a son and successor,

THOMAS WORTLEY, esq. of Wortley, whose short life was harassed by expensive lawsuits with the Talbots. He *m.* Margaret, daughter of Sir John Savile, of Tankersley and Thornhill, by whom, who wedded secondly, Richard Corbet, esq. he left at his decease, 11th April, 1543, a son and heir,

FRANCIS WORTLEY, esq. of Wortley, who according to the illuminated pedigree before referred to, "was brought up in learning at the Inne of Court, and was well versed in the laws, being on the queen's majesty's council of the North parts: he was also justice of the peace and justice of Coram, and custos rotulorum, and had great government in this West Riding, and was of singular great wisdom and manhood." A similar character is given of him by the Earl of Shrewsbury, in a letter to Walsingham, 1582, which mentions him as "a gentylman bothe wise and of very good credytt in the country;" and in another communication of the same nobleman, addressed to Burleigh, he is stated to be "of greate lyving and accounte." Mary Stuart was at that time a captive in Sheffield Castle, and the Earl of Shrewsbury her keeper, who then meditated a journey to London, proposed to commit the custody of the queen to Mr. Wortley. He *m.* first, in 1556, Mary, daughter and co-heir of Robert Swyft, esq. of Rotherham and Broomhall, and secondly, Frances, daughter of Thomas Burdet, esq. of Burthwaite, which lady survived and wedded, secondly, Francis Foljambe, of Aldwark. By his first wife, who died in 1561, Mr. Wortley had issue,

RICHARD, his heir.

John, of Langley, in Durham, *b.* 1st November,

Sir Edward Worsley, knt. of Gatcombe, who m. in 1737, Elizabeth, daughter of Sir John Miller, of Froyle, and had issue,

Edward-Meux, his heir.

James, rector of Gatcombe, who m. Miss Hales, and had issue, four daughters, and two sons, Edward Vaughan-Worsley, colonel R. A. and Thomas Worsley, colonel E. I. C. S.

Thomas, M.A. d. unm.

John, lieut. in the army, d. unm.

Henry, D.D. rector of Gatcombe, father of the Rev. Henry Worsley, LL.D. and other issue.

Jane, m. to the Rev. Arthur Hodgkinson,

Elizabeth, m. to Sir Samuel Marshall, K.B.

Anne, m. to Admiral R. R. Bligh.

Sir Edward died in August, 1762, and was s. by his son,

Edward-Meux Worsley, esq. of Gatcombe, b. in 1747, M.P. for Newtown. He m. first, Miss Elizabeth Crow, and by her, who died in 1771, had one daughter,

Elizabeth, m. in 1790, to Edmund John Glynn, esq. of Glynn, in Cornwall.

He m. secondly, in 1772, Elizabeth, eldest daughter of Leonard, Lord Holmes, by whom (who wedded, secondly, the Rev. Sir Henry Worsley Holmes, bart.) he left another daughter,

Jane, m. to Col. Alexander Campbell, younger son of Patrick Campbell, esq. of Ardchattan Priory, and had issue.

Thomas Worsley died in 1604, and was s. by his eldest son,

I. Richard Worsley, esq. of Appuldercombe, who was created a Baronet 29th June, 1611. He m. Frances, daughter of Sir Henry Neville, knt. of Billingbere, in Berkshire, and had issue,

Henry, his heir.

Richard, died unm.

Thomas, who m. Sarah Roe, of Shropshire, and was father of

George Worsley, esq. who m. Miss Lisle, of the Isle of Wight, and had a son,

The Rev. John Worsley, who m. Margaret, daughter of — Hancock, esq. of Wilts, and was s. by his son,

Robert Worsley, esq. of Pidford, who m. Jane, daughter of Henry Holmes, esq. of Newport, and sister of Thomas, Lord Holmes, of Kilmallock. By her he had a son,

The Rev. Henry Worsley, who assumed in 1804, pursuant to the will of his maternal uncle, Thomas Lord Holmes, the additional surname and arms of Holmes, and in the following year inherited as eighth baronet the old family title.

John, b. in 1617, died unm.

Anne, m. to Sir John Leigh, knt. of Bury, in Suffolk, and d. s. p.

Elizabeth, m. to Sir John Meux, bart. of Kingston.

Dorothy, died unm.

Sir Richard d. 27th June, 1621, and was s. by his son,

II. Sir Henry Worsley, of Appuldercombe, b. in 1612, high sheriff of Hants in 1656, who m. in 1634, Bridget, daughter of Sir Henry Wallop, knt. of Fairley Wallop, afterwards Lord Lymington, and had issue,

Henry, died young.

Robert (Sir), knighted at Whitehall, 29th December, 1664, successor to his father.

James (Sir), knt. of Pilewell, Hants, born 1645, who married, in 1668, Mary, daughter of Sir Nicholas Stuart, bart. of Hartley Maudiut, and had issue,

James, who succeeded as fifth Baronet.

Charles, a bencher of the Middle Temple, d. unm. in 1739.

Stuart, died s. p.

Sandys, m. to Peter Bettesworth, esq. of Brockenhurst, Hants.

Sir James died 17th March, 1695.

Bridget, m. to John Williams, esq. of Luel, Dorsetshire.

Jane, m. to Sir George Brown, knt. of Woolverton, Somersetshire.

Sir Henry died 11th September, 1666, and was s. by his son,

III. Sir Robert Worsley, of Appuldercombe, born in 1643, who m. in 1667, Mary, daughter of James Herbert, of Kingsey, Bucks, second son of Philip, Earl of Pembroke, and had issue,

Robert, his heir.

Henry, M.P. for Newton, in the Isle of Wight, envoy to the court of Portugal, in 1714, and governor of Barbadoes in 1721. He d. unm. 15th March, 1747.

Jane, m. to Sir Nathaniel Napier, bart. of Critchill.

Sir Robert died in 1676, and was s. by his son,

IV. Sir Robert Worsley, of Appuldercombe, b. in 1660, who m. in 1690, Frances, only daughter of Thomas, first Viscount Weymouth, and had issue,

Robert, b. in 1695, died unm. in 1714.

Thynne, b. in 1711, m. Henrietta Maria, daughter of Charles Wither, esq. of Hall Place, Hants, but d. s. p. in 1741. His widow wedded, secondly, Edmund Bramston, esq.

Frances, m. to John, Lord Carteret, afterwards Earl of Granville, and had issue,

Robert, Earl of Granville.

Grace, m. to Lionel, Earl of Dysart.

Louisa, m. to Thomas, second Viscount Weymouth.

Frances, m. to John, fourth Marquis of Tweeddale.

Georgiana-Caroline, m. first to Henry John Spencer, esq. and secondly to William, Earl Cowper.

Sir Robert died in August, 1747, and having outlived his sons, was s. by his cousin,

V. Sir James Worsley, of Pilewell, member in nine parliaments for the borough of Newton. He m. 15th February, 1714, Rachael, daughter of Thomas Merrick, esq. and dying in 1756, was s. by his son,

VI. Sir Thomas Worsley, of Appuldercombe, b. 22nd April, 1728, who m. in 1749, Elizabeth, daughter of John, Earl of Cork and Orrery, and by her ladyship, who died 10th January, 1800, had issue,

Richard, his heir.

Henrietta-Frances, b. 10th July, 1756, m. in 1784, the Hon. John Bridgman Simpson, second son of Henry, first Lord Bradford, and had an only daughter,

Henrietta-Anna-Maria-Charlotte, heiress to her maternal uncle, Sir Richard Worsley. She m. 11th August, 1806, the Hon. Charles Anderson Pelham, present Earl of Yarborough, and died 30th July, 1813, leaving issue.

Leonard, of Adwick, in Yorkshire, died 23rd August, 1509, leaving issue.

The eldest son,

Sir Christopher Wray, of Glentworth, born at Bedale, in Yorkshire, was educated at Magdalen College, Cambridge, and having studied at Lincoln's Inn, was called to the bar, at which he attained such eminence, that he became eventually (16 Elizabeth) lord chief justice of the Queen's Bench, and presided over that court with the highest reputation for seventeen years. An old writer describes him as an upright judge, who respected every man in his proper station, when he was off the bench, but when he was upon it, he had no such regard for the greatest of men, so as to bias his judgment; and Lloyd thus speaks of Sir Christopher, "Five particulars, I have heard old men say, he was choice in: 1. his friend, who was always wise and equal: 2. his wife: 3. his book: 4. his secrets: 5. his expression and garb. By four things, he would say, an estate was kept; 1. by understanding it: 2. by spending not until it comes: 3. by keeping old servants: 4. by a quarterly audit. He was mindful of what is past, observant of things present, and provident for things to come. No better instance whereof need be alledged, than his pathetic discourses in the behalf of those two great stays of this kingdom, husbandry and merchandise; for he had a clear discerning judgment, and that not only in points of law, which yet his arguments and decisions in that profession manifest without dispute; but in matters of policy and government; as also in the little mysteries of private manage, to which, when you add his happy faculty of communicating himself, by a free and graceful elocution, to charm and command his audience, assisted by the attractive dignity of his presence, you will not admire that he managed his justiceship with so much satisfaction to the court, and that he left it with so much applause from the country: for these two peculiarities he had, that none was more tender to the poor, or more civil in private; and yet none more stern to the rich, I mean, justices of the peace, officers, &c. or more severe in public. He delighted indeed to be loved, not reverenced; yet knew he well how to assert the dignity of his place and function, from the approaches of contempt." Sir Christopher had served for Boroughbridge in all the parliaments called by Queen Mary, and was chosen speaker of the House of Commons in the next reign. He m. Anne, daughter of Nicholas Girlington, esq. of Normanby, in Yorkshire, and had issue,

William, his heir.

Isabel, m. first to Godfrey Foljambe, esq.; secondly to Sir William Bowes, knt.; and thirdly to John, Lord Darcy.

Frances, m. first to Sir George St. Paul, bart. of Snarford, and secondly to Robert Rich, Earl of Warwick.

Sir Christopher died 8th May, 1592, and lies buried in the chancel of the church of Glentworth, under a splendid monument, whereon is the effigies, in full proportion, of a judge in his robes, with his lady by him, and this inscription:

Capital. Justiciar.
Quisquis es (o hospes!) manes reverere Sepultos:
Qui jacet hic, nostri Gloria Juris, erat
Christopherus Wrajus, re justus, Nomine verus;
Quique pia minuit, Cognitione, Fide.
En fuit: En non est: Rapidum rotat omnia Fatum
Heu moritur nobis: ipse sibi superest;
Terram Terra petit; Cinerem Cinis; Ætheraque Æther;
Spritus ætherei possidet Astra Poli.
Obiit Die Sept. Maii
Anno D. 1592,
Et Eliz.
Reg. 34.

WRA

The only son of this great lawyer,

I. Sir William Wray, of Glentworth, M.P. for Grimsby, and afterwards for Lincolnshire, was knighted by Queen Elizabeth, and created a Baronet by James I. in 1612. He m. first, Lucy, eldest daughter of Sir Edward Montague, knt. of Boughton, and had by her, who died in 1599, a numerous family, of whom the only sons that left issue were

John, his heir.

Edward, groom of the bedchamber to Charles I. who m. Elizabeth, only daughter and heir of Francis, Earl of Berkshire, Baron Norreys of Rycote, and had an only daughter and heir,

Bridget, m. first to Edward, second son of Edward, Earl of Dorset, by whom she had no issue, and secondly, Montague Bertie, Earl of Lindsey, by whom she had a son, James, Lord Norreys, of Rycote.

Sir William wedded, secondly, Frances, relict of Sir Nicholas Clifford, and daughter of Sir William Drury, knt. of Hawsted, in Suffolk, lord deputy of Ireland, by whom he had issue,

Christopher (Sir), knt. of Ashby, in Lincolnshire, M.P. married Albina, second daughter and co-heir of Edward Cecil, Viscount Wimbledon, third son of the Earl of Exeter, and had issue,

I. William (Sir), of Ashby, created a Baronet 27th June, 1660. He m. Olympia, daughter of Sir Humphrey Tufton, bart. and died in 1670, having had four sons and six daughters, viz.

Christopher (Sir), his heir, second baronet of Ashby, of whom presently as fourth Baronet of Glentworth.

Edward, William, Drury, } who d. s. p.

Margaret, m. to the Rev. Dr. Jeffries prebendary of Canterbury.

Tufton, m. to Sir James Montague, knt. lord chief baron of the Exchequer.

Drury, m. to Sir William Sanderson, bart. of Combe, in Greenwich.

————, m. to — Lewis, esq.

II. Edward, whose son,

Baptist-Edward, succeeded as fifth baronet of Glentworth.

III. Drury, who s. as sixth baronet.

IV. Cecil, who m. the daughter of Mr. Cressy of Brigsley, in Lincolnshire, and had a son,

William, who m. Isabella, daughter and co-heir of John Ullithorne, esq. of Slenningford, in Yorkshire, and had with four daughters, three sons,

John, who succeeded as ninth baronet.

William, d. s. p.

Cecil, who m. Frances Holmes, and had a son,

William Ullithorne, who [s.] as eleventh Baronet.

Charles, who d. in Spain.

Frances, m. to Sir Anthony Irby, knt. of Boston in Lincolnshire.

Sir William died 13th August, 1617, was interred in the church of Ashby, under a sumptuous marble monument, and was s. by his eldest son,

II. Sir John Wray, of Glentworth, who was knighted in the lifetime of his father, and served as member

1564, m. Bridget Frere, widow, daughter of Edward Lynsey, esq. of Selby, in Norfolk, and had an only daughter and heir,

MARY, m. to Francis Bunney, son and heir of Francis Bunney, prebendary of Durham.

William, b. 1566.

Thomas, b. 1569.

Elizabeth, b. 22nd April, 1563, m. to Richard Goodhall, of Lincolnshire.

Frances.

Jane, m. to Robert Brandling, esq. of Felling.

Mary, m. to — Winston.

The son and successor,

SIR RICHARD WORTLEY, of Wortley, received the honour of knighthood from *King* JAMES at York, 17th April, 1603, on his majesty's entrance into the kingdom. He m. Elizabeth, daughter of Edward Boughton, esq. of Cawston, in Warwickshire, and had by her (who wedded, secondly, William Cavendish, Earl of Devonshire,) three sons and five daughters, viz.

FRANCIS (Sir), his heir.

Edward (Sir), knt. m. Elizabeth, daughter of William Eldred, and widow of Sir Samuel Tryon, but *d. s. p.*

Thomas (Sir), knt. *d. s. p.*

Mary, m. to Henry Baron, of Hilton.

Anne, m. first to Sir Rotherham Willoughby, and secondly to Sir George Morton.

Elizabeth, m. to Sir Henry Crofts.

Eleanor, m. first to Sir Henry Lee, secondly to Edward, Earl of Sussex, thirdly to Robert, Earl of Warwick, and fourthly to Edward, Earl of Manchester.

Sarah, m. to Sir Sutton Coney.

Sir Richard died 25th July, 1603, was buried in St. George's Chapel, Windsor, and succeeded by his son,

I. SIR FRANCIS WORTLEY, knt. of Wortley, created BARONET 29th June, 1611. At the outbreak of the civil wars, Sir Francis, whose devotion to the royal cause shone conspicuous among the most faithful of the cavaliers, fortified his house at Wortley, and raised a troop of horse, with which he maintained a guerilla warfare, extremely harassing to his opponents. In 1644, he was taken prisoner at Walton House, near Wakefield, his estate sequestered, and he himself sent to the Tower, where he remained in captivity for many years, solacing the hours of his long confinement by literary occupations to which he was much attached. He wrote several small tracts principally connected with the occurrences and controversies of the times, and one larger work to prove that episcopacy is pure divine. The most curious of the former productions is, his "Characters and Elegies." Sir Francis m. first, Grace, daughter of Sir William Brouncker, of Melksham, Wilts, and had by her,

FRANCIS, his heir.

Margaret, m. to Sir Henry Griffiths, bart. of Burton Agnes, but *d. s. p.*

He m. secondly, Hester, daughter of George Smithies, alderman of London and widow of Alderman Eyre, of Alderman Street, by whom he had a daughter,

Sarah, m. to Roger Battridge or Battergh, esq.

Sir Francis *d.* in London, and was *s.* by his son,

II. SIR FRANCIS WORTLEY, of Wortley, aged twenty-two, 13 CHARLES I. He m. Frances, daughter and co-heir of Sir William Faunte, of Preston, in Leicestershire, but by her, who survived him, he left no issue, at his decease 14th March, 1665, when the BARONETCY became EXTINCT. With Sir Francis expired the line of Wortley, of Wortley, which had flourished through more than five centuries. His great inheritance passed under his will to his illegitimate daughter,

ANNE NEWCOMEN, *alias* WORTLEY, who m. the Hon. SIDNEY MONTAGUE, second son of Edward, first Earl of Sandwich, and had with other issue, a son,

EDWARD WORTLEY MONTAGUE, one of the lords commissioners of the Treasury, and ambassador to the Porte, m. LADY MARY PIERREPOINT, the celebrated Lady Mary Wortley Montague, eldest daughter of Evelyn, Duke of Kingston, and had a daughter and heir,*

MARY WORTLEY MONTAGUE, m. to John Stuart, Earl of Bute, and was created a peeress in her own right as Baroness Mount Stuart, of Wortley. Her ladyship's grandson, the present proprietor of the Wortley estates, is JAMES ARCHIBALD STUART WORTLEY, LORD WHARNCLIFFE.

Arms—Arg. on a bend between six martlets gu. three besants.

WRAY, OF GLENTWORTH.

CREATED 25th Nov. 1612.—EXTINCT 27th Aug. 1809.

WRAY, OF ASHBY.

CREATED 27th June, 1660.—EXTINCT ......

Lineage.

WILLIAM WRAY, son of Robert Wray, whose ancestors were anciently seated in the bishopric of Durham, and afterwards possessed estates in Richmond, Yorkshire, married the daughter and heir of Jackson, of Snydall, and had with other issue,

CHRISTOPHER, his heir.

Richard, ancestor of the WRAYS OF KELFIELD, the only branch of the family remaining, now represented by the REV. CECIL DANIEL WRAY, A.M. of Strangeways, Manchester. (See BURKE's *Commoners*, vol. iv.)

Thomas, of St. Nicholas, Richmondshire, who left by Ann Foster, three sons and a daughter, viz.

William, of St. Nicholas, living in 1615, whose son,

Thomas, of Beamish, Durham, sold his estates.

Thomas, named in the will of his uncle, Sir Christopher.

Robert.

Elizabeth, m. to A. Wagstaffe, of Hasland, Derbyshire.

* Mr. Wortley Montague disinherited his only son, Edward Wortley Montague, who had manifested very extraordinary excentricities, and whose varied life is well told in a work entitled "Literary Anecdotes of the 18th Century."

WRIGHT, OF DAGENHAMS.

Lineage.

John Wright, esq. of Kelvedon Hatch, living about the middle of the 17th century, had three sons, of whom the eldest, Robert, of Kelvedon Hatch, was ancestor of the Wrights of that place, the second of the Wrights of South Weald, and the third

John Wright, of Wright's Bridge, near Hornchurch, and of Gray's Inn, of the Wrights of Dagenhams. He died in 1644, leaving by Mary, his wife, daughter of John Mole, esq. and niece of Sir Thomas Cheke, a son and successor,

Laurence Wright, M.D. who died 3rd October, 1657, and was *s.* by his son,

I. Henry Wright, esq. of Dagenhams, in Essex, who was created a Baronet, 11th June, 1660. He *m.* Anne, daughter of John, Lord Crew, of Stene, and by her, who died 27th September, 1708, had issue,

- Henry, his heir.
- Anne, *m.* first to Sir Robert Pye, of Berkshire, and secondly to William Rider, esq.

Sir Henry died 5th February, 1663, and was *s.* by his son,

II. Sir Henry Wright, of Dagenhams, at whose decease under age and unm. in 1681, the Baronetcy became extinct.

Arms—Az. two bars arg. in chief three leopards' heads or.

WRIGHTE, OF CRANHAM HALL.

Created 15th Feb. 1660-1.—Extinct 10th Jan. 1737-8.

Lineage.

The Rev. Robert Wrighte, B.D. for thirty-four years rector of Dennington, in Suffolk, (second son of John Wrighte, of Wrighte's Bridge, Essex, and brother of the ancestor of the Wrightes, of Dagenhams,) *m.* Jane, daughter of John Butler, esq. of Sheby, in Essex, and sister of Sir Oliver Butler, of Sharnbrook, in Bedfordshire; by her he had issue,

- Euseby, barrister-at-law, who married thrice, but *d. s. p.*
- Nathan, of whom presently.
- Benjamin (Sir), knt. of Dennington, a merchant of London, who died in Spain, leaving an only daughter.
- Ezekiel, D.D. rector of Thurcaston, who *m.* Dorothy, second daughter of John Onebye, esq. and co-heir of her brother, Sir John Onebye, by whom (who died in 1691.) he left at his decease in 1688, a son and successor, the celebrated
  - Sir Nathan Wrighte, who succeeded Lord Somers in the custody of the great seal, as Lord Keeper, and continued in that elevated office until 1705. (For a continuation of Sir Nathan's line, until it merged in the Wyndhams of Cromer, see that family in Burke's *Commoners*, vol. ii. p. 345.)

The Rev. Robert Wrighte died in 1684. His second son,

Nathan Wrighte, a merchant and alderman of London, purchased the manor of Cranham, in Essex. He *m.* Anne Fleming, of Warley Place, and dying in 1657, was succeeded by his son,

I. Benjamin Wrighte, esq. of Cranham Hall, Essex, who was created a Baronet in 1660. He *m.* Jane, daughter of William Williams, merchant, of London, and dying in 1706, was *s.* by his son,

II. Sir Nathan Wrighte, of Cranham Hall, who *m.* first, Anne, daughter of John Merick, merchant; secondly, Elizabeth, daughter of Francis Bragg, esq. of Hatfield Peverell, in Essex; thirdly, Elizabeth, daughter of John Bowater, esq. of Coventry; and fourthly, Abigail, daughter of Samuel Trist, esq. of Culworth, in Northamptonshire. By the first he had a son, Nathan, his heir; and by the last, another son, Samuel, and a daughter, Elizabeth, *m.* to Gen. Oglethorpe. Sir Nathan died 16th October, 1727, aged sixty six, and was *s.* by his son,

III. Sir Nathan Wrighte, of Cranham Hall, who *m.* Margaret, daughter of Sir Francis Lawley, bart. of Spoonhill, in Shropshire, and had two daughters, his co-heirs, viz.

- Ann, *m.* to Thomas Lewis, esq. of Harpton Court, M.P. for the borough of Radnor, from the death of *Queen* Anne to the beginning of the reign of George III. At Mr. Lewis's demise, his Radnorshire estates devolved on his nephew, John Lewis, esq. father of the Right Hon. Thomas Frankland Lewis, now of Harpton Court. Mrs. Lewis survived her husband many years, and devised the estates which she inherited from her father, Sir Nathan Wrighte, at Lofts, near Malden, in Essex, to her nephew, Sir Thomas Hussey Apreece, bart.
- Dorothy, *m.* to Thomas Hussey Apreece, esq. and was mother of Thomas Hussey Apreece, created a Baronet in 1782. His son is the present Sir Hussey George Apreece, bart.

Sir Nathan died in 1737, aged fifty-three, and was *s.* by his half-brother,

IV. Sir Samuel Wrighte, who died unm. at Lisbon, 10th January, 1737-8, when the Baronetcy became extinct.

Arms—As Wright of Dagenham.

WROTH, OF BLENDEN HALL.

Lineage.

I. John Wroth, esq. of Blenden Hall, in Kent, descendant of an ancient family, was created a Baronet in 1660. He *m.* first, Anne, daughter of Toby, Lord Caulfeild, widow, first of William Gore, esq. ...

…r Lincolnshire in three parliaments, *temp.* Charles … He married Grisel, daughter and heir of Sir Hugh …ethell, knt. of Ellerton, in Yorkshire, and had …sue,

- i. John, his heir.
- ii. Christopher, *d. s. p.*
- iii. Theophilus, *d. s. p.*
- iv. William, *d. s. p.*
- v. Bethell, *d. s. p.*

- i. Frances, *m.* to John Hotham, esq.
- ii. Grissel, *m.* to Anthony Thorold, esq. of Marston, in Lincolnshire.
- iii. Theodosia, *m.* to Sir Richard Barker, knt.

…ir John was *s.* by his son,

…iii. Sir John Wray, of Glentworth,* who *m.* first, …lizabeth, daughter of Sir Henry Willoughby, bart. …f Risley, in Derbyshire, and widow of Sir Simeon …'Ewes, bart. by which lady he had no issue, and se…ondly, Sarah, daughter of Sir John Evelyn, knt. of …Vest Dean, in Wilts, by whom (who wedded, se…ondly, Thomas, Viscount Fanshaw, and thirdly, …eorge, Lord Castleton,) he had an only daughter and …eir,

Elizabeth, *m.* the Hon. Nicholas Saunderson, eldest son of George, Viscount Castleton, and had an only child, Wray Saunderson, who *m.* Mary, eldest daughter of the Earl of Rockingham, but died without issue during the lifetime of his mother. That lady, having thus no child to succeed her, entailed, by deed dated 29th October, 1709, her estates in Lincolnshire and Norfolk, first on Col. Christopher Wray, his sons and brothers, then on William Wray, his sons and brothers, and subsequently on George Wray, of Kelfield, his two sons, and their male heirs.

…ir John Wray was *s.* by his cousin,

…iv. Sir Christopher Wray, the second baronet of …ashby, at whose decease issueless, the Baronetcy of …ashby became extinct, while that of Glentworth …assed to his cousin,

…v. Sir Baptist Edward Wray, who also died *s. p.* …nd was *s.* by his uncle,

…vi. Sir Drury Wray, *b.* in Lincolnshire, 29th July, …633, who *m.* Anne, daughter and heir of Thomas …asey, esq. of Rathcannon, in the county of Limerick, …y Bridget, his wife, daughter and co-heir of Sir John …owdall, knt. and had, with several daughters, three …ons,

Christopher, his heir.
William, who predeceased his father.
Cecil, successor to his eldest brother.

…ir Drury died 30th October, 1710, was buried in the …hurch of Clonara, in the county of Limerick, and *s.* …y his son,

…vii. Sir Christopher Wray, lieut.-col. in the army, …who inherited his mother's estate in Ireland. He …ought on the side of William, at the Boyne, and in …he following reign, served with distinction in Spain, …Portugal, and Flanders, particularly at the siege of …Ostend. In 1710, twelve days after his father's de…ease, Sir Christopher died unm. at Portsmouth, while …reparing to embark with the fleet for Spain. He was …he first named in Mrs. Saunderson's deed of settle…ment, but that lady outlived him. His only surviving …rother and heir,

viii. Sir Cecil Wray, captain in the same regiment, served likewise in Flanders, Spain, and Portugal. He inherited, at the demise of Mrs. Saunderson, a considerable estate in the counties of Norfolk and York, and was high sheriff of the former shire in 1720. Sir Cecil wedded Mary, daughter of Edward Harrison, esq. of Morely, in the county of Antrim, by Johanna, his wife, daughter of Dr. Jeremiah Taylor, bishop of Dromore, but dying *s. p.* in May, 1736, was *s.* by his cousin,

ix. Sir John Wray, who *m.* Frances, daughter of Fairfax Norcliffe, esq. of Langton, in Yorkshire, and had issue,

Cecil, his heir.
John, died young.
Mary, on whom and her heirs the estates of her mother were entailed. She *m.* in 1760, Sir James Innes, bart. afterwards fifth Duke of Roxburghe, but died without issue, 20th July, 1807.
Isabella, *m.* to John Dalton, esq. and dying 29th May, 1780, left issue,

Thomas Dalton, who assumed in 1807, the surname of Norcliffe. His son and successor is the present Norcliffe Norcliffe, esq. of Langton.
John Dalton, who inherited Sleningford, in the county of York. (See Burke's *Commoners*, vol. i. p. 528.)
James Dalton, in holy orders, rector of Croft.
Frances-Elizabeth, *m.* to William Garforth, esq.
Isabella, *m.* to George Baker, esq. of Elemore Hall, Durham.

Frances, *m.* to John Arthington, esq. of Arthington, but *d. s. p.*

Sir John died 26th January, 1752, and was *s.* by his son,

x. Sir Cecil Wray, who *m.* Miss Esther Summers, but died without issue, 10th January, 1805,† having entailed his property on the second son of his second sister, John Dalton, esq. in case of failure of heirs male of his cousin and successor,

xi. Sir William Ullithorne Wray, rector of Darley, in Derbyshire. Sir William *m.* Frances Bromley, and had issue,

Cecil, born 6th April, 1768, *d. v. p.* unm. about 1790.
William-James, his heir.
Lucy, *b.* 17th May, 1773, *d. s. p.*
Mary-Ann, *b.* 2nd May, 1774, *m.* to the Rev. Mr. Morgan, and *d. s. p.*
Frances, *b.* 1st June, 1775.
Isabella, born 6th of May, 1777, died without issue.
Elizabeth, born 22nd May, 1778, died without issue.

Sir William died in 1808, and was succeeded by his son,

xii. Sir William-James Wray, who died without issue, in October, 1809, when the Baronetcy became extinct.

Arms—Az. on a chief or, three martlets gu.

* The estate of Glentworth, the mansion house of which was built out of the profits of the Royal Mint, granted to Sir Christopher Wray, by *Queen* Elizabeth, was conveyed to the Saundersons.

† In Michaelmas term, 1735, Sir Cecil passed a fine and suffered a recovery, and thus barred the estates which had descended to him from Mrs. Saunderson.

WYNDHAM, OF PILSDEN COURT.

CREATED 4th Aug. 1641. EXTINCT about 1663.

Lineage.

I. HUGH WYNDHAM, esq. of Pilsden Court, in the county of Dorset, fourth son of Edmond Wyndham, esq. of Kentsford, and grandson of Sir John Wyndham, of Orchard, in Somersetshire, was created a BARONET in 1641. He m. Mary, daughter of Christopher Alanson, esq. of London, but as he left daughters only, the title became EXTINCT at his decease.

Arms—Az. a chevron between three lions' heads erased.

WYNDHAM, OF TRENT.

CREATED 18th Nov. 1673.—EXTINCT in April, 1719.

Lineage.

SIR THOMAS WYNDHAM, knt. of Kentsford, eldest son of Edmond Wyndham, esq. of Kentsford, and grandson of Sir John Wyndham, knt. of Orchard Wyndham, m. Elizabeth, daughter of Richard Coningsby, esq. of Hampton Court, in the county of Hereford, and had several children, most of the sons engaged in the service of CHARLES I. and the fourth,

I. COL. FRANCIS WYNDHAM is memorable for having conducted CHARLES II. after the disastrous issue of the battle of Worcester, to his seat at Trent, where he entertained his majesty with the following remarkable words of his father, Sir Thomas Wyndham, "Who, not long before his death, in the year 1636, called unto him his five sons, (having not seen them together in some years before) and discoursed unto us, (said he) of the loving peace and prosperity this kingdom had enjoyed under its three last glorious monarchs; of the many miseries and calamities which lay sore upon our ancestors, by the several invasions and conquests of foreign nations, and likewise by intestine insurrections and rebellions. And notwithstanding the strange mutations and changes in England, he showed how it pleased God, in love to our nation, to preserve an undoubted succession of kings, to sit on the regal throne. He mentioned the healing conjunction of the two houses of York and Lancaster, and the blessed union of the two crowns of England and Scotland, stopping up those fountains, which by national feuds and quarrels kept open, had like to have drowned the whole island. He said he feared the beautiful garment of peace would shortly be torn in pieces, through the neglect of magistrates, the general corruption of manners, and the prevalence of a puritanical faction, which (if not prevented) would undermine the very pillars of government. My sons, we have seen serene and quiet times, but now prepare yourselves for cloudy and troublesome. I command you to honour and obey our gracious sovereign, and in all times adhere to the crown; and, though it *should hang upon a bush*, I charge you forsake it not. These words being spoken with much earnestness, both in gesture and manner extraordinary, he rose from his chair, and left us in a deep consultation what the meaning should be of 'the crown hanging upon a bush.' These words, sir, (said the colonel) made so firm an impression in all our breasts, that the many afflictions of these sad times, cannot rase out their indelible characters. Certainly, these are the days which my father pointed out in that expression, and I doubt not, God hath brought me through so many dangers, that I might shew myself both a dutiful son and a loyal subject, in faithfully endeavouring to serve your sacred majesty in this your greatest distress." Col. Wyndham, who became afterwards governor of Dunster Castle, was created a BARONET 18th November, 1673. He m. Anne, daughter and co-heir of Thomas Gerard, esq. of Trent, in Somersetshire, and had three sons, namely,

THOMAS, his heir.

Gerard, died unm.

FRANCIS, successor to his brother.

Sir Francis died in 1676, and was s. by his son,

II. SIR THOMAS WYNDHAM, of Trent, who m. Elizabeth, daughter of Sir Thomas Croke, knt. of Waterpery, Oxfordshire, and had an only daughter and heir,

ANNE, who m. William James, esq. of Ightham Court, in Kent, and had with two daughters, three sons, namely,

WILLIAM JAMES, of Ightham Court, high sheriff of Kent in 1732, whose son and heir Richard, died s. p. in 1817.

Richard James, of the Middle Temple, d. unmarried.

Demetrius James, colonel in the army, whose daughter, ELIZABETH, m. Charles Grevis, esq. formerly of Moseley Hall, Worcestershire, and had, with three daughters, one son,

DEMETRIUS GREVIS, esq. who assumed in 1817, the surname and arms of JAMES, and is the present DEMETRIUS GREVIS JAMES, esq. of Ightham Court. He served as high seriff of Kent in 1833. (See BURKE's *Commoners*, vol. i. p. 387.)

Sir Thomas Wyndham died about 1691, and was succeeded by his son,

III. SIR FRANCIS WYNDHAM, who m. first Elizabeth daughter of Sir Richard Onslow, bart. of Clandon, in Surrey; secondly, Hester, widow of Matthew Ingram, gent. and thirdly, Henrietta,* daughter of Thomas Wiggington, esq. of Ham, in Surrey, widow of Sir Richard Newdigate, bart. Sir Francis had by his first wife a son,

THOMAS, who died s. p. leaving a son, FRANCIS, successor to his grandfather, and a daughter, FRANCES, who m. Henry Bromley, esq. of Horseheath Hall and Holt Castle, who was elevated to the peerage as LORD MONTFORT in 1741. His lordship's grandson is Henry, present and third LORD MOUNTFORT. (See BURKE's *Peerage and Baronetage*.)

Sir Francis died at Chelsea, Middlesex, 22nd March 1716, and was s. by his grandson,

IV. SIR FRANCIS WYNDHAM, of Trent, at whose decease in minority in April, 1719, the BARONETCY became EXTINCT.

Arms—As WYNDHAM OF PILSDEN COURT.

* She wedded, thirdly, William Lowfield, esq.

WYNNE, OF LEESWOOD.

CREATED 9th Aug. 1731.

EXTINCT

Lineage.

I. GEORGE WYNNE, esq. of Leeswood, in Flintshire, son of Mr. Wnne, of Flint, who having discovered a rich mine on his estate, gained thereby a very considerable fortune, was created a BARONET in 1731, with remainder, in default of his own male issue, to his brother, John Wynne, esq. Sir George married Miss Lloyd, of Flintshire, and by her, who died 25th April, 1743, had one son and two daughters, namely,

GEORGE, who died *s. p.* unm.

Esther, } one of whom *m.* Richard Hill Waring,
Mary, } esq.

Sir George, who represented the borough of Flint in parliament, was *s.* at his decease by his brother,

II. SIR JOHN WYNNE, of Leeswood, who died in November, 1764, and was *s.* by his son,

III. SIR JOHN WYNNE, of Leeswood, with whom the BARONETCY EXPIRED.

Arms—Az. a chev. between three dolphins hauriant arg.

WYNNE, OF GWEDIR.

CREATED 29th June, 1611.

EXTINCT 7th Jan. 1719.

Lineage.

The Wynnes of Gwedir have had so able an historian in the person of Sir John Wynne, the first baronet, that it will suffice to refer to the work of that learned antiquary for the early ancestry from Owen Gwynedd, Prince of North Wales, in 1436, and commence our narrative with

JOHN WYNNE AP MEREDITH, of Gwedir, in Carnarvonshire, who died in 1553. He married Elen Lloyd, daughter of Morris ap John ap Meredith, of Ruedoc, and had five sons: Morris, his heir; Griffith, of Berthdda; Owen, of Caermelwr; Robert, of Convay; and John, D. D. The eldest,

MORRIS WYNNE, of Gwedir, was father of

I. SIR JOHN WYNNE, of Gwedir, *b.* in 1553, created BARONET in 1611, the well known author of the "History of the Gwedir family," which, while in MS. for above a century, was so prized in North Wales, that many in the principality thought it worthy the labour to make fair and complete transcripts of the whole. Sir John *m.* Sidney, daughter of Sir William Gerrard, chancellor of Ireland, and had, according to the inscription on his tomb at Llanrwst, eleven sons and two daughters. He *d.* 1st March, 1626,' much lamented by his family and neighbours, and was *s.* by his son,

II. SIR RICHARD WYNNE, of Gwedir, one of the grooms of the bedchamber to CHARLES I. when Prince of Wales, and afterwards treasurer to Queen Henrietta. Sir Richard accompanied the prince on his journey to Spain, and wrote a highly interesting narrative of the voyage, printed among Thomas Hearne's tracts. He married Anne, daughter and co-heir of Sir Francis Darcy, of Isleworth, in Middlesex, but dying without issue in 1649, aged sixty-one, was *s.* by his brother,

III. SIR OWEN WYNNE, of Gwedir, who *m.* Grace, daughter of Hugh Williams, of Werg, in Caernarvonshire, and died about 1660, leaving a son and successor,

IV. SIR RICHARD WYNNE, of Gwedir, who *m.* Sarah, daughter of Sir Thomas Middleton, bart. of Chirk Castle, in Denbighshire, but dying without male issue, was *s.* by (the only son of Henry, the tenth son of the first baronet,) his cousin,

V. SIR JOHN WYNNE, of Gwedir, who *m.* Jane, daughter and heir of Eyton Evans, esq. of Wynnstay, in Denbighshire, but died without issue, 7th January, 1719, aged ninety-one, the BARONETCY became EXTINCT. His great estates he devised to his kinsman,

SIR WATKIN WILLIAMS, bart. M. P. son and heir of Sir William Williams, bart. by Jane, his first wife, daughter and heir of Edward Thelwall, esq. of Plas y Ward, in Denbighshire, by Sydney, his wife, daughter and heir of William Wynne, esq. who was son of SIR JOHN WYNNE, the first baronet of Gwedir. Sir Watkin Williams, on inheriting, assumed the additional surname and arms of WYNNE. He *d.* in 1749, leaving a son and successor,

SIR WATKIN WILLIAMS-WYNNE, bart. M. P. for Denbighshire, father of the present

SIR WATKIN WILLIAMS-WYNNE, bart. M. P. (See BURKE's *Peerage and Baronetage.*)

Arms—Vert, three eagles displayed in fesse or.

WYTHAM, OF GOLDSBOROUGH.

CREATED 13th Dec. 1683.

EXTINCT 15th Nov. 1689.

Lineage.

In 1683 a BARONETCY was conferred on

I. JOHN WYTHAM, esq. of Goldsborough, in Yorkshire, but it became EXTINCT in six years after (15th November, 1689), at the decease issueless of Sir John.

Arms—Or, a bendlet gu. between three eaglets sa.

WYVILL, OF CONSTABLE BURTON.

CREATED Nov. 25th, 1611.

DORMANT since 1774.

Lineage.

This family (of knightly degree since the Conquest) is of Norman extraction, of the name of Vienville, which family is now in being in France.

SIR HUMPHRY D'WYVILL, knt. of Walworth and Slingsby Castle, came into England with WILLIAM the CONQUEROR.

SIR JOHN D'WYVILL, knt. his son, married a daughter of Sir John Fulthorpe, knt. and was father of

OLIVER D'WYVILL, whose son,

SIR JOHN D'WYVILL, knt. had a son,

SIR ROBERT D'WYVILL, knt. father of

SIR MARMADUKE WYVILL, knt. He married, in the reign of EDWARD I. a daughter of Sir John Elton, knt. and had a son,

ROBERT D'WYVILL, esq. to whom succeeded

SIR THOMAS WYVILL, knt. whose successor was

SIR THOMAS WYVILL, knt. He married a daughter of Sir Randulf Palmer, knt. and was succeeded by his son,

SIR MARMADUKE WYVILL, knt. father of

ROBERT WYVILL, esq. whose son,

SIR RICHARD WYVILL, knt. having, in the year 1461, taken part with HENRY VI. against the House of York, was slain at the battle of Towton, in Yorkshire, and his estate forfeited to EDWARD IV. His son,

CHRISTOPHER WYVILL, married a daughter of Richard Lassels, esq. and was *s.* by his son,

ROBERT WYVILL, esq. father of

ROBERT WYVILL, esq. who married Anne, daughter of Sir John Norton, knt. and was succeeded by his son,

SIR MARMADUKE WYVILL, knt. M.P. for Ripon in 1553, who *m.* first, Agnes, the daughter and heir of Sir Ralph Fitz Randolph, knt. of Spenithorne, Lord of Middleham, by Elizabeth his wife, one of the daughters and co-heirs of Ralph, Lord Scroope of Masham.* He married to his second wife, the widow of Sir Roger Bellingham, knt. and his third was Dorothy, relict of Sir William St. Quintin, knt.

CHRISTOPHER WYVILL, esq. his son and heir, by his first wife, (*temp. Queen* MARY,) married Margaret, daughter of the Hon. John Scroope, younger son of Henry, Lord Scrope, of Bolton, by Elizabeth his wife, daughter of Henry Piercy, Earl of Northumberland, and had a son and successor,

I. MARMADUKE WYVILL, esq. who received the honour of knighthood from *Queen* ELIZABETH, and was created a BARONET by *King* JAMES I. November 25, 1611. He married Magdalen, daughter of Sir Christopher Danby, knt. of Thorpe, in Yorkshire, and h[illegible] issue,

I. CHRISTOPHER, aged fifty in 1612, who *d.* [illegible] leaving by Jane, his wife, daughter of Sir R[illegible]bert Stapleton, knt. of Wighill, in Yorkshire,

MARMADUKE, successor to his grandfather.

Henry, *d.* unm.

William, who *m.* Mary, daughter of Leonard Musgrave, esq. of Johnby, son a[nd] heir of Sir William Musgrave, bart. [illegible] Hayton, and had a son,

Christopher, of Johnby, who *m.* Frances, daughter of Sir Timothy Fet[her]ston, knt. of Kirkswald, in Cumberland.

Edward or Edmund.

Elizabeth, *m.* to Bellingham, of Lincolnshire.

Olive, *m.* to Cuthbert Collingwood, esq [of] Ealington, in Northumberland.

Mary, *m.* first, to John Wylde, esq. of H[illegible]ton, and secondly, to Anthony, second s[on] of Sir Bertram Bulmer, knt.

Katharine, *m.* to John Wharton, esq. [of] Kirby Thore, Westmoreland.

Philippa, *m.* to Richard Sale, gent. of H[illegible]care, in Lancashire.

II. Marmaduke, of Croydon, in Surrey, living [in] 1623, who *m.* first, Judith, daughter of William Morley, of Glind, in Sussex, and secon[dly] Judith, daughter of William Braby, of Suf[fo]lk.

III. Thomas.

IV. Humphrey.

V. Francis, rector of Spennithorne, who died [in] 1649, leaving by Helen, his wife, daughter [of] Thomas Norton, esq. of Burneby, three sons,

Thomas, of Bellerby, in Yorkshire, who *m.* Mary, daughter of Christopher Place, esq. of Dinsdale, in Durham, and left an only daughter.

Edward who *m.* first, Elizabeth, daughter of Henry Pierson, esq. of Richmond, by whom he had one son, Edward, and secondly, Elizabeth, daughter of Peter Norton, esq. of Dishford, by whom he had another son, Francis.

Rowland, *d. s. p.*

VI. Robert.

VII. William, of York, barrister-at-law.

VIII. John, of Bardonin, in Yorkshire.

I. Elizabeth, *m.* to Christopher Phillipson, esq [of] Calgarth, in Westmoreland.

II. Maria, *m.* first to Francis Brigs, of Malton, and secondly to Thomas Percehay, esq. of Ritt[on], both in Yorkshire.

Sir Marmaduke died between November, 1616, and 12th March, 1617, and was *s.* by his grandson,

II. SIR MARMADUKE WYVILL, of Constable Burton, high sheriff of Yorkshire in the 9th of CHARLES I. During the troubles of that monarch's reign, Sir Marmaduke was a distinguished royalist, and sufferer, having been twice plundered by Cromwell's troops and finally compelled to pay £1343, composition for his estates. He married Isabel, daughter and heir [of] Sir William Gascoigne, knt. of Sedbury, in the county

* The claim to the barony of Scroope of Masham which was in abeyance between the families of Wyvill and Danby, rests since the demise of the late William Danby, esq. of Swinton Park, Yorkshire, without issue, in 18[illegible], with the representatives of the family of Wyvill.

of York, and had, with several other sons, who died unm.

I. CHRISTOPHER, his heir.

I. Mary, m. to Arthur Beckwith, esq. of Aldborough, Yorkshire.
II. Jane, m. to Robert Wyld, esq. of Hunton, in Yorkshire.
III. Isabel, m. to the Hon. James Darcy, of Sedbury Park, Yorkshire.
IV. Grace, m. to George Witham, esq. of Cliffe.
V. Olive, m. to George Meinill, esq. of Aldborough.
VI. Elizabeth, m. to Sir William Dalton, knt. of Hawkeswell.
VII. Anne, m. to Thomas, younger brother of Sir William Dalton, knt.
VIII. Dorothy, died unm.

Sir Marmaduke died in 1648, and was s. by his son,

III. SIR CHRISTOPHER WYVILL, of Constable Burton, who was elected M.P. for Richmond, in Yorkshire, at the Restoration. He m. Ursula, eldest daughter of Conyers, Lord Darcy, created Earl of Holderness, and had issue,

I. WILLIAM, his heir.
II. Francis, receiver general of the land tax for Yorkshire, Durham, and Northumberland, m. Anne, daughter of Sir William Cayley, bart. of Brompton, in Yorkshire, and died 22nd October, 1717, aged seventy, leaving three daughters, viz.

Ursula, m. to Leonard Childers, esq. of Carr House, in the county of York. (See BURKE'S *Commoners*, vol. ii. p. 229.)
Barbara, died unm.
Frances.

III. Christopher, D.D. dean of Ripon, who died in 1710, aged fifty-nine, leaving two sons, Christopher and William.

I. Dorothy, m. to Charles Tankard, esq. son and heir of Sir Charles Tankard, knt. of Whixley.
II. Barbara, m. to St. John Thompson, esq. of Crawley, Bedfordshire.

Sir Christopher died in 1665, and was s. by his son,

IV. SIR WILLIAM WYVILL, of Constable Burton, born in 1645, who m. Anne, only daughter of James Brooke, esq. of Ellingthorp, in Yorkshire, and had issue,

I. MARMADUKE, his heir.
II. D'Arcy, who died at Derby, 5th January, 1731, leaving three sons, viz.

1. William, who settled at Maryland, in America, and died there about the year 1750, leaving a son,

MARMADUKE, whose descendants if not barred by alienage, being American subjects, should enjoy the baronetcy.

2. Edward, general supervisor of Excise, at Edinburgh, who m. 18th December, 1737, Christian Catherine, daughter of William Clifton, esq. of that city, and died 12th March, 1791, leaving an only son,

CHRISTOPHER, of whom presently, as inheritor of Constable Burton, upon the demise, in 1774, of Sir Marmaduke, the seventh baronet.

3. Hale, of the city of York, m. and had issue.

I. Priscilla, m. to Major Kemp.
II. Ursula, d. unm.

Sir William died in 1684, and was s. by his son,

V. SIR MARMADUKE WYVILL, of Constable Burton, who was M.P. for Richmond, 7 WILLIAM III. and 1 *Queen* ANNE, and became subsequently a commissioner of Excise. He m. Henrietta-Maria, maid of honour to *Queens* CATHERINE and MARY, daughter of Sir Thomas Yarburgh, knt. of Balne Hall and Snaith, by Henrietta-Maria, his wife, daughter and co-heir of Colonel Thomas Blague, of Hollinger, in Suffolk, governor of Wallingford, (see BURKE'S *Commoners*, vol. iii. p. 663,) and had issue,

MARMADUKE, his heir.
Thomas, accomptant general of the Excise, d. unm. in 1731.
Christopher, a commissioner of Excise for North Britain, and comptroller of the Excise cash in England. He m. first in 1723, Elizabeth, daughter of Captain Stephen Martin Leake, of Beddington, in Surrey, and by her, who died 19th May, 1731, had a daughter,

ELIZABETH, m. to her cousin, the Rev. Christopher Wyvill, but d. s. p. 23rd July, 1783.

Christopher Wyvill m. secondly in 1738, Henrietta, second daughter and co-heir of Francis Asty, esq. of Black Notley, in Essex, and by her, who died in 1742, had issue,

MARMADUKE-ASTY, who succeeded as sixth baronet.

He m. thirdly, Anne Thayer, and died 26th April, 1752.

Anne, m. to John Wyvill, esq. of Walton-upon-Thames, Surrey, and d. s. p.
Margaret, m. to John Purcell, esq. and died in 1755, s. p.
Ursula, m. to Mr. Jones, of Furnival's Court, London.
Mary, m. to the Rev. Thomas Gee.

Sir Marmaduke died in October, 1722, and was s. by his son,

VI. SIR MARMADUKE WYVILL, of Constable Burton, b. in 1692, who m. Carey, daughter of Edward Coke, esq. of Holkham, in Norfolk, but dying s. p. in 1753-4, was s. by his nephew,

VII. SIR MARMADUKE-ASTY WYVILL, of Constable Burton, who died unm. at Bath, 23rd February, 1774, and was s. in his estates by his brother-in-law and cousin,

THE REV. CHRISTOPHER WYVILL, who m. two wives, by the first, Elizabeth, sister of Sir Marmaduke Wyvill, bart. he had no issue to survive, but by the second, he had,

MARMADUKE, his heir, now of Constable Burton. (See BURKE'S *Commoners*.)
Christopher, post captain R. N.
Edward, in holy orders, rector of Fingal and Spennythorne, who m. Frances-Pulleine, relict of Frederick Dodsworth, D.D.

Sarah, m. to the Hon. and Rev. Thomas Monson, rector of Bedale.
Elizabeth-Anne, m. to the Rev. John J. T. Monson.
Catherine.

Since the decease of Sir Marmaduke, the baronetcy has remained dormant: if alienage bar the inheritance of the branch settled in America, the title now vests in MARMADUKE WYVILL, esq. of Constable Burton.

Arms—Gu three chevronels interlaced vaire, and a chief or.

YATE, OF BUCKLAND.

CREATED 30th July, 1622. EXTINCT in 1690.

Lineage.

RICHARD YATE, esq. of Charney, in Berkshire, son of Edmond Yate, of the same place, and grandson of William Yate, also of Charney, m. a daughter of the family of Ashendon, and had issue,

EDMUND, of Stanlake, in Oxfordshire.
JOHN, of whom presently.
Margaret, m. to Robert Hyde, esq. of East Hendred.
Maud, m. first, to John Hawkins, esq. of Marcham; and secondly, to Thomas Latton.

The second son,

JOHN YATE, esq. of Charney, m. first, Joan, daughter and heir of Richard Goddard, esq. of Upham, Wilts; and secondly, Alice, daughter of Oliver Hyde, esq. of South Denchworth. By the latter he had a son, THOMAS, of Lyford, and twelve daughters, viz.

Dorothy, m. to John Cheney, esq. of West Woodhey.
Susanna, m. to John Warneford, esq. of Sevenhampton, Wilts.
Mary, m. to Robert Piggot, esq. of Buckinghamshire.
Ursula, m. to Henry Brouncker, esq. of Stoke, Wilts.
Martha, m. to James Braybrook, esq. of Sutton.
Winifred, m. to John Warden, of London, draper.
Catherine, m. to John Pates, of Buckingham.
Jane, m. first, to Oliver Welsborne, esq. of West Hanny; and secondly, to John Eyston, esq. of the East Hendred family.

By his first wife, John Yate had, with several other sons,

JAMES.
Richard, of Upham, Wilts.
Jane, m. to William Fettyplace, esq. of Charney.
Anne, m. to John Latton, esq. of Chilton, in Berkshire.
Elizabeth, m. to Thomas Spicer, esq. merchant of the staple.
Margaret, m. to William Martyn, esq. of Ockingham.

John Yate's son,

JAMES YATE, esq. of Buckland, in Berkshire, m. Mary, daughter of Richard Fettyplace, esq. of East Shefford, and had issue,

I. JAMES, his heir.
II. Thomas, of Shrivenham, who m. Anne, daughter of Richard Fettyplace, esq. and had issue.
III. Richard, of Longworth, m. and had issue.
IV. Philip.
V. Edward.
VI. Francis.
I. Elizabeth, a nun in Sion House.
II. Jane, m. to Philip Morrys, esq.
III. Eleanor, m. to Tobias Pleydell, esq. of Chipping Faringdon.
IV. Dorothy, m. to Thomas Everard, esq. of Aston Thorold.

The eldest son,

JOHN YATE, esq. of Buckland, m. Mary, daughter of William Justice, esq. of Reading, and with other issue, had a son and successor,

EDWARD YATE, esq. of Buckland, father of

I. EDWARD YATE, esq. of Buckland, who was created a BARONET 30th July, 1622. He m. Catherine, sister of Sir Henry Baker, bart. of Sisinghurst, in Kent, and died about the year 1645, leaving a son and successor,

II. SIR JOHN YATE, of Buckland, who m. Mary, daughter and co-heir of Humphrey Packington, esq. of Chaddesley Corbet, Worcestershire, and was s. by his son,

III. SIR CHARLES YATE, of Buckland, who married Frances, daughter of Sir Thomas Gage, bart. of Firle, and had issue,

JOHN, his heir.
MARY, m. to Sir Robert Throckmorton, bart. of Coughton, in Warwickshire; and from this marriage descends the present SIR CHARLES THROCKMORTON, bart.

Sir Charles d. about 1680, and was s. by his son,

IV. SIR JOHN YATE, of Buckland, at whose decease unm. at Paris, in 1690, the BARONETCY became EXTINCT.

Arms—Ar. a fesse embattled between three gates, sa.

YEAMANS, OF BRISTOL.

CREATED 12th Jan. 1664-5. EXTINCT 19th Feb. 17[illegible]

Lineage.

ROBERT YEAMANS, esq. alderman of Bristol, and sheriff in 1642, being zealously attached to the interests of CHARLES I. formed a design, in conjunction with several fellow citizens, to deliver up Bristol to the king's forces, and the night of the 7th March, 1643, was fixed for the execution of the plan. That evening, however, Colonel Nathaniel Fiennes obtained information of the conspiracy, and seized upon the principal leaders, the chief of whom were Mr. Robert Yeamans and Mr. George Boucher. The operations had been thus arranged:—After communication of councils, and many messages interchanged between Oxford and Bristol, it was resolved, that upon Monday, the 7th of March, in the night, Prince Rupert, with a strong party of the king's forces, should advance to Durdon-down, not a full mile from the city, and those within the city were to seize two of the ports, viz. Froomgate and Newgate, and having secured the guards there, were to open the said gates, and let in Prince Rupert, and his troops, who were to have notice given them to approach, by the ringing of St. John's and St. Michael's bells; the confederates were to be distinguished by white tape in their hats, and the word to be, Charles. According to this project, divers of them were met armed, at Mr. Yeaman's house, and others at Mr. Boucher's, and waiting the appointed hour (which was three in the morning) to fall upon their work. But that evening late, a little boy declared, that divers muskets were carried into Mr. Yeaman's house; whereupon a more diligent eye was kept upon them, and at last a guard ordered to search the house, who were first denied entrance, but afterwards let in, where they found a considerable number of men and arms; there was some small offer of resistance, but the most were endeavouring an escape over the top of the house, and divers were taken, both there and at Mr. Boucher's. Prince Rupert, with his forces, came that night to the Down, expecting, till five of the clock next morning, the signal and opening of the gates, but several pieces of ordnance being in the morning discharged that way, perceiving the design frustrated, his highness drew off. Whereupon several were apprehended, and Alderman Yeamans and Mr. Boucher were condemned by a council of war, for corresponding with Prince Rupert, and designing to deliver the city of Bristol into his hands. Great endeavours were used by the king and the generals of the royalists to save the lives of these gentlemen, as appears by the following letters in Mr. Rushworth's collections:

A letter from Patrick, Earl of Forth, Lord Etterick, and lord-lieutenant of all his Majesty's forces, sent by a drum, and directed to the commander-in-chief and the council of war, in the city of Bristol.

"I have been informed, that lately, at a council of war, you have condemned to death Robert Yeamans, late sheriff of the city of Bristol, who hath his majesty's commission for raising a regiment for his service, William Yeamans, his brother, George Boucher, and Edward Dacres, all for expressing their loyalty to his majesty, and endeavouring his service, according to their allegiance, and that you intend to proceed speedily against divers others in the like manner; I do therefore signify unto you, that I intend speedily to put Mr. Stephens, Mr. George, Captain Huntly, and others, taken in rebellion against his majesty, at Cirencester, into the same condition; and do further advertise you, that if you offer by that unjust judgment, to execute any of them you have so condemned, that those now in custody here, especially Mr. George, Mr. Stephens, and Captain Huntly, must expect no favour or mercy. Given under my hand at Oxford, this 16th of May, 1643."

"Charles Rex.

"Trusty and well beloved, we greet you well: whereas we are informed, that by the power and authority of certain factious and rebellious persons of that our city of Bristol, divers of our good subjects, namely, Robert Yeamans, George Boucher, William Yeamans, Edward Dacres, and others of that our city, are imprisoned for preserving their duty and loyalty to us, and for refusing to join in, or assist this horrid and odious rebellion against us; and that the said wicked and traitorous persons have presumed to condemn the said innocent men to die, and upon such their sentence, notoriously against the laws of God and man, they intend to execute and murder our said subjects; we have thought fit to signify to you, the mayor, alderman, sheriffs, and the rest of the body of the council of that our city, that if you suffer this horrid and execrable murder to be committed upon the persons aforesaid, and thereby call down the just judgment of God, and bring perpetual infamy upon that our city, we shall look upon it as the most barbarous and inhuman act that hath been yet committed against us, and upon you as the most desperate betrayers of us, and of the lives and liberties of your fellow subjects. And we therefore will and command you not to suffer any violence to be done upon the persons aforesaid, but that if any such be attempted against them, you raise all the power and strength of that our city, for their rescue; and to that purpose, we command all our good subjects of that our city to aid and assist you upon their allegiance, and as they hope for any grace and favour at our hands, and that you and they kill and slay all such, who shall attempt or endeavour to take away the lives of our said subjects: and hereof you may not fail at your utmost peril. Given at our court at Oxford, the 26th day of May, 1643.

"To our trusty and well beloved, the mayor, aldermen, and sheriffs, and the rest of the common council of our city of Bristol."

But these letters could not hinder the execution; for on Tuesday, the 30th May, 1643, Mr. Yeamans and Mr. Boucher were brought from the castle to the main court of guard, and there executed, by order of Nathaniel Fiennes, son to the Lord Say, and then governor of Bristol for the parliament.

Alderman Yeamans had two sons,

John, his heir.

Robert, created a Baronet in 1666 (see that title).

The elder,

I. John Yeamans, esq. of Bristol, who, in consideration of the loyalty and death of his father, was created a Baronet in 1664-5, and settled in Barbadoes. He *m.* first, a daughter of Mr. Limp, by whom he had a son, William, his heir; and secondly, Margaret, daughter of the Rev. John Forster, by whom he had another son,

Robert, who *m.* Elizabeth, daughter of Elisha Mellows, esq. and had three sons,

Robert, who *m.* Sarah, daughter of John Trent, esq. of Barbadoes, and had an only son, Robert, who *d.* 7th November, 1740, aged ten years. His widow *m.* secondly, the Rev. William Dowding.

John, who *m.* Mary, daughter of Alexander Walker, one of the judges in Barbadoes, and had a son, Walker.

Philip, who *m.* Mary, daughter of Joseph Gibbs, esq. of Barbadoes.

Sir John (who obtained a grant of forty-eight thousand acres of land in South Carolina, and settled there for a time) was *s.* at his decease by his son,

II. Sir William Yeamans, who *m.* Willoughby, daughter of Sir James Browne, knt. and left a son and successor,

III. Sir John Yeamans, who *m.* Margaret, daughter of Philip Gibbes, esq. of Barbadoes, and was *s.* by his son,

IV. Sir John Yeamans, who *m.* in Barbadoes, Anne, daughter of Mr. Scantlebury, and had an only son,

V. Sir John Yeamans, living in Barbadoes in 1771, with whose son,

VI. The Rev. Sir Robert Yeamans, who died *s. p.* 19th February, 1788, the Baronetcy became extinct.

Arms—Sa. a chev. between three chronells of spears arg.

YEAMANS, OF REDLAND.

Created 31st Dec. 1666.—Extinct in 1686-7.

Lineage.

I. Robert Yeamans, esq. of Redland, in Gloucestershire, second son of Alderman Yeamans, who was executed at Bristol, and like that ill-fated gentleman, an unflinching supporter of the royal cause, was created a BARONET in 1666. He m. a daughter of Sir Edward Stafford, knt. of Bradfield, Berks, but died without issue, 1686-7, when the title became EXTINCT.

Arms—As YEAMANS OF BRISTOL.

YELVERTON, OF EASTON MAUDUIT.

CREATED 30th June, 1641.

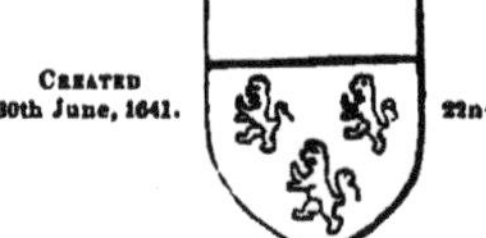

EXTINCT 22nd April, 1695.

Lineage.

Of this family, one of great antiquity in the county of Norfolk, was

ANDREW YELVERTON, living in the reign of EDWARD II. who was father of

ROBERT YELVERTON, seated *temp.* EDWARD III. at Rackheath, in the vicinity of Norwich. He married Cycely, daughter of Sir Thomas Bardolfe, and left a son and heir,

JOHN YELVERTON, of Rackheath, who had by his first wife, a son and successor,

> ROBERT, who died about the year 1420, leaving a son,
>
> > THOMAS, of Rackheath, who died *s. p.*

John Yelverton m. secondly, Elizabeth, daughter of John Read, of Rougham, in the county of Norfolk, and had a son,

SIR WILLIAM YELVERTON, a lawyer of great eminence, who was constituted one of the judges of the court of King's Bench in 22 HENRY VI. This learned person appears to have stood equally well with the monarchs of both the Roses, as we find him not only continued in his judicial office by *King* EDWARD IV. but made a knight of the Bath, in order to grace that prince's coronation; and upon the temporary restoration of *King* HENRY, appointed by patent, dated 9th October, 1470, one of the judges of the court of Common Pleas. He m. Agnes, daughter of Sir Oliver le Gross, of Crostwick, in the county of Norfolk, knt. and was s. by his son,

JOHN YELVERTON, esq. of Rackheath, who m. Margery, daughter of William Morley, esq. and had issue,

> WILLIAM (Sir), his successor.
>
> Anne, m. to Thomas Farmey, esq. of Helmingham.

He was s. by his son,

SIR WILLIAM YELVERTON, knt. who was retained by indenture, *anno* 1474, to serve the king (EDWARD IV.) in person in his wars in France, with two men at arms, and four archers. He m. first, Anne, daughter of John Paston, esq. of Paston Hall, in the county of Norfolk, by whom he had issue,

> WILLIAM, who died in his father's lifetime, *s. p.*
>
> Anne, m. to Thomas Jermy, esq. son of Sir John Jermy, knt.
>
> Margaret, m. to John Palgrave, esq. of Norwood Barmingham, in the county of Norfolk.
>
> Eleanor, m. to John Conyers, esq. son and heir of Sir Robert Conyers.

Sir William espoused, secondly, Eleanor, daughter of Sir Thomas Browse, knt. and had a son, his successor,

WILLIAM YELVERTON, esq. of Rougham and Rackheath. This gentleman m. Catherine, daughter of John Raves, esq. of the county of Essex, and had five sons, viz. WILLIAM, his successor, John, Nicholas, Edward, and Adam, and a daughter, Anne, m. to Matthew Canne, esq. of Wessenham, in Norfolk. He was s. at his decease by his eldest son,

WILLIAM YELVERTON, esq. of Rougham, who m. Margaret, daughter of Mr. Gamond, of London, and had two sons, WILLIAM and John, and three daughters, viz.

> Mary, m. first, to William Baker, esq.; and secondly, to Henry Wayte, esq.
>
> Susan, m. first, to Edward Eston, esq. of Rea-ham, in Norfolk; and secondly, to Edward Harvey, esq.
>
> Eleanor, m. to Richard Draper, esq. of Marham in the same county.

William Yelverton d. in the year 1541, and was s. by his elder son,

WILLIAM YELVERTON, esq. of Rougham. This gentleman m. first, Anne, daughter and heir of Sir Henry Fermor, knt. of East Barsham, in Norfolk, by whom he acquired a great increase to his landed possessions, and had issue,

> HENRY, who inherited Rougham, and the other estates of his father, as son and heir. He m. Bridget, daughter of Sir William Drury, of Hawsted, in Suffolk, knt. and had issue,
>
> > WILLIAM, his successor, created a BARONET in 1620. He m. Dionesse, daughter of Richard Stubbs, esq. of Sedgeford, in Norfolk and left
> >
> > > WILLIAM (Sir), second baronet of Rougham, who m. Ursula, daughter of Sir Thomas Richardson, knt. speaker of the House of Commons, and afterwards lord chief justice of the King's Bench, by whom he had, WILLIAM, and two daughters, Elizabeth and Ursula. He d. 19th Jun 1648, and was s. by his son,
> > >
> > > > WILLIAM (Sir), third baronet of Rougham, who died unm. in 1649 when that BARONETCY EXPIRED.
> >
> > Henry (Sir), m. Alice, daughter and co-heir of the Right Rev. William Barlow Bishop of Lincoln.
> >
> > Margaret, m. to Thomas Tyrrell, esq. of Gippinge, in the county of Suffolk.
>
> William.
>
> CHRISTOPHER, of whom presently.
>
> Humphrey.
>
> Launcelot.
>
> Winifred, m. to Owen Duckett, esq. of Wortinag in Norfolk.
>
> Anne, m. first, to Thomas Reade, esq. of Wisbyche; and secondly, to John Hawkins, esq. of Essex.
>
> Martha, m. first, to Thomas Fyncham, esq of Fyncham, in the county of Norfolk; and secondly, to John Higham, esq. of Gifford in Sussex.

Mr. Yelverton m. secondly, Jane, daughter of Edward Cocket, esq. of Ampton, in Suffolk, by whom he had

> Edward.
>
> Charles.
>
> William, m. to Grace, daughter of Mr. Newport of Buckingham.
>
> Jane, m. first, to Edmund Lummer, esq. of Mannington, in Norfolk; and secondly, to John Dodge, esq. of Wrotham, in Kent.
>
> Chrysold, m. first, to Thomas le Strange, son and

heir of Sir Nicholas le Strange; and secondly, to Sir Philip Woodhouse.

The third son of William Yelverton, by his first wife, Anne Fermor,

Christopher Yelverton, being bred to the bar, and called to the degree of serjeant-at-law, was constituted queen's serjeant, 31 Elizabeth. In some years afterwards he was chosen speaker of the House of Commons, and in the 44th of the same reign he was constituted one of the judges of the court of King's Bench. On the accession of *King* James his patent, as a judge, was renewed, and he was then made a knight. Sir Christopher m. Mary, daughter of Thomas Catesby, esq. of Whiston, in the county of Northampton, and had issue,

Henry, his successor.
Christopher (Sir).

Isabel, married to Sir Edward Cope, of Cannon's Ashy, in the county of Northampton.
Anne, m. first, to Thomas Sherland, esq. of the county of Suffolk; and secondly, to Sir Edward Cocket, knt. of Ampton, in the same shire.
Mary, m. to Sir William Gardiner, of Lagham, in Surrey.
Judith, m. to Edmund Abdy, esq. of Lincoln's Inn.

His lordship d. in 1607, at Easton-Mauduit, a seat which he had purchased in Northamptonshire, and was s. by his elder son,

Henry Yelverton, esq. of Easton-Mauduit. This gentleman having, like his father, adopted the profession of the law, was appointed solicitor-general in 1613, and knighted about the same period. In 1617 Sir Henry Yelverton was made attorney-general; previously, however, he is said to have displeased the king by refusing to appear against the Earl of Somerset, at his trial for the murder of Sir Thomas Overbury, and in the October of the year in which he was advanced to the attorney-generalship we find him writing a letter to his royal master, complaining of "his unhappiness to fall under his majesty's displeasure, who had made him almost the wonder of his favour; that he conceived it to arise from some accident, befel in the late business of the marriage of Sir John Villiers; as also from a report, as if he had uttered some speeches to the dishonour of the Earl of Buckingham." He pleaded his cause so successfully, however, that he very soon recovered any ground which he might have lost in James's opinion, but he was not so fortunate with the Duke of Buckingham, who seems, for a long time afterwards, to have regarded him with an evil eye. In 1620, principally through the machinations of that favoured nobleman, he was involved, with the lord mayor of London, and others, in a Star chamber prosecution, regarding the passing of certain clauses in a charter to the city of London, not authorised by the king's warrant; for this offence, although he made every submission, and that the charter was given up, he was adjudged to pay a fine of £4000, to be deprived of the office of attorney-general, and to be committed to the Tower. He was subsequently prosecuted before parliament upon another account, and the house of Lords, 16th May, 1621, proceeded to sentence, and declare, "that the said Sir Henry Yelverton, for his speeches, uttered here in court, which do touch the king's majesty's honour, shall be fined to the king in ten thousand marks, be imprisoned during pleasure, and make submission to the king; and for those which touched the marquess of Buckingham, he should be fined five thousand marks, &c." Upon which Buckingham stood up, and did freely remit his portion of the fine; and the prince and the house agreed to move his majesty to mitigate the other part of the judgment. What proportion of the fine was ultimately forgiven is nowhere mentioned, but his misfortunes very soon afterwards terminated. The Duke of Buckingham visited him *incognito* in the Tower, and Sir Henry making a sufficient apology to his grace, he was presently set at liberty, and became again a practising barrister, until April, 1625, when a gentleman from the duke brought him a warrant from the king, appointing him one of the judges of the court of Common Pleas. In this situation he remained until his decease, 24th January, 1629-30, when his remains were interred in the parish church of Easton-Mauduit. His lordship m. Margaret, daughter of Robert Beale, esq. clerk of the council to *Queen* Elizabeth, and was s. by his eldest son,

I. Sir Christopher Yelverton, knt. of Easton-Mauduit, who was created a Baronet 30th June, 1641. He m. in 1630, Anne, youngest daughter of Sir William Twisden, bart. of Roydon Hall, Kent, by whom he had issue,

Henry, his successor.

Anne, m. first, to Robert, Earl of Manchester; and secondly, to Charles, Earl of Halifax.

Sir Christopher d. 4th December, 1654, and was s. by his son,

II. Sir Henry Yelverton, member for Northamptonshire, in the parliament that voted the restoration of *King* Charles II. He m. Susan, Baroness Grey de Ruthyn, daughter and heiress of Charles Longueville, Lord Grey de Ruthyn, and great-grandaughter of Charles Grey, Earl of Kent, by whom he had issue,

Charles, his successor.
Henry, heir to his brother.
Christopher.

Frances, m. to Francis, Viscount Hatton.

Sir Henry d. 28th January, 1676, and was s. by his eldest son,

III. Sir Charles Yelverton, who, upon the decease of his mother, 28th January, 1676, became Baron Grey de Ruthyn. His lordship d. unm. of the small-pox, 17th May, 1679, and was s. by his brother,

IV. Sir Henry Yelverton, Lord Grey de Ruthyn. This nobleman claimed by inheritance from the Hastings, Earls of Pembroke, the right of carrying the golden spurs at the coronation of *King* James II. and his claim being admitted, he bore them accordingly. His lordship m. Barbara, daughter of John Talbot, esq. of Laycock, in the county of Wilts, and had, with other issue,

Talbot, his successor.
Henry, m. a daughter of Major Carle, and had an only daughter, Barbara, who d. young.

Barbara, m. to Reynolds Calthorpe, esq. of Elvesham, in the county of Northampton.

His lordship was advanced to the dignity of Viscount Longueville, 21st April, 1690. He d. in 1704, and was s. by his elder son,

V. Sir Talbot Yelverton, second Viscount Longueville, who was created, 26th September, 1717, Earl of Sussex, with remainder, in default of his own male issue, to his brother, the Hon. Henry Yelverton, and the heirs male of his body. His lordship was appointed deputy earl-marshal of England in 1725, and he officiated as such at the coronation of *King* George II. He was made a knight of the Bath upon the revival of that order, and subsequently sworn of the privy council. The earl m. Lucy, daughter of Henry Pelham, esq. of Lewes, in Sussex, clerk of the pells, and uncle of Thomas, Duke of Newcastle, by whom he had two sons,

George-Augustus, } successively inheritors of the
Henry, } honours.

The earl, who carried the golden spurs at the coronation of George I. *d.* 27th October, 1730, and was succeeded by his eldest son,

VI. Sir George-Augustus Yelverton, second Earl of Sussex. This nobleman was one of the lords of the bedchamber to Frederick, Prince of Wales, and afterwards to *King* George III. He *d.* unm. 8th January, 1758, and was *s.* by his brother,

VII. Sir Henry Yelverton, third Earl of Sussex. This nobleman *m.* first, Hester, daughter of John Hall, esq. of Mansfield Woodhouse, Notts, and had an only surviving daughter,

- Lady Barbara Yelverton, who *m.* Edward Thoroton Gould, esq. of Woodham-Mansfield, in the county of Notts, and dying in the lifetime of her father, 9th April, 1781, left issue,
  - Henry-Edward Gould, who, upon the death of his grandfather, the Earl of Sussex, became Lord Grey de Ruthyn, and assumed the surname of Yelverton. He *m.* in 1809, Anna-Maria, daughter of William Kellam, esq. and dying the next year, left an only daughter and heiress,
    - Barbara Yelverton, Baroness Grey de Ruthyn, who *m.* 18th August, 1831, George, present Marquess of Hastings.
  - Barbara Gould, *d.* unm.
  - Mary Gould, *m.* to the Hon. and Rev. Frederick Powys, son of Lord Lilford.

The earl espoused secondly, Mary, daughter of John Vaughan, esq. of Bristol, but had no issue. He died in 1799, when the Barony of Grey de Ruthyn devolved upon his grandson, Henry-Edward Gould, esq. who assumed the surname of Yelverton, as stated above, and the Baronetcy, together with the Viscounty of Longueville and the Earldom of Sussex, became extinct.

⁂ The family of Yelverton, Viscounts Avonmore, in Ireland, is a branch of this family.

Arms—Ar. three lions rampant, and a chief gu.

YELVERTON, OF ROUGHAM.

Created 31st May, 1620.—Extinct 15th Nov. 1649.

Lineage.

See Yelverton, of Easton Mauduit.

YONGE, OF CULLETON.

Created 26th Sept. 1661.

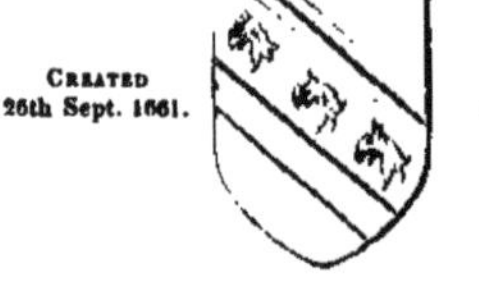

Extinct about 1810.

Lineage.

Thomas Yonge, mayor of Bristol 12 Henry IV. styles himself in his last will and testament, bearing date 14th March, 1426, burgess of Bristol, and orders his body to be buried before the altar of St. Nicholas, in the church of St. Thomas the Martyr. He left two sons, Thomas, of whom presently, and John (Sir), knt. lord mayor of London, and M.P. for that city 33 Henry VI. The elder son,

Thomas Yonge, a distinguished lawyer, and M.P. for Bristol, *temp.* Henry VI. was constituted 15 Edward IV. one of the judges of the court of King's Bench. He *d.* in 1476, was buried in Christ Church, London, and was *s.* by his eldest son,

Thomas Yonge, who had a mansion in Wyn Street, Bristol, and was also of Basilden, Berks, in the church of which place is a grave-stone, bearing a brass plate with a representation, at full length, of a man in armour, for

Roger Yonge, of Basilden, who died 3rd March, 1589, aged ninety-six, after he had continued in the commission of the peace for Berkshire, without any intermission, full sixty years. He is supposed to have been son of Thomas, and grandson of the judge. Contemporary with the said Roger Yonge, and probably his brother,

Walter Yonge, esq. is mentioned in the Visitation of Devonshire to be a younger son of the Yonges of Berkshire, and to have settled in Devon, *temp.* Henry VII. He *m.* twice, and in the latter part of his life resided at Sudburie, where his last will bears date, 2nd February, 1561. By his first wife he had issue,

- I. John, his heir.

- I. Julian, called Julian Berde, in her father's will.
- II. Joan, *m.* to Roger Hayman, esq.
- III. Jane, *m.* to Nicholas Westlake, esq.
- IV. Florence, *m.* to John Pitt, esq.

The only son and successor,

John Yonge, esq. inherited from his father the manors of Cobeton and Botteshorne Paulet, with considerable estates in Dorsetshire, and sat in parliament for the borough of Plymouth. He *m.* Joan, daughter and co-heir of John Colleton, esq. and had issue,

- I. Walter, died *s. p.*
- II. John, successor to his father.
- III. Robert, who *m.* Anne Hassard.

- I. Margaret, *m.* to Hercules Pyne, esq. of H[illegible] Devon.
- II. Alice.
- III. Agnes.
- IV. Helen.

The second, but elder surviving son,

John Yonge, esq. seated at Culliton, Devon, *m.* Alice Starre, and had, with two sons, John, who *d. s. p.* and Walter, his heir, five daughters, namely,

- Jane, *m.* to Richard Mallock, esq. of Axminster, Devon.
- Alice, *m.* to Humphrey Cokeram, esq.
- Anne, *m.* to Robert Hill, esq. of Hollylane, in Somersetshire.
- Jane, *m.* to William Hill, esq. of Pounsford, Somersetshire.
- Mary, *m.* to William Fry, esq. of Yarty, Devon.

The son and successor,

Walter Yonge, esq. of Upton Helion, in Devonshire, living in 1620, M.P. for Honiton, *m.* Jane, daughter and co-heir of Sir John Peryan, knt and had issue, John, his heir; Walter, who *m.* Alice, daughter of Joyles Green, esq. of Purbeck; and Jane, who died unm. The elder son,

I. Sir John Yonge, knt. of Culleton, M.P. for Plymouth, was one of those secluded by Cromwell who denied him and above a hundred entrance into the House of Commons; whereupon they had the courage to publish a remonstrance, asserting the legality of their right to sit in parliament. At the Restoration Sir John was created a Baronet. He *m.* Elizabeth, daughter of Sir William Strode, knt. of Newnham, in Devonshire, and had issue,

heir of Sir Nicholas le Strange; and secondly, to Sir Philip Woodhouse.

The third son of William Yelverton, by his first wife, Anne Fermor,

CHRISTOPHER YELVERTON, being bred to the bar, and called to the degree of serjeant-at-law, was constituted queen's serjeant, 31 ELIZABETH. In some years afterwards he was chosen speaker of the House of Commons, and in the 44th of the same reign he was constituted one of the judges of the court of King's Bench. On the accession of *King* JAMES his patent, as a judge, was renewed, and he was then made a knight. Sir Christopher *m.* Mary, daughter of Thomas Catesby, esq. of Whiston, in the county of Northampton, and had issue,

HENRY, his successor.
Christopher (Sir).

Isabel, married to Sir Edward Cope, of Cannon's Ashy, in the county of Northampton.
Anne, *m.* first, to Thomas Sherland, esq. of the county of Suffolk; and secondly, to Sir Edward Cocket, knt. of Ampton, in the same shire.
Mary, *m.* to Sir William Gardiner, of Lagham, in Surrey.
Judith, *m.* to Edmund Abdy, esq. of Lincoln's Inn.

His lordship *d.* in 1607, at Easton-Mauduit, a seat which he had purchased in Northamptonshire, and was *s.* by his elder son,

HENRY YELVERTON, esq. of Easton-Mauduit. This gentleman having, like his father, adopted the profession of the law, was appointed solicitor general in 1613, and knighted about the same period. In 1617 Sir Henry Yelverton was made attorney-general; previously, however, he is said to have displeased the king by refusing to appear against the Earl of Somerset, at his trial for the murder of Sir Thomas Overbury, and in the October of the year in which he was advanced to the attorney-generalship we find him writing a letter to his royal master, complaining of "his unhappiness to fall under his majesty's displeasure, who had made him almost the wonder of his favour; that he conceived it to arise from some accident, befel in the late business of the marriage of Sir John Villiers; as also from a report, as if he had uttered some speeches to the dishonour of the Earl of Buckingham." He pleaded his cause so successfully, however, that he very soon recovered any ground which he might have lost in JAMES's opinion, but he was not so fortunate with the Duke of Buckingham, who seems, for a long time afterwards, to have regarded him with an evil eye. In 1620, principally through the machinations of that favoured nobleman, he was involved, with the lord mayor of London, and others, in a Star chamber prosecution, regarding the passing of certain clauses in a charter to the city of London, not authorised by the king's warrant; for this offence, although he made every submission, and that the charter was given up, he was adjudged to pay a fine of £4000, to be deprived of the office of attorney general, and to be committed to the Tower. He was subsequently prosecuted before parliament upon another account, and the house of Lords, 16th May, 1621, proceeded to sentence, and declare, "that the said Sir Henry Yelverton, for his speeches, uttered here in court, which do touch the king's majesty's honour, shall be fined to the king in ten thousand marks, be imprisoned during pleasure, and make submission to the king; and for those which touched the Marquess of Buckingham, he should be fined five thousand marks, &c." Upon which Buckingham stood up, and did freely remit his portion of the fine; and the prince and the house agreed to move his majesty to mitigate the other part of the judgment. What proportion of the fine was ultimately forgiven is nowhere mentioned, but his misfortunes very soon afterwards terminated. The Duke of Buckingham visited him *incognito* in the Tower, and Sir Henry making a sufficient apology to his grace, he was presently set at liberty, and became again a practising barrister, until April, 1625, when a gentleman from the duke brought him a warrant from the king, appointing him one of the judges of the court of Common Pleas. In this situation he remained until his decease, 24th January, 1629-30, when his remains were interred in the parish church of Easton-Mauduit. His lordship *m.* Margaret, daughter of Robert Beale, esq. clerk of the council to *Queen* ELIZABETH, and was *s.* by his eldest son,

I. SIR CHRISTOPHER YELVERTON, knt. of Easton-Mauduit, who was created a BARONET 30th June, 1641. He *m.* in 1630, Anne, youngest daughter of Sir William Twisden, bart. of Roydon Hall, Kent, by whom he had issue,

HENRY, his successor.

Anne, *m.* first, to Robert, Earl of Manchester; and secondly, to Charles, Earl of Halifax.

Sir Christopher *d.* 4th December, 1654, and was *s.* by his son,

II. SIR HENRY YELVERTON, member for Northamptonshire, in the parliament that voted the restoration of *King* CHARLES II. He *m.* Susan, BARONESS GREY DE RUTHYN, daughter and heiress of Charles Longueville, Lord Grey de Ruthyn, and great-grandaughter of Charles Grey, Earl of Kent, by whom he had issue,

CHARLES, his successor.
Henry, heir to his brother.
Christopher.

Frances, *m.* to Francis, Viscount Hatton.

Sir Henry *d.* 28th January, 1676, and was *s.* by his eldest son,

III. SIR CHARLES YELVERTON, who, upon the decease of his mother, 28th January, 1676, became BARON GREY DE RUTHYN. His lordship *d.* unm. of the small-pox, 17th May, 1679, and was *s.* by his brother,

IV. SIR HENRY YELVERTON, Lord Grey de Ruthyn. This nobleman claimed by inheritance from the Hastings, Earls of Pembroke, the right of carrying the golden spurs at the coronation of *King* JAMES II. and his claim being admitted, he bore them accordingly. His lordship *m.* Barbara, daughter of John Talbot, esq. of Laycock, in the county of Wilts, and had, with other issue,

TALBOT, his successor.
Henry, *m.* a daughter of Major Carle, and had an only daughter, Barbara, who *d.* young.

Barbara, *m.* to Reynolds Calthorpe, esq. of Elvesham, in the county of Northampton.

His lordship was advanced to the dignity of VISCOUNT LONGUEVILLE, 21st April, 1690. He *d.* in 1704, and was *s.* by his elder son,

V. SIR TALBOT YELVERTON, second Viscount Longueville, who was created, 26th September, 1717, EARL OF SUSSEX, with remainder, in default of his own male issue, to his brother, the Hon. Henry Yelverton, and the heirs male of his body. His lordship was appointed deputy earl-marshal of England in 1725, and he officiated as such at the coronation of *King* GEORGE II. He was made a knight of the Bath upon the revival of that order, and subsequently sworn of the privy council. The earl *m.* Lucy, daughter of Henry Pelham, esq. of Lewes, in Sussex, clerk of the pells, and uncle of Thomas, Duke of Newcastle, by whom he had two sons,

GEORGE AUGUSTUS, } successively inheritors of the
HENRY. } honours.

WALTER, his heir.
Robert.
William, who m. Jane, daughter of Sir John Drake, bart. of Ashe.
George, who died young.

Jane, m. to Sir John Drake, bart. of Trill and Ashe.
Elizabeth, m. to Thomas Hodges, esq. of Shipton Moigne, Gloucestershire.

Sir John d. about 1663, and was s. by his son,

II. SIR WALTER YONGE, of Culleton, who m. Isabel, daughter of Sir John Davie, bart. of Creedy, in Devonshire, and had issue,

John, died unm. v. p.
WALTER, successor to his father.
Francis, died unm.
Charles, d. unm.

Isabella, m. to Richard Duke, esq. of Otterton, Devon.
Jane, d. unm.
Mary, m. to John Walrond, esq.
Elizabeth, m. to Bartholomew Beale, esq. of Heath House, Salop.
Sarah, m. to Robert Yate, esq. of Bristol.

Sir Walter died 21st November, 1670, and was s. by his son,

III. SIR WALTER YONGE, of Culleton, M. P. for Honiton, and one of the commissioners of the Customs, who m. first, Gertrude, daughter of Sir William Morrice, bart of Werrington, in Devon; and secondly, Gwen, daughter and co-heir of Sir Robert Williams, bart. of Penrhyn; by the latter of whom he left one son and three daughters, namely,

WILLIAM, his heir.

Gwen, m. to Arthur Arscot, esq. of Telcot, Devon, M. P.
Jane, who d. 20th May, 1783.
Frances, m. to Edward Sainthill, esq. of Bradninch.

Sir Walter died 18th July, 1731, and was s. by his son,

IV. THE RIGHT HON. SIR WILLIAM YONGE, M. P. for Honiton, constituted, in 1724, one of the lords commissioners of the Treasury; in 1728, one of the commissioners of the Admiralty; and subsequently secretary at war. In 1746, he became one of the joint vice-treasurers of Ireland, and in the same year acted as one of the committee of the Commons for managing the impeachment against Simon, Lord Lovat. Sir William m. first, Mary, daughter of Samuel Heathcote, esq. of Hackney, Middlesex, from whom he was divorced in 1724; and secondly, 14th September, 1729, Anna, daughter and co-heir of Thomas, Lord Howard, of Effingham, by whom he had issue,

GEORGE, his heir.
Howard, who d. young.

Anne.
Louisa, m. to Dr. Charles Howard, dean of Exeter.
Charlotte, m. to James Stuart Fulk, esq.
Amelia, m. to Sir Edward Lloyd, bart. of Pengwern.
Juliana, m. to William Sandford, esq. of Walford, Somersetshire.
Sophia.

Sir William died 10th August, 1755, and was s. by his elder son,

V. THE RIGHT HON. SIR GEORGE YONGE, of Culleton, M.P. for Honiton from 1754 till 1794, who filled successively the appointments of lord commissioner of the Admiralty, of secretary at war, master of the Mint, and governor-general of the Cape of Good Hope. He m. in 1765, Elizabeth, daughter and heir of Bouchier Clieve, esq. of Foots Cray, in Kent, but died s. p. in 1810, when the BARONETCY became EXTINCT.

Arms—Erm. on a bend between two cottises sa. three griffins' heads erased or.

YOUNG.

CREATED 10th March, 1628.—EXTINCT ......

Lineage.

I. RICHARD YOUNG, esq. gentleman of the privy chamber, was created a BARONET in 1628. He m. Martha, sister of Sir William Forth, knt. but dying without issue, the title became EXTINCT.

BARONETCIES

WHICH HAVE BECOME EXTINCT OR BEEN OMITTED DURING THE PROGRESS OF THE WORK.

BERRY, OF CATTON.

CREATED 12th Dec. 1806.—EXTINCT 13th Feb. 1831.

Lineage.

I. SIR EDWARD BERRY, of Catton, in the county of Norfolk, K.C.B. rear-admiral of the White, *b.* in 1768, was created a BARONET in 1806. He *m.* 12th December, 1797, Louisa, daughter of the Rev. Samuel Forster of Norwich, D.D. but had no issue,

This distinguished officer, who was the fourth son of the late Edward Berry, esq. a merchant in London, by Elizabeth, daughter of the Rev. Thomas Forster, of Barbadoes, F.R.S. having evinced an early predilection for the sea-service, was introduced into the royal navy, under the auspices of Lord Mulgrave, on the 5th February, 1779, when he wanted some months of being eleven years of age, and made his first voyage to the East Indies, in the Burford, of seventy guns. From this period, Sir Edward was engaged in continual active service, and reaped an abundant harvest of laurel, during the war previous to the short peace of Amiens, having been the associate of the gallant Nelson, at the Nile, and in other great achievements. Upon the renewal of hostilities, Captain Berry again sailing under the command of the hero of the Nile, engaged in the van division of the fleet in the memorable engagement off Cape Trafalgar, on the 21st of October 1805, and, as usual, sustained his high and bravely-earned reputation. After this engagement, Sir Edward, (who had received the honour of knighthood, on the 12th December, 1798,) proceeded to the West Indies, in the same ship, the Agamemnon, and participated in the victory gained by Sir Thomas Duckworth, 6th February, 1806, off St. Domingo. Upon his subsequent return home, Sir Edward received two medals from the king; one for this action, and another for Trafalgar; and, having previously obtained one for the Nile, he was the only captain in his majesty's service who had been honoured with three medals. He *d.* in 1831, when the BARONETCY became EXTINCT.

Arms—Ermine on a fesse, engr. az. three fleurs de lis or, in a chief two branches of palm, in saltier vert; in base a sphinx, couchant, ppr.

DOLBEN.

CREATED 1st April, 1704.—EXTINCT 27th Sept. 1837.

Lineage.

This ancient family is descended from that of D'Albini, Earls of Sussex and Barons Dutton, *temp.* HENRY II. The present genealogy ascends to the reign of EDWARD IV. at which time they had large possessions in Caernarvonshire and Denbighshire, and were connected by marriage with some of the first families in the Principality. In the line of descent they stand thus: *Hugh D'Albini*, *Humphrey Dalbin*, *John Dalbin*, *William Dalben*; this last was rector of Stanwick, in Northamptonshire, and nominated bishop of Rochester, but died before consecration. He was first cousin to David Doulben, or Dolben, rector of Hackney and bishop of Bangor.

JOHN DOLBEN, archbishop of York, prior to entering into holy orders, was a military officer, and distinguished himself upon active service during the civil wars, under the royal standard, particularly at the defence of York, where he was severely wounded. He was lord-high-almoner and clerk of the closet to CHARLES II. and, during the prohibition of the Liturgy, was accustomed to read it in a house opposite All Souls' College, of which a memorial is preserved in a fine painting, by Sir Peter Lily, at Finedon, a copy of which hangs in the hall of Christ Church, Oxford. He *m.* Mary, niece of Archbishop Sheldon, and was *s.* by his son,

I. GILBERT DOLBEN, one of the justices of the Court of Common Pleas in Ireland, who was created a BARONET, 1st April, 1704. Sir Gilbert, *m.* Anne, eldest daughter and co-heir of Tanfield Mulso, esq. of Finedon, in the county of Northampton, and dying in 1722, (two years after his retirement from the bench,) was *s.* by his only son,

II. THE REV. SIR JOHN DOLBEN, prebendary of Durham, *b.* 12th February, 1683-4, who *m.* Elizabeth, second daughter of William, Lord Digby, by whom he had,

- WILLIAM, his successor.
- Elizabeth, *m.* to John-Nicholls Raynsford, esq. of Brixworth, in Northamptonshire, and *d.* his widow in 1810.
- Frances, } *d.* unm.
- Anne, } *d.* unm.

He *d.* 20th November, 1756, and was *s.* by his son,

III. SIR WILLIAM DOLBEN. This gentleman, who represented the University of Oxford for more than thirty years in parliament, *m.* first, 17th May, 1748, Judith, daughter and sole heir of Somerset English, esq. by whom he had

- JOHN-ENGLISH, present baronet.
- Anne-Juliana, *d.* in 1804.

He wedded, secondly, 14th October, 1789, Charlotte, daughter of Gilbert Affleck, esq. of Dalham Hall, in Suffolk, and widow of John Scotchmer, esq. but by her, who *d.* 12th March, 1820, had no issue. He *d.* 20th March, 1814, and was *s.* by his son,

IV. SIR JOHN ENGLISH DOLBEN, *b.* in 1750, who *m.* in 1779, Hannah, daughter of William Hallet, esq. of Cannons, in Middlesex, and had issue,

- WILLIAM-SAUNDERS, who *m.* Frances, daughter of Captain Walter Saunders, and died in 1817, leaving two daughters.

Anne-Juliana, } one of whom is married.
Frances, }

Juliana.

Charlotte, *m.* in 1806, to the Rev. Samuel Woodfield Paul, and has issue.

Louisa.

Sir English died 27th September, 1837, when the BARONETCY became EXTINCT. "This remarkable personage," says a recent writer in the Gentleman's Magazine, "was much attached to classical literature and antiquities, and like his father, was a zealous supporter of the Established Church, but a sincere friend to toleration. Previously to his final retirement into the country, he lingered with much affection about the haunts of his youthful studies and amusements, being alike remarkable for his venerable deportment and harmless eccentricity. He was a constant visitor at the commemoration dinners at Christchurch; and he frequently joined the juvenile ranks at Westminster School, whom he would accompany to service at the Abbey, saying he was the youngest among them, beginning to count afresh from the age of seventy. He had his cards printed in black letter type, saying that he was himself "old English," and that was the most appropriate style for him. He carried so many small volumes about with him in his numerous and capacious pockets, that he appeared like a walking library; and his memory, particularly in classical quotations, was equally richly stored. About 1820, he visited Italy, taking with him Mr. G. Tytler, a Scotch artist, who afterwards published a large panoramic view of Edinburgh, and also several lithographic views in Italy, in which the figure of Sir English frequently occurs."

Arms—Sa. a helmet close between three pheons arg.

ELFORD, OF BICKHAM.

CREATED 26th Nov. 1800.—EXTINCT in 1837.

Lineage.

This family, of considerable antiquity in Devonshire, acquired the estate of Sheepstor, in that county, by marriage with Joan, daughter and co-heir of John Scudamore, of Scudamore, whose ancestors appear to have held that place as early as the reign of RICHARD II. JOHN ELFORD, of Sheepstor, son of Joan Scudamore, *d.* in 1517. From him descended

JOHN ELFORD, of Sheepstor, *b.* in 1604, who had for his second wife, Anne, daughter of John Northcote, of Hayne, in the county of Devon, by whom he had issue,

Walter, of Sheepstor, whose son John, *d. s. p.* in 1748, when that line became extinct.

Jonathan, of Bickham, in the county of Devon,

who *d.* in 1690, leaving a son John, M.P. for Saltash, who *d. s. p.* November, 1755.

WILLIAM.

The youngest son,

WILLIAM ELFORD, a merchant of Plymouth, *m.* Mary, daughter of John Tollard, esq. and left an only surviving son,

JOHN ELFORD, esq. of Plymouth, who *m.* Jenny, daughter of Thomas Cromphorne, esq. and dying in 1732, left issue,

Jonathan, *b.* in 1717, *d.* unm. in 1756.

LANCELOT, of whom presently.

Agnes, *m.* to William Wyatt, esq.

Jenny, *m.* to Thomas Veale, esq. of Coffleet.

Lucretia, *m.* to the Rev. John Bedford.

Sarah.

Amy, *d.* unm.

The second son,

THE REV. LANCELOT ELFORD, vicar of Plympton, in the county of Devon, *m.* Grace, daughter of Alexander Wills, of Kingsbridge, in the county of Devon, and *d.* in February, 1782, leaving issue,

WILLIAM, present baronet.

Jonathan, of Devenport, *m.* Mary, daughter of Henry Luxmore, esq. of Oakhampton, in the county of Devon.

Jenny, *m.* George Leach, esq. of Plymouth.

The elder son,

I. WILLIAM ELFORD, esq. of Bickham, in the county of Devon, F.R.S. was created a BARONET, 26th November, 1800. He *m.* first, Mary, daughter of the Rev. John Davis, of Plympton, by whom (who *d.* in 1817) he had issue,

Jonathan, *m.* in 1810, Charlotte, only daughter and heiress of John Wynne, esq. of Abercynlleth, in the county of Denbigh, and *d. s. p.* 11th March, 1823.

Grace-Chard.

Sir William *m.* secondly, Mrs. Walrond, relict of Colonel Walrond, and daughter and co-heiress of Humphrey Hall, esq. of Manadon, Devonshire. Sir William, who was recorder of Plymouth, *d.* in 1837, when the title became EXTINCT.

Arms—Per pale ar. and az. a lion rampant gu.

VAN FREISENDORF, OF HIRDECK.

CREATED 4th Oct. 1661.—EXTINCT ......

Lineage.

I. SIR JOHN FREDERICK VAN FREISENDORF, Lord of Kymp, in Sweden, counsellor to the king of that country, and ambassador to CHARLES II. was created a BARONET in 1661, but of him nothing further is known.

THE END.

C. Whittingham, Tooks Court, Chancery Lane.

BRITISH ORNITHOLOGY.

Just published, illustrated by numerous engravings, Vol. 1, 8vo. handsomely bound in cloth, price 16s.

A HISTORY OF BRITISH BIRDS, INDIGENOUS AND MIGRATORY:

Including their Organization, Habits, and Relations: Remarks on Classification and Nomenclature, an Account of the principal Organs of Birds, and Observations relative to Practical Ornithology: by WILLIAM MACGILLIVRAY, M.A., F.R.S.E., Member of the Natural History Societies of Edinburgh and Philadelphia: and Conservator of the Museum of the Royal College of Surgeons, Edinburgh.

The present volume contains the Introduction, embracing remarks on Classification and Nomenclature, and on the Structure of Birds; also descriptions of the Rasores, Scrapers, or Gallinaceous Birds, as Pheasants, Partridges, Grouse, Ptarmigan, &c.; Gemitores, Cooers, as Pigeons; Deglubitores, Huskers, or Conirostral Birds, as Finches, Sparrows, Linnets, &c.; Vagatores, Wanderers, as Crows, Magpies, Starlings, &c.

It is important to state that this is the only work which describes the Anatomical and Physiological structure of British Birds, which is of so much importance to every one who is desirous of studying the subject to advantage. It has been the object of the author, in the Introduction, to communicate as much information regarding the structure of birds, as may render the subsequent descriptions perfectly intelligible, even to the non-scientific reader. He states that many persons have been deterred from studying the anatomy of birds by a vague idea of its difficulty, but he assures them that such is not the case, and that even a slight general knowledge of their organization will give an interest to the details of their habits and economy, which can scarcely be felt, or at least adequately experienced, by one who only knows that they are organized beings. Such anatomical details, therefore, are introduced as are absolutely necessary to be known before any real knowledge of the relations of the species can be obtained. The entire series of the digestive apparatus, comprehending the bill, the tongue, the throat, the gullet, the crop, the proventriculus, the stomach or gizzard, the intestine, and its cœcal appendages, has been described in all cases, excepting those in which it was found impossible to procure recent specimens. The author has given descriptions, which he believes will be found more extended and more correct than any previously offered to the public. The ordinal, family and generic characters are described at length. The specific forms are minutely described, reference being made in each case to the general appearance, the bill, the feet, the wings, the tail, the plumage, the organs of sense, the intestinal canal, the sexual distinctions, the variations, the modes of walking and flying, the ordinary habits, the nestling, the food, and the various uses and relations of the bird treated of. The changes that take place in the plumage, the distribution of the species, their migrations, natural affinities, and other circumstances, are also described; and when occasions are offered, critical and explanatory remarks respecting families, genera, and species, are introduced.

It is contemplated that the work will extend to four volumes, each of which will be printed and illustrated uniformly with the present one.

Mr. Audubon, the celebrated American naturalist, in a letter to the publishers, remarks, "From the practical knowledge which I have acquired of the Birds of Europe, and more especially of those which inhabit Great Britain, either as constant residents or otherwise, I look on Mr. Macgillivray's History of British Birds, Indigenous and Migratory, as the best work on British Ornithological science with which I am acquainted."—*John J. Audubon, Feb.* 10, 1838.

The following are a few of the critical notices of Mr. Macgillivray's History of British Birds, Indigenous and Migratory, that have already appeared:—

"This work is a valuable addition to British Ornithology. Of all the portions of the science of Natural History, the knowledge of birds has hitherto been the least certain, and least definite; naturalists seem to have an extraordinary reluctance to act towards birds as they have to the other members of the animal kingdom: struck with the outward form of birds, they appear to have proceeded in the inspection of them no further than the plumage, beak, legs, or claws. Thus Linnæus grounds his system on the shape of the feet and bill—Vieillot, his upon the legs. Mr. Macgillivray is the first who has applied internal investigation to the study of birds, in its fullest extent; if he conclude his task with the same spirit, energy, and ability, that he has shewn in its commencement, he may fairly claim a place among the first Ornithologists of any age or time.—*Literary Gazette.*

"Mr. Macgillivray has not confined his labours to the study, the parlour, or the museum, taking his account of the structure and habits of birds from books, of their plumage from dried skins, and of their form and appearance from stuffed specimens stuck on perches. On the contrary, he has followed them to their haunts, he has observed them at all seasons, at all hours, and in all weathers, he has shot them, he has measured, he has dissected, he has anatomized them, and now, after a pleasing, though toilsome and protracted labour of twenty years, he has given part of the results to the world in a first volume, which contains four genera. The account of the habits of birds are written with the freshness, distinctness, and form, which characterize the original observer: the chapters on Practical Ornithology have a dramatic terseness and spirit about them, which reminds us of Izaac Walton."—*Spectator.*

"After a careful inspection of the work, we have no hesitation in saying, that it presents a much more complete and accurate account of those orders than any other work in existence. The descriptions are not derived from the works of other naturalists, but from personal inspection. The fidelity which this has given to his accounts, both of the organization and habits of the birds, is beyond all price."—*Chambers' Journal.*

Just published, in one volume, 12mo. with wood-cuts, Price 9s.

ELEMENTS OF PHYSIOLOGY;

Being an Account of the Laws and Principles of the Animal Economy, especially in Reference to the Constitution of Man. By Thomas Johnstone Aitkin, M.D., Lecturer on Physiology and Materia Medica, Fellow of the Royal College of Surgeons, Edinburgh, &c. &c.

It has been a matter of surprise, that in the advanced education of the present day so few attempts have been made to render the important study of Physiology a branch of general instruction—as a knowledge of the structure of the human body cannot but be considered by every cultivated, intelligent, and inquiring mind as a most desirable acquisition; to promote this object the author has been desirous to give such an account of the structure of the animal body, and especially of that of man, as may be readily understood by those who may not previously have directed their attention to investigations of this kind. He has freed his descriptions from unnecessary technical details, and such explanations as are not adapted to the purposes of general education; and he has also studiously made use of such language as is in accordance with the strictest propriety. Therefore he trusts that he has succeeded in producing a work which will enable any one of moderate acuteness of observation to become acquainted with the wonderful structure of their own bodies, and of the many beautiful illustrations of divine wisdom which that study will disclose to them.

NATURAL PHILOSOPHY.

Just published, in one volume, 12mo. with numerous figures, price 9s.

THE ELEMENTS OF PHYSICS.

By Thomas Webster, M.A. of Trinity College, Cambridge; Fellow of the Cambridge Philosophical Society, and Secretary to the Institution of Civil Engineers. This work contains, I. Introductory Observations. II. Properties of Bodies. III. Proportion and Constitution of Solids. IV. Laws of Equilibrium and Motion. V. Gravity. VI. Hydrostatics. VII. Capillary Theory. VIII. Acoustics. IX. Heat. X. Optics. XI. Electricity, Galvanism, and Magnetism. XII. Concluding Observations.

The object of the author has been to set forth a scheme of that part of Natural Philosophy, which is generally included in the term Physics, on a plan calculated to lead the student regularly through the various subjects, and to engender the habit of systematizing and of arranging his knowledge. It has been his especial aim in this work to familiarize the student with processes, reasonings, just inferences, and inductions, rather than to present to him a collection of facts; and he trusts that he has, in some measure, succeeded in compiling a Treatise exhibiting, in a mathematical form, but without mathematical technicalities and symbols, the various process by which the establishment of any proposition in Physics is arrived at, and the nature of the evidence which enables us to speak with confidence of the truth of any theory.

"This work merits considerable praise for simplicity of style and felicity of illustration; it is easier to read than Arnot's book, as it does not require the same study and fixity of attention, and it is therefore better suited to those who wish to acquire an elementary knowledge of Physical science."—*Athenæum.*

"This is an excellent work, and calculated to effect much good, more especially in these times, when a knowledge of the phenomena of nature is felt to be necessary to complete the education of the scholar, as well as to aid the views and promote the schemes of the artizan. The laws of mechanics, fluids, sound, heat, electricity and magnetism, are explained at considerable length, and illustrated throughout by easy and suitable diagrams, and the language, though in a great measure divested of mathematical technicalities, is clear and concise. It will be found no less advantageous to the mechanic in his workshop, or to the student previous to his entering on a course of philosophy in any of our Universities."—*Glasgow Courier.*

II.

Complete in one volume, with 185 wood-cuts, frontispiece and vignette,
Price, bound in cloth, 4s.

SCIENTIFIC DIALOGUES,

Intended for the Instruction and Entertainment of Young People; in which the first Principles of *Natural* and *Experimental Philosophy* are fully explained. By the Rev. J. Joyce.

This well-known and very much-admired elementary treatise on Natural Philosophy has never been surpassed. The object of the author has been to present a complete compendium of natural and experimental philosophy, not only adapted to the understandings of young people, but well calculated also to convey that familiar instruction which is necessary before they can attend public lectures with advantage.

III.

Just published, in one volume, with numerous Wood-cuts,

COMSTOCK'S SYSTEM OF NATURAL PHILOSOPHY;

In which the Elements of that Science are familiarly explained, and adapted to the Comprehension of Young Pupils. By JOHN L. COMSTOCK, M.D. A new edition, carefully revised, and enlarged with additions on the Air Pump, Steam Engine, &c. By GEORGE LEES, M.A. Lecturer on Natural Philosophy, &c. Edinburgh. With appropriate Questions on each page for the Examination of Scholars.

BOTANY.

A new edition, in one volume, 12mo. with 214 figures, Price 9s.

INTRODUCTION TO PHYSIOLOGICAL AND SYSTEMATICAL BOTANY.

By SIR JAMES EDWARD SMITH, M.D., F.R.S., late President of the Linnæan Society. A new Edition, with considerable Additions, by WILLIAM MACGILLIVRAY, A.M., F.R.S.E., &c., Editor of the new edition of Withering's Botany.

"The utility of this work has been amply evinced by the number of editions which it has gone through, and in having been very generally used by teachers of the science as a class-book. The exposition of the Linnæan system, which it contains, is confessed to be a master-piece, and the explanations of the various organs with reference to descriptive botany are clear and sufficiently minute for ordinary purposes. The editor has therefore only considered it necessary to add a chapter containing some remarks on the natural system, or that mode of arranging plants by which it is attempted to exhibit their mutual relations."—*The Editor.*

II.

The fourth edition, in one volume, 12mo., price, bound in cloth, 10s. 6d.

A SYSTEMATIC ARRANGEMENT OF BRITISH PLANTS.

By W. WITHERING, M.D. *Condensed and brought down to the present period.* Preceded by an Introduction to the Study of Botany, accompanied with 155 Figures and one coloured Plate. By WILLIAM MACGILLIVRAY, A.M., F.R.S.E., Conservator of the Royal College of Surgeons, Edinburgh.

This work comprises a description of the Plants of Great Britain and Ireland, and it has been the especial object of the author to free the descriptions as much as possible of foreign words, provided it could be done without sacrificing the technical terms, which are in every science necessary for preventing verbosity, and giving precision and perspicuity; also, by giving the descriptions sufficiently full, so as to enable the young botanist to determine every species that might come in his way without the assistance of others. The Cryptogamic plants, with the exception of the Ferns, have been omitted, as too difficult for the student, until he has rendered the more attractive species familiar.

In one volume, 12mo. price 7s. 6d.

PARKES'S CHEMICAL CATECHISM.

A new Edition, Revised throughout, Corrected, and considerably Enlarged, by William Barker, M.B., of Trinity College, Dublin.

As many important changes have taken place in the different branches of Chemistry, especially in nomenclature and classification, since the publication of the last edition prepared by Mr. Parkes, the present editor, as far as was consistent with retaining the character and plan of the original work, has altered and revised it throughout, so as to adapt it to the present state of Chemical Science.

Just published, in crown 8vo., with frontispiece, Price 7s.

ON THE BEAUTIFUL, THE PICTURESQUE, AND THE SUBLIME.

By the Rev. J. G. Macvicar, M.A.

"This volume proves the author to be an elegant and refined scholar, and a writer of research and thought. His style is lucid and easy, which renders it pleasing to the general reader, and its importance will enhance its value in the eyes of the scholar. He puts his readers in possession of notions of the beautiful and sublime at once clear and concise—its physics and philosophy be fully displays, and for the entire enjoyment of it he, in conclusion, strongly inculcates the necessity of religious meditation, and the sublime contemplation of the Godhead."—*Literary Gazette.*

In royal quarto, half-cloth, Price £1. 1s.

RUBIE'S BRITISH CELESTIAL ATLAS;

Being a complete Guide to the Attainment of a Practical Knowledge of the Heavenly Bodies, containing Twelve Royal Quarto Maps, or entire Views of the Starry Heavens, as they appear to the naked eye; adapted for every Night throughout the Year: on which are carefully laid down all the Stars visible in the British Empire, from the first to the fourth magnitude; with the boundaries of the Constellations accurately defined. Also three moveable plates, and a plate of Diagrams, to elucidate the Motions of the Earth and the Celestial Bodies. Accompanied by a familiar Treatise on Astronomy. By G. Rubie.

A new edition, 12mo. bound, Price 4s.

ETON GREEK GRAMMAR;

With copious English Notes, intended to explain the Principles on which many of the Rules were established. By the Rev. P. Homer, B.D., Thirty Years a Master in Rugby School.

Lately published, in 1 Vol. 8vo. price 9s. in cloth,

Dedicated by permission to his Grace the Archbishop of Canterbury.

BURNET'S EXPOSITION OF THE THIRTY-NINE ARTICLES OF THE CHURCH OF ENGLAND.

With an Appendix, containing the Confession of Augsburg, the Creed of Pope Pius IV., &c. Revised and corrected, with copious Notes and additional Scripture References, by the Rev. James Robert Page, A.M., of Queen's College, Cambridge, Minister of Carlisle Chapel.

*** In this Edition the text of Burnet has been preserved with strict fidelity: the numerous references to the Fathers, Councils, &c., have been verified, and, in many instances, so enlarged and corrected, that they may be found without difficulty: many Scripture references have been added: the most important Canons and Decrees of the Councils referred to have been given in the original; and, lastly, copious Notes have been added, containing an account of the lives and opinions of the principal heretics mentioned by Burnet, and a body of controversial divinity, chiefly selected from the most eminent Divines of the sixteenth and seventeenth centuries.

"The valuable References, Notes, and Indices, which accompany your edition, will give it a vast superiority over every other."—*The Lord Bishop of Winchester.*

"The Editor has given to our clergy and our students in theology an edition of this work, which must necessarily supersede every other, and we feel he deserves well at the hands of the Church of England, which he has so materially served."—*Church of England Quarterly Review.*

"It may be predicted that this edition of Bishop Burnet's Work will henceforth be one of the most popular. It is enriched with excellent Notes from Bishop Jewell, Hooker, &c. &c., and with very useful compendiums of information on ecclesiastical points, furnished by the Editor himself."—*British Magazine.*

Complete in one Vol. 8vo. with Portrait, Price 9s.

BISHOP BUTLER'S WORKS:

Containing the Analogy of Religion, and Sermons preached at the Rolls' Chapel; with Life by Dr. Halifax, Bishop of Gloucester.

"Whoever wishes to know the analogy of religion to the constitution and course of nature, has no where else to go to but to Butler—no man has attempted to carry it beyond the point where he left it. His work stands like one of those vast piles of architecture commenced in the middle ages, proofs of consummate skill, of vast power, of amazing wealth, yet in some respects incomplete or disproportioned, but which no one since has dared to remodel, and which no one, perhaps, has had either the wealth, power, or genius, to make more complete."—*Albert Barnes.*

"The Analogy of Religion has fixed the admiration of all competent judges for nearly a century, and will continue to be studied as long as the language in which he wrote endures."—*The Right Rev. Daniel Wilson, Bishop of Calcutta.*

"I have derived greater aid from the views and reasoning of Butler, than I have been able to find besides, in the whole range of our existent authorship. The Sermons may be safely pronounced the most precious repository of sound ethical principles extant in any language."—*Dr. Chalmers' Bridgewater Treatise.*

In one volume, 8vo. Price 4s. 6d.

BUTLER'S ANALOGY OF RELIGION,
And Life, by Dr. Halifax.

In one volume, 8vo. Price 4s. 6d.

BUTLER'S SERMONS, Preached at the Rolls' Chapel.

Complete in 1 Vol. 8vo. with Portrait, price 9s.

HORNE'S COMMENTARY ON THE PSALMS:

In which their literal or historical sense, as they relate to King David, and the People of Israel, is illustrated; and their application to Messiah, to the Church, and to Individuals, as members thereof, is pointed out.

"His Commentary on the Psalms has long been a refreshing and delightful companion in the Christian's retirement—it is spiritual and devotional."—*Bickersteth.*

"It will be known so long as piety and elegant learning are loved in England. It is altogether a beautiful work. The preface is a masterpiece of composition and good sense."—*W. Orme.*

Complete in 1 Vol. 8vo. Price 9s.

BISHOP HORSLEY'S SERMONS.

The whole of the Three Volumes is contained in this Edition.

"His powers of mind were of a high order; his Sermons and his other works will render assistance to the student chiefly in the way of criticism."—*Bickersteth.*

Complete in one Vol. 8vo. with Portrait, Price 9s.

BISHOP NEWTON'S DISSERTATION ON THE PROPHECIES,

Which have remarkably been fulfilled, and at this time are fulfilling, in the world. Edited by the Rev. W. S. Dobson, M.A., Peterhouse, Cambridge.

The great value of this celebrated Dissertation on the Prophecies, both to the learned and to the general reader of Scripture, has induced the Editor to spare no pains to render the present edition correct. For this purpose the text and notes have been closely revised, and the classical quotations and references compared with the original authorities. It is hoped, therefore, that this edition (which has been stereotyped) will be found worthy of public attention for its superior correctness, and as a valuable reprint of one of the most enlightened treatises on the subject of prophecy, which exists in the language.

Complete in one Vol. 8vo. Price 10s. 6d.

PEARSON'S EXPOSITION OF THE CREED.

With an Appendix, containing the principal Greek and Latin Creeds. Revised and corrected, by the Rev. W. S. Dobson, M.A., Peterhouse, Cambridge.

In this Edition great care has been taken to correct the numerous errors in the references to the texts of Scripture which had crept in by reason of the repeated editions through which this admirable Work has passed; and many references, as will be seen on turning to the Index of Texts, have been added.

The Quotations in the Notes have been almost universally identified, and the references to them adjoined.

The principal Symbola, or Creeds, of which the particular Articles have been cited by the Author, have been annexed; and wherever the original writers have given the Symbols in a scattered and disjointed manner, the detached parts have been brought into a successive and connected point of view. These have been added in chronological order in the form of an Appendix.

"An excellent work, containing a body of divinity."—*Bickersteth.*

Complete in one Vol. 8vo. Price 12s.

AMBROSE SERLE'S HORÆ SOLITARIÆ;

Or, Essays upon some remarkable Names and Titles of Jesus Christ and the Holy Spirit, occurring in the Old and New Testaments, and declarative of their essential Divinity and gracious Offices in the Salvation of Man. To which is annexed, an Essay, chiefly Historical, upon the Doctrine of the Trinity; and a brief account of the Heresies relative to the Doctrine of the Holy Spirit which have been published since the Christian Era.

"A very devotional and experimental work, and full of fine feeling."—*Bickersteth.*

The title Horæ Solitariæ was applied to these papers because they were the employment of many *Solitary Hours* of retreat from the business of the world. The two series of Essays beyond the particular subject of each concur in one common design, to shew that the doctrine of a Trinity of Persons in one and the *same* Jehovah is essential to the very being of the *Christian religion*; and that the practical use or *an experience* of this truth, uniting and combining all the other principles of the faith, is the proper constituent of the *Christian life.*

Royal 18mo. Portrait, Price 7s.

TAYLOR'S (Dr. Jeremy) HOLY LIVING AND DYING;

Together with Prayers, containing the whole Duty of a Christian.

A new edition, plates, 12mo. bound in sheep, Price 3s. 6d.

A short View of the whole SCRIPTURE HISTORY;

With a Continuation of the Jewish Affairs from the Old Testament till the time of Christ, and an Account of the chief Prophecies that relate to Him: represented in a way of Question and Answer. By Isaac Watts, D.D.

Lately published, in one volume, 18mo. cloth, Price 4s.

THE FEMALE STUDENT;

Or, Lectures to Young Ladies, on Female Education. For the use of Mothers, Teachers, and Pupils. By Mrs. Phelps, late Vice-Principal of Troy Female Seminary, America.

The object of this admirable work on Female Education is, "to give general instruction on subjects connected with literature, morals, and religion; to consider the nature and objects of education, the various branches of study, with their practical application, female manners and accomplishments, and the peculiar duties of woman in her domestic relations, towards society and towards her Maker."—*See Preface.*

"We have been exceedingly pleased with the strain of piety which pervades it. In almost every lecture the all-important subject of religion is pressed upon the attention. This, we think, is a most valuable and praiseworthy qualification in a book intended both as a guide to parents and teachers for the instruction of the young, and as a book for the learner's own perusal."—*Scottish Guardian.*

Second edition, neatly bound in silk, with gilt edges, Price 3s.

THE MORAL MUSE:

For Young Ladies. Comprising Education and Manners—Virtues and the Passions—Human Life—Nature and Time—Religion—Miscellanies. By Miss Emma Price.

The Editor has been careful in every one of the accompanying Selections, not only to present a *pleasing image* to the reader, but more especially to make the beauty subservient to the production of a salutary impression, and to convey whatever is adapted to embellish the manners and purify the morals of the rising generation.

In one volume, foolscap 8vo. bound in embossed roan, gilt leaves, Price 6s.

SUNDAY EVENINGS;

Or, an Easy Introduction to the Reading of the Bible, in language adapted to the capacity of Children. By a Lady.

"The author feels it necessary to state, that in looking anxiously for an interesting book which should serve to introduce her own children to the knowledge of Scripture history, in a manner at once attractive and easy, she was led to observe that most of the works published with this view are written in so abridged a form as to deprive the sacred story of those numerous charms with which it is clothed in the Bible itself—charms of which children are so far from being insensible, when presented to them in *language* adapted to their years, that no subject seems to possess for them half that lively interest which their young minds attach to the simple, the diversified, the picturesque, and affecting narratives which abound in the Word of God. Therefore, to supply such a defect has been the end at which the author has *aimed*. She is also anxious to state, that her object has not been to *supersede*, but to *assist*, the reading of the sacred volume: to furnish, as it were, a running exposition and development of the inspired narrative, by supplying at once that explanation or information which the mother or instructor would otherwise have to give, and, in many cases, to acquire from a variety of sources, at the expense of much time and trouble."—*See Preface.*

In one volume 12mo. bound in cloth, Price 6s.

EVENINGS AT HOME;

Consisting of a Variety of Miscellaneous Pieces for the Instruction and Amusement of Young Persons. By Dr. Aikin and Mrs. Barbauld. With Frontispiece and Vignette, and Twenty Illustrations, engraved on Steel.

"I am well convinced, that the child who, till its eighth or ninth year, is restricted to this book alone, for its literary amusement, will at the end of that period be found possessed of a greater number of clear and distinct ideas, and of a greater vigour and conception, than one that has run over all the instructive and entertaining stories that ever were written for children of that age."—*Miss Hamilton on Education.*

Printed in a large type and on thick paper. Price, half-bound, 2s. 6d.

BARBAULD'S LESSONS FOR CHILDREN:

With Ten Plates.

"It was found that, amidst the multitude of books professedly written for children, there is not one adapted to the comprehension of a child from two to three years old. Another great defect is the want of *good paper, a clear and large type,* and *large spaces.* They only who have actually taught young children, can be sensible how necessary these assistances are. To supply these deficiencies is the object of this book."—*Author's Preface.*

Frontispiece and Vignette, half-bound, Price 2s.

THE BLOSSOMS OF MORALITY.

Intended for the Amusement and Instruction of Young Ladies and Gentlemen.

Frontispiece and Vignette, half-bound, Price 2s.

THE LOOKING-GLASS FOR THE MIND;

Or, Intellectual Mirror; being an elegant Collection of the most delightful Little Stories and Interesting Tales.

Frontispiece and Vignette, half-bound, Price 2s.

MRS. TRIMMER'S EASY INTRODUCTION TO THE KNOWLEDGE OF NATURE,

And Reading the Holy Scriptures. Adapted to the Capacities of Children.

Illustrated with Twelve Plates, Price 3s. half-bound,

MRS. TRIMMER'S FABULOUS HISTORIES;

Or, the History of the Robins. Designed for the Instruction of Children respecting their Treatment of Animals.

In one volume, foolscap 8vo. with Portrait. Price, bound in cloth, 8s.

THE LIFE OF LORENZO DE' MEDICI.

By William Roscoe, Esq. F.L.S., &c. With a Memoir of the Author, by his Son, Thomas Roscoe, Esq.

In the present edition the text has been preserved entire, and the editor has taken great pains to correct the errors of former editions; but the Appendix, containing the Italian and Latin Illustrations, has been omitted as an unnecessary encumbrance to the work, and only such notes have been retained as were considered necessary to the understanding of the text.

In one volume, 12mo. bound in cloth, Price 6s.

THE SURPRISING ADVENTURES OF ROBINSON CRUSOE.

Complete Edition. With a Life of Defoe; with Frontispiece and Vignette, and Twenty Illustrations.

"Was there ever any thing written by mere man that the reader wished longer, excepting Robinson Crusoe, Don Quixote, and the Pilgrim's Progress?"—*Dr. Johnson.*

"How happy that this, the most moral of Romances, is not only the most charming of books, but the most instructive."—*A. Chalmers.*

"No fiction in any language was ever better supported than these Adventures of Robinson Crusoe."—*Dr. Blair.*

"Crusoe has obtained a ready passport to the mansions of the *rich* and the cottages of the *poor*, and communicated equal delight to all ranks and classes of the community Few works have been more generally read, or more justly admired; few that have yielded such incessant amusement, and, at the same time, have developed so many lessons of practical instruction."—*Sir W. Scott.*

In one volume, 12mo. bound in cloth, Price 6s.

THE HISTORY OF SANDFORD AND MERTON.

By Thomas Day, Esq.; with Frontispiece and Vignette, and Twenty Illustrations, engraved on Steel.

"This well-known and popular work has been read by many a boy with delight and instruction, and will continue to communicate equal delight to those that are to follow. It was the object of the author to convey to the youthful mind such useful impressions as were calculated to promote the formation of a generous, a contented, and a manly character—and it is even more adapted to the state of society at present than it was at the period when it was written."

In a small 32mo volume, with Portrait of Newton, and Vignette, bound in cloth and gilt edges, Price 2s.; in silk, 2s. 6d.; and in morocco, 3s. 6d.

OLNEY HYMNS,

By the Rev. John Newton and William Cowper, Esq.

Price 12s. bound in cloth, or handsomely bound in morocco, 16s.

SELECTIONS FROM THE ENGLISH POETS;

From Spenser to Beattie, with Twenty-five Illustrations, from Designs by H. Corbould, and engraved by C. Heath, C. Rolls, W. Finden, &c. This beautiful volume has been illustrated upon the plan of 'Rogers' Italy, and Poems,' and the 'Pilgrims of the Rhine.'

"In the beauty of its embellishments this volume deserves to be classed with the Annuals; while in its letter-press it is as undying as the language in which it is written. In the selection from the poets a sound judgment, a classical taste, and a poetic fancy, have been exercised."—*The Sun.*

"Great care has been exercised in selecting nothing unfit for the eye of youth; and as the authors are arranged in chronological order, and the samples of each poet stand together, it presents something like a notion of the progress of English Poetry, and its style in different ages. It is a sort of enduring Annual that may be presented at all times and seasons."—*Spectator.*

"Right glad are we to find that the sterling English Poets of former generations are not quite forgotten. This volume is one of the most pleasing remembrances of this agreeable fact that we have lately seen."—*Tait's Magazine.*

SHAKSPEARE'S COMPLETE WORKS.

With Portrait and Forty Illustrations, in one volume, Royal 8vo. Price £1. 11s. 6d. bound in cloth,

PLAYS AND POEMS OF SHAKSPEARE:

With Dr. Johnson's Preface; a Glossary; and an Account of each Play; and a Memoir of the Author, by the Rev. W. Harness, M.A.; *with Portrait, drawn from the Chandos Picture, and beautifully engraved by Cochrane;* and Forty Illustrations, engraved in the best manner, by C. Heath, C. Rolls, F. Bacon, &c., from Drawings by Smirke, Westall, Stephanoff, Corbould, and Wright.

The handsomest edition of Shakspeare that has ever been published in one volume.

With Portrait, medium 8vo. Price only 12s.

PLAYS AND POEMS OF SHAKSPEARE:

With Johnson's Preface, Glossary, &c.; and a Memoir of the Author, by the Rev. W. Harness, M.A.

With Portrait, medium 8vo, cloth, Price 12s.

SHAKSPEARE'S DRAMATIC WORKS:

With Memoir by the Rev. W. Harness, M.A.

THE PORTRAIT AND FORTY ILLUSTRATIONS OF SHAKSPEARE;

To Illustrate any edition. Royal 8vo. 21s.

ROBERTSON'S HISTORY OF THE DISCOVERY AND CONQUEST OF AMERICA. With an Account of his Life and Writings, by Dugald Stewart. With Two Maps, 5s.

"The most interesting and fascinating work of this historian, which joins the wonders of romance and the most exquisite graces of style to the philosophy of history. It is a model of historical excellence, and cannot fail to delight and instruct; and there is, perhaps, no book in the language better adapted for the purposes of private tuition, or as a class book in establishments for female education."

"This edition presents us with the connected narrative of the author in a slightly abridged form, avoiding prolixity, while the graphic descriptions of Robertson, where all stands out, as in a picture, are fully preserved."—*Literary Gazette.*

ROBERTSON'S HISTORY OF THE REIGN OF CHARLES V. EMPEROR OF GERMANY. With a View of the Progress of Society in Europe, from the Subversion of the Roman Empire to the beginning of the Sixteenth Century. Price 5s.

"One of the most pleasing and instructive accounts of the middle ages, and of the gradual rise of our present European polity and civilization, is to be found in Robertson's History of the Reign of Charles V."—*Chambers.*

TYTLER'S ELEMENTS OF GENERAL HISTORY, ANCIENT AND MODERN. To which are added, a Comparative View of Ancient and Modern Geography, and a Table of Chronology, brought down to the present time. By Alexander Fraser Tytler, Lord Woodhouselie. A new edition, complete in one volume, and carefully corrected and revised. With Maps, 4s.

This work contains the outlines of a course of Lectures on General History which were delivered by the author while Professor of Civil History and Greek and Roman Antiquities in the University of Edinburgh. The object of the work is to furnish a regular plan for the important study of history, and to unite with the detail of facts so much of reflection, as to aid the mind in the formation of rational views of the causes and consequences of events, as well as the policy of the actors. The author has also endeavoured to give a due share of attention to the state of the arts and sciences, the religion, laws, government, and manners of nations, which he has treated in distinct sections, and at particular periods.

BIOGRAPHY, AND VOYAGES AND TRAVELS.

BOURRIENNE'S MEMOIRS OF NAPOLEON BONAPARTE, abridged. Price 5s.

This is one of the most interesting Memoirs which is to be found in any language—and the translator trusts that he has succeeded in condensing the voluminous materials which were presented to him into one connected narrative of great interest.

"In this edition the greatest possible judgment has been used in the abridgement of the work, for all that is really interesting will be found in it. The volume is beautifully got up, and well deserves a place in every library where the work did not formerly appear on account of the expence."—*Bucks Herald.*

BRUCE'S TRAVELS THROUGH PART OF AFRICA, SYRIA, EGYPT AND ARABIA, INTO ABYSSINIA, to discover the Source of the Nile; with an Account of his Life. A new edition, carefully corrected and enlarged. Price 3s.

"I have conversed with the inhabitants of Abyssinia, who confirm all that Bruce has said in his Travels, which proves, beyond doubt, that his writings are not only correct as to the observance of truth, but that few travellers have written with more veracity than he has done; all the French travellers in Upper Egypt give praise and credit to his work. He is not only accurate in general facts, but in all the minute circumstances deduced from them."—*Dr. E. D. Clarke.*

CECIL'S LIFE OF THE REV. JOHN NEWTON; with Remarks on his Life, Connexions and Character. Price 2s.

The above Memoir was written to enable Christian parents to supply a book which might amuse their families, and yet tend to promote their best interests, by exhibiting the power of Divine grace in reclaiming from a course of profligacy and sin, one, who afterwards became an ornament to the church and to the Christian character.

COOK'S VOYAGES ROUND THE WORLD. With an Account of his Life, during the previous and intervening periods, by Dr. Kippis, F.R.S. &c. Price 3s.

"A fresh interest has now been given to the narrative of Cook, by the remarkable success which has lately attended the Missionary exertions in the islands which he discovered, in the conversion of an entire people from the fierceness of savage heathens to the mild and gentle influence of Christianity."

HOLCROFT'S LIFE OF BARON FREDERICK TRENCK; containing his Adventures, his Cruel and Excessive Sufferings during Ten Years' Imprisonment at the Fortress of Magdeburgh, by command of the late King of Prussia; also Anecdotes, Historical, Political, and Personal. Price 3s. 6d.

HUNTINGTON'S (Mrs. of Boston) MEMOIRS; consisting of Extracts from her Journals and Letters, with the Sermon on her Death. By the Rev. B. B. Wisner. Price 3s.

"Her religion was not confined to her closet, and the sanctuary. She endeavoured to carry it with her into all the business and circumstances of life. In the work of benevolence she has left her sex a noble example, and yet her exertions never produced any neglect of domestic duties, or any transgression of the bounds of strict propriety."—*The Rev. B. B. Wisner.*

VOLTAIRE'S HISTORY OF CHARLES THE TWELFTH, King of Sweden. Price 2s. 6d.

Almost all his actions, even those of his private life, border on the marvellous. He possessed all the virtues of a hero and a conqueror; but even these great qualities, any one of which would have been sufficient to immortalize another prince, proved pernicious to his country. From the history of his life it may be learned that a quiet and happy government is infinitely preferable to so much glory.

VOLTAIRE'S HISTORY OF PETER THE GREAT, Emperor of Russia. Price 3s.

POETRY.

BLAIR'S GRAVE; GRAY'S ELEGY; PORTEUS ON DEATH; and DODD'S PRISON THOUGHTS. With Memoirs of Blair and of Dr. Dodd. Price 2s.

BLOOMFIELD'S FARMER'S BOY; RURAL TALES; BALLADS and SONGS; and WILD FLOWERS, or Pastoral and Local Poetry. With Memoir of the Author. Price 2s.

BURNS' COMPLETE POETICAL WORKS. With Explanatory and Glossarial Notes; and the interesting Account of the Life of the Author, by James Currie, M.D. Price 5s.

This is the most complete edition which has been published, and contains the whole of the poetry comprised in the edition lately edited by Cunningham, as well as some additional pieces; and such notes have been added as are calculated to illustrate the manners and customs of Scotland, so as to render the whole more intelligible to the English reader.

"He owes nothing to the poetry of other lands—he is the offspring of the soil; he is as natural to Scotland as the heath is to her hills—his variety is equal to his originality; his humour, his gaiety, his tenderness, and his pathos, come all in a breath; they come freely, for they come of their own accord; the contrast is never offensive; the comic slides easily into the serious, the serious into the tender, and the tender into the pathetic."—*Allan Cunningham.*

COLLINS, GRAY, AND BEATTIE'S POETICAL WORKS, with Memoirs of the Authors. Price 2s. 6d.

"The poetical productions of Collins fill but a few pages, and are classed among the finest and most perfect productions in the language. The master-pieces of Gray will be read and loved as long as the 'still sad music of humanity' vibrates through the hearts of men;—and the Minstrel of Beattie may be classed among the most popular of English poems; the language is extremely elegant, the versification harmonious; it exhibits the richest poetic imagery, with a delightful flow of the most sublime, delicate, and pathetic sentiments; it breathes the spirit of the purest virtue, the soundest philosophy, and the most exquisite taste."—*S. C. Hall.*

COWPER'S COMPLETE POETICAL WORKS; including the Hymns and Translations from Madame Guion, Milton, &c. With a Memoir of the Author, by the Rev. Henry Stebbing, A. M. Price 5s.

This is the only complete edition which is printed in one volume.

"Morality never found in genius a more devoted advocate than Cowper, nor has moral wisdom, in its plain and severe precepts, been ever more successfully combined with the delicate spirit of poetry, than in his works. He was endowed with all the powers which a poet could want who was to be the moralist of the world—the reprover, but not the satirist, of men—the teacher of simple truths, which were to be rendered gracious without endangering their simplicity."—*Stebbing.*

COWPER'S POEMS. Part II. Containing Hymns, Translations from Madame Guion, Translations from Milton, and Minor Poems. Price 2s. 6d.

The poetry in this volume has been printed as a supplement to complete all the previous editions in the Classic size.

COWPER'S POEMS. With a Memoir by the Rev. H. Stebbing, A.M. Price 2s. 6d.

DODD'S BEAUTIES OF SHAKSPEARE. With a general Index. Price 3s.

"I greatly dislike beauties and selections in general; but make out your amplest catalogue of all the known faculties, and then compare with Shakspeare under each head all or any of the writers in prose and verse that ever lived! Who that is competent to judge doubts the result!"—*Coleridge.*

DRYDEN'S VIRGIL. With Life by Walsh. Price 3s. 6d.

"The most noble and spirited translation that I know in any language."—*Pope.*

FALCONER'S SHIPWRECK, with other Poems: and **SOMERVILE'S CHASE.** With Lives of the Authors. Price 2s.

GOLDSMITH'S POEMS, PLAYS, AND ESSAYS. With an Account of his Life and Writings, and a Critical Dissertation on his Poetry, by Dr. Aikin. Price 3s.

"He touched upon every kind of excellence, and that with such inimitable grace, that where he failed of originality most, he had ever a freshness and a charm. In this is the beauty of his poetry—his versification is remarkably elegant and sweet."—*S. C. Hall.*

KIRKE WHITE'S POETICAL WORKS AND LETTERS, with a Sketch of his Life. Price 2s. 6d.

MILTON'S POETICAL WORKS, complete, with Explanatory Notes, and a Life of the Author, by the Rev. H. Stebbing, A.M. Also, An Essay on the Poetical Genius of Milton, by Dr. Channing. Price 4s.

The Latin and Italian poems are included in this edition.

"Mr. Stebbing's notes will be found very useful in elucidating the learned allusions with which the text abounds, and they are also valuable for the correct appreciation with which the writer directs attention to the beauties of the Author."—*Printing Machine.*

MORE'S (HANNAH) POETICAL WORKS, complete, containing Sacred Dramas; Tragedies; Poems; Ballads; Hymns, &c. with a Memoir of the Author. Price 4s.

"This is a volume that ought to be in the possession of every lady; the object of the amiable author was ever to promote the love of piety and virtue, by placing them in broad contrast with impiety and vice, and to bring out in strong relief the indwelling beauty of a Christian life."

OSSIAN'S POEMS: translated by J. Macpherson, Esq. with Dissertations concerning the Era and Poems of Ossian; and Dr. Blair's Critical Dissertation. Price 3s.

"Ossian is sublime and pathetic in an eminent degree—and were this merit in other respects much less than it is, this alone ought to entitle him to high regard, that his writings are remarkably favourable to virtue. They awake the tenderest sympathies, and inspire the most generous actions. No reader can rise from him without being warmed with the sentiments of humanity, virtue, and honour, and we may boldly assign him a place among those whose works are to last for ages."—*Dr. Blair.*

POPE'S HOMER'S ILIAD. With Explanatory Notes, and Index of Persons; and Essay on the Life, Genius, and Writings, of Homer. Price 4s.

It has been attempted in the notes to supply the characters of all the heroes, and to convey some idea of the machinery made use of by Homer. The mythology, rites, customs, &c. of the heroic ages have also been explained, so far as the extent of the notes would admit; and particular care has been taken to direct the attention of the youthful reader to such passages as have been greatly admired in all ages.

"This deserves to be recommended as the best Pocket Edition of Pope's Iliad that has appeared."—*Printing Machine.*

POPE'S HOMER'S ODYSSEY. With Explanatory Notes and Index of Persons. Price 3s.

This is printed uniform with the Iliad, and the same object has been kept in view in selecting the notes.

SACRED POETRY. Selected by the Rev. H. Stebbing, A.M. New Edition, enlarged. Price 3s. 6d.

This collection has been drawn from the works of the most admired Poets in the language; the present edition contains upwards of 100 additional pages, and the Editor earnestly hopes that the publication may tend to purify and elevate the thoughts of those into whose hands it may fall.

SCOTT'S (Sir Walter) LAY OF THE LAST MINSTREL; BALLADS, AND LYRICAL PIECES. With Notes, and a Memoir of the Author. Price 2s. 6d.

THOMSON'S SEASONS, and Castle of Indolence. With a Life of the Author. Price 2s.

"His descriptions bring before us the whole magnificence of Nature, whether pleasing or dreadful. The gaiety of Spring, the splendour of Summer, the tranquillity of Autumn, and the horror of Winter, take in their turn possession of the mind."—*Johnson.*

YOUNG'S NIGHT THOUGHTS on Life, Death, and Immortality. Price 2s. 6d.

"Exhibits a very wide display of original poetry, variegated with deep reflections and striking allusions, a wilderness of thought, in which the fertility of fancy scatters flowers of every hue and of every odour."—*Johnson.*

EDUCATION.

CHAPONE ON THE MIND; DR. GREGORY'S LEGACY; AND PENNINGTON'S ADVICE TO HER DAUGHTERS. Price 2s. 6d.

"Mrs. Chapone's Letters are distinguished by sound sense, a liberal as well as a warm spirit of piety, and a philosophy applied to its best use—the culture of the heart and affections; and are the most unexceptionable treatises that can be put into the hands of female youth."—*Mrs. Barbauld.*

CHESTERFIELD'S PRINCIPLES OF POLITENESS, and YOUNG MAN'S OWN BOOK. Price 2s. 6d.

The '*Principles of Politeness*' consist of such selections only as apply to good breeding, and the manners, customs, and habits, of general society; and '*The Young Man's Own Book*,' which is now added as a suitable companion, was lately published in America; it is chiefly compiled from Paley, Watts, and others of our own writers, but many excellent observations are added, and the whole arranged under distinct heads, so as to form a useful manual.

EVENINGS AT HOME, consisting of a variety of Miscellaneous Pieces for the Instruction and Amusement of Young Persons. By Dr. Aikin and Mrs. Barbauld. Price 3s.

"This is one of the best books for young people from seven to ten years old, that has yet appeared in the world; and the mixture of scientific and moral lessons is so happily blended as to relieve the attention."—*Miss Edgeworth.*

JOYCE'S SCIENTIFIC DIALOGUES, intended for the Instruction and Entertainment of Young People; in which the first Principles of *Natural* and *Experimental Philosophy* are fully explained. Complete in one volume, with 185 Wood Cuts. Price 4s.

This is the best introduction to these subjects which has yet been published. The object of the author has been to present a complete compendium of natural and experimental philosophy, not only adapted to the understandings of young people, but well calculated also to convey that familiar instruction which is necessary before they can attend public lectures with advantage.

SMELLIE'S PHILOSOPHY OF NATURAL HISTORY: with an Introduction, and various additions and alterations, intended to adapt it to the present state of Knowledge, by John Ware, M.D. Price 3s.

The editor has availed himself of such modern discoveries and improvements in physiology and natural history as are connected with the subjects of which the book treats; and in the Introduction he has added a general view of animal and vegetable life, and a brief sketch of the structure and classification of the whole animal kingdom, which he trusts will be found of great assistance to young persons in learning the elements of Natural History.

WATTS ON THE IMPROVEMENT OF THE MIND. With a Discourse on the Education of Children and Youth. Price 3s.

"Whoever has the care of instructing others may be charged with deficiency in his duty if this book is not recommended."—*Dr. Johnson.*

RELIGION.

ABBOTT'S YOUNG CHRISTIAN; or, a Familiar Illustration of the Principles of Christian Duty. Price 2s. 6d.

"We strongly recommend this work as one of the most instructive, and at the same time amusing, that can be placed in a youth's hands."—*Dublin Christian Examiner.*

ABBOTT'S CORNER-STONE; or, a Familiar Illustration of the Principles of Christian Truth. Price 2s. 6d.

BAXTER'S SAINTS' EVERLASTING REST; or, a Treatise of the Blessed State of the Saints, in their enjoyment of God in Heaven. Price 2s.

"His practical writings are invaluable; powerful, awakening, with deep views of eternity, and the most heavenly meditations on a future state."—*Bickersteth.*

BUNYAN'S PILGRIM'S PROGRESS. Notes and Life by the Rev. Thomas Scott. Price 3s.

"The best evidence of its merit is the general and continued approbation of mankind."—*Johnson.*

BUNYAN'S GRACE ABOUNDING; WORLD TO COME, AND BARREN FIG-TREE. Price 3s.

The Grace Abounding is an invaluable piece of autobiography, and written with all the vigour of its remarkable author; and the other pieces which comprise this volume are much calculated to promote personal religion and holiness of life.

BUTLER'S ANALOGY OF RELIGION. Natural and Revealed, to the Constitution and Course of Nature; with a Preface and Life, by Bishop Halifax. Price 2s. 6d.

"I have derived greater aid from the views and reasonings of Butler, than I have been able to find besides in the whole range of our existent authorship."—*Dr. Chalmers.*

CLARKE'S SCRIPTURE PROMISES, in which the Promises of Scripture are arranged under their proper heads; representing, I. The Blessings Promised. II. The Duties to which Promises are made. Price 2s.

In this edition every passage of Scripture has been compared and verified.

"The volume is like an arranged museum of gems, and precious stones, and pearls of inestimable value. The divine promises comprehend a rich and endless variety."—*Dr. Wardlaw.*

DODDRIDGE'S RISE AND PROGRESS OF RELIGION IN THE SOUL. Price 2s.

HERVEY'S MEDITATIONS AND CONTEMPLATIONS; with a Sketch of the Author's Life. Price 3s.

PALEY'S EVIDENCES OF CHRISTIANITY. Price 2s. 6d.

"In this luminous and comprehensive work, the historical evidence for the truth of our Scriptures, selected from the volumes of Dr. Lardner, is arranged with clearness, and stated to the reader with the utmost force and precision."—*Rev. R. Lynam, M.A.*

PALEY'S NATURAL THEOLOGY. Price 2s. 6d.

"His Theology may be classed among the most interesting books of the English language, and contains many beautiful illustrations of the wisdom and goodness of God in the works of the creation."—*Rev. R. Lynam, M.A.*

SCOTT'S (Rev. Tho.) FORCE OF TRUTH: GROWTH IN GRACE: DISCOURSE UPON REPENTANCE: AND SERMON ON FINAL PERSEVERANCE. Price 2s. 6d.

"He was an eminently useful minister of the Gospel, and his sound, judicious, and practical writings form a most valuable accession to the theology of our country. The lessons of such a life and such an experience as he has honestly delineated, are highly instructive to every class of Christians, but to the sincere inquirer after truth we would especially recommend them."—*Dr. Chalmers.*

STURM'S REFLECTIONS ON THE WORKS OF GOD, and of His Providence throughout all Nature. Price 5s.

"The present work I venture to recommend to young people, with a firm confidence in its improving the mind and ameliorating the heart. It will be particularly useful to those whose reading is not very extensive, as containing much useful information in natural history and natural philosophy, conveyed in language intelligible to young children."—*The Translator.*

WILBERFORCE'S PRACTICAL VIEW OF THE PREVAILING RELIGIOUS SYSTEM of professed Christians, in the higher and middle Classes in this Country, contrasted with real Christianity. Price 2s. 6d.

"The attractive character of the work is universally allowed. Love is stamped on every page. It is not a dry disputation, a systematic treatise, a polemical discussion. It is a masterly, benevolent, tender appeal to the breast and conscience on the most important of all subjects."—*Daniel Wilson, Bishop of Calcutta.*

MISCELLANEOUS.

BARON MUNCHAUSEN'S SURPRISING TRAVELS AND ADVENTURES. Price 2s.

BURKE ON THE FRENCH REVOLUTION. Price 2s. 6d.

BURKE ON THE SUBLIME AND BEAUTIFUL. Price 2s.

CITIZEN OF THE WORLD. By Oliver Goldsmith. Price 3s.

DEFOE'S HISTORY OF THE GREAT PLAGUE OF LONDON in the year 1665, with an Introduction by the Rev. H. Stebbing, in which a short Account is given of the various visitations of Pestilence of which we have any knowledge. Price 2s. 6d.

ECONOMY OF HUMAN LIFE, by Dodsley. Price 2s.

FRANKLIN'S WORKS, consisting of Essays, Humorous, Moral, and Literary. With his Life, written by Himself. Price 2s. 6d.

GULLIVER'S TRAVELS into several remote Nations of the World, by Dean Swift. With a Memoir of the Author. Price 2s. 6d.

JOE MILLER'S BUDGET OF ANECDOTE AND WIT. Price 3s. 6d.

This is an entirely new selection under the above well-known title, and no piece of improper tendency has been admitted.

LOCKE'S CONDUCT OF THE UNDERSTANDING, AND BACON'S MORAL, ECONOMICAL, AND POLITICAL ESSAYS. Price 2s. 6d.

MASON ON SELF-KNOWLEDGE; MELMOTH'S GREAT IMPORTANCE OF A RELIGIOUS LIFE; and **DODSLEY'S ECONOMY OF HUMAN LIFE.** Price 2s. 6d.

PAUL AND VIRGINIA; ELIZABETH; OR, THE EXILES OF SIBERIA; and **THE INDIAN COTTAGE.** Price 2s. 6d.

RASSELAS, a TALE, by Dr. Johnson; and **DINARBAS,** a Tale; being a continuation of Rasselas. Price 2s. 6d.

ST. PIERRE'S STUDIES OF NATURE. Price 3s. 6d.

"I have read few performances with more complete satisfaction and with greater improvement, than the '*Studies of Nature:*' in no one have I found the useful and agreeable more happily blended."—*Dr. Hunter.*

TELEMACHUS, by Archbishop Fenelon. Price 3s.

It is deserving of particular remark that the Telemachus was written by its distinguished author to impress upon the youthful mind of the grandson of Lewis XIV. the principles of good government; and it may be questioned, if there is any work which is so well calculated to accomplish that object. It is a beautiful argument to persuade men to prefer the good of the public to private advantage, and to induce us to love the human race.

THINKS I TO MYSELF. A Serio-ludicro, Tragico-comico Tale, by the Rev. Dr. Nares. Price 2s. 6d.

VICAR OF WAKEFIELD, by Dr. Goldsmith. Price 2s.

"This Tale is the lasting monument of Goldsmith's genius, his great legacy of pleasure to generations and generations, past, present, and to come."—*Examiner.*

ZIMMERMAN ON SOLITUDE. With a Life of the Author. Price 3s.

"A work which will always be read with as much profit as pleasure, as it contains the most sublime conceptions, the greatest sagacity of observation, an extreme propriety of application, much ability in the choice of examples, and a constant anxiety for the interests of religion, with the sacred and solemn truths of which his mind was most devoutly impressed."—*Tissot.*

PRINTED BY A. SWEETING, 15, BARTLETT'S BUILDINGS, LONDON.

Lightning Source UK Ltd.
Milton Keynes UK
UKHW022025081121
393637UK00003B/154